MACARTHUR

DAILY BIBLE

SECOND EDITION

PRESENTED TO

_____

BY

_____

ON

_____

Your word is a lamp to my feet and a light to my path.

PSALM 119:105

The MacArthur Daily Bible, 2nd Edition
Copyright © 2003, 2022 by Thomas Nelson
Published in Nashville, Tennessee, by Thomas Nelson.
Thomas Nelson is a registered trademark of HarperCollins Christian Publishing, Inc.

Notes and commentary copyright © 2003 by John F. MacArthur, Jr.
All rights reserved.

Editorial development and research provided by Koechel Peterson & Associates, Inc., Minneapolis, Minnesota.

NEW AMERICAN STANDARD BIBLE
Copyright© 1960, 1962, 1963, 1968, 1971, 1972, 1973, 1975, 1977, 1995

by The Lockman Foundation
A Corporation Not for Profit
La Habra, CA
All rights reserved
www.lockman.org

The "NASB," "NAS," "New American Standard Bible," and "New American Standard" trademarks are registered in the United States Patent and Trademark Office by The Lockman Foundation. Use of these trademarks requires the permission of The Lockman Foundation.

Library of Congress Control Number: 2021950928

The text of the New American Standard Bible® may be quoted and/or reprinted up to and inclusive of five hundred (500) verses without express written permission of The Lockman Foundation, providing the verses do not amount to a complete book of the Bible nor do the verses quoted account for more than 25% of the total work in which they are quoted.

Notice of copyright must appear on the title or copyright page of the work as follows: "Scripture taken from the NEW AMERICAN STANDARD BIBLE®, Copyright © 1960, 1962, 1963, 1968, 1971, 1972, 1973, 1975, 1977, 1995 by The Lockman Foundation. Used by permission."

When quotations from the NASB® text are used in non-saleable media, such as church bulletins, orders of service, posters, transparencies or similar media, the abbreviation (NASB) may be used at the end of the quotation.

This permission to quote is limited to material which is wholly manufactured in compliance with the provisions of the copyright laws of the United States of America. The Lockman Foundation may terminate this permission at any time.

Quotations and/or reprints in excess of the above limitations, or other permission requests, must be directed to and approved in writing by The Lockman Foundation, PO Box 2279, La Habra, CA 90632-2279, www.lockman.org.

Printed in China

22 23 24 25 26 27 28 29 AMC 15 14 13 12 11 10 9 8 7 6 5 4 3 2

NEW AMERICAN STANDARD BIBLE

The

MACARTHUR DAILY BIBLE

READ *the* BIBLE *in* ONE YEAR *with* NOTES FROM

JOHN MACARTHUR

THOMAS NELSON
Since 1798

www.ThomasNelsonBibles.com

CONTENTS

MONTHS

OLD TESTAMENT

NEW TESTAMENT

FOREWORD

SCRIPTURAL PROMISE

"The grass withers, the flower fades,
but the word of our God stands forever."
Isaiah 40:8

The New American Standard Bible has been produced with the conviction that the words of Scripture as originally penned in the Hebrew, Aramaic, and Greek were inspired by God. Since they are the eternal Word of God, the Holy Scriptures speak with fresh power to each generation, to give wisdom that leads to salvation, that men may serve Christ to the glory of God.

The purpose of the Editorial Board in making this translation was to adhere as closely as possible to the original languages of the Holy Scriptures, and to make the translation in a fluent and readable style according to current English usage.

THE FOURFOLD AIM OF THE LOCKMAN FOUNDATION

1. These publications shall be true to the original Hebrew, Aramaic, and Greek.

2. They shall be grammatically correct.

3. They shall be understandable.

4. They shall give the Lord Jesus Christ His proper place, the place which the Word gives Him; therefore, no work will ever be personalized.

PREFACE TO THE
NEW AMERICAN STANDARD BIBLE

In the history of English Bible translations, the King James Version is the most prestigious. This time-honored version of 1611, itself a revision of the Bishops' Bible of 1568, became the basis for the English Revised Version appearing in 1881 (New Testament) and 1885 (Old Testament). The American counterpart of this last work was published in 1901 as the American Standard Version. The ASV, a product of both British and American scholarship, has been highly regarded for its scholarship and accuracy. Recognizing the values of the American Standard Version, The Lockman Foundation felt an urgency to preserve these and other lasting values of the ASV by incorporating recent discoveries of Hebrew and Greek textual sources and by rendering it into more current English. Therefore, in 1959 a new translation project was launched, based on the time-honored principles of translation of the ASV and KJV. The result is the New American Standard Bible.

Translation work for the NASB was begun in 1959. In the preparation of this work numerous other translations have been consulted along with the linguistic tools and literature of biblical scholarship. Decisions about English renderings were made by consensus of a team composed of educators and pastors. Subsequently, review and evaluation by other Hebrew and Greek scholars outside the Editorial Board were sought and carefully considered.

The Editorial Board has continued to function since publication of the complete Bible in 1971. This edition of the NASB represents revisions and refinements recommended over the last several years as well as thorough research based on modern English usage.

PRINCIPLES OF TRANSLATION

MODERN ENGLISH USAGE: The attempt has been made to render the grammar and terminology in contemporary English. When it was felt that the word-for-word literalness was unacceptable to the modern reader, a change was made in the direction of a more current English idiom. In the instances where this has been done, the more literal rendering has been indicated in the notes. There are a few exceptions to this procedure. In particular, frequently "And" is not translated at the beginning of sentences because of differences in style between ancient and modern writing. Punctuation is a relatively modern invention, and ancient writers often linked most of their sentences with "and" or other connectives. Also, the Hebrew idiom "answered and said" is sometimes reduced to "answered" or "said" as demanded by the context. For current English the idiom "it came about that" has not been translated in the New Testament except when a major transition is needed.

ALTERNATIVE READINGS: In addition to the more literal renderings, notations have been made to include alternate translations, reading of variant manuscripts and explanatory equivalents of the text. Only such notations have been used as have been felt justified in assisting the reader's comprehension of the terms used by the original author.

HEBREW TEXT: In the present translation the latest edition of Rudolf Kittel's BIBLIA HEBRAICA has been employed together with the most recent light from lexicography, cognate languages, and the Dead Sea Scrolls.

HEBREW TENSES: Consecution of tenses in Hebrew remains a puzzling factor in translation. The translators have been guided by the requirements of a literal translation, the sequence of tenses, and the immediate and broad contexts.

THE PROPER NAME OF GOD IN THE OLD TESTAMENT: In the Scriptures, the name of God is most significant and understandably so. It is inconceivable to think of spiritual matters without a proper designation for the Supreme Deity. Thus the most common name for the Deity is God, a translation of the original *Elohim*. One of the titles for God is Lord, a translation of *Adonai*. There is yet another name which is particularly assigned to God as His special or proper name, that is, the four letters YHWH (Exodus 3:14 and Isaiah 42:8). This name has not been pronounced by the Jews because of reverence for the great sacredness of the divine name. Therefore, it has been consistently translated LORD. The only exception to this translation of YHWH is when it occurs in immediate proximity to the word Lord, that is, *Adonai*. In that case it is regularly translated GOD in order to avoid confusion.

It is known that for many years YHWH has been transliterated as Yahweh, however no complete certainty attaches to this pronunciation.

GREEK TEXT: Consideration was given to the latest available manuscripts with a view to determining the best Greek text. In most instances the 26th edition of Eberhard Nestle's NOVUM TESTAMENTUM GRAECE was followed.

GREEK TENSES: A careful distinction has been made in the treatment of the Greek aorist tense (usually translated as the English past, "He did") and the Greek imperfect tense (normally rendered either as English past progressive, "He was doing"; or, if inceptive, as "He began to do" or "He started to do"; or else if customary past, as "He used to do"). "Began" is italicized if it renders an imperfect tense, in order to distinguish it from the Greek verb for "begin." In some contexts the difference between the Greek imperfect and the English past is conveyed better by the choice of vocabulary or by other words in the context, and in such cases the Greek imperfect may be rendered as a simple past tense (e.g. "had an illness for many years" would be preferable to "was having an illness for many years" and would be understood in the same way).

On the other hand, not all aorists have been rendered as English pasts ("He did"), for some of them are clearly to be rendered as English perfects ("He has done"), or even as past perfects ("He had done"), judging from the context in which they occur. Such aorists have been rendered as perfects or past perfects in this translation.

As for the distinction between aorist and present imperatives, the translators have usually rendered these imperatives in the customary manner, rather than attempting any such fine distinction as "Begin to do!" (for the aorist imperative), or, "Continually do!" (for the present imperative).

As for sequence of tenses, the translators took care to follow English rules rather than Greek in translating Greek presents, imperfects, and aorists. Thus, where English says, "We knew that he was doing," Greek puts it, "We knew that he does"; similarly, "We knew that he had done" is the Greek, "We knew that he did." Likewise, the English, "When he had come, they met him," is represented in Greek by, "When he came, they met him." In all cases a consistent transfer has been made from the Greek tense in the subordinate clause to the appropriate tense in English.

In the rendering of negative questions introduced by the particle *mē* (which always expects the answer "No") the wording has been altered from a mere, "Will he not do this?" to a more accurate, "He will not do this, will he?"

THE LOCKMAN FOUNDATION

EXPLANATION OF GENERAL FORMAT

PARAGRAPHS are designated by bold face verse numbers or letters.

QUOTATION MARKS are used in the text in accordance with modern English usage.

"THOU," "THEE" and "THY" are not used in this edition and have been rendered as "You" and "Your."

PERSONAL PRONOUNS are capitalized when pertaining to Deity.

ITALICS are used in the text to indicate words which are not found in the original Hebrew, Aramaic, or Greek but implied by it. Italics are used in the marginal notes to signify alternate readings for the text. Roman text in the marginal alternate readings is the same as italics in the Bible text.

SMALL CAPS in the New Testament are used in the text to indicate Old Testament quotations or obvious references to Old Testament texts. Variations of Old Testament wording are found in New Testament citations depending on whether the New Testament writer translated from a Hebrew text, used existing Greek or Aramaic translations, or paraphrased the material. It should be noted that modern rules for the indication of direct quotation were not used in biblical times; thus, the ancient writer would use exact quotations or references to quotation without specific indication of such.

ASTERISKS are used to mark verbs that are historical presents in the Greek which have been translated with an English past tense in order to conform to modern usage. The translators recognized that in some contexts the present tense seems more unexpected and unjustified to the English reader than a past tense would have been. But Greek authors frequently used the present tense for the sake of heightened vividness, thereby transporting their readers in imagination to the actual scene at the time of occurrence. However, the translators felt that it would be wise to change these historical presents to English past tenses.

ABBREVIATIONS AND
SPECIAL MARKINGS

A.D.	=	in the year of our Lord
a.k.a.	=	also known as
a.m.	=	midnight to noon
B.C.	=	before Christ
ca.	=	about, approximately
cf.	=	compare
chap., chaps.	=	chapter, chapters
contra.	=	contrast
e.g.	=	for example
et al.	=	and others
etc.	=	and so forth
f., ff.	=	following verse, following verses
i.e.	=	that is
Mt.	=	Mount
p.m.	=	noon to midnight
v., vv.	=	verse, verses
[ ]	=	brackets in text indicate words probably not in the original writings

WELCOME TO THE MACARTHUR DAILY BIBLE

No matter how much teaching and preaching you listen to, there can be no substitute for reading the Word of God daily yourself. The Bible is God's precious revelation of Himself to you. It's your point of contact with Him, where you learn the precious truth He has given to the Body of Christ. It's where you discover that history is His story, as you see the chain of events unfolding, always known to God, that led up to the birth, ministry, death, resurrection, and ascension of our Lord Jesus Christ. And it's where you learn what the future has in store in that wonderful day when the Lord returns.

This *MacArthur Daily Bible* provides a good way to develop a daily Bible reading habit. For each day of the year, it gives you a portion of the Old Testament, a bit from Psalms and Proverbs, and a portion of the New Testament, from the trusted New American Standard Bible translation.

It's all in Bible order: In each day's readings, you pick up where you left off the day before. If you stay in this *Daily Bible* every day for a year, you will have read through the entire Bible!

Along with each day's Scripture passages there are helpful comments and notes gleaned from the writings of John MacArthur.

WAYS TO WORK THE PLAN

There are several ways you might like to use the daily readings:

1. Bible in one year, once a day: Follow the plan. Read each day's readings during your daily Bible reading time, to finish the whole Bible in a year.
2. Bible in one year, twice a day: Like number 1 above, but in two sittings. Read the Psalms, Proverbs, and New Testament readings in the morning and the Old Testament reading in the evening.
3. Bible in two years: Read the Psalms, Proverbs, and New Testament readings the first year, then the Old Testament readings the second year.

KEY MEMORY PASSAGES

If you like to focus on specific Bible passages, we have also included a section that spotlights 52 key scriptures, with additional comments from Dr. MacArthur. These passages are also good ones to memorize. Learn them by heart, and at year's end, you'll have 52 of the Bible's most important passages committed to memory.

OUR PRAYER FOR YOU

May the Lord use your reading of His Word to strengthen and guide you in your faith as you live for Him each day. As you read the Bible daily, may you be blessed with the peace and reassurance that only God can give.

HOW TO USE YOUR NASB DAILY BIBLE

For each day of the year, there are four portions to read: a portion from the Old Testament, from Psalms, from Proverbs, and from the New Testament. By following this plan, at the end of one year you will have read through the entire Bible in consecutive daily installments.

If you aren't ready for the entire Bible in a year, an alternative two-year plan would be to read the portions from Psalms, Proverbs, and the New Testament the first year, and then the portions from the Old Testament the second year.

Either way, you will develop a habit of thorough, daily Bible reading that will bless you in life.

> "I rejoice at Your word,
>   as one who finds great spoil."
>
> *Psalm 119:162*

> "All Scripture is inspired by God and profitable for teaching, for reproof, for correction, for training in righteousness; so that the man of God may be adequate, equipped for every good work"
>
> *2 Timothy 3:16–17*

FIFTY-TWO KEY PASSAGES
OF THE BIBLE

Over the next year, you may wish to supplement your daily reading of Scripture with the following 52 weeks' worth of key passages of the Bible that have been selected and developed for you by Dr. John MacArthur. These passages provide a solid foundation upon which to build the Christian life, and gaining an understanding of these core biblical truths is the key to spiritual growth and development.

The intent is to provide you with the opportunity to focus on, and perhaps memorize, one important passage a week for a year. It is all a part of saturating and renewing your mind and thoughts with the Word of God. The page numbers where the passages are located among the daily readings are given so that you can study the context for the passages to ensure that you get the full meaning.

VERSES TO MEMORIZE

 WEEK 1

Bless the LORD, O my soul, and all that is within me, bless His holy name. Bless the LORD, O my soul, and forget none of His benefits; who pardons all your iniquities, who heals all your diseases; who redeems your life from the pit, who crowns you with lovingkindness and compassion—PSALM 103:1–4, page 855

King David learned the powerful habit of telling himself the truth. "Bless the LORD, O my soul." That's a good thing to tell yourself, isn't it? "And all that is within me, bless His holy name." That's a habit worth practicing. Train your soul to bless God. And how do you do that? By not forgetting His benefits. Whatever might be going wrong in your life, whatever might be a disappointment, even a serious illness or death, does not affect God's eternal blessing on you as His child. He has redeemed your life from destruction, and He crowns you with *lovingkindness*, which means grace and mercy. He pours out His tenderness. He heals all your diseases, not necessarily in time, but in eternity. And He forgives all your iniquities. Don't ever forget His benefits: forgiveness, absolute perfection in heaven, freedom from all sickness and death, abundant mercy, and

everything you ever need. May everything that is in you bless His holy name!

 WEEK 2

Thus says the LORD, "Let not a wise man boast of his wisdom, and let not the mighty man boast of his might, let not a rich man boast of his riches; but let him who boasts boast of this, that he understands and knows Me, that I am the LORD who exercises lovingkindness, justice and righteousness on earth; for I delight in these things," declares the LORD.—JEREMIAH 9:23–24, page 1018

What a wonderful promise, that God delights in those who understand and know Him. We live in a world full of people who glory in the big string of degrees after their names. They want people to be impressed by their achievements, insights, and wisdom. While some people glory in their physical strengths, others glory in the business they've built. We meet a lot of people who glory or boast in their riches. They proclaim it in the clothes they wear, the cars they drive, and the homes they own. That's just the way human, fallen, simple creatures are. But the Lord God says this: "If you're going to boast, boast in this, that you know and understand Me." Which is wonderful news! I know the God of the universe. Why would I glory in human wisdom and might and riches when I know the God of the universe? And, even more wonderfully, He knows me.

WEEK 3

And we know that God causes all things to work together for good to those who love God, to those who are called according to His purpose.—ROMANS 8:28, page 786

The best manuscript evidence of the original Greek records this verse this way: "We know that God causes all things to work together for good." Now, we understand that there is evil, not only in the world, but in us. It isn't saying that all things are good. It says that God causes all things to work together for good. This leads us to the profound element of God's supreme authority and power over all the issues of life to produce out of them

His own good purposes. God takes all the contingencies of life, all the choices, all the good, bad, and indifferent things, and weaves them together for ultimately a good purpose. That is the promise that God is giving to those who have been called to salvation. Every suffering, temptation, trial, even every sin, God works together into a tapestry that ultimately is for your good. You might not see it at the time. It's like looking at the back of a Persian rug. It's just a bunch of threads going into chaotic directions. But when you turn it over some day in eternity, you'll see how it all worked together for good.

 WEEK 4

For the word of God is living and active and sharper than any two-edged sword, and piercing as far as the division of soul and spirit, of both joints and marrow, and able to judge the thoughts and intentions of the heart.— HEBREWS 4:12, page 1121

Many people think of the Bible as a comforting book, but the Scripture claims to be a sword—alive, powerful, sharp. It cuts and penetrates way down into the depth of soul and spirit. It becomes a discerner of the thoughts and intents of the heart. Nothing cuts and penetrates like the truth of God. You could take all the psychology and philosophy in the world, and it cannot dismantle a man at the level of his soul as the Word of God can. And the reason is because nobody knows a man like God knows a man. The heart of every one of us is exposed to God, and the Bible reveals that penetrating insight into our souls. Yes, the Bible knows how to build us up, but it also knows how to convict and unmask our hypocrisy, how to cut into our pride and self-will, how to uncover our secret sins. But wherever God cuts, He heals, and whatever He reveals, He cleanses. And it's that kind of cleansing that makes me able to bear more fruit to my own joy and to the glory of God.

WEEK 5

*Or do you not know that your body is a temple of the Holy Spirit who is in you, whom you have from God, and that you are not your own? For you have been bought with a price: therefore glorify God in your body.—*1 CORINTHIANS 6:19-20, page 841

The Spirit of God lives in us. We literally are a temple in which God lives. We're not our own. We were bought, and the price was the precious blood of Jesus Christ as a Lamb without blemish and without spot. Therefore,

we have the obligation to use this Holy Spirit temple in such a way that brings honor to God.

I had a friend who was visiting a great cathedral in New York City. When he came to a shrine to St. Joseph, there was a sign hanging around St. Joseph's neck that read: *Do not worship here. This shrine is out of order.* My friend said to himself, "I wonder if there aren't many days when that sign should be hanging around my neck. Don't expect to see Christ here. This shrine is out of order."

Your body is that shrine. It is that temple to the Holy Spirit because He lives there. Sometimes I'm afraid He is obscured. Make sure your shrine is in order. Glorify God in your body and in your spirit which are God's.

WEEK 6

*Surely our griefs He Himself bore, and our sorrows He carried; yet we ourselves esteemed Him stricken, smitten of God, and afflicted. But He was pierced through for our transgressions, He was crushed for our iniquities; the chastening for our well-being fell upon Him, and by His scourging we are healed. All of us like sheep have gone astray, each of us has turned to his own way; but the Lord has caused the iniquity of us all to fall on Him.—*ISAIAH 53:4-6, page 975

Isaiah speaks of God placing all our sins on His Son, the Lord Jesus Christ. He bore the grief for our sin, carried the sorrow for our lawlessness, was wounded for our transgressions and bruised for our iniquities. But by whom, and why? He was stricken, smitten, and afflicted by God, because God is the Judge. God alone can determine the appropriate punishment for sin; and God gave that punishment to His Son. He did that because there was no other one who could take our place, no other spotless Lamb, no other perfect sacrifice. So in order for us to have peace with God, Jesus paid the price for our sins. By His wounds we are healed spiritually. Every one of us has followed his own sinful path, and the Lord gathered all of our iniquity and laid it on Him. This is the amazing reality of Jesus Christ. He offered Himself, the sinless One, for the sinful ones. Every person has sinned, and for everyone who puts their trust in Jesus Christ that sin is paid for.

WEEK 7

*For I am confident of this very thing, that He who began a good work in you will perfect it until the day of Christ Jesus.—*PHILIPPIANS 1:6, page 994

The Greek verb translated "has begun" is used only here and in Galatians 3:3, both times in reference to salvation. What it says is that when God begins a work of salvation in a person, He finishes it, He perfects it. You need to understand that salvation has three phases. There is justification, which occurs when you repent and put your faith in Jesus Christ. Then the second phase begins, which is sanctification. You are being continually separated from sin; that's an aspect of salvation. And the third phase is glorification. That occurs when we leave this world, enter into heaven, lose the residual fallen flesh, and the new creation is freed from any sinful impulses, from any reality of sin to enter into the full perfection and absolute holiness of eternal life. As a Christian, you have been justified. You are being sanctified, progressively set apart from sin by the work of the Holy Spirit through the Word. And you will one day be glorified, at which point you will be made like Jesus Christ. As much as glorified humanity can be like incarnate Deity, we will be like Jesus Christ!

 ## WEEK 8

By common confession, great is the mystery of godliness: He who was revealed in the flesh, was vindicated in the Spirit, seen by angels, proclaimed among the nations, believed on in the world, taken up in glory.—1 TIMOTHY 3:16, page 1064

This verse contains part of an early church hymn. It's uniformity, rhythm, and parallel as in the original language indicates this. Its six lines form a concise summary of the truth of the gospel. The "mystery of godliness" simply looks at Jesus Christ. The mystery is something that was hidden in the Old Testament age but is now revealed in the New Testament. And the greatest of mysteries was the mystery of God in human flesh, the mystery of Jesus Christ, the glorious reality of the Incarnation.

That becomes the theme for this early church hymn. God was manifested in human flesh through the virgin birth. He was righteous in His Spirit—perfectly righteous, perfectly holy. Angels holy and fallen acknowledged Him. He was preached among the nations. He was believed on by people in Galilee and Judea. After His resurrection, there were over 500 believers in Galilee. And when the church was founded on the Day of Pentecost, 3,000 believed on Him. At His ascension, He was received up into glory and seated at the right hand of the Father. So you have in that one verse a summation of the wonderful life of Jesus.

 ## WEEK 9

All Scripture is inspired by God and profitable for teaching, for reproof, for correction, for training in righteousness; so that the man of God may be adequate, equipped for every good work.—2 TIMOTHY 3:16-17, page 1084

If we ever hope to become spiritually strong and to do good works that glorify God, it all starts with teaching that confronts our sin and wrong thinking and then instructs us on how to walk in a righteous path. We find the truth that eliminates error, that brings truth and correct belief, and sets us in the path to righteousness in "all Scripture." All Scripture is given by inspiration of God and is profitable for that. Scripture brings us the sound teaching, the divine instruction that tears down what is wrong, builds up what is right, and puts us in the path of instruction to live a righteous life so that we can become mature and equipped to do the works that honor God. All Scripture is given by inspiration of God. It is, in the Greek, "God-breathed." Scripture is literally "out of the mouth of God." When you read the Bible, you are reading the very Word of God. God breathed it out; men wrote it down. And it is that powerful, living Word of God that brings to us the truth that equips us for every good work.

WEEK 10

The law of the LORD is perfect, restoring the soul; the testimony of the LORD is sure, making wise the simple. The precepts of the LORD are right, rejoicing the heart; the commandment of the LORD is pure, enlightening the eyes. The fear of the LORD is clean, enduring forever; the judgments of the LORD are true; they are righteous altogether.—PSALM 19:7-9, page 125

These verses contain six titles about the Scripture. As the law of the Lord, it is God's standard for man's conduct. As the testimony of the Lord, Scripture is God's self-disclosure that describes who He is. As the statutes of the Lord, it is the doctrines and principles the Lord wants us to know. As the commandment of the Lord, it is the binding and authoritative mandate God gives to us. As the fear of the Lord, it is a manual on appropriately fearing and worshiping God. And as the judgments of the Lord, the Scripture provides for us the verdicts of God Himself.

These verses also tell us that Scripture is perfect and totally transforms the inner person. It is sure and reliable and makes the simple wise. It is right, meaning a right path as opposed to a wrong path, and brings joys to the heart. It is pure or translucent and makes things clear; even the dark things become understandable. It is clean—without flaw or blemish—and is not subject to cultural interpretation because it is everlasting. And it is true, absolutely righteous. What an amazing Book!

WEEK 11

For by grace you have been saved through faith; and that not of yourselves, it is the gift of God; not as a result of works, so that no one may boast.—EPHESIANS 2:8-9, page 970

These verses gather together all of the elements necessary to understand the work of salvation. It is by grace…through faith… the gift of God, not of works, so that we have no reason to be proud about some achievement. In fact, the only way to be saved is by grace, and grace means "unmerited favor." God graciously saves us. It isn't because we have earned, deserved, or achieved it. In fact, Paul tells us that our salvation is "that not of yourselves." "That" refers to the entire previous statement of salvation—not only the grace, but the faith. Although we are required to believe for salvation, we are also dead in trespasses and sins, so we can't believe. It's impossible for us to do that. Therefore, it isn't just the grace that comes from God; it is also the faith. The whole work of salvation is a miracle of God. We receive the Lord Jesus Christ, but it is God who awakens us and gives us the power and the understanding and the faith to do just that. None of us can boast about any of it. God's grace is preeminent in every aspect of salvation.

WEEK 12

When you were dead in your transgressions and the uncircumcision of your flesh, He made you alive together with Him, having forgiven us all our transgressions, having canceled out the certificate of debt consisting of decrees against us, which was hostile to us; and He has taken it out of the way, having nailed it to the cross.—COLOSSIANS 2:13-14, page 1016

The language of these verses picks up on the legal concepts in the ancient world. When a person was crucified, the list of their crimes was nailed to the cross to demonstrate to everyone the reason they were there. With that imagery, the apostle Paul says the indictment against us as sinners, the handwriting of the laws we had broken, was taken and nailed to a cross. But we didn't have to die for them because Jesus was nailed there under our sins.

We were dead in sins. We were without cleansing. But we've been forgiven all our trespasses. We've been taken out of death and made alive because Jesus was nailed under our sins. He paid the penalty. Our crimes have been nailed to the cross so that the whole world could see the violations are placed on Jesus Christ, the sinless One, who satisfies the just wrath of God for us. And this is why there are so many songs and hymns written about the cross, because we can never stop singing its praises.

WEEK 13

Go therefore and make disciples of all the nations, baptizing them in the name of the Father and the Son and the Holy Spirit, teaching them to observe all that I commanded you; and lo, I am with you always, even to the end of the age.—MATTHEW 28:19-20, page 161

If you ever wondered what our responsibility is in the world, here is the answer. Go and make disciples of all nations. Jesus said that to the apostles, but the Great Commission extends to all of us. We are to make disciples of Christ from all the nations. In fact, in the Greek the only verb here is "make disciples." The rest of the verb forms are participles that modify the main verb. Going, baptizing, and teaching are components of making disciples. And you're not alone in this enterprise. "Lo, I am with you always, even to the end of the age." Until the time is completely done for evangelism, Jesus is with you helping you to do so. This is our commission and the reason God leaves us here on earth—to bring people to Christ from all the nations by going, baptizing, and then teaching them so that they can observe everything the Lord commanded. Make sure you're involved in this joyous duty.

WEEK 14

This book of the law shall not depart from your mouth, but you shall meditate on it day and night, so that you may be careful to do according to all that is written in it; for then you will make your way prosperous, and then you will have success.—JOSHUA 1:8, page 328

In the case of Joshua, the "book of the law" specifically referred to Genesis through

Deuteronomy as written by Moses. But it can be expanded, of course, to refer to all the Word of God. And it says that it should not depart from your mouth. You should be speaking the words of Scripture at all times. That will happen when you meditate in it day and night. It's a simple principle, isn't it? You saturate your mind and thoughts with the Word of God, and it comes out in your speech. When you're filled with the Word of God, that's what's going to come out of your mouth.

The verse also says that the purpose for this meditation is that you may observe to do according to all that is written in it. And that's what will happen. As you meditate or feed on the Word of God, it nourishes and shapes you as a person. It says that if you meditate, speak the Word, live the Word, you'll make your way prosperous and you'll have good success. The promise of God is a blessing on your spiritual effort and spiritual enterprise through the deep understanding and the application of Scripture.

WEEK 15

Therefore do not let sin reign in your mortal body so that you obey its lusts, and do not go on presenting the members of your body to sin as instruments of unrighteousness; but present yourselves to God as those alive from the dead, and your members as instruments of righteousness to God.—ROMANS 6:12–13, page 776

These verses speak about our physical body. Paul tells us that the only remaining repository where sin finds the believer vulnerable is in our humanness. It is physical, but it is also mental, because it mentions lusts. When you come to Christ, you are made a new creation. You are given a new nature with new desires, and you long to do what's right. The pattern of sin is broken, and you are no longer under the dominion of sin. But your new nature is still incarcerated in fallen humanness. That's going to be that way until we leave this world.

For all the wonders I'm looking forward to in heaven, what appeals most to me is the absence of sin. I hate the fact that there is residual sin in my life now. The appeal of heaven is to end the internal war with sin. But in the meantime, we're commanded to not let sin take over. Don't present your members as instruments of unrighteousness. Keep presenting yourself to God. Your members are instruments of righteousness to God. Fill your mind with biblical truth. And make sure that you stay in the presence of God so that His power and truth lead you to present yourself as an instrument of righteousness.

WEEK 16

And He was saying to them all, "If anyone wishes to come after Me, he must deny himself, and take up his cross daily and follow Me. For whoever wishes to save his life will lose it, but whoever loses his life for My sake, he is the one who will save it."—LUKE 9:23–24, page 82

With these words, Jesus clearly states the cost of following Him. This was Jesus' invitation to the crowd to follow Him; and the price, supreme. "If you want to come after Me, deny yourself." It's the end of you—your dreams, hopes, ambitions, goals. The gospel is not about self-fulfillment; it's about self-denial. In the Greek, the statement "deny himself" basically means "to refuse to associate with." That means that you're coming to Christ because you refuse to any longer associate with the person that you are. You're sick of yourself and your sin, and with desperation you willingly yield up that empty life you no longer want to associate with. You lose your life to gain it.

How extreme is this commitment? It involves taking up your cross daily. In the ancient world, the cross only meant one thing—a painful, horrible, shameful death. Jesus was saying, "If you want to follow Me, it's the end of you and not just your hopes and dreams. It may even cost you your physical life. But the infinite value of following Me is worth the high cost, because if you do lose your life for My sake, you'll save it forever." Ask yourself if you're truly following Jesus.

WEEK 17

For while we were still helpless, at the right time Christ died for the ungodly. For one will hardly die for a righteous man; though perhaps for the good man someone would dare even to die. But God demonstrates His own love toward us, in that while we were yet sinners, Christ died for us.—ROMANS 5:6–8, page 773

It's a powerful truth, isn't it? People rarely die for other people. Occasionally we read about someone giving his life for someone else. It's rare, even for the best of men, that someone would actually die on their behalf. It's notable when it happens. It is also true that sometimes for a good man someone will dare to die. But have you ever heard of anybody willing to die for a wicked, vile, evil man? That doesn't happen...unless you're Jesus Christ.

And what kind of love is it that causes Christ to die for the worst of us? That's the wonder of the love of God demonstrated toward us. Christ died for us. Christ died for the "ungodly." What a statement! It wasn't based on how worthy we were, how lovable we were, how godly we were. He died for the unworthy, the weak, the perverse. You can't say it any more directly than He died for the ungodly—not the righteous, not the good. He died for sinners, and He did it because of His love toward us. A love we didn't deserve produced a sacrifice we didn't deserve. But that's what grace does, and I hope you're overwhelmed with gratitude.

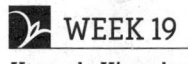

WEEK 18

Knowing that you were not redeemed with perishable things like silver or gold from your futile way of life inherited from your forefathers, but with precious blood, as of a lamb unblemished and spotless, the blood of Christ.—1 PETER 1:18–19, page 1183

Being redeemed is a tremendous concept. Redemption was a technical term for money paid to buy back a prisoner of war. It has the idea of paying a ransom to set someone free. We needed to be redeemed from the useless, aimless life passed down by tradition from our fathers. We needed to be rescued from that because the way of the world is the way of death and judgment.

We are redeemed by the precious blood of Christ. He alone was the acceptable sacrifice to God who paid the price for our sins. And He is pictured as a Lamb without blemish and without spot because throughout the Old Testament the whole sacrificial system of animals being offered as sin offerings to God all looked forward to the coming of the Lord Jesus Christ, who would be the final lamb. Which is why very soon after His death the city of Jerusalem was destroyed by the Romans in 70 A.D., and with that destruction, the entire sacrificial system came to an end. To this day there has never been a temple or a place for sacrifice, and none is needed because Jesus was the final sacrifice.

WEEK 19

He made Him who knew no sin to be sin on our behalf, so that we might become the righteousness of God in Him.—2 CORINTHIANS 5:21, page 907

The fifteen words in the original Greek in this verse express the doctrine of substitution like no other single verse in the Bible. God made the only person who knew no sin, the Lord Jesus Christ, to be sin for us. Some people mistakenly think this means that Jesus became a sinner—that, on the cross, He actually was punished because He was a sinner. The truth is that, on the cross, Jesus was as holy as He ever was in the eternity before or the eternity after. On the cross, God treated Jesus as if He had personally committed every sin ever committed by every person who would ever believe, though, in fact, He committed none of them. God put the punishment for our sins on the sinless Son.

The rest of the verse says that "we might become the righteousness of God in Him." That's the other side of substitution. God treated Jesus as a sinner so that He could treat us as if we were righteous. He was not a sinner, and we're not righteous. That's substitution. He fulfilled all righteousness so that His sinless life could be credited to your account. Pretty amazing, isn't it? On the cross, God treats Jesus as if He lived your life so that He can treat you as if you lived His life. That is the heart of the gospel.

WEEK 20

Blessed be the God and Father of our Lord Jesus Christ, who according to His great mercy has caused us to be born again to a living hope through the resurrection of Jesus Christ from the dead, to obtain an inheritance which is imperishable and undefiled and will not fade away, reserved in heaven for you.—1 PETER 1:3–4, page 1182

Throughout the Old Testament, God has a number of names. In the New Testament, He is most notably "the God and Father of our Lord Jesus Christ." He shares the same spiritual and eternal life, the same essential nature as Jesus Christ. He has begotten us again to a living hope as we put our trust in Jesus Christ. But everything that God has planned for those who belong to Him is not yet ours. And so we live in hope, a living hope of eternal life, because Christ rose from the dead. So we live by faith. We live today in the midst of God's blessings being poured out upon us, but there is a glorious reality yet ahead of us.

And then Peter adds that we have an inheritance that is incorruptible—not subject to termination, undefiled. It's not subject to any defect or tampering or fading away. But, rather, it is reserved intact in all its fullness, all its purity, all its glory in heaven for us. And so we not only enjoy what the Lord has done for us now, but we have our hope fixed on the day when the inheritance becomes a reality when we enter heaven.

WEEK 21

But the fruit of the Spirit is love, joy, peace, patience, kindness, goodness, faithfulness, gentleness, self-control; against such things there is no law.—GALATIANS 5:22–23, page 962

This scripture tells us that when the Holy Spirit is in full control of your life, this is what you're going to be like. These nine characteristics are interlinked, and the fruit produced is this package. It's like a tree that bears nine different kinds of fruit. If we are walking in the Spirit, there will be *agape* love, which is the love of the will. It's not the love of emotion or physical attraction or a family bond. It's the love of willful self-sacrifice. And there will be a deep-down satisfaction of joy and an inner calm of peace that results from the Spirit of God superintending everything. There will be the longsuffering or the patience to endure irritation and difficulty, and a kindness or tender concern toward others. There will be goodness, moral and spiritual excellence. There will be faithfulness, loyalty, and trustworthiness. And there will be gentleness or humility and self-control, the restraining of passions.

Paul adds that "against such things there is no law." Even if you had an external law, you couldn't force somebody to have this kind of character. You can't use the law to produce this. This fruit only flows up from within by the ministry of the Holy Spirit. And so how grateful should we be for that wonder-working Spirit, and how eager should we be to manifest that fruit as we walk in obedience to His revealed Word!

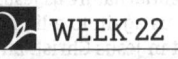

WEEK 22

Therefore, putting aside all malice and all deceit and hypocrisy and envy and all slander, like newborn babies, long for the pure milk of the word, so that by it you may grow in respect to salvation.—1 PETER 2:1–2, page 1186

Spiritual growth happens when you desire the pure milk of the Word like a newborn baby desires milk. A baby basically desires milk, and that's it. Frankly, they don't care about much of anything except milk. It's that singularity of life that's so remarkable and so unique.

As a baby grows older, life gets more complicated. It's not just milk anymore; it's not just food anymore. But Peter is saying that if you want to grow, you need to set aside everything else. You need to set aside all malice or evil, and anything that's deceitful. Set aside any hypocrisy, envy, any evil speaking. Strip yourself of all those things that are wrong and focus on one thing—the pure milk of the Word.

That's the challenge. If you want to grow strong in the faith, you need to be singularly focused on desiring the pure milk of the Word. Every time you have an opportunity to drink that milk, you should rush to be satisfied. That's how you'll grow.

WEEK 23

Trust in the LORD with all your heart and do not lean on your own understanding. In all your ways acknowledge Him, and He will make your paths straight.—PROVERBS 3:5–6, page 33

These verses get to the core of Christian living. Can you trust the Lord fully? "With all your heart" means with everything. No matter what comes—good, bad, or indifferent; no matter what the pain or suffering; no matter what the trial or disappointment, can you trust the Lord wholeheartedly? The alternative is to lean on your own understanding, which is to interpret everything from your perspective.

You need to remember this: God loves you, and His promise is that in all things He is working together for your good. You have to trust Him for that. Don't lean on your own understanding and trust your own interpretation. Consider the life of Job. He lost all his children, possessions, health, and his wife and friends failed him. But after all Job's questions and suffering, when he finally encounters God, he can only say, "I have heard of You by the hearing of the ear, but now my eye sees You. Therefore I…repent." It all came down to simply trusting in God and His goodness.

Don't lean on your own interpretation of the things that go on in life. Always trust the Lord. In everything acknowledge Him. He'll open up a path you never even expected. This is His promise.

WEEK 24

Beloved, now we are children of God, and it has not appeared as yet what we will be. We know that when He appears, we will be like Him, because we will see Him just as He is.

And everyone who has this hope fixed on Him purifies himself, just as He is pure.—1 JOHN 3:2-3, page 1221

Right now, if you believe in Jesus Christ, you are a child of God. But it hasn't been revealed what we shall be. We're sort of hidden at this time. But there's coming a day, the glorious manifestation of the children of God (Ro 8:21), when the whole world is going to find out who we really are. And when that happens, we're going to be like Him, for we shall see Him as He is. This incredible promise is our hope. Someday we're going to be like Jesus Christ. We'll not only experience it, but everyone will see it and the truth will then be revealed that we are the children of God.

If you live in the anticipation of the coming of Christ, it changes the way you live. How should it alter the way we live when we anticipate the imminent return of Jesus Christ? He could come at any time. But the fact that we know He's coming, and He is perfectly pure, and that when He does come, He's going to make us like Himself, that should be a marvelous motivation for our own purity. Make sure that when He does come, He finds you living in a pure way.

WEEK 25

Now to Him who is able to keep you from stumbling, and to make you stand in the presence of His glory blameless with great joy, to the only God our Savior, through Jesus Christ our Lord, be glory, majesty, dominion and authority, before all time and now and forever. Amen.—JUDE VV. 24-25, page 1237

These verses are a doxology or benediction. There are many of them scattered throughout the Bible. A doxology is simply a praise to God. It is a pronunciation of blessing. And when we praise God and think about the immensity of blessing that comes from Him, nothing is more wonderful than this thought: God is able to keep you from stumbling and to present you faultless before the presence of His glory with exceeding joy. It means God is not going to lose you or let go of you. You're never going to stumble and fall to the temptation of abandoning the faith, to deny Christ. He will keep you from that.

How can He do that? Well, one day when He does present you to Himself in the presence of His glory, your fallen humanness will have disappeared, and you will be brought into His glorious presence absolutely faultless. You will literally be made a perfectly holy person, and no wonder there will be exceeding joy.

The promise of God is that, if you are Christ's, He will keep you. Everyone the Father gives to Christ, Christ receives and keeps and raises to eternal glory. And so we praise our God for His keeping power.

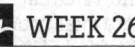 WEEK 26

By this the love of God was manifested in us, that God has sent His only begotten Son into the world so that we might live through Him. In this is love, not that we loved God, but that He loved us and sent His Son to be the propitiation for our sins.—1 JOHN 4:9-10, page 1224

The word "propitiation" means "satisfaction." That is essentially what Jesus came to do, to be a satisfaction for our sins. Who had to be satisfied? God had to be satisfied. After all, sin is a violation of the holy Law of God. Sin is a violation of God. It is an act of treachery against Him. God, then, if He is to forgive the sinner, must have that violation and that justice satisfied. Jesus comes to be that satisfaction. God was perfectly satisfied in His Son. Do you remember that the Father said at the baptism of Jesus, "This is My beloved Son, in whom I am well pleased"? He said the same thing again at the Transfiguration. The Father was perfectly satisfied with His Son so that His Son could be the perfect satisfaction for our sins.

How satisfied are you with Jesus? That's such an important question and such a basic spiritual reality. The Father is perfectly satisfied with the Son; the Son is perfectly satisfied with the Father. And how about you? Are you perfectly satisfied with Jesus Christ? Is He your purest and truest satisfaction? Do you find your highest joy in Him? If you do, it's going to have an impact on how you live your life. God is most pleased with us when we are most satisfied with His Son.

WEEK 27

For God so loved the world, that He gave His only begotten Son, that whoever believes in Him shall not perish, but have eternal life. For God did not send the Son into the world to judge the world, but that the world might be saved through Him.—JOHN 3:16-17, page 465

At the very heart of the message of God to us is a way to escape perishing. To "perish" connotes everlasting destruction, divine judgment and wrath, horrible punishment. Jesus said more about hell than He did about heaven. He talked about a fire never quenched, about a place where people experience permanent gnashing of teeth, loneliness, darkness, weeping, and wailing. That's perishing.

But God so loved the world that He sent His Son so that we don't have to perish, but we can have everlasting life. And that's not just a quantity of life; that's a quality of life. It isn't this temporal life; this kind of life forever. That would be a kind of hell in itself. It's another kind of life. God will give us eternal life, and that's why we have the word "saved" used here. It's the word "rescued." We are rescued from perishing and given not only a life different from this life, but a life also very different from the life of perishing. We are given everlasting life. It is God's kind of life. We literally participate in the bliss of divine immortality, the very life that belongs to God Himself. God gives us His own life, the very life that exists within His being and the being of the Son and the Holy Spirit. Rejoice always that you have been rescued by the love of God.

WEEK 28

Do not love the world nor the things in the world. If anyone loves the world, the love of the Father is not in him. For all that is in the world, the lust of the flesh and the lust of the eyes and the boastful pride of life, is not from the Father, but is from the world. The world is passing away, and also its lusts; but the one who does the will of God lives forever.
—1 JOHN 2:15-17, page 1218

So what is the "world"? John is saying: "Don't love the invisible spiritual system of evil dominated by Satan, because if you love that, the love of the Father is not in you." The "world" is that evil system that appeals to our passions, our vision, and our pride. The world comes at our self-centeredness. I want what I want. I want to fulfill my lust, my passion. I want what I can see, what I covet, and I want what I want for my own personal benefit and self-aggrandizement. That's pride. That's what the world is all about.

But that's not of the Father, and so as believers we don't love that. We are tempted by it, and sometimes we fall into sin. But when we do, we hate that sin. And that's because it's part of the passing world. We are those, rather, who are motivated and characterized by doing the will of God, and, therefore, we abide forever. Not because we do the will of God, but because as we do the will of God, it is manifest that we are His and are the possessors of eternal life.

WEEK 29

Be diligent to present yourself approved to God as a workman who does not need to be ashamed, accurately handling the word of truth.—2 TIMOTHY 2:15, page 1081

Christians desire to have God pleased with their lives. Certainly, you want to please the One who gave His Son for you. You want to please the One who loves you and promises to bless you and will someday give you an eternal reward and welcome you into His presence. Wanting to please God is just part of being a Christian.

But how do you present yourself to God for approval? Well, you have to be a worker who doesn't need to be ashamed. And the key to that is really important: Rightly dividing the word of truth. If I want God to approve my work, I need to rightly divide the word of truth or Scripture—all of it. To "rightly divide" means to "cut it straight." It refers to preciseness, exactness. For instance, if you were a leather worker such as Paul, cutting hides and making tents, you had to cut according to a pattern and sew the pattern together so that the tent was the way it should be. Precision and accuracy is the idea.

So if you want a life approved by God, and you want to be a worker who doesn't need to be ashamed, then heed these words: Handle accurately the Word of God in how you interpret and apply it.

WEEK 30

Instructing us to deny ungodliness and worldly desires and to live sensibly, righteously and godly in the present age, looking for the blessed hope and the appearing of the glory of our great God and Savior, Christ Jesus.—TITUS 2:12-13, page 1100

The Bible continually calls on us to live in the light of the return of Jesus Christ. He is coming, and we should love His appearing. No matter how much we may enjoy our lives, the fact is that the world at its best is far, far short of what heaven is going to be. Never become so involved in this world that heaven doesn't interest you anymore, because what God has prepared for us is infinitely beyond the best this life can offer.

But let's go beyond you. How long is Jesus Christ to endure the hostilities and hatred of this world, the demeaning, the denial of glory, the blasphemy of His name. How long must God the Father be blasphemed and maligned? How long does Satan run rampant over this planet doing everything he can to hinder God's work? How long should the Holy Spirit be grieved and quenched?

When you think about the Second Coming, the lofty thoughts are not just about you and me and heaven. It is longing for the final honoring of Jesus Christ and for the glorious appearing of our great God and Savior. Not just for my sake and what I'll receive, but for His.

 WEEK 31

O God, You are my God; I shall seek You earnestly; my soul thirsts for You, my flesh yearns for You, in a dry and weary land where there is no water. Thus I have seen You in the sanctuary, to see Your power and Your glory. Because Your lovingkindness is better than life, my lips will praise You.—PSALM 63:1–3, page 475

This is the heart of a true believer. This is the panting heart, the thirsty heart that can only be satisfied by the presence and the power of God. This is all about a pure desire for God. The psalmist rises in the morning, and the first thing he wants is God. His soul is thirsty. He's like a wanderer in the desert who longs for water. In fact, David wrote this psalm while hiding in the wilderness, but longing to be back worshiping in Jerusalem. What did he want to see? God's power manifest in his life. He wanted to experience God's lovingkindness and mercy.

God had a relationship with David, but here we find that David had a relationship with God, and God was the priority of his life. That's the way it should be for every believer. Right now, is God your deepest desire? "Oh, God, it's You I want in my life. I feel dry and thirsty. I need Your power, Your glory, Your lovingkindness. It's better to me than to live, and I want to praise You." Cultivate that by being in the Word of God. Read through the Psalms and find out the greatness of your God.

WEEK 32

And He has said to me, "My grace is sufficient for you, for power is perfected in weakness." Most gladly, therefore, I will rather boast about my weaknesses, so that the power of Christ may dwell in me. Therefore I am well content with weaknesses, with insults, with distresses, with persecutions, with difficulties, for Christ's sake; for when I am weak, then I am strong.
—2 CORINTHIANS 12:9–10, page 937

Some people read the apostle Paul's testimony here and think it sounds like a death wish. Why in the world does he say this? He says it because, despite all these painful experiences in his life, God has a purpose in it. God spoke to Paul's heart and said, "My grace is sufficient for you." God was saying that every difficult time, every weakness, reproach, need, persecution, and distress is an opportunity for Him to manifest sufficient grace. But you won't get the grace until you get there. And when you do, His strength is perfected in your weakness. When you go through these kinds of trials, you become dependent on Him.

What do you believe in God for that only He can do, so that when He does it, He gets all the credit? There are issues in life, such as the suffering Paul was enduring, that only God can alter, and when He does, you know He did it. Suffering, then, is a way for God to display His grace and power. Embrace weakness. No one is too weak to be powerful. Embrace the suffering and see the grace and strength of God perfected in it.

WEEK 33

The Lord is my shepherd, I shall not want. He makes me lie down in green pastures; He leads me beside quiet waters. He restores my soul; He guides me in the paths of righteousness for His name's sake. Even though I walk through the valley of the shadow of death, I fear no evil, for You are with me; Your rod and Your staff, they comfort me. You prepare a table before me in the presence of my enemies; You have anointed my head with oil; my cup overflows. Surely goodness and lovingkindness will follow me all the days of my life, and I will dwell in the house of the Lord forever.—PSALM 23, page 157

"Even though I walk through the valley of the shadow of death, I fear no evil." Sheep need to be fed. They need still water because they can't drink rushing water. They need to be led in safe places. And they need to be protected when they're in the shadow of death, which brings up a wonderful spiritual reality. We don't ever walk through the valley of death; we walk through the valley of the shadow of death. Think of it this way. As the sun is setting and a huge semi-truck sweeps past your car and casts its shadow over you, it is only the shadow running over you, not the truck itself. And so we fear no evil in the shadow of death. Death is but a harmless shadow for the sheep of the Good Shepherd. He takes care of us. He feeds us. He puts oil on our wounds. His goodness and mercy are available all the days of our life, and He will bring us into His eternal house forever.

🐾 WEEK 34

That if you confess with your mouth Jesus as Lord, and believe in your heart that God raised Him from the dead, you will be saved; for with the heart a person believes, resulting in righteousness, and with the mouth he confesses, resulting in salvation.—ROMANS 10:9-10, page 795

It is not enough to simply acknowledge that Jesus is God. The demons acknowledge that and tremble (Jas 2:19), but that doesn't save them. To confess with your mouth the Lord Jesus means that you hold the deep personal conviction that Jesus is your master, without reservation. It's not about letting Jesus in your life to make you more successful or your marriage better. It's about you coming before Jesus and beating your breast and saying, "God, be merciful to me, a sinner!" It's about you saying, "Jesus, I acknowledge You as my master and Lord, and I submit to whatever You desire."

The second aspect is to believe in your heart that Jesus died on the cross and rose from the dead and all that the Resurrection implies. You affirm both the deity and the sovereignty of Christ, His sinless life, substitutionary death, and literal bodily resurrection. You believe in your heart that God the Father put the stamp of divine approval on the perfect work of Jesus Christ. And you confess openly with your mouth unto salvation. And Jesus says, "Everyone who confesses Me before men, I will also confess him before My Father" (Mt 10:32).

🐾 WEEK 35

Let your light shine before men in such a way that they may see your good works, and glorify your Father who is in heaven.—MATTHEW 5:16, page 15

A German historian once said to a Christian, "Show me your redeemed life, and I might be inclined to be believe in your Redeemer." That's a pretty straightforward approach, isn't it? If I'm trying to tell you how great my doctor is, and I'm dying under his care, you might question his skill. This is something of the principle that's behind this verse. What good does it do to tell people how great our Savior is when they can't see the manifestation of His power in our lives? We must let the light shine.

What is "light" in the New Testament? Essentially, "light" means "eternal life." It's the life of God in us. It's the indwelling Christ, the indwelling Holy Spirit. In other words, "Let Christ shine through your life—the words you

say, your attitudes, the things you do." And when people see that, they're going to say you do have a great Savior. You do have a great Father in heaven. A godly life lays the platform down on which individual testimony becomes convincing.

On the other hand, it's so sad for somebody to proclaim Jesus Christ as Savior and then live a sinful life. Not only does it dishonor Christ, but it's ineffective in terms of convincing anyone else of the power of Jesus Christ. As witnesses, our responsibility is to tell the world that Jesus Christ can transform lives. That's only believable if they see a transformed life.

🐾 WEEK 36

I have been crucified with Christ; and it is no longer I who live, but Christ lives in me; and the life which I now live in the flesh I live by faith in the Son of God, who loved me and gave Himself up for me.—GALATIANS 2:20, page 948

To be "crucified with Christ" is a historical event that looks back at the cross. Literally, you and I, who believe in Jesus, were there at the cross as He bore our sins. Which is why Paul says we were buried with Him into death and rose with Him in newness of life (Ro 6). We were there. God literally placed us there even though we hadn't been born. Everybody who ever believed the truth of God, all the way back through the whole Old Testament, was there in Christ at His death. It's a glorious reality. You were there. Your sins were paid for. That's why you're not under condemnation.

Now we live this new life, and Paul says, "It's not really I who live it; it's Christ who lives in me." This is the glory of the mystery of Christ in us. Either you live this new life or you don't. Yet Paul says, "I live it, but Christ lives it." It takes all of us, but it's all of Him. Our old life is dead. We have a new life in Him. It takes all the discipline and obedience to live that life in the flesh by faith, and yet when it's all said and done, it's Christ Himself living in me.

🐾 WEEK 37

A new commandment I give to you, that you love one another, even as I have loved you, that you also love one another. By this all men will know that you are My disciples, if you have love for one another.—JOHN 13:34-35, page 549

Clearly, the mark of true Christianity is love for one another. This is the command of Christ to love, but it was not new. In the Book of

Deuteronomy, God commanded that we love Him and our neighbors. Yet Jesus' command regarding love presented a distinctly new standard. He said, "Love...as I have loved you." He gave a new model for this love, which He exemplified when He washed the disciples' feet. It was a common courtesy in the ancient world to provide a servant to wash feet. It was the lowest job on the servant ladder, yet Jesus stooped to do whatever they needed.

While that was a magnanimous gesture, it didn't come close to the lowliness of the One who went to the cross to bear the wrath of God for the sins of His own. He stooped all the way down, took upon Himself the form of a servant, was made in the likeness of man, went all the way down to a shameful death on the cross. So consider what Jesus meant when He told His disciples to love one another the way He loved them—sacrificially, selflessly, all the way down to most menial task and to giving your life for someone else. If you live like this, the world is going to know you're a disciple of Christ.

WEEK 38

Come to Me, all who are weary and heavy-laden, and I will give you rest. Take My yoke upon Me and learn from Me, for I am gentle and humble in heart, and you will find rest for your souls. For My yoke is easy and My burden is light.—MATTHEW 11:28-30, page 51

These words of Jesus were wonderfully good news to the Jewish people. They were loaded down with a heavy burden of trying to earn their salvation by keeping the law and all the ordinances and traditions that had developed in Judaism. This was a weight no one could bear. And there are countless people who are still under that burden. While there may be many religions by name and description, there are only two religious systems. There is the truth of the gospel that salvation comes apart from works by faith alone through grace. And there is every other system, by whatever name, that says by religious ceremony, by moral deeds, and by good works you earn your way to heaven. It provides no peace and no rest because no one can be perfect.

Jesus came along and said, "Come to Me, and I'll give you rest. Instead of this horrendous yoke that has been imposed upon you, take My yoke. I'm gentle, I'm lowly in heart, and I'll give you rest because My yoke is easy and My burden is light." That is the wonderful promise of salvation by grace through faith.

WEEK 39

In My Father's house are many dwelling places; if it were not so, I would have told you; for I go to prepare a place for you. If I go and prepare a place for you, I will come again and receive you to Myself, that where I am, there you may be also.—JOHN 14:2-3, page 552

Jesus, that last night before His death, gave His disciples many promises, and none more wonderful than that He was leaving for the purpose of preparing a place for them in heaven and that He would be back to take them there. When Jesus said, "In my Father's house are many mansions," the actual original language puts it this way: "In My Father's house are many rooms, many rooms." There's only one house—the Father's house—with many rooms. I'm not living 15 blocks from the Father's house; I'm in it. And so are you. I'm going to go there to be with the Lord. He will dwell forever with His people, and I shall dwell in His house.

What is the Lord Jesus doing right now? He's in heaven. One of the things He's doing is getting it ready for His children, and someday He's coming to take us all to be there. That looks at the Rapture when Jesus comes and snatches away His redeemed to heaven where we'll celebrate the marriage supper of the Lamb and receive our eternal rewards and find our room in the Father's house. And we'll dwell there throughout all of eternity, enjoying all the things that God has prepared for those who love Him.

WEEK 40

Finally, brethren, whatever is true, whatever is honorable, whatever is right, whatever is pure, whatever is lovely, whatever is of good repute, if there is any excellence and if anything worthy of praise, dwell on these things.—PHILIPPIANS 4:8, page 1007

We are the product of what we take in. If we take garbage in, garbage will come out. But Jesus said: "It is not what enters into the mouth that defiles the man, but what proceeds out of the mouth, this defiles the man" (Mt 15:11). The real problem is what's in us. It's that fallen flesh. Sin doesn't come from the outside in; it comes from the inside out. This verse tells us there are all kinds of things outside that excite that sin inside.

Paul is saying, "Look, if you want to live a life that honors God, meditate on godliness." "Whatever is true" encompasses all the revelation of God. Truth is found in God, in Christ, in the Holy Spirit, in the Scripture. "Whatever is honorable" means to meditate on what is worthy of respect, what is sacred as opposed to the profane. "Whatever is right" means to measure it by the divine standard of holiness. "Whatever is pure" means morally clean. "Whatever is lovely" means amiable or pleasing. "Whatever is of good reputet" is whatever is kind and gracious and edifying. So if there is any value in virtue, and if there is any value in a life that is worthy of praise, meditate on these things. Make sure the focus of your life is directed toward these things, and you will enjoy the wonderful fruit of this kind of godly thinking.

 ## WEEK 41

These things I have spoken to you, so that in Me you may have peace. In the world you have tribulation, but take courage; I have overcome the world.—JOHN 16:33, page 561

Jesus said this to His beloved apostles in the Upper Room the night of His betrayal. He was going away, and they were going to be worried, fearful, anxious, troubled. Through that night He made promises to ease their troubled hearts. He even said, "Let not your heart be troubled." And He promised them love and the Holy Spirit and answered prayer and peace. He said to them, "There's no reason to be troubled. All that I've told you is so that you might have peace in your heart because you know the Holy Spirit is there. You have nothing to be anxious about. In the world, you will have tribulation." That word actually means "trouble." It comes from a word that means "pressure." "You will be squeezed tightly by the difficulties of this life, but in the midst of it, be of good cheer because in the end I've overcome the world." That is to say there's nothing the world can do to you that wins ultimately. Momentary pain, a momentary disappointment, but the world's opposition has been rendered null and void. And even though the world continues to attack the people of God, such attacks fall harmlessly, for Christ's victory has already accomplished a smashing defeat of the whole world system.

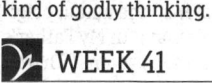 ## WEEK 42

Therefore I urge you, brethren, by the mercies of God, to present your bodies a living and holy sacrifice, acceptable to God, which is your spiritual service of worship. And do not be conformed to this world, but be transformed by the renewing of your mind, so that you may prove what the will of God is, that which is good and acceptable and perfect.—ROMANS 12:1-2, page 804

The goal of these two verses is to live a life that pleases God, a life in the center of God's will. How do you do that? By being transformed through the renewing of your mind. This principle is all through Scripture. Transformation occurs as the Holy Spirit changes your thinking. As you meditate on the Word of God, it takes root in your heart and shapes your thinking. You have to have a mind transformed by the renewing of biblical truth.

Don't let yourself think and act according to the system of beliefs and values around you. You cannot allow yourself to be shaped by the spirit of the age. And the key to all of that is to present yourself as a living sacrifice to God. Paul is saying you need to get up on the altar and hold back nothing. And you're going to have to stay there, because we have a habit of crawling back off again. Get up on that altar, offer yourself to God as your act of reasonable or logical or spiritual worship. Paul says, "I beseech you to do that." And he bases it all on the mercies of God which are yours in Christ. He's been good to you. Do this in return.

WEEK 43

Therefore, my beloved brethren, be steadfast, immovable, always abounding in the work of the Lord, knowing that your toil is not in vain in the Lord.—1 CORINTHIANS 15:58, page 885

We live in a capitalistic system, and we understand the principle of rewarding people for their work. It's very different from the communist world, where there are no rewards to motivate people. Fortunately, our Lord isn't like that. Whatever you do in His name will receive an appropriate reward. You can count on that. God makes His promise that if you're abounding in the work of the Lord—in other words, if you're going over the top in serving the Lord—your labor is not in vain in the Lord. No work done in His name is wasted, no work done in His name is ever unaccounted for, and all work done in His name is appropriately rewarded. That's His promise.

And what is that reward? It might not be money or acknowledgment here, but there will be acknowledgment in the time of rewards when we stand before the Lord and He rewards every man according to his work. So serve the Lord with all your heart and know that He's keeping a record of your faithfulness, and you'll enjoy His loving reward when you see Him face-to-face.

WEEK 44

How blessed is the man who does not walk in the counsel of the wicked, nor stand in the path of sinners, nor sit in the seat of scoffers! But his delight is in the law of the LORD, and in His law he meditates day and night. —PSALM 1:1–2, page 2

This is a promise for spiritual well-being—for deep-seated heart-blessing contentment, peace, and joy that's below the surface of circumstances. If you want to be blessed like that, the psalmist says, don't walk in the counsel of the ungodly. Don't listen to their spin, their solution, their assessment, their evaluation. Don't even walk with them, and don't stop and stand in the path of sinners. Don't even engage yourself with them casually, and don't let that conversation become deeper and more penetrating. And don't sit in the seat of the scornful. Don't take your seat in their classroom while they scoff at divine truth.

You want to be blessed? Then find your delight in the law of the Lord. Walk in the counsel of the godly. Stand in the path of the righteous. Sit in the seat of the holy. You want to give your life to the law of the Lord so that rather than ungodly, sinful, scornful ideas permeating your thoughts day and night, you're literally filled with the law of God. Meditate on it. Let it grip your heart. Find your delight in the law of the Lord and let that be the content of your thought day and night. This is the path to blessing.

WEEK 45

For I am convinced that neither death, nor life, nor angels, nor principalities, nor things present, nor things to come, nor powers, nor height, nor depth, nor any other created thing, will be able to separate us from the love of God, which is in Christ Jesus our Lord. —ROMANS 8:38–39, page 786

This is one of those really monumental biblical passages. The apostle could have written that nothing can separate us from the love of God, but somebody would have said, "But what about this?" So Paul spoke in expansive terms of what could not separate us from God's love. "I am absolutely sure that neither the realm of death nor life, which covers all of existence, can do it. Nor angels, nor principalities, nor powers—all spirit beings, whether holy or unholy. Nor things present; nor things to come, which covers all of time, both now and in the future. And just in case that doesn't cover it, there's nothing all the way up into infinity, there's nothing all the way down into infinite depth, and there isn't any other created thing that can separate us from the love of God which is in Christ Jesus."

There is nothing in the created universe that can change your eternal relationship to God if you are in Christ Jesus our Lord. You can know this: the One who justified you, the One who sanctifies you, will one day glorify you. He will bring all His sons to glory. This is because God loves us with an everlasting love, and we are hidden with Christ in God's love.

WEEK 46

Who may ascend into the hill of the Lord? And who may stand in His holy place? He who has clean hands and a pure heart, who has not lifted up his soul to falsehood and has not sworn deceitfully. He shall receive a blessing from the Lord and righteousness from the God of his salvation. —PSALM 24:3–5, page 160

In the city of Jerusalem, the steps are still there that led up through the wall into the temple mount, the steps that even Jesus went up into the temple to worship. Here the people ascended "the holy hill." And as they went, it's likely the priests would ask the questions recorded in Psalm 24. "Who may ascend into the hill of the Lord? Who may stand in His holy place?" And the people antiphonally would give answers. "He who has clean hands and a pure heart, who has not lifted up his soul to falsehood and has not sworn deceitfully. He shall receive a blessing from the Lord and righteousness from the God of his salvation."

Today we have worship bands and worship leaders, but do we ever ask ourselves: Do I have a right to come rushing into the holy presence of God? Because the Lord inhabits the praise of His people, He is there. Do I have a right to ascend into His presence? Not unless I come with clean hands and a pure heart; not if there is any sin in my life. If there is impurity, you will not receive blessing from the Lord and the mercies of His righteousness. To enjoy the blessing that God wants to give, make sure your heart is right as you enter His presence.

WEEK 47

No temptation has overtaken you but such as is common to man; and God is faithful, who will not allow you to be tempted beyond what you are able, but with the temptation will provide the way of escape also, so that you will be able to endure it.—1 CORINTHIANS 10:13, page 855

Despite what you may have heard, temptation is not about demons. It's just about being human. No temptation is ever going to come to you that is superhuman. You don't need to go through life in horror and dread of some demonic invasion. If you are a believer, you are Christ's. Greater is He that is in you than he that is in the world. God is faithful. He will not allow you to be tempted beyond what you are able.

And for a new Christian, it's different than for an older Christian. Some temptations that are very difficult for brand-new Christians who are just coming out of the world aren't a problem for an older believer who has walked with the Lord for years. But God is eminently, personally involved in our lives, sheltering us from the overwhelming temptation. And He says there will always be a way of escape, that we may be able to endure it. There's a path, and very often the path in the midst of the temptation is very clear to us. It's the path of resistance. It's the path of obedience. It's the path of prayer, of divine petition asking God to lead us out.

WEEK 48

I waited patiently for the LORD; and He inclined to me and heard my cry. He brought me up out of the pit of destruction, out of the miry clay, and He set my feet upon a rock making my footsteps firm. He put a new song in my mouth, a song of praise to our God; many will see and fear and will trust in the LORD.—PSALM 40:1-3, page 317

The psalmist actually says that praise is an evangelistic tool. He says when I have a new song in my mouth and I am praising God, many will see that and fear and trust in the Lord. There is a tremendous impact made upon the sinner by a believer filled with praise. We have a new song of redemption. The psalmist said, "I was in a horrible pit. I was in the miry clay." The picture is of hopelessness and helplessness, and the Lord "heard my cry...set my feet upon a rock making my footsteps firm." That's a picture of salvation. And the response to that is a song of praise. And the more we sing it, and the louder we sing it, the more who hear it. Many will see our confidence and our joy and be drawn to Christ.

We don't often think about praise as an evangelistic tool, but it is. Those around us who are in the miry clay will see in our deliverance their own hope. Be filled with praise for what God has done for you, and that may draw someone to open their heart to see Him do it for them.

WEEK 49

The LORD'S lovingkindnesses indeed never cease, for His compassions never fail. They are new every morning; great is Your faithfulness.—LAMENTATIONS 3:22-23, page 1105

Jeremiah tells us that the Lord is merciful. Mercy means withholding what we deserve, not giving us the punishment we really have earned. And it is through the Lord's mercies that we are not consumed. We deserve judgment from God because we have broken His law, spurned His love, offended Him, and dishonored Him. Every time we sin we do that. We should be consumed by His justice, but His justice is tempered by mercy. And His mercy is based on His compassion.

Fortunately for us, His compassions fail not. They are new every morning. God never runs out of the supply, and every day is a new day. Isn't that wonderful? You get up and it's a new day, and you can expect all the compassions of God are available for that day. All the mercies of God are available for that day. Great is His faithfulness. The bedrock of God's mercy and compassion is His covenant. When He makes a promise, He keeps it, and He has promised us mercy and compassion if we believe in Him, and He will be faithful to His covenant.

WEEK 50

But we all, with unveiled face, beholding as in a mirror the glory of the Lord, are being transformed into the same image from glory to glory, just as from the Lord, the Spirit.—2 CORINTHIANS 3:18, page 901

Believers today, unlike the saints of the Old Testament, are able to behold the glory of the Lord in an unveiled way. Moses saw a portion of the glory of God when he was on the mountain, but the people never saw the unveiled face of the glory of God because that awaited the arrival of the Lord Jesus Christ. We have the unveiled glory of the Lord manifest in the face of Jesus Christ. And when I say "glory," I mean all the attributes of God. They're revealed to us in the Old Testament, but they are manifest alive to us in Jesus Christ, so that the glory of God shines more wonderfully in Christ than any other place.

And as we look at Him and see Him revealed in the New Testament, we are being transformed into the same image from one level of glory to the next by the Holy Spirit. This describes the dynamics of sanctification. As you see the wonder of Christ and are lost in the vision of Christ, you will be imperceptibly transformed into His image. This is spiritual growth and maturity. How do you move up to higher levels of manifesting holiness and righteousness? It's the work of the Spirit which He does as Jesus Christ becomes our consuming vision.

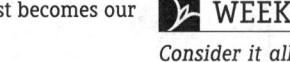

WEEK 51

So that you will prove yourselves to be blameless and innocent, children of God above reproach in the midst of a crooked and perverse generation, among whom you appear as lights in the world, holding fast the word of life, so that in the day of Christ I will have reason to glory because I did not run in vain nor toil in vain.—PHILIPPIANS 2:15-16, page 998

The "day of Christ" is the day we get to heaven and meet the Lord. What would make that a day of rejoicing for Paul is seeing the believers who were gathered together in the presence of the Lord and being rewarded because they had lived godly lives in the midst of a crooked and perverse generation, where they had faithfully been shining as lights in the world.

Paul said on another occasion to a group of believers, "You are my joy and crown of rejoicing. When I get to heaven, my joy is going to be in seeing you there and seeing you rewarded for your faithful service" (a paraphrase of 1Th 2:19). That's a wonderful eternal perspective. His only concern was to get into the presence of the Lord and know that his efforts had eternal consequences. That's why he wrote his letters, preached his gospel, and exhorted his churches. He wanted them to live blameless lives in the midst of what is a crooked, twisted, perverse world. And he wanted them to shine as lights in the world by holding forth the word of life, the word of Scripture. He wanted his people to live like that so that he could, with them, enjoy the eternal reward that the Lord would grant.

WEEK 52

Consider it all joy, my brethren, when you encounter various trials, knowing that the testing of your faith produces endurance. And let endurance have its perfect result, so that you may be perfect and complete, lacking in nothing.—JAMES 1:2-4, page 1164

As a Christian, I would like to be in a position where I'm lacking nothing. But spiritual perfection and maturity comes with pain. If there's going to be completeness, the only way to get there is through trials. You are strengthened by the development of spiritual endurance, and endurance is developed as you persevere through trouble. People say, "Lord, I want to be strong in the faith and bold for You." Get ready, because when the Lord answers that prayer, it's going to be the testing of your faith, taking you to the edge, that produces the endurance so critical to increasing spiritual strength.

I want to be all that God wants me to be for His glory and for my usefulness. I don't just grit my teeth and endure the trial. James says, "Consider it all joy." You can do that as you look past the trial to the goal, to the end, and that's where the joy comes from. The end of all our trials and all our suffering is our spiritual maturity. Here we are stronger than ever and less susceptible to besetting sins and debilitating temptations. I want that. I know you do, as well.

JANUARY 1

Genesis 1:1–2:25

1 In the beginning God created the heavens and the earth. ²The earth was formless and void, and darkness was over the surface of the deep, and the Spirit of God was moving over the surface of the waters. ³Then God said, "Let there be light"; and there was light. ⁴God saw that the light was good; and God separated the light from the darkness. ⁵God called the light day, and the darkness He called night. And there was evening and there was morning, one day.

1:5 one day. God established the pattern of creation in 7 days which constituted a complete week. "Day" can refer to: 1) the light portion of a 24-hour period (1:5, 14); 2) an extended period of time (2:4); or 3) the 24-hour period which basically refers to a full rotation of the earth on its axis, called evening and morning. "Day" with numerical adjectives in Hebrew always refers to a 24-hour period. The cycle of light and dark means that the earth was rotating on its axis, receiving light from a source on one side of the earth, even though the sun was not yet created (v. 16)

---

⁶Then God said, "Let there be an expanse in the midst of the waters, and let it separate the waters from the waters." ⁷God made the expanse, and separated the waters which were below the expanse from the waters which were above the expanse; and it was so. ⁸God called the expanse heaven. And there was evening and there was morning, a second day.

⁹Then God said, "Let the waters below the heavens be gathered into one place, and let the dry land appear"; and it was so. ¹⁰God called the dry land earth, and the gathering of the waters He called seas; and God saw that it was good. ¹¹Then God said, "Let the earth sprout vegetation, plants yielding seed, *and* fruit trees on the earth bearing fruit after their kind with seed in them"; and it was so. ¹²The earth brought forth vegetation, plants yielding seed after their kind, and trees bearing fruit with seed in them, after their kind; and God saw that it was good. ¹³There was evening and there was morning, a third day.

¹⁴Then God said, "Let there be lights in the expanse of the heavens to separate the day from the night, and let them be for signs and for seasons and for days and years; ¹⁵and let them be for lights in the expanse of the heavens to give light on the earth"; and it was so. ¹⁶God made the two great lights, the greater light to govern the day, and the lesser light to govern the night; *He made* the stars also. ¹⁷God placed them in the expanse of the heavens to give light on the earth, ¹⁸and to govern the day and the night, and to separate the light from the darkness; and God saw that it was good. ¹⁹There was evening and there was morning, a fourth day.

²⁰Then God said, "Let the waters teem with swarms of living creatures, and let birds fly above the earth in the open expanse of the heavens." ²¹God created the great sea monsters and every living creature that moves, with which the waters swarmed after their kind, and every winged bird after its kind; and God saw that it was good. ²²God blessed them, saying, "Be fruitful and multiply, and fill the waters in the seas, and let birds multiply on the earth." ²³There was evening and there was morning, a fifth day.

²⁴Then God said, "Let the earth bring forth living creatures after their kind: cattle and creeping things and beasts of the earth after their kind"; and it was so. ²⁵God made the beasts of the earth after their kind, and the cattle after their kind, and everything that creeps on the ground after its kind; and God saw that it was good.

²⁶Then God said, "Let Us make man in Our image, according to Our likeness; and let them rule over the fish of the sea and over the birds of the sky and over the cattle and over all the earth, and over every creeping thing that creeps on the earth." ²⁷God created man in His own image, in the image of God He created him; male and female He created them. ²⁸God blessed them; and God said to them, "Be fruitful and multiply, and fill the earth, and subdue it; and rule over the fish of the sea and over the birds of the sky and over every living thing that moves on the earth."

1:26 Us...Our. The first clear indication of the triunity of God. The very name of God, Elohim (1:1), is a plural form of El. **man.** The crowning point of creation, a living human, was made in God's image to rule creation. **Our image.** This defined man's unique relation to God. He was like God in that he could reason and had intellect, will, and emotion. When he was first created, he was like God because he was good and sinless.

---

²⁹Then God said, "Behold, I have given you every plant yielding seed that is on the surface of all the earth, and every tree which has fruit yielding seed; it shall be food for you; ³⁰and to every beast of the earth and to every bird of the sky and to every thing that moves on the earth which has life, *I have given* every green plant for food"; and it was so. ³¹God saw all that He had made, and behold, it was very good. And there was evening and there was morning, the sixth day.

2 Thus the heavens and the earth were completed, and all their hosts. ²By the seventh day God completed His work which He had done, and He rested on the seventh day from all His work which He had done. ³Then God blessed the seventh day and sanctified it, because in it He rested from all His work which God had created and made.

⁴This is the account of the heavens and the earth when they were created, in the day that the LORD God made earth and heaven. ⁵Now no shrub of the field was yet in the earth, and no plant of the field had yet sprouted, for the LORD God had not sent rain upon the earth, and there was no man to cultivate the ground. ⁶But a mist used to rise from the earth and water the whole surface of the ground. ⁷Then the LORD God formed man of dust from the ground, and breathed into his nostrils the breath of life; and man became a living being. ⁸The LORD God planted a garden toward the east, in Eden; and there He placed the man whom He had formed. ⁹Out of the ground the LORD God caused to grow every tree that is pleasing to the sight and good for food; the tree of life also in the midst of the garden, and the tree of the knowledge of good and evil.

¹⁰Now a river flowed out of Eden to water the garden; and from there it divided and became four rivers. ¹¹The name of the first is Pishon; it flows around the whole land of Havilah, where there is gold. ¹²The gold of that land is good; the bdellium and the onyx stone are there. ¹³The name of the second river is Gihon; it flows around the whole land of Cush. ¹⁴The name of the third river is Tigris; it flows east of Assyria. And the fourth river is the Euphrates.

¹⁵Then the LORD God took the man and put him into the garden of Eden to cultivate it and keep it. ¹⁶The LORD God commanded the man, saying, "From any tree of the garden you may eat freely; ¹⁷but from the tree of the knowledge of good and evil you shall not eat, for in the day that you eat from it you will surely die." ¹⁸Then the LORD God said, "It is not good for the man to be alone; I will make him a helper suitable for him." ¹⁹Out of the ground the LORD God formed every beast of the field and every bird of the sky, and brought *them* to the man to see what he would call them; and whatever the man called a living creature, that was its name. ²⁰The man gave names to all the cattle, and to the birds of the sky, and to every beast of the field, but for Adam there was not found a helper suitable for him. ²¹So the LORD God caused a deep sleep to fall upon the man, and he slept; then He took one of his ribs and closed up the flesh at that place. ²²The LORD God fashioned into a woman the rib which He had taken from the man, and brought her to the man. ²³The man said,

"This is now bone of my bones,
And flesh of my flesh;
She shall be called Woman,
Because she was taken out of Man."

²⁴For this reason a man shall leave his father and his mother, and be joined to his wife; and they shall become one flesh. ²⁵And the man and his wife were both naked and were not ashamed.

Psalm 1:1–6

The following expressions occur often in the Psalms:

Selah May mean *Pause, Crescendo* or *Musical Interlude*

Maskil Possibly, *Contemplative,* or *Didactic,* or *Skillful Psalm*

Mikhtam Possibly, *Epigrammatic Poem,* or *Atonement Psalm*

Sheol The nether world

How blessed is the man who does not walk in the counsel of the wicked,
Nor stand in the path of sinners,
Nor sit in the seat of scoffers!
2 But his delight is in the
   law of the LORD,
   And in His law he meditates
   day and night.
3 He will be like a tree *firmly*
   planted by streams of water,
   Which yields its fruit in its season
   And its leaf does not wither;
   And in whatever he does, he prospers.

4 The wicked are not so,
   But they are like chaff which
   the wind drives away.
5 Therefore the wicked will not
   stand in the judgment,
   Nor sinners in the assembly
   of the righteous.

⁶ For the LORD knows the
way of the righteous,
But the way of the wicked will perish.

Proverbs 1:1–7

1 The proverbs of Solomon the son of David,
king of Israel:

² To know wisdom and instruction,
To discern the sayings of
understanding,
³ To receive instruction in
wise behavior,
Righteousness, justice and equity;
⁴ To give prudence to the naive,
To the youth knowledge
and discretion,
⁵ A wise man will hear and
increase in learning,
And a man of understanding
will acquire wise counsel,
⁶ To understand a proverb
and a figure,
The words of the wise
and their riddles.

⁷ The fear of the LORD is the
beginning of knowledge;
Fools despise wisdom
and instruction.

Matthew 1:1–25

1 The record of the genealogy of Jesus the
Messiah, the son of David, the son of Abraham:

²Abraham was the father of Isaac, Isaac the
father of Jacob, and Jacob the father of Judah
and his brothers. ³ Judah was the father of
Perez and Zerah by Tamar, Perez was the father of Hezron, and Hezron the father of Ram.
⁴Ram was the father of Amminadab, Amminadab the father of Nahshon, and Nahshon
the father of Salmon. ⁵ Salmon was the father
of Boaz by Rahab, Boaz was the father of Obed
by Ruth, and Obed the father of Jesse. ⁶ Jesse
was the father of David the king.

David was the father of Solomon by Bathsheba who had been the wife of Uriah. ⁷ Solomon was the father of Rehoboam, Rehoboam
the father of Abijah, and Abijah the father
of Asa. ⁸ Asa was the father of Jehoshaphat,
Jehoshaphat the father of Joram, and Joram
the father of Uzziah. ⁹ Uzziah was the father
of Jotham, Jotham the father of Ahaz, and
Ahaz the father of Hezekiah. ¹⁰ Hezekiah was
the father of Manasseh, Manasseh the father
of Amon, and Amon the father of Josiah. ¹¹ Josiah became the father of Jeconiah and his

brothers, at the time of the deportation to
Babylon.
¹²After the deportation to Babylon: Jeconiah became the father of Shealtiel, and Shealtiel the father of Zerubbabel. ¹³ Zerubbabel
was the father of Abihud, Abihud the father
of Eliakim, and Eliakim the father of Azor.
¹⁴Azor was the father of Zadok, Zadok the father of Achim, and Achim the father of Eliud.
¹⁵ Eliud was the father of Eleazar, Eleazar the
father of Matthan, and Matthan the father of
Jacob. ¹⁶ Jacob was the father of Joseph the
husband of Mary, by whom Jesus was born,
who is called the Messiah.
¹⁷So all the generations from Abraham to
David are fourteen generations; from David
to the deportation to Babylon, fourteen generations; and from the deportation to Babylon
to the Messiah, fourteen generations.
¹⁸ Now the birth of Jesus Christ was as
follows: when His mother Mary had been betrothed to Joseph, before they came together
she was found to be with child by the Holy
Spirit. ¹⁹And Joseph her husband, being a
righteous man and not wanting to disgrace
her, planned to send her away secretly. ²⁰ But
when he had considered this, behold, an angel
of the Lord appeared to him in a dream, saying,
"Joseph, son of David, do not be afraid to take
Mary as your wife; for the Child who has been
conceived in her is of the Holy Spirit. ²¹ She
will bear a Son; and you shall call His name
Jesus, for He will save His people from their
sins." ²² Now all this took place to fulfill what
was spoken by the Lord through the prophet:
²³ "BEHOLD, THE VIRGIN SHALL BE WITH CHILD
AND SHALL BEAR A SON, AND THEY SHALL
CALL HIS NAME IMMANUEL," which translated
means, "GOD WITH US." ²⁴And Joseph awoke
from his sleep and did as the angel of the Lord
commanded him, and took *Mary* as his wife;
²⁵ but kept her a virgin until she gave birth to
a Son; and he called His name Jesus.

1:18 betrothed. Jewish betrothal was as binding as a modern marriage and could only be
broken through divorce. The betrothal couple
was legally considered husband and wife, even
though physical union had not yet taken place.

1:22 to fulfill. Matthew often referred to places
where Old Testament scriptures were fulfilled.
He quoted from the Old Testament more than
60 times, more frequently than any other New
Testament writer, except Paul in Romans.

DAY 1: How does the Bible challenge or agree with current scientific theories?

Scientific theories, by their very definition, are subject to change and adjustment. Scripture remains as God's revealed unchanging declaration of truth. The Bible was not written as a challenge to any particular scientific theory, but scientific theories have often been designed to challenge and undermine biblical statements. They either agree with scripture or are mistaken.

The description in Genesis 1:1 that "God created the heavens and the earth" yields three basic conclusions: 1) creation was a recent event measured in thousands not millions of years ago; 2) creation was *ex nihilo*, meaning that God created out of nothing; 3) creation was special, with light and time being the first of God's creative acts, since the day-count (Ge 1:5) began before the creation of sun and moon (Ge 1:16).

One key in evaluating scientific theories depends on our understanding of the biblical word "created." Although the Hebrew word used in Genesis 1:1 can be used to describe the act of shaping or altering existent matter (Is. 65:18), such is not the case with the Bible's first words. God spoke the heavens and earth into existence. Both context and the rest of Scripture bear witness to God's creativity without use of any preexisting material (Is. 40:28; 45:8, 12, 18; 48:13; Jer 10:16; Ac 17:24).

JANUARY 2

Genesis 3:1–4:26

3 Now the serpent was more crafty than any beast of the field which the LORD God had made. And he said to the woman, "Indeed, has God said, 'You shall not eat from any tree of the garden'?" ²The woman said to the serpent, "From the fruit of the trees of the garden we may eat; ³but from the fruit of the tree which is in the middle of the garden, God has said, 'You shall not eat from it or touch it, or you will die.'" ⁴The serpent said to the woman, "You surely will not die! ⁵For God knows that in the day you eat from it your eyes will be opened, and you will be like God, knowing good and evil." ⁶When the woman saw that the tree was good for food, and that it was a delight to the eyes, and that the tree was desirable to make *one* wise, she took from its fruit and ate; and she gave also to her husband with her, and he ate. ⁷Then the eyes of both of them were opened, and they knew that they were naked; and they sewed fig leaves together and made themselves loin coverings.

⁸They heard the sound of the LORD God walking in the garden in the cool of the day, and the man and his wife hid themselves from the presence of the LORD God among the trees of the garden. ⁹Then the LORD God called to the man, and said to him, "Where are you?" ¹⁰He said, "I heard the sound of You in the garden, and I was afraid because I was naked; so I hid myself." ¹¹And He said, "Who told you that you were naked? Have you eaten from the tree of which I commanded you not to eat?" ¹²The man said, "The woman whom You gave *to be* with me, she gave me from

the tree, and I ate." ¹³Then the LORD God said to the woman, "What is this you have done?" And the woman said, "The serpent deceived me, and I ate." ¹⁴The LORD God said to the serpent,

"Because you have done this,
Cursed are you more than all cattle,
And more than every
    beast of the field;
On your belly you will go,
And dust you will eat
All the days of your life;
¹⁵ And I will put enmity
Between you and the woman,
And between your seed and her seed;
He shall bruise you on the head,
And you shall bruise him on the heel."

¹⁶To the woman He said,

"I will greatly multiply
Your pain in childbirth,

3:15 bruise you on the head...bruise him on the heel. This is the first messianic prophecy, foretelling the coming of Jesus Christ. Ever since the Fall, Satan's "seed" (Satan and unbelievers, who are called the devil's children in Jn 8:44) has struggled against the woman's seed (Christ, a descendant of Eve, and His children). In the midst of this curse passage, God gives a message of hope—"He" is Christ, who will one day defeat Satan completely. Satan could only "bruise" Christ's heel (cause Him to suffer), while Christ will bruise Satan's head (destroy him with a fatal blow).

In pain you will bring forth children;
Yet your desire will be for
your husband,
And he will rule over you."

17 Then to Adam He said, "Because you have listened to the voice of your wife, and have eaten from the tree about which I commanded you, saying, 'You shall not eat from it';

Cursed is the ground because of you;
In toil you will eat of it
All the days of your life.
18 "Both thorns and thistles it
shall grow for you;
And you will eat the
plants of the field;
19 By the sweat of your face
You will eat bread,
Till you return to the ground,
Because from it you were taken;
For you are dust,
And to dust you shall return."

20 Now the man called his wife's name Eve, because she was the mother of all *the* living. 21 The LORD God made garments of skin for Adam and his wife, and clothed them.

22 Then the LORD God said, "Behold, the man has become like one of Us, knowing good and evil; and now, he might stretch out his hand, and take also from the tree of life, and eat, and live forever"— 23 therefore the LORD God sent him out from the garden of Eden, to cultivate the ground from which he was taken. 24 So He drove the man out; and at the east of the garden of Eden He stationed the cherubim and the flaming sword which turned every direction to guard the way to the tree of life.

4 Now the man had relations with his wife Eve, and she conceived and gave birth to Cain, and she said, "I have gotten a man-child with *the help of* the LORD." 2 Again, she gave birth to his brother Abel. And Abel was a keeper of flocks, but Cain was a tiller of the ground. 3 So it came about in the course of time that Cain brought an offering to the LORD of the fruit of the ground. 4 Abel, on his part also brought of the firstlings of his flock and of their fat portions. And the LORD had regard for Abel and for his offering; 5 but for Cain and for his offering He had no regard. So Cain became very angry, and his countenance fell. 6 Then the LORD said to Cain, "Why are you angry? And why has your countenance fallen? 7 If you do well, will not *your countenance* be lifted up? And if you do

4:4-5 Abel's offering was acceptable (Heb 11:4), not just because it was an animal, nor just because it was the very best of what he had, nor even that it was the culmination of a zealous heart for God; but, because it was in every way obediently given according to what God must have revealed (though not recorded in Genesis). Cain, disdaining the divine instruction, just brought what he wanted to bring: some of his crop.

not do well, sin is crouching at the door; and its desire is for you, but you must master it." 8 Cain told Abel his brother. And it came about when they were in the field, that Cain rose up against Abel his brother and killed him.

9 Then the LORD said to Cain, "Where is Abel your brother?" And he said, "I do not know. Am I my brother's keeper?" 10 He said, "What have you done? The voice of your brother's blood is crying to Me from the ground. 11 Now you are cursed from the ground, which has opened its mouth to receive your brother's blood from your hand. 12 When you cultivate the ground, it will no longer yield its strength to you; you will be a vagrant and a wanderer on the earth." 13 Cain said to the LORD, "My punishment is too great to bear! 14 Behold, You have driven me this day from the face of the ground; and from Your face I will be hidden, and I will be a vagrant and a wanderer on the earth, and whoever finds me will kill me." 15 So the LORD said to him, "Therefore whoever kills Cain, vengeance will be taken on him sevenfold." And the LORD appointed a sign for Cain, so that no one finding him would slay him.

16 Then Cain went out from the presence of the LORD, and settled in the land of Nod, east of Eden.

17 Cain had relations with his wife and she conceived, and gave birth to Enoch; and he built a city, and called the name of the city Enoch, after the name of his son. 18 Now to Enoch was born Irad, and Irad became the father of Mehujael, and Mehujael became the father of Methushael, and Methushael became the father of Lamech. 19 Lamech took to himself two wives: the name of the one was Adah, and the name of the other, Zillah. 20 Adah gave birth to Jabal; he was the father of those who dwell in tents and *have* livestock. 21 His brother's name was Jubal; he was the father of all those who play the lyre and pipe. 22 As for Zillah, she also gave birth to Tubal-cain, the forger of all implements of bronze and iron; and the sister of Tubal-cain was Naamah.

²³Lamech said to his wives,

> "Adah and Zillah,
> Listen to my voice,
> You wives of Lamech,
> Give heed to my speech,
> For I have killed a man for
>   wounding me;
> And a boy for striking me;
> ²⁴ If Cain is avenged sevenfold,
> Then Lamech seventy-sevenfold."

²⁵Adam had relations with his wife again; and she gave birth to a son, and named him Seth, for, *she said*, "God has appointed me another offspring in place of Abel, for Cain killed him." ²⁶To Seth, to him also a son was born; and he called his name Enosh. Then *men* began to call upon the name of the LORD.

Psalm 2:1-6

Why are the nations in an uproar
And the peoples devising
    a vain thing?
² The kings of the earth take their stand
And the rulers take counsel together
Against the LORD and against
    His Anointed, saying,
³ "Let us tear their fetters apart
And cast away their cords from us!"
⁴ He who sits in the heavens laughs,
The Lord scoffs at them.
⁵ Then He will speak to
    them in His anger
And terrify them in His fury, saying,
⁶ "But as for Me, I have
    installed My King
Upon Zion, My holy mountain."

Proverbs 1:8-9

⁸ Hear, my son, your father's
    instruction
And do not forsake your
    mother's teaching;

⁹ Indeed, they are a graceful
    wreath to your head
And ornaments about your
    neck.

Matthew 2:1-23

2 Now after Jesus was born in Bethlehem of Judea in the days of Herod the king, magi from the east arrived in Jerusalem, saying, ²"Where is He who has been born King of the Jews? For we saw His star in the east and have come to worship Him." ³When Herod the king heard *this,* he was troubled, and all Jerusalem with him. ⁴Gathering together all the chief priests and scribes of the people, he inquired of them where the Messiah was to be born. ⁵They said to him, "In Bethlehem of Judea; for this is what has been written by the prophet:

⁶ 'AND YOU, BETHLEHEM, LAND
    OF JUDAH,
ARE BY NO MEANS LEAST AMONG
    THE LEADERS OF JUDAH;
FOR OUT OF YOU SHALL COME
    FORTH A RULER
WHO WILL SHEPHERD MY
    PEOPLE ISRAEL.'"

⁷Then Herod secretly called the magi and determined from them the exact time the star appeared. ⁸And he sent them to Bethlehem and said, "Go and search carefully for the Child; and when you have found *Him,* report to me, so that I too may come and worship Him." ⁹After hearing the king, they went their way; and the star, which they had seen in the east, went on before them until it came and stood over *the place* where the Child was. ¹⁰When they saw the star, they rejoiced exceedingly with great joy. ¹¹After coming into the house they saw the Child with Mary His mother; and they fell to the ground and worshiped Him. Then, opening their treasures, they presented to Him gifts of gold, frankincense, and myrrh. ¹²And having been warned *by God* in a dream not to return to Herod, the magi left for their own country by another way.

¹³Now when they had gone, behold, an angel of the Lord *appeared to Joseph in a dream and said, "Get up! Take the Child and His mother and flee to Egypt, and remain there until I tell you; for Herod is going to search for the Child to destroy Him." ¹⁴So Joseph got up and took the Child and His mother while it was still night, and left for Egypt. ¹⁵He remained there until the death of Herod. *This was* to fulfill what had been

2:1 in the days of Herod the king. Herod the Great was the first in a dynasty of rulers and is thought to be a descendant of Esau. A ruthless and cunning ruler, he saw the beginning of the rebuilding of the Jerusalem temple under his reign. **magi from the east.** The number of men is not given, though the 3 gifts can be seen to represent one man each. These men were Magi magicians and astrologers not kings.

spoken by the Lord through the prophet: "Out of Egypt I called My Son."

16 Then when Herod saw that he had been tricked by the magi, he became very enraged, and sent and slew all the male children who were in Bethlehem and all its vicinity, from two years old and under, according to the time which he had determined from the magi. 17 Then what had been spoken through Jeremiah the prophet was fulfilled:

18 "A voice was heard in Ramah,
Weeping and great mourning,
Rachel weeping for her children;
And she refused to be comforted,
Because they were no more."

19 But when Herod died, behold, an angel of the Lord *appeared in a dream to Joseph in Egypt, and said, 20 "Get up, take the Child and His mother, and go into the land of Israel; for those who sought the Child's life are dead." 21 So Joseph got up, took the Child and His mother, and came into the land of Israel. 22 But when he heard that Archelaus was reigning over Judea in place of his father Herod, he was afraid to go there. Then after being warned by God in a dream, he left for the regions of Galilee, 23 and came and lived in a city called Nazareth. This was to fulfill what was spoken through the prophets: "He shall be called a Nazarene."

DAY 2: What do Christians mean when they talk about the Fall?

The Fall refers to that moment in time when human beings first disobeyed God. Genesis 3 tells the painful episode. What Eve set in motion, Adam confirmed and completed by joining her. They sinned together. The willful decision of Adam and Eve created a state of rebellion between the creation and her Creator.

The expression "the Fall" comes from the Bible itself. The apostle Paul uses the word in summarizing the human condition in Romans 3:23, "for all have sinned and fall short of the glory of God." It carries with it the sense of defeat and destruction. Great cities fell. So did people. But another fall preceded all these—the fall of the angel Lucifer, who became known as Satan (Is. 14:12–15). In the Fall, our first ancestors declared us on Satan's side.

The Bible makes it clear that the Fall brought sin into every subsequent person's life: "Therefore, just as through one man sin entered into the world, and death through sin, and so death spread to all men, because all sinned" (Ro 5:12). Our capacity for sin is inborn. We are sinners before we have the opportunity to sin. Not only are we sinners because we sin; we first sin because we are sinners. Why? Because we have all inherited the effects of Adam's fall.

 # JANUARY 3

Genesis 5:1–6:22

5 This is the book of the generations of Adam. In the day when God created man, He made him in the likeness of God. 2 He created them male and female, and He blessed them and named them Man in the day when they were created.

3 When Adam had lived one hundred and thirty years, he became the father of a son in his own likeness, according to his image, and named him Seth. 4 Then the days of Adam after he became the father of Seth were eight hundred years, and he had other sons and daughters. 5 So all the days that Adam lived were nine hundred and thirty years, and he died.

6 Seth lived one hundred and five years, and became the father of Enosh. 7 Then Seth lived eight hundred and seven years after he became the father of Enosh, and he had other sons and daughters. 8 So all the days of Seth were nine hundred and twelve years, and he died.

9 Enosh lived ninety years, and became the father of Kenan. 10 Then Enosh lived eight hundred and fifteen years after he became the father of Kenan, and he had other sons and daughters. 11 So all the days of Enosh were nine hundred and five years, and he died.

12 Kenan lived seventy years, and became the father of Mahalalel. 13 Then Kenan lived eight hundred and forty years after he became the father of Mahalalel, and he had other sons and daughters. 14 So all the days of Kenan were nine hundred and ten years, and he died.

15 Mahalalel lived sixty-five years, and became the father of Jared. 16 Then Mahalalel lived eight hundred and thirty years after he became the father of Jared, and he had other sons and daughters. 17 So all the days of Mahalalel were eight hundred and ninety-five years, and he died.

18 Jared lived one hundred and sixty-two years, and became the father of Enoch.

¹⁹Then Jared lived eight hundred years after he became the father of Enoch, and he had *other* sons and daughters. ²⁰So all the days of Jared were nine hundred and sixty-two years, and he died.

²¹Enoch lived sixty-five years, and became the father of Methuselah. ²²Then Enoch walked with God three hundred years after he became the father of Methuselah, and he had *other* sons and daughters. ²³So all the days of Enoch were three hundred and sixty-five years. ²⁴Enoch walked with God; and he was not, for God took him.

²⁵Methuselah lived one hundred and eighty-seven years, and became the father of Lamech. ²⁶Then Methuselah lived seven hundred and eighty-two years after he became the father of Lamech, and he had *other* sons and daughters. ²⁷So all the days of Methuselah were nine hundred and sixty-nine years, and he died.

²⁸Lamech lived one hundred and eighty-two years, and became the father of a son. ²⁹Now he called his name Noah, saying, "This one will rest us rest from our work and from the toil of our hands *arising* from the ground which the LORD has cursed." ³⁰Then Lamech lived five hundred and ninety-five years after he became the father of Noah, and he had *other* sons and daughters. ³¹So all the days of Lamech were seven hundred and seventy-seven years, and he died.

³²Noah was five hundred years old, and Noah became the father of Shem, Ham, and Japheth.

6 Now it came about, when men began to multiply on the face of the land, and daughters were born to them, ²that the sons of God saw that the daughters of men were beautiful; and they took wives for themselves, whomever they chose. ³Then the LORD said, "My Spirit shall not strive with man forever, because he also is flesh; nevertheless his days shall be one hundred and twenty years." ⁴The Nephilim were on the earth in those days, and also afterward, when the sons of God came in to the daughters of men, and they bore *children* to them. Those were the mighty men who *were* of old, men of renown.

⁵Then the LORD saw that the wickedness of man was great on the earth, and that every intent of the thoughts of his heart was only evil continually. ⁶The LORD was sorry that He had made man on the earth, and He was grieved in His heart. ⁷The LORD said, "I will blot out man whom I have created from the face of the land, from man to animals to creeping things and to birds of the sky; for I am sorry that I have made them." ⁸But Noah found favor in the eyes of the LORD.

⁹These are *the records of* the generations of Noah. Noah was a righteous man, blameless in his time; Noah walked with God. ¹⁰Noah became the father of three sons: Shem, Ham, and Japheth.

¹¹Now the earth was corrupt in the sight of God, and the earth was filled with violence. ¹²God looked on the earth, and behold, it was corrupt; for all flesh had corrupted their way upon the earth.

¹³Then God said to Noah, "The end of all flesh has come before Me; for the earth is filled with violence because of them; and behold, I am about to destroy them with the earth. ¹⁴Make for yourself an ark of gopher wood; you shall make the ark with rooms, and shall cover it inside and out with pitch. ¹⁵This is how you shall make it: the length of the ark three hundred cubits, its breadth fifty cubits, and its height thirty cubits. ¹⁶You shall make a window for the ark, and finish it to a cubit from the top; and set the door of the ark in the side of it; you shall make it with lower, second, and third decks. ¹⁷Behold, I, even I am bringing the flood of water upon the earth, to destroy all flesh in which is the breath of life, from under heaven; everything that is on the earth shall perish. ¹⁸But I will establish My covenant with you; and you shall enter the ark—you and your sons and your wife, and your sons' wives with you. ¹⁹And of every living thing of all flesh, you shall bring two of every *kind* into the ark, to keep *them* alive with you; they shall be male and female. ²⁰Of the birds after their kind, and of the animals after their kind, of every creeping thing of the ground after its kind, two of every *kind* will come to you to

6:15–16 While the ark was not designed for beauty or speed, these dimensions provided extraordinary stability in the tumultuous floodwaters. A cubit was about 18 inches long, making the ark 450 feet long, 75 feet wide, and 45 feet high. A gigantic box of that size would be very stable in the water, impossible to capsize. The volume of space in the ark was 1.4 million cubic feet, equal to the capacity of 522 standard railroad box cars. It had 3 stories, each 15 feet high; each deck was equipped with various rooms (literally "nests"). "Pitch" was a resin substance to seal the seams and cracks in the wood. The "window" may have actually been a low wall around the flat roof to catch water for all on the ark.

keep *them* alive. ²¹As for you, take for yourself some of all food which is edible, and gather *it* to yourself; and it shall be for food for you and for them." ²²Thus Noah did; according to all that God had commanded him, so he did.

Psalm 2:7–12

7 "I will surely tell of the
  decree of the LORD:
  He said to Me, 'You are My Son,
  Today I have begotten You.
8 'Ask of Me, and I will surely give the
  nations as Your inheritance,
  And the *very* ends of the earth
  as Your possession.
9 'You shall break them with
  a rod of iron,
  You shall shatter them like
  earthenware.' "

10 Now therefore, O kings,
  show discernment;
  Take warning, O judges
  of the earth.
11 Worship the LORD with reverence
  And rejoice with trembling.
12 Do homage to the Son, that
  He not become angry, and
  you perish *in* the way,
  For His wrath may soon
  be kindled.
  How blessed are all who
  take refuge in Him!

2:7 You are My Son. This recalls 2 Samuel 7:8–16 as the basis for the Davidic king. It is the first Old Testament reference to the Father/Son relationship—the paternal/filial roles—in the Trinity. **Today I have begotten You.** Rather than a reference to origin (there is no procreation within the Trinity), this vividly conveys the essential oneness shared between the Father and the Son. This verse is quoted in the New Testament with reference to the birth of Jesus (Heb 1:5–6) and also to His resurrection (Ac 13:33–34) as the earthly affirmations.

2:12 Do homage to the Son. This symbolic act would indicate allegiance and submission (1Sa 10:1; 1Ki 19:18). The word for "Son" here is not the Hebrew word for "son" that was used in v. 7, but rather its Aram. counterpart (Da 7:13), which is a term that would especially be suitable for these commands being addressed to "nations" (v. 1). **perish *in* the way.** These words pick up the major burden of Psalms 1.

Proverbs 1:10–19

10 My son, if sinners entice you,
  Do not consent.
11 If they say, "Come with us,
  Let us lie in wait for blood,
  Let us ambush the innocent
  without cause;
12 Let us swallow them alive like Sheol,
  Even whole, as those who
  go down to the pit;
13 We will find all *kinds* of
  precious wealth,
  We will fill our houses with spoil;
14 Throw in your lot with us,
  We shall all have one purse,"
15 My son, do not walk in the
  way with them.
  Keep your feet from their path,
16 For their feet run to evil
  And they hasten to shed blood.
17 Indeed, it is useless to
  spread the *baited* net
  In the sight of any bird;
18 But they lie in wait for
  their own blood;
  They ambush their own lives.
19 So are the ways of everyone
  who gains by violence;
  It takes away the life of its possessors.

Matthew 3:1–17

3 Now in those days John the Baptist *came, preaching in the wilderness of Judea, saying, ²"Repent, for the kingdom of heaven is at hand." ³For this is the one referred to by Isaiah the prophet when he said,

"THE VOICE OF ONE CRYING
  IN THE WILDERNESS,
  'MAKE READY THE WAY OF THE LORD,
  MAKE HIS PATHS STRAIGHT!' "

⁴Now John himself had a garment of camel's hair and a leather belt around his waist; and his food was locusts and wild honey. ⁵Then Jerusalem was going out to him, and all Judea and all the district around the Jordan; ⁶and they were being baptized by him in the Jordan River, as they confessed their sins.

⁷But when he saw many of the Pharisees and Sadducees coming for baptism, he said to them, "You brood of vipers, who warned you to flee from the wrath to come? ⁸Therefore bear fruit in keeping with repentance; ⁹and do not suppose that you can say to yourselves, 'We have Abraham for our father'; for I say to you that from these stones God is able to raise up children to Abraham. ¹⁰The axe is

already laid at the root of the trees; therefore every tree that does not bear good fruit is cut down and thrown into the fire.

¹¹ "As for me, I baptize you with water for repentance, but He who is coming after me is mightier than I, and I am not fit to remove His sandals; He will baptize you with the Holy Spirit and fire. ¹² His winnowing fork is in His hand, and He will thoroughly clear His threshing floor; and He will gather His wheat into the barn, but He will burn up the chaff with unquenchable fire."

¹³ Then Jesus *arrived from Galilee at the Jordan *coming* to John, to be baptized by him. ¹⁴ But John tried to prevent Him, saying, "I have need to be baptized by You, and do You come to me?" ¹⁵ But Jesus answering said to him, "Permit *it* at this time; for in this way it is fitting for us to fulfill all righteousness." Then he *permitted Him. ¹⁶ After being baptized, Jesus came up immediately from the water; and behold, the heavens were opened, and he saw the Spirit of God descending as a dove *and* lighting on Him, ¹⁷ and behold, a voice out of the heavens said, "This is My beloved Son, in whom I am well-pleased."

DAY 3: What is the difference between the Pharisees and Sadducees?

The Pharisees were a small (about 6,000), legalistic sect of the Jews. Their name means "separated ones," not in the sense of isolationists but in the puritanical sense, i.e., they were highly zealous for ritual and religious purity according to the Mosaic Law as well as their own traditions that they added to the Old Testament legislation. They represented the orthodox core of Judaism and very strongly influenced the common people of Israel. Jesus' interaction with the Pharisees was usually adversarial. He rebuked them for using human tradition to nullify Scripture (15:3-9), and especially for rank hypocrisy (15:7-8; 22:18; 23:13, 23, 25, 29; Lk 12:1).

The Sadducees were known for their denial of things supernatural. They denied the resurrection of the dead (22:23) and the existence of angels (Ac 23:8). Unlike the Pharisees, they rejected human tradition and scorned legalism. They accepted only the Pentateuch as authoritative. They tended to be wealthy, aristocratic, members of the priestly tribe, and in the days of Herod their sect controlled the temple, though they were fewer in number than the Pharisees.

Pharisees and Sadducees had little in common. Pharisees were ritualists; Sadducees were rationalists. Pharisees were legalists; Sadducees were liberals. Pharisees were separatists; Sadducees were compromisers and political opportunists. Yet they united together in their opposition of Christ (22:15-16, 23-35). John publicly addressed them as deadly snakes.

⅄ JANUARY 4

Genesis 7:1-8:22

7 Then the LORD said to Noah, "Enter the ark, you and all your household, for you *alone* I have seen *to be* righteous before Me in this time. ² You shall take with you of every clean animal by sevens, a male and his female; and of the animals that are not clean two, a male and his female; ³ also of the birds of the sky, by sevens, male and female, to keep offspring alive on the face of all the earth. ⁴ For after seven more days, I will send rain on the earth forty days and forty nights; and I will blot out from the face of the land every living thing that I have made." ⁵ Noah did according to all that the LORD had commanded him.

⁶ Now Noah was six hundred years old when the flood of water came upon the earth. ⁷ Then Noah and his sons and his wife and his sons' wives with him entered the ark because of the water of the flood. ⁸ Of clean animals and animals that are not clean and birds and everything that creeps on the ground, ⁹ there went into the ark to Noah by twos, male and female, as God had commanded Noah. ¹⁰ It came about after the seven days, that the water of the flood came upon the earth. ¹¹ In the six hundredth year of Noah's life, in the second month, on the seventeenth day of the month, on the same day all the fountains of the great deep burst open, and the floodgates of the sky were opened. ¹² The rain fell upon the earth for forty days and forty nights.

¹³ On the very same day Noah and Shem and Ham and Japheth, the sons of Noah, and Noah's wife and the three wives of his sons with them, entered the ark, ¹⁴ they and every beast after its kind, and all the cattle after their kind, and every creeping thing that creeps on the earth after its kind, and every bird after its kind, all sorts of birds. ¹⁵ So they went into the ark to Noah, by twos of all flesh in which was the breath of life. ¹⁶ Those that entered, male and female of all flesh, entered as God had commanded him; and the LORD closed *it* behind him.

¹⁷ Then the flood came upon the earth for forty days, and the water increased and lifted

7:11 all the fountains of the great deep burst open. The subterranean waters sprang up from inside the earth to form the seas and rivers (1:10; 2:10–14), which were not produced by rainfall (since there was none), but by deep fountains in the earth. **the floodgates of the sky.** The celestial waters in the canopy encircling the globe were dumped on the earth and joined with the terrestrial and the subterranean waters (1:7). This ended the water canopy surrounding the earth and unleashed the water in the earth; together these phenomena began the new system of hydrology that has since characterized the earth (Job 26:8; Ecc 1:7; Is 55:10; Am 9:6).

up the ark, so that it rose above the earth. [18] The water prevailed and increased greatly upon the earth, and the ark floated on the surface of the water. [19] The water prevailed more and more upon the earth, so that all the high mountains everywhere under the heavens were covered. [20] The water prevailed fifteen cubits higher, and the mountains were covered. [21] All flesh that moved on the earth perished, birds and cattle and beasts and every swarming thing that swarms upon the earth, and all mankind; [22] of all that was on the dry land, all in whose nostrils was the breath of the spirit of life, died. [23] Thus He blotted out every living thing that was upon the face of the land, from man to animals to creeping things and to birds of the sky, and they were blotted out from the earth; and only Noah was left, together with those that were with him in the ark. [24] The water prevailed upon the earth one hundred and fifty days.

8 But God remembered Noah and all the beasts and all the cattle that were with him in the ark; and God caused a wind to pass over the earth, and the water subsided. [2] Also the fountains of the deep and the floodgates of the sky were closed, and the rain from the sky was restrained; [3] and the water receded steadily from the earth, and at the end of one hundred and fifty days the water decreased. [4] In the seventh month, on the seventeenth day of the month, the ark rested upon the mountains of Ararat. [5] The water decreased steadily until the tenth month; in the tenth month, on the first day of the month, the tops of the mountains became visible.

[6] Then it came about at the end of forty days, that Noah opened the window of the ark which he had made; [7] and he sent out a raven, and it flew here and there until the water was dried up from the earth. [8] Then he sent out a dove from him, to see if the water was abated from the face of the land; [9] but the dove found no resting place for the sole of her foot, so she returned to him into the ark, for the water was on the surface of all the earth. Then he put out his hand and took her, and brought her into the ark to himself. [10] So he waited yet another seven days; and again he sent out the dove from the ark. [11] The dove came to him toward evening, and behold, in her beak was a freshly picked olive leaf. So Noah knew that the water was abated from the earth. [12] Then he waited yet another seven days, and sent out the dove; but she did not return to him again.

[13] Now it came about in the six hundred and first year, in the first *month,* on the first of the month, the water was dried up from the earth. Then Noah removed the covering of the ark, and looked, and behold, the surface of the ground was dried up. [14] In the second month, on the twenty-seventh day of the month, the earth was dry. [15] Then God spoke to Noah, saying, [16] "Go out of the ark, you and your wife and your sons and your sons' wives with you. [17] Bring out with you every living thing of all flesh that is with you, birds and animals and every creeping thing that creeps on the earth, that they may breed abundantly on the earth, and be fruitful and multiply on the earth." [18] So Noah went out, and his sons and his wife and his sons' wives with him. [19] Every beast, every creeping thing, and every bird, everything that moves on the earth, went out by their families from the ark.

[20] Then Noah built an altar to the LORD, and took of every clean animal and of every clean bird and offered burnt offerings on the altar. [21] The LORD smelled the soothing aroma; and the LORD said to Himself, "I will never again curse the ground on account of man, for the intent of man's heart is evil from his youth; and I will never again destroy every living thing, as I have done.

[22] "While the earth remains,
Seedtime and harvest,
And cold and heat,
And summer and winter,
And day and night
Shall not cease."

Psalm 3:1–4
A Psalm of David, when he fled from Absalom his son.

O LORD, how my adversaries have increased!
Many are rising up against me.

² Many are saying of my soul,
"There is no deliverance for him in
God."   *Selah*

³ But You, O LORD, are a
shield about me,
My glory, and the One
who lifts my head.
⁴ I was crying to the LORD
with my voice,
And He answered me from His holy
mountain.   *Selah*

Proverbs 1:20–22

²⁰ Wisdom shouts in the street,
She lifts her voice in the square;
²¹ At the head of the noisy
streets she cries out;
At the entrance of the gates in the
city she utters her sayings:
²² "How long, O naive ones, will you
love being simple-minded?
And scoffers delight
themselves in scoffing
And fools hate knowledge?

Matthew 4:1–25

4 Then Jesus was led up by the Spirit into the wilderness to be tempted by the devil. ²And after He had fasted forty days and forty nights, He then became hungry. ³And the tempter came and said to Him, "If You are the Son of God, command that these stones become bread." ⁴But He answered and said, "It is written, 'MAN SHALL NOT LIVE ON BREAD ALONE, BUT ON EVERY WORD THAT PROCEEDS OUT OF THE MOUTH OF GOD.'"

⁵Then the devil *took Him into the holy city and had Him stand on the pinnacle of the temple, ⁶and *said to Him, "If You are the Son of God, throw Yourself down; for it is written,

'HE WILL COMMAND HIS ANGELS
CONCERNING YOU';

and

'ON *their* HANDS THEY WILL BEAR
YOU UP,
SO THAT YOU WILL NOT STRIKE
YOUR FOOT AGAINST A STONE.'"

⁷Jesus said to him, "On the other hand, it is written, 'YOU SHALL NOT PUT THE LORD YOUR GOD TO THE TEST.'"

⁸Again, the devil *took Him to a very high mountain and *showed Him all the kingdoms of the world and their glory; ⁹and he said to

1:22 How long. Three questions reveal 3 classes of those needing wisdom, and the downward progression of sin: 1) the naive or simple-minded, who are ignorant; 2) scoffers or mockers, who commit more serious, determined acts; and 3) fools or obstinate unbelievers, who will not listen to the truth. Proverbs aims its wisdom primarily at the first group.

4:4 It is written. All 3 of Jesus' replies to the Devil were taken from Deuteronomy. This one, from Deuteronomy 8:3, states that God allowed Israel to hunger, so that He might feed them with manna and teach them to trust Him to provide for them. So the verse is directly applicable to Jesus' circumstances and a fitting reply to Satan's temptation. **EVERY WORD THAT PROCEEDS OUT OF THE MOUTH OF GOD.** A more important source of sustenance than food, it nurtures our spiritual needs in a way that benefits us eternally, rather than merely providing temporal relief from physical hunger.

Him, "All these things I will give You, if You fall down and worship me." ¹⁰Then Jesus *said to him, "Go, Satan! For it is written, 'YOU SHALL WORSHIP THE LORD YOUR GOD, AND SERVE HIM ONLY.'" ¹¹Then the devil *left Him; and behold, angels came and *began* to minister to Him.

¹²Now when Jesus heard that John had been taken into custody, He withdrew into Galilee; ¹³and leaving Nazareth, He came and settled in Capernaum, which is by the sea, in the region of Zebulun and Naphtali. ¹⁴*This was* to fulfill what was spoken through Isaiah the prophet:

¹⁵ "THE LAND OF ZEBULUN AND
THE LAND OF NAPHTALI,
BY THE WAY OF THE SEA, BEYOND THE
JORDAN, GALILEE OF THE GENTILES—
¹⁶ THE PEOPLE WHO WERE SITTING IN
DARKNESS SAW A GREAT LIGHT,
AND THOSE WHO WERE SITTING IN THE
LAND AND SHADOW OF DEATH,
UPON THEM A LIGHT DAWNED."

¹⁷From that time Jesus began to preach and say, "Repent, for the kingdom of heaven is at hand."

¹⁸Now as Jesus was walking by the Sea of Galilee, He saw two brothers, Simon who was called Peter, and Andrew his brother, casting a net into the sea; for they were fishermen. ¹⁹And He *said to them, "Follow Me, and I will make you fishers of men." ²⁰Immediately they left

their nets and followed Him. ²¹ Going on from there He saw two other brothers, James the *son* of Zebedee, and John his brother, in the boat with Zebedee their father, mending their nets; and He called them. ²² Immediately they left the boat and their father, and followed Him. ²³ Jesus was going throughout all Galilee, teaching in their synagogues and proclaiming the gospel of the kingdom, and healing every kind of disease and every kind of sickness among the people.

²⁴ The news about Him spread throughout all Syria; and they brought to Him all who were ill, those suffering with various diseases and pains, demoniacs, epileptics, paralytics; and He healed them. ²⁵ Large crowds followed Him from Galilee and *the* Decapolis and Jerusalem and Judea and *from* beyond the Jordan.

DAY 4: How significant is the Flood in the overall biblical history?

The Bible treats the Flood as a worldwide event directly brought by God as a judgment on the sin of humanity. The flood hangs like a warning cloud over all subsequent history. Fortunately, that cloud also holds a rainbow of God's promised grace.

Conditions in Noah's day were ripe for judgment. "Then the LORD saw that the wickedness of man was great on the earth, and that every intent of the thoughts of his heart was only evil continually" (Ge 6:5). This verse provides one of the strongest and clearest statements about man's sinful nature. Many other verses make it clear that God had every reason for radical action: Jeremiah 17:9–10; Matthew 12:34–35; 15:18–19; Mark 7:21; Luke 6:45. Other notable Scriptures on the worldwide flood brought by God include Job 12:15; 22:16; Psalms 29:10; 104:6–9; Isaiah 54:9; Matthew 24:37–39; Luke 17:26–27; Hebrews 11:7; 1 Peter 3:20; 2 Peter 2:5; 3:5–6.

The Flood illustrates several important aspects of God's character and God's relationship with His creation: 1) God retains ultimate control of world events; 2) God can and will judge sin; 3) God can and does exercise grace even in judgment; 4) An even more universal and final judgment will be carried out on the world based on God's timetable.

 # JANUARY 5

Genesis 9:1–10:32

9 And God blessed Noah and his sons and said to them, "Be fruitful and multiply, and fill the earth. ² The fear of you and the terror of you will be on every beast of the earth and on every bird of the sky; with everything that creeps on the ground, and all the fish of the sea, into your hand they are given. ³ Every moving thing that is alive shall be food for you; I give all to you, as *I gave* the green plant. ⁴ Only you shall not eat flesh with its life, *that is,* its blood. ⁵ Surely I will require your lifeblood; from every beast I will require it. And from *every* man, from every man's brother I will require the life of man.

⁶ "Whoever sheds man's blood,
By man his blood shall be shed,
For in the image of God
He made man."

9:6 For in the image of God. The reason man could kill animals, but neither animals nor man could kill man, is because man alone was created in God's image.

⁷ "As for you, be fruitful and multiply;
Populate the earth abundantly
and multiply in it."

⁸ Then God spoke to Noah and to his sons with him, saying, ⁹ "Now behold, I Myself do establish My covenant with you, and with your descendants after you; ¹⁰ and with every living creature that is with you, the birds, the cattle, and every beast of the earth with you; of all that comes out of the ark, even every beast of the earth. ¹¹ I establish My covenant with you; and all flesh shall never again be cut off by the water of the flood, neither shall there again be a flood to destroy the earth." ¹² God said, "This is the sign of the covenant which I am making between Me and you and every living creature that is with you, for all successive generations; ¹³ I set My bow in the cloud, and it shall be for a sign of a covenant between Me and the earth. ¹⁴ It shall come about, when I bring a cloud over the earth, that the bow will be seen in the cloud, ¹⁵ and I will remember My covenant, which is between Me and you and every living creature of all flesh; and never again shall the water become a flood to destroy all flesh. ¹⁶ When the bow is in the cloud, then I will look upon it, to remember the everlasting covenant between God and every living creature of all flesh that is on the earth." ¹⁷ And God said to

9:16 the everlasting covenant. This covenant with Noah is the first of 5 divinely originated covenants in Scripture explicitly described as "everlasting." The other 4 include: 1) Abrahamic (Ge 17:7); 2) Priestly (Nu 25:10–13); 3) Davidic (2Sa 23:5); and 4) New (Jer 32:40). The term "everlasting" can mean either 1) to the end of time and/or 2) through eternity future. It never looks back to eternity past. Of the 6 explicitly mentioned covenants of this kind in Scripture, only the Mosaic or Old Covenant was nullified.

Noah, "This is the sign of the covenant which I have established between Me and all flesh that is on the earth."

18 Now the sons of Noah who came out of the ark were Shem and Ham and Japheth; and Ham was the father of Canaan. 19 These three *were* the sons of Noah, and from these the whole earth was populated.

20 Then Noah began farming and planted a vineyard. 21 He drank of the wine and became drunk, and uncovered himself inside his tent. 22 Ham, the father of Canaan, saw the nakedness of his father, and told his two brothers outside. 23 But Shem and Japheth took a garment and laid it upon both their shoulders and walked backward and covered the nakedness of their father; and their faces were turned away, so that they did not see their father's nakedness. 24 When Noah awoke from his wine, he knew what his youngest son had done to him. 25 So he said,

"Cursed be Canaan;
A servant of servants
He shall be to his brothers."

26 He also said,

"Blessed be the LORD,
The God of Shem;
And let Canaan be his servant.
27 "May God enlarge Japheth,
And let him dwell in the
tents of Shem;
And let Canaan be his servant."

28 Noah lived three hundred and fifty years after the flood. 29 So all the days of Noah were nine hundred and fifty years, and he died.

10 Now these are *the records of* the generations of Shem, Ham, and Japheth, the sons of Noah; and sons were born to them after the flood.

2 The sons of Japheth *were* Gomer and Magog and Madai and Javan and Tubal and Meshech and Tiras. 3 The sons of Gomer *were* Ashkenaz and Riphath and Togarmah. 4 The sons of Javan *were* Elishah and Tarshish, Kittim and Dodanim. 5 From these the coastlands of the nations were separated into their lands, every one according to his language, according to their families, into their nations.

6 The sons of Ham *were* Cush and Mizraim and Put and Canaan. 7 The sons of Cush *were* Seba and Havilah and Sabtah and Raamah and Sabteca; and the sons of Raamah *were* Sheba and Dedan. 8 Now Cush became the father of Nimrod; he became a mighty one on the earth. 9 He was a mighty hunter before the LORD; therefore it is said, "Like Nimrod a mighty hunter before the LORD." 10 The beginning of his kingdom was Babel and Erech and Accad and Calneh, in the land of Shinar. 11 From that land he went forth into Assyria, and built Nineveh and Rehoboth-Ir and Calah, 12 and Resen between Nineveh and Calah; that is the great city. 13 Mizraim became the father of Ludim and Anamim and Lehabim and Naphtuhim 14 and Pathrusim and Casluhim (from which came the Philistines) and Caphtorim.

15 Canaan became the father of Sidon, his firstborn, and Heth 16 and the Jebusite and the Amorite and the Girgashite 17 and the Hivite and the Arkite and the Sinite 18 and the Arvadite and the Zemarite and the Hamathite; and afterward the families of the Canaanite were spread abroad. 19 The territory of the Canaanite extended from Sidon as you go toward Gerar, as far as Gaza; as you go toward Sodom and Gomorrah and Admah and Zeboiim, as far as Lasha. 20 These are the sons of Ham, according to their families, according to their languages, by their lands, by their nations.

21 Also to Shem, the father of all the children of Eber, *and* the older brother of Japheth, children were born. 22 The sons of Shem *were* Elam and Asshur and Arpachshad and Lud and Aram. 23 The sons of Aram *were* Uz and Hul and Gether and Mash. 24 Arpachshad became the father of Shelah; and Shelah became the father of Eber. 25 Two sons were born to Eber; the name of the one *was* Peleg, for in his days the earth was divided; and his brother's name *was* Joktan. 26 Joktan became the father of Almodad and Sheleph and Hazarmaveth and Jerah 27 and Hadoram and Uzal and Diklah 28 and Obal and Abimael and Sheba 29 and Ophir and Havilah and Jobab; all these were the sons of Joktan. 30 Now their settlement extended from Mesha as you go toward Sephar, the hill country of the east. 31 These are

the sons of Shem, according to their families, according to their languages, by their lands, according to their nations.

³² These are the families of the sons of Noah, according to their genealogies, by their nations; and out of these the nations were separated on the earth after the flood.

Psalm 3:5-8

⁵ I lay down and slept;
I awoke, for the LORD sustains me.
⁶ I will not be afraid of ten
thousands of people
Who have set themselves
against me round about.

⁷ Arise, O LORD; save me, O my God!
For You have smitten all my
enemies on the cheek;
You have shattered the
teeth of the wicked.
⁸ Salvation belongs to the LORD;
Your blessing *be* upon Your people!
Selah

Proverbs 1:23-27

²³ "Turn to my reproof,
Behold, I will pour out
my spirit on you;
I will make my words known to you.
²⁴ "Because I called and you refused,
I stretched out my hand and
no one paid attention;
²⁵ And you neglected all my counsel
And did not want my reproof;
²⁶ I will also laugh at your calamity;
I will mock when your dread comes,
²⁷ When your dread comes like a storm
And your calamity comes
like a whirlwind,
When distress and anguish
come upon you.

Matthew 5:1-26

5 When Jesus saw the crowds, He went up on the mountain; and after He sat down, His disciples came to Him. ²He opened His mouth and *began* to teach them, saying,

³ "Blessed are the poor in spirit, for theirs is the kingdom of heaven.

⁴ "Blessed are those who mourn, for they shall be comforted.

⁵ "Blessed are the gentle, for they shall inherit the earth.

⁶ "Blessed are those who hunger and thirst for righteousness, for they shall be satisfied.

⁷ "Blessed are the merciful, for they shall receive mercy.

5:3 Blessed. The word literally means "happy, fortunate, blissful." Here it speaks of more than a surface emotion. Jesus was describing the divinely bestowed well-being that belongs only to the faithful. The Beatitudes demonstrate that the way to heavenly blessedness is antithetical to the worldly path normally followed in pursuit of happiness. The worldly idea is that happiness is found in riches, merriment, abundance, leisure, and such things. The real truth is the very opposite. The Beatitudes give Jesus' description of the character of true faith. **poor in spirit.** The opposite of self-sufficiency. This speaks of the deep humility of recognizing one's utter spiritual bankruptcy apart from God. It describes those who are acutely conscious of their own lostness and hopelessness apart from divine grace (9:12; Lk 18:13). **theirs is the kingdom of heaven.** Notice that the truth of salvation by grace is clearly presupposed in this opening verse of the Sermon on the Mount. Jesus was teaching that the kingdom is a gracious gift to those who sense their own poverty of spirit.

⁸ "Blessed are the pure in heart, for they shall see God.

⁹ "Blessed are the peacemakers, for they shall be called sons of God.

¹⁰ "Blessed are those who have been persecuted for the sake of righteousness, for theirs is the kingdom of heaven.

¹¹ "Blessed are you when *people* insult you and persecute you, and falsely say all kinds of evil against you because of Me. ¹²Rejoice and be glad, for your reward in heaven is great; for in the same way they persecuted the prophets who were before you.

¹³ "You are the salt of the earth; but if the salt has become tasteless, how can it be made salty *again*? It is no longer good for anything, except to be thrown out and trampled under foot by men.

¹⁴ "You are the light of the world. A city set on a hill cannot be hidden; ¹⁵nor does *anyone* light a lamp and put it under a basket, but on the lampstand, and it gives light to all who are in the house. ¹⁶Let your light shine before men in such a way that they may see your good works, and glorify your Father who is in heaven.

¹⁷ "Do not think that I came to abolish the Law or the Prophets; I did not come to abolish but to fulfill. ¹⁸For truly I say to you, until heaven and earth pass away, not the smallest letter or stroke shall pass from the Law until

all is accomplished. ¹⁹Whoever then annuls one of the least of these commandments, and teaches others *to do* the same, shall be called least in the kingdom of heaven; but whoever keeps and teaches *them,* he shall be called great in the kingdom of heaven.

²⁰"For I say to you that unless your righteousness surpasses *that* of the scribes and Pharisees, you will not enter the kingdom of heaven.

²¹"You have heard that the ancients were told, 'You shall not commit murder' and 'Whoever commits murder shall be liable to the court.' ²²But I say to you that everyone who is angry with his brother shall be guilty before the court; and whoever says to his brother, 'You good-for-nothing,' shall be guilty before the supreme court; and whoever says, 'You fool,' shall be guilty *enough to go* into the fiery hell. ²³Therefore if you are presenting your offering at the altar, and there remember that your brother has something against you, ²⁴leave your offering there before the altar and go; first be reconciled to your brother, and then come and present your offering. ²⁵Make friends quickly with your opponent at law while you are with him on the way, so that your opponent may not hand you over to the judge, and the judge to the officer, and you be thrown into prison. ²⁶Truly I say to you, you will not come out of there until you have paid up the last cent.

DAY 5: Why did Jesus preach the Sermon on the Mount?

Matthew records five important discourses: the Sermon on the Mount (chaps. 5–7); the commissioning of the apostles (chap. 10); the parables about the kingdom of heaven (chap. 13); a discourse about the childlikeness of the believer (chap. 18); and the discourse on His second coming (chaps. 24–25). Each discourse ends with a variation of this phrase: "when Jesus had ended these sayings." That becomes a motif signaling a new narrative portion.

The Sermon on the Mount is a masterful exposition of the law and a potent assault on Pharisaic legalism, closing with a call to true faith and salvation (7:13–29). Matthew is keen to show the error of the Pharisees for the benefit of his Jewish audience—not for personal or self-aggrandizing reasons. Christ expounded the full meaning of the law, showing that its demands were humanly impossible (see 5:48). This is the proper use of the law with respect to salvation: It closes off every possible avenue of human merit and leaves sinners dependent on nothing but divine grace for salvation (see Ro 3:19–20; Gal 3:23–24). Christ plumbed the depth of the law, showing that its true demands went far beyond the surface meaning of the words (5:28, 39, 44) and set a standard that is higher than the most diligent students of the law had heretofore realized.

JANUARY 6

Genesis 11:1–12:20

11 Now the whole earth used the same language and the same words. ²It came about as they journeyed east, that they found a plain in the land of Shinar and settled there. ³They said to one another, "Come, let us make bricks and burn *them* thoroughly." And they used brick for stone, and they used tar for mortar. ⁴They said, "Come, let us build for ourselves a city, and a tower whose top *will reach* into heaven, and let us make for ourselves a name, otherwise we will be scattered abroad over the face of the whole earth." ⁵The LORD came down to see the city and the tower which the sons of men had built. ⁶The LORD said, "Behold, they are one people, and they all have the same language. And this is what they began to do, and now nothing which they purpose to do will be impossible for them. ⁷Come, let Us go down and there confuse their language, so that they will not understand one another's speech." ⁸So the LORD scattered them abroad from there over the face of the whole earth; and they stopped building the city. ⁹Therefore its name was called Babel, because there the LORD confused the language of the whole earth; and from there the LORD scattered them abroad over the face of the whole earth.

11:3–4 let us make bricks...build for ourselves a city, and a tower...make for ourselves a name. After God commanded the people to scatter to fill the earth, the people, under the leadership of the powerful Nimrod, disobeyed God's command to disperse. They stopped to build a city and tower in their own honor. The tower itself was not the singular act of rebellion. Rather, human pride caused them to rebel against God.

---

¹⁰ These are *the records of* the generations of Shem. Shem was one hundred years old, and became the father of Arpachshad two years after the flood; ¹¹ and Shem lived five hundred years after he became the father of Arpachshad, and he had *other* sons and daughters.

¹² Arpachshad lived thirty-five years, and became the father of Shelah; ¹³ and Arpach-shad lived four hundred and three years after he became the father of Shelah, and he had *other* sons and daughters.

¹⁴ Shelah lived thirty years, and became the father of Eber; ¹⁵ and Shelah lived four hundred and three years after he became the father of Eber, and he had *other* sons and daughters.

¹⁶ Eber lived thirty-four years, and became the father of Peleg; ¹⁷ and Eber lived four hundred and thirty years after he became the father of Peleg, and he had *other* sons and daughters.

¹⁸ Peleg lived thirty years, and became the father of Reu; ¹⁹ and Peleg lived two hundred and nine years after he became the father of Reu, and he had *other* sons and daughters.

²⁰ Reu lived thirty-two years, and became the father of Serug; ²¹ and Reu lived two hundred and seven years after he became the father of Serug, and he had *other* sons and daughters.

²² Serug lived thirty years, and became the father of Nahor; ²³ and Serug lived two hundred years after he became the father of Nahor, and he had *other* sons and daughters.

²⁴ Nahor lived twenty-nine years, and became the father of Terah; ²⁵ and Nahor lived one hundred and nineteen years after he became the father of Terah, and he had *other* sons and daughters.

²⁶ Terah lived seventy years, and became the father of Abram, Nahor and Haran.

²⁷ Now these are *the records of* the gener-ations of Terah. Terah became the father of Abram, Nahor and Haran; and Haran became the father of Lot. ²⁸ Haran died in the presence of his father Terah in the land of his birth, in Ur of the Chaldeans. ²⁹ Abram and Nahor took wives for themselves. The name of Abram's wife was Sarai; and the name of Nahor's wife was Milcah, the daughter of Haran, the father of Milcah and Iscah. ³⁰ Sarai was barren; she had no child.

³¹ Terah took Abram his son, and Lot the son of Haran, his grandson, and Sarai his daughter-in-law, his son Abram's wife; and they went out together from Ur of the Chal-deans in order to enter the land of Canaan;

and they went as far as Haran, and settled there. ³² The days of Terah were two hundred and five years; and Terah died in Haran.

12 Now the LORD said to Abram,

"Go forth from your country,
And from your relatives
And from your father's house,
To the land which I will show you;
² And I will make you a great nation,
And I will bless you,
And make your name great;
And so you shall be a blessing;
³ And I will bless those who bless you,
And the one who curses
you I will curse.
And in you all the families of
the earth will be blessed."

12:1–3 the LORD…to Abram. This passage con-tains the promise whose fulfillment extends all through Scripture. It is an everlasting cove-nant which includes four components: 1) seed (see Gal. 3:8, 16, referring to Christ); 2) land (15:18–21; 17:8); 3) a nation (12:2; 17:14); and 4) divine blessing and protection (12:3). The covenant is unconditional in the sense of its ultimate fulfillment of a kingdom and salva-tion. It has great national importance to Israel, as magnified by repeated references in the Old Testament, and great spiritual importance to all believers.

---

⁴ So Abram went forth as the LORD had spoken to him; and Lot went with him. Now Abram was seventy-five years old when he departed from Haran. ⁵ Abram took Sarai his wife and Lot his nephew, and all their posses-sions which they had accumulated, and the persons which they had acquired in Haran, and they set out for the land of Canaan; thus they came to the land of Canaan. ⁶ Abram passed through the land as far as the site of Shechem, to the oak of Moreh. Now the Canaanite *was* then in the land. ⁷ The LORD appeared to Abram and said, "To your descen-dants I will give this land." So he built an altar there to the LORD who had appeared to him. ⁸ Then he proceeded from there to the moun-tain on the east of Bethel, and pitched his tent, with Bethel on the west and Ai on the east; and there he built an altar to the LORD and called upon the name of the LORD. ⁹ Abram journeyed on, continuing toward the Negev.

¹⁰ Now there was a famine in the land; so Abram went down to Egypt to sojourn there,

for the famine was severe in the land. ¹¹ It came about when he came near to Egypt, that he said to Sarai his wife, "See now, I know that you are a beautiful woman; ¹² and when the Egyptians see you, they will say, 'This is his wife'; and they will kill me, but they will let you live. ¹³ Please say that you are my sister so that it may go well with me because of you, and that I may live on account of you." ¹⁴ It came about when Abram came into Egypt, the Egyptians saw that the woman was very beautiful. ¹⁵ Pharaoh's officials saw her and praised her to Pharaoh; and the woman was taken into Pharaoh's house. ¹⁶ Therefore he treated Abram well for her sake; and gave him sheep and oxen and donkeys and male and female servants and female donkeys and camels.

¹⁷ But the LORD struck Pharaoh and his house with great plagues because of Sarai, Abram's wife. ¹⁸ Then Pharaoh called Abram and said, "What is this you have done to me? Why did you not tell me that she was your wife? ¹⁹ Why did you say, 'She is my sister,' so that I took her for my wife? Now then, here is your wife, take her and go." ²⁰ Pharaoh commanded *his* men concerning him; and they escorted him away, with his wife and all that belonged to him.

Psalm 4:1–3

For the choir director; on stringed instruments. A Psalm of David.

Answer me when I call, O God of my righteousness!
You have relieved me in my distress;
Be gracious to me and
hear my prayer.

² O sons of men, how long will my honor become a reproach?
How long will you love what is worthless and aim at deception?   *Selah*
³ But know that the LORD has set apart the godly man for Himself;
The LORD hears when I call to Him.

4:1 **O God of my righteousness!** The ultimate basis for divine intervention resides in God, not in the psalmist. **distress.** This is an important word for trying circumstances in the psalms. It pictures the psalmist's plight as being in straits, i.e., painfully restricted. Here his testimony to God's historical salvation, "You have relieved me," conveys the picture that his Lord had provided space or room for him.

Proverbs 1:28–33

²⁸ "Then they will call on me,
but I will not answer;
They will seek me diligently
but they will not find me,
²⁹ Because they hated knowledge
And did not choose the
fear of the LORD.
³⁰ "They would not accept my counsel,
They spurned all my reproof.
³¹ "So they shall eat of the fruit
of their own way
And be satiated with their
own devices.
³² "For the waywardness of the
naive will kill them,
And the complacency of fools
will destroy them.
³³ "But he who listens to me
shall live securely
And will be at ease from
the dread of evil."

Matthew 5:27–48

²⁷ "You have heard that it was said, 'YOU SHALL NOT COMMIT ADULTERY'; ²⁸ but I say to you that everyone who looks at a woman with lust for her has already committed adultery with her in his heart. ²⁹ If your right eye makes you stumble, tear it out and throw it from you; for it is better for you to lose one of the parts of your body, than for your whole body to be thrown into hell. ³⁰ If your right hand makes you stumble, cut it off and throw it from you; for it is better for you to lose one of the parts of your body, than for your whole body to go into hell. ³¹ "It was said, 'WHOEVER SENDS HIS WIFE AWAY, LET HIM GIVE HER A CERTIFICATE OF DIVORCE'; ³² but I say to you that everyone who divorces his wife, except for *the* reason of unchastity, makes her commit adultery; and whoever marries a divorced woman commits adultery.

³³ "Again, you have heard that the ancients were told, 'YOU SHALL NOT MAKE FALSE VOWS, BUT SHALL FULFILL YOUR VOWS TO THE LORD.'

5:31 **It was said.** The rabbis wrongly understood Deuteronomy 24:1–4 to mean that divorce only required regulated paperwork and could be granted for anything that displeased a man. Moses provided this as a concession to protect the woman who was divorced, not to justify or legalize divorce under all circumstances.

³⁴But I say to you, make no oath at all, either by heaven, for it is the throne of God, ³⁵or by the earth, for it is the footstool of His feet, or by Jerusalem, for it is THE CITY OF THE GREAT KING. ³⁶Nor shall you make an oath by your head, for you cannot make one hair white or black. ³⁷But let your statement be, 'Yes, yes' or 'No, no'; anything beyond these is of evil.

³⁸"You have heard that it was said, 'AN EYE FOR AN EYE, AND A TOOTH FOR A TOOTH.' ³⁹But I say to you, do not resist an evil person; but whoever slaps you on your right cheek, turn the other to him also. ⁴⁰If anyone wants to sue you and take your shirt, let him have your coat also. ⁴¹Whoever forces you to go one mile, go with him two. ⁴²Give to him who asks of you, and do not turn away from him who wants to borrow from you.

⁴³"You have heard that it was said, 'YOU SHALL LOVE YOUR NEIGHBOR and hate your enemy.' ⁴⁴But I say to you, love your enemies and pray for those who persecute you, ⁴⁵so that you may be sons of your Father who is in heaven; for He causes His sun to rise on the evil and the good, and sends rain on the righteous and the unrighteous. ⁴⁶For if you love those who love you, what reward do you have? Do not even the tax collectors do the same? ⁴⁷If you greet only your brothers, what more are you doing than others? Do not even the Gentiles do the same? ⁴⁸Therefore you are to be perfect, as your heavenly Father is perfect.

DAY 6: Why did God cause the multiplication of languages and the dispersion of peoples?

After the Flood, human civilization again began to spread across the earth. Those who traveled east under Nimrod (10:8–10) settled for a while in a place called Shinar. Later, they decided to establish a city as a tribute to themselves and as a way to keep from spreading across the earth (11:4). This was a double prideful rebellion against God. First, their city, with its proposed tower, was to be a monument to their self-reliance. Second, the permanence of their settlement represented an effort to disobey God's direct command to inhabit the whole earth.

Because it was God's purpose to fill the earth with custodians, He responded to the people's prideful rebellion. They had chosen to settle; He forced them to scatter. Their cooperation and self-reliance had been based on their shared language. Instead of using all their resources to obey God, they misused them for disobedience. God chose to complicate communication by multiplying the languages. The location where this confusion took place became known as Babel (related to a Hebrew word meaning "to confuse"). Later it became Babylon, the constant enemy of God's people, and throughout Scripture the capital of human rebellion against God (Rev 16:19; 17:5).

 JANUARY 7

Genesis 13:1–14:24

13 So Abram went up from Egypt to the Negev, he and his wife and all that belonged to him, and Lot with him.

²Now Abram was very rich in livestock, in silver and in gold. ³He went on his journeys from the Negev as far as Bethel, to the place where his tent had been at the beginning, between Bethel and Ai, ⁴to the place of the altar which he had made there formerly; and there Abram called on the name of the LORD. ⁵Now Lot, who went with Abram, also had flocks and herds and tents. ⁶And the land could not sustain them while dwelling together, for their possessions were so great that they were not able to remain together. ⁷And there was strife between the herdsmen of Abram's livestock and the herdsmen of Lot's livestock. Now the Canaanite and the Perizzite were dwelling then in the land.

⁸So Abram said to Lot, "Please let there be no strife between you and me, nor between my herdsmen and your herdsmen, for we are brothers. ⁹Is not the whole land before you? Please separate from me; if to the left, then I will go to the right; or if to the right, then I will go to the left." ¹⁰Lot lifted up his eyes and saw all the valley of the Jordan, that it was well watered everywhere—this was before the LORD destroyed Sodom and Gomorrah—like the garden of the LORD, like the land of Egypt as you go to Zoar. ¹¹So Lot chose for himself all the valley of the Jordan, and Lot journeyed eastward. Thus they separated from each other. ¹²Abram settled in the land of Canaan,

---

13:8 we are brothers. Abram's whole reaction in resolving the strife between the two households and their personnel portrayed a different Abram than seen in Egypt; one whose attitude was not self-centered. Waving his right to seniority, he gave the choice to his nephew, Lot.

while Lot settled in the cities of the valley, and moved his tents as far as Sodom. ¹³ Now the men of Sodom were wicked exceedingly and sinners against the LORD.

¹⁴ The LORD said to Abram, after Lot had separated from him, "Now lift up your eyes and look from the place where you are, northward and southward and eastward and westward; ¹⁵ for all the land which you see, I will give it to you and to your descendants forever. ¹⁶ I will make your descendants as the dust of the earth, so that if anyone can number the dust of the earth, then your descendants can also be numbered. ¹⁷ Arise, walk about the land through its length and breadth; for I will give it to you." ¹⁸ Then Abram moved his tent and came and dwelt by the oaks of Mamre, which are in Hebron, and there he built an altar to the LORD.

14 And it came about in the days of Amraphel king of Shinar, Arioch king of Ellasar, Chedorlaomer king of Elam, and Tidal king of Goiim, ² *that* they made war with Bera king of Sodom, and with Birsha king of Gomorrah, Shinab king of Admah, and Shemeber king of Zeboiim, and the king of Bela (that is, Zoar). ³ All these came as allies to the valley of Siddim (that is, the Salt Sea). ⁴ Twelve years they had served Chedorlaomer, but the thirteenth year they rebelled. ⁵ In the fourteenth year Chedorlaomer and the kings that were with him, came and defeated the Rephaim in Ashteroth-karnaim and the Zuzim in Ham and the Emim in Shaveh-kiriathaim, ⁶ and the Horites in their Mount Seir, as far as El-paran, which is by the wilderness. ⁷ Then they turned back and came to En-mishpat (that is, Kadesh), and conquered all the country of the Amalekites, and also the Amorites, who lived in Hazazon-tamar. ⁸ And the king of Sodom and the king of Gomorrah and the king of Admah and the king of Zeboiim and the king of Bela (that is, Zoar) came out; and they arrayed for battle against them in the valley of Siddim, ⁹ against Chedorlaomer king of Elam and Tidal king of Goiim and Amraphel king of Shinar and Arioch king of Ellasar— four kings against five. ¹⁰ Now the valley of Siddim was full of tar pits; and the kings of Sodom and Gomorrah fled, and they fell into them. But those who survived fled to the hill country. ¹¹ Then they took all the goods of Sodom and Gomorrah and all their food supply, and departed. ¹² They also took Lot, Abram's nephew, and his possessions and departed, for he was living in Sodom. ¹³ Then a fugitive came and told Abram the

Hebrew. Now he was living by the oaks of Mamre the Amorite, brother of Eshcol and brother of Aner, and these were allies with Abram. ¹⁴ When Abram heard that his relative had been taken captive, he led out his trained men, born in his house, three hundred and eighteen, and went in pursuit as far as Dan. ¹⁵ He divided his forces against them by night, he and his servants, and defeated them, and pursued them as far as Hobah, which is north of Damascus. ¹⁶ He brought back all the goods, and also brought back his relative Lot with his possessions, and also the women, and the people.

¹⁷ Then after his return from the defeat of Chedorlaomer and the kings who were with him, the king of Sodom went out to meet him at the valley of Shaveh (that is, the King's Valley). ¹⁸ And Melchizedek king of Salem brought out bread and wine; now he was a priest of God Most High. ¹⁹ He blessed him and said,

> "Blessed be Abram of God Most High,
> Possessor of heaven and earth;
> ²⁰ And blessed be God Most High,
> Who has delivered your
> enemies into your hand."

He gave him a tenth of all. ²¹ The king of Sodom said to Abram, "Give the people to me and take the goods for yourself." ²² Abram said to the king of Sodom, "I have sworn to the

14:18 Melchizedek king of Salem. The lack of biographical and genealogical particulars for this ruler, whose name meant "righteous king" and who was a king-priest over ancient Jerusalem, allowed for later revelation to use him as a type of Christ (Ps 110:4; Heb 7:17, 21). His superior status in Abram's day is witnessed 1) by the king of Sodom, the first to meet Abram returning in victory, deferring to Melchizedek before continuing with his request (vv. 17, 21) and 2) by Abram, without demur, both accepting a blessing from and also giving a tithe to this priest-king (vv. 19–20). **priest of God Most High.** The use of El Elyon (Sovereign Lord) for God's name indicated that Melchizedek, who used this title two times (vv. 18–19), worshiped, served, and represented no Canaanite deity, but the same one whom Abram also called Yahweh El Elyon (v. 22). That this was so is confirmed by the added description, "Possessor of heaven and earth," being used by both Abram and Melchizedek (vv. 19, 22).

LORD God Most High, possessor of heaven and earth, 23 that I will not take a thread or a sandal thong or anything that is yours, for fear you would say, 'I have made Abram rich.' 24 I will take nothing except what the young men have eaten, and the share of the men who went with me, Aner, Eshcol, and Mamre; let them take their share."

Psalm 4:4-8

4 Tremble, and do not sin;
  Meditate in your heart upon
    your bed, and be still.   *Selah*
5 Offer the sacrifices of
    righteousness,
  And trust in the LORD.

6 Many are saying, "Who will
    show us *any* good?"
  Lift up the light of Your
    countenance upon us, O LORD!
7 You have put gladness in
    my heart,
  More than when their grain
    and new wine abound.
8 In peace I will both lie
    down and sleep,
  For You alone, O LORD, make
    me to dwell in safety.

Proverbs 2:1-5

2 My son, if you will receive my words
  And treasure my commandments
    within you,
2 Make your ear attentive to
    wisdom,
  Incline your heart to
    understanding;
3 For if you cry for discernment,
  Lift your voice for understanding;
4 If you seek her as silver
  And search for her as for
    hidden treasures;
5 Then you will discern the
    fear of the LORD
  And discover the knowledge
    of God.

2:1 my words. Solomon has taken God's law and made it his own by faith and obedience, as well as teaching. The wisdom of these words is available to those who, first of all, understand the rich value ("treasure") that wisdom possesses. Appropriating wisdom begins when one values it above all else.

Matthew 6:1-18

6 "Beware of practicing your righteousness before men to be noticed by them; otherwise you have no reward with your Father who is in heaven.

2 "So when you give to the poor, do not sound a trumpet before you, as the hypocrites do in the synagogues and in the streets, so that they may be honored by men. Truly I say to you, they have their reward in full. 3 But when you give to the poor, do not let your left hand know what your right hand is doing, 4 so that your giving will be in secret; and your Father who sees *what is done* in secret will reward you.

5 "When you pray, you are not to be like the hypocrites; for they love to stand and pray in the synagogues and on the street corners so that they may be seen by men. Truly I say to you, they have their reward in full. 6 But you, when you pray, go into your inner room, close your door and pray to your Father who is in secret, and your Father who sees *what is done* in secret will reward you.

7 "And when you are praying, do not use meaningless repetition as the Gentiles do, for they suppose that they will be heard for their many words. 8 So do not be like them; for your Father knows what you need before you ask Him.

9 "Pray, then, in this way:

  'Our Father who is in heaven,
    Hallowed be Your name.
10 'Your kingdom come.
  Your will be done,
    On earth as it is in heaven.
11 'Give us this day our daily bread.
12 'And forgive us our debts, as we
    also have forgiven our debtors.
13 'And do not lead us into temptation,
    but deliver us from evil. [For Yours
    is the kingdom and the power
    and the glory forever. Amen.']

14 For if you forgive others for their transgressions, your heavenly Father will also forgive you. 15 But if you do not forgive others, then your Father will not forgive your transgressions.

16 "Whenever you fast, do not put on a gloomy face as the hypocrites *do,* for they neglect their appearance so that they will be noticed by men when they are fasting. Truly I say to you, they have their reward in full. 17 But you, when you fast, anoint your head and wash your face 18 so that your fasting will not be noticed by men, but by your Father who is in secret; and your Father who sees *what is done* in secret will reward you.

DAY 7: What does the Lord's Prayer teach us about forgiveness?

The request, "Forgive us our debts" (6:12), is the heart of the prayer; it is what Jesus stressed in the words that followed the prayer (vv. 14–15; see Mk 11:25). The parallel passage in Luke 11:4 uses the word that means "sins," so that in context, spiritual debts are intended. Sinners are debtors to God in their violations of His laws.

When Jesus added that "if you do not forgive others, then your Father will not forgive your transgressions" (v. 15), this is not to suggest that God will withdraw justification from those who have already received the free pardon He extends to all believers. Forgiveness in that sense—a permanent and complete acquittal from the guilt and ultimate penalty of sin—belongs to all who are in Christ (see Jn 5:24; Ro 8:1; Eph 1:7). Yet, Scripture also teaches that God chastens His children who disobey (Heb 12:5–7). Believers are to confess their sins in order to obtain a day-to-day cleansing (1Jn 1:9). This sort of forgiveness is a simple washing from the worldly defilements of sin; not a repeat of the wholesale cleansing from sin's corruption that comes with justification. It is like a washing of the feet rather than a bath (Jn 13:10). Forgiveness in this latter sense is what God threatens to withhold from Christians who refuse to forgive others.

✝ JANUARY 8

Genesis 15:1–16:16

15 After these things the word of the LORD came to Abram in a vision, saying,

"Do not fear, Abram,
I am a shield to you;
Your reward shall be very great."

[2] Abram said, "O Lord GOD, what will You give me, since I am childless, and the heir of my house is Eliezer of Damascus?" [3] And Abram said, "Since You have given no offspring to me, one born in my house is my heir." [4] Then behold, the word of the LORD came to him, saying, "This man will not be your heir; but one who will come forth from your own body, he shall be your heir." [5] And He took him outside and said, "Now look toward the heavens, and count the stars, if you are able to count them." And He said to him, "So shall your descendants be." [6] Then he believed in the LORD; and He reckoned it to him as righteousness. [7] And He said to him, "I am the LORD who brought you out of Ur of the Chaldeans, to give you this land to possess it." [8] He said, "O Lord GOD, how may I know that I will possess it?" [9] So He said to him, "Bring Me a three year old heifer, and a three year old female goat, and a three year old ram, and a turtledove, and a young pigeon." [10] Then he brought all these to Him and cut them in two, and laid each half opposite the other; but he did not cut the birds. [11] The birds of prey came down upon the carcasses, and Abram drove them away.

[12] Now when the sun was going down, a deep sleep fell upon Abram; and behold, terror *and* great darkness fell upon him. [13] *God* said to Abram, "Know for certain that your descendants will be strangers in a land that is not theirs, where they will be enslaved and oppressed four hundred years. [14] But I will also judge the nation whom they will serve, and afterward they will come out with many possessions. [15] As for you, you shall go to your fathers in peace; you will be buried at a good old age. [16] Then in the fourth generation they will return here, for the iniquity of the Amorite is not yet complete."

[17] It came about when the sun had set, that it was very dark, and behold, *there appeared* a smoking oven and a flaming torch which passed between these pieces. [18] On that day the LORD made a covenant with Abram, saying,

"To your descendants I have
given this land,
From the river of Egypt as far as the
great river, the river Euphrates:

[19] the Kenite and the Kenizzite and the Kadmonite [20] and the Hittite and the Perizzite and the Rephaim [21] and the Amorite and the Canaanite and the Girgashite and the Jebusite."

16 Now Sarai, Abram's wife had borne him no *children,* and she had an Egyptian maid whose name was Hagar. [2] So Sarai said to Abram, "Now behold, the LORD has prevented me from bearing *children.* Please go in to my maid; perhaps I will obtain children through her." And Abram listened to the voice of Sarai. [3] After Abram had lived ten years in the land of Canaan, Abram's wife Sarai took Hagar the Egyptian, her maid, and gave her to her husband Abram as his wife. [4] He went in to Hagar, and she conceived; and when she saw that she had conceived, her mistress was despised in her sight. ⁵And Sarai said to Abram, "May the wrong done me be upon you. I gave my maid into your arms, but when she saw that she had conceived, I was despised in her sight. May the LORD judge between you and me." ⁶But Abram said to Sarai, "Behold, your maid is in your power; do to her what is good in your sight." So Sarai treated her harshly, and she fled from her presence.

⁷Now the angel of the LORD found her by a spring of water in the wilderness, by the spring on the way to Shur. ⁸He said, "Hagar, Sarai's maid, where have you come from and where are you going?" And she said, "I am fleeing from the presence of my mistress Sarai." ⁹Then the angel of the LORD said to her, "Return to your mistress, and submit yourself to her authority." ¹⁰Moreover, the angel of the LORD said to her, "I will greatly multiply your descendants so that they will be too many to count." ¹¹The angel of the LORD said to her further,

"Behold, you are with child,
And you will bear a son;
And you shall call his name Ishmael,
Because the LORD has given
heed to your affliction.
¹² "He will be a wild donkey of a man,
His hand *will be* against everyone,
And everyone's hand *will
be* against him;
And he will live to the east
of all his brothers."

¹³Then she called the name of the LORD who spoke to her, "You are a God who sees"; for she said, "Have I even remained alive here after seeing Him?" ¹⁴Therefore the well was called Beer-lahai-roi; behold, it is between Kadesh and Bered.

¹⁵So Hagar bore Abram a son; and Abram called the name of his son, whom Hagar bore, Ishmael. ¹⁶Abram was eighty-six years old when Hagar bore Ishmael to him.

Psalm 5:1–7

For the choir director; for flute accompaniment. A Psalm of David.

Give ear to my words, O LORD,
Consider my groaning.
² Heed the sound of my cry for
help, my King and my God,
For to You I pray.
³ In the morning, O LORD, You
will hear my voice;
In the morning I will order *my
prayer* to You and *eagerly* watch.

16:3 gave her to her husband. After 10 childless years (12:4), Sarai resorted to the custom of the day by which a barren wife could get a child through one of her own maidservants (v. 2, "I will obtain children through her"). Abram, ignoring divine reaction and assurance in response to his earlier attempt to appoint an heir (15:2–5), sinfully yielded to Sarai's insistence, and Ishmael was born (v. 15).

⁴ For You are not a God who takes
pleasure in wickedness;
No evil dwells with You.
⁵ The boastful shall not stand
before Your eyes;
You hate all who do iniquity.
⁶ You destroy those who
speak falsehood;
The LORD abhors the man of
bloodshed and deceit.
⁷ But as for me, by Your
abundant lovingkindness I
will enter Your house,
At Your holy temple I will bow
in reverence for You.

Proverbs 2:6–9

⁶ For the LORD gives wisdom;
From His mouth *come* knowledge
and understanding.
⁷ He stores up sound wisdom
for the upright;
He is a shield to those who
walk in integrity,
⁸ Guarding the paths of justice,
And He preserves the way
of His godly ones.
⁹ Then you will discern
righteousness and justice
And equity *and* every good course.

16:7 the angel of the LORD. This special individual spoke as though He were distinct from Yahweh, yet also spoke in the first person as though He were indeed to be identified as Yahweh Himself, with Hagar recognizing that in seeing this Angel, she had seen God (v. 13). Others had the same experience and came to the same conclusion (22:11–18; 31:11–13; Ex 3:2–5; Nu 22:22–35; Jdg 6:11–23; 13:2–5; 1Ki 19:5–7). The Angel of the Lord, who does not appear after the birth of Christ, is often identified as the preincarnate Christ.

Matthew 6:19–34

¹⁹ "Do not store up for yourselves treasures on earth, where moth and rust destroy, and where thieves break in and steal. ²⁰ But store up for yourselves treasures in heaven, where neither moth nor rust destroys, and where thieves do not break in or steal; ²¹ for where your treasure is, there your heart will be also.

²² "The eye is the lamp of the body; so then if your eye is clear, your whole body will be full of light. ²³ But if your eye is bad, your whole body will be full of darkness. If then the light that is in you is darkness, how great is the darkness!

²⁴ "No one can serve two masters; for either he will hate the one and love the other, or he will be devoted to one and despise the other. You cannot serve God and wealth.

²⁵ "For this reason I say to you, do not be worried about your life, *as to* what you will eat or what you will drink; nor for your body, *as to* what you will put on. Is not life more than food, and the body more than clothing? ²⁶ Look at the birds of the air, that they do not sow, nor reap nor gather into barns, and *yet* your heavenly Father feeds them. Are you not worth much more than they? ²⁷ And who of you by being worried can add a *single* hour to his life? ²⁸ And why are you worried about clothing? Observe how the lilies of the field grow; they do not toil nor do they spin, ²⁹ yet

6:22–23 This is an argument from the lesser to the greater. The analogy is simple. If your eye is bad, no light can come in and you are left with darkness because of that malady. How much worse when the problem is not merely related to external perception, but an internal corruption of one's whole nature, so that the darkness actually emanates from within and affects one's whole being. Jesus was indicting them for their superficial earthly religion that left their hearts dark.

I say to you that not even Solomon in all his glory clothed himself like one of these. ³⁰ But if God so clothes the grass of the field, which is *alive* today and tomorrow is thrown into the furnace, *will He* not much more *clothe* you? You of little faith! ³¹ Do not worry then, saying, 'What will we eat?' or 'What will we drink?' or 'What will we wear for clothing?' ³² For the Gentiles eagerly seek all these things; for your heavenly Father knows that you need all these things. ³³ But seek first His kingdom and His righteousness, and all these things will be added to you.

³⁴ "So do not worry about tomorrow; for tomorrow will care for itself. Each day has enough trouble of its own.

DAY 8: What does Abraham's faith teach us about justification?

In Genesis 15:6, we are told that when Abraham "believed" in the Lord, it was "reckoned" to him for "righteousness." The apostle Paul quoted these words as an illustration of faith over and against works (Ro 4:3, 9, 22; Gal 3:6). Abraham was regenerated by faith, and so are we!

This quotation is one of the clearest statements in all Scripture about justification. Abraham's faith is not a meritorious work. It is never the ground of justification—it is simply the channel through which it is received and it, too, is a gift. His faith was "reckoned" or "imputed" to him, which is a term used in both financial and legal settings. It means to take something that belongs to someone and credit to another's account. It is a one-sided transaction—Abraham did nothing to accumulate it: God simply credited it to him. In this case, God took His own righteousness and credited it to Abraham as if it were actually his. This God did because Abraham believed in Him.

The "righteousness" imputed to Abraham is unique: 1) God is its source (Is. 45:8); 2) it fulfills both the penalty and precept of God's law. Christ's death as a substitute pays the penalty exacted on those who failed to keep God's law, and His perfect obedience to every requirement of God's law fulfills God's demand for comprehensive righteousness (2Co 5:21; 1Pe 2:24; see Heb 9:28); and 3) because God's righteousness is eternal (Ps 119:142; Is 51:8; Da 9:24), the one who receives it from Him enjoys it forever.

JANUARY 9

Genesis 17:1–18:33

17 Now when Abram was ninety-nine years old, the LORD appeared to Abram and said to him,

"I am God Almighty;
Walk before Me, and be
blameless.
² "I will establish My covenant
between Me and you,
And I will multiply you
exceedingly."

[3] Abram fell on his face, and God talked with him, saying,

[4] "As for Me, behold, My
covenant is with you,
And you will be the father of
a multitude of nations.
[5] "No longer shall your name
be called Abram,
But your name shall be Abraham;
For I have made you the father
of a multitude of nations.

[6] I will make you exceedingly fruitful, and I will make nations of you, and kings will come forth from you. [7] I will establish My covenant between Me and you and your descendants after you throughout their generations for an everlasting covenant, to be God to you and to your descendants after you. [8] I will give to you and to your descendants after you, the land of your sojournings, all the land of Canaan, for an everlasting possession; and I will be their God."

[9] God said further to Abraham, "Now as for you, you shall keep My covenant, you and your descendants after you throughout their generations. [10] This is My covenant, which you shall keep, between Me and you and your descendants after you: every male among you shall be circumcised. [11] And you shall be circumcised in the flesh of your foreskin, and it shall be the sign of the covenant between Me and you. [12] And every male among you who is eight days old shall be circumcised throughout your generations, a *servant* who is born in the house or who is bought with money from any foreigner, who is not of your descendants. [13] A *servant* who is born in your house or who is bought with your money shall surely be circumcised; thus shall My covenant be in your flesh for an everlasting covenant. [14] But an uncircumcised male who is not circumcised in the flesh of his foreskin, that person shall be cut off from his people; he has broken My covenant."

[15] Then God said to Abraham, "As for Sarai your wife, you shall not call her name Sarai, but Sarah *shall be* her name. [16] I will bless her, and indeed I will give you a son by her. Then I will bless her, and she shall be *a mother of* nations; kings of peoples will come from her." [17] Then Abraham fell on his face and laughed, and said in his heart, "Will a child be born to a man one hundred years old? And will Sarah, who is ninety years old, bear *a child?*" [18] And Abraham said to God, "Oh that Ishmael might live before You!" [19] But God said, "No,

but Sarah your wife will bear you a son, and you shall call his name Isaac; and I will establish My covenant with him for an everlasting covenant for his descendants after him. [20] As for Ishmael, I have heard you; behold, I will bless him, and will make him fruitful and will multiply him exceedingly. He shall become the father of twelve princes, and I will make him a great nation. [21] But My covenant I will establish with Isaac, whom Sarah will bear to you at this season next year." [22] When He finished talking with him, God went up from Abraham.

17:15 Sarai…Sarah. Fittingly, since Sarai ("my princess") would be the ancestress of the promised nations and kings, God changed her name to Sarah, taking away the limiting personal pronoun "my," and calling her "princess" (v. 16).

17:19 call his name Isaac. The name of the promised son meant "he laughs," an appropriate reminder to Abraham of his initial, faithless reaction to God's promise.

[23] Then Abraham took Ishmael his son, and all *the servants* who were born in his house and all who were bought with his money, every male among the men of Abraham's household, and circumcised the flesh of their foreskin in the very same day, as God had said to him. [24] Now Abraham was ninety-nine years old when he was circumcised in the flesh of his foreskin. [25] And Ishmael his son was thirteen years old when he was circumcised in the flesh of his foreskin. [26] In the very same day Abraham was circumcised, and Ishmael his son. [27] All the men of his household, who were born in the house or bought with money from a foreigner, were circumcised with him.

18 Now the LORD appeared to him by the oaks of Mamre, while he was sitting at the tent door in the heat of the day. [2] When he lifted up his eyes and looked, behold, three men were standing opposite him; and when he saw *them,* he ran from the tent door to meet them and bowed himself to the earth, [3] and said, "My Lord, if now I have found favor in Your sight, please do not pass Your servant by. [4] Please let a little water be brought and wash your feet, and rest yourselves under the tree; [5] and I will bring a piece of bread, that you may refresh yourselves; after that you may go on, since you have visited your servant." And they said, "So do, as you have said." ⁶So Abraham hurried into the tent to Sarah, and said, "Quickly, prepare three measures of fine flour, knead *it* and make bread cakes." ⁷Abraham also ran to the herd, and took a tender and choice calf and gave *it* to the servant, and he hurried to prepare it. ⁸He took curds and milk and the calf which he had prepared, and placed *it* before them; and he was standing by them under the tree as they ate.

⁹Then they said to him, "Where is Sarah your wife?" And he said, "There, in the tent." ¹⁰He said, "I will surely return to you at this time next year; and behold, Sarah your wife will have a son." And Sarah was listening at the tent door, which was behind him. ¹¹Now Abraham and Sarah were old, advanced in age; Sarah was past childbearing. ¹²Sarah laughed to herself, saying, "After I have become old, shall I have pleasure, my lord being old also?" ¹³And the LORD said to Abraham, "Why did Sarah laugh, saying, 'Shall I indeed bear *a child*, when I am *so* old?' ¹⁴Is anything too difficult for the LORD? At the appointed time I will return to you, at this time next year, and Sarah will have a son." ¹⁵Sarah denied *it* however, saying, "I did not laugh"; for she was afraid. And He said, "No, but you did laugh."

¹⁶Then the men rose up from there, and looked down toward Sodom; and Abraham was walking with them to send them off. ¹⁷The LORD said, "Shall I hide from Abraham what I am about to do, ¹⁸since Abraham will surely become a great and mighty nation, and in him all the nations of the earth will be blessed? ¹⁹For I have chosen him, so that he may command his children and his household after him to keep the way of the LORD by doing righteousness and justice, so that the LORD may bring upon Abraham what He has spoken about him." ²⁰And the LORD said, "The outcry of Sodom and Gomorrah is indeed great, and their sin is exceedingly grave. ²¹I will go down now, and see if they have done entirely according to its outcry, which has come to Me; and if not, I will know."

²²Then the men turned away from there and went toward Sodom, while Abraham was still standing before the LORD. ²³Abraham came near and said, "Will You indeed sweep away the righteous with the wicked? ²⁴Suppose there are fifty righteous within the city; will You indeed sweep *it* away and not spare the place for the sake of the fifty righteous who are in it? ²⁵Far be it from You to do such a thing, to slay the righteous with the wicked, so that the righteous and the wicked are *treated* alike. Far be it from You! Shall not the Judge of all the earth deal justly?" ²⁶So the LORD said, "If I find in Sodom fifty righteous within the city, then I will spare the whole place on their account." ²⁷And Abraham replied, "Now behold, I have ventured to speak to the Lord, although I am *but* dust and ashes. ²⁸Suppose the fifty righteous are lacking five, will You destroy the whole city because of five?" And He said, "I will not destroy *it* if I find forty-five there." ²⁹He spoke to Him yet again and said, "Suppose forty are found there?" And He said, "I will not do *it* on account of the forty." ³⁰Then he said, "Oh may the Lord not be angry, and I shall speak; suppose thirty are found there?" And He said, "I will not do *it* if I find thirty there." ³¹And he said, "Now behold, I have ventured to speak to the Lord; suppose twenty are found there?" And He said, "I will not destroy *it* on account of the twenty." ³²Then he said, "Oh may the Lord not be angry, and I shall speak only this once; suppose ten are found there?" And He said, "I will not destroy *it* on account of the ten." ³³As soon as He had finished speaking to Abraham the LORD departed, and Abraham returned to his place.

Psalm 5:8–12

8   O LORD, lead me in Your
      righteousness because of my foes;
      Make Your way straight before me.
9   There is nothing reliable
      in what they say;
      Their inward part is destruction *itself.*
      Their throat is an open grave;
      They flatter with their tongue.
10   Hold them guilty, O God;
      By their own devices let them fall!
      In the multitude of their
      transgressions thrust them out,
      For they are rebellious against You.

11   But let all who take refuge
      in You be glad,
      Let them ever sing for joy;
      And may You shelter them,
      That those who love Your
      name may exult in You.
12   For it is You who blesses the
      righteous man, O LORD,
      You surround him with favor
      as with a shield.

Proverbs 2:10–22

10   For wisdom will enter your heart
      And knowledge will be
      pleasant to your soul;

11 Discretion will guard you,
   Understanding will watch
      over you,
12 To deliver you from the way
      of evil,
   From the man who speaks
      perverse things;
13 From those who leave the
      paths of uprightness
   To walk in the ways of darkness;
14 Who delight in doing evil
   And rejoice in the perversity
      of evil;
15 Whose paths are crooked,
   And who are devious in their ways;
16 To deliver you from the
      strange woman,
   From the adulteress who
      flatters with her words;
17 That leaves the companion
      of her youth
   And forgets the covenant
      of her God;
18 For her house sinks down
      to death
   And her tracks *lead* to the dead;
19 None who go to her return again,
   Nor do they reach the paths of life.
20 So you will walk in the
      way of good men
   And keep to the paths of
      the righteous.
21 For the upright will live in the land
   And the blameless will remain
      in it;
22 But the wicked will be cut
      off from the land
   And the treacherous will
      be uprooted from it.

Matthew 7:1–29

7 "Do not judge so that you will not be judged. ² For in the way you judge, you will be judged; and by your standard of measure, it will be measured to you. ³ Why do you look at the speck that is in your brother's eye, but do not notice the log that is in your own eye? ⁴ Or how can you say to your brother, 'Let me take the speck out of your eye,' and behold, the log is in your own eye? ⁵ You hypocrite, first take the log out of your own eye, and then you will see clearly to take the speck out of your brother's eye.

⁶ "Do not give what is holy to dogs, and do not throw your pearls before swine, or they will trample them under their feet, and turn and tear you to pieces.

⁷ "Ask, and it will be given to you; seek, and

7:1 Do not judge. As the context reveals, this does not prohibit all types of judging (v. 16). There is a righteous kind of judgment we are supposed to exercise with careful discernment (Jn 7:24). Censorious, hypocritical, self-righteous, or other kinds of unfair judgments are forbidden; but in order to fulfill the commandments that follow, it is necessary to discern dogs and swine (v. 6) from one's own brethren (vv. 3–5).

you will find; knock, and it will be opened to you. ⁸ For everyone who asks receives, and he who seeks finds, and to him who knocks it will be opened. ⁹ Or what man is there among you who, when his son asks for a loaf, will give him a stone? ¹⁰ Or if he asks for a fish, he will not give him a snake, will he? ¹¹ If you then, being evil, know how to give good gifts to your children, how much more will your Father who is in heaven give what is good to those who ask Him!

¹² "In everything, therefore, treat people the same way you want them to treat you, for this is the Law and the Prophets.

¹³ "Enter through the narrow gate; for the gate is wide and the way is broad that leads to destruction, and there are many who enter through it. ¹⁴ For the gate is small and the way is narrow that leads to life, and there are few who find it.

¹⁵ "Beware of the false prophets, who come to you in sheep's clothing, but inwardly are ravenous wolves. ¹⁶ You will know them by their fruits. Grapes are not gathered from thorn *bushes* nor figs from thistles, are they? ¹⁷ So every good tree bears good fruit, but the bad tree bears bad fruit. ¹⁸ A good tree cannot produce bad fruit, nor can a bad tree produce good fruit. ¹⁹ Every tree that does not bear good fruit is cut down and thrown into the fire. ²⁰ So then, you will know them by their fruits.

²¹ "Not everyone who says to Me, 'Lord, Lord,' will enter the kingdom of heaven, but he who does the will of My Father who is in heaven *will enter.* ²² Many will say to Me on that day, 'Lord, Lord, did we not prophesy in Your name, and in Your name cast out demons, and in Your name perform many miracles?' ²³ And then I will declare to them, 'I never knew you; DEPART FROM ME, YOU WHO PRACTICE LAWLESSNESS.'

²⁴ "Therefore everyone who hears these words of Mine and acts on them, may be compared to a wise man who built his house on

the rock. ²⁵And the rain fell, and the floods came, and the winds blew and slammed against that house; and yet it did not fall, for it had been founded on the rock. ²⁶Everyone who hears these words of Mine and does not act on them, will be like a foolish man who built his house on the sand. ²⁷The rain fell, and the floods came, and the winds blew and slammed against that house; and it fell—and great was its fall."

²⁸When Jesus had finished these words, the crowds were amazed at His teaching; ²⁹for He was teaching them as one having authority, and not as their scribes.

DAY 9: What did Jesus specify about the way to salvation?

In the closing section of the Sermon on the Mount (Mt 7:13–29), Jesus gave a clear gospel application. Here are two gates, two ways, two destinations, and two groups of people (vv. 13–14); two kinds of trees and two kinds of fruit (vv. 17–20); two groups at the judgment (vv. 21–23); and two kinds of builders, building on two kinds of foundations (vv. 24–28). Christ is drawing the line as clearly as possible between the way that leads to destruction and the way which leads to life.

Both the narrow gate and the wide gate (vv. 13–14) are assumed to provide the entrance to God's kingdom. Two ways are offered to people. The narrow gate is by faith, only through Christ, constricted and precise. It represents true salvation in God's way that leads to life eternal. The wide gate includes all religions of works and self-righteousness, with no single way (see Ac 4:12), but leads to hell, not heaven.

Christ continually emphasized the difficulty of following Him (10:38; 16:24–25; Jn 15:18–19; 16:1–3; see Ac 14:22). Salvation is by grace alone but is not easy. It calls for knowledge of the truth, repentance, submission to Christ as Lord, and a willingness to obey His will and Word.

 # JANUARY 10

Genesis 19:1–20:18

19 Now the two angels came to Sodom in the evening as Lot was sitting in the gate of Sodom. When Lot saw them, he rose to meet them and bowed down with his face to the ground. ²And he said, "Now behold, my lords, please turn aside into your servant's house, and spend the night, and wash your feet; then you may rise early and go on your way." They said however, "No, but we shall spend the night in the square." ³Yet he urged them strongly, so they turned aside to him and entered his house; and he prepared a feast for them, and baked unleavened bread, and they ate. ⁴Before they lay down, the men of the city, the men of Sodom, surrounded the house, both young and old, all the people from every quarter; ⁵and they called to Lot and said to him, "Where are the men who

---

19:5 have relations with them. They sought homosexual relations with the visitors. God's attitude toward this vile behavior became clear when He destroyed the city (vv. 23–29). (See Lv 18:22, 29; 20:13; Ro 1:26; 1Co 6:9; 1Ti 1:10 where all homosexual behavior is prohibited and condemned by God.)

came to you tonight? Bring them out to us that we may have relations with them." ⁶But Lot went out to them at the doorway, and shut the door behind him, ⁷and said, "Please, my brothers, do not act wickedly. ⁸Now behold, I have two daughters who have not had relations with man; please let me bring them out to you, and do to them whatever you like; only do nothing to these men, inasmuch as they have come under the shelter of my roof." ⁹But they said, "Stand aside." Furthermore, they said, "This one came in as an alien, and already he is acting like a judge; now we will treat you worse than them." So they pressed hard against Lot and came near to break the door. ¹⁰But the men reached out their hands and brought Lot into the house with them, and shut the door. ¹¹They struck the men who were at the doorway of the house with blindness, both small and great, so that they wearied themselves trying to find the doorway.

¹²Then the two men said to Lot, "Whom else have you here? A son-in-law, and your sons, and your daughters, and whomever you have in the city, bring them out of the place; ¹³for we are about to destroy this place, because their outcry has become so great before the LORD that the LORD has sent us to destroy it." ¹⁴Lot went out and spoke to his sons-in-law, who were to marry his daughters, and said, "Up, get out of this place, for the LORD will destroy the city." But he appeared to his sons-in-law to be jesting.

¹⁵When morning dawned, the angels urged Lot, saying, "Up, take your wife and your two daughters who are here, or you will be swept away in the punishment of the city." ¹⁶But he hesitated. So the men seized his hand and the hand of his wife and the hands of his two daughters, for the compassion of the LORD *was* upon him; and they brought him out, and put him outside the city. ¹⁷When they had brought them outside, one said, "Escape for your life! Do not look behind you, and do not stay anywhere in the valley; escape to the mountains, or you will be swept away." ¹⁸But Lot said to them, "Oh no, my lords! ¹⁹Now behold, your servant has found favor in your sight, and you have magnified your lovingkindness, which you have shown me by saving my life; but I cannot escape to the mountains, for the disaster will overtake me and I will die; ²⁰now behold, this town is near *enough* to flee to, and it is small. Please, let me escape there (is it not small?) that my life may be saved." ²¹He said to him, "Behold, I grant you this request also, not to overthrow the town of which you have spoken. ²²Hurry, escape there, for I cannot do anything until you arrive there." Therefore the name of the town was called Zoar.

²³The sun had risen over the earth when Lot came to Zoar. ²⁴Then the LORD rained on Sodom and Gomorrah brimstone and fire from the LORD out of heaven, ²⁵and He overthrew those cities, and all the valley, and all the inhabitants of the cities, and what grew on the ground. ²⁶But his wife, from behind him, looked *back,* and she became a pillar of salt.

²⁷Now Abraham arose early in the morning *and went* to the place where he had stood before the LORD; ²⁸and he looked down toward Sodom and Gomorrah, and toward all the land of the valley, and he saw, and behold, the smoke of the land ascended like the smoke of a furnace.

19:24 brimstone...from the LORD out of heaven. When morning came (v. 23) judgment fell. Any natural explanation about how the Lord used combustible sulfur deposits to destroy that locale falters on this emphatic indication of miraculous judgment. "Brimstone" could refer to any inflammable substance; perhaps a volcanic eruption and an earthquake with a violent electrical storm "overthrew" (v. 25) the area. That area is now believed to be under the south end of the Dead Sea. Burning gases, sulfur, and magma blown into the air all fell to bury the region.

²⁹Thus it came about, when God destroyed the cities of the valley, that God remembered Abraham, and sent Lot out of the midst of the overthrow, when He overthrew the cities in which Lot lived.

³⁰Lot went up from Zoar, and stayed in the mountains, and his two daughters with him; for he was afraid to stay in Zoar; and he stayed in a cave, he and his two daughters. ³¹Then the firstborn said to the younger, "Our father is old, and there is not a man on earth to come in to us after the manner of the earth. ³²Come, let us make our father drink wine, and let us lie with him that we may preserve our family through our father." ³³So they made their father drink wine that night, and the firstborn went in and lay with her father; and he did not know when she lay down or when she arose. ³⁴On the following day, the firstborn said to the younger, "Behold, I lay last night with my father; let us make him drink wine tonight also; then you go in and lie with him, that we may preserve our family through our father." ³⁵So they made their father drink wine that night also, and the younger arose and lay with him; and he did not know when she lay down or when she arose. ³⁶Thus both the daughters of Lot were with child by their father. ³⁷The firstborn bore a son, and called his name Moab; he is the father of the Moabites to this day. ³⁸As for the younger, she also bore a son, and called his name Ben-ammi; he is the father of the sons of Ammon to this day.

20 Now Abraham journeyed from there toward the land of the Negev, and settled between Kadesh and Shur; then he sojourned in Gerar. ²Abraham said of Sarah his wife, "She is my sister." So Abimelech king of Gerar sent and took Sarah. ³But God came to Abimelech in a dream of the night, and said to him, "Behold, you are a dead man because of the woman whom you have taken, for she is married." ⁴Now Abimelech had not come near her; and he said, "Lord, will You slay a nation, even *though* blameless? ⁵Did he not himself say to me, 'She is my sister'? And she herself said, 'He is my brother.' In the integrity of my heart and the innocence of my hands I have done this." ⁶Then God said to him in the dream, "Yes, I know that in the integrity of your heart you have done this, and I also kept you from sinning against Me; therefore I did not let you touch her. ⁷Now therefore, restore the man's wife, for he is a prophet, and he will pray for you and you will live. But if you do not restore *her,* know that you shall surely die, you and all who are yours."

⁸So Abimelech arose early in the morning

and called all his servants and told all these things in their hearing; and the men were greatly frightened. [9] Then Abimelech called Abraham and said to him, "What have you done to us? And how have I sinned against you, that you have brought on me and on my kingdom a great sin? You have done to me things that ought not to be done." [10] And Abimelech said to Abraham, "What have you encountered, that you have done this thing?" [11] Abraham said, "Because I thought, surely there is no fear of God in this place, and they will kill me because of my wife. [12] Besides, she actually is my sister, the daughter of my father, but not the daughter of my mother, and she became my wife; [13] and it came about, when God caused me to wander from my father's house, that I said to her, 'This is the kindness which you will show to me: everywhere we go, say of me, "He is my brother." ' " [14] Abimelech then took sheep and oxen and male and female servants, and gave them to Abraham, and restored his wife Sarah to him. [15] Abimelech said, "Behold, my land is before you; settle wherever you please." [16] To Sarah he said, "Behold, I have given your brother a thousand pieces of silver; behold, it is your vindication before all who are with you, and before all men you are cleared." [17] Abraham prayed to God, and God healed Abimelech and his wife and his maids, so that they bore *children*. [18] For the LORD had closed fast all the wombs of the household of Abimelech because of Sarah, Abraham's wife.

Psalm 6:1-5

For the choir director; with stringed instruments, upon an eight-string lyre. A Psalm of David.

O LORD, do not rebuke me
    in Your anger,
  Nor chasten me in Your wrath.
[2] Be gracious to me, O LORD,
    for I *am* pining away;
  Heal me, O LORD, for my
    bones are dismayed.
[3] And my soul is greatly
    dismayed;
  But You, O LORD—how long?

[4] Return, O LORD, rescue my soul;
  Save me because of Your
    lovingkindness.
[5] For there is no mention
    of You in death;
  In Sheol who will give You
    thanks?

Proverbs 3:1-4

3 My son, do not forget my teaching,
   But let your heart keep my
     commandments;
[2] For length of days and years of life
   And peace they will add to you.
[3] Do not let kindness and
     truth leave you;
   Bind them around your neck,
   Write them on the tablet
     of your heart.
[4] So you will find favor and good repute
   In the sight of God and man.

3:3 neck...heart. The virtues of mercy (the Hebrew word for "lovingkindness" and "loyal love") and truth that come from God are to become part of us—outwardly in our behavior for all to see as an adornment of spiritual beauty, and inwardly as the subject of our meditation (Dt 6:4-9). Such inward and outward mercy and truth is evidence of New Covenant salvation (Jer 31:33-34).

Matthew 8:1-17

8 When Jesus came down from the mountain, large crowds followed Him. [2] And a leper came to Him and bowed down before Him, and said, "Lord, if You are willing, You can make me clean." [3] Jesus stretched out His hand and touched him, saying, "I am willing; be cleansed." And immediately his leprosy was cleansed. [4] And Jesus *said to him, "See that you tell no one; but go, show yourself to the priest and present the offering that Moses commanded, as a testimony to them."

[5] And when Jesus entered Capernaum, a centurion came to Him, imploring Him, [6] and saying, "Lord, my servant is lying paralyzed at home, fearfully tormented." [7] Jesus *said to him, "I will come and heal him." [8] But the centurion said, "Lord, I am not worthy for You to come under my roof, but just say the word, and my servant will be healed. [9] For I also am a man under authority, with soldiers under me; and I say to this one, 'Go!' and he goes, and to another, 'Come!' and he comes, and to my slave, 'Do this!' and he does *it*." [10] Now when Jesus heard *this*, He marveled and said to those who were following, "Truly I say to you, I have not found such great faith with anyone in Israel. [11] I say to you that many will come from east and west, and recline *at the table* with Abraham, Isaac and Jacob in the kingdom of heaven; [12] but the sons of the kingdom will be

cast out into the outer darkness; in that place there will be weeping and gnashing of teeth." ¹³And Jesus said to the centurion, "Go; it shall be done for you as you have believed." And the servant was healed that *very* moment.

¹⁴When Jesus came into Peter's home, He saw his mother-in-law lying sick in bed with a fever. ¹⁵He touched her hand, and the fever left her; and she got up and waited on Him. ¹⁶When evening came, they brought to Him many who were demon-possessed; and He cast out the spirits with a word, and healed all who were ill. ¹⁷*This was* to fulfill what was spoken through Isaiah the prophet: "HE HIMSELF TOOK OUR INFIRMITIES AND CARRIED AWAY OUR DISEASES."

DAY 10: How can we study and apply some of the Proverbs if we don't understand them?

More often than not, those Proverbs that at first seem unclear or contradictory turn out, instead, to be elusive and deep. Proverbs sometimes do state obvious truths. Their meaning is crystal clear: "A foolish son is a grief to his father and bitterness to her who bore him" (17:25). But many proverbs require thoughtful meditation: "The lot is cast into the lap, but its every decision is from the LORD" (16:33) or "There is a way which seems right to a man, but its end is the way of death" (16:25). The fact that we may have to search the rest of the Scripture or work at thinking ought to make Proverbs dearer to us. If God has chosen this unusual approach to help us grow, why would we hesitate to give our full attention to Proverbs?

Given the context that surrounds Proverbs—the rest of God's Word—a student's failure to grasp a proverb ought not to lead to the conclusion that there's something wrong with this book. A better conclusion would be that the student doesn't know enough yet or hasn't paid enough attention. A wise person puts an elusive proverb on hold for further understanding rather than rejecting it as useless. God's further lessons in that person's life may well cast a new light on parts of the Bible that have been difficult to interpret.

 # JANUARY 11

Genesis 21:1–22:24

21 Then the LORD took note of Sarah as He had said, and the LORD did for Sarah as He had promised. ²So Sarah conceived and bore a son to Abraham in his old age, at the appointed time of which God had spoken to him. ³Abraham called the name of his son who was born to him, whom Sarah bore to him, Isaac. ⁴Then Abraham circumcised his son Isaac when he was eight days old, as God had commanded him. ⁵Now Abraham was one hundred years old when his son Isaac was born to him. ⁶Sarah said, "God has made laughter for me; everyone who hears will laugh with me." ⁷And she said, "Who would have said to Abraham that Sarah would nurse children? Yet I have borne him a son in his old age."

⁸The child grew and was weaned, and Abraham made a great feast on the day that Isaac was weaned. ⁹Now Sarah saw the son of Hagar the Egyptian, whom she had borne to Abraham, mocking. ¹⁰Therefore she said to Abraham, "Drive out this maid and her son, for the son of this maid shall not be an heir with my son Isaac." ¹¹The matter distressed Abraham greatly because of his son. ¹²But God said to Abraham, "Do not be distressed because of the lad and your maid; whatever Sarah tells you, listen to her, for through Isaac your descendants shall be named. ¹³And of the son of the maid I will make a nation also, because he is your descendant." ¹⁴So Abraham rose early in the morning and took bread and a skin of water and gave *them* to Hagar, putting *them* on her shoulder, and *gave her* the boy, and sent her away. And she departed

21:1 the LORD took note of Sarah. To the aged couple (vv. 2, 5, 7), exactly as promised, a son was born and the 25-year suspense was finally over with the laughter of derision turning to rejoicing (v. 6). The barrenness of Sarah (11:30) had ended.

21:10 Drive out...not be an heir. Legal codes of Abraham's day—e.g., of Nuzi and of Hammurabi—forbade the putting out of a handmaiden's son if a rightful, natural heir was born. Sarah's request, thus, offended social law, Abraham's sensibilities, and his love for Ishmael (v. 11). Abraham, however, was given divine approval and assurances to overcome his scruples before sending Hagar and Ishmael out into the wilderness (vv. 12–15).

and wandered about in the wilderness of Beersheba.

¹⁵When the water in the skin was used up, she left the boy under one of the bushes. ¹⁶Then she went and sat down opposite him, about a bowshot away, for she said, "Do not let me see the boy die." And she sat opposite him, and lifted up her voice and wept. ¹⁷God heard the lad crying; and the angel of God called to Hagar from heaven and said to her, "What is the matter with you, Hagar? Do not fear, for God has heard the voice of the lad where he is. ¹⁸Arise, lift up the lad, and hold him by the hand, for I will make a great nation of him." ¹⁹Then God opened her eyes and she saw a well of water; and she went and filled the skin with water and gave the lad a drink.

²⁰God was with the lad, and he grew; and he lived in the wilderness and became an archer. ²¹He lived in the wilderness of Paran, and his mother took a wife for him from the land of Egypt.

²²Now it came about at that time that Abimelech and Phicol, the commander of his army, spoke to Abraham, saying, "God is with you in all that you do; ²³now therefore, swear to me here by God that you will not deal falsely with me or with my offspring or with my posterity, but according to the kindness that I have shown to you, you shall show to me and to the land in which you have sojourned." ²⁴Abraham said, "I swear it." ²⁵But Abraham complained to Abimelech because of the well of water which the servants of Abimelech had seized. ²⁶And Abimelech said, "I do not know who has done this thing; you did not tell me, nor did I hear of it until today."

²⁷Abraham took sheep and oxen and gave them to Abimelech, and the two of them made a covenant. ²⁸Then Abraham set seven ewe lambs of the flock by themselves. ²⁹Abimelech said to Abraham, "What do these seven ewe lambs mean, which you have set by themselves?" ³⁰He said, "You shall take these seven ewe lambs from my hand so that it may be a witness to me, that I dug this well." ³¹Therefore he called that place Beersheba, because there the two of them took an oath. ³²So they made a covenant at Beersheba; and Abimelech and Phicol, the commander of his army, arose and returned to the land of the Philistines. ³³Abraham planted a tamarisk tree at Beersheba, and there he called on the name of the LORD, the Everlasting God. ³⁴And Abraham sojourned in the land of the Philistines for many days.

22 Now it came about after these things, that God tested Abraham, and said to him, "Abraham!" And he said, "Here I am." ²He said, "Take now your son, your only son, whom you love, Isaac, and go to the land of Moriah, and offer him there as a burnt offering on one of the mountains of which I will tell you." ³So Abraham rose early in the morning and saddled his donkey, and took two of his young men with him and Isaac his son; and he split wood for the burnt offering, and arose and went to the place of which God had told him. ⁴On the third day Abraham raised his eyes and saw the place from a distance. ⁵Abraham said to his young men, "Stay here with the donkey, and I and the lad will go over there; and we will worship and return to you." ⁶Abraham took the wood of the burnt offering and laid it on Isaac his son, and he took in his hand the fire and the knife. So the two of them walked on together. ⁷Isaac spoke to Abraham his father and said, "My father!" And he said, "Here I am, my son." And he said, "Behold, the fire and the wood, but where is the lamb for the burnt offering?" ⁸Abraham said, "God will provide for Himself the lamb for the burnt offering, my son." So the two of them walked on together.

⁹Then they came to the place of which God had told him; and Abraham built the altar there and arranged the wood, and bound his son Isaac and laid him on the altar, on top of the wood. ¹⁰Abraham stretched out his hand and took the knife to slay his son. ¹¹But the angel of the LORD called to him from heaven and said, "Abraham, Abraham!" And he said, "Here I am." ¹²He said, "Do not stretch out your hand against the lad, and do nothing to him; for now I know that you fear God, since you have not withheld your son, your only son, from Me." ¹³Then Abraham raised his eyes and looked, and behold, behind *him* a ram caught in the thicket by his horns; and Abraham went and took the ram and offered him up for a burnt offering in the place of his son. ¹⁴Abraham called the name of that place The LORD Will Provide, as it is said to this day, "In the mount of the LORD it will be provided."

¹⁵Then the angel of the LORD called to Abraham a second time from heaven, ¹⁶and said, "By Myself I have sworn, declares the LORD, because you have done this thing and have not withheld your son, your only son, ¹⁷indeed I will greatly bless you, and I will greatly multiply your seed as the stars of the heavens and as the sand which is on the seashore; and your seed shall possess the gate of their enemies. ¹⁸In your seed all the nations of

the earth shall be blessed, because you have obeyed My voice." [19] So Abraham returned to his young men, and they arose and went together to Beersheba; and Abraham lived at Beersheba.

[20] Now it came about after these things, that it was told Abraham, saying, "Behold, Milcah also has borne children to your brother Nahor: [21] Uz his firstborn and Buz his brother and Kemuel the father of Aram [22] and Chesed and Hazo and Pildash and Jidlaph and Bethuel." [23] Bethuel became the father of Rebekah; these eight Milcah bore to Nahor, Abraham's brother. [24] His concubine, whose name was Reumah, also bore Tebah and Gaham and Tahash and Maacah.

Psalm 6:6–10

[6] I am weary with my sighing;
　Every night I make my bed swim,
　I dissolve my couch with my tears.
[7] My eye has wasted away with grief;
　It has become old because
　　of all my adversaries.

[8] Depart from me, all you
　　who do iniquity,
　For the LORD has heard the
　　voice of my weeping.
[9] The LORD has heard my
　　supplication,
　The LORD receives my prayer.
[10] All my enemies will be ashamed
　　and greatly dismayed;
　They shall turn back, they will
　　suddenly be ashamed.

Proverbs 3:5–6

[5] Trust in the LORD with all your
　　heart
　And do not lean on your
　　own understanding.
[6] In all your ways acknowledge
　　Him,
　And He will make your paths straight.

Matthew 8:18–34

[18] Now when Jesus saw a crowd around Him, He gave orders to depart to the other side of the sea. [19] Then a scribe came and said to Him, "Teacher, I will follow You wherever You go." [20] Jesus *said to him, "The foxes have holes and the birds of the air *have* nests, but the Son of Man has nowhere to lay His head." [21] Another of the disciples said to Him, "Lord, permit me first to go and bury my father." [22] But Jesus *said to him, "Follow Me, and allow the dead to bury their own dead."

[23] When He got into the boat, His disciples followed Him. [24] And behold, there arose a great storm on the sea, so that the boat was being covered with the waves; but Jesus Himself was asleep. [25] And they came to *Him* and woke Him, saying, "Save us, Lord; we are perishing!" [26] He *said to them, "Why are you afraid, you men of little faith?" Then He got up and rebuked the winds and the sea, and it became perfectly calm. [27] The men were amazed, and said, "What kind of a man is this, that even the winds and the sea obey Him?"

[28] When He came to the other side into the country of the Gadarenes, two men who were demon-possessed met Him as they were coming out of the tombs. *They were* so extremely violent that no one could pass by that way. [29] And they cried out, saying, "What business do we have with each other, Son of God? Have You come here to torment us before the time?" [30] Now there was a herd of many swine feeding at a distance from them. [31] The demons *began* to entreat Him, saying, "If You *are going to* cast us out, send us into the herd of swine." [32] And He said to them, "Go!" And they came out and went into the swine, and the whole herd rushed down the steep bank into the sea and perished in the waters. [33] The herdsmen ran away, and went to the city and reported everything, including what had happened to the demoniacs. [34] And behold, the whole city came out to meet Jesus; and when they saw Him, they implored Him to leave their region.

8:21 permit me first to go and bury my father. This does not mean that the man's father was already dead. The phrase, "I must bury my father" was a common figure of speech meaning, "Let me wait until I receive my inheritance."

8:24 there arose a great storm. The Sea of Galilee is more than 690 ft. below sea level. To the north, Mt. Hermon rises 9,200 ft., and from May to Oct. strong winds often sweep through the narrow surrounding gorges into this valley, causing extremely sudden and violent storms. **Jesus…was asleep.** Just before the disciples saw one of the most awesome displays of His deity, they were given a touching picture of His humanity. He was so weary that not even the violent tossing of the boat awakened Him— even though the disciples feared they would drown (v. 25).

DAY 11: What does it mean to be demon-possessed?

Matthew 8:16 and 8:28 refer to individuals who were demon-possessed. This means "demonized," or under the internal control of a demon. All of the cases of demonization dealt with by Christ involved the actual indwelling of demons who utterly controlled the bodies of their victims, even to the point of speaking through them (Mk 5:5–9), causing derangement (Jn 10:20), violence (Lk 8:29), or rendering them mute (Mk 9:17–22).

From Matthew 8:29, it is evident that even the demons not only recognized the deity of Jesus, but also knew there was a divinely appointed time for their judgment, and He would be their judge. Their eschatology was factually correct, but it is one thing to know the truth and quite another thing to love it (see Jas 2:19). Luke 8:31 relates they pleaded not to be sent into the abyss, meaning the pit, the underworld, the prison of bound demons who disobeyed (2Pe 2:4; Jude v. 6). They knew Jesus had the power and authority to send them there if He desired.

Deliverance from demons and healing were a fulfillment of the words spoken by Isaiah the prophet concerning the atonement (Is. 53:4–5). Christ bore both the guilt and the curse of sin (see Gal 3:13). Both physical healing and ultimate victory over death are guaranteed by Christ's atoning work, but these will not be fully realized until the very end (1Co 15:26).

JANUARY 12

Genesis 23:1–24:67

23 Now Sarah lived one hundred and twenty-seven years; *these were* the years of the life of Sarah. ²Sarah died in Kiriath-arba (that is, Hebron) in the land of Canaan; and Abraham went in to mourn for Sarah and to weep for her. ³Then Abraham rose from before his dead, and spoke to the sons of Heth, saying, ⁴"I am a stranger and a sojourner among you; give me a burial site among you that I may bury my dead out of my sight." ⁵The sons of Heth answered Abraham, saying to him, ⁶"Hear us, my lord, you are a mighty prince among us; bury your dead in the choicest of our graves; none of us will refuse you his grave for burying your dead." ⁷So Abraham rose and bowed to the people of the land, the sons of Heth. ⁸And he spoke with them, saying, "If it is your wish *for me* to bury my dead out of my sight, hear me, and approach Ephron the son of Zohar for me, ⁹that he may give me the cave of Machpelah which he owns, which is at the end of his field; for the full price let him give it to me in your

23:1–2 Although Sarah's age—the only woman's age at death recorded in Scripture—might suggest her importance in God's plan, it more importantly reminds of the birth of her only son well beyond childbearing age (at 90 years of age, see 17:17) and of God's intervention to bring about the fulfillment of His word to her and Abraham. Sarah's death occurred ca. 2028 B.C.

presence for a burial site." ¹⁰Now Ephron was sitting among the sons of Heth; and Ephron the Hittite answered Abraham in the hearing of the sons of Heth; *even* of all who went in at the gate of his city, saying, ¹¹"No, my lord, hear me; I give you the field, and I give you the cave that is in it. In the presence of the sons of my people I give it to you; bury your dead." ¹²And Abraham bowed before the people of the land. ¹³He spoke to Ephron in the hearing of the people of the land, saying, "If you will only please listen to me; I will give the price of the field, accept *it* from me that I may bury my dead there." ¹⁴Then Ephron answered Abraham, saying to him, ¹⁵"My lord, listen to me; a piece of land worth four hundred shekels of silver, what is that between me and you? So bury your dead." ¹⁶Abraham listened to Ephron; and Abraham weighed out for Ephron the silver which he had named in the hearing of the sons of Heth, four hundred shekels of silver, commercial standard.

¹⁷So Ephron's field, which was in Machpelah, which faced Mamre, the field and cave which was in it, and all the trees which were in the field, that were within all the confines of its border, were deeded over ¹⁸to Abraham for a possession in the presence of the sons of Heth, before all who went in at the gate of his city. ¹⁹After this, Abraham buried Sarah his wife in the cave of the field at Machpelah facing Mamre (that is, Hebron) in the land of Canaan. ²⁰So the field and the cave that is in it, were deeded over to Abraham for a burial site by the sons of Heth.

24 Now Abraham was old, advanced in age; and the LORD had blessed Abraham in every way. ²Abraham said to his servant, the oldest of his household, who had charge of all that he owned, "Please place your

24:2–4 place your hand under my thigh, and… swear. A solemn pledge mentioning the Lord's name and formalized by an accepted customary gesture indicated just how serious an undertaking this was in Abraham's eyes. At his age (v. 1), Abraham was concerned to perpetuate his people and God's promise through the next generation, so he covenanted with his servant to return to Mesopotamia and bring back a wife for Isaac.

hand under my thigh, ³and I will make you swear by the LORD, the God of heaven and the God of earth, that you shall not take a wife for my son from the daughters of the Canaanites, among whom I live, ⁴but you will go to my country and to my relatives, and take a wife for my son Isaac." ⁵The servant said to him, "Suppose the woman is not willing to follow me to this land; should I take your son back to the land from where you came?" ⁶Then Abraham said to him, "Beware that you do not take my son back there! ⁷The LORD, the God of heaven, who took me from my father's house and from the land of my birth, and who spoke to me and who swore to me, saying, 'To your descendants I will give this land,' He will send His angel before you, and you will take a wife for my son from there. ⁸But if the woman is not willing to follow you, then you will be free from this my oath; only do not take my son back there." ⁹So the servant placed his hand under the thigh of Abraham his master, and swore to him concerning this matter.

¹⁰Then the servant took ten camels from the camels of his master, and set out with a variety of good things of his master's in his hand; and he arose and went to Mesopotamia, to the city of Nahor. ¹¹He made the camels kneel down outside the city by the well of water at evening time, the time when women go out to draw water. ¹²He said, "O LORD, the God of my master Abraham, please grant me success today, and show lovingkindness to my master Abraham. ¹³Behold, I am standing by the spring, and the daughters of the men of the city are coming out to draw water; ¹⁴now may it be that the girl to whom I say, 'Please let down your jar so that I may drink,' and who answers, 'Drink, and I will water your camels also'—*may* she *be the one* whom You have appointed for Your servant Isaac; and by this I will know that You have shown lovingkindness to my master."

¹⁵Before he had finished speaking, behold, Rebekah who was born to Bethuel the son of Milcah, the wife of Abraham's brother Nahor, came out with her jar on her shoulder. ¹⁶The girl was very beautiful, a virgin, and no man had had relations with her; and she went down to the spring and filled her jar and came up. ¹⁷Then the servant ran to meet her, and said, "Please let me drink a little water from your jar." ¹⁸She said, "Drink, my lord"; and she quickly lowered her jar to her hand, and gave him a drink. ¹⁹Now when she had finished giving him a drink, she said, "I will draw also for your camels until they have finished drinking." ²⁰So she quickly emptied her jar into the trough, and ran back to the well to draw, and she drew for all his camels. ²¹Meanwhile, the man was gazing at her in silence, to know whether the LORD had made his journey successful or not.

²²When the camels had finished drinking, the man took a gold ring weighing a half-shekel and two bracelets for her wrists weighing ten shekels in gold, ²³and said, "Whose daughter are you? Please tell me, is there room for us to lodge in your father's house?" ²⁴She said to him, "I am the daughter of Bethuel, the son of Milcah, whom she bore to Nahor." ²⁵Again she said to him, "We have plenty of both straw and feed, and room to lodge in." ²⁶Then the man bowed low and worshiped the LORD. ²⁷He said, "Blessed be the LORD, the God of my master Abraham, who has not forsaken His lovingkindness and His truth toward my master; as for me, the LORD has guided me in the way to the house of my master's brothers."

²⁸Then the girl ran and told her mother's household about these things. ²⁹Now Rebekah had a brother whose name was Laban; and Laban ran outside to the man at the spring. ³⁰When he saw the ring and the bracelets on his sister's wrists, and when he heard the words of Rebekah his sister, saying, "This is what the man said to me," he went to the man; and behold, he was standing by the camels at the spring. ³¹And he said, "Come in, blessed of the LORD! Why do you stand outside since I have prepared the house, and a place for the camels?" ³²So the man entered the house. Then Laban unloaded the camels, and he gave straw and feed to the camels, and water to wash his feet and the feet of the men who were with him. ³³But when *food* was set before him to eat, he said, "I will not eat until I have told my business." And he said, "Speak on." ³⁴So he said, "I am Abraham's servant. ³⁵The LORD has greatly blessed my master, so that he has become rich; and He has given him flocks and herds, and silver and gold, and servants and maids, and camels and donkeys. ³⁶Now Sarah

my master's wife bore a son to my master in her old age, and he has given him all that he has. 37 My master made me swear, saying, 'You shall not take a wife for my son from the daughters of the Canaanites, in whose land I live; 38 but you shall go to my father's house and to my relatives, and take a wife for my son.' 39 I said to my master, 'Suppose the woman does not follow me.' 40 He said to me, 'The LORD, before whom I have walked, will send His angel with you to make your journey successful, and you will take a wife for my son from my relatives and from my father's house; 41 then you will be free from my oath, when you come to my relatives; and if they do not give her to you, you will be free from my oath.'

42 "So I came today to the spring, and said, 'O LORD, the God of my master Abraham, if now You will make my journey on which I go successful; 43 behold, I am standing by the spring, and may it be that the maiden who comes out to draw, and to whom I say, "Please let me drink a little water from your jar"; 44 and she will say to me, "You drink, and I will draw for your camels also"; let her be the woman whom the LORD has appointed for my master's son.'

45 "Before I had finished speaking in my heart, behold, Rebekah came out with her jar on her shoulder, and went down to the spring and drew, and I said to her, 'Please let me drink.' 46 She quickly lowered her jar from her *shoulder*, and said, 'Drink, and I will water your camels also'; so I drank, and she watered the camels also. 47 Then I asked her, and said, 'Whose daughter are you?' And she said, 'The daughter of Bethuel, Nahor's son, whom Milcah bore to him'; and I put the ring on her nose, and the bracelets on her wrists. 48 And I bowed low and worshiped the LORD, and blessed the LORD, the God of my master Abraham, who had guided me in the right way to take the daughter of my master's kinsman for his son. 49 So now if you are going to deal kindly and truly with my master, tell me; and if not, let me know, that I may turn to the right hand or the left."

50 Then Laban and Bethuel replied, "The matter comes from the LORD; *so* we cannot speak to you bad or good. 51 Here is Rebekah before you, take *her* and go, and let her be the wife of your master's son, as the LORD has spoken."

52 When Abraham's servant heard their words, he bowed himself to the ground before the LORD. 53 The servant brought out articles of silver and articles of gold, and garments, and gave them to Rebekah; he also gave pre-

cious things to her brother and to her mother. 54 Then he and the men who were with him ate and drank and spent the night. When they arose in the morning, he said, "Send me away to my master." 55 But her brother and her mother said, "Let the girl stay with us *a few* days, say ten; afterward she may go." 56 He said to them, "Do not delay me, since the LORD has prospered my way. Send me away that I may go to my master." 57 And they said, "We will call the girl and consult her wishes." 58 Then they called Rebekah and said to her, "Will you go with this man?" And she said, "I will go." 59 Thus they sent away their sister Rebekah and her nurse with Abraham's servant and his men. 60 They blessed Rebekah and said to her,

> "May you, our sister,
> Become thousands of ten thousands,
> And may your descendants possess
> The gate of those who hate them."

61 Then Rebekah arose with her maids, and they mounted the camels and followed the man. So the servant took Rebekah and departed. 62 Now Isaac had come from going to Beer-lahai-roi; for he was living in the Negev. 63 Isaac went out to meditate in the field toward evening; and he lifted up his eyes and looked, and behold, camels were coming. 64 Rebekah lifted up her eyes, and when she saw Isaac she dismounted from the camel. 65 She said to the servant, "Who is that man walking in the field to meet us?" And the servant said, "He is my master." Then she took her veil and covered herself. 66 The servant told Isaac all the things that he had done. 67 Then Isaac brought her into his mother Sarah's tent, and he took Rebekah, and she became his wife, and he loved her; thus Isaac was comforted after his mother's death.

Psalm 7:1–5

A Shiggaion of David, which he sang
to the LORD concerning Cush, a Benjamite.

O LORD my God, in You I
   have taken refuge;
Save me from all those who
      pursue me, and deliver me,
2   Or he will tear my soul like a lion,
Dragging me away, while
      there is none to deliver.

3   O LORD my God, if I have done this,
If there is injustice in my hands,
4   If I have rewarded evil to my friend,
Or have plundered him who without
      cause was my adversary,

⁵ Let the enemy pursue my
    soul and overtake *it;*
   And let him trample my life
    down to the ground
   And lay my glory in the dust.   *Selah*

Proverbs 3:7-8

⁷ Do not be wise in your own eyes;
  Fear the LORD and turn
    away from evil.
⁸ It will be healing to your body
  And refreshment to your bones.

Matthew 9:1-17

9 Getting into a boat, Jesus crossed over *the sea* and came to His own city. ²And they brought to Him a paralytic lying on a bed. Seeing their faith, Jesus said to the paralytic, "Take courage, son; your sins are forgiven." ³And some of the scribes said to themselves, "This *fellow* blasphemes." ⁴And Jesus knowing their thoughts said, "Why are you thinking evil in your hearts? ⁵Which is easier, to say, 'Your sins are forgiven,' or to say, 'Get up, and walk'? ⁶But so that you may know that the Son of Man has authority on earth to forgive sins"—then He *said to the paralytic, "Get up, pick up your bed and go home." ⁷And he got up and went home. ⁸But when the crowds saw *this,* they were awestruck, and glorified God, who had given such authority to men.

⁹As Jesus went on from there, He saw a man called Matthew, sitting in the tax collector's booth; and He *said to him, "Follow Me!" And he got up and followed Him.

¹⁰Then it happened that as Jesus was reclining *at the table* in the house, behold, many tax collectors and sinners came and were dining with Jesus and His disciples. ¹¹When the Pharisees saw *this,* they said to His disciples, "Why is your Teacher eating with the tax col-

9:1 His own city. Capernaum is the city where Jesus settled. Jesus had left there to get away from the crowds for a time.

9:13 go and learn what this means. This phrase was commonly used as a rebuke for those who did not know something they should have known. The verse Jesus cites is Hosea 6:6, which emphasizes the absolute priority of the law's moral standards over the ceremonial requirements. The Pharisees tended to focus on the outward, ritual, and ceremonial aspects of God's law—to the neglect of its inward, eternal, and moral precepts. In doing so, they became harsh, judgmental, and self-righteously scornful of others. Jesus repeated this same criticism in 12:7.

lectors and sinners?" ¹²But when Jesus heard *this,* He said, "*It is* not those who are healthy who need a physician, but those who are sick. ¹³But go and learn what this means: 'I DESIRE COMPASSION, AND NOT SACRIFICE,' for I did not come to call the righteous, but sinners."

¹⁴Then the disciples of John *came to Him, asking, "Why do we and the Pharisees fast, but Your disciples do not fast?" ¹⁵And Jesus said to them, "The attendants of the bridegroom cannot mourn as long as the bridegroom is with them, can they? But the days will come when the bridegroom is taken away from them, and then they will fast. ¹⁶But no one puts a patch of unshrunk cloth on an old garment; for the patch pulls away from the garment, and a worse tear results. ¹⁷Nor do *people* put new wine into old wineskins; otherwise the wineskins burst, and the wine pours out and the wineskins are ruined; but they put new wine into fresh wineskins, and both are preserved."

DAY 12: Why were the scribes upset that Christ forgave the paralytic?

In Matthew 9:1-8, the fact that the man was brought on a bed indicates that his paralysis was severe. Christ ignored the paralysis and addressed the man's greater needs. Christ's words of forgiveness may indicate that the paralysis was a direct consequence of the man's own sin (Jn 9:1-3).

The scribes' outcry, "This Man blasphemes!" would be a true judgment about anyone but God incarnate, for only the One who has been sinned against has the prerogative to forgive. Jesus' words to the man were therefore an unequivocal claim of divine authority. That He asserted His prerogative that was God's alone was completely understood by the scribes.

Jesus then confronts the scribes directly. It is certainly easier to claim the power to pronounce absolution from sin than to demonstrate the power to heal. Christ actually proved His power to forgive by instantly healing the man of his paralysis. His ability to heal anyone and everyone at will—totally and immediately—was incontrovertible proof of His deity. If He could do the apparently harder, He could also do what seemed easier. The actual forgiving of the sins was in reality the more difficult task, however, because it ultimately required Him to sacrifice His life.

JANUARY 13

25 Now Abraham took another wife, whose name was Keturah. ²She bore to him Zimran and Jokshan and Medan and Midian and Ishbak and Shuah. ³Jokshan became the father of Sheba and Dedan. And the sons of Dedan were Asshurim and Letushim and Leummim. ⁴The sons of Midian were Ephah and Epher and Hanoch and Abida and Eldaah. All these were the sons of Keturah. ⁵Now Abraham gave all that he had to Isaac; ⁶but to the sons of his concubines, Abraham gave gifts while he was still living, and sent them away from his son Isaac eastward, to the land of the east.

⁷These are all the years of Abraham's life that he lived, one hundred and seventy-five years. ⁸Abraham breathed his last and died in a ripe old age, an old man and satisfied *with life;* and he was gathered to his people. ⁹Then his sons Isaac and Ishmael buried him in the cave of Machpelah, in the field of Ephron the son of Zohar the Hittite, facing Mamre, ¹⁰the field which Abraham purchased from the sons of Heth; there Abraham was buried with Sarah his wife. ¹¹It came about after the death of Abraham, that God blessed his son Isaac; and Isaac lived by Beer-lahai-roi.

¹²Now these are *the records of* the generations of Ishmael, Abraham's son, whom Hagar the Egyptian, Sarah's maid, bore to Abraham; ¹³and these are the names of the sons of Ishmael, by their names, in the order of their birth: Nebaioth, the firstborn of Ishmael, and Kedar and Adbeel and Mibsam ¹⁴and Mishma and Dumah and Massa, ¹⁵Hadad and Tema, Jetur, Naphish and Kedemah. ¹⁶These are the sons of Ishmael and these are their names, by their villages, and by their camps; twelve princes according to their tribes. ¹⁷These are the years of the life of Ishmael, one hundred and thirty-seven years; and he breathed his last and died, and was gathered to his people. ¹⁸They settled from Havilah to Shur which is east of Egypt as one goes toward Assyria; he settled in defiance of all his relatives.

¹⁹Now these are *the records of* the generations of Isaac, Abraham's son: Abraham became the father of Isaac; ²⁰and Isaac was forty years old when he took Rebekah, the daughter of Bethuel the Aramean of Paddan-aram, the sister of Laban the Aramean, to be his wife. ²¹Isaac prayed to the LORD on behalf of his wife, because she was barren; and the LORD answered him and Rebekah his wife conceived. ²²But the children struggled together within her; and she said, "If it is so, why then am I *this way?*" So she went to inquire of the LORD. ²³The LORD said to her,

"Two nations are in your womb;
And two peoples will be
  separated from your body;
And one people shall be
  stronger than the other;
And the older shall serve the younger."

²⁴When her days to be delivered were fulfilled, behold, there were twins in her womb. ²⁵Now the first came forth red, all over like a hairy garment; and they named him Esau. ²⁶Afterward his brother came forth with his hand holding on to Esau's heel, so his name was called Jacob; and Isaac was sixty years old when she gave birth to them.

²⁷When the boys grew up, Esau became a skillful hunter, a man of the field, but Jacob was a peaceful man, living in tents. ²⁸Now Isaac loved Esau, because he had a taste for game, but Rebekah loved Jacob. ²⁹When Jacob had cooked stew, Esau came in from the field and he was famished; ³⁰and Esau said to Jacob, "Please let me have a swallow of that red stuff there, for I am famished." Therefore his name was called Edom. ³¹But Jacob said, "First sell me your birthright." ³²Esau said, "Behold, I am about to die; so of what *use* then is the birthright to me?" ³³And Jacob said, "First swear to me";

25:23 the older shall serve the younger. This was contrary to the custom in patriarchal times when the elder son enjoyed the privileges of precedence in the household and at the father's death received a double share of the inheritance and became the recognized head of the family (Ex 22:29; Nu 8:14–17; Dt 21:17). Grave offenses could annul such primogeniture rights (Ge 35:22; 49:3–4; 1Ch 5:1) or the birthright could be sacrificed or legally transferred to another in the family, as in this case (vv. 29–34). In this case, God declared otherwise since His sovereign elective purposes did not necessarily have to follow custom (Ro 9:10–14, esp. v. 12).

25:8 gathered to his people. A euphemism for death, but also an expression of personal continuance beyond death, which denoted a reunion with previously departed friends (ca. 1990 B.C.).

so he swore to him, and sold his birthright to Jacob. ³⁴Then Jacob gave Esau bread and lentil stew; and he ate and drank, and rose and went on his way. Thus Esau despised his birthright.

26 Now there was a famine in the land, besides the previous famine that had occurred in the days of Abraham. So Isaac went to Gerar, to Abimelech king of the Philistines. ²The LORD appeared to him and said, "Do not go down to Egypt; stay in the land of which I shall tell you. ³Sojourn in this land and I will be with you and bless you, for to you and to your descendants I will give all these lands, and I will establish the oath which I swore to your father Abraham. ⁴I will multiply your descendants as the stars of heaven, and will give your descendants all these lands; and by your descendants all the nations of the earth shall be blessed; ⁵because Abraham obeyed Me and kept My charge, My commandments, My statutes and My laws."

⁶So Isaac lived in Gerar. ⁷When the men of the place asked about his wife, he said, "She is my sister," for he was afraid to say, "my wife," *thinking,* "the men of the place might kill me on account of Rebekah, for she is beautiful." ⁸It came about, when he had been there a long time, that Abimelech king of the Philistines looked out through a window, and saw, and behold, Isaac was caressing his wife Rebekah. ⁹Then Abimelech called Isaac and said, "Behold, certainly she is your wife! How then did you say, 'She is my sister'?" And Isaac said to him, "Because I said, 'I might die on account of her.'" ¹⁰Abimelech said, "What is this you have done to us? One of the people might easily have lain with your wife, and you would have brought guilt upon us." ¹¹So Abimelech charged all the people, saying, "He who touches this man or his wife shall surely be put to death."

¹²Now Isaac sowed in that land and reaped in the same year a hundredfold. And the LORD blessed him, ¹³and the man became rich, and continued to grow richer until he became very wealthy; ¹⁴for he had possessions of flocks and herds and a great household, so that the Philistines envied him. ¹⁵Now all the wells which his father's servants had dug in the days of Abraham his father, the Philistines stopped up by filling them with earth. ¹⁶Then Abimelech said to Isaac, "Go away from us, for you are too powerful for us." ¹⁷And Isaac departed from there and camped in the valley of Gerar, and settled there.

¹⁸Then Isaac dug again the wells of water which had been dug in the days of his father Abraham, for the Philistines had stopped them up after the death of Abraham; and he gave them the same names which his father had given them. ¹⁹But when Isaac's servants dug in the valley and found there a well of flowing water, ²⁰the herdsmen of Gerar quarreled with the herdsmen of Isaac, saying, "The water is ours!" So he named the well Esek, because they contended with him. ²¹Then they dug another well, and they quarreled over it too, so he named it Sitnah. ²²He moved away from there and dug another well, and they did not quarrel over it; so he named it Rehoboth, for he said, "At last the LORD has made room for us, and we will be fruitful in the land."

²³Then he went up from there to Beersheba. ²⁴The LORD appeared to him the same night and said,

"I am the God of your father Abraham;
    Do not fear, for I am with you.
I will bless you, and multiply
        your descendants,
    For the sake of My servant Abraham."

²⁵So he built an altar there and called upon the name of the LORD, and pitched his tent there; and there Isaac's servants dug a well. ²⁶Then Abimelech came to him from Gerar with his adviser Ahuzzath and Phicol the commander of his army. ²⁷Isaac said to them, "Why have you come to me, since you hate me and have sent me away from you?" ²⁸They said, "We see plainly that the LORD has been with you; so we said, 'Let there now be an oath between us, *even* between you and us, and let us make a covenant with you, ²⁹that you will do us no harm, just as we have not touched you and have done to you nothing but good and have sent you away in peace. You are now the blessed of the LORD.'" ³⁰Then he made them a feast, and they ate and drank. ³¹In the morning they arose early and exchanged oaths; then Isaac sent them away and they departed from him in peace. ³²Now it came about on the same day, that Isaac's servants came in and told him about the well which they had dug, and said to him, "We have found water." ³³So he called it Shibah; therefore the name of the city is Beersheba to this day.

³⁴When Esau was forty years old he married Judith the daughter of Beeri the Hittite, and Basemath the daughter of Elon the Hittite; ³⁵and they brought grief to Isaac and Rebekah.

Psalm 7:6–8

⁶ Arise, O LORD, in Your anger;
    Lift up Yourself against the
        rage of my adversaries,
    And arouse Yourself for me; You
        have appointed judgment.

7 Let the assembly of the
   peoples encompass You,
   And over them return on high.
8 The LORD judges the peoples;
   Vindicate me, O LORD, according
      to my righteousness and my
      integrity that is in me.

Proverbs 3:9-10

9 Honor the LORD from your wealth
   And from the first of all your produce;
10 So your barns will be filled with plenty
   And your vats will overflow
      with new wine.

Matthew 9:18-38

18 While He was saying these things to
them, a *synagogue* official came and bowed
down before Him, and said, "My daughter has
just died; but come and lay Your hand on her,
and she will live." 19 Jesus got up and *began* to
follow him, and *so did* His disciples.

20 And a woman who had been suffering
from a hemorrhage for twelve years, came
up behind Him and touched the fringe of His
cloak; 21 for she was saying to herself, "If I only
touch His garment, I will get well." 22 But Jesus
turning and seeing her said, "Daughter, take
courage; your faith has made you well." At
once the woman was made well.

23 When Jesus came into the official's house,
and saw the flute-players and the crowd in
noisy disorder, 24 He said, "Leave; for the girl
has not died, but is asleep." And they *began*
laughing at Him. 25 But when the crowd had
been sent out, He entered and took her by the
hand, and the girl got up. 26 This news spread
throughout all that land.

27 As Jesus went on from there, two blind
men followed Him, crying out, "Have mercy
on us, Son of David!" 28 When He entered the

3:9-10 Honor the LORD...wealth. A biblical
view of wealth demands using possessions
for honoring God. This is accomplished by
trusting God (v. 5); by giving the best to God
("first"; see Ex 22:29; 23:19; Dt 18:4); by being
fair (vv. 27-28); by giving generously (11:25);
and by expressing gratitude for all He gives
(Dt 6:10-12). The result of such faithfulness to
honor Him is prosperity and satisfaction.

house, the blind men came up to Him, and
Jesus *said to them, "Do you believe that I am
able to do this?" They *said to Him, "Yes, Lord."
29 Then He touched their eyes, saying, "It shall
be done to you according to your faith." 30 And
their eyes were opened. And Jesus sternly
warned them: "See that no one knows *about
this!*" 31 But they went out and spread the news
about Him throughout all that land.

32 As they were going out, a mute, demon-
possessed man was brought to Him. 33 After
the demon was cast out, the mute man spoke;
and the crowds were amazed, *and were* saying, "Nothing like this has ever been seen
in Israel." 34 But the Pharisees were saying,
"He casts out the demons by the ruler of the
demons."

35 Jesus was going through all the cities
and villages, teaching in their synagogues and
proclaiming the gospel of the kingdom, and
healing every kind of disease and every kind
of sickness.

36 Seeing the people, He felt compassion
for them, because they were distressed and
dispirited like sheep without a shepherd.
37 Then He *said to His disciples, "The harvest
is plentiful, but the workers are few. 38 Therefore beseech the Lord of the harvest to send
out workers into His harvest."

DAY 13: Why is compassion the key to Christian service?

In Matthew 9:35, it describes Jesus' ministry of teaching and preaching the gospel of the kingdom and of healing every sickness and every disease among the people. Jesus banished illness
in an unprecedented healing display, giving impressive evidence of His deity and making the
Jews' rejection all the more heinous.

In v. 36 it adds that Jesus "felt compassion" when He saw the multitudes. Here the humanity
of Christ allowed expression of His attitude toward sinners in terms of human passion. Whereas
God, who is immutable, is not subject to the rise and fall and change of emotions (Nu 23:19),
Christ, who was fully human with all the faculties of humanity, was on occasion moved to literal
tears over the plight of sinners (Lk 19:41). God Himself expressed similar compassion through
the prophets (Ex 33:19; Ps 86:15; Jer 9:1; 13:17; 14:17). He saw these people as weary and scattered.
Their spiritual needs were even more desperate than the need for physical healing.

Meeting those needs requires laborers (v. 37), which is where we come in. The Lord spoke of
the spiritual harvest of souls for salvation; but apart from being moved with the same compassion, our service will be in vain.

JANUARY 14

Genesis 27:1–28:22

27 Now it came about, when Isaac was old and his eyes were too dim to see, that he called his older son Esau and said to him, "My son." And he said to him, "Here I am." ² Isaac said, "Behold now, I am old *and* I do not know the day of my death. ³ Now then, please take your gear, your quiver and your bow, and go out to the field and hunt game for me; ⁴ and prepare a savory dish for me such as I love, and bring it to me that I may eat, so that my soul may bless you before I die."

⁵ Rebekah was listening while Isaac spoke to his son Esau. So when Esau went to the field to hunt for game to bring *home,* ⁶ Rebekah said to her son Jacob, "Behold, I heard your father speak to your brother Esau, saying, ⁷ 'Bring me *some* game and prepare a savory dish for me, that I may eat, and bless you in the presence of the LORD before my death.' ⁸ Now therefore, my son, listen to me as I command you. ⁹ Go now to the flock and bring me two choice young goats from there, that I may prepare them *as* a savory dish for your father, such as he loves. ¹⁰ Then you shall bring *it* to your father, that he may eat, so that he may bless you before his death." ¹¹ Jacob answered his mother Rebekah, "Behold, Esau my brother is a hairy man and I am a smooth man. ¹² Perhaps my father will feel me, then I will be as a deceiver in his sight, and I will bring upon myself a curse and not a blessing." ¹³ But his mother said to him, "Your curse be on me, my son; only obey my voice, and go, get *them* for me." ¹⁴ So he went and got *them,* and brought *them* to his mother; and his mother made savory food such as his father loved. ¹⁵ Then Rebekah took the best garments of Esau her elder son, which were with her in the house, and put them on Jacob her younger son. ¹⁶ And she put the skins of the young goats on his hands and on the smooth part of his neck. ¹⁷ She also gave the savory food and the bread, which she had made, to her son Jacob.

¹⁸ Then he came to his father and said, "My father." And he said, "Here I am. Who are you, my son?" ¹⁹ Jacob said to his father, "I am Esau your firstborn; I have done as you told me. Get up, please, sit and eat of my game, that you may bless me." ²⁰ Isaac said to his son, "How is it that you have *it* so quickly, my son?" And he said, "Because the LORD your God caused *it* to happen to me." ²¹ Then Isaac said to Jacob, "Please come close, that I may feel you, my son, whether you are really my son Esau or not." ²² So Jacob came close to Isaac his father, and he felt him and said, "The voice is the voice of Jacob, but the hands are the hands of Esau." ²³ He did not recognize him, because his hands were hairy like his brother Esau's hands; so he blessed him. ²⁴ And he said, "Are you really my son Esau?" And he said, "I am." ²⁵ So he said, "Bring *it* to me, and I will eat of my son's game, that I may bless you." And he brought *it* to him, and he ate; he also brought him wine and he drank. ²⁶ Then his father Isaac said to him, "Please come close and kiss me, my son." ²⁷ So he came close and kissed him; and when he smelled the smell of his garments, he blessed him and said,

"See, the smell of my son
    Is like the smell of a field which
        the LORD has blessed;
²⁸ Now may God give you of
        the dew of heaven,
    And of the fatness of the earth,
    And an abundance of grain
        and new wine;
²⁹ May peoples serve you,
    And nations bow down to you;
    Be master of your brothers,
    And may your mother's sons
        bow down to you.
    Cursed be those who curse you,
    And blessed be those who bless you."

³⁰ Now it came about, as soon as Isaac had finished blessing Jacob, and Jacob had hardly gone out from the presence of Isaac his father, that Esau his brother came in from his hunting. ³¹ Then he also made savory food, and brought it to his father; and he said to his father, "Let my father arise and eat of his son's game, that you may bless me." ³² Isaac his father said to him, "Who are you?" And he said, "I am your son, your firstborn, Esau." ³³ Then Isaac trembled violently, and said, "Who was he then that hunted game and brought *it* to me, so that I ate of all

27:33 Isaac trembled violently. Visibly shocked when the scandal was uncovered by the entrance of Esau, the father, remembering the Lord's words to Rebekah (25:23), refused to withdraw the blessing and emphatically affirmed its validity—"yes, and he shall be blessed" and a little later "Behold, I have made him your master" and also "your brother you shall serve" (vv. 37, 40). Sudden realization at having opposed God's will all those years likely made the shock more severe.

of it before you came, and blessed him? Yes, and he shall be blessed." ³⁴When Esau heard the words of his father, he cried out with an exceedingly great and bitter cry, and said to his father, "Bless me, *even* me also, O my father!" ³⁵And he said, "Your brother came deceitfully and has taken away your blessing." ³⁶Then he said, "Is he not rightly named Jacob, for he has supplanted me these two times? He took away my birthright, and behold, now he has taken away my blessing." And he said, "Have you not reserved a blessing for me?" ³⁷But Isaac replied to Esau, "Behold, I have made him your master, and all his relatives I have given to him as servants; and with grain and new wine I have sustained him. Now as for you then, what can I do, my son?" ³⁸Esau said to his father, "Do you have only one blessing, my father? Bless me, *even* me also, O my father." So Esau lifted his voice and wept.

³⁹Then Isaac his father answered and said to him,

> "Behold, away from the fertility of
>   the earth shall be your dwelling,
> And away from the dew of
>   heaven from above.
> ⁴⁰ "By your sword you shall live,
>   And your brother you shall serve;
> But it shall come about when
>   you become restless,
> That you will break his yoke
>   from your neck."

⁴¹So Esau bore a grudge against Jacob because of the blessing with which his father had blessed him; and Esau said to himself, "The days of mourning for my father are near; then I will kill my brother Jacob." ⁴²Now when the words of her elder son Esau were reported to Rebekah, she sent and called her younger son Jacob, and said to him, "Behold your brother Esau is consoling himself concerning you *by planning* to kill you. ⁴³Now therefore, my son, obey my voice, and arise, flee to Haran, to my brother Laban! ⁴⁴Stay with him a few days, until your brother's fury subsides, ⁴⁵until your brother's anger against you subsides and he forgets what you did to him. Then I will send and get you from there. Why should I be bereaved of you both in one day?"

⁴⁶Rebekah said to Isaac, "I am tired of living because of the daughters of Heth; if Jacob takes a wife from the daughters of Heth, like these, from the daughters of the land, what good will my life be to me?"

28 So Isaac called Jacob and blessed him and charged him, and said to him, "You shall not take a wife from the daughters of Canaan. ²Arise, go to Paddan-aram, to the house of Bethuel your mother's father; and from there take to yourself a wife from the daughters of Laban your mother's brother. ³May God Almighty bless you and make you fruitful and multiply you, that you may become a company of peoples. ⁴May He also give you the blessing of Abraham, to you and to your descendants with you, that you may possess the land of your sojournings, which God gave to Abraham." ⁵Then Isaac sent Jacob away, and he went to Paddan-aram to Laban, son of Bethuel the Aramean, the brother of Rebekah, the mother of Jacob and Esau.

⁶Now Esau saw that Isaac had blessed Jacob and sent him away to Paddan-aram to take to himself a wife from there, *and that* when he blessed him he charged him, saying, "You shall not take a wife from the daughters of Canaan," ⁷and that Jacob had obeyed his father and his mother and had gone to Paddan-aram. ⁸So Esau saw that the daughters of Canaan displeased his father Isaac; ⁹and Esau went to Ishmael, and married, besides the wives that he had, Mahalath the daughter of Ishmael, Abraham's son, the sister of Nebaioth.

¹⁰Then Jacob departed from Beersheba and went toward Haran. ¹¹He came to a certain place and spent the night there, because the sun had set; and he took one of the stones of the place and put it under his head, and lay down in that place. ¹²He had a dream, and behold, a ladder was set on the earth with its top reaching to heaven; and behold, the angels of God were ascending and descending on it. ¹³And behold, the LORD stood above it and said, "I am the LORD, the God of your father Abraham and the God of Isaac; the land on which you lie, I will give it to you and to your descendants. ¹⁴Your descendants will also be like the dust of the earth, and you will spread out to the west and to the east and to the north and to the south; and in you and in your descendants shall all the families of the earth be blessed. ¹⁵Behold, I am with you and will keep you wherever you go, and will bring you back to this land; for I will not leave you until I have done what I have promised you." ¹⁶Then Jacob awoke from his sleep and said, "Surely the LORD is in this place, and I did not know it." ¹⁷He was afraid and said, "How awesome is this place! This is none other than the house of God, and this is the gate of heaven."

¹⁸So Jacob rose early in the morning, and took the stone that he had put under his head and set it up as a pillar and poured oil on its top. ¹⁹He called the name of that place Bethel;

however, previously the name of the city had been Luz. ²⁰ Then Jacob made a vow, saying, "If God will be with me and will keep me on this journey that I take, and will give me food to eat and garments to wear, ²¹ and I return to my father's house in safety, then the LORD will be my God. ²² This stone, which I have set up as a pillar, will be God's house, and of all that You give me I will surely give a tenth to You."

Psalm 7:9–17

9 O let the evil of the wicked come
    to an end, but establish
    the righteous;
  For the righteous God tries
    the hearts and minds.
10 My shield is with God,
  Who saves the upright in heart.
11 God is a righteous judge,
  And a God who has
    indignation every day.
12 If a man does not repent, He
    will sharpen His sword;
  He has bent His bow and made it ready.
13 He has also prepared for
    Himself deadly weapons;
  He makes His arrows fiery shafts.
14 Behold, he travails with
    wickedness,
  And he conceives mischief and
    brings forth falsehood.
15 He has dug a pit and hollowed it out,
  And has fallen into the hole
    which he made.
16 His mischief will return
    upon his own head,
  And his violence will descend
    upon his own pate.

17 I will give thanks to the LORD
    according to His righteousness
  And will sing praise to the name
    of the LORD Most High.

Proverbs 3:11–12

11 My son, do not reject the
    discipline of the LORD
  Or loathe His reproof,
12 For whom the LORD loves He reproves,
  Even as a father *corrects* the
    son in whom he delights.

Matthew 10:1–20

10 Jesus summoned His twelve disciples and gave them authority over unclean spirits, to cast them out, and to heal every kind of disease and every kind of sickness.

3:11–12 not reject…discipline. Since even the wisest of God's children are subject to sin, there is necessity of God's fatherly discipline to increase wisdom and blessing. Such correction should not be resisted.

---

² Now the names of the twelve apostles are these: The first, Simon, who is called Peter, and Andrew his brother; and James the son of Zebedee, and John his brother; ³ Philip and Bartholomew; Thomas and Matthew the tax collector; James the son of Alphaeus, and Thaddaeus; ⁴ Simon the Zealot, and Judas Iscariot, the one who betrayed Him.

⁵ These twelve Jesus sent out after instructing them: "Do not go in *the* way of *the* Gentiles, and do not enter *any* city of the Samaritans; ⁶ but rather go to the lost sheep of the house of Israel. ⁷ And as you go, preach, saying, 'The kingdom of heaven is at hand.' ⁸ Heal *the* sick, raise *the* dead, cleanse *the* lepers, cast out demons. Freely you received, freely give. ⁹ Do not acquire gold, or silver, or copper for your money belts, ¹⁰ or a bag for *your* journey, or even two coats, or sandals, or a staff; for the worker is worthy of his support. ¹¹ And whatever city or village you enter, inquire who is worthy in it, and stay at his house until you leave *that city*. ¹² As you enter the house, give it your greeting. ¹³ If the house is worthy, give

---

10:1 gave them authority. Jesus delegated His power and authority to the apostles to show clearly that He and His kingdom were sovereign over the physical and spiritual realms, the effects of sin, and the efforts of Satan. This was an unheard of display of power, never before seen in all redemptive history, to announce Messiah's arrival and authenticate Him plus His apostles who preached His gospel. This power was a preview of the power Christ will exhibit in His earthly kingdom, when Satan will be bound (Rev 20) and the curse on physical life curtailed (Is 65:20–25).

10:8 Freely you received, freely give. Jesus was giving them great power, to heal the sick and raise the dead. If they sold these gifts for money, they could have made quite a fortune. But that would have obscured the message of grace Christ sent them to preach. So He forbade them to charge money for their ministry. Yet they were permitted to accept support to meet their basic needs, for a workman is worthy of such support (v. 10).

---

it your *blessing of* peace. But if it is not worthy, take back your *blessing of* peace. ¹⁴Whoever does not receive you, nor heed your words, as you go out of that house or that city, shake the dust off your feet. ¹⁵Truly I say to you, it will be more tolerable for *the* land of Sodom and Gomorrah in the day of judgment than for that city.

¹⁶"Behold, I send you out as sheep in the midst of wolves; so be shrewd as serpents and innocent as doves. ¹⁷But beware of men, for they will hand you over to *the* courts and scourge you in their synagogues; ¹⁸and you will even be brought before governors and kings for My sake, as a testimony to them and to the Gentiles. ¹⁹But when they hand you over, do not worry about how or what you are to say; for it will be given you in that hour what you are to say. ²⁰For it is not you who speak, but *it is* the Spirit of your Father who speaks in you.

DAY 14: What does Jacob's deception teach us about lying?

When Jacob said, "I will be as a deceiver in his sight" (Ge 27:12), his objection to his mother's proposal that he lie to his father makes it clear he fully understood. The differences between him and Esau would surely not fool his father and might result in blessing being replaced with a curse as a fitting punishment for deception. But when Rebekah accepted full responsibility for the scheme and the curse it might incur, Jacob acquiesced and followed Rebekah's instructions.

Even Isaac's perfectly legitimate question in v. 20 afforded Jacob an escape route—confess and stop the deceit! Instead, Jacob, with consummate ease, knowing he needed Isaac's irrevocable confirmation even though he had bought the birthright, ascribed success in the hunt to God's providence. A lie had to sustain a lie, and a tangled web had begun to be woven (vv. 21–24). That principle always follows any lie we tell.

Although Jacob received Isaac's blessing that day, the deceit caused severe consequences: 1) he never saw his mother after that; 2) Esau wanted him dead; 3) Laban, his uncle, deceived him; 4) his family life was full of conflict; and 5) he was exiled for years from his family. By the promise of God, he would have received the birthright (25:23). He didn't need to scheme this deception with his mother.

JANUARY 15

Genesis 29:1–30:43

29 Then Jacob went on his journey, and came to the land of the sons of the east. ²He looked, and saw a well in the field, and behold, three flocks of sheep were lying there beside it, for from that well they watered the flocks. Now the stone on the mouth of the well was large. ³When all the flocks were gathered there, they would then roll the stone from the mouth of the well and water the sheep, and put the stone back in its place on the mouth of the well.

⁴Jacob said to them, "My brothers, where are you from?" And they said, "We are from Haran." ⁵He said to them, "Do you know Laban the son of Nahor?" And they said, "We know *him*." ⁶And he said to them, "Is it well with him?" And they said, "It is well, and here is Rachel his daughter coming with the sheep." ⁷He said, "Behold, it is still high day; it is not time for the livestock to be gathered. Water the sheep, and go, pasture them." ⁸But they said, "We cannot, until all the flocks are gathered, and they roll the stone from the mouth of the well; then we water the sheep."

⁹While he was still speaking with them, Rachel came with her father's sheep, for she was a shepherdess. ¹⁰When Jacob saw Rachel the daughter of Laban his mother's brother, and the sheep of Laban his mother's brother, Jacob went up and rolled the stone from the mouth of the well and watered the flock of Laban his mother's brother. ¹¹Then Jacob kissed Rachel, and lifted his voice and wept. ¹²Jacob told Rachel that he was a relative of her father and that he was Rebekah's son, and she ran and told her father.

¹³So when Laban heard the news of Jacob his sister's son, he ran to meet him, and embraced him and kissed him and brought him to his house. Then he related to Laban all these things. ¹⁴Laban said to him, "Surely you are my bone and my flesh." And he stayed with him a month.

¹⁵Then Laban said to Jacob, "Because you are my relative, should you therefore serve me for nothing? Tell me, what shall your wages be?" ¹⁶Now Laban had two daughters; the name of the older was Leah, and the name of the younger was Rachel. ¹⁷And Leah's eyes were weak, but Rachel was beautiful of form and face. ¹⁸Now Jacob loved Rachel, so he said, "I will serve you seven years for your

29:17 eyes were weak. Probably means that they were a pale color rather than the dark and sparkling eyes most common. Such paleness was viewed as a blemish.

---

younger daughter Rachel." ¹⁹ Laban said, "It is better that I give her to you than to give her to another man; stay with me." ²⁰ So Jacob served seven years for Rachel and they seemed to him but a few days because of his love for her. ²¹ Then Jacob said to Laban, "Give *me* my wife, for my time is completed, that I may go in to her." ²² Laban gathered all the men of the place and made a feast. ²³ Now in the evening he took his daughter Leah, and brought her to him; and *Jacob* went in to her. ²⁴ Laban also gave his maid Zilpah to his daughter Leah as a maid. ²⁵ So it came about in the morning that, behold, it was Leah! And he said to Laban, "What is this you have done to me? Was it not for Rachel that I served with you? Why then have you deceived me?" ²⁶ But Laban said, "It is not the practice in our place to marry off the younger before the firstborn. ²⁷ Complete the week of this one, and we will give you the other also for the service which you shall serve with me for another seven years." ²⁸ Jacob did so and completed her week, and he gave him his daughter Rachel as his wife. ²⁹ Laban also gave his maid Bilhah to his daughter Rachel as her maid. ³⁰ So *Jacob* went in to Rachel also, and indeed he loved Rachel more than Leah, and he served with Laban for another seven years. ³¹ Now the LORD saw that Leah was unloved, and He opened her womb, but Rachel was barren. ³² Leah conceived and bore a son and named him Reuben, for she said, "Because the LORD has seen my affliction; surely now my husband will love me." ³³ Then she conceived again and bore a son and said, "Because the LORD has heard that I am unloved, He has therefore given me this *son* also." So she named him Simeon. ³⁴ She conceived again and bore a son and said, "Now this time my husband will become attached to me, because I have borne him three sons." Therefore he was named Levi. ³⁵ And she conceived again and bore a son and said, "This time I will praise the LORD." Therefore she named him Judah. Then she stopped bearing.

30 Now when Rachel saw that she bore Jacob no children, she became jealous of her sister; and she said to Jacob, "Give me children, or else I die." ² Then Jacob's anger burned against Rachel, and he said, "Am I in the place of God, who has withheld from you

---

30:2 Am I in the place of God…? Although spoken in a moment of frustration with Rachel's pleading for children and the envy with which it was expressed, Jacob's words do indicate an understanding that ultimately God opened and closed the womb.

---

the fruit of the womb?" ³ She said, "Here is my maid Bilhah, go in to her that she may bear on my knees, that through her I too may have children." ⁴ So she gave him her maid Bilhah as a wife, and Jacob went in to her. ⁵ Bilhah conceived and bore Jacob a son. ⁶ Then Rachel said, "God has vindicated me, and has indeed heard my voice and has given me a son." Therefore she named him Dan. ⁷ Rachel's maid Bilhah conceived again and bore Jacob a second son. ⁸ So Rachel said, "With mighty wrestlings I have wrestled with my sister, *and* I have indeed prevailed." And she named him Naphtali.

⁹ When Leah saw that she had stopped bearing, she took her maid Zilpah and gave her to Jacob as a wife. ¹⁰ Leah's maid Zilpah bore Jacob a son. ¹¹ Then Leah said, "How fortunate!" So she named him Gad. ¹² Leah's maid Zilpah bore Jacob a second son. ¹³ Then Leah said, "Happy am I! For women will call me happy." So she named him Asher. ¹⁴ Now in the days of wheat harvest Reuben went and found mandrakes in the field, and brought them to his mother Leah. Then Rachel said to Leah, "Please give me some of your son's mandrakes." ¹⁵ But she said to her, "Is it a small matter for you to take my husband? And would you take my son's mandrakes also?" So Rachel said, "Therefore he may lie with you tonight in return for your son's mandrakes." ¹⁶ When Jacob came in from the field in the evening, then Leah went out to meet him and said, "You must come in to me, for I have surely hired you with my son's mandrakes." So he lay with her that night. ¹⁷ God gave heed to Leah, and she conceived and bore Jacob a fifth son. ¹⁸ Then Leah said, "God has given me my wages because I gave my maid to my husband." So she named him Issachar. ¹⁹ Leah conceived again and bore a sixth son to Jacob. ²⁰ Then Leah said, "God has endowed me with a good gift; now my husband will dwell with me, because I have borne him six sons." So she named him Zebulun. ²¹ Afterward she bore a daughter and named her Dinah.

²² Then God remembered Rachel, and God gave heed to her and opened her womb. ²³ So she conceived and bore a son and said, "God

has taken away my reproach." ²⁴ She named him Joseph, saying, "May the LORD give me another son."

²⁵ Now it came about when Rachel had borne Joseph, that Jacob said to Laban, "Send me away, that I may go to my own place and to my own country. ²⁶ Give me my wives and my children for whom I have served you, and let me depart; for you yourself know my service which I have rendered you." ²⁷ But Laban said to him, "If now it pleases you, *stay with me;* I have divined that the LORD has blessed me on your account." ²⁸ He continued, "Name me your wages, and I will give it." ²⁹ But he said to him, "You yourself know how I have served you and how your cattle have fared with me. ³⁰ For you had little before I came and it has increased to a multitude, and the LORD has blessed you wherever I turned. But now, when shall I provide for my own household also?" ³¹ So he said, "What shall I give you?" And Jacob said, "You shall not give me anything. If you will do this *one* thing for me, I will again pasture *and* keep your flock: ³² let me pass through your entire flock today, removing from there every speckled and spotted sheep and every black one among the lambs and the spotted and speckled among the goats; and *such* shall be my wages. ³³ So my honesty will answer for me later, when you come concerning my wages. Every one that is not speckled and spotted among the goats and black among the lambs, *if found* with me, will be considered stolen." ³⁴ Laban said, "Good, let it be according to your word." ³⁵ So he removed on that day the striped and spotted male goats and all the speckled and spotted female goats, every one with white in it, and all the black ones among the sheep, and gave them into the care of his sons. ³⁶ And he put *a distance of* three days' journey between himself and Jacob, and Jacob fed the rest of Laban's flocks.

³⁷ Then Jacob took fresh rods of poplar and almond and plane trees, and peeled white stripes in them, exposing the white which *was* in the rods. ³⁸ He set the rods which he had peeled in front of the flocks in the gutters, *even* in the watering troughs, where the flocks came to drink; and they mated when they came to drink. ³⁹ So the flocks mated by the rods, and the flocks brought forth striped, speckled, and spotted. ⁴⁰ Jacob separated the lambs, and made the flocks face toward the striped and all the black in the flock of Laban; and he put his own herds apart, and did not put them with Laban's flock. ⁴¹ Moreover, whenever the stronger of the flock were mating, Jacob would place the rods in the sight of the flock in the gutters, so that they might mate by the rods; ⁴² but when the flock was feeble, he did not put *them* in; so the feebler were Laban's and the stronger Jacob's. ⁴³ So the man became exceedingly prosperous, and had large flocks and female and male servants and camels and donkeys.

Psalm 8:1–5

For the choir director; on the Gittith.
A Psalm of David.

O LORD, our Lord,
How majestic is Your name
in all the earth,
Who have displayed Your splendor
above the heavens!

² From the mouth of infants and nursing
babes You have established strength
Because of Your adversaries,
To make the enemy and the
revengeful cease.

³ When I consider Your heavens,
the work of Your fingers,
The moon and the stars, which
You have ordained;

⁴ What is man that You take
thought of him,
And the son of man that
You care for him?

⁵ Yet You have made him a
little lower than God,
And You crown him with
glory and majesty!

Proverbs 3:13–18

¹³ How blessed is the man
who finds wisdom
And the man who gains
understanding.

8:3 Your heavens, the work of Your fingers. The heavens are created by God (Pss 33:6, 9; 102:25; 136:5). The anthropomorphism "Your fingers" miniaturizes the magnitude of the universe in the presence of the Creator.

8:4 What is man. If the whole universe is diminutive in the sight of the Divine Creator, how much less is the significance of mankind! Even the word for "man" used in v. 4 alludes to his weakness (Pss 9:19–20; 90:3a; 103:15, etc.). **And the son of man.** This phrase also looks upon man as insignificant and transitory (e.g., Ps 90:3b). Yet, the Aram. counterpart of this phrase is found in Daniel 7:13, which has profound messianic overtones (see also Jesus' favorite self-designation in the New Testament, Son of Man).

14 For her profit is better than
  the profit of silver
  And her gain better than fine
    gold.
15 She is more precious than
    jewels;
  And nothing you desire
    compares with her.
16 Long life is in her right hand;
  In her left hand are riches
    and honor.
17 Her ways are pleasant ways
  And all her paths are peace.
18 She is a tree of life to those
    who take hold of her,
  And happy are all who hold
    her fast.

Matthew 10:21-42

21 "Brother will betray brother to death, and a father *his* child; and children will rise up against parents and cause them to be put to death. 22 You will be hated by all because of My name, but it is the one who has endured to the end who will be saved.

23 "But whenever they persecute you in one city, flee to the next; for truly I say to you, you will not finish *going through* the cities of Israel until the Son of Man comes.

24 "A disciple is not above his teacher, nor a slave above his master. 25 It is enough for the disciple that he become like his teacher, and the slave like his master. If they have called the head of the house Beelzebul, how much more *will they malign* the members of his household!

26 "Therefore do not fear them, for there is nothing concealed that will not be revealed, or hidden that will not be known. 27 What I tell you in the darkness, speak in the light; and what you hear *whispered* in *your* ear, proclaim upon the housetops. 28 Do not fear those who kill the body but are unable to kill the soul; but rather fear Him who is able to destroy both soul and body in hell. 29 Are not two sparrows sold for a cent? And *yet* not one of them will fall to the ground apart from your Father. 30 But the very hairs of your head are all numbered. 31 So do not fear; you are more valuable than many sparrows.

32 "Therefore everyone who confesses Me before men, I will also confess him before My Father who is in heaven. 33 But whoever denies Me before men, I will also deny him before My Father who is in heaven.

34 "Do not think that I came to bring peace on the earth; I did not come to bring peace, but a sword. 35 For I came to SET A MAN AGAINST HIS FATHER, AND A DAUGHTER AGAINST HER MOTHER, AND A DAUGHTER-IN-LAW AGAINST HER MOTHER-IN-LAW; 36 and A MAN'S ENEMIES WILL BE THE MEMBERS OF HIS HOUSEHOLD.

37 "He who loves father or mother more than Me is not worthy of Me; and he who loves son or daughter more than Me is not worthy of Me. 38 And he who does not take his cross and follow after Me is not worthy of Me. 39 He who has found his life will lose it, and he who has lost his life for My sake will find it.

40 "He who receives you receives Me, and he who receives Me receives Him who sent Me. 41 He who receives a prophet in *the* name of a prophet shall receive a prophet's reward; and he who receives a righteous man in the name of a righteous man shall receive a righteous man's reward. 42 And whoever in the name of a disciple gives to one of these little ones even a cup of cold water to drink, truly I say to you, he shall not lose his reward."

DAY 15: Should I expect to be persecuted for my faith?

In Matthew 10:32, Jesus makes the amazing promise that the person who acknowledges Him as Lord in life or in death, if necessary, is the one whom He will acknowledge personally before God as His own (Mt 13:20; 2Ti 2:10-13). Conversely, He describes the soul-damning denial of Christ of those who through fear, shame, neglect, or love of the world reject all evidence and revelation and decline to confess Christ as Savior and King.

Though the ultimate end of the gospel is peace with God (Jn 14:27; Ro 8:6), the immediate result of the gospel is frequently conflict (v. 34). Conversion to Christ can result in strained family relationships (vv. 35-36), persecution, and even martyrdom. Following Christ presupposes a willingness to endure such hardships (vv. 32-33, 37-39). Though He is called "Prince of Peace" (Is. 9:6), Christ will have no one deluded into thinking that He calls believers to a life devoid of all conflict.

When Jesus adds that a disciple must "take his cross" (v. 38), it is His first mention of the word "cross" to His disciples. To them it would have evoked a picture of a violent, degrading death. He was demanding total commitment from them—even unto physical death—and making this call to full surrender a part of the message they were to proclaim to others. For those who come to Christ with self-renouncing faith, there will be true and eternal life (v. 39).

JANUARY 16

Genesis 31:1–32:32

31 Now Jacob heard the words of Laban's sons, saying, "Jacob has taken away all that was our father's, and from what belonged to our father he has made all this wealth." ²Jacob saw the attitude of Laban, and behold, it was not *friendly* toward him as formerly. ³Then the LORD said to Jacob, "Return to the land of your fathers and to your relatives, and I will be with you." ⁴So Jacob sent and called Rachel and Leah to his flock in the field, ⁵and said to them, "I see your father's attitude, that it is not *friendly* toward me as formerly, but the God of my father has been with me. ⁶You know that I have served your father with all my strength. ⁷Yet your father has cheated me and changed my wages ten times; however, God did not allow him to hurt me. ⁸If he spoke thus, 'The speckled shall be your wages,' then all the flock brought forth speckled; and if he spoke thus, 'The striped shall be your wages,' then all the flock brought forth striped. ⁹Thus God has taken away your father's livestock and given *them* to me. ¹⁰And it came about at the time when the flock were mating that I lifted up my eyes and saw in a dream, and behold, the male goats which were mating *were* striped, speckled, and mottled. ¹¹Then the angel of God said to me in the dream, 'Jacob,' and I said, 'Here I am.' ¹²He said, 'Lift up now your eyes and see *that* all the male goats which are mating are striped, speckled, and mottled; for I have seen all that Laban has been doing to you. ¹³I am the God *of* Bethel, where you anointed a pillar, where you made a vow to Me; now arise, leave this land, and return to the land of your birth.'" ¹⁴Rachel and Leah said to him, "Do we still have any portion or inheritance in our father's house? ¹⁵Are we not reckoned by him as foreigners? For he has sold us, and has also entirely consumed our purchase price. ¹⁶Surely all the wealth which God has taken away from our father belongs to us and our children; now then, do whatever God has said to you."

¹⁷Then Jacob arose and put his children and his wives upon camels; ¹⁸and he drove away all his livestock and all his property which he had gathered, his acquired livestock which he had gathered in Paddan-aram, to go to the land of Canaan to his father Isaac. ¹⁹When Laban had gone to shear his flock, then Rachel stole the household idols that were her father's. ²⁰And Jacob deceived Laban the Aramean by not telling him that he was fleeing. ²¹So he fled with all that he had; and

---

31:19 household idols. Literally, teraphim (2Ki 23:24; Eze 21:21). These images or figurines of varying sizes, usually of nude goddesses with accentuated sexual features, either signaled special protection for, inheritance rights for, or guaranteed fertility for the bearer. Or, perhaps possession by Rachel would call for Jacob to be recognized as head of the household at Laban's death.

---

he arose and crossed the *Euphrates* River, and set his face toward the hill country of Gilead.

²²When it was told Laban on the third day that Jacob had fled, ²³then he took his kinsmen with him and pursued him *a distance of* seven days' journey, and he overtook him in the hill country of Gilead. ²⁴God came to Laban the Aramean in a dream of the night and said to him, "Be careful that you do not speak to Jacob either good or bad."

²⁵Laban caught up with Jacob. Now Jacob had pitched his tent in the hill country, and Laban with his kinsmen camped in the hill country of Gilead. ²⁶Then Laban said to Jacob, "What have you done by deceiving me and carrying away my daughters like captives of the sword? ²⁷Why did you flee secretly and deceive me, and did not tell me so that I might have sent you away with joy and with songs, with timbrel and with lyre; ²⁸and did not allow me to kiss my sons and my daughters? Now you have done foolishly. ²⁹It is in my power to do you harm, but the God of your father spoke to me last night, saying, 'Be careful not to speak either good or bad to Jacob.' ³⁰Now you have indeed gone away because you longed greatly for your father's house; *but* why did you steal my gods?" ³¹Then Jacob replied to Laban, "Because I was afraid, for I thought that you would take your daughters from me by force. ³²The one with whom you find your gods shall not live; in the presence of our kinsmen point out what is yours among my belongings and take *it* for yourself." For Jacob did not know that Rachel had stolen them.

³³So Laban went into Jacob's tent and into Leah's tent and into the tent of the two maids, but he did not find *them*. Then he went out of Leah's tent and entered Rachel's tent. ³⁴Now Rachel had taken the household idols and put them in the camel's saddle, and she sat on them. And Laban felt through all the tent but did not find *them*. ³⁵She said to her father, "Let not my lord be angry that I cannot rise before you, for the manner of women is upon me." So he searched but did not find the household idols.

36 Then Jacob became angry and contended with Laban; and Jacob said to Laban, "What is my transgression? What is my sin that you have hotly pursued me? 37 Though you have felt through all my goods, what have you found of all your household goods? Set *it* here before my kinsmen and your kinsmen, that they may decide between us two. 38 These twenty years I *have been* with you; your ewes and your female goats have not miscarried, nor have I eaten the rams of your flocks. 39 That which was torn *of beasts* I did not bring to you; I bore the loss of it myself. You required it of my hand *whether* stolen by day or stolen by night. 40 *Thus* I was: by day the heat consumed me and the frost by night, and my sleep fled from my eyes. 41 These twenty years I have been in your house; I served you fourteen years for your two daughters and six years for your flock, and you changed my wages ten times. 42 If the God of my father, the God of Abraham, and the fear of Isaac, had not been for me, surely now you would have sent me away empty-handed. God has seen my affliction and the toil of my hands, so He rendered judgment last night."

43 Then Laban replied to Jacob, "The daughters are my daughters, and the children are my children, and the flocks are my flocks, and all that you see is mine. But what can I do this day to these my daughters or to their children whom they have borne? 44 So now come, let us make a covenant, you and I, and let it be a witness between you and me." 45 Then Jacob took a stone and set it up *as* a pillar. 46 Jacob said to his kinsmen, "Gather stones." So they took stones and made a heap, and they ate there by the heap. 47 Now Laban called it Jegar-sahadutha, but Jacob called it Galeed. 48 Laban said, "This heap is a witness between you and me this day." Therefore it was named Galeed, 49 and Mizpah, for he said, "May the LORD watch between you and me when we are absent one from the other. 50 If you mistreat my daughters, or if you take wives besides my daughters, *although* no man is with us, see, God is witness between you and me." 51 Laban said to Jacob, "Behold this heap and behold the pillar which I have set between you and me. 52 This heap is a witness, and the pillar is a witness, that I will not pass by this heap to you for harm, and you will not pass by this heap and this pillar to me, for harm. 53 The God of Abraham and the God of Nahor, the God of their father, judge between us." So Jacob swore by the fear of his father Isaac. 54 Then Jacob offered a sacrifice on the mountain, and called his kinsmen to the meal; and they ate the meal and spent the night on the mountain. 55 Early in the morning Laban arose, and kissed his sons and his daughters and blessed them. Then Laban departed and returned to his place.

32 Now as Jacob went on his way, the angels of God met him. 2 Jacob said when he saw them, "This is God's camp." So he named that place Mahanaim.

3 Then Jacob sent messengers before him to his brother Esau in the land of Seir, the country of Edom. 4 He also commanded them saying, "Thus you shall say to my lord Esau: 'Thus says your servant Jacob, "I have sojourned with Laban, and stayed until now; 5 I have oxen and donkeys *and* flocks and male and female servants; and I have sent to tell my lord, that I may find favor in your sight."'"

6 The messengers returned to Jacob, saying, "We came to your brother Esau, and furthermore he is coming to meet you, and four hundred men are with him." 7 Then Jacob was greatly afraid and distressed; and he divided the people who were with him, and the flocks and the herds and the camels, into two companies; 8 for he said, "If Esau comes to the one company and attacks it, then the company which is left will escape."

9 Jacob said, "O God of my father Abraham and God of my father Isaac, O LORD, who said to me, 'Return to your country and to your relatives, and I will prosper you,' 10 I am unworthy of all the lovingkindness and of all the faithfulness which You have shown to Your servant; for with my staff *only* I crossed this Jordan, and now I have become two companies. 11 Deliver me, I pray, from the hand of my brother, from the hand of Esau; for I fear him, that he will come and attack me *and* the mothers with the children. 12 For You said, 'I will surely prosper you and make your descendants as the sand of the sea, which is too great to be numbered.'"

13 So he spent the night there. Then he selected from what he had with him a present for his brother Esau: 14 two hundred female goats and twenty male goats, two hundred ewes and twenty rams, 15 thirty milking camels and their colts, forty cows and ten bulls, twenty female donkeys and ten male donkeys. 16 He delivered *them* into the hand of his servants, every drove by itself, and said to his servants, "Pass on before me, and put a space between droves." 17 He commanded the one in front, saying, "When my brother Esau meets you and asks you, saying, 'To whom do you belong, and where are you going, and to whom do these *animals* in front of you belong?' 18 then you

shall say, '*These* belong to your servant Jacob; it is a present sent to my lord Esau. And behold, he also is behind us.'" ¹⁹ Then he commanded also the second and the third, and all those who followed the droves, saying, "After this manner you shall speak to Esau when you find him; ²⁰ and you shall say, 'Behold, your servant Jacob also is behind us.'" For he said, "I will appease him with the present that goes before me. Then afterward I will see his face; perhaps he will accept me." ²¹ So the present passed on before him, while he himself spent that night in the camp.

²² Now he arose that same night and took his two wives and his two maids and his eleven children, and crossed the ford of the Jabbok. ²³ He took them and sent them across the stream. And he sent across whatever he had. ²⁴ Then Jacob was left alone, and a man wrestled with him until daybreak. ²⁵ When he saw that he had not prevailed against him, he touched the socket of his thigh; so the socket of Jacob's thigh was dislocated while he wrestled with him. ²⁶ Then he said, "Let me go, for the dawn is breaking." But he said, "I will not let you go unless you bless me." ²⁷ So he said to him, "What is your name?" And he said, "Jacob." ²⁸ He said, "Your name shall no longer be Jacob, but Israel; for you have striven with God and with men and have prevailed." ²⁹ Then Jacob asked him and said, "Please tell me your name." But he said, "Why is it that you ask my name?" And he blessed him there. ³⁰ So Jacob named the place Peniel, for *he said,* "I have seen God face to face, yet my life has been preserved." ³¹ Now the sun rose upon him just as he crossed over Penuel, and he was limping on his thigh. ³² Therefore, to this day the sons of Israel do not eat the sinew of the hip which is on the socket of the thigh, because he touched the socket of Jacob's thigh in the sinew of the hip.

Psalm 8:6–9

⁶ You make him to rule over the
works of Your hands;
You have put all things under
his feet,
⁷ All sheep and oxen,
And also the beasts of the field,
⁸ The birds of the heavens and
the fish of the sea,
Whatever passes through
the paths of the seas.

⁹ O LORD, our Lord,
How majestic is Your name
in all the earth!

Proverbs 3:19–20

¹⁹ The LORD by wisdom
founded the earth,
By understanding He
established the heavens.
²⁰ By His knowledge the deeps
were broken up
And the skies drip with dew.

Matthew 11:1–30

11 When Jesus had finished giving instructions to His twelve disciples, He departed from there to teach and preach in their cities.

² Now when John, while imprisoned, heard of the works of Christ, he sent *word* by his disciples ³ and said to Him, "Are You the Expected One, or shall we look for someone else?" ⁴ Jesus answered and said to them, "Go and report to John what you hear and see: ⁵ *the* BLIND RECEIVE SIGHT and *the* lame walk, *the* lepers are cleansed and *the* deaf hear, *the* dead are raised up, and *the* POOR HAVE THE GOSPEL PREACHED TO THEM. ⁶ And blessed is he who does not take offense at Me."

⁷ As these men were going *away,* Jesus began to speak to the crowds about John, "What did you go out into the wilderness to see? A reed shaken by the wind? ⁸ But what did you go out to see? A man dressed in soft *clothing?* Those who wear soft *clothing* are in kings' palaces! ⁹ But what did you go out to see? A prophet? Yes, I tell you, and one who is more than a prophet. ¹⁰ This is the one about whom it is written,

'Behold, I SEND MY MESSENGER
AHEAD OF YOU,
WHO WILL PREPARE YOUR
WAY BEFORE YOU.'

¹¹ Truly I say to you, among those born of women there has not arisen *anyone* greater than John the Baptist! Yet the one who is least in the kingdom of heaven is greater than he. ¹² From the days of John the Baptist until now the kingdom of heaven suffers violence, and violent men take it by force. ¹³ For all the prophets and the Law prophesied until John. ¹⁴ And if you are willing to accept *it,* John himself is Elijah who was to come. ¹⁵ He who has ears to hear, let him hear.

¹⁶ "But to what shall I compare this generation? It is like children sitting in the market places, who call out to the other *children,* ¹⁷ and say, 'We played the flute for you, and you did not dance; we sang a dirge, and you did not mourn.' ¹⁸ For John came neither eating

11:12 the kingdom of heaven suffers violence.
From the time he began his preaching ministry, John the Baptist evoked a strong reaction. Having been imprisoned already, John ultimately fell victim to Herod's savagery. But the kingdom can never be subdued or opposed by human violence. Notice that where Matthew says, "the violent take it by force," Luke has, "everyone forcing his way into it" (Lk 16:16). So the sense of this verse may be rendered this way: "The kingdom presses ahead relentlessly, and only the relentless press their way into it." Thus again Christ is magnifying the difficulty of entering the kingdom.

---

nor drinking, and they say, 'He has a demon!' ¹⁹The Son of Man came eating and drinking, and they say, 'Behold, a gluttonous man and a drunkard, a friend of tax collectors and sinners!' Yet wisdom is vindicated by her deeds."

²⁰Then He began to denounce the cities in which most of His miracles were done, because they did not repent. ²¹"Woe to you, Chorazin! Woe to you, Bethsaida! For if the miracles had occurred in Tyre and Sidon which occurred in you, they would have repented long ago in sackcloth and ashes. ²²Nevertheless I say to you, it will be more tolerable for Tyre and Sidon in the day of judgment than for you. ²³And you, Capernaum, will not be exalted to heaven, will you? You will descend to Hades; for if the miracles had occurred in Sodom which occurred in you, it would have remained to this day. ²⁴Nevertheless I say to you that it will be more tolerable

for the land of Sodom in the day of judgment, than for you."

²⁵At that time Jesus said, "I praise You, Father, Lord of heaven and earth, that You have hidden these things from the wise and intelligent and have revealed them to infants. ²⁶Yes, Father, for this way was well-pleasing in Your sight. ²⁷All things have been handed over to Me by My Father; and no one knows the Son except the Father; nor does anyone know the Father except the Son, and anyone to whom the Son wills to reveal Him.

²⁸"Come to Me, all who are weary and heavy-laden, and I will give you rest. ²⁹Take My yoke upon you and learn from Me, for I am gentle and humble in heart, and YOU WILL FIND REST FOR YOUR SOULS. ³⁰For My yoke is easy and My burden is light."

11:28-30 Come to Me, all who are weary and heavy-laden. There is an echo of the first beatitude (5:3) in this passage. Note that this is an open invitation to all who hear—but phrased in such a way that the only ones who will respond to the invitation are those who are burdened by their own spiritual bankruptcy and the weight of trying to save themselves by keeping the law. The stubbornness of humanity's sinful rebellion is such that without a sovereignly bestowed spiritual awakening, all sinners refuse to acknowledge the depth of their spiritual poverty. That is why, as Jesus says in v. 27, our salvation is the sovereign work of God. But the truth of divine election in v. 27 is not incompatible with the free offer to all in vv. 28–30.

DAY 16: List the false gods in the Old Testament.

1. Rachel's household gods (Ge 31:19)
2. The golden calf at Sinai (Ex 32)
3. Nanna, the moon god of Ur, worshiped by Abraham before his salvation (Jos 24:2)
4. Asherah, or Ashtaroth, the chief goddess of Tyre, referred to as the lady of the sea (Jdg 6:24–32)
5. Dagon, the chief Philistine agriculture and sea god and father of Baal (Jdg 16:23–30)
6. Ashtoreth, a Canaanite goddess, another consort of Baal (1Sa 7:3–4)
7. Molech, the god of the Ammonites and the most horrible idol in the Scriptures (1Ki 11:7)
8. The two golden images made by King Jeroboam, set up at the shrines of Dan and Bethel (1Ki 12:28–31)
9. Baal, the chief deity of Canaan (1Ki 18:17–40; 2Ki 10:28; 11:18)
10. Rimmon, the Syrian god of Naaman the leper (2Ki 5:15–19)
11. Nishroch, the Assyrian god of Sennacherib (2Ki 19:37)
12. Nebo, the Babylonian god of wisdom and literature (Is. 46:1)
13. Merodach, also called Marduk, the chief god of the Babylonian pantheon (Jer 50:2)
14. Tammuz, the husband and brother of Ishtar (Asherah), goddess of fertility (Eze 8:14)
15. The golden image in the plain of Dura (Da 2)

JANUARY 17

Genesis 33:1–34:31

33 Then Jacob lifted his eyes and looked, and behold, Esau was coming, and four hundred men with him. So he divided the children among Leah and Rachel and the two maids. ²He put the maids and their children in front, and Leah and her children next, and Rachel and Joseph last. ³But he himself passed on ahead of them and bowed down to the ground seven times, until he came near to his brother.

⁴Then Esau ran to meet him and embraced him, and fell on his neck and kissed him, and they wept. ⁵He lifted his eyes and saw the women and the children, and said, "Who are these with you?" So he said, "The children whom God has graciously given your servant." ⁶Then the maids came near with their children, and they bowed down. ⁷Leah likewise came near with her children, and they bowed down; and afterward Joseph came near with Rachel, and they bowed down. ⁸And he said, "What do you mean by all this company which I have met?" And he said, "To find favor in the sight of my lord." ⁹But Esau said, "I have plenty, my brother; let what you have be your own." ¹⁰Jacob said, "No, please, if now I have found favor in your sight, then take my present from my hand, for I see your face as one sees the face of God, and you have received me favorably. ¹¹Please take my gift which has been brought to you, because God has dealt graciously with me and because I have plenty." Thus he urged him and he took *it*.

¹²Then Esau said, "Let us take our journey and go, and I will go before you." ¹³But he said to him, "My lord knows that the children are frail and that the flocks and herds which are nursing are a care to me. And if they are driven hard one day, all the flocks will die. ¹⁴Please let my lord pass on before his servant, and I will proceed at my leisure, according to the pace of the cattle that are before me and according to the pace of the children, until I come to my lord at Seir."

¹⁵Esau said, "Please let me leave with you some of the people who are with me." But he said, "What need is there? Let me find favor in the sight of my lord." ¹⁶So Esau returned that day on his way to Seir. ¹⁷Jacob journeyed to Succoth, and built for himself a house and made booths for his livestock; therefore the place is named Succoth.

¹⁸Now Jacob came safely to the city of Shechem, which is in the land of Canaan, when he came from Paddan-aram, and camped before the city. ¹⁹He bought the piece of land where he had pitched his tent from the hand of the sons of Hamor, Shechem's father, for one hundred pieces of money. ²⁰Then he erected there an altar and called it El-Elohe-Israel.

34 Now Dinah the daughter of Leah, whom she had borne to Jacob, went out to visit the daughters of the land. ²When Shechem the son of Hamor the Hivite, the prince of the land, saw her, he took her and lay with her by force. ³He was deeply attracted to Dinah the daughter of Jacob, and he loved the girl and spoke tenderly to her. ⁴So Shechem spoke to his father Hamor, saying, "Get me this young girl for a wife." ⁵Now Jacob heard that he had defiled Dinah his daughter; but his sons were with his livestock in the field, so Jacob kept silent until they came in. ⁶Then Hamor the father of Shechem went out to Jacob to speak with him. ⁷Now the sons of Jacob came in from the field when they heard *it*; and the men were grieved, and they were very angry because he had done a disgraceful thing in Israel by lying with Jacob's daughter, for such a thing ought not to be done.

⁸But Hamor spoke with them, saying, "The soul of my son Shechem longs for your daughter; please give her to him in marriage. ⁹Intermarry with us; give your daughters to us and take our daughters for yourselves. ¹⁰Thus you shall live with us, and the land shall be *open* before you; live and trade in it and acquire property in it." ¹¹Shechem also said to her father and to her brothers, "If I find favor in your sight, then I will give whatever you say to me. ¹²Ask me ever so much bridal payment and gift, and I will give according as you say to me; but give me the girl in marriage."

¹³But Jacob's sons answered Shechem and his father Hamor with deceit, because he had

---

33:3–4 Fearfully and deferentially, Jacob approached his brother as an inferior would a highly honored patron, while gladly and eagerly, Esau ran to greet his brother without restraint of emotion. "They wept" because, after 21 years of troubling separation, old memories were wiped away and murderous threats belonged to the distant past; hearts had been changed, brothers reconciled! See v. 10.

defiled Dinah their sister. ¹⁴They said to them, "We cannot do this thing, to give our sister to one who is uncircumcised, for that would be a disgrace to us. ¹⁵Only on this *condition* will we consent to you: if you will become like us, in that every male of you be circumcised, ¹⁶then we will give our daughters to you, and we will take your daughters for ourselves, and we will live with you and become one people. ¹⁷But if you will not listen to us to be circumcised, then we will take our daughter and go."

¹⁸Now their words seemed reasonable to Hamor and Shechem, Hamor's son. ¹⁹The young man did not delay to do the thing, because he was delighted with Jacob's daughter. Now he was more respected than all the household of his father. ²⁰So Hamor and his son Shechem came to the gate of their city and spoke to the men of their city, saying, ²¹"These men are friendly with us; therefore let them live in the land and trade in it, for behold, the land is large enough for them. Let us take their daughters in marriage, and give our daughters to them. ²²Only on this *condition* will the men consent to us to live with us, to become one people: that every male among us be circumcised as they are circumcised. ²³Will not their livestock and their property and all their animals be ours? Only let us consent to them, and they will live with us." ²⁴All who went out of the gate of his city listened to Hamor and to his son Shechem, and every male was circumcised, all who went out of the gate of his city.

²⁵Now it came about on the third day, when they were in pain, that two of Jacob's sons, Simeon and Levi, Dinah's brothers, each took his sword and came upon the city unawares, and killed every male. ²⁶They killed Hamor and his son Shechem with the edge of the sword, and took Dinah from Shechem's house, and went forth. ²⁷Jacob's sons came upon the slain and looted the city, because they had defiled their sister. ²⁸They took their flocks and their herds and their donkeys, and that which was in the city and that which was in the field; ²⁹and they captured and looted all their wealth and all their little ones and their wives, even all that *was* in the houses. ³⁰Then Jacob said to Simeon and Levi, "You have brought trouble on me by making me odious among the inhabitants of the land, among the Canaanites and the Perizzites; and my men being few in number, they will gather together against me and attack me and I will be destroyed, I and my household."

³¹But they said, "Should he treat our sister as a harlot?"

Psalm 9:1–5

> For the choir director; on Muth-
>   labben. A Psalm of David.

I will give thanks to the LORD
  with all my heart;
  I will tell of all Your wonders.
² I will be glad and exult in You;
  I will sing praise to Your
    name, O Most High.

³ When my enemies turn back,
  They stumble and perish before
    You.
⁴ For You have maintained
    my just cause;
  You have sat on the throne
    judging righteously.
⁵ You have rebuked the nations, You
    have destroyed the wicked;
  You have blotted out their
    name forever and ever.

Proverbs 3:21–26

²¹ My son, let them not vanish
    from your sight;
  Keep sound wisdom and
    discretion,
²² So they will be life to your soul
  And adornment to your neck.
²³ Then you will walk in
    your way securely
  And your foot will not stumble.
²⁴ When you lie down, you
    will not be afraid;
  When you lie down, your
    sleep will be sweet.
²⁵ Do not be afraid of sudden
    fear
  Nor of the onslaught of the
    wicked when it comes;
²⁶ For the LORD will be your
    confidence
  And will keep your foot
    from being caught.

3:22 life to your soul. The association of wisdom with the inner spiritual life unfolds throughout the book (4:10, 22; 7:2; 8:35; 9:11; 10:11, 16–17; 11:19, 30; 12:28; 13:14; 14:27; 15:4, 24; 16:22; 19:23; 21:21; 22:4). **adornment to your neck.** The wisdom of God will adorn one's life for all to see its beauty (1:9).

Matthew 12:1–21

12 At that time Jesus went through the grainfields on the Sabbath, and His disciples became hungry and began to pick the heads *of grain* and eat. ² But when the Pharisees saw *this,* they said to Him, "Look, Your disciples do what is not lawful to do on a Sabbath." ³ But He said to them, "Have you not read what David did when he became hungry, he and his companions, ⁴ how he entered the house of God, and they ate the consecrated bread, which was not lawful for him to eat nor for those with him, but for the priests alone? ⁵ Or have you not read in the Law, that on the Sabbath the priests in the temple break the Sabbath and are innocent? ⁶ But I say to you that something greater than the temple is here. ⁷ But if you had known what this means, 'I DESIRE COMPASSION, AND NOT A SACRIFICE,' you would not have condemned the innocent. ⁸ For the Son of Man is Lord of the Sabbath."

⁹ Departing from there, He went into their synagogue. ¹⁰ And a man *was there* whose hand was withered. And they questioned Jesus, asking, "Is it lawful to heal on the Sabbath?"—so that they might accuse Him. ¹¹ And He said to them, "What man is there among you who has a sheep, and if it falls into a pit on the Sabbath, will he not take hold of it and lift it out? ¹² How much more valuable then is a man than a sheep! So then, it is lawful to do good on the Sabbath." ¹³ Then He *said to the man, "Stretch out your hand!" He stretched it out, and it was restored to normal, like the other. ¹⁴ But the Pharisees went out and conspired against Him, *as to* how they might destroy Him.

¹⁵ But Jesus, aware of *this,* withdrew from there. Many followed Him, and He healed them all, ¹⁶ and warned them not to tell who

12:8 the Son of Man is Lord of the Sabbath. Christ has the prerogative to rule over not only their man-made sabbatarian rules, but also over the Sabbath itself—which was designed for worshiping God. Again, this was an inescapable claim of deity—and as such it prompted the Pharisees' violent outrage (v. 14).

12:15 He healed them all. In all of Old Testament history there was never a time or a person who exhibited such extensive healing power. Physical healings were very rare in the Old Testament. Christ chose to display His deity by healing, raising the dead, and liberating people from demons. That not only showed the Messiah's power over the physical and spiritual realms, but also demonstrated the compassion of God toward those affected by sin.

He was. ¹⁷ *This was* to fulfill what was spoken through Isaiah the prophet:

¹⁸ "BEHOLD, MY SERVANT WHOM
     I HAVE CHOSEN;
   MY BELOVED IN WHOM MY
     SOUL IS WELL-PLEASED;
   I WILL PUT MY SPIRIT UPON HIM,
   AND HE SHALL PROCLAIM
     JUSTICE TO THE GENTILES.
¹⁹ "HE WILL NOT QUARREL, NOR CRY OUT;
   NOR WILL ANYONE HEAR HIS
     VOICE IN THE STREETS.
²⁰ "A BATTERED REED HE WILL
     NOT BREAK OFF,
   AND A SMOLDERING WICK HE
     WILL NOT PUT OUT,
   UNTIL HE LEADS JUSTICE TO VICTORY.
²¹ "AND IN HIS NAME THE
     GENTILES WILL HOPE."

DAY 17: How are we to interpret the Bible when the ancient customs were so different from our own?

Three tools help us in the task of interpreting events that happened so long ago and so far away: 1) The best interpretive tool in understanding a Bible passage is its immediate context. Surrounding verses will often yield clues to the observant about foreign or unusual details in a particular account. 2) One part of the Bible often explains, expands, and comments on another part. An ever-growing familiarity with all of Scripture will equip a student with significant insight into the culture of those who lived the history. 3) Some insight can be gained from ancient sources outside of Scripture, but these only supplement our primary sources in the Bible itself.

Once we are at home in the exotic and unfamiliar contexts of Scripture, we meet people in the Bible pages who are very much like us. These are not aliens, but our ancestors across the ages. Their struggles are ours. Their failures are all familiar to us. The God who spoke to them still speaks to us.

JANUARY 18

Genesis 35:1–36:43

35 Then God said to Jacob, "Arise, go up to Bethel and live there, and make an altar there to God, who appeared to you when you fled from your brother Esau." [2] So Jacob said to his household and to all who were with him, "Put away the foreign gods which are among you, and purify yourselves and change your garments; [3] and let us arise and go up to Bethel, and I will make an altar there to God, who answered me in the day of my distress and has been with me wherever I have gone." [4] So they gave to Jacob all the foreign gods which they had and the rings which were in their ears, and Jacob hid them under the oak which was near Shechem.

[5] As they journeyed, there was a great terror upon the cities which were around them, and they did not pursue the sons of Jacob. [6] So Jacob came to Luz (that is, Bethel), which is in the land of Canaan, he and all the people who were with him. [7] He built an altar there, and called the place El-bethel, because there God had revealed Himself to him when he fled from his brother. [8] Now Deborah, Rebekah's nurse, died, and she was buried below Bethel under the oak; it was named Allon-bacuth.

[9] Then God appeared to Jacob again when he came from Paddan-aram, and He blessed him. [10] God said to him,

"Your name is Jacob;
You shall no longer be called
    Jacob,
But Israel shall be your name."

Thus He called him Israel. [11] God also said to him,

"I am God Almighty;
Be fruitful and multiply;
A nation and a company of
    nations shall come from you,
And kings shall come forth
    from you.
[12] "The land which I gave to
    Abraham and Isaac,
I will give it to you,
And I will give the land to your
    descendants after you."

[13] Then God went up from him in the place where He had spoken with him. [14] Jacob set up a pillar in the place where He had spoken

---

35:2–4 Put away the foreign gods. Moving to Bethel necessitated spiritual preparation beyond the level of an exercise in logistics. Possession of idolatrous symbols such as figurines, amulets, or cultic charms (v. 4, "rings…in their ears") were no longer tolerable, including Rachel's troubling teraphim (31:19). Idols buried out of sight, plus bathing and changing to clean clothes, all served to portray both cleansing from defilement by idolatry and consecration of the heart to the Lord. It had been 8 or 10 years since his return to Canaan and, appropriately, time enough to clean up all traces of idolatry.

35:5 a great terror. A supernaturally induced fear of Israel rendered the surrounding city-states unwilling and powerless to intervene and made Jacob's fear of their retaliation rather inconsequential (34:30).

---

with him, a pillar of stone, and he poured out a drink offering on it; he also poured oil on it. [15] So Jacob named the place where God had spoken with him, Bethel.

[16] Then they journeyed from Bethel; and when there was still some distance to go to Ephrath, Rachel began to give birth and she suffered severe labor. [17] When she was in severe labor the midwife said to her, "Do not fear, for now you have another son." [18] It came about as her soul was departing (for she died), that she named him Ben-oni; but his father called him Benjamin. [19] So Rachel died and was buried on the way to Ephrath (that is, Bethlehem). [20] Jacob set up a pillar over her grave; that is the pillar of Rachel's grave to this day. [21] Then Israel journeyed on and pitched his tent beyond the tower of Eder.

[22] It came about while Israel was dwelling in that land, that Reuben went and lay with Bilhah his father's concubine, and Israel heard *of it.*

Now there were twelve sons of Jacob— [23] the sons of Leah: Reuben, Jacob's firstborn, then Simeon and Levi and Judah and Issachar and Zebulun; [24] the sons of Rachel: Joseph and Benjamin; [25] and the sons of Bilhah, Rachel's maid: Dan and Naphtali; [26] and the sons of Zilpah, Leah's maid: Gad and Asher. These are the sons of Jacob who were born to him in Paddan-aram.

[27] Jacob came to his father Isaac at Mamre of Kiriath-arba (that is, Hebron), where Abraham and Isaac had sojourned.

[28] Now the days of Isaac were one hundred

and eighty years. ²⁹ Isaac breathed his last and died and was gathered to his people, an old man of ripe age; and his sons Esau and Jacob buried him.

36 Now these are *the records of* the generations of Esau (that is, Edom).

² Esau took his wives from the daughters of Canaan: Adah the daughter of Elon the Hittite, and Oholibamah the daughter of Anah and the granddaughter of Zibeon the Hivite; ³ also Basemath, Ishmael's daughter, the sister of Nebaioth. ⁴ Adah bore Eliphaz to Esau, and Basemath bore Reuel, ⁵ and Oholibamah bore Jeush and Jalam and Korah. These are the sons of Esau who were born to him in the land of Canaan.

⁶ Then Esau took his wives and his sons and his daughters and all his household, and his livestock and all his cattle and all his goods which he had acquired in the land of Canaan, and went to *another* land away from his brother Jacob. ⁷ For their property had become too great for them to live together, and the land where they sojourned could not sustain them because of their livestock. ⁸ So Esau lived in the hill country of Seir; Esau is Edom.

⁹ These then are *the records of* the generations of Esau the father of the Edomites in the hill country of Seir. ¹⁰ These are the names of Esau's sons: Eliphaz the son of Esau's wife Adah, Reuel the son of Esau's wife Basemath. ¹¹ The sons of Eliphaz were Teman, Omar, Zepho and Gatam and Kenaz. ¹² Timna was a concubine of Esau's son Eliphaz and she bore Amalek to Eliphaz. These are the sons of Esau's wife Adah. ¹³ These are the sons of Reuel: Nahath and Zerah, Shammah and Mizzah. These were the sons of Esau's wife Basemath. ¹⁴ These were the sons of Esau's wife Oholibamah, the daughter of Anah and the granddaughter of Zibeon: she bore to Esau, Jeush and Jalam and Korah.

¹⁵ These are the chiefs of the sons of Esau. The sons of Eliphaz, the firstborn of Esau, are chief Teman, chief Omar, chief Zepho, chief Kenaz, ¹⁶ chief Korah, chief Gatam, chief Amalek. These are the chiefs descended from Eliphaz in the land of Edom; these are the sons of Adah. ¹⁷ These are the sons of Reuel, Esau's son: chief Nahath, chief Zerah, chief Shammah, chief Mizzah. These are the chiefs descended from Reuel in the land of Edom; these are the sons of Esau's wife Basemath. ¹⁸ These are the sons of Esau's wife Oholibamah: chief Jeush, chief Jalam, chief Korah. These are the chiefs descended from Esau's wife Oholibamah, the

daughter of Anah. ¹⁹ These are the sons of Esau (that is, Edom), and these are their chiefs.

²⁰ These are the sons of Seir the Horite, the inhabitants of the land: Lotan and Shobal and Zibeon and Anah, ²¹ and Dishon and Ezer and Dishan. These are the chiefs descended from the Horites, the sons of Seir in the land of Edom. ²² The sons of Lotan were Hori and Hemam; and Lotan's sister was Timna. ²³ These are the sons of Shobal: Alvan and Manahath and Ebal, Shepho and Onam. ²⁴ These are the sons of Zibeon: Aiah and Anah—he is the Anah who found the hot springs in the wilderness when he was pasturing the donkeys of his father Zibeon. ²⁵ These are the children of Anah: Dishon, and Oholibamah, the daughter of Anah. ²⁶ These are the sons of Dishon: Hemdan and Eshban and Ithran and Cheran. ²⁷ These are the sons of Ezer: Bilhan and Zaavan and Akan. ²⁸ These are the sons of Dishan: Uz and Aran. ²⁹ These are the chiefs descended from the Horites: chief Lotan, chief Shobal, chief Zibeon, chief Anah, ³⁰ chief Dishon, chief Ezer, chief Dishan. These are the chiefs descended from the Horites, according to their *various* chiefs in the land of Seir.

³¹ Now these are the kings who reigned in the land of Edom before any king reigned over the sons of Israel. ³² Bela the son of Beor reigned in Edom, and the name of his city was Dinhabah. ³³ Then Bela died, and Jobab the son of Zerah of Bozrah became king in his place. ³⁴ Then Jobab died, and Husham of the land of the Temanites became king in his place. ³⁵ Then Husham died, and Hadad the son of Bedad, who defeated Midian in the field of Moab, became king in his place; and the name of his city was Avith. ³⁶ Then Hadad died, and Samlah of Masrekah became king in his place. ³⁷ Then Samlah died, and Shaul of Rehoboth on the *Euphrates* River became king in his place. ³⁸ Then Shaul died, and Baal-hanan the son of Achbor became king in his place. ³⁹ Then Baal-hanan the son of Achbor died, and Hadar became king in his place; and the name of his city was Pau; and his wife's name was Mehetabel, the daughter of Matred, daughter of Mezahab.

⁴⁰ Now these are the names of the chiefs descended from Esau, according to their families *and* their localities, by their names: chief Timna, chief Alvah, chief Jetheth, ⁴¹ chief Oholibamah, chief Elah, chief Pinon, ⁴² chief Kenaz, chief Teman, chief Mibzar, ⁴³ chief Magdiel, chief Iram. These are the chiefs of Edom (that is, Esau, the father of the Edomites), accord-

ing to their habitations in the land of their possession.

Psalm 9:6-10

6 The enemy has come to an
   end in perpetual ruins,
   And You have uprooted the cities;
   The very memory of them
   has perished.

7 But the LORD abides forever;
   He has established His
   throne for judgment,
8 And He will judge the world
   in righteousness;
   He will execute judgment for
   the peoples with equity.
9 The LORD also will be a stronghold
   for the oppressed,
   A stronghold in times of trouble;
10 And those who know Your name
   will put their trust in You,
   For You, O LORD, have not
   forsaken those who seek You.

Proverbs 3:27-30

27 Do not withhold good from
   those to whom it is due,
   When it is in your power to do *it*.
28 Do not say to your neighbor,
   "Go, and come back,
   And tomorrow I will give *it*,"
   When you have it with you.
29 Do not devise harm against
   your neighbor,
   While he lives securely beside you.
30 Do not contend with a man
   without cause,
   If he has done you no harm.

Matthew 12:22-50

22 Then a demon-possessed man *who was* blind and mute was brought to Jesus, and He healed him, so that the mute man spoke and saw. 23 All the crowds were amazed, and were saying, "This man cannot be the Son of David, can he?" 24 But when the Pharisees heard *this*, they said, "This man casts out demons only by Beelzebul the ruler of the demons." 25 And knowing their thoughts Jesus said to them, "Any kingdom divided against itself is laid waste; and any city or house divided against itself will not stand. 26 If Satan casts out Satan, he is divided against himself; how then will his kingdom stand? 27 If I by Beelzebul cast out demons, by whom do your sons cast *them* out? For this reason they will be your judges. 28 But if I cast out demons by

the Spirit of God, then the kingdom of God has come upon you. 29 Or how can anyone enter the strong man's house and carry off his property, unless he first binds the strong *man?* And then he will plunder his house. 30 He who is not with Me is against Me; and he who does not gather with Me scatters.

31 "Therefore I say to you, any sin and blasphemy shall be forgiven people, but blasphemy against the Spirit shall not be forgiven. 32 Whoever speaks a word against the Son of Man, it shall be forgiven him; but whoever speaks against the Holy Spirit, it shall not be forgiven him, either in this age or in the *age* to come.

33 "Either make the tree good and its fruit good, or make the tree bad and its fruit bad; for the tree is known by its fruit. 34 You brood of vipers, how can you, being evil, speak what is good? For the mouth speaks out of that which fills the heart. 35 The good man brings out of *his* good treasure what is good; and the evil man brings out of *his* evil treasure what is evil. 36 But I tell you that every careless word that people speak, they shall give an accounting for it in the day of judgment. 37 For by your words you will be justified, and by your words you will be condemned."

38 Then some of the scribes and Pharisees said to Him, "Teacher, we want to see a sign from You." 39 But He answered and said to them, "An evil and adulterous generation craves for a sign; and *yet* no sign will be given to it but the sign of Jonah the prophet; 40 for just as JONAH WAS THREE DAYS AND THREE NIGHTS IN THE BELLY OF THE SEA MONSTER, SO will the Son of Man be three days and three nights in the heart of the earth. 41 The men of Nineveh will stand up with this generation at the judgment, and will condemn it because they repented at the preaching of Jonah; and behold, something greater than Jonah is here. 42 *The* Queen of *the* South will rise up with this generation at the judgment and will condemn it, because she came from the ends of the earth to hear the wisdom of Solomon; and behold, something greater than Solomon is here.

43 "Now when the unclean spirit goes out of a man, it passes through waterless places seeking rest, and does not find *it*. 44 Then it says, 'I will return to my house from which I came'; and when it comes, it finds *it* unoccupied, swept, and put in order. 45 Then it goes and takes along with it seven other spirits more wicked than itself, and they go in and live there; and the last state of that man becomes worse than the first. That is the way it will also be with this evil generation."

⁴⁶While He was still speaking to the crowds, behold, His mother and brothers were standing outside, seeking to speak to Him. ⁴⁷Someone said to Him, "Behold, Your mother and Your brothers are standing outside seeking to speak to You." ⁴⁸But Jesus answered the one who was telling Him and said, "Who is My mother and who are My brothers?" ⁴⁹And stretching out His hand toward His disciples, He said, "Behold My mother and My brothers! ⁵⁰For whoever does the will of My Father who is in heaven, he is My brother and sister and mother."

12:46 brothers. These are actual siblings (half-brothers) of Jesus. Matthew explicitly connects them with Mary, indicating that they were not cousins or Joseph's sons from a previous marriage, as some of the church fathers imagined. They are mentioned in all the Gospels (Mk 3:31; Lk 8:19–21; Jn 7:3–5). Matthew and Mark give the names of 4 of Jesus' brothers, and mention that He had sisters as well (13:55; Mk 6:3).

DAY 18: What is the unforgivable sin that Jesus spoke of?

According to Jesus' words in Matthew 12:31, the unforgivable sin is the "blasphemy against the Spirit." The sin He was confronting was the Pharisees' deliberate rejection of that which they knew to be of God (see Jn 11:48; Ac 4:16). They could not deny the reality of what the Holy Spirit had done through Him, so they attributed to Satan a work that they knew was of God (v. 24; Mk 3:22).

Someone never exposed to Christ's divine power and presence might reject Him in ignorance and "it shall be forgiven him" (v. 32)—assuming the unbelief gives way to genuine repentance. Even a Pharisee such as Saul of Tarsus could be forgiven for speaking "against the Son of Man" or persecuting His followers—because his unbelief stemmed from ignorance (1Ti 1:13). But those who know His claims are true and reject Him anyway sin "against the Holy Spirit"—because it is the Holy Spirit who testifies of Christ and makes His truth known to us (Jn 15:26; 16:14–15). No forgiveness was possible for these Pharisees who witnessed His miracles firsthand, knew the truth of His claims, and still blasphemed the Holy Spirit—because they had already rejected the fullest possible revelation (Heb 6:4–6; 10:29).

 JANUARY 19

Genesis 37:1–38:30

37 Now Jacob lived in the land where his father had sojourned, in the land of Canaan. ²These are *the records of* the generations of Jacob.

Joseph, when seventeen years of age, was pasturing the flock with his brothers while he was *still* a youth, along with the sons of Bilhah and the sons of Zilpah, his father's wives. And Joseph brought back a bad report about them to their father. ³Now Israel loved Joseph more than all his sons, because he was the son of his old age; and he made him a varicolored tunic. ⁴His brothers saw that their father loved him more than all his brothers; and *so* they hated him and could not speak to him on friendly terms.

⁵Then Joseph had a dream, and when he told it to his brothers, they hated him even more. ⁶He said to them, "Please listen to this dream which I have had; ⁷for behold, we were binding sheaves in the field, and lo, my sheaf rose up and also stood erect; and behold, your sheaves gathered around and bowed down to my sheaf." ⁸Then his brothers said to him,

"Are you actually going to reign over us? Or are you really going to rule over us?" So they hated him even more for his dreams and for his words.

⁹Now he had still another dream, and related it to his brothers, and said, "Lo, I have had still another dream; and behold, the sun and the moon and eleven stars were bowing down to me." ¹⁰He related *it* to his father and to his brothers; and his father rebuked him and said to him, "What is this dream that you have had? Shall I and your mother and your brothers actually come to bow ourselves down before you to the ground?" ¹¹His brothers were jealous of him, but his father kept the saying *in mind*.

¹²Then his brothers went to pasture their

37:3-4 Overt favoritism of Joseph and tacit appointment of him as the primary son by the father conspired to estrange him from his brothers. They hated and envied him (vv. 4–5, 11) and could not interact with him without conflict and hostility. Joseph must have noticed the situation.

father's flock in Shechem. [13] Israel said to Joseph, "Are not your brothers pasturing *the flock* in Shechem? Come, and I will send you to them." And he said to him, "I will go." [14] Then he said to him, "Go now and see about the welfare of your brothers and the welfare of the flock, and bring word back to me." So he sent him from the valley of Hebron, and he came to Shechem.

[15] A man found him, and behold, he was wandering in the field; and the man asked him, "What are you looking for?" [16] He said, "I am looking for my brothers; please tell me where they are pasturing *the flock.*" [17] Then the man said, "They have moved from here; for I heard *them* say, 'Let us go to Dothan.'" So Joseph went after his brothers and found them at Dothan.

[18] When they saw him from a distance and before he came close to them, they plotted against him to put him to death. [19] They said to one another, "Here comes this dreamer! [20] Now then, come and let us kill him and throw him into one of the pits; and we will say, 'A wild beast devoured him.' Then let us see what will become of his dreams!" [21] But Reuben heard *this* and rescued him out of their hands and said, "Let us not take his life." [22] Reuben further said to them, "Shed no blood. Throw him into this pit that is in the wilderness, but do not lay hands on him"— that he might rescue him out of their hands, to restore him to his father. [23] So it came about, when Joseph reached his brothers, that they stripped Joseph of his tunic, the varicolored tunic that was on him; [24] and they took him and threw him into the pit. Now the pit was empty, without any water in it.

[25] Then they sat down to eat a meal. And as they raised their eyes and looked, behold, a caravan of Ishmaelites was coming from Gilead, with their camels bearing aromatic gum and balm and myrrh, on their way to bring *them* down to Egypt. [26] Judah said to his brothers, "What profit is it for us to kill our brother and cover up his blood? [27] Come and let us sell him to the Ishmaelites and not lay our hands on him, for he is our brother, our *own* flesh." And his brothers listened *to him.* [28] Then some Midianite traders passed by, so they pulled *him* up and lifted Joseph out of the pit, and sold him to the Ishmaelites for twenty *shekels* of silver. Thus they brought Joseph into Egypt.

[29] Now Reuben returned to the pit, and behold, Joseph was not in the pit; so he tore his garments. [30] He returned to his brothers and said, "The boy is not *there;* as for me, where

am I to go?" [31] So they took Joseph's tunic, and slaughtered a male goat and dipped the tunic in the blood; [32] and they sent the varicolored tunic and brought it to their father and said, "We found this; please examine *it* to *see* whether it is your son's tunic or not." [33] Then he examined it and said, "It is my son's tunic. A wild beast has devoured him; Joseph has surely been torn to pieces!" [34] So Jacob tore his clothes, and put sackcloth on his loins and mourned for his son many days. [35] Then all his sons and all his daughters arose to comfort him, but he refused to be comforted. And he said, "Surely I will go down to Sheol in mourning for my son." So his father wept for him. [36] Meanwhile, the Midianites sold him in Egypt to Potiphar, Pharaoh's officer, the captain of the bodyguard.

37:36 Potiphar. He was a prominent court official and high-ranking officer in Egypt, perhaps captain of the royal bodyguard (40:3–4). His name, a most unusual grammatical form for that period, either meant "the one whom the god Ra has given" or "the one who is placed on earth by Ra," making it a descriptive epithet more than a personal name.

38 And it came about at that time, that Judah departed from his brothers and visited a certain Adullamite, whose name was Hirah. [2] Judah saw there a daughter of a certain Canaanite whose name was Shua; and he took her and went in to her. [3] So she conceived and bore a son and he named him Er. [4] Then she conceived again and bore a son and named him Onan. [5] She bore still another son and named him Shelah; and it was at Chezib that she bore him.

[6] Now Judah took a wife for Er his firstborn, and her name *was* Tamar. [7] But Er, Judah's firstborn, was evil in the sight of the LORD, so the LORD took his life. [8] Then Judah said to Onan, "Go in to your brother's wife, and perform your duty as a brother-in-law to her, and raise up offspring for your brother." [9] Onan knew that the offspring would not be his; so when he went in to his brother's wife, he wasted his seed on the ground in order not to give offspring to his brother. [10] But what he did was displeasing in the sight of the LORD; so He took his life also. [11] Then Judah said to his daughter-in-law Tamar, "Remain a widow in your father's house until my son Shelah grows up"; for he thought, "*I am afraid that*

he too may die like his brothers." So Tamar went and lived in her father's house.

¹²Now after a considerable time Shua's daughter, the wife of Judah, died; and when the time of mourning was ended, Judah went up to his sheepshearers at Timnah, and his friend Hirah the Adullamite. ¹³It was told to Tamar, "Behold, your father-in-law is going up to Timnah to shear his sheep." ¹⁴So she removed her widow's garments and covered *herself* with a veil, and wrapped herself, and sat in the gateway of Enaim, which is on the road to Timnah; for she saw that Shelah had grown up, and she had not been given to him as a wife. ¹⁵When Judah saw her, he thought she *was* a harlot, for she had covered her face. ¹⁶So he turned aside to her by the road, and said, "Here now, let me come in to you"; for he did not know that she was his daughter-in-law. And she said, "What will you give me, that you may come in to me?" ¹⁷He said, therefore, "I will send you a young goat from the flock." She said, moreover, "Will you give a pledge until you send *it?*" ¹⁸He said, "What pledge shall I give you?" And she said, "Your seal and your cord, and your staff that is in your hand." So he gave *them* to her and went in to her, and she conceived by him. ¹⁹Then she arose and departed, and removed her veil and put on her widow's garments.

²⁰When Judah sent the young goat by his friend the Adullamite, to receive the pledge from the woman's hand, he did not find her. ²¹He asked the men of her place, saying, "Where is the temple prostitute who was by the road at Enaim?" But they said, "There has been no temple prostitute here." ²²So he returned to Judah, and said, "I did not find her; and furthermore, the men of the place said, 'There has been no temple prostitute here.'" ²³Then Judah said, "Let her keep them, otherwise we will become a laughingstock. After all, I sent this young goat, but you did not find her."

²⁴Now it was about three months later that Judah was informed, "Your daughter-in-law Tamar has played the harlot, and behold, she is also with child by harlotry." Then Judah said, "Bring her out and let her be burned!" ²⁵It was while she was being brought out that she sent to her father-in-law, saying, "I am with child by the man to whom these things belong." And she said, "Please examine and see, whose signet ring and cords and staff are these?" ²⁶Judah recognized *them,* and said, "She is more righteous than I, inasmuch as I did not give her to my son Shelah." And he did not have relations with her again.

²⁷It came about at the time she was giving birth, that behold, there were twins in her womb. ²⁸Moreover, it took place while she was giving birth, one put out a hand, and the midwife took and tied a scarlet *thread* on his hand, saying, "This one came out first." ²⁹But it came about as he drew back his hand, that behold, his brother came out. Then she said, "What a breach you have made for yourself!" So he was named Perez. ³⁰Afterward his brother came out who had the scarlet *thread* on his hand; and he was named Zerah.

Psalm 9:11-20

¹¹ Sing praises to the LORD,
  who dwells in Zion;
  Declare among the peoples His
    deeds.
¹² For He who requires blood
    remembers them;
  He does not forget the cry
    of the afflicted.
¹³ Be gracious to me, O LORD;
  See my affliction from
    those who hate me,
  You who lift me up from
    the gates of death,
¹⁴ That I may tell of all Your
    praises,
  That in the gates of the
    daughter of Zion
  I may rejoice in Your salvation.
¹⁵ The nations have sunk down in
    the pit which they have made;
  In the net which they hid, their
    own foot has been caught.
¹⁶ The LORD has made Himself
    known;
  He has executed judgment.
  In the work of his own hands
    the wicked is snared.
            Higgaion Selah

¹⁷ The wicked will return to Sheol,
  Even all the nations who forget
    God.
¹⁸ For the needy will not
    always be forgotten,
  Nor the hope of the afflicted
    perish forever.
¹⁹ Arise, O LORD, do not let man
    prevail;
  Let the nations be judged before
    You.
²⁰ Put them in fear, O LORD;
  Let the nations know that they
    are but men.   *Selah*

Proverbs 3:31–35

31 Do not envy a man of violence
And do not choose any of his ways.
32 For the devious are an
abomination to the LORD;
But He is intimate with the upright.
33 The curse of the LORD is on
the house of the wicked,
But He blesses the dwelling
of the righteous.
34 Though He scoffs at the scoffers,
Yet He gives grace to the afflicted.
35 The wise will inherit honor,
But fools display dishonor.

Matthew 13:1–30

13 That day Jesus went out of the house and was sitting by the sea. 2 And large crowds gathered to Him, so He got into a boat and sat down, and the whole crowd was standing on the beach.

3 And He spoke many things to them in parables, saying, "Behold, the sower went out to sow; 4 and as he sowed, some *seeds* fell beside the road, and the birds came and ate them up. 5 Others fell on the rocky places, where they did not have much soil; and immediately they sprang up, because they had no depth of soil. 6 But when the sun had risen, they were scorched; and because they had no root, they withered away. 7 Others fell among the thorns, and the thorns came up and choked them out. 8 And others fell on the good soil and *yielded a crop, some a hundredfold, some sixty, and some thirty. 9 He who has ears, let him hear."

13:3 **parables.** Parables were a common form of teaching in Judaism. The Greek term for "parable" appears 45 times in the LXX. A parable is a long analogy, often cast in the form of a story. Before this point in His ministry, Jesus had employed many graphic analogies (5:13–16), but their meaning was fairly clear in the context of His teaching. Parables required more explanation (v. 36) and Jesus employed them to obscure the truth from unbelievers while making it clearer to His disciples (vv. 11–12). For the remainder of His Galilean ministry, He did not speak to the multitudes except in parables (v. 34). Jesus' veiling the truth from unbelievers this way was both an act of judgment and an act of mercy. It was "judgment" because it kept them in the darkness that they loved (Jn 3:19), but it was "mercy" because they had already rejected the light, so any exposure to more truth would only increase their condemnation.

10 And the disciples came and said to Him, "Why do You speak to them in parables?" 11 Jesus answered them, "To you it has been granted to know the mysteries of the kingdom of heaven, but to them it has not been granted. 12 For whoever has, to him *more* shall be given, and he will have an abundance; but whoever does not have, even what he has shall be taken away from him. 13 Therefore I speak to them in parables; because while seeing they do not see, and while hearing they do not hear, nor do they understand. 14 In their case the prophecy of Isaiah is being fulfilled, which says,

'YOU WILL KEEP ON HEARING, BUT
WILL NOT UNDERSTAND;
YOU WILL KEEP ON SEEING, BUT
WILL NOT PERCEIVE;
15 FOR THE HEART OF THIS PEOPLE
HAS BECOME DULL,
WITH THEIR EARS THEY
SCARCELY HEAR,
AND THEY HAVE CLOSED THEIR EYES,
OTHERWISE THEY WOULD SEE
WITH THEIR EYES,
HEAR WITH THEIR EARS,
AND UNDERSTAND WITH THEIR
HEART AND RETURN,
AND I WOULD HEAL THEM.'

16 But blessed are your eyes, because they see; and your ears, because they hear. 17 For truly I say to you that many prophets and righteous men desired to see what you see, and did not see *it,* and to hear what you hear, and did not hear *it.*

18 "Hear then the parable of the sower. 19 When anyone hears the word of the kingdom and does not understand it, the evil *one* comes and snatches away what has been sown in his heart. This is the one on whom seed was sown beside the road. 20 The one on whom seed was sown on the rocky places, this is the man who hears the word and immediately receives it with joy; 21 yet he has no *firm* root in himself, but is *only* temporary, and when affliction or persecution arises because of the word, immediately he falls away. 22 And the one on whom seed was sown among the thorns, this is the man who hears the word, and the worry of the world and the deceitfulness of wealth choke the word, and it becomes unfruitful. 23 And the one on whom seed was sown on the good soil, this is the man who hears the word and understands it; who indeed bears fruit and brings forth, some a hundredfold, some sixty, and some thirty."

²⁴Jesus presented another parable to them, saying, "The kingdom of heaven may be compared to a man who sowed good seed in his field. ²⁵But while his men were sleeping, his enemy came and sowed tares among the wheat, and went away. ²⁶But when the wheat sprouted and bore grain, then the tares became evident also. ²⁷The slaves of the landowner came and said to him, 'Sir, did you not sow good seed in your field? How then does it have tares?' ²⁸And he said to them, 'An enemy has done this!' The slaves *said to him, 'Do you want us, then, to go and gather them up?' ²⁹But he *said, 'No; for while you are gathering up the tares, you may uproot the wheat with them. ³⁰Allow both to grow together until the harvest; and in the time of the harvest I will say to the reapers, "First gather up the tares and bind them in bundles to burn them up; but gather the wheat into my barn."'"

DAY 19: Why are some events in Matthew in a different order from the order in Mark or Luke?

In general, Matthew presents a topical or thematic approach to the life of Christ. He groups Jesus' teaching into five major discourses:

1. The Sermon on the Mount (chaps. 5–7)
2. The commissioning of the apostles (chap. 10)
3. The parables of the kingdom (chap. 13)
4. The childlikeness of the believer (chap. 18)
5. The discourse on His second coming (chaps. 24–25)

Matthew makes no attempt to follow a strict chronology. A comparison of the synoptic Gospels reveals that he freely placed things out of order. He was dealing with themes and broad concepts, not laying out a timeline. Mark's and Luke's Gospels follow a chronological order more closely.

JANUARY 20

Genesis 39:1–40:23

39 Now Joseph had been taken down to Egypt; and Potiphar, an Egyptian officer of Pharaoh, the captain of the bodyguard, bought him from the Ishmaelites, who had taken him down there. ²The LORD was with Joseph, so he became a successful man. And he was in the house of his master, the Egyptian. ³Now his master saw that the LORD was

39:2 The LORD was with Joseph. Any and all ideas that Joseph, twice a victim of injustice, had been abandoned by the Lord are summarily banished by the employment of phrases highlighting God's oversight of his circumstances, e.g., "with him" (vv. 3, 21), "caused all he did to prosper" (vv. 3, 23), "found/gave him favor" (vv. 4, 21), "blessed/blessing" (v. 5), and "extended kindness to him" (v. 21). Neither being unjustly sold into slavery and forcibly removed from the land (37:28), nor being unjustly accused of sexual harassment and imprisoned (vv. 13–18) were events signaling even a temporary loss of divine superintendence of Joseph's life and God's purpose for His people, Israel.

with him and *how* the LORD caused all that he did to prosper in his hand. ⁴So Joseph found favor in his sight and became his personal servant; and he made him overseer over his house, and all that he owned he put in his charge. ⁵It came about that from the time he made him overseer in his house and over all that he owned, the LORD blessed the Egyptian's house on account of Joseph; thus the LORD'S blessing was upon all that he owned, in the house and in the field. ⁶So he left everything he owned in Joseph's charge; and with him *there* he did not concern himself with anything except the food which he ate.

Now Joseph was handsome in form and appearance. ⁷It came about after these events that his master's wife looked with desire at Joseph, and she said, "Lie with me." ⁸But he refused and said to his master's wife, "Behold, with me *here*, my master does not concern himself with anything in the house, and he has put all that he owns in my charge. ⁹There is no one greater in this house than I, and he has withheld nothing from me except you, because you are his wife. How then could I do this great evil and sin against God?" ¹⁰As she spoke to Joseph day after day, he did not listen to her to lie beside her *or* be with her. ¹¹Now it happened one day that he went into the house to do his work, and none of the men of the household was there inside. ¹²She caught him by his garment, saying, "Lie with me!" And he left his garment in her hand and fled, and went outside. ¹³When she saw that he had left his garment in her hand and had fled outside, ¹⁴she called to the men of her household and said to them, "See, he has brought in a Hebrew to us to make sport of us; he came in to me to lie with me, and I screamed. ¹⁵When he heard that I raised my voice and screamed, he left his garment beside me and fled and went outside." ¹⁶So she left his garment beside her until his master came home. ¹⁷Then she spoke to him with these words, "The Hebrew slave, whom you brought to us, came in to me to make sport of me; ¹⁸and as I raised my voice and screamed, he left his garment beside me and fled outside."

¹⁹Now when his master heard the words of his wife, which she spoke to him, saying, "This is what your slave did to me," his anger burned. ²⁰So Joseph's master took him and put him into the jail, the place where the king's prisoners were confined; and he was there in the jail. ²¹But the LORD was with Joseph and extended kindness to him, and gave him favor in the sight of the chief jailer. ²²The chief jailer committed to Joseph's charge all the prisoners who were in the jail; so that whatever was done there, he was responsible for it. ²³The chief jailer did not supervise anything under Joseph's charge because the LORD was with him; and whatever he did, the LORD made to prosper.

40 Then it came about after these things, the cupbearer and the baker for the king of Egypt offended their lord, the king of Egypt. ²Pharaoh was furious with his two officials, the chief cupbearer and the chief baker. ³So he put them in confinement in the house of the captain of the bodyguard, in the jail, the same place where Joseph was imprisoned. ⁴The captain of the bodyguard put Joseph in charge of them, and he took care of them; and they were in confinement for some time. ⁵Then the cupbearer and the baker for the king of Egypt, who were confined in jail, both had a dream the same night, each man with his own dream and each dream with its own interpretation. ⁶When Joseph came to them in the morning and observed them, behold, they were dejected. ⁷He asked Pharaoh's officials who were with him in confinement in his master's house, "Why are your faces so sad today?" ⁸Then they said to him, "We have had a dream and there is no one to interpret it." Then Joseph said to them, "Do not interpretations belong to God? Tell it to me, please."

⁹So the chief cupbearer told his dream to Joseph, and said to him, "In my dream, behold, there was a vine in front of me; ¹⁰and on the vine were three branches. And as it was budding, its blossoms came out, and its clusters produced ripe grapes. ¹¹Now Pharaoh's cup was in my hand; so I took the grapes and squeezed them into Pharaoh's cup, and I put the cup into Pharaoh's hand." ¹²Then Joseph said to him, "This is the interpretation of it: the three branches are three days; ¹³within three more days Pharaoh will lift up your head and restore you to your office; and you will put Pharaoh's cup into his hand according to your former custom when you were his cupbearer. ¹⁴Only keep me in mind when it goes well with you, and please do me a kindness by mentioning me to Pharaoh and get me out of this house. ¹⁵For I was in fact kidnapped from the land of the Hebrews, and even here I have done nothing that they should have put me into the dungeon."

¹⁶When the chief baker saw that he had interpreted favorably, he said to Joseph, "I also saw in my dream, and behold, there were three baskets of white bread on my head; ¹⁷and in the top basket there were some of all sorts of baked food for Pharaoh, and the birds were eating them out of the basket on my head." ¹⁸Then Joseph answered and said, "This is its interpretation: the three baskets are three days; ¹⁹within three more days Pharaoh will lift up your head from you and will hang you on a tree, and the birds will eat your flesh off you."

²⁰Thus it came about on the third day, which was Pharaoh's birthday, that he made a feast for all his servants; and he lifted up the head of the chief cupbearer and the head of the chief baker among his servants. ²¹He restored the chief cupbearer to his office, and he put the cup into Pharaoh's hand; ²²but he hanged the chief baker, just as Joseph had interpreted to them. ²³Yet the chief cupbearer did not remember Joseph, but forgot him.

Psalm 10:1–11

Why do You stand afar off, O LORD?
Why do You hide Yourself
in times of trouble?
² In pride the wicked hotly
pursue the afflicted;
Let them be caught in the plots
which they have devised.

³ For the wicked boasts of
his heart's desire,
And the greedy man curses
and spurns the LORD.

⁴ The wicked, in the haughtiness of his
countenance, does not seek *Him*.
All his thoughts are,
"There is no God."

⁵ His ways prosper at all times;
Your judgments are on high,
out of his sight;
As for all his adversaries,
he snorts at them.

⁶ He says to himself, "I will
not be moved;
Throughout all generations I
will not be in adversity."

⁷ His mouth is full of curses and
deceit and oppression;
Under his tongue is mischief
and wickedness.

⁸ He sits in the lurking places
of the villages;
In the hiding places he
kills the innocent;
His eyes stealthily watch
for the unfortunate.

⁹ He lurks in a hiding place
as a lion in his lair;
He lurks to catch the afflicted;
He catches the afflicted when
he draws him into his net.

¹⁰ He crouches, he bows down,
And the unfortunate fall
by his mighty ones.

¹¹ He says to himself, "God has forgotten;
He has hidden His face; He
will never see it."

Proverbs 4:1-6

4 Hear, *O* sons, the instruction
of a father,
And give attention that you
may gain understanding,

² For I give you sound teaching;
Do not abandon my instruction.

³ When I was a son to my father,
Tender and the only son in
the sight of my mother,

⁴ Then he taught me and said to me,
"Let your heart hold fast my words;
Keep my commandments and live;

⁵ Acquire wisdom! Acquire
understanding!
Do not forget nor turn away from
the words of my mouth.

⁶ "Do not forsake her, and she
will guard you;
Love her, and she will watch
over you.

Matthew 13:31-58

³¹ He presented another parable to them,
saying, "The kingdom of heaven is like a mustard seed, which a man took and sowed in
his field; ³² and this is smaller than all *other*
seeds, but when it is full grown, it is larger
than the garden plants and becomes a tree,
so that THE BIRDS OF THE AIR come and NEST
IN ITS BRANCHES."

³³ He spoke another parable to them, "The
kingdom of heaven is like leaven, which a
woman took and hid in three pecks of flour
until it was all leavened."

³⁴ All these things Jesus spoke to the
crowds in parables, and He did not speak to
them without a parable. ³⁵ *This was* to fulfill
what was spoken through the prophet:

"I WILL OPEN MY MOUTH IN
PARABLES;
I WILL UTTER THINGS HIDDEN
SINCE THE FOUNDATION
OF THE WORLD."

³⁶ Then He left the crowds and went into
the house. And His disciples came to Him
and said, "Explain to us the parable of the
tares of the field." ³⁷ And He said, "The one
who sows the good seed is the Son of Man,
³⁸ and the field is the world; and *as for* the
good seed, these are the sons of the kingdom; and the tares are the sons of the evil
one; ³⁹ and the enemy who sowed them is the
devil, and the harvest is the end of the age;
and the reapers are angels. ⁴⁰ So just as the
tares are gathered up and burned with fire,
so shall it be at the end of the age. ⁴¹ The Son
of Man will send forth His angels, and they
will gather out of His kingdom all stumbling

4:2 sound teaching…my instruction. There is
no wisdom but that which is linked to sound
teaching, which should be the focal point of
all instruction (1Ti 1:10; 4:13, 16; 5:17; 2Ti 3:10, 16;
4:2; Titus 1:9; 2:1, 10).

13:37 The one who sows. The true sower of
salvation seed is the Lord Himself. He alone
can give the power in the heart to transform.
He is the One who saves sinners, even through
the preaching and witnessing of believers (Ro
10:14).

blocks, and those who commit lawlessness, 42 and will throw them into the furnace of fire; in that place there will be weeping and gnashing of teeth. 43 Then THE RIGHTEOUS WILL SHINE FORTH AS THE SUN in the kingdom of their Father. He who has ears, let him hear.

44 "The kingdom of heaven is like a treasure hidden in the field, which a man found and hid *again;* and from joy over it he goes and sells all that he has and buys that field.

45 "Again, the kingdom of heaven is like a merchant seeking fine pearls, 46 and upon finding one pearl of great value, he went and sold all that he had and bought it.

47 "Again, the kingdom of heaven is like a dragnet cast into the sea, and gathering *fish* of every kind; 48 and when it was filled, they drew it up on the beach; and they sat down and gathered the good *fish* into containers, but the bad they threw away. 49 So it will be at the end of the age; the angels will come forth and take out the wicked from among the righteous, 50 and will throw them into the furnace of fire; in that place there will be weeping and gnashing of teeth.

51 "Have you understood all these things?" They *said to Him, "Yes." 52 And Jesus said to them, "Therefore every scribe who has become a disciple of the kingdom of heaven is

13:57 A prophet...without honor...in his hometown. This is an ancient proverb paralleling the modern saying, "familiarity breeds contempt." They knew Jesus too well as a boy and a young man from their own town—and they concluded that He was nothing special. Verse 58 gives the sad result (Mk 6:4).

like a head of a household, who brings out of his treasure things new and old."

53 When Jesus had finished these parables, He departed from there. 54 He came to His hometown and *began* teaching them in their synagogue, so that they were astonished, and said, "Where *did* this man *get* this wisdom and *these* miraculous powers? 55 Is not this the carpenter's son? Is not His mother called Mary, and His brothers, James and Joseph and Simon and Judas? 56 And His sisters, are they not all with us? Where then *did* this man *get* all these things?" 57 And they took offense at Him. But Jesus said to them, "A prophet is not without honor except in his hometown and in his *own* household." 58 And He did not do many miracles there because of their unbelief.

DAY 20: What did Joseph understand about the interpretation of dreams?

Oneiromancy, the science or practice of interpreting dreams, flourished in ancient Egypt because dreams were thought to determine the future. Both Egypt and Babylon developed a professional class of dream interpreters. Deuteronomy 13:1–5 shows that such dream interpreters were part of ancient false religion and to be avoided by God's people. By some 500 years later, a detailed manual of dream interpretation had been compiled. Unlike Joseph, neither butler nor baker understood the significance of their dreams (see Ge 37:5–11), and the sadness they project in Genesis 40:5 expresses their belief that the dreams required an interpretation.

Joseph believed that when it came to dreams that the "interpretations belong to God" (v. 8). He was careful to give credit to his Lord (see 41:16). Daniel, the only other Hebrew whom God allowed to accurately interpret revelatory dreams, was just as careful to do so (Da 2:28). Significantly, God chose both men to play an important role for Israel while serving pagan monarchs and stepping forward at the critical moment to interpret their dreams and reveal their futures.

JANUARY 21

Genesis 41:1–42:38

41 Now it happened at the end of two full years that Pharaoh had a dream, and behold, he was standing by the Nile. 2 And lo, from the Nile there came up seven cows, sleek and fat; and they grazed in the marsh grass. 3 Then behold, seven other cows came up after them from the Nile, ugly and gaunt, and they stood by the *other* cows on the bank of the Nile. 4 The ugly and gaunt cows ate up

the seven sleek and fat cows. Then Pharaoh awoke. 5 He fell asleep and dreamed a second time; and behold, seven ears of grain came up on a single stalk, plump and good. 6 Then behold, seven ears, thin and scorched by the east wind, sprouted up after them. 7 The thin ears swallowed up the seven plump and full ears. Then Pharaoh awoke, and behold, *it was* a dream. 8 Now in the morning his spirit was troubled, so he sent and called for all the magicians of Egypt, and all its wise men. And Pharaoh told them his dreams, but there was no one who could interpret them to Pharaoh.

⁹Then the chief cupbearer spoke to Pharaoh, saying, "I would make mention today of my *own* offenses. ¹⁰Pharaoh was furious with his servants, and he put me in confinement in the house of the captain of the bodyguard, *both* me and the chief baker. ¹¹We had a dream on the same night, he and I; each of us dreamed according to the interpretation of his *own* dream. ¹²Now a Hebrew youth *was* with us there, a servant of the captain of the bodyguard, and we related *them* to him, and he interpreted our dreams for us. To each one he interpreted according to his *own* dream. ¹³And just as he interpreted for us, so it happened; he restored me in my office, but he hanged him."

¹⁴Then Pharaoh sent and called for Joseph, and they hurriedly brought him out of the dungeon; and when he had shaved himself and changed his clothes, he came to Pharaoh. ¹⁵Pharaoh said to Joseph, "I have had a dream, but no one can interpret it; and I have heard it said about you, that when you hear a dream you can interpret it." ¹⁶Joseph then answered Pharaoh, saying, "It is not in me; God will give Pharaoh a favorable answer." ¹⁷So Pharaoh spoke to Joseph, "In my dream, behold, I was standing on the bank of the Nile; ¹⁸and behold, seven cows, fat and sleek came up out of the Nile, and they grazed in the marsh grass. ¹⁹Lo, seven other cows came up after them, poor and very ugly and gaunt, such as I had never seen for ugliness in all the land of Egypt; ²⁰and the lean and ugly cows ate up the first seven fat cows. ²¹Yet when they had devoured them, it could not be detected that they had devoured them, for they were just as ugly as before. Then I awoke. ²²I saw also in my dream, and behold, seven ears, full and good, came up on a single stalk; ²³and lo, seven ears, withered, thin, *and* scorched by the east wind, sprouted up after them; ²⁴and the thin ears swallowed the seven good ears. Then I told it to the magicians, but there was no one who could explain it to me."

²⁵Now Joseph said to Pharaoh, "Pharaoh's dreams are one *and the same;* God has told to Pharaoh what He is about to do. ²⁶The seven good cows are seven years; and the seven good ears are seven years; the dreams are one *and the same.* ²⁷The seven lean and ugly cows that came up after them are seven years, and the seven thin ears scorched by the east wind will be seven years of famine. ²⁸It is as I have spoken to Pharaoh: God has shown to Pharaoh what He is about to do. ²⁹Behold, seven years of great abundance are coming in all the land of Egypt; ³⁰and after them seven years of famine will come, and all the abundance will be forgotten in the land of Egypt, and the famine will ravage the land. ³¹So the abundance will be unknown in the land because of that subsequent famine; for it *will be* very severe. ³²Now as for the repeating of the dream to Pharaoh twice, *it means* that the matter is determined by God, and God will quickly bring it about. ³³Now let Pharaoh look for a man discerning and wise, and set him over the land of Egypt. ³⁴Let Pharaoh take action to appoint overseers in charge of the land, and let him exact a fifth *of the produce* of the land of Egypt in the seven years of abundance. ³⁵Then let them gather all the food of these good years that are coming, and store up the grain for food in the cities under Pharaoh's authority, and let them guard *it.* ³⁶Let the food become as a reserve for the land for the seven years of famine which will occur in the land of Egypt, so that the land will not perish during the famine."

³⁷Now the proposal seemed good to Pharaoh and to all his servants. ³⁸Then Pharaoh said to his servants, "Can we find a man like this, in whom is a divine spirit?" ³⁹So Pharaoh said to Joseph, "Since God has informed you of all this, there is no one so discerning and wise as you are. ⁴⁰You shall be over my house, and according to your command all my people shall do homage; only in the throne I will be greater than you." ⁴¹Pharaoh said to Joseph, "See, I have set you over all the land of Egypt." ⁴²Then Pharaoh took off his signet ring from his hand and put it on Joseph's hand, and clothed him in garments of fine linen and put the gold necklace around his neck. ⁴³He had him ride in his second chariot; and they proclaimed before him, "Bow the knee!" And he set him over all the land of Egypt. ⁴⁴Moreover, Pharaoh said to Joseph, "*Though* I am Pharaoh, yet without your permission no one shall raise his hand or foot in all the land of Egypt." ⁴⁵Then Pharaoh named Joseph Zaphenath-paneah; and he gave him Asenath, the daughter of Potiphera priest of On, as his wife. And Joseph went forth over the land of Egypt.

41:42 signet ring…garments…gold necklace. Emblems of office and a reward of clothing and jewelry suitable to the new rank accompanied Pharaoh's appointment of Joseph as vizier, or prime minister, the second-in-command (v. 40; 45:8, 26). Joseph wore the royal seal on his finger, authorizing him to transact the affairs of state on behalf of Pharaoh himself.

⁴⁶ Now Joseph was thirty years old when he stood before Pharaoh, king of Egypt. And Joseph went out from the presence of Pharaoh and went through all the land of Egypt. ⁴⁷ During the seven years of plenty the land brought forth abundantly. ⁴⁸ So he gathered all the food of *these* seven years which occurred in the land of Egypt and placed the food in the cities; he placed in every city the food from its own surrounding fields. ⁴⁹ Thus Joseph stored up grain in great abundance like the sand of the sea, until he stopped measuring *it,* for it was beyond measure.

⁵⁰ Now before the year of famine came, two sons were born to Joseph, whom Asenath, the daughter of Potiphera priest of On, bore to him. ⁵¹ Joseph named the firstborn Manasseh, "For," *he said,* "God has made me forget all my trouble and all my father's household." ⁵² He named the second Ephraim, "For," *he said,* "God has made me fruitful in the land of my affliction."

⁵³ When the seven years of plenty which had been in the land of Egypt came to an end, ⁵⁴ and the seven years of famine began to come, just as Joseph had said, then there was famine in all the lands, but in all the land of Egypt there was bread. ⁵⁵ So when all the land of Egypt was famished, the people cried out to Pharaoh for bread; and Pharaoh said to all the Egyptians, "Go to Joseph; whatever he says to you, you shall do." ⁵⁶ When the famine was *spread* over all the face of the earth, then Joseph opened all the storehouses, and sold to the Egyptians; and the famine was severe in the land of Egypt. ⁵⁷ *The people of* all the earth came to Egypt to buy grain from Joseph, because the famine was severe in all the earth.

42 Now Jacob saw that there was grain in Egypt, and Jacob said to his sons, "Why are you staring at one another?" ² He said, "Behold, I have heard that there is grain in Egypt; go down there and buy *some* for us from that place, so that we may live and not die." ³ Then ten brothers of Joseph went down to buy grain from Egypt. ⁴ But Jacob did not send Joseph's brother Benjamin with his brothers, for he said, "I am afraid that harm may befall him." ⁵ So the sons of Israel came to buy grain among those who were coming, for the famine was in the land of Canaan *also.*

⁶ Now Joseph was the ruler over the land; he was the one who sold to all the people of the land. And Joseph's brothers came and bowed down to him with *their* faces to the ground. ⁷ When Joseph saw his brothers he recognized them, but he disguised himself to them and spoke to them harshly. And he said to them, "Where have you come from?"

42:6 bowed down. Without their appreciating it at the time, Joseph's dream became reality (37:5–8). Recognition of Joseph was unlikely because: 1) over 15 years had elapsed and the teenager sold into slavery had become a mature adult; 2) he had become Egyptian in appearance and dress; 3) he treated them without a hint of familiarity (vv. 7–8); and 4) they thought he was dead (v. 13).

And they said, "From the land of Canaan, to buy food."

⁸ But Joseph had recognized his brothers, although they did not recognize him. ⁹ Joseph remembered the dreams which he had about them, and said to them, "You are spies; you have come to look at the undefended parts of our land." ¹⁰ Then they said to him, "No, my lord, but your servants have come to buy food. ¹¹ We are all sons of one man; we are honest men, your servants are not spies." ¹² Yet he said to them, "No, but you have come to look at the undefended parts of our land!" ¹³ But they said, "Your servants are twelve brothers *in all,* the sons of one man in the land of Canaan; and behold, the youngest is with our father today, and one is no longer alive." ¹⁴ Joseph said to them, "It is as I said to you, you are spies; ¹⁵ by this you will be tested: by the life of Pharaoh, you shall not go from this place unless your youngest brother comes here! ¹⁶ Send one of you that he may get your brother, while you remain confined, that your words may be tested, whether there is truth in you. But if not, by the life of Pharaoh, surely you are spies." ¹⁷ So he put them all together in prison for three days.

¹⁸ Now Joseph said to them on the third day, "Do this and live, for I fear God: ¹⁹ if you are honest men, let one of your brothers be confined in your prison; but as for *the rest of* you, go, carry grain for the famine of your households, ²⁰ and bring your youngest brother to me, so your words may be verified, and you will not die." And they did so. ²¹ Then they said to one another, "Truly we are guilty concerning our brother, because we saw the distress of his soul when he pleaded with us, yet we would not listen; therefore this distress has come upon us." ²² Reuben answered them, saying, "Did I not tell you, 'Do not sin against the boy'; and you would not listen? Now comes the reckoning for his blood." ²³ They did not know, however, that Joseph understood, for there was an interpreter between them. ²⁴ He turned away from them and wept. But when

he returned to them and spoke to them, he took Simeon from them and bound him before their eyes. ²⁵Then Joseph gave orders to fill their bags with grain and to restore every man's money in his sack, and to give them provisions for the journey. And thus it was done for them.

²⁶So they loaded their donkeys with their grain and departed from there. ²⁷As one *of them* opened his sack to give his donkey fodder at the lodging place, he saw his money; and behold, it was in the mouth of his sack. ²⁸Then he said to his brothers, "My money has been returned, and behold, it is even in my sack." And their hearts sank, and they *turned* trembling to one another, saying, "What is this that God has done to us?"

²⁹When they came to their father Jacob in the land of Canaan, they told him all that had happened to them, saying, ³⁰"The man, the lord of the land, spoke harshly with us, and took us for spies of the country. ³¹But we said to him, 'We are honest men; we are not spies. ³²We are twelve brothers, sons of our father; one is no longer alive, and the youngest is with our father today in the land of Canaan.' ³³The man, the lord of the land, said to us, 'By this I will know that you are honest men: leave one of your brothers with me and take *grain for* the famine of your households, and go. ³⁴But bring your youngest brother to me that I may know that you are not spies, but honest men. I will give your brother to you, and you may trade in the land.'"

³⁵Now it came about as they were emptying their sacks, that behold, every man's bundle of money *was* in his sack; and when they and their father saw their bundles of money, they were dismayed. ³⁶Their father Jacob said to them, "You have bereaved me of my children: Joseph is no more, and Simeon is no more, and you would take Benjamin; all these things are against me." ³⁷Then Reuben spoke to his father, saying, "You may put my two sons to death if I do not bring him *back* to you; put him in my care, and I will return him to you." ³⁸But Jacob said, "My son shall not go down with you; for his brother is dead, and he alone is left. If harm should befall him on the journey you are taking, then you will bring my gray hair down to Sheol in sorrow."

Psalm 10:12–18

¹² Arise, O LORD; O God, lift
 up Your hand.
 Do not forget the afflicted.
¹³ Why has the wicked spurned God?
 He has said to himself, "You
 will not require *it.*"

10:14 helper of the orphan. God is pictured as Helper or Advocate again, but this time in association with orphans. He is the Defender par excellence of the defenseless (on the imagery, see Ex 22:21ff.; Dt 10:18ff.; 1Sa 1:17; Jer 7:6).

¹⁴ You have seen *it,* for You have
 beheld mischief and vexation
 to take it into Your hand.
 The unfortunate commits
 himself to You;
 You have been the helper
 of the orphan.
¹⁵ Break the arm of the wicked
 and the evildoer,
 Seek out his wickedness
 until You find none.
¹⁶ The LORD is King forever and ever;
 Nations have perished from His land.
¹⁷ O LORD, You have heard the
 desire of the humble;
 You will strengthen their heart,
 You will incline Your ear
¹⁸ To vindicate the orphan
 and the oppressed,
 So that man who is of the earth
 will no longer cause terror.

Proverbs 4:7–9

⁷ "The beginning of wisdom
 is: Acquire wisdom;
 And with all your acquiring,
 get understanding.
⁸ "Prize her, and she will exalt you;
 She will honor you if you embrace her.
⁹ "She will place on your head
 a garland of grace;
 She will present you with
 a crown of beauty."

Matthew 14:1–21

14 At that time Herod the tetrarch heard the news about Jesus, ²and said to his servants, "This is John the Baptist; he has risen from the dead, and that is why miraculous powers are at work in him."

³For when Herod had John arrested, he bound him and put him in prison because of Herodias, the wife of his brother Philip. ⁴For John had been saying to him, "It is not lawful for you to have her." ⁵Although Herod wanted to put him to death, he feared the crowd, because they regarded John as a prophet.

⁶But when Herod's birthday came, the

14:3 Herodias, the wife of his brother Philip.
Herodias was the daughter of Aristobulus, another son of Herod the Great; so when she married Philip, she was marrying her own father's brother. What precipitated the arrest of John the Baptist was that Herod Antipas (another of Herodias' uncles) talked Herodias into leaving her husband (his brother) in order to marry him (Mk 6:17)—thus compounding the incest, as well as violating Leviticus 18:16. John was outraged that a ruler in Israel would commit such a sin openly, so he rebuked Herod severely (v. 4). For this, he was imprisoned and later killed (Mk 6:14-29).

daughter of Herodias danced before *them* and pleased Herod, [7] so *much* that he promised with an oath to give her whatever she asked. [8] Having been prompted by her mother, she *said, "Give me here on a platter the head of John the Baptist." [9] Although he was grieved, the king commanded *it* to be given because of his oaths, and because of his dinner guests. [10] He sent and had John beheaded in the prison. [11] And his head was brought on a platter and given to the girl, and she brought it to her mother. [12] His

disciples came and took away the body and buried it; and they went and reported to Jesus.

[13] Now when Jesus heard *about John,* He withdrew from there in a boat to a secluded place by Himself; and when the people heard *of this,* they followed Him on foot from the cities. [14] When He went ashore, He saw a large crowd, and felt compassion for them and healed their sick.

[15] When it was evening, the disciples came to Him and said, "This place is desolate and the hour is already late; so send the crowds away, that they may go into the villages and buy food for themselves." [16] But Jesus said to them, "They do not need to go away; you give them *something* to eat!" [17] They *said to Him, "We have here only five loaves and two fish." [18] And He said, "Bring them here to Me." [19] Ordering the people to sit down on the grass, He took the five loaves and the two fish, and looking up toward heaven, He blessed *the food,* and breaking the loaves He gave them to the disciples, and the disciples *gave them* to the crowds, [20] and they all ate and were satisfied. They picked up what was left over of the broken pieces, twelve full baskets. [21] There were about five thousand men who ate, besides women and children.

DAY 21: How did Joseph's faithfulness lead to personal advancement?

Pharaoh's disturbing dreams in Genesis 41 were such that there was "no one who could interpret them" (v. 8). The combined expertise of a full council of Pharaoh's advisers and dream experts failed to provide an interpretation. Without knowing it, they had just set the stage for Joseph's entrance on the scene of Egyptian history. The chief butler spoke up and apprised Pharaoh of the Hebrew prisoner and his accurate interpretation of dreams two years earlier (vv. 10–13).

In the presence of Pharaoh, Joseph made his faith known: "It is not in me; God will give Pharaoh a favorable answer" (v. 16). Deprecating any innate ability, Joseph advised at the very outset that the answer Pharaoh desired could only come from God. And after hearing the dream described, Joseph's interpretation of what "God has told to Pharaoh" (v. 25) kept the focus fixed upon what God had determined for Egypt (vv. 28, 32).

After interpreting the dream, Joseph told Pharaoh how to survive the next 14 years. Incongruously, Joseph, a slave and a prisoner, appended to the interpretation a long-term strategy for establishing reserves to meet the future need and included advice on the quality of the man to head up the project. Famines had ravaged Egypt before, but this time divine warning permitted serious and sustained advance planning. To Pharaoh and his royal retinue, no other candidate but Joseph qualified for the task of working out this good plan, because they recognized that he spoke God-given revelation and insight (v. 39).

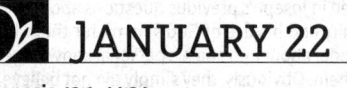

JANUARY 22

Genesis 43:1–44:34

43 Now the famine was severe in the land. [2] So it came about when they had finished eating the grain which they had brought from Egypt, that their father said to them, "Go back, buy us a little food."

[3] Judah spoke to him, however, saying, "The man solemnly warned us, 'You shall not see my face unless your brother is with you.' [4] If you send our brother with us, we will go down and buy you food. [5] But if you do not send *him,* we will not go down; for the man said to us, 'You will not see my face unless your brother is with you.'" [6] Then Israel said, "Why did you treat me so badly by telling the

man whether you still had *another* brother?" [7] But they said, "The man questioned particularly about us and our relatives, saying, 'Is your father still alive? Have you *another* brother?' So we answered his questions. Could we possibly know that he would say, 'Bring your brother down'?" [8] Judah said to his father Israel, "Send the lad with me and we will arise and go, that we may live and not die, we as well as you and our little ones. [9] I myself will be surety for him; you may hold me responsible for him. If I do not bring him *back* to you and set him before you, then let me bear the blame before you forever. [10] For if we had not delayed, surely by now we could have returned twice."

[11] Then their father Israel said to them, "If *it must be* so, then do this: take some of the best products of the land in your bags, and carry down to the man as a present, a little balm and a little honey, aromatic gum and myrrh, pistachio nuts and almonds. [12] Take double *the* money in your hand, and take back in your hand the money that was returned in the mouth of your sacks; perhaps it was a mistake. [13] Take your brother also, and arise, return to the man; [14] and may God Almighty grant you compassion in the sight of the man, so that he will release to you your other brother and Benjamin. And as for me, if I am bereaved of my children, I am bereaved." [15] So the men took this present, and they took double *the* money in their hand, and Benjamin; then they arose and went down to Egypt and stood before Joseph.

[16] When Joseph saw Benjamin with them, he said to his house steward, "Bring the men into the house, and slay an animal and make ready; for the men are to dine with me at noon." [17] So the man did as Joseph said, and brought the men to Joseph's house. [18] Now the men were afraid, because they were brought to Joseph's house; and they said, "*It is* because of the money that was returned in our sacks the first time that we are being brought in, that he may seek occasion against us and fall upon us, and take us for slaves with our donkeys." [19] So they came near to Joseph's house steward, and spoke to him at the entrance of the house, [20] and said, "Oh, my lord, we indeed came down the first time to buy food, [21] and it came about when we came to the lodging place, that we opened our sacks, and behold, each man's money was in the mouth of his sack, our money in full. So we have brought it back in our hand. [22] We have also brought down other money in our hand to buy food; we do not know who put our money in our

sacks." [23] He said, "Be at ease, do not be afraid. Your God and the God of your father has given you treasure in your sacks; I had your money." Then he brought Simeon out to them. [24] Then the man brought the men into Joseph's house and gave them water, and they washed their feet; and he gave their donkeys fodder. [25] So they prepared the present for Joseph's coming at noon; for they had heard that they were to eat a meal there.

[26] When Joseph came home, they brought into the house to him the present which was in their hand and bowed to the ground before him. [27] Then he asked them about their welfare, and said, "Is your old father well, of whom you spoke? Is he still alive?" [28] They said, "Your servant our father is well; he is still alive." They bowed down in homage. [29] As he lifted his eyes and saw his brother Benjamin, his mother's son, he said, "Is this your youngest brother, of whom you spoke to me?" And he said, "May God be gracious to you, my son." [30] Joseph hurried *out* for he was deeply stirred over his brother, and he sought *a place* to weep; and he entered his chamber and wept there. [31] Then he washed his face and came out; and he controlled himself and said, "Serve the meal." [32] So they served him by himself, and them by themselves, and the Egyptians who ate with him by themselves, because the Egyptians could not eat bread with the Hebrews, for that is loathsome to the Egyptians. [33] Now they were seated before him, the firstborn according to his birthright and the youngest according to his youth, and the men looked at one another in astonishment. [34] He took portions to them from his own table, but Benjamin's portion was five times as much as any of theirs. So they feasted and drank freely with him.

43:33 the firstborn...the youngest. To be seated at the table in birth order in the house of an Egyptian official was startling—how did he know this of them? Enough clues had been given in Joseph's previous questions about the family and his use of God's name for them to wonder about him and his personal knowledge of them. Obviously, they simply did not believe Joseph was alive (44:20) and certainly not as a personage of such immense influence and authority. They had probably laughed through the years at the memory of Joseph's dreams of superiority.

44

Then he commanded his house steward, saying, "Fill the men's sacks with food, as much as they can carry, and put each man's money in the mouth of his sack. ²Put my cup, the silver cup, in the mouth of the sack of the youngest, and his money for the grain." And he did as Joseph had told *him*. ³As soon as it was light, the men were sent away, they with their donkeys. ⁴They had *just* gone out of the city, *and* were not far off, when Joseph said to his house steward, "Up, follow the men; and when you overtake them, say to them, 'Why have you repaid evil for good? ⁵Is not this the one from which my lord drinks and which he indeed uses for divination? You have done wrong in doing this.'"

⁶So he overtook them and spoke these words to them. ⁷They said to him, "Why does my lord speak such words as these? Far be it from your servants to do such a thing. ⁸Behold, the money which we found in the mouth of our sacks we have brought back to you from the land of Canaan. How then could we steal silver or gold from your lord's house? ⁹With whomever of your servants it is found, let him die, and we also will be my lord's slaves." ¹⁰So he said, "Now let it also be according to your words; he with whom it is found shall be my slave, and *the rest of* you shall be innocent." ¹¹Then they hurried, each man lowered his sack to the ground, and each man opened his sack. ¹²He searched, beginning with the oldest and ending with the youngest, and the cup was found in Benjamin's sack. ¹³Then they tore their clothes, and when each man loaded his donkey, they returned to the city.

¹⁴When Judah and his brothers came to Joseph's house, he was still there, and they fell to the ground before him. ¹⁵Joseph said to them, "What is this deed that you have done? Do you not know that such a man as I can indeed practice divination?" ¹⁶So Judah said, "What can we say to my lord? What can we speak? And how can we justify ourselves? God has found out the iniquity of your servants; behold, we are my lord's slaves, both we and the one in whose possession the cup has been found." ¹⁷But he said, "Far be it from me to do this. The man in whose possession the cup has been found, he shall be my slave; but as for you, go up in peace to your father."

¹⁸Then Judah approached him, and said, "Oh my lord, may your servant please speak a word in my lord's ears, and do not be angry with your servant; for you are equal to Pharaoh. ¹⁹My lord asked his servants, saying, 'Have you a father or a brother?' ²⁰We said

44:13 tore their clothes. A well-known ancient Near Eastern custom of visibly portraying the pain of heart being experienced. They were very upset that Benjamin might become a slave in Egypt (v. 10). Benjamin appears to have been speechless. They had passed a second test of devotion to Benjamin (the first in v. 34).

44:18-34 An eloquent and contrite plea for mercy, replete with reference to the aged father's delight in and doting upon the youngest son (vv. 20, 30) and the fatal shock should he be lost (vv. 22, 29, 31, 34). Judah's evident compassion for Jacob and readiness to substitute himself for Benjamin in slavery finally overwhelmed Joseph—these were not the same brothers of yesteryear (45:1).

to my lord, 'We have an old father and a little child of *his* old age. Now his brother is dead, so he alone is left of his mother, and his father loves him.' ²¹Then you said to your servants, 'Bring him down to me that I may set my eyes on him.' ²²But we said to my lord, 'The lad cannot leave his father, for if he should leave his father, his father would die.' ²³You said to your servants, however, 'Unless your youngest brother comes down with you, you will not see my face again.' ²⁴Thus it came about when we went up to your servant my father, we told him the words of my lord. ²⁵Our father said, 'Go back, buy us a little food.' ²⁶But we said, 'We cannot go down. If our youngest brother is with us, then we will go down; for we cannot see the man's face unless our youngest brother is with us.' ²⁷Your servant my father said to us, 'You know that my wife bore me two sons; ²⁸and the one went out from me, and I said, "Surely he is torn in pieces," and I have not seen him since. ²⁹If you take this one also from me, and harm befalls him, you will bring my gray hair down to Sheol in sorrow.' ³⁰Now, therefore, when I come to your servant my father, and the lad is not with us, since his life is bound up in the lad's life, ³¹when he sees that the lad is not *with us,* he will die. Thus your servants will bring the gray hair of your servant our father down to Sheol in sorrow. ³²For your servant became surety for the lad to my father, saying, 'If I do not bring him *back* to you, then let me bear the blame before my father forever.' ³³Now, therefore, please let your servant remain instead of the lad a slave to my lord, and let the lad go up with his brothers. ³⁴For how shall I go up to my father if the lad is not with me—for fear that I see the evil that would overtake my father?"

Psalm 11:1–7

For the choir director. *A Psalm* of David.

I n the LORD I take refuge;
How can you say to my soul, "Flee
as a bird to your mountain;
2 For, behold, the wicked bend the bow,
They make ready their arrow
upon the string
To shoot in darkness at the
upright in heart.
3 "If the foundations are destroyed,
What can the righteous do?"

4 The LORD is in His holy temple; the
LORD'S throne is in heaven;
His eyes behold, His eyelids
test the sons of men.
5 The LORD tests the righteous
and the wicked,
And the one who loves
violence His soul hates.
6 Upon the wicked He will rain snares;
Fire and brimstone and burning wind
will be the portion of their cup.
7 For the LORD is righteous, He
loves righteousness;
The upright will behold His face.

Proverbs 4:10–13

10 Hear, my son, and accept my sayings
And the years of your life
will be many.
11 I have directed you in the
way of wisdom;
I have led you in upright paths.
12 When you walk, your steps
will not be impeded;
And if you run, you will not stumble.

13 Take hold of instruction; do not
let go.
Guard her, for she is your life.

Matthew 14:22–36

22 Immediately He made the disciples get into the boat and go ahead of Him to the other side, while He sent the crowds away. 23 After He had sent the crowds away, He went up on the mountain by Himself to pray; and when it was evening, He was there alone. 24 But the boat was already a long distance from the land, battered by the waves; for the wind was contrary. 25 And in the fourth watch of the night He came to them, walking on the sea. 26 When the disciples saw Him walking on the sea, they were terrified, and said, "It is a ghost!" And they cried out in fear. 27 But immediately Jesus spoke to them, saying, "Take courage, it is I; do not be afraid."

28 Peter said to Him, "Lord, if it is You, command me to come to You on the water." 29 And He said, "Come!" And Peter got out of the boat, and walked on the water and came toward Jesus. 30 But seeing the wind, he became frightened, and beginning to sink, he cried out, "Lord, save me!" 31 Immediately Jesus stretched out His hand and took hold of him, and *said to him, "You of little faith, why did you doubt?" 32 When they got into the boat, the wind stopped. 33 And those who were in the boat worshiped Him, saying, "You are certainly God's Son!"

34 When they had crossed over, they came to land at Gennesaret. 35 And when the men of that place recognized Him, they sent *word* into all that surrounding district and brought to Him all who were sick; 36 and they implored Him that they might just touch the fringe of His cloak; and as many as touched *it* were cured.

DAY 22: When the world seems to be falling apart, who can I trust?

In Psalm 11, the panic that launched its writing was not David's but that of his apparently well-meaning counselors. Their mood in the face of wicked persecution is panic, the desire to flee, but David's is peace. Their words are the expressions of committed but confused saints. Their philosophical problem is, "In view of the crumbling of the theocratic society, what can one righteous person, out of a shrinking remnant, do?"

David's immediate response to panic is to say, "In the LORD I take refuge." Literally, he said, "I put my trust in the Lord." God is the exclusive refuge for His persecuted children (see Pss 16:1; 36:7). After all, David adds, the Lord is "in His holy temple…in heaven." This emphasizes the transcendent throne room of God, yet God has sovereign sway over all the affairs of earth (see Hab 2:20). "His eyes behold…His eyelids test"—His transcendence previously depicted does not negate His eminence here presented from the perspective of the divine scrutiny of all men, including the righteous (see Jer 6:27–30; 17:10).

David had made up his mind to trust only in the Lord, and for good reason. In view of David's attitude, this psalm can be listed with the psalms of confidence (Pss 4, 16, 23, 27, 62, 125, 131).

JANUARY 23

Genesis 45:1–46:34

45 Then Joseph could not control himself before all those who stood by him, and he cried, "Have everyone go out from me." So there was no man with him when Joseph made himself known to his brothers. [2] He wept so loudly that the Egyptians heard *it,* and the household of Pharaoh heard *of it.* [3] Then Joseph said to his brothers, "I am Joseph! Is my father still alive?" But his brothers could not answer him, for they were dismayed at his presence.

[4] Then Joseph said to his brothers, "Please come closer to me." And they came closer. And he said, "I am your brother Joseph, whom you sold into Egypt. [5] Now do not be grieved or angry with yourselves, because you sold me here, for God sent me before you to preserve life. [6] For the famine *has been* in the land these two years, and there are still five years in which there will be neither plowing nor harvesting. [7] God sent me before you to preserve for you a remnant in the earth, and to keep you alive by a great deliverance. [8] Now, therefore, it was not you who sent me here, but God; and He has made me a father to Pharaoh and lord of all his household and ruler over all the land of Egypt. [9] Hurry and go up to my father, and say to him, 'Thus says your son Joseph, "God has made me lord of all Egypt; come down to me, do not delay. [10] You shall live in the land of Goshen, and you shall be near me, you and your children and your children's children and your flocks and your herds and all that you have. [11] There I will also provide for you, for there are still five years of famine *to come,* and you and your household and all that you have would be impoverished."' [12] Behold, your eyes see, and the eyes of my brother Benjamin *see,* that it is my mouth which is speaking to you. [13] Now you must tell my father of all my splendor in Egypt, and all that you have seen; and you must hurry and bring my father down here." [14] Then he fell on his brother Benjamin's neck and wept, and Benjamin wept on his neck. [15] He kissed all his brothers and wept on them, and afterward his brothers talked with him.

[16] Now when the news was heard in Pharaoh's house that Joseph's brothers had come, it pleased Pharaoh and his servants. [17] Then Pharaoh said to Joseph, "Say to your brothers, 'Do this: load your beasts and go to the land of Canaan, [18] and take your father and your households and come to me, and I will give you the best of the land of Egypt and you will eat the fat of the land.' [19] Now you are ordered, 'Do this: take wagons from the land of Egypt for your little ones and for your wives, and bring your father and come. [20] Do not concern yourselves with your goods, for the best of all the land of Egypt is yours.'"

[21] Then the sons of Israel did so; and Joseph gave them wagons according to the command of Pharaoh, and gave them provisions for the journey. [22] To each of them he gave changes of garments, but to Benjamin he gave three hundred *pieces of* silver and five changes of garments. [23] To his father he sent as follows: ten donkeys loaded with the best things of Egypt, and ten female donkeys loaded with grain and bread and sustenance for his father on the journey.

[24] So he sent his brothers away, and as they departed, he said to them, "Do not quarrel on the journey." [25] Then they went up from Egypt, and came to the land of Canaan to their father Jacob. [26] They told him, saying, "Joseph is still alive, and indeed he is ruler over all the land of Egypt." But he was stunned, for he did not believe them. [27] When they told him all the words of Joseph that he had spoken to them, and when he saw the wagons that Joseph had sent to carry him, the spirit of their father Jacob revived. [28] Then Israel said, "It is enough; my son Joseph is still alive. I will go and see him before I die."

46 So Israel set out with all that he had, and came to Beersheba, and offered sacrifices to the God of his father Isaac. [2] God spoke to Israel in visions of the night and said, "Jacob, Jacob." And he said, "Here I am." [3] He said, "I am God, the God of your father; do not be afraid to go down to Egypt, for I will make you a great nation there. [4] I will go down with you to Egypt, and I will also surely bring you up again; and Joseph will close your eyes."

[5] Then Jacob arose from Beersheba; and the sons of Israel carried their father Jacob and their little ones and their wives in the wagons which Pharaoh had sent to carry him. [6] They took their livestock and their property, which they had acquired in the land of Canaan, and

45:1–8 Stunned by the revelation of who it really was with whom they dealt, the brothers then heard expressed a masterpiece of recognition of and submission to the sovereignty of God, i.e., His providential rule over the affairs of life, both good and bad.

came to Egypt, Jacob and all his descendants with him: 7 his sons and his grandsons with him, his daughters and his granddaughters, and all his descendants he brought with him to Egypt.

8 Now these are the names of the sons of Israel, Jacob and his sons, who went to Egypt: Reuben, Jacob's firstborn. 9 The sons of Reuben: Hanoch and Pallu and Hezron and Carmi. 10 The sons of Simeon: Jemuel and Jamin and Ohad and Jachin and Zohar and Shaul the son of a Canaanite woman. 11 The sons of Levi: Gershon, Kohath, and Merari. 12 The sons of Judah: Er and Onan and Shelah and Perez and Zerah (but Er and Onan died in the land of Canaan). And the sons of Perez were Hezron and Hamul. 13 The sons of Issachar: Tola and Puvvah and Iob and Shimron. 14 The sons of Zebulun: Sered and Elon and Jahleel. 15 These are the sons of Leah, whom she bore to Jacob in Paddan-aram, with his daughter Dinah; all his sons and his daughters *numbered* thirty-three. 16 The sons of Gad: Ziphion and Haggi, Shuni and Ezbon, Eri and Arodi and Areli. 17 The sons of Asher: Imnah and Ishvah and Ishvi and Beriah and their sister Serah. And the sons of Beriah: Heber and Malchiel. 18 These are the sons of Zilpah, whom Laban gave to his daughter Leah; and she bore to Jacob these sixteen persons. 19 The sons of Jacob's wife Rachel: Joseph and Benjamin. 20 Now to Joseph in the land of Egypt were born Manasseh and Ephraim, whom Asenath, the daughter of Potiphera, priest of On, bore to him. 21 The sons of Benjamin: Bela and Becher and Ashbel, Gera and Naaman, Ehi and Rosh, Muppim and Huppim and Ard. 22 These are the sons of Rachel, who were born to Jacob; *there were* fourteen persons in all. 23 The sons of Dan: Hushim. 24 The sons of Naphtali: Jahzeel and Guni and Jezer and Shillem. 25 These are the sons of Bilhah, whom Laban gave to his daughter Rachel, and she bore these to Jacob; *there were* seven persons in all. 26 All the persons belonging to Jacob, who came to Egypt, his direct descendants, not including the wives of Jacob's sons, *were* sixty-six persons in all, 27 and the sons of Joseph, who were born to him in Egypt were two; all the persons of the house of Jacob, who came to Egypt, *were* seventy.

28 Now he sent Judah before him to Joseph, to point out *the way* before him to Goshen; and they came into the land of Goshen. 29 Joseph prepared his chariot and went up to Goshen to meet his father Israel; as soon as he appeared before him, he fell on his neck and wept on his neck a long time. 30 Then Israel said to Joseph, "Now let me die, since I have seen your face, that you are still alive." 31 Joseph said to his brothers and to his father's household, "I will go up and tell Pharaoh, and will say to him, 'My brothers and my father's household, who *were* in the land of Canaan, have come to me; 32 and the men are shepherds, for they have been keepers of livestock; and they have brought their flocks and their herds and all that they have.' 33 When Pharaoh calls you and says, 'What is your occupation?' 34 you shall say, 'Your servants have been keepers of livestock from our youth even until now, both we and our fathers,' that you may live in the land of Goshen; for every shepherd is loathsome to the Egyptians."

46:31-34 Joseph's instructions about his preparatory interview with Pharaoh were designed to secure his relatives a place somewhat separate from the mainstream of Egyptian society. The social stigma regarding the Hebrews (43:32), who were shepherds also (v. 34), played a crucial role in protecting Israel from intermingling and losing their identity in Egypt.

Psalm 12:1-8

For the choir director; upon an eight-stringed lyre. A Psalm of David.

H elp, LORD, for the godly
man ceases to be,
For the faithful disappear from
among the sons of men.
2 They speak falsehood to one
another;
With flattering lips and with a
double heart they speak.
3 May the LORD cut off all
flattering lips,
The tongue that speaks great
things;
4 Who have said, "With our
tongue we will prevail;
Our lips are our own; who
is lord over us?"
5 "Because of the devastation of
the afflicted, because of the
groaning of the needy,
Now I will arise," says the LORD;
"I will set him in the safety
for which he longs."

6 The words of the LORD
are pure words;

As silver tried in a furnace on the
earth, refined seven times.
7 You, O LORD, will keep them;
You will preserve him from
this generation forever.
8 The wicked strut about on
every side
When vileness is exalted
among the sons of men.

Proverbs 4:14–17

14 Do not enter the path of the
wicked
And do not proceed in the
way of evil men.
15 Avoid it, do not pass by it;
Turn away from it and pass on.
16 For they cannot sleep
unless they do evil;
And they are robbed of sleep
unless they make
someone stumble.
17 For they eat the bread
of wickedness
And drink the wine
of violence.

Matthew 15:1–20

15 Then some Pharisees and scribes *came
to Jesus from Jerusalem and said,
2 "Why do Your disciples break the tradition of
the elders? For they do not wash their hands
when they eat bread." 3 And He answered and
said to them, "Why do you yourselves transgress the commandment of God for the sake
of your tradition? 4 For God said, 'HONOR YOUR
FATHER AND MOTHER,' and, 'HE WHO SPEAKS
EVIL OF FATHER OR MOTHER IS TO BE PUT TO
DEATH.' 5 But you say, 'Whoever says to his
father or mother, "Whatever I have that would

help you has been given to God," 6 he is not to
honor his father or his mother.' And by this
you invalidated the word of God for the sake
of your tradition. 7 You hypocrites, rightly did
Isaiah prophesy of you:

8 'THIS PEOPLE HONORS ME
WITH THEIR LIPS,
BUT THEIR HEART IS FAR
AWAY FROM ME.
9 'BUT IN VAIN DO THEY WORSHIP ME,
TEACHING AS DOCTRINES THE
PRECEPTS OF MEN.'"

10 After Jesus called the crowd to Him, He
said to them, "Hear and understand. 11 It is not
what enters into the mouth that defiles the
man, but what proceeds out of the mouth,
this defiles the man."

12 Then the disciples *came and *said to
Him, "Do You know that the Pharisees were
offended when they heard this statement?"
13 But He answered and said, "Every plant
which My heavenly Father did not plant shall
be uprooted. 14 Let them alone; they are blind
guides of the blind. And if a blind man guides
a blind man, both will fall into a pit."
15 Peter said to Him, "Explain the parable to us." 16 Jesus said, "Are you still lacking in understanding also? 17 Do you not
understand that everything that goes into
the mouth passes into the stomach, and is
eliminated? 18 But the things that proceed
out of the mouth come from the heart, and
those defile the man. 19 For out of the heart
come evil thoughts, murders, adulteries,
fornications, thefts, false witness, slanders.
20 These are the things which defile the man;
but to eat with unwashed hands does not
defile the man."

DAY 23: What were the "traditions of the elders"?

The "tradition of the elders" (Mt 15:2) was a body of extrabiblical law that had existed only in
oral form and only since the time of the Babylonian captivity. Later it was committed to writing
in the Mishna near the end of the second century. The Law of Moses contained no commandment about washing one's hands before eating—except for priests who were required to wash
before eating holy offerings (Lv 22:6–7).

Jesus' problem with the Pharisees is that they used these traditions to dishonor their parents in a cleverly devised way (vv. 4–6). The commandments of God were clear (Ex 20:12; 21:17;
Dt 5:16); but to circumvent them, some people claimed they could not financially assist their
parents because they had dedicated a certain sum of money to God, who was greater than their
parents. The rabbis had approved this exception to the commandments of Moses and thus in
effect nullified God's law (v. 6).

Hypocritically, they "invalidated the word of God for the sake of" their traditions (v. 6).
"Invalidated" means, "to deprive of authority" or "to cancel." Jesus condemned this practice
by showing that the Pharisees and scribes were guilty of canceling out God's Word through
their tradition.

JANUARY 24

Genesis 47:1–48:22

47 Then Joseph went in and told Pharaoh, and said, "My father and my brothers and their flocks and their herds and all that they have, have come out of the land of Canaan; and behold, they are in the land of Goshen." ²He took five men from among his brothers and presented them to Pharaoh. ³Then Pharaoh said to his brothers, "What is your occupation?" So they said to Pharaoh, "Your servants are shepherds, both we and our fathers." ⁴They said to Pharaoh, "We have come to sojourn in the land, for there is no pasture for your servants' flocks, for the famine is severe in the land of Canaan. Now, therefore, please let your servants live in the land of Goshen." ⁵Then Pharaoh said to Joseph, "Your father and your brothers have come to you. ⁶The land of Egypt is at your disposal; settle your father and your brothers in the best of the land, let them live in the land of Goshen; and if you know any capable men among them, then put them in charge of my livestock."

⁷Then Joseph brought his father Jacob and presented him to Pharaoh; and Jacob blessed Pharaoh. ⁸Pharaoh said to Jacob, "How many years have you lived?" ⁹So Jacob said to Pharaoh, "The years of my sojourning are one hundred and thirty; few and unpleasant have been the years of my life, nor have they attained the years that my fathers lived during the days of their sojourning." ¹⁰And Jacob blessed Pharaoh, and went out from his presence. ¹¹So Joseph settled his father and his brothers and gave them a possession in the land of Egypt, in the best of the land, in the land of Rameses, as Pharaoh had ordered. ¹²Joseph provided his father and his brothers and all his father's household with food, according to their little ones.

¹³Now there was no food in all the land, because the famine was very severe, so that the land of Egypt and the land of Canaan languished because of the famine. ¹⁴Joseph gathered all the money that was found in the land of Egypt and in the land of Canaan for the grain which they bought, and Joseph brought the money into Pharaoh's house. ¹⁵When the money was all spent in the land of Egypt and in the land of Canaan, all the Egyptians came to Joseph and said, "Give us food, for why should we die in your presence? For *our* money is gone." ¹⁶Then Joseph said, "Give up your livestock, and I will give you *food* for your livestock, since *your* money is gone." ¹⁷So they brought their livestock to Joseph, and Joseph gave them food in exchange for the horses and the flocks and the herds and the donkeys; and he fed them with food in exchange for all their livestock that year. ¹⁸When that year was ended, they came to him the next year and said to him, "We will not hide from my lord that our money is all spent, and the cattle are my lord's. There is nothing left for my lord except our bodies and our lands. ¹⁹Why should we die before your eyes, both we and our land? Buy us and our land for food, and we and our land will be slaves to Pharaoh. So give us seed, that we may live and not die, and that the land may not be desolate."

²⁰So Joseph bought all the land of Egypt for Pharaoh, for every Egyptian sold his field, because the famine was severe upon them. Thus the land became Pharaoh's. ²¹As for the people, he removed them to the cities from one end of Egypt's border to the other. ²²Only the land of the priests he did not buy, for the priests had an allotment from Pharaoh, and they lived off the allotment which Pharaoh gave them. Therefore, they did not sell their land. ²³Then Joseph said to the people, "Behold, I have today bought you and your land for Pharaoh; now, *here* is seed for you, and you may sow the land. ²⁴At the harvest you shall give a fifth to Pharaoh, and four-fifths shall be your own for seed of the field and for your food and for those of your households and as food for your little ones." ²⁵So they said, "You have saved our lives! Let us find favor in the sight of my lord, and we will be Pharaoh's slaves." ²⁶Joseph made it a statute concerning the land of Egypt *valid* to this day, that Pharaoh should have the fifth; only the land of the priests did not become Pharaoh's.

²⁷Now Israel lived in the land of Egypt, in Goshen, and they acquired property in it and

47:25–26 The extra measures imposed by Joseph to control the impact of the famine, i.e., moving parts of the population into cities (v. 21) and demanding a one-fifth tax on crop yields (v. 24), did not affect his approval ratings (v. 25). Whatever the gain to Pharaoh, the people obviously understood that Joseph had not enriched himself at their expense.

were fruitful and became very numerous. 28 Jacob lived in the land of Egypt seventeen years; so the length of Jacob's life was one hundred and forty-seven years.

29 When the time for Israel to die drew near, he called his son Joseph and said to him, "Please, if I have found favor in your sight, place now your hand under my thigh and deal with me in kindness and faithfulness. Please do not bury me in Egypt, 30 but when I lie down with my fathers, you shall carry me out of Egypt and bury me in their burial place." And he said, "I will do as you have said." 31 He said, "Swear to me." So he swore to him. Then Israel bowed *in worship* at the head of the bed.

48 Now it came about after these things that Joseph was told, "Behold, your father is sick." So he took his two sons Manasseh and Ephraim with him. 2 When it was told to Jacob, "Behold, your son Joseph has come to you," Israel collected his strength and sat up in the bed. 3 Then Jacob said to Joseph, "God Almighty appeared to me at Luz in the land of Canaan and blessed me, 4 and He said to me, 'Behold, I will make you fruitful and numerous, and I will make you a company of peoples, and will give this land to your descendants after you for an everlasting possession.' 5 Now your two sons, who were born to you in the land of Egypt before I came to you in Egypt, are mine; Ephraim and Manasseh shall be mine, as Reuben and Simeon are. 6 But your offspring that have been born after them shall be yours; they shall be called by the names of their brothers in their inheritance. 7 Now as for me, when I came from Paddan, Rachel died, to my sorrow, in the land of Canaan on the journey, when there was still some distance to go to Ephrath; and I buried her there on the way to Ephrath (that is, Bethlehem)."

8 When Israel saw Joseph's sons, he said, "Who are these?" 9 Joseph said to his father, "They are my sons, whom God has given me here." So he said, "Bring them to me, please, that I may bless them." 10 Now the eyes of Israel were *so* dim from age *that* he could not see. Then Joseph brought them close to him, and he kissed them and embraced them. 11 Israel said to Joseph, "I never expected to see your face, and behold, God has let me see your children as well." 12 Then Joseph took them from his knees, and bowed with his face to the ground. 13 Joseph took them both, Ephraim with his right hand toward Israel's left, and Manasseh with his left hand toward

Israel's right, and brought them close to him. 14 But Israel stretched out his right hand and laid it on the head of Ephraim, who was the younger, and his left hand on Manasseh's head, crossing his hands, although Manasseh was the firstborn. 15 He blessed Joseph, and said,

> "The God before whom my
>   fathers Abraham and Isaac
>   walked,
> The God who has been my
>   shepherd all my life
>   to this day,
> 16 The angel who has redeemed
>   me from all evil,
> Bless the lads;
> And may my name live on
>   in them,
> And the names of my fathers
>   Abraham and Isaac;
> And may they grow into
>   a multitude in the midst
>   of the earth."

17 When Joseph saw that his father laid his right hand on Ephraim's head, it displeased him; and he grasped his father's hand to remove it from Ephraim's head to Manasseh's head. 18 Joseph said to his father, "Not so, my father, for this one is the firstborn. Place your right hand on his head." 19 But his father refused and said, "I know, my son, I know; he also will become a people and he also will be great. However, his younger brother shall be greater than he, and his descendants shall become a multitude of nations." 20 He blessed them that day, saying,

> "By you Israel will pronounce
>   blessing, saying,
> 'May God make you like Ephraim
>   and Manasseh!'"

Thus he put Ephraim before Manasseh. 21 Then Israel said to Joseph, "Behold, I am about to die, but God will be with you, and bring you back to the land of your fathers. 22 I give you one portion more than your brothers, which I took from the hand of the Amorite with my sword and my bow."

Psalm 13:1–6

For the choir director. A Psalm of David.

H ow long, O LORD? Will You forget me forever? How long will You hide Your face from me?

2 How long shall I take
counsel in my soul,
Having sorrow in my heart all
the day?
How long will my enemy
be exalted over me?

3 Consider *and* answer me,
O LORD my God;
Enlighten my eyes, or I will
sleep the *sleep of* death,

4 And my enemy will say, "I
have overcome him,"
And my adversaries will
rejoice when I am
shaken.

5 But I have trusted in Your
lovingkindness;
My heart shall rejoice in
Your salvation.

6 I will sing to the LORD,
Because He has dealt
bountifully with me.

Proverbs 4:18-19

18 But the path of the righteous
is like the light of dawn,
That shines brighter and
brighter until the
full day.

19 The way of the wicked
is like darkness;
They do not know over
what they stumble.

4:18 path of the...light of dawn. The path of
the believer is one of increasing light, just as a
sunrise begins with the faint glow of dawn and
proceeds to the splendor of noonday.

Matthew 15:21-39

21 Jesus went away from there, and withdrew into the district of Tyre and Sidon.
22 And a Canaanite woman from that region
came out and *began* to cry out, saying,
"Have mercy on me, Lord, Son of David;
my daughter is cruelly demon-possessed."
23 But He did not answer her a word. And His
disciples came and implored Him, saying,
"Send her away, because she keeps shouting
at us." 24 But He answered and said, "I was
sent only to the lost sheep of the house of
Israel." 25 But she came and *began* to bow
down before Him, saying, "Lord, help me!"
26 And He answered and said, "It is not good
to take the children's bread and throw it to
the dogs." 27 But she said, "Yes, Lord; but even
the dogs feed on the crumbs which fall from
their masters' table." 28 Then Jesus said to her,
"O woman, your faith is great; it shall be done
for you as you wish." And her daughter was
healed at once.

29 Departing from there, Jesus went along
by the Sea of Galilee, and having gone up on
the mountain, He was sitting there. 30 And
large crowds came to Him, bringing with
them *those who were* lame, crippled, blind,
mute, and many others, and they laid them
down at His feet; and He healed them. 31 So
the crowd marveled as they saw the mute
speaking, the crippled restored, and the lame
walking, and the blind seeing; and they glorified the God of Israel.

32 And Jesus called His disciples to Him,
and said, "I feel compassion for the people,
because they have remained with Me now
three days and have nothing to eat; and I
do not want to send them away hungry, for
they might faint on the way." 33 The disciples
*said to Him, "Where would we get so many
loaves in *this* desolate place to satisfy such
a large crowd?" 34 And Jesus *said to them,
"How many loaves do you have?" And they
said, "Seven, and a few small fish." 35 And
He directed the people to sit down on the
ground; 36 and He took the seven loaves and
the fish; and giving thanks, He broke them
and started giving them to the disciples, and
the disciples *gave them* to the people. 37 And
they all ate and were satisfied, and they
picked up what was left over of the broken
pieces, seven large baskets full. 38 And those
who ate were four thousand men, besides
women and children.

39 And sending away the crowds, Jesus
got into the boat and came to the region of
Magadan.

15:33 Where would we get so many loaves...?
No wonder our Lord called them men of little
faith (8:26; 14:31; 16:8; 17:20), when they asked
a question like that in the light of the recent
feeding of the 5,000 (14:13-21).

DAY 24: How was Joseph a type of Christ?		
Joseph	**Parallels**	**Jesus**
37:2	A shepherd of his father's family	John 10:11, 27–29
37:3	His father loved him dearly	Matthew 3:17
37:4	Hated by his brothers	John 7:4–5
37:13–14	Sent by father to brothers	Hebrews 2:11
37:20	Others plotted to harm them	John 11:53
37:23	Robes taken from them	John 19:23–24
37:26	Taken to Egypt	Matthew 2:14–15
37:28	Sold for the price of a slave	Matthew 26:15
39:7	Tempted	Matthew 4:1
39:16–18	Falsely accused	Matthew 26:59–60
38:20	Bound in chains	Matthew 27:2
40:2–3	Placed with two other prisoners, one who was saved and the other lost	Luke 23:32
41:41	Exalted after suffering	Philippians 2:9–11
41:46	Both 30 years old at the beginning of public recognition	Luke 3:23
42:24; 45:2, 14–15; 46:29	Both wept	John 11:35
45:1–15	Forgave those who wronged them	Luke 23:34
45:7	Saved their nation	Matthew 1:21
50:20	What men did to hurt them God turned to good	1 Corinthians 2:7–8

JANUARY 25

Genesis 49:1–50:26

49 Then Jacob summoned his sons and said, "Assemble yourselves that I may tell you what will befall you in the days to come.

2 "Gather together and hear,
    O sons of Jacob;
    And listen to Israel your father.

3 "Reuben, you are my firstborn;
    My might and the beginning
        of my strength,
    Preeminent in dignity and
        preeminent in power.
4 "Uncontrolled as water, you shall
        not have preeminence,
    Because you went up to
        your father's bed;
    Then you defiled *it*—he went
        up to my couch.

5 "Simeon and Levi are brothers;
    Their swords are implements
        of violence.
6 "Let my soul not enter into
        their council;
    Let not my glory be united
        with their assembly;
    Because in their anger they slew men,
    And in their self-will they lamed oxen.

7 "Cursed be their anger, for it is fierce;
    And their wrath, for it is cruel.
    I will disperse them in Jacob,
    And scatter them in Israel.

8 "Judah, your brothers shall
        praise you;
    Your hand shall be on the
        neck of your enemies;
    Your father's sons shall
        bow down to you.
9 "Judah is a lion's whelp;
    From the prey, my son,
        you have gone up.
    He couches, he lies down
        as a lion,
    And as a lion, who dares
        rouse him up?
10 "The scepter shall not
        depart from Judah,

49:1–28 With Judah and Joseph receiving the most attention (vv. 8–12, 22–26), the father's blessing portrayed the future history of each son, seemingly based upon their characters up to that time. The cryptic nature of the poetry demands rigorous analysis for correlating tribal history with Jacob's last word and testament. See Moses' blessing on the tribes in Deuteronomy 33, ca. 1405 B.C.

Nor the ruler's staff from
between his feet,
Until Shiloh comes,
And to him *shall be* the
obedience of the peoples.
11 "He ties *his* foal to the vine,
And his donkey's colt to
the choice vine;
He washes his garments in wine,
And his robes in the blood
of grapes.
12 "His eyes are dull from wine,
And his teeth white from milk.

13 "Zebulun will dwell at the seashore;
And he *shall be* a haven for ships,
And his flank *shall be* toward Sidon.

14 "Issachar is a strong donkey,
Lying down between the sheepfolds.
15 "When he saw that a resting
place was good
And that the land was pleasant,
He bowed his shoulder
to bear *burdens*,
And became a slave at forced labor.

16 "Dan shall judge his people,
As one of the tribes of Israel.
17 "Dan shall be a serpent in the way,
A horned snake in the path,
That bites the horse's heels,
So that his rider falls backward.
18 "For Your salvation I wait, O LORD.

19 "As for Gad, raiders shall raid him,
But he will raid *at* their heels.

20 "As for Asher, his food shall be rich,
And he will yield royal dainties.

21 "Naphtali is a doe let loose,
He gives beautiful words.

22 "Joseph is a fruitful bough,
A fruitful bough by a spring;
Its branches run over a wall.
23 "The archers bitterly attacked him,
And shot *at him* and harassed him;
24 But his bow remained firm,
And his arms were agile,
From the hands of the
Mighty One of Jacob
(From there is the Shepherd,
the Stone of Israel),
25 From the God of your father
who helps you,
And by the Almighty who blesses you

With blessings of heaven above,
Blessings of the deep
that lies beneath,
Blessings of the breasts
and of the womb.
26 "The blessings of your father
Have surpassed the blessings
of my ancestors
Up to the utmost bound of
the everlasting hills;
May they be on the head of Joseph,
And on the crown of the head
of the one distinguished
among his brothers.

27 "Benjamin is a ravenous wolf;
In the morning he devours the prey,
And in the evening he
divides the spoil."

28 All these are the twelve tribes of Israel, and this is what their father said to them when he blessed them. He blessed them, every one with the blessing appropriate to him. 29 Then he charged them and said to them, "I am about to be gathered to my people; bury me with my fathers in the cave that is in the field of Ephron the Hittite, 30 in the cave that is in the field of Machpelah, which is before Mamre, in the land of Canaan, which Abraham bought along with the field from Ephron the Hittite for a burial site. 31 There they buried Abraham and his wife Sarah, there they buried Isaac and his wife Rebekah, and there I buried Leah— 32 the field and the cave that is in it, purchased from the sons of Heth." 33 When Jacob finished charging his sons, he drew his feet into the bed and breathed his last, and was gathered to his people.

50 Then Joseph fell on his father's face, and wept over him and kissed him. 2 Joseph commanded his servants the physicians to embalm his father. So the physicians embalmed Israel. 3 Now forty days were required for it, for such is the period required for embalming. And the Egyptians wept for him seventy days.

4 When the days of mourning for him were past, Joseph spoke to the household of Pharaoh, saying, "If now I have found favor in your sight, please speak to Pharaoh, saying, 5 'My father made me swear, saying, "Behold, I am about to die; in my grave which I dug for myself in the land of Canaan, there you shall bury me." Now therefore, please let me go up and bury my father; then I will return.'" 6 Pharaoh said, "Go up and bury your father, as he made you swear."

⁷So Joseph went up to bury his father, and with him went up all the servants of Pharaoh, the elders of his household and all the elders of the land of Egypt, ⁸and all the household of Joseph and his brothers and his father's household; they left only their little ones and their flocks and their herds in the land of Goshen. ⁹There also went up with him both chariots and horsemen; and it was a very great company. ¹⁰When they came to the threshing floor of Atad, which is beyond the Jordan, they lamented there with a very great and sorrowful lamentation; and he observed seven days mourning for his father. ¹¹Now when the inhabitants of the land, the Canaanites, saw the mourning at the threshing floor of Atad, they said, "This is a grievous mourning for the Egyptians." Therefore it was named Abel-mizraim, which is beyond the Jordan. ¹²Thus his sons did for him as he had charged them; ¹³for his sons carried him to the land of Canaan and buried him in the cave of the field of Machpelah before Mamre, which Abraham had bought along with the field for a burial site from Ephron the Hittite. ¹⁴After he had buried his father, Joseph returned to Egypt, he and his brothers, and all who had gone up with him to bury his father.

¹⁵When Joseph's brothers saw that their father was dead, they said, "What if Joseph bears a grudge against us and pays us back in full for all the wrong which we did to him!" ¹⁶So they sent *a message* to Joseph, saying, "Your father charged before he died, saying, ¹⁷'Thus you shall say to Joseph, "Please forgive, I beg you, the transgression of your brothers and their sin, for they did you wrong."' And now, please forgive the transgression of the servants of the God of your father." And Joseph wept when they spoke to him. ¹⁸Then his brothers also came and fell down before him and said, "Behold, we are your servants." ¹⁹But Joseph said to them, "Do not be afraid, for am I in God's place? ²⁰As for you, you meant evil against me, *but* God meant it for good in order to bring about this present result, to preserve many people alive. ²¹So therefore, do not be afraid; I will provide for you and your little ones." So he comforted them and spoke kindly to them.

50:20 *but* God meant it for good. Joseph's wise, theological answer has gone down in history as the classic statement of God's sovereignty over the affairs of men.

²²Now Joseph stayed in Egypt, he and his father's household, and Joseph lived one hundred and ten years. ²³Joseph saw the third generation of Ephraim's sons; also the sons of Machir, the son of Manasseh, were born on Joseph's knees. ²⁴Joseph said to his brothers, "I am about to die, but God will surely take care of you and bring you up from this land to the land which He promised on oath to Abraham, to Isaac and to Jacob." ²⁵Then Joseph made the sons of Israel swear, saying, "God will surely take care of you, and you shall carry my bones up from here." ²⁶So Joseph died at the age of one hundred and ten years; and he was embalmed and placed in a coffin in Egypt.

Psalm 14:1–7

For the choir director. *A Psalm* of David.

The fool has said in his heart,
  "There is no God."
They are corrupt, they have
  committed abominable deeds;
There is no one who does good.
2 The LORD has looked down from
    heaven upon the sons of men
  To see if there are any
    who understand,
  Who seek after God.
3 They have all turned aside, together
    they have become corrupt;
  There is no one who does
    good, not even one.

4 Do all the workers of
    wickedness not know,
  Who eat up my people *as*
    they eat bread,
  And do not call upon the LORD?
5 There they are in great dread,
  For God is with the righteous
    generation.
6 You would put to shame the
    counsel of the afflicted,
  But the LORD is his refuge.

7 Oh, that the salvation of Israel
    would come out of Zion!
  When the LORD restores
    His captive people,
  Jacob will rejoice, Israel will be glad.

Proverbs 4:20–24

20 My son, give attention to my words;
  Incline your ear to my sayings.
21 Do not let them depart
    from your sight;
  Keep them in the midst of your heart.

4:21-23 heart. The "heart" commonly refers to the mind as the center of thinking and reason (3:3; 6:21; 7:3), but also includes the emotions (15:15, 30), the will (11:20; 14:14), and thus, the whole inner being (3:5). The heart is the depository of all wisdom and the source of whatever affects speech (v. 24), sight (v. 25), and conduct (vv. 26–27).

22 For they are life to those
     who find them
   And health to all their body.
23 Watch over your heart
     with all diligence,
   For from it *flow* the springs of life.
24 Put away from you a deceitful mouth
   And put devious speech far from you.

Matthew 16:1-28

16 The Pharisees and Sadducees came up, and testing Jesus, they asked Him to show them a sign from heaven. ² But He replied to them, "When it is evening, you say, '*It will be* fair weather, for the sky is red.' ³ And in the morning, '*There will be* a storm today, for the sky is red and threatening.' Do you know how to discern the appearance of the sky, but cannot *discern* the signs of the times? ⁴ An evil and adulterous generation seeks after a sign; and a sign will not be given it, except the sign of Jonah." And He left them and went away.

⁵ And the disciples came to the other side *of the sea,* but they had forgotten to bring *any* bread. ⁶ And Jesus said to them, "Watch out and beware of the leaven of the Pharisees and Sadducees." ⁷ They began to discuss *this* among themselves, saying, "*He said that* because we did not bring *any* bread." ⁸ But Jesus, aware of this, said, "You men of little faith, why do you discuss among yourselves that you have no bread? ⁹ Do you not yet understand or remember the five loaves of the five thousand, and how many baskets *full* you picked up? ¹⁰ Or the seven loaves of the four thousand, and how many large baskets *full* you picked up? ¹¹ How is it that you do not understand that I did not speak to you concerning bread? But beware of the leaven of the Pharisees and Sadducees." ¹² Then they understood that He did not say to beware of the leaven of bread, but of the teaching of the Pharisees and Sadducees.

¹³ Now when Jesus came into the district of Caesarea Philippi, He was asking His disciples, "Who do people say that the Son of Man is?" ¹⁴ And they said, "Some *say* John the Baptist; and others, Elijah; but still others, Jeremiah, or one of the prophets." ¹⁵ He *said to them, "But who do you say that I am?" ¹⁶ Simon Peter answered, "You are the Christ, the Son of the living God." ¹⁷ And Jesus said to him, "Blessed are you, Simon Barjona, because flesh and blood did not reveal *this* to you, but My Father who is in heaven. ¹⁸ I also say to you that you are Peter, and upon this rock I will build My church; and the gates of Hades will not overpower it. ¹⁹ I will give you the keys of the kingdom of heaven; and whatever you bind on earth shall have been bound in heaven, and whatever you loose on earth shall have been loosed in heaven." ²⁰ Then He warned the disciples that they should tell no one that He was the Christ.

²¹ From that time Jesus began to show His disciples that He must go to Jerusalem, and suffer many things from the elders and chief priests and scribes, and be killed, and be raised up on the third day. ²² Peter took Him aside and began to rebuke Him, saying, "God forbid *it,* Lord! This shall never happen to You." ²³ But He turned and said to Peter, "Get behind Me, Satan! You are a stumbling block to Me; for you are not setting your mind on God's interests, but man's."

²⁴ Then Jesus said to His disciples, "If anyone wishes to come after Me, he must deny himself, and take up his cross and follow Me. ²⁵ For whoever wishes to save his life will lose it; but whoever loses his life for My sake will find it. ²⁶ For what will it profit a man if he gains the whole world and forfeits his soul? Or what will a man give in exchange for his soul? ²⁷ For the Son of Man is going to come in the glory of His Father with His angels, and WILL THEN REPAY EVERY MAN ACCORDING TO HIS DEEDS.

²⁸ "Truly I say to you, there are some of those who are standing here who will not taste death until they see the Son of Man coming in His kingdom."

16:23 Get behind Me, Satan! The harshness of this rebuke contrasts sharply with Christ's words of commendation in vv. 17–19. Jesus suggested that Peter was being a mouthpiece for Satan. Jesus' death was part of God's sovereign plan (Ac 2:23; 4:27–28). "The LORD was pleased to crush Him" (Is 53:10). Christ had come with the express purpose of dying as an atonement for sin (Jn 12:27). And those who would thwart His mission were doing Satan's work.

DAY 25: Why was Peter's confession of Christ so significant in Matthew 16:16?

To call Jesus the Son of "the living God" was an Old Testament name for God. Never before had He explicitly taught Peter and the apostles the fullness of His identity. God the Father had opened Peter's eyes to the full significance of those claims (v. 17) and revealed to him who Jesus really was. Peter was not merely expressing an academic opinion about the identity of Christ; this was a confession of Peter's personal faith, made possible by a divinely regenerated heart.

Jesus said that "you are Peter, and upon this rock I will build My church" (v. 18). The word for "Peter," *Petros*, means a small stone (Jn 1:42). Jesus used a play on words here with *petra*, which means a foundation boulder (see 7:24–25). Since the New Testament makes it abundantly clear that Christ is both the foundation (Ac 4:11–12; 1Co 3:11) and the head (Eph 5:23) of the church, it is a mistake to think that here He is giving either of those roles to Peter. There is a sense in which the apostles played a foundational role in the building of the church (Eph 2:20), but the role of primacy is reserved for Christ alone, not assigned to Peter. So Jesus' words here are best interpreted as a simple play on words in that a boulderlike truth came from the mouth of one who was called a small stone. Peter himself explains the imagery in his first epistle: the church is built of "living stones" (1Pe 2:5) who, like Peter, confess that Jesus is the Christ, the Son of the living God. And Christ Himself is the chief, or the "VERY CORNER stone" (1Pe 2:6–7).

JANUARY 26

Exodus 1:1–2:25

1 Now these are the names of the sons of Israel who came to Egypt with Jacob; they came each one with his household: ² Reuben, Simeon, Levi and Judah; ³ Issachar, Zebulun and Benjamin; ⁴ Dan and Naphtali, Gad and Asher. ⁵ All the persons who came from the loins of Jacob were seventy in number, but Joseph was *already* in Egypt. ⁶ Joseph died, and all his brothers and all that generation. ⁷ But the sons of Israel were fruitful and increased greatly, and multiplied, and became exceedingly mighty, so that the land was filled with them.

⁸ Now a new king arose over Egypt, who did not know Joseph. ⁹ He said to his people, "Behold, the people of the sons of Israel are more and mightier than we. ¹⁰ Come, let us deal wisely with them, or else they will multiply and in the event of war, they will also join themselves to those who hate us, and fight against us and depart from the land." ¹¹ So they appointed taskmasters over them to

1:7 The growth of the nation (12:37) was phenomenal! It grew from 70 men to 603,000 males, 20 years of age and older, thus allowing for a total population of about 2 million (Nu 1:46) departing from Egypt. The seed of Abraham was no longer an extended family, but a nation. The promise that his descendants would be fruitful and multiply (Ge 35:11–12) had indeed been fulfilled in Egypt.

afflict them with hard labor. And they built for Pharaoh storage cities, Pithom and Raamses. ¹² But the more they afflicted them, the more they multiplied and the more they spread out, so that they were in dread of the sons of Israel. ¹³ The Egyptians compelled the sons of Israel to labor rigorously; ¹⁴ and they made their lives bitter with hard labor in mortar and bricks and at all *kinds* of labor in the field, all their labors which they rigorously imposed on them.

¹⁵ Then the king of Egypt spoke to the Hebrew midwives, one of whom was named Shiphrah and the other was named Puah; ¹⁶ and he said, "When you are helping the Hebrew women to give birth and see *them* upon the birthstool, if it is a son, then you shall put him to death; but if it is a daughter, then she shall live." ¹⁷ But the midwives feared God, and did not do as the king of Egypt had commanded them, but let the boys live. ¹⁸ So the king of Egypt called for the midwives and said to them, "Why have you done this thing, and let the boys live?" ¹⁹ The midwives said to Pharaoh, "Because the Hebrew women are not as the Egyptian women; for they are vigorous and give birth before the midwife can get to them." ²⁰ So God was good to the midwives, and the people multiplied, and became very mighty. ²¹ Because the midwives feared God, He established households for them. ²² Then Pharaoh commanded all his people, saying, "Every son who is born you are to cast into the Nile, and every daughter you are to keep alive."

2 Now a man from the house of Levi went and married a daughter of Levi. ² The woman conceived and bore a son; and when she saw that he was beautiful, she hid him

for three months. ³But when she could hide him no longer, she got him a wicker basket and covered it over with tar and pitch. Then she put the child into it and set *it* among the reeds by the bank of the Nile. ⁴His sister stood at a distance to find out what would happen to him.

⁵The daughter of Pharaoh came down to bathe at the Nile, with her maidens walking alongside the Nile; and she saw the basket among the reeds and sent her maid, and she brought it *to her.* ⁶When she opened *it,* she saw the child, and behold, *the* boy was crying. And she had pity on him and said, "This is one of the Hebrews' children." ⁷Then his sister said to Pharaoh's daughter, "Shall I go and call a nurse for you from the Hebrew women that she may nurse the child for you?" ⁸Pharaoh's daughter said to her, "Go *ahead.*" So the girl went and called the child's mother. ⁹Then Pharaoh's daughter said to her, "Take this child away and nurse him for me and I will give *you* your wages." So the woman took the child and nursed him. ¹⁰The child grew, and she brought him to Pharaoh's daughter and he became her son. And she named him Moses, and said, "Because I drew him out of the water."

¹¹Now it came about in those days, when Moses had grown up, that he went out to his brethren and looked on their hard labors; and he saw an Egyptian beating a Hebrew, one of his brethren. ¹²So he looked this way and that, and when he saw there was no one *around,* he struck down the Egyptian and hid him in the sand. ¹³He went out the next day, and behold, two Hebrews were fighting with each other; and he said to the offender, "Why are you striking your companion?" ¹⁴But he said, "Who made you a prince or a judge over

us? Are you intending to kill me as you killed the Egyptian?" Then Moses was afraid and said, "Surely the matter has become known." ¹⁵When Pharaoh heard of this matter, he tried to kill Moses. But Moses fled from the presence of Pharaoh and settled in the land of Midian, and he sat down by a well.

¹⁶Now the priest of Midian had seven daughters; and they came to draw water and filled the troughs to water their father's flock. ¹⁷Then the shepherds came and drove them away, but Moses stood up and helped them and watered their flock. ¹⁸When they came to Reuel their father, he said, "Why have you come *back* so soon today?" ¹⁹So they said, "An Egyptian delivered us from the hand of the shepherds, and what is more, he even drew the water for us and watered the flock." ²⁰He said to his daughters, "Where is he then? Why is it that you have left the man behind? Invite him to have something to eat." ²¹Moses was willing to dwell with the man, and he gave his daughter Zipporah to Moses. ²²Then she gave birth to a son, and he named him Gershom, for he said, "I have been a sojourner in a foreign land."

²³Now it came about in *the course of* those many days that the king of Egypt died. And the sons of Israel sighed because of the bondage, and they cried out; and their cry for help because of *their* bondage rose up to God. ²⁴So God heard their groaning; and God remembered His covenant with Abraham, Isaac, and Jacob. ²⁵God saw the sons of Israel, and God took notice *of them.*

Psalm 15:1–5

A Psalm of David.

O LORD, who may abide in Your tent?
　Who may dwell on Your holy hill?
² He who walks with integrity,
　and works righteousness,
　And speaks truth in his heart.
³ He does not slander with his tongue,
　Nor does evil to his neighbor,
　Nor takes up a reproach against his friend;
⁴ In whose eyes a reprobate is despised,
　But who honors those who fear the LORD;
　He swears to his own hurt and does not change;
⁵ He does not put out his money at interest,

2:10 became her son. The position of "son" undoubtedly granted Moses special privileges belonging to nobility, but none of these persuaded Moses to relinquish his native origin. Rather, as the New Testament advises, his spiritual maturity was such that when he came of age, he "refused to be called the son of Pharaoh's daughter" (Heb 11:24). The formal education in the court of that time meant that Moses would have learned reading, writing, arithmetic, and perhaps one or more of the languages of Canaan. He would also have participated in various outdoor sports, e.g., archery and horseback riding, two favorites of the 18th Dynasty court.

15:5 interest. Interest rates ran as high as 50 percent, but God's law put strict regulations on borrowing and lending. **He...will never be shaken.** This is an important promise in the light of its usage in Psalms and Proverbs (Pss 10:6; 13:4; 16:8; 46:5; 62:2, 6; Pr 10:30).

Nor does he take a bribe
    against the innocent.
He who does these things
    will never be shaken.

Proverbs 4:25–27

25 Let your eyes look directly
    ahead
And let your gaze be fixed
    straight in front of you.
26 Watch the path of your feet
And all your ways will be
    established.
27 Do not turn to the right nor
    to the left;
Turn your foot from evil.

Matthew 17:1–27

17 Six days later Jesus *took with Him Peter and James and John his brother, and *led them up on a high mountain by themselves. ² And He was transfigured before them; and His face shone like the sun, and His garments became as white as light. ³ And behold, Moses and Elijah appeared to them, talking with Him. ⁴ Peter said to Jesus, "Lord, it is good for us to be here; if You wish, I will make three tabernacles here, one for You, and one for Moses, and one for Elijah." ⁵ While he was still speaking, a bright cloud overshadowed them, and behold, a voice out of the cloud said, "This is My beloved Son, with whom I am well-pleased; listen to Him!" ⁶ When the disciples heard *this*, they fell face down to the ground and were terrified. ⁷ And Jesus came to *them* and touched them and said, "Get up, and do not be afraid." ⁸ And lifting up their eyes, they saw no one except Jesus Himself alone.

17:3 Moses and Elijah. Representing the Law and the Prophets respectively, both of which had foretold Christ's death, and that is what Luke says the 3 of them were discussing (Lk 9:31).

⁹ As they were coming down from the mountain, Jesus commanded them, saying, "Tell the vision to no one until the Son of Man has risen from the dead." ¹⁰ And His disciples asked Him, "Why then do the scribes say that Elijah must come first?" ¹¹ And He answered and said, "Elijah is coming and will restore all things; ¹² but I say to you that Elijah already came, and they did not recognize him, but did to him whatever they wished. So also the Son of Man is going to suffer at their hands." ¹³ Then the disciples understood that He had spoken to them about John the Baptist.

¹⁴ When they came to the crowd, a man came up to Jesus, falling on his knees before Him and saying, ¹⁵ "Lord, have mercy on my son, for he is a lunatic and is very ill; for he often falls into the fire and often into the water. ¹⁶ I brought him to Your disciples, and they could not cure him." ¹⁷ And Jesus answered and said, "You unbelieving and perverted generation, how long shall I be with you? How long shall I put up with you? Bring him here to Me." ¹⁸ And Jesus rebuked him, and the demon came out of him, and the boy was cured at once.

¹⁹ Then the disciples came to Jesus privately and said, "Why could we not drive it out?" ²⁰ And He *said to them, "Because of the littleness of your faith; for truly I say to you, if you have faith the size of a mustard seed, you will say to this mountain, 'Move from here to there,' and it will move; and nothing will be impossible to you. ²¹ [But this kind does not go out except by prayer and fasting."]

²² And while they were gathering together in Galilee, Jesus said to them, "The Son of Man is going to be delivered into the hands of men; ²³ and they will kill Him, and He will be raised on the third day." And they were deeply grieved.

²⁴ When they came to Capernaum, those who collected the two-drachma *tax* came to Peter and said, "Does your teacher not pay the two-drachma *tax*?" ²⁵ He *said, "Yes." And when he came into the house, Jesus spoke to him first, saying, "What do you think, Simon? From whom do the kings of the earth collect customs or poll-tax, from their sons or from strangers?" ²⁶ When Peter said, "From strangers," Jesus said to him, "Then the sons are exempt. ²⁷ However, so that we do not offend them, go to the sea and throw in a hook, and take the first fish that comes up; and when you open its mouth, you will find a shekel. Take that and give it to them for you and Me."

Jesus' disappointment with His disciples' inability to cast the demon out of the epileptic boy is readily felt in the words, "You unbelieving and perverted generation, how long shall I be with you?" (Mt 17:17).

Later, in privacy the disciples asked Jesus, "Why could we not drive it out?" (v. 19). When Christ sent the disciples out (Mt 10:6–8), He explicitly commissioned them to do these kinds of miracles. Less than a year later, they failed where they had once succeeded. Christ's explanation for their failure was that their faith was deficient (v. 20). The deficiency did not consist in a lack of confidence; they were surprised that they could not cast out this demon. The problem probably lay in a failure to make God—rather than their own gifts—the object of their confidence.

True faith, even "faith the size of a mustard seed" (v. 20), by Christ's definition, always involves surrender to the will of God. What He was teaching here is nothing like positive-thinking psychology. He was saying that both the source and the object of all genuine faith—even the weak, mustard seed variety—is God. "For nothing will be impossible with God" (Lk 1:37). Here, Christ assumes the qualifying thought that is explicitly added by 1 John 5:14: what we ask for must be "according to His will."

JANUARY 27

Exodus 3:1–4:31

3 Now Moses was pasturing the flock of Jethro his father-in-law, the priest of Midian; and he led the flock to the west side of the wilderness and came to Horeb, the mountain of God. ²The angel of the LORD appeared to him in a blazing fire from the midst of a bush; and he looked, and behold, the bush was burning with fire, yet the bush was not consumed. ³So Moses said, "I must turn aside now and see this marvelous sight, why the bush is not burned up." ⁴When the LORD saw that he turned aside to look, God called to him from the midst of the bush and said, "Moses, Moses!" And he said, "Here I am." ⁵Then He said, "Do not come near here; remove your sandals from your feet, for the place on which you are standing is holy ground." ⁶He said also, "I am the God of your father, the God of Abraham, the God of Isaac, and the God of Jacob." Then Moses hid his face, for he was afraid to look at God.

⁷The LORD said, "I have surely seen the affliction of My people who are in Egypt, and have given heed to their cry because of their taskmasters, for I am aware of their sufferings. ⁸So I have come down to deliver them from the power of the Egyptians, and to bring them up from that land to a good and spacious land, to a land flowing with milk and honey, to the place of the Canaanite and the Hittite and the Amorite and the Perizzite and the Hivite and the Jebusite. ⁹Now, behold, the cry of the sons of Israel has come to Me; furthermore, I have seen the oppression with which the Egyptians are oppressing them. ¹⁰Therefore, come now, and I will send you to Pharaoh, so that you may bring My people,

the sons of Israel, out of Egypt." ¹¹But Moses said to God, "Who am I, that I should go to Pharaoh, and that I should bring the sons of Israel out of Egypt?" ¹²And He said, "Certainly I will be with you, and this shall be the sign to you that it is I who have sent you: when you have brought the people out of Egypt, you shall worship God at this mountain."

¹³Then Moses said to God, "Behold, I am going to the sons of Israel, and I will say to them, 'The God of your fathers has sent me to you.' Now they may say to me, 'What is His name?' What shall I say to them?" ¹⁴God said to Moses, "I AM WHO I AM"; and He said, "Thus you shall say to the sons of Israel, 'I AM has sent me to you.'" ¹⁵God, furthermore, said to Moses, "Thus you shall say to the sons of Israel, 'The LORD, the God of your fathers, the God of Abraham, the God of Isaac, and the God of Jacob, has sent me to you.' This is My name forever, and this is My memorial-name to all generations. ¹⁶Go and gather the elders of Israel together and say to them, 'The LORD, the God of your fathers, the God of Abraham, Isaac and Jacob, has appeared to me, saying, "I am indeed concerned about you and what has been done to you in Egypt. ¹⁷So I said, I will bring you up out of the affliction of Egypt to the land of the Canaanite and the Hittite and the Amorite and the Perizzite and the Hivite and the Jebusite, to a land flowing with milk and honey."' ¹⁸They will pay heed to what you say; and you with the elders of Israel will come to the king of Egypt and you will say to him, 'The LORD, the God of the Hebrews, has met with us. So now, please, let us go a three days' journey into the wilderness, that we may sacrifice to the LORD our God.' ¹⁹But I know that the king of Egypt will not permit you to go, except under compulsion. ²⁰So I

will stretch out My hand and strike Egypt with all My miracles which I shall do in the midst of it; and after that he will let you go. ²¹ I will grant this people favor in the sight of the Egyptians; and it shall be that when you go, you will not go empty-handed. ²² But every woman shall ask of her neighbor and the woman who lives in her house, articles of silver and articles of gold, and clothing; and you will put them on your sons and daughters. Thus you will plunder the Egyptians."

4 Then Moses said, "What if they will not believe me or listen to what I say? For they may say, 'The LORD has not appeared to you.'" ² The LORD said to him, "What is that in your hand?" And he said, "A staff." ³ Then He said, "Throw it on the ground." So he threw it on the ground, and it became a serpent; and Moses fled from it. ⁴ But the LORD said to Moses, "Stretch out your hand and grasp *it* by its tail"—so he stretched out his hand and caught it, and it became a staff in his hand— ⁵ "that they may believe that the LORD, the God of their fathers, the God of Abraham, the God of Isaac, and the God of Jacob, has appeared to you."

⁶ The LORD furthermore said to him, "Now put your hand into your bosom." So he put his hand into his bosom, and when he took it out, behold, his hand was leprous like snow. ⁷ Then He said, "Put your hand into your bosom again." So he put his hand into his bosom again, and when he took it out of his bosom, behold, it was restored like *the rest of* his flesh. ⁸ "If they will not believe you or heed the witness of the first sign, they may believe the witness of the last sign. ⁹ But if they will not believe even these two signs or heed what you say, then you shall take some water from the Nile and pour it on the dry ground; and the water which you take from the Nile will become blood on the dry ground."

¹⁰ Then Moses said to the LORD, "Please, Lord, I have never been eloquent, neither recently nor in time past, nor since You have spoken to Your servant; for I am slow of speech and slow of tongue." ¹¹ The LORD said to him, "Who has made man's mouth? Or who makes *him* mute or deaf, or seeing or blind? Is it not I, the LORD? ¹² Now then go, and I, even I, will be with your mouth, and teach you what you are to say." ¹³ But he said, "Please, Lord, now send *the message* by whomever You will." ¹⁴ Then the anger of the LORD burned against Moses, and He said, "Is there not your brother Aaron the Levite? I know that he speaks fluently. And moreover, behold, he is coming out to meet you; when he sees you, he will be glad in his heart. ¹⁵ You are to speak to him and put the words in his mouth; and I, even I, will be with your mouth and his mouth, and I will teach you what you are to do. ¹⁶ Moreover, he shall speak for you to the people; and he will be as a mouth for you and you will be as God to him. ¹⁷ You shall take in your hand this staff, with which you shall perform the signs."

¹⁸ Then Moses departed and returned to Jethro his father-in-law and said to him, "Please, let me go, that I may return to my brethren who are in Egypt, and see if they are still alive." And Jethro said to Moses, "Go in peace." ¹⁹ Now the LORD said to Moses in Midian, "Go back to Egypt, for all the men who were seeking your life are dead." ²⁰ So Moses took his wife and his sons and mounted them on a donkey, and returned to the land of Egypt. Moses also took the staff of God in his hand.

²¹ The LORD said to Moses, "When you go back to Egypt see that you perform before Pharaoh all the wonders which I have put in your power; but I will harden his heart so that he will not let the people go. ²² Then you shall say to Pharaoh, 'Thus says the LORD,

4:21 I will harden his heart. The Lord's personal and direct involvement in the affairs of men so that His purposes might be done is revealed as God informed Moses what would take place. Pharaoh was also warned that his own refusal would bring judgment on him (v. 23). Previously Moses had been told that God was certain of Pharaoh's refusal (3:19). This interplay between God's hardening and Pharaoh's hardening his heart must be kept in balance. Ten times (4:21; 7:3; 9:12; 10:1, 20, 27; 11:10; 14:4, 8, 17) the historical record notes specifically that God hardened the king's heart, and ten times (7:13–14, 22; 8:15, 19, 32; 9:7, 34–35; 13:15) the record indicates the king hardened his own heart. The apostle Paul used this hardening as an example of God's inscrutable will and absolute power to intervene as He chooses, yet obviously never without loss of personal responsibility for actions taken (Ro 9:16–18). The theological conundrum posed by such interplay of God's acting and Pharaoh's acting can only be resolved by accepting the record as it stands and by taking refuge in the omniscience and omnipotence of the God who planned and brought about His deliverance of Israel from Egypt, and in so doing also judged Pharaoh's sinfulness.

"Israel is My son, My firstborn. ²³So I said to you, 'Let My son go that he may serve Me'; but you have refused to let him go. Behold, I will kill your son, your firstborn.'"

²⁴Now it came about at the lodging place on the way that the LORD met him and sought to put him to death. ²⁵Then Zipporah took a flint and cut off her son's foreskin and threw it at Moses' feet, and she said, "You are indeed a bridegroom of blood to me." ²⁶So He let him alone. At that time she said, "You are a bridegroom of blood"—because of the circumcision.

²⁷Now the LORD said to Aaron, "Go to meet Moses in the wilderness." So he went and met him at the mountain of God and kissed him. ²⁸Moses told Aaron all the words of the LORD with which He had sent him, and all the signs that He had commanded him to do. ²⁹Then Moses and Aaron went and assembled all the elders of the sons of Israel; ³⁰and Aaron spoke all the words which the LORD had spoken to Moses. He then performed the signs in the sight of the people. ³¹So the people believed; and when they heard that the LORD was concerned about the sons of Israel and that He had seen their affliction, then they bowed low and worshiped.

Psalm 16:1–6

A Mikhtam of David.

P reserve me, O God, for I
take refuge in You.
² I said to the LORD, "You are my Lord;
I have no good besides You."
³ As for the saints who are in the earth,
They are the majestic ones in
whom is all my delight.
⁴ The sorrows of those who
have bartered for another
god will be multiplied;
I shall not pour out their drink
offerings of blood,
Nor will I take their names
upon my lips.

⁵ The LORD is the portion of my
inheritance and my cup;
You support my lot.
⁶ The lines have fallen to me
in pleasant places;
Indeed, my heritage is
beautiful to me.

Proverbs 5:1–6

5 My son, give attention to my wisdom,
Incline your ear to my understanding;
² That you may observe discretion

And your lips may reserve
knowledge.
³ For the lips of an adulteress
drip honey
And smoother than oil is her speech;
⁴ But in the end she is bitter
as wormwood,
Sharp as a two-edged sword.
⁵ Her feet go down to death,
Her steps take hold of Sheol.
⁶ She does not ponder the path of life;
Her ways are unstable, she
does not know it.

Matthew 18:1–20

18 At that time the disciples came to Jesus and said, "Who then is greatest in the kingdom of heaven?" ²And He called a child to Himself and set him before them, ³and said, "Truly I say to you, unless you are converted and become like children, you will not enter the kingdom of heaven. ⁴Whoever then humbles himself as this child, he is the greatest in the kingdom of heaven. ⁵And whoever receives one such child in My name receives Me; ⁶but whoever causes one of these little ones who believe in Me to stumble, it would be better for him to have a heavy millstone hung around his neck, and to be drowned in the depth of the sea.

18:3 become like children. This is how Jesus characterized conversion. Like the Beatitudes, it pictures faith as the simple, helpless, trusting dependence of those who have no resources of their own. Like children, they have no achievements and no accomplishments to offer or commend themselves with.

⁷"Woe to the world because of its stumbling blocks! For it is inevitable that stumbling blocks come; but woe to that man through whom the stumbling block comes! ⁸"If your hand or your foot causes you to stumble, cut it off and throw it from you; it is better for you to enter life crippled or lame, than to have two hands or two feet and be cast into the eternal fire. ⁹If your eye causes you to stumble, pluck it out and throw it from you. It is better for you to enter life with one eye, than to have two eyes and be cast into the fiery hell. ¹⁰"See that you do not despise one of these little ones, for I say to you that their angels in heaven continually see the face of My Father

who is in heaven. [11] [For the Son of Man has come to save that which was lost.]

[12] "What do you think? If any man has a hundred sheep, and one of them has gone astray, does he not leave the ninety-nine on the mountains and go and search for the one that is straying? [13] If it turns out that he finds it, truly I say to you, he rejoices over it more than over the ninety-nine which have not gone astray. [14] So it is not *the* will of your Father who is in heaven that one of these little ones perish.

[15] "If your brother sins, go and show him his fault in private; if he listens to you, you have won your brother. [16] But if he does not listen *to you*, take one or two more with you, so that BY THE MOUTH OF TWO OR THREE WIT-NESSES EVERY FACT MAY BE CONFIRMED. [17] If he refuses to listen to them, tell it to the church; and if he refuses to listen even to the church, let him be to you as a Gentile and a tax collec-

tor. [18] Truly I say to you, whatever you bind on earth shall have been bound in heaven; and whatever you loose on earth shall have been loosed in heaven.

[19] "Again I say to you, that if two of you agree on earth about anything that they may ask, it shall be done for them by My Father who is in heaven. [20] For where two or three have gathered together in My name, I am there in their midst."

18:20 two or three. Jewish tradition requires at least 10 men (a *minyan*) to constitute a synagogue or even hold public prayer. Here, Christ promised to be present in the midst of an even smaller flock—"two or three witnesses" gathered in His name for the purpose of discipline.

DAY 27: Is it okay to question God?

Upon hearing that God was sending Moses to be the leader/deliverer of Israel (Ex 3:10), his response of "Who am I . . . ?" is an expression of inadequacy for such a serious mission. It sounded reasonable, for after 40 years of absence from Egypt, what could he, a mere shepherd of Midian, do upon return?

But was Moses crossing the line from reasonable inquiry to unreasonable doubt in 3:13? God's patient replies instructing Moses on what He would do and what the results would be, including Israel's being viewed with favor by the Egyptians (3:21), ought to caution the reader from hastily classifying Moses' attitude as altogether wrong from the very beginning of the interaction between him and the Lord. Yes, Israel might ask for God's name in validation of Moses' declaration that he had been sent by the God of their fathers. Asking "What is His name?" meant they sought for the relevancy of the name to their circumstances—the character, quality, or essence of a person. God's answer was: "I AM WHO I AM" (v. 14). This name for God points to His self—existence and eternality; it denotes "I am the One who is/will be." The significance in relation to "God of your fathers" is immediately discernible: He's the same God throughout the ages!

A response of divine anger comes only in 4:14 at the very end of Moses' questions and objections, where he moved beyond inquiry into objection.

JANUARY 28

Exodus 5:1–6:30

5 And afterward Moses and Aaron came and said to Pharaoh, "Thus says the LORD, the God of Israel, 'Let My people go that they may celebrate a feast to Me in the wilderness.'" [2] But Pharaoh said, "Who is the LORD that I should obey His voice to let Israel go? I do not know the LORD, and besides, I will not let Israel go." [3] Then they said, "The God of the Hebrews has met with us. Please, let us go a three days' journey into the wilderness that we may sacrifice to the LORD our God, otherwise He will fall upon us with pestilence or with the sword." [4] But the king of Egypt said

to them, "Moses and Aaron, why do you draw the people away from their work? Get *back* to your labors!" [5] Again Pharaoh said, "Look, the people of the land are now many, and you would have them cease from their labors!" [6] So the same day Pharaoh commanded the taskmasters over the people and their foremen, saying, [7] "You are no longer to give the

5:2 Who is the LORD...? In all likelihood Pharaoh knew of Israel's God, but his interrogative retort insolently and arrogantly rejected Him as having any power to make demands of Egypt's superior ruler.

people straw to make brick as previously; let them go and gather straw for themselves. ⁸ But the quota of bricks which they were making previously, you shall impose on them; you are not to reduce any of it. Because they are lazy, therefore they cry out, 'Let us go and sacrifice to our God.' ⁹ Let the labor be heavier on the men, and let them work at it so that they will pay no attention to false words."

¹⁰ So the taskmasters of the people and their foremen went out and spoke to the people, saying, "Thus says Pharaoh, 'I am not going to give you *any* straw. ¹¹ You go *and* get straw for yourselves wherever you can find *it*, but none of your labor will be reduced.'" ¹² So the people scattered through all the land of Egypt to gather stubble for straw. ¹³ The taskmasters pressed them, saying, "Complete your work quota, *your* daily amount, just as when you had straw." ¹⁴ Moreover, the foremen of the sons of Israel, whom Pharaoh's taskmasters had set over them, were beaten and were asked, "Why have you not completed your required amount either yesterday or today in making brick as previously?"

¹⁵ Then the foremen of the sons of Israel came and cried out to Pharaoh, saying, "Why do you deal this way with your servants? ¹⁶ There is no straw given to your servants, yet they keep saying to us, 'Make bricks!' And behold, your servants are being beaten; but it is the fault of your *own* people." ¹⁷ But he said, "You are lazy, *very* lazy; therefore you say, 'Let us go *and* sacrifice to the LORD.' ¹⁸ So go now *and* work; for you will be given no straw, yet you must deliver the quota of bricks." ¹⁹ The foremen of the sons of Israel saw that they were in trouble because they were told, "You must not reduce *your* daily amount of bricks." ²⁰ When they left Pharaoh's presence, they met Moses and Aaron as they were waiting for them. ²¹ They said to them, "May the LORD look upon you and judge *you,* for you have made us odious in Pharaoh's sight and in the sight of his servants, to put a sword in their hand to kill us."

²² Then Moses returned to the LORD and said, "O Lord, why have You brought harm to this people? Why did You ever send me? ²³ Ever since I came to Pharaoh to speak in Your name, he has done harm to this people, and You have not delivered Your people at all."

6 Then the LORD said to Moses, "Now you shall see what I will do to Pharaoh; for under compulsion he will let them go, and under compulsion he will drive them out of his land."

² God spoke further to Moses and said to

5:22–23 Moses returned to the LORD. Whether Moses and his brother remonstrated with the foremen about their strong and wrong evaluation remains a moot point. Rather, the focus is upon Moses, who remonstrated with the Lord in prayer. Evidently, Moses did not anticipate what effect Pharaoh's refusal and reaction would have upon his own people. Confrontation with Pharaoh so far had provoked both angry resentment of Israel by the Egyptians and of Moses by Israel—this was not the expected scenario!

him, "I am the LORD; ³ and I appeared to Abraham, Isaac, and Jacob, as God Almighty, but *by* My name, LORD, I did not make Myself known to them. ⁴ I also established My covenant with them, to give them the land of Canaan, the land in which they sojourned. ⁵ Furthermore I have heard the groaning of the sons of Israel, because the Egyptians are holding them in bondage, and I have remembered My covenant. ⁶ Say, therefore, to the sons of Israel, 'I am the LORD, and I will bring you out from under the burdens of the Egyptians, and I will deliver you from their bondage. I will also redeem you with an outstretched arm and with great judgments. ⁷ Then I will take you for My people, and I will be your God; and you shall know that I am the LORD your God, who brought you out from under the burdens of the Egyptians. ⁸ I will bring you to the land which I swore to give to Abraham, Isaac, and Jacob, and I will give it to you *for* a possession; I am the LORD.'" ⁹ So Moses spoke thus to the sons of Israel, but they did not listen to Moses on account of *their* despondency and cruel bondage.

¹⁰ Now the LORD spoke to Moses, saying, ¹¹ "Go, tell Pharaoh king of Egypt to let the sons of Israel go out of his land." ¹² But Moses spoke before the LORD, saying, "Behold, the sons of Israel have not listened to me; how then will Pharaoh listen to me, for I am unskilled in speech?" ¹³ Then the LORD spoke to Moses and to Aaron, and gave them a charge to the sons of Israel and to Pharaoh king of Egypt, to bring the sons of Israel out of the land of Egypt.

¹⁴ These are the heads of their fathers' households. The sons of Reuben, Israel's firstborn: Hanoch and Pallu, Hezron and Carmi; these are the families of Reuben. ¹⁵ The sons of Simeon: Jemuel and Jamin and Ohad and Jachin and Zohar and Shaul the son of a Canaanite woman; these are the families of

Simeon. [16] These are the names of the sons of Levi according to their generations: Gershon and Kohath and Merari; and the length of Levi's life was one hundred and thirty-seven years. [17] The sons of Gershon: Libni and Shimei, according to their families. [18] The sons of Kohath: Amram and Izhar and Hebron and Uzziel; and the length of Kohath's life was one hundred and thirty-three years. [19] The sons of Merari: Mahli and Mushi. These are the families of the Levites according to their generations. [20] Amram married his father's sister Jochebed, and she bore him Aaron and Moses; and the length of Amram's life was one hundred and thirty-seven years. [21] The sons of Izhar: Korah and Nepheg and Zichri. [22] The sons of Uzziel: Mishael and Elzaphan and Sithri. [23] Aaron married Elisheba, the daughter of Amminadab, the sister of Nahshon, and she bore him Nadab and Abihu, Eleazar and Ithamar. [24] The sons of Korah: Assir and Elkanah and Abiasaph; these are the families of the Korahites. [25] Aaron's son Eleazar married one of the daughters of Putiel, and she bore him Phinehas. These are the heads of the fathers' *households* of the Levites according to their families. [26] It was *the same* Aaron and Moses to whom the LORD said, "Bring out the sons of Israel from the land of Egypt according to their hosts." [27] They were the ones who spoke to Pharaoh king of Egypt about bringing out the sons of Israel from Egypt; it was *the same* Moses and Aaron.

[28] Now it came about on the day when the LORD spoke to Moses in the land of Egypt, [29] that the LORD spoke to Moses, saying, "I am the LORD; speak to Pharaoh king of Egypt all that I speak to you." [30] But Moses said before the LORD, "Behold, I am unskilled in speech; how then will Pharaoh listen to me?"

Psalm 16:7–11

[7] I will bless the LORD who
has counseled me;
Indeed, my mind instructs
me in the night.
[8] I have set the LORD
continually before me;
Because He is at my right hand,
I will not be shaken.
[9] Therefore my heart is glad
and my glory rejoices;
My flesh also will dwell securely.
[10] For You will not abandon
my soul to Sheol;
Nor will You allow Your Holy
One to undergo decay.
[11] You will make known to
me the path of life;
In Your presence is fullness of joy;
In Your right hand there are
pleasures forever.

Proverbs 5:7–14

[7] Now then, *my* sons, listen to me
And do not depart from the
words of my mouth.
[8] Keep your way far from her
And do not go near the
door of her house,
[9] Or you will give your vigor to others
And your years to the cruel one;
[10] And strangers will be filled
with your strength
And your hard-earned goods *will
go* to the house of an alien;
[11] And you groan at your final end,
When your flesh and your
body are consumed;
[12] And you say, "How I have
hated instruction!
And my heart spurned reproof!
[13] "I have not listened to the
voice of my teachers,
Nor inclined my ear to my instructors!
[14] "I was almost in utter ruin
In the midst of the assembly
and congregation."

Matthew 18:21–35

[21] Then Peter came and said to Him, "Lord, how often shall my brother sin against me and I forgive him? Up to seven times?" [22] Jesus *said to him, "I do not say to you, up to seven times, but up to seventy times seven.

[23] "For this reason the kingdom of heaven may be compared to a king who wished to settle accounts with his slaves. [24] When he had begun to settle *them,* one who owed him ten thousand talents was brought to him. [25] But since he did not have *the means* to repay, his lord commanded him to be sold, along with his wife and children and all that he had, and repayment to be made. [26] So the slave fell *to the ground* and prostrated himself before him, saying, 'Have patience with me and I will repay

18:24 ten thousand talents. This represents an incomprehensible amount of money. The talent was the largest denomination of currency, and "ten thousand" in common parlance signified an infinite number.

18:28 a hundred denarii. About 3 months' wages. This was not a negligible amount by normal standards, but it was a pittance in comparison to what the slave had been forgiven.

you everything.' ²⁷And the lord of that slave felt compassion and released him and forgave him the debt. ²⁸But that slave went out and found one of his fellow slaves who owed him a hundred denarii; and he seized him and *began* to choke *him,* saying, 'Pay back what you owe.' ²⁹So his fellow slave fell *to the ground* and *began* to plead with him, saying, 'Have

patience with me and I will repay you.' ³⁰But he was unwilling and went and threw him in prison until he should pay back what was owed. ³¹So when his fellow slaves saw what had happened, they were deeply grieved and came and reported to their lord all that had happened. ³²Then summoning him, his lord *said to him, 'You wicked slave, I forgave you all that debt because you pleaded with me. ³³Should you not also have had mercy on your fellow slave, in the same way that I had mercy on you?' ³⁴And his lord, moved with anger, handed him over to the torturers until he should repay all that was owed him. ³⁵My heavenly Father will also do the same to you, if each of you does not forgive his brother from your heart."

DAY 28: Are there other messianic prophecies in the Psalms other than Psalm 16:10?

Prophecy	Psalm	Fulfillment
1. God will announce Christ to be His Son	2:7	Matthew 3:17; Acts 13:33; Hebrews 1:5
2. All things will be put under Christ's feet	8:6	1 Corinthians 15:27; Hebrews 2:8.
3. Christ will be resurrected from the grave	16:10	Mark 16:6-7; Acts 13:35
4. God will forsake Christ in His moment of agony	22:1	Matthew 27:46; Mark 15:34
5. Christ will be scorned and ridiculed	22:7-8	Matthew 27:39-43; Luke 23:35
6. Christ's hands and feet will be pierced	22:16	John 20:25, 27; Acts 2:23
7. Others will gamble for Christ's clothes	22:18	Matthew 27:35, 36
8. Not one of Christ's bones will be broken	34:20	John 19:32-33, 36
9. Christ will be hated unjustly	35:19	John 15:25
10. Christ will come to do God's will	40:7-8	Hebrews 10:7
11. Christ will be betrayed by a friend	41:9	John 13:18
12. Christ's throne will be eternal	45:6	Hebrews 1:8
13. Christ will ascend to heaven	68:18	Ephesians 4:8
14. Zeal for God's temple will consume Christ	69:9	John 2:17
15. Christ will be given vinegar and gall	69:21	Matthew 27:34; John 19:28-30
16. Christ's betrayer will be replaced	109:8	Acts 1:20
17. Christ's enemies will bow down to Him	110:1	Acts 2:34-35
18. Christ will be a priest like Melchizedek	110:4	Hebrews 5:6; 6:20; 7:17
19. Christ will be the chief cornerstone	118:22	Matthew 21:42; Acts 4:11
20. Christ will come in the name of the Lord	118:26	Matthew 21:9

JANUARY 29

Exodus 7:1–8:32

7 Then the LORD said to Moses, "See, I make you *as* God to Pharaoh, and your brother Aaron shall be your prophet. ²You shall speak all that I command you, and your brother Aaron shall speak to Pharaoh that he let the sons of Israel go out of his land. ³But I will harden Pharaoh's heart that I may multiply My signs and My wonders in the land of Egypt. ⁴When Pharaoh does not listen to you, then I will lay My hand on Egypt and bring out My hosts, My people the

sons of Israel, from the land of Egypt by great judgments. ⁵The Egyptians shall know that I am the LORD, when I stretch out My hand on Egypt and bring out the sons of Israel from their midst." ⁶So Moses and Aaron did *it;* as the LORD commanded them, thus they did. ⁷Moses was eighty years old and Aaron eighty-three, when they spoke to Pharaoh.

⁸Now the LORD spoke to Moses and Aaron, saying, ⁹"When Pharaoh speaks to you, saying, 'Work a miracle,' then you shall say to Aaron, 'Take your staff and throw *it* down before Pharaoh, *that* it may become a serpent.'" ¹⁰So Moses and Aaron came to Pharaoh, and thus they did just as the LORD

had commanded; and Aaron threw his staff down before Pharaoh and his servants, and it became a serpent. ¹¹Then Pharaoh also called for *the* wise men and *the* sorcerers, and they also, the magicians of Egypt, did the same with their secret arts. ¹²For each one threw down his staff and they turned into serpents. But Aaron's staff swallowed up their staffs. ¹³Yet Pharaoh's heart was hardened, and he did not listen to them, as the LORD had said.

7:11 magicians. Magic and sorcery played a major role in the pantheistic religion of Egypt. Its ancient documents record the activities of the magicians, one of the most prominent being the charming of serpents. These men were also styled "wise men" and "sorcerers," i.e., the learned men of the day and the religious as well (the word for sorcery being derived from a word meaning "to offer prayers"). Two of these men were named Jannes and Jambres (2Ti 3:8). Any supernatural power came from Satan (2Co 11:13-15). **secret arts.** By means of their "witchcraft," the wise men, sorcerers, and magicians demonstrated their abilities to perform a similar feat. Whether by optical illusion, sleight of hand, or learned physical manipulation of a snake, all sufficiently skillful enough to totally fool Pharaoh and his servants, or by evil supernaturalism, the evaluation given in the inspired record is simply "they also…did the same." However, the turning of rods into snakes, and later turning water into blood (7:22) and calling forth frogs (8:7), were not the same as trying to create gnats from inanimate dust (8:18-19). At that point, the magicians had no option but to confess their failure.

¹⁴Then the LORD said to Moses, "Pharaoh's heart is stubborn; he refuses to let the people go. ¹⁵Go to Pharaoh in the morning as he is going out to the water, and station yourself to meet him on the bank of the Nile; and you shall take in your hand the staff that was turned into a serpent. ¹⁶You shall say to him, 'The LORD, the God of the Hebrews, sent me to you, saying, "Let My people go, that they may serve Me in the wilderness. But behold, you have not listened until now." ¹⁷Thus says the LORD, "By this you shall know that I am the LORD: behold, I will strike the water that is in the Nile with the staff that is in my hand, and it will be turned to blood. ¹⁸The fish that are in the Nile will die, and the Nile will become foul, and the Egyptians will find

difficulty in drinking water from the Nile." ' " ¹⁹Then the LORD said to Moses, "Say to Aaron, 'Take your staff and stretch out your hand over the waters of Egypt, over their rivers, over their streams, and over their pools, and over all their reservoirs of water, that they may become blood; and there will be blood throughout all the land of Egypt, both in *vessels of* wood and in *vessels of* stone.' "

²⁰So Moses and Aaron did even as the LORD had commanded. And he lifted up the staff and struck the water that *was* in the Nile, in the sight of Pharaoh and in the sight of his servants, and all the water that *was* in the Nile was turned to blood. ²¹The fish that *were* in the Nile died, and the Nile became foul, so that the Egyptians could not drink water from the Nile. And the blood was through all the land of Egypt. ²²But the magicians of Egypt did the same with their secret arts; and Pharaoh's heart was hardened, and he did not listen to them, as the LORD had said. ²³Then Pharaoh turned and went into his house with no concern even for this. ²⁴So all the Egyptians dug around the Nile for water to drink, for they could not drink of the water of the Nile. ²⁵Seven days passed after the LORD had struck the Nile.

8 Then the LORD said to Moses, "Go to Pharaoh and say to him, 'Thus says the LORD, "Let My people go, that they may serve Me. ²But if you refuse to let *them* go, behold, I will smite your whole territory with frogs. ³The Nile will swarm with frogs, which will come up and go into your house and into your bedroom and on your bed, and into the houses of your servants and on your people, and into your ovens and into your kneading bowls. ⁴So the frogs will come up on you and your people and all your servants." ' " ⁵Then the LORD said to Moses, "Say to Aaron, 'Stretch out your hand with your staff over the rivers, over the streams and over the pools, and make frogs come up on the land of Egypt.' " ⁶So Aaron stretched out his hand over the waters of Egypt, and the frogs came up and covered the land of Egypt. ⁷The magicians did the same with their secret arts, making frogs come up on the land of Egypt.

⁸Then Pharaoh called for Moses and Aaron and said, "Entreat the LORD that He remove the frogs from me and from my people; and I will let the people go, that they may sacrifice to the LORD." ⁹Moses said to Pharaoh, "The honor is yours to tell me: when shall I entreat for you and your servants and your people, that the frogs be destroyed from you and your houses, *that* they may be left only in the Nile?"

¹⁰Then he said, "Tomorrow." So he said, "*May it be* according to your word, that you may know that there is no one like the LORD our God. ¹¹The frogs will depart from you and your houses and your servants and your people; they will be left only in the Nile." ¹²Then Moses and Aaron went out from Pharaoh, and Moses cried to the LORD concerning the frogs which He had inflicted upon Pharaoh. ¹³The LORD did according to the word of Moses, and the frogs died out of the houses, the courts, and the fields. ¹⁴So they piled them in heaps, and the land became foul. ¹⁵But when Pharaoh saw that there was relief, he hardened his heart and did not listen to them, as the LORD had said.

¹⁶Then the LORD said to Moses, "Say to Aaron, 'Stretch out your staff and strike the dust of the earth, that it may become gnats through all the land of Egypt.'" ¹⁷They did so; and Aaron stretched out his hand with his staff, and struck the dust of the earth, and there were gnats on man and beast. All the dust of the earth became gnats through all the land of Egypt. ¹⁸The magicians tried with their secret arts to bring forth gnats, but they could not; so there were gnats on man and beast. ¹⁹Then the magicians said to Pharaoh, "This is the finger of God." But Pharaoh's heart was hardened, and he did not listen to them, as the LORD had said.

²⁰Now the LORD said to Moses, "Rise early in the morning and present yourself before Pharaoh, as he comes out to the water, and say to him, 'Thus says the LORD, "Let My people go, that they may serve Me. ²¹For if you do not let My people go, behold, I will send swarms of flies on you and on your servants and on your people and into your houses; and the houses of the Egyptians will be full of swarms of flies, and also the ground on which they *dwell*. ²²But on that day I will set apart the land of Goshen, where My people are living, so that no swarms of flies will be there, in order that you may know that I, the LORD, am in the midst of the land. ²³I will put a division between My people and your people. Tomorrow this sign will occur."'" ²⁴Then the LORD did so. And there came great swarms of flies into the house of Pharaoh and the houses of his servants and the land was laid waste because of the swarms of flies in all the land of Egypt.

²⁵Pharaoh called for Moses and Aaron and said, "Go, sacrifice to your God within the land." ²⁶But Moses said, "It is not right to do so, for we will sacrifice to the LORD our God what is an abomination to the Egyptians. If we sacrifice what is an abomination to the Egyptians before their eyes, will they not then stone us? ²⁷We must go a three days' journey into the wilderness and sacrifice to the LORD our God as He commands us." ²⁸Pharaoh said, "I will let you go, that you may sacrifice to the LORD your God in the wilderness; only you shall not go very far away. Make supplication for me." ²⁹Then Moses said, "Behold, I am going out from you, and I shall make supplication to the LORD that the swarms of flies may depart from Pharaoh, from his servants, and from his people tomorrow; only do not let Pharaoh deal deceitfully again in not letting the people go to sacrifice to the LORD."

³⁰So Moses went out from Pharaoh and made supplication to the LORD. ³¹The LORD did as Moses asked, and removed the swarms of flies from Pharaoh, from his servants and from his people; not one remained. ³²But Pharaoh hardened his heart this time also, and he did not let the people go.

Psalm 17:1–7

A Prayer of David.

Hear a just cause, O LORD,
 give heed to my cry;
 Give ear to my prayer, which is
  not from deceitful lips.
2 Let my judgment come forth
  from Your presence;
 Let Your eyes look with
  equity.
3 You have tried my heart;
 You have visited *me* by night;
 You have tested me and
  You find nothing;
 I have purposed that my mouth
  will not transgress.
4 As for the deeds of men, by
  the word of Your lips
 I have kept from the paths
  of the violent.
5 My steps have held fast
  to Your paths.
 My feet have not slipped.

6 I have called upon You, for You
  will answer me, O God;
 Incline Your ear to me,
  hear my speech.
7 Wondrously show Your
  lovingkindness,
 O Savior of those who take
  refuge at Your right hand
 From those who rise up
  against them.

Proverbs 5:15–20

15 Drink water from your own
    cistern
And fresh water from your
    own well.
16 Should your springs be
    dispersed abroad,
Streams of water in the streets?
17 Let them be yours alone
And not for strangers with you.
18 Let your fountain be blessed,
And rejoice in the wife of your
    youth.
19 *As* a loving hind and a graceful
    doe,
Let her breasts satisfy
    you at all times;
Be exhilarated always with
    her love.
20 For why should you, my son, be
    exhilarated with an adulteress
And embrace the bosom
    of a foreigner?

5:15–19 Using the imagery of water, the joy of a faithful marriage is contrasted with the disaster of infidelity (vv. 9–14). "Cistern" and "well" refer to the wife from whom the husband is to draw all his satisfying refreshment, sexually and affectionately (v. 19; see 9:17–18; SS 4:9–11).

Matthew 19:1–30

19 When Jesus had finished these words, He departed from Galilee and came into the region of Judea beyond the Jordan; 2 and large crowds followed Him, and He healed them there.

3 *Some* Pharisees came to Jesus, testing Him and asking, "Is it lawful *for a man* to divorce his wife for any reason at all?" 4 And He answered and said, "Have you not read that He who created *them* from the beginning MADE THEM MALE AND FEMALE, 5 and said, 'FOR THIS REASON A MAN SHALL LEAVE HIS FATHER AND MOTHER AND BE JOINED TO HIS WIFE, AND THE TWO SHALL BECOME ONE FLESH'? 6 So they are no longer two, but one flesh. What therefore God has joined together, let no man separate." 7 They *said to Him, "Why then did Moses command to GIVE HER A CERTIFICATE OF DIVORCE AND SEND *her* AWAY?" 8 He *said to them, "Because of your hardness of heart Moses permitted you to divorce your wives; but from the beginning it has not been this way. 9 And I say to you, whoever divorces his

19:7 Why then did Moses command to GIVE HER A CERTIFICATE OF DIVORCE…? The Pharisees misrepresented Deuteronomy 24:1–4. It was not a "command" for divorce, but a limitation on remarriage in the event of a divorce. While recognizing the legitimacy of divorce when a man "has found some indecency" (Deuteronomy 24:1) in his wife (sexual sin, by Jesus' interpretation in v. 9), Moses did not "command" divorce.

wife, except for immorality, and marries another woman commits adultery."

10 The disciples *said to Him, "If the relationship of the man with his wife is like this, it is better not to marry." 11 But He said to them, "Not all men *can* accept this statement, but *only* those to whom it has been given. 12 For there are eunuchs who were born that way from their mother's womb; and there are eunuchs who were made eunuchs by men; and there are *also* eunuchs who made themselves eunuchs for the sake of the kingdom of heaven. He who is able to accept *this,* let him accept *it.*"

13 Then *some* children were brought to Him so that He might lay His hands on them and pray; and the disciples rebuked them. 14 But Jesus said, "Let the children alone, and do not hinder them from coming to Me; for the kingdom of heaven belongs to such as these." 15 After laying His hands on them, He departed from there.

16 And someone came to Him and said, "Teacher, what good thing shall I do that I may obtain eternal life?" 17 And He said to him, "Why are you asking Me about what is good? There is *only* One who is good; but if you wish to enter into life, keep the commandments." 18 Then he *said to Him, "Which ones?" And Jesus said, "YOU SHALL NOT COMMIT MURDER; YOU SHALL NOT COMMIT ADULTERY; YOU SHALL NOT STEAL; YOU SHALL NOT BEAR FALSE WITNESS; 19 HONOR YOUR FATHER AND MOTHER; and YOU SHALL LOVE YOUR NEIGHBOR AS YOURSELF." 20 The young man *said to Him, "All these things I have kept; what am I still lacking?" 21 Jesus said to him, "If you wish to be complete, go *and* sell your possessions and give to *the* poor, and you will have treasure in heaven; and come, follow Me." 22 But when the young man heard this statement, he went away grieving; for he was one who owned much property.

23 And Jesus said to His disciples, "Truly I say to you, it is hard for a rich man to enter

the kingdom of heaven. ²⁴Again I say to you, it is easier for a camel to go through the eye of a needle, than for a rich man to enter the kingdom of God." ²⁵When the disciples heard *this*, they were very astonished and said, "Then who can be saved?" ²⁶And looking at *them* Jesus said to them, "With people this is impossible, but with God all things are possible."

²⁷Then Peter said to Him, "Behold, we have left everything and followed You; what then will there be for us?" ²⁸And Jesus said to them, "Truly I say to you, that you who have followed Me, in the regeneration when the Son of Man will sit on His glorious throne, you also shall sit upon twelve thrones, judging the twelve tribes of Israel. ²⁹And everyone who has left houses or brothers or sisters or father or mother or children or farms for My name's sake, will receive many times as much, and will inherit eternal life. ³⁰But many *who are* first will be last; and *the* last, first.

19:21 go *and* **sell your possessions and give to** *the* **poor.** Again, Jesus was not setting forth terms for salvation, but rather exposing the young man's true heart. His refusal to obey here revealed two things: 1) he was not blameless as far as the law was concerned, because he was guilty of loving himself and his possessions more than his neighbors (v. 19); and 2) he lacked true faith, which involves a willingness to surrender all at Christ's bidding (16:24). Jesus was not teaching salvation by philanthropy; but He was demanding that this young man give Him first place. The young man failed the test (v. 22). **come, follow Me.** This was the answer to the young man's question in v. 16. It was a call to faith. It is likely that the young man never even heard or contemplated it, though, because his own love of his possessions was such a stumbling block that he had already rejected Jesus' claim to lordship over his life. Thus, he walked away in unbelief.

DAY 29: Describe the ten plagues on Egypt.

The Plague	Egyptian Deity	The Effect
1. Blood (7:20)	Hapi	Pharaoh hardened (7:22)
2. Frogs (8:6)	Heqt	Pharaoh begs relief, promises freedom (8:8), but is hardened (8:15)
3. Lice (8:17)	Hathor, Nut	Pharaoh hardened (8:19)
4. Flies (8:24)	Shu, Isis	Pharaoh bargains (8:28), but is hardened (8:32)
5. Livestock diseased (9:6)	Apis	Pharaoh hardened (9:7)
6. Boils (9:10)	Sekhmet	Pharaoh hardened (9:12)
7. Hail (9:23)	Geb	Pharaoh begs relief (9:27), promises freedom (9:28), but is hardened (9:35)
8. Locusts (10:13)	Serapis	Pharaoh bargains (10:11), begs relief (10:17), but is hardened (10:20)
9. Darkness (10:22)	Ra	Pharaoh bargains (10:24), but is hardened (10:27)
10. Death of firstborn (12:29)		Pharaoh and Egyptians beg Israel to leave Egypt (12:31–33)

JANUARY 30

Exodus 9:1–10:29

9 Then the LORD said to Moses, "Go to Pharaoh and speak to him, 'Thus says the LORD, the God of the Hebrews, "Let My people go, that they may serve Me. ²For if you refuse to let *them* go and continue to hold them, ³behold, the hand of the LORD will come *with* a very severe pestilence on your livestock which are in the field, on the horses, on the donkeys, on the camels, on the herds, and on the flocks. ⁴But the LORD will make a distinction between the livestock of Israel and the livestock of Egypt, so that nothing will die of all that belongs to the sons of Israel."'" ⁵The LORD set a definite time, saying, "Tomorrow the LORD will do this thing in the land." ⁶So the LORD did this thing on the next day, and all the livestock of Egypt died; but of the livestock of the sons of Israel, not one died. ⁷Pharaoh sent, and behold, there was not even one of the livestock of Israel dead. But the heart of Pharaoh was hardened, and he did not let the people go.

⁸Then the LORD said to Moses and Aaron, "Take for yourselves handfuls of soot from a kiln, and let Moses throw it toward the sky in the sight of Pharaoh. ⁹It will become fine

dust over all the land of Egypt, and will become boils breaking out with sores on man and beast through all the land of Egypt." [10] So they took soot from a kiln, and stood before Pharaoh; and Moses threw it toward the sky, and it became boils breaking out with sores on man and beast. [11] The magicians could not stand before Moses because of the boils, for the boils were on the magicians as well as on all the Egyptians. [12] And the LORD hardened Pharaoh's heart, and he did not listen to them, just as the LORD had spoken to Moses.

[13] Then the LORD said to Moses, "Rise up early in the morning and stand before Pharaoh and say to him, 'Thus says the LORD, the God of the Hebrews, "Let My people go, that they may serve Me. [14] For this time I will send all My plagues on you and your servants and your people, so that you may know that there is no one like Me in all the earth. [15] For *if by* now I had put forth My hand and struck you and your people with pestilence, you would then have been cut off from the earth. [16] But, indeed, for this reason I have allowed you to remain, in order to show you My power and in order to proclaim My name through all the earth. [17] Still you exalt yourself against My people by not letting them go. [18] Behold, about this time tomorrow, I will send a very heavy hail, such as has not been *seen* in Egypt from the day it was founded until now. [19] Now therefore send, bring your livestock and whatever you have in the field to safety. Every man and beast that is found in the field and is not brought home, when the hail comes down on them, will die."'" [20] The one among the servants of Pharaoh who feared the word of the LORD made his servants and his livestock flee into the houses; [21] but he who paid no regard to the word of the LORD left his servants and his livestock in the field.

[22] Now the LORD said to Moses, "Stretch out your hand toward the sky, that hail may fall on all the land of Egypt, on man and on beast and on every plant of the field, throughout the land of Egypt." [23] Moses stretched out his staff toward the sky, and the LORD sent thunder and hail, and fire ran down to the earth. And the LORD rained hail on the land of Egypt. [24] So there was hail, and fire flashing continually in the midst of the hail, very severe, such as had not been in all the land of Egypt since it became a nation. [25] The hail struck all that was in the field through all the land of Egypt, both man and beast; the hail also struck every plant of the field and shattered every tree of the field. [26] Only in the land of Goshen, where the sons of Israel *were,* there was no hail.

[27] Then Pharaoh sent for Moses and Aaron, and said to them, "I have sinned this time; the LORD is the righteous one, and I and my people are the wicked ones. [28] Make supplication to the LORD, for there has been enough of God's thunder and hail; and I will let you go, and you shall stay no longer." [29] Moses said to him, "As soon as I go out of the city, I will spread out my hands to the LORD; the thunder will cease and there will be hail no longer, that you may know that the earth is the LORD'S. [30] But as for you and your servants, I know that you do not yet fear the LORD God." [31] (Now the flax and the barley were ruined, for the barley was in the ear and the flax was in bud. [32] But the wheat and the spelt were not ruined, for they *ripen* late.) [33] So Moses went out of the city from Pharaoh, and spread out his hands to the LORD; and the thunder and the hail ceased, and rain no longer poured on the earth. [34] But when Pharaoh saw that the rain and the hail and the thunder had ceased, he sinned again and hardened his heart, he and his servants. [35] Pharaoh's heart was hardened, and he did not let the sons of Israel go, just as the LORD had spoken through Moses.

10 Then the LORD said to Moses, "Go to Pharaoh, for I have hardened his heart and the heart of his servants, that I may perform these signs of Mine among them, [2] and that you may tell in the hearing of your son, and of your grandson, how I made a mockery of the Egyptians and how I performed My signs among them, that you may know that I am the LORD."

[3] Moses and Aaron went to Pharaoh and said to him, "Thus says the LORD, the God of the Hebrews, 'How long will you refuse to humble yourself before Me? Let My people go, that they may serve Me. [4] For if you refuse to let My people go, behold, tomorrow I will bring locusts into your territory. [5] They shall cover the surface of the land, so that no one will be able to see the land. They will also eat the rest of what has escaped—what is left to you from the hail—and they will eat every tree which sprouts for you out of the field. [6] Then your houses shall be filled and the houses of all your servants and the houses

9:14 My plagues. God's use of the possessive pronoun specified what should have become abundantly clear to Pharaoh by then, namely, that these were God's own workings.

of all the Egyptians, *something* which neither your fathers nor your grandfathers have seen, from the day that they came upon the earth until this day.'" And he turned and went out from Pharaoh. 7 Pharaoh's servants said to him, "How long will this man be a snare to us? Let the men go, that they may serve the LORD their God. Do you not realize that Egypt is destroyed?" 8 So Moses and Aaron were brought back to Pharaoh, and he said to them, "Go, serve the LORD your God! Who are the ones that are going?" 9 Moses said, "We shall go with our young and our old; with our sons and our daughters, with our flocks and our herds we shall go, for we must hold a feast to the LORD." 10 Then he said to them, "Thus may the LORD be with you, if ever I let you and your little ones go! Take heed, for evil is in your mind. 11 Not so! Go now, the men *among you,* and serve the LORD, for that is what you desire." So they were driven out from Pharaoh's presence.

12 Then the LORD said to Moses, "Stretch out your hand over the land of Egypt for the locusts, that they may come up on the land of Egypt and eat every plant of the land, *even* all that the hail has left." 13 So Moses stretched out his staff over the land of Egypt, and the LORD directed an east wind on the land all that day and all that night; and when it was morning, the east wind brought the locusts. 14 The locusts came up over all the land of Egypt and settled in all the territory of Egypt; *they were* very numerous. There had never been so *many* locusts, nor would there be so *many* again. 15 For they covered the surface of the whole land, so that the land was darkened; and they ate every plant of the land and all the fruit of the trees that the hail had left. Thus nothing green was left on tree or plant of the field through all the land of Egypt. 16 Then Pharaoh hurriedly called for Moses and Aaron, and he said, "I have sinned against the LORD your God and against you. 17 Now therefore, please forgive my sin only this once, and make supplication to the LORD your God, that He would only remove this death from me." 18 He went out from Pharaoh and made supplication to the LORD. 19 So the LORD shifted *the wind* to a very strong west

wind which took up the locusts and drove them into the Red Sea; not one locust was left in all the territory of Egypt. 20 But the LORD hardened Pharaoh's heart, and he did not let the sons of Israel go.

21 Then the LORD said to Moses, "Stretch out your hand toward the sky, that there may be darkness over the land of Egypt, even a darkness which may be felt." 22 So Moses stretched out his hand toward the sky, and there was thick darkness in all the land of Egypt for three days. 23 They did not see one another, nor did anyone rise from his place for three days, but all the sons of Israel had light in their dwellings. 24 Then Pharaoh called to Moses, and said, "Go, serve the LORD; only let your flocks and your herds be detained. Even your little ones may go with you." 25 But Moses said, "You must also let us have sacrifices and burnt offerings, that we may sacrifice *them* to the LORD our God. 26 Therefore, our livestock too shall go with us; not a hoof shall be left behind, for we shall take some of them to serve the LORD our God. And until we arrive there, we ourselves do not know with what we shall serve the LORD." 27 But the LORD hardened Pharaoh's heart, and he was not willing to let them go. 28 Then Pharaoh said to him, "Get away from me! Beware, do not see my face again, for in the day you see my face you shall die!" 29 Moses said, "You are right; I shall never see your face again!"

Psalm 17:8–15

8 Keep me as the apple of the eye;
  Hide me in the shadow
    of Your wings
9 From the wicked who despoil me,
  My deadly enemies who
    surround me.
10 They have closed their
    unfeeling *heart,*
  With their mouth they speak
    proudly.
11 They have now surrounded
    us in our steps;
  They set their eyes to cast *us*
    down to the ground.
12 He is like a lion that is eager
    to tear,
  And as a young lion lurking
    in hiding places.

13 Arise, O LORD, confront
    him, bring him low;
  Deliver my soul from the
    wicked with Your sword,

10:13 an east wind. God used natural means, most probably the spring hot wind, or "sirocco," to bring the locusts into the country from the Arabian Peninsula.

14 From men with Your hand,
O LORD,
From men of the world, whose
portion is in this life,
And whose belly You fill
with Your treasure;
They are satisfied with children,
And leave their abundance
to their babes.
15 As for me, I shall behold Your
face in righteousness;
I will be satisfied with Your
likeness when I awake.

Proverbs 5:21–23

21 For the ways of a man are before
the eyes of the LORD,
And He watches all his paths.
22 His own iniquities will
capture the wicked,
And he will be held with
the cords of his sin.
23 He will die for lack of instruction,
And in the greatness of his
folly he will go astray.

Matthew 20:1–16

20 "For the kingdom of heaven is like a landowner who went out early in the morning to hire laborers for his vineyard. 2 When he had agreed with the laborers for a denarius for the day, he sent them into his vineyard. 3 And he went out about the third hour and saw others standing idle in the market place; 4 and to those he said, 'You also go into the vineyard, and whatever is right I will give you.' And so they went. 5 Again he went out about the sixth and the ninth hour, and did the same thing. 6 And about the eleventh hour he went out and found others standing around; and he *said to them, 'Why have you been standing here idle all day long?' 7 They *said to him, 'Because no one hired us.' He *said to them, 'You go into the vineyard too.'

8 "When evening came, the owner of the vineyard *said to his foreman, 'Call the laborers and pay them their wages, beginning with the last group to the first.' 9 When those hired about the eleventh hour came, each one received a denarius. 10 When those hired first came, they thought that they would receive more; but each of them also received a denarius. 11 When they received it, they grumbled at the landowner, 12 saying, 'These last men have worked only one hour, and you have made them equal to us who have borne the burden and the scorching heat of the day.' 13 But he answered and said to one of them, 'Friend, I am doing you no wrong; did you not agree with me for a denarius? 14 Take what is yours and go, but I wish to give to this last man the same as to you. 15 Is it not lawful for me to do what I wish with what is my own? Or is your eye envious because I am generous?' 16 So the last shall be first, and the first last."

5:21–22 watches…held. The Lord sees all that man does and in mercy withholds immediate judgment, allowing the sinner time to repent or to be caught in his own sin (Nu 32:23; Pss 7:15–16; 57:6; Pr 1:17; Gal 6:7–8). Note the example of Haman (Est 5:9–14; 7:1–10).

20:16 last shall be first…first last. In other words, everyone finishes in a dead heat. No matter how long each of the workers worked, they each received a full day's wage. Similarly, the thief on the cross will enjoy the full blessings of heaven alongside those who have labored their whole lives for Christ. Such is the grace of God.

DAY 30: Why don't the Egyptian historical records acknowledge the events of the Exodus?

The absence of any Egyptian record of the devastation of Egypt by the 10 plagues and the major defeat of Pharaoh's elite army at the Red Sea should not give rise to speculation on whether the account is historically authentic. Egyptian historiography did not permit records of their pharaohs' embarrassments and ignominious defeats to be published. Interestingly, one of the subtle proofs of the truth of Scripture is the way in which it records both the triumphs and the tragedies of God's people. The Bible offers as many examples of failure as it does of faith.

Despite the absence of any extrabiblical, ancient Near Eastern records of the Hebrew bondage, the plagues, the Exodus, and the Conquest, archeological evidence corroborates Israel's dramatic exit from Egypt as occurring during the Eighteenth Dynasty (about 1445 B.C.), a setting of great political strength and economic strength in Egyptian history. Egypt was a world military, economic, and political superpower.

JANUARY 31

Exodus 11:1–12:51

11 Now the LORD said to Moses, "One more plague I will bring on Pharaoh and on Egypt; after that he will let you go from here. When he lets you go, he will surely drive you out from here completely. ²Speak now in the hearing of the people that each man ask from his neighbor and each woman from her neighbor for articles of silver and articles of gold." ³The LORD gave the people favor in the sight of the Egyptians. Furthermore, the man Moses *himself* was greatly esteemed in the land of Egypt, *both* in the sight of Pharaoh's servants and in the sight of the people.

⁴Moses said, "Thus says the LORD, 'About midnight I am going out into the midst of Egypt, ⁵and all the firstborn in the land of Egypt shall die, from the firstborn of the Pharaoh who sits on his throne, even to the firstborn of the slave girl who is behind the millstones; all the firstborn of the cattle as well. ⁶Moreover, there shall be a great cry in all the land of Egypt, such as there has not been *before* and such as shall never be again. ⁷But against any of the sons of Israel a dog will not *even* bark, whether against man or beast, that you may understand how the LORD makes a distinction between Egypt and Israel.' ⁸All these your servants will come down to me and bow themselves before me, saying, 'Go out, you and all the people who follow you,' and after that I will go out." And he went out from Pharaoh in hot anger.

⁹Then the LORD said to Moses, "Pharaoh will not listen to you, so that My wonders will be multiplied in the land of Egypt." ¹⁰Moses and Aaron performed all these wonders before Pharaoh; yet the LORD hardened Pha-

11:5 the firstborn. The firstborn held a particularly important position in the family and society, not only inheriting a double portion of the father's estate, but also representing special qualities of life and strength (Ge 49:3). In Egypt, the firstborn would ascend to the throne and continue the dynasty. Whatever significance might have been attached religiously, politically, dynastically, and socially, it was all stripped away by the extent and intensity of the plague—namely the execution of all the firstborn of all classes of the population including their animals.

raoh's heart, and he did not let the sons of Israel go out of his land.

12 Now the LORD said to Moses and Aaron in the land of Egypt, ²"This month shall be the beginning of months for you; it is to be the first month of the year to you. ³Speak to all the congregation of Israel, saying, 'On the tenth of this month they are each one to take a lamb for themselves, according to their fathers' households, a lamb for each household. ⁴Now if the household is too small for a lamb, then he and his neighbor nearest to his house are to take one according to the number of persons *in them;* according to what each man should eat, you are to divide the lamb. ⁵Your lamb shall be an unblemished male a year old; you may take it from the sheep or from the goats. ⁶You shall keep it until the fourteenth day of the same month, then the whole assembly of the congregation of Israel is to kill it at twilight. ⁷Moreover, they shall take some of the blood and put it on the two doorposts and on the lintel of the houses in which they eat it. ⁸They shall eat the flesh that *same* night, roasted with fire, and they shall eat it with unleavened bread and bitter herbs. ⁹Do not eat any of it raw or boiled at all with water, but rather roasted with fire, *both* its head and its legs along with its entrails. ¹⁰And you shall not leave any of it over until morning, but whatever is left of it until morning, you shall burn with fire. ¹¹Now you shall eat it in this manner: *with* your loins girded, your sandals on your feet, and your staff in your hand; and you shall eat it in haste—it is the LORD'S Passover. ¹²For I will go through the land of Egypt on that night, and will strike down all the firstborn in the land of Egypt, both man and beast; and against all the gods of Egypt I will execute judgments—I am the LORD. ¹³The blood shall be a sign for you on the houses where you live; and when I see the blood I will pass over you, and no plague will befall you to destroy *you* when I strike the land of Egypt.

¹⁴'Now this day will be a memorial to you, and you shall celebrate it *as* a feast to the LORD; throughout your generations you are to celebrate it *as* a permanent ordinance. ¹⁵Seven days you shall eat unleavened bread, but on the first day you shall remove leaven from your houses; for whoever eats anything leavened from the first day until the seventh day, that person shall be cut off from Israel. ¹⁶On the first day you shall have a holy assembly, and *another* holy assembly on the seventh day; no work at all shall be done on them, except what must be eaten by every

person, that alone may be prepared by you. [17] You shall also observe the *Feast of* Unleavened Bread, for on this very day I brought your hosts out of the land of Egypt; therefore you shall observe this day throughout your generations as a permanent ordinance. [18] In the first *month,* on the fourteenth day of the month at evening, you shall eat unleavened bread, until the twenty-first day of the month at evening. [19] Seven days there shall be no leaven found in your houses; for whoever eats what is leavened, that person shall be cut off from the congregation of Israel, whether *he is* an alien or a native of the land. [20] You shall not eat anything leavened; in all your dwellings you shall eat unleavened bread.' "

[21] Then Moses called for all the elders of Israel and said to them, "Go and take for yourselves lambs according to your families, and slay the Passover *lamb.* [22] You shall take a bunch of hyssop and dip it in the blood which is in the basin, and apply some of the blood that is in the basin to the lintel and the two doorposts; and none of you shall go outside the door of his house until morning. [23] For the LORD will pass through to smite the Egyptians; and when He sees the blood on the lintel and on the two doorposts, the LORD will pass over the door and will not allow the destroyer to come in to your houses to smite *you.* [24] And you shall observe this event as an ordinance for you and your children forever. [25] When you enter the land which the LORD will give you, as He has promised, you shall observe this rite. [26] And when your children say to you, 'What does this rite mean to you?' [27] you shall say, 'It is a Passover sacrifice to the LORD who passed over the houses of the sons of Israel in Egypt when He smote the Egyptians, but spared our homes.' " And the people bowed low and worshiped.

[28] Then the sons of Israel went and did *so;* just as the LORD had commanded Moses and Aaron, so they did.

[29] Now it came about at midnight that the LORD struck all the firstborn in the land of Egypt, from the firstborn of Pharaoh who sat on his throne to the firstborn of the captive who was in the dungeon, and all the firstborn of cattle. [30] Pharaoh arose in the night, he and all his servants and all the Egyptians, and there was a great cry in Egypt, for there was no home where there was not someone dead. [31] Then he called for Moses and Aaron at night and said, "Rise up, get out from among my people, both you and the sons of Israel; and go, worship the LORD, as you have said. [32] Take both your flocks and your herds, as you have said, and go, and bless me also." [33] The Egyptians urged the people, to send them out of the land in haste, for they said, "We will all be dead." [34] So the people took their dough before it was leavened, *with* their kneading bowls bound up in the clothes on their shoulders.

[35] Now the sons of Israel had done according to the word of Moses, for they had requested from the Egyptians articles of silver and articles of gold, and clothing; [36] and the LORD had given the people favor in the sight of the Egyptians, so that they let them have their request. Thus they plundered the Egyptians.

[37] Now the sons of Israel journeyed from Rameses to Succoth, about six hundred thousand men on foot, aside from children. [38] A mixed multitude also went up with them, along with flocks and herds, a very large number of livestock. [39] They baked the dough which they had brought out of Egypt into cakes of unleavened bread. For it had not become leavened, since they were driven out of Egypt and could not delay, nor had they prepared any provisions for themselves.

[40] Now the time that the sons of Israel lived in Egypt was four hundred and thirty years. [41] And at the end of four hundred and thirty years, to the very day, all the hosts of the LORD went out from the land of Egypt. [42] It is a night to be observed for the LORD for having brought them out from the land of Egypt; this night is for the LORD, to be observed by all the sons of Israel throughout their generations.

[43] The LORD said to Moses and Aaron, "This is the ordinance of the Passover: no foreigner is to eat of it; [44] but every man's slave purchased with money, after you have circumcised him, then he may eat of it. [45] A sojourner or a hired servant shall not eat of it. [46] It is to be eaten in a single house; you are not to bring forth any of the flesh outside of the house, nor are you to break any bone of it. [47] All the congregation of Israel are to celebrate this. [48] But if a stranger sojourns with you, and celebrates the Passover to the LORD, let all his males be circumcised, and then let him come near to celebrate it; and he shall be like a native of the land. But no uncircumcised person may eat of it. [49] The same law shall apply to the native as to the stranger who sojourns among you."

[50] Then all the sons of Israel did *so;* they did just as the LORD had commanded Moses and Aaron. [51] And on that same day the LORD brought the sons of Israel out of the land of Egypt by their hosts.

Psalm 18:1–12

For the choir director. A *Psalm* of David the servant of the LORD, who spoke to the LORD the words of this song in the day that the LORD delivered him from the hand of all his enemies and from the hand of Saul. And he said,

"I love You, O LORD, my strength."
² The LORD is my rock and my
    fortress and my deliverer,
My God, my rock, in whom
    I take refuge;
My shield and the horn of my
    salvation, my stronghold.
³ I call upon the LORD, who is
    worthy to be praised,
And I am saved from my enemies.

⁴ The cords of death encompassed me,
And the torrents of ungodliness
    terrified me.
⁵ The cords of Sheol surrounded me;
The snares of death confronted me.
⁶ In my distress I called upon the LORD,
And cried to my God for help;
He heard my voice out of His temple,
And my cry for help before
    Him came into His ears.

⁷ Then the earth shook and quaked;
And the foundations of the
    mountains were trembling
And were shaken, because
    He was angry.
⁸ Smoke went up out of His nostrils,
And fire from His mouth devoured;
Coals were kindled by it.
⁹ He bowed the heavens also,
    and came down
With thick darkness under His feet.
¹⁰ He rode upon a cherub and flew;
And He sped upon the
    wings of the wind.
¹¹ He made darkness His hiding
    place, His canopy around Him,
Darkness of waters, thick
    clouds of the skies.
¹² From the brightness before Him
    passed His thick clouds,
Hailstones and coals of fire.

Proverbs 6:1–5

6 My son, if you have become
    surety for your neighbor,
Have given a pledge for a stranger,
² *If* you have been snared with
    the words of your mouth,
Have been caught with the
    words of your mouth,

³ Do this then, my son, and
    deliver yourself;
Since you have come into the
    hand of your neighbor,
Go, humble yourself, and
    importune your neighbor.
⁴ Give no sleep to your eyes,
Nor slumber to your eyelids;
⁵ Deliver yourself like a gazelle
    from *the hunter's* hand
And like a bird from the
    hand of the fowler.

Matthew 20:17–34

6:2–4 snared...come into the hand. See 22:26–27. Anyone who becomes responsible for another person's debt is trapped and controlled because he has yielded control of what God has given him as a stewardship. The situation is so serious that it is imperative to take control of one's own God-given resources and get out of such an intolerable arrangement immediately ("deliver yourself," vv. 3–4) before coming to poverty or slavery. See Genesis 43:9; 44:32–33.

¹⁷As Jesus was about to go up to Jerusalem, He took the twelve *disciples* aside by themselves, and on the way He said to them, ¹⁸ "Behold, we are going up to Jerusalem; and the Son of Man will be delivered to the chief priests and scribes, and they will condemn Him to death, ¹⁹ and will hand Him over to the Gentiles to mock and scourge and crucify *Him*, and on the third day He will be raised up."

²⁰ Then the mother of the sons of Zebedee came to Jesus with her sons, bowing down and making a request of Him. ²¹ And He said to her, "What do you wish?" She *said to Him, "Command that in Your kingdom these two sons of mine may sit one on Your right and one on Your left." ²² But Jesus answered, "You do not know what you are asking. Are you able to drink the cup that I am about to drink?" They *said to Him, "We are able." ²³ He *said to them, "My cup you shall drink; but to sit on My right and on *My* left, this is not Mine to give, but it is for those for whom it has been prepared by My Father."

²⁴ And hearing *this*, the ten became indignant with the two brothers. ²⁵ But Jesus called them to Himself and said, "You know that the rulers of the Gentiles lord it over them, and *their* great men exercise authority over them. ²⁶ It is not this way among you, but whoever

wishes to become great among you shall be your servant, 27 and whoever wishes to be first among you shall be your slave; 28 just as the Son of Man did not come to be served, but to serve, and to give His life a ransom for many."

29 As they were leaving Jericho, a large crowd followed Him. 30 And two blind men sitting by the road, hearing that Jesus was passing by, cried out, "Lord, have mercy on us, Son of David!" 31 The crowd sternly told them to be quiet, but they cried out all the more, "Lord, Son of David, have mercy on us!" 32 And Jesus stopped and called them, and said, "What do you want Me to do for you?" 33 They *said to Him, "Lord, we want our eyes to be opened." 34 Moved with compassion, Jesus touched their eyes; and immediately they regained their sight and followed Him.

20:28 to give His life a ransom for many. The word translated "for" means "in the place of," underscoring the substitutionary nature of Christ's sacrifice. A "ransom" is a price paid to redeem a slave or a prisoner. Redemption does not involve a price paid to Satan. Rather, the ransom is offered to God—to satisfy His justice and wrath against sin. The price paid was Christ's own life—as a blood atonement (Lv 17:11; Heb 9:22). This, then, is the meaning of the cross: Christ subjected Himself to the divine punishment against sin on our behalf (Is 53:4–5). Suffering the brunt of divine wrath in the place of sinners was the "cup" He spoke of having to drink (v. 22).

DAY 31: Describe the chronology of the Exodus.		
Date	**Event**	**Reference**
Fifteenth day, first month, first year	Exodus	Exodus 12
Fifteenth day, second month, first year	Arrival in Wilderness of Sin	Exodus 16:1
Third month, first year	Arrival in Wilderness of Sinai	Exodus 19:1
First day, first month, second year	Erection of Tabernacle	Exodus 40:1, 17
	Dedication of Altar	Numbers 7:1
	Consecration of Levites	Numbers 8:1–26
Fourteenth day, first month, second year	Passover	Numbers 9:5
First day, second month, second year	Census	Numbers 1:1, 18
Fourteenth day, second month, second year	Supplemental Passover	Numbers 9:11
Twentieth day, second month, second year	Departure from Sinai	Numbers 10:11
First month, fortieth year	In Wilderness of Zin	Numbers 20:1, 22–29; 33:38
First day, fifth month, fortieth year	Death of Aaron	Numbers 20:22–29; 33:38
First day, eleventh month, fortieth year	Moses' Address	Deuteronomy 1:3

FEBRUARY 1

Exodus 13:1–14:31

13 Then the LORD spoke to Moses, saying, ² "Sanctify to Me every firstborn, the first offspring of every womb among the sons of Israel, both of man and beast; it belongs to Me."

³ Moses said to the people, "Remember this day in which you went out from Egypt, from the house of slavery; for by a powerful hand the LORD brought you out from this place. And nothing leavened shall be eaten. ⁴ On this day in the month of Abib, you are about to go forth. ⁵ It shall be when the LORD brings you to the land of the Canaanite, the Hittite, the Amorite, the Hivite and the Jebusite, which He swore to your fathers to give you, a land flowing with milk and honey, that you shall observe this rite in this month. ⁶ For seven days you shall eat unleavened bread, and on the seventh day there shall be a feast to the LORD. ⁷ Unleavened bread shall be eaten throughout the seven days; and nothing leavened shall be seen among you, nor shall any leaven be seen among you in all your borders. ⁸ You shall tell your son on that day, saying, 'It is because of what the LORD did for me when I came out of Egypt.' ⁹ And it shall serve as a sign to you on your hand, and as a reminder on your forehead, that the law of the LORD may be in your mouth; for with a powerful hand the LORD brought you out of Egypt. ¹⁰ Therefore, you shall keep this ordinance at its appointed time from year to year.

¹¹ "Now when the LORD brings you to the land of the Canaanite, as He swore to you and to your fathers, and gives it to you, ¹² you shall devote to the LORD the first offspring of every womb, and the first offspring of every beast that you own; the males belong to the LORD. ¹³ But every first offspring of a donkey you shall redeem with a lamb, but if you do not redeem *it*, then you shall break its neck; and every firstborn of man among your sons you shall redeem. ¹⁴ And it shall be when your son asks you in time to come, saying, 'What is this?' then you shall say to him, 'With a powerful hand the LORD brought us out of Egypt, from the house of slavery. ¹⁵ It came about, when Pharaoh was stubborn about letting us go, that the LORD killed every firstborn in the land of Egypt, both the firstborn of man and the firstborn of beast. Therefore, I sacrifice to the LORD the males, the first offspring of every womb, but every firstborn of my sons I redeem.' ¹⁶ So it shall serve as a sign on your hand and as phylacteries on your forehead, for with a powerful hand the LORD brought us out of Egypt."

¹⁷ Now when Pharaoh had let the people go, God did not lead them by the way of the land of the Philistines, even though it was near; for God said, "The people might change their minds when they see war, and return to Egypt." ¹⁸ Hence God led the people around by the way of the wilderness to the Red Sea; and the sons of Israel went up in martial array from the land of Egypt. ¹⁹ Moses took the bones of Joseph with him, for he had made the sons of Israel solemnly swear, saying, "God will surely take care of you, and you shall carry my bones from here with you." ²⁰ Then they set out from Succoth and camped in Etham on the edge of the wilderness. ²¹ The LORD was going before them in a pillar of cloud by day to lead them on the way, and in a pillar of fire by night to give them light, that they might travel by day and by night. ²² He did not take away the pillar of cloud by day, nor the pillar of fire by night, from before the people.

14 Now the LORD spoke to Moses, saying, ² "Tell the sons of Israel to turn back and camp before Pi-hahiroth, between Migdol and the sea; you shall camp in front of Baal-zephon, opposite it, by the sea. ³ For Pharaoh will say of the sons of Israel, 'They are wandering aimlessly in the land; the wilderness has shut them in.' ⁴ Thus I will harden Pharaoh's heart, and he will chase after them; and I will be honored through Pharaoh and all his army, and the Egyptians will know that I am the LORD." And they did so.

⁵ When the king of Egypt was told that the people had fled, Pharaoh and his servants had a change of heart toward the people, and they said, "What is this we have done, that we have let Israel go from serving us?" ⁶ So he made his chariot ready and took his people with him; ⁷ and he took six hundred select chariots, and all the *other* chariots of Egypt with officers over all of them. ⁸ The LORD hardened the heart of Pharaoh, king of Egypt, and he chased after the sons of Israel as the sons of Israel were going out boldly. ⁹ Then the Egyptians chased after them *with* all the horses *and* chariots of Pharaoh, his horsemen and his army, and they overtook them camping by the sea, beside Pi-hahiroth, in front of Baal-zephon.

¹⁰ As Pharaoh drew near, the sons of Israel looked, and behold, the Egyptians were marching after them, and they became very frightened; so the sons of Israel cried out to

the LORD. ¹¹Then they said to Moses, "Is it because there were no graves in Egypt that you have taken us away to die in the wilderness? Why have you dealt with us in this way, bringing us out of Egypt? ¹²Is this not the word that we spoke to you in Egypt, saying, 'Leave us alone that we may serve the Egyptians'? For it would have been better for us to serve the Egyptians than to die in the wilderness." ¹³But Moses said to the people, "Do not fear! Stand by and see the salvation of the LORD which He will accomplish for you today; for the Egyptians whom you have seen today, you will never see them again forever. ¹⁴The LORD will fight for you while you keep silent."

¹⁵Then the LORD said to Moses, "Why are you crying out to Me? Tell the sons of Israel to go forward. ¹⁶As for you, lift up your staff and stretch out your hand over the sea and divide it, and the sons of Israel shall go through the midst of the sea on dry land. ¹⁷As for Me, behold, I will harden the hearts of the Egyptians so that they will go in after them; and I will be honored through Pharaoh and all his army, through his chariots and his horsemen. ¹⁸Then the Egyptians will know that I am the LORD, when I am honored through Pharaoh, through his chariots and his horsemen."

¹⁹The angel of God, who had been going before the camp of Israel, moved and went behind them; and the pillar of cloud moved from before them and stood behind them. ²⁰So it came between the camp of Egypt and the camp of Israel; and there was the cloud along with the darkness, yet it gave light at night. Thus the one did not come near the other all night.

²¹Then Moses stretched out his hand over the sea; and the LORD swept the sea *back* by a strong east wind all night and turned the sea into dry land, so the waters were divided. ²²The sons of Israel went through the midst of the sea on the dry land, and the waters *were like* a wall to them on their right hand and on their left. ²³Then the Egyptians took up the pursuit, and all Pharaoh's horses, his chariots and his horsemen went in after them

14:21 strong east wind. God's use of natural phenomena does not detract in any way from the miraculous nature of what took place that night. The psalmist recorded this event as the Lord dividing the sea by His strength (Ps 74:13). The wind walled up the waters on either side of the pathway then opened (v. 22; 15:8; Ps 78:13).

into the midst of the sea. ²⁴At the morning watch, the LORD looked down on the army of the Egyptians through the pillar of fire and cloud and brought the army of the Egyptians into confusion. ²⁵He caused their chariot wheels to swerve, and He made them drive with difficulty; so the Egyptians said, "Let us flee from Israel, for the LORD is fighting for them against the Egyptians."

²⁶Then the LORD said to Moses, "Stretch out your hand over the sea so that the waters may come back over the Egyptians, over their chariots and their horsemen." ²⁷So Moses stretched out his hand over the sea, and the sea returned to its normal state at daybreak, while the Egyptians were fleeing right into it; then the LORD overthrew the Egyptians in the midst of the sea. ²⁸The waters returned and covered the chariots and the horsemen, even Pharaoh's entire army that had gone into the sea after them; not even one of them remained. ²⁹But the sons of Israel walked on dry land through the midst of the sea, and the waters *were like* a wall to them on their right hand and on their left.

³⁰Thus the LORD saved Israel that day from the hand of the Egyptians, and Israel saw the Egyptians dead on the seashore. ³¹When Israel saw the great power which the LORD had used against the Egyptians, the people feared the LORD, and they believed in the LORD and in His servant Moses.

Psalm 18:13–19

¹³ The LORD also thundered
        in the heavens,
    And the Most High uttered
        His voice,
    Hailstones and coals of fire.
¹⁴ He sent out His arrows,
        and scattered them,
    And lightning flashes in
        abundance, and routed them.
¹⁵ Then the channels of water
        appeared,
    And the foundations of the
        world were laid bare
    At Your rebuke, O LORD,
    At the blast of the breath
        of Your nostrils.

¹⁶ He sent from on high, He took me;
    He drew me out of many
        waters.
¹⁷ He delivered me from my
        strong enemy,
    And from those who hated me, for
        they were too mighty for me.

18 They confronted me in the
day of my calamity,
But the LORD was my stay.
19 He brought me forth also
into a broad place;
He rescued me, because He
delighted in me.

Proverbs 6:6–11

6 Go to the ant, O sluggard,
Observe her ways and be wise,
7 Which, having no chief,
Officer or ruler,
8 Prepares her food in the summer
And gathers her provision
in the harvest.
9 How long will you lie
down, O sluggard?
When will you arise from
your sleep?
10 "A little sleep, a little slumber,
A little folding of the hands
to rest"—
11 Your poverty will come in
like a vagabond
And your need like an armed
man.

6:6 ant...sluggard. See 30:25. The ant is an example of industry, diligence, and planning (vv. 7–8) and serves as a rebuke to a sluggard (a lazy person who lacks self-control). Wisdom sends a lazy man to learn from an ant (10:4, 26; 12:24; 13:4; 15:19; 19:15; 20:4; 26:14–16).

Matthew 21:1–22

21 When they had approached Jerusalem and had come to Bethphage, at the Mount of Olives, then Jesus sent two disciples, 2 saying to them, "Go into the village opposite you, and immediately you will find a donkey tied *there* and a colt with her; untie them and bring them to Me. 3 If anyone says anything to you, you shall say, 'The Lord has need of them,' and immediately he will send them." 4 This took place to fulfill what was spoken through the prophet:

5 "SAY TO THE DAUGHTER OF ZION,
'BEHOLD YOUR KING IS COMING
TO YOU,
GENTLE, AND MOUNTED ON
A DONKEY,
EVEN ON A COLT, THE FOAL OF
A BEAST OF BURDEN.'"

6 The disciples went and did just as Jesus had instructed them, 7 and brought the donkey and the colt, and laid their coats on them; and He sat on the coats. 8 Most of the crowd spread their coats in the road, and others were cutting branches from the trees and spreading them in the road. 9 The crowds going ahead of Him, and those who followed, were shouting,

"Hosanna to the Son of David;
BLESSED IS HE WHO COMES IN
THE NAME OF THE LORD;
Hosanna in the highest!"

10 When He had entered Jerusalem, all the city was stirred, saying, "Who is this?" 11 And the crowds were saying, "This is the prophet Jesus, from Nazareth in Galilee."

12 And Jesus entered the temple and drove out all those who were buying and selling in the temple, and overturned the tables of the money changers and the seats of those who were selling doves. 13 And He *said to them, "It is written, 'MY HOUSE SHALL BE CALLED A HOUSE OF PRAYER'; but you are making it a ROBBERS' DEN."

14 And *the* blind and *the* lame came to Him in the temple, and He healed them. 15 But when the chief priests and the scribes saw the wonderful things that He had done, and the children who were shouting in the temple, "Hosanna to the Son of David," they became indignant 16 and said to Him, "Do You hear what these *children* are saying?" And Jesus *said to them, "Yes; have you never read, 'OUT OF THE MOUTH OF INFANTS AND NURSING BABIES YOU HAVE PREPARED PRAISE FOR YOURSELF'?" 17 And He left them and went out of the city to Bethany, and spent the night there.

18 Now in the morning, when He was returning to the city, He became hungry. 19 Seeing a lone fig tree by the road, He came to it

21:9 Hosanna. This transliterates the Hebrew expression which is translated "Save now" in Psalms 118:25. **BLESSED IS HE.** This is an exact quotation from v. 26 of the same psalm. This, along with the messianic title "Son of David," make it clear that the crowd was acknowledging Christ's messianic claim. The date of this entry was Monday, 10 Nisan, A.D. 30, exactly 483 years after the decree of Artaxerxes mentioned in Daniel 9:24–26.

and found nothing on it except leaves only; and He *said to it, "No longer shall there ever be *any* fruit from you." And at once the fig tree withered.

²⁰ Seeing *this*, the disciples were amazed and asked, "How did the fig tree wither *all* at once?" ²¹ And Jesus answered and said to them, "Truly I say to you, if you have faith and do not doubt, you will not only do what was done to the fig tree, but even if you say to this mountain, 'Be taken up and cast into the sea,' it will happen. ²² And all things you ask in prayer, believing, you will receive."

21:21 if you have faith and do not doubt. This presupposes that the thing requested is actually God's will—for only God-given faith is so doubt-free (Mk 9:24). **it will happen.** A miracle on such a cosmic scale was precisely what the scribes and Pharisees wanted Christ to do, but He always declined. Here, He was speaking figuratively about the immeasurable power of God, unleashed in the lives of those with true faith.

DAY 1: Why did Jesus cleanse the temple in Matthew 21?

This was the second time Jesus cleansed the temple. John 2:14-16 describes a similar incident at the beginning of Christ's public ministry. He regarded both merchants and customers as guilty of desecrating the temple (Mt 21:12). Items being bought and sold included "doves" and other animals for sacrifice. Currency—exchange agents, or "money changers," present in droves, were needed because Roman coins and other forms of currency were deemed unacceptable for temple offerings. Evidently, both merchants and money changers were charging such excessive rates that the temple marketplace took on the atmosphere of a thieves' den (v. 13). Religion had become crass and materialistic.

In verse 13, Jesus uses two Old Testament prophecies, Isaiah 56:7 ("My house will be called a house of prayer for all the peoples") and Jeremiah 7:11 ("Has this house, which is called by My name, become a den of robbers in your sight?") to justify His actions. When the holiness of God and His worship was at stake, Jesus took fast and furious action. The "all" (v. 12) indicates that He drove out not only men but also animals. Yet, although His physical action was forceful, it was not cruel. The moderation of His actions is seen in the fact that no riotous uproar occurred; otherwise the especially large contingent of Roman troops in Jerusalem at that time because of the Passover crowds, would have swiftly reacted. Although the primary reference is to the actions of the Messiah in the millennial kingdom, Jesus' actions in cleansing the temple was an initial fulfillment of Malachi 3:1-3 (and Zec 14:20-21) that speak of the Messiah's purifying the religious worship of His people.

FEBRUARY 2

Exodus 15:1–16:36

15 Then Moses and the sons of Israel sang this song to the LORD, and said,

"I will sing to the LORD, for
   He is highly exalted;
The horse and its rider He
   has hurled into the sea.
² "The LORD is my strength and song,
   And He has become my salvation;
This is my God, and I will praise Him;
   My father's God, and I will extol Him.
³ "The LORD is a warrior;
   The LORD is His name.
⁴ "Pharaoh's chariots and his
      army He has cast into
      the sea;
   And the choicest of his officers
      are drowned in the Red Sea.

⁵ "The deeps cover them;
      They went down into the
      depths like a stone.
⁶ "Your right hand, O LORD, is
      majestic in power,
   Your right hand, O LORD,
      shatters the enemy.
⁷ "And in the greatness of Your
      excellence You overthrow those
      who rise up against You;
   You send forth Your burning anger,
      and it consumes them as chaff.
⁸ "At the blast of Your nostrils the
      waters were piled up,
   The flowing waters stood
      up like a heap;
   The deeps were congealed in
      the heart of the sea.
⁹ "The enemy said, 'I will pursue, I will
      overtake, I will divide the spoil;
   My desire shall be gratified
      against them;

I will draw out my sword, my
hand will destroy them.'
¹⁰ "You blew with Your wind,
the sea covered them;
They sank like lead in the
mighty waters.
¹¹ "Who is like You among
the gods, O LORD?
Who is like You, majestic in holiness,
Awesome in praises,
working wonders?
¹² "You stretched out Your right hand,
The earth swallowed them.
¹³ "In Your lovingkindness You
have led the people whom
You have redeemed;
In Your strength You have guided
them to Your holy habitation.
¹⁴ "The peoples have heard, they tremble;
Anguish has gripped the
inhabitants of Philistia.
¹⁵ "Then the chiefs of Edom
were dismayed;
The leaders of Moab,
trembling grips them;
All the inhabitants of Canaan
have melted away.
¹⁶ "Terror and dread fall upon them;
By the greatness of Your arm they
are motionless as stone;
Until Your people pass over,
O LORD,
Until the people pass over whom
You have purchased.
¹⁷ "You will bring them and plant
them in the mountain of
Your inheritance,
The place, O LORD, which You
have made for Your dwelling,
The sanctuary, O Lord, which
Your hands have established.
¹⁸ "The LORD shall reign
forever and ever."

¹⁹ For the horses of Pharaoh with his chariots and his horsemen went into the sea, and
the LORD brought back the waters of the sea
on them, but the sons of Israel walked on dry
land through the midst of the sea. ²⁰ Miriam the prophetess, Aaron's sister,
took the timbrel in her hand, and all the
women went out after her with timbrels and
with dancing. ²¹ Miriam answered them,

"Sing to the LORD, for He
is highly exalted;
The horse and his rider He
has hurled into the sea."

15:20 the prophetess. Miriam was the first
woman to be given this honor. She herself
claimed the Lord had spoken through her (Nu
12:2). She apparently played an important role
in these rescue events because the prophet
Micah states that God delivered Israel by the
hand of Moses, Aaron, and Miriam (Mic 6:4).
Other women to receive this rare honor were
Deborah (Jdg 4:4); Huldah (2Ki 22:14); Isaiah's
wife (Is 8:3); Anna (Lk 2:36); and Philip's four
daughters (Ac 21:9).

²² Then Moses led Israel from the Red Sea,
and they went out into the wilderness of Shur;
and they went three days in the wilderness and
found no water. ²³ When they came to Marah,
they could not drink the waters of Marah,
for they were bitter; therefore it was named
Marah. ²⁴ So the people grumbled at Moses,
saying, "What shall we drink?" ²⁵ Then he cried
out to the LORD, and the LORD showed him a
tree; and he threw *it* into the waters, and the
waters became sweet.

There He made for them a statute and regulation, and there He tested them. ²⁶ And He
said, "If you will give earnest heed to the voice
of the LORD your God, and do what is right in
His sight, and give ear to His commandments,
and keep all His statutes, I will put none of
the diseases on you which I have put on the
Egyptians; for I, the LORD, am your healer."
²⁷ Then they came to Elim where there
were twelve springs of water and seventy
date palms, and they camped there beside
the waters.

16 Then they set out from Elim, and all
the congregation of the sons of Israel
came to the wilderness of Sin, which is between Elim and Sinai, on the fifteenth day of
the second month after their departure from the
land of Egypt. ² The whole congregation of the
sons of Israel grumbled against Moses and
Aaron in the wilderness. ³ The sons of Israel
said to them, "Would that we had died by the
LORD'S hand in the land of Egypt, when we
sat by the pots of meat, when we ate bread
to the full; for you have brought us out into
this wilderness to kill this whole assembly
with hunger."
⁴ Then the LORD said to Moses, "Behold, I
will rain bread from heaven for you; and the
people shall go out and gather a day's portion
every day, that I may test them, whether or
not they will walk in My instruction. ⁵ On the
sixth day, when they prepare what they bring
in, it will be twice as much as they gather

daily." ⁶So Moses and Aaron said to all the sons of Israel, "At evening you will know that the LORD has brought you out of the land of Egypt; ⁷and in the morning you will see the glory of the LORD, for He hears your grumblings against the LORD; and what are we, that you grumble against us?" ⁸Moses said, "*This will happen* when the LORD gives you meat to eat in the evening, and bread to the full in the morning; for the LORD hears your grumblings which you grumble against Him. And what are we? Your grumblings are not against us but against the LORD."

⁹Then Moses said to Aaron, "Say to all the congregation of the sons of Israel, 'Come near before the LORD, for He has heard your grumblings.' " ¹⁰It came about as Aaron spoke to the whole congregation of the sons of Israel, that they looked toward the wilderness, and behold, the glory of the LORD appeared in the cloud. ¹¹And the LORD spoke to Moses, saying, ¹²"I have heard the grumblings of the sons of Israel; speak to them, saying, 'At twilight you shall eat meat, and in the morning you shall be filled with bread; and you shall know that I am the LORD your God.' "

¹³So it came about at evening that the quails came up and covered the camp, and in the morning there was a layer of dew around the camp. ¹⁴When the layer of dew evaporated, behold, on the surface of the wilderness there was a fine flake-like thing, fine as the frost on the ground. ¹⁵When the sons of Israel saw *it*, they said to one another, "What is it?" For they did not know what it was. And Moses said to them, "It is the bread which the LORD has given you to eat. ¹⁶This is what the LORD has commanded, 'Gather of it every man as much as he should eat; you shall take an omer apiece according to the number of persons each of you has in his tent.' " ¹⁷The sons of Israel did so, and *some* gathered much and *some* little. ¹⁸When they measured it with an omer, he who had gathered much had no excess, and he who had gathered little had no lack; every man gathered as much as he should eat. ¹⁹Moses said to them, "Let no man leave any of it until morning." ²⁰But they did not listen to Moses, and some left part of it until morning, and it bred worms and became foul; and Moses was angry with them. ²¹They gathered it morning by morning, every man as much as he should eat; but when the sun grew hot, it would melt.

²²Now on the sixth day they gathered twice as much bread, two omers for each one. When all the leaders of the congregation came and told Moses, ²³then he said to them, "This is what the LORD meant: Tomorrow is a sabbath observance, a holy sabbath to the LORD. Bake what you will bake and boil what you will boil, and all that is left over put aside to be kept until morning." ²⁴So they put it aside until morning, as Moses had ordered, and it did not become foul nor was there any worm in it. ²⁵Moses said, "Eat it today, for today is a sabbath to the LORD; today you will not find it in the field. ²⁶Six days you shall gather it, but on the seventh day, *the* sabbath, there will be none."

²⁷It came about on the seventh day that some of the people went out to gather, but they found none. ²⁸Then the LORD said to Moses, "How long do you refuse to keep My commandments and My instructions? ²⁹See, the LORD has given you the sabbath; therefore He gives you bread for two days on the sixth day. Remain every man in his place; let no man go out of his place on the seventh day." ³⁰So the people rested on the seventh day.

³¹The house of Israel named it manna, and it was like coriander seed, white, and its taste was like wafers with honey. ³²Then Moses said, "This is what the LORD has commanded, 'Let an omerful of it be kept throughout your generations, that they may see the bread that I fed you in the wilderness, when I brought you out of the land of Egypt.' " ³³Moses said to Aaron, "Take a jar and put an omerful of manna in it, and place it before the LORD to be kept throughout your generations." ³⁴As the LORD commanded Moses, so Aaron placed it before the Testimony, to be kept. ³⁵The sons of Israel ate the manna forty years, until they

16:31 manna. The arrival of the quails in much quantity (v. 13) was totally overshadowed by the arrival of manna the next morning. Despite the different descriptions given for its form and taste (vv. 14, 31), the name chosen for it derived from the question they asked. "Manna" was an older form of their question, "What is it?" The psalmist referred to manna as the "food from heaven" and "bread of angels" which rained down after God had opened the windows of heaven (Ps 78:23–25). Natural explanations for the manna, such as lichen growing on rocks or insect-excreted granules on tamarisk thickets, are totally inadequate to explain its presence in sufficient quantity on the ground under the dew every day except the Sabbath for the next 40 years (v. 35) to satisfy every family's hunger. It was supernaturally produced and supernaturally sustained to last for the Sabbath!

came to an inhabited land; they ate the manna until they came to the border of the land of Canaan. ³⁶ (Now an omer is a tenth of an ephah.)

Psalm 18:20-27

²⁰ The LORD has rewarded me
according to my righteousness;
According to the cleanness of my
hands He has recompensed me.
²¹ For I have kept the ways of the LORD,
And have not wickedly
departed from my God.
²² For all His ordinances
were before me,
And I did not put away His
statutes from me.
²³ I was also blameless with Him,
And I kept myself from my iniquity.
²⁴ Therefore the LORD has recompensed
me according to my righteousness,
According to the cleanness of
my hands in His eyes.

²⁵ With the kind You show Yourself kind;
With the blameless You show
Yourself blameless;
²⁶ With the pure You show Yourself pure,
And with the crooked You
show Yourself astute.
²⁷ For You save an afflicted people,
But haughty eyes You abase.

Proverbs 6:12-15

¹² A worthless person, a wicked man,
Is the one who walks with
a perverse mouth,
¹³ Who winks with his eyes, who
signals with his feet,
Who points with his fingers;
¹⁴ Who *with* perversity in his heart
continually devises evil,
Who spreads strife.
¹⁵ Therefore his calamity will
come suddenly;
Instantly he will be broken and
there will be no healing.

Matthew 21:23-46

²³ When He entered the temple, the chief priests and the elders of the people came to Him while He was teaching, and said, "By what authority are You doing these things, and who gave You this authority?" ²⁴ Jesus said to them, "I will also ask you one thing, which if you tell Me, I will also tell you by what authority I do these things. ²⁵ The baptism of John was from what *source,* from heaven or from men?" And they *began* rea-

soning among themselves, saying, "If we say, 'From heaven,' He will say to us, 'Then why did you not believe him?' ²⁶ But if we say, 'From men,' we fear the people; for they all regard John as a prophet." ²⁷ And answering Jesus, they said, "We do not know." He also said to them, "Neither will I tell you by what authority I do these things.

²⁸ "But what do you think? A man had two sons, and he came to the first and said, 'Son, go work today in the vineyard.' ²⁹ And he answered, 'I will not'; but afterward he regretted it and went. ³⁰ The man came to the second and said the same thing; and he answered, 'I *will,* sir'; but he did not go. ³¹ Which of the two did the will of his father?" They *said, "The first." Jesus *said to them, "Truly I say to you that the tax collectors and prostitutes will get into the kingdom of God before you. ³² For John came to you in the way of righteousness and you did not believe him; but the tax collectors and prostitutes did believe him; and you, seeing *this,* did not even feel remorse afterward so as to believe him.

³³ "Listen to another parable. There was a landowner who PLANTED A VINEYARD AND PUT A WALL AROUND IT AND DUG A WINE PRESS IN IT, AND BUILT A TOWER, and rented it out to vine-growers and went on a journey. ³⁴ When the harvest time approached, he sent his slaves to the vine-growers to receive his produce. ³⁵ The vine-growers took his slaves and beat one, and killed another, and stoned a third. ³⁶ Again he sent another group of slaves larger than the first; and they did the same thing to them. ³⁷ But afterward he sent his son to them, saying, 'They will respect my son.' ³⁸ But when the vine-growers saw the son, they said

21:25 The baptism of John was from what source...? Jesus caught the Jewish leaders in their own trap. They had no doubt hoped that He would answer by asserting that His authority came directly from God (as He had many times before—see Jn 5:19–23; 10:18). They then accused Him of blasphemy and used the charge as an excuse to kill Him—as they had also attempted to do before (Jn 5:18; 10:31–33). Here, however, He asked a question that placed them in an impossible dilemma, because John was widely revered by the people. They could not affirm John's ministry without condemning themselves. And if they denied John's legitimacy, they feared the response of the people (v. 26). In effect, Jesus exposed their own lack of any authority to examine Him.

among themselves, 'This is the heir; come, let us kill him and seize his inheritance.' ³⁹They took him, and threw him out of the vineyard and killed him. ⁴⁰Therefore when the owner of the vineyard comes, what will he do to those vine-growers?" ⁴¹They *said to Him, "He will bring those wretches to a wretched end, and will rent out the vineyard to other vine-growers who will pay him the proceeds at the *proper* seasons."

⁴²Jesus *said to them, "Did you never read in the Scriptures,

> 'THE STONE WHICH THE
>   BUILDERS REJECTED,
> THIS BECAME THE CHIEF CORNER *stone*;
> THIS CAME ABOUT FROM THE LORD,
> AND IT IS MARVELOUS IN OUR EYES'?

⁴³Therefore I say to you, the kingdom of God will be taken away from you and given to a people, producing the fruit of it. ⁴⁴And he who

21:42 THE STONE…REJECTED. This refers to His crucifixion; and the restoration of "the chief corner stone" anticipates His resurrection. **THE CHIEF CORNER *stone*.** To the superficial eye, this quotation from Psalms 118:22–23 is irrelevant to the parable that precedes it. But it is taken from a messianic psalm. Jesus cited it to suggest that the Son who was killed and thrown out of the vineyard was also "the chief corner stone" in God's redemptive plan.

falls on this stone will be broken to pieces; but on whomever it falls, it will scatter him like dust."

⁴⁵When the chief priests and the Pharisees heard His parables, they understood that He was speaking about them. ⁴⁶When they sought to seize Him, they feared the people, because they considered Him to be a prophet.

DAY 2: How are we to think about the astonishing miracles reported in Exodus?

The scientific materialism of many twenty-first-century people makes it difficult for them to consider any so-called miracles. If the laws of nature are considered supreme, the existence of a personal Supreme Being above the laws of nature and able to override them becomes inconceivable. Examples of miracles do little to convince someone who is already convinced that miracles are impossible.

Miracles can demonstrate God's existence; they don't prove it. Human beings display an amazing ability to come up with alternative explanations for God's activity in history. The situation is not that twenty-first-century people can't believe in miracles; rather, it is that twenty-first-century people often won't believe in miracles.

For Christians, the matter is settled by faith. In becoming Christians, we had to believe in the central miracle: God came in the flesh, Jesus Christ, who lived, died, and rose from the dead to reign eternally as Lord and Savior. In the light of that miracle, the miracles of Exodus become less a matter for speculation and more a matter of wonder and worship. They are examples of the lengths to which God went to communicate to people. Even twenty-first-century Christians are humbled and awestruck by God's amazing power!

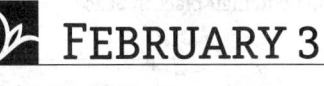

FEBRUARY 3

Exodus 17:1–18:27

17 Then all the congregation of the sons of Israel journeyed by stages from the wilderness of Sin, according to the command of the LORD, and camped at Rephidim, and there was no water for the people to drink. ²Therefore the people quarreled with Moses and said, "Give us water that we may drink." And Moses said to them, "Why do you quarrel with me? Why do you test the LORD?" ³But the people thirsted there for water; and they grumbled against Moses and said, "Why, now, have you brought us up from Egypt, to kill us and our children and our livestock with

thirst?" ⁴So Moses cried out to the LORD, saying, "What shall I do to this people? A little more and they will stone me." ⁵Then the LORD said to Moses, "Pass before the people and take with you some of the elders of Israel; and take in your hand your staff with which you struck the Nile, and go. ⁶Behold, I will stand before you there on the rock at Horeb; and you shall strike the rock, and water will come out of it, that the people may drink." And Moses did so in the sight of the elders of Israel. ⁷He named the place Massah and Meribah because of the quarrel of the sons of Israel, and because they tested the LORD, saying, "Is the LORD among us, or not?"

⁸Then Amalek came and fought against Israel at Rephidim. ⁹So Moses said to Joshua,

"Choose men for us and go out, fight against Amalek. Tomorrow I will station myself on the top of the hill with the staff of God in my hand." [10] Joshua did as Moses told him, and fought against Amalek; and Moses, Aaron, and Hur went up to the top of the hill. [11] So it came about when Moses held his hand up, that Israel prevailed, and when he let his hand down, Amalek prevailed. [12] But Moses' hands were heavy. Then they took a stone and put it under him, and he sat on it; and Aaron and Hur supported his hands, one on one side and one on the other. Thus his hands were steady until the sun set. [13] So Joshua overwhelmed Amalek and his people with the edge of the sword.

[14] Then the LORD said to Moses, "Write this in a book as a memorial and recite it to Joshua, that I will utterly blot out the memory of Amalek from under heaven." [15] Moses built an altar and named it The LORD is My Banner; [16] and he said, "The LORD has sworn; the LORD will have war against Amalek from generation to generation."

18 Now Jethro, the priest of Midian, Moses' father-in-law, heard of all that God had done for Moses and for Israel His people, how the LORD had brought Israel out of Egypt. [2] Jethro, Moses' father-in-law, took Moses' wife Zipporah, after he had sent her away, [3] and her two sons, of whom one was named Gershom, for Moses said, "I have been a sojourner in a foreign land." [4] The other was named Eliezer, for he said, "The God of my father was my help, and delivered me from the sword of Pharaoh."

[5] Then Jethro, Moses' father-in-law, came with his sons and his wife to Moses in the wilderness where he was camped, at the mount of God. [6] He sent word to Moses, "I, your father-in-law Jethro, am coming to you with your wife and her two sons with her." [7] Then Moses went out to meet his father-in-law, and he bowed down and kissed him; and they asked each other of their welfare and went into the tent. [8] Moses told his father-in-law all that the LORD had done to Pharaoh and to the Egyptians for Israel's sake, all the hardship that had befallen them on the journey, and how the LORD had delivered them. [9] Jethro rejoiced over all the goodness which the LORD had done to Israel, in delivering them from the hand of the Egyptians. [10] So Jethro said, "Blessed be the LORD who delivered you from the hand of the Egyptians and from the hand of Pharaoh, and who delivered the people from under the hand of the Egyptians. [11] Now I know that the LORD is greater than all the gods; indeed, it was proven when they dealt proudly against the people." [12] Then

Jethro, Moses' father-in-law, took a burnt offering and sacrifices for God, and Aaron came with all the elders of Israel to eat a meal with Moses' father-in-law before God.

[13] It came about the next day that Moses sat to judge the people, and the people stood about Moses from the morning until the evening. [14] Now when Moses' father-in-law saw all that he was doing for the people, he said, "What is this thing that you are doing for the people? Why do you alone sit as judge and all the people stand about you from morning until evening?" [15] Moses said to his father-in-law, "Because the people come to me to inquire of God. [16] When they have a dispute, it comes to me, and I judge between a man and his neighbor and make known the statutes of God and His laws." [17] Moses' father-in-law said to him, "The thing that you are doing is not good. [18] You will surely wear out, both yourself and these people who are with you, for the task is too heavy for you; you cannot do it alone. [19] Now listen to me: I will give you counsel, and God be with you. You be the people's representative before God, and you bring the disputes to God, [20] then teach them the statutes and the laws, and make known to them the way in which they are to walk and the work they are to do. [21] Furthermore, you shall select out of all the people able men who fear God, men of truth, those who hate dishonest gain; and you shall place these over them as leaders of thousands, of hundreds, of fifties and of tens. [22] Let them judge the people at all times; and let it be that every major dispute they will bring to you, but every minor dispute they themselves will judge. So it will be easier for you, and they will bear the burden with you. [23] If you do this thing and God so commands you, then you will be able to endure, and all these people also will go to their place in peace."

18:13–27 Jethro's practical wisdom was of immense benefit to Moses and Israel, and has been lauded as an example of delegation and management organization by efficiency experts for centuries—and still is. Woven into Jethro's advice were statements about God and the virtues of godly men that cause one to respect this man as having his newfound faith well integrated into his thinking. Indeed, he fully recognized that Moses needed divine permission to enact his advice (v. 23). Moses apparently did not immediately implement Jethro's solution, but waited until the law had been given (Dt 1:9–15).

²⁴So Moses listened to his father-in-law and did all that he had said. ²⁵Moses chose able men out of all Israel and made them heads over the people, leaders of thousands, of hundreds, of fifties and of tens. ²⁶They judged the people at all times; the difficult dispute they would bring to Moses, but every minor dispute they themselves would judge. ²⁷Then Moses bade his father-in-law farewell, and he went his way into his own land.

Psalm 18:28–36

²⁸ For You light my lamp;
The LORD my God illumines
my darkness.
²⁹ For by You I can run upon a troop;
And by my God I can leap over a wall.

³⁰ As for God, His way is blameless;
The word of the LORD is tried;
He is a shield to all who
take refuge in Him.
³¹ For who is God, but the LORD?
And who is a rock, except our God,
³² The God who girds me with strength
And makes my way blameless?
³³ He makes my feet like hinds' *feet,*
And sets me upon my high places.
³⁴ He trains my hands for battle,
So that my arms can bend
a bow of bronze.
³⁵ You have also given me the
shield of Your salvation,
And Your right hand upholds me;
And Your gentleness makes me great.
³⁶ You enlarge my steps under me,
And my feet have not slipped.

Proverbs 6:16–19

¹⁶ There are six things which
the LORD hates,
Yes, seven which are an
abomination to Him:
¹⁷ Haughty eyes, a lying tongue,
And hands that shed innocent blood,
¹⁸ A heart that devises wicked plans,
Feet that run rapidly to evil,
¹⁹ A false witness *who* utters lies,
And one who spreads strife
among brothers.

Matthew 22:1–22

22 Jesus spoke to them again in parables, saying, ²"The kingdom of heaven may be compared to a king who gave a wedding feast for his son. ³And he sent out his slaves to call those who had been invited to the wedding feast, and they were unwilling to come. ⁴Again he sent out other slaves saying, 'Tell those who have been invited, "Behold, I have prepared my dinner; my oxen and my fattened livestock are *all* butchered and everything is ready; come to the wedding feast."' ⁵But they paid no attention and went their way, one to his own farm, another to his business, ⁶and the rest seized his slaves and mistreated them and killed them. ⁷But the king was enraged, and he sent his armies and destroyed those murderers and set their city on fire. ⁸Then he *said to his slaves, 'The wedding is ready, but those who were invited were not worthy. ⁹Go therefore to the main highways, and as many as you find *there,* invite to the wedding feast.' ¹⁰Those slaves went out into the streets and gathered together all they found, both evil and good; and the wedding hall was filled with dinner guests.

¹¹"But when the king came in to look over the dinner guests, he saw a man there who was not dressed in wedding clothes, ¹²and he *said to him, 'Friend, how did you come in here without wedding clothes?' And the man was speechless. ¹³Then the king said to the servants, 'Bind him hand and foot, and throw him into the outer darkness; in that place there will be weeping and gnashing of teeth.' ¹⁴For many are called, but few *are* chosen."

¹⁵Then the Pharisees went and plotted together how they might trap Him in what He said. ¹⁶And they *sent their disciples to Him, along with the Herodians, saying, "Teacher, we know that You are truthful and teach the

---

22:13 outer darkness. This would describe the darkness farthest from the light, i.e., outer darkness. **weeping and gnashing of teeth.** This speaks of inconsolable grief and unremitting torment. Jesus commonly used the phrases in this verse to describe hell (13:42, 50; 24:51).

22:16 Herodians. A party of the Jews who supported the Roman-backed Herodian dynasty. The Herodians were not a religious party, like the Pharisees, but a political party, probably consisting largely of Sadducees (including the rulers of the temple). By contrast, the Pharisees hated Roman rule and the Herodian influence. The fact that these groups would conspire together to entrap Jesus reveals how seriously both groups viewed Him as a threat. Herod himself wanted Jesus dead (Lk 13:31), and the Pharisees were already plotting to kill Him as well (Jn 11:53). So they joined efforts to seek their common goal.

way of God in truth, and defer to no one; for You are not partial to any. [17]Tell us then, what do You think? Is it lawful to give a poll-tax to Caesar, or not?" [18]But Jesus perceived their malice, and said, "Why are you testing Me, you hypocrites? [19]Show Me the coin *used* for the poll-tax." And they brought Him a denarius.

[20]And He *said to them, "Whose likeness and inscription is this?" [21]They *said to Him, "Caesar's." Then He *said to them, "Then render to Caesar the things that are Caesar's; and to God the things that are God's." [22]And hearing *this*, they were amazed, and leaving Him, they went away.

DAY 3: Why was Moses' rod so important as Joshua went into battle? Did it have magic powers?

Joshua, the name of Moses' aide-de-camp, or personal minister (24:13; 33:11; Jos 1:1), appears for the first time in Exodus 17:9. His assignment to muster a task force was part of his being groomed for military leadership in Israel. Actually, at this stage his name was still Hoshea, which later changed to Joshua at Kadesh just before the reconnaissance mission in Canaan (Nu 13:16). At this stage, Israel could not be described as a seasoned army and was not even militarily well prepared and trained.

The staff, or "the staff of God," that Moses held up in his hands was no magic wand. Rather, it had been previously used to initiate, via God's chosen leader, the miracles that God did and about which He had informed Moses in advance. It became, therefore, the symbol of God's personal and powerful involvement, with Moses' outstretched arms perhaps signifying an appeal to God.

The ebb and flow of battle in correlation with Moses' uplifted or drooping arms imparted more than psychological encouragement as the soldiers looked up to their leader on the hilltop, and more than Moses' interceding for them. It demonstrated and acknowledged their having to depend upon God for victory in battle and not upon their own strength and zeal. It also confirmed the position of Moses both in relation to God and the nation's well-being and safety. They had angrily chided him for their problems (Ex 17:2), but God confirmed His appointment as leader.

FEBRUARY 4

Exodus 19:1–20:26

19 In the third month after the sons of Israel had gone out of the land of Egypt, on that very day they came into the wilderness of Sinai. [2]When they set out from Rephidim, they came to the wilderness of Sinai and camped in the wilderness; and there Israel camped in front of the mountain. [3]Moses went up to God, and the LORD called to him from the mountain, saying, "Thus you shall say to the house of Jacob and tell the sons of Israel: [4]'You yourselves have seen what I did to the Egyptians, and *how* I bore you on eagles' wings, and brought you to Myself. [5]Now then, if you will indeed obey My voice and keep My covenant, then you shall be My own possession among all the peoples, for all the earth is Mine; [6]and you shall be to Me a kingdom of priests and a holy nation.' These are the words that you shall speak to the sons of Israel."

[7]So Moses came and called the elders of the people, and set before them all these words which the LORD had commanded him. [8]All the people answered together and said, "All that the LORD has spoken we will do!" And

Moses brought back the words of the people to the LORD. [9]The LORD said to Moses, "Behold, I will come to you in a thick cloud, so that the people may hear when I speak with you and may also believe in you forever." Then Moses told the words of the people to the LORD.

[10]The LORD also said to Moses, "Go to the people and consecrate them today and tomorrow, and let them wash their garments; [11]and let them be ready for the third day, for on the third day the LORD will come down on Mount Sinai in the sight of all the people. [12]You shall set bounds for the people all around, saying, 'Beware that you do not go

19:4 bore you on eagles' wings. With a most appropriate metaphor, God described the Exodus and the journey to Sinai. Eagles were known to have carried their young out of the nests on their wings and taught them to fly, catching them when necessary on their outspread wings. Moses, in his final song, employed this metaphor of God's care for Israel and especially noted that there was only one Lord who did this (Dt 32:11–12).

up on the mountain or touch the border of it; whoever touches the mountain shall surely be put to death. ¹³ No hand shall touch him, but he shall surely be stoned or shot through; whether beast or man, he shall not live.' When the ram's horn sounds a long blast, they shall come up to the mountain." ¹⁴ So Moses went down from the mountain to the people and consecrated the people, and they washed their garments. ¹⁵ He said to the people, "Be ready for the third day; do not go near a woman."

¹⁶ So it came about on the third day, when it was morning, that there were thunder and lightning flashes and a thick cloud upon the mountain and a very loud trumpet sound, so that all the people who were in the camp trembled. ¹⁷ And Moses brought the people out of the camp to meet God, and they stood at the foot of the mountain. ¹⁸ Now Mount Sinai was all in smoke because the LORD descended upon it in fire; and its smoke ascended like the smoke of a furnace, and the whole mountain quaked violently. ¹⁹ When the sound of the trumpet grew louder and louder, Moses spoke and God answered him with thunder. ²⁰ The LORD came down on Mount Sinai, to the top of the mountain; and the LORD called Moses to the top of the mountain, and Moses went up. ²¹ Then the LORD spoke to Moses, "Go down, warn the people, so that they do not break through to the LORD to gaze, and many of them perish. ²² Also let the priests who come near to the LORD consecrate themselves, or else the LORD will break out against them." ²³ Moses said to the LORD, "The people cannot come up to Mount Sinai, for You warned us, saying, 'Set bounds about the mountain and consecrate it.'" ²⁴ Then the LORD said to him, "Go down and come up again, you and Aaron with you; but do not let the priests and the people break through to come up to the LORD, or He will break forth upon them." ²⁵ So Moses went down to the people and told them.

20 Then God spoke all these words, saying,

² "I am the LORD your God, who brought you out of the land of Egypt, out of the house of slavery.

³ "You shall have no other gods before Me.

⁴ "You shall not make for yourself an idol, or any likeness of what is in heaven above or on the earth beneath or in the water under the earth. ⁵ You shall not worship them or serve them; for I, the LORD your God, am a jealous God, visiting the iniquity of the fathers on the children, on the third and the fourth generations of those who hate Me, ⁶ but showing lovingkindness to thousands, to those who love Me and keep My commandments.

⁷ "You shall not take the name of the LORD your God in vain, for the LORD will not leave him unpunished who takes His name in vain.

⁸ "Remember the sabbath day, to keep it holy. ⁹ Six days you shall labor and do all your work, ¹⁰ but the seventh day is a sabbath of the LORD your God; in it you shall not do any work, you or your son or your daughter, your male or your female servant or your cattle or your sojourner who stays with you. ¹¹ For in six days the LORD made the heavens and the earth, the sea and all that is in them, and rested on the seventh day; therefore the LORD blessed the sabbath day and made it holy.

¹² "Honor your father and your mother, that your days may be prolonged in the land which the LORD your God gives you.

¹³ "You shall not murder.

¹⁴ "You shall not commit adultery.

¹⁵ "You shall not steal.

¹⁶ "You shall not bear false witness against your neighbor.

¹⁷ "You shall not covet your neighbor's house; you shall not covet your neighbor's wife or his male servant or his female servant or his ox or his donkey or anything that belongs to your neighbor."

¹⁸ All the people perceived the thunder and the lightning flashes and the sound of the trumpet and the mountain smoking; and when the people saw it, they trembled and stood at a distance. ¹⁹ Then they said to Moses, "Speak to us yourself and we will listen; but let not God speak to us, or we will die." ²⁰ Moses said to the people, "Do not be afraid; for God has come in order to test you, and in order that the fear of Him may remain with you, so that you may not sin." ²¹ So the people stood at a distance, while Moses approached the thick cloud where God was.

²² Then the LORD said to Moses, "Thus you shall say to the sons of Israel, 'You yourselves have seen that I have spoken to you from heaven. ²³ You shall not make other gods besides Me; gods of silver or gods of gold, you shall not make for yourselves. ²⁴ You shall make an altar of earth for Me, and you shall sacrifice on it your burnt offerings and your peace offerings, your sheep and your oxen; in every place where I cause My name to be remembered, I will come to you and bless you. ²⁵ If you make an altar of stone for Me, you shall not build it of cut stones, for if you wield your tool on it, you will profane it. ²⁶ And you shall not go up by steps to My altar, so that your nakedness will not be exposed on it.'

Psalm 18:37-45

37 I pursued my enemies and
   overtook them,
And I did not turn back until
   they were consumed.
38 I shattered them, so that they
   were not able to rise;
They fell under my feet.
39 For You have girded me with
   strength for battle;
You have subdued under me those
   who rose up against me.
40 You have also made my enemies
   turn their backs to me,
And I destroyed those who
   hated me.
41 They cried for help, but there
   was none to save,
Even to the LORD, but He
   did not answer them.
42 Then I beat them fine as the
   dust before the wind;
I emptied them out as the
   mire of the streets.

43 You have delivered me from
   the contentions of the
   people;
You have placed me as
   head of the nations;
A people whom I have not
   known serve me.
44 As soon as they hear, they
   obey me;
Foreigners submit to me.
45 Foreigners fade away,
And come trembling out
   of their fortresses.

Proverbs 6:20-25

20 My son, observe the commandment
   of your father
And do not forsake the
   teaching of your mother;
21 Bind them continually on
   your heart;
Tie them around your neck.
22 When you walk about, they
   will guide you;
When you sleep, they will
   watch over you;
And when you awake, they
   will talk to you.
23 For the commandment is
   a lamp and the teaching
   is light;
And reproofs for discipline
   are the way of life

24 To keep you from the evil woman,
   From the smooth tongue
   of the adulteress.
25 Do not desire her beauty
   in your heart,
Nor let her capture you
   with her eyelids.

6:25 desire. Sexual sin is rooted in desire
(imagination of the sinful act), as implied
in Exodus 20:17 and addressed by Christ in
Matthew 5:28. This initial attraction must be
consistently rejected (Jas 1:14-15).

Matthew 22:23-46

23 On that day *some* Sadducees (who say
there is no resurrection) came to Jesus and
questioned Him, 24 asking, "Teacher, Moses
said, 'IF A MAN DIES HAVING NO CHILDREN,
HIS BROTHER AS NEXT OF KIN SHALL MARRY
HIS WIFE, AND RAISE UP CHILDREN FOR HIS
BROTHER.' 25 Now there were seven brothers
with us; and the first married and died, and
having no children left his wife to his brother;
26 so also the second, and the third, down to
the seventh. 27 Last of all, the woman died.
28 In the resurrection, therefore, whose wife
of the seven will she be? For they all had
married her."
29 But Jesus answered and said to them,
"You are mistaken, not understanding the
Scriptures nor the power of God. 30 For in the
resurrection they neither marry nor are given
in marriage, but are like angels in heaven.
31 But regarding the resurrection of the dead,
have you not read what was spoken to you by
God: 32 'I AM THE GOD OF ABRAHAM, AND THE
GOD OF ISAAC, AND THE GOD OF JACOB'? He
is not the God of the dead but of the living."
33 When the crowds heard *this,* they were astonished at His teaching.
34 But when the Pharisees heard that Jesus
had silenced the Sadducees, they gathered
themselves together. 35 One of them, a lawyer, asked Him *a question,* testing Him,
36 "Teacher, which is the great commandment
in the Law?" 37 And He said to him, " 'YOU
SHALL LOVE THE LORD YOUR GOD WITH ALL
YOUR HEART, AND WITH ALL YOUR SOUL, AND
WITH ALL YOUR MIND.' 38 This is the great and
foremost commandment. 39 The second is like
it, 'YOU SHALL LOVE YOUR NEIGHBOR AS YOUR-
SELF.' 40 On these two commandments depend
the whole Law and the Prophets."
41 Now while the Pharisees were gath-

ered together, Jesus asked them a question: [42] "What do you think about the Christ, whose son is He?" They *said to Him, "*The son* of David." [43] He *said to them, "Then how does David in the Spirit call Him 'Lord,' saying,

[44] 'THE LORD SAID TO MY LORD,
"SIT AT MY RIGHT HAND,
UNTIL I PUT YOUR ENEMIES
BENEATH YOUR FEET"'?

[45] If David then calls Him 'Lord,' how is He his son?" [46] No one was able to answer Him a word, nor did anyone dare from that day on to ask Him another question.

22:45 David then calls Him "Lord." David would not have addressed a merely human descendant as "Lord." Here Jesus was not disputing whether "Son of David" was an appropriate title for the Messiah; after all, the title is based on what is revealed about the Messiah in the Old Testament (Is 11:1; Jer 23:5) and it is used as a messianic title in 1:1. But Jesus was pointing out that the title "son of David" did not begin to sum up all that is true about the Messiah who is also "son of God" (Lk 22:70). The inescapable implication is that Jesus was declaring His deity.

DAY 4: Are the Ten Commandments outmoded expectations or divine demands?

People make a serious error when they speak about "breaking the Ten Commandments." History amply displays the fact that people persist in breaking themselves on the Ten Commandments. They represent God's absolute and unchanging standard despite any arguments over their interpretation and application.

The title "Ten Commandments" comes from Moses (Ex 34:28). The emphasis on God Himself speaking and writing these words makes unacceptable any theories of Israel's borrowing legal patterns or concepts from surrounding nations.

The Ten Commandments may be grouped into two broad categories: the vertical-humanity's relationship to God (Ex 20:2–11); and the horizontal-humanity's relationship to the community (Ex 20:12–17). By these Ten Commandments, true theology and true worship, the name of God, family honor, life, marriage, property, truth, and virtue are well protected.

FEBRUARY 5

Exodus 21:1–22:31

21 "Now these are the ordinances which you are to set before them:

[2] "If you buy a Hebrew slave, he shall serve for six years; but on the seventh he shall go out as a free man without payment. [3] If he comes alone, he shall go out alone; if he is the husband of a wife, then his wife shall go out with him. [4] If his master gives him a wife, and she bears him sons or daughters, the wife and her children shall belong to her master, and he shall go out alone. [5] But if the slave plainly says, 'I love my master, my wife and my children; I will not go out as a free man,' [6] then his master shall bring him to God, then he shall bring him to the door or the doorpost. And his master shall pierce his ear with an awl; and he shall serve him permanently.

[7] "If a man sells his daughter as a female slave, she is not to go free as the male slaves do. [8] If she is displeasing in the eyes of her master who designated her for himself, then he shall let her be redeemed. He does not have authority to sell her to a foreign people because of his unfairness to her. [9] If he designates her for his son, he shall deal with her according to the custom of daughters. [10] If he takes to himself another woman, he may not reduce her food, her clothing, or her conjugal rights. [11] If he will not do these three *things* for her, then she shall go out for nothing, without *payment of* money.

[12] "He who strikes a man so that he dies shall surely be put to death. [13] But if he did not lie in wait *for him,* but God let *him* fall into his hand, then I will appoint you a place to which he may flee. [14] If, however, a man acts presumptuously toward his neighbor, so as to kill him craftily, you are to take him *even* from My altar, that he may die.

[15] "He who strikes his father or his mother shall surely be put to death.

[16] "He who kidnaps a man, whether he sells him or he is found in his possession, shall surely be put to death.

[17] "He who curses his father or his mother shall surely be put to death.

[18] "If men have a quarrel and one strikes the other with a stone or with *his* fist, and he does not die but remains in bed, [19] if he gets

up and walks around outside on his staff, then he who struck him shall go unpunished; he shall only pay for his loss of time, and shall take care of him until he is completely healed. [20] "If a man strikes his male or female slave with a rod and he dies at his hand, he shall be punished. [21] If, however, he survives a day or two, no vengeance shall be taken; for he is his property.

[22] "If men struggle with each other and strike a woman with child so that she gives birth prematurely, yet there is no injury, he shall surely be fined as the woman's husband may demand of him, and he shall pay as the judges decide. [23] But if there is any further injury, then you shall appoint as a penalty life for life, [24] eye for eye, tooth for tooth, hand for hand, foot for foot, [25] burn for burn, wound for wound, bruise for bruise.

[26] "If a man strikes the eye of his male or female slave, and destroys it, he shall let him go free on account of his eye. [27] And if he knocks out a tooth of his male or female slave, he shall let him go free on account of his tooth.

[28] "If an ox gores a man or a woman to death, the ox shall surely be stoned and its flesh shall not be eaten; but the owner of the ox shall go unpunished. [29] If, however, an ox was previously in the habit of goring and its owner has been warned, yet he does not confine it and it kills a man or a woman, the ox shall be stoned and its owner also shall be put to death. [30] If a ransom is demanded of him, then he shall give for the redemption of his life whatever is demanded of him. [31] Whether it gores a son or a daughter, it shall be done to him according to the same rule. [32] If the ox gores a male or female slave, the owner shall give his or her master thirty shekels of silver, and the ox shall be stoned.

[33] "If a man opens a pit, or digs a pit and does not cover it over, and an ox or a donkey falls into it, [34] the owner of the pit shall make restitution; he shall give money to its owner, and the dead animal shall become his. [35] If one man's ox hurts another's so that it dies, then they shall sell the live ox and divide its price equally; and also they shall divide the dead ox. [36] Or if it is known that the ox was previously in the habit of goring, yet its owner has not confined it, he shall surely pay ox for ox, and the dead animal shall become his.

22 "If a man steals an ox or a sheep and slaughters it or sells it, he shall pay five oxen for the ox and four sheep for the sheep.

[2] "If the thief is caught while breaking in and is struck so that he dies, there will be no bloodguiltiness on his account. [3] But if the sun has risen on him, there will be bloodguiltiness on his account. He shall surely make restitution; if he owns nothing, then he shall be sold for his theft. [4] If what he stole is actually found alive in his possession, whether an ox or a donkey or a sheep, he shall pay double.

[5] "If a man lets a field or vineyard be grazed bare and lets his animal loose so that it grazes in another man's field, he shall make restitution from the best of his own field and the best of his own vineyard.

[6] "If a fire breaks out and spreads to thorn bushes, so that stacked grain or the standing grain or the field itself is consumed, he who started the fire shall surely make restitution.

[7] "If a man gives his neighbor money or goods to keep for him and it is stolen from the man's house, if the thief is caught, he shall pay double. [8] If the thief is not caught, then the owner of the house shall appear before the judges, to determine whether he laid his hands on his neighbor's property. [9] For every breach of trust, whether it is for ox, for donkey, for sheep, for clothing, or for any lost thing about which one says, 'This is it,' the case of both parties shall come before the judges; he whom the judges condemn shall pay double to his neighbor.

[10] "If a man gives his neighbor a donkey, an ox, a sheep, or any animal to keep for him, and it dies or is hurt or is driven away while no one is looking, [11] an oath before the LORD shall be made by the two of them that he has not laid hands on his neighbor's property; and its owner shall accept it, and he shall not make restitution. [12] But if it is actually stolen from him, he shall make restitution to its owner. [13] If it is all torn to pieces, let him bring it as evidence; he shall not make restitution for what has been torn to pieces.

[14] "If a man borrows anything from his neighbor, and it is injured or dies while its owner is not with it, he shall make full restitution. [15] If its owner is with it, he shall not make restitution; if it is hired, it came for its hire.

[16] "If a man seduces a virgin who is not engaged, and lies with her, he must pay a dowry for her to be his wife. [17] If her father absolutely refuses to give her to him, he shall pay money equal to the dowry for virgins.

[18] "You shall not allow a sorceress to live.

[19] "Whoever lies with an animal shall surely be put to death.

[20] "He who sacrifices to any god, other than to the LORD alone, shall be utterly destroyed.

²¹ "You shall not wrong a stranger or oppress him, for you were strangers in the land of Egypt. ²² You shall not afflict any widow or orphan. ²³ If you afflict him at all, *and* if he does cry out to Me, I will surely hear his cry; ²⁴ and My anger will be kindled, and I will kill you with the sword, and your wives shall become widows and your children fatherless.

²⁵ "If you lend money to My people, to the poor among you, you are not to act as a creditor to him; you shall not charge him interest. ²⁶ If you ever take your neighbor's cloak as a pledge, you are to return it to him before the sun sets, ²⁷ for that is his only covering; it is his cloak for his body. What else shall he sleep in? And it shall come about that when he cries out to Me, I will hear *him,* for I am gracious.

²⁸ "You shall not curse God, nor curse a ruler of your people.

²⁹ "You shall not delay *the offering from* your harvest and your vintage. The firstborn of your sons you shall give to Me. ³⁰ You shall do the same with your oxen *and* with your sheep. It shall be with its mother seven days; on the eighth day you shall give it to Me.

³¹ "You shall be holy men to Me, therefore you shall not eat *any* flesh torn to pieces in the field; you shall throw it to the dogs.

Psalm 18:46–50

⁴⁶ The LORD lives, and blessed
  be my rock;
And exalted be the God
  of my salvation,
⁴⁷ The God who executes
  vengeance for me,
And subdues peoples under me.

22:22 widow or orphan. God reserved His special attention for widows and orphans who often had no one to care for them. He also reserved a special reaction, His wrath, for those abusing and exploiting them. This wrath would work out in military invasions as the sword reduced the abusers' families to the same status of being without spouse or parents.

22:25 interest. One way in which the people showed their concern for the poor and needy was to take no business advantage of them. Charging interest was allowable (Lv 25:35–37; Dt 23:19–20), but not when it was exorbitant or worsened the plight of the borrower. The psalmist identified a righteous man as one who lends money without interest (Ps 15:5).

⁴⁸ He delivers me from my enemies;
  Surely You lift me above those
    who rise up against me;
  You rescue me from the violent man.
⁴⁹ Therefore I will give thanks to You
    among the nations, O LORD,
  And I will sing praises to Your name.
⁵⁰ He gives great deliverance
    to His king,
  And shows lovingkindness
    to His anointed,
  To David and his descendants forever.

Proverbs 6:26–29

²⁶ For on account of a harlot *one is
    reduced* to a loaf of bread,
  And an adulteress hunts
    for the precious life.
²⁷ Can a man take fire in his bosom
  And his clothes not be burned?
²⁸ Or can a man walk on hot coals
  And his feet not be scorched?
²⁹ So is the one who goes in to
    his neighbor's wife;
  Whoever touches her will
    not go unpunished.

Matthew 23:1–22

23 Then Jesus spoke to the crowds and to His disciples, ² saying: "The scribes and the Pharisees have seated themselves in the chair of Moses; ³ therefore all that they tell you, do and observe, but do not do according to their deeds; for they say *things* and do not do *them.* ⁴ They tie up heavy burdens and lay them on men's shoulders, but they themselves are unwilling to move them with *so much as* a finger. ⁵ But they do all their deeds to be noticed by men; for they broaden their phylacteries and lengthen the tassels *of their garments.* ⁶ They love the place of honor at banquets and the chief seats in the synagogues, ⁷ and respectful greetings in the market places, and being called Rabbi by men. ⁸ But do not be called Rabbi; for One is your Teacher, and you are all brothers. ⁹ Do not call *anyone* on earth your father; for One is your Father, He who is in heaven. ¹⁰ Do not be called leaders; for One is your Leader, *that is,* Christ. ¹¹ But the greatest

6:26 loaf of bread. Here a loaf of bread demonstrates how the prostitute reduces the life of a man to insignificance, including the loss of his wealth (29:3), freedom, family, purity, dignity, and even his soul (v. 32).

among you shall be your servant. ¹²Whoever exalts himself shall be humbled; and whoever humbles himself shall be exalted.

¹³"But woe to you, scribes and Pharisees, hypocrites, because you shut off the kingdom of heaven from people; for you do not enter in yourselves, nor do you allow those who are entering to go in. ¹⁴[Woe to you, scribes and Pharisees, hypocrites, because you devour widows' houses, and for a pretense you make long prayers; therefore you will receive greater condemnation.]

¹⁵"Woe to you, scribes and Pharisees, hypocrites, because you travel around on sea and land to make one proselyte; and when he becomes one, you make him twice as much a son of hell as yourselves.

¹⁶"Woe to you, blind guides, who say, 'Whoever swears by the temple, *that* is nothing; but whoever swears by the gold of the temple is obligated.' ¹⁷You fools and blind men! Which is more important, the gold or the temple that sanctified the gold? ¹⁸And, 'Whoever swears by the altar, *that* is nothing, but whoever swears by the offering on it, he is obligated.' ¹⁹You blind men, which is more important, the offering, or the altar that sanctifies the offer-

23:5 phylacteries. Leather boxes containing a parchment on which is written in 4 columns (Ex 13:1-10, 11-16; Dt 6:4-9; 11:13-21). These are worn by men during prayer—one on the middle of the forehead and one on the left arm just above the elbow. The use of phylacteries was based on an overly literal interpretation of passages like Exodus 13:9-10; Deuteronomy 6:8. Evidently, the Pharisees would broaden the leather straps by which the phylacteries were bound to their arms and foreheads, in order to make the phylacteries more prominent. **the tassels** *of their garments.* Jesus Himself wore them, so it was not the tassels themselves that He condemned, only the mentality that would lengthen the tassels to make it appear that one was especially spiritual.

ing? ²⁰Therefore, whoever swears by the altar, swears *both* by the altar and by everything on it. ²¹And whoever swears by the temple, swears *both* by the temple and by Him who dwells within it. ²²And whoever swears by heaven, swears *both* by the throne of God and by Him who sits upon it.

DAY 5: Why did Jesus have such a hard time with the Pharisees?

Throughout Matthew 23, the words Jesus uses to characterize the Pharisees exposes their true nature. To say they "have seated themselves in the chair of Moses" (v. 2) is an expression equivalent to a university's "chair of philosophy." It meant they had the highest authority to instruct people in the law. The expression here may be translated, "[they] have seated themselves in Moses' seat"—stressing the fact that this was an imaginary authority they claimed for themselves. There was a legitimate sense in which the priests and Levites had authority to decide matters of the law (Dt 17:9), but the scribes and Pharisees had gone beyond any legitimate authority and were adding human tradition to the Word of God (Mt 15:3-9). For that Jesus condemned them (vv. 8-36).

As regards the Pharisees, Jesus tells the multitude to "do and observe" (v. 3) only what accords with the Word of God. The Pharisees were prone to bind "heavy burdens" (v. 4) of extra-biblical traditions and put them on others' shoulders. Jesus explicitly condemned that sort of legalism. The Pharisees would even widen their "phylacteries" and lengthen their "tassels" to make it appear that they were especially spiritual.

 # FEBRUARY 6

Exodus 23:1–24:18

23 "You shall not bear a false report; do not join your hand with a wicked man to be a malicious witness. ²You shall not follow the masses in doing evil, nor shall you testify in a dispute so as to turn aside after a multitude in order to pervert *justice;* ³nor shall you be partial to a poor man in his dispute.

⁴"If you meet your enemy's ox or his donkey wandering away, you shall surely return

it to him. ⁵If you see the donkey of one who hates you lying *helpless* under its load, you shall refrain from leaving it to him, you shall surely release *it* with him.

⁶"You shall not pervert the justice *due* to your needy *brother* in his dispute. ⁷Keep far from a false charge, and do not kill the innocent or the righteous, for I will not acquit the guilty.

⁸"You shall not take a bribe, for a bribe blinds the clear-sighted and subverts the cause of the just.

⁹"You shall not oppress a stranger, since

you yourselves know the feelings of a stranger, for you *also* were strangers in the land of Egypt.

¹⁰ "You shall sow your land for six years and gather in its yield, ¹¹but *on* the seventh year you shall let it rest and lie fallow, so that the needy of your people may eat; and whatever they leave the beast of the field may eat. You are to do the same with your vineyard *and* your olive grove.

¹² "Six days you are to do your work, but on the seventh day you shall cease *from labor* so that your ox and your donkey may rest, and the son of your female slave, as well as your stranger, may refresh themselves. ¹³ Now concerning everything which I have said to you, be on your guard; and do not mention the name of other gods, nor let *them* be heard from your mouth.

¹⁴ "Three times a year you shall celebrate a feast to Me. ¹⁵ You shall observe the Feast of Unleavened Bread; for seven days you are to eat unleavened bread, as I commanded you, at the appointed time in the month Abib, for in it you came out of Egypt. And none shall appear before Me empty-handed. ¹⁶ Also *you shall observe* the Feast of the Harvest *of* the first fruits of your labors *from* what you sow in the field; also the Feast of the Ingathering at the end of the year when you gather in *the fruit of* your labors from the field. ¹⁷ Three times a year all your males shall appear before the Lord GOD.

¹⁸ "You shall not offer the blood of My sacrifice with leavened bread; nor is the fat of My feast to remain overnight until morning. ¹⁹ "You shall bring the choice first fruits of your soil into the house of the LORD your God.

"You are not to boil a young goat in the milk of its mother.

²⁰ "Behold, I am going to send an angel before you to guard you along the way and to bring you into the place which I have prepared. ²¹ Be on your guard before him and obey his voice; do not be rebellious toward him, for he will not pardon your transgression, since My name is in him. ²² But if you truly obey his voice and do all that I say, then I will be an enemy to your enemies and an adversary to your adversaries. ²³ For My angel will go before you and bring you in to *the land of* the Amorites, the Hittites, the Perizzites, the Canaanites, the Hivites and the Jebusites; and I will completely destroy them. ²⁴ You shall not worship their gods, nor serve them, nor do according to their deeds; but you shall utterly overthrow them and break their *sacred* pillars in pieces. ²⁵ But you shall serve the LORD your

---

23:23 My angel. Usually taken to be a reference to the Angel of Yahweh, who is distinguished from the Lord who talks about Him as another person. Yet, He is identified with Him by reason of His forgiving sin and the Lord's name being in Him (v. 21). Neither Moses nor some other messenger or guide qualifies for such descriptions. The key to victory in the upcoming takeover of the land would not be Israel's military skill but the presence of this Angel, who is the preincarnate Christ.

God, and He will bless your bread and your water; and I will remove sickness from your midst. ²⁶ There shall be no one miscarrying or barren in your land; I will fulfill the number of your days. ²⁷ I will send My terror ahead of you, and throw into confusion all the people among whom you come, and I will make all your enemies turn *their* backs to you. ²⁸ I will send hornets ahead of you so that they will drive out the Hivites, the Canaanites, and the Hittites before you. ²⁹ I will not drive them out before you in a single year, that the land may not become desolate and the beasts of the field become too numerous for you. ³⁰ I will drive them out before you little by little, until you become fruitful and take possession of the land. ³¹ I will fix your boundary from the Red Sea to the sea of the Philistines, and from the wilderness to the River *Euphrates;* for I will deliver the inhabitants of the land into your hand, and you will drive them out before you. ³² You shall make no covenant with them or with their gods. ³³ They shall not live in your land, because they will make you sin against Me; for *if* you serve their gods, it will surely be a snare to you."

24 Then He said to Moses, "Come up to the LORD, you and Aaron, Nadab and Abihu and seventy of the elders of Israel, and you shall worship at a distance. ² Moses alone, however, shall come near to the LORD, but they shall not come near, nor shall the people come up with him."

³ Then Moses came and recounted to the people all the words of the LORD and all the ordinances; and all the people answered with one voice and said, "All the words which the LORD has spoken we will do!" ⁴ Moses wrote down all the words of the LORD. Then he arose early in the morning, and built an altar at the foot of the mountain with twelve pillars for the twelve tribes of Israel. ⁵ He sent young men of the sons of Israel, and they offered burnt offerings and sacrificed young bulls as

peace offerings to the LORD. ⁶ Moses took half of the blood and put *it* in basins, and the *other* half of the blood he sprinkled on the altar. ⁷ Then he took the book of the covenant and read *it* in the hearing of the people; and they said, "All that the LORD has spoken we will do, and we will be obedient!" ⁸ So Moses took the blood and sprinkled *it* on the people, and said, "Behold the blood of the covenant, which the LORD has made with you in accordance with all these words."

⁹ Then Moses went up with Aaron, Nadab and Abihu, and seventy of the elders of Israel, ¹⁰ and they saw the God of Israel; and under His feet there appeared to be a pavement of sapphire, as clear as the sky itself. ¹¹ Yet He did not stretch out His hand against the nobles of the sons of Israel; and they saw God, and they ate and drank.

¹² Now the LORD said to Moses, "Come up to Me on the mountain and remain there, and I will give you the stone tablets with the law and the commandment which I have written for their instruction." ¹³ So Moses arose with Joshua his servant, and Moses went up to the mountain of God. ¹⁴ But to the elders he said, "Wait here for us until we return to you. And behold, Aaron and Hur are with you; whoever has a legal matter, let him approach them." ¹⁵ Then Moses went up to the mountain, and the cloud covered the mountain. ¹⁶ The glory of the LORD rested on Mount Sinai, and the cloud covered it for six days; and on the seventh day He called to Moses from the midst of the cloud. ¹⁷ And to the eyes of the sons of Israel the appearance of the glory of the LORD was like a consuming fire on the mountain top. ¹⁸ Moses entered the midst of the cloud as he went up to the mountain; and Moses was on the mountain forty days and forty nights.

Psalm 19:1–6

For the choir director. A Psalm of David.

The heavens are telling of
the glory of God;
And their expanse is declaring
the work of His hands.
2 Day to day pours forth speech,
And night to night reveals knowledge.
3 There is no speech, nor
are there words;
Their voice is not heard.
4 Their line has gone out
through all the earth,
And their utterances to the
end of the world.
In them He has placed a
tent for the sun,

19:1–6 The testimony of the universe comes forth consistently and clearly, but sinful mankind persistently resists it. For this reason, general revelation cannot convert sinners, but it does make them highly accountable (Ro 1:18ff.). Salvation comes ultimately only through special revelation, i.e., as the Word of God is effectually applied by the Spirit of God.

5 Which is as a bridegroom
coming out of his chamber;
It rejoices as a strong man
to run his course.
6 Its rising is from one end
of the heavens,
And its circuit to the other
end of them;
And there is nothing hidden
from its heat.

Proverbs 6:30–31

30 Men do not despise a thief if
he steals
To satisfy himself when he
is hungry;
31 But when he is found, he
must repay sevenfold;
He must give all the substance
of his house.

Matthew 23:23–39

²³ "Woe to you, scribes and Pharisees, hypocrites! For you tithe mint and dill and cummin, and have neglected the weightier provisions of the law: justice and mercy and faithfulness; but these are the things you should have done without neglecting the others. ²⁴ You blind guides, who strain out a gnat and swallow a camel!

²⁵ "Woe to you, scribes and Pharisees, hypocrites! For you clean the outside of the cup and of the dish, but inside they are full of robbery and self-indulgence. ²⁶ You blind Pharisee, first clean the inside of the cup and of the dish, so that the outside of it may become clean also.

²⁷ "Woe to you, scribes and Pharisees, hypocrites! For you are like whitewashed tombs which on the outside appear beautiful, but inside they are full of dead men's bones and all uncleanness. ²⁸ So you, too, outwardly appear righteous to men, but inwardly you are full of hypocrisy and lawlessness.

²⁹ "Woe to you, scribes and Pharisees, hypocrites! For you build the tombs of the

prophets and adorn the monuments of the righteous, 30 and say, 'If we had been *living* in the days of our fathers, we would not have been partners with them in *shedding* the blood of the prophets.' 31 So you testify against yourselves, that you are sons of those who murdered the prophets. 32 Fill up, then, the measure *of the guilt* of your fathers. 33 You serpents, you brood of vipers, how will you escape the sentence of hell?

34 "Therefore, behold, I am sending you prophets and wise men and scribes; some of them you will kill and crucify, and some of them you will scourge in your synagogues, and persecute from city to city, 35 so that upon you may fall *the guilt* of all the righteous blood shed on earth, from the blood of righteous Abel to the blood of Zechariah, the son of Berechiah, whom you murdered between the temple and the altar. 36 Truly I say to you, all these things will come upon this generation.

37 "Jerusalem, Jerusalem, who kills the prophets and stones those who are sent to her! How often I wanted to gather your

23:25 you clean the outside. The Pharisees' focus on external issues lay at the heart of their error. Who would want to drink from a cup that had been washed on the outside but was still filthy inside? Yet the Pharisees lived their lives as if external appearance were more important than internal reality. That was the very essence of their hypocrisy, and Jesus rebuked them for it repeatedly.

23:39 you will not see Me. Christ's public teaching ministry was over. He withdrew from national Israel until the time yet future when they will recognize Him as Messiah (Ro 11:23–26). Then Christ quoted from Psalms 118:26.

children together, the way a hen gathers her chicks under her wings, and you were unwilling. 38 Behold, your house is being left to you desolate! 39 For I say to you, from now on you will not see Me until you say, 'BLESSED IS HE WHO COMES IN THE NAME OF THE LORD!'"

DAY 6: What broke Jesus' heart about His people?

Read Jesus' lament over Jerusalem in Matthew 23:37: "I wanted to gather your children together...and you were unwilling." God is utterly sovereign and therefore fully capable of bringing to pass what He desires (see Is. 46:10)—including the salvation of whomever He chooses (Eph 1:4–5). Yet, He sometimes expresses a wish for that which He does not sovereignly bring to pass (see Ge 6:6; Dt 5:29; Ps 81:13; Is. 48:18). Such expressions in no way suggest a limitation on the sovereignty of God or imply any actual change in Him (Nu 23:19). But these statements do reveal essential aspects of the divine character: He is full of compassion, sincerely good to all, desirous of good, not evil—and therefore not delighting in the destruction of the wicked (Eze 18:32; 33:11).

FEBRUARY 7

Exodus 25:1–26:37

25 Then the LORD spoke to Moses, saying, 2 "Tell the sons of Israel to raise a contribution for Me; from every man whose heart moves him you shall raise My contribution. 3 This is the contribution which you are to raise from them: gold, silver and bronze, 4 blue, purple and scarlet *material,* fine linen, goat *hair,* 5 rams' skins dyed red, porpoise skins, acacia wood, 6 oil for lighting, spices for the anointing oil and for the fragrant incense, 7 onyx stones and setting stones for the ephod and for the breastpiece. 8 Let them construct a sanctuary for Me, that I may dwell among them. 9 According to all that I am going to show you, *as* the pattern of the

tabernacle and the pattern of all its furniture, just so you shall construct *it.*

10 "They shall construct an ark of acacia wood two and a half cubits long, and one and a half cubits wide, and one and a half cubits high. 11 You shall overlay it with pure gold, inside and out you shall overlay it, and you shall make a gold molding around it. 12 You shall cast four gold rings for it and fasten them on its four feet, and two rings shall be on one side of it and two rings on the other side of it. 13 You shall make poles of acacia wood and overlay them with gold. 14 You shall put the poles into the rings on the sides of the ark, to carry the ark with them. 15 The poles shall remain in the rings of the ark; they shall not be removed from it. 16 You shall put into the ark the testimony which I shall give you.

¹⁷ "You shall make a mercy seat of pure gold, two and a half cubits long and one and a half cubits wide. ¹⁸ You shall make two cherubim of gold, make them of hammered work at the two ends of the mercy seat. ¹⁹ Make one cherub at one end and one cherub at the other end; you shall make the cherubim *of one piece* with the mercy seat at its two ends. ²⁰ The cherubim shall have *their* wings spread upward, covering the mercy seat with their wings and facing one another; the faces of the cherubim are to be *turned* toward the mercy seat. ²¹ You shall put the mercy seat on top of the ark, and in the ark you shall put the testimony which I will give to you. ²² There I will meet with you; and from above the mercy seat, from between the two cherubim which are upon the ark of the testimony, I will speak to you about all that I will give you in commandment for the sons of Israel.

25:17 mercy seat. The lid or cover of the ark was the "mercy seat" or the place at which atonement took place. Between the Shekinah glory cloud above the ark and the tablets of law inside the ark was the blood-sprinkled cover. Blood from the sacrifices stood between God and the broken law of God!

²³ "You shall make a table of acacia wood, two cubits long and one cubit wide and one and a half cubits high. ²⁴ You shall overlay it with pure gold and make a gold border around it. ²⁵ You shall make for it a rim of a handbreadth around *it;* and you shall make a gold border for the rim around it. ²⁶ You shall make four gold rings for it and put rings on the four corners which are on its four feet. ²⁷ The rings shall be close to the rim as holders for the poles to carry the table. ²⁸ You shall make the poles of acacia wood and overlay them with gold, so that with them the table may be carried. ²⁹ You shall make its dishes and its pans and its jars and its bowls with which to pour drink offerings; you shall make them of pure gold. ³⁰ You shall set the bread of the Presence on the table before Me at all times.

³¹ "Then you shall make a lampstand of pure gold. The lampstand *and* its base and its shaft are to be made of hammered work; its cups, its bulbs and its flowers shall be *of one piece* with it. ³² Six branches shall go out from its sides; three branches of the lampstand from its one side and three branches of the lampstand from its other side. ³³ Three

25:31 lampstand. Situated opposite the table of the bread of the Presence on the south side of the Holy Place stood an ornate lampstand, or menorah, patterned after a flowering almond tree. It provided light for the priests serving in the Holy Place. Care was taken, according to God's instructions (27:20–21; 30:7–8; Lv 24:1–4), to keep it well supplied with pure olive oil so that it would not be extinguished. The lampstand is seen as typifying the Lord Jesus Christ, who was the true Light which came into the world (Jn 1:6–9; 8:12).

cups *shall be* shaped like almond *blossoms* in the one branch, a bulb and a flower, and three cups shaped like almond *blossoms* in the other branch, a bulb and a flower—so for six branches going out from the lampstand; ³⁴ and in the lampstand four cups shaped like almond *blossoms,* its bulbs and its flowers. ³⁵ A bulb shall be under the *first* pair of branches *coming* out of it, and a bulb under the *second* pair of branches *coming* out of it, and a bulb under the *third* pair of branches *coming* out of it, for the six branches coming out of the lampstand. ³⁶ Their bulbs and their branches *shall be of one piece* with it; all of it shall be one piece of hammered work of pure gold. ³⁷ Then you shall make its lamps seven *in number;* and they shall mount its lamps so as to shed light on the space in front of it. ³⁸ Its snuffers and their trays *shall be* of pure gold. ³⁹ It shall be made from a talent of pure gold, with all these utensils. ⁴⁰ See that you make *them* after the pattern for them, which was shown to you on the mountain.

26 "Moreover you shall make the tabernacle with ten curtains of fine twisted linen and blue and purple and scarlet *material;* you shall make them with cherubim, the work of a skillful workman. ² The length of each curtain shall be twenty-eight cubits, and the width of each curtain four cubits; all the curtains shall have the same measurements. ³ Five curtains shall be joined to one another, and the other five curtains *shall be* joined to one another. ⁴ You shall make loops of blue on the edge of the outermost curtain in the *first* set, and likewise you shall make *them* on the edge of the curtain that is outermost in the second set. ⁵ You shall make fifty loops in the one curtain, and you shall make fifty loops on the edge of the curtain that is in the second set; the loops shall be opposite each other. ⁶ You shall make fifty clasps of gold, and join the curtains to one

another with the clasps so that the tabernacle will be a unit.

7 "Then you shall make curtains of goats' *hair* for a tent over the tabernacle; you shall make eleven curtains in all. 8 The length of each curtain *shall be* thirty cubits, and the width of each curtain four cubits; the eleven curtains shall have the same measurements. 9 You shall join five curtains by themselves and the *other* six curtains by themselves, and you shall double over the sixth curtain at the front of the tent. 10 You shall make fifty loops on the edge of the curtain that is outermost in the *first* set, and fifty loops on the edge of the curtain *that is outermost in* the second set. 11 "You shall make fifty clasps of bronze, and you shall put the clasps into the loops and join the tent together so that it will be a unit. 12 The overlapping part that is left over in the curtains of the tent, the half curtain that is left over, shall lap over the back of the tabernacle. 13 The cubit on one side and the cubit on the other, of what is left over in the length of the curtains of the tent, shall lap over the sides of the tabernacle on one side and on the other, to cover it. 14 You shall make a covering for the tent of rams' skins dyed red and a covering of porpoise skins above.

15 "Then you shall make the boards for the tabernacle of acacia wood, standing upright. 16 Ten cubits *shall be* the length of each board and one and a half cubits the width of each board. 17 *There shall be* two tenons for each board, fitted to one another; thus you shall do for all the boards of the tabernacle. 18 You shall make the boards for the tabernacle: twenty boards for the south side. 19 You shall make forty sockets of silver under the twenty boards, two sockets under one board for its two tenons and two sockets under another board for its two tenons; 20 and for the second side of the tabernacle, on the north side, twenty boards, 21 and their forty sockets of silver; two sockets under one board and two sockets under another board. 22 For the rear of the tabernacle, to the west, you shall make six boards. 23 You shall make two boards for the corners of the tabernacle at the rear. 24 They shall be double beneath, and together they shall be complete to its top to the first ring; thus it shall be with both of them: they shall form the two corners. 25 There shall be eight boards with their sockets of silver, sixteen sockets; two sockets under one board and two sockets under another board.

26 "Then you shall make bars of acacia wood, five for the boards of one side of the tabernacle, 27 and five bars for the boards of the other side of the tabernacle, and five bars for the boards of the side of the tabernacle for the rear *side* to the west. 28 The middle bar in the center of the boards shall pass through from end to end. 29 You shall overlay the boards with gold and make their rings of gold *as* holders for the bars; and you shall overlay the bars with gold. 30 Then you shall erect the tabernacle according to its plan which you have been shown in the mountain.

31 "You shall make a veil of blue and purple and scarlet *material* and fine twisted linen; it shall be made with cherubim, the work of a skillful workman. 32 You shall hang it on four pillars of acacia overlaid with gold, their hooks *also being of* gold, on four sockets of silver. 33 You shall hang up the veil under the clasps, and shall bring in the ark of the testimony there within the veil; and the veil shall serve for you as a partition between the holy place and the holy of holies. 34 You shall put the mercy seat on the ark of the testimony in the holy of holies. 35 You shall set the table outside the veil, and the lampstand opposite the table on the side of the tabernacle toward the south; and you shall put the table on the north side.

36 "You shall make a screen for the doorway of the tent of blue and purple and scarlet *material* and fine twisted linen, the work of a weaver. 37 You shall make five pillars of acacia for the screen and overlay them with gold, their hooks *also being of* gold; and you shall cast five sockets of bronze for them.

Psalm 19:7–14

7 The law of the LORD is perfect,
　　restoring the soul;
　The testimony of the LORD is sure,
　　making wise the simple.
8 The precepts of the LORD are
　　right, rejoicing the heart;
　The commandment of the LORD is
　　pure, enlightening the eyes.
9 The fear of the LORD is clean,
　　enduring forever;
　The judgments of the LORD are true;
　　they are righteous altogether.
10 They are more desirable than gold,
　　yes, than much fine gold;
　Sweeter also than honey and the
　　drippings of the honeycomb.
11 Moreover, by them Your
　　servant is warned;
　In keeping them there
　　is great reward.
12 Who can discern *his* errors?
　　Acquit me of hidden *faults.*

¹³ Also keep back Your servant
  from presumptuous *sins;*
Let them not rule over me;
Then I will be blameless,
And I shall be acquitted of
  great transgression.
¹⁴ Let the words of my mouth and
  the meditation of my heart
Be acceptable in Your sight,
O LORD, my rock and my
  Redeemer.

Proverbs 6:32-35

³² The one who commits adultery
  with a woman is lacking sense;
He who would destroy himself
  does it.
³³ Wounds and disgrace he will
  find,
And his reproach will not
  be blotted out.
³⁴ For jealousy enrages a man,
And he will not spare in the
  day of vengeance.
³⁵ He will not accept any ransom,
Nor will he be satisfied though
  you give many gifts.

Matthew 24:1-28

24 Jesus came out from the temple and was going away when His disciples came up to point out the temple buildings to Him. ² And He said to them, "Do you see all these things? Truly I say to you, not one stone here will be left upon another, which will not be torn down."

³ As He was sitting on the Mount of Olives, the disciples came to Him privately, saying, "Tell us, when will these things happen, and what *will be* the sign of Your coming, and of the end of the age?"

⁴ And Jesus answered and said to them, "See to it that no one misleads you. ⁵ For many will come in My name, saying, 'I am the Christ,' and will mislead many. ⁶ You will be hearing of wars and rumors of wars. See that you are not frightened, for *those things* must take place, but *that* is not yet the end. ⁷ For nation will rise against nation, and kingdom against kingdom, and in various places there will be famines and earthquakes. ⁸ But all these things are *merely* the beginning of birth pangs.

⁹ "Then they will deliver you to tribulation, and will kill you, and you will be hated by all nations because of My name. ¹⁰ At that time many will fall away and will betray one another and hate one another. ¹¹ Many false prophets will arise and will mislead many. ¹² Because lawlessness is increased, most people's love will grow cold. ¹³ But the one who endures to the end, he will be saved. ¹⁴ This gospel of the kingdom shall be preached in the whole world as a testimony to all the nations, and then the end will come.

¹⁵ "Therefore when you see the ABOMINATION OF DESOLATION which was spoken of through Daniel the prophet, standing in the holy place (let the reader understand), ¹⁶ then those who are in Judea must flee to the mountains. ¹⁷ Whoever is on the housetop must not go down to get the things out that are in his house. ¹⁸ Whoever is in the field must not turn back to get his cloak. ¹⁹ But woe to those who are pregnant and to those who are nursing babies in those days! ²⁰ But pray that your flight will not be in the winter, or on a Sabbath. ²¹ For then there will be a great tribulation, such as has not occurred since the beginning of the world until now, nor ever will. ²² Unless those days had been cut short, no life would have been saved; but for the sake of the elect those days will be cut short. ²³ Then if anyone says to you, 'Behold, here

24:2 not one stone here...left upon another. These words were literally fulfilled in A.D. 70. Titus, the Roman general, built large wooden scaffolds around the walls of the temple buildings, piled them high with wood and other flammable items, and set them ablaze. The heat from the fires was so intense that the stones crumbled. The rubble was then sifted to retrieve the melted gold, and the remaining ruins were "thrown down" into the Kidron Valley.

24:14 preached in the whole world. Despite all the tribulations that would come—the deception of false teachers, the wars, persecutions, natural disasters, defections from Christ, and all the obstacles to the spread of the gospel— the message ultimately penetrates every part of the globe. God is never without a witness, and He will proclaim the gospel from heaven itself if necessary (Rev 14:6). **then the end will come.** "The end" refers to the final, excruciating birth pangs. This is how Christ characterizes the time of Great Tribulation described in the verses that follow.

is the Christ,' or 'There *He is*,' do not believe *him*. [24]For false Christs and false prophets will arise and will show great signs and wonders, so as to mislead, if possible, even the elect. [25]Behold, I have told you in advance. [26]So if they say to you, 'Behold, He is in the wilderness,' do not go out, *or*, 'Behold, He is in the inner rooms,' do not believe *them*. [27]For just as the lightning comes from the east and flashes even to the west, so will the coming of the Son of Man be. [28]Wherever the corpse is, there the vultures will gather.

DAY 7: Why all the specific details about the tabernacle, and what do they mean for us today?

Ever since God dictated the blueprints of the tabernacle to Moses, people have wondered about the significance of the exact details. Several terms are used to indicate times in the Bible when events, persons, or things represent larger ideas: typology and foreshadowing. For example, the sacrifice of the lambs in the Old Testament had not only a limited immediate significance in understanding the cost of forgiveness, but this practice also foreshadowed the eventual sacrifice of the Lamb of God, Jesus, on the cross.

Because at least some parts of the tabernacle hold special significance—the ark representing God's covenant with His people—students of Scripture have looked for other possible deeper meanings. Ingenuity in linking every item of furniture and every piece of building material to Christ may appear most intriguing; but if New Testament statements and allusions do not support such linkage and typology, students ought to proceed with caution. The beauty and efficiency of the tabernacle's design presents a tribute to God's creative character, but those who look for hidden meaning in every tent peg and covering stitch run the risk of missing the big picture in the details. The New Testament points repeatedly to the awesome fact of God's presence with people as represented in the Tabernacle. Other New Testament lessons (particularly the Book of Hebrews) help identify the intended symbols and deeper meanings.

FEBRUARY 8

Exodus 27:1–28:43

27 "And you shall make the altar of acacia wood, five cubits long and five cubits wide; the altar shall be square, and its height shall be three cubits. [2]You shall make its horns on its four corners; its horns shall be of one piece with it, and you shall overlay it with bronze. [3]You shall make its pails for removing its ashes, and its shovels and its basins and its forks and its firepans; you shall make all its utensils of bronze. [4]You shall make for it a grating of network of bronze, and on the net you shall make four bronze rings at its four corners. [5]You shall put it beneath, under the ledge of the altar, so that the net will reach halfway up the altar. [6]You shall make poles for the altar, poles of acacia wood, and overlay them with bronze. [7]Its poles shall be inserted into the rings, so that the poles shall be on the two sides of the altar when it is carried. [8]You shall make it hollow with planks; as it was shown to you in the mountain, so they shall make *it*.

[9]"You shall make the court of the tabernacle. On the south side *there shall be* hangings for the court of fine twisted linen one hundred cubits long for one side; [10]and its pillars *shall be* twenty, with their twenty sockets of bronze; the hooks of the pillars and their bands *shall be* of silver. [11]Likewise for the north side in length *there shall be* hangings one hundred *cubits* long, and its twenty pillars with their twenty sockets of bronze; the hooks of the pillars and their bands *shall be* of silver. [12]*For* the width of the court on the west side *shall be* hangings of fifty cubits *with* their ten pillars and their ten sockets. [13]The width of the court on the east side *shall be* fifty cubits. [14]The hangings for the *one* side *of the gate shall be* fifteen cubits *with* their three pillars and their three sockets. [15]And for the other side *shall be* hangings of fifteen cubits *with* their three pillars and

27:9 the court of the tabernacle. The dimensions of the rectangular courtyard space, bordered by curtains and poles around the tabernacle were also precisely given (vv. 9–19; 150 ft. by 75 ft.). The outer hangings were high enough, 5 cubits or 7.5 ft., to block all view of the interior of the courtyard (v. 18). Entry into the courtyard of God's dwelling place was not gained just generally and freely from all quarters.

their three sockets. ¹⁶ For the gate of the court *there shall be* a screen of twenty cubits, of blue and purple and scarlet *material* and fine twisted linen, the work of a weaver, *with* their four pillars and their four sockets. ¹⁷ All the pillars around the court shall be furnished with silver bands *with* their hooks of silver and their sockets of bronze. ¹⁸ The length of the court *shall be* one hundred cubits, and the width fifty throughout, and the height five cubits of fine twisted linen, and their sockets of bronze. ¹⁹ All the utensils of the tabernacle *used* in all its service, and all its pegs, and all the pegs of the court, *shall be* of bronze.

²⁰ "You shall charge the sons of Israel, that they bring you clear oil of beaten olives for the light, to make a lamp burn continually. ²¹ In the tent of meeting, outside the veil which is before the testimony, Aaron and his sons shall keep it in order from evening to morning before the LORD; *it shall be* a perpetual statute throughout their generations for the sons of Israel.

28 "Then bring near to yourself Aaron your brother, and his sons with him, from among the sons of Israel, to minister as priest to Me—Aaron, Nadab and Abihu, Eleazar and Ithamar, Aaron's sons. ² You shall make holy garments for Aaron your brother, for glory and for beauty. ³ You shall speak to all the skillful persons whom I have endowed with the spirit of wisdom, that they make Aaron's garments to consecrate him, that he may minister as priest to Me. ⁴ These are the garments which they shall make: a breastpiece and an ephod and a robe and a tunic of checkered work, a turban and a sash,

28:1 minister as priest to Me. The 3-fold repetition of this phrase in the opening words about Aaron's priestly wardrobe would appear to stress the importance of his role in the religious life of the nation. Aaron's sons were part of the priesthood being set up. The Hebrew text groups the sons in two pairs, the first pair being Nadab and Abihu, both of whom died because of wanton disregard of God's instructions (Lv 10:1-2). Aaron and his descendants, as well as the tribe of Levi, were selected by God to be Israel's priests—they did not appoint themselves to the position. The law clearly defined their duties for worship and the sacrifices in the tabernacle and for the individual worshiper and the nation's covenantal relationship to God.

and they shall make holy garments for Aaron your brother and his sons, that he may minister as priest to Me. ⁵ They shall take the gold and the blue and the purple and the scarlet *material* and the fine linen.

⁶ "They shall also make the ephod of gold, of blue and purple *and* scarlet *material* and fine twisted linen, the work of the skillful workman. ⁷ It shall have two shoulder pieces joined to its two ends, that it may be joined. ⁸ The skillfully woven band, which is on it, shall be like its workmanship, of the same material: of gold, of blue and purple and scarlet *material* and fine twisted linen. ⁹ You shall take two onyx stones and engrave on them the names of the sons of Israel, ¹⁰ six of their names on the one stone and the names of the remaining six on the other stone, according to their birth. ¹¹ As a jeweler engraves a signet, you shall engrave the two stones according to the names of the sons of Israel; you shall set them in filigree *settings* of gold. ¹² You shall put the two stones on the shoulder pieces of the ephod, *as* stones of memorial for the sons of Israel, and Aaron shall bear their names before the LORD on his two shoulders for a memorial. ¹³ You shall make filigree *settings* of gold, ¹⁴ and two chains of pure gold; you shall make them of twisted cordage work, and you shall put the corded chains on the filigree *settings*.

¹⁵ "You shall make a breastpiece of judgment, the work of a skillful workman; like the work of the ephod you shall make it: of gold, of blue and purple and scarlet *material* and fine twisted linen you shall make it. ¹⁶ It shall be square *and* folded double, a span in length and a span in width. ¹⁷ You shall mount on it four rows of stones; the first row *shall be* a row of ruby, topaz and emerald; ¹⁸ and the second row a turquoise, a sapphire and a diamond; ¹⁹ and the third row a jacinth, an agate and an amethyst; ²⁰ and the fourth row a beryl and an onyx and a jasper; they shall be set in gold filigree. ²¹ The stones shall be according to the names of the sons of Israel: twelve, according to their names; they shall be *like* the engravings of a seal, each according to his name for the twelve tribes. ²² You shall make on the breastpiece chains of twisted cordage work in pure gold. ²³ You shall make on the breastpiece two rings of gold, and shall put the two rings on the two ends of the breastpiece. ²⁴ You shall put the two cords of gold on the two rings at the ends of the breastpiece. ²⁵ You shall put the *other* two ends of the two cords on the two filigree *settings*, and put them

on the shoulder pieces of the ephod, at the front of it. ²⁶ You shall make two rings of gold and shall place them on the two ends of the breastpiece, on the edge of it, which is toward the inner side of the ephod. ²⁷ You shall make two rings of gold and put them on the bottom of the two shoulder pieces of the ephod, on the front of it close to the place where it is joined, above the skillfully woven band of the ephod. ²⁸ They shall bind the breastpiece by its rings to the rings of the ephod with a blue cord, so that it will be on the skillfully woven band of the ephod, and that the breastpiece will not come loose from the ephod. ²⁹ Aaron shall carry the names of the sons of Israel in the breastpiece of judgment over his heart when he enters the holy place, for a memorial before the LORD continually. ³⁰ You shall put in the breastpiece of judgment the Urim and the Thummim, and they shall be over Aaron's heart when he goes in before the LORD; and Aaron shall carry the judgment of the sons of Israel over his heart before the LORD continually.

³¹ "You shall make the robe of the ephod all of blue. ³² There shall be an opening at its top in the middle of it; around its opening there shall be a binding of woven work, like the opening of a coat of mail, so that it will not be torn. ³³ You shall make on its hem pomegranates of blue and purple and scarlet *material,* all around on its hem, and bells of gold between them all around: ³⁴ a golden bell and a pomegranate, a golden bell and a pomegranate, all around on the hem of the robe. ³⁵ It shall be on Aaron when he ministers; and its tinkling shall be heard when he enters and leaves the holy place before the LORD, so that he will not die.

³⁶ "You shall also make a plate of pure gold and shall engrave on it, like the engravings of a seal, 'Holy to the LORD.' ³⁷ You shall fasten it on a blue cord, and it shall be on the turban; it shall be at the front of the turban. ³⁸ It shall be on Aaron's forehead, and Aaron shall take away the iniquity of the holy things which the sons of Israel consecrate, with regard to all their holy gifts; and it shall always be on his forehead, that they may be accepted before the LORD.

³⁹ "You shall weave the tunic of checkered work of fine linen, and shall make a turban of fine linen, and you shall make a sash, the work of a weaver.

⁴⁰ "For Aaron's sons you shall make tunics; you shall also make sashes for them, and you shall make caps for them, for glory and for beauty. ⁴¹ You shall put them on Aaron your brother and on his sons with him; and you shall anoint them and ordain them and consecrate them, that they may serve Me as priests. ⁴² You shall make for them linen breeches to cover *their* bare flesh; they shall reach from the loins even to the thighs. ⁴³ They shall be on Aaron and on his sons when they enter the tent of meeting, or when they approach the altar to minister in the holy place, so that they do not incur guilt and die. It *shall be* a statute forever to him and to his descendants after him.

Psalm 20:1–5

For the choir director. A Psalm of David.

May the LORD answer you
in the day of trouble!
May the name of the God of Jacob
set you *securely* on high!
² May He send you help
from the sanctuary
And support you from Zion!
³ May He remember all your
meal offerings
And find your burnt offering
acceptable!   *Selah*

⁴ May He grant you your heart's
desire
And fulfill all your counsel!
⁵ We will sing for joy over your
victory,
And in the name of our God we
will set up our banners.
May the LORD fulfill all your
petitions.

Proverbs 7:1–5

My son, keep my words
And treasure my commandments
within you.
² Keep my commandments
and live,
And my teaching as the
apple of your eye.
³ Bind them on your fingers;
Write them on the tablet
of your heart.

7:2 apple of your eye. This expression refers to the pupil of the eye which, because it is the source of sight, is carefully protected (Dt 32:10; Ps 17:8; Zec 2:8). The son is to guard and protect his father's teachings because they give him spiritual and moral sight.

⁴ Say to wisdom, "You are my
sister,"
And call understanding
your intimate friend;
⁵ That they may keep you
from an adulteress,
From the foreigner who
flatters with her words.

Matthew 24:29-51

²⁹ "But immediately after the tribulation of those days THE SUN WILL BE DARKENED, AND THE MOON WILL NOT GIVE ITS LIGHT, AND THE STARS WILL FALL from the sky, and the powers of the heavens will be shaken. ³⁰ And then the sign of the Son of Man will appear in the sky, and then all the tribes of the earth will mourn, and they will see the SON OF MAN COMING ON THE CLOUDS OF THE SKY with power and great glory. ³¹ And He will send forth His angels with A GREAT TRUMPET and THEY WILL GATHER TO-GETHER His elect from the four winds, from one end of the sky to the other.

³² "Now learn the parable from the fig tree: when its branch has already become tender and puts forth its leaves, you know that summer is near; ³³ so, you too, when you see all these things, recognize that He is near, *right* at the door. ³⁴ Truly I say to you, this genera-tion will not pass away until all these things take place. ³⁵ Heaven and earth will pass away, but My words will not pass away.

³⁶ "But of that day and hour no one knows, not even the angels of heaven, nor the Son, but the Father alone. ³⁷ For the coming of the Son of Man will be just like the days of Noah. ³⁸ For as in those days before the flood they were eating and drinking, marrying and giving in marriage, until the day that Noah entered the ark, ³⁹ and they did not under-stand until the flood came and took them all away; so will the coming of the Son of Man be. ⁴⁰ Then there will be two men in the field; one will be taken and one will be left. ⁴¹ Two

24:37 like the days of Noah. Jesus' emphasis here is not so much on the extreme wicked-ness of Noah's day (Ge 6:5), but on the people's preoccupation with mundane matters of ev-eryday life ("eating and drinking, marrying and giving in marriage"—v. 38), when judgment fell suddenly. They had received warnings, in the form of Noah's preaching (2Pe 2:5)—and the ark itself, which was a testimony to the judgment that was to come. But they were unconcerned about such matters and therefore were swept away unexpectedly in the midst of their daily activities.

women *will be* grinding at the mill; one will be taken and one will be left.

⁴² "Therefore be on the alert, for you do not know which day your Lord is coming. ⁴³ But be sure of this, that if the head of the house had known at what time of the night the thief was coming, he would have been on the alert and would not have allowed his house to be broken into. ⁴⁴ For this reason you also must be ready; for the Son of Man is coming at an hour when you do not think *He will.*

⁴⁵ "Who then is the faithful and sensible slave whom his master put in charge of his household to give them their food at the proper time? ⁴⁶ Blessed is that slave whom his master finds so doing when he comes. ⁴⁷ Truly I say to you that he will put him in charge of all his possessions. ⁴⁸ But if that evil slave says in his heart, 'My master is not coming for a long time,' ⁴⁹ and begins to beat his fellow slaves and eat and drink with drunkards; ⁵⁰ the master of that slave will come on a day when he does not expect *him* and at an hour which he does not know, ⁵¹ and will cut him in pieces and assign him a place with the hypocrites; in that place there will be weeping and gnashing of teeth.

DAY 8: How should Jesus' prophetic statements, many of which are found in Matthew 24 and 25, be interpreted?

The prophetic passages present a particular challenge for those seeking to understand a cor-rect interpretation of Jesus' words. The Olivet discourse (Matthew 24–25), for example, contains some details that evoke images of the violent destruction of Jerusalem in A.D. 70. Jesus' words in 24:34 have led some to conclude that all these things were fulfilled—albeit not literally—in the Roman conquest of that era. This view is known as "preterism." But this is a serious inter-pretive blunder, forcing the interpreter to read into these passages spiritualized, allegorical meanings unwarranted by normal exegetical study methods. The grammatical-historical her-meneutical approach to these passages is the approach to follow, and it yields a consistently futuristic interpretation of crucial prophecies.

FEBRUARY 9

Exodus 29:1–30:38

29 "Now this is what you shall do to them to consecrate them to minister as priests to Me: take one young bull and two rams without blemish, ²and unleavened bread and unleavened cakes mixed with oil, and unleavened wafers spread with oil; you shall make them of fine wheat flour. ³You shall put them in one basket, and present them in the basket along with the bull and the two rams. ⁴Then you shall bring Aaron and his sons to the doorway of the tent of meeting and wash them with water. ⁵You shall take the garments, and put on Aaron the tunic and the robe of the ephod and the ephod and the breastpiece, and gird him with the skillfully woven band of the ephod; ⁶and you shall set the turban on his head and put the holy crown on the turban. ⁷Then you shall take the anointing oil and pour it on his head and anoint him. ⁸You shall bring his sons and put tunics on them. ⁹You shall gird them with sashes, Aaron and his sons, and bind caps on them, and they shall have the priesthood by a perpetual statute. So you shall ordain Aaron and his sons.

¹⁰"Then you shall bring the bull before the tent of meeting, and Aaron and his sons shall lay their hands on the head of the bull. ¹¹You shall slaughter the bull before the LORD at the doorway of the tent of meeting. ¹²You shall take some of the blood of the bull and put *it* on the horns of the altar with your finger; and you shall pour out all the blood at the base of the altar. ¹³You shall take all the fat that covers the entrails and the lobe of the liver, and the two kidneys and the fat that is on them, and offer them up in smoke on the altar. ¹⁴But the flesh of the bull and its hide and its refuse, you shall burn with fire outside the camp; it is a sin offering.

¹⁵"You shall also take the one ram, and Aaron and his sons shall lay their hands on the head of the ram; ¹⁶and you shall slaughter the ram and shall take its blood and sprinkle it around on the altar. ¹⁷Then you shall cut the ram into its pieces, and wash its entrails and its legs, and put *them* with its pieces and its head. ¹⁸You shall offer up in smoke the whole ram on the altar; it is a burnt offering to the LORD: it is a soothing aroma, an offering by fire to the LORD.

¹⁹"Then you shall take the other ram, and Aaron and his sons shall lay their hands on the head of the ram. ²⁰You shall slaughter the ram, and take some of its blood and put *it* on the lobe of Aaron's right ear and on the lobes of his sons' right ears and on the thumbs of their right hands and on the big toes of their right feet, and sprinkle the *rest of the* blood around on the altar. ²¹Then you shall take some of the blood that is on the altar and some of the anointing oil, and sprinkle *it* on Aaron and on his garments and on his sons and on his sons' garments with him; so he and his garments shall be consecrated, as well as his sons and his sons' garments with him.

²²"You shall also take the fat from the ram and the fat tail, and the fat that covers the entrails and the lobe of the liver, and the two kidneys and the fat that is on them and the right thigh (for it is a ram of ordination), ²³and one cake of bread and one cake of bread *mixed with* oil and one wafer from the basket of unleavened bread which is *set* before the LORD; ²⁴and you shall put all these in the hands of Aaron and in the hands of his sons, and shall wave them as a wave offering before the LORD. ²⁵You shall take them from their hands, and offer them up in smoke on the altar on the burnt offering for a soothing aroma before the LORD; it is an offering by fire to the LORD.

²⁶"Then you shall take the breast of Aaron's ram of ordination, and wave it as a wave offering before the LORD; and it shall be your portion. ²⁷You shall consecrate the breast of the wave offering and the thigh of the heave offering which was waved and which was offered from the ram of ordination, from the one which was for Aaron and from the one which was for his sons. ²⁸It shall be for Aaron and his sons as *their* portion forever from the sons of Israel, for it is a heave offering; and it shall be a heave offering from the sons of Israel from the sacrifices of their peace offerings, *even* their heave offering to the LORD.

²⁹"The holy garments of Aaron shall be for his sons after him, that in them they may be anointed and ordained. ³⁰For seven days the one of his sons who is priest in his stead shall put them on when he enters the tent of meeting to minister in the holy place.

³¹"You shall take the ram of ordination and boil its flesh in a holy place. ³²Aaron and his sons shall eat the flesh of the ram and the bread that is in the basket, at the doorway of the tent of meeting. ³³Thus they shall eat those things by which atonement was made at their ordination *and* consecration; but a layman shall not eat *them*, because they are holy. ³⁴If any of the flesh of ordination or any of the bread remains until morning, then you

131

shall burn the remainder with fire; it shall not be eaten, because it is holy.

35 "Thus you shall do to Aaron and to his sons, according to all that I have commanded you; you shall ordain them through seven days. 36 Each day you shall offer a bull as a sin offering for atonement, and you shall purify the altar when you make atonement for it, and you shall anoint it to consecrate it. 37 For seven days you shall make atonement for the altar and consecrate it; then the altar shall be most holy, *and* whatever touches the altar shall be holy.

38 "Now this is what you shall offer on the altar: two one year old lambs each day, continuously. 39 The one lamb you shall offer in the morning and the other lamb you shall offer at twilight; 40 and there *shall be* one-tenth *of an ephah* of fine flour mixed with one-fourth of a hin of beaten oil, and one-fourth of a hin of wine for a drink offering with one lamb. 41 The other lamb you shall offer at twilight, and shall offer with it the same grain offering and the same drink offering as in the morning, for a soothing aroma, an offering by fire to the LORD. 42 It shall be a continual burnt offering throughout your generations at the doorway of the tent of meeting before the LORD, where I will meet with you, to speak to you there. 43 I will meet there with the sons of Israel, and it shall be consecrated by My glory. 44 I will consecrate the tent of meeting and the altar; I will also consecrate Aaron and his sons to minister as priests to Me. 45 I will dwell among the sons of Israel and will be their God. 46 They shall know that I am the LORD their God who brought them out of the land of Egypt, that I might dwell among them; I am the LORD their God.

30 "Moreover, you shall make an altar as a place for burning incense; you shall make it of acacia wood. 2 Its length *shall be* a cubit, and its width a cubit, it shall be square, and its height *shall be* two cubits; its horns *shall be* of one piece with it. 3 You shall

29:45 I will dwell. That He would be their God and they would be His people was one thing, but that He would also dwell or tabernacle with them was a very important reality in the experience of the new nation. They were to understand not only the transcendence of their God, whose dwelling place was in the heaven of heavens, but also the immanence of their God, whose dwelling place was with them. Their redemption from Egypt was for this purpose (v. 46).

overlay it with pure gold, its top and its sides all around, and its horns; and you shall make a gold molding all around for it. 4 You shall make two gold rings for it under its molding; you shall make *them* on its two side walls—on opposite sides—and they shall be holders for poles with which to carry it. 5 You shall make the poles of acacia wood and overlay them with gold. 6 You shall put this altar in front of the veil that is near the ark of the testimony, in front of the mercy seat that is over *the ark of* the testimony, where I will meet with you. 7 Aaron shall burn fragrant incense on it; he shall burn it every morning when he trims the lamps. 8 When Aaron trims the lamps at twilight, he shall burn incense. *There shall be* perpetual incense before the LORD throughout your generations. 9 You shall not offer any strange incense on this altar, or burnt offering or meal offering; and you shall not pour out a drink offering on it. 10 Aaron shall make atonement on its horns once a year; he shall make atonement on it with the blood of the sin offering of atonement once a year throughout your generations. It is most holy to the LORD."

11 The LORD also spoke to Moses, saying, 12 "When you take a census of the sons of Israel to number them, then each one of them shall give a ransom for himself to the LORD, when you number them, so that there will be no plague among them when you number them. 13 This is what everyone who is numbered shall give: half a shekel according to the shekel of the sanctuary (the shekel is twenty gerahs), half a shekel as a contribution to the LORD. 14 Everyone who is numbered, from twenty years old and over, shall give the contribution to the LORD. 15 The rich shall not pay more and the poor shall not pay less than the half shekel, when you give the contribution to the LORD to make atonement for yourselves. 16 You shall take the atonement money from the sons of Israel and shall give it for the service of the tent of meeting, that it may be a memorial for the sons of Israel before the LORD, to make atonement for yourselves."

17 The LORD spoke to Moses, saying, 18 "You shall also make a laver of bronze, with its base of bronze, for washing; and you shall put it between the tent of meeting and the altar, and you shall put water in it. 19 Aaron and his sons shall wash their hands and their feet from it; 20 when they enter the tent of meeting, they shall wash with water, so that they will not die; or when they approach the altar to minister, by offering up in smoke a fire *sacrifice* to the LORD. 21 So they shall wash their hands and their feet, so that they will not die; and it shall

be a perpetual statute for them, for Aaron and his descendants throughout their generations."

²² Moreover, the LORD spoke to Moses, saying, ²³ "Take also for yourself the finest of spices: of flowing myrrh five hundred *shekels,* and of fragrant cinnamon half as much, two hundred and fifty, and of fragrant cane two hundred and fifty, ²⁴ and of cassia five hundred, according to the shekel of the sanctuary, and of olive oil a hin. ²⁵ You shall make of these a holy anointing oil, a perfume mixture, the work of a perfumer; it shall be a holy anointing oil. ²⁶ With it you shall anoint the tent of meeting and the ark of the testimony, ²⁷ and the table and all its utensils, and the lampstand and its utensils, and the altar of incense, ²⁸ and the altar of burnt offering and all its utensils, and the laver and its stand. ²⁹ You shall also consecrate them, that they may be most holy; whatever touches them shall be holy. ³⁰ You shall anoint Aaron and his sons, and consecrate them, that they may minister as priests to Me. ³¹ You shall speak to the sons of Israel, saying, 'This shall be a holy anointing oil to Me throughout your generations. ³² It shall not be poured on anyone's body, nor shall you make *any* like it in the same proportions; it is holy, *and* it shall be holy to you. ³³ Whoever shall mix *any* like it or whoever puts any of it on a layman shall be cut off from his people.' "

³⁴ Then the LORD said to Moses, "Take for yourself spices, stacte and onycha and galbanum, spices with pure frankincense; there shall be an equal part of each. ³⁵ With it you shall make incense, a perfume, the work of a perfumer, salted, pure, *and* holy. ³⁶ You shall beat some of it very fine, and put part of it before the testimony in the tent of meeting where I will meet with you; it shall be most holy to you. ³⁷ The incense which you shall make, you shall not make in the same proportions for yourselves; it shall be holy to you for the LORD. ³⁸ Whoever shall make *any* like it, to use as perfume, shall be cut off from his people."

Psalm 20:6–9

⁶ Now I know that the LORD
　　saves His anointed;
He will answer him from
　　His holy heaven
With the saving strength
　　of His right hand.
⁷ Some *boast* in chariots and
　　some in horses,
But we will boast in the name
　　of the LORD, our God.

20:7 Some *boast* **in…**Trust, boast, and praise must not be directed to the wrong objects but only to God Himself (see, e.g., Dt 17:16; 20:1–4; Lv 26:7–8; Ps 33:16–17; Is 31:1–3; Jer 9:23–24; Zec 4:6).

⁸ They have bowed down and fallen,
　　But we have risen and stood upright.
⁹ Save, O LORD;
　　May the King answer us
　　　　in the day we call.

Proverbs 7:6–23

⁶ For at the window of my house
　　I looked out through my lattice,
⁷ And I saw among the naive,
　　And discerned among the youths
　　A young man lacking sense,
⁸ Passing through the street
　　near her corner;
　　And he takes the way to her house,
⁹ In the twilight, in the evening,
　　In the middle of the night
　　　　and *in* the darkness.
¹⁰ And behold, a woman
　　comes to meet him,
　　Dressed as a harlot and
　　　　cunning of heart.
¹¹ She is boisterous and rebellious,
　　Her feet do not remain at home;
¹² *She is* now in the streets,
　　now in the squares,
　　And lurks by every corner.
¹³ So she seizes him and kisses him
　　And with a brazen face
　　　　she says to him:
¹⁴ "I was due to offer peace offerings;
　　Today I have paid my vows.
¹⁵ "Therefore I have come
　　out to meet you,
To seek your presence earnestly,
　　and I have found you.
¹⁶ "I have spread my couch
　　with coverings,
With colored linens of Egypt.
¹⁷ "I have sprinkled my bed
　　With myrrh, aloes and cinnamon.

7:8 takes the way. Against the advice of 4:14–15, he put himself right in the harlot's place. "Fleeing immorality" (1Co 6:18) starts by not being in the harlot's neighborhood at night.

¹⁸ "Come, let us drink our fill of
      love until morning;
   Let us delight ourselves with
      caresses.
¹⁹ "For my husband is not at home,
   He has gone on a long journey;
²⁰ He has taken a bag of
      money with him,
   At the full moon he will come home."
²¹ With her many persuasions
      she entices him;
   With her flattering lips
      she seduces him.
²² Suddenly he follows her
   As an ox goes to the slaughter,
   Or as one in fetters to the
      discipline of a fool,
²³ Until an arrow pierces
      through his liver;
   As a bird hastens to the snare,
   So he does not know that it
      will cost him his life.

Matthew 25:1–30

25 "Then the kingdom of heaven will be comparable to ten virgins, who took their lamps and went out to meet the bridegroom. ² Five of them were foolish, and five were prudent. ³ For when the foolish took their lamps, they took no oil with them, ⁴ but the prudent took oil in flasks along with their lamps. ⁵ Now while the bridegroom was delaying, they all got drowsy and began to sleep. ⁶ But at midnight there was a shout, 'Behold, the bridegroom! Come out to meet him.' ⁷ Then all those virgins rose and trimmed their lamps. ⁸ The foolish said to the prudent, 'Give us some of your oil, for our lamps are going out.' ⁹ But the prudent answered, 'No, there will not be enough for us and you too; go instead to the dealers and buy some for yourselves.' ¹⁰ And while they were going away to make the purchase, the bridegroom came, and those who were ready went in with him to the wedding feast; and the door was shut. ¹¹ Later the other virgins also came, saying, 'Lord, lord, open up for us.' ¹² But he answered, 'Truly I say to you, I do not know you.' ¹³ Be on the alert then, for you do not know the day nor the hour.

¹⁴ "For it is just like a man about to go on a journey, who called his own slaves and entrusted his possessions to them. ¹⁵ To one he gave five talents, to another, two, and to another, one, each according to his own ability; and he went on his journey. ¹⁶ Immediately the one who had received the five talents went and traded with them, and gained five more talents. ¹⁷ In the same manner the one who

had received the two talents gained two more. ¹⁸ But he who received the one talent went away, and dug a hole in the ground and hid his master's money.

¹⁹ "Now after a long time the master of those slaves *came and *settled accounts with them. ²⁰ The one who had received the five talents came up and brought five more talents, saying, 'Master, you entrusted five talents to me. See, I have gained five more talents.' ²¹ His master said to him, 'Well done, good and faithful slave. You were faithful with a few things, I will put you in charge of many things; enter into the joy of your master.' ²² "Also the one who had received the two talents came up and said, 'Master, you entrusted two talents to me. See, I have gained two more talents.' ²³ His master said to him, 'Well done, good and faithful slave. You were faithful with a few things, I will put you in charge of many things; enter into the joy of your master.'

²⁴ "And the one also who had received the one talent came up and said, 'Master, I knew you to be a hard man, reaping where you did not sow and gathering where you scattered no seed. ²⁵ And I was afraid, and went away and hid your talent in the ground. See, you have what is yours.'

²⁶ "But his master answered and said to him, 'You wicked, lazy slave, you knew that I reap where I did not sow and gather where I scattered no seed. ²⁷ Then you ought to have put my money in the bank, and on my arrival I would have received my money back with interest. ²⁸ Therefore take away the talent from him, and give it to the one who has the ten talents.'

²⁹ "For to everyone who has, more shall be given, and he will have an abundance; but from the one who does not have, even what he does not have shall be taken away. ³⁰ Throw out the worthless slave into the outer darkness; in that place there will be weeping and gnashing of teeth.

25:15 talents. A talent was a measure of weight, not a specific coin, so that a talent of gold was more valuable than a talent of silver. A talent of silver (the word translated "money" in v. 18 is literally silver) was a considerable sum of money. The modern meaning of the word "talent," denoting a natural ability, stems from the fact that this parable is erroneously applied to the stewardship of one's natural gifts.

DAY 9: What do the parables of the 10 virgins and of the talents tell us about Christ's second coming?

The parable of the 10 virgins (Mt 25:1-13) is given to underscore the importance of being ready for Christ's return in any event—even if He delays longer than expected. The wedding would begin at the bride's house when the bridegroom arrived to observe the wedding ritual. Then a procession would follow as the bridegroom took the bride to his house for the completion of festivities. For a night wedding, "lamps," which were actually torches, were needed for the procession. For those not prepared when He does return, there will be no second chances (vv. 11-12).

The parable of the talents (Mt 25:14-30) illustrates the tragedy of wasted opportunity. The man who goes on the journey represents Christ, and the servants represent professing believers given different levels of responsibility. Faithfulness is what he demands of them (v. 23), but the parable suggests that all who are faithful will be fruitful to some degree. Both the man with five talents and the man with two received exactly the same reward, "the joy of your master," indicating that the reward is based on faithfulness, not results. The slothful servant (v. 24) does not represent a genuine believer, for it is obvious that this man had no true knowledge of the master. This fruitless person is unmasked as a hypocrite and utterly destroyed (v. 30).

FEBRUARY 10

Exodus 31:1-32:35

31 Now the LORD spoke to Moses, saying, ² "See, I have called by name Bezalel, the son of Uri, the son of Hur, of the tribe of Judah. ³ I have filled him with the Spirit of God in wisdom, in understanding, in knowledge, and in all *kinds of* craftsmanship, ⁴ to make artistic designs for work in gold, in silver, and in bronze, ⁵ and in the cutting of stones for settings, and in the carving of wood, that he may work in all *kinds of* craftsmanship. ⁶ And behold, I Myself have appointed with him Oholiab, the son of Ahisamach, of the tribe of Dan; and in the hearts of all who are skillful I have put skill, that they may make all that I have commanded you: ⁷ the tent of meeting, and the ark of testimony, and the mercy seat upon it, and all the furniture of the tent, ⁸ the table also and its utensils, and the pure *gold* lampstand with all its utensils, and the altar of incense, ⁹ the altar of burnt offering also with all its utensils, and the laver and its stand, ¹⁰ the woven garments as well, and the holy garments for Aaron the priest, and the garments of his sons, *with which* to carry on their priesthood; ¹¹ the anointing oil also, and the fragrant incense for the holy place, they are to make *them* according to all that I have commanded you."

¹² The LORD spoke to Moses, saying, ¹³ "But as for you, speak to the sons of Israel, saying, 'You shall surely observe My sabbaths; for *this* is a sign between Me and you throughout your generations, that you may know that I am the LORD who sanctifies you. ¹⁴ Therefore you are to observe the sabbath, for it is holy to you. Everyone who profanes it shall surely be put to death; for whoever does any work on it, that person shall be cut off from among his people. ¹⁵ For six days work may be done, but on the seventh day there is a sabbath of complete rest, holy to the LORD; whoever does any work on the sabbath day shall surely be put to death. ¹⁶ So the sons of Israel shall observe the sabbath, to celebrate the sabbath throughout their generations as a perpetual covenant.' ¹⁷ It is a sign between Me and the sons of Israel forever; for in six days the LORD made heaven and earth, but on the seventh day He ceased *from labor,* and was refreshed."

¹⁸ When He had finished speaking with him upon Mount Sinai, He gave Moses the two tablets of the testimony, tablets of stone, written by the finger of God.

32 Now when the people saw that Moses delayed to come down from the mountain, the people assembled about Aaron and said to him, "Come, make us a god who will go before us; as for this Moses, the man who brought us up from the land of Egypt, we do not know what has become of him." ² Aaron said to them, "Tear off the gold rings which are in the ears of your wives, your sons, and your daughters, and bring *them* to me." ³ Then all the people tore off the gold rings which were in their ears and brought *them* to Aaron. ⁴ He took *this* from their hand, and fashioned it with a graving tool and made it into a molten calf; and they said, "This is your god, O Israel, who brought you up from the land of Egypt." ⁵ Now when Aaron saw *this,* he built an altar before it; and Aaron made a proclamation and said, "Tomorrow *shall be* a feast to the LORD." ⁶ So the next day they rose early and offered burnt offerings, and brought peace offerings; and

135

32:4 a molten calf. The young bull, which Aaron caused to be fashioned, was a pagan religious symbol of virile power. A miniature form of the golden calf, although made of bronze and silver, was found at the site of the ancient Philistine city of Ashkelon. Since it dates to about 1550 B.C. it indicates that calf worship was known not only in Egypt, but also in Canaan prior to the time of Moses. In worshiping the calf, the Israelites violated the first 3 commandments (20:3-7).

32:6 rose up to play. The Hebrew word allows for the inclusion of drunken and immoral activities so common to idolatrous fertility cults in their revelry (see the description in vv. 7, 25). Syncretism had robbed the people of all ethical alertness and moral discernment (1Co 10:7).

the people sat down to eat and to drink, and rose up to play.

⁷ Then the LORD spoke to Moses, "Go down at once, for your people, whom you brought up from the land of Egypt, have corrupted *themselves.* ⁸ They have quickly turned aside from the way which I commanded them. They have made for themselves a molten calf, and have worshiped it and have sacrificed to it and said, 'This is your god, O Israel, who brought you up from the land of Egypt!'" ⁹ The LORD said to Moses, "I have seen this people, and behold, they are an obstinate people. ¹⁰ Now then let Me alone, that My anger may burn against them and that I may destroy them; and I will make of you a great nation."

¹¹ Then Moses entreated the LORD his God, and said, "O LORD, why does Your anger burn against Your people whom You have brought out from the land of Egypt with great power and with a mighty hand? ¹² Why should the Egyptians speak, saying, 'With evil *intent* He brought them out to kill them in the mountains and to destroy them from the face of the earth'? Turn from Your burning anger and change Your mind about *doing* harm to Your people. ¹³ Remember Abraham, Isaac, and Israel, Your servants to whom You swore by Yourself, and said to them, 'I will multiply your descendants as the stars of the heavens, and all this land of which I have spoken I will give to your descendants, and they shall inherit *it* forever.'" ¹⁴ So the LORD changed His mind about the harm which He said He would do to His people.

¹⁵ Then Moses turned and went down from the mountain with the two tablets of the testimony in his hand, tablets which were written on both sides; they were written on one *side* and the other. ¹⁶ The tablets were God's work, and the writing was God's writing engraved on the tablets. ¹⁷ Now when Joshua heard the sound of the people as they shouted, he said to Moses, "There is a sound of war in the camp." ¹⁸ But he said,

"It is not the sound of the
    cry of triumph,
Nor is it the sound of the cry
    of defeat;
But the sound of singing I hear."

¹⁹ It came about, as soon as Moses came near the camp, that he saw the calf and *the* dancing; and Moses' anger burned, and he threw the tablets from his hands and shattered them at the foot of the mountain. ²⁰ He took the calf which they had made and burned *it* with fire, and ground it to powder, and scattered it over the surface of the water and made the sons of Israel drink *it.*

²¹ Then Moses said to Aaron, "What did this people do to you, that you have brought *such* great sin upon them?" ²² Aaron said, "Do not let the anger of my lord burn; you know the people yourself, that they are prone to evil. ²³ For they said to me, 'Make a god for us who will go before us; for this Moses, the man who brought us up from the land of Egypt, we do not know what has become of him.' ²⁴ I said to them, 'Whoever has any gold, let them tear it off.' So they gave *it* to me, and I threw it into the fire, and out came this calf."

²⁵ Now when Moses saw that the people were out of control—for Aaron had let them get out of control to be a derision among their enemies— ²⁶ then Moses stood in the gate of the camp, and said, "Whoever is for the LORD, *come* to me!" And all the sons of Levi gathered together to him. ²⁷ He said to them, "Thus says the LORD, the God of Israel, 'Every man *of you* put his sword upon his thigh, and go back and forth from gate to gate in the camp, and kill every man his brother, and every man his friend, and every man his neighbor.'" ²⁸ So the sons of Levi did as Moses instructed, and about three thousand men of the people fell that day. ²⁹ Then Moses said, "Dedicate yourselves today to the LORD—for every man has been against his son and against his brother—in order that He may bestow a blessing upon you today."

³⁰ On the next day Moses said to the people, "You yourselves have committed a great sin; and now I am going up to the LORD, perhaps

I can make atonement for your sin." ³¹ Then Moses returned to the LORD, and said, "Alas, this people has committed a great sin, and they have made a god of gold for themselves. ³² But now, if You will, forgive their sin—and if not, please blot me out from Your book which You have written!" ³³ The LORD said to Moses, "Whoever has sinned against Me, I will blot him out of My book. ³⁴ But go now, lead the people where I told you. Behold, My angel shall go before you; nevertheless in the day when I punish, I will punish them for their sin." ³⁵ Then the LORD smote the people, because of what they did with the calf which Aaron had made.

32:32 blot me out from Your book. Nothing more strongly marked the love of Moses for his people than his sincere willingness to offer up his own life rather than see them disinherited and destroyed. The book to which Moses referred, the psalmist entitled "the book of life" (Ps 69:28). Untimely or premature death would constitute being blotted out of the book. The apostle Paul displayed a similar passionate devotion for his kinsmen (Ro 9:1–3).

Psalm 21:1–7

For the choir director. A Psalm of David.

O LORD, in Your strength the
   king will be glad,
And in Your salvation how
   greatly he will rejoice!
² You have given him his heart's
   desire,
And You have not withheld
   the request of his lips.   *Selah*
³ For You meet him with the
   blessings of good things;
You set a crown of fine
   gold on his head.
⁴ He asked life of You,
You gave it to him,
Length of days forever and ever.
⁵ His glory is great through
   Your salvation,
Splendor and majesty You
   place upon him.

21:3 You set a crown of fine gold on his head. This is symbolic of superlative blessing (note the reversal in Eze 21:25–27).

⁶ For You make him most
   blessed forever;
You make him joyful with
   gladness in Your presence.

⁷ For the king trusts in the LORD,
And through the lovingkindness
   of the Most High he
   will not be shaken.

Proverbs 7:24–27

²⁴ Now therefore, *my* sons, listen
   to me,
And pay attention to the
   words of my mouth.
²⁵ Do not let your heart turn
   aside to her ways,
Do not stray into her paths.
²⁶ For many are the victims
   she has cast down,
And numerous are all her slain.
²⁷ Her house is the way to Sheol,
Descending to the chambers
   of death.

Matthew 25:31–46

³¹ "But when the Son of Man comes in His glory, and all the angels with Him, then He will sit on His glorious throne. ³² All the nations will be gathered before Him; and He will separate them from one another, as the shepherd separates the sheep from the goats; ³³ and He will put the sheep on His right, and the goats on the left. ³⁴ "Then the King will say to those on His right, 'Come, you who are blessed of My Father, inherit the kingdom prepared for you from the foundation of the world. ³⁵ For I was hungry, and you gave Me *something* to eat; I was thirsty, and you gave Me *something* to drink; I was a stranger, and you invited Me in; ³⁶ naked, and you clothed Me; I was sick, and you visited Me; I was in prison, and you came to Me.' ³⁷ Then the righteous will answer Him, 'Lord, when did we see You hungry, and feed You, or thirsty, and give You *something* to drink? ³⁸ And when did we see You a stranger, and invite You in, or naked, and clothe You? ³⁹ When did we see You sick, or in prison, and come to You?' ⁴⁰ The King will answer and say to them, 'Truly I say to you, to the extent that you did it to one of these brothers of Mine, *even the least of them,* you did it to Me.'

⁴¹ "Then He will also say to those on His left, 'Depart from Me, accursed ones, into the eternal fire which has been prepared for the devil and his angels; ⁴² for I was hungry, and you gave Me *nothing* to eat; I was thirsty, and you

gave Me nothing to drink; ⁴³I was a stranger, and you did not invite Me in; naked, and you did not clothe Me; sick, and in prison, and you did not visit Me.' ⁴⁴Then they themselves also will answer, 'Lord, when did we see You hungry, or thirsty, or a stranger, or naked, or sick, or in prison, and did not take care of You?' ⁴⁵Then He will answer them, 'Truly I say to you, to the extent that you did not do it to one of the least of these, you did not do it to Me.' ⁴⁶These will go away into eternal punishment, but the righteous into eternal life."

DAY 10: Did Jesus Christ believe in everlasting punishment for the wicked?

Look at His words in Matthew 25:46: "These will go away into eternal punishment, but the righteous into eternal life." The same Greek word is used in both instances. The punishment of the wicked is as never-ending as the bliss of the righteous. The wicked are not given a second chance, nor are they annihilated. The punishment of the wicked dead is described through-out Scripture as "eternal fire" (v. 41); "unquenchable fire" (3:12); "disgrace and everlasting con-tempt" (Da 12:2); a place where "THEIR WORM DOES NOT DIE, AND THE FIRE IS NOT QUENCHED" (Mk 9:44-49); a place of "torment" and "flame" (Lk 16:23-24); "eternal destruction" (2Th 1:9); a place of torment with "fire and brimstone" where "the smoke of their torment goes up forever and ever" (Rev 14:10-11); and a "lake of fire and brimstone" where the wicked are "tormented day and night forever and ever" (Rev 20:10).

Here Jesus indicates that the punishment itself is everlasting—not merely the smoke and flames. The wicked are forever subject to the fury and the wrath of God. They consciously suffer shame and contempt and the assaults of an accusing conscience—along with the fiery wrath of an offended deity—for all of eternity. Even hell will acknowledge the perfect justice of God (Ps 76:10); those who are there will know that their punishment is just and that they alone are to blame (see Dt 32:3-5).

FEBRUARY 11

Exodus 33:1–34:35

33 Then the LORD spoke to Moses, "De-part, go up from here, you and the people whom you have brought up from the land of Egypt, to the land of which I swore to Abraham, Isaac, and Jacob, saying, 'To your descendants I will give it.' ²I will send an angel before you and I will drive out the Canaanite, the Amorite, the Hittite, the Per-izzite, the Hivite and the Jebusite. ³*Go up* to a land flowing with milk and honey; for I will not go up in your midst, because you are an obstinate people, and I might destroy you on the way."

⁴When the people heard this sad word, they went into mourning, and none of them put on his ornaments. ⁵For the LORD had said to Moses, "Say to the sons of Israel, 'You are an obstinate people; should I go up in your midst for one moment, I would destroy you. Now therefore, put off your ornaments from you, that I may know what I shall do with you.'" ⁶So the sons of Israel stripped them-selves of their ornaments, from Mount Horeb *onward.*

⁷Now Moses used to take the tent and pitch it outside the camp, a good distance from the camp, and he called it the tent of meeting. And everyone who sought the LORD would go out to the tent of meeting which was outside the camp. ⁸And it came about, whenever Moses went out to the tent, that all the people would arise and stand, each at the entrance of his tent, and gaze after Moses until he entered the tent. ⁹Whenever Moses entered the tent, the pillar of cloud would descend and stand at the entrance of the tent; and the LORD would speak with Moses. ¹⁰When all the people saw the pillar of cloud standing at the entrance of the tent, all the people would arise and worship, each at the entrance of his tent. ¹¹Thus the LORD used to speak to Moses face to face, just as a man speaks to his friend. When Moses re-turned to the camp, his servant Joshua, the son of Nun, a young man, would not depart from the tent.

¹²Then Moses said to the LORD, "See, You say to me, 'Bring up this people!' But You Yourself have not let me know whom You will send with me. Moreover, You have said, 'I have known you by name, and you have also found favor in My sight.' ¹³Now therefore, I pray You, if I have found favor in Your sight, let me know Your ways that I may know You, so that I may find favor in Your sight. Consider too, that this nation is Your people." ¹⁴And He said, "My presence shall go *with you,* and I will give you rest." ¹⁵Then he said to Him,

"If Your presence does not go *with us,* do not lead us up from here. ¹⁶ For how then can it be known that I have found favor in Your sight, I and Your people? Is it not by Your going with us, so that we, I and Your people, may be distinguished from all the *other* people who are upon the face of the earth?"

¹⁷ The LORD said to Moses, "I will also do this thing of which you have spoken; for you have found favor in My sight and I have known you by name." ¹⁸ Then Moses said, "I pray You, show me Your glory!" ¹⁹ And He said, "I Myself will make all My goodness pass before you, and will proclaim the name of the LORD before you; and I will be gracious to whom I will be gracious, and will show compassion on whom I will show compassion." ²⁰ But He said, "You cannot see My face, for no man can see Me and live!" ²¹ Then the LORD said, "Behold, there is a place by Me, and you shall stand *there* on the rock; ²² and it will come about, while My glory is passing by, that I will put you in the cleft of the rock and cover you with My hand until I have passed by. ²³ Then I will take My hand away and you shall see My back, but My face shall not be seen."

33:12–17 Again Moses entered earnestly and confidently into the role of intercessor before God for the nation whom he again referred to as "Your people" (vv. 13, 16). Moses clearly understood that without God's presence they would not be a people set apart from other nations, so why travel any farther? Moses' favored standing before the Lord comes out in the positive response to his intercession (v. 17).

34 Now the LORD said to Moses, "Cut out for yourself two stone tablets like the former ones, and I will write on the tablets the words that were on the former tablets which you shattered. ² So be ready by morning, and come up in the morning to Mount Sinai, and present yourself there to Me on the top of the mountain. ³ No man is to come up with you, nor let any man be seen anywhere on the mountain; even the flocks and the herds may not graze in front of that mountain." ⁴ So he cut out two stone tablets like the former ones, and Moses rose up early in the morning and went up to Mount Sinai, as the LORD had commanded him, and he took two stone tablets in his hand. ⁵ The LORD descended in the cloud and stood there with him as he called upon the name of the LORD. ⁶ Then the LORD passed by in front of him and proclaimed, "The LORD, the LORD God, compassionate and gracious, slow to anger, and abounding in lovingkindness and truth; ⁷ who keeps lovingkindness for thousands, who forgives iniquity, transgression and sin; yet He will by no means leave *the guilty* unpunished, visiting the iniquity of fathers on the children and on the grandchildren to the third and fourth generations." ⁸ Moses made haste to bow low toward the earth and worship. ⁹ He said, "If now I have found favor in Your sight, O Lord, I pray, let the Lord go along in our midst, even though the people are so obstinate, and pardon our iniquity and our sin, and take us as Your own possession."

¹⁰ Then God said, "Behold, I am going to make a covenant. Before all your people I will perform miracles which have not been produced in all the earth nor among any of the nations; and all the people among whom you live will see the working of the LORD, for it is a fearful thing that I am going to perform with you.

¹¹ "Be sure to observe what I am commanding you this day: behold, I am going to drive out the Amorite before you, and the Canaanite, the Hittite, the Perizzite, the Hivite and the Jebusite. ¹² Watch yourself that you make no covenant with the inhabitants of the land into which you are going, or it will become a snare in your midst. ¹³ But *rather,* you are to tear down their altars and smash their *sacred* pillars and cut down their Asherim ¹⁴ —for you shall not worship any other god, for the LORD, whose name is Jealous, is a jealous God— ¹⁵ otherwise you might make a covenant with the inhabitants of the land and they would play the harlot with their gods and sacrifice to their gods, and someone might invite you to eat of his sacrifice, ¹⁶ and you might take some of his daughters for your sons, and his daughters might play the harlot with their gods and cause your sons *also* to play the harlot with their gods. ¹⁷ You shall make for yourself no molten gods.

¹⁸ "You shall observe the Feast of Unleavened Bread. For seven days you are to eat unleavened bread, as I commanded you, at the appointed time in the month of Abib, for in the month of Abib you came out of Egypt.

¹⁹ "The first offspring from every womb belongs to Me, and all your male livestock, the first offspring from cattle and sheep. ²⁰ You shall redeem with a lamb the first offspring from a donkey; and if you do not redeem

it, then you shall break its neck. You shall redeem all the firstborn of your sons. None shall appear before Me empty-handed.

21 "You shall work six days, but on the seventh day you shall rest; *even* during plowing time and harvest you shall rest. 22 You shall celebrate the Feast of Weeks, *that is,* the first fruits of the wheat harvest, and the Feast of Ingathering at the turn of the year. 23 Three times a year all your males are to appear before the Lord GOD, the God of Israel. 24 For I will drive out nations before you and enlarge your borders, and no man shall covet your land when you go up three times a year to appear before the LORD your God.

25 "You shall not offer the blood of My sacrifice with leavened bread, nor is the sacrifice of the Feast of the Passover to be left over until morning.

26 "You shall bring the very first of the first fruits of your soil into the house of the LORD your God.

"You shall not boil a young goat in its mother's milk."

27 Then the LORD said to Moses, "Write down these words, for in accordance with these words I have made a covenant with you and with Israel." 28 So he was there with the LORD forty days and forty nights; he did not eat bread or drink water. And he wrote on the tablets the words of the covenant, the Ten Commandments.

29 It came about when Moses was coming down from Mount Sinai (and the two tablets of the testimony *were* in Moses' hand as he was coming down from the mountain), that Moses did not know that the skin of his face shone because of his speaking with Him. 30 So when Aaron and all the sons of Israel saw Moses, behold, the skin of his face shone, and they were afraid to come near him. 31 Then Moses called to them, and Aaron and all the rulers in the congregation returned to him; and Moses spoke to them. 32 Afterward all the sons of Israel came near, and he commanded them *to do* everything that the LORD had spoken to him on Mount Sinai. 33 When Moses had finished speaking with them, he put a veil over his face. 34 But whenever Moses went in before the LORD to speak with Him, he would take off the veil until he came out; and whenever he came out and spoke to the sons of Israel what he had been commanded, 35 the sons of Israel would see the face of Moses, that the skin of Moses' face shone. So Moses would replace the veil over his face until he went in to speak with Him.

Psalm 21:8–13

8 Your hand will find out
   all your enemies;
 Your right hand will find out
   those who hate you.
9 You will make them as a fiery oven
   in the time of your anger;
 The LORD will swallow them
   up in His wrath,
 And fire will devour them.
10 Their offspring You will
   destroy from the earth,
 And their descendants from
   among the sons of men.
11 Though they intended
   evil against You
 And devised a plot,
 They will not succeed.
12 For You will make them
   turn their back;
 You will aim with Your
   bowstrings at their faces.
13 Be exalted, O LORD, in Your
   strength;
 We will sing and praise
   Your power.

Proverbs 8:1–5

8 Does not wisdom call,
   And understanding lift up
   her voice?
2 On top of the heights beside
   the way,
 Where the paths meet, she
   takes her stand;
3 Beside the gates, at the
   opening to the city,
 At the entrance of the
   doors, she cries out:
4 "To you, O men, I call,
 And my voice is to the sons of men.
5 "O naive ones, understand prudence;
 And, O fools, understand wisdom.

Matthew 26:1–25

26 When Jesus had finished all these words, He said to His disciples, 2 "You know that after two days the Passover is coming, and the Son of Man is *to be* handed over for crucifixion."

3 Then the chief priests and the elders of the people were gathered together in the court of the high priest, named Caiaphas; 4 and they plotted together to seize Jesus by stealth and kill Him. 5 But they were saying, "Not during the festival, otherwise a riot might occur among the people."

6 Now when Jesus was in Bethany, at the

26:2 Passover. This was God's chosen time for Christ to die. He was the antitype to which the Passover Lamb had always referred. Christ had always avoided His enemies' plots to kill Him (Lk 4:29–30; Jn 5:18; 10:39), but now it was His time. The true Lamb of God would take away the sin of the world (Jn 1:29).

26:11 For you always have the poor with you. Jesus certainly was not disparaging ministry to the poor—especially so soon after the lesson of the sheep and goats judgment (25:35–36). However, He revealed here that there is a higher priority than any other earthly ministry, and that is worship rendered to Him. This would be an utter blasphemy for anyone less than God, so yet again He was implicitly affirming His deity.

home of Simon the leper, ⁷a woman came to Him with an alabaster vial of very costly perfume, and she poured it on His head as He reclined *at the table.* ⁸But the disciples were indignant when they saw *this,* and said, "Why this waste? ⁹For this *perfume* might have been sold for a high price and *the money* given to the poor." ¹⁰But Jesus, aware of this, said to them, "Why do you bother the woman? For she has done a good deed to Me. ¹¹For you always have the poor with you; but you do not always have Me. ¹²For when she poured this perfume on My body, she did it to prepare Me for burial. ¹³Truly I say to you, wherever this gospel is preached in the whole world, what this woman has done will also be spoken of in memory of her."

¹⁴Then one of the twelve, named Judas Iscariot, went to the chief priests ¹⁵and said, "What are you willing to give me to betray Him to you?" And they weighed out thirty pieces of silver to him. ¹⁶From then on he *began* looking for a good opportunity to betray Jesus.

¹⁷Now on the first *day* of Unleavened Bread the disciples came to Jesus and asked, "Where do You want us to prepare for You to eat the Passover?" ¹⁸And He said, "Go into the city to a certain man, and say to him, 'The Teacher says, "My time is near; I *am to* keep the Passover at your house with My disciples."'" ¹⁹The disciples did as Jesus had directed them; and they prepared the Passover.

²⁰Now when evening came, Jesus was reclining *at the table* with the twelve disciples. ²¹As they were eating, He said, "Truly I say to you that one of you will betray Me." ²²Being deeply grieved, they each one began to say to Him, "Surely not I, Lord?" ²³And He answered, "He who dipped his hand with Me in the bowl is the one who will betray Me. ²⁴The Son of Man *is to* go, just as it is written of Him; but woe to that man by whom the Son of Man is betrayed! It would have been good for that man if he had not been born." ²⁵And Judas, who was betraying Him, said, "Surely it is not I, Rabbi?" Jesus *said to him, "You have said *it* yourself."

DAY 11: How does Moses' veiled face represent the inadequacy of the Old Covenant?

The first time on Mount Sinai (Ex 24:12—32:14), unlike the second time (34:29–35), had not left Moses with a face which was reflecting some radiance associated with being in the presence of the Lord for an extended period of time.

The second time, in comparison with the first, was not interrupted by the Lord's sending Moses away because of sin in the camp (32:7–10). A compliant and not defiant people feared the evidence of God's presence. When not speaking to the Lord or authoritatively on His behalf to the people, Moses veiled his face.

The apostle Paul advised that the veil prevented the people from seeing a fading glory and related it to the inadequacy of the Old Covenant and the blindness of the Jews in his day (2Co 3:7–18). Paul says that "we all," not just Moses, or prophets, apostles, and preachers, but all believers are "with unveiled face." Believers in the New Covenant have nothing obstructing their vision of Christ and His glory as revealed in the Scripture. Though the vision is unobstructed and intimate ("beholding as in a mirror"), believers do not see a perfect representation of God's glory now, but will one day (see 1Co 13:12). As they gaze at the glory of the Lord, believers are continually being transformed into Christlikeness. The ultimate goal of the believer is to be like Christ (see Ro 8:29; Php 3:12–14; 1Jn 3:2), and by continually focusing on Him the Spirit transforms the believer more and more into His image. "From glory to glory"—from one level of manifesting Christ to another. The more believers grow in their knowledge of Christ, the more He is revealed in their lives (see Php 3:12–14).

FEBRUARY 12

Exodus 35:1–36:38

35 Then Moses assembled all the congregation of the sons of Israel, and said to them, "These are the things that the LORD has commanded you to do:

2 "For six days work may be done, but on the seventh day you shall have a holy day, a sabbath of complete rest to the LORD; whoever does any work on it shall be put to death. 3 You shall not kindle a fire in any of your dwellings on the sabbath day."

4 Moses spoke to all the congregation of the sons of Israel, saying, "This is the thing which the LORD has commanded, saying, 5 'Take from among you a contribution to the LORD; whoever is of a willing heart, let him bring it as the LORD'S contribution: gold, silver, and bronze, 6 and blue, purple and scarlet material, fine linen, goats' hair, 7 and rams' skins dyed red, and porpoise skins, and acacia wood, 8 and oil for lighting, and spices for the anointing oil, and for the fragrant incense, 9 and onyx stones and setting stones for the ephod and for the breastpiece.

10 'Let every skillful man among you come, and make all that the LORD has commanded: 11 the tabernacle, its tent and its covering, its hooks and its boards, its bars, its pillars, and its sockets; 12 the ark and its poles, the mercy seat, and the curtain of the screen; 13 the table and its poles, and all its utensils, and the bread of the Presence; 14 the lampstand also for the light and its utensils and its lamps and the oil for the light; 15 and the altar of incense and its poles, and the anointing oil and the fragrant incense, and the screen for the doorway at the entrance of the tabernacle; 16 the altar of burnt offering with its bronze grating, its poles, and all its utensils, the basin and its stand; 17 the hangings of the court, its pillars and its sockets, and the screen for the gate of the court; 18 the pegs of the tabernacle and the pegs of the court and their cords; 19 the woven garments for ministering in the holy place, the holy garments for Aaron the priest and the garments of his sons, to minister as priests.'"

20 Then all the congregation of the sons of Israel departed from Moses' presence. 21 Everyone whose heart stirred him and everyone whose spirit moved him came and brought the LORD'S contribution for the work of the tent of meeting and for all its service and for the holy garments. 22 Then all whose hearts moved them, both men and women, came and brought brooches and earrings and sig-

net rings and bracelets, all articles of gold; so did every man who presented an offering of gold to the LORD. 23 Every man, who had in his possession blue and purple and scarlet material and fine linen and goats' hair and rams' skins dyed red and porpoise skins, brought them. 24 Everyone who could make a contribution of silver and bronze brought the LORD'S contribution; and every man who had in his possession acacia wood for any work of the service brought it. 25 All the skilled women spun with their hands, and brought what they had spun, in blue and purple and scarlet material and in fine linen. 26 All the women whose heart stirred with a skill spun the goats' hair. 27 The rulers brought the onyx stones and the stones for setting for the ephod and for the breastpiece; 28 and the spice and the oil for the light and for the anointing oil and for the fragrant incense. 29 The Israelites, all the men and women, whose heart moved them to bring material for all the work, which the LORD had commanded through Moses to be done, brought a freewill offering to the LORD.

30 Then Moses said to the sons of Israel, "See, the LORD has called by name Bezalel the son of Uri, the son of Hur, of the tribe of Judah. 31 And He has filled him with the Spirit of God, in wisdom, in understanding and in knowledge and in all craftsmanship; 32 to make designs for working in gold and in silver and in bronze, 33 and in the cutting of stones for settings and in the carving of wood, so as to perform in every inventive work. 34 He also has put in his heart to teach, both he and Oholiab, the son of Ahisamach, of the tribe of Dan. 35 He has filled them with skill to perform every work of an engraver and of a designer and of an embroiderer, in blue and in purple and in scarlet material, and in fine linen, and of a weaver, as performers of every work and makers of designs.

36 "Now Bezalel and Oholiab, and every skillful person in whom the LORD has put skill and understanding to know how to perform all the work in the construction of the sanctuary, shall perform in accordance with all that the LORD has commanded."

2 Then Moses called Bezalel and Oholiab and every skillful person in whom the LORD had put skill, everyone whose heart stirred him, to come to the work to perform it. 3 They received from Moses all the contributions which the sons of Israel had brought to perform the work in the construction of the sanctuary. And they still continued bringing to him freewill offerings every morning. 4 And all the skillful men who were performing all the work of the

sanctuary came, each from the work which he was performing, [5] and they said to Moses, "The people are bringing much more than enough for the construction work which the LORD commanded us to perform." [6] So Moses issued a command, and a proclamation was circulated throughout the camp, saying, "Let no man or woman any longer perform work for the contributions of the sanctuary." Thus the people were restrained from bringing *any more*. [7] For the material they had was sufficient and more than enough for all the work, to perform it.

[8] All the skillful men among those who were performing the work made the tabernacle with ten curtains; of fine twisted linen and blue and purple and scarlet *material,* with cherubim, the work of a skillful workman, Bezalel made them. [9] The length of each curtain was twenty-eight cubits and the width of each curtain four cubits; all the curtains had the same measurements. [10] He joined five curtains to one another and *the other* five curtains he joined to one another. [11] He made loops of blue on the edge of the outermost curtain in the first set; he did likewise on the edge of the curtain that was outermost in the second set. [12] He made fifty loops in the one curtain and he made fifty loops on the edge of the curtain that was in the second set; the loops were opposite each other. [13] He made fifty clasps of gold and joined the curtains to one another with the clasps, so the tabernacle was a unit.

[14] Then he made curtains of goats' *hair* for a tent over the tabernacle; he made eleven curtains in all. [15] The length of each curtain *was* thirty cubits and four cubits the width of each curtain; the eleven curtains had the same measurements. [16] He joined five curtains by themselves and *the other* six curtains by themselves. [17] Moreover, he made fifty loops on the edge of the curtain that was outermost in the *first* set, and he made fifty loops on the edge of the curtain *that was outermost in* the second set. [18] He made fifty clasps of bronze to join the tent together so that it would be a unit. [19] He made a covering for the tent of rams' skins dyed red, and a covering of porpoise skins above.

[20] Then he made the boards for the tabernacle of acacia wood, standing upright. [21] Ten cubits *was* the length of each board and one and a half cubits the width of each board. [22] *There were* two tenons for each board, fitted to one another; thus he did for all the boards of the tabernacle. [23] He made the boards for the tabernacle: twenty boards for the south side; [24] and he made forty sockets of silver under the twenty boards; two sockets under

one board for its two tenons and two sockets under another board for its two tenons. [25] Then for the second side of the tabernacle, on the north side, he made twenty boards, [26] and their forty sockets of silver; two sockets under one board and two sockets under another board. [27] For the rear of the tabernacle, to the west, he made six boards. [28] He made two boards for the corners of the tabernacle at the rear. [29] They were double beneath, and together they were complete to its top to the first ring; thus he did with both of them for the two corners. [30] There were eight boards with their sockets of silver, sixteen sockets, two under every board. [31] Then he made bars of acacia wood, five for the boards of one side of the tabernacle, [32] and five bars for the boards of the other side of the tabernacle, and five bars for the boards of the tabernacle for the rear *side* to the west. [33] He made the middle bar to pass through in the center of the boards from end to end. [34] He overlaid the boards with gold and made their rings of gold *as* holders for the bars, and overlaid the bars with gold.

[35] Moreover, he made the veil of blue and purple and scarlet *material,* and fine twisted linen; he made it with cherubim, the work of a skillful workman. [36] He made four pillars of acacia for it, and overlaid them with gold, with their hooks of gold; and he cast four sockets of silver for them. [37] He made a screen for the doorway of the tent, of blue and purple and scarlet *material,* and fine twisted linen, the work of a weaver; [38] and *he made* its five pillars with their hooks, and he overlaid their tops and their bands with gold; but their five sockets were of bronze.

Psalm 22:1-8

For the choir director; upon Aijeleth Hashshahar. A Psalm of David.

M y God, my God, why have You forsaken me?
Far from my deliverance are the words of my groaning.

22:1 This heavy lament rivals Job 3; Psalm 69; Jeremiah 20:14-18. **My God, my God, why have You forsaken me?** The repeated noun of direct address to God reflects a personal molecule of hope in a seemingly hopeless situation. "Forsaken" is a strong expression for personal abandonment, intensely felt by David and supremely experienced by Christ on the cross (Mt 27:46).

2 O my God, I cry by day, but
   You do not answer;
   And by night, but I have no rest.
3 Yet You are holy,
   O You who are enthroned upon
   the praises of Israel.
4 In You our fathers trusted;
   They trusted and You delivered
   them.
5 To You they cried out and
   were delivered;
   In You they trusted and were
   not disappointed.

6 But I am a worm and not a man,
   A reproach of men and
   despised by the people.
7 All who see me sneer at me;
   They separate with the lip, they
   wag the head, *saying,*
8 "Commit *yourself* to the LORD;
   let Him deliver him;
   Let Him rescue him, because
   He delights in him."

Proverbs 8:6-11

6 "Listen, for I will speak noble
   things;
   And the opening of my lips
   will reveal right things.
7 "For my mouth will utter truth;
   And wickedness is an
   abomination to my lips.
8 "All the utterances of my mouth
   are in righteousness;
   There is nothing crooked or
   perverted in them.
9 "They are all straightforward to
   him who understands,
   And right to those who
   find knowledge.
10 "Take my instruction and not
   silver,
   And knowledge rather
   than choicest gold.
11 "For wisdom is better than
   jewels;
   And all desirable things cannot
   compare with her.

8:10-11 The most valuable reality a young person can attain is the insight to order his life by the standard of truth (see 3:14-15; 8:18-21; also Job 28:12-28; Ps 19:10).

Matthew 26:26-50

26 While they were eating, Jesus took *some* bread, and after a blessing, He broke *it* and gave *it* to the disciples, and said, "Take, eat; this is My body." 27 And when He had taken a cup and given thanks, He gave *it* to them, saying, "Drink from it, all of you; 28 for this is My blood of the covenant, which is poured out for many for forgiveness of sins. 29 But I say to you, I will not drink of this fruit of the vine from now on until that day when I drink it new with you in My Father's kingdom."

30 After singing a hymn, they went out to the Mount of Olives.

31 Then Jesus *said to them, "You will all fall away because of Me this night, for it is written, 'I WILL STRIKE DOWN THE SHEPHERD, AND THE SHEEP OF THE FLOCK SHALL BE SCATTERED.' 32 But after I have been raised, I will go ahead of you to Galilee." 33 But Peter said to Him, "*Even* though all may fall away because of You, I will never fall away." 34 Jesus said to him, "Truly I say to you that this *very* night, before a rooster crows, you will deny Me three times." 35 Peter *said to Him, "Even if I have to die with You, I will not deny You." All the disciples said the same thing too.

36 Then Jesus *came with them to a place called Gethsemane, and *said to His disciples, "Sit here while I go over there and pray." 37 And He took with Him Peter and the two sons of Zebedee, and began to be grieved and distressed. 38 Then He *said to them, "My soul is deeply grieved, to the point of death; remain here and keep watch with Me."

39 And He went a little beyond *them,* and fell on His face and prayed, saying, "My

26:39 this cup. See v. 42. A cup is often the symbol of divine wrath against sin in the Old Testament (Is 51:17, 22; Jer 25:15-17, 27-29; La 4:21-22; Eze 23:31-34; Hab 2:16). The next day Christ would "bear the sins of many" (Heb 9:28)—and the fullness of divine wrath would fall on Him (Is 53:10-11; 2Co 5:21). This was the price of the sin He bore, and He paid it in full. His cry of anguish in 27:46 reflects the extreme bitterness of the cup of wrath He was given. **not as I will, but as You will.** This implies no conflict between the Persons of the Godhead. Rather, it graphically reveals how Christ in His humanity voluntarily surrendered His will to the will of the Father in all things—precisely so that there would be no conflict between the divine will and His desires. See John 4:34; 6:38; 8:29; Philippians 2:8.

Father, if it is possible, let this cup pass from Me; yet not as I will, but as You will." ⁴⁰And He *came to the disciples and *found them sleeping, and *said to Peter, "So, you *men* could not keep watch with Me for one hour? ⁴¹Keep watching and praying that you may not enter into temptation; the spirit is willing, but the flesh is weak."

⁴²He went away again a second time and prayed, saying, "My Father, if this cannot pass away unless I drink it, Your will be done." ⁴³Again He came and found them sleeping, for their eyes were heavy. ⁴⁴And He left them again, and went away and prayed a third time, saying the same thing once more. ⁴⁵Then He *came to the disciples and *said to them, "Are

you still sleeping and resting? Behold, the hour is at hand and the Son of Man is being betrayed into the hands of sinners. ⁴⁶Get up, let us be going; behold, the one who betrays Me is at hand!"

⁴⁷While He was still speaking, behold, Judas, one of the twelve, came up accompanied by a large crowd with swords and clubs, *who came* from the chief priests and elders of the people. ⁴⁸Now he who was betraying Him gave them a sign, saying, "Whomever I kiss, He is the one; seize Him." ⁴⁹Immediately Judas went to Jesus and said, "Hail, Rabbi!" and kissed Him. ⁵⁰And Jesus said to him, "Friend, *do* what you have come for." Then they came and laid hands on Jesus and seized Him.

DAY 12: Why did Jesus institute the Lord's Supper?

In Matthew 26:26, "Jesus took some bread, and after a blessing, He broke it and gave it to the disciples, and said, 'Take, eat; this is My body,'" thus transforming His last Passover into the first observance of the Lord's Supper. He is the central antitype in both ceremonies, being represented symbolically by both the paschal lamb of the Passover and the elements in the communion service. His statement, "this is My body," could not possibly have been taken in any literal sense by the disciples present that evening. Such metaphorical language was a typical Hebraism. No eucharistic miracle of transubstantiation was implied, nor could the disciples have missed the symbolic intent of His statement, for His actual body—yet unbroken—was before their very eyes.

When He took the cup of wine, He said that this is "My blood of the covenant" (v. 28). Covenants were ratified with the blood of a sacrifice (Ge 8:20; 15:9–10). Jesus' words here echo Moses' pronouncement in Exodus 24:8. The blood of the New Covenant is not an animal's blood, but Christ's own blood, shed for the remission of sins. See Jeremiah 31:31–34; Hebrews 8:1–10:18, especially 8:6. Thus He established the observance as an ordinance for worship (1Co 11:23–26). Passover had looked forward to the sacrifice of Christ; He transformed it into an altogether different ceremony, which looks back in remembrance at His atoning death.

☙ FEBRUARY 13

Exodus 37:1–38:31

37 Now Bezalel made the ark of acacia wood; its length was two and a half cubits, and its width one and a half cubits, and its height one and a half cubits; ²and he overlaid it with pure gold inside and out, and made a gold molding for it all around. ³He cast four rings of gold for it on its four feet; even two rings on one side of it, and two rings on the other side of it. ⁴He made poles of acacia wood and overlaid them with gold. ⁵He put the poles into the rings on the sides of the ark, to carry it. ⁶He made a mercy seat of pure gold, two and a half cubits long and one and a half cubits wide. ⁷He made two cherubim of gold; he made them of hammered work at the two ends of the mercy seat; ⁸one cherub at the one end and one cherub at the other end;

he made the cherubim *of one piece* with the mercy seat at the two ends. ⁹The cherubim had *their* wings spread upward, covering the mercy seat with their wings, with their faces toward each other; the faces of the cherubim were toward the mercy seat.

¹⁰Then he made the table of acacia wood, two cubits long and a cubit wide and one and a half cubits high. ¹¹He overlaid it with pure gold, and made a gold molding for it all around. ¹²He made a rim for it of a handbreadth all around, and made a gold molding for its rim all around. ¹³He cast four gold rings for it and put the rings on the four corners that were on its four feet. ¹⁴Close by the rim were the rings, the holders for the poles to carry the table. ¹⁵He made the poles of acacia wood and overlaid them with gold, to carry the table. ¹⁶He made the utensils which were on the table, its dishes and its pans and its bowls and its jars, with which to pour out drink offerings, of pure gold.

¹⁷Then he made the lampstand of pure gold. He made the lampstand of hammered work, its base and its shaft; its cups, its bulbs and its flowers were *of one piece* with it. ¹⁸There were six branches going out of its sides; three branches of the lampstand from the one side of it and three branches of the lampstand from the other side of it; ¹⁹three cups shaped like almond *blossoms,* a bulb and a flower in one branch, and three cups shaped like almond *blossoms,* a bulb and a flower in the other branch—so for the six branches going out of the lampstand. ²⁰In the lampstand *there were* four cups shaped like almond *blossoms,* its bulbs and its flowers; ²¹and a bulb was under the *first* pair of branches *coming* out of it, and a bulb under the *second* pair of branches *coming* out of it, and a bulb under the *third* pair of branches *coming* out of it, for the six branches coming out of the lampstand. ²²Their bulbs and their branches were *of one piece* with it; the whole of it *was* a single hammered work of pure gold. ²³He made its seven lamps with its snuffers and its trays of pure gold. ²⁴He made it and all its utensils from a talent of pure gold.

²⁵Then he made the altar of incense of acacia wood: a cubit long and a cubit wide, square, and two cubits high; its horns were *of one piece* with it. ²⁶He overlaid it with pure gold, its top and its sides all around, and its horns; and he made a gold molding for it all around. ²⁷He made two golden rings for it under its molding, on its two sides—on opposite sides—as holders for poles with which to carry it. ²⁸He made the poles of acacia wood and overlaid them with gold. ²⁹And he made the holy anointing oil and the pure, fragrant incense of spices, the work of a perfumer.

38 Then he made the altar of burnt offering of acacia wood, five cubits long, and five cubits wide, square, and three cubits high. ²He made its horns on its four corners, its horns being *of one piece* with it, and he overlaid it with bronze. ³He made all the utensils of the altar, the pails and the shovels and the basins, the flesh hooks and the firepans; he made all its utensils of bronze. ⁴He made for the altar a grating of bronze network beneath, under its ledge, reaching halfway up. ⁵He cast four rings on the four ends of the bronze grating *as* holders for the poles. ⁶He made the poles of acacia wood and overlaid them with bronze. ⁷He inserted the poles into the rings on the sides of the altar, with which to carry it. He made it hollow with planks.

⁸Moreover, he made the laver of bronze with its base of bronze, from the mirrors of the serving women who served at the doorway of the tent of meeting.

⁹Then he made the court: for the south side the hangings of the court were of fine twisted linen, one hundred cubits; ¹⁰their twenty pillars, and their twenty sockets, *made* of bronze; the hooks of the pillars and their bands *were* of silver. ¹¹For the north side *there were* one hundred cubits; their twenty pillars and their twenty sockets *were* of bronze, the hooks of the pillars and their bands *were* of silver. ¹²For the west side *there were* hangings of fifty cubits *with* their ten pillars and their ten sockets; the hooks of the pillars and their bands *were* of silver. ¹³For the east side fifty cubits. ¹⁴The hangings for the one side *of the gate were* fifteen cubits, *with* their three pillars and their three sockets, ¹⁵and so for the other side. On both sides of the gate of the court *were* hangings of fifteen cubits, *with* their three pillars and their three sockets. ¹⁶All the hangings of the court all around *were* of fine twisted linen. ¹⁷The sockets for the pillars *were* of bronze, the hooks of the pillars and their bands, of silver; and the overlaying of their tops, of silver, and all the pillars of the court were furnished with silver bands. ¹⁸The screen of the gate of the court was the work of the weaver, of blue and purple and scarlet *material* and fine twisted linen. And the length *was* twenty cubits and the height *was* five cubits, corresponding to the hangings of the court. ¹⁹Their four pillars and their four sockets *were* of bronze; their hooks *were* of silver, and the overlaying of their tops and their bands *were* of silver. ²⁰All the pegs of the tabernacle and of the court all around *were* of bronze.

²¹This is the number of the things for the tabernacle, the tabernacle of the testimony, as they were numbered according to the command of Moses, for the service of the Levites, by the hand of Ithamar the son of Aaron the priest. ²²Now Bezalel the son of Uri, the son of Hur, of the tribe of Judah, made all that the LORD had commanded Moses. ²³With him *was* Oholiab the son of Ahisamach, of the tribe of Dan, an engraver and a skillful workman and a weaver in blue and in purple and in scarlet *material,* and fine linen.

²⁴All the gold that was used for the work, in all the work of the sanctuary, even the gold of the wave offering, was 29 talents and 730 shekels, according to the shekel of the sanctuary. ²⁵The silver of those of the congregation who were numbered was 100 talents and 1,775 shekels, according to the shekel of the sanctuary; ²⁶a beka a head (*that is,* half a shekel according to the shekel of the sanctu-

ary), for each one who passed over to those who were numbered, from twenty years old and upward, for 603,550 men. ²⁷ The hundred talents of silver were for casting the sockets of the sanctuary and the sockets of the veil; one hundred sockets for the hundred talents, a talent for a socket. ²⁸ Of the 1,775 *shekels,* he made hooks for the pillars and overlaid their tops and made bands for them. ²⁹ The bronze of the wave offering was 70 talents and 2,400 shekels. ³⁰ With it he made the sockets to the doorway of the tent of meeting, and the bronze altar and its bronze grating, and all the utensils of the altar, ³¹ and the sockets of the court all around and the sockets of the gate of the court, and all the pegs of the tabernacle and all the pegs of the court all around.

Psalm 22:9–15

9 Yet You are He who brought
    me forth from the womb;
  You made me trust *when* upon
    my mother's breasts.
¹⁰ Upon You I was cast from birth;
  You have been my God from
    my mother's womb.

¹¹ Be not far from me, for trouble is near;
  For there is none to help.
¹² Many bulls have surrounded me;
  Strong *bulls* of Bashan
    have encircled me.
¹³ They open wide their mouth at me,
  As a ravening and a roaring lion.
¹⁴ I am poured out like water,
  And all my bones are out of joint;
  My heart is like wax;
  It is melted within me.
¹⁵ My strength is dried up
    like a potsherd,
  And my tongue cleaves to my jaws;
  And You lay me in the dust of death.

Proverbs 8:12–21

¹² "I, wisdom, dwell with prudence,
  And I find knowledge *and* discretion.
¹³ "The fear of the LORD is to hate evil;
  Pride and arrogance and the evil way
  And the perverted mouth, I hate.
¹⁴ "Counsel is mine and sound wisdom;
  I am understanding, power is mine.
¹⁵ "By me kings reign,
  And rulers decree justice.
¹⁶ "By me princes rule, and nobles,
  All who judge rightly.
¹⁷ "I love those who love me;
  And those who diligently
    seek me will find me.

¹⁸ "Riches and honor are with me,
  Enduring wealth and righteousness.
¹⁹ "My fruit is better than gold,
    even pure gold,
  And my yield *better* than
    choicest silver.
²⁰ "I walk in the way of righteousness,
  In the midst of the paths of justice,
²¹ To endow those who love
    me with wealth,
  That I may fill their treasuries.

Matthew 26:51–75

⁵¹ And behold, one of those who were with Jesus reached and drew out his sword, and struck the slave of the high priest and cut off his ear. ⁵² Then Jesus *said to him, "Put your sword back into its place; for all those who take up the sword shall perish by the sword. ⁵³ Or do you think that I cannot appeal to My Father, and He will at once put at My disposal more than twelve legions of angels? ⁵⁴ How then will the Scriptures be fulfilled, *which say* that it must happen this way?"

⁵⁵ At that time Jesus said to the crowds, "Have you come out with swords and clubs to arrest Me as *you would* against a robber? Every day I used to sit in the temple teaching and you did not seize Me. ⁵⁶ But all this has taken place to fulfill the Scriptures of the prophets." Then all the disciples left Him and fled.

⁵⁷ Those who had seized Jesus led Him away to Caiaphas, the high priest, where the scribes and the elders were gathered together. ⁵⁸ But Peter was following Him at a distance as far as the courtyard of the high priest, and entered in, and sat down with the officers to see the outcome.

⁵⁹ Now the chief priests and the whole Council kept trying to obtain false testimony against Jesus, so that they might put Him to

26:57 Caiaphas, the high priest. From John 18:13, we learn that Christ was taken first to Annas (former High Priest and father-in-law to Caiaphas). He then was sent bound to Caiaphas' house (Jn 18:24). The conspiracy was well planned, so that "the scribes and the elders" (the Sanhedrin) were already "gathered" at Caiaphas' house and ready to try Jesus. The time was sometime between midnight and the first rooster's crowing (v. 74). Such a hearing was illegal on several counts: criminal trials were not to be held at night; and trials in capital cases could only be held at the temple and only in public.

death. ⁶⁰They did not find *any,* even though many false witnesses came forward. But later on two came forward, ⁶¹and said, "This man stated, 'I am able to destroy the temple of God and to rebuild it in three days.'" ⁶²The high priest stood up and said to Him, "Do You not answer? What is it that these men are testifying against You?" ⁶³But Jesus kept silent. And the high priest said to Him, "I adjure You by the living God, that You tell us whether You are the Christ, the Son of God." ⁶⁴Jesus *said to him, "You have said it *yourself;* nevertheless I tell you, hereafter you will see THE SON OF MAN SITTING AT THE RIGHT HAND OF POWER, and COMING ON THE CLOUDS OF HEAVEN."

⁶⁵Then the high priest tore his robes and said, "He has blasphemed! What further need do we have of witnesses? Behold, you have now heard the blasphemy; ⁶⁶what do you think?" They answered, "He deserves death!"

26:59 the whole Council. The great Sanhedrin was the Supreme Court of Israel, consisting of 71 members, presided over by the High Priest. They met daily in the temple to hold court, except on the Sabbath and other holy days. Technically, they did not have the power to administer capital punishment (Jn 18:31), but in the case of Stephen, for example, this was no deterrent to his stoning (Ac 6:12–14; 7:58–60). Roman governors evidently sometimes ignored such incidents as a matter of political expediency. In Jesus' case, the men who were trying Him were the same ones who had conspired against Him (Jn 11:47–50).

⁶⁷Then they spat in His face and beat Him with their fists; and others slapped Him, ⁶⁸and said, "Prophesy to us, You Christ; who is the one who hit You?"

⁶⁹Now Peter was sitting outside in the courtyard, and a servant-girl came to him and said, "You too were with Jesus the Galilean." ⁷⁰But he denied *it* before them all, saying, "I do not know what you are talking about." ⁷¹When he had gone out to the gateway, another *servant-girl* saw him and *said to those who were there, "This man was with Jesus of Nazareth." ⁷²And again he denied *it* with an oath, "I do not know the man." ⁷³A little later the bystanders came up and said to Peter, "Surely you too are *one* of them; for even the way you talk gives you away." ⁷⁴Then he began to curse and swear, "I do not know the man!" And immediately a rooster crowed. ⁷⁵And Peter remembered the word which Jesus had said, "Before a rooster crows, you will deny Me three times." And he went out and wept bitterly.

26:75 And Peter remembered. Luke 22:61 records that Jesus made eye contact with Peter at this very moment, which must have magnified Peter's already unbearable sense of shame. "He went out"—evidently departing from Caiaphas' house—"and wept bitterly." The true Peter is seen not in his denial but in his repentance. This account reminds us of not only our own weakness, but also the richness of divine grace (see also Jn 21:15–19).

DAY 13: Why did Jesus refuse to take up arms and fight?

When the multitude comes to arrest Jesus in Matthew 26, one of His disciples strikes out with a sword. John identifies the swordsman as Peter (Jn 18:10). Clearly, Peter was not aiming for the ear, but for the head. Jesus' response was immediate. "Put your sword back into its place; for all those who take up the sword shall perish by the sword" (v. 52). Peter's action was vigilantism. No matter how unjust the arrest of Jesus, Peter had no right to take the law into his own hands in order to stop it. Jesus' reply was a restatement of the Genesis 9:6 principle: "Whoever sheds man's blood, by man his blood shall be shed," an affirmation that capital punishment is an appropriate penalty for murder.

Jesus said that if it were a matter of force, His Father would send "more than twelve legions" (v. 53). A Roman legion was composed of 6,000 soldiers, so this would represent more than 72,000 angels. In 2 Kings 19:35, a single angel killed more than 185,000 men in a single night, so this many angels would make a formidable army.

But it wasn't about force; it was that the "Scriptures be fulfilled" (v. 54) God Himself had foreordained the very minutest details of how Jesus would die (Ac 2:23; 4:27–28). Dying was Christ's consummate act of submission to the Father's will. Jesus Himself was in absolute control (Jn 10:17–18). Yet it was not Jesus alone, but everyone around Him—His enemies included—who fulfilled precisely the details of the Old Testament prophecies. These events display His divine sovereignty.

FEBRUARY 14

Exodus 39:1–40:38

39 Moreover, from the blue and purple and scarlet *material,* they made finely woven garments for ministering in the holy place as well as the holy garments which were for Aaron, just as the LORD had commanded Moses.

2 He made the ephod of gold, *and* of blue and purple and scarlet *material,* and fine twisted linen. 3 Then they hammered out gold sheets and cut *them* into threads to be woven in *with* the blue and the purple and the scarlet *material,* and the fine linen, the work of a skillful workman. 4 They made attaching shoulder pieces for the ephod; it was attached at its two *upper* ends. 5 The skillfully woven band which was on it was like its workmanship, of the same material: of gold *and* of blue and purple and scarlet *material,* and fine twisted linen, just as the LORD had commanded Moses.

6 They made the onyx stones, set in gold filigree *settings;* they were engraved *like* the engravings of a signet, according to the names of the sons of Israel. 7 And he placed them on the shoulder pieces of the ephod, *as* memorial stones for the sons of Israel, just as the LORD had commanded Moses.

8 He made the breastpiece, the work of a skillful workman, like the workmanship of the ephod: of gold *and* of blue and purple and scarlet *material* and fine twisted linen. 9 It was square; they made the breastpiece folded double, a span long and a span wide when folded double. 10 And they mounted four rows of stones on it. The first row *was* a row of ruby, topaz, and emerald; 11 and the second row, a turquoise, a sapphire and a diamond; 12 and the third row, a jacinth, an agate, and an amethyst; 13 and the fourth row, a beryl, an onyx, and a jasper. They were set in gold filigree *settings* when they were mounted. 14 The stones were corresponding to the names of the sons of Israel; they were twelve, corresponding to their names, *engraved with* the engravings of a signet, each with its name for the twelve tribes. 15 They made on the breastpiece chains like cords, of twisted cordage work in pure gold. 16 They made two gold filigree *settings* and two gold rings, and put the two rings on the two ends of the breastpiece. 17 Then they put the two gold cords in the two rings at the ends of the breastpiece. 18 They put the *other* two ends of the two cords on the two filigree *settings,* and put them on the shoulder

pieces of the ephod at the front of it. 19 They made two gold rings and placed *them* on the two ends of the breastpiece, on its inner edge which was next to the ephod. 20 Furthermore, they made two gold rings and placed them on the bottom of the two shoulder pieces of the ephod, on the front of it, close to the place where it joined, above the woven band of the ephod. 21 They bound the breastpiece by its rings to the rings of the ephod with a blue cord, so that it would be on the woven band of the ephod, and that the breastpiece would not come loose from the ephod, just as the LORD had commanded Moses.

22 Then he made the robe of the ephod of woven work, all of blue; 23 and the opening of the robe was *at the top* in the center, as the opening of a coat of mail, with a binding all around its opening, so that it would not be torn. 24 They made pomegranates of blue and purple and scarlet *material and* twisted *linen* on the hem of the robe. 25 They also made bells of pure gold, and put the bells between the pomegranates all around on the hem of the robe, 26 alternating a bell and a pomegranate all around on the hem of the robe for the service, just as the LORD had commanded Moses.

27 They made the tunics of finely woven linen for Aaron and his sons, 28 and the turban of fine linen, and the decorated caps of fine linen, and the linen breeches of fine twisted linen, 29 and the sash of fine twisted linen, and blue and purple and scarlet *material,* the work of the weaver, just as the LORD had commanded Moses.

30 They made the plate of the holy crown of pure gold, and inscribed it like the engravings of a signet, "Holy to the LORD." 31 They fastened a blue cord to it, to fasten it on the turban above, just as the LORD had commanded Moses.

32 Thus all the work of the tabernacle of the tent of meeting was completed; and the sons of Israel did according to all that the LORD had commanded Moses; so they did. 33 They brought the tabernacle to Moses, the tent and all its furnishings: its clasps, its boards, its bars, and its pillars and its sockets; 34 and the covering of rams' skins dyed red, and the covering of porpoise skins, and the screening veil; 35 the ark of the testimony and its poles and the mercy seat; 36 the table, all its utensils, and the bread of the Presence; 37 the pure *gold* lampstand, with its arrangement of lamps and all its utensils, and the oil for the light; 38 and the gold altar, and the anointing oil and the fragrant incense, and the veil for the doorway of the tent; 39 the bronze altar and its

bronze grating, its poles and all its utensils, the laver and its stand; ⁴⁰ the hangings for the court, its pillars and its sockets, and the screen for the gate of the court, its cords and its pegs and all the equipment for the service of the tabernacle, for the tent of meeting; ⁴¹ the woven garments for ministering in the holy place and the holy garments for Aaron the priest and the garments of his sons, to minister as priests. ⁴² So the sons of Israel did all the work according to all that the LORD had commanded Moses. ⁴³ And Moses examined all the work and behold, they had done it; just as the LORD had commanded, this they had done. So Moses blessed them.

40 Then the LORD spoke to Moses, saying, ² "On the first day of the first month you shall set up the tabernacle of the tent of meeting. ³ You shall place the ark of the testimony there, and you shall screen the ark with the veil. ⁴ You shall bring in the table and arrange what belongs on it; and you shall bring in the lampstand and mount its lamps. ⁵ Moreover, you shall set the gold altar of incense before the ark of the testimony, and set up the veil for the doorway to the tabernacle. ⁶ You shall set the altar of burnt offering in front of the doorway of the tabernacle of the tent of meeting. ⁷ You shall set the laver between the tent of meeting and the altar and put water in it. ⁸ You shall set up the court all around and hang up the veil for the gateway of the court. ⁹ Then you shall take the anointing oil and anoint the tabernacle and all that is in it, and shall consecrate it and all its furnishings; and it shall be holy. ¹⁰ You shall anoint the altar of burnt offering and all its utensils, and consecrate the altar, and the altar shall be most holy. ¹¹ You shall anoint the laver and its stand, and consecrate it. ¹² Then you shall bring Aaron and his sons to the doorway of the tent of meeting and wash them with water. ¹³ You shall put the holy garments on Aaron and anoint him and consecrate him, that he may minister as a priest to Me. ¹⁴ You shall bring his sons and put tunics on them; ¹⁵ and you shall anoint them even as you have anointed their father, that they may minister as priests to Me; and their anointing will qualify them for a perpetual priesthood throughout their generations." ¹⁶ Thus Moses did; according to all that the LORD had commanded him, so he did.

¹⁷ Now in the first month of the second year, on the first *day* of the month, the tabernacle was erected. ¹⁸ Moses erected the tabernacle and laid its sockets, and set up its boards, and inserted its bars and erected its pillars. ¹⁹ He spread the tent over the tabernacle and put the covering of the tent on top of it, just as the LORD had commanded Moses. ²⁰ Then he took the testimony and put *it* into the ark, and attached the poles to the ark, and put the mercy seat on top of the ark. ²¹ He brought the ark into the tabernacle, and set up a veil for the screen, and screened off the ark of the testimony, just as the LORD had commanded Moses. ²² Then he put the table in the tent of meeting on the north side of the tabernacle, outside the veil. ²³ He set the arrangement of bread in order on it before the LORD, just as the LORD had commanded Moses. ²⁴ Then he placed the lampstand in the tent of meeting, opposite the table, on the south side of the tabernacle. ²⁵ He lighted the lamps before the LORD, just as the LORD had commanded Moses. ²⁶ Then he placed the gold altar in the tent of meeting in front of the veil; ²⁷ and he burned fragrant incense on it, just as the LORD had commanded Moses. ²⁸ Then he set up the veil for the doorway of the tabernacle. ²⁹ He set the altar of burnt offering *before* the doorway of the tabernacle of the tent of meeting, and offered on it the burnt offering and the meal offering, just as the LORD had commanded Moses. ³⁰ He placed the laver between the tent of meeting and the altar and put water in it for washing. ³¹ From it Moses and Aaron and his sons washed their hands and their feet. ³² When they entered the tent of meeting, and when they approached the altar, they washed, just as the LORD had commanded Moses. ³³ He erected the court all around the tabernacle and the altar, and hung up the veil for the gateway of the court. Thus Moses finished the work.

³⁴ Then the cloud covered the tent of meeting, and the glory of the LORD filled the tabernacle. ³⁵ Moses was not able to enter the tent of meeting because the cloud had settled on it, and the glory of the LORD filled the tabernacle. ³⁶ Throughout all their journeys whenever the cloud was taken up from over the tabernacle, the sons of Israel would set out; ³⁷ but if the cloud was not taken up, then they did not set out until the day when it was taken up. ³⁸ For throughout all their journeys, the cloud of the LORD was on the tabernacle by day, and there was fire in it by night, in the sight of all the house of Israel.

Psalm 22:16–21

¹⁶ For dogs have surrounded me;
A band of evildoers has
encompassed me;
They pierced my hands and my feet.

¹⁷ I can count all my bones.
    They look, they stare at me;
¹⁸ They divide my garments
        among them,
    And for my clothing they cast lots.

¹⁹ But You, O LORD, be not far off;
    O You my help, hasten to
        my assistance.
²⁰ Deliver my soul from the sword,
    My only *life* from the
        power of the dog.
²¹ Save me from the lion's mouth;
    From the horns of the wild
        oxen You answer me.

22:16 They pierced my hands and my feet. The Hebrew text reads "like a lion," i.e., these vicious attacking enemies, like animals, have torn me. Likely, a messianic prediction with reference to crucifixion (Is 53:5; Zec 12:10).

22:18 They divide...they cast. All 4 gospel writers appeal to this imagery in describing Christ's crucifixion (Mt 27:35; Mk 15:24; Lk 23:34; Jn 19:24).

Proverbs 8:22–31

²² "The LORD possessed me at the
        beginning of His way,
    Before His works of old.
²³ "From everlasting I was established,
    From the beginning, from the
        earliest times of the earth.
²⁴ "When there were no depths
    I was brought forth,
    When there were no springs
        abounding with water.
²⁵ "Before the mountains were settled,
    Before the hills I was brought forth;
²⁶ While He had not yet made
        the earth and the fields,
    Nor the first dust of the world.
²⁷ "When He established the
        heavens, I was there,
    When He inscribed a circle
        on the face of the deep,
²⁸ When He made firm the skies above,
    When the springs of the
        deep became fixed,
²⁹ When He set for the sea its boundary
    So that the water would not
        transgress His command,
    When He marked out the
        foundations of the earth;

8:27 circle on the face of the deep. The Hebrew word for "circle" indicates that the earth is a globe; therefore, the horizon is circular (Is 40:22). This "deep" that surrounds the earth was the original world ocean that covered the surface of the earth before it was fully formed and given life (Ge 1:2).

³⁰ Then I was beside Him, *as*
        a master workman;
    And I was daily *His* delight,
    Rejoicing always before Him,
³¹ Rejoicing in the world, His earth,
    And *having* my delight in
        the sons of men.

Matthew 27:1–26

27 Now when morning came, all the chief priests and the elders of the people conferred together against Jesus to put Him to death; ² and they bound Him, and led Him away and delivered Him to Pilate the governor.

³ Then when Judas, who had betrayed Him, saw that He had been condemned, he felt remorse and returned the thirty pieces of silver to the chief priests and elders, ⁴ saying, "I have sinned by betraying innocent blood." But they said, "What is that to us? See *to that* yourself!" ⁵ And he threw the pieces of silver into the temple sanctuary and departed; and he went away and hanged himself. ⁶ The chief priests took the pieces of silver and said, "It is not lawful to put them into the temple treasury, since it is the price of blood." ⁷ And they conferred together and with the money bought the Potter's Field as a burial place for strangers. ⁸ For this reason that field has been called the Field of Blood to this day. ⁹ Then that which was spoken through Jeremiah the prophet was fulfilled: "AND THEY TOOK THE THIRTY PIECES OF SILVER, THE PRICE OF THE ONE WHOSE PRICE HAD BEEN SET by the sons of Israel; ¹⁰ AND THEY GAVE THEM FOR THE POTTER'S FIELD, AS THE LORD DIRECTED ME."

¹¹ Now Jesus stood before the governor, and the governor questioned Him, saying, "Are You the King of the Jews?" And Jesus said to him, "*It is as* you say." ¹² And while He was being accused by the chief priests and elders, He did not answer. ¹³ Then Pilate *said to Him, "Do You not hear how many things they testify against You?" ¹⁴ And He did not answer him with regard to even a *single* charge, so the governor was quite amazed.

¹⁵Now at *the* feast the governor was accustomed to release for the people *any* one prisoner whom they wanted. ¹⁶At that time they were holding a notorious prisoner, called Barabbas. ¹⁷So when the people gathered together, Pilate said to them, "Whom do you want me to release for you? Barabbas, or Jesus who is called Christ?" ¹⁸For he knew that because of envy they had handed Him over.

¹⁹While he was sitting on the judgment seat, his wife sent him *a message,* saying, "Have nothing to do with that righteous Man; for last night I suffered greatly in a dream because of Him." ²⁰But the chief priests and the elders persuaded the crowds to ask for Barabbas and to put Jesus to death. ²¹But the governor said to them, "Which of the two do you want me to release for you?" And they said, "Barabbas." ²²Pilate *said to them, "Then what shall I do with Jesus who is called Christ?" They all *said, "Crucify Him!" ²³And he said, "Why, what evil has He done?" But they kept shouting all the more, saying, "Crucify Him!"

²⁴When Pilate saw that he was accomplishing nothing, but rather that a riot was starting, he took water and washed his hands in front of the crowd, saying, "I am innocent of this Man's blood; see *to that* yourselves." ²⁵And all the people said, "His blood shall be on us and on our children!" ²⁶Then he released Barabbas for them; but after having Jesus scourged, he handed Him over to be crucified.

27:26 scourged. The whip used for scourging consisted of several strands of leather attached to a wooden handle. Each strand had a bit of metal or bone attached to the end. The victim was bound to a post by the wrists, high over his head, so that the flesh of the back would be taut. An expert at wielding the scourge could literally tear the flesh from the back, lacerating muscles, and sometimes even exposing the kidneys or other internal organs. Scourging alone was fatal in some cases.

DAY 14: Does Matthew include any material not found in the other Gospels?

Matthew includes nine events in Jesus' life that are unique to his Gospel:

1. Joseph's dream (1:20–24).
2. Visit of the wise men (2:1–12).
3. Flight into Egypt (2:13–15).
4. Herod kills the children (2:16–18).
5. Judas repents (27:3–10; but see Ac 1:18–19).
6. The dream of Pilate's wife (27:19).
7. Other resurrections (27:52).
8. The bribery of the soldiers (28:11–15).
9. The Great Commission (28:19–20).

FEBRUARY 15

Leviticus 1:1–2:16

1 Then the LORD called to Moses and spoke to him from the tent of meeting, saying, ²"Speak to the sons of Israel and say to them, 'When any man of you brings an offering to the LORD, you shall bring your offering of animals from the herd or the flock. ³If his offering is a burnt offering from the herd, he shall offer it, a male without defect; he shall offer it at the doorway of the tent of meeting, that he may be accepted before the LORD. ⁴He shall lay his hand on the head of the burnt offering, that it may be accepted for him to make atonement on his behalf. ⁵He shall slay the young bull before the LORD; and Aaron's sons the priests shall offer up the blood and

sprinkle the blood around on the altar that is at the doorway of the tent of meeting. ⁶He shall then skin the burnt offering and cut it into its pieces. ⁷The sons of Aaron the priest shall put fire on the altar and arrange wood on the fire. ⁸Then Aaron's sons the priests shall arrange the pieces, the head and the suet over the wood which is on the fire that is on the altar. ⁹Its entrails, however, and its legs he shall wash with water. And the priest shall offer up in smoke all of it on the altar for a burnt offering, an offering by fire of a soothing aroma to the LORD.

¹⁰'But if his offering is from the flock, of the sheep or of the goats, for a burnt offering, he shall offer it a male without defect. ¹¹He shall slay it on the side of the altar northward before the LORD, and Aaron's sons the priests shall sprinkle its blood around on the altar.

1:4 lay his hand on the head. This symbolic gesture pictured the transfer of the sacrificer's sin to the sacrificial animal and was likely done with a prayer of repentance and request for forgiveness (Ps 51:18–19). **make atonement.** The word means "cover." The psalmist defines it by saying, "Blessed is he whose transgression is forgiven, whose sin *is* covered" (Ps 32:1). Theologically, the "atonement" of the Old Testament covered sin only temporarily, but it did not eliminate sin or later judgment (Heb 10:4). The one time sacrifice of Jesus Christ fully atoned for sin, thus satisfying God's wrath forever and insuring eternal salvation (Heb 9:12; 1Jn 2:2), even to those who put saving faith in God for their redemption before Christ's death on the cross (Ro 3:25–26; Heb 9:15). **on his behalf.** This was a substitutionary sacrifice that prefigured the ultimate substitute—Jesus Christ (Is 53; 2Co 5:21).

---

¹² He shall then cut it into its pieces with its head and its suet, and the priest shall arrange them on the wood which is on the fire that is on the altar. ¹³ The entrails, however, and the legs he shall wash with water. And the priest shall offer all of it, and offer it up in smoke on the altar; it is a burnt offering, an offering by fire of a soothing aroma to the LORD.

¹⁴ 'But if his offering to the LORD is a burnt offering of birds, then he shall bring his offering from the turtledoves or from young pigeons. ¹⁵ The priest shall bring it to the altar, and wring off its head and offer it up in smoke on the altar; and its blood is to be drained out on the side of the altar. ¹⁶ He shall also take away its crop with its feathers and cast it beside the altar eastward, to the place of the ashes. ¹⁷ Then he shall tear it by its wings, *but* shall not sever *it*. And the priest shall offer it up in smoke on the altar on the wood which is on the fire; it is a burnt offering, an offering by fire of a soothing aroma to the LORD.

2 'Now when anyone presents a grain offering as an offering to the LORD, his offering shall be of fine flour, and he shall pour oil on it and put frankincense on it. ² He shall then bring it to Aaron's sons the priests; and shall take from it his handful of its fine flour and of its oil with all of its frankincense. And the priest shall offer *it* up in smoke *as* its memorial portion on the altar, an offering by fire of a soothing aroma to the LORD. ³ The remainder of the grain offering belongs to Aaron and his sons: a thing most holy, of the offerings to the LORD by fire.

⁴ 'Now when you bring an offering of a grain offering baked in an oven, *it shall be* unleavened cakes of fine flour mixed with oil, or unleavened wafers spread with oil. ⁵ If your offering is a grain offering *made* on the griddle, *it shall be* of fine flour, unleavened, mixed with oil; ⁶ you shall break it into bits and pour oil on it; it is a grain offering. ⁷ Now if your offering is a grain offering *made* in a pan, it shall be made of fine flour with oil. ⁸ When you bring in the grain offering which is made of these things to the LORD, it shall be presented to the priest and he shall bring it to the altar. ⁹ The priest then shall take up from the grain offering its memorial portion, and shall offer *it* up in smoke on the altar *as* an offering by fire of a soothing aroma to the LORD. ¹⁰ The remainder of the grain offering belongs to Aaron and his sons: a thing most holy of the offerings to the LORD by fire.

¹¹ 'No grain offering, which you bring to the LORD, shall be made with leaven, for you shall not offer up in smoke any leaven or any honey as an offering by fire to the LORD. ¹² As an offering of first fruits you shall bring them to the LORD, but they shall not ascend for a soothing aroma on the altar. ¹³ Every grain offering of yours, moreover, you shall season with salt, so that the salt of the covenant of your God shall not be lacking from your grain offering; with all your offerings you shall offer salt.

¹⁴ 'Also if you bring a grain offering of early ripened things to the LORD, you shall bring fresh heads of grain roasted in the fire, grits of new growth, for the grain offering of your early ripened things. ¹⁵ You shall then put oil on it and lay incense on it; it is a grain offering. ¹⁶ The priest shall offer up in smoke its memorial portion, part of its grits and its oil with all its incense as an offering by fire to the LORD.

Psalm 22:22–31

²² I will tell of Your name
 to my brethren;
 In the midst of the assembly
  I will praise You.
²³ You who fear the LORD, praise Him;
 All you descendants of
  Jacob, glorify Him,
 And stand in awe of Him, all
  you descendants of Israel.
²⁴ For He has not despised nor abhorred
  the affliction of the afflicted;
 Nor has He hidden His face from him;
 But when he cried to Him
  for help, He heard.
²⁵ From You *comes* my praise
  in the great assembly;

I shall pay my vows before
those who fear Him.
²⁶ The afflicted will eat and be satisfied;
Those who seek Him will
praise the LORD.
Let your heart live forever!
²⁷ All the ends of the earth will
remember and turn to the LORD,
And all the families of the nations
will worship before You.
²⁸ For the kingdom is the LORD'S
And He rules over the nations.
²⁹ All the prosperous of the earth
will eat and worship,
All those who go down to the
dust will bow before Him,
Even he who cannot keep his soul alive.
³⁰ Posterity will serve Him;
It will be told of the Lord to
the *coming* generation.
³¹ They will come and will declare
His righteousness
To a people who will be born,
that He has performed *it.*

27:31 to crucify Him. Crucifixion was a form of punishment that had been passed down to the Romans from the Persians, Phoenicians, and Carthaginians. Roman crucifixion was a lingering doom—by design. Roman executioners had perfected the art of slow torture while keeping the victim alive. Some victims even lingered until they were eaten alive by birds of prey or wild beasts. Most hung on the cross for days before dying of exhaustion, dehydration, traumatic fever, or—most likely—suffocation. When the legs would no longer support the weight of the body, the diaphragm was constricted in a way that made breathing impossible. That is why breaking the legs would hasten death (Jn 19:31-33), but this was unnecessary in Jesus' case. The hands were usually nailed through the wrists, and the feet through the instep or the Achilles tendon (sometimes using one nail for both feet). None of these wounds would be fatal, but their pain would become unbearable as the hours dragged on. The most notable feature of crucifixion was the stigma of disgrace that was attached to it (Gal 3:13; 5:11; Heb 12:2). One indignity was the humiliation of carrying one's own cross, which might weigh as much as 200 pounds. Normally a quaternion, 4 soldiers, would escort the prisoner through the crowds to the place of crucifixion. A placard bearing the indictment would be hung around the person's neck.

Proverbs 8:32-36

³² "Now therefore, *O* sons, listen to me,
For blessed are they who
keep my ways.
³³ "Heed instruction and be wise,
And do not neglect *it.*
³⁴ "Blessed is the man who listens to me,
Watching daily at my gates,
Waiting at my doorposts.
³⁵ "For he who finds me finds life
And obtains favor from the LORD.
³⁶ "But he who sins against
me injures himself;
All those who hate me love death."

Matthew 27:27-54

²⁷ Then the soldiers of the governor took Jesus into the Praetorium and gathered the whole *Roman* cohort around Him. ²⁸ They stripped Him and put a scarlet robe on Him. ²⁹ And after twisting together a crown of thorns, they put it on His head, and a reed in His right hand; and they knelt down before Him and mocked Him, saying, "Hail, King of the Jews!" ³⁰ They spat on Him, and took the reed and *began* to beat Him on the head. ³¹ After they had mocked Him, they took the *scarlet* robe off Him and put His *own* garments back on Him, and led Him away to crucify Him.

³² As they were coming out, they found a man of Cyrene named Simon, whom they pressed into service to bear His cross.

³³ And when they came to a place called Golgotha, which means Place of a Skull, ³⁴ they gave Him wine to drink mixed with gall; and after tasting *it,* He was unwilling to drink.

³⁵ And when they had crucified Him, they divided up His garments among themselves by casting lots. ³⁶ And sitting down, they *began* to keep watch over Him there. ³⁷ And above His head they put up the charge against Him which read,

"THIS IS JESUS THE KING
OF THE JEWS."

³⁸ At that time two robbers *were crucified with Him, one on the right and one on the left. ³⁹ And those passing by were hurling abuse at Him, wagging their heads ⁴⁰ and saying, "You who *are going to* destroy the temple and rebuild it in three days, save Yourself! If You are the Son of God, come down from the cross." ⁴¹ In the same way the chief priests also, along with the scribes and elders, were mocking *Him* and saying, ⁴² "He saved others; He cannot save Himself. He is the King

of Israel; let Him now come down from the cross, and we will believe in Him. 43 HE TRUSTS IN GOD; LET GOD RESCUE *Him* now, IF HE DE-LIGHTS IN HIM; for He said, 'I am the Son of God.'" 44 The robbers who had been crucified with Him were also insulting Him with the same words.

45 Now from the sixth hour darkness fell upon all the land until the ninth hour. 46 About the ninth hour Jesus cried out with a loud voice, saying, "ELI, ELI, LAMA SABACHTHANI?" that is, "MY GOD, MY GOD, WHY HAVE YOU FOR-SAKEN ME?" 47 And some of those who were standing there, when they heard it, *began* saying, "This man is calling for Elijah." 48 Immediately one of them ran, and taking a sponge, he filled it with sour wine and put it on a reed, and gave Him a drink. 49 But the rest *of them* said, "Let us see whether Elijah will come to save Him." 50 And Jesus cried out again with a loud voice, and yielded up His spirit. 51 And behold, the veil of the temple was torn in two from top to bottom; and the earth shook

and the rocks were split. 52 The tombs were opened, and many bodies of the saints who had fallen asleep were raised; 53 and coming out of the tombs after His resurrection they entered the holy city and appeared to many. 54 Now the centurion, and those who were with him keeping guard over Jesus, when they saw the earthquake and the things that were happening, became very frightened and said, "Truly this was the Son of God!"

27:46 ELI, ELI, LAMA SABACHTHANI. "Eli" is Hebrew; the rest Aram. (Mk 15:34 gives the entire wail in Aramaic.) This cry is a fulfillment of Psalms 22:1, one of many striking parallels between that psalm and the specific events of the crucifixion. Christ at that moment was experiencing the abandonment and despair that resulted from the outpouring of divine wrath on Him as sin-bearer.

DAY 15: How is Christ seen in the Levitical offerings?

Offering	Christ's Provision	Christ's Character
1. Burnt Offering (Leviticus 1:3–17; 6:8–13)	atonement	Christ's sinless nature
2. Grain Offering (Leviticus 2:1–16; 6:14–23)	dedication/consecration	Christ was wholly devoted to the Father's purposes
3. Peace Offering (Leviticus 3:1–17; 7:11–36)	reconciliation/fellowship	Christ was at peace with God
4. Sin Offering (Leviticus 4:1–5:13; 6:24–30)	propitiation	Christ's substitutionary death
5. Trespass Offering (Leviticus 5:14–6:7; 7:1–10)	repentance	Christ paid it all for redemption

FEBRUARY 16

Leviticus 3:1–4:35

3 'Now if his offering is a sacrifice of peace offerings, if he is going to offer out of the herd, whether male or female, he shall offer it without defect before the LORD. 2 He shall lay his hand on the head of his offering and slay it at the doorway of the tent of meeting, and Aaron's sons the priests shall sprinkle the blood around on the altar. 3 From the sacrifice of the peace offerings he shall present an offering by fire to the LORD, the fat that covers the entrails and all the fat that is on the entrails, 4 and the two kidneys with the fat that is on them, which is on the loins, and the lobe of the liver, which he shall remove with the kidneys. 5 Then Aaron's sons shall offer *it*

up in smoke on the altar on the burnt offering, which is on the wood that is on the fire; it is an offering by fire of a soothing aroma to the LORD. 6 But if his offering for a sacrifice of peace offerings to the LORD is from the flock, he shall offer it, male or female, without defect. 7 If he is going to offer a lamb for his offering, then he shall offer it before the LORD, 8 and he shall lay his hand on the head of his offering and slay it before the tent of meet-ing, and Aaron's sons shall sprinkle its blood around on the altar. 9 From the sacrifice of peace offerings he shall bring as an offering by fire to the LORD, its fat, the entire fat tail which he shall remove close to the backbone, and the fat that covers the entrails and all the fat that is on the entrails, 10 and the two kidneys with the fat that is on them, which is on the loins, and the lobe of the liver, which he shall remove with the kidneys. ¹¹ Then the priest shall offer *it* up in smoke on the altar *as* food, an offering by fire to the LORD.

¹² 'Moreover, if his offering is a goat, then he shall offer it before the LORD, ¹³ and he shall lay his hand on its head and slay it before the tent of meeting, and the sons of Aaron shall sprinkle its blood around on the altar. ¹⁴ From it he shall present his offering as an offering by fire to the LORD, the fat that covers the entrails and all the fat that is on the entrails, ¹⁵ and the two kidneys with the fat that is on them, which is on the loins, and the lobe of the liver, which he shall remove with the kidneys. ¹⁶ The priest shall offer them up in smoke on the altar *as* food, an offering by fire for a soothing aroma; all fat is the LORD'S. ¹⁷ It is a perpetual statute throughout your generations in all your dwellings: you shall not eat any fat or any blood.'"

3:1–17 See 7:11–36 for the priests' instructions. The peace offering symbolizes the peace and fellowship between the true worshiper and God (as a voluntary offering). It was the third freewill offering resulting in a sweet aroma to the Lord (3:5), which served as the appropriate corollary to the burnt offering of atonement and the grain offering of consecration and dedication. It symbolized the fruit of redemptive reconciliation between a sinner and God (2Co 5:18).

4 Then the LORD spoke to Moses, saying, ² "Speak to the sons of Israel, saying, 'If a person sins unintentionally in any of the things which the LORD has commanded not to be done, and commits any of them, ³ if the anointed priest sins so as to bring guilt on the people, then let him offer to the LORD a bull without defect as a sin offering for the sin he has committed. ⁴ He shall bring the bull to the doorway of the tent of meeting before the LORD, and he shall lay his hand on the head of the bull and slay the bull before the LORD. ⁵ Then the anointed priest is to take some of the blood of the bull and bring it to the tent of meeting, ⁶ and the priest shall dip his finger in the blood and sprinkle some of the blood seven times before the LORD, in front of the veil of the sanctuary. ⁷ The priest shall also put some of the blood on the horns of the altar of fragrant incense which is before the LORD in the tent of meeting; and all the blood of the bull he shall pour out at the base of the altar

of burnt offering which is at the doorway of the tent of meeting. ⁸ He shall remove from it all the fat of the bull of the sin offering: the fat that covers the entrails, and all the fat which is on the entrails, ⁹ and the two kidneys with the fat that is on them, which is on the loins, and the lobe of the liver, which he shall remove with the kidneys ¹⁰ (just as it is removed from the ox of the sacrifice of peace offerings), and the priest is to offer them up in smoke on the altar of burnt offering. ¹¹ But the hide of the bull and all its flesh with its head and its legs and its entrails and its refuse, ¹² that is, all *the rest of* the bull, he is to bring out to a clean place outside the camp where the ashes are poured out, and burn it on wood with fire; where the ashes are poured out it shall be burned.

¹³ 'Now if the whole congregation of Israel commits error and the matter escapes the notice of the assembly, and they commit any of the things which the LORD has commanded not to be done, and they become guilty; ¹⁴ when the sin which they have committed becomes known, then the assembly shall offer a bull of the herd for a sin offering and bring it before the tent of meeting. ¹⁵ Then the elders of the congregation shall lay their hands on the head of the bull before the LORD, and the bull shall be slain before the LORD. ¹⁶ Then the anointed priest is to bring some of the blood of the bull to the tent of meeting; ¹⁷ and the priest shall dip his finger in the blood and sprinkle *it* seven times before the LORD, in front of the veil. ¹⁸ He shall put some of the blood on the horns of the altar which is before the LORD in the tent of meeting; and all the blood he shall pour out at the base of the altar of burnt offering which is at the doorway of the tent of meeting. ¹⁹ He shall remove all its fat from it and offer it up in smoke on the altar. ²⁰ He shall also do with the bull just as he did with the bull of the sin offering; thus he shall do with it. So the priest shall make atonement for them, and they will be forgiven. ²¹ Then he is to bring out the bull to *a place* outside the camp and burn it as he burned the first bull; it is the sin offering for the assembly.

²² 'When a leader sins and unintentionally does any one of all the things which the LORD his God has commanded not to be done, and he becomes guilty, ²³ if his sin which he has committed is made known to him, he shall bring for his offering a goat, a male without defect. ²⁴ He shall lay his hand on the head of the male goat and slay it in the place where they slay the burnt offering before the LORD; it is a sin offering. ²⁵ Then the priest is to take

some of the blood of the sin offering with his finger and put it on the horns of the altar of burnt offering; and *the rest of* its blood he shall pour out at the base of the altar of burnt offering. ²⁶All its fat he shall offer up in smoke on the altar as *in the case of* the fat of the sacrifice of peace offerings. Thus the priest shall make atonement for him in regard to his sin, and he will be forgiven.

²⁷'Now if anyone of the common people sins unintentionally in doing any of the things which the LORD has commanded not to be done, and becomes guilty, ²⁸if his sin which he has committed is made known to him, then he shall bring for his offering a goat, a female without defect, for his sin which he has committed. ²⁹He shall lay his hand on the head of the sin offering and slay the sin offering at the place of the burnt offering. ³⁰The priest shall take some of its blood with his finger and put it on the horns of the altar of burnt offering; and all *the rest of* its blood he shall pour out at the base of the altar. ³¹Then he shall remove all its fat, just as the fat was removed from the sacrifice of peace offerings; and the priest shall offer it up in smoke on the altar for a soothing aroma to the LORD. Thus the priest shall make atonement for him, and he will be forgiven.

³²'But if he brings a lamb as his offering for a sin offering, he shall bring it, a female without defect. ³³He shall lay his hand on the head of the sin offering and slay it for a sin offering in the place where they slay the burnt offering. ³⁴The priest is to take some of the blood of the sin offering with his finger and put it on the horns of the altar of burnt offering, and all *the rest of* its blood he shall pour out at the base of the altar. ³⁵Then he shall remove all its fat, just as the fat of the lamb is removed from the sacrifice of the peace offerings, and the priest shall offer them up in smoke on the altar, on the offerings by fire to the LORD. Thus the priest shall make atonement for him in regard to his sin which he has committed, and he will be forgiven.

Psalm 23:1–6

A Psalm of David.

The LORD is my shepherd,
I shall not want.
² He makes me lie down in
green pastures;
He leads me beside quiet waters.
³ He restores my soul;
He guides me in the paths
of righteousness
For His name's sake.

⁴ Even though I walk through the
valley of the shadow of death,
I fear no evil, for You are with me;
Your rod and Your staff,
they comfort me.
⁵ You prepare a table before me in
the presence of my enemies;
You have anointed my head with oil;
My cup overflows.
⁶ Surely goodness and
lovingkindness will follow
me all the days of my life,
And I will dwell in the house
of the LORD forever.

23:4 the valley of the shadow of death. Phraseology used to convey a perilously threatening environment (Job 10:21–22; 38:17; Pss 44:19; 107:10; Jer 2:6; Lk. 1:79). **Your rod and Your staff.** The shepherd's club and crook are viewed as comforting instruments of protection and direction, respectively.

Proverbs 9:1–6

9 Wisdom has built her house,
She has hewn out her seven pillars;
² She has prepared her food,
she has mixed her wine;
She has also set her table;
³ She has sent out her
maidens, she calls
From the tops of the
heights of the city:
⁴ "Whoever is naive, let him
turn in here!"
To him who lacks
understanding she says,
⁵ "Come, eat of my food
And drink of the wine I have
mixed.
⁶ "Forsake *your* folly and live,
And proceed in the way of
understanding."

Matthew 27:55–66

⁵⁵Many women were there looking on from a distance, who had followed Jesus from Galilee while ministering to Him. ⁵⁶Among them was Mary Magdalene, and Mary the mother of James and Joseph, and the mother of the sons of Zebedee.

⁵⁷When it was evening, there came a rich man from Arimathea, named Joseph, who himself had also become a disciple of Jesus. ⁵⁸This man went to Pilate and asked

27:56 Mary Magdalene. She had been delivered from 7 demons (Lk 8:2); the other "Mary" ("wife of Clopas," Jn 19:25—a variant of Alphaeus) was the mother of the apostle known as "James the Less" (Mk 15:40). **the mother of the sons of Zebedee.** Salome (Mk 15:40), mother of James and John. From John 19:26, we learn that Mary, the mother of Jesus, was also present at the cross—possibly standing apart from these 3, who were "looking on from a distance" (v. 55), as if they could not bear to watch His sufferings, but neither could they bear to leave Him.

27:57 Arimathea. A town about 15-20 miles northwest of Jerusalem. **Joseph.** Mark 15:43 and Luke 23:50-51 identify him as a member of the Sanhedrin, though Luke says "he had not consented to their plan and action" in condemning Christ. Joseph and Nicodemus (Jn 19:39), both being prominent Jewish leaders, buried Christ in Joseph's own "new tomb" (v. 60), thus fulfilling exactly the prophecy of Isaiah 53:9.

for the body of Jesus. Then Pilate ordered it to be given *to him.* ⁵⁹And Joseph took the body and wrapped it in a clean linen cloth, ⁶⁰and laid it in his own new tomb, which he had hewn out in the rock; and he rolled a large stone against the entrance of the tomb and went away. ⁶¹And Mary Magdalene was there, and the other Mary, sitting opposite the grave.

⁶²Now on the next day, the day after the preparation, the chief priests and the Pharisees gathered together with Pilate, ⁶³and said, "Sir, we remember that when He was still alive that deceiver said, 'After three days I *am* to rise again.' ⁶⁴Therefore, give orders for the grave to be made secure until the third day, otherwise His disciples may come and steal Him away and say to the people, 'He has risen from the dead,' and the last deception will be worse than the first." ⁶⁵Pilate said to them, "You have a guard; go, make it *as* secure as you know how." ⁶⁶And they went and made the grave secure, and along with the guard they set a seal on the stone.

DAY 16: Why are there so many uncomfortable expressions in the Psalms—for example in Psalms 23 and 139?

Because the Psalms genuinely reflect real life, we should expect that they will be uncomfortable in the same places that life is uncomfortable. According to the best-known Psalm 23, life isn't just about green pastures and still waters; it also includes death and enemies. The psalmists were convinced they knew the only true God. When someone was picking on them or their people, they would at times cry out for very specific judgment to be applied by God on their enemies. An amazing fact about the Psalms is their unblushing record of these cries to God that, if we are honest, echo some of our deepest hidden complaints before God.

In David's case, the role that he filled as the king and representative of God's people often blurs with his individual self-awareness. At times it is difficult to tell whether he is speaking for himself alone or for the people as a whole. This explains some of the vehemence behind the curse-pronouncing psalms. They unabashedly invoke God's righteous wrath and judgment against His enemies.

FEBRUARY 17

Leviticus 5:1-6:30

5 'Now if a person sins after he hears a public adjuration *to testify* when he is a witness, whether he has seen or *otherwise* known, if he does not tell *it,* then he will bear his guilt. ²Or if a person touches any unclean thing, whether a carcass of an unclean beast or the carcass of unclean cattle or a carcass of unclean swarming things, though it is hidden from him and he is unclean, then he will be guilty. ³Or if he touches human uncleanness, of whatever *sort* his uncleanness *may* be with which he becomes unclean, and it is

hidden from him, and then he comes to know *it,* he will be guilty. ⁴Or if a person swears thoughtlessly with his lips to do evil or to do good, in whatever matter a man may speak thoughtlessly with an oath, and it is hidden from him, and then he comes to know *it,* he will be guilty in one of these. ⁵So it shall be when he becomes guilty in one of these, that he shall confess that in which he has sinned. ⁶He shall also bring his guilt offering to the LORD for his sin which he has committed, a female from the flock, a lamb or a goat as a sin offering. So the priest shall make atonement on his behalf for his sin.

⁷'But if he cannot afford a lamb, then he shall bring to the LORD his guilt offering for

5:5 he shall confess. Confession must accompany the sacrifice as the outward expression of a repentant heart which openly acknowledged agreement with God concerning sin. Sacrifice minus true faith, repentance, and obedience was hypocrisy (Ps 26:4; Is 9:17; Am 5:21–26).

that in which he has sinned, two turtledoves or two young pigeons, one for a sin offering and the other for a burnt offering. 8 He shall bring them to the priest, who shall offer first that which is for the sin offering and shall nip its head at the front of its neck, but he shall not sever it. 9 He shall also sprinkle some of the blood of the sin offering on the side of the altar, while the rest of the blood shall be drained out at the base of the altar: it is a sin offering. 10 The second he shall then prepare as a burnt offering according to the ordinance. So the priest shall make atonement on his behalf for his sin which he has committed, and it will be forgiven him.

11 'But if his means are insufficient for two turtledoves or two young pigeons, then for his offering for that which he has sinned, he shall bring the tenth of an ephah of fine flour for a sin offering; he shall not put oil on it or place incense on it, for it is a sin offering. 12 He shall bring it to the priest, and the priest shall take his handful of it as its memorial portion and offer it up in smoke on the altar, with the offerings of the LORD by fire: it is a sin offering. 13 So the priest shall make atonement for him concerning his sin which he has committed from one of these, and it will be forgiven him; then the rest shall become the priest's, like the grain offering.'"

14 Then the LORD spoke to Moses, saying, 15 "If a person acts unfaithfully and sins unintentionally against the LORD'S holy things, then he shall bring his guilt offering to the LORD: a ram without defect from the flock, according to your valuation in silver by shekels, in terms of the shekel of the sanctuary, for a guilt offering. 16 He shall make restitution for that which he has sinned against the holy thing, and shall add to it a fifth part of it and give it to the priest. The priest shall then make atonement for him with the ram of the guilt offering, and it will be forgiven him.

17 "Now if a person sins and does any of the things which the LORD has commanded not to be done, though he was unaware, still he is guilty and shall bear his punishment. 18 He is then to bring to the priest a ram without defect from the flock, according to your valuation, for a guilt offering. So the priest shall make atonement for him concerning his error in which he sinned unintentionally and did not know it, and it will be forgiven him. 19 It is a guilt offering; he was certainly guilty before the LORD."

6 Then the LORD spoke to Moses, saying, 2 "When a person sins and acts unfaithfully against the LORD, and deceives his companion in regard to a deposit or a security entrusted to him, or through robbery, or if he has extorted from his companion, 3 or has found what was lost and lied about it and sworn falsely, so that he sins in regard to any one of the things a man may do; 4 then it shall be, when he sins and becomes guilty, that he shall restore what he took by robbery or what he got by extortion, or the deposit which was entrusted to him or the lost thing which he found, 5 or anything about which he swore falsely; he shall make restitution for it in full and add to it one-fifth more. He shall give it to the one to whom it belongs on the day he presents his guilt offering. 6 Then he shall bring to the priest his guilt offering to the LORD, a ram without defect from the flock, according to your valuation, for a guilt offering, 7 and the priest shall make atonement for him before the LORD, and he will be forgiven for any one of the things which he may have done to incur guilt."

8 Then the LORD spoke to Moses, saying, 9 "Command Aaron and his sons, saying, 'This is the law for the burnt offering: the burnt offering itself shall remain on the hearth on the altar all night until the morning, and the fire on the altar is to be kept burning on it. 10 The priest is to put on his linen robe, and he shall put on undergarments next to his flesh; and he shall take up the ashes to which the fire reduces the burnt offering on the altar and place them beside the altar. 11 Then he shall take off his garments and put on other garments, and carry the ashes outside the camp to a clean place. 12 The fire on the altar shall be kept burning on it. It shall not go out, but the priest shall burn wood on it every morning; and he shall lay out the burnt offering on it, and offer up in smoke the fat portions of the peace offerings on it. 13 Fire shall be kept burning continually on the altar; it is not to go out.

14 'Now this is the law of the grain offering: the sons of Aaron shall present it before the LORD in front of the altar. 15 Then one of them shall lift up from it a handful of the fine flour of the grain offering, with its oil and all the incense that is on the grain offering,

and he shall offer *it* up in smoke on the altar, a soothing aroma, as its memorial offering to the LORD. ¹⁶What is left of it Aaron and his sons are to eat. It shall be eaten as unleavened cakes in a holy place; they are to eat it in the court of the tent of meeting. ¹⁷It shall not be baked with leaven. I have given it as their share from My offerings by fire; it is most holy, like the sin offering and the guilt offering. ¹⁸Every male among the sons of Aaron may eat it; it is a permanent ordinance throughout your generations, from the offerings by fire to the LORD. Whoever touches them will become consecrated.'"

¹⁹Then the LORD spoke to Moses, saying, ²⁰"This is the offering which Aaron and his sons are to present to the LORD on the day when he is anointed; the tenth of an ephah of fine flour as a regular grain offering, half of it in the morning and half of it in the evening. ²¹It shall be prepared with oil on a griddle. When it is *well* stirred, you shall bring it. You shall present the grain offering in baked pieces as a soothing aroma to the LORD. ²²The anointed priest who will be in his place among his sons shall offer it. By a permanent ordinance it shall be entirely offered up in smoke to the LORD. ²³So every grain offering of the priest shall be burned entirely. It shall not be eaten."

²⁴Then the LORD spoke to Moses, saying, ²⁵"Speak to Aaron and to his sons, saying, 'This is the law of the sin offering: in the place where the burnt offering is slain the sin offering shall be slain before the LORD; it is most holy. ²⁶The priest who offers it for sin shall eat it. It shall be eaten in a holy place, in the court of the tent of meeting. ²⁷Anyone who touches its flesh will become consecrated; and when any of its blood splashes on a garment, in a holy place you shall wash what was splashed on. ²⁸Also the earthenware vessel in which it was boiled shall be broken; and if it was boiled in a bronze vessel, then it shall be scoured and rinsed in water. ²⁹Every male among the priests may eat of it; it is most holy. ³⁰But no sin offering of which any of the blood is brought into the tent of meeting to make atonement in the holy place shall be eaten; it shall be burned with fire.

Psalm 24:1–6

A Psalm of David.

The earth is the LORD'S,
　　and all it contains,
The world, and those who dwell in it.
² For He has founded it upon the seas
　　And established it upon the rivers.

³ Who may ascend into the
　　hill of the LORD?
And who may stand in His holy place?
⁴ He who has clean hands
　　and a pure heart,
Who has not lifted up his
　　soul to falsehood
And has not sworn deceitfully.

24:4 These sample qualities do not signify sinless perfection, but rather basic integrity of inward motive and outward manner.

⁵ He shall receive a blessing
　　from the LORD
And righteousness from the
　　God of his salvation.
⁶ This is the generation of
　　those who seek Him,
Who seek Your face—*even*
　　Jacob.　　　　　*Selah*

Proverbs 9:7–9

⁷ He who corrects a scoffer gets
　　dishonor for himself,
And he who reproves a wicked
　　man *gets* insults for himself.
⁸ Do not reprove a scoffer,
　　or he will hate you,
Reprove a wise man and
　　he will love you.
⁹ Give *instruction* to a wise man
　　and he will be still wiser,
Teach a righteous man and he
　　will increase *his* learning.

Matthew 28:1–20

28 Now after the Sabbath, as it began to dawn toward the first *day* of the week, Mary Magdalene and the other Mary came to look at the grave. ²And behold, a severe earthquake had occurred, for an angel of the Lord descended from heaven and came and rolled away the stone and sat upon it. ³And his appearance was like lightning, and his clothing as white as snow. ⁴The guards shook for fear of him and became like dead men. ⁵The angel said to the women, "Do not be afraid; for I know that you are looking for Jesus who has been crucified. ⁶He is not here, for He has risen, just as He said. Come, see the place where He was lying. ⁷Go quickly and tell His disciples that He has risen from the dead; and behold, He is going ahead of you into Galilee, there you will see Him; behold, I have told you."

28:1 it began to dawn toward the first *day* **of the week.** Sabbath officially ended with sundown on Saturday. At that time the women could purchase and prepare spices (Lk 24:1). The event described here occurred the next morning, at dawn on Sunday, the first day of the week. **other Mary.** The mother of James the Less.

28:4 became like dead men. This suggests that they were not merely paralyzed with fear, but completely unconscious, totally traumatized by what they had seen. The word translated "shook" has the same root as the word for "earthquake" in v. 2. The sudden appearance of this angel, at the same time the women arrived, was their first clue that anything extraordinary was happening.

[8] And they left the tomb quickly with fear and great joy and ran to report it to His disciples. [9] And behold, Jesus met them and greeted them. And they came up and took hold of His feet and worshiped Him. [10] Then Jesus *said to them, "Do not be afraid; go and take word to My brethren to leave for Galilee, and there they will see Me."

[11] Now while they were on their way, some of the guard came into the city and reported to the chief priests all that had happened. [12] And when they had assembled with the elders and consulted together, they gave a large sum of money to the soldiers, [13] and said, "You are to say, 'His disciples came by night and stole Him away while we were asleep.' [14] And if this should come to the governor's ears, we will win him over and keep you out of trouble." [15] And they took the money and did as they had been instructed; and this story was widely spread among the Jews, *and is* to this day.

[16] But the eleven disciples proceeded to Galilee, to the mountain which Jesus had designated. [17] When they saw Him, they worshiped *Him;* but some were doubtful. [18] And Jesus came up and spoke to them, saying, "All authority has been given to Me in heaven and on earth. [19] Go therefore and make disciples of all the nations, baptizing them in the name of the Father and the Son and the Holy Spirit, [20] teaching them to observe all that I commanded you; and lo, I am with you always, even to the end of the age."

28:18 All authority. See 11:27; John 3:35. Absolute sovereign authority—lordship over all—is handed to Christ, "in heaven and on earth." This is clear proof of His deity. The time of His humiliation was at an end, and God had exalted Him above all (Php 2:9-11).

DAY 17: How are the Old Testament sacrifices compared to Christ's sacrifice?			
Leviticus		**Hebrews**	
Old Covenant (temporary)	Hebrews 7:22; 8:6, 13; 10:20	1. New Covenant (permanent)	
Obsolete promises	Hebrews 8:6-13	2. Better promises	
A shadow	Hebrews 8:5; 9:23-24; 10:1	3. The reality	
Aaronic priesthood (many)	Hebrews 6:19-7:25	4. Melchizedekian priesthood (one)	
Sinful priesthood	Hebrews 7:26-27; 9:7	5. Sinless priest	
Limited-by-death priesthood	Hebrews 7:16-17, 23-24	6. Forever priesthood	
Daily sacrifices	Hebrews 7:27; 9:12, 25-26; 10:9-10, 12	7. Once-for-all sacrifice	
Animal sacrifices	Hebrews 9:11-15, 26; 10:4-10, 19	8. Sacrifice of God's Son	
Ongoing sacrifices	Hebrews 10:11-14, 18	9. Sacrifices no longer needed	
One-year atonement	Hebrews 7:25; 9:12, 15; 10:1-4, 12	10. Eternal propitiation	

FEBRUARY 18

Leviticus 7:1–8:36

7 'Now this is the law of the guilt offering; it is most holy. [2] In the place where they slay the burnt offering they are to slay the guilt offering, and he shall sprinkle its blood around on the altar. [3] Then he shall offer from it all its fat: the fat tail and the fat that covers the entrails, [4] and the two kidneys with the fat that is on them, which is on the loins, and the lobe on the liver he shall remove with the kidneys. [5] The priest shall offer them up in smoke on the

altar as an offering by fire to the LORD; it is a guilt offering. [6] Every male among the priests may eat of it. It shall be eaten in a holy place; it is most holy. [7] The guilt offering is like the sin offering, there is one law for them; the priest who makes atonement with it shall have it. [8] Also the priest who presents any man's burnt offering, that priest shall have for himself the skin of the burnt offering which he has presented. [9] Likewise, every grain offering that is baked in the oven and everything prepared in a pan or on a griddle shall belong to the priest who presents it. [10] Every grain offering, mixed with oil or dry, shall belong to all the sons of Aaron, to all alike.

[11] 'Now this is the law of the sacrifice of peace offerings which shall be presented to the LORD. [12] If he offers it by way of thanksgiving, then along with the sacrifice of thanksgiving he shall offer unleavened cakes mixed with oil, and unleavened wafers spread with oil, and cakes of well stirred fine flour mixed with oil. [13] With the sacrifice of his peace offerings for thanksgiving, he shall present his offering with cakes of leavened bread. [14] Of this he shall present one of every offering as a contribution to the LORD; it shall belong to the priest who sprinkles the blood of the peace offerings.

[15] 'Now as for the flesh of the sacrifice of his thanksgiving peace offerings, it shall be eaten on the day of his offering; he shall not leave any of it over until morning. [16] But if the sacrifice of his offering is a votive or a freewill offering, it shall be eaten on the day that he offers his sacrifice, and on the next day what is left of it may be eaten; [17] but what is left over from the flesh of the sacrifice on the third day shall be burned with fire. [18] So if any of the flesh of the sacrifice of his peace offerings should ever be eaten on the third day, he who offers it will not be accepted, and it will not be reckoned to his benefit. It shall be an offensive thing, and the person who eats of it will bear his own iniquity.

[19] 'Also the flesh that touches anything unclean shall not be eaten; it shall be burned with fire. As for other flesh, anyone who is clean may eat such flesh. [20] But the person who eats the flesh of the sacrifice of peace offerings which belong to the LORD, in his uncleanness, that person shall be cut off from his people. [21] When anyone touches anything unclean, whether human uncleanness, or an unclean animal, or any unclean detestable thing, and eats of the flesh of the sacrifice of peace offerings which belong to the LORD, that person shall be cut off from his people.'"

[22] Then the LORD spoke to Moses, saying, [23] "Speak to the sons of Israel, saying, 'You shall not eat any fat from an ox, a sheep or a goat. [24] Also the fat of an animal which dies and the fat of an animal torn by beasts may be put to any other use, but you must certainly not eat it. [25] For whoever eats the fat of the animal from which an offering by fire is offered to the LORD, even the person who eats shall be cut off from his people. [26] You are not to eat any blood, either of bird or animal, in any of your dwellings. [27] Any person who eats any blood, even that person shall be cut off from his people.'"

[28] Then the LORD spoke to Moses, saying, [29] "Speak to the sons of Israel, saying, 'He who offers the sacrifice of his peace offerings to the LORD shall bring his offering to the LORD from the sacrifice of his peace offerings. [30] His own hands are to bring offerings by fire to the LORD. He shall bring the fat with the breast, that the breast may be presented as a wave offering before the LORD. [31] The priest shall offer up the fat in smoke on the altar, but the breast shall belong to Aaron and his sons. [32] You shall give the right thigh to the priest as a contribution from the sacrifices of your peace offerings. [33] The one among the sons of Aaron who offers the blood of the peace offerings and the fat, the right thigh shall be his as his portion. [34] For I have taken the breast of the wave offering and the thigh of the contribution from the sons of Israel from the sacrifices of their peace offerings, and have given them to Aaron the priest and to his sons as their due forever from the sons of Israel.

[35] 'This is that which is consecrated to Aaron and that which is consecrated to his sons from the offerings by fire to the LORD, in that day when he presented them to serve as priests to the LORD. [36] These the LORD had commanded to be given them from the sons of Israel in the day that He anointed them. It is their due forever throughout their generations.'"

[37] This is the law of the burnt offering, the grain offering and the sin offering and the guilt offering and the ordination offering and the sacrifice of peace offerings, [38] which the LORD commanded Moses at Mount Sinai in the day that He commanded the sons of Israel to present their offerings to the LORD in the wilderness of Sinai.

8 Then the LORD spoke to Moses, saying, [2] "Take Aaron and his sons with him, and the garments and the anointing oil and the bull of the sin offering, and the two rams and the basket of unleavened bread, [3] and assemble all the congregation at the doorway of the tent of meeting." ⁴So Moses did just as the LORD commanded him. When the congregation was assembled at the doorway of the tent of meeting, ⁵Moses said to the congregation, "This is the thing which the LORD has commanded to do."

⁶Then Moses had Aaron and his sons come near and washed them with water. ⁷He put the tunic on him and girded him with the sash, and clothed him with the robe and put the ephod on him; and he girded him with the artistic band of the ephod, with which he tied it to him. ⁸He then placed the breastpiece on him, and in the breastpiece he put the Urim and the Thummim. ⁹He also placed the turban on his head, and on the turban, at its front, he placed the golden plate, the holy crown, just as the LORD had commanded Moses.

¹⁰Moses then took the anointing oil and anointed the tabernacle and all that was in it, and consecrated them. ¹¹He sprinkled some of it on the altar seven times and anointed the altar and all its utensils, and the basin and its stand, to consecrate them. ¹²Then he poured some of the anointing oil on Aaron's head and anointed him, to consecrate him. ¹³Next Moses had Aaron's sons come near and clothed them with tunics, and girded them with sashes and bound caps on them, just as the LORD had commanded Moses.

¹⁴Then he brought the bull of the sin offering, and Aaron and his sons laid their hands on the head of the bull of the sin offering. ¹⁵Next Moses slaughtered it and took the blood and with his finger put some of it around on the horns of the altar, and purified the altar. Then he poured out the rest of the blood at the base of the altar and consecrated it, to make atonement for it. ¹⁶He also took all the fat that was on the entrails and the lobe of the liver, and the two kidneys and their fat; and Moses offered it up in smoke on the altar. ¹⁷But the bull and its hide and its flesh and its refuse he burned in the fire outside the camp, just as the LORD had commanded Moses.

¹⁸Then he presented the ram of the burnt offering, and Aaron and his sons laid their hands on the head of the ram. ¹⁹Moses slaughtered it and sprinkled the blood around on the altar. ²⁰When he had cut the ram into its pieces, Moses offered up the head and the pieces and the suet in smoke. ²¹After he had washed the entrails and the legs with water, Moses offered up the whole ram in smoke on the altar. It was a burnt offering for a soothing aroma; it was an offering by fire to the LORD, just as the LORD had commanded Moses.

²²Then he presented the second ram, the ram of ordination, and Aaron and his sons laid their hands on the head of the ram. ²³Moses slaughtered it and took some of its blood and put it on the lobe of Aaron's right ear, and on the thumb of his right hand and on the big toe of his right foot. ²⁴He also had Aaron's sons come near; and Moses put some of the blood on the lobe of their right ear, and on the thumb of their right hand and on the big toe of their right foot. Moses then sprinkled the rest of the blood around on the altar. ²⁵He took the fat, and the fat tail, and all the fat that was on the entrails, and the lobe of the liver and the two kidneys and their fat and the right thigh. ²⁶From the basket of unleavened bread that was before the LORD, he took one unleavened cake and one cake of bread mixed with oil and one wafer, and placed them on the portions of fat and on the right thigh. ²⁷He then put all these on the hands of Aaron and on the hands of his sons and presented them as a wave offering before the LORD. ²⁸Then Moses took them from their hands and offered them up in smoke on the altar with the burnt offering. They were an ordination offering for a soothing aroma; it was an offering by fire to the LORD. ²⁹Moses also took the breast and presented it for a wave offering before the LORD; it was Moses' portion of the ram of ordination, just as the LORD had commanded Moses.

8:23-24 right ear...right hand...right foot. Using a part to represent the whole, Aaron and his sons were consecrated to listen to God's holy Word, to carry out His holy assignments, and to live holy lives.

³⁰So Moses took some of the anointing oil and some of the blood which was on the altar and sprinkled it on Aaron, on his garments, on his sons, and on the garments of his sons with him; and he consecrated Aaron, his garments, and his sons, and the garments of his sons with him.

³¹Then Moses said to Aaron and to his sons, "Boil the flesh at the doorway of the tent of meeting, and eat it there together with the bread which is in the basket of the ordination offering, just as I commanded, saying, 'Aaron and his sons shall eat it.' ³²The remainder of the flesh and of the bread you

shall burn in the fire. ³³You shall not go outside the doorway of the tent of meeting for seven days, until the day that the period of your ordination is fulfilled; for he will ordain you through seven days. ³⁴The LORD has commanded to do as has been done this day, to make atonement on your behalf. ³⁵At the doorway of the tent of meeting, moreover, you shall remain day and night for seven days and keep the charge of the LORD, so that you will not die, for so I have been commanded." ³⁶Thus Aaron and his sons did all the things which the LORD had commanded through Moses.

Psalm 24:7–10

7 Lift up your heads, O gates,
And be lifted up, O ancient doors,
That the King of glory may
come in!
8 Who is the King of glory?
The LORD strong and mighty,
The LORD mighty in battle.
9 Lift up your heads, O gates,
And lift *them* up, O ancient
doors,
That the King of glory may
come in!
10 Who is this King of glory?
The LORD of hosts,
He is the King of glory.   *Selah*

Proverbs 9:10–12

10 The fear of the LORD is the
beginning of wisdom,
And the knowledge of the Holy
One is understanding.
11 For by me your days will
be multiplied,
And years of life will be added
to you.
12 If you are wise, you are
wise for yourself,
And if you scoff, you
alone will bear it.

Mark 1:1–20

1 The beginning of the gospel of Jesus Christ, the Son of God.
²As it is written in Isaiah the prophet:

"BEHOLD, I SEND MY MESSENGER
AHEAD OF YOU,
WHO WILL PREPARE YOUR WAY;
3 THE VOICE OF ONE CRYING
IN THE WILDERNESS,
'MAKE READY THE WAY OF THE LORD,
MAKE HIS PATHS STRAIGHT.'"

⁴John the Baptist appeared in the wilderness preaching a baptism of repentance for the forgiveness of sins. ⁵And all the country of Judea was going out to him, and all the people of Jerusalem; and they were being baptized by him in the Jordan River, confessing their sins. ⁶John was clothed with camel's hair and *wore* a leather belt around his waist, and his diet was locusts and wild honey. ⁷And he was preaching, and saying, "After me One is coming who is mightier than I, and I am not fit to stoop down and untie the thong of His sandals. ⁸I baptized you with water; but He will baptize you with the Holy Spirit."

⁹In those days Jesus came from Nazareth in Galilee and was baptized by John in the Jordan. ¹⁰Immediately coming up out of the water, He saw the heavens opening, and the Spirit like a dove descending upon Him; ¹¹and a voice came out of the heavens: "You are My beloved Son, in You I am well-pleased."

¹²Immediately the Spirit *impelled Him to go* out into the wilderness. ¹³And He was in the wilderness forty days being tempted by Satan; and He was with the wild beasts, and the angels were ministering to Him.

¹⁴Now after John had been taken into custody, Jesus came into Galilee, preaching the gospel of God, ¹⁵and saying, "The time is fulfilled, and the kingdom of God is at hand; repent and believe in the gospel."

¹⁶As He was going along by the Sea of Galilee, He saw Simon and Andrew, the brother of

1:15 The time is fulfilled. Not time in a chronological sense, but the time for decisive action on God's part. With the arrival of the King, a new era in God's dealings with men had come. **the kingdom of God.** God's sovereign rule over the sphere of salvation; at present in the hearts of His people (Lk 17:21), and in the future, in a literal, earthly kingdom (Rev 20:4–6). **at hand.** Because the King was present. **repent and believe.** Repentance and faith are man's required responses to God's gracious offer of salvation (Ac 20:21).

1:17 Follow Me. Used frequently in the Gospels in reference to discipleship (2:14; 8:34; 10:21; Mt 4:19; 8:22; 9:9; 10:38; 16:24; 19:21; Lk 9:23, 59, 61; 18:22; Jn 1:43; 10:27; 12:26). **fishers of men.** Evangelism was the primary purpose for which Jesus called the apostles, and it remains the central mission for His people (Mt 28:19–20; Ac 1:8).

Simon, casting a net in the sea; for they were fishermen. ¹⁷ And Jesus said to them, "Follow Me, and I will make you become fishers of men." ¹⁸ Immediately they left their nets and followed Him. ¹⁹ Going on a little farther, He saw James the son of Zebedee, and John his brother, who were also in the boat mending the nets. ²⁰ Immediately He called them; and they left their father Zebedee in the boat with the hired servants, and went away to follow Him.

1:22 authority. Jesus' authoritative teaching, as the spoken Word of God, was in sharp contrast to that of the scribes (experts in the Old Testament Scriptures), who based their authority largely on that of other rabbis. Jesus' direct, personal, and forceful teaching was so foreign to their experience that those who heard Him were "amazed" (Titus 2:15).

DAY 18: What was the purpose of John's baptism?

The Gospels all introduce John the Baptist's ministry by quoting Isaiah 40:3 (see Mt 3:3; Lk 3:4; Jn 1:23). John was called "MY MESSENGER" (Mk 1:2), the divinely promised messenger, sent to prepare the way for the Messiah. In ancient times, a king's envoys would travel ahead of him, making sure the roads were safe and fit for him to travel on, as well as announcing his arrival.

As the last Old Testament prophet and the divinely ordained forerunner of the Messiah, John was the culmination of Old Testament history and prophecy (Lk 16:16) as well as the beginning of the historical record of the gospel of Jesus Christ. Not surprisingly, Jesus designated John as the greatest man who had lived until his time (Mt 11:11). John's baptism, being the distinctive mark of his ministry (Mk 1:4), differed from the ritual Jewish washings in that it was a one-time act. The Jews performed a similar one-time washing of Gentile proselytes, symbolizing their embracing of the true faith. That Jews would participate in such a rite was a startling admission that they needed to come to God through repentance and faith just like Gentiles.

FEBRUARY 19

Leviticus 9:1–10:20

9 Now it came about on the eighth day that Moses called Aaron and his sons and the elders of Israel; ² and he said to Aaron, "Take for yourself a calf, a bull, for a sin offering and a ram for a burnt offering, *both* without defect, and offer *them* before the LORD. ³ Then to the sons of Israel you shall speak, saying, 'Take a male goat for a sin offering, and a calf and a lamb, both one year old, without defect, for a burnt offering, ⁴ and an ox and a ram for peace offerings, to sacrifice before the LORD, and a grain offering mixed with oil; for today the LORD will appear to you.'" ⁵ So they took what Moses had commanded to the front of the tent of meeting, and the whole congregation came near and stood before the LORD. ⁶ Moses said, "This is the thing which the LORD has commanded you to do, that the glory of the LORD may appear to you." ⁷ Moses then said to Aaron, "Come near to the altar and offer your sin offering and your burnt offering, that you may make atonement for yourself and for the people; then make the offering for the people, that you may make atonement for them, just as the LORD has commanded."

⁸ So Aaron came near to the altar and slaughtered the calf of the sin offering which was for himself. ⁹ Aaron's sons presented the blood to him; and he dipped his finger in the blood and put *some* on the horns of the altar, and poured out *the rest* of the blood at the base of the altar. ¹⁰ The fat and the kidneys and the lobe of the liver of the sin offering, he then offered up in smoke on the altar just as the LORD had commanded Moses. ¹¹ The flesh and the skin, however, he burned with fire outside the camp.

¹² Then he slaughtered the burnt offering; and Aaron's sons handed the blood to him and he sprinkled it around on the altar. ¹³ They handed the burnt offering to him in pieces, with the head, and he offered *them* up in smoke on the altar. ¹⁴ He also washed the entrails and the legs, and offered *them* up in smoke with the burnt offering on the altar.

¹⁵ Then he presented the people's offering, and took the goat of the sin offering which was for the people, and slaughtered it and offered it for sin, like the first. ¹⁶ He also presented the burnt offering, and offered it according to the ordinance. ¹⁷ Next he presented the grain offering, and filled his hand with some of it and offered *it* up in smoke on the altar, besides the burnt offering of the morning.

[18] Then he slaughtered the ox and the ram, the sacrifice of peace offerings which was for the people; and Aaron's sons handed the blood to him and he sprinkled it around on the altar. [19] As for the portions of fat from the ox and from the ram, the fat tail, and the *fat* covering, and the kidneys and the lobe of the liver, [20] they now placed the portions of fat on the breasts; and he offered them up in smoke on the altar. [21] But the breasts and the right thigh Aaron presented as a wave offering before the LORD, just as Moses had commanded.

[22] Then Aaron lifted up his hands toward the people and blessed them, and he stepped down after making the sin offering and the burnt offering and the peace offerings. [23] Moses and Aaron went into the tent of meeting. When they came out and blessed the people, the glory of the LORD appeared to all the people. [24] Then fire came out from before the LORD and consumed the burnt offering and the portions of fat on the altar; and when all the people saw *it,* they shouted and fell on their faces.

10 Now Nadab and Abihu, the sons of Aaron, took their respective firepans, and after putting fire in them, placed incense on it and offered strange fire before the LORD, which He had not commanded them. [2] And fire came out from the presence of the LORD and consumed them, and they died before the LORD. [3] Then Moses said to Aaron, "It is what the LORD spoke, saying,

'By those who come near Me I
    will be treated as holy,
    And before all the people I
    will be honored.'"

So Aaron, therefore, kept silent.

[4] Moses called also to Mishael and Elzaphan, the sons of Aaron's uncle Uzziel, and said to them, "Come forward, carry your relatives away from the front of the sanctuary to the outside of the camp." [5] So they came forward and carried them still in their tunics to the outside of the camp, as Moses had said. [6] Then Moses said to Aaron and to his sons Eleazar and Ithamar, "Do not uncover your heads nor tear your clothes, so that you will not die and that He will not become wrathful against all the congregation. But your kinsmen, the whole house of Israel, shall bewail the burning which the LORD has brought about. [7] You shall not even go out from the doorway of the tent of meeting, or you will die; for the LORD'S anointing oil is upon you." So they did according to the word of Moses.

[8] The LORD then spoke to Aaron, saying, [9] "Do not drink wine or strong drink, neither you nor your sons with you, when you come into the tent of meeting, so that you will not die—it is a perpetual statute throughout your generations— [10] and so as to make a distinction between the holy and the profane, and between the unclean and the clean, [11] and so as to teach the sons of Israel all the statutes which the LORD has spoken to them through Moses."

[12] Then Moses spoke to Aaron, and to his surviving sons, Eleazar and Ithamar, "Take the grain offering that is left over from the LORD'S offerings by fire and eat it unleavened beside the altar, for it is most holy. [13] You shall eat it, moreover, in a holy place, because it is your due and your sons' due out of the LORD'S offerings by fire; for thus I have been commanded. [14] The breast of the wave offering, however, and the thigh of the offering you may eat in a clean place, you and your sons and your daughters with you; for they have been given as your due and your sons' due out of the sacrifices of the peace offerings of the sons of Israel. [15] The thigh offered by lifting up and the breast offered by waving they shall bring along with the offerings by fire of the portions of fat, to present as a wave offering before the LORD; so it shall be a thing perpetually due you and your sons with you, just as the LORD has commanded."

[16] But Moses searched carefully for the goat of the sin offering, and behold, it had been burned up! So he was angry with Aaron's surviving sons Eleazar and Ithamar, saying, [17] "Why did you not eat the sin offering at the holy place? For it is most holy, and He gave it to you to bear away the guilt of the congregation, to make atonement for them before the LORD. [18] Behold, since its blood had not been brought inside, into the sanctuary, you should certainly have eaten it in the sanctuary, just as I commanded." [19] But Aaron spoke to Moses, "Behold, this very day they presented their sin offering and their burnt offering before the LORD. When things like these happened to me, if I had eaten a sin offering today, would it have been good in the sight of the LORD?" [20] When Moses heard *that,* it seemed good in his sight.

Psalm 25:1–7

A Psalm of David.

To You, O LORD, I lift up my soul.
[2] O my God, in You I trust,
    Do not let me be ashamed;
    Do not let my enemies exult over me.

3 Indeed, none of those who wait
for You will be ashamed;
Those who deal treacherously
without cause will be ashamed.

4 Make me know Your ways, O LORD;
Teach me Your paths.

5 Lead me in Your truth and teach me,
For You are the God of my salvation;
For You I wait all the day.

6 Remember, O LORD, Your compassion
and Your lovingkindnesses,
For they have been from of old.

7 Do not remember the sins of my
youth or my transgressions;
According to Your lovingkindness
remember me,
For Your goodness' sake, O LORD.

25:6-7 Remember...Do not remember... remember. These are not concerns about God forgetting something, but the psalmist's prayer reminds the readers about God's gracious covenant promises and provisions, all of which are grounded upon His "goodness' sake" (see v. 11, "Your name's sake").

Proverbs 9:13-18

13 The woman of folly is boisterous,
She is naive and knows nothing.

14 She sits at the doorway
of her house,
On a seat by the high places
of the city,

15 Calling to those who pass by,
Who are making their paths
straight:

16 "Whoever is naive, let him
turn in here,"
And to him who lacks
understanding she says,

17 "Stolen water is sweet;
And bread *eaten* in secret is
pleasant."

18 But he does not know that
the dead are there,
That her guests are in the
depths of Sheol.

Mark 1:21-45

21 They *went into Capernaum; and immediately on the Sabbath He entered the synagogue and *began to teach. 22 They were amazed at His teaching; for He was teaching them as *one having authority, and not as the scribes. 23 Just then there was a man in their synagogue with an unclean spirit; and he cried out, 24 saying, "What business do we have with each other, Jesus of Nazareth? Have You come to destroy us? I know who You are—the Holy One of God!" 25 And Jesus rebuked him, saying, "Be quiet, and come out of him!" 26 Throwing him into convulsions, the unclean spirit cried out with a loud voice and came out of him. 27 They were all amazed, so that they debated among themselves, saying, "What is this? A new teaching with authority! He commands even the unclean spirits, and they obey Him." 28 Immediately the news about Him spread everywhere into all the surrounding district of Galilee.

29 And immediately after they came out of the synagogue, they came into the house of Simon and Andrew, with James and John. 30 Now Simon's mother-in-law was lying sick with a fever; and immediately they *spoke to Jesus about her. 31 And He came to her and raised her up, taking her by the hand, and the fever left her, and she waited on them.

32 When evening came, after the sun had set, they *began bringing to Him all who were ill and those who were demon-possessed. 33 And the whole city had gathered at the door. 34 And He healed many who were ill with various diseases, and cast out many demons; and He was not permitting the demons to speak, because they knew who He was.

35 In the early morning, while it was still dark, Jesus got up, left *the house,* and went away to a secluded place, and was praying there. 36 Simon and his companions searched for Him; 37 they found Him, and *said to Him, "Everyone is looking for You." 38 He *said to them, "Let us go somewhere else to the towns nearby, so that I may preach there also; for that is what I came for." 39 And He went into their synagogues throughout all Galilee, preaching and casting out the demons.

1:24 What business do we have with each other...? Or, possibly, "Why do You interfere with us?" The demon was acutely aware that he and Jesus belonged to two radically different kingdoms, and thus had nothing in common. That the demon used the plural pronoun "we" indicates he spoke for all the demons. **the Holy One of God.** See Psalm 16:10; Daniel 9:24; Luke 4:34; Acts 2:27; 3:14; 4:27; Revelation 3:7. Amazingly, the demon affirmed Jesus' sinlessness and deity—truths which many in Israel denied, and still deny.

⁴⁰And a leper *came to Jesus, beseeching Him and falling on his knees before Him, and saying, "If You are willing, You can make me clean." ⁴¹Moved with compassion, Jesus stretched out His hand and touched him, and *said to him, "I am willing; be cleansed." ⁴²Immediately the leprosy left him and he was cleansed. ⁴³And He sternly warned him and immediately sent him away, ⁴⁴and He *said to him, "See that you say nothing to anyone; but go, show yourself to the priest and offer for your cleansing what Moses commanded, as a testimony to them." ⁴⁵But he went out and began to proclaim it freely and to spread the news around, to such an extent that Jesus could no longer publicly enter a city, but stayed out in unpopulated areas; and they were coming to Him from everywhere.

1:40 leper. Lepers were considered ceremonially unclean, and were outcasts from society (Lv 13:11). While the Old Testament term for leprosy included other skin diseases, this man may have actually had true leprosy (Hansen's Disease), or else his cure would not have created such a sensation (v. 45).

1:41 compassion. Only Mark records Jesus' emotional reaction to the leper's desperate plight. The Greek word appears only in the Synoptic Gospels and (apart from parables) is used only in reference to Jesus. **touched him.** Unlike rabbis, who avoided lepers lest they become ceremonially defiled, Jesus expressed His compassion with a physical gesture.

DAY 19: What was the incident with Nadab and Abihu about?

In Leviticus 9:23, it states that "the glory of the LORD appeared." The Bible speaks often of the glory of God—the visible appearance of His beauty and perfection reduced to blazing light. His glory appeared to Moses (Ex 3:1–6; 24:15–17; 33:18–23). The glory of God also filled the tabernacle (Ex 40:34), led the people as a pillar of fire and cloud (Ex 40:35–38), and also filled the temple in Jerusalem (1Ki 8:10–11). When Aaron made the first sacrifice in the wilderness, as a priest, the "glory of the LORD appeared to all the people." In these manifestations, God was revealing His righteousness, holiness, truth, wisdom, and grace—the sum of all He is.

Nadab and Abihu were the two oldest sons of Aaron (10:1). The vessel in which the incense was burned in the Holy Place was to be used only for holy purposes. Though the exact infraction is not detailed, instead of taking the incense fire from the bronze altar, they had some other source and thus perpetrated a "strange" or profane act, especially considering the descent of the miraculous fire they had just seen. The same divine fire that accepted the sacrifices (9:24) consumed the errant priests. The sons of Aaron were guilty of violating both requirements of God's absolute standard: "treated as holy...be honored" (10:3). That was not unlike the later deaths of Uzzah (2Sa 6:6–7) or Ananias and Sapphira (Ac 5:5, 10).

FEBRUARY 20

Leviticus 11:1–12:8

11 The LORD spoke again to Moses and to Aaron, saying to them, ²"Speak to the sons of Israel, saying, 'These are the creatures which you may eat from all the animals that are on the earth. ³Whatever divides a hoof, thus making split hoofs, *and* chews the cud, among the animals, that you may eat. ⁴Nevertheless, you are not to eat of these, among those which chew the cud, or among those which divide the hoof: the camel, for though it chews cud, it does not divide the hoof, it is unclean to you. ⁵Likewise, the shaphan, for though it chews cud, it does not divide the hoof, it is unclean to you; ⁶the rabbit also, for though it chews cud, it does not divide the hoof, it is unclean to you; ⁷and the pig, for though it divides the hoof, thus making a split hoof, it does not chew cud, it is unclean to you. ⁸You shall not eat of their flesh nor touch their carcasses; they are unclean to you.

⁹'These you may eat, whatever is in the water: all that have fins and scales, those in the water, in the seas or in the rivers, you may eat. ¹⁰But whatever is in the seas and in the rivers that does not have fins and scales among all the teeming life of the water, and among all the living creatures that are in the water, they are detestable things to you, ¹¹and they shall be abhorrent to you; you may not eat of their flesh, and their carcasses you shall detest. ¹²Whatever in the water does not have fins and scales is abhorrent to you.

¹³'These, moreover, you shall detest among the birds; they are abhorrent, not to be eaten: the eagle and the vulture and the buzzard, ¹⁴and the kite and the falcon in its kind,

¹⁵ every raven in its kind, ¹⁶ and the ostrich and the owl and the sea gull and the hawk in its kind, ¹⁷ and the little owl and the cormorant and the great owl, ¹⁸ and the white owl and the pelican and the carrion vulture, ¹⁹ and the stork, the heron in its kinds, and the hoopoe, and the bat.

²⁰ 'All the winged insects that walk on *all* fours are detestable to you. ²¹ Yet these you may eat among all the winged insects which walk on *all* fours: those which have above their feet jointed legs with which to jump on the earth. ²² These of them you may eat: the locust in its kinds, and the devastating locust in its kinds, and the cricket in its kinds, and the grasshopper in its kinds. ²³ But all other winged insects which are four-footed are detestable to you.

²⁴ 'By these, moreover, you will be made unclean: whoever touches their carcasses becomes unclean until evening, ²⁵ and whoever picks up any of their carcasses shall wash his clothes and be unclean until evening. ²⁶ Concerning all the animals which divide the hoof but do not make a split *hoof,* or which do not chew cud, they are unclean to you: whoever touches them becomes unclean. ²⁷ Also whatever walks on its paws, among all the creatures that walk on *all* fours, are unclean to you; whoever touches their carcasses becomes unclean until evening, ²⁸ and the one who picks up their carcasses shall wash his clothes and be unclean until evening; they are unclean to you.

²⁹ 'Now these are to you the unclean among the swarming things which swarm on the earth: the mole, and the mouse, and the great lizard in its kinds, ³⁰ and the gecko, and the crocodile, and the lizard, and the sand reptile, and the chameleon. ³¹ These are to you the unclean among all the swarming things; whoever touches them when they are dead becomes unclean until evening. ³² Also anything on which one of them may fall when they are dead becomes unclean, including any wooden article, or clothing, or a skin, or a sack—any article of which use is made—it shall be put in the water and be unclean until evening, then it becomes clean. ³³ As for any earthenware vessel into which one of them may fall, whatever is in it becomes unclean and you shall break the vessel. ³⁴ Any of the food which may be eaten, on which water comes, shall become unclean, and any liquid which may be drunk in every vessel shall become unclean. ³⁵ Everything, moreover, on which part of their carcass may fall becomes unclean; an oven or a stove shall be smashed;

they are unclean and shall continue as unclean to you. ³⁶ Nevertheless a spring or a cistern collecting water shall be clean, though the one who touches their carcass shall be unclean. ³⁷ If a part of their carcass falls on any seed for sowing which is to be sown, it is clean. ³⁸ Though if water is put on the seed and a part of their carcass falls on it, it is unclean to you.

³⁹ 'Also if one of the animals dies which you have for food, the one who touches its carcass becomes unclean until evening. ⁴⁰ He too, who eats some of its carcass shall wash his clothes and be unclean until evening, and the one who picks up its carcass shall wash his clothes and be unclean until evening.

⁴¹ 'Now every swarming thing that swarms on the earth is detestable, not to be eaten. ⁴² Whatever crawls on its belly, and whatever walks on *all* fours, whatever has many feet, in respect to every swarming thing that swarms on the earth, you shall not eat them, for they are detestable. ⁴³ Do not render yourselves detestable through any of the swarming things that swarm; and you shall not make yourselves unclean with them so that you become unclean. ⁴⁴ For I am the LORD your God. Consecrate yourselves therefore, and be holy, for I am holy. And you shall not make yourselves unclean with any of the swarming things that swarm on the earth. ⁴⁵ For I am the LORD who brought you up from the land of Egypt to be your God; thus you shall be holy, for I am holy.'"

⁴⁶ This is the law regarding the animal and the bird, and every living thing that moves in the waters and everything that swarms on the earth, ⁴⁷ to make a distinction between the unclean and the clean, and between the edible creature and the creature which is not to be eaten.

12 Then the LORD spoke to Moses, saying: ² "Speak to the sons of Israel, saying:

'When a woman gives birth and bears a male *child,* then she shall be unclean for seven days, as in the days of her menstruation she shall be unclean. ³ On the eighth day the flesh of his foreskin shall be circumcised. ⁴ Then she shall remain in the blood of *her* purification for thirty-three days; she shall not touch any consecrated thing, nor enter the sanctuary until the days of her purification are completed. ⁵ But if she bears a female *child,* then she shall be unclean for two weeks, as in her menstruation; and she shall remain in the blood of *her* purification for sixty-six days.

⁶ 'When the days of her purification are

completed, for a son or for a daughter, she shall bring to the priest at the doorway of the tent of meeting a one year old lamb for a burnt offering and a young pigeon or a turtledove for a sin offering. 7 Then he shall offer it before the LORD and make atonement for her, and she shall be cleansed from the flow of her blood. This is the law for her who bears *a child, whether* a male or a female. 8 But if she cannot afford a lamb, then she shall take two turtledoves or two young pigeons, the one for a burnt offering and the other for a sin offering; and the priest shall make atonement for her, and she will be clean.'"

Psalm 25:8-15

8 Good and upright is the LORD;
  Therefore He instructs
    sinners in the way.
9 He leads the humble in justice,
  And He teaches the humble
    His way.
10 All the paths of the LORD are
    lovingkindness and truth
  To those who keep His covenant
    and His testimonies.
11 For Your name's sake, O LORD,
  Pardon my iniquity, for it is great.

12 Who is the man who fears
    the LORD?
  He will instruct him in the
    way he should choose.
13 His soul will abide in prosperity,
  And his descendants will
    inherit the land.
14 The secret of the LORD is for
    those who fear Him,
  And He will make them
    know His covenant.
15 My eyes are continually
    toward the LORD,
  For He will pluck my feet
    out of the net.

Proverbs 10:1-3

10 The proverbs of Solomon.

  A wise son makes a father glad,
  But a foolish son is a grief
    to his mother.
2 Ill-gotten gains do not profit,
  But righteousness delivers
    from death.
3 The LORD will not allow the
    righteous to hunger,
  But He will reject the craving
    of the wicked.

Mark 2:1-28

2 When He had come back to Capernaum several days afterward, it was heard that He was at home. 2 And many were gathered together, so that there was no longer room, not even near the door; and He was speaking the word to them. 3 And they *came, bringing to Him a paralytic, carried by four men. 4 Being unable to get to Him because of the crowd, they removed the roof above Him; and when they had dug an opening, they let down the pallet on which the paralytic was lying. 5 And Jesus seeing their faith *said to the paralytic, "Son, your sins are forgiven." 6 But some of the scribes were sitting there and reasoning in their hearts, 7 "Why does this man speak that way? He is blaspheming; who can forgive sins but God alone?" 8 Immediately Jesus, aware in His spirit that they were reasoning that way within themselves, *said to them, "Why are you reasoning about these things in your hearts? 9 Which is easier, to say to the paralytic, 'Your sins are forgiven'; or to say, 'Get up, and pick up your pallet and walk'? 10 But so that you may know that the Son of Man has authority on earth to forgive sins"—He *said to the paralytic, 11 "I say to you, get up, pick up your pallet and go home." 12 And he got up and immediately picked up the pallet and went out in the sight of everyone, so that they were all amazed and were glorifying God, saying, "We have never seen anything like this."

13 And He went out again by the seashore; and all the people were coming to Him, and He was teaching them. 14 As He passed by, He saw Levi the *son* of Alphaeus sitting in the tax booth, and He *said to him, "Follow Me!" And he got up and followed Him.

15 And it *happened that He was reclining *at the table* in his house, and many tax collectors and sinners were dining with Jesus and His disciples; for there were many of

2:5 Jesus seeing their faith. The aggressive, persistent effort of the paralytic's friends was visible evidence of their faith in Christ to heal. **Son, your sins are forgiven.** Many Jews in that day believed that all disease and affliction was a direct result of one's sins. This paralytic may have believed that as well; thus he would have welcomed forgiveness of his sins before healing. The Greek verb for "are forgiven" refers to sending or driving away (Ps 103:12; Jer 31:34; Mic 7:19). Thus Jesus dismissed the man's sin and freed him from the guilt of it.

them, and they were following Him. ¹⁶When the scribes of the Pharisees saw that He was eating with the sinners and tax collectors, they said to His disciples, "Why is He eating and drinking with tax collectors and sinners?" ¹⁷And hearing *this*, Jesus *said to them, "*It is* not those who are healthy who need a physician, but those who are sick; I did not come to call the righteous, but sinners."

¹⁸John's disciples and the Pharisees were fasting; and they *came and *said to Him, "Why do John's disciples and the disciples of the Pharisees fast, but Your disciples do not fast?" ¹⁹And Jesus said to them, "While the bridegroom is with them, the attendants of the bridegroom cannot fast, can they? So long as they have the bridegroom with them, they cannot fast. ²⁰But the days will come when the bridegroom is taken away from them, and then they will fast in that day.

²¹"No one sews a patch of unshrunk cloth on an old garment; otherwise the patch pulls away from it, the new from the old, and a worse tear results. ²²No one puts new wine into old wineskins; otherwise the wine will burst the skins, and the wine is lost and the skins *as well;* but *one puts* new wine into fresh wineskins."

²³And it happened that He was passing through the grainfields on the Sabbath, and His disciples began to make their way along while picking the heads *of grain.* ²⁴The Pharisees were saying to Him, "Look, why are they doing what is not lawful on the Sabbath?" ²⁵And He *said to them, "Have you never read what David did when he was in need and he

2:24 what is not lawful on the Sabbath. Rabbinical tradition had interpreted the rubbing of grain in the hands (Lk 6:1) as a form of threshing and had forbidden it. Reaping for profit on the Sabbath was forbidden by Mosaic law (Ex 34:21), but that was obviously not the situation here. Actually, the Pharisees' charge was itself sinful since they were holding their tradition on a par with God's Word.

2:27 The Sabbath was made for man. God instituted the Sabbath to benefit man by giving him a day to rest from his labors and to be a blessing to him. The Pharisees turned it into a burden and made man a slave to their myriad of man-made regulations.

2:28 Lord even of the Sabbath. Jesus claimed He was greater than the Sabbath, and thus was God. Based on that authority, Jesus could in fact reject the Pharisaic regulations concerning the Sabbath and restore God's original intention for Sabbath observance to be a blessing not a burden.

and his companions became hungry; ²⁶how he entered the house of God in the time of Abiathar *the* high priest, and ate the consecrated bread, which is not lawful for *anyone* to eat except the priests, and he also gave it to those who were with him?" ²⁷Jesus said to them, "The Sabbath was made for man, and not man for the Sabbath. ²⁸So the Son of Man is Lord even of the Sabbath."

DAY 20: Does God expect us to be holy?

In Leviticus 11:44-45, God says, "Consecrate yourselves therefore, and be holy, for I am holy." In all of this, God is teaching His people to live antithetically. That is, He is using these clean and unclean distinctions to separate Israel from other idolatrous nations who have no such restrictions, and He is illustrating by these prescriptions that His people must learn to live His way. Through dietary laws and rituals, God is teaching them the reality of living His way in everything. They are being taught to obey God in every seemingly mundane area of life, so as to learn how crucial obedience is. Sacrifices, rituals, diet, and even clothing and cooking are all carefully ordered by God to teach them that they are to live differently from everyone else. This is to be an external illustration for the separation from sin in their hearts. Because the Lord is their God, they are to be utterly distinct.

In v. 44, for the first time the statement "I am the LORD your God" is made as a reason for the required separation and holiness. After this verse, that phrase is mentioned about 50 more times in this book alone, along with the equally instructive claim, "I am holy." Because God is holy and is their God, the people are to be holy in outward ceremonial behavior as an external expression of the greater necessity of heart holiness. The connection between ceremonial holiness carries over into personal holiness. The only motivation given for all these laws is to learn to be holy because God is holy. The holiness theme is central to Leviticus (see 10:3; 19:2; 20:7, 26; 21:6-8).

FEBRUARY 21

Leviticus 13:1–59

13 Then the LORD spoke to Moses and to Aaron, saying, ² "When a man has on the skin of his body a swelling or a scab or a bright spot, and it becomes an infection of leprosy on the skin of his body, then he shall be brought to Aaron the priest or to one of his sons the priests. ³ The priest shall look at the mark on the skin of the body, and if the hair in the infection has turned white and the infection appears to be deeper than the skin of his body, it is an infection of leprosy; when the priest has looked at him, he shall pronounce him unclean. ⁴ But if the bright spot is white on the skin of his body, and it does not appear to be deeper than the skin, and the hair on it has not turned white, then the

13:2 bright spot. This probably refers to inflammation. **leprosy.** This is a term referring to various ancient skin disorders that were sometimes superficial, sometimes serious. It may have included modern leprosy (Hansen's disease). The symptoms described in vv. 2, 6, 10, 18, 30, and 39 are not sufficient for a diagnosis of the clinical condition. For the protection of the people, observation and isolation were demanded for all suspected cases of what could be a contagious disease. This biblical leprosy involved some whiteness (v. 3; Ex 4:6), which disfigured its victim but did not disable him. Naaman was able to exercise his functions as general of Syria's army, although a leper (2Ki 5:1, 27). Both Old Testament and New Testament lepers went almost everywhere, indicating that this disease was not the leprosy of today that cripples. A victim of this scaly disease was unclean as long as the infection was partial. Once the body was covered with it, he was clean and could enter the place of worship (vv. 12–17). Apparently, the complete covering meant the contagious period was over. The allusion to a boil (vv. 18–28) with inflamed or raw areas and whitened hairs may refer to a related infection that was contagious. When lepers were cured by Christ, they were neither lame nor deformed. They were never brought on beds. Similar skin conditions are described in vv. 29–37 and vv. 38–44 (some inflammation from infection). The aim of these laws was to protect the people from disease, but more importantly, to inculcate into them by vivid object lessons how God desired purity, holiness, and cleanness among His people.

priest shall isolate *him who has* the infection for seven days. ⁵ The priest shall look at him on the seventh day, and if in his eyes the infection has not changed *and* the infection has not spread on the skin, then the priest shall isolate him for seven more days. ⁶ The priest shall look at him again on the seventh day, and if the infection has faded and the mark has not spread on the skin, then the priest shall pronounce him clean; it is *only* a scab. And he shall wash his clothes and be clean.

⁷ "But if the scab spreads farther on the skin after he has shown himself to the priest for his cleansing, he shall appear again to the priest. ⁸ The priest shall look, and if the scab has spread on the skin, then the priest shall pronounce him unclean; it is leprosy.

⁹ "When the infection of leprosy is on a man, then he shall be brought to the priest. ¹⁰ The priest shall then look, and if there is a white swelling in the skin, and it has turned the hair white, and there is quick raw flesh in the swelling, ¹¹ it is a chronic leprosy on the skin of his body, and the priest shall pronounce him unclean; he shall not isolate him, for he is unclean. ¹² If the leprosy breaks out farther on the skin, and the leprosy covers all the skin of *him who has* the infection from his head even to his feet, as far as the priest can see, ¹³ then the priest shall look, and behold, *if* the leprosy has covered all his body, he shall pronounce clean *him who has* the infection; it has all turned white *and* he is clean. ¹⁴ But whenever raw flesh appears on him, he shall be unclean. ¹⁵ The priest shall look at the raw flesh, and he shall pronounce him unclean; the raw flesh is unclean, it is leprosy. ¹⁶ Or if the raw flesh turns again and is changed to white, then he shall come to the priest, ¹⁷ and the priest shall look at him, and behold, *if* the infection has turned to white, then the priest shall pronounce clean *him who has* the infection; he is clean.

¹⁸ "When the body has a boil on its skin and it is healed, ¹⁹ and in the place of the boil there is a white swelling or a reddish-white, bright spot, then it shall be shown to the priest; ²⁰ and the priest shall look, and behold, *if* it appears to be lower than the skin, and the hair on it has turned white, then the priest shall pronounce him unclean; it is the infection of leprosy, it has broken out in the boil. ²¹ But if the priest looks at it, and behold, there are no white hairs in it and it is not lower than the skin and is faded, then the priest shall isolate him for seven days; ²² and if it spreads farther on the skin, then the priest shall pronounce him unclean; it is an infection. ²³ But if the

bright spot remains in its place and does not spread, it is *only* the scar of the boil; and the priest shall pronounce him clean.

24 "Or if the body sustains in its skin a burn by fire, and the raw *flesh* of the burn becomes a bright spot, reddish-white, or white, 25 then the priest shall look at it. And if the hair in the bright spot has turned white and it appears to be deeper than the skin, it is leprosy; it has broken out in the burn. Therefore, the priest shall pronounce him unclean; it is an infection of leprosy. 26 But if the priest looks at it, and indeed, there is no white hair in the bright spot and it is no deeper than the skin, but is dim, then the priest shall isolate him for seven days; 27 and the priest shall look at him on the seventh day. If it spreads farther in the skin, then the priest shall pronounce him unclean; it is an infection of leprosy. 28 But if the bright spot remains in its place and has not spread in the skin, but is dim, it is the swelling from the burn; and the priest shall pronounce him clean, for it is *only* the scar of the burn.

29 "Now if a man or woman has an infection on the head or on the beard, 30 then the priest shall look at the infection, and if it appears to be deeper than the skin and there is thin yellowish hair in it, then the priest shall pronounce him unclean; it is a scale, it is leprosy of the head or of the beard. 31 But if the priest looks at the infection of the scale, and indeed, it appears to be no deeper than the skin and there is no black hair in it, then the priest shall isolate *the person* with the scaly infection for seven days. 32 On the seventh day the priest shall look at the infection, and if the scale has not spread and no yellowish hair has grown in it, and the appearance of the scale is no deeper than the skin, 33 then he shall shave himself, but he shall not shave the scale; and the priest shall isolate *the person* with the scale seven more days. 34 Then on the seventh day the priest shall look at the scale, and if the scale has not spread in the skin and it appears to be no deeper than the skin, the priest shall pronounce him clean; and he shall wash his clothes and be clean. 35 But if the scale spreads farther in the skin after his cleansing, 36 then the priest shall look at him, and if the scale has spread in the skin, the priest need not seek for the yellowish hair; he is unclean. 37 If in his sight the scale has remained, however, and black hair has grown in it, the scale has healed, he is clean; and the priest shall pronounce him clean.

38 "When a man or a woman has bright spots on the skin of the body, *even* white bright spots, 39 then the priest shall look, and if the bright spots on the skin of their bodies are a faint white, it is eczema that has broken out on the skin; he is clean.

40 "Now if a man loses the hair of his head, he is bald; he is clean. 41 If his head becomes bald at the front and sides, he is bald on the forehead; he is clean. 42 But if on the bald head or the bald forehead, there occurs a reddish-white infection, it is leprosy breaking out on his bald head or on his bald forehead. 43 Then the priest shall look at him; and if the swelling of the infection is reddish-white on his bald head or on his bald forehead, like the appearance of leprosy in the skin of the body, 44 he is a leprous man, he is unclean. The priest shall surely pronounce him unclean; his infection is on his head.

45 "As for the leper who has the infection, his clothes shall be torn, and the hair of his head shall be uncovered, and he shall cover his mustache and cry, 'Unclean! Unclean!' 46 He shall remain unclean all the days during which he has the infection; he is unclean. He shall live alone; his dwelling shall be outside the camp.

47 "When a garment has a mark of leprosy in it, whether it is a wool garment or a linen garment, 48 whether in warp or woof, of linen or of wool, whether in leather or in any article made of leather, 49 if the mark is greenish or reddish in the garment or in the leather, or in the warp or in the woof, or in any article of leather, it is a leprous mark and shall be shown to the priest. 50 Then the priest shall look at the mark and shall quarantine the article with the mark for seven days. 51 He shall then look at the mark on the seventh day; if the mark has spread in the garment, whether in the warp or in the woof, or in the leather, whatever the purpose for which the leather is used, the mark is a leprous malignancy, it is unclean. 52 So he shall burn the garment, whether the warp or the woof, in wool or in linen, or any article of leather in which the mark occurs, for it is a leprous malignancy; it shall be burned in the fire.

53 "But if the priest shall look, and indeed the mark has not spread in the garment, either in the warp or in the woof, or in any article of leather, 54 then the priest shall order them to wash the thing in which the mark occurs and he shall quarantine it for seven more days. 55 After the article with the mark has been washed, the priest shall again look, and if the mark has not changed its appearance, even though the mark has not spread, it is unclean; you shall burn it in the fire, whether

an eating away has produced bareness on the top or on the front of it.

⁵⁶ "Then if the priest looks, and if the mark has faded after it has been washed, then he shall tear it out of the garment or out of the leather, whether from the warp or from the woof; ⁵⁷ and if it appears again in the garment, whether in the warp or in the woof, or in any article of leather, it is an outbreak; the article with the mark shall be burned in the fire. ⁵⁸ The garment, whether the warp or the woof, or any article of leather from which the mark has departed when you washed it, it shall then be washed a second time and will be clean."

⁵⁹ This is the law for the mark of leprosy in a garment of wool or linen, whether in the warp or in the woof, or in any article of leather, for pronouncing it clean or unclean.

Psalm 25:16-22

¹⁶ Turn to me and be gracious to me,
For I am lonely and afflicted.
¹⁷ The troubles of my heart
are enlarged;
Bring me out of my distresses.
¹⁸ Look upon my affliction
and my trouble,
And forgive all my sins.
¹⁹ Look upon my enemies,
for they are many,
And they hate me with violent hatred.
²⁰ Guard my soul and deliver me;
Do not let me be ashamed, for
I take refuge in You.
²¹ Let integrity and uprightness
preserve me,
For I wait for You.
²² Redeem Israel, O God,
Out of all his troubles.

Proverbs 10:4-5

⁴ Poor is he who works with
a negligent hand,
But the hand of the diligent makes rich.
⁵ He who gathers in summer is
a son who acts wisely,
But he who sleeps in harvest is
a son who acts shamefully.

Mark 3:1-19

3 He entered again into a synagogue; and a man was there whose hand was withered. ² They were watching Him *to see* if He would heal him on the Sabbath, so that they might accuse Him. ³ He *said to the man with the withered hand, "Get up and come forward!" ⁴ And He *said to them, "Is it lawful to do good or to do harm on the Sabbath, to save a life or to kill?" But they kept silent. ⁵ After looking around at them with anger, grieved at their hardness of heart, He *said to the man, "Stretch out your hand." And he stretched it out, and his hand was restored. ⁶ The Pharisees went out and immediately *began* conspiring with the Herodians against Him, *as to* how they might destroy Him.

⁷ Jesus withdrew to the sea with His disciples; and a great multitude from Galilee followed; and *also* from Judea, ⁸ and from Jerusalem, and from Idumea, and beyond the Jordan, and the vicinity of Tyre and Sidon, a great number of people heard of all that He was doing and came to Him. ⁹ And He told His disciples that a boat should stand ready for Him because of the crowd, so that they would not crowd Him; ¹⁰ for He had healed many, with the result that all those who had afflictions pressed around Him in order to touch Him. ¹¹ Whenever the unclean spirits saw Him, they would fall down before Him and shout, "You are the Son of God!" ¹² And He earnestly warned them not to tell who He was.

¹³ And He *went up on the mountain and *summoned those whom He Himself wanted, and they came to Him. ¹⁴ And He appointed twelve, so that they would be with Him and that He *could* send them out to preach, ¹⁵ and to have authority to cast out the demons. ¹⁶ And He appointed the twelve: Simon (to whom He gave the name Peter), ¹⁷ and James, the *son* of Zebedee, and John the brother of James (to them He gave the name Boanerges, which means, "Sons of Thunder"); ¹⁸ and Andrew, and Philip, and Bartholomew, and Matthew, and Thomas, and James the son of Alphaeus, and Thaddaeus, and Simon the Zealot; ¹⁹ and Judas Iscariot, who betrayed Him.

3:13 summoned those whom He Himself wanted. The Greek verb "summoned" stresses that Jesus acted in His own sovereign interest when He chose the 12 disciples (Jn 15:16).

3:14 appointed twelve. Christ, by an explicit act of His will, formed a distinct group of 12 men who were among His followers. This new group constituted the foundation of His church (Eph 2:20).

3:15 have authority. This word is sometimes rendered "power." Along with the main task of preaching, Jesus gave the 12 the right to expel demons (Lk 9:1).

In Mark 3:1–6, Jesus was in a synagogue, where there was a man with a withered hand. This describes a condition of paralysis or deformity from an accident, a disease, or a congenital defect. It became another situation for the Pharisees to "accuse" Him (v. 2) of a violation of the Sabbath—an accusation they could bring before the Sanhedrin.

Jesus countered the Pharisees with a question that elevated the issue at hand from a legal to a moral problem. "Is it lawful to do good or to do harm on the Sabbath, to save a life or to kill?" Jesus asks (v. 4). He was forcing the Pharisees to examine their tradition regarding the Sabbath to see if it was consistent with God's Old Testament law. Christ used a device common in the Middle East—He framed the issue in terms of clear-cut extremes. The obvious implication is that failure to do good or save a life was wrong and not in keeping with God's original intention for the Sabbath. But the Pharisees kept silent, and by so doing implied that their Sabbath views and practices were false.

Jesus' "anger" (v. 5) with human sin reveals a healthy, moral nature. His reaction was consistent with His divine nature and proved that He is the righteous Son of God. This kind of holy indignation with sinful attitudes and practices was to be more fully demonstrated when Jesus cleansed the temple (see 11:15–18; Mt 21:12–13; Lk 19:45–48). The "hardness of hearts" refers to an inability to understand because of a rebellious attitude (Ps 95:8; Heb 3:8, 15). The Pharisees' hearts were becoming more and more obstinate and unresponsive to the truth (see 16:14; Ro 9:18).

FEBRUARY 22

Leviticus 14:1–57

14 Then the LORD spoke to Moses, saying, ² "This shall be the law of the leper in the day of his cleansing. Now he shall be brought to the priest, ³ and the priest shall go out to the outside of the camp. Thus the priest shall look, and if the infection of leprosy has been healed in the leper, ⁴ then the priest shall give orders to take two live clean birds and cedar wood and a scarlet string and hyssop for the one who is to be cleansed. ⁵ The priest shall also give orders to slay the one bird in an earthenware vessel over running water. ⁶ As for the live bird, he shall take it together with the cedar wood and the scarlet string and the hyssop, and shall dip them and the live bird in the blood of the bird that was slain over the running water. ⁷ He shall then sprinkle seven times the one who is to be cleansed from the leprosy and shall pronounce him clean, and shall let the live bird go free over the open field. ⁸ The one to be cleansed shall then wash his clothes and shave off all his hair and bathe in water and be clean. Now afterward, he may enter the camp, but he shall stay outside his tent for seven days. ⁹ It will be on the seventh day that he shall shave off all his hair: he shall shave his head and his beard and his eyebrows, even all his hair. He shall then wash his clothes and bathe his body in water and be clean.

¹⁰ "Now on the eighth day he is to take two male lambs without defect, and a yearling ewe lamb without defect, and three-tenths of an ephah of fine flour mixed with oil for a grain offering, and one log of oil; ¹¹ and the priest who pronounces him clean shall present the man to be cleansed and the aforesaid before the LORD at the doorway of the tent of meeting. ¹² Then the priest shall take the one male lamb and bring it for a guilt offering, with the log of oil, and present them as a wave offering before the LORD. ¹³ Next he shall slaughter the male lamb in the place where they slaughter the sin offering and the burnt offering, at the place of the sanctuary—for the guilt offering, like the sin offering, belongs to the priest; it is most holy. ¹⁴ The priest shall then take some of the blood of the guilt offering, and the priest shall put it on the lobe of the right ear of the one to be cleansed, and on the thumb of his right hand and on the big toe of his right foot. ¹⁵ The priest shall also take some of the log of oil, and pour it into his left palm; ¹⁶ the priest shall then dip his right-hand finger into the oil that is in his left palm, and with his finger sprinkle some of the oil seven times before the LORD. ¹⁷ Of the remaining oil which is in his palm, the priest shall put some on the right ear lobe of the one to be cleansed, and on the thumb of his right hand, and on the big toe of his right foot, on the blood of the guilt offering; ¹⁸ while the rest of the oil that is in the priest's palm, he shall put on the head of the one to be cleansed. So the priest

14:18 put on the head. This would not have been understood as an anointing for entry into an office, but rather a symbolic gesture of cleansing and healing. There could be a connection with the New Testament directive to anoint the sick for healing (Mk 6:13; 16:18; Jas 5:14).

shall make atonement on his behalf before the LORD. ¹⁹ The priest shall next offer the sin offering and make atonement for the one to be cleansed from his uncleanness. Then afterward, he shall slaughter the burnt offering. ²⁰ The priest shall offer up the burnt offering and the grain offering on the altar. Thus the priest shall make atonement for him, and he will be clean.

²¹ "But if he is poor and his means are insufficient, then he is to take one male lamb for a guilt offering as a wave offering to make atonement for him, and one-tenth *of an ephah* of fine flour mixed with oil for a grain offering, and a log of oil, ²² and two turtledoves or two young pigeons which are within his means, the one shall be a sin offering and the other a burnt offering. ²³ Then the eighth day he shall bring them for his cleansing to the priest, at the doorway of the tent of meeting, before the LORD. ²⁴ The priest shall take the lamb of the guilt offering and the log of oil, and the priest shall offer them for a wave offering before the LORD. ²⁵ Next he shall slaughter the lamb of the guilt offering; and the priest is to take some of the blood of the guilt offering and put *it* on the lobe of the right ear of the one to be cleansed and on the thumb of his right hand and on the big toe of his right foot. ²⁶ The priest shall also pour some of the oil into his left palm; ²⁷ and with his right-hand finger the priest shall sprinkle some of the oil that is in his left palm seven times before the LORD. ²⁸ The priest shall then put some of the oil that is in his palm on the lobe of the right ear of the one to be cleansed, and on the thumb of his right hand and on the big toe of his right foot, on the place of the blood of the guilt offering. ²⁹ Moreover, the rest of the oil that is in the priest's palm he shall put on the head of the one to be cleansed, to make atonement on his behalf before the LORD. ³⁰ He shall then offer one of the turtledoves or young pigeons, which are within his means. ³¹ *He shall offer* what he can afford, the one for a sin offering and the other for a burnt

offering, together with the grain offering. So the priest shall make atonement before the LORD on behalf of the one to be cleansed. ³² This is the law *for him* in whom there is an infection of leprosy, whose means are limited for his cleansing."

³³ The LORD further spoke to Moses and to Aaron, saying:

³⁴ "When you enter the land of Canaan, which I give you for a possession, and I put a mark of leprosy on a house in the land of your possession, ³⁵ then the one who owns the house shall come and tell the priest, saying, '*Something* like a mark *of leprosy* has become visible to me in the house.' ³⁶ The priest shall then command that they empty the house before the priest goes in to look at the mark, so that everything in the house need not become unclean; and afterward the priest shall go in to look at the house. ³⁷ So he shall look at the mark, and if the mark on the walls of the house has greenish or reddish depressions and appears deeper than the surface, ³⁸ then the priest shall come out of the house, to the doorway, and quarantine the house for seven days. ³⁹ The priest shall return on the seventh day and make an inspection. If the mark has indeed spread in the walls of the house, ⁴⁰ then the priest shall order them to tear out the stones with the mark in them and throw them away at an unclean place outside the city. ⁴¹ He shall have the house scraped all around inside, and they shall dump the plaster that they scrape off at an unclean place outside the city. ⁴² Then they shall take other stones and replace *those* stones, and he shall take other plaster and replaster the house.

⁴³ "If, however, the mark breaks out again in the house after he has torn out the stones and scraped the house, and after it has been replastered, ⁴⁴ then the priest shall come in and make an inspection. If he sees that the mark has indeed spread in the house, it is a malignant mark in the house; it is unclean. ⁴⁵ He shall therefore tear down the house, its stones, and its timbers, and all the plaster of the house, and he shall take *them* outside the city to an unclean place. ⁴⁶ Moreover, whoever goes into the house during the time that he has quarantined it, becomes unclean until evening. ⁴⁷ Likewise, whoever lies down in the house shall wash his clothes, and whoever eats in the house shall wash his clothes.

⁴⁸ "If, on the other hand, the priest comes in and makes an inspection and the mark has not indeed spread in the house after the house has been replastered, then the priest shall

pronounce the house clean because the mark has not reappeared. ⁴⁹To cleanse the house then, he shall take two birds and cedar wood and a scarlet string and hyssop, ⁵⁰and he shall slaughter the one bird in an earthenware vessel over running water. ⁵¹Then he shall take the cedar wood and the hyssop and the scarlet string, with the live bird, and dip them in the blood of the slain bird as well as in the running water, and sprinkle the house seven times. ⁵²He shall thus cleanse the house with the blood of the bird and with the running water, along with the live bird and with the cedar wood and with the hyssop and with the scarlet string. ⁵³However, he shall let the live bird go free outside the city into the open field. So he shall make atonement for the house, and it will be clean."

⁵⁴This is the law for any mark of leprosy— even for a scale, ⁵⁵and for the leprous garment or house, ⁵⁶and for a swelling, and for a scab, and for a bright spot— ⁵⁷to teach when they are unclean and when they are clean. This is the law of leprosy.

Psalm 26:1–5

A Psalm of David.

Vindicate me, O LORD, for I have
walked in my integrity,
And I have trusted in the LORD
without wavering.
² Examine me, O LORD, and
try me;
Test my mind and my heart.
³ For Your lovingkindness
is before my eyes,
And I have walked in Your
truth.
⁴ I do not sit with deceitful
men,
Nor will I go with pretenders.
⁵ I hate the assembly of
evildoers,
And I will not sit with the
wicked.

26:1 Vindicate me. Literally, "Judge me!" This refers to exoneration of some false accusations and/or charges under the protection of the covenant stipulations of the theocratic law (Pss 7:8; 35:24; 43:1). **my integrity.** Again, this is not a claim to perfection, but of innocence, particularly as viewed within the context of ungrounded "legal" charges (Ps 7:8; Pr 10:9; 19:1; 20:7; 28:6).

Proverbs 10:6–7

⁶ Blessings are on the head
of the righteous,
But the mouth of the wicked
conceals violence.
⁷ The memory of the
righteous is blessed,
But the name of the wicked
will rot.

Mark 3:20–35

²⁰And He *came home, and the crowd *gathered again, to such an extent that they could not even eat a meal. ²¹When His own people heard *of this,* they went out to take custody of Him; for they were saying, "He has lost His senses." ²²The scribes who came down from Jerusalem were saying, "He is possessed by Beelzebul," and "He casts out the demons by the ruler of the demons." ²³And He called them to Himself and began speaking to them in parables, "How can Satan cast out Satan? ²⁴If a kingdom is divided against itself, that kingdom cannot stand. ²⁵If a house is divided against itself, that house will not be able to stand. ²⁶If Satan has risen up against himself and is divided, he cannot stand, but he is finished! ²⁷But no one can enter the strong man's house and plunder his property unless he first binds the strong man, and then he will plunder his house.

²⁸"Truly I say to you, all sins shall be forgiven the sons of men, and whatever blasphemies they utter; ²⁹but whoever blasphemes against the Holy Spirit never has forgiveness, but is guilty of an eternal sin"— ³⁰because they were saying, "He has an unclean spirit."

³¹Then His mother and His brothers

3:21 His own people. In Greek, this expression was used in various ways to describe someone's friends or close associates. In the strictest sense, it meant family, which is probably the best understanding here. **take custody of Him.** Mark used this same term elsewhere to mean the arrest of a person (6:17; 12:12; 14:1, 44, 46, 51). Jesus' relatives evidently heard the report of v. 20 and came to Capernaum to restrain Him from His many activities and bring Him under their care and control, all supposedly for His own good. **lost His senses.** Jesus' family could only explain His unconventional lifestyle, with its willingness for others always to impose on Him, by saying He was irrational or had lost His mind.

*arrived, and standing outside they sent *word* to Him and called Him. ³²A crowd was sitting around Him, and they *said to Him, "Behold, Your mother and Your brothers are outside looking for You." ³³Answering them, He *said, "Who are My mother and My brothers?" ³⁴Looking about at those who were sitting around Him, He *said, "Behold My mother and My brothers! ³⁵For whoever does the will of God, he is My brother and sister and mother."

3:35 Jesus made a decisive and comprehensive statement on true Christian discipleship. Such discipleship involves a spiritual relationship that transcends the physical family and is open to all who are empowered by the Spirit of God to come to Christ in repentance and faith and enabled to live a life of obedience to God's Word.

DAY 22: How did Mark come to write one of the gospels if he wasn't one of the original disciples?

Although Mark was not one of the original apostles of Jesus, he was involved in many of the events recorded in the New Testament. He traveled as a close companion of the apostle Peter and appears repeatedly throughout the Book of Acts, where he is known as "John who was also called Mark" (Ac 12:12, 25; 15:37, 39). When Peter was miraculously freed from prison, his first action was to go to Mark's mother's home in Jerusalem (Ac 12:12).

John Mark was also a cousin of Barnabas (Col 4:10), and he joined Paul and Barnabas on their first missionary journey (Ac 12:25; 13:5). But Mark deserted the mission team while in Perga and returned to Jerusalem (Ac 13:13). Later, when Barnabas wanted to give Mark another opportunity to travel with Paul's second missionary team, Paul refused. The resulting friction between Paul and Barnabas led to their separation (Ac 15:38–40).

Eventually, Mark's youthful vacillation gave way to great strength and maturity. In time, he proved himself even to the apostle Paul. When Paul wrote to the Colossians, he told them that if John Mark came, they were to welcome him (Col 4:10). Paul even listed Mark as a fellow worker (Philem v. 24). Later, Paul told Timothy, "Pick up Mark and bring him with you, for he is useful to me for service" (2Ti 4:11).

FEBRUARY 23

Leviticus 15:1–16:34

15 The LORD also spoke to Moses and to Aaron, saying, ²"Speak to the sons of Israel, and say to them, 'When any man has a discharge from his body, his discharge is unclean. ³This, moreover, shall be his uncleanness in his discharge: it is his uncleanness whether his body allows its discharge to flow or whether his body obstructs its discharge. ⁴Every bed on which the person with the discharge lies becomes unclean, and everything on which he sits becomes unclean. ⁵Anyone, moreover, who touches his bed shall wash his clothes and bathe in water and be unclean until evening; ⁶and whoever sits on the thing on which the man with the discharge has been sitting, shall wash his clothes and bathe in water and be unclean until evening. ⁷Also whoever touches the person with the discharge shall wash his clothes and bathe in water and be unclean until evening. ⁸Or if the man with the discharge spits on one who is clean, he too shall wash his clothes and bathe in water and be

unclean until evening. ⁹Every saddle on which the person with the discharge rides becomes unclean. ¹⁰Whoever then touches any of the things which were under him shall be unclean until evening, and he who carries them shall wash his clothes and bathe in water and be unclean until evening. ¹¹Likewise, whomever the one with the discharge touches without having rinsed his hands in water shall wash his clothes and bathe in water and be unclean until evening. ¹²However, an earthenware vessel which the person with the discharge touches shall be broken, and every wooden vessel shall be rinsed in water.

¹³'Now when the man with the discharge becomes cleansed from his discharge, then he shall count off for himself seven days for his cleansing; he shall then wash his clothes and bathe his body in running water and will become clean. ¹⁴Then on the eighth day he shall take for himself two turtledoves or two young pigeons, and come before the LORD to the doorway of the tent of meeting and give them to the priest; ¹⁵and the priest shall offer them, one for a sin offering and the other for a burnt offering. So the priest shall make

atonement on his behalf before the LORD because of his discharge.

16 'Now if a man has a seminal emission, he shall bathe all his body in water and be unclean until evening. 17 As for any garment or any leather on which there is seminal emission, it shall be washed with water and be unclean until evening. 18 If a man lies with a woman *so that* there is a seminal emission, they shall both bathe in water and be unclean until evening.

19 'When a woman has a discharge, *if* her discharge in her body is blood, she shall continue in her menstrual impurity for seven days; and whoever touches her shall be unclean until evening. 20 Everything also on which she lies during her menstrual impurity shall be unclean, and everything on which she sits shall be unclean. 21 Anyone who touches her bed shall wash his clothes and bathe in water and be unclean until evening. 22 Whoever touches any thing on which she sits shall wash his clothes and bathe in water and be unclean until evening. 23 Whether it be on the bed or on the thing on which she is sitting, when he touches it, he shall be unclean until evening. 24 If a man actually lies with her so that her menstrual impurity is on him, he shall be unclean seven days, and every bed on which he lies shall be unclean.

25 'Now if a woman has a discharge of her blood many days, not at the period of her menstrual impurity, or if she has a discharge beyond that period, all the days of her impure discharge she shall continue as though in her menstrual impurity; she is unclean. 26 Any bed on which she lies all the days of her discharge shall be to her like her bed at menstruation; and every thing on which she sits shall be unclean, like her uncleanness at that time. 27 Likewise, whoever touches them shall be unclean and shall wash his clothes and bathe in water and be unclean until evening. 28 When she becomes clean from her discharge, she shall count off for herself seven days; and afterward she will be clean. 29 Then on the eighth day she shall take for herself two turtledoves or two young pigeons and bring them in to the priest, to the doorway of the tent of meeting. 30 The priest shall offer the one for a sin offering and the other for a burnt offering. So the priest shall make atonement on her behalf before the LORD because of her impure discharge.'

31 "Thus you shall keep the sons of Israel separated from their uncleanness, so that they will not die in their uncleanness by their defiling My tabernacle that is among them." 32 This is the law for the one with a discharge, and for the man who has a seminal emission so that he is unclean by it, 33 and for the woman who is ill because of menstrual impurity, and for the one who has a discharge, whether a male or a female, or a man who lies with an unclean woman.

16 Now the LORD spoke to Moses after the death of the two sons of Aaron, when they had approached the presence of the LORD and died. 2 The LORD said to Moses:

"Tell your brother Aaron that he shall not enter at any time into the holy place inside the veil, before the mercy seat which is on the ark, or he will die; for I will appear in the cloud over the mercy seat. 3 Aaron shall enter the holy place with this: with a bull for a sin offering and a ram for a burnt offering. 4 He shall put on the holy linen tunic, and the linen undergarments shall be next to his body, and he shall be girded with the linen sash and attired with the linen turban (these are holy garments). Then he shall bathe his body in water and put them on. 5 He shall take from the congregation of the sons of Israel two male goats for a sin offering and one ram for a burnt offering. 6 Then Aaron shall offer the bull for the sin offering which is for himself, that he may make atonement for himself and for his household. 7 He shall take the two goats and present them before the LORD at the doorway of the tent of meeting. 8 Aaron shall cast lots for the two goats, one lot for the LORD and the other lot for the scapegoat. 9 Then Aaron shall offer the goat on which the lot for the LORD fell, and make it a sin offering. 10 But the goat on which the lot for the scapegoat fell shall be presented alive before the LORD, to make atonement upon it, to send it into the wilderness as the scapegoat.

11 "Then Aaron shall offer the bull of the sin offering which is for himself and make atonement for himself and for his household, and he shall slaughter the bull of the sin offering which is for himself. 12 He shall take a firepan full of coals of fire from upon the altar before the LORD and two handfuls of finely ground sweet incense, and bring *it* inside the veil. 13 He shall put the incense on the fire before the LORD, that the cloud of

---

16:12 inside the veil. The veil separated all from the holy and consuming presence of God. It was this veil in Herod's temple that was torn open from top to bottom at the death of Christ, signifying access into God's presence through Jesus Christ (Mt 27:51; Mk 15:38; Lk 23:45).

incense may cover the mercy seat that is on *the ark of* the testimony, otherwise he will die. ¹⁴ Moreover, he shall take some of the blood of the bull and sprinkle *it* with his finger on the mercy seat on the east *side;* also in front of the mercy seat he shall sprinkle some of the blood with his finger seven times.

¹⁵ "Then he shall slaughter the goat of the sin offering which is for the people, and bring its blood inside the veil and do with its blood as he did with the blood of the bull, and sprinkle it on the mercy seat and in front of the mercy seat. ¹⁶ He shall make atonement for the holy place, because of the impurities of the sons of Israel and because of their transgressions in regard to all their sins; and thus he shall do for the tent of meeting which abides with them in the midst of their impurities. ¹⁷ When he goes in to make atonement in the holy place, no one shall be in the tent of meeting until he comes out, that he may make atonement for himself and for his household and for all the assembly of Israel. ¹⁸ Then he shall go out to the altar that is before the LORD and make atonement for it, and shall take some of the blood of the bull and of the blood of the goat and put it on the horns of the altar on all sides. ¹⁹ With his finger he shall sprinkle some of the blood on it seven times and cleanse it, and from the impurities of the sons of Israel consecrate it.

²⁰ "When he finishes atoning for the holy place and the tent of meeting and the altar, he shall offer the live goat. ²¹ Then Aaron shall lay both of his hands on the head of the live goat, and confess over it all the iniquities of the sons of Israel and all their transgressions in regard to all their sins; and he shall lay them on the head of the goat and send *it* away into the wilderness by the hand of a man who *stands* in readiness. ²² The goat shall bear on itself all their iniquities to a solitary land; and he shall release the goat in the wilderness.

²³ "Then Aaron shall come into the tent of meeting and take off the linen garments which he put on when he went into the holy place, and shall leave them there. ²⁴ He shall bathe his body with water in a holy place and put on his clothes, and come forth and offer his burnt offering and the burnt offering of the people and make atonement for himself and for the people. ²⁵ Then he shall offer up in smoke the fat of the sin offering on the altar. ²⁶ The one who released the goat as the scapegoat shall wash his clothes and bathe his body with water; then afterward he shall come into the camp. ²⁷ But the bull of the sin offering and the goat of the sin offering, whose blood was brought in to make atonement in the holy place, shall be taken outside the camp, and they shall burn their hides, their flesh, and their refuse in the fire. ²⁸ Then the one who burns them shall wash his clothes and bathe his body with water, then afterward he shall come into the camp.

²⁹ "*This* shall be a permanent statute for you: in the seventh month, on the tenth day of the month, you shall humble your souls and not do any work, whether the native, or the alien who sojourns among you; ³⁰ for it is on this day that atonement shall be made for you to cleanse you; you will be clean from all your sins before the LORD. ³¹ It is to be a sabbath of solemn rest for you, that you may humble your souls; it is a permanent statute. ³² So the priest who is anointed and ordained to serve as priest in his father's place shall make atonement: he shall thus put on the linen garments, the holy garments, ³³ and make atonement for the holy sanctuary, and he shall make atonement for the tent of meeting and for the altar. He shall also make atonement for the priests and for all the people of the assembly. ³⁴ Now you shall have this as a permanent statute, to make atonement for the sons of Israel for all their sins once every year." And just as the LORD had commanded Moses, *so* he did.

Psalm 26:6–12

⁶ I shall wash my hands in innocence,
And I will go about Your
altar, O LORD,
⁷ That I may proclaim with the
voice of thanksgiving

16:20–22 This "sin offering of atonement" portrayed Christ's substitutionary sacrifice (vv. 21–22) with the result that the sinner's sins were removed (v. 22). Christ lived out this representation when He cried from the cross, "My God, My God, why have You forsaken Me?" (Mt 27:46).

16:30 clean from all your sins. See Psalm 103:12; Isaiah 38:17; Micah 7:19. This day provided ceremonially cleansing for one year, and pictured the forgiveness of God available to all who believed and repented. Actual atonement was based on cleansing through the sacrifice of Christ (Ro 3:25–26; Heb 9:15).

And declare all Your wonders.

8 O LORD, I love the habitation
of Your house
And the place where Your
glory dwells.
9 Do not take my soul away
along with sinners,
Nor my life with men of bloodshed,
10 In whose hands is a wicked
scheme,
And whose right hand
is full of bribes.
11 But as for me, I shall walk
in my integrity;
Redeem me, and be gracious to me.
12 My foot stands on a level place;
In the congregations I shall
bless the LORD.

Proverbs 10:8

8 The wise of heart will
receive commands,
But a babbling fool will be ruined.

Mark 4:1–20

4 He began to teach again by the sea. And such a very large crowd gathered to Him that He got into a boat in the sea and sat down; and the whole crowd was by the sea on the land. 2 And He was teaching them many things in parables, and was saying to them in His teaching, 3 "Listen *to this!* Behold, the sower went out to sow; 4 as he was sowing, some *seed* fell beside the road, and the birds came and ate it up. 5 Other *seed* fell on the rocky *ground* where it did not have much soil; and immediately it sprang up because it had no depth of soil. 6 And after the sun had risen, it was scorched; and because it had no root, it withered away. 7 Other *seed* fell among the thorns, and the thorns came up and choked it, and it yielded no crop. 8 Other *seeds* fell into the good soil, and as they grew up and increased, they yielded a crop and

4:2 parables. A common method of teaching in Judaism, which Jesus employed to conceal the truth from unbelievers while explaining it to His disciples.

produced thirty, sixty, and a hundredfold." 9 And He was saying, "He who has ears to hear, let him hear."

10 As soon as He was alone, His followers, along with the twelve, *began* asking Him *about* the parables. 11 And He was saying to them, "To you has been given the mystery of the kingdom of God, but those who are outside get everything in parables, 12 so that WHILE SEEING, THEY MAY SEE AND NOT PERCEIVE, AND WHILE HEARING, THEY MAY HEAR AND NOT UNDERSTAND, OTHERWISE THEY MIGHT RETURN AND BE FORGIVEN."

13 And He *said to them, "Do you not understand this parable? How will you understand all the parables? 14 The sower sows the word. 15 These are the ones who are beside the road where the word is sown; and when they hear, immediately Satan comes and takes away the word which has been sown in them. 16 In a similar way these are the ones on whom seed was sown on the rocky *places,* who, when they hear the word, immediately receive it with joy; 17 and they have no *firm* root in themselves, but are *only* temporary; then, when affliction or persecution arises because of the word, immediately they fall away. 18 And others are the ones on whom seed was sown among the thorns; these are the ones who have heard the word, 19 but the worries of the world, and the deceitfulness of riches, and the desires for other things enter in and choke the word, and it becomes unfruitful. 20 And those are the ones on whom seed was sown on the good soil; and they hear the word and accept it and bear fruit, thirty, sixty, and a hundredfold."

DAY 23: What does the parable of the soils warn us about our heart?

Jesus made it clear that as the sower sows his seed, some of those seeds fall "beside the road" (Mk 4:4)—either a road near a field's edge or a path that traversed a field, both of which were hard surfaces due to constant foot traffic. Other seed falls on "rocky ground" (v. 5), where beds of solid rock lie under the surface of good soil. They are a little too deep for the plow to reach, and too shallow to allow a plant to reach water and develop a decent root system in the small amount of soil that covers them. Other seed falls among "thorns" (v. 7)—tough, thistle-bearing weeds that use up the available space, light, and water which good plants need.

Jesus warns in vv. 13—20 that our heart may be hard, like the stony ground, and the "word" of God never takes root in the soul and never transforms our life—there is only a temporary, surface change. Bring along the suffering, trials, and persecutions which result from one's association with God's Word and we fall away (Jn 8:31; 1Jn 2:19). Then there are the "worries of the world," or the distractions of the age. A preoccupation with the temporal issues of this present age blinds a person to any serious consideration of the gospel (Jas 4:4; 1Jn 2:15–16). And "the deceitfulness of riches" come our way. Not only can money and material possessions not satisfy the desires of the heart or bring the lasting happiness they deceptively promise, but they also blind those who pursue them to eternal, spiritual concerns (1Ti 6:9–10).

FEBRUARY 24

Leviticus 17:1–18:30

17 Then the LORD spoke to Moses, saying, ² "Speak to Aaron and to his sons and to all the sons of Israel and say to them, 'This is what the LORD has commanded, saying, ³ "Any man from the house of Israel who slaughters an ox or a lamb or a goat in the camp, or who slaughters it outside the camp, ⁴ and has not brought it to the doorway of the tent of meeting to present *it* as an offering to the LORD before the tabernacle of the LORD, bloodguiltiness is to be reckoned to that man. He has shed blood and that man shall be cut off from among his people. ⁵ The reason is so that the sons of Israel may bring their sacrifices which they were sacrificing in the open field, that they may bring them in to the LORD, at the doorway of the tent of meeting to the priest, and sacrifice them as sacrifices of peace offerings to the LORD. ⁶ The priest shall sprinkle the blood on the altar of the LORD at the doorway of the tent of meeting, and offer up the fat in smoke as a soothing aroma to the LORD. ⁷ They shall no longer sacrifice their sacrifices to the goat demons with which they play the harlot. This shall be a permanent statute to them throughout their generations." '

⁸ "Then you shall say to them, 'Any man from the house of Israel, or from the aliens who sojourn among them, who offers a burnt offering or sacrifice, ⁹ and does not bring it to the doorway of the tent of meeting to offer it to the LORD, that man also shall be cut off from his people.

¹⁰ 'And any man from the house of Israel, or from the aliens who sojourn among them, who eats any blood, I will set My face against that person who eats blood and will cut him off from among his people. ¹¹ For the life of the flesh is in the blood, and I have given it to you on the altar to make atonement for your souls; for it is the blood by reason of the life that makes atonement.' ¹² Therefore I said to the sons of Israel, 'No person among you may eat blood, nor may any alien who sojourns among you eat blood.' ¹³ So when any man

from the sons of Israel, or from the aliens who sojourn among them, in hunting catches a beast or a bird which may be eaten, he shall pour out its blood and cover it with earth.

¹⁴ "For *as for the* life of all flesh, its blood is *identified* with its life. Therefore I said to the sons of Israel, 'You are not to eat the blood of any flesh, for the life of all flesh is its blood; whoever eats it shall be cut off.' ¹⁵ When any person eats *an animal* which dies or is torn *by beasts,* whether he is a native or an alien, he shall wash his clothes and bathe in water, and remain unclean until evening; then he will become clean. ¹⁶ But if he does not wash *them* or bathe his body, then he shall bear his guilt."

17:11 life of the flesh is in the blood. This phrase is amplified by "its blood is *identified* with its life" (17:14). Blood carries life-sustaining elements to all parts of the body; therefore it represents the essence of life. In contrast, the shedding of blood represents the shedding of life, i.e., death (Ge 9:4). New Testament references to the shedding of the blood of Jesus Christ are references to His death. **blood...that makes atonement.** Since it contains the life, blood is sacred to God. Shed blood (death) from a substitute atones for or covers the sinner, who is then allowed to live.

18 Then the LORD spoke to Moses, saying, ² "Speak to the sons of Israel and say to them, 'I am the LORD your God. ³ You shall not do what is done in the land of Egypt where you lived, nor are you to do what is done in the land of Canaan where I am bringing you; you shall not walk in their statutes. ⁴ You are to perform My judgments and keep My statutes, to live in accord with them; I am the LORD your God. ⁵ So you shall keep My statutes and My judgments, by which a man may live if he does them; I am the LORD.

⁶ 'None of you shall approach any blood relative of his to uncover nakedness; I am the LORD. ⁷ You shall not uncover the nakedness of your father, that is, the nakedness of your

mother. She is your mother; you are not to uncover her nakedness. ⁸You shall not uncover the nakedness of your father's wife; it is your father's nakedness. ⁹The nakedness of your sister, *either* your father's daughter or your mother's daughter, whether born at home or born outside, their nakedness you shall not uncover. ¹⁰The nakedness of your son's daughter or your daughter's daughter, their nakedness you shall not uncover; for their nakedness is yours. ¹¹The nakedness of your father's wife's daughter, born to your father, she is your sister, you shall not uncover her nakedness. ¹²You shall not uncover the nakedness of your father's sister; she is your father's blood relative. ¹³You shall not uncover the nakedness of your mother's sister, for she is your mother's blood relative. ¹⁴You shall not uncover the nakedness of your father's brother; you shall not approach his wife, she is your aunt. ¹⁵You shall not uncover the nakedness of your daughter-in-law; she is your son's wife, you shall not uncover her nakedness. ¹⁶You shall not uncover the nakedness of your brother's wife; it is your brother's nakedness. ¹⁷You shall not uncover the nakedness of a woman and of her daughter, nor shall you take her son's daughter or her daughter's daughter, to uncover her nakedness; they are blood relatives. It is lewdness. ¹⁸You shall not marry a woman in addition to her sister as a rival while she is alive, to uncover her nakedness.

¹⁹'Also you shall not approach a woman to uncover her nakedness during her menstrual impurity. ²⁰You shall not have intercourse with your neighbor's wife, to be defiled with her. ²¹You shall not give any of your offspring to offer them to Molech, nor shall you profane the name of your God; I am the LORD. ²²You shall not lie with a male as one lies with a female; it is an abomination. ²³Also you shall not have intercourse with any animal to be defiled with it, nor shall any woman stand before an animal to mate with it; it is a perversion. ²⁴'Do not defile yourselves by any of these

18:21 Molech. This Semitic false deity (god of the Ammonites) was worshiped with child sacrifice (Lv 20:2–5; 1Ki 11:7; 2Ki 23:10; Jer 32:35). Since this chapter deals otherwise with sexual deviation, there is likely an unmentioned sexual perversion connected with this pagan ritual. Jews giving false gods homage gave foreigners occasion to blaspheme the true God.

things; for by all these the nations which I am casting out before you have become defiled. ²⁵For the land has become defiled, therefore I have brought its punishment upon it, so the land has spewed out its inhabitants. ²⁶But as for you, you are to keep My statutes and My judgments and shall not do any of these abominations, *neither* the native, nor the alien who sojourns among you ²⁷(for the men of the land who have been before you have done all these abominations, and the land has become defiled); ²⁸so that the land will not spew you out, should you defile it, as it has spewed out the nation which has been before you. ²⁹For whoever does any of these abominations, those persons who do *so* shall be cut off from among their people. ³⁰Thus you are to keep My charge, that you do not practice any of the abominable customs which have been practiced before you, so as not to defile yourselves with them; I am the LORD your God.'"

Psalm 27:1–3

A Psalm of David.

The LORD is my light and
  my salvation;
Whom shall I fear?
The LORD is the defense of my life;
Whom shall I dread?
² When evildoers came upon
  me to devour my flesh,
My adversaries and my enemies,
  they stumbled and fell.
³ Though a host encamp against me,
  My heart will not fear;
Though war arise against me,
In *spite of* this I shall be confident.

Proverbs 10:9

⁹ He who walks in integrity
  walks securely,
But he who perverts his ways
  will be found out.

Mark 4:21–41

²¹And He was saying to them, "A lamp is not brought to be put under a basket, is it, or under a bed? Is it not *brought* to be put on the lampstand? ²²For nothing is hidden, except

27:1 light. This important biblical word picture with exclusively positive connotations pictures the light of redemption in contrast to the darkness of condemnation (Pss 18:28; 36:9; 43:3; Is 60:1, 19–20; Mic 7:8; Jn 8:12; 12:46; 1Jn 1:5).

to be revealed; nor has *anything* been secret, but that it would come to light. ²³If anyone has ears to hear, let him hear." ²⁴And He was saying to them, "Take care what you listen to. By your standard of measure it will be measured to you; and more will be given you besides. ²⁵For whoever has, to him *more* shall be given; and whoever does not have, even what he has shall be taken away from him."

²⁶And He was saying, "The kingdom of God is like a man who casts seed upon the soil; ²⁷and he goes to bed at night and gets up by day, and the seed sprouts and grows—how, he himself does not know. ²⁸The soil produces crops by itself; first the blade, then the head, then the mature grain in the head. ²⁹But when the crop permits, he immediately puts in the sickle, because the harvest has come."

³⁰And He said, "How shall we picture the kingdom of God, or by what parable shall we present it? ³¹*It is* like a mustard seed, which, when sown upon the soil, though it is smaller than all the seeds that are upon the soil, ³²yet when it is sown, it grows up and becomes larger than all the garden plants and forms large branches; so that THE BIRDS OF THE AIR can NEST UNDER ITS SHADE."

³³With many such parables He was speaking the word to them, so far as they were able to hear it; ³⁴and He did not speak to them

4:31 a mustard seed. A reference to the common black mustard plant. The leaves were used as a vegetable and the seed as a condiment. It also had medicinal benefits. **smaller than all.** The mustard seed is not the smallest of all seeds in existence, but it was in comparison to all the other seeds the Jews sowed in Israel.

without a parable; but He was explaining everything privately to His own disciples.

³⁵On that day, when evening came, He *said to them, "Let us go over to the other side." ³⁶Leaving the crowd, they *took Him along with them in the boat, just as He was; and other boats were with Him. ³⁷And there *arose a fierce gale of wind, and the waves were breaking over the boat so much that the boat was already filling up. ³⁸Jesus Himself was in the stern, asleep on the cushion; and they *woke Him and *said to Him, "Teacher, do You not care that we are perishing?" ³⁹And He got up and rebuked the wind and said to the sea, "Hush, be still." And the wind died down and it became perfectly calm. ⁴⁰And He said to them, "Why are you afraid? Do you still have no faith?" ⁴¹They became very much afraid and said to one another, "Who then is this, that even the wind and the sea obey Him?"

DAY 24: Why would Jesus' own disciples fear Him?

In Mark 4:35, Jesus and His disciples were on the western shore of the Sea of Galilee. To escape the crowds for a brief respite, Jesus wanted to go to the eastern shore, which had no large cities and therefore fewer people. But as they crossed the lake, they were caught in a "fierce gale of wind" (v. 37). Wind is a common occurrence on that lake, about 690 feet below sea level and surrounded by hills. The Greek word can also mean "whirlwind." In this case, it was a storm so severe that it took on the properties of a hurricane. The disciples, used to being on the lake in the wind, thought this storm would drown them (v. 38).

Meanwhile, Jesus was asleep (v. 38). He was so exhausted from a full day of healing and preaching, even that storm could not wake Him up. Thus, they woke Him. He then rebuked the wind and said to the sea, "Hush, be still." Literally, it means to "be silent, be muzzled." Storms normally subside gradually, but when the Creator gave the order, the natural elements of this storm ceased immediately (v. 39).

At that point, we are told that "they became very much afraid" (v. 41). This was not fear of being harmed by the storm, but a reverence for the supernatural power Jesus had just displayed. The only thing more terrifying than having a storm outside the boat was having God in the boat! "Who then is this . . . ?" This statement betrayed the disciples' wonderment.

FEBRUARY 25

Leviticus 19:1–20:27

19 Then the LORD spoke to Moses, saying: ²"Speak to all the congregation of the sons of Israel and say to them, 'You shall be holy, for I the LORD your God am holy. ³Every

one of you shall reverence his mother and his father, and you shall keep My sabbaths; I am the LORD your God. ⁴Do not turn to idols or make for yourselves molten gods; I am the LORD your God.

⁵'Now when you offer a sacrifice of peace offerings to the LORD, you shall offer it so that you may be accepted. ⁶It shall be eaten

19:2 I the LORD your God am holy. This basic statement, which gives the reason for holy living among God's people, is the central theme in Leviticus (20:26). See 1Peter 1:16. Israel had been called to be a holy nation, and the perfectly holy character of God (Is 6:3) was the model after which the Israelites were to live (10:3; 20:26; 21:6–8).

the same day you offer *it,* and the next day; but what remains until the third day shall be burned with fire. ⁷So if it is eaten at all on the third day, it is an offense; it will not be accepted. ⁸Everyone who eats it will bear his iniquity, for he has profaned the holy thing of the LORD; and that person shall be cut off from his people.

⁹'Now when you reap the harvest of your land, you shall not reap to the very corners of your field, nor shall you gather the gleanings of your harvest. ¹⁰Nor shall you glean your vineyard, nor shall you gather the fallen fruit of your vineyard; you shall leave them for the needy and for the stranger. I am the LORD your God.

¹¹'You shall not steal, nor deal falsely, nor lie to one another. ¹²You shall not swear falsely by My name, so as to profane the name of your God; I am the LORD.

¹³'You shall not oppress your neighbor, nor rob *him.* The wages of a hired man are not to remain with you all night until morning. ¹⁴You shall not curse a deaf man, nor place a stumbling block before the blind, but you shall revere your God; I am the LORD.

¹⁵'You shall do no injustice in judgment; you shall not be partial to the poor nor defer to the great, but you are to judge your neighbor fairly. ¹⁶You shall not go about as a slanderer among your people, and you are not to act against the life of your neighbor; I am the LORD.

¹⁷'You shall not hate your fellow countryman in your heart; you may surely reprove your neighbor, but shall not incur sin because of him. ¹⁸You shall not take vengeance, nor bear any grudge against the sons of your people, but you shall love your neighbor as yourself; I am the LORD.

¹⁹'You are to keep My statutes. You shall not breed together two kinds of your cattle; you shall not sow your field with two kinds of seed, nor wear a garment upon you of two kinds of material mixed together.

²⁰'Now if a man lies carnally with a woman who is a slave acquired for *another* man, but who has in no way been redeemed nor given

her freedom, there shall be punishment; they shall not, *however,* be put to death, because she was not free. ²¹He shall bring his guilt offering to the LORD to the doorway of the tent of meeting, a ram for a guilt offering. ²²The priest shall also make atonement for him with the ram of the guilt offering before the LORD for his sin which he has committed, and the sin which he has committed will be forgiven him.

²³'When you enter the land and plant all kinds of trees for food, then you shall count their fruit as forbidden. Three years it shall be forbidden to you; *it* shall not be eaten. ²⁴But in the fourth year all its fruit shall be holy, an offering of praise to the LORD. ²⁵In the fifth year you are to eat of its fruit, that its yield may increase for you; I am the LORD your God.

²⁶'You shall not eat *anything* with the blood, nor practice divination or soothsaying. ²⁷You shall not round off the side-growth of your heads nor harm the edges of your beard. ²⁸You shall not make any cuts in your body for the dead nor make any tattoo marks on yourselves: I am the LORD.

19:26 divination or soothsaying. Attempting to tell the future with the help of snakes and clouds was a common ancient way of foretelling good or bad future. These were forbidden forms of witchcraft which involved demonic activity.

²⁹'Do not profane your daughter by making her a harlot, so that the land will not fall to harlotry and the land become full of lewdness. ³⁰You shall keep My sabbaths and revere My sanctuary; I am the LORD.

³¹'Do not turn to mediums or spiritists; do not seek them out to be defiled by them. I am the LORD your God.

³²'You shall rise up before the grayheaded and honor the aged, and you shall revere your God; I am the LORD.

³³'When a stranger resides with you in your land, you shall not do him wrong. ³⁴The stranger who resides with you shall be to you as the native among you, and you shall love him as yourself, for you were aliens in the land of Egypt; I am the LORD your God.

³⁵'You shall do no wrong in judgment, in measurement of weight, or capacity. ³⁶You shall have just balances, just weights, a just ephah, and a just hin; I am the LORD your God, who brought you out from the land of Egypt. ³⁷You shall thus observe all My statutes

and all My ordinances and do them; I am the LORD.'"

20 Then the LORD spoke to Moses, saying, ²"You shall also say to the sons of Israel:

'Any man from the sons of Israel or from the aliens sojourning in Israel who gives any of his offspring to Molech, shall surely be put to death; the people of the land shall stone him with stones. ³I will also set My face against that man and will cut him off from among his people, because he has given some of his offspring to Molech, so as to defile My sanctuary and to profane My holy name. ⁴If the people of the land, however, should ever disregard that man when he gives any of his offspring to Molech, so as not to put him to death, ⁵then I Myself will set My face against that man and against his family, and I will cut off from among their people both him and all those who play the harlot after him, by playing the harlot after Molech.

⁶'As for the person who turns to mediums and to spiritists, to play the harlot after them, I will also set My face against that person and will cut him off from among his people. ⁷You shall consecrate yourselves therefore and be holy, for I am the LORD your God. ⁸You shall keep My statutes and practice them; I am the LORD who sanctifies you.

⁹'If there is anyone who curses his father or his mother, he shall surely be put to death; he has cursed his father or his mother, his bloodguiltiness is upon him.

¹⁰'If there is a man who commits adultery with another man's wife, one who commits adultery with his friend's wife, the adulterer and the adulteress shall surely be put to death. ¹¹If there is a man who lies with his father's wife, he has uncovered his father's nakedness; both of them shall surely be put to death, their bloodguiltiness is upon them. ¹²If there is a man who lies with his daughter-in-law, both of them shall surely be put to death; they have committed incest, their bloodguiltiness is upon them. ¹³If there is a man who lies with a male as those who lie with a woman, both of them have committed a detestable act; they shall surely be put to death. Their bloodguiltiness is upon them. ¹⁴If there is a man who marries a woman and her mother, it is immorality; both he and they shall be burned with fire, so that there will be no immorality in your midst. ¹⁵If there is a man who lies with an animal, he shall surely be put to death; you shall also kill the animal. ¹⁶If there is a woman who approaches any animal to mate with it, you shall kill the woman and the animal; they shall surely be put to death. Their bloodguiltiness is upon them.

¹⁷'If there is a man who takes his sister, his father's daughter or his mother's daughter, so that he sees her nakedness and she sees his nakedness, it is a disgrace; and they shall be cut off in the sight of the sons of their people. He has uncovered his sister's nakedness; he bears his guilt. ¹⁸If there is a man who lies with a menstruous woman and uncovers her nakedness, he has laid bare her flow, and she has exposed the flow of her blood; thus both of them shall be cut off from among their people. ¹⁹You shall also not uncover the nakedness of your mother's sister or of your father's sister, for such a one has made naked his blood relative; they will bear their guilt. ²⁰If there is a man who lies with his uncle's wife he has uncovered his uncle's nakedness; they will bear their sin. They will die childless. ²¹If there is a man who takes his brother's wife, it is abhorrent; he has uncovered his brother's nakedness. They will be childless.

²²'You are therefore to keep all My statutes and all My ordinances and do them, so that the land to which I am bringing you to live will not spew you out. ²³Moreover, you shall not follow the customs of the nation which I will drive out before you, for they did all these things, and therefore I have abhorred them. ²⁴Hence I have said to you, "You are to possess their land, and I Myself will give it to you to possess it, a land flowing with milk and honey." I am the LORD your God, who has separated you from the peoples. ²⁵You are therefore to make a distinction between the clean animal and the unclean, and between the unclean bird and the clean; and you shall not make yourselves detestable by animal or by bird or by anything that creeps on the ground, which I have separated for you as unclean. ²⁶Thus you are to be holy to Me, for I the LORD am holy; and I have set you apart from the peoples to be Mine.

²⁷'Now a man or a woman who is a medium or a spiritist shall surely be put to death. They shall be stoned with stones, their bloodguiltiness is upon them.'"

Psalm 27:4–10

4   One thing I have asked from the
      LORD, that I shall seek:
  That I may dwell in the house of the
      LORD all the days of my life,
  To behold the beauty of the LORD
  And to meditate in His temple.

5 For in the day of trouble He will
    conceal me in His tabernacle;
  In the secret place of His
    tent He will hide me;
  He will lift me up on a rock.
6 And now my head will be lifted up
    above my enemies around me,
  And I will offer in His tent
    sacrifices with shouts of joy;
  I will sing, yes, I will sing
    praises to the LORD.

7 Hear, O LORD, when I cry
    with my voice,
  And be gracious to me and
    answer me.
8 *When You said*, "Seek My face,"
    my heart said to You,
  "Your face, O LORD, I shall seek."
9 Do not hide Your face from me,
  Do not turn Your servant
    away in anger;
  You have been my help;
  Do not abandon me nor forsake me,
  O God of my salvation!

27:8-9 Seek My face...Your face...Your face.
God's "face" indicates His personal presence
or simply His being (Pss 24:6; 105:4); and seeking His face is a primary characteristic of true
believers who desire fellowship with God (Dt
4:29; 2Ch 11:16; 20:4; Ps 40:16; Jer 50:4; Hos 3:5;
Zec 8:22).

10 For my father and my mother
    have forsaken me,
  But the LORD will take me up.

Proverbs 10:10-12

10 He who winks the eye causes
    trouble,
  And a babbling fool will be
    ruined.
11 The mouth of the righteous
    is a fountain of life,
  But the mouth of the wicked
    conceals violence.
12 Hatred stirs up strife,
  But love covers all
    transgressions.

Mark 5:1-20

5 They came to the other side of the sea, into
  the country of the Gerasenes. ²When He
got out of the boat, immediately a man from

the tombs with an unclean spirit met Him,
³and he had his dwelling among the tombs.
And no one was able to bind him anymore,
even with a chain; ⁴because he had often
been bound with shackles and chains, and
the chains had been torn apart by him and
the shackles broken in pieces, and no one was
strong enough to subdue him. ⁵Constantly,
night and day, he was screaming among the
tombs and in the mountains, and gashing
himself with stones. ⁶Seeing Jesus from a
distance, he ran up and bowed down before
Him; ⁷and shouting with a loud voice, he
*said, "What business do we have with each
other, Jesus, Son of the Most High God? I implore You by God, do not torment me!" ⁸For
He had been saying to him, "Come out of the
man, you unclean spirit!" ⁹And He was asking
him, "What is your name?" And he *said to
Him, "My name is Legion; for we are many."
¹⁰And he *began* to implore Him earnestly not
to send them out of the country. ¹¹Now there
was a large herd of swine feeding nearby on
the mountain. ¹²*The demons* implored Him,
saying, "Send us into the swine so that we may
enter them." ¹³Jesus gave them permission.
And coming out, the unclean spirits entered
the swine; and the herd rushed down the
steep bank into the sea, about two thousand
of them; and they were drowned in the sea.

¹⁴Their herdsmen ran away and reported it
in the city and in the country. And *the people*
came to see what it was that had happened.
¹⁵They *came to Jesus and *observed the man
who had been demon-possessed sitting down,
clothed and in his right mind, the very man
who had had the "legion"; and they became

5:5 screaming...gashing himself with stones.
"Screaming" describes a continual unearthly
scream uttered with intense emotion. The
"stones" likely were rocks made of flint with
sharp, jagged edges.

5:9 What is your name? Most likely, Jesus asked
this in view of the demon's appeal not to be tormented. However, He did not need to know the
demon's name in order to expel him. Rather,
Jesus posed the question to bring the reality
and complexity of this case into the open. **Legion.** A Latin term, by then common to Jews
and Greeks, that defined a Roman military unit
of 6,000 infantrymen. Such a name denotes
that the man was controlled by an extremely
large number of militant evil spirits, a truth
reiterated by the expression "for we are many."

frightened. ¹⁶ Those who had seen it described to them how it had happened to the demon-possessed man, and *all* about the swine. ¹⁷ And they began to implore Him to leave their region. ¹⁸ As He was getting into the boat, the man who had been demon-possessed was imploring Him that he might accompany Him. ¹⁹ And He did not let him, but He *said to him, "Go home to your people and report to them what great things the Lord has done for you, and *how* He had mercy on you." ²⁰ And he went away and began to proclaim in Decapolis what great things Jesus had done for him; and everyone was amazed.

DAY 25: What does the term "type of Christ" mean when used to describe someone in the Old Testament?

Certain persons and practices recorded in the Old Testament serve as hints, clues, and preillustrations of what Jesus Christ would accomplish by His life, death, and resurrection. In most cases, the similarities or parallels are pointed out in the New Testament. The following people are some of those mentioned as representing, in a narrow way, what Christ accomplished perfectly: (1) Adam (Ro 5:14; 1Co 15:45); (2) Abel (Ge 4:8, 10; Heb 12:24); (3) Aaron (Ex 28:1; Heb 5:4–5; 9:7, 24); (4) David (2Sa 8:15; Php 2:9); (5) Jonah (Jon 1:17; Mt 12:40); (6) Melchizedek (Ge 14:18–20; Heb 7:1–17); (7) Moses (Nu 12:7; Heb 3:2); (8) Noah (Ge 5:29; 2Co 1:5); (9) Samson (Jdg 16:30; Col 2:14–15); (10) Solomon (2Sa 7:12–13; 1Pe 2:5).

The following events and practices also prefigure Christ: (1) Ark (Ge 7:16; 1Pe 3:20, 21); (2) Atonement sacrifices (Lv 16:15–16; Heb 9:12, 24); (3) Bronze serpent (Nu 21:9; Jn 3:14–15); (4) Mercy seat (Ex 25:17–22; Ro 3:25; Heb 4:16); (5) Passover lamb (Ex 12:3–6, 46; Jn 19:36; 1Co 5:7); (6) Red heifer (Lv 3:1; Eph 2:14, 16); (7) Rock of Horeb (Ex 17:6; 1Co 10:4); (8) Scapegoat (Lv 16:20–22); (9) Tabernacle (Ex 40:2; Heb 9:11; Col 2:9); (10) Veil of the tabernacle (Ex 40:21; Heb 10:20).

 # FEBRUARY 26

Leviticus 21:1–22:33

21 Then the LORD said to Moses, "Speak to the priests, the sons of Aaron, and say to them:

'No one shall defile himself for a *dead* person among his people, ² except for his relatives who are nearest to him, his mother and his father and his son and his daughter and his brother, ³ also for his virgin sister, who is near to him because she has had no husband; for her he may defile himself. ⁴ He shall not defile himself as a relative by marriage among his people, and so profane himself. ⁵ They shall not make any baldness on their heads, nor shave off the edges of their beards, nor make any cuts in their flesh. ⁶ They shall be holy to their God and not profane the name of their God, for they present the offerings by fire to the LORD, the food of their God; so they shall be holy. ⁷ They shall not take a woman who is profaned by harlotry, nor shall they take a woman divorced from her husband; for he is holy to his God. ⁸ You shall consecrate him, therefore, for he offers the food of your God; he shall be holy to you; for I the LORD, who sanctifies you, am holy. ⁹ Also the daughter of any priest, if she profanes herself by harlotry, she profanes her father; she shall be burned with fire.

¹⁰ 'The priest who is the highest among his brothers, on whose head the anointing oil has been poured and who has been consecrated to wear the garments, shall not uncover his head nor tear his clothes; ¹¹ nor shall he approach any dead person, nor defile himself *even* for his father or his mother; ¹² nor shall he go out of the sanctuary nor profane the sanctuary of his God, for the consecration of the anointing oil of his God is on him; I am the LORD. ¹³ He shall take a wife in her virginity. ¹⁴ A widow, or a divorced woman, or one who is profaned by harlotry, these he may not take; but rather he is to marry a virgin of his own people, ¹⁵ so that he will not profane his offspring among his people; for I am the LORD who sanctifies him.'"

¹⁶ Then the LORD spoke to Moses, saying, ¹⁷ "Speak to Aaron, saying, 'No man of your offspring throughout their generations who has a defect shall approach to offer the food of his God. ¹⁸ For no one who has a defect shall approach: a blind man, or a lame man, or he who has a disfigured *face,* or any deformed *limb,* ¹⁹ or a man who has a broken foot or broken hand, ²⁰ or a hunchback or a dwarf, or *one who has* a defect in his eye or eczema or scabs or crushed testicles. ²¹ No

21:16–23 defect. Just as the sacrifice had to be without blemish, so did the one offering the sacrifice. As visible things exert strong impressions on the minds of people, any physical impurity or malformation tended to distract from the weight and authority of the sacred office, failed to externally exemplify the inward wholeness God sought, and failed to be a picture of Jesus Christ, the Perfect High Priest to come (Heb 7:26).

man among the descendants of Aaron the priest who has a defect is to come near to offer the LORD'S offerings by fire; *since* he has a defect, he shall not come near to offer the food of his God. ²²He may eat the food of his God, *both* of the most holy and of the holy, ²³only he shall not go in to the veil or come near the altar because he has a defect, so that he will not profane My sanctuaries. For I am the LORD who sanctifies them.'" ²⁴So Moses spoke to Aaron and to his sons and to all the sons of Israel.

22 Then the LORD spoke to Moses, saying, ² "Tell Aaron and his sons to be careful with the holy *gifts* of the sons of Israel, which they dedicate to Me, so as not to profane My holy name; I am the LORD. ³Say to them, 'If any man among all your descendants throughout your generations approaches the holy *gifts* which the sons of Israel dedicate to the LORD, while he has an uncleanness, that person shall be cut off from before Me; I am the LORD. ⁴No man of the descendants of Aaron, who is a leper or who has a discharge, may eat of the holy *gifts* until he is clean. And if one touches anything made unclean by a corpse or if a man has a seminal emission, ⁵or if a man touches any teeming things by which he is made unclean, or any man by whom he is made unclean, whatever his uncleanness; ⁶a person who touches any such shall be unclean until evening, and shall not eat of the holy *gifts* unless he has bathed his body in water. ⁷But when the sun sets, he will be clean, and afterward he shall eat of the holy *gifts*, for it is his food. ⁸He shall not eat *an animal* which dies or is torn *by beasts*, becoming unclean by it; I am the LORD. ⁹They shall therefore keep My charge, so that they will not bear sin because of it and die thereby because they profane it; I am the LORD who sanctifies them.

¹⁰'No layman, however, is to eat the holy *gift;* a sojourner with the priest or a hired man shall not eat of the holy *gift.* ¹¹But if a priest buys a slave as *his* property with his money, that one may eat of it, and those who are born in his house may eat of his food. ¹²If a priest's daughter is married to a layman, she shall not eat of the offering of the *gifts.* ¹³But if a priest's daughter becomes a widow or divorced, and has no child and returns to her father's house as in her youth, she shall eat of her father's food; but no layman shall eat of it. ¹⁴But if a man eats a holy *gift* unintentionally, then he shall add to it a fifth of it and shall give the holy *gift* to the priest. ¹⁵They shall not profane the holy *gifts* of the sons of Israel which they offer to the LORD, ¹⁶and *so* cause them to bear punishment for guilt by eating their holy *gifts;* for I am the LORD who sanctifies them.'"

¹⁷Then the LORD spoke to Moses, saying, ¹⁸"Speak to Aaron and to his sons and to all the sons of Israel and say to them, 'Any man of the house of Israel or of the aliens in Israel who presents his offering, whether it is any of their votive or any of their freewill offerings, which they present to the LORD for a burnt offering— ¹⁹for you to be accepted—*it must be* a male without defect from the cattle, the sheep, or the goats. ²⁰Whatever has a defect, you shall not offer, for it will not be accepted for you. ²¹When a man offers a sacrifice of peace offerings to the LORD to fulfill a special vow or for a freewill offering, of the herd or of the flock, it must be perfect to be accepted; there shall be no defect in it. ²²Those *that are* blind or fractured or maimed or having a running sore or eczema or scabs, you shall not offer to the LORD, nor make of them an offering by fire on the altar to the LORD. ²³In respect to an ox or a lamb which has an overgrown or stunted *member,* you may present it for a freewill offering, but for a vow it will not be accepted. ²⁴Also anything *with its testicles* bruised or crushed or torn or cut, you shall not offer to the LORD, or sacrifice in your land, ²⁵nor shall you accept any such from the hand of a foreigner for offering as the food of your God; for their corruption is in them, they have a defect, they shall not be accepted for you.'"

²⁶Then the LORD spoke to Moses, saying, ²⁷"When an ox or a sheep or a goat is born, it shall remain seven days with its mother, and from the eighth day on it shall be accepted as a sacrifice of an offering by fire to the LORD. ²⁸But, *whether* it is an ox or a sheep, you shall not kill *both* it and its young in one day. ²⁹When you sacrifice a sacrifice of thanksgiving to the LORD, you shall sacrifice it so that you may be accepted. ³⁰It shall be

eaten on the same day, you shall leave none of it until morning; I am the LORD. ³¹So you shall keep My commandments, and do them; I am the LORD.

³²"You shall not profane My holy name, but I will be sanctified among the sons of Israel; I am the LORD who sanctifies you, ³³who brought you out from the land of Egypt, to be your God; I am the LORD."

Psalm 27:11–14

¹¹ Teach me Your way, O LORD,
And lead me in a level path
Because of my foes.
¹² Do not deliver me over to the
desire of my adversaries,
For false witnesses have
risen against me,
And such as breathe out
violence.
¹³ *I would have despaired* unless I
had believed that I would see
the goodness of the LORD
In the land of the living.
¹⁴ Wait for the LORD;
Be strong and let your
heart take courage;
Yes, wait for the LORD.

Proverbs 10:13–16

¹³ On the lips of the discerning,
wisdom is found,
But a rod is for the back of him
who lacks understanding.
¹⁴ Wise men store up knowledge,
But with the mouth of the
foolish, ruin is at hand.
¹⁵ The rich man's wealth is his
fortress,
The ruin of the poor is their
poverty.
¹⁶ The wages of the righteous
is life,
The income of the wicked,
punishment.

Mark 5:21–43

²¹When Jesus had crossed over again in the boat to the other side, a large crowd gath-

10:13 rod. This first reference to corporal punishment applied to the backside (19:29; 26:3) recommends it as the most effective way of dealing with children and fools. See also 13:24; 18:6; 19:29; 22:15; 23:13–14; 26:3; 29:15.

ered around Him; and so He stayed by the seashore. ²²One of the synagogue officials named Jairus *came up, and on seeing Him, *fell at His feet ²³and *implored Him earnestly, saying, "My little daughter is at the point of death; *please* come and lay Your hands on her, so that she will get well and live." ²⁴And He went off with him; and a large crowd was following Him and pressing in on Him.

²⁵A woman who had had a hemorrhage for twelve years, ²⁶and had endured much at the hands of many physicians, and had spent all that she had and was not helped at all, but rather had grown worse— ²⁷after hearing about Jesus, she came up in the crowd behind *Him* and touched His cloak. ²⁸For she thought, "If I just touch His garments, I will get well." ²⁹Immediately the flow of her blood was dried up; and she felt in her body that she was healed of her affliction. ³⁰Immediately Jesus, perceiving in Himself that the power *proceeding* from Him had gone forth, turned around in the crowd and said, "Who touched My garments?" ³¹And His disciples said to Him, "You see the crowd pressing in on You, and You say, 'Who touched Me?'" ³²And He looked around to see the woman who had done this. ³³But the woman fearing and trembling, aware of what had happened to her, came and fell down before Him and told Him the whole truth. ³⁴And He said to her, "Daughter, your faith has made you well; go in peace and be healed of your affliction."

³⁵While He was still speaking, they *came from the *house of* the synagogue official, saying, "Your daughter has died; why trouble the Teacher anymore?" ³⁶But Jesus, overhearing what was being spoken, *said to the synagogue official, "Do not be afraid *any longer,* only believe." ³⁷And He allowed no one to accompany Him, except Peter and James and John the brother of James. ³⁸They *came to the house of the synagogue official; and He *saw a commotion, and *people* loudly weep-

5:26 endured much…many physicians. In New Testament times, it was common practice in difficult medical cases for people to consult many different doctors and receive a variety of treatments. The supposed cures were often conflicting, abusive, and many times made the ailment worse, not better. (Luke, the physician, in Lk 8:43 suggested the woman was not helped because her condition was incurable.)

5:38 weeping and wailing. In that culture, a sure sign that a death had occurred. Because burial followed soon after death, it was the people's only opportunity to mourn publicly. The wailing was especially loud and mostly from paid mourners.

ing and wailing. ³⁹And entering in, He *said to them, "Why make a commotion and weep? The child has not died, but is asleep." ⁴⁰They *began* laughing at Him. But putting them all out, He *took along the child's father and mother and His own companions, and *entered *the room* where the child was. ⁴¹Taking the child by the hand, He *said to her, "Talitha kum!" (which translated means, "Little girl, I say to you, get up!"). ⁴²Immediately the girl got up and *began* to walk, for she was twelve years old. And immediately they were completely astounded. ⁴³And He gave them strict orders that no one should know about this, and He said that *something* should be given her to eat.

DAY 26: What do the healings of Mark 5 teach us about faith?

Upon hearing about Jesus, the woman with the flow of blood said to herself, "If I just touch His garments, I will get well" (v. 28). Her faith in Jesus' healing powers was so great that she believed even indirect contact with Him through His garments would be enough to produce a cure. Jesus' response to her touch and healing was that "your faith has made you well" (v. 34). The form of the Greek verb translated "has made you well," which can also be rendered "has made you whole," indicates that her healing was complete. It is the same Greek word often translated "to save" and is the normal New Testament word for saving from sin, which strongly suggests that the woman's faith also led to spiritual salvation.

Jesus' response to the announced death of Jairus's daughter was simply, "Do not be afraid… only believe" (v. 36). The verb is a command for present, continuous action urging Jairus to maintain the faith he had initially demonstrated in coming to Jesus. Christ knew there was no other proper response to Jairus's helpless situation, and He was confident of faith's outcome (Lk 8:50). Even in the face of ridicule, Jesus said, "The child has not died, but is asleep" (v. 39). With this figurative expression, Jesus meant that the girl was not dead in the normal sense, because her condition was temporary and would be reversed (see note on Mt 9:24; see Jn 11:11–14; Ac 7:60; 13:36; 1Co 11:30; 15:6, 18, 20, 51; 1Th 4:13–14).

FEBRUARY 27

Leviticus 23:1–24:23

23 The LORD spoke again to Moses, saying, ² "Speak to the sons of Israel and say to them, 'The LORD'S appointed times which you shall proclaim as holy convocations—My appointed times are these:

³ 'For six days work may be done, but on the seventh day there is a sabbath of complete rest, a holy convocation. You shall not do any work; it is a sabbath to the LORD in all your dwellings.

23:2 proclaim as holy convocations. These festivals did not involve gatherings of all Israel in every case. Only the feasts of 1) Unleavened Bread; 2) Weeks; and 3) Tabernacles required that all males gather in Jerusalem (Ex 23:14–17; Dt 16:16–17).

⁴ 'These are the appointed times of the LORD, holy convocations which you shall proclaim at the times appointed for them. ⁵ In the first month, on the fourteenth day of the month at twilight is the LORD'S Passover. ⁶ Then on the fifteenth day of the same month there is the Feast of Unleavened Bread to the LORD; for seven days you shall eat unleavened bread. ⁷ On the first day you shall have a holy convocation; you shall not do any laborious work. ⁸ But for seven days you shall present an offering by fire to the LORD. On the seventh day is a holy convocation; you shall not do any laborious work.'"

⁹ Then the LORD spoke to Moses, saying, ¹⁰ "Speak to the sons of Israel and say to them, 'When you enter the land which I am going to give to you and reap its harvest, then you shall bring in the sheaf of the first fruits of your harvest to the priest. ¹¹ He shall wave the sheaf before the LORD for you to be accepted; on the day after the sabbath the priest shall wave it. ¹² Now on the day when you wave the sheaf, you shall offer a male lamb one year old without

defect for a burnt offering to the LORD. [13] Its grain offering shall then be two-tenths *of an ephah* of fine flour mixed with oil, an offering by fire to the LORD *for* a soothing aroma, with its drink offering, a fourth of a hin of wine. [14] Until this same day, until you have brought in the offering of your God, you shall eat neither bread nor roasted grain nor new growth. It is to be a perpetual statute throughout your generations in all your dwelling places.

[15] 'You shall also count for yourselves from the day after the sabbath, from the day when you brought in the sheaf of the wave offering; there shall be seven complete sabbaths. [16] You shall count fifty days to the day after the seventh sabbath; then you shall present a new grain offering to the LORD. [17] You shall bring in from your dwelling places two *loaves* of bread for a wave offering, made of two-tenths *of an ephah;* they shall be of a fine flour, baked with leaven as first fruits to the LORD. [18] Along with the bread you shall present seven one year old male lambs without defect, and a bull of the herd and two rams; they are to be a burnt offering to the LORD, with their grain offering and their drink offerings, an offering by fire of a soothing aroma to the LORD. [19] You shall also offer one male goat for a sin offering and two male lambs one year old for a sacrifice of peace offerings. [20] The priest shall then wave them with the bread of the first fruits for a wave offering with two lambs before the LORD; they are to be holy to the LORD for the priest. [21] On this same day you shall make a proclamation as well; you are to have a holy convocation. You shall do no laborious work. It is to be a perpetual statute in all your dwelling places throughout your generations.

[22] 'When you reap the harvest of your land, moreover, you shall not reap to the very corners of your field nor gather the gleaning of your harvest; you are to leave them for the needy and the alien. I am the LORD your God.'"

[23] Again the LORD spoke to Moses, saying, [24] "Speak to the sons of Israel, saying, 'In the seventh month on the first of the month you shall have a rest, a reminder by blowing *of trumpets,* a holy convocation. [25] You shall not do any laborious work, but you shall present an offering by fire to the LORD.'"

[26] The LORD spoke to Moses, saying, [27] "On exactly the tenth day of this seventh month is the day of atonement; it shall be a holy convocation for you, and you shall humble your souls and present an offering by fire to the LORD. [28] You shall not do any work on this same day, for it is a day of atonement, to make atonement on your behalf before the LORD your God. [29] If there is any person who will not humble himself on this same day, he shall be cut off from his people. [30] As for any person who does any work on this same day, that person I will destroy from among his people. [31] You shall do no work at all. It is to be a perpetual statute throughout your generations in all your dwelling places. [32] It is to be a sabbath of complete rest to you, and you shall humble your souls; on the ninth of the month at evening, from evening until evening you shall keep your sabbath."

[33] Again the LORD spoke to Moses, saying, [34] "Speak to the sons of Israel, saying, 'On the fifteenth of this seventh month is the Feast of Booths for seven days to the LORD. [35] On the first day is a holy convocation; you shall do no laborious work of any kind. [36] For seven days you shall present an offering by fire to the LORD. On the eighth day you shall have a holy convocation and present an offering by fire to the LORD; it is an assembly. You shall do no laborious work.

[37] 'These are the appointed times of the LORD which you shall proclaim as holy convocations, to present offerings by fire to the LORD—burnt offerings and grain offerings, sacrifices and drink offerings, *each* day's matter on its own day— [38] besides *those of* the sabbaths of the LORD, and besides your gifts and besides all your votive and freewill offerings, which you give to the LORD.

[39] 'On exactly the fifteenth day of the seventh month, when you have gathered in the crops of the land, you shall celebrate the feast of the LORD for seven days, with a rest on the first day and a rest on the eighth day. [40] Now on the first day you shall take for yourselves the foliage of beautiful trees, palm branches and boughs of leafy trees and willows of the brook, and you shall rejoice before the LORD your God for seven days. [41] You shall thus celebrate it *as* a feast to the LORD for seven days in the year. It *shall be* a perpetual statute throughout your generations; you shall celebrate it in the seventh month. [42] You shall live in booths for seven days; all the native-born in Israel shall live in booths, [43] so that your generations may know that I had the sons of Israel live in booths when I brought them out from the land of Egypt. I am the LORD your God.'" [44] So Moses declared to the sons of Israel the appointed times of the LORD.

24 Then the LORD spoke to Moses, saying, [2] "Command the sons of Israel that they bring to you clear oil from beaten olives for the light, to make a lamp burn continually.

3 Outside the veil of testimony in the tent of meeting, Aaron shall keep it in order from evening to morning before the LORD continually; *it shall be* a perpetual statute throughout your generations. 4 He shall keep the lamps in order on the pure *gold* lampstand before the LORD continually.

5 "Then you shall take fine flour and bake twelve cakes with it; two-tenths *of an ephah* shall be *in* each cake. 6 You shall set them *in* two rows, six *to* a row, on the pure *gold* table before the LORD. 7 You shall put pure frankincense on each row that it may be a memorial portion for the bread, *even* an offering by fire to the LORD. 8 Every sabbath day he shall set it in order before the LORD continually; it is an everlasting covenant for the sons of Israel. 9 It shall be for Aaron and his sons, and they shall eat it in a holy place; for it is most holy to him from the LORD'S offerings by fire, *his* portion forever."

10 Now the son of an Israelite woman, whose father was an Egyptian, went out among the sons of Israel; and the Israelite woman's son and a man of Israel struggled with each other in the camp. 11 The son of the Israelite woman blasphemed the Name and cursed. So they brought him to Moses. (Now his mother's name was Shelomith, the daughter of Dibri, of the tribe of Dan.) 12 They put him in custody so that the command of the LORD might be made clear to them.

13 Then the LORD spoke to Moses, saying, 14 "Bring the one who has cursed outside the camp, and let all who heard him lay their hands on his head; then let all the congregation stone him. 15 You shall speak to the sons of Israel, saying, 'If anyone curses his God, then he will bear his sin. 16 Moreover, the one who blasphemes the name of the LORD shall surely be put to death; all the congregation shall certainly stone him. The alien as well as the native, when he blasphemes the Name, shall be put to death.

17 'If a man takes the life of any human being, he shall surely be put to death. 18 The one who takes the life of an animal shall make it good, life for life. 19 If a man injures his neighbor, just as he has done, so it shall be done to him: 20 fracture for fracture, eye for eye, tooth for tooth; just as he has injured a man, so it shall be inflicted on him. 21 Thus the one who kills an animal shall make it good, but the one who kills a man shall be put to death. 22 There shall be one standard for you; it shall be for the stranger as well as the native, for I am the LORD your God.'" 23 Then Moses spoke to the sons of Israel, and

they brought the one who had cursed outside the camp and stoned him with stones. Thus the sons of Israel did, just as the LORD had commanded Moses.

Psalm 28:1-5

A Psalm of David.

To You, O LORD, I call;
My rock, do not be deaf
to me,
For if You are silent to me,
I will become like those who
go down to the pit.
2 Hear the voice of my supplications
when I cry to You for help,
When I lift up my hands toward
Your holy sanctuary.
3 Do not drag me away with
the wicked
And with those who work
iniquity,
Who speak peace with
their neighbors,
While evil is in their hearts.
4 Requite them according to their
work and according to the
evil of their practices;
Requite them according to the
deeds of their hands;
Repay them their recompense.
5 Because they do not regard
the works of the LORD
Nor the deeds of His hands,
He will tear them down and
not build them up.

Proverbs 10:17-18

17 He is *on* the path of life who
heeds instruction,
But he who ignores reproof
goes astray.
18 He who conceals hatred *has*
lying lips,
And he who spreads slander
is a fool.

Mark 6:1-29

6 Jesus went out from there and *came into His hometown; and His disciples *followed Him. 2 When the Sabbath came, He began to teach in the synagogue; and the many listeners were astonished, saying, "Where did this man *get* these things, and what is *this* wisdom given to Him, and such miracles as these performed by His hands? 3 Is not this the carpenter, the son of Mary, and brother of James and Joses and Judas and Simon? Are not His sisters here with us?" And

they took offense at Him. ⁴Jesus said to them, "A prophet is not without honor except in his hometown and among his *own* relatives and in his *own* household." ⁵And He could do no miracle there except that He laid His hands on a few sick people and healed them. ⁶And He wondered at their unbelief.

And He was going around the villages teaching.

⁷And He *summoned the twelve and began to send them out in pairs, and gave them authority over the unclean spirits; ⁸and He instructed them that they should take nothing for *their* journey, except a mere staff—no bread, no bag, no money in their belt— ⁹but *to* wear sandals; and *He added,* "Do not put on two tunics." ¹⁰And He said to them, "Wherever you enter a house, stay there until you leave town. ¹¹Any place that does not receive you or listen to you, as you go out from there, shake the dust off the soles of your feet for a testimony against them." ¹²They went out and preached that *men* should repent. ¹³And they were casting out many demons and were anointing with oil many sick people and healing them.

6:11 shake the dust off. A symbolic act that signified complete renunciation of further fellowship with those who rejected them. When the disciples made this gesture, it would show that the people had rejected Jesus and the gospel and were hence rejected by the disciples and by the Lord.

6:13 anointing with oil...sick. In Jesus' day olive oil was often used medicinally (Lk 10:34). But here it represented the power and presence of the Holy Spirit and was used symbolically in relation to supernatural healing (Is 11:2; Zec 4:1–6; Mt 25:2–4; Rev 1:4, 12). As a well-known healing agent, the oil was an appropriate, tangible medium the people could identify with as the disciples ministered to the sick among them.

---

¹⁴And King Herod heard *of it,* for His name had become well known; and *people* were saying, "John the Baptist has risen from the dead, and that is why these miraculous powers are at work in Him." ¹⁵But others were saying, "He is Elijah." And others were saying, *"He is* a prophet, like one of the prophets *of old."* ¹⁶But when Herod heard *of it,* he kept saying, "John, whom I beheaded, has risen!"

6:15 He is Elijah. This identification of Jesus, which probably had been discussed repeatedly among the Jews, was based on the Jewish expectation that the prophet Elijah would return prior to Messiah's coming. **a prophet... one of the prophets.** Some saw Jesus as the fulfillment of Deuteronomy 18:15, the messianic prophecy that looked to the One who, like Moses, would lead His people. Others were willing to identify Jesus only as a great prophet, or one who was resuming the suspended line of Old Testament prophets. These and the other opinions, although misplaced, show that the people still thought Jesus was special or somehow supernatural.

---

¹⁷For Herod himself had sent and had John arrested and bound in prison on account of Herodias, the wife of his brother Philip, because he had married her. ¹⁸For John had been saying to Herod, "It is not lawful for you to have your brother's wife." ¹⁹Herodias had a grudge against him and wanted to put him to death and could not *do so;* ²⁰for Herod was afraid of John, knowing that he was a righteous and holy man, and he kept him safe. And when he heard him, he was very perplexed; but he used to enjoy listening to him. ²¹A strategic day came when Herod on his birthday gave a banquet for his lords and military commanders and the leading men of Galilee; ²²and when the daughter of Herodias herself came in and danced, she pleased Herod and his dinner guests; and the king said to the girl, "Ask me for whatever you want and I will give it to you." ²³And he swore to her, "Whatever you ask of me, I will give it to you; up to half of my kingdom." ²⁴And she went out and said to her mother, "What shall I ask for?" And she said, "The head of John the Baptist." ²⁵Immediately she came in a hurry to the king and asked, saying, "I want you to give me at once the head of John the Baptist on a platter." ²⁶And although the king was very sorry, *yet* because of his oaths and because of his dinner guests, he was unwilling to refuse her. ²⁷Immediately the king sent an executioner and commanded *him* to bring *back* his head. And he went and had him beheaded in the prison, ²⁸and brought his head on a platter, and gave it to the girl; and the girl gave it to her mother. ²⁹When his disciples heard *about this,* they came and took away his body and laid it in a tomb.

DAY 27: What is the relationship of unbelief and Jesus' working in people's lives?

Although the people in Jesus' hometown of Nazareth were "astonished" by Jesus' wisdom and mighty works (Mk 6:2), their initial reaction gave way to skepticism and a critical attitude toward Jesus. They still thought of Jesus as a carpenter and the son of Mary with brothers and sisters (v. 3). The residents of Nazareth were deeply offended at Jesus' posturing Himself as some great teacher because of His ordinary background, His limited formal education, and His lack of an officially sanctioned religious position.

In the face of this, Jesus "could do no miracle there" (v. 5). This is not to suggest that His power was somehow diminished by their unbelief. It may suggest that because of their unbelief people were not coming to Him for healing or miracles the way they did in Capernaum and Jerusalem. Or, more importantly it may signify that Christ limited His ministry both as an act of mercy, so that the exposure to greater light would not result in a worse hardening that would only subject them to greater condemnation, and a judgment on their unbelief. He had the power to do more miracles, but not the will, because they rejected Him. Miracles belonged among those who were ready to believe.

"He wondered at their unbelief" (v. 6). "Wondered" means Jesus was completely astonished and amazed at Nazareth's reaction to Him, His teaching, and His miracles. He was not surprised at the fact of the people's unbelief, but at how they could reject Him while claiming to know all about Him.

FEBRUARY 28

Leviticus 25:1–55

25 The LORD then spoke to Moses at Mount Sinai, saying, 2 "Speak to the sons of Israel and say to them, 'When you come into the land which I shall give you, then the land shall have a sabbath to the LORD. 3 Six years you shall sow your field, and six years you shall prune your vineyard and gather in its crop, 4 but during the seventh year the land shall have a sabbath rest, a sabbath to the LORD; you shall not sow your field nor prune your vineyard. 5 Your harvest's aftergrowth you shall not reap, and your grapes of untrimmed vines you shall not gather; the land shall have a sabbatical year. 6 All of you shall have the sabbath *products* of the land for food; yourself, and your male and female slaves, and your hired man and your foreign resident, those who live as aliens with you. 7 Even your cattle and the animals that are in your land shall have all its crops to eat.

8 'You are also to count off seven sabbaths of years for yourself, seven times seven years, so that you have the time of the seven sabbaths of years, *namely,* forty-nine years. 9 You shall then sound a ram's horn abroad on the tenth day of the seventh month; on the day of atonement you shall sound a horn all through your land. 10 You shall thus consecrate the fiftieth year and proclaim a release through the land to all its inhabitants. It shall be a jubilee for you, and each of you shall return to his own property, and each of you shall return to his family. 11 You shall have the fiftieth year

as a jubilee; you shall not sow, nor reap its aftergrowth, nor gather in *from* its untrimmed vines. 12 For it is a jubilee; it shall be holy to you. You shall eat its crops out of the field.

13 'On this year of jubilee each of you shall return to his own property. 14 If you make a sale, moreover, to your friend or buy from your friend's hand, you shall not wrong one another. 15 Corresponding to the number of years after the jubilee, you shall buy from your friend; he is to sell to you according to the number of years of crops. 16 In proportion to the extent of the years you shall increase its price, and in proportion to the fewness of the years you shall diminish its price, for *it is* a number of crops he is selling to you. 17 So you shall not wrong one another, but you shall fear your God; for I am the LORD your God.

18 'You shall thus observe My statutes and keep My judgments, so as to carry them out, that you may live securely on the land. 19 Then the land will yield its produce, so that you can eat your fill and live securely on it. 20 But if you say, "What are we going to eat on the seventh

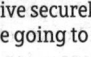

25:8–55 The Year of Jubilee involved a year of release from indebtedness (vv. 23–38) and bondage of all sorts (vv. 39–55). All prisoners and captives were set free, slaves released, and debtors absolved. All property reverted to original owners. This plan curbed inflation and moderated acquisitions. It also gave new opportunity to people who had fallen on hard times.

year if we do not sow or gather in our crops?" [21] then I will so order My blessing for you in the sixth year that it will bring forth the crop for three years. [22] When you are sowing the eighth year, you can still eat old things from the crop, eating the old until the ninth year when its crop comes in.

[23] 'The land, moreover, shall not be sold permanently, for the land is Mine; for you are but aliens and sojourners with Me. [24] Thus for every piece of your property, you are to provide for the redemption of the land.

[25] 'If a fellow countryman of yours becomes so poor he has to sell part of his property, then his nearest kinsman is to come and buy back what his relative has sold. [26] Or in case a man has no kinsman, but so recovers his means as to find sufficient for its redemption, [27] then he shall calculate the years since its sale and refund the balance to the man to whom he sold it, and so return to his property. [28] But if he has not found sufficient means to get it back for himself, then what he has sold shall remain in the hands of its purchaser until the year of jubilee; but at the jubilee it shall revert, that he may return to his property.

[29] 'Likewise, if a man sells a dwelling house in a walled city, then his redemption right remains valid until a full year from its sale; his right of redemption lasts a full year. [30] But if it is not bought back for him within the space of a full year, then the house that is in the walled city passes permanently to its purchaser throughout his generations; it does not revert in the jubilee. [31] The houses of the villages, however, which have no surrounding wall shall be considered as open fields; they have redemption rights and revert in the jubilee. [32] As for cities of the Levites, the Levites have a permanent right of redemption for the houses of the cities which are their possession. [33] What, therefore, belongs to the Levites may be redeemed and a house sale in the city of this possession reverts in the jubilee, for the houses of the cities of the Levites are their possession among the sons of Israel. [34] But pasture fields of their cities shall not be sold, for that is their perpetual possession.

[35] 'Now in case a countryman of yours becomes poor and his means with regard to you falter, then you are to sustain him, like a stranger or a sojourner, that he may live with you. [36] Do not take usurious interest from him, but revere your God, that your countryman may live with you. [37] You shall not give him your silver at interest, nor your food for gain. [38] I am the LORD your God, who brought you out of the land of Egypt to give you the land of Canaan and to be your God.

[39] 'If a countryman of yours becomes so poor with regard to you that he sells himself to you, you shall not subject him to a slave's service. [40] He shall be with you as a hired man, as if he were a sojourner; he shall serve with you until the year of jubilee. [41] He shall then go out from you, he and his sons with him, and shall go back to his family, that he may return to the property of his forefathers. [42] For they are My servants whom I brought out from the land of Egypt; they are not to be sold in a slave sale. [43] You shall not rule over him with severity, but are to revere your God. [44] As for your male and female slaves whom you may have—you may acquire male and female slaves from the pagan nations that are around you. [45] Then, too, it is out of the sons of the sojourners who live as aliens among you that you may gain acquisition, and out of their families who are with you, whom they will have produced in your land; they also may become your possession. [46] You may even bequeath them to your sons after you, to receive as a possession; you can use them as permanent slaves. But in respect to your countrymen, the sons of Israel, you shall not rule with severity over one another.

[47] 'Now if the means of a stranger or of a sojourner with you becomes sufficient, and a countryman of yours becomes so poor with regard to him as to sell himself to a stranger who is sojourning with you, or to the descendants of a stranger's family, [48] then he shall have redemption right after he has been sold. One of his brothers may redeem him, [49] or his uncle, or his uncle's son, may redeem him, or one of his blood relatives from his family may redeem him; or if he prospers, he may redeem himself. [50] He then with his purchaser shall calculate from the year when he sold himself to him up to the year of jubilee; and the price of his sale shall correspond to the number of years. It is like the days of a hired man that he shall be with him. [51] If there are still many years, he shall refund part of his purchase price in proportion to them for his own redemption; [52] and if few years remain until the year of jubilee, he shall so calculate with him. In proportion to his years he is to refund the amount for his redemption. [53] Like a man hired year by year he shall be with him; he shall not rule over him with severity in your sight. [54] Even if he is not redeemed by these means, he shall still go out in the year of jubilee, he and his sons with him. [55] For the sons of Israel are My servants; they are My

servants whom I brought out from the land of Egypt. I am the LORD your God.

Psalm 28:6–9

6 Blessed be the LORD,
   Because He has heard the voice
      of my supplication.
7 The LORD is my strength
      and my shield;
   My heart trusts in Him,
      and I am helped;
   Therefore my heart exults,
   And with my song I shall thank Him.
8 The LORD is their strength,
   And He is a saving defense
      to His anointed.
9 Save Your people and bless
      Your inheritance;
   Be their shepherd also, and
      carry them forever.

28:9 Your inheritance. God amazingly considers His people a most precious possession (Dt 7:6–16; 9:29; 1Sa 10:1; Pss 33:12; 94:5; Eph 1:18).

Proverbs 10:19–21

19 When there are many words,
      transgression is unavoidable,
   But he who restrains his lips is wise.
20 The tongue of the righteous
      is *as* choice silver,
   The heart of the wicked is *worth* little.
21 The lips of the righteous feed many,
   But fools die for lack of
      understanding.

Mark 6:30–56

30 The apostles *gathered together with Jesus; and they reported to Him all that they had done and taught. 31 And He *said to them, "Come away by yourselves to a secluded place and rest a while." (For there were many *people* coming and going, and they did not even have time to eat.) 32 They went away in the boat to a secluded place by themselves. 33 *The people* saw them going, and many recognized *them* and ran there together on foot from all the cities, and got there ahead of them. 34 When Jesus went ashore, He saw a large crowd, and He felt compassion for them because they were like sheep without a shepherd; and He began to teach them many things. 35 When it was already quite late, His disciples came to Him and said, "This place is desolate and it is already quite late; 36 send them away so that

they may go into the surrounding countryside and villages and buy themselves something to eat." 37 But He answered them, "You give them *something* to eat!" And they *said to Him, "Shall we go and spend two hundred denarii on bread and give them *something* to eat?" 38 And He *said to them, "How many loaves do you have? Go look!" And when they found out, they *said, "Five, and two fish." 39 And He commanded them all to sit down by groups on the green grass. 40 They sat down in groups of hundreds and of fifties. 41 And He took the five loaves and the two fish, and looking up toward heaven, He blessed *the food* and broke the loaves and He kept giving *them* to the disciples to set before them; and He divided up the two fish among them all. 42 They all ate and were satisfied, 43 and they picked up twelve full baskets of the broken pieces, and also of the fish. 44 There were five thousand men who ate the loaves.

45 Immediately Jesus made His disciples get into the boat and go ahead of *Him* to the other side to Bethsaida, while He Himself was sending the crowd away. 46 After bidding them farewell, He left for the mountain to pray.

47 When it was evening, the boat was in the middle of the sea, and He was alone on the land. 48 Seeing them straining at the oars, for the wind was against them, at about the fourth watch of the night He *came to them, walking on the sea; and He intended to pass by them. 49 But when they saw Him walking on the sea, they supposed that it was a ghost, and cried out; 50 for they all saw Him and were terrified. But immediately He spoke with them and *said to them, "Take courage; it is I, do not be afraid." 51 Then He got into

6:44 five thousand men. The Greek word for "men" means strictly males, so the numerical estimate did not include women and children (Mt 14:21). The women and children were traditionally seated separately from the men for meals. When everyone was added, there could have been at least 20,000.

6:50 Take courage. This command, always linked in the Gospels to a situation of fear and apprehension (10:49; Mt 9:2, 22; 14:27; Lk 8:48; Jn 16:33; Ac 23:11), urged the disciples to have a continuing attitude of courage. **it is I.** Literally "I AM." This statement clearly identified the figure as the Lord Jesus, not some phantom. It also echoed the Old Testament self-revelation of God (Ex 3:14).

the boat with them, and the wind stopped; and they were utterly astonished, [52] for they had not gained any insight from the *incident of* the loaves, but their heart was hardened.

[53] When they had crossed over they came to land at Gennesaret, and moored to the shore. [54] When they got out of the boat, immediately *the people* recognized Him, [55] and ran about that whole country and began to carry here and there on their pallets those who were sick, to the place they heard He was. [56] Wherever He entered villages, or cities, or countryside, they were laying the sick in the market places, and imploring Him that they might just touch the fringe of His cloak; and as many as touched it were being cured.

DAY 28: List all the Jewish feasts and dates.

Feast of	Month on Jewish Calendar	Day	Corresponding Month	References
Passover	Nisan	14	Mar.–Apr.	Exodus 12:1–14
				Matthew 26:17–20
*Unleavened Bread	Nisan	15–21	Mar.–Apr.	Exodus 12:15–20
Firstfruits	Nisan	16	Mar.–Apr.	Leviticus 23:9–14
	or Sivan	6	May–June	Numbers (28:26)
*Pentecost (Harvest or Weeks)	Sivan	6 (50 days after barley harvest)	May–June	Deuteronomy 16:9–12; Acts 2:1
Trumpets, Rosh Hashanah	Tishri	1, 2	Sept.–Oct.	Numbers 29:1–6
Day of Atonement, Yom Kippur	Tishri	10	Sept.–Oct.	Leviticus 23:26–32; Hebrews 9:7
*Tabernacles (Booths or Ingathering)	Tishri	15–22	Sept.–Oct.	Nehemiah 8:13–18; John 7:2
Dedication (Lights), Hanukkah	Chislev	25 (8 days)	Nov.–Dec.	John 10:22
Purim (Lots)	Adar	14–15	Feb.–Mar.	Esther 9:18–22

*The three major feasts for which all males of Israel were required to travel to the temple in Jerusalem (Ex 23:14–19).

MARCH 1

Leviticus 26:1–27:34

26 ¹'You shall not make for yourselves idols, nor shall you set up for yourselves an image or a *sacred* pillar, nor shall you place a figured stone in your land to bow down to it; for I am the LORD your God. ²You shall keep My sabbaths and reverence My sanctuary; I am the LORD. ³If you walk in My statutes and keep My commandments so as to carry them out, ⁴then I shall give you rains in their season, so that the land will yield its produce and the trees of the field will bear their fruit. ⁵Indeed, your threshing will last for you until grape gathering, and grape gathering will last until sowing time. You will thus eat your food to the full and live securely in your land. ⁶I shall also grant peace in the land, so that you may lie down with no one making *you* tremble. I shall also eliminate harmful beasts from the land, and no sword will pass through your land. ⁷But you will chase your enemies and they will fall before you by the sword; ⁸five of you will chase a hundred, and a hundred of you will chase ten thousand, and your enemies will fall before you by the sword. ⁹So I will turn toward you and make you fruitful and multiply you, and I will confirm My covenant with you. ¹⁰You will eat the old supply and clear out the old because of the new. ¹¹Moreover, I will make My dwelling among you, and My soul will not reject you. ¹²I will also walk among you and be your God, and you shall be My people. ¹³I am the LORD your God, who brought you out of the land of Egypt so that *you* would not be their slaves, and I broke the bars of your yoke and made you walk erect.

¹⁴'But if you do not obey Me and do not carry out all these commandments, ¹⁵if, instead, you reject My statutes, and if your soul abhors My ordinances so as not to carry out all My commandments, *and* so break My covenant, ¹⁶I, in turn, will do this to you: I will appoint over you a sudden terror, consumption and fever that will waste away the eyes and cause the soul to pine away; also, you will sow your seed uselessly, for your enemies will eat it up. ¹⁷I will set My face against you so that you will be struck down before your enemies; and those who hate you will rule over you, and you will flee when no one is pursuing you. ¹⁸If also after these things you do not obey Me, then I will punish you seven times more for your sins. ¹⁹I will also break down your pride of power; I will also make your sky like iron and your earth like bronze. ²⁰Your strength will be spent uselessly, for your land will not yield its produce and the trees of the land will not yield their fruit.

²¹'If then, you act with hostility against Me and are unwilling to obey Me, I will increase the plague on you seven times according to your sins. ²²I will let loose among you the beasts of the field, which will bereave you of your children and destroy your cattle and reduce your number so that your roads lie deserted.

²³'And if by these things you are not turned to Me, but act with hostility against Me, ²⁴then I will act with hostility against you; and I, even I, will strike you seven times for your sins. ²⁵I will also bring upon you a sword which will execute vengeance for the covenant; and when you gather together into your cities, I will send pestilence among you, so that you shall be delivered into enemy hands. ²⁶When I break your staff of bread, ten women will bake your bread in one oven, and they will bring back your bread in rationed amounts, so that you will eat and not be satisfied.

²⁷'Yet if in spite of this you do not obey Me, but act with hostility against Me, ²⁸then I will act with wrathful hostility against you, and I, even I, will punish you seven times for your sins. ²⁹Further, you will eat the flesh of your sons and the flesh of your daughters you will eat. ³⁰I then will destroy your high places, and cut down your incense altars, and heap your remains on the remains of your idols, for My soul shall abhor you. ³¹I will lay waste your

---

26:9 make you fruitful and multiply you… confirm My covenant with you. What God commanded at Creation and repeated after the Flood was contained in the covenant promise of seed (Ge 12:1–3), which He will fulfill to the nation of Israel as promised to Abraham (Ge 15:5–6).

26:12 your God…My people. The promise of an intimate covenant relationship with the God of the universe is given (2Co 6:16).

26:30 high places. These were natural shrines for the worship of idols. Solomon disobeyed God by worshiping Him on the high places (1Ki 3:4), and not long afterward, he was serving the gods of his foreign wives (1Ki 11:1–9).

cities as well and will make your sanctuaries desolate, and I will not smell your soothing aromas. ³²I will make the land desolate so that your enemies who settle in it will be appalled over it. ³³You, however, I will scatter among the nations and will draw out a sword after you, as your land becomes desolate and your cities become waste.

³⁴'Then the land will enjoy its sabbaths all the days of the desolation, while you are in your enemies' land; then the land will rest and enjoy its sabbaths. ³⁵All the days of *its* desolation it will observe the rest which it did not observe on your sabbaths, while you were living on it. ³⁶As for those of you who may be left, I will also bring weakness into their hearts in the lands of their enemies. And the sound of a driven leaf will chase them, and even when no one is pursuing they will flee as though from the sword, and they will fall. ³⁷They will therefore stumble over each other as if *running* from the sword, although no one is pursuing; and you will have *no strength* to stand up before your enemies. ³⁸But you will perish among the nations, and your enemies' land will consume you. ³⁹So those of you who may be left will rot away because of their iniquity in the lands of your enemies; and also because of the iniquities of their forefathers they will rot away with them.

⁴⁰'If they confess their iniquity and the iniquity of their forefathers, in their unfaithfulness which they committed against Me, and also in their acting with hostility against Me— ⁴¹I also was acting with hostility against them, to bring them into the land of their enemies—or if their uncircumcised heart becomes humbled so that they then make amends for their iniquity, ⁴²then I will remember My covenant with Jacob, and I will remember also My covenant with Isaac, and My covenant with Abraham as well, and I will remember the land. ⁴³For the land will be abandoned by them, and will make up for its sabbaths while it is made desolate without them. They, meanwhile, will be making amends for their iniquity, because they rejected My ordinances and their soul abhorred My statutes. ⁴⁴Yet in spite of this, when they are in the land of their enemies, I will not reject them, nor will I so abhor them as to destroy them, breaking My covenant with them; for I am the LORD their God. ⁴⁵But I will remember for them the covenant with their ancestors, whom I brought out of the land of Egypt in the sight of the nations, that I might be their God. I am the LORD.'"

⁴⁶These are the statutes and ordinances and laws which the LORD established between Himself and the sons of Israel through Moses at Mount Sinai.

27 Again, the LORD spoke to Moses, saying, ²"Speak to the sons of Israel and say to them, 'When a man makes a difficult vow, he *shall be valued* according to your valuation of persons belonging to the LORD. ³If your valuation is of the male from twenty years even to sixty years old, then your valuation shall be fifty shekels of silver, after the shekel of the sanctuary. ⁴Or if it is a female, then your valuation shall be thirty shekels. ⁵If it be from five years even to twenty years old then your valuation for the male shall be twenty shekels and for the female ten shekels. ⁶But if *they are* from a month even up to five years old, then your valuation shall be five shekels of silver for the male, and for the female your valuation shall be three shekels of silver. ⁷If *they are* from sixty years old and upward, if it is a male, then your valuation shall be fifteen shekels, and for the female ten shekels. ⁸But if he is poorer than your valuation, then he shall be placed before the priest and the priest shall value him; according to the means of the one who vowed, the priest shall value him.

⁹'Now if it is an animal of the kind which men can present as an offering to the LORD, any such that one gives to the LORD shall be holy. ¹⁰He shall not replace it or exchange it, a good for a bad, or a bad for a good; or if he does exchange animal for animal, then both it and its substitute shall become holy. ¹¹If, however, it is any unclean animal of the kind which men do not present as an offering to the LORD, then he shall place the animal before the priest. ¹²The priest shall value it as either good or bad; as you, the priest, value it, so it shall be. ¹³But if he should ever *wish to* redeem it, then he shall add one-fifth of it to your valuation.

¹⁴'Now if a man consecrates his house as holy to the LORD, then the priest shall value it as either good or bad; as the priest values it, so it shall stand. ¹⁵Yet if the one who consecrates it should *wish to* redeem his house, then he shall add one-fifth of your valuation price to it, so that it may be his.

¹⁶'Again, if a man consecrates to the LORD part of the fields of his own property, then your valuation shall be proportionate to the seed needed for it: a homer of barley seed at fifty shekels of silver. ¹⁷If he consecrates his field as of the year of jubilee, according to your valuation it shall stand. ¹⁸If he consecrates his field after the jubilee, however, then the priest shall calculate the price for him proportionate to the

years that are left until the year of jubilee; and it shall be deducted from your valuation. ¹⁹If the one who consecrates it should ever wish to redeem the field, then he shall add one-fifth of your valuation price to it, so that it may pass to him. ²⁰Yet if he will not redeem the field, but has sold the field to another man, it may no longer be redeemed; ²¹and when it reverts in the jubilee, the field shall be holy to the LORD, like a field set apart; it shall be for the priest as his property. ²²Or if he consecrates to the LORD a field which he has bought, which is not a part of the field of his own property, ²³then the priest shall calculate for him the amount of your valuation up to the year of jubilee; and he shall on that day give your valuation as holy to the LORD. ²⁴In the year of jubilee the field shall return to the one from whom he bought it, to whom the possession of the land belongs. ²⁵Every valuation of yours, moreover, shall be after the shekel of the sanctuary. The shekel shall be twenty gerahs.

²⁶'However, a firstborn among animals, which as a firstborn belongs to the LORD, no man may consecrate it; whether ox or sheep, it is the LORD'S. ²⁷But if *it is* among the unclean animals, then he shall redeem it according to your valuation and add to it one-fifth of it; and if it is not redeemed, then it shall be sold according to your valuation.

²⁸'Nevertheless, anything which a man sets apart to the LORD out of all that he has, of man or animal or of the fields of his own property, shall not be sold or redeemed. Anything devoted to destruction is most holy to the LORD. ²⁹No one who may have been set apart among men shall be ransomed; he shall surely be put to death.

³⁰'Thus all the tithe of the land, of the seed of the land or of the fruit of the tree, is the LORD'S; it is holy to the LORD. ³¹If, therefore, a man wishes to redeem part of his tithe, he shall add to it one-fifth of it. ³²For every tenth part of herd or flock, whatever passes under the rod, the tenth one shall be holy to the LORD. ³³He is not to be concerned whether *it is* good or bad, nor shall he exchange it; or if he does exchange it, then both it and its substitute shall become holy. It shall not be redeemed.'"

³⁴These are the commandments which the LORD commanded Moses for the sons of Israel at Mount Sinai.

Psalm 29:1-6

A Psalm of David.

Ascribe to the LORD, O sons
of the mighty,
Ascribe to the LORD glory
and strength.

29:1 sons of the mighty. Lit "sons of God" (see Ps 89:6 in its context of vv. 5–10; see the plural form of "gods" in Ex 15:11). The reference here in Psalms 29 is most likely to Yahweh's mighty angels.

² Ascribe to the LORD the glory
    due to His name;
    Worship the LORD in holy array.
³ The voice of the LORD is
    upon the waters;
    The God of glory thunders,
    The LORD is over many waters.
⁴ The voice of the LORD is powerful,
    The voice of the LORD is majestic.
⁵ The voice of the LORD
    breaks the cedars;
    Yes, the LORD breaks in pieces
    the cedars of Lebanon.
⁶ He makes Lebanon skip like a calf,
    And Sirion like a young wild ox.

Proverbs 10:22-25

²² It is the blessing of the LORD
    that makes rich,
    And He adds no sorrow to it.

10:22 rich. While having more than what one needs is not the object of wisdom, it is generally the result (Dt 6:11–15; 1Ki 3:10–14). **no sorrow.** None of the sorrow that is associated with ill-gotten wealth (13:11; 15:6; 16:19; 21:6; 28:6) is associated with wealth provided by the Lord.

²³ Doing wickedness is like
    sport to a fool,
    And *so is* wisdom to a man
    of understanding.
²⁴ What the wicked fears will
    come upon him,
    But the desire of the righteous
    will be granted.
²⁵ When the whirlwind passes,
    the wicked is no more,
    But the righteous *has* an
    everlasting foundation.

Mark 7:1-13

7 The Pharisees and some of the scribes gathered around Him when they had come from Jerusalem, ²and had seen that

some of His disciples were eating their bread with impure hands, that is, unwashed. ³(For the Pharisees and all the Jews do not eat unless they carefully wash their hands, *thus* observing the traditions of the elders; ⁴and *when they come* from the market place, they do not eat unless they cleanse themselves; and there are many other things which they have received in order to observe, such as the washing of cups and pitchers and copper pots.) ⁵The Pharisees and the scribes *asked Him, "Why do Your disciples not walk according to the tradition of the elders, but eat their bread with impure hands?" ⁶And He said to them, "Rightly did Isaiah prophesy of you hypocrites, as it is written:

'THIS PEOPLE HONORS ME
   WITH THEIR LIPS,
BUT THEIR HEART IS FAR
   AWAY FROM ME.

⁷ 'BUT IN VAIN DO THEY
   WORSHIP ME,
TEACHING AS DOCTRINES THE
   PRECEPTS OF MEN.'

⁸Neglecting the commandment of God, you hold to the tradition of men."

⁹He was also saying to them, "You are experts at setting aside the commandment of God in order to keep your tradition. ¹⁰For Moses said, 'HONOR YOUR FATHER AND YOUR MOTHER'; and, 'HE WHO SPEAKS EVIL OF FATHER OR MOTHER, IS TO BE PUT TO DEATH'; ¹¹but you say, 'If a man says to *his* father or *his* mother, whatever I have that would help you is Corban (that is to say, given *to God*),' ¹²you no longer permit him to do anything for *his* father or *his* mother; ¹³thus invalidating the word of God by your tradition which you have handed down; and you do many things such as that."

DAY 1: What did the washing of hands have to do with spirituality?

In Mark 7:1, a delegation of leading representatives of Judaism came from Jerusalem perhaps at the request of the Galilean Pharisees. They immediately found fault with the disciples of Jesus, accusing them of eating with hands that had not been ceremonially cleansed and, thus, that had not been separated from the defilement associated with their having touched anything profane (v. 2). This washing had nothing to do with cleaning dirty hands but with a ceremonial rinsing. The ceremony involved someone pouring water out of a jar onto another's hands, whose fingers must be pointing up. As long as the water dripped off at the wrist, the person could proceed to the next step. He then had water poured over both hands with the fingers pointing down. Then each hand was to be rubbed with the other fist. This was according to the "traditions of the elders"—a body of extrabiblical laws and interpretations of Scripture that had in actuality supplanted Scripture as the highest religious authority in Judaism.

The Pharisees and scribes went to the disciples' Master for an explanation of the disciples' allegedly disgraceful conduct. In reality, they were accusing Jesus of teaching His disciples to disobey the tradition of the elders (v. 5). Jesus' reply was to quote Isaiah 29:13, whose prophecy perfectly fit the actions of the Pharisees. Not only were their hearts far from God but they were "hypocrites," or spiritual phonies (v. 6). They followed the traditions of men because such teaching required only mechanical and thoughtless conformity without a pure heart. And in doing so, they had abandoned all the commandments contained in God's Word and substituted a humanly designed standard for God's standard (v. 8).

MARCH 2

Numbers 1:1–2:34

1 Then the LORD spoke to Moses in the wilderness of Sinai, in the tent of meeting, on the first of the second month, in the second year after they had come out of the land of Egypt, saying, ²"Take a census of all the congregation of the sons of Israel, by their families, by their fathers' households, according to the number of names, every male, head by head ³from twenty years old and upward, whoever *is able to* go out to war in Israel,

you and Aaron shall number them by their armies. ⁴With you, moreover, there shall be a man of each tribe, each one head of his father's household. ⁵These then are the names of the men who shall stand with you: of Reuben, Elizur the son of Shedeur; ⁶of Simeon, Shelumiel the son of Zurishaddai; ⁷of Judah, Nahshon the son of Amminadab; ⁸of Issachar, Nethanel the son of Zuar; ⁹of Zebulun, Eliab the son of Helon; ¹⁰of the sons of Joseph: of Ephraim, Elishama the son of Ammihud; of Manasseh, Gamaliel the son of Pedahzur; ¹¹of Benjamin, Abidan the son of Gideoni; ¹²of Dan, Ahiezer the son of Ammishaddai;

1:2 a census. In Exodus 30:11–16, the Lord had commanded that a census of the males in Israel over 20 (excluding the Levites) be taken for the purpose of determining the ransom money for the service of the tabernacle. The result of that census is recorded in Exodus 38:25–28. The total number, 603,550 (Ex 38:26), equals the number in 1:46.

1:3 go out to war. The purpose of this census was to form a roster of fighting men. The book of Numbers looks ahead to the invasion of the land promised to Abraham (Ge 12:1–3).

13 of Asher, Pagiel the son of Ochran; 14 of Gad, Eliasaph the son of Deuel; 15 of Naphtali, Ahira the son of Enan. 16 These are they who were called of the congregation, the leaders of their fathers' tribes; they were the heads of divisions of Israel."

17 So Moses and Aaron took these men who had been designated by name, 18 and they assembled all the congregation together on the first of the second month. Then they registered by ancestry in their families, by their fathers' households, according to the number of names, from twenty years old and upward, head by head, 19 just as the LORD had commanded Moses. So he numbered them in the wilderness of Sinai.

20 Now the sons of Reuben, Israel's first-born, their genealogical registration by their families, by their fathers' households, according to the number of names, head by head, every male from twenty years old and upward, whoever was able to go out to war, 21 their numbered men of the tribe of Reuben were 46,500.

22 Of the sons of Simeon, their genealogical registration by their families, by their fathers' households, their numbered men, according to the number of names, head by head, every male from twenty years old and upward, whoever was able to go out to war, 23 their numbered men of the tribe of Simeon were 59,300.

24 Of the sons of Gad, their genealogical registration by their families, by their fathers' households, according to the number of names, from twenty years old and upward, whoever was able to go out to war, 25 their numbered men of the tribe of Gad were 45,650.

26 Of the sons of Judah, their genealogical registration by their families, by their fa-

thers' households, according to the number of names, from twenty years old and upward, whoever was able to go out to war, 27 their numbered men of the tribe of Judah were 74,600.

28 Of the sons of Issachar, their genealogical registration by their families, by their fathers' households, according to the number of names, from twenty years old and upward, whoever was able to go out to war, 29 their numbered men of the tribe of Issachar were 54,400.

30 Of the sons of Zebulun, their genealogical registration by their families, by their fathers' households, according to the number of names, from twenty years old and upward, whoever was able to go out to war, 31 their numbered men of the tribe of Zebulun were 57,400.

32 Of the sons of Joseph, namely, of the sons of Ephraim, their genealogical registration by their families, by their fathers' households, according to the number of names, from twenty years old and upward, whoever was able to go out to war, 33 their numbered men of the tribe of Ephraim were 40,500.

34 Of the sons of Manasseh, their genealogical registration by their families, by their fathers' households, according to the number of names, from twenty years old and upward, whoever was able to go out to war, 35 their numbered men of the tribe of Manasseh were 32,200.

36 Of the sons of Benjamin, their genealogical registration by their families, by their fathers' households, according to the number of names, from twenty years old and upward, whoever was able to go out to war, 37 their numbered men of the tribe of Benjamin were 35,400.

38 Of the sons of Dan, their genealogical registration by their families, by their fathers' households, according to the number of names, from twenty years old and upward, whoever was able to go out to war, 39 their numbered men of the tribe of Dan were 62,700.

40 Of the sons of Asher, their genealogical registration by their families, by their fathers' households, according to the number of names, from twenty years old and upward, whoever was able to go out to war, 41 their numbered men of the tribe of Asher were 41,500.

42 Of the sons of Naphtali, their genealogical registration by their families, by their fathers' households, according to the number of names, from twenty years old and upward,

whoever *was able to* go out to war, ⁴³ their numbered men of the tribe of Naphtali *were* 53,400.

⁴⁴ These are the ones who were numbered, whom Moses and Aaron numbered, with the leaders of Israel, twelve men, each of whom was of his father's household. ⁴⁵ So all the numbered men of the sons of Israel by their fathers' households, from twenty years old and upward, whoever *was able to* go out to war in Israel, ⁴⁶ even all the numbered men were 603,550.

⁴⁷ The Levites, however, were not numbered among them by their fathers' tribe. ⁴⁸ For the LORD had spoken to Moses, saying, ⁴⁹ "Only the tribe of Levi you shall not number, nor shall you take their census among the sons of Israel. ⁵⁰ But you shall appoint the Levites over the tabernacle of the testimony, and over all its furnishings and over all that belongs to it. They shall carry the tabernacle and all its furnishings, and they shall take care of it; they shall also camp around the tabernacle. ⁵¹ So when the tabernacle is to set out, the Levites shall take it down; and when the tabernacle encamps, the Levites shall set it up. But the layman who comes near shall be put to death. ⁵² The sons of Israel shall camp, each man by his own camp, and each man by his own standard, according to their armies. ⁵³ But the Levites shall camp around the tabernacle of the testimony, so that there will be no wrath on the congregation of the sons of Israel. So the Levites shall keep charge of the tabernacle of the testimony." ⁵⁴ Thus the sons of Israel did; according to all which the LORD had commanded Moses, so they did.

1:51 **the layman.** This word often refers to the "alien" or "stranger." The non-Levite Israelite was like a "foreigner" to the transporting of the tabernacle and had to keep his distance lest he die.

2 Now the LORD spoke to Moses and to Aaron, saying, ² "The sons of Israel shall camp, each by his own standard, with the banners of their fathers' households; they shall camp around the tent of meeting at a distance. ³ Now those who camp on the east side toward the sunrise *shall be* of the standard of the camp of Judah, by their armies, and the leader of the sons of Judah: Nahshon the son of Amminadab, ⁴ and his army, even

their numbered men, 74,600. ⁵ Those who camp next to him *shall be* the tribe of Issachar, and the leader of the sons of Issachar: Nethanel the son of Zuar, ⁶ and his army, even their numbered men, 54,400. ⁷ *Then comes* the tribe of Zebulun, and the leader of the sons of Zebulun: Eliab the son of Helon, ⁸ and his army, even his numbered men, 57,400. ⁹ The total of the numbered men of the camp of Judah: 186,400, by their armies. They shall set out first.

¹⁰ "On the south side *shall be* the standard of the camp of Reuben by their armies, and the leader of the sons of Reuben: Elizur the son of Shedeur, ¹¹ and his army, even their numbered men, 46,500. ¹² Those who camp next to him *shall be* the tribe of Simeon, and the leader of the sons of Simeon: Shelumiel the son of Zurishaddai, ¹³ and his army, even their numbered men, 59,300. ¹⁴ Then *comes* the tribe of Gad, and the leader of the sons of Gad: Eliasaph the son of Deuel, ¹⁵ and his army, even their numbered men, 45,650. ¹⁶ The total of the numbered men of the camp of Reuben: 151,450 by their armies. And they shall set out second.

¹⁷ "Then the tent of meeting shall set out *with* the camp of the Levites in the midst of the camps; just as they camp, so they shall set out, every man in his place by their standards.

¹⁸ "On the west side *shall be* the standard of the camp of Ephraim by their armies, and the leader of the sons of Ephraim *shall be* Elishama the son of Ammihud, ¹⁹ and his army, even their numbered men, 40,500. ²⁰ Next to him *shall be* the tribe of Manasseh, and leader of the sons of Manasseh: Gamaliel the son of Pedahzur, ²¹ and his army, even their numbered men, 32,200. ²² Then *comes* the tribe of Benjamin, and the leader of the sons of Benjamin: Abidan the son of Gideoni, ²³ and his army, even their numbered men, 35,400. ²⁴ The total of the numbered men of the camp of Ephraim: 108,100, by their armies. And they shall set out third.

²⁵ "On the north side *shall be* the standard of the camp of Dan by their armies, and the leader of the sons of Dan: Ahiezer the son of Ammishaddai, ²⁶ and his army, even their numbered men, 62,700. ²⁷ Those who camp next to him *shall be* the tribe of Asher, and the leader of the sons of Asher: Pagiel the son of Ochran, ²⁸ and his army, even their numbered men, 41,500. ²⁹ Then *comes* the tribe of Naphtali, and the leader of the sons of Naphtali: Ahira the son of Enan, ³⁰ and his army, even their numbered men, 53,400. ³¹ The total of the numbered men of the camp of

Dan *was* 157,600. They shall set out last by their standards."

³²These are the numbered men of the sons of Israel by their fathers' households; the total of the numbered men of the camps by their armies, 603,550. ³³The Levites, however, were not numbered among the sons of Israel, just as the LORD had commanded Moses. ³⁴Thus the sons of Israel did; according to all that the LORD commanded Moses, so they camped by their standards, and so they set out, every one by his family according to his father's household.

Psalm 29:7–11

⁷ The voice of the LORD hews
out flames of fire.
⁸ The voice of the LORD shakes
the wilderness;
The LORD shakes the
wilderness of Kadesh.
⁹ The voice of the LORD makes
the deer to calve
And strips the forests bare;
And in His temple everything
says, "Glory!"

¹⁰ The LORD sat *as King* at the flood;
Yes, the LORD sits as King forever.
¹¹ The LORD will give strength
to His people;
The LORD will bless His
people with peace.

Proverbs 10:26–29

²⁶ Like vinegar to the teeth and
smoke to the eyes,
So is the lazy one to those
who send him.
²⁷ The fear of the LORD prolongs life,
But the years of the wicked
will be shortened.
²⁸ The hope of the righteous is gladness,
But the expectation of the
wicked perishes.
²⁹ The way of the LORD is a
stronghold to the upright,
But ruin to the workers of iniquity.

Mark 7:14–37

¹⁴After He called the crowd to Him again, He *began* saying to them, "Listen to Me, all of you, and understand: ¹⁵there is nothing outside the man which can defile him if it goes into him; but the things which proceed out of the man are what defile the man. ¹⁶[If anyone has ears to hear, let him hear."]

¹⁷When He had left the crowd *and* entered the house, His disciples questioned Him about the parable. ¹⁸And He *said to them, "Are you so lacking in understanding also? Do you not understand that whatever goes into the man from outside cannot defile him, ¹⁹because it does not go into his heart, but into his stomach, and is eliminated?" (*Thus He* declared all foods clean.) ²⁰And He was saying, "That which proceeds out of the man, that is what defiles the man. ²¹For from within, out of the heart of men, proceed the evil thoughts, fornications, thefts, murders, adulteries, ²²deeds of coveting *and* wickedness, *as well as* deceit, sensuality, envy, slander, pride *and* foolishness. ²³All these evil things proceed from within and defile the man."

7:19 Since food is merely physical, no one who eats it will defile his heart or inner person, which is spiritual. Physical pollution, no matter how corrupt, cannot cause spiritual or moral pollution. Neither can external ceremonies and rituals cleanse a person spiritually. ***Thus He declared all foods clean.*** By overturning the tradition of handwashing, Jesus in effect removed the restrictions regarding dietary laws.

7:20 That which proceeds out of the man. A person's defiled heart is expressed in both what he says and what he does.

---

²⁴Jesus got up and went away from there to the region of Tyre. And when He had entered a house, He wanted no one to know *of it;* yet He could not escape notice. ²⁵But after hearing of Him, a woman whose little daughter had an unclean spirit immediately came and fell at His feet. ²⁶Now the woman was a Gentile, of the Syrophoenician race. And she kept asking Him to cast the demon out of her daughter. ²⁷And He was saying to her, "Let the children be satisfied first, for it is not good to take the children's bread and throw it to the dogs." ²⁸But she answered and *said to Him, "Yes, Lord, *but* even the dogs under the table feed on the children's crumbs." ²⁹And He said to her, "Because of this answer go; the demon has gone out of your daughter." ³⁰And going back to her home, she found the child lying on the bed, the demon having left.

³¹Again He went out from the region of Tyre, and came through Sidon to the Sea of Galilee, within the region of Decapolis. ³²They *brought to Him one who was deaf and spoke with difficulty, and they *implored Him to lay

His hand on him. ³³Jesus took him aside from the crowd, by himself, and put His fingers into his ears, and after spitting, He touched his tongue *with the saliva;* ³⁴and looking up to heaven with a deep sigh, He *said to him, "Ephphatha!" that is, "Be opened!" ³⁵And his ears were opened, and the impediment of his tongue was removed, and he *began* speaking plainly. ³⁶And He gave them orders not to tell anyone; but the more He ordered them, the more widely they continued to proclaim it. ³⁷They were utterly astonished, saying, "He has done all things well; He makes even the deaf to hear and the mute to speak."

DAY 2: Did Moses perhaps inflate the numbers of Jews in the wilderness?

Twice during the wilderness wanderings, a census of the people of Israel was taken (Numbers 1:46; 26:51). Each time the resulting total count of fighting men exceeded 600,000. These numbers indicate a population for Israel in the wilderness of around 2.5 million people at any time. Viewed naturally, this total appears too high to sustain in wilderness conditions.

Before concluding that Moses inflated the numbers, several factors must be considered. First, the Lord supernaturally took care of Israel for 40 years (Dt 8:1-5). Miraculous provision of food was a daily event. Second, God also spelled out sanitary practices that prevented the kind of health crises that might have occurred under those conditions. Third, while Israel wandered in the wilderness for 40 years, they only moved camp about 40 times. Spending about a year in each campsite allowed for some normal life without creating a permanent settlement. This preserved some grazing for the herds while keeping the people's pollution to a manageable amount. Each census was meant to be an accurate accounting of God's people. They ought to be taken at face value.

MARCH 3

Numbers 3:1-4:49

3 Now these are *the records of* the generations of Aaron and Moses at the time when the LORD spoke with Moses on Mount Sinai. ²These then are the names of the sons of Aaron: Nadab the firstborn, and Abihu, Eleazar and Ithamar. ³These are the names of the sons of Aaron, the anointed priests, whom he ordained to serve as priests. ⁴But Nadab and Abihu died before the LORD when they offered strange fire before the LORD in the wilderness of Sinai; and they had no children. So Eleazar and Ithamar served as priests in the lifetime of their father Aaron.

3:1 Aaron and Moses. Because Aaron and his sons are emphasized in this chapter, Aaron is named first. **Mount Sinai.** The Lord had first communicated to Moses His choice of Aaron and his sons as priests in Exodus 28:1—29:46 while he was in the midst of the cloud on Mt. Sinai (Ex 24:18).

3:4 Eleazar and Ithamar. All of the future priests of Israel under the Mosaic Covenant were descendants of these two sons of Aaron. Eleazar and his descendants would later be singled out for great blessing (Nu 25:10-13).

⁵Then the LORD spoke to Moses, saying, ⁶"Bring the tribe of Levi near and set them before Aaron the priest, that they may serve him. ⁷They shall perform the duties for him and for the whole congregation before the tent of meeting, to do the service of the tabernacle. ⁸They shall also keep all the furnishings of the tent of meeting, along with the duties of the sons of Israel, to do the service of the tabernacle. ⁹You shall thus give the Levites to Aaron and to his sons; they are wholly given to him from among the sons of Israel. ¹⁰So you shall appoint Aaron and his sons that they may keep their priesthood, but the layman who comes near shall be put to death."

¹¹Again the LORD spoke to Moses, saying, ¹²"Now, behold, I have taken the Levites from among the sons of Israel instead of every firstborn, the first issue of the womb among the sons of Israel. So the Levites shall be Mine; ¹³For all the firstborn are Mine; on the day that I struck down all the firstborn in the land of Egypt, I sanctified to Myself all the firstborn in Israel, from man to beast. They shall be Mine; I am the LORD."

¹⁴Then the LORD spoke to Moses in the wilderness of Sinai, saying, ¹⁵"Number the sons of Levi by their fathers' households, by their families; every male from a month old and upward you shall number." ¹⁶So Moses numbered them according to the word of the LORD, just as he had been commanded. ¹⁷These then are the sons of Levi by their names: Gershon and Kohath and Merari.

18 These are the names of the sons of Gershon by their families: Libni and Shimei; 19 and the sons of Kohath by their families: Amram and Izhar, Hebron and Uzziel; 20 and the sons of Merari by their families: Mahli and Mushi. These are the families of the Levites according to their fathers' households.

21 Of Gershon *was* the family of the Libnites and the family of the Shimeites; these *were* the families of the Gershonites. 22 Their numbered men, in the numbering of every male from a month old and upward, *even* their numbered men *were* 7,500. 23 The families of the Gershonites were to camp behind the tabernacle westward, 24 and the leader of the fathers' households of the Gershonites *was* Eliasaph the son of Lael. 25 Now the duties of the sons of Gershon in the tent of meeting *involved* the tabernacle and the tent, its covering, and the screen for the doorway of the tent of meeting, 26 and the hangings of the court, and the screen for the doorway of the court which is around the tabernacle and the altar, and its cords, according to all the service concerning them.

27 Of Kohath *was* the family of the Amramites and the family of the Izharites and the family of the Hebronites and the family of the Uzzielites; these were the families of the Kohathites. 28 In the numbering of every male from a month old and upward, *there were* 8,600, performing the duties of the sanctuary. 29 The families of the sons of Kohath were to camp on the southward side of the tabernacle, 30 and the leader of the fathers' households of the Kohathite families was Elizaphan the son of Uzziel. 31 Now their duties *involved* the ark, the table, the lampstand, the altars, and the utensils of the sanctuary with which they minister, and the screen, and all the service concerning them; 32 and Eleazar the son of Aaron the priest *was* the chief of the leaders of Levi, *and had* the oversight of those who perform the duties of the sanctuary.

33 Of Merari *was* the family of the Mahlites and the family of the Mushites; these *were* the families of Merari. 34 Their numbered men in the numbering of every male from a month old and upward, *were* 6,200. 35 The leader of the fathers' households of the families of Merari *was* Zuriel the son of Abihail. They *were* to camp on the northward side of the tabernacle. 36 Now the appointed duties of the sons of Merari *involved* the frames of the tabernacle, its bars, its pillars, its sockets, all its equipment, and the service concerning them, 37 and the pillars around the court with their sockets and their pegs and their cords.

38 Now those who were to camp before the tabernacle eastward, before the tent of meeting toward the sunrise, are Moses and Aaron and his sons, performing the duties of the sanctuary for the obligation of the sons of Israel; but the layman coming near was to be put to death. 39 All the numbered men of the Levites, whom Moses and Aaron numbered at the command of the LORD by their families, every male from a month old and upward, *were* 22,000.

40 Then the LORD said to Moses, "Number every firstborn male of the sons of Israel from a month old and upward, and make a list of their names. 41 You shall take the Levites for Me, I am the LORD, instead of all the firstborn among the sons of Israel, and the cattle of the Levites instead of all the firstborn among the cattle of the sons of Israel." 42 So Moses numbered all the firstborn among the sons of Israel, just as the LORD had commanded him; 43 and all the firstborn males by the number of names from a month old and upward, for their numbered men were 22,273.

44 Then the LORD spoke to Moses, saying, 45 "Take the Levites instead of all the firstborn among the sons of Israel and the cattle of the Levites. And the Levites shall be Mine; I am the LORD. 46 For the ransom of the 273 of the firstborn of the sons of Israel who are in excess beyond the Levites, 47 you shall take five shekels apiece, per head; you shall take *them* in terms of the shekel of the sanctuary (the shekel is twenty gerahs), 48 and give the money, the ransom of those who are in excess among them, to Aaron and to his sons." 49 So Moses took the ransom money from those who were in excess, beyond those ransomed by the Levites; 50 from the firstborn of the sons of Israel he took the money in terms of the shekel of the sanctuary, 1,365. 51 Then Moses gave the ransom money to Aaron and to his sons, at the command of the LORD, just as the LORD had commanded Moses.

4 Then the LORD spoke to Moses and to Aaron, saying, 2 "Take a census of the descendants of Kohath from among the sons of Levi, by their families, by their fathers' households, 3 from thirty years and upward, even to fifty years old, all who enter the service to do the work in the tent of meeting. 4 This is the work of the descendants of Kohath in the tent of meeting, *concerning* the most holy things.

5 "When the camp sets out, Aaron and his sons shall go in and they shall take down the veil of the screen and cover the ark of the testimony with it; 6 and they shall lay a covering of porpoise skin on it, and shall spread over *it*

a cloth of pure blue, and shall insert its poles. [7] Over the table of the bread of the Presence they shall also spread a cloth of blue and put on it the dishes and the pans and the sacrificial bowls and the jars for the drink offering, and the continual bread shall be on it. [8] They shall spread over them a cloth of scarlet *material,* and cover the same with a covering of porpoise skin, and they shall insert its poles. [9] Then they shall take a blue cloth and cover the lampstand for the light, along with its lamps and its snuffers, and its trays and all its oil vessels, by which they serve it; [10] and they shall put it and all its utensils in a covering of porpoise skin, and shall put it on the carrying bars. [11] Over the golden altar they shall spread a blue cloth and cover it with a covering of porpoise skin, and shall insert its poles; [12] and they shall take all the utensils of service, with which they serve in the sanctuary, and put them in a blue cloth and cover them with a covering of porpoise skin, and put them on the carrying bars. [13] Then they shall take away the ashes from the altar, and spread a purple cloth over it. [14] They shall also put on it all its utensils by which they serve in connection with it: the firepans, the forks and shovels and the basins, all the utensils of the altar; and they shall spread a cover of porpoise skin over it and insert its poles. [15] When Aaron and his sons have finished covering the holy *objects* and all the furnishings of the sanctuary, when the camp is to set out, after that the sons of Kohath shall come to carry *them,* so that they will not touch the holy *objects* and die. These are the things in the tent of meeting which the sons of Kohath are to carry.

[16] "The responsibility of Eleazar the son of Aaron the priest is the oil for the light and the fragrant incense and the continual grain offering and the anointing oil—the responsibility of all the tabernacle and of all that is in it, with the sanctuary and its furnishings."

[17] Then the LORD spoke to Moses and to Aaron, saying, [18] "Do not let the tribe of the families of the Kohathites be cut off from among the Levites. [19] But do this to them that they may live and not die when they approach the most holy *objects:* Aaron and his sons shall go in and assign each of them to his work and to his load; [20] but they shall not go in to see the holy *objects* even for a moment, or they will die."

[21] Then the LORD spoke to Moses, saying, [22] "Take a census of the sons of Gershon also, by their fathers' households, by their families; [23] from thirty years and upward to fifty years old, you shall number them; all who enter to perform the service to do the work in the tent of meeting. [24] This is the service of the families of the Gershonites, in serving and in carrying: [25] they shall carry the curtains of the tabernacle and the tent of meeting *with* its covering and the covering of porpoise skin that is on top of it, and the screen for the doorway of the tent of meeting, [26] and the hangings of the court, and the screen for the doorway of the gate of the court which is around the tabernacle and the altar, and their cords and all the equipment for their service; and all that is to be done, they shall perform. [27] All the service of the sons of the Gershonites, in all their loads and in all their work, shall be *performed* at the command of Aaron and his sons; and you shall assign to them as a duty all their loads. [28] This is the service of the families of the sons of the Gershonites in the tent of meeting, and their duties *shall be* under the direction of Ithamar the son of Aaron the priest.

[29] "*As for* the sons of Merari, you shall number them by their families, by their fathers' households; [30] from thirty years and upward even to fifty years old, you shall number them, everyone who enters the service to do the work of the tent of meeting. [31] Now this is the duty of their loads, for all their service in the tent of meeting: the boards of the tabernacle and its bars and its pillars and its sockets, [32] and the pillars around the court and their sockets and their pegs and their cords, with all their equipment and with all their service; and you shall assign *each man* by name the items he is to carry. [33] This is the service of the families of the sons of Merari, according to all their service in the tent of meeting, under the direction of Ithamar the son of Aaron the priest."

[34] So Moses and Aaron and the leaders of the congregation numbered the sons of the Kohathites by their families and by their fathers' households, [35] from thirty years and upward even to fifty years old, everyone who entered the service for work in the tent of meeting. [36] Their numbered men by their families were 2,750. [37] These are the numbered men of the Kohathite families, everyone who was serving in the tent of meeting, whom Moses and Aaron numbered according to the commandment of the LORD through Moses.

[38] The numbered men of the sons of Gershon by their families and by their fathers' households, [39] from thirty years and upward even to fifty years old, everyone who entered the service for work in the tent of meeting. [40] Their numbered men by their families, by their fathers' households, were 2,630. [41] These are the

numbered men of the families of the sons of Gershon, everyone who was serving in the tent of meeting, whom Moses and Aaron numbered according to the commandment of the LORD.

⁴²The numbered men of the families of the sons of Merari by their families, by their fathers' households, ⁴³from thirty years and upward even to fifty years old, everyone who entered the service for work in the tent of meeting. ⁴⁴Their numbered men by their families were 3,200. ⁴⁵These are the numbered men of the families of the sons of Merari, whom Moses and Aaron numbered according to the commandment of the LORD through Moses.

⁴⁶All the numbered men of the Levites, whom Moses and Aaron and the leaders of Israel numbered, by their families and by their fathers' households, ⁴⁷from thirty years and upward even to fifty years old, everyone who could enter to do the work of service and the work of carrying in the tent of meeting. ⁴⁸Their numbered men were 8,580. ⁴⁹According to the commandment of the LORD through Moses, they were numbered, everyone by his serving or carrying; thus *these were* his numbered men, just as the LORD had commanded Moses.

Psalm 30:1–7

A Psalm; a Song at the Dedication of the House. *A Psalm* of David.

I will extol You, O LORD, for
  You have lifted me up,
And have not let my enemies
  rejoice over me.
² O LORD my God,
  I cried to You for help, and
  You healed me.
³ O LORD, You have brought up
  my soul from Sheol;
  You have kept me alive, that I
  would not go down to the pit.
⁴ Sing praise to the LORD,
  you His godly ones,
  And give thanks to His holy name.
⁵ For His anger is but for a moment,
  His favor is for a lifetime;
  Weeping may last for the night,
  But a shout of joy *comes*
  in the morning.

30:2–3 You healed me. God alone is the unique healer (Ex 15:26; Dt 32:39; Ps 107:20). David is extolling God for bringing him back from a near-death experience.

30:5 This stark contrast constitutes one of the most worshipful testimonies from the Scriptures (see the principle in Is 54:7–8; Jn 16:20–22; 2Co 4:17).

⁶ Now as for me, I said in
  my prosperity,
  "I will never be moved."
⁷ O LORD, by Your favor You have made
  my mountain to stand strong;
  You hid Your face, I was dismayed.

Proverbs 10:30–32

³⁰ The righteous will never be
  shaken,
  But the wicked will not
  dwell in the land.
³¹ The mouth of the righteous
  flows with wisdom,
  But the perverted tongue
  will be cut out.
³² The lips of the righteous bring
  forth what is acceptable,
  But the mouth of the wicked
  what is perverted.

Mark 8:1–21

8 In those days, when there was again a large crowd and they had nothing to eat, Jesus called His disciples and *said to them, ²"I feel compassion for the people because they have remained with Me now three days and have nothing to eat. ³If I send them away hungry to their homes, they will faint on the way; and some of them have come from a great distance." ⁴And His disciples answered Him, "Where will anyone be able *to find enough* bread here in *this* desolate place to satisfy these people?" ⁵And He was asking them, "How many loaves do you have?" And they said, "Seven." ⁶And He *directed the people to sit down on the ground; and taking the seven loaves, He gave thanks and broke

8:2 I feel compassion. Only here and in the parallel passage (Mt 15:32) did Jesus use this word of Himself. When He fed the 5,000, Jesus expressed "compassion" for the people's lost spiritual condition (6:34). Here, He expressed "compassion" for people's physical needs (Mt 6:8, 32). Jesus could empathize with their hunger, having experienced it Himself (Mt 4:2).

them, and started giving them to His disciples to serve to them, and they served them to the people. ⁷They also had a few small fish; and after He had blessed them, He ordered these to be served as well. ⁸And they ate and were satisfied; and they picked up seven large baskets full of what was left over of the broken pieces. ⁹About four thousand were *there*; and He sent them away. ¹⁰And immediately He entered the boat with His disciples and came to the district of Dalmanutha.

¹¹The Pharisees came out and began to argue with Him, seeking from Him a sign from heaven, to test Him. ¹²Sighing deeply in His spirit, He *said, "Why does this generation seek for a sign? Truly I say to you, no sign will be given to this generation." ¹³Leaving them, He again embarked and went away to the other side.

¹⁴And they had forgotten to take bread, and did not have more than one loaf in the boat with them. ¹⁵And He was giving orders to them, saying, "Watch out! Beware of the leaven of the Pharisees and the leaven of Herod." ¹⁶They *began* to discuss with one another *the fact* that they had no bread. ¹⁷And Jesus, aware of this, *said to them, "Why do you discuss *the fact* that you have no bread? Do you not yet see or understand? Do you have a hardened heart? ¹⁸HAVING EYES, DO YOU NOT SEE? AND HAVING EARS, DO YOU NOT HEAR? And do you not remember, ¹⁹when I broke the five loaves for the five thousand, how many baskets full of broken pieces you picked up?" They *said to Him, "Twelve." ²⁰"When *I broke* the seven for the four thousand, how many large baskets full of broken pieces did you pick up?" And they *said to Him, "Seven." ²¹And He was saying to them, "Do you not yet understand?"

DAY 3: What was the "leaven of the Pharisees and...of Herod" that Jesus warned about?

The skeptical Pharisees asked for a "sign from heaven" in Mark 8:11, demanding further miraculous proof of Jesus' messianic claims. Not content with the countless miracles He had performed on earth, they demanded some sort of astronomical miracle. Having already given them more than enough proof, Jesus refused to accommodate their spiritual blindness. The supreme sign verifying His claim to be the Son of God and Messiah was to be His resurrection (Mt 16:39–40).

Jesus warned the disciples about "the leaven of the Pharisees and...of Herod." "Leaven" is a yeast that multiplies quietly and permeates all that it contacts. In the New Testament, "leaven" most often symbolizes the evil influence of sin. The "leaven" of the Pharisees included both their false teaching (Mt 16:12) and their hypocritical behavior (Lk 12:1). The "leaven" of Herod Antipas was his immoral, corrupt conduct (see 6:17–29). The Pharisees and the Herodians were allied against Christ (3:6).

To Jesus' amazement, the disciples completely missed His point, thinking He was talking about physical bread. He was concerned with spiritual truth, not mundane physical matters. Jesus asks them, "Do you have a hardened heart?" (v. 17), which implies that they were rebellious, spiritually insensitive, and unable to understand spiritual truth. And He also reminded them of His ability to provide anything they might lack.

MARCH 4

Numbers 5:1–6:27

5 Then the LORD spoke to Moses, saying, ²"Command the sons of Israel that they send away from the camp every leper and everyone having a discharge and everyone who is unclean because of a *dead* person. ³You shall send away both male and female; you shall send them outside the camp so that they will not defile their camp where I dwell in their midst." ⁴The sons of Israel did so and sent them outside the camp; just as the LORD had spoken to Moses, thus the sons of Israel did.

⁵Then the LORD spoke to Moses, saying, ⁶"Speak to the sons of Israel, 'When a man or woman commits any of the sins of mankind, acting unfaithfully against the LORD, and that person is guilty, ⁷then he shall confess his sins which he has committed, and he shall make restitution in full for his wrong and add to it one-fifth of it, and give *it* to him whom he has wronged. ⁸But if the man has no relative to whom restitution may be made for the wrong, the restitution which is made for the wrong *must go* to the LORD for the priest, besides the ram of atonement, by which atonement is made for him. ⁹Also every contribution pertaining to all the holy *gifts* of the sons of Israel, which they offer to the priest, shall be his. ¹⁰So every man's holy *gifts* shall be his; whatever any man gives to the priest, it becomes his.'"

¹¹Then the LORD spoke to Moses, saying, ¹²"Speak to the sons of Israel and say to them, 'If any man's wife goes astray and is unfaithful to him, ¹³and a man has intercourse with her and it is hidden from the eyes of her husband and she is undetected, although she has defiled herself, and there is no witness against her and she has not been caught in the act, ¹⁴if a spirit of jealousy comes over him and he is jealous of his wife when she has defiled herself, or if a spirit of jealousy comes over him and he is jealous of his wife when she has not defiled herself, ¹⁵the man shall then bring his wife to the priest, and shall bring as an offering for her one-tenth of an ephah of barley meal; he shall not pour oil on it nor put frankincense on it, for it is a grain offering of jealousy, a grain offering of memorial, a reminder of iniquity.

¹⁶'Then the priest shall bring her near and have her stand before the LORD, ¹⁷and the priest shall take holy water in an earthenware vessel; and he shall take some of the dust that is on the floor of the tabernacle and put it into the water. ¹⁸The priest shall then have the woman stand before the LORD and let the hair of the woman's head go loose, and place the grain offering of memorial in her hands, which is the grain offering of jealousy, and in the hand of the priest is to be the water of bitterness that brings a curse. ¹⁹The priest shall have her take an oath and shall say to the woman, "If no man has lain with you and if you have not gone astray into uncleanness, being under the authority of your husband, be immune to this water of bitterness that brings a curse; ²⁰if you, however, have gone astray, being under the authority of your husband, and if you have defiled yourself and a man other than your husband has had intercourse with you" ²¹(then the priest shall have the woman swear with the oath of the curse, and the priest shall say to the woman), "the LORD make you a curse and an oath among your people by the LORD'S making your thigh waste away and your abdomen swell; ²²and this water that brings a curse shall go into your stomach, and make your abdomen swell and your thigh waste away." And the woman shall say, "Amen. Amen."

²³'The priest shall then write these curses on a scroll, and he shall wash them off into the water of bitterness. ²⁴Then he shall make the woman drink the water of bitterness that brings a curse, so that the water which brings a curse will go into her and cause bitterness. ²⁵The priest shall take the grain offering of jealousy from the woman's hand, and he shall wave the grain offering before the LORD and bring it to the altar; ²⁶and the priest shall take a handful of the grain offering as its memorial offering and offer it up in smoke on the altar, and afterward he shall make the woman drink the water. ²⁷When he has made her drink the water, then it shall come about, if she has defiled herself and has been unfaithful to her husband, that the water which brings a curse will go into her and cause bitterness, and her abdomen will swell and her thigh will waste away, and the woman will become a curse among her people. ²⁸But if the woman has not defiled herself and is clean, she will then be free and conceive children.

²⁹'This is the law of jealousy: when a wife, being under the authority of her husband, goes astray and defiles herself, ³⁰or when a spirit of jealousy comes over a man and he is jealous of his wife, he shall then make the woman stand before the LORD, and the priest shall apply all this law to her. ³¹Moreover, the man will be free from guilt, but that woman shall bear her guilt.'"

6 Again the LORD spoke to Moses, saying, ²"Speak to the sons of Israel and say to them, 'When a man or woman makes a special vow, the vow of a Nazirite, to dedicate himself to the LORD, ³he shall abstain from wine and strong drink; he shall drink no vinegar, whether made from wine or strong drink, nor shall he drink any grape juice nor eat fresh or dried grapes. ⁴All the days of his separation he shall not eat anything that is produced by the grape vine, from the seeds even to the skin.

6:2 the vow of a Nazirite. The word "vow" here is related to the word "wonder," which signifies something out of the ordinary. "Nazirite" transliterates a Hebrew term meaning "dedication by separation." The Nazirite separated himself to the Lord by separating himself from 1) grape products (6:3–4), 2) the cutting of one's hair (6:5), and 3) contact with a dead body (6:6–7). The High Priest was also forbidden 1) to drink wine while serving in the tabernacle (Lv 10:9), and 2) to touch dead bodies (Lv 21:11). Further, both the High Priest's crown (Ex 29:6; 39:30; Lv 8:9) and the Nazirite's head (6:9, 18) are referred to by the same Hebrew word. The Nazirite's hair was like the High Priest's crown. Like the High Priest, the Nazirite was holy to the Lord (6:8; cf: Ex 28:36) all the days (6:4–6, 8) of his vow.

5'All the days of his vow of separation no razor shall pass over his head. He shall be holy until the days are fulfilled for which he separated himself to the LORD; he shall let the locks of hair on his head grow long.

6'All the days of his separation to the LORD he shall not go near to a dead person. 7He shall not make himself unclean for his father or for his mother, for his brother or for his sister, when they die, because his separation to God is on his head. 8All the days of his separation he is holy to the LORD.

9'But if a man dies very suddenly beside him and he defiles his dedicated head *of hair,* then he shall shave his head on the day when he becomes clean; he shall shave it on the seventh day. 10Then on the eighth day he shall bring two turtledoves or two young pigeons to the priest, to the doorway of the tent of meeting. 11The priest shall offer one for a sin offering and *the* other for a burnt offering, and make atonement for him concerning his sin because of the *dead* person. And that same day he shall consecrate his head, 12and shall dedicate to the LORD his days as a Nazirite, and shall bring a male lamb a year old for a guilt offering; but the former days will be void because his separation was defiled.

13'Now this is the law of the Nazirite when the days of his separation are fulfilled, he shall bring the offering to the doorway of the tent of meeting. 14He shall present his offering to the LORD: one male lamb a year old without defect for a burnt offering and one ewe-lamb a year old without defect for a sin offering and one ram without defect for a peace offering, 15and a basket of unleavened cakes of fine flour mixed with oil and unleavened wafers spread with oil, along with their grain offering and their drink offering. 16Then the priest shall present *them* before the LORD and shall offer his sin offering and his burnt offering. 17He shall also offer the ram for a sacrifice of peace offerings to the LORD, together with the basket of unleavened cakes; the priest shall likewise offer its grain offering and its drink offering. 18The Nazirite shall then shave his dedicated head *of hair* at the doorway of the tent of meeting, and take the dedicated hair of his head and put *it* on the fire which is under the sacrifice of peace offerings. 19The priest shall take the ram's shoulder *when it has been* boiled, and one unleavened cake out of the basket and one unleavened wafer, and shall put *them* on the hands of the Nazirite after he has shaved his dedicated *hair.* 20Then the priest shall wave them for a wave offering before the LORD. It

is holy for the priest, together with the breast offered by waving and the thigh offered by lifting up; and afterward the Nazirite may drink wine.'

21"This is the law of the Nazirite who vows his offering to the LORD according to his separation, in addition to what *else* he can afford; according to his vow which he takes, so he shall do according to the law of his separation."

22Then the LORD spoke to Moses, saying, 23"Speak to Aaron and to his sons, saying, 'Thus you shall bless the sons of Israel. You shall say to them:

24 The LORD bless you, and keep you;

25 The LORD make His face shine on you,
And be gracious to you;

26 The LORD lift up His
countenance on you,
And give you peace.'

27So they shall invoke My name on the sons of Israel, and I *then* will bless them."

Psalm 30:8–12

8 To You, O LORD, I called,
And to the Lord I made supplication:
9 "What profit is there in my blood,
if I go down to the pit?
Will the dust praise You? Will it
declare Your faithfulness?

10 "Hear, O LORD, and be gracious
to me;
O LORD, be my helper."
11 You have turned for me my
mourning into dancing;
You have loosed my sackcloth and
girded me with gladness,
12 That *my* soul may sing praise
to You and not be silent.
O LORD my God, I will give
thanks to You forever.

Proverbs 11:1–3

11 A false balance is an
abomination to the LORD,
But a just weight is His delight.
2 When pride comes, then
comes dishonor,
But with the humble is wisdom.
3 The integrity of the upright
will guide them,
But the crookedness of the
treacherous will destroy them.

11:2 pride. From a root meaning "to boil," or "to run over," indicating an overwhelmingly arrogant attitude or behavior. It is used of ordinary men (Dt 17:12–13); kings (Ne 9:10); Israel (Ne 9:16, 29); false prophets (Dt 18:20); and murderers (Ex 21:14). **the humble.** A rare word, which appears in Micah 6:8: "walk humbly with your God." This humble and teachable spirit is first of all directed toward God (15:33; 16:18–19; 18:12; 22:4).

Mark 8:22–38

²²And they *came to Bethsaida. And they *brought a blind man to Jesus and *implored Him to touch him. ²³Taking the blind man by the hand, He brought him out of the village; and after spitting on his eyes and laying His hands on him, He asked him, "Do you see anything?" ²⁴And he looked up and said, "I see men, for I see *them* like trees, walking around." ²⁵Then again He laid His hands on his eyes; and he looked intently and was restored, and *began* to see everything clearly. ²⁶And He sent him to his home, saying, "Do not even enter the village."

²⁷Jesus went out, along with His disciples, to the villages of Caesarea Philippi; and on the way He questioned His disciples, saying to them, "Who do people say that I am?" ²⁸They told Him, saying, "John the Baptist; and others

8:23 spitting on his eyes. This action and Jesus' touching his eyes with His hands (v. 25) were apparently meant to reassure the blind man (who would naturally depend on his other senses, such as touch) that Jesus would heal his eyes (7:33; Jn 9:6).

say Elijah; but others, one of the prophets." ²⁹And He *continued* by questioning them, "But who do you say that I am?" Peter *answered and *said to Him, "You are the Christ." ³⁰And He warned them to tell no one about Him.

³¹And He began to teach them that the Son of Man must suffer many things and be rejected by the elders and the chief priests and the scribes, and be killed, and after three days rise again. ³²And He was stating the matter plainly. And Peter took Him aside and began to rebuke Him. ³³But turning around and seeing His disciples, He rebuked Peter and *said, "Get behind Me, Satan; for you are not setting your mind on God's interests, but man's."

³⁴And He summoned the crowd with His disciples, and said to them, "If anyone wishes to come after Me, he must deny himself, and take up his cross and follow Me. ³⁵For whoever wishes to save his life will lose it, but whoever loses his life for My sake and the gospel's will save it. ³⁶For what does it profit a man to gain the whole world, and forfeit his soul? ³⁷For what will a man give in exchange for his soul? ³⁸For whoever is ashamed of Me and My words in this adulterous and sinful generation, the Son of Man will also be ashamed of him when He comes in the glory of His Father with the holy angels."

8:30 tell no one. Jesus' messianic mission cannot be understood apart from the cross, which the disciples did not yet understand (vv. 31–33; 9:30–32). For them to have proclaimed Jesus as Messiah at this point would have only furthered the misunderstanding that the Messiah was to be a political-military deliverer. The fallout was that the Jewish people, desperate to be rid of the yoke of Rome, would seek to make Jesus king by force (Jn 6:15; see 12:12–19).

DAY 4: What does it mean to be a disciple of Jesus Christ?

In Mark 8:34, Jesus Christ makes it clear that no one who is unwilling to "deny himself" can legitimately claim to be a disciple. When He adds that one must "take up his cross," He reveals the extent of self-denial—to the point of death, if necessary. The extent of desperation on the part of the penitent sinner who is aware he can't save himself reaches the place where nothing is held back as He follows Jesus Christ (see Mt 19:21–22).

Jesus says that whoever "loses his life for My sake and the gospel's will save it" (v. 35). This paradoxical saying reveals an important spiritual truth: those who pursue a life of ease, comfort, and acceptance by the world will not find eternal life. On the other hand, those who give up their lives for the sake of Christ and the gospel will find it.

To have all that the world has to offer yet not have Christ is to be eternally bankrupt. All the world's goods will not compensate for losing one's soul eternally (v. 36). It is the "soul," the real person, who will live forever in heaven or hell. Those who reject the demands of discipleship prove themselves to be ashamed of Jesus Christ and the truth He taught.

MARCH 5

Numbers 7:1–8:26

7 Now on the day that Moses had finished setting up the tabernacle, he anointed it and consecrated it with all its furnishings and the altar and all its utensils; he anointed them and consecrated them also. ²Then the leaders of Israel, the heads of their fathers' households, made an offering (they were the leaders of the tribes; they were the ones who were over the numbered men). ³When they brought their offering before the LORD, six covered carts and twelve oxen, a cart for *every* two of the leaders and an ox for each one, then they presented them before the tabernacle. ⁴Then the LORD spoke to Moses, saying, ⁵"Accept *these things* from them, that they may be used in the service of the tent of meeting, and you shall give them to the Levites, *to* each man according to his service." ⁶So Moses took the carts and the oxen and gave them to the Levites. ⁷Two carts and four oxen he gave to the sons of Gershon, according to their service, ⁸and four carts and eight oxen he gave to the sons of Merari, according to their service, under the direction of Ithamar the son of Aaron the priest. ⁹But he did not give *any* to the sons of Kohath because theirs *was* the service of the holy *objects, which* they carried on the shoulder.

¹⁰The leaders offered the dedication *offering* for the altar when it was anointed, so the leaders offered their offering before the altar. ¹¹Then the LORD said to Moses, "Let them present their offering, one leader each day, for the dedication of the altar."

¹²Now the one who presented his offering on the first day was Nahshon the son of Amminadab, of the tribe of Judah; ¹³and his offering *was* one silver dish whose weight *was* one hundred and thirty *shekels,* one silver bowl of seventy shekels, according to the shekel of the sanctuary, both of them full of fine flour mixed with oil for a grain offering; ¹⁴one gold pan of ten *shekels,* full of incense; ¹⁵one bull, one ram, one male lamb one year old, for a burnt offering; ¹⁶one male goat for a sin offering; ¹⁷and for the sacrifice of peace offerings, two oxen, five rams, five male goats, five male lambs one year old. This *was* the offering of Nahshon the son of Amminadab.

¹⁸On the second day Nethanel the son of Zuar, leader of Issachar, presented *an offering;* ¹⁹he presented as his offering one silver dish whose weight *was* one hundred and thirty *shekels,* one silver bowl of seventy shekels, according to the shekel of the sanctuary, both of them full of fine flour mixed with oil for a grain offering; ²⁰one gold pan of ten *shekels,* full of incense; ²¹one bull, one ram, one male lamb one year old, for a burnt offering; ²²one male goat for a sin offering; ²³and for the sacrifice of peace offerings, two oxen, five rams, five male goats, five male lambs one year old. This *was* the offering of Nethanel the son of Zuar.

²⁴On the third day *it was* Eliab the son of Helon, leader of the sons of Zebulun; ²⁵his offering *was* one silver dish whose weight *was* one hundred and thirty *shekels,* one silver bowl of seventy shekels, according to the shekel of the sanctuary, both of them full of fine flour mixed with oil for a grain offering; ²⁶one gold pan of ten *shekels,* full of incense; ²⁷one young bull, one ram, one male lamb one year old, for a burnt offering; ²⁸one male goat for a sin offering; ²⁹and for the sacrifice of peace offerings, two oxen, five rams, five male goats, five male lambs one year old. This *was* the offering of Eliab the son of Helon.

³⁰On the fourth day *it was* Elizur the son of Shedeur, leader of the sons of Reuben; ³¹his offering *was* one silver dish whose weight *was* one hundred and thirty *shekels,* one silver bowl of seventy shekels, according to the shekel of the sanctuary, both of them full of fine flour mixed with oil for a grain offering; ³²one gold pan of ten *shekels,* full of incense; ³³one bull, one ram, one male lamb one year old, for a burnt offering; ³⁴one male goat for a sin offering; ³⁵and for the sacrifice of peace offerings, two oxen, five rams, five male goats, five male lambs one year old. This *was* the offering of Elizur the son of Shedeur.

³⁶On the fifth day *it was* Shelumiel the son of Zurishaddai, leader of the children of Simeon; ³⁷his offering *was* one silver dish whose weight *was* one hundred and thirty *shekels,* one silver bowl of seventy shekels, according to the shekel of the sanctuary, both of them full of fine flour mixed with oil for a grain offering; ³⁸one gold pan of ten *shekels,* full of incense; ³⁹one bull, one ram, one male lamb one year old, for a burnt offering; ⁴⁰one male goat for a sin offering; ⁴¹and for the sacrifice of peace offerings, two oxen, five rams, five male goats, five male lambs one year old. This *was* the offering of Shelumiel the son of Zurishaddai.

⁴²On the sixth day *it was* Eliasaph the son of Deuel, leader of the sons of Gad; ⁴³his offering *was* one silver dish whose weight *was* one hundred and thirty *shekels,* one silver bowl of seventy shekels, according to the shekel of

the sanctuary, both of them full of fine flour mixed with oil for a grain offering; 44 one gold pan of ten *shekels,* full of incense; 45 one bull, one ram, one male lamb one year old, for a burnt offering; 46 one male goat for a sin offering; 47 and for the sacrifice of peace offerings, two oxen, five rams, five male goats, five male lambs one year old. This *was* the offering of Eliasaph the son of Deuel.

48 On the seventh day *it was* Elishama the son of Ammihud, leader of the sons of Ephraim; 49 his offering *was* one silver dish whose weight *was* one hundred and thirty *shekels,* one silver bowl of seventy shekels, according to the shekel of the sanctuary, both of them full of fine flour mixed with oil for a grain offering; 50 one gold pan of ten *shekels,* full of incense; 51 one bull, one ram, one male lamb one year old, for a burnt offering; 52 one male goat for a sin offering; 53 and for the sacrifice of peace offerings, two oxen, five rams, five male goats, five male lambs one year old. This *was* the offering of Elishama the son of Ammihud.

54 On the eighth day *it was* Gamaliel the son of Pedahzur, leader of the sons of Manasseh; 55 his offering *was* one silver dish whose weight *was* one hundred and thirty *shekels,* one silver bowl of seventy shekels, according to the shekel of the sanctuary, both of them full of fine flour mixed with oil for a grain offering; 56 one gold pan of ten *shekels,* full of incense; 57 one bull, one ram, one male lamb one year old, for a burnt offering; 58 one male goat for a sin offering; 59 and for the sacrifice of peace offerings, two oxen, five rams, five male goats, five male lambs one year old. This *was* the offering of Gamaliel the son of Pedahzur.

60 On the ninth day *it was* Abidan the son of Gideoni, leader of the sons of Benjamin; 61 his offering *was* one hundred and thirty *shekels,* one silver bowl of seventy shekels, according to the shekel of the sanctuary, both of them full of fine flour mixed with oil for a grain offering; 62 one gold pan of ten *shekels,* full of incense; 63 one bull, one ram, one male lamb one year old, for a burnt offering; 64 one male goat for a sin offering; 65 and for the sacrifice of peace offerings, two oxen, five rams, five male goats, five male lambs one year old. This *was* the offering of Abidan the son of Gideoni.

66 On the tenth day *it was* Ahiezer the son of Ammishaddai, leader of the sons of Dan; 67 his offering *was* one silver dish whose weight *was* one hundred and thirty *shekels,* one silver bowl of seventy shekels, according

to the shekel of the sanctuary, both of them full of fine flour mixed with oil for a grain offering; 68 one gold pan of ten *shekels,* full of incense; 69 one bull, one ram, one male lamb one year old, for a burnt offering; 70 one male goat for a sin offering; 71 and for the sacrifice of peace offerings, two oxen, five rams, five male goats, five male lambs one year old. This *was* the offering of Ahiezer the son of Ammishaddai.

72 On the eleventh day *it was* Pagiel the son of Ochran, leader of the sons of Asher; 73 his offering *was* one silver dish whose weight *was* one hundred and thirty *shekels,* one silver bowl of seventy shekels, according to the shekel of the sanctuary, both of them full of fine flour mixed with oil for a grain offering; 74 one gold pan of ten *shekels,* full of incense; 75 one bull, one ram, one male lamb one year old, for a burnt offering; 76 one male goat for a sin offering; 77 and for the sacrifice of peace offerings, two oxen, five rams, five male goats, five male lambs one year old. This *was* the offering of Pagiel the son of Ochran.

78 On the twelfth day *it was* Ahira the son of Enan, leader of the sons of Naphtali; 79 his offering *was* one silver dish whose weight *was* one hundred and thirty *shekels,* one silver bowl of seventy shekels, according to the shekel of the sanctuary, both of them full of fine flour mixed with oil for a grain offering; 80 one gold pan of ten *shekels,* full of incense; 81 one bull, one ram, one male lamb one year old, for a burnt offering; 82 one male goat for a sin offering; 83 and for the sacrifice of peace offerings, two oxen, five rams, five male goats, five male lambs one year old. This *was* the offering of Ahira the son of Enan.

84 This *was* the dedication *offering* for the altar from the leaders of Israel when it was anointed: twelve silver dishes, twelve silver bowls, twelve gold pans, 85 each silver dish *weighing* one hundred and thirty *shekels* and each bowl seventy; all the silver of the utensils *was* 2,400 *shekels,* according to the shekel of the sanctuary; 86 the twelve gold pans, full of incense, *weighing* ten *shekels* apiece, according to the shekel of the sanctuary, all the gold of the pans 120 *shekels;* 87 all the oxen for the burnt offering twelve bulls, *all* the rams twelve, the male lambs one year old with their grain offering twelve, and the male goats for a sin offering twelve; 88 and all the oxen for the sacrifice of peace offerings 24 bulls, *all* the rams 60, the male goats 60, the male lambs one year old 60. This *was* the dedication *offering* for the altar after it was anointed.

[89] Now when Moses went into the tent of meeting to speak with Him, he heard the voice speaking to him from above the mercy seat that was on the ark of the testimony, from between the two cherubim, so He spoke to him.

7:89 He spoke to him. With the completion of the tabernacle, the Lord communicated His Word to Moses from the mercy seat in the Holy of Holies (Lv 1:1; Nu 1:1).

---

8 Then the LORD spoke to Moses, saying, [2] "Speak to Aaron and say to him, 'When you mount the lamps, the seven lamps will give light in the front of the lampstand.'" [3] Aaron therefore did so; he mounted its lamps at the front of the lampstand, just as the LORD had commanded Moses. [4] Now this was the workmanship of the lampstand, hammered work of gold; from its base to its flowers it was hammered work; according to the pattern which the LORD had shown Moses, so he made the lampstand.

[5] Again the LORD spoke to Moses, saying, [6] "Take the Levites from among the sons of Israel and cleanse them. [7] Thus you shall do to them, for their cleansing: *sprinkle* purifying water on them, and let them use a razor over their whole body and wash their clothes, and they will be clean. [8] Then let them take a bull with its grain offering, fine flour mixed with oil; and a second bull you shall take for a sin offering. [9] So you shall present the Levites before the tent of meeting. You shall also assemble the whole congregation of the sons of Israel, [10] and present the Levites before the LORD; and the sons of Israel shall lay their hands on the Levites. [11] Aaron then shall present the Levites before the LORD as a wave offering from the sons of Israel, that they may qualify to perform the service of the LORD. [12] Now the Levites shall lay their hands on the heads of the bulls; then offer the one for a sin offering and the other for a burnt offering to the LORD, to make atonement for the Levites. [13] You shall have the Levites stand before Aaron and before his sons so as to present them as a wave offering to the LORD. [14] "Thus you shall separate the Levites from among the sons of Israel, and the Levites shall be Mine. [15] Then after that the Levites may go in to serve the tent of meeting. But you shall cleanse them and present them as a wave offering; [16] for they are wholly given to Me from among the sons of Israel. I have taken them for Myself instead of every first issue of the womb, the firstborn of all the sons of Israel. [17] For every firstborn among the sons of Israel is Mine, among the men and among the animals; on the day that I struck down all the firstborn in the land of Egypt I sanctified them for Myself. [18] But I have taken the Levites instead of every firstborn among the sons of Israel. [19] I have given the Levites as a gift to Aaron and to his sons from among the sons of Israel, to perform the service of the sons of Israel at the tent of meeting and to make atonement on behalf of the sons of Israel, so that there will be no plague among the sons of Israel by their coming near to the sanctuary."

[20] Thus did Moses and Aaron and all the congregation of the sons of Israel to the Levites; according to all that the LORD had commanded Moses concerning the Levites, so the sons of Israel did to them. [21] The Levites, too, purified themselves from sin and washed their clothes; and Aaron presented them as a wave offering before the LORD. Aaron also made atonement for them to cleanse them. [22] Then after that the Levites went in to perform their service in the tent of meeting before Aaron and before his sons; just as the LORD had commanded Moses concerning the Levites, so they did to them.

[23] Now the LORD spoke to Moses, saying, [24] "This is what *applies* to the Levites: from twenty-five years old and upward they shall enter to perform service in the work of the tent of meeting. [25] But at the age of fifty years they shall retire from service in the work and not work any more. [26] They may, however, assist their brothers in the tent of meeting, to keep an obligation, but they *themselves* shall do no work. Thus you shall deal with the Levites concerning their obligations."

Psalm 31:1–5

For the choir director. A Psalm of David.

In You, O LORD, I have taken refuge;
Let me never be ashamed;
In Your righteousness deliver me.
[2] Incline Your ear to me,
rescue me quickly;
Be to me a rock of strength,
A stronghold to save me.
[3] For You are my rock and my fortress;
For Your name's sake You will lead me and guide me.
[4] You will pull me out of the net which they have secretly laid for me,
For You are my strength.

⁵ Into Your hand I commit my spirit;
    You have ransomed me,
        O LORD, God of truth.

Proverbs 11:4–6

⁴ Riches do not profit in
    the day of wrath,
    But righteousness delivers
    from death.
⁵ The righteousness of the blameless
    will smooth his way,
    But the wicked will fall by
    his own wickedness.
⁶ The righteousness of the
    upright will deliver them,
    But the treacherous will be
    caught by *their own* greed.

31:5 Into Your hand. This is applied to both the lesser David and the Greater David (Lk 23:46); here it involves the common denominator of trust. This is a metaphor depicting God's power and control (see v. 15a; contra. vv. 8, 15b).

11:4 day of wrath. Money buys no escape from death in the day of final accounting to God, the divine Judge (Is 10:3; Eze 7:19; Zep 1:18; Lk 12:16–21).

Mark 9:1–29

9 And Jesus was saying to them, "Truly I say to you, there are some of those who are standing here who will not taste death until they see the kingdom of God after it has come with power."

² Six days later, Jesus *took with Him Peter and James and John, and *brought them up on a high mountain by themselves. And He was transfigured before them; ³ and His garments became radiant and exceedingly white, as no launderer on earth can whiten them. ⁴ Elijah appeared to them along with Moses; and they were talking with Jesus. ⁵ Peter *said to Jesus, "Rabbi, it is good for us to be here; let us make three tabernacles, one for You, and one for Moses, and one for Elijah." ⁶ For he did not know what to answer; for they became terrified. ⁷ Then a cloud formed, overshadowing them, and a voice came out of the cloud, "This is My beloved Son, listen to Him!" ⁸ All at once they looked around and saw no one with them anymore, except Jesus alone.

⁹ As they were coming down from the mountain, He gave them orders not to relate to anyone what they had seen, until the Son of Man rose from the dead. ¹⁰ They seized upon that statement, discussing with one another what rising from the dead meant. ¹¹ They asked Him, saying, "*Why is it* that the scribes say that Elijah must come first?" ¹² And He said to them, "Elijah does first come and restore all things. And *yet* how is it written of the Son of Man that He will suffer many things and be treated with contempt? ¹³ But I say to you that Elijah has indeed come, and they did to him whatever they wished, just as it is written of him."

¹⁴ When they came *back* to the disciples, they saw a large crowd around them, and *some* scribes arguing with them. ¹⁵ Immediately, when the entire crowd saw Him, they were amazed and *began* running up to greet Him. ¹⁶ And He asked them, "What are you discussing with them?" ¹⁷ And one of the crowd answered Him, "Teacher, I brought You my son, possessed with a spirit which makes him mute; ¹⁸ and whenever it seizes him, it slams him *to the ground* and he foams *at the mouth,* and grinds his teeth and stiffens out. I told Your disciples to cast it out, and they could not *do it.*" ¹⁹ And He *answered them and *said, "O unbelieving generation, how long shall I be with you? How long shall I put up with you? Bring him to Me!" ²⁰ They brought the boy to Him. When he saw Him, immediately the spirit threw him into a convulsion, and falling to the ground, he *began* rolling around and foaming *at the mouth.* ²¹ And He asked his father, "How long has this been happening to him?" And he said, "From childhood. ²² It has often thrown him both into the fire and into the water to destroy him. But if You can do anything, take pity on us and help us!" ²³ And Jesus said to him, " 'If You can?' All things are possible to him who believes." ²⁴ Immediately the boy's father cried out and said, "I do believe; help my unbelief." ²⁵ When

9:22 to destroy him. This demon was an especially violent and dangerous one. Open fires and unfenced bodies of water were common in first-century Israel, providing ample opportunity for the demon's attempts to destroy the child. The father's statement added to the pathos of the situation. The boy himself was probably disfigured from burn scars, and possibly further ostracized because of them. His situation also created a hardship for his family, who would have had to watch the boy constantly to protect him from harm.

Jesus saw that a crowd was rapidly gathering, He rebuked the unclean spirit, saying to it, "You deaf and mute spirit, I command you, come out of him and do not enter him again." 26 After crying out and throwing him into terrible convulsions, it came out; and the boy became so much like a corpse that most of them said, "He is dead!" 27 But Jesus took him by the hand and raised him; and he got up. 28 When He came into the house, His disciples began questioning Him privately, "Why could we not drive it out?" 29 And He said to them, "This kind cannot come out by anything but prayer."

DAY 5: What was the purpose of Jesus' Transfiguration?

Matthew and Mark place the Transfiguration six days after Jesus' promise that some disciples would "see the kingdom of God after it has come with power" (Mk 9:1). Peter, James, and John, as the inner circle of Jesus' disciples, were allowed to witness this great event on "a high mountain" (Mk 9:2), most likely Mt. Hermon, the highest mountain in the vicinity of Caesarea Philippi (see 8:27). Jesus was "transfigured," meaning "to change in form" or "to be transformed," in front of them. In some inexplicable way, Jesus manifested some of His divine glory to the 3 disciples (see 2Pe 1:16). The divine glory emanating from Jesus made even His clothing radiate brilliant white light (Mk 9:3). Light is often associated with God's visible presence (see Ps 104:2; Da 7:9; 1Ti 6:16; Rev 1:14; 21:23).

Also appearing with Jesus were "Elijah...with Moses." They were symbolic of the Prophets and the Law, the two great divisions of the Old Testament. They "were talking with Jesus" (Mk 9:4), and the subject was His coming death (Lk 9:31). Then "a cloud formed, overshadowing them" (v. 7). This is the glory cloud, Shekinah, which throughout the Old Testament was symbolic of God's presence (Ex 13:21; 33:18–23; 40:34–35; Nu 9:15; 14:14; Dt 1:33). And "a voice came out of the cloud," which was the Father's voice, saying, "This is My beloved Son" (v. 7)—repeating the affirmation of His love for the Son first given at Jesus' baptism (Mk 1:11). "Listen to Him!" says the Father. Jesus, the One to whom the Law and Prophets pointed (see Dt 18:15), is the One whom the disciples are to listen to and obey (see Heb 1:1–2).

✷ MARCH 6

Numbers 9:1–10:36

9 Thus the LORD spoke to Moses in the wilderness of Sinai, in the first month of the second year after they had come out of the land of Egypt, saying, ² "Now, let the sons of Israel observe the Passover at its appointed time. ³ On the fourteenth day of this month, at twilight, you shall observe it at its appointed time; you shall observe it according to all its statutes and according to all its ordinances." ⁴ So Moses told the sons of Israel to observe the Passover. ⁵ They observed the Passover in the first month, on the fourteenth day of the month, at twilight, in the wilderness of Sinai; according to all that the LORD had commanded Moses, so the sons of Israel did. ⁶ But there were some men who were unclean because of the dead person, so that they could not observe Passover on that day; so they came before Moses and Aaron on that day. ⁷ Those men said to him, "Though we are unclean because of the dead person, why are we restrained from presenting the offering of the LORD at its appointed time among the sons of Israel?" ⁸ Moses therefore said to them, "Wait, and I will listen to what the LORD will command concerning you."

⁹ Then the LORD spoke to Moses, saying, ¹⁰ "Speak to the sons of Israel, saying, 'If any one of you or of your generations becomes unclean because of a dead person, or is on a distant journey, he may, however, observe the Passover to the LORD. ¹¹ In the second month on the fourteenth day at twilight, they shall observe it; they shall eat it with unleavened bread and bitter herbs. ¹² They shall leave none of it until morning, nor break a bone of it; according to all the statute of the Passover they shall observe it. ¹³ But the man who is clean and is not on a journey, and yet neglects to observe the Passover, that person shall then be cut off from his people, for he did not present the offering of the LORD at its appointed time. That man will bear his sin. ¹⁴ If an alien sojourns among you and observes the Passover to the LORD, according to the statute of the Passover and according to its ordinance, so he shall do; you shall have one statute, both for the alien and for the native of the land.'"

¹⁵ Now on the day that the tabernacle was erected the cloud covered the tabernacle, the tent of the testimony, and in the evening it was like the appearance of fire over the tabernacle,

until morning. ¹⁶So it was continuously; the cloud would cover it *by day,* and the appearance of fire by night. ¹⁷Whenever the cloud was lifted from over the tent, afterward the sons of Israel would then set out; and in the place where the cloud settled down, there the sons of Israel would camp. ¹⁸At the command of the LORD the sons of Israel would

9:15 tabernacle was erected. The presence of the Lord arrived when the tabernacle was completed and raised up on the first day of the first month of the second year after they had come out of Egypt.

9:16 cloud...fire. The presence of the Lord which was seen in the cloud by day became a fire that was seen at night (Lv 16:2).

set out, and at the command of the LORD they would camp; as long as the cloud settled over the tabernacle, they remained camped. ¹⁹Even when the cloud lingered over the tabernacle for many days, the sons of Israel would keep the LORD'S charge and not set out. ²⁰If sometimes the cloud remained a few days over the tabernacle, according to the command of the LORD they remained camped. Then according to the command of the LORD they set out. ²¹If sometimes the cloud remained from evening until morning, when the cloud was lifted in the morning, they would move out; or *if it remained* in the daytime and at night, whenever the cloud was lifted, they would set out. ²²Whether it was two days or a month or a year that the cloud lingered over the tabernacle, staying above it, the sons of Israel remained camped and did not set out; but when it was lifted, they did set out. ²³At the command of the LORD they camped, and at the command of the LORD they set out; they kept the LORD'S charge, according to the command of the LORD through Moses.

10 The LORD spoke further to Moses, saying, ²"Make yourself two trumpets of silver, of hammered work you shall make them; and you shall use them for summoning the congregation and for having the camps set out. ³When both are blown, all the congregation shall gather themselves to you at the doorway of the tent of meeting. ⁴Yet if *only* one is blown, then the leaders, the heads of the divisions of Israel, shall assemble before you. ⁵But when you blow an alarm, the camps that are pitched on the east side shall set out.

⁶When you blow an alarm the second time, the camps that are pitched on the south side shall set out; an alarm is to be blown for them to set out. ⁷When convening the assembly, however, you shall blow without sounding an alarm. ⁸The priestly sons of Aaron, moreover, shall blow the trumpets; and this shall be for you a perpetual statute throughout your generations. ⁹When you go to war in your land against the adversary who attacks you, then you shall sound an alarm with the trumpets, that you may be remembered before the LORD your God, and be saved from your enemies. ¹⁰Also in the day of your gladness and in your appointed feasts, and on the first *days* of your months, you shall blow the trumpets over your burnt offerings, and over the sacrifices of your peace offerings; and they shall be as a reminder of you before your God. I am the LORD your God."

¹¹Now in the second year, in the second month, on the twentieth of the month, the cloud was lifted from over the tabernacle of the testimony; ¹²and the sons of Israel set out on their journeys from the wilderness of Sinai. Then the cloud settled down in the wilderness of Paran. ¹³So they moved out for the first time according to the commandment of the LORD through Moses. ¹⁴The standard of the camp of the sons of Judah, according to their armies, set out first, with Nahshon the son of Amminadab, over its army, ¹⁵and Nethanel the son of Zuar, over the tribal army of the sons of Issachar; ¹⁶and Eliab the son of Helon over the tribal army of the sons of Zebulun.

¹⁷Then the tabernacle was taken down; and the sons of Gershon and the sons of Merari, who were carrying the tabernacle, set out. ¹⁸Next the standard of the camp of Reuben, according to their armies, set out with Elizur the son of Shedeur, over its army, ¹⁹and Shelumiel the son of Zurishaddai over the tribal army of the sons of Simeon, ²⁰and Eliasaph the son of Deuel was over the tribal army of the sons of Gad.

²¹Then the Kohathites set out, carrying the holy *objects;* and the tabernacle was set up before their arrival. ²²Next the standard of the camp of the sons of Ephraim, according to their armies, was set out, with Elishama the son of Ammihud over its army, ²³and Gamaliel the son of Pedahzur over the tribal army of the sons of Manasseh; ²⁴and Abidan the son of Gideoni over the tribal army of the sons of Benjamin.

²⁵Then the standard of the camp of the sons of Dan, according to their armies, *which*

formed the rear guard for all the camps, set out, with Ahiezer the son of Ammishaddai over its army, 26 and Pagiel the son of Ochran over the tribal army of the sons of Asher; 27 and Ahira the son of Enan over the tribal army of the sons of Naphtali. 28 This was the order of march of the sons of Israel by their armies as they set out.

29 Then Moses said to Hobab the son of Reuel the Midianite, Moses' father-in-law, "We are setting out to the place of which the LORD said, 'I will give it to you'; come with us and we will do you good, for the LORD has promised good concerning Israel." 30 But he said to him, "I will not come, but rather will go to my *own* land and relatives." 31 Then he said, "Please do not leave us, inasmuch as you know where we should camp in the wilderness, and you will be as eyes for us. 32 So it will be, if you go with us, that whatever good the LORD does for us, we will do for you."

33 Thus they set out from the mount of the LORD three days' journey, with the ark of the covenant of the LORD journeying in front of them for the three days, to seek out a resting place for them. 34 The cloud of the LORD was over them by day when they set out from the camp.

35 Then it came about when the ark set out that Moses said,

> "Rise up, O LORD!
> And let Your enemies be scattered,
> And let those who hate You
> flee before You."

36 When it came to rest, he said,

> "Return, O LORD,
> *To* the myriad thousands of Israel."

Psalm 31:6–14

6 I hate those who regard vain idols,
But I trust in the LORD.
7 I will rejoice and be glad in
Your lovingkindness,
Because You have seen my affliction;
You have known the
troubles of my soul,

31:6 I hate. See Psalms 26:5 on the proper basis for such hatred (Ps 139:21). **vain idols.** This is a common designation for false gods (Dt 32:21; 1Ki 16:13; Jer 10:15; 14:22; 16:19; 18:15; Jon 2:8). On the "idiocy" of idolatry, see Habakkuk 2:18–20.

8 And You have not given me over
into the hand of the enemy;
You have set my feet in a large place.

9 Be gracious to me, O LORD,
for I am in distress;
My eye is wasted away from grief,
my soul and my body *also.*
10 For my life is spent with sorrow
And my years with sighing;
My strength has failed
because of my iniquity,
And my body has wasted away.
11 Because of all my adversaries, I
have become a reproach,
Especially to my neighbors,
And an object of dread to
my acquaintances;
Those who see me in the
street flee from me.
12 I am forgotten as a dead
man, out of mind;
I am like a broken vessel.
13 For I have heard the slander of many,
Terror is on every side;
While they took counsel
together against me,
They schemed to take away my life.
14 But as for me, I trust in You, O LORD,
I say, "You are my God."

Proverbs 11:7–11

7 When a wicked man dies, *his*
expectation will perish,
And the hope of strong men perishes.
8 The righteous is delivered
from trouble,
But the wicked takes his place.
9 With *his* mouth the godless man
destroys his neighbor,
But through knowledge the
righteous will be delivered.
10 When it goes well with the
righteous, the city rejoices,
And when the wicked perish,
there is joyful shouting.
11 By the blessing of the upright
a city is exalted,
But by the mouth of the
wicked it is torn down.

Mark 9:30–50

30 From there they went out and *began* to go through Galilee, and He did not want anyone to know *about it.* 31 For He was teaching His disciples and telling them, "The Son of Man is to be delivered into the hands of men,

and they will kill Him; and when He has been killed, He will rise three days later." [32] But they did not understand *this* statement, and they were afraid to ask Him.

[33] They came to Capernaum; and when He was in the house, He *began* to question them, "What were you discussing on the way?" [34] But they kept silent, for on the way they had discussed with one another which *of them was* the greatest. [35] Sitting down, He called the twelve and *said to them, "If anyone wants to be first, he shall be last of all and servant of all." [36] Taking a child, He set him before them, and taking him in His arms, He said to them, [37] "Whoever receives one child like this in My name receives Me; and whoever receives Me does not receive Me, but Him who sent Me."

[38] John said to Him, "Teacher, we saw someone casting out demons in Your name, and we tried to prevent him because he was not following us." [39] But Jesus said, "Do not hinder him, for there is no one who will perform a miracle in My name, and be able soon afterward to speak evil of Me. [40] For he who is not against us is for us. [41] For whoever gives you a cup of water to drink because of your name as *followers* of Christ, truly I say to you, he will not lose his reward.

[42] "Whoever causes one of these little ones who believe to stumble, it would be better for him if, with a heavy millstone hung around his neck, he had been cast into the sea. [43] If your hand causes you to stumble, cut it off; it is better for you to enter life crippled, than, having your two hands, to go into hell, into the unquenchable fire, [44] [where THEIR WORM DOES NOT DIE, AND THE FIRE IS NOT QUENCHED.] [45] If your foot causes you to stumble, cut it off; it is better for you to enter life lame, than, hav-ing your two feet, to be cast into hell, [46] [where THEIR WORM DOES NOT DIE, AND THE FIRE IS NOT QUENCHED.] [47] If your eye causes you to stumble, throw it out; it is better for you to enter the kingdom of God with one eye, than, having two eyes, to be cast into hell, [48] where THEIR WORM DOES NOT DIE, AND THE FIRE IS NOT QUENCHED.

[49] "For everyone will be salted with fire. [50] Salt is good; but if the salt becomes unsalty, with what will you make it salty *again?* Have salt in yourselves, and be at peace with one another."

9:43 cut it off. Jesus' words are to be taken figuratively; no amount of self-mutilation can deal with sin, which is an issue of the heart. The Lord is emphasizing the seriousness of sin and the need to do whatever is necessary to deal with it. **life.** The contrast of "life" with "hell" indicates that Jesus was referring to eternal life. **hell.** The Greek word refers to the Valley of Hinnom near Jerusalem, a garbage dump where fires constantly burned, furnishing a graphic symbol of eternal torment. **the unquenchable fire.** That the punishment of hell lasts for eternity is the unmistakable teaching of Scripture (Da 12:2; Mt 25:41; 2Th 1:9; Rev 14:10–11; 20:10).

9:50 Salt is good. Salt was an essential item in first-century Israel. In a hot climate, without refrigeration, salt was the practical means of preserving food. **Have salt in yourselves.** The work of the Word (Col 3:16) and the Spirit (Gal 5:22–23) produce godly character, enabling a person to act as a preservative in society.

DAY 6: What essential element is Christ looking for in our character?

To be directly confronted by Christ with sin in your heart, as the disciples were in Mark 9:33, must have been powerfully convicting and embarrassing. We are told that "they kept silent"—they were speechless at His inquiry. They were caught in a dispute over "which of them was the greatest" (v. 34), possibly triggered by the privilege granted Peter, James, and John to witness the Transfiguration. The disciples' quarrel highlights their failure to apply Jesus' explicit teaching on humility (Mt 5:3) and the example of His own suffering and death (vv. 31–32; 8:30–33). It also prompted them to ask Jesus to settle the issue, which He did—though not as they had expected.

Jesus "[sat] down" (v. 35)—rabbis usually sat down to teach—and said that "if anyone wants to be first," as the disciples undeniably did (v. 34; see 10:35–37), "he shall be last of all and servant of all." The disciples' concept of greatness and leadership, drawn from their culture, needed to be completely reversed. Not those who lord their position over others are great in God's kingdom, but those who humbly serve others (see 10:31, 43–45; Mt 19:30–20:16; 23:11–12; Lk 13:30; 14:8–11; 18:14; 22:24–27).

Then Jesus took "a child" (v. 36)—the Greek word indicates an infant or toddler. If the house they were in was Peter's, this may have been one of his children. The child became in Jesus' masterful teaching an example of believers who have humbled themselves and become like trusting children.

MARCH 7

Numbers 11:1–12:16

11 Now the people became like those who complain of adversity in the hearing of the LORD; and when the LORD heard *it*, His anger was kindled, and the fire of the LORD burned among them and consumed *some* of the outskirts of the camp. ²The people therefore cried out to Moses, and Moses prayed to the LORD and the fire died out. ³So the name of that place was called Taberah, because the fire of the LORD burned among them.

⁴The rabble who were among them had greedy desires; and also the sons of Israel wept again and said, "Who will give us meat to eat? ⁵We remember the fish which we used to eat free in Egypt, the cucumbers and the melons and the leeks and the onions and the garlic, ⁶but now our appetite is gone. There is nothing at all to look at except this manna."

⁷Now the manna was like coriander seed, and its appearance like that of bdellium. ⁸The people would go about and gather *it* and grind *it* between two millstones or beat *it* in the mortar, and boil *it* in the pot and make cakes with it; and its taste was as the taste of cakes baked with oil. ⁹When the dew fell on the camp at night, the manna would fall with it.

¹⁰Now Moses heard the people weeping throughout their families, each man at the doorway of his tent; and the anger of the LORD was kindled greatly, and Moses was displeased. ¹¹So Moses said to the LORD, "Why have You been so hard on Your servant? And why have I not found favor in Your sight, that You have laid the burden of all this people on me? ¹²Was it I who conceived all this people? Was it I who brought them forth, that You should say to me, 'Carry them in your bosom as a nurse carries a nursing infant, to the land which You swore to their fathers'? ¹³Where am I to get meat to give to all this people? For they weep before me, saying, 'Give us meat that we may eat!' ¹⁴I alone am not able to carry all this people, because it is too burdensome for me. ¹⁵So if You are going to deal thus with me, please kill me at once, if I have found favor in Your sight, and do not let me see my wretchedness."

¹⁶The LORD therefore said to Moses, "Gather for Me seventy men from the elders of Israel, whom you know to be the elders of the people and their officers and bring them to the tent of meeting, and let them take their stand there with you. ¹⁷Then I will come down and speak with you there, and I will take of the Spirit who is upon you, and will put *Him* upon them; and they shall bear the burden of the people with you, so that you will not bear *it* all alone. ¹⁸Say to the people, 'Consecrate yourselves for tomorrow, and you shall eat meat; for you have wept in the ears of the LORD, saying, "Oh that someone would give us meat to eat! For we

11:17 the Spirit. This refers to the Spirit of God. It was by means of the Holy Spirit that Moses was able to lead Israel. In v. 25, the Lord gave the Spirit to the 70 men in fulfillment of the word He gave to Moses.

were well-off in Egypt." Therefore the LORD will give you meat and you shall eat. ¹⁹You shall eat, not one day, nor two days, nor five days, nor ten days, nor twenty days, ²⁰but a whole month, until it comes out of your nostrils and becomes loathsome to you; because you have rejected the LORD who is among you and have wept before Him, saying, "Why did we ever leave Egypt?" ' " ²¹But Moses said, "The people, among whom I am, are 600,000 on foot; yet You have said, 'I will give them meat, so that they may eat for a whole month.' ²²Should flocks and herds be slaughtered for them, to be sufficient for them? Or should all the fish of the sea be gathered together for them, to be sufficient for them?" ²³The LORD said to Moses, "Is the LORD'S power limited? Now you shall see whether My word will come true for you or not."

²⁴So Moses went out and told the people the words of the LORD. Also, he gathered seventy men of the elders of the people, and stationed them around the tent. ²⁵Then the LORD came down in the cloud and spoke to him; and He took of the Spirit who was upon him and placed *Him* upon the seventy elders. And when the Spirit rested upon them, they prophesied. But they did not do *it* again.

²⁶But two men had remained in the camp; the name of one was Eldad and the name of the other Medad. And the Spirit rested upon them (now they were among those who had been registered, but had not gone out to the tent), and they prophesied in the camp. ²⁷So a young man ran and told Moses and said, "Eldad and Medad are prophesying in the camp." ²⁸Then Joshua the son of Nun, the attendant of Moses from his youth, said, "Moses, my lord, restrain them." ²⁹But Moses said to him, "Are you jealous for my sake? Would that all the LORD'S people were prophets, that

11:29 that the LORD would put His Spirit upon them! Moses desired and anticipated the day when all of God's people would have His Spirit within them. By this, he looked forward to the New Covenant. (See Eze 36:22–27; Jer 31:31ff.; Joel 2:28.)

the LORD would put His Spirit upon them!" ³⁰Then Moses returned to the camp, *both* he and the elders of Israel.

³¹Now there went forth a wind from the LORD and it brought quail from the sea, and let *them* fall beside the camp, about a day's journey on this side and a day's journey on the other side, all around the camp and about two cubits *deep* on the surface of the ground. ³²The people spent all day and all night and all the next day, and gathered the quail (he who gathered least gathered ten homers) and they spread *them* out for themselves all around the camp. ³³While the meat was still between their teeth, before it was chewed, the anger of the LORD was kindled against the people, and the LORD struck the people with a very severe plague. ³⁴So the name of that place was called Kibroth-hattaavah, because there they buried the people who had been greedy. ³⁵From Kibroth-hattaavah the people set out for Hazeroth, and they remained at Hazeroth.

12 Then Miriam and Aaron spoke against Moses because of the Cushite woman whom he had married (for he had married a Cushite woman); ²and they said, "Has the LORD indeed spoken only through Moses? Has He not spoken through us as well?" And the LORD heard it. ³(Now the man Moses was very humble, more than any man who was on the face of the earth.) ⁴Suddenly the LORD said to Moses and Aaron and to Miriam, "You three come out to the tent of meeting." So the three of them came out. ⁵Then the LORD came down in a pillar of cloud and stood at the doorway of the tent, and He called Aaron and Miriam. When they had both come forward, ⁶He said,

> "Hear now My words:
> If there is a prophet among you,
> I, the LORD, shall make Myself
> known to him in a vision.
> I shall speak with him in
> a dream.
> ⁷ "Not so, with My servant
> Moses,
> He is faithful in all My
> household;

⁸ With him I speak mouth to mouth,
Even openly, and not in dark
sayings,
And he beholds the form
of the LORD.
Why then were you not afraid
To speak against My servant,
against Moses?"

⁹So the anger of the LORD burned against them and He departed. ¹⁰But when the cloud had withdrawn from over the tent, behold, Miriam *was* leprous, as *white as* snow. As Aaron turned toward Miriam, behold, she *was* leprous. ¹¹Then Aaron said to Moses, "Oh, my lord, I beg you, do not account *this* sin to us, in which we have acted foolishly and in which we have sinned. ¹²Oh, do not let her be like one dead, whose flesh is half eaten away when he comes from his mother's womb!" ¹³Moses cried out to the LORD, saying, "O God, heal her, I pray!" ¹⁴But the LORD said to Moses, "If her father had but spit in her face, would she not bear her shame for seven days? Let her be shut up for seven days outside the camp, and afterward she may be received again." ¹⁵So Miriam was shut up outside the camp for seven days, and the people did not move on until Miriam was received again.

¹⁶Afterward, however, the people moved out from Hazeroth and camped in the wilderness of Paran.

Psalm 31:15–18

¹⁵ My times are in Your hand;
Deliver me from the hand of
my enemies and from those
who persecute me.
¹⁶ Make Your face to shine
upon Your servant;
Save me in Your lovingkindness.
¹⁷ Let me not be put to shame,
O LORD, for I call upon You;
Let the wicked be put
to shame, let them be
silent in Sheol.
¹⁸ Let the lying lips be mute,
Which speak arrogantly
against the righteous
With pride and contempt.

Proverbs 11:12–14

¹² He who despises his
neighbor lacks sense,
But a man of understanding
keeps silent.
¹³ He who goes about as a
talebearer reveals secrets,

But he who is trustworthy
conceals a matter.
¹⁴ Where there is no guidance
the people fall,
But in abundance of counselors
there is victory.

Mark 10:1–31

10 Getting up, He *went from there to the region of Judea and beyond the Jordan; crowds *gathered around Him again, and, according to His custom, He once more *began* to teach them.

² *Some* Pharisees came up to Jesus, testing Him, and *began* to question Him whether it was lawful for a man to divorce a wife. ³ And He answered and said to them, "What did Moses command you?" ⁴ They said, "Moses permitted *a man* TO WRITE A CERTIFICATE OF DIVORCE AND SEND *her* AWAY." ⁵ But Jesus said to them, "Because of your hardness of heart he wrote you this commandment. ⁶ But from the beginning of creation, *God* MADE THEM MALE AND FEMALE. ⁷ FOR THIS REASON A MAN SHALL LEAVE HIS FATHER AND MOTHER, ⁸ AND THE TWO SHALL BECOME ONE FLESH; so they are no longer two, but one flesh. ⁹ What therefore God has joined together, let no man separate."

¹⁰ In the house the disciples *began* questioning Him about this again. ¹¹ And He *said to them, "Whoever divorces his wife and marries another woman commits adultery against her; ¹² and if she herself divorces her husband and marries another man, she is committing adultery."

¹³ And they were bringing children to Him so that He might touch them; but the disciples rebuked them. ¹⁴ But when Jesus saw this, He was indignant and said to them, "Permit the children to come to Me; do not hinder them; for the kingdom of God belongs to such as these. ¹⁵ Truly I say to you, whoever does not receive the kingdom of God like a child will not enter it *at all*." ¹⁶ And He took them in His arms and *began* blessing them, laying His hands on them.

¹⁷ As He was setting out on a journey, a man ran up to Him and knelt before Him, and asked Him, "Good Teacher, what shall I do to inherit eternal life?" ¹⁸ And Jesus said to him, "Why do you call Me good? No one is good except God alone. ¹⁹ You know the commandments, 'DO NOT MURDER, DO NOT COMMIT ADULTERY, DO NOT STEAL, DO NOT BEAR FALSE WITNESS, Do not defraud, HONOR YOUR FATHER AND MOTHER.'" ²⁰ And he said to Him, "Teacher, I have kept all these things from my youth up." ²¹ Looking at him, Jesus felt a love for him and said to him, "One thing you lack: go and sell all you possess and give to the poor, and you will have treasure in heaven; and come, follow Me." ²² But at these words he was saddened, and he went away grieving, for he was one who owned much property.

10:21 Jesus felt a love for him. Jesus felt great compassion for this sincere truth-seeker who was so hopelessly lost. And out of that great love He told the rich young man to **sell all you possess.** Jesus was not making either philanthropy or poverty a requirement for salvation, but exposing the young man's heart. He was not blameless, as he maintained (v. 20), since he loved his possessions more than his neighbors (Lv 19:18). More importantly, he refused to obey Christ's direct command, choosing to serve riches instead of God (Mt 6:24). The issue was to determine whether he would submit to the Lordship of Christ no matter what He asked of him. So, as he would not acknowledge his sin and repent, neither would he submit to the Sovereign Savior. Such unwillingness on both counts kept him from the eternal life he sought. **treasure in heaven.** Salvation and all its benefits, given by the Father who dwells there, both in this life and the life to come (cf. Mt 13:44–46).

²³ And Jesus, looking around, *said to His disciples, "How hard it will be for those who are wealthy to enter the kingdom of God!" ²⁴ The disciples were amazed at His words. But Jesus *answered again and *said to them, "Children, how hard it is to enter the kingdom of God! ²⁵ It is easier for a camel to go through the eye of a needle than for a rich man to enter the kingdom of God." ²⁶ They were even more astonished and said to Him, "Then who can be saved?" ²⁷ Looking at them, Jesus *said, "With people it is impossible, but not with God; for all things are possible with God."

²⁸ Peter began to say to Him, "Behold, we have left everything and followed You." ²⁹ Jesus said, "Truly I say to you, there is no one who has left house or brothers or sisters or mother or father or children or farms, for My sake and for the gospel's sake, ³⁰ but that he will receive a hundred times as much now in the present age, houses and brothers and sisters and mothers and children and farms, along with persecutions; and in the age to come, eternal life. ³¹ But many *who are* first will be last, and the last, first."

Watching the rich young ruler walk away sorrowful in Mark 10:23, Jesus said, "How hard it will be for those who are wealthy to enter the kingdom of God!" "Hard" in this context means impossible (see v. 25). Wealth tends to breed self-sufficiency and a false sense of security, leading those who have them to imagine they do not need divine resources (see Lk 16:13; contra. Lk 19:2; see 1Ti 6:9, 17–18).

Jesus adds that it is "easier for a camel to go through the eye of a needle" (v. 25). The Persians expressed impossibility by saying it would be easier to put an elephant through the eye of a needle. This was a Jewish colloquial adaptation of that expression denoting impossibility (the largest animal in Palestine was a camel). Many improbable interpretations have arisen that attempt to soften this phrase, but Jesus' use of this illustration was to explicitly say that salvation by human effort is impossible—it is wholly by God's grace.

The Jews believed that with alms a man purchased salvation (as recorded in the Talmud), so the more wealth one had, the more alms he could give, the more sacrifices and offerings he could offer, thus purchasing redemption. The disciples' question, "Who then can be saved?" (v. 26), makes it clear that they understood what Jesus meant—that not even the rich could buy salvation. Jesus' emphatic teaching that even the rich could not be saved by their own efforts left the bewildered disciples wondering what chance the poor stood. "With people it is impossible, but not with God," Jesus added (v. 27). It is impossible for anyone to be saved by his own efforts, since salvation is entirely a gracious, sovereign work of God.

MARCH 8

Numbers 13:1–14:45

13 Then the LORD spoke to Moses saying, 2 "Send out for yourself men so that they may spy out the land of Canaan, which I am going to give to the sons of Israel; you shall send a man from each of their fathers' tribes, every one a leader among them." 3 So Moses sent them from the wilderness of Paran at the command of the LORD, all of them men who were heads of the sons of Israel. 4 These then were their names: from the tribe of Reuben, Shammua the son of Zaccur; 5 from the tribe of Simeon, Shaphat the son of Hori; 6 from the tribe of Judah, Caleb the son of Jephunneh; 7 from the tribe of Issachar, Igal the son of Joseph; 8 from the tribe of Ephraim, Hoshea the son of Nun; 9 from the tribe of Benjamin, Palti the son of Raphu; 10 from the tribe of Zebulun, Gaddiel the son of Sodi; 11 from the tribe of Joseph, from the tribe of Manasseh, Gaddi the son of Susi; 12 from the tribe of Dan, Ammiel the son of Gemalli; 13 from the tribe of Asher, Sethur the son of Michael; 14 from the tribe of

Naphtali, Nahbi the son of Vophsi; 15 from the tribe of Gad, Geuel the son of Machi. 16 These are the names of the men whom Moses sent to spy out the land; but Moses called Hoshea the son of Nun, Joshua.

17 When Moses sent them to spy out the land of Canaan, he said to them, "Go up there into the Negev; then go up into the hill country. 18 See what the land is like, and whether the people who live in it are strong or weak, whether they are few or many. 19 How is the land in which they live, is it good or bad? And how are the cities in which they live, are they like open camps or with fortifications? 20 How is the land, is it fat or lean? Are there trees in it or not? Make an effort then to get some of the fruit of the land." Now the time was the time of the first ripe grapes.

21 So they went up and spied out the land from the wilderness of Zin as far as Rehob, at Lebo-hamath. 22 When they had gone up into the Negev, they came to Hebron where Ahiman, Sheshai and Talmai, the descendants of Anak were. (Now Hebron was built seven years before Zoan in Egypt.) 23 Then they came to the valley of Eshcol and from there cut down a branch with a single cluster of grapes; and they carried it on a pole between two men, with some of the pomegranates and the figs. 24 That place was called the valley of Eshcol, because of the cluster which the sons of Israel cut down from there. 25 When they returned from spying out the land, at the end of forty days, 26 they proceeded to come to Moses and Aaron and

13:1 the LORD spoke to Moses. According to Deuteronomy 1:22–23, the people had first requested the spies be sent out after Moses challenged them to take the land. Here, the Lord affirmed the peoples' desire and commanded Moses to send them.

to all the congregation of the sons of Israel in the wilderness of Paran, at Kadesh; and they brought back word to them and to all the congregation and showed them the fruit of the land. ²⁷ Thus they told him, and said, "We went in to the land where you sent us; and it certainly does flow with milk and honey, and this is its fruit. ²⁸ Nevertheless, the people who live in the land are strong, and the cities are fortified *and* very large; and moreover, we saw the descendants of Anak there. ²⁹ Amalek is living in the land of the Negev and the Hittites and the Jebusites and the Amorites are living in the hill country, and the Canaanites are living by the sea and by the side of the Jordan."

³⁰ Then Caleb quieted the people before Moses and said, "We should by all means go up and take possession of it, for we will surely overcome it." ³¹ But the men who had gone up with him said, "We are not able to go up against the people, for they are too strong for us." ³² So they gave out to the sons of Israel a bad report of the land which they had spied out, saying, "The land through which we have gone, in spying it out, is a land that devours its inhabitants; and all the people whom we saw in it are men of *great* size. ³³ There also we saw the Nephilim (the sons of Anak are part of the Nephilim); and we became like grasshoppers in our own sight, and so we were in their sight."

14 Then all the congregation lifted up their voices and cried, and the people wept that night. ² All the sons of Israel grumbled against Moses and Aaron; and the whole congregation said to them, "Would that we had died in the land of Egypt! Or would that we had died in this wilderness! ³ Why is the LORD bringing us into this land, to fall by the sword? Our wives and our little ones will become plunder; would it not be better for us to return to Egypt?" ⁴ So they said to one another, "Let us appoint a leader and return to Egypt."

⁵ Then Moses and Aaron fell on their faces in the presence of all the assembly of the congregation of the sons of Israel. ⁶ Joshua the son of Nun and Caleb the son of Jephunneh, of those who had spied out the land, tore their clothes; ⁷ and they spoke to all the congregation of the sons of Israel, saying, "The land which we passed through to spy out is an exceedingly good land. ⁸ If the LORD is pleased with us, then He will bring us into this land and give it to us—a land which flows with milk and honey. ⁹ Only do not rebel against the LORD; and do not fear the people of the

land, for they will be our prey. Their protection has been removed from them, and the LORD is with us; do not fear them." ¹⁰ But all the congregation said to stone them with stones. Then the glory of the LORD appeared in the tent of meeting to all the sons of Israel.

¹¹ The LORD said to Moses, "How long will this people spurn Me? And how long will they not believe in Me, despite all the signs which I have performed in their midst? ¹² I will smite them with pestilence and dispossess them, and I will make you into a nation greater and mightier than they."

¹³ But Moses said to the LORD, "Then the Egyptians will hear of it, for by Your strength You brought up this people from their midst, ¹⁴ and they will tell *it* to the inhabitants of this land. They have heard that You, O LORD, are in the midst of this people, for You, O LORD, are seen eye to eye, while Your cloud stands over them; and You go before them in a pillar of cloud by day and in a pillar of fire by night. ¹⁵ Now if You slay this people as one man, then the nations who have heard of Your fame will say, ¹⁶ 'Because the LORD could not bring this people into the land which He promised them by oath, therefore He slaughtered them in the wilderness.' ¹⁷ But now, I pray, let the power of the Lord be great, just as You have declared, ¹⁸ 'The LORD is slow to anger and abundant in lovingkindness, forgiving iniquity and transgression; but He will by no means clear *the guilty,* visiting the iniquity of the fathers on the children to the third and the fourth *generations.*' ¹⁹ Pardon, I pray, the iniquity of this people according to the greatness of Your lovingkindness, just as You also have forgiven this people, from Egypt even until now."

²⁰ So the LORD said, "I have pardoned *them* according to your word; ²¹ but indeed, as I live, all the earth will be filled with the glory of the LORD. ²² Surely all the men who have seen My glory and My signs which I performed in Egypt and in the wilderness, yet have put Me to the test these ten times and have not listened to My voice, ²³ shall by no means see the land which I swore to their fathers, nor shall any of those who spurned Me see it. ²⁴ But My servant Caleb, because he has had a different spirit and has followed Me fully, I will bring into the land which he entered, and his descendants shall take possession of it. ²⁵ Now the Amalekites and the Canaanites live in the valleys; turn tomorrow and set out to the wilderness by the way of the Red Sea."

²⁶ The LORD spoke to Moses and Aaron, saying, ²⁷ "How long *shall I bear* with this evil congregation who are grumbling against

Me? I have heard the complaints of the sons of Israel, which they are making against Me. ²⁸ Say to them, 'As I live,' says the LORD, 'just as you have spoken in My hearing, so I will surely do to you; ²⁹ your corpses will fall in this wilderness, even all your numbered men, according to your complete number from twenty years old and upward, who have grumbled against Me. ³⁰ Surely you shall not come into the land in which I swore to settle you, except Caleb the son of Jephunneh and Joshua the son of Nun. ³¹ Your children, however, whom you said would become a prey—I will bring them in, and they will know the land which you have rejected. ³² But as for you, your corpses will fall in this wilderness. ³³ Your sons shall be shepherds for forty years in the wilderness, and they will suffer *for* your unfaithfulness, until your corpses lie in the wilderness. ³⁴ According to the number of days which you spied out the land, forty days, for every day you shall bear your guilt a year, *even* forty years, and you will know My opposition. ³⁵ I, the LORD, have spoken, surely this I will do to all this evil congregation who are gathered together against Me. In this wilderness they shall be destroyed, and there they will die.' "

³⁶ As for the men whom Moses sent to spy out the land and who returned and made all the congregation grumble against him by bringing out a bad report concerning the land, ³⁷ even those men who brought out the very bad report of the land died by a plague before the LORD. ³⁸ But Joshua the son of Nun and Caleb the son of Jephunneh remained alive out of those men who went to spy out the land.

³⁹ When Moses spoke these words to all the sons of Israel, the people mourned greatly. ⁴⁰ In the morning, however, they rose up early and went up to the ridge of the hill country, saying, "Here we are; we have indeed sinned, but we will go up to the place which the LORD has promised." ⁴¹ But Moses said, "Why then are you transgressing the commandment of the LORD, when it will not succeed? ⁴² Do not go up, or you will be struck down before your enemies, for the LORD is not among you. ⁴³ For the Amalekites and the Canaanites will be there in front of you, and you will fall by the sword, inasmuch as you have turned back from following the LORD. And the LORD will not be with you." ⁴⁴ But they went up heedlessly to the ridge of the hill country; neither the ark of the covenant of the LORD nor Moses left the camp. ⁴⁵ Then the Amalekites and the Canaanites who lived in that hill country came down, and struck them and beat them down as far as Hormah.

Psalm 31:19–24

¹⁹ How great is Your goodness,
    Which You have stored up for
        those who fear You,
    Which You have wrought for those
        who take refuge in You,
    Before the sons of men!
²⁰ You hide them in the secret
        place of Your presence from
        the conspiracies of man;
    You keep them secretly in a shelter
        from the strife of tongues.
²¹ Blessed be the LORD,
    For He has made marvelous
        His lovingkindness to me
        in a besieged city.
²² As for me, I said in my alarm,
    "I am cut off from before Your eyes";
    Nevertheless You heard the
        voice of my supplications
        When I cried to You.

²³ O love the LORD, all you
        His godly ones!
    The LORD preserves the faithful
    And fully recompenses
        the proud doer.
²⁴ Be strong and let your
        heart take courage,
    All you who hope in the LORD.

31:23 love the LORD. Biblical love includes an attitudinal response and demonstrated obedience (Dt 6:4–5; 10:12; Jn 14:15, 21; 15:10; 2Jn 6). The assurance of both reward and retribution is a biblical maxim (e.g., Dt 7:9–10).

Proverbs 11:15

¹⁵ He who is guarantor for a stranger
        will surely suffer for it,
    But he who hates being a
        guarantor is secure.

Mark 10:32–52

³² They were on the road going up to Jerusalem, and Jesus was walking on ahead of them; and they were amazed, and those who followed were fearful. And again He took the twelve aside and began to tell them what was going to happen to Him, ³³ saying, "Behold, we are going up to Jerusalem, and the Son of Man will be delivered to the chief priests and the

scribes; and they will condemn Him to death and will hand Him over to the Gentiles. 34 They will mock Him and spit on Him, and scourge Him and kill *Him,* and three days later He will rise again."

35 James and John, the two sons of Zebedee, *came up to Jesus, saying, "Teacher, we want You to do for us whatever we ask of You." 36 And He said to them, "What do you want Me to do for you?" 37 They said to Him, "Grant that we may sit, one on Your right and one on *Your* left, in Your glory." 38 But Jesus said to them, "You do not know what you are asking. Are you able to drink the cup that I drink, or to be baptized with the baptism with which I am baptized?" 39 They said to Him, "We are able." And Jesus said to them, "The cup that I drink you shall drink; and you shall be baptized with the baptism with which I am baptized. 40 But to sit on My right or on *My* left, this is not Mine to give; but it is for those for whom it has been prepared."

41 Hearing *this,* the ten began to feel indignant with James and John. 42 Calling them to Himself, Jesus *said to them, "You know that those who are recognized as rulers of the Gentiles lord it over them; and their great men exercise authority over them. 43 But it is not this way among you, but whoever wishes to become great among you shall be your servant; 44 and whoever wishes to be first among you shall be slave of all. 45 For even the Son of Man did not come to be served, but to serve, and to give His life a ransom for many."

46 Then they *came to Jericho. And as He was leaving Jericho with His disciples and a large crowd, a blind beggar *named* Bartimaeus, the son of Timaeus, was sitting by the road. 47 When he heard that it was Jesus the

10:45 Son of Man...did not come to be served. Jesus was the supreme example of servant leadership (Jn 13:13-15). The King of kings and Lord of lords (Rev 19:16) relinquished His privileges (Php 2:5-8) and gave His life as a selfless sacrifice in serving others. **ransom for many.** "Ransom" refers to the price paid to free a slave or a prisoner; "for" means "in place of." Christ's substitutionary death on behalf of those who would put their faith in Him is the most glorious, blessed truth in all of Scripture (Ro 8:1-3; 1Co 6:20; Gal 3:13; 4:5; Eph 1:7; Titus 2:14; 1Pe 1:18-19). The ransom was not paid to Satan, as some erroneous theories of the atonement teach. Satan is presented in Scripture as a foe to be defeated, not a ruler to be placated. The ransom price was paid to God to satisfy His justice and holy wrath against sin. In paying it, Christ "bore our sins in His body on the cross" (1Pe 2:24).

Nazarene, he began to cry out and say, "Jesus, Son of David, have mercy on me!" 48 Many were sternly telling him to be quiet, but he kept crying out all the more, "Son of David, have mercy on me!" 49 And Jesus stopped and said, "Call him here." So they *called the blind man, saying to him, "Take courage, stand up! He is calling for you." 50 Throwing aside his cloak, he jumped up and came to Jesus. 51 And answering him, Jesus said, "What do you want Me to do for you?" And the blind man said to Him, "Rabboni, I *want* to regain my sight!" 52 And Jesus said to him, "Go; your faith has made you well." Immediately he regained his sight and *began* following Him on the road.

DAY 8: If the report of the spies was true, why was it a "bad report"?

The spies were specifically called to explore the land that God had promised to Israel. This exploration gave valuable information to Moses for the conquest ahead. And while it was true that the land was flowing with milk and honey, it was also true that "the descendants of Anak" were in the fortified city of Hebron (Nu 13:22). Anak was probably the ancestor of Ahiman, Sheshai, and Talmai. They were noted for their height and strength (Dt 2:21; 9:2). And "the people... are strong" (v. 28), as in too strong to be conquered (v. 31). "Nephilim," or giants, were in the land (v. 33). This term was used in Genesis 6:4 for a group of strong men who lived on the earth before the Flood. The descendants of Anak were, in exaggeration, compared to these giants, which led the spies to view themselves as grasshoppers before them.

In v. 30, Caleb concurred with the report of the other spies, but called the people to go up and take the land, knowing that with God's help they were able to overcome the strong people. The report of the 10 spies was evil because it exaggerated the dangers of the people in the land, sought to stir up and instill fear in the people of Israel, and, most importantly, it expressed their faithless attitude toward God and His promises (v. 32). The result was that "all the congregation...wept" over the circumstances (14:1) and "grumbled" to the point that they wished they had died in Egypt or the wilderness (v. 2). It was such a "bad report" that they were prepared to "appoint a leader and return to Egypt" (v. 4).

MARCH 9

Numbers 15:1–16:50

15 Now the LORD spoke to Moses, saying, [2] "Speak to the sons of Israel and say to them, 'When you enter the land where you are to live, which I am giving you, [3] then make an offering by fire to the LORD, a burnt offering or a sacrifice to fulfill a special vow, or as a freewill offering or in your appointed times, to make a soothing aroma to the LORD, from the herd or from the flock. [4] The one who presents his offering shall present to the LORD a grain offering of one-tenth *of an ephah* of fine flour mixed with one-fourth of a hin of oil, [5] and you shall prepare wine for the drink offering, one-fourth of a hin, with the burnt offering or for the sacrifice, for each lamb. [6] Or for a ram you shall prepare as a grain offering two-tenths *of an ephah* of fine flour mixed with one-third of a hin of oil; [7] and for the drink offering you shall offer one-third of a hin of wine as a soothing aroma to the LORD. [8] When you prepare a bull as a burnt offering or a sacrifice, to fulfill a special vow, or for peace offerings to the LORD, [9] then you shall offer with the bull a grain offering of three-tenths *of an ephah* of fine flour mixed with one-half a hin of oil; [10] and you shall offer as the drink offering one-half a hin of wine as an offering by fire, as a soothing aroma to the LORD.

[11] 'Thus it shall be done for each ox, or for each ram, or for each of the male lambs, or of the goats. [12] According to the number that you prepare, so you shall do for everyone according to their number. [13] All who are native shall do these things in this manner, in presenting an offering by fire, as a soothing aroma to the LORD. [14] If an alien sojourns with you, or one who may be among you throughout your generations, and he *wishes to* make an offering by fire, as a soothing aroma to the LORD, just as you do so he shall do. [15] *As for* the assembly, there shall be one statute for you and for the alien who sojourns *with you,* a perpetual statute throughout your generations; as you are, so shall the alien be before the LORD. [16] There is to be one law and one ordinance for you and for the alien who sojourns with you.'"

[17] Then the LORD spoke to Moses, saying, [18] "Speak to the sons of Israel and say to them, 'When you enter the land where I bring you, [19] then it shall be, that when you eat of the food of the land, you shall lift up an offering to the LORD. [20] Of the first of your dough you shall lift up a cake as an offering; as the offering of the threshing floor, so you shall lift it up. [21] From the first of your dough you shall give to the LORD an offering throughout your generations.

[22] 'But when you unwittingly fail and do not observe all these commandments, which the LORD has spoken to Moses, [23] *even* all that the LORD has commanded you through Moses, from the day when the LORD gave commandment and onward throughout your generations, [24] then it shall be, if it is done unintentionally, without the knowledge of the congregation, that all the congregation shall offer one bull for a burnt offering, as a soothing aroma to the LORD, with its grain offering and its drink offering, according to the ordinance, and one male goat for a sin offering. [25] Then the priest shall make atonement for all the congregation of the sons of Israel, and they will be forgiven; for it was an error, and they have brought their offering, an offering by fire to the LORD, and their sin offering before the LORD, for their error. [26] So all the congregation of the sons of Israel will be forgiven, with the alien who sojourns among them, for *it happened* to all the people through error.

[27] 'Also if one person sins unintentionally, then he shall offer a one year old female goat for a sin offering. [28] The priest shall make atonement before the LORD for the person who goes astray when he sins unintentionally, making atonement for him that he may be forgiven. [29] You shall have one law for him who does *anything* unintentionally, for him who is native among the sons of Israel and for the alien who sojourns among them. [30] But the person who does *anything* defiantly, whether he is native or an alien, that one is blaspheming the LORD; and that person shall be cut off from among his people. [31] Because he has despised the word of the LORD and has broken His commandment, that person shall be completely cut off; his guilt *will be* on him.'"

[32] Now while the sons of Israel were in the wilderness, they found a man gathering wood on the sabbath day. [33] Those who found him gathering wood brought him to Moses and Aaron and to all the congregation; [34] and they put him in custody because it had not been declared what should be done to him. [35] Then the LORD said to Moses, "The man shall surely be put to death; all the congregation shall stone him with stones outside the camp." [36] So all the congregation brought him outside the camp and stoned him to death with stones, just as the LORD had commanded Moses.

37 The LORD also spoke to Moses, saying, 38 "Speak to the sons of Israel, and tell them that they shall make for themselves tassels on the corners of their garments throughout their generations, and that they shall put on the tassel of each corner a cord of blue. 39 It shall be a tassel for you to look at and remember all the commandments of the LORD, so as to do them and not follow after your own heart and your own eyes, after which you played the harlot, 40 so that you may remember to do all My commandments and be holy to your God. 41 I am the LORD your God who brought you out from the land of Egypt to be your God; I am the LORD your God."

16 Now Korah the son of Izhar, the son of Kohath, the son of Levi, with Dathan and Abiram, the sons of Eliab, and On the son of Peleth, sons of Reuben, took *action*, 2 and they rose up before Moses, together with some of the sons of Israel, two hundred and fifty leaders of the congregation, chosen in the assembly, men of renown. 3 They assembled together against Moses and Aaron, and said to them, "You have gone far enough, for all the congregation are holy, every one of them, and the LORD is in their midst; so why do you exalt yourselves above the assembly of the LORD?"

4 When Moses heard *this*, he fell on his face; 5 and he spoke to Korah and all his company, saying, "Tomorrow morning the LORD will show who is His, and who is holy, and will bring *him* near to Himself; even the one whom He will choose, He will bring near to Himself. 6 Do this: take censers for yourselves, Korah and all your company, 7 and put fire in them, and lay incense upon them in the presence of the LORD tomorrow; and the man whom the LORD chooses *shall be* the one who is holy. You have gone far enough, you sons of Levi!"

8 Then Moses said to Korah, "Hear now, you sons of Levi, 9 is it not enough for you that the God of Israel has separated you from the *rest of* the congregation of Israel, to bring you near to Himself, to do the service of the tabernacle of the LORD, and to stand before the congregation to minister to them; 10 and that He has brought you near, *Korah*, and all your brothers, sons of Levi, with you? And are you seeking for the priesthood also? 11 Therefore you and all your company are gathered together against the LORD; but as for Aaron, who is he that you grumble against him?"

12 Then Moses sent a summons to Dathan and Abiram, the sons of Eliab; but they said, "We will not come up. 13 Is it not enough that you have brought us up out of a land flowing with milk and honey to have us die in the wilderness, but you would also lord it over us? 14 Indeed, you have not brought us into a land flowing with milk and honey, nor have you given us an inheritance of fields and vineyards. Would you put out the eyes of these men? We will not come up!"

15 Then Moses became very angry and said to the LORD, "Do not regard their offering! I have not taken a single donkey from them, nor have I done harm to any of them." 16 Moses said to Korah, "You and all your company be present before the LORD tomorrow, both you and they along with Aaron. 17 Each of you take his firepan and put incense on it, and each of you bring his censer before the LORD, two hundred and fifty firepans; also you and Aaron *shall* each *bring* his firepan." 18 So they each took his *own* censer and put fire on it, and laid incense on it; and they stood at the doorway of the tent of meeting, with Moses and Aaron. 19 Thus Korah assembled all the congregation against them at the doorway of the tent of meeting. And the glory of the LORD appeared to all the congregation.

20 Then the LORD spoke to Moses and Aaron, saying, 21 "Separate yourselves from among this congregation, that I may consume them instantly." 22 But they fell on their faces and said, "O God, God of the spirits of all flesh, when one man sins, will You be angry with the entire congregation?"

16:22 God of the spirits of all flesh. This phrase appears only here and in 27:16. Moses called on omniscient God who knows the heart of everyone to judge those who had sinned, and those only.

---

23 Then the LORD spoke to Moses, saying, 24 "Speak to the congregation, saying, 'Get back from around the dwellings of Korah, Dathan and Abiram.'"

25 Then Moses arose and went to Dathan and Abiram, with the elders of Israel following him, 26 and he spoke to the congregation, saying, "Depart now from the tents of these wicked men, and touch nothing that belongs to them, or you will be swept away in all their sin." 27 So they got back from around the dwellings of Korah, Dathan and Abiram; and Dathan and Abiram came out *and* stood at the doorway of their tents, along with their wives and their sons and their little ones.

28 Moses said, "By this you shall know that the LORD has sent me to do all these deeds; for this is not my doing. 29 If these men die the death of all men or if they suffer the fate of all men, *then* the LORD has not sent me. 30 But if the LORD brings about an entirely new thing and the ground opens its mouth and swallows them up with all that is theirs, and they descend alive into Sheol, then you will understand that these men have spurned the LORD."

16:30 an entirely new thing. This supernatural opening of the earth to swallow the rebels was a sign of God's wrath and the vindication of Moses and Aaron.

31 As he finished speaking all these words, the ground that was under them split open; 32 and the earth opened its mouth and swallowed them up, and their households, and all the men who belonged to Korah with *their* possessions. 33 So they and all that belonged to them went down alive to Sheol; and the earth closed over them, and they perished from the midst of the assembly. 34 All Israel who *were* around them fled at their outcry, for they said, "The earth may swallow us up!" 35 Fire also came forth from the LORD and consumed the two hundred and fifty men who were offering the incense.

36 Then the LORD spoke to Moses, saying, 37 "Say to Eleazar, the son of Aaron the priest, that he shall take up the censers out of the midst of the blaze, for they are holy; and you scatter the burning coals abroad. 38 As for the censers of these men who have sinned at the cost of their lives, let them be made into hammered sheets for a plating of the altar, since they did present them before the LORD and they are holy; and they shall be for a sign to the sons of Israel." 39 So Eleazar the priest took the bronze censers which the men who were burned had offered, and they hammered them out as a plating for the altar, 40 as a reminder to the sons of Israel that no layman who is not of the descendants of Aaron should come near to burn incense before the LORD; so that he will not become like Korah and his company—just as the LORD had spoken to him through Moses.

41 But on the next day all the congregation of the sons of Israel grumbled against Moses and Aaron, saying, "You are the ones who have caused the death of the LORD'S people." 42 It came about, however, when the congregation had assembled against Moses and Aaron, that they turned toward the tent of meeting, and behold, the cloud covered it and the glory of the LORD appeared. 43 Then Moses and Aaron came to the front of the tent of meeting, 44 and the LORD spoke to Moses, saying, 45 "Get away from among this congregation, that I may consume them instantly." Then they fell on their faces. 46 Moses said to Aaron, "Take your censer and put in it fire from the altar, and lay incense *on it;* then bring it quickly to the congregation and make atonement for them, for wrath has gone forth from the LORD, the plague has begun!" 47 Then Aaron took *it* as Moses had spoken, and ran into the midst of the assembly, for behold, the plague had begun among the people. So he put *on* the incense and made atonement for the people. 48 He took his stand between the dead and the living, so that the plague was checked. 49 But those who died by the plague were 14,700, besides those who died on account of Korah. 50 Then Aaron returned to Moses at the doorway of the tent of meeting, for the plague had been checked.

Psalm 32:1–5
A Psalm of David. A Maskil.

How blessed is he whose
   transgression is forgiven,
Whose sin is covered!
2 How blessed is the man to whom the
      LORD does not impute iniquity,
   And in whose spirit there is no deceit!

3 When I kept silent *about my sin,*
      my body wasted away
   Through my groaning all day long.
4 For day and night Your hand
      was heavy upon me;
   My vitality was drained away *as* with
      the fever heat of summer.   *Selah*
5 I acknowledged my sin to You,
   And my iniquity I did not hide;
   I said, "I will confess my
      transgressions to the LORD";
   And You forgave the guilt of my sin.
                                    Selah

Proverbs 11:16–18
16 A gracious woman attains honor,
   And ruthless men attain riches.
17 The merciful man does himself good,
   But the cruel man does himself harm.
18 The wicked earns deceptive wages,
   But he who sows righteousness
   gets a true reward.

Mark 11:1–19

11 As they *approached Jerusalem, at Bethphage and Bethany, near the Mount of Olives, He *sent two of His disciples, ² and *said to them, "Go into the village opposite you, and immediately as you enter it, you will find a colt tied *there,* on which no one yet has ever sat; untie it and bring it *here.* ³ If anyone says to you, 'Why are you doing this?' you say, 'The Lord has need of it'; and immediately he will send it back here." ⁴ They went away and found a colt tied at the door, outside in the street; and they *untied it. ⁵ Some of the bystanders were saying to them, "What are you doing, untying the colt?" ⁶ They spoke to them just as Jesus had told *them,* and they gave them permission. ⁷ They *brought the colt to Jesus and put their coats on it; and He sat on it. ⁸ And many spread their coats in the road, and others *spread* leafy branches which they had cut from the fields. ⁹ Those who went in front and those who followed were shouting:

"Hosanna!
BLESSED IS HE WHO COMES IN
    THE NAME OF THE LORD;
¹⁰ Blessed *is* the coming kingdom
    of our father David;
Hosanna in the highest!"

¹¹ Jesus entered Jerusalem *and came* into the temple; and after looking around at everything, He left for Bethany with the twelve, since it was already late.

¹² On the next day, when they had left Beth-

11:10 the coming kingdom of our father David. This tribute, recorded only by Mark, acknowledges Jesus as bringing in the messianic kingdom promised to David's Son. The crowd paraphrased the quote from Psalms 118:26 (v. 9) in anticipation that Jesus was fulfilling prophecy by bringing in the kingdom.

any, He became hungry. ¹³ Seeing at a distance a fig tree in leaf, He went *to see* if perhaps He would find anything on it; and when He came to it, He found nothing but leaves, for it was not the season for figs. ¹⁴ He said to it, "May no one ever eat fruit from you again!" And His disciples were listening.

¹⁵ Then they *came to Jerusalem. And He entered the temple and began to drive out those who were buying and selling in the temple, and overturned the tables of the money changers and the seats of those who were selling doves; ¹⁶ and He would not permit anyone to carry merchandise through the temple. ¹⁷ And He *began* to teach and say to them, "Is it not written, 'MY HOUSE SHALL BE CALLED A HOUSE OF PRAYER FOR ALL THE NATIONS'? But you have made it a ROBBERS' DEN." ¹⁸ The chief priests and the scribes heard *this,* and *began* seeking how to destroy Him; for they were afraid of Him, for the whole crowd was astonished at His teaching.

¹⁹ When evening came, they would go out of the city.

DAY 9: Why did Jesus curse the fig tree in Mark 11:12–14?

Fig trees were common as a source of food. Three years were required from planting until fruit bearing. After that, a tree could be harvested twice a year, usually yielding much fruit. The figs normally grew with the leaves. This tree had leaves but, strangely, no fruit. That this tree was along the side of the road (see Mt 21:19) implies it was public property. It was also apparently in good soil because its foliage was ahead of season and ahead of the surrounding fig trees. The abundance of leaves held out promise that the tree might also be ahead of schedule with its fruit. That it was "not the season for figs" (v. 13) recognizes that the next normal fig season was in June, more than a month away. This phrase, unique to Mark, emphasizes the unusual nature of this fig tree.

Jesus' direct address to the tree personified it and condemned it for not providing what its appearance promised. "May no one ever eat fruit from you again!" (v. 14). This incident was not the acting out of the parable of the fig tree (Lk 13:6–9), which was a warning against spiritual fruitlessness. Here, Jesus cursed the tree for its misleading appearance that suggested great productivity without providing it. It should have been full of fruit, but was barren. The fig tree was frequently an Old Testament type of the Jewish nation (Hos 9:10; Na 3:12; Zec 3:10)—and the barren fig tree often symbolizes divine judgment on Israel because of her spiritual fruitlessness despite an abundance of spiritual advantages (Jer 8:13; Joel 1:12). In this instance Jesus used the tree by the road as a purposeful divine object lesson concerning Israel's spiritual hypocrisy and fruitlessness, exemplified in the rejection of their Messiah. It was not an impetuous act of frustration as some have stated.

MARCH 10

Numbers 17:1–18:32

17 Then the LORD spoke to Moses, saying, ² "Speak to the sons of Israel, and get from them a rod for each father's household: twelve rods, from all their leaders according to their fathers' households. You shall write each name on his rod, ³ and write Aaron's name on the rod of Levi; for there is one rod for the head *of each* of their fathers' households. ⁴ You shall then deposit them in the tent of meeting in front of the testimony, where I meet with you. ⁵ It will come about that the rod of the man whom I choose will sprout. Thus I will lessen from upon Myself the grumblings of the sons of Israel, who are grumbling against you." ⁶ Moses therefore spoke to the sons of Israel, and all their leaders gave him a rod apiece, for each leader according to their fathers' households, twelve rods, with the rod of Aaron among their rods. ⁷ So Moses deposited the rods before the LORD in the tent of the testimony.

⁸ Now on the next day Moses went into the tent of the testimony; and behold, the rod of Aaron for the house of Levi had sprouted and put forth buds and produced blossoms, and it bore ripe almonds. ⁹ Moses then brought out all the rods from the presence of the LORD to all the sons of Israel; and they looked, and each man took his rod. ¹⁰ But the LORD said to Moses, "Put back the rod of Aaron before the testimony to be kept as a sign against the rebels, that you may put an end to their grumblings against Me, so that they will not die." ¹¹ Thus Moses did; just as the LORD had commanded him, so he did.

17:8 the rod of Aaron. God had stated that the stick of the man He had chosen would blossom (17:5). The stick of Aaron had not only blossomed, but had yielded ripe almonds. Thus God had exceeded the demands of the test, so there would be no uncertainty of the fact that Aaron had been chosen as High Priest.

¹² Then the sons of Israel spoke to Moses, saying, "Behold, we perish, we are dying, we are all dying! ¹³ Everyone who comes near, who comes near to the tabernacle of the LORD, must die. Are we to perish completely?"

18 So the LORD said to Aaron, "You and your sons and your father's household with you shall bear the guilt in connection with the sanctuary, and you and your sons with you shall bear the guilt in connection with your priesthood. ² But bring with you also your brothers, the tribe of Levi, the tribe of your father, that they may be joined with you and serve you, while you and your sons with you are before the tent of the testimony. ³ And they shall thus attend to your obligation and the obligation of all the tent, but they shall not come near to the furnishings of the sanctuary and the altar, or both they and you will die. ⁴ They shall be joined with you and attend to the obligations of the tent of meeting, for all the service of the tent; but an outsider may not come near you. ⁵ So you shall attend to the obligations of the sanctuary and the obligations of the altar, so that there will no longer be wrath on the sons of Israel. ⁶ Behold, I Myself have taken your fellow Levites from among the sons of Israel; they are a gift to you, dedicated to the LORD, to perform the service for the tent of meeting. ⁷ But you and your sons with you shall attend to your priesthood for everything concerning the altar and inside the veil, and you are to perform service. I am giving you the priesthood as a bestowed service, but the outsider who comes near shall be put to death."

⁸ Then the LORD spoke to Aaron, "Now behold, I Myself have given you charge of My offerings, even all the holy gifts of the sons of Israel I have given them to you as a portion and to your sons as a perpetual allotment. ⁹ This shall be yours from the most holy *gifts reserved* from the fire; every offering of theirs, even every grain offering and every sin offering and every guilt offering, which they shall render to Me, shall be most holy for you and for your sons. ¹⁰ As the most holy *gifts* you shall eat it; every male shall eat it. It shall be holy to you. ¹¹ This also is yours, the offering of their gift, even all the wave offerings of the sons of Israel; I have given them to you and to your sons and daughters with you as a perpetual allotment. Everyone of your household who is clean may eat it. ¹² All the best of the fresh oil and all the best of the fresh wine and of the grain, the first fruits of those which they give to the LORD, I give them to you. ¹³ The first ripe fruits of all that is in their land, which they bring to the LORD, shall be yours; everyone of your household who is clean may eat it. ¹⁴ Every devoted thing in Israel shall be yours. ¹⁵ Every first issue of the womb of all flesh, whether man or animal, which they offer to the LORD, shall be yours; nevertheless the firstborn of man you shall surely redeem, and the firstborn

of unclean animals you shall redeem. ¹⁶As to their redemption price, from a month old you shall redeem them, by your valuation, five shekels in silver, according to the shekel of the sanctuary, which is twenty gerahs. ¹⁷But the firstborn of an ox or the firstborn of a sheep or the firstborn of a goat, you shall not redeem; they are holy. You shall sprinkle their blood on the altar and shall offer up their fat in smoke *as* an offering by fire, for a soothing aroma to the LORD. ¹⁸Their meat shall be yours; it shall be yours like the breast of a wave offering and like the right thigh. ¹⁹All the offerings of the holy *gifts,* which the sons of Israel offer to the LORD, I have given to you and your sons and your daughters with you, as a perpetual allotment. It is an everlasting covenant of salt before the LORD to you and your descendants with you." ²⁰Then the LORD said to Aaron, "You shall have no inheritance in their land nor own any portion among them; I am your portion and your inheritance among the sons of Israel.

18:19 an everlasting covenant of salt. Salt, which does not burn, was a metaphor to speak of durability. As salt keeps its flavor, so the Lord's covenant with the priesthood was durable. The Lord would provide through the offerings of His people for His priests forever.

²¹"To the sons of Levi, behold, I have given all the tithe in Israel for an inheritance, in return for their service which they perform, the service of the tent of meeting. ²²The sons of Israel shall not come near the tent of meeting again, or they will bear sin and die. ²³Only the Levites shall perform the service of the tent of meeting, and they shall bear their iniquity; it shall be a perpetual statute throughout your generations, and among the sons of Israel they shall have no inheritance. ²⁴For the tithe of the sons of Israel, which they offer as an offering to the LORD, I have given to the Levites for an inheritance; therefore I have said concerning them, 'They shall have no inheritance among the sons of Israel.'"

²⁵Then the LORD spoke to Moses, saying, ²⁶"Moreover, you shall speak to the Levites and say to them, 'When you take from the sons of Israel the tithe which I have given you from them for your inheritance, then you shall present an offering from it to the LORD, a tithe of the tithe. ²⁷Your offering shall be reckoned to you as the grain from the thresh-

ing floor or the full produce from the wine vat. ²⁸So you shall also present an offering to the LORD from your tithes, which you receive from the sons of Israel; and from it you shall give the LORD'S offering to Aaron the priest. ²⁹Out of all your gifts you shall present every offering due to the LORD, from all the best of them, the sacred part from them.' ³⁰You shall say to them, 'When you have offered from it the best of it, then *the rest* shall be reckoned to the Levites as the product of the threshing floor, and as the product of the wine vat. ³¹You may eat it anywhere, you and your households, for it is your compensation in return for your service in the tent of meeting. ³²You will bear no sin by reason of it when you have offered the best of it. But you shall not profane the sacred gifts of the sons of Israel, or you will die.'"

Psalm 32:6–11

⁶ Therefore, let everyone who is
 godly pray to You in a time
  when You may be found;
 Surely in a flood of great waters
  they will not reach him.
⁷ You are my hiding place; You
  preserve me from trouble;
 You surround me with songs of
  deliverance. *Selah*

⁸ I will instruct you and teach you in
  the way which you should go;
 I will counsel you with
  My eye upon you.
⁹ Do not be as the horse or
  as the mule which have
  no understanding,
 Whose trappings include bit and
  bridle to hold them in check,
 Otherwise they will not
  come near to you.
¹⁰ Many are the sorrows of the wicked,
 But he who trusts in the
  LORD, lovingkindness
  shall surround him.
¹¹ Be glad in the LORD and rejoice,
  you righteous ones;
 And shout for joy, all you who
  are upright in heart.

Proverbs 11:19–21

¹⁹ He who is steadfast in righteousness
  will attain to life,
 And he who pursues evil *will
  bring about* his own death.
²⁰ The perverse in heart are an
  abomination to the LORD,

11:20 abomination. Defined throughout Scripture as attitudes, this involves words and behaviors which God hates.

But the blameless in *their*
  walk are His delight.
²¹ Assuredly, the evil man will
    not go unpunished,
  But the descendants of the
    righteous will be delivered.

Mark 11:20–33

²⁰ As they were passing by in the morning, they saw the fig tree withered from the roots up. ²¹ Being reminded, Peter *said to Him, "Rabbi, look, the fig tree which You cursed has withered." ²² And Jesus *answered saying to them, "Have faith in God. ²³ Truly I say to you, whoever says to this mountain, 'Be taken up and cast into the sea,' and does not doubt in his heart, but believes that what he says is going to happen, it will be *granted* him. ²⁴ Therefore I say to you, all things for which you pray and ask, believe that you have received them, and they will be *granted* you. ²⁵ Whenever you stand praying, forgive, if you have anything against anyone, so that your Father who is in heaven will also forgive you your transgressions. ²⁶ [But if you do not forgive, neither will your Father who is in heaven forgive your transgressions."]

²⁷ They *came again to Jerusalem. And as He was walking in the temple, the chief priests and the scribes and the elders *came to Him, ²⁸ and *began saying to Him, "By what authority are You doing these things, or who gave You this authority to do these things?" ²⁹ And Jesus said to them, "I will ask you one question, and you answer Me, and *then* I will tell you by what authority I do these things. ³⁰ Was the baptism of John from heaven, or from men? Answer Me." ³¹ They *began reasoning among themselves, saying, "If we say, 'From heaven,' He will say, 'Then why did you not believe him?' ³² But shall we say, 'From men'?"—they were afraid of the people, for everyone considered John to have been a real prophet. ³³ Answering Jesus, they *said, "We do not know." And Jesus *said to them, "Nor will I tell you by what authority I do these things."

11:25 stand praying. The traditional Jewish prayer posture (1Sa 1:26; 1Ki 8:14, 22; Ne 9:4; Mt 6:5; Lk 18:11, 13). Kneeling or lying with one's face on the ground was used during extraordinary circumstances or for extremely urgent requests (1Ki 8:54; Ezr 9:5; Da 6:10; Mt 26:39; Ac 7:60). **anything against anyone.** An all-inclusive statement that includes both sins and simple dislikes, which cause the believer to hold something against another person. "Anyone" incorporates believers and unbelievers. **forgive.** Jesus states the believer's ongoing duty to have a forgiving attitude. Successful prayer requires forgiveness as well as faith.

DAY 10: How does one's faith move mountains?

When an amazed Peter noted to Jesus that the fig tree had withered, Jesus' response was simply that they should "have faith in God" (Mk 11:22). This was a gentle rebuke for the disciples' lack of faith in the power of His word. Such faith believes in God's revealed truth, His power, and seeks to do His will (see 1Jn 5:14; Mt 21:21).

The expression Jesus used, "this mountain…into the sea" (v. 23), was related to a common metaphor of that day, "rooter up of mountains," which was used in Jewish literature of great rabbis and spiritual leaders who could solve difficult problems and seemingly do the impossible. Obviously, Jesus did not literally uproot mountains. In fact, He refused to do such spectacular miracles for the unbelieving Jewish leaders (Mt 12:38). Jesus' point is that, if believers sincerely trust in God and truly realize the unlimited power that is available through such faith in Him, they will see His mighty powers at work (see Jn 14:13–14).

"all things for which you pray and ask, believe that you have received them, and they will be granted you" (v. 24). This places no limits on a believer's prayers, as long as they are according to God's will and purpose. This therefore means that man's faith and prayer are not inconsistent with God's sovereignty. And it is not the believer's responsibility to figure out how that can be true, but simply to be faithful and obedient to the clear teaching on prayer, as Jesus gives it in this passage. God's will is being unfolded through all of redemptive history by means of the prayers of His people—as His saving purpose is coming to pass through the faith of those who hear the gospel and repent. See James 5:16.

MARCH 11

Numbers 19:1–20:29

19 Then the LORD spoke to Moses and Aaron, saying, ² "This is the statute of the law which the LORD has commanded, saying, 'Speak to the sons of Israel that they bring you an unblemished red heifer in which is no defect *and* on which a yoke has never been placed. ³ You shall give it to Eleazar the priest, and it shall be brought outside the camp and be slaughtered in his presence. ⁴ Next Eleazar the priest shall take some of its blood with his finger and sprinkle some of its blood toward the front of the tent of meeting seven times. ⁵ Then the heifer shall be burned in his sight; its hide and its flesh and its blood, with its refuse, shall be burned. ⁶ The priest shall take cedar wood and hyssop and scarlet *material* and cast it into the midst of the burning heifer. ⁷ The priest shall then wash his clothes and bathe his body in water, and afterward come into the camp, but the priest shall be unclean until evening. ⁸ The one who burns it shall also wash his clothes in water and bathe his body in water, and shall be unclean until evening. ⁹ Now a man who is clean shall gather up the ashes of the heifer and deposit them outside the camp in a clean place, and the congregation of the sons of Israel shall keep it as water to remove impurity; it is purification from sin. ¹⁰ The one who gathers the ashes of the heifer shall wash his clothes and be unclean until evening; and it shall be a perpetual statute to the sons of Israel and to the alien who sojourns among them.

¹¹ 'The one who touches the corpse of any person shall be unclean for seven days. ¹² That one shall purify himself from uncleanness with the water on the third day and on the seventh day, *and then* he will be clean; but if he does not purify himself on the third day and on the seventh day, he will not be clean. ¹³ Anyone who touches a corpse, the body of a man who has died, and does not purify himself, defiles the tabernacle of the LORD; and that person shall be cut off from Israel. Because the water for impurity was not sprinkled on him, he shall be unclean; his uncleanness is still on him.

¹⁴ 'This is the law when a man dies in a tent: everyone who comes into the tent and everyone who is in the tent shall be unclean for seven days. ¹⁵ Every open vessel, which has no covering tied down on it, shall be unclean. ¹⁶ Also, anyone who in the open field touches one who has been slain with a sword or who has died *naturally,* or a human bone or a grave, shall be unclean for seven days. ¹⁷ Then for the unclean *person* they shall take some of the ashes of the burnt purification from sin and flowing water shall be added to them in a vessel. ¹⁸ A clean person shall take hyssop and dip *it* in the water, and sprinkle *it* on the tent and on all the furnishings and on the persons who were there, and on the one who touched the bone or the one slain or the one dying *naturally* or the grave. ¹⁹ Then the clean *person* shall sprinkle on the unclean on the third day and on the seventh day; and on the seventh day he shall purify him from uncleanness, and he shall wash his clothes and bathe *himself* in water and shall be clean by evening.

²⁰ 'But the man who is unclean and does not purify himself from uncleanness, that person shall be cut off from the midst of the assembly, because he has defiled the sanctuary of the LORD; the water for impurity has not been sprinkled on him, he is unclean. ²¹ So it shall be a perpetual statute for them. And he who sprinkles the water for impurity shall wash his clothes, and he who touches the water for impurity shall be unclean until evening. ²² Furthermore, anything that the unclean *person* touches shall be unclean; and the person who touches *it* shall be unclean until evening.' "

20 Then the sons of Israel, the whole congregation, came to the wilderness of Zin in the first month; and the people stayed at Kadesh. Now Miriam died there and was buried there.

² There was no water for the congregation, and they assembled themselves against Moses and Aaron. ³ The people thus contended with Moses and spoke, saying, "If only we had perished when our brothers perished before the LORD! ⁴ Why then have you brought the LORD'S assembly into this wilderness, for us and our beasts to die here? ⁵ Why have you made us come up from Egypt, to bring us in to this wretched place? It is not a place of grain or figs or vines or pomegranates, nor is there water to drink." ⁶ Then Moses and Aaron came in from the presence of the assembly to the doorway of the tent of meeting and fell on their faces. Then the glory of the LORD appeared to them; ⁷ and the LORD spoke to Moses, saying, ⁸ "Take the rod; and you and your brother Aaron assemble the congregation and speak to the rock before their eyes, that it may yield its water. You shall thus bring forth water for them out of the rock and let the congregation and their beasts drink."

⁹ So Moses took the rod from before the

LORD, just as He had commanded him; ¹⁰ and Moses and Aaron gathered the assembly before the rock. And he said to them, "Listen now, you rebels; shall we bring forth water for you out of this rock?" ¹¹ Then Moses lifted up his hand and struck the rock twice with his rod; and water came forth abundantly, and the congregation and their beasts drank. ¹² But the LORD said to Moses and Aaron, "Because you have not believed Me, to treat Me as holy in the sight of the sons of Israel, therefore you shall not bring this assembly into the land which I have given them." ¹³ Those *were* the waters of Meribah, because the sons of Israel contended with the LORD, and He proved Himself holy among them.

20:8 speak to the rock. Though God told Moses to take his rod with which He had performed many wonders in the past (Ex 4:1–5; 7:19–21; 14:16; 17:5–6), he was only to speak to the rock for it to yield water.

20:10 you rebels. Instead of speaking to the rock, Moses spoke to the people, accusing them of being rebels against God. By his actions, Moses joined the people in rebellion against God (27:14).

¹⁴ From Kadesh Moses then sent messengers to the king of Edom: "Thus your brother Israel has said, 'You know all the hardship that has befallen us; ¹⁵ that our fathers went down to Egypt, and we stayed in Egypt a long time, and the Egyptians treated us and our fathers badly. ¹⁶ But when we cried out to the LORD, He heard our voice and sent an angel and brought us out from Egypt; now behold, we are at Kadesh, a town on the edge of your territory. ¹⁷ Please let us pass through your land. We will not pass through field or through vineyard; we will not even drink water from a well. We will go along the king's highway, not turning to the right or left, until we pass through your territory.'"
¹⁸ Edom, however, said to him, "You shall not pass through us, or I will come out with the sword against you." ¹⁹ Again, the sons of Israel said to him, "We will go up by the highway, and if I and my livestock do drink any of your water, then I will pay its price. Let me only pass through on my feet, nothing *else.*" ²⁰ But he said, "You shall not pass through." And Edom came out against him with a heavy force and with a strong hand. ²¹ Thus Edom

refused to allow Israel to pass through his territory; so Israel turned away from him.

²² Now when they set out from Kadesh, the sons of Israel, the whole congregation, came to Mount Hor. ²³ Then the LORD spoke to Moses and Aaron at Mount Hor by the border of the land of Edom, saying, ²⁴ "Aaron will be gathered to his people; for he shall not enter the land which I have given to the sons of Israel, because you rebelled against My command at the waters of Meribah. ²⁵ Take Aaron and his son Eleazar and bring them up to Mount Hor; ²⁶ and strip Aaron of his garments and put them on his son Eleazar. So Aaron will be gathered *to his people,* and will die there." ²⁷ So Moses did just as the LORD had commanded, and they went up to Mount Hor in the sight of all the congregation. ²⁸ After Moses had stripped Aaron of his garments and put them on his son Eleazar, Aaron died there on the mountain top. Then Moses and Eleazar came down from the mountain. ²⁹ When all the congregation saw that Aaron had died, all the house of Israel wept for Aaron thirty days.

Psalm 33:1–9

S ing for joy in the LORD,
  O you righteous ones;
  Praise is becoming to the upright.
² Give thanks to the LORD with the lyre;
  Sing praises to Him with a
    harp of ten strings.
³ Sing to Him a new song;
  Play skillfully with a shout of joy.
⁴ For the word of the LORD is upright,
  And all His work is *done*
    in faithfulness.
⁵ He loves righteousness and justice;
  The earth is full of the
    lovingkindness of the LORD.

⁶ By the word of the LORD the
    heavens were made,
  And by the breath of His
    mouth all their host.

33:3 a new song. I.e., a new occasion and impulse for expressing fresh praise to God (Pss 96:1; 98:1; 149:1).

33:6 host. This designation refers to stellar and planetary bodies (Is 40:26; 45:12) and/or heaven's complement of angels (Ps 103:20–22). The former emphasis is more prominent in the immediate context.

7 He gathers the waters of the
sea together as a heap;
He lays up the deeps in
storehouses.
8 Let all the earth fear the LORD;
Let all the inhabitants of the
world stand in awe of Him.
9 For He spoke, and it was done;
He commanded, and it stood fast.

Proverbs 11:22–24

22 As a ring of gold in a swine's
snout
So is a beautiful woman
who lacks discretion.
23 The desire of the righteous
is only good,
But the expectation of the
wicked is wrath.
24 There is one who scatters, and
yet increases all the more,
And there is one who withholds
what is justly due, and yet
it results only in want.

Mark 12:1–27

12 And He began to speak to them in parables: "A man PLANTED A VINEYARD AND PUT A WALL AROUND IT, AND DUG A VAT UNDER THE WINE PRESS AND BUILT A TOWER, and rented it out to vine-growers and went on a journey. 2 At the harvest time he sent a slave to the vine-growers, in order to receive some of the produce of the vineyard from the vine-growers. 3 They took him, and beat him and sent him away empty-handed. 4 Again he sent them another slave, and they wounded him in the head, and treated him shamefully. 5 And he sent another, and that one they killed; and so with many others, beating some and killing others. 6 He had one more to send, a beloved son; he sent him last of all to them, saying, 'They will respect my son.' 7 But those vine-growers said to one another, 'This is the heir; come, let us kill him, and the inheritance will be ours!' 8 They took him, and killed him and threw him out of the vineyard. 9 What will the owner of the vineyard do? He will come and destroy the vine-growers, and will give the vineyard to others. 10 Have you not even read this Scripture:

'THE STONE WHICH THE
BUILDERS REJECTED,
THIS BECAME THE CHIEF CORNER
stone;
11 THIS CAME ABOUT FROM THE LORD,
AND IT IS MARVELOUS IN OUR EYES'?"

12 And they were seeking to seize Him, and yet they feared the people, for they understood that He spoke the parable against them. And so they left Him and went away.

13 Then they *sent some of the Pharisees and Herodians to Him in order to trap Him in a statement. 14 They *came and *said to Him, "Teacher, we know that You are truthful and defer to no one; for You are not partial to any, but teach the way of God in truth. Is it lawful to pay a poll-tax to Caesar, or not? 15 Shall we pay or shall we not pay?" But He, knowing their hypocrisy, said to them, "Why are you testing Me? Bring Me a denarius to look at." 16 They brought one. And He *said to them, "Whose likeness and inscription is this?" And they said to Him, "Caesar's." 17 And Jesus said to them, "Render to Caesar the things that are Caesar's, and to God the things that are God's." And they were amazed at Him.

18 Some Sadducees (who say that there is no resurrection) *came to Jesus, and began questioning Him, saying, 19 "Teacher, Moses wrote for us that IF A MAN'S BROTHER DIES and leaves behind a wife AND LEAVES NO CHILD, HIS BROTHER SHOULD MARRY THE WIFE AND RAISE UP CHILDREN TO HIS BROTHER. 20 There were seven brothers; and the first took a wife, and died leaving no children. 21 The second one married her, and died leaving behind no children; and the third likewise; 22 and so all seven left no children. Last of all the woman died also. 23 In the resurrection, when they rise again, which one's wife will she be? For all seven had married her." 24 Jesus said to them, "Is this not the reason you are mistaken, that you do not understand the Scriptures or the power of God? 25 For when they rise from the dead, they neither marry nor are given in marriage, but are like angels in heaven. 26 But regarding the fact that the dead rise again, have you not read in the book of Moses, in the passage about the burning bush, how God spoke to him, saying, 'I AM THE GOD OF ABRAHAM, AND THE GOD OF ISAAC, AND THE GOD OF JACOB'? 27 He is not the God of the dead, but of the living; you are greatly mistaken."

12:24 the power of God. Their ignorance of the Scriptures extended to their lack of understanding regarding the miracles God performed throughout the Old Testament. Such knowledge would have enabled them to believe in God's power to raise the dead.

In Mark 12:13, the Pharisees and the Herodians came together to try to catch Jesus off guard by a seemingly sincere question: "Is it lawful to pay a poll-tax to Caesar, or not? Shall we pay or shall we not pay?" The Herodians were a political party of Jews who backed Herod Antipas, who in turn was but a puppet of Rome. The Greek word for "taxes" was borrowed from the Latin word that gives us the English word "census." The Romans counted all the citizens and made each one pay an annual poll tax of one denarius.

Jesus was fully aware of their hypocrisy, using a feigned interest in His teaching to hide their true intention to trap Him. "Why are you testing Me?" (v. 15), He asked, and His response was to ask for a denarius. This small silver coin, minted by the Roman emperor, was the equivalent of a day's wage for a common laborer or soldier. On one side of the denarius was likely the image of the current emperor, Tiberius. If the coin was minted by Tiberius, it would have read, "Tiberius Caesar Augustus, the son of the Divine Augustus" on one side and "Chief Priest" on the other.

Based on the image on the denarius, Jesus answered, "Render to Caesar the things that are Caesar's." The Greek word for "render" means "to pay or give back," which implies a debt. All who lived within the realm of Caesar were obligated to return to him the tax that was owed him. It was not optional. Thus, Jesus declared that all citizens are under divine obligation to pay taxes to whatever government is over them (see Ro 13:1–7; 1Pe 2:13–17).

MARCH 12

Numbers 21:1–22:41

21 When the Canaanite, the king of Arad, who lived in the Negev, heard that Israel was coming by the way of Atharim, then he fought against Israel and took some of them captive. ²So Israel made a vow to the LORD and said, "If You will indeed deliver this people into my hand, then I will utterly destroy their cities." ³The LORD heard the voice of Israel and delivered up the Canaanites; then they utterly destroyed them and their cities. Thus the name of the place was called Hormah.

⁴Then they set out from Mount Hor by the way of the Red Sea, to go around the land of Edom; and the people became impatient because of the journey. ⁵The people spoke against God and Moses, "Why have you brought us up out of Egypt to die in the wilderness? For there is no food and no water, and we loathe this miserable food." ⁶The LORD sent fiery serpents among the people and they bit the people, so that many people of Israel died. ⁷So the people came to Moses and said, "We have sinned, because we have spoken against the LORD and you; intercede with the LORD, that He may remove the serpents from us." And Moses interceded for the people. ⁸Then the LORD said to Moses, "Make a fiery serpent, and set it on a standard; and it shall come about, that everyone who is bitten, when he looks at it, he will live." ⁹And Moses made a bronze serpent and set it on the standard; and it came about, that if a serpent bit any man, when he looked to the bronze serpent, he lived.

¹⁰Now the sons of Israel moved out and camped in Oboth. ¹¹They journeyed from Oboth and camped at Iye-abarim, in the wilderness which is opposite Moab, to the east. ¹²From there they set out and camped in Wadi Zered. ¹³From there they journeyed and camped on the other side of the Arnon, which is in the wilderness that comes out of the border of the Amorites, for the Arnon is the border of Moab, between Moab and the Amorites. ¹⁴Therefore it is said in the Book of the Wars of the LORD,

"Waheb in Suphah,
And the wadis of the Arnon,
¹⁵ And the slope of the wadis
That extends to the site of Ar,
And leans to the border of Moab."

¹⁶From there they continued to Beer, that is the well where the LORD said to Moses, "Assemble the people, that I may give them water." ¹⁷Then Israel sang this song:

"Spring up, O well! Sing to it!
¹⁸ "The well, which the leaders sank,
Which the nobles of the people dug,
With the scepter and with their staffs."

And from the wilderness they continued to Mattanah, ¹⁹and from Mattanah to Nahaliel, and from Nahaliel to Bamoth, ²⁰and from Bamoth to the valley that is in the land of Moab, at the top of Pisgah which overlooks the wasteland.

²¹Then Israel sent messengers to Sihon, king of the Amorites, saying, ²²"Let me pass

through your land. We will not turn off into field or vineyard; we will not drink water from wells. We will go by the king's highway until we have passed through your border." ²³ But Sihon would not permit Israel to pass through his border. So Sihon gathered all his people and went out against Israel in the wilderness, and came to Jahaz and fought against Israel. ²⁴ Then Israel struck him with the edge of the sword, and took possession of his land from the Arnon to the Jabbok, as far as the sons of Ammon; for the border of the sons of Ammon *was* Jazer. ²⁵ Israel took all these cities and Israel lived in all the cities of the Amorites, in Heshbon, and in all her villages. ²⁶ For Heshbon was the city of Sihon, king of the Amorites, who had fought against the former king of Moab and had taken all his land out of his hand, as far as the Arnon. ²⁷ Therefore those who use proverbs say,

> "Come to Heshbon! Let it be
> built!
> So let the city of Sihon be
> established.
> ²⁸ "For a fire went forth from
> Heshbon,
> A flame from the town of Sihon;
> It devoured Ar of Moab,
> The dominant heights of the
> Arnon.
> ²⁹ "Woe to you, O Moab!
> You are ruined, O people of
> Chemosh!
> He has given his sons as fugitives,
> And his daughters into captivity,
> To an Amorite king, Sihon.
> ³⁰ "But we have cast them down,
> Heshbon is ruined as far as
> Dibon,
> Then we have laid waste
> even to Nophah,
> Which *reaches* to Medeba."

³¹ Thus Israel lived in the land of the Amorites. ³² Moses sent to spy out Jazer, and they captured its villages and dispossessed the Amorites who *were* there.

³³ Then they turned and went up by the way of Bashan, and Og the king of Bashan went out with all his people, for battle at Edrei. ³⁴ But the LORD said to Moses, "Do not fear him, for I have given him into your hand, and all his people and his land; and you shall do to him as you did to Sihon, king of the Amorites, who lived at Heshbon." ³⁵ So they killed him and his sons and all his people,

until there was no remnant left him; and they possessed his land.

22 Then the sons of Israel journeyed, and camped in the plains of Moab beyond the Jordan *opposite* Jericho.

² Now Balak the son of Zippor saw all that Israel had done to the Amorites. ³ So Moab was in great fear because of the people, for they were numerous; and Moab was in dread of the sons of Israel. ⁴ Moab said to the elders of Midian, "Now this horde will lick up all that is around us, as the ox licks up the grass of the field." And Balak the son of Zippor was king of Moab at that time. ⁵ So he sent messengers to Balaam the son of Beor, at Pethor, which is near the River, *in* the land of the sons of his people, to call him, saying, "Behold, a people came out of Egypt; behold, they cover the surface of the land, and they are living opposite me. ⁶ Now, therefore, please come, curse this people for me since they are too mighty for me; perhaps I may be able to defeat them and drive them out of the land. For I know that he whom you bless is blessed, and he whom you curse is cursed."

22:5 Balaam. Balaam was from Pethor, a city on the Euphrates River, perhaps near Mari, where the existence of a cult of prophets whose activities resembled those of Balaam have been found. Balaam practiced magic and divination (24:1) and eventually led Israel into apostasy (31:16). Later Scripture identifies Balaam as a false prophet (Dt 23:3–6; Jos 13:22; 24:9–10; Ne 13:1–3; Mic 6:5; 2Pe 2:15–16; Jude 11; Rev 2:14).

⁷ So the elders of Moab and the elders of Midian departed with the *fees for* divination in their hand; and they came to Balaam and repeated Balak's words to him. ⁸ He said to them, "Spend the night here, and I will bring word back to you as the LORD may speak to me." And the leaders of Moab stayed with Balaam. ⁹ Then God came to Balaam and said, "Who are these men with you?" ¹⁰ Balaam said to God, "Balak the son of Zippor, king of Moab, has sent *word* to me, ¹¹ 'Behold, there is a people who came out of Egypt and they cover the surface of the land; now come, curse them for me; perhaps I may be able to fight against them and drive them out.'" ¹² God said to Balaam, "Do not go with them; you shall not curse the people, for they are blessed." ¹³ So Balaam arose in the morning and said to Balak's leaders, "Go back to your

land, for the LORD has refused to let me go with you." [14] The leaders of Moab arose and went to Balak and said, "Balaam refused to come with us."

[15] Then Balak again sent leaders, more numerous and more distinguished than the former. [16] They came to Balaam and said to him, "Thus says Balak the son of Zippor, 'Let nothing, I beg you, hinder you from coming to me; [17] for I will indeed honor you richly, and I will do whatever you say to me. Please come then, curse this people for me.'" [18] Balaam replied to the servants of Balak, "Though Balak were to give me his house full of silver and gold, I could not do anything, either small or great, contrary to the command of the LORD my God. [19] Now please, you also stay here tonight, and I will find out what else the LORD will speak to me." [20] God came to Balaam at night and said to him, "If the men have come to call you, rise up *and* go with them; but only the word which I speak to you shall you do."

[21] So Balaam arose in the morning, and saddled his donkey and went with the leaders of Moab. [22] But God was angry because he was going, and the angel of the LORD took his stand in the way as an adversary against him. Now he was riding on his donkey and his two servants were with him. [23] When the donkey saw the angel of the LORD standing in the way with his drawn sword in his hand, the donkey turned off from the way and went into the field; but Balaam struck the donkey to turn her back into the way. [24] Then the angel of the LORD stood in a narrow path of the vineyards, *with* a wall on this side and a wall on that side. [25] When the donkey saw the angel of the LORD, she pressed herself to the wall and pressed Balaam's foot against the wall, so he struck her again. [26] The angel of the LORD went further, and stood in a narrow place where there was no way to turn to the right hand or the left. [27] When the donkey saw the angel of the LORD, she lay down under Balaam; so Balaam was angry and struck the donkey with his stick. [28] And the LORD opened the mouth of the donkey, and she said to Balaam, "What have I done to you, that you have struck me these three times?" [29] Then Balaam said to the donkey, "Because you have made a mockery of me! If there had been a sword in my hand, I would have killed you by now." [30] The donkey said to Balaam, "Am I not your donkey on which you have ridden all your life to this day? Have I ever been accustomed to do so to you?" And he said, "No."

[31] Then the LORD opened the eyes of Balaam, and he saw the angel of the LORD standing in the way with his drawn sword in his hand; and he bowed all the way to the ground. [32] The angel of the LORD said to him, "Why have you struck your donkey these three times? Behold, I have come out as an adversary, because your way was contrary to me. [33] But the donkey saw me and turned aside from me these three times. If she had not turned aside from me, I would surely have killed you just now, and let her live." [34] Balaam said to the angel of the LORD, "I have sinned, for I did not know that you were standing in the way against me. Now then, if it is displeasing to you, I will turn back." [35] But the angel of the LORD said to Balaam, "Go with the men, but you shall speak only the word which I tell you." So Balaam went along with the leaders of Balak.

[36] When Balak heard that Balaam was coming, he went out to meet him at the city of Moab, which is on the Arnon border, at the extreme end of the border. [37] Then Balak said to Balaam, "Did I not urgently send to you to call you? Why did you not come to me? Am I really unable to honor you?" [38] So Balaam said to Balak, "Behold, I have come now to you! Am I able to speak anything at all? The word that God puts in my mouth, that I shall speak." [39] And Balaam went with Balak, and they came to Kiriath-huzoth. [40] Balak sacrificed oxen and sheep, and sent *some* to Balaam and the leaders who were with him.

[41] Then it came about in the morning that Balak took Balaam and brought him up to the high places of Baal, and he saw from there a portion of the people.

Psalm 33:10–17

[10] The LORD nullifies the
counsel of the nations;
He frustrates the plans of the
peoples.
[11] The counsel of the LORD
stands forever,
The plans of His heart from
generation to generation.
[12] Blessed is the nation whose
God is the LORD,
The people whom He has chosen
for His own inheritance.

[13] The LORD looks from heaven;
He sees all the sons of men;
[14] From His dwelling place He
looks out
On all the inhabitants
of the earth,

¹⁵ He who fashions the
hearts of them all,
He who understands all their
works.
¹⁶ The king is not saved by
a mighty army;
A warrior is not delivered
by great strength.
¹⁷ A horse is a false hope for victory;
Nor does it deliver anyone
by its great strength.

Proverbs 11:25–26

²⁵ The generous man will be
prosperous,
And he who waters will
himself be watered.
²⁶ He who withholds grain, the
people will curse him,
But blessing will be on the
head of him who sells *it*.

Mark 12:28–44

²⁸ One of the scribes came and heard them arguing, and recognizing that He had answered them well, asked Him, "What commandment is the foremost of all?" ²⁹ Jesus answered, "The foremost is, 'HEAR, O ISRAEL! THE LORD OUR GOD IS ONE LORD; ³⁰ AND YOU SHALL LOVE THE LORD YOUR GOD WITH ALL YOUR HEART, AND WITH ALL YOUR SOUL, AND WITH ALL YOUR MIND, AND WITH ALL YOUR STRENGTH.' ³¹ The second is this, 'YOU SHALL LOVE YOUR NEIGHBOR AS YOURSELF.' There is no other commandment greater than these." ³² The scribe said to Him, "Right, Teacher; You have truly stated that HE IS ONE, AND THERE IS NO ONE ELSE BESIDES HIM; ³³ AND TO LOVE HIM WITH ALL THE HEART AND WITH ALL THE UN-

DERSTANDING AND WITH ALL THE STRENGTH, AND TO LOVE ONE'S NEIGHBOR AS HIMSELF, is much more than all burnt offerings and sacrifices." ³⁴ When Jesus saw that he had answered intelligently, He said to him, "You are not far from the kingdom of God." After that, no one would venture to ask Him any more questions.

³⁵ And Jesus *began* to say, as He taught in the temple, "How *is it that* the scribes say that the Christ is the son of David? ³⁶ David himself said in the Holy Spirit,

'THE LORD SAID TO MY LORD,
"SIT AT MY RIGHT HAND,
UNTIL I PUT YOUR ENEMIES
BENEATH YOUR FEET."'

³⁷ David himself calls Him 'Lord'; so in what sense is He his son?" And the large crowd enjoyed listening to Him.

³⁸ In His teaching He was saying: "Beware of the scribes who like to walk around in long robes, and *like* respectful greetings in the market places, ³⁹ and chief seats in the synagogues and places of honor at banquets, ⁴⁰ who devour widows' houses, and for appearance's sake offer long prayers; these will receive greater condemnation."

⁴¹ And He sat down opposite the treasury, and *began* observing how the people were putting money into the treasury; and many rich people were putting in large sums. ⁴² A poor widow came and put in two small copper coins, which amount to a cent. ⁴³ Calling His disciples to Him, He said to them, "Truly I say to you, this poor widow put in more than all the contributors to the treasury; ⁴⁴ for they all put in out of their surplus, but she, out of her poverty, put in all she owned, all she had to live on."

12:28 What commandment is the foremost…? The rabbis had determined that there were 613 commandments contained in the Pentateuch, one for each letter of the Ten Commandments. Of the 613 commandments, 248 were seen as affirmative and 365 as negative. Those laws were also divided into heavy and light categories, with the heavy laws being more binding than the light ones. The scribes and rabbis, however, had been unable to agree on which were heavy and which were light. This orientation to the law led the Pharisees to think Jesus had devised His own theory. So the Pharisees asked this particular question to get Jesus to incriminate Himself by revealing His unorthodox and unilateral beliefs.

12:40 devour widows' houses. Jesus exposed the greedy, unscrupulous practice of the scribes. Scribes often served as estate planners for widows, which gave them the opportunity to convince distraught widows that they would be serving God by supporting the temple or the scribe's own holy work. In either case, the scribe benefited monetarily and effectively robbed the widow of her husband's legacy to her. **long prayers.** The Pharisees attempted to flaunt their piety by praying for long periods. Their motive was not devotion to God, but a desire to be revered by the people.

DAY 12: Wasn't it idol worship for the Israelites to look at the bronze serpent in Numbers 21:4–9?

The circumstances leading up to the casting of the bronze serpent were all too familiar. The people were tired and discouraged. They were angry with God and complained to Moses. They were convinced that things couldn't get any worse, but God showed them otherwise. He sent "fiery serpents" among the people and some of the Israelites died. Others suffered excruciating bites.

Realizing their mistake, the people came in repentance to Moses and begged for help. They were not worshiping the bronze serpent but were acting in faith, in obedience to God's and Moses' directions.

In John 3:14, Jesus said, "So must the Son of Man be lifted up." This is a veiled prediction of His death on the cross. It is in reference to the story of where the Israelite people who looked at the serpent lifted up by Moses were healed. The point of this illustration or analogy is in the "lifted up." Just as Moses lifted up the snake on the pole so that all who looked upon it might live physically, those who look to Christ, who was "lifted up" on the cross for the sins of the world, will live spiritually and eternally.

MARCH 13

Numbers 23:1–24:25

23 Then Balaam said to Balak, "Build seven altars for me here, and prepare seven bulls and seven rams for me here." ² Balak did just as Balaam had spoken, and Balak and Balaam offered up a bull and a ram on each altar. ³ Then Balaam said to Balak, "Stand beside your burnt offering, and I will go; perhaps the LORD will come to meet me, and whatever He shows me I will tell you." So he went to a bare hill.

⁴ Now God met Balaam, and he said to Him, "I have set up the seven altars, and I have offered up a bull and a ram on each altar." ⁵ Then the LORD put a word in Balaam's mouth and said, "Return to Balak, and you shall speak thus." ⁶ So he returned to him, and behold, he was standing beside his burnt offering, he and all the leaders of Moab. ⁷ He took up his discourse and said,

23:5 the LORD put a word in Balaam's mouth. Even though Balak and Balaam offered sacrifices on pagan altars, it was the Lord who gave Balaam his oracle.

"From Aram Balak has brought me,
Moab's king from the
mountains of the East,
'Come curse Jacob for me,
And come, denounce Israel!'
⁸ "How shall I curse whom
God has not cursed?
And how can I denounce whom
the LORD has not denounced?

⁹ "As I see him from the top of the rocks,
And I look at him from the hills;
Behold, a people *who* dwells apart,
And will not be reckoned
among the nations.
¹⁰ "Who can count the dust of Jacob,
Or number the fourth part of Israel?
Let me die the death of the upright,
And let my end be like his!"

¹¹ Then Balak said to Balaam, "What have you done to me? I took you to curse my enemies, but behold, you have actually blessed them!" ¹² He replied, "Must I not be careful to speak what the LORD puts in my mouth?" ¹³ Then Balak said to him, "Please come with me to another place from where you may see them, although you will only see the extreme end of them and will not see all of them; and curse them for me from there." ¹⁴ So he took him to the field of Zophim, to the top of Pisgah, and built seven altars and offered a bull and a ram on *each* altar. ¹⁵ And he said to Balak, "Stand here beside your burnt offering while I myself meet *the LORD* over there." ¹⁶ Then the LORD met Balaam and put a word in his mouth and said, "Return to Balak, and thus you shall speak." ¹⁷ He came to him, and behold, he was standing beside his burnt offering, and the leaders of Moab with him. And Balak said to him, "What has the LORD spoken?" ¹⁸ Then he took up his discourse and said,

"Arise, O Balak, and hear;
Give ear to me, O son of Zippor!
¹⁹ "God is not a man, that He should lie,
Nor a son of man, that He
should repent;
Has He said, and will He not do it?

Or has He spoken, and will
He not make it good?

20 "Behold, I have received *a
command* to bless;
When He has blessed, then
I cannot revoke it.

21 "He has not observed
misfortune in Jacob;
Nor has He seen trouble in Israel;
The LORD his God is with him,
And the shout of a king
is among them.

22 "God brings them out of Egypt,
He is for them like the
horns of the wild ox.

23 "For there is no omen against Jacob,
Nor is there any divination
against Israel;
At the proper time it shall
be said to Jacob
And to Israel, what God has done!

24 "Behold, a people rises like a lioness,
And as a lion it lifts itself;
It will not lie down until it
devours the prey,
And drinks the blood of the slain."

25 Then Balak said to Balaam, "Do not curse them at all nor bless them at all!" 26 But Balaam replied to Balak, "Did I not tell you, 'Whatever the LORD speaks, that I must do'?" 27 Then Balak said to Balaam, "Please come, I will take you to another place; perhaps it will be agreeable with God that you curse them for me from there." 28 So Balak took Balaam to the top of Peor which overlooks the wasteland. 29 Balaam said to Balak, "Build seven altars for me here and prepare seven bulls and seven rams for me here." 30 Balak did just as Balaam had said, and offered up a bull and a ram on *each* altar.

24 When Balaam saw that it pleased the LORD to bless Israel, he did not go as at other times to seek omens but he set his face toward the wilderness. 2 And Balaam lifted up his eyes and saw Israel camping tribe by

24:2 the Spirit of God came upon him. This terminology was regularly used in the Old Testament for those whom God uniquely prepared to do His work (Jdg 3:10). Unlike the previous two oracles, Balaam does not involve himself in divination before giving this third oracle. He is empowered with the Holy Spirit to utter God's message accurately.

tribe; and the Spirit of God came upon him. 3 He took up his discourse and said,

"The oracle of Balaam the son of Beor,
And the oracle of the man
whose eye is opened;

4 The oracle of him who hears
the words of God,
Who sees the vision of the Almighty,
Falling down, yet having
his eyes uncovered,

5 How fair are your tents, O Jacob,
Your dwellings, O Israel!

6 "Like valleys that stretch out,
Like gardens beside the river,
Like aloes planted by the LORD,
Like cedars beside the waters.

7 "Water will flow from his buckets,
And his seed *will be* by many waters,
And his king shall be
higher than Agag,
And his kingdom shall be exalted.

8 "God brings him out of Egypt,
He is for him like the horns
of the wild ox.
He will devour the nations
who are his adversaries,
And will crush their bones in pieces,
And shatter *them* with his arrows.

9 "He couches, he lies down as a lion,
And as a lion, who dares rouse him?
Blessed is everyone who blesses you,
And cursed is everyone
who curses you."

10 Then Balak's anger burned against Balaam, and he struck his hands together; and Balak said to Balaam, "I called you to curse my enemies, but behold, you have persisted in blessing them these three times! 11 Therefore, flee to your place now. I said I would honor you greatly, but behold, the LORD has held you back from honor." 12 Balaam said to Balak, "Did I not tell your messengers whom you had sent to me, saying, 13 'Though Balak were to give me his house full of silver and gold, I could not do anything contrary to the command of the LORD, either good or bad, of my own accord. What the LORD speaks, that I will speak'? 14 And now, behold, I am going to my people; come, *and* I will advise you what this people will do to your people in the days to come."

15 He took up his discourse and said,

"The oracle of Balaam the son of Beor,
And the oracle of the man
whose eye is opened,

16 The oracle of him who hears
  the words of God,
And knows the knowledge
  of the Most High,
Who sees the vision of the Almighty,
Falling down, yet having
  his eyes uncovered.
17 "I see him, but not now;
I behold him, but not near;
A star shall come forth from Jacob,
A scepter shall rise from Israel,
And shall crush through the
  forehead of Moab,
And tear down all the sons of Sheth.
18 "Edom shall be a possession,
Seir, its enemies, also will
  be a possession,
While Israel performs valiantly.
19 "One from Jacob shall have dominion,
And will destroy the remnant
  from the city."

20 And he looked at Amalek and took up his discourse and said,

"Amalek was the first of the
  nations,
But his end *shall be* destruction."

21 And he looked at the Kenite, and took up his discourse and said,

"Your dwelling place is enduring,
And your nest is set in the cliff.
22 "Nevertheless Kain will be consumed;
How long will Asshur keep
  you captive?"

23 Then he took up his discourse and said,

"Alas, who can live except
  God has ordained it?
24 "But ships *shall come* from
  the coast of Kittim,
And they shall afflict Asshur
  and will afflict Eber;
So they also *will come* to
  destruction."

25 Then Balaam arose and departed and returned to his place, and Balak also went his way.

Psalm 33:18–22

18 Behold, the eye of the LORD is
  on those who fear Him,
On those who hope for His
  lovingkindness,
19 To deliver their soul from death
And to keep them alive in famine.
20 Our soul waits for the LORD;
He is our help and our shield.
21 For our heart rejoices in Him,
Because we trust in His holy
  name.
22 Let Your lovingkindness,
O LORD, be upon us,
According as we have hoped
  in You.

Proverbs 11:27

27 He who diligently seeks
  good seeks favor,
But he who seeks evil, evil
  will come to him.

Mark 13:1–23

13 As He was going out of the temple, one of His disciples *said to Him, "Teacher, behold what wonderful stones and what wonderful buildings!" 2 And Jesus said to him, "Do you see these great buildings? Not one stone will be left upon another which will not be torn down."

3 As He was sitting on the Mount of Olives opposite the temple, Peter and James and John and Andrew were questioning Him privately, 4 "Tell us, when will these things be, and what *will be* the sign when all these things are going to be fulfilled?" 5 And Jesus began to say to them, "See to it that no one misleads you. 6 Many will come in My name, saying, 'I am *He!*' and will mislead many. 7 When you hear of wars and rumors of wars, do not be frightened; *those things* must take place; but *that is* not yet the end.

13:2 **Jesus said.** In response to the disciple's admiration, Jesus again predicted that the temple would be destroyed. About 40 years later, in A.D. 70, the Romans ransacked Jerusalem, killed a million Jews, and demolished the temple. **Not one stone.** The only stones left undisturbed were huge foundation stones that were not actually a part of the temple edifice but formed footings for the retaining wall under the entire temple mount. These can be viewed today in the "Rabbi's Tunnel" which runs north-south along the western wall. It is a portion of the western side of the retaining wall that today is called the Wailing Wall. More of that retaining wall, including the steps used to ascend and descend from the temple mount, has also been uncovered on the southern side.

8 For nation will rise up against nation, and kingdom against kingdom; there will be earthquakes in various places; there will *also* be famines. These things are *merely* the beginning of birth pangs.

9 "But be on your guard; for they will deliver you to *the* courts, and you will be flogged in *the* synagogues, and you will stand before governors and kings for My sake, as a testimony to them. 10 The gospel must first be preached to all the nations. 11 When they arrest you and hand you over, do not worry beforehand about what you are to say, but say whatever is given you in that hour; for it is not you who speak, but *it is* the Holy Spirit. 12 Brother

13:8 the beginning of birth pangs. The Lord was referring to the pain a woman experiences in childbirth. Birth pains signal the end of pregnancy—they are infrequent at first and gradually increase just before the child is born. Likewise, the signs of vv. 6–8 will be infrequent, relatively speaking, in the beginning and will escalate to massive and tragic proportions just prior to Christ's second coming (1Th 5:3; Mt 24:8).

will betray brother to death, and a father *his* child; and children will rise up against parents and have them put to death. 13 You will be hated by all because of My name, but the one who endures to the end, he will be saved.

14 "But when you see the ABOMINATION OF DESOLATION standing where it should not be (let the reader understand), then those who are in Judea must flee to the mountains. 15 The one who is on the housetop must not go down, or go in to get anything out of his house; 16 and the one who is in the field must not turn back to get his coat. 17 But woe to those who are pregnant and to those who are nursing babies in those days! 18 But pray that it may not happen in the winter. 19 For those days will be a *time of* tribulation such as has not occurred since the beginning of the creation which God created until now, and never will. 20 Unless the Lord had shortened *those* days, no life would have been saved; but for the sake of the elect, whom He chose, He shortened the days. 21 And then if anyone says to you, 'Behold, here is the Christ'; or, 'Behold, *He is* there'; do not believe *him;* 22 for false Christs and false prophets will arise, and will show signs and wonders, in order to lead astray, if possible, the elect. 23 But take heed; behold, I have told you everything in advance.

DAY 13: How does one makes sense of Balaam and his talking donkey?

Balaam, whose story is recorded in Numbers 22:2—24:25, does seem to receive special treatment in the biblical story. Even though Balaam claimed to know the Lord (Nu 22:18), Scripture consistently refers to him as a false prophet (2Pe 2:15–16; Jude 11). Apparently God placed such a priority on the message that the character of the messenger became a secondary consideration. The Lord used Balaam as His mouthpiece to speak the true words He put in his mouth. God had a purpose for Balaam despite the pagan prophet's own plans.

When it comes to the talking donkey, several observations come to mind. First, this incident was not recorded as a commonplace occurrence but as something unusual and noteworthy. Second, one can just as easily wonder why God didn't (or doesn't) use talking animals more often—we'd all probably be better off. Third, why not recognize God's sense of humor in this account? Fourth, God's display of patience and persistence in these events ought to provoke in us a sense of humble worship. And, fifth, the incident, as unusual as it may be, should be accepted at face value.

MARCH 14

Numbers 25:1–26:65

25 While Israel remained at Shittim, the people began to play the harlot with the daughters of Moab. 2 For they invited the people to the sacrifices of their gods, and the people ate and bowed down to their gods. 3 So Israel joined themselves to Baal of Peor, and the LORD was angry against Israel. 4 The LORD said to Moses, "Take all the leaders of

the people and execute them in broad daylight before the LORD, so that the fierce anger of the LORD may turn away from Israel." 5 So Moses said to the judges of Israel, "Each of you slay his men who have joined themselves to Baal of Peor."

6 Then behold, one of the sons of Israel came and brought to his relatives a Midianite woman, in the sight of Moses and in the sight of all the congregation of the sons of Israel, while they were weeping at the doorway of the tent of meeting. 7 When Phine-

25:3 joined themselves to Baal of Peor. Israel engaged in acts of sexual immorality with the women of Moab. Since this was part of the pagan cult that was worshiped by the Moabites, the Israelites joined in these idolatrous practices. The Israelites yoked themselves to the false god of the Moabites and the Midianites, referred to as Baal of Peor. This was a violation of the first commandment.

has the son of Eleazar, the son of Aaron the priest, saw it, he arose from the midst of the congregation and took a spear in his hand, [8] and he went after the man of Israel into the tent and pierced both of them through, the man of Israel and the woman, through the body. So the plague on the sons of Israel was checked. [9] Those who died by the plague were 24,000.

[10] Then the LORD spoke to Moses, saying, [11] "Phinehas the son of Eleazar, the son of Aaron the priest, has turned away My wrath from the sons of Israel in that he was jealous with My jealousy among them, so that I did not destroy the sons of Israel in My jealousy. [12] Therefore say, 'Behold, I give him My covenant of peace; [13] and it shall be for him and his descendants after him, a covenant of a perpetual priesthood, because he was jealous for his God and made atonement for the sons of Israel.'"

[14] Now the name of the slain man of Israel who was slain with the Midianite woman, was Zimri the son of Salu, a leader of a father's household among the Simeonites. [15] The name of the Midianite woman who was slain was Cozbi the daughter of Zur, who was head of the people of a father's household in Midian.

[16] Then the LORD spoke to Moses, saying, [17] "Be hostile to the Midianites and strike them; [18] for they have been hostile to you with their tricks, with which they have deceived you in the affair of Peor and in the affair of Cozbi, the daughter of the leader of Midian, their

25:10–13 Because of Phinehas' zeal for God's holiness, the Lord made "a covenant of a perpetual priesthood" with him so that through his family line would come all future, legitimate High Priests (Ps 106:30–31). This promise will extend even into the millennial kingdom (Eze 40:46; 44:10, 15; 48:11).

sister who was slain on the day of the plague because of Peor."

26 Then it came about after the plague, that the LORD spoke to Moses and to Eleazar the son of Aaron the priest, saying, [2] "Take a census of all the congregation of the sons of Israel from twenty years old and upward, by their fathers' households, whoever is able to go out to war in Israel." [3] So Moses and Eleazar the priest spoke with them in the plains of Moab by the Jordan at Jericho, saying, [4] "Take a census of the people from twenty years old and upward, as the LORD has commanded Moses."

Now the sons of Israel who came out of the land of Egypt were:

[5] Reuben, Israel's firstborn, the sons of Reuben: of Hanoch, the family of the Hanochites; of Pallu, the family of the Palluites; [6] of Hezron, the family of the Hezronites; of Carmi, the family of the Carmites. [7] These are the families of the Reubenites, and those who were numbered of them were 43,730. [8] The son of Pallu: Eliab. [9] The sons of Eliab: Nemuel and Dathan and Abiram. These are the Dathan and Abiram who were called by the congregation, who contended against Moses and against Aaron in the company of Korah, when they contended against the LORD, [10] and the earth opened its mouth and swallowed them up along with Korah, when that company died, when the fire devoured 250 men, so that they became a warning. [11] The sons of Korah, however, did not die.

[12] The sons of Simeon according to their families: of Nemuel, the family of the Nemuelites; of Jamin, the family of the Jaminites; of Jachin, the family of the Jachinites; [13] of Zerah, the family of the Zerahites; of Shaul, the family of the Shaulites. [14] These are the families of the Simeonites, 22,200.

[15] The sons of Gad according to their families: of Zephon, the family of the Zephonites; of Haggi, the family of the Haggites; of Shuni, the family of the Shunites; [16] of Ozni, the family of the Oznites; of Eri, the family of the Erites; [17] of Arod, the family of the Arodites; of Areli, the family of the Arelites. [18] These are the families of the sons of Gad according to those who were numbered of them, 40,500.

[19] The sons of Judah were Er and Onan, but Er and Onan died in the land of Canaan. [20] The sons of Judah according to their families were: of Shelah, the family of the Shelanites; of Perez, the family of the Perezites; of Zerah, the family of the Zerahites. [21] The sons of Perez were: of Hezron, the family of the Hezronites; of Hamul, the family of the Hamulites. [22] These

are the families of Judah according to those who were numbered of them, 76,500.

23 The sons of Issachar according to their families: of Tola, the family of the Tolaites; of Puvah, the family of the Punites; 24 of Jashub, the family of the Jashubites; of Shimron, the family of the Shimronites. 25 These are the families of Issachar according to those who were numbered of them, 64,300.

26 The sons of Zebulun according to their families: of Sered, the family of the Seredites; of Elon, the family of the Elonites; of Jahleel, the family of the Jahleelites. 27 These are the families of the Zebulunites according to those who were numbered of them, 60,500.

28 The sons of Joseph according to their families: Manasseh and Ephraim. 29 The sons of Manasseh: of Machir, the family of the Machirites; and Machir became the father of Gilead: of Gilead, the family of the Gileadites. 30 These are the sons of Gilead: of Iezer, the family of the Iezerites; of Helek, the family of the Helekites; 31 and of Asriel, the family of the Asrielites; and of Shechem, the family of the Shechemites; 32 and of Shemida, the family of the Shemidaites; and of Hepher, the family of the Hepherites. 33 Now Zelophehad the son of Hepher had no sons, but only daughters; and the names of the daughters of Zelophehad were Mahlah, Noah, Hoglah, Milcah and Tirzah. 34 These are the families of Manasseh; and those who were numbered of them were 52,700.

35 These are the sons of Ephraim according to their families: of Shuthelah, the family of the Shuthelahites; of Becher, the family of the Becherites; of Tahan, the family of the Tahanites. 36 These are the sons of Shuthelah: of Eran, the family of the Eranites. 37 These are the families of the sons of Ephraim according to those who were numbered of them, 32,500. These are the sons of Joseph according to their families.

38 The sons of Benjamin according to their families: of Bela, the family of the Belaites; of Ashbel, the family of the Ashbelites; of Ahiram, the family of the Ahiramites; 39 of Shephupham, the family of the Shuphamites; of Hupham, the family of the Huphamites. 40 The sons of Bela were Ard and Naaman: of Ard, the family of the Ardites; of Naaman, the family of the Naamites. 41 These are the sons of Benjamin according to their families; and those who were numbered of them were 45,600.

42 These are the sons of Dan according to their families: of Shuham, the family of the Shuhamites. These are the families of Dan according to their families. 43 All the families of the Shuhamites, according to those who were numbered of them, were 64,400.

44 The sons of Asher according to their families: of Imnah, the family of the Imnites; of Ishvi, the family of the Ishvites; of Beriah, the family of the Beriites. 45 Of the sons of Beriah: of Heber, the family of the Heberites; of Malchiel, the family of the Malchielites. 46 The name of the daughter of Asher was Serah. 47 These are the families of the sons of Asher according to those who were numbered of them, 53,400.

48 The sons of Naphtali according to their families: of Jahzeel, the family of the Jahzeelites; of Guni, the family of the Gunites; 49 of Jezer, the family of the Jezerites; of Shillem, the family of the Shillemites. 50 These are the families of Naphtali according to their families; and those who were numbered of them were 45,400.

51 These are those who were numbered of the sons of Israel, 601,730.

52 Then the LORD spoke to Moses, saying, 53 "Among these the land shall be divided for an inheritance according to the number of names. 54 To the larger group you shall increase their inheritance, and to the smaller group you shall diminish their inheritance; each shall be given their inheritance according to those who were numbered of them. 55 But the land shall be divided by lot. They shall receive their inheritance according to the names of the tribes of their fathers. 56 According to the selection by lot, their inheritance shall be divided between the larger and the smaller groups."

57 These are those who were numbered of the Levites according to their families: of Gershon, the family of the Gershonites; of Kohath, the family of the Kohathites; of Merari, the family of the Merarites. 58 These are the families of Levi: the family of the Libnites, the family of the Hebronites, the family of the Mahlites, the family of the Mushites, the family of the Korahites. Kohath became the father of Amram. 59 The name of Amram's wife was Jochebed, the daughter of Levi, who was born to Levi in Egypt; and she bore to Amram: Aaron and Moses and their sister Miriam. 60 To Aaron were born Nadab and Abihu, Eleazar and Ithamar. 61 But Nadab and Abihu died when they offered strange fire before the LORD. 62 Those who were numbered of them were 23,000, every male from a month old and upward, for they were not numbered among the sons of Israel since no inheritance was given to them among the sons of Israel.

⁶³ These are those who were numbered by Moses and Eleazar the priest, who numbered the sons of Israel in the plains of Moab by the Jordan at Jericho. ⁶⁴ But among these there was not a man of those who were numbered by Moses and Aaron the priest, who numbered the sons of Israel in the wilderness of Sinai. ⁶⁵ For the LORD had said of them, "They shall surely die in the wilderness." And not a man was left of them, except Caleb the son of Jephunneh and Joshua the son of Nun.

Psalm 34:1–7

A Psalm of David when he feigned
madness before Abimelech, who
drove him away and he departed.

I will bless the LORD at all times;
His praise shall continually
be in my mouth.
² My soul will make its
boast in the LORD;
The humble will hear it and
rejoice.
³ O magnify the LORD with me,
And let us exalt His name
together.

⁴ I sought the LORD, and
He answered me,
And delivered me from all
my fears.
⁵ They looked to Him and were
radiant,
And their faces will never
be ashamed.
⁶ This poor man cried, and
the LORD heard him
And saved him out of all his
troubles.
⁷ The angel of the LORD encamps
around those who fear Him,
And rescues them.

Proverbs 11:28

²⁸ He who trusts in his riches
will fall,
But the righteous will flourish
like the *green* leaf.

34:7 The angel of the LORD. A special manifestation of Yahweh Himself at strategic historical junctures (Ge 16:7ff.; 18; 19; 31:11ff.; Jos 5; Jdg 6; 13). A strong case can be made that these were pre-incarnate appearances of the Lord Jesus Christ.

13:26 SON OF MAN COMING IN CLOUDS with great power and glory. Jesus will return to earth in the same manner in which He left it (Ac 1:9–11; see Da 7:13–14; Rev 1:7). The psalmist said that God uses "clouds" as His chariot (Ps 104:3), and Isaiah 19:1 pictures the Lord riding on a cloud. Although these "clouds" could be natural, they more likely describe the supernatural "glory cloud" that represented God's presence in Old Testament Israel. While Christ possesses "great power and glory," His return will be accompanied with visible manifestations of that power and glory (Rev 6:15–17; 11:15–19; 16:17–21; 19:11–16)—He will redeem the elect, restore the devastated earth, and establish His rule on earth.

Mark 13:24–37

²⁴ "But in those days, after that tribulation, THE SUN WILL BE DARKENED AND THE MOON WILL NOT GIVE ITS LIGHT, ²⁵ AND THE STARS WILL BE FALLING from heaven, and the powers that are in the heavens will be shaken. ²⁶ Then they will see THE SON OF MAN COMING IN CLOUDS with great power and glory. ²⁷ And then He will send forth the angels, and will gather together His elect from the four winds, from the farthest end of the earth to the farthest end of heaven.

²⁸ "Now learn the parable from the fig tree: when its branch has already become tender and puts forth its leaves, you know that summer is near. ²⁹ Even so, you too, when you see these things happening, recognize that He is near, *right* at the door. ³⁰ Truly I say to you, this generation will not pass away until all these things take place. ³¹ Heaven and earth will pass away, but My words will not pass away. ³² But of that day or hour no one knows, not even the angels in heaven, nor the Son, but the Father *alone*.

³³ "Take heed, keep on the alert; for you do not know when the *appointed* time will come. ³⁴ *It is* like a man away on a journey, *who* upon leaving his house and putting his slaves in charge, *assigning* to each one his task, also commanded the doorkeeper to stay on the alert. ³⁵ Therefore, be on the alert—for you do not know when the master of the house is coming, whether in the evening, at midnight, or when the rooster crows, or in the morning— ³⁶ in case he should come suddenly and find you asleep. ³⁷ What I say to you I say to all, 'Be on the alert!'"

✒ MARCH 15

Numbers 27:1–28:31

27 Then the daughters of Zelophehad, the son of Hepher, the son of Gilead, the son of Machir, the son of Manasseh, of the families of Manasseh the son of Joseph, came near; and these are the names of his daughters: Mahlah, Noah and Hoglah and Milcah and Tirzah. ²They stood before Moses and before Eleazar the priest and before the leaders and all the congregation, at the doorway of the tent of meeting, saying, ³"Our father died in the wilderness, yet he was not among the company of those who gathered themselves together against the LORD in the company of Korah; but he died in his own sin, and he had no sons. ⁴Why should the name of our father be withdrawn from among his family because he had no son? Give us a possession among our father's brothers." ⁵So Moses brought their case before the LORD.

⁶Then the LORD spoke to Moses, saying, ⁷"The daughters of Zelophehad are right in *their* statements. You shall surely give them a hereditary possession among their father's brothers, and you shall transfer the inheritance of their father to them. ⁸Further, you shall speak to the sons of Israel, saying, 'If a man dies and has no son, then you shall transfer his inheritance to his daughter. ⁹If he has no daughter, then you shall give his inheritance to his brothers. ¹⁰If he has no brothers, then you shall give his inheritance to his father's brothers. ¹¹If his father has no brothers, then you shall give his inheritance to his nearest relative in his own family, and he shall possess it; and it shall be a statutory ordinance to the sons of Israel, just as the LORD commanded Moses.'"

¹²Then the LORD said to Moses, "Go up to this mountain of Abarim, and see the land which I have given to the sons of Israel. ¹³When you have seen it, you too will be gathered to your people, as Aaron your brother was; ¹⁴for in the wilderness of Zin, during the strife of the congregation, you rebelled against My command to treat Me as holy before their eyes at the water." (These are the waters of Meribah of Kadesh in the wilderness of Zin.)

¹⁵Then Moses spoke to the LORD, saying, ¹⁶"May the LORD, the God of the spirits of all flesh, appoint a man over the congregation, ¹⁷who will go out and come in before them, and who will lead them out and bring them in, so that the congregation of the LORD will not be like sheep which have no shepherd." ¹⁸So the LORD said to Moses, "Take Joshua the son of Nun, a man in whom is the Spirit, and lay your hand on him; ¹⁹and have him stand before Eleazar the priest and before all the congregation, and commission him in their sight. ²⁰You shall put some of your authority on him, in order that all the congregation of the sons of Israel may obey *him*. ²¹Moreover, he shall stand before Eleazar the priest, who shall inquire for him by the judgment of the Urim before the LORD. At his command they shall go out and at his command they shall come in, *both* he and the sons of Israel with him, even all the congregation." ²²Moses did just as the LORD commanded him; and he took Joshua and set him before Eleazar the priest and before all the congregation. ²³Then he laid his hands on him and commissioned him, just as the LORD had spoken through Moses.

27:18 lay your hand on him. Joshua already had the inner endowment for leadership. He was empowered by the Holy Spirit. This inner endowment was to be recognized by an external ceremony. Moses publicly laid his hands upon Joshua. This act signified the transfer of Moses' leadership to Joshua. The laying on of hands can accompany a dedication to an office (Nu 8:10).

27:21 Eleazar...shall inquire for him. Moses had been able to communicate directly with God (12:8), but Joshua would receive the Word from the Lord through the High Priest. **Urim.** See Exodus 28:30 for this part of the High Priest's breastpiece (Ex 39:8–21) as a means of determining God's will (Dt 33:8; 1Sa 28:6).

28 Then the LORD spoke to Moses, saying, ²"Command the sons of Israel and say to them, 'You shall be careful to present My offering, My food for My offerings by fire, of a soothing aroma to Me, at their appointed time.' ³You shall say to them, 'This is the offering by fire which you shall offer to the LORD: two male lambs one year old without defect *as* a continual burnt offering every day. ⁴You shall offer the one lamb in the morning and the other lamb you shall offer at twilight; ⁵also a tenth of an ephah of fine flour for a grain offering, mixed with a fourth of a hin of beaten oil. ⁶It is a continual burnt offering which was ordained in Mount Sinai as a soothing aroma, an offering by fire to the LORD. ⁷Then the drink offering with it *shall* be a fourth of a hin for each lamb, in the holy place you shall pour out a drink offering of strong drink to the LORD. ⁸The other lamb you shall offer at twilight; as the grain offering of the morning and as its drink offering, you shall offer it, an offering by fire, a soothing aroma to the LORD.

⁹'Then on the sabbath day two male lambs one year old without defect, and two-tenths *of an ephah* of fine flour mixed with oil as a grain offering, and its drink offering: ¹⁰ *This is* the burnt offering of every sabbath in addition to the continual burnt offering and its drink offering.

¹¹'Then at the beginning of each of your months you shall present a burnt offering to the LORD: two bulls and one ram, seven male lambs one year old without defect; ¹² and three-tenths *of an ephah* of fine flour mixed with oil for a grain offering, for each bull; and two-tenths of fine flour mixed with oil for a grain offering, for the one ram; ¹³ and a tenth *of an ephah* of fine flour mixed with oil for a grain offering for each lamb, for a burnt offering of a soothing aroma, an offering by fire to the LORD. ¹⁴Their drink offerings shall be half a hin of wine for a bull and a third of a hin for the ram and a fourth of a hin for a lamb; this is the burnt offering of each month throughout the months of the year. ¹⁵And one male goat for a sin offering to the LORD; it shall be offered with its drink offering in addition to the continual burnt offering.

¹⁶'Then on the fourteenth day of the first month shall be the LORD'S Passover. ¹⁷On the fifteenth day of this month *shall be* a feast, unleavened bread *shall be* eaten for seven days. ¹⁸On the first day *shall be* a holy convocation; you shall do no laborious work. ¹⁹You shall present an offering by fire, a burnt offering to the LORD: two bulls and one ram and seven male lambs one year old, having them without defect. ²⁰For their grain offering, you shall offer fine flour mixed with oil: three-tenths *of an ephah* for a bull and two-tenths for the ram. ²¹A tenth *of an ephah* you shall offer for each of the seven lambs; ²² and one male goat for a sin offering to make atonement for you. ²³You shall present these besides the burnt offering of the morning, which is for a continual burnt offering. ²⁴After this manner you shall present daily, for seven days, the food of the offering by fire, of a soothing aroma to the LORD; it shall be presented with its drink offering in addition to the continual burnt offering. ²⁵On the seventh day you shall have a holy convocation; you shall do no laborious work.

²⁶'Also on the day of the first fruits, when you present a new grain offering to the LORD in your *Feast of* Weeks, you shall have a holy convocation; you shall do no laborious work. ²⁷You shall offer a burnt offering for a soothing aroma to the LORD: two young bulls, one ram, seven male lambs one year old; ²⁸ and their grain offering, fine flour mixed with oil: three-tenths *of an ephah* for each bull, two-tenths for the one ram, ²⁹ a tenth for each of the seven lambs; ³⁰ *also* one male goat to make atonement for you. ³¹ Besides the continual burnt offering and its grain offering, you shall present *them* with their drink offerings. They shall be without defect.

Psalm 34:8–14

⁸ O taste and see that the LORD is good;
How blessed is the man who
takes refuge in Him!
⁹ O fear the LORD, you His saints;
For to those who fear Him
there is no want.
¹⁰ The young lions do lack
and suffer hunger;
But they who seek the LORD shall not
be in want of any good thing.
¹¹ Come, you children, listen to me;
I will teach you the fear of the LORD.
¹² Who is the man who desires life
And loves *length of* days that
he may see good?
¹³ Keep your tongue from evil
And your lips from speaking deceit.
¹⁴ Depart from evil and do good;
Seek peace and pursue it.

Proverbs 11:29

²⁹ He who troubles his own
house will inherit wind,
And the foolish will be servant
to the wisehearted.

11:29 inherit wind. The one who mismanages his house will see all he has blown away, and he will have nothing left in the end. He will serve the one who manages well (15:27).

Mark 14:1–26

14 Now the Passover and Unleavened Bread were two days away; and the chief priests and the scribes were seeking how to seize Him by stealth and kill *Him;* ² for they were saying, "Not during the festival, otherwise there might be a riot of the people." ³While He was in Bethany at the home of

Simon the leper, and reclining *at the table,* there came a woman with an alabaster vial of very costly perfume of pure nard; *and* she broke the vial and poured it over His head. [4] But some were indignantly *remarking* to one another, "Why has this perfume been wasted? [5] For this perfume might have been sold for over three hundred denarii, and *the money* given to the poor." And they were scolding her. [6] But Jesus said, "Let her alone; why do you bother her? She has done a good deed to Me. [7] For you always have the poor with you, and whenever you wish you can do good to them; but you do not always have Me. [8] She has done what she could; she has anointed My body beforehand for the burial. [9] Truly I say to you, wherever the gospel is preached in the whole world, what this woman has done will also be spoken of in memory of her."

[10] Then Judas Iscariot, who was one of the twelve, went off to the chief priests in order to betray Him to them. [11] They were glad when they heard *this,* and promised to give him money. And he *began* seeking how to betray Him at an opportune time.

[12] On the first day of Unleavened Bread, when the Passover *lamb* was being sacrificed, His disciples *said to Him, "Where do You want us to go and prepare for You to eat the Passover?" [13] And He *sent two of His disciples and *said to them, "Go into the city, and a man will meet you carrying a pitcher of water; follow him; [14] and wherever he enters, say to the owner of the house, 'The Teacher says, "Where is My guest room in which I may eat the Passover with My disciples?" ' [15] And he himself will show you a large upper room furnished *and* ready; prepare for us there." [16] The disciples went out and came to the city, and found *it* just as He had told them; and they prepared the Passover.

[17] When it was evening He *came with the twelve. [18] As they were reclining *at the table

14:12 Unleavened Bread. Passover and the Feast of Unleavened Bread were so closely associated that both terms were used interchangeably to refer to the 8-day celebration that began with the Passover. Although Unleavened Bread is used here, Mark's clear intention is the preparation for Passover. **the Passover *lamb* was being sacrificed.** The lambs were killed on 14 Nisan at twilight (Ex 12:6), a Hebrew term meaning "between the two evenings," or between 3:00 and 5:00 p.m. After the lamb was slaughtered and some of its blood sprinkled on the altar, the lamb was taken home, roasted whole, and eaten in the evening meal with unleavened bread, bitter herbs, *charoseth* (a paste made of crushed apples, dates, pomegranates, and nuts, into which they dipped bread), and wine.

and eating, Jesus said, "Truly I say to you that one of you will betray Me—one who is eating with Me." [19] They began to be grieved and to say to Him one by one, "Surely not I?" [20] And He said to them, "*It is* one of the twelve, one who dips with Me in the bowl. [21] For the Son of Man *is to* go just as it is written of Him; but woe to that man by whom the Son of Man is betrayed! *It would have been* good for that man if he had not been born."

[22] While they were eating, He took *some* bread, and after a blessing He broke *it,* and gave *it* to them, and said, "Take *it;* this is My body." [23] And when He had taken a cup *and* given thanks, He gave *it* to them, and they all drank from it. [24] And He said to them, "This is My blood of the covenant, which is poured out for many. [25] Truly I say to you, I will never again drink of the fruit of the vine until that day when I drink it new in the kingdom of God." [26] After singing a hymn, they went out to the Mount of Olives.

DAY 15: Why did Mary's anointing of Jesus spark a controversy?

In Mark 14:3, Jesus was in the home of Simon the leper at Bethany. "A woman," who is identified in John 12:3 as Mary, the sister of Martha and Lazarus, brought an alabaster flask—a long-necked bottle made out of a special variety of marble, a material which proved to be the best container for preserving expensive perfumes and oils. The flask contained "pure nard." The oil was derived from the nard plant, which was native to India. That it was pure meant it was genuine and unadulterated, which is what made it so costly. She may have simply broken the neck of the bottle so that she could pour out the contents more quickly, an expression of her sincere and total devotion to the Lord.

Some who were there became indignant (v. 4). John 12:4–5 says that Judas was the instigator, and Matthew 26:8 indicates that all the disciples, following Judas's lead, were angry with Mary's waste of a very valuable commodity. It was valued at three hundred denarii (v. 5). Since a denarius was a day's wage for a common laborer, it represented almost a year's work for such a person. This money could have been "given to the poor." While 11 of the disciples would have agreed to this use of the money, the fact is the poor may never have seen it. Since Judas was in reality a thief masquerading as the treasurer of the 12, he could have embezzled all of it (Jn 12:6).

In any case, Jesus' answer was that "you always have the poor with you" (v. 7). Opportunities to minister to the poor are "always" available, but Jesus would be in their presence for only a limited time. This was not a time for meeting the needs of the poor and the sick—it was a time for sacrificial worship of the One who would soon suffer and be crucified.

MARCH 16

Numbers 29:1–30:16

29 'Now in the seventh month, on the first day of the month, you shall also have a holy convocation; you shall do no laborious work. It will be to you a day for blowing trumpets. ²You shall offer a burnt offering as a soothing aroma to the LORD: one bull, one ram, *and* seven male lambs one year old without defect; ³also their grain offering, fine flour mixed with oil: three-tenths *of an ephah* for the bull, two-tenths for the ram, ⁴and one-tenth for each of the seven lambs. ⁵*Offer* one male goat for a sin offering, to make atonement for you, ⁶besides the burnt offering of the new moon and its grain offering, and the continual burnt offering and its grain offering, and their drink offerings, according to their ordinance, for a soothing aroma, an offering by fire to the LORD.

⁷'Then on the tenth day of this seventh month you shall have a holy convocation, and you shall humble yourselves; you shall not do any work. ⁸You shall present a burnt offering to the LORD *as* a soothing aroma: one bull, one ram, seven male lambs one year old, having them without defect; ⁹and their grain offering, fine flour mixed with oil: three-tenths *of an ephah* for the bull, two-tenths for the one ram, ¹⁰a tenth for each of the seven lambs; ¹¹one male goat for a sin offering, besides the sin offering of atonement and the continual burnt offering and its grain offering, and their drink offerings.

¹²'Then on the fifteenth day of the seventh month you shall have a holy convocation; you shall do no laborious work, and you shall observe a feast to the LORD for seven days. ¹³You shall present a burnt offering, an offering by fire as a soothing aroma to the LORD: thirteen bulls, two rams, fourteen male lambs one year old, which are without defect; ¹⁴and their grain offering, fine flour mixed with oil: three-tenths *of an ephah* for each of the thirteen bulls, two-tenths for each of the two rams, ¹⁵and a tenth for each of the fourteen lambs; ¹⁶and one male goat for a sin offering,

besides the continual burnt offering, its grain offering and its drink offering.

¹⁷'Then on the second day: twelve bulls, two rams, fourteen male lambs one year old without defect; ¹⁸and their grain offering and their drink offerings for the bulls, for the rams and for the lambs, by their number according to the ordinance; ¹⁹and one male goat for a sin offering, besides the continual burnt offering and its grain offering, and their drink offerings.

²⁰'Then on the third day: eleven bulls, two rams, fourteen male lambs one year old without defect; ²¹and their grain offering and their drink offerings for the bulls, for the rams and for the lambs, by their number according to the ordinance; ²²and one male goat for a sin offering, besides the continual burnt offering and its grain offering and its drink offering.

²³'Then on the fourth day: ten bulls, two rams, fourteen male lambs one year old without defect; ²⁴their grain offering and their drink offerings for the bulls, for the rams and for the lambs, by their number according to the ordinance; ²⁵and one male goat for a sin offering, besides the continual burnt offering, its grain offering and its drink offering.

²⁶'Then on the fifth day: nine bulls, two rams, fourteen male lambs one year old without defect; ²⁷and their grain offering and their drink offerings for the bulls, for the rams and for the lambs, by their number according to the ordinance; ²⁸and one male goat for a sin offering, besides the continual burnt offering and its grain offering and its drink offering.

²⁹'Then on the sixth day: eight bulls, two rams, fourteen male lambs one year old without defect; ³⁰and their grain offering and their drink offerings for the bulls, for the rams and for the lambs, by their number according to the ordinance; ³¹and one male goat for a sin offering, besides the continual burnt offering, its grain offering and its drink offerings.

³²'Then on the seventh day: seven bulls, two rams, fourteen male lambs one year old without defect; ³³and their grain offering and their drink offerings for the bulls, for the rams

and for the lambs, by their number according to the ordinance; ³⁴ and one male goat for a sin offering, besides the continual burnt offering, its grain offering and its drink offering.

³⁵ 'On the eighth day you shall have a solemn assembly; you shall do no laborious work. ³⁶ But you shall present a burnt offering, an offering by fire, as a soothing aroma to the LORD: one bull, one ram, seven male lambs one year old without defect; ³⁷ their grain offering and their drink offerings for the bull, for the ram and for the lambs, by their number according to the ordinance; ³⁸ and one male goat for a sin offering, besides the continual burnt offering and its grain offering and its drink offering.

³⁹ 'You shall present these to the LORD at your appointed times, besides your votive offerings and your freewill offerings, for your burnt offerings and for your grain offerings and for your drink offerings and for your peace offerings.'" ⁴⁰ Moses spoke to the sons of Israel in accordance with all that the LORD had commanded Moses.

30 Then Moses spoke to the heads of the tribes of the sons of Israel, saying, "This is the word which the LORD has commanded. ² If a man makes a vow to the LORD, or takes an oath to bind himself with a binding obligation, he shall not violate his word; he shall do according to all that proceeds out of his mouth.

³ "Also if a woman makes a vow to the LORD, and binds herself by an obligation in her father's house in her youth, ⁴ and her father hears her vow and her obligation by which she has bound herself, and her father says nothing to her, then all her vows shall stand and every obligation by which she has bound herself shall stand. ⁵ But if her father should forbid her on the day he hears of it, none of her vows or her obligations by which she has bound herself shall stand; and the LORD will forgive her because her father had forbidden her.

⁶ "However, if she should marry while under her vows or the rash statement of her lips by which she has bound herself, ⁷ and her husband hears of it and says nothing to her on the day he hears it, then her vows shall stand and her obligations by which she has bound herself shall stand. ⁸ But if on the day her husband hears of it, he forbids her, then he shall annul her vow which she is under and the rash statement of her lips by which she has bound herself; and the LORD will forgive her.

⁹ "But the vow of a widow or of a divorced woman, everything by which she has bound

herself, shall stand against her. ¹⁰ However, if she vowed in her husband's house, or bound herself by an obligation with an oath, ¹¹ and her husband heard *it,* but said nothing to her *and* did not forbid her, then all her vows shall stand and every obligation by which she bound herself shall stand. ¹² But if her husband indeed annuls them on the day he hears *them,* then whatever proceeds out of her lips concerning her vows or concerning the obligation of herself shall not stand; her husband has annulled them, and the LORD will forgive her.

¹³ "Every vow and every binding oath to humble herself, her husband may confirm it or her husband may annul it. ¹⁴ But if her husband indeed says nothing to her from day to day, then he confirms all her vows or all her obligations which are on her; he has confirmed them, because he said nothing to her on the day he heard them. ¹⁵ But if he indeed annuls them after he has heard them, then he shall bear her guilt."

¹⁶ These are the statutes which the LORD commanded Moses, *as* between a man and his wife, *and as* between a father and his daughter, *while she is* in her youth in her father's house.

Psalm 34:15–22

¹⁵ The eyes of the LORD are
    toward the righteous
    And His ears are *open* to their cry.
¹⁶ The face of the LORD is
    against evildoers,
    To cut off the memory of
    them from the earth.
¹⁷ *The righteous* cry, and the LORD hears
    And delivers them out of
    all their troubles.
¹⁸ The LORD is near to the brokenhearted
    And saves those who are
    crushed in spirit.

¹⁹ Many are the afflictions
    of the righteous,
    But the LORD delivers him
    out of them all.
²⁰ He keeps all his bones,
    Not one of them is broken.

34:18 brokenhearted…crushed in spirit. These are graphic idioms that describe dependent disciples (Pss 51:17; 147:3; Is 57:15; 61:1; 66:2; Mt 5:3).

²¹ Evil shall slay the wicked,
And those who hate the righteous
will be condemned.
²² The LORD redeems the soul
of His servants,
And none of those who take refuge
in Him will be condemned.

Proverbs 11:30-31

³⁰ The fruit of the righteous
is a tree of life,
And he who is wise wins souls.
³¹ If the righteous will be
rewarded in the earth,
How much more the wicked
and the sinner!

11:30 wins souls. Literally, "to take lives," in the sense of doing them good or influencing them with wisdom's ways (Lk 5:10). The word is also used for capturing people for evil purposes as in 6:25; Psalm 31:13; Ezekiel 13:18.

11:31 rewarded. God's final blessing and reward to the "righteous," and His judgment and punishment of the "wicked" and "sinners" come after life on this earth has ended. But there are foretastes of both during life on the earth, as the righteous experience God's personal care and goodness, while the wicked are void of it.

Mark 14:27-52

²⁷ And Jesus *said to them, "You will all fall away, because it is written, 'I WILL STRIKE DOWN THE SHEPHERD, AND THE SHEEP SHALL BE SCATTERED.' ²⁸ But after I have been raised, I will go ahead of you to Galilee." ²⁹ But Peter said to Him, "*Even* though all may fall away, yet I will not." ³⁰ And Jesus *said to him, "Truly I say to you, that this very night, before a rooster crows twice, you yourself will deny Me three times." ³¹ But *Peter* kept saying insistently, "*Even* if I have to die with You, I will not deny You!" And they all were saying the same thing also.

³² They *came to a place named Gethsemane; and He *said to His disciples, "Sit here until I have prayed." ³³ And He *took with Him Peter and James and John, and began to be very distressed and troubled. ³⁴ And He *said to them, "My soul is deeply grieved to the point of death; remain here and keep watch." ³⁵ And He went a little beyond *them,* and fell to the ground and *began* to pray that if it were possible, the hour might pass Him by. ³⁶ And He was saying, "Abba! Father! All things are

14:32 Gethsemane. The name means "oil press," and referred to a garden filled with olive trees on a slope of the Mt. of Olives. Jesus frequented this spot with the disciples when He wanted to get away from the crowds to pray (Jn 18:1-2; Mt 26:36).

14:36 Abba! An endearing, intimate Aram. term that is essentially equivalent to the Eng. word "Daddy" (Ro 8:15; Gal 4:6). **All things are possible.** Jesus knew that it was in the scope of God's power and omniscience to provide an alternate plan of salvation, if He desired. **cup.** This was the cup of divine wrath referred to in the Old Testament (Ps 75:8; Is 51:17; Jer 49:12). Christ was to endure the fury of God over sin, Satan, the power of death, and the guilt of iniquity. **not what I will, but what You will.** This reveals Jesus' total resolution and resignation to do the will of God. He came into the world to do God's will, and that remained His commitment while here (Mt 26:39; Jn 6:38-40).

possible for You; remove this cup from Me; yet not what I will, but what You will." ³⁷ And He *came and *found them sleeping, and *said to Peter, "Simon, are you asleep? Could you not keep watch for one hour? ³⁸ Keep watching and praying that you may not come into temptation; the spirit is willing, but the flesh is weak." ³⁹ Again He went away and prayed, saying the same words. ⁴⁰ And again He came and found them sleeping, for their eyes were very heavy; and they did not know what to answer Him. ⁴¹ And He *came the third time, and *said to them, "Are you still sleeping and resting? It is enough; the hour has come; behold, the Son of Man is being betrayed into the hands of sinners. ⁴² Get up, let us be going; behold, the one who betrays Me is at hand!"

⁴³ Immediately while He was still speaking, Judas, one of the twelve, *came up accompanied by a crowd with swords and clubs, *who were* from the chief priests and the scribes and the elders. ⁴⁴ Now he who was betraying Him had given them a signal, saying, "Whomever I kiss, He is the one; seize Him and lead Him away under guard." ⁴⁵ After coming, Judas immediately went to Him, saying, "Rabbi!" and kissed Him. ⁴⁶ They laid hands on Him and seized Him. ⁴⁷ But one of those who stood by drew his sword, and struck the slave of the high priest and cut off his ear. ⁴⁸ And Jesus said to them, "Have you come out with swords and clubs to arrest Me, as *you would* against a robber? ⁴⁹ Every day I

was with you in the temple teaching, and you did not seize Me; but *this has taken place* to fulfill the Scriptures." ⁵⁰ And they all left Him and fled.

⁵¹ A young man was following Him, wearing *nothing but* a linen sheet over *his* naked *body;* and they *seized him. ⁵² But he pulled free of the linen sheet and escaped naked.

DAY 16: Who was involved in the arrest of Jesus?

"Judas, one of the twelve," was the betrayer (Mk 14:43). All the Gospel writers refer to him this way (vv. 10, 20; Mt 26:14, 47; Lk 22:47; Jn 6:71); and in so doing, they display remarkable restraint in describing and evaluating Judas. Especially in this context, such a simple description actually heightens the evil of his crime more than any series of derogatory epithets or negative criticisms could do. It also points out the precise fulfillment of Jesus' announcement in vv. 18–20.

"A crowd with swords and clubs" also was there. This "crowd" was a carefully selected group whose sole purpose was arresting Jesus so He could be put to death. A cohort (600 men at full strength) of Roman soldiers (Jn 18:3, 12) was in this crowd because the Jewish leaders (see Lk 22:52) who organized the throng needed permission from Rome to carry out the death penalty and feared the crowds. The "swords" were the regular small hand weapons of the Romans, and the wood "clubs" were ordinary weapons carried by the Jewish temple police.

Then there were the "chief priests...elders...scribes." Although 3 distinct sections of the Sanhedrin, they were acting in unity. These Jewish leaders had evidently for some time hoped to accuse Jesus of rebellion against Rome. Then, His execution could be blamed on the Romans and the leaders could escape potential reprisals from those Jews who admired Jesus. The Sanhedrin likely had hurried to Pontius Pilate, the Roman governor, to ask immediate use of his soldiers, or perhaps acted on a prearranged agreement for troop use on short notice. Whatever the case, the leaders procured the assistance of the Roman military from Fort Antonia in Jerusalem.

MARCH 17

Numbers 31:1–32:42

31 Then the LORD spoke to Moses, saying, ² "Take full vengeance for the sons of Israel on the Midianites; afterward you will be gathered to your people." ³ Moses spoke to the people, saying, "Arm men from among you for the war, that they may go against Midian to execute the LORD'S vengeance on Midian. ⁴ A thousand from each tribe of all the tribes of Israel you shall send to the war." ⁵ So there were furnished from the thousands of Israel, a thousand from each tribe, twelve thousand armed for war. ⁶ Moses sent them, a thousand from each tribe, to the war, and Phinehas the son of Eleazar the priest, to the war with them, and the holy vessels and the trumpets for the alarm in his hand. ⁷ So they made war against Midian, just as the LORD had commanded Moses, and they killed every male. ⁸ They killed the kings of Midian along with the *rest of* their slain: Evi and Rekem and Zur and Hur and Reba, the five kings of Midian; they also killed Balaam the son of Beor with the sword. ⁹ The sons of Israel captured the women of Midian and their little ones; and all their cattle and all their flocks and all their goods they plundered. ¹⁰ Then they burned all their cities where they lived and all their camps with fire. ¹¹ They took all the spoil and

all the prey, both of man and of beast. ¹² They brought the captives and the prey and the spoil to Moses, and to Eleazar the priest and to the congregation of the sons of Israel, to the camp at the plains of Moab, which are by the Jordan *opposite* Jericho.

¹³ Moses and Eleazar the priest and all the leaders of the congregation went out to meet them outside the camp. ¹⁴ Moses was angry with the officers of the army, the captains of thousands and the captains of hundreds, who had come from service in the war. ¹⁵ And Moses said to them, "Have you spared all the women? ¹⁶ Behold, these caused the sons of Israel, through the counsel of Balaam, to trespass against the LORD in the matter of Peor, so the plague was among the congregation of the LORD. ¹⁷ Now therefore, kill every male among the little ones, and kill every woman who has known man intimately. ¹⁸ But all the girls who have not known man intimately, spare for yourselves. ¹⁹ And you, camp outside the camp seven days; whoever has killed any person and whoever has touched any slain, purify yourselves, you and your captives, on the third day and on the seventh day. ²⁰ You shall purify for yourselves every garment and every article of leather and all the work of goats' *hair,* and all articles of wood."

²¹ Then Eleazar the priest said to the men of war who had gone to battle, "This is the statute of the law which the LORD has com-

manded Moses: [22] only the gold and the silver, the bronze, the iron, the tin and the lead, [23] everything that can stand the fire, you shall pass through the fire, and it shall be clean, but it shall be purified with water for impurity. But whatever cannot stand the fire you shall pass through the water. [24] And you shall wash your clothes on the seventh day and be clean, and afterward you may enter the camp."

[25] Then the LORD spoke to Moses, saying, [26] "You and Eleazar the priest and the heads of the fathers' *households* of the congregation take a count of the booty that was captured, both of man and of animal; [27] and divide the booty between the warriors who went out to battle and all the congregation. [28] Levy a tax for the LORD from the men of war who went out to battle, one in five hundred of the persons and of the cattle and of the donkeys and of the sheep; [29] take it from their half and give it to Eleazar the priest, as an offering to the LORD. [30] From the sons of Israel's half, you shall take one drawn out of every fifty of the persons, of the cattle, of the donkeys and of the sheep, from all the animals, and give them to the Levites who keep charge of the tabernacle of the LORD." [31] Moses and Eleazar the priest did just as the LORD had commanded Moses.

[32] Now the booty that remained from the spoil which the men of war had plundered was 675,000 sheep, [33] and 72,000 cattle, [34] and 61,000 donkeys, [35] and of human beings, of the women who had not known man intimately, all the persons were 32,000.

[36] The half, the portion of those who went out to war, was *as follows:* the number of sheep was 337,500, [37] and the LORD'S levy of the sheep was 675; [38] and the cattle were 36,000, from which the LORD'S levy was 72; [39] and the donkeys were 30,500, from which the LORD'S levy was 61; [40] and the human beings were 16,000, from whom the LORD'S levy was 32 persons. [41] Moses gave the levy *which was* the LORD'S offering to Eleazar the priest, just as the LORD had commanded Moses.

[42] As for the sons of Israel's half, which Moses separated from the men who had gone to war— [43] now the congregation's half was 337,500 sheep, [44] and 36,000 cattle, [45] and 30,500 donkeys, [46] and the human beings were 16,000— [47] and from the sons of Israel's half, Moses took one drawn out of every fifty, both of man and of animals, and gave them to the Levites, who kept charge of the tabernacle of the LORD, just as the LORD had commanded Moses.

[48] Then the officers who were over the thousands of the army, the captains of thousands and the captains of hundreds, approached Moses, [49] and they said to Moses, "Your servants have taken a census of men of war who are in our charge, and no man of us is missing. [50] So we have brought as an offering to the LORD what each man found, articles of gold, armlets and bracelets, signet rings, earrings and necklaces, to make atonement for ourselves before the LORD." [51] Moses and Eleazar the priest took the gold from them, all kinds of wrought articles. [52] All the gold of the offering which they offered up to the LORD, from the captains of thousands and the captains of hundreds, was 16,750 shekels. [53] The men of war had taken booty, every man for himself. [54] So Moses and Eleazar the priest took the gold from the captains of thousands and of hundreds, and brought it to the tent of meeting as a memorial for the sons of Israel before the LORD.

32 Now the sons of Reuben and the sons of Gad had an exceedingly large number of livestock. So when they saw the land of Jazer and the land of Gilead, that it was indeed a place suitable for livestock, [2] the sons of Gad and the sons of Reuben came and spoke to Moses and to Eleazar the priest and to the leaders of the congregation, saying, [3] "Ataroth, Dibon, Jazer, Nimrah, Heshbon, Elealeh, Sebam, Nebo and Beon, [4] the land which the LORD conquered before the congregation of Israel, is a land for livestock, and your servants have livestock." [5] They said, "If we have found favor in your sight, let this land be given to your servants as a possession; do not take us across the Jordan."

[6] But Moses said to the sons of Gad and to the sons of Reuben, "Shall your brothers go to war while you yourselves sit here? [7] Now why are you discouraging the sons of Israel from crossing over into the land which the LORD has given them? [8] This is what your fathers did when I sent them from Kadesh-barnea to see the land. [9] For when they went up to the valley of Eshcol and saw the land, they discouraged the sons of Israel so that they did not go into

---

32:8 This is what your fathers did. Moses feared that if these two tribes were comfortably settled, they would not join with the other 10 tribes in conquering Canaan, and that could be the beginning of a general revolt against entering the land. As the 10 spies had dissuaded the people at Kadesh nearly 40 years earlier from conquering the land (vv. 9–13; 13:26—14:4), the refusal of these two tribes could cause the people to fail again (v. 15).

---

the land which the LORD had given them. ¹⁰ So the LORD'S anger burned in that day, and He swore, saying, ¹¹ 'None of the men who came up from Egypt, from twenty years old and upward, shall see the land which I swore to Abraham, to Isaac and to Jacob; for they did not follow Me fully, ¹² except Caleb the son of Jephunneh the Kenizzite and Joshua the son of Nun, for they have followed the LORD fully.' ¹³ So the LORD'S anger burned against Israel, and He made them wander in the wilderness forty years, until the entire generation of those who had done evil in the sight of the LORD was destroyed. ¹⁴ Now behold, you have risen up in your fathers' place, a brood of sinful men, to add still more to the burning anger of the LORD against Israel. ¹⁵ For if you turn away from following Him, He will once more abandon them in the wilderness, and you will destroy all these people."

¹⁶ Then they came near to him and said, "We will build here sheepfolds for our livestock and cities for our little ones; ¹⁷ but we ourselves will be armed ready *to go* before the sons of Israel, until we have brought them to their place, while our little ones live in the fortified cities because of the inhabitants of the land. ¹⁸ We will not return to our homes until every one of the sons of Israel has possessed his inheritance. ¹⁹ For we will not have an inheritance with them on the other side of the Jordan and beyond, because our inheritance has fallen to us on this side of the Jordan toward the east."

²⁰ So Moses said to them, "If you will do this, if you will arm yourselves before the LORD for the war, ²¹ and all of you armed men cross over the Jordan before the LORD until He has driven His enemies out from before Him, ²² and the land is subdued before the LORD, then afterward you shall return and be free of obligation toward the LORD and toward Israel, and this land shall be yours for a possession before the LORD. ²³ But if you will not do so, behold, you have sinned against the LORD, and be sure your sin will find you out. ²⁴ Build yourselves cities for your little ones, and sheepfolds for your sheep, and do what you have promised."

²⁵ The sons of Gad and the sons of Reuben spoke to Moses, saying, "Your servants will do just as my lord commands. ²⁶ Our little ones, our wives, our livestock and all our cattle shall remain there in the cities of Gilead; ²⁷ while your servants, everyone who is armed for war, will cross over in the presence of the LORD to battle, just as my lord says."

²⁸ So Moses gave command concerning them to Eleazar the priest, and to Joshua the son of Nun, and to the heads of the fathers' *households* of the tribes of the sons of Israel. ²⁹ Moses said to them, "If the sons of Gad and the sons of Reuben, everyone who is armed for battle, will cross with you over the Jordan in the presence of the LORD, and the land is subdued before you, then you shall give them the land of Gilead for a possession; ³⁰ but if they will not cross over with you armed, they shall have possessions among you in the land of Canaan." ³¹ The sons of Gad and the sons of Reuben answered, saying, "As the LORD has said to your servants, so we will do. ³² We ourselves will cross over armed in the presence of the LORD into the land of Canaan, and the possession of our inheritance *shall remain* with us across the Jordan."

³³ So Moses gave to them, to the sons of Gad and to the sons of Reuben and to the half-tribe of Joseph's son Manasseh, the kingdom of Sihon, king of the Amorites and the kingdom of Og, the king of Bashan, the land with its cities with *their* territories, the cities of the surrounding land. ³⁴ The sons of Gad built Dibon and Ataroth and Aroer, ³⁵ and Atroth-shophan and Jazer and Jogbehah, ³⁶ and Beth-nimrah and Beth-haran as fortified cities, and sheepfolds for sheep. ³⁷ The sons of Reuben built Heshbon and Elealeh and Kiriathaim, ³⁸ and Nebo and Baal-meon—*their* names being changed—and Sibmah, and they gave *other* names to the cities which they built. ³⁹ The sons of Machir the son of Manasseh went to Gilead and took it, and dispossessed the Amorites who were in it. ⁴⁰ So Moses gave Gilead to Machir the son of Manasseh, and he lived in it. ⁴¹ Jair the son of Manasseh went and took its towns, and called them Havvoth-jair. ⁴² Nobah went and took Kenath and its villages, and called it Nobah after his own name.

32:23 your sin will find you out. The two tribes committed themselves to provide their warriors for the conquest of the land. This agreement satisfied Moses, although he added that nonparticipation would be sin, and God would certainly find and judge the tribes for their sin.

Psalm 35:1–8

A Psalm of David.

C ontend, O LORD, with those
who contend with me;
Fight against those who
fight against me.
² Take hold of buckler and shield
And rise up for my help.

3 Draw also the spear and the battle-axe
to meet those who pursue me;
Say to my soul, "I am your salvation."
4 Let those be ashamed and
dishonored who seek my life;
Let those be turned back and
humiliated who devise
evil against me.
5 Let them be like chaff
before the wind,
With the angel of the LORD
driving *them* on.
6 Let their way be dark and slippery,
With the angel of the LORD
pursuing them.
7 For without cause they hid
their net for me;
Without cause they dug
a pit for my soul.
8 Let destruction come upon
him unawares,
And let the net which he
hid catch himself;
Into that very destruction let him fall.

Proverbs 12:1

12 Whoever loves discipline
loves knowledge,
But he who hates reproof is stupid.

Mark 14:53-72

53 They led Jesus away to the high priest;
and all the chief priests and the elders and
the scribes *gathered together. 54 Peter had
followed Him at a distance, right into the
courtyard of the high priest; and he was sitting with the officers and warming himself
at the fire. 55 Now the chief priests and the
whole Council kept trying to obtain testimony against Jesus to put Him to death, and
they were not finding any. 56 For many were
giving false testimony against Him, but their
testimony was not consistent. 57 Some stood
up and *began* to give false testimony against
Him, saying, 58 "We heard Him say, 'I will
destroy this temple made with hands, and
in three days I will build another made without hands.'" 59 Not even in this respect was
their testimony consistent. 60 The high priest
stood up and *came* forward and questioned
Jesus, saying, "Do You not answer? What
is it that these men are testifying against
You?" 61 But He kept silent and did not answer. Again the high priest was questioning
Him, and saying to Him, "Are You the Christ,
the Son of the Blessed *One*?" 62 And Jesus
said, "I am; and you shall see THE SON OF
MAN SITTING AT THE RIGHT HAND OF POWER,
and COMING WITH THE CLOUDS OF HEAVEN."
63 Tearing his clothes, the high priest *said,
"What further need do we have of witnesses?
64 You have heard the blasphemy; how does it
seem to you?" And they all condemned Him
to be deserving of death. 65 Some began to
spit at Him, and to blindfold Him, and to
beat Him with their fists, and to say to Him,
"Prophesy!" And the officers received Him
with slaps *in the face.*
66 As Peter was below in the courtyard,
one of the servant-girls of the high priest
*came, 67 and seeing Peter warming himself,
she looked at him and *said, "You also were
with Jesus the Nazarene." 68 But he denied
it, saying, "I neither know nor understand
what you are talking about." And he went
out onto the porch. 69 The servant-girl saw
him, and began once more to say to the bystanders, "This is *one* of them!" 70 But again
he denied it. And after a little while the bystanders were again saying to Peter, "Surely
you are *one* of them, for you are a Galilean
too." 71 But he began to curse and swear, "I do
not know this man you are talking about!"
72 Immediately a rooster crowed a second
time. And Peter remembered how Jesus had
made the remark to him, "Before a rooster
crows twice, you will deny Me three times."
And he began to weep.

14:56 Because Jesus was innocent, the Jewish leaders could not convict Him except by
relying on perjured testimony and perverted
justice. The Jews were intent on doing whatever was necessary, even if they had to violate
every biblical and rabbinical rule. **many were
giving false testimony against Him.** There
was no lack of people to come forward at the
Sanhedrin's invitation to consciously present
false, lying testimony. **was not consistent.** The
testimonies were grossly inconsistent. The law,
however, required exact agreement between
two witnesses (Dt 17:6; 19:15).

14:65 spit at Him...beat Him. For the Jews,
to "spit" in another's face was the grossest,
most hateful form of personal insult (Nu
12:14; Dt 25:9). Their brutal cruelty reached
a climax and revealed the great depravity of
their hearts when they "beat Him," or hit Him
with clenched fists. **Prophesy!** They jeeringly
and disrespectfully ordered Jesus to use the
prophetic powers He claimed to have—even
in the frivolous manner of telling them who
struck Him (Mt 26:68).

DAY 17: Did Jesus claim to be God during His trial?

In Mark 14:61, when Caiaphas, the high priest, asked Jesus if He was the "Christ," the term refers to Jesus' claim to be the promised Messiah. The "Son of the Blessed One" clearly refers to Jesus' claim to Deity. This is the only New Testament use of the expression, and it is an example of Jewish wording that avoided using God's name. Jesus' acceptance of messiahship and Deity (see Lk 4:18–21; Jn 4:25–26; 5:17, 18; 8:58) had always brought vigorous opposition from the Jewish leaders (Jn 5:19–47; 8:16–19; 10:29–39). Clearly, the high priest was asking this question in hopes that Jesus would affirm it and open Himself to the formal charge of blasphemy.

Jesus' response that "I am" (v. 62) was an explicit, unambiguous declaration that He was and is both the Messiah and "the Son of Man"—Jesus used this commonly acknowledged messianic title of Himself more than 80 times in the Gospels, here in a reference to Psalm 110:1 and Daniel 7:13 (see Rev 1:13; 14:14). He added that His glorified position is next to the throne of God, "THE RIGHT HAND OF POWER." Jesus' "Power" is another reference to God.

That Jesus' declaration was understood is seen when the high priest "[tore] his clothes" (v. 63), a ceremonial, and in this case contrived, display of grief and indignation over the presumed dishonoring of God's name by Jesus (see Ge 37:29; Lv 10:6; Job 1:20; Ac 14:13, 19). Strictly speaking, Jesus' words were not "blasphemy" (v. 64) or defiant irreverence of God (Lv 24:10–23), but Caiaphas regarded them as such because Jesus claimed for Himself equal power and prerogative with God.

MARCH 18

Numbers 33:1–34:29

33 These are the journeys of the sons of Israel, by which they came out from the land of Egypt by their armies, under the leadership of Moses and Aaron. ² Moses recorded their starting places according to their journeys by the command of the LORD, and these are their journeys according to their starting places. ³ They journeyed from Rameses in the first month, on the fifteenth day of the first month; on the next day after the Passover the sons of Israel started out boldly in the sight of all the Egyptians, ⁴ while the Egyptians were burying all their firstborn whom the LORD had struck down among them. The LORD had also executed judgments on their gods.

⁵ Then the sons of Israel journeyed from Rameses and camped in Succoth. ⁶ They journeyed from Succoth and camped in Etham, which is on the edge of the wilderness. ⁷ They journeyed from Etham and turned back to Pi-hahiroth, which faces Baal-zephon, and they camped before Migdol. ⁸ They journeyed from before Hahiroth and passed through the midst of the sea into the wilderness; and they went three days' journey in the wilderness of Etham and camped at Marah. ⁹ They journeyed from Marah and came to Elim; and in Elim there were twelve springs of water and seventy palm trees, and they camped there. ¹⁰ They journeyed from Elim and camped by the Red Sea. ¹¹ They journeyed from the Red Sea and camped in the wilderness of Sin. ¹² They journeyed from the wilderness of Sin and camped at Dophkah.

¹³ They journeyed from Dophkah and camped at Alush. ¹⁴ They journeyed from Alush and camped at Rephidim; now it was there that the people had no water to drink. ¹⁵ They journeyed from Rephidim and camped in the wilderness of Sinai. ¹⁶ They journeyed from the wilderness of Sinai and camped at Kibroth-hattaavah.

¹⁷ They journeyed from Kibroth-hattaavah and camped at Hazeroth. ¹⁸ They journeyed from Hazeroth and camped at Rithmah. ¹⁹ They journeyed from Rithmah and camped at Rimmon-perez. ²⁰ They journeyed from Rimmon-perez and camped at Libnah. ²¹ They journeyed from Libnah and camped at Rissah. ²² They journeyed from Rissah and camped in Kehelathah. ²³ They journeyed from Kehelathah and camped at Mount Shepher. ²⁴ They journeyed from Mount Shepher and camped at Haradah. ²⁵ They journeyed from Haradah and camped at Makheloth. ²⁶ They journeyed from Makheloth and camped at Tahath. ²⁷ They journeyed from Tahath and camped at Terah. ²⁸ They journeyed from Terah and camped at Mithkah. ²⁹ They journeyed from Mithkah and camped at Hashmonah. ³⁰ They journeyed from Hashmonah and camped at Moseroth. ³¹ They journeyed from Moseroth and camped at Bene-jaakan. ³² They journeyed from Bene-jaakan and camped at Hor-haggidgad. ³³ They journeyed from Hor-haggidgad and camped at Jotbathah. ³⁴ They journeyed from Jotbathah and camped at Abronah. ³⁵ They journeyed from Abronah and camped at Ezion-geber. ³⁶ They journeyed from Ezion-geber and camped in the wilderness of Zin, that is, Kadesh. ³⁷ They journeyed from Kadesh and camped at Mount Hor, at the edge of the land of Edom.

[38]Then Aaron the priest went up to Mount Hor at the command of the LORD, and died there in the fortieth year after the sons of Israel had come from the land of Egypt, on the first *day* in the fifth month. [39]Aaron was one hundred twenty-three years old when he died on Mount Hor.

[40]Now the Canaanite, the king of Arad who lived in the Negev in the land of Canaan, heard of the coming of the sons of Israel.

[41]Then they journeyed from Mount Hor and camped at Zalmonah. [42]They journeyed from Zalmonah and camped at Punon. [43]They journeyed from Punon and camped at Oboth. [44]They journeyed from Oboth and camped at Iye-abarim, at the border of Moab. [45]They journeyed from Iyim and camped at Dibon-gad. [46]They journeyed from Dibon-gad and camped at Almon-diblathaim. [47]They journeyed from Almon-diblathaim and camped in the mountains of Abarim, before Nebo. [48]They journeyed from the mountains of Abarim and camped in the plains of Moab by the Jordan *opposite* Jericho. [49]They camped by the Jordan, from Beth-jeshimoth as far as Abel-shittim in the plains of Moab.

[50]Then the LORD spoke to Moses in the plains of Moab by the Jordan *opposite* Jericho, saying, [51]"Speak to the sons of Israel and say to them, 'When you cross over the Jordan into the land of Canaan, [52]then you shall drive out all the inhabitants of the land from before you, and destroy all their figured stones, and destroy all their molten images and demolish all their high places; [53]and you shall take possession of the land and live in it, for I have given the land to you to possess it. [54]You shall inherit the land by lot according to your families; to the larger you shall give more inheritance, and to the smaller you shall give less inheritance. Wherever the lot falls to anyone, that shall be his. You shall inherit according to the tribes of your fathers. [55]But if you do not drive out the inhabitants of the land from before you, then it shall come about that those whom you let remain of them *will become* as pricks in your eyes and as thorns in your sides, and they will trouble you in the land in which you live. [56]And as I plan to do to them, so I will do to you.'"

33:56 as I plan to do to them, so I will do to you. If Israel failed to obey God, she would be the object of God's punishment in exactly the same way as the Canaanites were.

---

34 Then the LORD spoke to Moses, saying, [2]"Command the sons of Israel and say to them, 'When you enter the land of Canaan, this is the land that shall fall to you as an inheritance, *even the* land of Canaan according to its borders. [3]Your southern sector shall extend from the wilderness of Zin along the side of Edom, and your southern border shall extend from the end of the Salt Sea eastward. [4]Then your border shall turn *direction* from the south to the ascent of Akrabbim and continue to Zin, and its termination shall be to the south of Kadesh-barnea; and it shall reach Hazaraddar and continue to Azmon. [5]The border shall turn *direction* from Azmon to the brook of Egypt, and its termination shall be at the sea.

[6]'As for the western border, you shall have the Great Sea, that is, *its* coastline; this shall be your west border.

[7]'And this shall be your north border: you shall draw your *border* line from the Great Sea to Mount Hor. [8]You shall draw a line from Mount Hor to the Lebo-hamath, and the termination of the border shall be at Zedad; [9]and the border shall proceed to Ziphron, and its termination shall be at Hazar-enan. This shall be your north border.

[10]'For your eastern border you shall also draw a line from Hazar-enan to Shepham, [11]and the border shall go down from Shepham to Riblah on the east side of Ain; and the border shall go down and reach to the slope on the east side of the Sea of Chinnereth. [12]And the border shall go down to the Jordan and its termination shall be at the Salt Sea. This shall be your land according to its borders all around.'"

[13]So Moses commanded the sons of Israel, saying, "This is the land that you are to apportion by lot among you as a possession, which the LORD has commanded to give to the nine and a half tribes. [14]For the tribe of the sons of Reuben have received *theirs* according to their fathers' households, and the tribe of the sons of Gad according to their fathers' households, and the half-tribe of Manasseh have received their possession. [15]The two and a half tribes have received their possession across the Jordan opposite Jericho, eastward toward the sunrising."

[16]Then the LORD spoke to Moses, saying, [17]"These are the names of the men who shall apportion the land to you for inheritance: Eleazar the priest and Joshua the son of Nun. [18]You shall take one leader of every tribe to apportion the land for inheritance. [19]These are the names of the men: of the tribe of

Judah, Caleb the son of Jephunneh. ²⁰Of the tribe of the sons of Simeon, Samuel the son of Ammihud. ²¹Of the tribe of Benjamin, Elidad the son of Chislon. ²²Of the tribe of the sons of Dan a leader, Bukki the son of Jogli. ²³Of the sons of Joseph: of the tribe of the sons of Manasseh a leader, Hanniel the son of Ephod. ²⁴Of the tribe of the sons of Ephraim a leader, Kemuel the son of Shiphtan. ²⁵Of the tribe of the sons of Zebulun a leader, Elizaphan the son of Parnach. ²⁶Of the tribe of the sons of Issachar a leader, Paltiel the son of Azzan. ²⁷Of the tribe of the sons of Asher a leader, Ahihud the son of Shelomi. ²⁸Of the tribe of the sons of Naphtali a leader, Pedahel the son of Ammihud." ²⁹These are those whom the LORD commanded to apportion the inheritance to the sons of Israel in the land of Canaan.

Psalm 35:9–16

9   And my soul shall rejoice in the LORD;
It shall exult in His salvation.
¹⁰ All my bones shall say, "LORD,
who is like You,
Who delivers the afflicted from
him who is too strong for him,
And the afflicted and the needy
from him who robs him?"

35:10 LORD, who is like You. This had become a canonized expression of awe at the uniqueness of Israel's great God (Ex 15:11; Mic 7:18).

¹¹ Malicious witnesses rise up;
They ask me of things that
I do not know.
¹² They repay me evil for good,
To the bereavement of my soul.
¹³ But as for me, when they were sick,
my clothing was sackcloth;
I humbled my soul with fasting,
And my prayer kept returning
to my bosom.
¹⁴ I went about as though it were
my friend or brother;
I bowed down mourning, as one
who sorrows for a mother.
¹⁵ But at my stumbling they rejoiced
and gathered themselves
together;
The smiters whom I did not know
gathered together against me,
They slandered me without ceasing.
¹⁶ Like godless jesters at a feast,
They gnashed at me with their teeth.

Proverbs 12:2

²   A good man will obtain
favor from the LORD,
But He will condemn a man
who devises evil.

Mark 15:1–26

15 Early in the morning the chief priests with the elders and scribes and the whole Council, immediately held a consultation; and binding Jesus, they led Him away and delivered Him to Pilate. ²Pilate questioned Him, "Are You the King of the Jews?" And He *answered him, "*It is as* you say." ³The chief priests *began* to accuse Him harshly. ⁴Then Pilate questioned Him again, saying, "Do You not answer? See how many charges they bring against You!" ⁵But Jesus made no further answer; so Pilate was amazed.

⁶Now at *the* feast he used to release for them *any* one prisoner whom they requested. ⁷The man named Barabbas had been imprisoned with the insurrectionists who had committed murder in the insurrection. ⁸The crowd went up and began asking him *to do* as he had been accustomed to do for them. ⁹Pilate answered them, saying, "Do you want me to release for you the King of the Jews?" ¹⁰For he was aware that the chief priests had handed Him over because of envy. ¹¹But the chief priests stirred up the crowd *to ask* him to release Barabbas for them instead. ¹²Answering again, Pilate said to them, "Then what shall I do with Him whom you call the King of the Jews?" ¹³They shouted back, "Crucify Him!" ¹⁴But Pilate said to them, "Why, what evil has He done?" But they shouted all the more, "Crucify Him!" ¹⁵Wishing to satisfy the crowd, Pilate released Barabbas for them, and after having Jesus scourged, he handed Him over to be crucified.

¹⁶The soldiers took Him away into the palace (that is, the Praetorium), and they *called together the whole *Roman* cohort. ¹⁷They *dressed Him up in purple, and after twisting a crown of thorns, they put it on Him; ¹⁸and

15:7 Barabbas. A robber (Jn 18:40) and murderer (Lk 23:18–19) in some way involved as an anti-Roman insurrectionist. Whether his involvement was motivated by political conviction or personal greed is not known. It is impossible to identify the specific insurrection in question, but such uprisings were common in Jesus' day and were precursors of the wholesale revolt of A.D. 66–70.

they began to acclaim Him, "Hail, King of the Jews!" ¹⁹They kept beating His head with a reed, and spitting on Him, and kneeling and bowing before Him. ²⁰After they had mocked Him, they took the purple robe off Him and put His *own* garments on Him. And they *led Him out to crucify Him.

²¹They *pressed into service a passer-by coming from the country, Simon of Cyrene (the father of Alexander and Rufus), to bear His cross.

²²Then they *brought Him to the place Golgotha, which is translated, Place of a Skull. ²³They tried to give Him wine mixed with myrrh; but He did not take it. ²⁴And they *crucified Him, and *divided up His garments among themselves, casting lots for them *to decide* what each man should take. ²⁵It was the third hour when they crucified Him. ²⁶The inscription of the charge against Him read,

"THE KING OF THE JEWS."

15:17 dressed Him up in purple...crown of thorns. "Purple" was the color traditionally worn by royalty. The "crown of thorns" was in mockery of a royal crown. The callous soldiers decided to hold a mock coronation of Jesus as king of the Jews.

15:21 Condemned prisoners were required to carry the heavy crossbeam of their cross to the execution site. Exhausted from a sleepless night and severely wounded and weakened by His scourging, Jesus was unable to continue. The Roman guards conscripted Simon, apparently at random, to carry Jesus' crossbeam the rest of the way. Simon, from the North African city of Cyrene, was on his way into Jerusalem. The identification of him as "the father of Alexander and Rufus" (Ro 16:13) is evidence of Mark's connection with the church at Rome.

DAY 18: What are some general, time-tested principles that will help rightly interpret Proverbs?

One of the most common characteristics of Proverbs is the use of parallelism—placing truths side by side so that the second statement expands, completes, defines, and emphasizes the first. Sometimes a logical conclusion is reached; at other times, a logical contrast is demonstrated.

The following tools will assist a student in gaining greater confidence as he or she interprets these Proverbs: 1) determine what facts, principles, or circumstances make up the parallel ideas in that proverb—what two central concepts or persons are being compared or contrasted; 2) identify the figures of speech and rephrase the thought without those figures—for example, restate the idea behind "put a knife to your throat" (23:1-3); 3) summarize the lesson or principle of the proverb in a few words; 4) describe the behavior that is being taught or encouraged; and 5) think of examples from elsewhere in Scripture that illustrate the truth of that proverb.

MARCH 19

Numbers 35:1–36:13

35 Now the LORD spoke to Moses in the plains of Moab by the Jordan *opposite* Jericho, saying, ²"Command the sons of Israel that they give to the Levites from the inheritance of their possession cities to live in; and you shall give to the Levites pasture lands around the cities. ³The cities shall be theirs to live in; and their pasture lands shall be for their cattle and for their herds and for all their beasts.

⁴"The pasture lands of the cities which you shall give to the Levites *shall extend* from the wall of the city outward a thousand cubits around. ⁵You shall also measure outside the city on the east side two thousand cubits, and on the south side two thousand cubits, and on the west side two thousand cubits, and on the north side two thousand cubits, with the city in the center. This shall become theirs as pasture lands for the cities. ⁶The cities which you shall give to the Levites *shall be* the six cities of refuge, which you shall give for the manslayer to flee to; and in addition to them you shall give forty-two cities. ⁷All the cities which you shall give to the Levites *shall be* forty-eight cities, together with their pasture lands. ⁸As for the cities which you shall give from the possession of the sons of Israel, you shall take more from the larger and you shall take less from the smaller; each shall give some of his cities to the Levites in proportion to his possession which he inherits."

⁹Then the LORD spoke to Moses, saying, ¹⁰"Speak to the sons of Israel and say to them, 'When you cross the Jordan into the land of Canaan, ¹¹then you shall select for yourselves cities

to be your cities of refuge, that the manslayer who has killed any person unintentionally may flee there. ¹²The cities shall be to you as a refuge from the avenger, so that the manslayer will not die until he stands before the congregation for trial. ¹³The cities which you are to give shall be your six cities of refuge. ¹⁴You shall give three cities across the Jordan and three cities in the land of Canaan; they are to be cities of refuge. ¹⁵These six cities shall be for refuge for the sons of Israel, and for the alien and for the sojourner among them; that anyone who kills a person unintentionally may flee there.

35:12 the avenger. The meaning of this term is "near of kin." It refers to the person chosen by a family to deal with a loss suffered in that family. Here the close relative of a homicide victim would seek to avenge his death, but not until proper judgment was made.

¹⁶'But if he struck him down with an iron object, so that he died, he is a murderer; the murderer shall surely be put to death. ¹⁷If he struck him down with a stone in the hand, by which he will die, and *as a result* he died, he is a murderer; the murderer shall surely be put to death. ¹⁸Or if he struck him with a wooden object in the hand, by which he might die, and *as a result* he died, he is a murderer; the murderer shall surely be put to death. ¹⁹The blood avenger himself shall put the murderer to death; he shall put him to death when he meets him. ²⁰If he pushed him of hatred, or threw something at him lying in wait and *as a result* he died, ²¹or if he struck him down with his hand in enmity, and *as a result* he died, the one who struck him shall surely be put to death, he is a murderer; the blood avenger shall put the murderer to death when he meets him. ²²'But if he pushed him suddenly without enmity, or threw something at him without lying in wait, ²³or with any deadly object of stone, and without seeing it dropped on him so that he died, while he was not his enemy nor seeking his injury, ²⁴then the congregation shall judge between the slayer and the blood avenger according to these ordinances. ²⁵The congregation shall deliver the manslayer from the hand of the blood avenger, and the congregation shall restore him to his city of refuge to which he fled; and he shall live in it until the death of the high priest who was anointed with the holy oil. ²⁶But if the manslayer at any time goes beyond the border of his city of

refuge to which he may flee, ²⁷and the blood avenger finds him outside the border of his city of refuge, and the blood avenger kills the manslayer, he will not be guilty of blood ²⁸because he should have remained in his city of refuge until the death of the high priest. But after the death of the high priest the manslayer shall return to the land of his possession. ²⁹'These things shall be for a statutory ordinance to you throughout your generations in all your dwellings. ³⁰'If anyone kills a person, the murderer shall be put to death at the evidence of witnesses, but no person shall be put to death on the testimony of one witness. ³¹Moreover, you shall not take ransom for the life of a murderer who is guilty of death, but he shall surely be put to death. ³²You shall not take ransom for him who has fled to his city of refuge, that he may return to live in the land before the death of the priest. ³³So you shall not pollute the land in which you are; for blood pollutes the land and no expiation can be made for the land for the blood that is shed on it, except by the blood of him who shed it. ³⁴You shall not defile the land in which you live, in the midst of which I dwell; for I the LORD am dwelling in the midst of the sons of Israel.'"

35:33 blood pollutes the land. Though murder and inadvertent killing polluted the land, murder was atoned for by the death of the murderer. Failure to observe these principles would make the land unclean. If the whole land became unclean, then the Lord would no longer be able to dwell in their midst.

36 And the heads of the fathers' *households* of the family of the sons of Gilead, the son of Machir, the son of Manasseh, of the families of the sons of Joseph, came near and spoke before Moses and before the leaders, the heads of the fathers' *households* of the sons of Israel, ²and they said, "The LORD commanded my lord to give the land by lot to the sons of Israel as an inheritance, and my lord was commanded by the LORD to give the inheritance of Zelophehad our brother to his daughters. ³But if they marry one of the sons of the *other* tribes of the sons of Israel, their inheritance will be withdrawn from the inheritance of our fathers and will be added to the inheritance of the tribe to which they belong; thus it will be withdrawn from our allotted inheritance. ⁴When the jubilee of the sons of Israel comes, then their inheritance will be added to the inheritance of the tribe to which they belong; so their inheritance will be withdrawn from the inheritance of the tribe of our fathers."

⁵ Then Moses commanded the sons of Israel according to the word of the LORD, saying, "The tribe of the sons of Joseph are right in *their* statements. ⁶ This is what the LORD has commanded concerning the daughters of Zelophehad, saying, 'Let them marry whom they wish; only they must marry within the family of the tribe of their father.' ⁷ Thus no inheritance of the sons of Israel shall be transferred from tribe to tribe, for the sons of Israel shall each hold to the inheritance of the tribe of his fathers. ⁸ Every daughter who comes into possession of an inheritance of any tribe of the sons of Israel shall be wife to one of the family of the tribe of her father, so that the sons of Israel each may possess the inheritance of his fathers. ⁹ Thus no inheritance shall be transferred from one tribe to another tribe, for the tribes of the sons of Israel shall each hold to his own inheritance."

¹⁰ Just as the LORD had commanded Moses, so the daughters of Zelophehad did: ¹¹ Mahlah, Tirzah, Hoglah, Milcah and Noah, the daughters of Zelophehad married their uncles' sons. ¹² They married *those* from the families of the sons of Manasseh the son of Joseph, and their inheritance remained with the tribe of the family of their father.

¹³ These are the commandments and the ordinances which the LORD commanded to the sons of Israel through Moses in the plains of Moab by the Jordan *opposite* Jericho.

Psalm 35:17–28

¹⁷ Lord, how long will You look on?
Rescue my soul from their ravages,
My only *life* from the lions.
¹⁸ I will give You thanks in the
great congregation;
I will praise You among a
mighty throng.
¹⁹ Do not let those who are wrongfully
my enemies rejoice over me;
Nor let those who hate me without
cause wink maliciously.
²⁰ For they do not speak peace,
But they devise deceitful words
against those who are
quiet in the land.
²¹ They opened their mouth
wide against me;
They said, "Aha, aha, our
eyes have seen it!"

35:21–22 our eyes have seen it! You have seen it, O LORD. What David's enemy allegedly saw, the Lord has seen perfectly. David knew that his God would vindicate him based upon the true evidence, all in his favor.

²² You have seen it, O LORD,
do not keep silent;
O Lord, do not be far from me.
²³ Stir up Yourself, and awake to my right
And to my cause, my God and my Lord.
²⁴ Judge me, O LORD my God, according
to Your righteousness,
And do not let them rejoice over me.
²⁵ Do not let them say in their
heart, "Aha, our desire!"
Do not let them say, "We have
swallowed him up!"
²⁶ Let those be ashamed and
humiliated altogether who
rejoice at my distress;
Let those be clothed with shame
and dishonor who magnify
themselves over me.
²⁷ Let them shout for joy and rejoice,
who favor my vindication;
And let them say continually,
"The LORD be magnified,
Who delights in the prosperity
of His servant."
²⁸ And my tongue shall declare
Your righteousness
And Your praise all day long.

15:26 inscription of the charge. The crime for which a condemned man was executed was written on a wooden board, which was fastened to the cross above his head. Jesus' inscription was written in Latin, Hebrew, and Greek (Jn 19:20). **THE KING OF THE JEWS.** Since Pilate had repeatedly declared Jesus to be innocent of any crime (Lk 23:4, 14–15, 22), he ordered this inscription written for Him. While Pilate's intent was probably neither to mock nor to honor Jesus, he certainly intended it as an affront to the Jewish authorities, who had given him so much trouble. When the outraged Jewish leaders demanded the wording be changed, Pilate bluntly refused. A comparison of all 4 gospel accounts reveals that the full inscription read THIS IS JESUS OF NAZARETH, THE KING OF THE JEWS.

Proverbs 12:3

3 A man will not be established
 by wickedness,
But the root of the righteous
 will not be moved.

Mark 15:27–47

27 They *crucified two robbers with Him, one on His right and one on His left. 28 [And the Scripture was fulfilled which says, "And He was numbered with transgressors."] 29 Those passing by were hurling abuse at Him, wagging their heads, and saying, "Ha! You who *are going to* destroy the temple and rebuild it in three days, 30 save Yourself, and come down from the cross!" 31 In the same way the chief priests also, along with the scribes, were mocking *Him* among themselves and saying, "He saved others; He cannot save Himself. 32 Let *this* Christ, the King of Israel, now come down from the cross, so that we may see and believe!" Those who were crucified with Him were also insulting Him.

33 When the sixth hour came, darkness fell over the whole land until the ninth hour. 34 At the ninth hour Jesus cried out with a loud voice, "ELOI, ELOI, LAMA SABACHTHANI?" which is translated, "MY GOD, MY GOD, WHY HAVE YOU FORSAKEN ME?" 35 When some of the bystanders heard it, they *began* saying, "Behold, He is calling for Elijah." 36 Someone ran and filled a sponge with sour wine, put it on a reed, and gave Him a drink, saying, "Let us see whether Elijah will come to take Him down." 37 And Jesus uttered a loud cry, and breathed His last. 38 And the veil of the temple was torn in two from top to bottom. 39 When the cen-

---

15:38 the veil of the temple was torn in two. The massive curtain separating the Holy of Holies from the rest of the sanctuary (Ex 26:31–33; 40:20–21; Lv 16:2; Heb 9:3). This rending signified that the way into God's presence was open by the death of His Son.

---

turion, who was standing right in front of Him, saw the way He breathed His last, he said, "Truly this man was the Son of God!"

40 There were also *some* women looking on from a distance, among whom *were* Mary Magdalene, and Mary the mother of James the Less and Joses, and Salome. 41 When He was in Galilee, they used to follow Him and minister to Him; and *there were* many other women who came up with Him to Jerusalem.

42 When evening had already come, because it was the preparation day, that is, the day before the Sabbath, 43 Joseph of Arimathea came, a prominent member of the Council, who himself was waiting for the kingdom of God; and he gathered up courage and went in before Pilate, and asked for the body of Jesus. 44 Pilate wondered if He was dead by this time, and summoning the centurion, he questioned him as to whether He was already dead. 45 And ascertaining this from the centurion, he granted the body to Joseph. 46 Joseph bought a linen cloth, took Him down, wrapped Him in the linen cloth and laid Him in a tomb which had been hewn out in the rock; and he rolled a stone against the entrance of the tomb. 47 Mary Magdalene and Mary the *mother* of Joses were looking on *to see* where He was laid.

DAY 19: What happened to Jesus after His death?

Joseph of Arimathea, a prominent member of the "Council" (or the Sanhedrin), who had opposed Jesus' condemnation (Lk 23:51), took courage and came forward (Mk 15:43). Pilate would not likely have been pleased to see a member of the Sanhedrin, after that group had forced him to crucify an innocent man. Further, Joseph's public identification with Jesus would enrage the other members of the Sanhedrin. Nevertheless, he "asked for the body of Jesus."

"Pilate wondered" that Jesus was already dead (v. 44). Victims of crucifixion often lingered for days, hence Pilate's surprise that Jesus was dead after only 6 hours. Before granting Jesus' body to Joseph, Pilate checked with the "centurion" in charge of the crucifixion to verify that Jesus was really dead. Having received confirmation from the centurion that Jesus was dead, Pilate granted Jesus' body to Joseph (v. 45). By that act, the Romans officially pronounced Jesus dead.

Then Jesus' body was wrapped in the linen (v. 46). The Jews did not embalm corpses but wrapped them in perfumed burial cloths. Nicodemus, another prominent member of the Sanhedrin (see Jn 7:50), assisted Joseph in caring for the body of Jesus (Jn 19:39–40). These men, who had kept their allegiance to Jesus secret during His lifetime, then came forward publicly to bury Him, while the disciples, who had openly followed Jesus, hid (Jn 20:19). Then they laid Jesus in a "tomb… hewn out in the rock." This "tomb" was located near Golgotha (Jn 19:42). Matthew adds that it was Joseph's own tomb (Mt 27:60), while Luke and John note that no one as yet had been buried in it (Lk 23:53; Jn 19:41).

MARCH 20

Deuteronomy 1:1–2:37

1 These are the words which Moses spoke to all Israel across the Jordan in the wilderness, in the Arabah opposite Suph, between Paran and Tophel and Laban and Hazeroth and Dizahab. ² It is eleven days' *journey* from Horeb by the way of Mount Seir to Kadesh-barnea. ³ In the fortieth year, on the first *day* of the eleventh month, Moses spoke to the children of Israel, according to all that the LORD had commanded him *to give* to them, ⁴ after he had defeated Sihon the king of the Amorites, who lived in Heshbon, and Og the king of Bashan, who lived in Ashtaroth and Edrei. ⁵ Across the Jordan in the land of Moab, Moses undertook to expound this law, saying,

⁶ "The LORD our God spoke to us at Horeb, saying, 'You have stayed long enough at this mountain. ⁷ Turn and set your journey, and go to the hill country of the Amorites, and to all their neighbors in the Arabah, in the hill country and in the lowland and in the Negev and by the seacoast, the land of the Canaanites, and Lebanon, as far as the great river, the river Euphrates. ⁸ See, I have placed the land before you; go in and possess the land which the LORD swore to give to your fathers, to Abraham, to Isaac, and to Jacob, to them and their descendants after them.'

⁹ "I spoke to you at that time, saying, 'I am not able to bear *the burden* of you alone. ¹⁰ The

---

1:7–8 the land. The land which the Lord set before Israel to go in and possess was clearly described in v. 7. The hill country of the Amorites referred to the mountainous territory west of the Dead Sea. The Arabah was the land in the rift valley from the Sea of Galilee in the north to the Dead Sea in the south. The hill country referred to the hills that run through the center of the land north and south. These hills are to the west of the Sea of Galilee and the Jordan River. The lowland referred to the low rolling hills that sloped toward the Mediterranean coast (Shephelah). The Negev described the dry wasteland stretching southward from Beersheba to the wilderness. The seacoast referred to the land along the Mediterranean Sea. The boundaries of the land of the Canaanites were given in Numbers 34:1–15. Lebanon to the north marked the northwestern boundary on the coast. The northeast boundary of the land was the Euphrates River. See Numbers 34:1–12.

LORD your God has multiplied you, and behold, you are this day like the stars of heaven in number. ¹¹ May the LORD, the God of your fathers, increase you a thousand-fold more than you are and bless you, just as He has

---

1:10 the stars of heaven. The Lord had promised Abraham that his descendants would be as numerous as the stars in the sky (Ge 15:5; 22:17). The nation's growth proved both God's intention and ability to fulfill His original promises to Abraham.

---

promised you! ¹² How can I alone bear the load and burden of you and your strife? ¹³ Choose wise and discerning and experienced men from your tribes, and I will appoint them as your heads.' ¹⁴ You answered me and said, 'The thing which you have said to do is good.' ¹⁵ So I took the heads of your tribes, wise and experienced men, and appointed them heads over you, leaders of thousands and of hundreds, of fifties and of tens, and officers for your tribes.

¹⁶ "Then I charged your judges at that time, saying, 'Hear *the cases* between your fellow countrymen, and judge righteously between a man and his fellow countryman, or the alien who is with him. ¹⁷ You shall not show partiality in judgment; you shall hear the small and the great alike. You shall not fear man, for the judgment is God's. The case that is too hard for you, you shall bring to me, and I will hear it.' ¹⁸ I commanded you at that time all the things that you should do.

¹⁹ "Then we set out from Horeb, and went through all that great and terrible wilderness which you saw on the way to the hill country of the Amorites, just as the LORD our God had commanded us; and we came to Kadesh-barnea. ²⁰ I said to you, 'You have come to the hill country of the Amorites which the LORD our God is about to give us. ²¹ See, the LORD your God has placed the land before you; go up, take possession, as the LORD, the God of your fathers, has spoken to you. Do not fear or be dismayed.'

²² "Then all of you approached me and said, 'Let us send men before us, that they may search out the land for us, and bring back to us word of the way by which we should go up and the cities which we shall enter.' ²³ The thing pleased me and I took twelve of your men, one man for each tribe. ²⁴ They turned and went up into the hill country, and came to the valley of Eshcol and spied it out. ²⁵ Then

they took *some* of the fruit of the land in their hands and brought it down to us; and they brought us back a report and said, 'It is a good land which the LORD our God is about to give us.'

²⁶ "Yet you were not willing to go up, but rebelled against the command of the LORD your God; ²⁷ and you grumbled in your tents and said, 'Because the LORD hates us, He has brought us out of the land of Egypt to deliver us into the hand of the Amorites to destroy us. ²⁸ Where can we go up? Our brethren have made our hearts melt, saying, "The people are bigger and taller than we; the cities are large and fortified to heaven. And besides, we saw the sons of the Anakim there."' ²⁹ Then I said to you, 'Do not be shocked, nor fear them. ³⁰ The LORD your God who goes before you will Himself fight on your behalf, just as He did for you in Egypt before your eyes, ³¹ and in the wilderness where you saw how the LORD your God carried you, just as a man carries his son, in all the way which you have walked until you came to this place.' ³² But for all this, you did not trust the LORD your God, ³³ who goes before you on *your* way, to seek out a place for you to encamp, in fire by night and cloud by day, to show you the way in which you should go.

³⁴ "Then the LORD heard the sound of your words, and He was angry and took an oath, saying, ³⁵ 'Not one of these men, this evil generation, shall see the good land which I swore to give your fathers, ³⁶ except Caleb the son of Jephunneh; he shall see it, and to him and to his sons I will give the land on which he has set foot, because he has followed the LORD fully.' ³⁷ The LORD was angry with me also on your account, saying, 'Not even you shall enter there. ³⁸ Joshua the son of Nun, who stands before you, he shall enter there; encourage him, for he will cause Israel to inherit it. ³⁹ Moreover, your little ones who you said would become a prey, and your sons, who this day have no knowledge of good or evil, shall enter there, and I will give it to them and they shall possess it. ⁴⁰ But as for you, turn around and set out for the wilderness by the way to the Red Sea.'

⁴¹ "Then you said to me, 'We have sinned against the LORD; we will indeed go up and fight, just as the LORD our God commanded us.' And every man of you girded on his weapons of war, and regarded it as easy to go up into the hill country. ⁴² And the LORD said to me, 'Say to them, "Do not go up nor fight, for I am not among you; otherwise you will be defeated before your enemies."' ⁴³ So I spoke

to you, but you would not listen. Instead you rebelled against the command of the LORD, and acted presumptuously and went up into the hill country. ⁴⁴ The Amorites who lived in that hill country came out against you and chased you as bees do, and crushed you from Seir to Hormah. ⁴⁵ Then you returned and wept before the LORD; but the LORD did not listen to your voice nor give ear to you. ⁴⁶ So you remained in Kadesh many days, the days that you spent *there*.

2 "Then we turned and set out for the wilderness by the way to the Red Sea, as the LORD spoke to me, and circled Mount Seir for many days. ² And the LORD spoke to me, saying, ³ 'You have circled this mountain long enough. *Now* turn north, ⁴ and command the people, saying, "You will pass through the territory of your brothers the sons of Esau who live in Seir; and they will be afraid of you. So be very careful; ⁵ do not provoke them, for I will not give you any of their land, even *as little as* a footstep because I have given Mount Seir to Esau as a possession. ⁶ You shall buy food from them with money so that you may eat, and you shall also purchase water from them with money so that you may drink. ⁷ For the LORD your God has blessed you in all that you have done; He has known your wanderings through this great wilderness. These forty years the LORD your God has been with you; you have not lacked a thing."'

⁸ "So we passed beyond our brothers the sons of Esau, who live in Seir, away from the Arabah road, away from Elath and from Ezion-geber. And we turned and passed through by the way of the wilderness of Moab. ⁹ Then the LORD said to me, 'Do not harass Moab, nor provoke them to war, for I will not give you any of their land as a possession, because I have given Ar to the sons of Lot as a possession.' ¹⁰ (The Emim lived there formerly, a people as great, numerous, and tall as the Anakim. ¹¹ Like the Anakim, they are also regarded as Rephaim, but the Moabites call them Emim. ¹² The Horites formerly lived in Seir, but the sons of Esau dispossessed them and destroyed them from before them and settled in their place, just as Israel did to the land of their possession which the LORD gave to them.) ¹³ 'Now arise and cross over the brook Zered yourselves.' So we crossed over the brook Zered. ¹⁴ Now the time that it took for us to come from Kadesh-barnea until we crossed over the brook Zered was thirty-eight years, until all the generation of the men of war perished from within the camp, as the LORD had sworn to them. ¹⁵ Moreover the hand of

the LORD was against them, to destroy them from within the camp until they all perished.

16 "So it came about when all the men of war had finally perished from among the people, 17 that the LORD spoke to me, saying, 18 'Today you shall cross over Ar, the border of Moab. 19 When you come opposite the sons of Ammon, do not harass them nor provoke them, for I will not give you any of the land of the sons of Ammon as a possession, because I have given it to the sons of Lot as a possession.' 20 (It is also regarded as the land of the Rephaim, for Rephaim formerly lived in it, but the Ammonites call them Zamzummin, 21 a people as great, numerous, and tall as the Anakim, but the LORD destroyed them before them. And they dispossessed them and settled in their place, 22 just as He did for the sons of Esau, who live in Seir, when He destroyed the Horites from before them; they dispossessed them and settled in their place even to this day. 23 And the Avvim, who lived in villages as far as Gaza, the Caphtorim who came from Caphtor, destroyed them and lived in their place.) 24 'Arise, set out, and pass through the valley of Arnon. Look! I have given Sihon the Amorite, king of Heshbon, and his land into your hand; begin to take possession and contend with him in battle. 25 This day I will begin to put the dread and fear of you upon the peoples everywhere under the heavens, who, when they hear the report of you, will tremble and be in anguish because of you.'

26 "So I sent messengers from the wilderness of Kedemoth to Sihon king of Heshbon with words of peace, saying, 27 'Let me pass through your land, I will travel only on the highway; I will not turn aside to the right or to the left. 28 You will sell me food for money so that I may eat, and give me water for money so that I may drink, only let me pass through on foot, 29 just as the sons of Esau who live in Seir and the Moabites who live in Ar did for me, until I cross over the Jordan into the land which the LORD our God is giving to us.' 30 But Sihon king of Heshbon was not willing for us to pass through his land; for the LORD your God hardened his spirit and made his heart obstinate, in order to deliver him into your hand, as he is today. 31 The LORD said to me, 'See, I have begun to deliver Sihon and his land over to you. Begin to occupy, that you may possess his land.'

32 "Then Sihon with all his people came out to meet us in battle at Jahaz. 33 The LORD our God delivered him over to us, and we defeated him with his sons and all his people. 34 So we captured all his cities at that time and utterly destroyed the men, women and children of every city. We left no survivor. 35 We took only the animals as our booty and the spoil of the cities which we had captured. 36 From Aroer which is on the edge of the valley of Arnon and from the city which is in the valley, even to Gilead, there was no city that was too high for us; the LORD our God delivered all over to us. 37 Only you did not go near to the land of the sons of Ammon, all along the river Jabbok and the cities of the hill country, and wherever the LORD our God had commanded us.

Psalm 36:1–6

For the choir director. A Psalm
of David the servant of the LORD.

Transgression speaks to the
    ungodly within his heart;
There is no fear of God before his eyes.
2 For it flatters him in his own eyes
    Concerning the discovery of his
      iniquity and the hatred of it.
3 The words of his mouth are
    wickedness and deceit;
  He has ceased to be wise
    and to do good.
4 He plans wickedness upon his bed;
  He sets himself on a path
    that is not good;
  He does not despise evil.

5 Your lovingkindness, O LORD,
    extends to the heavens,
  Your faithfulness reaches to the skies.
6 Your righteousness is like
    the mountains of God;
  Your judgments are like a great deep.
  O LORD, You preserve man and beast.

Proverbs 12:4–6

4 An excellent wife is the
    crown of her husband,
  But she who shames him is like
    rottenness in his bones.
5 The thoughts of the righteous are just,
  But the counsels of the
    wicked are deceitful.
6 The words of the wicked lie
    in wait for blood,
  But the mouth of the upright
    will deliver them.

Mark 16:1–20

16 When the Sabbath was over, Mary Magdalene, and Mary the mother of James, and Salome, bought spices, so that they might come and anoint Him. 2 Very early on the first day of the week, they *came to the tomb when

the sun had risen. ³They were saying to one another, "Who will roll away the stone for us from the entrance of the tomb?" ⁴Looking up, they *saw that the stone had been rolled away, although it was extremely large. ⁵Entering the tomb, they saw a young man sitting at the right, wearing a white robe; and they were amazed. ⁶And he *said to them, "Do not be amazed; you are looking for Jesus the Nazarene, who has been crucified. He has risen; He is not here; behold, *here is* the place where they laid Him. ⁷But go, tell His disciples and Peter, 'He is going ahead of you to Galilee; there you will see Him, just as He told you.'" ⁸They went out and fled from the tomb, for trembling and astonishment had gripped them; and they said nothing to anyone, for they were afraid.

⁹[Now after He had risen early on the first day of the week, He first appeared to Mary

16:3 Who will roll away the stone…? Only Mark records this discussion on the way to the tomb. The women realized they had no men with them to move the heavy stone (v. 4) away from the entrance to the tomb. Since they last visited the tomb on Friday evening, they did not know it had been sealed and a guard posted, which took place on Saturday (Mt 27:62–66).

16:4 the stone had been rolled away. This was not to let Jesus out, but to let the witnesses in. The earthquake when the angel rolled away the stone (Mt 28:2) may have affected only the area around the tomb, since the women apparently did not feel it.

Magdalene, from whom He had cast out seven demons. ¹⁰She went and reported to those who had been with Him, while they were mourning and weeping. ¹¹When they heard that He was alive and had been seen by her, they refused to believe it.

¹²After that, He appeared in a different form to two of them while they were walking along on their way to the country. ¹³They went away and reported it to the others, but they did not believe them either.

¹⁴Afterward He appeared to the eleven themselves as they were reclining *at the table;* and He reproached them for their unbelief and hardness of heart, because they had not believed those who had seen Him after He had risen. ¹⁵And He said to them, "Go into all the world and preach the gospel to all creation. ¹⁶He who has believed and has been baptized shall be saved; but he who has disbelieved shall be condemned. ¹⁷These signs will accompany those who have believed: in My name they will cast out demons, they will speak with new tongues; ¹⁸they will pick up serpents, and if they drink any deadly *poison,* it will not hurt them; they will lay hands on the sick, and they will recover."

¹⁹So then, when the Lord Jesus had spoken to them, He was received up into heaven and sat down at the right hand of God. ²⁰And they went out and preached everywhere, while the Lord worked with them, and confirmed the word by the signs that followed.]

[*And they promptly reported all these instructions to Peter and his companions. And after that, Jesus Himself sent out through them from east to west the sacred and imperishable proclamation of eternal salvation.*]

DAY 20: Were the last 12 verses of Mark 16 originally in the Gospel?

The external evidence strongly suggests these verses were not originally part of Mark's Gospel. While the majority of Greek manuscripts contain these verses, the earliest and most reliable do not. A shorter ending also existed, but it is not included in the text. Further, some that include the passage note that it was missing from older Greek manuscripts, while others have scribal marks indicating the passage was considered spurious. The fourth-century church fathers Eusebius and Jerome noted that almost all of the Greek manuscripts available to them lacked vv. 9–20.

The internal evidence from this passage also weighs heavily against Mark's authorship. The grammatical transition between vv. 8 and 9 is abrupt and awkward. The vocabulary in these verses does not match the rest of Mark. Even the events and people mentioned in these verses appear in awkward fashion. For example, Mary Magdalene is introduced as if she were a new person on the scene rather than someone Mark had mentioned three times (v. 1; 15:40, 47). Clearly, Mark 16:9–20 represents an early attempt to complete Mark's Gospel.

While for the most part summarizing truths taught elsewhere in Scripture, these verses should always be compared with the rest of Scripture, and no doctrines should be formulated based solely on them. Further, in spite of all these considerations of the likely unreliability of this section, it is possible to be wrong on the issue. It is good to consider the meaning of this passage and leave it in the text, just as with John 7:53–8:11.

MARCH 21

Deuteronomy 3:1–4:49

3 "Then we turned and went up the road to Bashan, and Og, king of Bashan, with all his people came out to meet us in battle at Edrei. ² But the LORD said to me, 'Do not fear him, for I have delivered him and all his people and his land into your hand; and you shall do to him just as you did to Sihon king of the Amorites, who lived at Heshbon.' ³ So the LORD our God delivered Og also, king of Bashan, with all his people into our hand, and we smote them until no survivor was left. ⁴ We captured all his cities at that time; there was not a city which we did not take from them: sixty cities, all the region of Argob, the kingdom of Og in Bashan. ⁵ All these were cities fortified with high walls, gates and bars, besides a great many unwalled towns. ⁶ We utterly destroyed them, as we did to Sihon king of Heshbon, utterly destroying the men, women and children of every city. ⁷ But all the animals and the spoil of the cities we took as our booty.

⁸ "Thus we took the land at that time from the hand of the two kings of the Amorites who were beyond the Jordan, from the valley of Arnon to Mount Hermon ⁹ (Sidonians call Hermon Sirion, and the Amorites call it Senir): ¹⁰ all the cities of the plateau and all Gilead and all Bashan, as far as Salecah and Edrei, cities of the kingdom of Og in Bashan. ¹¹ (For only Og king of Bashan was left of the remnant of the Rephaim. Behold, his bedstead was an iron bedstead; it is in Rabbah of the sons of Ammon. Its length was nine cubits and its width four cubits by ordinary cubit.)

¹² "So we took possession of this land at that time. From Aroer, which is by the valley of Arnon, and half the hill country of Gilead and its cities I gave to the Reubenites and to the Gadites. ¹³ The rest of Gilead and all Bashan, the kingdom of Og, I gave to the half-tribe of Manasseh, all the region of Argob (concerning all Bashan, it is called the land of Rephaim. ¹⁴ Jair the son of Manasseh took all the region of Argob as far as the border of the Geshurites and the Maacathites, and called it, *that is,* Bashan, after his own name, Havvoth-jair, *as it is* to this day.) ¹⁵ To Machir I gave Gilead. ¹⁶ To the Reubenites and to the Gadites I gave from Gilead even as far as the valley of Arnon, the middle of the valley as a border and as far as the river Jabbok, the border of the sons of Ammon; ¹⁷ the Arabah also, with the Jordan as *a* border, from Chinnereth even as far as the sea of the Arabah, the Salt Sea, at the foot of the slopes of Pisgah on the east.

¹⁸ "Then I commanded you at that time, saying, 'The LORD your God has given you this land to possess it; all you valiant men shall cross over armed before your brothers, the sons of Israel. ¹⁹ But your wives and your little ones and your livestock (I know that you have much livestock) shall remain in your cities which I have given you, ²⁰ until the LORD gives rest to your fellow countrymen as to you, and they also possess the land which the LORD your God will give them beyond the Jordan. Then you may return every man to his possession which I have given you.' ²¹ I commanded Joshua at that time, saying, 'Your eyes have seen all that the LORD your God has done to these two kings; so the LORD shall do to all the kingdoms into which you are about to cross. ²² Do not fear them, for the LORD your God is the one fighting for you.'

²³ "I also pleaded with the LORD at that time, saying, ²⁴ 'O Lord GOD, You have begun to show Your servant Your greatness and Your strong hand; for what god is there in heaven or on earth who can do such works and mighty acts as Yours? ²⁵ Let me, I pray, cross over and see the fair land that is beyond the Jordan, that good hill country and Lebanon.' ²⁶ But the LORD was angry with me on your account, and would not listen to me; and the LORD said to me, 'Enough! Speak to Me no more of this matter. ²⁷ Go up to the top of Pisgah and lift up your eyes to the west and north and south and east, and see *it* with your eyes, for you shall not cross over this Jordan. ²⁸ But charge Joshua and encourage him and strengthen him, for he shall go across at the head of this people, and he will give them as an inheritance the land which you will see.' ²⁹ So we remained in the valley opposite Beth-peor.

4 "Now, O Israel, listen to the statutes and the judgments which I am teaching you to perform, so that you may live and go in and take possession of the land which the

3:11 an iron bedstead. The bedstead may actually have been a coffin, which would have been large enough to also hold tomb objects. The size of the "bedstead," 13.5 by 6 ft., emphasized the largeness of Og, who was a giant (the last of the Rephaim, a race of giants). As God had given Israel victory over the giant Og, so He would give them victory over the giants in the land.

LORD, the God of your fathers, is giving you. ²You shall not add to the word which I am commanding you, nor take away from it, that you may keep the commandments of the LORD your God which I command you. ³Your eyes have seen what the LORD has done in the case of Baal-peor, for all the men who followed Baal-peor, the LORD your God has destroyed them from among you. ⁴But you who held fast to the LORD your God are alive today, every one of you.

4:2 You shall not add...nor take away from. The Word that God had given to Israel through Moses was complete and sufficient to direct the people. Thus, this law, the gift of God at Horeb, could not be supplemented or reduced. Anything that adulterated or contradicted God's law would not be tolerated (12:32; Pr 30:6; Rev 22:18–19).

⁵"See, I have taught you statutes and judgments just as the LORD my God commanded me, that you should do thus in the land where you are entering to possess it. ⁶So keep and do *them*, for that is your wisdom and your understanding in the sight of the peoples who will hear all these statutes and say, 'Surely this great nation is a wise and understanding people.' ⁷For what great nation is there that has a god so near to it as is the LORD our God whenever we call on Him? ⁸Or what great nation is there that has statutes and judgments as righteous as this whole law which I am setting before you today?

⁹"Only give heed to yourself and keep your soul diligently, so that you do not forget the things which your eyes have seen and they do not depart from your heart all the days of your life; but make them known to your sons and your grandsons. ¹⁰Remember the day you stood before the LORD your God at Horeb, when the LORD said to me, 'Assemble the people to Me, that I may let them hear My words so they may learn to fear Me all the days they live on the earth, and that they may teach their children.' ¹¹You came near and stood at the foot of the mountain, and the mountain burned with fire to the *very* heart of the heavens: darkness, cloud and thick gloom. ¹²Then the LORD spoke to you from the midst of the fire; you heard the sound of words, but you saw no form—only a voice. ¹³So He declared to you His covenant which He commanded you to perform, *that is,* the Ten Commandments;

and He wrote them on two tablets of stone. ¹⁴The LORD commanded me at that time to teach you statutes and judgments, that you might perform them in the land where you are going over to possess it.

¹⁵"So watch yourselves carefully, since you did not see any form on the day the LORD spoke to you at Horeb from the midst of the fire, ¹⁶so that you do not act corruptly and make a graven image for yourselves in the form of any figure, the likeness of male or female, ¹⁷the likeness of any animal that is on the earth, the likeness of any winged bird that flies in the sky, ¹⁸the likeness of anything that creeps on the ground, the likeness of any fish that is in the water below the earth. ¹⁹And *beware* not to lift up your eyes to heaven and see the sun and the moon and the stars, all the host of heaven, and be drawn away and worship them and serve them, those which the LORD your God has allotted to all the peoples under the whole heaven. ²⁰But the LORD has taken you and brought you out of the iron furnace, from Egypt, to be a people for His own possession, as today.

²¹"Now the LORD was angry with me on your account, and swore that I would not cross the Jordan, and that I would not enter the good land which the LORD your God is giving you as an inheritance. ²²For I will die in this land, I shall not cross the Jordan, but you shall cross and take possession of this good land. ²³So watch yourselves, that you do not forget the covenant of the LORD your God which He made with you, and make for yourselves a graven image in the form of anything *against* which the LORD your God has commanded you. ²⁴For the LORD your God is a consuming fire, a jealous God.

²⁵"When you become the father of children and children's children and have remained long in the land, and act corruptly, and make an idol in the form of anything, and do that which is evil in the sight of the LORD your God *so as* to provoke Him to anger, ²⁶I call heaven and earth to witness against you today, that you will surely perish quickly from the land where you are going over the Jordan to possess it. You shall not live long on it, but will be utterly destroyed. ²⁷The LORD will scatter you among the peoples, and you will be left few in number among the nations where the LORD drives you. ²⁸There you will serve gods, the work of man's hands, wood and stone, which neither see nor hear nor eat nor smell. ²⁹But from there you will seek the LORD your God, and you will find *Him* if you search for Him with all your heart and all your soul. ³⁰When you are in distress

and all these things have come upon you, in the latter days you will return to the LORD your God and listen to His voice. [31] For the LORD your God is a compassionate God; He will not fail you nor destroy you nor forget the covenant with your fathers which He swore to them.

[32] "Indeed, ask now concerning the former days which were before you, since the day that God created man on the earth, and *inquire* from one end of the heavens to the other. Has *anything* been done like this great thing, or has *anything* been heard like it? [33] Has *any* people heard the voice of God speaking from the midst of the fire, as you have heard *it,* and survived? [34] Or has a god tried to go to take for himself a nation from within *another* nation by trials, by signs and wonders and by war and by a mighty hand and by an outstretched arm and by great terrors, as the LORD your God did for you in Egypt before your eyes? [35] To you it was shown that you might know that the LORD, He is God; there is no other besides Him. [36] Out of the heavens He let you hear His voice to discipline you; and on earth He let you see His great fire, and you heard His words from the midst of the fire. [37] Because He loved your fathers, therefore He chose their descendants after them. And He personally brought you from Egypt by His great power, [38] driving out from before you nations greater and mightier than you, to bring you in *and* to give you their land for an inheritance, as it is today. [39] Know therefore today, and take it to your heart, that the LORD, He is God in heaven above and on the earth below; there is no other. [40] So you shall keep His statutes and His commandments which I am giving you today, that it may go well with you and with your children after you, and that you may live long on the land which the LORD your God is giving you for all time."

[41] Then Moses set apart three cities across the Jordan to the east, [42] that a manslayer might flee there, who unintentionally slew his neighbor without having enmity toward him in time past; and by fleeing to one of these cities he might live: [43] Bezer in the wilderness on the plateau for the Reubenites, and Ramoth in Gilead for the Gadites, and Golan in Bashan for the Manassites.

[44] Now this is the law which Moses set before the sons of Israel; [45] these are the testimonies and the statutes and the ordinances which Moses spoke to the sons of Israel, when they came out from Egypt, [46] across the Jordan, in the valley opposite Beth-peor, in the land of Sihon king of the Amorites who lived at Heshbon, whom Moses and the sons of Israel defeated when they came out from Egypt. [47] They took possession of his land and the land of Og king of Bashan, the two kings of the Amorites, *who were* across the Jordan to the east, [48] from Aroer, which is on the edge of the valley of Arnon, even as far as Mount Sion (that is, Hermon), [49] with all the Arabah across the Jordan to the east, even as far as the sea of the Arabah, at the foot of the slopes of Pisgah.

Psalm 36:7–12

[7] How precious is Your
   lovingkindness, O God!
And the children of men take refuge
   in the shadow of Your wings.
[8] They drink their fill of the
   abundance of Your house;
And You give them to drink of
   the river of Your delights.
[9] For with You is the fountain of life;
In Your light we see light.
[10] O continue Your lovingkindness
   to those who know You,
And Your righteousness to
   the upright in heart.
[11] Let not the foot of pride come upon me,
And let not the hand of the
   wicked drive me away.
[12] There the doers of iniquity have fallen;
They have been thrust down
   and cannot rise.

Proverbs 12:7

[7] The wicked are overthrown
   and are no more,
But the house of the
   righteous will stand.

Luke 1:1–20

1 Inasmuch as many have undertaken to compile an account of the things accomplished among us, [2] just as they were handed down to us by those who from the beginning were eyewitnesses and servants of the word, [3] it seemed fitting for me as well, having investigated everything carefully from the beginning, to write *it* out for you in consecutive order, most excellent Theophilus; [4] so that you may know the exact truth about the things you have been taught.

[5] In the days of Herod, king of Judea, there was a priest named Zacharias, of the division of Abijah; and he had a wife from the daughters of Aaron, and her name was Elizabeth. [6] They were both righteous in the sight of God, walking blamelessly in all the commandments

1:1 many. Although Luke wrote direct divine revelation inspired by the Holy Spirit, he acknowledged the works of others who had set down in writing events from Christ's life. All those sources have been long lost, except for the inspired Gospels. Since Matthew and Mark were most likely written before Luke, it has been suggested that either one or both of those may have been among Luke's sources when he did his research. It is also known that he was personally acquainted with many firsthand witnesses to the events of Christ's life. And it is possible that some of his sources were word-of-mouth reports. About 60 percent of the material in Mark is repeated in Luke, and Luke seems to follow Mark's order of events closely. **compile an account.** Luke proposed to narrate the ministry of Christ in an authoritative, logical, and factual order (though not always strictly chronological—v. 3). **the things accomplished.** I.e., the Old Testament messianic promises fulfilled in Christ. **among us.** I.e., in our generation. This phrase does not mean Luke was personally an eyewitness to the life of Christ.

---

and requirements of the Lord. ⁷ But they had no child, because Elizabeth was barren, and they were both advanced in years.

⁸ Now it happened *that* while he was performing his priestly service before God in the *appointed* order of his division, ⁹ according to the custom of the priestly office, he was chosen by lot to enter the temple of the Lord and burn incense. ¹⁰ And the whole multitude of the people were in prayer outside at the hour of the incense offering. ¹¹ And an angel of the

Lord appeared to him, standing to the right of the altar of incense. ¹² Zacharias was troubled when he saw *the angel,* and fear gripped him. ¹³ But the angel said to him, "Do not be afraid, Zacharias, for your petition has been heard, and your wife Elizabeth will bear you a son, and you will give him the name John. ¹⁴ You will have joy and gladness, and many will rejoice at his birth. ¹⁵ For he will be great in the sight of the Lord; and he will drink no wine or liquor, and he will be filled with the Holy Spirit while yet in his mother's womb. ¹⁶ And he will turn many of the sons of Israel back to the Lord their God. ¹⁷ It is he who will go *as a forerunner* before Him in the spirit and power of Elijah, TO TURN THE HEARTS OF THE FATHERS BACK TO THE CHILDREN, and the disobedient to the attitude of the righteous, so as to make ready a people prepared for the Lord."

¹⁸ Zacharias said to the angel, "How will I know this *for certain?* For I am an old man and my wife is advanced in years." ¹⁹ The angel answered and said to him, "I am Gabriel, who stands in the presence of God, and I have been sent to speak to you and to bring you this good news. ²⁰ And behold, you shall be silent and unable to speak until the day when these things take place, because you did not believe my words, which will be fulfilled in their proper time."

1:19 Gabriel. Literally "strong man of God." Gabriel also appears in Daniel 8:16; 9:21. He is one of only two holy angels whose names are given in Scripture, the other being Michael (Da 10:13, 21; Jude 9; Rev 12:7).

DAY 21: Who was the writer Luke?

According to tradition, Luke was a Gentile. The apostle Paul seems to confirm this, distinguishing Luke from those who were "from the circumcision" (Col 4:11, 14). That would make Luke the only Gentile to pen any books of Scripture. He is responsible for a significant portion of the New Testament, having written both this Gospel and the Book of Acts.

Very little is known about Luke. He almost never included personal details about himself, and nothing definite is known about his background or his conversion. Both Eusebius and Jerome identified him as a native of Antioch (which may explain why so much of the Book of Acts centers on Antioch—see Ac 11:19–27; 13:1–3; 14:26; 15:22–23, 30–35; 18:22–23). Luke was a frequent companion of the apostle Paul, at least from the time of Paul's Macedonian vision (Ac 16:9–10) right up to the time of Paul's martyrdom (2Ti 4:11).

The apostle Paul referred to Luke as a physician (Col 4:14). Luke's interest in medical phenomena is evident in the high profile he gave to Jesus' healing ministry (e.g., 4:38–40; 5:15–25; 6:17–19; 7:11–15; 8:43–47, 49–56; 9:2, 6, 11; 13:11–13; 14:2–4; 17:12–14; 22:50, 51). In Luke's day, physicians did not have a unique vocabulary of technical terminology; so, when Luke discusses healings and other medical issues, his language is not markedly different from that of the other Gospel writers.

MARCH 22

Deuteronomy 5:1–6:25

5 Then Moses summoned all Israel and said to them:

"Hear, O Israel, the statutes and the ordinances which I am speaking today in your hearing, that you may learn them and observe them carefully. ²The LORD our God made a covenant with us at Horeb. ³The LORD did not make this covenant with our fathers, but with us, *with* all those of us alive here today. ⁴The LORD spoke to you face to face at the mountain from the midst of the fire, ⁵ *while* I was standing between the LORD and you at that time, to declare to you the word of the LORD; for you were afraid because of the fire and did not go up the mountain. He said,

⁶'I am the LORD your God who brought you out of the land of Egypt, out of the house of slavery.

⁷'You shall have no other gods before Me.

⁸'You shall not make for yourself an idol, *or* any likeness *of* what is in heaven above or on the earth beneath or in the water under the earth. ⁹You shall not worship them or serve them; for I, the LORD your God, am a jealous God, visiting the iniquity of the fathers on the children, and on the third and the fourth *generations* of those who hate Me, ¹⁰but showing lovingkindness to thousands, to those who love Me and keep My commandments.

¹¹'You shall not take the name of the LORD your God in vain, for the LORD will not leave him unpunished who takes His name in vain.

¹²'Observe the sabbath day to keep it holy, as the LORD your God commanded you. ¹³Six days you shall labor and do all your work, ¹⁴but the seventh day is a sabbath of the LORD your God; *in it* you shall not do any work, you or your son or your daughter or your male servant or your female servant or your ox or your donkey or any of your cattle or your sojourner who stays with you, so that your male servant and your female servant may rest as well as you. ¹⁵You shall remember that you were a slave in the land of Egypt, and the LORD your God brought you out of there by a mighty hand and by an outstretched arm; therefore the LORD your God commanded you to observe the sabbath day.

¹⁶'Honor your father and your mother, as the LORD your God has commanded you, that your days may be prolonged and that it may go well with you on the land which the LORD your God gives you.

¹⁷'You shall not murder.

¹⁸'You shall not commit adultery.

¹⁹'You shall not steal.

²⁰'You shall not bear false witness against your neighbor.

²¹'You shall not covet your neighbor's wife, and you shall not desire your neighbor's house, his field or his male servant or his female servant, his ox or his donkey or anything that belongs to your neighbor.'

²²"These words the LORD spoke to all your assembly at the mountain from the midst of the fire, *of* the cloud and *of* the thick gloom, with a great voice, and He added no more. He wrote them on two tablets of stone and

5:22 and He added no more. These Ten Commandments alone were identified as direct quotations by God. The rest of the stipulations of the covenant were given to Moses, who in turn gave them to the Israelites. These basic rules, which reflect God's character, continue to be a means by which God reveals the sinful deeds of the flesh (Ro 7:7–14; Gal 3:19–24; 5:13–26). They are also a holy standard for conduct that the saved live by through the Spirit's power, with the exception of keeping the Sabbath (Col 2:16–17).

gave them to me. ²³And when you heard the voice from the midst of the darkness, while the mountain was burning with fire, you came near to me, all the heads of your tribes and your elders. ²⁴You said, 'Behold, the LORD our God has shown us His glory and His greatness, and we have heard His voice from the midst of the fire; we have seen today that God speaks with man, yet he lives. ²⁵Now then why should we die? For this great fire will consume us; if we hear the voice of the LORD our God any longer, then we will die. ²⁶For who is there of all flesh who has heard the voice of the living God speaking from the midst of the fire, as we *have,* and lived? ²⁷Go near and hear all that the LORD our God says; then speak to us all that the LORD our God speaks to you, and we will hear and do *it.*'

²⁸"The LORD heard the voice of your words when you spoke to me, and the LORD said to me, 'I have heard the voice of the words of this people which they have spoken to you. They have done well in all that they have spoken. ²⁹Oh that they had such a heart in them, that they would fear Me and keep all My commandments always, that it may be well with them and with their sons forever! ³⁰Go, say to them, "Return to your tents." ³¹But as for you, stand here by Me, that I may speak

to you all the commandments and the statutes and the judgments which you shall teach them, that they may observe *them* in the land which I give them to possess.' ³²So you shall observe to do just as the LORD your God has commanded you; you shall not turn aside to the right or to the left. ³³You shall walk in all the way which the LORD your God has commanded you, that you may live and that it may be well with you, and that you may prolong *your* days in the land which you will possess.

6 "Now this is the commandment, the statutes and the judgments which the LORD your God has commanded *me* to teach you, that you might do *them* in the land where you are going over to possess it, ²so that you and your son and your grandson might fear the LORD your God, to keep all His statutes and His commandments which I command you, all the days of your life, and that your days may be prolonged. ³O Israel, you should listen and be careful to do *it,* that it may be well with you and that you may multiply greatly, just as the LORD, the God of your fathers, has promised you, *in* a land flowing with milk and honey.

⁴"Hear, O Israel! The LORD is our God, the LORD is one! ⁵You shall love the LORD your God with all your heart and with all your soul and with all your might. ⁶These words, which I am commanding you today, shall be on your heart. ⁷You shall teach them diligently to your sons and shall talk of them when you sit in your house and when you walk by the way and when you lie down and when you rise up. ⁸You shall bind them as a sign on your hand and they shall be as frontals on your forehead. ⁹You shall write them on the doorposts of your house and on your gates.

¹⁰"Then it shall come about when the LORD your God brings you into the land which He swore to your fathers, Abraham, Isaac and Jacob, to give you, great and splendid cities which you did not build, ¹¹and houses full of all good things which you did not fill, and hewn cisterns which you did not dig, vineyards and olive trees which you did not plant, and you eat and are satisfied, ¹²then watch yourself, that you do not forget the LORD who brought you from the land of Egypt, out of the house of slavery. ¹³You shall fear *only* the LORD your God; and you shall worship Him and swear by His name. ¹⁴You shall not follow other gods, any of the gods of the peoples who surround you, ¹⁵for the LORD your God in the midst of you is a jealous God; otherwise the anger of the LORD your God will be kindled against you, and He will wipe you off the face of the earth. ¹⁶"You shall not put the LORD your God to

the test, as you tested *Him* at Massah. ¹⁷You should diligently keep the commandments of the LORD your God, and His testimonies and His statutes which He has commanded you. ¹⁸You shall do what is right and good in the sight of the LORD, that it may be well with you and that you may go in and possess the good land which the LORD swore to *give* your fathers, ¹⁹by driving out all your enemies from before you, as the LORD has spoken.

²⁰"When your son asks you in time to come, saying, 'What *do* the testimonies and the statutes and the judgments *mean* which the LORD our God commanded you?' ²¹then you shall say to your son, 'We were slaves to Pharaoh in Egypt, and the LORD brought us from Egypt with a mighty hand. ²²Moreover, the LORD showed great and distressing signs and wonders before our eyes against Egypt, Pharaoh and all his household; ²³He brought us out from there in order to bring us in, to give us the land which He had sworn to our fathers.' ²⁴So the LORD commanded us to observe all these statutes, to fear the LORD our God for our good always and for our survival, as *it is* today. ²⁵It will be righteousness for us if we are careful to observe all this commandment before the LORD our God, just as He commanded us.

Psalm 37:1-4

A Psalm of David.

D o not fret because of evildoers,
Be not envious toward wrongdoers.
² For they will wither quickly
   like the grass
And fade like the green herb.
³ Trust in the LORD and do good;
Dwell in the land and
   cultivate faithfulness.
⁴ Delight yourself in the LORD;
And He will give you the
   desires of your heart.

Proverbs 12:8

⁸ A man will be praised
   according to his insight,
But one of perverse mind
   will be despised.

Luke 1:21-38

²¹The people were waiting for Zacharias, and were wondering at his delay in the temple. ²²But when he came out, he was unable to speak to them; and they realized that he had seen a vision in the temple; and he kept making signs to them, and remained mute. ²³When the days of his priestly service were ended, he went back home.

²⁴After these days Elizabeth his wife became pregnant, and she kept herself in seclusion for five months, saying, ²⁵"This is the way the Lord has dealt with me in the days when He looked *with favor* upon *me,* to take away my disgrace among men."

²⁶Now in the sixth month the angel Gabriel was sent from God to a city in Galilee called Nazareth, ²⁷to a virgin engaged to a man whose name was Joseph, of the descendants of David; and the virgin's name was Mary. ²⁸And coming in, he said to her, "Greetings, favored one! The Lord *is* with you." ²⁹But she was very perplexed at *this* statement, and kept pondering what kind of salutation this was. ³⁰The angel said to her, "Do not be afraid, Mary; for you have found favor with God. ³¹And behold, you will conceive in your womb and bear a son, and you shall name Him Jesus. ³²He will be great and will be called the Son of the Most High; and the Lord God will give Him the throne of His father David; ³³and He will reign over the house of Jacob forever,

and His kingdom will have no end." ³⁴Mary said to the angel, "How can this be, since I am a virgin?" ³⁵The angel answered and said to her, "The Holy Spirit will come upon you, and the power of the Most High will overshadow you; and for that reason the holy Child shall be called the Son of God. ³⁶And behold, even your relative Elizabeth has also conceived a son in her old age; and she who was called barren is now in her sixth month. ³⁷For nothing will be impossible with God." ³⁸And Mary said, "Behold, the bondslave of the Lord; may it be done to me according to your word." And the angel departed from her.

1:34 I am a virgin. Mary understood that the angel was speaking of an immediate conception, and she and Joseph were still in the midst of the long betrothal, or engagement period (Mt 1:18), before the actual marriage and consummation. Her question was borne out of wonder, not doubt, nor disbelief, so the angel did not rebuke her as he had Zacharias (v. 20).

1:38 may it be done to me according to your word. Mary was in an extremely embarrassing and difficult position. Betrothed to Joseph, she faced the stigma of unwed motherhood. Joseph would obviously have known that the child was not his. She knew she would be accused of adultery—an offense punishable by stoning (Dt 22:13–21; see Jn 8:3–5). Yet she willingly and graciously submitted to the will of God.

1:27 a virgin. The importance of the virgin birth cannot be overstated. A right view of the incarnation hinges on the truth that Jesus was virgin-born. Both Luke and Matthew expressly state that Mary was a virgin when Jesus was conceived (Mt 1:23). The Holy Spirit wrought the conception through supernatural means (v. 35; Mt 1:18). The nature of Christ's conception testifies of both His deity and His sinlessness.

DAY 22: What was the greatest of God's commandments?

Deuteronomy 6:4–9, known as the *Shema* (Hebrew for "hear"), has become the Jewish confession of faith, recited twice daily by the devout, along with 11:13–21 and Numbers 15:37–41. "Hear, O Israel! The LORD…LORD is one!" (v. 4). The intent of these words was to give a clear statement of the truth of monotheism, that there is only one God. Thus, it has also been translated "The Lord is our God, the Lord alone." The word used for "one" in this passage does not mean "singleness," but "unity." The same word is used in Genesis 2:24, where the husband and wife were said to be "one flesh." Thus, while this verse was intended as a clear and concise statement of monotheism, it does not exclude the concept of the Trinity.

"You shall love the LORD your God with all your heart and with all your soul and with all your might" (v. 5). First in the list of all that was essential for the Jew was an unreserved, wholehearted commitment expressed in love to God. Since this relationship of love for God could not be represented in any material way as with idols, it had to be demonstrated in obedience to God's law in daily life. See 11:16–21; Matthew 22:37; Luke 10:27.

"These words…on your heart" (v. 6). The people were to think about these commandments and meditate on them so that obedience would not be a matter of formal legalism, but a response based upon understanding. The law written upon the heart would be an essential characteristic of the later New Covenant (Jer 31:33). And "teach them diligently to your sons" (v. 7). The commandments were to be the subject of conversation, both inside and outside the home, from the beginning of the day to its end.

MARCH 23

Deuteronomy 7:1–8:20

7 "When the LORD your God brings you into the land where you are entering to possess it, and clears away many nations before you, the Hittites and the Girgashites and the Amorites and the Canaanites and the Perizzites and the Hivites and the Jebusites, seven nations greater and stronger than you, ²and when the LORD your God delivers them before you and you defeat them, then you shall utterly destroy them. You shall make no covenant with them and show no favor to them. ³Furthermore, you

---

7:2 utterly destroy them. All the men, women and children were to be put to death. Even though this action seems extreme, the following need to be kept in mind: 1) the Canaanites deserved to die for their sin (9:4–5; see Ge 15:16); 2) the Canaanites persisted in their hatred of God (7:10); and 3) the Canaanites constituted a moral cancer that had the potential of introducing idolatry and immorality which would spread rapidly among the Israelites (20:17–18).

---

shall not intermarry with them; you shall not give your daughters to their sons, nor shall you take their daughters for your sons. ⁴For they will turn your sons away from following Me to serve other gods; then the anger of the LORD will be kindled against you and He will quickly destroy you. ⁵But thus you shall do to them: you shall tear down their altars, and smash their *sacred* pillars, and hew down their Asherim, and burn their graven images with fire. ⁶For you are a holy people to the LORD your God; the LORD your God has chosen you to be a people for His own possession out of all the peoples who are on the face of the earth.

⁷"The LORD did not set His love on you nor choose you because you were more in num-

---

7:6 a holy people to the LORD your God. The basis for the command to destroy the Canaanites is found in God's election of Israel. God had set apart Israel for His own special use and they were His treasured possession. As God's people, Israel needed to be separated from the moral pollution of the Canaanites.

---

ber than any of the peoples, for you were the fewest of all peoples, ⁸but because the LORD loved you and kept the oath which He swore to your forefathers, the LORD brought you out by a mighty hand and redeemed you from the house of slavery, from the hand of Pharaoh king of Egypt. ⁹Know therefore that the LORD your God, He is God, the faithful God, who keeps His covenant and His lovingkindness to a thousandth generation with those who love Him and keep His commandments; ¹⁰but repays those who hate Him to their faces, to destroy them; He will not delay with him who hates Him, He will repay him to his face. ¹¹Therefore, you shall keep the commandment and the statutes and the judgments which I am commanding you today, to do them.

¹²"Then it shall come about, because you listen to these judgments and keep and do them, that the LORD your God will keep with you His covenant and His lovingkindness which He swore to your forefathers. ¹³He will love you and bless you and multiply you; He will also bless the fruit of your womb and the fruit of your ground, your grain and your new wine and your oil, the increase of your herd and the young of your flock, in the land which He swore to your forefathers to give you. ¹⁴You shall be blessed above all peoples; there will be no male or female barren among you or among your cattle. ¹⁵The LORD will remove from you all sickness; and He will not put on you any of the harmful diseases of Egypt which you have known, but He will lay them on all who hate you. ¹⁶You shall consume all the peoples whom the LORD your God will deliver to you; your eye shall not pity them, nor shall you serve their gods, for that *would be* a snare to you.

¹⁷"If you should say in your heart, 'These nations are greater than I; how can I dispossess them?' ¹⁸you shall not be afraid of them; you shall well remember what the LORD your God did to Pharaoh and to all Egypt: ¹⁹the great trials which your eyes saw and the signs and the wonders and the mighty hand and the outstretched arm by which the LORD your God brought you out. So shall the LORD your God do to all the peoples of whom you are afraid. ²⁰Moreover, the LORD your God will send the hornet against them, until those who are left and hide themselves from you perish. ²¹You shall not dread them, for the LORD your God is in your midst, a great and awesome God. ²²The LORD your God will clear away these nations before you little by little; you will not be able to put an end to them quickly, for the wild beasts would grow too numerous for you. ²³But the LORD your God

will deliver them before you, and will throw them into great confusion until they are destroyed. ²⁴He will deliver their kings into your hand so that you will make their name perish from under heaven; no man will be able to stand before you until you have destroyed them. ²⁵The graven images of their gods you are to burn with fire; you shall not covet the silver or the gold that is on them, nor take it for yourselves, or you will be snared by it, for it is an abomination to the LORD your God. ²⁶You shall not bring an abomination into your house, and like it come under the ban; you shall utterly detest it and you shall utterly abhor it, for it is something banned.

8 "All the commandments that I am commanding you today you shall be careful to do, that you may live and multiply, and go in and possess the land which the LORD swore *to give* to your forefathers. ²You shall remember all the way which the LORD your God has led you in the wilderness these forty years, that He might humble you, testing you, to know what was in your heart, whether you will keep His commandments or not. ³He humbled you and let you be hungry, and fed you with manna which you did not know, nor did your fathers know, that He might make you understand that man does not live by bread alone, but man lives by everything that proceeds out of the mouth of the LORD. ⁴Your clothing did not wear out on you, nor did your foot swell these forty years. ⁵Thus you are to know in your heart that the LORD your God was disciplining you just as a man disciplines his son. ⁶Therefore, you shall keep the commandments of the LORD your God, to walk in His ways and to fear Him. ⁷For the LORD your God is bringing you into a good land, a land of brooks of water, of fountains and springs, flowing forth in valleys and hills; ⁸a land of wheat and barley, of vines and fig trees and pomegranates, a land of olive oil and honey; ⁹a land where you will eat food without scarcity, in which you will not lack anything; a land whose stones are iron, and out of whose hills you can dig copper. ¹⁰When you have eaten and are satisfied, you shall bless the LORD your God for the good land which He has given you.

¹¹"Beware that you do not forget the LORD your God by not keeping His commandments and His ordinances and His statutes which I am commanding you today; ¹²otherwise, when you have eaten and are satisfied, and have built good houses and lived *in them,* ¹³and when your herds and your flocks multiply, and your silver and gold multiply, and all that you have multiplies, ¹⁴then your heart

8:11 do not forget the LORD your God. Sufficient food would lead to the satisfaction of Israel in the land (vv. 10, 12). This satisfaction and security could lead to Israel forgetting God. Forgetting God means no longer having Him in the daily thoughts of one's life. This forgetfulness would lead to a disobedience of His commandments. Whereas, in the wilderness, Israel had to depend on God for the necessities of life, in the rich land there would be a tempting sense of self-sufficiency.

will become proud and you will forget the LORD your God who brought you out from the land of Egypt, out of the house of slavery. ¹⁵He led you through the great and terrible wilderness, *with its* fiery serpents and scorpions and thirsty ground where there was no water; He brought water for you out of the rock of flint. ¹⁶In the wilderness He fed you manna which your fathers did not know, that He might humble you and that He might test you, to do good for you in the end. ¹⁷Otherwise, you may say in your heart, 'My power and the strength of my hand made me this wealth.' ¹⁸But you shall remember the LORD your God, for it is He who is giving you power to make wealth, that He may confirm His covenant which He swore to your fathers, as *it is* this day. ¹⁹It shall come about if you ever forget the LORD your God and go after other gods and serve them and worship them, I testify against you today that you will surely perish. ²⁰Like the nations that the LORD makes to perish before you, so you shall perish; because you would not listen to the voice of the LORD your God.

Psalm 37:5–11

⁵ Commit your way to the LORD,
  Trust also in Him, and He will do it.
⁶ He will bring forth your
    righteousness as the light
  And your judgment as the noonday.

⁷ Rest in the LORD and wait
    patiently for Him;
  Do not fret because of him
    who prospers in his way,
  Because of the man who carries
    out wicked schemes.
⁸ Cease from anger and forsake wrath;
  Do not fret; *it leads* only to evildoing.
⁹ For evildoers will be cut off,
  But those who wait for the LORD,
    they will inherit the land.

¹⁰ Yet a little while and the wicked
man will be no more;
And you will look carefully for his
place and he will not be *there*.
¹¹ But the humble will inherit the land
And will delight themselves
in abundant prosperity.

Proverbs 12:9–10

⁹ Better is he who is lightly
esteemed and has a servant
Than he who honors himself
and lacks bread.
¹⁰ A righteous man has regard
for the life of his animal,
But *even* the compassion of
the wicked is cruel.

Luke 1:39–56

³⁹ Now at this time Mary arose and went in a hurry to the hill country, to a city of Judah, ⁴⁰ and entered the house of Zacharias and greeted Elizabeth. ⁴¹ When Elizabeth heard Mary's greeting, the baby leaped in her womb; and Elizabeth was filled with the Holy Spirit. ⁴² And she cried out with a loud voice and said, "Blessed *are* you among women, and blessed *is* the fruit of your womb! ⁴³ And how has it *happened* to me, that the mother of my Lord would come to me? ⁴⁴ For behold, when the sound of your greeting reached my ears, the baby leaped in my womb for joy. ⁴⁵ And blessed *is* she who believed that there would be a fulfillment of what had been spoken to her by the Lord."

⁴⁶ And Mary said:

"My soul exalts the Lord,
⁴⁷ And my spirit has rejoiced
in God my Savior.
⁴⁸ "For He has had regard for the
humble state of His bondslave;

For behold, from this time on all
generations will count me blessed.
⁴⁹ "For the Mighty One has done
great things for me;
And holy is His name.
⁵⁰ "AND HIS MERCY IS UPON GENERATION
AFTER GENERATION
TOWARD THOSE WHO FEAR HIM.
⁵¹ "He has done mighty deeds
with His arm;
He has scattered *those who were* proud
in the thoughts of their heart.
⁵² "He has brought down rulers
from *their* thrones,
And has exalted those who
were humble.
⁵³ "HE HAS FILLED THE HUNGRY
WITH GOOD THINGS;
And sent away the rich empty-handed.
⁵⁴ "He has given help to Israel His servant,
In remembrance of His mercy,
⁵⁵ As He spoke to our fathers,
To Abraham and his
descendants forever."

⁵⁶ And Mary stayed with her about three months, and *then* returned to her home.

1:47 my Savior. Mary referred to God as "Savior," indicating both that she recognized her own need of a Savior, and that she knew the true God as her Savior. Nothing here or anywhere else in Scripture indicates Mary thought of herself as "immaculate" (free from the taint of original sin). Quite the opposite is true; she employed language typical of someone whose only hope for salvation is divine grace. Nothing in this passage lends support to the notion that Mary herself ought to be an object of adoration.

DAY 23: Is Deuteronomy simply Moses' version of the secular covenants and treaties of his day, or does it represent a unique revelation from God?

The format that Moses used in recording not only the material in Deuteronomy but also the rest of the Pentateuch bears some resemblance to other official documents from a particular time in history. This fact can be used by historians in trying to establish a date for the book. This fact can also be used by those who question God's unique revelation when they claim that Moses must have merely been copying the style of other nations of his time.

The people whom God enlisted to record His revelation did not shed their personalities, education, or style as they wrote for God. Moses had the equivalent of advanced degrees in the best training Egypt had to offer young princes (Ac 7:22). If we think of the Pentateuch as Moses' God-guided journaling during the wilderness wanderings, it will not seem unusual that his writing style bears similarities to the official and political writings of his day. What sets Moses' writings, along with the rest of Scripture, apart is not so much the style but their authoritative and God-inspired content.

MARCH 24

Deuteronomy 9:1–10:22

9 "Hear, O Israel! You are crossing over the Jordan today to go in to dispossess nations greater and mightier than you, great cities fortified to heaven, ² a people great and tall, the sons of the Anakim, whom you know and of whom you have heard *it said,* 'Who can stand before the sons of Anak?' ³ Know therefore today that it is the LORD your God who is crossing over before you as a consuming fire. He will destroy them and He will subdue them before you, so that you may drive them out and destroy them quickly, just as the LORD has spoken to you.

⁴ "Do not say in your heart when the LORD your God has driven them out before you, 'Because of my righteousness the LORD has brought me in to possess this land,' but *it is* because of the wickedness of these nations *that* the LORD is dispossessing them before you. ⁵ It is not for your righteousness or for

---

9:3 a consuming fire. The Lord was pictured as a fire which burned everything in its path. So the Lord would go over into Canaan and exterminate Canaanites. **destroy them quickly.** Israel was to be the human agent of the Lord's destruction of the Canaanites. The military strength of the Canaanites would be destroyed quickly (Jos 6:1—11:23), though the complete subjugation of the land would take time (7:22; Jos 13:1).

9:4 Because of my righteousness. Three times in vv. 4–6, Moses emphasized that the victory was not because of Israel's goodness, but was entirely the work of God. It was the wickedness of the Canaanites that led to their expulsion from the land (Ro 10:6).

---

the uprightness of your heart that you are going to possess their land, but *it is* because of the wickedness of these nations *that* the LORD your God is driving them out before you, in order to confirm the oath which the LORD swore to your fathers, to Abraham, Isaac and Jacob.

⁶ "Know, then, *it is* not because of your righteousness *that* the LORD your God is giving you this good land to possess, for you are a stubborn people. ⁷ Remember, do not forget how you provoked the LORD your God to wrath in the wilderness; from the day that

you left the land of Egypt until you arrived at this place, you have been rebellious against the LORD. ⁸ Even at Horeb you provoked the LORD to wrath, and the LORD was so angry with you that He would have destroyed you. ⁹ When I went up to the mountain to receive the tablets of stone, the tablets of the covenant which the LORD had made with you, then I remained on the mountain forty days and nights; I neither ate bread nor drank water. ¹⁰ The LORD gave me the two tablets of stone written by the finger of God; and on them *were* all the words which the LORD had spoken with you at the mountain from the midst of the fire on the day of the assembly. ¹¹ It came about at the end of forty days and nights that the LORD gave me the two tablets of stone, the tablets of the covenant. ¹² Then the LORD said to me, 'Arise, go down from here quickly, for your people whom you brought out of Egypt have acted corruptly. They have quickly turned aside from the way which I commanded them; they have made a molten image for themselves.' ¹³ The LORD spoke further to me, saying, 'I have seen this people, and indeed, it is a stubborn people. ¹⁴ Let Me alone, that I may destroy them and blot out their name from under heaven; and I will make of you a nation mightier and greater than they.'

¹⁵ "So I turned and came down from the mountain while the mountain was burning with fire, and the two tablets of the covenant were in my two hands. ¹⁶ And I saw that you had sinned against the LORD your God. You had made for yourselves a molten calf; you had turned aside quickly from the way which the LORD had commanded you. ¹⁷ I took hold of the two tablets and threw them from my hands and smashed them before your eyes. ¹⁸ I fell down before the LORD, as at the first, forty days and nights; I neither ate bread nor drank water, because of all your sin which you had committed in doing what was evil in the sight of the LORD to provoke Him to anger. ¹⁹ For I was afraid of the anger and hot displeasure with which the LORD was wrathful against you in order to destroy you, but the LORD listened to me that time also. ²⁰ The LORD was angry enough with Aaron to destroy him; so I also prayed for Aaron at the same time. ²¹ I took your sinful *thing,* the calf which you had made, and burned it with fire and crushed it, grinding it very small until it was as fine as dust; and I threw its dust into the brook that came down from the mountain.

²² "Again at Taberah and at Massah and at Kibroth-hattaavah you provoked the LORD

to wrath. [23] When the LORD sent you from Kadesh-barnea, saying, 'Go up and possess the land which I have given you,' then you rebelled against the command of the LORD your God; you neither believed Him nor listened to His voice. [24] You have been rebellious against the LORD from the day I knew you.

[25] "So I fell down before the LORD the forty days and nights, which I did because the LORD had said He would destroy you. [26] I prayed to the LORD and said, 'O Lord GOD, do not destroy Your people, even Your inheritance, whom You have redeemed through Your greatness, whom You have brought out of Egypt with a mighty hand. [27] Remember Your servants, Abraham, Isaac, and Jacob; do not look at the stubbornness of this people or at their wickedness or their sin. [28] Otherwise the land from which You brought us may say, "Because the LORD was not able to bring them into the land which He had promised them and because He hated them He has brought them out to slay them in the wilderness." [29] Yet they are Your people, even Your inheritance, whom You have brought out by Your great power and Your outstretched arm.'

10 "At that time the LORD said to me, 'Cut out for yourself two tablets of stone like the former ones, and come up to Me on the mountain, and make an ark of wood for yourself. [2] I will write on the tablets the words that were on the former tablets which you shattered, and you shall put them in the ark.' [3] So I made an ark of acacia wood and cut out two tablets of stone like the former ones, and went up on the mountain with the two tablets in my hand. [4] He wrote on the tablets, like the former writing, the Ten Commandments which the LORD had spoken to you on the mountain from the midst of the fire on the day of the assembly; and the LORD gave them to me. [5] Then I turned and came down from the mountain and put the tablets in the ark which I had made; and there they are, as the LORD commanded me."

[6] (Now the sons of Israel set out from Beeroth Bene-jaakan to Moserah. There Aaron died and there he was buried and Eleazar his son ministered as priest in his place. [7] From there they set out to Gudgodah, and from Gudgodah to Jotbathah, a land of brooks of water. [8] At that time the LORD set apart the tribe of Levi to carry the ark of the covenant of the LORD, to stand before the LORD to serve Him and to bless in His name until this day. [9] Therefore, Levi does not have a portion or inheritance with his brothers; the LORD is his inheritance, just as the LORD your God spoke to him.)

[10] "I, moreover, stayed on the mountain forty days and forty nights like the first time, and the LORD listened to me that time also; the LORD was not willing to destroy you. [11] Then the LORD said to me, 'Arise, proceed on your journey ahead of the people, that they may go in and possess the land which I swore to their fathers to give them.'

[12] "Now, Israel, what does the LORD your God require from you, but to fear the LORD your God, to walk in all His ways and love Him, and to serve the LORD your God with all your heart and with all your soul, [13] and to keep the LORD'S commandments and His statutes which I am commanding you today for your good? [14] Behold, to the LORD your God belong heaven and the highest heavens, the earth and all that is in it. [15] Yet on your fathers did the LORD set His affection to love them, and He chose their descendants after them, even you above all peoples, as it is this day. [16] So circumcise your heart, and stiffen your neck no longer. [17] For the LORD your God is the God of gods and the Lord of lords, the great, the mighty, and the awesome God who does not show partiality nor take a bribe. [18] He executes justice for the orphan and the widow, and shows His love for the alien by giving him food and clothing. [19] So show your love for the alien, for you were aliens in the land of Egypt. [20] You shall fear the LORD your God; you shall serve Him and cling to Him, and you shall swear by His name. [21] He is your praise and He is your God, who has done these great and awesome things for you which your eyes have seen. [22] Your fathers went down to Egypt seventy persons in all, and now the LORD your God has made you as numerous as the stars of heaven.

Psalm 37:12–17

[12] The wicked plots against
       the righteous
      And gnashes at him with his teeth.
[13] The Lord laughs at him,
      For He sees his day is coming.
[14] The wicked have drawn the
       sword and bent their bow
      To cast down the afflicted
       and the needy,
      To slay those who are
       upright in conduct.
[15] Their sword will enter
       their own heart,
      And their bows will be broken.

[16] Better is the little of the righteous
      Than the abundance of many wicked.

10:16 So circumcise your heart. Moses called the Israelites to cut away all the sin in their hearts, as the circumcision surgery cut away the skin. This would leave them with a clean relationship to God (30:6; Lv 26:40–41; Jer 4:4; 9:25; Ro 2:29).

---

17 For the arms of the wicked
   will be broken,
   But the LORD sustains the
   righteous.

Proverbs 12:11

11 He who tills his land will
   have plenty of bread,
   But he who pursues worthless
   things lacks sense.

Luke 1:57–80

57 Now the time had come for Elizabeth to give birth, and she gave birth to a son. 58 Her neighbors and her relatives heard that the Lord had displayed His great mercy toward her; and they were rejoicing with her.

59 And it happened that on the eighth day they came to circumcise the child, and they were going to call him Zacharias, after his father. 60 But his mother answered and said, "No indeed; but he shall be called John." 61 And they said to her, "There is no one among your relatives who is called by that name." 62 And they made signs to his father, as to what he wanted him called. 63 And he asked for a tablet and wrote as follows, "His name is John." And they were all astonished. 64 And at once his mouth was opened and his tongue *loosed,* and he *began* to speak in praise of God. 65 Fear came on all those living around them; and all these matters were being talked about in all the hill country of Judea. 66 All who heard them kept them in mind, saying, "What then will this child *turn out to* be?" For the hand of the Lord was certainly with him.

67 And his father Zacharias was filled with the Holy Spirit, and prophesied, saying:

68 "Blessed *be* the Lord God
   of Israel,
   For He has visited us and
   accomplished redemption
   for His people,
69 And has raised up a horn
   of salvation for us
   In the house of David His
   servant—

1:80 lived in the deserts. Several groups of ascetics inhabited the wilderness regions east of Jerusalem. One was the famous Qumran community, source of the Dead Sea Scrolls. John's parents, already old when he was born, might have given him over to the care of someone with ties to such a community. In a similar way, Hannah consecrated Samuel to the Lord by entrusting him to Eli (1Sa 1:22–28). However, there is nothing concrete in Scripture to suggest that John was part of any such group. On the contrary, he is painted as a solitary figure, in the spirit of Elijah.

---

70 As He spoke by the mouth of His
   holy prophets from of old—
71 Salvation FROM OUR ENEMIES,
   And FROM THE HAND OF
   ALL WHO HATE US;
72 To show mercy toward our
   fathers,
   And to remember His holy
   covenant,
73 The oath which He swore to
   Abraham our father,
74 To grant us that we, being
   rescued from the hand
   of our enemies,
   Might serve Him without
   fear,
75 In holiness and righteousness
   before Him all our days.
76 "And you, child, will be called
   the prophet of the Most
   High;
   For you will go on BEFORE
   THE LORD TO PREPARE HIS
   WAYS;
77 To give to His people *the*
   knowledge of salvation
   By the forgiveness of their
   sins,
78 Because of the tender
   mercy of our God,
   With which the Sunrise from
   on high will visit us,
79 TO SHINE UPON THOSE WHO
   SIT IN DARKNESS AND THE
   SHADOW OF DEATH,
   To guide our feet into the
   way of peace."

80 And the child continued to grow and to become strong in spirit, and he lived in the deserts until the day of his public appearance to Israel.

DAY 24: For whom did Luke write?

Luke, like Mark, and in contrast to Matthew, appears to target a Gentile readership. He identified locations that would have been familiar to all Jews (4:31; 23:51; 24:13), suggesting that his audience went beyond those who already had knowledge of Palestinian geography. He usually preferred Greek terminology over Hebraisms (e.g., "Calvary" instead of "Golgotha" in 23:33). The other Gospels all use occasional Semitic terms such as "Abba" (Mk 14:36), "rabbi" (Mt 23:7–8; Jn 1:38, 49), and "hosanna" (Mt 21:9; Mk 11:9–10; Jn 12:13)—but Luke either omitted them or used Greek equivalents.

Luke quoted the Old Testament more sparingly than Matthew; and when citing Old Testament passages, he nearly always employed the Septuagint, a Greek translation of the Hebrew Scriptures. Furthermore, most of Luke's Old Testament citations are allusions rather than direct quotations, and many of them appear in Jesus' words rather than Luke's narration (2:23–24; 3:4–6; 4:4, 8, 10–12, 18–19; 7:27; 10:27; 18:20; 19:46; 20:17–18, 37, 42–43; 22:37).

Luke, more than any of the other Gospel writers, highlighted the universal scope of the gospel invitation. He portrayed Jesus as the Son of Man, rejected by Israel, and then offered to the world. He repeatedly related accounts of Gentiles, Samaritans, and other outcasts who found grace in Jesus' eyes. This emphasis is precisely what we would expect from a close companion of the "apostle of Gentiles" (Ro 11:13).

MARCH 25

Deuteronomy 11:1–12:32

11 "You shall therefore love the LORD your God, and always keep His charge, His statutes, His ordinances, and His commandments. ² Know this day that I *am* not *speaking* with your sons who have not known and who have not seen the discipline of the LORD your God—His greatness, His mighty hand and His outstretched arm, ³ and His signs and His works which He did in the midst of Egypt to Pharaoh the king of Egypt and to all his land; ⁴ and what He did to Egypt's army, to its horses and its chariots, when He made the water of the Red Sea to engulf them while they were pursuing you, and the LORD completely destroyed them; ⁵ and what He did to you in the wilderness until you came to this place; ⁶ and what He did to Dathan and Abiram, the sons of Eliab, the son of Reuben, when the earth opened its mouth and swallowed them, their households, their tents, and every living thing that followed them, among all Israel— ⁷ but your own eyes have seen all the great work of the LORD which He did.

⁸ "You shall therefore keep every commandment which I am commanding you today, so that you may be strong and go in and possess the land into which you are about to cross to possess it; ⁹ so that you may prolong *your* days on the land which the LORD swore to your fathers to give to them and to their descendants, a land flowing with milk and honey. ¹⁰ For the land, into which you are entering to possess it, is not like the land of Egypt from which you came, where you used to sow your seed and water it with your foot like a vegetable garden. ¹¹ But the land into which you are about to cross to possess it, a land of hills and valleys, drinks water from the rain of heaven, ¹² a land for which the LORD your God cares; the eyes of the LORD your God are always on it, from the beginning even to the end of the year.

¹³ "It shall come about, if you listen obediently to my commandments which I am commanding you today, to love the LORD your God and to serve Him with all your heart and all your soul, ¹⁴ that He will give the rain for your land in its season, the early and late rain, that you may gather in your grain and your new wine and your oil. ¹⁵ He will give grass in your fields for your cattle, and you will eat and be satisfied. ¹⁶ Beware that your hearts are not deceived, and that you do not turn away and serve other gods and worship them. ¹⁷ Or the anger of the LORD will be kindled against you, and He will shut up the heavens so that there will be no rain and the ground will not yield its fruit; and you will perish quickly from the good land which the LORD is giving you.

¹⁸ "You shall therefore impress these words of mine on your heart and on your soul; and you shall bind them as a sign on your hand, and they shall be as frontals on your forehead. ¹⁹ You shall teach them to your sons, talking of them when you sit in your house and when you walk along the road and when you lie down and when you rise up. ²⁰ You shall write them on the doorposts of your house and on your gates, ²¹ so that your days and the days of your sons may be multiplied on the land which the LORD swore to your fathers to give them, as long as the heavens *remain* above

the earth. ²² For if you are careful to keep all this commandment which I am commanding you to do, to love the LORD your God, to walk in all His ways and hold fast to Him, ²³ then the LORD will drive out all these nations from before you, and you will dispossess nations greater and mightier than you. ²⁴ Every place on which the sole of your foot treads shall be yours; your border will be from the wilderness to Lebanon, *and* from the river, the river Euphrates, as far as the western sea. ²⁵ No man will be able to stand before you; the LORD your God will lay the dread of you and the fear of you on all the land on which you set foot, as He has spoken to you.

11:24 Every place...your foot treads. In response to the obedience of Israel (vv. 22–23), the Lord promised to give to Israel all of the land they personally traversed to the extent of the boundaries that He had given. This same promise was repeated in Joshua 1:3–5. Had Israel obeyed God faithfully, her boundaries would have been enlarged to fulfill the promise made to Abraham (Ge 15:18). But because of Israel's disobedience, the complete promise of the whole land still remains, to be fulfilled in the future kingdom of Messiah (Eze 36:8–38).

---

²⁶ "See, I am setting before you today a blessing and a curse: ²⁷ the blessing, if you listen to the commandments of the LORD your God, which I am commanding you today; ²⁸ and the curse, if you do not listen to the commandments of the LORD your God, but turn aside from the way which I am commanding you today, by following other gods which you have not known.

²⁹ "It shall come about, when the LORD your God brings you into the land where you are entering to possess it, that you shall place the blessing on Mount Gerizim and the curse on Mount Ebal. ³⁰ Are they not across the Jordan, west of the way toward the sunset, in the land of the Canaanites who live in the Arabah, opposite Gilgal, beside the oaks of Moreh? ³¹ For you are about to cross the Jordan to go in to possess the land which the LORD your God is giving you, and you shall possess it and live in it, ³² and you shall be careful to do all the statutes and the judgments which I am setting before you today.

12 "These are the statutes and the judgments which you shall carefully observe in the land which the LORD, the God of your fathers, has given you to possess as long as you live on the earth. ² You shall utterly destroy all the places where the nations whom you shall dispossess serve their gods, on the high mountains and on the hills and under every green tree. ³ You shall tear down their altars and smash their *sacred* pillars and burn their Asherim with fire, and you shall cut down the engraved images of their gods and obliterate their name from that place. ⁴ You shall not act like this toward the LORD your God. ⁵ But you shall seek *the LORD* at the place which the LORD your God will choose from all your tribes, to establish His name there for His dwelling, and there you shall come. ⁶ There you shall bring your burnt offerings, your sacrifices, your tithes, the contribution of your hand, your votive offerings, your freewill offerings, and the firstborn of your herd and of your flock. ⁷ There also you and your households shall eat before the LORD your God, and rejoice in all your undertakings in which the LORD your God has blessed you.

⁸ "You shall not do at all what we are doing here today, every man *doing* whatever is right in his own eyes; ⁹ for you have not as yet come to the resting place and the inheritance which the LORD your God is giving you. ¹⁰ When you cross the Jordan and live in the land which the LORD your God is giving you to inherit, and He gives you rest from all your enemies around *you* so that you live in security, ¹¹ then it shall come about that the place in which the LORD your God will choose for His name to dwell, there you shall bring all that I command you: your burnt offerings and your sacrifices, your tithes and the contribution of your hand, and all your choice votive offerings which you will vow to the LORD. ¹² And you shall rejoice before the LORD your God, you and your sons and daughters, your male and female servants, and the Levite who is within your gates, since he has no portion or inheritance with you.

¹³ "Be careful that you do not offer your burnt offerings in every *cultic* place you see, ¹⁴ but in the place which the LORD chooses in one of your tribes, there you shall offer your burnt offerings, and there you shall do all that I command you.

¹⁵ "However, you may slaughter and eat meat within any of your gates, whatever you desire, according to the blessing of the LORD your God which He has given you; the unclean and the clean may eat of it, as of the gazelle and the deer. ¹⁶ Only you shall not eat the blood; you are to pour it out on the ground like water. ¹⁷ You are not allowed to eat within your gates the tithe of your grain or new wine or oil, or the firstborn of your herd or flock, or any of

your votive offerings which you vow, or your freewill offerings, or the contribution of your hand. [18] But you shall eat them before the LORD your God in the place which the LORD your God will choose, you and your son and daughter, and your male and female servants, and the Levite who is within your gates; and you shall rejoice before the LORD your God in all your undertakings. [19] Be careful that you do not forsake the Levite as long as you live in your land.

[20] "When the LORD your God extends your border as He has promised you, and you say, 'I will eat meat,' because you desire to eat meat, then you may eat meat, whatever you desire. [21] If the place which the LORD your God chooses to put His name is too far from you, then you may slaughter of your herd and flock which the LORD has given you, as I have commanded you; and you may eat within your gates whatever you desire. [22] Just as a gazelle or a deer is eaten, so you will eat it; the unclean and the clean alike may eat of it. [23] Only be sure not to eat the blood, for the blood is the life, and you shall not eat the life with the flesh. [24] You shall not eat it; you shall pour it out on the ground like water. [25] You shall not eat it, so that it may be well with you and your sons after you, for you will be doing what is right in the sight of the LORD. [26] Only your holy things which you may have and your votive offerings, you shall take and go to the place which the LORD chooses. [27] And you shall offer your burnt offerings, the flesh and the blood, on the altar of the LORD your God; and the blood of your sacrifices shall be poured out on the altar of the LORD your God, and you shall eat the flesh.

[28] "Be careful to listen to all these words which I command you, so that it may be well with you and your sons after you forever, for you will be doing what is good and right in the sight of the LORD your God.

[29] "When the LORD your God cuts off before you the nations which you are going in to dispossess, and you dispossess them and dwell in their land, [30] beware that you are not ensnared to follow them, after they are destroyed before you, and that you do not inquire after their gods, saying, 'How do these nations serve their gods, that I also may do likewise?' [31] You shall not behave thus toward the LORD your God, for every abominable act which the LORD hates they have done for their gods; for they even burn their sons and daughters in the fire to their gods.

[32] "Whatever I command you, you shall be careful to do; you shall not add to nor take away from it.

Psalm 37:18-22

[18] The LORD knows the days
    of the blameless,
And their inheritance will be forever.
[19] They will not be ashamed
    in the time of evil,
And in the days of famine they
    will have abundance.
[20] But the wicked will perish;
And the enemies of the LORD will be
    like the glory of the pastures,
They vanish—like smoke
    they vanish away.
[21] The wicked borrows and
    does not pay back,
But the righteous is gracious
    and gives.
[22] For those blessed by Him
    will inherit the land,
But those cursed by Him will
    be cut off.

Proverbs 12:12-14

[12] The wicked man desires the
    booty of evil men,
But the root of the righteous
    yields *fruit*.
[13] An evil man is ensnared by the
    transgression of his lips,
But the righteous will
    escape from trouble.
[14] A man will be satisfied with good
    by the fruit of his words,
And the deeds of a man's hands
    will return to him.

12:14 fruit of his words. This deals with the power of words; the reward of wise words is like the reward for physical labor (10:11; 15:4; 18:4).

Luke 2:1-24

2 Now in those days a decree went out from Caesar Augustus, that a census be taken of all the inhabited earth. [2] This was the first census taken while Quirinius was governor of Syria. [3] And everyone was on his way to register for the census, each to his own city. [4] Joseph also went up from Galilee, from the city of Nazareth, to Judea, to the city of David which is called Bethlehem, because he was of the house and family of David, [5] in order to register along with Mary, who was engaged to him, and was with child. [6] While they were there, the days were completed

for her to give birth. ⁷And she gave birth to her firstborn son; and she wrapped Him in cloths, and laid Him in a manger, because there was no room for them in the inn.

⁸In the same region there were *some* shepherds staying out in the fields and keeping watch over their flock by night. ⁹And an angel of the Lord suddenly stood before them, and the glory of the Lord shone around them; and they were terribly frightened. ¹⁰But the angel said to them, "Do not be afraid; for behold, I bring you good news of great joy which will be for all the people; ¹¹for today in the city of David there has been born for you a Savior, who is Christ the Lord. ¹²This *will be* a sign for you: you will find a baby wrapped in cloths and lying in a manger." ¹³And suddenly there appeared with the angel a multitude of the heavenly host praising God and saying,

2:11 city of David. I.e., Bethlehem, the town where David was born—not the City of David, which was on the southern slope of Mt. Zion (2Sa 5:7-9). **a Savior.** This is one of only two places in the Gospels where Christ is referred to as "Savior"—the other being John 4:42, where the men of Sychar confessed Him as "Savior of the world." **Christ.** "Christ" is the Greek equivalent of "Messiah". **Lord.** The Greek word can mean "master"—but it is also the word used to translate the covenant name of God. Here (and in most of its New Testament occurrences), it is used in the latter sense, as a title of deity.

¹⁴"Glory to God in the highest,
And on earth peace among
men with whom He is
pleased."

¹⁵When the angels had gone away from them into heaven, the shepherds *began* saying to one another, "Let us go straight to Bethlehem then, and see this thing that has happened which the Lord has made known to us." ¹⁶So they came in a hurry and found their way to Mary and Joseph, and the baby as He lay in the manger. ¹⁷When they had seen this, they made known the statement which had been told them about this Child. ¹⁸And all who heard it wondered at the things which were told them by the shepherds. ¹⁹But Mary treasured all these things, pondering them in her heart. ²⁰The shepherds went back, glorifying and praising God for all that they had heard and seen, just as had been told them.

²¹And when eight days had passed, before His circumcision, His name was *then* called Jesus, the name given by the angel before He was conceived in the womb.

²²And when the days for their purification according to the law of Moses were completed, they brought Him up to Jerusalem to present Him to the Lord ²³(as it is written in the Law of the Lord, "EVERY *firstborn* MALE THAT OPENS THE WOMB SHALL BE CALLED HOLY TO THE LORD"), ²⁴and to offer a sacrifice according to what was said in the Law of the Lord, "A PAIR OF TURTLEDOVES OR TWO YOUNG PIGEONS."

DAY 25: Why was there an emphasis on prescribed places of worship in the Old Testament?

In Deuteronomy 12:1-32, Moses begins by repeating his instructions concerning what to do with the false worship centers after Israel had taken possession of the land of the Canaanites (see 7:1-6). They were to destroy them completely. In v. 2, he speaks about "the high mountains...hills...every green tree." The Canaanite sanctuaries to be destroyed were located in places believed to have particular religious significance. The mountain or hill was thought to be the home of a god; and by ascending the mountain, the worshiper was in some symbolic sense closer to the deity. Certain trees were considered to be sacred and symbolized fertility, a dominant theme in Canaanite religion. And in v. 3, Moses addresses "their altars...pillars...Asherim... engraved images." These were elements of Canaanite worship, which included human sacrifice (v. 31). If they remained, the people might mix the worship of God with those places (v. 4).

In contrast to false worship centers, the Israelites are told "you shall seek the LORD at the place which the LORD your God will choose from all your tribes, to establish His name there for His dwelling" (v. 5). Various places of worship were chosen after the people settled in Canaan, such as Mt. Ebal (27:1-8; Jos 8:30-35), Shechem (Jos 24:1-28), and Shiloh (Jos 18:1), which was the center of worship through the period of Judges (Jdg 21:19). The tabernacle, the Lord's dwelling place, was located in Canaan, where the Lord chose to dwell. The central importance of the tabernacle was in direct contrast to the multiple places (see v. 2) where the Canaanites practiced their worship of idols. Eventually, the tabernacle was brought to Jerusalem by David (2Sa 6:12-19).

MARCH 26

Deuteronomy 13:1–14:29

13 "If a prophet or a dreamer of dreams arises among you and gives you a sign or a wonder, ²and the sign or the wonder comes true, concerning which he spoke to you, saying, 'Let us go after other gods (whom you have not known) and let us serve them,' ³you shall not listen to the words of that prophet or that dreamer of dreams; for the LORD your God is testing you to find out if you love the LORD your God with all your heart and with all your soul. ⁴You shall follow the LORD your God and fear Him; and you shall keep His commandments, listen to His voice, serve Him, and cling to Him. ⁵But that prophet or that dreamer of dreams shall be put to death, because he has counseled rebellion against the LORD your God who brought you from the land of Egypt and redeemed you from the house of slavery, to seduce you from the way in which the LORD your God commanded you to walk. So you shall purge the evil from among you.

⁶"If your brother, your mother's son, or your son or daughter, or the wife you cherish, or your friend who is as your own soul, entice you secretly, saying, 'Let us go and serve other gods' (whom neither you nor your fathers have known, ⁷of the gods of the peoples

13:2 the sign or the wonder comes true. Miraculous signs alone were never meant to be a test of truth (see Pharaoh's magicians in Ex 7–10). A prophet or a dreamer's prediction may come true, but if his message contradicted God's commands, the people were to trust God and His Word rather than such experience. **Let us go after other gods.** The explicit temptation was to renounce allegiance to the Lord and go after other gods. The result of this apostasy would be the serving of these false gods by worshiping them, which would be in direct contradiction to the first commandment (5:7).

13:5 purge the evil from among you. The object of the severe penalty was not only the punishment of the evildoer, but also the preservation of the community. Paul must have had this text in mind when he gave a similar command to the Corinthian church (see 1Co 5:13; also Dt 17:7; 19:19; 21:21; 22:21; 24:7).

who are around you, near you or far from you, from one end of the earth to the other end), ⁸you shall not yield to him or listen to him; and your eye shall not pity him, nor shall you spare or conceal him. ⁹But you shall surely kill him; your hand shall be first against him to put him to death, and afterwards the hand of all the people. ¹⁰So you shall stone him to death because he has sought to seduce you from the LORD your God who brought you out from the land of Egypt, out of the house of slavery. ¹¹Then all Israel will hear and be afraid, and will never again do such a wicked thing among you.

¹²"If you hear in one of your cities, which the LORD your God is giving you to live in, *anyone* saying *that* ¹³some worthless men have gone out from among you and have seduced the inhabitants of their city, saying, 'Let us go and serve other gods' (whom you have not known), ¹⁴then you shall investigate and search out and inquire thoroughly. If it is true *and* the matter established that this abomination has been done among you, ¹⁵you shall surely strike the inhabitants of that city with the edge of the sword, utterly destroying it and all that is in it and its cattle with the edge of the sword. ¹⁶Then you shall gather all its booty into the middle of its open square and burn the city and all its booty with fire as a whole burnt offering to the LORD your God; and it shall be a ruin forever. It shall never be rebuilt. ¹⁷Nothing from that which is put under the ban shall cling to your hand, in order that the LORD may turn from His burning anger and show mercy to you, and have compassion on you and make you increase, just as He has sworn to your fathers, ¹⁸if you will listen to the voice of the LORD your God, keeping all His commandments which I am commanding you today, and doing what is right in the sight of the LORD your God.

14 "You are the sons of the LORD your God; you shall not cut yourselves nor shave your forehead for the sake of the dead. ²For you are a holy people to the LORD your God, and the LORD has chosen you to be a people for His own possession out of all the peoples who are on the face of the earth.

³"You shall not eat any detestable thing. ⁴These are the animals which you may eat: the ox, the sheep, the goat, ⁵the deer, the gazelle, the roebuck, the wild goat, the ibex, the antelope and the mountain sheep. ⁶Any animal that divides the hoof and has the hoof split in two *and* chews the cud, among the animals, that you may eat. ⁷Nevertheless, you

are not to eat of these among those which chew the cud, or among those that divide the hoof in two: the camel and the rabbit and the shaphan, for though they chew the cud, they do not divide the hoof; they are unclean for you. ⁸ The pig, because it divides the hoof but *does* not *chew* the cud, it is unclean for you. You shall not eat any of their flesh nor touch their carcasses.

⁹ "These you may eat of all that are in water: anything that has fins and scales you may eat, ¹⁰ but anything that does not have fins and scales you shall not eat; it is unclean for you.

¹¹ "You may eat any clean bird. ¹² But these are the ones which you shall not eat: the eagle and the vulture and the buzzard, ¹³ and the red kite, the falcon, and the kite in their kinds, ¹⁴ and every raven in its kind, ¹⁵ and the ostrich, the owl, the sea gull, and the hawk in their kinds, ¹⁶ the little owl, the great owl, the white owl, ¹⁷ the pelican, the carrion vulture, the cormorant, ¹⁸ the stork, and the heron in their kinds, and the hoopoe and the bat. ¹⁹ And all the teeming life with wings are unclean to you; they shall not be eaten. ²⁰ You may eat any clean bird.

²¹ "You shall not eat anything which dies *of itself.* You may give it to the alien who is in your town, so that he may eat it, or you may sell it to a foreigner, for you are a holy people to the LORD your God. You shall not boil a young goat in its mother's milk.

²² "You shall surely tithe all the produce from what you sow, which comes out of the field every year. ²³ You shall eat in the presence of the LORD your God, at the place where He chooses to establish His name, the tithe of your grain, your new wine, your oil, and the firstborn of your herd and your flock, so that you may learn to fear the LORD your God always. ²⁴ If the distance is so great for you that you are not able to bring the *tithe,* since the place where the LORD your God chooses to set His name is too far away from you when the LORD your God blesses you, ²⁵ then you shall exchange *it* for money, and bind the money in your hand and go to the place which the LORD your God chooses. ²⁶ You may spend the money for whatever your heart desires: for oxen, or sheep, or wine, or strong drink, or whatever your heart desires; and there you shall eat in the presence of the LORD your God and rejoice, you and your household. ²⁷ Also you shall not neglect the Levite who is in your town, for he has no portion or inheritance among you.

²⁸ "At the end of every third year you shall bring out all the tithe of your produce in that year, and shall deposit *it* in your town. ²⁹ The Levite, because he has no portion or inheritance among you, and the alien, the orphan and the widow who are in your town, shall come and eat and be satisfied, in order that the LORD your God may bless you in all the work of your hand which you do.

Psalm 37:23–29

²³ The steps of a man are
    established by the LORD,
And He delights in his way.
²⁴ When he falls, he will not
    be hurled headlong,
Because the LORD is the One
    who holds his hand.
²⁵ I have been young and now
    I am old,
Yet I have not seen the
    righteous forsaken
Or his descendants begging
    bread.
²⁶ All day long he is gracious
    and lends,
And his descendants are a
    blessing.

²⁷ Depart from evil and do
    good,
So you will abide forever.
²⁸ For the LORD loves justice
And does not forsake His
    godly ones;
They are preserved forever,
But the descendants of the
    wicked will be cut off.
²⁹ The righteous will inherit
    the land
And dwell in it forever.

Proverbs 12:15–16

¹⁵ The way of a fool is right
    in his own eyes,
But a wise man is he who
    listens to counsel.
¹⁶ A fool's anger is known at once,
    But a prudent man conceals
    dishonor.

Luke 2:25–52

²⁵ And there was a man in Jerusalem whose name was Simeon; and this man was righteous and devout, looking for the consolation of Israel; and the Holy Spirit was upon him. ²⁶ And it had been revealed to him by the Holy Spirit that he would not see death before he had seen the Lord's Christ. ²⁷ And he came

2:26 it had been revealed to him. It is significant that with messianic expectation running so high (3:15), and with the many Old Testament prophecies that spoke of His coming, still only a handful of people realized the significance of Christ's birth. Most of them, including Simeon, received some angelic message or other special revelation to make the fulfillment of the Old Testament prophecies clear.

in the Spirit into the temple; and when the parents brought in the child Jesus, to carry out for Him the custom of the Law, 28 then he took Him into his arms, and blessed God, and said,

29 "Now Lord, You are releasing
Your bond-servant to
depart in peace,
According to Your word;
30 For my eyes have seen Your
salvation,
31 Which You have prepared
in the presence of all
peoples,
32 A LIGHT OF REVELATION
TO THE GENTILES,
And the glory of Your people
Israel."

33 And His father and mother were amazed at the things which were being said about Him. 34 And Simeon blessed them and said to Mary His mother, "Behold, this *Child* is appointed for the fall and rise of many in Israel, and for a sign to be opposed— 35 and a sword will pierce even your own soul—to the end that thoughts from many hearts may be revealed."

36 And there was a prophetess, Anna the daughter of Phanuel, of the tribe of Asher. She was advanced in years and had lived with *her* husband seven years after her marriage, 37 and then as a widow to the age of eighty-four. She never left the temple, serving night and day with fastings and prayers. 38 At that very moment she came up and *began* giving thanks to God, and continued to speak of Him to all those who were looking for the redemption of Jerusalem.

39 When they had performed everything according to the Law of the Lord, they returned to Galilee, to their own city of Nazareth. 40 The Child continued to grow and become strong,

2:36 a prophetess. This refers to a woman who spoke God's Word. She was a teacher of the OT, not a source of revelation. The Old Testament mentions only 3 women who prophesied: Miriam (Ex 15:20); Deborah (Jdg 4:4); Huldah (2Ki 22:14; 2Ch 34:22). One other, the "prophetess" Noadiah, was evidently a false prophet, grouped by Nehemiah with his enemies. Isaiah 8:3 refers to the prophet's wife as a "prophetess"—but there is no evidence Isaiah's wife prophesied. Perhaps she is so-called because the child she bore was given a name that was prophetic (Is 8:3–4). This use of the title for Isaiah's wife also shows that the title does not necessarily indicate an ongoing revelatory prophetic ministry. Rabbinical tradition also regarded Sarah, Hannah, Abigail, and Esther as prophetesses (apparently to make an even 7 with Miriam, Deborah, and Huldah). In the NT, the daughters of Philip prophesied (Ac 21:9).

increasing in wisdom; and the grace of God was upon Him. 41 Now His parents went to Jerusalem every year at the Feast of the Passover. 42 And when He became twelve, they went up *there* according to the custom of the Feast; 43 and as they were returning, after spending the full number of days, the boy Jesus stayed behind in Jerusalem. But His parents were unaware of it, 44 but supposed Him to be in the caravan, and went a day's journey; and they *began* looking for Him among their relatives and acquaintances. 45 When they did not find Him, they returned to Jerusalem looking for Him. 46 Then, after three days they found Him in the temple, sitting in the midst of the teachers, both listening to them and asking them questions. 47 And all who heard Him were amazed at His understanding and His answers. 48 When they saw Him, they were astonished; and His mother said to Him, "Son, why have You treated us this way? Behold, Your father and I have been anxiously looking for You." 49 And He said to them, "Why is it that you were looking for Me? Did you not know that I had to be in My Father's *house?*" 50 But they did not understand the statement which He had made to them. 51 And He went down with them and came to Nazareth, and He continued in subjection to them; and His mother treasured all *these* things in her heart.

52 And Jesus kept increasing in wisdom and stature, and in favor with God and men.

When Jesus was 12 years old, He celebrated His first Feast of the Passover in preparation for that rite of passage into adulthood (*Bar mitzvah*). After the celebration, it says that "Jesus stayed behind" (v. 43). In stark contrast to the apocryphal gospels' spurious tales of youthful miracles and supernatural exploits, this lone biblical insight into the youth of Jesus portrays Him as a typical boy in a typical family. His lingering was neither mischievous nor disobedient—it was owing to a simple mistaken presumption on His parents' part (v. 44) that He was left behind.

Obviously Joseph and Mary were traveling with a large caravan of friends and relatives from Nazareth. Men and women in such a group might have been separated by some distance, and it appears each parent thought He was with the other. The reference to "three days" (v. 46) probably means they realized He was missing at the end of a full day's travel. That required another full day's journey back to Jerusalem, and the better part of another day was spent seeking Him. They found Jesus among the teachers in the temple, "listening to them and asking them questions." He was utterly respectful; but even at that young age, His questions showed a wisdom that put the teachers to shame (v. 47).

In the exchange of words that follow, Mary's words convey a tone of exasperation normal for any mother under such circumstances, but misplaced in this case. He was not hiding from them or defying their authority. In fact, He had done precisely what any child should do under such circumstances (being left by His parents)—He went to a safe, public place, in the presence of trusted adults, where His parents could be expected to come looking for Him (v. 49). Jesus' reference to "My Father's house" reveals a genuine amazement that they did not know where to look for Him. This also reveals that, even at so young an age, He had a clear consciousness of His identity and mission. However, He "continued in subjection to them" (v. 51). His relationship with His heavenly Father did not override or nullify His duty to His earthly parents. His obedience to the fifth commandment was an essential part of the perfect legal obedience He rendered on our behalf (Heb 4:4; 5:8–9).

 # MARCH 27

Deuteronomy 15:1–16:22

15 "At the end of *every* seven years you shall grant a remission *of debts.* ²This is the manner of remission: every creditor shall release what he has loaned to his neighbor; he shall not exact it of his neighbor and his brother, because the LORD'S remission has been proclaimed. ³From a foreigner you may exact *it,* but your hand shall release whatever of yours is with your brother. ⁴However, there will be no poor among you, since the LORD will surely bless you in the land which the LORD your God is giving you as an inheritance to possess, ⁵if only you listen obediently to the voice of the LORD your God, to observe carefully all this commandment which I am commanding you today. ⁶For the LORD your God will bless you as He has promised you, and you will lend to many nations, but you will not borrow; and you will rule over many nations, but they will not rule over you.

⁷"If there is a poor man with you, one of your brothers, in any of your towns in your land which the LORD your God is giving you, you shall not harden your heart, nor close your hand from your poor brother; ⁸but you shall freely open your hand to him, and shall generously lend him sufficient for his need *in* whatever he lacks. ⁹Beware that there is no base thought in your heart, saying, 'The seventh year, the year of remission, is near,' and your eye is hostile toward your poor brother, and you give him nothing; then he may cry to the LORD against you, and it will be a sin in you. ¹⁰You shall generously give to him, and your heart shall not be grieved when you give to him, because for this thing the LORD your God will bless you in all your work and in all your undertakings. ¹¹For the poor will never cease *to be* in the land; therefore I command you, saying, 'You shall freely open your hand to your brother, to your needy and poor in your land.'

¹²"If your kinsman, a Hebrew man or woman, is sold to you, then he shall serve you six years, but in the seventh year you shall set him free. ¹³When you set him free, you shall not send him away empty-handed. ¹⁴You shall furnish him liberally from your flock and from your threshing floor and from your wine vat; you shall give to him as the LORD your God has blessed you. ¹⁵You shall remember that you were a slave in the land of Egypt, and the LORD your God redeemed you; therefore I command you this today. ¹⁶It shall come about if he says to you, 'I will not go out from you,' because he loves you

and your household, since he fares well with you; [17] then you shall take an awl and pierce it through his ear into the door, and he shall be your servant forever. Also you shall do likewise to your maidservant.

[18] "It shall not seem hard to you when you set him free, for he has given you six years *with* double the service of a hired man; so the LORD your God will bless you in whatever you do.

[19] "You shall consecrate to the LORD your God all the firstborn males that are born of your herd and of your flock; you shall not work with the firstborn of your herd, nor shear the firstborn of your flock. [20] You and your household shall eat it every year before the LORD your God in the place which the LORD chooses. [21] But if it has any defect, *such as* lameness or blindness, *or* any serious defect, you shall not sacrifice it to the LORD your God. [22] You shall eat it within your gates; the unclean and the clean alike *may eat it,* as a gazelle or a deer. [23] Only you shall not eat its blood; you are to pour it out on the ground like water.

16 "Observe the month of Abib and celebrate the Passover to the LORD your God, for in the month of Abib the LORD your God brought you out of Egypt by night. [2] You shall sacrifice the Passover to the LORD your God from the flock and the herd, in the place where the LORD chooses to establish His name. [3] You shall not eat leavened bread with it; seven days you shall eat with it unleavened bread, the bread of affliction (for you came out of the land of Egypt in haste), so that you may remember all the days of your life the day when you came out of the land of Egypt. [4] For seven days no leaven shall be seen with you in all your territory, and none of the flesh which you sacrifice on the evening of the first day shall remain overnight until morning. [5] You are not allowed to sacrifice the Passover in any of your towns which the LORD your God is giving you; [6] but at the place where the LORD your God chooses to establish His name, you shall sacrifice the Passover in the evening at sunset, at the time that you came out of Egypt. [7] You shall cook and eat *it* in the place which the LORD your God chooses. In the morning you are to return to your tents. [8] Six days you shall eat unleavened bread, and on the seventh day there shall be a solemn assembly to the LORD your God; you shall do no work *on it.*

[9] "You shall count seven weeks for yourself; you shall begin to count seven weeks from the time you begin to put the sickle to the standing grain. [10] Then you shall celebrate the Feast of Weeks to the LORD your God with a tribute of a freewill offering of your hand, which you shall give just as the LORD your God blesses you; [11] and you shall rejoice before the LORD your God, you and your son and your daughter and your male and female servants and the Levite who is in your town, and the stranger and the orphan and the widow who are in your midst, in the place where the LORD your God chooses to establish His name. [12] You shall remember that you were a slave in Egypt, and you shall be careful to observe these statutes.

[13] "You shall celebrate the Feast of Booths seven days after you have gathered in from your threshing floor and your wine vat; [14] and you shall rejoice in your feast, you and your son and your daughter and your male and female servants and the Levite and the stranger and the orphan and the widow who are in your towns. [15] Seven days you shall celebrate a feast to the LORD your God in the place which the LORD chooses, because the LORD your God will bless you in all your produce and in all the work of your hands, so that you will be altogether joyful.

[16] "Three times in a year all your males shall appear before the LORD your God in the place which He chooses, at the Feast of Unleavened Bread and at the Feast of Weeks and at the Feast of Booths, and they shall not appear before the LORD empty-handed. [17] Every man shall give as he is able, according to the blessing of the LORD your God which He has given you.

[18] "You shall appoint for yourself judges and officers in all your towns which the LORD your God is giving you, according to your tribes, and they shall judge the people with righteous judgment. [19] You shall not distort justice; you shall not be partial, and you shall not take a bribe, for a bribe blinds the eyes of the wise and perverts the words of the righteous. [20] Justice, *and only* justice, you shall pursue, that you may live and possess the land which the LORD your God is giving you.

[21] "You shall not plant for yourself an Asherah of any kind of tree beside the altar of the LORD your God, which you shall make for

---

16:21–22 Asherah...*sacred* pillar. Asherah was the name of a Canaanite goddess, represented by a wooden pole, image or tree. A stone pillar symbolic of male fertility was prevalent in the Canaanite religion. These were forbidden by the first two commandments (Ex 20:3–6; Dt 5:7–10).

yourself. ²² You shall not set up for yourself a *sacred* pillar which the LORD your God hates.

Psalm 37:30-36

³⁰ The mouth of the righteous
　　utters wisdom,
　　And his tongue speaks justice.
³¹ The law of his God is in his heart;
　　His steps do not slip.
³² The wicked spies upon the righteous
　　And seeks to kill him.
³³ The LORD will not leave
　　　him in his hand
　　Or let him be condemned
　　　when he is judged.
³⁴ Wait for the LORD and keep His way,
　　And He will exalt you to
　　　inherit the land;
　　When the wicked are cut
　　　off, you will see it.

³⁵ I have seen a wicked, violent man
　　Spreading himself like a luxuriant
　　　tree in its native soil.
³⁶ Then he passed away, and
　　　lo, he was no more;
　　I sought for him, but he
　　　could not be found.

Proverbs 12:17-19

¹⁷ He who speaks truth tells
　　what is right,
　　But a false witness, deceit.
¹⁸ There is one who speaks rashly
　　like the thrusts of a sword,
　　But the tongue of the wise
　　brings healing.

12:18 speaks...thrusts. The contrast here is between cutting words that are spoken "rashly" (Ps 106:33) and thoughtful words that bring health (Eph 4:29-30).

¹⁹ Truthful lips will be
　　established forever,
　　But a lying tongue is only
　　　for a moment.

Luke 3:1-38

3 Now in the fifteenth year of the reign of Tiberius Caesar, when Pontius Pilate was governor of Judea, and Herod was tetrarch of Galilee, and his brother Philip was tetrarch of the region of Ituraea and Trachonitis, and Lysanias was tetrarch of Abilene, ² in the high priesthood of Annas and Caiaphas, the word of God came to John, the son of Zacharias, in the wilderness. ³ And he came into all the district around the Jordan, preaching a baptism of repentance for the forgiveness of sins; ⁴ as it is written in the book of the words of Isaiah the prophet,

3:2 high priesthood of Annas and Caiaphas. According to Josephus, Annas served as High Priest A.D. 6-15, when he was deposed by Roman officials. He nonetheless retained *de facto* power, as seen in the fact that his successors included 5 of his sons and Caiaphas, a son-in-law (Mt 26:3). Caiaphas was the actual High Priest during the time Luke describes, but Annas still controlled the office. This is seen clearly in the fact that Christ was taken to Annas first after His arrest, then to Caiaphas (Mt 26:57).

3:4 MAKE HIS PATHS STRAIGHT. Quoted from Isaiah 40:3-5. A monarch traveling in wilderness regions would have a crew of workmen go ahead to make sure the road was clear of debris, obstructions, potholes, and other hazards that made the journey difficult. In a spiritual sense, John was calling the people of Israel to prepare their hearts for the coming of their Messiah.

"THE VOICE OF ONE CRYING
　　IN THE WILDERNESS,
　'MAKE READY THE WAY OF THE LORD,
　　MAKE HIS PATHS STRAIGHT.
⁵ 'EVERY RAVINE WILL BE FILLED,
　　AND EVERY MOUNTAIN AND HILL
　　　WILL BE BROUGHT LOW;
　　THE CROOKED WILL BECOME STRAIGHT,
　　AND THE ROUGH ROADS SMOOTH;
⁶ AND ALL FLESH WILL SEE THE
　　SALVATION OF GOD.'"

⁷ So he *began* saying to the crowds who were going out to be baptized by him, "You brood of vipers, who warned you to flee from the wrath to come? ⁸ Therefore bear fruits in keeping with repentance, and do not begin to say to yourselves, 'We have Abraham for our father,' for I say to you that from these stones God is able to raise up children to Abraham. ⁹ Indeed the axe is already laid at the root of the trees; so every tree that does not bear good fruit is cut down and thrown into the fire."

¹⁰ And the crowds were questioning him,

saying, "Then what shall we do?" ¹¹And he would answer and say to them, "The man who has two tunics is to share with him who has none; and he who has food is to do likewise." ¹²And some tax collectors also came to be baptized, and they said to him, "Teacher, what shall we do?" ¹³And he said to them, "Collect no more than what you have been ordered to." ¹⁴Some soldiers were questioning him, saying, "And what about us, what shall we do?" And he said to them, "Do not take money from anyone by force, or accuse anyone falsely, and be content with your wages."

¹⁵Now while the people were in a state of expectation and all were wondering in their hearts about John, as to whether he was the Christ, ¹⁶John answered and said to them all, "As for me, I baptize you with water; but One is coming who is mightier than I, and I am not fit to untie the thong of His sandals; He will baptize you with the Holy Spirit and fire. ¹⁷His winnowing fork is in His hand to thoroughly clear His threshing floor, and to gather the wheat into His barn; but He will burn up the chaff with unquenchable fire."

¹⁸So with many other exhortations he preached the gospel to the people. ¹⁹But when Herod the tetrarch was reprimanded by him because of Herodias, his brother's wife, and because of all the wicked things which Herod had done, ²⁰Herod also added this to them all: he locked John up in prison.

²¹Now when all the people were baptized, Jesus was also baptized, and while He was praying, heaven was opened, ²²and the Holy Spirit descended upon Him in bodily form like a dove, and a voice came out of heaven, "You are My beloved Son, in You I am well-pleased."

²³When He began His ministry, Jesus Himself was about thirty years of age, being, as was supposed, the son of Joseph, the son of Eli, ²⁴the son of Matthat, the son of Levi, the son of Melchi, the son of Jannai, the son of Joseph, ²⁵the son of Mattathias, the son of Amos, the son of Nahum, the son of Hesli, the son of Naggai, ²⁶the son of Maath, the son of Mattathias, the son of Semein, the son of Josech, the son of Joda, ²⁷the son of Joanan, the son of Rhesa, the son of Zerubbabel, the son of Shealtiel, the son of Neri, ²⁸the son of Melchi, the son of Addi, the son of Cosam, the son of Elmadam, the son of Er, ²⁹the son of Joshua, the son of Eliezer, the son of Jorim, the son of Matthat, the son of Levi, ³⁰the son of Simeon, the son of Judah, the son of Joseph, the son of Jonam, the son of Eliakim, ³¹the son of Melea, the son of Menna, the son of Mattatha, the son of Nathan, the son of David, ³²the son of Jesse, the son of Obed, the son of Boaz, the son of Salmon, the son of Nahshon, ³³the son of Amminadab, the son of Admin, the son of Ram, the son of Hezron, the son of Perez, the son of Judah, ³⁴the son of Jacob, the son of Isaac, the son of Abraham, the son of Terah, the son of Nahor, ³⁵the son of Serug, the son of Reu, the son of Peleg, the son of Heber, the son of Shelah, ³⁶the son of Cainan, the son of Arphaxad, the son of Shem, the son of Noah, the son of Lamech, ³⁷the son of Methuselah, the son of Enoch, the son of Jared, the son of Mahalaleel, the son of Cainan, ³⁸the son of Enosh, the son of Seth, the son of Adam, the son of God.

DAY 27: How were God's people to treat the poor?

As the Israelites prepared to enter the Promised Land, Deuteronomy 15:4 has an interesting statement: "However, there will be no poor among you . . ." Idealistically, there was the possibility that poverty would be eradicated in the land "since the LORD will surely bless you in the land." The fullness of that blessing, however, would be contingent on the completeness of Israel's obedience. Thus, vv. 4–6 were an encouragement to strive for a reduction of poverty while at the same time they stressed the abundance of the provision God would make in the Promised Land.

God specifically warns them about hardening their hearts against the poor, but to "freely open your hand to him, and shall generously lend him sufficient for his need" (v. 8). The attitude of the Israelites toward the poor in their community was to be one of warmth and generosity. The poor were given whatever was necessary to meet their needs, even with the realization that such "loans" would never need to be paid back.

"For the poor will never cease to be in the land," Moses adds (v. 11). Realistically (in contrast to v. 4), the disobedience toward the Lord on Israel's part meant that there would always be poor people in the land of Israel. Jesus repeated this truism in Matthew 26:11. Even if a Hebrew was sold into a period of servitude for his debts, his master "shall not send him away empty-handed" (Dt 15:13). When a slave had completed his time of service, his former owner was to make ample provision for him so that he would not begin his state of new freedom in destitution.

MARCH 28

Deuteronomy 17:1–18:22

17 "You shall not sacrifice to the LORD your God an ox or a sheep which has a blemish *or* any defect, for that is a detestable thing to the LORD your God.

² "If there is found in your midst, in any of your towns, which the LORD your God is giving you, a man or a woman who does what is evil in the sight of the LORD your God, by transgressing His covenant, ³ and has gone and served other gods and worshiped them, or the sun or the moon or any of the heavenly host, which I have not commanded, ⁴ and if it is told you and you have heard of it, then you shall inquire thoroughly. Behold, if it is true and the thing certain that this detestable thing has been done in Israel, ⁵ then you shall bring out that man or that woman who has done this evil deed to your gates, *that is,* the man or the woman, and you shall stone them to death. ⁶ On the evidence of two witnesses or three witnesses, he who is to die shall be put to death; he shall not be put to death on the evidence of one witness. ⁷ The hand of the witnesses shall be first against him to put him to death, and afterward the hand of all the people. So you shall purge the evil from your midst.

⁸ "If any case is too difficult for you to decide, between one kind of homicide or another, between one kind of lawsuit or another, and between one kind of assault or another, being cases of dispute in your courts, then you shall arise and go up to the place which the LORD your God chooses. ⁹ So you shall come to the Levitical priest or the judge who is *in office* in those days, and you shall inquire *of them* and they will declare to you the verdict in the case. ¹⁰ You shall do according to the terms of the verdict which they declare to you from that place which the LORD chooses; and you shall be careful to observe according to all that they teach you. ¹¹ According to the terms of the law which they teach you, and according to the verdict which they tell you, you shall do; you shall not turn aside from the word which they declare to you, to the right or the left. ¹² The man who acts presumptuously by not listening to the priest who stands there to serve the LORD your God, nor to the judge, that man shall die; thus you shall purge the evil from Israel. ¹³ Then all the people will hear and be afraid, and will not act presumptuously again.

¹⁴ "When you enter the land which the LORD your God gives you, and you possess it and live in it, and you say, 'I will set a king over me like all the nations who are around me,' ¹⁵ you shall surely set a king over you whom the LORD your God chooses, *one* from among your countrymen you shall set as king over yourselves; you may not put a foreigner over yourselves who is not your countryman. ¹⁶ Moreover, he shall not multiply horses for himself, nor shall he cause the people to return to Egypt to multiply horses, since the LORD has said to you, 'You shall never again return that way.' ¹⁷ He shall not multiply wives for himself, or else his heart will turn away; nor shall he greatly increase silver and gold for himself.

17:16–17 multiply…multiply…multiply. Restrictions were placed on the king: 1) he must not acquire many horses; 2) he must not take multiple wives; and 3) he must not accumulate much silver and gold. The king was not to rely on military strength, political alliances, or wealth for his position and authority, but he was to look to the Lord. Solomon violated all of those prohibitions, while his father, David, violated the last two. Solomon's wives brought idolatry into Jerusalem, which resulted in the kingdom being divided (1Ki 11:1–43).

¹⁸ "Now it shall come about when he sits on the throne of his kingdom, he shall write for himself a copy of this law on a scroll in the presence of the Levitical priests. ¹⁹ It shall be with him and he shall read it all the days of his life, that he may learn to fear the LORD his God, by carefully observing all the words of this law and these statutes, ²⁰ that his heart may not be lifted up above his countrymen and that he may not turn aside from the commandment, to the right or the left, so that he and his sons may continue long in his kingdom in the midst of Israel.

18 "The Levitical priests, the whole tribe of Levi, shall have no portion or inheritance with Israel; they shall eat the LORD'S offerings by fire and His portion. ² They shall have no inheritance among their countrymen; the LORD is their inheritance, as He promised them.

³ "Now this shall be the priests' due from the people, from those who offer a sacrifice, either an ox or a sheep, of which they shall give to the priest the shoulder and the two cheeks and the stomach. ⁴ You shall give him the first fruits of your grain, your new wine, and your oil, and the first shearing of your sheep. ⁵ For the LORD your God has chosen

him and his sons from all your tribes, to stand and serve in the name of the LORD forever.

6 "Now if a Levite comes from any of your towns throughout Israel where he resides, and comes whenever he desires to the place which the LORD chooses, 7 then he shall serve in the name of the LORD his God, like all his fellow Levites who stand there before the LORD. 8 They shall eat equal portions, except *what they receive* from the sale of their fathers' *estates.*

9 "When you enter the land which the LORD your God gives you, you shall not learn to imitate the detestable things of those nations. 10 There shall not be found among you anyone who makes his son or his daughter pass through the fire, one who uses divination, one who practices witchcraft, or one who interprets omens, or a sorcerer, 11 or one who casts a spell, or a medium, or a spiritist, or one who calls up the dead. 12 For whoever does these things is detestable to the LORD; and because of these detestable things the LORD your God will drive them out before you. 13 You shall be blameless before the LORD your God. 14 For those nations, which you shall dispossess, listen to those who practice witchcraft and to diviners, but as for you, the LORD your God has not allowed you *to do* so.

15 "The LORD your God will raise up for you a prophet like me from among you, from your countrymen, you shall listen to him. 16 This is according to all that you asked of the LORD your God in Horeb on the day of the assembly, saying, 'Let me not hear again the voice of the LORD my God, let me not see this great fire anymore, or I will die.' 17 The LORD said to me, 'They have spoken well. 18 I will raise up a prophet from among their countrymen like you, and I will put My words in his mouth, and he shall speak to them all that I command him. 19 It shall come about that whoever will not listen to My words which he shall speak in My name, I Myself will require *it* of him. 20 But the prophet who speaks a word presumptuously in My name which I have not commanded him to speak, or which he speaks in the name of other gods, that prophet shall die.' 21 You may say in your heart, 'How will we know the word which the LORD has not spoken?' 22 When a prophet speaks in the name of the LORD, if the thing does not come about or come true, that is the thing which the LORD has not spoken. The prophet has spoken it presumptuously; you shall not be afraid of him.

Psalm 37:37-40

37 Mark the blameless man, and behold the upright;
For the man of peace will have a posterity.
38 But transgressors will be altogether destroyed;
The posterity of the wicked will be cut off.
39 But the salvation of the righteous is from the LORD;
He is their strength in time of trouble.
40 The LORD helps them and delivers them;
He delivers them from the wicked and saves them,
Because they take refuge in Him.

Proverbs 12:20-22

20 Deceit is in the heart of those who devise evil,
But counselors of peace have joy.
21 No harm befalls the righteous,
But the wicked are filled with trouble.
22 Lying lips are an abomination to the LORD,
But those who deal faithfully are His delight.

Luke 4:1-30

4 Jesus, full of the Holy Spirit, returned from the Jordan and was led around by the Spirit in the wilderness 2 for forty days, being tempted by the devil. And He ate nothing during those days, and when they had ended, He became hungry. 3 And the devil said to Him, "If You are the Son of God, tell this stone to become bread." 4 And Jesus answered him, "It is written, 'MAN SHALL NOT LIVE ON BREAD ALONE.'"

5 And he led Him up and showed Him all the kingdoms of the world in a moment of time. 6 And the devil said to Him, "I will give You all this domain and its glory; for it has been handed over to me, and I give it to whomever I wish. 7 Therefore if You worship before me, it shall all be Yours." 8 Jesus answered him, "It is written, 'YOU SHALL WORSHIP THE LORD YOUR GOD AND SERVE HIM ONLY.'"

9 And he led Him to Jerusalem and had Him stand on the pinnacle of the temple, and said to Him, "If You are the Son of God, throw Yourself down from here; 10 for it is written,

'HE WILL COMMAND HIS ANGELS
CONCERNING YOU TO GUARD YOU,'

11 and,

'ON *their* HANDS THEY
WILL BEAR YOU UP,

SO THAT YOU WILL NOT STRIKE
YOUR FOOT AGAINST A STONE.'"

¹²And Jesus answered and said to him, "It is said, 'YOU SHALL NOT PUT THE LORD YOUR GOD TO THE TEST.'"

¹³When the devil had finished every temptation, he left Him until an opportune time.

¹⁴And Jesus returned to Galilee in the power of the Spirit, and news about Him spread through all the surrounding district. ¹⁵And He *began* teaching in their synagogues and was praised by all.

¹⁶And He came to Nazareth, where He had been brought up; and as was His custom, He entered the synagogue on the Sabbath, and stood up to read. ¹⁷And the book of the prophet Isaiah was handed to Him. And He opened the book and found the place where it was written,

¹⁸ "THE SPIRIT OF THE LORD IS UPON ME,
BECAUSE HE ANOINTED ME TO PREACH
THE GOSPEL TO THE POOR.
HE HAS SENT ME TO PROCLAIM
RELEASE TO THE CAPTIVES,
AND RECOVERY OF SIGHT TO THE BLIND,
TO SET FREE THOSE WHO
ARE OPPRESSED,
¹⁹ TO PROCLAIM THE FAVORABLE
YEAR OF THE LORD."

²⁰And He closed the book, gave it back to the attendant and sat down; and the eyes of all in the synagogue were fixed on Him. ²¹And He began to say to them, "Today this Scripture has been fulfilled in your hearing." ²²And all were speaking well of Him, and wondering at the gracious words which were falling from His lips; and they were saying, "Is this not Joseph's son?" ²³And He said to them, "No doubt you will quote this proverb to Me, 'Physician, heal yourself! Whatever we heard was done at Capernaum, do here in your hometown as

4:21 this Scripture has been fulfilled. This was an unambiguous claim that He was the Messiah who fulfilled the prophecy. They correctly understood His meaning but could not accept such lofty claims from One whom they knew so well as the carpenter's son (v. 22; see Mt 13:55).

well.'" ²⁴And He said, "Truly I say to you, no prophet is welcome in his hometown. ²⁵But I say to you in truth, there were many widows in Israel in the days of Elijah, when the sky was shut up for three years and six months, when a great famine came over all the land; ²⁶and yet Elijah was sent to none of them, but only to Zarephath, *in the land* of Sidon, to a woman who was a widow. ²⁷And there were many lepers in Israel in the time of Elisha the prophet; and none of them was cleansed, but only Naaman the Syrian." ²⁸And all *the people* in the synagogue were filled with rage as they heard these things; ²⁹and they got up and drove Him out of the city, and led Him to the brow of the hill on which their city had been built, in order to throw Him down the cliff. ³⁰But passing through their midst, He went His way.

4:28 filled with rage. This is Luke's first mention of hostile opposition to Christ's ministry. What seems to have sparked the Nazarenes' fury was Christ's suggestion that divine grace might be withheld from them yet extended to Gentiles.

4:30 passing through their midst. The implication is that this was a miraculous escape—the first of several similar incidents in which He escaped a premature death at the hands of a mob (Jn 7:30; 8:59; 10:39).

DAY 28: Who is the Prophet that Moses refers to in Deuteronomy 18:15–19?

Read through 18:15–19 again where Moses promises that "the LORD your God will raise up for you a prophet like me from among you." The singular pronoun emphasizes the ultimate Prophet who was to come. Both the Old Testament (34:10) and the New Testament (Ac 3:22–23; 7:37) interpret this passage as a reference to the coming Messiah, who, like Moses, would receive and preach divine revelation and lead His people (Jn 1:21, 25, 43–45; 6:14; 7:40). In fact, Jesus was like Moses in several other ways: 1) He was spared death as a baby (Ex 2; Mt 2:13–23); 2) He renounced a royal court (Php 2:5–8; Heb 11:24–27); 3) He had compassion on His people (Nu 27:17; Mt 9:36); 4) He made intercession for the people (Dt 9:18; Heb 7:25); 5) He spoke with God face-to-face (Ex 34:29–30; 2Co 3:7); and 6) He was the mediator of a covenant (Dt 29:1; Heb 8:6–7).

In contrast to the true Prophet, Moses predicted there would be false prophets who would come to Israel, speaking not in the name of the Lord, but in the name of false gods (vv. 20–22).

How could the people tell if a prophet was authentically speaking for God? Moses said, "If the thing does not come about," it was not from God. The characteristic of false prophets is the failure of their predictions to always come true. Sometimes false prophets speak and it happens as they said, but they are representing false gods and trying to turn people from the true God—they must be rejected and executed (13:1–5). Other times, false prophets are more subtle and identify with the true God but speak lies. If ever a prophecy of such a prophet fails, he is shown to be false (Jer 28:15–17; 29:30–32).

MARCH 29

Deuteronomy 19:1–20:20

19 "When the LORD your God cuts off the nations, whose land the LORD your God gives you, and you dispossess them and settle in their cities and in their houses, ²you shall set aside three cities for yourself in the midst of your land, which the LORD your God gives you to possess. ³You shall prepare the roads for yourself, and divide into three parts the territory of your land which the LORD your God will give you as a possession, so that any manslayer may flee there.

⁴"Now this is the case of the manslayer who may flee there and live: when he kills his friend unintentionally, not hating him previously— ⁵as when *a man* goes into the forest with his friend to cut wood, and his hand swings the axe to cut down the tree, and the iron *head* slips off the handle and strikes his friend so that he dies—he may flee to one of these cities and live; ⁶otherwise the avenger of blood might pursue the manslayer in the heat of his anger, and overtake him, because the way is long, and take his life, though he was not deserving of death, since he had not hated him previously. ⁷Therefore, I command you, saying, 'You shall set aside three cities for yourself.'

⁸"If the LORD your God enlarges your territory, just as He has sworn to your fathers, and gives you all the land which He promised to give your fathers— ⁹if you carefully observe all this commandment which I command you today, to love the LORD your God, and to walk in His ways always—then you shall add three more cities for yourself, besides these three. ¹⁰So innocent blood will not be shed in the midst of your land which the LORD your God gives you as an inheritance, and bloodguiltiness be on you.

¹¹"But if there is a man who hates his neighbor and lies in wait for him and rises up against him and strikes him so that he dies, and he flees to one of these cities, ¹²then the elders of his city shall send and take him from there and deliver him into the hand of the avenger of blood, that he may die. ¹³You shall not pity him, but you shall purge the blood of the innocent from Israel, that it may go well with you.

¹⁴"You shall not move your neighbor's boundary mark, which the ancestors have set, in your inheritance which you will inherit in the land that the LORD your God gives you to possess.

¹⁵"A single witness shall not rise up against a man on account of any iniquity or any sin which he has committed; on the evidence of two or three witnesses a matter shall be confirmed. ¹⁶If a malicious witness rises up against a man to accuse him of wrongdoing, ¹⁷then both the men who have the dispute shall stand before the LORD, before the priests and the judges who will be *in office* in those days. ¹⁸The judges shall investigate thoroughly, and if the witness is a false witness *and* he has accused his brother falsely, ¹⁹then you shall do to him just as he had intended to do to his brother. Thus you shall purge the evil from among you. ²⁰The rest will hear and be afraid, and will never again do such an evil thing among you. ²¹Thus you shall not show pity: life for life, eye for eye, tooth for tooth, hand for hand, foot for foot.

20 "When you go out to battle against your enemies and see horses and chariots *and* people more numerous than you, do not be afraid of them; for the LORD your God, who brought you up from the land of Egypt, is with you. ²When you are approaching the battle, the priest shall come near and speak to the people. ³He shall say to them, 'Hear, O Israel, you are approaching

20:1 do not be afraid. When Israelites went into battle, they were never to fear an enemy's horses or chariots because the outcome of a battle would never be determined by mere military strength. The command not to be afraid was based on God's power and faithfulness, which had already been proved to Israel in their deliverance from Egypt.

the battle against your enemies today. Do not be fainthearted. Do not be afraid, or panic, or tremble before them, ⁴for the LORD your God is the one who goes with you, to fight for you against your enemies, to save you.' ⁵The officers also shall speak to the people, saying, 'Who is the man that has built a new house and has not dedicated it? Let him depart and return to his house, otherwise he might die in the battle and another man would dedicate it. ⁶Who is the man that has planted a vineyard and has not begun to use its fruit? Let him depart and return to his house, otherwise he might die in the battle and another man would begin to use its fruit. ⁷And who is the man that is engaged to a woman and has not married her? Let him depart and return to his house, otherwise he might die in the battle and another man would marry her.' ⁸Then the officers shall speak further to the people and say, 'Who is the man that is afraid and fainthearted? Let him depart and return to his house, so that he might not make his brothers' hearts melt like his heart.' ⁹When the officers have finished speaking to the people, they shall appoint commanders of armies at the head of the people.

20:5–8 Let him depart and return to his house. Four exemptions from service in Israel's volunteer army were cited to illustrate the principle that anyone whose heart was not in the fight should not be there. Those who had other matters on their minds or were afraid were allowed to leave the army and return to their homes, since they would be useless in battle and even influence others to lose courage (v. 8).

---

¹⁰"When you approach a city to fight against it, you shall offer it terms of peace. ¹¹If it agrees to make peace with you and opens to you, then all the people who are found in it shall become your forced labor and shall serve you. ¹²However, if it does not make peace with you, but makes war against you, then you shall besiege it. ¹³When the LORD your God gives it into your hand, you shall strike all the men in it with the edge of the sword. ¹⁴Only the women and the children and the animals and all that is in the city, all its spoil, you shall take as booty for yourself; and you shall use the spoil of your enemies which the LORD your God has given you. ¹⁵Thus you shall do to all the cities that are very far from you, which are not of the cities

of these nations nearby. ¹⁶Only in the cities of these peoples that the LORD your God is giving you as an inheritance, you shall not leave alive anything that breathes. ¹⁷But you shall utterly destroy them, the Hittite and the Amorite, the Canaanite and the Perizzite, the Hivite and the Jebusite, as the LORD your God has commanded you, ¹⁸so that they may not teach you to do according to all their detestable things which they have done for their gods, so that you would sin against the LORD your God.

¹⁹"When you besiege a city a long time, to make war against it in order to capture it, you shall not destroy its trees by swinging an axe against them; for you may eat from them, and you shall not cut them down. For is the tree of the field a man, that it should be besieged by you? ²⁰Only the trees which you know are not fruit trees you shall destroy and cut down, that you may construct siegeworks against the city that is making war with you until it falls.

Psalm 38:1–8

A Psalm of David, for a memorial.

O LORD, rebuke me not in Your wrath,
And chasten me not in
  Your burning anger.
² For Your arrows have sunk
  deep into me,
And Your hand has pressed
  down on me.
³ There is no soundness in my flesh
  because of Your indignation;
There is no health in my bones
  because of my sin.
⁴ For my iniquities are gone
  over my head;
As a heavy burden they weigh
  too much for me.
⁵ My wounds grow foul *and* fester
Because of my folly.
⁶ I am bent over and greatly
  bowed down;
I go mourning all day long.
⁷ For my loins are filled with
  burning,
And there is no soundness
  in my flesh.
⁸ I am benumbed and badly crushed;
I groan because of the
  agitation of my heart.

Proverbs 12:23–25

²³ A prudent man conceals knowledge,
But the heart of fools proclaims folly.
²⁴ The hand of the diligent will rule,

12:23 conceals. Unlike the fool who makes all hear his folly, the wise person is a model of restraint and humility, speaking what he knows at an appropriate time (29:11).

> But the slack *hand* will be
> put to forced labor.
> ²⁵ Anxiety in a man's heart
> weighs it down,
> But a good word makes
> it glad.

Luke 4:31–44

³¹And He came down to Capernaum, a city of Galilee, and He was teaching them on the Sabbath; ³²and they were amazed at His teaching, for His message was with authority. ³³In the synagogue there was a man possessed by the spirit of an unclean demon, and he cried out with a loud voice, ³⁴"Let us alone! What business do we have with each other, Jesus of Nazareth? Have You come to destroy us? I know who You are—the Holy One of God!" ³⁵But Jesus rebuked him, saying, "Be quiet and come out of him!" And when the demon had thrown him down in the midst *of the people,* he came out of him without doing him any harm. ³⁶And amazement came upon them all, and they *began* talking with one another saying, "What is this message? For with authority and power He commands the unclean spirits and they come out." ³⁷And the report about Him was spreading into every locality in the surrounding district.

³⁸Then He got up and *left* the synagogue, and entered Simon's home. Now Simon's mother-in-law was suffering from a high fever, and they asked Him to help her. ³⁹And standing over her, He rebuked the fever, and it left her; and she immediately got up and waited on them.

⁴⁰While the sun was setting, all those who had any *who were* sick with various diseases brought them to Him; and laying His hands on each one of them, He was healing them. ⁴¹Demons also were coming out of many, shouting, "You are the Son of God!" But rebuking them, He would not allow them to speak, because they knew Him to be the Christ.

⁴²When day came, Jesus left and went to a secluded place; and the crowds were searching for Him, and came to Him and tried to keep Him from going away from them. ⁴³But He said to them, "I must preach the kingdom of God to the other cities also, for I was sent for this purpose." ⁴⁴So He kept on preaching in the synagogues of Judea.

4:38 Simon's mother-in-law. Peter was married (1Co 9:5), though no details about his wife are given anywhere in Scripture. **a high fever.** Matthew 8:14–15 and Mark 1:30–31 also report this miracle. But only Luke, the physician, remarks that the fever was "high," and makes note of the means Jesus used to heal her (v. 39).

DAY 29: What did the law warn about bringing false witness against another person?

In Deuteronomy 19:15, the law required that "on the evidence of two or three witnesses a matter shall be confirmed." More than one witness was necessary to convict a man of a crime. This principle was to act as a safeguard against the false witness who might bring an untruthful charge against a fellow Israelite. By requiring more than one witness, greater accuracy and objectivity was gained (Dt 17:6; Mt 18:15–17; 2Co 13:1).

However, it was possible that "a malicious witness [might rise] up against a man to accuse him of wrongdoing" (v. 16). In some cases, there would only be one witness who brought a charge against someone. When such a case was taken to the central tribunal of priests and judges for trial, and upon investigation the testimony of the witness was found to be false, the accuser received the punishment appropriate for the alleged crime (v. 19). Others looking on would be taught to "hear and be afraid, and will never again do such an evil thing among you" (v. 20). When the fate of the false witness became known in Israel, it would serve as a deterrent against giving false testimony in Israel's courts.

In Israel, the principle of legal justice (called *lex talionis,* "law of retaliation") or "eye for eye" (v. 21) was given to encourage appropriate punishment of a criminal in cases where there might be a tendency to be either too lenient or too strict (Ex 21:23–25; Lv 24:17–22). Jesus confronted the Jews of His day for taking this law out of the courts and using it for purposes of personal vengeance (Mt 5:38–42).

MARCH 30

21 "If a slain person is found lying in the open country in the land which the LORD your God gives you to possess, *and* it is not known who has struck him, ² then your elders and your judges shall go out and measure *the distance* to the cities which are around the slain one. ³ It shall be that the city which is nearest to the slain man, that is, the elders of that city, shall take a heifer of the herd, which has not been worked and which has not pulled in a yoke; ⁴ and the elders of that city shall bring the heifer down to a valley with running water, which has not been plowed or sown, and shall break the heifer's neck there in the valley. ⁵ Then the priests, the sons of Levi, shall come near, for the LORD your God has chosen them to serve Him and to bless in the name of the LORD; and every dispute and every assault shall be settled by them. ⁶ All the elders of that city which is nearest to the slain man shall wash their hands over the heifer whose neck was broken in the valley; ⁷ and they shall answer and say, 'Our hands did not shed this blood, nor did our eyes see *it*. ⁸ Forgive Your people Israel whom You have redeemed, O LORD, and do not place the guilt of innocent blood in the midst of Your people Israel.' And the bloodguiltiness shall be forgiven them. ⁹ So you shall remove the guilt of innocent blood from your midst, when you do what is right in the eyes of the LORD.

¹⁰ "When you go out to battle against your enemies, and the LORD your God delivers them into your hands and you take them away captive, ¹¹ and see among the captives a beautiful woman, and have a desire for her and would take her as a wife for yourself, ¹² then you shall bring her home to your house, and she shall shave her head and trim her nails. ¹³ She shall also remove the clothes of her captivity and shall remain in your house, and mourn her father and mother a full month; and after that you may go in to her and be her husband and she shall be your wife. ¹⁴ It shall be, if you are not pleased with her, then you shall let her go wherever she wishes; but you shall certainly not sell her for money, you shall not mistreat her, because you have humbled her.

¹⁵ "If a man has two wives, the one loved and the other unloved, and *both* the loved and the unloved have borne him sons, if the firstborn son belongs to the unloved, ¹⁶ then it shall be in the day he wills what he has to his sons, he cannot make the son of the loved the firstborn before the son of the unloved, who is the firstborn. ¹⁷ But he shall acknowledge the firstborn, the son of the unloved, by giving him a double portion of all that he has, for he is the beginning of his strength; to him belongs the right of the firstborn.

¹⁸ "If any man has a stubborn and rebellious son who will not obey his father or his mother, and when they chastise him, he will not even listen to them, ¹⁹ then his father and mother shall seize him, and bring him out to the elders of his city at the gateway of his hometown. ²⁰ They shall say to the elders of his city, 'This son of ours is stubborn and rebellious, he will not obey us, he is a glutton and a drunkard.' ²¹ Then all the men of his city shall stone him to death; so you shall remove the evil from your midst, and all Israel will hear *of it* and fear.

²² "If a man has committed a sin worthy of death and he is put to death, and you hang him on a tree, ²³ his corpse shall not hang all night on the tree, but you shall surely bury him on the same day (for he who is hanged is accursed of God), so that you do not defile your land which the LORD your God gives you as an inheritance.

22 "You shall not see your countryman's ox or his sheep straying away, and pay no attention to them; you shall certainly bring them back to your countryman. ² If your countryman is not near you, or if you do not know him, then you shall bring it home to your house, and it shall remain with you until your countryman looks for it; then you shall restore it to him. ³ Thus you shall do with his donkey, and you shall do the same with his garment, and you shall do likewise with anything lost by your countryman, which he has lost and you have found. You are not allowed to neglect *them*. ⁴ You shall not see your countryman's donkey or his ox fallen down on the way, and pay no attention to them; you shall certainly help him to raise *them* up.

⁵ "A woman shall not wear man's clothing, nor shall a man put on a woman's clothing; for whoever does these things is an abomination to the LORD your God.

⁶ "If you happen to come upon a bird's nest along the way, in any tree or on the ground, with young ones or eggs, and the mother sitting on the young or on the eggs, you shall not take the mother with the young; ⁷ you shall certainly let the mother go, but the young you may take for yourself, in order that it may be well with you and that you may prolong your days.

22:5 nor shall a man put on a woman's clothing. Found only here in the Pentateuch, this statute prohibited a man from wearing any item of feminine clothing or ornamentation, or a woman from wearing any item of masculine clothing or ornamentation. The same word translated "abomination" was used to describe God's view of homosexuality (Lv 18:22; 20:13). This instance specifically outlawed transvestism. The creation order distinctions between male and female were to be maintained without exception (Ge 1:27).

8 "When you build a new house, you shall make a parapet for your roof, so that you will not bring bloodguilt on your house if anyone falls from it.

9 "You shall not sow your vineyard with two kinds of seed, or all the produce of the seed which you have sown and the increase of the vineyard will become defiled.

10 "You shall not plow with an ox and a donkey together.

11 "You shall not wear a material mixed of wool and linen together.

12 "You shall make yourself tassels on the four corners of your garment with which you cover yourself.

13 "If any man takes a wife and goes in to her and *then* turns against her, 14 and charges her with shameful deeds and publicly defames her, and says, 'I took this woman, *but* when I came near her, I did not find her a virgin,' 15 then the girl's father and her mother shall take and bring out the *evidence* of the girl's virginity to the elders of the city at the gate. 16 The girl's father shall say to the elders, 'I gave my daughter to this man for a wife, but he turned against her; 17 and behold, he has charged her with shameful deeds, saying, "I did not find your daughter a virgin." And this is the evidence of my daughter's virginity.' And they shall spread the garment before the elders of the city. 18 So the elders of that city shall take the man and chastise him, 19 and they shall fine him a hundred *shekels* of silver and give it to the girl's father, because he publicly defamed a virgin of Israel. And she shall remain his wife; he cannot divorce her all his days.

20 "But if this charge is true, that the girl was not found a virgin, 21 then they shall bring out the girl to the doorway of her father's house, and the men of her city shall stone her to death because she has committed an act of folly in Israel by playing the harlot in her father's house; thus you shall purge the evil from among you.

22 "If a man is found lying with a married woman, then both of them shall die, the man who lay with the woman, and the woman; thus you shall purge the evil from Israel.

23 "If there is a girl who is a virgin engaged to a man, and *another* man finds her in the city and lies with her, 24 then you shall bring them both out to the gate of that city and you shall stone them to death; the girl, because she did not cry out in the city, and the man, because he has violated his neighbor's wife. Thus you shall purge the evil from among you.

25 "But if in the field the man finds the girl who is engaged, and the man forces her and lies with her, then only the man who lies with her shall die. 26 But you shall do nothing to the girl; there is no sin in the girl worthy of death, for just as a man rises against his neighbor and murders him, so is this case. 27 When he found her in the field, the engaged girl cried out, but there was no one to save her.

28 "If a man finds a girl who is a virgin, who is not engaged, and seizes her and lies with her and they are discovered, 29 then the man who lay with her shall give to the girl's father fifty *shekels* of silver, and she shall become his wife because he has violated her; he cannot divorce her all his days.

30 "A man shall not take his father's wife so that he will not uncover his father's skirt.

22:22–29 Adultery was punished by death for the two found in the act. If the adulterous persons were a man with a woman who was pledged to be married to someone else, this consental act led to the death of both parties (vv. 23–24). However, if the man forced (i.e., raped) the woman, then only the man's life was required (vv. 25–27). If the woman was a virgin not pledged in marriage, then the man had to pay a fine, marry the girl, and keep her as his wife as long as he lived (vv. 28–29).

Psalm 38:9–22

9   Lord, all my desire is before You;
    And my sighing is not
       hidden from You.
10   My heart throbs, my strength fails me;
    And the light of my eyes, even
       that has gone from me.
11   My loved ones and my friends
       stand aloof from my plague;
    And my kinsmen stand afar off.

12 Those who seek my life
  lay snares *for me;*
And those who seek to injure me
  have threatened destruction,
And they devise treachery
  all day long.

13 But I, like a deaf man, do
    not hear;
And *I am* like a mute man who
  does not open his mouth.
14 Yes, I am like a man who
    does not hear,
And in whose mouth are
  no arguments.
15 For I hope in You, O LORD;
You will answer, O Lord my God.
16 For I said, "May they not
    rejoice over me,
Who, when my foot slips, would
  magnify themselves
  against me."
17 For I am ready to fall,
And my sorrow is continually
  before me.
18 For I confess my iniquity;
I am full of anxiety because
  of my sin.
19 But my enemies are
    vigorous *and* strong,
And many are those who
  hate me wrongfully.
20 And those who repay evil
    for good,
They oppose me, because I
  follow what is good.
21 Do not forsake me, O LORD;
O my God, do not be far from me!
22 Make haste to help me,
O Lord, my salvation!

Proverbs 12:26–28

26 The righteous is a guide
    to his neighbor,
But the way of the wicked
  leads them astray.
27 A lazy man does not roast his prey,
But the precious possession
  of a man *is* diligence.
28 In the way of righteousness is life,
And in *its* pathway there is no death.

Luke 5:1–16

5 Now it happened that while the crowd was pressing around Him and listening to the word of God, He was standing by the lake of Gennesaret; 2 and He saw two boats lying at the edge of the lake; but the fisher-men had gotten out of them and were washing their nets. 3 And He got into one of the boats, which was Simon's, and asked him to put out a little way from the land. And He sat down and *began* teaching the people from the boat. 4 When He had finished speaking, He said to Simon, "Put out into the deep water and let down your nets for a catch." 5 Simon

5:4 let down your nets. Normally, the fish that were netted in shallow water at night would migrate during the daylight hours to waters too deep to reach easily with nets, which is why Peter fished at night. Peter no doubt thought Jesus' directive made no sense, but he obeyed anyway, and was rewarded for his obedience (v. 6).

answered and said, "Master, we worked hard all night and caught nothing, but I will do as You say *and* let down the nets." 6 When they had done this, they enclosed a great quantity of fish, and their nets *began* to break; 7 so they signaled to their partners in the other boat for them to come and help them. And they came and filled both of the boats, so that they began to sink. 8 But when Simon Peter saw *that,* he fell down at Jesus' feet, saying, "Go away from me Lord, for I am a sinful man!" 9 For amazement had seized him and all his companions because of the catch of fish which they had taken; 10 and so also *were* James and John, sons of Zebedee, who were partners with Simon. And Jesus said to Simon, "Do not fear, from now on you will be catching men." 11 When they had brought their boats to land, they left everything and followed Him.
12 While He was in one of the cities, behold, *there was* a man covered with leprosy; and when he saw Jesus, he fell on his face and implored Him, saying, "Lord, if You are willing, You can make me clean." 13 And He stretched out His hand and touched him, saying, "I am willing; be cleansed." And immediately the leprosy left him. 14 And He ordered him to tell no one, "But go and show yourself to the priest and make an offering for your cleansing, just as Moses commanded, as a testimony to them." 15 But the news about Him was spreading even farther, and large crowds were gathering to hear *Him* and to be healed of their sicknesses. 16 But Jesus Himself would *often* slip away to the wilderness and pray.

DAY 30: What specific crimes were listed in the Old Testament as deserving the death penalty?	
Crime	**Scripture Reference**
1. Premeditated Murder	Genesis 9:6; Exodus 21:12–14, 22–23
2. Kidnapping	Exodus 21:16; Deuteronomy 24:7
3. Striking or Cursing Parents	Exodus 21:15; Leviticus 20:9; Proverbs 20:20; Matthew 15:4; Mark 7:10
4. Magic and Divination	Exodus 22:18
5. Bestiality	Exodus 22:19; Leviticus 20:15–16
6. Sacrificing to False Gods	Exodus 22:20
7. Profaning the Sabbath	Exodus 35:2; Numbers 15:32–36
8. Offering Human Sacrifice	Leviticus 20:2
9. Adultery	Leviticus 20:10–21; Deuteronomy 22:22
10. Incest	Leviticus 20:11–12, 14
11. Homosexuality	Leviticus 20:13
12. Blasphemy	Leviticus 24:11–14, 16, 23
13. False Prophecy	Deuteronomy 13:1–10
14. Incorrigible Rebelliousness	Deuteronomy 17:12; 21:18–21
15. Fornication	Deuteronomy 22:20–21
16. Rape of Betrothed Virgin	Deuteronomy 22:23–27

MARCH 31

Deuteronomy 23:1–24:22

23 "No one who is emasculated or has his male organ cut off shall enter the assembly of the LORD. ² No one of illegitimate birth shall enter the assembly of the LORD; none of his *descendants,* even to the tenth generation, shall enter the assembly of the LORD. ³ No Ammonite or Moabite shall enter the assembly of the LORD; none of their *descendants,* even to the tenth generation, shall ever enter the assembly of the LORD, ⁴ because they did not meet you with food and water on the way when you came out of Egypt, and because they hired against you Balaam the son of Beor from Pethor of Mesopotamia, to curse you. ⁵ Nevertheless, the LORD your God was not willing to listen to Balaam, but the LORD your God turned the curse into a blessing for you because the LORD your God loves you. ⁶ You shall never seek their peace or their prosperity all your days.

⁷ "You shall not detest an Edomite, for he is your brother; you shall not detest an Egyptian, because you were an alien in his land. ⁸ The sons of the third generation who are born to them may enter the assembly of the LORD.

⁹ "When you go out as an army against your enemies, you shall keep yourself from every evil thing. ¹⁰ "If there is among you any man who is unclean because of a nocturnal emission, then he must go outside the camp; he may not reenter the camp. ¹¹ But it shall be when evening approaches, he shall bathe himself with water, and at sundown he may reenter the camp.

¹² "You shall also have a place outside the camp and go out there, ¹³ and you shall have a spade among your tools, and it shall be when you sit down outside, you shall dig with it and shall turn to cover up your excrement. ¹⁴ Since the LORD your God walks in the midst of your camp to deliver you and to defeat your enemies before you, therefore your camp must be holy; and He must not see anything indecent among you or He will turn away from you.

¹⁵ "You shall not hand over to his master a slave who has escaped from his master to you. ¹⁶ He shall live with you in your midst, in the place which he shall choose in one of your towns where it pleases him; you shall not mistreat him.

¹⁷ "None of the daughters of Israel shall be a cult prostitute, nor shall any of the sons of Israel be a cult prostitute. ¹⁸ You shall not bring the hire of a harlot or the wages of a dog into the house of the LORD your God for any votive offering, for both of these are an abomination to the LORD your God.

¹⁹ "You shall not charge interest to your countrymen: interest on money, food, *or* anything that may be loaned at interest. ²⁰ You may charge interest to a foreigner, but to your countrymen you shall not charge interest, so

that the LORD your God may bless you in all that you undertake in the land which you are about to enter to possess.

21 "When you make a vow to the LORD your God, you shall not delay to pay it, for it would be sin in you, and the LORD your God will surely require it of you. 22 However, if you refrain from vowing, it would not be sin in you. 23 You shall be careful to perform what goes out from your lips, just as you have voluntarily vowed to the LORD your God, what you have promised.

24 "When you enter your neighbor's vineyard, then you may eat grapes until you are fully satisfied, but you shall not put any in your basket.

25 "When you enter your neighbor's standing grain, then you may pluck the heads with your hand, but you shall not wield a sickle in your neighbor's standing grain.

24 "When a man takes a wife and marries her, and it happens that she finds no favor in his eyes because he has found some indecency in her, and he writes her a certificate of divorce and puts *it* in her hand and sends her out from his house, 2 and she leaves his house and goes and becomes another man's *wife*, 3 and if the latter husband turns against her and writes her a certificate of divorce and puts *it* in her hand and sends her out of his house, or if the latter husband dies who took her to be his wife, 4 *then* her former husband who sent her away is not allowed to take her again to be his wife, since she has been defiled; for that is an abomination before the LORD, and you shall not bring sin on the land which the LORD your God gives you as an inheritance.

5 "When a man takes a new wife, he shall not go out with the army nor be charged with any duty; he shall be free at home one year and shall give happiness to his wife whom he has taken.

6 "No one shall take a handmill or an upper millstone in pledge, for he would be taking a life in pledge.

7 "If a man is caught kidnapping any of his countrymen of the sons of Israel, and he deals with him violently or sells him, then that thief shall die; so you shall purge the evil from among you.

8 "Be careful against an infection of leprosy, that you diligently observe and do according to all that the Levitical priests teach you; as I have commanded them, so you shall be careful to do. 9 Remember what the LORD your God did to Miriam on the way as you came out of Egypt.

10 "When you make your neighbor a loan of any sort, you shall not enter his house to take his pledge. 11 You shall remain outside, and the man to whom you make the loan shall bring the pledge out to you. 12 If he is a poor man, you shall not sleep with his pledge. 13 When the sun goes down you shall surely return the pledge to him, that he may sleep in his cloak and bless you; and it will be righteousness for you before the LORD your God.

14 "You shall not oppress a hired servant *who is* poor and needy, whether *he is* one of your countrymen or one of your aliens who is in your land in your towns. 15 You shall give him his wages on his day before the sun sets, for he is poor and sets his heart on it; so that he will not cry against you to the LORD and it become sin in you.

16 "Fathers shall not be put to death for *their* sons, nor shall sons be put to death for *their* fathers; everyone shall be put to death for his own sin.

17 "You shall not pervert the justice due an alien *or* an orphan, nor take a widow's garment in pledge. 18 But you shall remember that you were a slave in Egypt, and that the LORD your God redeemed you from there; therefore I am commanding you to do this thing.

19 "When you reap your harvest in your field and have forgotten a sheaf in the field, you shall not go back to get it; it shall be for the alien, for the orphan, and for the widow, in order that the LORD your God may bless you in all the work of your hands. 20 When you beat your olive tree, you shall not go over the boughs again; it shall be for the alien, for the orphan, and for the widow.

21 "When you gather the grapes of your vineyard, you shall not go over it again; it shall be for the alien, for the orphan, and for the widow. 22 You shall remember that you were a slave in the land of Egypt; therefore I am commanding you to do this thing.

Psalm 39:1-6

For the choir director, for Jeduthun.
A Psalm of David.

I said, "I will guard my ways
That I may not sin with my tongue;
I will guard my mouth as
with a muzzle
While the wicked are in my presence."
2 I was mute and silent,
I refrained *even* from good,
And my sorrow grew worse.
3 My heart was hot within me,
While I was musing the fire burned;

Then I spoke with my tongue:
4 "LORD, make me to know my end
And what is the extent
of my days;
Let me know how transient I am.
5 "Behold, You have made my
days *as* handbreadths,
And my lifetime as nothing
in Your sight;
Surely every man at his best is
a mere breath.   *Selah*
6 "Surely every man walks
about as a phantom;
Surely they make an uproar
for nothing;
He amasses *riches* and does not
know who will gather them.

39:5 handbreadths. He measures the length of his life with the smallest popular measuring unit of ancient times (1Ki 7:26); see "four fingers" (i.e., about 2.9 in.) in Jeremiah 52:21. **And my lifetime as nothing in Your sight.** On "measuring" God's age, see Psalms 90:2. **breath.** For the same Hebrew word, see Ecclesiastes 1:2ff., "vanity" (a total of 31 occurrences of this term are in Ecc); Psalm 144:4. On the concept in the New Testament, see James 4:14.

Proverbs 13:1–3

13 A wise son *accepts his*
father's discipline,
But a scoffer does not listen
to rebuke.
2 From the fruit of a man's
mouth he enjoys good,
But the desire of the
treacherous is violence.
3 The one who guards his mouth
preserves his life;
The one who opens wide his
lips comes to ruin.

Luke 5:17–39

17 One day He was teaching; and there were *some* Pharisees and teachers of the law sitting *there,* who had come from every village of Galilee and Judea and *from* Jerusalem; and the power of the Lord was *present* for Him to perform healing. 18 And *some* men *were* carrying on a bed a man who was paralyzed; and they were trying to bring him in and to set him down in front of Him. 19 But not finding any *way* to bring him in because of the crowd, they went up on the roof and let

him down through the tiles with his stretcher, into the middle *of the crowd,* in front of Jesus. 20 Seeing their faith, He said, "Friend, your sins are forgiven you." 21 The scribes and the Pharisees began to reason, saying, "Who is this *man* who speaks blasphemies? Who can forgive sins, but God alone?" 22 But Jesus, aware of their reasonings, answered and said to them, "Why are you reasoning in your hearts? 23 Which is easier, to say, 'Your sins have been forgiven you,' or to say, 'Get up and walk'? 24 But, so that you may know that the Son of Man has authority on earth to forgive sins,"—He said to the paralytic—"I say to you, get up, and pick up your stretcher and go home." 25 Immediately he got up before them, and picked up what he had been lying on, and went home glorifying God. 26 They were all struck with astonishment and *began* glorifying God; and they were filled with fear, saying, "We have seen remarkable things today."

27 After that He went out and noticed a tax collector named Levi sitting in the tax booth, and He said to him, "Follow Me." 28 And he left everything behind, and got up and *began* to follow Him.

29 And Levi gave a big reception for Him in his house; and there was a great crowd of tax collectors and other *people* who were reclining *at the table* with them. 30 The Pharisees and their scribes *began* grumbling at His disciples, saying, "Why do you eat and drink with the tax collectors and sinners?" 31 And Jesus answered and said to them, "*It is* not those who are well who need a physician, but those who are sick. 32 I have not come to call the righteous but sinners to repentance." 33 And they said to Him, "The disciples of John often fast and offer prayers, the *disciples* of the Pharisees also do the same, but Yours eat and drink." 34 And Jesus said to them, "You cannot make the attendants of the bridegroom fast while the bridegroom is with them, can you? 35 But *the* days will

---

5:26 remarkable things. The response is curiously noncommittal—not void of wonder and amazement, but utterly void of true faith.

5:30 eat and drink. Consorting with outcasts on any level—even merely speaking to them— was bad enough. Eating and drinking with them implied a level of friendship that was abhorrent to the Pharisees (7:34; 15:2; 19:7).

come; and when the bridegroom is taken away from them, then they will fast in those days." [36] And He was also telling them a parable: "No one tears a piece of cloth from a new garment and puts it on an old garment; otherwise he will both tear the new, and the piece from the new will not match the old. [37] And no one puts new wine into old wineskins; otherwise the new wine will burst the skins and it will be spilled out, and the skins will be ruined. [38] But new wine must be put into fresh wineskins. [39] And no one, after drinking old *wine* wishes for new; for he says, 'The old is good *enough.*'"

5:33 often fast. Jesus did fast on at least one occasion (Mt 4:2)—but privately, in accordance with His own teaching (Mt 6:16–18). The law also prescribed a fast on the Day of Atonement (Lv 16:29–31; 23:27)—but all other fasts were supposed to be voluntary, for specific reasons such as penitence and earnest prayer. The fact that these Pharisees raised this question shows that they thought of fasting as a public exercise to display one's own spirituality. Yet, the Old Testament also rebuked hypocritical fasting (Is 58:3–6).

DAY 31: What does Deuteronomy 24:1–4 say about divorce and remarriage?

This passage does not command, commend, condone, or even suggest divorce. Rather, it recognizes that divorce occurs and permits it only on restricted grounds. The case presented here is designed to convey the fact that divorcing produced defilement. Notice the following sequence:

1. if a man finds an uncleanness (some impurity or something vile, see 23:14) in his wife, other than adultery, which was punished by execution (see 22:22);
2. if he legally divorces her (although God hates divorce, as Mal 2:16 says; He has designed marriage for life, as Ge 2:24 declares; and He allowed divorce because of hard hearts, as Mt 19:8 reveals);
3. if she then marries another man;
4. if the new husband then dies or divorces her, then that woman could not return to her first husband (v. 4). This is so because she was "defiled" with such a defilement that is an abomination to the Lord and a sinful pollution of the Promised Land.

What constitutes that defilement? Only one thing is possible—she was defiled in the remarriage because there was no ground for the divorce. So when she remarried, she became an adulteress (Mt 5:31–32) and is thus defiled so that her former husband can't take her back. Illegitimate divorce proliferates adultery.

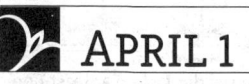

APRIL 1

Deuteronomy 25:1–26:19

25 "If there is a dispute between men and they go to court, and the judges decide their case, and they justify the righteous and condemn the wicked, ²then it shall be if the wicked man deserves to be beaten, the judge shall then make him lie down and be beaten in his presence with the number of stripes according to his guilt. ³He may beat him forty times *but* no more, so that he does not beat him with many more stripes than these and your brother is not degraded in your eyes.

⁴"You shall not muzzle the ox while he is threshing.

⁵"When brothers live together and one of them dies and has no son, the wife of the deceased shall not be *married* outside *the family* to a strange man. Her husband's brother shall go in to her and take her to himself as wife and perform the duty of a husband's brother to her. ⁶It shall be that the firstborn whom she bears shall assume the name of his dead brother, so that his name will not be blotted out from Israel. ⁷But if the man does not desire to take his brother's wife, then his brother's wife shall go up to the gate to the elders and say, 'My husband's brother refuses to establish a name for his brother in Israel; he is not willing to perform the duty of a husband's brother to me.' ⁸Then the elders of his city shall summon him and speak to him. And *if* he persists and says, 'I do not desire to take her,' ⁹then his brother's wife shall come to him in the sight of the elders, and pull his sandal off his foot and spit in his face; and she shall declare, 'Thus it is done to the man who does not build up his brother's house.' ¹⁰In Israel his name shall be called, 'The house of him whose sandal is removed.'

¹¹"If *two* men, a man and his countryman, are struggling together, and the wife of one comes near to deliver her husband from the hand of the one who is striking him, and puts out her hand and seizes his genitals, ¹²then you shall cut off her hand; you shall not show pity.

¹³"You shall not have in your bag differing weights, a large and a small. ¹⁴You shall not have in your house differing measures, a large and a small. ¹⁵You shall have a full and just weight; you shall have a full and just measure, that your days may be prolonged in the land which the LORD your God gives you. ¹⁶For everyone who does these things, everyone who acts unjustly is an abomination to the LORD your God.

¹⁷"Remember what Amalek did to you along the way when you came out from Egypt, ¹⁸how he met you along the way and attacked among you all the stragglers at your rear when you were faint and weary; and he did not fear God. ¹⁹Therefore it shall come about when the LORD your God has given you rest from all your surrounding enemies, in the land which the LORD your God gives you as an inheritance to possess, you shall blot out the memory of Amalek from under heaven; you must not forget.

26 "Then it shall be, when you enter the land which the LORD your God gives you as an inheritance, and you possess it and live in it, ²that you shall take some of the first of all the produce of the ground which you bring in from your land that the LORD your God gives you, and you shall put *it* in a basket and go to the place where the LORD your God chooses to establish His name. ³You shall go to the priest who is in office at that time and say to him, 'I declare this day to the LORD my God that I have entered the land which the LORD swore to our fathers to give us.' ⁴Then the priest shall take the basket from your hand and set it down before the altar of the LORD your God. ⁵You shall answer and say before the LORD your God, 'My father was a wandering Aramean, and he went down to Egypt and sojourned there, few in number; but there he became a great, mighty and populous nation. ⁶And the Egyptians treated us harshly and afflicted us, and imposed hard labor on us. ⁷Then we cried to the LORD, the God of our fathers, and the LORD heard our voice and saw our affliction and our toil and our oppression; ⁸and the LORD brought us out of Egypt with a mighty hand and an outstretched arm and with great terror and with signs and wonders; ⁹and He has brought us to this place and has given us this land, a land flowing with milk and honey. ¹⁰Now behold, I have brought the first of the produce of the ground which You, O LORD have given me.' And you shall set it down before the LORD your God, and worship before the LORD your God; ¹¹and you and the Levite and the alien who is among you shall rejoice in all the good which the LORD your God has given you and your household.

¹²"When you have finished paying all the tithe of your increase in the third year, the year of tithing, then you shall give it to the Levite, to the stranger, to the orphan and to the widow, that they may eat in your towns and be satisfied. ¹³You shall say before the LORD your God, 'I have removed the sacred *portion* from

my house, and also have given it to the Levite and the alien, the orphan and the widow, according to all Your commandments which You have commanded me; I have not transgressed or forgotten any of Your commandments. ¹⁴ I have not eaten of it while mourning, nor have I removed any of it while I was unclean, nor offered any of it to the dead. I have listened to the voice of the LORD my God; I have done according to all that You have commanded me. ¹⁵ Look down from Your holy habitation, from heaven, and bless Your people Israel, and the ground which You have given us, a land flowing with milk and honey, as You swore to our fathers.'

26:13–14 You shall say before the LORD your God. The confession to be made in connection with the offering of this first tithe consisted of a statement of obedience (vv. 13–14) and a prayer for God's blessing (v. 15). In this manner, the Israelite confessed his continual dependence on God and lived in obedient expectation of God's continued gracious blessing.

26:15 Look down from…heaven. This was the first reference to God's dwelling place being in heaven. From His abode in heaven, God had given the Israelites the land flowing with milk and honey as He had promised to the patriarchs. His continued blessing on both the people and the land was requested.

¹⁶ "This day the LORD your God commands you to do these statutes and ordinances. You shall therefore be careful to do them with all your heart and with all your soul. ¹⁷ You have today declared the LORD to be your God, and that you would walk in His ways and keep His statutes, His commandments and His ordinances, and listen to His voice. ¹⁸ The LORD has today declared you to be His people, a treasured possession, as He promised you, and that you should keep all His commandments; ¹⁹ and that He will set you high above all nations which He has made, for praise, fame, and honor; and that you shall be a consecrated people to the LORD your God, as He has spoken."

Psalm 39:7–11

⁷ "And now, Lord, for what do
　　I wait?
　My hope is in You.

⁸ "Deliver me from all my
　　transgressions;
　Make me not the reproach
　　of the foolish.
⁹ "I have become mute, I do
　　not open my mouth,
　Because it is You who have
　　done *it*.
¹⁰ "Remove Your plague from me;
　Because of the opposition of
　　Your hand I am perishing.
¹¹ "With reproofs You chasten
　　a man for iniquity;
　You consume as a moth what
　　is precious to him;
　Surely every man is a
　　mere breath.　　　　*Selah*

39:11 as a moth. The moth normally represented one of the most destructive creatures, but here the delicacy of the moth is intended (Job 13:28; Is 50:9; 51:8; Mt 6:19ff.).

Proverbs 13:4–6

⁴ The soul of the sluggard
　　craves and *gets* nothing,
　But the soul of the diligent
　　is made fat.
⁵ A righteous man hates
　　falsehood,
　But a wicked man acts
　　disgustingly and shamefully.
⁶ Righteousness guards the one
　　whose way is blameless,
　But wickedness subverts
　　the sinner.

Luke 6:1–26

6 Now it happened that He was passing through *some* grainfields on a Sabbath; and His disciples were picking the heads of grain, rubbing them in their hands, and eating *the grain.* ² But some of the Pharisees said, "Why do you do what is not lawful on the Sabbath?" ³ And Jesus answering them said, "Have you not even read what David did when he was hungry, he and those who were with him, ⁴ how he entered the house of God, and took and ate the consecrated bread which is not lawful for any to eat except the priests alone, and gave it to his companions?" ⁵ And He was saying to them, "The Son of Man is Lord of the Sabbath."

⁶ On another Sabbath He entered the synagogue and was teaching; and there was a

man there whose right hand was withered. 7 The scribes and the Pharisees were watching Him closely *to see* if He healed on the Sabbath, so that they might find *reason* to accuse Him. 8 But He knew what they were thinking, and He said to the man with the withered hand, "Get up and come forward!" And he got up and came forward. 9 And Jesus said to them, "I ask you, is it lawful to do good or to do harm on the Sabbath, to save a life or to destroy it?" 10 After looking around at them all, He said to him, "Stretch out your hand!" And he did *so;* and his hand was restored. 11 But they themselves were filled with rage, and discussed together what they might do to Jesus.

12 It was at this time that He went off to the mountain to pray, and He spent the whole night in prayer to God. 13 And when day came, He called His disciples to Him and chose twelve of them, whom He also named as apostles: 14 Simon, whom He also named Peter, and Andrew his brother; and James and John; and Philip and Bartholomew; 15 and Matthew and Thomas; James *the son* of Alphaeus, and Simon who was called the Zealot; 16 Judas *the son* of James, and Judas Iscariot, who became a traitor.

17 Jesus came down with them and stood on a level place; and *there was* a large crowd of His disciples, and a great throng of people from all Judea and Jerusalem and the coastal region of Tyre and Sidon, 18 who had come to hear Him and to be healed of their diseases; and those who were troubled with unclean spirits were being cured. 19 And all the people were trying to touch Him, for power was coming from Him and healing *them* all.

6:11 filled with rage. A curious response in the face of so glorious a miracle. Such irrational hatred was their response to having been publicly humiliated—something they hated worse than anything (Mt 23:6-7). They were unable to answer His reasoning (vv. 9-10). And furthermore, by healing the man only with a command, He had performed no actual "work" that they could charge Him with. Desperately seeking a reason to accuse Him (v. 7), they could find none. Their response was blind fury.

6:12 spent the whole night in prayer. Luke frequently shows Jesus praying—and particularly before major events in His ministry. See 3:21; 5:16; 9:18, 28-29; 11:1; 22:32, 40-46.

20 And turning His gaze toward His disciples, He *began* to say, "Blessed *are* you *who are* poor, for yours is the kingdom of God. 21 Blessed *are* you who hunger now, for you shall be satisfied. Blessed *are* you who weep now, for you shall laugh. 22 Blessed are you when men hate you, and ostracize you, and insult you, and scorn your name as evil, for the sake of the Son of Man. 23 Be glad in that day and leap *for joy,* for behold, your reward is great in heaven. For in the same way their fathers used to treat the prophets. 24 But woe to you who are rich, for you are receiving your comfort in full. 25 Woe to you who are well-fed now, for you shall be hungry. Woe *to you* who laugh now, for you shall mourn and weep. 26 Woe *to you* when all men speak well of you, for their fathers used to treat the false prophets in the same way.

DAY 1: How similar is the sermon in Luke 6:17–49 to the Sermon on the Mount?

The similarity of the Sermon on the Plateau in Luke to the Sermon on the Mount (Mt 5:1—7:29) is remarkable. It is possible, of course, that Jesus simply preached the same sermon on more than one occasion. (It is evident that He often used the same material more than once—e.g., 12:58–59; see Mt 5:25–26.) It appears more likely, however, that these are variant accounts of the same event. Luke's version is abbreviated somewhat, because he omitted sections from the sermon that are uniquely Jewish (particularly Christ's exposition of the law). Aside from that, the two sermons follow exactly the same flow of thought, beginning with the Beatitudes and ending with the parable about building on the rock. Differences in wording between the two accounts are undoubtedly owing to the fact that the sermon was originally delivered in Aramaic. Luke and Matthew translate into Greek with slight variances. Of course, both translations are equally inspired and authoritative.

Luke tells us the sermon was given on "a level place" (v. 17), after coming down from a mountain. In Matthew 5:1, it says "on the mountain." These harmonize easily if Luke is referring to either a plateau or a level place on the mountainside. Indeed, there is such a place at the site near Capernaum where tradition says this sermon was delivered.

APRIL 2

Deuteronomy 27:1–28:68

27 Then Moses and the elders of Israel charged the people, saying, "Keep all the commandments which I command you today. ² So it shall be on the day when you cross the Jordan to the land which the LORD your God gives you, that you shall set up for yourself large stones and coat them with lime ³ and write on them all the words of this law, when you cross over, so that you may enter the land which the LORD your God gives you, a land flowing with milk and honey, as the LORD, the God of your fathers, promised you. ⁴ So it shall be when you cross the Jordan, you shall set up on Mount Ebal, these stones, as I am commanding you today, and you shall coat them with lime. ⁵ Moreover, you shall build there an altar to the LORD your God, an altar of stones; you shall not wield an iron *tool* on them. ⁶ You shall build the altar of the LORD your God of uncut stones, and you shall offer on it burnt offerings to the LORD your God; ⁷ and you shall sacrifice peace offerings and eat there, and rejoice before the LORD your God. ⁸ You shall write on the stones all the words of this law very distinctly."

⁹ Then Moses and the Levitical priests spoke to all Israel, saying, "Be silent and listen, O Israel! This day you have become a people for the LORD your God. ¹⁰ You shall therefore obey the LORD your God, and do His commandments and His statutes which I command you today."

¹¹ Moses also charged the people on that day, saying, ¹² "When you cross the Jordan, these shall stand on Mount Gerizim to bless the people: Simeon, Levi, Judah, Issachar, Joseph, and Benjamin. ¹³ For the curse, these shall stand on Mount Ebal: Reuben, Gad, Asher, Zebulun, Dan, and Naphtali. ¹⁴ The Levites shall then answer and say to all the men of Israel with a loud voice,

¹⁵ 'Cursed is the man who makes an idol or a molten image, an abomination to the LORD, the work of the hands of the craftsman, and sets *it* up in secret.' And all the people shall answer and say, 'Amen.'

¹⁶ 'Cursed is he who dishonors his father or mother.' And all the people shall say, 'Amen.'

¹⁷ 'Cursed is he who moves his neighbor's boundary mark.' And all the people shall say, 'Amen.'

¹⁸ 'Cursed is he who misleads a blind *person* on the road.' And all the people shall say, 'Amen.'

¹⁹ 'Cursed is he who distorts the justice due an alien, orphan, and widow.' And all the people shall say, 'Amen.'

²⁰ 'Cursed is he who lies with his father's wife, because he has uncovered his father's skirt.' And all the people shall say, 'Amen.'

²¹ 'Cursed is he who lies with any animal.' And all the people shall say, 'Amen.'

²² 'Cursed is he who lies with his sister, the daughter of his father or of his mother.' And all the people shall say, 'Amen.'

²³ 'Cursed is he who lies with his mother-in-law.' And all the people shall say, 'Amen.'

²⁴ 'Cursed is he who strikes his neighbor in secret.' And all the people shall say, 'Amen.'

²⁵ 'Cursed is he who accepts a bribe to strike down an innocent person.' And all the people shall say, 'Amen.'

²⁶ 'Cursed is he who does not confirm the words of this law by doing them.' And all the people shall say, 'Amen.'

28 "Now it shall be, if you diligently obey the LORD your God, being careful to do all His commandments which I command you today, the LORD your God will set you high above all the nations of the earth. ² All these blessings will come upon you and overtake you if you obey the LORD your God:

³ "Blessed *shall* you *be* in the city, and blessed *shall* you *be* in the country.

⁴ "Blessed *shall be* the offspring of your body and the produce of your ground and the

28:1 high above all the nations. If Israel obeyed the Lord, ultimate blessing would be given in the form of preeminence above all the nations of the world (26:19). The indispensable condition for obtaining this blessing was salvation, resulting in obedience to the Lord, in the form of keeping His commandments. This blessing will ultimately come to pass in the millennial kingdom, particularly designed to exalt Israel's King, the Messiah, and His nation (Zec 13:1—14:21; Ro 11:25–27).

28:1–2 diligently obey the LORD your God. "Diligently obey" stressed the need for complete obedience on the part of Israel. The people could not legally or personally merit God's goodness and blessing, but their constant desire to obey, worship, and maintain a right relation to Him was evidence of their true faith in and love for Him (6:5). It was also evidence of God's gracious work in their hearts.

offspring of your beasts, the increase of your herd and the young of your flock. ⁵ "Blessed *shall be* your basket and your kneading bowl.

⁶ "Blessed *shall* you *be* when you come in, and blessed *shall* you *be* when you go out.

⁷ "The LORD shall cause your enemies who rise up against you to be defeated before you; they will come out against you one way and will flee before you seven ways. ⁸ The LORD will command the blessing upon you in your barns and in all that you put your hand to, and He will bless you in the land which the LORD your God gives you. ⁹ The LORD will establish you as a holy people to Himself, as He swore to you, if you keep the commandments of the LORD your God and walk in His ways. ¹⁰ So all the peoples of the earth will see that you are called by the name of the LORD, and they will be afraid of you. ¹¹ The LORD will make you abound in prosperity, in the offspring of your body and in the offspring of your beast and in the produce of your ground, in the land which the LORD swore to your fathers to give you. ¹² The LORD will open for you His good storehouse, the heavens, to give rain to your land in its season and to bless all the work of your hand; and you shall lend to many nations, but you shall not borrow. ¹³ The LORD will make you the head and not the tail, and you only will be above, and you will not be underneath, if you listen to the commandments of the LORD your God, which I charge you today, to observe *them* carefully, ¹⁴ and do not turn aside from any of the words which I command you today, to the right or to the left, to go after other gods to serve them.

¹⁵ "But it shall come about, if you do not obey the LORD your God, to observe to do all His commandments and His statutes with which I charge you today, that all these curses will come upon you and overtake you:

¹⁶ "Cursed *shall* you *be* in the city, and cursed *shall* you *be* in the country.

¹⁷ "Cursed *shall be* your basket and your kneading bowl.

¹⁸ "Cursed *shall be* the offspring of your body and the produce of your ground, the increase of your herd and the young of your flock.

¹⁹ "Cursed *shall* you *be* when you come in, and cursed *shall* you *be* when you go out.

²⁰ "The LORD will send upon you curses, confusion, and rebuke, in all you undertake to do, until you are destroyed and until you perish quickly, on account of the evil of your deeds, because you have forsaken Me. ²¹ The LORD will make the pestilence cling to you until He has consumed you from the land where you are entering to possess it. ²² The LORD will smite you with consumption and with fever and with inflammation and with fiery heat and with the sword and with blight and with mildew, and they will pursue you until you perish. ²³ The heaven which is over your head shall be bronze, and the earth which is under you, iron. ²⁴ The LORD will make the rain of your land powder and dust; from heaven it shall come down on you until you are destroyed.

²⁵ "The LORD shall cause you to be defeated before your enemies; you will go out one way against them, but you will flee seven ways before them, and you will be *an example of* terror to all the kingdoms of the earth. ²⁶ Your carcasses will be food to all birds of the sky and to the beasts of the earth, and there will be no one to frighten *them* away.

²⁷ "The LORD will smite you with the boils of Egypt and with tumors and with the scab and with the itch, from which you cannot be healed. ²⁸ The LORD will smite you with madness and with blindness and with bewilderment of heart; ²⁹ and you will grope at noon, as the blind man gropes in darkness, and you will not prosper in your ways; but you shall only be oppressed and robbed continually, with none to save you. ³⁰ You shall betroth a wife, but another man will violate her; you shall build a house, but you will not live in it; you shall plant a vineyard, but you will not use its fruit. ³¹ Your ox shall be slaughtered before your eyes, but you will not eat of it; your donkey shall be torn away from you, and will not be restored to you; your sheep shall be given to your enemies, and you will have none to save you. ³² Your sons and your daughters shall be given to another people, while your eyes look on and yearn for them continually; but there will be nothing you can do. ³³ A people whom you do not know shall eat up the produce of your ground and all your labors, and you will never be anything but oppressed and crushed continually. ³⁴ You shall be driven mad by the sight of what you see. ³⁵ The LORD will strike you on the knees and legs with sore boils, from which you cannot be healed, from the sole of your foot to the crown of your head. ³⁶ The LORD will bring you and your king, whom you set over you, to a nation which neither you nor your fathers have known, and there you shall serve other gods, wood and stone. ³⁷ You shall become a horror, a proverb, and a taunt among all the people where the LORD drives you.

³⁸ "You shall bring out much seed to the field but you will gather in little, for the locust will consume it. ³⁹ You shall plant and cultivate vineyards, but you will neither drink of the wine nor gather *the grapes,* for the worm will devour them. ⁴⁰ You shall have olive trees throughout your territory but you will not anoint yourself with the oil, for your olives will drop off. ⁴¹ You shall have sons and daughters but they will not be yours, for they will go into captivity. ⁴² The cricket shall possess all your trees and the produce of your ground. ⁴³ The alien who is among you shall rise above you higher and higher, but you will go down lower and lower. ⁴⁴ He shall lend to you, but you will not lend to him; he shall be the head, and you will be the tail.

⁴⁵ "So all these curses shall come on you and pursue you and overtake you until you are destroyed, because you would not obey the LORD your God by keeping His commandments and His statutes which He commanded you. ⁴⁶ They shall become a sign and a wonder on you and your descendants forever.

⁴⁷ "Because you did not serve the LORD your God with joy and a glad heart, for the abundance of all things; ⁴⁸ therefore you shall serve your enemies whom the LORD will send against you, in hunger, in thirst, in nakedness, and in the lack of all things; and He will put an iron yoke on your neck until He has destroyed you.

⁴⁹ "The LORD will bring a nation against you from afar, from the end of the earth, as the eagle swoops down, a nation whose language you shall not understand, ⁵⁰ a nation of fierce countenance who will have no respect for the old, nor show favor to the young. ⁵¹ Moreover, it shall eat the offspring of your herd and the produce of your ground until you are destroyed, who also leaves you no grain, new wine, or oil, nor the increase of your herd or the young of your flock until they have caused you to perish. ⁵² It shall besiege you in all your towns until your high and fortified walls in which you trusted come down throughout your land, and it shall besiege you in all your towns throughout your land which the LORD your God has given you. ⁵³ Then you shall eat the offspring of your own body, the flesh of your sons and of your daughters whom the LORD your God has given you, during the siege and the distress by which your enemy will oppress you. ⁵⁴ The man who is refined and very delicate among you shall be hostile toward his brother and toward the wife he cherishes and toward the rest of his children who remain, ⁵⁵ so that he

will not give *even* one of them any of the flesh of his children which he will eat, since he has nothing *else* left, during the siege and the distress by which your enemy will oppress you in all your towns. ⁵⁶ The refined and delicate woman among you, who would not venture to set the sole of her foot on the ground for delicateness and refinement, shall be hostile toward the husband she cherishes and toward her son and daughter, ⁵⁷ and toward her afterbirth which issues from between her legs and toward her children whom she bears; for she will eat them secretly for lack of anything *else,* during the siege and the distress by which your enemy will oppress you in your towns.

⁵⁸ "If you are not careful to observe all the words of this law which are written in this book, to fear this honored and awesome name, the LORD your God, ⁵⁹ then the LORD will bring extraordinary plagues on you and your descendants, even severe and lasting plagues, and miserable and chronic sicknesses. ⁶⁰ He will bring back on you all the diseases of Egypt of which you were afraid, and they will cling to you. ⁶¹ Also every sickness and every plague which, not written in the book of this law, the LORD will bring on you until you are destroyed. ⁶² Then you shall be left few in number, whereas you were as numerous as the stars of heaven, because you did not obey the LORD your God. ⁶³ It shall come about that as the LORD delighted over you to prosper you, and multiply you, so the LORD will delight over you to make you perish and destroy you; and you will be torn from the land where you are entering to possess it. ⁶⁴ Moreover, the LORD will scatter you among all peoples, from one end of the earth to the other end of the earth; and there you shall serve other gods, wood and stone, which you or your fathers have not known. ⁶⁵ Among those nations you shall find no rest, and there will be no resting place for the sole of your foot; but there the LORD will give you a trembling heart, failing of eyes, and despair of soul. ⁶⁶ So your life shall hang in doubt before you; and you will be in dread night and day, and shall have no assurance of your life. ⁶⁷ In the morning you shall say, 'Would that it were evening!' And at evening you shall say, 'Would that it were morning!' because of the dread of your heart which you dread, and for the sight of your eyes which you will see. ⁶⁸ The LORD will bring you back to Egypt in ships, by the way about which I spoke to you, 'You will never see it again!' And there you will offer yourselves for sale

to your enemies as male and female slaves, but there will be no buyer."

Psalm 39:12-13

12 "Hear my prayer, O LORD, and
   give ear to my cry;
Do not be silent at my tears;
For I am a stranger with You,
A sojourner like all my fathers.
13 "Turn Your gaze away from me,
   that I may smile *again*
Before I depart and am
   no more."

Proverbs 13:7-8

7 There is one who pretends to
   be rich, but has nothing;
Another pretends to be poor,
   but has great wealth.
8 The ransom of a man's
   life is his wealth,
But the poor hears no
   rebuke.

13:8 ransom...wealth...poor...rebuke. Riches deliver some people from punishment, while others suffer, because they will not heed the rebuke of laziness, which keeps them poor.

Luke 6:27-49

27 "But I say to you who hear, love your enemies, do good to those who hate you, 28 bless those who curse you, pray for those who mistreat you. 29 Whoever hits you on the cheek, offer him the other also; and whoever takes away your coat, do not withhold your shirt from him either. 30 Give to everyone who asks of you, and whoever takes away what is yours, do not demand it back. 31 Treat others the same way you want them to treat you. 32 If you love those who love you, what credit is *that* to you? For even sinners love those who love them. 33 If you do good to those who do good to you, what credit is *that* to you? For even sinners do the same. 34 If you lend to those from whom you expect to receive, what credit is *that* to you? Even sinners lend to sinners in order to receive back the same *amount.* 35 But love your enemies, and do good, and lend, expecting nothing in return; and your reward will be great, and you will be sons of the Most High; for He Himself is kind to ungrateful and evil *men.* 36 Be merciful, just as your Father is merciful. 37 "Do not judge, and you will not be judged;

and do not condemn, and you will not be condemned; pardon, and you will be pardoned. 38 Give, and it will be given to you. They will pour into your lap a good measure—pressed down, shaken together, *and* running over. For by your standard of measure it will be measured to you in return."

39 And He also spoke a parable to them: "A blind man cannot guide a blind man, can he? Will they not both fall into a pit? 40 A pupil is not above his teacher; but everyone, after he has been fully trained, will be like his teacher. 41 Why do you look at the speck that is in your brother's eye, but do not notice the log that is in your own eye? 42 Or how can you say to your brother, 'Brother, let me take out the speck that is in your eye,' when you yourself do not see the log that is in your own eye? You hypocrite, first take the log out of your own eye, and then you will see clearly to take out the speck that is in your brother's eye. 43 For there is no good tree which produces bad fruit, nor, on the other hand, a bad tree which produces good fruit. 44 For each tree is known by its own fruit. For men do not gather figs from thorns, nor do they pick grapes from a briar bush. 45 The good man out of the good treasure of his heart brings forth what is good; and the evil *man* out of the evil *treasure* brings forth what is evil; for his mouth speaks from that which fills his heart.

46 "Why do you call Me, 'Lord, Lord,' and do not do what I say? 47 Everyone who comes to Me and hears My words and acts on them, I will show you whom he is like: 48 he is like a man building a house, who dug deep and laid a foundation on the rock; and when a flood occurred, the torrent burst against that house and could not shake it, because it had been well built. 49 But the one who has heard and has not acted *accordingly,* is like a man who built a house on the ground without any foundation; and the torrent burst against it and immediately it collapsed, and the ruin of that house was great."

6:41 speck...log. The humor of the imagery was no doubt intentional. Christ often employed hyperbole to paint comical images (18:25; Mt 23:24).

6:46 you call Me, 'Lord, Lord.' It is not sufficient to give lip service to Christ's lordship. Genuine faith produces obedience. A tree is known by its fruits (v. 44). See Matthew 7:21-23.

DAY 2: What did God promise would happen to Israel if they disobeyed the law?

Their obedience centers around "honored and awesome name, the LORD your God," as described in Deuteronomy 28:58 and would lead to fearing the Lord, whose "name" represents His presence and character. The title "LORD (Yahweh)" revealed the glory and greatness of God (see Ex 3:15). Significantly, the phrase "the LORD your God" is used approximately 280 times in the Book of Deuteronomy. The full measure of the divine curse would come on Israel when its disobedience had been hardened into disregard for the glorious and awesome character of God. In vv. 15, 45, Moses described curses for disobedience; hence, the worst of the curses come when disobedience is hardened into failure to fear God. Only God's grace would save a small remnant (v. 62), thus keeping Israel from being annihilated (see Mal 2:2). In contrast to the promise made to Abraham in Genesis 15:5, the physical seed of Abraham under God's curse would be reduced. As God had multiplied the seed of the patriarchs in Egypt (see Ex 1:7), He would decimate their numbers to make them as nothing until His restoration of the nation in a future day (see 30:5).

In v. 64, it warns that "the LORD will scatter you." The Jews remaining after the curses fall would be dispersed by the Lord ultimately to serve false gods, restlessly and fearfully throughout all the nations of the earth (see Ne 1:8–9; Jer 30:11; Eze 11:16). This dispersion began with the captivity of the northern kingdom, Israel (722 B.C.), then the southern kingdom, Judah (586 B.C.), and is still a reality today. In the future earthly kingdom of Messiah, Israel will experience its regathering in faith, salvation, and righteousness. (See Is. 59:19–21; Jer 31:31–34; Eze 36:8—37:14; Zec 12:10—14:21.)

In fact, Israel would be so abandoned by God that she would not even be able to sell herself into slavery (v. 68). The curse of God would bring Israel into a seemingly hopeless condition (see Hos 8:13; 9:3). The specific mention of Egypt could be symbolic for any lands where the Jews have been taken into bondage or sold as slaves. But it is true that after the destruction of Jerusalem in A.D. 70, which was a judgment on the apostasy of Israel and their rejection and execution of the Messiah, this prophecy was actually fulfilled. The Roman general Titus, who conquered Jerusalem and Israel, sent 17,000 adult Jews to Egypt to perform hard labor there and had those who were under 17 years old publicly sold. Under the Roman emperor Hadrian, countless Jews were sold and suffered such bondage and cruelty.

APRIL 3

Deuteronomy 29:1–30:20

29 These are the words of the covenant which the LORD commanded Moses to make with the sons of Israel in the land of Moab, besides the covenant which He had made with them at Horeb. ²And Moses summoned all Israel and said to them, "You have seen all that the LORD did before your eyes in the land of Egypt to Pharaoh and all his servants and all his land; ³the great trials which your eyes have seen, those great signs and wonders. ⁴Yet to this day the LORD has not given you a heart to know, nor eyes to see, nor ears to hear. ⁵I have led you forty years in the wilderness; your clothes have not worn out on you, and your sandal has not worn out on your foot. ⁶You have not eaten bread, nor have you drunk wine or strong drink, in order that you might know that I am the LORD your God. ⁷When you reached this place, Sihon the king of Heshbon and Og the king of Bashan came out to meet us for battle, but we defeated them; ⁸and we

took their land and gave it as an inheritance to the Reubenites, the Gadites, and the half-tribe of the Manassites. ⁹So keep the words of this covenant to do them, that you may prosper in all that you do.

¹⁰"You stand today, all of you, before the LORD your God: your chiefs, your tribes, your elders and your officers, *even* all the men of Israel, ¹¹your little ones, your wives, and the alien who is within your camps, from the one

---

29:4 the LORD has not given you...eyes to see. In spite of all they had experienced (vv. 2–3), Israel was spiritually blind to the significance of what the Lord had done for them, lacking spiritual understanding, even as Moses was speaking. This spiritual blindness of Israel continues to the present day (Ro 11:8), and it will not be reversed until Israel's future day of salvation (Ro 11:25–27). The Lord had not given them an understanding heart, simply because the people had not penitently sought it (2Ch 7:14).

who chops your wood to the one who draws your water, 12 that you may enter into the covenant with the LORD your God, and into His oath which the LORD your God is making with you today, 13 in order that He may establish you today as His people and that He may be your God, just as He spoke to you and as He swore to your fathers, to Abraham, Isaac, and Jacob.

14 "Now not with you alone am I making this covenant and this oath, 15 but both with those who stand here with us today in the presence of the LORD our God and with those who are not with us here today 16 (for you know how we lived in the land of Egypt, and how we came through the midst of the nations through which you passed; 17 moreover, you have seen their abominations and their idols of wood, stone, silver, and gold, which they had with them); 18 so that there will not be among you a man or woman, or family or tribe, whose heart turns away today from the LORD our God, to go and serve the gods of those nations; that there will not be among you a root bearing poisonous fruit and wormwood. 19 It shall be when he hears the words of this curse, that he will boast, saying, 'I have peace though I walk in the stubbornness of my heart in order to destroy the watered land with the dry.' 20 The LORD shall never be willing to forgive him, but rather the anger of the LORD and His jealousy will burn against that man, and every curse which is written in this book will rest on him, and the LORD will blot out his name from under heaven. 21 Then the LORD will single him out for adversity from all the tribes of Israel, according to all the curses of the covenant which are written in this book of the law.

22 "Now the generation to come, your sons who rise up after you and the foreigner who comes from a distant land, when they see the plagues of the land and the diseases with which the LORD has afflicted it, will say, 23 'All its land is brimstone and salt, a burning waste, unsown and unproductive, and no grass grows in it, like the overthrow of Sodom and Gomorrah, Admah and Zeboiim, which the LORD overthrew in His anger and in His wrath.' 24 All the nations will say, 'Why has the LORD done thus to this land? Why this great outburst of anger?' 25 Then men will say, 'Because they forsook the covenant of the LORD, the God of their fathers, which He made with them when He brought them out of the land of Egypt. 26 They went and served other gods and worshiped them, gods whom they have not known and whom He had not

allotted to them. 27 Therefore, the anger of the LORD burned against that land, to bring upon it every curse which is written in this book; 28 and the LORD uprooted them from their land in anger and in fury and in great wrath, and cast them into another land, as it is this day.'

29 "The secret things belong to the LORD our God, but the things revealed belong to us and to our sons forever, that we may observe all the words of this law.

29:29 The secret things…the things revealed. God has not revealed all that could be disclosed from His infinite mind. What He has unveiled stands sufficient for salvation, maturation in the faith, and glorifying God by obedience to His Word. While there are secret things unknown, believers will be held accountable to obey only what they do know accented by the divine threat of judgment for continued sinful disobedience.

30 "So it shall be when all of these things have come upon you, the blessing and the curse which I have set before you, and you call them to mind in all nations where the LORD your God has banished you, 2 and you return to the LORD your God and obey Him with all your heart and soul according to all that I command you today, you and your sons, 3 then the LORD your God will restore you from captivity, and have compassion on you, and will gather you again from all the peoples where the LORD your God has scattered you. 4 If your outcasts are at the ends of the earth, from there the LORD your God will gather you, and from there He will bring you back. 5 The LORD your God will bring you into the land which your fathers possessed, and you shall possess it; and He will prosper you and multiply you more than your fathers.

6 "Moreover the LORD your God will circumcise your heart and the heart of your descendants, to love the LORD your God with all your heart and with all your soul, so that you may live. 7 The LORD your God will inflict all these curses on your enemies and on those who hate you, who persecuted you. 8 And you shall again obey the LORD, and observe all His commandments which I command you today. 9 Then the LORD your God will prosper you abundantly in all the work of your hand, in the offspring of your body and in the offspring of your cattle and in the produce of

30:4-5 The gathering of Jews out of all the countries of the earth will follow Israel's final redemption. Restoration to the land will be in fulfillment of the promise of the covenant given to Abraham (Ge 12:7; 13:15; 15:18-21; 17:8) and so often reiterated by Moses and the prophets.

30:6 the LORD...will circumcise your heart. See 10:16. This work of God in the innermost being of the individual is the true salvation that grants a new will to obey Him in place of the former spiritual insensitivity and stubbornness (Jer 4:4; 9:25; Ro 2:28-29). This new heart will allow the Israelite to love the Lord wholeheartedly, and is the essential feature of the New Covenant (29:4, 18; 30:10, 17; Jer 31:31-34; 32:37-42; Eze 11:19; 36:26).

---

your ground, for the LORD will again rejoice over you for good, just as He rejoiced over your fathers; [10] if you obey the LORD your God to keep His commandments and His statutes which are written in this book of the law, if you turn to the LORD your God with all your heart and soul.

[11] "For this commandment which I command you today is not too difficult for you, nor is it out of reach. [12] It is not in heaven, that you should say, 'Who will go up to heaven for us to get it for us and make us hear it, that we may observe it?' [13] Nor is it beyond the sea, that you should say, 'Who will cross the sea for us to get it for us and make us hear it, that we may observe it?' [14] But the word is very near you, in your mouth and in your heart, that you may observe it.

[15] "See, I have set before you today life and prosperity, and death and adversity; [16] in that I command you today to love the LORD your God, to walk in His ways and to keep His commandments and His statutes and His judgments, that you may live and multiply, and that the LORD your God may bless you in the land where you are entering to possess it. [17] But if your heart turns away and you will not obey, but are drawn away and worship other gods and serve them, [18] I declare to you today that you shall surely perish. You will not prolong your days in the land where you are crossing the Jordan to enter and possess it. [19] I call heaven and earth to witness against you today, that I have set before you life and death, the blessing and the curse. So choose life in order that you may live, you and your descendants, [20] by loving the LORD your God,

by obeying His voice, and by holding fast to Him; for this is your life and the length of your days, that you may live in the land which the LORD swore to your fathers, to Abraham, Isaac, and Jacob, to give them."

Psalm 40:1-5

For the choir director. A Psalm of David.

I waited patiently for the LORD;
And He inclined to me
and heard my cry.
[2] He brought me up out of the pit of
destruction, out of the miry clay,
And He set my feet upon a rock
making my footsteps firm.
[3] He put a new song in my mouth,
a song of praise to our God;
Many will see and fear
And will trust in the LORD.

[4] How blessed is the man who has
made the LORD his trust,
And has not turned to the proud, nor
to those who lapse into falsehood.
[5] Many, O LORD my God, are the
wonders which You have done,
And Your thoughts toward us;
There is none to compare with You.
If I would declare and speak of them,
They would be too
numerous to count.

Proverbs 13:9-10

[9] The light of the righteous rejoices,
But the lamp of the wicked goes out.
[10] Through insolence comes
nothing but strife,
But wisdom is with those
who receive counsel.

Luke 7:1-30

7 When He had completed all His discourse in the hearing of the people, He went to Capernaum.

[2] And a centurion's slave, who was highly regarded by him, was sick and about to die. [3] When he heard about Jesus, he sent some Jewish elders asking Him to come and save the life of his slave. [4] When they came to Jesus, they earnestly implored Him, saying, "He is worthy for You to grant this to him; [5] for he loves our nation and it was he who built us our synagogue." [6] Now Jesus *started* on His way with them; and when He was not far from the house, the centurion sent friends, saying to Him, "Lord, do not trouble Yourself further, for I am not worthy for You to come under my roof; [7] for this reason I did not even consider

myself worthy to come to You, but *just* say the word, and my servant will be healed. ⁸For I also am a man placed under authority, with soldiers under me; and I say to this one, 'Go!' and he goes, and to another, 'Come!' and he comes, and to my slave, 'Do this!' and he does it." ⁹Now when Jesus heard this, He marveled at him, and turned and said to the crowd that was following Him, "I say to you, not even in Israel have I found such great faith." ¹⁰When those who had been sent returned to the house, they found the slave in good health.

¹¹Soon afterwards He went to a city called Nain; and His disciples were going along with Him, accompanied by a large crowd. ¹²Now as He approached the gate of the city, a dead man was being carried out, the only son of his mother, and she was a widow; and a sizeable crowd from the city was with her. ¹³When the Lord saw her, He felt compassion for her, and said to her, "Do not weep." ¹⁴And He came up and touched the coffin; and the bearers came to a halt. And He said, "Young man, I say to you, arise!" ¹⁵The dead man sat up and began to speak. And *Jesus* gave him back to his mother. ¹⁶Fear gripped them all, and they *began* glorifying God, saying, "A great prophet has arisen among us!" and, "God has visited His people!" ¹⁷This report concerning Him went out all over Judea and in all the surrounding district.

¹⁸The disciples of John reported to him about all these things. ¹⁹Summoning two of his disciples, John sent them to the Lord, saying, "Are You the Expected One, or do we look for someone else?" ²⁰When the men came to Him, they said, "John the Baptist has sent us to You, to ask, 'Are You the Expected One, or do we look for someone else?'" ²¹At that very time He cured many *people* of diseases and afflictions and evil spirits; and He gave sight to many *who were* blind. ²²And He answered and said to them, "Go and report to John what you have seen and heard: the BLIND RECEIVE SIGHT, the

---

7:14 touched the coffin. A ceremonially defiling act, normally. Jesus graphically illustrated how impervious He was to such defilements. When He touched the coffin, its defilement did not taint Him; rather, His power immediately dispelled the presence of all death and defilement. This was the first of 3 times Jesus raised people from the dead (8:49–56; Jn 11:20–44). Verse 22 implies that Christ also raised others who are not specifically mentioned.

---

lame walk, *the* lepers are cleansed, and *the* deaf hear, *the* dead are raised up, *the* POOR HAVE THE GOSPEL PREACHED TO THEM. ²³Blessed is he who does not take offense at Me."

²⁴When the messengers of John had left, He began to speak to the crowds about John, "What did you go out into the wilderness to see? A reed shaken by the wind? ²⁵But what did you go out to see? A man dressed in soft clothing? Those who are splendidly clothed and live in luxury are *found* in royal palaces! ²⁶But what did you go out to see? A prophet? Yes, I say to you, and one who is more than a prophet. ²⁷This is the one about whom it is written,

'BEHOLD, I SEND MY MESSENGER
AHEAD OF YOU,
WHO WILL PREPARE YOUR
WAY BEFORE YOU.'

²⁸I say to you, among those born of women there is no one greater than John; yet he who is least in the kingdom of God is greater than he." ²⁹When all the people and the tax collectors heard *this,* they acknowledged God's justice, having been baptized with the baptism of John. ³⁰But the Pharisees and the lawyers rejected God's purpose for themselves, not having been baptized by John.

DAY 3: Why are our choices in life so important?

In Deuteronomy 30:11–14, after remembering the failures of the past and the prospects for the future, Moses earnestly admonished the people to make the right choice. The issue facing them was to enjoy salvation and blessing by loving God so wholeheartedly that they would willingly live in obedience to His word. The choice was simple, yet profound. It was stated in simple terms so that they could understand and grasp what God expected of them (v. 11). Although God had spoken from heaven, He had spoken through Moses in words every person could understand (v. 12). Neither did they have to search at some point beyond the sea (v. 13). The truth was there, through Moses, now in their hearts and minds (v. 14). All the truth necessary for choosing to love and obey God and thus avoid disobedience and cursing, they had heard and known (v. 15).

In v. 15, Moses pinpoints the choice—to love and obey God is life and good; to reject God is death and evil. If they chose to love God and obey His word, they would enjoy all God's blessings (v. 16). If they refused to love and obey Him, they would be severely and immediately punished (vv. 17–18). Paul, in speaking about salvation in the New Testament, makes use of this appeal made by Moses (Ro 10:1–13). Like Moses, Paul is saying that the message of salvation is plain and understandable.

So "choose life" (v. 19). Moses forces the decision, exhorting Israel on the plains of Moab before God (heaven) and man (earth) to choose, by believing in and loving God, the life available through the New Covenant (see v. 6). Sadly, Israel failed to respond to this call to the right choice (see 31:16–18, 27–29). Choosing life or death was also emphasized by Jesus. The one who believed in Him had the promise of eternal life, while the one who refused to believe faced eternal death (see Jn 3:1–36). Every person faces this same choice.

APRIL 4

Deuteronomy 31:1–32:52

31 So Moses went and spoke these words to all Israel. ²And he said to them, "I am a hundred and twenty years old today; I am no longer able to come and go, and the LORD has said to me, 'You shall not cross this Jordan.' ³It is the LORD your God who will cross ahead of you; He will destroy these nations before you, and you shall dispossess them. Joshua is the one who will cross ahead of you, just as the LORD has spoken. ⁴The LORD will do to them just as He did to Sihon and Og, the kings of the Amorites, and to their land, when He destroyed them. ⁵The LORD will deliver them up before you, and you shall do to them according to all the commandments which I have commanded you. ⁶Be strong and courageous, do not be afraid or tremble at them, for the LORD your God is the one who goes with you. He will not fail you or forsake you."

⁷Then Moses called to Joshua and said to him in the sight of all Israel, "Be strong and courageous, for you shall go with this people into the land which the LORD has sworn to their fathers to give them, and you shall give it to them as an inheritance. ⁸The LORD is the one who goes ahead of you; He will be with you. He will not fail you or forsake you. Do not fear or be dismayed."

⁹So Moses wrote this law and gave it to the priests, the sons of Levi who carried the ark of the covenant of the LORD, and to all the elders of Israel. ¹⁰Then Moses commanded them, saying, "At the end of *every* seven years, at the time of the year of remission of debts, at the Feast of Booths, ¹¹when all Israel comes to appear before the LORD your God at the place which He will choose, you shall read this law in front of all Israel in their hearing. ¹²Assemble the people, the men and the women and children and the alien who is in your town, so that they may hear and learn and fear the LORD your God, and be careful to observe all the words of this law. ¹³Their children, who have not known, will hear and learn to fear the LORD your God, as long as you live on the land which you are about to cross the Jordan to possess."

¹⁴Then the LORD said to Moses, "Behold, the time for you to die is near; call Joshua, and present yourselves at the tent of meeting, that I may commission him." So Moses and Joshua went and presented themselves at the tent of meeting. ¹⁵The LORD appeared in the tent in a pillar of cloud, and the pillar of cloud stood at the doorway of the tent. ¹⁶The LORD said to Moses, "Behold, you are about to lie down with your fathers; and this people will arise and play the harlot with the strange gods of the land, into the midst of which they are going, and will forsake Me and break My covenant which I have made with them. ¹⁷Then My anger will be kindled against them in that day, and I will forsake them and hide My face from them, and they will be consumed, and many evils and troubles will come upon them; so that they will say in that day, 'Is it not because our God is not among us that these evils have come upon

31:6-8 Be strong and courageous. The strength and courage of the warriors of Israel would come from their confidence that their God was with them and would not forsake them. In vv. 7–8, Moses repeated the substance of his exhortation, this time addressing it specifically to Joshua in the presence of the people to encourage him and to remind the people that Joshua's leadership was being assumed with the full approval of God. This principle for faith and confidence is repeated in 31:23; Joshua 1:5–7; 2 Samuel 10:12; 2 Kings 2:2; 1 Chronicles 22:11–13; 2 Chronicles 32:1–8; Psalm 27:14. The writer of Hebrews quotes vv. 6, 8 in 13:5.

us?' ¹⁸ But I will surely hide My face in that day because of all the evil which they will do, for they will turn to other gods.

¹⁹ "Now therefore, write this song for yourselves, and teach it to the sons of Israel; put it on their lips, so that this song may be a witness for Me against the sons of Israel. ²⁰ For when I bring them into the land flowing with milk and honey, which I swore to their fathers, and they have eaten and are satisfied and become prosperous, then they will turn to other gods and serve them, and spurn Me and break My covenant. ²¹ Then it shall come about, when many evils and troubles have come upon them, that this song will testify before them as a witness (for it shall not be forgotten from the lips of their descendants); for I know their intent which they are developing today, before I have brought them into the land which I swore." ²² So Moses wrote this song the same day, and taught it to the sons of Israel.

²³ Then He commissioned Joshua the son of Nun, and said, "Be strong and courageous, for you shall bring the sons of Israel into the land which I swore to them, and I will be with you."

²⁴ It came about, when Moses finished writing the words of this law in a book until they were complete, ²⁵ that Moses commanded the Levites who carried the ark of the covenant of the LORD, saying, ²⁶ "Take this book of the law and place it beside the ark of the covenant of the LORD your God, that it may remain there as a witness against you. ²⁷ For I know your rebellion and your stubbornness; behold, while I am still alive with you today, you have been rebellious against the LORD; how much more, then, after my death? ²⁸ Assemble to me all the elders of your tribes and your officers, that I may speak these words in their hearing and call the heavens and the earth to witness against them. ²⁹ For I know that after my death you will act corruptly and turn from the way which I have commanded you; and evil will befall you in the latter days, for you will do that which is evil in the sight of the LORD, provoking Him to anger with the work of your hands."

³⁰ Then Moses spoke in the hearing of all the assembly of Israel the words of this song, until they were complete:

32

"Give ear, O heavens,
and let me speak;
And let the earth hear the
words of my mouth.
² "Let my teaching drop as the rain,
My speech distill as the dew,
As the droplets on the fresh grass
And as the showers on the herb.

³ "For I proclaim the name of the LORD;
Ascribe greatness to our God!
⁴ "The Rock! His work is perfect,
For all His ways are just;
A God of faithfulness and
without injustice,
Righteous and upright is He.
⁵ "They have acted corruptly
toward Him,
They are not His children,
because of their defect;
But are a perverse and
crooked generation.
⁶ "Do you thus repay the LORD,
O foolish and unwise people?
Is not He your Father who
has bought you?
He has made you and established you.
⁷ "Remember the days of old,
Consider the years of all generations.
Ask your father, and he
will inform you,
Your elders, and they will tell you.
⁸ "When the Most High gave the
nations their inheritance,
When He separated the sons of man,
He set the boundaries of the peoples
According to the number
of the sons of Israel.
⁹ "For the LORD'S portion is His people;
Jacob is the allotment of
His inheritance.
¹⁰ "He found him in a desert land,
And in the howling waste
of a wilderness;
He encircled him, He cared for him,
He guarded him as the
pupil of His eye.
¹¹ "Like an eagle that stirs up its nest,
That hovers over its young,
He spread His wings and caught them,
He carried them on His pinions.
¹² "The LORD alone guided him,
And there was no foreign
god with him.
¹³ "He made him ride on the high
places of the earth,
And he ate the produce of the field;
And He made him suck
honey from the rock,
And oil from the flinty rock,
¹⁴ Curds of cows, and milk of the flock,
With fat of lambs,
And rams, the breed of
Bashan, and goats,
With the finest of the wheat—
And of the blood of grapes
you drank wine.

15 "But Jeshurun grew fat and kicked—
You are grown fat, thick, and sleek—
Then he forsook God who made him,
And scorned the Rock of his salvation.
16 "They made Him jealous
with strange *gods;*
With abominations they
provoked Him to anger.
17 "They sacrificed to demons
who were not God,
To gods whom they have not known,
New *gods* who came lately,
Whom your fathers did not dread.
18 "You neglected the Rock
who begot you,
And forgot the God who
gave you birth.

19 "The LORD saw *this,* and spurned *them*
Because of the provocation of
His sons and daughters.
20 "Then He said, 'I will hide
My face from them,
I will see what their end *shall be;*
For they are a perverse generation,
Sons in whom is no faithfulness.
21 'They have made Me jealous
with *what* is not God;
They have provoked Me to
anger with their idols.
So I will make them jealous with
those who are not a people;
I will provoke them to anger
with a foolish nation,
22 For a fire is kindled in My anger,
And burns to the lowest part
of Sheol,
And consumes the earth
with its yield,
And sets on fire the foundations
of the mountains.
23 'I will heap misfortunes on them;
I will use My arrows on them.
24 'They *will be* wasted by famine,
and consumed by plague
And bitter destruction;
And the teeth of beasts I
will send upon them,
With the venom of crawling
things of the dust.
25 'Outside the sword will bereave,
And inside terror—
Both young man and virgin,
The nursling with the
man of gray hair.
26 'I would have said, "I will
cut them to pieces,

I will remove the memory
of them from men,"
27 Had I not feared the provocation
by the enemy,
That their adversaries
would misjudge,
That they would say, "Our
hand is triumphant,
And the LORD has not done all this."'
28 "For they are a nation
lacking in counsel,
And there is no understanding
in them.
29 "Would that they were wise, that
they understood this,
That they would discern their future!
30 "How could one chase a thousand,
And two put ten thousand to flight,
Unless their Rock had sold them,
And the LORD had given them up?
31 "Indeed their rock is not like our Rock,
Even our enemies themselves
judge this.
32 "For their vine is from the
vine of Sodom,
And from the fields of Gomorrah;
Their grapes are grapes of poison,
Their clusters, bitter.
33 "Their wine is the venom of serpents,
And the deadly poison of cobras.

34 'Is it not laid up in store with Me,
Sealed up in My treasuries?
35 'Vengeance is Mine, and retribution,
In due time their foot will slip;
For the day of their calamity is near,
And the impending things are
hastening upon them.'
36 "For the LORD will vindicate
His people,
And will have compassion
on His servants,
When He sees that *their*
strength is gone,
And there is none *remaining,*
bond or free.
37 "And He will say, 'Where
are their gods,
The rock in which they sought refuge?
38 'Who ate the fat of their sacrifices,
And drank the wine of their
drink offering?
Let them rise up and help you,
Let them be your hiding place!
39 'See now that I, I am He,
And there is no god besides Me;
It is I who put to death and give life.

I have wounded and it is I who heal,
And there is no one who can
deliver from My hand.
⁴⁰ 'Indeed, I lift up My hand to heaven,
And say, as I live forever,
⁴¹ If I sharpen My flashing sword,
And My hand takes hold on justice,
I will render vengeance
on My adversaries,
And I will repay those who hate Me.
⁴² 'I will make My arrows
drunk with blood,
And My sword will devour flesh,
With the blood of the slain
and the captives,
From the long-haired leaders
of the enemy.'
⁴³ "Rejoice, O nations, *with* His people;
For He will avenge the blood
of His servants,
And will render vengeance
on His adversaries,
And will atone for His land
and His people."

⁴⁴ Then Moses came and spoke all the words of this song in the hearing of the people, he, with Joshua the son of Nun. ⁴⁵ When Moses had finished speaking all these words to all Israel, ⁴⁶ he said to them, "Take to your heart all the words with which I am warning you today, which you shall command your sons to observe carefully, *even* all the words of this law. ⁴⁷ For it is not an idle word for you; indeed it is your life. And by this word you will prolong your days in the land, which you are about to cross the Jordan to possess."

⁴⁸ The LORD spoke to Moses that very same day, saying, ⁴⁹ "Go up to this mountain of the Abarim, Mount Nebo, which is in the land of Moab opposite Jericho, and look at the land of Canaan, which I am giving to the sons of Israel for a possession. ⁵⁰ Then die on the mountain where you ascend, and be gathered to your people, as Aaron your brother died on Mount Hor and was gathered to his people, ⁵¹ because you broke faith with Me in the midst of the sons of Israel at the waters of Meribah-kadesh, in the wilderness of Zin, because you did not treat Me as holy in the midst of the sons of Israel. ⁵² For you shall see the land at a distance, but you shall not go there, into the land which I am giving the sons of Israel."

Psalm 40:6-12

⁶ Sacrifice and meal offering
You have not desired;
My ears You have opened;
Burnt offering and sin offering
You have not required.
⁷ Then I said, "Behold, I come;
In the scroll of the book it
is written of me.
⁸ "I delight to do Your will,
O my God;
Your Law is within my heart."

⁹ I have proclaimed glad tidings
of righteousness in the
great congregation;
Behold, I will not restrain my lips,
O LORD, You know.
¹⁰ I have not hidden Your
righteousness within my heart;
I have spoken of Your faithfulness
and Your salvation;
I have not concealed Your
lovingkindness and Your truth
from the great congregation.

¹¹ You, O LORD, will not withhold
Your compassion from me;
Your lovingkindness and Your truth
will continually preserve me.

32:43 Rejoice, O nations, *with* His people. As a result of the execution of God's vengeance, all nations will be called upon to praise with Israel the Lord who will have provided redemptively for them in Christ and also provided a new beginning in the land. This atonement for the land is the satisfaction of God's wrath by the sacrifice of His enemies in judgment. The atonement for the people is by the sacrifice of Jesus Christ on the cross (Ps 79:9). Paul quotes this passage in Romans 15:10, as does the writer of Hebrews (1:6).

40:6 Sacrifice and meal offering You have not desired. He is not negating the commandment to offer sacrifices, but is emphasizing their being offered with the right attitude of heart (contra. Saul, 1Sa 15:22–23; note the emphases on proper spiritual prerequisites for sacrifices in Pss 19:14; 50:7–15; 51:15–17; 69:30–31; Is 1:10–15; Jer 7:21–26; Hos 6:6; Am 5:21–24; Mic 6:6–8; Mt 23:23). **My ears You have opened.** Literally "ears" or "two ears You have dug for me." This pictures obedience and dedication.

12 For evils beyond number
    have surrounded me;
My iniquities have overtaken me,
    so that I am not able to see;
They are more numerous than
    the hairs of my head,
And my heart has failed me.

Proverbs 13:11–12

11 Wealth *obtained* by fraud dwindles,
But the one who gathers by
    labor increases *it.*
12 Hope deferred makes the heart sick,
But desire fulfilled is a tree
    of life.

Luke 7:31–50

31 "To what then shall I compare the men of this generation, and what are they like? 32 They are like children who sit in the market place and call to one another, and they say, 'We played the flute for you, and you did not dance; we sang a dirge, and you did not weep.' 33 For John the Baptist has come eating no bread and drinking no wine, and you say, 'He has a demon!' 34 The Son of Man has come eating and drinking, and you say, 'Behold, a gluttonous man and a drunkard, a friend of tax collectors and sinners!' 35 Yet wisdom is vindicated by all her children."

7:32 like children. Christ used strong derision to rebuke the Pharisees. He suggested they were behaving childishly, determined not to be pleased, whether invited to "dance" (a reference to Christ's joyous style of ministry, "eating and drinking" with sinners—v. 34), or urged to "weep" (a reference to John the Baptist's call to repentance, and John's more austere manner of ministry—v. 33).

36 Now one of the Pharisees was requesting Him to dine with him, and He entered the Pharisee's house and reclined *at the table.* 37 And there was a woman in the city who was a sinner; and when she learned that He was reclining *at the table* in the Pharisee's house, she brought an alabaster vial of perfume, 38 and standing behind *Him* at His feet, weeping, she began to wet His feet with her tears, and kept wiping them with the hair of her head, and kissing His feet and anointing them with the perfume. 39 Now when the Pharisee who had invited Him saw this, he said to himself, "If this man were a prophet He would know who and what sort of person this woman is who is touching Him, that she is a sinner." 40 And Jesus answered him, "Simon, I have something to say to you." And he replied, "Say it, Teacher." 41 "A moneylender had two debtors: one owed five hundred denarii, and the other fifty. 42 When they were unable to repay, he graciously forgave them both. So which of them will love him more?" 43 Simon answered and said, "I suppose the one whom he forgave more." And He said to him, "You have judged correctly." 44 Turning toward the woman, He said to Simon, "Do you see this woman? I entered your house; you gave Me no water for My feet, but she has wet My feet with her tears and wiped them with her hair. 45 You gave Me no kiss; but she, since the time I came in, has not ceased to kiss My feet. 46 You did not anoint My head with oil, but she anointed My feet with perfume. 47 For this reason I say to you, her sins, which are many, have been forgiven, for she loved much; but he who is forgiven little, loves little." 48 Then He said to her, "Your sins have been forgiven." 49 Those who were reclining *at the table* with Him began to say to themselves, "Who is this *man* who even forgives sins?" 50 And He said to the woman, "Your faith has saved you; go in peace."

DAY 4: How is God characterized in the Song of Moses in Deuteronomy 32?

The Song of Moses is a call to Israel to always "ascribe greatness to our God" (v. 3). This command refers to the greatness of God revealed in His acts of omnipotence. Read through the song and note the descriptions of God.

"The Rock" (v. 4). This word, representing the stability and permanence of God, was placed at the beginning of the verse for emphasis and was followed by a series of phrases which elaborated the attributes of God as the Rock of Israel. It is one of the principle themes in this song (see vv. 15, 18, 30–31), stressing the unchanging nature of God in contrast with the fickle nature of the people.

"Your Father" (v. 6). The foolishness and stupidity of Israel would be seen in the fact that they would rebel against God who as a Father had brought them forth and formed them into a nation. As Father, He was the progenitor and originator of the nation and the One who had matured and sustained it. This idea of God as Father of the nation is emphasized in the Old Testament (see 1Ch 29:10; Is. 63:16; 64:8; Mal 2:10) while the idea of God as Father of individual believers is developed in the New Testament (see Ro 8:15; Gal 4:6).

"The Most High" (vv. 8–9). This title for God emphasized His sovereignty and authority over all the nations (see Ge 11:9; 10:32; 14:18; Nu 24:16) with the amazing revelation that, in the whole plan for the world, God had as His goal the salvation of His chosen people. God ordained a plan where the number of nations (70, according to Ge 10) corresponded to the number of the children of Israel (70, according to Ge 46:27). Further, as God gave the nations their lands, He established their boundaries, leaving Israel enough land to sustain their expected population.

"Hovers over its young" (v. 11). The Lord exercised His loving care for Israel like an eagle caring for its young, especially as they were taught to fly. As they began to fly and had little strength, they would start to fall. At that point, an eagle would stop their fall by spreading its wings so they could land on them. So the Lord has carried Israel and not let the nation fall. He has been training Israel to fly on His wings of love and omnipotence.

APRIL 5

Deuteronomy 33:1–34:12

33 Now this is the blessing with which Moses the man of God blessed the sons of Israel before his death. ²He said,

"The LORD came from Sinai,
And dawned on them from Seir;
He shone forth from Mount Paran,
And He came from the midst of
    ten thousand holy ones;
At His right hand there was
    flashing lightning for them.
³ "Indeed, He loves the people;
All Your holy ones are in Your
    hand,
And they followed in Your steps;
Everyone receives of Your words.
⁴ "Moses charged us with a law,
A possession for the
    assembly of Jacob.
⁵ "And He was king in Jeshurun,
When the heads of the people
    were gathered,
The tribes of Israel together.

⁶ "May Reuben live and not die,
Nor his men be few."

33:5 king in Jeshurun. Literally, "he was king." It is possible that this refers back to Moses in v. 4. However, it is more likely speaking of God since: 1) Moses is never called "king" elsewhere in Scripture; 2) Moses was not anointed to be king as were the other human kings of Israel; 3) Israel forsook God as their king when they chose Saul to be king (1Sa 8:7); and 4) God is elsewhere actually declared to be king over Jeshurun (Is 44:1–6).

⁷And this regarding Judah; so he said,

"Hear, O LORD, the voice of Judah,
And bring him to his people.
With his hands he
    contended for them,
And may You be a help against
    his adversaries."

⁸Of Levi he said,

"*Let* Your Thummim and Your Urim
    belong to Your godly man,
Whom You proved at Massah,
With whom You contended at
    the waters of Meribah;
⁹ Who said of his father and
    his mother,
'I did not consider them';
And he did not acknowledge
    his brothers,
Nor did he regard his own sons,
For they observed Your word,
And kept Your covenant.
¹⁰ "They shall teach Your
    ordinances to Jacob,
And Your law to Israel.
They shall put incense before You,
And whole burnt offerings
    on Your altar.
¹¹ "O LORD, bless his substance,
And accept the work of his hands;
Shatter the loins of those who
    rise up against him,
And those who hate him, so that
    they will not rise *again*."

¹²Of Benjamin he said,

"May the beloved of the LORD
    dwell in security by Him,
Who shields him all the day,
And he dwells between
    His shoulders."

¹³ Of Joseph he said,

"Blessed of the LORD *be* his land,
With the choice things of
heaven, with the dew,
And from the deep lying beneath,
¹⁴ And with the choice yield of the sun,
And with the choice produce
of the months.
¹⁵ "And with the best things of
the ancient mountains,
And with the choice things of
the everlasting hills,
¹⁶ And with the choice things of
the earth and its fullness,
And the favor of Him who
dwelt in the bush.
Let it come to the head of Joseph,
And to the crown of the head
of the one distinguished
among his brothers.
¹⁷ "As the firstborn of his ox,
majesty is his,
And his horns are the horns
of the wild ox;
With them he will push the peoples,
All at once, *to* the ends of the earth.
And those are the ten
thousands of Ephraim,
And those are the thousands
of Manasseh."

¹⁸ Of Zebulun he said,

"Rejoice, Zebulun, in your going forth,
And, Issachar, in your tents.
¹⁹ "They will call peoples *to*
the mountain;
There they will offer
righteous sacrifices;
For they will draw out the
abundance of the seas,
And the hidden treasures of the sand."

²⁰ Of Gad he said,

"Blessed is the one who enlarges Gad;
He lies down as a lion,
And tears the arm, also the
crown of the head.
²¹ "Then he provided the first
part for himself,
For there the ruler's portion
was reserved;
And he came *with* the
leaders of the people;
He executed the justice of the LORD,
And His ordinances with Israel."

²² Of Dan he said,

"Dan is a lion's whelp,
That leaps forth from Bashan."

²³ Of Naphtali he said,

"O Naphtali, satisfied with favor,
And full of the blessing of the LORD,
Take possession of the sea
and the south."

²⁴ Of Asher he said,

"More blessed than sons is Asher;
May he be favored by his brothers,
And may he dip his foot in oil.
²⁵ "Your locks will be iron and bronze,
And according to your days, so
will your leisurely walk be.

²⁶ "There is none like the
God of Jeshurun,
Who rides the heavens to
your help,
And through the skies in His
majesty.
²⁷ "The eternal God is a dwelling
place,
And underneath are the
everlasting arms;
And He drove out the enemy
from before you,
And said, 'Destroy!'
²⁸ "So Israel dwells in security,
The fountain of Jacob secluded,
In a land of grain and new wine;
His heavens also drop down dew.
²⁹ "Blessed are you, O Israel;
Who is like you, a people
saved by the LORD,
Who is the shield of your help
And the sword of your majesty!
So your enemies will
cringe before you,
And you will tread upon
their high places."

34 Now Moses went up from the plains of Moab to Mount Nebo, to the top of Pisgah, which is opposite Jericho. And the LORD showed him all the land, Gilead as far as Dan, ² and all Naphtali and the land of Ephraim and Manasseh, and all the land of Judah as far as the western sea, ³ and the Negev and the plain in the valley of Jericho, the city of palm trees, as far as Zoar. ⁴ Then the LORD said to him, "This is the land which I swore to Abraham,

Isaac, and Jacob, saying, 'I will give it to your descendants'; I have let you see *it* with your eyes, but you shall not go over there." ⁵ So Moses the servant of the LORD died there in the land of Moab, according to the word of the LORD. ⁶ And He buried him in the valley in the land of Moab, opposite Beth-peor; but no man knows his burial place to this day. ⁷ Although Moses was one hundred and twenty years old when he died, his eye was not dim, nor his vigor abated. ⁸ So the sons of Israel wept for Moses in the plains of Moab thirty days; then the days of weeping *and* mourning for Moses came to an end.

⁹ Now Joshua the son of Nun was filled with the spirit of wisdom, for Moses had laid his hands on him; and the sons of Israel listened to him and did as the LORD had commanded Moses. ¹⁰ Since that time no prophet has risen in Israel like Moses, whom the LORD knew face to face, ¹¹ for all the signs and wonders which the LORD sent him to perform in the land of Egypt against Pharaoh, all his servants, and all his land, ¹² and for all the mighty power and for all the great terror which Moses performed in the sight of all Israel.

Psalm 40:13-17

¹³ Be pleased, O LORD, to deliver me;
Make haste, O LORD, to help me.
¹⁴ Let those be ashamed and
humiliated together
Who seek my life to destroy it;
Let those be turned back
and dishonored
Who delight in my hurt.
¹⁵ Let those be appalled because
of their shame
Who say to me, "Aha, aha!"
¹⁶ Let all who seek You rejoice
and be glad in You;
Let those who love Your
salvation say continually,
"The LORD be magnified!"
¹⁷ Since I am afflicted and needy,
Let the Lord be mindful of me.
You are my help and my deliverer;
Do not delay, O my God.

Proverbs 13:13-14

¹³ The one who despises the word
will be in debt to it,
But the one who fears the
commandment will be rewarded.
¹⁴ The teaching of the wise is
a fountain of life,
To turn aside from the
snares of death.

Luke 8:1-25

8 Soon afterwards, He *began* going around from one city and village to another, proclaiming and preaching the kingdom of God. The twelve were with Him, ² and *also* some women who had been healed of evil spirits and sicknesses: Mary who was called Magdalene, from whom seven demons had gone out, ³ and Joanna the wife of Chuza, Herod's steward, and Susanna, and many others who were contributing to their support out of their private means.

8:2 some women. Rabbis normally did not have women as disciples. **Mary...called Magdalene.** Her name probably derives from the Galilean town of Magdala. Some believe she is the woman described in 7:37-50, but it seems highly unlikely that Luke would introduce her here by name for the first time if she were the main figure in the account he just completed. Also, while it is clear that she had suffered at the hands of "demons," there is no reason whatsoever to think that she had ever been a prostitute.

8:3 Joanna. This woman is also mentioned in 24:10, but nowhere else in Scripture. It is possible that she was a source for some of the details Luke recounts about Herod (23:8, 12). **Susanna.** Aside from this reference, she is nowhere mentioned in Scripture. She is probably someone Luke knew personally. **out of their private means.** It was a Jewish custom for disciples to support rabbis in this way. (See 10:7; 1Co 9:4-11; Gal 6:6; 1Ti 5:17-18.)

⁴ When a large crowd was coming together, and those from the various cities were journeying to Him, He spoke by way of a parable: ⁵ "The sower went out to sow his seed; and as he sowed, some fell beside the road, and it was trampled under foot and the birds of the air ate it up. ⁶ Other *seed* fell on rocky *soil,* and as soon as it grew up, it withered away, because it had no moisture. ⁷ Other *seed* fell among the thorns; and the thorns grew up with it and choked it out. ⁸ Other *seed* fell into the good soil, and grew up, and produced a crop a hundred times as great." As He said these things, He would call out, "He who has ears to hear, let him hear."

⁹ His disciples *began* questioning Him as to what this parable meant. ¹⁰ And He said, "To you it has been granted to know the mysteries of the kingdom of God, but to

the rest *it is* in parables, so that SEEING THEY MAY NOT SEE, AND HEARING THEY MAY NOT UNDERSTAND. ¹¹ "Now the parable is this: the seed is the word of God. ¹² Those beside the road are those who have heard; then the devil comes and takes away the word from their heart, so that they will not believe and be saved. ¹³ Those on the rocky *soil are* those who, when they hear, receive the word with joy; and these have no *firm* root; they believe for a while, and in time of temptation fall away. ¹⁴ The *seed* which fell among the thorns, these are the ones who have heard, and as they go on their way they are choked with worries and riches and pleasures of *this* life, and bring no fruit to maturity. ¹⁵ But the *seed* in the good soil, these are the ones who have heard the word in an honest and good heart, and hold it fast, and bear fruit with perseverance.

¹⁶ "Now no one after lighting a lamp covers it over with a container, or puts it under a bed; but he puts it on a lampstand, so that those who come in may see the light. ¹⁷ For nothing is hidden that will not become evident, nor *anything* secret that will not be known and come to light. ¹⁸ So take care how you listen; for whoever has, to him *more* shall be given; and whoever does not have, even what he thinks he has shall be taken away from him."

¹⁹ And His mother and brothers came to Him, and they were unable to get to Him be-

cause of the crowd. ²⁰ And it was reported to Him, "Your mother and Your brothers are standing outside, wishing to see You." ²¹ But He answered and said to them, "My mother and My brothers are these who hear the word of God and do it."

²² Now on one of *those* days Jesus and His disciples got into a boat, and He said to them, "Let us go over to the other side of the lake." So they launched out. ²³ But as they were sailing along He fell asleep; and a fierce gale of wind descended on the lake, and they *began* to be swamped and to be in danger. ²⁴ They came to Jesus and woke Him up, saying, "Master, Master, we are perishing!" And He got up and rebuked the wind and the surging waves, and they stopped, and it became calm. ²⁵ And He said to them, "Where is your faith?" They were fearful and amazed, saying to one another, "Who then is this, that He commands even the winds and the water, and they obey Him?"

8:18 take care how you listen. One's response to the light in this life is crucial, because at the throne of judgment there will be no opportunity to embrace truth that was formerly spurned (Rev 20:11–15). Those who scorn the light of the gospel now will have all light removed from them in eternity. See 19:26; Matthew 25:29.

DAY 5: How is Moses described at the end of his life?

He is called "the man of God" in Deuteronomy 33:1. This is the first use of this phrase in Scripture. Subsequently, some 70 times in the Old Testament, messengers of God (especially prophets) are called a "man of God" (1Sa 2:27; 9:6; 1Ki 13:1; 17:18; 2Ki 4:7). The New Testament uses this title for Timothy (1Ti 6:11; 2Ti 3:17). Moses was viewed among such prophets in this conclusion to the book (see 34:10).

In Deuteronomy 34:1–4, he went to the top of Pisgah where "the LORD showed him" the panorama of the land the Lord had promised to give (the land of Canaan) to the patriarchs and their seed in Genesis 12:7; 13:15; 15:18–21; 26:4; 28:13–14. Remarkably, it adds that "He buried him" (v. 6). The context indicates that the Lord is the One who buried Moses, and man did not have a part in it. See Jude v. 9, which recounts Michael's and Satan's dispute over Moses' body.

At the end, Moses' physical vision and physical health were "not dim…abated" (v. 7). It was not death by natural causes that kept Moses from leading Israel into the Promised Land. It was his unfaithfulness to the Lord at Meribah (see Nu 20:12). Before he passed on, Moses "laid his hands" on Joshua (v. 9), which was a confirmation of the military and administrative ability necessary to the task the Lord had given Joshua. It also confirmed that Joshua had the spiritual wisdom to rely on and to be committed to the Lord.

Moses was the greatest of all the Old Testament prophets (v. 10), one whom the Lord knew intimately. Not until John the Baptist was there another prophet greater than Moses (see Mt 11:11). After John, the Prophet came of whom Moses wrote (see Jn 1:21, 25; 6:14 with Dt 18:15, 18; Ac 3:22; 7:37). Moses next appeared on the Mt. of Transfiguration together with Elijah and Jesus Christ (Mt 17:3; Mk 9:4; Lk 9:30–31).

APRIL 6

Joshua 1:1–2:24

1 Now it came about after the death of Moses the servant of the LORD, that the LORD spoke to Joshua the son of Nun, Moses' servant, saying, ²"Moses My servant is dead; now therefore arise, cross this Jordan, you and all this people, to the land which I am giving to them, to the sons of Israel. ³Every place on which the sole of your foot treads, I have given it to you, just as I spoke to Moses. ⁴From the wilderness and this Lebanon, even as far as the great river, the river Euphrates, all the land of the Hittites, and as far as the Great Sea toward the setting of the sun will be your territory. ⁵No man will *be able to* stand before you all the days of your life. Just as I have been with Moses, I will be with you; I will not fail you or forsake you. ⁶Be strong and courageous, for you shall give this people possession of the land which I swore to their fathers to give them. ⁷Only be strong and very courageous; be careful to do according to all the law which Moses My servant commanded you; do not turn from it to the right or to the left, so that you may have success wherever you go. ⁸This book of the law shall not depart from your mouth, but you shall meditate on it day and night, so that you may be careful to do according to all that is written in it; for then you will make your way prosperous, and then you will have success. ⁹Have I not commanded you? Be strong and courageous! Do not tremble or be dismayed, for the LORD your God is with you wherever you go."

¹⁰Then Joshua commanded the officers of the people, saying, ¹¹"Pass through the midst of the camp and command the people, saying, 'Prepare provisions for yourselves, for within

1:8 This book of the law. A reference to Scripture, specifically Genesis through Deuteronomy, written by Moses (Ex 17:14; Dt 31:9–11, 24). **meditate on it.** To read with thoughtfulness, to linger over God's Word. The parts of Scripture they possessed have always been the main spiritual food of those who served Him, e.g., Job (Job 23:12); the psalmist (Ps 1:1–3); Jeremiah (Jer 15:16); and Jesus (Jn 4:34). **prosperous... success.** The promise of God's blessing on the great responsibility God has given Joshua. The principle here is central to all spiritual effort and enterprise, namely the deep understanding and application of Scripture at all times.

1:9 LORD...is with you. This assurance has always been the staying sufficiency for His servants such as: Abraham (Ge 15:1); Moses and his people (Ex 14:13); Isaiah (Is 41:10); Jeremiah (Jer 1:7–8); and Christians through the centuries (Mt 28:20; Heb 13:5).

three days you are to cross this Jordan, to go in to possess the land which the LORD your God is giving you, to possess it.'"

¹²To the Reubenites and to the Gadites and to the half-tribe of Manasseh, Joshua said, ¹³"Remember the word which Moses the servant of the LORD commanded you, saying, 'The LORD your God gives you rest and will give you this land.' ¹⁴Your wives, your little ones, and your cattle shall remain in the land which Moses gave you beyond the Jordan, but you shall cross before your brothers in battle array, all your valiant warriors, and shall help them, ¹⁵until the LORD gives your brothers rest, as *He gives* you, and they also possess the land which the LORD your God is giving them. Then you shall return to your own land, and possess that which Moses the servant of the LORD gave you beyond the Jordan toward the sunrise."

¹⁶They answered Joshua, saying, "All that you have commanded us we will do, and wherever you send us we will go. ¹⁷Just as we obeyed Moses in all things, so we will obey you; only may the LORD your God be with you as He was with Moses. ¹⁸Anyone who rebels against your command and does not obey your words in all that you command him, shall be put to death; only be strong and courageous."

2 Then Joshua the son of Nun sent two men as spies secretly from Shittim, saying, "Go, view the land, especially Jericho." So they went and came into the house of a harlot whose name was Rahab, and lodged there. ²It was told the king of Jericho, saying, "Behold, men from the sons of Israel have come here tonight to search out the land." ³And the king of Jericho sent *word* to Rahab, saying, "Bring out the men who have come to you, who have entered your house, for they have come to search out all the land." ⁴But the woman had taken the two men and hidden them, and she said, "Yes, the men came to me, but I did not know where they were from. ⁵It came about when *it was time* to shut the gate at dark, that the men went out; I do not know where the men went. Pursue them quickly, for you will overtake them." ⁶But she had brought

2:1 two men as spies. These scouts would inform Joshua on various features of the topography, food, drinking water, and defenses to be overcome in the invasion. **house of a harlot.** Their purpose was not impure; rather, the spies sought a place where they would not be conspicuous. Resorting to such a house would be a good cover, from where they might learn something of Jericho. Also, a house on the city wall (v. 15) would allow a quick getaway. In spite of this precaution, their presence became known (vv. 2–3). God, in His sovereign providence, wanted them there for the salvation of the harlot. She would provide an example of His saving by faith a woman at the bottom of the social strata, as He saved Abraham at the top (Jas 2:18–25). Most importantly, by God's grace she was in the Messianic line (Mt 1:5).

them up to the roof and hidden them in the stalks of flax which she had laid in order on the roof. [7]So the men pursued them on the road to the Jordan to the fords; and as soon as those who were pursuing them had gone out, they shut the gate.

[8]Now before they lay down, she came up to them on the roof, [9]and said to the men, "I know that the LORD has given you the land, and that the terror of you has fallen on us, and that all the inhabitants of the land have melted away before you. [10]For we have heard how the LORD dried up the water of the Red Sea before you when you came out of Egypt, and what you did to the two kings of the Amorites who were beyond the Jordan, to Sihon and Og, whom you utterly destroyed. [11]When we heard *it*, our hearts melted and no courage remained in any man any longer because of you; for the LORD your God, He is God in heaven above and on earth beneath. [12]Now therefore, please swear to me by the LORD, since I have dealt kindly with you, that you also will deal kindly with my father's household, and give me a pledge of truth, [13]and spare my father and my mother and my brothers and my sisters, with all who belong to them, and deliver our lives from death." [14]So the men said to her, "Our life for yours if you do not tell this business of ours; and it shall come about when the LORD gives us the land that we will deal kindly and faithfully with you."

[15]Then she let them down by a rope through the window, for her house was on the city wall, so that she was living on the wall. [16]She said to them, "Go to the hill country, so that the pursuers will not happen upon

you, and hide yourselves there for three days until the pursuers return. Then afterward you may go on your way." [17]The men said to her, "We *shall be* free from this oath to you which you have made us swear, [18]unless, when we come into the land, you tie this cord of scarlet thread in the window through which you let us down, and gather to yourself into the house your father and your mother and your brothers and all your father's household. [19]It shall come about that anyone who goes out of the doors of your house into the street, his blood *shall be* on his own head, and we *shall be* free; but anyone who is with you in the house, his blood *shall be* on our head if a hand is *laid* on him. [20]But if you tell this business of ours, then we shall be free from the oath which you have made us swear." [21]She said, "According to your words, so be it." So she sent them away, and they departed; and she tied the scarlet cord in the window.

[22]They departed and came to the hill country, and remained there for three days until the pursuers returned. Now the pursuers had sought *them* all along the road, but had not found *them*. [23]Then the two men returned and came down from the hill country and crossed over and came to Joshua the son of Nun, and they related to him all that had happened to them. [24]They said to Joshua, "Surely the LORD has given all the land into our hands; moreover, all the inhabitants of the land have melted away before us."

Psalm 41:1–13

For the choir director. A Psalm of David.

How blessed is he who
   considers the helpless;
   The LORD will deliver him
    in a day of trouble.
[2] The LORD will protect him
    and keep him alive,
   And he shall be called blessed
    upon the earth;
   And do not give him over to
    the desire of his enemies.
[3] The LORD will sustain him
    upon his sickbed;
   In his illness, You restore
    him to health.

[4] As for me, I said, "O LORD,
    be gracious to me;
   Heal my soul, for I have
    sinned against You."
[5] My enemies speak evil against me,
   "When will he die, and his
    name perish?"

⁶ And when he comes to see *me,*
    he speaks falsehood;
    His heart gathers wickedness to itself;
    When he goes outside, he tells it.
⁷ All who hate me whisper
    together against me;
    Against me they devise
    my hurt, *saying,*
⁸ "A wicked thing is poured
    out upon him,
    That when he lies down, he
    will not rise up again."
⁹ Even my close friend in
    whom I trusted,
    Who ate my bread,
    Has lifted up his heel against me.

¹⁰ But You, O LORD, be gracious
    to me and raise me up,
    That I may repay them.
¹¹ By this I know that You are
    pleased with me,
    Because my enemy does not
    shout in triumph over me.
¹² As for me, You uphold me
    in my integrity,
    And You set me in Your
    presence forever.

¹³ Blessed be the LORD, the God of Israel,
    From everlasting to everlasting.
    Amen and Amen.

41:13 Blessed be. The essence of the Hebrew root of "amen" is "it is true," i.e., reliable, confirmed, verified. Note that Book I of the Psalms (Pss 1–41) closes with a doxology; see the endings of the other 4 books (Pss 72:18–19; 89:52; 106:48; 150:6).

Proverbs 13:15–16

¹⁵ Good understanding produces favor,
    But the way of the
    treacherous is hard.
¹⁶ Every prudent man acts
    with knowledge,
    But a fool displays folly.

Luke 8:26–56

²⁶ Then they sailed to the country of the Gerasenes, which is opposite Galilee. ²⁷ And when He came out onto the land, He was met by a man from the city who was possessed with demons; and who had not put on any clothing for a long time, and was not living in a house, but in the tombs. ²⁸ Seeing Jesus, he cried out and fell before Him, and said in a loud voice, "What business do we have with each other, Jesus, Son of the Most High God? I beg You, do not torment me." ²⁹ For He had commanded the unclean spirit to come out of the man. For it had seized him many times; and he was bound with chains and shackles and kept under guard, and *yet* he would break his bonds and be driven by the demon into the desert. ³⁰ And Jesus asked him, "What is your name?" And he said, "Legion"; for many demons had entered him. ³¹ They were imploring Him not to command them to go away into the abyss.

³² Now there was a herd of many swine feeding there on the mountain; and *the demons* implored Him to permit them to enter the swine. And He gave them permission. ³³ And the demons came out of the man and entered the swine; and the herd rushed down the steep bank into the lake and was drowned. ³⁴ When the herdsmen saw what had happened, they ran away and reported it in the city and *out* in the country. ³⁵ *The people* went out to see what had happened; and they came to Jesus, and found the man from whom the demons had gone out, sitting down at the feet of Jesus, clothed and in his right mind; and they became frightened. ³⁶ Those who had seen it reported to them how the man who was demon-possessed had been made well. ³⁷ And all the people of the country of the Gerasenes and the surrounding district asked Him to leave them, for they were gripped with great fear; and He got into a boat and returned. ³⁸ But the man from whom the demons had gone out was begging Him that he might accompany Him; but He sent him away, saying, ³⁹ "Return to your house and describe what great things God has done for you." So he went away, proclaiming throughout the whole city what great things Jesus had done for him.

⁴⁰ And as Jesus returned, the people welcomed Him, for they had all been waiting for Him. ⁴¹ And there came a man named Jairus, and he was an official of the synagogue; and he fell at Jesus' feet, and *began* to implore Him to come to his house; ⁴² for he had an only daughter, about twelve years old, and she was dying. But as He went, the crowds were pressing against Him.

⁴³ And a woman who had a hemorrhage for twelve years, and could not be healed by anyone, ⁴⁴ came up behind Him and touched the fringe of His cloak, and immediately her hemorrhage stopped. ⁴⁵ And Jesus said, "Who

is the one who touched Me?" And while they were all denying it, Peter said, "Master, the people are crowding and pressing in on You." ⁴⁶ But Jesus said, "Someone did touch Me, for I was aware that power had gone out of Me." ⁴⁷ When the woman saw that she had not escaped notice, she came trembling and fell down before Him, and declared in the presence of all the people the reason why she had touched Him, and how she had been immediately healed. ⁴⁸ And He said to her, "Daughter, your faith has made you well; go in peace."

⁴⁹ While He was still speaking, someone *came from the house of the synagogue official, saying, "Your daughter has died; do not trouble the Teacher anymore." ⁵⁰ But when Jesus heard this, He answered him, "Do not be afraid any longer; only believe, and she will be made well." ⁵¹ When He came to the house, He did not allow anyone to enter with Him, except Peter and John and James, and the girl's father and mother. ⁵² Now they were all weeping and lamenting for her; but He said, "Stop weeping, for she has not died, but is asleep." ⁵³ And they began laughing at Him, knowing that she had died. ⁵⁴ He, however, took her by the hand and called, saying, "Child, arise!" ⁵⁵ And her spirit returned, and she got up immediately; and He gave orders for something to be given her to eat. ⁵⁶ Her parents were amazed; but He instructed them to tell no one what had happened.

DAY 6: What prepared Joshua for leading the nation of Israel?

1. Exodus 17:9-10, 13-14—Joshua led the victorious battle against the Amalekites.
2. Exodus 24:13—Joshua, the servant of Moses, accompanied the Jewish leader to the mountain of God (see 32:17).
3. Numbers 11:28—Joshua was the attendant of Moses from his youth.
4. Numbers 13:16—Moses changed his name from Hoshea ("salvation") to Joshua ("the Lord saves").
5. Numbers 14:6-10, 30, 38—Joshua, along with Caleb, spied out the land of Canaan with 10 others. Only Joshua and Caleb urged the nation to possess the land and, thus, only they of the 12 actually entered Canaan.
6. Numbers 27:18—Joshua was indwelt by the Holy Spirit.
7. Numbers 27:18-23—Joshua was commissioned for spiritual service the first time, to assist Moses.
8. Numbers 32:12—Joshua followed the Lord fully.
9. Deuteronomy 31:23—Joshua was commissioned a second time, to replace Moses.
10. Deuteronomy 34:9—Joshua was filled with the spirit of wisdom.

APRIL 7

Joshua 3:1-4:24

3 Then Joshua rose early in the morning; and he and all the sons of Israel set out from Shittim and came to the Jordan, and they lodged there before they crossed. ² At the end of three days the officers went through the midst of the camp; ³ and they commanded the people, saying, "When you see the ark of the covenant of the LORD your God with the Levitical priests carrying it, then you shall set out from your place and go after it. ⁴ However, there shall be between you and it a distance of about 2,000 cubits by measure. Do not come near it, that you may know the way by which you shall go, for you have not passed this way before."

⁵ Then Joshua said to the people, "Consecrate yourselves, for tomorrow the LORD will do wonders among you." ⁶ And Joshua spoke to the priests, saying, "Take up the ark of the covenant and cross over ahead of the people." So they took up the ark of the covenant and went ahead of the people.

⁷ Now the LORD said to Joshua, "This day I will begin to exalt you in the sight of all Israel, that they may know that just as I have been with Moses, I will be with you. ⁸ You shall, moreover, command the priests who are carrying the ark of the covenant, saying, 'When you come to the edge of the waters of the Jordan, you shall stand still in the Jordan.'" ⁹ Then Joshua said to the sons of Israel, "Come here, and hear the words of the LORD your God." ¹⁰ Joshua said, "By this you shall know that the living God is among you, and that He will assuredly dispossess from before you the Canaanite, the Hittite, the Hivite, the Perizzite, the Girgashite, the Amorite, and the Jebusite. ¹¹ Behold, the ark of the covenant of the Lord of all the earth is crossing over ahead of you into the Jordan.

3:10 Canaanite people to be killed or defeated were sinful to the point of extreme (Ge 15:16; Lv 18:24–25). God, as moral judge, has the right to deal with all people, as at the end (Rev 20:11–15) or any other time when He deems it appropriate for His purposes. The question is not why God chose to destroy these sinners, but why He had let them live so long, and why all sinners are not destroyed far sooner than they are. It is grace that allows any sinner to draw one more breath of life (Ge 2:17; Eze 18:20; Ro 6:23).

[12] Now then, take for yourselves twelve men from the tribes of Israel, one man for each tribe. [13] It shall come about when the soles of the feet of the priests who carry the ark of the LORD, the Lord of all the earth, rest in the waters of the Jordan, the waters of the Jordan will be cut off, *and* the waters which are flowing down from above will stand in one heap."

[14] So when the people set out from their tents to cross the Jordan with the priests carrying the ark of the covenant before the people, [15] and when those who carried the ark came into the Jordan, and the feet of the priests carrying the ark were dipped in the edge of the water (for the Jordan overflows all its banks all the days of harvest), [16] the waters which were flowing down from above stood *and* rose up in one heap, a great distance away at Adam, the city that is beside Zarethan; and those which were flowing down toward the sea of the Arabah, the Salt Sea, were completely cut off. So the people crossed opposite Jericho. [17] And the priests who carried the ark of the covenant of the LORD stood firm on dry ground in the middle of the Jordan while all Israel crossed on dry ground, until all the nation had finished crossing the Jordan.

3:16 rose up in one heap. The God of all power, who created heaven, earth, and all else according to Genesis 1, worked miracles here. The waters were dammed up at Adam, a city 15 miles north of the crossing, and also in tributary creeks. Once the miracle was completed, God permitted waters to flow again (4:18) after all the people had walked to the other side on dry ground (3:17). As the Exodus had begun (Ex 14), so it ended.

4 Now when all the nation had finished crossing the Jordan, the LORD spoke to Joshua, saying, [2] "Take for yourselves twelve men from the people, one man from each tribe, [3] and command them, saying, 'Take up for yourselves twelve stones from here out of the middle of the Jordan, from the place where the priests' feet are standing firm, and carry them over with you and lay them down in the lodging place where you will lodge tonight.'" [4] So Joshua called the twelve men whom he had appointed from the sons of Israel, one man from each tribe; [5] and Joshua said to them, "Cross again to the ark of the LORD your God into the middle of the Jordan, and each of you take up a stone on his shoulder, according to the number of the tribes of the sons of Israel. [6] Let this be a sign among you, so that when your children ask later, saying, 'What do these stones mean to you?' [7] then you shall say to them, 'Because the waters of the Jordan were cut off before the ark of the covenant of the LORD; when it crossed the Jordan, the waters of the Jordan were cut off.' So these stones shall become a memorial to the sons of Israel forever."

[8] Thus the sons of Israel did as Joshua commanded, and took up twelve stones from the middle of the Jordan, just as the LORD spoke to Joshua, according to the number of the tribes of the sons of Israel; and they carried them over with them to the lodging place and put them down there. [9] Then Joshua set up twelve stones in the middle of the Jordan at the place where the feet of the priests who carried the ark of the covenant were standing, and they are there to this day. [10] For the priests who carried the ark were standing in the middle of the Jordan until everything was completed that the LORD had commanded Joshua to speak to the people, according to all that Moses had commanded Joshua. And the people hurried and crossed; [11] and when all the people had finished crossing, the ark of the LORD and the priests crossed before the people. [12] The sons of Reuben and the sons of Gad and the half-tribe of Manasseh crossed over in battle array before the sons of Israel, just as Moses had spoken to them; [13] about 40,000 equipped for war, crossed for battle before the LORD to the desert plains of Jericho.

[14] On that day the LORD exalted Joshua in the sight of all Israel; so that they revered him, just as they had revered Moses all the days of his life.

[15] Now the LORD said to Joshua, [16] "Command the priests who carry the ark of the

testimony that they come up from the Jordan." ¹⁷ So Joshua commanded the priests, saying, "Come up from the Jordan." ¹⁸ It came about when the priests who carried the ark of the covenant of the LORD had come up from the middle of the Jordan, and the soles of the priests' feet were lifted up to the dry ground, that the waters of the Jordan returned to their place, and went over all its banks as before.

¹⁹ Now the people came up from the Jordan on the tenth of the first month and camped at Gilgal on the eastern edge of Jericho. ²⁰ Those twelve stones which they had taken from the Jordan, Joshua set up at Gilgal. ²¹ He said to the sons of Israel, "When your children ask their fathers in time to come, saying, 'What are these stones?' ²² then you shall inform your children, saying, 'Israel crossed this Jordan on dry ground.' ²³ For the LORD your God dried up the waters of the Jordan before you until you had crossed, just as the LORD your God had done to the Red Sea, which He dried up before us until we had crossed; ²⁴ that all the peoples of the earth may know that the hand of the LORD is mighty, so that you may fear the LORD your God forever."

Psalm 42:1–5

For the choir director. A Maskil
of the sons of Korah.

As the deer pants for the
water brooks,
So my soul pants for You, O God.
² My soul thirsts for God,
for the living God;
When shall I come and
appear before God?
³ My tears have been my
food day and night,
While *they* say to me all day
long, "Where is your God?"
⁴ These things I remember and I
pour out my soul within me.
For I used to go along with the
throng *and* lead them in
procession to the house of God,

42:4 These things I remember and I pour out my soul. Such language also characterizes Jeremiah's Lamentations, indicating a heavy dirge. On "pouring out one's soul" or "heart," see 1 Samuel 1:15; Psalm 62:8; Lamentations 2:19. These are attempts at trying to unburden oneself from intolerable pain, grief, and agony.

With the voice of joy and
thanksgiving, a multitude
keeping festival.

⁵ Why are you in despair, O my soul?
And *why* have you become
disturbed within me?
Hope in God, for I shall
again praise Him
For the help of His presence.

Proverbs 13:17–18

¹⁷ A wicked messenger falls
into adversity,
But a faithful envoy *brings* healing.
¹⁸ Poverty and shame *will come* to
him who neglects discipline,
But he who regards reproof
will be honored.

Luke 9:1–17

9 And He called the twelve together, and gave them power and authority over all the demons and to heal diseases. ² And He sent them out to proclaim the kingdom of God and to perform healing. ³ And He said to them, "Take nothing for *your* journey, neither a staff, nor a bag, nor bread, nor money; and do not *even* have two tunics apiece. ⁴ Whatever house you enter, stay there until you leave that city. ⁵ And as for those who do not receive you, as you go out from that city, shake the dust off your feet as a testimony against them." ⁶ Departing, they *began* going throughout the villages, preaching the gospel and healing everywhere.

⁷ Now Herod the tetrarch heard of all that was happening; and he was greatly perplexed, because it was said by some that John had risen from the dead, ⁸ and by some that Elijah had appeared, and by others that one

9:3 Take nothing. Slight differences between Matthew, Mark, and Luke have troubled some. Matthew 10:9–10 and this text say the disciples were not to take staffs; but Mark 6:8 prohibited everything "except a...staff." Mark 6:9 also instructed them to "wear sandals"; but in Matthew 10:10 sandals were included in the things they were not to carry. Actually, however, what Mathew 10:10 and this verse prohibited was the packing of extra staffs and sandals. The disciples were not to be carrying baggage for the journey, but merely to go with the clothes on their backs.

of the prophets of old had risen again. ⁹Herod said, "I myself had John beheaded; but who is this man about whom I hear such things?" And he kept trying to see Him.

¹⁰When the apostles returned, they gave an account to Him of all that they had done. Taking them with Him, He withdrew by Himself to a city called Bethsaida. ¹¹But the crowds were aware of this and followed Him; and welcoming them, He *began* speaking to them about the kingdom of God and curing those who had need of healing.

¹²Now the day was ending, and the twelve came and said to Him, "Send the crowd away, that they may go into the surrounding villages and countryside and find lodging and get something to eat; for here we are in a desolate place." ¹³But He said to them, "You give them *something* to eat!" And they said, "We have no more than five loaves and two fish, unless perhaps we go and buy food for all these people." ¹⁴(For there were about five thousand men.) And He said to His disciples, "Have them sit down *to eat* in groups of about fifty each." ¹⁵They did so, and had them all sit down. ¹⁶Then He took the five loaves and the two fish, and looking up to heaven, He blessed them, and broke *them*, and kept giving *them* to the disciples to set before the people. ¹⁷And they all ate and were satisfied; and the broken pieces which they had left over were picked up, twelve baskets *full*.

DAY 7: How do the Proverbs apply to specific life decisions and experiences?

Proverbs are divine guidelines and wise observations that teach underlying principles of life (24:3–4). They are not inflexible laws or absolute promises. This is because they are applied in life situations that are rarely clear-cut or uncomplicated by other conditions. The consequences of a fool's behavior as described in Proverbs apply to the complete fool. Most people are only occasionally foolish and therefore experience the occasional consequences of foolish behavior. It becomes apparent that the proverbs usually do have exceptions due to the uncertainty of life and the unpredictable behavior of fallen people.

The marvelous challenge and principle expressed in 3:5–6 puts a heavy emphasis on trusting the Lord with "all your heart" and "in all your ways [acknowledging] Him." Even partly practicing the conditions of those phrases represents a major challenge. Because of God's grace, we don't have to perfectly carry out the conditions in order to experience the truth that "He will make your paths straight."

God does not guarantee uniform outcome or application for each proverb. By studying them and applying them, a believer is allowed to contemplate God's mind, character, attributes, works, and blessings. In Jesus Christ are hidden all the treasures of wisdom and knowledge which are only partly expressed in Proverbs (Col 2:3).

APRIL 8

Joshua 5:1–6:27

5 Now it came about when all the kings of the Amorites who *were* beyond the Jordan to the west, and all the kings of the Canaanites who *were* by the sea, heard how the LORD had dried up the waters of the Jordan before the sons of Israel until they had crossed, that their hearts melted, and there was no spirit in them any longer because of the sons of Israel.

²At that time the LORD said to Joshua, "Make for yourself flint knives and circumcise again the sons of Israel the second time." ³So Joshua made himself flint knives and circumcised the sons of Israel at Gibeath-haaraloth. ⁴This is the reason why Joshua circumcised them: all the people who came out of Egypt who were males, all the men of war, died in the wilderness along the way after they came out of Egypt. ⁵For all the people who came out were circumcised, but all the people who were born in the wilderness along the way as they came out of Egypt had not been circumcised. ⁶For the sons of Israel walked forty years in the wilderness, until all the nation, *that is,* the men of war who came out of Egypt, perished because they did not listen to the voice of the

5:2 circumcise. God commanded Joshua to see that this was done to all males under 40. These were sons of the generation who died in the wilderness, survivors (vv. 6–7) from the new generation God spared in Numbers 13–14. This surgical sign of a faith commitment to the Abrahamic Covenant (Genesis 17:9–14) had been ignored during the wilderness trek. Now God wanted it reinstated, so the Israelites would start out right in the land they were possessing.

LORD, to whom the LORD had sworn that He would not let them see the land which the LORD had sworn to their fathers to give us, a land flowing with milk and honey. 7 Their children whom He raised up in their place, Joshua circumcised; for they were uncircumcised, because they had not circumcised them along the way.

8 Now when they had finished circumcising all the nation, they remained in their places in the camp until they were healed. 9 Then the LORD said to Joshua, "Today I have rolled away the reproach of Egypt from you." So the name of that place is called Gilgal to this day.

10 While the sons of Israel camped at Gilgal they observed the Passover on the evening of the fourteenth day of the month on the desert plains of Jericho. 11 On the day after the Passover, on that very day, they ate some of the produce of the land, unleavened cakes and parched *grain*. 12 The manna ceased on the day after they had eaten some of the produce of the land, so that the sons of Israel no longer had manna, but they ate some of the yield of the land of Canaan during that year.

13 Now it came about when Joshua was by Jericho, that he lifted up his eyes and looked, and behold, a man was standing opposite him with his sword drawn in his hand, and Joshua went to him and said to him, "Are you for us or for our adversaries?" 14 He said, "No; rather I indeed come now *as* captain of the host of the LORD." And Joshua fell on his face to the earth, and bowed down, and said to him, "What has my lord to say to his servant?" 15 The captain of the LORD'S host said to Joshua, "Remove your sandals from your feet, for the place where you are standing is holy." And Joshua did so.

6 Now Jericho was tightly shut because of the sons of Israel; no one went out and no one came in. 2 The LORD said to Joshua, "See, I have given Jericho into your hand, with its king *and* the valiant warriors. 3 You shall march around the city, all the men of war circling the city once. You shall do so for six days. 4 Also seven priests shall carry seven trumpets of rams' horns before the ark; then on the seventh day you shall march around the city seven times, and the priests shall blow the trumpets. 5 It shall be that when they make a long blast with the ram's horn, and when you hear the sound of the trumpet, all the people shall shout with a great shout; and the wall of the city will fall down flat, and the people will go up every man straight ahead."

6 So Joshua the son of Nun called the priests and said to them, "Take up the ark of the covenant, and let seven priests carry seven trumpets of rams' horns before the ark of the LORD." 7 Then he said to the people, "Go forward, and march around the city, and let the armed men go on before the ark of the LORD." 8 And it was *so*, that when Joshua had spoken to the people, the seven priests carrying the seven trumpets of rams' horns before the LORD went forward and blew the trumpets; and the ark of the covenant of the LORD followed them. 9 The armed men went before the priests who blew the trumpets, and the rear guard came after the ark, while they continued to blow the trumpets. 10 But Joshua commanded the people, saying, "You shall not shout nor let your voice be heard nor let a word proceed out of your mouth, until the day I tell you, 'Shout!' Then you shall shout!" 11 So he had the ark of the LORD taken around the city, circling *it* once; then they came into the camp and spent the night in the camp.

12 Now Joshua rose early in the morning, and the priests took up the ark of the LORD. 13 The seven priests carrying the seven trumpets of rams' horns before the ark of the LORD went on continually, and blew the trumpets; and the armed men went before them and the rear guard came after the ark of the LORD, while they continued to blow the trumpets. 14 Thus the second day they marched around the city once and returned to the camp; they did so for six days.

15 Then on the seventh day they rose early at the dawning of the day and marched around the city in the same manner seven times; only on that day they marched around the city seven times. 16 At the seventh time, when the priests blew the trumpets, Joshua said to the people, "Shout! For the LORD has given you the city. 17 The city shall be under the ban, it and all that is in it belongs to the LORD; only Rahab the harlot and all who are with her in the house shall live, because she hid the messengers whom we sent. 18 But as for you, only keep yourselves from the things under the ban, so that you do not covet *them* and take some of the things under the ban, and make the camp of Israel accursed and bring trouble on it. 19 But all the silver and gold and articles of bronze and iron are holy to the LORD; they shall go into the treasury of the LORD." 20 So the people shouted, and *priests* blew the trumpets; and when the people heard the sound of the trumpet, the people shouted with a great shout and the wall fell down flat, so that the people went up into the city, every man straight ahead, and they took the city. 21 They utterly destroyed everything

335

in the city, both man and woman, young and old, and ox and sheep and donkey, with the edge of the sword. ²²Joshua said to the two men who had spied out the land, "Go into the harlot's house and bring the woman and all she has out of there, as you have sworn to her." ²³So the young men who were spies went in and brought out Rahab and her father and her mother and her brothers and all she had; they also brought out all her relatives and placed them outside the camp of Israel. ²⁴They burned the city with fire, and all that was in it. Only the silver and gold, and articles of bronze and iron, they put into the treasury of the house of the LORD. ²⁵However, Rahab the harlot and her father's household and all she had, Joshua spared; and she has lived in the midst of Israel to this day, for she hid the messengers whom Joshua sent to spy out Jericho. ²⁶Then Joshua made them take an oath at that time, saying, "Cursed before the LORD is the man who rises up and builds this city Jericho; with *the loss of* his firstborn he shall lay its foundation, and with *the loss of* his youngest son he shall set up its gates." ²⁷So the LORD was with Joshua, and his fame was in all the land.

Psalm 42:6–11

⁶ O my God, my soul is in
despair within me;
Therefore I remember You from
the land of the Jordan
And the peaks of Hermon,
from Mount Mizar.
⁷ Deep calls to deep at the sound
of Your waterfalls;
All Your breakers and Your
waves have rolled over me.
⁸ The LORD will command His
lovingkindness in the daytime;
And His song will be with
me in the night,
A prayer to the God of my life.
⁹ I will say to God my rock, "Why
have You forgotten me?

42:8 The LORD will command His lovingkind-ness. This statement of confidence interrupts his laments (see their continuance in vv. 9–10), providing a few gracious gulps of divine "air" under the cascading inundations of his trials and tormentors.

Why do I go mourning because of
the oppression of the enemy?"
¹⁰ As a shattering of my bones,
my adversaries revile me,
While they say to me all day
long, "Where is your God?"
¹¹ Why are you in despair, O my soul?
And why have you become
disturbed within me?
Hope in God, for I shall
yet praise Him,
The help of my countenance
and my God.

Proverbs 13:19–21

¹⁹ Desire realized is sweet to the soul,
But it is an abomination to fools
to turn away from evil.
²⁰ He who walks with wise
men will be wise,
But the companion of fools
will suffer harm.
²¹ Adversity pursues sinners,
But the righteous will be
rewarded with prosperity.

13:20 walks...companion. This speaks of the power of association to shape character. See 1:10, 18; 2:12; 4:14; 16:29; 22:24–25; 23:20; 28:7, 19; Psalm 1.

Luke 9:18–36

¹⁸And it happened that while He was praying alone, the disciples were with Him, and He questioned them, saying, "Who do the people say that I am?" ¹⁹They answered and said, "John the Baptist, and others *say* Elijah; but others, that one of the prophets of old has risen again." ²⁰And He said to them, "But who do you say that I am?" And Peter answered and said, "The Christ of God." ²¹But He warned them and instructed *them* not to tell this to anyone, ²²saying, "The Son of Man must suffer many things and be rejected by the elders and chief priests and scribes, and be killed and be raised up on the third day." ²³And He was saying to *them* all, "If anyone wishes to come after Me, he must deny himself, and take up his cross daily and follow Me. ²⁴For whoever wishes to save his life will lose it, but whoever loses his life for My sake, he is the one who will save it. ²⁵For what is a man profited if he gains the whole world, and loses or forfeits himself? ²⁶For whoever is ashamed of Me and My words, the Son of

9:23 cross. Self-denial was a common thread in Christ's teaching to His disciples (14:26–27; Mt 10:38; 16:24; Mk 8:34; Jn 12:24–26). The kind of self-denial He sought was not a reclusive asceticism, but a willingness to obey His commandments, serve one another, and suffer—perhaps even die—for His sake.

9:29 while He was praying. As at His baptism, while He was praying, the Father's voice came from heaven. **gleaming.** Literally "emitting light." This word is used only here in the New Testament. It suggests a brilliant flashing light, similar to lightning.

Man will be ashamed of him when He comes in His glory, and *the glory* of the Father and of the holy angels. ²⁷But I say to you truthfully, there are some of those standing here who will not taste death until they see the kingdom of God."

²⁸Some eight days after these sayings, He took along Peter and John and James, and went up on the mountain to pray. ²⁹And while He was praying, the appearance of His face became different, and His clothing *became* white *and* gleaming. ³⁰And behold, two men were talking with Him; and they were Moses and Elijah, ³¹who, appearing in glory, were speaking of His departure which He was about to accomplish at Jerusalem.

³²Now Peter and his companions had been overcome with sleep; but when they were fully awake, they saw His glory and the two men standing with Him. ³³And as these were leaving Him, Peter said to Jesus, "Master, it is good for us to be here; let us make three tabernacles: one for You, and one for Moses, and one for Elijah"—not realizing what he was saying. ³⁴While he was saying this, a cloud formed and *began* to overshadow them; and they were afraid as they entered the cloud. ³⁵Then a voice came out of the cloud, saying, "This is My Son, *My* Chosen One; listen to Him!" ³⁶And when the voice had spoken, Jesus was found alone. And they kept silent, and reported to no one in those days any of the things which they had seen.

DAY 8: Why did God bless Rahab the prostitute?

Rahab's life was not spared because of her lie. It was spared because she put her faith in God. Rahab was given a gracious opportunity to side with God by protecting the two Israelite spies, and she acted within her circumstances. She lied daringly and elaborately. Perhaps her initial response was simply a habit of her profession. From the perspective of the king of Jericho, Rahab would have been guilty of treason, not just lying. She had a new allegiance, and she didn't yet know that the God she now wanted to trust had a rule about lying.

While those around her feared what the God of Israel might do, Rahab feared enough to boldly trust Him as the one true God, "for the LORD your God, He is God in heaven above and on earth beneath" (2:11). She understood that God wasn't a local or a national god. She knew enough to act.

The spies were impressed and indebted. When Rahab asked them for protection, they recognized their obligation. They were exact in promising to preserve the lives of those in her house, indicated by the scarlet cord from the window.

The radical change that came into Rahab's life when those spies knocked on her door can be seen in several ways. She risked her life to trust God. The Book of Ruth, along with Matthew 1:5, also reveals that Rahab married and became the great-great-grandmother of King David and one of the ancestors of Jesus. Centuries later, Rahab was one of the women listed in Hebrews 11 because of her faith.

APRIL 9

Joshua 7:1–8:35

7 But the sons of Israel acted unfaithfully in regard to the things under the ban, for Achan, the son of Carmi, the son of Zabdi, the son of Zerah, from the tribe of Judah, took some of the things under the ban, therefore the anger of the LORD burned against the sons of Israel.

²Now Joshua sent men from Jericho to Ai, which is near Beth-aven, east of Bethel, and said to them, "Go up and spy out the land." So the men went up and spied out Ai. ³They returned to Joshua and said to him, "Do not let all the people go up; *only* about two or three thousand men need go up to

Ai; do not make all the people toil up there, for they are few." ⁴So about three thousand men from the people went up there, but they fled from the men of Ai. ⁵The men of Ai struck down about thirty-six of their men, and pursued them from the gate as far as Shebarim and struck them down on the descent, so the hearts of the people melted and became as water.

⁶Then Joshua tore his clothes and fell to the earth on his face before the ark of the LORD until the evening, *both* he and the elders of Israel; and they put dust on their heads. ⁷Joshua said, "Alas, O Lord GOD, why did You ever bring this people over the Jordan, *only* to deliver us into the hand of the Amorites, to destroy us? If only we had been willing to dwell beyond the Jordan! ⁸O Lord, what can I say since Israel has turned *their* back before their enemies? ⁹For the Canaanites and all the inhabitants of the land will hear of it, and they will surround us and cut off our name from the earth. And what will You do for Your great name?"

7:9 what will You do for Your great name? The main issue is the glory and honor of God (see Daniel's prayer in Da 9:16–19).

---

¹⁰So the LORD said to Joshua, "Rise up! Why is it that you have fallen on your face? ¹¹Israel has sinned, and they have also transgressed My covenant which I commanded them. And they have even taken some of the things under the ban and have both stolen and deceived. Moreover, they have also put *them* among their own things. ¹²Therefore the sons of Israel cannot stand before their enemies; they turn *their* backs before their enemies, for they have become accursed. I will not be with you anymore unless you destroy the things under the ban from your midst. ¹³Rise up! Consecrate the people and say, 'Consecrate yourselves for tomorrow, for thus the LORD, the God of Israel, has said, "There are things under the ban in your midst, O Israel. You cannot stand before your enemies until you have removed the things under the ban from your midst." ¹⁴In the morning then you shall come near by your tribes. And it shall be that the tribe which the LORD takes *by lot* shall come near by families, and the family which the LORD takes shall come near by households, and the household which the LORD takes shall

come near man by man. ¹⁵It shall be that the one who is taken with the things under the ban shall be burned with fire, he and all that belongs to him, because he has transgressed the covenant of the LORD, and because he has committed a disgraceful thing in Israel.'"

¹⁶So Joshua arose early in the morning and brought Israel near by tribes, and the tribe of Judah was taken. ¹⁷He brought the family of Judah near, and he took the family of the Zerahites; and he brought the family of the Zerahites near man by man, and Zabdi was taken. ¹⁸He brought his household near man by man; and Achan, son of Carmi, son of Zabdi, son of Zerah, from the tribe of Judah, was taken. ¹⁹Then Joshua said to Achan, "My son, I implore you, give glory to the LORD, the God of Israel, and give praise to Him; and tell me now what you have done. Do not hide it from me." ²⁰So Achan answered Joshua and said, "Truly, I have sinned against the LORD, the God of Israel, and this is what I did: ²¹when I saw among the spoil a beautiful mantle from Shinar and two hundred shekels of silver and a bar of gold fifty shekels in weight, then I coveted them and took them; and behold, they are concealed in the earth inside my tent with the silver underneath it."

²²So Joshua sent messengers, and they ran to the tent; and behold, it was concealed in his tent with the silver underneath it. ²³They took them from inside the tent and brought them to Joshua and to all the sons of Israel, and they poured them out before the LORD. ²⁴Then Joshua and all Israel with him, took Achan the son of Zerah, the silver, the mantle, the bar of gold, his sons, his daughters, his oxen, his donkeys, his sheep, his tent and all that belonged to him; and they brought them up to the valley of Achor. ²⁵Joshua said, "Why have you troubled us? The LORD will trouble you this day." And all Israel stoned them with stones; and they burned them with fire after they had stoned them with stones. ²⁶They raised over him a great heap of stones that stands to this day, and the LORD turned from the fierceness of His anger. Therefore the name of that place has been called the valley of Achor to this day.

8 Now the LORD said to Joshua, "Do not fear or be dismayed. Take all the people of war with you and arise, go up to Ai; see, I have given into your hand the king of Ai, his people, his city, and his land. ²You shall do to Ai and its king just as you did to Jericho and its king; you shall take only its spoil and its cattle as plunder for yourselves. Set an ambush for the city behind it."

³ So Joshua rose with all the people of war to go up to Ai; and Joshua chose 30,000 men, valiant warriors, and sent them out at night. ⁴ He commanded them, saying, "See, you are going to ambush the city from behind it. Do not go very far from the city, but all of you be ready. ⁵ Then I and all the people who are with me will approach the city. And when they come out to meet us as at the first, we will flee before them. ⁶ They will come out after us until we have drawn them away from the city, for they will say, 'They are fleeing before us as at the first.' So we will flee before them. ⁷ And you shall rise from your ambush and take possession of the city, for the LORD your God will deliver it into your hand. ⁸ Then it will be when you have seized the city, that you shall set the city on fire. You shall do it according to the word of the LORD. See, I have commanded you." ⁹ So Joshua sent them away, and they went to the place of ambush and remained between Bethel and Ai, on the west side of Ai; but Joshua spent that night among the people.

¹⁰ Now Joshua rose early in the morning and mustered the people, and he went up with the elders of Israel before the people to Ai. ¹¹ Then all the people of war who were with him went up and drew near and arrived in front of the city, and camped on the north side of Ai. Now there was a valley between him and Ai. ¹² And he took about 5,000 men and set them in ambush between Bethel and Ai, on the west side of the city. ¹³ So they stationed the people, all the army that was on the north side of the city, and its rear guard on the west side of the city, and Joshua spent that night in the midst of the valley. ¹⁴ It came about when the king of Ai saw it, that the men of the city hurried and rose up early and went out to meet Israel in battle, he and all his people at the appointed place before the desert plain. But he did not know that there was an ambush against him behind the city. ¹⁵ Joshua and all Israel pretended to be beaten before them, and fled by the way of the wilderness. ¹⁶ And all the people who were in the city were called together to pursue them, and they pursued Joshua and were drawn away from the city. ¹⁷ So not a man was left in Ai or Bethel who had not gone out after Israel, and they left the city unguarded and pursued Israel.

¹⁸ Then the LORD said to Joshua, "Stretch out the javelin that is in your hand toward Ai, for I will give it into your hand." So Joshua stretched out the javelin that was in his hand toward the city. ¹⁹ The men in ambush rose quickly from their place, and when he had stretched out his hand, they ran and entered the city and captured it, and they quickly set the city on fire. ²⁰ When the men of Ai turned back and looked, behold, the smoke of the city ascended to the sky, and they had no place to flee this way or that, for the people who had been fleeing to the wilderness turned against the pursuers. ²¹ When Joshua and all Israel saw that the men in ambush had captured the city and that the smoke of the city ascended, they turned back and slew the men of Ai. ²² The others came out from the city to encounter them, so that they were trapped in the midst of Israel, some on this side and some on that side; and they slew them until no one was left of those who survived or escaped. ²³ But they took alive the king of Ai and brought him to Joshua.

²⁴ Now when Israel had finished killing all the inhabitants of Ai in the field in the wilderness where they pursued them, and all of them were fallen by the edge of the sword until they were destroyed, then all Israel returned to Ai and struck it with the edge of the sword. ²⁵ All who fell that day, both men and women, were 12,000—all the people of Ai. ²⁶ For Joshua did not withdraw his hand with which he stretched out the javelin until he had utterly destroyed all the inhabitants of Ai. ²⁷ Israel took only the cattle and the spoil of that city as plunder for themselves, according to the word of the LORD which He had commanded Joshua. ²⁸ So Joshua burned Ai and made it a heap forever, a desolation until this day. ²⁹ He hanged the king of Ai on a tree until evening; and at sunset Joshua gave command and they took his body down from the tree and threw it at the entrance of the city gate, and raised over it a great heap of stones that stands to this day.

³⁰ Then Joshua built an altar to the LORD, the God of Israel, in Mount Ebal, ³¹ just as Moses the servant of the LORD had commanded the sons of Israel, as it is written in the book of the law of Moses, an altar of uncut stones on which no man had wielded an iron tool; and they offered burnt offerings on it to the LORD, and sacrificed peace offerings. ³² He wrote there on the stones a copy of the law of Moses, which he had written, in the presence of the sons of Israel. ³³ All Israel with their elders and officers and their judges were standing on both sides of the ark before the Levitical priests who carried the ark of the covenant of the LORD, the

stranger as well as the native. Half of them *stood* in front of Mount Gerizim and half of them in front of Mount Ebal, just as Moses the servant of the LORD had given command at first to bless the people of Israel. [34] Then afterward he read all the words of the law, the blessing and the curse, according to all that is written in the book of the law. [35] There was not a word of all that Moses had commanded which Joshua did not read before all the assembly of Israel with the women and the little ones and the strangers who were living among them.

Psalm 43:1-5

Vindicate me, O God, and plead
　my case against an ungodly
　nation;
O deliver me from the deceitful
　and unjust man!
[2] For You are the God of my strength;
　why have You rejected me?
Why do I go mourning because
　of the oppression of the
　enemy?

[3] O send out Your light and Your
　truth, let them lead me;
Let them bring me to Your
　holy hill
And to Your dwelling places.
[4] Then I will go to the altar
　of God,
To God my exceeding joy;
And upon the lyre I shall praise
　You, O God, my God.

[5] Why are you in despair,
　O my soul?
And why are you disturbed
　within me?
Hope in God, for I shall
　again praise Him,
The help of my countenance
　and my God.

43:3 Your light and Your truth, let them lead me. These are bold personifications for divine guidance. He desired that these "messenger-attributes" divinely direct (see such "leading" and "guiding" in Ge 24:48; Pss 78:14, 53, 72; 107:30; Is 57:18) so as to bring him successfully to his destination, i.e., Israel's designated place for worship.

Proverbs 13:22-23

[22] A good man leaves an inheritance
　to his children's children,
And the wealth of the sinner is
　stored up for the righteous.
[23] Abundant food *is in* the fallow
　ground of the poor,
But it is swept away by injustice.

Luke 9:37-62

[37] On the next day, when they came down from the mountain, a large crowd met Him. [38] And a man from the crowd shouted, saying, "Teacher, I beg You to look at my son, for he is my only *boy;* [39] and a spirit seizes him, and he suddenly screams, and it throws him into a convulsion with foaming *at the mouth;* and only with difficulty does it leave him, mauling him *as it leaves.* [40] I begged Your disciples to cast it out, and they could not." [41] And Jesus answered and said, "You unbelieving and perverted generation, how long shall I be with you and put up with you? Bring your son here." [42] While he was still approaching, the demon slammed him *to the ground* and threw him into a convulsion. But Jesus rebuked the unclean spirit, and healed the boy and gave him back to his father. [43] And they were all amazed at the greatness of God.

But while everyone was marveling at all that He was doing, He said to His disciples, [44] "Let these words sink into your ears; for the Son of Man is going to be delivered into the hands of men." [45] But they did not understand this statement, and it was concealed from them so that they would not perceive it; and they were afraid to ask Him about this statement.

[46] An argument started among them as to which of them might be the greatest. [47] But Jesus, knowing what they were thinking in their heart, took a child and stood him by His side, [48] and said to them, "Whoever receives this child in My name receives Me, and whoever receives Me receives Him who sent Me; for the one who is least among all of you, this is the one who is great."

[49] John answered and said, "Master, we saw someone casting out demons in Your name; and we tried to prevent him because he does not follow along with us." [50] But Jesus said to him, "Do not hinder *him;* for he who is not against you is for you."

[51] When the days were approaching for His ascension, He was determined to go to Jerusalem; [52] and He sent messengers on ahead of Him, and they went and entered a village of the Samaritans to make arrangements for Him. [53] But they did not receive Him, because

9:51 was determined to go to Jerusalem. This begins a major section of Luke's Gospel. From here to 19:27, Christ's face was set toward Jerusalem, and Luke's narrative is a travelogue of that long journey to the cross. This was a dramatic turning point in Christ's ministry. After this, Galilee was no longer His base of operation. Although 17:11–37 describes a return visit to Galilee, Luke included everything between this point and that short Galilean sojourn as part of the journey to Jerusalem. We know from a comparison of the Gospels that, during this period of Christ's ministry, He made short visits to Jerusalem to celebrate feasts. Nonetheless, those brief visits were only interludes in this period of ministry that would culminate in a final journey to Jerusalem for the purpose of dying there. Thus, Luke underscored this turning point in Christ's ministry more dramatically than any of the other Gospels, by showing Christ's determination to complete His mission of going to the cross.

He was traveling toward Jerusalem. ⁵⁴ When His disciples James and John saw *this,* they said, "Lord, do You want us to command fire to come down from heaven and consume them?" ⁵⁵ But He turned and rebuked them, [and said, "You do not know what kind of spirit you are of; ⁵⁶ for the Son of Man did not come to destroy men's lives, but to save them."] And they went on to another village.

⁵⁷ As they were going along the road, someone said to Him, "I will follow You wherever You go." ⁵⁸ And Jesus said to him, "The foxes have holes and the birds of the air *have* nests, but the Son of Man has nowhere to lay His head." ⁵⁹ And He said to another, "Follow Me." But he said, "Lord, permit me first to go and bury my father." ⁶⁰ But He said to him, "Allow the dead to bury their own dead; but as for you, go and proclaim everywhere the kingdom of God." ⁶¹ Another also said, "I will follow You, Lord; but first permit me to say good-bye to those at home." ⁶² But Jesus said to him, "No one, after putting his hand to the plow and looking back, is fit for the kingdom of God."

DAY 9: How should we respond to all forms of religious persecution?

Luke 9:51–56 show us Jesus' response to persecution. The Samaritans were descendants of Jewish mixed marriages from the days of captivity. They were rivals of the Jewish nation and had devised their own worship, a hybrid of Judaism and paganism, with a temple of their own on Mt. Gerizim. They were considered unclean by the Jews and were so hated that most Jewish travelers from Galilee to Judah took the longer route east of the Jordan to avoid traveling through Samaria.

The fact that Jesus was traveling to Jerusalem for worship implied rejection of the temple on Mt. Gerizim and a contempt for Samaritan worship. This was a strong point of contention between Jews and Samaritans (see Jn 4:20–22), and the Samaritan village would not take Him in (v. 53). James and John, whom Jesus nicknamed the "Sons of Thunder" (Mk 3:17), then suggested they call down fire from heaven as Elijah once did (v. 54). To which Christ "rebuked them" (v. 55).

Christ's response to the Samaritans exemplifies the attitude the church ought to have with regard to all forms of religious persecution. The Samaritans' worship was pagan at heart, plainly wrong. Compounding that was their intolerance. Yet, the Lord would not retaliate with force against them. Nor did He even revile them verbally. He had come to save, not to destroy, and so His response was grace rather than destructive fury (v. 56). Nonetheless, Christ's words of disapproval here must not be taken as condemnation of Elijah's actions in 1 Kings 18:38–40 or 2 Kings 1:10–12. Elijah was commissioned to a special ministry as prophet in a theocracy, and it was his God-ordained task to confront an evil monarch (Ahab) who was attempting to usurp God's authority. Elijah acted with an authority comparable to that of modern civil authorities (see Ro 13:4)—not in a capacity that parallels that of ministers of the gospel.

APRIL 10

Joshua 9:1–10:43

9 Now it came about when all the kings who were beyond the Jordan, in the hill country and in the lowland and on all the coast of the Great Sea toward Lebanon, the Hittite

and the Amorite, the Canaanite, the Perizzite, the Hivite and the Jebusite, heard of it, ² that they gathered themselves together with one accord to fight with Joshua and with Israel.

³ When the inhabitants of Gibeon heard what Joshua had done to Jericho and to Ai, ⁴ they also acted craftily and set out as envoys, and took worn-out sacks on their

donkeys, and wineskins worn-out and torn and mended, [5] and worn-out and patched sandals on their feet, and worn-out clothes on themselves; and all the bread of their provision was dry *and* had become crumbled. [6] They went to Joshua to the camp at Gilgal and said to him and to the men of Israel, "We have come from a far country; now therefore, make a covenant with us." [7] The men of Israel said to the Hivites, "Perhaps you are living within our land; how then shall we make a covenant with you?" [8] But they said to Joshua, "We are your servants." Then Joshua said to them, "Who are you and where do you come from?" [9] They said to him, "Your servants have come from a very far country because of the fame of the LORD your God; for we have heard the report of Him and all that He did in Egypt, [10] and all that He did to the two kings of the Amorites who were beyond the Jordan, to Sihon king of Heshbon and to Og king of Bashan who was at Ashtaroth. [11] So our elders and all the inhabitants of our country spoke to us, saying, 'Take provisions in your hand for the journey, and go to meet them and say to them, "We are your servants; now then, make a covenant with us."' [12] This our bread *was* warm *when* we took it for our provisions out of our houses on the day that we left to come to you; but now behold, it is dry and has become crumbled. [13] These wineskins which we filled were new, and behold, they are torn; and these our clothes and our sandals are worn out because of the very long journey." [14] So the men *of Israel* took some of their provisions, and did not ask for the counsel of the LORD. [15] Joshua made peace with them and made a covenant with them, to let them live; and the leaders of the congregation swore *an oath* to them.

[16] It came about at the end of three days after they had made a covenant with them, that they heard that they were neighbors and that they were living within their land. [17] Then the sons of Israel set out and came to their cities on the third day. Now their cities *were* Gibeon and Chephirah and Beeroth and Kiriath-jearim. [18] The sons of Israel did not strike them because the leaders of the congregation had sworn to them by the LORD the God of Israel. And the whole congregation grumbled against the leaders. [19] But all the leaders said to the whole congregation, "We have sworn to them by the LORD, the God of Israel, and now we cannot touch them. [20] This we will do to them, even let them live, so that wrath will not be upon us for the oath which we swore to them." [21] The leaders said to them, "Let them live." So they became hewers of wood and drawers of water for the whole congregation, just as the leaders had spoken to them.

[22] Then Joshua called for them and spoke to them, saying, "Why have you deceived us, saying, 'We are very far from you,' when you are living within our land? [23] Now therefore, you are cursed, and you shall never cease being slaves, both hewers of wood and drawers of water for the house of my God." [24] So they answered Joshua and said, "Because it was certainly told your servants that the LORD your God had commanded His servant Moses to give you all the land, and to destroy all the inhabitants of the land before you; therefore we feared greatly for our lives because of you, and have done this thing. [25] Now behold, we are in your hands; do as it seems good and right in your sight to do to us." [26] Thus he did to them, and delivered them from the hands of the sons of Israel, and they did not kill them. [27] But Joshua made them that day hewers of wood and drawers of water for the congregation and for the altar of the LORD, to this day, in the place which He would choose.

10 Now it came about when Adoni-zedek king of Jerusalem heard that Joshua had captured Ai, and had utterly destroyed it (just as he had done to Jericho and its king, so he had done to Ai and its king), and that the inhabitants of Gibeon had made peace with Israel and were within their land, [2] that he feared greatly, because Gibeon *was* a great city, like one of the royal cities, and because it was greater than Ai, and all its men *were* mighty. [3] Therefore Adoni-zedek king of Jerusalem sent *word* to Hoham king of Hebron and to Piram king of Jarmuth and to Japhia king of Lachish and to Debir king of Eglon, saying, [4] "Come up to me and help me, and let us attack Gibeon, for it has made peace with Joshua and with the sons of Israel." [5] So the five kings of the Amorites, the king of Jerusalem, the king of Hebron, the king of Jarmuth, the king of Lachish, *and* the king of Eglon, gathered together and went up, they with all their armies, and camped by Gibeon and fought against it.

[6] Then the men of Gibeon sent *word* to Joshua to the camp at Gilgal, saying, "Do not abandon your servants; come up to us quickly and save us and help us, for all the kings of the Amorites that live in the hill country have assembled against us." [7] So Joshua went up from Gilgal, he and all the

people of war with him and all the valiant warriors. [8] The LORD said to Joshua, "Do not fear them, for I have given them into your hands; not one of them shall stand before you." [9] So Joshua came upon them suddenly by marching all night from Gilgal. [10] And the LORD confounded them before Israel, and He slew them with a great slaughter at Gibeon, and pursued them by the way of the ascent of Beth-horon and struck them as far as Azekah and Makkedah. [11] As they fled from before Israel, *while* they were at the descent of Beth-horon, the LORD threw large stones from heaven on them as far as Azekah, and they died; *there were* more who died from the hailstones than those whom the sons of Israel killed with the sword.

10:11 The hailstones were miraculous. Note their: 1) source, God; 2) size, large; 3) slaughter, more by stones than by sword; 4) selectivity, only on the enemy; 5) swath, "as far as Azekah"; 6) situation, during a trek down a slope and while God caused the sun to stand still; and 7) similarity to miraculous stones God will fling down during the future wrath (Rev 16:21).

[12] Then Joshua spoke to the LORD in the day when the LORD delivered up the Amorites before the sons of Israel, and he said in the sight of Israel,

"O sun, stand still at Gibeon,
And O moon in the valley of Aijalon."
[13] So the sun stood still, and
the moon stopped,
Until the nation avenged
themselves of their enemies.

Is it not written in the book of Jashar? And the sun stopped in the middle of the sky and did not hasten to go *down* for about a whole day. [14] There was no day like that before it or after it, when the LORD listened to the voice of a man; for the LORD fought for Israel.

[15] Then Joshua and all Israel with him returned to the camp to Gilgal.

[16] Now these five kings had fled and hidden themselves in the cave at Makkedah. [17] It was told Joshua, saying, "The five kings have been found hidden in the cave at Makkedah." [18] Joshua said, "Roll large stones against the mouth of the cave, and assign men by it to guard them, [19] but do not stay *there* yourselves; pursue your enemies and attack them

10:12-14 sun stood still, and the moon stopped. Some say an eclipse hid the sun, keeping its heat from Joshua's worn soldiers and allowing coolness for battle. Others suppose a local (not universal) refraction of the sun's rays such as the local darkness in Egypt (Ex 10:21-23). Another view has it as only language of observation; i.e., it only seemed to Joshua's men that the sun and moon stopped as God helped them do in one literal 24-hour day what would normally take longer. Others view it as lavish poetic description, not literal fact. However, such ideas fail to do justice to 10:12-14, and needlessly question God's power as Creator. This is best accepted as an outright, monumental miracle. Joshua, moved by the Lord's will, commanded the sun to delay (Hebrew, "be still, silent, leave off"). The earth actually stopped rotating or, more likely, the sun moved in the same way to keep perfect pace with the battlefield. The moon also ceased its orbiting. This permitted Joshua's troops time to finish the battle with complete victory (v. 11).

in the rear. Do not allow them to enter their cities, for the LORD your God has delivered them into your hand." [20] It came about when Joshua and the sons of Israel had finished slaying them with a very great slaughter, until they were destroyed, and the survivors *who* remained of them had entered the fortified cities, [21] that all the people returned to the camp to Joshua at Makkedah in peace. No one uttered a word against any of the sons of Israel.

[22] Then Joshua said, "Open the mouth of the cave and bring these five kings out to me from the cave." [23] They did so, and brought these five kings out to him from the cave: the king of Jerusalem, the king of Hebron, the king of Jarmuth, the king of Lachish, *and* the king of Eglon. [24] When they brought these kings out to Joshua, Joshua called for all the men of Israel, and said to the chiefs of the men of war who had gone with him, "Come near, put your feet on the necks of these kings." So they came near and put their feet on their necks. [25] Joshua then said to them, "Do not fear or be dismayed! Be strong and courageous, for thus the LORD will do to all your enemies with whom you fight." [26] So afterward Joshua struck them and put them to death, and he hanged them on five trees; and they hung on the trees until evening. [27] It came about at sunset that Joshua gave a command, and they took them down

from the trees and threw them into the cave where they had hidden themselves, and put large stones over the mouth of the cave, to this very day.

²⁸ Now Joshua captured Makkedah on that day, and struck it and its king with the edge of the sword; he utterly destroyed it and every person who was in it. He left no survivor. Thus he did to the king of Makkedah just as he had done to the king of Jericho.

²⁹ Then Joshua and all Israel with him passed on from Makkedah to Libnah, and fought against Libnah. ³⁰ The LORD gave it also with its king into the hands of Israel, and he struck it and every person who was in it with the edge of the sword. He left no survivor in it. Thus he did to its king just as he had done to the king of Jericho.

³¹ And Joshua and all Israel with him passed on from Libnah to Lachish, and they camped by it and fought against it. ³² The LORD gave Lachish into the hands of Israel; and he captured it on the second day, and struck it and every person who was in it with the edge of the sword, according to all that he had done to Libnah.

³³ Then Horam king of Gezer came up to help Lachish, and Joshua defeated him and his people until he had left him no survivor.

³⁴ And Joshua and all Israel with him passed on from Lachish to Eglon, and they camped by it and fought against it. ³⁵ They captured it on that day and struck it with the edge of the sword; and he utterly destroyed that day every person who was in it, according to all that he had done to Lachish.

³⁶ Then Joshua and all Israel with him went up from Eglon to Hebron, and they fought against it. ³⁷ They captured it and struck it and its king and all its cities and all the persons who were in it with the edge of the sword. He left no survivor, according to all that he had done to Eglon. And he utterly destroyed it and every person who was in it.

³⁸ Then Joshua and all Israel with him returned to Debir, and they fought against it. ³⁹ He captured it and its king and all its cities, and they struck them with the edge of the sword, and utterly destroyed every person who was in it. He left no survivor. Just as he had done to Hebron, so he did to Debir and its king, as he had also done to Libnah and its king.

⁴⁰ Thus Joshua struck all the land, the hill country and the Negev and the lowland and the slopes and all their kings. He left no survivor, but he utterly destroyed all who breathed, just as the LORD, the God of Israel, had commanded. ⁴¹ Joshua struck them from Kadesh-barnea even as far as Gaza, and all the country of Goshen even as far as Gibeon. ⁴² Joshua captured all these kings and their lands at one time, because the LORD, the God of Israel, fought for Israel. ⁴³ So Joshua and all Israel with him returned to the camp at Gilgal.

Psalm 44:1-3

For the choir director. A Maskil of the sons of Korah.

O God, we have heard with
    our ears,
Our fathers have told us
The work that You did in their
    days,
In the days of old.
² You with Your own hand
    drove out the nations;
Then You planted them;
You afflicted the peoples,
Then You spread them abroad.
³ For by their own sword they
    did not possess the land,
And their own arm did not
    save them,
But Your right hand and Your
    arm and the light of Your
    presence,
For You favored them.

Proverbs 13:24-25

²⁴ He who withholds his rod
    hates his son,
But he who loves him
    disciplines him diligently.
²⁵ The righteous has enough to
    satisfy his appetite,
But the stomach of the
    wicked is in need.

13:24 rod...disciplines...diligently. Early childhood teaching requires both parental discipline, including corporal punishment (10:13; 19:18; 22:15; 29:15, 17), and balanced kindness and love. There is great hope that the use of the "divine ordinance" of the rod will produce godly virtue (23:13-14) and parental joy (10:1; 15:20; 17:21; 23:15-16, 24-25; 28:7; 29:1, 15, 17). Such discipline must have the right motivation (Heb 12:5-11) and appropriate severity (Eph 6:4). One who has genuine affection for his child, but withholds corporal punishment, will produce the same kind of child as a parent who hates his offspring.

Luke 10:1-24

10 Now after this the Lord appointed seventy others, and sent them in pairs ahead of Him to every city and place where He Himself was going to come. ²And He was saying to them, "The harvest is plentiful, but the laborers are few; therefore beseech the Lord of the harvest to send out laborers into His harvest. ³Go; behold, I send you out as lambs in the midst of wolves. ⁴Carry no money belt, no bag, no shoes; and greet no one on the way. ⁵Whatever house you enter, first say, 'Peace *be* to this house.' ⁶If a man of peace is there, your peace will rest on him; but if not, it will return to you. ⁷Stay in that house, eating and drinking what they give you; for the laborer is worthy of his wages. Do not keep moving from house to house. ⁸Whatever city you enter and they receive you, eat what is set before you; ⁹and heal those in it who are sick, and say to them, 'The kingdom of God has come near to you.' ¹⁰But whatever city you enter and they do not receive you, go out into its streets and say, ¹¹'Even the dust of your city which clings to our feet we wipe off *in protest* against you; yet be sure of this, that the kingdom of God has come near.' ¹²I say to you, it will be more tolerable in that day for Sodom than for that city.

¹³"Woe to you, Chorazin! Woe to you, Bethsaida! For if the miracles had been performed in Tyre and Sidon which occurred in you, they would have repented long ago, sitting in sackcloth and ashes. ¹⁴But it will be more tolerable for Tyre and Sidon in the judgment than for you. ¹⁵And you, Capernaum, will not be exalted to heaven, will you? You will be brought down to Hades!

¹⁶"The one who listens to you listens to Me, and the one who rejects you rejects Me; and he who rejects Me rejects the One who sent Me."

¹⁷The seventy returned with joy, saying, "Lord, even the demons are subject to us in Your name." ¹⁸And He said to them, "I was watching Satan fall from heaven like lightning. ¹⁹Behold, I have given you authority to tread on serpents and scorpions, and over all the power of the enemy, and nothing will injure you. ²⁰Nevertheless do not rejoice in this, that the spirits are subject to you, but rejoice that your names are recorded in heaven."

²¹At that very time He rejoiced greatly in the Holy Spirit, and said, "I praise You, O Father, Lord of heaven and earth, that You have hidden these things from *the* wise and intelligent and have revealed them to infants. Yes, Father, for this way was well-pleasing in Your sight. ²²All things have been handed over to Me by My Father, and no one knows who the Son is except the Father, and who the Father is except the Son, and anyone to whom the Son wills to reveal *Him.*"

²³Turning to the disciples, He said privately, "Blessed *are* the eyes which see the things you see, ²⁴for I say to you, that many prophets and kings wished to see the things which you see, and did not see *them,* and to hear the things which you hear, and did not hear *them.*"

DAY 10: What authority are Christians given over demonic power?

The commissioning of the 70 disciples is recorded only in Luke 10:1. Moses also appointed 70 elders as his representatives (Nu 11:16, 24–26). The 12 disciples had been sent into Galilee (9:1–6); the 70 were sent into every city and place where Jesus was about to go—i.e., into Judea, and possibly Perea. They were to go out 2 by 2, as the 12 had been sent (Mk 6:7; see Ecc 4:9, 11; Ac 13:2; 15:27, 39–40; 19:22; Rev 11:3). Jesus warned them in Luke 10:3 that they would face hostility (see Eze 2:3–6; Jn 15:20) and spiritual danger (see Mt 7:15; Jn 10:12). Yet we are told they "returned with joy" (v. 17). How long the mission lasted is not recorded. It may have been several weeks.

Regarding their experience, Jesus said, "I was watching Satan fall from heaven like lightning" (v. 18). In this context, it appears Jesus' meaning was, "Don't be so surprised that the demons are subject to you. I saw their commander cast out of heaven, so it is no wonder if his minions are cast out on earth. After all, I am the source of the authority that makes them subject to you" (see vv. 19–20). He may also have intended a subtle reminder and warning against pride—the reason for Satan's fall (see 1Ti 3:6). Jesus gave them "authority to tread on serpents and scorpions." These appear to be figurative terms for demonic powers (see Ro 16:20).

Nevertheless, Jesus says, "Do not rejoice in this" (v. 20). Rather than being so enthralled with extraordinary manifestations such as power over demons and the ability to work miracles, they should have realized that the greatest wonder of all is the reality of salvation—the whole point of the gospel message and the central issue to which all the miracles pointed—"Your names are written in heaven."

APRIL 11

Joshua 11:1–12:24

11 Then it came about, when Jabin king of Hazor heard *of it*, that he sent to Jobab king of Madon and to the king of Shimron and to the king of Achshaph, ²and to the kings who were of the north in the hill country, and in the Arabah—south of Chinneroth and in the lowland and on the heights of Dor on the west— ³to the Canaanite on the east and on the west, and the Amorite and the Hittite and the Perizzite and the Jebusite in the hill country, and the Hivite at the foot of Hermon in the land of Mizpeh. ⁴They came out, they and all their armies with them, *as* many people as the sand that is on the seashore, with very many horses and chariots. ⁵So all of these kings having agreed to meet, came and encamped together at the waters of Merom, to fight against Israel.

⁶Then the LORD said to Joshua, "Do not be afraid because of them, for tomorrow at this time I will deliver all of them slain before Israel; you shall hamstring their horses and burn their chariots with fire." ⁷So Joshua and all the people of war with him came upon them suddenly by the waters of Merom, and attacked them. ⁸The LORD delivered them into the hand of Israel, so that they defeated them, and pursued them as far as Great Sidon and Misrephoth-maim and the valley of Mizpeh to the east; and they struck them until no survivor was left to them. ⁹Joshua did to them as the LORD had told him; he hamstrung their horses and burned their chariots with fire.

¹⁰Then Joshua turned back at that time, and captured Hazor and struck its king with the sword; for Hazor formerly was the head of all these kingdoms. ¹¹They struck every person who was in it with the edge of the sword, utterly destroying *them;* there was no one left who breathed. And he burned Hazor with fire. ¹²Joshua captured all the cities of these kings, and all their kings, and he struck them with the edge of the sword, *and* utterly destroyed them; just as Moses the servant of the LORD had commanded. ¹³However, Israel did not burn any cities that stood on their mounds, except Hazor alone, *which* Joshua burned. ¹⁴All the spoil of these cities and the cattle, the sons of Israel took as their plunder; but they struck every man with the edge of the sword, until they had destroyed them. They left no one who breathed. ¹⁵Just as the LORD had commanded Moses his servant, so Moses commanded Joshua, and so Joshua did; he left nothing undone of all that the LORD had commanded Moses.

¹⁶Thus Joshua took all that land: the hill country and all the Negev, all that land of Goshen, the lowland, the Arabah, the hill country of Israel and its lowland ¹⁷from Mount Halak, that rises toward Seir, even as far as Baal-gad in the valley of Lebanon at the foot of Mount Hermon. And he captured all their kings and struck them down and put them to death. ¹⁸Joshua waged war a long time with all these kings. ¹⁹There was not a city which made peace with the sons of Israel except the Hivites living in Gibeon; they took them all in battle. ²⁰For it was of the LORD to harden their hearts, to meet Israel in battle in order that he might utterly destroy them, that they might receive no mercy, but that he might destroy them, just as the LORD had commanded Moses.

²¹Then Joshua came at that time and cut off the Anakim from the hill country, from Hebron, from Debir, from Anab and from all the hill country of Judah and from all the hill country of Israel. Joshua utterly destroyed them with their cities. ²²There were no Anakim left in the land of the sons of Israel; only in Gaza, in Gath, and in Ashdod some remained. ²³So Joshua took the whole land, according to all that the LORD had spoken to Moses, and Joshua gave it for an inheritance to Israel according to their divisions by their tribes. Thus the land had rest from war.

11:18 war a long time. The conquest took approximately 7 years. Only Gibeon submitted without a fight (v. 19).

11:20 it was of the LORD to harden their hearts. God turned the Canaanites' hearts to fight in order that Israel might be His judging instrument to destroy them. They were willfully guilty of rejecting the true God with consequent great wickedness, and were as unfit to remain in the land as vomit spewed out of the mouth (Lv 18:24–25).

11:21 Anakim. Enemies who dwelt in the southern area which Joshua had defeated. They descended from Anak ("long-necked"), and were related to the giants who made Israel's spies feel small as grasshoppers by comparison (Nu 13:28–33). Their territory was later given to Caleb as a reward for his loyalty (14:6–15).

---

12 Now these are the kings of the land whom the sons of Israel defeated, and whose land they possessed beyond the Jordan toward the sunrise, from the valley of the Arnon as far as Mount Hermon, and all the Arabah to the east: ² Sihon king of the Amorites, who lived in Heshbon, *and* ruled from Aroer, which is on the edge of the valley of the Arnon, both the middle of the valley and half of Gilead, even as far as the brook Jabbok, the border of the sons of Ammon; ³ and the Arabah as far as the Sea of Chinneroth toward the east, and as far as the sea of the Arabah, *even* the Salt Sea, eastward toward Beth-jeshimoth, and on the south, at the foot of the slopes of Pisgah; ⁴ and the territory of Og king of Bashan, one of the remnant of Rephaim, who lived at Ashtaroth and at Edrei, ⁵ and ruled over Mount Hermon and Salecah and all Bashan, as far as the border of the Geshurites and the Maacathites, and half of Gilead, *as far as* the border of Sihon king of Heshbon. ⁶ Moses the servant of the LORD and the sons of Israel defeated them; and Moses the servant of the LORD gave it to the Reubenites and the Gadites and the half-tribe of Manasseh as a possession.

⁷ Now these are the kings of the land whom Joshua and the sons of Israel defeated beyond the Jordan toward the west, from Baalgad in the valley of Lebanon even as far as Mount Halak, which rises toward Seir; and Joshua gave it to the tribes of Israel as a possession according to their divisions, ⁸ in the hill country, in the lowland, in the Arabah, on the slopes, and in the wilderness, and in the Negev; the Hittite, the Amorite and the Canaanite, the Perizzite, the Hivite and the Jebusite: ⁹ the king of Jericho, one; the king of Ai, which is beside Bethel, one; ¹⁰ the king of Jerusalem, one; the king of Hebron, one; ¹¹ the king of Jarmuth, one; the king of Lachish, one; ¹² the king of Eglon, one; the king of Gezer, one; ¹³ the king of Debir, one; the king of Geder, one; ¹⁴ the king of Hormah, one; the king of Arad, one; ¹⁵ the king of Libnah, one; the king of Adullam, one; ¹⁶ the king of Makkedah, one; the king of Bethel, one; ¹⁷ the king of Tappuah, one; the king of Hepher, one; ¹⁸ the king of Aphek, one; the king of Lasharon, one; ¹⁹ the king of Madon, one; the king of Hazor, one; ²⁰ the king of Shimron-meron, one; the king of Achshaph, one; ²¹ the king of Taanach, one; the king of Megiddo, one; ²² the king of Kedesh, one; the king of Jokneam in Carmel, one; ²³ the king of Dor in the heights of Dor, one; the king of Goiim in Gilgal, one; ²⁴ the king of Tirzah, one: in all, thirty-one kings.

Psalm 44:4–19

⁴ You are my King, O God;
  Command victories for Jacob.
⁵ Through You we will push
    back our adversaries;
  Through Your name we will
    trample down those who
    rise up against us.
⁶ For I will not trust in my bow,
  Nor will my sword save me.
⁷ But You have saved us from
    our adversaries,
  And You have put to shame
    those who hate us.
⁸ In God we have boasted all
    day long,
  And we will give thanks to
    Your name forever.   *Selah*

⁹ Yet You have rejected *us* and
    brought us to dishonor,
  And do not go out with our armies.
¹⁰ You cause us to turn back
    from the adversary;
  And those who hate us have
    taken spoil for themselves.
¹¹ You give us as sheep to be eaten
  And have scattered us
    among the nations.
¹² You sell Your people cheaply,
  And have not profited by their sale.
¹³ You make us a reproach
    to our neighbors,
  A scoffing and a derision
    to those around us.
¹⁴ You make us a byword
    among the nations,
  A laughingstock among the peoples.
¹⁵ All day long my dishonor is
    before me
  And my humiliation has
    overwhelmed me,
¹⁶ Because of the voice of him who
    reproaches and reviles,
  Because of the presence of the
    enemy and the avenger.

¹⁷ All this has come upon us, but
    we have not forgotten You,
  And we have not dealt falsely
    with Your covenant.
¹⁸ Our heart has not turned back,
  And our steps have not
    deviated from Your way,
¹⁹ Yet You have crushed us in
    a place of jackals
  And covered us with the
    shadow of death.

Proverbs 14:1-2

14 The wise woman builds her house,
But the foolish tears it down
with her own hands.
2 He who walks in his uprightness
fears the LORD,
But he who is devious in his
ways despises Him.

Luke 10:25-42

25 And a lawyer stood up and put Him to the test, saying, "Teacher, what shall I do to inherit eternal life?" 26 And He said to him, "What is written in the Law? How does it read to you?" 27 And he answered, "YOU SHALL LOVE THE LORD YOUR GOD WITH ALL YOUR HEART, AND WITH ALL YOUR SOUL, AND WITH ALL YOUR STRENGTH, AND WITH ALL YOUR MIND; AND YOUR NEIGHBOR AS YOURSELF." 28 And He said to him, "You have answered correctly; DO THIS AND YOU WILL LIVE." 29 But wishing to justify himself, he said to Jesus, "And who is my neighbor?" 30 Jesus replied and said, "A man was going down from Jerusalem to Jericho, and fell among robbers, and they stripped him and beat him, and went away leaving him half dead. 31 And by chance a priest was going down on that road, and when he saw him, he passed by on the other side. 32 Likewise a Levite also, when he came to the place and saw him, passed by on the other side. 33 But a Samaritan, who was on a journey, came upon him; and when he saw him, he felt compassion, 34 and came to him and bandaged up his wounds, pouring oil and wine on *them;* and he put him on his own beast, and brought him to an inn and took care of him. 35 On the next day he took out two denarii and gave them to the innkeeper and said, 'Take care of him; and whatever more you spend, when I return I will repay you.' 36 Which of these three do you think proved to be a neighbor to the man who fell into the robbers' *hands?*" 37 And he said, "The one who showed mercy toward him." Then Jesus said to him, "Go and do the same."

38 Now as they were traveling along, He entered a village; and a woman named Martha welcomed Him into her home. 39 She had a sister called Mary, who was seated at the Lord's feet, listening to His word. 40 But Martha was distracted with all her preparations; and she came up *to Him* and said, "Lord, do You not care that my sister has left me to do all the serving alone? Then tell her to help me." 41 But the Lord answered and said to her, "Martha, Martha, you are worried and bothered about so many things; 42 but *only* one thing is necessary, for Mary has chosen the good part, which shall not be taken away from her."

10:42 one thing...good part. Jesus was not speaking of the number of dishes to be served. The one thing necessary was exemplified by Mary, i.e., an attitude of worship and meditation, listening with an open mind and heart to Jesus' words.

DAY 11: If we are to love our neighbor, who is our neighbor?

The lawyer who asked Jesus what he must do to inherit eternal life in Luke 10:25 knew the commandments well enough. But when he asked Jesus, "Who is my neighbor?" we are told that he was "wishing to justify himself" (v. 29). It revealed the man's self-righteous character, as well as his desire to test Christ.

The prevailing opinion among scribes and Pharisees was that one's neighbors were the righteous alone. According to them, the wicked—including rank sinners (such as tax collectors and prostitutes), Gentiles, and especially Samaritans—were to be hated because they were the enemies of God. They cited Psalm 139:21-22 to justify their position. As that passage suggests, hatred of evil is the natural corollary of loving righteousness. But the truly righteous person's "hatred" for sinners is not a malevolent enmity. It is a righteous abhorrence of all that is base and corrupt—not a spiteful, personal loathing of individuals. Godly hatred is marked by a brokenhearted grieving over the condition of the sinner. And as Jesus taught here and elsewhere (6:27-36; Mt 5:44-48), it is also tempered by a genuine love. The Pharisees had elevated hostility toward the wicked to the status of a virtue, in effect nullifying the second Great Commandment. Jesus' answer to this lawyer demolished the Pharisaical excuse for hating one's enemies.

Contrasting the Levite, a religious person who assisted the priests in the work of the temple, with a despised Samaritan, who rescued the wounded person, Jesus reversed the lawyer's original question (v. 29). The lawyer assumed it was up to others to prove themselves neighbor to him. Jesus' reply makes it clear that each has a responsibility to be a neighbor—especially to those who are in need.

APRIL 12

Joshua 13:1–14:15

13 Now Joshua was old *and* advanced in years when the LORD said to him, "You are old *and* advanced in years, and very much of the land remains to be possessed. ² This is the land that remains: all the regions *of* the Philistines and all *those of* the Geshurites; ³ from the Shihor which is east of Egypt, even as far as the border of Ekron to the north (it is counted as Canaanite); the five lords of the Philistines: the Gazite, the Ashdodite, the Ashkelonite, the Gittite, the Ekronite; and the Avvite ⁴ to the south, all the land of the Canaanite, and Mearah that belongs to the Sidonians, as far as Aphek, to the border of the Amorite; ⁵ and the land of the Gebalite, and all of Lebanon, toward the east, from Baal-gad below Mount Hermon as far as Lebo-hamath. ⁶ All the inhabitants of the hill country from Lebanon as far as Misrephoth-maim, all the Sidonians, I will drive them out from before the sons of Israel; only allot it to Israel for an inheritance as I have commanded you. ⁷ Now therefore, apportion this land for an inheritance to the nine tribes and the half-tribe of Manasseh."

⁸ With the other half-tribe, the Reubenites and the Gadites received their inheritance which Moses gave them beyond the Jordan to the east, just as Moses the servant of the LORD gave to them; ⁹ from Aroer, which is on the edge of the valley of the Arnon, with the city which is in the middle of the valley, and all the plain of Medeba, as far as Dibon; ¹⁰ and all the cities of Sihon king of the Amorites, who reigned in Heshbon, as far as the border of the sons of Ammon; ¹¹ and Gilead, and the territory of the Geshurites and Maacathites, and all Mount Hermon, and all Bashan as far as Salecah; ¹² all the kingdom of Og in Bashan, who reigned in Ashtaroth and in Edrei (he alone was left of the remnant of the Rephaim); for Moses struck them and dispossessed them. ¹³ But the sons of Israel did not dispossess the Geshurites or the Maacathites; for Geshur and Maacath live among Israel until this day. ¹⁴ Only to the tribe of Levi he did not give an inheritance; the offerings by fire to the LORD, the God of Israel, are their inheritance, as He spoke to him.

¹⁵ So Moses gave *an inheritance* to the tribe of the sons of Reuben according to their families. ¹⁶ Their territory was from Aroer, which is on the edge of the valley of the Arnon, with the city which is in the middle of the valley and all the plain by Medeba; ¹⁷ Heshbon, and all its cities which are on the plain: Dibon and Bamoth-baal and Beth-baal-meon, ¹⁸ and Jahaz and Kedemoth and Mephaath, ¹⁹ and Kiriathaim and Sibmah and Zereth-shahar on the hill of the valley, ²⁰ and Beth-peor and the slopes of Pisgah and Beth-jeshimoth, ²¹ even all the cities of the plain and all the kingdom of Sihon king of the Amorites who reigned in Heshbon, whom Moses struck with the chiefs of Midian, Evi and Rekem and Zur and Hur and Reba, the princes of Sihon, who lived in the land. ²² The sons of Israel also killed Balaam the son of Beor, the diviner, with the sword among *the rest of* their slain. ²³ The border of the sons of Reuben was the Jordan. This was the inheritance of the sons of Reuben according to their families, the cities and their villages.

13:22 Israel also killed Balaam. This Israelite slaying of the infamous false prophet occurred at an unidentified point during the conquest (Nu 21–25; 31:16; Jos 24:9–10; 2Pe 2:15–16; Jude 11; Rev 2:14).

²⁴ Moses also gave *an inheritance* to the tribe of Gad, to the sons of Gad, according to their families. ²⁵ Their territory was Jazer, and all the cities of Gilead, and half the land of the sons of Ammon, as far as Aroer which is before Rabbah; ²⁶ and from Heshbon as far as Ramath-mizpeh and Betonim, and from Mahanaim as far as the border of Debir; ²⁷ and in the valley, Beth-haram and Beth-nimrah and Succoth and Zaphon, the rest of the kingdom of Sihon king of Heshbon, with the Jordan as a border, as far as the *lower* end of the Sea of Chinnereth beyond the Jordan to the east. ²⁸ This is the inheritance of the sons of Gad according to their families, the cities and their villages.

²⁹ Moses also gave *an inheritance* to the half-tribe of Manasseh; and it was for the half-tribe of the sons of Manasseh according to their families. ³⁰ Their territory was from Mahanaim, all Bashan, all the kingdom of Og king of Bashan, and all the towns of Jair, which are in Bashan, sixty cities; ³¹ also half of Gilead, with Ashtaroth and Edrei, the cities of the kingdom of Og in Bashan, *were* for the sons of Machir the son of Manasseh, for half of the sons of Machir according to their families.

³² These are *the territories* which Moses apportioned for an inheritance in the plains of Moab, beyond the Jordan at Jericho to the east. ³³ But to the tribe of Levi, Moses did not give an inheritance; the LORD, the God of Israel, is their inheritance, as He had promised to them.

14 Now these are *the territories* which the sons of Israel inherited in the land of Canaan, which Eleazar the priest, and Joshua the son of Nun, and the heads of the households of the tribes of the sons of Israel apportioned to them for an inheritance, ²by the lot of their inheritance, as the LORD commanded through Moses, for the nine tribes and the half-tribe. ³For Moses had given the inheritance of the two tribes and the half-tribe beyond the Jordan; but he did not give an inheritance to the Levites among them. ⁴For the sons of Joseph were two tribes, Manasseh and Ephraim, and they did not give a portion to the Levites in the land, except cities to live in, with their pasture lands for their livestock and for their property. ⁵Thus the sons of Israel did just as the LORD had commanded Moses, and they divided the land.

⁶Then the sons of Judah drew near to Joshua in Gilgal, and Caleb the son of Jephunneh the Kenizzite said to him, "You know the word which the LORD spoke to Moses the man of God concerning you and me in Kadesh-barnea. ⁷I was forty years old when Moses the servant of the LORD sent me from Kadesh-barnea to spy out the land, and I brought word back to him as *it was* in my heart. ⁸Nevertheless my brethren who went up with me made the heart of the people melt with fear; but I followed the LORD my God fully. ⁹So Moses swore on that day, saying, 'Surely the land on which your foot has trodden will be an inheritance to you and to your children forever, because you have followed the LORD my God fully.' ¹⁰Now behold, the LORD has let me live, just as He spoke, these forty-five years, from the time that the LORD spoke this word to Moses, when Israel walked in the wilderness; and now behold, I am eighty-five years old today. ¹¹I am still as strong today as I was in the day Moses sent me; as my strength was then, so my strength is now, for war and for going out and coming in. ¹²Now then, give me this hill country about which the LORD spoke on that day, for you heard on that day that Anakim *were* there, with great fortified cities; perhaps the LORD will be with me, and I will drive them out as the LORD has spoken."

¹³So Joshua blessed him and gave Hebron to Caleb the son of Jephunneh for an inheritance. ¹⁴Therefore, Hebron became the inheritance of Caleb the son of Jephunneh the Kenizzite until this day, because he followed the LORD God of Israel fully. ¹⁵Now the name of Hebron was formerly Kiriath-arba; *for Arba* was the greatest man among the Anakim. Then the land had rest from war.

Psalm 44:20–26

²⁰ If we had forgotten the
name of our God
Or extended our hands
to a strange god,
²¹ Would not God find this out?
For He knows the secrets
of the heart.
²² But for Your sake we are
killed all day long;
We are considered as sheep
to be slaughtered.

44:22 But for Your sake. They had no specific answers; only this inescapable conclusion that, by God's sovereign will, they were allowed to be destroyed by their enemies. See Paul's quote of this verse in Romans 8:36 and its general principle in Matthew 5:10–12; 1 Peter 3:13–17; 4:12–16.

²³ Arouse Yourself, why do
You sleep, O Lord?
Awake, do not reject us forever.
²⁴ Why do You hide Your face
And forget our affliction
and our oppression?
²⁵ For our soul has sunk
down into the dust;
Our body cleaves to the earth.
²⁶ Rise up, be our help,
And redeem us for the sake of
Your lovingkindness.

Proverbs 14:3

³ In the mouth of the foolish
is a rod for *his* back,
But the lips of the wise
will protect them.

Luke 11:1–28

11 It happened that while Jesus was praying in a certain place, after He had finished, one of His disciples said to Him, "Lord, teach us to pray just as John also taught his disciples." ²And He said to them, "When you pray, say:

11:1 Lord, teach us to pray. Rabbis often composed prayers for their disciples to recite. Having seen Jesus pray many times, they knew of His love for prayer, and they knew prayer was not just the reciting of words.

'Father, hallowed be Your name.
Your kingdom come.
³ 'Give us each day our daily bread.
⁴ 'And forgive us our sins,
For we ourselves also forgive
everyone who is indebted to us.
And lead us not into temptation.' "

⁵Then He said to them, "Suppose one of you has a friend, and goes to him at midnight and says to him, 'Friend, lend me three loaves; ⁶for a friend of mine has come to me from a journey, and I have nothing to set before him'; ⁷and from inside he answers and says, 'Do not bother me; the door has already been shut and my children and I are in bed; I cannot get up and give you *anything*.' ⁸I tell you, even though he will not get up and give him *anything* because he is his friend, yet because of his persistence he will get up and give him as much as he needs.

⁹"So I say to you, ask, and it will be given to you; seek, and you will find; knock, and it will be opened to you. ¹⁰For everyone who asks, receives; and he who seeks, finds; and to him who knocks, it will be opened. ¹¹Now suppose one of you fathers is asked by his son for a fish; he will not give him a snake instead of a fish, will he? ¹²Or *if* he is asked for an egg, he will not give him a scorpion, will he? ¹³If you then, being evil, know how to give good gifts to your children, how much more will *your* heavenly Father give the Holy Spirit to those who ask Him?"

¹⁴And He was casting out a demon, and it was mute; when the demon had gone out, the mute man spoke; and the crowds were amazed. ¹⁵But some of them said, "He casts out demons by Beelzebul, the ruler of the demons." ¹⁶Others, to test *Him*, were demanding of Him a sign from heaven. ¹⁷But He knew their thoughts and said to them, "Any kingdom divided against itself is laid waste; and a house *divided* against itself falls. ¹⁸If Satan also is divided against himself, how will his kingdom stand? For you say that I cast out demons by Beelzebul. ¹⁹And if I by Beelzebul cast out demons, by whom do your sons cast them out? So they will be your judges. ²⁰But if I cast out demons by the finger of God, then the kingdom of God has come upon you. ²¹When a strong *man*, fully armed, guards his own house, his possessions are undisturbed. ²²But when someone stronger than he attacks him and overpowers him, he takes away from him all his armor on which he had relied and distributes his plunder. ²³He who is not with Me is against Me; and he who does not gather with Me, scatters.

²⁴"When the unclean spirit goes out of a man, it passes through waterless places seeking rest, and not finding any, it says, 'I will return to my house from which I came.' ²⁵And when it comes, it finds it swept and put in order. ²⁶Then it goes and takes *along* seven other spirits more evil than itself, and they go in and live there; and the last state of that man becomes worse than the first."

²⁷While Jesus was saying these things, one of the women in the crowd raised her voice and said to Him, "Blessed is the womb that bore You and the breasts at which You nursed." ²⁸But He said, "On the contrary, blessed are those who hear the word of God and observe it."

11:28 On the contrary. This has the sense of, "Yes, but rather..." While not denying the blessedness of Mary, Christ did not countenance any tendency to elevate Mary as an object of veneration. Mary's relationship to Him as His physical mother did not confer on her any greater honor than the blessedness of those who hear and obey the Word of God.

DAY 12: How far would some go to explain away Jesus' power?

Having just watched Jesus cast a demon out of a person, some people said, "He casts out demons by Beelzebul, the ruler of the demons" (Lk 11:15). Originally this referred to Baal-Zebul ("Baal, the prince"), chief god of the Philistine city of Ekron. The Israelites disdainfully referred to him as Baal-Zebub ("Lord of Flies").

Jesus reminded them that "any kingdom divided against itself is laid waste" (v. 17). This may have been a subtle jab at the Jewish nation, a kingdom divided in the time of Jeroboam, and still marked by various kinds of bitter internal strife and factionalism, right up to the destruction of Jerusalem in A.D. 70. He also questioned them: "By whom do your sons cast them out?" (v. 19). There were Jewish exorcists who claimed power to cast out demons (Ac 19:13–15). Jesus' point was that if such exorcisms could be done via satanic power, the Pharisaical exorcists must be suspect, as well. And in fact, the evidence in Acts 19 suggests that the sons of Sceva were charlatans who employed fraud and trickery to fabricate phony exorcisms. "They will be your judges" (v. 19), i.e., witnesses against you. This seems to suggest that the fraudulent exorcisms (which had their approval) stood as a testimony against the Pharisees themselves, who disapproved of Christ's genuine exorcisms.

"But if I cast out demons by the finger of God, then the kingdom of God has come upon you" (v. 20). In Exodus 8:19, the phony magicians of Egypt were forced to confess that Moses' miracles were genuine works of God, not mere trickery such as they had performed. Here Jesus made a similar comparison between His exorcisms and the work of the Jewish exorcists.

APRIL 13

Joshua 15:1–16:10

15 Now the lot for the tribe of the sons of Judah according to their families reached the border of Edom, southward to the wilderness of Zin at the extreme south. ² Their south border was from the lower end of the Salt Sea, from the bay that turns to the south. ³ Then it proceeded southward to the ascent of Akrabbim and continued to Zin, then went up by the south of Kadesh-barnea and continued to Hezron, and went up to Addar and turned about to Karka. ⁴ It continued to Azmon and proceeded to the brook of Egypt, and the border ended at the sea. This shall be your south border. ⁵ The east border was the Salt Sea, as far as the mouth of the Jordan. And the border of the north side was from the bay of the sea at the mouth of the Jordan. ⁶ Then the border went up to Beth-hoglah, and continued on the north of Beth-arabah, and the border went up to the stone of Bohan the son of Reuben. ⁷ The border went up to Debir from the valley of Achor, and turned northward toward Gilgal which is opposite the ascent of Adummim, which is on the south of the valley; and the border continued to the waters of En-shemesh and it ended at En-rogel. ⁸ Then the border went up the valley of Ben-hinnom to the slope of the Jebusite on the south (that is, Jerusalem); and the border went up to the top of the mountain which is before the valley of Hinnom to the west, which is at the end of the valley of Rephaim toward the north. ⁹ From the top of the mountain the border curved to the spring of the waters of Nephtoah and proceeded to the cities of Mount Ephron, then the border curved to Baalah (that is, Kiriath-jearim). ¹⁰ The border turned about from Baalah westward to Mount Seir, and continued to the slope of Mount Jearim on the north (that is, Chesalon), and went down to Beth-shemesh and continued through Timnah. ¹¹ The border proceeded to the side of Ekron northward. Then the border curved to Shikkeron and continued to Mount Baalah and proceeded to Jabneel, and the border ended at the sea. ¹² The west border was at the Great Sea, even its coastline. This is the border around the sons of Judah according to their families.

¹³ Now he gave to Caleb the son of Jephunneh a portion among the sons of Judah, according to the command of the LORD to Joshua, namely, Kiriath-arba, Arba being the father of Anak (that is, Hebron). ¹⁴ Caleb drove out from there the three sons of Anak: Sheshai and Ahiman and Talmai, the children of Anak. ¹⁵ Then he went up from there against the inhabitants of Debir; now the name of Debir formerly was Kiriath-sepher. ¹⁶ And Caleb said, "The one who attacks Kiriath-sepher and captures it, I will give him Achsah my daughter as a wife." ¹⁷ Othniel the son of Kenaz, the brother of Caleb, captured it; so he gave him Achsah his daughter as a wife. ¹⁸ It came about that when she came to him, she persuaded him to ask her father for a field. So she alighted from the donkey, and Caleb said to her, "What do you want?" ¹⁹ Then she said, "Give me a blessing; since you have given me the land of the Negev, give me also springs of water." So he gave her the upper springs and the lower springs.

²⁰ This is the inheritance of the tribe of the sons of Judah according to their families.

²¹ Now the cities at the extremity of the tribe of the sons of Judah toward the border of Edom in the south were Kabzeel and Eder and Jagur, ²² and Kinah and Dimonah and Adadah, ²³ and Kedesh and Hazor and Ithnan, ²⁴ Ziph and Telem and Bealoth, ²⁵ and Hazor-hadattah and Kerioth-hezron (that is, Hazor), ²⁶ Amam and Shema and Moladah, ²⁷ and Hazar-gaddah and Heshmon and Beth-pelet, ²⁸ and Hazar-shual and Beersheba and Biziothiah, ²⁹ Baalah and Iim and Ezem, ³⁰ and Eltolad and Chesil and Hormah, ³¹ and Ziklag and Madmannah and Sansannah, ³² and Lebaoth and Shilhim and Ain and Rimmon; in all, twenty-nine cities with their villages.

³³ In the lowland: Eshtaol and Zorah and Ashnah, ³⁴ and Zanoah and En-gannim, Tappuah and Enam, ³⁵ Jarmuth and Adullam, Socoh and Azekah, ³⁶ and Shaaraim and Adithaim and Gederah and Gederothaim; fourteen cities with their villages.

³⁷ Zenan and Hadashah and Migdal-gad,

38 and Dilean and Mizpeh and Joktheel, 39 Lachish and Bozkath and Eglon, 40 and Cabbon and Lahmas and Chitlish, 41 and Gederoth, Beth-dagon and Naamah and Makkedah; sixteen cities with their villages.

42 Libnah and Ether and Ashan, 43 and Iphtah and Ashnah and Nezib, 44 and Keilah and Achzib and Mareshah; nine cities with their villages.

45 Ekron, with its towns and its villages; 46 from Ekron even to the sea, all that were by the side of Ashdod, with their villages.

47 Ashdod, its towns and its villages; Gaza, its towns and its villages; as far as the brook of Egypt and the Great Sea, even *its* coastline.

48 In the hill country: Shamir and Jattir and Socoh, 49 and Dannah and Kiriath-sannah (that is, Debir), 50 and Anab and Eshtemoh and Anim, 51 and Goshen and Holon and Giloh; eleven cities with their villages.

52 Arab and Dumah and Eshan, 53 and Janum and Beth-tappuah and Aphekah, 54 and Humtah and Kiriath-arba (that is, Hebron), and Zior; nine cities with their villages.

55 Maon, Carmel and Ziph and Juttah, 56 and Jezreel and Jokdeam and Zanoah, 57 Kain, Gibeah and Timnah; ten cities with their villages.

58 Halhul, Beth-zur and Gedor, 59 and Maarath and Beth-anoth and Eltekon; six cities with their villages.

60 Kiriath-baal (that is, Kiriath-jearim), and Rabbah; two cities with their villages.

61 In the wilderness: Beth-arabah, Middin and Secacah, 62 and Nibshan and the City of Salt and Engedi; six cities with their villages.

63 Now as for the Jebusites, the inhabitants of Jerusalem, the sons of Judah could not drive them out; so the Jebusites live with the sons of Judah at Jerusalem until this day.

16 Then the lot for the sons of Joseph went from the Jordan at Jericho to the waters of Jericho on the east into the wilderness, going up from Jericho through the hill country to Bethel. 2 It went from Bethel to Luz, and continued to the border of the Archites at Ataroth. 3 It went down westward to the territory of the Japhletites, as far as the territory of lower Beth-horon even to Gezer, and it ended at the sea.

4 The sons of Joseph, Manasseh and Ephraim, received their inheritance. 5 Now *this* was the territory of the sons of Ephraim according to their families: the border of their inheritance eastward was Ataroth-addar, as far as upper Beth-horon. 6 Then the border went westward at Michmethath on the north, and the border turned about eastward to

Taanath-shiloh and continued *beyond* it to the east of Janoah. 7 It went down from Janoah to Ataroth and to Naarah, then reached Jericho and came out at the Jordan. 8 From Tappuah the border continued westward to the brook of Kanah, and it ended at the sea. This is the inheritance of the tribe of the sons of Ephraim according to their families, 9 *together* with the cities which were set apart for the sons of Ephraim in the midst of the inheritance of the sons of Manasseh, all the cities with their villages. 10 But they did not drive out the Canaanites who lived in Gezer, so the Canaanites live in the midst of Ephraim to this day, and they became forced laborers.

16:10 Ephraim did not drive the Canaanites from their area. This is the first mention of the fatal policy of neglecting to exterminate the idolaters (Dt 20:16).

Psalm 45:1–5

For the choir director; according to the Shoshannim. A Maskil of the sons of Korah. A Song of Love.

M y heart overflows with
   a good theme;
   I address my verses to the King;
   My tongue is the pen of
      a ready writer.
2 You are fairer than the sons of men;
   Grace is poured upon Your lips;
   Therefore God has blessed
      You forever.
3 Gird Your sword on *Your*
      thigh, O Mighty One,
   In Your splendor and Your
      majesty!
4 And in Your majesty ride
      on victoriously,
   For the cause of truth and
      meekness *and* righteousness;
   Let Your right hand teach
      You awesome things.

45:1 My heart overflows...My tongue. The psalmist is overwhelmed with emotion upon the occasion of the king's marriage; consequently, he puts his stirred-up mind and feelings into words. In v. 2ff. his tongue is the brush that he uses to paint vivid word pictures.

5 Your arrows are sharp;
  The peoples fall under You;
  Your arrows are in the heart
     of the King's enemies.

Proverbs 14:4–5

4 Where no oxen are, the
     manger is clean,
  But much revenue *comes* by
     the strength of the ox.
5 A trustworthy witness
     will not lie,
  But a false witness utters lies.

Luke 11:29–54

29 As the crowds were increasing, He began to say, "This generation is a wicked generation; it seeks for a sign, and *yet* no sign will be given to it but the sign of Jonah. 30 For just as Jonah became a sign to the Ninevites, so will the Son of Man be to this generation. 31 The Queen of the South will rise up with the men of this generation at the judgment and condemn them, because she came from the ends of the earth to hear the wisdom of Solomon; and behold, something greater than Solomon is here. 32 The men of Nineveh will stand up with this generation at the judgment and condemn it, because they repented at the preaching of Jonah; and behold, something greater than Jonah is here.

33 "No one, after lighting a lamp, puts it away in a cellar nor under a basket, but on the lampstand, so that those who enter may see the light. 34 The eye is the lamp of your body; when your eye is clear, your whole body also is full of light; but when it is bad, your body also is full of darkness. 35 Then watch out that the light in you is not darkness. 36 If therefore your whole body is full of light, with no dark part in it, it will be wholly illumined, as when the lamp illumines you with its rays."

37 Now when He had spoken, a Pharisee *asked Him to have lunch with him; and He went in, and reclined *at the table.* 38 When the Pharisee saw it, he was surprised that He had not first ceremonially washed before the meal. 39 But the Lord said to him, "Now you Pharisees clean the outside of the cup and of the platter; but inside of you, you are full of robbery and wickedness. 40 You foolish ones, did not He who made the outside make the inside also? 41 But give that which is within as charity, and then all things are clean for you.

42 "But woe to you Pharisees! For you pay tithe of mint and rue and every *kind of* garden herb, and *yet* disregard justice and the love of

---

11:34 the lamp of your body. This is a different metaphor from the one in v. 33. There the lamp speaks of the Word of God; here the eye is the "lamp"—i.e., the source of light—for the body. **when your eye...is bad.** The problem was their perception, not a lack of light. They did not need a sign; they needed hearts to believe the great display of divine power they had already seen.

11:38 He had not first ceremonially washed. The Pharisee was concerned with ceremony, not hygiene. The Greek word for "washed" refers to a ceremonial ablution. Nothing in the law commanded such washings, but the Pharisees practiced them, believing the ritual cleansed them of any accidental ceremonial defilement.

God; but these are the things you should have done without neglecting the others. 43 Woe to you Pharisees! For you love the chief seats in the synagogues and the respectful greetings in the market places. 44 Woe to you! For you are like concealed tombs, and the people who walk over *them* are unaware *of it."*

45 One of the lawyers *said to Him in reply, "Teacher, when You say this, You insult us too." 46 But He said, "Woe to you lawyers as well! For you weigh men down with burdens hard to bear, while you yourselves will not even touch the burdens with one of your fingers. 47 Woe to you! For you build the tombs of the prophets, and *it was* your fathers *who* killed them. 48 So you are witnesses and approve the deeds of your fathers; because it was they who killed them, and you build *their tombs.* 49 For this reason also the wisdom of God said, 'I will send to them prophets and apostles, and *some* of them they will kill and *some* they will persecute, 50 so that the blood of all the prophets, shed since the foundation of the world, may be charged against this generation, 51 from the blood of Abel to the blood of Zechariah, who was killed between the altar and the house *of God;* yes, I tell you, it shall be charged against this generation.' 52 Woe to you lawyers! For you have taken away the key of knowledge; you yourselves did not enter, and you hindered those who were entering."

53 When He left there, the scribes and the Pharisees began to be very hostile and to question Him closely on many subjects, 54 plotting against Him to catch *Him* in something He might say.

The Book of Joshua begins with God's commissioning of Israel's new leader. God described Joshua's mission—to go in and possess the Land (1:2–6). God hinged Joshua's success on three key factors: 1) God's own presence (v. 5); 2) Joshua's personal strength and courage (vv. 7, 9); and 3) Joshua's attention to and application of God's word (vv. 7–8).

God spelled out this third factor with some detail for it was to be the basis for all of Joshua's actions. God's word was to be Joshua's constant conversation, continual meditation, and unswerving application. The phrase "This book of the law shall not depart from your mouth" (v. 8) deserves added attention. While a first impression might lead to the conclusion that Joshua was not supposed to talk about the Book of the Law, the direct opposite is the case: he was not supposed to stop talking about it.

Biblical meditation begins with the thoughtful, lingering reading of God's Word. It progresses to familiarity and memorization. In order to "meditate on it day and night" (v. 8), the Book of the Law would have been in Joshua. The purpose has been achieved when meditation leads us to "be careful to do according to all that is written in it" (v. 8).

"Then," God told Joshua, "you will make your way prosperous, and then you will have success" (v. 8). Joshua found the ultimate measure of prosperity and success—knowing how God wants His people to live and then living that way. God repeatedly assured Joshua of His own presence "wherever you go." What greater measurement of success could there be than to honor the ever-present God with our obedience?

APRIL 14

Joshua 17:1–18:28

17 Now *this* was the lot for the tribe of Manasseh, for he was the firstborn of Joseph. To Machir the firstborn of Manasseh, the father of Gilead, were allotted Gilead and Bashan, because he was a man of war. ² So *the lot* was *made* for the rest of the sons of Manasseh according to their families: for the sons of Abiezer and for the sons of Helek and for the sons of Asriel and for the sons of Shechem and for the sons of Hepher and for the sons of Shemida; these *were* the male descendants of Manasseh the son of Joseph according to their families.

³ However, Zelophehad, the son of Hepher, the son of Gilead, the son of Machir, the son of Manasseh, had no sons, only daughters; and these are the names of his daughters: Mahlah and Noah, Hoglah, Milcah and Tirzah. ⁴ They came near before Eleazar the priest and before Joshua the son of Nun and before the leaders, saying, "The LORD commanded Moses to give us an inheritance among our brothers." So according to the command of the LORD he gave them an inheritance among their father's brothers. ⁵ Thus there fell ten portions to Manasseh, besides the land of Gilead and Bashan, which is beyond the Jordan, ⁶ because the daughters of Manasseh received an inheritance among his sons. And the land of Gilead belonged to the rest of the sons of Manasseh.

⁷ The border of Manasseh ran from Asher to Michmethath which was east of Shechem; then the border went southward to the inhabitants of En-tappuah. ⁸ The land of Tappuah belonged to Manasseh, but Tappuah on the border of Manasseh *belonged* to the sons of Ephraim. ⁹ The border went down to the brook of Kanah, southward of the brook (these cities *belonged* to Ephraim among the cities of Manasseh), and the border of Manasseh *was* on the north side of the brook and it ended at the sea. ¹⁰ The south side *belonged* to Ephraim and the north side to Manasseh, and the sea was their border; and they reached to Asher on the north and to Issachar on the east. ¹¹ In Issachar and in Asher, Manasseh had Beth-shean and its towns and Ibleam and its towns, and the inhabitants of Dor and its towns, and the inhabitants of En-dor and its towns, the inhabitants of Taanach and its towns, and the inhabitants of Megiddo and its towns, the third is Napheth. ¹² But the sons of Manasseh could not take possession of these cities, because the Canaanites persisted in living in that land. ¹³ It came about when the sons of Israel became strong, they put the Canaanites to forced labor, but they did not drive them out completely.

¹⁴ Then the sons of Joseph spoke to Joshua, saying, "Why have you given me only one lot and one portion for an inheritance, since I am a numerous people whom the LORD has thus far blessed?" ¹⁵ Joshua said to them, "If you are a numerous people, go up to the forest and clear a place for yourself there in the land of the Perizzites and of the Rephaim, since the hill country of Ephraim is

too narrow for you." ¹⁶The sons of Joseph said, "The hill country is not enough for us, and all the Canaanites who live in the valley land have chariots of iron, both those who are in Beth-shean and its towns and those who are in the valley of Jezreel." ¹⁷Joshua spoke to the house of Joseph, to Ephraim and Manasseh, saying, "You are a numerous people and have great power; you shall not have one lot *only*, ¹⁸ but the hill country shall be yours. For though it is a forest, you shall clear it, and to its farthest borders it shall be yours; for you shall drive out the Canaanites, even though they have chariots of iron *and* though they are strong."

17:12–18 sons of Manasseh. Tribesmen of Manasseh complained that Joshua did not allot them land sufficient to their numbers and that the Canaanites were too tough for them to drive out altogether. He permitted them extra land in forested hills that they could clear. Joshua told them that they could drive out the Canaanites for God had promised to be with them in victory against chariots (Dt 20:1).

18 Then the whole congregation of the sons of Israel assembled themselves at Shiloh, and set up the tent of meeting there; and the land was subdued before them.

²There remained among the sons of Israel seven tribes who had not divided their inheritance. ³So Joshua said to the sons of Israel, "How long will you put off entering to take possession of the land which the LORD, the God of your fathers, has given you? ⁴Provide for yourselves three men from each tribe that I may send them, and that they may arise and walk through the land and write a description of it according to their inheritance; then they shall return to me. ⁵They shall divide it into seven portions; Judah shall stay in its territory on the south, and the house of Joseph shall stay in their territory on the north. ⁶You shall describe the land in seven divisions, and bring *the description* here to me. I will cast lots for you here before the LORD our God. ⁷For the Levites have no portion among you, because the priesthood of the LORD is their inheritance. Gad and Reuben and the half-tribe of Manasseh also have received their inheritance eastward beyond the Jordan, which Moses the servant of the LORD gave them."

⁸Then the men arose and went, and Joshua commanded those who went to describe the land, saying, "Go and walk through the land and describe it, and return to me; then I will cast lots for you here before the LORD in Shiloh." ⁹So the men went and passed through the land, and described it by cities in seven divisions in a book; and they came to Joshua to the camp at Shiloh. ¹⁰And Joshua cast lots for them in Shiloh before the LORD, and there Joshua divided the land to the sons of Israel according to their divisions.

¹¹Now the lot of the tribe of the sons of Benjamin came up according to their families, and the territory of their lot lay between the sons of Judah and the sons of Joseph. ¹²Their border on the north side was from the Jordan, then the border went up to the side of Jericho on the north, and went up through the hill country westward, and it ended at the wilderness of Beth-aven. ¹³From there the border continued to Luz, to the side of Luz (that is, Bethel) southward; and the border went down to Ataroth-addar, near the hill which *lies* on the south of lower Beth-horon. ¹⁴The border extended *from there* and turned round on the west side southward, from the hill which *lies* before Beth-horon southward; and it ended at Kiriath-baal (that is, Kiriath-jearim), a city of the sons of Judah. This *was* the west side. ¹⁵Then the south side *was* from the edge of Kiriath-jearim, and the border went westward and went to the fountain of the waters of Nephtoah. ¹⁶The border went down to the edge of the hill which is in the valley of Ben-hinnom, which is in the valley of Rephaim northward; and it went down to the valley of Hinnom, to the slope of the Jebusite southward, and went down to En-rogel. ¹⁷It extended northward and went to En-shemesh and went to Geliloth, which is opposite the ascent of Adummim, and it went down to the stone of Bohan the son of Reuben. ¹⁸It continued to the side in front of the Arabah northward and went down to the Arabah. ¹⁹The border continued to the side of Beth-hoglah northward; and the border ended at the north bay of the Salt Sea, at the south end of the Jordan. This *was* the south border. ²⁰Moreover, the Jordan was its border on the east side. This *was* the inheritance of the sons of Benjamin, according to their families *and* according to its borders all around.

²¹Now the cities of the tribe of the sons of Benjamin according to their families were Jericho and Beth-hoglah and Emek-keziz, ²²and Beth-arabah and Zemaraim and Bethel, ²³and

Avvim and Parah and Ophrah, 24 and Chephar-ammoni and Ophni and Geba; twelve cities with their villages. 25 Gibeon and Ramah and Beeroth, 26 and Mizpeh and Chephirah and Mozah, 27 and Rekem and Irpeel and Taralah, 28 and Zelah, Haeleph and the Jebusite (that is, Jerusalem), Gibeah, Kiriath; fourteen cities with their villages. This is the inheritance of the sons of Benjamin according to their families.

Psalm 45:6–17

⁶ Your throne, O God, is
    forever and ever;
  A scepter of uprightness is the
    scepter of Your kingdom.
⁷ You have loved righteousness
    and hated wickedness;
  Therefore God, Your God,
    has anointed You
  With the oil of joy above
    Your fellows.

45:6–7 Your throne, O God. Since this king-groom was likely a member of the Davidic dynasty (e.g., 2Sa 7), there was a near and immediate application (1Ch 28:5; 29:23). Through progressive revelation (i.e., Heb 1:8–9), we learn of the ultimate application to "a greater than Solomon" who is God—the Lord Jesus Christ.

⁸ All Your garments are *fragrant
    with* myrrh and aloes *and*
    cassia;
  Out of ivory palaces stringed
    instruments have made
    You glad.
⁹ Kings' daughters are among
    Your noble ladies;
  At Your right hand stands the
    queen in gold from Ophir.

¹⁰ Listen, O daughter, give attention
    and incline your ear:
  Forget your people and
    your father's house;
¹¹ Then the King will desire
    your beauty.
  Because He is your Lord,
    bow down to Him.
¹² The daughter of Tyre *will
    come* with a gift;
  The rich among the people
    will seek your favor.

¹³ The King's daughter is all
    glorious within;
  Her clothing is interwoven
    with gold.
¹⁴ She will be led to the King in
    embroidered work;
  The virgins, her companions
    who follow her,
  Will be brought to You.
¹⁵ They will be led forth with
    gladness and rejoicing;
  They will enter into the King's
    palace.

¹⁶ In place of your fathers
    will be your sons;
  You shall make them princes
    in all the earth.
¹⁷ I will cause Your name to be
    remembered in all
    generations;
  Therefore the peoples will give
    You thanks forever and ever.

Proverbs 14:6

⁶ A scoffer seeks wisdom
    and *finds* none,
  But knowledge is easy to one
    who has understanding.

Luke 12:1–32

12 Under these circumstances, after so many thousands of people had gathered together that they were stepping on one another, He began saying to His disciples first *of all,* "Beware of the leaven of the Pharisees, which is hypocrisy. ² But there is nothing covered up that will not be revealed, and hidden that will not be known. ³ Accordingly, whatever you have said in the dark will be heard in the light, and what you have whispered in the inner rooms will be proclaimed upon the housetops.

⁴ "I say to you, My friends, do not be afraid of those who kill the body and after that have no more that they can do. ⁵ But I will warn you whom to fear: fear the One who, after He has killed, has authority to cast into hell; yes, I tell you, fear Him! ⁶ Are not five sparrows sold for two cents? *Yet* not one of them is forgotten before God. ⁷ Indeed, the very hairs of your head are all numbered. Do not fear; you are more valuable than many sparrows.

⁸ "And I say to you, everyone who confesses Me before men, the Son of Man will confess him also before the angels of God; ⁹ but he who denies Me before men will be denied before the angels of God. ¹⁰ And everyone

12:11 do not worry. I.e., do not be anxious. This does not suggest that ministers and teachers should forego preparation in their normal spiritual duties. To cite this passage and others like it (21:12–15; Mt 10:19) to justify the neglect of study and meditation is to twist the meaning of Scripture. This verse is meant as a comfort for those under life-threatening persecution, not an excuse for laziness in ministry. The exact same expression is used in v. 22, speaking of concern for one's material necessities. In neither context was Jesus condemning legitimate toil and preparation. He was promising the Holy Spirit's aid for times of persecution when there can be no preparation.

who speaks a word against the Son of Man, it will be forgiven him; but he who blasphemes against the Holy Spirit, it will not be forgiven him. ¹¹When they bring you before the synagogues and the rulers and the authorities, do not worry about how or what you are to speak in your defense, or what you are to say; ¹²for the Holy Spirit will teach you in that very hour what you ought to say."

¹³Someone in the crowd said to Him, "Teacher, tell my brother to divide the *family* inheritance with me." ¹⁴But He said to him, "Man, who appointed Me a judge or arbitrator over you?" ¹⁵Then He said to them, "Beware, and be on your guard against every form of greed; for not *even* when one has an abundance does his life consist of his possessions." ¹⁶And He told them a parable, saying, "The land of a rich man was very productive. ¹⁷And he began reasoning to himself, saying, 'What shall I do, since I

have no place to store my crops?' ¹⁸Then he said, 'This is what I will do: I will tear down my barns and build larger ones, and there I will store all my grain and my goods. ¹⁹And I will say to my soul, "Soul, you have many goods laid up for many years *to come;* take your ease, eat, drink *and* be merry."' ²⁰But God said to him, 'You fool! This *very* night your soul is required of you; and *now* who will own what you have prepared?' ²¹So is the man who stores up treasure for himself, and is not rich toward God."

²²And He said to His disciples, "For this reason I say to you, do not worry about *your* life, *as to* what you will eat; nor for your body, *as to* what you will put on. ²³For life is more than food, and the body more than clothing. ²⁴Consider the ravens, for they neither sow nor reap; they have no storeroom nor barn, and *yet* God feeds them; how much more valuable you are than the birds! ²⁵And which of you by worrying can add a *single* hour to his life's span? ²⁶If then you cannot do even a very little thing, why do you worry about other matters? ²⁷Consider the lilies, how they grow: they neither toil nor spin; but I tell you, not even Solomon in all his glory clothed himself like one of these. ²⁸But if God so clothes the grass in the field, which is *alive* today and tomorrow is thrown into the furnace, how much more *will He clothe* you? You men of little faith! ²⁹And do not seek what you will eat and what you will drink, and do not keep worrying. ³⁰For all these things the nations of the world eagerly seek; but your Father knows that you need these things. ³¹But seek His kingdom, and these things will be added to you. ³²Do not be afraid, little flock, for your Father has chosen gladly to give you the kingdom.

DAY 14: What passages in Luke are unique to his Gospel?

Luke included 12 events or major passages not found in the other Gospels:

1. Events preceding the birth of John the Baptist and Jesus (1:5–80).
2. Scenes from Jesus' childhood (2:1–52).
3. Herod imprisons John the Baptist (3:19–20).
4. The people of Nazareth reject Jesus (4:16–30).
5. The first disciples are called (5:1–11).
6. A widow's son is raised (7:11–17).
7. A woman anoints Jesus' feet (7:36–50).
8. Certain women minister to Christ (8:1–3).
9. Events, teaching, and miracles during the months leading up to Christ's death (10:1—18:14).
10. Christ abides with Zacchaeus (19:1–27).
11. Herod tries Christ (23:6–12).
12. Some of Jesus' final words before His ascension (24:44–49).

APRIL 15

Joshua 19:1–20:9

19 Then the second lot fell to Simeon, to the tribe of the sons of Simeon according to their families, and their inheritance was in the midst of the inheritance of the sons of Judah. ²So they had as their inheritance Beersheba or Sheba and Moladah, ³and Hazar-shual and Balah and Ezem, ⁴and Eltolad and Bethul and Hormah, ⁵and Ziklag and Beth-marcaboth and Hazar-susah, ⁶and Bethlebaoth and Sharuhen; thirteen cities with their villages; ⁷Ain, Rimmon and Ether and Ashan; four cities with their villages; ⁸and all the villages which *were* around these cities as far as Baalath-beer, Ramah of the Negev. This *was* the inheritance of the tribe of the sons of Simeon according to their families. ⁹The inheritance of the sons of Simeon *was taken* from the portion of the sons of Judah, for the share of the sons of Judah was too large for them; so the sons of Simeon received *an* inheritance in the midst of Judah's inheritance.

¹⁰Now the third lot came up for the sons of Zebulun according to their families. And the territory of their inheritance was as far as Sarid. ¹¹Then their border went up to the west and to Maralah, it then touched Dabbesheth and reached to the brook that is before Jokneam. ¹²Then it turned from Sarid to the east toward the sunrise as far as the border of Chisloth-tabor, and it proceeded to Daberath and up to Japhia. ¹³From there it continued eastward toward the sunrise to Gath-hepher, to Eth-kazin, and it proceeded to Rimmon which stretches to Neah. ¹⁴The border circled around it on the north to Hannathon, and it ended at the valley of Iphtahel. ¹⁵*Included* also *were* Kattah and Nahalal and Shimron and Idalah and Bethlehem; twelve cities with their villages. ¹⁶This *was* the inheritance of the sons of Zebulun according to their families, these cities with their villages.

¹⁷The fourth lot fell to Issachar, to the sons of Issachar according to their families. ¹⁸Their territory was to Jezreel and *included* Chesulloth and Shunem, ¹⁹and Hapharaim and Shion and Anaharath, ²⁰and Rabbith and Kishion and Ebez, ²¹and Remeth and En-gannim and En-haddah and Beth-pazzez. ²²The border reached to Tabor and Shahazumah and Beth-shemesh, and their border ended at the Jordan; sixteen cities with their villages. ²³This *was* the inheritance of the tribe of the sons of Issachar according to their families, the cities with their villages.

²⁴Now the fifth lot fell to the tribe of the sons of Asher according to their families. ²⁵Their territory was Helkath and Hali and Beten and Achshaph, ²⁶and Allammelech and Amad and Mishal; and it reached to Carmel on the west and to Shihor-libnath. ²⁷It turned toward the east to Beth-dagon and reached to Zebulun, and to the valley of Iphtahel northward to Beth-emek and Neiel; then it proceeded on north to Cabul, ²⁸and Ebron and Rehob and Hammon and Kanah, as far as Great Sidon. ²⁹The border turned to Ramah and to the fortified city of Tyre; then the border turned to Hosah, and it ended at the sea by the region of Achzib. ³⁰*Included* also *were* Ummah, and Aphek and Rehob; twenty-two cities with their villages. ³¹This *was* the inheritance of the tribe of the sons of Asher according to their families, these cities with their villages.

³²The sixth lot fell to the sons of Naphtali; to the sons of Naphtali according to their families. ³³Their border was from Heleph, from the oak in Zaanannim and Adami-nekeb and Jabneel, as far as Lakkum, and it ended at the Jordan. ³⁴Then the border turned westward to Aznoth-tabor and proceeded from there to Hukkok; and it reached to Zebulun on the south and touched Asher on the west, and to Judah at the Jordan toward the east. ³⁵The fortified cities *were* Ziddim, Zer and Hammath, Rakkath and Chinnereth, ³⁶and Adamah and Ramah and Hazor, ³⁷and Kedesh and Edrei and En-hazor, ³⁸and Yiron and Migdal-el, Horem and Beth-anath and Beth-shemesh; nineteen cities with their villages. ³⁹This *was* the inheritance of the tribe of the sons of Naphtali according to their families, the cities with their villages.

⁴⁰The seventh lot fell to the tribe of the sons of Dan according to their families. ⁴¹The territory of their inheritance was Zorah and Eshtaol and Ir-shemesh, ⁴²and Shaalabbin and Aijalon and Ithlah, ⁴³and Elon and Timnah and Ekron, ⁴⁴and Eltekeh and Gibbethon and Baalath, ⁴⁵and Jehud and Bene-berak and Gath-rimmon, ⁴⁶and Me-jarkon and Rakkon, with the territory over against Joppa. ⁴⁷The territory of the sons of Dan proceeded beyond them; for the sons of Dan went up and fought with Leshem and captured it. Then they struck it with the edge of the sword and possessed it and settled in it; and they called Leshem Dan after the name of Dan their father. ⁴⁸This *was* the inheritance of the tribe of the sons of Dan according to their families, these cities with their villages.

⁴⁹When they finished apportioning the

land for inheritance by its borders, the sons of Israel gave an inheritance in their midst to Joshua the son of Nun. ⁵⁰ In accordance with the command of the LORD they gave him the city for which he asked, Timnath-serah in the hill country of Ephraim. So he built the city and settled in it.

⁵¹ These are the inheritances which Eleazar the priest, and Joshua the son of Nun, and the heads of the households of the tribes of the sons of Israel distributed by lot in Shiloh before the LORD at the doorway of the tent of meeting. So they finished dividing the land.

20 Then the LORD spoke to Joshua, saying, ² "Speak to the sons of Israel, saying, 'Designate the cities of refuge, of which I spoke to you through Moses, ³ that the manslayer who kills any person unintentionally, without premeditation, may flee there, and they shall become your refuge from the avenger of blood. ⁴ He shall flee to one of these cities, and shall stand at the entrance of the gate of the city and state his case in the hearing of the elders of that city; and they shall take him into the city to them and give him a place, so that he may dwell among them. ⁵ Now if the avenger of blood pursues him, then they shall not deliver the manslayer into his hand, because he struck his neighbor without premeditation and did not hate him beforehand. ⁶ He shall dwell in that city until he stands before the congregation for judgment, until the death of the one who is high priest in those days. Then the manslayer shall return to his own city and to his own house, to the city from which he fled.' "

⁷ So they set apart Kedesh in Galilee in the hill country of Naphtali and Shechem in the hill country of Ephraim, and Kiriath-arba (that is, Hebron) in the hill country of Judah.

⁸ Beyond the Jordan east of Jericho, they designated Bezer in the wilderness on the plain from the tribe of Reuben, and Ramoth in Gilead from the tribe of Gad, and Golan in Bashan from the tribe of Manasseh. ⁹ These were the appointed cities for all the sons of Israel and for the stranger who sojourns among them, that whoever kills any person unintentionally may flee there, and not die by the hand of the avenger of blood until he stands before the congregation.

Psalm 46:1–6

For the choir director. *A Psalm* of the sons of Korah, set to Alamoth. A Song.

G od is our refuge and strength,
A very present help in trouble.
² Therefore we will not fear, though
the earth should change
And though the mountains slip
into the heart of the sea;
³ Though its waters roar *and*
foam,
Though the mountains quake
at its swelling pride. *Selah*

⁴ There is a river whose streams
make glad the city of God,
The holy dwelling places
of the Most High.
⁵ God is in the midst of her, she
will not be moved;
God will help her when
morning dawns.
⁶ The nations made an uproar,
the kingdoms tottered;
He raised His voice, the earth
melted.

Proverbs 14:7–11

⁷ Leave the presence of a fool,
Or you will not discern
words of knowledge.
⁸ The wisdom of the sensible is
to understand his way,
But the foolishness of fools
is deceit.
⁹ Fools mock at sin,
But among the upright
there is good will.

20:2–9 cities of refuge. Moses had spoken God's Word to name 6 cities in Israel as refuge centers. A person who inadvertently killed another could flee to the nearest of these for protection (Nu 35:9–34). Three lay west of the Jordan, and 3 lay to the east, each reachable in a day for those in its area. The slayer could flee there to escape pursuit by a family member seeking to exact private justice. Authorities at the refuge protected him and escorted him to a trial. If found innocent, he was guarded at the refuge until the death of the current High Priest, a kind of statute of limitations (Jos 20:6). He could then return home. If found guilty of murder, he suffered due punishment.

14:10 At its depth, suffering and rejoicing are personal and private. No one is able to communicate them fully (1Sa 1:10; 1Ki 8:38; Mt 2:18; 26:39–42, 75).

10 The heart knows its own bitterness,
    And a stranger does not share
        its joy.
11 The house of the wicked
        will be destroyed,
    But the tent of the upright
        will flourish.

Luke 12:33–59

33 "Sell your possessions and give to charity; make yourselves money belts which do not wear out, an unfailing treasure in heaven, where no thief comes near nor moth destroys. 34 For where your treasure is, there your heart will be also.

35 "Be dressed in readiness, and *keep* your lamps lit. 36 Be like men who are waiting for their master when he returns from the wedding feast, so that they may immediately open *the door* to him when he comes and knocks. 37 Blessed are those slaves whom the master will find on the alert when he comes; truly I say to you, that he will gird himself *to serve,* and have them recline *at the table,* and will come up and wait on them. 38 Whether he comes in the second watch, or even in the third, and finds *them* so, blessed are those *slaves.*

39 "But be sure of this, that if the head of the house had known at what hour the thief was coming, he would not have allowed his house to be broken into. 40 You too, be ready; for the Son of Man is coming at an hour that you do not expect."

12:33 Sell your possessions and give to charity. Those who amassed earthly possessions, falsely thinking their security lay in material resources (vv. 16–20), needed to lay up treasure in heaven instead. Believers in the early church did sell their goods to meet the basic needs of poorer brethren (Ac 2:44–45; 4:32–37). But this commandment is not to be twisted into an absolute prohibition of all earthly possessions. In fact, Peter's words to Ananias in Acts 5:4 make it clear that the selling of one's possessions was optional. **money belts which do not wear out.** These belts that do not wear out (so as to lose the money) are defined as "treasure in the heavens that does not fail." The surest place to put one's money is in such a belt—in heaven, where it is safe from thieves and decay as well.

12:34 your heart will be also. Where one puts his money reveals the priorities of his heart. See 16:1–13; Matthew 6:21.

41 Peter said, "Lord, are You addressing this parable to us, or to everyone *else* as well?" 42 And the Lord said, "Who then is the faithful and sensible steward, whom his master will put in charge of his servants, to give them their rations at the proper time? 43 Blessed is that slave whom his master finds so doing when he comes. 44 Truly I say to you that he will put him in charge of all his possessions. 45 But if that slave says in his heart, 'My master will be a long time in coming,' and begins to beat the slaves, *both* men and women, and to eat and drink and get drunk; 46 the master of that slave will come on a day when he does not expect *him* and at an hour he does not know, and will cut him in pieces, and assign him a place with the unbelievers. 47 And that slave who knew his master's will and did not get ready or act in accord with his will, will receive many lashes, 48 but the one who did not know *it,* and committed deeds worthy of a flogging, will receive but few. From everyone who has been given much, much will be required; and to whom they entrusted much, of him they will ask all the more.

49 "I have come to cast fire upon the earth; and how I wish it were already kindled! 50 But I have a baptism to undergo, and how distressed I am until it is accomplished! 51 Do you suppose that I came to grant peace on earth? I tell you, no, but rather division; 52 for from now on five *members* in one household will be divided, three against two and two against three. 53 They will be divided, father against son and son against father, mother against daughter and daughter against mother, mother-in-law against daughter-in-law and daughter-in-law against mother-in-law."

54 And He was also saying to the crowds, "When you see a cloud rising in the west, immediately you say, 'A shower is coming,' and so it turns out. 55 And when *you see* a south wind blowing, you say, 'It will be a hot day,' and it turns out *that way.* 56 You hypocrites! You know how to analyze the appearance of the earth and the sky, but why do you not analyze this present time?

57 "And why do you not even on your own initiative judge what is right? 58 For while you are going with your opponent to appear before the magistrate, on *your* way *there* make an effort to settle with him, so that he may not drag you before the judge, and the judge turn you over to the officer, and the officer throw you into prison. 59 I say to you, you will not get out of there until you have paid the very last cent."

Psalm 46 was the scriptural catalyst for Martin Luther's great hymn "A Mighty Fortress Is Our God." This psalm extols the adequacy of God in facing threats from nature and the nations. God indeed protects (see vv. 1, 7, 11) His people upon the earth (see vv. 2, 6, 8–10). The major burden of Psalm 46 is that God provides stability for His people who live in two exceedingly unstable environments.

Specifically, "Though the earth should change" (v. 2); i.e., When earth changes and when mountains move or shake or totter or slip (see the language of Is. 24:19–20; 54:10; Hag 2:6). These are poetic allusions to earthquakes. Since "the earth" and "mountains" are regarded by men as symbols of stability, when they "dance," great terror normally ensues. But when the most stable becomes unstable, there should be "no fear" because of the transcendent stability of God. And "though its waters roar" (v. 3). This is an illustration of powerfully surging and potentially destructive floods of waters. These will not erode God's protective fortifications.

"There is a river whose streams make glad the city of God" (v. 4). Refreshing waters contrast with those threatening torrents of v. 3. See the garden of paradise concept often mentioned in ancient Near Eastern literature, but most importantly, see the biblical revelation, noting especially the "bookends" of Genesis 2:10 and Revelation 22:1–2. "She will not be moved" (vv. 5–6). These verses pick up some of the key terms about moving, slipping, tottering, sliding, and roaring from vv. 1–3. However, here, because of the presence of God, the forces of nature and the nations are no longer a threat to the people of God who dwell with Him.

APRIL 16

Joshua 21:1–22:34

21 Then the heads of households of the Levites approached Eleazar the priest, and Joshua the son of Nun, and the heads of households of the tribes of the sons of Israel. ²They spoke to them at Shiloh in the land of Canaan, saying, "The LORD commanded through Moses to give us cities to live in, with their pasture lands for our cattle." ³So the sons of Israel gave the Levites from their inheritance these cities with their pasture lands, according to the command of the LORD. ⁴Then the lot came out for the families of the Kohathites. And the sons of Aaron the priest, who were of the Levites, received thirteen cities by lot from the tribe of Judah and from the tribe of the Simeonites and from the tribe of Benjamin.

⁵The rest of the sons of Kohath received ten cities by lot from the families of the tribe of Ephraim and from the tribe of Dan and from the half-tribe of Manasseh.

⁶The sons of Gershon received thirteen cities by lot from the families of the tribe of Issachar and from the tribe of Asher and from the tribe of Naphtali and from the half-tribe of Manasseh in Bashan.

⁷The sons of Merari according to their families received twelve cities from the tribe of Reuben and from the tribe of Gad and from the tribe of Zebulun.

⁸Now the sons of Israel gave by lot to the Levites these cities with their pasture lands, as the LORD had commanded through Moses.

⁹They gave these cities which are *here* mentioned by name from the tribe of the sons of Judah and from the tribe of the sons of Simeon; ¹⁰and they were for the sons of Aaron, one of the families of the Kohathites, of the sons of Levi, for the lot was theirs first. ¹¹Thus they gave them Kiriath-arba, *Arba being* the father of Anak (that is, Hebron), in the hill country of Judah, with its surrounding pasture lands. ¹²But the fields of the city and its villages they gave to Caleb the son of Jephunneh as his possession.

¹³So to the sons of Aaron the priest they gave Hebron, the city of refuge for the manslayer, with its pasture lands, and Libnah with its pasture lands, ¹⁴and Jattir with its pasture lands and Eshtemoa with its pasture lands, ¹⁵and Holon with its pasture lands and Debir with its pasture lands, ¹⁶and Ain with its pasture lands and Juttah with its pasture lands and Beth-shemesh with its pasture lands; nine cities from these two tribes. ¹⁷From the tribe of Benjamin, Gibeon with its pasture lands, Geba with its pasture lands, ¹⁸Anathoth with its pasture lands and Almon with its pasture lands; four cities. ¹⁹All the cities of the sons of Aaron, the priests, were thirteen cities with their pasture lands.

²⁰Then the cities from the tribe of Ephraim were allotted to the families of the sons of Kohath, the Levites, *even to* the rest of the sons of Kohath. ²¹They gave them Shechem, the city of refuge for the manslayer, with its pasture lands, in the hill country of Ephraim, and Gezer with its pasture lands, ²²and Kibzaim with its pasture lands and Beth-horon

with its pasture lands; four cities. ²³ From the tribe of Dan, Elteke with its pasture lands, Gibbethon with its pasture lands, ²⁴ Aijalon with its pasture lands, Gath-rimmon with its pasture lands; four cities. ²⁵ From the half-tribe of Manasseh, *they allotted* Taanach with its pasture lands and Gath-rimmon with its pasture lands; two cities. ²⁶ All the cities with their pasture lands for the families of the rest of the sons of Kohath were ten.

²⁷ To the sons of Gershon, one of the families of the Levites, from the half-tribe of Manasseh, *they gave* Golan in Bashan, the city of refuge for the manslayer, with its pasture lands, and Be-eshterah with its pasture lands; two cities. ²⁸ From the tribe of Issachar, *they gave* Kishion with its pasture lands, Daberath with its pasture lands, ²⁹ Jarmuth with its pasture lands, En-gannim with its pasture lands; four cities. ³⁰ From the tribe of Asher, *they gave* Mishal with its pasture lands, Abdon with its pasture lands, ³¹ Helkath with its pasture lands and Rehob with its pasture lands; four cities. ³² From the tribe of Naphtali, *they gave* Kedesh in Galilee, the city of refuge for the manslayer, with its pasture lands and Hammoth-dor with its pasture lands and Kartan with its pasture lands; three cities. ³³ All the cities of the Gershonites according to their families were thirteen cities with their pasture lands.

³⁴ To the families of the sons of Merari, the rest of the Levites, *they gave* from the tribe of Zebulun, Jokneam with its pasture lands and Kartah with its pasture lands. ³⁵ Dimnah with its pasture lands, Nahalal with its pasture lands; four cities. ³⁶ From the tribe of Reuben, *they gave* Bezer with its pasture lands and Jahaz with its pasture lands, ³⁷ Kedemoth with its pasture lands and Mephaath with its pasture lands; four cities. ³⁸ From the tribe of Gad, *they gave* Ramoth in Gilead, the city of refuge for the manslayer, with its pasture lands and Mahanaim with its pasture lands, ³⁹ Heshbon with its pasture lands, Jazer with its pasture lands; four cities in all. ⁴⁰ All *these were* the cities of the sons of Merari according to their families, the rest of the families of the Levites; and their lot was twelve cities.

⁴¹ All the cities of the Levites in the midst of the possession of the sons of Israel were forty-eight cities with their pasture lands. ⁴² These cities each had its surrounding pasture lands; thus *it was* with all these cities.

⁴³ So the LORD gave Israel all the land which He had sworn to give to their fathers, and they possessed it and lived in it. ⁴⁴ And the LORD gave them rest on every side, accord-

---

21:43–45 So the LORD gave Israel all the land. This sums up God's fulfillment of His covenant promise to give Abraham's people the land (Ge 12:7; Jos 1:2, 5–9). God also kept His Word in giving the people rest (Dt 12:9–10). In a valid sense, the Canaanites were in check, under military conquest as God had pledged (Jos 1:5), not posing an immediate threat. Not every enemy had been driven out, however, leaving some to stir up trouble later. But God's people failed to exercise their responsibility and possess their land to the full degree in various areas.

---

ing to all that He had sworn to their fathers, and no one of all their enemies stood before them; the LORD gave all their enemies into their hand. ⁴⁵ Not one of the good promises which the LORD had made to the house of Israel failed; all came to pass.

22 Then Joshua summoned the Reubenites and the Gadites and the half-tribe of Manasseh, ² and said to them, "You have kept all that Moses the servant of the LORD commanded you, and have listened to my voice in all that I commanded you. ³ You have not forsaken your brothers these many days to this day, but have kept the charge of the commandment of the LORD your God. ⁴ And now the LORD your God has given rest to your brothers, as He spoke to them; therefore turn now and go to your tents, to the land of your possession, which Moses the servant of the LORD gave you beyond the Jordan. ⁵ Only be very careful to observe the commandment and the law which Moses the servant of the LORD commanded you, to love the LORD your God and walk in all His ways and keep His commandments and hold fast to Him and serve Him with all your heart and with all your soul." ⁶ So Joshua blessed them and sent them away, and they went to their tents.

⁷ Now to the one half-tribe of Manasseh Moses had given *a possession* in Bashan, but to the other half Joshua gave *a possession* among their brothers westward beyond the Jordan. So when Joshua sent them away to their tents, he blessed them, ⁸ and said to them, "Return to your tents with great riches and with very much livestock, with silver, gold, bronze, iron, and with very many clothes; divide the spoil of your enemies with your brothers." ⁹ The sons of Reuben and the sons of Gad and the half-tribe of Manasseh returned *home* and departed from the sons of Israel at Shiloh which is in the land of Canaan, to go to the land of Gilead, to the land

of their possession which they had possessed, according to the command of the LORD through Moses.

[10] When they came to the region of the Jordan which is in the land of Canaan, the sons of Reuben and the sons of Gad and the half-tribe of Manasseh built an altar there by the Jordan, a large altar in appearance. [11] And the sons of Israel heard *it* said, "Behold, the sons of Reuben and the sons of Gad and the half-tribe of Manasseh have built an altar at the frontier of the land of Canaan, in the region of the Jordan, on the side *belonging to* the sons of Israel." [12] When the sons of Israel heard *of it,* the whole congregation of the sons of Israel gathered themselves at Shiloh to go up against them in war.

[13] Then the sons of Israel sent to the sons of Reuben and to the sons of Gad and to the half-tribe of Manasseh, into the land of Gilead, Phinehas the son of Eleazar the priest, [14] and with him ten chiefs, one chief for each father's household from each of the tribes of Israel; and each one of them *was* the head of his father's household among the thousands of Israel. [15] They came to the sons of Reuben and to the sons of Gad and to the half-tribe of Manasseh, to the land of Gilead, and they spoke with them saying, [16] "Thus says the whole congregation of the LORD, 'What is this unfaithful act which you have committed against the God of Israel, turning away from following the LORD this day, by building yourselves an altar, to rebel against the LORD this day? [17] Is not the iniquity of Peor enough for us, from which we have not cleansed ourselves to this day, although a plague came on the congregation of the LORD, [18] that you must turn away this day from following the LORD? If you rebel against the LORD today, He will be angry with the whole congregation of Israel tomorrow. [19] If, however, the land of your possession is unclean, then cross into the land of the possession of the LORD, where the LORD'S tabernacle stands, and take possession among us. Only do not rebel against the LORD, or rebel against us by building an altar for yourselves, besides the altar of the LORD our God. [20] Did not Achan the son of Zerah act unfaithfully in the things under the ban, and wrath fall on all the congregation of Israel? And that man did not perish alone in his iniquity.'"

[21] Then the sons of Reuben and the sons of Gad and the half-tribe of Manasseh answered and spoke to the heads of the families of Israel. [22] "The Mighty One, God, the LORD, the Mighty One, God, the LORD! He knows, and

may Israel itself know. If *it was* in rebellion, or if in an unfaithful act against the LORD do not save us this day! [23] If we have built us an altar to turn away from following the LORD, or if to offer a burnt offering or grain offering on it, or if to offer sacrifices of peace offerings on it, may the LORD Himself require it. [24] But truly we have done this out of concern, for a reason, saying, 'In time to come your sons may say to our sons, "What have you to do with the LORD, the God of Israel? [25] For the LORD has made the Jordan a border between us and you, *you* sons of Reuben and sons of Gad; you have no portion in the LORD." So your sons may make our sons stop fearing the LORD.'

[26] "Therefore we said, 'Let us build an altar, not for burnt offering or for sacrifice; [27] rather it shall be a witness between us and you and between our generations after us, that we are to perform the service of the LORD before Him with our burnt offerings, and with our sacrifices and with our peace offerings, so that your sons will not say to our sons in time to come, "You have no portion in the LORD."' [28] Therefore we said, 'It shall also come about if they say *this* to us or to our generations in time to come, then we shall say, "See the copy of the altar of the LORD which our fathers made, not for burnt offering or for sacrifice; rather it is a witness between us and you."' [29] Far be it from us that we should rebel against the LORD and turn away from following the LORD this day, by building an altar for burnt offering, for grain offering or for sacrifice, besides the altar of the LORD our God which is before His tabernacle."

[30] So when Phinehas the priest and the leaders of the congregation, even the heads of the families of Israel who *were* with him, heard the words which the sons of Reuben and the sons of Gad and the sons of Manasseh spoke, it pleased them. [31] And Phinehas the son of Eleazar the priest said to the sons of Reuben and to the sons of Gad and to the sons of Manasseh, "Today we know that the LORD is in our midst, because you have not committed this unfaithful act against the LORD; now you have delivered the sons of Israel from the hand of the LORD."

[32] Then Phinehas the son of Eleazar the priest and the leaders returned from the sons of Reuben and from the sons of Gad, from the land of Gilead to the land of Canaan, to the sons of Israel, and brought back word to them. [33] The word pleased the sons of Israel, and the sons of Israel blessed God; and they did not speak of going up against them in

war to destroy the land in which the sons of Reuben and the sons of Gad were living. ³⁴The sons of Reuben and the sons of Gad called the altar *Witness;* "For," *they said,* "it is a witness between us that the LORD is God."

Psalm 46:7–11

7 The LORD of hosts is with us;
  The God of Jacob is our
    stronghold. *Selah*

8 Come, behold the works of the LORD,
  Who has wrought desolations
    in the earth.
9 He makes wars to cease to
    the end of the earth;
  He breaks the bow and cuts
    the spear in two;
  He burns the chariots with fire.
10 "Cease *striving* and know
    that I am God;
  I will be exalted among the nations,
  I will be exalted in the earth."
11 The LORD of hosts is with us;
  The God of Jacob is our
    stronghold. *Selah*

46:7 The LORD of hosts is with us. The precious personal presence (see "God with us" in Is 7:14; 8:8, 10) of the Divine Warrior (see "LORD of hosts" or "armies," e.g., Pss 24:10; 48:8; 59:5) secures the safety of His people.

46:10 Cease *striving* and know that I am God. These twin commands to not panic and to recognize His sovereignty are probably directed to both His nation for comfort and all other nations for warning.

Proverbs 14:12–13

12 There is a way *which seems*
    right to a man,
  But its end is the way of death.
13 Even in laughter the heart
    may be in pain,
  And the end of joy may be grief.

Luke 13:1–21

13 Now on the same occasion there were some present who reported to Him about the Galileans whose blood Pilate had mixed with their sacrifices. ²And Jesus said to them, "Do you suppose that these Galileans were *greater* sinners than all *other* Galileans because they suffered this *fate?* ³I tell you, no,

but unless you repent, you will all likewise perish. ⁴Or do you suppose that those eighteen on whom the tower in Siloam fell and killed them were *worse* culprits than all the men who live in Jerusalem? ⁵I tell you, no, but unless you repent, you will all likewise perish."

⁶And He *began* telling this parable: "A man had a fig tree which had been planted in his vineyard; and he came looking for fruit on it and did not find any. ⁷And he said to the vineyard-keeper, 'Behold, for three years I have come looking for fruit on this fig tree without finding any. Cut it down! Why does it even use up the ground?' ⁸And he answered and said to him, 'Let it alone, sir, for this year too, until I dig around it and put in fertilizer; ⁹and if it bears fruit next year, *fine;* but if not, cut it down.' "

¹⁰And He was teaching in one of the synagogues on the Sabbath. ¹¹And there was a woman who for eighteen years had had a sickness caused by a spirit; and she was bent double, and could not straighten up at all. ¹²When Jesus saw her, He called her over and said to her, "Woman, you are freed from your sickness." ¹³And He laid His hands on her; and immediately she was made erect again and *began* glorifying God. ¹⁴But the synagogue official, indignant because Jesus had healed on the Sabbath, *began* saying to the crowd in response, "There are six days in which work should be done; so come during them and get healed, and not on the Sabbath day." ¹⁵But the Lord answered him and said, "You hypocrites, does not each of you on the Sabbath untie his ox or his donkey from the stall and lead him away to water *him?* ¹⁶And this woman, a daughter of Abraham as she is, whom Satan has bound for eighteen long years, should she not have been released from

13:11 had a sickness caused by a spirit. This suggests that her physical ailment, which left her unable to stand erect, was caused by an evil spirit. However, Christ did not have to confront and drive out a demon, but simply declared her loosed (v. 12), so her case appears somewhat different from other cases of demonic possession He often encountered.

13:12 He called her over. The healing was unsolicited; He took the initiative (7:12–14). Furthermore, no special faith was required on her part or anyone else's. Jesus sometimes called for faith, but not always (8:48; Mk 5:34).

this bond on the Sabbath day?" ¹⁷As He said this, all His opponents were being humiliated; and the entire crowd was rejoicing over all the glorious things being done by Him.

¹⁸So He was saying, "What is the kingdom of God like, and to what shall I compare it? ¹⁹It is like a mustard seed, which a man took and threw into his own garden; and it grew and became a tree, and THE BIRDS OF THE AIR NESTED IN ITS BRANCHES."

²⁰And again He said, "To what shall I compare the kingdom of God? ²¹It is like leaven, which a woman took and hid in three pecks of flour until it was all leavened."

DAY 16: Are catastrophes a sign of God's judgment?

Upon hearing about an incident where Galileans were sought out and killed in the temple by Roman authorities while in the process of offering a sacrifice, perhaps because they were seditious zealots, Jesus asked His listeners, "Do you suppose that these Galileans were greater sinners…because they suffered this fate?" (Lk 13:2). It was the belief of many that disaster and sudden death always signified divine displeasure over particular sins (see Job 4:7). Those who suffered in uncommon ways were therefore assumed to be guilty of some more severe immorality (see Jn 9:2).

Jesus did not deny the connection between catastrophe and human evil, for all such afflictions ultimately stem from the curse of humanity's fallenness (Ge 3:17–19). Furthermore, specific calamities may indeed be the fruit of certain iniquities (Pr 24:16). But Christ challenged the people's notion that they were morally superior to those who suffered in such catastrophes. He called all to repent (v. 3), for all were in danger of sudden destruction. No one is guaranteed time to prepare for death, so now is the time for repentance for all (see 2Co 6:2).

Jesus also mentions another disaster in Siloam, where evidently one of the towers guarding an aqueduct collapsed, perhaps while under construction, killing some people (v. 4). Again, the question in the minds of people was regarding the connection between calamity and iniquity ("greater sinners"). Jesus responded by saying that such a calamity was not God's way to single out an especially evil group for death, but a means of warning to all sinners.

APRIL 17

Joshua 23:1–24:33

23 Now it came about after many days, when the LORD had given rest to Israel from all their enemies on every side, and Joshua was old, advanced in years, ²that Joshua called for all Israel, for their elders and their heads and their judges and their officers, and said to them, "I am old, advanced in years. ³And you have seen all that the LORD your God has done to all these nations because of you, for the LORD your God is He who has been fighting for you. ⁴See, I have apportioned to you these nations which remain as an inheritance for your tribes, with all the nations which I have cut off, from the Jordan even to the Great Sea toward the setting of the sun. ⁵The LORD your God, He will thrust them out from before you and drive them out from before you; and you will possess their land, just as the LORD your God promised you. ⁶Be very firm, then, to keep and do all that is written in the book of the law of Moses, so that you may not turn aside from it to the right hand or to the left, ⁷so that you will not associate with these nations, these which remain among you, or mention the name of their gods, or make anyone swear by them, or serve them, or bow down to them. ⁸But you are to cling to the LORD your God, as you have done to this day. ⁹For the LORD has driven out great and strong nations from before you; and as for you, no man has stood before you to this day. ¹⁰One of your men puts to flight a thousand, for the LORD your God is He who fights for you, just as He promised you. ¹¹So take diligent heed to yourselves to love the LORD your God. ¹²For if you ever go back and cling to the rest of these nations, these which remain among you, and intermarry with them, so that you associate with them and they with you, ¹³know with certainty that the LORD your God will not continue to drive these nations out from before you; but they will be a snare and a trap to you, and a whip on your sides and thorns in your eyes, until you perish from off this good land which the LORD your God has given you.

¹⁴"Now behold, today I am going the way of all the earth, and you know in all your hearts and in all your souls that not one word of all the good words which the LORD your God spoke concerning you has failed; all have been fulfilled for you, not one of them has failed. ¹⁵It shall come about that just as all the good words which the LORD your God spoke

to you have come upon you, so the LORD will bring upon you all the threats, until He has destroyed you from off this good land which the LORD your God has given you. [16] When you transgress the covenant of the LORD your God, which He commanded you, and go and serve other gods and bow down to them, then the anger of the LORD will burn against you, and you will perish quickly from off the good land which He has given you."

24 Then Joshua gathered all the tribes of Israel to Shechem, and called for the elders of Israel and for their heads and their judges and their officers; and they presented themselves before God. [2] Joshua said to all the people, "Thus says the LORD, the God of Israel, 'From ancient times your fathers lived beyond the River, *namely,* Terah, the father of Abraham and the father of Nahor, and they served other gods. [3] Then I took your father Abraham from beyond the River, and led him through all the land of Canaan, and multiplied his descendants and gave him Isaac. [4] To Isaac I gave Jacob and Esau, and to Esau I gave Mount Seir to possess it; but Jacob and his sons went down to Egypt. [5] Then I sent Moses and Aaron, and I plagued Egypt by what I did in its midst; and afterward I brought you out. [6] I brought your fathers out of Egypt, and you came to the sea; and Egypt pursued your fathers with chariots and horsemen to the Red Sea. [7] But when they cried out to the LORD, He put darkness between you and the Egyptians, and brought the sea upon them and covered them; and your own eyes saw what I did in Egypt. And you lived in the wilderness for a long time. [8] Then I brought you into the land of the Amorites who lived beyond the Jordan, and they fought with you; and I gave them into your hand, and you took possession of their land when I destroyed them before you. [9] Then Balak the son of Zippor, king of Moab, arose and fought against Israel, and he sent and summoned Balaam the son of Beor to curse you. [10] But I was not willing to listen to Balaam. So he had to bless you, and I delivered you from his hand. [11] You crossed the Jordan and came to Jericho; and the citizens of Jericho fought against you, *and* the Amorite and the Perizzite and the Canaanite and the Hittite and the Girgashite, the Hivite and the Jebusite. Thus I gave them into your hand. [12] Then I sent the hornet before you and it drove out the two kings of the Amorites from before you, *but* not by your sword or your bow. [13] I gave you a land on which you had not labored, and cities which you had not built, and you have lived in them; you are

eating of vineyards and olive groves which you did not plant.'

[14] "Now, therefore, fear the LORD and serve Him in sincerity and truth; and put away the gods which your fathers served beyond the River and in Egypt, and serve the LORD. [15] If it is disagreeable in your sight to serve the LORD, choose for yourselves today whom you will serve: whether the gods which your fathers served which were beyond the River, or the gods of the Amorites in whose land you are living; but as for me and my house, we will serve the LORD."

24:15 choose...today whom you will serve. Joshua's fatherly model (reminiscent of Abraham's, Ge 18:19) was for himself and his family to serve the Lord, not false gods. He called others in Israel to this, and they committed themselves to serve the Lord also (vv. 21, 24).

---

[16] The people answered and said, "Far be it from us that we should forsake the LORD to serve other gods; [17] for the LORD our God is He who brought us and our fathers up out of the land of Egypt, from the house of bondage, and who did these great signs in our sight and preserved us through all the way in which we went and among all the peoples through whose midst we passed. [18] The LORD drove out from before us all the peoples, even the Amorites who lived in the land. We also will serve the LORD, for He is our God."

[19] Then Joshua said to the people, "You will not be able to serve the LORD, for He is a holy God. He is a jealous God; He will not forgive your transgression or your sins. [20] If you forsake the LORD and serve foreign gods, then He will turn and do you harm and consume you after He has done good to you." [21] The people said to Joshua, "No, but we will serve the LORD." [22] Joshua said to the people, "You are witnesses against yourselves that you have chosen for yourselves the LORD, to serve Him." And they said, "We are witnesses." [23] "Now therefore, put away the foreign gods which are in your midst, and incline your hearts to the LORD, the God of Israel." [24] The people said to Joshua, "We will serve the LORD our God and we will obey His voice." [25] So Joshua made a covenant with the people that day, and made for them a statute and an ordinance in Shechem. [26] And Joshua wrote these words in the book of the law of God; and he took a large stone and

set it up there under the oak that was by the sanctuary of the LORD. ²⁷ Joshua said to all the people, "Behold, this stone shall be for a witness against us, for it has heard all the words of the LORD which He spoke to us; thus it shall be for a witness against you, so that you do not deny your God." ²⁸ Then Joshua dismissed the people, each to his inheritance.

²⁹ It came about after these things that Joshua the son of Nun, the servant of the LORD, died, being one hundred and ten years old. ³⁰ And they buried him in the territory of his inheritance in Timnath-serah, which is in the hill country of Ephraim, on the north of Mount Gaash.

³¹ Israel served the LORD all the days of Joshua and all the days of the elders who survived Joshua, and had known all the deeds of the LORD which He had done for Israel.

³² Now they buried the bones of Joseph, which the sons of Israel brought up from Egypt, at Shechem, in the piece of ground which Jacob had bought from the sons of Hamor the father of Shechem for one hundred pieces of money; and they became the inheritance of Joseph's sons. ³³ And Eleazar the son of Aaron died; and they buried him at Gibeah of Phinehas his son, which was given him in the hill country of Ephraim.

Psalm 47:1–9

For the choir director. A Psalm of the sons of Korah.

O clap your hands, all peoples; Shout to God with the voice of joy.
2 For the LORD Most High is to be feared, A great King over all the earth.
3 He subdues peoples under us And nations under our feet.
4 He chooses our inheritance for us, The glory of Jacob whom He loves. *Selah*
5 God has ascended with a shout, The LORD, with the sound of a trumpet.
6 Sing praises to God, sing praises; Sing praises to our King, sing praises.
7 For God is the King of all the earth; Sing praises with a skillful psalm.
8 God reigns over the nations, God sits on His holy throne.

9 The princes of the people have assembled themselves *as* the people of the God of Abraham, For the shields of the earth belong to God; He is highly exalted.

Proverbs 14:14

14 The backslider in heart will have his fill of his own ways, But a good man will *be* satisfied with his.

Luke 13:22–35

²² And He was passing through from one city and village to another, teaching, and proceeding on His way to Jerusalem. ²³ And someone said to Him, "Lord, are there *just* a few who are being saved?" And He said to them, ²⁴ "Strive to enter through the narrow door; for many, I tell you, will seek to enter and will not be able. ²⁵ Once the head of the house gets up and shuts the door, and you begin to stand outside and knock on the door, saying, 'Lord, open up to us!' then He will answer and say to you, 'I do not know where you are from.' ²⁶ Then you will begin to say, 'We ate and drank in Your presence, and You taught in our streets'; ²⁷ and

14:14 backslider in heart. This term, so often used by the prophets (Is 57:17; Jer 3:6, 8, 11–12, 14, 22; 8:5; 31:22; 49:4; Hos 11:7; 14:4), is here used in such a way as to clarify who is a backslider. He belongs in the category of the fool, the wicked, and the disobedient, and he is contrasted with the godly wise. It is a word that the prophets used of apostate unbelievers.

13:23 are there *just* a few who are being saved? That question may have been prompted by a number of factors. The great multitudes that had once followed Christ were subsiding to a faithful few (Jn 6:66). Great crowds still came to hear (14:25), but committed followers were increasingly scarce. Moreover, Christ's messages often seemed designed to discourage the half-hearted. And He Himself had stated that the way is so narrow that few find it (Mt 7:14). This contradicted the Jewish belief that all Jews, except for tax collectors and other notorious sinners, would be saved. Christ's reply once again underscored the difficulty of entering at the narrow gate. After the resurrection, only 120 disciples gathered in the upper room in Jerusalem (Ac 1:15), and only about 500 in Galilee (Mt 28:16).

He will say, 'I tell you, I do not know where you are from; DEPART FROM ME, ALL YOU EVILDO- ERS.' ²⁸ In that place there will be weeping and gnashing of teeth when you see Abraham and Isaac and Jacob and all the prophets in the kingdom of God, but yourselves being thrown out. ²⁹ And they will come from east and west and from north and south, and will recline *at the table* in the kingdom of God. ³⁰ And behold, *some* are last who will be first and *some* are first who will be last."

³¹ Just at that time some Pharisees approached, saying to Him, "Go away, leave here, for Herod wants to kill You." ³² And He said to them, "Go and tell that fox, 'Behold, I cast out demons and perform cures today and tomorrow, and the third *day* I reach My goal.' ³³ Nevertheless I must journey on today and tomorrow and the next *day;* for it cannot be that a prophet would perish outside

13:29 they will come. By including people from the 4 corners of the earth, Jesus made it clear that even Gentiles would be invited to the heavenly banquet table. This was contrary to prevailing rabbinical thought, but perfectly consistent with the Old Testament Scriptures (Ps 107:3; Is 66:18–19; Mal 1:11).

of Jerusalem. ³⁴ O Jerusalem, Jerusalem, *the city* that kills the prophets and stones those sent to her! How often I wanted to gather your children together, just as a hen *gathers* her brood under her wings, and you would not *have it!* ³⁵ Behold, your house is left to you *desolate;* and I say to you, you will not see Me until *the time* comes when you say, 'BLESSED IS HE WHO COMES IN THE NAME OF THE LORD!' "

DAY 17: Why would Jesus call Herod a "fox" in Luke 13:32?

Some have suggested that Jesus' use of this expression is hard to reconcile with Exodus 22:28; Ecclesiastes 10:20; and Acts 23:5. However, those verses apply to everyday discourse. Prophets, speaking as mouthpieces of God and with divine authority, were often commissioned to rebuke leaders publicly (see Is. 1:23; Eze 22:27; Hos 7:3–7; Zep 3:3). Since Jesus spoke with perfect divine authority, He had every right to speak of Herod in such terms. Rabbinical writings often used "the fox". to signify someone who was both crafty and worthless. The Pharisees, who trembled at Herod's power, must have been astonished at Christ's boldness.

Jesus' message to Herod was: "Behold, I cast out demons and perform cures today and tomorrow, and the third day I reach My goal" (v. 32). This expression signified only that Christ was on His own divine timetable; it was not meant to lay out a literal 3-day schedule. Expressions like this were common in Semitic usage and seldom were employed in a literal sense to specify precise intervals of time. To "reach My goal," i.e., by death, in the finishing of His work. (See Heb 2:10; Jn 17:4–5; 19:30.) Herod was threatening to kill Him, but no one could kill Christ before His time (Jn 10:17–18).

Jesus adds that "it cannot be that a prophet would perish outside of Jerusalem" (v. 33). Not all prophets who were martyred died in Jerusalem, of course. This saying was probably a familiar proverb. The statement is full of irony, noting that most of the Old Testament prophets were martyred at the hands of the Jewish people, not by foreign enemies. Luke's inclusion of this saying underscores his theme in this section of his Gospel—Jesus' relentless journey to Jerusalem for the purpose of dying.

APRIL 18

Judges 1:1–2:23

1 Now it came about after the death of Joshua that the sons of Israel inquired of the LORD, saying, "Who shall go up first for us against the Canaanites, to fight against them?" ² The LORD said, "Judah shall go up; behold, I have given the land into his hand." ³ Then Judah said to Simeon his brother, "Come up with me into the territory allotted me, that we may fight against the Canaanites; and I in turn will go with you into the territory allotted you." So

Simeon went with him. ⁴ Judah went up, and the LORD gave the Canaanites and the Perizzites into their hands, and they defeated ten thousand men at Bezek. ⁵ They found Adoni-bezek in Bezek and fought against him, and they defeated the Canaanites and the Perizzites. ⁶ But Adoni-bezek fled; and they pursued him and caught him and cut off his thumbs and big toes. ⁷ Adoni-bezek said, "Seventy kings with their thumbs and their big toes cut off used to gather up *scraps* under my table; as I have done, so God has repaid me." So they brought him to Jerusalem and he died there.

⁸ Then the sons of Judah fought against

Jerusalem and captured it and struck it with the edge of the sword and set the city on fire. ⁹Afterward the sons of Judah went down to fight against the Canaanites living in the hill country and in the Negev and in the lowland. ¹⁰So Judah went against the Canaanites who lived in Hebron (now the name of Hebron formerly *was* Kiriath-arba); and they struck Sheshai and Ahiman and Talmai.

¹¹Then from there he went against the inhabitants of Debir (now the name of Debir formerly *was* Kiriath-sepher). ¹²And Caleb said, "The one who attacks Kiriath-sepher and captures it, I will even give him my daughter Achsah for a wife." ¹³Othniel the son of Kenaz, Caleb's younger brother, captured it; so he gave him his daughter Achsah for a wife. ¹⁴Then it came about when she came *to him,* that she persuaded him to ask her father for a field. Then she alighted from her donkey, and Caleb said to her, "What do you want?" ¹⁵She said to him, "Give me a blessing, since you have given me the land of the Negev, give me also springs of water." So Caleb gave her the upper springs and the lower springs.

¹⁶The descendants of the Kenite, Moses' father-in-law, went up from the city of palms with the sons of Judah, to the wilderness of Judah which is in the south of Arad; and they went and lived with the people. ¹⁷Then Judah went with Simeon his brother, and they struck the Canaanites living in Zephath, and utterly destroyed it. So the name of the city was called Hormah. ¹⁸And Judah took Gaza with its territory and Ashkelon with its territory and Ekron with its territory. ¹⁹Now the LORD was with Judah, and they took possession of the hill country; but they could not drive out the inhabitants of the valley because they had iron chariots. ²⁰Then they gave Hebron to Caleb, as Moses had promised; and he drove out from

---

1:19 they could not drive out. "They" of Judah could not. They had been promised by Joshua that they could conquer the lowland (Jos 17:16, 18) and should have remembered Joshua 11:4–9. This is a recurring failure among the tribes to rise to full trust and obedience for victory by God's power. Compromising for less than what God was able to give (Jos 1:6–9) began even in Joshua's day (Jdg 2:2–6) and earlier (Nu 13–14). In another sense, God permitted enemies to hold out as a test to display whether His people would obey Him (2:20–23; 3:1, 4). Another factor involved keeping the wild animal count from rising too fast (Dt 7:22).

---

there the three sons of Anak. ²¹But the sons of Benjamin did not drive out the Jebusites who lived in Jerusalem; so the Jebusites have lived with the sons of Benjamin in Jerusalem to this day.

²²Likewise the house of Joseph went up against Bethel, and the LORD was with them. ²³The house of Joseph spied out Bethel (now the name of the city was formerly Luz). ²⁴The spies saw a man coming out of the city and they said to him, "Please show us the entrance to the city and we will treat you kindly." ²⁵So he showed them the entrance to the city, and they struck the city with the edge of the sword, but they let the man and all his family go free. ²⁶The man went into the land of the Hittites and built a city and named it Luz which is its name to this day.

²⁷But Manasseh did not take possession of Beth-shean and its villages, or Taanach and its villages, or the inhabitants of Dor and its villages, or the inhabitants of Ibleam and its villages, or the inhabitants of Megiddo and its villages; so the Canaanites persisted in living in that land. ²⁸It came about when Israel became strong, that they put the Canaanites to forced labor, but they did not drive them out completely.

²⁹Ephraim did not drive out the Canaanites who were living in Gezer; so the Canaanites lived in Gezer among them.

³⁰Zebulun did not drive out the inhabitants of Kitron, or the inhabitants of Nahalol; so the Canaanites lived among them and became subject to forced labor.

³¹Asher did not drive out the inhabitants of Acco, or the inhabitants of Sidon, or of Ahlab, or of Achzib, or of Helbah, or of Aphik, or of Rehob. ³²So the Asherites lived among the Canaanites, the inhabitants of the land; for they did not drive them out.

³³Naphtali did not drive out the inhabitants of Beth-shemesh, or the inhabitants of Beth-anath, but lived among the Canaanites, the inhabitants of the land; and the inhabitants of Beth-shemesh and Beth-anath became forced labor for them.

³⁴Then the Amorites forced the sons of Dan into the hill country, for they did not allow them to come down to the valley; ³⁵yet the Amorites persisted in living in Mount Heres, in Aijalon and in Shaalbim; but when the power of the house of Joseph grew strong, they became forced labor. ³⁶The border of the Amorites ran from the ascent of Akrabbim, from Sela and upward.

2 Now the angel of the LORD came up from Gilgal to Bochim. And he said, "I brought you up out of Egypt and led you into the land

2:1 the angel of the LORD. One of 3 pre-incarnate theophanies by the Lord Jesus Christ in Judges (6:11–18; 13:3–23). This same Divine Messenger had earlier led Israel out of Egypt (Ex 14:19). **I will never break My covenant with you.** God would be faithful until the end, but the people would forfeit blessing for trouble, due to their disobedience (v. 3).

which I have sworn to your fathers; and I said, 'I will never break My covenant with you, ²and as for you, you shall make no covenant with the inhabitants of this land; you shall tear down their altars.' But you have not obeyed Me; what is this you have done? ³Therefore I also said, 'I will not drive them out before you; but they will become *as thorns* in your sides and their gods will be a snare to you.'" ⁴When the angel of the LORD spoke these words to all the sons of Israel, the people lifted up their voices and wept. ⁵So they named that place Bochim; and there they sacrificed to the LORD.

⁶When Joshua had dismissed the people, the sons of Israel went each to his inheritance to possess the land. ⁷The people served the LORD all the days of Joshua, and all the days of the elders who survived Joshua, who had seen all the great work of the LORD which He had done for Israel. ⁸Then Joshua the son of Nun, the servant of the LORD, died at the age of one hundred and ten. ⁹And they buried him in the territory of his inheritance in Timnath-heres, in the hill country of Ephraim, north of Mount Gaash. ¹⁰All that generation also were gathered to their fathers; and there arose another generation after them who did not know the LORD, nor yet the work which He had done for Israel.

¹¹Then the sons of Israel did evil in the sight of the LORD and served the Baals, ¹²and they forsook the LORD, the God of their fathers, who had brought them out of the land of Egypt, and followed other gods from *among* the gods of the peoples who were around them, and bowed themselves down to them; thus they provoked the LORD to anger. ¹³So they forsook the LORD and served Baal and the Ashtaroth. ¹⁴The anger of the LORD burned against Israel, and He gave them into the hands of plunderers who plundered them; and He sold them into the hands of their enemies around *them,* so that they could no longer stand before their enemies. ¹⁵Wherever they went, the hand of the LORD was against them for evil, as the LORD

had spoken and as the LORD had sworn to them, so that they were severely distressed.

¹⁶Then the LORD raised up judges who delivered them from the hands of those who plundered them. ¹⁷Yet they did not listen to their judges, for they played the harlot after other gods and bowed themselves down to them. They turned aside quickly from the way in which their fathers had walked in obeying the commandments of the LORD; they did not do as *their fathers.* ¹⁸When the LORD raised up judges for them, the LORD was with the judge and delivered them from the hand of their enemies all the days of the judge; for the LORD was moved to pity by their groaning because of those who oppressed them and afflicted them. ¹⁹But it came about when the judge died, that they would turn back and act more corruptly than their fathers, in following other gods to serve them and bow down to them; they did not abandon their practices or their stubborn ways. ²⁰So the anger of the LORD burned against Israel, and He said, "Because this nation has transgressed My covenant which I commanded their fathers and has not listened to My voice, ²¹I also will no longer drive out before them any of the nations which Joshua left when he died, ²²in order to test Israel by them, whether they will keep the way of the LORD to walk in it as their fathers did, or not." ²³So the LORD allowed those nations to remain, not driving them out quickly; and He did not give them into the hand of Joshua.

Psalm 48:1–8

A Song; a Psalm of the sons of Korah.

G reat is the LORD, and
    greatly to be praised,
  In the city of our God, His
    holy mountain.
² Beautiful in elevation, the
    joy of the whole earth,
  Is Mount Zion *in* the far north,
    The city of the great King.
³ God, in her palaces,
  Has made Himself known
    as a stronghold.

⁴ For, lo, the kings assembled
    themselves,
  They passed by together.
⁵ They saw *it,* then they were amazed;
  They were terrified, they
    fled in alarm.
⁶ Panic seized them there,
  Anguish, as of a woman in childbirth.
⁷ With the east wind
  You break the ships of Tarshish.

48:2 the joy of the whole earth. See the judgment context of Lamentations 2:15. **the far north.** "North" is an interpretive translation of a word term that occurs as a Semitic place name, i.e., "Zaphon." In Canaanite mythology Zaphon was an ancient Near Eastern equivalent to Mt. Olympus, the dwelling place of pagan gods. If this was the psalmist's intention in Psalms 48:2, the reference becomes a polemical description of the Lord; He is not only King of kings but also is God of all so-called gods. **The city of the great King.** See Psalms 47:2 and Matthew 5:34–35. God Himself has always been the King of kings.

8   As we have heard, so have we seen
     In the city of the LORD of hosts,
       in the city of our God;
     God will establish her forever.   *Selah*

Proverbs 14:15–17

15   The naive believes everything,
     But the sensible man
       considers his steps.
16   A wise man is cautious and
       turns away from evil,
     But a fool is arrogant and careless.
17   A quick-tempered man acts foolishly,
     And a man of evil devices is hated.

Luke 14:1–24

14 It happened that when He went into the house of one of the leaders of the Pharisees on *the* Sabbath to eat bread, they were watching Him closely. [2] And there in front of Him was a man suffering from dropsy. [3] And Jesus answered and spoke to the lawyers and Pharisees, saying, "Is it lawful to heal on the Sabbath, or not?" [4] But they kept silent. And He took hold of him and healed him, and sent him away. [5] And He said to them, "Which one of you will have a son or an ox fall into a well, and will not immediately pull him out on a Sabbath day?" [6] And they could make no reply to this.

[7] And He *began* speaking a parable to the invited guests when He noticed how they had been picking out the places of honor *at the table,* saying to them, [8] "When you are invited by someone to a wedding feast, do not take the place of honor, for someone more distinguished than you may have been invited by him, [9] and he who invited you both will come and say to you, 'Give *your* place to this man,' and then in disgrace you proceed to occupy the last place. [10] But when you are invited, go and recline at the last place, so that when the one who has invited you comes, he may say to you, 'Friend, move up

higher'; then you will have honor in the sight of all who are at the table with you. [11] For everyone who exalts himself will be humbled, and he who humbles himself will be exalted."

[12] And He also went on to say to the one who had invited Him, "When you give a luncheon or a dinner, do not invite your friends or your brothers or your relatives or rich neighbors, otherwise they may also invite you in return and *that* will be your repayment. [13] But when you give a reception, invite *the* poor, *the* crippled, *the* lame, *the* blind, [14] and you will be blessed, since they do not have *the means* to repay you; for you will be repaid at the resurrection of the righteous."

[15] When one of those who were reclining *at the table* with Him heard this, he said to Him, "Blessed is everyone who will eat bread in the kingdom of God!" [16] But He said to him, "A man was giving a big dinner, and he invited many; [17] and at the dinner hour he sent his slave to say to those who had been invited, 'Come; for everything is ready now.' [18] But they all alike began to make excuses. The first one said to him, 'I have bought a piece of land and I need to go out and look at it; please consider me excused.' [19] Another one said, 'I have bought five yoke of oxen, and I am going to try them out; please consider me excused.' [20] Another one said, 'I have married a wife, and for that reason I cannot come.' [21] And the slave came *back* and reported this to his master. Then the head of the household became angry and said to his slave, 'Go out at once into the streets and lanes of the city and bring in here the poor and crippled and blind and lame.' [22] And the slave said, 'Master, what you commanded has been done, and still there is room.' [23] And the master said to the slave, 'Go out into the highways and along the hedges, and compel *them* to come in, so that my house may be filled. [24] For I tell you, none of those men who were invited shall taste of my dinner.'"

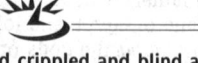

14:21 the poor and crippled and blind and lame. I.e., people the Pharisees tended to regard as unclean or unworthy. The religious leaders condemned Jesus for His associations with prostitutes and tax collectors (5:29–30; 15:1; Mt 9:10–11; 11:19; 21:31–32; Mk 2:15–16).

14:23 into the highways and along the hedges. This evidently represents the Gentile regions. **compel *them* to come in.** I.e., not by force or violence, but by earnest persuasion.

"There arose another generation after them who did not know the Lord, nor yet the work which He had done" (Jdg 2:10). The first people in the land had vivid recollections of all the miracles and judgments and were devoted to faith, duty, and purity. The new generation were ignorant of the experiences of their parents and yielded more easily to corruption. To a marked degree the people of this new generation were not true believers.

The new generation "followed other gods" (v. 12). Idol worship, such as the golden calf in the wilderness (Ex 32), flared up again. Spurious gods of Canaan were plentiful. El was the supreme Canaanite deity, a god of uncontrolled lust and a bloody tyrant, as shown in writings found at Ras Shamra in northern Syria. His name means "strong, powerful." Baal, son and successor of El, was "lord of heaven," a farm god of rain and storm, his name meaning "lord, possessor." His cult at Phoenicia included animal sacrifices, ritual meals, and licentious dances. Chambers catered to sacred prostitution by men and women (see 1Ki 14:23-24; 2Ki 23:7). Anath, sister-wife of Baal, also called Ashtoreth (Astarte), patroness of sex and war, was called "virgin" and "holy," but was actually a "sacred prostitute." Many other gods besides these also attracted worship.

"The anger of the LORD burned" against them (v. 14), which was followed by plunderers and calamities designed as chastisement to lead the people to repentance. During these times, "the LORD raised up judges" (v. 16). A "judge" or deliverer guided military expeditions against foes and arbitrated judicial matters (see 4:5). There was no succession or national rule. They were local deliverers, lifted up to leadership by God when the deplorable condition of Israel in the region around them prompted God to rescue the people.

APRIL 19

Judges 3:1–4:24

3 Now these are the nations which the LORD left, to test Israel by them (*that is,* all who had not experienced any of the wars of Canaan; ² only in order that the generations of the sons of Israel might be taught war, those who had not experienced it formerly). ³ *These nations are:* the five lords of the Philistines and all the Canaanites and the Sidonians and the Hivites who lived in Mount Lebanon, from Mount Baal-hermon as far as Lebo-hamath. ⁴ They were for testing Israel, to find out if they would obey the commandments of the LORD, which He had commanded their fathers through Moses. ⁵ The sons of Israel lived among the Canaanites, the Hittites, the Amorites, the Perizzites, the Hivites, and the Jebusites; ⁶ and they took their daughters for themselves as wives, and gave their own daughters to their sons, and served their gods.

⁷ The sons of Israel did what was evil in the sight of the LORD, and forgot the LORD their God and served the Baals and the Asheroth. ⁸ Then the anger of the LORD was kindled against Israel, so that He sold them into the hands of Cushan-rishathaim king of Mesopotamia; and the sons of Israel served Cushan-rishathaim eight years. ⁹ When the sons of Israel cried to the LORD, the LORD raised up a deliverer for the sons of Israel to deliver them, Othniel the son of Kenaz, Caleb's younger

brother. ¹⁰ The Spirit of the LORD came upon him, and he judged Israel. When he went out to war, the LORD gave Cushan-rishathaim king of Mesopotamia into his hand, so that he prevailed over Cushan-rishathaim. ¹¹ Then the land had rest forty years. And Othniel the son of Kenaz died.

3:10 The Spirit of the LORD came. Certain judges were expressly said to have the Spirit of the Lord come upon them (6:34; 11:29; 13:25; 14:6, 19; 15:14); others apparently also had this experience. This is a common Old Testament expression signifying a unique act of God which conferred power and wisdom for victory. But this did not guarantee that the will of God would be done in absolutely all details, as is apparent in Gideon (8:24–27, 30), Jephthah (11:34–40), and Samson (16:1).

¹² Now the sons of Israel again did evil in the sight of the LORD. So the LORD strengthened Eglon the king of Moab against Israel, because they had done evil in the sight of the LORD. ¹³ And he gathered to himself the sons of Ammon and Amalek; and he went and defeated Israel, and they possessed the city of the palm trees. ¹⁴ The sons of Israel served Eglon the king of Moab eighteen years.

¹⁵ But when the sons of Israel cried to the LORD, the LORD raised up a deliverer for them, Ehud the son of Gera, the Benjamite, a

left-handed man. And the sons of Israel sent tribute by him to Eglon the king of Moab. [16] Ehud made himself a sword which had two edges, a cubit in length, and he bound it on his right thigh under his cloak. [17] He presented the tribute to Eglon king of Moab. Now Eglon was a very fat man. [18] It came about when he had finished presenting the tribute, that he sent away the people who had carried the tribute. [19] But he himself turned back from the idols which were at Gilgal, and said, "I have a secret message for you, O king." And he said, "Keep silence." And all who attended him left him. [20] Ehud came to him while he was sitting alone in his cool roof chamber. And Ehud said, "I have a message from God for you." And he arose from his seat. [21] Ehud stretched out his left hand, took the sword from his right thigh and thrust it into his belly. [22] The handle also went in after the blade, and the fat closed over the blade, for he did not draw the sword out of his belly; and the refuse came out. [23] Then Ehud went out into the vestibule and shut the doors of the roof chamber behind him, and locked *them*.

[24] When he had gone out, his servants came and looked, and behold, the doors of the roof chamber were locked; and they said, "He is only relieving himself in the cool room." [25] They waited until they became anxious; but behold, he did not open the doors of the roof chamber. Therefore they took the key and opened them, and behold, their master had fallen to the floor dead.

[26] Now Ehud escaped while they were delaying, and he passed by the idols and escaped to Seirah. [27] It came about when he had arrived, that he blew the trumpet in the hill country of Ephraim; and the sons of Israel went down with him from the hill country, and he *was* in front of them. [28] He said to them, "Pursue *them*, for the LORD has given your enemies the Moabites into your hands." So they went down after him and seized the fords of the Jordan opposite Moab, and did not allow anyone to cross. [29] They struck down at that time about ten thousand Moabites, all robust and valiant men; and no one escaped. [30] So Moab was subdued that day under the hand of Israel. And the land was undisturbed for eighty years.

[31] After him came Shamgar the son of Anath, who struck down six hundred Philistines with an oxgoad; and he also saved Israel.

3:31 Shamgar. His extraordinary exploit causes one to think of Samson (15:16). **an oxgoad.** This was a stout stick about 8–10 ft. long and 6 in. around, with a sharp metal tip to prod or turn oxen. The other end was a flat, curved blade for cleaning a plow.

4 Then the sons of Israel again did evil in the sight of the LORD, after Ehud died. [2] And the LORD sold them into the hand of Jabin king of Canaan, who reigned in Hazor; and the commander of his army was Sisera, who lived in Harosheth-hagoyim. [3] The sons of Israel cried to the LORD; for he had nine hundred iron chariots, and he oppressed the sons of Israel severely for twenty years.

[4] Now Deborah, a prophetess, the wife of Lappidoth, was judging Israel at that time. [5] She used to sit under the palm tree of Deborah between Ramah and Bethel in the hill country of Ephraim; and the sons of Israel came up to her for judgment. [6] Now she sent and summoned Barak the son of Abinoam from Kedesh-naphtali, and said to him, "Behold, the LORD, the God of Israel, has commanded, 'Go and march to Mount Tabor, and take with you ten thousand men from the sons of Naphtali and from the sons of

4:4 Deborah, a prophetess. She was an unusual woman of wisdom and influence who did the tasks of a judge, except for military leadership. God can use women mightily for civil, religious, or other tasks, e.g., Huldah the prophetess (2Ki 22:14), Philip's daughters in prophesying (Ac 21:8–9), and Phoebe a deaconess (Ro 16:1). Deborah's rise to such a role is the exception in the book because of Barak's failure to show the courage to lead courageously (vv. 8, 14). God rebuked his cowardice by the pledge that a woman would slay Sisera (v. 9).

3:20 "I have a message from God for you." Ehud claimed he came to do God's will in answer to prayer (v. 15). Calmly and confidently, Ehud acted and later credited the defeat of the wicked king to God (v. 28; see Ps 75:6–7, 10; Da 4:25), though it was by means of Ehud, as Jael used her way (4:21) and Israel's armies used the sword (4:16). By God's power, Ehud's army would slay a greater number (v. 29). Men's evil provokes God's judgment (Lv 18:25).

Zebulun. ⁷I will draw out to you Sisera, the commander of Jabin's army, with his chariots and his many *troops* to the river Kishon, and I will give him into your hand.'" ⁸Then Barak said to her, "If you will go with me, then I will go; but if you will not go with me, I will not go." ⁹She said, "I will surely go with you; nevertheless, the honor shall not be yours on the journey that you are about to take, for the LORD will sell Sisera into the hands of a woman." Then Deborah arose and went with Barak to Kedesh. ¹⁰Barak called Zebulun and Naphtali together to Kedesh, and ten thousand men went up with him; Deborah also went up with him.

¹¹Now Heber the Kenite had separated himself from the Kenites, from the sons of Hobab the father-in-law of Moses, and had pitched his tent as far away as the oak in Zaanannim, which is near Kedesh.

¹²Then they told Sisera that Barak the son of Abinoam had gone up to Mount Tabor. ¹³Sisera called together all his chariots, nine hundred iron chariots, and all the people who *were* with him, from Harosheth-hagoyim to the river Kishon. ¹⁴Deborah said to Barak, "Arise! For this is the day in which the LORD has given Sisera into your hands; behold, the LORD has gone out before you." So Barak went down from Mount Tabor with ten thousand men following him. ¹⁵The LORD routed Sisera and all *his* chariots and all *his* army with the edge of the sword before Barak; and Sisera alighted from *his* chariot and fled away on foot. ¹⁶But Barak pursued the chariots and the army as far as Harosheth-hagoyim, and all the army of Sisera fell by the edge of the sword; not even one was left.

¹⁷Now Sisera fled away on foot to the tent of Jael the wife of Heber the Kenite, for *there was* peace between Jabin the king of Hazor and the house of Heber the Kenite. ¹⁸Jael went out to meet Sisera, and said to him, "Turn aside, my master, turn aside to me! Do not be afraid." And he turned aside to her into the tent, and she covered him with a rug. ¹⁹He said to her, "Please give me a little water to drink, for I am thirsty." So she opened a bottle of milk and gave him a drink; then she covered him. ²⁰He said to her, "Stand in the doorway of the tent, and it shall be if anyone comes and inquires of you, and says, 'Is there anyone here?' that you shall say, 'No.'" ²¹But Jael, Heber's wife, took a tent peg and seized a hammer in her hand, and went secretly to him and drove the peg into his temple, and it went through into the ground; for he was sound asleep and exhausted. So he died.

²²And behold, as Barak pursued Sisera, Jael came out to meet him and said to him, "Come, and I will show you the man whom you are seeking." And he entered with her, and behold Sisera was lying dead with the tent peg in his temple.

²³So God subdued on that day Jabin the king of Canaan before the sons of Israel. ²⁴The hand of the sons of Israel pressed heavier and heavier upon Jabin the king of Canaan, until they had destroyed Jabin the king of Canaan.

Psalm 48:9–14

⁹ We have thought on Your
  lovingkindness, O God,
  In the midst of Your temple.
¹⁰ As is Your name, O God,
  So is Your praise to the
    ends of the earth;
  Your right hand is full of
    righteousness.
¹¹ Let Mount Zion be glad,
  Let the daughters of Judah rejoice
  Because of Your judgments.
¹² Walk about Zion and go around her;
  Count her towers;
¹³ Consider her ramparts;
  Go through her palaces,
  That you may tell *it* to the
    next generation.
¹⁴ For such is God,
  Our God forever and ever;
  He will guide us until death.

Proverbs 14:18–19

¹⁸ The naive inherit foolishness,
  But the sensible are crowned
    with knowledge.
¹⁹ The evil will bow down
    before the good,
  And the wicked at the gates
    of the righteous.

14:19 evil will bow. The ancient custom was for the inferior to prostrate himself before the superior or wait humbly before the great one's gate seeking favor. Good will humble evil.

Luke 14:25–35

²⁵Now large crowds were going along with Him; and He turned and said to them, ²⁶"If anyone comes to Me, and does not hate his own father and mother and wife and children and brothers and sisters, yes, and even his own life, he cannot be My disciple. ²⁷Whoever does not

carry his own cross and come after Me cannot be My disciple. ²⁸ For which one of you, when he wants to build a tower, does not first sit down and calculate the cost to see if he has enough to complete it? ²⁹ Otherwise, when he has laid a foundation and is not able to finish, all who observe it begin to ridicule him, ³⁰ saying, 'This man began to build and was not able to finish.' ³¹ Or what king, when he sets out to meet another king in battle, will not first sit down and consider whether he is strong enough with ten thousand *men* to encounter the one coming against him with twenty thousand? ³² Or else, while the other is still far away, he sends a delegation and asks for terms of peace. ³³ So then, none of you can be My disciple who does not give up all his own possessions.

³⁴ "Therefore, salt is good; but if even salt has become tasteless, with what will it be seasoned? ³⁵ It is useless either for the soil or for the manure pile; it is thrown out. He who has ears to hear, let him hear."

DAY 19: How deep of a commitment does Christ ask of His followers?

From the teaching in Luke 14:25–35, it is clear that Christ's aim was not to gather appreciative crowds, but to make true disciples. He never adapted His message to majority preferences, but always plainly declared the high cost of discipleship. Here He made several bold demands that would discourage the halfhearted.

"Hate" (v. 26). A similar statement in Matthew 10:37 is the key to understanding this difficult command. The "hatred" called for here is actually a lesser love. Jesus was calling His disciples to cultivate such a devotion to Him that their attachment to everything else—including their own lives—would seem like hatred by comparison. See 16:13; Genesis 29:30–31 for similar usages of the word "hate."

"Carry his cross" (v. 27). I.e., willingly. This parallels the idea of hating one's own life in v. 26.

"Calculate the cost" (v. 28). The multitudes were positive but uncommitted. Far from making it easy for them to respond positively, He set the cost of discipleship as high as possible and encouraged them to do a careful inventory before declaring their willingness to follow.

"Give up all" (v. 33). Only those willing to carefully assess the cost and invest all they had in His kingdom were worthy to enter. This speaks of something far more than mere abandonment of one's material possessions. It is an absolute, unconditional surrender. His disciples were permitted to retain no privileges and make no demands. They were to safeguard no cherished sins, treasure no earthly possessions, and cling to no secret self-indulgences. Their commitment to Him must be without reservation.

 # APRIL 20

Judges 5:1–6:40

5 Then Deborah and Barak the son of Abinoam sang on that day, saying,

2 "That the leaders led in Israel,
   That the people volunteered,
   Bless the LORD!
3 "Hear, O kings; give ear, O rulers!
   I—to the LORD, I will sing,
   I will sing praise to the LORD,
   the God of Israel.
4 "LORD, when You went out from Seir,
   When You marched from
   the field of Edom,
   The earth quaked, the
   heavens also dripped,
   Even the clouds dripped water.
5 "The mountains quaked at the
   presence of the LORD,
   This Sinai, at the presence of the
   LORD, the God of Israel.

6 "In the days of Shamgar
   the son of Anath,
   In the days of Jael, the
   highways were deserted,
   And travelers went by
   roundabout ways.
7 "The peasantry ceased, they
   ceased in Israel,
   Until I, Deborah, arose,
   Until I arose, a mother in Israel.
8 "New gods were chosen;
   Then war *was* in the gates.
   Not a shield or a spear was seen
   Among forty thousand in Israel.
9 "My heart *goes out* to the
   commanders of Israel,
   The volunteers among the people;
   Bless the LORD!
10 "You who ride on white donkeys,
   You who sit on *rich* carpets,
   And you who travel on
   the road—sing!
11 "At the sound of those who divide
   flocks among the watering places,

There they shall recount the
    righteous deeds of the LORD,
The righteous deeds for His
    peasantry in Israel.
Then the people of the LORD
    went down to the gates.

12 "Awake, awake, Deborah;
Awake, awake, sing a song!
Arise, Barak, and take away your
    captives, O son of Abinoam.

13 "Then survivors came down
    to the nobles;
The people of the LORD came
    down to me as warriors.

14 "From Ephraim those whose root
    is in Amalek *came down,*
Following you, Benjamin,
    with your peoples;
From Machir commanders
    came down,
And from Zebulun those who
    wield the staff of office.

15 "And the princes of Issachar
    were with Deborah;
As *was* Issachar, so *was* Barak;
Into the valley they rushed
    at his heels;
Among the divisions of Reuben
    There were great resolves of heart.

16 "Why did you sit among
    the sheepfolds,
To hear the piping for the flocks?
Among the divisions of Reuben
    There were great searchings
    of heart.

17 "Gilead remained across the Jordan;
And why did Dan stay in ships?
Asher sat at the seashore,
And remained by its landings.

18 "Zebulun *was* a people who despised
    their lives *even* to death,
And Naphtali also, on the
    high places of the field.

19 "The kings came *and* fought;
Then fought the kings of Canaan
At Taanach near the waters
    of Megiddo;
They took no plunder in silver.

20 "The stars fought from heaven,
From their courses they
    fought against Sisera.

21 "The torrent of Kishon
    swept them away,
The ancient torrent, the
    torrent Kishon.
O my soul, march on with strength.

22 "Then the horses' hoofs beat
From the dashing, the dashing
    of his valiant steeds.

23 'Curse Meroz,' said the
    angel of the LORD,
'Utterly curse its inhabitants;
Because they did not come to
    the help of the LORD,
To the help of the LORD
    against the warriors.'

24 "Most blessed of women is Jael,
The wife of Heber the Kenite;
Most blessed is she of
    women in the tent.

25 "He asked for water *and*
    she gave him milk;
In a magnificent bowl she
    brought him curds.

26 "She reached out her hand
    for the tent peg,
And her right hand for the
    workmen's hammer.
Then she struck Sisera, she
    smashed his head;
And she shattered and
    pierced his temple.

27 "Between her feet he bowed,
    he fell, he lay;
Between her feet he bowed, he fell;
Where he bowed, there he fell dead.

28 "Out of the window she
    looked and lamented,
The mother of Sisera
    through the lattice,
'Why does his chariot
    delay in coming?
Why do the hoofbeats of
    his chariots tarry?'

29 "Her wise princesses would
    answer her,
Indeed she repeats her
    words to herself,

30 'Are they not finding, are they
    not dividing the spoil?
A maiden, two maidens
    for every warrior;
To Sisera a spoil of dyed work,
A spoil of dyed work embroidered,
Dyed work of double embroidery
    on the neck of the spoiler?'

31 "Thus let all Your enemies
    perish, O LORD;
But let those who love Him be like
    the rising of the sun in its might."

And the land was undisturbed for forty years.

6 Then the sons of Israel did what was evil in the sight of the LORD; and the LORD gave them into the hands of Midian seven years. ²The power of Midian prevailed against Israel. Because of Midian the sons of Israel made for themselves the dens which were in the mountains and the caves and the strongholds. ³For it was when Israel had sown, that the Midianites would come up with the Amalekites and the sons of the east and go against them. ⁴So they would camp against them and destroy the produce of the earth as far as Gaza, and leave no sustenance in Israel as well as no sheep, ox, or donkey. ⁵For they would come up with their livestock and their tents, they would come in like locusts for number, both they and their camels were innumerable; and they came into the land to devastate it. ⁶So Israel was brought very low because of Midian, and the sons of Israel cried to the LORD.

⁷Now it came about when the sons of Israel cried to the LORD on account of Midian, ⁸that the LORD sent a prophet to the sons of Israel, and he said to them, "Thus says the LORD, the God of Israel, 'It was I who brought you up from Egypt and brought you out from the house of slavery. ⁹I delivered you from the hands of the Egyptians and from the hands of all your oppressors, and dispossessed them before you and gave you their land, ¹⁰and I said to you, "I am the LORD your God; you shall not fear the gods of the Amorites in whose land you live. But you have not obeyed Me."'"

6:8 the LORD sent a prophet. He used prophets in isolated cases before Samuel, the band of prophets Samuel probably founded (1Sa 10:5), and later such prophets as Elijah, Elisha, and the writing prophets—major and minor. Here the prophet is sent to bring the divine curse because of their infidelity (v. 10).

¹¹Then the angel of the LORD came and sat under the oak that was in Ophrah, which belonged to Joash the Abiezrite as his son Gideon was beating out wheat in the wine press in order to save *it* from the Midianites. ¹²The angel of the LORD appeared to him and said to him, "The LORD is with you, O valiant warrior." ¹³Then Gideon said to him, "O my lord, if the LORD is with us, why then has all this happened to us? And where are all His miracles which our fathers told us about, saying, 'Did not the LORD bring us up from Egypt?' But now the LORD has abandoned us and given us into the hand of Midian." ¹⁴The LORD looked at him and said, "Go in this your strength and deliver Israel from the hand of Midian. Have I not sent you?" ¹⁵He said to Him, "O Lord, how shall I deliver Israel? Behold, my family is the least in Manasseh, and I am the youngest in my father's house." ¹⁶But the LORD said to him, "Surely I will be with you, and you shall defeat Midian as one man." ¹⁷So Gideon said to Him, "If now I have found favor in Your sight, then show me a sign that it is You who speak with me. ¹⁸Please do not depart from here, until I come *back* to You, and bring out my offering and lay it before You." And He said, "I will remain until you return."

¹⁹Then Gideon went in and prepared a young goat and unleavened bread from an ephah of flour; he put the meat in a basket and the broth in a pot, and brought *them* out to him under the oak and presented *them*. ²⁰The angel of God said to him, "Take the meat and the unleavened bread and lay them on this rock, and pour out the broth." And he did so. ²¹Then the angel of the LORD put out the end of the staff that was in his hand and touched the meat and the unleavened bread; and fire sprang up from the rock and consumed the meat and the unleavened bread. Then the angel of the LORD vanished from his sight. ²²When Gideon saw that he was the angel of the LORD, he said, "Alas, O Lord GOD! For now I have seen the angel of the LORD face to face." ²³The LORD said to him, "Peace to you, do not fear; you shall not die." ²⁴Then Gideon built an altar there to the LORD and named it The LORD is Peace. To this day it is still in Ophrah of the Abiezrites.

²⁵Now on the same night the LORD said to him, "Take your father's bull and a second bull seven years old, and pull down the altar of Baal which belongs to your father, and cut down the Asherah that is beside it; ²⁶and build an altar to the LORD your God on the top of this stronghold in an orderly manner, and take a second bull and offer a burnt offering with the wood of the Asherah which you shall cut down." ²⁷Then Gideon took ten men of his servants and did as the LORD had spoken to him; and because he was too afraid of his father's household and the men of the city to do it by day, he did it by night.

²⁸When the men of the city arose early in the morning, behold, the altar of Baal was torn down, and the Asherah which was beside it was cut down, and the second bull was offered on the altar which had been built.

²⁹They said to one another, "Who did this thing?" And when they searched about and inquired, they said, "Gideon the son of Joash did this thing." ³⁰Then the men of the city said to Joash, "Bring out your son, that he may die, for he has torn down the altar of Baal, and indeed, he has cut down the Asherah which was beside it." ³¹But Joash said to all who stood against him, "Will you contend for Baal, or will you deliver him? Whoever will plead for him shall be put to death by morning. If he is a god, let him contend for himself, because someone has torn down his altar." ³²Therefore on that day he named him Jerubbaal, that is to say, "Let Baal contend against him," because he had torn down his altar.

³³Then all the Midianites and the Amalekites and the sons of the east assembled themselves; and they crossed over and camped in the valley of Jezreel. ³⁴So the Spirit of the LORD came upon Gideon; and he blew a trumpet, and the Abiezrites were called together to follow him. ³⁵He sent messengers throughout Manasseh, and they also were called together to follow him; and he sent messengers to Asher, Zebulun, and Naphtali, and they came up to meet them.

³⁶Then Gideon said to God, "If You will deliver Israel through me, as You have spoken, ³⁷behold, I will put a fleece of wool on the threshing floor. If there is dew on the fleece only, and it is dry on all the ground, then I will know that You will deliver Israel through me, as You have spoken." ³⁸And it was so. When he arose early the next morning and squeezed the fleece, he drained the dew from the fleece, a bowl full of water. ³⁹Then Gideon said to God, "Do not let Your anger burn against me that I may speak once more; please let me make a test once more with the fleece, let it now be dry only on the fleece, and let there be dew on all the ground." ⁴⁰God did so that night; for it was dry only on the fleece, and dew was on all the ground.

Psalm 49:1–9

For the choir director. A Psalm
of the sons of Korah.

Hear this, all peoples;
  Give ear, all inhabitants of
    the world,
² Both low and high,
  Rich and poor together.
³ My mouth will speak wisdom,
  And the meditation of my heart
    will be understanding.
⁴ I will incline my ear to a proverb;
  I will express my riddle on the harp.

49:6 those who trust in their wealth. Mankind's propensity to trust in his own material goods is well attested in Scripture (e.g., Ps 52:7; Jer 17:5). Biblically this is exposed as the epitome of stupidity (see, e.g., Pr 23:4–5; Lk 12:16ff.).

⁵ Why should I fear in days of adversity,
  When the iniquity of my
    foes surrounds me,
⁶ Even those who trust in their wealth
  And boast in the abundance
    of their riches?
⁷ No man can by any means
  redeem *his* brother
  Or give to God a ransom for him—
⁸ For the redemption of
    his soul is costly,
  And he should cease *trying* forever—
⁹ That he should live on eternally,
  That he should not undergo decay.

Proverbs 14:20–21

²⁰ The poor is hated even
    by his neighbor,
  But those who love the rich are many.
²¹ He who despises his neighbor sins,
  But happy is he who is
    gracious to the poor.

14:20 This sad-but-true picture of human nature is not given approvingly, but only as a fact.

Luke 15:1–10

15 Now all the tax collectors and the sinners were coming near Him to listen to Him. ²Both the Pharisees and the scribes *began* to grumble, saying, "This man receives sinners and eats with them."

³So He told them this parable, saying, ⁴"What man among you, if he has a hundred sheep and has lost one of them, does not leave the ninety-nine in the open pasture and go after the one which is lost until he finds it? ⁵When he has found it, he lays it on his shoulders, rejoicing. ⁶And when he comes home, he calls together his friends and his neighbors, saying to them, 'Rejoice with me, for I have found my sheep which was lost!' ⁷I tell you that in the same way, there will be *more* joy in heaven over one sinner who repents than over ninety-nine righteous persons who need no repentance.

8 "Or what woman, if she has ten silver coins and loses one coin, does not light a lamp and sweep the house and search carefully until she finds it? 9 When she has found it, she calls together her friends and neighbors, saying, 'Rejoice with me, for I have found the coin which I had lost!' 10 In the same way, I tell you, there is joy in the presence of the angels of God over one sinner who repents."

DAY 20: Was it right for Gideon to ask God for signs?

In Judges 6:11, Gideon received a visitation from the "angel of the LORD." This is identified as "the LORD" Himself (vv. 14, 16, 23, 25, 27). See Genesis 16:7–14; 18:1; 32:24–30 for other appearances. Conditions in the land were grim due to the Midianites, which led Gideon to express his frustration that the Lord had forsaken them utterly.

Like Moses (Ex 33), Gideon desired a sign when the Lord directed him to rise up and lead a deliverance (v. 17). In both incidents, revelation was so rare and wickedness so prevalent that they desired full assurance. God graciously gave it. In vv. 18–23, the fire from God brought the realization of the presence of God to Gideon, filling him with awe and even the fear of death. When he saw the Lord, he knew the Lord had also seen him in his fallenness. Thus, he feared the death that sinners should die before Holy God. But God graciously promised life (v. 23).

In vv. 36–40, Gideon's two requests for signs in the fleece should be viewed as weak faith. Even Gideon recognized this when he said, "Do not let Your anger burn against me" (v. 39), since God had already specifically promised His presence and victory (vv. 12, 14, 16). But they were also legitimate requests for confirmation of victory against seemingly impossible odds (6:5; 7:2, 12). God nowhere reprimanded Gideon, but was very compassionate in giving what his inadequacy requested. In 7:10–15, God volunteered a sign to boost Gideon's faith.

 # APRIL 21

Judges 7:1–8:35

7 Then Jerubbaal (that is, Gideon) and all the people who were with him, rose early and camped beside the spring of Harod; and the camp of Midian was on the north side of them by the hill of Moreh in the valley.

2 The LORD said to Gideon, "The people who are with you are too many for Me to give Midian into their hands, for Israel would become boastful, saying, 'My own power has delivered me.' 3 Now therefore come, proclaim in the hearing of the people, saying, 'Whoever is afraid and trembling, let him return and depart from Mount Gilead.'" So 22,000 people returned, but 10,000 remained.

4 Then the LORD said to Gideon, "The people are still too many; bring them down to the water and I will test them for you there. Therefore it shall be that he of whom I say to you, 'This one shall go with you,' he shall go with you; but everyone of whom I say to you, 'This one shall not go with you,' he shall not go." 5 So he brought the people down to the water. And the LORD said to Gideon, "You shall separate everyone who laps the water with his tongue as a dog laps, as well as everyone who kneels to drink." 6 Now the number of those who lapped, putting their hand to their mouth, was 300 men; but all the rest of the people kneeled to drink water. 7 The LORD said

to Gideon, "I will deliver you with the 300 men who lapped and will give the Midianites into your hands; so let all the *other* people go, each man to his home." 8 So the 300 men took the people's provisions and their trumpets into their hands. And Gideon sent all the *other* men of Israel, each to his tent, but retained the 300 men; and the camp of Midian was below him in the valley.

9 Now the same night it came about that the LORD said to him, "Arise, go down against the camp, for I have given it into your hands. 10 But if you are afraid to go down, go with Purah your servant down to the camp, 11 and you will hear what they say; and afterward your hands will be strengthened that you may go down against the camp." So he went with Purah his servant down to the outposts of the army that was in the camp. 12 Now the Midianites and the Amalekites and all the sons of the east were lying in the valley as numerous as locusts; and their camels were without number, as numerous as the sand on the seashore. 13 When Gideon came, behold, a man was relating a dream to his friend. And he said, "Behold, I had a dream; a loaf of barley bread was tumbling into the camp of Midian, and it came to the tent and struck it so that it fell, and turned it upside down so that the tent lay flat." 14 His friend replied, "This is nothing less than the sword of Gideon the son of Joash, a man of Israel; God has given Midian and all the camp into his hand."

¹⁵When Gideon heard the account of the dream and its interpretation, he bowed in worship. He returned to the camp of Israel and said, "Arise, for the LORD has given the camp of Midian into your hands." ¹⁶He divided the 300 men into three companies, and he put trumpets and empty pitchers into the hands of all of them, with torches inside the pitchers. ¹⁷He said to them, "Look at me and do likewise. And behold, when I come to the outskirts of the camp, do as I do. ¹⁸When I and all who are with me blow the trumpet, then you also blow the trumpets all around the camp and say, 'For the LORD and for Gideon.'"

¹⁹So Gideon and the hundred men who were with him came to the outskirts of the camp at the beginning of the middle watch, when they had just posted the watch; and they blew the trumpets and smashed the pitchers that were in their hands. ²⁰When the three companies blew the trumpets and broke the pitchers, they held the torches in their left hands and the trumpets in their right hands for blowing, and cried, "A sword for the LORD and for Gideon!" ²¹Each stood in

---

7:20 A sword for the LORD and for Gideon! Here was the power of God in harmony with the obedience of man. Such shouts reminded the enemies that the threat of the sword of Gideon and of God was for real. The impression was one of doom and terror.

---

his place around the camp; and all the army ran, crying out as they fled. ²²When they blew 300 trumpets, the LORD set the sword of one against another even throughout the whole army; and the army fled as far as Beth-shittah toward Zererah, as far as the edge of Abel-meholah, by Tabbath. ²³The men of Israel were summoned from Naphtali and Asher and all Manasseh, and they pursued Midian.

²⁴Gideon sent messengers throughout all the hill country of Ephraim, saying, "Come down against Midian and take the waters before them, as far as Beth-barah and the Jordan." So all the men of Ephraim were summoned and they took the waters as far as Beth-barah and the Jordan. ²⁵They captured the two leaders of Midian, Oreb and Zeeb, and they killed Oreb at the rock of Oreb, and they killed Zeeb at the wine press of Zeeb, while they pursued Midian; and they brought the heads of Oreb and Zeeb to Gideon from across the Jordan.

8 Then the men of Ephraim said to him, "What is this thing you have done to us, not calling us when you went to fight against Midian?" And they contended with him vigorously. ²But he said to them, "What have I done now in comparison with you? Is not the gleaning *of the grapes* of Ephraim better than the vintage of Abiezer? ³God has given the leaders of Midian, Oreb and Zeeb into your hands; and what was I able to do in comparison with you?" Then their anger toward him subsided when he said that.

⁴Then Gideon and the 300 men who were with him came to the Jordan and crossed over, weary yet pursuing. ⁵He said to the men of Succoth, "Please give loaves of bread to the people who are following me, for they are weary, and I am pursuing Zebah and Zalmunna, the kings of Midian." ⁶The leaders of Succoth said, "Are the hands of Zebah and Zalmunna already in your hands, that we should give bread to your army?" ⁷Gideon said, "All right, when the LORD has given Zebah and Zalmunna into my hand, then I will thrash your bodies with the thorns of the wilderness and with briers." ⁸He went up from there to Penuel and spoke similarly to them; and the men of Penuel answered him just as the men of Succoth had answered. ⁹So he spoke also to the men of Penuel, saying, "When I return safely, I will tear down this tower."

¹⁰Now Zebah and Zalmunna were in Karkor, and their armies with them, about 15,000 men, all who were left of the entire army of the sons of the east; for the fallen were 120,000 swordsmen. ¹¹Gideon went up by the way of those who lived in tents on the east of Nobah and Jogbehah, and attacked the camp when the camp was unsuspecting. ¹²When Zebah and Zalmunna fled, he pursued them and captured the two kings of Midian, Zebah and Zalmunna, and routed the whole army.

¹³Then Gideon the son of Joash returned from the battle by the ascent of Heres. ¹⁴And he captured a youth from Succoth and questioned him. Then *the youth* wrote down for him the princes of Succoth and its elders, seventy-seven men. ¹⁵He came to the men of Succoth and said, "Behold Zebah and Zalmunna, concerning whom you taunted me, saying, 'Are the hands of Zebah and Zalmunna already in your hand, that we should give bread to your men who are weary?'" ¹⁶He took the elders of the city, and thorns of the wilderness and briers, and he disciplined the men of Succoth with them. ¹⁷He tore down the tower of Penuel and killed the men of the city.

¹⁸Then he said to Zebah and Zalmunna,

"What kind of men *were* they whom you killed at Tabor?" And they said, "They were like you, each one resembling the son of a king." ¹⁹ He said, "They *were* my brothers, the sons of my mother. *As* the LORD lives, if only you had let them live, I would not kill you." ²⁰ So he said to Jether his firstborn, "Rise, kill them." But the youth did not draw his sword, for he was afraid, because he was still a youth. ²¹ Then Zebah and Zalmunna said, "Rise up yourself, and fall on us; for as the man, so is his strength." So Gideon arose and killed Zebah and Zalmunna, and took the crescent ornaments which were on their camels' necks. ²² Then the men of Israel said to Gideon, "Rule over us, both you and your son, also your son's son, for you have delivered us from the hand of Midian." ²³ But Gideon said to them, "I will not rule over you, nor shall my son rule over you; the LORD shall rule over you." ²⁴ Yet Gideon said to them, "I would request of you, that each of you give me an earring from his spoil." (For they had gold earrings, because they were Ishmaelites.) ²⁵ They said, "We will surely give *them*." So they spread out a garment, and every one of them threw an earring there from his spoil. ²⁶ The weight of the gold earrings that he requested was 1,700 *shekels* of gold, besides the crescent ornaments and the pendants and the purple robes which *were* on the kings of Midian, and besides the neck bands that *were* on their camels' necks. ²⁷ Gideon made it into an ephod, and placed it in his city, Ophrah, and all Israel played the harlot with it there, so that it became a snare to Gideon and his household. ²⁸ So Midian was subdued before the sons of Israel, and they did not lift up their heads anymore. And the land was undisturbed for forty years in the days of Gideon.

²⁹ Then Jerubbaal the son of Joash went and lived in his own house. ³⁰ Now Gideon had seventy sons who were his direct descendants, for he had many wives. ³¹ His concubine who was in Shechem also bore him a son, and he named him Abimelech. ³² And Gideon the son of Joash died at a ripe old age and was buried in the tomb of his father Joash, in Ophrah of the Abiezrites.

³³ Then it came about, as soon as Gideon was dead, that the sons of Israel again played the harlot with the Baals, and made Baal-berith their god. ³⁴ Thus the sons of Israel did not remember the LORD their God, who had delivered them from the hands of all their enemies on every side; ³⁵ nor did they show kindness to the household of Jerubbaal (*that is,* Gideon) in accord with all the good that he had done to Israel.

Psalm 49:10–20

¹⁰ For he sees *that even* wise men die;
   The stupid and the senseless
      alike perish
   And leave their wealth to others.
¹¹ Their inner thought is *that*
      their houses are forever
   And their dwelling places
      to all generations;
   They have called their lands
      after their own names.
¹² But man in *his* pomp will
      not endure;
   He is like the beasts that perish.

¹³ This is the way of those
      who are foolish,
   And of those after them who
      approve their words.   *Selah*
¹⁴ As sheep they are appointed
      for Sheol;
   Death shall be their shepherd;
   And the upright shall rule over
      them in the morning,
   And their form shall be for
      Sheol to consume
   So that they have no habitation.
¹⁵ But God will redeem my soul
      from the power of Sheol,
   For He will receive me.   *Selah*

¹⁶ Do not be afraid when a
      man becomes rich,
   When the glory of his
      house is increased;
¹⁷ For when he dies he will
      carry nothing away;
   His glory will not descend after him.

8:24–27 Gideon made...an ephod. This was certainly a sad end to Gideon's influence as he, perhaps in an expression of pride, sought to lift himself up in the eyes of the people. Gideon intended nothing more than to make a breastpiece as David did (1Ch 15:27) to indicate civil, not priestly rule. It was never intended to set up idolatrous worship, but to be a symbol of civil power. That no evil was intended can be noted from the subduing of Midian (v. 28), quietness from wars (v. 28), and the fact that idolatry came after Gideon's death (v. 33) as well as the commendation of Gideon (v. 35).

49:15 But God will redeem my soul...He will receive me. This is one of the greatest affirmations of confidence in God in the Psalms. Although the faithless person cannot buy his way out of death (v. 7ff.), the faithful one is redeemed by the only Redeemer, God Himself. (On the significance of the word "receive," see Ge 5:24; 2Ki 2:10; Ps 73:24; Heb 11:5.) So in v. 15 the psalmist expresses his confidence in God, that He would raise him to eternal life.

18 Though while he lives he
   congratulates himself—
   And though *men* praise you when
   you do well for yourself—
19 He shall go to the generation
   of his fathers;
   They will never see the light.
20 Man in *his* pomp, yet without
   understanding,
   Is like the beasts that perish.

Proverbs 14:22-24

22 Will they not go astray
   who devise evil?
   But kindness and truth *will be*
   to those who devise good.
23 In all labor there is profit,
   But mere talk *leads* only to poverty.
24 The crown of the wise is their riches,
   But the folly of fools is foolishness.

Luke 15:11-32

11 And He said, "A man had two sons. 12 The younger of them said to his father, 'Father, give me the share of the estate that falls to me.' So he divided his wealth between them. 13 And not many days later, the younger son gathered everything together and went on a journey into a distant country, and there he squandered his estate with loose living. 14 Now when he had spent everything, a severe famine occurred in that country, and he began to be impoverished. 15 So he went and hired himself out to one of the citizens of that country, and he sent him into his fields to feed swine. 16 And he would have gladly filled his stomach with the pods that the swine were eating, and no one was giving *anything* to him. 17 But when he came to his senses, he said, 'How many of my father's hired men have more than enough bread, but I am dying here with hunger! 18 I will get up and go to my father, and will say to him, "Father, I have sinned against heaven, and in your sight; 19 I am no longer worthy to be called your son;

make me as one of your hired men." ' 20 So he got up and came to his father. But while he was still a long way off, his father saw him and felt compassion *for him,* and ran and embraced him and kissed him. 21 And the son said to him, 'Father, I have sinned against heaven and in your sight; I am no longer worthy to be called your son.' 22 But the father said to his slaves, 'Quickly bring out the best robe and put it on him, and put a ring on his hand and sandals on his feet; 23 and bring the fattened calf, kill it, and let us eat and celebrate; 24 for this son of mine was dead and has come to life again; he was lost and has been found.' And they began to celebrate.

25 "Now his older son was in the field, and when he came and approached the house, he heard music and dancing. 26 And he summoned one of the servants and *began* inquiring what these things could be. 27 And he said to him, 'Your brother has come, and your father has killed the fattened calf because he has received him back safe and sound.' 28 But he became angry and was not willing to go in; and his father came out and *began* pleading with him. 29 But he answered and said to his father, 'Look! For so many years I have been serving you and I have never neglected a command of yours; and *yet* you have never given me a young goat, so that I might celebrate with my friends; 30 but when this son of yours came, who has devoured your wealth with prostitutes, you killed the fattened calf for him.' 31 And he said to him, 'Son, you have always been with me, and all that is mine is yours. 32 But we had to celebrate and rejoice, for this brother of yours was dead and *has begun* to live, and *was* lost and has been found.' "

15:29 I have never neglected a command of yours. Unlikely, given the boy's obvious contempt for his father, shown by his refusal to participate in the father's great joy. This statement reveals the telltale problem with all religious hypocrites. They will not recognize their sin and repent. The elder son's comment reeks of the same spirit as the words of the Pharisee in 18:11. **you have never given me a young goat.** All those years of service to the father appear to have been motivated too much by concern for what he could get for himself. This son's self-righteous behavior was more socially acceptable than the younger brother's debauchery, but it was equally dishonoring to the father—and called for repentance.

DAY 21: What is the main feature of the parable of the prodigal son?

The parable in Luke 15:11–32, unlike most parables, has more than one lesson. The prodigal is an example of sound repentance. The elder brother illustrates the wickedness of the Pharisees' self-righteousness, prejudice, and indifference toward repenting sinners. And the father pictures God, eager to forgive and longing for the return of the sinner. The main feature, however, is the joy of God, the celebrations that fill heaven when a sinner repents.

For the son to demand "the share of the estate that falls to me" (v. 12) is tantamount to saying he wished his father were dead. He was not entitled to any inheritance while his father still lived. Yet the father graciously fulfilled the request, giving him his full portion, which would have been one-third of the entire estate—because the right of the firstborn (Dt 21:17) gave the elder brother a double portion. This act pictures all sinners (related to God the Father by creation), who waste their potential privileges and refuse any relationship with Him, choosing instead a life of sinful self-indulgence. The Greek word for "prodigal" means "dissolute" and conveys the idea of an utterly debauched lifestyle. "To feed swine" (v. 15) was the worst sort of degradation imaginable for Jesus' Jewish audience; swine were the worst sort of unclean animals. His situation could hardly have been more desperate.

Nevertheless, when "his father saw him and felt compassion for him, and ran and embraced him and kissed him" (v. 20). Clearly, the father had been waiting and looking for his son's return. The father's eagerness and joy at his son's return is unmistakable. This is the magnificent attribute of God that sets Him apart from all the false gods invented by men and demons. He is not indifferent or hostile, but a Savior by nature, longing to see sinners repent and rejoicing when they do. From Genesis 3:8 to Revelation 22:17, from the Fall to the Consummation, God has been and will be seeking to save sinners and rejoices each time one repents and is converted.

APRIL 22

Judges 9:1–10:18

9 And Abimelech the son of Jerubbaal went to Shechem to his mother's relatives, and spoke to them and to the whole clan of the household of his mother's father, saying, ² "Speak, now, in the hearing of all the leaders of Shechem, 'Which is better for you, that seventy men, all the sons of Jerubbaal, rule over you, or that one man rule over you?' Also, remember that I am your bone and your flesh." ³ And his mother's relatives spoke all these words on his behalf in the hearing of all the leaders of Shechem; and they were inclined to follow Abimelech, for they said, "He is our relative." ⁴ They gave him seventy *pieces* of silver from the house of Baal-berith with which Abimelech hired worthless and reckless fellows, and they followed him. ⁵ Then he went to his father's house at Ophrah and killed his brothers the sons of Jerubbaal, seventy men, on one stone. But Jotham the youngest son of Jerubbaal was left, for he hid himself. ⁶ All the men of Shechem and all Beth-millo assembled together, and they went and made Abimelech king, by the oak of the pillar which was in Shechem.

⁷ Now when they told Jotham, he went and stood on the top of Mount Gerizim, and lifted his voice and called out. Thus he said to them, "Listen to me, O men of Shechem, that God may listen to you. ⁸ Once the trees went forth to anoint a king over them, and they said to the olive tree, 'Reign over us!' ⁹ But the olive tree said to them, 'Shall I leave my fatness with which God and men are honored, and go to wave over the trees?' ¹⁰ Then the trees said to the fig tree, 'You come, reign over us!' ¹¹ But the fig tree said to them, 'Shall I leave my sweetness and my good fruit, and go to wave over the trees?' ¹² Then the trees said to the vine, 'You come, reign over us!' ¹³ But the vine said to them, 'Shall I leave my new wine, which cheers God and men, and go to wave over the trees?' ¹⁴ Finally all the trees said to the bramble, 'You come, reign over us!' ¹⁵ The bramble said to the trees, 'If in truth you are anointing me as king over you, come and take refuge in my shade; but if not, may fire come out from the bramble and consume the cedars of Lebanon.'

¹⁶ "Now therefore, if you have dealt in truth and integrity in making Abimelech king, and if you have dealt well with Jerubbaal and his house, and have dealt with him as he deserved— ¹⁷ for my father fought for you and risked his life and delivered you from the hand of Midian; ¹⁸ but you have risen against my father's house today and have killed his sons, seventy men, on one stone, and have made Abimelech, the son of his maidservant, king over the men of Shechem, because he is your relative— ¹⁹ if then you have dealt in truth and integrity with Jerubbaal and his

house this day, rejoice in Abimelech, and let him also rejoice in you. ²⁰ But if not, let fire come out from Abimelech and consume the men of Shechem and Beth-millo; and let fire come out from the men of Shechem and from Beth-millo, and consume Abimelech." ²¹ Then Jotham escaped and fled, and went to Beer and remained there because of Abimelech his brother.

²² Now Abimelech ruled over Israel three years. ²³ Then God sent an evil spirit between Abimelech and the men of Shechem; and the men of Shechem dealt treacherously with Abimelech, ²⁴ so that the violence done to the seventy sons of Jerubbaal might come, and their blood might be laid on Abimelech their brother, who killed them, and on the men of Shechem, who strengthened his hands to kill his brothers. ²⁵ The men of Shechem set men in ambush against him on the tops of the mountains, and they robbed all who might pass by them along the road; and it was told to Abimelech.

²⁶ Now Gaal the son of Ebed came with his relatives, and crossed over into Shechem; and the men of Shechem put their trust in him. ²⁷ They went out into the field and gathered *the grapes of* their vineyards and trod *them*, and held a festival; and they went into the house of their god, and ate and drank and cursed Abimelech. ²⁸ Then Gaal the son of Ebed said, "Who is Abimelech, and who is Shechem, that we should serve him? Is he not the son of Jerubbaal, and *is* Zebul *not* his lieutenant? Serve the men of Hamor the father of Shechem; but why should we serve him? ²⁹ Would, therefore, that this people were under my authority! Then I would remove Abimelech." And he said to Abimelech, "Increase your army and come out."

³⁰ When Zebul the ruler of the city heard the words of Gaal the son of Ebed, his anger burned. ³¹ He sent messengers to Abimelech deceitfully, saying, "Behold, Gaal the son of Ebed and his relatives have come to Shechem; and behold, they are stirring up the city against you. ³² Now therefore, arise by night, you and the people who are with you, and lie in wait in the field. ³³ In the morning, as soon as the sun is up, you shall rise early and rush upon the city; and behold, when he and the people who are with him come out against you, you shall do to them whatever you can."

³⁴ So Abimelech and all the people who *were* with him arose by night and lay in wait against Shechem in four companies. ³⁵ Now Gaal the son of Ebed went out and stood in the entrance of the city gate; and Abimelech and the people who *were* with him arose from the ambush. ³⁶ When Gaal saw the people, he said to Zebul, "Look, people are coming down from the tops of the mountains." But Zebul said to him, "You are seeing the shadow of the mountains as *if they were* men." ³⁷ Gaal spoke again and said, "Behold, people are coming down from the highest part of the land, and one company comes by the way of the diviners' oak." ³⁸ Then Zebul said to him, "Where is your boasting now with which you said, 'Who is Abimelech that we should serve him?' Is this not the people whom you despised? Go out now and fight with them!" ³⁹ So Gaal went out before the leaders of Shechem and fought with Abimelech. ⁴⁰ Abimelech chased him, and he fled before him; and many fell wounded up to the entrance of the gate. ⁴¹ Then Abimelech remained at Arumah, but Zebul drove out Gaal and his relatives so that they could not remain in Shechem.

⁴² Now it came about the next day, that the people went out to the field, and it was told to Abimelech. ⁴³ So he took his people and divided them into three companies, and lay in wait in the field; when he looked and saw the people coming out from the city, he arose against them and slew them. ⁴⁴ Then Abimelech and the company who was with him dashed forward and stood in the entrance of the city gate; the other two companies then dashed against all who *were* in the field and slew them. ⁴⁵ Abimelech fought against the city all that day, and he captured the city and killed the people who *were* in it; then he razed the city and sowed it with salt.

⁴⁶ When all the leaders of the tower of Shechem heard of *it,* they entered the inner chamber of the temple of El-berith. ⁴⁷ It was told Abimelech that all the leaders of the tower of Shechem were gathered together. ⁴⁸ So Abimelech went up to Mount Zalmon, he and all the people who *were* with him; and Abimelech took an axe in his hand and cut down a branch from the trees, and lifted it and laid *it* on his shoulder. Then he said to the people who *were* with him, "What you have seen me do, hurry *and* do likewise." ⁴⁹ All the people also cut down each one his branch and followed Abimelech, and put *them* on the inner chamber and set the inner chamber on fire over those *inside,* so that all the men of the tower of Shechem also died, about a thousand men and women.

⁵⁰ Then Abimelech went to Thebez, and he camped against Thebez and captured it. ⁵¹ But there was a strong tower in the center

of the city, and all the men and women with all the leaders of the city fled there and shut themselves in; and they went up on the roof of the tower. ⁵²So Abimelech came to the tower and fought against it, and approached the entrance of the tower to burn it with fire. ⁵³But a certain woman threw an upper millstone on Abimelech's head, crushing his skull. ⁵⁴Then he called quickly to the young man, his armor bearer, and said to him, "Draw your sword and kill me, so that it will not be said of me, 'A woman slew him.'" So the young man pierced him through, and he died. ⁵⁵When the men of Israel saw that Abimelech was dead, each departed to his home. ⁵⁶Thus God repaid the wickedness of Abimelech, which he had done to his father in killing his seventy brothers. ⁵⁷Also God returned all the wickedness of the men of Shechem on their heads, and the curse of Jotham the son of Jerubbaal came upon them.

10 Now after Abimelech died, Tola the son of Puah, the son of Dodo, a man of Issachar, arose to save Israel; and he lived in Shamir in the hill country of Ephraim. ²He judged Israel twenty-three years. Then he died and was buried in Shamir.

³After him, Jair the Gileadite arose and judged Israel twenty-two years. ⁴He had thirty sons who rode on thirty donkeys, and they had thirty cities in the land of Gilead that are called Havvoth-jair to this day. ⁵And Jair died and was buried in Kamon.

⁶Then the sons of Israel again did evil in the sight of the LORD, served the Baals and the Ashtaroth, the gods of Aram, the gods of Sidon, the gods of Moab, the gods of the sons of Ammon, and the gods of the Philistines; thus they forsook the LORD and did not serve Him. ⁷The anger of the LORD burned against Israel, and He sold them into the hands of the Philistines and into the hands of the sons of Ammon. ⁸They afflicted and crushed the sons of Israel that year; for eighteen years they *afflicted* all the sons of Israel who were beyond the Jordan in Gilead in the land of the Amorites. ⁹The sons of Ammon crossed the Jordan to fight also against Judah, Benjamin, and the house of Ephraim, so that Israel was greatly distressed.

¹⁰Then the sons of Israel cried out to the LORD, saying, "We have sinned against You, for indeed, we have forsaken our God and served the Baals." ¹¹The LORD said to the sons of Israel, "*Did I* not *deliver you* from the Egyptians, the Amorites, the sons of Ammon, and the Philistines? ¹²Also when the Sidonians, the Amalekites and the Maonites oppressed

you, you cried out to Me, and I delivered you from their hands. ¹³Yet you have forsaken Me and served other gods; therefore I will no longer deliver you. ¹⁴Go and cry out to the gods which you have chosen; let them deliver you in the time of your distress." ¹⁵The sons of Israel said to the LORD, "We have sinned, do to us whatever seems good to You; only please deliver us this day." ¹⁶So they put away the foreign gods from among them and served the LORD; and He could bear the misery of Israel no longer.

¹⁷Then the sons of Ammon were summoned and they camped in Gilead. And the sons of Israel gathered together and camped in Mizpah. ¹⁸The people, the leaders of Gilead, said to one another, "Who is the man who will begin to fight against the sons of Ammon? He shall become head over all the inhabitants of Gilead."

Psalm 50:1–6

A Psalm of Asaph.

The Mighty One, God, the
  LORD, has spoken,
And summoned the earth from the
  rising of the sun to its setting.
² Out of Zion, the perfection
  of beauty,
God has shone forth.
³ May our God come and
  not keep silence;
Fire devours before Him,
And it is very tempestuous
  around Him.
⁴ He summons the heavens above,
And the earth, to judge His
  people:
⁵ "Gather My godly ones to Me,
Those who have made a covenant
  with Me by sacrifice."
⁶ And the heavens declare
His righteousness,
For God Himself is judge.   *Selah*

50:1 The Mighty One, God, the LORD. The Divine Judge is introduced with three significant Old Testament names. The first two are the short and longer forms of the most common word for "God" in the OT, and the third is the name for Israel's God par excellence, i.e., Yahweh (see its historical origin in Ex 3:14). **from the rising of the sun to its setting.** A common Old Testament idiom conveying from east to west, i.e., all over the planet.

Proverbs 14:25–27

²⁵ A truthful witness saves lives,
But he who utters lies is treacherous.
²⁶ In the fear of the LORD there
is strong confidence,
And his children will have refuge.
²⁷ The fear of the LORD is a
fountain of life,
That one may avoid the
snares of death.

Luke 16:1–31

16 Now He was also saying to the disciples, "There was a rich man who had a manager, and this *manager* was reported to him as squandering his possessions. ²And he called him and said to him, 'What is this I hear about you? Give an accounting of your management, for you can no longer be manager.' ³The manager said to himself, 'What shall I do, since my master is taking the management away from me? I am not strong enough to dig; I am ashamed to beg. ⁴I know what I shall do, so that when I am removed from the management people will welcome me into their homes.' ⁵And he summoned each one of his master's debtors, and he *began* saying to the first, 'How much do you owe my master?' ⁶And he said, 'A hundred measures of oil.' And he said to him, 'Take your bill, and sit down quickly and write fifty.' ⁷Then he said to another, 'And how much do you owe?' And he said, 'A hundred measures of wheat.' He *said to him, 'Take your bill, and write eighty.' ⁸And his master praised the unrighteous manager because he had acted shrewdly; for the sons of this age are more shrewd in relation to their own kind than the sons of light. ⁹And I say to you, make friends for yourselves by means of the wealth of unrighteousness, so that when it fails, they will receive you into the eternal dwellings.

¹⁰ "He who is faithful in a very little thing is faithful also in much; and he who is unrighteous in a very little thing is unrighteous also in much. ¹¹Therefore if you have not been faithful in the *use of* unrighteous wealth, who will entrust the true *riches* to you? ¹²And if you have not been faithful in *the use of* that which is another's, who will give you that which is your own? ¹³No servant can serve two masters; for either he will hate the one and love the other, or else he will be devoted to one and despise the other. You cannot serve God and wealth."

¹⁴Now the Pharisees, who were lovers of money, were listening to all these things and were scoffing at Him. ¹⁵And He said to them,

16:13 You cannot serve God and wealth. Many of the Pharisees taught that devotion to money and devotion to God were perfectly compatible (v. 14). This went hand in hand with the commonly held notion that earthly riches signified divine blessing. Rich people were therefore regarded as God's favorites. While not condemning wealth per se, Christ denounced both love of wealth and devotion to mammon.

16:15 justify yourselves. The Pharisees' belief was that their own goodness was what justified them (Ro 10:3). This is the very definition of "self-righteousness." But, as Jesus suggested, their righteousness was flawed, being an external veneer only. That might be enough to justify them before men, but not before God, because He knew their hearts. He repeatedly exposed their habit of seeking the approval of people (Mt 6:2, 5, 16; 23:28).

"You are those who justify yourselves in the sight of men, but God knows your hearts; for that which is highly esteemed among men is detestable in the sight of God.

¹⁶ "The Law and the Prophets *were proclaimed* until John; since that time the gospel of the kingdom of God has been preached, and everyone is forcing his way into it. ¹⁷But it is easier for heaven and earth to pass away than for one stroke of a letter of the Law to fail.

¹⁸ "Everyone who divorces his wife and marries another commits adultery, and he who marries one who is divorced from a husband commits adultery.

¹⁹ "Now there was a rich man, and he habitually dressed in purple and fine linen, joyously living in splendor every day. ²⁰And a poor man named Lazarus was laid at his gate, covered with sores, ²¹and longing to be fed with the *crumbs* which were falling from the rich man's table; besides, even the dogs were coming and licking his sores. ²²Now the poor man died and was carried away by the angels to Abraham's bosom; and the rich man also died and was buried. ²³In Hades he lifted up his eyes, being in torment, and *saw Abraham far away and Lazarus in his bosom. ²⁴And he cried out and said, 'Father Abraham, have mercy on me, and send Lazarus so that he may dip the tip of his finger in water and cool off my tongue, for I am in agony in this flame.' ²⁵But Abraham said, 'Child, remember that during your life you received your good things, and likewise Lazarus bad things; but now he is being comforted here,

and you are in agony. ²⁶And besides all this, between us and you there is a great chasm fixed, so that those who wish to come over from here to you will not be able, and *that* none may cross over from there to us.' ²⁷And he said, 'Then I beg you, father, that you send him to my father's house— ²⁸for I have five brothers—in order that he may warn them, so that they will not also come to this place of torment.' ²⁹But Abraham *said, 'They have Moses and the Prophets; let them hear them.' ³⁰But he said, 'No, father Abraham, but if someone goes to them from the dead, they will repent!' ³¹But he said to him, 'If they do not listen to Moses and the Prophets, they will not be persuaded even if someone rises from the dead.' "

16:31 they will not be persuaded. This speaks powerfully of the singular sufficiency of Scripture to overcome unbelief. The gospel itself is the power of God unto salvation (Ro 1:16). Since unbelief is at heart a moral, rather than an intellectual, problem, no amount of evidences will ever turn unbelief to faith. But the revealed Word of God has inherent power to do so (Jn 6:63; Heb 4:12; Jas 1:18; 1Pe 1:23).

DAY 22: Why would the parable of the rich man scandalize the Pharisees?

The parable of the rich man and Lazarus (Lk 16:19–31) was employed in the same fashion as all Christ's parables, to teach a lesson, in this case for the benefit of the Pharisees. The mention of table scraps, sores, and dogs all made this poor man appear odious in the eyes of the Pharisees (v. 21). They were inclined to see all such things as proof of divine disfavor.

The idea was that Lazarus was given a place of high honor, reclining next to Abraham at the heavenly banquet, "Abraham's bosom" (v. 22). This same expression (found only here in Scripture) was used in the Talmud as a figure for heaven. Yet the rich man was "in Hades" (v. 23). The suggestion that a rich man would be excluded from heaven would have scandalized the Pharisees. Especially galling was the idea that a beggar who ate scraps from his table was granted the place of honor next to Abraham.

"Hades" was the Greek term for the abode of the dead. In the Greek Old Testament, it was used to translate the Hebrew *Sheol,* which referred to the realm of the dead in general, without necessarily distinguishing between righteous or unrighteous souls. However, in New Testament usage, "Hades" always refers to the place of the wicked prior to final judgment in hell. The imagery Jesus used fit the erroneous common rabbinical idea that Sheol had two parts, one for the souls of the righteous and the other for the souls of the wicked—separated by an impassable gulf. But there is no reason to suppose, as some do, that "Abraham's bosom" spoke of a temporary prison for the souls of Old Testament saints, who were brought to heaven only after He had actually atoned for their sins. Scripture consistently teaches that the spirits of the righteous dead go immediately into the presence of God (see 23:43; 2Co 5:8; Php 1:23). And the presence of Moses and Elijah on the Mount of Transfiguration (9:30) belies the notion that they were confined in a compartment of Sheol until Christ finished His work.

 # APRIL 23

Judges 11:1–12:15

11 Now Jephthah the Gileadite was a valiant warrior, but he was the son of a harlot. And Gilead was the father of Jephthah. ²Gilead's wife bore him sons; and when his wife's sons grew up, they drove Jephthah out and said to him, "You shall not have an inheritance in our father's house, for you are the son of another woman." ³So Jephthah fled from his brothers and lived in the land of Tob; and worthless fellows gathered themselves about Jephthah, and they went out with him.

⁴It came about after a while that the sons of Ammon fought against Israel. ⁵When the sons of Ammon fought against Israel, the elders of Gilead went to get Jephthah from the land of Tob; ⁶and they said to Jephthah, "Come and be our chief that we may fight against the sons of Ammon." ⁷Then Jephthah said to the elders of Gilead, "Did you not hate me and drive me from my father's house? So why have you come to me now when you are in trouble?" ⁸The elders of Gilead said to Jephthah, "For this reason we have now returned to you, that you may go with us and fight with the sons of Ammon and become head over all the inhabitants of Gilead." ⁹So Jephthah said to the elders of Gilead, "If you take me back to fight against the sons of Ammon and the

LORD gives them up to me, will I become your head?" ¹⁰ The elders of Gilead said to Jephthah, "The LORD is witness between us; surely we will do as you have said." ¹¹ Then Jephthah went with the elders of Gilead, and the people made him head and chief over them; and Jephthah spoke all his words before the LORD at Mizpah.

¹² Now Jephthah sent messengers to the king of the sons of Ammon, saying, "What is between you and me, that you have come to me to fight against my land?" ¹³ The king of the sons of Ammon said to the messengers of Jephthah, "Because Israel took away my land when they came up from Egypt, from the Arnon as far as the Jabbok and the Jordan; therefore, return them peaceably now." ¹⁴ But Jephthah sent messengers again to the king of the sons of Ammon, ¹⁵ and they said to him, "Thus says Jephthah, 'Israel did not take away the land of Moab nor the land of the sons of Ammon. ¹⁶ For when they came up from Egypt, and Israel went through the wilderness to the Red Sea and came to Kadesh, ¹⁷ then Israel sent messengers to the king of Edom, saying, "Please let us pass through your land," but the king of Edom would not listen. And they also sent to the king of Moab, but he would not consent. So Israel remained at Kadesh. ¹⁸ Then they went through the wilderness and around the land of Edom and the land of Moab, and came to the east side of the land of Moab, and they camped beyond the Arnon; but they did not enter the territory of Moab, for the Arnon *was* the border of Moab. ¹⁹ And Israel sent messengers to Sihon king of the Amorites, the king of Heshbon, and Israel said to him, "Please let us pass through your land to our place." ²⁰ But Sihon did not trust Israel to pass through his territory; so Sihon gathered all his people and camped in Jahaz and fought with Israel. ²¹ The LORD, the God of Israel, gave Sihon and all his people into the hand of Israel, and they defeated them; so Israel possessed all the land of the Amorites, the inhabitants of that country. ²² So they possessed all the territory of the Amorites, from the Arnon as far as the Jabbok, and from the wilderness as far as the Jordan. ²³ Since now the LORD, the God of Israel, drove out the Amorites from before His people Israel, are you then to possess it? ²⁴ Do you not possess what Chemosh your god gives you to possess? So whatever the LORD our God has driven out before us, we will possess it. ²⁵ Now are you any better than Balak the son of Zippor, king of Moab?

Did he ever strive with Israel, or did he ever fight against them? ²⁶ While Israel lived in Heshbon and its villages, and in Aroer and its villages, and in all the cities that are on the banks of the Arnon, three hundred years, why did you not recover them within that time? ²⁷ I therefore have not sinned against you, but you are doing me wrong by making war against me; may the LORD, the Judge, judge today between the sons of Israel and the sons of Ammon.'" ²⁸ But the king of the sons of Ammon disregarded the message which Jephthah sent him.

²⁹ Now the Spirit of the LORD came upon Jephthah, so that he passed through Gilead and Manasseh; then he passed through Mizpah of Gilead, and from Mizpah of Gilead he went on to the sons of Ammon. ³⁰ Jephthah made a vow to the LORD and said, "If You will indeed give the sons of Ammon into my hand, ³¹ then it shall be that whatever comes out of the doors of my house to meet me when I return in peace from the sons of Ammon, it shall be the LORD'S, and I will offer it up as a burnt offering." ³² So Jephthah crossed over to the sons of Ammon to fight against them; and the LORD gave them into his hand. ³³ He struck them with a very great slaughter from Aroer to the entrance of Minnith, twenty cities, and as far as Abel-keramim. So the sons of Ammon were subdued before the sons of Israel.

³⁴ When Jephthah came to his house at Mizpah, behold, his daughter was coming out to meet him with tambourines and with dancing. Now she was his one *and* only child; besides her he had no son or daughter.

11:31 I will offer it. Some interpreters reason that Jephthah offered his daughter as a living sacrifice in perpetual virginity. With this idea, v. 31 is made to mean "shall be the LORD's" or "I will offer it up as a burnt offering." The view sees only perpetual virginity in vv. 37–40, and rejects his offering a human sacrifice as being against God's revealed will (Dt 12:31). On the other hand, since he was 1) beyond the Jordan, 2) far from the tabernacle, 3) a hypocrite in religious devotion, 4) familiar with human sacrifice among other nations, 5) influenced by such superstition, and 6) wanting victory badly, he likely meant a burnt offering. The translation in v. 31 is "and," not "or." His act came in an era of bizarre things, even inconsistency by leaders whom God otherwise empowered (Gideon in 8:27).

³⁵When he saw her, he tore his clothes and said, "Alas, my daughter! You have brought me very low, and you are among those who trouble me; for I have given my word to the LORD, and I cannot take it back." ³⁶So she said to him, "My father, you have given your word to the LORD; do to me as you have said, since the LORD has avenged you of your enemies, the sons of Ammon." ³⁷She said to her father, "Let this thing be done for me; let me alone two months, that I may go to the mountains and weep because of my virginity, I and my companions." ³⁸Then he said, "Go." So he sent her away for two months; and she left with her companions, and wept on the mountains because of her virginity. ³⁹At the end of two months she returned to her father, who did to her according to the vow which he had made; and she had no relations with a man. Thus it became a custom in Israel, ⁴⁰that the daughters of Israel went yearly to commemorate the daughter of Jephthah the Gileadite four days in the year.

12 Then the men of Ephraim were summoned, and they crossed to Zaphon and said to Jephthah, "Why did you cross over to fight against the sons of Ammon without calling us to go with you? We will burn your house down on you." ²Jephthah said to them, "I and my people were at great strife with the sons of Ammon; when I called you, you did not deliver me from their hand. ³When I saw that you would not deliver me, I took my life in my hands and crossed over against the sons of Ammon, and the LORD gave them into my hand. Why then have you come up to me this day to fight against me?" ⁴Then Jephthah gathered all the men of Gilead and fought Ephraim; and the men of Gilead defeated Ephraim, because they said, "You are fugitives of Ephraim, O Gileadites, in the midst of Ephraim and in the midst of Manasseh." ⁵The Gileadites captured the fords of the Jordan opposite Ephraim. And it happened when any of the fugitives of Ephraim said, "Let me cross over," the men of Gilead would say to him, "Are you an Ephraimite?" If he said, "No," ⁶then they would say to him, "Say now, 'Shibboleth.'" But he said, "Sibboleth," for he could not pronounce it correctly. Then they seized him and slew him at the fords of the Jordan. Thus there fell at that time 42,000 of Ephraim.

⁷Jephthah judged Israel six years. Then Jephthah the Gileadite died and was buried in one of the cities of Gilead.

⁸Now Ibzan of Bethlehem judged Israel after him. ⁹He had thirty sons, and thirty daughters whom he gave in marriage outside the family, and he brought in thirty daughters from outside for his sons. And he judged Israel seven years. ¹⁰Then Ibzan died and was buried in Bethlehem.

¹¹Now Elon the Zebulunite judged Israel after him; and he judged Israel ten years. ¹²Then Elon the Zebulunite died and was buried at Aijalon in the land of Zebulun.

¹³Now Abdon the son of Hillel the Pirathonite judged Israel after him. ¹⁴He had forty sons and thirty grandsons who rode on seventy donkeys; and he judged Israel eight years. ¹⁵Then Abdon the son of Hillel the Pirathonite died and was buried at Pirathon in the land of Ephraim, in the hill country of the Amalekites.

Psalm 50:7–15

7 "Hear, O My people, and I will
    speak;
  O Israel, I will testify against
    you;
  I am God, your God.
8 "I do not reprove you for
    your sacrifices,
  And your burnt offerings are
    continually before Me.
9 "I shall take no young bull
    out of your house
  Nor male goats out of your
    folds.
10 "For every beast of the forest
    is Mine,
  The cattle on a thousand hills.
11 "I know every bird of the
    mountains,
  And everything that moves
    in the field is Mine.
12 "If I were hungry I would not
    tell you,
  For the world is Mine, and
    all it contains.

※

50:8 I do not reprove you for your sacrifices. The Divine Judge's condemnations are directed not at the act of sacrifice but at the people's attitude in sacrificing (1Sa 15:22; Pss 40:6–8; 51:17; 69:30; Is 1:12; Jer 7:21–26; Hos 6:6; Mic 6:6–8).

50:9–13 shall take no young bull out of your house. God refuses mere ritual; it is an abomination to Him. He, unlike the pagan deities, needs nothing; He created everything and owns everything.

[13] "Shall I eat the flesh of bulls
Or drink the blood of male
goats?
[14] "Offer to God a sacrifice
of thanksgiving
And pay your vows to the
Most High;
[15] Call upon Me in the day
of trouble;
I shall rescue you, and you
will honor Me."

Proverbs 14:28

[28] In a multitude of people
is a king's glory,
But in the dearth of people
is a prince's ruin.

Luke 17:1-19

17 He said to His disciples, "It is inevitable that stumbling blocks come, but woe to him through whom they come! [2] It would be better for him if a millstone were hung around his neck and he were thrown into the sea, than that he would cause one of these little ones to stumble. [3] Be on your guard! If your brother sins, rebuke him; and if he repents, forgive him. [4] And if he sins against you seven times a day, and returns to you seven times, saying, 'I repent,' forgive him."

[5] The apostles said to the Lord, "Increase our faith!" [6] And the Lord said, "If you had faith like a mustard seed, you would say to this mulberry tree, 'Be uprooted and be planted in the sea'; and it would obey you.

[7] "Which of you, having a slave plowing or tending sheep, will say to him when he has come in from the field, 'Come immediately and sit down to eat'? [8] But will he not say to

him, 'Prepare something for me to eat, and *properly* clothe yourself and serve me while I eat and drink; and afterward you may eat and drink'? [9] He does not thank the slave because he did the things which were commanded, does he? [10] So you too, when you do all the things which are commanded you, say, 'We are unworthy slaves; we have done *only* that which we ought to have done.' "

[11] While He was on the way to Jerusalem, He was passing between Samaria and Galilee. [12] As He entered a village, ten leprous men who stood at a distance met Him; [13] and they raised their voices, saying, "Jesus, Master, have mercy on us!" [14] When He saw them, He said to them, "Go and show yourselves to the priests." And as they were going, they were cleansed. [15] Now one of them, when he saw that he had been healed, turned back, glorifying God with a loud voice, [16] and he fell on his face at His feet, giving thanks to Him. And he was a Samaritan. [17] Then Jesus answered and said, "Were there not ten cleansed? But the nine—where are they? [18] Was no one found who returned to give glory to God, except this foreigner?" [19] And He said to him, "Stand up and go; your faith has made you well."

17:16 he was a Samaritan. Jesus' sending the lepers to show themselves to the priest suggests that they were Jewish. This Samaritan had been permitted to associate with them when all were ceremonially unclean, but in their healing, they did not share his deep gratitude.

DAY 23: Why does God make use of leaders who display such obvious weaknesses?

It is true that judges such as Gideon, Jephthah, and Samson exhibited gross failures, as well as successes. But as long as God chooses to use people at all, He will end up using people with obvious weaknesses. No one escapes that category. The point is that God uses people in His plans in spite of it.

This does not excuse the sins of a leader. Note for example that Moses forfeited his opportunity to enter the Promised Land because of an angry outburst (Nu 20:10; Dt 3:24-27). Jephthah made a rash vow for which his daughter had to bear the primary consequence (Jdg 11:29-40). What probably ought to attract our attention to these servants of God is not so much their weaknesses, or even the great accomplishments, but the fact that they remained faithful to God despite their failures.

When we study the lives of the judges, we discover ourselves. The shared victories, defeats, mistakes, and right choices form a common link across the centuries and turn our attention to the God who worked in their lives. The invitation from the ancients remains silently compelling: If we are to live as boldly for God, surely we would discover each day that same kind of God's immediate presence that was such a part of their experience.

APRIL 24

Judges 13:1-14:20

13 Now the sons of Israel again did evil in the sight of the LORD, so that the LORD gave them into the hands of the Philistines forty years. ² There was a certain man of Zorah, of the family of the Danites, whose name was Manoah; and his wife was barren and had borne no *children*. ³ Then the angel of the LORD appeared to the woman and said to her, "Behold now, you are barren and have borne no *children*, but you shall conceive and give birth to a son. ⁴ Now therefore, be careful not to drink wine or strong drink, nor eat any unclean thing. ⁵ For behold, you shall conceive and give birth to a son, and no razor shall come upon his head, for the boy shall be a Nazirite to God from the womb; and he shall begin to deliver Israel from the hands of the Philistines." ⁶ Then the woman came and told

> **13:5 Nazirite.** The word is from the Hebrew "to separate." For rigid Nazirite restrictions, such as here in Samson's case, see Numbers 6:1-8. God gave 2 restrictions: no wine (v. 4) and no razor cutting the hair (v. 5). An additional restriction for a Nazirite was not to touch a dead body (Nu 6:6). Such outward actions indicated an inner dedication to God.

her husband, saying, "A man of God came to me and his appearance was like the appearance of the angel of God, very awesome. And I did not ask him where he *came* from, nor did he tell me his name. ⁷ But he said to me, 'Behold, you shall conceive and give birth to a son, and now you shall not drink wine or strong drink nor eat any unclean thing, for the boy shall be a Nazirite to God from the womb to the day of his death.'" ⁸ Then Manoah entreated the LORD and said, "O Lord, please let the man of God whom You have sent come to us again that he may teach us what to do for the boy who is to be born." ⁹ God listened to the voice of Manoah; and the angel of God came again to the woman as she was sitting in the field, but Manoah her husband was not with her. ¹⁰ So the woman ran quickly and told her husband, "Behold, the man who came the *other* day has appeared to me." ¹¹ Then Manoah arose and followed his wife, and when

he came to the man he said to him, "Are you the man who spoke to the woman?" And he said, "I am." ¹² Manoah said, "Now when your words come *to pass,* what shall be the boy's mode of life and his vocation?" ¹³ So the angel of the LORD said to Manoah, "Let the woman pay attention to all that I said. ¹⁴ She should not eat anything that comes from the vine nor drink wine or strong drink, nor eat any unclean thing; let her observe all that I commanded."

¹⁵ Then Manoah said to the angel of the LORD, "Please let us detain you so that we may prepare a young goat for you." ¹⁶ The angel of the LORD said to Manoah, "Though you detain me, I will not eat your food, but if you prepare a burnt offering, *then* offer it to the LORD." For Manoah did not know that he was the angel of the LORD. ¹⁷ Manoah said to the angel of the LORD, "What is your name, so that when your words come *to pass,* we may honor you?" ¹⁸ But the angel of the LORD said to him, "Why do you ask my name, seeing it is wonderful?" ¹⁹ So Manoah took the young goat with the grain offering and offered it on the rock to the LORD, and He performed wonders while Manoah and his wife looked on. ²⁰ For it came about when the flame went up from the altar toward heaven, that the angel of the LORD ascended in the flame of the altar. When Manoah and his wife saw *this,* they fell on their faces to the ground.

²¹ Now the angel of the LORD did not appear to Manoah or his wife again. Then Manoah knew that he was the angel of the LORD. ²² So Manoah said to his wife, "We will surely die, for we have seen God." ²³ But his wife said to him, "If the LORD had desired to kill us, He would not have accepted a burnt offering and a grain offering from our hands, nor would He have shown us all these things, nor would He have let us hear *things* like this at this time."

²⁴ Then the woman gave birth to a son and named him Samson; and the child grew up and the LORD blessed him. ²⁵ And the Spirit of the LORD began to stir him in Mahaneh-dan, between Zorah and Eshtaol.

14 Then Samson went down to Timnah and saw a woman in Timnah, *one* of the daughters of the Philistines. ² So he came back and told his father and mother, "I saw a woman in Timnah, *one* of the daughters of the Philistines; now therefore, get her for me as a wife." ³ Then his father and his mother said to him, "Is there no woman among the daughters of your relatives, or among all our people, that you go to take a wife from the uncircumcised Philistines?" But Samson said to

14:1–4 she looks good to me. The Philistines were not among the 7 nations of Canaan which Israel was specifically forbidden to marry. Nonetheless Samson's choice was seriously weak. Samson sins here, but God is sovereign and was able to turn the situation to please Him (v. 14). He was not at a loss, but used the opportunity to work against the wicked Philistines and provided gracious help to His people. He achieved destruction of these people, not by an army, but by the miraculous power of one man.

his father, "Get her for me, for she looks good to me." ⁴However, his father and mother did not know that it was of the LORD, for He was seeking an occasion against the Philistines. Now at that time the Philistines were ruling over Israel.

⁵Then Samson went down to Timnah with his father and mother, and came as far as the vineyards of Timnah; and behold, a young lion *came* roaring toward him. ⁶The Spirit of the LORD came upon him mightily, so that he tore him as one tears a young goat though he had nothing in his hand; but he did not tell his father or mother what he had done. ⁷So he went down and talked to the woman; and she looked good to Samson. ⁸When he returned later to take her, he turned aside to look at the carcass of the lion; and behold, a swarm of bees and honey were in the body of the lion. ⁹So he scraped the honey into his hands and went on, eating as he went. When he came to his father and mother, he gave *some* to them and they ate *it;* but he did not tell them that he had scraped the honey out of the body of the lion.

¹⁰Then his father went down to the woman; and Samson made a feast there, for the young men customarily did this. ¹¹When they saw him, they brought thirty companions to be with him. ¹²Then Samson said to them, "Let me now propound a riddle to you; if you will indeed tell it to me within the seven days of the feast, and find it out, then I will give you thirty linen wraps and thirty changes of clothes. ¹³But if you are unable to tell me, then you shall give me thirty linen wraps and thirty changes of clothes." And they said to him, "Propound your riddle, that we may hear it." ¹⁴So he said to them,

"Out of the eater came
    something to eat,

And out of the strong came
    something sweet."

But they could not tell the riddle in three days.

¹⁵Then it came about on the fourth day that they said to Samson's wife, "Entice your husband, so that he will tell us the riddle, or we will burn you and your father's house with fire. Have you invited us to impoverish us? Is this not *so?*" ¹⁶Samson's wife wept before him and said, "You only hate me, and you do not love me; you have propounded a riddle to the sons of my people, and have not told *it* to me." And he said to her, "Behold, I have not told *it* to my father or mother; so should I tell you?" ¹⁷However she wept before him seven days while their feast lasted. And on the seventh day he told her because she pressed him so hard. She then told the riddle to the sons of her people. ¹⁸So the men of the city said to him on the seventh day before the sun went down,

"What is sweeter than honey?
    And what is stronger than
    a lion?"

And he said to them,

"If you had not plowed with
    my heifer,
You would not have found
    out my riddle."

¹⁹Then the Spirit of the LORD came upon him mightily, and he went down to Ashkelon and killed thirty of them and took their spoil and gave the changes *of clothes* to those who told the riddle. And his anger burned, and he went up to his father's house. ²⁰But Samson's wife was *given* to his companion who had been his friend.

Psalm 50:16–23

16 But to the wicked God says,
    "What right have you to
        tell of My statutes
    And to take My covenant
        in your mouth?
17 "For you hate discipline,
    And you cast My words behind
        you.
18 "When you see a thief, you
        are pleased with him,
    And you associate with
        adulterers.
19 "You let your mouth loose
        in evil

And your tongue frames deceit.
²⁰ "You sit and speak against
your brother;
You slander your own
mother's son.
²¹ "These things you have done
and I kept silence;
You thought that I was just
like you;
I will reprove you and state
the case in order before
your eyes.

²² "Now consider this, you
who forget God,
Or I will tear *you* in pieces,
and there will be none
to deliver.
²³ "He who offers a sacrifice of
thanksgiving honors Me;
And to him who orders *his*
way *aright*
I shall show the salvation
of God."

Proverbs 14:29-30

²⁹ He who is slow to anger has
great understanding,
But he who is quick-tempered
exalts folly.
³⁰ A tranquil heart is life to the
body,
But passion is rottenness
to the bones.

Luke 17:20-37

²⁰ Now having been questioned by the Pharisees as to when the kingdom of God was coming, He answered them and said, "The kingdom of God is not coming with signs to be observed; ²¹ nor will they say, 'Look, here *it is!*' or, 'There *it is!*' For behold, the kingdom of God is in your midst."
²² And He said to the disciples, "The days will come when you will long to see one of the days of the Son of Man, and you will not see it. ²³ They will say to you, 'Look there! Look here!' Do not go away, and do not run after *them.* ²⁴ For just like the lightning, when it flashes out of one part of the sky, shines to the other part of the sky, so will the Son of Man be in His day. ²⁵ But first He must suffer many things and be rejected by this generation. ²⁶ And just as it happened in the days of Noah, so it will be also in the days of the Son of Man: ²⁷ they were eating, they were drinking, they were marrying, they were being given in marriage, until the day that

17:20 when the kingdom of God was coming. They may have asked the question mockingly, having already concluded that He was not the Messiah. **not coming with signs to be observed.** The Pharisees believed that the Messiah's triumph would be immediate. They were looking for Him to come, overthrow Rome, and set up the millennial kingdom. Christ's program was altogether different. He was inaugurating an era in which the kingdom would be manifest in the rule of God in men's hearts through faith in the Savior (v. 21; see Ro 14:17). That kingdom was neither confined to a particular geographical location nor visible to human eyes. It would come quietly, invisibly, and without the normal pomp and splendor associated with the arrival of a king. Jesus did not suggest that the Old Testament promises of an earthly kingdom were hereby nullified. Rather, that earthly, visible manifestation of the kingdom is yet to come (Rev 20:1-6).

17:22 The days will come. This introduces a brief discourse that has some similarities to the Olivet Discourse of Matthew 24-25. **you will long to see one of the days of the Son of Man.** I.e., desire to have Him physically present. This suggests a longing for His return to set things right (Rev 6:9-11; 22:20).

Noah entered the ark, and the flood came and destroyed them all. ²⁸ It was the same as happened in the days of Lot: they were eating, they were drinking, they were buying, they were selling, they were planting, they were building; ²⁹ but on the day that Lot went out from Sodom it rained fire and brimstone from heaven and destroyed them all. ³⁰ It will be just the same on the day that the Son of Man is revealed. ³¹ On that day, the one who is on the housetop and whose goods are in the house must not go down to take them out; and likewise the one who is in the field must not turn back. ³² Remember Lot's wife. ³³ Whoever seeks to keep his life will lose it, and whoever loses *his life* will preserve it. ³⁴ I tell you, on that night there will be two in one bed; one will be taken and the other will be left. ³⁵ There will be two women grinding at the same place; one will be taken and the other will be left. ³⁶ [Two men will be in the field; one will be taken and the other will be left.] ³⁷ And answering they *said to Him, "Where, Lord?" And He said to them, "Where the body *is,* there also the vultures will be gathered."

Although Luke, more than any of the other Gospel writers, highlighted the universal scope of the gospel invitation, some have questioned why a companion of Paul's would use so little of Paul's language in explaining the process of salvation. But a difference in vocabulary does not necessarily imply a difference in thought or underlying theology.

Luke certainly wrote in his own style. He was an astute observer and careful thinker. In writing the Gospel, he was careful not to insert Pauline language back into the Gospel account. The theology of Luke's record parallels Paul's exactly. Luke repeatedly related accounts of Gentiles, Samaritans, and other outcasts who found grace in Jesus' eyes. This emphasis not only records Jesus' appeal, but also proves to be precisely what we would expect from the close companion of the "apostle of the Gentiles" (Ro 11:13).

A compelling illustration of this parallel involves Luke's treatment of the centerpiece of Paul's doctrine-justification by faith. Luke highlighted and illustrated justification by faith in many of the incidents and parables he related in his Gospel. For example, the account of the Pharisee and the publican (18:9–14), the familiar story of the prodigal son (15:11–32), the incident at Simon's house (7:36–50), and the salvation of Zaccheaus (19:1–10) all serve to demonstrate that Jesus taught justification by faith long before Paul wrote about it.

 APRIL 25

Judges 15:1–16:31

15 But after a while, in the time of wheat harvest, Samson visited his wife with a young goat, and said, "I will go in to my wife in *her* room." But her father did not let him enter. ² Her father said, "I really thought that you hated her intensely; so I gave her to your companion. Is not her younger sister more beautiful than she? Please let her be yours instead." ³ Samson then said to them, "This time I shall be blameless in regard to the Philistines when I do them harm." ⁴ Samson went and caught three hundred foxes, and took torches, and turned *the foxes* tail to tail and put one torch in the middle between two tails. ⁵ When he had set fire to the torches, he released the foxes into the standing grain of the Philistines, thus burning up both the shocks and the standing grain, along with the vineyards *and* groves. ⁶ Then the Philistines said, "Who did this?" And they said, "Samson, the son-in-law of the Timnite, because he took his wife and gave her to his companion." So the Philistines came up and burned her and her father with fire. ⁷ Samson said to them, "Since you act like this, I will surely take revenge on you, but after that I will quit." ⁸ He struck them ruthlessly with a great slaughter; and he went down and lived in the cleft of the rock of Etam.

⁹ Then the Philistines went up and camped in Judah, and spread out in Lehi. ¹⁰ The men of Judah said, "Why have you come up against us?" And they said, "We have come up to bind Samson in order to do to him as he did to us." ¹¹ Then 3,000 men of Judah went down to the cleft of the rock of Etam and said to Samson, "Do you not know that the Philistines are rulers over us? What then is this that you have done to us?" And he said to them, "As they did to me, so I have done to them." ¹² They said to him, "We have come down to bind you so that we may give you into the hands of the Philistines." And Samson said to them, "Swear to me that you will not kill me." ¹³ So they said to him, "No, but we will bind you fast and give you into their hands; yet surely we will not kill you." Then they bound him with two new ropes and brought him up from the rock.

¹⁴ When he came to Lehi, the Philistines shouted as they met him. And the Spirit of the LORD came upon him mightily so that the ropes that were on his arms were as flax that is burned with fire, and his bonds dropped from his hands. ¹⁵ He found a fresh jawbone of a donkey, so he reached out and took it and killed a thousand men with it. ¹⁶ Then Samson said,

"With the jawbone of a donkey,
Heaps upon heaps,
With the jawbone of a donkey
I have killed a thousand men."

¹⁷ When he had finished speaking, he threw the jawbone from his hand; and he named that place Ramath-lehi. ¹⁸ Then he became very thirsty, and he called to the LORD and said, "You have given this great deliverance by the hand of Your servant, and now shall I die of thirst and fall into the hands of the uncircumcised?" ¹⁹ But God split the hollow place that is in Lehi so that water came out of it. When he drank, his strength returned and he revived.

Therefore he named it En-hakkore, which is in Lehi to this day. ²⁰ So he judged Israel twenty years in the days of the Philistines.

16 Now Samson went to Gaza and saw a harlot there, and went in to her. ² When *it was told* to the Gazites, saying, "Samson has come here," they surrounded *the place* and lay in wait for him all night at the gate of the city. And they kept silent all night, saying, "*Let us wait* until the morning light, then we will kill him." ³ Now Samson lay until midnight, and at midnight he arose and took hold of the doors of the city gate and the two posts and pulled them up along with the bars; then he put them on his shoulders and carried them up to the top of the mountain which is opposite Hebron.

⁴ After this it came about that he loved a woman in the valley of Sorek, whose name was Delilah. ⁵ The lords of the Philistines came up to her and said to her, "Entice him, and see where his great strength *lies* and how we may overpower him that we may bind him to afflict him. Then we will each give you eleven hundred *pieces* of silver." ⁶ So Delilah said to Samson, "Please tell me where your great strength is and how you may be bound to afflict you." ⁷ Samson said to her, "If they bind me with seven fresh cords that have not been dried, then I will become weak and be like any *other* man." ⁸ Then the lords of the Philistines brought up to her seven fresh cords that had not been dried, and she bound him with them. ⁹ Now she had *men* lying in wait in an inner room. And she said to him, "The Philistines are upon you, Samson!" But he snapped the cords as a string of tow snaps when it touches fire. So his strength was not discovered.

¹⁰ Then Delilah said to Samson, "Behold, you have deceived me and told me lies; now please tell me how you may be bound." ¹¹ He said to her, "If they bind me tightly with new ropes which have not been used, then I will become weak and be like any *other* man." ¹² So Delilah took new ropes and bound him with them and said to him, "The Philistines are upon you, Samson!" For the *men* were lying in wait in the inner room. But he snapped the ropes from his arms like a thread.

¹³ Then Delilah said to Samson, "Up to now you have deceived me and told me lies; tell me how you may be bound." And he said to her, "If you weave the seven locks of my hair with the web [and fasten it with a pin, then I will become weak and be like any other man." ¹⁴ So while he slept, Delilah took the seven locks of his hair and wove them into the web]. And she fastened *it* with the pin and said to him, "The Philistines are upon you, Samson!" But he awoke from his sleep and pulled out the pin of the loom and the web.

¹⁵ Then she said to him, "How can you say, 'I love you,' when your heart is not with me? You have deceived me these three times and have not told me where your great strength is." ¹⁶ It came about when she pressed him daily with her words and urged him, that his soul was annoyed to death. ¹⁷ So he told her all *that was* in his heart and said to her, "A razor has never come on my head, for I have been a Nazirite to God from my mother's womb. If I am shaved, then my strength will leave me and I will become weak and be like any *other* man."

¹⁸ When Delilah saw that he had told her all *that was* in his heart, she sent and called the lords of the Philistines, saying, "Come up once more, for he has told me all *that is* in his heart." Then the lords of the Philistines came up to her and brought the money in their hands. ¹⁹ She made him sleep on her knees, and called for a man and had him shave off the seven locks of his hair. Then she began to afflict him, and his strength left him. ²⁰ She said, "The Philistines are upon you, Samson!" And he awoke from his sleep and said, "I will go out as at other times and shake myself free." But he did not know that the LORD had departed from him. ²¹ Then the Philistines seized him and gouged out his eyes; and they brought him down to Gaza and bound him with bronze chains, and he was a grinder in the prison. ²² However, the hair of his head began to grow again after it was shaved off.

²³ Now the lords of the Philistines assembled to offer a great sacrifice to Dagon their god, and to rejoice, for they said,

> "Our god has given Samson our
>   enemy into our hands."

²⁴ When the people saw him, they praised their god, for they said,

> "Our god has given our enemy
>   into our hands,
> Even the destroyer of our country,
>   Who has slain many of us."

16:20 he did not know that the LORD had departed from him. Here was the tragedy of the wrath of abandonment. His sin had caused him to forfeit the power of God's presence. This principle is seen throughout Scripture (Ge 6:3; Pr 1:24–31; Mt 15:14; Ro 1:24–32).

16:24 they praised their god. It is tragic when a person's sin contributes to the unsaved community giving praise to a false god, for God alone is worthy of praise.

51:1 lovingkindness. Even though he had sinned horribly, David knew that forgiveness was available, based on God's covenant love.

51:4 Against You, You only. David realized what every believer seeking forgiveness must; even though he had tragically wronged Bathsheba and Uriah, his ultimate crime was against God and His holy law (2Sa 11:27).

25 It so happened when they were in high spirits, that they said, "Call for Samson, that he may amuse us." So they called for Samson from the prison, and he entertained them. And they made him stand between the pillars. 26 Then Samson said to the boy who was holding his hand, "Let me feel the pillars on which the house rests, that I may lean against them." 27 Now the house was full of men and women, and all the lords of the Philistines were there. And about 3,000 men and women were on the roof looking on while Samson was amusing *them*.

28 Then Samson called to the LORD and said, "O Lord GOD, please remember me and please strengthen me just this time, O God, that I may at once be avenged of the Philistines for my two eyes." 29 Samson grasped the two middle pillars on which the house rested, and braced himself against them, the one with his right hand and the other with his left. 30 And Samson said, "Let me die with the Philistines!" And he bent with all his might so that the house fell on the lords and all the people who were in it. So the dead whom he killed at his death were more than those whom he killed in his life. 31 Then his brothers and all his father's household came down, took him, brought him up and buried him between Zorah and Eshtaol in the tomb of Manoah his father. Thus he had judged Israel twenty years.

5 Behold, I was brought
    forth in iniquity,
  And in sin my mother conceived me.
6 Behold, You desire truth in
    the innermost being,
  And in the hidden part You will
    make me know wisdom.

51:5 brought forth in iniquity. David also acknowledged that his sin was not God's fault in any way (vv. 4b, 6), nor was it some aberration. Rather, the source of David's sin was a fallen, sinful disposition, his since conception.

Proverbs 14:31–32

31 He who oppresses the poor
    taunts his Maker,
  But he who is gracious to the
    needy honors Him.
32 The wicked is thrust down
    by his wrongdoing,
  But the righteous has a
    refuge when he dies.

Psalm 51:1–6

For the choir director. A Psalm of David, when Nathan the prophet came to him, after he had gone in to Bathsheba.

B e gracious to me, O God, according
    to Your lovingkindness;
  According to the greatness
    of Your compassion blot
    out my transgressions.
2 Wash me thoroughly from my iniquity
  And cleanse me from my sin.
3 For I know my transgressions,
  And my sin is ever before me.
4 Against You, You only, I have sinned
  And done what is evil in Your sight,
  So that You are justified
    when You speak
  And blameless when You judge.

Luke 18:1–27

18 Now He was telling them a parable to show that at all times they ought to pray and not to lose heart, 2 saying, "In a certain city there was a judge who did not fear God and did not respect man. 3 There was a widow in that city, and she kept coming to him, saying, 'Give me legal protection from my opponent.' 4 For a while he was unwilling; but afterward he said to himself, 'Even though I do not fear God nor respect man, 5 yet because this widow bothers me, I will give her legal protection, otherwise by continually coming she will wear me out.'" 6 And the Lord said, "Hear what the unrighteous judge *said; 7 now, will not God bring about justice for His elect who cry to Him day and night, and will He delay long over them? 8 I

tell you that He will bring about justice for them quickly. However, when the Son of Man comes, will He find faith on the earth?"

9 And He also told this parable to some people who trusted in themselves that they were righteous, and viewed others with contempt: 10 "Two men went up into the temple to pray, one a Pharisee and the other a tax collector. 11 The Pharisee stood and was praying this to himself: 'God, I thank You that I am not like other people: swindlers, unjust, adulterers, or even like this tax collector. 12 I fast twice a week; I pay tithes of all that I get.' 13 But the tax collector, standing some distance away, was even unwilling to lift up his eyes to heaven, but was beating his breast, saying, 'God, be merciful to me, the sinner!' 14 I tell you, this man went to his house justified rather than the other; for everyone who exalts himself will be humbled, but he who humbles himself will be exalted."

15 And they were bringing even their babies to Him so that He would touch them, but when the disciples saw it, they *began* rebuking them. 16 But Jesus called for them, saying, "Permit the children to come to Me, and do not hinder them, for the kingdom of God belongs to such as these. 17 Truly I say to you, whoever does not receive the kingdom of God like a child will not enter it *at all.*"

18 A ruler questioned Him, saying, "Good Teacher, what shall I do to inherit eternal life?" 19 And Jesus said to him, "Why do you call Me good? No one is good except God alone. 20 You know the commandments, 'DO NOT COMMIT ADULTERY, DO NOT MURDER, DO NOT STEAL, DO NOT BEAR FALSE WITNESS, HONOR YOUR FATHER AND MOTHER.'" 21 And he said, "All these things I have kept from *my* youth." 22 When Jesus heard *this,* He said to him, "One thing you still lack; sell all that you possess and distribute it to the poor, and you shall have treasure in heaven; and come, follow Me." 23 But when he had heard these things, he became very sad, for he was extremely rich. 24 And Jesus looked at him and said, "How hard it is for those who are wealthy to enter the kingdom of God! 25 For it is easier for a camel to go through the eye of a needle than for a rich man to enter the kingdom of God." 26 They who heard it said, "Then who can be saved?" 27 But He said, "The things that are impossible with people are possible with God."

DAY 25: Why is human righteousness so insufficient for salvation?

The parable of the Pharisee and the tax collector in Luke 18:9–14 is rich with truth about the doctrine of justification by faith. It illustrates perfectly how a sinner who is utterly devoid of personal righteousness may be declared righteous before God instantaneously through an act of repentant faith. The parable is addressed to Pharisees who trusted their own righteousness (vv. 10–11). Such confidence in one's inherent righteousness is a damning hope (see Ro 10:3; Php 3:9), because human righteousness—even the righteousness of the most fastidious Pharisee—falls short of the divine standard (Mt 5:48). Scripture consistently teaches that sinners are justified when God's perfect righteousness is imputed to their account (see Ge 15:6; Ro 4:4–5; 2Co 5:21; Php 3:4–9)—and it was only on that basis that this tax collector (or anyone else) could be saved.

For the Pharisee to fast twice a week (v. 12) was more than is required by any biblical standard. By exalting his own works, the Pharisee revealed that his entire hope lay in his not being as bad as someone else. He utterly lacked any sense of his own unworthiness and sin.

The tax collector's humility is notable in everything about his posture and behavior (v. 13). Here was a man who had been made to face the reality of his own sin, and his only response was abject humility and repentance. He contrasts with the Pharisee in virtually every detail. "God, be merciful to me, the sinner!" He had no hope but the mercy of God. This is the point to which the law aims to bring every sinner (see Ro 3:19–20; 7:13; Gal 3:22–24). He was "justified" (v. 14), i.e., reckoned righteous before God by means of an imputed righteousness.

APRIL 26

Judges 17:1–19:30

17 Now there was a man of the hill country of Ephraim whose name was Micah. 2 He said to his mother, "The eleven hundred *pieces* of silver which were taken from you, about which you uttered a curse in my hearing, behold, the silver is with me; I took it." And his mother said, "Blessed be my son by the LORD." 3 He then returned the eleven hundred *pieces* of silver to his mother, and his mother said, "I wholly dedicate the silver from my hand to the LORD for my son to make a graven image and a molten image; now therefore, I will return them to you." 4 So when he returned the silver to his mother, his mother

took two hundred *pieces* of silver and gave them to the silversmith who made them into a graven image and a molten image, and they were in the house of Micah. ⁵And the man Micah had a shrine and he made an ephod and household idols and consecrated one of his sons, that he might become his priest. ⁶In those days there was no king in Israel; every man did what was right in his own eyes.

⁷Now there was a young man from Bethlehem in Judah, of the family of Judah, who was a Levite; and he was staying there. ⁸Then the man departed from the city, from Bethlehem in Judah, to stay wherever he might find *a place;* and as he made his journey, he came to the hill country of Ephraim to the house of Micah. ⁹Micah said to him, "Where do you come from?" And he said to him, "I am a Levite from Bethlehem in Judah, and I am going to stay wherever I may find *a place.*" ¹⁰Micah then said to him, "Dwell with me and be a father and a priest to me, and I will give you ten *pieces* of silver a year, a suit of clothes, and your maintenance." So the Levite went *in.* ¹¹The Levite agreed to live with the man, and the young man became to him like one of his sons. ¹²So Micah consecrated the Levite, and the young man became his priest and lived in the house of Micah. ¹³Then Micah said, "Now I know that the LORD will prosper me, seeing I have a Levite as priest."

18 In those days there was no king of Israel; and in those days the tribe of the Danites was seeking an inheritance for themselves to live in, for until that day an inheritance had not been allotted to them as a possession among the tribes of Israel. ²So the sons of Dan sent from their family five men out of their whole number, valiant men from Zorah and Eshtaol, to spy out the land and to search it; and they said to them, "Go, search the land." And they came to the hill country of Ephraim, to the house of Micah, and lodged there. ³When they were near the house of Micah, they recognized the voice of the young man, the Levite; and they turned aside there and said to him, "Who brought you here? And what are you doing in this *place?* And what do you have here?" ⁴He said to them, "Thus and so has Micah done to me, and he has hired me and I have become his priest." ⁵They said to him, "Inquire of God, please, that we may know whether our way on which we are going will be prosperous." ⁶The priest said to them, "Go in peace; your way in which you are going has the LORD'S approval."

⁷Then the five men departed and came to Laish and saw the people who were in it living in security, after the manner of the Sidonians, quiet and secure; for there was no ruler humiliating *them* for anything in the land, and they were far from the Sidonians and had no dealings with anyone. ⁸When they came back to their brothers at Zorah and Eshtaol, their brothers said to them, "What *do* you *report?*" ⁹They said, "Arise, and let us go up against them; for we have seen the land, and behold, it is very good. And will you sit still? Do not delay to go, to enter, to possess the land. ¹⁰When you enter, you will come to a secure people with a spacious land; for God has given it into your hand, a place where there is no lack of anything that is on the earth."

¹¹Then from the family of the Danites, from Zorah and from Eshtaol, six hundred men armed with weapons of war set out. ¹²They went up and camped at Kiriath-jearim in Judah. Therefore they called that place Mahaneh-dan to this day; behold, it is west of Kiriath-jearim. ¹³They passed from there to the hill country of Ephraim and came to the house of Micah.

¹⁴Then the five men who went to spy out the country of Laish said to their kinsmen, "Do you know that there are in these houses an ephod and household idols and a graven image and a molten image? Now therefore, consider what you should do." ¹⁵They turned aside there and came to the house of the young man, the Levite, to the house of Micah, and asked him of his welfare. ¹⁶The six hundred men armed with their weapons of war, who were of the sons of Dan, stood by the entrance of the gate. ¹⁷Now the five men who went to spy out the land went up *and* entered there, *and* took the graven image and the ephod and household idols and the molten image, while the priest stood by the entrance of the gate with the six hundred men armed with weapons of war. ¹⁸When these went into Micah's house and took the graven image, the ephod and household idols and the molten image, the priest said to them, "What are you doing?" ¹⁹They said to him, "Be silent, put your hand over your mouth and come with us, and be to us a father and a priest. Is it better for you to be a priest to the house of one man, or to be priest to a tribe and a family in Israel?" ²⁰The priest's heart was glad, and he took the ephod and household idols and the graven image and went among the people.

²¹Then they turned and departed, and put the little ones and the livestock and the valuables in front of them. ²²When they had gone some distance from the house of Micah, the

men who *were* in the houses near Micah's house assembled and overtook the sons of Dan. ²³They cried to the sons of Dan, who turned around and said to Micah, "What is *the matter* with you, that you have assembled together?" ²⁴He said, "You have taken away my gods which I made, and the priest, and have gone away, and what do I have besides? So how can you say to me, 'What is *the matter* with you?'" ²⁵The sons of Dan said to him, "Do not let your voice be heard among us, or else fierce men will fall upon you and you will lose your life, with the lives of your household." ²⁶So the sons of Dan went on their way; and when Micah saw that they were too strong for him, he turned and went back to his house.

²⁷Then they took what Micah had made and the priest who had belonged to him, and came to Laish, to a people quiet and secure, and struck them with the edge of the sword; and they burned the city with fire. ²⁸And there was no one to deliver *them,* because it was far from Sidon and they had no dealings with anyone, and it was in the valley which is near Beth-rehob. And they rebuilt the city and lived in it. ²⁹They called the name of the city Dan, after the name of Dan their father who was born in Israel; however, the name of the city formerly was Laish. ³⁰The sons of Dan set up for themselves the graven image; and Jonathan, the son of Gershom, the son of Manasseh, he and his sons were priests to the tribe of the Danites until the day of the captivity of the land. ³¹So they set up for themselves Micah's graven image which he had made, all the time that the house of God was at Shiloh.

19 Now it came about in those days, when there was no king in Israel, that there was a certain Levite staying in the remote part of the hill country of Ephraim, who took a concubine for himself from Bethlehem in Judah. ²But his concubine played the harlot against him, and she went away from him to her father's house in Bethlehem in Judah, and was there for a period of four months. ³Then her husband arose and went after her to speak tenderly to her in order to bring her back, taking with him his servant and a pair of donkeys. So she brought him into her father's house, and when the girl's father saw him, he was glad to meet him. ⁴His father-in-law, the girl's father, detained him; and he remained with him three days. So they ate and drank and lodged there. ⁵Now on the fourth day they got up early in the morning, and he prepared to go; and the girl's father said to his son-in-law, "Sustain yourself with a piece of bread, and afterward you may go." ⁶So both of them sat down and ate and drank together; and the girl's father said to the man, "Please be willing to spend the night, and let your heart be merry." ⁷Then the man arose to go, but his father-in-law urged him so that he spent the night there again. ⁸On the fifth day he arose to go early in the morning, and the girl's father said, "Please sustain yourself, and wait until afternoon"; so both of them ate. ⁹When the man arose to go along with his concubine and servant, his father-in-law, the girl's father, said to him, "Behold now, the day has drawn to a close; please spend the night. Lo, the day is coming to an end; spend the night here that your heart may be merry. Then tomorrow you may arise early for your journey so that you may go home."

¹⁰But the man was not willing to spend the night, so he arose and departed and came to *a place* opposite Jebus (that is, Jerusalem). And there were with him a pair of saddled donkeys; his concubine also was with him. ¹¹When they *were* near Jebus, the day was almost gone; and the servant said to his master, "Please come, and let us turn aside into this city of the Jebusites and spend the night in it." ¹²However, his master said to him, "We will not turn aside into the city of foreigners who are not of the sons of Israel; but we will go on as far as Gibeah." ¹³He said to his servant, "Come and let us approach one of these places; and we will spend the night in Gibeah or Ramah." ¹⁴So they passed along and went their way, and the sun set on them near Gibeah which belongs to Benjamin. ¹⁵They turned aside there in order to enter *and* lodge in Gibeah. When they entered, they sat down in the open square of the city, for no one took them into *his* house to spend the night.

¹⁶Then behold, an old man was coming out of the field from his work at evening. Now the man was from the hill country of Ephraim, and he was staying in Gibeah, but the men of the place were Benjamites. ¹⁷And he lifted up his eyes and saw the traveler in the open square of the city; and the old man said, "Where are you going, and where do you come from?" ¹⁸He said to him, "We are passing from Bethlehem in Judah to the remote part of the hill country of Ephraim, *for* I am from there, and I went to Bethlehem in Judah. But I am *now* going to my house, and no man will take me into his house. ¹⁹Yet there is both straw and fodder for our donkeys, and also bread and wine for me, your

maidservant, and the young man who is with your servants; there is no lack of anything." ²⁰The old man said, "Peace to you. Only let me *take care of* all your needs; however, do not spend the night in the open square." ²¹So he took him into his house and gave the donkeys fodder, and they washed their feet and ate and drank.

²²While they were celebrating, behold, the men of the city, certain worthless fellows, surrounded the house, pounding the door; and they spoke to the owner of the house, the old man, saying, "Bring out the man who came into your house that we may have relations with him." ²³Then the man, the owner of the house, went out to them and said to them, "No, my fellows, please do not act so wickedly; since this man has come into my house, do not commit this act of folly. ²⁴Here is my virgin daughter and his concubine. Please let me bring them out that you may ravish them and do to them whatever you wish. But do not commit such an act of folly against this man." ²⁵But the men would not listen to him. So the man seized his concubine and brought *her* out to them; and they raped her and abused her all night until morning, then let her go at the approach of dawn. ²⁶As the day began to dawn, the woman came and fell down at the doorway of the man's house where her master was, until *full* daylight.

²⁷When her master arose in the morning and opened the doors of the house and went out to go on his way, then behold, his

19:22 worthless fellows. Literally "sons of Belial," i.e., base and perverse men, who desired to commit sodomy against the Levite. The phrase elsewhere is used for idolaters (Dt 13:13), neglecters of the poor (Dt 15:9), drunks (1Sa 1:16), immoral people (1Sa 2:12), and rebels against the civil authority (2Sa 20:1; Pr 19:28). "Belial" can be traced to the false god Baal, and is also a term for yoke (they cast off the yoke of decency), and a term for entangling or injuring. It is used in the New Testament of Satan (2Co 6:15).

19:25 the man seized his concubine and brought *her* out to them. This is unthinkable weakness and cowardice for any man, especially a priest of God. Apparently he even slept through the night, or stayed in bed out of fear, since he didn't see her again until he awakened and prepared to leave (v. 28).

concubine was lying at the doorway of the house with her hands on the threshold. ²⁸He said to her, "Get up and let us go," but there was no answer. Then he placed her on the donkey; and the man arose and went to his home. ²⁹When he entered his house, he took a knife and laid hold of his concubine and cut her in twelve pieces, limb by limb, and sent her throughout the territory of Israel. ³⁰All who saw *it* said, "Nothing like this has *ever* happened or been seen from the day when the sons of Israel came up from the land of Egypt to this day. Consider it, take counsel and speak up!"

Psalm 51:7–11

⁷ Purify me with hyssop, and
  I shall be clean;
  Wash me, and I shall be
  whiter than snow.

51:7 hyssop. Old Testament priests used hyssop, a leafy plant, to sprinkle blood or water on a person being ceremonially cleansed from defilements such as leprosy or touching a dead body (Lv 14:6ff.; Nu 19:16–19). Here hyssop is a figure for David's longing to be spiritually cleansed from his moral defilement. In forgiveness, God washes away sin (Ps 103:12; Is 1:16; Mic 7:19).

⁸ Make me to hear joy and
  gladness,
  Let the bones which You
  have broken rejoice.
⁹ Hide Your face from my sins
  And blot out all my iniquities.
¹⁰ Create in me a clean heart,
  O God,
  And renew a steadfast
  spirit within me.
¹¹ Do not cast me away from
  Your presence
  And do not take Your Holy
  Spirit from me.

Proverbs 14:33–35

³³ Wisdom rests in the heart of one
  who has understanding,
  But in the hearts of fools
  it is made known.
³⁴ Righteousness exalts a nation,
  But sin is a disgrace to *any*
  people.

14:33 is made known. Wisdom is quietly preserved in the heart of the wise for the time of proper use, while fools are eager to blurt out their folly (12:23; 13:16; 15:2, 14).

35 The king's favor is toward a
     servant who acts wisely,
   But his anger is toward him
     who acts shamefully.

Luke 18:28-43

28 Peter said, "Behold, we have left our own *homes* and followed You." 29 And He said to them, "Truly I say to you, there is no one who has left house or wife or brothers or parents or children, for the sake of the kingdom of God, 30 who will not receive many times as much at this time and in the age to come, eternal life."

31 Then He took the twelve aside and said to them, "Behold, we are going up to Jerusalem, and all things which are written through the prophets about the Son of Man will be accomplished. 32 For He will be handed over to the Gentiles, and will be mocked and mistreated and spit upon, 33 and after they have scourged Him, they will kill Him; and the third day He will rise again." 34 But the disciples understood none of these things, and *the meaning of* this statement was hidden from them, and they did not comprehend the things that were said.

35 As Jesus was approaching Jericho, a blind man was sitting by the road begging. 36 Now hearing a crowd going by, he *began* to inquire what this was. 37 They told him that Jesus of Nazareth was passing by. 38 And he called out, saying, "Jesus, Son of David, have mercy on me!" 39 Those who led the way were sternly telling him to be quiet; but he kept crying out all the more, "Son of David, have mercy on me!" 40 And Jesus stopped and commanded that he be brought to Him; and when he came near, He questioned him, 41 "What do you want Me to do for you?" And he said, "Lord, *I want* to regain my sight!" 42 And Jesus said to him, "Receive your sight; your faith has made you well." 43 Immediately he regained his sight and *began* following Him, glorifying God; and when all the people saw it, they gave praise to God.

DAY 26: What did the anointing of the Holy Spirit mean in the Old Testament?

Old Testament Israel had mediators who stood between God and His people. To empower the Old Testament mediators, the Holy Spirit gave special administrative ability to carry out the management of the nation and military skills which enabled them to defeat the theocracy's enemies. The Lord first anointed Moses with this ministry of the Spirit, and then in a truly dramatic scene, took some of this ministry of the Spirit and shared it with the 70 elders. Thus, they were enabled to help Moses administer Israel (Nu 11:17-25).

Also Joshua (Dt 34:9), the judges (Jdg 3:10; 6:34), and the kings of united Israel and the southern kingdom were anointed with this special ministry of the Spirit. When the Spirit of the Lord came upon King Saul, for example, "God changed his heart" (1Sa 10:6-10). This does not mean that he was regenerated at this point in his life, but that he was given skills to be a king. Later the theocratic anointing was taken from Saul and given to David (1Sa 16:1-14). Saul, from that time on, became a totally incapable leader.

King David no doubt had this special ministry of the Spirit in mind in his prayer of repentance in Psalm 51. He was not afraid of losing his salvation when he prayed, "Do not take Your Holy Spirit from me" (Ps 51:11), but rather was concerned that God would remove this spiritual wisdom and administrative skill from him. David had earlier seen such the tragedy in the life of Saul when that king of Israel lost the anointing of the Holy Spirit. David was thus pleading with God not to remove His hand of guidance.

King Solomon also perceived his youthful inabilities at the beginning of his reign and requested God to give him special wisdom in administering Israel. God was greatly pleased with this request and granted an extra measure to the young man (1Ki 3:7-12, 28; 4:29-34). Although the Old Testament is silent in this regard about the kings who succeeded Solomon, the theocratic anointing of the Spirit likely came on all the descendants of David in connection with the Davidic Covenant.

When the theocracy went out of existence as Judah was carried away into captivity and the last Davidic king was disempowered, the theocratic anointing was no longer given (Eze 8-11). The kings of the northern tribes, on the other hand, being essentially apostate and not in the Davidic line, never had the benefit of this special ministry of the Spirit.

APRIL 27

Judges 20:1–21:25

20 Then all the sons of Israel from Dan to Beersheba, including the land of Gilead, came out, and the congregation assembled as one man to the LORD at Mizpah. ²The chiefs of all the people, even of all the tribes of Israel, took their stand in the assembly of the people of God, 400,000 foot soldiers who drew the sword. ³(Now the sons of Benjamin heard that the sons of Israel had gone up to Mizpah.) And the sons of Israel said, "Tell us, how did this wickedness take place?" ⁴So the Levite, the husband of the woman who was murdered, answered and said, "I came with my concubine to spend the night at Gibeah which belongs to Benjamin. ⁵But the men of Gibeah rose up against me and surrounded the house at night because of me. They intended to kill me; instead, they ravished my concubine so that she died. ⁶And I took hold of my concubine and cut her in pieces and sent her throughout the land of Israel's inheritance; for they have committed a lewd and disgraceful act in Israel. ⁷Behold, all you sons of Israel, give your advice and counsel here."

⁸Then all the people arose as one man, saying, "Not one of us will go to his tent, nor will any of us return to his house. ⁹But now this is the thing which we will do to Gibeah; we will go up against it by lot. ¹⁰And we will take 10 men out of 100 throughout the tribes of Israel, and 100 out of 1,000, and 1,000 out of 10,000 to supply food for the people, that when they come to Gibeah of Benjamin, they may punish them for all the disgraceful acts that they have committed in Israel." ¹¹Thus all the men of Israel were gathered against the city, united as one man.

¹²Then the tribes of Israel sent men through the entire tribe of Benjamin, saying, "What is this wickedness that has taken place among you? ¹³Now then, deliver up the men, the worthless fellows in Gibeah, that we may put them to death and remove this wickedness from Israel." But the sons of Benjamin would not listen to the voice of their brothers, the sons of Israel. ¹⁴The sons of Benjamin gathered from the cities to Gibeah, to go out to battle against the sons of Israel. ¹⁵From the cities on that day the sons of Benjamin were numbered, 26,000 men who draw the sword, besides the inhabitants of Gibeah who were numbered, 700 choice men. ¹⁶Out of all these people 700 choice men were left-handed; each one could sling a stone at a hair and not miss.

¹⁷Then the men of Israel besides Benjamin were numbered, 400,000 men who draw the sword; all these were men of war.

¹⁸Now the sons of Israel arose, went up to Bethel, and inquired of God and said, "Who shall go up first for us to battle against the sons of Benjamin?" Then the LORD said, "Judah shall go up first."

20:18 inquired of God. The Lord gave His counsel from the location of the ark at Shiloh, probably through the Urim and Thummim (vv. 27–28). The tribe of Judah was responsible to lead in battle since God had chosen a leadership role for that tribe (Ge 49:8–12; 1Ch 5:1–2).

¹⁹So the sons of Israel arose in the morning and camped against Gibeah. ²⁰The men of Israel went out to battle against Benjamin, and the men of Israel arrayed for battle against them at Gibeah. ²¹Then the sons of Benjamin came out of Gibeah and felled to the ground on that day 22,000 men of Israel. ²²But the people, the men of Israel, encouraged themselves and arrayed for battle again in the place where they had arrayed themselves the first day. ²³The sons of Israel went up and wept before the LORD until evening, and inquired of the LORD, saying, "Shall we again draw near for battle against the sons of my brother Benjamin?" And the LORD said, "Go up against him." ²⁴Then the sons of Israel came against the sons of Benjamin the second day. ²⁵Benjamin went out against them from Gibeah the second day and felled to the ground again 18,000 men of the sons of Israel; all these drew the sword. ²⁶Then all the sons of Israel and all the people went up and came to Bethel and wept; thus they remained there before the LORD and fasted that day until evening. And they offered

20:22–25 Twice the Lord allowed great defeat and death to Israel to bring them to their spiritual senses regarding the cost of tolerating apostasy. Also, while they sought counsel, they placed too much reliance on their own prowess and on satisfying their own outrage. Finally, when desperate enough, they fasted and offered sacrifices (v. 26). The Lord then gave victory with a strategy similar to that at Ai (Jos 8).

burnt offerings and peace offerings before the LORD. ²⁷The sons of Israel inquired of the LORD (for the ark of the covenant of God *was* there in those days, ²⁸ and Phinehas the son of Eleazar, Aaron's son, stood before it to *minister* in those days), saying, "Shall I yet again go out to battle against the sons of my brother Benjamin, or shall I cease?" And the LORD said, "Go up, for tomorrow I will deliver them into your hand."

²⁹ So Israel set men in ambush around Gibeah. ³⁰ The sons of Israel went up against the sons of Benjamin on the third day and arrayed themselves against Gibeah as at other times. ³¹ The sons of Benjamin went out against the people and were drawn away from the city, and they began to strike and kill some of the people as at other times, on the highways, one of which goes up to Bethel and the other to Gibeah, *and* in the field, about thirty men of Israel. ³² The sons of Benjamin said, "They are struck down before us, as at the first." But the sons of Israel said, "Let us flee that we may draw them away from the city to the highways." ³³ Then all the men of Israel arose from their place and arrayed themselves at Baal-tamar; and the men of Israel in ambush broke out of their place, even out of Maareh-geba. ³⁴ When ten thousand choice men from all Israel came against Gibeah, the battle became fierce; but Benjamin did not know that disaster was close to them. ³⁵ And the LORD struck Benjamin before Israel, so that the sons of Israel destroyed 25,100 men of Benjamin that day, all who draw the sword.

³⁶ So the sons of Benjamin saw that they were defeated. When the men of Israel gave ground to Benjamin because they relied on the men in ambush whom they had set against Gibeah, ³⁷ the men in ambush hurried and rushed against Gibeah; the men in ambush also deployed and struck all the city with the edge of the sword. ³⁸ Now the appointed sign between the men of Israel and the men in ambush was that they would make a great cloud of smoke rise from the city. ³⁹ Then the men of Israel turned in the battle, and Benjamin began to strike and kill about thirty men of Israel, for they said, "Surely they are defeated before us, as in the first battle." ⁴⁰ But when the cloud began to rise from the city in a column of smoke, Benjamin looked behind them; and behold, the whole city was going up *in smoke* to heaven. ⁴¹ Then the men of Israel turned, and the men of Benjamin were terrified; for they saw that disaster was close to them. ⁴² Therefore, they turned their backs before the men of Israel toward the direction of the wilderness, but

the battle overtook them while those who came out of the cities destroyed them in the midst of them. ⁴³ They surrounded Benjamin, pursued them without rest *and* trod them down opposite Gibeah toward the east. ⁴⁴ Thus 18,000 men of Benjamin fell; all these were valiant warriors. ⁴⁵ The rest turned and fled toward the wilderness to the rock of Rimmon, but they caught 5,000 of them on the highways and overtook them at Gidom and killed 2,000 of them. ⁴⁶ So all of Benjamin who fell that day were 25,000 men who draw the sword; all these were valiant warriors. ⁴⁷ But 600 men turned and fled toward the wilderness to the rock of Rimmon, and they remained at the rock of Rimmon four months. ⁴⁸ The men of Israel then turned back against the sons of Benjamin and struck them with the edge of the sword, both the entire city with the cattle and all that they found; they also set on fire all the cities which they found.

21 Now the men of Israel had sworn in Mizpah, saying, "None of us shall give his daughter to Benjamin in marriage." ² So the people came to Bethel and sat there before God until evening, and lifted up their voices and wept bitterly. ³ They said, "Why, O LORD, God of Israel, has this come about in Israel, so that one tribe should be *missing* today in Israel?" ⁴ It came about the next day that the people arose early and built an altar there and offered burnt offerings and peace offerings.

⁵ Then the sons of Israel said, "Who is there among all the tribes of Israel who did not come up in the assembly to the LORD?" For they had taken a great oath concerning him who did not come up to the LORD at Mizpah, saying, "He shall surely be put to death." ⁶ And the sons of Israel were sorry for their brother Benjamin and said, "One tribe is cut off from Israel today. ⁷ What shall we do for wives for those who are left, since we have sworn by the LORD not to give them any of our daughters in marriage?"

⁸ And they said, "What one is there of the tribes of Israel who did not come up to the LORD at Mizpah?" And behold, no one had come to the camp from Jabesh-gilead to the assembly. ⁹ For when the people were numbered, behold, not one of the inhabitants of Jabesh-gilead was there. ¹⁰ And the congregation sent 12,000 of the valiant warriors there, and commanded them, saying, "Go and strike the inhabitants of Jabesh-gilead with the edge of the sword, with the women and the little ones. ¹¹ This is the thing that you shall do: you shall utterly destroy every man and every woman who has lain with a man." ¹² And they found

among the inhabitants of Jabesh-gilead 400 young virgins who had not known a man by lying with him; and they brought them to the camp at Shiloh, which is in the land of Canaan. [13] Then the whole congregation sent *word* and spoke to the sons of Benjamin who were at the rock of Rimmon, and proclaimed peace to them. [14] Benjamin returned at that time, and they gave them the women whom they had kept alive from the women of Jabesh-gilead; yet they were not enough for them. [15] And the people were sorry for Benjamin because the LORD had made a breach in the tribes of Israel.

[16] Then the elders of the congregation said, "What shall we do for wives for those who are left, since the women are destroyed out of Benjamin?" [17] They said, "*There must be* an inheritance for the survivors of Benjamin, so that a tribe will not be blotted out from Israel. [18] But we cannot give them wives of our daughters." For the sons of Israel had sworn, saying, "Cursed is he who gives a wife to Benjamin."

[19] So they said, "Behold, there is a feast of the LORD from year to year in Shiloh, which is on the north side of Bethel, on the east side of the highway that goes up from Bethel to Shechem, and on the south side of Lebonah." [20] And they commanded the sons of Benjamin, saying, "Go and lie in wait in the vineyards, [21] and watch; and behold, if the daughters of Shiloh come out to take part in the dances, then you shall come out of the vineyards and each of you shall catch his wife from the daughters of Shiloh, and go to the land of Benjamin. [22] It shall come about, when their fathers or their brothers come to complain to us, that we shall say to them, 'Give them to us voluntarily, because we did not take for each man *of Benjamin* a wife in battle, nor did you give *them* to them, *else* you would now be guilty.'" [23] The sons of Benjamin did so, and took wives according to their number from those who danced, whom they carried away. And they went and returned to their inheritance and rebuilt the cities and lived in them. [24] The sons of Israel departed from there at that time, every man to his tribe and family, and each one of them went out from there to his inheritance.

[25] In those days there was no king in Israel; everyone did what was right in his own eyes.

Psalm 51:12–19

[12] Restore to me the joy of
    Your salvation
And sustain me with a willing spirit.
[13] *Then* I will teach transgressors
    Your ways,
And sinners will be converted to You.

21:25 Judges 17–21 vividly demonstrates how bizarre and deep sin can become when people throw off the authority of God as mediated through the king (17:6). This was the appropriate, but tragic, conclusion to a bleak period of Israelite history (Dt 12:8).

[14] Deliver me from bloodguiltiness,
    O God, the God of my salvation;
Then my tongue will joyfully
    sing of Your righteousness.
[15] O Lord, open my lips,
That my mouth may declare
    Your praise.
[16] For You do not delight in sacrifice,
    otherwise I would give it;
You are not pleased with
    burnt offering.
[17] The sacrifices of God are
    a broken spirit;
A broken and a contrite heart,
    O God, You will not despise.

[18] By Your favor do good to Zion;
Build the walls of Jerusalem.
[19] Then You will delight in
    righteous sacrifices,
In burnt offering and whole
    burnt offering;
Then young bulls will be
    offered on Your altar.

Proverbs 15:1–3

15 A gentle answer turns away
    wrath,
But a harsh word stirs up anger.
[2] The tongue of the wise makes
    knowledge acceptable,
But the mouth of fools spouts folly.
[3] The eyes of the LORD are
    in every place,
Watching the evil and the good.

Luke 19:1–27

19 He entered Jericho and was passing
    through. [2] And there was a man called by the name of Zaccheus; he was a chief tax collector and he was rich. [3] Zaccheus was trying to see who Jesus was, and was unable because of the crowd, for he was small in stature. [4] So he ran on ahead and climbed up into a sycamore tree in order to see Him, for He was about to pass through that way. [5] When Jesus came to the place, He looked up and said to him, "Zaccheus, hurry and come down,

for today I must stay at your house." ⁶And he hurried and came down and received Him gladly. ⁷When they saw it, they all *began* to grumble, saying, "He has gone to be the guest of a man who is a sinner." ⁸Zaccheus stopped and said to the Lord, "Behold, Lord, half of my possessions I will give to the poor, and if I have defrauded anyone of anything, I will give back four times as much." ⁹And Jesus said to him, "Today salvation has come to this house, because he, too, is a son of Abraham. ¹⁰For the Son of Man has come to seek and to save that which was lost."

¹¹While they were listening to these things, Jesus went on to tell a parable, because He was near Jerusalem, and they supposed that the kingdom of God was going to appear immediately. ¹²So He said, "A nobleman went to a distant country to receive a kingdom for himself, and *then* return. ¹³And he called ten of his slaves, and gave them ten minas and said to them, 'Do business *with this* until I come *back.*' ¹⁴But his citizens hated him and sent a delegation after him, saying, 'We do not want this man to reign over us.' ¹⁵When he returned, after receiving the kingdom, he ordered that these slaves, to whom he had given the money, be called to him so that he might know what business they had done. ¹⁶The first appeared, saying, 'Master, your mina has made ten minas more.' ¹⁷And he said to him, 'Well done, good slave, because you have been faithful in a very little thing, you are to be in authority over ten cities.' ¹⁸The second came, saying, 'Your mina, master, has made five minas.' ¹⁹And he said to him also, 'And you are to be over five cities.' ²⁰Another came, saying, 'Master, here is your mina, which I kept put away in a handkerchief; ²¹for I was afraid of you, because you are an exacting man; you take up what you did not lay down and reap what you did not sow.' ²²He *said to him, 'By your own words I will judge you, you worthless slave. Did you know that I am an exacting man, taking up what I did not lay down and reaping what I did not sow? ²³Then why did you not put my money in the bank, and having come, I would have collected it with interest?' ²⁴Then he said to the bystanders, 'Take the mina away from him and give it to the one who has the ten minas.' ²⁵And they said to him, 'Master, he has ten minas *already.*' ²⁶'I tell you that to everyone who has, more shall be given, but from the one who does not have, even what he does have shall be taken away. ²⁷But these enemies of mine, who did not want me to reign over them, bring them here and slay them in my presence.' "

19:17 faithful in a very little. Those with relatively small gifts and opportunities are just as responsible to use them faithfully as those who are given much more. **over ten cities.** The reward is incomparably greater than the 10 minas warranted. Note also that the rewards were apportioned according to the servants' diligence: the one who gained 10 minas was given 10 cities, the one who gained 5 minas, 5 cities (v. 19), and so on.

DAY 27: How did Zaccheus personify why Jesus came to this world?

Zaccheus was a chief tax collector, who probably oversaw a large tax district and had other tax collectors working for him (Lk 19:2). Jericho alone was a prosperous trading center, so it is certain that Zaccheus was a wealthy man. Zaccheus was among "the crowd" in Jericho who lined the street to see Jesus pass through. They had undoubtedly heard about the recent raising of Lazarus in Bethany, less than 15 miles away (Jn 11). That, combined with His fame as a healer and teacher, stirred the entire city when word arrived that He was coming. Zaccheus was so desperate to see Christ that he took an undignified position for someone of his rank (v. 4).

Both the religious elite and the common people hated Zaccheus. They did not understand, and in their blind pride refused to see, what possible righteous purpose Jesus had in visiting such a notorious sinner (v. 7). But He had come to seek and to save the lost, which is exactly what happened here (v. 10).

Not only did Zaccheus receive Jesus joyfully (v. 6), but his willingness to make restitution was proof that his conversion was genuine (v. 8). It was the fruit, not the condition, of his salvation. The law required a penalty of one-fifth as restitution for money acquired by fraud (Lv 6:5; Nu 5:6–7), so Zaccheus was doing more than was required. Zaccheus judged his own crime severely, acknowledging that he was as guilty as the lowest common robber. Since much of his wealth had probably been acquired fraudulently, this was a costly commitment. On top of that, he gave half his goods to the poor. But Zaccheus had just found incomprehensible spiritual riches and did not mind the loss of material wealth.

APRIL 28

Ruth 1:1–2:23

1 Now it came about in the days when the judges governed, that there was a famine in the land. And a certain man of Bethlehem in Judah went to sojourn in the land of Moab with his wife and his two sons. ²The name of the man *was* Elimelech, and the name of his wife, Naomi; and the names of his two sons *were* Mahlon and Chilion, Ephrathites of Bethlehem in Judah. Now they entered the land of Moab and remained there. ³Then Elimelech, Naomi's husband, died; and she was left with her two sons. ⁴They took for themselves Moabite women *as* wives; the name of the one was Orpah and the name of the other Ruth. And they lived there about ten years. ⁵Then both Mahlon and Chilion also died, and the woman was bereft of her two children and her husband.

⁶Then she arose with her daughters-in-law that she might return from the land of Moab, for she had heard in the land of Moab that the LORD had visited His people in giving them food. ⁷So she departed from the place where she was, and her two daughters-in-law with her; and they went on the way to return to the land of Judah. ⁸And Naomi said to her two daughters-in-law, "Go, return each of you to her mother's house. May the LORD deal kindly with you as you have dealt with the dead and with me. ⁹May the LORD grant that you may find rest, each in the house of her husband." Then she kissed them, and they lifted up their voices and wept. ¹⁰And they said to her, "*No,* but we will surely return with you to your people." ¹¹But Naomi said, "Return, my daughters. Why should you go with me? Have I yet sons in my womb, that they may be your husbands? ¹²Return, my daughters! Go, for I am too old to have a husband. If I said I have hope, if I should even have a husband tonight and also bear sons, ¹³would you therefore wait until they were grown? Would you therefore refrain from marrying? No, my daughters; for it is harder for me than for you, for the hand of the LORD has gone forth against me." ¹⁴And they lifted up their voices and wept again; and Orpah kissed her mother-in-law, but Ruth clung to her.

¹⁵Then she said, "Behold, your sister-in-law has gone back to her people and her gods; return after your sister-in-law." ¹⁶But Ruth said, "Do not urge me to leave you *or* turn back from following you; for where you go, I will go, and where you lodge, I will lodge.

Your people *shall be* my people, and your God, my God. ¹⁷Where you die, I will die, and there I will be buried. Thus may the LORD do to me, and worse, if *anything but* death parts you and me." ¹⁸When she saw that she was determined to go with her, she said no more to her.

1:16 and your God, my God. This testimony evidenced Ruth's conversion from worshiping Chemosh to Jehovah of Israel (1Th 1:9–10).

¹⁹So they both went until they came to Bethlehem. And when they had come to Bethlehem, all the city was stirred because of them, and the women said, "Is this Naomi?" ²⁰She said to them, "Do not call me Naomi; call me Mara, for the Almighty has dealt very bitterly with me. ²¹I went out full, but the LORD has brought me back empty. Why do you call me Naomi, since the LORD has witnessed against me and the Almighty has afflicted me?"

²²So Naomi returned, and with her Ruth the Moabitess, her daughter-in-law, who returned from the land of Moab. And they came to Bethlehem at the beginning of barley harvest.

2 Now Naomi had a kinsman of her husband, a man of great wealth, of the family of Elimelech, whose name was Boaz. ²And Ruth the Moabitess said to Naomi, "Please let me go to the field and glean among the ears of grain after one in whose sight I may find favor." And she said to her, "Go, my daughter." ³So she departed and went and gleaned in the field after the reapers; and she happened to come to the portion of the field belonging to Boaz, who was of the family of Elimelech. ⁴Now behold, Boaz came from Bethlehem and said to the reapers, "May the LORD be with you." And they said to him, "May the LORD bless you." ⁵Then Boaz said to his servant who was in charge of the reapers, "Whose young woman is this?" ⁶The servant in charge of the reapers replied, "She is the young Moabite woman who returned with Naomi from the land of Moab. ⁷And she said, 'Please let me glean and gather after the reapers among the sheaves.' Thus she came and has remained from the morning until now; she has been sitting in the house for a little while."

⁸Then Boaz said to Ruth, "Listen carefully, my daughter. Do not go to glean in another field; furthermore, do not go on from this

one, but stay here with my maids. [9] Let your eyes be on the field which they reap, and go after them. Indeed, I have commanded the servants not to touch you. When you are thirsty, go to the water jars and drink from what the servants draw." [10] Then she fell on her face, bowing to the ground and said to him, "Why have I found favor in your sight that you should take notice of me, since I am a foreigner?" [11] Boaz replied to her, "All that you have done for your mother-in-law after the death of your husband has been fully reported to me, and how you left your father and your mother and the land of your birth, and came to a people that you did not previously know. [12] May the LORD reward your work, and your wages be full from the LORD, the God of Israel, under whose wings you have come to seek refuge." [13] Then she said, "I have found favor in your sight, my lord, for you have comforted me and indeed have spoken kindly to your maidservant, though I am not like one of your maidservants."

2:12 wings...refuge. Scripture pictures God as catching Israel up on His wings in the Exodus (Ex 19:4; Dt 32:11). God is here portrayed as a mother bird sheltering the young and fragile with her wings (Pss 17:8; 36:7; 57:1; 61:4; 63:7; 91:1, 4). Boaz blessed Ruth in light of her new-found commitment to and dependence on the Lord. Later, he would become God's answer to this prayer (3:9).

[14] At mealtime Boaz said to her, "Come here, that you may eat of the bread and dip your piece of bread in the vinegar." So she sat beside the reapers; and he served her roasted grain, and she ate and was satisfied and had some left. [15] When she rose to glean, Boaz commanded his servants, saying, "Let her glean even among the sheaves, and do not insult her. [16] Also you shall purposely pull out for her some grain from the bundles and leave it that she may glean, and do not rebuke her." [17] So she gleaned in the field until evening. Then she beat out what she had gleaned, and it was about an ephah of barley. [18] She took it up and went into the city, and her mother-in-law saw what she had gleaned. She also took it out and gave Naomi what she had left after she was satisfied. [19] Her mother-in-law then said to her, "Where did you glean today and where did you work? May he who took notice of you be blessed." So she told her

mother-in-law with whom she had worked and said, "The name of the man with whom I worked today is Boaz." [20] Naomi said to her daughter-in-law, "May he be blessed of the LORD who has not withdrawn his kindness to the living and to the dead." Again Naomi said to her, "The man is our relative, he is one of our closest relatives." [21] Then Ruth the Moabitess said, "Furthermore, he said to me, 'You should stay close to my servants until they have finished all my harvest.'" [22] Naomi said to Ruth her daughter-in-law, "It is good, my daughter, that you go out with his maids, so that others do not fall upon you in another field." [23] So she stayed close by the maids of Boaz in order to glean until the end of the barley harvest and the wheat harvest. And she lived with her mother-in-law.

Psalm 52:1–5

For the choir director. A Maskil of David, when Doeg the Edomite came and told Saul and said to him, "David has come to the house of Ahimelech."

Why do you boast in evil, O mighty man?
The lovingkindness of God
    endures all day long.
[2] Your tongue devises destruction,
    Like a sharp razor, O worker of deceit.

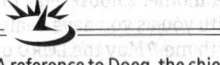

52:1 mighty man. A reference to Doeg, the chief of Saul's shepherds, who reported to Saul that the priests of Nob had aided David when he was a fugitive (1Sa 22:9, 18–19).

[3] You love evil more than good,
    Falsehood more than speaking
        what is right.   *Selah*
[4] You love all words that devour,
    O deceitful tongue.

[5] But God will break you down forever;
    He will snatch you up and tear
        you away from your tent,
    And uproot you from the land
        of the living.   *Selah*

Proverbs 15:4–5

[4] A soothing tongue is a tree of life,
    But perversion in it crushes the spirit.
[5] A fool rejects his father's discipline,
    But he who regards
        reproof is sensible.

Luke 19:28-48

²⁸After He had said these things, He was going on ahead, going up to Jerusalem.

²⁹When He approached Bethphage and Bethany, near the mount that is called Olivet, He sent two of the disciples, ³⁰saying, "Go into the village ahead of *you*; there, as you enter, you will find a colt tied on which no one yet has ever sat; untie it and bring it *here*. ³¹If anyone asks you, 'Why are you untying it?' you shall say, 'The Lord has need of it.'" ³²So those who were sent away and found it just as He had told them. ³³As they were untying the colt, its owners said to them, "Why are you untying the colt?" ³⁴They said, "The Lord has need of it." ³⁵They brought it to Jesus, and they threw their coats on the colt and put Jesus *on it*. ³⁶As He was going, they were spreading their coats on the road. ³⁷As soon as He was approaching, near the descent of the Mount of Olives, the whole crowd of the disciples began to praise God joyfully with a loud voice for all the miracles which they had seen, ³⁸shouting:

"BLESSED IS THE KING WHO COMES
    IN THE NAME OF THE LORD;
Peace in heaven and glory
    in the highest!"

³⁹Some of the Pharisees in the crowd said to Him, "Teacher, rebuke Your disciples." ⁴⁰But Jesus answered, "I tell you, if these become silent, the stones will cry out!"

⁴¹When He approached *Jerusalem*, He saw the city and wept over it, ⁴²saying, "If you had known in this day, even you, the things which make for peace! But now they have been hidden from your eyes. ⁴³For the days will come

19:40 the stones will cry out! This was a strong claim of deity, and perhaps a reference to the words of Habakkuk 2:11. Scripture often speaks of inanimate nature praising God. (See Pss 96:11; 98:7-9; 114:7; Is 55:12.) See also the words of John the Baptist in Matthew 3:9; note the fulfillment of Jesus' words in Matthew 27:51.

19:41-42 Only Luke recorded the weeping of Jesus over the city of Jerusalem. Christ grieved over Jerusalem on at least two other occasions (13:34; Mt 23:37). The timing of this lament may seem incongruous with the triumphal entry, but it reveals that Jesus knew the true superficiality of the peoples' hearts, and His mood was anything but giddy as He rode into the city. The same crowd would soon cry for His death (23:21).

---

upon you when your enemies will throw up a barricade against you, and surround you and hem you in on every side, ⁴⁴and they will level you to the ground and your children within you, and they will not leave in you one stone upon another, because you did not recognize the time of your visitation."

⁴⁵Jesus entered the temple and began to drive out those who were selling, ⁴⁶saying to them, "It is written, 'AND MY HOUSE SHALL BE A HOUSE OF PRAYER,' but you have made it a ROBBERS' DEN."

⁴⁷And He was teaching daily in the temple; but the chief priests and the scribes and the leading men among the people were trying to destroy Him, ⁴⁸and they could not find anything that they might do, for all the people were hanging on to every word He said.

DAY 28: Why is the "kinsman-redeemer" a prominent part in the story of Ruth?

In Ruth 2:20, the great kinsman-redeemer theme of Ruth begins (cf. 3:9, 12; 4:1, 3, 6, 8, 14). A close relative could redeem 1) a family member sold into slavery (Lv 25:47-49), 2) land which needed to be sold under economic hardship (Lv 25:23-28), and/or 3) the family name by virtue of a levirate marriage (Dt 25:5-10). This earthly custom pictures the reality of God the Redeemer doing a greater work (Pss 19:14; 78:35; Is. 41:14; 43:14) by reclaiming those who needed to be spiritually redeemed out of slavery to sin (Ps 107:2; Is. 62:12). Thus, Boaz pictures Christ, who as a Brother (Heb 2:17) redeemed those who 1) were slaves to sin (Ro 6:15-18), 2) had lost all earthly possessions/privilege in the Fall (Ge 3:17-19), and 3) had been alienated by sin from God (2Co 5:18-21). Boaz stands in the direct line of Christ (Mt 1:5; Lk 3:32). This turn of events marks the point where Naomi's human emptiness (1:21) begins to be refilled by the Lord. Her night of earthly doubt has been broken by the dawning of new hope (cf. Ro 8:28-39).

When Boaz negotiated with another relative about the settlement of Elimelech and Naomi's estate in Ruth 4:1-12, he referred to a law established by Moses in Deuteronomy 25:5-10. That law set out specific actions to be taken by the surviving family if a married son were to die without a son to inherit or carry on his name. Another (presumably unmarried) man in the family was to marry the widow. The first resulting child would inherit the estate of the man who had died.

APRIL 29

Ruth 3:1–4:22

3 Then Naomi her mother-in-law said to her, "My daughter, shall I not seek security for you, that it may be well with you? ²Now is not Boaz our kinsman, with whose maids you were? Behold, he winnows barley at the threshing floor tonight. ³Wash yourself therefore, and anoint yourself and put on your *best* clothes, and go down to the threshing floor; *but* do not make yourself known to the man until he has finished eating and drinking. ⁴It shall be when he lies down, that you shall notice the place where he lies, and you shall go and uncover his feet and lie down; then he will tell you what you shall do." ⁵She said to her, "All that you say I will do."

⁶So she went down to the threshing floor and did according to all that her mother-in-law had commanded her. ⁷When Boaz had eaten and drunk and his heart was merry, he went to lie down at the end of the heap of grain; and she came secretly, and uncovered his feet and lay down. ⁸It happened in the middle of the night that the man was startled and bent forward; and behold, a woman was lying at his feet. ⁹He said, "Who are you?" And she answered, "I am Ruth your maid. So spread your covering over your maid, for you are a close relative." ¹⁰Then he said, "May you be blessed of the LORD, my daughter. You have shown your last kindness to be better than the first by not going after young men, whether poor or rich. ¹¹Now, my daughter, do not fear. I will do for you whatever you ask, for all my people in the city know that you are a woman of excellence. ¹²Now it is true I am a close relative; however, there is a relative closer than I. ¹³Remain this night, and when morning comes, if he will redeem you, good; let him redeem you. But if he does not wish to redeem you, then I will redeem you, as the LORD lives. Lie down until morning."

¹⁴So she lay at his feet until morning and rose before one could recognize another; and he said, "Let it not be known that the woman came to the threshing floor." ¹⁵Again he said, "Give me the cloak that is on you and hold it." So she held it, and he measured six *measures* of barley and laid *it* on her. Then she went into the city. ¹⁶When she came to her mother-in-law, she said, "How did it go, my daughter?" And she told her all that the man had done for her. ¹⁷She said, "These six *measures* of barley he gave to me, for he said, 'Do not go to your mother-in-law empty-handed.'" ¹⁸Then she

said, "Wait, my daughter, until you know how the matter turns out; for the man will not rest until he has settled it today."

4 Now Boaz went up to the gate and sat down there, and behold, the close relative of whom Boaz spoke was passing by, so he said, "Turn aside, friend, sit down here." And he turned aside and sat down. ²He took ten men of the elders of the city and said, "Sit down here." So they sat down. ³Then he said to the closest relative, "Naomi, who has come back from the land of Moab, has to sell the piece of land which belonged to our brother Elimelech. ⁴So I thought to inform you, saying, 'Buy *it* before those who are sitting *here*, and before the elders of my people. If you will redeem *it*, redeem *it*; but if not, tell me that I may know; for there is no one but you to redeem *it*, and I am after you.'" And he said, "I will redeem *it*." ⁵Then Boaz said, "On the day you buy the field from the hand of Naomi, you must also acquire Ruth the Moabitess, the widow of the deceased, in order to raise up the name of the deceased on his inheritance." ⁶The closest relative said, "I cannot redeem *it* for myself, because I would jeopardize my own inheritance. Redeem *it* for yourself; you *may have* my right of redemption, for I cannot redeem *it*."

⁷Now this was *the custom* in former times in Israel concerning the redemption and the exchange *of land* to confirm any matter: a man removed his sandal and gave it to another; and this was the *manner of* attestation in Israel. ⁸So the closest relative said to Boaz, "Buy *it* for yourself." And he removed his sandal. ⁹Then Boaz said to the elders and all the people, "You are witnesses today that I have bought from the hand of Naomi all that belonged to Elimelech and all that belonged to Chilion and Mahlon. ¹⁰Moreover, I have acquired Ruth the Moabitess, the widow of Mahlon, to be my wife in order to raise up the name of the deceased on his inheritance, so that the name of the deceased will not be

4:7 removed his sandal. The Scripture writer explained to his own generation what had been a custom in former generations. This kind of tradition appears in Deuteronomy 25:5–10 and apparently continued at least to the time of Amos (2:6; 8:6). The closer relative legally transferred his right to the property as symbolized by the sandal, most likely that of the nearer relative.

cut off from his brothers or from the court of his *birth* place; you are witnesses today." [11] All the people who were in the court, and the elders, said, "*We are* witnesses. May the LORD make the woman who is coming into your home like Rachel and Leah, both of whom built the house of Israel; and may you achieve wealth in Ephrathah and become famous in Bethlehem. [12] Moreover, may your house be like the house of Perez whom Tamar bore to Judah, through the offspring which the LORD will give you by this young woman."

[13] So Boaz took Ruth, and she became his wife, and he went in to her. And the LORD enabled her to conceive, and she gave birth to a son. [14] Then the women said to Naomi, "Blessed is the LORD who has not left you without a redeemer today, and may his name become famous in Israel. [15] May he also be to you a restorer of life and a sustainer of your old age; for your daughter-in-law, who loves you and is better to you than seven sons, has given birth to him." [16] Then Naomi took the child and laid him in her lap, and became his nurse. [17] The neighbor women gave him a name, saying, "A son has been born to Naomi!" So they named him Obed. He is the father of Jesse, the father of David.

[18] Now these are the generations of Perez: to Perez was born Hezron, [19] and to Hezron was born Ram, and to Ram, Amminadab, [20] and to Amminadab was born Nahshon, and to Nahshon, Salmon, [21] and to Salmon was born Boaz, and to Boaz, Obed, [22] and to Obed was born Jesse, and to Jesse, David.

4:22 David. Looking back at Ruth from a New Testament perspective, latent messianic implications become more apparent (Mt 1:1). The fruit which is promised later on in the Davidic Covenant (2Sa 7:1–17) finds its seedbed here. The hope of a messianic king and kingdom (2Sa 7:12–14) will be fulfilled in the Lord Jesus Christ (Rev 19–20) through the lineage of David's grandfather Obed, who was born to Boaz and Ruth the Moabitess.

Psalm 52:6–9

6   The righteous will see and fear,
    And will laugh at him, *saying*,
7   "Behold, the man who would
        not make God his refuge,
    But trusted in the abundance
        of his riches
    And was strong in his *evil* desire."

8   But as for me, I am like a green
        olive tree in the house of God;
    I trust in the lovingkindness
        of God forever and ever.
9   I will give You thanks forever,
        because You have done *it*,
    And I will wait on Your name,
        for *it is* good, in the presence
        of Your godly ones.

52:8 green olive tree. The psalmist exults (through this simile) that the one who trusts in the mercy of God is productive and secure.

Proverbs 15:6–7

6   Great wealth is *in* the house
        of the righteous,
    But trouble is in the income
        of the wicked.
7   The lips of the wise spread
        knowledge,
    But the hearts of fools are not so.

Luke 20:1–26

20 On one of the days while He was teaching the people in the temple and preaching the gospel, the chief priests and the scribes with the elders confronted *Him,* [2] and they spoke, saying to Him, "Tell us by what authority You are doing these things, or who is the one who gave You this authority?" [3] Jesus answered and said to them, "I will also ask you a question, and you tell Me: [4] Was the baptism of John from heaven or from men?" [5] They reasoned among themselves, saying, "If we say, 'From heaven,' He will say, 'Why did you not believe him?' [6] But if we say, 'From men,' all the people will stone us to death, for

20:5 Why did you not believe him? John had clearly testified that Jesus was the Messiah. If John was a prophet whose words were true, they ought to believe his testimony about Christ. On the other hand, it would have been political folly for the Pharisees to attack the legitimacy of John the Baptist or deny his authority as a prophet of God. John was enormously popular with the people, and a martyr at the hands of the despised Herod. For the Pharisees to question John's authority was to attack a national hero, and they knew better than that. So they pleaded ignorance (v. 7).

they are convinced that John was a prophet." ⁷So they answered that they did not know where *it came* from. ⁸And Jesus said to them, "Nor will I tell you by what authority I do these things."

⁹And He began to tell the people this parable: "A man planted a vineyard and rented it out to vine-growers, and went on a journey for a long time. ¹⁰At the *harvest* time he sent a slave to the vine-growers, so that they would give him *some* of the produce of the vineyard; but the vine-growers beat him and sent him away empty-handed. ¹¹And he proceeded to send another slave; and they beat him also and treated him shamefully and sent him away empty-handed. ¹²And he proceeded to send a third; and this one also they wounded and cast out. ¹³The owner of the vineyard said, 'What shall I do? I will send my beloved son; perhaps they will respect him.' ¹⁴But when the vine-growers saw him, they reasoned with one another, saying, 'This is the heir; let us kill him so that the inheritance will be ours.' ¹⁵So they threw him out of the vineyard and killed him. What, then, will the owner of the vineyard do to them? ¹⁶He will come and destroy these vine-growers and will give the vineyard to others." When they heard it, they said, "May it never be!" ¹⁷But Jesus looked at them and said, "What then is this that is written:

'THE STONE WHICH THE
  BUILDERS REJECTED,
THIS BECAME THE CHIEF
  CORNER *stone*'?

¹⁸Everyone who falls on that stone will be broken to pieces; but on whomever it falls, it will scatter him like dust."

¹⁹The scribes and the chief priests tried to lay hands on Him that very hour, and they feared the people; for they understood that He spoke this parable against them. ²⁰So they watched Him, and sent spies who pretended to be righteous, in order that they might catch Him in some statement, so that they *could* deliver Him to the rule and the authority of the governor. ²¹They questioned Him, saying, "Teacher, we know that You speak and teach correctly, and You are not partial to any, but teach the way of God in truth. ²²Is it lawful for us to pay taxes to Caesar, or not?" ²³But He detected their trickery and said to them, ²⁴"Show Me a denarius. Whose likeness and inscription does it have?" They said, "Caesar's." ²⁵And He said to them, "Then render to Caesar the things that are Caesar's, and to God the things that are God's." ²⁶And they were unable to catch Him in a saying in the presence of the people; and being amazed at His answer, they became silent.

DAY 29: How does Ruth exemplify the Proverbs 31 wife?

The "excellent," or virtuous, wife of Proverbs 31:10 is personified by "excellent" Ruth of whom the same Hebrew word is used (Ru 3:11). With amazing parallel, they share at least 8 character traits (see below). One wonders (in concert with Jewish tradition) if King Lemuel's mother might not have been Bathsheba, who orally passed the family heritage of Ruth's spotless reputation along to David's son Solomon. Lemuel, which means "devoted to God," could have been a family name for Solomon (see Jedidiah, 2Sa 12:25), who then could have penned Proverbs 31:10–31 with Ruth in mind:

1. Devoted to her family (Ru 1:15–18 // Pr 31:10–12, 23).
2. Delighted in her work (Ru 2:2 // Pr 31:13).
3. Diligent in her labor (Ru 2:7, 17, 23 // Pr 31:14–18, 19–21, 24, 27).
4. Dedicated to godly speech (Ru 2:10, 13 // Pr 31:26).
5. Dependent on God (Ru 2:12 // Pr 31:25b, 30).
6. Dressed with care (Ru 3:3 // Pr 31:22, 25a).
7. Discreet with men (Ru 3:6–13 // Pr 31:11–12, 23).
8. Delivered blessings (Ru 4:14–15 // Pr 31:28–29, 31)

APRIL 30

1 Samuel 1:1–3:21

1 Now there was a certain man from Ramathaim-zophim from the hill country of Ephraim, and his name was Elkanah the son of Jeroham, the son of Elihu, the son of Tohu, the son of Zuph, an Ephraimite. ²He had two wives: the name of one was Hannah and the name of the other Peninnah; and Peninnah had children, but Hannah had no children.

³Now this man would go up from his city yearly to worship and to sacrifice to the LORD of hosts in Shiloh. And the two sons

of Eli, Hophni and Phinehas, were priests to the LORD there. 4When the day came that Elkanah sacrificed, he would give portions to Peninnah his wife and to all her sons and her daughters; 5but to Hannah he would give a double portion, for he loved Hannah, but the LORD had closed her womb. 6Her rival, however, would provoke her bitterly to irritate her, because the LORD had closed her womb. 7It happened year after year, as often as she went up to the house of the LORD, she would provoke her; so she wept and would not eat. 8Then Elkanah her husband said to her, "Hannah, why do you weep and why do you not eat and why is your heart sad? Am I not better to you than ten sons?"

9Then Hannah rose after eating and drinking in Shiloh. Now Eli the priest was sitting on the seat by the doorpost of the temple of the LORD. 10She, greatly distressed, prayed to the LORD and wept bitterly. 11She made a vow and said, "O LORD of hosts, if You will indeed look on the affliction of Your maidservant and remember me, and not forget Your maidservant, but will give Your maidservant a son, then I will give him to the LORD all the days of his life, and a razor shall never come on his head."

12Now it came about, as she continued praying before the LORD, that Eli was watching her mouth. 13As for Hannah, she was speaking in her heart, only her lips were moving, but her voice was not heard. So Eli thought she was drunk. 14Then Eli said to her, "How long will you make yourself drunk? Put away your wine from you." 15But Hannah replied, "No, my lord, I am a woman oppressed in spirit; I have drunk neither wine nor strong drink, but I have poured out my soul before the LORD. 16Do not consider your maidservant as a worthless woman, for I have spoken until now out of my great concern and provocation." 17Then Eli answered and said, "Go in peace; and may the God of Israel grant your petition that you have asked of Him." 18She said, "Let your maidservant find favor in your sight." So the woman went her way and ate, and her face was no longer *sad*.

19Then they arose early in the morning and worshiped before the LORD, and returned again to their house in Ramah. And Elkanah had relations with Hannah his wife, and the LORD remembered her. 20It came about in due time, after Hannah had conceived, that she gave birth to a son; and she named him Samuel, *saying*, "Because I have asked him of the LORD."

21Then the man Elkanah went up with all his household to offer to the LORD the yearly sacrifice and *pay* his vow. 22But Hannah did not go up, for she said to her husband, "*I will not go up* until the child is weaned; then I will bring him, that he may appear before the LORD and stay there forever." 23Elkanah her husband said to her, "Do what seems best to you. Remain until you have weaned him; only may the LORD confirm His word." So the woman remained and nursed her son until she weaned him. 24Now when she had weaned him, she took him up with her, with a three-year-old bull and one ephah of flour and a jug of wine, and brought him to the house of the LORD in Shiloh, although the child was young. 25Then they slaughtered the bull, and brought the boy to Eli. 26She said, "Oh, my lord! As your soul lives, my lord, I am the woman who stood here beside you, praying to the LORD. 27For this boy I prayed, and the LORD has given me my petition which I asked of Him. 28So I have also dedicated him to the LORD; as long as he lives he is dedicated to the LORD." And he worshiped the LORD there.

2 Then Hannah prayed and said,

"My heart exults in the LORD;
My horn is exalted in the LORD,
My mouth speaks boldly
    against my enemies,
Because I rejoice in Your salvation.
2 "There is no one holy like the LORD,
Indeed, there is no one besides You,
Nor is there any rock like our God.
3 "Boast no more so very proudly,
Do not let arrogance come
    out of your mouth;
For the LORD is a God of knowledge,
And with Him actions are
    weighed.
4 "The bows of the mighty are
    shattered,
But the feeble gird on strength.
5 "Those who were full hire
    themselves out for bread,
But those who were hungry
    cease *to hunger*.
Even the barren gives birth to
    seven,
But she who has many
    children languishes.
6 "The LORD kills and makes alive;
He brings down to Sheol
    and raises up.
7 "The LORD makes poor and rich;
He brings low, He also exalts.
8 "He raises the poor from the
    dust,

He lifts the needy from the ash heap
To make them sit with nobles,
And inherit a seat of honor;
For the pillars of the earth
  are the LORD'S,
And He set the world on them.
9 "He keeps the feet of His godly
    ones,
But the wicked ones are
    silenced in darkness;
For not by might shall a man
    prevail.
10 "Those who contend with the
    LORD will be shattered;
Against them He will thunder
    in the heavens,
The LORD will judge the
    ends of the earth;
And He will give strength
    to His king,
And will exalt the horn
    of His anointed."

11 Then Elkanah went to his home at Ramah. But the boy ministered to the LORD before Eli the priest.

12 Now the sons of Eli were worthless men; they did not know the LORD 13 and the custom of the priests with the people. When any man was offering a sacrifice, the priest's servant would come while the meat was boiling, with a three-pronged fork in his hand. 14 Then he would thrust it into the pan, or kettle, or caldron, or pot; all that the fork brought up the priest would take for himself. Thus they did in Shiloh to all the Israelites who came there. 15 Also, before they burned the fat, the priest's servant would come and say to the man who was sacrificing, "Give the priest meat for roasting, as he will not take boiled meat from you, only raw." 16 If the man said to him, "They must surely burn the fat first, and then take as much as you desire," then he would say, "No, but you shall give it to me now; and if not, I will take it by force." 17 Thus the sin of the young men was very great before the LORD, for the men despised the offering of the LORD.

18 Now Samuel was ministering before the LORD, as a boy wearing a linen ephod. 19 And his mother would make him a little robe and bring it to him from year to year when she would come up with her husband to offer the yearly sacrifice. 20 Then Eli would bless Elkanah and his wife and say, "May the LORD give you children from this woman in place of the one she dedicated to the LORD." And they went to their own home.

21 The LORD visited Hannah; and she conceived and gave birth to three sons and two daughters. And the boy Samuel grew before the LORD.

22 Now Eli was very old; and he heard all that his sons were doing to all Israel, and how they lay with the women who served at the doorway of the tent of meeting. 23 He said to them, "Why do you do such things, the evil things that I hear from all these people? 24 No, my sons; for the report is not good which I hear the LORD'S people circulating. 25 If one man sins against another, God will mediate for him; but if a man sins against the LORD, who can intercede for him?" But they would not listen to the voice of their father, for the LORD desired to put them to death.

26 Now the boy Samuel was growing in stature and in favor both with the LORD and with men.

27 Then a man of God came to Eli and said to him, "Thus says the LORD, 'Did I not indeed reveal Myself to the house of your father when they were in Egypt in bondage to Pharaoh's house? 28 Did I not choose them from all the tribes of Israel to be My priests, to go up to My altar, to burn incense, to carry an ephod before Me; and did I not give to the house of your father all the fire offerings of the sons of Israel? 29 Why do you kick at My sacrifice and at My offering which I have commanded in My dwelling, and honor your sons above Me, by making yourselves fat with the choicest of every offering of My people Israel?' 30 Therefore the LORD God of Israel declares, 'I did indeed say that your house and the house of your father should walk before Me forever'; but now the LORD declares, 'Far be it from Me—for those who honor Me I will honor, and those who despise Me will be lightly esteemed. 31 Behold, the days are coming when I will break your strength and the strength of your father's house so that there will not be an old man in your house. 32 You will see the distress of My dwelling, in spite of all the good that I do for Israel; and an old man will not be in your house forever. 33 Yet I will not cut off every man of yours from My altar so that your eyes will fail from weeping and your soul grieve, and all the increase of your house will die in the prime of life. 34 This will be the sign to you which will come concerning your two sons, Hophni and Phinehas: on the same day both of them will die. 35 But I will raise up for Myself a faithful priest who will do according to what is in My heart and in My soul; and I will build him an enduring house, and he will walk before My anointed always. 36 Everyone

who is left in your house will come and bow down to him for a piece of silver or a loaf of bread and say, "Please assign me to one of the priest's offices so that I may eat a piece of bread."'"

3 Now the boy Samuel was ministering to the LORD before Eli. And word from the LORD was rare in those days, visions were infrequent.

3:1 the boy Samuel. Samuel was no longer a child (2:21, 26). While Jewish historian Josephus suggested he was 12 years of age, he was probably a teenager at this time. The same Hebrew term translated here "boy" was used of David when he slew Goliath (17:33). **word from the LORD was rare.** The time of the judges was a period of extremely limited prophetic activity. The few visions that God did give were not widely known. **visions.** A divine revelation mediated through an auditory or visual encounter.

²It happened at that time as Eli was lying down in his place (now his eyesight had begun to grow dim *and* he could not see *well*), ³and the lamp of God had not yet gone out, and Samuel was lying down in the temple of the LORD where the ark of God *was*, ⁴that the LORD called Samuel; and he said, "Here I am." ⁵Then he ran to Eli and said, "Here I am, for you called me." But he said, "I did not call, lie down again." So he went and lay down. ⁶The LORD called yet again, "Samuel!" So Samuel arose and went to Eli and said, "Here I am, for you called me." But he answered, "I did not call, my son, lie down again." ⁷Now Samuel did not yet know the LORD, nor had the word of the LORD yet been revealed to him. ⁸So the LORD called Samuel again for the third time. And he arose and went to Eli and said, "Here I am, for you called me." Then Eli discerned that the LORD was calling the boy. ⁹And Eli said to Samuel, "Go lie down, and it shall be if He calls you, that you shall say, 'Speak, LORD, for Your servant is listening.' " So Samuel went and lay down in his place.

¹⁰Then the LORD came and stood and called as at other times, "Samuel! Samuel!" And Samuel said, "Speak, for Your servant is listening." ¹¹The LORD said to Samuel, "Behold, I am about to do a thing in Israel at which both ears of everyone who hears it will tingle. ¹²In that day I will carry out against Eli all that I have spoken concerning his house, from beginning to end. ¹³For I have told him that I am about to judge his house forever for the iniquity which he knew, because his sons brought a curse on themselves and he did not rebuke them. ¹⁴Therefore I have sworn to the house of Eli that the iniquity of Eli's house shall not be atoned for by sacrifice or offering forever."

¹⁵So Samuel lay down until morning. Then he opened the doors of the house of the LORD. But Samuel was afraid to tell the vision to Eli. ¹⁶Then Eli called Samuel and said, "Samuel, my son." And he said, "Here I am." ¹⁷He said, "What is the word that He spoke to you? Please do not hide it from me. May God do so to you, and more also, if you hide anything from me of all the words that He spoke to you." ¹⁸So Samuel told him everything and hid nothing from him. And he said, "It is the LORD; let Him do what seems good to Him."

¹⁹Thus Samuel grew and the LORD was with him and let none of his words fail. ²⁰All Israel from Dan even to Beersheba knew that Samuel was confirmed as a prophet of the LORD. ²¹And the LORD appeared again at Shiloh, because the LORD revealed Himself to Samuel at Shiloh by the word of the LORD.

3:19 the LORD was with him. The Lord's presence was with Samuel, as it would be later with David (16:18; 18:12). The Lord's presence validated His choice of a man for His service. **let none of his words fail.** Everything Samuel said with divine authorization came true. This fulfillment of Samuel's word proved that he was a true prophet of God (Dt 18:21–22).

Psalm 53:1–6

For the choir director; according to Mahalath. A Maskil of David.

The fool has said in his heart,
    "There is no God,"
They are corrupt, and have
    committed abominable
    injustice;
There is no one who does
    good.
² God has looked down from
    heaven upon the sons
    of men
To see if there is anyone
    who understands,
Who seeks after God.

³ Every one of them has turned
   aside; together they have
   become corrupt;
 There is no one who does
   good, not even one.

⁴ Have the workers of wickedness
   no knowledge,
 Who eat up My people *as*
   though they ate bread
 And have not called upon God?

⁵ There they were in great fear
   where no fear had been;
 For God scattered the bones
   of him who encamped
   against you;
 You put *them* to shame, because
   God had rejected them.

⁶ Oh, that the salvation of Israel
   would come out of Zion!
 When God restores His captive
   people,
 Let Jacob rejoice, let Israel be
   glad.

Proverbs 15:8–11

⁸ The sacrifice of the wicked
   is an abomination to
   the LORD,
 But the prayer of the upright
   is His delight.

⁹ The way of the wicked is an
   abomination to the LORD,
 But He loves one who pursues
   righteousness.

¹⁰ Grievous punishment is for
   him who forsakes
   the way;
 He who hates reproof will
   die.

¹¹ Sheol and Abaddon *lie open*
   before the LORD,
 How much more the hearts
   of men!

Luke 20:27–47

²⁷ Now there came to Him some of the Sadducees (who say that there is no resurrection), ²⁸ and they questioned Him, saying, "Teacher, Moses wrote for us that IF A MAN'S BROTHER

15:11 Sheol and Abaddon. See 27:20. Hell or Sheol is the place of the dead. "Abaddon" or destruction refers to the experience of eternal punishment. See Job 26:6.

DIES, HAVING A WIFE, AND HE IS CHILDLESS, HIS BROTHER SHOULD MARRY THE WIFE AND RAISE UP CHILDREN TO HIS BROTHER. ²⁹ Now there were seven brothers; and the first took a wife and died childless; ³⁰ and the second ³¹ and the third married her; and in the same way all seven died, leaving no children. ³² Finally the woman died also. ³³ In the resurrection therefore, which one's wife will she be? For all seven had married her."

³⁴ Jesus said to them, "The sons of this age marry and are given in marriage, ³⁵ but those who are considered worthy to attain to that age and the resurrection from the dead, neither marry nor are given in marriage; ³⁶ for they cannot even die anymore, because they are like angels, and are sons of God, being sons of the resurrection. ³⁷ But that the dead are raised, even Moses showed, in the *passage about the burning* bush, where he calls the Lord THE GOD OF ABRAHAM, AND THE GOD OF ISAAC, AND THE GOD OF JACOB. ³⁸ Now He is not the God of the dead but of the living; for all live to Him." ³⁹ Some of the scribes answered and said, "Teacher, You have spoken well." ⁴⁰ For they did not have courage to question Him any longer about anything.

⁴¹ Then He said to them, "How *is it that* they say the Christ is David's son? ⁴² For David himself says in the book of Psalms,

'THE LORD SAID TO MY LORD,
   "SIT AT MY RIGHT HAND,
⁴³ UNTIL I MAKE YOUR ENEMIES A
      FOOTSTOOL FOR YOUR FEET." '

⁴⁴ Therefore David calls Him 'Lord,' and how is He his son?"

⁴⁵ And while all the people were listening, He said to the disciples, ⁴⁶ "Beware of the scribes, who like to walk around in long robes,

20:37 *passage about the burning* **bush.** Exodus 3:1—4:17. In that passage God identified Himself to Moses as the God of Abraham, Isaac, and Jacob—using the present tense. He didn't say He *was* their God, but "I AM" their God, indicating that their existence had not ended with their deaths.

20:40 not have courage to question Him. The more questions Jesus answered the clearer it became that His understanding and authority were vastly superior to that of the scribes and Pharisees.

and love respectful greetings in the market places, and chief seats in the synagogues and places of honor at banquets, 47who devour widows' houses, and for appearance's sake offer long prayers. These will receive greater condemnation."

DAY 30: What do the two prayers of Hannah teach us about prayer?

In 1 Samuel 1:10–11, Hannah vowed while "greatly distressed" to give the Lord her son in return for God's favor in giving her that son. She prayed as a "maidservant"—a humble, submissive way of referring to herself in the presence of her superior, sovereign God. "Remember me," she requested, asking for special attention and care from the Lord. She would give the child to the Lord "all the days of his life," which was in contrast to the normal Nazirite vow, which was only for a specified period of time (see Nu 6:4–5, 8).

In contrast to the prayer that came from her bitterness, Hannah prayed from joy in 2:1–10. The prominent idea in Hannah's prayer is that the Lord is a righteous Judge. He had brought down the proud (Peninnah) and exalted the humble (Hannah). The prayer has four sections: 1) Hannah prayed to the Lord for His salvation (vv. 1–2); 2) Hannah warned the proud of the Lord's humbling (vv. 3–8d); 3) Hannah affirmed the Lord's faithful care for His saints (vv. 8e–9b); 4) Hannah petitioned the Lord to judge the world and to prosper His anointed king (vv. 10d—e). This prayer has a number of striking verbal similarities with David's song of 2 Samuel 22:2–51: "horn" (2:1; 22:3), "rock" (2:2; 22:2–3), salvation/deliverance (2:1–2; 22:2–3), grave/Sheol (2:6; 22:6), "thunder" (2:10; 22:14), "king" (2:10; 22:51), and "anointed" (2:10; 22:51).

MAY 1

1 Samuel 4:1–5:12

4 Thus the word of Samuel came to all Israel. Now Israel went out to meet the Philistines in battle and camped beside Ebenezer while the Philistines camped in Aphek. ²The Philistines drew up in battle array to meet Israel. When the battle spread, Israel was defeated before the Philistines who killed about four thousand men on the battlefield. ³When the people came into the camp, the elders of Israel said, "Why has the LORD defeated us today before the Philistines? Let us take to ourselves from Shiloh the ark of the covenant of the LORD, that it may come among us and deliver us from the power of our enemies." ⁴So the people sent to Shiloh, and from there they carried the ark of the covenant of the LORD of hosts who sits *above* the cherubim; and the two sons of Eli, Hophni and Phinehas, *were* there with the ark of the covenant of God.

4:4 sits *above* the cherubim. A repeated phrase used to describe the Lord (2Sa 6:2; 2Ki 19:15; 1Ch 13:6; Pss 80:1; 99:1; Is 37:16). It spoke of His sovereign majesty. **Hophni and Phinehas.** These were the two wicked sons of Eli (2:12–17, 27–36), of whom it was said that they "did not know the LORD" (2:12). The fact that they were mentioned together recalls the prophecy that they would die together (2:34).

⁵As the ark of the covenant of the LORD came into the camp, all Israel shouted with a great shout, so that the earth resounded. ⁶When the Philistines heard the noise of the shout, they said, "What *does* the noise of this great shout in the camp of the Hebrews *mean?*" Then they understood that the ark of the LORD had come into the camp. ⁷The Philistines were afraid, for they said, "God has come into the camp." And they said, "Woe to us! For nothing like this has happened before. ⁸Woe to us! Who shall deliver us from the hand of these mighty gods? These are the gods who smote the Egyptians with all *kinds of* plagues in the wilderness. ⁹Take courage and be men, O Philistines, or you will become slaves to the Hebrews, as they have been slaves to you; therefore, be men and fight."

¹⁰So the Philistines fought and Israel was defeated, and every man fled to his tent; and the slaughter was very great, for there fell of Israel thirty thousand foot soldiers. ¹¹And the ark of God was taken; and the two sons of Eli, Hophni and Phinehas, died.

4:11 the ark of God was taken. In spite of their hopes to manipulate God into giving them the victory, Israel was defeated and the ark fell into the hands of the Philistines. The view of having the ark of God being equivalent to having control of God, possessed both by Israel and then the Philistines, is to be contrasted with the power and providence of God in the remaining narrative.

¹²Now a man of Benjamin ran from the battle line and came to Shiloh the same day with his clothes torn and dust on his head. ¹³When he came, behold, Eli was sitting on *his* seat by the road eagerly watching, because his heart was trembling for the ark of God. So the man came to tell *it* in the city, and all the city cried out. ¹⁴When Eli heard the noise of the outcry, he said, "What *does* the noise of this commotion *mean?*" Then the man came hurriedly and told Eli. ¹⁵Now Eli was ninety-eight years old, and his eyes were set so that he could not see. ¹⁶The man said to Eli, "I am the one who came from the battle line. Indeed, I escaped from the battle line today." And he said, "How did things go, my son?" ¹⁷Then the one who brought the news replied, "Israel has fled before the Philistines and there has also been a great slaughter among the people, and your two sons also, Hophni and Phinehas, are dead, and the ark of God has been taken." ¹⁸When he mentioned the ark of God, Eli fell off the seat backward beside the gate, and his neck was broken and he died, for he was old and heavy. Thus he judged Israel forty years.

¹⁹Now his daughter-in-law, Phinehas's wife, was pregnant and about to give birth; and when she heard the news that the ark of God was taken and that her father-in-law and her husband had died, she kneeled down and gave birth, for her pains came upon her. ²⁰And about the time of her death the women who stood by her said to her, "Do not be afraid, for you have given birth to a son." But she did not answer or pay attention. ²¹And she called the boy Ichabod, saying, "The glory has departed from Israel," because the ark of God was taken and because of her father-in-law and her husband. ²²She said, "The glory has departed from Israel, for the ark of God was taken."

4:21 Ichabod…The glory has departed. Due primarily to the loss of the ark, the symbol of God's presence, Phinehas' wife names her child Ichabod, meaning either "Where is the glory?" or "no glory." To the Hebrew, "glory" was often used to refer to God's presence; hence, the text means "Where is God?" The word "departed" carries the idea of having gone into exile. Thus, to the people of Israel, the capturing of the ark was a symbol that God had gone into exile. Although this was the mindset of Israel, the text narrative will reveal that God was present, even when He disciplined His people.

5 Now the Philistines took the ark of God and brought it from Ebenezer to Ashdod. ² Then the Philistines took the ark of God and brought it to the house of Dagon and set it by Dagon. ³ When the Ashdodites arose early the next morning, behold, Dagon had fallen on his face to the ground before the ark of the LORD. So they took Dagon and set him in his place again. ⁴ But when they arose early the next morning, behold, Dagon had fallen on his face to the ground before the ark of the LORD. And the head of Dagon and both the palms of his hands *were* cut off on the threshold; only the trunk of Dagon was left to him. ⁵ Therefore neither the priests of Dagon nor all who enter Dagon's house tread on the threshold of Dagon in Ashdod to this day.

⁶ Now the hand of the LORD was heavy on the Ashdodites, and He ravaged them and smote them with tumors, both Ashdod and its territories. ⁷ When the men of Ashdod saw that it was so, they said, "The ark of the God of Israel must not remain with us, for His hand is severe on us and on Dagon our god." ⁸ So they sent and gathered all the lords of the Philistines to them and said, "What shall we do with the ark of the God of Israel?" And they said, "Let the ark of the God of Israel be brought around to Gath." And they brought the ark of the God of Israel *around*. ⁹ After they had brought it around, the hand of the LORD was against the city with very great confusion; and He smote the men of the city, both young and old, so that tumors broke out on them. ¹⁰ So they sent the ark of God to Ekron. And as the ark of God came to Ekron the Ekronites cried out, saying, "They have brought the ark of the God of Israel around to us, to kill us and our people." ¹¹ They sent therefore and gathered all the lords of the Philistines and said, "Send away the ark of the God of Israel, and let it return to its own place, so that it will not kill

us and our people." For there was a deadly confusion throughout the city; the hand of God was very heavy there. ¹² And the men who did not die were smitten with tumors and the cry of the city went up to heaven.

Psalm 54:1–7

> For the choir director; on stringed instruments. A Maskil of David, when the Ziphites came and said to Saul, "Is not David hiding himself among us?"

S ave me, O God, by Your name,
And vindicate me by Your power.
² Hear my prayer, O God;
Give ear to the words of my mouth.
³ For strangers have risen against me
And violent men have sought my life;
They have not set God before them. *Selah*

54:1 by Your name. In the ancient world, a person's name was essentially the person himself. Here, God's name includes His covenant protection. **vindicate.** David requests that God will execute justice for him, as in a court trial when a defendant is declared not guilty.

⁴ Behold, God is my helper;
The Lord is the sustainer of my soul.
⁵ He will recompense the evil to my foes;
Destroy them in Your faithfulness.

⁶ Willingly I will sacrifice to You;
I will give thanks to Your name,
O LORD, for it is good.
⁷ For He has delivered me from all trouble,
And my eye has looked *with satisfaction* upon my enemies.

Proverbs 15:12–13

¹² A scoffer does not love one who reproves him,
He will not go to the wise.
¹³ A joyful heart makes a cheerful face,
But when the heart is sad, the spirit is broken.

Luke 21:1-19

21 And He looked up and saw the rich putting their gifts into the treasury. ²And He saw a poor widow putting in two small copper coins. ³And He said, "Truly I say to you, this poor widow put in more than all *of them;* ⁴for they all out of their surplus put into the offering; but she out of her poverty put in all that she had to live on."

⁵And while some were talking about the temple, that it was adorned with beautiful stones and votive gifts, He said, ⁶"*As for* these things which you are looking at, the days will come in which there will not be left one stone upon another which will not be torn down."

21:1 the treasury. Thirteen chests with funnel-shaped openings stood in the court of the women. Each was labeled for a specific use, and donations were given accordingly.

21:5 votive gifts. Wealthy people gave gifts of gold sculptures, golden plaques, and other treasures to the temple. Herod had donated a golden vine with clusters of golden grapes nearly 6 feet tall. The gifts were displayed on the walls and suspended in the portico. They constituted an unimaginable collection of wealth. All of these riches were looted by the Romans when the temple was destroyed (v. 6).

⁷They questioned Him, saying, "Teacher, when therefore will these things happen? And what *will be* the sign when these things are about to take place?" ⁸And He said, "See to it that you are not misled; for many will come in My name, saying, 'I am *He*,' and, 'The time is near.' Do not go after them. ⁹When you hear of wars and disturbances, do not be terrified; for these things must take place first, but the end *does* not *follow* immediately."

¹⁰Then He continued by saying to them, "Nation will rise against nation and kingdom against kingdom, ¹¹and there will be great earthquakes, and in various places plagues and famines; and there will be terrors and great signs from heaven.

¹²"But before all these things, they will lay their hands on you and will persecute you, delivering you to the synagogues and prisons, bringing you before kings and governors for My name's sake. ¹³It will lead to an opportunity for your testimony. ¹⁴So make up your minds not to prepare beforehand to defend yourselves; ¹⁵for I will give you utterance and wisdom which none of your opponents will be able to resist or refute. ¹⁶But you will be betrayed even by parents and brothers and relatives and friends, and they will put *some* of you to death, ¹⁷and you will be hated by all because of My name. ¹⁸Yet not a hair of your head will perish. ¹⁹By your endurance you will gain your lives.

DAY 1: Contrast the pagan god of the Philistines and the living God.

In Judges 5:2, Dagon is mentioned. Ugaritic literature identifies this deity as a god of grain or vegetation, whose image had the lower body of a fish and upper body of a man. Dagon seems to have been the leader of the Philistine pantheon (Jdg 16:23) and is noted to be the father of Baal. The placing of the ark of God in the temple of Dagon was supposed to be a sign of Dagon's power and Yahweh's inferiority, a visual representation that the god of the Philistines was victorious over the God of the Hebrews.

The next morning the Philistines found Dagon had "fallen on his face" (1Sa 5:3). Ironically, God Himself overturned the supposed supremacy of Dagon by having Dagon fallen over, as if paying homage to the Lord. The same thing happened the next morning, but this time the "head...hands were cut off" (v. 4). The first display of God's authority over Dagon was not perceived. God's second display of authority, the cutting off of Dagon's head and hands, was a common sign that the enemy was dead (Jdg 7:25; 8:6; 1Sa 17:54; 31:9; 2Sa 4:12), and was to be understood as God's divine judgment on the false idol. Because the head and hands of Dagon fell on the threshold, superstition developed that it was cursed; therefore, the Philistines would not tread on it (v. 5).

In contrast to the hands of Dagon being cut off, symbolizing his helplessness against the power of Yahweh, the Lord was pictured to be actively involved in judging the Philistines. "The hand of the LORD was heavy" on the people (v. 6). The imagery of God's hand is found throughout the ark narrative (4:8; 5:6, 7, 9, 11; 6:3, 5, 9). It has been suggested that "tumors" refers to the sores or boils caused by an epidemic of the bubonic plague carried by rats (6:4–5). The spread of the disease and its deadly effect (5:6, 9, 12; 6:11, 17) make this a likely view.

MAY 2

1 Samuel 6:1–7:17

6 Now the ark of the LORD had been in the country of the Philistines seven months. ²And the Philistines called for the priests and the diviners, saying, "What shall we do with the ark of the LORD? Tell us how we shall send it to its place." ³They said, "If you send away the ark of the God of Israel, do not send it empty; but you shall surely return to Him a guilt offering. Then you will be healed and it will be known to you why His hand is not removed from you." ⁴Then they said, "What shall be the guilt offering which we shall return to Him?" And they said, "Five golden tumors and five golden mice *according to* the number of the lords of the Philistines, for one plague was on all of you and on your lords. ⁵So you shall make likenesses of your tumors and likenesses of your mice that ravage the land, and you shall give glory to the God of Israel; perhaps He will ease His hand from you, your gods, and your land. ⁶Why then do you harden your hearts as the Egyptians and Pharaoh hardened their hearts? When He had severely dealt with them, did they not allow the people to go, and they departed? ⁷Now therefore, take and prepare a new cart and two milch cows on which there has never been a yoke; and hitch the cows to the cart and take their calves home, away from them. ⁸Take the ark of the LORD and place it on the cart; and put the articles of gold which you return to Him as a guilt offering in a box by its side. Then send it away that it may go. ⁹Watch, if it goes up by the way of its own territory to Beth-shemesh, then He has done us this great evil. But if not, then we will know that it was not His hand that struck us; it happened to us by chance."

¹⁰Then the men did so, and took two milch cows and hitched them to the cart, and shut up their calves at home. ¹¹They put the ark of the LORD on the cart, and the box with the golden mice and the likenesses of their tumors. ¹²And the cows took the straight way in the direction of Beth-shemesh; they went along the highway, lowing as they went, and did not turn aside to the right or to the left. And the lords of the Philistines followed them to the border of Beth-shemesh.

¹³Now *the people of* Beth-shemesh were reaping their wheat harvest in the valley, and they raised their eyes and saw the ark and were glad to see *it.* ¹⁴The cart came into the field of Joshua the Beth-shemite and stood there where there *was* a large stone; and they split the wood of the cart and offered the cows as a burnt offering to the LORD. ¹⁵The Levites took down the ark of the LORD and the box that was with it, in which were the articles of gold, and put them on the large stone; and the men of Beth-shemesh offered burnt offerings and sacrificed sacrifices that day to the LORD. ¹⁶When the five lords of the Philistines saw it, they returned to Ekron that day.

¹⁷These are the golden tumors which the Philistines returned for a guilt offering to the LORD: one for Ashdod, one for Gaza, one for Ashkelon, one for Gath, one for Ekron; ¹⁸and the golden mice, *according* to the number of all the cities of the Philistines belonging to the five lords, both of fortified cities and of country villages. The large stone on which they set the ark of the LORD *is a witness* to this day in the field of Joshua the Beth-shemite.

¹⁹He struck down some of the men of Beth-shemesh because they had looked into the ark of the LORD. He struck down of all the people, 50,070 men, and the people mourned because the LORD had struck the people with a great slaughter. ²⁰The men of Beth-shemesh said, "Who is able to stand before the LORD, this holy God? And to whom shall He go up from us?" ²¹So they sent messengers to the inhabitants of Kiriath-jearim, saying, "The Philistines have brought back the ark of the LORD; come down and take it up to you."

7 And the men of Kiriath-jearim came and took the ark of the LORD and brought it into the house of Abinadab on the hill, and consecrated Eleazar his son to keep the ark of the LORD. ²From the day that the ark remained at Kiriath-jearim, the time was long, for it was twenty years; and all the house of Israel lamented after the LORD.

6:19 looked into the ark. This action on the part of the men of Beth-shemesh constituted the sin of presumption. This is first addressed in Numbers 4:20 and is mentioned again in 2 Samuel 6:6–7. **fifty thousand and seventy men.** Some debate whether this figure is too large. However, retaining the larger number is more consistent with the context of "a great slaughter," and the reference to 30,000 in 4:10 (see 11:8). However, a scribal error could have occurred, in which case the number would omit the 50,000 and likely be "seventy," as in Josephus.

³ Then Samuel spoke to all the house of Israel, saying, "If you return to the LORD with all your heart, remove the foreign gods and the Ashtaroth from among you and direct your hearts to the LORD and serve Him alone; and He will deliver you from the hand of the Philistines." ⁴ So the sons of Israel removed the Baals and the Ashtaroth and served the LORD alone.

⁵ Then Samuel said, "Gather all Israel to Mizpah and I will pray to the LORD for you." ⁶ They gathered to Mizpah, and drew water and poured it out before the LORD, and fasted on that day and said there, "We have sinned against the LORD." And Samuel judged the sons of Israel at Mizpah.

7:6 drew water and poured it out before the LORD. The pouring out of water before the Lord was a sign of repentance. This act is repeated in 2 Samuel 23:16. **We have sinned against the LORD.** The symbol of Samuel pouring out the water and the acknowledgment of the people reveal a situation where true repentance had taken place. The condition of the heart superseded the importance or righteousness of the ritual. **Samuel judged.** At this point Samuel is introduced as the judge of Israel. His judgeship encompassed both domestic leadership and the conduct of war. The word links the text back to the last comment about Eli who judged 40 years (4:18). Samuel is shown to be the one taking over Eli's judgeship. He served as the last judge before the first king (1Sa 8:5).

⁷ Now when the Philistines heard that the sons of Israel had gathered to Mizpah, the lords of the Philistines went up against Israel. And when the sons of Israel heard it, they were afraid of the Philistines. ⁸ Then the sons of Israel said to Samuel, "Do not cease to cry to the LORD our God for us, that He may save us from the hand of the Philistines." ⁹ Samuel took a suckling lamb and offered it for a whole burnt offering to the LORD; and Samuel cried to the LORD for Israel and the LORD answered him. ¹⁰ Now Samuel was offering up the burnt offering, and the Philistines drew near to battle against Israel. But the LORD thundered with a great thunder on that day against the Philistines and confused them, so that they were routed before Israel. ¹¹ The men of Israel went out of Mizpah and pursued the Philistines, and struck them down as far as below Beth-car.

¹² Then Samuel took a stone and set it between Mizpah and Shen, and named it Ebenezer, saying, "Thus far the LORD has helped us." ¹³ So the Philistines were subdued and they did not come anymore within the border of Israel. And the hand of the LORD was against the Philistines all the days of Samuel. ¹⁴ The cities which the Philistines had taken from Israel were restored to Israel, from Ekron even to Gath; and Israel delivered their territory from the hand of the Philistines. So there was peace between Israel and the Amorites.

¹⁵ Now Samuel judged Israel all the days of his life. ¹⁶ He used to go annually on circuit to Bethel and Gilgal and Mizpah, and he judged Israel in all these places. ¹⁷ Then his return *was* to Ramah, for his house *was* there, and there he judged Israel; and he built there an altar to the LORD.

7:16 on circuit. The circuit was an annual trip made by Samuel; he would travel to Bethel, Gilgal, Mizpah, and return once again to Ramah, which allowed him to manage the affairs of the people.

Psalm 55:1–8

For the choir director; on stringed instruments. A Maskil of David.

Give ear to my prayer, O God;
And do not hide Yourself
from my supplication.
2   Give heed to me and answer me;
I am restless in my complaint
and am surely distracted,
3   Because of the voice of the enemy,
Because of the pressure of the wicked;
For they bring down trouble
upon me
And in anger they bear a
grudge against me.

4   My heart is in anguish within me,
And the terrors of death
have fallen upon me.
5   Fear and trembling come upon me,
And horror has overwhelmed me.
6   I said, "Oh, that I had
wings like a dove!
I would fly away and be at rest.
7   "Behold, I would wander far away,
I would lodge in the wilderness.
Selah
8   "I would hasten to my place of refuge
From the stormy wind *and* tempest."

Proverbs 15:14

¹⁴ The mind of the intelligent
   seeks knowledge,
   But the mouth of fools feeds on folly.

Luke 21:20–38

²⁰ "But when you see Jerusalem surrounded by armies, then recognize that her desolation is near. ²¹ Then those who are in Judea must flee to the mountains, and those who are in the midst of the city must leave, and those who are in the country must not enter the

21:20 Jerusalem surrounded by armies. A comparison with Matthew 24:15–16 and Mark 13:14 suggests that this sign is closely associated with "the abomination of desolation" (Mt 24:15; Da 9:27; 11:31). This sign of Jerusalem under siege was previewed in A.D. 70, but awaits its fulfillment in the future.

city; ²² because these are days of vengeance, so that all things which are written will be fulfilled. ²³ Woe to those who are pregnant and to those who are nursing babies in those days; for there will be great distress upon the land and wrath to this people; ²⁴ and they will fall by the edge of the sword, and will be led captive into all the nations; and Jerusalem will be trampled under foot by the Gentiles until the times of the Gentiles are fulfilled.

²⁵ "There will be signs in sun and moon and stars, and on the earth dismay among nations, in perplexity at the roaring of the sea and the waves, ²⁶ men fainting from fear and the expectation of the things which are coming upon the world; for the powers of the heavens will be shaken. ²⁷ Then they will see THE SON OF MAN COMING IN A CLOUD with power and great glory. ²⁸ But when these

21:24 the times of the Gentiles. This expression is unique to Luke. It identifies the era from Israel's captivity (ca. 586 B.C. to Babylon; see 2Ki 25) to her restoration in the kingdom (Rev 20:1–6). It has been a time during which, in accord with God's purpose, Gentiles have dominated or threatened Jerusalem. The era has also been marked by vast spiritual privileges for the Gentile nations (Is 66:12; Mal 1:11; Mt 24:14; Mk 13:10).

things begin to take place, straighten up and lift up your heads, because your redemption is drawing near."

²⁹ Then He told them a parable: "Behold the fig tree and all the trees; ³⁰ as soon as they put forth *leaves*, you see it and know for yourselves that summer is now near. ³¹ So you also, when you see these things happening, recognize that the kingdom of God is near. ³² Truly I say to you, this generation will not pass away until all things take place. ³³ Heaven and earth will pass away, but My words will not pass away.

³⁴ "Be on guard, so that your hearts will not be weighted down with dissipation and drunkenness and the worries of life, and that day will not come on you suddenly like a trap; ³⁵ for it will come upon all those who dwell on the face of all the earth. ³⁶ But keep on the alert at all times, praying that you may have strength to escape all these things that are about to take place, and to stand before the Son of Man."

³⁷ Now during the day He was teaching in the temple, but at evening He would go out and spend the night on the mount that is called Olivet. ³⁸ And all the people would get up early in the morning *to come* to Him in the temple to listen to Him.

DAY 2: How did the Philistines attempt to stop the plague?

"The priests and the diviners" (1Sa 6:2) of the Philistines were summoned to figure out how to appease God so that He would stop the plague. They understood that they had offended God. Their diviners decided to rightfully appease His wrath by sending the ark back to Israel. These pagans recognized their sin and the need for manifest repentance, which they did according to their religious tradition by means of a "guilt offering" (v. 3) to compensate for their trespass of dishonoring the God of Israel. It was their custom to make models of their sores (and the rats which brought the plague), in hopes that the deity would recognize that they knew why he was angry and remove the evil which had fallen upon them (v. 4).

"Give glory to the God of Israel…He will ease His hand" (v. 5). While sympathetic magic was the Philistine custom, this statement expressly affirms the intention behind the offerings: They were to halt the dishonor, confess their sin, and give glory to the God of Israel by acknowledging who it was that they had offended and who was the supreme Deity. The diviners correlate the Philistines' actions of not recognizing God with those of Pharaoh and the Egyptians. "Why then do you harden your hearts?" (v. 6). This is the same word "harden" that was used in Exodus 7:14; 8:15, 32. It is an interesting correlation, because the dominant purpose in Exodus 5–14 is that the Egyptians might "know that I am the LORD" (Ex 7:5).

To know without a doubt that the God of Israel was behind all of their troubles, the diviners devised a plan that would reveal whether God was the One responsible. Using cows that had never been yoked (v. 7) meant using animals that were untrained to pull a cart and probably would not go anywhere. The second element in their plan was to use nursing cows taken away from their calves. For the cows unnaturally to head off in the opposite direction from their calves would be a clear sign that the cause of their judgment was supernatural, which is precisely what happened (v. 12).

MAY 3

1 Samuel 8:1–9:27

8 And it came about when Samuel was old that he appointed his sons judges over Israel. ² Now the name of his firstborn was Joel, and the name of his second, Abijah; *they* were judging in Beersheba. ³ His sons, however, did not walk in his ways, but turned aside after dishonest gain and took bribes and perverted justice.

⁴ Then all the elders of Israel gathered together and came to Samuel at Ramah; ⁵ and they said to him, "Behold, you have grown old, and your sons do not walk in your ways. Now appoint a king for us to judge us like all the nations." ⁶ But the thing was displeasing in the sight of Samuel when they said, "Give us a king to judge us." And Samuel prayed to the LORD. ⁷ The LORD said to Samuel, "Listen to the voice of the people in regard to all that they say to you, for they have not rejected you, but they have rejected Me from being king over them. ⁸ Like all the deeds which they have done since the day that I brought them up from Egypt even to this day—in that they have forsaken Me and served other gods—so they are doing to you also. ⁹ Now then, listen to their voice; however, you shall solemnly warn them and tell them of the procedure of the king who will reign over them."

¹⁰ So Samuel spoke all the words of the LORD to the people who had asked of him a king. ¹¹ He said, "This will be the procedure of the king who will reign over you: he will take your sons and place *them* for himself in his chariots and among his horsemen and they will run before his chariots. ¹² He will appoint for himself commanders of thousands and of fifties, and *some* to do his plowing and to reap his harvest and to make his weapons of war and equipment for his chariots. ¹³ He will also take your daughters for perfumers and cooks and bakers. ¹⁴ He will take the best of your fields and your vineyards and your olive groves and give *them* to his servants. ¹⁵ He will take a tenth of your seed and of your vineyards and give to his officers and to his servants. ¹⁶ He will also take your male servants and your female servants and your best young men and your donkeys and use *them* for his work. ¹⁷ He will take a tenth of your flocks, and you yourselves will become his servants. ¹⁸ Then you will cry out in that day because of your king whom you have chosen for yourselves, but the LORD will not answer you in that day."

¹⁹ Nevertheless, the people refused to listen to the voice of Samuel, and they said, "No, but there shall be a king over us, ²⁰ that we also may be like all the nations, that our king may judge us and go out before us and fight our battles." ²¹ Now after Samuel had heard all the words of the people, he repeated them in the LORD'S hearing. ²² The LORD said to Samuel, "Listen to their voice and appoint them a king." So Samuel said to the men of Israel, "Go every man to his city."

9 Now there was a man of Benjamin whose name was Kish the son of Abiel, the son of Zeror, the son of Becorath, the son of Aphiah, the son of a Benjamite, a mighty man of valor. ² He had a son whose name was Saul, a choice and handsome *man,* and there was not a more handsome person than he among the sons of Israel; from his shoulders and up he was taller than any of the people.

³ Now the donkeys of Kish, Saul's father, were lost. So Kish said to his son Saul, "Take now with you one of the servants, and arise, go search for the donkeys." ⁴ He passed through the hill country of Ephraim and passed through the land of Shalishah, but they did not find *them.* Then they passed through the land of Shaalim, but *they were* not *there.* Then he passed through the land of the Benjamites, but they did not find *them.*

⁵ When they came to the land of Zuph, Saul said to his servant who was with him, "Come, and let us return, or else my father will cease

to be concerned about the donkeys and will become anxious for us." ⁶He said to him, "Behold now, there is a man of God in this city, and the man is held in honor; all that he says surely comes true. Now let us go there, perhaps he can tell us about our journey on which we have set out." ⁷Then Saul said to his servant, "But behold, if we go, what shall we bring the man? For the bread is gone from our sack and there is no present to bring to the man of God. What do we have?" ⁸The servant answered Saul again and said, "Behold, I have in my hand a fourth of a shekel of silver; I will give *it* to the man of God and he will tell us our way." ⁹(Formerly in Israel, when a man went to inquire of God, he used to say, "Come, and let us go to the seer"; for *he who is called* a prophet now was formerly called a seer.) ¹⁰Then Saul said to his servant, "Well said; come, let us go." So they went to the city where the man of God was.

¹¹As they went up the slope to the city, they found young women going out to draw water and said to them, "Is the seer here?" ¹²They answered them and said, "He is; see, *he is* ahead of you. Hurry now, for he has come into the city today, for the people have a sacrifice on the high place today. ¹³As soon as you enter the city you will find him before he goes up to the high place to eat, for the people will not eat until he comes, because he must bless the sacrifice; afterward those who are invited will eat. Now therefore, go up for you will find him at once." ¹⁴So they went up to the city. As they came into the city, behold, Samuel was coming out toward them to go up to the high place.

¹⁵Now a day before Saul's coming, the LORD had revealed *this* to Samuel saying, ¹⁶"About this time tomorrow I will send you a man from the land of Benjamin, and you shall anoint him to be prince over My people Israel; and he will deliver My people from the hand of the Philistines. For I have regarded My people, because their cry has come to Me." ¹⁷When Samuel saw Saul, the LORD said to him, "Behold, the man of whom I spoke to you! This one shall rule over My people." ¹⁸Then Saul approached Samuel in the gate and said, "Please tell me where the seer's house is." ¹⁹Samuel answered Saul and said, "I am the seer. Go up before me to the high place, for you shall eat with me today; and in the morning I will let you go, and will tell you all that is on your mind. ²⁰As for your donkeys which were lost three days ago, do not set your mind on them, for they have been found. And for whom is all that is desirable in Israel? Is it not for you and for all your

father's household?" ²¹Saul replied, "Am I not a Benjamite, of the smallest of the tribes of Israel, and my family the least of all the families of the tribe of Benjamin? Why then do you speak to me in this way?"

²²Then Samuel took Saul and his servant and brought them into the hall and gave them a place at the head of those who were invited, who were about thirty men. ²³Samuel said to the cook, "Bring the portion that I gave you, concerning which I said to you, 'Set it aside.'" ²⁴Then the cook took up the leg with what was on it and set *it* before Saul. And *Samuel* said, "Here is what has been reserved! Set *it* before you *and* eat, because it has been kept for you until the appointed time, since I said I have invited the people." So Saul ate with Samuel that day.

²⁵When they came down from the high place into the city, *Samuel* spoke with Saul on the roof. ²⁶And they arose early; and at daybreak Samuel called to Saul on the roof, saying, "Get up, that I may send you away." So Saul arose, and both he and Samuel went out into the street. ²⁷As they were going down to the edge of the city, Samuel said to Saul, "Say to the servant that he might go ahead of us and pass on, but you remain standing now, that I may proclaim the word of God to you."

9:16 anoint him. This represents a setting apart for service to the Lord, which occurs in 10:1. **prince.** Literally "one given prominence, one placed in front." The title referred to "one designated to rule" (1Ki 1:35; 2Ch 11:22). **their cry has come to Me.** The people had been crying out for deliverance from the Philistines, their longstanding rivals, just as they did for liberation from Egypt (Ex 2:25; 3:9).

9:17 This one shall rule over My people. God identified Saul to Samuel, assuring there was no mistaking whom God was choosing to be king.

Psalm 55:9–15

9 Confuse, O Lord, divide their tongues,
  For I have seen violence
    and strife in the city.
10 Day and night they go around
    her upon her walls,
  And iniquity and mischief
    are in her midst.
11 Destruction is in her midst;
  Oppression and deceit do not
    depart from her streets.

¹² For it is not an enemy who
   reproaches me,
   Then I could bear *it;*
   Nor is it one who hates me who has
   exalted himself against me,
   Then I could hide myself from him.
¹³ But it is you, a man my equal,
   My companion and my familiar friend;
¹⁴ We who had sweet fellowship together
   Walked in the house of
   God in the throng.
¹⁵ Let death come deceitfully upon them;
   Let them go down alive to Sheol,
   For evil is in their dwelling,
   in their midst.

Proverbs 15:15–17

¹⁵ All the days of the afflicted are bad,
   But a cheerful heart *has*
   a continual feast.
¹⁶ Better is a little with the
   fear of the LORD
   Than great treasure and
   turmoil with it.
¹⁷ Better is a dish of vegetables
   where love is
   Than a fattened ox *served* with hatred.

Luke 22:1–23

22 Now the Feast of Unleavened Bread, which is called the Passover, was approaching. ² The chief priests and the scribes were seeking how they might put Him to death; for they were afraid of the people. ³ And Satan entered into Judas who was called Iscariot, belonging to the number of the twelve. ⁴ And he went away and discussed with the chief priests and officers how he might betray Him to them. ⁵ They were glad and agreed to give him money. ⁶ So he consented, and *began* seeking a good opportunity to betray Him to them apart from the crowd. ⁷ Then came the *first* day of Unleavened Bread on which the Passover *lamb* had to be sacrificed. ⁸ And Jesus sent Peter and John, saying, "Go and prepare the Passover for us, so that we may eat it." ⁹ They said to Him,

22:3 Satan entered. I.e., Judas was possessed by Satan himself. Satan evidently gained direct control over Judas on two occasions—once just before Judas arranged his betrayal with the chief priests, and again during the Last Supper (Jn 13:27), immediately before the betrayal was actually carried out.

"Where do You want us to prepare it?" ¹⁰ And He said to them, "When you have entered the city, a man will meet you carrying a pitcher of water; follow him into the house that he enters. ¹¹ And you shall say to the owner of the house, 'The Teacher says to you, "Where is the guest room in which I may eat the Passover with My disciples?"' ¹² And he will show you a large, furnished upper room; prepare it there." ¹³ And they left and found *everything* just as He had told them; and they prepared the Passover.

22:12 a large, furnished upper room. One of many such rooms for rent in Jerusalem that were maintained for the express purpose of providing pilgrims a place to celebrate feasts. The furnishings undoubtedly included everything necessary to prepare and serve a meal.

¹⁴ When the hour had come, He reclined *at the table,* and the apostles with Him. ¹⁵ And He said to them, "I have earnestly desired to eat this Passover with you before I suffer; ¹⁶ for I say to you, I shall never again eat it until it is fulfilled in the kingdom of God." ¹⁷ And when He had taken a cup *and* given thanks, He said, "Take this and share it among yourselves; ¹⁸ for I say to you, I will not drink of the fruit of the vine from now on until the kingdom of God comes." ¹⁹ And when He had taken *some* bread *and* given thanks, He broke it and gave it to them, saying, "This is My body which is given for you; do this in remembrance of Me." ²⁰ And in the same way *He took* the cup after they had eaten, saying, "This cup which is poured out for you is the new covenant in My blood. ²¹ But behold, the hand of the one betraying Me is with Mine on the table. ²² For indeed, the Son of Man is going as it has been determined; but woe to that man by whom He is betrayed!" ²³ And they began to discuss among themselves which one of them it might be who was going to do this thing.

22:22 as it has been determined. Every detail of the crucifixion of Christ was under the sovereign control of God and in accord with His eternal purposes. See Acts 2:23; 4:26–28. **but woe.** The fact that Judas' betrayal was part of God's plan does not free him from the guilt of a crime he entered into willfully. God's sovereignty is never a legitimate excuse for human guilt.

DAY 3: What was wrong with Israel wanting a king?

"Now appoint a king for us . . . like all the nations" (1 Samuel 8:5). When Israel entered the land, they encountered Canaanite city-states that were led by kings (Jos 12:7–24) and were later enslaved by nations that were led by kings (Jdg 3:8, 12; 4:2; 8:5; 11:12). However, at the time of the judges, there was no king in Israel (Jdg 17:6; 18:1; 19:1; 21:25).

According to Deuteronomy 17:14, God knew this would be their desire and He would allow it to occur. "Listen to the voice of the people," the Lord told Samuel (v. 7) and give them a king. "They have not rejected you, but...Me." The nature of this rejection of the Lord by Israel is explained in vv. 19–20.

Samuel obeyed the Lord by warning them of the behavior of a human king in vv. 10–18. A king would: 1) draft young men and women for his service (vv. 11–13); 2) tax the people's crops and flocks (vv. 14–15, 17a); 3) appropriate the best of their animals and servants (v. 16); and 4) place limitations on their personal freedom (v. 17b). Additionally, Samuel told them "you will cry out...because of your king" (v. 18). They would later cry out for freedom from his rule (1Ki 12:4), but "the LORD will not answer you." In contrast to the Lord's response to Israel during the period of the judges (Jdg 2:18), the Lord would refuse to deliver the people out of the hand of their king who oppressed them.

In spite of Samuel's warnings, the people demanded a king who will "fight our battles" (v. 20). Up until this point, the Lord Himself had fought the battles for Israel and given continual victory (Jos 10:14; 1Sa 7:10). Israel no longer wanted the Lord to be their warrior—replacing Him with a human king was their desire. It was in this way that Israel rejected the Lord. The problem was not in having a king, but rather, the reason the people wanted a king was to be like other nations. They also foolishly assumed there would be some greater power in a king leading them in battle.

 # MAY 4

1 Samuel 10:1–11:15

10 Then Samuel took the flask of oil, poured it on his head, kissed him and said, "Has not the LORD anointed you a ruler over His inheritance? [2] When you go from me today, then you will find two men close to Rachel's tomb in the territory of Benjamin at Zelzah; and they will say to you, 'The donkeys which you went to look for have been found. Now behold, your father has ceased to be concerned about the donkeys and is anxious for you, saying, "What shall I do about my son?"' [3] Then you will go on further from there, and you will come as far as the oak of Tabor, and there three men going up to God at Bethel will meet you, one carrying three young goats, another carrying three loaves of bread, and another carrying a jug of wine;

[4] and they will greet you and give you two *loaves* of bread, which you will accept from their hand. [5] Afterward you will come to the hill of God where the Philistine garrison is; and it shall be as soon as you have come there to the city, that you will meet a group of prophets coming down from the high place with harp, tambourine, flute, and a lyre before them, and they will be prophesying. [6] Then the Spirit of the LORD will come upon you mightily, and you shall prophesy with them and be changed into another man. [7] It shall be when these signs come to you, do for yourself what the occasion requires, for God is with you. [8] And you shall go down before me to Gilgal; and behold, I will come down to you to offer burnt offerings and sacrifice peace offerings. You shall wait seven days until I come to you and show you what you should do."

10:1 the LORD anointed you a ruler. The Lord chose Saul to be the leader of Israel and communicated His choice through the private anointing by Samuel, signifying a setting aside for God's service. **His inheritance.** The inheritance was God's nation, Israel, in the sense that she uniquely belonged to Him (Dt 4:20; 9:26).

10:6 the Spirit of the LORD will come upon you. The Holy Spirit would enable Saul to declare the Word of the Lord with the prophets. **changed into another man.** With this empowerment by the Holy Spirit, Saul would emerge another man (10:9), equipped in the manner of Gideon and Jephthah for deeds of valor (v. 9; Jdg 6:34; 11:29).

⁹Then it happened when he turned his back to leave Samuel, God changed his heart; and all those signs came about on that day. ¹⁰When they came to the hill there, behold, a group of prophets met him; and the Spirit of God came upon him mightily, so that he prophesied among them. ¹¹It came about, when all who knew him previously saw that he prophesied now with the prophets, that the people said to one another, "What has happened to the son of Kish? Is Saul also among the prophets?" ¹²A man there said, "Now, who is their father?" Therefore it became a proverb: "Is Saul also among the prophets?" ¹³When he had finished prophesying, he came to the high place.

¹⁴Now Saul's uncle said to him and his servant, "Where did you go?" And he said, "To look for the donkeys. When we saw that they could not be found, we went to Samuel." ¹⁵Saul's uncle said, "Please tell me what Samuel said to you." ¹⁶So Saul said to his uncle, "He told us plainly that the donkeys had been found." But he did not tell him about the matter of the kingdom which Samuel had mentioned.

¹⁷Thereafter Samuel called the people together to the LORD at Mizpah; ¹⁸and he said to the sons of Israel, "Thus says the LORD, the God of Israel, 'I brought Israel up from Egypt, and I delivered you from the hand of the Egyptians and from the power of all the kingdoms that were oppressing you.' ¹⁹But you have today rejected your God, who delivers you from all your calamities and your distresses; yet you have said, 'No, but set a king over us!' Now therefore, present yourselves before the LORD by your tribes and by your clans."

²⁰Thus Samuel brought all the tribes of Israel near, and the tribe of Benjamin was taken by lot. ²¹Then he brought the tribe of Benjamin near by its families, and the Matrite family was taken. And Saul the son of Kish was taken; but when they looked for him, he could not be found. ²²Therefore they inquired further of the LORD, "Has the man come here yet?" So the LORD said, "Behold, he is hiding himself by the baggage." ²³So they ran and took him from there, and when he stood among the people, he was taller than any of the people from his shoulders upward. ²⁴Samuel said to all the people, "Do you see him whom the LORD has chosen? Surely there is no one like him among all the people." So all the people shouted and said, "*Long* live the king!"

²⁵Then Samuel told the people the ordinances of the kingdom, and wrote *them* in the book and placed *it* before the LORD. And Samuel sent all the people away, each one to his house. ²⁶Saul also went to his house at Gibeah; and the valiant *men* whose hearts God had touched went with him. ²⁷But certain worthless men said, "How can this one deliver us?" And they despised him and did not bring him any present. But he kept silent.

11 Now Nahash the Ammonite came up and besieged Jabesh-gilead; and all the men of Jabesh said to Nahash, "Make a covenant with us and we will serve you." ²But Nahash the Ammonite said to them, "I will make *it* with you on this condition, that I will gouge out the right eye of every one of you, thus I will make it a reproach on all Israel." ³The elders of Jabesh said to him, "Let us alone for seven days, that we may send messengers throughout the territory of Israel. Then, if there is no one to deliver us, we will come out to you." ⁴Then the messengers came to Gibeah of Saul and spoke these words in the hearing of the people, and all the people lifted up their voices and wept.

⁵Now behold, Saul was coming from the field behind the oxen, and he said, "What is *the matter* with the people that they weep?" So they related to him the words of the men of Jabesh. ⁶Then the Spirit of God came upon Saul mightily when he heard these words, and he became very angry. ⁷He took a yoke of oxen and cut them in pieces, and sent *them* throughout the territory of Israel by the hand of messengers, saying, "Whoever does not come out after Saul and after Samuel, so shall it be done to his oxen." Then the dread of the LORD fell on the people, and they came out as one man. ⁸He numbered them in Bezek; and the sons of Israel were 300,000, and the men of Judah 30,000. ⁹They said to the messengers who had come, "Thus you shall say to the men of Jabesh-gilead, 'Tomorrow, by the time the sun is hot, you will have deliverance.'" So the messengers went and told the men of Jabesh; and they were glad. ¹⁰Then the men of Jabesh said, "Tomorrow we will come out to you, and you may do to us whatever seems good to you." ¹¹The next morning Saul put the people in three companies; and they came into the

55:22 Cast your burden upon the LORD. The word for "burden" implies one's circumstances, one's lot. The psalmist promises that the Lord will uphold the believer in the struggles of life.

midst of the camp at the morning watch and struck down the Ammonites until the heat of the day. Those who survived were scattered, so that no two of them were left together.

[12] Then the people said to Samuel, "Who is he that said, 'Shall Saul reign over us?' Bring the men, that we may put them to death." [13] But Saul said, "Not a man shall be put to death this day, for today the LORD has accomplished deliverance in Israel."

[14] Then Samuel said to the people, "Come and let us go to Gilgal and renew the kingdom there." [15] So all the people went to Gilgal, and there they made Saul king before the LORD in Gilgal. There they also offered sacrifices of peace offerings before the LORD; and there Saul and all the men of Israel rejoiced greatly.

11:15 they made Saul king before the LORD. All the people came to crown Saul king that day. The process of entering the kingship was the same for both Saul and David: 1) commissioned by the Lord (9:1—10:16; 16:1-13); 2) confirmed by military victory (10:17—11:11; 16:14—2Sa 1:27); and 3) crowned (11:12-15; 2Sa 2:4; 5:3). **peace offerings.** Sacrifices of thanksgiving (Lv 7:13). **rejoiced greatly.** Along with the victory over the Ammonites, there was a great celebration over the nation being united.

Psalm 55:16-23

[16] As for me, I shall call upon God,
And the LORD will save me.
[17] Evening and morning and at noon,
I will complain and murmur,
And He will hear my voice.
[18] He will redeem my soul in peace from
the battle which is against me,
For they are many who
strive with me.
[19] God will hear and answer them—
Even the one who sits enthroned
from of old— Selah
With whom there is no change,
And who do not fear God.
[20] He has put forth his hands against
those who were at peace with him;
He has violated his covenant.
[21] His speech was smoother than butter,
But his heart was war;
His words were softer than oil,
Yet they were drawn swords.
[22] Cast your burden upon the LORD
and He will sustain you;

He will never allow the
righteous to be shaken.
[23] But You, O God, will bring them
down to the pit of destruction;
Men of bloodshed and deceit will
not live out half their days.
But I will trust in You.

Proverbs 15:18-20

[18] A hot-tempered man stirs up strife,
But the slow to anger calms a dispute.
[19] The way of the lazy is as
a hedge of thorns,
But the path of the upright
is a highway.
[20] A wise son makes a father glad,
But a foolish man despises
his mother.

Luke 22:24-46

[24] And there arose also a dispute among them as to which one of them was regarded to be greatest. [25] And He said to them, "The kings of the Gentiles lord it over them; and those who have authority over them are called 'Benefactors.' [26] But it is not this way with you, but the one who is the greatest among you must become like the youngest, and the leader like the servant. [27] For who is greater, the one who reclines at the table or the one who serves? Is it not the one who reclines at the table? But I am among you as the one who serves.

[28] "You are those who have stood by Me in My trials; [29] and just as My Father has granted Me a kingdom, I grant you [30] that you may eat and drink at My table in My kingdom, and you will sit on thrones judging the twelve tribes of Israel.

[31] "Simon, Simon, behold, Satan has demanded permission to sift you like wheat; [32] but I have prayed for you, that your faith may not fail; and you, when once you have turned again, strengthen your brothers." [33] But he said to Him, "Lord, with You I am ready to go both to prison and to death!" [34] And He said, "I say to you, Peter, the rooster will not crow today until you have denied three times that you know Me."

[35] And He said to them, "When I sent you out without money belt and bag and sandals, you did not lack anything, did you?" They said, "No, nothing." [36] And He said to them, "But now, whoever has a money belt is to take it along, likewise also a bag, and whoever has no sword is to sell his coat and buy one. [37] For I tell you that this which is written must be fulfilled in Me, 'AND HE WAS NUMBERED WITH

TRANSGRESSORS'; for that which refers to Me has *its* fulfillment." 38 They said, "Lord, look, here are two swords." And He said to them, "It is enough."

39 And He came out and proceeded as was His custom to the Mount of Olives; and the disciples also followed Him. 40 When He arrived at the place, He said to them, "Pray that you may not enter into temptation." 41 And He withdrew from them about a stone's throw, and He knelt down and *began* to pray, 42 saying, "Father, if You are willing, remove this cup from Me; yet not My will, but Yours be done." 43 Now an angel from heaven appeared to Him, strengthening Him. 44 And being in agony He was praying very fervently; and His sweat became like drops of blood, falling down upon the ground.

22:44 like drops of blood. This suggests a dangerous condition known as *hematidrosis*, the effusion of blood in one's perspiration. It can be caused by extreme anguish or physical strain. Subcutaneous capillaries dilate and burst, mingling blood with sweat. Christ Himself stated that His distress had brought Him to the threshold of death (Mt 26:38; Mk 14:34; Heb 12:3-4).

45 When He rose from prayer, He came to the disciples and found them sleeping from sorrow, 46 and said to them, "Why are you sleeping? Get up and pray that you may not enter into temptation."

DAY 4: How can we face temptation with confidence?

Shortly after a dispute among the disciples as to which one should be considered the greatest (Lk 22:24), Jesus specifically addresses Peter as "Simon, Simon" (v. 31). The repetition of the name (see 10:41; Ac 9:4) implied an earnest and somber tone of warning. Christ Himself had given Simon the name Peter (6:14), but here He reverted to his old name, perhaps to intensify His rebuke about Peter's fleshly overconfidence. The context also suggests that Peter may have been one of the more vocal participants in the dispute of v. 24.

"Satan," Jesus told him, "has demanded permission to sift you." Though addressed specifically to Peter, this warning embraced the other disciples as well. The pronoun "you" is plural in the Greek text. "To sift you like wheat." The imagery is apt. It suggests that such trials, though unsettling and undesirable, have a necessary refining effect.

Nevertheless, Jesus said, "I have prayed for you" (v. 32). The pronoun "you" is singular. Although it is clear that He prayed for all of them (Jn 17:6-19), He personally assured Peter of His prayers and of Peter's ultimate victory, even encouraging Peter to be an encourager to the others. "That your faith may not fail." Peter himself failed miserably, but his faith was never overthrown (see Jn 21:18-19).

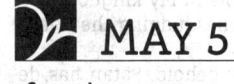

MAY 5

1 Samuel 12:1–13:23

12 Then Samuel said to all Israel, "Behold, I have listened to your voice in all that you said to me and I have appointed a king over you. 2 Now, here is the king walking before you, but I am old and gray, and behold my sons are with you. And I have walked before you from my youth even to this day. 3 Here I am; bear witness against me before the LORD and His anointed. Whose ox have I taken, or whose donkey have I taken, or whom have I defrauded? Whom have I oppressed, or from whose hand have I taken a bribe to blind my eyes with it? I will restore *it* to you." 4 They said, "You have not defrauded us or oppressed us or taken anything from any man's hand." 5 He said to them, "The LORD is witness against you, and His anointed is witness this day that you have found nothing in my hand." And they said, "*He is* witness."

6 Then Samuel said to the people, "It is the LORD who appointed Moses and Aaron and who brought your fathers up from the land of Egypt. 7 So now, take your stand, that I may plead with you before the LORD concerning all the righteous acts of the LORD which He did for you and your fathers. 8 When Jacob went into Egypt and your fathers cried out to the LORD, then the LORD sent Moses and Aaron who brought your fathers out of Egypt and settled them in this place. 9 But they forgot the LORD their God, so He sold them into the hand of Sisera, captain of the army of Hazor, and into the hand of the Philistines and into the hand of the king of Moab, and they fought against them. 10 They cried out to the LORD and said, 'We have sinned because we have forsaken the LORD and have served the Baals and the Ashtaroth; but now deliver us from the

hands of our enemies, and we will serve You.' ¹¹Then the LORD sent Jerubbaal and Bedan and Jephthah and Samuel, and delivered you from the hands of your enemies all around, so that you lived in security. ¹²When you saw that Nahash the king of the sons of Ammon came against you, you said to me, 'No, but a king shall reign over us,' although the LORD your God *was* your king. ¹³Now therefore, here is

12:12 When you saw that Nahash the king of the sons of Ammon came against you. According to the DSS and Josephus, Nahash was campaigning over a large area. It was that Ammonite threat that seemingly provoked Israel to demand a human king (8:1–20). **the LORD your God *was* your king.** The clearest indictment of Israel for choosing a mere man to fight for her instead of the Lord God (8:20).

the king whom you have chosen, whom you have asked for, and behold, the LORD has set a king over you. ¹⁴If you will fear the LORD and serve Him, and listen to His voice and not rebel against the command of the LORD, then both you and also the king who reigns over you will follow the LORD your God. ¹⁵If you will not listen to the voice of the LORD, but rebel against the command of the LORD, then the hand of the LORD will be against you, *as it was* against your fathers. ¹⁶Even now, take your stand and see this great thing which the LORD will do before your eyes. ¹⁷Is it not the wheat harvest today? I will call to the LORD, that He may send thunder and rain. Then you will know and see that your wickedness is great which you have done in the sight of the LORD by asking for yourselves a king." ¹⁸So Samuel called to the LORD, and the LORD sent thunder and rain that day; and all the people greatly feared the LORD and Samuel.

¹⁹Then all the people said to Samuel, "Pray for your servants to the LORD your God, so that we may not die, for we have added to all our sins *this* evil by asking for ourselves a king." ²⁰Samuel said to the people, "Do not fear. You have committed all this evil, yet do not turn aside from following the LORD, but serve the LORD with all your heart. ²¹You must not turn aside, for *then you would go* after futile things which can not profit or deliver, because they are futile. ²²For the LORD will not abandon His people on account of His great name, because the LORD has been pleased to make you a people for Himself. ²³Moreover, as for me, far be it

from me that I should sin against the LORD by ceasing to pray for you; but I will instruct you in the good and right way. ²⁴Only fear the LORD and serve Him in truth with all your heart; for consider what great things He has done for you. ²⁵But if you still do wickedly, both you and your king will be swept away."

13 Saul was *thirty* years old when he began to reign, and he reigned *forty* two years over Israel.

²Now Saul chose for himself 3,000 men of Israel, of which 2,000 were with Saul in Michmash and in the hill country of Bethel, while 1,000 were with Jonathan at Gibeah of Benjamin. But he sent away the rest of the people, each to his tent. ³Jonathan smote the garrison of the Philistines that was in Geba, and the Philistines heard of *it*. Then Saul blew the trumpet throughout the land, saying, "Let the Hebrews hear." ⁴All Israel heard the news that Saul had smitten the garrison of the Philistines, and also that Israel had become odious to the Philistines. The people were then summoned to Saul at Gilgal.

⁵Now the Philistines assembled to fight with Israel, 30,000 chariots and 6,000 horsemen, and people like the sand which is on the seashore in abundance; and they came up and camped in Michmash, east of Beth-aven. ⁶When the men of Israel saw that they were in a strait (for the people were hard-pressed), then the people hid themselves in caves, in thickets, in cliffs, in cellars, and in pits. ⁷Also *some of* the Hebrews crossed the Jordan into the land of Gad and Gilead. But as for Saul, he *was* still in Gilgal, and all the people followed him trembling.

⁸Now he waited seven days, according to the appointed time set by Samuel, but Samuel did not come to Gilgal; and the people were scattering from him. ⁹So Saul said, "Bring to me the burnt offering and the peace offerings." And he offered the burnt offering. ¹⁰As soon as he finished offering the burnt offering, behold, Samuel came; and Saul went out to meet him *and* to greet him. ¹¹But Samuel said, "What have you done?" And Saul said, "Because I saw that the people were scattering from me, and that you did not come within the appointed days, and that the Philistines were assembling at Michmash, ¹²therefore I said, 'Now the Philistines will come down against me at Gilgal, and I have not asked the favor of the LORD.' So I forced myself and offered the burnt offering." ¹³Samuel said to Saul, "You have acted foolishly; you have not kept the commandment of the LORD your God, which He commanded you, for now the LORD would have established your kingdom over Israel forever. ¹⁴But now

your kingdom shall not endure. The LORD has sought out for Himself a man after His own heart, and the LORD has appointed him as ruler over His people, because you have not kept what the LORD commanded you."

¹⁵ Then Samuel arose and went up from Gilgal to Gibeah of Benjamin. And Saul numbered the people who were present with him, about six hundred men. ¹⁶ Now Saul and his son Jonathan and the people who were present with them were staying in Geba of Benjamin while the Philistines camped at Michmash. ¹⁷ And the raiders came from the camp of the Philistines in three companies: one company turned toward Ophrah, to the land of Shual, ¹⁸ and another company turned toward Beth-horon, and another company turned toward the border which overlooks the valley of Zeboim toward the wilderness.

¹⁹ Now no blacksmith could be found in all the land of Israel, for the Philistines said, "Otherwise the Hebrews will make swords or spears." ²⁰ So all Israel went down to the Philistines, each to sharpen his plowshare, his mattock, his axe, and his hoe. ²¹ The charge was two-thirds of a shekel for the plowshares, the mattocks, the forks, and the axes, and to fix the hoes. ²² So it came about on the day of battle that neither sword nor spear was found in the hands of any of the people who were with Saul and Jonathan, but they were found with Saul and his son Jonathan. ²³ And the garrison of the Philistines went out to the pass of Michmash.

13:19 no blacksmith. The Philistines had superior iron and metal-working craftsmen until David's time (1Ch 22:3), accounting for their formidable military force.

Psalm 56:1–13

For the choir director; according to Jonath elem rehokim. A Mikhtam of David, when the Philistines seized him in Gath.

Be gracious to me, O God, for man has trampled upon me; Fighting all day long he oppresses me.
² My foes have trampled upon me all day long, For they are many who fight proudly against me.
³ When I am afraid, I will put my trust in You.
⁴ In God, whose word I praise, In God I have put my trust; I shall not be afraid.

What can mere man do to me?
⁵ All day long they distort my words; All their thoughts are against me for evil.
⁶ They attack, they lurk, They watch my steps, As they have waited to take my life.
⁷ Because of wickedness, cast them forth, In anger put down the peoples, O God!

⁸ You have taken account of my wanderings; Put my tears in Your bottle. Are they not in Your book?
⁹ Then my enemies will turn back in the day when I call; This I know, that God is for me.

56:8 my tears…Your bottle. David asked God to keep a remembrance of all of his sufferings so that God would eventually vindicate him.

¹⁰ In God, whose word I praise, In the LORD, whose word I praise,
¹¹ In God I have put my trust, I shall not be afraid. What can man do to me?
¹² Your vows are binding upon me, O God; I will render thank offerings to You.
¹³ For You have delivered my soul from death, Indeed my feet from stumbling, So that I may walk before God In the light of the living.

Proverbs 15:21–23

²¹ Folly is joy to him who lacks sense, But a man of understanding walks straight.
²² Without consultation, plans are frustrated, But with many counselors they succeed.
²³ A man has joy in an apt answer, And how delightful is a timely word!

Luke 22:47–71

⁴⁷ While He was still speaking, behold, a crowd came, and the one called Judas, one of the twelve, was preceding them; and he approached Jesus to kiss Him. ⁴⁸ But Jesus said to him, "Judas, are you betraying the Son of Man with a kiss?" ⁴⁹ When those who were around Him saw what was going to happen, they said, "Lord, shall we strike with the sword?" ⁵⁰ And one of them struck the slave

of the high priest and cut off his right ear. [51] But Jesus answered and said, "Stop! No more of this." And He touched his ear and healed him. [52] Then Jesus said to the chief priests and officers of the temple and elders who had come against Him, "Have you come out with swords and clubs as you would against a robber? [53] While I was with you daily in the temple, you did not lay hands on Me; but this hour and the power of darkness are yours."

[54] Having arrested Him, they led Him *away* and brought Him to the house of the high priest; but Peter was following at a distance. [55] After they had kindled a fire in the middle of the courtyard and had sat down together, Peter was sitting among them. [56] And a servant-girl, seeing him as he sat in the firelight and looking intently at him, said, "This man was with Him too." [57] But he denied *it*, saying, "Woman, I do not know Him." [58] A little later, another saw him and said, "You are *one* of them too!" But Peter said, "Man, I am not!" [59] After about an hour had passed, another man *began* to insist, saying, "Certainly this man also was with Him, for he is a Galilean too." [60] But Peter said, "Man, I do not know what you are talking about." Immediately, while he was still speaking, a rooster crowed. [61] The Lord turned and looked at Peter. And Peter remembered the word of the Lord, how He had told him, "Before a rooster crows today, you will deny Me three times." [62] And he went out and wept bitterly.

[63] Now the men who were holding Jesus in custody were mocking Him and beating Him, [64] and they blindfolded Him and were asking Him, saying, "Prophesy, who is the one who hit You?" [65] And they were saying many other things against Him, blaspheming.

22:51 touched his ear and healed him. This is the only instance in all of Scripture where Christ healed a flesh wound. The miracle is also unique in that Christ healed an enemy, unasked, and without any evidence of faith in the recipient. It is also remarkable that such a dramatic miracle had no effect whatsoever on the hearts of those men. Neither had the explosive power of Jesus' words, which knocked them to the ground (Jn 18:6). They carried on with the arrest as if nothing peculiar had happened (v. 54).

22:53 this hour…darkness are yours. I.e., nighttime, the hour of darkness. They had not the courage to confront Jesus in the presence of the crowds at the temple, where He had openly taught each day. Their skulking tactics betrayed the truth about their hearts. Nighttime was a fitting hour for the servants of the power of darkness (Satan) to be afoot (Jn 3:20–21; Eph 5:8, 12–15; 1Th 5:5–7).

[66] When it was day, the Council of elders of the people assembled, both chief priests and scribes, and they led Him away to their council *chamber,* saying, [67] "If You are the Christ, tell us." But He said to them, "If I tell you, you will not believe; [68] and if I ask a question, you will not answer. [69] But from now on THE SON OF MAN WILL BE SEATED AT THE RIGHT HAND of the power OF GOD." [70] And they all said, "Are You the Son of God, then?" And He said to them, "Yes, I am." [71] Then they said, "What further need do we have of testimony? For we have heard it ourselves from His own mouth."

DAY 5: Why was Saul judged so severely?

When Saul was anointed king by Samuel, Saul was commanded to wait 7 days to meet Samuel in Gilgal. Samuel would offer burnt offerings and peace offerings, and he would show Saul what he should do (1Sa 10:8). After 7 days of waiting and Samuel had not come, the people were scattered (1Sa 13:8). Saul's men were deserting him because of anxiety and fear over the coming battle.

Rather than continue to wait, Saul "offered the burnt offering" (v. 9). Saul's sin was not specifically that he made a sacrifice (see 2Sa 24:25; 1Ki 8:62–64), but that he did not wait for priestly assistance from Samuel. He wished to rule as an autocrat, who possessed absolute power in civil and sacred matters. Samuel had waited the 7 days as a test of Saul's character and obedience to God, but Saul failed it by invading the priestly office himself.

Confronted by Samuel, Saul's response was "Because I saw . . ." (v. 11). Saul reacted disobediently based upon what he saw and not by faith. He feared losing his men and did not properly consider what God would have him do. Consequently, Samuel places the responsibility fully on Saul's shoulders: "You have not kept the commandment" (v. 13). "Now your kingdom shall not endure" (v. 14). Instead of Saul, God was going to choose one whose heart was like His own, i.e., one who had a will to obey God. Paul quotes this passage in Acts 13:22 of David. Someone else, namely David, had already been chosen to be God's leader over His people.

MAY 6

1 Samuel 14:1–15:35

14 Now the day came that Jonathan, the son of Saul, said to the young man who was carrying his armor, "Come and let us cross over to the Philistines' garrison that is on the other side." But he did not tell his father. ² Saul was staying in the outskirts of Gibeah under the pomegranate tree which is in Migron. And the people who *were* with him *were* about six hundred men, ³ and Ahijah, the son of Ahitub, Ichabod's brother, the son of Phinehas, the son of Eli, the priest of the LORD at Shiloh, was wearing an ephod. And the people did not know that Jonathan had gone. ⁴ Between the passes by which Jonathan sought to cross over to the Philistines' garrison, there was a sharp crag on the one side and a sharp crag on the other side, and the name of the one was Bozez, and the name of the other Seneh. ⁵ The one crag rose on the north opposite Michmash, and the other on the south opposite Geba.

⁶ Then Jonathan said to the young man who was carrying his armor, "Come and let us cross over to the garrison of these uncircumcised; perhaps the LORD will work for us, for the LORD is not restrained to save by many or by few." ⁷ His armor bearer said to him, "Do all that is in your heart; turn yourself, *and* here I am with you according to your desire." ⁸ Then Jonathan said, "Behold, we will cross over to the men and reveal ourselves to them. ⁹ If they say to us, 'Wait until we come to you'; then we will stand in our place and not go up to them. ¹⁰ But if they say, 'Come up to us,' then we will go up, for the LORD has given them into our hands; and this shall be the sign to us." ¹¹ When both of them revealed themselves to the garrison of the Philistines, the Philistines said, "Behold, Hebrews are coming out of the holes where they have hidden themselves." ¹² So the men of the garrison hailed Jonathan and his armor bearer and said, "Come up to us and we will tell you something." And Jonathan said to his armor bearer, "Come up after me, for the LORD has given them into the hands of Israel." ¹³ Then Jonathan climbed up on his hands and feet, with his armor bearer behind him; and they fell before Jonathan, and his armor bearer put some to death after him. ¹⁴ That first slaughter which Jonathan and his armor bearer made was about twenty men within about half a furrow in an acre of land. ¹⁵ And there was a trembling in the camp, in the field, and among all the people.

14:15 the earth quaked. The earthquake affirms the fact that divine intervention aided Jonathan and his armor bearer in their raid. The earthquake caused a panic among the Philistines. God would have intervened on Saul's behalf in such a manner had he chosen to be faithfully patient (13:9).

Even the garrison and the raiders trembled, and the earth quaked so that it became a great trembling. ¹⁶ Now Saul's watchmen in Gibeah of Benjamin looked, and behold, the multitude melted away; and they went here and *there.* ¹⁷ Saul said to the people who *were* with him, "Number now and see who has gone from us." And when they had numbered, behold, Jonathan and his armor bearer were not *there.* ¹⁸ Then Saul said to Ahijah, "Bring the ark of God here." For the ark of God was at that time with the sons of Israel. ¹⁹ While Saul talked to the priest, the commotion in the camp of the Philistines continued and increased; so Saul said to the priest, "Withdraw your hand." ²⁰ Then Saul and all the people who *were* with him rallied and came to the battle; and behold, every man's sword was against his fellow, *and there was* very great confusion. ²¹ Now the Hebrews *who* were with the Philistines previously, who went up with them all around in the camp, even they also *turned* to be with the Israelites who *were* with Saul and Jonathan. ²² When all the men of Israel who had hidden themselves in the hill country of Ephraim heard that the Philistines had fled, even they also pursued them closely in the battle. ²³ So the LORD delivered Israel that day, and the battle spread beyond Beth-aven.

²⁴ Now the men of Israel were hard-pressed on that day, for Saul had put the people under oath, saying, "Cursed be the man who eats food before evening, and until I have avenged myself on my enemies." So none of the people tasted food. ²⁵ All *the people of* the land entered the forest, and there was honey on the ground. ²⁶ When the people entered the forest, behold, *there was* a flow of honey; but no man put his hand to his mouth, for the people feared the oath. ²⁷ But Jonathan had not heard when his father put the people under oath; therefore, he put out the end of the staff that *was* in his hand and dipped it in the honeycomb, and put his hand to his mouth, and his eyes brightened. ²⁸ Then one of the people said, "Your father strictly put

the people under oath, saying, 'Cursed be the man who eats food today.'" And the people were weary. [29] Then Jonathan said, "My father has troubled the land. See now, how my eyes have brightened because I tasted a little of this honey. [30] How much more, if only the people had eaten freely today of the spoil of their enemies which they found! For now the slaughter among the Philistines has not been great."

[31] They struck among the Philistines that day from Michmash to Aijalon. And the people were very weary. [32] The people rushed greedily upon the spoil, and took sheep and oxen and calves, and slew *them* on the ground; and the people ate *them* with the blood. [33] Then they told Saul, saying, "Behold, the people are sinning against the LORD by eating with the blood." And he said, "You have acted treacherously; roll a great stone to me today." [34] Saul said, "Disperse yourselves among the people and say to them, 'Each one of you bring me his ox or his sheep, and slaughter *it* here and eat; and do not sin against the LORD by eating with the blood.'" So all the people that night brought each one his ox with him and slaughtered *it* there. [35] And Saul built an altar to the LORD; it was the first altar that he built to the LORD.

[36] Then Saul said, "Let us go down after the Philistines by night and take spoil among them until the morning light, and let us not leave a man of them." And they said, "Do whatever seems good to you." So the priest said, "Let us draw near to God here." [37] Saul inquired of God, "Shall I go down after the Philistines? Will You give them into the hand of Israel?" But He did not answer him on that day. [38] Saul said, "Draw near here, all you chiefs of the people, and investigate and see how this sin has happened today. [39] For as the LORD lives, who delivers Israel, though it is in Jonathan my son, he shall surely die." But not one of all the people answered him. [40] Then he said to all Israel, "You shall be on one side and I and Jonathan my son will be on the other side." And the people said to Saul, "Do what seems good to you." [41] Therefore, Saul said to the LORD, the God of Israel, "Give

14:37 Saul inquired of God. At the request of Ahijah, Saul inquired of the Lord regarding his battle plan. **He did not answer him.** Because of the sin that Saul had caused in his army, God did not answer his inquiry. This would not be the last time that the Lord would refuse to respond to sinful Saul (28:6).

a perfect *lot.*" And Jonathan and Saul were taken, but the people escaped. [42] Saul said, "Cast *lots* between me and Jonathan my son." And Jonathan was taken.

[43] Then Saul said to Jonathan, "Tell me what you have done." So Jonathan told him and said, "I indeed tasted a little honey with the end of the staff that was in my hand. Here I am, I must die!" [44] Saul said, "May God do this *to me* and more also, for you shall surely die, Jonathan." [45] But the people said to Saul, "Must Jonathan die, who has brought about this great deliverance in Israel? Far from it! As the LORD lives, not one hair of his head shall fall to the ground, for he has worked with God this day." So the people rescued Jonathan and he did not die. [46] Then Saul went up from pursuing the Philistines, and the Philistines went to their own place.

[47] Now when Saul had taken the kingdom over Israel, he fought against all his enemies on every side, against Moab, the sons of Ammon, Edom, the kings of Zobah, and the Philistines; and wherever he turned, he inflicted punishment. [48] He acted valiantly and defeated the Amalekites, and delivered Israel from the hands of those who plundered them.

[49] Now the sons of Saul were Jonathan and Ishvi and Malchi-shua; and the names of his two daughters *were these:* the name of the firstborn Merab and the name of the younger Michal. [50] The name of Saul's wife was Ahinoam the daughter of Ahimaaz. And the name of the captain of his army was Abner the son of Ner, Saul's uncle. [51] Kish *was* the father of Saul, and Ner the father of Abner *was* the son of Abiel.

[52] Now the war against the Philistines was severe all the days of Saul; and when Saul saw any mighty man or any valiant man, he attached him to his staff.

15 Then Samuel said to Saul, "The LORD sent me to anoint you as king over His people, over Israel; now therefore, listen to the words of the LORD. [2] Thus says the LORD of hosts, 'I will punish Amalek *for* what he did to Israel, how he set himself against him on the way while he was coming up from Egypt. [3] Now go and strike Amalek and utterly destroy all that he has, and do not spare him; but put to death both man and woman, child and infant, ox and sheep, camel and donkey.'"

[4] Then Saul summoned the people and numbered them in Telaim, 200,000 foot soldiers and 10,000 men of Judah. [5] Saul came to the city of Amalek and set an ambush in the valley. [6] Saul said to the Kenites, "Go, depart, go down from among the Amalekites, so that I do not destroy you with them; for you

showed kindness to all the sons of Israel when they came up from Egypt." So the Kenites departed from among the Amalekites. [7] So Saul defeated the Amalekites, from Havilah as you go to Shur, which is east of Egypt. [8] He captured Agag the king of the Amalekites alive, and utterly destroyed all the people with the edge of the sword. [9] But Saul and the people spared Agag and the best of the sheep, the oxen, the fatlings, the lambs, and all that was good, and were not willing to destroy them utterly; but everything despised and worthless, that they utterly destroyed.

[10] Then the word of the LORD came to Samuel, saying, [11] "I regret that I have made Saul king, for he has turned back from following Me and has not carried out My commands." And Samuel was distressed and cried out to the LORD all night. [12] Samuel rose early in the morning to meet Saul; and it was told Samuel, saying, "Saul came to Carmel, and behold, he set up a monument for himself, then turned and proceeded on down to Gilgal." [13] Samuel came to Saul, and Saul said to him, "Blessed are you of the LORD! I have carried out the command of the LORD." [14] But Samuel said, "What then is this bleating of the sheep in my ears, and the lowing of the oxen which I hear?" [15] Saul said, "They have brought them from the Amalekites, for the people spared the best of the sheep and oxen, to sacrifice to the LORD your God; but the rest we have utterly destroyed." [16] Then Samuel said to Saul, "Wait, and let me tell you what the LORD said to me last night." And he said to him, "Speak!"

[17] Samuel said, "Is it not true, though you were little in your own eyes, you were *made* the head of the tribes of Israel? And the LORD anointed you king over Israel, [18] and the LORD sent you on a mission, and said, 'Go and utterly destroy the sinners, the Amalekites, and fight against them until they are exterminated.' [19] Why then did you not obey the voice of the LORD, but rushed upon the spoil and did what was evil in the sight of the LORD?" [20] Then Saul said to Samuel, "I did obey the voice of the LORD, and went on the mission on which the LORD sent me, and have brought back Agag the king of Amalek, and have utterly destroyed the Amalekites. [21] But the people took *some* of the spoil, sheep and oxen, the choicest of the things devoted to destruction, to sacrifice to the LORD your God at Gilgal." [22] Samuel said,

"Has the LORD as much delight in
    burnt offerings and sacrifices
As in obeying the voice of the LORD?

Behold, to obey is better than sacrifice,
    And to heed than the fat of rams.
[23] "For rebellion is as the sin
        of divination,
    And insubordination is as
        iniquity and idolatry.
Because you have rejected
        the word of the LORD,
He has also rejected you
        from *being* king."

[24] Then Saul said to Samuel, "I have sinned; I have indeed transgressed the command of the LORD and your words, because I feared the people and listened to their voice. [25] Now therefore, please pardon my sin and return with me, that I may worship the LORD." [26] But Samuel said to Saul, "I will not return with you; for you have rejected the word of the LORD, and the LORD has rejected you from being king over Israel." [27] As Samuel turned to go, *Saul* seized the edge of his robe, and it tore. [28] So Samuel said to him, "The LORD has torn the kingdom of Israel from you today and has given it to your neighbor, who is better than you. [29] Also the Glory of Israel will not lie or change His mind; for He is not a man that He should change His mind." [30] Then he said, "I have sinned; *but* please honor me now before the elders of my people and before Israel, and go back with me, that I may worship the LORD your God." [31] So Samuel went back following Saul, and Saul worshiped the LORD.

[32] Then Samuel said, "Bring me Agag, the king of the Amalekites." And Agag came to him cheerfully. And Agag said, "Surely the bitterness of death is past." [33] But Samuel said, "As your sword has made women childless, so shall your mother be childless among women." And Samuel hewed Agag to pieces before the LORD at Gilgal.

[34] Then Samuel went to Ramah, but Saul went up to his house at Gibeah of Saul. [35] Samuel did not see Saul again until the day of his death; for Samuel grieved over Saul. And the LORD regretted that He had made Saul king over Israel.

Psalm 57:1–3

For the choir director; *set to* Altashheth. A Mikhtam of David, when
he fled from Saul in the cave.

B e gracious to me, O God,
    be gracious to me,
For my soul takes refuge in You;
And in the shadow of Your
        wings I will take refuge
Until destruction passes by.

57:1 the shadow of Your wings. Metaphorically, God cares for His own as a mother bird protects its young. Symbolically, there may be a reference here to the cherubim wings on the ark of the covenant where God was specifically present (Ex 37:1–16; Pss 17:8; 36:7; 61:4; 63:7; 91:1, 4). **I will take refuge.** When life becomes bizarre, only one's relationship with his God calms the soul.

23:8 had wanted to see Him. Herod's interest in Christ was fueled by the fact that Christ reminded him of his late nemesis, John the Baptist (9:7–9). At one time Herod had apparently threatened to kill Jesus (13:31–33), but with Christ in Judea rather than Galilee and Perea (where Herod ruled), the king's concern seems to have been nothing more than an eager curiosity.

23:9 answered him nothing. It is significant that in all Jesus' various interrogations, Herod was the only one to whom He refused to speak. See Matthew 7:6. Herod had summarily rejected the truth when he heard it from John the Baptist, so it would have been pointless for Jesus to answer him. See Isaiah 53:7; Psalms 38:13–14; 39:1–2, 9; 1 Peter 2:23.

2 I will cry to God Most High,
To God who accomplishes
all things for me.
3 He will send from heaven and save me;
He reproaches him who
trembles upon me.   *Selah*
God will send forth His
lovingkindness and His truth.

Proverbs 15:24–25

24 The path of life *leads*
upward for the wise
That he may keep away
from Sheol below.
25 The LORD will tear down the
house of the proud,
But He will establish the
boundary of the widow.

Luke 23:1–25

23 Then the whole body of them got up and brought Him before Pilate. ²And they began to accuse Him, saying, "We found this man misleading our nation and forbidding to pay taxes to Caesar, and saying that He Himself is Christ, a King." ³So Pilate asked Him, saying, "Are You the King of the Jews?" And He answered him and said, "*It is as* you say." ⁴Then Pilate said to the chief priests and the crowds, "I find no guilt in this man." ⁵But they kept on insisting, saying, "He stirs up the people, teaching all over Judea, starting from Galilee even as far as this place."

⁶When Pilate heard it, he asked whether the man was a Galilean. ⁷And when he learned that He belonged to Herod's jurisdiction, he sent Him to Herod, who himself also was in Jerusalem at that time.

⁸Now Herod was very glad when he saw Jesus; for he had wanted to see Him for a long time, because he had been hearing about Him and was hoping to see some sign performed by Him. ⁹And he questioned Him at some length; but He answered him nothing. ¹⁰And the chief priests and the scribes were standing there, accusing Him vehemently. ¹¹And

Herod with his soldiers, after treating Him with contempt and mocking Him, dressed Him in a gorgeous robe and sent Him back to Pilate. ¹²Now Herod and Pilate became friends with one another that very day; for before they had been enemies with each other.

¹³Pilate summoned the chief priests and the rulers and the people, ¹⁴and said to them, "You brought this man to me as one who incites the people to rebellion, and behold, having examined Him before you, I have found no guilt in this man regarding the charges which you make against Him. ¹⁵No, nor has Herod, for he sent Him back to us; and behold, nothing deserving death has been done by Him. ¹⁶Therefore I will punish Him and release Him." ¹⁷[Now he was obliged to release to them at the feast one prisoner.]

¹⁸But they cried out all together, saying, "Away with this man, and release for us Barabbas!" ¹⁹(He was one who had been thrown into prison for an insurrection made in the city, and for murder.) ²⁰Pilate, wanting to release Jesus, addressed them again, ²¹but they kept on calling out, saying, "Crucify, crucify Him!" ²²And he said to them the third time, "Why, what evil has this man done? I have found in Him no guilt *demanding* death; therefore I will punish Him and release Him." ²³But they were insistent, with loud voices asking that He be crucified. And their voices *began* to prevail. ²⁴And Pilate pronounced sentence that their demand be granted. ²⁵And he released the man they were asking for who had been thrown into prison for insurrection and murder, but he delivered Jesus to their will.

DAY 6: Why is obedience so important?

Samuel's specific command to Saul was to destroy all the Amalekites and their animals, but instead he spared their king and the best of the animals (1Sa 15:3, 9). But when confronted by Samuel, Saul's response was: "I have carried out the command of the LORD" (v. 13). Saul, either ignorantly or deceitfully, maintained that he did what was commanded (15:20). Saul also began to place blame on others (vv. 11–12), making room for his own excuses just as he had done earlier. Then he tried to justify his sin by saying that the animals would be used to sacrifice to the God of Samuel. Saul's blatant disobedience at least pained his conscience so that he could not claim God as his God. Instead of confessing his sin and repenting, Saul continued to justify himself.

"Behold," Samuel told Saul, "to obey is better than sacrifice" (v. 22). This is an essential Old Testament truth. Samuel stated that God desires heart obedience over the ritual sacrifice of animals (Ps 51:16–17; Is. 1:10–17). The sacrificial system was never intended to function in place of living an obedient life, but was rather to be an expression of it (Hos 6:6; Am 5:21–27; Mic 6:6–8).

Saul needed to see that his real worship was indicated by his behavior and not by his sacrifices. He demonstrated himself to be an idolater whose idol was himself. He had failed the conditions (12:13–15) which would have brought blessing on the nation. His disobedience here was on the same level as witchcraft and idolatry, sins worthy of death (v. 23). "Because you have rejected the word of the LORD, He also has rejected you." A universal principle is given here that those who continually reject God will one day be rejected by Him. The sins of Saul caused God to immediately depose Saul and his descendants forever from the throne of Israel.

MAY 7

1 Samuel 16:1–17:58

16 Now the LORD said to Samuel, "How long will you grieve over Saul, since I have rejected him from being king over Israel? Fill your horn with oil and go; I will send you to Jesse the Bethlehemite, for I have selected a king for Myself among his sons." ² But Samuel said, "How can I go? When Saul hears *of it,* he will kill me." And the LORD said, "Take a heifer with you and say, 'I have come to sacrifice to the LORD.' ³ You shall invite Jesse to the sacrifice, and I will show you what you shall do; and you shall anoint for Me the one whom I designate to you." ⁴ So Samuel did what the LORD said, and came to Bethlehem. And the elders of the city came trembling to meet him and said, "Do you come in peace?" ⁵ He said, "In peace; I have come to sacrifice to the LORD. Consecrate yourselves and come with me to the sacrifice." He also consecrated Jesse and his sons and invited them to the sacrifice.

⁶ When they entered, he looked at Eliab and thought, "Surely the LORD'S anointed is before Him." ⁷ But the LORD said to Samuel, "Do not look at his appearance or at the height of his stature, because I have rejected him; for God *sees* not as man sees, for man looks at the outward appearance, but the LORD looks at the heart." ⁸ Then Jesse called Abinadab and made him pass before Samuel. And he said, "The LORD has not chosen this one either." ⁹ Next Jesse made Shammah pass by. And he said, "The LORD has not chosen this one

16:7 his appearance...height of his stature. Samuel needed to be reminded that God's anointed was not chosen because of physical attributes. This was initially a difficult concept for Samuel as he was accustomed to a king whose only positive attributes were physical. **the LORD looks at the heart.** The Hebrew concept of "heart" embodies emotions, will, intellect, and desires. The life of the man will reflect his heart (Mt 12:34–35).

either." ¹⁰ Thus Jesse made seven of his sons pass before Samuel. But Samuel said to Jesse, "The LORD has not chosen these." ¹¹ And Samuel said to Jesse, "Are these all the children?" And he said, "There remains yet the youngest, and behold, he is tending the sheep." Then Samuel said to Jesse, "Send and bring him; for we will not sit down until he comes here." ¹² So he sent and brought him in. Now he was ruddy, with beautiful eyes and a handsome appearance. And the LORD said, "Arise, anoint him; for this is he." ¹³ Then Samuel took the horn of oil and anointed him in the midst of his brothers; and the Spirit of the LORD came mightily upon David from that day forward. And Samuel arose and went to Ramah.

¹⁴ Now the Spirit of the LORD departed from Saul, and an evil spirit from the LORD terrorized him. ¹⁵ Saul's servants then said to him, "Behold now, an evil spirit from God is terrorizing you. ¹⁶ Let our lord now command your servants who are before you. Let them seek a man who is a skillful player on the harp;

and it shall come about when the evil spirit from God is on you, that he shall play *the harp* with his hand, and you will be well." ¹⁷So Saul said to his servants, "Provide for me now a man who can play well and bring *him* to me." ¹⁸Then one of the young men said, "Behold, I have seen a son of Jesse the Bethlehemite who is a skillful musician, a mighty man of valor, a warrior, one prudent in speech, and a handsome man; and the LORD is with him." ¹⁹So Saul sent messengers to Jesse and said, "Send me your son David who is with the flock." ²⁰Jesse took a donkey *loaded with* bread and a jug of wine and a young goat, and sent *them* to Saul by David his son. ²¹Then David came to Saul and attended him; and Saul loved him greatly, and he became his armor bearer. ²²Saul sent to Jesse, saying, "Let David now stand before me, for he has found favor in my sight." ²³So it came about whenever the *evil* spirit from God came to Saul, David would take the harp and play *it* with his hand; and Saul would be refreshed and be well, and the evil spirit would depart from him.

17 Now the Philistines gathered their armies for battle; and they were gathered at Socoh which belongs to Judah, and they camped between Socoh and Azekah, in Ephes-dammim. ²Saul and the men of Israel were gathered and camped in the valley of Elah, and drew up in battle array to encounter the Philistines. ³The Philistines stood on the mountain on one side while Israel stood on the mountain on the other side, with the valley between them. ⁴Then a champion came out from the armies of the Philistines named Goliath, from Gath, whose height was six cubits and a span. ⁵*He had* a bronze helmet on his head, and he was clothed with scale-armor which weighed five thousand shekels of bronze. ⁶He also *had* bronze greaves on his legs and a bronze javelin *slung* between his shoulders. ⁷The shaft of his spear was like a weaver's beam, and the head of his spear *weighed* six hundred shekels of iron; his shield-carrier also walked before him. ⁸He

17:4 champion. Literally "the man between two." An appropriate appellation as Goliath stood between the two armies of the Philistines and Israel, and offered his challenge to a "duel" of hand-to-hand combat, the outcome of which would settle the battle for both sides. **six cubits and a span.** One cubit measures approximately 18 in. and one span about 9 in., making Goliath about 9 ft. 9 in. in height.

stood and shouted to the ranks of Israel and said to them, "Why do you come out to draw up in battle array? Am I not the Philistine and you servants of Saul? Choose a man for yourselves and let him come down to me. ⁹If he is able to fight with me and kill me, then we will become your servants; but if I prevail against him and kill him, then you shall become our servants and serve us." ¹⁰Again the Philistine said, "I defy the ranks of Israel this day; give me a man that we may fight together." ¹¹When Saul and all Israel heard these words of the Philistine, they were dismayed and greatly afraid.

¹²Now David was the son of the Ephrathite of Bethlehem in Judah, whose name was Jesse, and he had eight sons. And Jesse was old in the days of Saul, advanced *in years* among men. ¹³The three older sons of Jesse had gone after Saul to the battle. And the names of his three sons who went to the battle were Eliab the firstborn, and the second to him Abinadab, and the third Shammah. ¹⁴David was the youngest. Now the three oldest followed Saul, ¹⁵but David went back and forth from Saul to tend his father's flock at Bethlehem. ¹⁶The Philistine came forward morning and evening for forty days and took his stand.

¹⁷Then Jesse said to David his son, "Take now for your brothers an ephah of this roasted grain and these ten loaves and run to the camp to your brothers. ¹⁸Bring also these ten cuts of cheese to the commander of *their* thousand, and look into the welfare of your brothers, and bring back news of them. ¹⁹For Saul and they and all the men of Israel are in the valley of Elah, fighting with the Philistines." ²⁰So David arose early in the morning and left the flock with a keeper and took *the supplies* and went as Jesse had commanded him. And he came to the circle of the camp while the army was going out in battle array shouting the war cry. ²¹Israel and the Philistines drew up in battle array, army against army. ²²Then David left his baggage in the care of the baggage keeper, and ran to the battle line and entered in order to greet his brothers. ²³As he was talking with them, behold, the champion, the Philistine from Gath named Goliath, was coming up from the army of the Philistines, and he spoke these same words; and David heard *them*.

²⁴When all the men of Israel saw the man, they fled from him and were greatly afraid. ²⁵The men of Israel said, "Have you seen this man who is coming up? Surely he is coming up to defy Israel. And it will be that the king will enrich the man who kills him with great riches and will give him his daughter and make his father's house free in Israel."

²⁶Then David spoke to the men who were standing by him, saying, "What will be done for the man who kills this Philistine and takes away the reproach from Israel? For who is this uncircumcised Philistine, that he should taunt the armies of the living God?" ²⁷The people answered him in accord with this word, saying, "Thus it will be done for the man who kills him."

²⁸Now Eliab his oldest brother heard when he spoke to the men; and Eliab's anger burned against David and he said, "Why have you come down? And with whom have you left those few sheep in the wilderness? I know your insolence and the wickedness of your heart; for you have come down in order to see the battle." ²⁹But David said, "What have I done now? Was it not just a question?" ³⁰Then he turned away from him to another and said the same thing; and the people answered the same thing as before.

³¹When the words which David spoke were heard, they told *them* to Saul, and he sent for him. ³²David said to Saul, "Let no man's heart fail on account of him; your servant will go and fight with this Philistine." ³³Then Saul said to David, "You are not able to go against this Philistine to fight with him; for you are *but* a youth while he has been a warrior from his youth." ³⁴But David said to Saul, "Your servant was tending his father's sheep. When a lion or a bear came and took a lamb from the flock, ³⁵I went out after him and attacked him, and rescued *it* from his mouth; and when he rose up against me, I seized *him* by his beard and struck him and killed him. ³⁶Your servant has killed both the lion and the bear; and this uncircumcised Philistine will be like one of them, since he has taunted the armies of the living God." ³⁷And David said, "The LORD who delivered me from the paw of the lion and from the paw of the bear, He will deliver me from the hand of this Philistine." And Saul said to David, "Go, and may the LORD be with you." ³⁸Then Saul clothed David with his garments and put a bronze helmet on his head, and he clothed him with armor. ³⁹David girded his sword over his armor and tried to walk, for he had not tested *them.* So David

17:32 Let no man's heart fail. Joshua and Caleb exhorted Israel in the same fashion regarding the giant Anakim 400 years prior (Nu 13:30; 14:8–9). The heathens' hearts fail at the name of the Lord God of Israel (Jos 2:11).

17:37 The LORD...He will deliver me. Just as Jonathan believed earlier (14:6). David had a wholehearted faith in the God of Israel. **the LORD be with you.** One of the first explicit indications in the text that Saul knew that the Lord was with David (15:28).

said to Saul, "I cannot go with these, for I have not tested *them.*" And David took them off. ⁴⁰He took his stick in his hand and chose for himself five smooth stones from the brook, and put them in the shepherd's bag which he had, even in *his* pouch, and his sling was in his hand; and he approached the Philistine. ⁴¹Then the Philistine came on and approached David, with the shield-bearer in front of him. ⁴²When the Philistine looked and saw David, he disdained him; for he was *but* a youth, and ruddy, with a handsome appearance. ⁴³The Philistine said to David, "Am I a dog, that you come to me with sticks?" And the Philistine cursed David by his gods. ⁴⁴The Philistine also said to David, "Come to me, and I will give your flesh to the birds of the sky and the beasts of the field." ⁴⁵Then David said to the Philistine, "You come to me with a sword, a spear, and a javelin, but I come to you in the name of the LORD of hosts, the God of the armies of Israel, whom you have taunted. ⁴⁶This day the LORD will deliver you up into my hands, and I will strike you down and remove your head from you. And I will give the dead bodies of the army of the Philistines this day to the birds of the sky and the wild beasts of the earth, that all the earth may know that there is a God in Israel, ⁴⁷and that all this assembly may know that the LORD does not deliver by sword or by spear; for the battle is the LORD'S and He will give you into our hands."

⁴⁸Then it happened when the Philistine rose and came and drew near to meet David, that David ran quickly toward the battle line to meet the Philistine. ⁴⁹And David put his hand into his bag and took from it a stone and slung *it,* and struck the Philistine on his forehead. And the stone sank into his forehead, so that he fell on his face to the ground.

⁵⁰Thus David prevailed over the Philistine with a sling and a stone, and he struck the Philistine and killed him; but there was no sword in David's hand. ⁵¹Then David ran and stood over the Philistine and took his sword and drew it out of its sheath and killed him, and cut off his head with it. When the Philistines saw that their champion was dead,

they fled. ⁵²The men of Israel and Judah arose and shouted and pursued the Philistines as far as the valley, and to the gates of Ekron. And the slain Philistines lay along the way to Shaaraim, even to Gath and Ekron. ⁵³The sons of Israel returned from chasing the Philistines and plundered their camps. ⁵⁴Then David took the Philistine's head and brought it to Jerusalem, but he put his weapons in his tent.

⁵⁵Now when Saul saw David going out against the Philistine, he said to Abner the commander of the army, "Abner, whose son is this young man?" And Abner said, "By your life, O king, I do not know." ⁵⁶The king said, "You inquire whose son the youth is." ⁵⁷So when David returned from killing the Philistine, Abner took him and brought him before Saul with the Philistine's head in his hand. ⁵⁸Saul said to him, "Whose son are you, young man?" And David answered, "I am the son of your servant Jesse the Bethlehemite."

Psalm 57:4-11

4 My soul is among lions;
  I must lie among those who
    breathe forth fire,
  Even the sons of men, whose
    teeth are spears and arrows
  And their tongue a sharp sword.
5 Be exalted above the heavens, O God;
  Let Your glory *be* above all the earth.
6 They have prepared a net for my steps;
  My soul is bowed down;
  They dug a pit before me;
  They *themselves* have fallen
    into the midst of it.   *Selah*

7 My heart is steadfast, O God,
    my heart is steadfast;
  I will sing, yes, I will sing praises!
8 Awake, my glory!
  Awake, harp and lyre!
  I will awaken the dawn.
9 I will give thanks to You, O Lord,
    among the peoples;
  I will sing praises to You
    among the nations.
10 For Your lovingkindness is
    great to the heavens
  And Your truth to the clouds.
11 Be exalted above the heavens, O God;
  Let Your glory *be* above all the earth.

Proverbs 15:26

26 Evil plans are an abomination
    to the LORD,
  But pleasant words are pure.

Luke 23:26-56

²⁶When they led Him away, they seized a man, Simon of Cyrene, coming in from the country, and placed on him the cross to carry behind Jesus.

²⁷And following Him was a large crowd of the people, and of women who were mourning and lamenting Him. ²⁸But Jesus turning to them said, "Daughters of Jerusalem, stop weeping for Me, but weep for yourselves and for your children. ²⁹For behold, the days are coming when they will say, 'Blessed are the barren, and the wombs that never bore, and the breasts that never nursed.' ³⁰Then they will begin to say to the mountains, 'Fall on us,' and to the hills, 'Cover us.' ³¹For if they do these things when the tree is green, what will happen when it is dry?"

³²Two others also, who were criminals, were being led away to be put to death with Him.

³³When they came to the place called The Skull, there they crucified Him and the criminals, one on the right and the other on the left. ³⁴But Jesus was saying, "Father, forgive them; for they do not know what they are doing." And they cast lots, dividing up His garments among themselves. ³⁵And the people stood by, looking on. And even the rulers were sneering at Him, saying, "He saved others; let Him save Himself if this is the Christ of God, His Chosen One." ³⁶The soldiers also mocked Him, coming up to Him, offering Him sour wine, ³⁷and saying, "If You are the King of the Jews, save Yourself!" ³⁸Now there was also an inscription above Him,

"THIS IS THE KING OF THE JEWS."

³⁹One of the criminals who were hanged *there* was hurling abuse at Him, saying, "Are You not the Christ? Save Yourself and us!" ⁴⁰But the other answered, and rebuking him said, "Do you not even fear God, since you are under the same sentence of condemnation? ⁴¹And we indeed *are suffering* justly, for we are receiving what we deserve for our deeds; but this man has done nothing wrong." ⁴²And he was saying, "Jesus, remember me when You come in Your kingdom!" ⁴³And He said to him, "Truly I say to you, today you shall be with Me in Paradise."

⁴⁴It was now about the sixth hour, and darkness fell over the whole land until the ninth hour, ⁴⁵because the sun was obscured; and the veil of the temple was torn in two. ⁴⁶And Jesus, crying out with a loud voice, said, "Father, into Your hands I commit

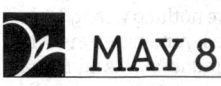

23:42 Jesus, remember me. The penitent thief's prayer reflected his belief that the soul lives on after death; that Christ had a right to rule over a kingdom of the souls of men; and that He would soon enter that kingdom despite His impending death. His request to be remembered was a plea for mercy, which also reveals that the thief understood he had no hope but divine grace, and that the dispensing of that grace lay in Jesus' power. All of this demonstrates true faith on the part of the dying thief, and Christ graciously affirmed the man's salvation (v. 43).

MY SPIRIT." Having said this, He breathed His last. ⁴⁷Now when the centurion saw what had happened, he *began* praising God, saying, "Certainly this man was innocent." ⁴⁸And all the crowds who came together for this specta-

cle, when they observed what had happened, *began* to return, beating their breasts. ⁴⁹And all His acquaintances and the women who accompanied Him from Galilee were standing at a distance, seeing these things.

⁵⁰And a man named Joseph, who was a member of the Council, a good and righteous man ⁵¹(he had not consented to their plan and action), *a man* from Arimathea, a city of the Jews, who was waiting for the kingdom of God; ⁵²this man went to Pilate and asked for the body of Jesus. ⁵³And he took it down and wrapped it in a linen cloth, and laid Him in a tomb cut into the rock, where no one had ever lain. ⁵⁴It was the preparation day, and the Sabbath was about to begin. ⁵⁵Now the women who had come with Him out of Galilee followed, and saw the tomb and how His body was laid. ⁵⁶Then they returned and prepared spices and perfumes.

And on the Sabbath they rested according to the commandment.

DAY 7: Contrast the spiritual anointings of David and Saul.

David was first anointed by Samuel "in the midst of his brothers" (1Sa 16:13). David's first anointing was before his family/house. His second anointing would be before the assembly of his tribe, Judah; and his third anointing would be before the nation Israel. At this time, "the Spirit of the LORD came mightily upon David." This familiar Old Testament expression relates to empowerment for some God-given task (see 10:6, 11; 11:6; 19:20, 23; 2Sa 23:2; 2Ch 20:14; Is. 11:2; 61:1; Eze 11:5; 37:1). David's anointing was an external symbol of an inward work of God. The operation of the Holy Spirit in this case was not for regeneration, but for empowerment to perform his (David's) role in God's program for Israel. After David sinned with Bathsheba (2Sa 11–12), he prayed, "Do not take Your Holy Spirit from me" (Ps 51:11).

When David's ascent to the throne began, Saul's slow and painful descent began also. "The Spirit of the LORD departed from Saul" (1Sa 16:14). Without God's empowering Holy Spirit, Saul was effectively no longer king over Israel (15:28), although his physical removal from the throne, and his death, happened many years later. "And an evil spirit from the LORD terrorized him." God, in His sovereignty, allowed an evil spirit to torment Saul (see Jdg 9:23; 1Ki 22:19–23; Job 1:6–12) for His purpose of establishing the throne of David. This spirit, a messenger from Satan, is to be distinguished from a troubled emotional state brought on by indwelling sin or the harmful consequences of the sinful acts of others (e.g., spirit of jealousy, Nu 5:14). This demon spirit attacked Saul from without, for there is no evidence that the demon indwelt Saul. Saul, whose inward constitution was already prone to questionable judgment and the fear of men, began to experience God's judgment in the form of severe bouts of depression, anger, and delusion, initiated and aggravated by the evil spirit assigned to him. There are several New Testament occasions where God turned people over to demons or Satan for judgment (see Ac 5:1–3; 1Co 5:1–7; 1Ti 1:18–20).

MAY 8

1 Samuel 18:1–19:24

18 Now it came about when he had finished speaking to Saul, that the soul of Jonathan was knit to the soul of David, and Jonathan loved him as himself. ²Saul took him that day and did not let him return to his father's house. ³Then Jonathan made a

covenant with David because he loved him as himself. ⁴Jonathan stripped himself of the robe that was on him and gave it to David, with his armor, including his sword and his bow and his belt. ⁵So David went out wherever Saul sent him, *and* prospered; and Saul set him over the men of war. And it was pleasing in the sight of all the people and also in the sight of Saul's servants.

⁶It happened as they were coming, when

18:1 Jonathan loved him. Jonathan loved David with a loyalty and devotion indicative of covenantal love (18:3). Hiram of Tyre had much the same covenantal love for David (2Sa 5:11; 1Ki 5:1; 9:11). David's later reign from Jerusalem is marked by loyalty to his covenant with Jonathan (2Sa 9:1).

David returned from killing the Philistine, that the women came out of all the cities of Israel, singing and dancing, to meet King Saul, with tambourines, with joy and with musical instruments. ⁷The women sang as they played, and said,

"Saul has slain his thousands,
And David his ten thousands."

⁸Then Saul became very angry, for this saying displeased him; and he said, "They have ascribed to David ten thousands, but to me they have ascribed thousands. Now what more can he have but the kingdom?" ⁹Saul looked at David with suspicion from that day on.

¹⁰Now it came about on the next day that an evil spirit from God came mightily upon Saul, and he raved in the midst of the house, while David was playing *the harp* with his hand, as usual; and a spear *was* in Saul's hand. ¹¹Saul hurled the spear for he thought, "I will pin David to the wall." But David escaped from his presence twice.

¹²Now Saul was afraid of David, for the LORD was with him but had departed from Saul. ¹³Therefore Saul removed him from his presence and appointed him as his commander of a thousand; and he went out and came in before the people. ¹⁴David was prospering in all his ways for the LORD *was* with him. ¹⁵When Saul saw that he was prospering greatly, he dreaded him. ¹⁶But all Israel and Judah loved David, and he went out and came in before them.

¹⁷Then Saul said to David, "Here is my older daughter Merab; I will give her to you as a wife, only be a valiant man for me and fight the LORD'S battles." For Saul thought, "My hand shall not be against him, but let the hand of the Philistines be against him." ¹⁸But David said to Saul, "Who am I, and what is my life *or* my father's family in Israel, that I should be the king's son-in-law?" ¹⁹So it came about at the time when Merab, Saul's daughter, should have been given to David, that she was given to Adriel the Meholathite for a wife.

²⁰Now Michal, Saul's daughter, loved David. When they told Saul, the thing was agreeable to him. ²¹Saul thought, "I will give her to him that she may become a snare to him, and that the hand of the Philistines may be against him." Therefore Saul said to David, "For a second time you may be my son-in-law today." ²²Then Saul commanded his servants, "Speak to David secretly, saying, 'Behold, the king delights in you, and all his servants love you; now therefore, become the king's son-in-law.'" ²³So Saul's servants spoke these words to David. But David said, "Is it trivial in your sight to become the king's son-in-law, since I am a poor man and lightly esteemed?" ²⁴The servants of Saul reported to him according to these words *which* David spoke. ²⁵Saul then said, "Thus you shall say to David, 'The king does not desire any dowry except a hundred foreskins of the Philistines, to take vengeance on the king's enemies.'" Now Saul planned to make David fall by the hand of the Philistines. ²⁶When his servants told David these words, it pleased David to become the king's son-in-law. Before the days had expired ²⁷David rose up and went, he and his men, and struck down two hundred men among the Philistines. Then David brought their foreskins, and they gave them in full number to the king, that he might become the king's son-in-law. So Saul gave him Michal his daughter for a wife. ²⁸When Saul saw and knew that the LORD was with David, and *that* Michal, Saul's daughter, loved him, ²⁹then Saul was even more afraid of David. Thus Saul was David's enemy continually.

³⁰Then the commanders of the Philistines went out *to battle,* and it happened as often as they went out, that David behaved himself more wisely than all the servants of Saul. So his name was highly esteemed.

19 Now Saul told Jonathan his son and all his servants to put David to death. But Jonathan, Saul's son, greatly delighted in David. ²So Jonathan told David saying, "Saul my father is seeking to put you to death. Now therefore, please be on guard in the morning, and stay in a secret place and hide yourself. ³I will go out and stand beside my father in the field where you are, and I will speak with my father about you; if I find out anything, then I will tell you." ⁴Then Jonathan spoke well of David to Saul his father and said to him, "Do not let the king sin against his servant David, since he has not sinned against you, and since his deeds *have been* very beneficial to you. ⁵For he took his life in his hand and struck the Philistine, and the LORD brought about a great deliverance for all Israel; you saw *it* and rejoiced. Why then will you sin against innocent blood by putting David to death without a cause?" [6] Saul listened to the voice of Jonathan, and Saul vowed, "As the LORD lives, he shall not be put to death." [7] Then Jonathan called David, and Jonathan told him all these words. And Jonathan brought David to Saul, and he was in his presence as formerly.

[8] When there was war again, David went out and fought with the Philistines and defeated them with great slaughter, so that they fled before him. [9] Now there was an evil spirit from the LORD on Saul as he was sitting in his house with his spear in his hand, and David was playing *the harp* with *his* hand. [10] Saul tried to pin David to the wall with the spear, but he slipped away out of Saul's presence, so that he stuck the spear into the wall. And David fled and escaped that night.

[11] Then Saul sent messengers to David's house to watch him, in order to put him to death in the morning. But Michal, David's wife, told him, saying, "If you do not save your life tonight, tomorrow you will be put to death." [12] So Michal let David down through a window, and he went out and fled and escaped. [13] Michal took the household idol and laid *it* on the bed, and put a quilt of goats' *hair* at its head, and covered *it* with clothes. [14] When Saul sent messengers to take David, she said, "He is sick." [15] Then Saul sent messengers to see David, saying, "Bring him up to me on his bed, that I may put him to death." [16] When the messengers entered, behold, the household idol *was* on the bed with the quilt of goats' *hair* at its head. [17] So Saul said to Michal, "Why have you deceived me like this and let my enemy go, so that he has escaped?" And Michal said to Saul, "He said to me, 'Let me go! Why should I put you to death?' "

[18] Now David fled and escaped and came to Samuel at Ramah, and told him all that Saul had done to him. And he and Samuel went and stayed in Naioth. [19] It was told Saul, saying, "Behold, David is at Naioth in Ramah." [20] Then Saul sent messengers to take David, but when they saw the company of the prophets prophesying, with Samuel standing *and* presiding over them, the Spirit of God came upon the messengers of Saul; and they also prophesied. [21] When it was told Saul, he sent other messengers, and they also prophesied. So Saul sent messengers again the third time, and they also prophesied. [22] Then he himself went to Ramah and came as far as the large well that is in Secu; and he asked and said,

"Where are Samuel and David?" And *someone* said, "Behold, they are at Naioth in Ramah." [23] He proceeded there to Naioth in Ramah; and the Spirit of God came upon him also, so that he went along prophesying continually until he came to Naioth in Ramah. [24] He also stripped off his clothes, and he too prophesied before Samuel and lay down naked all that day and all that night. Therefore they say, "Is Saul also among the prophets?"

19:23 the Spirit of God came upon him. This was the last time the Spirit of the Lord would rest on Saul. God turned Saul's heart to prophesy and not to harm David.

19:24 stripped off his clothes. Saul removed his armor and royal garments (see Jonathan, 18:4), prompted by the Spirit of God, thus signifying God's rejection of Saul as king over Israel. **lay down naked.** Without the royal garments, Saul was figuratively "naked," perhaps so overwhelmed by the Spirit of God as to be in a deep sleep. Other than Saul's utter despair and pitiful state at the home of the witch at En-dor (28:20) and his end at Mt. Gilboa (31:4–6), this episode represents one of the severest humblings in Saul's life. **Is Saul also among the prophets?** This is a final editorial comment tying together the Spirit of God's presence at Saul's inauguration (10:10–11), and the final departure of the same at his rejection (19:24).

Psalm 58:1–11

> For the choir director; *set to* Altashheth. A Mikhtam of David.

Do you indeed speak
   righteousness, O gods?
Do you judge uprightly,
   O sons of men?
[2] No, in heart you work
   unrighteousness;
On earth you weigh out the
   violence of your hands.
[3] The wicked are estranged
   from the womb;
These who speak lies go
   astray from birth.
[4] They have venom like the
   venom of a serpent;
Like a deaf cobra that stops
   up its ear,
[5] So that it does not hear the
   voice of charmers,
Or a skillful caster of spells.

58:4 They have venom. The words and actions of these tyrants are like poisonous venom in a serpent's fangs. **deaf cobra.** Like a cobra which cannot hear its charmer are these stubborn rulers, who ignore all encouragements to righteousness.

6 O God, shatter their teeth
    in their mouth;
  Break out the fangs of the
    young lions, O LORD.
7 Let them flow away like
    water that runs off;
  When he aims his arrows, let
    them be as headless shafts.
8 *Let them be* as a snail which
    melts away as it goes along,
  Like the miscarriages of a woman
    which never see the sun.
9 Before your pots can feel
    the fire of thorns
  He will sweep them away with
    a whirlwind, the green
    and the burning alike.
10 The righteous will rejoice when
    he sees the vengeance;
  He will wash his feet in the
    blood of the wicked.
11 And men will say, "Surely there is
    a reward for the righteous;
  Surely there is a God who
    judges on earth!"

Proverbs 15:27–30

27 He who profits illicitly
    troubles his own house,
  But he who hates bribes will live.
28 The heart of the righteous
    ponders how to answer,
  But the mouth of the wicked
    pours out evil things.
29 The LORD is far from the wicked,
  But He hears the prayer
    of the righteous.
30 Bright eyes gladden the heart;
  Good news puts fat on the bones.

Luke 24:1–35

24 But on the first day of the week, at early dawn, they came to the tomb bringing the spices which they had prepared. 2 And they found the stone rolled away from the tomb, 3 but when they entered, they did not find the body of the Lord Jesus. 4 While they were perplexed about this, behold, two men suddenly stood near them in dazzling clothing; 5 and as *the women* were terrified and bowed their faces to the ground, *the men* said to them, "Why do you seek the living One among the dead? 6 He is not here, but He has risen. Remember how He spoke to you while He was still in Galilee, 7 saying that the Son of Man must be delivered into the hands of sinful men, and be crucified, and the third day rise again." 8 And they remembered His words, 9 and returned from the tomb and reported all these things to the eleven and to all the rest. 10 Now they were Mary Magdalene and Joanna and Mary the *mother* of James; also the other women with them were telling these things to the apostles. 11 But these words appeared to them as nonsense, and they would not believe them. 12 But Peter got up and ran to the tomb; stooping and looking in, he *saw the linen wrappings only; and he went away to his home, marveling at what had happened.

13 And behold, two of them were going that very day to a village named Emmaus, which was about seven miles from Jerusalem. 14 And they were talking with each other about all these things which had taken place. 15 While they were talking and discussing, Jesus Himself approached and *began* traveling with them. 16 But their eyes were prevented from recognizing Him. 17 And He said to them, "What are these words that you are exchanging with one another as you are walking?" And they stood still, looking sad. 18 One *of them,* named Cleopas, answered and said to Him, "Are You the only one visiting Jerusalem and unaware of the things which have happened here in these days?" 19 And He said to them, "What things?" And they said to Him, "The things about Jesus the Nazarene, who was a prophet mighty in deed and word in the sight of God and all the people, 20 and how the chief priests and our rulers delivered Him to the sentence of death, and crucified Him. 21 But we were hoping that it was He who was going to redeem Israel. Indeed, besides all this, it is the third day since these things happened. 22 But also some women among us amazed us. When they were at the tomb early in the morning, 23 and did not find His body, they came, saying that they had also seen a vision of angels who said that He was alive. 24 Some of those who were with us went to the tomb and found it just exactly as the women also had said; but Him they did not see." 25 And He said to them, "O foolish men and slow of heart to believe in all that the

prophets have spoken! ²⁶Was it not necessary for the Christ to suffer these things and to enter into His glory?" ²⁷Then beginning with Moses and with all the prophets, He explained to them the things concerning Himself in all the Scriptures.

²⁸And they approached the village where they were going, and He acted as though He were going farther. ²⁹But they urged Him, saying, "Stay with us, for it is *getting* toward evening, and the day is now nearly over." So He went in to stay with them. ³⁰When He had reclined *at the table* with them, He took the bread and blessed *it*, and breaking *it*, He began giving *it* to them. ³¹Then their eyes were opened and they recognized Him; and He vanished from their sight. ³²They said to one another, "Were not our hearts burning within us while He was speaking to us on the road, while He was explaining the Scriptures to us?" ³³And they got up that very hour and returned to Jerusalem, and found gathered together the eleven and those who were with them, ³⁴saying, "The Lord has really risen and has appeared to Simon." ³⁵They *began* to relate their experiences on the road and how He was recognized by them in the breaking of the bread.

DAY 8: What happened on the day that Christ was resurrected from the dead?

Early in the morning, certain women came to the tomb "bringing the spices which they had prepared" (Lk 24:1). But they found "the stone rolled away" (v. 2). Matthew 28:2–4 records that an earthquake occurred, and an angel rolled the stone away. The Roman guards fainted with fear. Mark, Luke, and John make no mention of the guards, so it appears they fled when they awoke to find the empty tomb. The women must have arrived shortly after.

Finding the stone rolled away, the women entered the tomb, but found it empty (v. 3). While they were still in the tomb, the angels suddenly appeared (v. 4; Mk 16:5). Only Luke mentioned both angels. Mark was concerned only with the one who spoke for the duo. Such minor differences in the Gospel accounts are all reconcilable.

The angel who spoke reminded them of Jesus' promises (vv. 6–8), then sent them to find Peter and the disciples to report that Jesus was risen (Mt 28:7–8; Mk 16:7–8). The women did as they were told (vv. 9–11). The disciples were skeptical at first (v. 11), but ran to where the tomb was, John arriving first (Jn 20:4), but Peter actually entering the tomb first (Jn 20:6). They saw the linen wrappings intact but empty, proof that Jesus was risen (v. 12; Jn 20:6–8). They left immediately (v. 12; Jn 20:10).

Meanwhile, Mary Magdalene returned to the tomb and was standing outside weeping when Christ suddenly appeared to her (Jn 20:11–18). That was His first appearance (Mk 16:9). Sometime soon after that, He met the other women on the road and appeared to them, as well (Mt 28:9–10). Later that day He appeared to two of the disciples on the road to Emmaus (vv. 13–32) and to Peter (v. 34).

MAY 9

1 Samuel 20:1–21:15

20 Then David fled from Naioth in Ramah, and came and said to Jonathan, "What have I done? What is my iniquity? And what is my sin before your father, that he is seeking my life?" ²He said to him, "Far from it, you shall not die. Behold, my father does nothing either great or small without disclosing it to me. So why should my father hide this thing from me? It is not so!" ³Yet David vowed again, saying, "Your father knows well that I have found favor in your sight, and he has said, 'Do not let Jonathan know this, or he will be grieved.' But truly as the LORD lives and as your soul lives, there is hardly a step between me and death." ⁴Then Jonathan said to David, "Whatever you say, I will do for you." ⁵So David said to Jonathan, "Behold, tomorrow is the new moon, and I ought to sit down to eat with the king. But let me go, that I may hide myself in the field until the third evening. ⁶If your father misses me at all, then say, 'David earnestly asked *leave* of me to run to Bethlehem his city, because it is the yearly sacrifice there for the whole family.' ⁷If he says, 'It is good,' your servant *will be* safe; but if he is very angry, know that he has decided on evil. ⁸Therefore deal kindly with your servant, for you have brought your servant into a covenant of the LORD with you. But if there is iniquity in me, put me to death yourself; for why then should you bring me to your father?" ⁹Jonathan said, "Far be it from you! For if I should indeed learn that evil has been decided by my father to come

upon you, then would I not tell you about it?" ¹⁰Then David said to Jonathan, "Who will tell me if your father answers you harshly?" ¹¹Jonathan said to David, "Come, and let us go out into the field." So both of them went out to the field.

¹²Then Jonathan said to David, "The LORD, the God of Israel, *be witness!* When I have sounded out my father about this time tomorrow, *or* the third day, behold, if there is good *feeling* toward David, shall I not then send to you and make it known to you? ¹³If it please my father *to do* you harm, may the LORD do so to Jonathan and more also, if I do not make it known to you and send you away, that you may go in safety. And may the LORD be with you as He has been with my father. ¹⁴If I am still alive, will you not show me the lovingkindness of the LORD, that I may not die? ¹⁵You shall not cut off your lovingkindness from my house forever, not even when the LORD cuts off every one of the enemies of David from the face of the earth." ¹⁶So Jonathan made a *covenant* with the house of David, *saying,* "May the LORD require *it* at the hands of David's enemies." ¹⁷Jonathan made David vow again because of his love for him, because he loved him as he loved his own life.

¹⁸Then Jonathan said to him, "Tomorrow is the new moon, and you will be missed because your seat will be empty. ¹⁹When you have stayed for three days, you shall go down quickly and come to the place where you hid yourself on that eventful day, and you shall remain by the stone Ezel. ²⁰I will shoot three arrows to the side, as though I shot at a target. ²¹And behold, I will send the lad, *saying,* 'Go, find the arrows.' If I specifically say to the lad, 'Behold, the arrows are on this side of you, get them,' then come; for there is safety for you and no harm, as the LORD lives. ²²But if I say to the youth, 'Behold, the arrows are beyond you,' go, for the LORD has sent you away. ²³As for the agreement of which you and I have spoken, behold, the LORD is between you and me forever."

²⁴So David hid in the field; and when the new moon came, the king sat down to eat food. ²⁵The king sat on his seat as usual, the seat by the wall; then Jonathan rose up and Abner sat down by Saul's side, but David's place was empty. ²⁶Nevertheless Saul did not speak anything that day, for he thought, "It is an accident, he is not clean, surely *he is* not clean." ²⁷It came about the next day, the second *day* of the new moon, that David's place was empty; so Saul said to Jonathan his son, "Why has the son of Jesse not come to the meal, either yesterday or today?" ²⁸Jonathan then answered Saul, "David earnestly asked leave of me *to go* to Bethlehem, ²⁹for he said, 'Please let me go, since our family has a sacrifice in the city, and my brother has commanded me to attend. And now, if I have found favor in your sight, please let me get away that I may see my brothers.' For this reason he has not come to the king's table."

³⁰Then Saul's anger burned against Jonathan and he said to him, "You son of a perverse, rebellious woman! Do I not know that you are choosing the son of Jesse to your own shame and to the shame of your mother's nakedness? ³¹For as long as the son of Jesse lives on the earth, neither you nor your kingdom will be established. Therefore now, send and bring him to me, for he must surely die." ³²But Jonathan answered Saul his father and said to him, "Why should he be put to death? What has he done?" ³³Then Saul hurled his spear at him to strike him down; so Jonathan knew that his father had decided to put David to death. ³⁴Then Jonathan arose from the table in fierce anger, and did not eat food on the second day of the new moon, for he was grieved over David because his father had dishonored him.

³⁵Now it came about in the morning that Jonathan went out into the field for the appointment with David, and a little lad *was* with him. ³⁶He said to his lad, "Run, find now the arrows which I am about to shoot." As the lad was running, he shot an arrow past him. ³⁷When the lad reached the place of the arrow which Jonathan had shot, Jonathan called after the lad and said, "Is not the arrow beyond you?" ³⁸And Jonathan called after the lad, "Hurry, be quick, do not stay!" And Jonathan's lad picked up the arrow and came to his master. ³⁹But the lad was not aware of anything; only Jonathan and David knew about the matter. ⁴⁰Then Jonathan gave his weapons to his lad and said to him, "Go, bring *them* to the city." ⁴¹When the lad was gone, David rose from the south side and fell on his face to the ground, and bowed three times. And they kissed each other and wept together, but David *wept* the more. ⁴²Jonathan said to David, "Go in safety, inasmuch as we have sworn to each other in the name of the LORD, saying, 'The LORD will be between me and you, and between my descendants and your descendants forever.'" Then he rose and departed, while Jonathan went into the city.

21 Then David came to Nob to Ahimelech the priest; and Ahimelech came trembling to meet David and said to him, "Why are you alone and no one with you?" ² David said to Ahimelech the priest, "The king has commissioned me with a matter and has said to me, 'Let no one know anything about the matter on which I am sending you and with which I have commissioned you; and I have directed the young men to a certain place.' ³ Now therefore, what do you have on hand? Give me five loaves of bread, or whatever can be found." ⁴ The priest answered David and said, "There is no ordinary bread on hand, but there is consecrated bread; if only the young men have kept themselves from women." ⁵ David answered the priest and said to him, "Surely women have been kept from us as previously when I set out and the vessels of the young men were holy, though it was an ordinary journey; how much more then today will their vessels *be holy?*" ⁶ So the priest gave him consecrated *bread;* for there was no bread there but the bread of the Presence which was removed from before the LORD, in order to put hot bread *in its place* when it was taken away.

21:2 The king has commissioned me. David, fearing someone might tell Saul where he was, deceived Ahimelech the priest into thinking that he was on official business for the king. He supposed, as many do, that it is excusable to lie for the purpose of saving one's life. But what is essentially sinful can never, because of circumstances, change its immoral character (Ps 119:29). David's lying led tragically to the deaths of the priests (22:9–18).

21:6 consecrated *bread.* Since that bread was no longer on the Lord's table, having been replaced by hot bread, it was to be eaten by the priests and in these exigencies, by David under the law of necessity and mercy. The removal of the old bread and the replacing with new was done on the Sabbath (Lv 24:8).

⁷ Now one of the servants of Saul was there that day, detained before the LORD; and his name was Doeg the Edomite, the chief of Saul's shepherds.

⁸ David said to Ahimelech, "Now is there not a spear or a sword on hand? For I brought neither my sword nor my weapons with me, because the king's matter was urgent." ⁹ Then the priest said, "The sword of Goliath the Philistine, whom you killed in the valley of Elah, behold, it is wrapped in a cloth behind the ephod; if you would take it for yourself, take *it.* For there is no other except it here." And David said, "There is none like it; give it to me."

¹⁰ Then David arose and fled that day from Saul, and went to Achish king of Gath. ¹¹ But the servants of Achish said to him, "Is this not David the king of the land? Did they not sing of this one as they danced, saying,

'Saul has slain his thousands,
And David his ten thousands'?"

¹² David took these words to heart and greatly feared Achish king of Gath. ¹³ So he disguised his sanity before them, and acted insanely in their hands, and scribbled on the doors of the gate, and let his saliva run down into his beard. ¹⁴ Then Achish said to his servants,

21:13 disguised his sanity. David feared for his life, lacked trust in God to deliver him, and feigned insanity to persuade Achish to send him away. See the titles of Pss 34–56. Drooling in one's beard was considered in the East an intolerable indignity, as was spitting in another's beard.

"Behold, you see the man behaving as a madman. Why do you bring him to me? ¹⁵ Do I lack madmen, that you have brought this one to act the madman in my presence? Shall this one come into my house?"

Psalm 59:1–5

For the choir director; *set to* Altashheth. A Mikhtam of David, when Saul sent *men* and they watched the house in order to kill him.

Deliver me from my
enemies, O my God;
Set me *securely* on high
away from those who
rise up against me.
² Deliver me from those
who do iniquity
And save me from men
of bloodshed.
³ For behold, they have set an
ambush for my life;
Fierce men launch an
attack against me,

Not for my transgression nor
for my sin, O LORD,
4 For no guilt of *mine*, they run and
set themselves against me.
Arouse Yourself to help me,
and see!
5 You, O LORD God of hosts,
the God of Israel,
Awake to punish all the nations;
Do not be gracious to any
who are treacherous in
iniquity.   Selah

Proverbs 15:31-33

31 He whose ear listens to the
life-giving reproof
Will dwell among the wise.
32 He who neglects discipline
despises himself,
But he who listens to reproof
acquires understanding.
33 The fear of the LORD is the
instruction for wisdom,
And before honor *comes*
humility.

Luke 24:36-53

36While they were telling these things,
He Himself stood in their midst and *said
to them, "Peace be to you." 37But they were
startled and frightened and thought that they
were seeing a spirit. 38And He said to them,
"Why are you troubled, and why do doubts
arise in your hearts? 39See My hands and
My feet, that it is I Myself; touch Me and see,
for a spirit does not have flesh and bones as
you see that I have." 40And when He had said
this, He showed them His hands and His feet.
41While they still could not believe *it* because

of their joy and amazement, He said to them,
"Have you anything here to eat?" 42They gave
Him a piece of a broiled fish; 43and He took
it and ate *it* before them.

44Now He said to them, "These are My words
which I spoke to you while I was still with you,
that all things which are written about Me in
the Law of Moses and the Prophets and the
Psalms must be fulfilled." 45Then He opened
their minds to understand the Scriptures,
46and He said to them, "Thus it is written, that
the Christ would suffer and rise again from
the dead the third day, 47and that repentance
for forgiveness of sins would be proclaimed
in His name to all the nations, beginning
from Jerusalem. 48You are witnesses of these
things. 49And behold, I am sending forth the
promise of My Father upon you; but you are
to stay in the city until you are clothed with
power from on high."

50And He led them out as far as Bethany,
and He lifted up His hands and blessed them.
51While He was blessing them, He parted from
them and was carried up into heaven. 52And
they, after worshiping Him, returned to Jerusalem with great joy, 53and were continually
in the temple praising God.

24:45 opened their minds. He undoubtedly
taught them from the OT, as He had on the
road to Emmaus. But the gist of the expression
also seems to convey a supernatural opening of
their minds to receive the truths He unfolded.
Whereas their understanding was once dull
(9:45), they finally saw clearly (Ps 119:18; Is
29:18-19; 2Co 3:14-16).

DAY 9: What was the resurrected body of Christ like?

In Luke 24:31, it tells us that after the two men had traveled with Jesus on the road to Emmaus,
"their eyes were opened," i.e., by God. They had been sovereignly kept from recognizing Him
until this point (v. 16). His resurrection body was glorified and altered from its previous appearance (see John's description in Rev 1:13-16), and this surely explains why even Mary did not
recognize Him at first (Jn 20:14-16). But in this case, God actively intervened to keep them from
recognizing Him until it was time for Him to depart.

"He vanished from their sight." His resurrection body, though real and tangible (Jn 20:27)—
and even capable of ingesting earthly food (vv. 42-43)—nonetheless possessed certain properties that indicate it was glorified, altered in a mysterious way (1Co 15:35-54; Php 3:21). Christ
could appear and disappear bodily, as seen in this text. His body could pass through solid
objects—such as the graveclothes (v. 12) or the walls and doors of a closed room (Jn 20:19,
26). He could apparently travel great distances in a moment, for by the time these disciples
returned to Jerusalem, Christ had already appeared to Peter (v. 34). The fact that He ascended
into heaven bodily demonstrated that His resurrection body was already fit for heaven. Yet it
was His body, the same one that was missing from the tomb, even retaining identifying features such as the nail wounds (Jn 20:25-27). He was no ghost or phantom.

MAY 10

1 Samuel 22:1–23:29

22 So David departed from there and escaped to the cave of Adullam; and when his brothers and all his father's household heard *of it,* they went down there to him. [2] Everyone who was in distress, and everyone who was in debt, and everyone who was discontented gathered to him; and he became captain over them. Now there were about four hundred men with him.

22:1 cave of Adullam. A cave near Adullam was David's refuge. Adullam, which may mean "refuge," was located in the western foothills of Judah (Jos 15:33), about 17 miles southwest of Jerusalem and 10 miles southeast of Gath. See titles of Pss 57,142, which could possibly refer to 1 Samuel 24:3. **brothers and all his father's household.** David's family members went down from Bethlehem to join David in Adullam, a journey of about 12 miles

---

[3] And David went from there to Mizpah of Moab; and he said to the king of Moab, "Please let my father and my mother come *and stay* with you until I know what God will do for me." [4] Then he left them with the king of Moab; and they stayed with him all the time that David was in the stronghold. [5] The prophet Gad said to David, "Do not stay in the stronghold; depart, and go into the land of Judah." So David departed and went into the forest of Hereth.

[6] Then Saul heard that David and the men who were with him had been discovered. Now Saul was sitting in Gibeah, under the tamarisk tree on the height with his spear in his hand, and all his servants were standing around him. [7] Saul said to his servants who stood around him, "Hear now, O Benjamites! Will the son of Jesse also give to all of you fields and vineyards? Will he make you all commanders of thousands and commanders of hundreds? [8] For all of you have conspired against me so that there is no one who discloses to me when my son makes *a covenant* with the son of Jesse, and there is none of you who is sorry for me or discloses to me that my son has stirred up my servant against me to lie in ambush, as *it is* this day." [9] Then Doeg the Edomite, who was standing by the servants of Saul, said, "I saw the son of Jesse coming to Nob, to Ahimelech

the son of Ahitub. [10] He inquired of the LORD for him, gave him provisions, and gave him the sword of Goliath the Philistine."

[11] Then the king sent someone to summon Ahimelech the priest, the son of Ahitub, and all his father's household, the priests who were in Nob; and all of them came to the king. [12] Saul said, "Listen now, son of Ahitub." And he answered, "Here I am, my lord." [13] Saul then said to him, "Why have you and the son of Jesse conspired against me, in that you have given him bread and a sword and have inquired of God for him, so that he would rise up against me by lying in ambush as *it is* this day?"

[14] Then Ahimelech answered the king and said, "And who among all your servants is as faithful as David, even the king's son-in-law, who is captain over your guard, and is honored in your house? [15] Did I *just* begin to inquire of God for him today? Far be it from me! Do not let the king impute anything to his servant *or* to any of the household of my father, for your servant knows nothing at all of this whole affair." [16] But the king said, "You shall surely die, Ahimelech, you and all your father's household!" [17] And the king said to the guards who were attending him, "Turn around and put the priests of the LORD to death, because their hand also is with David and because they knew that he was fleeing and did not reveal it to me." But the servants of the king were not willing to put forth their hands to attack the priests of the LORD. [18] Then the king said to Doeg, "You turn around and attack the priests." And Doeg the Edomite turned around and attacked the priests, and he killed that day eighty-five men who wore the linen ephod. [19] And he struck Nob the city of the priests with the edge of the sword, both men and women, children and infants; also oxen, donkeys, and sheep *he struck* with the edge of the sword.

[20] But one son of Ahimelech the son of Ahitub, named Abiathar, escaped and fled after David. [21] Abiathar told David that Saul had killed the priests of the LORD. [22] Then David said to Abiathar, "I knew on that day, when Doeg the Edomite was there, that he would surely tell Saul. I have brought about *the death* of every person in your father's household. [23] Stay with me; do not be afraid, for he who seeks my life seeks your life, for you are safe with me."

23 Then they told David, saying, "Behold, the Philistines are fighting against Keilah and are plundering the threshing floors." [2] So David inquired of the LORD, saying, "Shall I go and attack these Philistines?"

And the LORD said to David, "Go and attack the Philistines and deliver Keilah." ³But David's men said to him, "Behold, we are afraid here in Judah. How much more then if we go to Keilah against the ranks of the Philistines?" ⁴Then David inquired of the LORD once more. And the LORD answered him and said, "Arise, go down to Keilah, for I will give the Philistines into your hand." ⁵So David and his men went to Keilah and fought with the Philistines; and he led away their livestock and struck them with a great slaughter. Thus David delivered the inhabitants of Keilah.

⁶Now it came about, when Abiathar the son of Ahimelech fled to David at Keilah, that he came down with an ephod in his hand. ⁷When it was told Saul that David had come to Keilah, Saul said, "God has delivered him into my hand, for he shut himself in by entering a city with double gates and bars." ⁸So Saul summoned all the people for war, to go down to Keilah to besiege David and his men. ⁹Now David knew that Saul was plotting evil against him; so he said to Abiathar the priest, "Bring the ephod here." ¹⁰Then David said, "O LORD God of Israel, Your servant has heard for certain that Saul is seeking to come to Keilah to destroy the city on my account. ¹¹Will the men of Keilah surrender me into his hand? Will Saul come down just as Your servant has heard? O LORD God of Israel, I pray, tell Your servant." And the LORD said, "He will come down." ¹²Then David said, "Will the men of Keilah surrender me and my men into the hand of Saul?" And the LORD said, "They will surrender you." ¹³Then David and his men, about six hundred, arose and departed from Keilah, and they went wherever they could go. When it was told Saul that David had escaped from Keilah, he gave up the pursuit. ¹⁴David stayed in the wilderness in the strongholds, and remained in the hill country in the wilderness of Ziph. And Saul sought him every day, but God did not deliver him into his hand.

¹⁵Now David became aware that Saul had come out to seek his life while David was in the wilderness of Ziph at Horesh. ¹⁶And Jonathan, Saul's son, arose and went to David at Horesh, and encouraged him in God. ¹⁷Thus he said to him, "Do not be afraid, because the hand of Saul my father will not find you, and you will be king over Israel and I will be next to you; and Saul my father knows that also." ¹⁸So the two of them made a covenant before the LORD; and David stayed at Horesh while Jonathan went to his house.

¹⁹Then Ziphites came up to Saul at Gibeah, saying, "Is David not hiding with us in the strongholds at Horesh, on the hill of Hachilah, which is on the south of Jeshimon? ²⁰Now then, O king, come down according to all the desire of your soul to do so; and our part *shall be* to surrender him into the king's hand." ²¹Saul said, "May you be blessed of the LORD, for you have had compassion on me. ²²Go now, make more sure, and investigate and see his place where his haunt is, *and* who has seen him there; for I am told that he is very cunning. ²³So look, and learn about all the hiding places where he hides himself and return to me with certainty, and I will go with you; and if he is in the land, I will search him out among all the thousands of Judah."

²⁴Then they arose and went to Ziph before Saul. Now David and his men were in the wilderness of Maon, in the Arabah to the south of Jeshimon. ²⁵When Saul and his men went to seek *him*, they told David, and he came down to the rock and stayed in the wilderness of Maon. And when Saul heard *it*, he pursued David in the wilderness of Maon. ²⁶Saul went on one side of the mountain, and David and his men on the other side of the mountain; and David was hurrying to get away from Saul, for Saul and his men were surrounding David and his men to seize them. ²⁷But a messenger came to Saul, saying, "Hurry and come, for the Philistines have made a raid on the land." ²⁸So Saul returned from pursuing David and went to meet the Philistines; therefore they called that place the Rock of Escape. ²⁹David went up from there and stayed in the strongholds of Engedi.

Psalm 59:6–17

⁶ They return at evening,
    they howl like a dog,
And go around the city.
⁷ Behold, they belch forth
    with their mouth;
Swords are in their lips,
For, *they say*, "Who hears?"
⁸ But You, O LORD, laugh at them;
You scoff at all the nations.

⁹ *Because of* his strength I
    will watch for You,
For God is my stronghold.
¹⁰ My God in His lovingkindness
    will meet me;
God will let me look *triumphantly*
    upon my foes.
¹¹ Do not slay them, or my
    people will forget;
Scatter them by Your power,
    and bring them down,
O Lord, our shield.

¹² *On account of* the sin of their mouth
  and the words of their lips,
Let them even be caught
  in their pride,
And on account of curses and
  lies which they utter.
¹³ Destroy *them* in wrath, destroy
  them that they may be no more;
That *men* may know that
  God rules in Jacob
To the ends of the earth.   *Selah*
¹⁴ They return at evening,
  they howl like a dog,
And go around the city.
¹⁵ They wander about for food
And growl if they are not satisfied.

¹⁶ But as for me, I shall sing
  of Your strength;
Yes, I shall joyfully sing of Your
  lovingkindness in the morning,
For You have been my stronghold
And a refuge in the day
  of my distress.
¹⁷ O my strength, I will sing
  praises to You;
For God is my stronghold, the God
  who shows me lovingkindness.

Proverbs 16:1–2

16 The plans of the heart belong
     to man,
But the answer of the tongue
  is from the LORD.
² All the ways of a man are
  clean in his own sight,
But the LORD weighs the motives.

John 1:1–28

1 In the beginning was the Word, and the
Word was with God, and the Word was
God. ² He was in the beginning with God.
³ All things came into being through Him,
and apart from Him nothing came into being
that has come into being. ⁴ In Him was life,
and the life was the Light of men. ⁵ The Light
shines in the darkness, and the darkness did
not comprehend it.

⁶ There came a man sent from God, whose
name was John. ⁷ He came as a witness, to testify about the Light, so that all might believe
through him. ⁸ He was not the Light, but *he
came* to testify about the Light.

⁹ There was the true Light which, coming
into the world, enlightens every man. ¹⁰ He
was in the world, and the world was made
through Him, and the world did not know
Him. ¹¹ He came to His own, and those who
were His own did not receive Him. ¹² But as
many as received Him, to them He gave the
right to become children of God, *even* to those
who believe in His name, ¹³ who were born,
not of blood nor of the will of the flesh nor
of the will of man, but of God.

¹⁴ And the Word became flesh, and dwelt
among us, and we saw His glory, glory as
of the only begotten from the Father, full
of grace and truth. ¹⁵ John *testified about
Him and cried out, saying, "This was He of
whom I said, 'He who comes after me has
a higher rank than I, for He existed before
me.'" ¹⁶ For of His fullness we have all received, and grace upon grace. ¹⁷ For the Law
was given through Moses; grace and truth
were realized through Jesus Christ. ¹⁸ No one

**1:12 as many as received Him...to those who
believe in His name.** The second phrase describes the first. To receive Him who is the
Word of God means to acknowledge His claims,
place one's faith in Him, and thereby yield allegiance to Him. **gave.** The term emphasizes the
grace of God involved in the gift of salvation
(Eph 2:8–10). **the right.** Those who receive
Jesus, the Word, receive full authority to claim
the exalted title of "children of God." **His name.**
Denotes the character of the person himself.

1:14 the Word became flesh. While Christ as
God was uncreated and eternal, the word "became" emphasizes Christ's taking on humanity
(Heb 1:1–3; 2:14–18). This reality is surely the
most profound ever because it indicates that
the Infinite became finite; the Eternal was conformed to time; the Invisible became visible;
the supernatural One reduced Himself to the
natural. In the incarnation, however, the Word
did not cease to be God but became God in
human flesh, i.e., undiminished deity in human
form as a man (1Ti 3:16). **dwelt.** Meaning "to
pitch a tabernacle," or "live in a tent." The term
recalls to mind the Old Testament tabernacle
where God met with Israel before the temple
was constructed (Ex 25:8). It was called the
"tent of meeting" (Ex 33:7) where "the LORD
used to speak to Moses face to face, just as
a man speaks to his friend" (Ex 33:11). In the
New Testament, God chose to dwell among His
people in a far more personal way through becoming a man. In the OT, when the tabernacle
was completed, God's Shekinah presence filled
the entire structure (Ex 40:34; 1Ki 8:10). When
the Word became flesh, the glorious presence
of deity was embodied in Him (Col 2:9).

has seen God at any time; the only begotten God who is in the bosom of the Father, He has explained *Him*.

[19] This is the testimony of John, when the Jews sent to him priests and Levites from Jerusalem to ask him, "Who are you?" [20] And he confessed and did not deny, but confessed, "I am not the Christ." [21] They asked him, "What then? Are you Elijah?" And he *said, "I am not." "Are you the Prophet?" And he answered, "No." [22] Then they said to him, "Who are you, so that we may give an answer to those who sent us? What do you say about yourself?"

[23] He said, "I am A VOICE OF ONE CRYING IN THE WILDERNESS, 'MAKE STRAIGHT THE WAY OF THE LORD,' as Isaiah the prophet said."

[24] Now they had been sent from the Pharisees. [25] They asked him, and said to him, "Why then are you baptizing, if you are not the Christ, nor Elijah, nor the Prophet?" [26] John answered them saying, "I baptize in water, *but* among you stands One whom you do not know. [27] *It is* He who comes after me, the thong of whose sandal I am not worthy to untie." [28] These things took place in Bethany beyond the Jordan, where John was baptizing.

DAY 10: Note the powerful words loaded into John 1:1.

"In the beginning." In contrast to 1 John 1:1 where John used a similar phrase ("from the beginning") to refer to the starting point of Jesus' ministry and gospel preaching, this phrase parallels Genesis 1:1 where the same phrase is used. John used the phrase in an absolute sense to refer to the beginning of the time-space-material universe. "Was." The verb highlights the eternal preexistence of the Word, i.e., Jesus Christ. Before the universe began, the Second Person of the Trinity always existed; i.e., He always was (see 8:58). This word is used in contrast with the verb "was made" (or "were made") in v. 3, which indicate a beginning in time. Because of John's theme that Jesus Christ is the eternal God, the Second Person of the Trinity, he did not include a genealogy as Matthew and Luke did. In terms of Jesus' humanity, He had a human genealogy; but in terms of His deity, He has no genealogy.

"The Word." John borrowed the use of the term "Word" not only from the vocabulary of the Old Testament but also from Greek philosophy, in which the term was essentially impersonal, signifying the rational principle of "divine reason," "mind," or even "wisdom." John, however, imbued the term entirely with Old Testament and Christian meaning (e.g., Ge 1:3 where God's Word brought the world into being; Pss 33:6; 107:20; Pr 8:27 where God's Word is His powerful self-expression in creation, wisdom, revelation, and salvation) and made it refer to a person, i.e., Jesus Christ. Greek philosophical usage, therefore, is not the exclusive background of John's thought. Strategically, the term "Word" serves as a bridge-word to reach not only Jews but also the unsaved Greeks. John chose this concept because both Jews and Greeks were familiar with it.

"The Word was with God." The Word, as the Second Person of the Trinity, was in intimate fellowship with God the Father throughout all eternity. Yet, although the Word enjoyed the splendors of heaven and eternity with the Father (Is. 6:1–13; see 12:41; 17:5), He willingly gave up His heavenly status, taking the form of a man, and became subject to the death of the cross (Php 2:6–8). "Was God." The Greek construction emphasizes that the Word had all the essence or attributes of Deity, i.e., Jesus the Messiah was fully God (Col 2:9). Even in His incarnation when He emptied Himself, He did not cease to be God but took on a genuine human nature/body and voluntarily refrained from the independent exercise of the attributes of Deity.

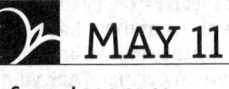

MAY 11

1 Samuel 24:1–25:44

24 Now when Saul returned from pursuing the Philistines, he was told, saying, "Behold, David is in the wilderness of Engedi." [2] Then Saul took three thousand chosen men from all Israel and went to seek David and his men in front of the Rocks of the Wild Goats. [3] He came to the sheepfolds on the way, where there *was* a cave; and Saul went in to relieve himself. Now David and his men were sitting in the inner recesses of the cave. [4] The men

of David said to him, "Behold, *this is* the day of which the LORD said to you, 'Behold; I am about to give your enemy into your hand,

24:4 the day of which the LORD said to you. David's men perhaps believed that God had providentially placed Saul in the same cave where they were hiding so David could kill the king. However, nothing revelatory had previously been said by the Lord that indicated He wanted David to lift a hand against Saul.

and you shall do to him as it seems good to you.' " Then David arose and cut off the edge of Saul's robe secretly. [5] It came about afterward that David's conscience bothered him because he had cut off the edge of Saul's *robe*. [6] So he said to his men, "Far be it from me because of the LORD that I should do this thing to my lord, the LORD'S anointed, to stretch out my hand against him, since he is the LORD'S anointed." [7] David persuaded his men with *these* words and did not allow them to rise up against Saul. And Saul arose, left the cave, and went on *his* way.

24:5 David's conscience bothered him. David was able to cut off a piece of Saul's robe undetected. However, touching Saul's clothing was tantamount to touching his person, and David's conscience troubled him on this account.

24:6 LORD's anointed. David recognized that the Lord Himself had placed Saul into the kingship. Thus the judgment and removal of Saul had to be left to the Lord.

[8] Now afterward David arose and went out of the cave and called after Saul, saying, "My lord the king!" And when Saul looked behind him, David bowed with his face to the ground and prostrated himself. [9] David said to Saul, "Why do you listen to the words of men, saying, 'Behold, David seeks to harm you'? [10] Behold, this day your eyes have seen that the LORD had given you today into my hand in the cave, and some said to kill you, but *my eye* had pity on you; and I said, 'I will not stretch out my hand against my lord, for he is the LORD'S anointed.' [11] Now, my father, see! Indeed, see the edge of your robe in my hand! For in that I cut off the edge of your robe and did not kill you, know and perceive that there is no evil or rebellion in my hands, and I have not sinned against you, though you are lying in wait for my life to take it. [12] May the LORD judge between you and me, and may the LORD avenge me on you; but my hand shall not be against you. [13] As the proverb of the ancients says, 'Out of the wicked comes forth wickedness'; but my hand shall not be against you. [14] After whom has the king of Israel come out? Whom are you pursuing? A dead dog, a single flea? [15] The LORD therefore be judge and decide between you and me; and may He see and plead my cause and deliver me from your hand."

[16] When David had finished speaking these words to Saul, Saul said, "Is this your voice, my son David?" Then Saul lifted up his voice and wept. [17] He said to David, "You are more righteous than I; for you have dealt well with me, while I have dealt wickedly with you. [18] You have declared today that you have done good to me, that the LORD delivered me into your hand and *yet* you did not kill me. [19] For if a man finds his enemy, will he let him go away safely? May the LORD therefore reward you with good in return for what you have done to me this day. [20] Now, behold, I know that you will surely be king, and that the kingdom of Israel will be established in your hand. [21] So now swear to me by the LORD that you will not cut off my descendants after me and that you will not destroy my name from my father's household." [22] David swore to Saul. And Saul went to his home, but David and his men went up to the stronghold.

25 Then Samuel died; and all Israel gathered together and mourned for him, and buried him at his house in Ramah. And David arose and went down to the wilderness of Paran.

[2] Now *there was* a man in Maon whose business was in Carmel; and the man was very rich, and he had three thousand sheep and a thousand goats. And it came about while he was shearing his sheep in Carmel [3] (now the man's name was Nabal, and his wife's name was Abigail. And the woman was intelligent and beautiful in appearance, but the man was harsh and evil in *his* dealings, and he was a Calebite), [4] that David heard in the wilderness that Nabal was shearing his sheep. [5] So David sent ten young men; and David said to the young men, "Go up to Carmel, visit Nabal and greet him in my name; [6] and thus you shall say, 'Have a long life, peace be to you, and peace be to your house, and peace be to all that you have. [7] Now I have heard that you have shearers; now your shepherds have been with us and we have not insulted them, nor have they missed anything all the days they were in Carmel. [8] Ask your young men and they will tell you. Therefore let *my* young men find favor in your eyes, for we have come on a festive day. Please give whatever you find at hand to your servants and to your son David.' "

[9] When David's young men came, they spoke to Nabal according to all these words in David's name; then they waited. [10] But Nabal answered David's servants and said, "Who is David? And who is the son of Jesse? There are many servants today who are each breaking

away from his master. ¹¹ Shall I then take my bread and my water and my meat that I have slaughtered for my shearers, and give it to men whose origin I do not know?" ¹² So David's young men retraced their way and went back; and they came and told him according to all these words. ¹³ David said to his men, "Each *of you* gird on his sword." So each man girded on his sword. And David also girded on his sword, and about four hundred men went up behind David while two hundred stayed with the baggage.

¹⁴ But one of the young men told Abigail, Nabal's wife, saying, "Behold, David sent messengers from the wilderness to greet our master, and he scorned them. ¹⁵ Yet the men were very good to us, and we were not insulted, nor did we miss anything as long as we went about with them, while we were in the fields. ¹⁶ They were a wall to us both by night and by day, all the time we were with them tending the sheep. ¹⁷ Now therefore, know and consider what you should do, for evil is plotted against our master and against all his household; and he is such a worthless man that no one can speak to him."

¹⁸ Then Abigail hurried and took two hundred *loaves* of bread and two jugs of wine and five sheep already prepared and five measures of roasted grain and a hundred clusters of raisins and two hundred cakes of figs, and loaded *them* on donkeys. ¹⁹ She said to her young men, "Go on before me; behold, I am coming after you." But she did not tell her husband Nabal. ²⁰ It came about as she was riding on her donkey and coming down by the hidden part of the mountain, that behold, David and his men were coming down toward her; so she met them. ²¹ Now David had said, "Surely in vain I have guarded all that this *man* has in the wilderness, so that nothing was missed of all that belonged to him; and he has returned me evil for good. ²² May God do so to the enemies of David, and more also, if by morning I leave *as much as* one male of any who belong to him."

²³ When Abigail saw David, she hurried and dismounted from her donkey, and fell on her face before David and bowed herself to the ground. ²⁴ She fell at his feet and said, "On me alone, my lord, be the blame. And please let your maidservant speak to you, and listen to the words of your maidservant. ²⁵ Please do not let my lord pay attention to this worthless man, Nabal, for as his name is, so is he. Nabal is his name and folly is with him; but I your maidservant did not see the young men of my lord whom you sent.

²⁶ "Now therefore, my lord, as the LORD lives, and as your soul lives, since the LORD has restrained you from shedding blood, and from avenging yourself by your own hand, now then let your enemies and those who seek evil against my lord, be as Nabal. ²⁷ Now let this gift which your maidservant has brought to my lord be given to the young men who accompany my lord. ²⁸ Please forgive the transgression of your maidservant; for the LORD will certainly make for my lord an enduring house, because my lord is fighting the battles of the LORD, and evil will not be found in you all your days. ²⁹ Should anyone rise up to pursue you and to seek your life, then the life of my lord shall be bound in the bundle of the living with the LORD your God; but the lives of your enemies He will sling out as from the hollow of a sling. ³⁰ And when the LORD does for my lord according to all the good that He has spoken concerning you, and appoints you ruler over Israel, ³¹ this will not cause grief or a troubled heart to my lord, both by having shed blood without cause and by my lord having avenged himself. When the LORD deals well with my lord, then remember your maidservant."

³² Then David said to Abigail, "Blessed be the LORD God of Israel, who sent you this day to meet me, ³³ and blessed be your discernment, and blessed be you, who have kept me this day from bloodshed and from avenging myself by my own hand. ³⁴ Nevertheless, as the LORD God of Israel lives, who has restrained me from harming you, unless you had come quickly to meet me, surely there would not have been left to Nabal until the morning light *as much as* one male." ³⁵ So David received from her hand what she had brought him and said to her, "Go up to your house in peace. See, I have listened to you and granted your request."

³⁶ Then Abigail came to Nabal, and behold, he was holding a feast in his house, like the feast of a king. And Nabal's heart was merry within him, for he was very drunk; so she did not tell him anything at all until the morning light. ³⁷ But in the morning, when the wine had gone out of Nabal, his wife told him these things, and his heart died within him so that he became *as* a stone. ³⁸ About ten days later, the LORD struck Nabal and he died.

³⁹ When David heard that Nabal was dead, he said, "Blessed be the LORD, who has pleaded the cause of my reproach from the hand of Nabal and has kept back His servant from evil. The LORD has also returned the evildoing of Nabal on his own head." Then

David sent a proposal to Abigail, to take her as his wife. 40 When the servants of David came to Abigail at Carmel, they spoke to her, saying, "David has sent us to you to take you as his wife." 41 She arose and bowed with her face to the ground and said, "Behold, your maidservant is a maid to wash the feet of my lord's servants." 42 Then Abigail quickly arose, and rode on a donkey, with her five maidens who attended her; and she followed the messengers of David and became his wife.

43 David had also taken Ahinoam of Jezreel, and they both became his wives.

44 Now Saul had given Michal his daughter, David's wife, to Palti the son of Laish, who was from Gallim.

Psalm 60:1–5

For the choir director; according to Shushan Eduth. A Mikhtam of David, to teach; when he struggled with Aram-naharaim and with Aram-zobah, and Joab returned, and smote twelve thousand of Edom in the Valley of Salt.

O God, You have rejected us.
    You have broken us;
You have been angry; O, restore us.
2 You have made the land quake,
    You have split it open;
    Heal its breaches, for it totters.
3 You have made Your people
    experience hardship;
    You have given us wine to drink
    that makes us stagger.
4 You have given a banner to
    those who fear You,
    That it may be displayed
    because of the truth.   Selah
5 That Your beloved may be delivered,
    Save with Your right hand,
    and answer us!

Proverbs 16:3

3 Commit your works to the LORD
    And your plans will be established.

John 1:29–51

29 The next day he *saw Jesus coming to him and *said, "Behold, the Lamb of God who takes away the sin of the world! 30 This is He on behalf of whom I said, 'After me comes

16:3 Commit. Literally "roll upon" in the sense of both total trust (3:5–6) and submission to the will of God (Pss 22:8; 37:5; 119:133); He will fulfill your righteous plans.

a Man who has a higher rank than I, for He existed before me.' 31 I did not recognize Him, but so that He might be manifested to Israel, I came baptizing in water." 32 John testified saying, "I have seen the Spirit descending as a dove out of heaven, and He remained upon Him. 33 I did not recognize Him, but He who sent me to baptize in water said to me, 'He upon whom you see the Spirit descending and remaining upon Him, this is the One who baptizes in the Holy Spirit.' 34 I myself have seen, and have testified that this is the Son of God."

35 Again the next day John was standing with two of his disciples, 36 and he looked at Jesus as He walked, and *said, "Behold, the Lamb of God!" 37 The two disciples heard him speak, and they followed Jesus. 38 And Jesus turned and saw them following, and *said to them, "What do you seek?" They said to Him, "Rabbi (which translated means Teacher), where are You staying?" 39 He *said to them, "Come, and you will see." So they came and saw where He was staying; and they stayed with Him that day, for it was about the tenth hour. 40 One of the two who heard John *speak* and followed Him, was Andrew, Simon Peter's brother. 41 He *found first his own brother Simon and *said to him, "We have found the Messiah" (which translated means Christ). 42 He brought him to Jesus. Jesus looked at him and said, "You are Simon the son of John; you shall be called Cephas" (which is translated Peter).

43 The next day He purposed to go into Galilee, and He *found Philip. And Jesus *said to him, "Follow Me." 44 Now Philip was from

1:41 Messiah. The term "Messiah" is a transliteration of a Hebrew or Aram. verbal adjective that means "Anointed One." It comes from a verb that means "to anoint" someone as an action involved in consecrating that person to a particular office or function. While the term at first applied to the king of Israel ("the LORD's anointed"—1Sa 16:6), the High Priest ("the anointed priest," Lv 4:3) and, in one passage, the patriarchs ("My anointed ones," Ps 105:15), the term eventually came to point above all to the prophesied "Coming One" or "Messiah" in His role as prophet, priest, and king. The term "Christ," a Greek word (verbal adjective) that comes from a verb meaning "to anoint," is used in translating the Hebrew term, so that the terms "Messiah" or "Christ" are titles and not personal names of Jesus.

Bethsaida, of the city of Andrew and Peter. ⁴⁵Philip *found Nathanael and *said to him, "We have found Him of whom Moses in the Law and *also* the Prophets wrote—Jesus of Nazareth, the son of Joseph." ⁴⁶Nathanael said to him, "Can any good thing come out of Nazareth?" Philip *said to him, "Come and see." ⁴⁷Jesus saw Nathanael coming to Him, and *said of him, "Behold, an Israelite indeed, in whom there is no deceit!" ⁴⁸Nathanael *said to Him, "How do You know me?" Jesus answered and said to him, "Before Philip called you, when you were under the fig tree, I saw you." ⁴⁹Nathanael answered Him, "Rabbi, You are the Son of God; You are the King of Israel." ⁵⁰Jesus answered and said to him, "Because I said to you that I saw you under the fig tree, do you believe? You will see greater things than these." ⁵¹And He *said to him, "Truly, truly, I say to you, you will see the heavens opened and the angels of God ascending and descending on the Son of Man."

DAY 11: How did John the Baptist characterize Jesus Christ?

John the Baptist's witness to Jesus in John 1 introduces a lengthy list of titles applied to Jesus: Lamb of God (vv. 29, 36), Rabbi (vv. 38, 49), Messiah/Christ (v. 41), Son of God (vv. 34, 49), King of Israel (v. 49), Son of Man (v. 51), and "Him of whom Moses in the Law and also the prophets wrote" (v. 45).

In John 1:29, John the Baptist refers to Jesus as "The Lamb of God." The use of a lamb for sacrifice was very familiar to Jews. A lamb was used as a sacrifice during Passover (Ex 12:1–36); a lamb was led to the slaughter in the prophecies of Isaiah (Is. 53:7); a lamb was offered in the daily sacrifices of Israel (Lv 14:12–21; Heb 10:5–7). John the Baptist used this expression as a reference to the ultimate sacrifice of Jesus on the cross to atone for the sins of the world, a theme which John the apostle carries throughout his writings (19:36; see Rev 5:1–6; 7:17; 17:14) and that appears in other New Testament writings (e.g., 1Pe 1:19).

"Who takes away the sin of the world." In this context "world" has the connotation of humanity in general, not specifically every person. The use of the singular "sin" in conjunction with "of the world" indicates that Jesus' sacrifice for sin potentially reaches all human beings without distinction (1Jn 2:2). John makes clear, however, that its efficacious effect is only for those who receive Christ (vv. 11–12).

John adds that "I saw the Spirit descending...upon Him" (v. 32). God had previously communicated to John that this sign was to indicate the promised Messiah (v. 33), so when John witnessed this act, he was able to identify the Messiah as Jesus (Mt 3:16; Mk 1:10; Lk 3:22). "I myself have seen, and have testified that this is the Son of God" (v. 34). Although, in a limited sense, believers can be called "children of God" (v. 12; Mt 5:9; Ro 8:14), John uses this phrase with the full force as a title that points to the unique oneness and intimacy that Jesus sustains to the Father as "Son." The term carries the idea of the deity of Jesus as Messiah (v. 49; 5:16–30; 2Sa 7:14; Ps 2:7; Heb 1:1–9).

 # MAY 12

1 Samuel 26:1–27:12

26 Then the Ziphites came to Saul at Gibeah, saying, "Is not David hiding on the hill of Hachilah, *which is* before Jeshimon?" ²So Saul arose and went down to the wilderness of Ziph, having with him three thousand chosen men of Israel, to search for David in the wilderness of Ziph. ³Saul camped in the hill of Hachilah, which is before Jeshimon, beside the road, and David was staying in the wilderness. When he saw that Saul came after him into the wilderness, ⁴David sent out spies, and he knew that Saul was definitely coming. ⁵David then arose and came to the place where Saul had camped. And David saw the place where Saul lay, and Abner the son of Ner, the commander of his army; and Saul was lying in the circle of the camp, and the people were camped around him.

⁶Then David said to Ahimelech the Hittite and to Abishai the son of Zeruiah, Joab's brother, saying, "Who will go down with me to Saul in the camp?" And Abishai said, "I will go down with you." ⁷So David and Abishai came to the people by night, and behold, Saul lay sleeping inside the circle of the camp with his spear stuck in the ground at his head; and Abner and the people were lying around him. ⁸Then Abishai said to David, "Today God has delivered your enemy into your hand; now therefore, please let me strike him with the spear to the ground with one stroke, and I will not strike him the second time." ⁹But David said to Abishai, "Do not destroy him, for who can stretch out his hand against the LORD'S

anointed and be without guilt?" ¹⁰David also said, "As the LORD lives, surely the LORD will strike him, or his day will come that he dies, or he will go down into battle and perish. ¹¹The LORD forbid that I should stretch out my hand against the LORD'S anointed; but now please take the spear that is at his head and the jug of water, and let us go." ¹²So David took the spear and the jug of water from *beside* Saul's head, and they went away, but no one saw or knew *it*, nor did any awake, for they were all asleep, because a sound sleep from the LORD had fallen on them.

¹³Then David crossed over to the other side and stood on top of the mountain at a distance *with* a large area between them. ¹⁴David called to the people and to Abner the son of Ner, saying, "Will you not answer, Abner?" Then Abner replied, "Who are you who calls to the king?" ¹⁵So David said to Abner, "Are you not a man? And who is like you in Israel? Why then have you not guarded your lord the king? For one of the people came to destroy the king your lord. ¹⁶This thing that you have done is not good. As the LORD lives, *all* of you must surely die, because you did not guard your lord, the LORD'S anointed. And now, see where the king's spear is and the jug of water that was at his head."

¹⁷Then Saul recognized David's voice and said, "Is this your voice, my son David?" And David said, "It is my voice, my lord the king." ¹⁸He also said, "Why then is my lord pursuing his servant? For what have I done? Or what evil is in my hand? ¹⁹Now therefore, please let my lord the king listen to the words of his servant. If the LORD has stirred you up against me, let Him accept an offering; but if it is men, cursed are they before the LORD, for they have driven me out today so that I would have no attachment with the inheritance of the LORD, saying, 'Go, serve other gods.' ²⁰Now then, do not let my blood fall to the ground away from the presence of the LORD; for the king of Israel has come out to search for a single flea, just as one hunts a partridge in the mountains."

²¹Then Saul said, "I have sinned. Return, my son David, for I will not harm you again because my life was precious in your sight this day. Behold, I have played the fool and have committed a serious error." ²²David replied, "Behold the spear of the king! Now let one of the young men come over and take it. ²³The LORD will repay each man *for* his righteousness and his faithfulness; for the LORD delivered you into *my* hand today, but I refused to stretch out my hand against the

26:21 I have sinned. As in 24:17, Saul confessed his sin and wrongdoing. Although Saul may have been sincere, he could not be trusted and David wisely did not accept his invitation to return with him. **I have played the fool.** Saul had been foolish in his actions toward David, as had Nabal.

LORD'S anointed. ²⁴Now behold, as your life was highly valued in my sight this day, so may my life be highly valued in the sight of the LORD, and may He deliver me from all distress." ²⁵Then Saul said to David, "Blessed are you, my son David; you will both accomplish much and surely prevail." So David went on his way, and Saul returned to his place.

27 Then David said to himself, "Now I will perish one day by the hand of Saul. There is nothing better for me than to escape into the land of the Philistines. Saul then will despair of searching for me anymore in all the territory of Israel, and I will escape from his hand." ²So David arose and crossed over, he and the six hundred men who were with him, to Achish the son of Maoch, king of Gath. ³And David lived with Achish at Gath, he and his men, each with his household, *even* David with his two wives, Ahinoam the Jezreelitess, and Abigail the Carmelitess, Nabal's widow. ⁴Now it was told Saul that David had fled to Gath, so he no longer searched for him.

27:1 by the hand of Saul. In direct contrast to Saul's word that David would prevail (26:25), David thought that Saul would ultimately kill him. This anxious thinking and the fear that fell upon him explain David's actions in this chapter. God had told him to stay in Judah (22:5), but he was afraid and sought protection again among the Philistine enemies of Israel (21:10–15).

⁵Then David said to Achish, "If now I have found favor in your sight, let them give me a place in one of the cities in the country, that I may live there; for why should your servant live in the royal city with you?" ⁶So Achish gave him Ziklag that day; therefore Ziklag has belonged to the kings of Judah to this day. ⁷The number of days that David lived in the country of the Philistines was a year and four months.

8 Now David and his men went up and raided the Geshurites and the Girzites and the Amalekites; for they were the inhabitants of the land from ancient times, as you come to Shur even as far as the land of Egypt. 9 David attacked the land and did not leave a man or a woman alive, and he took away the sheep, the cattle, the donkeys, the camels, and the clothing. Then he returned and came to Achish. 10 Now Achish said, "Where have you made a raid today?" And David said, "Against the Negev of Judah and against the Negev of the Jerahmeelites and against the Negev of the Kenites." 11 David did not leave a man or a woman alive to bring to Gath, saying, "Otherwise they will tell about us, saying, 'So has David done and so *has been* his practice all the time he has lived in the country of the Philistines.'" 12 So Achish believed David, saying, "He has surely made himself odious among his people Israel; therefore he will become my servant forever."

Psalm 60:6-12

6   God has spoken in His holiness:
     "I will exult, I will portion out
        Shechem and measure out
           the valley of Succoth.
7   "Gilead is Mine, and Manasseh
        is Mine;
     Ephraim also is the helmet
        of My head;
     Judah is My scepter.
8   "Moab is My washbowl;
     Over Edom I shall throw My shoe;
     Shout loud, O Philistia,
        because of Me!"

9   Who will bring me into
        the besieged city?
     Who will lead me to Edom?
10 Have not You Yourself,
        O God, rejected us?
     And will You not go forth with
        our armies, O God?
11 O give us help against the adversary,
     For deliverance by man is in vain.
12 Through God we shall do valiantly,
     And it is He who will tread
        down our adversaries.

Proverbs 16:4-5

4   The LORD has made everything
        for its own purpose,
     Even the wicked for the day of evil.
5   Everyone who is proud in heart is
        an abomination to the LORD;
     Assuredly, he will not be unpunished.

John 2:1-25

2 On the third day there was a wedding in Cana of Galilee, and the mother of Jesus was there; 2 and both Jesus and His disciples were invited to the wedding. 3 When the wine ran out, the mother of Jesus *said to Him,

2:2 both Jesus and His disciples were invited. The fact that Jesus, His mother, and His disciples all attended the wedding suggests that the wedding may have been for a relative or close family friend. The disciples who accompanied Him are the 5 mentioned in chap. 1: Andrew, Simon Peter, Philip, Nathanael, and the unnamed disciple (1:35) who was surely John, who also witnessed this miracle.

"They have no wine." 4 And Jesus *said to her, "Woman, what does that have to do with us? My hour has not yet come." 5 His mother *said to the servants, "Whatever He says to you, do it." 6 Now there were six stone waterpots set there for the Jewish custom of purification, containing twenty or thirty gallons each. 7 Jesus *said to them, "Fill the waterpots with water." So they filled them up to the brim. 8 And He *said to them, "Draw *some* out now and take it to the headwaiter." So they took it *to him.* 9 When the headwaiter tasted the water which had become wine, and did not know where it came from (but the servants who had drawn the water knew), the headwaiter *called the bridegroom, 10 and *said to him, "Every man serves the good wine first, and when *the people* have drunk freely, *then he serves* the poorer *wine; but* you have kept the good wine until now." 11 This beginning of *His* signs Jesus did in Cana of Galilee, and manifested His glory, and His disciples believed in Him.

12 After this He went down to Capernaum, He and His mother and *His* brothers and His disciples; and they stayed there a few days.

13 The Passover of the Jews was near, and Jesus went up to Jerusalem. 14 And He found in the temple those who were selling oxen and sheep and doves, and the money changers seated *at their tables.* 15 And He made a scourge of cords, and drove *them* all out of the temple, with the sheep and the oxen; and He poured out the coins of the money changers and overturned their tables; 16 and to those who were selling the doves He said, "Take these things away; stop making My Father's house a place of business." 17 His

disciples remembered that it was written, "ZEAL FOR YOUR HOUSE WILL CONSUME ME." [18] The Jews then said to Him, "What sign do You show us as your authority for doing these things?" [19] Jesus answered them, "Destroy this temple, and in three days I will raise it up." [20] The Jews then said, "It took forty-six years to build this temple, and will You raise it up in three days?" [21] But He was speaking of the temple of His body. [22] So when He was raised from the dead, His disciples remembered that He said this; and they believed the Scripture and the word which Jesus had spoken.

[23] Now when He was in Jerusalem at the Passover, during the feast, many believed in His name, observing His signs which He was doing. [24] But Jesus, on His part, was not entrusting Himself to them, for He knew all men, [25] and because He did not need anyone to testify concerning man, for He Himself knew what was in man.

2:23–24 many believed in His name....But Jesus...was not entrusting Himself to them. John based these two phrases on the same Greek verb for "believe." This verse subtly reveals the true nature of belief from a biblical standpoint. Because of what they knew of Jesus from His miraculous signs, many came to believe in Him. However, Jesus made it His habit not to wholeheartedly "entrust" or "commit" Himself to them because He knew their hearts. Verse 24 indicates that Jesus looked for genuine conversion rather than enthusiasm for the spectacular. The latter verse also leaves a subtle doubt as to the genuineness of the conversion of some (8:31–32). This emphatic contrast between vv. 23–24 in terms of type of trust, therefore, reveals that, literally, "belief into His name" involved much more than intellectual assent. It called for whole-hearted commitment of one's life as Jesus' disciple (Mt 10:37; 16:24–26).

DAY 12: What did Jesus mean by His comments about the temple in John 2?

In John 2:18, the Jews demanded that Jesus show some type of miraculous sign that would indicate His authority for the actions that He had just taken in regulating the activities of the temple. Their demand of a sign reveals that they had not grasped the significance of Jesus' rebuke that centered in their need for proper attitudes and holiness in worship. Such an action itself constituted a "sign" of Jesus' person and authority. Moreover, they were requesting from Jesus a crass display of miracles on demand, further displaying their unbelief.

"Destroy this temple, and in three days I will raise it up" (v. 19). At His trial, the authorities charged Jesus (Mk 14:29, 58) with making a threatening statement against the temple, revealing that they did not understand Jesus' response here. Once again John's Gospel supplements the other Gospels at this point by indicating that Jesus enigmatically referred to His resurrection. As with His usage of parables, Jesus' cryptic statement most likely was designed to reveal the truth to His disciples but conceal its meaning from unbelievers who questioned Him (Mt 13:10–11). Only after His resurrection, however, did the disciples understand the real significance of this statement (v. 22; Mt 12:40). Importantly, through the death and resurrection of Christ, temple worship in Jerusalem was destroyed (see 4:21) and reinstituted in the hearts of those who were built into a spiritual temple called the church (Eph 2:19–22).

"It took forty-six years to build this temple" (v. 20). This was not a reference to the Solomonic temple, since it had been destroyed during the Babylonian conquest in 586 B.C. When the captives returned from Babylon, Zerubbabel and Joshua began rebuilding the temple (Ezr 1–4). Encouraged by the prophets Haggai and Zechariah (Ezr 5:1–6:18), the Jews completed the work in 516 B.C. In 20/19 B.C., Herod the Great began a reconstruction and expansion. Workers completed the main part of the project in 10 years, but other parts were still being constructed even at the time Jesus cleansed the temple. The famous "Wailing Wall" is built on part of the Herodian temple foundation.

MAY 13

1 Samuel 28:1-25

28 Now it came about in those days that the Philistines gathered their armed camps for war, to fight against Israel. And

Achish said to David, "Know assuredly that you will go out with me in the camp, you and your men." [2] David said to Achish, "Very well, you shall know what your servant can do." So Achish said to David, "Very well, I will make you my bodyguard for life."

[3] Now Samuel was dead, and all Israel had

28:3 mediums and spiritists. By divine law, they were banned from Israel (Dt 18:11), and Israel was not to be defiled by them (Lv 19:31). Turning to them was tantamount to playing the harlot and would result in God setting His face against the person and cutting him off from among His people (Lv 20:6). Mediums and spiritists were to be put to death by stoning (Lv 20:27). Even Saul understood this and had previously dealt with the issue (v. 9).

28:12 the woman saw Samuel. Though questions have arisen as to the nature of Samuel's appearance, the text clearly indicates that Samuel, not an apparition, was evident to the eyes of the medium. God miraculously permitted the actual spirit of Samuel to speak (vv. 16–19). Because she understood her inability to raise the dead in this manner, she immediately knew 1) that it must have been by the power of God and 2) that her disguised inquirer must be Saul.

lamented him and buried him in Ramah, his own city. And Saul had removed from the land those who were mediums and spiritists. ⁴So the Philistines gathered together and came and camped in Shunem; and Saul gathered all Israel together and they camped in Gilboa. ⁵When Saul saw the camp of the Philistines, he was afraid and his heart trembled greatly. ⁶When Saul inquired of the LORD, the LORD did not answer him, either by dreams or by Urim or by prophets. ⁷Then Saul said to his servants, "Seek for me a woman who is a medium, that I may go to her and inquire of her." And his servants said to him, "Behold, there is a woman who is a medium at En-dor."

⁸Then Saul disguised himself by putting on other clothes, and went, he and two men with him, and they came to the woman by night; and he said, "Conjure up for me, please, and bring up for me whom I shall name to you." ⁹But the woman said to him, "Behold, you know what Saul has done, how he has cut off those who are mediums and spiritists from the land. Why are you then laying a snare for my life to bring about my death?" ¹⁰Saul vowed to her by the LORD, saying, "As the LORD lives, no punishment shall come upon you for this thing." ¹¹Then the woman said, "Whom shall I bring up for you?" And he said, "Bring up Samuel for me." ¹²When the woman saw Samuel, she cried out with a loud voice; and the woman spoke to Saul, saying, "Why have you deceived me? For you are Saul." ¹³The king said to her, "Do not be afraid; but what do you see?" And the woman said to Saul, "I see a divine being coming up out of the earth." ¹⁴He said to her, "What is his form?" And she said, "An old man is coming up, and he is wrapped with a robe." And Saul knew that it was Samuel, and he bowed with his face to the ground and did homage.

¹⁵Then Samuel said to Saul, "Why have you disturbed me by bringing me up?" And

Saul answered, "I am greatly distressed; for the Philistines are waging war against me, and God has departed from me and no longer answers me, either through prophets or by dreams; therefore I have called you, that you may make known to me what I should do." ¹⁶Samuel said, "Why then do you ask me, since the LORD has departed from you and has become your adversary? ¹⁷The LORD has done accordingly as He spoke through me; for the LORD has torn the kingdom out of your hand and given it to your neighbor, to David. ¹⁸As you did not obey the LORD and did not execute His fierce wrath on Amalek, so the LORD has done this thing to you this day. ¹⁹Moreover the LORD will also give over Israel along with you into the hands of the Philistines, therefore tomorrow you and your sons will be with me. Indeed the LORD will give over the army of Israel into the hands of the Philistines!"

²⁰Then Saul immediately fell full length upon the ground and was very afraid because of the words of Samuel; also there was no strength in him, for he had eaten no food all day and all night. ²¹The woman came to Saul and saw that he was terrified, and said to him, "Behold, your maidservant has obeyed you, and I have taken my life in my hand and have listened to your words which you spoke to me. ²²So now also, please listen to the voice of your maidservant, and let me set a piece of bread before you that *you may* eat and have strength when you go on *your* way." ²³But he refused and said, "I will not eat." However, his servants together with the woman urged him, and he listened to them. So he arose from the ground and sat on the bed. ²⁴The woman had a fattened calf in the house, and she quickly slaughtered it; and she took flour, kneaded it and baked unleavened bread from it. ²⁵She brought *it* before Saul and his servants, and they ate. Then they arose and went away that night.

Psalm 61:1-4

For the choir director; on a stringed
instrument. *A Psalm* of David.

Hear my cry, O God;
Give heed to my prayer.
2 From the end of the earth I call to
You when my heart is faint;
Lead me to the rock that
is higher than I.
3 For You have been a refuge for me,
A tower of strength
against the enemy.
4 Let me dwell in Your tent forever;
Let me take refuge in the shelter
of Your wings. *Selah*

Proverbs 16:6

6 By lovingkindness and truth
iniquity is atoned for,
And by the fear of the LORD
one keeps away from evil.

John 3:1-15

3 Now there was a man of the Pharisees,
named Nicodemus, a ruler of the Jews;
2 this man came to Jesus by night and said
to Him, "Rabbi, we know that You have come
from God *as* a teacher; for no one can do these
signs that You do unless God is with him."
3 Jesus answered and said to him, "Truly, truly,
I say to you, unless one is born again he cannot see the kingdom of God."
4 Nicodemus *said to Him, "How can a man
be born when he is old? He cannot enter a
second time into his mother's womb and be
born, can he?" 5 Jesus answered, "Truly, truly, I
say to you, unless one is born of water and the
Spirit he cannot enter into the kingdom of God.
6 That which is born of the flesh is flesh, and

that which is born of the Spirit is spirit. 7 Do
not be amazed that I said to you, 'You must be
born again.' 8 The wind blows where it wishes
and you hear the sound of it, but do not know
where it comes from and where it is going; so
is everyone who is born of the Spirit."

9 Nicodemus said to Him, "How can these
things be?" 10 Jesus answered and said to him,
"Are you the teacher of Israel and do not understand these things? 11 Truly, truly, I say to
you, we speak of what we know and testify
of what we have seen, and you do not accept
our testimony. 12 If I told you earthly things
and you do not believe, how will you believe
if I tell you heavenly things? 13 No one has
ascended into heaven, but He who descended
from heaven: the Son of Man. 14 As Moses lifted
up the serpent in the wilderness, even so must
the Son of Man be lifted up; 15 so that whoever
believes will in Him have eternal life.

3:15 eternal life. This is the first of 17 references
to "eternal life" in John's Gospel. The same Greek
phrase is translated in some versions as "everlasting life." The two expressions appear in the New
Testament nearly 50 times. Eternal life refers not
only to eternal quantity but divine quality of life.
It means literally "life of the age to come" and
refers therefore to resurrection and heavenly existence in perfect glory and holiness. This life for
believers in the Lord Jesus is experienced before
heaven is reached. This "eternal life" is in essence
nothing less than participation in the eternal life
of the Living Word, Jesus Christ. It is the life of
God in every believer, yet not fully manifest until
the resurrection (Ro 8:19-23; Php 3:20-21).

DAY 13: What does it mean to be "born again"?

In John 3:3, Jesus answered a question that Nicodemus does not even ask. He read Nicodemus's
heart and came to the very core of his problem, i.e., the need for spiritual transformation or
regeneration produced by the Holy Spirit. He tells Nicodemus that he must be "born again."
The phrase literally means "born from above." New birth is an act of God whereby eternal life
is imparted to the believer (2Co 5:17; Titus 3:5; 1Pe 1:3; 1Jn 2:29; 3:9; 4:7; 5:1, 4, 18). Chapter 1:12-13
indicates that "born again" also carries the idea "to become children of God" through trust in
the name of the incarnate Word.

Unless one is born again, he "cannot see the kingdom of God." In context, this is primarily a
reference to participation in the millennial kingdom at the end of the age, fervently anticipated
by the Pharisees and other Jews. Since the Pharisees were supernaturalists, they naturally and
eagerly expected the coming of the prophesied resurrection of the saints and institution of
the messianic kingdom (Is. 11:1-16; Da 12:2). Their problem was that they thought that mere
physical lineage and keeping of religious externals qualified them for entrance into the kingdom rather than the needed spiritual transformation which Jesus emphasized (see 8:33-39; Gal
6:15). The coming of the kingdom at the end of the age can be described as the "regeneration"
of the world (Mt 19:28), but regeneration of the individual is required before the end of the
world in order to enter the kingdom.

Restating it, Jesus said that one must be "born of water and the Spirit" (v. 5). Jesus referred not to literal water here but to the need for "cleansing" (see Eze 36:24–27). When water is used figuratively in the Old Testament, it consistently refers to renewal or spiritual cleansing, especially when used in conjunction with "spirit" (Nu 19:17–19; Ps 51:9–10; Is. 32:15; 44:3–5; 55:1–3; Jer 2:13; Joel 2:28–29). Thus, Jesus made reference to the spiritual washing or purification of the soul, accomplished by the Holy Spirit through the Word of God at the moment of salvation (Eph 5:26; Titus 3:5), required for belonging to His kingdom.

MAY 14

1 Samuel 29:1–31:13

29 Now the Philistines gathered together all their armies to Aphek, while the Israelites were camping by the spring which is in Jezreel. ² And the lords of the Philistines were proceeding on by hundreds and by thousands, and David and his men were proceeding on in the rear with Achish. ³ Then the commanders of the Philistines said, "What *are* these Hebrews *doing here*?" And Achish said to the commanders of the Philistines, "Is this not David, the servant of Saul the king of Israel, who has been with me these days, or *rather* these years, and I have found no fault in him from the day he deserted *to me* to this day?" ⁴ But the commanders of the Philistines were angry with him, and the commanders of the Philistines said to him, "Make the man go back, that he may return to his place where you have assigned him, and do not let him go down to battle with us, or in the battle he may become an adversary to us. For with what could this *man* make himself acceptable to his lord? *Would it* not *be* with the heads of these men? ⁵ Is this not David, of whom they sing in the dances, saying,

'Saul has slain his thousands,
And David his ten thousands'?"

⁶ Then Achish called David and said to him, "*As* the LORD lives, you *have been* upright, and your going out and your coming in with me in the army are pleasing in my sight; for I have not found evil in you from the day of your coming to me to this day. Nevertheless, you are not pleasing in the sight of the lords. ⁷ Now therefore return and go in peace, that you may not displease the lords of the Philistines." ⁸ David said to Achish, "But what have I done? And what have you found in your servant from the day when I came before you to this day, that I may not go and fight against the enemies of my lord the king?" ⁹ But Achish replied to David, "I know that you are pleasing in my sight, like an angel of God; nevertheless the commanders of the Philistines have said, 'He must not go up with us to the battle.' ¹⁰ Now then arise early in the morning with the servants of your lord who have come with you, and as soon as you have arisen early in the morning and have light, depart." ¹¹ So David arose early, he and his men, to depart in the morning to return to the land of the Philistines. And the Philistines went up to Jezreel.

30 Then it happened when David and his men came to Ziklag on the third day, that the Amalekites had made a raid on the Negev and on Ziklag, and had overthrown Ziklag and burned it with fire; ² and they took captive the women *and all* who were in it, both small and great, without killing anyone, and carried *them* off and went their way. ³ When David and his men came to the city, behold, it was burned with fire, and their wives and their sons and their daughters had been taken captive. ⁴ Then David and the people who were with him lifted their voices and wept until there was no strength in them to weep. ⁵ Now David's two wives had been taken captive, Ahinoam the Jezreelitess and Abigail the widow of Nabal the Carmelite. ⁶ Moreover David was greatly distressed because the people spoke of stoning him, for all the people were embittered, each one because of his sons and his daughters. But David strengthened himself in the LORD his God.

⁷ Then David said to Abiathar the priest, the son of Ahimelech, "Please bring me the

30:6 distressed…embittered. Arriving home to the reality of their great tragedy caused David immense distress and provoked the wickedness of his men to entertain the treasonous idea of stoning him. Having not inquired of the Lord before his departure to support Achish in battle, David was in need of God's getting his attention. **strengthened himself in the LORD his God.** This was the key to David being a man after God's heart (1Sa 13:14; Ac 13:22).

ephod." So Abiathar brought the ephod to David. ⁸David inquired of the LORD, saying, "Shall I pursue this band? Shall I overtake them?" And He said to him, "Pursue, for you will surely overtake them, and you will surely rescue *all*." ⁹So David went, he and the six hundred men who were with him, and came to the brook Besor, *where* those left behind remained. ¹⁰But David pursued, he and four hundred men, for two hundred who were too exhausted to cross the brook Besor remained *behind*.

¹¹Now they found an Egyptian in the field and brought him to David, and gave him bread and he ate, and they provided him water to drink. ¹²They gave him a piece of fig cake and two clusters of raisins, and he ate; then his spirit revived. For he had not eaten bread or drunk water for three days and three nights. ¹³David said to him, "To whom do you belong? And where are you from?" And he said, "I am a young man of Egypt, a servant of an Amalekite; and my master left me behind when I fell sick three days ago. ¹⁴We made a raid on the Negev of the Cherethites, and on that which belongs to Judah, and on the Negev of Caleb, and we burned Ziklag with fire." ¹⁵Then David said to him, "Will you bring me down to this band?" And he said, "Swear to me by God that you will not kill me or deliver me into the hands of my master, and I will bring you down to this band."

¹⁶When he had brought him down, behold, they were spread over all the land, eating and drinking and dancing because of all the great spoil that they had taken from the land of the Philistines and from the land of Judah. ¹⁷David slaughtered them from the twilight until the evening of the next day; and not a man of them escaped, except four hundred young men who rode on camels and fled. ¹⁸So David recovered all that the Amalekites had taken, and rescued his two wives. ¹⁹But nothing of theirs was missing, whether small or great, sons or daughters, spoil or anything that they had taken for themselves; David brought *it* all back. ²⁰So David had captured all the sheep and the cattle *which the people*

30:19 nothing...was missing. In spite of David's previous failures, God showed Himself to be more than gracious and abundant in His stewardship of the wives, children, livestock, and possessions of David and his men.

drove ahead of the *other* livestock, and they said, "This is David's spoil."

²¹When David came to the two hundred men who were too exhausted to follow David, who had also been left at the brook Besor, and they went out to meet David and to meet the people who were with him, then David approached the people and greeted them. ²²Then all the wicked and worthless men among those who went with David said, "Because they did not go with us, we will not give them any of the spoil that we have recovered, except to every man his wife and his children, that they may lead *them* away and depart." ²³Then David said, "You must not do so, my brothers, with what the LORD has given us, who has kept us and delivered into our hand the band that came against us. ²⁴And who will listen to you in this matter? For as his share is who goes down to the battle, so shall his share be who stays by the baggage; they shall share alike." ²⁵So it has been from that day forward, that he made it a statute and an ordinance for Israel to this day.

²⁶Now when David came to Ziklag, he sent *some* of the spoil to the elders of Judah, to his friends, saying, "Behold, a gift for you from the spoil of the enemies of the LORD: ²⁷to those who were in Bethel, and to those who were in Ramoth of the Negev, and to those who were in Jattir, ²⁸and to those who were in Aroer, and to those who were in Siphmoth, and to those who were in Eshtemoa, ²⁹and to those who were in Racal, and to those who were in the cities of the Jerahmeelites, and to those who were in the cities of the Kenites, ³⁰and to those who were in Hormah, and to those who were in Borashan, and to those who were in Athach, ³¹and to those who were in Hebron, and to all the places where David himself and his men were accustomed to go."

31 Now the Philistines were fighting against Israel, and the men of Israel fled from before the Philistines and fell slain on Mount Gilboa. ²The Philistines overtook Saul and his sons; and the Philistines killed Jonathan and Abinadab and Malchi-shua the sons of Saul. ³The battle went heavily against Saul, and the archers hit him; and he was badly wounded by the archers. ⁴Then Saul said to his armor bearer, "Draw your sword and pierce me through with it, otherwise these uncircumcised will come and pierce me through and make sport of me." But his armor bearer would not, for he was greatly afraid. So Saul took his sword and fell on it. ⁵When his armor bearer saw that Saul was dead, he also fell on his sword and died with

31:4 these uncircumcised. A common term of derision used among Israelites to designate non-Israelites. Circumcision was given as the sign of the Abrahamic Covenant in Genesis17:10–14. **make sport.** Having engaged in several battles against the Philistines, Saul had succeeded in provoking their hatred and resentment. As the king, Saul had certainly received especially cruel treatment from the hands of his enemies, who would have likely made sport of him and tortured him before his death. **Saul took his sword and fell on it.** Though Saul's suicide is considered by some to be an act of heroism, Saul should have found his strength and courage in God as David did in 23:16 and 30:6 to fight to the end or to surrender. Saul's suicide is the ultimate expression of his faithlessness towards God at this moment in his life.

him. ⁶Thus Saul died with his three sons, his armor bearer, and all his men on that day together.

⁷When the men of Israel who were on the other side of the valley, with those who were beyond the Jordan, saw that the men of Israel had fled and that Saul and his sons were dead, they abandoned the cities and fled; then the Philistines came and lived in them.

⁸It came about on the next day when the Philistines came to strip the slain, that they found Saul and his three sons fallen on Mount Gilboa. ⁹They cut off his head and stripped off his weapons, and sent *them* throughout the land of the Philistines, to carry the good news to the house of their idols and to the people. ¹⁰They put his weapons in the temple of Ashtaroth, and they fastened his body to the wall of Beth-shan. ¹¹Now when the inhabitants of Jabesh-gilead heard what the Philistines had done to Saul, ¹²all the valiant men rose and walked all night, and took the body of Saul and the bodies of his sons from the wall of Beth-shan, and they came to Jabesh and burned them there. ¹³They took their bones and buried them under the tamarisk tree at Jabesh, and fasted seven days.

Psalm 61:5–8

⁵ For You have heard my vows, O God;
  You have given *me* the inheritance
    of those who fear Your name.
⁶ You will prolong the king's life;
  His years will be as many
    generations.
⁷ He will abide before God forever;

Appoint lovingkindness and truth
    that they may preserve him.
⁸ So I will sing praise to
    Your name forever,
  That I may pay my vows day by day.

Proverbs 16:7–9

⁷ When a man's ways are
    pleasing to the LORD,
  He makes even his enemies to
    be at peace with him.
⁸ Better is a little with righteousness
  Than great income with injustice.
⁹ The mind of man plans his way,
  But the LORD directs his steps.

61:7 forever. The Davidic Covenant guaranteed that on the basis of God's merciful and faithful dealings with David and the nation, David's descendants would rule on the throne of Israel forever (2Sa 7; Pss 40:11; 89:4, 33–37).

16:9 Sovereign God overrules the plans of men to fulfill His purposes. (See Ge 50:20; 1Ki 12:15; Ps 119:133; Jer 10:23; Da 5:23–30; 1Co 3:19–20.)

John 3:16–36

¹⁶"For God so loved the world, that He gave His only begotten Son, that whoever believes in Him shall not perish, but have eternal life. ¹⁷For God did not send the Son into the world to judge the world, but that the world might be saved through Him. ¹⁸He who believes in Him is not judged; he who does not believe has been judged already, because he has not believed in the name of the only begotten Son of God. ¹⁹This is the judgment, that the Light has come into the world, and men loved the darkness rather than the Light, for their deeds were evil. ²⁰For everyone who does evil hates the Light, and does not come to the Light for fear that his deeds will be exposed. ²¹But he who practices the truth comes to the Light, so

3:16 For God so loved the world. The Son's mission is bound up in the supreme love of God for the evil, sinful "world" of humanity (6:32, 51; 12:47) that is in rebellion against Him. The word "so" emphasizes the intensity or greatness of His love. The Father gave His unique and beloved Son to die on behalf of sinful men (2Co 5:21).

that his deeds may be manifested as having been wrought in God."

²²After these things Jesus and His disciples came into the land of Judea, and there He was spending time with them and baptizing. ²³John also was baptizing in Aenon near Salim, because there was much water there; and *people* were coming and were being baptized— ²⁴for John had not yet been thrown into prison.

²⁵Therefore there arose a discussion on the part of John's disciples with a Jew about purification. ²⁶And they came to John and said to him, "Rabbi, He who was with you beyond the Jordan, to whom you have testified, behold, He is baptizing and all are coming to Him." ²⁷John answered and said, "A man can receive nothing unless it has been given him from heaven. ²⁸You yourselves are my witnesses that I said, 'I am not the Christ,' but, 'I have been sent ahead of Him.' ²⁹He who has the bride is the bridegroom; but the friend of the bridegroom, who stands and hears him, rejoices greatly because of the bridegroom's voice. So this joy of mine has been made full. ³⁰He must increase, but I must decrease.

³¹"He who comes from above is above all, he who is of the earth is from the earth and speaks of the earth. He who comes from heaven is above all. ³²What He has seen and heard, of that He testifies; and no one receives His testimony. ³³He who has received His testimony has set his seal to *this*, that God is true. ³⁴For He whom God has sent speaks the words of God; for He gives the Spirit without measure. ³⁵The Father loves the Son and has given all things into His hand. ³⁶He who believes in the Son has eternal life; but he who does not obey the Son will not see life, but the wrath of God abides on him."

DAY 14: How did John the Baptist respond to the growing ministry of Christ?

The potential conflict between John and Jesus as depicted in John 3:26 was heightened by the fact that both were engaged in ministry in close proximity to each other. Because baptism is mentioned in v. 22, Jesus may have been close to Jericho near the fords of the Jordan, while John was a short distance north baptizing at Aenon. John's followers were especially disturbed by the fact that so many were flocking to Jesus whereas formerly they had come to John.

John's response was to emphasize God's sovereign authority in granting any ministry opportunity (v. 27). It must be "given him from heaven." And he conveyed his understanding of his own role through the use of a parable (v. 29). The "friend of the bridegroom" was the ancient equivalent of the best man who organized the details and presided over the Judean wedding. This friend found his greatest joy in watching the ceremony proceed without problems. Most likely, John was also alluding to Old Testament passages where faithful Israel is depicted as the bride of the Lord (Is. 62:4–5; Jer 2:2; Hos 2:16–20).

In vv. 31–36, John the Baptist gave 5 reasons for Christ's superiority to him: 1) Christ had a heavenly origin (v. 31); 2) Christ knew what was true by firsthand experience (v. 32); 3) Christ's testimony always agreed with God (v. 33); 4) Christ experienced the Holy Spirit in an unlimited manner (v. 34); and 5) Christ was supreme because the Father sovereignly had granted that status to Him (v. 35).

In a fitting climax to the chapter (v. 36), John the Baptist laid out two alternatives, genuine faith and defiant disobedience, thereby bringing to the forefront the threat of looming judgment. As John faded from the forefront, he offered an invitation to faith in the Son and clearly expressed the ultimate consequence of failure to believe, i.e., "the wrath of God."

 # MAY 15

2 Samuel 1:1–2:32

1 Now it came about after the death of Saul, when David had returned from the slaughter of the Amalekites, that David remained two days in Ziklag. ²On the third day, behold, a man came out of the camp from Saul, with his clothes torn and dust on his head. And it came about when he came to David that he fell to the ground and prostrated himself. ³Then David said to him, "From where do you come?" And he said to him, "I have escaped from the camp of Israel." ⁴David said to him, "How did things go? Please tell me." And he said, "The people have fled from the battle, and also many of the people have fallen and are dead; and Saul and Jonathan his son are dead also." ⁵So David said to the young man who told him, "How do you know that Saul and his son Jonathan are dead?" ⁶The young man who told him said, "By chance I happened to be on Mount Gilboa, and behold, Saul was leaning on his spear. And behold, the chariots and the horsemen pursued him

closely. ⁷When he looked behind him, he saw me and called to me. And I said, 'Here I am.' ⁸He said to me, 'Who are you?' And I answered him, 'I am an Amalekite.' ⁹Then he said to me, 'Please stand beside me and kill me, for agony has seized me because my life still lingers in me.' ¹⁰So I stood beside him and killed him, because I knew that he could not live after he had fallen. And I took the crown which *was* on his head and the bracelet which *was* on his arm, and I have brought them here to my lord."

¹¹Then David took hold of his clothes and tore them, and *so* also *did* all the men who *were* with him. ¹²They mourned and wept and fasted until evening for Saul and his son Jonathan and for the people of the LORD and the house of Israel, because they had fallen by the sword. ¹³David said to the young man who told him, "Where are you from?" And he answered, "I am the son of an alien, an Amalekite." ¹⁴Then David said to him, "How is it you were not afraid to stretch out your hand to destroy the LORD'S anointed?" ¹⁵And David called one of the young men and said, "Go, cut him down." So he struck him and he died. ¹⁶David said to him, "Your blood is on your head, for your mouth has testified against you, saying, 'I have killed the LORD'S anointed.'"

¹⁷Then David chanted with this lament over Saul and Jonathan his son, ¹⁸and he told *them* to teach the sons of Judah *the song of* the bow; behold, it is written in the book of Jashar.

¹⁹ "Your beauty, O Israel, is slain
    on your high places!
  How have the mighty fallen!
²⁰ "Tell *it* not in Gath,
    Proclaim it not in the
    streets of Ashkelon,

Or the daughters of the
    Philistines will rejoice,
The daughters of the
    uncircumcised will exult.
²¹ "O mountains of Gilboa,
  Let not dew or rain be on you,
    nor fields of offerings;
  For there the shield of the
    mighty was defiled,
  The shield of Saul, not
    anointed with oil.
²² "From the blood of the slain,
    from the fat of the mighty,
  The bow of Jonathan did
    not turn back,
  And the sword of Saul did
    not return empty.
²³ "Saul and Jonathan, beloved
    and pleasant in their life,
  And in their death they
    were not parted;
  They were swifter than eagles,
  They were stronger than lions.
²⁴ "O daughters of Israel, weep
    over Saul,
  Who clothed you luxuriously
    in scarlet,
  Who put ornaments of gold
    on your apparel.
²⁵ "How have the mighty fallen in
    the midst of the battle!
  Jonathan is slain on your high
    places.
²⁶ "I am distressed for you, my
    brother Jonathan;
  You have been very pleasant
    to me.
  Your love to me was more
    wonderful
  Than the love of women.
²⁷ "How have the mighty fallen,
    And the weapons of war
    perished!"

1:19 Your beauty, O Israel. Literally the gazelle or antelope of Israel, the chosen symbol of youthful elegance and symmetry, most likely referring to Jonathan. Thus, the song began and ended with Saul's noble son (vv. 25–26). **high places.** These were open-air worship sites generally established at high elevations. In this case the high place was Mt. Gilboa, where Saul had died. **How have the mighty fallen!** They were not only Israel's slain "beauty," but Saul and Jonathan were mighty men who had fallen in battle. This phrase is repeated as a refrain in vv. 25 and 27.

2 Then it came about afterwards that David inquired of the LORD, saying, "Shall I go up to one of the cities of Judah?" And the LORD said to him, "Go up." So David said, "Where shall I go up?" And He said, "To Hebron." ²So David went up there, and his two wives also, Ahinoam the Jezreelitess and Abigail the widow of Nabal the Carmelite. ³And David brought up his men who *were* with him, each with his household; and they lived in the cities of Hebron. ⁴Then the men of Judah came and there anointed David king over the house of Judah.

And they told David, saying, "It was the

2:4 anointed David king. David had already been privately anointed king by Samuel (1Sa 16:3). This anointing recognized his rule in the southern area of Judah. Later he would be anointed as king over all Israel (2Sa 5:3). **men of Jabesh-gilead.** Jabesh, a city of Israel east of the Jordan, demonstrated its loyalty to Saul by giving him a proper burial (1Sa 31:11–13).

---

men of Jabesh-gilead who buried Saul." ⁵ David sent messengers to the men of Jabesh-gilead, and said to them, "May you be blessed of the LORD because you have shown this kindness to Saul your lord, and have buried him. ⁶ Now may the LORD show lovingkindness and truth to you; and I also will show this goodness to you, because you have done this thing. ⁷ Now therefore, let your hands be strong and be valiant; for Saul your lord is dead, and also the house of Judah has anointed me king over them."

⁸ But Abner the son of Ner, commander of Saul's army, had taken Ish-bosheth the son of Saul and brought him over to Mahanaim. ⁹ He made him king over Gilead, over the Ashurites, over Jezreel, over Ephraim, and over Benjamin, even over all Israel. ¹⁰ Ish-bosheth, Saul's son, was forty years old when he became king over Israel, and he was king for two years. The house of Judah, however, followed David. ¹¹ The time that David was king in Hebron over the house of Judah was seven years and six months.

¹² Now Abner the son of Ner, went out from Mahanaim to Gibeon with the servants of Ish-bosheth the son of Saul. ¹³ And Joab the son of Zeruiah and the servants of David went out and met them by the pool of Gibeon; and they sat down, one on the one side of the pool and the other on the other side of the pool. ¹⁴ Then Abner said to Joab, "Now let the young men arise and hold a contest before us." And Joab said, "Let them arise." ¹⁵ So they arose and went over by count, twelve for Benjamin and Ish-bosheth the son of Saul, and twelve of the servants of David. ¹⁶ Each one of them seized his opponent by the head and *thrust* his sword in his opponent's side; so they fell down together. Therefore that place was called Helkath-hazzurim, which is in Gibeon. ¹⁷ That day the battle was very severe, and Abner and the men of Israel were beaten before the servants of David.

¹⁸ Now the three sons of Zeruiah were there, Joab and Abishai and Asahel; and Asahel *was as* swift-footed as one of the gazelles which is in the field. ¹⁹ Asahel pursued Abner and did not turn to the right or to the left from following Abner. ²⁰ Then Abner looked behind him and said, "Is that you, Asahel?" And he answered, "It is I." ²¹ So Abner said to him, "Turn to your right or to your left, and take hold of one of the young men for yourself, and take for yourself his spoil." But Asahel was not willing to turn aside from following him. ²² Abner repeated again to Asahel, "Turn aside from following me. Why should I strike you to the ground? How then could I lift up my face to your brother Joab?" ²³ However, he refused to turn aside; therefore Abner struck him in the belly with the butt end of the spear, so that the spear came out at his back. And he fell there and died on the spot. And it came about that all who came to the place where Asahel had fallen and died, stood still.

²⁴ But Joab and Abishai pursued Abner, and when the sun was going down, they came to the hill of Ammah, which is in front of Giah by the way of the wilderness of Gibeon. ²⁵ The sons of Benjamin gathered together behind Abner and became one band, and they stood on the top of a certain hill. ²⁶ Then Abner called to Joab and said, "Shall the sword devour forever? Do you not know that it will be bitter in the end? How long will you refrain from telling the people to turn back from following their brothers?" ²⁷ Joab said, "As God lives, if you had not spoken, surely then the people would have gone away in the morning, each from following his brother." ²⁸ So Joab blew the trumpet; and all the people halted and pursued Israel no longer, nor did they continue to fight anymore. ²⁹ Abner and his men then went through the Arabah all that night; so they crossed the Jordan, walked all morning, and came to Mahanaim.

³⁰ Then Joab returned from following Abner; when he had gathered all the people together, nineteen of David's servants besides Asahel were missing. ³¹ But the servants of David had struck down many of Benjamin and Abner's men, *so that* three hundred and sixty men died. ³² And they took up Asahel and buried him in his father's tomb which was in Bethlehem. Then Joab and his men went all night until the day dawned at Hebron.

Psalm 62:1–4

For the choir director; according
to Jeduthun. A Psalm of David.

M y soul *waits* in silence for God only;
From Him is my salvation.
² He only is my rock and my salvation,
My stronghold; I shall not
be greatly shaken.

³ How long will you assail a man,
That you may murder *him,* all of you,
Like a leaning wall, like a
   tottering fence?
⁴ They have counseled only to thrust
   him down from his high position;
They delight in falsehood;
They bless with their mouth,
But inwardly they curse.   *Selah*

Proverbs 16:10–12

¹⁰ A divine decision is in the
   lips of the king;
His mouth should not
   err in judgment.
¹¹ A just balance and scales
   belong to the LORD;
All the weights of the bag
   are His concern.
¹² It is an abomination for kings
   to commit wicked acts,
For a throne is established
   on righteousness.

John 4:1–30

4 Therefore when the Lord knew that the
Pharisees had heard that Jesus was making and baptizing more disciples than John ²(although Jesus Himself was not baptizing, but His disciples were), ³He left Judea and went away again into Galilee. ⁴And He had to pass through Samaria. ⁵So He *came to a city of Samaria called Sychar, near the parcel of ground that Jacob gave to his son Joseph; ⁶and Jacob's well was there. So Jesus, being wearied from His journey, was sitting thus by the well. It was about the sixth hour.

⁷There *came a woman of Samaria to draw water. Jesus *said to her, "Give Me a drink." ⁸For His disciples had gone away into the city to buy food. ⁹Therefore the Samaritan woman *said to Him, "How is it that You, being a Jew, ask me for a drink since I am a Samaritan woman?" (For Jews have no dealings with Samaritans.) ¹⁰Jesus answered and said to her, "If you knew the gift of God, and who it is who says to you, 'Give Me a drink,' you would have asked Him, and He would have given you living water." ¹¹She *said to Him, "Sir, You have nothing to draw with and the well is deep; where then do You get that living water? ¹²You are not greater than our father Jacob, are You, who gave us the well, and drank of it himself and his sons and his cattle?" ¹³Jesus answered and said to her, "Everyone who drinks of this water will thirst again; ¹⁴but whoever drinks of the water that I will give him shall never thirst; but the water

4:4 Samaria. When the nation of Israel split politically after Solomon's rule, King Omri named the capital of the northern kingdom of Israel "Samaria" (1Ki 16:24). The name eventually referred to the entire district and sometimes to the entire northern kingdom, which had been taken captive (capital, Samaria) by Assyria in 722 B.C. (2Ki 17:1–6). While Assyria led most of the populace of the 10 northern tribes away (into the region which today is northern Iraq), it left a sizable population of Jews in the northern Samaritan region and transported many non-Jews into Samaria. These groups intermingled to form a mixed race through intermarriage. Eventually, tension developed between the Jews who returned from captivity and the Samaritans. The Samaritans withdrew from the worship of Yahweh at Jerusalem and established their worship at Mt. Gerizim in Samaria (vv. 20–22). Samaritans regarded only the Pentateuch as authoritative. As a result of this history, Jews repudiated Samaritans and considered them heretical. Intense ethnic and cultural tensions raged historically between the two groups so that both avoided contact as much as possible (v. 9; Ezr 4:1–24; Ne 4:1–6; Lk 10:25–37).

4:10 living water. The Old Testament is the background for this term, which has important metaphorical significance. In Jeremiah 2:13, Yahweh decries the disobedient Jews for rejecting Him, the "fountain of living waters." The Old Testament prophets looked forward to a time when "living waters will flow out of Jerusalem" (Eze 47:9; Zec 14:8). The Old Testament metaphor spoke of the knowledge of God and His grace which provides cleansing, spiritual life, and the transforming power of the Holy Spirit (Is 1:16–18; 12:3; 44:3; Eze 36:25–27). John applies these themes to Jesus Christ as the living water which is symbolic of eternal life mediated by the Holy Spirit from Him (v. 14; 6:35; 7:37–39). Jesus used the woman's need for physical water to sustain life in this arid region in order to serve as an object lesson for her need for spiritual transformation.

that I will give him will become in him a well of water springing up to eternal life."

¹⁵The woman *said to Him, "Sir, give me this water, so I will not be thirsty nor come all the way here to draw." ¹⁶He *said to her, "Go, call your husband and come here." ¹⁷The woman answered and said, "I have no husband." Jesus *said to her, "You have correctly said, 'I have no husband'; ¹⁸for you have had five husbands, and the one whom you now

have is not your husband; this you have said truly." [19] The woman *said to Him, "Sir, I perceive that You are a prophet. [20] Our fathers worshiped in this mountain, and you *people* say that in Jerusalem is the place where men ought to worship." [21] Jesus *said to her, "Woman, believe Me, an hour is coming when neither in this mountain nor in Jerusalem will you worship the Father. [22] You worship what you do not know; we worship what we know, for salvation is from the Jews. [23] But an hour is coming, and now is, when the true worshipers will worship the Father in spirit and truth; for such people the Father seeks to be His worshipers. [24] God is spirit,

and those who worship Him must worship in spirit and truth." [25] The woman *said to Him, "I know that Messiah is coming (He who is called Christ); when that One comes, He will declare all things to us." [26] Jesus *said to her, "I who speak to you am *He*."

[27] At this point His disciples came, and they were amazed that He had been speaking with a woman, yet no one said, "What do You seek?" or, "Why do You speak with her?" [28] So the woman left her waterpot, and went into the city and *said to the men, [29] "Come, see a man who told me all the things that I *have* done; this is not the Christ, is it?" [30] They went out of the city, and were coming to Him.

DAY 15: What aspect of worship toward God is absolutely essential?

In His conversation with the Samaritan woman in John 4:24, Jesus reminded her that "God is spirit." This verse represents the classical statement on the nature of God as Spirit. The phrase means that God is invisible (Col 1:15; 1Ti 1:17; Heb 11:27) as opposed to the physical or material nature of man (1:18; 3:6). The word order of this phrase puts an emphasis on "spirit," and the statement is essentially emphatic. Man could never comprehend the invisible God unless He revealed Himself, as He did in Scripture and the Incarnation.

"Must worship." Jesus is not speaking of a desirable element in worship but that which is absolutely necessary. "In spirit and truth." The word "spirit" does not refer to the Holy Spirit but to the human spirit. Jesus' point here is that a person must worship not simply by external conformity to religious rituals and places (outwardly) but inwardly ("in spirit") with the proper heart attitude. The reference to "truth" refers to worship of God consistent with the revealed Scripture and centered on the "Word made flesh" who ultimately revealed His Father (see 14:6).

The Samaritans also anticipated Messiah's coming. The Samaritan woman responded, pushing toward the future. "I who speak to you am He"—Jesus forthrightly declared Himself to be Messiah, though His habit was to avoid such declarations to His own Jewish people, who had such crassly political and militaristic views regarding Messiah (10:24; Mk 9:41). The "He" in this translation is not in the original Greek for Jesus literally said "I who speak to you am." The usage of "I am" is reminiscent of 8:58. This claim constitutes the main point of the story regarding the Samaritan woman, upon which all worship is centered.

MAY 16

2 Samuel 3:1–4:12

3 Now there was a long war between the house of Saul and the house of David; and David grew steadily stronger, but the house of Saul grew weaker continually.

[2] Sons were born to David at Hebron: his firstborn was Amnon, by Ahinoam the Jezreelitess; [3] and his second, Chileab, by Abigail the widow of Nabal the Carmelite; and the third, Absalom the son of Maacah, the daughter of Talmai, king of Geshur; [4] and the fourth, Adonijah the son of Haggith; and the fifth, Shephatiah the son of Abital; [5] and the sixth, Ithream, by David's wife Eglah. These were born to David at Hebron.

[6] It came about while there was war be-

tween the house of Saul and the house of David that Abner was making himself strong in the house of Saul. [7] Now Saul had a concubine whose name was Rizpah, the daughter of Aiah; and Ish-bosheth said to Abner, "Why have you gone in to my father's concubine?" [8] Then Abner was very angry over the words of Ish-bosheth and said, "Am I a dog's head that belongs to Judah? Today I show kindness to the house of Saul your father, to his brothers and to his friends, and have not delivered you into the hands of David; and yet today you charge me with a guilt concerning the woman. [9] May God do so to Abner, and more also, if as the LORD has sworn to David, I do not accomplish this for him, [10] to transfer the kingdom from the house of Saul and to establish the throne of David over Israel and over Judah, from Dan even to Beersheba." [11] And he could no longer answer Abner a word, because he was afraid of him.

¹²Then Abner sent messengers to David in his place, saying, "Whose is the land? Make your covenant with me, and behold, my hand shall be with you to bring all Israel over to you." ¹³He said, "Good! I will make a covenant with you, but I demand one thing of you, namely, you shall not see my face unless you first bring Michal, Saul's daughter, when you come to see me." ¹⁴So David sent messengers to Ish-bosheth, Saul's son, saying, "Give me my wife Michal, to whom I was betrothed for a hundred foreskins of the Philistines." ¹⁵Ish-bosheth sent and took her from her husband, from Paltiel the son of Laish. ¹⁶But her husband went with her, weeping as he went, and followed her as far as Bahurim. Then Abner said to him, "Go, return." So he returned.

¹⁷Now Abner had consultation with the elders of Israel, saying, "In times past you were seeking for David to be king over you. ¹⁸Now then, do it! For the LORD has spoken of David, saying, 'By the hand of My servant David I will save My people Israel from the hand of the Philistines and from the hand of all their enemies.'" ¹⁹Abner also spoke in the hearing of Benjamin; and in addition Abner went to speak in the hearing of David in Hebron all that seemed good to Israel and to the whole house of Benjamin.

²⁰Then Abner and twenty men with him came to David at Hebron. And David made a feast for Abner and the men who were with him. ²¹Abner said to David, "Let me arise and go and gather all Israel to my lord the king, that they may make a covenant with you, and that you may be king over all that your soul desires." So David sent Abner away, and he went in peace.

²²And behold, the servants of David and Joab came from a raid and brought much spoil with them; but Abner was not with David in Hebron, for he had sent him away, and he had gone in peace. ²³When Joab and all the army that was with him arrived, they told Joab, saying, "Abner the son of Ner came to the king, and he has sent him away, and he has gone in peace." ²⁴Then Joab came to the king and said, "What have you done? Behold, Abner came to you; why then have you sent him away and he is already gone? ²⁵You know Abner the son of Ner, that he came to deceive you and to learn of your going out and coming in and to find out all that you are doing."

²⁶When Joab came out from David, he sent messengers after Abner, and they brought him back from the well of Sirah; but David

3:25 Abner...came to deceive you. It is ironic that Joab accused Abner of deception in spying on David in v. 25 when in v. 26 he deceived David by not telling him of his request to have Abner returned to Hebron. Joab used this deception to slay Abner out of personal vengeance for the death of his brother Asahel (v. 27; see 2:19–23).

did not know it. ²⁷So when Abner returned to Hebron, Joab took him aside into the middle of the gate to speak with him privately, and there he struck him in the belly so that he died on account of the blood of Asahel his brother. ²⁸Afterward when David heard it, he said, "I and my kingdom are innocent before the LORD forever of the blood of Abner the son of Ner. ²⁹May it fall on the head of Joab and on all his father's house; and may there not fail from the house of Joab one who has a discharge, or who is a leper, or who takes hold of a distaff, or who falls by the sword, or who lacks bread." ³⁰So Joab and Abishai his brother killed Abner because he had put their brother Asahel to death in the battle at Gibeon.

³¹Then David said to Joab and to all the people who were with him, "Tear your clothes and gird on sackcloth and lament before Abner." And King David walked behind the bier. ³²Thus they buried Abner in Hebron; and the king lifted up his voice and wept at the grave of Abner, and all the people wept. ³³The king chanted a *lament* for Abner and said,

"Should Abner die as a fool dies?
³⁴"Your hands were not bound, nor
  your feet put in fetters;
As one falls before the wicked,
  you have fallen."

And all the people wept again over him. ³⁵Then all the people came to persuade David to eat bread while it was still day; but David vowed, saying, "May God do so to me, and more also, if I taste bread or anything else before the sun goes down." ³⁶Now all the people took note of it, and it pleased them, just as everything the king did pleased all the people. ³⁷So all the people and all Israel understood that day that it had not been the will of the king to put Abner the son of Ner to death. ³⁸Then the king said to his servants, "Do you not know that a prince and a great man has fallen this day in Israel? ³⁹I am weak today, though anointed king; and these men the sons of Zeruiah are too difficult for me. May the LORD repay the evildoer according to his evil."

4 Now when Ish-bosheth, Saul's son, heard that Abner had died in Hebron, he lost courage, and all Israel was disturbed. ² Saul's son *had* two men who were commanders of bands: the name of the one was Baanah and the name of the other Rechab, sons of Rimmon the Beerothite, of the sons of Benjamin (for Beeroth is also considered *part* of Benjamin, ³ and the Beerothites fled to Gittaim and have been aliens there until this day).

⁴ Now Jonathan, Saul's son, had a son crippled in his feet. He was five years old when the report of Saul and Jonathan came from Jezreel, and his nurse took him up and fled. And it happened that in her hurry to flee, he fell and became lame. And his name was Mephibosheth.

4:4 Mephibosheth. He may be introduced here to demonstrate that his youth and physical handicap disqualified him from being considered for ruling Israel. He would have been only 12 years old at the time of Ish-bosheth's death. For the history of this man, see 9:6–13; 16:1–4; 19:24–30; 21:7.

⁵ So the sons of Rimmon the Beerothite, Rechab and Baanah, departed and came to the house of Ish-bosheth in the heat of the day while he was taking his midday rest. ⁶ They came to the middle of the house as if to get wheat, and they struck him in the belly; and Rechab and Baanah his brother escaped. ⁷ Now when they came into the house, as he was lying on his bed in his bedroom, they struck him and killed him and beheaded him. And they took his head and traveled by way of the Arabah all night. ⁸ Then they brought the head of Ish-bosheth to David at Hebron and said to the king, "Behold, the head of Ish-bosheth the son of Saul, your enemy, who sought your life; thus the LORD has given my lord the king vengeance this day on Saul and his descendants."

⁹ David answered Rechab and Baanah his brother, sons of Rimmon the Beerothite, and said to them, "As the LORD lives, who has redeemed my life from all distress, ¹⁰ when one told me, saying, 'Behold, Saul is dead,' and thought he was bringing good news, I seized him and killed him in Ziklag, which was the reward I gave him for *his* news. ¹¹ How

much more, when wicked men have killed a righteous man in his own house on his bed, shall I not now require his blood from your hand and destroy you from the earth?" ¹² Then David commanded the young men, and they killed them and cut off their hands and feet and hung them up beside the pool in Hebron. But they took the head of Ish-bosheth and buried it in the grave of Abner in Hebron.

Psalm 62:5–12

⁵ My soul, wait in silence for God only,
  For my hope is from Him.
⁶ He only is my rock and my salvation,
  My stronghold; I shall not be shaken.
⁷ On God my salvation and
    my glory *rest;*
  The rock of my strength,
    my refuge is in God.
⁸ Trust in Him at all times, O people;
  Pour out your heart before Him;
  God is a refuge for us.   *Selah*

⁹ Men of low degree are only vanity
    and men of rank are a lie;
  In the balances they go up;
  They are together lighter than breath.
¹⁰ Do not trust in oppression
  And do not vainly hope in robbery;
  If riches increase, do not set
    your heart *upon them.*

¹¹ Once God has spoken;
  Twice I have heard this:
  That power belongs to God;
¹² And lovingkindness is Yours, O Lord,
  For You recompense a man
    according to his work.

Proverbs 16:13–15

¹³ Righteous lips are the
    delight of kings,
  And he who speaks right is loved.
¹⁴ The fury of a king is *like*
    messengers of death,
  But a wise man will appease it.
¹⁵ In the light of a king's face is life,
  And his favor is like a cloud
    with the spring rain.

16:15 cloud with the spring rain. The late spring rain, which matured the crop, fell before the harvest (2Sa 23:3–4; Ps 72:6) and is here compared to the king's power to grace his subjects with encouragement.

John 4:31-54

³¹Meanwhile the disciples were urging Him, saying, "Rabbi, eat." ³²But He said to them, "I have food to eat that you do not know about." ³³So the disciples were saying to one another, "No one brought Him *anything* to eat, did he?" ³⁴Jesus *said to them, "My food is to do the will of Him who sent Me and to accomplish His work. ³⁵Do you not say, 'There are yet four months, and *then* comes the harvest'? Behold, I say to you, lift up your eyes and look on the fields, that they are white for harvest. ³⁶Already he who reaps is receiving wages and is gathering fruit for life eternal; so that he who sows and he who reaps may rejoice together. ³⁷For in this *case* the saying is true, 'One sows and another reaps.' ³⁸I sent you to reap that for which you have not labored; others have labored and you have entered into their labor."

³⁹From that city many of the Samaritans believed in Him because of the word of the woman who testified, "He told me all the things that I *have* done." ⁴⁰So when the Samaritans came to Jesus, they were asking Him to stay with them; and He stayed there two days. ⁴¹Many more believed because of His word; ⁴²and they were saying to the woman, "It is no longer because of what you said that we believe, for we have heard for ourselves and know that this One is indeed the Savior of the world."

⁴³After the two days He went forth from there into Galilee. ⁴⁴For Jesus Himself testified that a prophet has no honor in his own country. ⁴⁵So when He came to Galilee, the Galileans received Him, having seen all the things that He did in Jerusalem at the feast; for they themselves also went to the feast.

⁴⁶Therefore He came again to Cana of Galilee where He had made the water wine. And there was a royal official whose son was sick at Capernaum. ⁴⁷When he heard that Jesus had come out of Judea into Galilee, he went

to Him and was imploring *Him* to come down and heal his son; for he was at the point of death. ⁴⁸So Jesus said to him, "Unless you *people* see signs and wonders, you *simply* will not believe." ⁴⁹The royal official *said to Him, "Sir, come down before my child dies." ⁵⁰Jesus *said to him, "Go; your son lives." The man believed the word that Jesus spoke to him and started off. ⁵¹As he was now going down, *his* slaves met him, saying that his son was living. ⁵²So he inquired of them the hour when he began to get better. Then they said to him, "Yesterday at the seventh hour the fever left him." ⁵³So the father knew that *it was* at that hour in which Jesus said to him, "Your son lives"; and he himself believed and his whole household. ⁵⁴This is again a second sign that Jesus performed when He had come out of Judea into Galilee.

4:44 a prophet has no honor in his own country. This proverb (also in Mt 13:57; Mk 6:4) contrasts the believing response of the Samaritans (v. 39) with the characteristic unbelief of Jesus' own people in Galilee (and Judea) whose reticent faith depended so much on Jesus' performance of miracles (v. 48). While in Samaria, Jesus had enjoyed His first unqualified and unopposed success. His own people's hearts were not open to Him, but exhibited reluctance and hardness.

4:48 Unless you *people* see signs and wonders. The "you" is plural. Jesus addresses these words to the Galileans as a whole and not just to the royal official (vv. 45-46). The response of the Galileans was fundamentally flawed because it disregarded the person of Christ and centered in the need for a constant display of miraculous signs. Such an attitude represents the deepest state of unbelief.

DAY 16: What is a believer's role in the evangelism of the world?

In the context of the Samaritan woman and village coming to faith in Christ, Jesus spoke of the harvest and the need for workers in John 4:35. Jesus used the fact that they were surrounded by crops growing in the field and waiting to be harvested as an object lesson to illustrate His urgency about reaching the lost, which the "harvest" symbolized. The event probably happened in December or January, which was 4 months before the normal spring harvest (mid-April). Crops were planted in November, and by December or January the grain would be sprouting up in vibrant green color. Jesus points out the Samaritan woman and people of Sychar ("lift up your eyes") who were at that moment coming upon the scene (v. 30) looking like a ripened "harvest" that urgently need to be "gather[ed]," i.e., evangelized. "White for harvest." Their white clothing seen above the growing grain may have looked like white heads on the stalks, an indication of readiness for harvest. Jesus knew the hearts of all (2:24), so was able to state their readiness for salvation (vv. 39-41).

This episode represents the first instance of cross-cultural evangelism (Ac 1:8). In vv. 36-38, the Lord's call to His disciples to do the work of evangelism both then and now contains promises of reward ("wages"), fruit that brings eternal joy (v. 36), and the mutual partnership of shared privilege (vv. 37–38).

When He talked with the Samaritan woman, Jesus was performing the will of the Father and thereby received greater sustenance and satisfaction than any mere physical food could offer Him (v. 34). Obedience to and dependence upon God's will summed up Jesus' whole life (Eph 5:17). Certainly, the same is true for any follower of Christ.

MAY 17

2 Samuel 5:1–6:23

5 Then all the tribes of Israel came to David at Hebron and said, "Behold, we are your bone and your flesh. ²Previously, when Saul was king over us, you were the one who led Israel out and in. And the LORD said to you, 'You will shepherd My people Israel, and you will be a ruler over Israel.'" ³So all the elders of Israel came to the king at Hebron, and King David made a covenant with them before the LORD at Hebron; then they anointed David king over Israel. ⁴David was thirty years old when he became king, *and* he reigned forty years. ⁵At Hebron he reigned over Judah seven years and six months, and in Jerusalem he reigned thirty-three years over all Israel and Judah.

5:1–2 all the tribes of Israel. The term "all" is used 3 times (vv. 1, 3, 5) to emphasize that the kingdom established under King David was truly a united monarchy. The "elders" of Israel (v. 3), representing the "tribes" (v. 1), came to David at Hebron with the express purpose of submitting to his rule. Three reasons were given by the Israelites for wanting to make David king: 1) he was an Israelite brother (Dt 17:15); 2) he was Israel's best warrior and commander; and 3) he had been chosen by the Lord to be the king of Israel.

⁶Now the king and his men went to Jerusalem against the Jebusites, the inhabitants of the land, and they said to David, "You shall not come in here, but the blind and lame will turn you away"; thinking, "David cannot enter here." ⁷Nevertheless, David captured the stronghold of Zion, that is the city of David. ⁸David said on that day, "Whoever would strike the Jebusites, let him reach the lame and the blind, who are hated by David's soul, through the water tunnel." Therefore they say, "The blind or the lame shall not come into the

house." ⁹So David lived in the stronghold and called it the city of David. And David built all around from the Millo and inward. ¹⁰David became greater and greater, for the LORD God of hosts was with him.

¹¹Then Hiram king of Tyre sent messengers to David with cedar trees and carpenters and stonemasons; and they built a house for David. ¹²And David realized that the LORD had established him as king over Israel, and that He had exalted his kingdom for the sake of His people Israel.

¹³Meanwhile David took more concubines and wives from Jerusalem, after he came from Hebron; and more sons and daughters were born to David. ¹⁴Now these are the names of those who were born to him in Jerusalem: Shammua, Shobab, Nathan, Solomon, ¹⁵Ibhar, Elishua, Nepheg, Japhia, ¹⁶Elishama, Eliada and Eliphelet.

¹⁷When the Philistines heard that they had anointed David king over Israel, all the Philistines went up to seek out David; and when David heard *of it,* he went down to the stronghold. ¹⁸Now the Philistines came and spread themselves out in the valley of Rephaim. ¹⁹Then David inquired of the LORD, saying, "Shall I go up against the Philistines? Will You give them into my hand?" And the LORD said to David, "Go up, for I will certainly give the Philistines into your hand." ²⁰So David came to Baal-perazim and defeated them there; and he said, "The LORD has broken through my enemies before me like the breakthrough of waters." Therefore he named that place Baal-perazim. ²¹They abandoned their idols there, so David and his men carried them away.

²²Now the Philistines came up once again and spread themselves out in the valley of Rephaim. ²³When David inquired of the LORD, He said, "You shall not go *directly* up; circle around behind them and come at them in front of the balsam trees. ²⁴It shall be, when you hear the sound of marching in the tops of the balsam trees, then you shall act promptly, for then the LORD will have gone out before you to strike the army of the Philistines." ²⁵Then David did so, just as the LORD had

commanded him, and struck down the Philistines from Geba as far as Gezer.

6 Now David again gathered all the chosen men of Israel, thirty thousand. ² And David arose and went with all the people who were with him to Baale-judah, to bring up from there the ark of God which is called by the Name, the very name of the LORD of hosts who is enthroned *above* the cherubim. ³ They placed the ark of God on a new cart that they might bring it from the house of Abinadab which was on the hill; and Uzzah and Ahio, the sons of Abinadab, were leading the new cart. ⁴ So they brought it with the ark of God from the house of Abinadab, which was on the hill; and Ahio was walking ahead of the ark. ⁵ Meanwhile, David and all the house of Israel were celebrating before the LORD with all kinds of *instruments made of* fir wood, and with lyres, harps, tambourines, castanets and cymbals.

⁶ But when they came to the threshing floor of Nacon, Uzzah reached out toward the ark of God and took hold of it, for the oxen nearly upset *it*. ⁷ And the anger of the LORD burned against Uzzah, and God struck him down there for his irreverence; and he died there by the ark of God. ⁸ David became angry because of the LORD'S outburst against Uzzah, and that place is called Perez-uzzah to this day. ⁹ So David was afraid of the LORD that day; and he said, "How can the ark of the LORD come to me?" ¹⁰ And David was unwilling to move the ark of the LORD into the city of David with him; but David took it aside to the house of Obed-edom the Gittite. ¹¹ Thus the ark of the LORD remained in the house of Obed-edom the Gittite three months, and the LORD blessed Obed-edom and all his household.

¹² Now it was told King David, saying, "The LORD has blessed the house of Obed-edom and all that belongs to him, on account of the ark of God." David went and brought up the ark of God from the house of Obed-edom into the city of David with gladness. ¹³ And so it was, that when the bearers of the ark of the LORD had gone six paces, he sacrificed an ox and a fatling. ¹⁴ And David was dancing before the LORD with all *his* might, and David was wearing a linen ephod. ¹⁵ So David and all the house of Israel were bringing up the ark of the LORD with shouting and the sound of the trumpet.

¹⁶ Then it happened *as* the ark of the LORD came into the city of David that Michal the daughter of Saul looked out of the window and saw King David leaping and dancing before the LORD; and she despised him in her heart.

¹⁷ So they brought in the ark of the LORD and set it in its place inside the tent which David had pitched for it; and David offered burnt offerings and peace offerings before the LORD. ¹⁸ When David had finished offering the burnt offering and the peace offering, he blessed the people in the name of the LORD of hosts. ¹⁹ Further, he distributed to all the people, to all the multitude of Israel, both to men and women, a cake of bread and one of dates and one of raisins to each one. Then all the people departed each to his house.

²⁰ But when David returned to bless his household, Michal the daughter of Saul came out to meet David and said, "How the king of Israel distinguished himself today! He uncovered himself today in the eyes of his servants' maids as one of the foolish ones shamelessly uncovers himself!" ²¹ So David said to Michal, "*It was* before the LORD, who chose me above your father and above all his house, to appoint me ruler over the people of the LORD, over Israel; therefore I will celebrate before the LORD. ²² I will be more lightly esteemed than this and will be humble in my own eyes, but with the maids of whom you have spoken, with them I will be distinguished." ²³ Michal the daughter of Saul had no child to the day of her death.

Psalm 63:1–11

A Psalm of David, when he was
in the wilderness of Judah.

O God, You are my God; I shall
seek You earnestly;
My soul thirsts for You, my
flesh yearns for You,
In a dry and weary land where
there is no water.
² Thus I have seen You in the sanctuary,
To see Your power and Your glory.
³ Because Your lovingkindness
is better than life,
My lips will praise You.

63:1 I shall seek You earnestly. Eagerness to be with the Lord in every situation is more in view than the time of day. **My soul thirsts.** David longs for God's presence like a wanderer in a desert longs for water. **In a dry and weary land.** David writes this psalm while hiding in the wilderness of Judea, but longing to be back worshiping in Jerusalem.

4 So I will bless You as long
  as I live;
  I will lift up my hands in
  Your name.
5 My soul is satisfied as with
  marrow and fatness,
  And my mouth offers praises
  with joyful lips.

6 When I remember You on my bed,
  I meditate on You in the
  night watches,
7 For You have been my help,
  And in the shadow of Your
  wings I sing for joy.
8 My soul clings to You;
  Your right hand upholds me.

9 But those who seek my
  life to destroy it,
  Will go into the depths of the earth.
10 They will be delivered over to
  the power of the sword;
  They will be a prey for foxes.
11 But the king will rejoice in God;
  Everyone who swears by
  Him will glory,
  For the mouths of those who
  speak lies will be stopped.

Proverbs 16:16–17

16 How much better it is to get
  wisdom than gold!
  And to get understanding is to
  be chosen above silver.
17 The highway of the upright
  is to depart from evil;
  He who watches his way
  preserves his life.

John 5:1–23

5 After these things there was a feast of the Jews, and Jesus went up to Jerusalem.
2 Now there is in Jerusalem by the sheep *gate* a pool, which is called in Hebrew Bethesda, having five porticoes. 3 In these lay a multitude of those who were sick, blind, lame, and withered, [waiting for the moving of the waters; 4 for an angel of the Lord went down at certain seasons into the pool and stirred up the water; whoever then first, after the stirring up of the water, stepped in was made well from whatever disease with which he was afflicted.] 5 A man was there who had been ill for thirty-eight years. 6 When Jesus saw him lying *there,* and knew that he had already been a long time *in that condition,* He *said to him, "Do you wish to get well?"

7 The sick man answered Him, "Sir, I have no man to put me into the pool when the water is stirred up, but while I am coming, another steps down before me." 8 Jesus *said to him, "Get up, pick up your pallet and walk." 9 Immediately the man became well, and picked up his pallet and *began* to walk.

Now it was the Sabbath on that day. 10 So the Jews were saying to the man who was cured, "It is the Sabbath, and it is not permissible for you to carry your pallet." 11 But he answered them, "He who made me well was the one who said to me, 'Pick up your pallet and walk.' " 12 They asked him, "Who is the man who said to you, 'Pick up *your pallet* and walk'?" 13 But the man who was healed did not know who it was, for Jesus had slipped away while there was a crowd in *that* place. 14 Afterward Jesus *found him in the temple and said to him, "Behold, you have become well; do not sin anymore, so that

5:10–11 The Old Testament had forbidden work on the Sabbath but did not stipulate what "work" was specifically indicated (Ex 20:8–11). The assumption in Scripture seems to be that "work" was one's customary employment, but rabbinical opinion had developed oral tradition beyond the Old Testament which stipulated 39 activities forbidden (Mishnah *Shabbath* 7:2; 10:5), including carrying anything from one domain to another. Thus, the man had broken oral tradition, not Old Testament law.

5:14 do not sin anymore, so that nothing worse happens to you. The basic thrust of Jesus' comments here indicates that sin has its inevitable consequences (Gal 6:7–8). Although Scripture makes clear that not all disease is a consequence of sin (9:1–3; Lk 13:1–5), illness at times may be directly tied into one's moral turpitude (1Co 11:29–30; Jas 5:15). Jesus may specifically have chosen this man in order to highlight this point.

nothing worse happens to you." 15 The man went away, and told the Jews that it was Jesus who had made him well. 16 For this reason the Jews were persecuting Jesus, because He was doing these things on the Sabbath. 17 But He answered them, "My Father is working until now, and I Myself am working." 18 For this reason therefore the Jews were seeking all the more to kill Him, because He not only was breaking the Sabbath, but also was calling God His own Father, making Himself equal with God.

[19]Therefore Jesus answered and was saying to them, "Truly, truly, I say to you, the Son can do nothing of Himself, unless *it is* something He sees the Father doing; for whatever the Father does, these things the Son also does in like manner. [20]For the Father loves the Son, and shows Him all things that He Himself is doing; and *the Father* will show Him greater works than these, so that you will marvel. [21]For just as the Father raises the dead and gives them life, even so the Son also gives life to whom He wishes. [22]For not even the Father judges anyone, but He has given all judgment to the Son, [23]so that all will honor the Son even as they honor the Father. He who does not honor the Son does not honor the Father who sent Him.

DAY 17: Why did Jesus not back down to religious hypocrisy?

A careful reading of John 5:17–47 reveals the ultimate reason Jesus confronted the Jews' religious hypocrisy, i.e., the opportunity to declare who He was. This section is Christ's own personal statement of His deity. As such, it is one of the greatest Christological discourses in Scripture. Herein Jesus makes 5 claims to equality with God: 1) He is equal with God in His person (vv. 17–18); 2) He is equal with God in His works (vv. 19–20); 3) He is equal with God in His power and sovereignty (v. 21); 4) He is equal with God in His judgment (v. 22); and 5) He is equal with God in His honor (v. 23).

In v. 17, Jesus' point is that whether He broke the Sabbath or not, God was working continuously and, since Jesus Himself worked continuously, He also must be God. Furthermore, God does not need a day of rest for He never wearies (Is. 40:28). For Jesus' self-defense to be valid, the same factors that apply to God must also apply to Him. Jesus is Lord of the Sabbath! (Mt 12:8). Interestingly, even the rabbis admitted that God's work had not ceased after the Sabbath because He sustains the universe.

In response to Jewish hostility at the implications of His assertions of equality with God (v. 18), Jesus became even more fearless, forceful, and emphatic. "Truly, truly" (v. 19) is an emphatic way of saying "I'm telling you the truth." Jesus essentially tied His activities of healing on the Sabbath directly to the Father. The Son never took independent action that set Him against the Father because the Son only did those things that were coincident with and coextensive with all that the Father does. Jesus thus implied that the only One who could do what the Father does must be as great as the Father.

MAY 18

2 Samuel 7:1–8:18

7 Now it came about when the king lived in his house, and the LORD had given him rest on every side from all his enemies, [2]that the king said to Nathan the prophet, "See now, I dwell in a house of cedar, but the ark of God dwells within tent curtains." [3]Nathan said to the king, "Go, do all that is in your mind, for the LORD is with you."

[4]But in the same night the word of the LORD came to Nathan, saying, [5]"Go and say to My servant David, 'Thus says the LORD, "Are you the one who should build Me a house to dwell in? [6]For I have not dwelt in a house since the day I brought up the sons of Israel from Egypt, even to this day; but I have been moving about in a tent, even in a tabernacle. [7]Wherever I have gone with all the sons of Israel, did I speak a word with one of the tribes of Israel, which I commanded to shepherd My people Israel, saying, 'Why have you not built Me a house of cedar?'"' [8]Now therefore, thus you shall say to My servant David, 'Thus says the LORD of hosts, "I took you from the pasture, from following the sheep, to be ruler over My people Israel. [9]I have been with you wherever you have gone and have cut off all your enemies from before you; and I will make you a great name, like the names of the great men who are on the earth. [10]I will also appoint a place for My people Israel and will plant them, that they may live in their own place and not be disturbed again, nor will the wicked afflict them any more as formerly, [11]even from the day that I commanded judges to be over My people Israel; and I will give you rest from all your enemies. The LORD also declares to you that the LORD will make a house for you. [12]When your days are complete and you lie down with your fathers, I will raise up your descendant after you, who will come forth from you, and I will establish his kingdom. [13]He shall build a house for My name, and I will establish the throne of his kingdom forever. [14]I will be a father to him and he will be a son to Me; when he commits iniquity, I will correct him with the rod of men and the strokes of the sons of men, [15]but My

7:14 a father....son. These words are directly related to Jesus the Messiah in Hebrews 1:5. In Semitic thought, since the son had the full character of the father, the future seed (or foremost Descendant) of David would have the same essence of God. That Jesus Christ was God incarnate is the central theme of John's gospel. **when he commits iniquity.** As a human father disciplines his sons, so the Lord would discipline David's descendants, if they committed iniquity. This has reference to the intermediary seed until Messiah's arrival (any king of David's line from Solomon on). However, the ultimate Seed of David will not be a sinner like David and his descendants were, as recorded in Samuel and Kings (2Co 5:21). Significantly, Chronicles, focusing more directly on the Messiah, does not include this statement in its record of Nathan's words (1Ch 17:13).

lovingkindness shall not depart from him, as I took it away from Saul, whom I removed from before you. ¹⁶Your house and your kingdom shall endure before Me forever; your throne shall be established forever."'" ¹⁷In accordance with all these words and all this vision, so Nathan spoke to David.

¹⁸Then David the king went in and sat before the LORD, and he said, "Who am I, O Lord GOD, and what is my house, that You have brought me this far? ¹⁹And yet this was insignificant in Your eyes, O Lord GOD, for You have spoken also of the house of Your servant concerning the distant future. And this is the custom of man, O Lord GOD. ²⁰Again what more can David say to You? For You know Your servant, O Lord GOD! ²¹For the sake of Your word, and according to Your own heart, You have done all this greatness to let Your servant know. ²²For this reason You are great, O Lord GOD; for there is none like You, and there is no

7:16 Your house...your kingdom...your throne. Luke 1:32b, 33 indicates that these 3 terms are fulfilled in Jesus, "... and the Lord God will give Him the throne of His father David; and He will reign over the house of Jacob forever, and His kingdom will have no end." **forever.** This word conveys the idea of 1) an indeterminately long time or 2) into eternity future. It does not mean that there cannot be interruptions, but rather that the outcome is guaranteed. Christ's Davidic reign will conclude human history.

God besides You, according to all that we have heard with our ears. ²³And what one nation on the earth is like Your people Israel, whom God went to redeem for Himself as a people and to make a name for Himself, and to do a great thing for You and awesome things for Your land, before Your people whom You have redeemed for Yourself from Egypt, from nations and their gods? ²⁴For You have established for Yourself Your people Israel as Your own people forever, and You, O LORD, have become their God. ²⁵Now therefore, O LORD God, the word that You have spoken concerning Your servant and his house, confirm it forever, and do as You have spoken, ²⁶that Your name may be magnified forever, by saying, 'The LORD of hosts is God over Israel'; and may the house of Your servant David be established before You. ²⁷For You, O LORD of hosts, the God of Israel, have made a revelation to Your servant, saying, 'I will build you a house'; therefore Your servant has found courage to pray this prayer to You. ²⁸Now, O Lord GOD, You are God, and Your words are truth, and You have promised this good thing to Your servant. ²⁹Now therefore, may it please You to bless the house of Your servant, that it may continue forever before You. For You, O Lord GOD, have spoken; and with Your blessing may the house of Your servant be blessed forever."

8 Now after this it came about that David defeated the Philistines and subdued them; and David took control of the chief city from the hand of the Philistines.

²He defeated Moab, and measured them with the line, making them lie down on the ground; and he measured two lines to put to death and one full line to keep alive. And the Moabites became servants to David, bringing tribute.

³Then David defeated Hadadezer, the son of Rehob king of Zobah, as he went to restore his rule at the River. ⁴David captured from him 1,700 horsemen and 20,000 foot soldiers; and David hamstrung the chariot horses, but reserved enough of them for 100 chariots. ⁵When the Arameans of Damascus came to help Hadadezer, king of Zobah, David killed 22,000 Arameans. ⁶Then David put garrisons among the Arameans of Damascus, and the Arameans became servants to David, bringing tribute. And the LORD helped David wherever he went. ⁷David took the shields of gold which were carried by the servants of Hadadezer and brought them to Jerusalem. ⁸From Betah and from Berothai, cities of Hadadezer, King David took a very large amount of bronze.

⁹Now when Toi king of Hamath heard that

David had defeated all the army of Hadadezer, ¹⁰ Toi sent Joram his son to King David to greet him and bless him, because he had fought against Hadadezer and defeated him; for Hadadezer had been at war with Toi. And *Joram* brought with him articles of silver, of gold and of bronze. ¹¹ King David also dedicated these to the LORD, with the silver and gold that he had dedicated from all the nations which he had subdued: ¹² from Aram and Moab and the sons of Ammon and the Philistines and Amalek, and from the spoil of Hadadezer, son of Rehob, king of Zobah.

¹³ So David made a name *for himself* when he returned from killing 18,000 Arameans in the Valley of Salt. ¹⁴ He put garrisons in Edom. In all Edom he put garrisons, and all the Edomites became servants to David. And the LORD helped David wherever he went.

¹⁵ So David reigned over all Israel; and David administered justice and righteousness for all his people. ¹⁶ Joab the son of Zeruiah *was* over the army, and Jehoshaphat the son of Ahilud *was* recorder. ¹⁷ Zadok the son of Ahitub and Ahimelech the son of Abiathar *were* priests, and Seraiah *was* secretary. ¹⁸ Benaiah the son of Jehoiada was over the Cherethites and the Pelethites; and David's sons were chief ministers.

Psalm 64:1-10

For the choir director. A Psalm of David.

Hear my voice, O God, in
  my complaint;
Preserve my life from
  dread of the enemy.

64:1 Preserve...from dread. The psalmist recognized that the fear of an enemy can be as destructive as an actual assault.

---

² Hide me from the secret
  counsel of evildoers,
From the tumult of those
  who do iniquity,
³ Who have sharpened their
  tongue like a sword.
They aimed bitter speech
  as their arrow,
⁴ To shoot from concealment
  at the blameless;
Suddenly they shoot at him,
  and do not fear.
⁵ They hold fast to themselves
  an evil purpose;

They talk of laying snares secretly;
They say, "Who can see them?"
⁶ They devise injustices, *saying,*
  "We are ready with a
    well-conceived plot";
For the inward thought and the
  heart of a man are deep.

⁷ But God will shoot at them
    with an arrow;
Suddenly they will be wounded.
⁸ So they will make him stumble;
Their own tongue is against them;
All who see them will shake the head.
⁹ Then all men will fear,
And they will declare the work of God,
And will consider what He has done.
¹⁰ The righteous man will be glad in the
    LORD and will take refuge in Him;
And all the upright in heart will glory.

Proverbs 16:18-19

¹⁸ Pride *goes* before destruction,
And a haughty spirit
    before stumbling.
¹⁹ It is better to be humble in
    spirit with the lowly
Than to divide the spoil
    with the proud.

John 5:24-47

²⁴ "Truly, truly, I say to you, he who hears My word, and believes Him who sent Me, has eternal life, and does not come into judgment, but has passed out of death into life. ²⁵ Truly, truly, I say to you, an hour is coming and now is, when the dead will hear the voice of the Son of God, and those who hear will live. ²⁶ For just as the Father has life in Himself, even so He gave to the Son also to have life in Himself; ²⁷ and He gave Him authority to execute judgment, because He is *the* Son of Man. ²⁸ Do not marvel at this; for an hour is coming, in which all who are in the tombs will hear His voice, ²⁹ and will come forth; those who did the good *deeds* to a resurrection of life, those who committed the evil *deeds* to a resurrection of judgment.

³⁰ "I can do nothing on My own initiative. As I hear, I judge; and My judgment is just, because I do not seek My own will, but the will of Him who sent Me.

³¹ "If I *alone* testify about Myself, My testimony is not true. ³² There is another who testifies of Me, and I know that the testimony which He gives about Me is true. ³³ You have sent to John, and he has testified to the truth. ³⁴ But the testimony which I receive is not from man, but

I say these things so that you may be saved. ³⁵He was the lamp that was burning and was shining and you were willing to rejoice for a while in his light. ³⁶But the testimony which I have is greater than *the testimony of* John; for the works which the Father has given Me to accomplish—the very works that I do—testify about Me, that the Father has sent Me. ³⁷And the Father who sent Me, He has testified of Me. You have neither heard His voice at any time nor seen His form. ³⁸You do not have His word abiding in you, for you do not believe Him whom He sent. ³⁹You search the Scriptures because you think that in them you have eternal life; it is these that testify about Me; ⁴⁰and you are unwilling to come to Me so that you may have life. ⁴¹I do not receive glory from men; ⁴²but I know you, that you do not have the love of God in yourselves. ⁴³I have come in My Father's name, and you do not receive Me; if another comes in his own name, you will receive him. ⁴⁴How can you believe, when you receive glory from one another and you do not seek the glory that is from the *one and only* God? ⁴⁵Do not think that I will accuse you before the Father; the one who accuses you

5:36 the very works that I do. See 10:25. The miracles of Jesus were witness to His deity and messiahship. Such miracles are the major signs recorded by John in this Gospel, so as to fulfill his purpose in 20:30–31.

5:39 You search. Although the verb "search" could also be understood as a command (i.e., "Search the Scriptures!"), most prefer this translation as an indicative. The verb implies diligent scrutiny in investigating the Scriptures to find "eternal life." However, Jesus points out that with all their fastidious effort, they miserably failed in their understanding of the true way to eternal life through the Son of God. **testify about Me.** See v. 45. Christ is the main theme of Scripture.

is Moses, in whom you have set your hope. ⁴⁶For if you believed Moses, you would believe Me, for he wrote about Me. ⁴⁷But if you do not believe his writings, how will you believe My words?"

DAY 18: What was the Davidic Covenant?

Second Samuel 7:1–17 record the establishment of the Davidic Covenant, God's unconditional promise to David and his posterity. While not called a covenant here, it is later (23:5). This promise is an important key to understanding God's irrevocable pledge of a king from the line of David to rule forever (v. 16). It has been estimated that over 40 individual biblical passages are directly related to these verses (see Pss 89; 110; 132); thus, this text is a major highlight in the Old Testament. The ultimate fulfillment comes at Christ's Second Advent when He sets up His millennial kingdom on earth (see Eze 37; Zec 14; Rev 19). This is the fourth of 5 irrevocable, unconditional covenants made by God. The first 3 include: 1) the Noahic Covenant (Ge 9:8–17); 2) the Abrahamic Covenant (Ge 15:12–21); and 3) the Levitical or Priestly Covenant (Nu 3:1–18; 18:1–20; 25:10–13). The New Covenant, which actually provided redemption, was revealed later through Jeremiah (Jer 31:31–34) and accomplished by the death and resurrection of Jesus Christ.

Specifically, 2 Samuel 7:8–16 state the promises the Lord gave to David. Verses 8–11a give the promises to be realized during David's lifetime. Verses 11b–16 state the promises that would be fulfilled after David's death. During David's lifetime, the Lord: 1) gave David "a great name"; 2) appointed a place for Israel; and 3) gave David "rest" from all his enemies. After David's death, the Lord gave David: 1) a son to sit on his national throne, whom the Lord would oversee as a father with necessary chastening, discipline, and mercy (Solomon); and 2) a Son who would rule a kingdom that will be established forever (Messiah). This prophecy referred in its immediacy to Solomon and to the temporal kingdom of David's family in the land. But in a larger and more sublime sense, it refers to David's greater Son of another nature, Jesus Christ (Heb 1:8).

MAY 19

2 Samuel 9:1–10:19

9 Then David said, "Is there yet anyone left of the house of Saul, that I may show him kindness for Jonathan's sake?" ²Now there was a servant of the house of Saul whose name was Ziba, and they called him to David; and the king said to him, "Are you Ziba?" And he said, "*I am* your servant." ³The king said, "Is there not yet anyone of the house of Saul to whom I may show the kindness of God?" And Ziba said to the king, "There is still a son of Jonathan who is crippled in both feet." ⁴So the king said to him, "Where is he?" And Ziba

said to the king, "Behold, he is in the house of Machir the son of Ammiel in Lo-debar." ⁵Then King David sent and brought him from the house of Machir the son of Ammiel, from Lo-debar. ⁶Mephibosheth, the son of Jonathan the son of Saul, came to David and fell on his face and prostrated himself. And David said, "Mephibosheth." And he said, "Here is your servant!" ⁷David said to him, "Do not fear, for I will surely show kindness to you for the sake of your father Jonathan, and will restore to you all the land of your grandfather Saul; and you shall eat at my table regularly." ⁸Again he prostrated himself and said, "What is your servant, that you should regard a dead dog like me?"

9:8 dead dog. A "dead dog" was considered contemptible and useless. Mephibosheth saw himself as such in that he knew that he had not merited David's kindness and that there was no way for him to repay it. David's offer was an extraordinary expression of grace and beauty to his covenant with Jonathan (1Sa 18:3; 20:15, 42).

⁹Then the king called Saul's servant Ziba and said to him, "All that belonged to Saul and to all his house I have given to your master's grandson. ¹⁰You and your sons and your servants shall cultivate the land for him, and you shall bring in *the produce* so that your master's grandson may have food; nevertheless Mephibosheth your master's grandson shall eat at my table regularly." Now Ziba had fifteen sons and twenty servants. ¹¹Then Ziba said to the king, "According to all that my lord the king commands his servant so your servant will do." So Mephibosheth ate at David's table as one of the king's sons. ¹²Mephibosheth had a young son whose name was Mica. And all who lived in the house of Ziba were servants to Mephibosheth. ¹³So Mephibosheth lived in Jerusalem, for he ate at the king's table regularly. Now he was lame in both feet.

10 Now it happened afterwards that the king of the Ammonites died, and Hanun his son became king in his place. ²Then David said, "I will show kindness to Hanun the son of Nahash, just as his father showed kindness to me." So David sent some of his servants to console him concerning his father. But when David's servants came to the land of the Ammonites, ³the princes of

the Ammonites said to Hanun their lord, "Do you think that David is honoring your father because he has sent consolers to you? Has David not sent his servants to you in order to search the city, to spy it out and overthrow it?" ⁴So Hanun took David's servants and shaved off half of their beards, and cut off their garments in the middle as far as their hips, and sent them away. ⁵When they told *it* to David, he sent to meet them, for the men were greatly humiliated. And the king said, "Stay at Jericho until your beards grow, and *then* return."

10:4 shaved off half of their beards. Forced shaving was considered an insult and a sign of submission (Is 7:20). **cut off their garments... as far as their hips.** To those who wore long garments in that time, exposure of the buttocks was a shameful practice inflicted on prisoners of war (Is 20:4). Perhaps this was partly the concern of Michal in regard to David's dancing (6:14, 20).

⁶Now when the sons of Ammon saw that they had become odious to David, the sons of Ammon sent and hired the Arameans of Beth-rehob and the Arameans of Zobah, 20,000 foot soldiers, and the king of Maacah with 1,000 men, and the men of Tob with 12,000 men. ⁷When David heard *of it,* he sent Joab and all the army, the mighty men. ⁸The sons of Ammon came out and drew up in battle array at the entrance of the city, while the Arameans of Zobah and of Rehob and the men of Tob and Maacah *were* by themselves in the field.

⁹Now when Joab saw that the battle was set against him in front and in the rear, he selected from all the choice men of Israel, and arrayed *them* against the Arameans. ¹⁰But the remainder of the people he placed in the hand of Abishai his brother, and he arrayed *them* against the sons of Ammon. ¹¹He said, "If the Arameans are too strong for me, then you shall help me, but if the sons of Ammon are too strong for you, then I will come to help you. ¹²Be strong, and let us show ourselves courageous for the sake of our people and for the cities of our God; and may the LORD do what is good in His sight." ¹³So Joab and the people who were with him drew near to the battle against the Arameans, and they fled before him. ¹⁴When the sons of Ammon saw that the Arameans fled, they *also* fled

before Abishai and entered the city. Then Joab returned from *fighting* against the sons of Ammon and came to Jerusalem.

[15] When the Arameans saw that they had been defeated by Israel, they gathered themselves together. [16] And Hadadezer sent and brought out the Arameans who were beyond the River, and they came to Helam; and Shobach the commander of the army of Hadadezer led them. [17] Now when it was told David, he gathered all Israel together and crossed the Jordan, and came to Helam. And the Arameans arrayed themselves to meet David and fought against him. [18] But the Arameans fled before Israel, and David killed 700 charioteers of the Arameans and 40,000 horsemen and struck down Shobach the commander of their army, and he died there. [19] When all the kings, servants of Hadadezer, saw that they were defeated by Israel, they made peace with Israel and served them. So the Arameans feared to help the sons of Ammon anymore.

Psalm 65:1-8

For the choir director. A Psalm of David. A Song.

There will be silence before You, *and* praise in Zion, O God, And to You the vow will be performed.
[2] O You who hear prayer, To You all men come.
[3] Iniquities prevail against me; As for our transgressions, You forgive them.
[4] How blessed is the one whom You choose and bring near *to You* To dwell in Your courts. We will be satisfied with the goodness of Your house, Your holy temple.

[5] By awesome *deeds* You answer us in righteousness, O God of our salvation, You who are the trust of all the ends of the earth and of the farthest sea;
[6] Who establishes the mountains by His strength, Being girded with might;
[7] Who stills the roaring of the seas, The roaring of their waves, And the tumult of the peoples.
[8] They who dwell in the ends *of the earth* stand in awe of Your signs; You make the dawn and the sunset shout for joy.

Proverbs 16:20-21

[20] He who gives attention to the word will find good, And blessed is he who trusts in the LORD.
[21] The wise in heart will be called understanding, And sweetness of speech increases persuasiveness.

16:21 sweetness of speech. "Honeyed words," which reflect intelligence, judiciousness, and discernment in speech. This refers to eloquent discourse from the wise (v. 24).

John 6:1-21

6 After these things Jesus went away to the other side of the Sea of Galilee (or Tiberias). [2] A large crowd followed Him, because they saw the signs which He was performing on those who were sick. [3] Then Jesus went up on the mountain, and there He sat down with His disciples. [4] Now the Passover, the feast of the Jews, was near. [5] Therefore Jesus, lifting up His eyes and seeing that a large crowd was coming to Him, *said to Philip, "Where are we to buy bread, so that these may eat?" [6] This He was saying to test him, for He Himself knew what He was intending to do. [7] Philip answered Him, "Two hundred denarii worth of bread is not sufficient for them, for everyone to receive a little." [8] One of His disciples, Andrew, Simon Peter's brother, *said to Him, [9] "There is a lad here who has five barley loaves and two fish, but what are these for so many people?" [10] Jesus said, "Have the people sit down." Now there was much grass in the place. So the men sat down, in number about five thousand. [11] Jesus then took the loaves, and having given thanks, He distributed to those who were seated; likewise also of the fish as much as they wanted. [12] When they were filled, He *said to His disciples, "Gather up the leftover fragments so that nothing will be lost." [13] So they gathered them up, and filled twelve baskets with fragments from the five barley loaves which were left over by those who had eaten. [14] Therefore when the people saw the sign which He had performed, they said, "This is truly the Prophet who is to come into the world."

[15] So Jesus, perceiving that they were intending to come and take Him by force to make Him king, withdrew again to the mountain by Himself alone.

[16] Now when evening came, His disciples

went down to the sea, [17] and after getting into a boat, they *started to* cross the sea to Capernaum. It had already become dark, and Jesus had not yet come to them. [18] The sea *began* to be stirred up because a strong wind was blowing. [19] Then, when they had rowed about three or four miles, they *saw Jesus walking on the sea and drawing near to the boat; and they were frightened. [20] But He *said to them, "It is I; do not be afraid." [21] So they were willing to receive Him into the boat, and immediately the boat was at the land to which they were going.

6:19-20 Jesus walking on the sea. The Synoptics reveal that in fear and the darkness, they thought He was a ghost (Mt 14:26; Mk 6:49). The Son of God, who made the world, was in control of its forces; and, in this case, He suspended the law of gravity. The act was not frivolous on Jesus' part, for it constituted a dramatic object lesson to the disciples of Jesus' true identity as the sovereign Lord of all creation (1:3).

DAY 19: Why were the crowds who followed Jesus a potential liability?

In John 6:2, it says that the multitudes followed Jesus "because they saw the signs." The crowds followed not out of belief but out of curiosity concerning the miracles that He performed (v. 26). However, in spite of the crowd's crass motivations, Jesus, having compassion on them, healed their sick and fed them (Mt 13:14; Mk 6:34).

The crowd's declaration of Jesus as "the Prophet" (v. 14) is a reference to Deuteronomy 18:15. Sadly, these comments, coming right after Jesus healed and fed them, indicate that the people desired a Messiah who met their physical, rather than spiritual, needs. Apparently, no recognition existed for the need of spiritual repentance and preparation for the kingdom (Mt 4:17). They wanted an earthly, political Messiah to meet all their needs and to deliver them from Roman oppression. Their reaction typifies many who want a "Christ" that makes no demands of them (Mt 10:34-39; 16:24-26), but of whom they can make their selfish personal requests.

Jesus, "perceiving that they were intending to come and take Him by force to make Him king" (v. 15). John supplemented the information in Matthew and Mark by indicating that the reason Jesus dismissed the disciples and withdrew from the crowd into a mountain alone was because of His supernatural knowledge of their intention to make Him king in light of His healing and feeding of them. The crowd, incited by mob enthusiasm, was ready to proceed with crassly political intentions that would have jeopardized God's will.

MAY 20

2 Samuel 11:1-12:31

11 Then it happened in the spring, at the time when kings go out *to battle,* that David sent Joab and his servants with him and all Israel, and they destroyed the sons of Ammon and besieged Rabbah. But David stayed at Jerusalem.

[2] Now when evening came David arose from his bed and walked around on the roof of the king's house, and from the roof he saw a woman bathing; and the woman was very beautiful in appearance. [3] So David sent and inquired about the woman. And one said, "Is this not Bathsheba, the daughter of Eliam, the wife of Uriah the Hittite?" [4] David sent messengers and took her, and when she came to him, he lay with her; and when she had purified herself from her uncleanness, she returned to her house. [5] The woman conceived; and she sent and told David, and said, "I am pregnant."

[6] Then David sent to Joab, *saying,* "Send me Uriah the Hittite." So Joab sent Uriah to David. [7] When Uriah came to him, David asked concerning the welfare of Joab and the people

11:3 Bathsheba. Not until 12:24 is her name used again. Rather, to intensify the sin of adultery, it is emphasized that she was the wife of Uriah (vv. 3, 26; 12:10, 15). Even the New Testament says "the wife of Uriah" (Mt 1:6). See Exodus 20:17. **Eliam.** The father of Bathsheba was one of David's mighty men (23:34). Since Eliam was the son of Ahithophel, Bathsheba was Ahithophel's granddaughter (15:12; 16:15). This could explain why Ahithophel, one of David's counselors (15:12), later gave his allegiance to Absalom in his revolt against David. **Uriah.** Also one of David's mighty men (23:39). Although a Hittite (Ge 15:20; Ex 3:8, 17), Uriah bore a Hebrew name meaning "the Lord is my light," indicating he was a worshiper of the one true God.

and the state of the war. ⁸ Then David said to Uriah, "Go down to your house, and wash your feet." And Uriah went out of the king's house, and a present from the king was sent out after him. ⁹ But Uriah slept at the door of the king's house with all the servants of his lord, and did not go down to his house. ¹⁰ Now when they told David, saying, "Uriah did not go down to his house," David said to Uriah, "Have you not come from a journey? Why did you not go down to your house?" ¹¹ Uriah said to David, "The ark and Israel and Judah are staying in temporary shelters, and my lord Joab and the servants of my lord are camping in the open field. Shall I then go to my house to eat and to drink and to lie with my wife? By your life and the life of your soul, I will not do this thing." ¹² Then David said to Uriah, "Stay here today also, and tomorrow I will let you go." So Uriah remained in Jerusalem that day and the next. ¹³ Now David called him, and he ate and drank before him, and he made him drunk; and in the evening he went out to lie on his bed with his lord's servants, but he did not go down to his house.

¹⁴ Now in the morning David wrote a letter to Joab and sent it by the hand of Uriah. ¹⁵ He had written in the letter, saying, "Place Uriah in the front line of the fiercest battle and withdraw from him, so that he may be struck down and die." ¹⁶ So it was as Joab kept

11:15 he may...die. Failing twice to cover up his sin with Bathsheba, the frustrated and panicked David plotted the murder of Uriah by taking advantage of Uriah's unswerving loyalty to him as king, even having Uriah deliver his own death warrant. Thus David engaged in another crime deserving of capital punishment (Lv 24:17). This is graphic proof of the extremes people go to in pursuit of sin and in the absence of restraining grace.

watch on the city, that he put Uriah at the place where he knew there were valiant men. ¹⁷ The men of the city went out and fought against Joab, and some of the people among David's servants fell; and Uriah the Hittite also died. ¹⁸ Then Joab sent and reported to David all the events of the war. ¹⁹ He charged the messenger, saying, "When you have finished telling all the events of the war to the king, ²⁰ and if it happens that the king's wrath rises and he says to you, 'Why did you go so near to the city to fight? Did you not know that

they would shoot from the wall? ²¹ Who struck down Abimelech the son of Jerubbesheth? Did not a woman throw an upper millstone on him from the wall so that he died at Thebez? Why did you go so near the wall?'—then you shall say, 'Your servant Uriah the Hittite is dead also.'"

²² So the messenger departed and came and reported to David all that Joab had sent him to tell. ²³ The messenger said to David, "The men prevailed against us and came out against us in the field, but we pressed them as far as the entrance of the gate. ²⁴ Moreover, the archers shot at your servants from the wall; so some of the king's servants are dead, and your servant Uriah the Hittite is also dead." ²⁵ Then David said to the messenger, "Thus you shall say to Joab, 'Do not let this thing displease you, for the sword devours one as well as another; make your battle against the city stronger and overthrow it'; and so encourage him."

²⁶ Now when the wife of Uriah heard that Uriah her husband was dead, she mourned for her husband. ²⁷ When the time of mourning was over, David sent and brought her to his house and she became his wife; then she bore him a son. But the thing that David had done was evil in the sight of the LORD.

12 Then the LORD sent Nathan to David. And he came to him and said,

"There were two men in one city, the
    one rich and the other poor.
² "The rich man had a great
    many flocks and herds.
³ "But the poor man had nothing
    except one little ewe lamb
Which he bought and nourished;
And it grew up together with
    him and his children.
It would eat of his bread and drink
    of his cup and lie in his bosom,
And was like a daughter to him.
⁴ "Now a traveler came to the rich man,
And he was unwilling to take from
    his own flock or his own herd,
To prepare for the wayfarer
    who had come to him;
Rather he took the poor man's ewe
    lamb and prepared it for the
    man who had come to him."

⁵ Then David's anger burned greatly against the man, and he said to Nathan, "As the LORD lives, surely the man who has done this deserves to die. ⁶ He must make restitution for the lamb fourfold, because he did this thing and had no compassion."

⁷Nathan then said to David, "You are the man! Thus says the LORD God of Israel, 'It is I who anointed you king over Israel and it is I who delivered you from the hand of Saul. ⁸I also gave you your master's house and your master's wives into your care, and I gave you the house of Israel and Judah; and if *that had been* too little, I would have added to you many more things like these! ⁹Why have you despised the word of the LORD by doing evil in His sight? You have struck down Uriah the Hittite with the sword, have taken his wife to be your wife, and have killed him with the sword of the sons of Ammon. ¹⁰Now therefore, the sword shall never depart from your house, because you have despised Me and have taken the wife of Uriah the Hittite to be your wife.' ¹¹Thus says the LORD, 'Behold, I will raise up evil against you from your own household; I will even take your wives before your eyes and give *them* to your companion, and he will lie with your wives in broad daylight. ¹²Indeed you did it secretly, but I will do this thing before all Israel, and under the sun.' " ¹³Then David said to Nathan, "I have sinned against the LORD." And Nathan said to David, "The LORD also has taken away your sin; you shall not die. ¹⁴However, because by this deed you have given occasion to the enemies of the LORD to blaspheme, the child also that is born to you shall surely die." ¹⁵So Nathan went to his house.

Then the LORD struck the child that Uriah's widow bore to David, so that he was *very* sick. ¹⁶David therefore inquired of God for the child; and David fasted and went and lay all night on the ground. ¹⁷The elders of his household stood beside him in order to raise him up from the ground, but he was unwilling and would not eat food with them. ¹⁸Then it happened on the seventh day that the child died. And the servants of David were afraid to tell him that the child was dead, for they said, "Behold, while the child was *still* alive, we spoke to him and he did not listen to our voice. How then can we tell him that the child is dead, since he might do *himself* harm!" ¹⁹But when David saw that his servants were whispering together, David perceived that the child was dead; so David said to his servants, "Is the child dead?" And they said, "He is dead." ²⁰So David arose from the ground, washed, anointed *himself*, and changed his clothes; and he came into the house of the LORD and worshiped. Then he came to his own house, and when he requested, they set food before him and he ate.

²¹Then his servants said to him, "What is this thing that you have done? While the child was alive, you fasted and wept; but when the child died, you arose and ate food." ²²He said, "While the child was *still* alive, I fasted and wept; for I said, 'Who knows, the LORD may be gracious to me, that the child may live.' ²³But now he has died; why should I fast? Can I bring him back again? I will go to him, but he will not return to me."

²⁴Then David comforted his wife Bathsheba, and went in to her and lay with her; and she gave birth to a son, and he named him Solomon. Now the LORD loved him ²⁵and sent *word* through Nathan the prophet, and he named him Jedidiah for the LORD'S sake.

²⁶Now Joab fought against Rabbah of the sons of Ammon and captured the royal city. ²⁷Joab sent messengers to David and said, "I have fought against Rabbah, I have even captured the city of waters. ²⁸Now therefore, gather the rest of the people together and camp against the city and capture it, or I will capture the city myself and it will be named after me." ²⁹So David gathered all the people and went to Rabbah, fought against it and captured it. ³⁰Then he took the crown of their king from his head; and its weight *was* a talent of gold, and *in it was* a precious stone; and it was *placed* on David's head. And he brought out the spoil of the city in great amounts. ³¹He also brought out the people who were in it, and set *them* under saws, sharp iron instruments, and iron axes, and made them pass through the brickkiln. And thus he did to all the cities of the sons of Ammon. Then David and all the people returned *to* Jerusalem.

Psalm 65:9–13

⁹ You visit the earth and
     cause it to overflow;
 You greatly enrich it;
 The stream of God is full of water;
 You prepare their grain, for thus
     You prepare the earth.
¹⁰ You water its furrows abundantly,
 You settle its ridges,
 You soften it with showers,
 You bless its growth.
¹¹ You have crowned the year
     with Your bounty,
 And Your paths drip *with* fatness.
¹² The pastures of the wilderness drip,
 And the hills gird themselves
     with rejoicing.
¹³ The meadows are clothed with flocks
 And the valleys are covered
     with grain;
 They shout for joy, yes, they sing.

Proverbs 16:22–24

²² Understanding is a fountain
of life to one who has it,
But the discipline of fools is folly.
²³ The heart of the wise
instructs his mouth
And adds persuasiveness to his lips.
²⁴ Pleasant words are a honeycomb,
Sweet to the soul and
healing to the bones.

John 6:22–51

²² The next day the crowd that stood on the other side of the sea saw that there was no other small boat there, except one, and that Jesus had not entered with His disciples into the boat, but *that* His disciples had gone away alone. ²³ There came other small boats from Tiberias near to the place where they ate the bread after the Lord had given thanks. ²⁴ So when the crowd saw that Jesus was not there, nor His disciples, they themselves got into the small boats, and came to Capernaum seeking Jesus. ²⁵ When they found Him on the other side of the sea, they said to Him, "Rabbi, when did You get here?"

²⁶ Jesus answered them and said, "Truly, truly, I say to you, you seek Me, not because you saw signs, but because you ate of the loaves and were filled. ²⁷ Do not work for the food which perishes, but for the food which endures to eternal life, which the Son of Man will give to you, for on Him the Father, God, has set His seal." ²⁸ Therefore they said to Him, "What shall we do, so that we may work the works of God?" ²⁹ Jesus answered and said to them, "This is the work of God, that you believe in Him whom He has sent." ³⁰ So they said to Him, "What then do You do for a sign, so that we may see, and believe You? What work do You perform? ³¹ Our fathers ate the manna in the wilderness; as it is written, 'HE GAVE THEM BREAD OUT OF HEAVEN TO EAT.'" ³² Jesus then said to them, "Truly, truly, I say to you, it is not Moses who has given you the bread out of heaven, but it is My Father who gives you the true bread out of heaven. ³³ For the bread of God is that which comes down out of heaven, and gives life to the world." ³⁴ Then they said to Him, "Lord, always give us this bread."

³⁵ Jesus said to them, "I am the bread of life; he who comes to Me will not hunger, and he who believes in Me will never thirst. ³⁶ But I said to you that you have seen Me, and yet do not believe. ³⁷ All that the Father gives Me will come to Me, and the one who comes to Me I will certainly not cast out. ³⁸ For I have come down from heaven, not to do My own will, but the will of Him who sent Me. ³⁹ This is the will of Him who sent Me, that of all that He has given Me I lose nothing, but raise it up on the last day. ⁴⁰ For this is the will of My Father, that everyone who beholds the Son and believes in Him will have eternal life, and I Myself will raise him up on the last day."

6:40 everyone who beholds the Son and believes in Him. This verse emphasizes human responsibility in salvation. Although God is sovereign, He works through faith, so that a person must believe in Jesus as the Messiah and Son of God who alone offers the only way of salvation (14:6). However, even faith is a gift of God (Ro 12:3; Eph 2:8–9). Intellectually harmonizing the sovereignty of God and the responsibility of man is impossible humanly, but perfectly resolved in the infinite mind of God.

⁴¹ Therefore the Jews were grumbling about Him, because He said, "I am the bread that came down out of heaven." ⁴² They were saying, "Is not this Jesus, the son of Joseph, whose father and mother we know? How does He now say, 'I have come down out of heaven'?" ⁴³ Jesus answered and said to them, "Do not grumble among yourselves. ⁴⁴ No one can come to Me unless the Father who sent Me draws him; and I will raise him up on the last day. ⁴⁵ It is written in the prophets, 'AND THEY SHALL ALL BE TAUGHT OF GOD.' Everyone who has heard and learned from the Father, comes to Me. ⁴⁶ Not that anyone has seen the Father, except the One who is from God; He has seen the Father. ⁴⁷ Truly, truly, I say to you, he who believes has eternal life. ⁴⁸ I am the bread of life. ⁴⁹ Your fathers ate the manna in the wilderness, and they died. ⁵⁰ This is the bread which comes down out of heaven, so that one may eat of it and not die. ⁵¹ I am the living bread that came down out of heaven; if anyone eats of this bread, he will live forever; and the bread also which I will give for the life of the world is My flesh."

6:51 This pronouncement exactly reiterates vv. 33, 35, 47, 48. **bread…is My flesh.** Jesus refers here prophetically to His impending sacrifice upon the cross (2Co 5:21; 1Pe 2:24). Jesus voluntarily laid down His life for evil, sinful mankind (10:18; 1Jn 2:2).

DAY 20: How do Jesus' "I am" statements in the Book of John express His saving relationship toward the world?

After the miraculous feeding of the 5,000, Jesus was challenged by the crowd to perform an even greater miracle in John 6:30. "Our fathers ate the manna," they said (v. 31), implying that Jesus' miraculous feeding was a small miracle compared to what Moses did. In order for them to believe in Him, they would need to see Him feed the nation of Israel on the same scale that God did when He sent manna and fed the entire nation of Israel during their wilderness wanderings for 40 years (Ex 16:11–36). They were demanding that Jesus outdo Moses if they were to believe in Him.

Jesus responded that the manna God gave was temporary and perished and was only a meager shadow of what God offered them in the true bread, Himself, who gives spiritual and eternal life to mankind ("world"). He is the "true bread out of heaven," and in case that wasn't understood, He added, "I am the bread of life" (v. 35).

Twenty-three times in all we find our Lord's meaningful "I AM" in the Greek text of this Gospel (4:26; 6:20, 35, 41, 48, 51; 8:12, 18, 24, 28, 58; 10:7, 9, 11, 14; 11:25; 13:19; 14:6; 15:1, 5; 18:5–6, 8). In several of these, He joins His "I am" with seven tremendous metaphors which are expressive of His saving relationship toward the world.

"I am the bread of life" (6:35, 48, 51; see v. 41).
"I am the Light of the world" (8:12).
"I am the door of the sheep" (10:7; see v. 9).
"I am the good Shepherd" (10:11, 14).
"I am the resurrection and the life" (11:25).
"I am the way, and the truth, and the life" (14:6).
"I am the true vine" (15:1, 5).

MAY 21

2 Samuel 13:1–14:33

13 Now it was after this that Absalom the son of David had a beautiful sister whose name was Tamar, and Amnon the son of David loved her. ²Amnon was so frustrated because of his sister Tamar that he made himself ill, for she was a virgin, and it seemed hard to Amnon to do anything to her. ³But Amnon had a friend whose name was Jonadab, the son of Shimeah, David's brother; and Jonadab was a very shrewd man. ⁴He said to him, "O son of the king, why are you so depressed morning after morning? Will you not tell me?" Then Amnon said to him, "I am in love with Tamar, the sister of my brother Absalom." ⁵Jonadab then said to him, "Lie down on your bed and pretend to be ill; when your father comes to see you, say to him, 'Please let my sister Tamar come and give me some food to eat, and let her prepare the food in my sight, that I may see it and eat from her hand.'" ⁶So Amnon lay down and pretended to be ill; when the king came to see him, Amnon said to the king, "Please let my sister Tamar come and make me a couple of cakes in my sight, that I may eat from her hand."

⁷Then David sent to the house for Tamar, saying, "Go now to your brother Amnon's house, and prepare food for him." ⁸So Tamar went to her brother Amnon's house, and he was lying down. And she took dough, kneaded it, made cakes in his sight, and baked the cakes. ⁹She took the pan and dished them out before him, but he refused to eat. And Amnon said, "Have everyone go out from me." So everyone went out from him. ¹⁰Then Amnon said to Tamar, "Bring the food into the bedroom, that I may eat from your hand." So Tamar took the cakes which she had made and brought them into the bedroom to her brother Amnon. ¹¹When she brought them to him to eat, he took hold of her and said to her, "Come, lie with me, my sister." ¹²But she answered him, "No, my brother, do not violate me, for such a thing is not done in Israel; do not do this disgraceful thing! ¹³As for me, where could I get rid of my reproach? And as for you, you will be like one of the fools in Israel. Now therefore, please speak to the king, for he will not withhold me from you." ¹⁴However, he would not listen to her; since he was stronger than she, he violated her and lay with her.

¹⁵Then Amnon hated her with a very great hatred; for the hatred with which he hated her was greater than the love with which he had loved her. And Amnon said to her, "Get up, go away!" ¹⁶But she said to him, "No, because this wrong in sending me away is greater than the other that you have done to me!" Yet

13:15 hated her. Amnon's "love" (v. 1) was nothing but sensual desire that, once gratified, turned to hatred. His sudden revulsion was the result of her unwilling resistance, the atrocity of what he had done, feelings of remorse, and dread of exposure and punishment. All of these rendered her intolerably undesirable to him.

he would not listen to her. ¹⁷Then he called his young man who attended him and said, "Now throw this woman out of my *presence,* and lock the door behind her." ¹⁸Now she had on a long-sleeved garment; for in this manner the virgin daughters of the king dressed themselves in robes. Then his attendant took her out and locked the door behind her. ¹⁹Tamar put ashes on her head and tore her long-sleeved garment which *was* on her; and she put her hand on her head and went away, crying aloud as she went.

²⁰Then Absalom her brother said to her, "Has Amnon your brother been with you? But now keep silent, my sister, he is your brother; do not take this matter to heart." So Tamar remained and was desolate in her brother Absalom's house. ²¹Now when King David heard of all these matters, he was very angry. ²²But Absalom did not speak to Amnon either good or bad; for Absalom hated Amnon because he had violated his sister Tamar.

²³Now it came about after two full years that Absalom had sheepshearers in Baalhazor, which is near Ephraim, and Absalom invited all the king's sons. ²⁴Absalom came to the king and said, "Behold now, your servant has sheepshearers; please let the king and his servants go with your servant." ²⁵But the king said to Absalom, "No, my son, we should not all go, for we will be burdensome to you." Although he urged him, he would not go, but blessed him. ²⁶Then Absalom said, "If not, please let my brother Amnon go with us." And the king said to him, "Why should he go with you?" ²⁷But when Absalom urged him, he let Amnon and all the king's sons go with him.

²⁸Absalom commanded his servants, saying, "See now, when Amnon's heart is merry with wine, and when I say to you, 'Strike Amnon,' then put him to death. Do not fear; have not I myself commanded you? Be courageous and be valiant." ²⁹The servants of Absalom did to Amnon just as Absalom had commanded. Then all the king's sons arose and each mounted his mule and fled. ³⁰Now it was while they were on the way

that the report came to David, saying, "Absalom has struck down all the king's sons, and not one of them is left." ³¹Then the king arose, tore his clothes and lay on the ground; and all his servants were standing by with clothes torn. ³²Jonadab, the son of Shimeah, David's brother, responded, "Do not let my lord suppose they have put to death all the young men, the king's sons, for Amnon alone is dead; because by the intent of Absalom this has been determined since the day that he violated his sister Tamar. ³³Now therefore, do not let my lord the king take the report to heart, namely, 'all the king's sons are dead,' for only Amnon is dead."

³⁴Now Absalom had fled. And the young man who was the watchman raised his eyes and looked, and behold, many people were coming from the road behind him by the side of the mountain. ³⁵Jonadab said to the king, "Behold, the king's sons have come; according to your servant's word, so it happened." ³⁶As soon as he had finished speaking, behold, the king's sons came and lifted their voices and wept; and also the king and all his servants wept very bitterly.

³⁷Now Absalom fled and went to Talmai the son of Ammihud, the king of Geshur. And *David* mourned for his son every day. ³⁸So Absalom had fled and gone to Geshur, and was there three years. ³⁹*The heart of* King David longed to go out to Absalom; for he was comforted concerning Amnon, since he was dead.

14 Now Joab the son of Zeruiah perceived that the king's heart *was inclined* toward Absalom. ²So Joab sent to Tekoa and brought a wise woman from there and said to her, "Please pretend to be a mourner, and put on mourning garments now, and do not anoint yourself with oil, but be like a woman who has been mourning for the dead many days; ³then go to the king and speak to him in this manner." So Joab put the words in her mouth.

⁴Now when the woman of Tekoa spoke to the king, she fell on her face to the ground and prostrated herself and said, "Help, O king." ⁵The king said to her, "What is your trouble?" And she answered, "Truly I am a widow, for my husband is dead. ⁶Your maidservant had two sons, but the two of them struggled together in the field, and there was no one to separate them, so one struck the other and killed him. ⁷Now behold, the whole family has risen against your maidservant, and they say, 'Hand over the one who struck his brother, that we may put him to death for the life of

his brother whom he killed, and destroy the heir also.' Thus they will extinguish my coal which is left, so as to leave my husband neither name nor remnant on the face of the earth."

[8] Then the king said to the woman, "Go to your house, and I will give orders concerning you." [9] The woman of Tekoa said to the king, "O my lord, the king, the iniquity is on me and my father's house, but the king and his throne are guiltless." [10] So the king said, "Whoever speaks to you, bring him to me, and he will not touch you anymore." [11] Then she said, "Please let the king remember the LORD your God, *so that* the avenger of blood will not continue to destroy, otherwise they will destroy my son." And he said, "As the LORD lives, not one hair of your son shall fall to the ground."

[12] Then the woman said, "Please let your maidservant speak a word to my lord the king." And he said, "Speak." [13] The woman said, "Why then have you planned such a thing against the people of God? For in speaking this word the king is as one who is guilty, *in that* the king does not bring back his banished one. [14] For we will surely die and are like water

---

14:13 against the people of God. The woman asserted that by allowing Absalom to remain in exile, David had jeopardized the future welfare of Israel. If he would be so generous to a son he did not know in a family he did not know, would he not forgive his own son?

---

spilled on the ground which cannot be gathered up again. Yet God does not take away life, but plans ways so that the banished one will not be cast out from him. [15] Now the reason I have come to speak this word to my lord the king is that the people have made me afraid; so your maidservant said, 'Let me now speak to the king, perhaps the king will perform the request of his maidservant. [16] For the king will hear and deliver his maidservant from the hand of the man who would destroy both me and my son from the inheritance of God.' [17] Then your maidservant said, 'Please let the word of my lord the king be comforting, for as the angel of God, so is my lord the king to discern good and evil. And may the LORD your God be with you.'"

[18] Then the king answered and said to the woman, "Please do not hide anything from me that I am about to ask you." And the woman

said, "Let my lord the king please speak." [19] So the king said, "Is the hand of Joab with you in all this?" And the woman replied, "As your soul lives, my lord the king, no one can turn to the right or to the left from anything that my lord the king has spoken. Indeed, it was your servant Joab who commanded me, and it was he who put all these words in the mouth of your maidservant; [20] in order to change the appearance of things your servant Joab has done this thing. But my lord is wise, like the wisdom of the angel of God, to know all that is in the earth."

[21] Then the king said to Joab, "Behold now, I will surely do this thing; go therefore, bring back the young man Absalom." [22] Joab fell on his face to the ground, prostrated himself and blessed the king; then Joab said, "Today your servant knows that I have found favor in your sight, O my lord, the king, in that the king has performed the request of his servant." [23] So Joab arose and went to Geshur and brought Absalom to Jerusalem. [24] However the king said, "Let him turn to his own house, and let him not see my face." So Absalom turned to his own house and did not see the king's face.

[25] Now in all Israel was no one as handsome as Absalom, so highly praised; from the sole of his foot to the crown of his head there was no defect in him. [26] When he cut the hair of his head (and it was at the end of every year that he cut *it,* for it was heavy on him so he cut it), he weighed the hair of his head at 200 shekels by the king's weight. [27] To Absalom there were born three sons, and one daughter whose name was Tamar; she was a woman of beautiful appearance.

[28] Now Absalom lived two full years in Jerusalem, and did not see the king's face. [29] Then Absalom sent for Joab, to send him to the king, but he would not come to him. So he sent again a second time, but he would not come. [30] Therefore he said to his servants, "See, Joab's field is next to mine, and he has barley there; go and set it on fire." So Absalom's servants set the field on fire. [31] Then Joab arose, came to Absalom at his house and said to him, "Why have your servants set my field on fire?" [32] Absalom answered Joab, "Behold, I sent for you, saying, 'Come here, that I may send you to the king, to say, "Why have I come from Geshur? It would be better for me still to be there."' Now therefore, let me see the king's face, and if there is iniquity in me, let him put me to death." [33] So when Joab came to the king and told him, he called for Absalom. Thus he came to

the king and prostrated himself on his face to the ground before the king, and the king kissed Absalom.

Psalm 66:1-7

For the choir director. A Song. A Psalm.

Shout joyfully to God, all the earth;

2 Sing the glory of His name;
   Make His praise glorious.
3 Say to God, "How awesome
   are Your works!
   Because of the greatness of Your
      power Your enemies will give
      feigned obedience to You.
4 "All the earth will worship You,
   And will sing praises to You;
   They will sing praises to
      Your name."   *Selah*

66:4 All the earth will worship You. This praise is not only an acknowledgment of God's universal Lordship, but also an intimation of the people's belief in a future worldwide kingdom where God will be worshiped (Is 66:23; Zec 14:16; Php 2:10–11).

---

5 Come and see the works of God,
   Who is awesome in *His* deeds
      toward the sons of men.
6 He turned the sea into dry land;
   They passed through the
      river on foot;
   There let us rejoice in Him!
7 He rules by His might forever;
   His eyes keep watch on the
      nations;
   Let not the rebellious exalt
      themselves.   *Selah*

Proverbs 16:25-26

25 There is a way *which seems*
   right to a man,
   But its end is the way of death.
26 A worker's appetite works
   for him,
   For his hunger urges him *on.*

John 6:52-71

52 Then the Jews *began* to argue with one another, saying, "How can this man give us *His* flesh to eat?" 53 So Jesus said to them, "Truly, truly, I say to you, unless you eat the flesh of the Son of Man and drink His blood, you have no life in yourselves. 54 He who eats My flesh and drinks My blood has eternal life, and I will raise him up on the last day. 55 For My flesh is true food, and My blood is true drink. 56 He who eats My flesh and drinks My blood abides in Me, and I in him. 57 As the living Father sent Me, and I live because of the Father, so he who eats Me, he also will live because of Me. 58 This is the bread which came down out of heaven; not as the fathers ate and died; he who eats this bread will live forever." 59 These things He said in the synagogue as He taught in Capernaum.

60 Therefore many of His disciples, when they heard *this* said, "This is a difficult statement; who can listen to it?" 61 But Jesus, conscious that His disciples grumbled at this, said to them, "Does this cause you to stumble? 62 *What* then if you see the Son of Man ascending to where He was before? 63 It is the Spirit who gives life; the flesh profits nothing; the words that I have spoken to you are spirit and are life. 64 But there are some of you who do not believe." For Jesus knew from the beginning who they were who did not believe, and who it was that would betray Him. 65 And He was saying, "For this reason I have said to you, that no one can come to Me unless it has been granted him from the Father."

6:64 Jesus knew. Reminiscent of John's words in 2:23–25, Jesus knew the hearts of men, including those disciples who followed Him. He supernaturally knew that many did not believe in Him as Messiah and Son of God so He did not entrust Himself to them. These false disciples were simply attracted to the physical phenomena (e.g., miracles and food), and failed to understand the true significance of Jesus' teaching (v. 61).

---

66 As a result of this many of His disciples withdrew and were not walking with Him anymore. 67 So Jesus said to the twelve, "You do not want to go away also, do you?" 68 Simon Peter answered Him, "Lord, to whom shall we go? You have words of eternal life. 69 We have believed and have come to know that You are the Holy One of God." 70 Jesus answered them, "Did I Myself not choose you, the twelve, and *yet* one of you is a devil?" 71 Now He meant Judas *the son* of Simon Iscariot, for he, one of the twelve, was going to betray Him.

DAY 21: If we accept the scholarly view that the surviving ancient manuscripts of 1 and 2 Samuel were poorly preserved, what should be our attitude toward these books?

Given the challenges involved in hand-copying and preserving scrolls, it is a wonder that we have the ancient documents that we do have. Our attitude ought to lean more toward amazement that we have such few discrepancies rather than toward concern over the ones that puzzle and challenge us.

Many of the discoveries in the science of analyzing ancient manuscripts involve the typical errors that commonly appear when handwritten documents are copied. For example, when two lines of text end with the same word or words, the eye of the copyist tends to skip the second line, deleting it completely. Careful comparisons between manuscripts and reconstruction of the text often reveal these simple errors.

In the case of 1 and 2 Samuel we have two ancient text families: 1) the Masoretic text in the Hebrew language and 2) the LXX (Septuagint) text in Greek that was translated by Jewish scholars in about 100 B.C. Comparing the two, it is clear that the two differ in more places with the Samuel books than with other Old Testament books. There are frequent disagreements between the texts when it comes to numbers. In settling these discrepancies, the age and language of the Masoretic text is generally considered a closer version of the original manuscript unless grammar and context indicate a copying error.

When thinking about the possibility of textual errors in the Scriptures, it is crucial to remember this: The central doctrines of the Christian faith are never based on a single verse of Scripture, nor do they rely on a disputed section of Scripture. God's plan of salvation and the main outline of Christian teaching can be found throughout Scripture.

 # MAY 22

2 Samuel 15:1–16:23

15 Now it came about after this that Absalom provided for himself a chariot and horses and fifty men as runners before him. ² Absalom used to rise early and stand beside the way to the gate; and when any man had a suit to come to the king for judgment, Absalom would call to him and say, "From what city are you?" And he would say, "Your servant is from one of the tribes of Israel." ³ Then Absalom would say to him, "See, your claims are good and right, but no man listens to you on the part of the king." ⁴ Moreover, Absalom would say, "Oh that one would appoint

15:1–6 stole away the hearts. Public hearings were always conducted early in the morning in a court held outside by the city gates. Absalom positioned himself there to win favor. Because King David was busy with other matters or with wars, and was also aging, many matters were left unresolved, building a deep feeling of resentment among the people. Absalom used that situation to undermine his father, by gratifying all he could with a favorable settlement and showing them all warm cordiality. Thus, he won the people to himself, without them knowing his wicked ambition.

me judge in the land, then every man who has any suit or cause could come to me and I would give him justice." ⁵ And when a man came near to prostrate himself before him, he would put out his hand and take hold of him and kiss him. ⁶ In this manner Absalom dealt with all Israel who came to the king for judgment; so Absalom stole away the hearts of the men of Israel.

⁷ Now it came about at the end of forty years that Absalom said to the king, "Please let me go and pay my vow which I have vowed to the LORD, in Hebron. ⁸ For your servant vowed a vow while I was living at Geshur in Aram, saying, 'If the LORD shall indeed bring me back to Jerusalem, then I will serve the LORD.'" ⁹ The king said to him, "Go in peace." So he arose and went to Hebron. ¹⁰ But Absalom sent spies throughout all the tribes of Israel, saying, "As soon as you hear the sound of the trumpet, then you shall say, 'Absalom is king in Hebron.'" ¹¹ Then two hundred men went with Absalom from Jerusalem, who were invited and went innocently, and they did not know anything. ¹² And Absalom sent for Ahithophel the Gilonite, David's counselor, from his city Giloh, while he was offering the sacrifices. And the conspiracy was strong, for the people increased continually with Absalom.

¹³ Then a messenger came to David, saying, "The hearts of the men of Israel are with Absalom." ¹⁴ David said to all his servants who were with him at Jerusalem, "Arise and let us

15:10–12 Absalom formed a conspiracy, which included taking some of the leading men to create the impression that the king supported this action and was in his old age sharing the kingdom. All of this was a subtle disguise so Absalom could have freedom to plan his revolution. Absalom was able to do this against his father not merely because of his cleverness, but also because of the laxness of his father (1Ki 1:6).

flee, for *otherwise* none of us will escape from Absalom. Go in haste, or he will overtake us quickly and bring down calamity on us and strike the city with the edge of the sword." ¹⁵ Then the king's servants said to the king, "Behold, your servants *are ready to do* whatever my lord the king chooses." ¹⁶ So the king went out and all his household with him. But the king left ten concubines to keep the house. ¹⁷ The king went out and all the people with him, and they stopped at the last house. ¹⁸ Now all his servants passed on beside him, all the Cherethites, all the Pelethites and all the Gittites, six hundred men who had come with him from Gath, passed on before the king.

¹⁹ Then the king said to Ittai the Gittite, "Why will you also go with us? Return and remain with the king, for you are a foreigner and also an exile; *return* to your own place. ²⁰ You came *only* yesterday, and shall I today make you wander with us, while I go where I will? Return and take back your brothers; mercy and truth be with you." ²¹ But Ittai answered the king and said, "As the LORD lives, and as my lord the king lives, surely wherever my lord the king may be, whether for death or for life, there also your servant will be." ²² Therefore David said to Ittai, "Go and pass over." So Ittai the Gittite passed over with all his men and all the little ones who *were* with him. ²³ While all the country was weeping with a loud voice, all the people passed over. The king also passed over the brook Kidron, and all the people passed over toward the way of the wilderness.

²⁴ Now behold, Zadok also *came,* and all the Levites with him carrying the ark of the covenant of God. And they set down the ark of God, and Abiathar came up until all the people had finished passing from the city. ²⁵ The king said to Zadok, "Return the ark of God to the city. If I find favor in the sight of the LORD, then He will bring me back again and show me both it and His habitation. ²⁶ But if He should say thus, 'I have no delight in you,' behold, here I

am, let Him do to me as seems good to Him." ²⁷ The king said also to Zadok the priest, "Are you *not* a seer? Return to the city in peace and your two sons with you, your son Ahimaaz and Jonathan the son of Abiathar. ²⁸ See, I am going to wait at the fords of the wilderness until word comes from you to inform me." ²⁹ Therefore Zadok and Abiathar returned the ark of God to Jerusalem and remained there.

³⁰ And David went up the ascent of the *Mount of* Olives, and wept as he went, and his head was covered and he walked barefoot. Then all the people who were with him each covered his head and went up weeping as they went. ³¹ Now someone told David, saying, "Ahithophel is among the conspirators with Absalom." And David said, "O LORD, I pray, make the counsel of Ahithophel foolishness."

³² It happened as David was coming to the summit, where God was worshiped, that behold, Hushai the Archite met him with his coat torn and dust on his head. ³³ David said to him, "If you pass over with me, then you will be a burden to me. ³⁴ But if you return to the city, and say to Absalom, 'I will be your servant, O king; as I have been your father's servant in time past, so I will now be your servant,' then you can thwart the counsel of Ahithophel for me. ³⁵ Are not Zadok and Abiathar the priests with you there? So it shall be that whatever you hear from the king's house, you shall report to Zadok and Abiathar the priests. ³⁶ Behold their two sons are with them there, Ahimaaz, Zadok's son and Jonathan, Abiathar's son; and by them you shall send me everything that you hear." ³⁷ So Hushai, David's friend, came into the city, and Absalom came into Jerusalem.

16 Now when David had passed a little beyond the summit, behold, Ziba the servant of Mephibosheth met him with a couple of saddled donkeys, and on them *were* two hundred loaves of bread, a hundred clusters of raisins, a hundred summer fruits, and a jug of wine. ² The king said to Ziba, "Why do you have these?" And Ziba said, "The donkeys are for the king's household to ride, and the bread and summer fruit for the young men to eat, and the wine, for whoever is faint in the wilderness to drink." ³ Then the king said, "And where is your master's son?" And Ziba said to the king, "Behold, he is staying in Jerusalem, for he said, 'Today the house of Israel will restore the kingdom of my father to me.'" ⁴ So the king said to Ziba, "Behold, all that belongs to Mephibosheth is yours." And Ziba said, "I prostrate myself; let me find favor in your sight, O my lord, the king!"

⁵When King David came to Bahurim, behold, there came out from there a man of the family of the house of Saul whose name was Shimei, the son of Gera; he came out cursing continually as he came. ⁶He threw stones at David and at all the servants of King David; and all the people and all the mighty men were at his right hand and at his left. ⁷Thus Shimei said when he cursed, "Get out, get out, you man of bloodshed, and worthless fellow! ⁸The LORD has returned upon you all the bloodshed of the house of Saul, in whose place you have reigned; and the LORD has given the kingdom into the hand of your son Absalom. And behold, you are *taken* in your own evil, for you are a man of bloodshed!"

⁹Then Abishai the son of Zeruiah said to the king, "Why should this dead dog curse my lord the king? Let me go over now and cut off his head." ¹⁰But the king said, "What have I to do with you, O sons of Zeruiah? If he curses, and if the LORD has told him, 'Curse David,' then who shall say, 'Why have you done so?'" ¹¹Then David said to Abishai and to all his servants, "Behold, my son who came out from me seeks my life; how much more now this Benjamite? Let him alone and let him curse, for the LORD has told him. ¹²Perhaps the LORD will look on my affliction and return good to me instead of his cursing this day." ¹³So David and his men went on the way; and Shimei went along on the hillside parallel with him and as he went he cursed and cast stones and threw dust at him. ¹⁴The king and all the people who were with him arrived weary and he refreshed himself there.

¹⁵Then Absalom and all the people, the men of Israel, entered Jerusalem, and Ahithophel with him. ¹⁶Now it came about when Hushai the Archite, David's friend, came to Absalom, that Hushai said to Absalom, "*Long* live the king! *Long* live the king!" ¹⁷Absalom said to Hushai, "Is this your loyalty to your friend? Why did you not go with your friend?" ¹⁸Then Hushai said to Absalom, "No! For whom the LORD, this people, and all the men of Israel have chosen, his I will be, and with him I will remain. ¹⁹Besides, whom should I serve? *Should I* not *serve* in the presence of his son? As I have served in your father's presence, so I will be in your presence."

²⁰Then Absalom said to Ahithophel, "Give your advice. What shall we do?" ²¹Ahithophel said to Absalom, "Go in to your father's concubines, whom he has left to keep the house; then all Israel will hear that you have made yourself odious to your father. The hands of all who are with you will also be strength-ened." ²²So they pitched a tent for Absalom on the roof, and Absalom went in to his father's concubines in the sight of all Israel. ²³The advice of Ahithophel, which he gave in those days, *was* as if one inquired of the word of God; so was all the advice of Ahithophel *regarded* by both David and Absalom.

Psalm 66:8–15

⁸ Bless our God, O peoples,
 And sound His praise abroad,
⁹ Who keeps us in life
 And does not allow our feet to slip.
¹⁰ For You have tried us, O God;
 You have refined us as
 silver is refined.
¹¹ You brought us into the net;
 You laid an oppressive
 burden upon our loins.
¹² You made men ride over our heads;
 We went through fire and
 through water,
 Yet You brought us out into
 a place of abundance.
¹³ I shall come into Your house
 with burnt offerings;
 I shall pay You my vows,
¹⁴ Which my lips uttered
 And my mouth spoke when
 I was in distress.
¹⁵ I shall offer to You burnt
 offerings of fat beasts,
 With the smoke of rams;
 I shall make *an offering of* bulls
 with male goats. *Selah*

Proverbs 16:27–30

²⁷ A worthless man digs up evil,
 While his words are like
 scorching fire.
²⁸ A perverse man spreads strife,
 And a slanderer separates
 intimate friends.
²⁹ A man of violence entices
 his neighbor
 And leads him in a way
 that is not good.
³⁰ He who winks his eyes *does so*
 to devise perverse things;
 He who compresses his lips
 brings evil to pass.

John 7:1–24

7 After these things Jesus was walking in Galilee, for He was unwilling to walk in Judea because the Jews were seeking to kill Him. ²Now the feast of the Jews, the Feast of Booths, was near. ³Therefore His brothers

said to Him, "Leave here and go into Judea, so that Your disciples also may see Your works which You are doing. ⁴For no one does anything in secret when he himself seeks to be *known* publicly. If You do these things, show Yourself to the world." ⁵For not even His brothers were believing in Him. ⁶So Jesus *said to them, "My time is not yet here, but your time is always opportune. ⁷The world cannot hate you, but it hates Me because I testify of it, that its deeds are evil. ⁸Go up to the feast yourselves; I do not go up to this feast because My time has not yet fully come." ⁹Having said these things to them, He stayed in Galilee.

7:4 to be *known* publicly ....show Yourself to the world. Jesus' brothers wanted Him to put on a display of His miracles. Although the text does not clearly state their motivation, perhaps they made the request for two reasons: 1) they wanted to see the miracles for themselves to determine their genuineness, and 2) they may have had similar crass political motives as did the people, namely that He would become their social and political Messiah. Jerusalem's acceptance of Him was to be the acid test for them as to whether His own family would believe in Him as Messiah.

¹⁰But when His brothers had gone up to the feast, then He Himself also went up, not publicly, but as if, in secret. ¹¹So the Jews were seeking Him at the feast and were saying, "Where is He?" ¹²There was much grumbling among the crowds concerning Him; some were saying, "He is a good man"; others were saying, "No, on the contrary, He leads the people astray." ¹³Yet no one was speaking openly of Him for fear of the Jews.

¹⁴But when it was now the midst of the feast Jesus went up into the temple, and *began to* teach. ¹⁵The Jews then were astonished, saying, "How has this man become learned, having never been educated?" ¹⁶So Jesus answered them and said, "My teaching is not Mine, but His who sent Me. ¹⁷If anyone is willing to do His will, he will know of the teaching, whether it is of God or *whether* I speak from Myself. ¹⁸He who speaks from himself seeks his own glory; but He who is seeking the glory of the One who sent Him, He is true, and there is no unrighteousness in Him.

7:17 If anyone is willing to do His will, he will know. Those who are fundamentally committed to doing the will of God will be guided by Him in the affirmation of His truth. God's truth is self-authenticating through the teaching ministry of the Holy Spirit (16:13; 1Jn 2:20, 27).

¹⁹"Did not Moses give you the Law, and *yet* none of you carries out the Law? Why do you seek to kill Me?" ²⁰The crowd answered, "You have a demon! Who seeks to kill You?" ²¹Jesus answered them, "I did one deed, and you all marvel. ²²For this reason Moses has given you circumcision (not because it is from Moses, but from the fathers), and on *the* Sabbath you circumcise a man. ²³If a man receives circumcision on *the* Sabbath so that the Law of Moses will not be broken, are you angry with Me because I made an entire man well on *the* Sabbath? ²⁴Do not judge according to appearance, but judge with righteous judgment."

DAY 22: How confused were the Jewish people about who Jesus was?

John 7:12–27 reflects the confusion among the people. In vv. 12–13 the crowds, made up of Judeans, Galileans, and Diaspora (scattered) Jews, expressed various opinions regarding Christ. The spectrum ranged from superficial acceptance ("He is a good man") to cynical rejection ("He leads the people astray"). The Jewish Talmud reveals that the latter view of deception became the predominant opinion of many Jews.

Jesus' knowledge of Scripture was supernatural. The people "astonished" (v. 15) that someone who had never studied at any great rabbinical centers or under any great rabbis could display such profound mastery of Scripture. Both the content and manner of Jesus' teachings were qualitatively different from those of any other teacher. And the people were surprised that, in spite of the ominous threat from the religious authorities (vv. 20, 32), Jesus boldly proclaimed His identity (v. 26).

"The rulers do not really know that this is the Christ, do they?" they asked. The question indicates the level of confusion and uncertainty as to who Jesus was and what to do about Him. They did not really have any firm convictions regarding Jesus' identity. They were also perplexed at the religious leaders' failure to arrest and silence Him if He really were a fraud. Such dense confusion caused the crowd to wonder if the religious authorities in private concluded that He was indeed the Christ. Mass confusion among all groups reigned regarding Jesus.

"No one knows where He is from" (v. 27). Only information regarding the Messiah's birthplace was revealed in Scripture (Mic 5:2; Mt 2:5–6). Beyond that, a tradition had developed in Jewish circles that the Messiah would appear suddenly to the people, based on a misinterpretation of Isaiah 53:8 and Malachi 3:1. In light of this, the meaning of this phrase most likely is that the identity of the Messiah would be wholly unknown until He suddenly appeared in Israel and accomplished Israel's redemption. In contrast, Jesus had lived His life in Nazareth and was known (at least superficially) to the people (v. 28).

MAY 23

2 Samuel 17:1–18:33

17 Furthermore, Ahithophel said to Absalom, "Please let me choose 12,000 men that I may arise and pursue David tonight. ² I will come upon him while he is weary and exhausted and terrify him, so that all the people who are with him will flee. Then I will strike down the king alone, ³ and I will bring back all the people to you. The return of everyone depends on the man you seek; *then* all the people will be at peace." ⁴ So the plan pleased Absalom and all the elders of Israel.

⁵ Then Absalom said, "Now call Hushai the Archite also, and let us hear what he has to say." ⁶ When Hushai had come to Absalom, Absalom said to him, "Ahithophel has spoken thus. Shall we carry out his plan? If not, you speak." ⁷ So Hushai said to Absalom, "This time the advice that Ahithophel has given is not good." ⁸ Moreover, Hushai said, "You know your father and his men, that they are mighty men and they are fierce, like a bear robbed of her cubs in the field. And your father is an expert in warfare, and will not spend the night with the people. ⁹ Behold, he has now hidden himself in one of the caves or in another place; and it will be when he falls on them at the first attack, that whoever hears *it* will say, 'There has been a slaughter among the people who follow Absalom.' ¹⁰ And even the one who is valiant, whose heart is like the heart of a lion, will completely lose heart; for all Israel knows that your father is a mighty man and those who are with him are valiant men. ¹¹ But I counsel that all Israel be surely gathered to you, from Dan even to Beersheba, as the sand that is by the sea in abundance, and that you personally go into battle. ¹² So we shall come to him in one of the places where he can be found, and we will fall on him as the dew falls on the ground; and of him and of all the men who are with him, not even one will be left. ¹³ If he withdraws into a city, then all Israel shall bring ropes to

that city, and we will drag it into the valley until not even a small stone is found there." ¹⁴ Then Absalom and all the men of Israel said, "The counsel of Hushai the Archite is better than the counsel of Ahithophel." For the LORD had ordained to thwart the good counsel of Ahithophel, so that the LORD might bring calamity on Absalom.

17:7–13 Providentially, the Lord took control of the situation through the counsel of Hushai (15:32) who advised Absalom in such a way as to give David time to prepare for war with Absalom. Hushai's plan seemed best to the elders. It had two features: 1) the need for an army larger than 12,000 (v. 1), so that Absalom would not lose, and 2) the king leading the army into battle (an appeal to Absalom's arrogance).

17:14 the LORD had ordained. The text notes that Ahithophel's advice was rejected by Absalom because the Lord had determined to defeat the rebellion of Absalom, as prayed for by David (15:31). God's providence was controlling all the intrigues among the usurper's counselors.

¹⁵ Then Hushai said to Zadok and to Abiathar the priests, "This is what Ahithophel counseled Absalom and the elders of Israel, and this is what I have counseled. ¹⁶ Now therefore, send quickly and tell David, saying, 'Do not spend the night at the fords of the wilderness, but by all means cross over, or else the king and all the people who are with him will be destroyed.'" ¹⁷ Now Jonathan and Ahimaaz were staying at En-rogel, and a maidservant would go and tell them, and they would go and tell King David, for they could not be seen entering the city. ¹⁸ But a lad did see them and told Absalom; so the two of them departed quickly and came to the house of a man in Bahurim, who had a well in his courtyard, and

they went down into it. [19] And the woman took a covering and spread it over the well's mouth and scattered grain on it, so that nothing was known. [20] Then Absalom's servants came to the woman at the house and said, "Where are Ahimaaz and Jonathan?" And the woman said to them, "They have crossed the brook of water." And when they searched and could not find *them*, they returned to Jerusalem.

[21] It came about after they had departed that they came up out of the well and went and told King David; and they said to David, "Arise and cross over the water quickly for thus Ahithophel has counseled against you." [22] Then David and all the people who *were* with him arose and crossed the Jordan; and by dawn not even one remained who had not crossed the Jordan.

[23] Now when Ahithophel saw that his counsel was not followed, he saddled *his* donkey and arose and went to his home, to his city, and set his house in order, and strangled himself; thus he died and was buried in the grave of his father.

[24] Then David came to Mahanaim. And Absalom crossed the Jordan, he and all the men of Israel with him. [25] Absalom set Amasa over the army in place of Joab. Now Amasa was the son of a man whose name was Ithra the Israelite, who went in to Abigail the daughter of Nahash, sister of Zeruiah, Joab's mother. [26] And Israel and Absalom camped in the land of Gilead.

[27] Now when David had come to Mahanaim, Shobi the son of Nahash from Rabbah of the sons of Ammon, Machir the son of Ammiel from Lo-debar, and Barzillai the Gileadite from Rogelim, [28] brought beds, basins, pottery, wheat, barley, flour, parched *grain*, beans, lentils, parched *seeds*, [29] honey, curds, sheep, and cheese of the herd, for David and for the people who *were* with him, to eat; for they said, "The people are hungry and weary and thirsty in the wilderness."

18 Then David numbered the people who were with him and set over them commanders of thousands and commanders of hundreds. [2] David sent the people out, one third under the command of Joab, one third under the command of Abishai the son of Zeruiah, Joab's brother, and one third under the command of Ittai the Gittite. And the king said to the people, "I myself will surely go out with you also." [3] But the people said, "You should not go out; for if we indeed flee, they will not care about us; even if half of us die, they will not care about us. But you are worth ten thousand of us; therefore now it is better that you *be ready* to help us from the city."

[4] Then the king said to them, "Whatever seems best to you I will do." So the king stood beside the gate, and all the people went out by hundreds and thousands. [5] The king charged Joab and Abishai and Ittai, saying, "*Deal* gently for my sake with the young man Absalom." And all the people heard when the king charged all the commanders concerning Absalom.

[6] Then the people went out into the field against Israel, and the battle took place in the forest of Ephraim. [7] The people of Israel were defeated there before the servants of David, and the slaughter there that day was great, 20,000 men. [8] For the battle there was spread over the whole countryside, and the forest devoured more people that day than the sword devoured.

[9] Now Absalom happened to meet the servants of David. For Absalom was riding on *his* mule, and the mule went under the thick branches of a great oak. And his head caught fast in the oak, so he was left hanging between heaven and earth, while the mule that was under him kept going. [10] When a certain man saw *it*, he told Joab and said, "Behold, I saw Absalom hanging in an oak." [11] Then Joab said to the man who had told him, "Now behold, you saw *him!* Why then did you not strike him there to the ground? And I would have given you ten *pieces* of silver and a belt." [12] The man said to Joab, "Even if I should receive a thousand *pieces of* silver in my hand, I would not put out my hand against the king's son; for in our hearing the king charged you and Abishai and Ittai, saying, 'Protect for me the young man Absalom!' [13] Otherwise, if I had dealt treacherously against his life (and there is nothing hidden from the king), then you yourself would have stood aloof." [14] Then Joab said, "I will not waste time here with you." So he took three spears in his hand and thrust them through the heart of Absalom while he was yet alive in the midst of the oak. [15] And ten young men who carried Joab's armor gathered around and struck Absalom and killed him.

[16] Then Joab blew the trumpet, and the people returned from pursuing Israel, for Joab restrained the people. [17] They took Absalom and cast him into a deep pit in the forest and erected over him a very great heap of stones. And all Israel fled, each to his tent. [18] Now Absalom in his lifetime had taken and set up for himself a pillar which is in the King's Valley, for he said, "I have no son to preserve my name." So he named the pillar after his own name, and it is called Absalom's Monument to this day.

[19] Then Ahimaaz the son of Zadok said, "Please let me run and bring the king news

that the LORD has freed him from the hand of his enemies." ²⁰ But Joab said to him, "You are not the man to carry news this day, but you shall carry news another day; however, you shall carry no news today because the king's son is dead." ²¹ Then Joab said to the Cushite, "Go, tell the king what you have seen." So the Cushite bowed to Joab and ran. ²² Now Ahimaaz the son of Zadok said once more to Joab, "But whatever happens, please let me also run after the Cushite." And Joab said, "Why would you run, my son, since you will have no reward for going?" ²³ "But whatever happens," he said, "I will run." So he said to him, "Run." Then Ahimaaz ran by way of the plain and passed up the Cushite.

²⁴ Now David was sitting between the two gates; and the watchman went up to the roof of the gate by the wall, and raised his eyes and looked, and behold, a man running by himself. ²⁵ The watchman called and told the king. And the king said, "If he is by himself there is good news in his mouth." And he came nearer and nearer. ²⁶ Then the watchman saw another man running; and the watchman called to the gatekeeper and said, "Behold, another man running by himself." And the king said, "This one also is bringing good news." ²⁷ The watchman said, "I think the running of the first one is like the running of Ahimaaz the son of Zadok." And the king said, "This is a good man and comes with good news."

²⁸ Ahimaaz called and said to the king, "All is well." And he prostrated himself before the king with his face to the ground. And he said, "Blessed is the LORD your God, who has delivered up the men who lifted their hands against my lord the king." ²⁹ The king said, "Is it well with the young man Absalom?" And Ahimaaz answered, "When Joab sent the king's servant, and your servant, I saw a great tumult, but I did not know what it was." ³⁰ Then the king said, "Turn aside and stand here." So he turned aside and stood still.

³¹ Behold, the Cushite arrived, and the Cushite said, "Let my lord the king receive good news, for the LORD has freed you this day from the hand of all those who rose up against you." ³² Then the king said to the Cushite, "Is it well with the young man Absalom?" And the Cushite answered, "Let the enemies of my lord the king, and all who rise up against you for evil, be as that young man!"

³³ The king was deeply moved and went up to the chamber over the gate and wept. And thus he said as he walked, "O my son Absalom, my son, my son Absalom! Would I had died instead of you, O Absalom, my son, my son!"

18:33 my son. Repeated 5 times in this verse, David lamented the death of Absalom, his son (19:5). In spite of all the harm that Absalom had caused, David was preoccupied with his personal loss in a melancholy way that seems to be consistent with his weakness as a father. It was an unwarranted zeal for such a worthless son, and a warning about the pitiful results of sin.

Psalm 66:16-20

¹⁶ Come and hear, all who fear God,
And I will tell of what He
has done for my soul.
¹⁷ I cried to Him with my mouth,
And He was extolled with my tongue.
¹⁸ If I regard wickedness in my heart,
The Lord will not hear;
¹⁹ But certainly God has heard;
He has given heed to the
voice of my prayer.
²⁰ Blessed be God,
Who has not turned away my prayer
Nor His lovingkindness from me.

Proverbs 16:31-32

³¹ A gray head is a crown of glory;
It is found in the way of
righteousness.
³² He who is slow to anger is
better than the mighty,
And he who rules his spirit, than
he who captures a city.

John 7:25-53

²⁵ So some of the people of Jerusalem were saying, "Is this not the man whom they are seeking to kill? ²⁶ Look, He is speaking publicly, and they are saying nothing to Him. The rulers do not really know that this is the Christ, do they? ²⁷ However, we know where this man is from; but whenever the Christ may come, no one knows where He is from." ²⁸ Then Jesus cried out in the temple, teaching and saying, "You both know Me and know where I am from; and I have not come of Myself, but He who sent Me is true, whom you do not know. ²⁹ I know Him, because I am from Him, and He sent Me." ³⁰ So they were seeking to seize Him; and no man laid his hand on Him, because His hour had not yet come. ³¹ But many of the crowd believed in Him; and they were saying, "When the Christ comes, He will not perform more signs than those which this man has, will He?"

³² The Pharisees heard the crowd muttering

7:31 many...believed. Divided conviction existed among the people regarding Jesus. While some wanted to seize Him, a small remnant of genuine believers existed among the crowds. The question here anticipates a negative answer, i.e., the Messiah could do no greater kinds of miracles than those Jesus had done.

these things about Him, and the chief priests and the Pharisees sent officers to seize Him. ³³Therefore Jesus said, "For a little while longer I am with you, then I go to Him who sent Me. ³⁴You will seek Me, and will not find Me; and where I am, you cannot come." ³⁵The Jews then said to one another, "Where does this man intend to go that we will not find Him? He is not intending to go to the Dispersion among the Greeks, and teach the Greeks, is He? ³⁶What is this statement that He said, 'You will seek Me, and will not find Me; and where I am, you cannot come'?"

³⁷Now on the last day, the great *day* of the feast, Jesus stood and cried out, saying, "If anyone is thirsty, let him come to Me and drink. ³⁸He who believes in Me, as the Scripture said, 'From his innermost being will flow rivers of living water.'" ³⁹But this He spoke of the Spirit, whom those who believed in Him were to receive; for the Spirit was not yet *given*, because Jesus was not yet glorified.

⁴⁰*Some* of the people therefore, when they heard these words, were saying, "This certainly is the Prophet." ⁴¹Others were saying, "This is the Christ." Still others were saying, "Surely the Christ is not going to come from Galilee, is He? ⁴²Has not the Scripture said

that the Christ comes from the descendants of David, and from Bethlehem, the village where David was?" ⁴³So a division occurred in the crowd because of Him. ⁴⁴Some of them wanted to seize Him, but no one laid hands on Him.

⁴⁵The officers then came to the chief priests and Pharisees, and they said to them, "Why did you not bring Him?" ⁴⁶The officers answered, "Never has a man spoken the way this man speaks." ⁴⁷The Pharisees then answered them, "You have not also been led astray, have you? ⁴⁸No one of the rulers or Pharisees has believed in Him, has he? ⁴⁹But this crowd which does not know the Law is accursed." ⁵⁰Nicodemus (he who came to Him before, being one of them) *said to them, ⁵¹"Our Law does not judge a man unless it first hears from him and knows what he is doing, does it?" ⁵²They answered him, "You are not also from Galilee, are you? Search, and see that no prophet arises out of Galilee." ⁵³[Everyone went to his home.

7:37–52 This section catalogues the different reactions of people to Jesus' claims. These reactions have become universal patterns for reactions to Him through the ages. This section may be divided into the claim of Christ (vv. 37–39) and the reactions to Christ (vv. 40–52). The reactions may be subdivided into 5 sections: 1) the reaction of the convinced (vv. 40–41a); 2) the reaction of the contrary (vv. 41b–42); 3) the reaction of the hostile (vv. 43–44); 4) the reaction of the confused (vv. 45–46); and 5) the reaction of the religious authorities (vv. 47–52).

DAY 23: What does the "living water" have to do with Jesus?

A tradition grew up in the few centuries before Jesus that on the 7 days of the Feast of Tabernacles, a golden container filled with water from the pool of Siloam was carried in procession by the high priest back to the temple. As the procession came to the Watergate on the south side of the inner temple court, 3 trumpet blasts were made to mark the joy of the occasion and the people recited Isaiah 12:3, "With joy you will draw water from the wells of salvation." At the temple, while onlookers watched, the priests would march around the altar with the water container while the temple choir sang the Hallel (Pss 113–118). The water was offered in sacrifice to God at the time of the morning sacrifice. The use of the water symbolized the blessing of adequate rainfall for crops.

In John 7:37, Jesus used this event as an object lesson and opportunity to make a very public invitation on the last day of the feast for His people to accept Him as the living water. His words recall Isaiah 55:1. "If anyone is *thirsty*, let him *come* to Me and *drink*" (emphasis added). These 3 words summarize the gospel invitation. A recognition of need leads to an approach to the source of provision, followed by receiving what is needed. The thirsty, needy soul feels the craving to come to the Savior and drink, i.e., receive the salvation that He offers.

"From his innermost being will flow rivers of living water" (v. 38). The water-pouring rite was also associated within Jewish tradition as a foreshadowing of the eschatological rivers of living water foreseen in Ezekiel 47:1–9 and Zechariah 13:1. The significance of Jesus' invitation centers in the fact that He was the fulfillment of all the Feast of Tabernacles anticipated, i.e., He was the One who provided the living water that gives eternal life to man (4:10–11). By this "He spoke of the Spirit" (v. 39). The impartation of the Holy Spirit is the source of spiritual and eternal life.

MAY 24

2 Samuel 19:1–20:26

19 Then it was told Joab, "Behold, the king is weeping and mourns for Absalom." ²The victory that day was turned to mourning for all the people, for the people heard *it* said that day, "The king is grieved for his son." ³So the people went by stealth into the city that day, as people who are humiliated steal away when they flee in battle. ⁴The king covered his face and cried out with a loud voice, "O my son Absalom, O Absalom, my son, my son!" ⁵Then Joab came into the house to the king and said, "Today you have covered with shame the faces of all your servants, who today have saved your life and the lives of your sons and daughters, the lives of your wives, and the lives of your concubines, ⁶by loving those who hate you, and by hating those who love you. For you have shown today that princes and servants are nothing to you; for I know this day that if Absalom were alive and all of us were dead today, then you would be pleased. ⁷Now therefore arise, go out and speak kindly to your servants, for I swear by the LORD, if you do not go out, surely not a man will pass the night with you, and this will be worse for you than all the evil that has come upon you from your youth until now." ⁸So the king arose and sat in the gate. When they told all the people, saying, "Behold, the king is sitting in the gate," then all the people came before the king.

Now Israel had fled, each to his tent. ⁹All the people were quarreling throughout all the

19:7 not a man will pass the night with you. Joab, who was the esteemed general of the army, was a dangerous person because of that power. He was also dangerous to David because he had disobeyed his command to spare Absalom, and killed him with no remorse. When he warned David that he would be in deep trouble if he did not immediately express appreciation to his men for their victory, David knew he could be in serious danger.

tribes of Israel, saying, "The king delivered us from the hand of our enemies and saved us from the hand of the Philistines, but now he has fled out of the land from Absalom. ¹⁰However, Absalom, whom we anointed over us, has died in battle. Now then, why are you silent about bringing the king back?"

¹¹Then King David sent to Zadok and Abiathar the priests, saying, "Speak to the elders of Judah, saying, 'Why are you the last to bring the king back to his house, since the word of all Israel has come to the king, *even* to his house? ¹²You are my brothers; you are my bone and my flesh. Why then should you be the last to bring back the king?' ¹³Say to Amasa, 'Are you not my bone and my flesh? May God do so to me, and more also, if you will not be commander of the army before me continually in place of Joab.'" ¹⁴Thus he

19:13 Amasa...commander of the army...in place of Joab. David appointed Amasa commander of his army, hoping to secure the allegiance of those who had followed Amasa when he led Absalom's forces, especially those of Judah. This appointment did persuade the tribe of Judah to support David's return to the kingship (v. 14) and secured the animosity of Joab against Amasa for taking his position (20:8–10).

turned the hearts of all the men of Judah as one man, so that they sent *word* to the king, *saying*, "Return, you and all your servants." ¹⁵The king then returned and came as far as the Jordan. And Judah came to Gilgal in order to go to meet the king, to bring the king across the Jordan.

¹⁶Then Shimei the son of Gera, the Benjamite who was from Bahurim, hurried and came down with the men of Judah to meet King David. ¹⁷There were a thousand men of Benjamin with him, with Ziba the servant of the house of Saul, and his fifteen sons and his twenty servants with him; and they rushed to the Jordan before the king. ¹⁸Then they kept crossing the ford to bring over the king's household, and to do what was good in his

sight. And Shimei the son of Gera fell down before the king as he was about to cross the Jordan. ¹⁹ So he said to the king, "Let not my lord consider me guilty, nor remember what your servant did wrong on the day when my lord the king came out from Jerusalem, so that the king would take *it* to heart. ²⁰ For your servant knows that I have sinned; therefore behold, I have come today, the first of all the house of Joseph to go down to meet my lord the king." ²¹ But Abishai the son of Zeruiah said, "Should not Shimei be put to death for this, because he cursed the LORD'S anointed?" ²² David then said, "What have I to do with you, O sons of Zeruiah, that you should this day be an adversary to me? Should any man be put to death in Israel today? For do I not know that I am king over Israel today?" ²³ The king said to Shimei, "You shall not die." Thus the king swore to him.

²⁴ Then Mephibosheth the son of Saul came down to meet the king; and he had neither cared for his feet, nor trimmed his mustache, nor washed his clothes, from the day the king departed until the day he came *home* in peace. ²⁵ It was when he came from Jerusalem to meet the king, that the king said to him, "Why did you not go with me, Mephibosheth?" ²⁶ So he answered, "O my lord, the king, my servant deceived me; for your servant said, 'I will saddle a donkey for myself that I may ride on it and go with the king,' because your servant is lame. ²⁷ Moreover, he has slandered your servant to my lord the king; but my lord the king is like the angel of God, therefore do what is good in your sight. ²⁸ For all my father's household was nothing but dead men before my lord the king; yet you set your servant among those who ate at your own table. What right do I have yet that I should complain anymore to the king?" ²⁹ So the king said to him, "Why do you still speak of your affairs? I have decided, 'You and Ziba shall divide the land.'" ³⁰ Mephibosheth said to the king, "Let him even take it all, since my lord the king has come safely to his own house."

³¹ Now Barzillai the Gileadite had come down from Rogelim; and he went on to the Jordan with the king to escort him over the Jordan. ³² Now Barzillai was very old, being eighty years old; and he had sustained the king while he stayed at Mahanaim, for he was a very great man. ³³ The king said to Barzillai, "You cross over with me and I will sustain you in Jerusalem with me." ³⁴ But Barzillai said to the king, "How long have I yet to live, that I should go up with the king to Jerusalem? ³⁵ I

20:11 one of Joab's young men. Joab was reinstated as commander of David's army by his troops. It is a striking illustration of Joab's influence over the army that he could murder the commander whom David had chosen, a killing right before their eyes, and they would follow him unanimously as their leader in pursuit of Sheba.

am now eighty years old. Can I distinguish between good and bad? Or can your servant taste what I eat or what I drink? Or can I hear anymore the voice of singing men and women? Why then should your servant be an added burden to my lord the king? ³⁶ Your servant would merely cross over the Jordan with the king. Why should the king compensate me *with* this reward? ³⁷ Please let your servant return, that I may die in my own city near the grave of my father and my mother. However, here is your servant Chimham, let him cross over with my lord the king, and do for him what is good in your sight. ³⁸ The king answered, "Chimham shall cross over with me, and I will do for him what is good in your sight; and whatever you require of me, I will do for you." ³⁹ All the people crossed over the Jordan and the king crossed too. The king then kissed Barzillai and blessed him, and he returned to his place.

⁴⁰ Now the king went on to Gilgal, and Chimham went on with him; and all the people of Judah and also half the people of Israel accompanied the king. ⁴¹ And behold, all the men of Israel came to the king and said to the king, "Why had our brothers the men of Judah stolen you away, and brought the king and his household and all David's men with him over the Jordan?" ⁴² Then all the men of Judah answered the men of Israel, "Because the king is a close relative to us. Why then are you angry about this matter? Have we eaten at all at the king's *expense,* or has anything been taken for us?" ⁴³ But the men of Israel answered the men of Judah and said, "We have ten parts in the king, therefore we also have more *claim* on David than you. Why then did you treat us with contempt? Was it not our advice first to bring back our king?" Yet the words of the men of Judah were harsher than the words of the men of Israel.

20 Now a worthless fellow happened to be there whose name was Sheba, the son of Bichri, a Benjamite; and he blew the trumpet and said,

"We have no portion in David,
Nor do we have inheritance
in the son of Jesse;
Every man to his tents, O Israel!"

2 So all the men of Israel withdrew from following David *and* followed Sheba the son of Bichri; but the men of Judah remained steadfast to their king, from the Jordan even to Jerusalem.

3 Then David came to his house at Jerusalem, and the king took the ten women, the concubines whom he had left to keep the house, and placed them under guard and provided them with sustenance, but did not go in to them. So they were shut up until the day of their death, living as widows.

4 Then the king said to Amasa, "Call out the men of Judah for me within three days, and be present here yourself." 5 So Amasa went to call out *the men of* Judah, but he delayed longer than the set time which he had appointed him. 6 And David said to Abishai, "Now Sheba the son of Bichri will do us more harm than Absalom; take your lord's servants and pursue him, so that he does not find for himself fortified cities and escape from our sight." 7 So Joab's men went out after him, along with the Cherethites and the Pelethites and all the mighty men; and they went out from Jerusalem to pursue Sheba the son of Bichri. 8 When they were at the large stone which is in Gibeon, Amasa came to meet them. Now Joab was dressed in his military attire, and over it was a belt with a sword in its sheath fastened at his waist; and as he went forward, it fell out. 9 Joab said to Amasa, "Is it well with you, my brother?" And Joab took Amasa by the beard with his right hand to kiss him. 10 But Amasa was not on guard against the sword which was in Joab's hand so he struck him in the belly with it and poured out his inward parts on the ground, and did not *strike* him again, and he died. Then Joab and Abishai his brother pursued Sheba the son of Bichri. 11 Now there stood by him one of Joab's young men, and said, "Whoever favors Joab and whoever is for David, *let him* follow Joab." 12 But Amasa lay wallowing in *his* blood in the middle of the highway. And when the man saw that all the people stood still, he removed Amasa from the highway into the field and threw a garment over him when he saw that everyone who came by him stood still. 13 As soon as he was removed from the highway, all the men passed on after Joab to pursue Sheba the son of Bichri.

14 Now he went through all the tribes of Israel to Abel, even Beth-maacah, and all the Berites; and they were gathered together and also went after him. 15 They came and besieged him in Abel Beth-maacah, and they cast up a siege ramp against the city, and it stood by the rampart; and all the people who were with Joab were wreaking destruction in order to topple the wall. 16 Then a wise woman called from the city, "Hear, hear! Please tell Joab, 'Come here that I may speak with you.'" 17 So he approached her, and the woman said, "Are you Joab?" And he answered, "I am." Then she said to him, "Listen to the words of your maidservant." And he answered, "I am listening." 18 Then she spoke, saying, "Formerly they used to say, 'They will surely ask *advice* at Abel,' and thus they ended *the dispute.* 19 I am of those who are peaceable *and* faithful in Israel. You are seeking to destroy a city, even a mother in Israel. Why would you swallow up the inheritance of the LORD?" 20 Joab replied, "Far be it, far be it from me that I should swallow up or destroy! 21 Such is not the case. But a man from the hill country of Ephraim, Sheba the son of Bichri by name, has lifted up his hand against King David. Only hand him over, and I will depart from the city." And the woman said to Joab, "Behold, his head will be thrown to you over the wall." 22 Then the woman wisely came to all the people. And they cut off the head of Sheba the son of Bichri and threw it to Joab. So he blew the trumpet, and they were dispersed from the city, each to his tent. Joab also returned to the king at Jerusalem.

23 Now Joab was over the whole army of Israel, and Benaiah the son of Jehoiada was over the Cherethites and the Pelethites; 24 and Adoram was over the forced labor, and Jehoshaphat the son of Ahilud was the recorder; 25 and Sheva was scribe, and Zadok and Abiathar were priests; 26 and Ira the Jairite was also a priest to David.

Psalm 67:1–7

For the choir director; with stringed
instruments. A Psalm. A Song.

God be gracious to us and bless us,
And cause His face to shine
upon us—   *Selah*
2 That Your way may be
known on the earth,
Your salvation among all nations.
3 Let the peoples praise You, O God;
Let all the peoples praise You.
4 Let the nations be glad and sing for joy;
For You will judge the peoples
with uprightness
And guide the nations
on the earth.   *Selah*

⁵ Let the peoples praise You, O God;
Let all the peoples praise You.
⁶ The earth has yielded its produce;
God, our God, blesses us.
⁷ God blesses us,
That all the ends of the
earth may fear Him.

Proverbs 16:33–17:1

³³ The lot is cast into the lap,
But its every decision is
from the LORD.

16:33 lot. Casting lots was a method often used to reveal God's purposes in a matter (Jos 14:1–2; 1Sa 14:38–43; 1Ch 25:8–31; Jon 1:7; Ac 1:26). The High Priest may have carried lots in his sacred vest, along with the Urim and Thummim.

17 Better is a dry morsel and
quietness with it
Than a house full of
feasting with strife.

John 8:1–30

8 But Jesus went to the Mount of Olives. ² Early in the morning He came again into the temple, and all the people were coming to Him; and He sat down and *began* to teach them. ³ The scribes and the Pharisees *brought a woman caught in adultery, and having set her in the center *of the court,* ⁴ they *said to Him, "Teacher, this woman has been caught in adultery, in the very act. ⁵ Now in the Law Moses commanded us to stone such women; what then do You say?" ⁶ They were saying this, testing Him, so that they might have grounds for accusing Him. But Jesus stooped down and with His finger wrote on the ground. ⁷ But when they persisted in asking Him, He straightened up, and said to them, "He who is without sin among you, let him *be the* first to throw a stone at her." ⁸ Again He stooped down and wrote on the ground. ⁹ When they heard it, they *began* to go out one by one, beginning with the older ones, and He was left alone, and the woman, where she was, in the center *of the court.* ¹⁰ Straightening up, Jesus said to her, "Woman, where are they? Did no one condemn you?" ¹¹ She said, "No one, Lord." And Jesus said, "I do not condemn you, either. Go. From now on sin no more."]

¹² Then Jesus again spoke to them, saying, "I am the Light of the world; he who follows Me will not walk in the darkness, but will have the Light of life." ¹³ So the Pharisees said to Him, "You are testifying about Yourself; Your testimony is not true." ¹⁴ Jesus answered and said to them, "Even if I testify about Myself, My testimony is true, for I know where I came from and where I am going; but you do not know where I come from or where I am going. ¹⁵ You judge according to the flesh; I am not judging anyone. ¹⁶ But even if I do judge, My judgment is true; for I am not alone *in it,* but I and the Father who sent Me. ¹⁷ Even in your law it has been written that the testimony of two men is true. ¹⁸ I am He who testifies about Myself, and the Father who sent Me testifies about Me." ¹⁹ So they were saying to Him, "Where is Your Father?" Jesus answered, "You know neither Me nor My Father; if you knew Me, you would know My Father also." ²⁰ These words He spoke in the treasury, as He taught in the temple; and no one seized Him, because His hour had not yet come.

²¹ Then He said again to them, "I go away, and you will seek Me, and will die in your sin; where I am going, you cannot come." ²² So the Jews were saying, "Surely He will not kill Himself, will He, since He says, 'Where I am going, you cannot come'?" ²³ And He was saying to them, "You are from below, I am from above; you are of this world, I am not of this world. ²⁴ Therefore I said to you that you will die in your sins; for unless you believe that I am *He,* you will die in your sins." ²⁵ So they were saying to Him, "Who are You?" Jesus said to them, "What have I been saying to you *from* the beginning? ²⁶ I have many things to speak and to judge concerning you, but He

8:24 unless you believe. Jesus emphasized that the fatal, unforgivable, and eternal sin is failure to believe in Him as Messiah and Son of God. In truth, all other sins can be forgiven if this one is repented of. **I am He.** The word *"He"* is not part of the original statement. Jesus' words were not constructed normally but were influenced by Old Testament Hebrew usage. It is an absolute usage meaning "I AM" and has immense theological significance. The reference may be to both Exodus 3:14 where the Lord declared His name as "I AM" and to Isaiah 40–55 where the phrase "I am" occurs repeatedly (especially 43:10, 13, 25; 46:4; 48:12). In this, Jesus referred to Himself as the God (Yahweh—the Lord) of the OT, and directly claimed full deity for Himself, prompting the Jews' question of v. 25.

who sent Me is true; and the things which I heard from Him, these I speak to the world." [27] They did not realize that He had been speaking to them about the Father. [28] So Jesus said, "When you lift up the Son of Man, then you will know that I am *He,* and I do nothing on My own initiative, but I speak these things as the Father taught Me. [29] And He who sent Me is with Me; He has not left Me alone, for I always do the things that are pleasing to Him." [30] As He spoke these things, many came to believe in Him.

DAY 24: How is Jesus the light of the world?

In John 8:12–21, the word "again" indicates that Jesus spoke once more to the people at this same Feast of Tabernacles (7:2, 10). While Jesus first used the water-drawing rite (7:37–39) as a metaphor to portray the ultimate spiritual truth of Himself as Messiah who fulfills all that the feast anticipated, He then turned to another rite that traditionally occurred at the feast: the lighting ceremony. During Tabernacles, 4 large lamps in the temple's court of women were lit and an exuberant nightly celebration took place under their light with people dancing through the night and holding burning torches in their hands while singing songs and praises. The Levitical orchestras also played.

Jesus took this opportunity of the lighting celebration to portray another spiritual analogy for the people: "I am the Light of the world" (v. 12). This is the second "I am" statement (6:35). John has already used the "Light" metaphor for Jesus (1:4). Jesus' metaphor here is steeped in Old Testament allusions (Ex 13:21–22; 14:19–25; Pss 27:1; 119:105; Pr 6:23; Eze 1:4, 13, 26–28; Hab 3:3–4). The phrase highlights Jesus' role as Messiah and Son of God (Ps 27:1; Mal 4:2). The Old Testament indicates that the coming age of Messiah would be a time when the Lord would be a light for His people (Is. 60:19–22; see Rev 21:23–24), as well as for the whole earth (Is. 42:6; 49:6). Zechariah 14:5b–8 has an emphasis on God as the light of the world who gives living waters to His people. This latter passage probably formed the liturgical readings for the Feast of Tabernacles.

"He who follows Me will not walk in the darkness, but will have the Light of life." The word "follows" conveys the idea of someone who gives himself completely to the person followed. No half-hearted followers exist in Jesus' mind (Mt 8:18–22; 10:38–39). A veiled reference exists here to the Jews, following the pillar of cloud and fire that led them during the Exodus (Ex 13:21).

MAY 25

2 Samuel 21:1–22:51

21 Now there was a famine in the days of David for three years, year after year; and David sought the presence of the LORD. And the LORD said, "It is for Saul and his bloody house, because he put the Gibeonites to death." [2] So the king called the Gibeonites and spoke to them (now the Gibeonites were not of the sons of Israel but of the remnant of the Amorites, and the sons of Israel made a covenant with them, but Saul had sought to kill them in his zeal for the sons of Israel and Judah). [3] Thus David said to the Gibeonites, "What should I do for you? And how can I make atonement that you may bless the inheritance of the LORD?" [4] Then the Gibeonites said to him, "We have no *concern* of silver or gold with Saul or his house, nor is it for us to put any man to death in Israel." And he said, "I will do for you whatever you say." [5] So they said to the king, "The man who consumed us and who planned to exterminate us from remaining within any border of Israel, [6] let seven men from his sons be given to us, and we will hang them before the LORD in Gibeah of Saul, the chosen of the LORD." And the king said, "I will give *them.*"

[7] But the king spared Mephibosheth, the son of Jonathan the son of Saul, because of the oath of the LORD which was between them,

21:1–2 Saul and his bloody house. By divine revelation David learned that the famine was a result of sin committed by Saul; namely that he had slain the Gibeonites. There is no further reference to this event. Saul was probably trying to do as God commanded and rid the land of the remnant of heathen in order that Israel might prosper (v. 2). But in his zeal he had committed a serious sin; he had broken a covenant that had been made 400 years before between Joshua and the Gibeonites, who were in the land when Israel took possession of it. They deceived Joshua into making the covenant, but it was, nevertheless, a covenant (Jos 9:3–27). Covenant keeping was no small matter to God (Jos 9:20).

between David and Saul's son Jonathan. ⁸ So the king took the two sons of Rizpah the daughter of Aiah, Armoni and Mephibosheth whom she had borne to Saul, and the five sons of Merab the daughter of Saul, whom she had borne to Adriel the son of Barzillai the Meholathite. ⁹ Then he gave them into the hands of the Gibeonites, and they hanged them in the mountain before the LORD, so that the seven of them fell together; and they were put to death in the first days of harvest at the beginning of barley harvest.

¹⁰ And Rizpah the daughter of Aiah took sackcloth and spread it for herself on the rock, from the beginning of harvest until it rained on them from the sky; and she allowed neither the birds of the sky to rest on them by day nor the beasts of the field by night. ¹¹ When it was told David what Rizpah the daughter of Aiah, the concubine of Saul, had done, ¹² then David went and took the bones of Saul and the bones of Jonathan his son from the men of Jabesh-gilead, who had stolen them from the open square of Beth-shan, where the Philistines had hanged them on the day the Philistines struck down Saul in Gilboa. ¹³ He brought up the bones of Saul and the bones of Jonathan his son from there, and they gathered the bones of those who had been hanged. ¹⁴ They buried the bones of Saul and Jonathan his son in the country of Benjamin in Zela, in the grave of Kish his father; thus they did all that the king commanded, and after that God was moved by prayer for the land.

¹⁵ Now when the Philistines were at war again with Israel, David went down and his servants with him; and as they fought against the Philistines, David became weary. ¹⁶ Then Ishbi-benob, who was among the descendants of the giant, the weight of whose spear was three hundred *shekels* of bronze in weight, was girded with a new *sword*, and he intended to kill David. ¹⁷ But Abishai the son of Zeruiah helped him, and struck the Philistine and killed him. Then the men of David swore to him, saying, "You shall not go out again with us to battle, so that you do not extinguish the lamp of Israel."

¹⁸ Now it came about after this that there was war again with the Philistines at Gob; then Sibbecai the Hushathite struck down Saph, who was among the descendants of the giant. ¹⁹ There was war with the Philistines again at Gob, and Elhanan the son of Jaare-oregim the Bethlehemite killed Goliath the Gittite, the shaft of whose spear was like a weaver's beam. ²⁰ There was war at Gath again, where there was a man of *great* stature

who had six fingers on each hand and six toes on each foot, twenty-four in number; and he also had been born to the giant. ²¹ When he defied Israel, Jonathan the son of Shimei, David's brother, struck him down. ²² These four were born to the giant in Gath, and they fell by the hand of David and by the hand of his servants.

22 And David spoke the words of this song to the LORD in the day that the LORD delivered him from the hand of all his enemies and from the hand of Saul. ² He said,

"The LORD is my rock and my
    fortress and my deliverer;
³ My God, my rock, in whom
    I take refuge,
My shield and the horn of my
    salvation, my stronghold
    and my refuge;
My savior, You save me from violence.
⁴ "I call upon the LORD, who is
    worthy to be praised,
And I am saved from my enemies.
⁵ "For the waves of death
    encompassed me;
The torrents of destruction
    overwhelmed me;
⁶ The cords of Sheol surrounded me;
The snares of death confronted me.
⁷ "In my distress I called upon the LORD,
Yes, I cried to my God;
And from His temple He
    heard my voice,
And my cry for help *came*
    into His ears.
⁸ "Then the earth shook and quaked,
The foundations of heaven
    were trembling
And were shaken, because
    He was angry.
⁹ "Smoke went up out of His nostrils,
Fire from His mouth devoured;
Coals were kindled by it.
¹⁰ "He bowed the heavens also,
    and came down
With thick darkness under His feet.
¹¹ "And He rode on a cherub and flew;
And He appeared on the
    wings of the wind.
¹² "And He made darkness
    canopies around Him,
A mass of waters, thick
    clouds of the sky.
¹³ "From the brightness before Him
Coals of fire were kindled.
¹⁴ "The LORD thundered from heaven,
And the Most High uttered His voice.

¹⁵ "And He sent out arrows,
and scattered them,
Lightning, and routed them.
¹⁶ "Then the channels of the
sea appeared,
The foundations of the
world were laid bare
By the rebuke of the LORD,
At the blast of the breath
of His nostrils.
¹⁷ "He sent from on high, He took me;
He drew me out of many waters.
¹⁸ "He delivered me from my
strong enemy,
From those who hated me, for
they were too strong for me.
¹⁹ "They confronted me in the
day of my calamity,
But the LORD was my support.
²⁰ "He also brought me forth
into a broad place;
He rescued me, because He
delighted in me.
²¹ "The LORD has rewarded me
according to my righteousness;
According to the cleanness of my
hands He has recompensed me.
²² "For I have kept the ways of the LORD,
And have not acted wickedly
against my God.
²³ "For all His ordinances
were before me,
And as for His statutes, I did
not depart from them.
²⁴ "I was also blameless toward Him,
And I kept myself from my iniquity.
²⁵ "Therefore the LORD has recompensed
me according to my righteousness,
According to my cleanness
before His eyes.
²⁶ "With the kind You show Yourself kind,
With the blameless You show
Yourself blameless;
²⁷ With the pure You show Yourself pure,
And with the perverted You
show Yourself astute.
²⁸ "And You save an afflicted people;
But Your eyes are on the
haughty whom You abase.
²⁹ "For You are my lamp, O LORD;
And the LORD illumines my darkness.
³⁰ "For by You I can run upon a troop;
By my God I can leap over a wall.
³¹ "As for God, His way is blameless;
The word of the LORD is tested;
He is a shield to all who
take refuge in Him.
³² "For who is God, besides the LORD?

And who is a rock, besides our God?
³³ "God is my strong fortress;
And He sets the blameless in His way.
³⁴ "He makes my feet like hinds' feet,
And sets me on my high places.
³⁵ "He trains my hands for battle,
So that my arms can bend
a bow of bronze.
³⁶ "You have also given me the
shield of Your salvation,
And Your help makes me great.
³⁷ "You enlarge my steps under me,
And my feet have not slipped.
³⁸ "I pursued my enemies and
destroyed them,
And I did not turn back until
they were consumed.
³⁹ "And I have devoured them
and shattered them, so
that they did not rise;
And they fell under my feet.
⁴⁰ "For You have girded me with
strength for battle;
You have subdued under me those
who rose up against me.
⁴¹ "You have also made my enemies
turn their backs to me,
And I destroyed those who hated me.
⁴² "They looked, but there
was none to save;
Even to the LORD, but He
did not answer them.
⁴³ "Then I pulverized them as
the dust of the earth;
I crushed and stamped them
as the mire of the streets.
⁴⁴ "You have also delivered me from
the contentions of my people;
You have kept me as head
of the nations;
A people whom I have not
known serve me.
⁴⁵ "Foreigners pretend obedience to me;
As soon as they hear, they obey me.
⁴⁶ "Foreigners lose heart,
And come trembling out
of their fortresses.
⁴⁷ "The LORD lives, and blessed
be my rock;
And exalted be God, the
rock of my salvation,
⁴⁸ The God who executes
vengeance for me,
And brings down peoples under me,
⁴⁹ Who also brings me out
from my enemies;
You even lift me above those
who rise up against me;

You rescue me from the violent man.
⁵⁰ "Therefore I will give thanks to You,
O LORD, among the nations,
And I will sing praises to Your name.
⁵¹ "*He* is a tower of deliverance
to His king,
And shows lovingkindness
to His anointed,
To David and his descendants
forever."

22:1–51 David's song of praise here is almost identical to Psalms 18. This song also has many verbal links to Hannah's prayer and together with it forms the framework for the books of Samuel. This song focuses on the Lord's deliverance of David from all his enemies, in response to which David praised the Lord, his deliverer (vv. 2–4). The major part of the song (vv. 5–46) states the reason for this praise of the Lord. David first describes how the Lord had delivered him from his enemies (vv. 5–20), then declares why the Lord had delivered him from his enemies (vv. 21–28), then states the extent of the Lord's deliverance from his enemies (vv. 29–46). The song concludes with David's resolve to praise his delivering Lord, even among the Gentiles (vv. 47–51).

Psalm 68:1–6

For the choir director. A Psalm
of David. A Song.

Let God arise, let His enemies
be scattered,
And let those who hate Him
flee before Him.
² As smoke is driven away,
so drive *them* away;
As wax melts before the fire,
So let the wicked perish before God.
³ But let the righteous be glad;
let them exult before God;
Yes, let them rejoice with gladness.
⁴ Sing to God, sing praises to
His name;
Lift up *a song* for Him who
rides through the deserts,
Whose name is the LORD,
and exult before Him.

⁵ A father of the fatherless and
a judge for the widows,
Is God in His holy habitation.
⁶ God makes a home for the lonely;
He leads out the prisoners
into prosperity,

Only the rebellious dwell
in a parched land.

Proverbs 17:2–4

² A servant who acts wisely will rule
over a son who acts shamefully,
And will share in the inheritance
among brothers.
³ The refining pot is for silver
and the furnace for gold,
But the LORD tests hearts.
⁴ An evildoer listens to wicked lips;
A liar pays attention to a
destructive tongue.

John 8:31–59

³¹ So Jesus was saying to those Jews who had believed Him, "If you continue in My word, *then* you are truly disciples of Mine; ³² and you will know the truth, and the truth will make you free." ³³ They answered Him, "We are Abraham's descendants and have never yet been enslaved to anyone; how is it that You say, 'You will become free'?"

³⁴ Jesus answered them, "Truly, truly, I say to you, everyone who commits sin is the slave of sin. ³⁵ The slave does not remain in the house forever; the son does remain forever. ³⁶ So if the Son makes you free, you will be free indeed. ³⁷ I know that you are Abraham's descendants; yet you seek to kill Me, because My word has no place in you. ³⁸ I speak the things which I have seen with *My* Father; therefore you also do the things which you heard from *your* father."

³⁹ They answered and said to Him, "Abraham is our father." Jesus *said to them, "If you are Abraham's children, do the deeds of Abraham. ⁴⁰ But as it is, you are seeking to kill Me, a man who has told you the truth, which I heard from God; this Abraham did not do. ⁴¹ You are doing the deeds of your father." They said to Him, "We were not born of fornication; we have one Father: God." ⁴² Jesus said to them, "If God were your Father, you would love Me, for I proceeded forth and have come from God, for I have not even come on My own initiative, but He sent Me. ⁴³ Why do you not understand what I am saying? *It is* because you cannot hear My word. ⁴⁴ You are of *your* father the devil, and you want to do the desires of your father. He was a murderer from the beginning, and does not stand in the truth because there is no truth in him. Whenever he speaks a lie, he speaks from his own *nature,* for he is a liar and the father of lies. ⁴⁵ But because I speak the truth, you do not believe Me. ⁴⁶ Which one of you convicts Me of sin? If I speak truth, why do you not believe Me? ⁴⁷ He who is of God

8:39 If you are Abraham's children. The construction of this phrase indicates that Jesus was denying that mere physical lineage was sufficient for salvation (Php 3:4-9). The sense would be "if you are Abraham's children, but you are not, then you would act like Abraham did." Just as children inherit genetic characteristics from their parents, so also those who are truly Abraham's offspring will act like Abraham, i.e., imitate Abraham's faith and obedience (Ro 4:16; Gal 3:6-9; Heb 11:8-19; Jas 2:21-24). **deeds of Abraham.** Abraham's faith was demonstrated through his obedience to God (Jas 2:21-24). Jesus' point was that the conduct of the unbelieving Jews was diametrically opposed to the conduct of Abraham, who lived a life of obedience to all that God had commanded. Their conduct toward Jesus demonstrated that their real father was Satan (vv. 41, 44).

"Now we know that You have a demon. Abraham died, and the prophets *also;* and You say, 'If anyone keeps My word, he will never taste of death.' ⁵³Surely You are not greater than our father Abraham, who died? The prophets died too; whom do You make Yourself out to be?" ⁵⁴Jesus answered, "If I glorify Myself, My glory is nothing; it is My Father who glorifies Me, of whom you say, 'He is our God'; ⁵⁵and you have not come to know Him, but I know Him; and if I say that I do not know Him, I will be a liar like you, but I do know Him and keep His word. ⁵⁶Your father Abraham rejoiced to see My day, and he saw *it* and was glad." ⁵⁷So the Jews said to Him, "You are not yet fifty years old, and have You seen Abraham?" ⁵⁸Jesus said to them, "Truly, truly, I say to you, before Abraham was born, I am." ⁵⁹Therefore they picked up stones to throw at Him, but Jesus hid Himself and went out of the temple.

hears the words of God; for this reason you do not hear *them,* because you are not of God."

⁴⁸The Jews answered and said to Him, "Do we not say rightly that You are a Samaritan and have a demon?" ⁴⁹Jesus answered, "I do not have a demon; but I honor My Father, and you dishonor Me. ⁵⁰But I do not seek My glory; there is One who seeks and judges. ⁵¹Truly, truly, I say to you, if anyone keeps My word he will never see death." ⁵²The Jews said to Him,

8:58 Truly, truly… I am. Here Jesus declared Himself to be Yahweh, i.e., the Lord of the Old Testament. Basic to the expression are such passages as Exodus 3:14; Deuteronomy 32:39; Isaiah 41:4; 43:10, where God declared Himself to be the eternally preexistent God who revealed Himself in the Old Testament to the Jews.

DAY 25: What are the steps toward true Christian discipleship?

John 8:31-36 is a pivotal section of Scripture in understanding genuine salvation and true discipleship. John emphasized these realities by stressing truth and freedom. The focus in the passage is upon those who were exercising the beginnings of faith in Jesus as Messiah and Son of God. Jesus desired them to move on in their faith. Saving faith is not fickle but firm and settled. Such maturity expresses itself in full commitment to the truth in Jesus Christ resulting in genuine freedom.

The first step in the progress toward true discipleship is belief in Jesus Christ as Messiah and Son of God (v. 31). "If you continue in My word, then you are truly disciples of Mine" reveals the second step in the progress toward true discipleship. Perseverance in obedience to Scripture (Mt 28:19-20) is the fruit or evidence of genuine faith (Eph 2:10). The word "continue" means to habitually abide in Jesus' words. A genuine believer holds fast, obeys, and practices Jesus' teaching. The one who continues in His teaching has both the Father and the Son (2Jn 9; Heb 3:14; Rev 2:26). Real disciples are both learners (the basic meaning of the word) and faithful followers.

"The truth" (v. 32) has reference not only to the facts surrounding Jesus as the Messiah and Son of God but also to the teaching that He brought. A genuinely saved and obedient follower of the Lord Jesus will know divine truth and both freedom from sin (v. 34) and the search for reality. This divine truth comes not merely by intellectual assent (1Co 2:14) but by saving commitment to Christ (Titus 1:1-2).

"Everyone who commits sin" (v. 34). The kind of slavery that Jesus had in mind was not physical slavery but slavery to sin (Ro 6:17-18). The idea of "commits sin" means to practice sin habitually (1Jn 3:4, 8-9). The ultimate bondage is not political or economic enslavement but spiritual bondage to sin and rebellion against God. Thus, this also explains why Jesus would not let Himself be reduced to merely a political Messiah (6:14-15).

MAY 26

23 Now these are the last words of David.

David the son of Jesse declares,
The man who was raised
     on high declares,
The anointed of the God of Jacob,
And the sweet psalmist of Israel,
² "The Spirit of the LORD spoke by me,
And His word was on my tongue.
³ "The God of Israel said,
The Rock of Israel spoke to me,
'He who rules over men righteously,
Who rules in the fear of God,
⁴ Is as the light of the morning
     when the sun rises,
A morning without clouds,
When the tender grass *springs*
     out of the earth,
Through sunshine after rain.'
⁵ "Truly is not my house so with God?
For He has made an everlasting
     covenant with me,
Ordered in all things, and secured;
For all my salvation and all *my* desire,
Will He not indeed make *it* grow?
⁶ "But the worthless, every one of them
     will be thrust away like thorns,
Because they cannot be taken in hand;
⁷ But the man who touches them
Must be armed with iron and
     the shaft of a spear,
And they will be completely burned
     with fire in *their* place."

⁸ These are the names of the mighty men whom David had: Josheb-basshebeth a Tahchemonite, chief of the captains, he was *called* Adino the Eznite, because of eight hundred slain *by him* at one time; ⁹ and after him was Eleazar the son of Dodo the Ahohite, one of the three mighty men with David when they defied the Philistines who were gathered there to battle and the men of Israel had withdrawn. ¹⁰ He arose and struck the Philistines until his hand was weary and clung to the sword, and the LORD brought about a great victory that day; and the people returned after him only to strip *the slain.* ¹¹ Now after him was Shammah the son of Agee a Hararite. And the Philistines were gathered into a troop where there was a plot of ground full of lentils, and the people fled from the Philistines. ¹² But he took his stand in the midst of the plot, defended it and struck the Philistines; and the LORD brought about a great victory.

¹³ Then three of the thirty chief men went down and came to David in the harvest time to the cave of Adullam, while the troop of the Philistines was camping in the valley of Rephaim. ¹⁴ David was then in the stronghold, while the garrison of the Philistines was then in Bethlehem. ¹⁵ David had a craving and said, "Oh that someone would give me water to drink from the well of Bethlehem which is by the gate!" ¹⁶ So the three mighty men broke through the camp of the Philistines, and drew water from the well of Bethlehem which was by the gate, and took *it* and brought *it* to David. Nevertheless he would not drink it, but poured it out to the LORD; ¹⁷ and he said, "Be it far from me, O LORD, that I should do this. *Shall I drink* the blood of the men who went in *jeopardy* of their lives?" Therefore he would not drink it. These things the three mighty men did.

¹⁸ Abishai, the brother of Joab, the son of Zeruiah, was chief of the thirty. And he swung his spear against three hundred and killed *them,* and had a name as well as the three. ¹⁹ He was most honored of the thirty, therefore he became their commander; however, he did not attain to the three.

²⁰ Then Benaiah the son of Jehoiada, the son of a valiant man of Kabzeel, who had done mighty deeds, killed the two *sons of* Ariel of Moab. He also went down and killed a lion in the middle of a pit on a snowy day. ²¹ He killed an Egyptian, an impressive man. Now the Egyptian *had* a spear in his hand, but he went down to him with a club and snatched the spear from the Egyptian's hand and killed him with his own spear. ²² These *things* Benaiah the son of Jehoiada did, and had a name as well as the three mighty men. ²³ He was honored among the thirty, but he did not attain to the three. And David appointed him over his guard.

²⁴ Asahel the brother of Joab was among the thirty; Elhanan the son of Dodo of Bethlehem, ²⁵ Shammah the Harodite, Elika the Harodite, ²⁶ Helez the Paltite, Ira the son of Ikkesh the Tekoite, ²⁷ Abiezer the Anathothite, Mebunnai the Hushathite, ²⁸ Zalmon the Ahohite, Maharai the Netophathite, ²⁹ Heleb the son of Baanah the Netophathite, Ittai the son of Ribai of Gibeah of the sons of Benjamin, ³⁰ Benaiah a Pirathonite, Hiddai of the brooks of Gaash, ³¹ Abi-albon the Arbathite, Azmaveth the Barhumite, ³² Eliahba the Shaalbonite, the sons of Jashen, Jonathan, ³³ Shammah the Hararite, Ahiam the son of Sharar the Ararite,

³⁴ Eliphelet the son of Ahasbai, the son of the Maacathite, Eliam the son of Ahithophel the Gilonite, ³⁵ Hezro the Carmelite, Paarai the Arbite, ³⁶ Igal the son of Nathan of Zobah, Bani the Gadite, ³⁷ Zelek the Ammonite, Naharai the Beerothite, armor bearers of Joab the son of Zeruiah, ³⁸ Ira the Ithrite, Gareb the Ithrite, ³⁹ Uriah the Hittite; thirty-seven in all.

24 Now again the anger of the LORD burned against Israel, and it incited David against them to say, "Go, number Israel and Judah." ² The king said to Joab the commander of the army who was with him, "Go about now through all the tribes of Israel, from Dan to Beersheba, and register the people, that I may know the number of the people." ³ But Joab said to the king, "Now may the LORD your God add to the people a hundred times as many as they are, while the eyes of my lord the king *still* see; but why does my lord the king delight in this thing?" ⁴ Nevertheless, the king's word prevailed against Joab and against the commanders of the army. So Joab and the commanders of the army went out from the presence of the king to register the people of Israel. ⁵ They crossed the Jordan and camped in Aroer, on the right side of the city that is in the middle of the valley of Gad and toward Jazer. ⁶ Then they came to Gilead

---

24:1 again. A second outbreak of the divine wrath occurred after the 3-year famine recorded in 21:1. **against Israel.** The inciting of David to conduct a census was a punishment on Israel from the Lord for some unspecified sins. Perhaps sins of pride and ambition had led him to increase the size of his army unnecessarily and place heavy burdens of support on the people. Whatever the sin, it is clear God was dissatisfied with David's motives, goals, and actions and brought judgment. **it incited David.** Satan incited David to take this census, and the Lord sovereignly and permissively used Satan to accomplish His will (1 Chr. 21:1). **number Israel and Judah.** A census was usually for military purposes, which seems to be the case here (v. 9). Numbering the potential army of Israel had been done in the past (Nu 1:1–2; 26:1–4). However, this census of Israel's potential army did not have the sanction of the Lord and proceeded from wrong motives. David either wanted to glory in the size of his fighting force or take more territory than what the Lord had granted him. He shifted his trust from God to military power (this is a constant theme in the Psalms; see 20:7; 25:2; 44:6).

and to the land of Tahtim-hodshi, and they came to Dan-jaan and around to Sidon, ⁷ and came to the fortress of Tyre and to all the cities of the Hivites and of the Canaanites, and they went out to the south of Judah, *to* Beersheba. ⁸ So when they had gone about through the whole land, they came to Jerusalem at the end of nine months and twenty days. ⁹ And Joab gave the number of the registration of the people to the king; and there were in Israel eight hundred thousand valiant men who drew the sword, and the men of Judah were five hundred thousand men.

¹⁰ Now David's heart troubled him after he had numbered the people. So David said to the LORD, "I have sinned greatly in what I have done. But now, O LORD, please take away the iniquity of Your servant, for I have acted very foolishly." ¹¹ When David arose in the morning, the word of the LORD came to the prophet Gad, David's seer, saying, ¹² "Go and speak to David, 'Thus the LORD says, "I am offering you three things; choose for yourself one of them, which I will do to you." '" ¹³ So Gad came to David and told him, and said to him, "Shall seven years of famine come to you in your land? Or will you flee three months before your foes while they pursue you? Or shall there be three days' pestilence in your land? Now consider and see what answer I shall return to Him who sent me." ¹⁴ Then David said to Gad, "I am in great distress. Let us now fall into the hand of the LORD for His mercies are great, but do not let me fall into the hand of man."

¹⁵ So the LORD sent a pestilence upon Israel from the morning until the appointed time, and seventy thousand men of the people from Dan to Beersheba died. ¹⁶ When the angel stretched out his hand toward Jerusalem to destroy it, the LORD relented from the calamity and said to the angel who destroyed the people, "It is enough! Now relax your hand!" And the angel of the LORD was by the threshing floor of Araunah the Jebusite. ¹⁷ Then David spoke to the LORD when he saw the angel who was striking down the people, and said, "Behold, it is I who have sinned, and it is I who have done wrong; but these sheep, what have they done? Please let Your hand be against me and against my father's house."

¹⁸ So Gad came to David that day and said to him, "Go up, erect an altar to the LORD on the threshing floor of Araunah the Jebusite. ¹⁹ David went up according to the word of Gad, just as the LORD had commanded. ²⁰ Araunah looked down and saw the king and his servants crossing over toward him; and Araunah went out and bowed his face to the ground

before the king. ²¹ Then Araunah said, "Why has my lord the king come to his servant?" And David said, "To buy the threshing floor from you, in order to build an altar to the LORD, that the plague may be held back from the people." ²² Araunah said to David, "Let my lord the king take and offer up what is good in his sight. Look, the oxen for the burnt offering, the threshing sledges and the yokes of the oxen for the wood. ²³ Everything, O king, Araunah gives to the king." And Araunah said to the king, "May the LORD your God accept you." ²⁴ However, the king said to Araunah, "No, but I will surely buy *it* from you for a price, for I will not offer burnt offerings to the LORD my God which cost me nothing." So David bought the threshing floor and the oxen for fifty shekels of silver. ²⁵ David built there an altar to the LORD and offered burnt offerings and peace offerings. Thus the LORD was moved by prayer for the land, and the plague was held back from Israel.

Psalm 68:7–10

⁷ O God, when You went forth
     before Your people,
   When You marched through
     the wilderness,   *Selah*
⁸ The earth quaked;
   The heavens also dropped *rain*
     at the presence of God;
   Sinai itself *quaked* at the presence
     of God, the God of Israel.
⁹ You shed abroad a plentiful
     rain, O God;
   You confirmed Your inheritance
     when it was parched.
¹⁰ Your creatures settled in it;
   You provided in Your goodness
     for the poor, O God.

Proverbs 17:5–6

⁵ He who mocks the poor
     taunts his Maker;
   He who rejoices at calamity
     will not go unpunished.
⁶ Grandchildren are the
     crown of old men,
   And the glory of sons is their
     fathers.

John 9:1–23

9 As He passed by, He saw a man blind from birth. ² And His disciples asked Him, "Rabbi, who sinned, this man or his parents, that he would be born blind?" ³ Jesus answered, "*It was* neither *that* this man sinned, nor his parents; but *it was* so

9:2 who sinned. While sin may be a cause of suffering, as clearly indicated in Scripture (5:14; Nu 12; 1Co 11:30; Jas 5:15), it is not always the case necessarily (Job; 2Co 12:7; Gal 4:13). The disciples assumed, like most Jews of their day, that sin was the primary, if not exclusive, cause of all suffering. In this instance, however, Jesus made it clear that personal sin was not the reason for the blindness (v. 3).

9:3 Jesus did not deny the general connection between sin and suffering, but He refuted the idea that personal acts of sin were the direct cause. God's sovereignty and purposes play a part in such matters, as is clear from Job 1 and 2.

that the works of God might be displayed in him. ⁴ We must work the works of Him who sent Me as long as it is day; night is coming when no one can work. ⁵ While I am in the world, I am the Light of the world." ⁶ When He had said this, He spat on the ground, and made clay of the spittle, and applied the clay to his eyes, ⁷ and said to him, "Go, wash in the pool of Siloam" (which is translated, Sent). So he went away and washed, and came *back* seeing. ⁸ Therefore the neighbors, and those who previously saw him as a beggar, were saying, "Is not this the one who used to sit and beg?" ⁹ Others were saying, "This is he," *still* others were saying, "No, but he is like him." He kept saying, "I am the one." ¹⁰ So they were saying to him, "How then were your eyes opened?" ¹¹ He answered, "The man who is called Jesus made clay, and anointed my eyes, and said to me, 'Go to Siloam and wash'; so I went away and washed, and I received sight." ¹² They said to him, "Where is He?" He *said, "I do not know."

¹³ They *brought to the Pharisees the man who was formerly blind. ¹⁴ Now it was a Sabbath on the day when Jesus made the clay and opened his eyes. ¹⁵ Then the Pharisees also were asking him again how he received his sight. And he said to them, "He applied clay to my eyes, and I washed, and I see." ¹⁶ Therefore some of the Pharisees were saying, "This man is not from God, because He does not keep the Sabbath." But others were saying, "How can a man who is a sinner perform such signs?" And there was a division among them. ¹⁷ So they *said to the blind man again, "What do you say about Him, since He opened your eyes?" And he said, "He is a prophet."

9:17 He is a prophet. While the blind man saw clearly that Jesus was more than a mere man, the sighted but obstinate Pharisees were spiritually blind to that truth (v. 39). Blindness in the Bible is a metaphor for spiritual darkness, i.e., inability to discern God or His truth (2Co 4:3–6; Col 1:12–14).

[18] The Jews then did not believe *it* of him, that he had been blind and had received sight, until they called the parents of the very one who had received his sight, [19] and questioned them, saying, "Is this your son, who you say was born blind? Then how does he now see?" [20] His parents answered them and said, "We know that this is our son, and that he was born blind; [21] but how he now sees, we do not know; or who opened his eyes, we do not know. Ask him; he is of age, he will speak for himself." [22] His parents said this because they were afraid of the Jews; for the Jews had already agreed that if anyone confessed Him to be Christ, he was to be put out of the synagogue. [23] For this reason his parents said, "He is of age; ask him."

DAY 26: What does the healing of the blind man in John 9 teach us about unbelief?

In ancient times, severe physical deformities, such as congenital blindness (vv. 8–9), sentenced a person to begging as the only means of support (Ac 3:1–7). The drastic change in the healed man caused many to faithlessly believe that he was not the person born blind.

If you read through vv. 13–34, this section in the story of the healing of the blind man reveals some key characteristics of willful unbelief: 1) unbelief sets false standards; 2) unbelief always wants more evidence but never has enough; 3) unbelief does biased research on a purely subjective basis; 4) unbelief rejects the facts; and 5) unbelief is self-centered. John included this section on the dialogue of the Pharisees with the blind man most likely for two reasons: 1) the dialogue carefully demonstrates the character of willful and fixed unbelief, and 2) the story confirms the first great schism between the synagogue and Christ's new followers. The blind man was the first known person thrown out of the synagogue because he chose to follow Christ (see 16:1–3).

Even though the neighbors had confirmed that the man had in fact been blind (v. 9), that was not evidence enough. So the authorities called the parents (v. 18). While neighbors may have been mistaken as to the man's identity, the parents would know if this was their own son. And the authorities considered the witness of the healed man worthless.

MAY 27

1 Kings 1:1–2:46

1 Now King David was old, advanced in age; and they covered him with clothes, but he could not keep warm. [2] So his servants said to him, "Let them seek a young virgin for my lord the king, and let her attend the king and become his nurse; and let her lie in your bosom, that my lord the king may keep warm." [3] So they searched for a beautiful girl throughout all the territory of Israel, and found Abishag the Shunammite, and brought her to the king. [4] The girl was very beautiful; and she became the king's nurse and served him, but the king did not cohabit with her. [5] Now Adonijah the son of Haggith exalted himself, saying, "I will be king." So he prepared for himself chariots and horsemen with fifty men to run before him. [6] His father had never crossed him at any time by asking, "Why have you done so?" And he was also a very handsome man, and he was born after Absalom.

[7] He had conferred with Joab the son of Zeruiah and with Abiathar the priest; and following Adonijah they helped him. [8] But Zadok the priest, Benaiah the son of Jehoiada, Nathan the prophet, Shimei, Rei, and the mighty men who belonged to David, were not with Adonijah. [9] Adonijah sacrificed sheep and oxen and fatlings by the stone of Zoheleth, which is beside En-rogel; and he invited all his brothers,

1:5 Adonijah. Adonijah was the fourth son of David (2Sa 3:4) and probably the oldest living son, since Amnon (2Sa 13:28–29) and Absalom (2Sa 18:14–15) had been killed, and Chileab apparently died in his youth, since there is no mention of him beyond his birth. As David's oldest surviving heir, Adonijah attempted to claim the kingship. **chariots and horsemen.** Like Absalom (2Sa 15:1), Adonijah sought to confirm and support his claim to kingship by raising a small army.

the king's sons, and all the men of Judah, the king's servants. [10] But he did not invite Nathan the prophet, Benaiah, the mighty men, and Solomon his brother.

[11] Then Nathan spoke to Bathsheba the mother of Solomon, saying, "Have you not heard that Adonijah the son of Haggith has become king, and David our lord does not know it? [12] So now come, please let me give you counsel and save your life and the life of your son Solomon. [13] Go at once to King David and say to him, 'Have you not, my lord, O king, sworn to your maidservant, saying, "Surely Solomon your son shall be king after me, and he shall sit on my throne"? Why then has Adonijah become king?' [14] Behold, while you are still there speaking with the king, I will come in after you and confirm your words."

1:13 **Have you not…sworn.** This oath was given privately (unrecorded in Scripture) by David, perhaps to both Nathan and Bathsheba. Solomon's choice by the Lord was implicit in his name Jedidiah, meaning "beloved of the LORD" (2Sa 12:24–25) and explicit in David's declaration to Solomon (1Ch 22:6–13).

[15] So Bathsheba went in to the king in the bedroom. Now the king was very old, and Abishag the Shunammite was ministering to the king. [16] Then Bathsheba bowed and prostrated herself before the king. And the king said, "What do you wish?" [17] She said to him, "My lord, you swore to your maidservant by the LORD your God, saying, 'Surely your son Solomon shall be king after me and he shall sit on my throne.' [18] Now, behold, Adonijah is king; and now, my lord the king, you do not know it. [19] He has sacrificed oxen and fatlings and sheep in abundance, and has invited all the sons of the king and Abiathar the priest and Joab the commander of the army, but he has not invited Solomon your servant. [20] As for you now, my lord the king, the eyes of all Israel are on you, to tell them who shall sit on the throne of my lord the king after him. [21] Otherwise it will come about, as soon as my lord the king sleeps with his fathers, that I and my son Solomon will be considered offenders."

[22] Behold, while she was still speaking with the king, Nathan the prophet came in. [23] They told the king, saying, "Here is Nathan the prophet." And when he came in before the king, he prostrated himself before the king with his face to the ground. [24] Then Nathan said, "My lord the king, have you said, 'Adonijah shall be king after me, and he shall sit on my throne'? [25] For he has gone down today and has sacrificed oxen and fatlings and sheep in abundance, and has invited all the king's sons and the commanders of the army and Abiathar the priest, and behold, they are eating and drinking before him; and they say, 'Long live King Adonijah!' [26] But me, even me your servant, and Zadok the priest and Benaiah the son of Jehoiada and your servant Solomon, he has not invited. [27] Has this thing been done by my lord the king, and you have not shown to your servants who should sit on the throne of my lord the king after him?"

[28] Then King David said, "Call Bathsheba to me." And she came into the king's presence and stood before the king. [29] The king vowed and said, "As the LORD lives, who has redeemed my life from all distress, [30] surely as I vowed to you by the LORD the God of Israel, saying, 'Your son Solomon shall be king after me, and he shall sit on my throne in my place'; I will indeed do so this day." [31] Then Bathsheba bowed with her face to the ground, and prostrated herself before the king and said, "May my lord King David live forever."

[32] Then King David said, "Call to me Zadok the priest, Nathan the prophet, and Benaiah the son of Jehoiada." And they came into the king's presence. [33] The king said to them, "Take with you the servants of your lord, and have my son Solomon ride on my own mule, and bring him down to Gihon. [34] Let Zadok the priest and Nathan the prophet anoint him there as king over Israel, and blow the trumpet and say, 'Long live King Solomon!' [35] Then you shall come up after him, and he shall come and sit on my throne and be king in my place; for I have appointed him to be ruler over Israel and Judah." [36] Benaiah the son of Jehoiada answered the king and said, "Amen! Thus may the LORD, the God of my lord the king, say. [37] As the LORD has been with my lord the king, so may He be with Solomon, and make his throne greater than the throne of my lord King David!"

[38] So Zadok the priest, Nathan the prophet, Benaiah the son of Jehoiada, the Cherethites, and the Pelethites went down and had Solomon ride on King David's mule, and brought him to Gihon. [39] Zadok the priest then took the horn of oil from the tent and anointed Solomon. Then they blew the trumpet, and all the people said, "Long live King Solomon!" [40] All the people went up after him, and the people were playing on flutes and rejoicing with great joy, so that the earth shook at their noise.

⁴¹Now Adonijah and all the guests who *were* with him heard *it* as they finished eating. When Joab heard the sound of the trumpet, he said, "Why is the city making such an uproar?" ⁴²While he was still speaking, behold, Jonathan the son of Abiathar the priest came. Then Adonijah said, "Come in, for you are a valiant man and bring good news." ⁴³But Jonathan replied to Adonijah, "No! Our lord King David has made Solomon king. ⁴⁴The king has also sent with him Zadok the priest, Nathan the prophet, Benaiah the son of Jehoiada, the Cherethites, and the Pelethites; and they have made him ride on the king's mule. ⁴⁵Zadok the priest and Nathan the prophet have anointed him king in Gihon, and they have come up from there rejoicing, so that the city is in an uproar. This is the noise which you have heard. ⁴⁶Besides, Solomon has even taken his seat on the throne of the kingdom. ⁴⁷Moreover, the king's servants came to bless our lord King David, saying, 'May your God make the name of Solomon better than your name and his throne greater than your throne!' And the king bowed himself on the bed. ⁴⁸The king has also said thus, 'Blessed be the LORD, the God of Israel, who has granted one to sit on my throne today while my own eyes see *it*.' "

⁴⁹Then all the guests of Adonijah were terrified; and they arose and each went on his way. ⁵⁰And Adonijah was afraid of Solomon, and he arose, went and took hold of the horns of the altar. ⁵¹Now it was told Solomon, saying, "Behold, Adonijah is afraid of King Solomon, for behold, he has taken hold of the horns of the altar, saying, 'Let King Solomon swear to me today that he will not put his servant to death with the sword.' " ⁵²Solomon said, "If he is a worthy man, not one of his hairs will fall to the ground; but if wickedness is found in him, he will die." ⁵³So King Solomon sent, and they brought him down from the altar. And he came and prostrated himself before King Solomon, and Solomon said to him, "Go to your house."

2 As David's time to die drew near, he charged Solomon his son, saying, ²"I am going the way of all the earth. Be strong, therefore, and show yourself a man. ³Keep the charge of the LORD your God, to walk in His ways, to keep His statutes, His commandments, His ordinances, and His testimonies, according to what is written in the Law of Moses, that you may succeed in all that you do and wherever you turn, ⁴so that the LORD may carry out His promise which He spoke concerning me, saying, 'If your sons are careful of their way, to walk before Me in truth

2:4 His promise. The unconditional Davidic Covenant was made by God with David in 2 Samuel 7:4–17 and confirmed to Solomon in 1 Kings 9:5, promising the perpetuation of the Davidic dynasty over Israel. **If your sons are careful of their way.** David declared that the king's obedience to the law of Moses was a necessary condition for the fulfillment of the divine promise. The book of Kings demonstrates that none of the descendants of David remained faithful to God's law; none of them met the conditions for the fulfillment of the divine promise. Rather, David's words provided a basis for explaining the Exile. Thus, the ultimate and final King of Israel would appear at a later, undesignated time.

with all their heart and with all their soul, you shall not lack a man on the throne of Israel.'

⁵"Now you also know what Joab the son of Zeruiah did to me, what he did to the two commanders of the armies of Israel, to Abner the son of Ner, and to Amasa the son of Jether, whom he killed; he also shed the blood of war in peace. And he put the blood of war on his belt about his waist, and on his sandals on his feet. ⁶So act according to your wisdom, and do not let his gray hair go down to Sheol in peace. ⁷But show kindness to the sons of Barzillai the Gileadite, and let them be among those who eat at your table; for they assisted me when I fled from Absalom your brother. ⁸Behold, there is with you Shimei the son of Gera the Benjamite, of Bahurim; now it was he who cursed me with a violent curse on the day I went to Mahanaim. But when he came down to me at the Jordan, I swore to him by the LORD, saying, 'I will not put you to death with the sword.' ⁹Now therefore, do not let him go unpunished, for you are a wise man; and you will know what you ought to do to him, and you will bring his gray hair down to Sheol with blood."

¹⁰Then David slept with his fathers and was buried in the city of David. ¹¹The days that David reigned over Israel *were* forty years: seven years he reigned in Hebron and thirty-three years he reigned in Jerusalem. ¹²And Solomon sat on the throne of David his father, and his kingdom was firmly established.

¹³Now Adonijah the son of Haggith came to Bathsheba the mother of Solomon. And she said, "Do you come peacefully?" And he said, "Peacefully." ¹⁴Then he said, "I have something *to say* to you." And she said, "Speak." ¹⁵So he said, "You know that the kingdom was mine

and that all Israel expected me to be king; however, the kingdom has turned about and become my brother's, for it was his from the LORD. ¹⁶ Now I am making one request of you; do not refuse me." And she said to him, "Speak." ¹⁷ Then he said, "Please speak to Solomon the king, for he will not refuse you, that he may give me Abishag the Shunammite as a wife." ¹⁸ Bathsheba said, "Very well; I will speak to the king for you."

¹⁹ So Bathsheba went to King Solomon to speak to him for Adonijah. And the king arose to meet her, bowed before her, and sat on his throne; then he had a throne set for the king's mother, and she sat on his right. ²⁰ Then she said, "I am making one small request of you; do not refuse me." And the king said to her, "Ask, my mother, for I will not refuse you." ²¹ So she said, "Let Abishag the Shunammite be given to Adonijah your brother as a wife." ²² King Solomon answered and said to his mother, "And why are you asking Abishag the Shunammite for Adonijah? Ask for him also the kingdom—for he is my older brother—even for him, for Abiathar the priest, and for Joab the son of Zeruiah!" ²³ Then King Solomon swore by the LORD, saying, "May God do so to me and more also, if Adonijah has not spoken this word against his own life. ²⁴ Now therefore, as the LORD lives, who has established me and set me on the throne of David my father and who has made me a house as He promised, surely Adonijah shall be put to death today." ²⁵ So King Solomon sent Benaiah the son of Jehoiada; and he fell upon him so that he died.

²⁶ Then to Abiathar the priest the king said, "Go to Anathoth to your own field, for you deserve to die; but I will not put you to death at this time, because you carried the ark of the Lord GOD before my father David, and because you were afflicted in everything with which my father was afflicted." ²⁷ So Solomon dismissed Abiathar from being priest to the LORD, in order to fulfill the word of the LORD, which He had spoken concerning the house of Eli in Shiloh.

²⁸ Now the news came to Joab, for Joab had followed Adonijah, although he had not followed Absalom. And Joab fled to the tent of the LORD and took hold of the horns of the altar. ²⁹ It was told King Solomon that Joab had fled to the tent of the LORD, and behold, he is beside the altar. Then Solomon sent Benaiah the son of Jehoiada, saying, "Go, fall upon him." ³⁰ So Benaiah came to the tent of the LORD and said to him, "Thus the king has said, 'Come out.'" But he said, "No, for I will die here." And Benaiah brought the king word again, saying, "Thus

spoke Joab, and thus he answered me." ³¹ The king said to him, "Do as he has spoken and fall upon him and bury him, that you may remove from me and from my father's house the blood which Joab shed without cause. ³² The LORD will return his blood on his own head, because he fell upon two men more righteous and better than he and killed them with the sword, while my father David did not know it: Abner the son of Ner, commander of the army of Israel, and Amasa the son of Jether, commander of the army of Judah. ³³ So shall their blood return on the head of Joab and on the head of his descendants forever; but to David and his descendants and his house and his throne, may there be peace from the LORD forever." ³⁴ Then Benaiah the son of Jehoiada went up and fell upon him and put him to death, and he was buried at his own house in the wilderness. ³⁵ The king appointed Benaiah the son of Jehoiada over the army in his place, and the king appointed Zadok the priest in the place of Abiathar.

³⁶ Now the king sent and called for Shimei and said to him, "Build for yourself a house in Jerusalem and live there, and do not go out from there to any place. ³⁷ For on the day you go out and cross over the brook Kidron, you will know for certain that you shall surely die; your blood shall be on your own head." ³⁸ Shimei then said to the king, "The word is good. As my lord the king has said, so your servant will do." So Shimei lived in Jerusalem many days.

³⁹ But it came about at the end of three years, that two of the servants of Shimei ran away to Achish son of Maacah, king of Gath. And they told Shimei, saying, "Behold, your servants are in Gath." ⁴⁰ Then Shimei arose and saddled his donkey, and went to Gath to Achish to look for his servants. And Shimei went and brought his servants from Gath. ⁴¹ It was told Solomon that Shimei had gone from Jerusalem to Gath, and had returned. ⁴² So the king sent and called for Shimei and said to him, "Did I not make you swear by the LORD and solemnly warn you, saying, 'You will know for certain that on the day you depart and go anywhere, you shall surely die'? And you said to me, 'The word which I have heard is good.' ⁴³ Why then have you not kept the oath of the LORD, and the command which I have laid on you?" ⁴⁴ The king also said to Shimei, "You know all the evil which you acknowledge in your heart, which you did to my father David; therefore the LORD shall return your evil on your own head. ⁴⁵ But King Solomon shall be blessed, and the throne of David shall be established before the LORD

forever." ⁴⁶ So the king commanded Benaiah the son of Jehoiada, and he went out and fell upon him so that he died.

Thus the kingdom was established in the hands of Solomon.

Psalm 68:11–14

¹¹ The Lord gives the command;
The women who proclaim the
good tidings are a great host:

¹² "Kings of armies flee, they flee,
And she who remains at home
will divide the spoil!"

¹³ When you lie down among
the sheepfolds,
You are like the wings of a
dove covered with silver,
And its pinions with glistening gold.

¹⁴ When the Almighty scattered
the kings there,
It was snowing in Zalmon.

Proverbs 17:7–9

⁷ Excellent speech is not
fitting for a fool,
Much less are lying lips to a prince.

⁸ A bribe is a charm in the
sight of its owner;
Wherever he turns, he prospers.

⁹ He who conceals a
transgression seeks love,
But he who repeats a matter
separates intimate friends.

John 9:24–41

²⁴ So a second time they called the man who had been blind, and said to him, "Give glory to God; we know that this man is a sinner." ²⁵ He then answered, "Whether He is a sinner, I do not know; one thing I do know, that though I was blind, now I see." ²⁶ So they said to him, "What did He do to you? How did He open your eyes?" ²⁷ He answered them, "I told you already and you did not listen; why do you want to hear *it* again? You do not want to become His disciples too, do you?" ²⁸ They reviled him and said, "You are His disciple, but we are disciples of Moses. ²⁹ We know that God has spoken to Moses, but as for this man, we do not know where He is from." ³⁰ The man answered and said to them, "Well, here is an amazing thing, that you do not know where He is from, and *yet* He opened my eyes. ³¹ We know that God does not hear sinners; but if anyone is God-fearing and does His will, He hears him. ³² Since the beginning of time it has never been heard that anyone opened the eyes of a person born blind. ³³ If this man were not from God, He could do nothing." ³⁴ They answered him, "You were born entirely in sins, and are you teaching us?" So they put him out.

³⁵ Jesus heard that they had put him out, and finding him, He said, "Do you believe in the Son of Man?" ³⁶ He answered, "Who is He, Lord, that I may believe in Him?" ³⁷ Jesus said to him, "You have both seen Him, and He is the one who is talking with you." ³⁸ And he said, "Lord, I believe." And he worshiped Him. ³⁹ And Jesus said, "For judgment I came into this world, so that those who do not see may see, and that those who see may become blind." ⁴⁰ Those of the Pharisees who were with Him heard these things and said to Him, "We are not blind too, are we?" ⁴¹ Jesus said to them, "If you were blind, you would have no sin; but since you say, 'We see,' your sin remains.

9:35 Do you believe...? Jesus invited the man to put his trust in Him as the One who revealed God to man. Jesus placed great emphasis on public acknowledgment of who He was and confession of faith in Him (Mt 10:32; Lk 12:8). **Son of Man.** See 1:51; 3:13–14; 5:27; 6:27, 53, 62; 8:28.

9:41 your sin remains. Jesus had particular reference to the sin of unbelief and rejection of Him as Messiah and Son of God. If they knew their lostness and darkness and cried out for spiritual light, they would no longer be guilty of the sin of unbelief in Christ. But satisfied that their darkness was light, and continuing in rejection of Christ, their sin remained.

DAY 27: How did the simple logic of the healed man outwit the religious authorities?

In John 9, the religious authorities wanted the man to own up and admit the truth that Jesus was a sinner because He violated their traditions and threatened their influence (see Jos 7:19). "Give glory to God; we know that this man is a sinner" (v. 24). Enough unanimity existed among the religious authorities to conclude that Jesus was a sinner (8:46). Because of this already predetermined opinion, they refused to accept any of the testimony that a miracle had actually taken place.

In order to forcefully emphasize their hypocrisy, the healed man resorted to biting sarcasm when he suggested they desired to be Jesus' disciples (v. 27).

"You are His disciple, but we are disciples of Moses" (v. 28). At this point, the meeting degenerated into a shouting match of insults. The healed man's wit had exposed the bias of his inquisitors. As far as the authorities were concerned, the conflict between Jesus and Moses was irreconcilable. If the healed man defended Jesus, then such defense could only mean that he was Jesus' disciple.

In vv. 30–33, the healed man demonstrated more spiritual insight and common sense than all of the religious authorities combined who sat in judgment of Jesus and him. His penetrating wit focused in on their intractable unbelief. His logic was that such an extraordinary miracle could only indicate that Jesus was from God, for the Jews believed that God responds in proportion to the righteousness of the one praying (Job 27:9; 35:13; Pss 66:18; 109:7; Pr 15:29; Is. 1:15; see 14:13–14; 16:23–27; 1Jn 3:21–22). The greatness of the miracle could only indicate that Jesus was actually from God.

"You were born entirely in sins, and are you teaching us?" (v. 34). The Pharisees were incensed with the man, and their anger prevented them from seeing the penetrating insight that the uneducated healed man had demonstrated. The phrase also revealed their ignorance of Scripture, for the Old Testament indicated that the coming messianic age would be evidenced by restoration of sight to the blind (Is. 29:18; 35:5; 42:7; Mt 11:4–5; Lk 4:18–19).

MAY 28

1 Kings 3:1–4:34

3 Then Solomon formed a marriage alliance with Pharaoh king of Egypt, and took Pharaoh's daughter and brought her to the city of David until he had finished building his own house and the house of the LORD and the wall around Jerusalem. ²The people were still sacrificing on the high places, because there was no house built for the name of the LORD until those days.

³Now Solomon loved the LORD, walking in the statutes of his father David, except he sacrificed and burned incense on the high places. ⁴The king went to Gibeon to sacrifice there, for that was the great high place; Solomon offered a thousand burnt offerings on that altar. ⁵In Gibeon the LORD appeared to Solomon in a dream at night; and God said, "Ask what *you wish* Me to give you." ⁶Then Solomon said, "You have shown great lovingkindness to Your servant David my father, according as he walked before You in truth and righteousness and uprightness of heart toward You; and You have reserved for him this great lovingkindness, that You have given him a son to sit on his throne, as *it is* this day. ⁷Now, O LORD my God, You have made Your servant king in place of my father David, yet I am but a little child; I do not know how to go out or come in. ⁸Your servant is in the midst of Your people which You have chosen, a great people who are too many to be numbered or counted. ⁹So give Your servant an understanding heart to judge Your people to discern between good and evil. For who is able to judge this great people of Yours?"

¹⁰It was pleasing in the sight of the Lord

3:7 little child. Since Solomon was probably only about 20 years of age, he readily admitted his lack of qualification and experience to be king (1Ch 22:5; 29:1).

3:8 a great people. Based on the census, which recorded 800,000 men of fighting age in Israel and 500,000 in Judah (2Sa 24:9), the total population was over 4 million, approximately double what it had been at the time of the Conquest (Nu 26:1–65).

3:9 an understanding heart. Humbly admitting his need, Solomon sought "a listening heart" to govern God's people with wisdom.

3:10 pleasing in the sight of the Lord. The Lord was delighted that Solomon had not asked for personal benefits, e.g., long life, wealth, or the death of his enemies.

that Solomon had asked this thing. ¹¹God said to him, "Because you have asked this thing and have not asked for yourself long life, nor have you asked riches for yourself, nor have you asked for the life of your enemies, but have asked for yourself discernment to understand justice, ¹²behold, I have done according to your words. Behold, I have given you a wise and discerning heart, so that there has been no one like you before you, nor shall one like you arise after you. ¹³I have also given you what you have not asked, both riches and honor, so that there will not be any among the kings like you all your days. ¹⁴If you walk in My ways, keeping My statutes and commandments, as your father David walked, then I will prolong your days."

¹⁵Then Solomon awoke, and behold, it was a dream. And he came to Jerusalem and stood before the ark of the covenant of the Lord, and offered burnt offerings and made peace offerings, and made a feast for all his servants. ¹⁶Then two women who were harlots came to the king and stood before him. ¹⁷The one woman said, "Oh, my lord, this woman and I live in the same house; and I gave birth to a child while she *was* in the house. ¹⁸It happened on the third day after I gave birth, that this woman also gave birth to a child, and we were together. There was no stranger with us in the house, only the two of us in the house. ¹⁹This woman's son died in the night, because she lay on it. ²⁰So she arose in the middle of the night and took my son from beside me while your maidservant slept, and laid him in her bosom, and laid her dead son in my bosom. ²¹When I rose in the morning to nurse my son, behold, he was dead; but when I looked at him carefully in the morning, behold, he was not my son, whom I had borne." ²²Then the other woman said, "No! For the living one is my son, and the dead one is your son." But the first woman said, "No! For the dead one is your son, and the living one is my son." Thus they spoke before the king.

²³Then the king said, "The one says, 'This is my son who is living, and your son is the dead one'; and the other says, 'No! For your son is the dead one, and my son is the living one.'" ²⁴The king said, "Get me a sword." So they brought a sword before the king. ²⁵The king said, "Divide the living child in two, and give half to the one and half to the other." ²⁶Then the woman whose child *was* the living one spoke to the king, for she was deeply stirred over her son and said, "Oh, my lord, give her the living child, and by no means kill him." But the other said, "He shall be neither mine nor yours; divide *him!*" ²⁷Then the king said, "Give the first woman the living child, and by no means kill him. She is his mother." ²⁸When all Israel heard of the judgment which the king had handed down, they feared the king, for they saw that the wisdom of God was in him to administer justice.

4 Now King Solomon was king over all Israel. ²These were his officials: Azariah the son of Zadok *was* the priest; ³Elihoreph and Ahijah, the sons of Shisha *were* secretaries; Jehoshaphat the son of Ahilud *was* the recorder; ⁴and Benaiah the son of Jehoiada *was* over the army; and Zadok and Abiathar *were* priests; ⁵and Azariah the son of Nathan *was* over the deputies; and Zabud the son of Nathan, a priest, *was* the king's friend; ⁶and

Ahishar was over the household; and Adoniram the son of Abda *was* over the men subject to forced labor.

⁷Solomon had twelve deputies over all Israel, who provided for the king and his household; each man had to provide for a month in the year. ⁸These are their names: Ben-hur, in the hill country of Ephraim; ⁹Ben-deker in Makaz and Shaalbim and Beth-shemesh and Elonbeth-hanan; ¹⁰Ben-hesed, in Arubboth (Socoh *was* his and all the land of Hepher); ¹¹Ben-abinadab, *in* all the height of Dor (Taphath the daughter of Solomon was his wife); ¹²Baana the son of Ahilud, *in* Taanach and Megiddo, and all Beth-shean which is beside Zarethan below Jezreel, from Beth-shean to Abel-meholah as far as the other side of Jokmeam; ¹³Ben-geber, in Ramoth-gilead (the towns of Jair, the son of Manasseh, which are in Gilead were his: the region of Argob, which is in Bashan, sixty great cities with walls and bronze bars *were* his); ¹⁴Ahinadab the son of Iddo, *in* Mahanaim; ¹⁵Ahimaaz, in Naphtali (he also married Basemath the daughter of Solomon); ¹⁶Baana the son of Hushai, in Asher and Bealoth; ¹⁷Jehoshaphat the son of Paruah, in Issachar; ¹⁸Shimei the son of Ela, in Benjamin; ¹⁹Geber the son of Uri, in the land of Gilead, the country of Sihon king of the Amorites and of Og king of Bashan; and *he was* the only deputy who *was* in the land.

²⁰Judah and Israel *were* as numerous as the sand that is on the seashore in abundance; *they* were eating and drinking and rejoicing.

²¹Now Solomon ruled over all the kingdoms from the River *to* the land of the Philistines and to the border of Egypt; *they* brought tribute and served Solomon all the days of his life.

²²Solomon's provision for one day was thirty kors of fine flour and sixty kors of meal, ²³ten fat oxen, twenty pasture-fed oxen, a hundred sheep besides deer, gazelles, roebucks, and fattened fowl. ²⁴For he had dominion over everything west of the River, from Tiphsah even to Gaza, over all the kings west of the River; and he had peace on all sides around about him. ²⁵So Judah and Israel lived in safety, every man under his vine and his fig tree, from Dan even to Beersheba, all the days of Solomon. ²⁶Solomon had 40,000 stalls of horses for his chariots, and 12,000 horsemen. ²⁷Those deputies provided for King Solomon and all who came to King Solomon's table, each in his month; they left nothing lacking. ²⁸They also brought barley and straw for the horses and swift steeds to the place where it should be, each according to his charge.

²⁹ Now God gave Solomon wisdom and very great discernment and breadth of mind, like the sand that is on the seashore. ³⁰ Solomon's wisdom surpassed the wisdom of all the sons of the east and all the wisdom of Egypt. ³¹ For he was wiser than all men, than Ethan the Ezrahite, Heman, Calcol and Darda, the sons of Mahol; and his fame was *known* in all the surrounding nations. ³² He also spoke 3,000 proverbs, and his songs were 1,005. ³³ He spoke of trees, from the cedar that is in Lebanon even to the hyssop that grows on the wall; he spoke also of animals and birds and creeping things and fish. ³⁴ Men came from all peoples to hear the wisdom of Solomon, from all the kings of the earth who had heard of his wisdom.

Psalm 68:15–20

¹⁵ A mountain of God is the
      mountain of Bashan;
    A mountain *of many* peaks is
      the mountain of Bashan.
¹⁶ Why do you look with envy,
      O mountains with *many*
      peaks,
    At the mountain which God has
      desired for His abode?
    Surely the LORD will dwell
      there forever.
¹⁷ The chariots of God are myriads,
      thousands upon thousands;
    The Lord is among them *as*
      at Sinai, in holiness.
¹⁸ You have ascended on high, You
      have led captive *Your* captives;
    You have received gifts
      among men,
    Even *among* the rebellious also,
      that the LORD God may
      dwell *there*.
¹⁹ Blessed be the Lord, who
      daily bears our burden,
    The God *who* is our salvation.   *Selah*
²⁰ God is to us a God of deliverances;
    And to GOD the Lord belong
      escapes from death.

Proverbs 17:10–12

¹⁰ A rebuke goes deeper into one
      who has understanding
    Than a hundred blows into
      a fool.
¹¹ A rebellious man seeks
      only evil,
    So a cruel messenger will
      be sent against him.

¹² Let a man meet a bear
      robbed of her cubs,
    Rather than a fool in his folly.

John 10:1–21

10 "Truly, truly, I say to you, he who does not enter by the door into the fold of the sheep, but climbs up some other way, he is a thief and a robber. ² But he who enters by the door is a shepherd of the sheep. ³ To him the doorkeeper opens, and the sheep hear his voice, and he calls his own sheep by name and leads them out. ⁴ When he puts forth all his own, he goes ahead of them, and the sheep follow him because they know his voice. ⁵ A stranger they simply will not follow, but will flee from him, because they do not know the voice of strangers." ⁶ This figure of speech Jesus spoke to them, but they did not understand what those things were which He had been saying to them.

⁷ So Jesus said to them again, "Truly, truly, I say to you, I am the door of the sheep. ⁸ All who came before Me are thieves and robbers, but the sheep did not hear them. ⁹ I am the door; if anyone enters through Me, he will be saved, and will go in and out and find pasture. ¹⁰ The thief comes only to steal and kill and destroy; I came that they may have life, and have *it* abundantly.

10:7–10 I am the door. This is the third of 7 "I am" statements of Jesus (6:35; 8:12). Here, He changes the metaphor slightly. While in vv. 1–5 He was the shepherd, here He is the gate. While in vv. 1–5, the shepherd led the sheep out of the sheep fold, here He is the entrance to the fold (v. 9) that leads to proper pasture. This section echoes Jesus' words in 14:6 that He is the only way to the Father. His point is that He serves as the sole means to approach the Father and partake of God's promised salvation. As some Near Eastern shepherds slept in the gateway to guard the sheep, Jesus here pictures Himself as the gate.

¹¹ "I am the good shepherd; the good shepherd lays down His life for the sheep. ¹² He who is a hired hand, and not a shepherd, who is not the owner of the sheep, sees the wolf coming, and leaves the sheep and flees, and the wolf snatches them and scatters *them*. ¹³ *He flees* because he is a hired hand and is not concerned about the sheep. ¹⁴ I am the good shepherd, and I know My own and My

own know Me, [15] even as the Father knows Me and I know the Father; and I lay down My life for the sheep. [16] I have other sheep, which are not of this fold; I must bring them also, and they will hear My voice; and they will become one flock *with* one shepherd. [17] For this reason the Father loves Me, because I lay down My life so that I may take it again. [18] No one has taken it away from Me, but I lay it down on My own initiative. I have authority to lay it down, and I have authority to take it up again. This commandment I received from My Father."

[19] A division occurred again among the Jews because of these words. [20] Many of them were saying, "He has a demon and is insane. Why do you listen to Him?" [21] Others were saying, "These are not the sayings of one demon-possessed. A demon cannot open the eyes of the blind, can he?"

10:17-18 take it again. Jesus repeated this phrase twice in these two verses, indicating that His sacrificial death was not the end. His resurrection followed in demonstration of His messiahship and deity (Ro 1:4). His death and resurrection resulted in His ultimate glorification (12:23; 17:5) and the outpouring of the Holy Spirit (7:37-39; Ac 2:16-39).

DAY 28: What does it mean to have Jesus as the "Good Shepherd"?

In John 10:1-39, Jesus' discourse on Himself as the "Good Shepherd" flowed directly from chapter 9, as Jesus continued to talk to the very same people. The problem of chapter 9 was that Israel was led by false shepherds who drew them astray from the true knowledge and kingdom of Messiah (9:39-41). In chapter 10, Jesus declared Himself to be the "Good Shepherd" who was appointed by His Father as Savior and King, in contrast to the false shepherds of Israel who were self-appointed and self-righteous (Ps 23:1; Is. 40:11; Jer 3:15; see Is. 56:9-12; Jer 23:1-4; 25:32-38; Eze 34:1-31; Zec 11:16).

Jesus spoke in vv. 1-30 using a sustained metaphor based on first-century sheep ranching. The sheep were kept in a pen, which had a gate through which the sheep entered and left. The shepherd engaged a "doorkeeper" (v. 3) or "hired hand" (v. 12) as an undershepherd to guard the gate. The shepherd entered through that gate. He whose interest was stealing or wounding the sheep would choose another way to attempt entrance. The words of Ezekiel 34 most likely form the background to Jesus' teaching since God decried the false shepherds of Israel (i.e., the spiritual leaders of the nation) for not caring properly for the flock of Israel (i.e., the nation). The Gospels themselves contain extensive sheep/shepherd imagery (Mt 9:36; Mk 6:34; 14:27; Lk 15:1-7).

The doorkeeper was a hired undershepherd who recognized the true shepherd of the flock, opened the gate for Him, assisted the shepherd in caring for the flock, and especially guarded them at night (v. 3). "The sheep hear his voice." Near Eastern shepherds stand at different locations outside the sheep pen, sounding out their own unique calls which their sheep recognize. As a result, the sheep gather around the shepherd. "He calls his own sheep by name." This shepherd goes even further by calling each sheep by its own special name. Jesus' point is that He comes to the fold of Israel and calls out His own sheep individually to come into His own messianic fold. The assumption is that they are already in some way His sheep even before He calls them by name (vv. 25-27; 6:37, 39, 44, 64-65; 17:6, 9, 24; 18:9).

Unlike Western shepherds who drive the sheep from the side or behind, often using sheep dogs, Near Eastern shepherds lead their flocks, their voice calling them to move on (vv. 4-5). This draws a remarkable picture of the master/disciple relationship. New Testament spiritual leadership is always by example, i.e., a call to imitate conduct (1Ti 4:12; 1Pe 5:1-3).

MAY 29

1 Kings 5:1-6:38

5 Now Hiram king of Tyre sent his servants to Solomon, when he heard that they had anointed him king in place of his father, for Hiram had always been a friend of David. [2] Then Solomon sent *word* to Hiram, saying,

[3] "You know that David my father was unable to build a house for the name of the LORD his God because of the wars which surrounded him, until the LORD put them under the soles of his feet. [4] But now the LORD my God has given me rest on every side; there is neither adversary nor misfortune. [5] Behold, I intend to build a house for the name of the LORD my God, as the LORD spoke to David my father,

saying, 'Your son, whom I will set on your throne in your place, he will build the house for My name.' 6 Now therefore, command that they cut for me cedars from Lebanon, and my servants will be with your servants; and I will give you wages for your servants according to all that you say, for you know that there is no one among us who knows how to cut timber like the Sidonians."

5:6 cedars from Lebanon. The cedars of Lebanon symbolized majesty and might (Ps 92:12; Eze 31:3). Because it was durable, resistant to rot and worms, closely-grained, and could be polished to a fine shine, its wood was regarded as the best timber for building. The logs were tied together and floated down the Mediterranean to Joppa (v. 9; 2Ch 2:16), from where they could be transported to Jerusalem, 35 miles inland.

7 When Hiram heard the words of Solomon, he rejoiced greatly and said, "Blessed be the LORD today, who has given to David a wise son over this great people." 8 So Hiram sent word to Solomon, saying, "I have heard the message which you have sent me; I will do what you desire concerning the cedar and cypress timber. 9 My servants will bring them down from Lebanon to the sea; and I will make them into rafts to go by sea to the place where you direct me, and I will have them broken up there, and you shall carry them away. Then you shall accomplish my desire by giving food to my household." 10 So Hiram gave Solomon as much as he desired of the cedar and cypress timber. 11 Solomon then gave Hiram 20,000 kors of wheat as food for his household, and twenty kors of beaten oil; thus Solomon would give Hiram year by year. 12 The LORD gave wisdom to Solomon, just as He promised him; and there was peace between Hiram and Solomon, and the two of them made a covenant.

13 Now King Solomon levied forced laborers from all Israel; and the forced laborers numbered 30,000 men. 14 He sent them to Lebanon, 10,000 a month in relays; they were in Lebanon a month and two months at home. And Adoniram was over the forced laborers. 15 Now Solomon had 70,000 transporters, and 80,000 hewers of stone in the mountains, 16 besides Solomon's 3,300 chief deputies who were over the project and who ruled over the people who were doing the

6:16 the most holy place. This inner sanctuary, partitioned off from the main hall by cedar planks, was a perfect cube about 30 ft. on a side (v. 20) and was the most sacred area of the temple. The Most Holy Place is further described in vv. 19–28. The tabernacle also had a "most holy place" (Ex 26:33–34).

work. 17 Then the king commanded, and they quarried great stones, costly stones, to lay the foundation of the house with cut stones. 18 So Solomon's builders and Hiram's builders and the Gebalites cut them, and prepared the timbers and the stones to build the house.

6 Now it came about in the four hundred and eightieth year after the sons of Israel came out of the land of Egypt, in the fourth year of Solomon's reign over Israel, in the month of Ziv which is the second month, that he began to build the house of the LORD. 2 As for the house which King Solomon built for the LORD, its length was sixty cubits and its width twenty cubits and its height thirty cubits. 3 The porch in front of the nave of the house was twenty cubits in length, corresponding to the width of the house, and its depth along the front of the house was ten cubits. 4 Also for the house he made windows with artistic frames. 5 Against the wall of the house he built stories encompassing the walls of the house around both the nave and the inner sanctuary; thus he made side chambers all around. 6 The lowest story was five cubits wide, and the middle was six cubits wide, and the third was seven cubits wide; for on the outside he made offsets in the wall of the house all around in order that the beams would not be inserted in the walls of the house.

7 The house, while it was being built, was built of stone prepared at the quarry, and there was neither hammer nor axe nor any iron tool heard in the house while it was being built.

8 The doorway for the lowest side chamber was on the right side of the house; and they would go up by winding stairs to the middle story, and from the middle to the third. 9 So he built the house and finished it; and he covered the house with beams and planks of cedar. 10 He also built the stories against the whole house, each five cubits high; and they were fastened to the house with timbers of cedar.

11 Now the word of the LORD came to Solomon saying, 12 "Concerning this house

which you are building, if you will walk in My statutes and execute My ordinances and keep all My commandments by walking in them, then I will carry out My word with you which I spoke to David your father. ¹³ I will dwell among the sons of Israel, and will not forsake My people Israel."

¹⁴ So Solomon built the house and finished it. ¹⁵ Then he built the walls of the house on the inside with boards of cedar; from the floor of the house to the ceiling he overlaid *the walls* on the inside with wood, and he overlaid the floor of the house with boards of cypress. ¹⁶ He built twenty cubits on the rear part of the house with boards of cedar from the floor to the ceiling; he built *them* for it on the inside as an inner sanctuary, *even* as the most holy place. ¹⁷ The house, that is, the nave in front of *the inner sanctuary,* was forty cubits *long.* ¹⁸ There was cedar on the house within, carved *in the shape* of gourds and open flowers; all was cedar, there was no stone seen. ¹⁹ Then he prepared an inner sanctuary within the house in order to place there the ark of the covenant of the LORD. ²⁰ The inner sanctuary *was* twenty cubits in length, twenty cubits in width, and twenty cubits in height, and he overlaid it with pure gold. He also overlaid the altar with cedar. ²¹ So Solomon overlaid the inside of the house with pure gold. And he drew chains of gold across the front of the inner sanctuary, and he overlaid it with gold. ²² He overlaid the whole house with gold, until all the house was finished. Also the whole altar which was by the inner sanctuary he overlaid with gold.

²³ Also in the inner sanctuary he made two cherubim of olive wood, each ten cubits high. ²⁴ Five cubits *was* the one wing of the cherub and five cubits the other wing of the cherub; from the end of one wing to the end of the other wing *were* ten cubits. ²⁵ The other cherub *was* ten cubits; both the cherubim were of the same measure and the same form. ²⁶ The height of the one cherub *was* ten cubits, and so *was* the other cherub. ²⁷ He placed the cherubim in the midst of the inner house, and the wings of the cherubim were spread out, so that the wing of the one was touching the *one* wall, and the wing of the other cherub was touching the other wall. So their wings were touching each other in the center of the house. ²⁸ He also overlaid the cherubim with gold.

²⁹ Then he carved all the walls of the house round about with carved engravings of cherubim, palm trees, and open flowers, inner and outer *sanctuaries.* ³⁰ He overlaid the floor of the house with gold, inner and outer *sanctuaries.*

³¹ For the entrance of the inner sanctuary he made doors of olive wood, the lintel *and* five-sided doorposts. ³² So *he made* two doors of olive wood, and he carved on them carvings of cherubim, palm trees, and open flowers, and overlaid them with gold; and he spread the gold on the cherubim and on the palm trees.

³³ So also he made for the entrance of the nave four-sided doorposts of olive wood ³⁴ and two doors of cypress wood; the two leaves of the one door turned on pivots, and the two leaves of the other door turned on pivots. ³⁵ He carved *on it* cherubim, palm trees, and open flowers; and he overlaid *them* with gold evenly applied on the engraved work. ³⁶ He built the inner court with three rows of cut stone and a row of cedar beams.

³⁷ In the fourth year the foundation of the house of the LORD was laid, in the month of Ziv. ³⁸ In the eleventh year, in the month of Bul, which is the eighth month, the house was finished throughout all its parts and according to all its plans. So he was seven years in building it.

Psalm 68:21–27

21 Surely God will shatter the
    head of His enemies,
The hairy crown of him who
    goes on in his guilty deeds.
22 The Lord said, "I will bring
    them back from Bashan,
I will bring *them* back from
    the depths of the sea;
23 That your foot may shatter
    them in blood,
The tongue of your dogs *may have*
    its portion from *your* enemies."

24 They have seen Your
    procession, O God,
The procession of my God, my
    King, into the sanctuary.
25 The singers went on, the
    musicians after *them,*
In the midst of the maidens
    beating tambourines.
26 Bless God in the congregations,
    Even the LORD, *you who are* of
    the fountain of Israel.
27 There is Benjamin, the
    youngest, ruling them,
The princes of Judah *in* their throng,
The princes of Zebulun, the
    princes of Naphtali.

Proverbs 17:13–15

13 He who returns evil for good,
Evil will not depart from his house.

14 The beginning of strife is
like letting out water,
So abandon the quarrel
before it breaks out.

15 He who justifies the wicked and he
who condemns the righteous,
Both of them alike are an
abomination to the LORD.

17:13 evil for good. Solomon knew this proverb well, since his father mistreated Uriah (2Sa 12:10–31). Contrast this with the man who repays evil with good (20:22; Mt 5:43–48; 1Pe 3:9).

John 10:22–42

22 At that time the Feast of the Dedication took place at Jerusalem; 23 it was winter, and Jesus was walking in the temple in the portico of Solomon. 24 The Jews then gathered around Him, and were saying to Him, "How long will You keep us in suspense? If You are the Christ, tell us plainly." 25 Jesus answered them, "I told you, and you do not believe; the works that I do in My Father's name, these testify of Me. 26 But you do not believe because you are not of My sheep. 27 My sheep hear My voice, and I know them, and they follow Me; 28 and I give eternal life to them, and they will never perish; and no one will snatch them out of My hand. 29 My Father, who has given *them* to Me, is greater than all; and no one is able to snatch *them* out of the Father's hand. 30 I and the Father are one." 31 The Jews picked up stones again to stone

Him. 32 Jesus answered them, "I showed you many good works from the Father; for which of them are you stoning Me?" 33 The Jews answered Him, "For a good work we do not stone You, but for blasphemy; and because You, being a man, make Yourself out *to be* God." 34 Jesus answered them, "Has it not been written in your Law, 'I SAID, YOU ARE GODS'? 35 If he called them gods, to whom the word of God came (and the Scripture cannot be broken), 36 do you say of Him, whom the Father sanctified and sent into the world, 'You are blaspheming,' because I said, 'I am the Son of God'? 37 If I do not do the works of My Father, do not believe Me; 38 but if I do them, though you do not believe Me, believe the works, so that you may know and understand that the Father is in Me, and I in the Father." 39 Therefore they were seeking again to seize Him, and He eluded their grasp.

40 And He went away again beyond the Jordan to the place where John was first baptizing, and He was staying there. 41 Many came to Him and were saying, "While John performed no sign, yet everything John said about this man was true." 42 Many believed in Him there.

10:38 believe the works. Jesus did not expect to be believed merely on His own assertions. Since He did the same things that the Father does (5:19), His enemies should consider this in their evaluation of Him. The implication is, however, that they were so ignorant of God that they could not recognize the works of the Father or the One whom the Father sent (also 14:10–11).

DAY 29: How secure is the believer in Christ?

In John 10:24, the Jews surrounded Him and said, "If You are the Christ, tell us plainly." In light of the context of vv. 31–39, the Jews were not seeking merely for clarity and understanding regarding who Jesus was, but rather wanted Him to declare openly that He was Messiah in order to justify attacking Him.

Jesus' response is that He has told them and that His works confirm the truth of who He is. The problem is that they do not believe because they "are not of My sheep" (v. 26). This clearly indicates that God has chosen His sheep and it is they who believe and follow.

But for those who do believe and follow Christ, "I give eternal life to them, and they will never perish" (v. 28). The security of Jesus' sheep rests with Him as the Good Shepherd, who has the power to keep them safe. Neither thieves and robbers (vv. 1, 8) nor the wolf (v. 12) can harm them. Verse 29 makes clear that the Father ultimately stands behind the sheep's security, for no one is able to steal from God, who is in sovereign control of all things (Col 3:3; Ro 8:31–39). No stronger passage in the Old Testament or New Testament exists for the absolute, eternal security of every true Christian.

"I and the Father are one" (v. 30). Both Father and Son are committed to the perfect protection and preservation of Jesus' sheep. The sentence, stressing the united purpose and action of both in the security and safety of the flock, presupposes unity of nature and essence (see 5:17–23; 17:22).

MAY 30

1 Kings 7:1–8:66

7 Now Solomon was building his own house thirteen years, and he finished all his house. ² He built the house of the forest of Lebanon; its length was 100 cubits and its width 50 cubits and its height 30 cubits, on four rows of cedar pillars with cedar beams on the pillars. ³ It was paneled with cedar above the side chambers which were on the 45 pillars, 15 in each row. ⁴ *There were artistic window* frames in three rows, and window was opposite window in three ranks. ⁵ All the doorways and doorposts *had* squared *artistic* frames, and window was opposite window in three ranks.

⁶ Then he made the hall of pillars; its length was 50 cubits and its width 30 cubits, and a porch *was* in front of them and pillars and a threshold in front of them.

⁷ He made the hall of the throne where he was to judge, the hall of judgment, and it was paneled with cedar from floor to floor.

⁸ His house where he was to live, the other court inward from the hall, was of the same workmanship. He also made a house like this hall for Pharaoh's daughter, whom Solomon had married.

⁹ All these were of costly stones, of stone cut according to measure, sawed with saws, inside and outside; even from the foundation to the coping, and so on the outside to the great court.

¹⁰ The foundation was of costly stones, *even* large stones, stones of ten cubits and stones of eight cubits. ¹¹ And above were costly stones, stone cut according to measure, and cedar. ¹² So the great court all around *had* three rows of cut stone and a row of cedar beams even as the inner court of the house of the LORD, and the porch of the house.

¹³ Now King Solomon sent and brought Hiram from Tyre. ¹⁴ He was a widow's son from the tribe of Naphtali, and his father was a man of Tyre, a worker in bronze; and he was filled with wisdom and understanding and skill for doing any work in bronze. So he came to King Solomon and performed all his work.

¹⁵ He fashioned the two pillars of bronze; eighteen cubits was the height of one pillar, and a line of twelve cubits measured the circumference of both. ¹⁶ He also made two capitals of molten bronze to set on the tops of the pillars; the height of the one capital was five cubits and the height of the other capital was five cubits. ¹⁷ *There were* nets of network and twisted threads of chainwork for the capitals which were on the top of the pillars; seven for the one capital and seven for the other capital. ¹⁸ So he made the pillars, and two rows around on the one network to cover the capitals which were on the top of the pomegranates; and so he did for the other capital. ¹⁹ The capitals which *were* on the top of the pillars in the porch were of lily design, four cubits. ²⁰ *There were* capitals on the two pillars, even above *and* close to the rounded projection which was beside the network; and the pomegranates *numbered* two hundred in rows around both capitals. ²¹ Thus he set up the pillars at the porch of the nave; and he set up the right pillar and named it Jachin, and he set up the left pillar and named it Boaz. ²² On the top of the pillars was lily design. So the work of the pillars was finished.

²³ Now he made the sea of cast *metal* ten cubits from brim to brim, circular in form, and its height was five cubits, and thirty cubits in circumference. ²⁴ Under its brim gourds went around encircling it ten to a cubit, completely surrounding the sea; the gourds were in two rows, cast with the rest. ²⁵ It stood on twelve oxen, three facing north, three facing west, three facing south, and three facing east; and the sea *was set* on top of them, and all their rear parts *turned* inward. ²⁶ It was a handbreadth thick, and its brim was made like the brim of a cup, *as* a lily blossom; it could hold two thousand baths.

²⁷ Then he made the ten stands of bronze; the length of each stand was four cubits and its width four cubits and its height three cubits. ²⁸ This was the design of the stands: they had borders, even borders between the frames, ²⁹ and on the borders which were between the frames *were* lions, oxen and cherubim; and on the frames there *was* a pedestal above, and beneath the lions and oxen *were* wreaths of hanging work. ³⁰ Now each stand had four bronze wheels with bronze axles, and its four feet had supports; beneath the basin *were* cast supports with wreaths at each side. ³¹ Its opening inside the crown at the top *was* a cubit, and its opening *was* round like the design of a pedestal, a cubit and a half; and also on its opening *there were* engravings, and their borders were square, not round. ³² The four wheels *were* underneath the borders, and the axles of the wheels *were* on the stand. And the height of a wheel *was* a cubit and a half. ³³ The workmanship of the wheels *was* like the workmanship of a chariot wheel. Their axles, their rims, their spokes, and their hubs *were* all cast. ³⁴ Now

there were four supports at the four corners of each stand; its supports were part of the stand itself. ³⁵ On the top of the stand there was a circular form half a cubit high, and on the top of the stand its stays and its borders were part of it. ³⁶ He engraved on the plates of its stays and on its borders, cherubim, lions and palm trees, according to the clear space on each, with wreaths all around. ³⁷ He made the ten stands like this: all of them had one casting, one measure and one form.

³⁸ He made ten basins of bronze, one basin held forty baths; each basin was four cubits, and on each of the ten stands was one basin. ³⁹ Then he set the stands, five on the right side of the house and five on the left side of the house; and he set the sea of cast metal on the right side of the house eastward toward the south.

⁴⁰ Now Hiram made the basins and the shovels and the bowls. So Hiram finished doing all the work which he performed for King Solomon in the house of the LORD: ⁴¹ the two pillars and the two bowls of the capitals which were on the top of the two pillars, and the two networks to cover the two bowls of the capitals which were on the top of the pillars; ⁴² and the four hundred pomegranates for the two networks, two rows of pomegranates for each network to cover the two bowls of the capitals which were on the tops of the pillars; ⁴³ and the ten stands with the ten basins on the stands; ⁴⁴ and the one sea and the twelve oxen under the sea; ⁴⁵ and the pails and the shovels and the bowls; even all these utensils which Hiram made for King Solomon in the house of the LORD were of polished bronze. ⁴⁶ In the plain of the Jordan the king cast them, in the clay ground between Succoth and Zarethan. ⁴⁷ Solomon left all the utensils unweighed, because they were too many; the weight of the bronze could not be ascertained.

⁴⁸ Solomon made all the furniture which was in the house of the LORD: the golden altar and the golden table on which was the bread of the Presence; ⁴⁹ and the lampstands, five on the right side and five on the left, in front of the inner sanctuary, of pure gold; and the flowers and the lamps and the tongs, of gold; ⁵⁰ and the cups and the snuffers and the bowls and the spoons and the firepans, of pure gold; and the hinges both for the doors of the inner house, the most holy place, and for the doors of the house, that is, of the nave, of gold.

⁵¹ Thus all the work that King Solomon performed in the house of the LORD was finished. And Solomon brought in the things dedicated by his father David, the silver and the gold and the utensils, and he put them in the treasuries of the house of the LORD.

8 Then Solomon assembled the elders of Israel and all the heads of the tribes, the leaders of the fathers' households of the sons of Israel, to King Solomon in Jerusalem, to bring up the ark of the covenant of the LORD from the city of David, which is Zion. ² All the men of Israel assembled themselves to King Solomon at the feast, in the month Ethanim, which is the seventh month. ³ Then all the elders of Israel came, and the priests took up the ark. ⁴ They brought up the ark of the LORD and the tent of meeting and all the holy utensils, which were in the tent, and the priests and the Levites brought them up. ⁵ And King Solomon and all the congregation of Israel, who were assembled to him, were with him before the ark, sacrificing so many sheep and oxen they could not be counted or numbered. ⁶ Then the priests brought the ark of the covenant of the LORD to its place, into the inner sanctuary of the house, to the most holy place, under the wings of the cherubim. ⁷ For the cherubim spread their wings over the place of the ark, and the cherubim made a covering over the ark and its poles from above. ⁸ But the poles were so long that the ends of the poles could be seen from the holy place before the inner sanctuary, but they could not be seen outside; they are there to this day. ⁹ There was nothing in the ark except the two tablets of stone which Moses put there at Horeb, where the LORD made a covenant with the sons of Israel, when they came out of the land of Egypt. ¹⁰ It happened that when the priests came from the holy place, the cloud filled the house of the LORD, ¹¹ so that the priests could not stand to minister because of the cloud, for the glory of the LORD filled the house of the LORD.

¹² Then Solomon said,

"The LORD has said that He would
    dwell in the thick cloud.
¹³ "I have surely built You a lofty house,
    A place for Your dwelling forever."

8:10 the cloud. The cloud was "the glory of the LORD" (v. 11), the visible symbol of God's presence. It signaled the Lord's approval of this new temple. A similar manifestation took place when the tabernacle was dedicated (Ex 40:34–35).

¹⁴ Then the king faced about and blessed all the assembly of Israel, while all the assembly of Israel was standing. ¹⁵ He said, "Blessed be the LORD, the God of Israel, who spoke with His mouth to my father David and has fulfilled *it* with His hand, saying, ¹⁶ 'Since the day that I brought My people Israel from Egypt, I did not choose a city out of all the tribes of Israel *in which* to build a house that My name might be there, but I chose David to be over My people Israel.' ¹⁷ Now it was in the heart of my father David to build a house for the name of the LORD, the God of Israel. ¹⁸ But the LORD said to my father David, 'Because it was in your heart to build a house for My name, you did well that it was in your heart. ¹⁹ Nevertheless you shall not build the house, but your son who will be born to you, he will build the house for My name.' ²⁰ Now the LORD has fulfilled His word which He spoke; for I have risen in place of my father David and sit on the throne of Israel, as the LORD promised, and have built the house for the name of the LORD, the God of Israel. ²¹ There I have set a place for the ark, in which is the covenant of the LORD, which He made with our fathers when He brought them from the land of Egypt."

²² Then Solomon stood before the altar of the LORD in the presence of all the assembly of Israel and spread out his hands toward heaven. ²³ He said, "O LORD, the God of Israel, there is no God like You in heaven above or on earth beneath, keeping covenant and *showing* lovingkindness to Your servants who walk before You with all their heart, ²⁴ who have kept with Your servant, my father David, that which You have promised him; indeed, You have spoken with Your mouth and have fulfilled it with Your hand as it is this day. ²⁵ Now therefore, O LORD, the God of Israel, keep with Your servant David my father that which You have promised him, saying, 'You shall not lack a man to sit on the throne of Israel, if only your sons take heed to their way to walk before Me as you have walked.' ²⁶ Now therefore, O God of Israel, let Your word, I pray, be confirmed which You have spoken to Your servant, my father David.

²⁷ "But will God indeed dwell on the earth? Behold, heaven and the highest heaven cannot contain You, how much less this house which I have built! ²⁸ Yet have regard to the prayer of Your servant and to his supplication, O LORD my God, to listen to the cry and to the prayer which Your servant prays before You today; ²⁹ that Your eyes may be open toward this house night and day, toward the place of which You have said, 'My name shall be there,' to listen to the prayer which Your servant shall pray toward this place. ³⁰ Listen to the supplication of Your servant and of Your people Israel, when they pray toward this place; hear in heaven Your dwelling place; hear and forgive.

³¹ "If a man sins against his neighbor and is made to take an oath, and he comes *and* takes an oath before Your altar in this house, ³² then hear in heaven and act and judge Your servants, condemning the wicked by bringing his way on his own head and justifying the righteous by giving him according to his righteousness.

³³ "When Your people Israel are defeated before an enemy, because they have sinned against You, if they turn to You again and confess Your name and pray and make supplication to You in this house, ³⁴ then hear in heaven, and forgive the sin of Your people Israel, and bring them back to the land which You gave to their fathers.

³⁵ "When the heavens are shut up and there is no rain, because they have sinned against You, and they pray toward this place and confess Your name and turn from their sin when You afflict them, ³⁶ then hear in heaven and forgive the sin of Your servants and of Your people Israel, indeed, teach them the good way in which they should walk. And send rain on Your land, which You have given Your people for an inheritance.

³⁷ "If there is famine in the land, if there is pestilence, if there is blight *or* mildew, locust *or* grasshopper, if their enemy besieges them in the land of their cities, whatever plague, whatever sickness *there is,* ³⁸ whatever prayer or supplication is made by any man *or* by all Your people Israel, each knowing the affliction of his own heart, and spreading his hands toward this house; ³⁹ then hear in heaven Your dwelling place, and forgive and act and render to each according to all his ways, whose heart You know, for You alone know the hearts of all the sons of men, ⁴⁰ that they may fear You all the days that they live in the land which You have given to our fathers.

⁴¹ "Also concerning the foreigner who is not of Your people Israel, when he comes from a far country for Your name's sake ⁴² (for they will hear of Your great name and Your mighty hand, and of Your outstretched arm); when he comes and prays toward this house, ⁴³ hear in heaven Your dwelling place, and do according to all for which the foreigner calls to You, in order that all the peoples of the earth may know Your name, to fear You, as *do*

Your people Israel, and that they may know that this house which I have built is called by Your name.

44 "When Your people go out to battle against their enemy, by whatever way You shall send them, and they pray to the LORD toward the city which You have chosen and the house which I have built for Your name, 45 then hear in heaven their prayer and their supplication, and maintain their cause.

46 "When they sin against You (for there is no man who does not sin) and You are angry with them and deliver them to an enemy, so that they take them away captive to the land of the enemy, far off or near; 47 if they take thought in the land where they have been taken captive, and repent and make supplication to You in the land of those who have taken them captive, saying, 'We have sinned and have committed iniquity, we have acted wickedly'; 48 if they return to You with all their heart and with all their soul in the land of their enemies who have taken them captive, and pray to You toward their land which You have given to their fathers, the city which You have chosen, and the house which I have built for Your name; 49 then hear their prayer and their supplication in heaven Your dwelling place, and maintain their cause, 50 and forgive Your people who have sinned against You and all their transgressions which they have transgressed against You, and make them *objects of* compassion before those who have taken

8:22–53 Solomon then moved to the altar of burnt offering to offer a lengthy prayer of consecration to the Lord. First, he affirmed that no god could compare to Israel's God, the Lord (vv. 23–24). Second, he asked the Lord for His continued presence and protection (vv. 25–30). Third, he listed 7 typical Israelite prayers that would require the Lord's response (vv. 31–54). These supplications recalled the detailed list of curses that Deuteronomy 28:15–68 ascribed for the breaking of the law. Specifically, Solomon prayed that the Lord would judge between the wicked and the righteous (vv. 31–32); the Lord would forgive the sins that had caused defeat in battle (vv. 33–34); the Lord would forgive the sins that had brought on drought (vv. 35–36); the Lord would forgive the sins that had resulted in national calamities (vv. 37–40); the Lord would show mercy to God-fearing foreigners (vv. 41–43); the Lord would give victory in battle (vv. 44–45); and the Lord would bring restoration after captivity (vv. 46–54).

them captive, that they may have compassion on them 51 (for they are Your people and Your inheritance which You have brought forth from Egypt, from the midst of the iron furnace), 52 that Your eyes may be open to the supplication of Your servant and to the supplication of Your people Israel, to listen to them whenever they call to You. 53 For You have separated them from all the peoples of the earth as Your inheritance, as You spoke through Moses Your servant, when You brought our fathers forth from Egypt, O Lord GOD."

54 When Solomon had finished praying this entire prayer and supplication to the LORD, he arose from before the altar of the LORD, from kneeling on his knees with his hands spread toward heaven. 55 And he stood and blessed all the assembly of Israel with a loud voice, saying:

56 "Blessed be the LORD, who has given rest to His people Israel, according to all that He promised; not one word has failed of all His good promise, which He promised through Moses His servant. 57 May the LORD our God be with us, as He was with our fathers; may He not leave us or forsake us, 58 that He may incline our hearts to Himself, to walk in all His ways and to keep His commandments and His statutes and His ordinances, which He commanded our fathers. 59 And may these words of mine, with which I have made supplication before the LORD, be near to the LORD our God day and night, that He may maintain the cause of His servant and the cause of His people Israel, as each day requires, 60 so that all the peoples of the earth may know that the LORD is God; there is no one else. 61 Let your heart therefore be wholly devoted to the LORD our God, to walk in His statutes and to keep His commandments, as at this day."

62 Now the king and all Israel with him offered sacrifice before the LORD. 63 Solomon offered for the sacrifice of peace offerings, which he offered to the LORD, 22,000 oxen and 120,000 sheep. So the king and all the sons of Israel dedicated the house of the LORD. 64 On the same day the king consecrated the middle of the court that *was* before the house of the LORD, because there he offered the burnt offering and the grain offering and the fat of the peace offerings; for the bronze altar that *was* before the LORD *was* too small to hold the burnt offering and the grain offering and the fat of the peace offerings.

65 So Solomon observed the feast at that time, and all Israel with him, a great assembly from the entrance of Hamath to the brook of Egypt, before the LORD our God, for seven

days and seven *more* days, *even* fourteen days. ⁶⁶On the eighth day he sent the people away and they blessed the king. Then they went to their tents joyful and glad of heart for all the goodness that the LORD had shown to David His servant and to Israel His people.

Psalm 68:28-35

²⁸ Your God has commanded
    your strength;
  Show Yourself strong, O God, who
    have acted on our behalf.
²⁹ Because of Your temple at Jerusalem
  Kings will bring gifts to You.
³⁰ Rebuke the beasts in the reeds,
  The herd of bulls with the
    calves of the peoples,
  Trampling under foot the
    pieces of silver;
  He has scattered the peoples
    who delight in war.
³¹ Envoys will come out of Egypt;
  Ethiopia will quickly stretch
    out her hands to God.

³² Sing to God, O kingdoms of the earth,
  Sing praises to the Lord,   *Selah*
³³ To Him who rides upon the
    highest heavens, which are
    from ancient times;
  Behold, He speaks forth with
    His voice, a mighty voice.
³⁴ Ascribe strength to God;
  His majesty is over Israel
  And His strength is in the skies.
³⁵ O God, *You are* awesome
    from Your sanctuary.
  The God of Israel Himself gives
    strength and power to the people.
  Blessed be God!

Proverbs 17:16-17

¹⁶ Why is there a price in the hand
    of a fool to buy wisdom,
  When he has no sense?
¹⁷ A friend loves at all times,
  And a brother is born for adversity.

17:17 The difference between a friend and brother is noted here. A true friend is a constant source of love, while a brother in one's family may not be close but is drawn near to help in trouble. Friends are closer than brothers because they are available all the time, not just in the crisis. See 18:24.

John 11:1-27

11 Now a certain man was sick, Lazarus of Bethany, the village of Mary and her sister Martha. ²It was the Mary who anointed the Lord with ointment, and wiped His feet with her hair, whose brother Lazarus was sick. ³So the sisters sent *word* to Him, saying, "Lord, behold, he whom You love is sick." ⁴But when Jesus heard *this*, He said, "This sickness is not to end in death, but for the glory of God, so that the Son of God may be glorified by it." ⁵Now Jesus loved Martha and her sister and Lazarus. ⁶So when He heard that he was sick, He then stayed two days *longer* in the place where He was. ⁷Then after this He *said to the disciples, "Let us go to Judea again." ⁸The disciples *said to Him, "Rabbi, the Jews were just now seeking to stone You, and are You going there again?" ⁹Jesus answered, "Are there not twelve hours in the day? If anyone walks in the day, he does not stumble, because he sees the light of this world. ¹⁰But if anyone walks in the night, he stumbles, because the light is not in him." ¹¹This He said, and after that He *said to them, "Our friend Lazarus has fallen asleep; but I go, so that I may awaken him out of sleep." ¹²The disciples then said to Him, "Lord, if he has fallen asleep, he will recover." ¹³Now Jesus had spoken of his death, but they thought that He was speaking of literal sleep. ¹⁴So Jesus then said to them plainly, "Lazarus is dead, ¹⁵and I am glad for your sakes that I was not there, so that you may believe; but let us go to him." ¹⁶Therefore Thomas, who is called Didymus, said to *his* fellow disciples, "Let us also go, so that we may die with Him."

¹⁷So when Jesus came, He found that he had already been in the tomb four days. ¹⁸Now Bethany was near Jerusalem, about two miles off; ¹⁹and many of the Jews had

11:17 in the tomb. The term "tomb" means a stone sepulcher. In the eastern Mediterranean basin such a grave was common. Either a cave or rock area would be hewn out, the floor inside leveled and graded to make a shallow descent. Shelves were cut out or constructed inside the area in order to bury additional family members. A rock was rolled in front to prevent wild animals or grave robbers from entering. The evangelist made special mention of the fourth day in order to stress the magnitude of the miracle, for the Jews did not embalm, and by then the body would have been in a state of rapid decomposition.

come to Martha and Mary, to console them concerning *their* brother. ²⁰ Martha therefore, when she heard that Jesus was coming, went to meet Him, but Mary stayed at the house. ²¹ Martha then said to Jesus, "Lord, if You had been here, my brother would not have died. ²² Even now I know that whatever You ask of God, God will give You." ²³ Jesus *said to her, "Your brother will rise again." ²⁴ Martha *said to Him, "I know that he will rise again in the resurrection on the last day." ²⁵ Jesus said to her, "I am the resurrection and the life; he who believes in Me will live even if he dies, ²⁶ and everyone who lives and believes in Me will never die. Do you believe this?" ²⁷ She *said to Him, "Yes, Lord; I have believed that You are the Christ, the Son of God, *even* He who comes into the world."

DAY 30: Why did Jesus delay when He heard that Lazarus was sick?

The resurrection of Lazarus in John 11 is the climactic and most dramatic sign in this Gospel and the capstone of Christ's public ministry. Six miracles have already been presented (water into wine [2:1–11], healing of the nobleman's son [4:46–54], restoring the impotent man [5:1–15], multiplying the loaves and fishes [6:1–14], walking on the water [6:15–21], and curing the man born blind [9:1–12]). Lazarus's resurrection is more potent than all those and even more monumental than the raising of the widow's son in Nain (Lk 7:11–16) or Jairus's daughter (Lk 8:40–56) because those two resurrections occurred immediately after death. Lazarus was raised after 4 days of being in the grave with the process of decomposition already having started (v. 39).

Upon hearing that Lazarus is sick, Jesus' immediate response is that it is "for the glory of God, so that the Son of God may be glorified by it" (v. 4). This phrase reveals the real purpose behind Lazarus's sickness, i.e., not death, but that the Son of God might be glorified through his resurrection. So He stayed two more days. The decision to delay coming did not bring about Lazarus's death, since Jesus already supernaturally knew his plight. Most likely by the time the messenger arrived to inform Jesus, Lazarus was already dead. The delay was because He loved the family (v. 5) and that love would be clear as He greatly strengthened their faith by raising Lazarus from the dead. The delay also ensured that Lazarus had been dead long enough that no one could misinterpret the miracle as a fraud or mere resuscitation.

Coming to Martha, Jesus said, "I am the resurrection and the life" (v. 25). This is the fifth in a series of 7 great "I am" statements of Jesus (6:35; 8:12; 10:7, 9; 10:11, 14). With this statement, Jesus moved Mary from an abstract belief in the resurrection that will take place "on the last day" (v. 24; see 5:28–29) to a personalized trust in Him who alone can raise the dead. No resurrection or eternal life exists outside of the Son of God. Time ("on the last day") is no barrier to the One who has the power of resurrection and life (1:4) for He can give life at any time.

MAY 31

1 Kings 9:1–10:29

9 Now it came about when Solomon had finished building the house of the LORD, and the king's house, and all that Solomon desired to do, ² that the LORD appeared to Solomon a second time, as He had appeared to him at Gibeon. ³ The LORD said to him, "I have heard your prayer and your supplication, which you have made before Me; I have consecrated this house which you have built by putting My name there forever, and My eyes and My heart will be there perpetually. ⁴ As for you, if you will walk before Me as your father David walked, in integrity of heart and uprightness, doing according to all that I have commanded you *and* will keep My statutes and My ordinances, ⁵ then I will establish the throne of your kingdom over Israel forever, just as I promised to your father

9:3 consecrated. The Lord made the temple holy by being present in the cloud (8:10). As proof of the temple's consecration, the Lord told Solomon that He had put His name there (3:2). **forever.** God was not saying He will dwell in that building forever, since in less than 400 years it was destroyed by the Babylonians (vv. 7–9). He was saying that Jerusalem and the temple mount are to be His earthly throne as long as the earth remains, through the millennial kingdom (Is 2:1–4; Zec 14:16). Even during the New Heaven and New Earth, the eternal state, there will be the heavenly Jerusalem, where God will eternally dwell (Rev 21:1–2). **eyes...heart.** These symbolized, respectively, the Lord's constant attention toward and deep affection for Israel. By implication, He promised them access to His presence and answers to their prayers.

David, saying, 'You shall not lack a man on the throne of Israel.'

6 "But if you or your sons indeed turn away from following Me, and do not keep My commandments and My statutes which I have set before you, and go and serve other gods and worship them, 7 then I will cut off Israel from the land which I have given them, and the house which I have consecrated for My name, I will cast out of My sight. So Israel will become a proverb and a byword among all peoples. 8 And this house will become a heap of ruins; everyone who passes by will be astonished and hiss and say, 'Why has the LORD done thus to this land and to this house?' 9 And they will say, 'Because they forsook the LORD their God, who brought their fathers out of the land of Egypt, and adopted other gods and worshiped them and served them, therefore the LORD has brought all this adversity on them.' "

10 It came about at the end of twenty years in which Solomon had built the two houses, the house of the LORD and the king's house 11 (Hiram king of Tyre had supplied Solomon with cedar and cypress timber and gold according to all his desire), then King Solomon gave Hiram twenty cities in the land of Galilee. 12 So Hiram came out from Tyre to see the cities which Solomon had given him, and they did not please him. 13 He said, "What are these cities which you have given me, my brother?" So they were called the land of Cabul to this day. 14 And Hiram sent to the king 120 talents of gold.

15 Now this is the account of the forced labor which King Solomon levied to build the house of the LORD, his own house, the Millo, the wall of Jerusalem, Hazor, Megiddo, and Gezer. 16 For Pharaoh king of Egypt had gone up and captured Gezer and burned it with fire, and killed the Canaanites who lived in the city, and had given it as a dowry to his daughter, Solomon's wife. 17 So Solomon rebuilt Gezer and the lower Beth-horon 18 and Baalath and Tamar in the wilderness, in the land of Judah, 19 and all the storage cities which Solomon had, even the cities for his chariots and the cities for his horsemen, and all that it pleased Solomon to build in Jerusalem, in Lebanon, and in all the land under his rule. 20 As for all the people who were left of the Amorites, the Hittites, the Perizzites, the Hivites and the Jebusites, who were not of the sons of Israel, 21 their descendants who were left after them in the land whom the sons of Israel were unable to destroy utterly, from them Solomon levied forced laborers, even to

this day. 22 But Solomon did not make slaves of the sons of Israel; for they were men of war, his servants, his princes, his captains, his chariot commanders, and his horsemen. 23 These were the chief officers who were over Solomon's work, five hundred and fifty, who ruled over the people doing the work.

24 As soon as Pharaoh's daughter came up from the city of David to her house which Solomon had built for her, then he built the Millo. 25 Now three times in a year Solomon offered burnt offerings and peace offerings on the altar which he built to the LORD, burning incense with them on the altar which was before the LORD. So he finished the house.

26 King Solomon also built a fleet of ships in Ezion-geber, which is near Eloth on the shore of the Red Sea, in the land of Edom. 27 And Hiram sent his servants with the fleet, sailors who knew the sea, along with the servants of Solomon. 28 They went to Ophir and took four hundred and twenty talents of gold from there, and brought it to King Solomon.

10 Now when the queen of Sheba heard about the fame of Solomon concerning the name of the LORD, she came to test him with difficult questions. 2 So she came to Jerusalem with a very large retinue, with camels carrying spices and very much gold

10:1 Sheba. Sheba was located in southwestern Arabia, about 1,200 miles from Jerusalem. concerning the name of the LORD. The primary motive for the queen's visit was to verify Solomon's reputation for wisdom and devotion to the Lord. difficult questions. Riddles designed to stump the hearer (Jdg 14:12).

and precious stones. When she came to Solomon, she spoke with him about all that was in her heart. 3 Solomon answered all her questions; nothing was hidden from the king which he did not explain to her. 4 When the queen of Sheba perceived all the wisdom of Solomon, the house that he had built, 5 the food of his table, the seating of his servants, the attendance of his waiters and their attire, his cupbearers, and his stairway by which he went up to the house of the LORD, there was no more spirit in her. 6 Then she said to the king, "It was a true report which I heard in my own land about your words and your wisdom. 7 Nevertheless I did not believe the reports, until I came and my eyes had seen it. And behold, the half was not told me. You exceed *in* wisdom and prosperity the report which I heard. ⁸ How blessed are your men, how blessed are these your servants who stand before you continually *and* hear your wisdom. ⁹ Blessed be the LORD your God who delighted in you to set you on the throne of Israel; because the LORD loved Israel forever, therefore He made you king, to do justice and righteousness." ¹⁰ She gave the king a hundred and twenty talents of gold, and a very great *amount* of spices and precious stones. Never again did such abundance of spices come in as that which the queen of Sheba gave King Solomon.

¹¹ Also the ships of Hiram, which brought gold from Ophir, brought in from Ophir a very great *number of* almug trees and precious stones. ¹² The king made of the almug trees supports for the house of the LORD and for the king's house, also lyres and harps for the singers; such almug trees have not come in *again* nor have they been seen to this day.

¹³ King Solomon gave to the queen of Sheba all her desire which she requested, besides what he gave her according to his royal bounty. Then she turned and went to her own land together with her servants.

¹⁴ Now the weight of gold which came in to Solomon in one year was 666 talents of gold, ¹⁵ besides *that* from the traders and the wares of the merchants and all the kings of the Arabs and the governors of the country. ¹⁶ King Solomon made 200 large shields of beaten gold, using 600 *shekels of* gold on each large shield. ¹⁷ *He made* 300 shields of beaten gold, using three minas of gold on each shield, and the king put them in the house of the forest of Lebanon. ¹⁸ Moreover, the king made a great throne of ivory and overlaid it with refined gold. ¹⁹ *There were* six steps to the throne and a round top to the throne at its rear, and arms on each side of the seat, and two lions standing beside the arms. ²⁰ Twelve lions were standing there on the six steps on the one side and on the other; nothing like *it* was made for any other kingdom. ²¹ All King Solomon's drinking vessels *were* of gold, and all the vessels of the house of the forest of Lebanon *were* of pure gold. None was of silver; it was not considered valuable in the days of Solomon. ²² For the king had at sea the ships of Tarshish with the ships of Hiram; once every three years the ships of Tarshish came bringing gold and silver, ivory and apes and peacocks.

²³ So King Solomon became greater than all the kings of the earth in riches and in wisdom. ²⁴ All the earth was seeking the presence of Solomon, to hear his wisdom which God had put in his heart. ²⁵ They brought every man his gift, articles of silver and gold, garments, weapons, spices, horses, and mules, so much year by year.

10:25 silver and gold...horses. The wisdom God had given to Solomon (v. 24) caused many rulers, like the queen of Sheba (vv. 1–13), to bring presents to Solomon as they sought to buy his wisdom to be applied in their own nations. These gifts led Solomon to multiply for himself horses, as well as silver and gold, precisely that which God's king was warned against in Deuteronomy 17:16–17. Solomon became ensnared by the blessings of his own wisdom and disobeyed God's commands.

---

²⁶ Now Solomon gathered chariots and horsemen; and he had 1,400 chariots and 12,000 horsemen, and he stationed them in the chariot cities and with the king in Jerusalem. ²⁷ The king made silver *as common* as stones in Jerusalem, and he made cedars as plentiful as sycamore trees that are in the lowland. ²⁸ Also Solomon's import of horses was from Egypt and Kue, *and* the king's merchants procured *them* from Kue for a price. ²⁹ A chariot was imported from Egypt for 600 *shekels* of silver, and a horse for 150; and by the same means they exported them to all the kings of the Hittites and to the kings of the Arameans.

Psalm 69:1–4

For the choir director; according
to Shoshannim. *A Psalm* of David.

S ave me, O God,
For the waters have
threatened my life.
² I have sunk in deep mire, and
there is no foothold;
I have come into deep waters,
and a flood overflows me.
³ I am weary with my crying;
my throat is parched;
My eyes fail while I wait for my God.
⁴ Those who hate me without
a cause are more than
the hairs of my head;
Those who would destroy
me are powerful, being
wrongfully my enemies;
What I did not steal, I then
have to restore.

Proverbs 17:18-19

18 A man lacking in sense pledges
And becomes guarantor in the
presence of his neighbor.
19 He who loves transgression
loves strife;
He who raises his door
seeks destruction.

John 11:28-57

28 When she had said this, she went away and called Mary her sister, saying secretly, "The Teacher is here and is calling for you." 29 And when she heard it, she *got up quickly and was coming to Him.

30 Now Jesus had not yet come into the village, but was still in the place where Martha met Him. 31 Then the Jews who were with her in the house, and consoling her, when they saw that Mary got up quickly and went out, they followed her, supposing that she was going to the tomb to weep there. 32 Therefore, when Mary came where Jesus was, she saw Him, and fell at His feet, saying to Him, "Lord, if You had been here, my brother would not have died." 33 When Jesus therefore saw her weeping, and the Jews who came with her *also* weeping, He was deeply moved in spirit and was troubled, 34 and said, "Where have you laid him?" They *said to Him, "Lord, come and see." 35 Jesus wept. 36 So the Jews were saying, "See how He loved him!" 37 But some of them said, "Could not this man, who opened the eyes of the blind man, have kept this man also from dying?"

38 So Jesus, again being deeply moved within, *came to the tomb. Now it was a cave, and a stone was lying against it. 39 Jesus *said, "Remove the stone." Martha, the sister of the deceased, *said to Him, "Lord, by this time there will be a stench, for he has been *dead* four days." 40 Jesus *said to her, "Did I not say to you that if you believe, you will see the glory of God?" 41 So they removed the stone. Then Jesus raised His eyes, and said, "Father, I thank You that You have heard Me. 42 I knew that You always hear Me; but because of the people standing around I said it, so that they may believe that You sent Me." 43 When He had said these things, He cried out with a loud voice, "Lazarus, come forth." 44 The man who had died came forth, bound hand and foot with wrappings, and his face was wrapped around with a cloth. Jesus *said to them, "Unbind him, and let him go."

45 Therefore many of the Jews who came to Mary, and saw what He had done, believed in Him. 46 But some of them went to the Phar- isees and told them the things which Jesus had done.

47 Therefore the chief priests and the Phar- isees convened a council, and were saying, "What are we doing? For this man is perform- ing many signs. 48 If we let Him *go on* like this, all men will believe in Him, and the Romans will come and take away both our place and our nation." 49 But one of them, Caiaphas, who was high priest that year, said to them, "You know nothing at all, 50 nor do you take into account that it is expedient for you that one man die for the people, and that the whole nation not perish." 51 Now he did not say this on his own initiative, but being high priest that year, he prophesied that Jesus was going to die for the nation, 52 and not for the nation only, but in order that He might also gather together into one the children of God who are scattered abroad. 53 So from that day on they planned together to kill Him.

54 Therefore Jesus no longer continued to walk publicly among the Jews, but went away from there to the country near the wilder- ness, into a city called Ephraim; and there He stayed with the disciples.

55 Now the Passover of the Jews was near, and many went up to Jerusalem out of the country before the Passover to purify them- selves. 56 So they were seeking for Jesus, and were saying to one another as they stood in the temple, "What do you think; that He will not come to the feast at all?" 57 Now the chief priests and the Pharisees had given orders that if anyone knew where He was, he was to report it, so that they might seize Him.

11:50 one man die for the people. He only meant that Jesus should be executed in order to spare their own positions and nation from Roman reprisals, but Caiaphas unwittingly used sacrificial, substitutionary language and prophesied the death of Christ for sinners.

11:51 he prophesied. Caiaphas did not realize the implications of what he spoke. While he ut- tered blasphemy against Christ, God parodied his statement into truth (Ps 76:10). The respon- sibility for the wicked meaning of his words belonged to Caiaphas, but God's providence directed the choice of words so as to express the heart of God's glorious plan of salvation (Ac 4:27-28). He actually was used by God as a prophet because he was the High Priest and originally the High Priest was the means of God's will being revealed (2Sa 15:27).

DAY 31: What so troubled Christ at the death of His friend Lazarus?

Jesus was met by Mary, who fell brokenhearted at His feet and "the Jews who came with her also weeping" (Jn 11:33). According to Jewish oral tradition, the funeral custom indicated that even a poor family must hire at least two flute players and a professional wailing woman to mourn the dead. Because the family may have been well-to-do, a rather large group appears present.

"He was deeply moved in the spirit and was troubled." The phrase here does not mean merely that Jesus was deeply touched or moved with sympathy at the sight. The Greek term "moved" always suggests anger, outrage, or emotional indignation (v. 38; Mt 9:30; Mk 1:43; 14:5). Most likely Jesus was angered at the emotional grief of the people because it implicitly revealed unbelief in the resurrection and the temporary nature of death. The group was acting like pagans who had no hope (1Th 4:13). While grief is understandable, the group was acting in despair, thus indicating a tacit denial of the resurrection and the Scripture that promised it. Jesus may also have been angered because He was indignant at the pain and sorrow in death that sin brought into the human condition.

"Jesus wept" (v. 35). The Greek word here has the connotation of silently bursting into tears in contrast to the loud lament of the group. His tears here were not generated out of mourning, since He was to raise Lazarus, but out of grief for a fallen world entangled in sin-caused sorrow and death. He was "a man of sorrows and acquainted with grief" (Is. 53:3; see Jn 3:16).

Jesus' prayer in vv. 41, 42 was not really a petition, but thanksgiving to the Father. The reason for the miracle was to authenticate His claims to be the Messiah and Son of God.

JUNE 1

1 Kings 11:1–12:33

11 Now King Solomon loved many foreign women along with the daughter of Pharaoh: Moabite, Ammonite, Edomite, Sidonian, and Hittite women, ² from the nations concerning which the LORD had said to the sons of Israel, "You shall not associate with them, nor shall they associate with you, *for* they will surely turn your heart away after their gods." Solomon held fast to these in love. ³ He had seven hundred wives, princesses, and three hundred concubines, and his wives turned his heart away. ⁴ For when Solomon was old, his wives turned his heart away after other gods; and his heart was not wholly devoted to the LORD his God, as the heart of David his father *had been.* ⁵ For Solomon went after Ashtoreth the goddess of the Sidonians and after Milcom the detestable idol of the Ammonites. ⁶ Solomon did what was evil in the sight of the LORD, and did not follow the LORD fully, as David his father *had done.* ⁷ Then Solomon built a high place for Chemosh the detestable idol of Moab, on the mountain which is east of Jerusalem, and for Molech the detestable idol of the sons of Ammon. ⁸ Thus also he did for all his foreign wives, who burned incense and sacrificed to their gods.

⁹ Now the LORD was angry with Solomon because his heart was turned away from the LORD, the God of Israel, who had appeared to him twice, ¹⁰ and had commanded him concerning this thing, that he should not go after other gods; but he did not observe what the LORD had commanded. ¹¹ So the LORD said to Solomon, "Because you have done this, and you have not kept My covenant and My statutes, which I have commanded you, I will surely tear the kingdom from you, and will give it to your servant. ¹² Nevertheless I will not do it in your days for the sake of your father David, *but* I will tear it out of the hand of your son. ¹³ However, I will not tear away all the kingdom, *but* I will give one tribe to your son for the sake of My servant David and for the sake of Jerusalem which I have chosen."

¹⁴ Then the LORD raised up an adversary to Solomon, Hadad the Edomite; he was of the royal line in Edom. ¹⁵ For it came about, when David was in Edom, and Joab the commander of the army had gone up to bury the slain, and had struck down every male in Edom ¹⁶ (for Joab and all Israel stayed there six months, until he had cut off every male in Edom), ¹⁷ that Hadad fled to Egypt, he and certain Edomites of his father's servants with him, while Hadad *was* a young boy. ¹⁸ They arose from Midian and came to Paran; and they took men with them from Paran and came to Egypt, to Pharaoh king of Egypt, who gave him a house and assigned him food and gave him land. ¹⁹ Now Hadad found great favor before Pharaoh, so that he gave him in marriage the sister of his own wife, the sister of Tahpenes the queen. ²⁰ The sister of Tahpenes bore his son Genubath, whom Tahpenes weaned in Pharaoh's house; and Genubath was in Pharaoh's house among the sons of Pharaoh. ²¹ But when Hadad heard in Egypt that David slept with his fathers and that Joab the commander of the army was dead, Hadad said to Pharaoh, "Send me away, that I may go to my own country." ²² Then Pharaoh said to him, "But what have you lacked with me, that behold, you are seeking to go to your own country?" And he answered, "Nothing; nevertheless you must surely let me go."

²³ God also raised up *another* adversary to him, Rezon the son of Eliada, who had fled from his lord Hadadezer king of Zobah. ²⁴ He gathered men to himself and became leader of a marauding band, after David slew them of *Zobah;* and they went to Damascus and stayed there, and reigned in Damascus. ²⁵ So he was an adversary to Israel all the days of Solomon, along with the evil that Hadad *did;* and he abhorred Israel and reigned over Aram.

²⁶ Then Jeroboam the son of Nebat, an Ephraimite of Zeredah, Solomon's servant, whose mother's name was Zeruah, a widow, also rebelled against the king. ²⁷ Now this was the reason why he rebelled against the king:

11:26 Jeroboam the son of Nebat. In contrast to Hadad and Rezon, who were external adversaries of Solomon, God raised up Jeroboam from a town in Ephraim as an internal adversary. Jeroboam was from Ephraim, the leading tribe of Israel's northern 10 tribes. He was a young man of talent and energy who, having been appointed by Solomon as leader over the building works around Jerusalem, rose to public notice.

Solomon built the Millo, *and* closed up the breach of the city of his father David. ²⁸ Now the man Jeroboam was a valiant warrior, and when Solomon saw that the young man was industrious, he appointed him over all the forced labor of the house of Joseph. ²⁹ It came about at that time, when Jeroboam went out of Jerusalem, that the prophet Ahijah the Shilonite found him on the road. Now Ahijah had clothed himself with a new cloak; and both of them were alone in the field. ³⁰ Then Ahijah took hold of the new cloak which was on him and tore it into twelve pieces. ³¹ He said to Jeroboam, "Take for yourself ten pieces; for thus says the LORD, the God of Israel, 'Behold, I will tear the kingdom out of the hand of Solomon and give you ten tribes ³² (but he will have one tribe, for the sake of My servant David and for the sake of Jerusalem, the city which I have chosen from all the tribes of Israel), ³³ because they have forsaken Me, and have worshiped Ashtoreth the goddess of the Sidonians, Chemosh the god of Moab, and Milcom the god of the sons of Ammon; and they have not walked in My ways, doing what is right in My sight and *observing* My statutes and My ordinances, as his father David *did*. ³⁴ Nevertheless I will not take the whole kingdom out of his hand, but I will make him ruler all the days of his life, for the sake of My servant David whom I chose, who observed My commandments and My statutes; ³⁵ but I will take the kingdom from his son's hand and give it to you, *even* ten tribes. ³⁶ But to his son I will give one tribe, that My servant David may have a lamp always before Me in Jerusalem, the city where I have chosen for Myself to put My name. ³⁷ I will take you, and you shall reign over whatever you desire, and you shall be king over Israel. ³⁸ Then it will be, that if you listen to all that I command you and walk in My ways, and do what is right in My sight by observing My statutes and My commandments, as My servant David did, then I will be with you and build you an enduring house as I built for David, and I will give Israel to you. ³⁹ Thus I will afflict the descendants of David for this, but not always.'" ⁴⁰ Solomon sought

therefore to put Jeroboam to death; but Jeroboam arose and fled to Egypt to Shishak king of Egypt, and he was in Egypt until the death of Solomon.

⁴¹ Now the rest of the acts of Solomon and whatever he did, and his wisdom, are they not written in the book of the acts of Solomon? ⁴² Thus the time that Solomon reigned in Jerusalem over all Israel was forty years. ⁴³ And Solomon slept with his fathers and was buried in the city of his father David, and his son Rehoboam reigned in his place.

12 Then Rehoboam went to Shechem, for all Israel had come to Shechem to make him king. ² Now when Jeroboam the son of Nebat heard *of it,* he was living in Egypt (for he was yet in Egypt, where he had fled from the presence of King Solomon). ³ Then they sent and called him, and Jeroboam and all the assembly of Israel came and spoke to Rehoboam, saying, ⁴ "Your father made our yoke hard; now therefore lighten the hard service of your father and his heavy yoke which he put on us, and we will serve you." ⁵ Then he said to them, "Depart for three days, then return to me." So the people departed.

⁶ King Rehoboam consulted with the elders who had served his father Solomon while he was still alive, saying, "How do you counsel *me* to answer this people?" ⁷ Then they spoke to him, saying, "If you will be a servant to this people today, and will serve them and grant them their petition, and speak good words to them, then they will be your servants forever." ⁸ But he forsook the counsel of the elders which they had given him, and consulted with the young men who grew up with him and served him. ⁹ So he said to them, "What counsel do you give that we may answer this people who have spoken to me, saying, 'Lighten the yoke which your father put on us'?" ¹⁰ The young men who grew up with him spoke to him, saying, "Thus you shall say to this people who spoke to you, saying, 'Your father made our yoke heavy, now you make it lighter for us!' But you shall speak to them, 'My little finger is thicker than my father's loins! ¹¹ Whereas my father loaded you with a heavy yoke, I will add to your yoke; my father disciplined you with whips, but I will discipline you with scorpions.'"

¹² Then Jeroboam and all the people came to Rehoboam on the third day as the king had directed, saying, "Return to me on the third day." ¹³ The king answered the people harshly, for he forsook the advice of the elders which they had given him, ¹⁴ and he spoke to them according to the advice of the young men,

11:38 if you listen to all that I command you. The Lord gave to Jeroboam the same promise that He had made to David—an enduring royal dynasty over Israel, the 10 northern tribes, if he obeyed God's law. The Lord imposed on Jeroboam the same conditions for his kingship that He had imposed on David (2:3–4; 3:14).

11:39 but not always. This statement implied that the kingdom's division was not to be permanent and that David's house would ultimately rule all the tribes of Israel again (Eze 37:15–28).

saying, "My father made your yoke heavy, but I will add to your yoke; my father disciplined you with whips, but I will discipline you with scorpions." ¹⁵ So the king did not listen to the people; for it was a turn *of events* from the LORD, that He might establish His word, which the LORD spoke through Ahijah the Shilonite to Jeroboam the son of Nebat.

¹⁶ When all Israel *saw* that the king did not listen to them, the people answered the king, saying,

"What portion do we have in David?
We have no inheritance in
the son of Jesse;
To your tents, O Israel!
Now look after your own
house, David!"

So Israel departed to their tents. ¹⁷ But as for the sons of Israel who lived in the cities of Judah, Rehoboam reigned over them. ¹⁸ Then King Rehoboam sent Adoram, who was over the forced labor, and all Israel stoned him to death. And King Rehoboam made haste to mount his chariot to flee to Jerusalem. ¹⁹ So Israel has been in rebellion against the house of David to this day.

²⁰ It came about when all Israel heard that Jeroboam had returned, that they sent and called him to the assembly and made him king over all Israel. None but the tribe of Judah followed the house of David.

²¹ Now when Rehoboam had come to Jerusalem, he assembled all the house of Judah and the tribe of Benjamin, 180,000 chosen men who were warriors, to fight against the house of Israel to restore the kingdom to Rehoboam the son of Solomon. ²² But the word of God came to Shemaiah the man of God, saying, ²³ "Speak to Rehoboam the son of Solomon, king of Judah, and to all the house of Judah and Benjamin, and to the rest of the people, saying, ²⁴ 'Thus says the LORD, "You must not go up and fight against your relatives the sons of Israel; return every man to his house, for this thing has come from Me."'" So they listened to the word of the LORD, and returned and went *their way* according to the word of the LORD.

²⁵ Then Jeroboam built Shechem in the hill country of Ephraim, and lived there. And he went out from there and built Penuel. ²⁶ Jeroboam said in his heart, "Now the kingdom will return to the house of David. ²⁷ If this people go up to offer sacrifices in the house of the LORD at Jerusalem, then the heart of this people will return to their lord, *even* to

12:26 return to the house of David. The Lord had ordained a political, not a religious, division of Solomon's kingdom. The Lord had promised Jeroboam political control of the 10 northern tribes (11:31, 35, 37). However, Jeroboam was to religiously follow the Mosaic law, which demanded that he follow the Lord's sacrificial system at the temple in Jerusalem (11:38). Having received the kingdom from God, he should have relied on divine protection, but he did not. Seeking to keep his subjects from being influenced by Rehoboam when they went to Jerusalem to worship, he set up worship in the north (vv. 27–28).

Rehoboam king of Judah; and they will kill me and return to Rehoboam king of Judah." ²⁸ So the king consulted, and made two golden calves, and he said to them, "It is too much for you to go up to Jerusalem; behold your gods, O Israel, that brought you up from the land of Egypt." ²⁹ He set one in Bethel, and the other he put in Dan. ³⁰ Now this thing became a sin, for the people went *to worship* before the one as far as Dan. ³¹ And he made houses on high places, and made priests from among all the people who were not of the sons of Levi. ³² Jeroboam instituted a feast in the eighth month on the fifteenth day of the month, like the feast which is in Judah, and he went up to the altar; thus he did in Bethel, sacrificing to the calves which he had made. And he stationed in Bethel the priests of the high places which he had made. ³³ Then he went up to the altar which he had made in Bethel on the fifteenth day in the eighth month, even in the month which he had devised in his own heart; and he instituted a feast for the sons of Israel and went up to the altar to burn incense.

Psalm 69:5–15

⁵ O God, it is You who knows my folly,
And my wrongs are not
hidden from You.
⁶ May those who wait for You
not be ashamed through
me, O Lord GOD of hosts;
May those who seek You not
be dishonored through
me, O God of Israel,
⁷ Because for Your sake I have
borne reproach;
Dishonor has covered my face.
⁸ I have become estranged
from my brothers
And an alien to my mother's sons.

9 For zeal for Your house
   has consumed me,
   And the reproaches of those who
      reproach You have fallen on me.
10 When I wept in my soul with fasting,
   It became my reproach.

69:9 has consumed me. The psalmist has brought hatred and hostility on himself by his unyielding insistence that the behavior of the people measure up to their outward claim of devotion to God. Whenever God was dishonored he felt the pain, because he loved God so greatly. Jesus claimed for Himself this attitude, as indicated in John 2:17; Romans 15:3.

11 When I made sackcloth my clothing,
   I became a byword to them.
12 Those who sit in the gate
      talk about me,
   And I *am* the song of the
      drunkards.
13 But as for me, my prayer is to You,
      O LORD, at an acceptable time;
   O God, in the greatness of
      Your lovingkindness,
   Answer me with Your saving truth.
14 Deliver me from the mire
      and do not let me sink;
   May I be delivered from my foes
      and from the deep waters.
15 May the flood of water
      not overflow me
   Nor the deep swallow me up,
   Nor the pit shut its mouth on me.

Proverbs 17:20–22

20 He who has a crooked mind
      finds no good,
   And he who is perverted in his
      language falls into evil.
21 He who sires a fool *does*
      so to his sorrow,
   And the father of a fool has no joy.
22 A joyful heart is good medicine,
   But a broken spirit dries up the bones.

John 12:1–26

12 Jesus, therefore, six days before the Passover, came to Bethany where Lazarus was, whom Jesus had raised from the dead. ² So they made Him a supper there, and Martha was serving; but Lazarus was one of those reclining *at the table* with Him. ³ Mary

then took a pound of very costly perfume of pure nard, and anointed the feet of Jesus and wiped His feet with her hair; and the house was filled with the fragrance of the perfume. ⁴ But Judas Iscariot, one of His disciples, who was intending to betray Him, *said, ⁵ "Why was this perfume not sold for three hundred denarii and given to poor *people?"* ⁶ Now he said this, not because he was concerned about the poor, but because he was a thief, and as he had the money box, he used to pilfer what was put into it. ⁷ Therefore Jesus said, "Let her alone, so that she may keep it for the day of My burial. ⁸ For you always have the poor with you, but you do not always have Me."

⁹ The large crowd of the Jews then learned that He was there; and they came, not for Jesus' sake only, but that they might also see Lazarus, whom He raised from the dead. ¹⁰ But the chief priests planned to put Lazarus to death also; ¹¹ because on account of him many of the Jews were going away and were believing in Jesus.

¹² On the next day the large crowd who had come to the feast, when they heard that Jesus was coming to Jerusalem, ¹³ took the branches of the palm trees and went out to meet Him, and *began* to shout, "Hosanna! BLESSED IS HE WHO COMES IN THE NAME OF THE LORD, even the King of Israel." ¹⁴ Jesus, finding a young donkey, sat on it; as it is written, ¹⁵ "FEAR NOT, DAUGHTER OF ZION; BEHOLD, YOUR KING IS COMING, SEATED ON A DONKEY'S COLT." ¹⁶ These things His disciples did not understand at the first; but when Jesus was glorified, then they remembered that these things were written of Him, and that they had done these things to Him. ¹⁷ So the people, who were with Him when He called Lazarus out of the tomb and raised him from the dead, continued to testify *about Him.* ¹⁸ For this reason also the people went and met Him, because they heard that He had performed this sign. ¹⁹ So the Pharisees said to one another, "You see that you are not doing any good; look, the world has gone after Him."

²⁰ Now there were some Greeks among

12:19 the world has gone after Him. "The world" means the people in general, as opposed to everyone in particular. Clearly, most people in the world did not even know of Jesus at that time, and many in Israel did not believe in Him. Often, "world" is used in this general sense (v. 47; 1:29; 3:17; 4:42; 14:22; 17:9, 21).

those who were going up to worship at the feast; [21] these then came to Philip, who was from Bethsaida of Galilee, and *began to* ask him, saying, "Sir, we wish to see Jesus." [22] Philip *came and *told Andrew; Andrew and Philip *came and *told Jesus. [23] And Jesus *answered them, saying, "The hour has come for the Son of Man to be glorified. [24] Truly, truly, I say to you, unless a grain of wheat falls into the earth and dies, it remains alone; but if it dies, it bears much fruit. [25] He who loves his life loses it, and he who hates his life in this world will keep it to life eternal. [26] If anyone serves Me, he must follow Me; and where I am, there My servant will be also; if anyone serves Me, the Father will honor him.

DAY 1: What was Solomon's main downfall?

"Now King Solomon loved many foreign women" (1Ki 11:1). Many of Solomon's marriages were for the purpose of ratifying treaties with other nations, a common practice in the ancient Near East. The practice of multiplying royal wives, prohibited in Deuteronomy 17:17 because the practice would turn the king's heart away from the Lord, proved to be accurate in the experience of Solomon. His love for his wives (vv. 1–2) led him to abandon his loyalty to the Lord and worship other gods (vv. 3–6). No sadder picture can be imagined than the ugly apostasy of his later years (over 50), which can be traced back to his sins with foreign wives. Polygamy was tolerated among the ancient Hebrews, though most in the East had only one wife. A number of wives was seen as a sign of wealth and importance. The king desired to have a larger harem than any of his subjects, and Solomon resorted to this form of state magnificence. But it was a sin directly violating God's law, and the very result which that law was designed to prevent happened.

"Solomon did what was evil in the sight of the LORD" (v. 6). The particular evil of Solomon was his tolerance of and personal practice of idolatry. These same words were used throughout the Book of Kings to describe the rulers who promoted and practiced idolatry (15:26, 34; 16:19, 25, 30; 22:52; 2Ki 3:2; 8:18, 27; 13:2, 11; 14:24; 15:9, 18, 24, 28; 17:2; 21:2, 20; 23:32; 24:9, 19). Solomon became an open idolater, worshiping images of wood and stone in the sight of the temple which, in his early years, he had erected to the one true God.

The Lord appeared to him twice (vv. 9–10). Once was at Gibeon (3:5), the next at Jerusalem (9:2). On both occasions, God had warned Solomon, so he had no excuses. "Because you have done this…I will surely tear the kingdom from you" (v. 11). Solomon failed to obey the commandments to honor God (Ex 20:3–6), which were part of the Mosaic Covenant. Obedience to that Covenant was necessary for receiving the blessings of the Davidic Covenant (2:3–4). The Lord's tearing of the kingdom from Solomon was announced in Ahijah's symbolic action of tearing his garment in vv. 29–39.

JUNE 2

1 Kings 13:1–14:31

13 Now behold, there came a man of God from Judah to Bethel by the word of the LORD, while Jeroboam was standing by the altar to burn incense. [2] He cried against the altar by the word of the LORD, and said, "O altar, altar, thus says the LORD, 'Behold, a son shall be born to the house of David, Josiah by name; and on you he shall sacrifice the priests of the high places who burn incense on you, and human bones shall be burned on you.'" [3] Then he gave a sign the same day, saying, "This is the sign which the LORD has spoken, 'Behold, the altar shall be split apart and the ashes which are on it shall be poured out.'" [4] Now when the king heard the saying of the man of God, which he cried against the altar in Bethel, Jeroboam stretched out his hand from the altar, saying, "Seize him." But his hand which he stretched out against him dried up, so that he could not draw it back to himself. [5] The altar also was split apart and the ashes were poured out from the altar, according to the sign which the man of God had given by the word of the LORD. [6] The king said to the man of God, "Please entreat the LORD your God, and pray for me, that my hand may be restored to me." So the man of God entreated the LORD, and the king's hand was restored to him, and it became as it was before. [7] Then the king said to the man of God, "Come home with me and refresh yourself, and I will give you a reward." [8] But the man of God said to the king, "If you were to give me half your house I would not go with you, nor would I eat bread or drink water in this place. [9] For so it was commanded me by the word of the LORD, saying, 'You shall eat no bread, nor drink water, nor return by the way which you came.'" [10] So he went another way and did not return by the way which he came to Bethel.

¹¹ Now an old prophet was living in Bethel; and his sons came and told him all the deeds which the man of God had done that day in Bethel; the words which he had spoken to the king, these also they related to their father. ¹² Their father said to them, "Which way did he go?" Now his sons had seen the way which the man of God who came from Judah had gone. ¹³ Then he said to his sons, "Saddle the donkey for me." So they saddled the donkey for him and he rode away on it. ¹⁴ So he went after the man of God and found him sitting under an oak; and he said to him, "Are you the man of God who came from Judah?" And he said, "I am." ¹⁵ Then he said to him, "Come home with me and eat bread." ¹⁶ He said, "I cannot return with you, nor go with you, nor will I eat bread or drink water with you in this place. ¹⁷ For a command *came* to me by the word of the LORD, 'You shall eat no bread, nor drink water there; do not return by going the way which you came.'" ¹⁸ He said to him, "I also am a prophet like you, and an angel spoke to me by the word of the LORD, saying, 'Bring him back with you to your house, that he may eat bread and drink water.'" *But* he lied to him. ¹⁹ So he went back with him, and ate bread in his house and drank water.

13:18 he lied to him. Why the old prophet deceived the man of God the text does not state. It may be that his own sons were worshipers at Bethel or perhaps priests, and this man wanted to gain favor with the king by showing up the man of God as an imposter who acted contrary to his own claim to have heard from God. Accustomed to receiving direct revelations, the Judean prophet should have regarded the supposed angelic message with suspicion and sought divine verification of this revised order.

---

²⁰ Now it came about, as they were sitting down at the table, that the word of the LORD came to the prophet who had brought him back; ²¹ and he cried to the man of God who came from Judah, saying, "Thus says the LORD, 'Because you have disobeyed the command of the LORD, and have not observed the commandment which the LORD your God commanded you, ²² but have returned and eaten bread and drunk water in the place of which He said to you, "Eat no bread and drink no water"; your body shall not come to the grave of your fathers.'" ²³ It came about after

he had eaten bread and after he had drunk, that he saddled the donkey for him, for the prophet whom he had brought back. ²⁴ Now when he had gone, a lion met him on the way and killed him, and his body was thrown on the road, with the donkey standing beside it; the lion also was standing beside the body. ²⁵ And behold, men passed by and saw the body thrown on the road, and the lion standing beside the body; so they came and told *it* in the city where the old prophet lived.

²⁶ Now when the prophet who brought him back from the way heard *it,* he said, "It is the man of God, who disobeyed the command of the LORD; therefore the LORD has given him to the lion, which has torn him and killed him, according to the word of the LORD which He spoke to him." ²⁷ Then he spoke to his sons, saying, "Saddle the donkey for me." And they saddled *it.* ²⁸ He went and found his body thrown on the road with the donkey and the lion standing beside the body; the lion had not eaten the body nor torn the donkey. ²⁹ So the prophet took up the body of the man of God and laid it on the donkey and brought it back, and he came to the city of the old prophet to mourn and to bury him. ³⁰ He laid his body in his own grave, and they mourned over him, *saying,* "Alas, my brother!" ³¹ After he had buried him, he spoke to his sons, saying, "When I die, bury me in the grave in which the man of God is buried; lay my bones beside his bones. ³² For the thing shall surely come to pass which he cried by the word of the LORD against the altar in Bethel and against all the houses of the high places which are in the cities of Samaria."

³³ After this event Jeroboam did not return from his evil way, but again he made priests of the high places from among all the people; any who would, he ordained, to be priests of the high places. ³⁴ This event became sin to the house of Jeroboam, even to blot *it* out and destroy *it* from off the face of the earth.

14 At that time Abijah the son of Jeroboam became sick. ² Jeroboam said to his wife, "Arise now, and disguise yourself so that they will not know that you are the wife of Jeroboam, and go to Shiloh; behold, Ahijah the prophet is there, who spoke concerning me *that I would be* king over this people. ³ Take ten loaves with you, *some* cakes and a jar of honey, and go to him. He will tell you what will happen to the boy."

⁴ Jeroboam's wife did so, and arose and went to Shiloh, and came to the house of Ahijah. Now Ahijah could not see, for his eyes were dim because of his age. ⁵ Now the

LORD had said to Ahijah, "Behold, the wife of Jeroboam is coming to inquire of you concerning her son, for he is sick. You shall say thus and thus to her, for it will be when she arrives that she will pretend to be another woman."

6 When Ahijah heard the sound of her feet coming in the doorway, he said, "Come in, wife of Jeroboam, why do you pretend to be another woman? For I am sent to you *with* a harsh *message.* 7 Go, say to Jeroboam, 'Thus says the LORD God of Israel, "Because I exalted you from among the people and made you leader over My people Israel, 8 and tore the kingdom away from the house of David and gave it to you—yet you have not been like My servant David, who kept My commandments and who followed Me with all his heart, to do only that which was right in My sight; 9 you also have done more evil than all who were before you, and have gone and made for yourself other gods and molten images to provoke Me to anger, and have cast Me behind your back— 10 therefore behold, I am bringing calamity on the house of Jeroboam, and will cut off from Jeroboam every male person, both bond and free in Israel, and I will make a clean sweep of the house of Jeroboam, as one sweeps away dung until it is all gone. 11 Anyone belonging to Jeroboam who dies in the city the dogs will eat. And he who dies in the field the birds of the heavens will eat; for the LORD has spoken *it.*" ' 12 Now you, arise, go to your house. When your feet enter the city the child will die. 13 All Israel shall mourn for him and bury him, for he alone of Jeroboam's *family* will come to the grave, because in him something good was found toward the LORD God of Israel in the house of Jeroboam. 14 Moreover, the LORD will raise up for Himself a king over Israel who will cut off the house of Jeroboam this day and from now on.

15 "For the LORD will strike Israel, as a reed is shaken in the water; and He will uproot Israel from this good land which He gave to their fathers, and will scatter them beyond the *Euphrates* River, because they have made their Asherim, provoking the LORD to anger. 16 He will give up Israel on account of the sins of Jeroboam, which he committed and with which he made Israel to sin."

17 Then Jeroboam's wife arose and departed and came to Tirzah. As she was entering the threshold of the house, the child died. 18 All Israel buried him and mourned for him, according to the word of the LORD which He spoke through His servant Ahijah the prophet.

14:15 Ahijah announced God's stern judgment on Israel for joining Jeroboam's apostasy. Struck by the Lord, Israel would sway like a reed in a rushing river, a biblical metaphor for political instability (Mt 11:7; Lk 7:24). One day, the Lord would uproot Israel from Palestinian soil and scatter it in exile east of the Euphrates. The fulfillment of this prophecy is recorded in 2 Kings 17:23.

19 Now the rest of the acts of Jeroboam, how he made war and how he reigned, behold, they are written in the Book of the Chronicles of the Kings of Israel. 20 The time that Jeroboam reigned *was* twenty-two years; and he slept with his fathers, and Nadab his son reigned in his place.

21 Now Rehoboam the son of Solomon reigned in Judah. Rehoboam was forty-one years old when he became king, and he reigned seventeen years in Jerusalem, the city which the LORD had chosen from all the tribes of Israel to put His name there. And his mother's name was Naamah the Ammonitess. 22 Judah did evil in the sight of the LORD, and they provoked Him to jealousy more than all that their fathers had done, with the sins which they committed. 23 For they also built for themselves high places and *sacred* pillars and Asherim on every high hill and beneath every luxuriant tree. 24 There were also male cult prostitutes in the land. They did according to all the abominations of the nations which the LORD dispossessed before the sons of Israel.

25 Now it happened in the fifth year of King Rehoboam, that Shishak the king of Egypt came up against Jerusalem. 26 He took away the treasures of the house of the LORD and the treasures of the king's house, and he took everything, even taking all the shields of gold which Solomon had made. 27 So King Rehoboam made shields of bronze in their place, and committed them to the care of the commanders of the guard who guarded the doorway of the king's house. 28 Then it happened as often as the king entered the house of the LORD, that the guards would carry them and would bring them back into the guards' room.

29 Now the rest of the acts of Rehoboam and all that he did, are they not written in the Book of the Chronicles of the Kings of Judah? 30 There was war between Rehoboam and Jeroboam continually. 31 And Rehoboam

slept with his fathers and was buried with his fathers in the city of David; and his mother's name was Naamah the Ammonitess. And Abijam his son became king in his place.

Psalm 69:16-21

16 Answer me, O LORD, for Your
     lovingkindness is good;
   According to the greatness of
     Your compassion, turn to me,
17 And do not hide Your face
     from Your servant,
   For I am in distress;
     answer me quickly.
18 Oh draw near to my soul
     and redeem it;
   Ransom me because of my enemies!
19 You know my reproach and my
     shame and my dishonor;
   All my adversaries are before You.
20 Reproach has broken my
     heart and I am so sick.
   And I looked for sympathy,
     but there was none,
   And for comforters, but I found none.
21 They also gave me gall for my food
   And for my thirst they gave
     me vinegar to drink.

69:21 gall...vinegar. Gall was a poisonous herb. Here it serves as a metaphor for betrayal. Friends who should provide sustenance to the psalmist had turned against him. Gall in vinegar was actually offered to Christ while He was on the cross (Mt 27:34).

Proverbs 17:23-24

23 A wicked man receives a
     bribe from the bosom
   To pervert the ways of justice.
24 Wisdom is in the presence of the
     one who has understanding,
   But the eyes of a fool are on
     the ends of the earth.

John 12:27-50

27 "Now My soul has become troubled; and what shall I say, 'Father, save Me from this hour'? But for this purpose I came to this hour. 28 Father, glorify Your name." Then a voice came out of heaven: "I have both glorified it, and will glorify it again." 29 So the crowd *of people* who stood by and heard it were saying that it had thundered; others were saying, "An angel has spoken to Him." 30 Jesus answered and said, "This voice has not come for My sake, but for your sakes. 31 Now judgment is upon this world; now the ruler of this world will be cast out. 32 And I, if I am lifted up from the earth, will draw all men to Myself." 33 But He was saying this to indicate the kind of death by which He was to die. 34 The crowd then answered Him, "We have heard out of the Law that the Christ is to remain forever; and how can You say, 'The Son of Man must be lifted up'? Who is this Son of Man?" 35 So Jesus said to them, "For a little while longer the Light is among you. Walk while you have the Light, so that darkness will not overtake you; he who walks in the darkness does not know where he goes. 36 While you have the Light, believe in the Light, so that you may become sons of Light."

These things Jesus spoke, and He went away and hid Himself from them. 37 But though He had performed so many signs before them, *yet* they were not believing in Him. 38 *This was* to fulfill the word of Isaiah the prophet which he spoke: "LORD, WHO HAS BELIEVED OUR REPORT? AND TO WHOM HAS THE ARM OF THE LORD BEEN REVEALED?" 39 For this reason they could not believe, for Isaiah said again, 40 "HE HAS BLINDED THEIR EYES AND HE HARDENED THEIR HEART, SO THAT THEY WOULD NOT SEE WITH THEIR EYES AND PERCEIVE WITH THEIR HEART, AND BE CONVERTED AND I HEAL THEM." 41 These things Isaiah said because he saw His glory, and he spoke of Him. 42 Nevertheless many even of the rulers believed in Him, but because of the Pharisees they were not confessing *Him,* for fear that they would be put out of the synagogue; 43 for they loved the approval of men rather than the approval of God.

44 And Jesus cried out and said, "He who believes in Me, does not believe in Me but in

12:42-43 The indictment of vv. 37-41 is followed by the exceptions of vv. 42-43 (see 1:10-11 vs. 1:12-13). While the people seemed to trust Jesus with much more candor and fervency, the leaders of Israel who believed in Him demonstrated inadequate, irresolute, even spurious faith. The faith of the latter was so weak that they refused to take any position that would threaten their position in the synagogue. This is one of the saddest statements about spiritual leadership, for they preferred the praises of men above the praises of God in their refusal to publicly acknowledge Jesus as Messiah and Son of God.

Him who sent Me. [45] He who sees Me sees the One who sent Me. [46] I have come *as* Light into the world, so that everyone who believes in Me will not remain in darkness. [47] If anyone hears My sayings and does not keep them, I do not judge him; for I did not come to judge the world, but to save the world. [48] He who rejects Me and does not receive My sayings, has one who judges him; the word I spoke is what will judge him at the last day. [49] For I did not speak on My own initiative, but the Father Himself who sent Me has given Me a commandment *as to* what to say and what to speak. [50] I know that His commandment is eternal life; therefore the things I speak, I speak just as the Father has told Me."

DAY 2: As Jesus approached His death, what kept Him going?

In John 12:23, Jesus knew that "the hour" had come for His death. Considering what was ahead, He confessed, "Now My soul has become troubled" (v. 27). The term used here is strong and signifies horror, anxiety, and agitation. Jesus' contemplation of taking on the wrath of God for the sins of the world caused revulsion in the sinless Savior (2Co 5:21).

What kept Him going was the principle that Jesus lived by and would die by: "Father, glorify Your name" (v. 28). See 7:18; 8:29, 50. The fact that the Father answered the Son in an audible voice signifies its importance: "I have both glorified it, and will glorify." This is only one of three instances during Jesus' ministry when this took place (Mt 3:17—His baptism; 17:5—His transfiguration).

Jesus acknowledged that "the ruler of this world" was involved (v. 31). This is a reference to Satan (see 14:30; 16:11; Mt 4:8–9; Lk 4:6–7; 2Co 4:4; Eph 2:2; 6:12). Although the Cross might have appeared to signal Satan's victory over God, in reality it marked Satan's defeat (Ro 16:20; Heb 2:14). This would occur as Jesus was "lifted up from the earth" (v. 32), referring to His crucifixion (v. 33; 18:32). This is a veiled prediction of Jesus' death on the cross. Jesus referred to the story of Numbers 21:5–9 where the Israelite people who looked at the serpent lifted up by Moses were healed. The point of this illustration or analogy is in the "lifted up." Just as Moses lifted up the snake on the pole so that all who looked upon it might live physically, those who look to Christ, who was lifted up on the cross for the sins of the world, will live spiritually and eternally.

The people's response was to ask Him, "We have heard out of the Law that the Christ is to remain forever; and how can You say, 'The Son of Man must be lifted up'?" (v. 34). The term "Law" was used broadly enough to include not only the 5 books of Moses but also the whole of the Old Testament (Ro 10:4). Perhaps they had in mind Isaiah 9:7 which promised that Messiah's kingdom would last forever or Ezekiel 37:25 where God promised that the final David would be Israel's prince forever (Ps 89:35–37). To their question, Jesus offered them a final invitation to focus on His theme of believing in the Messiah and Son of God (vv. 35–36).

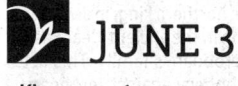

JUNE 3

1 Kings 15:1–16:34

15 Now in the eighteenth year of King Jeroboam, the son of Nebat, Abijam became king over Judah. [2] He reigned three years in Jerusalem; and his mother's name was Maacah the daughter of Abishalom. [3] He walked in all the sins of his father which he had committed before him; and his heart was not wholly devoted to the LORD his God, like the heart of his father David. [4] But for David's sake the LORD his God gave him a lamp in Jerusalem, to raise up his son after him and to establish Jerusalem; [5] because David did what was right in the sight of the LORD, and had not turned aside from anything that He commanded him all the days of his life, except in the case of Uriah the Hittite. [6] There was war between Rehoboam and Jeroboam all the days of his life.

[7] Now the rest of the acts of Abijam and all that he did, are they not written in the Book of the Chronicles of the Kings of Judah? And there was war between Abijam and Jeroboam. [8] And Abijam slept with his fathers and they buried him in the city of David; and Asa his son became king in his place.

[9] So in the twentieth year of Jeroboam the king of Israel, Asa began to reign as king of Judah. [10] He reigned forty-one years in Jerusalem; and his mother's name was Maacah the daughter of Abishalom. [11] Asa did what was right in the sight of the LORD, like David his father. [12] He also put away the male cult prostitutes from the land and removed all the idols which his fathers had made. [13] He also removed Maacah his mother from *being* queen mother, because she had made a horrid image as an Asherah; and Asa cut down her horrid image and burned *it* at the brook Kidron. [14] But the high places

were not taken away; nevertheless the heart of Asa was wholly devoted to the LORD all his days. ¹⁵ He brought into the house of the LORD the dedicated things of his father and his own dedicated things: silver and gold and utensils.

15:11–15 Asa did 4 good things: 1) he removed the sacred prostitutes (v. 12); 2) he rid the land of all the idols made by his predecessors (v. 12); 3) he removed the corrupt queen mother and burned the idol she had made; and 4) he placed "dedicated things," items that he and his father had dedicated to the Lord, back in the temple (v. 15). Though he never engaged in idolatry, Asa's failure was his toleration of "the high places" (v. 14).

15:13 horrid image. This term is derived from the verb "to shudder" (Job 9:6). It suggests a shocking, perhaps even a sexually explicit, idol. Asa removed his mother ("grandmother" in some translations), Maacah, the official queen mother, because of her association with this idol.

¹⁶ Now there was war between Asa and Baasha king of Israel all their days. ¹⁷ Baasha king of Israel went up against Judah and fortified Ramah in order to prevent *anyone* from going out or coming in to Asa king of Judah. ¹⁸ Then Asa took all the silver and the gold which were left in the treasuries of the house of the LORD and the treasuries of the king's house, and delivered them into the hand of his servants. And King Asa sent them to Ben-hadad the son of Tabrimmon, the son of Hezion, king of Aram, who lived in Damascus, saying, ¹⁹ "*Let there be* a treaty between you and me, *as* between my father and your father. Behold, I have sent you a present of silver and gold; go, break your treaty with Baasha king of Israel so that he will withdraw from me." ²⁰ So Ben-hadad listened to King Asa and sent the commanders of his armies against the cities of Israel, and conquered Ijon, Dan, Abel-beth-maacah and all Chinneroth, besides all the land of Naphtali. ²¹ When Baasha heard *of it,* he ceased fortifying Ramah and remained in Tirzah. ²² Then King Asa made a proclamation to all Judah—none was exempt—and they carried away the stones of Ramah and its timber with which Baasha had built. And King Asa built with them Geba of Benjamin and Mizpah.

²³ Now the rest of all the acts of Asa and all his might and all that he did and the cities which he built, are they not written in the Book of the Chronicles of the Kings of Judah? But in the time of his old age he was diseased in his feet. ²⁴ And Asa slept with his fathers and was buried with his fathers in the city of David his father; and Jehoshaphat his son reigned in his place.

²⁵ Now Nadab the son of Jeroboam became king over Israel in the second year of Asa king of Judah, and he reigned over Israel two years. ²⁶ He did evil in the sight of the LORD, and walked in the way of his father and in his sin which he made Israel sin. ²⁷ Then Baasha the son of Ahijah of the house of Issachar conspired against him, and Baasha struck him down at Gibbethon, which belonged to the Philistines, while Nadab and all Israel were laying siege to Gibbethon. ²⁸ So Baasha killed him in the third year of Asa king of Judah and reigned in his place. ²⁹ It came about as soon as he was king, he struck down all the household of Jeroboam. He did not leave to Jeroboam any persons alive, until he had destroyed them, according to the word of the LORD, which He spoke by His servant Ahijah the Shilonite, ³⁰ *and* because of the sins of Jeroboam which he sinned, and which he made Israel sin, because of his provocation with which he provoked the LORD God of Israel to anger.

15:29 he struck down all the household of Jeroboam. Baasha, the northern king, in a vicious practice too common in the ancient Near East, annihilated all of Jeroboam's family. This act fulfilled Ahijah's prophecy against Jeroboam (14:9–11). However, Baasha went beyond the words of the prophecy, since 14:10 specified judgment only on every male, while Baasha killed all men, women, and children.

³¹ Now the rest of the acts of Nadab and all that he did, are they not written in the Book of the Chronicles of the Kings of Israel? ³² There was war between Asa and Baasha king of Israel all their days. ³³ In the third year of Asa king of Judah, Baasha the son of Ahijah became king over all Israel at Tirzah, *and reigned* twenty-four years. ³⁴ He did evil in the sight of the LORD, and walked in the way of Jeroboam and in his sin which he made Israel sin.

16 Now the word of the LORD came to Jehu the son of Hanani against Baasha, saying, ²"Inasmuch as I exalted you from the dust and made you leader over My people Israel, and you have walked in the way of Jeroboam and have made My people Israel sin, provoking Me to anger with their sins, ³behold, I will consume Baasha and his house, and I will make your house like the house of Jeroboam the son of Nebat. ⁴Anyone of Baasha who dies in the city the dogs will eat, and anyone of his who dies in the field the birds of the heavens will eat."

⁵Now the rest of the acts of Baasha and what he did and his might, are they not written in the Book of the Chronicles of the Kings of Israel? ⁶And Baasha slept with his fathers and was buried in Tirzah, and Elah his son became king in his place. ⁷Moreover, the word of the LORD through the prophet Jehu the son of Hanani also came against Baasha and his household, both because of all the evil which he did in the sight of the LORD, provoking Him to anger with the work of his hands, in being like the house of Jeroboam, and because he struck it.

⁸In the twenty-sixth year of Asa king of Judah, Elah the son of Baasha became king over Israel at Tirzah, *and reigned* two years. ⁹His servant Zimri, commander of half his chariots, conspired against him. Now he *was* at Tirzah drinking himself drunk in the house of Arza, who *was* over the household at Tirzah. ¹⁰Then Zimri went in and struck him and put him to death in the twenty-seventh year of Asa king of Judah, and became king in his place. ¹¹It came about when he became king, as soon as he sat on his throne, that he killed all the household of Baasha; he did not leave a single male, neither of his relatives nor of his friends.

¹²Thus Zimri destroyed all the household of Baasha, according to the word of the LORD, which He spoke against Baasha through Jehu the prophet, ¹³for all the sins of Baasha and the sins of Elah his son, which they sinned and which they made Israel sin, provoking the LORD God of Israel to anger with their idols. ¹⁴Now the rest of the acts of Elah and all that he did, are they not written in the Book of the Chronicles of the Kings of Israel?

¹⁵In the twenty-seventh year of Asa king of Judah, Zimri reigned seven days at Tirzah. Now the people were camped against Gibbethon, which belonged to the Philistines. ¹⁶The people who were camped heard it said, "Zimri has conspired and has also struck down the king." Therefore all Israel made Omri, the commander of the army, king over Israel that day in the camp. ¹⁷Then Omri and all Israel with him went up from Gibbethon and besieged Tirzah. ¹⁸When Zimri saw that the city was taken, he went into the citadel of the king's house and burned the king's house over him with fire, and died, ¹⁹because of his sins which he sinned, doing evil in the sight of the LORD, walking in the way of Jeroboam, and in his sin which he did, making Israel sin. ²⁰Now the rest of the acts of Zimri and his conspiracy which he carried out, are they not written in the Book of the Chronicles of the Kings of Israel?

²¹Then the people of Israel were divided into two parts: half of the people followed Tibni the son of Ginath, to make him king; the *other* half followed Omri. ²²But the people who followed Omri prevailed over the people who followed Tibni the son of Ginath. And Tibni died and Omri became king. ²³In the thirty-first year of Asa king of Judah, Omri became king over Israel *and reigned* twelve years; he reigned six years at Tirzah. ²⁴He bought the hill Samaria from Shemer for two talents of silver; and he built on the hill, and named the city which he built Samaria, after the name of Shemer, the owner of the hill.

²⁵Omri did evil in the sight of the LORD, and acted more wickedly than all who *were* before him. ²⁶For he walked in all the way of Jeroboam the son of Nebat and in his sins which he made Israel sin, provoking the LORD God of Israel with their idols. ²⁷Now the rest of the acts of Omri which he did and his might which he showed, are they not written in the Book of the Chronicles of the Kings of Israel? ²⁸So Omri slept with his fathers and was buried in Samaria; and Ahab his son became king in his place.

²⁹Now Ahab the son of Omri became king over Israel in the thirty-eighth year of Asa king of Judah, and Ahab the son of Omri reigned over Israel in Samaria twenty-two years. ³⁰Ahab the son of Omri did evil in the sight of the LORD more than all who were before him.

16:30 evil…more than all who were before him. With Ahab, Israel's spiritual decay reached its lowest point. He was even worse than his father, Omri, who was more wicked than all before him (v. 25). Ahab's evil consisted of perpetuating all the sins of Jeroboam and promoting the worship of Baal in Israel (vv. 31–32). Of all Israel's kings, Ahab outraged the Lord most (v. 33).

³¹ It came about, as though it had been a trivial thing for him to walk in the sins of Jeroboam the son of Nebat, that he married Jezebel the daughter of Ethbaal king of the Sidonians, and went to serve Baal and worshiped him. ³² So he erected an altar for Baal in the house of Baal which he built in Samaria. ³³ Ahab also made the Asherah. Thus Ahab did more to provoke the LORD God of Israel than all the kings of Israel who were before him. ³⁴ In his days Hiel the Bethelite built Jericho; he laid its foundations with the *loss of* Abiram his firstborn, and set up its gates with the *loss of* his youngest son Segub, according to the word of the LORD, which He spoke by Joshua the son of Nun.

Psalm 69:22-28

²² May their table before them
become a snare;
And when they are in peace,
may it become a trap.
²³ May their eyes grow dim so
that they cannot see,
And make their loins
shake continually.
²⁴ Pour out Your indignation
on them,
And may Your burning
anger overtake them.
²⁵ May their camp be desolate;
May none dwell in their
tents.
²⁶ For they have persecuted
him whom You Yourself
have smitten,
And they tell of the pain
of those whom You have
wounded.
²⁷ Add iniquity to their
iniquity,
And may they not come into
Your righteousness.
²⁸ May they be blotted out
of the book of life
And may they not be recorded
with the righteous.

69:26 him whom You...have smitten. Those hostile to the psalmist were ridiculing him as one suffering from God's chastisement. In its messianic application, the suffering of the Messiah was a part of God's plan from eternity past (Is 53:10).

Proverbs 17:25-26

²⁵ A foolish son is a grief to his father
And bitterness to her who bore him.
²⁶ It is also not good to fine
the righteous,
Nor to strike the noble for
their uprightness.

17:26 fine...strike. Here is a clear statement on political and religious injustice, focusing on the equally bad mistreatment of the innocent and the noble.

John 13:1-20

13 Now before the Feast of the Passover, Jesus knowing that His hour had come that He would depart out of this world to the Father, having loved His own who were in the world, He loved them to the end. ² During supper, the devil having already put into the heart of Judas Iscariot, *the son* of Simon, to betray Him, ³ *Jesus,* knowing that the Father had given all things into His hands, and that He had come forth from God and was going back to God, ⁴ *got up from supper, and *laid aside His garments; and taking a towel, He girded Himself. ⁵ Then He *poured water into the basin, and began to wash the disciples' feet and to wipe them with the towel with which He was girded. ⁶ So He *came to Simon Peter. He *said to Him, "Lord, do You wash my feet?" ⁷ Jesus answered and said to him, "What I do you do not realize now, but you will understand hereafter." ⁸ Peter *said to Him, "Never shall You wash my feet!" Jesus answered him, "If I do not wash you, you have no part with Me." ⁹ Simon Peter *said to Him, "Lord, *then wash* not only my feet, but also my hands and my head." ¹⁰ Jesus *said to him, "He who has bathed needs only to wash his feet, but is completely clean; and you are clean, but not all *of you.*" ¹¹ For He knew the one who was betraying Him; for this reason He said, "Not all of you are clean."

¹² So when He had washed their feet, and taken His garments and reclined *at the table* again, He said to them, "Do you know what I have done to you? ¹³ You call Me Teacher and Lord; and you are right, for *so* I am. ¹⁴ If I then, the Lord and the Teacher, washed your feet, you also ought to wash one another's feet. ¹⁵ For I gave you an example that you also should do as I did to you. ¹⁶ Truly, truly, I say to you, a slave is not greater than his master,

nor *is* one who is sent greater than the one who sent him. ¹⁷ If you know these things, you are blessed if you do them. ¹⁸ I do not speak of all of you. I know the ones I have chosen; but *it is* that the Scripture may be fulfilled, 'HE WHO EATS MY BREAD HAS LIFTED UP HIS HEEL AGAINST ME.' ¹⁹ From now on I am telling you before *it* comes to pass, so that when it does occur, you may believe that I am *He.* ²⁰ Truly, truly, I say to you, he who receives whomever I send receives Me; and he who receives Me receives Him who sent Me."

DAY 3: Why was Jesus' washing of the disciples' feet so powerful a lesson?

The dusty and dirty conditions of the region necessitated the need for footwashing. Although the disciples most likely would have been happy to wash Jesus' feet, they could not conceive of washing one another's feet (Jn 13:4–17). This was because in the society of the time footwashing was reserved for the lowliest of menial servants. Peers did not wash one another's feet, except very rarely and as a mark of great love. Luke points out (22:24) that they were arguing about who was the greatest of them, so that none was willing to stoop to wash feet. When Jesus moved to wash their feet, they were shocked. His actions serve also as symbolic of spiritual cleansing (vv. 6–9) and a model of Christian humility (vv. 12–17). Through this action Jesus taught the lesson of selfless service that was supremely exemplified by His death on the cross.

These proceedings embarrassed all of the disciples (vv. 6–10). While others remained silent, Peter spoke up in indignation that Jesus would stoop so low as to wash his feet. He failed to see beyond the humble service itself to the symbolism of spiritual cleansing involved (v. 7; 1Jn 1:7–9). Jesus' response made the real point of His actions clear: Unless the Lamb of God cleanses a person's sin (i.e., as portrayed in the symbolism of washing), one can have no part with Him. The cleansing that Christ does at salvation never needs to be repeated—atonement is complete at that point. But all who have been cleansed by God's gracious justification need constant washing in the experiential sense as they battle sin in the flesh. Believers are justified and granted imputed righteousness (Php 3:8–9), but still need sanctification and personal righteousness (Php 3:12–14).

Jesus said, "I gave you an example" (v. 15). The word used here suggests both example and pattern. Jesus' purpose in this action was to establish the model of loving humility. "If you know these things, you are blessed if you do them" (v. 17). Joy is always tied to obedience to God's revealed Word.

JUNE 4

1 Kings 17:1–18:46

17 Now Elijah the Tishbite, who was of the settlers of Gilead, said to Ahab, "As the LORD, the God of Israel lives, before whom I stand, surely there shall be neither dew nor rain these years, except by my word." ² The word of the LORD came to him, saying, ³ "Go away from here and turn eastward, and hide yourself by the brook Cherith, which is east of the Jordan. ⁴ It shall be that you will drink of the brook, and I have commanded the ravens to provide for you there." ⁵ So he went and did according to the word of the LORD, for he went and lived by the brook Cherith, which is east of the Jordan. ⁶ The ravens brought him bread and meat in the morning and bread and meat in the evening, and he would drink from the brook. ⁷ It happened after a while that the brook dried up, because there was no rain in the land.

⁸ Then the word of the LORD came to him, saying, ⁹ "Arise, go to Zarephath, which belongs to Sidon, and stay there; behold, I have commanded a widow there to provide for you." ¹⁰ So he arose and went to Zarephath, and when he came to the gate of the city, behold, a widow was there gathering sticks;

17:1 Elijah. His name means "the LORD is God." The prophet Elijah's ministry corresponded to his name: He was sent by God to confront Baalism and to declare to Israel that the Lord was God and there was no other. **Tishbite.** Elijah lived in a town called Tishbe, east of the Jordan River in the vicinity of the Jabbok River. **neither dew nor rain.** The autumn and spring rains and summer dew were necessities for the crops of Israel. The Lord had threatened to withhold these from the land if His people turned from Him to serve other gods (Lv 26:18–19; Dt 11:16–17; 28:23–24). Elijah had prayed for the drought (Jas 5:17) and God answered. It lasted 3 years and 6 months according to James (5:17). The drought proved that Baal, the god of the rains and fertility, was impotent before the Lord.

and he called to her and said, "Please get me a little water in a jar, that I may drink." ¹¹As she was going to get *it*, he called to her and said, "Please bring me a piece of bread in your hand." ¹²But she said, "As the LORD your God lives, I have no bread, only a handful of flour in the bowl and a little oil in the jar; and behold, I am gathering a few sticks that I may go in and prepare for me and my son, that we may eat it and die." ¹³Then Elijah said to her, "Do not fear; go, do as you have said, but make me a little bread cake from it first and bring *it* out to me, and afterward you may make *one* for yourself and for your son. ¹⁴For thus says the LORD God of Israel, 'The bowl of flour shall not be exhausted, nor shall the jar of oil be empty, until the day that the LORD sends rain on the face of the earth.'" ¹⁵So she went and did according to the word of Elijah, and she and he and her household ate for *many* days. ¹⁶The bowl of flour was not exhausted nor did the jar of oil become empty, according to the word of the LORD which He spoke through Elijah.

¹⁷Now it came about after these things that the son of the woman, the mistress of the house, became sick; and his sickness was so severe that there was no breath left in him. ¹⁸So she said to Elijah, "What do I have to do with you, O man of God? You have come to me to bring my iniquity to remembrance and to put my son to death!" ¹⁹He said to her, "Give me your son." Then he took him from her bosom and carried him up to the upper room where he was living, and laid him on his own bed. ²⁰He called to the LORD and said, "O LORD my God, have You also brought calamity to the widow with whom I am staying, by causing her son to die?" ²¹Then he stretched himself upon the child three times, and called to the LORD and said, "O LORD my God, I pray You, let this child's life return to him." ²²The LORD heard the voice of Elijah, and the life of the child returned to him and he revived. ²³Elijah took the child and brought him down from the upper room into the house and gave him to his mother; and Elijah said, "See, your son is alive." ²⁴Then the woman said to Elijah, "Now I know that you are a man of God and that the word of the LORD in your mouth is truth."

18 Now it happened *after* many days that the word of the LORD came to Elijah in the third year, saying, "Go, show yourself to Ahab, and I will send rain on the face of the earth." ²So Elijah went to show himself to Ahab. Now the famine *was* severe in Samaria. ³Ahab called Obadiah who *was* over the household. (Now Obadiah feared the

18:3 Obadiah. His name means "servant of the LORD." He was the manager of Ahab's royal palace and a devout worshiper of the Lord, who had demonstrated his devotion to the Lord by protecting 100 of the Lord's prophets from death by Jezebel (vv. 4, 13) which had put him on tenuous ground with Ahab.

LORD greatly; ⁴for when Jezebel destroyed the prophets of the LORD, Obadiah took a hundred prophets and hid them by fifties in a cave, and provided them with bread and water.) ⁵Then Ahab said to Obadiah, "Go through the land to all the springs of water and to all the valleys; perhaps we will find grass and keep the horses and mules alive, and not have to kill some of the cattle." ⁶So they divided the land between them to survey it; Ahab went one way by himself and Obadiah went another way by himself.

⁷Now as Obadiah was on the way, behold, Elijah met him, and he recognized him and fell on his face and said, "Is this you, Elijah my master?" ⁸He said to him, "It is I. Go, say to your master, 'Behold, Elijah *is here*.'" ⁹He said, "What sin have I committed, that you are giving your servant into the hand of Ahab to put me to death? ¹⁰As the LORD your God lives, there is no nation or kingdom where my master has not sent to search for you; and when they said, 'He is not *here*,' he made the kingdom or nation swear that they could not find you. ¹¹And now you are saying, 'Go, say to your master, "Behold, Elijah *is here*."' ¹²It will come about when I leave you that the Spirit of the LORD will carry you where I do not know; so when I come and tell Ahab and he cannot find you, he will kill me, although *I* your servant have feared the LORD from my youth. ¹³Has it not been told to my master what I did when Jezebel killed the prophets of the LORD, that I hid a hundred prophets

18:12 the Spirit of the LORD will carry you. The servant had been asked to tell Ahab that Elijah was present to speak with him (vv. 7, 18), but he was afraid because Ahab was seeking Elijah so intensely. Since Elijah had disappeared from sight earlier (17:5), Obadiah was afraid that the Holy Spirit would carry Elijah away again (2Ki 2:16) and the irrational Ahab would kill him for the false report of Elijah's presence.

of the LORD by fifties in a cave, and provided them with bread and water? ¹⁴And now you are saying, 'Go, say to your master, "Behold, Elijah *is here*"'; he will then kill me." ¹⁵Elijah said, "As the LORD of hosts lives, before whom I stand, I will surely show myself to him today." ¹⁶So Obadiah went to meet Ahab and told him; and Ahab went to meet Elijah.

¹⁷When Ahab saw Elijah, Ahab said to him, "Is this you, you troubler of Israel?" ¹⁸He said, "I have not troubled Israel, but you and your father's house *have*, because you have forsaken the commandments of the LORD and you have followed the Baals. ¹⁹Now then send *and* gather to me all Israel at Mount Carmel, *together* with 450 prophets of Baal and 400 prophets of the Asherah, who eat at Jezebel's table."

²⁰So Ahab sent *a message* among all the sons of Israel and brought the prophets together at Mount Carmel. ²¹Elijah came near to all the people and said, "How long *will* you hesitate between two opinions? If the LORD is God, follow Him; but if Baal, follow him." But the people did not answer him a word. ²²Then Elijah said to the people, "I alone am left a prophet of the LORD, but Baal's prophets are 450 men. ²³Now let them give us two oxen; and let them choose one ox for themselves and cut it up, and place it on the wood, but put no fire *under it;* and I will prepare the other ox and lay it on the wood, and I will not put a fire *under it.* ²⁴Then you call on the name of your god, and I will call on the name of the LORD, and the God who answers by fire, He is God." And all the people said, "That is a good idea."

²⁵So Elijah said to the prophets of Baal, "Choose one ox for yourselves and prepare it

18:21 hesitate between two opinions. Literally "limp along on or between two twigs." Israel had not totally rejected the Lord, but was seeking to combine worship of Him with the worship of Baal. The issue posed by Elijah was that Israel had to choose who was God, the Lord or Baal, and then serve God wholeheartedly. Rather than decide by his message, Elijah sought a visible sign from heaven.

18:24 the God who answers by fire. Since Baal's followers believed that he controlled the thunder, lightning, and storms, and the Lord's followers declared the same (Pss 18:14; 29:3–9; 104:3), this would prove to be a fair test to show who was God.

first for you are many, and call on the name of your god, but put no fire *under it.*" ²⁶Then they took the ox which was given them and they prepared it and called on the name of Baal from morning until noon saying, "O Baal, answer us." But there was no voice and no one answered. And they leaped about the altar which they made. ²⁷It came about at noon, that Elijah mocked them and said, "Call out with a loud voice, for he is a god; either he is occupied or gone aside, or is on a journey, or perhaps he is asleep and needs to be awakened." ²⁸So they cried with a loud voice and cut themselves according to their custom with swords and lances until the blood gushed out on them. ²⁹When midday was past, they raved until the time of the offering of the *evening* sacrifice; but there was no voice, no one answered, and no one paid attention.

³⁰Then Elijah said to all the people, "Come near to me." So all the people came near to him. And he repaired the altar of the LORD which had been torn down. ³¹Elijah took twelve stones according to the number of the tribes of the sons of Jacob, to whom the word of the LORD had come, saying, "Israel shall be your name." ³²So with the stones he built an altar in the name of the LORD, and he made a trench around the altar, large enough to hold two measures of seed. ³³Then he arranged the wood and cut the ox in pieces and laid *it* on the wood. ³⁴And he said, "Fill four pitchers with water and pour *it* on the burnt offering and on the wood." And he said, "Do it a second time," and they did it a second time. And he said, "Do it a third time," and they did it a third time. ³⁵The water flowed around the altar and he also filled the trench with water. ³⁶At the time of the offering of the *evening* sacrifice, Elijah the prophet came near and said, "O LORD, the God of Abraham, Isaac and Israel, today let it be known that You are God in Israel and that I am Your servant and I have done all these things at Your word. ³⁷Answer me, O LORD, answer me, that this people may know that You, O LORD, are God, and *that* You have turned their heart back again." ³⁸Then the fire of the LORD fell and consumed the burnt offering and the wood and the stones and the dust, and licked up the water that was in the trench. ³⁹When all the people saw it, they fell on their faces; and they said, "The LORD, He is God; the LORD, He is God." ⁴⁰Then Elijah said to them, "Seize the prophets of Baal; do not let one of them escape." So they seized them; and Elijah brought them down to the brook Kishon, and slew them there.

⁴¹ Now Elijah said to Ahab, "Go up, eat and drink; for there is the sound of the roar of a *heavy* shower." ⁴² So Ahab went up to eat and drink. But Elijah went up to the top of Carmel; and he crouched down on the earth and put his face between his knees. ⁴³ He said to his servant, "Go up now, look toward the sea." So he went up and looked and said, "There is nothing." And he said, "Go back" seven times. ⁴⁴ It came about at the seventh *time*, that he said, "Behold, a cloud as small as a man's hand is coming up from the sea." And he said, "Go up, say to Ahab, 'Prepare *your chariot* and go down, so that the *heavy* shower does not stop you.' " ⁴⁵ In a little while the sky grew black with clouds and wind, and there was a heavy shower. And Ahab rode and went to Jezreel. ⁴⁶ Then the hand of the LORD was on Elijah, and he girded up his loins and outran Ahab to Jezreel.

Psalm 69:29–36

²⁹ But I am afflicted and
    in pain;
May Your salvation, O God, set
    me *securely* on high.
³⁰ I will praise the name of
    God with song
And magnify Him with
    thanksgiving.
³¹ And it will please the LORD
    better than an ox
Or a young bull with horns
    and hoofs.
³² The humble have seen *it and*
    are glad;
You who seek God, let
    your heart revive.
³³ For the LORD hears the needy
And does not despise His
    who are prisoners.
³⁴ Let heaven and earth praise
    Him,
The seas and everything
    that moves in them.
³⁵ For God will save Zion and
    build the cities of Judah,
That they may dwell there
    and possess it.
³⁶ The descendants of His
    servants will inherit it,
And those who love His
    name will dwell in it.

Proverbs 17:27–28

²⁷ He who restrains his words
    has knowledge,

And he who has a cool spirit is
    a man of understanding.
²⁸ Even a fool, when he keeps silent, is
    considered
    wise;
When he closes his lips, he is
    considered prudent.

John 13:21–38

²¹ When Jesus had said this, He became troubled in spirit, and testified and said, "Truly, truly, I say to you, that one of you will betray Me." ²² The disciples *began* looking at one another, at a loss *to know* of which one He was speaking. ²³ There was reclining on Jesus' bosom one of His disciples, whom Jesus loved. ²⁴ So Simon Peter *gestured to him, and *said to him, "Tell *us* who it is of whom He is speaking." ²⁵ He, leaning back thus on Jesus' bosom, *said to Him, "Lord, who is it?" ²⁶ Jesus then *answered, "That is the one for whom I shall dip the morsel and give it to him." So when He had dipped the morsel, He *took and *gave it to Judas, *the son* of Simon Iscariot. ²⁷ After the morsel, Satan then entered into him. Therefore Jesus *said to him, "What you do, do quickly." ²⁸ Now no one of those reclining *at the table* knew for what purpose He had said this to him. ²⁹ For some were supposing, because Judas had the money box, that Jesus was saying to him, "Buy the things we have need of for the feast"; or else, that he should give something to the poor. ³⁰ So after receiving the morsel he went out immediately; and it was night.

³¹ Therefore when he had gone out, Jesus *said, "Now is the Son of Man glorified, and God is glorified in Him; ³² if God is glorified in Him, God will also glorify Him in Himself, and will glorify Him immediately. ³³ Little children, I am with you a little while longer. You will seek Me; and as I said to the Jews, now I

13:26 He...gave it to Judas. The host at a feast (whose role was filled by Jesus) would dip into a common bowl and pull out a particularly tasty bit and pass it to a guest as a special mark of honor or friendship. Because Jesus passed it so easily to Judas, it has been suggested that he was seated near the Lord in a place of honor. Jesus was demonstrating a final gesture of His love for Judas even though he would betray Him.

also say to you, 'Where I am going, you can-not come.' ³⁴A new commandment I give to you, that you love one another, even as I have loved you, that you also love one another. ³⁵By this all men will know that you are My disci-ples, if you have love for one another."

³⁶Simon Peter *said to Him, "Lord, where are You going?" Jesus answered, "Where I go, you cannot follow Me now; but you will follow later." ³⁷Peter *said to Him, "Lord, why can I not follow You right now? I will lay down my life for You." ³⁸Jesus *answered, "Will you lay down your life for Me? Truly, truly, I say to you, a rooster will not crow until you deny Me three times.

13:34 A new commandment...as I have loved you. The commandment to love was not new. Deuteronomy 6:5 commanded love for God, and Leviticus 19:18 commanded loving one's neigh-bor as oneself (Mt 22:34–40; Ro 13:8–10; Gal 5:14; Jas 2:8). However, Jesus' command regarding love presented a distinctly new standard for two reasons: 1) it was sacrificial love modeled after His love ("as I have loved you"; see 15:13), and 2) it is produced through the New Covenant by the transforming power of the Holy Spirit (Jer 31:29–34; Eze 36:24–26; Gal 5:22).

DAY 4: How do scholars conclude that the expression "whom Jesus loved" was John's way of referring to himself?

Three obvious clues about John's Gospel help identify the unnamed disciple who called himself the disciple "whom Jesus loved" (13:23; 20:2; 21:7, 20; also 19:26).

Early church fathers invariably identify the apostle John as the author of this Gospel. John is frequently mentioned by the other Gospel writers as an active participant among the disciples of Jesus, yet John's name is absent from the fourth Gospel.

If four people take a trip together and each carries a camera, the group-shots each person takes will naturally not include them. In fact, someone else could probably guess who took which pictures by which member of the group was absent. The Gospel of John functions this way—John's absence by name shouts his presence.

As for his signature phrase, the words "whom Jesus loved" convey both a sense of the apos-tle's humility and the depth of his relationship to Jesus. The phrase doesn't mean that John thought of himself as the only disciple Jesus loved. It simply expresses with disarming honesty the wonder of this disciple over the fact that the Lord loved him!

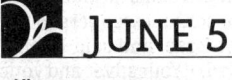

JUNE 5

1 Kings 19:1–20:43

19 Now Ahab told Jezebel all that Elijah had done, and how he had killed all the prophets with the sword. ²Then Jezebel sent a messenger to Elijah, saying, "So may the gods do to me and even more, if I do not make your life as the life of one of them by tomorrow about this time." ³And he was afraid and arose and ran for his life and came to Beersheba, which belongs to Judah, and left his servant there. ⁴But he himself went a day's journey into the wilderness, and came and sat down under a juniper tree; and he requested for himself that he might die, and said, "It is enough; now, O LORD, take my life, for I am not better than my fathers." ⁵He lay down and slept under a juniper tree; and behold, there was an angel touching him, and he said to him, "Arise, eat." ⁶Then he looked and behold, there was at his head a bread cake *baked on* hot stones, and a jar of water. So he ate and

drank and lay down again. ⁷The angel of the LORD came again a second time and touched him and said, "Arise, eat, because the journey

19:3 he was afraid. His hope shattered, Elijah fled as a prophet, broken by Jezebel's threats (v. 2), her unrepentant Baalism, and her con-tinuing power over Israel. Elijah expected Je-zebel to surrender; when she did not capitulate, he became a discouraged man (vv. 4, 10, 14).

19:4 juniper tree. A desert bush that grew to a height of 10 ft. It had slender branches featur-ing small leaves and fragrant blossoms. **take my life.** Since Israelites believed that suicide was an affront to the Lord, it was not an option, whatever the distress. So Elijah asked the Lord for death (Jon 4:3, 8) because he viewed the situation as hopeless. Job (Job 6:8–9), Moses (Nu 11:10–15), and Jeremiah (Jer 20:14–18) had also reacted in similar fashion during their ministries.

is too great for you." ⁸So he arose and ate and drank, and went in the strength of that food forty days and forty nights to Horeb, the mountain of God.

⁹Then he came there to a cave and lodged there; and behold, the word of the LORD *came* to him, and He said to him, "What are you doing here, Elijah?" ¹⁰He said, "I have been very zealous for the LORD, the God of hosts; for the sons of Israel have forsaken Your covenant, torn down Your altars and killed Your prophets with the sword. And I alone am left; and they seek my life, to take it away."

¹¹So He said, "Go forth and stand on the mountain before the LORD." And behold, the LORD was passing by! And a great and strong wind was rending the mountains and breaking in pieces the rocks before the LORD; *but* the LORD *was* not in the wind. And after the wind an earthquake, *but* the LORD *was* not in the earthquake. ¹²After the earthquake a fire,

19:11 the LORD was passing by. The 3 phenomena, wind, earthquake, and fire, announced the imminent arrival of the Lord (Ex 19:16–19; Ps 18:7–15; Hab 3:3–6). The Lord's self-revelation to Elijah came in a faint, whispering voice (v. 12). The lesson for Elijah was that Almighty God was quietly, sometimes imperceptibly, doing His work in Israel (v. 18).

but the LORD *was* not in the fire; and after the fire a sound of a gentle blowing. ¹³When Elijah heard *it,* he wrapped his face in his mantle and went out and stood in the entrance of the cave. And behold, a voice *came* to him and said, "What are you doing here, Elijah?" ¹⁴Then he said, "I have been very zealous for the LORD, the God of hosts; for the sons of Israel have forsaken Your covenant, torn down Your altars and killed Your prophets with the sword. And I alone am left; and they seek my life, to take it away."

¹⁵The LORD said to him, "Go, return on your way to the wilderness of Damascus, and when you have arrived, you shall anoint Hazael king over Aram; ¹⁶and Jehu the son of Nimshi you shall anoint king over Israel; and Elisha the son of Shaphat of Abel-meholah you shall anoint as prophet in your place. ¹⁷It shall come about, the one who escapes from the sword of Hazael, Jehu shall put to death, and the one who escapes from the sword of Jehu, Elisha shall put to death. ¹⁸Yet I will leave 7,000 in Israel, all the knees that have

not bowed to Baal and every mouth that has not kissed him."

¹⁹So he departed from there and found Elisha the son of Shaphat, while he was plowing with twelve pairs *of oxen* before him, and he with the twelfth. And Elijah passed over to him and threw his mantle on him. ²⁰He left the oxen and ran after Elijah and said, "Please let me kiss my father and my mother, then I will follow you." And he said to him, "Go back again, for what have I done to you?" ²¹So he returned from following him, and took the pair of oxen and sacrificed them and boiled their flesh with the implements of the oxen, and gave *it* to the people and they ate. Then he arose and followed Elijah and ministered to him.

19:19 Elisha. This name means "my God is salvation" and belonged to Elisha, the successor to Elijah (2Ki 2:9–15). **twelve pairs *of oxen.*** It was a common practice for several teams of oxen, each with its own plow and driver, to work together in a row. After letting the others pass, Elijah threw his mantle around the last man, Elisha, thus designating him as his successor.

20 Now Ben-hadad king of Aram gathered all his army, and there *were* thirty-two kings with him, and horses and chariots. And he went up and besieged Samaria and fought against it. ²Then he sent messengers to the city to Ahab king of Israel and said to him, "Thus says Ben-hadad, ³'Your silver and your gold are mine; your most beautiful wives and children are also mine.'" ⁴The king of Israel replied, "It is according to your word, my lord, O king; I am yours, and all that I have." ⁵Then the messengers returned and said, "Thus says Ben-hadad, 'Surely, I sent to you saying, "You shall give me your silver and your gold and your wives and your children," ⁶but about this time tomorrow I will send my servants to you, and they will search your house and the houses of your servants; and whatever is desirable in your eyes, they will take in their hand and carry away.'"

⁷Then the king of Israel called all the elders of the land and said, "Please observe and see how this man is looking for trouble; for he sent to me for my wives and my children and my silver and my gold, and I did not refuse him." ⁸All the elders and all the people said to him, "Do not listen or consent." ⁹So he said to the messengers of Ben-hadad, "Tell

my lord the king, 'All that you sent for to your servant at the first I will do, but this thing I cannot do.'" And the messengers departed and brought him word again. ¹⁰Ben-hadad sent to him and said, "May the gods do so to me and more also, if the dust of Samaria will suffice for handfuls for all the people who follow me." ¹¹Then the king of Israel replied, "Tell *him*, 'Let not him who girds on *his armor* boast like him who takes *it* off.'" ¹²When *Ben-hadad* heard this message, as he was drinking with the kings in the temporary shelters, he said to his servants, "Station *yourselves.*" So they stationed *themselves* against the city.

¹³Now behold, a prophet approached Ahab king of Israel and said, "Thus says the LORD, 'Have you seen all this great multitude? Behold, I will deliver them into your hand today, and you shall know that I am the LORD.'" ¹⁴Ahab said, "By whom?" So he said, "Thus says the LORD, 'By the young men of the rulers of the provinces.'" Then he said, "Who shall begin the battle?" And he answered, "You." ¹⁵Then he mustered the young men of the rulers of the provinces, and there were 232; and after them he mustered all the people, *even* all the sons of Israel, 7,000.

¹⁶They went out at noon, while Ben-hadad was drinking himself drunk in the temporary shelters with the thirty-two kings who helped him. ¹⁷The young men of the rulers of the provinces went out first; and Ben-hadad sent out and they told him, saying, "Men have come out from Samaria." ¹⁸Then he said, "If they have come out for peace, take them alive; or if they have come out for war, take them alive."

¹⁹So these went out from the city, the young men of the rulers of the provinces, and the army which followed them. ²⁰They killed each his man; and the Arameans fled and Israel pursued them, and Ben-hadad king of Aram escaped on a horse with horsemen. ²¹The king of Israel went out and struck the horses and chariots, and killed the Arameans with a great slaughter.

²²Then the prophet came near to the king of Israel and said to him, "Go, strengthen yourself and observe and see what you have to do; for at the turn of the year the king of Aram will come up against you."

²³Now the servants of the king of Aram said to him, "Their gods are gods of the mountains, therefore they were stronger than we; but rather let us fight against them in the plain, *and* surely we will be stronger than they. ²⁴Do this thing: remove the kings, each

from his place, and put captains in their place, ²⁵and muster an army like the army that you have lost, horse for horse, and chariot for chariot. Then we will fight against them in the plain, and surely we will be stronger than they." And he listened to their voice and did so.

²⁶At the turn of the year, Ben-hadad mustered the Arameans and went up to Aphek to fight against Israel. ²⁷The sons of Israel were mustered and were provisioned and went to meet them; and the sons of Israel camped before them like two little flocks of goats, but the Arameans filled the country. ²⁸Then a man of God came near and spoke to the king of Israel and said, "Thus says the LORD, 'Because the Arameans have said, "The LORD is a god of *the* mountains, but He is not a god of *the* valleys," therefore I will give all this great multitude into your hand, and you shall know that I am the LORD.'" ²⁹So they camped one over against the other seven days. And on the seventh day the battle was joined, and the sons of Israel killed *of* the Arameans 100,000 foot soldiers in one day. ³⁰But the rest fled to Aphek into the city, and the wall fell on 27,000 men who were left. And Ben-hadad fled and came into the city into an inner chamber.

³¹His servants said to him, "Behold now, we have heard that the kings of the house of Israel are merciful kings, please let us put sackcloth on our loins and ropes on our heads, and go out to the king of Israel; perhaps he will save your life." ³²So they girded sackcloth on their loins and *put* ropes on their heads, and came to the king of Israel and said, "Your servant Ben-hadad says, 'Please let me live.'" And he said, "Is he still alive? He is my brother." ³³Now the men took this as an omen, and quickly catching his word said, "Your brother Ben-hadad." Then he said, "Go, bring him." Then Ben-hadad came out to him, and he took him up into the chariot. ³⁴*Ben-hadad* said to him, "The cities which my father took from your father I will restore, and you shall make streets for yourself in Damascus, as my father made in Samaria." *Ahab said,* "And I will let you go with this covenant." So he made a covenant with him and let him go.

³⁵Now a certain man of the sons of the prophets said to another by the word of the LORD, "Please strike me." But the man refused to strike him. ³⁶Then he said to him, "Because you have not listened to the voice of the LORD, behold, as soon as you have departed from me, a lion will kill you." And as soon as he

had departed from him a lion found him and killed him. ³⁷Then he found another man and said, "Please strike me." And the man struck him, wounding him. ³⁸So the prophet departed and waited for the king by the way, and disguised himself with a bandage over his eyes. ³⁹As the king passed by, he cried to the king and said, "Your servant went out into the midst of the battle; and behold, a man turned aside and brought a man to me and said, 'Guard this man; if for any reason he is missing, then your life shall be for his life, or else you shall pay a talent of silver.' ⁴⁰While your servant was busy here and there, he was gone." And the king of Israel said to him, "So shall your judgment be; you yourself have decided it." ⁴¹Then he hastily took the bandage away from his eyes, and the king of Israel recognized him that he was of the prophets. ⁴²He said to him, "Thus says the LORD, 'Because you have let go out of your hand the man whom I had devoted to destruction, therefore your life shall go for his life, and your people for his people.'" ⁴³So the king of Israel went to his house sullen and vexed, and came to Samaria.

Psalm 70:1–5

For the choir director. *A Psalm*
of David; for a memorial.

O God, *hasten* to deliver me;
O LORD, hasten to my help!
² Let those be ashamed and
humiliated
Who seek my life;
Let those be turned back
and dishonored
Who delight in my hurt.
³ Let those be turned back
because of their shame
Who say, "Aha, aha!"

⁴ Let all who seek You rejoice
and be glad in You;
And let those who love Your
salvation say continually,
"Let God be magnified."
⁵ But I am afflicted and needy;
Hasten to me, O God!
You are my help and my
deliverer;
O LORD, do not delay.

Proverbs 18:1–2

18 He who separates himself
seeks *his own* desire,
He quarrels against all
sound wisdom.

² A fool does not delight in
understanding,
But only in revealing his
own mind.

John 14:1–31

14 "Do not let your heart be troubled; believe in God, believe also in Me. ²In My Father's house are many dwelling places; if it were not so, I would have told you; for I go to prepare a place for you. ³If I go and prepare a place for you, I will come again and receive you to Myself, that where I am, *there* you may be also. ⁴And you know the way where I am going." ⁵Thomas *said to Him, "Lord, we do not know where You are going, how do we know the way?" ⁶Jesus *said to him, "I am the way, and the truth, and the life; no one comes to the Father but through Me. ⁷If you had known Me, you would have known My Father also; from now on you know Him, and have seen Him."

14:6 This is the sixth "I am" statement of Jesus in John (6:35; 8:12; 10:7, 9; 10:11, 14; 11:25; 15:1, 5). In response to Thomas' query (v. 4), Jesus declared that He is the way to God because He is the truth of God (1:14) and the life of God (1:4; 3:15; 11:25). In this verse, the exclusiveness of Jesus as the only approach to the Father is emphatic. Only one way, not many ways, exist to God, i.e., Jesus Christ (10:7–9; Mt 7:13–14; Lk 13:24; Ac 4:12).

⁸Philip *said to Him, "Lord, show us the Father, and it is enough for us." ⁹Jesus *said to him, "Have I been so long with you, and *yet* you have not come to know Me, Philip? He who has seen Me has seen the Father; how *can* you say, 'Show us the Father'? ¹⁰Do you not believe that I am in the Father, and the Father is in Me? The words that I say to you I do not speak on My own initiative, but the Father abiding in Me does His works. ¹¹Believe Me that I am in the Father and the Father is in Me; otherwise believe because of the works themselves. ¹²Truly, truly, I say to you, he who believes in Me, the works that I do, he will do also; and greater *works* than these he will do; because I go to the Father. ¹³Whatever you ask in My name, that will I do, so that the Father may be glorified in the Son. ¹⁴If you ask Me anything in My name, I will do *it*.
¹⁵"If you love Me, you will keep My com-

14:12 greater *works* than these he will do. Jesus did not mean greater works in power, but in extent. They would become witnesses to all the world through the power of the indwelling and infilling of the Holy Spirit (Ac 1:8) and would bring many to salvation because of the Comforter dwelling in them. The focus is on spiritual rather than physical miracles. The book of Acts constitutes the beginning historical record of the impact that the Spirit-empowered disciples had on the world (Ac 17:6).

mandments. ¹⁶ I will ask the Father, and He will give you another Helper, that He may be with you forever; ¹⁷ *that is* the Spirit of truth, whom the world cannot receive, because it does not see Him or know Him, *but* you know Him because He abides with you and will be in you. ¹⁸ "I will not leave you as orphans; I will come to you. ¹⁹ After a little while the world will no longer see Me, but you *will* see Me; because I live, you will live also. ²⁰ In that day you will know that I am in My Father, and you in Me, and I in you. ²¹ He who has My commandments and keeps them is the one who loves Me; and he who loves Me will be loved by My Father, and I will love him

and will disclose Myself to him." ²² Judas (not Iscariot) *said to Him, "Lord, what then has happened that You are going to disclose Yourself to us and not to the world?" ²³ Jesus answered and said to him, "If anyone loves Me, he will keep My word; and My Father will love him, and We will come to him and make Our abode with him. ²⁴ He who does not love Me does not keep My words; and the word which you hear is not Mine, but the Father's who sent Me.

²⁵ "These things I have spoken to you while abiding with you. ²⁶ But the Helper, the Holy Spirit, whom the Father will send in My name, He will teach you all things, and bring to your remembrance all that I said to you. ²⁷ Peace I leave with you; My peace I give to you; not as the world gives do I give to you. Do not let your heart be troubled, nor let it be fearful. ²⁸ You heard that I said to you, 'I go away, and I will come to you.' If you loved Me, you would have rejoiced because I go to the Father, for the Father is greater than I. ²⁹ Now I have told you before it happens, so that when it happens, you may believe. ³⁰ I will not speak much more with you, for the ruler of the world is coming, and he has nothing in Me; ³¹ but so that the world may know that I love the Father, I do exactly as the Father commanded Me. Get up, let us go from here.

DAY 5: How is the role of the Holy Spirit explained in John 14?

Jesus said, "I will ask the Father, and He will give you another Helper, that He may be with you forever" (v. 16). The priestly and intercessory work of Christ began with the request that the Father send the Holy Spirit to indwell in the people of faith (7:39; 15:26; 16:7; 20:22; Ac 1:8; 2:4, 33). The Greek word specifically means "another of the same kind," i.e., someone like Jesus Himself who will take His place and do His work. The Spirit of Christ is the Third Person of the Trinity, having the same essence of Deity as Jesus and as perfectly one with Him as He is with the Father. A "Helper" literally means one called alongside to help and has the idea of someone who encourages and exhorts. Abiding has to do with His permanent residence in believers (Ro 8:9; 1Co 6:19–20; 12:13).

He is the "Spirit of truth" (v. 17) in that He is the source of truth and communicates the truth to His own (v. 26; 16:12–15). Apart from Him, men cannot know God's truth (1Co 2:12–16; 1Jn 2:20, 27). He "abides with you and will be in you." This indicates some distinction between the ministry of the Holy Spirit to believers before and after Pentecost. While clearly the Holy Spirit has been with all who have ever believed throughout redemptive history as the source of truth, faith, and life, Jesus is saying something new is coming in His ministry. John 7:37–39 indicates this unique ministry would be like rivers of living water. Acts 19:1–7 introduces some Old Covenant believers who had not received the Holy Spirit in this unique fullness and intimacy.

He "will teach you all things" (v. 26). The Holy Spirit energized the hearts and minds of the apostles in their ministry, helping them to produce the New Testament scriptures. The disciples had failed to understand many things about Jesus and what He taught; but because of this supernatural work, they came to an inerrant and accurate understanding of the Lord and His work and recorded it in the Gospels and the rest of the New Testament scriptures (2Ti 3:16; 2Pe 1:20–21).

JUNE 6

1 Kings 21:1–22:53

21 Now it came about after these things that Naboth the Jezreelite had a vineyard which *was* in Jezreel beside the palace of Ahab king of Samaria. ²Ahab spoke to Naboth, saying, "Give me your vineyard, that I may have it for a vegetable garden because it is close beside my house, and I will give you a better vineyard than it in its place; if you like, I will give you the price of it in money." ³But Naboth said to Ahab, "The LORD forbid me that I should give you the inheritance of my fathers." ⁴So Ahab came into his house sullen and vexed because of the word which Naboth the Jezreelite had spoken to him; for he said, "I will not give you the inheritance of my fathers." And he lay down on his bed and turned away his face and ate no food.

21:3 The LORD forbid. Naboth's words implied that trading or selling his property would be a disregard of the law and thus displeasing in God's eyes (1Sa 24:6; 26:11; 2Sa 23:17). The reason was that the vineyard was his ancestral property. The Lord, the owner of all of the land of Israel, had forbidden Israelite families to surrender ownership of family lands permanently (Lv 25:23–28; Nu 36:7–9). Out of loyalty to God, Naboth declined Ahab's offer.

⁵But Jezebel his wife came to him and said to him, "How is it that your spirit is so sullen that you are not eating food?" ⁶So he said to her, "Because I spoke to Naboth the Jezreelite and said to him, 'Give me your vineyard for money; or else, if it pleases you, I will give you a vineyard in its place.' But he said, 'I will not give you my vineyard.'" ⁷Jezebel his wife said to him, "Do you now reign over Israel? Arise, eat bread, and let your heart be joyful; I will give you the vineyard of Naboth the Jezreelite."

⁸So she wrote letters in Ahab's name and sealed them with his seal, and sent letters to the elders and to the nobles who were living with Naboth in his city. ⁹Now she wrote in the letters, saying, "Proclaim a fast and seat Naboth at the head of the people; ¹⁰and seat two worthless men before him, and let them testify against him, saying, 'You cursed God and the king.' Then take him out and stone him to death."

¹¹So the men of his city, the elders and the nobles who lived in his city, did as Jezebel had sent *word* to them, just as it was written in the letters which she had sent them. ¹²They proclaimed a fast and seated Naboth at the head of the people. ¹³Then the two worthless men came in and sat before him; and the worthless men testified against him, even against Naboth, before the people, saying, "Naboth cursed God and the king." So they took him outside the city and stoned him to death with stones. ¹⁴Then they sent *word* to Jezebel, saying, "Naboth has been stoned and is dead."

¹⁵When Jezebel heard that Naboth had been stoned and was dead, Jezebel said to Ahab, "Arise, take possession of the vineyard of Naboth, the Jezreelite, which he refused to give you for money; for Naboth is not alive, but dead." ¹⁶When Ahab heard that Naboth was dead, Ahab arose to go down to the vineyard of Naboth the Jezreelite, to take possession of it.

¹⁷Then the word of the LORD came to Elijah the Tishbite, saying, ¹⁸"Arise, go down to meet Ahab king of Israel, who is in Samaria; behold, he is in the vineyard of Naboth where he has gone down to take possession of it. ¹⁹You shall speak to him, saying, 'Thus says the LORD, "Have you murdered and also taken possession?"' And you shall speak to him, saying, 'Thus says the LORD, "In the place where the dogs licked up the blood of Naboth the dogs will lick up your blood, even yours."'"

²⁰Ahab said to Elijah, "Have you found me, O my enemy?" And he answered, "I have found *you,* because you have sold yourself to do evil in the sight of the LORD. ²¹Behold, I will bring evil upon you, and will utterly sweep you away, and will cut off from Ahab every male, both bond and free in Israel; ²²and I will make your house like the house of Jeroboam the son of Nebat, and like the house of Baasha the son of Ahijah, because of the provocation with which you have provoked *Me* to anger, and *because* you have made Israel sin. ²³Of Jezebel also has the LORD spoken, saying, 'The dogs will eat Jezebel in the district of Jezreel.' ²⁴The one belonging to Ahab, who dies in the city, the dogs will eat, and the one who dies in the field the birds of heaven will eat."

²⁵Surely there was no one like Ahab who sold himself to do evil in the sight of the LORD, because Jezebel his wife incited him. ²⁶He acted very abominably in following idols, according to all that the Amorites had done,

whom the LORD cast out before the sons of Israel.

27 It came about when Ahab heard these words, that he tore his clothes and put on sackcloth and fasted, and he lay in sackcloth and went about despondently. 28 Then the word of the LORD came to Elijah the Tishbite, saying, 29 "Do you see how Ahab has humbled himself before Me? Because he has humbled himself before Me, I will not bring the evil in his days, but I will bring the evil upon his house in his son's days."

22 Three years passed without war between Aram and Israel. 2 In the third year Jehoshaphat the king of Judah came down to the king of Israel. 3 Now the king of Israel said to his servants, "Do you know that Ramoth-gilead belongs to us, and we are still doing nothing to take it out of the hand of the king of Aram?" 4 And he said to Jehoshaphat, "Will you go with me to battle at Ramoth-gilead?" And Jehoshaphat said to the king of Israel, "I am as you are, my people as your people, my horses as your horses."

5 Moreover, Jehoshaphat said to the king of Israel, "Please inquire first for the word of the LORD." 6 Then the king of Israel gathered the prophets together, about four hundred men, and said to them, "Shall I go against Ramoth-gilead to battle or shall I refrain?" And they said, "Go up, for the Lord will give it into the

22:6 prophets. These 400 prophets of Ahab were not true prophets of the Lord. They worshiped at Bethel in the golden-calf center set up by Jeroboam (12:28–29) and were supported by Ahab, whose religious policy also permitted Baal worship. Their words were designed to please Ahab (v. 8), so they refused to begin with the authoritative "thus says the Lord" and did not use the covenant name for Israel's God, "Lord."

hand of the king." 7 But Jehoshaphat said, "Is there not yet a prophet of the LORD here that we may inquire of him?" 8 The king of Israel said to Jehoshaphat, "There is yet one man by whom we may inquire of the LORD, but I hate him, because he does not prophesy good concerning me, but evil. He is Micaiah son of Imlah." But Jehoshaphat said, "Let not the king say so." 9 Then the king of Israel called an officer and said, "Bring quickly Micaiah son of Imlah." 10 Now the king of Israel and Jehoshaphat king of Judah were sitting each

on his throne, arrayed in their robes, at the threshing floor at the entrance of the gate of Samaria; and all the prophets were prophesying before them. 11 Then Zedekiah the son of Chenaanah made horns of iron for himself and said, "Thus says the LORD, 'With these you will gore the Arameans until they are consumed.'" 12 All the prophets were prophesying thus, saying, "Go up to Ramoth-gilead and prosper, for the LORD will give it into the hand of the king."

13 Then the messenger who went to summon Micaiah spoke to him saying, "Behold now, the words of the prophets are uniformly favorable to the king. Please let your word be like the word of one of them, and speak favorably." 14 But Micaiah said, "As the LORD lives, what the LORD says to me, that I shall speak."

15 When he came to the king, the king said to him, "Micaiah, shall we go to Ramoth-gilead to battle, or shall we refrain?" And he answered him, "Go up and succeed, and the LORD will give it into the hand of the king." 16 Then the king said to him, "How many times must I adjure you to speak to me nothing but the truth in the name of the LORD?" 17 So he said,

"I saw all Israel
Scattered on the mountains,
Like sheep which have no shepherd.
And the LORD said,
'These have no master.
Let each of them return to his house in peace.'"

18 Then the king of Israel said to Jehoshaphat, "Did I not tell you that he would not prophesy good concerning me, but evil?"

19 Micaiah said, "Therefore, hear the word of the LORD. I saw the LORD sitting on His throne, and all the host of heaven standing by Him on His right and on His left. 20 The LORD said, 'Who will entice Ahab to go up and fall at Ramoth-gilead?' And one said this while another said that. 21 Then a spirit came forward and stood before the LORD and said, 'I will entice him.' 22 The LORD said to him, 'How?' And he said, 'I will go out and be a deceiving spirit in the mouth of all his prophets.' Then He said, 'You are to entice him and also prevail. Go and do so.' 23 Now therefore, behold, the LORD has put a deceiving spirit in the mouth of all these your prophets; and the LORD has proclaimed disaster against you."

²⁴Then Zedekiah the son of Chenaanah came near and struck Micaiah on the cheek and said, "How did the Spirit of the LORD pass from me to speak to you?" ²⁵Micaiah said, "Behold, you shall see on that day when you enter an inner room to hide yourself." ²⁶Then the king of Israel said, "Take Micaiah and return him to Amon the governor of the city and to Joash the king's son; ²⁷and say, 'Thus says the king, "Put this man in prison and feed him sparingly with bread and water until I return safely."'" ²⁸Micaiah said, "If you indeed return safely the LORD has not spoken by me." And he said, "Listen, all you people."

²⁹So the king of Israel and Jehoshaphat king of Judah went up against Ramoth-gilead. ³⁰The king of Israel said to Jehoshaphat, "I will disguise myself and go into the battle, but you put on your robes." So the king of Israel disguised himself and went into the battle. ³¹Now the king of Aram had commanded the thirty-two captains of his chariots, saying, "Do not fight with small or great, but with the king of Israel alone." ³²So when the captains of the chariots saw Jehoshaphat, they said, "Surely it is the king of Israel," and they turned aside to fight against him, and Jehoshaphat cried out. ³³When the captains of the chariots saw that it was not the king of Israel, they turned back from pursuing him.

³⁴Now a certain man drew his bow at random and struck the king of Israel in a joint of the armor. So he said to the driver of his chariot, "Turn around and take me out of the fight; for I am severely wounded." ³⁵The battle raged that day, and the king was propped up in his chariot in front of the Arameans, and died at evening, and the blood from the wound ran into the bottom of the chariot. ³⁶Then a cry passed throughout the army close to sunset, saying, "Every man to his city and every man to his country."

³⁷So the king died and was brought to Samaria, and they buried the king in Samaria. ³⁸They washed the chariot by the pool of Samaria, and the dogs licked up his blood (now the harlots bathed themselves *there*), according to the word of the LORD which He spoke. ³⁹Now the rest of the acts of Ahab and all that he did and the ivory house which he built and all the cities which he built, are they not written in the Book of the Chronicles of the Kings of Israel? ⁴⁰So Ahab slept with his fathers, and Ahaziah his son became king in his place.

⁴¹Now Jehoshaphat the son of Asa became king over Judah in the fourth year of Ahab king of Israel. ⁴²Jehoshaphat was thirty-five years old when he became king, and he reigned twenty-five years in Jerusalem. And his mother's name was Azubah the daughter of Shilhi. ⁴³He walked in all the way of Asa his father; he did not turn aside from it, doing right in the sight of the LORD. However, the high places were not taken away; the people still sacrificed and burnt incense on the high places. ⁴⁴Jehoshaphat also made peace with the king of Israel.

⁴⁵Now the rest of the acts of Jehoshaphat, and his might which he showed and how he warred, are they not written in the Book of the Chronicles of the Kings of Judah? ⁴⁶The remnant of the sodomites who remained in the days of his father Asa, he expelled from the land.

⁴⁷Now there was no king in Edom; a deputy was king. ⁴⁸Jehoshaphat made ships of Tarshish to go to Ophir for gold, but they did not go for the ships were broken at Ezion-geber. ⁴⁹Then Ahaziah the son of Ahab said to Jehoshaphat, "Let my servants go with your servants in the ships." But Jehoshaphat was not willing. ⁵⁰And Jehoshaphat slept with his fathers and was buried with his fathers in the city of his father David, and Jehoram his son became king in his place.

⁵¹Ahaziah the son of Ahab became king over Israel in Samaria in the seventeenth year of Jehoshaphat king of Judah, and he reigned two years over Israel. ⁵²He did evil in the sight of the LORD and walked in the way of his father and in the way of his mother and in the way of Jeroboam the son of Nebat, who caused Israel to sin. ⁵³So he served Baal and worshiped him and provoked the LORD God of Israel to anger, according to all that his father had done.

Psalm 71:1–8

In You, O LORD, I have taken refuge;
  Let me never be ashamed.
² In Your righteousness deliver
    me and rescue me;
  Incline Your ear to me and
    save me.
³ Be to me a rock of habitation to
    which I may continually come;
  You have given commandment
    to save me,
  For You are my rock and my
    fortress.
⁴ Rescue me, O my God, out of
    the hand of the wicked,
  Out of the grasp of the wrongdoer
    and ruthless man,
⁵ For You are my hope;

O Lord GOD, *You are* my
confidence from my youth.
6 By You I have been sustained
from *my* birth;
You are He who took me from
my mother's womb;
My praise is continually of You.

7 I have become a marvel to many,
For You are my strong refuge.
8 My mouth is filled with Your
praise
And with Your glory all day
long.

Proverbs 18:3-5

3 When a wicked man comes,
contempt also comes,
And with dishonor *comes*
scorn.
4 The words of a man's mouth
are deep waters;
The fountain of wisdom is
a bubbling brook.
5 To show partiality to the
wicked is not good,
Nor to thrust aside the
righteous in judgment.

John 15:1-27

15 "I am the true vine, and My Father is the vinedresser. 2 Every branch in Me that does not bear fruit, He takes away; and every *branch* that bears fruit, He prunes it so that it may bear more fruit. 3 You are already clean because of the word which I have spoken to you. 4 Abide in Me, and I in you. As the branch cannot bear fruit of itself unless it abides in the vine, so neither *can* you unless you abide in Me. 5 I am the vine, you are the branches; he who abides in Me and I in him, he bears much fruit, for apart from Me you can do nothing. 6 If anyone does not abide in Me, he is thrown away as a branch and dries up; and they gather them, and cast them into the fire and they are burned. 7 If you abide in Me, and My words abide in you, ask whatever you wish, and it will be done for you. 8 My Father is glorified by this, that you bear much fruit, and *so* prove to be My disciples. 9 Just as the Father has loved Me, I have also loved you; abide in My love. 10 If you keep My commandments, you will abide in My love; just as I have kept My Father's commandments and abide in His love. 11 These things I have spoken to you so that My joy may be in you, and *that* your joy may be made full.

12 "This is My commandment, that you love one another, just as I have loved you. 13 Greater love has no one than this, that one lay down his life for his friends. 14 You are My friends if you do what I command you. 15 No longer do I call you slaves, for the slave does not know what his master is doing; but I have called you friends, for all things that I have heard from My Father I have made known to you. 16 You did not choose Me but I chose you, and appointed you that you would go and bear fruit, and *that* your fruit would remain, so that whatever you ask of the Father in My name He may give to you. 17 This I command you, that you love one another.

15:14-15 friends. Just as Abraham was called the "friend" of God (2Ch 20:7; Jas 2:23) because he enjoyed extraordinary access to the mind of God through God's revelation to him which he believed, so also those who follow Christ are privileged with extraordinary revelation through the Messiah and Son of God and, believing, become "friends" of God also. It was for His "friends" that the Lord laid down His life (v. 13; 10:11, 15, 17).

---

18 "If the world hates you, you know that it has hated Me before *it hated* you. 19 If you were of the world, the world would love its own; but because you are not of the world, but I chose you out of the world, because of this the world hates you. 20 Remember the word that I said to you, 'A slave is not greater than his master.' If they persecuted Me, they will also persecute you; if they kept My word, they will keep yours also. 21 But all these things they will do to you for My name's sake, because they do not know the One who sent Me. 22 If I had not come and spoken to them, they would not have sin, but now they have no excuse for their sin. 23 He who hates Me hates My Father also. 24 If I had not done among them the works which no one else did, they would not have sin; but now they have both seen and hated Me and My Father as well. 25 But *they have done this* to fulfill the word that is written in their Law, 'THEY HATED ME WITHOUT A CAUSE.' 26 "When the Helper comes, whom I will send to you from the Father, *that is* the Spirit of truth who proceeds from the Father, He will testify about Me, 27 and you *will* testify also, because you have been with Me from the beginning.

DAY 6: What serious warning is sounded in the lesson of the vine and branches?

In John 15:1-17, Jesus used the extended metaphor of the vine and branches to set forth the basis of Christian living. Jesus used the imagery of agricultural life at the time, i.e., vines and vine crops (see also Mt 20:1-16; 21:23-41; Mk 12:1-9; Lk 13:6-9; 20:9-16). In the Old Testament, the vine is used commonly as a symbol for Israel (Ps 80:9-16; Is. 5:1-7; 27:2-6; Jer 2:21; 12:10; Eze 15:1-8; 17:1-21; 19:10-14; Hos 10:1-2). He specifically identified Himself as the true vine and the Father as the vinedresser or caretaker of the vine.

The vine has two types of branches: 1) branches that bear fruit (vv. 2, 8), and 2) branches that do not (vv. 2, 6). The branches that bear fruit are genuine believers. Though in immediate context the focus is upon the 11 faithful disciples, the imagery also encompasses all believers down through the ages. The branches that do not bear fruit are those who profess to believe, but their lack of fruit indicates genuine salvation has never taken place and they have no life from the vine. Especially in the immediate context, Judas was in view, but the imagery extends from him to all those who make a profession of faith in Christ but do not actually possess salvation. The image of non-fruit-bearing branches being burned pictures eschatological judgment and eternal rejection (Eze 15:6-8).

"Abide in Me," Jesus said (vv. 4-6). The word "abide" means to remain or stay around. The remaining is evidence that salvation has already taken place (1Jn 2:19) and not vice versa. The fruit or evidence of salvation is continuance in service to Him and in His teaching (8:31; 1Jn 2:24; Col 1:23). The abiding believer is the only legitimate believer. Abiding and believing actually are addressing the same issue of genuine salvation (Heb 3:6-19). "Abide in My love" (vv. 9-10; Jude 21). This is not emotional or mystical, but defined in v. 10 as obedience. Jesus set the model by His perfect obedience to the Father, which we are to use as the pattern for our obedience to Him.

♫ JUNE 7

2 Kings 1:1-2:25

1 Now Moab rebelled against Israel after the death of Ahab. ²And Ahaziah fell through the lattice in his upper chamber which *was* in Samaria, and became ill. So he sent messengers and said to them, "Go, inquire of Baal-zebub, the god of Ekron, whether I will recover from this sickness." ³But the angel of the LORD said to Elijah the Tishbite, "Arise, go up to meet the messengers of the king of Samaria and say to them, 'Is it because there is no God in Israel *that* you are going to inquire of Baal-zebub, the god of Ekron?' ⁴Now therefore thus says the LORD, 'You shall not come down from the bed where you have gone up, but you shall surely die.'" Then Elijah departed.

⁵When the messengers returned to him he said to them, "Why have you returned?" ⁶They said to him, "A man came up to meet us and said to us, 'Go, return to the king who sent you and say to him, "Thus says the LORD, 'Is it because there is no God in Israel *that* you are sending to inquire of Baal-zebub, the god of Ekron? Therefore you shall not come down from the bed where you have gone up, but shall surely die.'"'" ⁷He said to them, "What kind of man was he who came up to meet you and spoke these words to you?" ⁸They

answered him, "He *was* a hairy man with a leather girdle bound about his loins." And he said, "It is Elijah the Tishbite."

⁹Then *the king* sent to him a captain of fifty with his fifty. And he went up to him, and behold, he was sitting on the top of the hill. And he said to him, "O man of God, the king says, 'Come down.'" ¹⁰Elijah replied to the captain of fifty, "If I am a man of God, let fire come down from heaven and consume you and your fifty." Then fire came down from heaven and consumed him and his fifty.

¹¹So he again sent to him another captain of fifty with his fifty. And he said to him, "O man of God, thus says the king, 'Come down quickly.'" ¹²Elijah replied to them, "If I am a man of God, let fire come down from heaven and consume you and your fifty." Then the fire of God came down from heaven and consumed him and his fifty.

¹³So he again sent the captain of a third fifty with his fifty. When the third captain of fifty went up, he came and bowed down on his knees before Elijah, and begged him and said to him, "O man of God, please let my life and the lives of these fifty servants of yours be precious in your sight. ¹⁴Behold fire came down from heaven and consumed the first two captains of fifty with their fifties; but now let my life be precious in your sight." ¹⁵The angel of the LORD said to Elijah, "Go down with him; do not be afraid of him."

So he arose and went down with him to the king. ¹⁶ Then he said to him, "Thus says the LORD, 'Because you have sent messengers to inquire of Baal-zebub, the god of Ekron—is it because there is no God in Israel to inquire of His word?—therefore you shall not come down from the bed where you have gone up, but shall surely die.'"

¹⁷ So Ahaziah died according to the word of the LORD which Elijah had spoken. And because he had no son, Jehoram became king in his place in the second year of Jehoram the son of Jehoshaphat, king of Judah. ¹⁸ Now the rest of the acts of Ahaziah which he did, are they not written in the Book of the Chronicles of the Kings of Israel?

2 And it came about when the LORD was about to take up Elijah by a whirlwind to heaven, that Elijah went with Elisha from Gilgal. ² Elijah said to Elisha, "Stay here please, for the LORD has sent me as far as Bethel." But Elisha said, "As the LORD lives and as you yourself live, I will not leave you." So they went down to Bethel. ³ Then the sons of the prophets who were at Bethel came out to Elisha and said to him, "Do you know that the LORD will take away your master from over you today?" And he said, "Yes, I know; be still."

⁴ Elijah said to him, "Elisha, please stay

2:1 by a whirlwind. Literally "in the whirlwind." This was a reference to the specific storm with lightning and thunder in which Elijah was taken to heaven (v. 11). The Lord's presence was connected with a whirlwind in Job 38:1; 40:6; Jeremiah 23:19; 25:32; 30:23; Zechariah 9:14. **Elisha.** The record of this prophet, who was the successor to Elijah, begins in 1 Kings 19:16 and extends to his death in 2 Kings 13:20.

2:3 the sons of the prophets. See 1 Kings 20:35. **take away.** The same term was used of Enoch's translation to heaven in Genesis 5:24. The question from the sons of the prophets implied that the Lord had revealed Elijah's imminent departure to them. Elisha's response that he didn't need to hear about it ("be still") explicitly stated that Elijah's departure had been revealed by the Lord to him also (v. 5). **from over you.** I.e., from supervising you, an allusion to the habit of students sitting beneath the feet of their master, elevated on a platform. Elisha would soon change from being Elijah's assistant to serving as the leader among the prophets.

here, for the LORD has sent me to Jericho." But he said, "As the LORD lives, and as you yourself live, I will not leave you." So they came to Jericho. ⁵ The sons of the prophets who were at Jericho approached Elisha and said to him, "Do you know that the LORD will take away your master from over you today?" And he answered, "Yes, I know; be still." ⁶ Then Elijah said to him, "Please stay here, for the LORD has sent me to the Jordan." And he said, "As the LORD lives, and as you yourself live, I will not leave you." So the two of them went on.

⁷ Now fifty men of the sons of the prophets went and stood opposite them at a distance, while the two of them stood by the Jordan. ⁸ Elijah took his mantle and folded it together and struck the waters, and they were divided here and there, so that the two of them crossed over on dry ground.

⁹ When they had crossed over, Elijah said to Elisha, "Ask what I shall do for you before I am taken from you." And Elisha said, "Please, let a double portion of your spirit be upon me." ¹⁰ He said, "You have asked a hard thing. Nevertheless, if you see me when I am taken from you, it shall be so for you; but if not, it shall not be so." ¹¹ As they were going along and talking, behold, there appeared a chariot of fire and horses of fire which separated the two of them. And Elijah went up by a whirlwind to heaven. ¹² Elisha saw it and cried out, "My father, my father, the

2:11 chariot of fire and horses of fire. The horse-drawn chariot was the fastest means of transport and the mightiest means of warfare in that day. Thus, the chariot and horses symbolized God's powerful protection, which was the true safety of Israel (v. 12). As earthly kingdoms are dependent for their defense on such military force as represented by horses and chariots, one single prophet had done more by God's power to preserve his nation than all their military preparations.

chariots of Israel and its horsemen!" And he saw Elijah no more. Then he took hold of his own clothes and tore them in two pieces. ¹³ He also took up the mantle of Elijah that fell from him and returned and stood by the bank of the Jordan. ¹⁴ He took the mantle of Elijah that fell from him and struck the waters and said, "Where is the LORD, the God of Elijah?" And when he also had struck the waters, they were divided here and there; and Elisha crossed over.

¹⁵ Now when the sons of the prophets who *were* at Jericho opposite *him* saw him, they said, "The spirit of Elijah rests on Elisha." And they came to meet him and bowed themselves to the ground before him. ¹⁶ They said to him, "Behold now, there are with your servants fifty strong men, please let them go and search for your master; perhaps the Spirit of the LORD has taken him up and cast him on some mountain or into some valley." And he said, "You shall not send." ¹⁷ But when they urged him until he was ashamed, he said, "Send." They sent therefore fifty men; and they searched three days but did not find him. ¹⁸ They returned to him while he was staying at Jericho; and he said to them, "Did I not say to you, 'Do not go'?"

¹⁹ Then the men of the city said to Elisha, "Behold now, the situation of this city is pleasant, as my lord sees; but the water is bad and the land is unfruitful." ²⁰ He said, "Bring me a new jar, and put salt in it." So they brought *it* to him. ²¹ He went out to the spring of water and threw salt in it and said, "Thus says the LORD, 'I have purified these waters; there shall not be from there death or unfruitfulness any longer.' " ²² So the waters have been purified to this day, according to the word of Elisha which he spoke.

²³ Then he went up from there to Bethel; and as he was going up by the way, young lads came out from the city and mocked him and said to him, "Go up, you baldhead; go up, you baldhead!" ²⁴ When he looked behind him and saw them, he cursed them in the name of the LORD. Then two female bears came out of the woods and tore up forty-two lads of their number. ²⁵ He went from there to Mount Carmel, and from there he returned to Samaria.

2:24 cursed. Because these young people of about 20 years of age or older (the same term is used of Solomon in 1Ki 3:7) so despised the prophet of the Lord, Elisha called upon the Lord to deal with the rebels as He saw fit. The Lord's punishment was the mauling of 42 youths by two female bears. The penalty was clearly justified, for to ridicule Elisha was to ridicule the Lord Himself. The gravity of the penalty mirrored the gravity of the crime. The appalling judgment was God's warning to any and all who attempted to interfere with the newly invested prophet's ministry.

Psalm 71:9–16

⁹ Do not cast me off in the
    time of old age;
  Do not forsake me when
    my strength fails.
¹⁰ For my enemies have
    spoken against me;
  And those who watch for my life
    have consulted together,
¹¹ Saying, "God has forsaken him;
  Pursue and seize him, for there
    is no one to deliver."

¹² O God, do not be far from me;
  O my God, hasten to my help!
¹³ Let those who are adversaries of my
    soul be ashamed *and* consumed;
  Let them be covered with
    reproach and dishonor,
    who seek to injure me.
¹⁴ But as for me, I will hope continually,
  And will praise You yet
    more and more.
¹⁵ My mouth shall tell of Your
    righteousness
  And of Your salvation all day long;
  For I do not know the sum *of them.*
¹⁶ I will come with the mighty
    deeds of the Lord GOD;
  I will make mention of Your
    righteousness, Yours alone.

Proverbs 18:6–8

⁶ A fool's lips bring strife,
  And his mouth calls for blows.
⁷ A fool's mouth is his ruin,
  And his lips are the snare of his soul.
⁸ The words of a whisperer are
    like dainty morsels,
  And they go down into the
    innermost parts of the body.

John 16:1–33

16 "These things I have spoken to you so that you may be kept from stumbling. ² They will make you outcasts from the synagogue, but an hour is coming for everyone who kills you to think that he is offering service to God. ³ These things they will do because they have not known the Father or Me. ⁴ But these things I have spoken to you, so that when their hour comes, you may remember that I told you of them. These things I did not say to you at the beginning, because I was with you.

⁵ "But now I am going to Him who sent Me; and none of you asks Me, 'Where are You going?' ⁶ But because I have said these things

to you, sorrow has filled your heart. ⁷But I tell you the truth, it is to your advantage that I go away; for if I do not go away, the Helper will not come to you; but if I go, I will send Him to you. ⁸And He, when He comes, will convict the world concerning sin and righteousness and judgment; ⁹concerning sin, because they do not believe in Me; ¹⁰and concerning righteousness, because I go to the Father and you no longer see Me; ¹¹and concerning judgment, because the ruler of this world has been judged.

¹²"I have many more things to say to you, but you cannot bear *them* now. ¹³But when He, the Spirit of truth, comes, He will guide you into all the truth; for He will not speak on His own initiative, but whatever He hears, He will speak; and He will disclose to you what is to come. ¹⁴He will glorify Me, for He will take of Mine and will disclose *it* to you. ¹⁵All things that the Father has are Mine; therefore I said that He takes of Mine and will disclose *it* to you.

¹⁶"A little while, and you will no longer see Me; and again a little while, and you will see Me." ¹⁷*Some* of His disciples then said to one another, "What is this thing He is telling us, 'A little while, and you will not see Me; and again a little while, and you will see Me'; and, 'because I go to the Father'?" ¹⁸So they were saying, "What is this that He says, 'A little while'? We do not know what He is talking about." ¹⁹Jesus knew that they wished to question Him, and He said to them, "Are you deliberating together about this, that I said, 'A little while, and you will not see Me, and again a little while, and you will see Me'? ²⁰Truly, truly, I say to you, that you will weep and lament, but the world will rejoice; you will grieve, but your grief will be turned into joy. ²¹Whenever a woman is in labor she has pain, because her hour has come; but when she gives birth to the child, she no longer remembers the anguish because of the joy that a child has been born into the world. ²²Therefore you too have grief now; but I will see you again, and your heart will rejoice, and no one *will* take your joy away from you. ²³In that day you will not question Me about anything.

Truly, truly, I say to you, if you ask the Father for anything in My name, He will give it to you. ²⁴Until now you have asked for nothing in My name; ask and you will receive, so that your joy may be made full.

²⁵"These things I have spoken to you in figurative language; an hour is coming when I will no longer speak to you in figurative language, but will tell you plainly of the Father. ²⁶In that day you will ask in My name, and I do not say to you that I will request of

16:25 in figurative language. The word means "veiled, pointed statement" that is pregnant with meaning, i.e., something that is obscure. What seemed hard to understand for the disciples during the life of Jesus would become clear after His death, resurrection, and the coming of the Holy Spirit (vv. 13–14; 14:26; 15:26–27). They would actually understand the ministry of Christ better than they had while they were with Him, as the Spirit inspired them to write the Gospels and Epistles and ministered in and through them.

the Father on your behalf; ²⁷for the Father Himself loves you, because you have loved Me and have believed that I came forth from the Father. ²⁸I came forth from the Father and have come into the world; I am leaving the world again and going to the Father."

²⁹His disciples *said, "Lo, now You are speaking plainly and are not using a figure of speech. ³⁰Now we know that You know all things, and have no need for anyone to question You; by this we believe that You came from God." ³¹Jesus answered them, "Do you now believe? ³²Behold, an hour is coming, and has *already* come, for you to be scattered, each to his own *home,* and to leave Me alone; and *yet* I am not alone, because the Father is with Me. ³³These things I have spoken to you, so that in Me you may have peace. In the world you have tribulation, but take courage; I have overcome the world."

DAY 7: What very specific ministry does the Holy Spirit have on people's lives?

In John 16:8, the coming of the Holy Spirit at Pentecost was approximately 40 or more days away at this point (Ac 2:1–13). Jesus says that the Holy Spirit's ministry is to "convict" people. This word has two meanings: 1) the judicial act of conviction with a view toward sentencing (i.e., a courtroom term—conviction of sin) or 2) the act of convincing. Here the second idea is best, since the purpose of the Holy Spirit is not condemnation but conviction of the need for the Savior. The Son does the judgment, with the Father (5:22, 27, 30). In v. 14, it is said that He will reveal the glories of Christ to His people. He will also inspire the writing of the New Testament, guiding the apostles to write it (v. 13), and He will reveal things to come, through the New Testament prophecies (v. 13).

The Holy Spirit convicts of "sin" (v. 9). The singular indicates that a specific sin is in view; i.e., that of not believing in Jesus as Messiah and Son of God. This is the only sin, ultimately, that damns people to hell. Though all men are depraved, cursed by their violation of God's law, and sinful by nature, what ultimately damns them to hell is their unwillingness to believe in the Lord Jesus Christ as Savior (8:24).

He convicts of "righteousness" (v. 10). The Holy Spirit's purpose here is to shatter the pretensions of self-righteousness (hypocrisy), exposing the darkness of the heart. While Jesus was on the earth, He performed this task especially toward the shallowness and emptiness of Judaism that had degenerated into legalistic modes without life-giving reality. With Jesus gone to the Father, the Holy Spirit continues His convicting role.

And of "judgment" (v. 11). The judgment here in context is that of the world under Satan's control. Its judgments are blind, faulty, and evil as evidenced in their verdict on Christ. The world can't make righteous judgments (7:24), but the Spirit of Christ does (8:16). All Satan's adjudications are lies (8:44–47), so the Spirit convicts men of their false judgment of Christ. Satan, the ruler of the world (14:30; Eph 2:1–3) who, as the god of this world, has perverted the world's judgment and turned people from believing in Jesus as the Messiah and Son of God (2Co 4:4), was defeated at the Cross. While Christ's death looked like Satan's greatest victory, it actually was Satan's destruction (Col 2:15; Heb 2:14–15; Rev 20:10). The Spirit will lead sinners to true judgment.

JUNE 8

2 Kings 3:1–4:44

3 Now Jehoram the son of Ahab became king over Israel at Samaria in the eighteenth year of Jehoshaphat king of Judah, and reigned twelve years. ² He did evil in the sight of the LORD, though not like his father and his mother; for he put away the *sacred* pillar of Baal which his father had made. ³ Nevertheless, he clung to the sins of Jeroboam the son of Nebat, which he made Israel sin; he did not depart from them.

⁴ Now Mesha king of Moab was a sheep breeder, and used to pay the king of Israel 100,000 lambs and the wool of 100,000 rams. ⁵ But when Ahab died, the king of Moab rebelled against the king of Israel. ⁶ And King Jehoram went out of Samaria at that time and mustered all Israel. ⁷ Then he went and sent *word* to Jehoshaphat the king of Judah, saying, "The king of Moab has rebelled against me. Will you go with me to fight against Moab?" And he said, "I will go up; I am as you are, my people as your people, my horses as your horses." ⁸ He said, "Which way shall we go up?" And he answered, "The way of the wilderness of Edom."

⁹ So the king of Israel went with the king of Judah and the king of Edom; and they made a circuit of seven days' journey, and there was no water for the army or for the cattle that followed them. ¹⁰ Then the king of Israel said, "Alas! For the LORD has called these three kings to give them into the hand of Moab."

¹¹ But Jehoshaphat said, "Is there not a prophet of the LORD here, that we may inquire of the LORD by him?" And one of the king of Israel's servants answered and said, "Elisha the son of Shaphat is here, who used to pour water on the hands of Elijah." ¹² Jehoshaphat said, "The word of the LORD is with him." So the king of Israel and Jehoshaphat and the king of Edom went down to him.

¹³ Now Elisha said to the king of Israel, "What do I have to do with you? Go to the prophets of your father and to the prophets of your mother." And the king of Israel said to him, "No, for the LORD has called these three kings *together* to give them into the hand of Moab." ¹⁴ Elisha said, "As the LORD of hosts lives, before whom I stand, were it not that I regard the presence of Jehoshaphat the king of Judah, I would not look at you nor see you. ¹⁵ But now bring me a minstrel." And it came about, when the minstrel played, that the hand of the LORD came upon him. ¹⁶ He said, "Thus says the LORD, 'Make this valley full of trenches.' ¹⁷ For thus says the LORD, 'You shall not see wind nor shall you see rain; yet that valley shall be filled with water, so that you shall drink, both you and

3:15 a minstrel. The music was used to accompany praise and prayer, which calmed the mind of the prophet that he might clearly hear the word of the Lord. Music often accompanied prophecies in the Old Testament (1Ch 25:1).

your cattle and your beasts. ¹⁸This is but a slight thing in the sight of the LORD; He will also give the Moabites into your hand. ¹⁹Then you shall strike every fortified city and every choice city, and fell every good tree and stop all springs of water, and mar every good piece of land with stones.' " ²⁰It happened in the morning about the time of offering the sacrifice, that behold, water came by the way of Edom, and the country was filled with water.

²¹Now all the Moabites heard that the kings had come up to fight against them. And all who were able to put on armor and older were summoned and stood on the border. ²²They rose early in the morning, and the sun shone on the water, and the Moabites saw the water opposite *them* as red as blood. ²³Then they said, "This is blood; the kings have surely fought together, and they have slain one another. Now therefore, Moab, to the spoil!" ²⁴But when they came to the camp of Israel, the Israelites arose and struck the Moabites, so that they fled before them; and they went forward into the land, slaughtering the Moabites. ²⁵Thus they destroyed the cities; and each one threw a stone on every piece of good land and filled it. So they stopped all the springs of water and felled all the good trees, until in Kir-haraseth *only* they left its stones; however, the slingers went about *it* and struck it. ²⁶When the king of Moab saw that the battle was too fierce for him, he took with him 700 men who drew swords, to break through to the king of Edom; but they could not. ²⁷Then he took his oldest son who was to reign in his place, and offered him as a burnt offering on the wall. And there came great wrath against Israel; and they departed from him and returned to their own land.

4 Now a certain woman of the wives of the sons of the prophets cried out to Elisha, "Your servant my husband is dead, and you know that your servant feared the LORD; and the creditor has come to take my two children to be his slaves." ²Elisha said to her, "What shall I do for you? Tell me, what do you have in the house?" And she said, "Your maidservant has nothing in the house except a jar of oil." ³Then he said, "Go, borrow vessels at large for yourself from all your neighbors, *even* empty vessels; do not get a few. ⁴And you shall go in and shut the door behind you and your sons, and pour out into all these vessels, and you shall set aside what is full." ⁵So she went from him and shut the door behind her and her sons; they were bringing *the vessels* to her and she poured. ⁶When the vessels were full, she said to her son, "Bring

4:4 shut the door behind you. Since the widow's need was private, the provision was to be private also. Further, the absence of Elisha demonstrated that the miracle happened only by God's power. God's power multiplied "little" into "much," filling all the vessels to meet the widow's need (1Ki 17:7–16).

me another vessel." And he said to her, "There is not one vessel more." And the oil stopped. ⁷Then she came and told the man of God. And he said, "Go, sell the oil and pay your debt, and you *and* your sons can live on the rest."

⁸Now there came a day when Elisha passed over to Shunem, where there was a prominent woman, and she persuaded him to eat food. And so it was, as often as he passed by, he turned in there to eat food. ⁹She said to her husband, "Behold now, I perceive that this is a holy man of God passing by us continually. ¹⁰Please, let us make a little walled upper chamber and let us set a bed for him there, and a table and a chair and a lampstand; and it shall be, when he comes to us, *that* he can turn in there."

¹¹One day he came there and turned in to the upper chamber and rested. ¹²Then he said to Gehazi his servant, "Call this Shunammite." And when he had called her, she stood before him. ¹³He said to him, "Say now to her, 'Behold, you have been careful for us with all this care; what can I do for you? Would you be spoken for to the king or to the captain of the army?' " And she answered, "I live among my own people." ¹⁴So he said, "What then is to be done for her?" And Gehazi answered, "Truly she has no son and her husband is old." ¹⁵He said, "Call her." When he had called her, she stood in the doorway. ¹⁶Then he said, "At this season next year you will embrace a son." And she said, "No, my lord, O man of God, do not lie to your maidservant."

¹⁷The woman conceived and bore a son at that season the next year, as Elisha had said to her.

¹⁸When the child was grown, the day came that he went out to his father to the reapers. ¹⁹He said to his father, "My head, my head." And he said to his servant, "Carry him to his mother." ²⁰When he had taken him and brought him to his mother, he sat on her lap until noon, and *then* died. ²¹She went up and laid him on the bed of the man of God, and shut *the door* behind him and went out. ²²Then she called to her husband and said,

"Please send me one of the servants and one of the donkeys, that I may run to the man of God and return." ²³He said, "Why will you go to him today? It is neither new moon nor sabbath." And she said, "*It will be* well." ²⁴Then she saddled a donkey and said to her servant, "Drive and go forward; do not slow down the pace for me unless I tell you." ²⁵So she went and came to the man of God to Mount Carmel.

When the man of God saw her at a distance, he said to Gehazi his servant, "Behold, there is the Shunammite. ²⁶Please run now to meet her and say to her, 'Is it well with you? Is it well with your husband? Is it well with the child?'" And she answered, "It is well." ²⁷When she came to the man of God to the hill, she caught hold of his feet. And Gehazi came near to push her away; but the man of God said, "Let her alone, for her soul is troubled within her; and the LORD has hidden it from me and has not told me." ²⁸Then she said, "Did I ask for a son from my lord? Did I not say, 'Do not deceive me'?"

²⁹Then he said to Gehazi, "Gird up your loins and take my staff in your hand, and go your way; if you meet any man, do not salute him, and if anyone salutes you, do not answer him; and lay my staff on the lad's face." ³⁰The mother of the lad said, "As the LORD lives and as you yourself live, I will not leave you." And he arose and followed her. ³¹Then Gehazi passed on before them and laid the staff on the lad's face, but there was no sound or response. So he returned to meet him and told him, "The lad has not awakened."

³²When Elisha came into the house, behold the lad was dead and laid on his bed. ³³So he entered and shut the door behind them both and prayed to the LORD. ³⁴And he went up and lay on the child, and put his mouth on his mouth and his eyes on his eyes and his hands on his hands, and he stretched himself on him; and the flesh of the child became warm. ³⁵Then he returned and walked in the house once back and forth, and went up and stretched himself on him; and the lad sneezed seven times and the lad opened his eyes. ³⁶He called Gehazi and said, "Call this Shunammite." So he called her. And when she came in to him, he said, "Take up your son." ³⁷Then she went in and fell at his feet and bowed herself to the ground, and she took up her son and went out.

³⁸When Elisha returned to Gilgal, *there was* a famine in the land. As the sons of the prophets were sitting before him, he said to his servant, "Put on the large pot and boil stew for the sons of the prophets." ³⁹Then one went out into the field to gather herbs, and found a wild vine and gathered from it his lap full of wild gourds, and came and sliced them into the pot of stew, for they did not know *what they were*. ⁴⁰So they poured *it* out for the men to eat. And as they were eating of the stew, they cried out and said, "O man of God, there is death in the pot." And they were unable to eat. ⁴¹But he said, "Now bring meal." He threw it into the pot and said, "Pour *it* out for the people that they may eat." Then there was no harm in the pot.

⁴²Now a man came from Baal-shalishah, and brought the man of God bread of the first fruits, twenty loaves of barley and fresh ears of grain in his sack. And he said, "Give *them* to the people that they may eat." ⁴³His attendant said, "What, will I set this before a hundred men?" But he said, "Give *them* to the people that they may eat, for thus says the LORD, 'They shall eat and have *some* left over.'" ⁴⁴So he set *it* before them, and they ate and had *some* left over, according to the word of the LORD.

Psalm 71:17–24

17 O God, You have taught me
from my youth,
And I still declare Your
wondrous deeds.
18 And even when *I am* old and gray,
O God, do not forsake me,
Until I declare Your strength
to *this* generation,
Your power to all who are
to come.
19 For Your righteousness, O God,
reaches to the heavens,
You who have done great things;
O God, who is like You?
20 You who have shown me many
troubles and distresses
Will revive me again,
And will bring me up again from
the depths of the earth.
21 May You increase my greatness
And turn *to* comfort me.
22 I will also praise You with
a harp,
Even Your truth, O my God;
To You I will sing praises
with the lyre,
O Holy One of Israel.
23 My lips will shout for joy when
I sing praises to You;
And my soul, which You
have redeemed.

24 My tongue also will utter Your
righteousness all day long;
For they are ashamed, for they
are humiliated who seek
my hurt.

Proverbs 18:9

9 He also who is slack in his work
Is brother to him who
destroys.

John 17:1–26

17 Jesus spoke these things; and lifting up His eyes to heaven, He said, "Father, the hour has come; glorify Your Son, that the Son may glorify You, ² even as You gave Him authority over all flesh, that to all whom You have given Him, He may give eternal life. ³ This is eternal life, that they may know You, the only true God, and Jesus Christ whom You have sent. ⁴ I glorified You on the earth, having accomplished the work which You have given Me to do. ⁵ Now, Father, glorify Me together with Yourself, with the glory which I had with You before the world was.

⁶ "I have manifested Your name to the men whom You gave Me out of the world; they were Yours and You gave them to Me, and they have kept Your word. ⁷ Now they have come to know that everything You have given Me is from You; ⁸ for the words which You gave Me I have given to them; and they received *them* and truly understood that I came forth from You, and they believed that You sent Me. ⁹ I ask on their behalf; I do not ask on behalf of the world, but of those whom You have given Me; for they are Yours; ¹⁰ and all things that are Mine are Yours, and Yours are Mine; and I have been glorified in them. ¹¹ I am no longer in the world; and *yet* they themselves are in the world, and I come to You. Holy Father, keep them in Your name, *the name* which You have given Me, that they may be one even as We *are*. ¹² While I was with them, I was keeping them in Your name which You have given Me; and I guarded them and not one of them perished but the son of perdition, so that the Scripture would be fulfilled. ¹³ But now I come to You; and these things I speak in the world so that they may have My joy made full in themselves. ¹⁴ I have given them Your word; and the world has hated them, because they are not of the world, even as I am not of the world. ¹⁵ I do not ask You to take them out of the world, but to keep them from the evil *one*. ¹⁶ They are not of the world, even as I am not of the world. ¹⁷ Sanctify them in the truth; Your word is

17:17 Sanctify. This verb also occurs in John's Gospel at v. 19; 10:36. The idea of sanctification is the setting apart of something for a particular use. Accordingly, believers are set apart for God and His purposes alone so that the believer does only what God wants and hates all that God hates (Lv 11:44–45; 1 Peter 1:16). Sanctification is accomplished by means of the truth, which is the revelation that the Son gave regarding all that the Father commanded Him to communicate and is now contained in the Scriptures left by the apostles.

truth. ¹⁸ As You sent Me into the world, I also have sent them into the world. ¹⁹ For their sakes I sanctify Myself, that they themselves also may be sanctified in truth.

²⁰ "I do not ask on behalf of these alone, but for those also who believe in Me through their word; ²¹ that they may all be one; even as You, Father, *are* in Me and I in You, that they also may be in Us, so that the world may believe

17:21 they may all be one. The basis of this unity centers in adherence to the revelation the Father mediated to His first disciples through His Son. Believers are also to be united in the common belief of the truth that was received in the Word of God (Php 2:2). This is not still a wish, but it became a reality when the Spirit came (Ac 2:4; 1Co 12:13). It is not experiential unity, but the unity of common eternal life shared by all who believe the truth, and it results in the one body of Christ all sharing His life.

that You sent Me. ²² The glory which You have given Me I have given to them, that they may be one, just as We are one; ²³ I in them and You in Me, that they may be perfected in unity, so that the world may know that You sent Me, and loved them, even as You have loved Me. ²⁴ Father, I desire that they also, whom You have given Me, be with Me where I am, so that they may see My glory which You have given Me, for You loved Me before the foundation of the world.

²⁵ "O righteous Father, although the world has not known You, yet I have known You; and these have known that You sent Me; ²⁶ and I have made Your name known to them, and will make it known, so that the love with which You loved Me may be in them, and I in them."

DAY 8: What was Jesus' prayer in John 17 about?

Although Matthew 6:9–13 and Luke 11:2–4 have become known popularly as the Lord's Prayer, that prayer was actually a prayer taught to the disciples by Jesus as a pattern for their prayers. The prayer recorded in John 17:1–26 is truly the Lord's Prayer, exhibiting the face-to-face communion the Son had with the Father. Very little is recorded of the content of Jesus' frequent prayers to the Father (Mt 14:23; Lk 5:16), so this prayer reveals some of the precious content of the Son's communion and intercession with Him.

This chapter is a transitional chapter, marking the end of Jesus' earthly ministry and the beginning of His intercessory ministry for believers (Heb 7:25). In many respects, the prayer is a summary of John's entire Gospel. Its principle themes include: 1) Jesus' obedience to His Father; 2) the glorification of His Father through His death and exaltation; 3) the revelation of God in Jesus Christ; 4) the choosing of the disciples out of the world; 5) their mission to the world; 6) their unity modeled on the unity of the Father and Son; and 7) the believer's final destiny in the presence of the Father and Son. The chapter divides into three parts: 1) Jesus' prayer for Himself (vv. 1–5); 2) Jesus' prayer for the apostles (vv. 6–19); and 3) Jesus' prayer for all New Testament believers who will form the church (vv. 20–26).

Jesus speaks to His Father that the hour of His death has come (v. 1). "Glorify Your Son." The very event that would glorify the Son was His death. By it, He has received the adoration, worship, and love of millions whose sins He bore. He accepted this path to glory, knowing that by it He would be exalted to the Father. The goal is that the Father may be glorified for His redemptive plan in the Son.

Note Jesus' concern that the Father keep His disciples "from the evil one" (v. 15). The reference here refers to protection from Satan and all the wicked forces following him (Mt 6:13; 1Jn 2:13–14; 3:12; 5:18–19). Though Jesus' sacrifice on the cross was the defeat of Satan, he is still loose and orchestrating his evil system against believers. He seeks to destroy believers (1Pe 5:8; Eph 6:12), but God is their strong protector (12:31; 16:11; Ps 27:1–3; 2Co 4:4; Jude 24–25).

JUNE 9

2 Kings 5:1–6:33

5 Now Naaman, captain of the army of the king of Aram, was a great man with his master, and highly respected, because by him the LORD had given victory to Aram. The man was also a valiant warrior, *but he was* a leper. ² Now the Arameans had gone out in bands and had taken captive a little girl from the land of Israel; and she waited on Naaman's wife. ³ She said to her mistress, "I wish that my master were with the prophet who is in Samaria! Then he would cure him of his leprosy." ⁴ Naaman went in and told his master, saying, "Thus and thus spoke the girl who is from the land of Israel." ⁵ Then the king of Aram said, "Go now, and I will send a letter to the king of Israel." He departed and took with him ten talents of silver and six thousand *shekels* of gold and ten changes of clothes.

⁶ He brought the letter to the king of Israel, saying, "And now as this letter comes to you, behold, I have sent Naaman my servant to you, that you may cure him of his leprosy." ⁷ When the king of Israel read the letter, he tore his clothes and said, "Am I God, to kill and to make alive, that this man is sending *word* to me to cure a man of his leprosy? But consider now, and see how he is seeking a quarrel against me."

⁸ It happened when Elisha the man of God heard that the king of Israel had torn his clothes, that he sent *word* to the king, saying, "Why have you torn your clothes? Now let him come to me, and he shall know that there is a prophet in Israel." ⁹ So Naaman came with his horses and his chariots and stood at the doorway of the house of Elisha. ¹⁰ Elisha sent a messenger to him, saying, "Go and wash in the Jordan seven times, and your flesh will be restored to you and *you will* be clean." ¹¹ But Naaman was furious and went away and said, "Behold, I thought, 'He will surely come out to me and stand and call on the name of the LORD his God, and wave his hand over the place and cure the leper.' ¹² Are not Abanah and Pharpar, the rivers of Damascus, better than all the waters of Israel? Could I not wash in them and be clean?" So he turned and went away in a rage. ¹³ Then his servants came near and spoke to him and said, "My father, had the prophet told you *to do some* great thing, would you not have done *it?* How much more *then,* when he says to you, 'Wash, and be clean'?" ¹⁴ So he went down and dipped *himself* seven times in the Jordan, according to the word of the man of God; and his flesh was restored like the flesh of a little child and he was clean.

¹⁵When he returned to the man of God with all his company, and came and stood before him, he said, "Behold now, I know that there is no God in all the earth, but in Israel; so please take a present from your servant now." ¹⁶But he said, "As the LORD lives, before whom I stand, I will take nothing." And he urged him to take *it*, but he refused. ¹⁷Naaman said, "If not, please let your servant at least be given two mules' load of earth; for your servant will no longer offer burnt offering nor will he sacrifice to other gods, but to the LORD.

5:17 two mules' load of earth. In the ancient Near East it was thought that a god could be worshiped only on the soil of the nation to which he was bound. Therefore, Naaman wanted a load of Israelite soil on which to make burnt offerings and sacrifices to the Lord when he returned to Damascus. This request confirmed how Naaman had changed—whereas he had previously disparaged Israel's river, now he wanted to take a pile of Israel's soil to Damascus.

¹⁸In this matter may the LORD pardon your servant: when my master goes into the house of Rimmon to worship there, and he leans on my hand and I bow myself in the house of Rimmon, when I bow myself in the house of Rimmon, the LORD pardon your servant in this matter." ¹⁹He said to him, "Go in peace." So he departed from him some distance.

²⁰But Gehazi, the servant of Elisha the man of God, thought, "Behold, my master has spared this Naaman the Aramean, by not receiving from his hands what he brought. As the LORD lives, I will run after him and take something from him." ²¹So Gehazi pursued Naaman. When Naaman saw one running after him, he came down from the chariot to meet him and said, "Is all well?" ²²He said, "All is well. My master has sent me, saying, 'Behold, just now two young men of the sons of the prophets have come to me from the hill country of Ephraim. Please give them a talent of silver and two changes of clothes.'" ²³Naaman said, "Be pleased to take two talents." And he urged him, and bound two talents of silver in two bags with two changes of clothes and gave them to two of his servants; and they carried *them* before him. ²⁴When he came to the hill, he took them from their hand and deposited them in the house, and he sent the men away, and they departed. ²⁵But he went in and stood before his master. And Elisha said to him, "Where have you been, Gehazi?" And he said, "Your servant went nowhere."

²⁶Then he said to him, "Did not my heart go *with you*, when the man turned from his chariot to meet you? Is it a time to receive money and to receive clothes and olive groves and vineyards and sheep and oxen and male and female servants? ²⁷Therefore, the leprosy of Naaman shall cling to you and to your descendants forever." So he went out from his presence a leper *as white* as snow.

5:27 leprosy...shall cling to you. Gehazi's greed had cast a shadow over the integrity of Elisha's prophetic office. This made him no better in the people's thinking than Israel's false prophets, who prophesied for material gain, the very thing he wanted to avoid (vv. 15–16). Gehazi's act betrayed a lack of faith in the Lord's ability to provide. As a result, Elisha condemned Gehazi and his descendants to suffer Naaman's skin disease forever. The punishment was a twist for Gehazi, who had gone to "take something" from Naaman (v. 20), but what he received was Naaman's disease.

6 Now the sons of the prophets said to Elisha, "Behold now, the place before you where we are living is too limited for us. ²Please let us go to the Jordan and each of us take from there a beam, and let us make a place there for ourselves where we may live." So he said, "Go." ³Then one said, "Please be willing to go with your servants." And he answered, "I shall go." ⁴So he went with them; and when they came to the Jordan, they cut down trees. ⁵But as one was felling a beam, the axe head fell into the water; and he cried out and said, "Alas, my master! For it was borrowed." ⁶Then the man of God said, "Where did it fall?" And when he showed him the place, he cut off a stick and threw *it* in there, and made the iron float. ⁷He said, "Take it

6:5 axe head...borrowed. Iron was expensive and relatively rare in Israel at that time and the student-prophet was very poor. The axe head was loaned to the prophet since he could not have afforded it on his own and would have had no means to reimburse the owner for it.

up for yourself." So he put out his hand and took it.

⁸ Now the king of Aram was warring against Israel; and he counseled with his servants saying, "In such and such a place shall be my camp." ⁹ The man of God sent *word* to the king of Israel saying, "Beware that you do not pass this place, for the Arameans are coming down there." ¹⁰ The king of Israel sent to the place about which the man of God had told him; thus he warned him, so that he guarded himself there, more than once or twice.

¹¹ Now the heart of the king of Aram was enraged over this thing; and he called his servants and said to them, "Will you tell me which of us is for the king of Israel?" ¹² One of his servants said, "No, my lord, O king; but Elisha, the prophet who is in Israel, tells the king of Israel the words that you speak in your bedroom." ¹³ So he said, "Go and see where he is, that I may send and take him." And it was told him, saying, "Behold, he is in Dothan." ¹⁴ He sent horses and chariots and a great army there, and they came by night and surrounded the city.

¹⁵ Now when the attendant of the man of God had risen early and gone out, behold, an army with horses and chariots was circling the city. And his servant said to him, "Alas, my master! What shall we do?" ¹⁶ So he answered, "Do not fear, for those who are with us are more than those who are with them." ¹⁷ Then Elisha prayed and said, "O LORD, I pray, open his eyes that he may see." And the LORD opened the servant's eyes and he saw; and behold, the mountain was full of horses and chariots of fire all around Elisha. ¹⁸ When they came down to him, Elisha prayed to the LORD and said, "Strike this people with blindness, I pray." So He struck them with blindness according to the word of Elisha. ¹⁹ Then Elisha said to them, "This is not the way, nor is this the city; follow me and I will bring you to the man whom you seek." And he brought them to Samaria.

²⁰ When they had come into Samaria, Elisha said, "O LORD, open the eyes of these *men*, that they may see." So the LORD opened their eyes and they saw; and behold, they were in the midst of Samaria. ²¹ Then the king of Israel when he saw them, said to Elisha, "My father, shall I kill them? Shall I kill them?" ²² He answered, "You shall not kill *them*. Would you kill those you have taken captive with your sword and with your bow? Set bread and water before them, that they may eat and drink and go to their master." ²³ So he prepared a great feast for them; and when they had eaten and drunk he

sent them away, and they went to their master. And the marauding bands of Arameans did not come again into the land of Israel.

²⁴ Now it came about after this, that Benhadad king of Aram gathered all his army and went up and besieged Samaria. ²⁵ There was a great famine in Samaria; and behold, they besieged it, until a donkey's head was sold for eighty *shekels* of silver, and a fourth of a kab of dove's dung for five *shekels* of silver. ²⁶ As the king of Israel was passing by on the wall a woman cried out to him, saying, "Help, my lord, O king!" ²⁷ He said, "If the LORD does not help you, from where shall I help you? From the threshing floor, or from the wine press?" ²⁸ And the king said to her, "What is the matter with you?" And she answered, "This woman said to me, 'Give your son that we may eat him today, and we will eat my son tomorrow.' ²⁹ So we boiled my son and ate him; and I said to her on the next day, 'Give your son, that we may eat him'; but she has hidden her son." ³⁰ When the king heard the words of the woman, he tore his clothes—now he was passing by on the wall—and the people looked, and behold, he had sackcloth beneath on his body. ³¹ Then he said, "May God do so to me and more also, if the head of Elisha the son of Shaphat remains on him today."

³² Now Elisha was sitting in his house, and the elders were sitting with him. And *the king* sent a man from his presence; but before the messenger came to him, he said to the elders, "Do you see how this son of a murderer has sent to take away my head? Look, when the messenger comes, shut the door and hold the door shut against him. Is not the sound of his master's feet behind him?" ³³ While he was still talking with them, behold, the messenger came down to him and he said, "Behold, this evil is from the LORD; why should I wait for the LORD any longer?"

Psalm 72:1–7

A Psalm of Solomon.

Give the king Your judgments, O God,
And Your righteousness
    to the king's son.
2   May he judge Your people
        with righteousness
    And Your afflicted with justice.
3   Let the mountains bring
        peace to the people,
    And the hills, in righteousness.
4   May he vindicate the afflicted
        of the people,
    Save the children of the needy
    And crush the oppressor.

⁵ Let them fear You while
  the sun *endures,*
  And as long as the moon,
  throughout all generations.
⁶ May he come down like rain
  upon the mown grass,
  Like showers that water the earth.
⁷ In his days may the
  righteous flourish,
  And abundance of peace till
  the moon is no more.

Proverbs 18:10–11

¹⁰ The name of the LORD is
  a strong tower;
  The righteous runs into it and is safe.
¹¹ A rich man's wealth is his strong city,
  And like a high wall in his
  own imagination.

John 18:1–18

18 When Jesus had spoken these words, He went forth with His disciples over the ravine of the Kidron, where there was a garden, in which He entered with His disciples. ² Now Judas also, who was betraying Him, knew the place, for Jesus had often met there with His disciples. ³ Judas then, having received the *Roman* cohort and officers from the chief priests and the Pharisees, *came there with lanterns and torches and weapons. ⁴ So Jesus, knowing all the things that were coming upon Him, went forth and *said to them, "Whom do you seek?" ⁵ They answered Him, "Jesus the Nazarene." He *said to them, "I am *He.*" And Judas also, who was betraying Him, was standing with them. ⁶ So when He said to them, "I am *He,*" they drew back and fell to the ground. ⁷ Therefore He again asked them, "Whom do you seek?" And they said,

"Jesus the Nazarene." ⁸ Jesus answered, "I told you that I am *He;* so if you seek Me, let these go their way," ⁹ to fulfill the word which He spoke, "Of those whom You have given Me I lost not one." ¹⁰ Simon Peter then, having a sword, drew it and struck the high priest's slave, and cut off his right ear; and the slave's name was Malchus. ¹¹ So Jesus said to Peter, "Put the sword into the sheath; the cup which the Father has given Me, shall I not drink it?"

¹² So the *Roman* cohort and the commander and the officers of the Jews, arrested Jesus and bound Him, ¹³ and led Him to Annas first; for he was father-in-law of Caiaphas, who was high priest that year. ¹⁴ Now Caiaphas was the one who had advised the Jews that it was expedient for one man to die on behalf of the people.

¹⁵ Simon Peter was following Jesus, and *so was* another disciple. Now that disciple was known to the high priest, and entered with Jesus into the court of the high priest, ¹⁶ but Peter was standing at the door outside. So the other disciple, who was known to the high priest, went out and spoke to the doorkeeper, and brought Peter in. ¹⁷ Then the slave-girl who kept the door *said to Peter, "You are not also *one* of this man's disciples, are you?" He *said, "I am not." ¹⁸ Now the slaves and the officers were standing *there,* having made a charcoal fire, for it was cold and they were warming themselves; and Peter was also with them, standing and warming himself.

18:4–8 Whom do you seek? By twice asking that question (vv. 4, 7), to which they replied, "Jesus the Nazarene" (vv. 5, 7), Jesus was forcing them to acknowledge that they had no authority to take His disciples. In fact, He demanded that they let the disciples go (v. 8). The force of His demand was established by the power of His words. When He spoke, "I am *He*" (v. 6), a designation He had used before to declare Himself God (8:28, 58; see 6:35; 8:12; 10:7, 9, 11, 14; 11:25; 14:6; 15:1, 5), they were jolted backward and to the ground (v. 6). This power display and the authoritative demand not to take the disciples were of immense significance, as the next verse indicates.

18:13 Annas first. Annas held the High Priesthood office from A.D. 6–15 when Valerius Gratus, Pilate's predecessor, removed him from office. In spite of this, Annas continued to wield influence over the office, most likely because he was still regarded as the true High Priest and also because no fewer than 5 of his sons, and his son-in-law Caiaphas, held the office at one time or another. Two trials occurred: one Jewish and one Roman. The Jewish phase began with the informal examination by Annas (vv. 12–14, 19–23), probably giving time for the members of the Sanhedrin to hurriedly gather together. A session before the Sanhedrin was next (Mt 26:57–68) at which consensus was reached to send Jesus to Pilate (Mt 27:1–2). The Roman phase began with a first examination before Pilate (vv. 28–38a; Mt 27:11–14), and then Herod Antipas ("that fox"—Lk 13:32) interrogated Him (Lk 23:6–12). Lastly, Jesus appeared again before Pilate (vv. 38b—19:16; Mt 27:15–31).

In 2 Kings 5:1, four phrases describe the importance of Naaman: 1) he was the supreme commander of the army of Syria as indicated by the term "captain," used of an army's highest ranking officer (Ge 21:22; 1Sa 12:9; 1Ch 27:34); 2) he was a great man, a man of high social standing and prominence; 3) he was an honorable man in the eyes of his master, a man highly regarded by the king of Syria because of the military victories he had won; and 4) he was a mighty man of valor, a term used in the Old Testament for both a man of great wealth (Ru 2:1) and a courageous warrior (Jdg 6:12; 11:1). Severely mitigating against all of this was the fact that he suffered from leprosy, a serious skin disease (v. 27). Naaman's military success was attributable to the God of Israel, who is sovereign over all the nations (Is. 10:13; Am 9:7).

Because of his personal greatness (v. 1), his huge gift of ten talents of silver, six thousand *shekels* of gold (about 750 pounds of silver and 150 pounds of gold in v. 5), and diplomatic letter (v. 6), Naaman expected that Elisha would "surely come out to me" (v. 11). He expected personal attention to his need. However, Elisha did not even go out to meet him. Instead, he sent his instructions for healing through a messenger (v. 10). Naaman was angry because he anticipated a personal cleansing ceremony from the prophet himself. Besides, if Naaman needed to wash in a river, two Syrian rivers were superior to the muddy Jordan. However, it was obedience to God's word that was the issue, not the quality of the water.

Fortunately, Naaman had a servant who pointed out to him that he had been willing to do anything, no matter how hard, to be cured. He should be even more willing, therefore, to do something as easy as washing in a muddy river. Naaman's healing restored his flesh to that "of a little child" (v. 14). Upon his healing, Naaman returned from the Jordan River to Elisha's house in Samaria to give confession of his new belief: "there is no God…but in Israel" (v. 15).

JUNE 10

2 Kings 7:1–8:29

7 Then Elisha said, "Listen to the word of the LORD; thus says the LORD, 'Tomorrow about this time a measure of fine flour will be *sold* for a shekel, and two measures of barley for a shekel, in the gate of Samaria.'" ² The royal officer on whose hand the king was leaning answered the man of God and said, "Behold, if the LORD should make windows in heaven, could this thing be?" Then he said, "Behold, you will see it with your own eyes, but you will not eat of it."

³ Now there were four leprous men at the entrance of the gate; and they said to one another, "Why do we sit here until we die? ⁴ If we say, 'We will enter the city,' then the famine is in the city and we will die there; and if we sit here, we die also. Now therefore come, and let us go over to the camp of the Arameans. If they spare us, we will live; and if they kill us, we will but die." ⁵ They arose at twilight to go to the camp of the Arameans; when they came to the outskirts of the camp of the Arameans, behold, there was no one there. ⁶ For the Lord had caused the army of the Arameans to hear a sound of chariots and a sound of horses, *even* the sound of a great army, so that they said to one another, "Behold, the king of Israel has hired against us the kings of the Hittites and the kings of the

7:6 the Hittites and…Egyptians. Sometime before the arrival of the lepers, the Lord had made the Syrians hear the terrifying sound of a huge army approaching. They thought the Israelite king had hired two massive foreign armies to attack them. The Hittites were descendants of the once-great Hittite empire who lived in small groups across northern Syria (1Ki 10:29). Egypt was in decline at this time, but its army would still have represented a great danger to the Syrians.

Egyptians, to come upon us." ⁷ Therefore they arose and fled in the twilight, and left their tents and their horses and their donkeys, *even* the camp just as it was, and fled for their life. ⁸ When these lepers came to the outskirts of the camp, they entered one tent and ate and drank, and carried from there silver and gold and clothes, and went and hid *them;* and they returned and entered another tent and carried from there *also,* and went and hid *them.*

⁹ Then they said to one another, "We are not doing right. This day is a day of good news, but we are keeping silent; if we wait until morning light, punishment will overtake us. Now therefore come, let us go and tell the king's household." ¹⁰ So they came and called to the gatekeepers of the city, and they told them, saying, "We came to the camp of the Arameans, and behold, there was no one

there, nor the voice of man, only the horses tied and the donkeys tied, and the tents just as they were." ¹¹The gatekeepers called and told *it* within the king's household. ¹²Then the king arose in the night and said to his servants, "I will now tell you what the Arameans have done to us. They know that we are hungry; therefore they have gone from the camp to hide themselves in the field, saying, 'When they come out of the city, we will capture them alive and get into the city.' " ¹³One of his servants said, "Please, let some *men* take five of the horses which remain, which are left in the city. Behold, they *will be in any case* like all the multitude of Israel who are left in it; behold, they *will be in any case* like all the multitude of Israel who have already perished, so let us send and see." ¹⁴They took therefore two chariots with horses, and the king sent after the army of the Arameans, saying, "Go and see." ¹⁵They went after them to the Jordan, and behold, all the way was full of clothes and equipment which the Arameans had thrown away in their haste. Then the messengers returned and told the king.

¹⁶So the people went out and plundered the camp of the Arameans. Then a measure of fine flour *was sold* for a shekel and two measures of barley for a shekel, according to the word of the LORD. ¹⁷Now the king appointed the royal officer on whose hand he leaned to have charge of the gate; but the people trampled on him at the gate, and he died just as the man of God had said, who spoke when the king came down to him. ¹⁸It happened just as the man of God had spoken to the king, saying, "Two measures of barley for a shekel and a measure of fine flour for a shekel, will be *sold* tomorrow about this time at the gate of Samaria." ¹⁹Then the royal officer answered the man of God and said, "Now behold, if the LORD should make windows in heaven, could such a thing be?" And he said, "Behold, you will see it with your own eyes, but you will not eat of it." ²⁰And so it happened to him, for the people trampled on him at the gate and he died.

8 Now Elisha spoke to the woman whose son he had restored to life, saying, "Arise and go with your household, and sojourn wherever you can sojourn; for the LORD has called for a famine, and it will even come on the land for seven years." ²So the woman arose and did according to the word of the man of God, and she went with her household and sojourned in the land of the Philistines seven years. ³At the end of seven years, the woman returned from the land of the Phi-

listines; and she went out to appeal to the king for her house and for her field. ⁴Now the king was talking with Gehazi, the servant of the man of God, saying, "Please relate to me all the great things that Elisha has done." ⁵As he was relating to the king how he had restored to life the one who was dead, behold, the woman whose son he had restored to life appealed to the king for her house and for her field. And Gehazi said, "My lord, O king, this is the woman and this is her son, whom Elisha restored to life." ⁶When the king asked the woman, she related *it* to him. So the king appointed for her a certain officer, saying, "Restore all that was hers and all the produce of the field from the day that she left the land even until now."

⁷Then Elisha came to Damascus. Now Ben-hadad king of Aram was sick, and it was told him, saying, "The man of God has come here." ⁸The king said to Hazael, "Take a gift in your hand and go to meet the man of God, and inquire of the LORD by him, saying, 'Will I recover from this sickness?' " ⁹So Hazael went to meet him and took a gift in his hand, even every kind of good thing of Damascus, forty camels' loads; and he came and stood before him and said, "Your son Ben-hadad king of Aram has sent me to you, saying, 'Will I recover from this sickness?' " ¹⁰Then Elisha said to him, "Go, say to him, 'You will surely recover,' but the LORD has shown me that he will certainly die." ¹¹He fixed his gaze steadily *on him* until he was ashamed, and the man of God wept. ¹²Hazael said, "Why does my lord weep?" Then he answered, "Because I know the evil that you will do to the sons of Israel: their strongholds you will set on fire, and their young men you will kill with the sword, and their little ones you will dash in pieces,

---

8:10 recover…die. Ben-hadad wanted to know whether or not he would recover from his present illness. In response, Elisha affirmed two interrelated things: 1) Ben-hadad would be restored to health; his present sickness would not be the means of his death. 2) Ben-hadad would surely die by some other means.

8:11 he was ashamed. With a fixed gaze, Elisha stared at Hazael because it had been revealed to him what Hazael would do, including the murder of Ben-hadad (v. 15). Hazael was embarrassed, knowing that Elisha knew of his plan to assassinate the Syrian king.

and their women with child you will rip up."
¹³ Then Hazael said, "But what is your servant, *who is but* a dog, that he should do this great thing?" And Elisha answered, "The LORD has shown me that you will be king over Aram." ¹⁴ So he departed from Elisha and returned to his master, who said to him, "What did Elisha say to you?" And he answered, "He told me that you would surely recover." ¹⁵ On the following day, he took the cover and dipped it in water and spread it on his face, so that he died. And Hazael became king in his place.

¹⁶ Now in the fifth year of Joram the son of Ahab king of Israel, Jehoshaphat being then the king of Judah, Jehoram the son of Jehoshaphat king of Judah became king. ¹⁷ He was thirty-two years old when he became king, and he reigned eight years in Jerusalem. ¹⁸ He walked in the way of the kings of Israel, just as the house of Ahab had done, for the daughter of Ahab became his wife; and he did evil in the sight of the LORD. ¹⁹ However, the LORD was not willing to destroy Judah, for the sake of David His servant, since He had promised him to give a lamp to him through his sons always.

²⁰ In his days Edom revolted from under the hand of Judah, and made a king over themselves. ²¹ Then Joram crossed over to Zair, and all his chariots with him. And he arose by night and struck the Edomites who had surrounded him and the captains of the chariots; but *his* army fled to their tents. ²² So Edom revolted against Judah to this day. Then Libnah revolted at the same time. ²³ The rest of the acts of Joram and all that he did, are they not written in the Book of the Chronicles of the Kings of Judah? ²⁴ So Joram slept with his fathers and was buried with his fathers in the city of David; and Ahaziah his son became king in his place.

²⁵ In the twelfth year of Joram the son of Ahab king of Israel, Ahaziah the son of Jehoram king of Judah began to reign. ²⁶ Ahaziah *was* twenty-two years old when he became king, and he reigned one year in Jerusalem. And his mother's name *was* Athaliah the granddaughter of Omri king of Israel. ²⁷ He walked in the way of the house of Ahab and did evil in the sight of the LORD, like the house of Ahab *had done,* because he was a son-in-law of the house of Ahab.

²⁸ Then he went with Joram the son of Ahab to war against Hazael king of Aram at Ramoth-gilead, and the Arameans wounded Joram. ²⁹ So King Joram returned to be healed in Jezreel of the wounds which the Arameans had inflicted on him at Ramah when he fought against Hazael king of Aram. Then Ahaziah the son of Jehoram king of Judah went down to see Joram the son of Ahab in Jezreel because he was sick.

Psalm 72:8-16

⁸ May he also rule from sea to sea
And from the River to the
ends of the earth.
⁹ Let the nomads of the desert
bow before him,
And his enemies lick the dust.
¹⁰ Let the kings of Tarshish and of
the islands bring presents;
The kings of Sheba and
Seba offer gifts.

72:10 Tarshish...Seba. Countries near and far which brought tribute to Solomon (1Ki 4:21; 10:1, 23–24; Is 60:4–7; Jer 6:20). Tarshish is probably in Spain; Sheba, a kingdom in southern Arabia (modern Yemen); and Seba, a North African nation.

¹¹ And let all kings bow
down before him,
All nations serve him.

¹² For he will deliver the needy
when he cries for help,
The afflicted also, and him
who has no helper.
¹³ He will have compassion on
the poor and needy,
And the lives of the needy
he will save.
¹⁴ He will rescue their life from
oppression and violence,
And their blood will be
precious in his sight;
¹⁵ So may he live, and may the
gold of Sheba be given
to him;
And let them pray for
him continually;
Let them bless him all day long.

¹⁶ May there be abundance of
grain in the earth on top
of the mountains;
Its fruit will wave like *the
cedars of* Lebanon;
And may those from the city
flourish like vegetation
of the earth.

Proverbs 18:12-13

¹² Before destruction the heart
of man is haughty,
But humility *goes* before honor.
¹³ He who gives an answer
before he hears,
It is folly and shame to him.

John 18:19-40

¹⁹ The high priest then questioned Jesus about His disciples, and about His teaching. ²⁰ Jesus answered him, "I have spoken openly to the world; I always taught in synagogues and in the temple, where all the Jews come together; and I spoke nothing in secret. ²¹ Why do you question Me? Question those who have heard what I spoke to them; they know what I said." ²² When He had said this, one of the officers standing nearby struck Jesus, saying, "Is that the way You answer the high priest?" ²³ Jesus answered him, "If I have spoken wrongly, testify of the wrong; but if rightly, why do you strike Me?" ²⁴ So Annas sent Him bound to Caiaphas the high priest.

²⁵ Now Simon Peter was standing and warming himself. So they said to him, "You are not also *one* of His disciples, are you?" He denied *it,* and said, "I am not." ²⁶ One of the slaves of the high priest, being a relative of the one whose ear Peter cut off, *said, "Did I not see you in the garden with Him?" ²⁷ Peter then denied *it* again, and immediately a rooster crowed.

²⁸ Then they *led Jesus from Caiaphas into the Praetorium, and it was early; and they themselves did not enter into the Praetorium so that they would not be defiled, but might eat the Passover. ²⁹ Therefore Pilate went out to them and *said, "What accusation do you bring against this Man?" ³⁰ They answered and said to him, "If this Man were not an evildoer, we would not have delivered Him to you." ³¹ So Pilate said to them, "Take Him yourselves, and judge Him according to your law." The Jews said to him, "We are not permitted to put anyone to death," ³² to fulfill the word of Jesus which He spoke, signifying by what kind of death He was about to die.

³³ Therefore Pilate entered again into the Praetorium, and summoned Jesus and said to Him, "Are You the King of the Jews?" ³⁴ Jesus answered, "Are you saying this on your own initiative, or did others tell you about Me?" ³⁵ Pilate answered, "I am not a Jew, am I? Your own nation and the chief priests delivered You to me; what have You done?" ³⁶ Jesus answered, "My kingdom is not of this world. If My kingdom were of this world, then My servants would be fighting so that I would not be handed over to the Jews; but as it is, My kingdom is not of this realm." ³⁷ Therefore Pilate said to Him, "So You are a king?" Jesus answered, "You say *correctly* that I am a king. For this I have been born, and for this I have come into the world, to testify to the truth. Everyone who is of the truth hears My voice." ³⁸ Pilate *said to Him, "What is truth?"

And when he had said this, he went out again to the Jews and *said to them, "I find no guilt in Him. ³⁹ But you have a custom that I release someone for you at the Passover; do you wish then that I release for you the King of the Jews?" ⁴⁰ So they cried out again, saying, "Not this Man, but Barabbas." Now Barabbas was a robber.

18:36 My kingdom is not of this realm. By this phrase, Jesus meant that His kingdom is not connected to earthly political and national entities, nor does it have its origin in the evil world system that is in rebellion against God. If His kingdom was of this world, He would have fought. The kingships of this world preserve themselves by fighting with force. Messiah's kingdom does not originate in the efforts of man, but with the Son of Man forcefully and decisively conquering sin in the lives of His people and someday conquering the evil world system at His second coming when He establishes the earthly form of His kingdom. His kingdom was no threat to the national identity of Israel or the political and military identity of Rome. It exists in the spiritual dimension until the end of the age (Rev 11:15).

DAY 10: Why was the trial of Jesus conducted by the Romans rather than the Sanhedrin?

Jesus was led from the trial before Caiaphas to the Praetorium in John 18:28. This was the headquarters of the commanding officer of the Roman military camp or the headquarters of the Roman military governor (i.e., Pilate). Pilate's normal headquarters was in Caesarea, in the palace that Herod the Great had built for himself. However, Pilate and his predecessors made it a point to be in Jerusalem during the feasts in order to quell any riots. Jerusalem became his *praetorium* or headquarters. It was "early" morning. The word is ambiguous. Most likely, it refers to around 6:00 a.m. since many Roman officials began their day very early and finished by 10:00 or 11:00 a.m. Those who brought Jesus did not go into the Praetorium "so that they would not be defiled." Jewish oral law gives evidence that a Jew who entered the dwelling places of Gentiles became ceremonially unclean. Their remaining outside in the colonnade avoided that pollution. John loads this statement with great irony by noting the chief priests' scrupulousness in the matter of ceremonial cleansing, when all the time they were incurring incomparably greater moral defilement by their proceedings against Jesus.

"What accusation . . . ?" (v. 29). This question formally opened the Roman civil phase of proceedings against Jesus. The fact that Roman troops were used at the arrest proves that the Jewish authorities communicated something about this case to Pilate in advance. Although they most likely had expected Pilate to confirm their judgment against Jesus and order His death sentence, Pilate ordered instead a fresh hearing in His presence.

When Pilate told them to take Jesus back and try Him themselves, the Jews objected on the basis that "We are not permitted to put anyone to death" (v. 31). When Rome took over Judea and began direct rule through a prefect in A.D. 6, capital jurisdiction (i.e., the right to execute) was taken away from the Jews and given to the Roman governor. Capital punishment was the most jealously guarded of all the attributes in Roman provincial administration.

By a Roman crucifixion, it also fulfilled "the word of Jesus" (v. 32) that He would die by being lifted up (3:14; 8:28; 12:32–33). If the Jews had executed Him, it would have been by throwing Him down and stoning Him. But God providentially controlled all the political procedures to assure that, when sentence was finally passed, He would be crucified by the Romans and not stoned by the Jews, as was Stephen (Ac 7:59).

JUNE 11

2 Kings 9:1–10:36

9 Now Elisha the prophet called one of the sons of the prophets and said to him, "Gird up your loins, and take this flask of oil in your hand and go to Ramoth-gilead. ² When you arrive there, search out Jehu the son of Jehoshaphat the son of Nimshi, and go in and bid him arise from among his brothers, and bring him to an inner room. ³ Then take the flask of oil and pour it on his head and say, 'Thus says the LORD, "I have anointed you king over Israel."' Then open the door and flee and do not wait."

⁴ So the young man, the servant of the prophet, went to Ramoth-gilead. ⁵ When he came, behold, the captains of the army were sitting, and he said, "I have a word for you, O captain." And Jehu said, "For which one of

9:2 Jehu. The Lord had previously told Elijah that Jehu would become king over Israel and kill those involved in the worship of Baal (1Ki 19:17). The fulfillment of the prophecy is recorded from 9:1—10:31. **inner room.** A private room that could be closed off to the public. Elisha commissioned one of the younger prophets to anoint Jehu alone behind closed doors. The rite was to be a secret affair without Elisha present so that Jehoram would not suspect that a coup was coming.

9:3 anointed you king over Israel. The anointing with olive oil by a prophet of the Lord confirmed that God Himself had earlier chosen that man to be king (1Sa 10:1; 16:13). This action of anointing by a commissioned prophet indicated divine investiture with God's sovereign power to Jehu. **flee and do not wait.** The need for haste by the young prophet underscored the danger of the assignment. A prophet in the midst of Israel's army camp would alert the pro-Jehoram elements to the possibility of the coup.

us?" And he said, "For you, O captain." ⁶ He arose and went into the house, and he poured the oil on his head and said to him, "Thus says the LORD, the God of Israel, 'I have anointed you king over the people of the LORD, even over Israel. ⁷ You shall strike the house of Ahab your master, that I may avenge the blood of My servants the prophets, and the blood of all the servants of the LORD, at the hand of Jezebel. ⁸ For the whole house of Ahab shall perish, and I will cut off from Ahab every male person both bond and free in Israel. ⁹ I will make the house of Ahab like the house of Jeroboam the son of Nebat, and like the house of Baasha the son of Ahijah. ¹⁰ The dogs shall eat Jezebel in the territory of Jezreel, and none shall bury her.'" Then he opened the door and fled.

¹¹ Now Jehu came out to the servants of his master, and one said to him, "Is all well? Why did this mad fellow come to you?" And

he said to them, "You know *very well* the man and his talk." ¹²They said, "It is a lie, tell us now." And he said, "Thus and thus he said to me, 'Thus says the LORD, "I have anointed you king over Israel." ' " ¹³Then they hurried and each man took his garment and placed it under him on the bare steps, and blew the trumpet, saying, "Jehu is king!"

¹⁴So Jehu the son of Jehoshaphat the son of Nimshi conspired against Joram. Now Joram with all Israel was defending Ramoth-gilead against Hazael king of Aram, ¹⁵but King Joram had returned to Jezreel to be healed of the wounds which the Arameans had inflicted on him when he fought with Hazael king of Aram. So Jehu said, "If this is your mind, *then* let no one escape *or* leave the city to go tell *it* in Jezreel." ¹⁶Then Jehu rode in a chariot and went to Jezreel, for Joram was lying there. Ahaziah king of Judah had come down to see Joram.

¹⁷Now the watchman was standing on the tower in Jezreel and he saw the company of Jehu as he came, and said, "I see a company." And Joram said, "Take a horseman and send him to meet them and let him say, 'Is it peace?' " ¹⁸So a horseman went to meet him and said, "Thus says the king, 'Is it peace?' " And Jehu said, "What have you to do with peace? Turn behind me." And the watchman reported, "The messenger came to them, but he did not return." ¹⁹Then he sent out a second horseman, who came to them and said, "Thus says the king, 'Is it peace?' " And Jehu answered, "What have you to do with peace? Turn behind me." ²⁰The watchman reported, "He came even to them, and he did not return; and the driving is like the driving of Jehu the son of Nimshi, for he drives furiously."

²¹Then Joram said, "Get ready." And they made his chariot ready. Joram king of Israel and Ahaziah king of Judah went out, each in his chariot, and they went out to meet Jehu and found him in the property of Naboth the Jezreelite. ²²When Joram saw Jehu, he said, "Is it peace, Jehu?" And he answered, "What peace, so long as the harlotries of your mother Jezebel and her witchcrafts are so many?" ²³So Joram reined about and fled and said to Ahaziah, "*There is* treachery, O Ahaziah!" ²⁴And Jehu drew his bow with his full strength and shot Joram between his arms; and the arrow went through his heart and he sank in his chariot. ²⁵Then *Jehu* said to Bidkar his officer, "Take *him* up and cast him into the property of the field of Naboth the Jezreelite, for I remember when you and I were riding together after Ahab his father,

that the LORD laid this oracle against him: ²⁶'Surely I have seen yesterday the blood of Naboth and the blood of his sons,' says the LORD, 'and I will repay you in this property,' says the LORD. Now then, take and cast him into the property, according to the word of the LORD."

²⁷When Ahaziah the king of Judah saw *this,* he fled by the way of the garden house. And Jehu pursued him and said, "Shoot him too, in the chariot." *So they shot him* at the ascent of Gur, which is at Ibleam. But he fled to Megiddo and died there. ²⁸Then his servants carried him in a chariot to Jerusalem and buried him in his grave with his fathers in the city of David.

²⁹Now in the eleventh year of Joram, the son of Ahab, Ahaziah became king over Judah.

³⁰When Jehu came to Jezreel, Jezebel heard *of it,* and she painted her eyes and adorned her head and looked out the window. ³¹As Jehu

9:30 painted her eyes. The painting of the eyelids with a black powder mixed with oil and applied with a brush darkened them to give an enlarged effect. Jezebel's appearance at the window gave the air of a royal audience to awe Jehu.

entered the gate, she said, "Is it well, Zimri, your master's murderer?" ³²Then he lifted up his face to the window and said, "Who is on my side? Who?" And two or three officials looked down at him. ³³He said, "Throw her down." So they threw her down, and some of her blood was sprinkled on the wall and on the horses, and he trampled her under foot. ³⁴When he came in, he ate and drank; and he said, "See now to this cursed woman and bury her, for she is a king's daughter." ³⁵They went to bury her, but they found nothing more of her than the skull and the feet and the palms of her hands. ³⁶Therefore they returned and told him. And he said, "This is the word of the LORD, which He spoke by His servant Elijah the Tishbite, saying, 'In the property of Jezreel the dogs shall eat the flesh of Jezebel; ³⁷and the corpse of Jezebel will be as dung on the face of the field in the property of Jezreel, so they cannot say, "This is Jezebel." ' "

10 Now Ahab had seventy sons in Samaria. And Jehu wrote letters and sent *them* to Samaria, to the rulers of Jezreel, the elders, and to the guardians of *the children of* Ahab, saying, ²"Now, when this letter comes to you, since your master's sons are with you, as well as the chariots and horses and a fortified city and the weapons, ³ select the best and fittest of your master's sons, and set *him* on his father's throne, and fight for your master's house." ⁴ But they feared greatly and said, "Behold, the two kings did not stand before him; how then can we stand?" ⁵ And the one who *was* over the household, and he who *was* over the city, the elders, and the guardians of *the children,* sent *word* to Jehu, saying, "We are your servants, all that you say to us we will do, we will not make any man king; do what is good in your sight." ⁶ Then he wrote a letter to them a second time saying, "If you are on my side, and you will listen to my voice, take the heads of the men, your master's sons, and come to me at Jezreel tomorrow about this time." Now the king's sons, seventy persons, *were* with the great men of the city, *who* were rearing them. ⁷ When the letter came to them, they took the king's sons and slaughtered *them,* seventy persons, and put their heads in baskets, and sent *them* to him at Jezreel. ⁸ When the messenger came and told him, saying, "They have brought the heads of the king's sons," he said, "Put them in two heaps at the entrance of the gate until morning." ⁹ Now in the morning he went out and stood and said to all the people, "You are innocent; behold, I conspired against my master and killed him, but who killed all these? ¹⁰ Know then that there shall fall to the earth nothing of the word of the LORD, which the LORD spoke concerning the house of Ahab, for the LORD has done what He spoke through His servant Elijah." ¹¹ So Jehu killed all who remained of the house of Ahab in Jezreel, and all his great men and his acquaintances and his priests, until he left him without a survivor.

¹² Then he arose and departed and went to Samaria. On the way while he was at Beth-eked of the shepherds, ¹³ Jehu met the relatives of Ahaziah king of Judah and said, "Who are you?" And they answered, "We are the relatives of Ahaziah; and we have come down to greet the sons of the king and the sons of the queen mother." ¹⁴ He said, "Take them alive." So they took them alive and killed them at the pit of Beth-eked, forty-two men; and he left none of them.

¹⁵ Now when he had departed from there, he met Jehonadab the son of Rechab *coming* to meet him; and he greeted him and said to him, "Is your heart right, as my heart is with your heart?" And Jehonadab answered, "It is." *Jehu said,* "If it is, give *me* your hand." And he gave him his hand, and he took him

up to him into the chariot. ¹⁶ He said, "Come with me and see my zeal for the LORD." So he made him ride in his chariot. ¹⁷ When he came to Samaria, he killed all who remained to Ahab in Samaria, until he had destroyed him, according to the word of the LORD which He spoke to Elijah.

¹⁸ Then Jehu gathered all the people and said to them, "Ahab served Baal a little; Jehu will serve him much. ¹⁹ Now, summon all the prophets of Baal, all his worshipers and all his priests; let no one be missing, for I have a great sacrifice for Baal; whoever is missing shall not live." But Jehu did it in cunning, so that he might destroy the worshipers of Baal. ²⁰ And Jehu said, "Sanctify a solemn assembly for Baal." And they proclaimed *it.* ²¹ Then Jehu sent throughout Israel and all the worshipers of Baal came, so that there was not a man left who did not come. And when they went into the house of Baal, the house of Baal was filled from one end to the other. ²² He said to the one who *was* in charge of the wardrobe, "Bring out garments for all the worshipers of Baal." So he brought out garments for them. ²³ Jehu went into the house of Baal with Jehonadab the son of Rechab; and he said to the worshipers of Baal, "Search and see that there is here with you none of the servants of the LORD, but only the worshipers of Baal." ²⁴ Then they went in to offer sacrifices and burnt offerings.

Now Jehu had stationed for himself eighty men outside, and he had said, "The one who permits any of the men whom I bring into your hands to escape shall give up his life in exchange." ²⁵ Then it came about, as soon as he had finished offering the burnt offering, that Jehu said to the guard and to the royal officers, "Go in, kill them; let none come out." And they killed them with the edge of the sword; and the guard and the royal officers threw *them* out, and went to the inner room of the house of Baal. ²⁶ They brought out the *sacred* pillars of the house of Baal and burned them. ²⁷ They also broke down the *sacred* pillar of Baal and broke down the house of Baal, and made it a latrine to this day.

²⁸ Thus Jehu eradicated Baal out of Israel. ²⁹ However, *as for* the sins of Jeroboam the son of Nebat, which he made Israel sin, from these Jehu did not depart, *even* the golden calves that *were* at Bethel and that *were* at Dan. ³⁰ The LORD said to Jehu, "Because you have done well in executing what is right in My eyes, *and* have done to the house of Ahab according to all that *was* in My heart, your

sons of the fourth generation shall sit on the throne of Israel." ³¹ But Jehu was not careful to walk in the law of the LORD, the God of Israel, with all his heart; he did not depart from the sins of Jeroboam, which he made Israel sin.

³² In those days the LORD began to cut off *portions* from Israel; and Hazael defeated them throughout the territory of Israel: ³³ from the Jordan eastward, all the land of Gilead, the Gadites and the Reubenites and the Manassites, from Aroer, which is by the valley of the Arnon, even Gilead and Bashan. ³⁴ Now the rest of the acts of Jehu and all that he did and all his might, are they not written in the Book of the Chronicles of the Kings of Israel? ³⁵ And Jehu slept with his fathers, and they buried him in Samaria. And Jehoahaz his son became king in his place. ³⁶ Now the time which Jehu reigned over Israel in Samaria *was* twenty-eight years.

Psalm 72:17–20

¹⁷ May his name endure forever;
May his name increase as
long as the sun *shines;*
And let *men* bless themselves
by him;
Let all nations call him blessed.

¹⁸ Blessed be the LORD God,
the God of Israel,
Who alone works wonders.
¹⁹ And blessed be His glorious
name forever;
And may the whole earth be
filled with His glory.
Amen, and Amen.

²⁰ The prayers of David the son
of Jesse are ended.

Proverbs 18:14–15

¹⁴ The spirit of a man can
endure his sickness,
But *as for* a broken spirit
who can bear it?
¹⁵ The mind of the prudent
acquires knowledge,
And the ear of the wise
seeks knowledge.

John 19:1–22

19 Pilate then took Jesus and scourged Him. ² And the soldiers twisted together a crown of thorns and put it on His head, and put a purple robe on Him; ³ and they *began* to come up to Him and say, "Hail, King of the Jews!" and to give Him slaps *in the face.*

⁴ Pilate came out again and *said to them, "Behold, I am bringing Him out to you so that you may know that I find no guilt in Him." ⁵ Jesus then came out, wearing the crown of thorns and the purple robe. *Pilate* *said to them, "Behold, the Man!" ⁶ So when the chief priests and the officers saw Him, they cried out saying, "Crucify, crucify!" Pilate *said to them, "Take Him yourselves and crucify Him, for I find no guilt in Him." ⁷ The Jews answered him, "We have a law, and by that law He ought to die because He made Himself out *to be* the Son of God."

⁸ Therefore when Pilate heard this statement, he was *even* more afraid; ⁹ and he entered into the Praetorium again and *said to Jesus, "Where are You from?" But Jesus gave him no answer. ¹⁰ So Pilate *said to Him, "You do not speak to me? Do You not know that I have authority to release You, and I have authority to crucify You?" ¹¹ Jesus answered, "You would have no authority over Me, unless it had been given you from above; for this reason he who delivered Me to you has *the* greater sin." ¹² As a result of this Pilate made efforts to release Him, but the Jews cried out saying, "If you release this Man, you are no friend of Caesar; everyone who makes himself out *to be* a king opposes Caesar."

19:12 no friend of Caesar. This statement by the Jews was loaded with irony, for the Jews' hatred of Rome certainly indicated they too were no friends of Caesar. But they knew Pilate feared Tiberius Caesar (the Roman emperor at the time of Jesus' crucifixion) since he had a highly suspicious personality and exacted ruthless punishment. Pilate had already created upheaval in Jerusalem by several foolish acts that had infuriated the Jews, and so was under the scrutiny of Rome to see if his ineptness continued. The Jews were intimidating him by threatening another upheaval that could spell the end of his power in Jerusalem, if he did not execute Jesus.

¹³ Therefore when Pilate heard these words, he brought Jesus out, and sat down on the judgment seat at a place called The Pavement, but in Hebrew, Gabbatha. ¹⁴ Now it was the day of preparation for the Passover; it was about the sixth hour. And he *said to the Jews, "Behold, your King!" ¹⁵ So they cried out, "Away with *Him,* away with *Him,* crucify Him!" Pilate *said to them, "Shall I crucify your King?"

The chief priests answered, "We have no king but Caesar." ¹⁶ So he then handed Him over to them to be crucified.

¹⁷ They took Jesus, therefore, and He went out, bearing His own cross, to the place called the Place of a Skull, which is called in Hebrew, Golgotha. ¹⁸ There they crucified Him, and with Him two other men, one on either side, and Jesus in between. ¹⁹ Pilate also wrote an inscription and put it on the cross. It was written,

> "JESUS THE NAZARENE, THE
> KING OF THE JEWS."

²⁰ Therefore many of the Jews read this inscription, for the place where Jesus was crucified was near the city; and it was written in Hebrew, Latin *and* in Greek. ²¹ So the chief priests of the Jews were saying to Pilate, "Do not write, 'The King of the Jews'; but that He said, 'I am King of the Jews.' " ²² Pilate answered, "What I have written I have written."

19:18 crucified Him. Jesus was made to lie on the ground while His arms were stretched out and nailed to the horizontal beam that He carried. The beam was then hoisted up, along with the victim, and fastened to the vertical beam. His feet were nailed to the vertical beam to which sometimes was attached a piece of wood that served as a kind of seat that partially supported the weight of the body. The latter, however, was designed to prolong and increase the agony, not relieve it. Having been stripped naked and beaten, Jesus could hang in the hot sun for hours if not days. To breathe, it was necessary to push with the legs and pull with the arms, creating excruciating pain. Terrible muscle spasms wracked the entire body; but since collapse meant asphyxiation, the struggle for life continued. **two other men.** Matthew (27:38) and Luke (23:33) use the same word for these two as John used for Barabbas, i.e., guerrilla fighters.

DAY 11: Describe the abuse that Christ endured during the trial?

In John 19:1, it says that "Pilate then took Jesus and scourged Him." Pilate appears to have flogged Jesus as a strategy to set Him free (vv. 4–6). He was hoping that the Jews would be appeased by this action and that sympathy for Jesus' suffering would result in their desire that He be released (Lk 23:13–16). Scourging was a horribly cruel act in which the victim was stripped, tied to a post and beaten by several torturers, i.e., soldiers who alternated when exhausted. For victims who were not Roman citizens, the preferred instrument was a short wooden handle to which several leather thongs were attached. Each leather thong had pieces of bones or metal on the end. The beatings were so savage that sometimes victims died. The body could be torn or lacerated to such an extent that muscles, veins, or bones were exposed. Such flogging often preceded execution in order to weaken and dehumanize the victim (Is. 53:5). Apparently, however, Pilate intended this to create sympathy for Jesus.

Then there was the "crown of thorns" (v. 2). This crown was made from the long spikes (up to 12 inches) of a date palm formed into an imitation of the radiating crowns which oriental kings wore. The long thorns would have cut deeply into Jesus' head, adding to the pain and bleeding. The use of the "purple robe" represented royalty. The robe probably was a military cloak flung around Jesus' shoulders, intended to mock His claim to be King of the Jews.

Pilate declared to the people, "I find no guilt in Him" (v. 4), and when he brought Jesus out, he cried, "Behold, the Man!" (v. 5). Pilate dramatically presented Jesus after His torturous treatment by the soldiers. Jesus would have been swollen, bruised, and bleeding. Pilate displayed Jesus as a beaten and pathetic figure, hoping to gain the people's choice of Jesus for release. Pilate's phrase is filled with sarcasm since he was attempting to impress upon the Jewish authorities that Jesus was not the dangerous man that they had made Him out to be.

JUNE 12

2 Kings 11:1–13:25

11 When Athaliah the mother of Ahaziah saw that her son was dead, she rose and destroyed all the royal offspring. ² But Jehosheba, the daughter of King Joram, sister of Ahaziah, took Joash the son of Ahaziah and stole him from among the king's sons who were being put to death, and placed him and his nurse in the bedroom. So they hid him from Athaliah, and he was not put to death. ³ So he was hidden with her in the house of the LORD six years, while Athaliah was reigning over the land.

⁴ Now in the seventh year Jehoiada sent and brought the captains of hundreds of the

Carites and of the guard, and brought them to him in the house of the LORD. Then he made a covenant with them and put them under oath in the house of the LORD, and showed them the king's son. ⁵ He commanded them, saying, "This is the thing that you shall do: one third of you, who come in on the sabbath and keep watch over the king's house ⁶ (one third also *shall be* at the gate Sur, and one third at the gate behind the guards), shall keep watch over the house for defense. ⁷ Two parts of you, *even* all who go out on the sabbath, shall also keep watch over the house of the LORD for the king. ⁸ Then you shall surround the king, each with his weapons in his hand; and whoever comes within the ranks shall be put to death. And be with the king when he goes out and when he comes in."

⁹ So the captains of hundreds did according to all that Jehoiada the priest commanded. And each one of them took his men who were to come in on the sabbath, with those who were to go out on the sabbath, and came to Jehoiada the priest. ¹⁰ The priest gave to the captains of hundreds the spears and shields that *had been* King David's, which *were* in the house of the LORD. ¹¹ The guards stood each with his weapons in his hand, from the right side of the house to the left side of the house, by the altar and by the house, around the king. ¹² Then he brought the king's son out and put the crown on him and *gave him* the testimony; and they made him king and anointed him, and they clapped their hands and said, "*Long* live the king!"

¹³ When Athaliah heard the noise of the guard *and of* the people, she came to the people in the house of the LORD. ¹⁴ She looked and behold, the king was standing by the pillar, according to the custom, with the captains and the trumpeters beside the king; and all the people of the land rejoiced and blew trumpets. Then Athaliah tore her clothes and cried, "Treason! Treason!" ¹⁵ And Jehoiada the priest commanded the captains of hundreds who were appointed over the army and said to them, "Bring her out between the ranks, and whoever follows her put to death with the sword." For the priest said, "Let her not be put to death in the house of the LORD." ¹⁶ So they seized her, and when she arrived at the horses' entrance of the king's house, she was put to death there.

¹⁷ Then Jehoiada made a covenant between the LORD and the king and the people, that they would be the LORD'S people, also between the king and the people. ¹⁸ All the people of the land went to the house of Baal,

11:17 a covenant. The renewal of the agreement between the people and the Lord and between the house of David and the people was appropriate because of the disruption under Athaliah. A similar ceremony was held later, during the reign of Josiah (23:1–3).

and tore it down; his altars and his images they broke in pieces thoroughly, and killed Mattan the priest of Baal before the altars. And the priest appointed officers over the house of the LORD. ¹⁹ He took the captains of hundreds and the Carites and the guards and all the people of the land; and they brought the king down from the house of the LORD, and came by the way of the gate of the guards to the king's house. And he sat on the throne of the kings. ²⁰ So all the people of the land rejoiced and the city was quiet. For they had put Athaliah to death with the sword at the king's house.

²¹ Jehoash was seven years old when he became king.

12 In the seventh year of Jehu, Jehoash became king, and he reigned forty years in Jerusalem; and his mother's name was Zibiah of Beersheba. ² Jehoash did right in the sight of the LORD all his days in which Jehoiada the priest instructed him. ³ Only the high places were not taken away; the people still sacrificed and burned incense on the high places.

⁴ Then Jehoash said to the priests, "All the money of the sacred things which is brought into the house of the LORD, in current money, *both* the money of each man's assessment *and* all the money which any man's heart prompts him to bring into the house of the LORD, ⁵ let the priests take it for themselves, each from his acquaintance; and they shall repair the damages of the house wherever any damage may be found."

⁶ But it came about that in the twenty-third year of King Jehoash the priests had not repaired the damages of the house. ⁷ Then King Jehoash called for Jehoiada the priest, and for the *other* priests and said to them, "Why do you not repair the damages of the house? Now therefore take no *more* money from your acquaintances, but pay it for the damages of the house." ⁸ So the priests agreed that they would take no *more* money from the people, nor repair the damages of the house.

⁹ But Jehoiada the priest took a chest and bored a hole in its lid and put it beside the altar, on the right side as one comes

into the house of the LORD; and the priests who guarded the threshold put in it all the money which was brought into the house of the LORD. ¹⁰ When they saw that there was much money in the chest, the king's scribe and the high priest came up and tied *it* in bags and counted the money which was found in the house of the LORD. ¹¹ They gave the money which was weighed out into the hands of those who did the work, who had the oversight of the house of the LORD; and they paid it out to the carpenters and the builders who worked on the house of the LORD; ¹² and to the masons and the stonecutters, and for buying timber and hewn stone to repair the damages to the house of the LORD, and for all that was laid out for the house to repair it. ¹³ But there were not made for the house of the LORD silver cups, snuffers, bowls, trumpets, any vessels of gold, or vessels of silver from the money which was brought into the house of the LORD; ¹⁴ for they gave that to those who did the work, and with it they repaired the house of the LORD. ¹⁵ Moreover, they did not require an accounting from the men into whose hand they gave the money to pay to those who did the work, for they dealt faithfully. ¹⁶ The money from the guilt offerings and the money from the sin offerings was not brought into the house of the LORD; it was for the priests.

¹⁷ Then Hazael king of Aram went up and fought against Gath and captured it, and Hazael set his face to go up to Jerusalem. ¹⁸ Jehoash king of Judah took all the sacred things that Jehoshaphat and Jehoram and Ahaziah, his fathers, kings of Judah, had dedicated, and his own sacred things and all the gold that was found among the treasuries of the house of the LORD and of the king's house, and sent *them* to Hazael king of Aram. Then he went away from Jerusalem.

¹⁹ Now the rest of the acts of Joash and all that he did, are they not written in the Book of the Chronicles of the Kings of Judah? ²⁰ His servants arose and made a conspiracy and struck down Joash at the house of Millo *as he was* going down to Silla. ²¹ For Jozacar the son of Shimeath and Jehozabad the son of Shomer, his servants, struck *him* and he died; and they buried him with his fathers in the city of David, and Amaziah his son became king in his place.

13 In the twenty-third year of Joash son of Ahaziah, king of Judah, Jehoahaz the son of Jehu became king over Israel at Samaria, *and he reigned* seventeen years. ² He did evil in the sight of the LORD, and followed the sins of Jeroboam the son of Nebat, with which he made Israel sin; he did not turn from them. ³ So the anger of the LORD was kindled against Israel, and He gave them continually into the hand of Hazael king of Aram, and into the hand of Ben-hadad the son of Hazael. ⁴ Then Jehoahaz entreated the favor of the LORD, and the LORD listened to him; for He saw the oppression of Israel, how the king of Aram oppressed them. ⁵ The LORD gave Israel a deliverer, so that they escaped from under the hand of the Arameans; and the sons of Israel lived in their tents as formerly. ⁶ Nevertheless they did not turn away from the sins of the house of Jeroboam, with which he made Israel sin, but walked in them; and the Asherah also remained standing in Samaria. ⁷ For he left to Jehoahaz of the army not more than fifty horsemen and ten chariots and 10,000 footmen, for the king of Aram had destroyed them and made them like the dust at threshing. ⁸ Now the rest of the acts of Jehoahaz, and all that he did and his might, are they not written in the Book of the Chronicles of the Kings of Israel? ⁹ And Jehoahaz slept with his fathers, and they buried him in Samaria; and Joash his son became king in his place.

¹⁰ In the thirty-seventh year of Joash king of Judah, Jehoash the son of Jehoahaz became king over Israel in Samaria, *and reigned* sixteen years. ¹¹ He did evil in the sight of the LORD; he did not turn away from all the sins of Jeroboam the son of Nebat, with which he made Israel sin, but he walked in them. ¹² Now the rest of the acts of Joash and all that he did and his might with which he fought against Amaziah king of Judah, are they not written in the Book of the Chronicles of the Kings of Israel? ¹³ So Joash slept with his fathers, and Jeroboam sat on his throne; and Joash was buried in Samaria with the kings of Israel.

¹⁴ When Elisha became sick with the illness of which he was to die, Joash the king of Israel came down to him and wept over him and said, "My father, my father, the chariots of Israel and its horsemen!" ¹⁵ Elisha said to him, "Take a bow and arrows." So he took a bow and arrows. ¹⁶ Then he said to the king of Israel, "Put your hand on the bow." And he put his hand *on it,* then Elisha laid his hands on the king's hands. ¹⁷ He said, "Open the window toward the east," and he opened *it.* Then Elisha said, "Shoot!" And he shot. And he said, "The LORD'S arrow of victory, even the arrow of victory over Aram; for you will defeat the Arameans at Aphek until you have destroyed *them.*" ¹⁸ Then he said, "Take the

arrows," and he took them. And he said to the king of Israel, "Strike the ground," and he struck *it* three times and stopped. ¹⁹ So the man of God was angry with him and said, "You should have struck five or six times, then you would have struck Aram until you would have destroyed *it*. But now you shall strike Aram *only* three times."

²⁰ Elisha died, and they buried him. Now the bands of the Moabites would invade the land in the spring of the year. ²¹ As they were burying a man, behold, they saw a marauding band; and they cast the man into the grave of Elisha. And when the man touched the bones of Elisha he revived and stood up on his feet.

13:21 he revived. A dead man returned to life after touching Elisha's bones. This miracle was a sign that God's power continued to work in relationship to Elisha even after his death. What God had promised to Jehoash through Elisha when he was alive would surely come to pass after the prophet's death (vv. 19, 25) in the defeat of the enemy, the recovery of the cities that had been taken, and their restoration to the kingdom of Israel (vv. 22–25).

²² Now Hazael king of Aram had oppressed Israel all the days of Jehoahaz. ²³ But the LORD was gracious to them and had compassion on them and turned to them because of His covenant with Abraham, Isaac, and Jacob, and would not destroy them or cast them from His presence until now.

²⁴ When Hazael king of Aram died, Benhadad his son became king in his place. ²⁵ Then Jehoash the son of Jehoahaz took again from the hand of Ben-hadad the son of Hazael the cities which he had taken in war from the hand of Jehoahaz his father. Three times Joash defeated him and recovered the cities of Israel.

Psalm 73:1–9

A Psalm of Asaph.

S urely God is good to Israel,
To those who are pure in heart!
² But as for me, my feet came
close to stumbling,
My steps had almost slipped.
³ For I was envious of the arrogant
As I saw the prosperity of the
wicked.
⁴ For there are no pains in their death,
And their body is fat.

⁵ They are not in trouble *as other*
men,
Nor are they plagued like mankind.
⁶ Therefore pride is their necklace;
The garment of violence covers them.
⁷ Their eye bulges from fatness;
The imaginations of *their*
heart run riot.
⁸ They mock and wickedly
speak of oppression;
They speak from on high.
⁹ They have set their mouth
against the heavens,
And their tongue parades
through the earth.

Proverbs 18:16–17

¹⁶ A man's gift makes room for him
And brings him before great men.
¹⁷ The first to plead his case *seems*
right,
Until another comes and
examines him.

18:16 man's gift. This is not the word for a bribe (17:23), but rather the word for a present given to someone (see Jacob's gift, Ge 32:20–21; Joseph's gift, Ge 43:11; David's gift, 1Sa 17:17–18; and Abigail's gift, 1Sa 25:27).

John 19:23–42

²³ Then the soldiers, when they had crucified Jesus, took His outer garments and made four parts, a part to every soldier and *also* the tunic; now the tunic was seamless, woven in one piece. ²⁴ So they said to one another, "Let us not tear it, but cast lots for it, *to decide* whose it shall be"; *this was* to fulfill the Scripture: "THEY DIVIDED MY OUTER GARMENTS AMONG THEM, AND FOR MY CLOTHING THEY CAST LOTS." ²⁵ Therefore the soldiers did these things.

19:23 His outer garments...and *also* **the tunic.** By custom, the clothes of the condemned person were the property of the executioners. The division of the garments suggests that the execution squad was made up of 4 soldiers (Ac 12:4). The tunic was worn next to the skin. The plural "garments" probably refers to other clothes, including an outer garment, belt, sandals, and head covering.

19:24 John cites Psalms 22:18. In the psalm, David, beset by physical distress and mockery by his opponents, used the symbolism of the common practice in an execution scene in which the executioner divided the victim's clothes to portray the depth of his trouble. It is notable that David precisely described a form of execution that he had never seen. The passage was typologically prophetic of Jesus, David's heir to the messianic throne (Mt 27:46; Mk 15:34).

But standing by the cross of Jesus were His mother, and His mother's sister, Mary the *wife* of Clopas, and Mary Magdalene. [26]When Jesus then saw His mother, and the disciple whom He loved standing nearby, He *said to His mother, "Woman, behold, your son!" [27]Then He *said to the disciple, "Behold, your mother!" From that hour the disciple took her into his own *household.*

[28]After this, Jesus, knowing that all things had already been accomplished, to fulfill the Scripture, *said, "I am thirsty." [29]A jar full of sour wine was standing there; so they put a sponge full of the sour wine upon *a branch of* hyssop and brought it up to His mouth. [30]Therefore when Jesus had received the sour wine, He said, "It is finished!" And He bowed His head and gave up His spirit.

[31]Then the Jews, because it was the day of preparation, so that the bodies would not remain on the cross on the Sabbath (for that Sabbath was a high day), asked Pilate that their legs might be broken, and *that* they might be taken away. [32]So the soldiers came, and broke the legs of the first man and of the other who was crucified with Him; [33]but coming to Jesus, when they saw that He was already dead, they did not break His legs. [34]But one of the soldiers pierced His side with a spear, and immediately blood and water came out. [35]And he who has seen has testified, and his testimony is true; and he knows that he is telling the truth, so that you also may believe. [36]For these things came to pass to fulfill the Scripture, "NOT A BONE OF HIM SHALL BE BROKEN." [37]And again another Scripture says, "THEY SHALL LOOK ON HIM WHOM THEY PIERCED."

[38]After these things Joseph of Arimathea, being a disciple of Jesus, but a secret *one* for fear of the Jews, asked Pilate that he might take away the body of Jesus; and Pilate granted permission. So he came and took away His body. [39]Nicodemus, who had first come to Him by night, also came, bringing a mixture of myrrh and aloes, about a hundred pounds *weight.* [40]So they took the body of Jesus and bound it in linen wrappings with the spices, as is the burial custom of the Jews. [41]Now in the place where He was crucified there was a garden, and in the garden a new tomb in which no one had yet been laid. [42]Therefore because of the Jewish day of preparation, since the tomb was nearby, they laid Jesus there.

DAY 12: Was there any question as to whether Jesus died or not?

In His death on the cross, Jesus finally cried out, "It is finished!" (Jn 19:30). The verb here carries the idea of fulfilling one's task and, in religious contexts, has the idea of fulfilling one's religious obligations. The entire work of redemption had been brought to completion. The single Greek word here (translated "it is finished") has been found in the papyri being placed on receipts for taxes meaning paid in full (Col 3:13–14). He "gave up His spirit." The sentence signaled that Jesus handed over His spirit as an act of His will. No one took His life from Him, for He voluntarily and willingly gave it up (10:17–18).

It was "the day of preparation" (v. 31). This refers to Friday, the day before or the preparation day for the Sabbath. "Bodies would not remain on the cross on the Sabbath." The normal Roman practice was to leave crucified men and women on the cross until they died (and this could take days) and then leave their rotting bodies hanging there to be devoured by vultures. The Mosaic Law insisted that anyone being impaled (usually after execution) should not remain there overnight (Dt 21:22–23). Such a person was under God's curse, and to leave him exposed would be to desecrate the land in their minds. So "[the Jews] asked Pilate that their legs might be broken." In order to hasten death for certain reasons, soldiers would smash the legs of the victim with an iron mallet. Not only did this action induce shock and additional loss of blood, but it prevented the victim from pushing with his legs to keep breathing, and thus the victim died due to asphyxiation.

However, the soldier's stabbing of Jesus' side caused significant penetration because of the sudden flow of blood and water (v. 34). Either the spear pierced Jesus' heart or the chest cavity was pierced at the bottom. In either event, John mentioned the outflow of blood and water to emphasize that Jesus was unquestionably dead.

JUNE 13

14 In the second year of Joash son of Joahaz king of Israel, Amaziah the son of Joash king of Judah became king. ²He was twenty-five years old when he became king, and he reigned twenty-nine years in Jerusalem. And his mother's name was Jehoaddin of Jerusalem. ³He did right in the sight of the LORD, yet not like David his father; he did according to all that Joash his father had done. ⁴Only the high places were not taken away; the people still sacrificed and burned incense on the high places. ⁵Now it came about, as soon as the kingdom was firmly in his hand, that he killed his servants who had slain the king his father. ⁶But the sons of the slayers he did not put to death, according to what is written in the book of the Law of Moses, as the LORD commanded, saying, "The fathers shall not be put to death for the sons, nor the sons be put to death for the fathers; but each shall be put to death for his own sin."

⁷He killed *of* Edom in the Valley of Salt 10,000 and took Sela by war, and named it Joktheel to this day.

⁸Then Amaziah sent messengers to Jehoash, the son of Jehoahaz son of Jehu, king of Israel, saying, "Come, let us face each other." ⁹Jehoash king of Israel sent to Amaziah king of Judah, saying, "The thorn bush which was in Lebanon sent to the cedar which was in Lebanon, saying, 'Give your daughter to my son in marriage.' But there passed by a wild beast that was in Lebanon, and trampled the thorn bush. ¹⁰You have indeed defeated Edom, and your heart has become proud. Enjoy your glory and stay at home; for why should you provoke trouble so that you, even you, would fall, and Judah with you?"

¹¹But Amaziah would not listen. So Jehoash king of Israel went up; and he and Amaziah king of Judah faced each other at Bethshemesh, which belongs to Judah. ¹²Judah was defeated by Israel, and they fled each to his tent. ¹³Then Jehoash king of Israel captured Amaziah king of Judah, the son of Jehoash the son of Ahaziah, at Beth-shemesh, and came to Jerusalem and tore down the wall of Jerusalem from the Gate of Ephraim to the Corner Gate, 400 cubits. ¹⁴He took all the gold and silver and all the utensils which were found in the house of the LORD, and in the treasuries of the king's house, the hostages also, and returned to Samaria.

¹⁵Now the rest of the acts of Jehoash which he did, and his might and how he fought with Amaziah king of Judah, are they not written in the Book of the Chronicles of the Kings of Israel? ¹⁶So Jehoash slept with his fathers and was buried in Samaria with the kings of Israel; and Jeroboam his son became king in his place.

¹⁷Amaziah the son of Joash king of Judah lived fifteen years after the death of Jehoash son of Jehoahaz king of Israel. ¹⁸Now the rest of the acts of Amaziah, are they not written in the Book of the Chronicles of the Kings of Judah? ¹⁹They conspired against him in Jerusalem, and he fled to Lachish; but they sent after him to Lachish and killed him there. ²⁰Then they brought him on horses and he was buried at Jerusalem with his fathers in the city of David. ²¹All the people of Judah took Azariah, who *was* sixteen years old, and made him king in the place of his father Amaziah. ²²He built Elath and restored it to Judah after the king slept with his fathers.

²³In the fifteenth year of Amaziah the son of Joash king of Judah, Jeroboam the son of Joash king of Israel became king in Samaria, *and reigned* forty-one years. ²⁴He did evil in the sight of the LORD; he did not depart from all the sins of Jeroboam the son of Nebat, which he made Israel sin. ²⁵He restored the border of Israel from the entrance of Hamath as far as the Sea of the Arabah, according to the word of the LORD, the God of Israel,

14:1—15:38 This section quickly surveys the kings and selected events of the northern and southern kingdoms from 796 to 735 B.C. In contrast to the previous 19 chapters (1Ki 17:1—2Ki 13:25), which narrated 90 years of history (885–796 B.C.) with a concentration on the ministries of Elijah and Elisha during the final 65 years of that period (860–796 B.C.), 62 years are covered in these two chapters. The previous section concluded with a shadow of hope: officially sanctioned Baal worship had been eradicated in both Israel (10:18–28) and Judah (11:17–18); the temple of the Lord in Jerusalem had been repaired (12:9–15); and the Syrian threat to Israel had been overcome (13:25). However, this section emphasizes that the fundamental problems still remained: the false religion established by Jeroboam I continued in Israel even with the change of royal families (14:24—15:9, 18, 24, 28), and the high places were not removed in Judah even though there were only good kings there during those years (14:4; 15:4, 35).

14:25 restored the border of Israel. Jeroboam II's greatest accomplishment was the restoration of Israel's boundaries to approximately their extent in Solomon's time, excluding the territory belonging to Judah. The northern boundary was the entrance of Hamath, the same as Solomon's (1Ki 8:65) and the southern boundary was the Sea of the Arabah, the Dead Sea (Jos 3:16; 12:3). Jeroboam II took Hamath, a major city located on the Orontes River, about 160 miles north of the Sea of Galilee. He also controlled Damascus, indicating that the Transjordan territory south to Moab was also under his authority. These victories of Jeroboam II were accomplished because the Syrians had been weakened by attacks from the Assyrians, while Assyria herself was weak at this time, suffering from threats on her northern border, internal dissension, and a series of weak kings. **Jonah.** The territorial extension of Jeroboam II was in accordance with the will of the Lord as revealed through the prophet Jonah. This was the same Jonah who traveled to Nineveh with God's message of repentance for the Assyrians.

which He spoke through His servant Jonah the son of Amittai, the prophet, who was of Gath-hepher. ²⁶ For the LORD saw the affliction of Israel, *which was* very bitter; for there was neither bond nor free, nor was there any helper for Israel. ²⁷ The LORD did not say that He would blot out the name of Israel from under heaven, but He saved them by the hand of Jeroboam the son of Joash.

²⁸ Now the rest of the acts of Jeroboam and all that he did and his might, how he fought and how he recovered for Israel, Damascus and Hamath, *which had belonged* to Judah, are they not written in the Book of the Chronicles of the Kings of Israel? ²⁹ And Jeroboam slept with his fathers, even with the kings of Israel, and Zechariah his son became king in his place.

Psalm 73:10–20

¹⁰ Therefore his people return
 to this place,
 And waters of abundance
  are drunk by them.
¹¹ They say, "How does God know?
 And is there knowledge
  with the Most High?"
¹² Behold, these are the wicked;
 And always at ease, they have
  increased *in* wealth.

¹³ Surely in vain I have kept
 my heart pure
 And washed my hands in innocence;
¹⁴ For I have been stricken all day long
 And chastened every morning.

¹⁵ If I had said, "I will speak thus,"
 Behold, I would have betrayed the
  generation of Your children.
¹⁶ When I pondered to understand this,
 It was troublesome in my sight
¹⁷ Until I came into the
  sanctuary of God;
 Then I perceived their end.
¹⁸ Surely You set them in
 slippery places;
 You cast them down to destruction.
¹⁹ How they are destroyed in a moment!
 They are utterly swept away
  by sudden terrors!
²⁰ Like a dream when one awakes,
 O Lord, when aroused, You
  will despise their form.

Proverbs 18:18–19

¹⁸ The *cast* lot puts an end to strife
 And decides between the
  mighty ones.
¹⁹ A brother offended *is harder to
 be won* than a strong city,
 And contentions are like
  the bars of a citadel.

18:19 There are no feuds as difficult to resolve as those with relatives; no barriers are so hard to bring down. Hence, great care should be taken to avoid such conflicts

John 20:1–31

20 Now on the first *day* of the week Mary Magdalene *came early to the tomb, while it *was still dark, and *saw the stone *already* taken away from the tomb. ² So she *ran and *came to Simon Peter and to the other disciple whom Jesus loved, and *said to them, "They have taken away the Lord out of the tomb, and we do not know where they have laid Him." ³ So Peter and the other disciple went forth, and they were going to the tomb. ⁴ The two were running together; and the other disciple ran ahead faster than Peter and came to the tomb first; ⁵ and stooping and looking in, he *saw the linen wrappings lying *there;* but he did not go in. ⁶ And so Simon Peter also *came, following him, and entered

the tomb; and he *saw the linen wrappings lying *there*, ⁷and the face-cloth which had been on His head, not lying with the linen wrappings, but rolled up in a place by itself. ⁸So the other disciple who had first come to the tomb then also entered, and he saw and believed. ⁹For as yet they did not understand the Scripture, that He must rise again from the dead. ¹⁰So the disciples went away again to their own homes.

20:9 did not understand the Scripture. Neither Peter nor John understood that Scripture said Jesus would rise (Ps 16:10). This is evident by the reports of Luke (24:25-27, 32, 44-47). Jesus had foretold His resurrection (2:19; Mt 16:21; Mk 8:31; 9:31; Lk 9:22), but they would not accept it (Mt 16:22; Lk 9:44-45). By the time John wrote this gospel, the church had developed an understanding of the Old Testament prediction of Messiah's resurrection.

¹¹But Mary was standing outside the tomb weeping; and so, as she wept, she stooped and looked into the tomb; ¹²and she *saw two angels in white sitting, one at the head and one at the feet, where the body of Jesus had been lying. ¹³And they *said to her, "Woman, why are you weeping?" She *said to them, "Because they have taken away my Lord, and I do not know where they have laid Him." ¹⁴When she had said this, she turned around and *saw Jesus standing *there*, and did not know that it was Jesus. ¹⁵Jesus *said to her, "Woman, why are you weeping? Whom are you seeking?" Supposing Him to be the gardener, she *said to Him, "Sir, if you have carried Him away, tell me where you have laid Him, and I will take Him away." ¹⁶Jesus *said to her, "Mary!" She turned and *said to Him in Hebrew, "Rabboni!" (which means, Teacher). ¹⁷Jesus *said to her, "Stop clinging to Me, for I have not yet ascended to the Father; but go to

My brethren and say to them, 'I ascend to My Father and your Father, and My God and your God.'" ¹⁸Mary Magdalene *came, announcing to the disciples, "I have seen the Lord," and *that* He had said these things to her.

¹⁹So when it was evening on that day, the first *day* of the week, and when the doors were shut where the disciples were, for fear of the Jews, Jesus came and stood in their midst and *said to them, "Peace *be* with you." ²⁰And when He had said this, He showed them both His hands and His side. The disciples then rejoiced when they saw the Lord. ²¹So Jesus said to them again, "Peace *be* with you; as the Father has sent Me, I also send you." ²²And when He had said this, He breathed on them and *said to them, "Receive the Holy Spirit. ²³If you forgive the sins of any, *their sins* have been forgiven them; if you retain the *sins* of any, they have been retained."

²⁴But Thomas, one of the twelve, called Didymus, was not with them when Jesus came. ²⁵So the other disciples were saying to him, "We have seen the Lord!" But he said to them, "Unless I see in His hands the imprint of the nails, and put my finger into the place of the nails, and put my hand into His side, I will not believe."

²⁶After eight days His disciples were again inside, and Thomas with them. Jesus *came, the doors having been shut, and stood in their midst and said, "Peace *be* with you." ²⁷Then He *said to Thomas, "Reach here with your finger, and see My hands; and reach here your hand and put it into My side; and do not be unbelieving, but believing." ²⁸Thomas answered and said to Him, "My Lord and my God!" ²⁹Jesus *said to him, "Because you have seen Me, have you believed? Blessed *are* they who did not see, and *yet* believed."

³⁰Therefore many other signs Jesus also performed in the presence of the disciples, which are not written in this book; ³¹but these have been written so that you may believe that Jesus is the Christ, the Son of God; and that believing you may have life in His name.

DAY 13: Describe the resurrection appearances of Jesus to His followers.

John 20 records the appearances of Jesus to His own followers: 1) the appearance to Mary Magdalene (vv. 1-18); 2) the appearance to the 10 disciples (vv. 19-23); and 3) the appearance to Thomas (vv. 24-29). Jesus did not appear to unbelievers (see 14:19; 16:16, 22) because the evidence of His resurrection would not have convinced them as the miracles had not (Lk 16:31). The god of this world had blinded them and prevented their belief (2Co 4:4). Jesus, therefore, appears exclusively to His own in order to confirm their faith in the living Christ. Such appearances were so profound that they transformed the disciples from cowardly men hiding in fear to bold witnesses for Jesus (e.g., Peter; see 18:27; Ac 2:14-39). Once again John's purpose in recording these resurrection appearances was to demonstrate that Jesus' physical and bodily resurrection was the crowning proof that He truly is the Messiah and Son of God who laid down His life for His own (10:17–18; 15:13; Ro 1:4).

In particular, His appearance to Thomas, who has already been portrayed as loyal but pessimistic, is insightful (vv. 24–26). Jesus did not rebuke Thomas for his failure, but instead compassionately offered him proof of His resurrection. Jesus lovingly met him at the point of his weakness (2Ti 2:13). Thomas's actions indicated that Jesus had to convince the disciples rather forcefully of His resurrection, i.e., they were not gullible people predisposed to believing in resurrection. The point is they would not have fabricated it or hallucinated it, since they were so reluctant to believe even with the evidence they could see.

With the words "My Lord and my God!" (v. 28), Thomas declared his firm belief in the resurrection and, therefore, the deity of Jesus the Messiah and Son of God (Titus 2:13). This is the greatest confession a person can make. Thomas's confession functions as the fitting capstone of John's purpose in writing (vv. 30–31).

JUNE 14

2 Kings 15:1–16:20

15 In the twenty-seventh year of Jeroboam king of Israel, Azariah son of Amaziah king of Judah became king. ² He was sixteen years old when he became king, and he reigned fifty-two years in Jerusalem; and his mother's name was Jecoliah of Jerusalem. ³ He did right in the sight of the LORD, according to all that his father Amaziah had done. ⁴ Only the high places were not taken away; the people still sacrificed and burned incense on the high places. ⁵ The LORD struck the king, so that he was a leper to the day of his death. And he lived in a separate house, while Jotham the king's son was over the household, judging the people of the land. ⁶ Now the rest of the acts of Azariah and all that he did, are they not written in the Book of the Chronicles of the Kings of Judah? ⁷ And Azariah slept with his fathers, and they buried him with his fathers in the city of David, and Jotham his son became king in his place.

⁸ In the thirty-eighth year of Azariah king of Judah, Zechariah the son of Jeroboam became king over Israel in Samaria for six months. ⁹ He did evil in the sight of the LORD, as his fathers had done; he did not depart from the sins of Jeroboam the son of Nebat, which he made Israel sin. ¹⁰ Then Shallum the son of Jabesh conspired against him and struck him before the people and killed him, and reigned in his place. ¹¹ Now the rest of the acts of Zechariah, behold they are written in the Book of the Chronicles of the Kings of Israel. ¹² This is the word of the LORD which He spoke to Jehu, saying, "Your sons to the fourth generation shall sit on the throne of Israel." And so it was.

¹³ Shallum son of Jabesh became king in the thirty-ninth year of Uzziah king of Judah, and he reigned one month in Samaria. ¹⁴ Then Menahem son of Gadi went up from Tirzah and came to Samaria, and struck Shallum son of Jabesh in Samaria, and killed him and became king in his place. ¹⁵ Now the rest of the acts of Shallum and his conspiracy which he made, behold they are written in the Book of the Chronicles of the Kings of Israel. ¹⁶ Then Menahem struck Tiphsah and all who were in it and its borders from Tirzah, because they did not open to him; therefore he struck it and ripped up all its women who were with child.

¹⁷ In the thirty-ninth year of Azariah king of Judah, Menahem son of Gadi became king over Israel and reigned ten years in Samaria. ¹⁸ He did evil in the sight of the LORD; he did not depart all his days from the sins of Jeroboam the son of Nebat, which he made Israel sin.

¹⁹ Pul, king of Assyria, came against the land, and Menahem gave Pul a thousand talents of silver so that his hand might be with him to strengthen the kingdom under his rule. ²⁰ Then Menahem exacted the money from Israel, even from all the mighty men of wealth, from each man fifty shekels of silver to pay the king of Assyria. So the king of Assyria returned and did not remain there in the land. ²¹ Now the rest of the acts of Menahem and all that he did, are they not written in the Book of the Chronicles of the Kings of Israel? ²² And Menahem slept with his fathers, and Pekahiah his son became king in his place.

²³ In the fiftieth year of Azariah king of Judah, Pekahiah son of Menahem became king over Israel in Samaria, and reigned two years. ²⁴ He did evil in the sight of the LORD; he did not depart from the sins of Jeroboam son of Nebat, which he made Israel sin. ²⁵ Then Pekah son of Remaliah, his officer, conspired against him and struck him in Samaria, in the castle of the king's house with Argob and Arieh; and with him were fifty men of the Gileadites, and he killed him and became king in his place. ²⁶ Now the rest

of the acts of Pekahiah and all that he did, behold they are written in the Book of the Chronicles of the Kings of Israel.

²⁷ In the fifty-second year of Azariah king of Judah, Pekah son of Remaliah became king over Israel in Samaria, *and reigned* twenty years. ²⁸ He did evil in the sight of the LORD; he did not depart from the sins of Jeroboam son of Nebat, which he made Israel sin.

²⁹ In the days of Pekah king of Israel, Tiglath-pileser king of Assyria came and captured Ijon and Abel-beth-maacah and Janoah and Kedesh and Hazor and Gilead and Galilee, all the land of Naphtali; and he carried them captive to Assyria. ³⁰ And Hoshea the son of Elah made a conspiracy against Pekah the son of Remaliah, and struck him and put him to death and became king in his place, in the twentieth year of Jotham the son of Uzziah. ³¹ Now the rest of the acts of Pekah and all that he did, behold, they are written in the Book of the Chronicles of the Kings of Israel.

³² In the second year of Pekah the son of Remaliah king of Israel, Jotham the son of Uzziah king of Judah became king. ³³ He was twenty-five years old when he became king, and he reigned sixteen years in Jerusalem; and his mother's name *was* Jerusha the daughter of Zadok. ³⁴ He did what was right in the sight of the LORD; he did according to all that his father Uzziah had done. ³⁵ Only the high places were not taken away; the people still sacrificed and burned incense on the high places. He built the upper gate of the house of the LORD. ³⁶ Now the rest of the acts of Jotham and all that he did, are they not written in the Book of the Chronicles of the Kings of Judah? ³⁷ In those days the LORD began to send Rezin king of Aram and Pekah the son of Remaliah against Judah. ³⁸ And Jotham slept with his fathers, and he was buried with his fathers in the city of David his father; and Ahaz his son became king in his place.

16 In the seventeenth year of Pekah the son of Remaliah, Ahaz the son of Jotham, king of Judah, became king. ² Ahaz *was* twenty years old when he became king, and he reigned sixteen years in Jerusalem; and he did not do what was right in the sight of the LORD his God, as his father David *had done.* ³ But he walked in the way of the kings of Israel, and even made his son pass through the fire, according to the abominations of the nations whom the LORD had driven out from before the sons of Israel. ⁴ He sacrificed and burned incense on the high places and on the hills and under every green tree.

⁵ Then Rezin king of Aram and Pekah son

16:3 walked in the way of the kings of Israel. This does not necessarily mean that Ahaz participated in the calf worship introduced by Jeroboam I at Bethel and Dan, but that he increasingly brought pagan, idolatrous practices into the worship of the Lord in Jerusalem. These are specified in vv. 10–16 and parallel those of Jeroboam I in the northern kingdom. This included idols to Baal (2Ch 28:2). **made his son pass through the fire.** As a part of the ritual worship of Molech, the god of the Moabites, children were sacrificed by fire (3:27). This horrific practice was continually condemned in the Old Testament (Lv 18:21; 20:2–5; Dt 18:10; Jer 7:31; 19:5; 32:35).

of Remaliah, king of Israel, came up to Jerusalem to *wage* war; and they besieged Ahaz, but could not overcome him. ⁶ At that time Rezin king of Aram recovered Elath for Aram, and cleared the Judeans out of Elath entirely; and the Arameans came to Elath and have lived there to this day.

⁷ So Ahaz sent messengers to Tiglath-pileser king of Assyria, saying, "I am your servant and your son; come up and deliver me from the hand of the king of Aram and from the hand of the king of Israel, who are rising up against me." ⁸ Ahaz took the silver and gold that was found in the house of the LORD and in the treasuries of the king's house, and sent a present to the king of Assyria. ⁹ So the king of Assyria listened to him; and the king of Assyria went up against Damascus and captured it, and carried *the people of* it away into exile to Kir, and put Rezin to death.

¹⁰ Now King Ahaz went to Damascus to meet Tiglath-pileser king of Assyria, and saw the altar which *was* at Damascus; and King

16:10 the altar. When Ahaz traveled to Damascus to meet Tiglath-pileser III, he saw a large altar (v. 15) which was most likely Assyrian. Ahaz sent a sketch of this altar to Urijah the High Priest in Jerusalem and Urijah built an altar just like it. The serious iniquity in this was meddling with and changing, according to personal taste, the furnishings of the temple, the design for which had been given by God (Ex 25:40; 26:30; 27:1–8; 1Ch 28:19). This was like building an idol in the temple, done to please the pagan Assyrian king, whom Ahaz served instead of God.

Ahaz sent to Urijah the priest the pattern of the altar and its model, according to all its workmanship. [11] So Urijah the priest built an altar; according to all that King Ahaz had sent from Damascus, thus Urijah the priest made *it*, before the coming of King Ahaz from Damascus. [12] When the king came from Damascus, the king saw the altar; then the king approached the altar and went up to it, [13] and burned his burnt offering and his meal offering, and poured his drink offering and sprinkled the blood of his peace offerings on the altar. [14] The bronze altar, which *was* before the LORD, he brought from the front of the house, from between *his* altar and the house of the LORD, and he put it on the north side of *his* altar. [15] Then King Ahaz commanded Urijah the priest, saying, "Upon the great altar burn the morning burnt offering and the evening meal offering and the king's burnt offering and his meal offering, with the burnt offering of all the people of the land and their meal offering and their drink offerings; and sprinkle on it all the blood of the burnt offering and all the blood of the sacrifice. But the bronze altar shall be for me to inquire *by*." [16] So Urijah the priest did according to all that King Ahaz commanded.

[17] Then King Ahaz cut off the borders of the stands, and removed the laver from them; he also took down the sea from the bronze oxen which were under it and put it on a pavement of stone. [18] The covered way for the sabbath which they had built in the house, and the outer entry of the king, he removed from the house of the LORD because of the king of Assyria. [19] Now the rest of the acts of Ahaz which he did, are they not written in the Book of the Chronicles of the Kings of Judah? [20] So Ahaz slept with his fathers, and was buried with his fathers in the city of David; and his son Hezekiah reigned in his place.

Psalm 73:21–28

[21] When my heart was embittered
And I was pierced within,
[22] Then I was senseless and ignorant;
I was *like* a beast before You.
[23] Nevertheless I am
continually with You;
You have taken hold of my right hand.
[24] With Your counsel You will guide me,
And afterward receive me to glory.

[25] Whom have I in heaven *but You?*
And besides You, I desire
nothing on earth.
[26] My flesh and my heart may fail,

But God is the strength of my
heart and my portion forever.
[27] For, behold, those who are far
from You will perish;
You have destroyed all those
who are unfaithful to You.
[28] But as for me, the nearness
of God is my good;
I have made the Lord GOD my refuge,
That I may tell of all Your works.

Proverbs 18:20–21

[20] With the fruit of a man's mouth
his stomach will be satisfied;
He will be satisfied *with* the
product of his lips.
[21] Death and life are in the
power of the tongue,
And those who love it will eat its fruit.

18:21 Death and life. The greatest good and the greatest harm are in the power of the tongue (Jas 3:6–10).

John 21:1–25

21 After these things Jesus manifested Himself again to the disciples at the Sea of Tiberias, and He manifested *Himself* in this way. [2] Simon Peter, and Thomas called Didymus, and Nathanael of Cana in Galilee, and the *sons* of Zebedee, and two others of His disciples were together. [3] Simon Peter *said to them, "I am going fishing." They *said to him, "We will also come with you." They went out and got into the boat; and that night they caught nothing.

[4] But when the day was now breaking, Jesus stood on the beach; yet the disciples did not know that it was Jesus. [5] So Jesus *said to them, "Children, you do not have any fish, do you?" They answered Him, "No." [6] And He said to them, "Cast the net on the right-hand side of the boat and you will find *a catch*." So they cast, and then they were not able to haul it in because of the great number of fish. [7] Therefore that disciple whom Jesus loved *said to Peter, "It is the Lord." So when Simon Peter heard that it was the Lord, he put his outer garment on (for he was stripped *for work*), and threw himself into the sea. [8] But the other disciples came in the little boat, for they were not far from the land, but about one hundred yards away, dragging the net *full* of fish.

[9] So when they got out on the land, they *saw a charcoal fire *already* laid and fish

placed on it, and bread. ¹⁰ Jesus *said to them, "Bring some of the fish which you have now caught." ¹¹ Simon Peter went up and drew the net to land, full of large fish, a hundred and fifty-three; and although there were so many, the net was not torn. ¹² Jesus *said to them, "Come *and* have breakfast." None of the disciples ventured to question Him, "Who are You?" knowing that it was the Lord. ¹³ Jesus *came and *took the bread and *gave *it* to them, and the fish likewise. ¹⁴ This is now the third time that Jesus was manifested to the disciples, after He was raised from the dead.

¹⁵ So when they had finished breakfast, Jesus *said to Simon Peter, "Simon, *son* of John, do you love Me more than these?" He *said to Him, "Yes, Lord; You know that I love You." He *said to him, "Tend My lambs." ¹⁶ He *said to him again a second time, "Simon, *son* of John, do you love Me?" He *said to Him, "Yes, Lord; You know that I love You." He *said to him, "Shepherd My sheep." ¹⁷ He *said to him the third time, "Simon, *son* of John, do you love Me?" Peter was grieved because He said to him the third time, "Do you love Me?" And he said to Him, "Lord, You know all things; You know that I love You." Jesus *said to him, "Tend My sheep. ¹⁸ Truly, truly, I say to you, when you were younger, you used to gird yourself and walk wherever you wished; but when you grow old, you will stretch out your hands and someone else will gird you, and bring you where you do not wish to *go*." ¹⁹ Now this He said, signifying by what kind of death he would glorify God. And when He had spoken this, He *said to him, "Follow Me!"

²⁰ Peter, turning around, *saw the disciple

21:18-19 A prophecy of Peter's martyrdom. Jesus' call of devotion to Him would also mean that Peter's devotion would entail his own death (Mt 10:37-39). Whenever any Christian follows Christ, he must be prepared to suffer and die (Mt 16:24-26). Peter lived 3 decades serving the Lord and anticipating the death that was before him (2Pe 1:12-15), but he wrote that such suffering and death for the Lord brings praise to God (1Pe 4:14-16). Church tradition records that Peter suffered martyrdom under Nero (ca. A.D. 67-68), being crucified upside down, because he refused to be crucified like his Lord.

whom Jesus loved following *them;* the one who also had leaned back on His bosom at the supper and said, "Lord, who is the one who betrays You?" ²¹ So Peter seeing him *said to Jesus, "Lord, and what about this man?" ²² Jesus *said to him, "If I want him to remain until I come, what *is that* to you? You follow Me!" ²³ Therefore this saying went out among the brethren that that disciple would not die; yet Jesus did not say to him that he would not die, but *only,* "If I want him to remain until I come, what *is that* to you?"

²⁴ This is the disciple who is testifying to these things and wrote these things, and we know that his testimony is true.

²⁵ And there are also many other things which Jesus did, which if they *were written in detail, I suppose that even the world itself *would not contain the books that *would be written.

DAY 14: How does Jesus deal with Peter's denial of Him during the trial?

In John 21:15-17, the meaning of this section hinges upon the usage of two synonyms for love. In terms of interpretation, when two synonyms are placed in close proximity in context, a difference in meaning, however slight, is emphasized. When Jesus asked Peter if he loved Him, He used a word for love that signified total commitment. Peter responded with a word for love that signified his love for Jesus, but not necessarily his total commitment. This was not because he was reluctant to express that greater love, but because he had been disobedient and denied the Lord in the past. He was, perhaps, now reluctant to make a claim of supreme devotion when, in the past, his life did not support such a claim. Jesus pressed home to Peter the need for unswerving devotion by repeatedly asking Peter if he loved Him supremely. The essential message here is that Jesus demands total commitment from His followers. Their love for Him must place Him above their love for all else. Jesus confronted Peter with love because He wanted Peter to lead the apostles (Mt 16:18), but in order for Peter to be an effective shepherd, his overwhelming drive must exemplify supreme love for his Lord.

In v. 15, when Jesus asked him if he loved Him "more than these," He probably refers to the fish (v. 11) representing Peter's profession as a fisherman, for he had gone back to it while waiting for Jesus (v. 3). Jesus wanted Peter to love Him so supremely as to forsake all that he was familiar with and be exclusively devoted to being a fisher of men (Mt 4:19). The phrase may refer to the other disciples, since Peter had claimed he would be more devoted than all the others (Mt 26:33). "Tend My lambs." The word "tend" conveys the idea of being devoted to the

Lord's service as an undershepherd who cares for His flock (1Pe 5:1–4). The word has the idea of constantly feeding and nourishing the sheep. This served as a reminder that the primary duty of the messenger of Jesus Christ is to teach the word of God (2Ti 4:2). Acts 1–13 records Peter's obedience to this commission.

In v. 17, "Peter was grieved." The third time Jesus asked Peter, He used Peter's word for love that signified something less than total devotion, questioning even that level of love Peter thought he was safe in claiming. The lessons driven home to Peter grieved his heart, so that he sought for a proper understanding of his heart, not by what he said or had done, but based on the Lord's omniscience (2:24–25).

JUNE 15

2 Kings 17:1–18:37

17 In the twelfth year of Ahaz king of Judah, Hoshea the son of Elah became king over Israel in Samaria, *and reigned* nine years. ²He did evil in the sight of the LORD, only not as the kings of Israel who were before him. ³Shalmaneser king of Assyria came up against him, and Hoshea became his servant and paid him tribute. ⁴But the king of Assyria found conspiracy in Hoshea, who had sent messengers to So king of Egypt and had offered no tribute to the king of Assyria, as *he had done* year by year; so the king of Assyria shut him up and bound him in prison.

⁵Then the king of Assyria invaded the whole land and went up to Samaria and besieged it three years. ⁶In the ninth year of Hoshea, the king of Assyria captured Samaria and carried Israel away into exile to Assyria, and settled them in Halah and Habor, *on* the river of Gozan, and in the cities of the Medes.

⁷Now *this* came about because the sons of Israel had sinned against the LORD their God, who had brought them up from the land of Egypt from under the hand of Pharaoh, king of Egypt, and they had feared other gods ⁸and walked in the customs of the nations whom the LORD had driven out before the sons of Israel, and *in the customs* of the kings of Israel which they had introduced. ⁹The sons of Israel did things secretly which were not right against the LORD their God. Moreover, they built for themselves high places in all their towns, from watchtower to fortified city. ¹⁰They set for themselves *sacred* pillars and Asherim on every high hill and under every green tree, ¹¹and there they burned incense on all the high places as the nations *did* which the LORD had carried away to exile before them; and they did evil things provoking the LORD. ¹²They served idols, concerning which the LORD had said to them, "You shall not do this thing." ¹³Yet the LORD warned Israel and Judah through all His prophets *and* every

seer, saying, "Turn from your evil ways and keep My commandments, My statutes according to all the law which I commanded your fathers, and which I sent to you through My servants the prophets." ¹⁴However, they did not listen, but stiffened their neck like their fathers, who did not believe in the LORD their God. ¹⁵They rejected His statutes and His covenant which He made with their fathers and His warnings with which He warned them. And they followed vanity and became vain, and *went* after the nations which surrounded them, concerning which the LORD had commanded them not to do like them. ¹⁶They forsook all the commandments of the LORD their God and made for themselves molten images, *even* two calves, and made an Asherah and worshiped all the host of heaven and served Baal. ¹⁷Then they made their sons and their daughters pass through the fire, and practiced divination and enchantments, and sold themselves to do evil in the sight of the LORD, provoking Him. ¹⁸So the LORD was very angry with Israel and removed them from His sight; none was left except the tribe of Judah.

¹⁹Also Judah did not keep the commandments of the LORD their God, but walked in the customs which Israel had introduced. ²⁰The LORD rejected all the descendants of Israel and afflicted them and gave them into the hand of plunderers, until He had cast them out of His sight.

²¹When He had torn Israel from the house of David, they made Jeroboam the son of Nebat king. Then Jeroboam drove Israel away from following the LORD and made them commit a great sin. ²²The sons of Israel walked in all the sins of Jeroboam which he did; they did not depart from them ²³until the LORD removed Israel from His sight, as He spoke through all His servants the prophets. So Israel was carried away into exile from their own land to Assyria until this day.

²⁴The king of Assyria brought *men* from Babylon and from Cuthah and from Avva and from Hamath and Sepharvaim, and settled *them* in the cities of Samaria in place of the

sons of Israel. So they possessed Samaria and lived in its cities. ²⁵ At the beginning of their living there, they did not fear the LORD; therefore the LORD sent lions among them which killed some of them. ²⁶ So they spoke to the king of Assyria, saying, "The nations whom you have carried away into exile in the cities of Samaria do not know the custom of the god of the land; so he has sent lions among them, and behold, they kill them because they do not know the custom of the god of the land."

²⁷ Then the king of Assyria commanded, saying, "Take there one of the priests whom you carried away into exile and let him go and live there; and let him teach them the custom of the god of the land." ²⁸ So one of the priests whom they had carried away into exile from Samaria came and lived at Bethel, and taught them how they should fear the LORD.

²⁹ But every nation still made gods of its own and put them in the houses of the high places which the people of Samaria had made, every nation in their cities in which they lived. ³⁰ The men of Babylon made Succoth-benoth, the men of Cuth made Nergal, the men of Hamath made Ashima, ³¹ and the Avvites made Nibhaz and Tartak; and the Sepharvites burned their children in the fire to Adrammelech and Anammelech the gods of Sepharvaim. ³² They also feared the LORD and appointed from among themselves priests of the high places, who acted for them in the houses of the high places. ³³ They feared the LORD and served their own gods according to the custom of the nations from among whom they had been carried away into exile.

³⁴ To this day they do according to the earlier customs: they do not fear the LORD, nor do they follow their statutes or their ordinances or the law, or the commandments which the LORD commanded the sons of Jacob, whom He named Israel; ³⁵ with whom the LORD made a covenant and commanded them, saying, "You shall not fear other gods, nor bow down yourselves to them nor serve them nor sacrifice to them. ³⁶ But the LORD, who brought you up from the land of Egypt with great power and with an outstretched arm, Him you shall fear, and to Him you shall bow yourselves down, and to Him you shall sacrifice. ³⁷ The statutes and the ordinances and the law and the commandment which He wrote for you, you shall observe to do forever; and you shall not fear other gods. ³⁸ The covenant that I have made with you, you shall not forget, nor shall you fear other gods. ³⁹ But the LORD your God you shall fear; and He will deliver you from the hand of all

your enemies." ⁴⁰ However, they did not listen, but they did according to their earlier custom. ⁴¹ So while these nations feared the LORD, they also served their idols; their children likewise and their grandchildren, as their fathers did, so they do to this day.

18 Now it came about in the third year of Hoshea, the son of Elah king of Israel, that Hezekiah the son of Ahaz king of Judah became king. ² He was twenty-five years old when he became king, and he reigned twenty-nine years in Jerusalem; and his mother's name was Abi the daughter of Zechariah. ³ He did right in the sight of the LORD, according to all that his father David had done. ⁴ He removed the high places and broke down the *sacred* pillars and cut down the Asherah. He also broke in pieces the bronze serpent that Moses had made, for until those days the sons of Israel burned incense to it; and it was called Nehushtan. ⁵ He trusted in the LORD, the God of Israel; so that after him there was none like him among all the kings of Judah, nor *among those* who were before him. ⁶ For

18:5 He trusted in the LORD, the God of Israel. The most noble quality of Hezekiah (in dramatic contrast to his father, Ahaz) was that he relied on the Lord as his exclusive hope in every situation. What distinguished him from all other kings of Judah (after the division of the kingdom) was his firm trust in the Lord during a severe national crisis (18:17–19:34). Despite troublesome events, Hezekiah clung tightly to the Lord, faithfully following Him and obeying His commands (v. 6). As a result, the Lord was with him and gave him success (v. 7).

he clung to the LORD; he did not depart from following Him, but kept His commandments, which the LORD had commanded Moses. ⁷ And the LORD was with him; wherever he went he prospered. And he rebelled against the king of Assyria and did not serve him. ⁸ He defeated the Philistines as far as Gaza and its territory, from watchtower to fortified city.

⁹ Now in the fourth year of King Hezekiah, which was the seventh year of Hoshea son of Elah king of Israel, Shalmaneser king of Assyria came up against Samaria and besieged it. ¹⁰ At the end of three years they captured it; in the sixth year of Hezekiah, which was the ninth year of Hoshea king of Israel, Samaria was captured. ¹¹ Then the king of Assyria carried Israel away into exile to

Assyria, and put them in Halah and on the Habor, the river of Gozan, and in the cities of the Medes, [12] because they did not obey the voice of the LORD their God, but transgressed His covenant, *even* all that Moses the servant of the LORD commanded; they would neither listen nor do *it*.

[13] Now in the fourteenth year of King Hezekiah, Sennacherib king of Assyria came up against all the fortified cities of Judah and seized them. [14] Then Hezekiah king of Judah sent to the king of Assyria at Lachish, saying, "I have done wrong. Withdraw from me; whatever you impose on me I will bear." So the king of Assyria required of Hezekiah king of Judah three hundred talents of silver and thirty talents of gold. [15] Hezekiah gave *him* all the silver which was found in the house of the LORD, and in the treasuries of the king's house. [16] At that time Hezekiah cut off *the gold from* the doors of the temple of the LORD, and *from* the doorposts which Hezekiah king of Judah had overlaid, and gave it to the king of Assyria.

[17] Then the king of Assyria sent Tartan and Rab-saris and Rabshakeh from Lachish to King Hezekiah with a large army to Jerusalem. So they went up and came to Jerusalem. And when they went up, they came and stood by the conduit of the upper pool, which is on the highway of the fuller's field. [18] When they called to the king, Eliakim the son of Hilkiah, who was over the household, and Shebnah the scribe and Joah the son of Asaph the recorder, came out to them.

[19] Then Rabshakeh said to them, "Say now to Hezekiah, 'Thus says the great king, the king of Assyria, "What is this confidence that you have? [20] You say (but *they are* only empty words), '*I have* counsel and strength for the war.' Now on whom do you rely, that you have rebelled against me? [21] Now behold, you rely on the staff of this crushed reed, *even* on Egypt; on which if a man leans, it will go into his hand and pierce it. So is Pharaoh king of Egypt to all who rely on him. [22] But if you say to me, 'We trust in the LORD our God,' is it not He whose high places and whose altars Hezekiah has taken away, and has said to Judah and to Jerusalem, 'You shall worship before this altar in Jerusalem'? [23] Now therefore, come, make a bargain with my master the king of Assyria, and I will give you two thousand horses, if you are able on your part to set riders on them. [24] How then can you repulse one official of the least of my master's servants, and rely on Egypt for chariots and for horsemen? [25] Have I now come up without

the LORD's approval against this place to destroy it? The LORD said to me, 'Go up against this land and destroy it.'"'"

[26] Then Eliakim the son of Hilkiah, and Shebnah and Joah, said to Rabshakeh, "Speak now to your servants in Aramaic, for we understand *it;* and do not speak with us in Judean in the hearing of the people who are on the wall." [27] But Rabshakeh said to them, "Has my master sent me only to your master and to you to speak these words, *and* not to the men who sit on the wall, *doomed* to eat their own dung and drink their own urine with you?"

[28] Then Rabshakeh stood and cried with a loud voice in Judean, saying, "Hear the word of the great king, the king of Assyria. [29] Thus says the king, 'Do not let Hezekiah deceive you, for he will not be able to deliver you from my hand; [30] nor let Hezekiah make you trust in the LORD, saying, "The LORD will surely deliver us, and this city will not be given into the hand of the king of Assyria." [31] Do not listen to Hezekiah, for thus says the king of Assyria, "Make your peace with me and come out to me, and eat each of his vine and each of his fig tree and drink each of the waters of his own cistern, [32] until I come and take you away to a land like your own land, a land of grain and new wine, a land of bread and vineyards, a land of olive trees and honey, that you may live and not die." But do not listen to Hezekiah when he misleads you, saying, "The LORD will deliver us." [33] Has any one of the gods of the nations delivered his land from the hand of the king of Assyria? [34] Where are the gods of Hamath and Arpad? Where are the gods of Sepharvaim, Hena and Ivvah? Have they delivered Samaria from my hand? [35] Who among all the gods of the lands have delivered their land from my hand, that the LORD should deliver Jerusalem from my hand?'"

[36] But the people were silent and answered him not a word, for the king's commandment was, "Do not answer him." [37] Then Eliakim the son of Hilkiah, who was over the household, and Shebna the scribe and Joah the son of Asaph, the recorder, came to Hezekiah with their clothes torn and told him the words of Rabshakeh.

Psalm 74:1–8

A Maskil of Asaph.

O God, why have You
 rejected *us* forever?
Why does Your anger smoke against
 the sheep of Your pasture?
[2] Remember Your congregation, which
  You have purchased of old,

Which You have redeemed to be
the tribe of Your inheritance;
And this Mount Zion, where
You have dwelt.
3 Turn Your footsteps toward
the perpetual ruins;
The enemy has damaged everything
within the sanctuary.
4 Your adversaries have roared in the
midst of Your meeting place;
They have set up their own
standards for signs.
5 It seems as if one had lifted up
His axe in a forest of trees.
6 And now all its carved work
They smash with hatchet
and hammers.
7 They have burned Your
sanctuary to the ground;
They have defiled the dwelling
place of Your name.
8 They said in their heart, "Let us
completely subdue them."
They have burned all the meeting
places of God in the land.

Proverbs 18:22-24

22 He who finds a wife finds
a good thing
And obtains favor from the LORD.
23 The poor man utters supplications,
But the rich man answers roughly.
24 A man of *too many* friends
comes to ruin,
But there is a friend who sticks
closer than a brother.

18:24 *comes* to ruin. The person who makes
friends too easily and indiscriminately does
so to his own destruction. On the other hand,
a friend chosen wisely is more loyal than a
brother. **friend.** This is a strong word meaning
"one who loves" and was used of Abraham,
God's friend (2Ch 20:7; Is 41:8; see 1Sa 18:1;
2Sa 1:26).

Acts 1:1-26

1 The first account I composed, Theophilus,
about all that Jesus began to do and teach,
2 until the day when He was taken up *to heaven*,
after He had by the Holy Spirit given orders to
the apostles whom He had chosen. 3 To these He
also presented Himself alive after His suffering, by many convincing proofs, appearing to
them over *a period of* forty days and speaking

**1:3 presented Himself...by many convincing
proofs.** See John 20:30; 1 Corinthians 15:5-8.
To give the apostles confidence to present His
message, Jesus entered a locked room (Jn 20:19),
showed His crucifixion wounds (Lk 24:39), and
ate and drank with the disciples (Lk 24:41-43).
forty days. The time period between Jesus' resurrection and ascension during which He appeared
at intervals to the apostles and others (1Co 15:5-8)
and provided convincing evidence of His resurrection. **kingdom of God.** See 8:12; 14:22; 19:8;
20:25; 28:23, 31. Here this expression refers to
the sphere of salvation, the gracious domain of
divine rule over believers' hearts (1Co 6:9; Eph 5:5;
see 17:7; Col 1:13-14; Rev 11:15; 12:10). This was the
dominant theme during Christ's earthly ministry
(Mt 4:23; 9:35; Mk 1:15; Lk 4:43; 9:2; Jn 3:3-21).

of the things concerning the kingdom of God.
4 Gathering them together, He commanded
them not to leave Jerusalem, but to wait for
what the Father had promised, "Which," *He
said,* "you heard of from Me; 5 for John baptized
with water, but you will be baptized with the
Holy Spirit not many days from now."

6 So when they had come together, they
were asking Him, saying, "Lord, is it at this
time You are restoring the kingdom to Israel?"
7 He said to them, "It is not for you to know
times or epochs which the Father has fixed
by His own authority; 8 but you will receive
power when the Holy Spirit has come upon
you; and you shall be My witnesses both in
Jerusalem, and in all Judea and Samaria, and
even to the remotest part of the earth." 9 And
after He had said these things, He was lifted

1:8 The apostles' mission of spreading the gospel was the major reason the Holy Spirit empowered them. This event dramatically altered
world history, and the gospel message eventually reached all parts of the earth (Mt 28:19-20).
receive power. The apostles had already experienced the Holy Spirit's saving, guiding,
teaching, and miracle-working power. Soon
they would receive His indwelling presence
and a new dimension of power for witness (2:4;
1Co 6:19-20; Eph 3:16, 20). **witnesses.** People
who tell the truth about Jesus Christ (Jn 14:26;
1Pe 3:15). The Greek word means "one who dies
for his faith" because that was commonly the
price of witnessing. **Judea.** The region in which
Jerusalem was located. **Samaria.** The region
immediately to the north of Judea.

up while they were looking on, and a cloud received Him out of their sight. ¹⁰And as they were gazing intently into the sky while He was going, behold, two men in white clothing stood beside them. ¹¹They also said, "Men of Galilee, why do you stand looking into the sky? This Jesus, who has been taken up from you into heaven, will come in just the same way as you have watched Him go into heaven."

¹²Then they returned to Jerusalem from the mount called Olivet, which is near Jerusalem, a Sabbath day's journey away. ¹³When they had entered the city, they went up to the upper room where they were staying; that is, Peter and John and James and Andrew, Philip and Thomas, Bartholomew and Matthew, James the son of Alphaeus, and Simon the Zealot, and Judas the son of James. ¹⁴These all with one mind were continually devoting themselves to prayer, along with the women, and Mary the mother of Jesus, and with His brothers.

¹⁵At this time Peter stood up in the midst of the brethren (a gathering of about one hundred and twenty persons was there together), and said, ¹⁶"Brethren, the Scripture had to be fulfilled, which the Holy Spirit foretold by the mouth of David concerning Judas, who became a guide to those who arrested Jesus. ¹⁷For he was counted among us and received his share in this ministry." ¹⁸(Now this man acquired a field with the price of his wickedness, and fall-ing headlong, he burst open in the middle and all his intestines gushed out. ¹⁹And it became known to all who were living in Jerusalem; so that in their own language that field was called Hakeldama, that is, Field of Blood.) ²⁰"For it is written in the book of Psalms,

'LET HIS HOMESTEAD BE
    MADE DESOLATE,
AND LET NO ONE DWELL IN IT';

and,

'LET ANOTHER MAN TAKE HIS OFFICE.'

²¹Therefore it is necessary that of the men who have accompanied us all the time that the Lord Jesus went in and out among us— ²²beginning with the baptism of John until the day that He was taken up from us—one of these must become a witness with us of His resurrection." ²³So they put forward two men, Joseph called Barsabbas (who was also called Justus), and Matthias. ²⁴And they prayed and said, "You, Lord, who know the hearts of all men, show which one of these two You have chosen ²⁵to occupy this ministry and apostleship from which Judas turned aside to go to his own place." ²⁶And they drew lots for them, and the lot fell to Matthias; and he was added to the eleven apostles.

DAY 15: When and why did the northern kingdom of Israel come to an end?

In 2 Kings 17:6, it says that the "king of Assyria captured Samaria and carried Israel away into exile to Assyria." The capture of Samaria by Sargon II marked the end of the northern kingdom in 722 B.C. According to Assyrian records, the Assyrians deported 27,290 inhabitants of Israel to distant locations. The relocation of populations was characteristic of Assyrian policy during that era. The Israelites were resettled in the upper Tigris-Euphrates Valley and never returned to the Promised Land. "Halah" was a city northeast of Nineveh. The "Habor" River was a northern tributary of the Euphrates. The "cities of the Medes" were northeast of Nineveh. Samaria was resettled with foreigners (v. 24). God did what He said He would do in Deuteronomy 28. The Jews were carried as far east as Susa, where the Book of Esther later took place.

In vv. 7–23, the writer departs from quoting his written sources and gives his own explanation for the captivity of Israel. Judah is included, though her captivity did not occur until 605/604–586 B.C. at the hands of the Babylonians. Her sins were the same. Here is a very full and impressive vindication of God's action in punishing His privileged but rebellious and apostate people. In v. 7, he begins by stating that the Israelites had sinned against the Lord who had redeemed them from Egypt. Gross perversion of the worship of God and national propensity to idolatry finally exhausted divine patience. The idolatry of Israel is described in vv. 7–12. In response to Israel's actions, the Lord sent His prophets to Israel and Judah with a message of repentance (v. 13). However, the people failed to respond to the prophets' messages, because, like their fathers, they did not have faith in the Lord (v. 14). Their lack of faith resulted in disobedience to the Lord's commands and the further pursuit of idolatry (vv. 15–17). The idolatry of Israel (and Judah) brought forth the anger of the Lord, which resulted in exile (v. 18). The "great sin" of both Israel and Judah was their continual following of the sinful pattern of Jeroboam I, departing from the Lord and practicing idolatry, thus bringing down the judgment of captivity predicted by the prophets (vv. 19–23).

JUNE 16

2 Kings 19:1–21:26

19 And when King Hezekiah heard *it,* he tore his clothes, covered himself with sackcloth and entered the house of the LORD. ²Then he sent Eliakim who was over the household with Shebna the scribe and the elders of the priests, covered with sackcloth, to Isaiah the prophet the son of Amoz. ³They said to him, "Thus says Hezekiah, 'This day is a day of distress, rebuke, and rejection; for children have come to birth and there is no strength to *deliver.* ⁴Perhaps the LORD your God will hear all the words of Rabshakeh, whom his master the king of Assyria has sent to reproach the living God, and will rebuke the words which the LORD your God has heard. Therefore, offer a prayer for the remnant that is left.'" ⁵So the servants of King Hezekiah came to Isaiah. ⁶Isaiah said to them, "Thus you shall say to your master, 'Thus says the LORD, "Do not be afraid because of the words that you have heard, with which the servants of the king of Assyria have blasphemed Me. ⁷Behold, I will put a spirit in him so that he will hear a rumor and return to his own land. And I will make him fall by the sword in his own land." '"

⁸Then Rabshakeh returned and found the king of Assyria fighting against Libnah, for he had heard that the king had left Lachish. ⁹When he heard *them* say concerning Tirhakah king of Cush, "Behold, he has come out to fight against you," he sent messengers again to Hezekiah saying, ¹⁰"Thus you shall say to Hezekiah king of Judah, 'Do not let your God in whom you trust deceive you saying, "Jerusalem will not be given into the hand of the king of Assyria." ¹¹Behold, you have heard what the kings of Assyria have done to all the lands, destroying them completely. So will you be spared? ¹²Did the gods of those nations which my fathers destroyed deliver them, *even* Gozan and Haran and Rezeph and the sons of Eden who *were* in Telassar? ¹³Where is the king of Hamath, the king of Arpad, the king of the city of Sepharvaim, and *of* Hena and Ivvah?'"

¹⁴Then Hezekiah took the letter from the hand of the messengers and read it, and he went up to the house of the LORD and spread it out before the LORD. ¹⁵Hezekiah prayed before the LORD and said, "O LORD, the God of Israel, who are enthroned *above* the cherubim, You are the God, You alone, of all the kingdoms of the earth. You have made heaven and earth. ¹⁶Incline Your ear, O LORD, and hear; open Your eyes, O LORD, and see; and listen to the words of Sennacherib, which he has sent to reproach the living God. ¹⁷Truly, O LORD, the kings of Assyria have devastated the nations and their lands ¹⁸and have cast their gods into the fire, for they were not gods but the work of men's hands, wood and stone. So they have destroyed them. ¹⁹Now, O LORD our God, I pray, deliver us from his hand that all the kingdoms of the earth may know that You alone, O LORD, are God."

²⁰Then Isaiah the son of Amoz sent to Hezekiah saying, "Thus says the LORD, the God of Israel, 'Because you have prayed to Me about Sennacherib king of Assyria, I have heard *you.*' ²¹This is the word that the LORD has spoken against him:

'She has despised you
  and mocked you,
The virgin daughter of Zion;
She has shaken *her* head behind you,
  The daughter of Jerusalem!
²² 'Whom have you reproached
  and blasphemed?
And against whom have you
  raised *your* voice,
And haughtily lifted up your eyes?
  Against the Holy One of Israel!
²³ 'Through your messengers you
  have reproached the Lord,
And you have said, "With
  my many chariots
I came up to the heights
  of the mountains,
To the remotest parts of Lebanon;
And I cut down its tall cedars
  and its choice cypresses.
And I entered its farthest lodging
  place, its thickest forest.
²⁴ "I dug *wells* and drank foreign waters,
And with the sole of my
  feet I dried up
All the rivers of Egypt."

²⁵ 'Have you not heard?
Long ago I did it;
From ancient times I planned it.
Now I have brought it to pass,
That you should turn fortified
  cities into ruinous heaps.
²⁶ 'Therefore their inhabitants
  were short of strength,
They were dismayed and
  put to shame;
They were as the vegetation of the
  field and as the green herb,

As grass on the housetops is
    scorched before it is grown up.
²⁷ 'But I know your sitting down,
    And your going out and
        your coming in,
    And your raging against Me.
²⁸ 'Because of your raging against Me,
    And because your arrogance
        has come up to My ears,
    Therefore I will put My
        hook in your nose,
    And My bridle in your lips,
    And I will turn you back by the
        way which you came.

²⁹ 'Then this shall be the sign for you: you will eat this year what grows of itself, in the second year what springs from the same, and in the third year sow, reap, plant vineyards, and eat their fruit. ³⁰ The surviving remnant of the house of Judah will again take root downward and bear fruit upward. ³¹ For out of Jerusalem will go forth a remnant, and out of Mount Zion survivors. The zeal of the LORD will perform this.

³² 'Therefore thus says the LORD concerning the king of Assyria, "He will not come to this city or shoot an arrow there; and he will not come before it with a shield or throw up a siege ramp against it. ³³ By the way that he came, by the same he will return, and he shall not come to this city," declares the LORD. ³⁴ 'For I will defend this city to save it for My own sake and for My servant David's sake.' "

³⁵ Then it happened that night that the angel of the LORD went out and struck 185,000 in the camp of the Assyrians; and when men rose early in the morning, behold, all of them were dead. ³⁶ So Sennacherib king of Assyria departed and returned *home,* and lived at Nineveh. ³⁷ It came about as he was worshiping in the house of Nisroch his god, that Adrammelech and Sharezer killed him with the sword; and they escaped into the land of Ararat. And Esarhaddon his son became king in his place.

20 In those days Hezekiah became mortally ill. And Isaiah the prophet the son of Amoz came to him and said to him, "Thus says the LORD, 'Set your house in order, for you shall die and not live.' " ² Then he turned his face to the wall and prayed to the LORD, saying, ³ "Remember now, O LORD, I beseech You, how I have walked before You in truth and with a whole heart and have done what is good in Your sight." And Hezekiah wept bitterly. ⁴ Before Isaiah had gone out of the middle court, the word of the LORD came

to him, saying, ⁵ "Return and say to Hezekiah the leader of My people, 'Thus says the LORD, the God of your father David, "I have heard your prayer, I have seen your tears; behold, I will heal you. On the third day you shall go up to the house of the LORD. ⁶ I will add fifteen years to your life, and I will deliver you and this city from the hand of the king of Assyria; and I will defend this city for My own sake and for My servant David's sake." ' " ⁷ Then Isaiah said, "Take a cake of figs." And they took and laid *it* on the boil, and he recovered.

⁸ Now Hezekiah said to Isaiah, "What will be the sign that the LORD will heal me, and that I shall go up to the house of the LORD the third day?" ⁹ Isaiah said, "This shall be the sign to you from the LORD, that the LORD will do the thing that He has spoken: shall the shadow go forward ten steps or go back ten steps?" ¹⁰ So Hezekiah answered, "It is easy for the shadow to decline ten steps; no, but let the shadow turn backward ten steps." ¹¹ Isaiah the prophet cried to the LORD, and He brought the shadow on the stairway back ten steps by which it had gone down on the stairway of Ahaz.

¹² At that time Berodach-baladan a son of Baladan, king of Babylon, sent letters and a present to Hezekiah, for he heard that Hezekiah had been sick. ¹³ Hezekiah listened to them, and showed them all his treasure house, the silver and the gold and the spices and the precious oil and the house of his armor and all that was found in his treasuries. There was nothing in his house nor in all his dominion that Hezekiah did not show them. ¹⁴ Then Isaiah the prophet came to King Hezekiah and said to him, "What did these men say, and from where have they come to you?" And Hezekiah said, "They have come from a far country, from Babylon." ¹⁵ He said, "What have they seen in your house?" So Hezekiah answered, "They have seen all that is in my house; there is nothing among my treasuries that I have not shown them."

¹⁶ Then Isaiah said to Hezekiah, "Hear the word of the LORD. ¹⁷ 'Behold, the days are coming when all that is in your house, and all that your fathers have laid up in store to this day

20:16–17 word of the LORD...carried to Babylon. Isaiah predicted the Babylonian captivity that would come over a century later (586 B.C.), another prophecy historically fulfilled in all of its expected detail.

20:17 nothing shall be left. Hezekiah's sin of parading his wealth before the visitors backfired, though this sin was only symptomatic of the ultimate reason for the captivity. The major cause was the corrupt leadership of Manasseh, Hezekiah's son (21:11–15).

will be carried to Babylon; nothing shall be left,' says the LORD. ¹⁸ 'Some of your sons who shall issue from you, whom you will beget, will be taken away; and they will become officials in the palace of the king of Babylon.'" ¹⁹ Then Hezekiah said to Isaiah, "The word of the LORD which you have spoken is good." For he thought, "Is it not so, if there will be peace and truth in my days?"

²⁰ Now the rest of the acts of Hezekiah and all his might, and how he made the pool and the conduit and brought water into the city, are they not written in the Book of the Chronicles of the Kings of Judah? ²¹ So Hezekiah slept with his fathers, and Manasseh his son became king in his place.

21 Manasseh was twelve years old when he became king, and he reigned fifty-five years in Jerusalem; and his mother's name was Hephzibah. ² He did evil in the sight of the LORD, according to the abominations of the nations whom the LORD dispossessed before the sons of Israel. ³ For he rebuilt the high places which Hezekiah his father had destroyed; and he erected altars for Baal and made an Asherah, as Ahab king of Israel had done, and worshiped all the host of heaven and served them. ⁴ He built altars in the house of the LORD, of which the LORD had said, "In Jerusalem I will put My name." ⁵ For he built altars for all the host of heaven in the two courts of the house of the LORD. ⁶ He made his son pass through the fire, practiced witchcraft and used divination, and dealt with mediums and spiritists. He did much evil in the sight of the LORD provoking *Him to anger.* ⁷ Then he set the carved image of Asherah that he had made, in the house of which the LORD said to David and to his son Solomon, "In this house and in Jerusalem, which I have chosen from all the tribes of Israel, I will put My name forever. ⁸ And I will not make the feet of Israel wander anymore from the land which I gave their fathers, if only they will observe to do according to all that I have commanded them, and according to all the law that My servant Moses commanded them." ⁹ But they did not listen, and Manasseh seduced them to do evil

more than the nations whom the LORD destroyed before the sons of Israel.

¹⁰ Now the LORD spoke through His servants the prophets, saying, ¹¹ "Because Manasseh king of Judah has done these abominations, having done wickedly more than all the Amorites did who *were* before him, and has also made Judah sin with his idols; ¹² therefore thus says the LORD, the God of Israel, 'Behold, I am bringing *such* calamity on Jerusalem and Judah, that whoever hears of it, both his ears will tingle. ¹³ I will stretch over Jerusalem the line of Samaria and the plummet of the house of Ahab, and I will wipe Jerusalem as one wipes a dish, wiping it and

21:13 the plummet. These were weighted lines dropped from walls to see whether they were structurally straight (Is 28:17; Am 7:7–8). Walls out of line were torn down. The Lord had measured Jerusalem by the standard of His Word and had determined that the fate of Samaria (Israel) was also to befall Jerusalem. **wipe Jerusalem.** As one would wipe food off a dish, the Lord would wipe Jerusalem clean off the earth, i.e., obliterate her, and leave her turned upside down, empty, and useless.

turning it upside down. ¹⁴ I will abandon the remnant of My inheritance and deliver them into the hand of their enemies, and they will become as plunder and spoil to all their enemies; ¹⁵ because they have done evil in My sight, and have been provoking Me to anger since the day their fathers came from Egypt, even to this day.'"

¹⁶ Moreover, Manasseh shed very much innocent blood until he had filled Jerusalem from one end to another; besides his sin with which he made Judah sin, in doing evil in the sight of the LORD. ¹⁷ Now the rest of the acts of Manasseh and all that he did and his sin which he committed, are they not written in the Book of the Chronicles of the Kings of Judah? ¹⁸ And Manasseh slept with his fathers and was buried in the garden of his own house, in the garden of Uzza, and Amon his son became king in his place.

¹⁹ Amon was twenty-two years old when he became king, and he reigned two years in Jerusalem; and his mother's name *was* Meshullemeth the daughter of Haruz of Jotbah. ²⁰ He did evil in the sight of the LORD, as Manasseh his father had done. ²¹ For he walked in all the way that his father had walked, and served

the idols that his father had served and worshiped them. ²²So he forsook the LORD, the God of his fathers, and did not walk in the way of the LORD. ²³The servants of Amon conspired against him and killed the king in his own house. ²⁴Then the people of the land killed all those who had conspired against King Amon, and the people of the land made Josiah his son king in his place. ²⁵Now the rest of the acts of Amon which he did, are they not written in the Book of the Chronicles of the Kings of Judah? ²⁶He was buried in his grave in the garden of Uzza, and Josiah his son became king in his place.

Psalm 74:9–17

⁹ We do not see our signs;
    There is no longer any prophet,
    Nor is there any among us
      who knows how long.
¹⁰ How long, O God, will the
    adversary revile,
    And the enemy spurn Your
    name forever?
¹¹ Why do You withdraw Your hand,
    even Your right hand?
    From within Your bosom,
    destroy *them!*

¹² Yet God is my king from of old,
    Who works deeds of deliverance
    in the midst of the earth.
¹³ You divided the sea by Your
    strength;
    You broke the heads of the sea
    monsters in the waters.
¹⁴ You crushed the heads of Leviathan;
    You gave him as food for the
    creatures of the wilderness.
¹⁵ You broke open springs and
    torrents;
    You dried up ever-flowing streams.
¹⁶ Yours is the day, Yours
    also is the night;
    You have prepared the
    light and the sun.
¹⁷ You have established all the
    boundaries of the earth;
    You have made summer and winter.

Proverbs 19:1–2

19 Better is a poor man who
    walks in his integrity
    Than he who is perverse in
    speech and is a fool.
² Also it is not good for a person
    to be without knowledge,
    And he who hurries his footsteps errs.

Acts 2:1–21

2 When the day of Pentecost had come, they were all together in one place. ²And suddenly there came from heaven a noise like a violent rushing wind, and it filled the whole house where they were sitting. ³And there appeared to them tongues as of fire distributing themselves, and they rested on each one of them. ⁴And they were all filled with the Holy Spirit and began to speak with other tongues, as the Spirit was giving them utterance.

2:3 The disciples could not comprehend the significance of the Spirit's arrival without the Lord sovereignly illustrating what was occurring with a visible phenomenon. **tongues as of fire.** Just as the sound, like wind, was symbolic, these were not literal flames of fire but supernatural indicators, like fire, that God had sent the Holy Spirit upon each believer. In Scripture, fire often denoted the divine presence (Ex 3:2–6). God's use of a fire-like appearance here parallels what He did with the dove when Jesus was baptized (Mt 3:11; Lk 3:16).

⁵Now there were Jews living in Jerusalem, devout men from every nation under heaven. ⁶And when this sound occurred, the crowd came together, and were bewildered because each one of them was hearing them speak in his own language. ⁷They were amazed and astonished, saying, "Why, are not all these who are speaking Galileans? ⁸And how is it that we each hear *them* in our own language to which we were born? ⁹Parthians and Medes and Elamites, and residents of Mesopotamia, Judea and Cappadocia, Pontus and Asia, ¹⁰Phrygia and Pamphylia, Egypt and the districts of Libya around Cyrene, and visitors from Rome, both Jews and proselytes, ¹¹Cretans and Arabs—we hear them in our *own* tongues speaking of the mighty deeds of God." ¹²And they all continued in

2:7 Galileans. Inhabitants of the mostly rural area of northern Israel around the Sea of Galilee. Galilean Jews spoke with a distinct regional accent and were considered to be unsophisticated and uneducated by the southern Judean Jews. When Galileans were seen to be speaking so many different languages, the Judean Jews were astonished.

amazement and great perplexity, saying to one another, "What does this mean?" [13] But others were mocking and saying, "They are full of sweet wine."

[14] But Peter, taking his stand with the eleven, raised his voice and declared to them: "Men of Judea and all you who live in Jerusalem, let this be known to you and give heed to my words. [15] For these men are not drunk, as you suppose, for it is *only* the third hour of the day; [16] but this is what was spoken of through the prophet Joel:

[17] 'AND IT SHALL BE IN THE
    LAST DAYS,' God says,
  'THAT I WILL POUR FORTH OF MY
    SPIRIT ON ALL MANKIND;
  AND YOUR SONS AND YOUR
    DAUGHTERS SHALL PROPHESY,
  AND YOUR YOUNG MEN
    SHALL SEE VISIONS,

  AND YOUR OLD MEN SHALL
    DREAM DREAMS;
[18] EVEN ON MY BONDSLAVES,
    BOTH MEN AND WOMEN,
  I WILL IN THOSE DAYS POUR
    FORTH OF MY SPIRIT
  And they shall prophesy.
[19] 'AND I WILL GRANT WONDERS
    IN THE SKY ABOVE
  AND SIGNS ON THE EARTH
    BELOW,
  BLOOD, AND FIRE, AND
    VAPOR OF SMOKE.
[20] 'THE SUN WILL BE TURNED
    INTO DARKNESS
  AND THE MOON INTO BLOOD,
  BEFORE THE GREAT AND GLORIOUS
    DAY OF THE LORD SHALL COME.
[21] 'AND IT SHALL BE THAT EVERYONE
    WHO CALLS ON THE NAME OF
    THE LORD WILL BE SAVED.'

DAY 16: What can we learn about the Holy Spirit's special role from the Book of Acts?

One of the cautions we must exercise in studying and teaching from the Book of Acts has to do with the difference between description and prescription. The difference plays an important role in interpreting the historical biblical books. The Bible's description of an event does not imply that the event or action can, should, or will be repeated.

The role of the Holy Spirit in His arrival as the promised Helper (Jn 14:17), which Acts describes as a startling audiovisual event (2:1-13), had some partial and selected repetitions (8:14-19; 10:44-48; 19:1-7). These were special cases in which believers are reported to have received or been filled with the Holy Spirit. In each of these cases, the sound of a rushing mighty wind and the tongues as of fire that were present in the original event (2:1-13) were absent, but the people spoke in tongues they did not know (but others recognized). These events should not be taken as the basis for teaching that believers today should expect the same tongue-evidence to accompany the filling of Holy Spirit. Even in Acts itself, genuine conversions did not necessarily lead to extraordinary filling by the Holy Spirit. For example, a crowd of three thousand people believed and were baptized on the same Day of Pentecost (2:41) that started so dramatically, yet there is no mention of tongues. So, why in some cases did tongues accompany the confirmation of faith? That this actually occurred likely demonstrated that believers were being drawn from very different groups into the church. Each new group received a special welcome from the Holy Spirit. Thus, Samaritans (8:14-19), Gentiles (10:44-48), and believers from the old covenant (19:1-7) were added to the church, and the unity of the church was established. To demonstrate that unity, it was imperative to have some replication in each instance of what had occurred at Pentecost with the believing Jews, such as the presence of the apostles and the coming of the Spirit, manifestly indicated through speaking in the languages of Pentecost.

✍ JUNE 17

2 Kings 22:1–24:20

22 Josiah was eight years old when he became king, and he reigned thirty-one years in Jerusalem; and his mother's name *was* Jedidah the daughter of Adaiah of Bozkath. [2] He did right in the sight of the LORD and walked in all the way of his father David, nor did he turn aside to the right or to the left.

[3] Now in the eighteenth year of King Josiah, the king sent Shaphan, the son of Azaliah the son of Meshullam the scribe, to the house of the LORD saying, [4] "Go up to Hilkiah the high priest that he may count the money brought in to the house of the LORD which the doorkeepers have gathered from the people. [5] Let them deliver it into the hand of the workmen

who have the oversight of the house of the LORD, and let them give it to the workmen who are in the house of the LORD to repair the damages of the house, ⁶to the carpenters and the builders and the masons and for buying timber and hewn stone to repair the house. ⁷Only no accounting shall be made with them for the money delivered into their hands, for they deal faithfully."

⁸Then Hilkiah the high priest said to Shaphan the scribe, "I have found the book of the law in the house of the LORD." And Hilkiah gave the book to Shaphan who read it. ⁹Shaphan the scribe came to the king and brought back word to the king and said, "Your servants have emptied out the money that was found in the house, and have delivered it into the hand of the workmen who have the oversight of the house of the LORD." ¹⁰Moreover, Shaphan the scribe told the king saying, "Hilkiah the priest has given me a book." And Shaphan read it in the presence of the king.

22:8 the book of the law. A scroll containing the Torah (the Pentateuch), the revelation of God through Moses to Israel (23:2; Dt 28:61). Manasseh may have destroyed all the copies of God's law that were not hidden. This could have been the official copy laid beside the ark of the covenant in the Most Holy Place (Dt 31:25–26). It may have been removed from its place under Ahaz, Manasseh, or Amon (2Ch 35:3), but was found during repair work.

---

¹¹When the king heard the words of the book of the law, he tore his clothes. ¹²Then the king commanded Hilkiah the priest, Ahikam the son of Shaphan, Achbor the son of Micaiah, Shaphan the scribe, and Asaiah the king's servant saying, ¹³"Go, inquire of the LORD for me and the people and all Judah concerning the words of this book that has been found, for great is the wrath of the LORD that burns against us, because our fathers have not listened to the words of this book, to do according to all that is written concerning us."

¹⁴So Hilkiah the priest, Ahikam, Achbor, Shaphan, and Asaiah went to Huldah the prophetess, the wife of Shallum the son of Tikvah, the son of Harhas, keeper of the wardrobe (now she lived in Jerusalem in the Second Quarter); and they spoke to her. ¹⁵She said to them, "Thus says the LORD God of Israel, 'Tell the man who sent you to me, ¹⁶thus says the LORD, "Behold, I bring evil on this place

and on its inhabitants, *even* all the words of the book which the king of Judah has read. ¹⁷Because they have forsaken Me and have burned incense to other gods that they might provoke Me to anger with all the work of their hands, therefore My wrath burns against this place, and it shall not be quenched." ' ¹⁸But to the king of Judah who sent you to inquire of the LORD thus shall you say to him, 'Thus says the LORD God of Israel, "*Regarding* the words which you have heard, ¹⁹because your heart was tender and you humbled yourself before the LORD when you heard what I spoke against this place and against its inhabitants that they should become a desolation and a curse, and you have torn your clothes and wept before Me, I truly have heard you," declares the LORD. ²⁰"Therefore, behold, I will gather you to your fathers, and you will be gathered to your grave in peace, and your eyes will not see all the evil which I will bring on this place." ' " So they brought back word to the king.

23 Then the king sent, and they gathered to him all the elders of Judah and of Jerusalem. ²The king went up to the house of the LORD and all the men of Judah and all the inhabitants of Jerusalem with him, and the priests and the prophets and all the people, both small and great; and he read in their hearing all the words of the book of the covenant which was found in the house of the LORD. ³The king stood by the pillar and made a covenant before the LORD, to walk after the LORD, and to keep His commandments and His testimonies and His statutes with all *his* heart and all *his* soul, to carry out the words of this covenant that were written in this book. And all the people entered into the covenant.

⁴Then the king commanded Hilkiah the high priest and the priests of the second order and the doorkeepers, to bring out of the temple of the LORD all the vessels that were made for Baal, for Asherah, and for all the host of heaven; and he burned them outside Jerusalem in the fields of the Kidron, and carried their ashes to Bethel. ⁵He did away with the idolatrous priests whom the kings of Judah had appointed to burn incense in the high places in the cities of Judah and in the surrounding area of Jerusalem, also those who burned incense to Baal, to the sun and to the moon and to the constellations and to all the host of heaven. ⁶He brought out the Asherah from the house of the LORD outside Jerusalem to the brook Kidron, and burned it at the brook Kidron, and ground *it* to dust, and threw its dust on the graves of the common

people. ⁷He also broke down the houses of the *male* cult prostitutes which *were* in the house of the LORD, where the women were weaving hangings for the Asherah. ⁸Then he brought all the priests from the cities of Judah, and defiled the high places where the priests had burned incense, from Geba to Beersheba; and he broke down the high places of the gates which *were* at the entrance of the gate of Joshua the governor of the city, which *were* on one's left at the city gate. ⁹Nevertheless the priests of the high places did not go up to the altar of the LORD in Jerusalem, but they ate unleavened bread among their brothers. ¹⁰He also defiled Topheth, which is in the valley of the son of Hinnom, that no man might make his son or his daughter pass through the fire for Molech. ¹¹He did away with the horses which the kings of Judah had given to the sun, at the entrance of the house of the LORD, by the chamber of Nathan-melech the official, which *was* in the precincts; and he burned the chariots of the sun with fire. ¹²The altars which *were* on the roof, the upper chamber of Ahaz, which the kings of Judah had made, and the altars which Manasseh had made in the two courts of the house of the LORD, the king broke down; and he smashed them there and threw their dust into the brook Kidron. ¹³The high places which *were* before Jerusalem, which *were* on the right of the mount of destruction which Solomon the king of Israel had built for Ashtoreth the abomination of the Sidonians, and for Chemosh the abomination of Moab, and for Milcom the abomination of the sons of Ammon, the king defiled. ¹⁴He broke in pieces the *sacred* pillars and cut down the Asherim and filled their places with human bones.

¹⁵Furthermore, the altar that *was* at Bethel *and* the high place which Jeroboam the son of Nebat, who made Israel sin, had made, even that altar and the high place he broke down. Then he demolished its stones, ground them to dust, and burned the Asherah. ¹⁶Now when Josiah turned, he saw the graves that *were* there on the mountain, and he sent and took the bones from the graves and burned *them* on the altar and defiled it according to the word of the LORD which the man of God proclaimed, who proclaimed these things. ¹⁷Then he said, "What is this monument that I see?" And the men of the city told him, "It is the grave of the man of God who came from Judah and proclaimed these things which you have done against the altar of Bethel." ¹⁸He said, "Let him alone; let no one disturb his bones." So they left his bones undisturbed with the bones of the prophet who came from

Samaria. ¹⁹Josiah also removed all the houses of the high places which *were* in the cities of Samaria, which the kings of Israel had made provoking the LORD; and he did to them just as he had done in Bethel. ²⁰All the priests of the high places who *were* there he slaughtered on the altars and burned human bones on them; then he returned to Jerusalem.

²¹Then the king commanded all the people saying, "Celebrate the Passover to the LORD your God as it is written in this book of the covenant." ²²Surely such a Passover had not been celebrated from the days of the judges who judged Israel, nor in all the days of the kings of Israel and of the kings of Judah. ²³But in the eighteenth year of King Josiah, this Passover was observed to the LORD in Jerusalem.

²⁴Moreover, Josiah removed the mediums and the spiritists and the teraphim and the idols and all the abominations that were seen in the land of Judah and in Jerusalem, that he might confirm the words of the law which were written in the book that Hilkiah the priest found in the house of the LORD. ²⁵Before him there was no king like him who turned to the LORD with all his heart and with all his soul and with all his might, according to all the law of Moses; nor did any like him arise after him.

23:25 no king like him. Of all the kings in David's line, including David himself, no king more closely approximated the royal ideal of Deuteronomy 17:14–20 than Josiah (Mt 22:37). Yet, even Josiah fell short of complete obedience because he had multiple wives (vv. 31, 36). However, even this righteous king could not turn away the Lord's wrath because of Manasseh's sin (vv. 26–27).

²⁶However, the LORD did not turn from the fierceness of His great wrath with which His anger burned against Judah, because of all the provocations with which Manasseh had provoked Him. ²⁷The LORD said, "I will remove Judah also from My sight, as I have removed Israel. And I will cast off Jerusalem, this city which I have chosen, and the temple of which I said, 'My name shall be there.'" ²⁸Now the rest of the acts of Josiah and all that he did, are they not written in the Book of the Chronicles of the Kings of Judah? ²⁹In his days Pharaoh Neco king of Egypt went up to the king of Assyria to the river Euphrates. And King Josiah went to meet him, and

when *Pharaoh Neco* saw him he killed him at Megiddo. ³⁰ His servants drove his body in a chariot from Megiddo, and brought him to Jerusalem and buried him in his own tomb. Then the people of the land took Jehoahaz the son of Josiah and anointed him and made him king in place of his father.

³¹ Jehoahaz was twenty-three years old when he became king, and he reigned three months in Jerusalem; and his mother's name was Hamutal the daughter of Jeremiah of Libnah. ³² He did evil in the sight of the LORD, according to all that his fathers had done. ³³ Pharaoh Neco imprisoned him at Riblah in the land of Hamath, that he might not reign in Jerusalem; and he imposed on the land a fine of one hundred talents of silver and a talent of gold. ³⁴ Pharaoh Neco made Eliakim the son of Josiah king in the place of Josiah his father, and changed his name to Jehoiakim. But he took Jehoahaz away and brought *him* to Egypt, and he died there. ³⁵ So Jehoiakim gave the silver and gold to Pharaoh, but he taxed the land in order to give the money at the command of Pharaoh. He exacted the silver and gold from the people of the land, each according to his valuation, to give it to Pharaoh Neco.

³⁶ Jehoiakim was twenty-five years old when he became king, and he reigned eleven years in Jerusalem; and his mother's name *was* Zebidah the daughter of Pedaiah of Rumah. ³⁷ He did evil in the sight of the LORD, according to all that his fathers had done.

24 In his days Nebuchadnezzar king of Babylon came up, and Jehoiakim became his servant *for* three years; then he turned and rebelled against him. ² The LORD sent against him bands of Chaldeans, bands of Arameans, bands of Moabites, and bands of Ammonites. So He sent them against Judah to destroy it, according to the word of the LORD which He had spoken through His servants the prophets. ³ Surely at the command of the LORD it came upon Judah, to remove *them* from His sight because of the sins of Manasseh, according to all that he had done, ⁴ and also for the innocent blood which he shed, for he filled Jerusalem with innocent blood; and the LORD would not forgive. ⁵ Now the rest of the acts of Jehoiakim and all that he did, are they not written in the Book of the Chronicles of the Kings of Judah? ⁶ So Jehoiakim slept with his fathers, and Jehoiachin his son became king in his place. ⁷ The king of Egypt did not come out of his land again, for the king of Babylon had taken all that belonged to the king of Egypt from the brook of Egypt to the river Euphrates.

24:1 Nebuchadnezzar. Nebuchadnezzar II was the son of Nabopolassar, king of Babylon from 626–605 B.C. As crown prince, Nebuchadnezzar had led his father's army against Pharaoh Neco and the Egyptians at Carchemish on the Euphrates River in northern Syria (605 B.C.). By defeating the Egyptians, Babylon was established as the strongest nation in the ancient Near East. Egypt and its vassals, including Judah, became vassals of Babylon with this victory. Nebuchadnezzar followed up his victory at Carchemish by invading the land of Judah. Later, in 605 B.C., Nebuchadnezzar took some captives to Babylon, including Daniel and his friends (Da 1:1–3). Toward the end of 605 B.C., Nabopolassar died and Nebuchadnezzar succeeded him as king of Babylon, 3 years after Jehoiakim had taken the throne in Judah (Jer 25:1). Nebuchadnezzar reigned from 605–562 B.C. **three years.** Nebuchadnezzar returned to the west in 604 B.C. and took tribute from all of the kings of the west, including Jehoiakim of Judah. Jehoiakim submitted to Babylonian rule from 604–602 B.C. In 602 B.C., Jehoiakim rebelled against Babylon, disregarding the advice of the prophet Jeremiah (Jer 27:9–11).

⁸ Jehoiachin was eighteen years old when he became king, and he reigned three months in Jerusalem; and his mother's name *was* Nehushta the daughter of Elnathan of Jerusalem. ⁹ He did evil in the sight of the LORD, according to all that his father had done.

¹⁰ At that time the servants of Nebuchadnezzar king of Babylon went up to Jerusalem, and the city came under siege. ¹¹ And Nebuchadnezzar the king of Babylon came to the city, while his servants were besieging it. ¹² Jehoiachin the king of Judah went out to the king of Babylon, he and his mother and his servants and his captains and his officials. So the king of Babylon took him captive in the eighth year of his reign. ¹³ He carried out from there all the treasures of the house of the LORD, and the treasures of the king's house, and cut in pieces all the vessels of gold which Solomon king of Israel had made in the temple of the LORD, just as the LORD had said. ¹⁴ Then he led away into exile all Jerusalem and all the captains and all the mighty men of valor, ten thousand captives, and all the craftsmen and the smiths. None remained except the poorest people of the land.

¹⁵ So he led Jehoiachin away into exile to Babylon; also the king's mother and the king's wives and his officials and the leading men of

24:14-16 In 597 B.C., Nebuchadnezzar took an additional 10,000 Judeans as captives to Babylon, in particular the leaders of the nation. This included the leaders of the military and those whose skills would support the military. Included in this deportation was the prophet Ezekiel (Eze 1:1-3). Only the lower classes remained behind in Jerusalem. The Babylonian policy of captivity was different from that of the Assyrians, who took most of the people into exile and resettled the land of Israel with foreigners (17:24). The Babylonians took only the leaders and the strong, while leaving the weak and poor, elevating those left to leadership and thereby earning their loyalty. Those taken to Babylon were allowed to work and live in the mainstream of society. This kept the captive Jews together, so it would be possible for them to return, as recorded in Ezra.

the land, he led away into exile from Jerusalem to Babylon. ¹⁶All the men of valor, seven thousand, and the craftsmen and the smiths, one thousand, all strong and fit for war, and these the king of Babylon brought into exile to Babylon. ¹⁷Then the king of Babylon made his uncle Mattaniah king in his place, and changed his name to Zedekiah.

¹⁸Zedekiah was twenty-one years old when he became king, and he reigned eleven years in Jerusalem; and his mother's name was Hamutal the daughter of Jeremiah of Libnah. ¹⁹He did evil in the sight of the LORD, according to all that Jehoiakim had done. ²⁰For through the anger of the LORD *this* came about in Jerusalem and Judah until He cast them out from His presence. And Zedekiah rebelled against the king of Babylon.

Psalm 74:18-23

¹⁸ Remember this, O LORD, that
the enemy has reviled,
And a foolish people has
spurned Your name.
¹⁹ Do not deliver the soul of Your
turtledove to the wild beast;
Do not forget the life of Your
afflicted forever.
²⁰ Consider the covenant;
For the dark places of the land
are full of the habitations
of violence.
²¹ Let not the oppressed return
dishonored;
Let the afflicted and needy
praise Your name.

²² Arise, O God, *and* plead
Your own cause;
Remember how the foolish man
reproaches You all day long.
²³ Do not forget the voice of
Your adversaries,
The uproar of those who rise against
You which ascends continually.

Proverbs 19:3

³ The foolishness of man ruins his way,
And his heart rages against the LORD.

Acts 2:22-47

²² "Men of Israel, listen to these words: Jesus the Nazarene, a man attested to you by God with miracles and wonders and signs which God performed through Him in your midst, just as you yourselves know— ²³this *Man,* delivered over by the predetermined plan and foreknowledge of God, you nailed to a cross by the hands of godless men and put *Him* to death. ²⁴But God raised Him up again, putting an end to the agony of death, since it was impossible for Him to be held in its power. ²⁵For David says of Him,

'I SAW THE LORD ALWAYS
IN MY PRESENCE;
FOR HE IS AT MY RIGHT HAND, SO
THAT I WILL NOT BE SHAKEN.
²⁶ 'THEREFORE MY HEART WAS GLAD
AND MY TONGUE EXULTED;
MOREOVER MY FLESH ALSO
WILL LIVE IN HOPE;
²⁷ BECAUSE YOU WILL NOT ABANDON
MY SOUL TO HADES,
NOR ALLOW YOUR HOLY ONE
TO UNDERGO DECAY.
²⁸ 'YOU HAVE MADE KNOWN TO
ME THE WAYS OF LIFE;
YOU WILL MAKE ME FULL OF GLADNESS
WITH YOUR PRESENCE.'

²⁹"Brethren, I may confidently say to you regarding the patriarch David that he both died and was buried, and his tomb is with us to this day. ³⁰And so, because he was a prophet and knew that GOD HAD SWORN TO HIM WITH AN OATH TO SEAT *one* OF HIS DESCENDANTS ON HIS THRONE, ³¹he looked ahead and spoke of the resurrection of the Christ, that HE WAS NEITHER ABANDONED TO HADES, NOR DID His flesh SUFFER DECAY. ³²This Jesus God raised up again, to which we are all witnesses. ³³Therefore having been exalted to the right hand of God, and having received from the Father the promise

of the Holy Spirit, He has poured forth this which you both see and hear. ³⁴For it was not David who ascended into heaven, but he himself says:

'THE LORD SAID TO MY LORD,
"SIT AT MY RIGHT HAND,
³⁵ UNTIL I MAKE YOUR ENEMIES A
    FOOTSTOOL FOR YOUR FEET."'

³⁶Therefore let all the house of Israel know for certain that God has made Him both Lord and Christ—this Jesus whom you crucified."

³⁷Now when they heard *this,* they were pierced to the heart, and said to Peter and the rest of the apostles, "Brethren, what shall we do?" ³⁸Peter *said* to them, "Repent, and each of you be baptized in the name of Jesus Christ for the forgiveness of your sins; and you will receive the gift of the Holy Spirit. ³⁹For the promise is for you and your children and for all who are far off, as many as the Lord our God will call to Himself." ⁴⁰And with many other words he solemnly testified and kept on exhorting them, saying, "Be saved from this perverse generation!" ⁴¹So then, those who had received his word were baptized; and that day there were added about three thousand souls. ⁴²They were continually devoting themselves to the apostles' teaching and to fellowship, to the breaking of bread and to prayer.

2:42 apostles' teaching. The foundational content for the believer's spiritual growth and maturity was the Scripture, God's revealed truth, which the apostles received and taught faithfully. **fellowship.** Literally, "partnership," or "sharing." Because Christians become partners with Jesus Christ and all other believers (1Jn 1:3), it is their spiritual duty to stimulate one another to righteousness and obedience (Ro 12:10; 13:8; 15:5; Gal 5:13; Eph 4:2, 25; 5:21; Col 3:9; 1Th 4:9; Heb 3:13; 10:24–25; 1Pe 4:9–10). **breaking of bread.** A reference to the Lord's Table, or Communion, which is mandatory for all Christians to observe (1Co 11:24–29).

⁴³Everyone kept feeling a sense of awe; and many wonders and signs were taking place through the apostles. ⁴⁴And all those who had believed were together and had all things in common; ⁴⁵and they *began* selling their property and possessions and were sharing them with all, as anyone might have need. ⁴⁶Day by day continuing with one mind in the temple, and breaking bread from house to house, they were taking their meals together with gladness and sincerity of heart, ⁴⁷praising God and having favor with all the people. And the Lord was adding to their number day by day those who were being saved.

DAY 17: In response to Peter's sermon, what instructions were given on how to become a Christian?

Those who listened to that powerful sermon were "pierced to the heart" (v. 37). The Greek word for pierce means "cut" or "stab," and thus denotes something sudden and unexpected. In grief, remorse, and intense spiritual conviction, Peter's listeners were stunned by his indictment that they had killed their Messiah.

"Repent" (v. 38). This refers to a change of mind and purpose that turns an individual from sin to God (1Th 1:9). Such change involves more than fearing the consequences of God's judgment. Genuine repentance knows that the evil of sin must be forsaken and the Person and work of Christ totally and singularly embraced. Peter exhorted his hearers to repent; otherwise, they would not experience true conversion.

"Be baptized." This Greek word means "be dipped" or "immersed" in water. Peter was obeying Christ's command from Matthew 28:19 and urging the people who repented and turned to the Lord Christ for salvation to identify, through the waters of baptism, with His death, burial, and resurrection (19:5; Ro 6:3–4; 1Co 12:13; Gal 3:27). This is the first time the apostles publicly enjoined people to obey that ceremony. Prior to this, many Jews had experienced the baptism of John the Baptist and were also familiar with the baptism of Gentile converts to Judaism (proselytes).

"In the name of Jesus Christ." For the new believer, it was a crucial but costly identification to accept. "For the forgiveness of your sins." This might better be translated "because of the forgiveness of sins." Baptism does not produce forgiveness and cleansing from sin. The reality of forgiveness precedes the rite of baptism (v. 41). Genuine repentance brings from God the forgiveness (remission) of sins (Eph 1:7); and because of that, the new believer was to be baptized.

"Receive the gift of the Holy Spirit." The one-time act by which God places His Spirit into the believer's life.

JUNE 18

2 Kings 25:1–30

25 Now in the ninth year of his reign, on the tenth day of the tenth month, Nebuchadnezzar king of Babylon came, he and all his army, against Jerusalem, camped against it and built a siege wall all around it. ² So the city was under siege until the eleventh year of King Zedekiah. ³ On the ninth day of the *fourth* month the famine was so severe in the city that there was no food for the people of the land. ⁴ Then the city was broken into, and all the men of war *fled* by night by way of the gate between the two walls beside the king's garden, though the Chaldeans were all around the city. And they went by way of the Arabah. ⁵ But the army of the Chaldeans pursued the king and overtook him in the plains of Jericho and all his army was scattered from him. ⁶ Then they captured the king and brought him to the king of Babylon at Riblah, and he passed sentence on him. ⁷ They slaughtered the sons of Zedekiah before his eyes, then put out the eyes of Zedekiah and bound him with bronze fetters and brought him to Babylon.

⁸ Now on the seventh day of the fifth month, which was the nineteenth year of King Nebuchadnezzar, king of Babylon, Nebuzaradan the captain of the guard, a servant of the king of Babylon, came to Jerusalem. ⁹ He burned the house of the LORD, the king's house, and all the houses of Jerusalem; even every great house he burned with fire. ¹⁰ So all the army of the Chaldeans who *were with* the captain of the guard broke down the walls around Jerusalem. ¹¹ Then the rest of the people who were left in the city and the deserters who had deserted to the king of Babylon and the rest of the people, Nebuzaradan the captain of the guard carried away into exile. ¹² But the captain of the guard left some of the poorest of the land to be vinedressers and plowmen.

¹³ Now the bronze pillars which were in the house of the LORD, and the stands and the bronze sea which were in the house of the LORD, the Chaldeans broke in pieces and carried the bronze to Babylon. ¹⁴ They took away the pots, the shovels, the snuffers, the spoons, and all the bronze vessels which were used in *temple* service. ¹⁵ The captain of the guard also took away the firepans and the basins, what was fine gold and what was fine silver. ¹⁶ The two pillars, the one sea, and the stands which Solomon had made for the house of the LORD—the bronze of all these ves-

sels was beyond weight. ¹⁷ The height of the one pillar was eighteen cubits, and a bronze capital was on it; the height of the capital was three cubits, with a network and pomegranates on the capital all around, all of bronze. And the second pillar was like these with network.

¹⁸ Then the captain of the guard took Seraiah the chief priest and Zephaniah the second priest, with the three officers of the temple. ¹⁹ From the city he took one official who was overseer of the men of war, and five of the king's advisers who were found in the city; and the scribe of the captain of the army who mustered the people of the land; and sixty men of the people of the land who were found in the city. ²⁰ Nebuzaradan the captain of the guard took them and brought them to the king of Babylon at Riblah. ²¹ Then the king of Babylon struck them down and put them to death at Riblah in the land of Hamath. So Judah was led away into exile from its land.

²² Now *as for* the people who were left in the land of Judah, whom Nebuchadnezzar king of Babylon had left, he appointed Gedaliah the son of Ahikam, the son of Shaphan over them. ²³ When all the captains of the forces, they and *their* men, heard that the king of Babylon had appointed Gedaliah *governor,* they came to Gedaliah to Mizpah, namely, Ishmael the son of Nethaniah, and Johanan the son of Kareah, and Seraiah the son of Tanhumeth the Netophathite, and Jaazaniah the son of the Maacathite, they and their men. ²⁴ Gedaliah swore to them and their men and said to them, "Do not be afraid of the servants of the Chaldeans; live in the land and serve the king of Babylon, and it will be well with you."

²⁵ But it came about in the seventh month, that Ishmael the son of Nethaniah, the son of Elishama, of the royal family, came with ten men and struck Gedaliah down so that he died along with the Jews and the Chaldeans who were with him at Mizpah. ²⁶ Then all the people, both small and great, and the captains of the forces arose and went to Egypt; for they were afraid of the Chaldeans.

²⁷ Now it came about in the thirty-seventh year of the exile of Jehoiachin king of Judah, in the twelfth month, on the twenty-seventh *day* of the month, that Evil-merodach king of Babylon, in the year that he became king, released Jehoiachin king of Judah from prison; ²⁸ and he spoke kindly to him and set his throne above the throne of the kings who *were* with him in Babylon. ²⁹ Jehoiachin changed his prison clothes and had his meals in the king's presence regularly all the days

of his life; [30] and for his allowance, a regular allowance was given him by the king, a portion for each day, all the days of his life.

Psalm 75:1–10

For the choir director; *set to* Al-tashsheth. A Psalm of Asaph, A Song.

We give thanks to You,
O God, we give thanks,
For Your name is near;
Men declare Your wondrous works.

75:1 Your name is near. God's name represents His presence. The history of God's supernatural interventions on behalf of His people demonstrated that God was personally immanent. But Old Testament saints did not have the fullness from permanent, personal indwelling of the Holy Spirit (Jn 14:1, 16–17; 1Co 3:16; 6:19).

---

² "When I select an appointed time,
It is I who judge with equity.
³ "The earth and all who dwell in it melt;
It is I who have firmly set
its pillars. ***Selah***
⁴ "I said to the boastful, 'Do not boast,'
And to the wicked, 'Do not
lift up the horn;
⁵ Do not lift up your horn on high,
Do not speak with insolent pride.'"

⁶ For not from the east, nor
from the west,
Nor from the desert *comes* exaltation;
⁷ But God is the Judge;
He puts down one and exalts another.
⁸ For a cup is in the hand of the
LORD, and the wine foams;
It is well mixed, and He
pours out of this;
Surely all the wicked of the
earth must drain *and*
drink down its dregs.

⁹ But as for me, I will declare *it* forever;
I will sing praises to the God of Jacob.
¹⁰ And all the horns of the
wicked He will cut off,
But the horns of the righteous
will be lifted up.

Proverbs 19:4–5

⁴ Wealth adds many friends,
But a poor man is separated
from his friend.

⁵ A false witness will not
go unpunished,
And he who tells lies will not escape.

Acts 3:1–26

3 Now Peter and John were going up to the temple at the ninth *hour*, the hour of prayer. ² And a man who had been lame from his mother's womb was being carried along, whom they used to set down every day at the gate of the temple which is called Beautiful, in order to beg alms of those who were entering the temple. ³ When he saw Peter and John about to go into the temple, he *began* asking to receive alms. ⁴ But Peter, along with John, fixed his gaze on him and said, "Look at us!" ⁵ And he *began* to give them his attention, expecting to receive something from them. ⁶ But Peter said, "I do not possess silver and gold, but what I do have I give to you: In the name of Jesus Christ the Nazarene—walk!" ⁷ And seizing him by the right hand, he raised him up; and immediately his feet and his ankles were strengthened. ⁸ With a leap he stood upright and *began* to walk; and he entered the temple with them, walking and leaping and praising God. ⁹ And all the people saw him walking and praising God; ¹⁰ and they were taking note of him as being the one who used to sit at the Beautiful Gate of the temple to *beg* alms, and they were filled with wonder and amazement at what had happened to him.

¹¹ While he was clinging to Peter and John, all the people ran together to them at the so-called portico of Solomon, full of amazement. ¹² But when Peter saw *this*, he replied to the people, "Men of Israel, why are you amazed at this, or why do you gaze at us, as if by our own power or piety we had made him walk? ¹³ The God of Abraham, Isaac and Jacob, the God of our fathers, has glorified His servant Jesus, *the one* whom you delivered and disowned in the presence of Pilate, when he had decided to release Him. ¹⁴ But you disowned the Holy and Righteous One and asked for a murderer to be granted to you, ¹⁵ but put to death the Prince of life, *the one* whom God raised from the dead, *a fact* to which we are witnesses. ¹⁶ And on the basis of faith in His name, *it is* the name of Jesus which has strengthened this man whom you see and know; and the faith which *comes* through Him has given him this perfect health in the presence of you all.

¹⁷ "And now, brethren, I know that you acted in ignorance, just as your rulers did also. ¹⁸ But the things which God announced beforehand by the mouth of all the prophets, that His Christ would suffer, He has thus fulfilled.

3:13 The God of Abraham, Isaac and Jacob. A description of God familiar to Peter's Jewish audience (Ex 3:6, 15; 1Ki 18:36; 1Ch 29:18; 2Ch 30:6; Mt 22:32). He used this formula, which stressed God's covenant faithfulness, to demonstrate that he declared the same God and Messiah whom the prophets had proclaimed. **His servant Jesus.** Peter depicted Jesus as God's personal representative. This is an unusual New Testament title for Jesus, used only 4 other places (v. 26; 4:27, 30; Mt 12:18), but a more familiar Old Testament name for Messiah (Is 42:1–4, 19; 49:5–7; 52:13–53:12; see Mt 20:28; Jn 6:38; 8:28; 13:1–7). **Pilate...decided to release Him.** Pontius Pilate, the Roman governor at Jesus' trial, came from a national tradition that strongly supported justice (16:37–38; 22:25–29; 25:16). He knew Jesus' crucifixion would be unjust and therefore declared Him innocent 6 times (Lk 23:4, 14–15, 22; Jn 18:38; 19:4, 6) and repeatedly sought to release Him (Lk 23:13–22; Jn 19:12–13).

3:15 put to death...God raised...we are witnesses. Peter's confident and forceful declaration (1Co 15:3–7) was a clear defense of and provided further evidence for Christ's resurrection. Peter's claim was undeniable; the Jews never showed any evidence, such as Jesus' corpse, to disprove it. **Prince of life.** The Greek word for "prince" means originator, pioneer, or beginner of something. It describes Jesus as the Divine Originator of life (Ps 36:9; Heb 2:10; 12:2; 1Jn 5:11, 20).

[19]Therefore repent and return, so that your sins may be wiped away, in order that times of refreshing may come from the presence of the Lord; [20]and that He may send Jesus, the Christ appointed for you, [21]whom heaven must receive until the period of restoration of all things about which God spoke by the mouth of His holy prophets from ancient time. [22]Moses said, 'THE LORD GOD WILL RAISE UP FOR YOU A PROPHET LIKE ME FROM YOUR BRETHREN; TO HIM YOU SHALL GIVE HEED to everything He says to you. [23]And it will be that every soul that does not heed that prophet shall be utterly destroyed from among the people.' [24]And likewise, all the prophets who have spoken, from Samuel and his successors onward, also announced these days. [25]It is you who are the sons of the prophets and of the covenant which God made with your fathers, saying to Abraham, 'AND IN YOUR SEED ALL THE FAMILIES OF THE EARTH SHALL BE BLESSED.' [26]For you first, God raised up His Servant and sent Him to bless you by turning every one of you from your wicked ways."

3:19 repent and return. "Return" is a frequent New Testament word that relates to sinners turning to God (9:35; 14:15; 26:18, 20; Lk 1:16–17; 2Co 3:16; 1Pe 2:25). **your sins...wiped away.** See Psalm 51:9; Isaiah 43:25; 44:22. "Wiped away" compares forgiveness to the complete wiping away of ink from the surface of a document (Col 2:14).

DAY 18: How did Judah and Jerusalem finally fall?

Responding to King Zedekiah's rebellion in 2 Kings 24:20, Nebuchadnezzar sent his whole army to lay siege against the city of Jerusalem (2Ki 25:1). The siege began in January 588 B.C. and lasted until July 586 B.C. In August 586 B.C., one month after the Babylonian breakthrough of Jerusalem's walls (25:2–4), Nebuzaradan, the commander of Nebuchadnezzar's own imperial guard, was sent by the king to oversee the destruction of Jerusalem. The dismantling and destruction of Jerusalem was accomplished by the Babylonians in an orderly progression (v. 8).

First, Jerusalem's most important buildings were burned (v. 9). Second, the Babylonian army tore down Jerusalem's outer walls, the city's main defense (v. 10). Third, Nebuzaradan organized and led a forced march of remaining Judeans into exile in Babylon (vv. 11–12). The exiles included survivors from Jerusalem and those who had surrendered to the Babylonians before the capture of the city. Only poor, unskilled laborers were left behind to tend the vineyards and farm the fields. Fourth, the items made with precious metals in the temple were carried away to Babylon (vv. 13–17). Fifth, Nebuzaradan took Jerusalem's remaining leaders to Riblah, where Nebuchadnezzar had them executed. This insured that they would never lead another rebellion against Babylon (vv. 18–21).

"So Judah was led away into exile from its land" (v. 21). Exile was the ultimate curse brought upon Judah because of her disobedience to the Mosaic Covenant (Lv 26:33; Dt 28:36, 64). The Book of Lamentations records the sorrow of Jeremiah over this destruction of Jerusalem.

JUNE 19

1 Chronicles 1:1–2:55

1 Adam, Seth, Enosh, ² Kenan, Mahalalel, Jared, ³ Enoch, Methuselah, Lamech, ⁴ Noah, Shem, Ham and Japheth.

⁵ The sons of Japheth *were* Gomer, Magog, Madai, Javan, Tubal, Meshech and Tiras. ⁶ The sons of Gomer *were* Ashkenaz, Diphath, and Togarmah. ⁷ The sons of Javan *were* Elishah, Tarshish, Kittim and Rodanim.

⁸ The sons of Ham *were* Cush, Mizraim, Put, and Canaan. ⁹ The sons of Cush *were* Seba, Havilah, Sabta, Raama and Sabteca; and the sons of Raamah *were* Sheba and Dedan. ¹⁰ Cush became the father of Nimrod; he began to be a mighty one in the earth.

¹¹ Mizraim became the father of the people of Lud, Anam, Lehab, Naphtuh, ¹² Pathrus, Casluh, from which the Philistines came, and Caphtor.

¹³ Canaan became the father of Sidon, his firstborn, Heth, ¹⁴ and the Jebusites, the Amorites, the Girgashites, ¹⁵ the Hivites, the Arkites, the Sinites, ¹⁶ the Arvadites, the Zemarites and the Hamathites.

¹⁷ The sons of Shem *were* Elam, Asshur, Arpachshad, Lud, Aram, Uz, Hul, Gether and Meshech. ¹⁸ Arpachshad became the father of Shelah and Shelah became the father of Eber. ¹⁹ Two sons were born to Eber, the name of the one was Peleg, for in his days the earth was divided, and his brother's name was Joktan. ²⁰ Joktan became the father of Almodad, Sheleph, Hazarmaveth, Jerah, ²¹ Hadoram, Uzal, Diklah, ²² Ebal, Abimael, Sheba, ²³ Ophir, Havilah and Jobab; all these *were* the sons of Joktan.

²⁴ Shem, Arpachshad, Shelah, ²⁵ Eber, Peleg, Reu, ²⁶ Serug, Nahor, Terah, ²⁷ Abram, that is Abraham.

²⁸ The sons of Abraham *were* Isaac and Ishmael. ²⁹ These are their genealogies: the first-born of Ishmael *was* Nebaioth, then Kedar, Adbeel, Mibsam, ³⁰ Mishma, Dumah, Massa, Hadad, Tema, ³¹ Jetur, Naphish and Kedemah; these *were* the sons of Ishmael. ³² The sons of Keturah, Abraham's concubine, *whom* she bore, *were* Zimran, Jokshan, Medan, Midian, Ishbak and Shuah. And the sons of Jokshan *were* Sheba and Dedan. ³³ The sons of Midian were Ephah, Epher, Hanoch, Abida and Eldaah. All these were the sons of Keturah.

³⁴ Abraham became the father of Isaac. The sons of Isaac *were* Esau and Israel. ³⁵ The sons of Esau *were* Eliphaz, Reuel, Jeush, Jalam and Korah. ³⁶ The sons of Eliphaz *were* Teman,

Omar, Zephi, Gatam, Kenaz, Timna and Amalek. ³⁷ The sons of Reuel *were* Nahath, Zerah, Shammah and Mizzah. ³⁸ The sons of Seir *were* Lotan, Shobal, Zibeon, Anah, Dishon, Ezer and Dishan. ³⁹ The sons of Lotan *were* Hori and Homam; and Lotan's sister *was* Timna. ⁴⁰ The sons of Shobal *were* Alian, Manahath, Ebal, Shephi and Onam. And the sons of Zibeon *were* Aiah and Anah. ⁴¹ The son of Anah *was* Dishon. And the sons of Dishon *were* Hamran, Eshban, Ithran and Cheran. ⁴² The sons of Ezer *were* Bilhan, Zaavan and Jaakan. The sons of Dishan *were* Uz and Aran.

⁴³ Now these are the kings who reigned in the land of Edom before any king of the sons of Israel reigned. Bela was the son of Beor, and the name of his city was Dinhabah. ⁴⁴ When Bela died, Jobab the son of Zerah of Bozrah became king in his place. ⁴⁵ When Jobab died, Husham of the land of the Temanites became king in his place. ⁴⁶ When Husham died, Hadad the son of Bedad, who defeated Midian in the field of Moab, became king in his place; and the name of his city *was* Avith. ⁴⁷ When Hadad died, Samlah of Masrekah became king in his place. ⁴⁸ When Samlah died, Shaul of Rehoboth by the River became king in his place. ⁴⁹ When Shaul died, Baal-hanan the son of Achbor became king in his place. ⁵⁰ When Baal-hanan died, Hadad became king in his place; and the name of his city was Pai, and his wife's name was Mehetabel, the daughter of Matred, the daughter of Mezahab. ⁵¹ Then Hadad died.

Now the chiefs of Edom were: chief Timna, chief Aliah, chief Jetheth, ⁵² chief Oholibamah, chief Elah, chief Pinon, ⁵³ chief Kenaz, chief Teman, chief Mibzar, ⁵⁴ chief Magdiel, chief Iram. These *were* the chiefs of Edom.

2 These are the sons of Israel: Reuben, Simeon, Levi, Judah, Issachar, Zebulun, ² Dan, Joseph, Benjamin, Naphtali, Gad and Asher.

³ The sons of Judah *were* Er, Onan and Shelah; *these* three were born to him by Bath-shua the Canaanitess. And Er, Judah's firstborn, was wicked in the sight of the LORD, so He put him to death. ⁴ Tamar his daughter-in-law bore him Perez and Zerah. Judah had five sons in all.

⁵ The sons of Perez *were* Hezron and Hamul. ⁶ The sons of Zerah *were* Zimri, Ethan, Heman, Calcol and Dara; five of them in all. ⁷ The son of Carmi *was* Achar, the troubler of Israel, who violated the ban. ⁸ The son of Ethan *was* Azariah.

⁹ Now the sons of Hezron, who were born to him *were* Jerahmeel, Ram and Chelubai. ¹⁰ Ram became the father of Amminadab, and

Amminadab became the father of Nahshon, leader of the sons of Judah; ¹¹Nahshon became the father of Salma, Salma became the father of Boaz, ¹²Boaz became the father of Obed, and Obed became the father of Jesse; ¹³and Jesse became the father of Eliab his firstborn, then Abinadab the second, Shimea the third, ¹⁴Nethanel the fourth, Raddai the fifth, ¹⁵Ozem the sixth, David the seventh; ¹⁶and their sisters were Zeruiah and Abigail. And the three sons of Zeruiah were Abshai, Joab and Asahel. ¹⁷Abigail bore Amasa, and the father of Amasa was Jether the Ishmaelite.

¹⁸Now Caleb the son of Hezron had sons by Azubah his wife, and by Jerioth; and these were her sons: Jesher, Shobab, and Ardon. ¹⁹When Azubah died, Caleb married Ephrath, who bore him Hur. ²⁰Hur became the father of Uri, and Uri became the father of Bezalel.

²¹Afterward Hezron went in to the daughter of Machir the father of Gilead, whom he married when he was sixty years old; and she bore him Segub. ²²Segub became the father of Jair, who had twenty-three cities in the land of Gilead. ²³But Geshur and Aram took the towns of Jair from them, with Kenath and its villages, even sixty cities. All these were the sons of Machir, the father of Gilead. ²⁴After the death of Hezron in Caleb-ephrathah, Abijah, Hezron's wife, bore him Ashhur the father of Tekoa.

²⁵Now the sons of Jerahmeel the firstborn of Hezron were Ram the firstborn, then Bunah, Oren, Ozem and Ahijah. ²⁶Jerahmeel had another wife, whose name was Atarah; she was the mother of Onam. ²⁷The sons of Ram, the firstborn of Jerahmeel, were Maaz, Jamin and Eker. ²⁸The sons of Onam were Shammai and Jada. And the sons of Shammai were Nadab and Abishur. ²⁹The name of Abishur's wife was Abihail, and she bore him Ahban and Molid. ³⁰The sons of Nadab were Seled and Appaim, and Seled died without sons. ³¹The son of Appaim was Ishi. And the son of Ishi was Sheshan. And the son of Sheshan was Ahlai. ³²The sons of Jada the brother of Shammai were Jether and Jonathan, and Jether died without sons. ³³The sons of Jonathan were Peleth and Zaza. These were the sons of Jerahmeel. ³⁴Now Sheshan had no sons, only daughters. And Sheshan had an Egyptian servant whose name was Jarha. ³⁵Sheshan gave his daughter to Jarha his servant in marriage, and she bore him Attai. ³⁶Attai became the father of Nathan, and Nathan became the father of Zabad, ³⁷and Zabad became the father of Ephlal, and Ephlal became the father of Obed, ³⁸and Obed be-

came the father of Jehu, and Jehu became the father of Azariah, ³⁹and Azariah became the father of Helez, and Helez became the father of Eleasah, ⁴⁰and Eleasah became the father of Sismai, and Sismai became the father of Shallum, ⁴¹and Shallum became the father of Jekamiah, and Jekamiah became the father of Elishama.

⁴²Now the sons of Caleb, the brother of Jerahmeel, were Mesha his firstborn, who was the father of Ziph; and his son was Mareshah, the father of Hebron. ⁴³The sons of Hebron were Korah and Tappuah and Rekem and Shema. ⁴⁴Shema became the father of Raham, the father of Jorkeam; and Rekem became the father of Shammai. ⁴⁵The son of Shammai was Maon, and Maon was the father of Bethzur. ⁴⁶Ephah, Caleb's concubine, bore Haran, Moza and Gazez; and Haran became the father of Gazez. ⁴⁷The sons of Jahdai were Regem, Jotham, Geshan, Pelet, Ephah and Shaaph. ⁴⁸Maacah, Caleb's concubine, bore Sheber and Tirhanah. ⁴⁹She also bore Shaaph the father of Madmannah, Sheva the father of Machbena and the father of Gibea; and the daughter of Caleb was Achsah. ⁵⁰These were the sons of Caleb.

The sons of Hur, the firstborn of Ephrathah, were Shobal the father of Kiriath-jearim, ⁵¹Salma the father of Bethlehem and Hareph the father of Beth-gader. ⁵²Shobal the father of Kiriath-jearim had sons: Haroeh, half of the Manahathites, ⁵³and the families of Kiriath-jearim: the Ithrites, the Puthites, the Shumathites and the Mishraites; from these came the Zorathites and the Eshtaolites. ⁵⁴The sons of Salma were Bethlehem and the Netophathites, Atroth-beth-joab and half of the Manahathites, the Zorites. ⁵⁵The families of scribes who lived at Jabez were the Tirathites, the Shimeathites and the Sucathites. Those are the Kenites who came from Hammath, the father of the house of Rechab.

Psalm 76:1–6

For the choir director; on stringed instruments. A Psalm of Asaph, a Song.

God is known in Judah;
His name is great in Israel.
² His tabernacle is in Salem;
His dwelling place also is in Zion.
³ There He broke the flaming arrows,
The shield and the sword and
the weapons of war.   *Selah*

⁴ You are resplendent,
More majestic than the
mountains of prey.

⁵ The stouthearted were plundered,
They sank into sleep;
And none of the warriors
could use his hands.
⁶ At Your rebuke, O God of Jacob,
Both rider and horse were
cast into a dead sleep.

Proverbs 19:6–7

⁶ Many will seek the favor
of a generous man,
And every man is a friend to
him who gives gifts.
⁷ All the brothers of a poor
man hate him;
How much more do his
friends abandon him!
He pursues *them with* words,
but they are gone.

Acts 4:1–22

4 As they were speaking to the people, the priests and the captain of the temple *guard* and the Sadducees came up to them, ² being greatly disturbed because they were teaching the people and proclaiming in Jesus the resurrection from the dead. ³ And they laid hands on them and put them in jail until the next day, for it was already evening. ⁴ But many of those who had heard the message believed; and the number of the men came to be about five thousand.

⁵ On the next day, their rulers and elders

4:1 priests. The office of priest in the Old Testament began with Aaron and his sons (Lv 8). They became the human intermediaries between holy God and sinful humanity. They were characterized by 3 qualities: 1) they were chosen and set apart for priestly service by God; 2) they were to be holy in character; and 3) they were the only ones allowed to come near to God on behalf of the people with the High Priest being the chief go-between on the Day of Atonement (Lv 16). See Numbers 16:5. **the captain of the temple *guard*.** Chief of the temple police force (composed of Levites) and second-ranking official to the High Priest. The Romans had delegated the temple-policing responsibility to the Jews.

4:2 proclaiming in Jesus the resurrection. This part of the apostles' message was the most objectionable to the Jewish leaders. They had executed Christ as a blasphemer, and now Peter and John were proclaiming His resurrection.

and scribes were gathered together in Jerusalem; ⁶ and Annas the high priest *was there*, and Caiaphas and John and Alexander, and all who were of high-priestly descent. ⁷ When they had placed them in the center, they *began to* inquire, "By what power, or in what name, have you done this?" ⁸ Then Peter, filled with the Holy Spirit, said to them, "Rulers and elders of the people, ⁹ if we are on trial today for a benefit done to a sick man, as to how this man has been made well, ¹⁰ let it be known to all of you and to all the people of Israel, that by the name of Jesus Christ the Nazarene, whom you crucified, whom God raised from the dead—by this *name* this man stands here before you in good health. ¹¹ He is the STONE WHICH WAS REJECTED by you, THE BUILDERS, *but* WHICH BECAME THE CHIEF CORNER *stone*. ¹² And there is salvation in no one else; for there is no other name under heaven that has been given among men by which we must be saved."

4:8 filled with the Holy Spirit. Because Peter was under the control of the Spirit, he was able to face persecution and preach the gospel with power (Lk 12:11–12

4:12 no other name. This refers to the exclusivism of salvation by faith in Jesus Christ. There are only two religious paths: the broad way of works salvation leading to eternal death, and the narrow way of faith in Jesus, leading to eternal life (Mt 7:13–14; see Jn 10:7–8; 14:6). Sadly, the Sanhedrin and its followers were on the first path.

¹³ Now as they observed the confidence of Peter and John and understood that they were uneducated and untrained men, they were amazed, and *began* to recognize them as having been with Jesus. ¹⁴ And seeing the man who had been healed standing with them, they had nothing to say in reply. ¹⁵ But when they had ordered them to leave the Council, they *began* to confer with one another, ¹⁶ saying, "What shall we do with these

4:13 uneducated and untrained men. Peter and John were not educated in the rabbinical schools and had no formal training in Old Testament theology.

men? For the fact that a noteworthy miracle has taken place through them is apparent to all who live in Jerusalem, and we cannot deny it. ¹⁷ But so that it will not spread any further among the people, let us warn them to speak no longer to any man in this name." ¹⁸ And when they had summoned them, they commanded them not to speak or teach at all in the name of Jesus. ¹⁹ But Peter and John answered and said to them, "Whether it is right in the sight of God to give heed to you rather than to God, you be the judge; ²⁰ for we cannot stop speaking about what we have seen and heard." ²¹ When they had threatened them further, they let them go (finding no basis on which to punish them) on account of the people, because they were all glorifying God for what had happened; ²² for the man was more than forty years old on whom this miracle of healing had been performed.

DAY 19: List the ministries of the Holy Spirit.	
Baptismal Medium	1 Corinthians 12:13
Calls to Ministry	Acts 13:2-4
Channel of Divine Revelation	2 Samuel 23:2; Nehemiah 9:30; Zechariah 7:12; John 14:17
Empowers	Exodus 31:1-2; Judges 13:25; Acts 1:8
Fills	Luke 4:1; Acts 2:4; Ephesians 5:18
Guarantees	2 Corinthians 1:22; 5:5; Ephesians 1:14
Guards	2 Timothy 1:14
Helps	John 14:16, 26; 15:26; 16:7
Illuminates	1 Corinthians 2:10-13
Indwells	Romans 8:9-11; 1 Corinthians 3:16; 6:19
Intercedes	Romans 8:26-27
Produces Fruit	Galatians 5:22-23
Provides Spiritual Character	Galatians 5:16, 18, 25
Regenerates	John 3:5-6, 8
Restrains/Convicts of Sin	Genesis 6:3; John 16:8-10; Acts 7:51
Sanctifies	Romans 15:16; 1 Corinthians 6:11; 2 Thessalonians 2:13
Seals	2 Corinthians 1:22; Ephesians 1:14; 4:30
Selects Overseers	Acts 20:28
Source of Fellowship	2 Corinthians 13:14; Philippians 2:1
Source of Liberty	2 Corinthians 3:17-18
Source of Power	Ephesians 3:16
Source of Unity	Ephesians 4:3-4
Source of Spiritual Gifts	1 Corinthians 12:4-11
Teaches	John 14:26; Acts 15:28; 1 John 2:20, 27

JUNE 20

1 Chronicles 3:1-4:43

3 Now these were the sons of David who were born to him in Hebron: the first-born *was* Amnon, by Ahinoam the Jezreelitess; the second *was* Daniel, by Abigail the Carmelitess; ² the third *was* Absalom the son

---

3:1 David. The chief reason for such detailed genealogies is that they affirm the line of Christ from Adam (Lk 3:38) through Abraham and David (Mt 1:1), thus emphasizing the kingdom intentions of God in Christ.

---

of Maacah, the daughter of Talmai king of Geshur; the fourth *was* Adonijah the son of Haggith; ³ the fifth *was* Shephatiah, by Abital; the sixth *was* Ithream, by his wife Eglah. ⁴ Six were born to him in Hebron, and there he reigned seven years and six months. And in Jerusalem he reigned thirty-three years. ⁵ These were born to him in Jerusalem: Shimea, Shobab, Nathan and Solomon, four, by Bath-shua the daughter of Ammiel; ⁶ and Ibhar, Elishama, Eliphelet, ⁷ Nogah, Nepheg and Japhia, ⁸ Elishama, Eliada and Eliphelet, nine. ⁹ All *these were* the sons of David, besides the sons of the concubines; and Tamar *was* their sister.

¹⁰ Now Solomon's son *was* Rehoboam, Abijah *was* his son, Asa his son, Jehoshaphat his son, ¹¹ Joram his son, Ahaziah his son, Joash

his son, ¹²Amaziah his son, Azariah his son, Jotham his son, ¹³Ahaz his son, Hezekiah his son, Manasseh his son, ¹⁴Amon his son, Josiah his son. ¹⁵The sons of Josiah were Johanan the firstborn, and the second was Jehoiakim, the third Zedekiah, the fourth Shallum. ¹⁶The sons of Jehoiakim were Jeconiah his son, Zedekiah his son. ¹⁷The sons of Jeconiah, the prisoner, were Shealtiel his son, ¹⁸and Malchiram, Pedaiah, Shenazzar, Jekamiah, Hoshama and Nedabiah. ¹⁹The sons of Pedaiah were Zerubbabel and Shimei. And the sons of Zerubbabel were Meshullam and Hananiah, and Shelomith was their sister; ²⁰and Hashubah, Ohel, Berechiah, Hasadiah and Jushab-hesed, five. ²¹The sons of Hananiah were Pelatiah and Jeshaiah, the sons of Rephaiah, the sons of Arnan, the sons of Obadiah, the sons of Shecaniah. ²²The descendants of Shecaniah were Shemaiah, and the sons of Shemaiah: Hattush, Igal, Bariah, Neariah and Shaphat, six. ²³The sons of Neariah were Elioenai, Hizkiah and Azrikam, three. ²⁴The sons of Elioenai were Hodaviah, Eliashib, Pelaiah, Akkub, Johanan, Delaiah and Anani, seven.

4 The sons of Judah were Perez, Hezron, Carmi, Hur and Shobal. ²Reaiah the son of Shobal became the father of Jahath, and Jahath became the father of Ahumai and Lahad. These were the families of the Zorathites. ³These were the sons of Etam: Jezreel, Ishma and Idbash; and the name of their sister was Hazzelelponi. ⁴Penuel was the father of Gedor, and Ezer the father of Hushah. These were the sons of Hur, the firstborn of Ephrathah, the father of Bethlehem. ⁵Ashhur, the father of Tekoa, had two wives, Helah and Naarah. ⁶Naarah bore him Ahuzzam, Hepher, Temeni and Haahashtari. These were the sons of Naarah. ⁷The sons of Helah were Zereth, Izhar and Ethnan. ⁸Koz became the father of Anub and Zobebah, and the families of Aharhel the son of Harum. ⁹Jabez was more honorable than his brothers, and his mother named him Jabez saying, "Because I bore him with pain." ¹⁰Now Jabez called on the God of Israel, saying, "Oh that You would bless me indeed and enlarge my border, and that Your hand might be with me, and that You would keep me from harm that it may not pain me!" And God granted him what he requested.

¹¹Chelub the brother of Shuhah became the father of Mehir, who was the father of Eshton. ¹²Eshton became the father of Beth-rapha and Paseah, and Tehinnah the father of Ir-nahash. These are the men of Recah.

¹³Now the sons of Kenaz were Othniel and Seraiah. And the sons of Othniel were Hathath and Meonothai. ¹⁴Meonothai became the father of Ophrah, and Seraiah became the father of Joab the father of Ge-harashim, for they were craftsmen. ¹⁵The sons of Caleb the son of Jephunneh were Iru, Elah and Naam; and the son of Elah was Kenaz. ¹⁶The sons of Jehallelel were Ziph and Ziphah, Tiria and Asarel. ¹⁷The sons of Ezrah were Jether, Mered, Epher and Jalon. (And these are the sons of Bithia the daughter of Pharaoh, whom Mered took) and she conceived and bore Miriam, Shammai and Ishbah the father of Eshtemoa. ¹⁸His Jewish wife bore Jered the father of Gedor, and Heber the father of Soco, and Jekuthiel the father of Zanoah. ¹⁹The sons of the wife of Hodiah, the sister of Naham, were the fathers of Keilah the Garmite and Eshtemoa the Maacathite. ²⁰The sons of Shimon were Amnon and Rinnah, Benhanan and Tilon. And the sons of Ishi were Zoheth and Ben-zoheth. ²¹The sons of Shelah the son of Judah were Er the father of Lecah and Laadah the father of Mareshah, and the families of the house of the linen workers at Beth-ashbea; ²²and Jokim, the men of Cozeba, Joash, Saraph, who ruled in Moab, and Jashubi-lehem. And the records are ancient. ²³These were the potters and the inhabitants of Netaim and Gederah; they lived there with the king for his work.

²⁴The sons of Simeon were Nemuel and Jamin, Jarib, Zerah, Shaul; ²⁵Shallum his son, Mibsam his son, Mishma his son. ²⁶The sons of Mishma were Hammuel his son, Zaccur his son, Shimei his son. ²⁷Now Shimei had sixteen sons and six daughters; but his brothers did not have many sons, nor did all their family multiply like the sons of Judah. ²⁸They lived at Beersheba, Moladah and Hazar-shual, ²⁹at Bilhah, Ezem, Tolad, ³⁰Bethuel, Hormah, Ziklag, ³¹Beth-marcaboth, Hazar-susim, Beth-biri and Shaaraim. These were their cities until the reign of David. ³²Their villages were Etam, Ain, Rimmon, Tochen and Ashan, five cities; ³³and all their villages that were around the same cities as far as Baal. These were their settlements, and they have their genealogy.

³⁴Meshobab and Jamlech and Joshah the son of Amaziah, ³⁵and Joel and Jehu the son of Joshibiah, the son of Seraiah, the son of Asiel, ³⁶and Elioenai, Jaakobah, Jeshohaiah, Asaiah, Adiel, Jesimiel, Benaiah, ³⁷Ziza the son of Shiphi, the son of Allon, the son of Jedaiah, the son of Shimri, the son of Shemaiah; ³⁸these mentioned by name were leaders in their families; and their fathers' houses increased greatly. ³⁹They went to the entrance of Gedor, even to the east side of the valley, to seek pasture for their flocks.

⁴⁰They found rich and good pasture, and the land was broad and quiet and peaceful; for those who lived there formerly *were* Hamites. ⁴¹These, recorded by name, came in the days of Hezekiah king of Judah, and attacked their tents and the Meunites who were found there, and destroyed them utterly to this day, and lived in their place, because there was pasture there for their flocks. ⁴²From them, from the sons of Simeon, five hundred men went to Mount Seir, with Pelatiah, Neariah, Rephaiah and Uzziel, the sons of Ishi, as their leaders. ⁴³They destroyed the remnant of the Amalekites who escaped, and have lived there to this day.

Psalm 76:7-12

⁷ You, even You, are to be feared;
　　And who may stand in Your presence
　　　when once You are angry?

⁸ You caused judgment to be
　　heard from heaven;
　　The earth feared and was still
⁹ When God arose to judgment,
　　To save all the humble
　　　of the earth.　　　　　　*Selah*
¹⁰ For the wrath of man shall
　　praise You;
　　With a remnant of wrath You
　　　will gird Yourself.

¹¹ Make vows to the LORD your
　　God and fulfill *them;*
　　Let all who are around Him bring
　　　gifts to Him who is to be feared.
¹² He will cut off the spirit of princes;
　　He is feared by the kings of the earth.

───────────────────────

76:10 wrath of man shall praise You. The railings against God and His people are turned into praise to God when God providentially brings the wicked down (Is 36:4–20; Ac 2:23; Ro 8:28).

76:12 cut off the spirit of princes. God shatters the attitude of proud governmental leaders who rebel against Him.

Proverbs 19:8-9

⁸ He who gets wisdom loves
　　his own soul;
　　He who keeps understanding
　　　will find good.

⁹ A false witness will not
　　go unpunished,
　　And he who tells lies will perish.

Acts 4:23-37

²³When they had been released, they went to their own *companions* and reported all that the chief priests and the elders had said to them. ²⁴And when they heard *this,* they lifted their voices to God with one accord and said, "O Lord, it is You who MADE THE HEAVEN AND THE EARTH AND THE SEA, AND ALL THAT IS IN THEM, ²⁵who by the Holy Spirit, *through* the mouth of our father David Your servant, said,

'WHY DID THE GENTILES RAGE,
　　AND THE PEOPLES DEVISE
　　　FUTILE THINGS?
²⁶ 'THE KINGS OF THE EARTH
　　　TOOK THEIR STAND,
　　AND THE RULERS WERE
　　　GATHERED TOGETHER
　　AGAINST THE LORD AND
　　　AGAINST HIS CHRIST.'

²⁷For truly in this city there were gathered together against Your holy servant Jesus, whom You anointed, both Herod and Pontius Pilate, along with the Gentiles and the peoples of Israel, ²⁸to do whatever Your hand and Your purpose predestined to occur. ²⁹And now, Lord, take note of their threats, and grant that Your bond-servants may speak Your word with all confidence, ³⁰while You extend Your hand to heal, and signs and wonders take place through the name of Your holy servant Jesus." ³¹And when they had prayed, the place where they had gathered together was shaken, and they were all filled with the Holy Spirit and *began* to speak the word of God with boldness.

³²And the congregation of those who believed were of one heart and soul; and not one *of them* claimed that anything belonging to him was his own, but all things were common property to them. ³³And with great power the apostles were giving testimony to

───────────────────────

4:24-30 Peter and John's experience did not frighten or discourage the other disciples, but exhilarated them. They took confidence in God's sovereign control of all events, even their sufferings. Furthermore, they were comforted that the opposition whom they were facing was foreseen in the Old Testament (vv. 25–26).

4:32-35 all things were common property. Believers understood that all they had belonged to God, and therefore when a brother or sister had a need, those who could meet it were obligated to do so (Jas 2:15-16; 1Jn 3:17). The method was to give the money to the apostles who would distribute it (vv. 35, 37).

4:33 abundant grace. This means "favor" and carries a twofold meaning here: 1) favor from the people outside the church. Because of the believers' love and unity, the common people were impressed (2:47); and 2) favor from God who was granting blessing.

---

the resurrection of the Lord Jesus, and abundant grace was upon them all. ³⁴ For there was not a needy person among them, for all who were owners of land or houses would sell them and bring the proceeds of the sales

³⁵ and lay them at the apostles' feet, and they would be distributed to each as any had need.

³⁶ Now Joseph, a Levite of Cyprian birth, who was also called Barnabas by the apostles (which translated means Son of Encouragement), ³⁷ and who owned a tract of land, sold it and brought the money and laid it at the apostles' feet.

4:36 Joseph, a Levite...called Barnabas. Luke introduces Barnabas as a role model from among those who donated property proceeds. Barnabas was a member of the priestly tribe of the Levites and a native of the island of Cyprus. He becomes an associate of Paul and a prominent figure later in the book (9:26-27; 11:22-24, 30; chaps. 13-15). **Cyprian.** Barnabas was from Cyprus, the third largest island in the Mediterranean after Sicily and Sardinia, located some 60 miles west off the Syrian coast.

DAY 20: List the major sermons in Acts.		
Sermon	**Theme**	**Reference**
Peter to crowds at Pentecost	Peter's explanation of the meaning of Pentecost	Acts 2:14-40
Peter to crowds at the temple	The Jewish people should repent	Acts 3:12-26
Peter to the Sanhedrin	Testimony that a helpless man was healed	Acts 4:5-12
Stephen to the Sanhedrin	Stephen accuses the Jews of killing the Messiah	Acts 7:2-53
Peter to Gentiles	Gentiles can be saved in the same manner as Jews	Acts 10:28-47
Peter to church at Jerusalem	A defense of Peter's ministry to the Gentiles	Acts 11:4-18
Paul to synagogue at Antioch	Jesus was the Messiah of Old Testament prophecies	Acts 13:16-41
Peter to Jerusalem Council	Salvation by grace available to all	Acts 15:7-11
James to Jerusalem Council	Gentile converts do not require circumcision	Acts 15:13-21
Paul to Ephesian elders	Remain faithful in spite of persecution	Acts 20:17-35
Paul to crowd at Jerusalem	Paul's conversion and mission to the Gentiles	Acts 22:1-21
Paul to Sanhedrin	Paul's defense of the gospel	Acts 23:1-6
Paul to King Agrippa	Paul's conversion and zeal for the gospel	Acts 26:2-23
Paul to Jewish leaders at Rome	Paul's statement about his Jewish heritage	Acts 28:17-20

JUNE 21

1 Chronicles 5:1-6:81

5 Now the sons of Reuben the firstborn of Israel (for he was the firstborn, but because he defiled his father's bed, his birthright was given to the sons of Joseph the son of Israel; so that he is not enrolled in the genealogy according to the birthright. ² Though Judah prevailed over his brothers, and from him *came* the leader, yet the birthright belonged to Joseph), ³ the sons of Reuben the firstborn of Israel *were* Hanoch and Pallu, Hezron and Carmi. ⁴ The sons of Joel *were* Shemaiah his son, Gog his son, Shimei his son, ⁵ Micah his son, Reaiah his son, Baal his son, ⁶ Beerah his son, whom Tilgath-pilneser king of Assyria carried away into exile; he was leader of the Reubenites. ⁷ His kinsmen by their families, in the genealogy of their generations, *were* Jeiel the chief, then Zechariah ⁸ and Bela the son of Azaz, the son of Shema, the son of Joel, who lived in Aroer, even to Nebo and Baal-meon. ⁹ To the east he settled as far as the entrance of the wilderness from the river

Euphrates, because their cattle had increased in the land of Gilead. ¹⁰ In the days of Saul they made war with the Hagrites, who fell by their hand, so that they occupied their tents throughout all the land east of Gilead. ¹¹ Now the sons of Gad lived opposite them in the land of Bashan as far as Salecah. ¹² Joel *was* the chief and Shapham the second, then Janai and Shaphat in Bashan. ¹³ Their kinsmen of their fathers' households *were* Michael, Meshullam, Sheba, Jorai, Jacan, Zia and Eber, seven. ¹⁴ These *were* the sons of Abihail, the son of Huri, the son of Jaroah, the son of Gilead, the son of Michael, the son of Jeshishai, the son of Jahdo, the son of Buz; ¹⁵ Ahi the son of Abdiel, the son of Guni, *was* head of their fathers' households. ¹⁶ They lived in Gilead, in Bashan and in its towns, and in all the pasture lands of Sharon, as far as their borders. ¹⁷ All of these were enrolled in the genealogies in the days of Jotham king of Judah and in the days of Jeroboam king of Israel.

¹⁸ The sons of Reuben and the Gadites and the half-tribe of Manasseh, *consisting* of valiant men, men who bore shield and sword and shot with bow and *were* skillful in battle, *were* 44,760, who went to war. ¹⁹ They made war against the Hagrites, Jetur, Naphish and Nodab. ²⁰ They were helped against them, and the Hagrites and all who *were* with them were given into their hand; for they cried out to God in the battle, and He answered their prayers because they trusted in Him. ²¹ They took away their cattle: their 50,000 camels, 250,000 sheep, 2,000 donkeys; and 100,000 men. ²² For many fell slain, because the war *was* of God. And they settled in their place until the exile.

²³ Now the sons of the half-tribe of Manasseh lived in the land; from Bashan to Baal-hermon and Senir and Mount Hermon they were numerous. ²⁴ These were the heads of their fathers' households, even Epher, Ishi, Eliel, Azriel, Jeremiah, Hodaviah and Jahdiel, mighty men of valor, famous men, heads of their fathers' households.

²⁵ But they acted treacherously against the God of their fathers and played the harlot after the gods of the peoples of the land, whom God had destroyed before them. ²⁶ So the God of Israel stirred up the spirit of Pul, king of Assyria, even the spirit of Tilgath-pilneser king of Assyria, and he carried them away into exile, namely the Reubenites, the Gadites and the half-tribe of Manasseh, and brought them to Halah, Habor, Hara and to the river of Gozan, to this day.

6 The sons of Levi *were* Gershon, Kohath and Merari. ² The sons of Kohath *were* Amram, Izhar, Hebron and Uzziel. ³ The children of Amram *were* Aaron, Moses and Miriam. And the sons of Aaron *were* Nadab, Abihu, Eleazar and Ithamar. ⁴ Eleazar became the father of Phinehas, *and* Phinehas became the father of Abishua, ⁵ and Abishua became the father of Bukki, and Bukki became the father of Uzzi, ⁶ and Uzzi became the father of Zerahiah, and Zerahiah became the father of Meraioth, ⁷ Meraioth became the father of Amariah, and Amariah became the father of Ahitub, ⁸ and Ahitub became the father of Zadok, and Zadok became the father of Ahimaaz, ⁹ and Ahimaaz became the father of Azariah, and Azariah be-

6:8 Zadok. By the time of David's reign, the High Priestly line had wrongly been shifted to the sons of Ithamar as represented by Abiathar. When Abiathar sided with Adonijah rather than Solomon, Zadok became the ruling High Priest (1Ki 2:26–27) and restored the high-priesthood to the Levitical line through Phinehas (Nu 25:10–13).

came the father of Johanan, ¹⁰ and Johanan became the father of Azariah (it was he who served as the priest in the house which Solomon built in Jerusalem), ¹¹ and Azariah became the father of Amariah, and Amariah became the father of Ahitub, ¹² and Ahitub became the father of Zadok, and Zadok became the father of Shallum, ¹³ and Shallum became the father of Hilkiah, and Hilkiah became the father of Azariah, ¹⁴ and Azariah became the father of Seraiah, and Seraiah became the father of Jehozadak; ¹⁵ and Jehozadak went *along* when the LORD carried Judah and Jerusalem away into exile by Nebuchadnezzar.

¹⁶ The sons of Levi *were* Gershom, Kohath and Merari. ¹⁷ These are the names of the sons of Gershom: Libni and Shimei. ¹⁸ The sons of Kohath *were* Amram, Izhar, Hebron and Uzziel. ¹⁹ The sons of Merari *were* Mahli and Mushi. And these are the families of the Levites according to their fathers' *households*. ²⁰ Of Gershom: Libni his son, Jahath his son, Zimmah his son, ²¹ Joah his son, Iddo his son, Zerah his son, Jeatherai his son. ²² The sons of Kohath *were* Amminadab his son, Korah his son, Assir his son, ²³ Elkanah his son, Ebiasaph his son and Assir his son, ²⁴ Tahath his son, Uriel his son, Uzziah his son and Shaul his son. ²⁵ The sons of Elkanah *were* Amasai and

Ahimoth. [26]As for Elkanah, the sons of El-kanah were Zophai his son and Nahath his son, [27]Eliab his son, Jeroham his son, Elkanah his son. [28]The sons of Samuel were Joel the firstborn, and Abijah the second. [29]The sons of Merari were Mahli, Libni his son, Shimei his son, Uzzah his son, [30]Shimea his son, Haggiah his son, Asaiah his son.

6:27-28 Samuel, a Levite, by exceptional, divine direction, offered priestly sacrifices (1Sa 7:9; 10:8; 11:14-15). The fact that Elkanah was from Ephraim (1Sa 1:1) indicates where he lived, not his family history (Nu 35:6-8).

[31]Now these are those whom David ap-pointed over the service of song in the house of the LORD, after the ark rested there. [32]They ministered with song before the tabernacle of the tent of meeting, until Solomon had built the house of the LORD in Jerusalem; and they served in their office according to their order. [33]These are those who served with their sons: From the sons of the Kohathites were Heman the singer, the son of Joel, the son of Samuel, [34]the son of Elkanah, the son of Jeroham, the son of Eliel, the son of Toah, [35]the son of Zuph, the son of Elkanah, the son of Mahath, the son of Amasai, [36]the son of Elkanah, the son of Joel, the son of Azariah, the son of Zephaniah, [37]the son of Tahath, the son of Assir, the son of Ebiasaph, the son of Korah, [38]the son of Izhar, the son of Kohath, the son of Levi, the son of Israel. [39]Heman's brother Asaph stood at his right hand, even Asaph the son of Berechiah, the son of Shimea, [40]the son of Michael, the son of Baaseiah, the son of Malchijah, [41]the son of Ethni, the son of Zerah, the son of Adaiah, [42]the son of Ethan, the son of Zimmah, the son of Shimei, [43]the son of Jahath, the son of Gershom, the son of Levi. [44]On the left hand were their kinsmen the sons of Merari: Ethan the son of Kishi, the son of Abdi, the son of Malluch, [45]the son of Hashabiah, the son of Amaziah, the son of Hilkiah, [46]the son of Amzi, the son of Bani, the son of Shemer, [47]the son of Mahli, the son of Mushi, the son of Merari, the son of Levi. [48]Their kinsmen the Levites were appointed for all the service of the tabernacle of the house of God.

[49]But Aaron and his sons offered on the altar of burnt offering and on the altar of in-cense, for all the work of the most holy place, and to make atonement for Israel, according to all that Moses the servant of God had com-manded. [50]These are the sons of Aaron: Elea-zar his son, Phinehas his son, Abishua his son, [51]Bukki his son, Uzzi his son, Zerahiah his son, [52]Meraioth his son, Amariah his son, Ahitub his son, [53]Zadok his son, Ahimaaz his son.

[54]Now these are their settlements accord-ing to their camps within their borders. To the sons of Aaron of the families of the Kohathites (for theirs was the first lot), [55]to them they gave Hebron in the land of Judah and its pas-ture lands around it; [56]but the fields of the city and its villages, they gave to Caleb the son of Jephunneh. [57]To the sons of Aaron they gave the following cities of refuge: Hebron, Libnah also with its pasture lands, Jattir, Eshtemoa with its pasture lands, [58]Hilen with its pasture lands, Debir with its pasture lands, [59]Ashan with its pasture lands and Beth-shemesh with its pasture lands; [60]and from the tribe of Ben-jamin: Geba with its pasture lands, Allemeth with its pasture lands, and Anathoth with its pasture lands. All their cities throughout their families were thirteen cities.

[61]Then to the rest of the sons of Kohath were given by lot, from the family of the tribe, from the half-tribe, the half of Manasseh, ten cities. [62]To the sons of Gershom, according to their families, were given from the tribe of Issachar and from the tribe of Asher, the tribe of Naph-tali, and the tribe of Manasseh, thirteen cities in Bashan. [63]To the sons of Merari were given by lot, according to their families, from the tribe of Reuben, the tribe of Gad and the tribe of Zebulun, twelve cities. [64]So the sons of Israel gave to the Levites the cities with their pasture lands. [65]They gave by lot from the tribe of the sons of Judah, the tribe of the sons of Simeon and the tribe of the sons of Benjamin, these cities which are mentioned by name.

[66]Now some of the families of the sons of Kohath had cities of their territory from the tribe of Ephraim. [67]They gave to them the following cities of refuge: Shechem in the hill country of Ephraim with its pasture lands, Gezer also with its pasture lands, [68]Jokmeam with its pasture lands, Beth-horon with its pasture lands, [69]Aijalon with its pasture lands and Gath-rimmon with its pasture lands; [70]and from the half-tribe of Manasseh: Aner with its pasture lands and Bileam with its pasture lands, for the rest of the family of the sons of Kohath.

[71]To the sons of Gershom were given, from the family of the half-tribe of Manasseh: Golan in Bashan with its pasture lands and Ashtaroth with its pasture lands; [72]and from the tribe of Issachar: Kedesh with its pasture lands, Daberath with its pasture lands [73]and Ramoth with its pasture lands, Anem with its

pasture lands; [74] and from the tribe of Asher: Mashal with its pasture lands, Abdon with its pasture lands, [75] Hukok with its pasture lands and Rehob with its pasture lands; [76] and from the tribe of Naphtali: Kedesh in Galilee with its pasture lands, Hammon with its pasture lands and Kiriathaim with its pasture lands.

[77] To the rest of *the Levites,* the sons of Merari, *were given,* from the tribe of Zebulun: Rimmono with its pasture lands, Tabor with its pasture lands; [78] and beyond the Jordan at Jericho, on the east side of the Jordan, *were given them,* from the tribe of Reuben: Bezer in the wilderness with its pasture lands, Jahzah with its pasture lands, [79] Kedemoth with its pasture lands and Mephaath with its pasture lands; [80] and from the tribe of Gad: Ramoth in Gilead with its pasture lands, Mahanaim with its pasture lands, [81] Heshbon with its pasture lands and Jazer with its pasture lands.

Psalm 77:1–3

For the choir director; according to Jeduthun. A Psalm of Asaph.

M y voice *rises* to God, and
I will cry aloud;
My voice *rises* to God, and
He will hear me.
[2] In the day of my trouble I
sought the Lord;
In the night my hand was stretched
out without weariness;
My soul refused to be comforted.
[3] *When* I remember God,
then I am disturbed;
When I sigh, then my spirit
grows faint.   *Selah*

Proverbs 19:10–12

[10] Luxury is not fitting for a fool;
Much less for a slave to
rule over princes.
[11] A man's discretion makes
him slow to anger,
And it is his glory to overlook
a transgression.
[12] The king's wrath is like the
roaring of a lion,
But his favor is like dew on the grass.

Acts 5:1–21a

5 But a man named Ananias, with his wife Sapphira, sold a piece of property, [2] and kept back *some* of the price for himself, with his wife's full knowledge, and bringing a portion of it, he laid it at the apostles' feet. [3] But Peter said, "Ananias, why has Satan filled your heart to lie to the Holy Spirit and to keep

back *some* of the price of the land? [4] While it remained *unsold,* did it not remain your own? And after it was sold, was it not under your control? Why is it that you have conceived this deed in your heart? You have not lied to men but to God." [5] And as he heard these words, Ananias fell down and breathed his last; and great fear came over all who heard of it. [6] The young men got up and covered him up, and after carrying him out, they buried him.

[7] Now there elapsed an interval of about three hours, and his wife came in, not knowing what had happened. [8] And Peter responded to her, "Tell me whether you sold the land for such and such a price?" And she said, "Yes, that was the price." [9] Then Peter *said* to her, "Why is it that you have agreed together to put the Spirit of the Lord to the test? Behold, the feet of those who have buried your husband are at the door, and they will carry you out *as well.*" [10] And immediately she fell at his feet and breathed her last, and the young men came in and found her dead, and they carried her out and buried her beside her husband. [11] And great fear came over the whole church, and over all who heard of these things.

5:11 church. This is the first use of "church" in Acts, although it is the most common word used to describe the assembly of those who had believed (cf. 4:32).

[12] At the hands of the apostles many signs and wonders were taking place among the people; and they were all with one accord in Solomon's portico. [13] But none of the rest dared to associate with them; however, the people held them in high esteem. [14] And all the more believers in the Lord, multitudes of men and women, were constantly added to *their number,* [15] to such an extent that they even carried

5:15 Peter...his shadow. The people truly believed he had divine healing power and that it might even extend to them through his shadow (3:1-10). But Scripture does not say Peter's shadow ever healed anyone; in fact, the healing power of God through him seemed to go far beyond his shadow (v. 16, "people...all being healed"). This outpouring of healing was an answer to the prayer in 4:29-30.

the sick out into the streets and laid them on cots and pallets, so that when Peter came by at least his shadow might fall on any one of them. ¹⁶ Also the people from the cities in the vicinity of Jerusalem were coming together, bringing people who were sick or afflicted with unclean spirits, and they were all being healed.

¹⁷ But the high priest rose up, along with all his associates (that is the sect of the Sadducees), and they were filled with jealousy. ¹⁸ They laid hands on the apostles and put them in a public jail. ¹⁹ But during the night an angel of the Lord opened the gates of the prison, and taking them out he said, ²⁰ "Go, stand and speak to the people in the temple the whole message of this Life." ²¹ Upon hear-ing *this*, they entered into the temple about daybreak and *began* to teach.

5:16 unclean spirits. They are demons, fallen angels (Rev 12:3) who are so designated because of their vile wickedness. They frequently live inside unbelievers, particularly those who vent their wicked nature.

5:20 the whole message of this Life. The gospel (Php 2:16; 1Jn 1:1–4). Jesus Christ came into this world to provide abundant and eternal life to spiritually dead people (Jn 1:4; 11:25; 1Jn 5:20).

DAY 21: Why the severity of judgment upon Ananias and Sapphira?

The account of Ananias and Sapphira as shown in Acts 5 represents the classic example of hypocrisy among Christians who faked their spirituality to impress others (Mt 6:1–6, 16–18; 15:7; 23:13–36). They were in the "congregation of those who believed" (4:32) and were involved with the Holy Spirit (v. 3) but remained hypocrites. They sold a possession and "kept back some of the price" (v. 2). This was not a sin in and of itself. However, they had promised, perhaps publicly, that they were giving the full amount received to the Lord. Their outward sin was lying about how much they were giving to the church, but the deeper, more devastating sin was their spiritual hypocrisy based on selfishness.

Peter addressed Ananias with the words: "Satan filled your heart to lie to the Holy Spirit" (v. 3). Ananias and Sapphira were satanically inspired in contrast to Barnabas's Spirit-filled gesture (4:37). Ananias must have promised the Lord he would give the whole amount. He lied to the ever-present Holy Spirit in him (1Co 6:19–20) and in the church (Eph 2:21–22). And hearing Peter's words, Ananias fell down and died. The Jews did not embalm, but customarily buried the dead the same day, especially someone who died by divine judgment (see Dt 21:22–23).

"And great fear came over all who heard of it" (v. 5). They were afraid about the seriousness of hypocrisy and sin in the church. The people learned that death can be the consequence of sin (1Co 11:30–32; 1Jn 5:16). That fear extended beyond those present to all who heard about the divine judgment (v. 11).

Then the same judgment fell upon Sapphira. Peter said that they had "agreed together to put the Spirit of the Lord to the test" (v. 9). Sapphira had gone too far in presuming upon God's forbearance. The folly of such blatant human presumption had to be shown as a sin, hence the ultimate divine chastening that followed.

JUNE 22

1 Chronicles 7:1–8:40

7 Now the sons of Issachar *were* four: Tola, Puah, Jashub and Shimron. ² The sons of Tola *were* Uzzi, Rephaiah, Jeriel, Jahmai, Ibsam and Samuel, heads of their fathers' households. *The sons* of Tola *were* mighty men of valor in their generations; their number in the days of David was 22,600. ³ The son of Uzzi *was* Izrahiah. And the sons of Izrahiah *were* Michael, Obadiah, Joel, Isshiah; all five of them *were* chief men. ⁴ With them by their generations according to their fathers' households were 36,000 troops of the army for war, for they had many wives and sons. ⁵ Their relatives among all the families of Issachar *were* mighty men of valor, enrolled by genealogy, in all 87,000.

⁶ *The sons of* Benjamin *were* three: Bela and Becher and Jediael. ⁷ The sons of Bela were five: Ezbon, Uzzi, Uzziel, Jerimoth and Iri. They *were* heads of fathers' households, mighty men of valor, and were 22,034 enrolled by genealogy. ⁸ The sons of Becher *were* Zemirah, Joash, Eliezer, Elioenai, Omri, Jeremoth, Abijah, Anathoth and Alemeth. All these *were* the sons of Becher. ⁹ They were enrolled by genealogy, according to their generations, heads of their fathers' households, 20,200 mighty men of valor.

¹⁰ The son of Jediael *was* Bilhan. And the sons of Bilhan *were* Jeush, Benjamin, Ehud, Chenaanah, Zethan, Tarshish and Ahishahar. ¹¹ All these *were* sons of Jediael, according to the heads of their fathers' households, 17,200 mighty men of valor, who were ready to go out with the army to war. ¹² Shuppim and Huppim *were* the sons of Ir; Hushim *was* the son of Aher.

¹³ The sons of Naphtali *were* Jahziel, Guni, Jezer, and Shallum, the sons of Bilhah.

¹⁴ The sons of Manasseh *were* Asriel, whom his Aramean concubine bore; she bore Machir the father of Gilead. ¹⁵ Machir took a wife for Huppim and Shuppim, whose sister's name was Maacah. And the name of the second was Zelophehad, and Zelophehad had daughters. ¹⁶ Maacah the wife of Machir bore a son, and she named him Peresh; and the name of his brother *was* Sheresh, and his sons *were* Ulam and Rakem. ¹⁷ The son of Ulam *was* Bedan. These *were* the sons of Gilead the son of Machir, the son of Manasseh. ¹⁸ His sister Hammolecheth bore Ishhod and Abiezer and Mahlah. ¹⁹ The sons of Shemida were Ahian and Shechem and Likhi and Aniam.

²⁰ The sons of Ephraim *were* Shuthelah and Bered his son, Tahath his son, Eleadah his son, Tahath his son, ²¹ Zabad his son, Shuthelah his son, and Ezer and Elead whom the men of Gath who were born in the land killed, because they came down to take their livestock. ²² Their father Ephraim mourned many days, and his relatives came to comfort him. ²³ Then he went in to his wife, and she conceived and bore a son, and he named him Beriah, because misfortune had come upon his house. ²⁴ His daughter was Sheerah, who built lower and upper Beth-horon, also Uzzen-sheerah. ²⁵ Rephah was his son *along* with Resheph, Telah his son, Tahan his son, ²⁶ Ladan his son, Ammihud his son, Elishama his son, ²⁷ Non his son and Joshua his son.

²⁸ Their possessions and settlements *were* Bethel with its towns, and to the east Naaran, and to the west Gezer with its towns, and Shechem with its towns as far as Ayyah with its towns, ²⁹ and along the borders of the sons of Manasseh, Beth-shean with its towns, Taanach with its towns, Megiddo with its towns, Dor with its towns. In these lived the sons of Joseph the son of Israel.

³⁰ The sons of Asher *were* Imnah, Ishvah, Ishvi and Beriah, and Serah their sister. ³¹ The sons of Beriah *were* Heber and Malchiel, who was the father of Birzaith. ³² Heber became the father of Japhlet, Shomer and Hotham, and Shua their sister. ³³ The sons of Japhlet *were* Pasach, Bimhal and Ashvath. These were the sons of Japhlet. ³⁴ The sons of Shemer *were* Ahi and Rohgah, Jehubbah and Aram. ³⁵ The sons of his brother Helem *were* Zophah, Imna, Shelesh and Amal. ³⁶ The sons of Zophah *were* Suah, Harnepher, Shual, Beri and Imrah, ³⁷ Bezer, Hod, Shamma, Shilshah, Ithran and Beera. ³⁸ The sons of Jether *were* Jephunneh, Pispa and Ara. ³⁹ The sons of Ulla *were* Arah, Hanniel and Rizia. ⁴⁰ All these *were* the sons of Asher, heads of the fathers' houses, choice and mighty men of valor, heads of the princes. And the number of them enrolled by genealogy for service in war was 26,000 men.

8 And Benjamin became the father of Bela his firstborn, Ashbel the second, Aharah the third, ² Nohah the fourth and Rapha the fifth. ³ Bela had sons: Addar, Gera, Abihud, ⁴ Abishua, Naaman, Ahoah, ⁵ Gera, Shephuphan and Huram. ⁶ These are the sons of Ehud: these are the heads of fathers' *households* of the inhabitants of Geba, and they carried them into exile to Manahath, ⁷ namely, Naaman, Ahijah and Gera—he carried them into exile; and he became the father of Uzza and Ahihud. ⁸ Shaharaim became the father of children in the country of Moab after he had sent away Hushim and Baara his wives. ⁹ By Hodesh his wife he became the father of Jobab, Zibia, Mesha, Malcam, ¹⁰ Jeuz, Sachia, Mirmah. These were his sons, heads of fathers' *households.* ¹¹ By Hushim he became the father of Abitub and Elpaal. ¹² The sons of Elpaal *were* Eber, Misham, and Shemed, who built Ono and Lod, with its towns; ¹³ and Beriah and Shema, who were heads of fathers' *households* of the inhabitants of Aijalon, who put to flight the inhabitants of Gath; ¹⁴ and Ahio, Shashak and Jeremoth. ¹⁵ Zebadiah, Arad, Eder, ¹⁶ Michael, Ishpah and Joha *were* the sons of Beriah. ¹⁷ Zebadiah, Meshullam, Hizki, Heber, ¹⁸ Ishmerai, Izliah and Jobab *were* the sons of Elpaal. ¹⁹ Jakim, Zichri, Zabdi, ²⁰ Elienai, Zillethai, Eliel, ²¹ Adaiah, Beraiah and Shimrath *were* the sons of Shimei. ²² Ishpan, Eber, Eliel, ²³ Abdon, Zichri, Hanan, ²⁴ Hananiah, Elam, Anthothijah, ²⁵ Iphdeiah and Penuel *were* the sons of Shashak. ²⁶ Shamsherai, Shehariah, Athaliah, ²⁷ Jaareshiah, Elijah and Zichri *were* the sons of Jeroham. ²⁸ These were heads of the fathers' *households* according to their generations, chief men who lived in Jerusalem.

²⁹ Now in Gibeon, *Jeiel,* the father of Gibeon lived, and his wife's name was Maacah; ³⁰ and his firstborn son *was* Abdon, then Zur, Kish,

Baal, Nadab, ³¹ Gedor, Ahio and Zecher. ³² Mikloth became the father of Shimeah. And they also lived with their relatives in Jerusalem opposite their *other* relatives. ³³ Ner became the father of Kish, and Kish became the father of Saul, and Saul became the father of Jonathan, Malchi-shua, Abinadab and Eshbaal. ³⁴ The son of Jonathan *was* Merib-baal, and Merib-baal became the father of Micah. ³⁵ The sons of Micah *were* Pithon, Melech, Tarea and Ahaz. ³⁶ Ahaz became the father of Jehoaddah, and Jehoaddah became the father of Alemeth, Azmaveth and Zimri; and Zimri became the father of Moza. ³⁷ Moza became the father of Binea; Raphah *was* his son, Eleasah his son, Azel his son. ³⁸ Azel had six sons, and these *were* their names: Azrikam, Bocheru, Ishmael, Sheariah, Obadiah and Hanan. All these *were* the sons of Azel. ³⁹ The sons of Eshek his brother *were* Ulam his firstborn, Jeush the second and Eliphelet the third. ⁴⁰ The sons of Ulam were mighty men of valor, archers, and had many sons and grandsons, 150 *of them*. All these *were* of the sons of Benjamin.

Psalm 77:4–9

⁴ You have held my eyelids *open;*
  I am so troubled that I cannot speak.
⁵ I have considered the days of old,
  The years of long ago.
⁶ I will remember my song
    in the night;
  I will meditate with my heart,
  And my spirit ponders:

⁷ Will the Lord reject forever?
  And will He never be favorable
    again?
⁸ Has His lovingkindness
    ceased forever?
  Has *His* promise come to
    an end forever?
⁹ Has God forgotten to be gracious,
  Or has He in anger withdrawn
    His compassion?   *Selah*

77:4 held my eyelids open. The psalmist was so upset that he could neither sleep nor talk rationally.

77:6 my song in the night. The remembrance of happier times only deepened his depression. **spirit ponders.** His spirit continually meditated on possible solutions to his problems.

Proverbs 19:13–14

¹³ A foolish son is destruction
    to his father,
  And the contentions of a wife
    are a constant dripping.
¹⁴ House and wealth are an
    inheritance from fathers,
  But a prudent wife is from the LORD.

19:13 constant dripping. An obstinate, argumentative woman is literally like a leak so unrelenting that one has to run from it or go mad. Here are two ways to devastate a man: an ungodly son and an irritating wife.

19:14 One receives inheritance as a family blessing (a result of human birth), but a wise wife (31:10–31) is a result of divine blessing.

Acts 5:21b–42

Now when the high priest and his associates came, they called the Council together, even all the Senate of the sons of Israel, and sent *orders* to the prison house for them to be brought. ²² But the officers who came did not find them in the prison; and they returned and reported back, ²³ saying, "We found the prison house locked quite securely and the guards standing at the doors; but when we had opened up, we found no one inside." ²⁴ Now when the captain of the temple *guard* and the chief priests heard these words, they were greatly perplexed about them as to what would come of this. ²⁵ But someone came and reported to them, "The men whom you put in prison are standing in the temple and teaching the people!" ²⁶ Then the captain went along with the officers and *proceeded* to bring them *back* without violence (for they were afraid of the people, that they might be stoned).

²⁷ When they had brought them, they stood them before the Council. The high priest questioned them, ²⁸ saying, "We gave you strict orders not to continue teaching in this name, and yet, you have filled Jerusalem with your teaching and intend to bring this man's blood upon us." ²⁹ But Peter and the apostles answered, "We must obey God rather than men. ³⁰ The God of our fathers raised up Jesus, whom you had put to death by hanging Him on a cross. ³¹ He is the one whom God exalted to His right hand as a Prince and a Savior, to grant repentance to Israel, and forgiveness of sins. ³² And we are witnesses of these things;

and *so is* the Holy Spirit, whom God has given to those who obey Him."

33 But when they heard this, they were cut to the quick and intended to kill them. 34 But a Pharisee named Gamaliel, a teacher of the Law, respected by all the people, stood up in the Council and gave orders to put the men outside for a short time. 35 And he said to them, "Men of Israel, take care what you propose to do with these men. 36 For some time ago Theudas rose up, claiming to be somebody, and a group of about four hundred men joined up with him. But he was killed, and all who followed him were dispersed and came to nothing. 37 After this man, Judas of Galilee rose up in the days of the census and drew away *some* people after him; he too per-

ished, and all those who followed him were scattered. 38 So in the present case, I say to you, stay away from these men and let them alone, for if this plan or action is of men, it will be overthrown; 39 but if it is of God, you will not be able to overthrow them; or else you may even be found fighting against God."

40 They took his advice; and after calling the apostles in, they flogged them and ordered them not to speak in the name of Jesus, and *then* released them. 41 So they went on their way from the presence of the Council, rejoicing that they had been considered worthy to suffer shame for *His* name. 42 And every day, in the temple and from house to house, they kept right on teaching and preaching Jesus *as* the Christ.

DAY 22: How was the church in Jerusalem spared initially from persecution?

In Acts 5:28, the high priest reminds Peter and the other apostles: "We gave you strict orders not to continue teaching in this name, and yet, you have filled Jerusalem with your teaching." The gospel of Jesus Christ (2:14-40; 4:12-13). "And intend to bring this man's blood on us." The Sanhedrin had apparently forgotten the brash statement its supporters had made before Pilate that the responsibility for Jesus' death should be on them and their children (Mt 27:25).

The apostles' response was so fearlessly delivered that the Jews were infuriated and plotted to kill them. Then Gamaliel stood up in the Sanhedrin. Like his grandfather, the prominent rabbi Hillel, Gamaliel was the most noted rabbi of his time and led the liberal faction of the Pharisees. His most famous student was the apostle Paul (22:3). He argued that they needed to take heed as to what they were plotting. He mentioned Theudas (v. 36), an otherwise unknown individual who led a revolt in Judea in the early years of the first century, not to be confused with a later Theudas cited in Josephus as a revolutionary.

And Gamaliel reminded them of how Judas of Galilee rose up (v. 37). He was the founder of the Zealots who led another revolt in Palestine early in the first century. Zealots, a party of Jews who were fanatical nationalists, believed that radical action was required to overthrow the Roman power in Palestine. They even sought to take up arms against Rome.

Gamaliel's counsel was to "let them alone" (v. 38); for if it was the work of men, it would come to nothing. But if it was of God, none could overcome it. Fortunately, the members of the Sanhedrin heeded Gamaliel's words concerning the apostles and restricted their punishment to beating them.

✴ JUNE 23

1 Chronicles 9:1-10:14

9 So all Israel was enrolled by genealogies; and behold, they are written in the Book of the Kings of Israel. And Judah was carried away into exile to Babylon for their unfaithfulness.

2 Now the first who lived in their possessions in their cities *were* Israel, the priests, the Levites and the temple servants. 3 Some of the sons of Judah, of the sons of Benjamin and of the sons of Ephraim and Manasseh lived in Jerusalem: 4 Uthai the son of Ammihud, the son of Omri, the son of Imri, the son of Bani, from the sons of Perez the son

of Judah. 5 From the Shilonites *were* Asaiah the firstborn and his sons. 6 From the sons of Zerah *were* Jeuel and their relatives, 690 *of them.* 7 From the sons of Benjamin *were* Sallu the son of Meshullam, the son of Hodaviah, the son of Hassenuah, 8 and Ibneiah the son of Jeroham, and Elah the son of Uzzi, the son of Michri, and Meshullam the son of Shephatiah, the son of Reuel, the son of Ibnijah; 9 and their relatives according to their generations, 956. All these *were* heads of fathers' *households* according to their fathers' houses.

10 From the priests *were* Jedaiah, Jehoiarib, Jachin, 11 and Azariah the son of Hilkiah, the son of Meshullam, the son of Zadok, the son of Meraioth, the son of Ahitub, the chief officer

of the house of God; [12] and Adaiah the son of Jeroham, the son of Pashhur, the son of Malchijah, and Maasai the son of Adiel, the son of Jahzerah, the son of Meshullam, the son of Meshillemith, the son of Immer; [13] and their relatives, heads of their fathers' households, 1,760 very able men for the work of the service of the house of God.

[14] Of the Levites were Shemaiah the son of Hasshub, the son of Azrikam, the son of Hashabiah, of the sons of Merari; [15] and Bakbakkar, Heresh and Galal and Mattaniah the son of Mica, the son of Zichri, the son of Asaph, [16] and Obadiah the son of Shemaiah, the son of Galal, the son of Jeduthun, and Berechiah the son of Asa, the son of Elkanah, who lived in the villages of the Netophathites.

[17] Now the gatekeepers were Shallum and Akkub and Talmon and Ahiman and their relatives (Shallum the chief [18] being stationed until now at the king's gate to the east). These were the gatekeepers for the camp of the sons of Levi. [19] Shallum the son of Kore, the son of Ebiasaph, the son of Korah, and his relatives of his father's house, the Korahites, were over the work of the service, keepers of the thresholds of the tent; and their fathers had been over the camp of the LORD, keepers of the entrance. [20] Phinehas the son of Eleazar was ruler over them previously, and the LORD was with him. [21] Zechariah the son of Meshelemiah was gatekeeper of the entrance of the tent of meeting. [22] All these who were chosen to be gatekeepers at the thresholds were 212. These were enrolled by genealogy in their villages, whom David and Samuel the seer appointed in their office of trust. [23] So they and their sons had charge of the gates of the house of the LORD, even the house of the tent, as guards. [24] The gatekeepers were on the four sides, to the east, west, north and south. [25] Their relatives in their villages were to come in every seven days from time to time to be with them; [26] for the four chief gatekeepers who were Levites, were in an office of trust, and were over the chambers and over the treasuries in the house of God. [27] They spent the night around the house of God, because the watch was committed to them; and they were in charge of opening it morning by morning.

[28] Now some of them had charge of the utensils of service, for they counted them when they brought them in and when they took them out. [29] Some of them also were appointed over the furniture and over all the utensils of the sanctuary and over the fine flour and the wine and the oil and the frankincense and the spices. [30] Some of the sons of the priests prepared the mixing of the spices. [31] Mattithiah, one of the Levites, who was the firstborn of Shallum the Korahite, had the responsibility over the things which were baked in pans. [32] Some of their relatives of the sons of the Kohathites were over the showbread to prepare it every sabbath.

[33] Now these are the singers, heads of fathers' households of the Levites, who lived in the chambers of the temple free from other service; for they were engaged in their work day and night. [34] These were heads of fathers' households of the Levites according to their generations, chief men, who lived in Jerusalem.

[35] In Gibeon Jeiel the father of Gibeon lived, and his wife's name was Maacah, [36] and his firstborn son was Abdon, then Zur, Kish, Baal, Ner, Nadab, [37] Gedor, Ahio, Zechariah and Mikloth. [38] Mikloth became the father of Shimeam. And they also lived with their relatives in Jerusalem opposite their other relatives. [39] Ner became the father of Kish, and Kish became the father of Saul, and Saul became the father of Jonathan, Malchi-shua, Abinadab and Eshbaal. [40] The son of Jonathan was Merib-baal; and Merib-baal became the father of Micah. [41] The sons of Micah were Pithon, Melech, Tahrea and Ahaz. [42] Ahaz became the father of Jarah, and Jarah became the father of Alemeth, Azmaveth and Zimri; and Zimri became the father of Moza, [43] and Moza became the father of Binea and Rephaiah his son, Eleasah his son, Azel his son. [44] Azel had six sons whose names are these: Azrikam, Bocheru and Ishmael and Sheariah and Obadiah and Hanan. These were the sons of Azel.

10 Now the Philistines fought against Israel; and the men of Israel fled before the Philistines and fell slain on Mount Gilboa. [2] The Philistines closely pursued Saul and his sons, and the Philistines struck down Jonathan, Abinadab and Malchi-shua, the sons of Saul. [3] The battle became heavy against Saul, and the archers overtook him; and he was wounded by the archers. [4] Then Saul said to his armor bearer, "Draw your sword and thrust me through with it, otherwise these uncircumcised will come and abuse me." But his armor bearer would not, for he was greatly afraid. Therefore Saul took his sword and fell on it. [5] When his armor bearer saw that Saul was dead, he likewise fell on his sword and died. [6] Thus Saul died with his three sons, and all those of his house died together.

⁷When all the men of Israel who were in the valley saw that they had fled, and that Saul and his sons were dead, they forsook their cities and fled; and the Philistines came and lived in them.

⁸It came about the next day, when the Philistines came to strip the slain, that they found Saul and his sons fallen on Mount Gilboa. ⁹So they stripped him and took his head and his armor and sent *messengers* around the land of the Philistines to carry the good news to their idols and to the people. ¹⁰They put his armor in the house of their gods and fastened his head in the house of Dagon. ¹¹When all Jabesh-gilead heard all that the Philistines had done to Saul, ¹²all the valiant men arose and took away the body of Saul and the bodies of his sons and brought them to Jabesh, and they buried their bones under the oak in Jabesh, and fasted seven days.

¹³So Saul died for his trespass which he committed against the LORD, because of the word of the LORD which he did not keep; and also because he asked counsel of a medium, making inquiry *of it,* ¹⁴and did not inquire of the LORD. Therefore He killed him and turned the kingdom to David the son of Jesse.

Psalm 77:10–15

¹⁰ Then I said, "It is my grief,
   That the right hand of the
      Most High has changed."

¹¹ I shall remember the
      deeds of the LORD;
   Surely I will remember Your
      wonders of old.
¹² I will meditate on all Your work
   And muse on Your deeds.
¹³ Your way, O God, is holy;
   What god is great like our God?

77:10 This psalm illustrates one cure for depression. The psalmist does not explain the cause of his despair, but he was definitely locked into gloom. When he thought about God, it only caused him to complain bitterly. But beginning in v. 10, the psalmist's mood starts to change because he commits himself to focusing on God's goodness and past acts of deliverance. His lament then changes into a hymn of praise. **right hand of the Most High.** The psalmist began to remember the times when God used His right hand (power) to strengthen and protect him.

¹⁴ You are the God who works wonders;
   You have made known Your
      strength among the peoples.
¹⁵ You have by Your power
      redeemed Your people,
   The sons of Jacob and Joseph.   *Selah*

Proverbs 19:15–16

¹⁵ Laziness casts into a deep sleep,
   And an idle man will suffer hunger.
¹⁶ He who keeps the commandment
      keeps his soul,
   But he who is careless of
      conduct will die.

19:16 commandment. Wisdom is equated with God's commandments. In a sense, Proverbs contains the applications and implications of all that is in God's moral law.

Acts 6:1–15

6 Now at this time while the disciples were increasing *in number,* a complaint arose on the part of the Hellenistic *Jews* against the *native* Hebrews, because their widows were being overlooked in the daily serving *of food.* ²So the twelve summoned the congregation of the disciples and said, "It is not desirable for us to neglect the word of God in order to serve tables. ³Therefore, brethren, select from among you seven men of good reputation, full of the Spirit and of wisdom, whom we may put in charge of this task. ⁴But we will devote ourselves to prayer and to the ministry of the word." ⁵The statement found approval with the whole congregation; and they chose Stephen, a man full of faith and of the Holy Spirit, and Philip, Prochorus, Nicanor, Timon, Parmenas and Nicolas, a proselyte from Antioch. ⁶And these they brought before the apostles; and after praying, they laid their hands on them.

⁷The word of God kept on spreading; and the number of the disciples continued to increase greatly in Jerusalem, and a great

6:7 One of Luke's periodic statements summarizing the growth of the church and the spread of the gospel (2:41, 47; 4:4; 5:14; 9:31; 12:24; 13:49; 16:5; 19:20). **great many of the priests.** The conversion of large numbers of priests may account for the vicious opposition that arose against Stephen.

many of the priests were becoming obedient to the faith.

⁸ And Stephen, full of grace and power, was performing great wonders and signs among the people. ⁹ But some men from what was called the Synagogue of the Freedmen, *including* both Cyrenians and Alexandrians, and some from Cilicia and Asia, rose up and argued with Stephen. ¹⁰ But they were unable

6:8 wonders and signs. Acts 4:30; 5:12; 14:3; 15:12. Wonders is the amazement people experience when witnessing supernatural works (miracles). Signs point to the power of God behind miracles marvels have no value unless they point to God and His truth. Such works were often done by the Holy Spirit through the apostles (5:12–16) and their associates (6:8) to authenticate them as the messengers of God's truth (2Co 12:12; Heb 2:3–4).

to cope with the wisdom and the Spirit with which he was speaking. ¹¹ Then they secretly induced men to say, "We have heard him speak blasphemous words against Moses and *against* God." ¹² And they stirred up the people, the elders and the scribes, and they came up to him and dragged him away and brought him before the Council. ¹³ They put forward false witnesses who said, "This man incessantly speaks against this holy place and the Law; ¹⁴ for we have heard him say that this Nazarene, Jesus, will destroy this place and alter the customs which Moses handed down to us." ¹⁵ And fixing their gaze on him, all who were sitting in the Council saw his face like the face of an angel.

6:15 face of an angel. Pure, calm, unruffled composure, reflecting the presence of God (Ex 34:29–35).

DAY 23: How did the apostles deal with the first major problem within the church?

By Acts 6:1 the church could have reached over 20,000 men and women. At that time "a complaint arose on the part of the Hellenistic Jews against the native Hebrews." Hebrews were the native Jewish population of Palestine; Hellenists were Jews from the Diaspora. The Hellenists' absorption of aspects of Greek culture made them suspect to the Palestinian Jews. The Hellenists believed their widows were not receiving an adequate share of the food the church provided for their care (1Ti 5:3–16).

The apostles considered the problem and said they could not "neglect the word of God in order to serve tables" (v. 2). The word translated "tables" can refer to tables used in monetary matters (Mt 21:12; Mk 11:15; Jn 2:15), as well as those used for serving meals. To be involved either in financial matters or in serving meals would take the 12 away from their first priority. Prayer and the ministry of the word (v. 2) define the highest priorities of church leaders (v. 4).

Rather, they told the church to pick out "seven men" to take care of it (v. 3). These were not deacons in terms of the later church office (1Ti 3:8–13), although they performed some of the same duties. Stephen and Philip (the only ones of the 7 mentioned elsewhere in Scripture) clearly were evangelists, not deacons. Acts later mentions elders (14:23; 20:17), but not deacons.

The 7 men chosen by the church all had Greek names, implying they were all Hellenists. The church, in a display of love and unity, may have chosen them to rectify the apparent imbalance involving the Hellenistic widows. "After praying [the apostles] laid their hands on them" (v. 6). This expression was used of Jesus when He healed and sometimes indicated being taken prisoner. In the Old Testament, offerers of sacrifices laid their hands on the animal as an expression of identification (Lv 8:14, 18, 22; Heb 6:2). But in the symbolic sense, it signified the affirmation, support, and identification with someone and his ministry (see 1Ti 4:14; 5:22; 2Ti 1:6; Nu 27:23).

🦌 JUNE 24

1 Chronicles 11:1–12:40

11 Then all Israel gathered to David at Hebron and said, "Behold, we are your bone and your flesh. ² In times past, even when Saul was king, you *were* the one who led out and brought in Israel; and the LORD your God said

to you, 'You shall shepherd My people Israel, and you shall be prince over My people Israel.'" ³ So all the elders of Israel came to the king at Hebron, and David made a covenant with them in Hebron before the LORD; and they anointed David king over Israel, according to the word of the LORD through Samuel.

⁴ Then David and all Israel went to Jerusalem (that is, Jebus); and the Jebusites, the

inhabitants of the land, *were* there. ⁵ The inhabitants of Jebus said to David, "You shall not enter here." Nevertheless David captured the stronghold of Zion (that is, the city of David). ⁶ Now David had said, "Whoever strikes down a Jebusite first shall be chief and commander." Joab the son of Zeruiah went up first, so he became chief. ⁷ Then David dwelt in the stronghold; therefore it was called the city of David. ⁸ He built the city all around, from the Millo even to the surrounding area; and Joab repaired the rest of the city. ⁹ David became greater and greater, for the LORD of hosts *was* with him.

¹⁰ Now these are the heads of the mighty men whom David had, who gave him strong support in his kingdom, together with all Israel, to make him king, according to the word of the LORD concerning Israel. ¹¹ These *constitute* the list of the mighty men whom David had: Jashobeam, the son of a Hachmonite, the chief of the thirty; he lifted up his spear against three hundred whom he killed at one time.

¹² After him was Eleazar the son of Dodo, the Ahohite, who *was* one of the three mighty men. ¹³ He was with David at Pasdammim when the Philistines were gathered together there to battle, and there was a plot of ground full of barley; and the people fled before the Philistines. ¹⁴ They took their stand in the midst of the plot and defended it, and struck down the Philistines; and the LORD saved them by a great victory.

¹⁵ Now three of the thirty chief men went down to the rock to David, into the cave of Adullam, while the army of the Philistines was camping in the valley of Rephaim. ¹⁶ David was then in the stronghold, while the garrison of the Philistines *was* then in Bethlehem. ¹⁷ David had a craving and said, "Oh that someone would give me water to drink from the well of Bethlehem, which is by the gate!" ¹⁸ So the three broke through the camp of the Philistines and drew water from the well of Bethlehem which *was* by the gate, and took *it* and brought *it* to David; nevertheless David would not drink it, but poured it out to the LORD; ¹⁹ and he said, "Be it far from me before my God that I should do this. Shall I drink the blood of these men *who went* at the risk of their lives? For at the risk of their lives they brought it." Therefore he would not drink it. These things the three mighty men did.

²⁰ As for Abshai the brother of Joab, he was chief of the thirty, and he swung his spear against three hundred and killed them; and he

had a name as well as the thirty. ²¹ Of the three in the second *rank* he was the most honored and became their commander; however, he did not attain to the *first* three.

²² Benaiah the son of Jehoiada, the son of a valiant man of Kabzeel, mighty in deeds, struck down the two *sons* of Ariel of Moab. He also went down and killed a lion inside a pit on a snowy day. ²³ He killed an Egyptian, a man of *great* stature five cubits tall. Now in the Egyptian's hand *was* a spear like a weaver's beam, but he went down to him with a club and snatched the spear from the Egyptian's hand and killed him with his own spear. ²⁴ These *things* Benaiah the son of Jehoiada did, and had a name as well as the three mighty men. ²⁵ Behold, he was honored among the thirty, but he did not attain to the three; and David appointed him over his guard.

²⁶ Now the mighty men of the armies *were* Asahel the brother of Joab, Elhanan the son of Dodo of Bethlehem, ²⁷ Shammoth the Harorite, Helez the Pelonite, ²⁸ Ira the son of Ikkesh the Tekoite, Abiezer the Anathothite, ²⁹ Sibbecai the Hushathite, Ilai the Ahohite, ³⁰ Maharai the Netophathite, Heled the son of Baanah the Netophathite, ³¹ Ithai the son of Ribai of Gibeah of the sons of Benjamin, Benaiah the Pirathonite, ³² Hurai of the brooks of Gaash, Abiel the Arbathite, ³³ Azmaveth the Baharumite, Eliahba the Shaalbonite, ³⁴ the sons of Hashem the Gizonite, Jonathan the son of Shagee the Hararite, ³⁵ Ahiam the son of Sacar the Hararite, Eliphal the son of Ur, ³⁶ Hepher the Mecherathite, Ahijah the Pelonite, ³⁷ Hezro the Carmelite, Naarai the son of Ezbai, ³⁸ Joel the brother of Nathan, Mibhar the son of Hagri, ³⁹ Zelek the Ammonite, Naharai the Berothite, the armor bearer of Joab the son of Zeruiah, ⁴⁰ Ira the Ithrite, Gareb the Ithrite, ⁴¹ Uriah the Hittite, Zabad the son of Ahlai, ⁴² Adina the son of Shiza the Reubenite, a chief of the Reubenites, and thirty with him, ⁴³ Hanan the son of Maacah and Joshaphat the Mithnite, ⁴⁴ Uzzia the Ashterathite, Shama and Jeiel the sons of Hotham the Aroerite, ⁴⁵ Jediael the son of Shimri and Joha his brother, the Tizite, ⁴⁶ Eliel the Mahavite and Jeribai and Joshaviah, the sons of Elnaam, and Ithmah the Moabite, ⁴⁷ Eliel and Obed and Jaasiel the Mezobaite.

12 Now these are the ones who came to David at Ziklag, while he was still restricted because of Saul the son of Kish; and they were among the mighty men who helped *him* in war. ² They were equipped with bows, using both the right hand and the left to sling stones and to shoot arrows from the bow; they were Saul's kinsmen from Benjamin. ³ The chief was Ahiezer, then Joash, the sons of Shemaah the Gibeathite; and Jeziel and Pelet, the sons of Azmaveth, and Beracah and Jehu the Anathothite, ⁴ and Ishmaiah the Gibeonite, a mighty man among the thirty, and over the thirty. Then Jeremiah, Jahaziel, Johanan, Jozabad the Gederathite, ⁵ Eluzai, Jerimoth, Bealiah, Shemariah, Shephatiah the Haruphite, ⁶ Elkanah, Isshiah, Azarel, Joezer, Jashobeam, the Korahites, ⁷ and Joelah and Zebadiah, the sons of Jeroham of Gedor.

⁸ From the Gadites there came over to David in the stronghold in the wilderness, mighty men of valor, men trained for war, who could handle shield and spear, and whose faces were like the faces of lions, and they were as swift as the gazelles on the mountains. ⁹ Ezer was the first, Obadiah the second, Eliab the third, ¹⁰ Mishmannah the fourth, Jeremiah the fifth, ¹¹ Attai the sixth, Eliel the seventh, ¹² Johanan the eighth, Elzabad the ninth, ¹³ Jeremiah the tenth, Machbannai the eleventh. ¹⁴ These of the sons of Gad were captains of the army; he who was least was equal to a hundred and the greatest to a thousand. ¹⁵ These are the ones who crossed the Jordan in the first month when it was overflowing all its banks and they put to flight all those in the valleys, both to the east and to the west.

¹⁶ Then some of the sons of Benjamin and Judah came to the stronghold to David. ¹⁷ David went out to meet them, and said to them, "If you come peacefully to me to help me, my heart shall be united with you; but if to betray me to my adversaries, since there is no wrong in my hands, may the God of our fathers look on it and decide." ¹⁸ Then the Spirit came upon Amasai, who was the chief of the thirty, and he said,

"We are yours, O David,
And with you, O son of Jesse!
Peace, peace to you,
And peace to him who helps you;
Indeed, your God helps you!"

Then David received them and made them captains of the band.

12:18 the Spirit. A temporary empowerment by the Holy Spirit to assure David that the Benjamites and Judahites were loyal to him and that the cause was blessed by God.

¹⁹ From Manasseh also some defected to David when he was about to go to battle with the Philistines against Saul. But they did not help them, for the lords of the Philistines after consultation sent him away, saying, "At the cost of our heads he may defect to his master Saul." ²⁰ As he went to Ziklag there defected to him from Manasseh: Adnah, Jozabad, Jediael, Michael, Jozabad, Elihu and Zillethai, captains of thousands who belonged to Manasseh. ²¹ They helped David against the band of raiders, for they were all mighty men of valor, and were captains in the army. ²² For day by day men came to David to help him, until there was a great army like the army of God.

²³ Now these are the numbers of the divisions equipped for war, who came to David at Hebron, to turn the kingdom of Saul to him, according to the word of the LORD. ²⁴ The sons of Judah who bore shield and spear were 6,800, equipped for war. ²⁵ Of the sons of Simeon, mighty men of valor for war, 7,100. ²⁶ Of the sons of Levi 4,600. ²⁷ Now Jehoiada was the leader of the house of Aaron, and with him were 3,700, ²⁸ also Zadok, a young man mighty of valor, and of his father's house twenty-two captains. ²⁹ Of the sons of Benjamin, Saul's kinsmen, 3,000; for until now the greatest part of them had kept their allegiance to the house of Saul. ³⁰ Of the sons of Ephraim 20,800, mighty men of valor, famous men in their fathers' households. ³¹ Of the half-tribe of Manasseh 18,000, who were designated by name to come and make David king. ³² Of the sons of Issachar, men who understood the times, with knowledge of what Israel should do, their chiefs were two hundred; and all their kinsmen were at their command. ³³ Of Zebulun, there were 50,000 who went out in the army, who could draw up in battle formation with all kinds of weapons of war and helped David with an undivided heart. ³⁴ Of Naphtali there were 1,000 captains, and with them 37,000 with shield and spear. ³⁵ Of the Danites who could draw up in battle formation, there were 28,600. ³⁶ Of Asher there were 40,000 who went out in the army to draw up in battle formation. ³⁷ From the other side of the Jordan, of the Reubenites and the Gadites and of the half-tribe of Manasseh, there were 120,000 with all kinds of weapons of war for the battle.

³⁸ All these, being men of war who could draw up in battle formation, came to Hebron with a perfect heart to make David king over all Israel; and all the rest also of Israel were of one mind to make David king. ³⁹ They were

there with David three days, eating and drinking, for their kinsmen had prepared for them. [40] Moreover those who were near to them, *even* as far as Issachar and Zebulun and Naphtali, brought food on donkeys, camels, mules and on oxen, great quantities of flour cakes, fig cakes and bunches of raisins, wine, oil, oxen and sheep. There was joy indeed in Israel.

Psalm 77:16–20

[16] The waters saw You, O God;
  The waters saw You, they
    were in anguish;
  The deeps also trembled.
[17] The clouds poured out water;
  The skies gave forth a sound;
  Your arrows flashed here and
    there.
[18] The sound of Your thunder
    was in the whirlwind;
  The lightnings lit up the world;
  The earth trembled and shook.
[19] Your way was in the sea
  And Your paths in the mighty
    waters,
  And Your footprints may
    not be known.
[20] You led Your people like a flock
  By the hand of Moses and Aaron.

Proverbs 19:17–19

[17] One who is gracious to a poor
    man lends to the LORD,
  And He will repay him for
    his good deed.
[18] Discipline your son while
    there is hope,
  And do not desire his death.
[19] *A man of* great anger will
    bear the penalty,
  For if you rescue *him,* you will
    only have to do it again.

Acts 7:1–16

7 The high priest said, "Are these things so?" [2] And he said, "Hear me, brethren and fathers! The God of glory appeared to our father Abraham when he was in Mesopotamia, before he lived in Haran, [3] and said to him, 'LEAVE YOUR COUNTRY AND YOUR RELATIVES, AND COME INTO THE LAND THAT I WILL SHOW YOU.' [4] Then he left the land of the Chaldeans and settled in Haran. From there, after his father died, *God* had him move to this country in which you are now living. [5] But He gave him no inheritance in it, not even a foot of ground, and *yet,* even when he had no child,

He promised that HE WOULD GIVE IT TO HIM AS A POSSESSION, AND TO HIS DESCENDANTS AFTER HIM. [6] But God spoke to this effect, that his DESCENDANTS WOULD BE ALIENS IN A FOREIGN LAND, AND THAT THEY WOULD BE ENSLAVED AND MISTREATED FOR FOUR HUNDRED YEARS. [7] 'AND WHATEVER NATION TO WHICH THEY WILL BE IN BONDAGE I MYSELF WILL JUDGE,' said God, 'AND AFTER THAT THEY WILL COME OUT AND SERVE ME IN THIS PLACE.' [8] And He gave him the covenant of circumcision; and so *Abraham* became the father of Isaac, and circumcised him on the eighth day; and Isaac *became the father of* Jacob, and Jacob *of* the twelve patriarchs.

[9] "The patriarchs became jealous of Joseph and sold him into Egypt. *Yet* God was with him, [10] and rescued him from all his afflictions, and granted him favor and wisdom in the sight of Pharaoh, king of Egypt, and he made him governor over Egypt and all his household.

[11] "Now a famine came over all Egypt and Canaan, and great affliction *with it,* and our fathers could find no food. [12] But when Jacob heard that there was grain in Egypt, he sent our fathers *there* the first time. [13] On the second *visit* Joseph made himself known to his brothers, and Joseph's family was disclosed to Pharaoh. [14] Then Joseph sent *word* and invited Jacob his father and all his relatives to come to him, seventy-five persons *in all.* [15] And Jacob went down to Egypt and *there* he and our fathers died. [16] *From there* they were removed to Shechem and laid in the tomb which Abraham had purchased for a sum of money from the sons of Hamor in Shechem.

7:2–53 Stephen's response does not seem to answer the High Priest's question. Instead, he gave a masterful, detailed defense of the Christian faith from the Old Testament and concluded by condemning the Jewish leaders for rejecting Jesus.

7:2 The God of glory. A title used only here and in Psalm 29:3. God's glory is the sum of His attributes (Ex 33:18–19). **Abraham...Mesopotamia, before he lived in Haran.** Genesis 12:1–4 refers to the repeat of this call after Abraham had settled in Haran (ca. 500 miles northwest of Ur). Evidently, God had originally called Abraham while he was living in Ur (Ge 15:7; Ne 9:7), then repeated that call at Haran.

The inspiration of Scripture (2Ti 3:16) was sometimes accomplished through direct revelation from God without a human writer, e.g., the Mosaic Law. At other times, God used human sources, as mentioned in Luke 1:1-4. Such was the experience of the chronicler as evidenced by the many contributing sources. Whether the material came through direct revelation or by existing resources, God's inspiration through the Holy Spirit prevented the original human authors of Scripture from any error (2Pe 1:19-21). Although relatively few scribal errors have been made in copying Scripture, they can be identified and corrected. Thus, the original, inerrant content of the Bible has been preserved.

1. Book of the Kings of Israel/Judah (1Ch 9:1; 2Ch 16:11; 20:34; 25:26; 27:7; 28:26; 32:32; 35:27; 36:8)
2. The Chronicles of David (1Ch 27:24)
3. Book of Samuel (1Ch 29:29)
4. Book of Nathan (1Ch 29:29; 2Ch 9:29)
5. Book of Gad (1Ch 29:29)
6. Prophecy of Ahijah the Shilonite (2Ch 9:29)
7. Visions of Iddo (2Ch 9:29)
8. Records of Shemaiah (2Ch 12:15)
9. Records of Iddo (2Ch 12:15)
10. Annals of Iddo (2Ch 13:22)
11. Annals of Jehu (2Ch 20:34)
12. Commentary on the Book of the Kings (2Ch 24:27)
13. Acts of Uzziah by Isaiah (2Ch 26:22)
14. Letters/Message of Sennacherib (2Ch 32:10-17)
15. Vision of Isaiah (2Ch 32:32)
16. Words of the Seers (2Ch 33:18)
17. Sayings of Hozai (2Ch 33:19)
18. Written instructions of David and Solomon (2Ch 35:4)
19. The Laments (2Ch 35:25)

JUNE 25

1 Chronicles 13:1-14:17

13 Then David consulted with the captains of the thousands and the hundreds, even with every leader. ² David said to all the assembly of Israel, "If it seems good to you, and if it is from the LORD our God, let us send everywhere to our kinsmen who remain in all the land of Israel, also to the priests and Levites who are with them in their cities with pasture lands, that they may meet with us; ³ and let us bring back the ark of our God to us, for we did not seek it in the days of Saul." ⁴ Then all the assembly said that they would

---

13:3 the ark of our God. Not only had the ark been stolen and profaned by the Philistines (1Sa 5-6), but when it was returned, Saul neglected to seek God's instruction for it. Scripture records only one occasion when Saul sought God's ark after its return (1Sa 14:18).

---

do so, for the thing was right in the eyes of all the people.

⁵ So David assembled all Israel together, from the Shihor of Egypt even to the entrance of Hamath, to bring the ark of God from Kiriath-jearim. ⁶ David and all Israel went up to Baalah, *that is,* to Kiriath-jearim, which belongs to Judah, to bring up from there the ark of God, the LORD who is enthroned *above* the cherubim, where His name is called. ⁷ They carried the ark of God on a new cart from the house of Abinadab, and Uzza and Ahio drove the cart. ⁸ David and all Israel were celebrating before God with all *their* might, even with songs and with lyres, harps, tambourines, cymbals and with trumpets.

⁹ When they came to the threshing floor of Chidon, Uzza put out his hand to hold the ark, because the oxen nearly upset *it*. ¹⁰ The anger of the LORD burned against Uzza, so He struck him down because he put out his hand to the ark; and he died there before God. ¹¹ Then David became angry because of the LORD'S outburst against Uzza; and he called that place Perez-uzza to this day. ¹² David was afraid of God that day, saying, "How can I bring the ark of God *home* to

me?" [13] So David did not take the ark with him to the city of David, but took it aside to the house of Obed-edom the Gittite. [14] Thus the ark of God remained with the family of Obed-edom in his house three months; and the LORD blessed the family of Obed-edom with all that he had.

14 Now Hiram king of Tyre sent messengers to David with cedar trees, masons and carpenters, to build a house for him. [2] And David realized that the LORD had established him as king over Israel, *and* that his kingdom was highly exalted, for the sake of His people Israel.

[3] Then David took more wives at Jerusalem, and David became the father of more sons and daughters. [4] These are the names of the children born *to him* in Jerusalem: Shammua, Shobab, Nathan, Solomon, [5] Ibhar, Elishua, Elpelet, [6] Nogah, Nepheg, Japhia, [7] Elishama, Beeliada and Eliphelet.

[8] When the Philistines heard that David had been anointed king over all Israel, all the Philistines went up in search of David; and David heard of it and went out against them. [9] Now the Philistines had come and made a raid in the valley of Rephaim. [10] David inquired of God, saying, "Shall I go up against the Philistines? And will You give them into my hand?" Then the LORD said to him, "Go up, for I will give them into your hand." [11] So they came up to Baal-perazim, and David defeated them there; and David said, "God has broken through my enemies by my hand, like the breakthrough of waters." Therefore they named that place Baal-perazim. [12] They abandoned their gods there; so David gave the order and they were burned with fire.

[13] The Philistines made yet another raid in the valley. [14] David inquired again of God, and God said to him, "You shall not go up after them; circle around behind them and come at them in front of the balsam trees. [15] It shall be when you hear the sound of marching in the tops of the balsam trees, then you shall go out to battle, for God will have gone out before you to strike the army of the Philistines."

14:8–17 The Philistines desired to ruin David before the throne was consolidated. Their plan was to kill David, but God gave him victory over the Philistines (unlike Saul) and thus declared both to the Philistines and Israel His support of Israel's new king.

[16] David did just as God had commanded him, and they struck down the army of the Philistines from Gibeon even as far as Gezer. [17] Then the fame of David went out into all the lands; and the LORD brought the fear of him on all the nations.

Psalm 78:1–11

A Maskil of Asaph.

L isten, O my people, to my
  instruction;
  Incline your ears to the
    words of my mouth.
[2] I will open my mouth in a parable;
  I will utter dark sayings of old,
[3] Which we have heard and known,
  And our fathers have told us.
[4] We will not conceal them
    from their children,
  But tell to the generation to come
    the praises of the LORD,
  And His strength and His wondrous
    works that He has done.

78:2 parable. The word is used here in the broader sense of a story with moral and spiritual applications. **dark sayings.** Puzzling, ambiguous information. The lessons of history are not easily discerned correctly. For an infallible interpretation of history, there must be a prophet. The specific puzzle in Israel's history is the nation's rebellious spirit in spite of God's grace.

[5] For He established a
    testimony in Jacob
  And appointed a law in Israel,
  Which He commanded our
    fathers
  That they should teach them
    to their children,
[6] That the generation to come
    might know, *even* the
    children *yet* to be born,
  That they may arise and tell
    them to their children,
[7] That they should put their
    confidence in God
  And not forget the works
    of God,
  But keep His commandments,
[8] And not be like their fathers,
  A stubborn and rebellious
    generation,

A generation that did not
    prepare its heart
And whose spirit was not
    faithful to God.

9 The sons of Ephraim were archers
    equipped with bows,
    Yet they turned back in
    the day of battle.
10 They did not keep the covenant
    of God
And refused to walk in His law;
11 They forgot His deeds
And His miracles that He
    had shown them.

Proverbs 19:20–21

20 Listen to counsel and
    accept discipline,
That you may be wise the
    rest of your days.
21 Many plans are in a man's
    heart,
But the counsel of the
    LORD will stand.

Acts 7:17–43

17 "But as the time of the promise was approaching which God had assured to Abraham, the people increased and multiplied in Egypt, 18 until THERE AROSE ANOTHER KING OVER EGYPT WHO KNEW NOTHING ABOUT JOSEPH. 19 It was he who took shrewd advantage of our race and mistreated our fathers so that they would expose their infants and they would not survive. 20 It was at this time that Moses was born; and he was lovely in the sight of God, and he was nurtured three months in his father's home. 21 And after he had been set outside, Pharaoh's daughter took him away and nurtured him as her own son. 22 Moses was educated in all the learning of the Egyptians, and he was a man of power in words and deeds. 23 But when he was approaching the age of forty, it entered his mind to visit his brethren, the sons of Israel. 24 And when he saw one

7:23 approaching the age of forty. Moses' life may be divided into three 40-year periods. The first 40 years encompassed his birth and life in Pharaoh's court; the second his exile in Midian (vv. 29–30); and the third revolved around the events of the Exodus and the years of Israel's wilderness wandering (v. 36).

of them being treated unjustly, he defended him and took vengeance for the oppressed by striking down the Egyptian. 25 And he supposed that his brethren understood that God was granting them deliverance through him, but they did not understand. 26 On the following day he appeared to them as they were fighting together, and he tried to reconcile them in peace, saying, 'Men, you are brethren, why do you injure one another?' 27 But the one who was injuring his neighbor pushed him away, saying, 'WHO MADE YOU A RULER AND JUDGE OVER US? 28 YOU DO NOT MEAN TO KILL ME AS YOU KILLED THE EGYPTIAN YESTERDAY, DO YOU?' 29 At this remark, MOSES FLED AND BECAME AN ALIEN IN THE LAND OF MIDIAN, where he became the father of two sons.

30 "After forty years had passed, AN ANGEL APPEARED TO HIM IN THE WILDERNESS OF MOUNT Sinai, IN THE FLAME OF A BURNING THORN BUSH. 31 When Moses saw it, he marveled at the sight; and as he approached to look *more* closely, there came the voice of the Lord: 32 'I AM THE GOD OF YOUR FATHERS, THE GOD OF ABRAHAM AND ISAAC AND JACOB.' Moses shook with fear and would not venture to look. 33 BUT THE LORD SAID TO HIM, 'TAKE OFF THE SANDALS FROM YOUR FEET, FOR THE PLACE ON WHICH YOU ARE STANDING IS HOLY GROUND. 34 I HAVE CERTAINLY SEEN THE OPPRESSION OF MY people IN EGYPT AND HAVE HEARD THEIR GROANS, AND I HAVE COME DOWN TO RESCUE THEM; COME NOW, AND I WILL SEND YOU TO EGYPT.'

35 "This Moses whom they disowned, saying, 'WHO MADE YOU A RULER AND A JUDGE?' is the one whom God sent *to be* both a ruler and a deliverer with the help of the angel who appeared to him in the thorn bush. 36 This man led them out, performing wonders and signs in the land of Egypt and in the Red Sea and in the wilderness for forty years. 37 This is the Moses who said to the sons of Israel, 'GOD WILL RAISE UP FOR YOU A PROPHET LIKE ME FROM YOUR BRETHREN.' 38 This is the one who was in the congregation in the wilderness together with the angel who was speaking to him on Mount Sinai, and *who was* with our fathers; and he received living oracles to pass on to you. 39 Our fathers were unwilling to be obedient to him, but repudiated him and in their hearts turned back to Egypt, 40 SAYING TO AARON, 'MAKE FOR US GODS WHO WILL GO BEFORE US; FOR THIS MOSES WHO LED US OUT OF THE LAND OF EGYPT—WE DO NOT KNOW WHAT HAPPENED TO HIM.' 41 At that time they made a calf and

brought a sacrifice to the idol, and were rejoicing in the works of their hands. ⁴²But God turned away and delivered them up to serve the host of heaven; as it is written in the book of the prophets, 'IT WAS NOT TO ME THAT YOU OFFERED VICTIMS AND SACRIFICES FORTY YEARS IN THE WILDERNESS, WAS IT, O HOUSE OF ISRAEL? ⁴³YOU ALSO TOOK ALONG THE TABERNACLE OF MOLOCH AND THE STAR OF THE GOD ROMPHA, THE IMAGES WHICH YOU MADE TO WORSHIP. I ALSO WILL REMOVE YOU BEYOND BABYLON.'

7:43 BABYLON. Amos wrote Damascus (Am 5:27), while Stephen said Babylon. Amos was prophesying the captivity of the northern kingdom in Assyria, a deportation beyond Damascus. Later the southern kingdom was taken captive to Babylon. Stephen, inspired to do so, extended the prophecy to embrace the judgment on the whole nation, summarizing their idolatrous history and its results.

DAY 25: What does it mean that God "gave them up" in Acts 7:42?

"But God turned away and delivered them up to serve the host of heaven." Here Stephen quoted from Amos 5:25–27. It means that God judicially abandoned the people to their sin and idolatry (Hos 4:17). The worship of the sun, moon, and stars began in the wilderness and lasted through the Babylonian captivity (Dt 4:19; 17:3; 2Ki 17:16; 21:3–5; 23:4; 2Ch 33:3, 5; Jer 8:2; 19:13; Zep 1:5).

Similarly, in Romans 1:24, it states that "God gave them over in the lusts of their hearts to impurity." The Greek word used is for handing over a prisoner to his sentence. When men consistently abandon God, He will abandon them (Jdg 10:13; 2Ch 15:2; 24:20; Ps 81:11–12; Mt 15:14). He accomplishes this 1) indirectly and immediately, by removing His restraint and allowing their sin to run its inevitable course and 2) directly and eventually, by specific acts of divine judgment and punishment. "Impurity" is a general term often used of decaying matter, like the contents of a grave. It speaks here of sexual immorality (2Co 12:21; Gal 5:19–23; Eph 5:3; 1Th 4:7), which begins in the heart and moves to the shame of the body.

And "God gave them over to degrading passions" (Ro 1:26). This is identified in vv. 26–27 as homosexuality, a sin roundly condemned in Scripture (Ge 19; Lv 18:22; 1Co 6:9–11; Gal 5:19–21; Eph 5:3–5; 1Ti 1:9, 10; Jude v. 7). Rather than the normal Greek term for "women," this is a general word for female. Paul mentions women first to show the extent of debauchery under the wrath of abandonment because, in most cultures, women are the last to be affected by moral collapse.

And "God gave them over to a depraved mind" (v. 28). This translates a Greek word that means "not passing the test." It was often used to describe useless, worthless metals, discarded because they contained too much impurity. God has tested man's minds and found them worthless and useless (Jer 6:30).

 JUNE 26

1 Chronicles 15:1–16:43

15 Now *David* built houses for himself in the city of David; and he prepared a place for the ark of God and pitched a tent for it. ²Then David said, "No one is to carry the ark of God but the Levites; for the LORD chose them to carry the ark of God and to minister to Him forever." ³And David assembled all Israel at Jerusalem to bring up the ark of the LORD to its place which he had prepared for it. ⁴David gathered together the sons of Aaron and the Levites; ⁵of the sons of Kohath, Uriel the chief, and 120 of his relatives; ⁶of the sons of Merari, Asaiah the chief, and 220 of his relatives; ⁷of the sons of Gershom, Joel the chief, and 130 of his relatives; ⁸of the sons of Elizaphan, Shemaiah the chief, and 200 of

his relatives; ⁹of the sons of Hebron, Eliel the chief, and 80 of his relatives; ¹⁰of the sons of Uzziel, Amminadab the chief, and 112 of his relatives.

¹¹Then David called for Zadok and Abiathar the priests, and for the Levites, for Uriel, Asaiah, Joel, Shemaiah, Eliel and Amminadab,

15:1 *David* built houses for himself. He was able by the alliance and help of Hiram (18:1) to build a palace for himself and separate houses for his wives and their children. While the ark remained near Jerusalem at the home of Obed-edom for 3 months (13:13–14), David constructed a new tabernacle in Jerusalem to fulfill God's Word in Deuteronomy 12:5–7 of a permanent residency.

15:11 Zadok...Abiathar. These two High Priests, heads of the two priestly houses of Eleazar and Ithamar, were colleagues in the high-priesthood (2Sa 20:25). They served the Lord simultaneously in David's reign. Zadok attended the tabernacle in Gibeon (1Ch 16:39), while Abiathar served the temporary place of the ark in Jerusalem. Ultimately, Zadok prevailed (1Ki 2:26–27).

[12] and said to them, "You are the heads of the fathers' *households* of the Levites; consecrate yourselves both you and your relatives, that you may bring up the ark of the LORD God of Israel to *the place* that I have prepared for it. [13] Because you did not *carry it* at the first, the LORD our God made an outburst on us, for we did not seek Him according to the ordinance." [14] So the priests and the Levites consecrated themselves to bring up the ark of the LORD God of Israel. [15] The sons of the Levites carried the ark of God on their shoulders with the poles thereon, as Moses had commanded according to the word of the LORD.

[16] Then David spoke to the chiefs of the Levites to appoint their relatives the singers, with instruments of music, harps, lyres, loud-sounding cymbals, to raise sounds of joy. [17] So the Levites appointed Heman the son of Joel, and from his relatives, Asaph the son of Berechiah; and from the sons of Merari their relatives, Ethan the son of Kushaiah, [18] and with them their relatives of the second rank, Zechariah, Ben, Jaaziel, Shemiramoth, Jehiel, Unni, Eliab, Benaiah, Maaseiah, Mattithiah, Eliphelehu, Mikneiah, Obed-edom and Jeiel, the gatekeepers. [19] So the singers, Heman, Asaph and Ethan *were appointed* to sound aloud cymbals of bronze; [20] and Zechariah, Aziel, Shemiramoth, Jehiel, Unni, Eliab, Maaseiah and Benaiah, with harps *tuned* to alamoth; [21] and Mattithiah, Eliphelehu, Mikneiah, Obed-edom, Jeiel and Azaziah, to lead with lyres tuned to the sheminith. [22] Chenaniah, chief of the Levites, was *in charge of* the singing; he gave instruction in singing because he was skillful. [23] Berechiah and Elkanah were gatekeepers for the ark. [24] Shebaniah, Joshaphat, Nethanel, Amasai, Zechariah, Benaiah and Eliezer, the priests, blew the trumpets before the ark of God. Obed-edom and Jehiah also *were* gatekeepers for the ark. [25] So *it was* David, with the elders of Israel and the captains over thousands, who went to bring up the ark of the covenant of the LORD from the house of Obed-edom with joy. [26] Because God was helping the Levites who were carrying the ark of the covenant of the LORD, they sacrificed seven bulls and seven rams. [27] Now David was clothed with a robe of fine linen with all the Levites who were carrying the ark, and the singers and Chenaniah the leader of the singing *with* the singers. David also wore an ephod of linen. [28] Thus all Israel brought up the ark of the covenant of the LORD with shouting, and with sound of the horn, with trumpets, with loud-sounding cymbals, with harps and lyres.

[29] It happened when the ark of the covenant of the LORD came to the city of David, that Michal the daughter of Saul looked out of the window and saw King David leaping and celebrating; and she despised him in her heart.

16 And they brought in the ark of God and placed it inside the tent which David had pitched for it, and they offered burnt offerings and peace offerings before God. [2] When David had finished offering the burnt offering and the peace offerings, he blessed the people in the name of the LORD. [3] He distributed to everyone of Israel, both man and woman, to everyone a loaf of bread and a portion *of meat* and a raisin cake.

[4] He appointed some of the Levites *as* ministers before the ark of the LORD, even to celebrate and to thank and praise the LORD God of Israel: [5] Asaph the chief, and second to him Zechariah, *then* Jeiel, Shemiramoth, Jehiel, Mattithiah, Eliab, Benaiah, Obed-edom and Jeiel, with musical instruments, harps, lyres; also Asaph *played* loud-sounding cymbals, [6] and Benaiah and Jahaziel the priests *blew* trumpets continually before the ark of the covenant of God.

[7] Then on that day David first assigned Asaph and his relatives to give thanks to the LORD.

[8]   Oh give thanks to the LORD,
         call upon His name;
      Make known His deeds
         among the peoples.
[9]   Sing to Him, sing praises to Him;
      Speak of all His wonders.
[10] Glory in His holy name;
      Let the heart of those who
         seek the LORD be glad.
[11] Seek the LORD and His strength;
      Seek His face continually.
[12] Remember His wonderful deeds
         which He has done,
      His marvels and the judgments
         from His mouth,

13 O seed of Israel His servant,
Sons of Jacob, His chosen ones!
14 He is the LORD our God;
His judgments are in all the earth.
15 Remember His covenant forever,
The word which He commanded
to a thousand generations,
16 *The covenant* which He
made with Abraham,
And His oath to Isaac.
17 He also confirmed it to
Jacob for a statute,
To Israel as an everlasting
covenant,
18 Saying, "To you I will give
the land of Canaan,
As the portion of your
inheritance."
19 When they were only a
few in number,
Very few, and strangers in it,
20 And they wandered about
from nation to nation,
And from *one* kingdom to
another people,
21 He permitted no man to
oppress them,
And He reproved kings for
their sakes, *saying,*
22 "Do not touch My anointed ones,
And do My prophets no harm."
23 Sing to the LORD, all the earth;
Proclaim good tidings of His
salvation from day to day.
24 Tell of His glory among the
nations,
His wonderful deeds among
all the peoples.
25 For great is the LORD, and
greatly to be praised;
He also is to be feared above
all gods.
26 For all the gods of the
peoples are idols,
But the LORD made the heavens.
27 Splendor and majesty are
before Him,
Strength and joy are in His place.
28 Ascribe to the LORD, O families
of the peoples,
Ascribe to the LORD glory
and strength.
29 Ascribe to the LORD the
glory due His name;
Bring an offering, and
come before Him;
Worship the LORD in holy
array.

30 Tremble before Him, all the earth;
Indeed, the world is firmly
established, it will not be moved.
31 Let the heavens be glad, and
let the earth rejoice;
And let them say among the
nations, "The LORD reigns."
32 Let the sea roar, and all it contains;
Let the field exult, and all that is in it.
33 Then the trees of the forest will
sing for joy before the LORD;
For He is coming to judge the earth.
34 O give thanks to the LORD,
for *He is* good;
For His lovingkindness is everlasting.
35 Then say, "Save us, O God
of our salvation,
And gather us and deliver
us from the nations,
To give thanks to Your holy name,
And glory in Your praise."
36 Blessed be the LORD, the God of Israel,
From everlasting even to
everlasting.

Then all the people said, "Amen," and praised the LORD.

37 So he left Asaph and his relatives there before the ark of the covenant of the LORD to minister before the ark continually, as every day's work required; 38 and Obed-edom with his 68 relatives; Obed-edom, also the son of Jeduthun, and Hosah as gatekeepers. 39 *He left* Zadok the priest and his relatives the priests before the tabernacle of the LORD in the high place which *was* at Gibeon, 40 to offer burnt offerings to the LORD on the altar of burnt offering continually morning and evening, even according to all that is written in the law of the LORD, which He commanded Israel. 41 With them *were* Heman and Jeduthun, and the rest who were chosen, who were designated by name, to give thanks to the LORD, because His lovingkindness is everlasting. 42 And with them *were* Heman and Jeduthun *with* trumpets and cymbals for those who should sound aloud, and *with* instruments *for* the songs of God, and the sons of Jeduthun for the gate.

43 Then all the people departed each to his house, and David returned to bless his household.

Psalm 78:12–16

12 He wrought wonders
before their fathers
In the land of Egypt, in
the field of Zoan.

¹³ He divided the sea and caused
  them to pass through,
And He made the waters
  stand up like a heap.
¹⁴ Then He led them with
  the cloud by day
And all the night with a light
  of fire.
¹⁵ He split the rocks in the
  wilderness
And gave *them* abundant drink
  like the ocean depths.
¹⁶ He brought forth streams
  also from the rock

78:13 waters stand up like a heap. The parting of the Red Sea at the beginning of the Exodus, which allowed Israel to escape from the Egyptian armies, was always considered by the Old Testament saints to be the most spectacular miracle of their history (Ex 14).

78:15 split the rocks. Twice in the wilderness, when Israel desperately needed a great water supply, God brought water out of rocks (Ex 17:6; Nu 20:11).

And caused waters to run
  down like rivers.

Proverbs 19:22-24

²² What is desirable in a man
  is his kindness,
And *it is* better to be a poor
  man than a liar.
²³ The fear of the LORD *leads*
  to life,
So that one may sleep satisfied,
  untouched by evil.
²⁴ The sluggard buries his
  hand in the dish,
But will not even bring it
  back to his mouth.

Acts 7:44-60

⁴⁴ "Our fathers had the tabernacle of testimony in the wilderness, just as He who spoke to Moses directed *him* to make it according to the pattern which he had seen. ⁴⁵ And having received it in their turn, our fathers brought it in with Joshua upon dispossessing the nations whom God drove out before our fathers, until the time of David. ⁴⁶ *David* found favor in God's sight, and asked that he might find a dwelling place for the God of Jacob. ⁴⁷ But it was Sol-

7:44-50 To counter the false charge that he blasphemed the temple (6:13-14), Stephen recounted its history to show his respect for it.

omon who built a house for Him. ⁴⁸ However, the Most High does not dwell in *houses* made by *human* hands; as the prophet says:

⁴⁹ 'HEAVEN IS MY THRONE,
  AND EARTH IS THE FOOTSTOOL
    OF MY FEET;
  WHAT KIND OF HOUSE WILL YOU
    BUILD FOR ME?' says the Lord,
  'OR WHAT PLACE IS THERE
    FOR MY REPOSE?
⁵⁰ 'WAS IT NOT MY HAND WHICH
    MADE ALL THESE THINGS?'

7:49-50 Quoted from Isaiah 66:1-2. Stephen's point is that God is greater than the temple, and thus the Jewish leaders were guilty of blaspheming by confining God to it.

⁵¹ "You men who are stiff-necked and uncircumcised in heart and ears are always resisting the Holy Spirit; you are doing just as your fathers did. ⁵² Which one of the prophets did your fathers not persecute? They killed those who had previously announced the coming of the Righteous One, whose betrayers and murderers you have now become; ⁵³ you who received the law as ordained by angels, and *yet* did not keep it."

⁵⁴ Now when they heard this, they were cut to the quick, and they *began* gnashing their teeth at him. ⁵⁵ But being full of the Holy Spirit, he gazed intently into heaven and saw the glory of God, and Jesus standing at the right hand of God; ⁵⁶ and he said, "Behold, I see the heavens opened up and the Son of Man standing at the right hand of God." ⁵⁷ But they cried out with a loud voice, and covered their ears and rushed at him with one impulse. ⁵⁸ When they had driven him out of the city, they *began* stoning *him;* and the witnesses laid aside their robes at the feet of a young man named Saul. ⁵⁹ They went on stoning Stephen as he called on *the Lord* and said, "Lord Jesus, receive my spirit!" ⁶⁰ Then falling on his knees, he cried out with a loud voice, "Lord, do not hold this sin against them!" Having said this, he fell asleep.

In the climax of Stephen's sermon (Ac 7:51–53), he indicted the Jewish leaders for rejecting God in the same way that their ancestors had rejected Him in the Old Testament. He told the members of the esteemed Sanhedrin that they were "obstinate" like their fathers (Ex 32:9; 33:5) and "uncircumcised in heart and ears." Thus they were as unclean before God as the uncircumcised Gentiles (Dt 10:16; Jer 4:4; Ro 2:28–9). "You are always resisting the Holy Spirit" by rejecting the Spirit's messengers and their message. And when he spoke of the "Righteous One," Stephen reminds them that they betrayed and murdered Him (v. 52). His words were reminiscent of those from Jesus' sermon in Matthew 23:13–39.

The reaction of the Sanhedrin was that they "began gnashing their teeth at him" (v. 54). That is the fullness of anger and frustration and was in contrast to Stephen, who "being full of the Holy Spirit, he gazed intently into heaven and saw the glory of God, and Jesus standing at the right hand of God" (v. 55). Isaiah (Is. 6:1–3), Ezekiel (Eze 1:26–28), Paul (2Co 12:2–4), and John (Rev 1:10) also received visions of God's glory in heaven.

Stephen's words were so appalling that they took him out of the city and "began stoning him." This was the punishment prescribed in the law for blasphemy (Lv 24:16); however, this was not a formal execution but an act of mob violence. And those who participated "laid aside their robes at the feet of...Saul" (v. 58). Paul's first appearance in Scripture. That he was near enough to the action to be holding the clothes of Stephen's killers reflects his deep involvement in the sordid affair. And Paul heard those marvelous words of Stephen: "Do not hold this sin against them!" (v. 60). As had Jesus before him (Lk 23:34), Stephen prayed for God to forgive his killers.

☙ JUNE 27

1 Chronicles 17:1–18:17

17 And it came about, when David dwelt in his house, that David said to Nathan the prophet, "Behold, I am dwelling in a house of cedar, but the ark of the covenant of the LORD is under curtains." ²Then Nathan said to David, "Do all that is in your heart, for God is with you."

³It came about the same night that the word of God came to Nathan, saying, ⁴"Go and tell David My servant, 'Thus says the LORD, "You shall not build a house for Me to dwell in; ⁵for I have not dwelt in a house since the day that I brought up Israel to this day, but I have gone from tent to tent and from one dwelling place to another. ⁶In all places where I have walked with all Israel, have I spoken a word with any of the judges of Israel, whom I commanded to shepherd My people, saying, 'Why have you not built for Me a house of cedar?' " ⁷Now, therefore, thus shall you say to My servant David, 'Thus says the LORD of hosts, "I took you from the pasture, from following the sheep, to be leader over My people Israel. ⁸I have been with you wherever you have gone, and have cut off all your enemies from before you; and I will make you a name like the name of the great ones who are in the earth. ⁹I will appoint a place for My people Israel, and will plant them, so that they may dwell in their own place and not be moved

again; and the wicked will not waste them anymore as formerly, ¹⁰even from the day that I commanded judges to be over My people Israel. And I will subdue all your enemies.

Moreover, I tell you that the LORD will build a house for you. ¹¹When your days are fulfilled that you must go to be with your fathers, that I will set up one of your descendants after you, who will be of your sons; and I will establish his kingdom. ¹²He shall build for Me a house, and I will establish his throne forever. ¹³I will be his father and he shall be My son; and I will not take My lovingkindness away from him, as I took it from him who was before you. ¹⁴But I will settle him in My house and in My kingdom forever, and his throne shall be established forever." ' " ¹⁵According to all these words and according to all this vision, so Nathan spoke to David.

¹⁶Then David the king went in and sat before the LORD and said, "Who am I, O LORD God, and what is my house that You have brought me this far? ¹⁷This was a small thing in Your eyes, O God; but You have spoken of Your servant's house for a great while to come, and have regarded me according to the standard of a man of high degree, O LORD God. ¹⁸What more can David still say to You concerning the honor bestowed on Your servant? For You know Your servant. ¹⁹O LORD, for Your servant's sake, and according to Your own heart, You have wrought all this greatness, to make known all these great things. ²⁰O LORD, there is none like You, nor is there

any God besides You, according to all that we have heard with our ears. ²¹ And what one nation in the earth is like Your people Israel, whom God went to redeem for Himself *as* a people, to make You a name by great and terrible things, in driving out nations from before Your people, whom You redeemed out of Egypt? ²² For Your people Israel You made Your own people forever, and You, O LORD, became their God.

²³ "Now, O LORD, let the word that You have spoken concerning Your servant and concerning his house be established forever, and do as You have spoken. ²⁴ Let Your name be established and magnified forever, saying, 'The LORD of hosts is the God of Israel, *even* a God to Israel; and the house of David Your servant is established before You.' ²⁵ For You, O my God, have revealed to Your servant that You will build for him a house; therefore Your servant has found *courage* to pray before You. ²⁶ Now, O LORD, You are God, and have promised this good thing to Your servant. ²⁷ And now it has pleased You to bless the house of Your servant, that it may continue forever before You; for You, O LORD, have blessed, and it is blessed forever."

The Davidic Covenant in Chronicles
For an exposition of the details and significance of the Davidic Covenant, see the notes on 2 Samuel 7.

1. 1 Chronicles 17:7–27 — God to Nathan to David
2. 1 Chronicles 22:6–16 — David to Solomon
3. 1 Chronicles 28:6–7 — David to Solomon
4. 2 Chronicles 6:8–9, 16–17 — Solomon to the nation
5. 2 Chronicles 7:17, 18 — God to Solomon
6. 2 Chronicles 13:4–5 — Abijah to Jeroboam
7. 2 Chronicles 21:7 — Chronicle's commentary

18 Now after this it came about that David defeated the Philistines and subdued them and took Gath and its towns from the hand of the Philistines. ² He defeated Moab, and the Moabites became servants to David, bringing tribute.

³ David also defeated Hadadezer king of Zobah *as far as* Hamath, as he went to establish his rule to the Euphrates River. ⁴ David took from him 1,000 chariots and 7,000 horsemen and 20,000 foot soldiers, and David hamstrung all the chariot horses, but reserved *enough* of them for 100 chariots.

⁵ When the Arameans of Damascus came to help Hadadezer king of Zobah, David killed 22,000 men of the Arameans. ⁶ Then David put *garrisons* among the Arameans of Damascus; and the Arameans became servants to David, bringing tribute. And the LORD helped David wherever he went. ⁷ David took the shields of gold which were carried by the servants of Hadadezer and brought them to Jerusalem. ⁸ Also from Tibhath and from Cun, cities of Hadadezer, David took a very large amount of bronze, with which Solomon made the bronze sea and the pillars and the bronze utensils.

⁹ Now when Tou king of Hamath heard that David had defeated all the army of Hadadezer king of Zobah, ¹⁰ he sent Hadoram his son to King David to greet him and to bless him, because he had fought against Hadadezer and had defeated him; for Hadadezer had been at war with Tou. And *Hadoram brought* all kinds of articles of gold and silver and bronze. ¹¹ King David also dedicated these to the LORD with the silver and the gold which he had carried away from all the nations: from Edom, Moab, the sons of Ammon, the Philistines, and from Amalek.

¹² Moreover Abishai the son of Zeruiah defeated 18,000 Edomites in the Valley of Salt. ¹³ Then he put garrisons in Edom, and all the Edomites became servants to David. And the LORD helped David wherever he went.

¹⁴ So David reigned over all Israel; and he administered justice and righteousness for all his people. ¹⁵ Joab the son of Zeruiah *was* over the army, and Jehoshaphat the son of Ahilud *was* recorder; ¹⁶ and Zadok the son of Ahitub and Abimelech the son of Abiathar *were* priests, and Shavsha *was* secretary; ¹⁷ and Benaiah the son of Jehoiada *was* over the Cherethites and the Pelethites, and the sons of David *were* chiefs at the king's side.

Psalm 78:17–25

¹⁷ Yet they still continued to
    sin against Him,
   To rebel against the Most
    High in the desert.
¹⁸ And in their heart they
    put God to the test
   By asking food according
    to their desire.

78:18 food according to their desire. Instead of being grateful for God's marvelous provisions of manna, the Israelites complained against God and Moses. God sent them meat, but also judged them (Nu 11).

¹⁹ Then they spoke against God;
They said, "Can God prepare a
table in the wilderness?
²⁰ "Behold, He struck the rock so
that waters gushed out,
And streams were overflowing;
Can He give bread also?
Will He provide meat for His people?"

²¹ Therefore the LORD heard
and was full of wrath;
And a fire was kindled against Jacob
And anger also mounted
against Israel,
²² Because they did not believe in God
And did not trust in His salvation.
²³ Yet He commanded the clouds above
And opened the doors of heaven;
²⁴ He rained down manna
upon them to eat
And gave them food from heaven.
²⁵ Man did eat the bread of angels;
He sent them food in abundance.

Proverbs 19:25-26

²⁵ Strike a scoffer and the naive
may become shrewd,
But reprove one who has
understanding and he
will gain knowledge.
²⁶ He who assaults *his* father *and*
drives *his* mother away
Is a shameful and disgraceful son.

19:25 scoffer...naive...understanding. Three classes of people are noted: 1) scoffers are rebuked for learning nothing; 2) naive people are warned by observing the rebuke of the scoffer; and 3) the understanding deepen their wisdom from any reproof.

Acts 8:1-25

8 Saul was in hearty agreement with putting him to death.

And on that day a great persecution began against the church in Jerusalem, and they were all scattered throughout the regions of Judea and Samaria, except the apostles. ² *Some* devout men buried Stephen, and made loud lamentation over him. ³ But Saul *began* ravaging the church, entering house after house, and dragging off men and women, he would put them in prison.

⁴ Therefore, those who had been scattered went about preaching the word. ⁵ Philip went

8:1 in...agreement. Paul's murderous hatred of all believers was manifested here in his attitude toward Stephen (1Ti 1:13-15). **scattered.** Led by a Jew named Saul of Tarsus, the persecution scattered the Jerusalem fellowship and led to the first missionary outreach of the church. Not all members of the Jerusalem church were forced to flee; the Hellenists, because Stephen was likely one, bore the brunt of the persecution (11:19-20). **except the apostles.** They remained because of their devotion to Christ, to care for those at Jerusalem, and to continue evangelizing the region (9:26-27).

8:3 ravaging the church. "Ravaging" was used in extrabiblical writings to refer to the destruction of a city or mangling by a wild animal.

down to the city of Samaria and *began* proclaiming Christ to them. ⁶ The crowds with one accord were giving attention to what was said by Philip, as they heard and saw the signs which he was performing. ⁷ For *in the case of* many who had unclean spirits, they were coming out *of them* shouting with a loud voice; and many who had been paralyzed and lame were healed. ⁸ So there was much rejoicing in that city.

⁹ Now there was a man named Simon, who formerly was practicing magic in the city and astonishing the people of Samaria, claiming to be someone great; ¹⁰ and they all, from smallest to greatest, were giving attention to him, saying, "This man is what is called the Great Power of God." ¹¹ And they were giving him attention because he had for a long time astonished them with his magic arts. ¹² But when they believed Philip preaching the good news about the kingdom of God and the name of Jesus Christ, they were being baptized, men and women alike. ¹³ Even Simon himself believed; and after being baptized, he continued on with Philip, and as he observed signs and great miracles taking place, he was constantly amazed.

8:10-11 the Great Power of God. Simon claimed to be united to God. The early church Fathers claimed he was one of the founders of Gnosticism, which asserted there were a series of divine emanations reaching up to God. They were called "Powers," and the people believed he was at the top of the ladder.

¹⁴ Now when the apostles in Jerusalem heard that Samaria had received the word of God, they sent them Peter and John, ¹⁵ who came down and prayed for them that they might receive the Holy Spirit. ¹⁶ For He had not yet fallen upon any of them; they had simply been baptized in the name of the Lord Jesus. ¹⁷ Then they *began* laying their hands on them, and they were receiving the Holy Spirit. ¹⁸ Now when Simon saw that the Spirit was bestowed through the laying on of the apostles' hands, he offered them money, ¹⁹ saying, "Give this authority to me as well, so that everyone on whom I lay my hands may receive the Holy Spirit." ²⁰ But Peter said to him, "May your silver perish with you, be-cause you thought you could obtain the gift of God with money! ²¹ You have no part or portion in this matter, for your heart is not right before God. ²² Therefore repent of this wickedness of yours, and pray the Lord that, if possible, the intention of your heart may be forgiven you. ²³ For I see that you are in the gall of bitterness and in the bondage of iniquity." ²⁴ But Simon answered and said, "Pray to the Lord for me yourselves, so that nothing of what you have said may come upon me."

²⁵ So, when they had solemnly testified and spoken the word of the Lord, they started back to Jerusalem, and were preaching the gospel to many villages of the Samaritans.

DAY 27: Is the Holy Spirit received subsequent to salvation?

In Acts 8:15, Peter and John were sent to Samaria to pray for those who had responded to the preaching of Philip (Ac 8:4–13) that they might receive the Holy Spirit. "For He had not yet fallen upon any of them" (v. 16). This verse does not support the false notion that Christians receive the Holy Spirit subsequent to salvation. This was a transitional period in which confirmation by the apostles was necessary to verify the inclusion of a new group of people into the church. Because of the animosity that existed between Jews and Samaritans, it was essential for the Samaritans to receive the Spirit in the presence of the leaders of the Jerusalem church, for the purpose of maintaining a unified church. The delay also revealed the Samaritans' need to come under apostolic authority. The same transitional event occurred when the Gentiles were added to the church (11:44–46; 15:6–12; 19:6).

So "they laid began laying their hands on them, and they were receiving the Holy Spirit" (v. 17). This signified apostolic affirmation and solidarity. That this actually occurred likely demonstrated that believers also spoke in tongues here, just as those who received the Spirit did on the Day of Pentecost, as the Gentiles did when they received the Spirit (10:46), and as those followers of John did (19:6). As Samaritans, Gentiles, and believers from the Old Covenant were added to the church, the unity of the church was established. No longer could one nation (Israel) be God's witness people, but the church made up of Jews, Gentiles, half-breed Samari-tans, and Old Testament saints who became New Testament believers (19:1–7). To demonstrate the unity, it was imperative that there be some replication in each instance of what had occurred at Pentecost with the believing Jews, such as the presence of the apostles and the coming of the Spirit manifestly indicated through speaking in the languages of Pentecost (2:5–12).

⌖ JUNE 28

1 Chronicles 19:1–20:8

19 Now it came about after this, that Na-hash the king of the sons of Ammon died, and his son became king in his place. ² Then David said, "I will show kindness to Hanun the son of Nahash, because his father showed kindness to me." So David sent mes-sengers to console him concerning his father. And David's servants came into the land of the sons of Ammon to Hanun to console him. ³ But the princes of the sons of Ammon said to Hanun, "Do you think that David is honoring your father, in that he has sent comforters to you? Have not his servants come to you to search and to overthrow and to spy out the land?" ⁴ So Hanun took David's servants and shaved them and cut off their garments in the middle as far as their hips, and sent them away. ⁵ Then *certain persons* went and told David about the men. And he sent to meet them, for the men were greatly humiliated. And the king said, "Stay at Jericho until your beards grow, and *then* return."

⁶ When the sons of Ammon saw that they had made themselves odious to David, Hanun and the sons of Ammon sent 1,000 talents of silver to hire for themselves chariots and horsemen from Mesopotamia, from Aram-maacah and from Zobah. ⁷ So they hired for themselves 32,000 chariots, and the king of Maacah and his people, who came and camped

before Medeba. And the sons of Ammon gathered together from their cities and came to battle. ⁸When David heard of it, he sent Joab and all the army, the mighty men. ⁹The sons of Ammon came out and drew up in battle array at the entrance of the city, and the kings who had come were by themselves in the field.

¹⁰Now when Joab saw that the battle was set against him in front and in the rear, he selected from all the choice men of Israel and they arrayed themselves against the Arameans. ¹¹But the remainder of the people he placed in the hand of Abshai his brother; and they arrayed themselves against the sons of Ammon. ¹²He said, "If the Arameans are too strong for me, then you shall help me; but if the sons of Ammon are too strong for you, then I will help you. ¹³Be strong, and let us show ourselves courageous for the sake of our people and for the cities of our God; and may the LORD do what is good in His sight." ¹⁴So Joab and the people who were with him drew near to the battle against the Arameans, and they fled before him. ¹⁵When the sons of Ammon saw that the Arameans fled, they also fled before Abshai his brother and entered the city. Then Joab came to Jerusalem.

¹⁶When the Arameans saw that they had been defeated by Israel, they sent messengers and brought out the Arameans who were beyond the River, with Shophach the commander of the army of Hadadezer leading them. ¹⁷When it was told David, he gathered all Israel together and crossed the Jordan, and came upon them and drew up in formation against them. And when David drew up in battle array against the Arameans, they fought against him. ¹⁸The Arameans fled before Israel, and David killed of the Arameans 7,000 charioteers and 40,000 foot soldiers, and put to death Shophach the commander of the army. ¹⁹So when the servants of Hadadezer saw that they were defeated by Israel, they made peace with David and served him. Thus the Arameans were not willing to help the sons of Ammon anymore.

20 Then it happened in the spring, at the time when kings go out to battle, that Joab led out the army and ravaged the land of the sons of Ammon, and came and besieged Rabbah. But David stayed at Jerusalem. And Joab struck Rabbah and overthrew it. ²David took the crown of their king from his head, and he found it to weigh a talent of gold, and there was a precious stone in it; and it was placed on David's head. And he brought out the spoil of the city, a very great amount. ³He brought out the people who were in it, and cut

them with saws and with sharp instruments and with axes. And thus David did to all the cities of the sons of Ammon. Then David and all the people returned to Jerusalem.

⁴Now it came about after this, that war broke out at Gezer with the Philistines; then Sibbecai the Hushathite killed Sippai, one of the descendants of the giants, and they were subdued. ⁵And there was war with the

20:1–3 The chronicler was not inspired by God to mention David's sin with Bathsheba and subsequent sins recorded in 2Sa 11:2—12:23. The adultery and murder occurred at this time, while David stayed in Jerusalem instead of going to battle. The story was likely omitted because the book was written to focus on God's permanent interest in His people, Israel, and the perpetuity of David's kingdom.

20:4–8 See 2 Samuel 21:15–22. The chronicler chose not to write of some of the darker days in David's reign, especially the revolt of David's son Absalom, for the same reason the iniquity of the king with Bathsheba was left out. This section describes the defeat of 4 Philistine giants at the hands of David and his men. Though these events cannot be located chronologically with any certainty, the narratives of victory provide a fitting preface to David's song of praise, which magnifies God's deliverance (2Sa 22:1–51).

Philistines again, and Elhanan the son of Jair killed Lahmi the brother of Goliath the Gittite, the shaft of whose spear was like a weaver's beam. ⁶Again there was war at Gath, where there was a man of great stature who had twenty-four fingers and toes, six fingers on each hand and six toes on each foot; and he also was descended from the giants. ⁷When he taunted Israel, Jonathan the son of Shimea, David's brother, killed him. ⁸These were descended from the giants in Gath, and they fell by the hand of David and by the hand of his servants.

Psalm 78:26–33

²⁶ He caused the east wind to
   blow in the heavens
   And by His power He directed
   the south wind.
²⁷ When He rained meat upon
   them like the dust,
   Even winged fowl like the
   sand of the seas,

28 Then He let *them* fall in the
   midst of their camp,
   Round about their dwellings.
29 So they ate and were well filled,
   And their desire He gave to them.
30 Before they had satisfied their desire,
   While their food was in their mouths,
31 The anger of God rose against them
   And killed some of their stoutest ones,
   And subdued the choice
      men of Israel.
32 In spite of all this they still sinned
   And did not believe in His
      wonderful works.
33 So He brought their days
      to an end in futility
   And their years in sudden terror.

Proverbs 19:27-29

27 Cease listening, my son, to discipline,
   And you will stray from the
      words of knowledge.
28 A rascally witness makes a
      mockery of justice,
   And the mouth of the wicked
      spreads iniquity.
29 Judgments are prepared for scoffers,
   And blows for the back of fools.

Acts 8:26-40

26 But an angel of the Lord spoke to Philip saying, "Get up and go south to the road that descends from Jerusalem to Gaza." (This is a desert *road*.) 27 So he got up and went; and there was an Ethiopian eunuch, a court official of Candace, queen of the Ethiopians, who was in charge of all her treasure; and he had come to Jerusalem to worship, 28 and he was returning and sitting in his chariot, and was reading the prophet Isaiah. 29 Then the Spirit said to Philip, "Go up and join this chariot." 30 Philip ran up and heard him reading Isaiah the prophet, and said, "Do you understand what you are reading?" 31 And he said, "Well, how could I, unless someone guides me?" And he invited Philip to come up and sit with him. 32 Now the passage of Scripture which he was reading was this:

"HE WAS LED AS A SHEEP TO SLAUGHTER;
   AND AS A LAMB BEFORE ITS
      SHEARER IS SILENT,
   SO HE DOES NOT OPEN HIS MOUTH.
33 "IN HUMILIATION HIS JUDGMENT
      WAS TAKEN AWAY;
   WHO WILL RELATE HIS GENERATION?
   FOR HIS LIFE IS REMOVED
      FROM THE EARTH."

34 The eunuch answered Philip and said, "Please *tell me*, of whom does the prophet say this? Of himself or of someone else?" 35 Then Philip opened his mouth, and beginning from this Scripture he preached Jesus to him. 36 As they went along the road they came to some water; and the eunuch *said, "Look! Water! What prevents me from being baptized?" 37 [And Philip said, "If you believe with all your heart, you may." And he answered and said, "I believe that Jesus Christ is the Son of God."] 38 And he ordered the chariot to stop; and they both went down into the water, Philip as well as the eunuch, and he baptized him. 39 When they came up out of the water, the Spirit of the Lord snatched Philip away; and the eunuch no longer saw him, but went on his way rejoicing. 40 But Philip found himself at Azotus, and as he passed through he kept preaching the gospel to all the cities until he came to Caesarea.

DAY 28: How did Philip bring the gospel to the Ethiopian eunuch?

Philip, who had been involved with the evangelization of the Samaritans, was told by an angel of the Lord to go to an undisclosed location along the road that went down from Jerusalem to Gaza (Ac 8:26). Gaza was one of 5 chief cities of the Philistines. The original city was destroyed in the first century B.C. and a new city was built near the coast.

There Philip met an Ethiopian eunuch. Ethiopia in those days was a large kingdom located south of Egypt. A eunuch can refer to one who was emasculated or generally, to a government official. It is likely he was both since Luke refers to him as a eunuch and as one who held a position of authority in the queen's court—that of treasurer, much like a Minister of Finance or Secretary of the Treasury. As a physical eunuch, he would have been denied access to the temple (Dt 23:1) and the opportunity to become a full proselyte to Judaism.

The eunuch was reading Isaiah (Ac 8:28). He knew the importance of seeking God through the Scripture. And the verses he was reading were found in Isaiah 53:7-8. The eunuch's question to Philip was "of whom does the prophet say this? Of himself or of someone else?" (v. 34). His confusion was understandable. Even the Jewish religious experts were divided on the meaning of this passage. Some believed the slaughtered sheep represented Israel, others thought Isaiah was referring to himself, and others thought the Messiah was Isaiah's subject.

Philip preached Jesus to the eunuch, who immediately responded with the wish to be baptized. After the baptism, it says that "Spirit of the Lord snatched Philip away" (v. 39). Elijah (1Ki 18:12; 2Ki 2:16) and Ezekiel (Eze 3:12, 14; 8:3) were also snatched away in a miraculous fashion. This was a powerful confirmation to the caravan that Philip was God's representative.

JUNE 29

1 Chronicles 21:1–22:19

21 Then Satan stood up against Israel and moved David to number Israel. ² So David said to Joab and to the princes of the people, "Go, number Israel from Beersheba even to Dan, and bring me *word* that I may know their number." ³ Joab said, "May the LORD add to His people a hundred times as many as they are! But, my lord the king, are they not all my lord's servants? Why does my lord seek this thing? Why should he be a cause of guilt to Israel?" ⁴ Nevertheless, the king's word prevailed against Joab. Therefore, Joab departed and went throughout all Israel, and came to Jerusalem. ⁵ Joab gave the number of the census of *all* the people to David. And all Israel were 1,100,000 men who drew the sword; and Judah *was* 470,000 men who drew the sword. ⁶ But he did not number Levi and Benjamin among them, for the king's command was abhorrent to Joab.

⁷ God was displeased with this thing, so

21:1 Satan...moved. Second Samuel 24:1 reports that "the anger of the LORD burned against Israel," and this "incited" David to take the census. This apparent discrepancy is resolved by understanding that God sovereignly and permissively uses Satan to achieve His purposes. God uses Satan to judge sinners (Mk 4:15; 2Co 4:4), to refine saints (Job 1:8–2:10; Lk 22:31–32), to discipline those in the church (1Co 5:1–5; 1Ti 1:20), and to further purify obedient believers (2Co 12:7–10). Neither God nor Satan forced David to sin (Jas 1:13–15), but God allowed Satan to tempt David, and he chose to sin. The sin surfaced his proud heart and God dealt with him for it. **number Israel.** David's census brought tragedy because, unlike the census in Moses' time (Nu 1–2) which God had commanded, this census by David was to gratify his pride in the great strength of his army and consequent military power. He was also putting more trust in his forces than in his God. He was taking credit for his victories by the building of his great army. This angered God, who moved Satan to bring the sin to a head.

He struck Israel. ⁸ David said to God, "I have sinned greatly, in that I have done this thing. But now, please take away the iniquity of Your servant, for I have done very foolishly."

⁹ The LORD spoke to Gad, David's seer, saying, ¹⁰ "Go and speak to David, saying, 'Thus says the LORD, "I offer you three things; choose for yourself one of them, which I will do to you."'" ¹¹ So Gad came to David and said to him, "Thus says the LORD, 'Take for yourself ¹² either three years of famine, or three months to be swept away before your foes, while the sword of your enemies overtakes *you*, or else three days of the sword of the LORD, even pestilence in the land, and the angel of the LORD destroying throughout all the territory of Israel.' Now, therefore, consider what answer I shall return to Him who sent me." ¹³ David said to Gad, "I am in great distress; please let me fall into the hand of the LORD, for His mercies are very great. But do not let me fall into the hand of man."

¹⁴ So the LORD sent a pestilence on Israel; 70,000 men of Israel fell. ¹⁵ And God sent an angel to Jerusalem to destroy it; but as he was about to destroy *it*, the LORD saw and was sorry over the calamity, and said to the destroying angel, "It is enough; now relax your hand." And the angel of the LORD was standing by the threshing floor of Ornan the Jebusite. ¹⁶ Then David lifted up his eyes and saw the angel of the LORD standing between earth and heaven, with his drawn sword in his hand stretched out over Jerusalem. Then David and the elders, covered with sackcloth, fell on their faces. ¹⁷ David said to God, "Is it not I who commanded to count the people? Indeed, I am the one who has sinned and done very wickedly, but these sheep, what have they done? O LORD my God, please let Your hand be against me and my father's household, but not against Your people that they should be plagued."

¹⁸ Then the angel of the LORD commanded Gad to say to David, that David should go up and build an altar to the LORD on the threshing floor of Ornan the Jebusite. ¹⁹ So David went up at the word of Gad, which he spoke in the name of the LORD. ²⁰ Now Ornan turned back and saw the angel, and his four sons *who were* with him hid themselves. And Ornan was threshing wheat. ²¹ As David came to Ornan,

21:16 the giant. The Hebrew term used in vv. 16, 18, 20, 22 is *rapha*. This was not the name of an individual, but a term used collectively for the "Rephaim" who inhabited the land of Canaan and were noted for their inordinate size (Ge 15:19-21; Nu 13:33; Dt 2:11; 3:11, 13). The term "Rephaim" was used of the people called the "Anakim" (Dt 2:10-11, 20-21), distinguished for their size and strength. According to Joshua 11:21-22, the "Anakim" were driven from the hill country of Israel and Judah, but remained in the Philistine cities of Gaza, Gath, and Ashdod. Though the Philistines had succumbed to the power of Israel's army, the appearance of some great champion revived their courage and invited their hope for victory against the Israelite invaders.

Ornan looked and saw David, and went out from the threshing floor and prostrated himself before David with his face to the ground. [22] Then David said to Ornan, "Give me the site of *this* threshing floor, that I may build on it an altar to the LORD; for the full price you shall give it to me, that the plague may be restrained from the people." [23] Ornan said to David, "Take *it* for yourself; and let my lord the king do what is good in his sight. See, I will give the oxen for burnt offerings and the threshing sledges for wood and the wheat for the grain offering; I will give *it* all." [24] But King David said to Ornan, "No, but I will surely buy *it* for the full price; for I will not take what is yours for the LORD, or offer a burnt offering which costs me nothing." [25] So David gave Ornan 600 shekels of gold by weight for the site. [26] Then David built an altar to the LORD there and offered burnt offerings and peace offerings. And he called to the LORD and He answered him with fire from heaven on the altar of burnt offering. [27] The LORD commanded the angel, and he put his sword back in its sheath.

[28] At that time, when David saw that the LORD had answered him on the threshing floor of Ornan the Jebusite, he offered sacrifice there. [29] For the tabernacle of the LORD, which Moses had made in the wilderness, and the altar of burnt offering *were* in the high place at Gibeon at that time. [30] But David could not go before it to inquire of God, for he was terrified by the sword of the angel of the LORD.

22 Then David said, "This is the house of the LORD God, and this is the altar of burnt offering for Israel."

[2] So David gave orders to gather the for-

eigners who were in the land of Israel, and he set stonecutters to hew out stones to build the house of God. [3] David prepared large quantities of iron to make the nails for the doors of the gates and for the clamps, and more bronze than could be weighed; [4] and timbers of cedar logs beyond number, for the Sidonians and Tyrians brought large quantities of cedar timber to David. [5] David said, "My son Solomon is young and inexperienced, and the house that is to be built for the LORD shall be exceedingly magnificent, famous and glorious throughout all lands. *Therefore* now I will make preparation for it." So David made ample preparations before his death.

22:5 young. Solomon was born early in David's reign (ca. 1000-990 B.C.) and was at this time 20 to 30 years of age. The magnificent and complex challenge of building such a monumental edifice with all its elements required an experienced leader for preparation. **magnificent.** David understood that the temple needed to reflect on earth something of God's heavenly majesty, so he devoted himself to the collection of the plans and materials, tapping the vast amount of spoils from people he had conquered and cities he had sacked (vv. 14-16).

---

[6] Then he called for his son Solomon, and charged him to build a house for the LORD God of Israel. [7] David said to Solomon, "My son, I had intended to build a house to the name of the LORD my God. [8] But the word of the LORD came to me, saying, 'You have shed much blood and have waged great wars; you shall not build a house to My name, because you have shed *so* much blood on the earth before Me. [9] Behold, a son will be born to you, who shall be a man of rest; and I will give him rest from all his enemies on every side; for his name shall be Solomon, and I will give peace and quiet to Israel in his days. [10] He shall build a house for My name, and he shall be My son and I will be his father; and I will establish the throne of his kingdom over Israel forever.' [11] Now, my son, the LORD be with you that you may be successful, and build the house of the LORD your God just as He has spoken concerning you. [12] Only the LORD give you discretion and understanding, and give you charge over Israel, so that you may keep the law of the LORD your God. [13] Then you will prosper, if you are careful to observe the statutes and the ordinances which the LORD

commanded Moses concerning Israel. Be strong and courageous, do not fear nor be dismayed. ¹⁴ Now behold, with great pains I have prepared for the house of the LORD 100,000 talents of gold and 1,000,000 talents of silver, and bronze and iron beyond weight, for they are in great quantity; also timber and stone I have prepared, and you may add to them. ¹⁵ Moreover, there are many workmen with you, stonecutters and masons of stone and carpenters, and all men who are skillful

22:11–13 David's spiritual charge to Solomon resembles the Lord's exhortation to Joshua (Jos 1:6–9). Solomon asked God for and received the very "discretion and understanding" his father, David, desired for him (1Ki 3:3–14; 2Ch 1:7–12). He learned the value of such spiritual counsel and passed it on in Ecclesiastes 12:1, 13.

22:14 prepared…100,000 talents of gold. Assuming a talent weighed about 75 lbs., this would be approximately 3,750 tons, a staggering amount of gold. **and 1,000,000 talents of silver.** This would be approximately 37,500 tons of silver.

in every kind of work. ¹⁶ Of the gold, the silver and the bronze and the iron there is no limit. Arise and work, and may the LORD be with you."

¹⁷ David also commanded all the leaders of Israel to help his son Solomon, *saying,* ¹⁸ "Is not the LORD your God with you? And has He not given you rest on every side? For He has given the inhabitants of the land into my hand, and the land is subdued before the LORD and before His people. ¹⁹ Now set your heart and your soul to seek the LORD your God; arise, therefore, and build the sanctuary of the LORD God, so that you may bring the ark of the covenant of the LORD and the holy vessels of God into the house that is to be built for the name of the LORD."

Psalm 78:34–39

³⁴ When He killed them, then
    they sought Him,
And returned and searched
    diligently for God;
³⁵ And they remembered that
    God was their rock,
And the Most High God
    their Redeemer.

³⁶ But they deceived Him
    with their mouth
And lied to Him with their
    tongue.
³⁷ For their heart was not
    steadfast toward Him,
Nor were they faithful
    in His covenant.
³⁸ But He, being compassionate,
    forgave *their* iniquity and
    did not destroy *them;*
And often He restrained
    His anger
And did not arouse all
    His wrath.
³⁹ Thus He remembered that
    they were but flesh,
A wind that passes and
    does not return.

Proverbs 20:1–2

20 Wine is a mocker, strong
    drink a brawler,
And whoever is intoxicated
    by it is not wise.
² The terror of a king is like
    the growling of a lion;
He who provokes him to anger
    forfeits his own life.

20:1 Wine…strong drink. This begins a new theme of temperance (23:20–21, 29–35; 31:4–5). Wine was grape juice mixed with water to dilute it, but strong drink was unmixed. While the use of these beverages is not specifically condemned (Dt 14:26), being intoxicated always is (Is 28:7). Rulers were not to drink, so their judgment would not be clouded nor their behavior less than exemplary (31:4–5). **mocker…brawler.** "Mocker" is the same word as "scoffer" in 19:25, 29; a brawler is violent, loud, and uncontrolled. Both words describe the personality of the drunkard.

Acts 9:1–22

9 Now Saul, still breathing threats and murder against the disciples of the Lord, went to the high priest, ² and asked for letters from him to the synagogues at Damascus, so that if he found any belonging to the Way, both men and women, he might bring them bound to Jerusalem. ³ As he was traveling, it happened that he was approaching Damascus, and suddenly a light from heaven flashed around him; ⁴ and he fell to the ground and heard a voice saying to him, "Saul, Saul, why are you persecuting Me?" ⁵And he said, "Who are You, Lord?" And He *said,* "I am Jesus whom you are persecuting, ⁶but get up and enter the city, and it will be told you what you must do." ⁷The men who traveled with him stood speechless, hearing the voice but seeing no one. ⁸Saul got up from the ground, and though his eyes were open, he could see nothing; and leading him by the hand, they brought him into Damascus. ⁹And he was three days without sight, and neither ate nor drank.

¹⁰Now there was a disciple at Damascus named Ananias; and the Lord said to him in a vision, "Ananias." And he said, "Here I am, Lord." ¹¹And the Lord *said* to him, "Get up and go to the street called Straight, and inquire at the house of Judas for a man from Tarsus named Saul, for he is praying, ¹²and he has seen in a vision a man named Ananias come in and lay his hands on him, so that he might regain his sight." ¹³But Ananias answered, "Lord, I have heard from many about this man, how much harm he did to Your saints at Jerusalem; ¹⁴and here he has authority from the chief priests to bind all who call on Your name." ¹⁵But the Lord said to him, "Go,

for he is a chosen instrument of Mine, to bear My name before the Gentiles and kings and the sons of Israel; ¹⁶for I will show him how much he must suffer for My name's sake." ¹⁷So Ananias departed and entered the house, and after laying his hands on him said, "Brother Saul, the Lord Jesus, who appeared to you on the road by which you were coming, has sent me so that you may regain your sight and be filled with the Holy Spirit." ¹⁸And immediately there fell from his eyes something like scales, and he regained his sight, and he got up and was baptized; ¹⁹and he took food and was strengthened.

Now for several days he was with the disciples who were at Damascus, ²⁰and immediately he *began* to proclaim Jesus in the synagogues, saying, "He is the Son of God." ²¹All those hearing him continued to be amazed, and were saying, "Is this not he who in Jerusalem destroyed those who called on this name, and *who* had come here for the purpose of bringing them bound before the chief priests?" ²²But Saul kept increasing in strength and confounding the Jews who lived at Damascus by proving that this *Jesus* is the Christ.

DAY 29: How did the apostle Paul come to faith in Jesus Christ?

The apostle Paul was originally named Saul, after the first king of Israel. He was born a Jew, studied in Jerusalem under Gamaliel (Ac 22:3), and became a Pharisee (23:6). He was also a Roman citizen, a right he inherited from his father (22:8). Acts 9:1–19 records the external facts of his conversion (see also 22:1–22; 26:9–20). Philippians 3:1–14 records the internal spiritual conversion.

At the time of his conversion Saul was "still breathing threats and murder" against Christians (Ac 9:1; see also 1Ti 1:12–13; 1Co 15:9). He was in Damascus, the capital of Syria, which apparently had a large population of Jews, including Hellenist believers who fled Jerusalem to avoid persecution (Ac 9:2). He had letters authorizing him to seek out those "belonging to the Way." This description of Christianity, derived from Jesus' description of Himself (Jn 14:6), appears several times in Acts (19:9, 23; 22:4; 24:14, 22).

The "light from heaven" (v. 3) that struck him was the appearance of Jesus Christ in glory (22:6; 26:13) and was visible only to Saul (26:9). The voice that asked him, "Why are you persecuting Me?" was that of Jesus (v. 5). An inseparable union exists between Christ and His followers. Saul's persecution represented a direct attack on Christ. Saul arose from that encounter, blinded by the light, and went in obedience to await the next step (v. 6).

Meanwhile, Ananias was being given divine instructions concerning Paul and Paul's ministry. He is told that Saul is a "chosen instrument," literally "a vessel of election" (v. 15). There was perfect continuity between Paul's salvation and his service; God chose him to convey His grace to all men (Gal 1:1; 1Ti 2:7; 2Ti 1:11). Paul used this same word 4 times (Ro 9:21, 23; 2Co 4:7; 2Ti 2:21). "Before the Gentiles and kings and the sons of Israel" (v. 15). Paul began his ministry preaching to Jews (13:14; 14:1; 17:1, 10; 18:4; 19:8), but his primary calling was to Gentiles (Ro 11:13; 15:16). God also called him to minister to kings such as Agrippa (25:23—26:32) and likely Caesar (25:10–12; 2Ti 4:16–17).

Ananias went to Paul and "after laying his hands on him," he prayed for Paul's healing and that he would "be filled with the Holy Spirit" (v. 17). He was then filled with the Spirit and empowered for service (2:4, 14; 4:8, 31; 6:5, 8).

JUNE 30

1 Chronicles 23:1–25:31

23 Now when David reached old age, he made his son Solomon king over Israel. ²And he gathered together all the leaders of Israel with the priests and the Levites. ³The Levites were numbered from thirty years old and upward, and their number by census of men was 38,000. ⁴Of these, 24,000 were to oversee the work of the house of the LORD; and 6,000 were officers and judges, ⁵and 4,000 were gatekeepers, and 4,000 were praising the LORD with the instruments which David made for giving praise. ⁶David divided them into divisions according to the sons of Levi: Gershon, Kohath, and Merari.

⁷Of the Gershonites were Ladan and Shimei. ⁸The sons of Ladan were Jehiel the first and Zetham and Joel, three. ⁹The sons of Shimei were Shelomoth and Haziel and Haran, three. These were the heads of the fathers' households of Ladan. ¹⁰The sons of Shimei were Jahath, Zina, Jeush and Beriah. These four were the sons of Shimei. ¹¹Jahath was the first and Zizah the second; but Jeush and Beriah did not have many sons, so they became a father's household, one class.

¹²The sons of Kohath were four: Amram, Izhar, Hebron and Uzziel. ¹³The sons of Amram were Aaron and Moses. And Aaron was set apart to sanctify him as most holy, he and his sons forever, to burn incense before the LORD, to minister to Him and to bless in His name forever. ¹⁴But as for Moses the man of God, his sons were named among the tribe of Levi. ¹⁵The sons of Moses were Gershom and Eliezer. ¹⁶The son of Gershom was Shebuel the chief. ¹⁷The son of Eliezer was Rehabiah the chief; and Eliezer had no other sons, but the sons of Rehabiah were very many. ¹⁸The son of Izhar was Shelomith the chief. ¹⁹The sons of Hebron were Jeriah the first, Amariah the second, Jahaziel the third and Jekameam the fourth. ²⁰The sons of Uzziel were Micah the first and Isshiah the second.

²¹The sons of Merari were Mahli and Mushi. The sons of Mahli were Eleazar and Kish. ²²Eleazar died and had no sons, but daughters only, so their brothers, the sons of Kish, took them as wives. ²³The sons of Mushi were three: Mahli, Eder and Jeremoth.

²⁴These were the sons of Levi according to their fathers' households, even the heads of the fathers' households of those of them who were counted, in the number of names by their census, doing the work for the service of the house of the LORD, from twenty years old and upward. ²⁵For David said, "The LORD God of Israel has given rest to His people, and He dwells in Jerusalem forever. ²⁶Also, the Levites will no longer need to carry the tabernacle and all its utensils for its service." ²⁷For by the last words of David the sons of Levi were numbered from twenty years old and upward. ²⁸For their office is to assist the sons of Aaron with the service of the house of the LORD, in the courts and in the chambers and in the purifying of all holy things, even the work of the service of the house of God, ²⁹and with the showbread, and the fine flour for a grain offering, and unleavened wafers, or what is baked in the pan or what is well-mixed, and all measures of volume and size. ³⁰They are to stand every morning to thank and to praise the LORD, and likewise at evening, ³¹and to offer all burnt offerings to the LORD, on the sabbaths, the new moons and the fixed festivals in the number set by the ordinance concerning them, continually before the LORD. ³²Thus they are to keep charge of the tent of meeting, and charge of the holy place, and charge of the sons of Aaron their relatives, for the service of the house of the LORD.

24 Now the divisions of the descendants of Aaron were these: the sons of Aaron were Nadab, Abihu, Eleazar and Ithamar. ²But Nadab and Abihu died before their father and had no sons. So Eleazar and Ithamar served as priests. ³David, with Zadok of the sons of Eleazar and Ahimelech of the sons of Ithamar, divided them according to their offices for their ministry. ⁴Since more chief men were found from the descendants of Eleazar than the descendants of Ithamar, they divided them thus: there were sixteen heads of fathers' households of the descendants of Eleazar and eight of the descendants of Ithamar, according to their fathers' households. ⁵Thus they were divided by lot, the one as the other; for they were officers of the sanctuary and officers of God, both from the descendants of Eleazar and the descendants of Ithamar. ⁶Shemaiah, the son of Nethanel the scribe, from the Levites, recorded them in the presence of the king, the princes, Zadok the priest, Ahimelech the son of Abiathar, and the heads of the fathers' households of the priests and of the Levites; one father's household taken for Eleazar and one taken for Ithamar.

⁷Now the first lot came out for Jehoiarib, the second for Jedaiah, ⁸the third for Harim, the fourth for Seorim, ⁹the fifth for Malchijah,

the sixth for Mijamin, ¹⁰the seventh for Hakkoz, the eighth for Abijah, ¹¹the ninth for Jeshua, the tenth for Shecaniah, ¹²the eleventh for Eliashib, the twelfth for Jakim, ¹³the thirteenth for Huppah, the fourteenth for Jeshebeab, ¹⁴the fifteenth for Bilgah, the sixteenth for Immer, ¹⁵the seventeenth for Hezir, the eighteenth for Happizzez, ¹⁶the nineteenth for Pethahiah, the twentieth for Jehezkel, ¹⁷the twenty-first for Jachin, the twenty-second for Gamul, ¹⁸the twenty-third for Delaiah, the twenty-fourth for Maaziah. ¹⁹These were their offices for their ministry when *they* came in to the house of the LORD according to the ordinance *given* to them through Aaron their father, just as the LORD God of Israel had commanded him.

²⁰Now for the rest of the sons of Levi: of the sons of Amram, Shubael; of the sons of Shubael, Jehdeiah. ²¹Of Rehabiah: of the sons of Rehabiah, Isshiah the first. ²²Of the Izharites, Shelomoth; of the sons of Shelomoth, Jahath. ²³The sons *of Hebron:* Jeriah *the first,* Amariah the second, Jahaziel the third, Jekameam the fourth. ²⁴*Of* the sons of Uzziel, Micah; of the sons of Micah, Shamir. ²⁵The brother of Micah, Isshiah; of the sons of Isshiah, Zechariah. ²⁶The sons of Merari, Mahli and Mushi; the sons of Jaaziah, Beno. ²⁷The sons of Merari: by Jaaziah *were* Beno, Shoham, Zaccur and Ibri. ²⁸By Mahli: Eleazar, who had no sons. ²⁹By Kish: the sons of Kish, Jerahmeel. ³⁰The sons of Mushi: Mahli, Eder and Jerimoth. These *were* the sons of the Levites according to their fathers' households. ³¹These also cast lots just as their relatives the sons of Aaron in the presence of David the king, Zadok, Ahimelech, and the heads of the fathers' *households* of the priests and of the Levites—the head of fathers' *households* as well as those of his younger brother.

25 Moreover, David and the commanders of the army set apart for the service *some* of the sons of Asaph and of Heman and of Jeduthun, who *were* to prophesy with lyres, harps and cymbals; and the number of those who performed their service was: ²Of the sons of Asaph: Zaccur, Joseph, Nethaniah and Asharelah; the sons of Asaph *were* under the direction of Asaph, who prophesied under the direction of the king. ³Of Jeduthun, the sons of Jeduthun: Gedaliah, Zeri, Jeshaiah, Shimei, Hashabiah and Mattithiah, six, under the direction of their father Jeduthun with the harp, who prophesied in giving thanks and praising the LORD. ⁴Of Heman, the sons of Heman: Bukkiah, Mattaniah, Uzziel, Shebuel and Jerimoth, Hananiah, Hanani, Eliathath,

25:1 the commanders of the army. David relied on his mighty men for help (11:10). **Asaph... Heman...Jeduthun.** David's 3 chief ministers of music (6:31–48). **prophesy.** This is not necessarily to be taken in a revelatory sense, but rather in the sense of proclamation and exhortation through the lyrics of their music (25:2–3). Prophesying is not necessarily predicting the future or even speaking direct revelation. It is proclaiming truth (v. 5) to people (1Co 14:3), and music is a vehicle for such proclamation in praise (v. 3). David and the leaders selected those most capable (v. 7) of leading the people to worship God through their music.

Giddalti and Romamti-ezer, Joshbekashah, Mallothi, Hothir, Mahazioth. ⁵All these *were* the sons of Heman the king's seer to exalt him according to the words of God, for God gave fourteen sons and three daughters to Heman. ⁶All these were under the direction of their father to sing in the house of the LORD, with cymbals, harps and lyres, for the service of the house of God. Asaph, Jeduthun and Heman *were* under the direction of the king. ⁷Their number who were trained in singing to the LORD, with their relatives, all who were skillful, *was* 288. ⁸They cast lots for their duties, all alike, the small as well as the great, the teacher *as well* as the pupil.

⁹Now the first lot came out for Asaph to Joseph, the second for Gedaliah, he with his relatives and sons *were* twelve; ¹⁰the third to Zaccur, his sons and his relatives, twelve; ¹¹the fourth to Izri, his sons and his relatives, twelve; ¹²the fifth to Nethaniah, his sons and his relatives, twelve; ¹³the sixth to Bukkiah, his sons and his relatives, twelve; ¹⁴the seventh to Jesharelah, his sons and his relatives, twelve; ¹⁵the eighth to Jeshaiah, his sons and his relatives, twelve; ¹⁶the ninth to Mattaniah, his sons and his relatives, twelve; ¹⁷the tenth to Shimei, his sons and his relatives, twelve; ¹⁸the eleventh to Azarel, his sons and his relatives, twelve; ¹⁹the twelfth to Hashabiah, his sons and his relatives, twelve; ²⁰for the thirteenth, Shubael, his sons and his relatives, twelve; ²¹for the fourteenth, Mattithiah, his sons and his relatives, twelve; ²²for the fifteenth to Jeremoth, his sons and his relatives, twelve; ²³for the sixteenth to Hananiah, his sons and his relatives, twelve; ²⁴for the seventeenth to Joshbekashah, his sons and his relatives, twelve; ²⁵for the eighteenth to Hanani, his sons and his relatives, twelve; ²⁶for the nineteenth to Mallothi, his sons and

his relatives, twelve; ²⁷ for the twentieth to Eliathah, his sons and his relatives, twelve; ²⁸ for the twenty-first to Hothir, his sons and his relatives, twelve; ²⁹ for the twenty-second to Giddalti, his sons and his relatives, twelve; ³⁰ for the twenty-third to Mahazioth, his sons and his relatives, twelve; ³¹ for the twenty-fourth to Romamti-ezer, his sons and his relatives, twelve.

Psalm 78:40–55

⁴⁰ How often they rebelled against
   Him in the wilderness
   And grieved Him in the desert!
⁴¹ Again and again they tempted God,
   And pained the Holy One of Israel.
⁴² They did not remember His power,
   The day when He redeemed
      them from the adversary,

78:41 pained the Holy One. The Israelites did this by doubting God's power.

78:42 did not remember His power. The generations of Israelites which left Egypt and eventually died in the wilderness were characterized by ignoring God's previous acts of power and faithfulness. The following verses (vv. 43–55) rehearse the plagues and miracles of the Exodus from Egypt, which marvelously demonstrated God's omnipotence and covenant love.

⁴³ When He performed His
   signs in Egypt
   And His marvels in the field
      of Zoan,
⁴⁴ And turned their rivers to blood,
   And their streams, they
      could not drink.
⁴⁵ He sent among them swarms of
   flies which devoured them,
   And frogs which destroyed them.
⁴⁶ He gave also their crops to
   the grasshopper
   And the product of their
      labor to the locust.
⁴⁷ He destroyed their vines
   with hailstones
   And their sycamore trees with frost.
⁴⁸ He gave over their cattle
   also to the hailstones
   And their herds to bolts of lightning.
⁴⁹ He sent upon them His
   burning anger,

Fury and indignation and trouble,
   A band of destroying angels.
⁵⁰ He leveled a path for His anger;
   He did not spare their
      soul from death,
   But gave over their life to the plague,
⁵¹ And smote all the firstborn in Egypt,
   The first *issue* of their virility
      in the tents of Ham.
⁵² But He led forth His own
   people like sheep
   And guided them in the
      wilderness like a flock;
⁵³ He led them safely, so that
   they did not fear;
   But the sea engulfed their enemies.

⁵⁴ So He brought them to His holy land,
   To this hill country which His
      right hand had gained.
⁵⁵ He also drove out the
   nations before them
   And apportioned them for an
      inheritance by measurement,
   And made the tribes of Israel
      dwell in their tents.

Proverbs 20:3

³ Keeping away from strife is
   an honor for a man,
   But any fool will quarrel.

Acts 9:23–43

²³ When many days had elapsed, the Jews plotted together to do away with him, ²⁴ but their plot became known to Saul. They were also watching the gates day and night so that they might put him to death; ²⁵ but his disciples took him by night and let him down through *an opening in* the wall, lowering him in a large basket.

²⁶ When he came to Jerusalem, he was trying to associate with the disciples; but they were all afraid of him, not believing that he was a disciple. ²⁷ But Barnabas took hold of him and brought him to the apostles and described to them how he had seen the Lord on the road, and that He had talked to him, and how at Damascus he had spoken out boldly in the name of Jesus. ²⁸ And he was with them, moving about freely in Jerusalem, speaking out boldly in the name of the Lord. ²⁹ And he was talking and arguing with the Hellenistic *Jews;* but they were attempting to put him to death. ³⁰ But when the brethren learned *of it,* they brought him down to Caesarea and sent him away to Tarsus.

³¹ So the church throughout all Judea and

Galilee and Samaria enjoyed peace, being built up; and going on in the fear of the Lord and in the comfort of the Holy Spirit, it continued to increase.

32 Now as Peter was traveling through all *those regions,* he came down also to the saints who lived at Lydda. 33 There he found a man named Aeneas, who had been bedridden eight years, for he was paralyzed. 34 Peter said to him, "Aeneas, Jesus Christ heals you; get up and make your bed." Immediately he got up. 35 And all who lived at Lydda and Sharon saw him, and they turned to the Lord.

36 Now in Joppa there was a disciple named Tabitha (which translated *in Greek* is called Dorcas); this woman was abounding with deeds of kindness and charity which she continually did. 37 And it happened at that time that she fell sick and died; and when they had washed her body, they laid it in an upper room. 38 Since Lydda was near Joppa, the disciples, having heard that Peter was there, sent two men to him, imploring him, "Do not delay in coming to us." 39 So Peter arose and went with them. When he arrived, they brought him into the upper room; and all the widows

9:30 Caesarea. See 8:40. An important port city on the Mediterranean located 30 miles north of Joppa. As the capital of the Roman province of Judea and the home of the Roman procurator, it served as the headquarters of a large Roman garrison. **sent him away to Tarsus.** Paul disappeared from prominent ministry for several years, although he possibly founded some churches around Syria and Cilicia (15:23; Gal 1:21).

stood beside him, weeping and showing all the tunics and garments that Dorcas used to make while she was with them. 40 But Peter sent them all out and knelt down and prayed, and turning to the body, he said, "Tabitha, arise." And she opened her eyes, and when she saw Peter, she sat up. 41 And he gave her his hand and raised her up; and calling the saints and widows, he presented her alive. 42 It became known all over Joppa, and many believed in the Lord. 43 And Peter stayed many days in Joppa with a tanner *named* Simon.

DAY 30: How were the duties of the temple divided up?		
Administrative Duties	Supervisors	1 Chronicles 23:4–5
	Bailiffs	1 Chronicles 23:4–5
	Judges	1 Chronicles 23:4–5
	Public administrators	1 Chronicles 26:29–30
Ministerial Duties	Priests	1 Chronicles 24:1–2
	Prophets	1 Chronicles 25:1
	Assistants for sacrifices	1 Chronicles 23:29–31
	Assistants for purification ceremonies	1 Chronicles 23:27–28
Service Duties	Bakers of the Bread of the Presence	1 Chronicles 23:29
	Those who checked the weights and measures	1 Chronicles 23:29
	Custodians	1 Chronicles 23:28
Financial Duties	Those who cared for the treasury	1 Chronicles 26:20
	Those who cared for dedicated items	1 Chronicles 26:26–28
Artistic Duties	Musicians	1 Chronicles 25:6
	Singers	1 Chronicles 25:7
Protective Duties	Temple guards	1 Chronicles 23:5
	Guards for the gates and storehouses	1 Chronicles 26:12–18
Individual Assignments	Recording secretary	1 Chronicles 24:6
	Chaplain to the king	1 Chronicles 25:4
	Private prophet to the king	1 Chronicles 25:2
	Captain of the guard	1 Chronicles 26:1
	Chief officer of the treasury	1 Chronicles 26:23–24

JULY 1

1 Chronicles 26:1–27:34

26 For the divisions of the gatekeepers *there were* of the Korahites, Meshelemiah the son of Kore, of the sons of Asaph. ²Meshelemiah had sons: Zechariah the firstborn, Jediael the second, Zebadiah the third, Jathniel the fourth, ³Elam the fifth, Johanan the sixth, Eliehoenai the seventh. ⁴Obed-edom had sons: Shemaiah the firstborn, Jehozabad the second, Joah the third, Sacar the fourth, Nethanel the fifth, ⁵Ammiel the sixth, Issachar the seventh *and* Peullethai the eighth; God had indeed blessed him. ⁶Also to his son Shemaiah sons were born who ruled over the house of their father, for they were mighty men of valor. ⁷The sons of Shemaiah *were* Othni, Rephael, Obed and Elzabad, whose brothers, Elihu and Semachiah, were valiant men. ⁸All these *were* of the sons of Obed-edom; they and their sons and their relatives *were* able men with strength for the service, 62 from Obed-edom. ⁹Meshelemiah had sons and relatives, 18 valiant men. ¹⁰Also Hosah, *one* of the sons of Merari had sons: Shimri the first (although he was not the firstborn, his father made him first), ¹¹Hilkiah the second, Tebaliah the third, Zechariah the fourth; all the sons and relatives of Hosah *were* 13.

¹²To these divisions of the gatekeepers, the chief men, *were given* duties like their relatives to minister in the house of the LORD. ¹³They cast lots, the small and the great alike, according to their fathers' households, for every gate. ¹⁴The lot to the east fell to Shelemiah. Then they cast lots *for* his son Zechariah, a counselor with insight, and his lot came out to the north. ¹⁵For Obed-edom *it fell* to the south, and to his sons went the storehouse. ¹⁶For Shuppim and Hosah *it was* to the west, by the gate of Shallecheth, on the ascending highway. Guard corresponded to guard. ¹⁷On the east there were six Levites, on the north four daily, on the south four daily, and at the storehouse two by two. ¹⁸At the Parbar on the west *there were* four at the highway and two at the Parbar. ¹⁹These were the divisions of the gatekeepers of the sons of Korah and of the sons of Merari.

²⁰The Levites, their relatives, had charge of the treasures of the house of God and of the treasures of the dedicated gifts. ²¹The sons of Ladan, the sons of the Gershonites belonging to Ladan, *namely,* the Jehielites, *were* the heads of the fathers' *households,* belonging to Ladan the Gershonite.

26:1–19 The temple gatekeepers (guards) had other duties, such as checking out equipment and utensils; storing, ordering and maintaining food for the priests and sacrifices; caring for the temple furniture; mixing the incense daily burned; and accounting for gifts brought. Their "duties" (v. 12) are given in 1 Chronicles 9:17–27.

26:20 treasures. The Levites watched over the store of valuables given to the Lord. This is a general reference to all the precious things committed to their trust, including contributions from David and the people, as well as war spoils given by triumphant soldiers (vv. 26–27).

---

²²The sons of Jehieli, Zetham and Joel his brother, had charge of the treasures of the house of the LORD. ²³As for the Amramites, the Izharites, the Hebronites and the Uzzielites, ²⁴Shebuel the son of Gershom, the son of Moses, was officer over the treasures. ²⁵His relatives by Eliezer *were* Rehabiah his son, Jeshaiah his son, Joram his son, Zichri his son and Shelomoth his son. ²⁶This Shelomoth and his relatives had charge of all the treasures of the dedicated gifts which King David and the heads of the fathers' *households,* the commanders of thousands and hundreds, and the commanders of the army, had dedicated. ²⁷They dedicated part of the spoil won in battles to repair the house of the LORD. ²⁸And all that Samuel the seer had dedicated and Saul the son of Kish, Abner the son of Ner and Joab the son of Zeruiah, everyone who had dedicated *anything, all of this* was in the care of Shelomoth and his relatives.

²⁹As for the Izharites, Chenaniah and his sons were *assigned* to outside duties for Israel, as officers and judges. ³⁰As for the Hebronites, Hashabiah and his relatives, 1,700 capable men, had charge of the affairs of Israel west of the Jordan, for all the work of the LORD and the service of the king. ³¹As for the Hebronites, Jerijah the chief (these Hebronites were investigated according to their genealogies and fathers' *households,* in the fortieth year of David's reign, and men of outstanding capability were found among them at Jazer of

---

26:29–32 officers and judges. There were 6,000 magistrates exercising judicial functions throughout the land.

Gilead) ³²and his relatives, capable men, *were* 2,700 in number, heads of fathers' *households.* And King David made them overseers of the Reubenites, the Gadites and the half-tribe of the Manassites concerning all the affairs of God and of the king.

27 Now *this is* the enumeration of the sons of Israel, the heads of fathers' *households,* the commanders of thousands and of hundreds, and their officers who served the king in all the affairs of the divisions which came in and went out month by month throughout all the months of the year, each division *numbering* 24,000:

²Jashobeam the son of Zabdiel had charge of the first division for the first month; and in his division *were* 24,000. ³*He was* from the sons of Perez, *and was* chief of all the commanders of the army for the first month. ⁴Dodai the Ahohite and his division had charge of the division for the second month, Mikloth *being* the chief officer; and in his division *were* 24,000. ⁵The third commander of the army for the third month *was* Benaiah, the son of Jehoiada the priest, *as* chief; and in his division *were* 24,000. ⁶This Benaiah *was* the mighty man of the thirty, and had charge of thirty; and over his division was Ammizabad his son. ⁷The fourth for the fourth month *was* Asahel the brother of Joab, and Zebadiah his son after him; and in his division *were* 24,000. ⁸The fifth for the fifth month *was* the commander Shamhuth the Izrahite; and in his division *were* 24,000. ⁹The sixth for the sixth month *was* Ira the son of Ikkesh the Tekoite; and in his division *were* 24,000. ¹⁰The seventh for the seventh month *was* Helez the Pelonite of the sons of Ephraim; and in his division *were* 24,000. ¹¹The eighth for the eighth month *was* Sibbecai the Hushathite of the Zerahites; and in his division *were* 24,000. ¹²The ninth for the ninth month *was* Abiezer the Anathothite of the Benjamites; and in his division *were* 24,000. ¹³The tenth for the tenth month *was* Maharai the Netophathite of the Zerahites; and in his division *were* 24,000. ¹⁴The eleventh for the eleventh

27:1–15 This section enumerates the standing army of Israel (288,000 men), which had responsibility to guard the nation and temple. They were divided into 12 divisions, each of which served for one month during the year. When full war occurred, a larger force could be called into action.

month *was* Benaiah the Pirathonite of the sons of Ephraim; and in his division *were* 24,000. ¹⁵The twelfth for the twelfth month *was* Heldai the Netophathite of Othniel; and in his division *were* 24,000.

¹⁶Now in charge of the tribes of Israel: chief officer for the Reubenites was Eliezer the son of Zichri; for the Simeonites, Shephatiah the son of Maacah; ¹⁷for Levi, Hashabiah the son of Kemuel; for Aaron, Zadok; ¹⁸for Judah, Elihu, *one* of David's brothers; for Issachar, Omri the son of Michael; ¹⁹for Zebulun, Ishmaiah the son of Obadiah; for Naphtali, Jeremoth the son of Azriel; ²⁰for the sons of Ephraim, Hoshea the son of Azaziah; for the half-tribe of Manasseh, Joel the son of Pedaiah; ²¹for the half-tribe of Manasseh in Gilead, Iddo the son of Zechariah; for Benjamin, Jaasiel the son of Abner; ²²for Dan, Azarel the son of Jeroham. These *were* the princes of the tribes of Israel. ²³But David did not count those twenty years of age and under, because the LORD had said He would multiply Israel as the stars of heaven. ²⁴Joab the son of Zeruiah had begun to count *them,* but did not finish; and because of this, wrath came upon Israel, and the number was not included in the account of the chronicles of King David.

²⁵Now Azmaveth the son of Adiel had charge of the king's storehouses. And Jonathan the son of Uzziah had charge of the storehouses in the country, in the cities, in the villages and in the towers. ²⁶Ezri the son of Chelub had charge of the agricultural workers who tilled the soil. ²⁷Shimei the Ramathite had charge of the vineyards; and Zabdi the Shiphmite had charge of the produce of the vineyards *stored* in the wine cellars. ²⁸Baal-hanan the Gederite had charge of the olive and sycamore trees in the Shephelah; and Joash had charge of the stores of oil. ²⁹Shitrai the Sharonite had charge of the cattle which were grazing in Sharon; and Shaphat the son of Adlai had charge of the cattle in the valleys. ³⁰Obil the Ishmaelite had charge of the camels; and Jehdeiah the Meronothite had charge of the donkeys. ³¹Jaziz the Hagrite had charge of the flocks. All these were overseers of the property which belonged to King David.

³²Also Jonathan, David's uncle, *was* a counselor, a man of understanding, and a scribe; and Jehiel the son of Hachmoni tutored the king's sons. ³³Ahithophel *was* counselor to the king; and Hushai the Archite *was* the king's friend. ³⁴Jehoiada the son of Benaiah, and Abiathar succeeded Ahithophel; and Joab was the commander of the king's army.

Psalm 78:56–66

56 Yet they tempted and rebelled
   against the Most High God
   And did not keep His testimonies,
57 But turned back and acted
   treacherously like their fathers;
   They turned aside like a
   treacherous bow.
58 For they provoked Him with
   their high places
   And aroused His jealousy with
   their graven images.
59 When God heard, He was
   filled with wrath
   And greatly abhorred Israel;
60 So that He abandoned the
   dwelling place at Shiloh,
   The tent which He had
   pitched among men,

78:60 dwelling place at Shiloh. Shiloh was an early location of Jehovah worship in the Promised Land. The capture and removal of the ark from Shiloh by the Philistines symbolized God's judgment.

61 And gave up His strength to
   captivity
   And His glory into the hand
   of the adversary.
62 He also delivered His
   people to the sword,
   And was filled with wrath
   at His inheritance.
63 Fire devoured His young men,
   And His virgins had no
   wedding songs.
64 His priests fell by the sword,
   And His widows could not weep.

65 Then the Lord awoke as if from sleep,
   Like a warrior overcome by wine.
66 He drove His adversaries backward;
   He put on them an
   everlasting reproach.

Proverbs 20:4–5

4 The sluggard does not plow
   after the autumn,
   So he begs during the harvest
   and has nothing.
5 A plan in the heart of a man
   is like deep water,
   But a man of understanding
   draws it out.

20:5 deep water. The wise man has keen discernment reaching to the deepest intentions of the heart to grasp wise counsel (18:4; Heb 4:12).

Acts 10:1–23a

10 Now *there was* a man at Caesarea named Cornelius, a centurion of what was called the Italian cohort, 2 a devout man and one who feared God with all his household, and gave many alms to the *Jewish* people and prayed to God continually. 3 About the ninth hour of the day he clearly saw in a vision an angel of God who had *just* come in and said to him, "Cornelius!" 4 And fixing his gaze on him and being much alarmed, he said, "What is it, Lord?" And he said to him, "Your prayers and alms have ascended as a memorial before God. 5 Now dispatch *some* men to Joppa and send for a man *named* Simon, who is also called Peter; 6 he is staying with a tanner *named* Simon, whose house is by the sea." 7 When the angel who was speaking to him had left, he summoned two of his servants and a devout soldier of those who were his personal attendants, 8 and after he had explained everything to them, he sent them to Joppa.

9 On the next day, as they were on their way and approaching the city, Peter went up on the housetop about the sixth hour to pray. 10 But he became hungry and was desiring to eat; but while they were making preparations, he fell into a trance; 11 and he *saw the sky opened up, and an object like a great sheet coming down, lowered by four corners to the ground, 12 and there were in it all *kinds of* four-footed animals and crawling creatures of the earth and birds of the air. 13 A voice came to him, "Get up, Peter, kill and eat!" 14 But Peter said, "By no means, Lord, for I have never eaten anything unholy and unclean." 15 Again a voice *came* to him a second time, "What God has cleansed, no *longer* consider unholy." 16 This happened three times, and immediately the object was taken up into the sky.

17 Now while Peter was greatly perplexed in mind as to what the vision which he had seen might be, behold, the men who had been sent by Cornelius, having asked directions for Simon's house, appeared at the gate; 18 and calling out, they were asking whether Simon, who was also called Peter, was staying there. 19 While Peter was reflecting on the vision, the Spirit said to him, "Behold, three men are looking for you. 20 But get up, go downstairs and accompany them without misgivings, for

I have sent them Myself." ²¹Peter went down to the men and said, "Behold, I am the one you are looking for; what is the reason for which you have come?" ²²They said, "Cornelius, a centurion, a righteous and God-fearing man well spoken of by the entire nation of the Jews, was *divinely* directed by a holy angel to send for you *to come* to his house and hear a message from you." ²³So he invited them in and gave them lodging.

DAY 1: Who was Cornelius, and why was he so important?

In Acts 10:1, it states that Cornelius was a centurion—one of 60 officers in a Roman legion, each of whom commanded 100 men. He was of the "Italian Regiment" or "Italian Cohort." Ten cohorts of 600 men each made up a legion.

Cornelius was a "devout man and one who feared God" (v. 2). This is a technical term used by Jews to refer to Gentiles who had abandoned their pagan religion in favor of worshiping the Lord God. Such a person, while following the ethics of the Old Testament, had not become a full proselyte to Judaism through circumcision. Cornelius was a Gentile who was about to receive the saving knowledge of God in Christ. Cornelius was told in a vision that his prayers, devotion, faith, and goodness were like a fragrant offering rising up to God, "a memorial" (v. 4). He was even given specific directions on how to reach Peter.

The next day "Peter went up on the housetop...to pray" (v. 9). All kinds of worship occurred on the flat roofs of Jewish homes (2Ki 23:12; Jer 19:13; 32:29). In a trance Peter sees a great sheet descending from heaven, and "there were in it all kinds of four-footed animals," both clean and unclean animals (v. 12). To keep the Israelites separate from their idolatrous neighbors, God set specific dietary restrictions regarding the consumption of such animals (Lv 11:25–26). But a voice speaks to him and says, "Get up, Peter, kill and eat!" (v. 13). With the coming of the New Covenant and the calling of the church, God ended the dietary restrictions (Mk 7:19). "What God has cleansed, no longer consider unholy" (v. 15). More than just abolishing the Old Testament dietary restrictions, God made unity possible in the church of both Jews, symbolized by the clean animals, and Gentiles, symbolized by the unclean animals, through the comprehensive sacrificial death of Christ (Eph 2:14).

The vision and the confirmation by the Holy Spirit (v. 19) made it crystal clear to Peter that the gospel was for all people. The proof is that when the men from Cornelius arrived, he "invited them in" (v. 23). Self-respecting Jews did not invite any Gentiles into their home, especially soldiers of the hated Roman army.

JULY 2

1 Chronicles 28:1–29:30

28 Now David assembled at Jerusalem all the officials of Israel, the princes of the tribes, and the commanders of the divisions that served the king, and the commanders of thousands, and the commanders of hundreds, and the overseers of all the property and livestock belonging to the king and his sons, with the officials and the mighty men, even all the valiant men. ²Then King David rose to his feet and said, "Listen to me, my brethren and my people; I *had* intended to build a permanent home for the ark of the covenant of the LORD and for the footstool of our God. So I had made preparations to build *it.* ³But God said to me, 'You shall not build a house for My name because you are a man of war and have shed blood.' ⁴Yet, the LORD, the God of Israel, chose me from all the house of my father to be king over Israel forever. For He has chosen Judah to be a leader; and in the house of Judah, my father's house, and among the sons of my father He took pleasure in me to make *me* king over all Israel. ⁵Of all my sons (for the LORD has given me many sons), He has chosen my son Solomon to sit on the throne of the kingdom of the LORD over Israel. ⁶He said to me, 'Your son Solomon is the one who shall build My house and My courts; for I have chosen him to be a son to Me, and I will be a father to him. ⁷I will establish his kingdom forever if he resolutely performs My commandments and My ordi-

28:2–8 For the assembly's sake, David testified to the Davidic Covenant originally given by God to him in 2 Samuel 7 (17:7–27; 22:6–16). David makes it clear that Solomon was God's choice (v. 5) as had been frequently intimated (2Sa 12:24–25; 1Ki 1:13), just as the coming Christ will be God's chosen Son to ultimately fulfill the kingdom promise.

nances, as is done now.' [8] So now, in the sight of all Israel, the assembly of the LORD, and in the hearing of our God, observe and seek after all the commandments of the LORD your God so that you may possess the good land and bequeath *it* to your sons after you forever.

[9] "As for you, my son Solomon, know the God of your father, and serve Him with a whole heart and a willing mind; for the LORD searches all hearts, and understands every intent of the thoughts. If you seek Him, He will let you find Him; but if you forsake Him, He will reject you forever. [10] Consider now, for the LORD has chosen you to build a house for the sanctuary; be courageous and act."

[11] Then David gave to his son Solomon the plan of the porch *of the temple,* its buildings, its storehouses, its upper rooms, its inner rooms and the room for the mercy seat; [12] and the plan of all that he had in mind, for the courts of the house of the LORD, and for all the surrounding rooms, for the storehouses of the house of God and for the storehouses of the dedicated things; [13] also for the divisions of the priests and the Levites and for all the work of the service of the house of the LORD and for all the utensils of service in the house of the LORD; [14] for the golden *utensils,* the weight of gold for all utensils for every kind of service; for the silver utensils, the weight *of silver* for all utensils for every kind of service; [15] and the weight *of gold* for the golden lampstands and their golden lamps, with the weight of each lampstand and its lamps; and *the weight of silver* for the silver lampstands, with the weight of each lampstand and its lamps according to the use of each lampstand; [16] and the gold by weight for the tables of showbread, for each table; and silver for the silver tables; [17] and the forks, the basins, and the pitchers of pure gold; and for the golden bowls with the weight for each bowl; and for the silver bowls with the weight for each bowl; [18] and for the altar of incense refined gold by weight; and gold for the model of the chariot, *even* the cherubim that spread out *their wings* and covered the ark of the covenant of the LORD.

[19] "All *this,*" said *David,* "the LORD made me understand in writing by His hand upon me, all the details of this pattern."

[20] Then David said to his son Solomon, "Be strong and courageous, and act; do not fear nor be dismayed, for the LORD God, my God, is with you. He will not fail you nor forsake you until all the work for the service of the house of the LORD is finished. [21] Now behold, *there are* the divisions of the priests and the

---

28:19 in writing. David wrote down the plans under the Holy Spirit's divine inspiration (non-canonical, written revelation). This divine privilege was much like that of Moses for the tabernacle (Ex 25:9, 40; 27:8; Heb 8:5).

28:20–21 Solomon's associates in the building project were God, the owner and general contractor (28:20), plus the human workforce (28:21).

Levites for all the service of the house of God, and every willing man of any skill will be with you in all the work for all kinds of service. The officials also and all the people will be entirely at your command."

29 Then King David said to the entire assembly, "My son Solomon, whom alone God has chosen, is still young and inexperienced and the work is great; for the temple is not for man, but for the LORD God. [2] Now with all my ability I have provided for the house of my God the gold for the *things of* gold, and the silver for the *things of* silver, and the bronze for the *things of* bronze, the iron for the *things of* iron, and wood for the *things of* wood, onyx stones and inlaid *stones,* stones of antimony and stones of various colors, and all kinds of precious stones and alabaster in abundance. [3] Moreover, in my delight in the house of my God, the treasure I have of gold and silver, I give to the house of my God, over and above all that I have already provided for the holy temple, [4] *namely,* 3,000 talents of gold, of the gold of Ophir, and 7,000 talents of refined silver, to overlay the walls of the buildings; [5] of gold for the *things of* gold and of silver for the *things of* silver, that is, for all the work done by the craftsmen. Who then is willing to consecrate himself this day to the LORD?"

[6] Then the rulers of the fathers' *households,* and the princes of the tribes of Israel, and the commanders of thousands and of hundreds, with the overseers over the king's work, offered willingly; [7] and for the service for the house of God they gave 5,000 talents and 10,000 darics of gold, and 10,000 talents of silver, and 18,000 talents of brass, and 100,000 talents of iron. [8] Whoever possessed *precious* stones gave them to the treasury of the house of the LORD, in care of Jehiel the Gershonite. [9] Then the people rejoiced because they had offered so willingly, for they made their offering to the LORD with a whole heart, and King David also rejoiced greatly.

¹⁰ So David blessed the LORD in the sight of all the assembly; and David said, "Blessed are You, O LORD God of Israel our father, forever and ever. ¹¹ Yours, O LORD, is the greatness and the power and the glory and the victory and the majesty, indeed everything that is in the heavens and the earth; Yours is the dominion, O LORD, and You exalt Yourself as head over all. ¹² Both riches and honor *come* from You, and You rule over all, and in Your hand is power and might; and it lies in Your hand to make great and to strengthen everyone. ¹³ Now therefore, our God, we thank You, and praise Your glorious name.

¹⁴ "But who am I and who are my people that we should be able to offer as generously as this? For all things come from You, and from Your hand we have given You. ¹⁵ For we are sojourners before You, and tenants, as all our fathers were; our days on the earth are like a shadow, and there is no hope. ¹⁶ O LORD our God, all this abundance that we have provided to build You a house for Your holy name, it is from Your hand, and all is Yours. ¹⁷ Since I know, O my God, that You try the heart and delight in uprightness, I, in the integrity of my heart, have willingly offered all these *things;* so now with joy I have seen Your people, who are present here, make *their* offerings willingly to You. ¹⁸ O LORD, the God of Abraham, Isaac and Israel, our fathers, preserve this forever in the intentions of the heart of Your people, and direct their heart to You; ¹⁹ and give to my son Solomon a perfect heart to keep Your commandments, Your testimonies and Your statutes, and to do *them* all, and to build the temple, for which I have made provision."

²⁰ Then David said to all the assembly, "Now bless the LORD your God." And all the assembly blessed the LORD, the God of their fathers, and bowed low and did homage to the LORD and to the king. ²¹ On the next day they made sacrifices to the LORD and offered burnt offerings to the LORD, 1,000 bulls, 1,000 rams *and* 1,000 lambs, with their drink offerings and sacrifices in abundance for all Israel. ²² So they ate and drank that day before the LORD with great gladness.

And they made Solomon the son of David king a second time, and they anointed *him* as ruler for the LORD and Zadok as priest. ²³ Then Solomon sat on the throne of the LORD as king instead of David his father; and he prospered, and all Israel obeyed him. ²⁴ All the officials, the mighty men, and also all the sons of King David pledged allegiance to King Solomon. ²⁵ The LORD highly exalted Solomon in the sight of all Israel, and bestowed on him royal majesty which had not been on any king before him in Israel.

²⁶ Now David the son of Jesse reigned over all Israel. ²⁷ The period which he reigned over Israel *was* forty years; he reigned in Hebron seven years and in Jerusalem thirty-three *years.* ²⁸ Then he died in a ripe old age, full of days, riches and honor; and his son Solomon reigned in his place. ²⁹ Now the acts of King David, from first to last, are written in the chronicles of Samuel the seer, in the chronicles of Nathan the prophet and in the chronicles of Gad the seer, ³⁰ with all his reign, his power, and the circumstances which came on him, on Israel, and on all the kingdoms of the lands.

Psalm 78:67–72

⁶⁷ He also rejected the tent of Joseph,
  And did not choose the
    tribe of Ephraim,
⁶⁸ But chose the tribe of Judah,
  Mount Zion which He loved.
⁶⁹ And He built His sanctuary
    like the heights,
  Like the earth which He has
    founded forever.
⁷⁰ He also chose David His servant
  And took him from the sheepfolds;
⁷¹ From the care of the ewes with
    suckling lambs He brought him
  To shepherd Jacob His people,
  And Israel His inheritance.
⁷² So he shepherded them according
    to the integrity of his heart,
  And guided them with
    his skillful hands.

Proverbs 20:6–7

⁶ Many a man proclaims
    his own loyalty,
  But who can find a trustworthy man?
⁷ A righteous man who walks
    in his integrity—
  How blessed are his sons after him.

Acts 10:23b–48

And on the next day he got up and went away with them, and some of the brethren from Joppa accompanied him. ²⁴ On the following day he entered Caesarea. Now Cornelius was waiting for them and had called together his relatives and close friends. ²⁵ When Peter entered, Cornelius met him, and fell at his feet and worshiped *him.* ²⁶ But Peter raised him up, saying, "Stand up; I too am *just* a man." ²⁷ As he talked with him, he entered and *found many people assembled. ²⁸And he said to them, "You yourselves know how unlawful it is for a man who is a Jew to associate with a foreigner or to visit him; and *yet* God has shown me that I should not call any man unholy or unclean. ²⁹That is why I came without even raising any objection when I was sent for. So I ask for what reason you have sent for me."

10:28 unlawful. Literally "breaking a taboo." Peter followed the Jewish standards and traditions his whole life. His comments reveal his acceptance of a new standard in which Jews no longer were to consider Gentiles profane.

³⁰Cornelius said, "Four days ago to this hour, I was praying in my house during the ninth hour; and behold, a man stood before me in shining garments, ³¹and he *said, 'Cornelius, your prayer has been heard and your alms have been remembered before God. ³²Therefore send to Joppa and invite Simon, who is also called Peter, to come to you; he is staying at the house of Simon *the* tanner by the sea.' ³³So I sent for you immediately, and you have been kind enough to come. Now then, we are all here present before God to hear all that you have been commanded by the Lord."

³⁴Opening his mouth, Peter said:

"I most certainly understand *now* that God is not one to show partiality, ³⁵but in every nation the man who fears Him and does what is right is welcome to Him. ³⁶The word which He sent to the sons of Israel, preaching peace through Jesus Christ (He is Lord of all)— ³⁷you yourselves know the thing which took place throughout all Judea, starting from Galilee, after the baptism which John proclaimed. ³⁸*You know of* Jesus of Nazareth, how God anointed Him with the Holy Spirit and with

10:34 God is not one to show partiality. Taught in both the Old Testament (Dt 10:17; 2Ch 19:7; Job 34:19) and New Testament (Ro 2:11; 3:29–30; Jas 2:1). The reality of this truth was taking on new dimensions for Peter.

10:36 preaching peace. Christ, by paying the price of sin through His sacrificial death, established peace between man and God (Ro 5:1–11).

power, and *how* He went about doing good and healing all who were oppressed by the devil, for God was with Him. ³⁹We are witnesses of all the things He did both in the land of the Jews and in Jerusalem. They also put Him to death by hanging Him on a cross. ⁴⁰God raised Him up on the third day and granted that He become visible, ⁴¹not to all the people, but to witnesses who were chosen beforehand by God, *that is,* to us who ate and drank with Him after He arose from the dead. ⁴²And He ordered us to preach to the people, and solemnly to testify that this is the One who has been appointed by God as Judge of the living and the dead. ⁴³Of Him all the prophets bear witness that through His name everyone who believes in Him receives forgiveness of sins."

⁴⁴While Peter was still speaking these words, the Holy Spirit fell upon all those who were listening to the message. ⁴⁵All the circumcised believers who came with Peter were amazed, because the gift of the Holy Spirit had been poured out on the Gentiles also. ⁴⁶For they were hearing them speaking with tongues and exalting God. Then Peter answered, ⁴⁷"Surely no one can refuse the water for these to be baptized who have received the Holy Spirit just as we *did,* can he?" ⁴⁸And he ordered them to be baptized in the name of Jesus Christ. Then they asked him to stay on for a few days.

DAY 2: What does God desire in our giving?

King David called for consecrated giving to the building of the temple, based on his personal example of generosity (1Ch 29:3–4). David gave his personal fortune to the temple building, a fortune almost immeasurable. He says, "the treasure I have of gold and silver, I give to the house of my God, over and above all that I have already provided for the holy temple, namely, 3,000 talents of gold, of the gold of Ophir." Assuming a talent weighed about 75 pounds, this amounts to almost 112 tons of gold. This was held to be the purest and finest in the world (Job 22:24; 28:16; Is. 13:12). Plus the 7,000 talents of silver, which would be 260 tons, the total worth of such precious metals has been estimated in the billions of dollars.

As he addresses the people, David notes the word "willingly" (vv. 6–9). Here is the key to all freewill giving, i.e., giving what one desires to give. Tithes were required for taxation, to fund the theocracy, similar to taxation today. The law required that to be paid. This, however, is the voluntary giving from the heart to the Lord. The New Testament speaks of this (Lk 6:38; 2Co 9:1–8) and never demands that a tithe be given to God, but that taxes be paid to one's government (Ro 13:6–7). Paying taxes and giving God whatever one is willing to give, based on devotion to Him and His glory, is biblical giving.

The people rejoiced in their offering to the temple which was "5,000 talents...of gold" (1Ch 29:7). This amounts to 187 tons of gold. Add to that 375 tons of silver, 675 tons of bronze, and 3,750 tons of iron. The sum of all this is staggering and has been estimated into the billions of dollars. David responds to the phenomenal offering expressing amazing sacrifices of wealth with praise in which he acknowledges that all things belong to and come from God (vv. 10–15). David says that opportunities for giving to God are tests of the character: "try the heart" of a believer's devotion to the Lord (v. 17). The king acknowledges that the attitude of one's heart is significantly more important than the amount of offering in one's hand.

JULY 3

2 Chronicles 1:1–2:18

1 Now Solomon the son of David established himself securely over his kingdom, and the LORD his God *was* with him and exalted him greatly.

2 Solomon spoke to all Israel, to the commanders of thousands and of hundreds and to the judges and to every leader in all Israel, the heads of the fathers' *households.* 3 Then Solomon and all the assembly with him went to the high place which was at Gibeon, for God's tent of meeting was there, which Moses the servant of the LORD had made in the wilderness. 4 However, David had brought up the ark of God from Kiriath-jearim to the place he had prepared for it, for he had pitched a tent for it in Jerusalem. 5 Now the bronze altar, which Bezalel the son of Uri, the son of Hur, had made, was there before the tabernacle of the LORD, and Solomon and the assembly sought it out. 6 Solomon went up there before the LORD to the bronze altar which *was* at the tent of meeting, and offered a thousand burnt offerings on it.

7 In that night God appeared to Solomon and said to him, "Ask what I shall give you." 8 Solomon said to God, "You have dealt with my father David with great lovingkindness, and have made me king in his place. 9 Now, O LORD God, Your promise to my father David is fulfilled, for You have made me king over a people as numerous as the dust of the earth. 10 Give me now wisdom and knowledge, that I may go out and come in before this people, for who can rule this great people of Yours?" 11 God said to Solomon, "Because you had this in mind, and did not ask for riches, wealth or honor, or the life of those who hate you, nor have you even asked for long life, but you have asked for yourself wisdom and knowl-

edge that you may rule My people over whom I have made you king, 12 wisdom and knowledge have been granted to you. And I will give you riches and wealth and honor, such as none of the kings who were before you has possessed nor those who will come after you." 13 So Solomon went from the high place which was at Gibeon, from the tent of meeting, to Jerusalem, and he reigned over Israel.

14 Solomon amassed chariots and horsemen. He had 1,400 chariots and 12,000 horsemen, and he stationed them in the chariot cities and with the king at Jerusalem. 15 The king made silver and gold as plentiful in Jerusalem as stones, and he made cedars as plentiful as sycamores in the lowland. 16 Solomon's horses were imported from Egypt and from Kue; the king's traders procured them from Kue for a price. 17 They imported chariots from Egypt for 600 *shekels* of silver apiece and horses for 150 apiece, and by the same means they exported them to all the kings of the Hittites and the kings of Aram.

1:17 chariots...for 600 *shekels*. Assuming a shekel weighs .4 oz., this represents 15 lbs. of silver for one chariot. **horses for 150 apiece.** Assuming the weight is in shekels, this would be about 3.75 lbs. of silver. Deuteronomy 17:16 warned against the king's amassing horses.

---

2 Now Solomon decided to build a house for the name of the LORD and a royal palace for himself. 2 So Solomon assigned 70,000 men to carry loads and 80,000 men to quarry *stone* in the mountains and 3,600 to supervise them.

3 Then Solomon sent *word* to Huram the king of Tyre, saying, "As you dealt with David my father and sent him cedars to

2:1 house for the name of the LORD. God's covenant name, Yahweh or Jehovah (Ex 3:14), is in mind. David wanted to do this, but was not allowed to do any more than plan and prepare (1Ch 23–26; 28:11–13), purchase the land (2Sa 24:18–25; 1Ch 22), and gather the materials (1Ch 22:14–16).

---

build him a house to dwell in, so do for me. [4] Behold, I am about to build a house for the name of the LORD my God, dedicating it to Him, to burn fragrant incense before Him and *to set out* the showbread continually, and to offer burnt offerings morning and evening, on sabbaths and on new moons and on the appointed feasts of the LORD our God, this *being required* forever in Israel. [5] The house which I am about to build *will be* great, for greater is our God than all the gods. [6] But who is able to build a house for Him, for the heavens and the highest heavens cannot contain Him? So who am I, that I should build a house for Him, except to burn *incense* before Him? [7] Now send me a skilled man to work in gold, silver, brass and iron, and in purple, crimson and violet *fabrics,* and who knows how to make engravings, to *work* with the skilled men whom I have in Judah and Jerusalem, whom David my father provided. [8] Send me also cedar, cypress and algum timber from Lebanon, for I know that your servants know how to cut timber of Lebanon; and indeed my servants *will work* with your servants, [9] to prepare timber in abundance for me, for the house which I am about to build *will be* great and wonderful. [10] Now behold, I will give to your servants, the woodsmen who cut the timber, 20,000 kors of crushed wheat and 20,000 kors of barley, and 20,000 baths of wine and 20,000 baths of oil."

[11] Then Huram, king of Tyre, answered in a letter sent to Solomon: "Because the LORD loves His people, He has made you king over them." [12] Then Huram continued, "Blessed be the LORD, the God of Israel, who has made heaven and earth, who has given King David a wise son, endowed with discretion and understanding, who will build a house for the LORD and a royal palace for himself. [13] "Now I am sending Huram-abi, a skilled man, endowed with understanding, [14] the son of a Danite woman and a Tyrian father, who knows how to work in gold, silver, bronze, iron, stone and wood, *and* in purple, violet,

linen and crimson fabrics, and *who knows how* to make all kinds of engravings and to execute any design which may be assigned to him, *to work* with your skilled men and with those of my lord David your father. [15] Now then, let my lord send to his servants wheat and barley, oil and wine, of which he has spoken. [16] We will cut whatever timber you need from Lebanon and bring it to you on rafts by sea to Joppa, so that you may carry it up to Jerusalem."

[17] Solomon numbered all the aliens who *were* in the land of Israel, following the census which his father David had taken; and 153,600 were found. [18] He appointed 70,000 of them to carry loads and 80,000 to quarry *stones* in the mountains and 3,600 supervisors to make the people work.

Psalm 79:1–4

A Psalm of Asaph.

O God, the nations have invaded
   Your inheritance;
They have defiled Your holy temple;
   They have laid Jerusalem in ruins.
[2] They have given the dead bodies
      of Your servants for food to
      the birds of the heavens,
   The flesh of Your godly ones to
      the beasts of the earth.
[3] They have poured out their
      blood like water round
      about Jerusalem;
   And there was no one to bury
      them.
[4] We have become a reproach
      to our neighbors,
   A scoffing and derision to
      those around us.

79:1–13 The historical basis for this lament psalm was probably Nebuchadnezzar's destruction of the temple in 586 B.C. (Ps 74; 2Ki 25:8–21; La 1–5). The psalm contains prayer for the nation's spiritual needs, curses against the enemies of God's people, and praises in anticipation of God's actions. The psalm helps the believer express his anguish in a disaster when it seems as though God is aloof.

79:1 nations. In this context, the word refers to heathen, pagan people. **inheritance.** The inheritance of God was national Israel, and specifically its capital city, Jerusalem, where the temple was located.

Proverbs 20:8-9

8 A king who sits on the
     throne of justice
   Disperses all evil with his eyes.
9 Who can say, "I have
     cleansed my heart,
   I am pure from my sin"?

Acts 11:1-30

11 Now the apostles and the brethren who were throughout Judea heard that the Gentiles also had received the word of God. ² And when Peter came up to Jerusalem, those who were circumcised took issue with him, ³ saying, "You went to uncircumcised men and ate with them." ⁴ But Peter began *speaking*

11:3 ate with them. The Jewish believers were outraged over such a blatant breach of Jewish custom. It was difficult for them to conceive that Jesus could be equally Lord of Gentile believers.

and *proceeded* to explain to them in orderly sequence, saying, ⁵ "I was in the city of Joppa praying; and in a trance I saw a vision, an object coming down like a great sheet lowered by four corners from the sky; and it came right down to me, ⁶ and when I had fixed my gaze on it and was observing it I saw the four-footed animals of the earth and the wild beasts and the crawling creatures and the birds of the air. ⁷ I also heard a voice saying to me, 'Get up, Peter; kill and eat.' ⁸ But I said, 'By no means, Lord, for nothing unholy or unclean has ever entered my mouth.' ⁹ But a voice from heaven answered a second time, 'What God has cleansed, no longer consider unholy.' ¹⁰ This happened three times, and everything was drawn back up into the sky. ¹¹ And behold, at that moment three men appeared at the house in which we were *staying*, having been sent to me from Caesarea. ¹² The Spirit told me to go with them without misgivings. These six brethren also went with me and we entered the man's house. ¹³ And he reported to us how he had seen the angel standing in his house, and saying, 'Send to Joppa and have Simon, who is also called Peter, brought here; ¹⁴ and he will speak words to you by which you will be saved, you and all your household.' ¹⁵ And as I began to speak, the Holy Spirit fell upon them just as *He did* upon us at the beginning. ¹⁶ And I remembered the word of the Lord, how He used to say, 'John baptized with water,

but you will be baptized with the Holy Spirit.' ¹⁷ Therefore if God gave to them the same gift as *He gave* to us also after believing in the Lord Jesus Christ, who was I that I could stand in God's way?" ¹⁸ When they heard this, they quieted down and glorified God, saying, "Well then, God has granted to the Gentiles also the repentance *that leads* to life."

11:18 God has granted to the Gentiles also the repentance…to life. One of the most shocking admissions in Jewish history, but an event that the Old Testament had prophesied (Is 42:1, 6; 49:6; Ac 2:38).

¹⁹ So then those who were scattered because of the persecution that occurred in connection with Stephen made their way to Phoenicia and Cyprus and Antioch, speaking the word to no one except to Jews alone. ²⁰ But there were some of them, men of Cyprus and Cyrene, who came to Antioch and *began* speaking to the Greeks also, preaching the Lord Jesus. ²¹ And the hand of the Lord was with them, and a large number who believed turned to the Lord. ²² The news about them reached the ears of the church at Jerusalem, and they sent Barnabas off to Antioch. ²³ Then when he arrived and witnessed the grace of God, he rejoiced and *began* to encourage them all with resolute heart to remain *true* to the Lord; ²⁴ for he was a good man, and full of the Holy Spirit and of faith. And considerable numbers were brought to the Lord. ²⁵ And he left for Tarsus to look for Saul; ²⁶ and when he had found him, he brought him to Antioch. And for an entire year they met with the church and taught considerable numbers; and the disciples were first called Christians in Antioch.

11:27 prophets. Preachers of the New Testament (1Co 14:32; Eph 2:20).

11:28 Agabus. One of the Jerusalem prophets who years later played an important part in Paul's ministry (21:10-11). **a great famine.** Several ancient writers (Tacitus [*Annals* XI.43], Josephus [*Antiquities* XX.ii.5], and Suetonius [*Claudius* 18]) affirm the occurrence of great famines in Israel ca. A.D. 45-46. **all over the world.** The famine reached beyond the region of Israel. **Claudius.** Emperor of Rome (A.D. 41-54).

²⁷ Now at this time some prophets came down from Jerusalem to Antioch. ²⁸ One of them named Agabus stood up and *began* to indicate by the Spirit that there would certainly be a great famine all over the world. And this took place in the *reign* of Claudius.

²⁹ And in the proportion that any of the disciples had means, each of them determined to send *a contribution* for the relief of the brethren living in Judea. ³⁰ And this they did, sending it in charge of Barnabas and Saul to the elders.

DAY 3: How does the baptism with the Holy Spirit (1Co 12:13) relate to the Spirit's activities in the Book of Acts?

Acts describes a number of occasions in which the Holy Spirit "fell on" or "filled" or "came upon" people (2:4; 10:44; 19:6). Here in Acts 11:16, 17, Peter recounts how the Holy Spirit fell upon the Gentiles just as it had the early Jewish disciples. Peter identifies these actions by God as a fulfillment of Joel's prophecy (Joel 2:28–32).

Viewed from the perspective of the entire New Testament, these experiences were neither the same nor replacements for what John the Baptist (Mk 1:8) and Paul described as the baptism with the Holy Spirit (1Co 12:13). The *baptism* with the Spirit is the one-time act by which God places believers into His body. The *filling* is a repeated reality of Spirit-controlled behavior that God commands believers to maintain (Eph 5:18). Peter and others who experienced the special filling on Pentecost Day (2:4) were filled with the Spirit again and again (4:8, 31; 6:5; 7:55) and so boldly spoke the word of God. That was just the beginning. The fullness of the Spirit affects all areas of life, not just speaking boldly (Eph 5:18–33).

JULY 4

2 Chronicles 3:1–4:22

3 Then Solomon began to build the house of the LORD in Jerusalem on Mount Moriah, where *the LORD* had appeared to his father David, at the place that David had prepared on the threshing floor of Ornan the Jebusite. ² He began to build on the second *day* in the second month of the fourth year of his reign. ³ Now these are the foundations which Solomon laid for building the house of God. The length in cubits, according to the old standard *was* sixty cubits, and the width twenty cubits. ⁴ The porch which was in front of the house was as long as the width of the house, twenty cubits, and the height 120; and inside he overlaid it with pure gold. ⁵ He overlaid the main room with cypress wood and overlaid it with fine gold, and ornamented it with palm trees and chains. ⁶ Further, he adorned the house with precious stones; and the gold was gold from Parvaim. ⁷ He also overlaid the house with gold—the beams, the thresholds and its walls and its doors; and he carved cherubim on the walls.

⁸ Now he made the room of the holy of holies: its length across the width of the house *was* twenty cubits, and its width *was* twenty cubits; and he overlaid it with fine gold, *amounting* to 600 talents. ⁹ The weight of the nails was fifty shekels of gold. He also overlaid the upper rooms with gold.

¹⁰ Then he made two sculptured cherubim in the room of the holy of holies and overlaid them with gold. ¹¹ The wingspan of the cherubim *was* twenty cubits; the wing of one, of five cubits, touched the wall of the house, and *its* other wing, of five cubits, touched the wing of the other cherub. ¹² The wing of the other cherub, of five cubits, touched the wall of the house; and *its* other wing of five cubits was attached to the wing of the first cherub. ¹³ The wings of these cherubim extended twenty cubits, and they stood on their feet facing the *main* room. ¹⁴ He made the veil of violet, purple, crimson and fine linen, and he worked cherubim on it.

¹⁵ He also made two pillars for the front of the house, thirty-five cubits high, and the capital on the top of each *was* five cubits.

3:10–13 two sculptured cherubim. This freestanding set of cherubim was in addition to the more diminutive set on the ark itself.

3:14 veil. The veil separated the Holy Place from the Holy of Holies, which was entered once annually by the High Priest on the Day of Atonement (Lv 16). This highly limited access to the presence of God was eliminated by the death of Christ, when the veil in Herod's temple was torn in two from top to bottom (Mt 27:51). It signified that believers had immediate, full access to God's presence through their Mediator and High Priest Jesus Christ, who was the perfect, once-for-all sacrifice (Heb 3:14–16; 9:19–22).

[16] He made chains in the inner sanctuary and placed *them* on the tops of the pillars; and he made one hundred pomegranates and placed *them* on the chains. [17] He erected the pillars in front of the temple, one on the right and the other on the left, and named the one on the right Jachin and the one on the left Boaz.

4 Then he made a bronze altar, twenty cubits in length and twenty cubits in width and ten cubits in height. [2] Also he made the cast *metal* sea, ten cubits from brim to brim, circular in form, and its height *was* five cubits and its circumference thirty cubits. [3] Now figures like oxen *were* under it *and* all around it, ten cubits, entirely encircling the sea. The oxen *were* in two rows, cast in one piece.

4:1 bronze altar. This is the main altar on which sacrifices were offered (the millennial temple altar, Eze 43:13–17). For comparison to the tabernacle's altar, see Exodus 27:1–8; 38:1–7. If the cubit of 18 in. was used rather than the royal cubit of 21 in., it would make the altar 30 ft. by 30 ft. by 15 ft. high.

4:2 made the...sea. This large laver was used for ritual cleansing. In Ezekiel's millennial temple, the laver will apparently be replaced by the waters that flow through the temple (Eze 47:1–12).

---

[4] It stood on twelve oxen, three facing the north, three facing west, three facing south and three facing east; and the sea *was set* on top of them and all their hindquarters turned inwards. [5] It was a handbreadth thick, and its brim was made like the brim of a cup, *like* a lily blossom; it could hold 3,000 baths. [6] He also made ten basins in which to wash, and he set five on the right side and five on the left to rinse things for the burnt offering; but the sea *was* for the priests to wash in.

[7] Then he made the ten golden lampstands in the way prescribed for them and he set them in the temple, five on the right side and five on the left. [8] He also made ten tables and placed them in the temple, five on the right side and five on the left. And he made one hundred golden bowls. [9] Then he made the court of the priests and the great court and doors for the court, and overlaid their doors with bronze. [10] He set the sea on the right side *of the house* toward the southeast.

[11] Huram also made the pails, the shovels and the bowls. So Huram finished doing the work which he performed for King Solomon in the house of God: [12] the two pillars, the bowls and the two capitals on top of the pillars, and the two networks to cover the two bowls of the capitals which were on top of the pillars, [13] and the four hundred pomegranates for the two networks, two rows of pomegranates for each network to cover the two bowls of the capitals which were on the pillars. [14] He also made the stands and he made the basins on the stands, [15] *and* the one sea with the twelve oxen under it. [16] The pails, the shovels, the forks and all its utensils, Huram-abi made of polished bronze for King Solomon for the house of the LORD. [17] On the plain of the Jordan the king cast them in the clay ground between Succoth and Zeredah. [18] Thus Solomon made all these utensils in great quantities, for the weight of the bronze could not be found out.

[19] Solomon also made all the things that *were* in the house of God: even the golden altar, the tables with the bread of the Presence on them, [20] the lampstands with their lamps of pure gold, to burn in front of the inner sanctuary in the way prescribed; [21] the flowers, the lamps, and the tongs of gold, of purest gold; [22] and the snuffers, the bowls, the spoons and the firepans of pure gold; and the entrance of the house, its inner doors for the holy of holies and the doors of the house, *that is,* of the nave, of gold.

Psalm 79:5–10

[5] How long, O LORD? Will You
      be angry forever?
     Will Your jealousy burn like fire?
[6] Pour out Your wrath upon the
      nations which do not know You,
     And upon the kingdoms which
      do not call upon Your name.
[7] For they have devoured Jacob
     And laid waste his habitation.

[8] Do not remember the iniquities
      of *our* forefathers against us;
     Let Your compassion come
      quickly to meet us,
     For we are brought very low.
[9] Help us, O God of our salvation,
      for the glory of Your name;
     And deliver us and forgive our
      sins for Your name's sake.
[10] Why should the nations say,
      "Where is their God?"
     Let there be known among
      the nations in our sight,
     Vengeance for the blood of
      Your servants which
      has been shed.

79:9 forgive. The word, found 3 times in the Psalms (65:3; 78:38), means to cover away sin and its effects. In the Old Testament, atonement was symbolized in sacrificial ritual, though actual forgiveness of sin was ultimately based on the death of Christ applied to the penitent sinner (Heb 9). **for Your name's sake.** A defeat of a nation was believed to be a defeat of its god. A mark of spiritual maturity is one's concern for the reputation of God.

Proverbs 20:10-12

10 Differing weights and
    differing measures,
    Both of them are abominable
    to the LORD.
11 It is by his deeds that a lad
    distinguishes himself
    If his conduct is pure and right.
12 The hearing ear and the seeing eye,
    The LORD has made both of them.

Acts 12:1-25

12 Now about that time Herod the king laid hands on some who belonged to the church in order to mistreat them. ²And he had James the brother of John put to death with a sword. ³When he saw that it pleased the Jews, he proceeded to arrest Peter also. Now it was during the days of Unleavened Bread. ⁴When he had seized him, he put him in prison, delivering him to four squads of soldiers to guard him, intending after the Passover to bring him out before the people. ⁵So Peter was kept in the prison, but prayer for him was being made fervently by the church to God.

⁶On the very night when Herod was about to bring him forward, Peter was sleeping between two soldiers, bound with two chains, and guards in front of the door were watching over the prison. ⁷And behold, an angel of the Lord suddenly appeared and a light shone in the cell; and he struck Peter's side and woke him up, saying, "Get up quickly." And his chains fell off his hands. ⁸And the angel said to him, "Gird yourself and put on your sandals." And he did so. And he *said to him, "Wrap your cloak around you and follow me." ⁹And he went out and continued to follow, and he did not know that what was being done by the angel was real, but thought he was seeing a vision. ¹⁰When they had passed the first and second guard, they came to the iron gate that leads into the city, which opened for them by itself; and they went out and went along one street,

and immediately the angel departed from him. ¹¹When Peter came to himself, he said, "Now I know for sure that the Lord has sent forth His angel and rescued me from the hand of Herod and from all that the Jewish people were expecting." ¹²And when he realized *this,* he went to the house of Mary, the mother of John who was also called Mark, where many were gathered together and were praying. ¹³When he knocked at the door of the gate, a servant-girl named Rhoda came to answer. ¹⁴When she recognized Peter's voice, because of her joy she did not open the gate, but ran in and announced that Peter was standing in front of the gate. ¹⁵They said to her, "You are out of your mind!" But she kept insisting that it was so. They kept saying, "It is his angel." ¹⁶But Peter continued knocking; and when they had opened *the door,* they saw him and were amazed. ¹⁷But motioning to them with his hand to be silent, he described to them how the Lord had led him out of the prison. And he said, "Report these things to James and the brethren." Then he left and went to another place.

¹⁸Now when day came, there was no small disturbance among the soldiers *as to* what could have become of Peter. ¹⁹When Herod had searched for him and had not found him, he examined the guards and ordered that they be led away *to execution.* Then he went down from Judea to Caesarea and was spending time there.

²⁰Now he was very angry with the people

12:12 Mary. Mark is called the cousin of Barnabas in Colossians 4:10, so she was his aunt. **John... Mark.** Cousin of Barnabas (Col 4:10), acquaintance of Peter in his youth (1Pe 5:13), he accompanied Barnabas and Paul to Antioch (v. 25) and later to Cyprus (13:4-5). He deserted them at Perga (13:13) and Paul refused to take him on his second missionary journey because of that desertion (15:36-41). He accompanied Barnabas to Cyprus (15:39). He disappeared until he was seen with Paul at Rome as an accepted companion and coworker (Col 4:10; Phm 24). During Paul's second imprisonment at Rome, Paul sought John Mark's presence as useful to him (2Ti 4:11). He wrote the second gospel that bears his name, being enriched in his task by the aid of Peter (1Pe 5:13).

12:17 James. The Lord's brother, now head of the Jerusalem church. **he left.** Except for a brief appearance in chap. 15, Peter fades from the scene as the rest of Acts revolves around Paul and his ministry.

of Tyre and Sidon; and with one accord they came to him, and having won over Blastus the king's chamberlain, they were asking for peace, because their country was fed by the king's country. ²¹ On an appointed day Herod, having put on his royal apparel, took his seat on the rostrum and *began* delivering an address to them. ²² The people kept crying out, "The voice of a god and not of a man!"

²³ And immediately an angel of the Lord struck him because he did not give God the glory, and he was eaten by worms and died.

²⁴ But the word of the Lord continued to grow and to be multiplied.

²⁵ And Barnabas and Saul returned from Jerusalem when they had fulfilled their mission, taking along with *them* John, who was also called Mark.

DAY 4: Who was the Herod of Acts 12 who violently persecuted the church?

"Herod the king" of v. 1 was Herod Agrippa I, who reigned from A.D. 37 to 44 and was the grandson of Herod the Great. He ran up numerous debts in Rome and fled to Palestine. Imprisoned by Emperor Tiberius after some careless comments, he eventually was released following Tiberius's death, and was made ruler of northern Palestine, to which Judea and Samaria were added in A.D. 41. As a hedge against his shaky relationship with Rome, he curried favor with the Jews by persecuting Christians.

He killed James the brother of John with the sword (v. 2). James was the first of the apostles to be martyred. The manner of his execution indicates James was accused of leading people to follow false gods (Dt 13:12–15). He also imprisoned Peter and put him in the custody of "four squads" (v. 4). Each squad contained 4 soldiers and rotated the watch on Peter. At all times 2 guards were chained to him in his cell, while the other 2 stood guard outside the cell door (v. 6).

After Peter's rescue by an angel, Herod "led away to execution" the guards who were in charge (v. 19). According to Justinian's *Code* (ix. 4:4), a guard who allowed a prisoner to escape would suffer the same fatal penalty that awaited the prisoner.

Later, Herod came under the judgment of God. "On an appointed day" (v. 21), at a feast in honor of Herod's patron, the Roman emperor Claudius, Herod came out in "his royal apparel." According to Josephus, he wore a garment made of silver. When the people began shouting, "The voice of a god and not of a man!" we are told that Herod "did not give God the glory" (v. 22), the crime for which Herod was struck down by an angel (A.D. 44). "And he was eaten by worms" (v. 23). According to Josephus, Herod endured terrible pain for 5 days before he died.

𝒥 JULY 5

2 Chronicles 5:1–6:42

5 Thus all the work that Solomon performed for the house of the LORD was finished. And Solomon brought in the things that David his father had dedicated, even the silver and the gold and all the utensils, *and* put *them* in the treasuries of the house of God.

² Then Solomon assembled to Jerusalem the elders of Israel and all the heads of the tribes, the leaders of the fathers' *households* of the sons of Israel, to bring up the ark of the covenant of the LORD out of the city of David, which is Zion. ³ All the men of Israel assembled themselves to the king at the feast, that is *in* the seventh month. ⁴ Then all the elders of Israel came, and the Levites took up the ark. ⁵ They brought up the ark and the tent of meeting and all the holy utensils which *were* in the tent; the Levitical priests brought them up. ⁶ And King Solomon and all the congregation of Israel who were assembled with him before the ark, were sacrificing so many sheep and oxen that they could not be counted or numbered. ⁷ Then the priests brought the ark of the covenant of the LORD to its place, into the inner sanctuary of the house, to the holy of holies, under the wings of the cherubim. ⁸ For the cherubim spread

5:1 The temple took 7 years, 6 months to build and was completed in Solomon's 11th year (959 B.C.) in the eighth month (1Ki 6:38). Since it was dedicated in the seventh month (5:3), its dedication occurred 11 months later to coincide with the Feast of Booths, or Tabernacles. Why is there so much emphasis in the Old Testament on the temple? 1) It was the center of worship that called people to correct belief through the generations. 2) It was the symbol of God's presence with His people. 3) It was the symbol of forgiveness and grace, reminding the people of the seriousness of sin and the availability of mercy. 4) It prepared the people for the true Lamb of God, Jesus Christ, who would take away sin. 5) It was a place of prayer.

their wings over the place of the ark, so that the cherubim made a covering over the ark and its poles. ⁹ The poles were so long that the ends of the poles of the ark could be seen in front of the inner sanctuary, but they could not be seen outside; and they are there to this day. ¹⁰ There was nothing in the ark except the two tablets which Moses put *there* at Horeb, where the LORD made a covenant with the sons of Israel, when they came out of Egypt.

¹¹ When the priests came forth from the holy place (for all the priests who were present had sanctified themselves, without regard to divisions), ¹² and all the Levitical singers, Asaph, Heman, Jeduthun, and their sons and kinsmen, clothed in fine linen, with cymbals, harps and lyres, standing east of the altar, and with them one hundred and twenty priests blowing trumpets ¹³ in unison when the trumpeters and the singers were to make themselves heard with one voice to praise and to glorify the LORD, and when they lifted up their voice accompanied by trumpets and cymbals and instruments of music, and when they praised the LORD *saying,* "He indeed is good for His lovingkindness is everlasting," then the house, the house of the LORD, was filled with a cloud, ¹⁴ so that the priests could not stand to minister because of the cloud, for the glory of the LORD filled the house of God.

5:13–14 the glory of the LORD. The Lord's presence indwelt the temple and the first service of worship was held. In the same manner He descended on the tabernacle (Ex 40:34–38). He will do likewise on the millennial temple (Eze 43:1–5). His glory is representative of His person (Ex 33), and entering the temple signified His presence.

6 Then Solomon said,

"The LORD has said that He would
    dwell in the thick cloud.
² "I have built You a lofty house,
And a place for Your
    dwelling forever."

³ Then the king faced about and blessed all the assembly of Israel, while all the assembly of Israel was standing. ⁴ He said, "Blessed be the LORD, the God of Israel, who spoke with His mouth to my father David and has fulfilled *it* with His hands, saying, ⁵ 'Since the day that I brought My people from the land of Egypt, I did not choose a city out of all the tribes of Israel *in which* to build a house that My name might be there, nor did I choose any man for a leader over My people Israel; ⁶ but I have chosen Jerusalem that My name might be there, and I have chosen David to be over My people Israel.' ⁷ Now it was in the heart of my father David to build a house for the name of the LORD, the God of Israel. ⁸ But the LORD said to my father David, 'Because it was in your heart to build a house for My name, you did well that it was in your heart. ⁹ Nevertheless you shall not build the house, but your son who will be born to you, he shall build the house for My name.' ¹⁰ Now the LORD has fulfilled His word which He spoke; for I have risen in the place of my father David and sit on the throne of Israel, as the LORD promised, and have built the house for the name of the LORD, the God of Israel. ¹¹ There I have set the ark in which is the covenant of the LORD, which He made with the sons of Israel."

¹² Then he stood before the altar of the LORD in the presence of all the assembly of Israel and spread out his hands. ¹³ Now Solomon had made a bronze platform, five cubits long, five cubits wide and three cubits high, and had set it in the midst of the court; and he stood on it, knelt on his knees in the presence of all the assembly of Israel and spread out his hands toward heaven. ¹⁴ He said, "O LORD, the God of Israel, there is no god like You in heaven or on earth, keeping covenant and *showing* lovingkindness to Your servants who walk before You with all their heart; ¹⁵ who has kept with Your servant David, my father, that which You have promised him; indeed You have spoken with Your mouth and have fulfilled it with Your hand, as it is this day. ¹⁶ Now therefore, O LORD, the God of Israel, keep with Your servant David, my father, that which You have promised him, saying, 'You shall not lack a man to sit on the throne of Israel, if only your sons take heed to their way, to walk in My law as you have walked before Me.' ¹⁷ Now therefore, O LORD, the God of Israel, let Your word be confirmed which You have spoken to Your servant David.

¹⁸ "But will God indeed dwell with mankind on the earth? Behold, heaven and the highest heaven cannot contain You; how much less this house which I have built. ¹⁹ Yet have regard to the prayer of Your servant and to his supplication, O LORD my God, to listen to the cry and to the prayer which Your servant prays before You; ²⁰ that Your eye may be open toward this house day and night, toward the place of which You have said that *You would* put Your name there, to listen to the prayer

which Your servant shall pray toward this place. [21] Listen to the supplications of Your servant and of Your people Israel when they pray toward this place; hear from Your dwelling place, from heaven; hear and forgive.

[22] "If a man sins against his neighbor and is made to take an oath, and he comes *and* takes an oath before Your altar in this house, [23] then hear from heaven and act and judge Your servants, punishing the wicked by bringing his way on his own head and justifying the righteous by giving him according to his righteousness.

[24] "If Your people Israel are defeated before an enemy because they have sinned against You, and they return *to You* and confess Your name, and pray and make supplication before You in this house, [25] then hear from heaven and forgive the sin of Your people Israel, and bring them back to the land which You have given to them and to their fathers.

[26] "When the heavens are shut up and there is no rain because they have sinned against You, and they pray toward this place and confess Your name, and turn from their sin when You afflict them; [27] then hear in heaven and forgive the sin of Your servants and Your people Israel, indeed, teach them the good way in which they should walk. And send rain on Your land which You have given to Your people for an inheritance.

[28] "If there is famine in the land, if there is pestilence, if there is blight or mildew, if there is locust or grasshopper, if their enemies besiege them in the land of their cities, whatever plague or whatever sickness *there is,* [29] whatever prayer or supplication is made by any man or by all Your people Israel, each knowing his own affliction and his own pain, and spreading his hands toward this house, [30] then hear from heaven Your dwelling place, and forgive, and render to each according to all his ways, whose heart You know for You alone know the hearts of the sons of men, [31] that they may fear You, to walk in Your ways as long as they live in the land which You have given to our fathers.

[32] "Also concerning the foreigner who is not from Your people Israel, when he comes from a far country for Your great name's sake and Your mighty hand and Your outstretched arm, when they come and pray toward this house, [33] then hear from heaven, from Your dwelling place, and do according to all for which the foreigner calls to You, in order that all the peoples of the earth may know Your name, and fear You as *do* Your people Israel, and that they may know that this house which I have built is called by Your name.

[34] "When Your people go out to battle against their enemies, by whatever way You shall send them, and they pray to You toward this city which You have chosen and the house which I have built for Your name, [35] then hear from heaven their prayer and their supplication, and maintain their cause.

[36] "When they sin against You (for there is no man who does not sin) and You are angry with them and deliver them to an enemy, so that they take them away captive to a land far off or near, [37] if they take thought in the land where they are taken captive, and repent and make supplication to You in the land of their captivity, saying, 'We have sinned, we have committed iniquity and have acted wickedly'; [38] if they return to You with all their heart and with all their soul in the land of their captivity, where they have been taken captive, and pray toward their land which You have given to their fathers and the city which You have chosen, and toward the house which I have built for Your name, [39] then hear from heaven, from Your dwelling place, their prayer and supplications, and maintain their cause and forgive Your people who have sinned against You.

[40] "Now, O my God, I pray, let Your eyes be open and Your ears attentive to the prayer *offered* in this place.

[41] "Now therefore arise, O LORD God, to Your resting place, You and the ark of Your might; let Your priests, O LORD God, be clothed with salvation and let Your godly ones rejoice in what is good.

[42] "O LORD God, do not turn away the face of Your anointed; remember *Your* lovingkindness to Your servant David."

Psalm 79:11–13

[11] Let the groaning of the prisoner
    come before You;
    According to the greatness of
      Your power preserve those
      who are doomed to die.
[12] And return to our neighbors
    sevenfold into their bosom
    The reproach with which they
      have reproached You, O Lord.
[13] So we Your people and the
    sheep of Your pasture
    Will give thanks to You forever;
    To all generations we will
      tell of Your praise.

Proverbs 20:13–14

[13] Do not love sleep, or you
    will become poor;
    Open your eyes, *and* you will
    be satisfied with food.

¹⁴ "Bad, bad," says the buyer,
But when he goes his way,
then he boasts.

Acts 13:1–25

13 Now there were at Antioch, in the church that was *there*, prophets and teachers: Barnabas, and Simeon who was called Niger, and Lucius of Cyrene, and Manaen who had been brought up with Herod the tetrarch, and Saul. ² While they were ministering to the Lord and fasting, the Holy Spirit said, "Set apart for Me Barnabas and Saul for the work to which I have called them." ³ Then, when they had fasted and prayed and laid their hands on them, they sent them away.

⁴ So, being sent out by the Holy Spirit, they went down to Seleucia and from there they sailed to Cyprus. ⁵ When they reached Salamis, they *began* to proclaim the word of God in the synagogues of the Jews; and they also had John as their helper. ⁶ When they had gone through the whole island as far as Paphos, they found a magician, a Jewish false prophet whose name was Bar-Jesus, ⁷ who was with the proconsul, Sergius Paulus, a man of intelligence. This man summoned Barnabas and Saul and sought to hear the word of God. ⁸ But Elymas the magician (for so his name is translated) was opposing them, seeking to turn the

13:6 Paphos. The capital of Cyprus and thus the seat of the Roman government. It also was a great center for the worship of Aphrodite (Venus), and thus a hotbed for all kinds of immorality. **a magician... Jewish.** "Magician" originally carried no evil connotation, but later was used to describe all kinds of practitioners and dabblers in the occult. This particular magician put his knowledge to evil use.

proconsul away from the faith. ⁹ But Saul, who was also *known as* Paul, filled with the Holy Spirit, fixed his gaze on him, ¹⁰ and said, "You who are full of all deceit and fraud, you son of the devil, you enemy of all righteousness, will you not cease to make crooked the straight ways of the Lord? ¹¹ Now, behold, the hand of the Lord is upon you, and you will be blind and not see the sun for a time." And immediately a mist and a darkness fell upon him, and he went about seeking those who would lead him by the hand. ¹² Then the proconsul believed when he saw what had happened, being amazed at the teaching of the Lord.

¹³ Now Paul and his companions put out to sea from Paphos and came to Perga in Pamphylia; but John left them and returned to Jerusalem. ¹⁴ But going on from Perga, they arrived at Pisidian Antioch, and on the Sabbath day they went into the synagogue and sat down. ¹⁵ After the reading of the Law and the Prophets the synagogue officials sent to them, saying, "Brethren, if you have any word of exhortation for the people, say it." ¹⁶ Paul stood up, and motioning with his hand said,

"Men of Israel, and you who fear God, listen: ¹⁷ The God of this people Israel chose our fathers and made the people great during their stay in the land of Egypt, and with an uplifted arm He led them out from it. ¹⁸ For a period of about forty years He put up with them in the wilderness. ¹⁹ When He had destroyed seven nations in the land of Canaan, He distributed their land as an inheritance—*all of which took* about four hundred and fifty years. ²⁰ After these things He gave *them* judges until Samuel the prophet. ²¹ Then they asked for a king, and God gave them Saul the son of Kish, a man of the tribe of Benjamin, for forty years. ²² After He had removed him, He raised up David to be their king, concerning whom He also testified and said, 'I HAVE FOUND DAVID the son of Jesse, A MAN AFTER My HEART, who will do all My will.' ²³ From the descendants of this man, according to promise, God has brought to Israel a Savior, Jesus, ²⁴ after John had proclaimed before His coming a baptism of repentance to all the people of Israel. ²⁵ And while John was completing his course, he kept saying, 'What do you suppose that I am? I am not *He*. But behold, one is coming after me the sandals of whose feet I am not worthy to untie.'

13:15 reading of the Law and the Prophets. The reading of the Scriptures. This occupied the third part in the liturgy of the synagogue, after the recitation of the *shema* (Dt 6:4) and further prayers, but before the teaching, which was usually based on what had been read from the Scriptures. **synagogue officials.** Those who had general oversight of the synagogue, including designating who would read from the Scriptures.

13:22 A MAN AFTER MY HEART. Some would question the reality of this designation for David since he proved to be such a sinner at times (1Sa 11:1–4; 12:9; 21:10—22:1). No man after God's own heart is perfect; yet he will recognize sin and repent of it, as did David (Pss 32, 38, 51).

Chapter 13 marks a turning point in Acts in that the first 12 chapters focus on Peter while the remaining chapters revolve around Paul. With Peter, the emphasis is the Jewish church in Jerusalem and Judea; with Paul, the focus is the spread of the Gentile church throughout the Roman world, which began at the church in Antioch. In this church were certain "prophets" (v. 1). These men had a significant role in the apostolic church (1Co 12:28; Eph 2:20). They were preachers of God's Word and were responsible in the early years of the church to instruct local congregations. On some occasions, they received new revelation that was of a practical nature (11:28; 21:10), a function that ended with the cessation of the temporary sign gifts. Their office was also replaced by pastor-teachers and evangelists (Eph 4:11).

The leaders in the church in Antioch "were ministering to the Lord" (v. 2). This is from a Greek word which in Scripture describes priestly service. Serving in leadership in the church is an act of worship to God and consists of offering spiritual sacrifices to Him, including prayer, oversight of the flock, plus preaching and teaching the Word. And they fasted. This is often connected with vigilant, passionate prayer (Ne 1:4; Ps 35:13; Da 9:3; Mt 17:21; Lk 2:37) and includes either a loss of desire for food or the purposeful setting aside of eating to concentrate on spiritual issues (Mt 6:16–17).

While they worshiped, the Holy Spirit issued the first missionary outreach: "Set apart for Me Barnabas and Saul for the work to which I have called them" (v. 2). Saul and Barnabas chose to begin their missionary outreach in Cyprus because it was Barnabas's home, which was only a two-day journey from Antioch and had a large Jewish population. Here Paul established the custom of preaching to the Jews first whenever he entered a new city because he had an open door, as a Jew, to speak and introduce the gospel. Also, if he preached to Gentiles first, the Jews would never have listened to him.

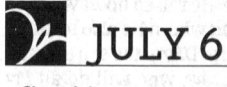 ## JULY 6

2 Chronicles 7:1–8:18

7 Now when Solomon had finished praying, fire came down from heaven and consumed the burnt offering and the sacrifices, and the glory of the LORD filled the house. ² The priests could not enter into the house of the LORD because the glory of the LORD filled the LORD'S house. ³ All the sons of Israel, seeing the fire come down and the glory of the LORD upon the house, bowed down on the pavement with their faces to the ground, and they worshiped and gave praise to the LORD, *saying*, "Truly He is good, truly His lovingkindness is everlasting."

⁴ Then the king and all the people offered sacrifice before the LORD. ⁵ King Solomon offered a sacrifice of 22,000 oxen and 120,000 sheep. Thus the king and all the people dedicated the house of God. ⁶ The priests stood at their posts, and the Levites also, with the instruments of music to the LORD, which King David had made for giving praise to the LORD—"for His lovingkindness is everlasting"—whenever he gave praise by their means, while the priests on the other side blew trumpets; and all Israel was standing.

⁷ Then Solomon consecrated the middle of the court that *was* before the house of the LORD, for there he offered the burnt offerings and the fat of the peace offerings because the bronze altar which Solomon had made was not able to contain the burnt offering, the grain offering and the fat.

⁸ So Solomon observed the feast at that time for seven days, and all Israel with him, a very great assembly *who came* from the entrance of Hamath to the brook of Egypt. ⁹ On the eighth day they held a solemn assembly, for the dedication of the altar they observed seven days and the feast seven days. ¹⁰ Then on the twenty-third day of the seventh month he sent the people to their tents, rejoicing and happy of heart because of the goodness that the LORD had shown to David and to Solomon and to His people Israel.

¹¹ Thus Solomon finished the house of the LORD and the king's palace, and successfully completed all that he had planned on doing in the house of the LORD and in his palace.

¹² Then the LORD appeared to Solomon at night and said to him, "I have heard your prayer and have chosen this place for Myself as a house of sacrifice. ¹³ If I shut up the heavens so that there is no rain, or if I command the locust to devour the land, or if I send pestilence among My people, ¹⁴ and My people who are called by My name humble themselves and pray and seek My face and turn from their wicked ways, then I will hear from heaven, will forgive their sin and will heal their land. ¹⁵ Now My eyes will be open and My ears at-

tentive to the prayer *offered* in this place. [16] For now I have chosen and consecrated this house that My name may be there forever, and My eyes and My heart will be there perpetually. [17] As for you, if you walk before Me as your father David walked, even to do according to all that I have commanded you, and will keep My statutes and My ordinances, [18] then I will establish your royal throne as I covenanted with your father David, saying, 'You shall not lack a man *to be* ruler in Israel.'

7:17–18 if…then. If there was obedience on the part of the nation, the kingdom would be established and they would have "a man *to be* ruler." Their disobedience was legendary and so was the destruction of their kingdom and their dispersion. When Israel is saved (Zec 12:14; Ro 11:25–27), then their King Messiah will set up this glorious kingdom (Rev 20:1ff.).

[19] "But if you turn away and forsake My statutes and My commandments which I have set before you, and go and serve other gods and worship them, [20] then I will uproot you from My land which I have given you, and this house which I have consecrated for My name I will cast out of My sight and I will make it a proverb and a byword among all peoples. [21] As for this house, which was exalted, everyone who passes by it will be astonished and say, 'Why has the LORD done thus to this land and to this house?' [22] And they will say, 'Because they forsook the LORD, the God of their fathers who brought them from the land of Egypt, and they adopted other gods and worshiped them and served them; therefore He has brought all this adversity on them.'"

8 Now it came about at the end of the twenty years in which Solomon had built the house of the LORD and his own house [2] that he built the cities which Huram had given to him, and settled the sons of Israel there. [3] Then Solomon went to Hamath-zobah and captured it. [4] He built Tadmor in the wilderness and all the storage cities which he had built in Hamath. [5] He also built upper Beth-horon and lower Beth-horon, fortified cities *with* walls, gates and bars; [6] and Baalath and all the storage cities that Solomon had, and all the cities for his chariots and cities for his horsemen, and all that it pleased Solomon to build in Jerusalem, in Lebanon, and in all the land under his rule. [7] All of the people who were left of the

Hittites, the Amorites, the Perizzites, the Hivites and the Jebusites, who were not of Israel, [8] namely, from their descendants who were left after them in the land whom the sons of Israel had not destroyed, them Solomon raised as forced laborers to this day. [9] But Solomon did not make slaves for his work from the sons of Israel; they were men of war, his chief captains and commanders of his chariots and his horsemen. [10] These were the chief officers of King Solomon, two hundred and fifty who ruled over the people.

[11] Then Solomon brought Pharaoh's daughter up from the city of David to the house which he had built for her, for he said, "My wife shall not dwell in the house of David king of Israel, because the places are holy where the ark of the LORD has entered."

8:11 Pharaoh's daughter. See 1 Kings 9:24. First Kings 3:1 mentions the marriage and the fact that Solomon brought her to Jerusalem until he could build a house for her. Until that palace was built, Solomon lived in David's palace, but did not allow her to do so, because she was a heathen and because the ark of God had once been in David's house. He surely knew his marriage to this pagan did not please God (Dt 7:3–4). Eventually his pagan wives caused tragic consequences (1Ki 11:1–11).

[12] Then Solomon offered burnt offerings to the LORD on the altar of the LORD which he had built before the porch; [13] and *did so* according to the daily rule, offering *them* up according to the commandment of Moses, for the sabbaths, the new moons and the three annual feasts—the Feast of Unleavened Bread, the Feast of Weeks and the Feast of Booths. [14] Now according to the ordinance of his father David, he appointed the divisions of the priests for their service, and the Levites for their duties of praise and ministering before the priests according to the daily rule, and the gatekeepers by their divisions at every gate; for David the man of God had so commanded. [15] And they did not depart from the commandment of the king to the priests and Levites in any manner or concerning the storehouses. [16] Thus all the work of Solomon was carried out from the day of the foundation of the house of the LORD, and until it was finished. So the house of the LORD was completed. [17] Then Solomon went to Ezion-geber and to Eloth on the seashore in the land of Edom.

¹⁸ And Huram by his servants sent him ships and servants who knew the sea; and they went with Solomon's servants to Ophir, and took from there four hundred and fifty talents of gold and brought them to King Solomon.

Psalm 80:1–6

For the choir director; *set to* El Shoshannim; Eduth. A Psalm of Asaph.

Oh, give ear, Shepherd of Israel,
You who lead Joseph like a flock;
You who are enthroned *above*
the cherubim, shine forth!
² Before Ephraim and Benjamin
and Manasseh, stir up Your power
And come to save us!
³ O God, restore us
And cause Your face to shine *upon us,* and we will be saved.

⁴ O LORD God *of* hosts,
How long will You be angry with
the prayer of Your people?
⁵ You have fed them with
the bread of tears,
And You have made them
to drink tears in large measure.
⁶ You make us an object of
contention to our neighbors,
And our enemies laugh
among themselves.

Proverbs 20:15

¹⁵ There is gold, and an
abundance of jewels;
But the lips of knowledge are
a more precious thing.

Acts 13:26–52

²⁶ "Brethren, sons of Abraham's family, and those among you who fear God, to us the message of this salvation has been sent. ²⁷ For those who live in Jerusalem, and their rulers, recognizing neither Him nor the utterances of the prophets which are read every Sabbath, fulfilled *these* by condemning *Him.* ²⁸ And though they found no ground for *putting Him to* death, they asked Pilate that He be executed. ²⁹ When they had carried out all that was written concerning Him, they took Him down from the cross and laid Him in a tomb. ³⁰ But God raised Him from the dead; ³¹ and for many days He appeared to those who came up with Him from Galilee to Jerusalem, the very ones who are now His witnesses to the people. ³² And we preach to you the good news of the

13:29–30 cross...tomb...God raised. The Old Testament predicted the crucifixion of Christ on a cross (Ps 22; Dt 21), at the time when this particular form of execution was not used. His burial in a "tomb" was also prophesied (Is 53:9), yet victims of crucifixions were commonly tossed into mass graves. The climax of Paul's message was the resurrection of Christ, the ultimate proof that Jesus is the Messiah, and the fulfillment of 3 specific prophecies (*vv.* 33–35).

promise made to the fathers, ³³ that God has fulfilled this *promise* to our children in that He raised up Jesus, as it is also written in the second Psalm, 'YOU ARE MY SON; TODAY I HAVE BEGOTTEN YOU.' ³⁴ *As for the fact* that He raised Him up from the dead, no longer to return to decay, He has spoken in this way: 'I WILL GIVE YOU THE HOLY *and* SURE *blessings* OF DAVID.' ³⁵ Therefore He also says in another *Psalm,* 'YOU WILL NOT ALLOW YOUR HOLY ONE TO UNDERGO DECAY.' ³⁶ For David, after he had served the purpose of God in his own generation, fell asleep, and was laid among his fathers and underwent decay; ³⁷ but He whom God raised did not undergo decay. ³⁸ Therefore let it be known to you, brethren, that through Him forgiveness of sins is proclaimed to you, ³⁹ and through Him everyone who believes is freed from all things, from which you could not be freed through the Law of Moses. ⁴⁰ Therefore take heed, so that the thing spoken of in the Prophets may not come upon *you:*

13:39 you could not be freed through the Law of Moses. Keeping the law of Moses did not free anyone from their sins (Ro 3:28; 1Co 1:30; Gal 2:16; 3:11; Php 3:9). But the atoning death of Jesus completely satisfied the demands of God's law, making forgiveness of all sins available to all who believe (Gal 3:16; Col 2:13–14). Only the forgiveness Christ offers can free people from their sins (Ro 3:20, 22).

⁴¹ 'BEHOLD, YOU SCOFFERS, AND
MARVEL, AND PERISH;
FOR I AM ACCOMPLISHING A
WORK IN YOUR DAYS,
A WORK WHICH YOU WILL NEVER
BELIEVE, THOUGH SOMEONE
SHOULD DESCRIBE IT TO YOU.' "

⁴²As Paul and Barnabas were going out, the people kept begging that these things might be spoken to them the next Sabbath. ⁴³Now when *the meeting of* the synagogue had broken up, many of the Jews and of the God-fearing proselytes followed Paul and Barnabas, who, speaking to them, were urging them to continue in the grace of God.

13:43 God-fearing proselytes. Full converts to Judaism who had been circumcised. **continue in the grace of God.** Those who are truly saved persevere and validate the reality of their salvation by continuing in the grace of God (Jn 8:31; 15:1–6; Col 1:21–23; 1Jn 2:19). With such encouragement, Paul and Barnabas hoped to prevent those who were intellectually convinced of the truths of the gospel, yet had stopped short of saving faith, from reverting to legalism rather than embracing Christ completely.

⁴⁴The next Sabbath nearly the whole city assembled to hear the word of the Lord. ⁴⁵But when the Jews saw the crowds, they were filled with jealousy and *began* contradicting the things spoken by Paul, and were blaspheming. ⁴⁶Paul and Barnabas spoke out boldly and said, "It was necessary that the word of God be spoken to you first; since you repudiate it and judge yourselves unworthy of eternal life, behold, we are turning to the Gentiles. ⁴⁷For so the Lord has commanded us,

> 'I HAVE PLACED YOU AS A LIGHT
>   FOR THE GENTILES,
> THAT YOU MAY BRING SALVATION
>   TO THE END OF THE EARTH.'"

⁴⁸When the Gentiles heard this, they *began* rejoicing and glorifying the word of the Lord; and as many as had been appointed to eternal life believed. ⁴⁹And the word of the Lord was being spread through the whole region. ⁵⁰But the Jews incited the devout women of prominence and the leading men of the city, and instigated a persecution against Paul and Barnabas, and drove them out of their district. ⁵¹But they shook off the dust of their feet *in protest* against them and went to Iconium. ⁵²And the disciples were continually filled with joy and with the Holy Spirit.

13:51 shook off the dust of their feet. The Jews' antagonism toward Gentiles extended to their unwillingness to even bring Gentile dust into Israel. The symbolism of Paul and Barnabas' act is clear that they considered the Jews at Antioch no better than heathen. There could have been no stronger condemnation.

DAY 6: How does a verse such as 2 Chronicles 7:14 relate to country such as America?

"If…My people who are called by My name humble themselves and pray and seek My face and turn from their wicked ways, then I will hear from heaven, will forgive their sin and will heal their land."

Unlike ancient Israel, America is not a covenant nation. God has made no promise to our physical ancestors that guarantees our national status. If Israel had to fulfill the conditions for divine blessing, even though God had covenanted with them as His chosen people, America certainly has no inviolable claim on the blessing of God. As long as unbelief and disobedience to the Word of God color the soul of our nation, we simply cannot expect the blessing of God. Israel didn't get it in her unbelief.

But for those of us who are Christians, the covenant blessings do apply. "If you belong to Christ, then you are Abraham's descendants, heirs according to promise" (Gal 3:29). All the promises of salvation, mercy, forgiveness of sins, and spiritual prosperity are ours to claim as long as we remain faithful to God.

That is why the spiritual state of the church in our nation is the key to the blessing of the nation as a whole. If God is going to bless America, it will not be for the sake of the nation itself. He blesses the nation, and has always done so, for the sake of His people. If we who are called by His name are not fulfilling the conditions for divine blessing, there is no hope whatsoever for the rest of the nation.

On the other hand, if the church is fit to receive God's blessing, the whole nation will be the beneficiary of that, because the Word of God will be proclaimed with power, God will add to His church, and spiritual blessings of all kinds will result. And those are the truest blessings of all.

JULY 7

2 Chronicles 9:1–10:19

9 Now when the queen of Sheba heard of the fame of Solomon, she came to Jerusalem to test Solomon with difficult questions. She had a very large retinue, with camels carrying spices and a large amount of gold and precious stones; and when she came to Solomon, she spoke with him about all that was on her heart. ² Solomon answered all her questions; nothing was hidden from Solomon which he did not explain to her. ³ When the queen of Sheba had seen the wisdom of Solomon, the house which he had built, ⁴ the food at his table, the seating of his servants, the attendance of his ministers and their attire, his cupbearers and their attire, and his stairway by which he went up to the house of the LORD, she was breathless. ⁵ Then she said to the king, "It was a true report which I heard in my own land about your words and your wisdom. ⁶ Nevertheless I did not believe their reports until I came and my eyes had seen it. And behold, the half of the greatness of your wisdom was not told me. You surpass the report that I heard. ⁷ How blessed are your men, how blessed are these your servants who stand before you continually and hear your wisdom. ⁸ Blessed be the LORD your God who delighted in you, setting you on His throne as king for the LORD your God; because your God loved Israel establishing them forever, therefore He made you king over them, to do justice and righteousness." ⁹ Then she gave the king one hundred and twenty talents of gold and a very great *amount of* spices and precious stones; there had never been spice like that which the queen of Sheba gave to King Solomon.

¹⁰ The servants of Huram and the servants of Solomon who brought gold from Ophir, also brought algum trees and precious stones. ¹¹ From the algum trees the king made steps for the house of the LORD and for the king's palace, and lyres and harps for the singers; and none like that was seen before in the land of Judah.

¹² King Solomon gave to the queen of Sheba all her desire which she requested besides *a return for* what she had brought to the king. Then she turned and went to her own land with her servants.

¹³ Now the weight of gold which came to Solomon in one year was 666 talents of gold, ¹⁴ besides that which the traders and merchants brought; and all the kings of Arabia and the governors of the country brought gold and silver to Solomon. ¹⁵ King Solomon made 200 large shields of beaten gold, using 600 *shekels* of beaten gold on each large shield. ¹⁶ He made 300 shields of beaten gold, using three hundred shekels of gold on each shield, and the king put them in the house of the forest of Lebanon.

¹⁷ Moreover, the king made a great throne of ivory and overlaid it with pure gold. ¹⁸ *There were* six steps to the throne and a footstool in gold attached to the throne, and arms on each side of the seat, and two lions standing beside the arms. ¹⁹ Twelve lions were standing there on the six steps on the one side and on the other; nothing like *it* was made for any *other* kingdom. ²⁰ All King Solomon's drinking vessels *were* of gold, and all the vessels of the house of the forest of Lebanon *were* of pure gold; silver was not considered valuable in the days of Solomon. ²¹ For the king had ships which went to Tarshish with the servants of Huram; once every three years the ships of Tarshish came bringing gold and silver, ivory and apes and peacocks.

²² So King Solomon became greater than all the kings of the earth in riches and wisdom. ²³ And all the kings of the earth were seeking the presence of Solomon, to hear his wisdom which God had put in his heart. ²⁴ They brought every man his gift, articles of silver and gold, garments, weapons, spices, horses and mules, so much year by year.

²⁵ Now Solomon had 4,000 stalls for horses and chariots and 12,000 horsemen, and he stationed them in the chariot cities and with the king in Jerusalem. ²⁶ He was the ruler over all the kings from the Euphrates River even to the land of the Philistines, and as far as the border of Egypt. ²⁷ The king made silver *as common* as stones in Jerusalem, and he made cedars as plentiful as sycamore trees that are in the lowland. ²⁸ And they were bringing horses for Solomon from Egypt and from all countries.

²⁹ Now the rest of the acts of Solomon, from first to last, are they not written in the records of Nathan the prophet, and in the prophecy

9:29 In later years, he turned away from God and, due to the influence of his wives, he led the nation into idolatry. This split the kingdom and sowed the seeds that led to its defeat and dispersion. The Chronicles do not record this sad end to Solomon's life because the focus is on encouraging the returning Jews from Babylon with God's pledge to them for a glorious future in the Davidic Covenant.

of Ahijah the Shilonite, and in the visions of Iddo the seer concerning Jeroboam the son of Nebat? ³⁰ Solomon reigned forty years in Jerusalem over all Israel. ³¹ And Solomon slept with his fathers and was buried in the city of his father David; and his son Rehoboam reigned in his place.

10 Then Rehoboam went to Shechem, for all Israel had come to Shechem to make him king. ² When Jeroboam the son of Nebat heard *of it* (for he was in Egypt where he had fled from the presence of King Solomon), Jeroboam returned from Egypt. ³ So they sent and summoned him. When Jeroboam and all Israel came, they spoke to Rehoboam, saying, ⁴ "Your father made our yoke hard; now therefore lighten the hard service of your father and his heavy yoke which he put on us, and we will serve you." ⁵ He said to them, "Return to me again in three days." So the people departed.

⁶ Then King Rehoboam consulted with the elders who had served his father Solomon while he was still alive, saying, "How do you counsel *me* to answer this people?" ⁷ They spoke to him, saying, "If you will be kind to this people and please them and speak good words to them, then they will be your servants forever." ⁸ But he forsook the counsel of the elders which they had given him, and consulted with the young men who grew up with him and served him. ⁹ So he said to them, "What counsel do you give that we may answer this people, who have spoken to me, saying, 'Lighten the yoke which your father put on us'?" ¹⁰ The young men who grew up with him spoke to him, saying, "Thus you shall say to the people who spoke to you, saying, 'Your father made our yoke heavy, but you make it lighter for us.' Thus you shall say to them, 'My little finger is thicker than my father's loins! ¹¹ Whereas my father loaded you with a heavy yoke, I will add to your yoke; my father disciplined you with whips, but I *will discipline you* with scorpions.'"

¹² So Jeroboam and all the people came to Rehoboam on the third day as the king had directed, saying, "Return to me on the third day." ¹³ The king answered them harshly, and King Rehoboam forsook the counsel of the elders. ¹⁴ He spoke to them according to the advice of the young men, saying, "My father made your yoke heavy, but I will add to it; my father disciplined you with whips, but I *will discipline you* with scorpions." ¹⁵ So the king did not listen to the people, for it was a turn *of events* from God that the LORD might establish His word, which He spoke through

Ahijah the Shilonite to Jeroboam the son of Nebat.

¹⁶ When all Israel *saw* that the king did not listen to them the people answered the king, saying,

> "What portion do we have in David?
> *We have* no inheritance in
>   the son of Jesse.
> Every man to your tents, O Israel;
> Now look after your own
>   house, David."

So all Israel departed to their tents. ¹⁷ But as for the sons of Israel who lived in the cities of Judah, Rehoboam reigned over them. ¹⁸ Then King Rehoboam sent Hadoram, who was over the forced labor, and the sons of Israel stoned him to death. And King Rehoboam made haste to mount his chariot to flee to Jerusalem. ¹⁹ So Israel has been in rebellion against the house of David to this day.

Psalm 80:7–13

7   O God *of* hosts, restore us
> And cause Your face to shine *upon*
>   *us,* and we will be saved.

8   You removed a vine from Egypt;
> You drove out the nations
>   and planted it.

80:8 vine from Egypt. The vine is a metaphor for Israel, whom God delivered out of Egypt and nurtured into a powerful nation (Is 5:1–7; 27:2–6; Mt 21:33–40).

9   You cleared *the ground* before it,
> And it took deep root and
>   filled the land.

10 The mountains were covered
>   with its shadow,
> And the cedars of God
>   with its boughs.

11 It was sending out its
>   branches to the sea
> And its shoots to the River.

12 Why have You broken
>   down its hedges,
> So that all who pass *that*
>   way pick its *fruit?*

13 A boar from the forest eats it
>   away
> And whatever moves in
>   the field feeds on it.

Proverbs 20:16-18

16 Take his garment when he becomes
surety for a stranger;
And for foreigners, hold
him in pledge.

17 Bread obtained by falsehood
is sweet to a man,
But afterward his mouth will
be filled with gravel.

18 Prepare plans by consultation,
And make war by wise guidance.

20:16 Garments were common security for a
loan, but they always had to be returned by
sundown (Ex 22:26-27; Dt 24:10-13). Anyone
who foolishly has taken on the responsibility
for the debt of a stranger will likely never be
paid back, so he will never pay his creditor
unless his own garment is taken as security.

Acts 14:1-28

14 In Iconium they entered the synagogue
of the Jews together, and spoke in such
a manner that a large number of people believed, both of Jews and of Greeks. 2 But the
Jews who disbelieved stirred up the minds of
the Gentiles and embittered them against the
brethren. 3 Therefore they spent a long time
there speaking boldly *with reliance* upon the
Lord, who was testifying to the word of His
grace, granting that signs and wonders be
done by their hands. 4 But the people of the
city were divided; and some sided with the
Jews, and some with the apostles. 5 And when
an attempt was made by both the Gentiles and
the Jews with their rulers, to mistreat and
stone them, 6 they became aware of it and fled
to the cities of Lycaonia, Lystra and Derbe,
and the surrounding region; 7 and there they
continued to preach the gospel.

8 At Lystra a man was sitting who had no
strength in his feet, lame from his mother's

14:4 apostles. Barnabas was not an apostle in
the same sense as Paul and the 12 since he was
not an eyewitness of the resurrected Christ
nor had he been called by Him. It is best to
translate "apostles" here as "messengers" (2Co
8:23; Php 2:25). The verb means "to send." The
12 and Paul were "apostles of Christ," (2Co 11:13;
1Th 2:6), while Barnabas and others were "messengers of the churches" (2Co 8:23).

womb, who had never walked. 9 This man was
listening to Paul as he spoke, who, when he
had fixed his gaze on him and had seen that
he had faith to be made well, 10 said with a
loud voice, "Stand upright on your feet." And
he leaped up and *began* to walk. 11 When the
crowds saw what Paul had done, they raised
their voice, saying in the Lycaonian language,
"The gods have become like men and have
come down to us." 12 And they *began* calling Barnabas, Zeus, and Paul, Hermes, because he was the chief speaker. 13 The priest
of Zeus, whose *temple* was just outside the
city, brought oxen and garlands to the gates,
and wanted to offer sacrifice with the crowds.
14 But when the apostles Barnabas and Paul
heard of it, they tore their robes and rushed
out into the crowd, crying out 15 and saying,
"Men, why are you doing these things? We
are also men of the same nature as you, and
preach the gospel to you that you should turn
from these vain things to a living God, WHO
MADE THE HEAVEN AND THE EARTH AND THE
SEA AND ALL THAT IS IN THEM. 16 In the generations gone by He permitted all the nations to
go their own ways; 17 and yet He did not leave
Himself without witness, in that He did good
and gave you rains from heaven and fruitful
seasons, satisfying your hearts with food and
gladness." 18 *Even* saying these things, with
difficulty they restrained the crowds from
offering sacrifice to them.

19 But Jews came from Antioch and Iconium, and having won over the crowds, they
stoned Paul and dragged him out of the city,
supposing him to be dead. 20 But while the
disciples stood around him, he got up and
entered the city. The next day he went away
with Barnabas to Derbe. 21 After they had
preached the gospel to that city and had made
many disciples, they returned to Lystra and

14:15-17 Because the crowd at Lystra was pagan
and had no knowledge of the OT, Paul adjusted
his message to fit the audience. Instead of
proclaiming the God of Abraham, Isaac, and
Jacob, he appealed to the universal and rational knowledge of the One who created the
world (17:22-26; Jon 1:9).

14:17 did not leave Himself without witness.
God's providence and His creative power
testify to man's reason of His existence (Ro
1:18-20), as does man's own conscience, which
contains His moral law (Ro 2:13-15).

to Iconium and to Antioch, [22] strengthening the souls of the disciples, encouraging them to continue in the faith, and *saying,* "Through many tribulations we must enter the kingdom of God." [23] When they had appointed elders for them in every church, having prayed with fasting, they commended them to the Lord in whom they had believed.

[24] They passed through Pisidia and came into Pamphylia. [25] When they had spoken the word in Perga, they went down to Attalia. [26] From there they sailed to Antioch, from which they had been commended to the grace of God for the work that they had accomplished. [27] When they had arrived and gathered the church together, they *began* to report all things that God had done with them and how He had opened a door of faith to the Gentiles. [28] And they spent a long time with the disciples.

DAY 7: How does Acts 14 demonstrate the varied reactions for preaching the gospel of Christ?

The city of Iconium was a cultural melting pot of native Phrygians, Greeks, Jews, and Roman colonists. A great multitude came to faith as Paul and Barnabas spoke "boldly with reliance upon the Lord, who was testifying to the word of His grace, granting that signs and wonders be done by their hands" (v. 3). Acts of such divine power confirmed that Paul and Barnabas spoke for God. Nevertheless, the gospel message divided the city and a violent attempt was made by both the Gentiles and Jews, with their rulers, to abuse and stone them (v. 5). This proves that their Jewish opponents were the instigators, since stoning was a Jewish form of execution, usually for blasphemy.

Fleeing Iconium, they went to Lystra and Derbe, cities of Lycaonia (v. 6). Lycaonia was a district in the Roman province of Galatia. Lystra was about 18 miles from Iconium and was the home of Lois, Eunice, and Timothy (16:1; 2Ti 1:5). The strange reaction by the people of Lystra to the healing of the cripple, who had never walked (v. 8), had its roots in local folklore. According to tradition, the gods Zeus and Hermes visited Lystra incognito, asking for food and lodging. All turned them away except for a peasant named Philemon and his wife, Baucis. The gods took vengeance by drowning everyone in a flood. But they turned the lowly cottage of Philemon and Baucis into a temple, where they were to serve as priest and priestess. Not wanting to repeat their ancestors' mistake, the people of Lystra believed Barnabas to be Zeus and Paul to be Hermes.

"But Jews came from Antioch and Iconium . . . they stoned Paul...supposing him to be dead" (v. 19). Paul did not die from the stoning as some claim, who link it to his third—heaven experience in 2 Corinthians 12. "Supposing" usually means "to suppose something that is not true." The main New Testament use of this word argues that the crowd's supposition was incorrect and that Paul was not dead. Another argument in favor of this position is that if Paul was resurrected, why didn't Luke mention it? Also, the dates of Paul's third—heaven experience and the time of the stoning do not reconcile.

✍ JULY 8

2 Chronicles 11:1–12:16

11 Now when Rehoboam had come to Jerusalem, he assembled the house of Judah and Benjamin, 180,000 chosen men who were warriors, to fight against Israel to restore the kingdom to Rehoboam. [2] But the word of the LORD came to Shemaiah the man of God, saying, [3] "Speak to Rehoboam the son of Solomon, king of Judah, and to all Israel in Judah and Benjamin, saying, [4] 'Thus says the LORD, "You shall not go up or fight against your relatives; return every man to his house, for this thing is from Me."'" So they listened to the words of the LORD and returned from going against Jeroboam.

[5] Rehoboam lived in Jerusalem and built cities for defense in Judah. [6] Thus he built Bethlehem, Etam, Tekoa, [7] Beth-zur, Soco, Adullam, [8] Gath, Mareshah, Ziph, [9] Adoraim, Lachish, Azekah, [10] Zorah, Aijalon and Hebron, which are fortified cities in Judah and in Benjamin. [11] He also strengthened the fortresses and put officers in them and stores of food, oil and wine. [12] *He put* shields and spears in every city and strengthened them greatly. So he held Judah and Benjamin.

[13] Moreover, the priests and the Levites who were in all Israel stood with him from all their districts. [14] For the Levites left their pasture lands and their property and came to Judah and Jerusalem, for Jeroboam and his sons had excluded them from serving as priests to the LORD. [15] He set up priests of his own for the

high places, for the satyrs and for the calves which he had made. [16] Those from all the tribes of Israel who set their hearts on seeking the LORD God of Israel followed them to Jerusalem, to sacrifice to the LORD God of their fathers. [17] They strengthened the kingdom of Judah and supported Rehoboam the son of Solomon for three years, for they walked in the way of David and Solomon for three years.

[18] Then Rehoboam took as a wife Mahalath the daughter of Jerimoth the son of David *and of* Abihail the daughter of Eliab the son of Jesse, [19] and she bore him sons: Jeush, Shemariah and Zaham. [20] After her he took Maacah the daughter of Absalom, and she bore him Abijah, Attai, Ziza and Shelomith. [21] Rehoboam loved Maacah the daughter of Absalom more than all his *other* wives and concubines. For he had taken eighteen wives and sixty concubines and fathered twenty-eight sons and sixty daughters. [22] Rehoboam appointed Abijah the son of Maacah as head and leader among his brothers, for he *intended* to make him king. [23] He acted wisely and distributed some of his sons through all the territories of Judah and Benjamin to all the fortified cities, and he gave them food in abundance. And he sought many wives *for them.*

12 When the kingdom of Rehoboam was established and strong, he and all Israel with him forsook the law of the LORD. [2] And it came about in King Rehoboam's fifth year, because they had been unfaithful to the LORD, that Shishak king of Egypt came up against Jerusalem [3] with 1,200 chariots and 60,000 horsemen. And the people who came with him from Egypt were without number: the Lubim, the Sukkiim and the Ethiopians. [4] He captured the fortified cities of Judah and came as far as Jerusalem. [5] Then Shemaiah the prophet came to Rehoboam and the princes of Judah who had gathered at Jerusalem because of Shishak, and he said to them, "Thus

12:2–5 Shishak. He ruled over Egypt ca. 945–924 B.C. An Egyptian record of this invasion written on stone has been found, recording that Shishak's army penetrated all the way north to the Sea of Galilee. He wanted to restore Egypt's once-great power, but was unable to conquer both Israel and Judah. However, he was able to destroy cities in Judah and gain some control of trade routes. Judah came under Egyptian control.

says the LORD, 'You have forsaken Me, so I also have forsaken you to Shishak.' " [6] So the princes of Israel and the king humbled themselves and said, "The LORD is righteous."

[7] When the LORD saw that they humbled themselves, the word of the LORD came to Shemaiah, saying, "They have humbled themselves *so* I will not destroy them, but I will grant them some *measure* of deliverance, and My wrath shall not be poured out on Jerusalem by means of Shishak. [8] But they will become his slaves so that they may learn *the difference between* My service and the service of the kingdoms of the countries."

12:6–7 humbled themselves. In the face of the Egyptian conqueror, the leaders responded to the Word of God through the prophet (v. 5) and repented, so that God would end His wrath worked through Shishak.

12:8 But. A fitting punishment arose to remind the Jews of their heritage in relationship to Egypt. This was the first major military encounter with Egypt since the Exodus had ended hundreds of years of slavery there. A taste of being enslaved again to a people from whom God had given liberation was bitter. The message was crystal clear—if the Jews would forsake the true worship of God, they would also lose His protective hand of blessing. It was much better to serve God than to have to serve "kingdoms of the countries."

[9] So Shishak king of Egypt came up against Jerusalem, and took the treasures of the house of the LORD and the treasures of the king's palace. He took everything; he even took the golden shields which Solomon had made. [10] Then King Rehoboam made shields of bronze in their place and committed them to the care of the commanders of the guard who guarded the door of the king's house. [11] As often as the king entered the house of the LORD, the guards came and carried them and *then* brought them back into the guards' room. [12] And when he humbled himself, the anger of the LORD turned away from him, so as not to destroy *him* completely; and also conditions were good in Judah.

[13] So King Rehoboam strengthened himself in Jerusalem and reigned. Now Rehoboam was forty-one years old when he began to reign, and he reigned seventeen years in Jerusalem, the city which the LORD had chosen from all the tribes of Israel, to put His name

there. And his mother's name was Naamah the Ammonitess. ¹⁴ He did evil because he did not set his heart to seek the LORD.

¹⁵ Now the acts of Rehoboam, from first to last, are they not written in the records of Shemaiah the prophet and of Iddo the seer, according to genealogical enrollment? And *there were* wars between Rehoboam and Jeroboam continually. ¹⁶ And Rehoboam slept with his fathers and was buried in the city of David; and his son Abijah became king in his place.

Psalm 80:14–19

¹⁴ O God *of* hosts, turn again
　　now, we beseech You;
　Look down from heaven and see,
　　and take care of this vine,
¹⁵ Even the shoot which Your
　　right hand has planted,
　And on the son whom You have
　　strengthened for Yourself.
¹⁶ It is burned with fire, it is cut down;
　They perish at the rebuke of
　　Your countenance.
¹⁷ Let Your hand be upon the
　　man of Your right hand,
　Upon the son of man whom You
　　made strong for Yourself.

80:17 son of man. In this context, this phrase is primarily a reference to Israel. In a secondary sense, the "son of man" may allude to the Davidic dynasty and even extend to the Messiah, since He is so frequently called by that title in the New Testament.

¹⁸ Then we shall not turn back from You;
　Revive us, and we will call
　　upon Your name.
¹⁹ O LORD God of hosts, restore us;
　Cause Your face to shine *upon us,* and we will be saved.

Proverbs 20:19–21

¹⁹ He who goes about as a
　　slanderer reveals secrets,
　Therefore do not associate
　　with a gossip.
²⁰ He who curses his father
　　or his mother,
　His lamp will go out in
　　time of darkness.
²¹ An inheritance gained hurriedly
　　at the beginning
　Will not be blessed in the end.

20:21 gained hurriedly. This implies an unjust method in gaining the inheritance, so that it will be lost by the same unjust ways or by punishment.

Acts 15:1–21

15 Some men came down from Judea and *began* teaching the brethren, "Unless you are circumcised according to the custom of Moses, you cannot be saved." ² And when Paul and Barnabas had great dissension and debate with them, *the brethren* determined that Paul and Barnabas and some others of them should go up to Jerusalem to the apostles and elders concerning this issue. ³ Therefore, being sent on their way by the church, they were passing through both Phoenicia and Samaria, describing in detail the conversion of the Gentiles, and were bringing great joy to all the brethren. ⁴ When they arrived at Jerusalem, they were received by the church and the apostles and the elders, and they reported all that God had done with them. ⁵ But some of the sect of the Pharisees who had believed stood up, saying, "It is necessary to circumcise them and to direct them to observe the Law of Moses."

⁶ The apostles and the elders came together to look into this matter. ⁷ After there had been much debate, Peter stood up and said to them, "Brethren, you know that in the early days God made a choice among you, that by my mouth the Gentiles would hear the word of the gospel and believe. ⁸ And God, who knows the heart, testified to them giving them the Holy Spirit, just as He also did to us; ⁹ and He made no distinction between us and them, cleansing their hearts by faith. ¹⁰ Now therefore why do you put God to the test by placing upon the neck of the disciples a yoke which neither our fathers nor we have been able to bear? ¹¹ But we believe that we are saved through the grace of the Lord Jesus, in the same way as they also are."

¹² All the people kept silent, and they were listening to Barnabas and Paul as they were relating what signs and wonders God had done through them among the Gentiles. ¹³ After they had stopped speaking, James answered, saying, "Brethren, listen to me. ¹⁴ Simeon has related how God first concerned Himself about taking from among the Gentiles a people for His name. ¹⁵ With this the words of the Prophets agree, just as it is written,

¹⁶ 'AFTER THESE THINGS I will return,
AND I WILL REBUILD THE TABERNACLE
OF DAVID WHICH HAS FALLEN,
AND I WILL REBUILD ITS RUINS,
AND I WILL RESTORE IT,
¹⁷ SO THAT THE REST OF MANKIND
MAY SEEK THE LORD,
AND ALL THE GENTILES WHO
ARE CALLED BY MY NAME,'
¹⁸ SAYS THE LORD, WHO MAKES
THESE THINGS KNOWN
FROM LONG AGO.

¹⁹ Therefore it is my judgment that we do not trouble those who are turning to God from among the Gentiles, ²⁰ but that we write to them that they abstain from things contami-nated by idols and from fornication and from what is strangled and from blood. ²¹ For Moses from ancient generations has in every city those who preach him, since he is read in the synagogues every Sabbath."

15:19 we do not trouble. The Greek word for "trouble" means "to throw something in the path of someone to annoy them." The decision of the Jerusalem Council, after considering all the evidence, was that keeping the law and observing rituals were not requirements for salvation. The Judaizers were to cease troubling and annoying the Gentiles.

DAY 8: Why is the first church council in Acts 15 the most important ever held?

Throughout its history, the church's leaders have met to settle doctrinal issues. Historians point to 7 ecumenical councils in the church's early history, especially the Councils of Nicea (A.D. 325) and Chalcedon (A.D. 451). Yet the most important council was the first one—the Jerusalem Council—because it established the answer to the most vital doctrinal question of all: "What must a person do to be saved?" The apostles and elders defied efforts to impose legalism and ritualism as necessary prerequisites for salvation. They forever affirmed that salvation is totally by grace through faith in Christ alone.

The Judaizers were false teachers who were self-appointed guardians of legalism. They taught a doctrine of salvation by works through the act of circumcision (v. 1). In answer to this, Peter rose up and gave the first of 3 speeches at the Council that amount to one of the strongest defenses of salvation by grace through faith alone contained in Scripture. Peter began his defense by reviewing how God saved Gentiles in the early days of the church without a require-ment of circumcision, law keeping, or ritual—referring to the salvation of Cornelius and his household (10:44–48; 11:17–18). If God did not require any additional qualifications for salvation, neither should the legalists.

The Judaizers could have argued that Cornelius and the others could not have been saved because they did not meet the legalistic requirements. To thwart that potential argument, Peter reiterates that God gave them the Holy Spirit, thus proving the genuineness of their salvation (v. 8). Peter warns the Judaizers that they are putting a yoke on the neck of the disci-ples—a description of the law and the legalism of the scribes and Pharisees (Mt 23:4; Lk 11:46). The legalists expected the Gentiles to carry a load they themselves were unwilling to bear. "But we believe that we are saved through the grace of the Lord Jesus" (v. 11). His declaration is a resounding affirmation of salvation by grace through faith alone.

 JULY 9

2 Chronicles 13:1–14:15

13 In the eighteenth year of King Jeroboam, Abijah became king over Judah. ² He reigned three years in Jerusalem; and his mother's name was Micaiah the daughter of Uriel of Gibeah.

Now there was war between Abijah and Jeroboam. ³ Abijah began the battle with an army of valiant warriors, 400,000 chosen men, while Jeroboam drew up in battle for-mation against him with 800,000 chosen men *who were* valiant warriors.

⁴ Then Abijah stood on Mount Zemaraim, which is in the hill country of Ephraim, and said, "Listen to me, Jeroboam and all Israel: ⁵ Do you not know that the LORD God of Israel gave the rule over Israel forever to David and his sons by a covenant of salt? ⁶ Yet Jeroboam the son of Nebat, the servant of Solomon the son of David, rose up and rebelled against his master, ⁷ and worthless men gathered about him, scoundrels, who proved too strong for Rehoboam, the son of Solomon, when he was

young and timid and could not hold his own against them.

8 "So now you intend to resist the kingdom of the LORD through the sons of David, being a great multitude and *having* with you the golden calves which Jeroboam made for gods for you. 9 Have you not driven out the priests of the LORD, the sons of Aaron and the Levites, and made for yourselves priests like the peoples of *other* lands? Whoever comes to consecrate himself with a young bull and seven rams, even he may become a priest of *what are* no gods. 10 But as for us, the LORD is our God, and we have not forsaken Him; and the sons of Aaron are ministering to the LORD as priests, and the Levites attend to their work. 11 Every morning and evening they burn to the LORD burnt offerings and fragrant incense, and the showbread is *set* on the clean table, and the golden lampstand with its lamps is *ready* to light every evening; for we keep the charge of the LORD our God, but you have forsaken Him. 12 Now behold, God is with us at *our* head and His priests with the signal trumpets to sound the alarm against you. O sons of Israel, do not fight against the LORD God of your fathers, for you will not succeed."

13 But Jeroboam had set an ambush to come from the rear, so that *Israel* was in front of Judah and the ambush was behind them. 14 When Judah turned around, behold, they were attacked both front and rear; so they cried to the LORD, and the priests blew the trumpets. 15 Then the men of Judah raised a war cry, and when the men of Judah raised the war cry, then it was that God routed Jeroboam and all Israel before Abijah and Judah. 16 When the sons of Israel fled before Judah, God gave them into their hand. 17 Abijah and his people defeated them with a great slaughter, so that

13:15 God routed Jeroboam and all Israel. At the time of certain defeat, with 400,000 troops behind and the same number in front, Judah was saved by divine intervention. What God did is unknown, but the army of Israel began to flee (v. 16), and the soldiers of Judah massacred 500,000 of them in an unimaginable blood bath (v. 17).

13:17 Before the battle, Jeroboam outnumbered Abijah two to one (13:3). After the fray, in which the Lord intervened on behalf of Judah, Abijah outnumbered Jeroboam 4 to 3.

500,000 chosen men of Israel fell slain. 18 Thus the sons of Israel were subdued at that time, and the sons of Judah conquered because they trusted in the LORD, the God of their fathers. 19 Abijah pursued Jeroboam and captured from him *several* cities, Bethel with its villages, Jeshanah with its villages and Ephron with its villages. 20 Jeroboam did not again recover strength in the days of Abijah; and the LORD struck him and he died.

21 But Abijah became powerful; and took fourteen wives to himself, and became the father of twenty-two sons and sixteen daughters. 22 Now the rest of the acts of Abijah, and his ways and his words are written in the treatise of the prophet Iddo.

14 So Abijah slept with his fathers, and they buried him in the city of David, and his son Asa became king in his place. The land was undisturbed for ten years during his days.

2 Asa did good and right in the sight of the LORD his God, 3 for he removed the foreign altars and high places, tore down the *sacred* pillars, cut down the Asherim, 4 and commanded Judah to seek the LORD God of their fathers and to observe the law and the commandment. 5 He also removed the high places and the incense altars from all the cities of Judah. And the kingdom was undisturbed under him. 6 He built fortified cities in Judah, since the land was undisturbed, and there was no one at war with him during those years, because the LORD had given him rest. 7 For he said to Judah, "Let us build these cities and surround *them* with walls and towers, gates and bars. The land is still ours because we have sought the LORD our God; we have sought Him, and He has given us rest on every side." So they built and prospered. 8 Now Asa had an army of 300,000 from Judah, bearing large shields and spears, and 280,000 from Benjamin, bearing shields and wielding bows; all of them were valiant warriors.

9 Now Zerah the Ethiopian came out against them with an army of a million men and 300 chariots, and he came to Mareshah. 10 So Asa went out to meet him, and they drew up in battle formation in the valley of Zephathah at Mareshah. 11 Then Asa called to the LORD his God and said, "LORD, there is no one besides You to help *in the battle* between the powerful and those who have no strength; so help us, O LORD our God, for we trust in You, and in Your name have come against this multitude. O LORD, You are our God; let not man prevail against You." 12 So the LORD

routed the Ethiopians before Asa and before Judah, and the Ethiopians fled. [13] Asa and the people who *were* with him pursued them as far as Gerar; and so many Ethiopians fell that they could not recover, for they were shattered before the LORD and before His army. And they carried away very much plunder. [14] They destroyed all the cities around Gerar, for the dread of the LORD had fallen on them; and they despoiled all the cities, for there was much plunder in them. [15] They also struck down those who owned livestock, and they carried away large numbers of sheep and camels. Then they returned to Jerusalem.

Psalm 81:1-5

For the choir director; on the Gittith.
A Psalm of Asaph.

Sing for joy to God our strength;
Shout joyfully to the God
of Jacob.
[2] Raise a song, strike the
timbrel,
The sweet sounding lyre
with the harp.
[3] Blow the trumpet at the
new moon,
At the full moon, on our
feast day.
[4] For it is a statute for Israel,
An ordinance of the God
of Jacob.
[5] He established it for a
testimony in Joseph
When he went throughout
the land of Egypt.
I heard a language that
I did not know:

Proverbs 20:22-23

[22] Do not say, "I will repay evil";
Wait for the LORD, and
He will save you.

81:3 new moon...full moon. The seventh month of Israel's year (Tishri; Sept./Oct.) culminated the festival year with a succession of celebrations. The month began with the blowing of the trumpets, continued with the Day of Atonement on the tenth day, and celebrated the Feast of Booths, or Tabernacles, on the fifteenth day when the moon was full. The Feast of Tabernacles praised God for His care in the wilderness wanderings, and also pointed to the coming kingdom (Mt 17:1-4).

[23] Differing weights are an
abomination to the LORD,
And a false scale is not good.

Acts 15:22-41

[22] Then it seemed good to the apostles and the elders, with the whole church, to choose men from among them to send to Antioch with Paul and Barnabas—Judas called Barsabbas, and Silas, leading men among the brethren, [23] and they sent this letter by them,

"The apostles and the brethren who are elders, to the brethren in Antioch and Syria and Cilicia who are from the Gentiles, greetings. [24] Since we have heard that some of our number to whom we gave no instruction have disturbed you with *their* words, unsettling your souls, [25] it seemed good to us, having become of one mind, to select men to send to you with our beloved Barnabas and Paul, [26] men who have risked their lives for the name of our Lord Jesus Christ. [27] Therefore we have sent Judas and Silas, who themselves will also report the same things by word *of mouth*. [28] For it seemed good to the Holy Spirit and to us to lay upon you no greater burden than these essentials: [29] that you abstain from things sacrificed to idols and from blood and from things strangled and from fornication; if you keep yourselves free from such things, you will do well. Farewell."

15:24 disturbed...unsettling. "Disturbed" is a different Greek word from the one in v. 19, meaning "to deeply upset," "to deeply trouble," "to perplex," or "to create fear." The Greek word for "unsettling" was used in extrabiblical writings to speak of someone going bankrupt. Together these words aptly describe the chaos caused by the Judaizers.

[30] So when they were sent away, they went down to Antioch; and having gathered the congregation together, they delivered the letter. [31] When they had read it, they rejoiced because of its encouragement. [32] Judas and Silas, also being prophets themselves, encouraged and strengthened the brethren with a lengthy message. [33] After they had spent time *there*, they were sent away from the brethren in peace to those who had sent them out. [34] [But it seemed good to Silas to remain there.] [35] But

Paul and Barnabas stayed in Antioch, teaching and preaching with many others also, the word of the Lord.

³⁶After some days Paul said to Barnabas, "Let us return and visit the brethren in every city in which we proclaimed the word of the Lord, *and see* how they are." ³⁷Barnabas wanted to take John, called Mark, along with them also. ³⁸But Paul kept insisting that they should not take him along who had deserted them in Pamphylia and had not gone with them to the work. ³⁹And there occurred such a sharp disagreement that they separated from one another, and Barnabas took Mark with him and sailed away to Cyprus. ⁴⁰But Paul chose Silas and left, being committed by

15:36 *see* how they are. In addition to proclaiming the gospel, Paul also recognized his responsibility to mature the new believers in their faith (Mt 28:19–20; Eph 4:12–13; Php 1:8; Col 1:28; 1Th 2:17). So he planned his second missionary journey to retrace his first one.

the brethren to the grace of the Lord. ⁴¹And he was traveling through Syria and Cilicia, strengthening the churches.

15:39 disagreement...separated. This was not an amicable parting—they were in sharp disagreement regarding John Mark. The weight of the evidence favors Paul's decision, especially since he was an apostle of Jesus Christ. That alone should have caused Barnabas to submit to his authority. But they eventually did reconcile (1Co 9:6).

15:40 Silas. He was perfectly suited to be Paul's companion, since he was a prophet and could proclaim and teach the Word. Being a Jew gave him access to the synagogues. Because he was a Roman citizen (16:37), he enjoyed the same benefits and protection as Paul. His status as a respected leader in the Jerusalem fellowship helped to reinforce Paul's teaching that Gentile salvation was by grace alone through faith alone.

DAY 9: How did a godly king respond to crises?

Second Chronicles 14:1—16:14 records the reign of Asa in Judah (ca. 911–870 B.C.). First Kings 15:11 says that Asa did as his forefather David had done—honoring God while building the kingdom (vv. 6–8). Times of peace were used for strengthening. "Asa did good and right in the sight of the LORD his God" (v. 2). He removed elements of false worship that had accumulated over the years of Solomon, Rehoboam, and Abijah (1Ki 15:12–13). Apparently, he did not remove all the high places or, once removed, they reappeared (1Ki 15:14; 1Ch 15:6). His son Jehoshaphat later had to remove them (2Ch 17:6), although not completely (2Ch 20:33). This was done in an effort to comply with Deuteronomy 12:2–3.

Asa had an army of 580,000 men "bearing shields and wielding bows; all of them were valiant warriors" (v. 8). Yet a major threat developed from Zerah, the Ethiopian, probably on behalf of the Egyptian Pharaoh, who was attempting to regain control as Shishak had during the days of Rehoboam (2Ch 12:7–8), ca. 901–900 B.C. The Ethiopians came against them with "an army of a million men and 300 chariots" (v. 9). Asa's appeal to God centered on God's omnipotence and reputation and is well worth memorizing. "LORD, there is no one besides You to help in the battle between the powerful and those who have no strength; so help us . . . O LORD, You are our God; let not man prevail against You" (v. 11). God's response was to strike the Ethiopian army and overthrow them. "And they carried away very much plunder" (v. 13). It appears that this great horde was a nomadic people who moved with all their possessions and had set up their camp near Gerar. The spoils of Judah's victory were immense.

⌇ JULY 10

2 Chronicles 15:1–16:14

15 Now the Spirit of God came on Azariah the son of Oded, ²and he went out to meet Asa and said to him, "Listen to me, Asa, and all Judah and Benjamin: the LORD is with you when you are with Him. And if you seek Him, He will let you find Him; but if you forsake Him, He will forsake you. ³For many days Israel was without the true God and without a teaching priest and without law. ⁴But in their distress they turned to the LORD God of Israel, and they sought Him, and He let them find Him. ⁵In those times there

15:1 Spirit of God. An act of the Holy Spirit, common in the Old Testament enabling servants of God to speak or act uniquely for Him. **Azariah.** This man was a prophet mentioned only here, who met Asa as he returned from the victory and spoke to him before all his army.

15:2 The spiritual truth here is basic, namely that God is present and powerful in defense of His obedient people. While good Asa ruled for 41 years, 8 wicked kings ruled in Israel, including Jeroboam, who along with the others, was a negative illustration of this truth.

was no peace to him who went out or to him who came in, for many disturbances afflicted all the inhabitants of the lands. ⁶ Nation was crushed by nation, and city by city, for God troubled them with every kind of distress. ⁷ But you, be strong and do not lose courage, for there is reward for your work."

⁸ Now when Asa heard these words and the prophecy which Azariah the son of Oded the prophet spoke, he took courage and removed the abominable idols from all the land of Judah and Benjamin and from the cities which he had captured in the hill country of Ephraim. He then restored the altar of the LORD which was in front of the porch of the LORD. ⁹ He gathered all Judah and Benjamin and those from Ephraim, Manasseh and Simeon who resided with them, for many defected to him from Israel when they saw that the LORD his God was with him. ¹⁰ So they assembled at Jerusalem in the third month of the fifteenth year of Asa's reign. ¹¹ They sacrificed to the LORD that day 700 oxen and 7,000 sheep from the spoil they had brought. ¹² They entered into the covenant to seek the LORD God of their fathers with all their heart and soul; ¹³ and whoever would not seek the LORD God of Israel should be put to death, whether small or great, man or woman. ¹⁴ Moreover, they made an oath to the LORD with a loud voice, with shouting, with trumpets and with horns. ¹⁵ All Judah rejoiced concerning the oath, for they had sworn with their whole heart and had sought Him earnestly, and He let them find Him. So the LORD gave them rest on every side.

¹⁶ He also removed Maacah, the mother of King Asa, from the *position of* queen mother, because she had made a horrid image as an Asherah, and Asa cut down her horrid image, crushed *it* and burned *it* at the brook Kidron.

¹⁷ But the high places were not removed from Israel; nevertheless Asa's heart was blameless all his days. ¹⁸ He brought into the house of God the dedicated things of his father and his own dedicated things: silver and gold and utensils. ¹⁹ And there was no more war until the thirty-fifth year of Asa's reign.

16 In the thirty-sixth year of Asa's reign Baasha king of Israel came up against Judah and fortified Ramah in order to prevent *anyone* from going out or coming in to Asa king of Judah. ² Then Asa brought out silver and gold from the treasuries of the house of the LORD and the king's house, and sent them to Ben-hadad king of Aram, who lived in Damascus, saying, ³ "*Let there be* a treaty between you and me, *as* between my father and your father. Behold, I have sent you silver and gold; go, break your treaty with Baasha king of Israel so that he will withdraw from me." ⁴ So Ben-hadad listened to King Asa and sent the commanders of his armies against the cities of Israel, and they conquered Ijon, Dan, Abel-maim and all the store cities of Naphtali. ⁵ When Baasha heard *of it*, he ceased fortifying Ramah and stopped his work. ⁶ Then King Asa brought all Judah, and they carried away the stones of Ramah and its timber with which Baasha had been building, and with them he fortified Geba and Mizpah.

⁷ At that time Hanani the seer came to Asa king of Judah and said to him, "Because you have relied on the king of Aram and have not relied on the LORD your God, therefore the army of the king of Aram has escaped out of your hand. ⁸ Were not the Ethiopians and the Lubim an immense army with very many chariots and horsemen? Yet because

16:7 Hanani. God used this prophet to rebuke Asa 1) for his wicked appropriation of temple treasures devoted to God to purchase power, and 2) for his faithless dependence on a pagan king instead of the Lord, in contrast to before when opposed by Egypt (2Ch 14:9–15). **army of the king of Aram has escaped.** Asa forfeited by this sin the opportunity of gaining victory not only over Israel, but also Aram, or Syria. This could have been a greater victory than over the Ethiopians, which would have deprived Syria of any future successful attacks on Judah. Though God had delivered them when they were outnumbered (13:3ff.; 14:9ff.), the king showed his own spiritual decline both in lack of trust and in his treatment of the prophet of God who spoke truth (v. 10).

you relied on the LORD, He delivered them into your hand. ⁹For the eyes of the LORD move to and fro throughout the earth that He may strongly support those whose heart is completely His. You have acted foolishly in this. Indeed, from now on you will surely have wars." ¹⁰Then Asa was angry with the seer and put him in prison, for he was enraged at him for this. And Asa oppressed some of the people at the same time.

¹¹Now, the acts of Asa from first to last, behold, they are written in the Book of the Kings of Judah and Israel. ¹²In the thirty-ninth year of his reign Asa became diseased in his feet. His disease was severe, yet even in his disease he did not seek the LORD, but the physicians. ¹³So Asa slept with his fathers, having died in the forty-first year of his reign. ¹⁴They buried him in his own tomb which he had cut out for himself in the city of David, and they laid him in the resting place which he had filled with spices of various kinds blended by the perfumers' art; and they made a very great fire for him.

Psalm 81:6–10

6 "I relieved his shoulder of
    the burden,
  His hands were freed from
    the basket.
7 "You called in trouble and
    I rescued you;
  I answered you in the hiding
    place of thunder;
  I proved you at the waters
    of Meribah.   *Selah*
8 "Hear, O My people, and I
    will admonish you;
  O Israel, if you would listen
    to Me!
9 "Let there be no strange
    god among you;
  Nor shall you worship
    any foreign god.
10 "I, the LORD, am your God,
  Who brought you up from
    the land of Egypt;
  Open your mouth wide
    and I will fill it.

Proverbs 20:24–25

24 Man's steps are *ordained* by
    the LORD,
  How then can man
    understand his way?
25 It is a trap for a man to say
    rashly, "It is holy!"
  And after the vows to make inquiry.

Acts 16:1–18

16 Paul came also to Derbe and to Lystra. And a disciple was there, named Timothy, the son of a Jewish woman who was a believer, but his father was a Greek, ²and he was well spoken of by the brethren who were in Lystra and Iconium. ³Paul wanted this man to go with him; and he took him and circumcised him because of the Jews who were in those parts, for they all knew that his father was a Greek. ⁴Now while they were passing through the cities, they

16:1 a disciple…Timothy. A young man (late teens or early 20s) of high regard, a "true child in the faith" (1Ti 1:2; see 2Ti 1:2), who eventually became Paul's right-hand man (1Co 4:17; 1Th 3:2; Php 2:19). In essence, he became John Mark's replacement. After being commissioned by the elders of the local church (1Ti 4:14; 2Ti 1:6), he joined Paul and Silas. **his father was a Greek.** The grammar likely suggests his father was dead. By being both Jew and Gentile, Timothy had access to both cultures—an indispensable asset for missionary service.

16:3 circumcised him. This was done to aid his acceptance by the Jews and provide full access to the synagogues he would be visiting with Paul and Silas. If Timothy had not been circumcised, the Jews could have assumed he had renounced his Jewish heritage and had chosen to live as a Gentile.

were delivering the decrees which had been decided upon by the apostles and elders who were in Jerusalem, for them to observe. ⁵So the churches were being strengthened in the faith, and were increasing in number daily.

⁶They passed through the Phrygian and Galatian region, having been forbidden by the Holy Spirit to speak the word in Asia; ⁷and after they came to Mysia, they were trying to go into Bithynia, and the Spirit of Jesus did not permit them; ⁸and passing by Mysia, they came down to Troas. ⁹A vision appeared to Paul in the night: a man of Macedonia was standing and appealing to him, and saying,

16:6 Holy Spirit…Asia. Paul was not allowed to fulfill his intention to minister in Asia Minor (modern Turkey) and to such cities as Ephesus, Smyrna, Philadelphia, Laodicea, Colosse, Sardis, Pergamos, and Thyatira.

—— ☀ ——

16:9 Macedonia. The region located across the Aegean Sea on the mainland of Greece. The cities of Philippi and Thessalonica were located there. Most significantly, going there was to take the gospel from Asia into Europe.

"Come over to Macedonia and help us." ¹⁰ When he had seen the vision, immediately we sought to go into Macedonia, concluding that God had called us to preach the gospel to them.

¹¹ So putting out to sea from Troas, we ran a straight course to Samothrace, and on the day following to Neapolis; ¹² and from there to Philippi, which is a leading city of the district of Macedonia, a *Roman* colony; and we were staying in this city for some days. ¹³ And on the Sabbath day we went outside the gate to a riverside, where we were supposing that there would be a place of prayer; and we

sat down and began speaking to the women who had assembled. ¹⁴ A woman named Lydia, from the city of Thyatira, a seller of purple fabrics, a worshiper of God, was listening; and the Lord opened her heart to respond to the things spoken by Paul. ¹⁵ And when she and her household had been baptized, she urged us, saying, "If you have judged me to be faithful to the Lord, come into my house and stay." And she prevailed upon us.

¹⁶ It happened that as we were going to the place of prayer, a slave-girl having a spirit of divination met us, who was bringing her masters much profit by fortune-telling. ¹⁷ Following after Paul and us, she kept crying out, saying, "These men are bond-servants of the Most High God, who are proclaiming to you the way of salvation." ¹⁸ She continued doing this for many days. But Paul was greatly annoyed, and turned and said to the spirit, "I command you in the name of Jesus Christ to come out of her!" And it came out at that very moment.

DAY 10: How did Lydia and the demon-possessed girl in Philippi respond differently to the gospel?

When Paul arrived in Philippi (Ac 16:12), evidently the Jewish community did not have the minimum of 10 Jewish men who were heads of households required to form a synagogue. In such cases, a place of prayer under the open sky and near a river or sea was adopted as a meeting place. Most likely this spot was located where the road leading out of the city crossed the Gangites River. Paul spoke "to the women who had assembled" (v. 13). In further evidence of the small number of Jewish men, it was women who met to pray, read from the Old Testament law, and discuss what they read.

Lydia was from the city of Thyatira, which was located in the Roman province of Lydia, thus the name "Lydia" was probably associated with her place of origin. She was a "seller of purple fabrics" (v. 14). Because purple dye was extremely expensive, purple garments were usually worn by royalty and the wealthy. As a result, Lydia's business turned a nice profit, which enabled her to have a house large enough to accommodate the missionary team (v. 15) and the new church at Philippi (v. 40). "A worshiper of God." Like Cornelius, she believed in the God of Israel but had not become a full proselyte (10:2). The Lord opened her heart, and she and her household were baptized.

Also in Philippi was a "slave-girl having a spirit of divination" (v. 16), literally, "a python spirit." That expression comes from Greek mythology. Python was a snake that guarded the oracle at Delphi. Essentially, this girl was a medium in contact with demons who could supposedly predict the future. For several days she followed Paul and rightly cried out in the streets, "These men are bond-servants of the Most High God" (v. 17). El Elyon, the Absolutely Sovereign God, is an Old Testament title (used about 50 times) for the God of Israel (Ge 14:18–22; Ps 78:35; Da 5:18). But the spirit was wrong, and Paul finally turned and said to the spirit, "I command you in the name of Jesus Christ to come out of her!" (v. 18). The demon left the girl in obedience to Paul's command and his apostolic authority. The ability to cast out demons was a special ability of Christ's apostles (Mk 3:15; 2Co 12:12).

⅃ JULY 11

2 Chronicles 17:1–18:34

17 Jehoshaphat his son then became king in his place, and made his position over Israel firm. ² He placed troops in all the fortified cities of Judah, and set garrisons in the

land of Judah and in the cities of Ephraim which Asa his father had captured. ³ The LORD was with Jehoshaphat because he followed the example of his father David's earlier days and did not seek the Baals, ⁴ but sought the God of his father, followed His commandments, and did not act as Israel did. ⁵ So the LORD established the kingdom in his control, and all Judah brought tribute to Jehoshaphat, and he had great riches and honor. ⁶He took great pride in the ways of the LORD and again removed the high places and the Asherim from Judah.

⁷Then in the third year of his reign he sent his officials, Ben-hail, Obadiah, Zechariah, Nethanel and Micaiah, to teach in the cities of Judah; ⁸and with them the Levites, Shemaiah, Nethaniah, Zebadiah, Asahel, Shemiramoth, Jehonathan, Adonijah, Tobijah and Tobadonijah, the Levites; and with them Elishama and Jehoram, the priests. ⁹They taught in Judah, *having* the book of the law of the LORD with them; and they went throughout all the cities of Judah and taught among the people.

17:3–9 Jehoshaphat made three strategic moves, spiritually speaking: 1) he obeyed the Lord (17:3–6); 2) he removed false worship from the land (17:6); and 3) he sent out teachers who taught the people the law of the Lord (17:7–9).

¹⁰Now the dread of the LORD was on all the kingdoms of the lands which *were* around Judah, so that they did not make war against Jehoshaphat. ¹¹Some of the Philistines brought gifts and silver as tribute to Jehoshaphat; the Arabians also brought him flocks, 7,700 rams and 7,700 male goats. ¹²So Jehoshaphat grew greater and greater, and he built fortresses and store cities in Judah. ¹³He had large supplies in the cities of Judah, and warriors, valiant men, in Jerusalem.

17:12–13 These verses indicate the massive wealth that developed under divine blessing (18:1), as well as formidable military power (vv. 14–19).

¹⁴This was their muster according to their fathers' households: of Judah, commanders of thousands, Adnah *was* the commander, and with him 300,000 valiant warriors; ¹⁵and next to him *was* Johanan the commander, and with him 280,000; ¹⁶and next to him Amasiah the son of Zichri, who volunteered for the LORD, and with him 200,000 valiant warriors; ¹⁷and of Benjamin, Eliada a valiant warrior, and with him 200,000 armed with bow and shield; ¹⁸and next to him Jehozabad, and with him 180,000 equipped for war. ¹⁹These are they who served the king, apart from those whom the king put in the fortified cities through all Judah.

18 Now Jehoshaphat had great riches and honor; and he allied himself by marriage with Ahab. ²Some years later he went down to *visit* Ahab at Samaria. And Ahab slaughtered many sheep and oxen for him and the people who were with him, and induced him to go up against Ramoth-gilead. ³Ahab king of Israel said to Jehoshaphat king of Judah, "Will you go with me *against* Ramoth-gilead?" And he said to him, "I am as you are, and my people as your people, and *we will be* with you in the battle."

⁴Moreover, Jehoshaphat said to the king of Israel, "Please inquire first for the word of the LORD." ⁵Then the king of Israel assembled the prophets, four hundred men, and said to them, "Shall we go against Ramoth-gilead to battle, or shall I refrain?" And they said, "Go up, for God will give *it* into the hand of the king." ⁶But Jehoshaphat said, "Is there not yet a prophet of the LORD here that we may inquire of him?" ⁷The king of Israel said to Jehoshaphat, "There is yet one man by whom we may inquire of the LORD, but I hate him, for he never prophesies good concerning me but always evil. He is Micaiah, son of Imla." But Jehoshaphat said, "Let not the king say so." ⁸Then the king of Israel called an officer and said, "Bring quickly Micaiah, Imla's son." ⁹Now the king of Israel and Jehoshaphat the king of Judah were sitting each on his throne, arrayed in *their* robes, and *they* were sitting at the threshing floor at the entrance of the gate of Samaria; and all the prophets were prophesying before them. ¹⁰Zedekiah the son of Chenaanah made horns of iron for himself and said, "Thus says the LORD, 'With these you shall gore the Arameans until they are consumed.'" ¹¹All the prophets were prophesying thus, saying, "Go up to Ramoth-gilead and succeed, for the LORD will give *it* into the hand of the king."

¹²Then the messenger who went to summon Micaiah spoke to him saying, "Behold, the words of the prophets are uniformly favorable to the king. So please let your word be like one of them and speak favorably." ¹³But Micaiah said, "As the LORD lives, what my God says, that I will speak." ¹⁴When he came to the king, the king said to him, "Micaiah, shall we go to Ramoth-gilead to battle, or shall I refrain?" He said, "Go up and succeed, for they will be given into your hand." ¹⁵Then the king said to him, "How many times must I adjure you to speak to

me nothing but the truth in the name of the LORD?" ¹⁶ So he said,

"I saw all Israel
Scattered on the mountains,
Like sheep which have no shepherd;
And the LORD said,
'These have no master.
Let each of them return to
his house in peace.' "

¹⁷ Then the king of Israel said to Jehoshaphat, "Did I not tell you that he would not prophesy good concerning me, but evil?"

¹⁸ Micaiah said, "Therefore, hear the word of the LORD. I saw the LORD sitting on His throne, and all the host of heaven standing on His right and on His left. ¹⁹ The LORD said, 'Who will entice Ahab king of Israel to go up and fall at Ramoth-gilead?' And one said this while another said that. ²⁰ Then a spirit came forward and stood before the LORD and said, 'I will entice him.' And the LORD said to him, 'How?' ²¹ He said, 'I will go and be a deceiving spirit in the mouth of all his prophets.' Then He said, 'You are to entice *him* and prevail also. Go and do so.' ²² Now therefore, behold, the LORD has put a deceiving spirit in the mouth of these your prophets, for the LORD has proclaimed disaster against you."

²³ Then Zedekiah the son of Chenaanah came near and struck Micaiah on the cheek and said, "How did the Spirit of the LORD pass from me to speak to you?" ²⁴ Micaiah said, "Behold, you will see on that day when you enter an inner room to hide yourself." ²⁵ Then the king of Israel said, "Take Micaiah and return him to Amon the governor of the city and to Joash the king's son; ²⁶ and say, 'Thus says the king, "Put this *man* in prison and feed him sparingly with bread and water until I return safely." ' " ²⁷ Micaiah said, "If you indeed return safely, the LORD has not spoken by me." And he said, "Listen, all you people."

²⁸ So the king of Israel and Jehoshaphat king of Judah went up against Ramoth-gilead. ²⁹ The king of Israel said to Jehoshaphat, "I will disguise myself and go into battle, but you put on your robes." So the king of Israel disguised himself, and they went into battle. ³⁰ Now the king of Aram had commanded the captains of his chariots, saying, "Do not fight with small or great, but with the king of Israel alone." ³¹ So when the captains of the chariots saw Jehoshaphat, they said, "It is the king of Israel," and they turned aside to fight against him. But Jehoshaphat cried out, and the LORD helped him, and God diverted them from him.

³² When the captains of the chariots saw that it was not the king of Israel, they turned back from pursuing him. ³³ A certain man drew his bow at random and struck the king of Israel in a joint of the armor. So he said to the driver of the chariot, "Turn around and take me out of the fight, for I am severely wounded." ³⁴ The battle raged that day, and the king of Israel propped himself up in his chariot in front of the Arameans until the evening; and at sunset he died.

Psalm 81:11–16

¹¹ "But My people did not
listen to My voice,
And Israel did not obey Me.
¹² "So I gave them over to the
stubbornness of their heart,
To walk in their own devices.
¹³ "Oh that My people would listen to Me,
That Israel would walk in My ways!
¹⁴ "I would quickly subdue their enemies
And turn My hand against
their adversaries.
¹⁵ "Those who hate the LORD would
pretend obedience to Him,
And their time *of punishment*
would be forever.
¹⁶ "But I would feed you with the
finest of the wheat,
And with honey from the rock
I would satisfy you."

81:16 honey from the rock. This phrase was first used by Moses in his song of praise (Dt 32:13). Though honey is sometimes found in the clefts of rocks, the intent of the figure here is more likely to valuable food provided from unlikely places.

Proverbs 20:26–28

²⁶ A wise king winnows the wicked,
And drives the *threshing*
wheel over them.
²⁷ The spirit of man is the
lamp of the LORD,
Searching all the innermost
parts of his being.

20:27 the lamp of the LORD. The "spirit" represents the conscience of man which searches every secret place.

²⁸ Loyalty and truth preserve the king,
   And he upholds his throne
      by righteousness.

Acts 16:19-40

¹⁹ But when her masters saw that their hope of profit was gone, they seized Paul and Silas and dragged them into the market place before the authorities, ²⁰ and when they had brought them to the chief magistrates, they said, "These men are throwing our city into confusion, being Jews, ²¹ and are proclaiming customs which it is not lawful for us to accept or to observe, being Romans." ²² The crowd rose up together against them, and the chief magistrates tore their robes off them and proceeded to order *them* to be beaten with rods. ²³ When they had struck them with many blows, they threw them into prison, commanding the jailer to guard them securely; ²⁴ and he, having received such a command, threw them into the inner prison and fastened their feet in the stocks.

²⁵ But about midnight Paul and Silas were praying and singing hymns of praise to God, and the prisoners were listening to them; ²⁶ and suddenly there came a great earthquake, so that the foundations of the prison house were shaken; and immediately all the doors were opened and everyone's chains were unfastened. ²⁷ When the jailer awoke and saw the prison doors opened, he drew his sword and was about to kill himself,

16:24 inner prison…in the stocks. The most secure part of the prison. The jailer took further precautions by putting their feet "in the stocks." This particular security measure was designed to produce painful cramping so the prisoner's legs were spread as far apart as possible.

16:27 prison doors opened…about to kill himself. Instead of waiting to face humiliation and a painful execution. A Roman soldier who let a prisoner escape paid for his negligence with his life (12:19; 27:42).

supposing that the prisoners had escaped. ²⁸ But Paul cried out with a loud voice, saying, "Do not harm yourself, for we are all here!" ²⁹ And he called for lights and rushed in, and trembling with fear he fell down before Paul and Silas, ³⁰ and after he brought them out, he said, "Sirs, what must I do to be saved?" ³¹ They said, "Believe in the Lord Jesus, and you will be saved, you and your household."

16:31 Believe in the Lord Jesus. One must believe He is who He claimed to be (Jn 20:31) and believe in what He did (1Co 15:3-4; Ro 1:16). **you and your household.** All of his family, servants, and guests who could comprehend the gospel and believe heard the gospel and believed. This does not include infants. See v. 15.

³² And they spoke the word of the Lord to him together with all who were in his house. ³³ And he took them that *very* hour of the night and washed their wounds, and immediately he was baptized, he and all his *household.* ³⁴ And he brought them into his house and set food before them, and rejoiced greatly, having believed in God with his whole household.

³⁵ Now when day came, the chief magistrates sent their policemen, saying, "Release those men." ³⁶ And the jailer reported these words to Paul, *saying,* "The chief magistrates have sent to release you. Therefore come out now and go in peace." ³⁷ But Paul said to them, "They have beaten us in public without trial, men who are Romans, and have thrown us into prison; and now are they sending us away secretly? No indeed! But let them come themselves and bring us out." ³⁸ The policemen reported these words to the chief magistrates. They were afraid when they heard that they were Romans, ³⁹ and they came and appealed to them, and when they had brought them out, they kept begging them to leave the city. ⁴⁰ They went out of the prison and entered *the house of* Lydia, and when they saw the brethren, they encouraged them and departed.

DAY 11: How did Roman law affect Paul and the preaching of the gospel?

The city of Philippi, which was located 10 miles inland from Neapolis, was named for Philip II of Macedon (the father of Alexander the Great). It was a Roman colony (Ac 16:2). Philippi became a Roman colony in 31 B.C., so it carried the right of freedom (it was self-governing and independent of the provincial government), the right of exemption from tax, and the right of holding land in full ownership.

In Acts 16:21, Paul and those with him are accused before the city magistrates as trouble-makers who "are proclaiming customs…not lawful for us…Romans." It was technically true that Roman citizens were not to engage in any foreign religion that had not been sanctioned by the state. But it was a false charge that they were creating chaos. Every Roman colony had two magistrates serving as judges. In this case, they did not uphold Roman justice: They did not investigate the charges, conduct a proper hearing, or give Paul and Silas the chance to defend themselves. Instead, the magistrates had them beaten with rods. This was an illegal punishment since they had not been convicted of any crime. The officers (v. 35) under the command of the magistrates administered the beating with rods tied together in a bundle. Paul received the same punishment on two other occasions (2Co 11:25).

Later, when Paul told them they were "Romans" (v. 37), it was a real problem. To inflict corporal punishment on a Roman citizen was a serious crime and made more so since Paul and Barnabas did not receive a trial. As a result, the magistrates faced the possibility of being removed from office and having Philippi's privileges as a Roman colony revoked.

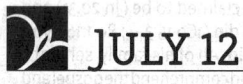

JULY 12

2 Chronicles 19:1–20:37

19 Then Jehoshaphat the king of Judah returned in safety to his house in Jerusalem. ² Jehu the son of Hanani the seer went out to meet him and said to King Jehoshaphat, "Should you help the wicked and love those who hate the LORD and so *bring* wrath on yourself from the LORD? ³ But there is *some* good in you, for you have removed the Asheroth from the land and you have set your heart to seek God."

19:1-3 Having faced possible death that was diverted by God (18:31), Jehoshaphat was rebuked because of his alliances. The prophet condemned the king's alliance with God's enemy, Ahab (1Ki 22:2), yet there was mercy mingled with wrath because of the king's concern personally and nationally for the true worship of God.

⁴ So Jehoshaphat lived in Jerusalem and went out again among the people from Beersheba to the hill country of Ephraim and brought them back to the LORD, the God of their fathers. ⁵ He appointed judges in the land in all the fortified cities of Judah, city by city. ⁶ He said to the judges, "Consider what you are doing, for you do not judge for man but for the LORD who is with you when you render judgment. ⁷ Now then let the fear of the LORD be upon you; be very careful what you do, for the LORD our God will have no part in unrighteousness or partiality or the taking of a bribe."

⁸ In Jerusalem also Jehoshaphat appointed some of the Levites and priests, and some of the heads of the fathers' *households* of Israel, for the judgment of the LORD and to judge disputes among the inhabitants of Jerusalem. ⁹ Then he charged them saying, "Thus you shall do in the fear of the LORD, faithfully and wholeheartedly. ¹⁰ Whenever any dispute comes to you from your brethren who live in their cities, between blood and blood, between law and commandment, statutes and ordinances, you shall warn them so that they may not be guilty before the LORD, and wrath may *not* come on you and your brethren. Thus you shall do and you will not be guilty. ¹¹ Behold, Amariah the chief priest will be over you in all that pertains to the LORD, and Zebadiah the son of Ishmael, the ruler of the house of Judah, in all that pertains to the king. Also the Levites shall be officers before you. Act resolutely, and the LORD be with the upright."

20 Now it came about after this that the sons of Moab and the sons of Ammon, together with some of the Meunites, came to make war against Jehoshaphat. ² Then some came and reported to Jehoshaphat, saying, "A great multitude is coming against you from beyond the sea, out of Aram and behold, they are in Hazazon-tamar (that is Engedi)." ³ Jehoshaphat was afraid and turned his attention to seek the LORD, and proclaimed a fast throughout all Judah. ⁴ So Judah gathered together to seek help from the LORD; they even came from all the cities of Judah to seek the LORD.

⁵ Then Jehoshaphat stood in the assembly of Judah and Jerusalem, in the house of the LORD before the new court, ⁶ and he said, "O LORD, the God of our fathers, are You not God in the heavens? And are You not ruler over all the kingdoms of the nations? Power and might are in Your hand so that no one can stand against You. ⁷ Did You not, O our God, drive out the inhabitants of this land before Your people Israel and give it to the descendants of Abraham Your friend forever? ⁸ They have lived in it, and have built

You a sanctuary there for Your name, saying, 9 'Should evil come upon us, the sword, *or* judgment, or pestilence, or famine, we will stand before this house and before You (for Your name is in this house) and cry to You in our distress, and You will hear and deliver us.' 10 Now behold, the sons of Ammon and Moab and Mount Seir, whom You did not let Israel invade when they came out of the land of Egypt (they turned aside from them and did not destroy them), 11 see *how* they are rewarding us by coming to drive us out from Your possession which You have given us as an inheritance. 12 O our God, will You not judge them? For we are powerless before this great multitude who are coming against us; nor do we know what to do, but our eyes are on You."

13 All Judah was standing before the LORD, with their infants, their wives and their children. 14 Then in the midst of the assembly the Spirit of the LORD came upon Jahaziel the son of Zechariah, the son of Benaiah, the son of Jeiel, the son of Mattaniah, the Levite of the sons of Asaph; 15 and he said, "Listen, all Judah and the inhabitants of Jerusalem and King Jehoshaphat: thus says the LORD to you, 'Do not fear or be dismayed because of this great multitude, for the battle is not yours but God's. 16 Tomorrow go down against them. Behold, they will come up by the ascent of Ziz, and you will find them at the end of the valley in front of the wilderness of Jeruel. 17 You *need* not fight in this *battle;* station yourselves, stand and see the salvation of the LORD on your behalf, O Judah and Jerusalem.' Do not fear or be dismayed; tomorrow go out to face them, for the LORD is with you."

18 Jehoshaphat bowed his head with *his* face to the ground, and all Judah and the inhabitants of Jerusalem fell down before the LORD, worshiping the LORD. 19 The Levites, from the sons of the Kohathites and of the sons of the Korahites, stood up to praise the LORD God of Israel, with a very loud voice.

20 They rose early in the morning and went out to the wilderness of Tekoa; and when they went out, Jehoshaphat stood and said, "Listen to me, O Judah and inhabitants of Jerusalem, put your trust in the LORD your God and you will be established. Put your trust in His prophets and succeed." 21 When he had consulted with the people, he appointed those who sang to the LORD and those who praised *Him* in holy attire, as they went out before the army and said, "Give thanks to the LORD, for His lovingkindness is everlasting." 22 When they began singing and praising, the LORD set ambushes against the sons of Ammon, Moab and Mount Seir, who had come against Judah; so they were routed. 23 For the sons of Ammon and Moab rose up against the inhabitants of Mount Seir destroying *them* completely; and when they had finished with the inhabitants of Seir, they helped to destroy one another.

24 When Judah came to the lookout of the wilderness, they looked toward the multitude, and behold, they *were* corpses lying on the ground, and no one had escaped. 25 When Jehoshaphat and his people came to take their spoil, they found much among them, *including* goods, garments and valuable things which they took for themselves, more than they could carry. And they were three days taking the spoil because there was so much. 26 Then on the fourth day they assembled in the valley of Beracah, for there they blessed the LORD. Therefore they have named that place "The Valley of Beracah" until today. 27 Every man of Judah and Jerusalem returned with Jehoshaphat at their head, returning to Jerusalem with joy, for the LORD had made them to rejoice over their enemies. 28 They came to Jerusalem with harps, lyres and trumpets to the house of the LORD. 29 And the dread of God was on all the kingdoms of the lands when they heard that the LORD had fought against the enemies of Israel. 30 So the kingdom of Jehoshaphat was at peace, for his God gave him rest on all sides.

31 Now Jehoshaphat reigned over Judah. He *was* thirty-five years old when he became king, and he reigned in Jerusalem twenty-five years. And his mother's name *was* Azubah the daughter of Shilhi. 32 He walked in the way of his father Asa and did not depart from it, doing right in the sight of the LORD. 33 The high places, however, were not removed; the people had not yet directed their hearts to the God of their fathers.

34 Now the rest of the acts of Jehoshaphat, first to last, behold, they are written in the annals of Jehu the son of Hanani, which is recorded in the Book of the Kings of Israel.

35 After this Jehoshaphat king of Judah allied himself with Ahaziah king of Israel. He acted wickedly in so doing. 36 So he allied himself with him to make ships to go to Tarshish, and they made the ships in Eziongeber. 37 Then Eliezer the son of Dodavahu of Mareshah prophesied against Jehoshaphat saying, "Because you have allied yourself with Ahaziah, the LORD has destroyed your works." So the ships were broken and could not go to Tarshish.

Psalm 82:1-8

A Psalm of Asaph.

G od takes His stand in His
own congregation;
He judges in the midst of the rulers.
2 How long will you judge unjustly
And show partiality to the
wicked?   *Selah*

82:1 His own congregation. The scene opens
with God having called the world leaders together. **midst of the rulers.** The best interpretation is that these are human leaders, such as
judges, kings, legislators, and presidents (Ex
22:8–9, 28; Jdg 5:8–9). God the Great Judge,
presides over these lesser judges.

3 Vindicate the weak and fatherless;
Do justice to the afflicted and destitute.
4 Rescue the weak and needy;
Deliver *them* out of the
hand of the wicked.

5 They do not know nor do
they understand;
They walk about in darkness;
All the foundations of the
earth are shaken.
6 I said, "You are gods,
And all of you are sons of the Most High.
7 "Nevertheless you will die like men
And fall like *any* one of the princes."
8 Arise, O God, judge the earth!
For it is You who possesses
all the nations.

82:6 I said. Kings and judges are set up ultimately by the decree of God (Ps 2:6). God, in
effect, invests His authority in human leaders
for the stability of the universe (Ro 13:1–7). But
God may revoke this authority (v. 7). **You are
gods.** Jesus, in quoting this phrase in John
10:34, supported the interpretation that the
"gods" were human beings. In a play on words,
He claims that if human leaders can be called
"gods," certainly the Messiah can be called God.

82:8 You who possess all the nations. The
psalmist prayerfully anticipates the future
when God will set up His kingdom and restore
order and perfect justice to a sin-cursed world
(Pss 96–97; Is 11:1–5).

Proverbs 20:29-30

29 The glory of young men
is their strength,
And the honor of old men
is their gray hair.
30 Stripes that wound scour
away evil,
And strokes *reach* the
innermost parts.

Acts 17:1-15

17 Now when they had traveled through
Amphipolis and Apollonia, they came
to Thessalonica, where there was a synagogue of the Jews. 2 And according to Paul's
custom, he went to them, and for three Sabbaths reasoned with them from the Scriptures, 3 explaining and giving evidence that
the Christ had to suffer and rise again from
the dead, and *saying*, "This Jesus whom I
am proclaiming to you is the Christ." 4 And
some of them were persuaded and joined
Paul and Silas, along with a large number
of the God-fearing Greeks and a number of
the leading women. 5 But the Jews, becoming
jealous and taking along some wicked men
from the market place, formed a mob and
set the city in an uproar; and attacking the
house of Jason, they were seeking to bring
them out to the people. 6 When they did not
find them, they *began* dragging Jason and
some brethren before the city authorities,
shouting, "These men who have upset the
world have come here also; 7 and Jason has
welcomed them, and they all act contrary
to the decrees of Caesar, saying that there
is another king, Jesus." 8 They stirred up the
crowd and the city authorities who heard
these things. 9 And when they had received
a pledge from Jason and the others, they
released them.
10 The brethren immediately sent Paul and
Silas away by night to Berea, and when they
arrived, they went into the synagogue of the
Jews. 11 Now these were more noble-minded
than those in Thessalonica, for they received
the word with great eagerness, examining
the Scriptures daily *to see* whether these
things were so. 12 Therefore many of them
believed, along with a number of prominent

17:7 contrary to the decrees of Caesar. One of
the most serious crimes in the Roman Empire
was to acknowledge allegiance to any king but
Caesar (Jn 19:15).

Greek women and men. ¹³ But when the Jews of Thessalonica found out that the word of God had been proclaimed by Paul in Berea also, they came there as well, agitating and stirring up the crowds. ¹⁴ Then immediately the brethren sent Paul out to go as far as the sea; and Silas and Timothy remained there. ¹⁵ Now those who escorted Paul brought him as far as Athens; and receiving a command for Silas and Timothy to come to him as soon as possible, they left.

17:15 Athens. The cultural center of Greece. At its zenith, Athens was home to the most renowned philosophers in history, including Socrates, Plato, and Aristotle, who was arguably the most influential philosopher of all. Two other significant philosophers taught there: Epicurus, founder of Epicureanism, and Zeno, founder of Stoicism—two of the dominant philosophies in that day (v. 18).

DAY 12: How did Jehoshaphat express his faith in the face of adversity?

Second Chronicles 20:1-30 is one of the great stories of faith in the Old Testament. Attacked by a great multitude from Moab and Ammon, Jehoshaphat made the appropriate spiritual response, i.e., the king and the nation appealed to God in prayer and fasting. The fast was national, including even the children (v. 13). Jehoshaphat stood in the redecorated center court praying for the nation, appealing to the promises, the glory, and the reputation of God which were at stake since He was identified with Judah (vv. 5–12). In his prayer he acknowledged God's sovereignty (v. 6), God's covenant (v. 7), God's presence (vv. 8– 9), God's goodness (v. 10), God's possession (v. 11), and their utter dependence on Him (v. 12).

The Lord responded immediately, sending a message of confidence through the prophet Jahaziel. "Do not fear or be dismayed because of this great multitude, for the battle is not yours but God's. Tomorrow go down against them…You need not fight in this battle; station yourselves, stand and see the salvation of the LORD" (v. 15–17).

Here was the praise of faith (vv. 18–21). They were confident enough in God's promise of victory to begin the praise before the battle was won. So great was their trust that the choir marched in front of the army, singing psalms. People were appointed who "praised Him in holy attire" (v. 21). Another rendering of this phrase is "the beauty of holiness." And, yes, the Lord is beautiful in holiness (Ex 15:11; Ps 27:4), but the text here was translated "in holy attire," which was referring to the manner in which the Levite singers were clothed in symbolic sacred clothing (1Ch 16:29) in honor of the Lord's holiness.

Similar to God's intervention in Gideon's day (Jdg 7:15–23), God caused confusion among the enemy, who mistakenly turned upon themselves and slaughtered each other (vv. 22–24). Some think this may have been done by angels who appeared and set off this uncontrolled and deadly panic. The destruction was complete before Jehoshaphat and his army ever met the enemy (v. 24).

JULY 13

2 Chronicles 21:1–22:12

21 Then Jehoshaphat slept with his fathers and was buried with his fathers in the city of David, and Jehoram his son became king in his place. ² He had brothers, the sons of Jehoshaphat: Azariah, Jehiel, Zechariah, Azaryahu, Michael and Shephatiah. All these were the sons of Jehoshaphat king of Israel. ³ Their father gave them many gifts of silver, gold and precious things, with fortified cities in Judah, but he gave the kingdom to Jehoram because he was the firstborn.

⁴ Now when Jehoram had taken over the kingdom of his father and made himself secure, he killed all his brothers with the sword, and some of the rulers of Israel also. ⁵ Jehoram *was* thirty-two years old when he became king, and he reigned eight years in Jerusalem. ⁶ He walked in the way of the kings of Israel, just as the house of Ahab did (for Ahab's daughter was his wife), and he did evil in the sight of the LORD. ⁷ Yet the LORD was not willing to destroy the house of David because of the covenant which He had made with David, and since He had promised to give a lamp to him and his sons forever.

⁸ In his days Edom revolted against the rule of Judah and set up a king over themselves. ⁹ Then Jehoram crossed over with his commanders and all his chariots with him. And he arose by night and struck down the Edomites who were surrounding him and the commanders of the chariots. ¹⁰ So Edom

revolted against Judah to this day. Then Libnah revolted at the same time against his rule, because he had forsaken the LORD God of his fathers. ¹¹Moreover, he made high places in the mountains of Judah, and caused the inhabitants of Jerusalem to play the harlot and led Judah astray.

¹²Then a letter came to him from Elijah the prophet saying, "Thus says the LORD God of your father David, 'Because you have not walked in the ways of Jehoshaphat your father and the ways of Asa king of Judah, ¹³but have walked in the way of the kings of Israel, and have caused Judah and the inhabitants of Jerusalem to play the harlot as the house of Ahab played the harlot, and you have also killed your brothers, your own family, who were better than you, ¹⁴behold, the LORD is going to strike your people, your sons, your wives and all your possessions with a great calamity; ¹⁵and you will suffer severe sickness, a disease of your bowels, until your bowels come out because of the sickness, day by day.'"

21:11 led Judah astray. Undoubtedly he was influenced by his marriage to Ahab's daughter (v. 6) and was influenced in the alliance just like his father (2Ch 18:1). They had not learned from Solomon's sinful example (1Ki 11:3–4). His wicked wife, Athaliah, later became ruler over Judah and tried to wipe out David's royal line (2Ch 22:10).

21:12–15 Elijah, best known for his confrontations with Israel's Ahab and Jezebel (1Ki 17—2Ki 2:11), confronted prophetically Jehoram's sins of idolatry and murder (21:13). The consequences from God's judgment extended beyond himself to his family and the nation (21:14–15). This event undoubtedly occurred in the early years of Jehoram's co-regency with his father Jehoshaphat and shortly before Elijah's departure to heaven, ca. 848 B.C. (2Ki 2:11–12).

---

¹⁶Then the LORD stirred up against Jehoram the spirit of the Philistines and the Arabs who bordered the Ethiopians; ¹⁷and they came against Judah and invaded it, and carried away all the possessions found in the king's house together with his sons and his wives, so that no son was left to him except Jehoahaz, the youngest of his sons.

¹⁸So after all this the LORD smote him in his bowels with an incurable sickness. ¹⁹Now it came about in the course of time, at the end of two years, that his bowels came out because of his sickness and he died in great pain. And his people made no fire for him like the fire for his fathers. ²⁰He was thirty-two years old when he became king, and he reigned in Jerusalem eight years; and he departed with no one's regret, and they buried him in the city of David, but not in the tombs of the kings.

22 Then the inhabitants of Jerusalem made Ahaziah, his youngest son, king in his place, for the band of men who came with the Arabs to the camp had slain all the older *sons.* So Ahaziah the son of Jehoram king of Judah began to reign. ²Ahaziah *was* twenty-two years old when he became king, and he reigned one year in Jerusalem. And his mother's name was Athaliah, the granddaughter of Omri. ³He also walked in the ways of the house of Ahab, for his mother was his counselor to do wickedly. ⁴He did evil in the sight of the LORD like the house of Ahab, for they were his counselors after the death of his father, to his destruction. ⁵He also walked according to their counsel, and went with Jehoram the son of Ahab king of Israel to wage war against Hazael king of Aram at Ramothgilead. But the Arameans wounded Joram. ⁶So he returned to be healed in Jezreel of the wounds which they had inflicted on him at Ramah, when he fought against Hazael king of Aram. And Ahaziah, the son of Jehoram king of Judah, went down to see Jehoram the son of Ahab in Jezreel, because he was sick.

⁷Now the destruction of Ahaziah was from God, in that he went to Joram. For when he came, he went out with Jehoram against Jehu the son of Nimshi, whom the LORD had anointed to cut off the house of Ahab. ⁸It came about when Jehu was executing judgment on the house of Ahab, he found the princes of Judah and the sons of Ahaziah's brothers ministering to Ahaziah, and slew them. ⁹He also sought Ahaziah, and they caught him while he was hiding in Samaria; they brought him to Jehu, put him to death and buried him. For they said, "He is the son of Jehoshaphat, who sought the LORD with all his heart." So there was no one of the house of Ahaziah to retain the power of the kingdom.

¹⁰Now when Athaliah the mother of Ahaziah saw that her son was dead, she rose and destroyed all the royal offspring of the house of Judah. ¹¹But Jehoshabeath the king's daughter took Joash the son of Ahaziah, and stole him from among the king's sons who were being put to death, and placed him and

his nurse in the bedroom. So Jehoshabeath, the daughter of King Jehoram, the wife of Jehoiada the priest (for she was the sister of Ahaziah), hid him from Athaliah so that she would not put him to death. ¹²He was hidden with them in the house of God six years while Athaliah reigned over the land.

Psalm 83:1–8

A Song, a Psalm of Asaph.

O God, do not remain quiet;
Do not be silent and,
O God, do not be still.
² For behold, Your enemies
make an uproar,
And those who hate You have
exalted themselves.
³ They make shrewd plans
against Your people,
And conspire together against
Your treasured ones.
⁴ They have said, "Come, and let us
wipe them out as a nation,
That the name of Israel be
remembered no more."

83:4 wipe them out. The hostile nations, under Satan's influence, repudiated God's promise to preserve forever the nation of Israel (Ge 17:7–8; Ps 89:34–37).

---

⁵ For they have conspired
together with one mind;
Against You they make a covenant:
⁶ The tents of Edom and
the Ishmaelites,
Moab and the Hagrites;
⁷ Gebal and Ammon and Amalek,
Philistia with the inhabitants of Tyre;
⁸ Assyria also has joined with them;
They have become a help to the
children of Lot. **Selah**

Proverbs 21:1

21 The king's heart is *like* channels of
water in the hand of the LORD;
He turns it wherever He wishes.

Acts 17:16–34

¹⁶ Now while Paul was waiting for them at Athens, his spirit was being provoked within him as he was observing the city full of idols. ¹⁷ So he was reasoning in the synagogue with the Jews and the God-fearing *Gentiles,* and in the market place every day with those who

happened to be present. ¹⁸ And also some of the Epicurean and Stoic philosophers were conversing with him. Some were saying, "What would this idle babbler wish to say?" Others, "He seems to be a proclaimer of strange deities,"—because he was preaching Jesus and the resurrection. ¹⁹ And they took him and brought him to the Areopagus, saying, "May we know what this new teaching is which you are proclaiming? ²⁰ For you are bringing some strange things to our ears; so we want to know what these things mean." ²¹ (Now all the Athenians and the strangers visiting there used to spend their time in nothing other than telling or hearing something new.)

17:18 Epicurean and Stoic philosophers. Epicurean philosophy taught that the chief end of man was the avoidance of pain. Epicureans were materialists—they did not deny the existence of God, but they believed He did not become involved with the affairs of men. When a person died, they believed his body and soul disintegrated. Stoic philosophy taught self-mastery—that the goal in life was to reach a place of indifference to pleasure or pain. **babbler.** Literally "seed picker." Some of the philosophers viewed Paul as an amateur philosopher—one who had no ideas of his own but only picked among prevailing philosophies and constructed one with no depth.

---

²² So Paul stood in the midst of the Areopagus and said, "Men of Athens, I observe that you are very religious in all respects. ²³ For while I was passing through and examining the objects of your worship, I also found an altar with this inscription,

'TO AN UNKNOWN GOD.'

Therefore what you worship in ignorance, this I proclaim to you. ²⁴ The God who made the world and all things in it, since He is Lord of heaven and earth, does not dwell in temples made with hands; ²⁵ nor is He served by human hands, as though He needed anything, since He Himself gives to all *people* life and breath and all things; ²⁶ and He made from one *man* every nation of mankind to live on all the face of the earth, having determined *their* appointed times and the boundaries of their habitation, ²⁷ that they would seek God, if perhaps they might grope for Him and find

Him, though He is not far from each one of us; ²⁸ for in Him we live and move and exist, as even some of your own poets have said, 'For we also are His children.' ²⁹ Being then the children of God, we ought not to think that the Divine Nature is like gold or silver or stone, an image formed by the art and thought of man. ³⁰ Therefore having overlooked the times of ignorance, God is now declaring to men that all *people* everywhere should repent, ³¹ because He has fixed a day in which He will judge the world in righteousness through a Man whom He has appointed, having furnished proof to all men by raising Him from the dead."

³² Now when they heard of the resurrection of the dead, some *began* to sneer, but others said, "We shall hear you again concerning this." ³³ So Paul went out of their midst. ³⁴ But

17:28 in Him we live and move and exist. A quote from the Cretan poet Epimenides.

17:29 the children of God. A quote from Aratus, who came from Paul's home region of Cilicia. **not...like gold or silver.** If man is the offspring of God, as the Greek poet suggested, it is foolish to think that God could be nothing more than a man-made idol. Such reasoning points out the absurdity of idolatry (Is 44:9–20).

some men joined him and believed, among whom also were Dionysius the Areopagite and a woman named Damaris and others with them.

DAY 13: How did Paul address the philosophers of Athens?

In preaching to them Jesus and the resurrection, Paul was brought to the Areopagus (Ac 17:19). This was a court named for the hill on which it once met. Paul was not being formally tried; only being asked to defend his teaching.

Paul immediately mentioned the inscription on one other object of worship: TO THE UNKNOWN GOD. The Athenians were supernaturalists—they believed in supernatural powers that intervened in the course of natural laws. They at least acknowledged the existence of someone beyond their ability to understand who had made all things. Paul thus had the opportunity to introduce them to the Creator-God who could be known. When evangelizing pagans, Paul started from creation, the general revelation of God (14:15–17). When evangelizing Jews, he started from the Old Testament (vv. 10–13).

Declaring to them the "God who made the world" (v. 24) flatly contradicted both the Epicureans, who believed matter was eternal and therefore had no creator, and the Stoics, who as pantheists believed God was part of everything and could not have created Himself. And adding that "He made from one man every nation of mankind" (v. 26) also confronted them directly. All men are equal in God's sight since all came from one man, Adam. This teaching was a blow to the national pride of the Greeks, who believed all non-Greeks were barbarians. "Having determined their appointed times and the boundaries of their habitation." God sovereignly controls the rise and fall of nations and empires (Da 2:36–45; Lk 21:24). God is responsible for establishing nations as to their racial identity and their specific geographical locations (Dt 32:8) and determining the extent of their conquests (Is. 10:12–15).

God's objective for man in revealing Himself as the creator, ruler, and controller of the world was that they "would seek God" (v. 27). Men have no excuse for not knowing about God because He has revealed Himself in man's conscience and in the physical world (Ro 1:19–20; 2:15).

JULY 14

2 Chronicles 23:1–24:27

23 Now in the seventh year Jehoiada strengthened himself, and took captains of hundreds: Azariah the son of Jeroham, Ishmael the son of Johanan, Azariah the son of Obed, Maaseiah the son of Adaiah, and Elishaphat the son of Zichri, *and they entered* into a covenant with him. ² They went throughout Judah and gathered the Levites from all the cities of Judah, and the heads of the fathers' *households* of Israel, and they came to Jerusalem. ³ Then all the assembly made a covenant with the king in the house of God. And Jehoiada said to them, "Behold, the king's son shall reign, as the LORD has spoken concerning the sons of David. ⁴ This is the thing which you shall do: one third of you, of the priests and Levites who come in on the sabbath, *shall be* gatekeepers, ⁵ and one third *shall be* at the king's house, and a third at the Gate of the Foundation; and all the people *shall be* in the courts of the house of the LORD. ⁶ But let no one enter the house

23:3 as the LORD has spoken. This is one of the most dramatic moments in messianic history. The human offspring of David have been reduced to one—Joash. If he had died, there would have been no human heir to the Davidic throne, and it would have meant the destruction of the line of the Messiah. However, God remedied the situation by providentially protecting Joash (22:10–12) and eliminating Athaliah (23:12–21).

of the LORD except the priests and the ministering Levites; they may enter, for they are holy. And let all the people keep the charge of the LORD. ⁷The Levites will surround the king, each man with his weapons in his hand; and whoever enters the house, let him be killed. Thus be with the king when he comes in and when he goes out."

⁸So the Levites and all Judah did according to all that Jehoiada the priest commanded. And each one of them took his men who were to come in on the sabbath, with those who were to go out on the sabbath, for Jehoiada the priest did not dismiss *any of* the divisions. ⁹Then Jehoiada the priest gave to the captains of hundreds the spears and the large and small shields which had been King David's, which were in the house of God. ¹⁰He stationed all the people, each man with his weapon in his hand, from the right side of the house to the left side of the house, by the altar and by the house, around the king. ¹¹Then they brought out the king's son and put the crown on him, and *gave him* the testimony and made him king. And Jehoiada and his sons anointed him and said, "*Long* live the king!"

¹²When Athaliah heard the noise of the people running and praising the king, she came into the house of the LORD to the people. ¹³She looked, and behold, the king was standing by his pillar at the entrance, and the captains and the trumpeters *were* beside the king. And all the people of the land rejoiced and blew trumpets, the singers with *their* musical instruments leading the praise. Then Athaliah tore her clothes and said, "Treason! Treason!" ¹⁴Jehoiada the priest brought out the captains of hundreds who were appointed over the army and said to them, "Bring her out between the ranks; and whoever follows her, put to death with the sword." For the priest said, "Let her not be put to death in the house of the LORD." ¹⁵So they seized her,

and when she arrived at the entrance of the Horse Gate of the king's house, they put her to death there.

¹⁶Then Jehoiada made a covenant between himself and all the people and the king, that they would be the LORD'S people. ¹⁷And all the people went to the house of Baal and tore it down, and they broke in pieces his altars and his images, and killed Mattan the priest of Baal before the altars. ¹⁸Moreover, Jehoiada placed the offices of the house of the LORD under the authority of the Levitical priests, whom David had assigned over the house of the LORD, to offer the burnt offerings of the LORD, as it is written in the law of Moses— with rejoicing and singing according to the order of David. ¹⁹He stationed the gatekeepers of the house of the LORD, so that no one would enter *who was* in any way unclean. ²⁰He took the captains of hundreds, the nobles, the rulers of the people and all the people of the land, and brought the king down from the house of the LORD, and came through the upper gate to the king's house. And they placed the king upon the royal throne. ²¹So all of the people of the land rejoiced and the city was quiet. For they had put Athaliah to death with the sword.

24 Joash *was* seven years old when he became king, and he reigned forty years in Jerusalem; and his mother's name *was* Zibiah from Beersheba. ²Joash did what was right in the sight of the LORD all the days of Jehoiada the priest. ³Jehoiada took two wives for him, and he became the father of sons and daughters.

⁴Now it came about after this that Joash decided to restore the house of the LORD. ⁵He gathered the priests and Levites and said to them, "Go out to the cities of Judah and collect money from all Israel to repair the house of your God annually, and you shall do the matter quickly." But the Levites did not act quickly. ⁶So the king summoned Jehoiada the chief *priest* and said to him, "Why have you not required the Levites to bring in from Judah and from Jerusalem the levy *fixed by* Moses the servant of the LORD on the congregation of Israel for the tent of the testimony?" ⁷For the sons of the wicked Athaliah had broken into the house of God and even used the holy things of the house of the LORD for the Baals.

⁸So the king commanded, and they made a chest and set it outside by the gate of the house of the LORD. ⁹They made a proclamation in Judah and Jerusalem to bring to the LORD the levy *fixed by* Moses the servant of God on Israel in the wilderness. ¹⁰All

the officers and all the people rejoiced and brought in their levies and dropped *them* into the chest until they had finished. ¹¹It came about whenever the chest was brought in to the king's officer by the Levites, and when they saw that there was much money, then the king's scribe and the chief priest's officer would come, empty the chest, take it, and return it to its place. Thus they did daily and collected much money. ¹²The king and Jehoiada gave it to those who did the work of the service of the house of the LORD; and they hired masons and carpenters to restore the house of the LORD, and also workers in iron and bronze to repair the house of the LORD. ¹³So the workmen labored, and the repair work progressed in their hands, and they restored the house of God according to its specifications and strengthened it. ¹⁴When they had finished, they brought the rest of the money before the king and Jehoiada; and it was made into utensils for the house of the LORD, utensils for the service and the burnt offering, and pans and utensils of gold and silver. And they offered burnt offerings in the house of the LORD continually all the days of Jehoiada.

¹⁵Now when Jehoiada reached a ripe old age he died; he was one hundred and thirty years old at his death. ¹⁶They buried him in the city of David among the kings, because he had done well in Israel and to God and His house.

24:15-16 Jehoiada. This man was the High Priest of Athaliah's and Joash's reigns (2Ch 23:1—24:16), who championed God's cause of righteousness during days of evil by: 1) leading the fight against idols; 2) permitting the coup against Athaliah; and 3) granting the throne to Joash to bring about the subsequent revival.

¹⁷But after the death of Jehoiada the officials of Judah came and bowed down to the king, and the king listened to them. ¹⁸They abandoned the house of the LORD, the God of their fathers, and served the Asherim and the idols; so wrath came upon Judah and Jerusalem for this their guilt. ¹⁹Yet He sent prophets to them to bring them back to the LORD; though they testified against them, they would not listen.

²⁰Then the Spirit of God came on Zechariah the son of Jehoiada the priest; and he stood above the people and said to them, "Thus God has said, 'Why do you transgress the commandments of the LORD and do not prosper? Because you have forsaken the LORD, He has also forsaken you.'" ²¹So they conspired against him and at the command of the king they stoned him to death in the court of the house of the LORD. ²²Thus Joash the king did not remember the kindness which his father Jehoiada had shown him, but he murdered his son. And as he died he said, "May the LORD see and avenge!"

²³Now it happened at the turn of the year that the army of the Arameans came up against him; and they came to Judah and Jerusalem, destroyed all the officials of the people from among the people, and sent all their spoil to the king of Damascus. ²⁴Indeed the army of the Arameans came with a small number of men; yet the LORD delivered a very great army into their hands, because they had forsaken the LORD, the God of their fathers. Thus they executed judgment on Joash.

²⁵When they had departed from him (for they left him very sick), his own servants conspired against him because of the blood of the son of Jehoiada the priest, and murdered him on his bed. So he died, and they buried him in the city of David, but they did not bury him in the tombs of the kings. ²⁶Now these are those who conspired against him: Zabad the son of Shimeath the Ammonitess, and Jehozabad the son of Shimrith the Moabitess. ²⁷As to his sons and the many oracles against him and the rebuilding of the house of God, behold, they are written in the treatise of the Book of the Kings. Then Amaziah his son became king in his place.

Psalm 83:9-18

9 Deal with them as with Midian,
  As with Sisera *and* Jabin at
     the torrent of Kishon,
10 Who were destroyed at En-dor,
  Who became as dung for the ground.
11 Make their nobles like Oreb
     and Zeeb
  And all their princes like
     Zebah and Zalmunna,
12 Who said, "Let us possess
     for ourselves
  The pastures of God."

13 O my God, make them like
     the whirling dust,
  Like chaff before the wind.
14 Like fire that burns the forest
  And like a flame that sets the
     mountains on fire,

¹⁵ So pursue them with Your tempest
And terrify them with Your storm.
¹⁶ Fill their faces with dishonor,
That they may seek Your
name, O LORD.
¹⁷ Let them be ashamed and
dismayed forever,
And let them be humiliated
and perish,
¹⁸ That they may know that You alone,
whose name is the LORD,
Are the Most High over all the earth.

83:18 know…Most High. The purpose of the maledictions against the hostile nations is neither personal nor national, but spiritual: that the nations may know and glorify God. **You alone…the LORD.** The Gentile nations need to know that the God of the Bible is the only God.

Proverbs 21:2–3

² Every man's way is right
in his own eyes,
But the LORD weighs the hearts.
³ To do righteousness and justice
Is desired by the LORD
more than sacrifice.

Acts 18:1–28

18 After these things he left Athens and went to Corinth. ² And he found a Jew named Aquila, a native of Pontus, having recently come from Italy with his wife Priscilla, because Claudius had commanded all the Jews to leave Rome. He came to them, ³ and because he was of the same trade, he stayed with them and they were working, for by trade they were tent-makers. ⁴ And he was reasoning in the synagogue every Sabbath and trying to persuade Jews and Greeks.

⁵ But when Silas and Timothy came down from Macedonia, Paul *began* devoting himself completely to the word, solemnly testifying to the Jews that Jesus was the Christ. ⁶ But when they resisted and blasphemed, he shook out his garments and said to them, "Your blood *be* on your own heads! I am clean. From now on I will go to the Gentiles." ⁷ Then he left there and went to the house of a man named Titius Justus, a worshiper of God, whose house was next to the synagogue. ⁸ Crispus, the leader of the synagogue, believed in the Lord with all his household, and many of the Corinthians when they heard were believing and being baptized. ⁹ And the Lord said to Paul in the night by a vision, "Do not be afraid *any longer,* but go on speaking and do not be silent; ¹⁰ for I am with you, and no man will attack you in order to harm you, for I have many people in this city." ¹¹ And he settled *there* a year and six months, teaching the word of God among them.

¹² But while Gallio was proconsul of Achaia, the Jews with one accord rose up against Paul and brought him before the judgment seat, ¹³ saying, "This man persuades men to worship God contrary to the law." ¹⁴ But when Paul was about to open his mouth, Gallio said to the Jews, "If it were a matter of wrong or of vicious crime, O Jews, it would be reasonable for me to put up with you; ¹⁵ but if there are questions about words and names and your own law, look after it yourselves; I am unwilling to be a judge of these matters." ¹⁶ And he drove them away from the judgment seat. ¹⁷ And they all took hold of Sosthenes, the leader of the synagogue, and *began* beating him in front of the judgment seat. But Gallio was not concerned about any of these things.

18:1 Corinth. The leading political and commercial center in Greece. It was located at a strategic point on the isthmus of Corinth, which connected the Peloponnesian peninsula with the rest of Greece. Virtually all traffic between northern and southern Greece had to pass through the city. Because Corinth was a trade center and host to all sorts of travelers, it had an unsettled population that was extremely debauched. It also housed the temple of Aphrodite, the goddess of love. One thousand temple priestesses, who were ritual prostitutes, came each evening into the city to practice their trade.

18:8 Crispus, the leader of the synagogue. The conversion of this respected leader must have sent shock waves throughout the Jewish community.

18:13 contrary to the law. While Judaism was not an official religion, it was officially tolerated in the Roman world, and Christianity was viewed as a sect of Judaism. The Jews in Corinth claimed that Paul's teaching was external to Judaism, and therefore should be banned. Had Gallio ruled in the Jews' favor, Christianity could have been outlawed throughout the Empire.

[18] Paul, having remained many days longer, took leave of the brethren and put out to sea for Syria, and with him were Priscilla and Aquila. In Cenchrea he had his hair cut, for he was keeping a vow. [19] They came to Ephesus, and he left them there. Now he himself entered the synagogue and reasoned with the Jews. [20] When they asked him to stay for a longer time, he did not consent, [21] but taking leave of them and saying, "I will return to you again if God wills," he set sail from Ephesus. [22] When he had landed at Caesarea, he went up and greeted the church, and went down to Antioch. [23] And having spent some time *there*, he left and passed successively through the Galatian region and Phrygia, strengthening all the disciples.

[24] Now a Jew named Apollos, an Alexandrian by birth, an eloquent man, came to Ephesus; and he was mighty in the Scriptures. [25] This man had been instructed in the way of the Lord; and being fervent in spirit, he was speaking and teaching accurately the things concerning Jesus, being acquainted only with the baptism of John; [26] and he began to speak out boldly in the synagogue. But when Priscilla and Aquila heard him, they took him aside and explained to him the way of God more accurately. [27] And when he wanted to go across to Achaia, the brethren encouraged him and wrote to the disciples to welcome him; and when he had arrived, he greatly helped those who had believed through grace, [28] for he powerfully refuted the Jews in public, demonstrating by the Scriptures that Jesus was the Christ.

DAY 14: How did Aquila and Priscilla help Apollos?

In Acts 18:24, Apollos came to Ephesus and clearly was an Old Testament saint and follower of John the Baptist (v. 25). He came from Alexandria, an important city in Egypt located near the mouth of the Nile. In the first century, it had a large Jewish population. Thus Apollos, though born outside of Israel, was reared in a Jewish cultural setting. It states that he was "mighty in the Scriptures," referring to Apollos's knowledge of the Old Testament Scriptures. That knowledge, combined with his eloquence, allowed him to crush his Jewish opponents in a later debate (v. 28).

He had been instructed in "the way of the Lord" (v. 25). This did not include the Christian faith (v. 26). The Old Testament uses the phrase to describe the spiritual and moral standards God required His people to observe. "Being acquainted only with the baptism of John." Despite his knowledge of the Old Testament, Apollos did not fully understand Christian truth. John's baptism was to prepare Israel for the Messiah's arrival. Apollos accepted that message, even acknowledging that Jesus of Nazareth was Israel's Messiah. He did not, however, understand such basic Christian truths as the significance of Christ's death and resurrection, the ministry of the Holy Spirit, and the church as God's new witness people. He was a redeemed Old Testament believer (v. 24).

Fortunately, Aquila and Priscilla completed Apollos's training in divine truth by instructing him in the fullness of the Christian faith (v. 26). After further instruction, he became a powerful Christian preacher. His ministry profoundly influenced the Corinthians (1Co 1:12). Aquila and Priscilla were a husband and wife team who became Paul's close friends and even risked their lives for him (Ro 16:3–4).

JULY 15

2 Chronicles 25:1–27:9

25 Amaziah was twenty-five years old when he became king, and he reigned twenty-nine years in Jerusalem. And his mother's name was Jehoaddan of Jerusalem. [2] He did right in the sight of the LORD, yet not with a whole heart. [3] Now it came about as soon as the kingdom was firmly in his grasp, that he killed his servants who had slain his father the king. [4] However, he did not put their children to death, but *did* as it is written in the law in the book of Moses, which the LORD commanded, saying, "Fathers shall not be put to death for sons, nor sons be put to death for fathers, but each shall be put to death for his own sin."

[5] Moreover, Amaziah assembled Judah and appointed them according to *their* fathers' households under commanders of thousands and commanders of hundreds throughout Judah and Benjamin; and he took a census of those from twenty years old and upward and found them to be 300,000 choice men, *able* to go to war *and* handle spear and shield. [6] He hired also 100,000 valiant warriors out of Israel for one hundred talents of silver. [7] But a man of God came to him saying, "O king, do

not let the army of Israel go with you, for the LORD is not with Israel *nor with* any of the sons of Ephraim. ⁸ But if you do go, do *it,* be strong for the battle; *yet* God will bring you down before the enemy, for God has power to help and to bring down." ⁹ Amaziah said

25:7 man of God. This is a technical term used about 70 times in the OT, always referring to one who spoke for God. He warned Amaziah not to make idolatrous Israel his ally because the Lord was not with Ephraim, i.e., Israel, the capital of idolatry.

25:8 God has power. The man of God reminded the king sarcastically that he would need to be strong, since God wouldn't help.

to the man of God, "But what *shall we* do for the hundred talents which I have given to the troops of Israel?" And the man of God answered, "The LORD has much more to give you than this." ¹⁰ Then Amaziah dismissed them, the troops which came to him from Ephraim, to go home; so their anger burned against Judah and they returned home in fierce anger.

¹¹ Now Amaziah strengthened himself and led his people forth, and went to the Valley of Salt and struck down 10,000 of the sons of Seir. ¹² The sons of Judah also captured 10,000 alive and brought them to the top of the cliff and threw them down from the top of the cliff, so that they were all dashed to pieces. ¹³ But the troops whom Amaziah sent back from going with him to battle, raided the cities of Judah, from Samaria to Beth-horon, and struck down 3,000 of them and plundered much spoil.

¹⁴ Now after Amaziah came from slaughtering the Edomites, he brought the gods of the sons of Seir, set them up as his gods, bowed down before them and burned incense to them. ¹⁵ Then the anger of the LORD burned against Amaziah, and He sent him a prophet who said to him, "Why have you sought the gods of the people who have not delivered their own people from your hand?" ¹⁶ As he was talking with him, the king said to him, "Have we appointed you a royal counselor? Stop! Why should you be struck down?" Then the prophet stopped and said, "I know that God has planned to destroy you, because you have done this and have not listened to my counsel."

25:14–16 Amaziah did the unthinkable from both a biblical and political perspective—he embraced the false gods of the people whom he had just defeated. Perhaps he did this because he was seduced by the wicked pleasures of idolatry and because he thought it would help him in assuring no future threat from Edom. However, it only brought destruction to the king, who just wanted to silence the voice of God.

¹⁷ Then Amaziah king of Judah took counsel and sent to Joash the son of Jehoahaz the son of Jehu, the king of Israel, saying, "Come, let us face each other." ¹⁸ Joash the king of Israel sent to Amaziah king of Judah, saying, "The thorn bush which was in Lebanon sent to the cedar which was in Lebanon, saying, 'Give your daughter to my son in marriage.' But there passed by a wild beast that was in Lebanon and trampled the thorn bush. ¹⁹ You said, 'Behold, you have defeated Edom.' And your heart has become proud in boasting. Now stay at home; for why should you provoke trouble so that you, even you, would fall and Judah with you?"

²⁰ But Amaziah would not listen, for it was from God, that He might deliver them into the hand *of Joash* because they had sought the gods of Edom. ²¹ So Joash king of Israel went up, and he and Amaziah king of Judah faced each other at Beth-shemesh, which belonged to Judah. ²² Judah was defeated by Israel, and they fled each to his tent. ²³ Then Joash king of Israel captured Amaziah king of Judah, the son of Joash the son of Jehoahaz, at Beth-shemesh, and brought him to Jerusalem and tore down the wall of Jerusalem from the Gate of Ephraim to the Corner Gate, 400 cubits. ²⁴ *He took* all the gold and silver and all the utensils which were found in the house of God with Obed-edom, and the treasures of the king's house, the hostages also, and returned to Samaria.

²⁵ And Amaziah, the son of Joash king of Judah, lived fifteen years after the death of Joash, son of Jehoahaz, king of Israel. ²⁶ Now the rest of the acts of Amaziah, from first to last, behold, are they not written in the Book of the Kings of Judah and Israel? ²⁷ From the time that Amaziah turned away from following the LORD they conspired against him in Jerusalem, and he fled to Lachish; but they sent after him to Lachish and killed him there. ²⁸ Then they brought him on horses

and buried him with his fathers in the city of Judah.

26 And all the people of Judah took Uzziah, who *was* sixteen years old, and made him king in the place of his father Amaziah. ² He built Eloth and restored it to Judah after the king slept with his fathers. ³ Uzziah was sixteen years old when he became king, and he reigned fifty-two years in Jerusalem; and his mother's name was Jechiliah of Jerusalem. ⁴ He did right in the sight of the LORD according to all that his father Amaziah had done. ⁵ He continued to seek God in the days of Zechariah, who had understanding through the vision of God; and as long as he sought the LORD, God prospered him.

⁶ Now he went out and warred against the Philistines, and broke down the wall of Gath and the wall of Jabneh and the wall of Ashdod; and he built cities in *the area of* Ashdod and among the Philistines. ⁷ God helped him against the Philistines, and against the Arabians who lived in Gur-baal, and the Meunites. ⁸ The Ammonites also gave tribute to Uzziah, and his fame extended to the border of Egypt, for he became very strong. ⁹ Moreover, Uzziah built towers in Jerusalem at the Corner Gate and at the Valley Gate and at the corner buttress and fortified them. ¹⁰ He built towers in the wilderness and hewed many cisterns, for he had much livestock, both in the lowland and in the plain. *He also had* plowmen and vinedressers in the hill country and the fertile fields, for he loved the soil. ¹¹ Moreover, Uzziah had an army ready for battle, which entered combat by divisions according to the number of their muster, prepared by Jeiel the scribe and Maaseiah the official, under the direction of Hananiah, one of the king's officers. ¹² The total number of the heads of the households, of valiant warriors, was 2,600. ¹³ Under their direction was an elite army of 307,500, who could wage war with great power, to help the king against the enemy. ¹⁴ Moreover, Uzziah prepared for all the army shields, spears, helmets, body armor, bows and sling stones. ¹⁵ In Jerusalem he made engines *of war* invented by skillful men to be on the towers and on the corners for the purpose of shooting arrows and great stones. Hence his fame spread afar, for he was marvelously helped until he *was* strong.

¹⁶ But when he became strong, his heart was so proud that he acted corruptly, and he was unfaithful to the LORD his God, for he entered the temple of the LORD to burn incense on the altar of incense. ¹⁷ Then Azariah the priest entered after him and with him eighty priests of the LORD, valiant men. ¹⁸ They opposed Uzziah the king and said to him, "It is not for you, Uzziah, to burn incense to the LORD, but for the priests, the sons of Aaron who are consecrated to burn incense. Get out of the sanctuary, for you have been unfaithful and will have no honor from the LORD God." ¹⁹ But Uzziah, with a censer in his hand for burning incense, was enraged; and while he was enraged with the priests, the leprosy broke out on his forehead before the priests in the house of the LORD, beside the altar of incense. ²⁰ Azariah the chief priest and all the priests looked at him, and behold, he *was* leprous on his forehead; and they hurried him out of there, and he himself also hastened to get out because the LORD had smitten him. ²¹ King Uzziah was a leper to the day of his death; and he lived in a separate house, being a leper, for he was cut off from the house of the LORD. And Jotham his son *was* over the king's house judging the people of the land.

²² Now the rest of the acts of Uzziah, first to last, the prophet Isaiah, the son of Amoz, has written. ²³ So Uzziah slept with his fathers, and they buried him with his fathers in the field of the grave which belonged to the kings, for they said, "He is a leper." And Jotham his son became king in his place.

27 Jotham was twenty-five years old when he became king, and he reigned sixteen years in Jerusalem. And his mother's name was Jerushah the daughter of Zadok. ² He did right in the sight of the LORD, according to all that his father Uzziah had done; however he did not enter the temple of the LORD. But the people continued acting corruptly. ³ He built the upper gate of the house of the LORD, and he built extensively the wall of Ophel. ⁴ Moreover, he built cities in the hill country of Judah, and he built fortresses and towers on the wooded *hills*. ⁵ He fought also with the king of the Ammonites and prevailed over them so that the Ammonites gave him during that year one hundred talents of silver, ten thousand kors of wheat and ten thousand of barley. The Ammonites also paid him this *amount* in the second and in the third year. ⁶ So Jotham became mighty because he ordered his ways before the LORD his God. ⁷ Now the rest of the acts of Jotham, even all his wars and his acts, behold, they are written in the Book of the Kings of Israel and Judah. ⁸ He was twenty-five years old when he became king, and he reigned sixteen years in Jerusalem. ⁹ And Jotham slept with his fathers, and they buried him in the city of David; and Ahaz his son became king in his place.

Psalm 84:1-7

For the choir director; on the Gittith.
A Psalm of the sons of Korah.

How lovely are Your dwelling
     places,
  O LORD of hosts!
2 My soul longed and even yearned
     for the courts of the LORD;
  My heart and my flesh sing
     for joy to the living God.
3 The bird also has found a house,
  And the swallow a nest for
     herself, where she may
     lay her young,
  Even Your altars, O LORD of
     hosts,
  My King and my God.
4 How blessed are those who
     dwell in Your house!
  They are ever praising You.   Selah

5 How blessed is the man whose
     strength is in You,
  In whose heart are the
     highways to Zion!
6 Passing through the valley of
     Baca they make it a spring;
  The early rain also covers
     it with blessings.
7 They go from strength to
     strength,
  Every one of them appears
     before God in Zion.

Proverbs 21:4-5

4 Haughty eyes and a proud
     heart,
  The lamp of the wicked, is sin.
5 The plans of the diligent lead
     surely to advantage,
  But everyone who is hasty
     comes surely to poverty.

Acts 19:1-20

19 It happened that while Apollos was at Corinth, Paul passed through the upper country and came to Ephesus, and found some disciples. 2 He said to them, "Did you receive the Holy Spirit when you believed?" And they said to him, "No, we have not even heard whether there is a Holy Spirit." 3 And he said, "Into what then were you baptized?" And they said, "Into John's baptism." 4 Paul said, "John baptized with the baptism of repentance, telling the people to believe in Him

who was coming after him, that is, in Jesus." 5 When they heard this, they were baptized in the name of the Lord Jesus. 6 And when Paul had laid his hands upon them, the Holy Spirit came on them, and they began speaking with tongues and prophesying. 7 There were in all about twelve men.

8 And he entered the synagogue and continued speaking out boldly for three months, reasoning and persuading them about the kingdom of God. 9 But when some were becoming hardened and disobedient, speaking evil of the Way before the people, he withdrew from them and took away the disciples, reasoning daily in the school of Tyrannus. 10 This took place for two years, so that all who lived in Asia heard the word of the Lord, both Jews and Greeks.

11 God was performing extraordinary miracles by the hands of Paul, 12 so that handkerchiefs or aprons were even carried from his body to the sick, and the diseases left them and the evil spirits went out. 13 But also some of the Jewish exorcists, who went from place to place, attempted to name over those who had the evil spirits the name of the Lord Jesus, saying, "I adjure you by Jesus whom Paul preaches." 14 Seven sons of one Sceva, a Jewish chief priest, were doing this. 15 And the evil spirit answered and said to them, "I recognize Jesus, and I know about Paul, but who are you?" 16 And the man, in whom was the evil spirit, leaped on them and subdued all of them and overpowered them, so that they fled out of that house naked and wounded. 17 This became known to all, both Jews and Greeks, who lived in Ephesus; and

19:13 Jewish exorcists. Simon Magus (8:9–25) and Bar-Jesus (13:6–12) were other possible examples of such charlatans (Mt 12:27). In contrast to the absolute authority exercised by Jesus and the apostles over demons, those exorcists sought to expel the demons by attempting to call on a more potent spirit being—in this case the Lord Jesus.

19:15 recognize Jesus, and I know about Paul. Recognizing that the exorcists had no authority over him (unlike Jesus and Paul), the demon rejected their attempt to expel him from his victim. This confirms that the power to cast out demons belonged to Jesus and the apostles and no one else. Even the demons give testimony to that.

fear fell upon them all and the name of the Lord Jesus was being magnified. ¹⁸ Many also of those who had believed kept coming, confessing and disclosing their practices. ¹⁹ And many of those who practiced magic brought their books together and *began* burning them in the sight of everyone; and they counted up the price of them and found it fifty thousand pieces of silver. ²⁰ So the word of the Lord was growing mightily and prevailing.

19:19 books. Of secret magical spells. Burning them proved the genuineness of the magicians' repentance. Having destroyed these books, they could not easily resume their practices. **fifty thousand pieces of silver.** Fifty thousand days' wages for a common laborer—an astonishing sum of money given to indicate how widespread the practice of magic was in Ephesus.

DAY 15: How could the "disciples" of Acts 19:1 not have received the Holy Spirit?

Coming to Ephesus, Paul found "some disciples." They were of John the Baptist (v. 3), hence Old Testament seekers. That they did not yet fully understand the Christian faith is evident from their reply to Paul's question (v. 2). The word "disciple" means "learner," or "follower," and does not always refer to Christians (Mt 9:14; 11:2; Mk 2:18; Lk 5:33; 7:18–19; 11:1; Jn 1:35; 6:66). Followers of John the Baptist, like this group, existed into the second century.

"Did you receive the Holy Spirit when you believed?" (v. 2). The question reflects Paul's uncertainty about their spiritual status. Since all Christians receive the Holy Spirit at the moment of salvation, their answer revealed they were not yet fully Christians. They had not yet received Christian baptism (having been baptized only "into John's baptism"), which further evidenced that they were not Christians. These disciples did not realize Jesus of Nazareth was the One to whom John's baptism pointed. Paul gave them instruction not on how to receive the Spirit, but about Jesus Christ. "They were baptized in the name of the Lord Jesus" (v. 5). They believed Paul's presentation of the gospel and came to saving faith in the Lord Jesus Christ (2:41). Although required of all Christians, baptism does not save.

Then "Paul...laid his hands upon them" (v. 6). This signified their inclusion into the church. Apostles were also present when the church was born (chap. 2), and when the Samaritans (chap. 8) and Gentiles (chap. 10) were included. In each case, God's purpose was to emphasize the unity of the church. And they "began speaking with tongues and prophesying." This served as proof that they were part of the church. They also needed tangible evidence that the Holy Spirit now indwelt them, since they had not heard that He had come (v. 2).

JULY 16

2 Chronicles 28:1–29:36

28 Ahaz *was* twenty years old when he became king, and he reigned sixteen years in Jerusalem; and he did not do right in the sight of the LORD as David his father *had* done. ² But he walked in the ways of the kings of Israel; he also made molten images for the Baals. ³ Moreover, he burned incense in the valley of Ben-hinnom and burned his sons in fire, according to the abominations of the nations whom the LORD had driven out before the sons of Israel. ⁴ He sacrificed and burned incense on the high places, on the hills and under every green tree.

⁵ Wherefore, the LORD his God delivered him into the hand of the king of Aram; and they defeated him and carried away from him a great number of captives and brought *them* to Damascus. And he was also delivered into the hand of the king of Israel, who inflicted

him with heavy casualties. ⁶ For Pekah the son of Remaliah slew in Judah 120,000 in one day, all valiant men, because they had forsaken the LORD God of their fathers. ⁷ And Zichri, a mighty man of Ephraim, slew Maaseiah the king's son and Azrikam the ruler of the house and Elkanah the second to the king.

⁸ The sons of Israel carried away captive of their brethren 200,000 women, sons and daughters; and they took also a great deal of

28:9 Oded. An otherwise unknown prophet, with the same name as an earlier Oded (15:1, 8). The prophet said that Israel had won the victory because God was judging Judah. But he protested the viciousness of the killing and the effort to enslave them (v. 10) and warned them of God's wrath for such action (v. 11). Amazingly the apostate and hostile Israelites complied with the prophet's warning (vv. 12–15).

spoil from them, and brought the spoil to Samaria. ⁹But a prophet of the LORD was there, whose name *was* Oded; and he went out to meet the army which came to Samaria and said to them, "Behold, because the LORD, the God of your fathers, was angry with Judah, He has delivered them into your hand, and you have slain them in a rage *which* has even reached heaven. ¹⁰Now you are proposing to subjugate for yourselves the people of Judah and Jerusalem for male and female slaves. Surely, *do* you not *have* transgressions of your own against the LORD your God? ¹¹Now therefore, listen to me and return the captives whom you captured from your brothers, for the burning anger of the LORD is against you." ¹²Then some of the heads of the sons of Ephraim—Azariah the son of Johanan, Berechiah the son of Meshillemoth, Jehizkiah the son of Shallum, and Amasa the son of Hadlai—arose against those who were coming from the battle, ¹³and said to them, "You must not bring the captives in here, for you are proposing *to bring* upon us guilt against the LORD adding to our sins and our guilt; for our guilt is great so that *His* burning anger is against Israel." ¹⁴So the armed men left the captives and the spoil before the officers and all the assembly. ¹⁵Then the men who were designated by name arose, took the captives, and they clothed all their naked ones from the spoil; and they gave them clothes and sandals, fed them and gave them drink, anointed them *with oil*, led all their feeble ones on donkeys, and brought them to Jericho, the city of palm trees, to their brothers; then they returned to Samaria.

¹⁶At that time King Ahaz sent to the kings of Assyria for help. ¹⁷For again the Edomites had come and attacked Judah and carried away captives. ¹⁸The Philistines also had invaded the cities of the lowland and of the Negev of Judah, and had taken Beth-shemesh, Aijalon, Gederoth, and Soco with its villages, Timnah with its villages, and Gimzo with its villages, and they settled there. ¹⁹For the LORD humbled Judah because of Ahaz king of Israel, for he had brought about a lack of restraint in Judah and was very unfaithful to the LORD. ²⁰So Tilgath-pilneser king of Assyria came against him and afflicted him instead of strengthening him. ²¹Although Ahaz took a portion out of the house of the LORD and out of the palace of the king and of the princes, and gave *it* to the king of Assyria, it did not help him.

²²Now in the time of his distress this same King Ahaz became yet more unfaithful to the LORD. ²³For he sacrificed to the gods of Damascus which had defeated him, and said, "Because the gods of the kings of Aram helped them, I will sacrifice to them that they may help me." But they became the downfall of him and all Israel. ²⁴Moreover, when Ahaz gathered together the utensils of the house of God, he cut the utensils of the house of God in pieces; and he closed the doors of the house of the LORD and made altars for himself in every corner of Jerusalem. ²⁵In every city of Judah he made high places to burn incense to other gods, and provoked the LORD, the God of his fathers, to anger. ²⁶Now the rest of his acts and all his ways, from first to last, behold, they are written in the Book of the Kings of Judah and Israel. ²⁷So Ahaz slept with his fathers, and they buried him in the city, in Jerusalem, for they did not bring him into the tombs of the kings of Israel; and Hezekiah his son reigned in his place.

29 Hezekiah became king *when he was* twenty-five years old; and he reigned twenty-nine years in Jerusalem. And his mother's name *was* Abijah, the daughter of Zechariah. ²He did right in the sight of the LORD, according to all that his father David had done.

³In the first year of his reign, in the first month, he opened the doors of the house of the LORD and repaired them. ⁴He brought

---

29:3 first year...first month. Hezekiah addressed the spiritual problems first, which reflected his life priorities. Hezekiah correctly diagnosed Judah's ills—she had abandoned the true worship of God. So the king stepped in to reverse the policy of his father (28:22–25) and to repair the temple and return proper temple worship as God had prescribed in His Word (vv. 3–7). He knew such a revival of devotion to God would turn God's wrath away from Judah (v. 10).

---

in the priests and the Levites and gathered them into the square on the east. ⁵Then he said to them, "Listen to me, O Levites. Consecrate yourselves now, and consecrate the house of the LORD, the God of your fathers, and carry the uncleanness out from the holy place. ⁶For our fathers have been unfaithful and have done evil in the sight of the LORD our God, and have forsaken Him and turned their faces away from the dwelling place of the LORD, and have turned *their* backs. ⁷They have also shut the doors of the porch and put out the lamps, and have not burned incense or offered burnt offerings in the holy place to the God of Israel. ⁸ Therefore the wrath of the LORD was against Judah and Jerusalem, and He has made them an object of terror, of horror, and of hissing, as you see with your own eyes. ⁹ For behold, our fathers have fallen by the sword, and our sons and our daughters and our wives are in captivity for this. ¹⁰ Now it is in my heart to make a covenant with the LORD God of Israel, that His burning anger may turn away from us. ¹¹ My sons, do not be negligent now, for the LORD has chosen you to stand before Him, to minister to Him, and to be His ministers and burn incense."

¹² Then the Levites arose: Mahath, the son of Amasai and Joel the son of Azariah, from the sons of the Kohathites; and from the sons of Merari, Kish the son of Abdi and Azariah the son of Jehallelel; and from the Gershonites, Joah the son of Zimmah and Eden the son of Joah; ¹³ and from the sons of Elizaphan, Shimri and Jeiel; and from the sons of Asaph, Zechariah and Mattaniah; ¹⁴ and from the sons of Heman, Jehiel and Shimei; and from the sons of Jeduthun, Shemaiah and Uzziel. ¹⁵ They assembled their brothers, consecrated themselves, and went in to cleanse the house of the LORD, according to the commandment of the king by the words of the LORD. ¹⁶ So the priests went in to the inner part of the house of the LORD to cleanse it, and every unclean thing which they found in the temple of the LORD they brought out to the court of the house of the LORD. Then the Levites received it to carry out to the Kidron valley. ¹⁷ Now they began the consecration on the first *day* of the first month, and on the eighth day of the month they entered the porch of the LORD. Then they consecrated the house of the LORD in eight days, and finished on the sixteenth day of the first month. ¹⁸ Then they went in to King Hezekiah and said, "We have cleansed the whole house of the LORD, the altar of burnt offering with all of its utensils, and the table of showbread with all of its utensils. ¹⁹ Moreover, all the utensils which King Ahaz had discarded during his reign in his unfaithfulness, we have prepared and consecrated; and behold, they are before the altar of the LORD."

²⁰ Then King Hezekiah arose early and assembled the princes of the city and went up to the house of the LORD. ²¹ They brought seven bulls, seven rams, seven lambs and seven male goats for a sin offering for the kingdom, the sanctuary, and Judah. And he ordered the priests, the sons of Aaron, to offer *them* on the altar of the LORD. ²² So they slaughtered the bulls, and the priests took the blood and sprinkled it on the altar. They also slaughtered the rams and sprinkled the blood on the altar; they slaughtered the lambs also and sprinkled the blood on the altar. ²³ Then they brought the male goats of the sin offering before the king and the assembly, and they laid their hands on them. ²⁴ The priests slaughtered them and purged the altar with their blood to atone for all Israel, for the king ordered the burnt offering and the sin offering for all Israel.

²⁵ He then stationed the Levites in the house of the LORD with cymbals, with harps and with lyres, according to the command of David and of Gad the king's seer, and of Nathan the prophet; for the command was from the LORD through His prophets. ²⁶ The Levites stood with the *musical* instruments of David, and the priests with the trumpets. ²⁷ Then Hezekiah gave the order to offer the burnt offering on the altar. When the burnt offering began, the song to the LORD also began with the trumpets, *accompanied* by the instruments of David, king of Israel. ²⁸ While the whole assembly worshiped, the singers also sang and the trumpets sounded; all this *continued* until the burnt offering was finished.

²⁹ Now at the completion of the burnt offerings, the king and all who were present with him bowed down and worshiped. ³⁰ Moreover, King Hezekiah and the officials ordered the Levites to sing praises to the LORD with the words of David and Asaph the seer. So they sang praises with joy, and bowed down and worshiped.

³¹ Then Hezekiah said, "Now *that* you have consecrated yourselves to the LORD, come near and bring sacrifices and thank offerings to the house of the LORD." And the assembly brought sacrifices and thank offerings, and all those who were willing *brought* burnt offerings. ³² The number of the burnt offerings which the assembly brought was 70 bulls, 100 rams, and 200 lambs; all these were for a burnt offering to the LORD. ³³ The consecrated things were 600 bulls and 3,000 sheep. ³⁴ But the priests were too few, so that they were unable to skin all the burnt offerings; therefore their brothers the Levites helped them until the work was completed and until the *other* priests had consecrated themselves. For the Levites were more conscientious to consecrate themselves than the priests. ³⁵ There *were* also many burnt offerings with the fat

of the peace offerings and with the libations for the burnt offerings. Thus the service of the house of the LORD was established *again*. ³⁶Then Hezekiah and all the people rejoiced over what God had prepared for the people, because the thing came about suddenly.

Psalm 84:8-12

⁸ O LORD God of hosts, hear my prayer;
　　Give ear, O God of Jacob! 　　　*Selah*
⁹ Behold our shield, O God,
　　And look upon the face of
　　　Your anointed.

84:9 Behold our shield. A metaphor for the king, who also would have participated in a festival at the temple (Ps 47:9; Hos 4:18). **the face of Your anointed.** The king is regularly described as God's "anointed" (Pss 2:2; 18:50; 20:6; 28:8; 89:38, 51). The psalmist thus prays that God would look upon the king with favor, blessing his reign with prosperity.

¹⁰ For a day in Your courts is better
　　than a thousand *outside*.
　I would rather stand at the threshold
　　of the house of my God
　Than dwell in the tents of wickedness.
¹¹ For the LORD God is a sun and shield;
　　The LORD gives grace and glory;
　　No good thing does He withhold
　　　from those who walk uprightly.
¹² O LORD of hosts,
　　How blessed is the man
　　　who trusts in You!

Proverbs 21:6-8

⁶ The acquisition of treasures
　　by a lying tongue
　Is a fleeting vapor, the
　　pursuit of death.
⁷ The violence of the wicked
　　will drag them away,
　Because they refuse to
　　act with justice.
⁸ The way of a guilty man is crooked,
　　But as for the pure, his
　　　conduct is upright.

Acts 19:21-41

²¹Now after these things were finished, Paul purposed in the Spirit to go to Jerusalem after he had passed through Macedonia and Achaia, saying, "After I have been there, I must also see Rome." ²²And having sent into

19:21 I must also see Rome. Paul had not visited the Imperial capital, but because of the strategic importance of the church there, he could stay away no longer. In addition, Paul intended to use Rome as a jumping-off point for ministry in the strategic region of Spain (Ro 15:22–24). This simple declaration marked a turning point in Acts; from this point on, Rome became Paul's goal. He would ultimately arrive there as a Roman prisoner (28:16).

Macedonia two of those who ministered to him, Timothy and Erastus, he himself stayed in Asia for a while.

²³About that time there occurred no small disturbance concerning the Way. ²⁴For a man named Demetrius, a silversmith, who made silver shrines of Artemis, was bringing no little business to the craftsmen; ²⁵these he gathered together with the workmen of similar *trades,* and said, "Men, you know that our prosperity depends upon this business. ²⁶You see and hear that not only in Ephesus, but in almost all of Asia, this Paul has persuaded and turned away a considerable number of people, saying that gods made with hands are no gods *at all*. ²⁷Not only is there danger that this trade of ours fall into disrepute, but also that the temple of the great goddess Artemis be regarded as worthless and that she whom all of Asia and the world worship will even be dethroned from her magnificence."

²⁸When they heard *this* and were filled with rage, they *began* crying out, saying, "Great is Artemis of the Ephesians!" ²⁹The city was filled with the confusion, and they rushed with one accord into the theater, dragging along Gaius and Aristarchus, Paul's traveling companions from Macedonia. ³⁰And when Paul wanted to go into the assembly, the disciples would not let him. ³¹Also some of the Asiarchs who were friends of his sent to him and repeatedly urged him

19:31 Asiarchs. These members of the aristocracy were dedicated to promoting Roman interests. Though only one Asiarch ruled at a time, they bore the title for life. That such powerful, influential men were Paul's friends shows that they did not regard him or his message as criminal. Hence, there was no legitimate cause for the riot.

not to venture into the theater. ³²So then, some were shouting one thing and some another, for the assembly was in confusion and the majority did not know for what reason they had come together. ³³Some of the crowd concluded *it was* Alexander, since the Jews had put him forward; and having motioned with his hand, Alexander was intending to make a defense to the assembly. ³⁴But when they recognized that he was a Jew, a *single*

19:33 Alexander. Probably not the false teacher later active at Ephesus (1Ti 1:20), or the individual who opposed Paul at Rome (2Ti 4:14), since the name was common. He was either a Christian Jew or a spokesman for Ephesus' Jewish community. Either way, the Jews' motive for putting him forward was the same—to disassociate themselves from the Christians and avoid a massacre of the Jews. **make a defense.** Either of the Christians, or the Jews, depending on which group he represented.

outcry arose from them all as they shouted for about two hours, "Great is Artemis of the Ephesians!" ³⁵After quieting the crowd, the town clerk *said, "Men of Ephesus, what man is there after all who does not know that the city of the Ephesians is guardian of the temple of the great Artemis and of the *image* which fell down from heaven? ³⁶So, since these are undeniable facts, you ought to keep calm and to do nothing rash. ³⁷For you have brought these men *here* who are neither robbers of temples nor blasphemers of our goddess. ³⁸So then, if Demetrius and the craftsmen who are with him have a complaint against any man, the courts are in session and proconsuls are *available;* let them bring charges against one another. ³⁹But if you want anything beyond this, it shall be settled in the lawful assembly. ⁴⁰For indeed we are in danger of being accused of a riot in connection with today's events, since there is no *real* cause *for it,* and in this connection we will be unable to account for this disorderly gathering." ⁴¹After saying this he dismissed the assembly.

DAY 16: How profound an impact can the gospel have on a society?

Reading Acts 19:1–20, it is clear that the gospel made a tremendous impact on Ephesus. Paul's two years of ministry here along with "extraordinary miracles," the very public deliverance of a man from an evil spirit, and burning of magic books had left their mark. "So the word of the Lord was growing mightily and prevailing" (v. 20).

So much so that Demetrius, a silversmith, took action against them. He was a maker of "silver shrines of Artemis" (v. 24), the goddess Artemis (also known as Diana). These shrines were used as household idols and in the worship at the temple of Diana. Worship of her, centered at the great temple of Diana at Ephesus (one of the Seven Wonders of the Ancient World), was widespread throughout the Roman Empire. It is likely that the riot described in this passage took place during the annual spring festival held in her honor at Ephesus. The statement "was bringing no little business" suggests Demetrius may have been the head of the silversmiths' guild—which would explain his taking the lead in opposing the Christian preachers.

Demetrius cleverly played upon his hearers' fears of financial ruin, religious zeal, and concern for their city's prestige. The Christian preachers, he argued, threatened the continued prosperity of Ephesus. His audience's violent reaction shows they took the threat seriously (v. 28). That was the impact of the gospel on their daily lives. The frenzied mob gathered in the theater clearly threatened the lives of Gaius and Aristarchus because of their role in the delivery of the Christian message.

JULY 17

2 Chronicles 30:1–31:21

30 Now Hezekiah sent to all Israel and Judah and wrote letters also to Ephraim and Manasseh, that they should come to the house of the LORD at Jerusalem to celebrate the Passover to the LORD God of Israel. ²For the king and his princes and

all the assembly in Jerusalem had decided to celebrate the Passover in the second month, ³since they could not celebrate it at that time, because the priests had not consecrated themselves in sufficient numbers, nor had the people been gathered to Jerusalem. ⁴Thus the thing was right in the sight of the king and all the assembly. ⁵So they established a decree to circulate a proclamation throughout all Israel from Beersheba even to Dan, that they should come to celebrate the Passover to the LORD God of Israel at Jerusalem. For they had not celebrated *it* in great numbers as it was prescribed. [6] The couriers went throughout all Israel and Judah with the letters from the hand of the king and his princes, even according to the command of the king, saying, "O sons of Israel, return to the LORD God of Abraham, Isaac and Israel, that He may return to those of you who escaped *and* are left from the hand of the kings of Assyria. [7] Do

30:6 return. The nation was required by law to annually celebrate 3 feasts in Jerusalem: 1) Passover; 2) Weeks, or Pentecost; and 3) Booths, or Tabernacles (Ex 23; Lv 23; Nu 28–29; Dt 16). God would have returned to bless the people of the northern apostate and idolatrous kingdom of Israel if they had returned to Him.

not be like your fathers and your brothers, who were unfaithful to the LORD God of their fathers, so that He made them a horror, as you see. [8] Now do not stiffen your neck like your fathers, but yield to the LORD and enter His sanctuary which He has consecrated forever, and serve the LORD your God, that His burning anger may turn away from you. [9] For if you return to the LORD, your brothers and your sons *will find* compassion before those who led them captive and will return to this land. For the LORD your God is gracious and compassionate, and will not turn *His* face away from you if you return to Him."

[10] So the couriers passed from city to city through the country of Ephraim and Manasseh, and as far as Zebulun, but they laughed them to scorn and mocked them. [11] Nevertheless some men of Asher, Manasseh and Zebulun humbled themselves and came to Jerusalem. [12] The hand of God was also on Judah to give them one heart to do what the king and the princes commanded by the word of the LORD.

[13] Now many people were gathered at Jerusalem to celebrate the Feast of Unleavened Bread in the second month, a very large assembly. [14] They arose and removed the altars which *were* in Jerusalem; they also removed all the incense altars and cast *them* into the brook Kidron. [15] Then they slaughtered the Passover *lambs* on the fourteenth of the second month. And the priests and Levites were ashamed of themselves, and consecrated themselves and brought burnt

offerings to the house of the LORD. [16] They stood at their stations after their custom, according to the law of Moses the man of God; the priests sprinkled the blood *which they received* from the hand of the Levites. [17] For *there were* many in the assembly who had not consecrated themselves; therefore, the Levites *were* over the slaughter of the Passover *lambs* for everyone who *was* unclean, in order to consecrate *them* to the LORD. [18] For a multitude of the people, *even* many from Ephraim and Manasseh, Issachar and Zebulun, had not purified themselves, yet they ate the Passover otherwise than prescribed. For Hezekiah prayed for them, saying, "May the good LORD pardon [19] everyone who prepares his heart to seek God, the LORD God of his fathers, though not according to the purification *rules* of the sanctuary." [20] So the LORD heard Hezekiah and healed the people. [21] The sons of Israel present in Jerusalem celebrated the Feast of Unleavened Bread *for* seven days with great joy, and the Levites and the priests praised the LORD day after day with loud instruments to the LORD. [22] Then Hezekiah spoke encouragingly to all the Levites who showed good insight *in the things* of the LORD. So they ate for the appointed seven days, sacrificing peace offerings and giving thanks to the LORD God of their fathers.

[23] Then the whole assembly decided to celebrate *the feast* another seven days, so they celebrated the seven days with joy. [24] For Hezekiah king of Judah had contributed to the assembly 1,000 bulls and 7,000 sheep, and the princes had contributed to the assembly 1,000 bulls and 10,000 sheep; and a large number of priests consecrated themselves. [25] All the assembly of Judah rejoiced, with the priests and the Levites and all the assembly that came from Israel, both the sojourners who came from the land of Israel and those living in Judah. [26] So there was great joy in Jerusalem, because there was nothing like this in Jerusalem since the days of Solomon

30:1–27 Hezekiah reached back to restore the Passover (Ex 12:1–20; Lv 23:1–8) which apparently had not been properly and regularly observed in some time, perhaps since the division of the kingdom 215 years earlier (v. 5). The Passover would later be revived again by Josiah (2Ch 35:1–9) and Zerubbabel (Ezr 6:19–22). It celebrated God's forgiveness and redemption of His believing people.

30:26 nothing like this. A telling statement about the spiritual degeneracy of the divided kingdom since the time of Solomon over 215 years earlier.

the son of David, king of Israel. ²⁷Then the Levitical priests arose and blessed the people; and their voice was heard and their prayer came to His holy dwelling place, to heaven.

31 Now when all this was finished, all Israel who were present went out to the cities of Judah, broke the pillars in pieces, cut down the Asherim and pulled down the high places and the altars throughout all Judah and Benjamin, as well as in Ephraim and Manasseh, until they had destroyed them all. Then all the sons of Israel returned to their cities, each to his possession.

²And Hezekiah appointed the divisions of the priests and the Levites by their divisions, each according to his service, *both* the priests and the Levites, for burnt offerings and for peace offerings, to minister and to give thanks and to praise in the gates of the camp of the LORD. ³*He* also *appointed* the king's portion of his goods for the burnt offerings, *namely,* for the morning and evening burnt offerings, and the burnt offerings for the sabbaths and for the new moons and for the fixed festivals, as it is written in the law of the LORD. ⁴Also he commanded the people who lived in Jerusalem to give the portion due to the priests and the Levites, that they might devote themselves to the law of the LORD. ⁵As soon as the order spread, the sons of Israel provided in abundance the first fruits of grain, new wine, oil, honey and of all the produce of the field; and they brought in abundantly the tithe of all. ⁶The sons of Israel and Judah who lived in the cities of Judah also brought in the tithe of oxen and sheep, and the tithe of sacred gifts which were consecrated to the LORD their God, and placed *them* in heaps. ⁷In the third month they began to make the heaps, and finished *them* by the seventh month. ⁸When Hezekiah and the rulers came and saw the heaps, they blessed the LORD and His people Israel. ⁹Then Hezekiah questioned the priests and the Levites concerning the heaps. ¹⁰Azariah the chief priest of the house of Zadok said to him, "Since the contributions began to be brought into the house of the LORD, we have had enough to eat with plenty left over, for the LORD has blessed His people, and this great quantity is left over."

31:6 tithe. Since the priests and Levites served the nation, they were to be supported by the people through the taxation of the tithe. According to Leviticus 27:30–33 and Numbers 18:21, 24, the people were to give the tenth (tithe) to supply all the needs of the Levites. Malachi 3:8 says they were robbing God when they did not give the tithe. Deuteronomy 12:6–7 called for a second tithe that was to support the nation's devotion to the temple by being used for the national festivals at the temple in Jerusalem. This was called the festival tithe. Deuteronomy 14:28–29 called for a third tithe every 3 years for the poor. The sum of this tax plan totaled about 23 percent annually.

¹¹Then Hezekiah commanded *them* to prepare rooms in the house of the LORD, and they prepared *them.* ¹²They faithfully brought in the contributions and the tithes and the consecrated things; and Conaniah the Levite *was* the officer in charge of them and his brother Shimei *was* second. ¹³Jehiel, Azaziah, Nahath, Asahel, Jerimoth, Jozabad, Eliel, Ismachiah, Mahath and Benaiah *were* overseers under the authority of Conaniah and Shimei his brother by the appointment of King Hezekiah, and Azariah *was* the *chief* officer of the house of God. ¹⁴Kore the son of Imnah the Levite, the keeper of the eastern *gate, was* over the freewill offerings of God, to apportion the contributions for the LORD and the most holy things. ¹⁵Under his authority *were* Eden, Miniamin, Jeshua, Shemaiah, Amariah and Shecaniah in the cities of the priests, to distribute faithfully *their portions* to their brothers by divisions, whether great or small, ¹⁶without regard to their genealogical enrollment, to the males from thirty years old and upward—everyone who entered the house of the LORD for his daily obligations— for their work in their duties according to their divisions; ¹⁷as well as the priests who were enrolled genealogically according to their fathers' households, and the Levites from twenty years old and upwards, by their duties *and* their divisions. ¹⁸The genealogical enrollment *included* all their little children, their wives, their sons and their daughters, for the whole assembly, for they consecrated themselves faithfully in holiness. ¹⁹Also for the sons of Aaron the priests *who were* in the pasture lands of their cities, or in each and every city, *there were* men who were designated by name to distribute portions to every male among the priests and to ev-

eryone genealogically enrolled among the Levites.

²⁰ Thus Hezekiah did throughout all Judah; and he did what *was* good, right and true before the LORD his God. ²¹ Every work which he began in the service of the house of God in law and in commandment, seeking his God, he did with all his heart and prospered.

Psalm 85:1–7

For the choir director. A Psalm
of the sons of Korah.

O LORD, You showed favor
to Your land;
You restored the captivity of Jacob.
² You forgave the iniquity
of Your people;
You covered all their sin.   *Selah*
³ You withdrew all Your fury;
You turned away from Your
burning anger.

⁴ Restore us, O God of our salvation,
And cause Your indignation
toward us to cease.
⁵ Will You be angry with us forever?
Will You prolong Your anger
to all generations?
⁶ Will You not Yourself revive us again,
That Your people may rejoice in You?
⁷ Show us Your lovingkindness,
O LORD,
And grant us Your salvation.

Proverbs 21:9–11

⁹ It is better to live in a corner of a roof
Than in a house shared with
a contentious woman.
¹⁰ The soul of the wicked desires evil;
His neighbor finds no
favor in his eyes.
¹¹ When the scoffer is punished,
the naive becomes wise;
But when the wise is instructed,
he receives knowledge.

Acts 20:1–16

20 After the uproar had ceased, Paul sent for the disciples, and when he had exhorted them and taken his leave of them, he left to go to Macedonia. ²When he had gone through those districts and had given them much exhortation, he came to Greece. ³And *there* he spent three months, and when a plot was formed against him by the Jews as he was about to set sail for Syria, he decided to return through Macedonia. ⁴And he was accompanied by Sopater of Berea, *the son* of

20:3 three months. Most or all of it were likely spent in Corinth. **a plot...against him by the Jews.** See 9:20, 23; 13:45; 14:2, 19; 17:5–9, 13; 18:6, 12–13; 19:9; 21:27–36; 23:12–15. Tragically, most of the opposition to Paul's ministry stemmed from his fellow countrymen (2Co 11:26). The Jewish community of Corinth hated Paul because of its humiliating debacle before Gallio (18:12–17), and the stunning conversions of two of its most prominent leaders, Crispus (18:8) and Sosthenes (18:17; 1Co 1:1). Luke does not record the details of the Jews' plot, but it undoubtedly involved murdering Paul during the voyage to Syria. The apostle would have been an easy target on a small ship packed with Jewish pilgrims. Because of that danger, Paul canceled his plans to sail from Greece to Syria. Instead, he decided to go north into Macedonia, cross the Aegean Sea to Asia Minor, and catch another ship from there. That delay cost Paul his opportunity to reach Jerusalem in time for Passover; but he hurried to be there in time for Pentecost (v. 16).

Pyrrhus, and by Aristarchus and Secundus of the Thessalonians, and Gaius of Derbe, and Timothy, and Tychicus and Trophimus of Asia. ⁵ But these had gone on ahead and were waiting for us at Troas. ⁶ We sailed from Philippi after the days of Unleavened Bread, and came to them at Troas within five days; and there we stayed seven days.

⁷ On the first day of the week, when we were gathered together to break bread, Paul *began* talking to them, intending to leave the next day, and he prolonged his message until midnight. ⁸ There were many lamps in the upper room where we were gathered together. ⁹ And there was a young man named Eutychus sitting on the window sill, sinking into a deep sleep; and as Paul kept on talking, he was overcome by sleep and fell down from the third floor and was picked up dead. ¹⁰ But Paul went down and fell upon him, and after embracing him, he said, "Do not be troubled, for his life is in him." ¹¹ When he had gone *back*

20:9 young man. The Greek word suggests he was between 7 and 14 years old. His youth, the fumes from the lamps, and the lateness of the hour (v. 7) gradually overcame his resistance. He dozed off, fell out of the open window, and was killed.

20:10 his life is in him. This does not mean that he had not died, but that his life had been restored. As a physician, Luke knew whether someone had died, as he plainly states (v. 9) was the case with Eutychus.

up and had broken the bread and eaten, he talked with them a long while until daybreak, and then left. ¹²They took away the boy alive, and were greatly comforted.

¹³But we, going ahead to the ship, set sail for Assos, intending from there to take Paul on board; for so he had arranged it, intending himself to go by land. ¹⁴And when he met us at Assos, we took him on board and came to Mitylene. ¹⁵Sailing from there, we arrived the following day opposite Chios; and the next day we crossed over to Samos; and the day following we came to Miletus. ¹⁶For Paul had decided to sail past Ephesus so that he would not have to spend time in Asia; for he was hurrying to be in Jerusalem, if possible, on the day of Pentecost.

DAY 17: Why did the church gather to worship on Sunday?

"On the first day of the week" (Ac 20:7). Sunday was the day the church gathered for worship, because it was the day of Christ's resurrection (Mt 28:1; Mk 16:2, 9; Lk 24:1; John 20:1, 19; 1Co 16:2). The writings of the early church fathers confirm that the church continued to meet on Sunday after the close of the New Testament period. Scripture does not require Christians to observe the Saturday Sabbath:

1. The Sabbath was the sign of the Mosaic Covenant (Ex 31:16, 17; Ne 9:14; Eze 20:12), whereas Christians are under the New Covenant (2Co 3; Heb 8);
2. there is no New Testament command to keep the Sabbath;
3. the first command to keep the Sabbath was not until the time of Moses (Ex 20:8);
4. 4. the Jerusalem Council (chap. 15) did not order Gentile believers to keep the Sabbath;
5. Paul never cautioned Christians about breaking the Sabbath; and
6. the New Testament explicitly teaches that Sabbath keeping was not a requirement (Ro 14:5; Gal 4:10–11; Col 2:16–17).

JULY 18

2 Chronicles 32:1–33:25

32 After these acts of faithfulness Sennacherib king of Assyria came and invaded Judah and besieged the fortified cities, and thought to break into them for himself. ²Now when Hezekiah saw that Sennacherib had come and that he intended to make war on Jerusalem, ³he decided with his officers and his warriors to cut off the *supply of* water from the springs which *were* outside the city, and they helped him. ⁴So many people assembled and stopped up all the springs and the stream which flowed through the region, saying, "Why should the kings of Assyria come and find abundant water?" ⁵And he took courage and rebuilt all the wall that had been broken down and erected towers on it, and *built* another outside wall and strengthened the Millo *in* the city of David, and made weapons and shields in great number. ⁶He appointed military officers over the people and gathered them to him in the square at the city gate, and spoke encouragingly to them, saying, ⁷"Be strong and courageous, do not fear or be dismayed because of the king of Assyria nor because of all the horde that is with him; for the one with us is greater than the one with him. ⁸With him is *only* an arm of flesh, but with us is the LORD our God to help us and to fight our battles." And the people relied on the words of Hezekiah king of Judah.

⁹After this Sennacherib king of Assyria sent his servants to Jerusalem while he *was* besieging Lachish with all his forces with him, against Hezekiah king of Judah and against all Judah who *were* at Jerusalem, saying, ¹⁰"Thus says Sennacherib king of Assyria, 'On what are you trusting that you are remaining in Jerusalem under siege? ¹¹Is not Hezekiah misleading you to give yourselves over to die by hunger and by thirst, saying, "The LORD our God will deliver us from the hand of the king of Assyria"? ¹²Has not the same Hezekiah taken away His high places and His altars, and said to Judah and Jerusalem, "You shall worship before one altar, and on it you shall burn incense"? ¹³Do you not know what I and my fathers have done to all the peoples of the lands? Were the gods of the nations of the lands able at all to deliver their land from my hand? ¹⁴Who *was there* among

all the gods of those nations which my fathers utterly destroyed who could deliver his people out of my hand, that your God should be able to deliver you from my hand? ¹⁵ Now therefore, do not let Hezekiah deceive you or mislead you like this, and do not believe him, for no god of any nation or kingdom was able to deliver his people from my hand or from the hand of my fathers. How much less will your God deliver you from my hand?'"

¹⁶ His servants spoke further against the LORD God and against His servant Hezekiah. ¹⁷ He also wrote letters to insult the LORD God of Israel, and to speak against Him, saying, "As the gods of the nations of the lands have not delivered their people from my hand, so the God of Hezekiah will not deliver His people from my hand." ¹⁸ They called this out with a loud voice in the language of Judah to the people of Jerusalem who were on the wall, to frighten and terrify them, so that they might take the city. ¹⁹ They spoke of the God of Jerusalem as of the gods of the peoples of the earth, the work of men's hands.

²⁰ But King Hezekiah and Isaiah the prophet, the son of Amoz, prayed about this and cried out to heaven. ²¹ And the LORD sent an angel who destroyed every mighty warrior, commander and officer in the camp of the king of Assyria. So he returned in shame to his own land. And when he had entered the temple of his god, some of his own children killed him there with the sword. ²² So the LORD saved Hezekiah and the inhabitants of Jerusalem from the hand of Sennacherib the king of Assyria and from the hand of all *others,* and guided them on every side. ²³ And many were bringing gifts to the LORD at Jerusalem and choice presents to Hezekiah king of Judah, so that he was exalted in the sight of all nations thereafter.

²⁴ In those days Hezekiah became mortally ill; and he prayed to the LORD, and the LORD spoke to him and gave him a sign. ²⁵ But Hezekiah gave no return for the benefit he received, because his heart was proud; therefore wrath came on him and on Judah and Jerusalem. ²⁶ However, Hezekiah humbled the pride of his heart, both he and the inhabitants of Jerusalem, so that the wrath of the LORD did not come on them in the days of Hezekiah.

²⁷ Now Hezekiah had immense riches and honor; and he made for himself treasuries for silver, gold, precious stones, spices, shields and all kinds of valuable articles, ²⁸ storehouses also for the produce of grain, wine and oil, pens for all kinds of cattle and sheepfolds for the flocks. ²⁹ He made cities for himself

and acquired flocks and herds in abundance, for God had given him very great wealth. ³⁰ It was Hezekiah who stopped the upper outlet of the waters of Gihon and directed them to the west side of the city of David. And Hezekiah prospered in all that he did. ³¹ Even *in the matter of* the envoys of the rulers of Babylon, who sent to him to inquire of the wonder that had happened in the land, God left him *alone only* to test him, that He might know all that was in his heart.

32:30 A 1,700 ft. long tunnel cut through solid rock (below Jerusalem) redirected water from the spring Gihon outside of Jerusalem (to the E) toward the south of Jerusalem into the pool of Siloam within the city to provide water in time of siege. The tunnel was a remarkable feat of engineering and boring skill, often 60 ft. below the ground and large enough to walk through. It was discovered in 1838, but not until 1909 was it cleared of the debris left by the destruction of Jerusalem back in 586 B.C. This may not have been the first water shaft, since David may have entered Jerusalem 300 years earlier through a water shaft (2Sa 5:6–8).

---

³² Now the rest of the acts of Hezekiah and his deeds of devotion, behold, they are written in the vision of Isaiah the prophet, the son of Amoz, in the Book of the Kings of Judah and Israel. ³³ So Hezekiah slept with his fathers, and they buried him in the upper section of the tombs of the sons of David; and all Judah and the inhabitants of Jerusalem honored him at his death. And his son Manasseh became king in his place.

33 Manasseh was twelve years old when he became king, and he reigned fifty-five years in Jerusalem. ² He did evil in the sight of the LORD according to the abominations of the nations whom the LORD dispossessed before the sons of Israel. ³ For he rebuilt the high places which Hezekiah his father had broken down; he also erected altars for the Baals and made Asherim, and worshiped all the host of heaven and served them. ⁴ He built altars in the house of the LORD of which the LORD had said, "My name shall be in Jerusalem forever." ⁵ For he built altars for all the host of heaven in the two courts of the house of the LORD. ⁶ He made his sons pass through the fire in the valley of Ben-hinnom; and he practiced witchcraft, used divination, practiced sorcery and dealt with mediums and spiritists. He did much evil in the sight of the LORD, provoking Him *to anger*. ⁷Then he put the carved image of the idol which he had made in the house of God, of which God had said to David and to Solomon his son, "In this house and in Jerusalem, which I have chosen from all the tribes of Israel, I will put My name forever; ⁸and I will not again remove the foot of Israel from the land which I have appointed for your fathers, if only they will observe to do all that I have commanded them according to all the law, the statutes and the ordinances *given* through Moses." ⁹Thus Manasseh misled Judah and the inhabitants of Jerusalem to do more evil than the nations whom the LORD destroyed before the sons of Israel.

¹⁰The LORD spoke to Manasseh and his people, but they paid no attention. ¹¹Therefore the LORD brought the commanders of the army of the king of Assyria against them, and they captured Manasseh with hooks, bound him with bronze *chains* and took him to Babylon. ¹²When he was in distress, he entreated the LORD his God and humbled himself greatly before the God of his fathers. ¹³When he prayed to Him, He was moved by his entreaty and heard his supplication, and brought him again to Jerusalem to his kingdom. Then Manasseh knew that the LORD *was* God.

33:12–13 Manasseh. This king was very wicked and idolatrous, a murderer of his children, and a desecrater of the temple. God graciously forgave this "chief of sinners" (1Ti 1:15) when he repented. He did what he could to reverse the effect of his life (vv. 15–17). Although the people worshiped God and not idols, they were doing it in the wrong place and wrong way. God had commanded them to offer sacrifices only in certain places (Dt 12:13–14) to keep them from corrupting the prescribed forms and to protect them from pagan religious influence. Disobedience to God's requirements in this matter surely contributed to the decline under the next king, Amon (vv. 21–25), whose corruption his successor, Josiah, had to eliminate (34:3–7).

¹⁴Now after this he built the outer wall of the city of David on the west side of Gihon, in the valley, even to the entrance of the Fish Gate; and he encircled the Ophel *with it* and made it very high. Then he put army commanders in all the fortified cities of Judah. ¹⁵He also removed the foreign gods and the idol from the house of the LORD, as well as all the altars which he had built on the mountain of the house of the LORD and in Jerusalem, and he threw *them* outside the city. ¹⁶He set up the altar of the LORD and sacrificed peace offerings and thank offerings on it; and he ordered Judah to serve the LORD God of Israel. ¹⁷Nevertheless the people still sacrificed in the high places, *although* only to the LORD their God.

¹⁸Now the rest of the acts of Manasseh even his prayer to his God, and the words of the seers who spoke to him in the name of the LORD God of Israel, behold, they are among the records of the kings of Israel. ¹⁹His prayer also and *how God* was entreated by him, and all his sin, his unfaithfulness, and the sites on which he built high places and erected the Asherim and the carved images, before he humbled himself, behold, they are written in the records of the Hozai. ²⁰So Manasseh slept with his fathers, and they buried him in his own house. And Amon his son became king in his place.

²¹Amon *was* twenty-two years old when he became king, and he reigned two years in Jerusalem. ²²He did evil in the sight of the LORD as Manasseh his father had done, and Amon sacrificed to all the carved images which his father Manasseh had made, and he served them. ²³Moreover, he did not humble himself before the LORD as his father Manasseh had done, but Amon multiplied guilt. ²⁴Finally his servants conspired against him and put him to death in his own house. ²⁵But the people of the land killed all the conspirators against King Amon, and the people of the land made Josiah his son king in his place.

Psalm 85:8–13

8 I will hear what God the
       LORD will say;
     For He will speak peace to His
       people, to His godly ones;
     But let them not turn back to folly.
9 Surely His salvation is near
       to those who fear Him,
     That glory may dwell in our land.
10 Lovingkindness and truth
       have met together;
     Righteousness and peace
       have kissed each other.
11 Truth springs from the earth,
     And righteousness looks
       down from heaven.
12 Indeed, the LORD will give
       what is good,
     And our land will yield its
       produce.

85:9 salvation...who fear Him. Only those who renounce their sinful autonomy and put their complete trust in the living God will participate in the blessings of salvation and the future kingdom (Jn 3:3–5). **glory may dwell in our land.** The departure of the glory of God, which signified His presence, is described in Ezekiel 10–11. He withdrew His glory because of the apostasy of the nation immediately preceding the Babylonian Exile (Eze 8–11). The return of the glory of the Lord in the future millennial temple is foretold in Ezekiel 43:1–4

85:10 Lovingkindness...truth...Righteousness...peace. These 4 spiritual qualities characterizing the atmosphere of the future kingdom of Christ will relate to each other in perfect harmony and will saturate kingdom life (vv. 10, 13).

---

¹³ Righteousness will go before Him
And will make His footsteps
into a way.

Proverbs 21:12

¹² The righteous one considers
the house of the wicked,
Turning the wicked to ruin.

Acts 20:17–38

¹⁷ From Miletus he sent to Ephesus and called to him the elders of the church. ¹⁸ And when they had come to him, he said to them, "You yourselves know, from the first day that I set foot in Asia, how I was with you the whole time, ¹⁹ serving the Lord with all humility and with tears and with trials which came upon me through the plots of the Jews; ²⁰ how I did not shrink from declaring to you anything that was profitable, and teaching you publicly and from house to house, ²¹ solemnly testifying to both Jews and Greeks of repentance toward God and faith in our Lord Jesus Christ. ²² And now, behold, bound by the Spirit, I am on my way to Jerusalem, not

20:19 with tears. Paul wept because of: 1) those who did not know Christ (Ro 9:2–3); 2) struggling, immature believers (2Co 2:4); and 3) the threat of false teachers (v. 29–30). **plots of the Jews.** Ironically, it was the plot of the Jews at Corinth that allowed the Ephesian elders this opportunity to spend time with Paul.

20:22 bound by the Spirit. Paul's deep sense of duty toward the Master who had redeemed him and called him to service drove him onward despite the threat of danger and hardship (v. 23).

20:23 Holy Spirit...testifies. Paul knew he faced persecution in Jerusalem (Ro 15:31), though he would not know the details until he heard Agabus' prophecy (21:10–11).

---

knowing what will happen to me there, ²³ except that the Holy Spirit solemnly testifies to me in every city, saying that bonds and afflictions await me. ²⁴ But I do not consider my life of any account as dear to myself, so that I may finish my course and the ministry which I received from the Lord Jesus, to testify solemnly of the gospel of the grace of God.

²⁵ "And now, behold, I know that all of you, among whom I went about preaching the kingdom, will no longer see my face. ²⁶ Therefore, I testify to you this day that I am innocent of the blood of all men. ²⁷ For I did not shrink from declaring to you the whole purpose of God. ²⁸ Be on guard for yourselves and for all the flock, among which the Holy Spirit has made you overseers, to shepherd the church of God which He purchased with His own blood. ²⁹ I know that after my departure savage wolves will come in among you, not sparing the flock; ³⁰ and from among your own selves men will arise, speaking perverse things, to draw away the disciples after them. ³¹ Therefore be on the alert, remembering that night and day for a period of three years I did not cease to admonish each one with tears. ³² And now I commend you to God and to the word of His grace, which is able to build *you* up and to give *you* the inheritance among all those who are sanctified. ³³ I have coveted no one's silver or gold or clothes. ³⁴ You yourselves know that these hands ministered to my *own* needs and to the men who were with me. ³⁵ In everything I showed you that by working hard in this manner you must help the weak and remember the words of the Lord Jesus, that He Himself said, 'It is more blessed to give than to receive.'"

³⁶ When he had said these things, he knelt down and prayed with them all. ³⁷ And they *began* to weep aloud and embraced Paul, and repeatedly kissed him, ³⁸ grieving especially over the word which he had spoken, that they would not see his face again. And they were accompanying him to the ship.

Paul told the Ephesians that he had declared to them "the whole purpose of God" (Ac 20:27). The entire plan and purpose of God for man's salvation in all its fullness: divine truths of creation, election, redemption, justification, adoption, conversion, sanctification, holy living, and glorification. And now that he was leaving, he gives them a warning.

False teachers were already plaguing the churches of Galatia (Gal 1:6) and the Corinthian church (2Co 11:4). "Be on guard for yourselves" (v. 28), a warning that proved true by later events at Ephesus (1Ti 1:3–7, 19–20; 6:20–21; Rev 2:2). Paul repeated this call to self-examination to Timothy when his young son in the faith served as pastor of the Ephesian congregation (1Ti 4:16; 2Ti 2:20–21). The "overseers" are the same as elders and pastors. The word stresses the leaders' responsibility to watch over and protect their congregations—an appropriate usage in the context of a warning against false teachers. Church rule, which minimizes the biblical authority of elders in favor of a cultural, democratic process, is foreign to the New Testament (1Th 5:12, 13; Heb 13:17).

He warns of "savage wolves" (v. 29)—a term borrowed from Jesus (Mt 7:15; 10:16). This metaphor stresses the extreme danger false teachers pose to the church. "From among your own selves" (v. 30). Even more deadly than attacks from outside the church are the defections of those (especially leaders) within the church (1Ti 1:20; 2Ti 1:15; 2:17; Jude 3, 4, 10–13). These wolves would speak "perverse things." The Greek word means "distorted" or "twisted." False teachers twist God's Word for their own evil ends (13:10; 2Pe 3:16).

"And now I commend you to God and to the word of His grace, which is able to build you up" (v. 32). The Scriptures, the record of God's gracious dealings with mankind, is the source of spiritual growth for all Christians. And since the church is "the pillar and support of the truth" (1Ti 3:15), its leaders must be familiar with that truth.

JULY 19

2 Chronicles 34:1–36:23

34 Josiah was eight years old when he became king, and he reigned thirty-one years in Jerusalem. ²He did right in the sight of the LORD, and walked in the ways of his father David and did not turn aside to the right or to the left. ³For in the eighth year of his reign while he was still a youth, he began to seek the God of his father David; and in the twelfth year he began to purge Judah and Jerusalem of the high places, the Asherim, the carved images and the molten images. ⁴They tore down the altars of the Baals in his presence, and the incense altars that were high above them he chopped down; also the Asherim, the carved images and the molten images he broke in pieces and ground to powder and scattered it on the graves of those who had sacrificed to them. ⁵Then he burned the bones of the priests on their altars and purged Judah and Jerusalem. ⁶In the cities of Manasseh, Ephraim, Simeon, even as far as Naphtali, in their surrounding ruins, ⁷he also tore down the altars and beat the Asherim and the carved images into powder, and chopped down all the incense altars throughout the land of Israel. Then he returned to Jerusalem.

⁸Now in the eighteenth year of his reign, when he had purged the land and the house, he sent Shaphan the son of Azaliah, and Maaseiah an official of the city, and Joah the son of Joahaz the recorder, to repair the house of the LORD his God. ⁹They came to Hilkiah the high priest and delivered the money that was brought into the house of God, which the Levites, the doorkeepers, had collected from Manasseh and Ephraim, and from all the remnant of Israel, and from all Judah and Benjamin and the inhabitants of Jerusalem. ¹⁰Then they gave it into the hands of the workmen who had the oversight of the house of the LORD, and the workmen who were working in the house of the LORD used it to restore and repair the house. ¹¹They in turn gave it to the carpenters and to the builders to buy quarried stone and timber for couplings and to make beams for the houses which the kings of Judah had let go to ruin. ¹²The men did the work faithfully with foremen over them to supervise: Jahath and Obadiah, the Levites of the sons of Merari, Zechariah and Meshullam of the sons of the Kohathites, and the Levites, all who were skillful with musical instruments. ¹³They were also over the burden bearers, and supervised all the workmen from job to job; and some of the Levites were scribes and officials and gatekeepers.

¹⁴When they were bringing out the money which had been brought into the house of the LORD, Hilkiah the priest found the book of the

law of the LORD *given* by Moses. [15] Hilkiah responded and said to Shaphan the scribe, "I have found the book of the law in the house of the LORD." And Hilkiah gave the book to Shaphan. [16] Then Shaphan brought the book to the king and reported further word to the king, saying, "Everything that was entrusted to your servants they are doing. [17] They have also emptied out the money which was found in the house of the LORD, and have delivered it into the hands of the supervisors and the workmen." [18] Moreover, Shaphan the scribe told the king saying, "Hilkiah the priest gave me a book." And Shaphan read from it in the presence of the king.

[19] When the king heard the words of the law, he tore his clothes. [20] Then the king commanded Hilkiah, Ahikam the son of Shaphan, Abdon the son of Micah, Shaphan the scribe, and Asaiah the king's servant, saying, [21] "Go, inquire of the LORD for me and for those who are left in Israel and in Judah, concerning the words of the book which has been found; for great is the wrath of the LORD which is poured out on us because our fathers have not observed the word of the LORD, to do according to all that is written in this book."

[22] So Hilkiah and *those* whom the king had told went to Huldah the prophetess, the wife of Shallum the son of Tokhath, the son of Hasrah, the keeper of the wardrobe (now she lived in Jerusalem in the Second Quarter); and they spoke to her regarding this. [23] She said to them, "Thus says the LORD, the God of Israel, 'Tell the man who sent you to Me, [24] thus says the LORD, "Behold, I am bringing evil on this place and on its inhabitants, *even* all the curses written in the book which they have read in the presence of the king of Judah. [25] Because they have forsaken Me and have burned incense to other gods, that they might provoke Me to anger with all the works of their hands; therefore My wrath will be poured out on this place and it shall not be quenched." ' [26] But to the king of Judah who sent you to inquire of the LORD, thus you will say to him, 'Thus says the LORD God of Israel *regarding* the words which you have heard, [27] "Because your heart was tender and you humbled yourself before God when you heard His words against this place and against its inhabitants, and *because* you humbled yourself before Me, tore your clothes and wept before Me, I truly have heard you," declares the LORD. [28] "Behold, I will gather you to your fathers and you shall be gathered to your grave in peace, so your eyes will not see all the evil which I will bring on this place and

on its inhabitants." ' " And they brought back word to the king.

[29] Then the king sent and gathered all the elders of Judah and Jerusalem. [30] The king went up to the house of the LORD and all the men of Judah, the inhabitants of Jerusalem, the priests, the Levites and all the people, from the greatest to the least; and he read in their hearing all the words of the book of the covenant which was found in the house of the LORD. [31] Then the king stood in his place and made a covenant before the LORD to walk after the LORD, and to keep His commandments and His testimonies and His statutes with all his heart and with all his soul, to perform the words of the covenant written in this book. [32] Moreover, he made all who were present in Jerusalem and Benjamin to stand *with him*. So the inhabitants of Jerusalem did according to the covenant of God, the God of their fathers. [33] Josiah removed all the abominations from all the lands belonging to the sons of Israel, and made all who were present in Israel to serve the LORD their God. Throughout his lifetime they did not turn from following the LORD God of their fathers.

35 Then Josiah celebrated the Passover to the LORD in Jerusalem, and they slaughtered the Passover *animals* on the fourteenth *day* of the first month. [2] He set the priests in their offices and encouraged them in the service of the house of the LORD. [3] He also said to the Levites who taught all Israel *and* who were holy to the LORD, "Put the holy ark in the house which Solomon the son of David king of Israel built; it will be a burden on *your* shoulders no longer. Now serve the LORD your God and His people Israel. [4] Prepare *yourselves* by your fathers' households in your divisions, according to the writing

35:3 the holy ark. The ark of the covenant which was to remain in the Most Holy Place had been removed, probably by Manasseh, who set a carved image in its place (33:7). The law for the carrying of the ark during the tabernacle days, when it was portable, called for poles to be placed through rings on the sides, and Levites (Kohathites) to carry it by the poles without touching it (Ex 25:14–15). Uzza(h) died for touching the ark while he was improperly transporting the ark on a cart (1Ch 13:6–10). Now that the temple was built and the ark had a permanent place, it no longer needed to be transported in the old way.

of David king of Israel and according to the writing of his son Solomon. ⁵ Moreover, stand in the holy place according to the sections of the fathers' households of your brethren the lay people, and according to the Levites, by division of a father's household. ⁶ Now slaughter the Passover *animals,* sanctify yourselves and prepare for your brethren to do according to the word of the LORD by Moses."

⁷ Josiah contributed to the lay people, to all who were present, flocks of lambs and young goats, all for the Passover offerings, numbering 30,000 plus 3,000 bulls; these were from the king's possessions. ⁸ His officers also contributed a freewill offering to the people, the priests and the Levites. Hilkiah and Zechariah and Jehiel, the officials of the house of God, gave to the priests for the Passover offerings 2,600 *from the flocks* and 300 bulls. ⁹ Conaniah also, and Shemaiah and Nethanel, his brothers, and Hashabiah and Jeiel and Jozabad, the officers of the Levites, contributed to the Levites for the Passover offerings 5,000 *from the flocks* and 500 bulls.

¹⁰ So the service was prepared, and the priests stood at their stations and the Levites by their divisions according to the king's command. ¹¹ They slaughtered the Passover *animals,* and while the priests sprinkled the blood *received* from their hand, the Levites skinned *them.* ¹² Then they removed the burnt offerings that *they* might give them to the sections of the fathers' households of the lay people to present to the LORD, as it is written in the book of Moses. *They did* this also with the bulls. ¹³ So they roasted the Passover *animals* on the fire according to the ordinance, and they boiled the holy things in pots, in kettles, in pans, and carried *them* speedily to all the lay people. ¹⁴ Afterwards they prepared for themselves and for the priests, because the priests, the sons of Aaron, *were* offering the burnt offerings and the fat until night; therefore the Levites prepared for themselves and for the priests, the sons of Aaron. ¹⁵ The singers, the sons of Asaph, *were* also at their stations according to the command of David, Asaph, Heman, and Jeduthun the king's seer; and the gatekeepers at each gate did not have to depart from their service, because the Levites their brethren prepared for them.

¹⁶ So all the service of the LORD was prepared on that day to celebrate the Passover, and to offer burnt offerings on the altar of the LORD according to the command of King Josiah. ¹⁷ Thus the sons of Israel who were present celebrated the Passover at that time, and the Feast of Unleavened Bread seven days.

¹⁸ There had not been celebrated a Passover like it in Israel since the days of Samuel the prophet; nor had any of the kings of Israel celebrated such a Passover as Josiah did with the priests, the Levites, all Judah and Israel who were present, and the inhabitants of Jerusalem. ¹⁹ In the eighteenth year of Josiah's reign this Passover was celebrated.

²⁰ After all this, when Josiah had set the temple in order, Neco king of Egypt came up to make war at Carchemish on the Euphrates, and Josiah went out to engage him. ²¹ But Neco sent messengers to him, saying, "What have we to do with each other, O King of Judah? *I am* not *coming* against you today but against the house with which I am at war, and God has ordered me to hurry. Stop for your own sake from *interfering with* God who is with me, so

35:21 God has ordered me. He is referring to the true God; whether he had a true revelation or not is unknown. Josiah had no way to know either, and it is apparent he did not believe that Neco spoke the Word of God. There is no reason to assume his death was punishment for refusing to believe. He probably thought Neco was lying and, once victorious with Assyria over Babylon, they would together be back to assault Israel.

that He will not destroy you." ²² However, Josiah would not turn away from him, but disguised himself in order to make war with him; nor did he listen to the words of Neco from the mouth of God, but came to make war on the plain of Megiddo. ²³ The archers shot King Josiah, and the king said to his servants, "Take me away, for I am badly wounded." ²⁴ So his servants took him out of the chariot and carried him in the second chariot which he had, and brought him to Jerusalem where he died and was buried in the tombs of his fathers. All Judah and Jerusalem mourned for Josiah. ²⁵ Then Jeremiah chanted a lament for Josiah. And all the male and female singers speak about Josiah in their lamentations to this day. And they made them an ordinance in Israel; behold, they are also written in the Lamentations. ²⁶ Now the rest of the acts of Josiah and his deeds of devotion as written in the law of the LORD, ²⁷ and his acts, first to last, behold, they are written in the Book of the Kings of Israel and Judah.

36 Then the people of the land took Joahaz the son of Josiah, and made him king in place of his father in Jerusalem. ² Joahaz was twenty-three years old when he became king, and he reigned three months in Jerusalem. ³Then the king of Egypt deposed him at Jerusalem, and imposed on the land a fine of one hundred talents of silver and one talent of gold. ⁴The king of Egypt made Eliakim his brother king over Judah and Jerusalem, and changed his name to Jehoiakim. But Neco took Joahaz his brother and brought him to Egypt.

⁵Jehoiakim was twenty-five years old when he became king, and he reigned eleven years in Jerusalem; and he did evil in the sight of the LORD his God. ⁶Nebuchadnezzar king of Babylon came up against him and bound him with bronze *chains* to take him to Babylon. ⁷Nebuchadnezzar also brought *some* of the articles of the house of the LORD to Babylon and put them in his temple at Babylon. ⁸Now the rest of the acts of Jehoiakim and the abominations which he did, and what was found against him, behold, they are written in the Book of the Kings of Israel and Judah. And Jehoiachin his son became king in his place.

⁹Jehoiachin was eight years old when he became king, and he reigned three months and ten days in Jerusalem, and he did evil in the sight of the LORD. ¹⁰At the turn of the year King Nebuchadnezzar sent and brought him to Babylon with the valuable articles of the house of the LORD, and he made his kinsman Zedekiah king over Judah and Jerusalem.

¹¹Zedekiah was twenty-one years old when he became king, and he reigned eleven years in Jerusalem. ¹²He did evil in the sight of the LORD his God; he did not humble himself before Jeremiah the prophet who spoke for the LORD. ¹³He also rebelled against King Nebuchadnezzar who had made him swear *allegiance* by God. But he stiffened his neck and hardened his heart against turning to the LORD God of Israel. ¹⁴Furthermore, all the officials of the priests and the people were very unfaithful *following* all the abominations of the nations; and they defiled the house of the LORD which He had sanctified in Jerusalem. ¹⁵The LORD, the God of their fathers, sent *word* to them again and again by His messengers, because He had compassion on His people and on His dwelling place; ¹⁶but they *continually* mocked the messengers of God, despised His words and scoffed at His prophets, until the wrath of the LORD arose against His people, until there was no remedy. ¹⁷Therefore He brought up against them the king of the Chaldeans who slew their young men with the sword in the house of their sanctuary, and had no compassion on young man or virgin, old man or infirm; He gave *them* all

into his hand. ¹⁸All the articles of the house of God, great and small, and the treasures of the house of the LORD, and the treasures of the king and of his officers, he brought *them* all to Babylon. ¹⁹Then they burned the house of God and broke down the wall of Jerusalem, and burned all its fortified buildings with fire and destroyed all its valuable articles. ²⁰Those who had escaped from the sword he carried away to Babylon; and they were servants to him and to his sons until the rule of the kingdom of Persia, ²¹to fulfill the word of the LORD by the mouth of Jeremiah, until the land had enjoyed its sabbaths. All the days of its desolation it kept sabbath until seventy years were complete.

🔥

36:11-21 The reign of Zedekiah, a.k.a. Mattaniah (ca. 597–586 B.C.). Jeremiah prophesied during this reign (Jer 1:3) and wrote Lamentations to mourn the destruction of Jerusalem and the temple in 586 B.C. Ezekiel received his commission during this reign (Eze 1:1) and prophesied from 592 B.C. to his death in 560 B.C.

²²Now in the first year of Cyrus king of Persia—in order to fulfill the word of the LORD by the mouth of Jeremiah—the LORD stirred up the spirit of Cyrus king of Persia, so that he sent a proclamation throughout his kingdom, and also *put it* in writing, saying, ²³"Thus says Cyrus king of Persia, 'The LORD, the God of heaven, has given me all the kingdoms of the earth, and He has appointed me to build Him a house in Jerusalem, which is in Judah. Whoever there is among you of all His people, may the LORD his God be with him, and let him go up!'"

Psalm 86:1-5

A Prayer of David.

Incline Your ear, O LORD,
   and answer me;
   For I am afflicted and needy.
² Preserve my soul, for I
   am a godly man;
   O You my God, save Your
   servant who trusts in You.
³ Be gracious to me, O Lord,
   For to You I cry all day long.
⁴ Make glad the soul of Your servant,
   For to You, O Lord, I lift up my soul.
⁵ For You, Lord, are good, and
   ready to forgive,
   And abundant in lovingkindness
   to all who call upon You.

Proverbs 21:13-14

¹³ He who shuts his ear to
the cry of the poor
Will also cry himself and
not be answered.

¹⁴ A gift in secret subdues anger,
And a bribe in the bosom,
strong wrath.

Acts 21:1-16

21 When we had parted from them and had set sail, we ran a straight course to Cos and the next day to Rhodes and from there to Patara; ²and having found a ship crossing over to Phoenicia, we went aboard and set sail. ³When we came in sight of Cyprus,

21:2 found a ship...to Phoenicia. Realizing he would never reach Jerusalem in time for Pentecost if he continued to hug the coast, Paul decided to risk sailing directly across the Mediterranean Sea to Tyre (v. 3). The ship they embarked on would have been considerably larger than the small coastal vessels on which they had been sailing. The ship that later took Paul on his ill-fated voyage to Rome held 276 people (27:37); this one was probably of comparable size.

leaving it on the left, we kept sailing to Syria and landed at Tyre; for there the ship was to unload its cargo. ⁴After looking up the disciples, we stayed there seven days; and they kept telling Paul through the Spirit not to set foot in Jerusalem. ⁵When our days there were ended, we left and started on our journey, while they all, with wives and children, escorted us until *we were* out of the city. After kneeling down on the beach and praying, we said farewell to one another. ⁶Then we went on board the ship, and they returned home again.

⁷When we had finished the voyage from Tyre, we arrived at Ptolemais, and after greeting the brethren, we stayed with them for a day. ⁸On the next day we left and came to Caesarea, and entering the house of Philip the evangelist, who was one of the seven, we stayed with him. ⁹Now this man had four virgin daughters who were prophetesses.

21:9 virgin daughters. That they were virgins may indicate that they had been called by God for special ministry (1Co 7:34). The early church regarded these women as important sources of information in the early years of the church. **prophetesses.** Luke does not reveal the nature of their prophecy. They may have had an ongoing prophetic ministry, or prophesied only once. Since women are not to be preachers or teachers in the church (1Co 14:34-36; 1Ti 2:11-12), they probably ministered to individuals.

¹⁰As we were staying there for some days, a prophet named Agabus came down from Judea. ¹¹And coming to us, he took Paul's belt and bound his own feet and hands, and said, "This is what the Holy Spirit says: 'In this way the Jews at Jerusalem will bind the man who owns this belt and deliver him into the hands of the Gentiles.'" ¹²When we had heard this, we as well as the local residents *began* begging him not to go up to Jerusalem. ¹³Then Paul answered, "What are you doing, weeping and breaking my heart? For I am ready not only to be bound, but even to die at Jerusalem for the name of the Lord Jesus." ¹⁴And since he would not be persuaded, we fell silent, remarking, "The will of the Lord be done!"

¹⁵After these days we got ready and started on our way up to Jerusalem. ¹⁶*Some* of the disciples from Caesarea also came with us, taking us to Mnason of Cyprus, a disciple of long standing with whom we were to lodge.

DAY 19: Why did Paul not heed all the warnings about going to Jerusalem?

The church in Tyre had been founded by some of those who fled Jerusalem after Stephen's martyrdom (Ac 11:19)—a persecution Paul himself had spearheaded. When Paul arrived there, the disciples there told Paul "not to set foot in Jerusalem" (21:4). This was not a command from the Spirit for Paul not to go to Jerusalem. Rather, the Spirit had revealed to the believers at Tyre that Paul would face suffering in Jerusalem. Understandably, they tried to dissuade him from going there. Paul's mission to Jerusalem had been given him by the Lord Jesus (20:24); the Spirit would never command him to abandon it.

Later, a prophet named Agabus (11:28) met Paul in Caesarea. Although it was located in Judea, the Jews considered Caesarea, seat of the Roman government, to be a foreign city. Old Testament prophets sometimes acted out their prophecies (1Ki 11:29-39; Is. 20:2-6; Jer 13:1-11;

Eze 4–5), and Agabus's action of binding his hands and feet with Paul's belt foreshadowed Paul's arrest and imprisonment by the Romans (Ac 21:11). Though falsely accused by the Jews (vv. 27–28), Paul was arrested and imprisoned by the Romans (vv. 31–33).

Hearing these warnings, it is not surprising that both Paul's friends (Luke and the others traveling with him) and the Caesarean Christians pleaded with Paul to not go. Paul's response is to say, "I am ready not only to be bound, but even to die at Jerusalem for the name of the Lord Jesus" (v. 13). Jesus' name represents all that He is. That said from Paul, his friends' response was, "The will of the Lord be done!" (v. 14)—a confident expression of trust that God's will is best (1Sa 3:18; Mt 6:10; Lk 22:42; Jas 4:13–15).

JULY 20

Ezra 1:1–2:70

1 Now in the first year of Cyrus king of Persia, in order to fulfill the word of the LORD by the mouth of Jeremiah, the LORD stirred up the spirit of Cyrus king of Persia, so that he sent a proclamation throughout all his kingdom, and also *put it* in writing, saying: ² "Thus says Cyrus king of Persia, 'The LORD, the God of heaven, has given me all the kingdoms of the earth and He has appointed me to build Him a house in Jerusalem, which is in Judah. ³ Whoever there is among you of all His people, may his God be with him! Let him go up to Jerusalem which is in Judah and rebuild the house of the LORD, the God of Israel; He is the God who is in Jerusalem. ⁴ Every survivor, at whatever place he may live, let the men of that place support him with silver and gold, with goods and cattle, together with a freewill offering for the house of God which is in Jerusalem.' "

⁵ Then the heads of fathers' *households* of Judah and Benjamin and the priests and the Levites arose, even everyone whose spirit God had stirred to go up and rebuild the house of the LORD which is in Jerusalem. ⁶ All those about them encouraged them with articles of silver, with gold, with goods, with cattle and with valuables, aside from all that was given as a freewill offering. ⁷ Also King Cyrus brought out the articles of the house of the LORD, which Nebuchadnezzar had carried

away from Jerusalem and put in the house of his gods; ⁸ and Cyrus, king of Persia, had them brought out by the hand of Mithredath the treasurer, and he counted them out to Sheshbazzar, the prince of Judah. ⁹ Now this *was* their number: 30 gold dishes, 1,000 silver dishes, 29 duplicates; ¹⁰ 30 gold bowls, 410 silver bowls of a second *kind and* 1,000 other articles. ¹¹ All the articles of gold and silver *numbered* 5,400. Sheshbazzar brought them all up with the exiles who went up from Babylon to Jerusalem.

2 Now these are the people of the province who came up out of the captivity of the exiles whom Nebuchadnezzar the king of Babylon had carried away to Babylon, and returned to Jerusalem and Judah, each to his city. ² These came with Zerubbabel, Jeshua, Nehemiah, Seraiah, Reelaiah, Mordecai, Bilshan, Mispar, Bigvai, Rehum *and* Baanah.

The number of the men of the people of Israel: ³ the sons of Parosh, 2,172; ⁴ the sons of Shephatiah, 372; ⁵ the sons of Arah, 775; ⁶ the sons of Pahath-moab of the sons of Jeshua

2:2 Zerubbabel. This man was the rightful leader of Judah in that he was of the lineage of David through Jehoiachin (1Ch 3:17). He did not serve as king (see the curse on Jehoiachin's line, Jer 22:24–30), but was still in the messianic line because the curse was bypassed (Mt 1:12; Lk 3:27). The curse of the messianic line for Christ was bypassed in Luke's genealogy by tracing the lineage through David's son Nathan. His name means "offspring of Babylon," indicating his place of birth. He, rather than Cyrus' political appointee Sheshbazzar (1:11), led Judah according to God's will. **Jeshua.** The High Priest of the first return whose name means "Jehovah saves." He is called Joshua in Haggai 1:1 and Zec 3:1. His father Jozadak (Ezr 3:2) had been exiled (1Ch 6:15). He came from the lineage of Levi, Aaron, Eleazar, and Phinehas; thus he was legitimately in the line of the High Priest (Nu 25:10–13).

1:5 whose spirit God had stirred. The primary underlying message of Ezra and Nehemiah is that the sovereign hand of God is at work in perfect keeping with His plan at His appointed times. The 70 years of captivity were complete, so God stirred up not only the spirit of Cyrus to make the decree, but His own people to go and build up Jerusalem and the temple (1:1).

and Joab, 2,812; [7] the sons of Elam, 1,254; [8] the sons of Zattu, 945; [9] the sons of Zaccai, 760; [10] the sons of Bani, 642; [11] the sons of Bebai, 623; [12] the sons of Azgad, 1,222; [13] the sons of Adonikam, 666; [14] the sons of Bigvai, 2,056; [15] the sons of Adin, 454; [16] the sons of Ater of Hezekiah, 98; [17] the sons of Bezai, 323; [18] the sons of Jorah, 112; [19] the sons of Hashum, 223; [20] the sons of Gibbar, 95; [21] the men of Bethlehem, 123; [22] the men of Netophah, 56; [23] the men of Anathoth, 128; [24] the sons of Azmaveth, 42; [25] the sons of Kiriath-arim, Chephirah and Beeroth, 743; [26] the sons of Ramah and Geba, 621; [27] the men of Michmas, 122; [28] the men of Bethel and Ai, 223; [29] the sons of Nebo, 52; [30] the sons of Magbish, 156; [31] the sons of the other Elam, 1,254; [32] the sons of Harim, 320; [33] the sons of Lod, Hadid and Ono, 725; [34] the men of Jericho, 345; [35] the sons of Senaah, 3,630.

[36] The priests: the sons of Jedaiah of the house of Jeshua, 973; [37] the sons of Immer, 1,052; [38] the sons of Pashhur, 1,247; [39] the sons of Harim, 1,017.

[40] The Levites: the sons of Jeshua and Kadmiel, of the sons of Hodaviah, 74. [41] The singers: the sons of Asaph, 128. [42] The sons of the gatekeepers: the sons of Shallum, the sons of Ater, the sons of Talmon, the sons of Akkub, the sons of Hatita, the sons of Shobai, in all 139.

[43] The temple servants: the sons of Ziha, the sons of Hasupha, the sons of Tabbaoth, [44] the sons of Keros, the sons of Siaha, the sons of Padon, [45] the sons of Lebanah, the sons of Hagabah, the sons of Akkub, [46] the sons of Hagab, the sons of Shalmai, the sons of Hanan, [47] the sons of Giddel, the sons of Gahar, the sons of Reaiah, [48] the sons of Rezin, the sons of Nekoda, the sons of Gazzam, [49] the sons of Uzza, the sons of Paseah, the sons of Besai, [50] the sons of Asnah, the sons of Meunim, the sons of Nephisim, [51] the sons of Bakbuk, the sons of Hakupha, the sons of Harhur, [52] the sons of Bazluth, the sons of Mehida, the sons of Harsha, [53] the sons of Barkos, the sons of Sisera, the sons of Temah, [54] the sons of Neziah, the sons of Hatipha.

[55] The sons of Solomon's servants: the sons of Sotai, the sons of Hassophereth, the sons of Peruda, [56] the sons of Jaalah, the sons of Darkon, the sons of Giddel, [57] the sons of Shephatiah, the sons of Hattil, the sons of Pochereth-hazzebaim, the sons of Ami.

[58] All the temple servants and the sons of Solomon's servants were 392.

[59] Now these are those who came up from Tel-melah, Tel-harsha, Cherub, Addan *and* Immer, but they were not able to give evidence of their fathers' households and their descendants, whether they were of Israel: [60] the sons of Delaiah, the sons of Tobiah, the sons of Nekoda, 652. [61] Of the sons of the priests: the sons of Habaiah, the sons of Hakkoz, the sons of Barzillai, who took a wife from the daughters of Barzillai the Gileadite, and he was called by their name. [62] These searched *among* their ancestral registration, but they could not be located; therefore they were considered unclean *and excluded* from the priesthood. [63] The governor said to them that they should not eat from the most holy things until a priest stood up with Urim and Thummim.

[64] The whole assembly numbered 42,360, [65] besides their male and female servants who numbered 7,337; and they had 200 singing men and women. [66] Their horses were 736; their mules, 245; [67] their camels, 435; *their* donkeys, 6,720.

[68] Some of the heads of fathers' *households*, when they arrived at the house of the LORD which is in Jerusalem, offered willingly for the house of God to restore it on its foundation. [69] According to their ability they gave to the treasury for the work 61,000 gold drachmas and 5,000 silver minas and 100 priestly garments.

[70] Now the priests and the Levites, some of the people, the singers, the gatekeepers and the temple servants lived in their cities, and all Israel in their cities.

Psalm 86:6–10

6 Give ear, O LORD, to my prayer;
   And give heed to the voice
     of my supplications!
7 In the day of my trouble I
     shall call upon You,
   For You will answer me.
8 There is no one like You among
     the gods, O Lord,
   Nor are there any works like Yours.
9 All nations whom You have
     made shall come and worship
     before You, O Lord,
   And they shall glorify Your name.
10 For You are great and do
     wondrous deeds;
   You alone are God.

Proverbs 21:15–16

15 The exercise of justice is joy
     for the righteous,
   But is terror to the workers
     of iniquity.

¹⁶ A man who wanders from the
way of understanding
Will rest in the assembly of the dead.

Acts 21:17-40

¹⁷After we arrived in Jerusalem, the brethren received us gladly. ¹⁸And the following day Paul went in with us to James, and all the elders were present. ¹⁹After he had greeted them, he *began* to relate one by one the things which God had done among the Gentiles through his ministry. ²⁰And when they heard it they *began* glorifying God; and they said to him, "You see, brother, how many thousands there are among the Jews of those who have believed, and they are all zealous for the Law; ²¹and they have been told about you, that you are teaching all the Jews who are among the Gentiles to forsake Moses, telling them not to circumcise their children nor to walk according to the customs. ²²What, then, is *to be done?* They will certainly hear that you have come. ²³Therefore do this that we tell you. We have four men who are under a vow; ²⁴take them and purify yourself along with them, and pay their expenses so that they may shave their heads; and all will know that there is nothing to the things which they have been told about you, but that you yourself also walk orderly, keeping the Law. ²⁵But concerning the Gentiles who have believed, we wrote, having decided that they should abstain from meat sacrificed to idols and from blood and from what is strangled and from fornication." ²⁶Then Paul took the men, and the next day, purifying himself along with them, went into the temple giving notice of the completion of the days of purification, until the sacrifice was offered for each one of them.

²⁷When the seven days were almost over,

21:24 purify yourself. Having just returned from an extended stay in Gentile lands, Paul was considered ceremonially unclean. He therefore needed to undergo ritual purification before participating (as their sponsor) in the ceremony marking the end of the 4 men's vows. **pay their expenses.** For the temple ceremony in which the 4 would shave their heads, and the sacrifices associated with the Nazirite vow. Paying those expenses for another was considered an act of piety, and by so doing, Paul would give further proof that he had not forsaken his Jewish heritage. **shave their heads.** A practice commonly associated with a Nazirite vow (Nu 6:18).

the Jews from Asia, upon seeing him in the temple, *began* to stir up all the crowd and laid hands on him, ²⁸crying out, "Men of Israel, come to our aid! This is the man who preaches to all men everywhere against our people and the Law and this place; and besides he has even brought Greeks into the temple and has defiled this holy place." ²⁹For they had previously seen Trophimus the Ephesian in the city with him, and they supposed that Paul had brought him into the temple. ³⁰Then all the city was provoked, and the people rushed together, and taking hold of Paul they dragged him out of the temple, and immediately the doors were shut. ³¹While they were seeking to

21:28 our people and the Law and this place. Paul's enemies leveled 3 false charges against him. They claimed that he taught Jews to forsake their heritage—the same lie told by the Judaizers. The second charge, that Paul opposed the law, was a very dangerous one, albeit false, in this setting. Originally, Pentecost was a celebration of the firstfruits of the harvest. But by this time, it had become a celebration of Moses' receiving the law on Mt. Sinai. Thus, the Jewish people were especially zealous for the law during this feast. The third charge, of blaspheming or defiling the temple, had helped bring about the deaths of Jesus (Mk 14:57–58) and Stephen (6:13). All 3 charges were, of course, totally false.

21:30 doors were shut. This was done by the temple guards, since Paul's death on the temple grounds would defile the temple (2Ki 11:15). They made no effort, however, to rescue the apostle from the crowd, which was intent on beating him to death.

kill him, a report came up to the commander of the *Roman* cohort that all Jerusalem was in confusion. ³²At once he took along *some* soldiers and centurions and ran down to them; and when they saw the commander and the soldiers, they stopped beating Paul. ³³Then the commander came up and took hold of him, and ordered him to be bound with two chains; and he *began* asking who he was and what he had done. ³⁴But among the crowd some were shouting one thing *and* some another, and when he could not find out the facts because of the uproar, he ordered him to be brought into the barracks. ³⁵When he got to the stairs, he was carried by the soldiers because of the violence of the mob; ³⁶for the multitude of the people kept following them, shouting, "Away with him!"

37 As Paul was about to be brought into the barracks, he said to the commander, "May I say something to you?" And he *said, "Do you know Greek? 38 Then you are not the Egyptian who some time ago stirred up a revolt and led the four thousand men of the Assassins out into the wilderness?" 39 But Paul said, "I am a Jew of Tarsus in Cilicia, a citizen of no insignificant city; and I beg you, allow me to speak to the people." 40 When he had given him permission, Paul, standing on the stairs, motioned to the people with his hand; and when there was a great hush, he spoke to them in the Hebrew dialect, saying,

---

DAY 20: How did God sovereignly restore the Jews to the land?

It was through a proclamation by Cyrus king of Persia. The Lord had prophesied through Isaiah, who said of Cyrus, "'He is My shepherd...and he declares of Jerusalem, 'She will be built,' and of the temple, 'Your foundation will be laid'" (Is. 44:28). The historian Josephus records an account of the day when Daniel read Isaiah's prophecy to Cyrus, and in response he was moved to declare the proclamation of Ezra 1:2–4 (538 B.C.). "In order to fulfill the word of the LORD by the mouth of Jeremiah." Jeremiah had prophesied the return of the exiles after a 70-year captivity in Babylon (Jer 25:11; 29:10–14; Da 9:2). This was no isolated event, but rather an outworking of the covenant promises made to Abraham in Genesis 12:1–3.

We are told that "the LORD stirred up the spirit of Cyrus." A strong expression of the fact that God sovereignly works in the lives of kings to affect His purposes (Pr 21:1; Da 2:21; 4:17). Cyrus made a proclamation, which was the most common form of spoken, public communication, usually from the central administration. The king would dispatch a herald, perhaps with a written document, into the city. In order to address the people, he would either go to the city gate, where people often congregated for social discourse, or gather the people together in a square, occasionally by the blowing of a horn. The herald would then make the proclamation to the people. A document called the Cyrus Cylinder, recovered in reasonably good condition by archeologists, commissions people from many lands to return to their cities to rebuild the temples to their gods, apparently as some sort of general policy of Cyrus. Whether or not this document was an extension of the proclamation made to the exiles in this passage must remain a matter of speculation.

It is possible that Daniel played a part in the Jews' receiving such favorable treatment (Da 6:25–28). According to the Jewish historian Josephus, he was Cyrus's prime minister who shared Isaiah's prophecies with Cyrus (Is. 44:28; 46:1–4). The existence of such documents, written over a century before Cyrus was born, led him to acknowledge that all his power came from the God of Israel and prompted him to fulfill the prophecy.

JULY 21

Ezra 3:1–4:24

3 Now when the seventh month came, and the sons of Israel were in the cities, the people gathered together as one man to Jerusalem. 2 Then Jeshua the son of Jozadak and his brothers the priests, and Zerubbabel the son of Shealtiel and his brothers arose and built the altar of the God of Israel to offer burnt offerings on it, as it is written in the law of Moses, the man of God. 3 So they set up the altar on its foundation, for they were terrified because of the peoples of the lands; and they offered burnt offerings on it to the LORD, burnt offerings morning and evening. 4 They celebrated the Feast of Booths, as it is written, and offered the fixed number of burnt offerings daily, according to the ordinance, as each day required; 5 and afterward there was a continual burnt offering, also for the new moons and for all the fixed festivals of the LORD that were consecrated, and from everyone who offered a freewill offering to the LORD. 6 From the first day of the seventh month they began to offer burnt offerings to the LORD, but the foundation of the temple of the LORD had not been laid. 7 Then they gave money to the masons and carpenters, and food, drink and oil to the Sidonians and to the Tyrians, to bring cedar wood from Lebanon to the sea at Joppa, according to the permission they had from Cyrus king of Persia.

8 Now in the second year of their coming to the house of God at Jerusalem in the second month, Zerubbabel the son of Shealtiel and Jeshua the son of Jozadak and the rest of their brothers the priests and the Levites, and all who came from the captivity to Jerusalem, began the work and appointed the Levites from twenty years and older to oversee the

work of the house of the LORD. ⁹ Then Jeshua *with* his sons and brothers stood united *with* Kadmiel and his sons, the sons of Judah *and* the sons of Henadad *with* their sons and brothers the Levites, to oversee the workmen in the temple of God.

¹⁰ Now when the builders had laid the foundation of the temple of the LORD, the priests stood in their apparel with trumpets, and the Levites, the sons of Asaph, with cymbals, to praise the LORD according to the directions of King David of Israel. ¹¹ They sang, praising and giving thanks to the LORD, *saying,* "For He is good, for His lovingkindness is upon Israel forever." And all the people shouted with a great shout when they praised the LORD because the foundation of the house of the LORD was laid. ¹² Yet many of the priests and Levites and heads of fathers' *households,* the old men who had seen the first temple, wept with a loud voice when the foundation of this house was laid before their eyes, while many shouted aloud for joy, ¹³ so that the people

3:12 the first temple. The temple built by Solomon (1Ki 5–7). **wept with a loud voice.** The first temple had been destroyed 50 years earlier. The old men, who would have been about 60 years or older, knew that this second temple did not begin to match the splendor of Solomon's temple nor did the presence of God reside within it (Hag 2:1–4; Zec 4:9–10). The nation was small and weak, the temple smaller and less beautiful by far. There were no riches as in David and Solomon's days. The ark was gone. But most disappointing was the absence of God's Shekinah glory. Thus the weeping. **shouted…for joy.** For those who did not have a point of comparison, this was a great moment. Possibly Psalms 126 was written and sung for this occasion.

could not distinguish the sound of the shout of joy from the sound of the weeping of the people, for the people shouted with a loud shout, and the sound was heard far away.

4 Now when the enemies of Judah and Benjamin heard that the people of the exile were building a temple to the LORD God of Israel, ² they approached Zerubbabel and the heads of fathers' *households,* and said to them, "Let us build with you, for we, like you, seek your God; and we have been sacrificing to Him since the days of Esarhaddon king of Assyria, who brought us up here." ³ But Zerubbabel and Jeshua and the rest of the

heads of fathers' *households* of Israel said to them, "You have nothing in common with us in building a house to our God; but we ourselves will together build to the LORD God of Israel, as King Cyrus, the king of Persia has commanded us."

⁴ Then the people of the land discouraged the people of Judah, and frightened them from building, ⁵ and hired counselors against them to frustrate their counsel all the days of Cyrus king of Persia, even until the reign of Darius king of Persia.

⁶ Now in the reign of Ahasuerus, in the beginning of his reign, they wrote an accusation against the inhabitants of Judah and Jerusalem.

⁷ And in the days of Artaxerxes, Bishlam, Mithredath, Tabeel and the rest of his colleagues wrote to Artaxerxes king of Persia; and the text of the letter was written in Aramaic and translated *from* Aramaic. ⁸ Rehum the commander and Shimshai the scribe wrote a letter against Jerusalem to King Artaxerxes, as follows— ⁹ then *wrote* Rehum the commander and Shimshai the scribe and the rest of their colleagues, the judges and the lesser governors, the officials, the secretaries, the men of Erech, the Babylonians, the men of Susa, that is, the Elamites, ¹⁰ and the rest of the nations which the great and honorable Osnappar deported and settled in the city of Samaria, and in the rest of the region beyond the River. Now ¹¹ this is the copy of the letter which they sent to him:

"To King Artaxerxes: Your servants, the men in the region beyond the River, and now ¹² let it be known to the king that the Jews who came up from you have come to us at Jerusalem; they are rebuilding the rebellious and evil city and are finishing the walls and repairing the foundations. ¹³ Now let it be known to the king, that if that city is rebuilt and the walls are finished, they will not pay tribute, custom or toll, and it will damage the revenue of the kings. ¹⁴ Now because we are in the service of the palace, and it is not fitting for us to see the king's dishonor, therefore we have sent and informed the king, ¹⁵ so that a search may be made in the record books of your fathers. And you will discover in the record books and learn that that city is a rebellious city and damaging to kings and provinces, and that they have incited revolt within it in past days; therefore that city was laid waste. ¹⁶ We inform the king that if that city is rebuilt and the walls finished, as a result you will have no possession in *the province* beyond the River."

4:6–23 This section represents later opposition which Ezra chose to put here as a parenthetical continuation of the theme "opposition to resettling and rebuilding Judah." He first referred to the opposition from Israel's enemies under King Ahasuerus (a regal title) or Xerxes (ca. 486–464 B.C.), who ruled at the time of Esther (4:6). Ezra 4:7–23 then recounts opposition in Nehemiah's day under Artaxerxes I (ca. 464–423 B.C.) expressed in a detailed letter of accusation against the Jews (vv. 7–16). It was successful in stopping the work, as the king's reply indicates (vv. 17–23). Most likely, this opposition is that also spoken of in Nehemiah 1:3. All this was the ongoing occurrence of severe animosity between the Israelites and Samaritans, which was later aggravated when the Samaritans built a rival temple on Mt. Gerizim (Jn 4:9). The opposition to Zerubbabel picks up again at 4:24—5:2 during the reign of Darius I, who actually reigned before either Ahasuerus or Artaxerxes.

[17] *Then* the king sent an answer to Rehum the commander, to Shimshai the scribe, and to the rest of their colleagues who live in Samaria and in the rest of *the provinces* beyond the River: "Peace. And now [18] the document which you sent to us has been translated and read before me. [19] A decree has been issued by me, and a search has been made and it has been discovered that that city has risen up against the kings in past days, that rebellion and revolt have been perpetrated in it, [20] that mighty kings have ruled over Jerusalem, governing all *the provinces* beyond the River, and that tribute, custom and toll were paid to them. [21] So, now issue a decree to make these men stop *work,* that this city may not be rebuilt until a decree is issued by me. [22] Beware of being negligent in carrying out this *matter;* why should damage increase to the detriment of the kings?"

[23] Then as soon as the copy of King Artaxerxes' document was read before Rehum and

4:21 now issue a decree. No small order for one or two workers, but rather the efforts of 50,000 were called to a halt. The king was commissioning a decree of great significance. The original language calls for the difference. This decree would not lose its authority until the king established a new decree.

Shimshai the scribe and their colleagues, they went in haste to Jerusalem to the Jews and stopped them by force of arms.

[24] Then work on the house of God in Jerusalem ceased, and it was stopped until the second year of the reign of Darius king of Persia.

Psalm 86:11–17

[11] Teach me Your way, O LORD;
I will walk in Your truth;
Unite my heart to fear Your name.
[12] I will give thanks to You, O Lord
my God, with all my heart,
And will glorify Your name forever.
[13] For Your lovingkindness
toward me is great,
And You have delivered my soul
from the depths of Sheol.

[14] O God, arrogant men have
risen up against me,
And a band of violent men
have sought my life,
And they have not set
You before them.
[15] But You, O Lord, are a God
merciful and gracious,
Slow to anger and abundant in
lovingkindness and truth.
[16] Turn to me, and be gracious to me;
Oh grant Your strength
to Your servant,
And save the son of Your handmaid.
[17] Show me a sign for good,
That those who hate me may
see *it* and be ashamed,
Because You, O LORD, have helped
me and comforted me.

Proverbs 21:17–18

[17] He who loves pleasure *will
become* a poor man;
He who loves wine and oil
will not become rich.
[18] The wicked is a ransom
for the righteous,
And the treacherous is in the
place of the upright.

Acts 22:1–30

22 "Brethren and fathers, hear my defense which I now *offer* to you."
[2] And when they heard that he was addressing them in the Hebrew dialect, they became even more quiet; and he *said,
[3] "I am a Jew, born in Tarsus of Cilicia, but brought up in this city, educated under Gamaliel, strictly according to the law of our

22:3 I am a Jew. A response to the false charges raised by the Asian Jews. **born in Tarsus.** Tarsus was the chief city of Cilicia. **brought up in this city.** Paul was born among the Hellenistic Jews of the Diaspora, but had been brought up in Jerusalem. **Gamaliel.** That Paul had studied under the most celebrated rabbi of that day was further evidence that the charges against him were absurd. **law of our fathers.** As a student of Gamaliel, Paul received extensive training both in the Old Testament law and in the rabbinic traditions. Also, though he did not mention it to the crowd, he also had been a Pharisee. In light of all that, the charge that Paul opposed the law was ridiculous.

fathers, being zealous for God just as you all are today. ⁴ I persecuted this Way to the death, binding and putting both men and women into prisons, ⁵ as also the high priest and all the Council of the elders can testify. From them I also received letters to the brethren, and started off for Damascus in order to bring even those who were there to Jerusalem as prisoners to be punished.

⁶ "But it happened that as I was on my way, approaching Damascus about noontime, a very bright light suddenly flashed from heaven all around me, ⁷ and I fell to the ground and heard a voice saying to me, 'Saul, Saul, why are you persecuting Me?' ⁸ And I answered, 'Who are You, Lord?' And He said to me, 'I am Jesus the Nazarene, whom you are persecuting.' ⁹ And those who were with me saw the light, to be sure, but did not understand the voice of the One who was speaking to me. ¹⁰ And I said, 'What shall I do, Lord?' And the Lord said to me, 'Get up and go on into Damascus, and there you will be told of all that has been appointed for you to do.' ¹¹ But since I could not see because of the brightness of that light, I was led by the hand by those who were with me and came into Damascus.

¹² "A certain Ananias, a man who was devout by the standard of the Law, *and* well spoken of by all the Jews who lived there, ¹³ came to me, and standing near said to me, 'Brother Saul, receive your sight!' And at that very time I looked up at him. ¹⁴ And he said, 'The God of our fathers has appointed you to know His will and to see the Righteous One and to hear an utterance from His mouth. ¹⁵ For you will be a witness for Him to all men of what you have seen and heard. ¹⁶ Now why do you delay? Get up and be baptized, and wash away your sins, calling on His name.'

¹⁷ "It happened when I returned to Jerusalem and was praying in the temple, that I fell into a trance, ¹⁸ and I saw Him saying to me, 'Make haste, and get out of Jerusalem quickly, because they will not accept your testimony about Me.' ¹⁹ And I said, 'Lord, they themselves understand that in one synagogue after another I used to imprison and beat those who believed in You. ²⁰ And when the blood of Your witness Stephen was being shed, I also was standing by approving, and watching out for the coats of those who were slaying him.' ²¹ And He said to me, 'Go! For I will send you far away to the Gentiles.' "

²² They listened to him up to this statement, and *then* they raised their voices and said, "Away with such a fellow from the earth, for he should not be allowed to live!" ²³ And as they were crying out and throwing off their cloaks and tossing dust into the air, ²⁴ the

22:21–23 Paul's insistence that the Lord had sent him to minister to the despised Gentiles was too much for the crowd. They viewed the teaching that Gentiles could be saved without first becoming Jewish proselytes (thus granting them equal status with the Jewish people before God) as intolerable blasphemy.

commander ordered him to be brought into the barracks, stating that he should be examined by scourging so that he might find out the reason why they were shouting against him that way. ²⁵ But when they stretched him out with thongs, Paul said to the centurion who was standing by, "Is it lawful for you to scourge a man who is a Roman and uncondemned?" ²⁶ When the centurion heard *this,* he went to the commander and told him, saying, "What are you about to do? For this man is a Roman." ²⁷ The commander came and said to him, "Tell me, are you a Roman?" And he said, "Yes." ²⁸ The commander answered, "I acquired this citizenship with a large sum of money." And Paul said, "But I was actually born *a citizen.*" ²⁹ Therefore those who were about to examine him immediately let go of him; and the commander also was afraid when he found out that he was a Roman, and because he had put him in chains.

³⁰ But on the next day, wishing to know for certain why he had been accused by the Jews, he released him and ordered the chief priests and all the Council to assemble, and brought Paul down and set him before them.

In Ezra 3:3, it mentions "the people of the lands." These were the settlers who had come to occupy the land during the 70 years of Israel's absence. They were deportees brought in from other countries by the Assyrians and the Babylonians. These inhabitants saw the Jews as a threat and quickly wanted to undermine their allegiance to God (4:1, 2). These are called "the enemies"—Israel's enemies in the region, who resisted their reestablishment of the temple.

These enemies came to the Jews offering their assistance, saying, "We have been sacrificing to Him" (v. 2). This false claim represented the syncretistic worship of the Samaritans, whose ancestry came from intermarriage with foreign immigrants in Samaria after 722 B.C. (4:10). In the British Museum is a large cylinder; and inscribed on it are the annals of Esarhaddon, an Assyrian king (ca. 681–669 B.C.), who deported a large population of Israelites from Palestine. A consequent settlement of Babylonian colonists took their place and intermarried with remaining Jewish women and their descendants. The result was the mongrel race called Samaritans. They had developed a superstitious form of worshiping God (2Ki 17:26–34).

Idolatry had been the chief cause for Judah's deportation to Babylon, and they wanted to avoid it altogether. While they still had their spiritual problems (Ezr 9–10), they rejected any form of mixed religion, particularly this offer of cooperation which had sabotage as its goal (vv. 4–5). "King Cyrus...commanded us." This note gave authority to their refusal.

Nevertheless, the enemies hired counselors who managed to "frustrate" the work on the temple. This caused a 16-year delay (ca. 536–520 B.C.). As a result, the people took more interest in their personal affairs than in spiritual matters (Hag 1:2–6).

JULY 22

Ezra 5:1–6:22

5 When the prophets, Haggai the prophet and Zechariah the son of Iddo, prophesied to the Jews who were in Judah and Jerusalem in the name of the God of Israel, who was over them, ² then Zerubbabel the son of Shealtiel and Jeshua the son of Jozadak arose and began to rebuild the house of God which is in Jerusalem; and the prophets of God were with them supporting them.

³ At that time Tattenai, the governor of *the province* beyond the River, and Shethar-bozenai and their colleagues came to them

5:1 Haggai...and Zechariah. The book of Haggai is styled as a "royal administrative correspondence" (Hag 1:13) sent from the Sovereign King of the Universe through the "messenger of the LORD," Haggai (Hag 1:13). Part of its message is addressed specifically to Zerubbabel, the political leader, and Joshua, the religious leader, telling them to "take courage...and work" on the temple because God was with them (Hag 2:4). These two prophets gave severe reproaches and threats if the people did not return to the building and promised national prosperity if they did. Not long after the exiles heard this message, the temple work began afresh after a 16-year hiatus.

and spoke to them thus, "Who issued you a decree to rebuild this temple and to finish this structure?" ⁴ Then we told them accordingly what the names of the men were who were reconstructing this building. ⁵ But the eye of their God was on the elders of the Jews, and they did not stop them until a report could come to Darius, and then a written reply be returned concerning it.

5:5 But the eye of their God was on the elders. God's hand of protection which led this endeavor allowed the work to continue while official communication was going on with Darius, the Persian king.

⁶ *This is* the copy of the letter which Tattenai, the governor of *the province* beyond the River, and Shethar-bozenai and his colleagues the officials, who were beyond the River, sent to Darius the king. ⁷ They sent a report to him in which it was written thus: "To Darius the king, all peace. ⁸ Let it be known to the king that we have gone to the province of Judah, to the house of the great God, which is being built with huge stones, and beams are being laid in the walls; and this work is going on with great care and is succeeding in their hands. ⁹ Then we asked those elders and said to them thus, 'Who issued you a decree to rebuild this temple and to finish this

structure?' ¹⁰ We also asked them their names so as to inform you, and that we might write down the names of the men who were at their head. ¹¹ Thus they answered us, saying, 'We are the servants of the God of heaven and earth and are rebuilding the temple that was built many years ago, which a great king of Israel built and finished. ¹² But because our fathers had provoked the God of heaven to wrath, He gave them into the hand of Nebuchadnezzar king of Babylon, the Chaldean, *who* destroyed this temple and deported the people to Babylon. ¹³ However, in the first year of Cyrus king of Babylon, King Cyrus issued a decree to rebuild this house of God. ¹⁴ Also the gold and silver utensils of the house of God which Nebuchadnezzar had taken from the temple in Jerusalem, and brought them to the temple of Babylon, these King Cyrus took from the temple of Babylon and they were given to one whose name was Sheshbazzar, whom he had appointed governor. ¹⁵ He said to him, "Take these utensils, go *and* deposit them in the temple in Jerusalem and let the house of God be rebuilt in its place." ¹⁶ Then that Sheshbazzar came *and* laid the foundations of the house of God in Jerusalem; and from then until now it has been under construction and it is not *yet* completed.' ¹⁷ Now if it pleases the king, let a search be conducted in the king's treasure house, which is there in Babylon, if it be that a decree was issued by King Cyrus to rebuild this house of God at Jerusalem; and let the king send to us his decision concerning this *matter*."

6 Then King Darius issued a decree, and search was made in the archives, where the treasures were stored in Babylon. ² In Ecbatana in the fortress, which is in the province of Media, a scroll was found and there was written in it as follows: "Memorandum— ³ In the first year of King Cyrus, Cyrus the king issued a decree: '*Concerning* the house of God at Jerusalem, let the temple, the place where sacrifices are offered, be rebuilt and let its foundations be retained, its height being 60 cubits and its width 60 cubits; ⁴ with three layers of huge stones and one layer of timbers. And let the cost be paid from the royal treasury. ⁵ Also let the gold and silver utensils of the house of God, which Nebuchadnezzar took from the temple in Jerusalem and brought to Babylon, be returned and brought to their places in the temple in Jerusalem; and you shall put *them* in the house of God.'

⁶ "Now *therefore*, Tattenai, governor of *the province* beyond the River, Shethar-bozenai and your colleagues, the officials of *the prov*-

inces beyond the River, keep away from there. ⁷ Leave this work on the house of God alone; let the governor of the Jews and the elders of the Jews rebuild this house of God on its site. ⁸ Moreover, I issue a decree concerning what you are to do for these elders of Judah in the rebuilding of this house of God: the full cost is to be paid to these people from the royal treasury out of the taxes of *the provinces* beyond the River, and that without delay. ⁹ Whatever is needed, both young bulls, rams, and lambs for a burnt offering to the God of heaven, and wheat, salt, wine and anointing oil, as the priests in Jerusalem request, *it* is to be given to them daily without fail, ¹⁰ that they may offer acceptable sacrifices to the God of heaven and pray for the life of the king and his sons. ¹¹ And I issued a decree that any man who violates this edict, a timber shall be drawn from his house and he shall be impaled on it and his house shall be made a refuse heap on account of this. ¹² May the God who has caused His name to dwell there overthrow any king or people who attempts to change *it*, so as to destroy this house of God in Jerusalem. I, Darius, have issued *this* decree, let *it* be carried out with all diligence!"

¹³ Then Tattenai, the governor of *the province* beyond the River, Shethar-bozenai and their colleagues carried out *the decree* with all diligence, just as King Darius had sent. ¹⁴ And the elders of the Jews were successful in building through the prophesying of Haggai the prophet and Zechariah the son of Iddo. And they finished building according to the command of the God of Israel and the decree of Cyrus, Darius, and Artaxerxes king of Persia. ¹⁵ This temple was completed on the third day of the month Adar; it was the sixth year of the reign of King Darius.

¹⁶ And the sons of Israel, the priests, the

6:14 the command of the God of Israel...the decree of Cyrus. This is not the normal term for command, but it is the same word translated "decree" or "administrative order" throughout the book. The message here is powerful. It was the decree from God, the Sovereign of the universe, which gave administrative authority to rebuild the temple. The decrees (same word) of 3 of the greatest monarchs in the history of the ancient Near East were only a secondary issue. God rules the universe and He raises up kings, then pulls them from their thrones when they have served His administration.

Levites and the rest of the exiles, celebrated the dedication of this house of God with joy. [17] They offered for the dedication of this temple of God 100 bulls, 200 rams, 400 lambs, and as a sin offering for all Israel 12 male goats, corresponding to the number of the tribes of Israel. [18] Then they appointed the priests to their divisions and the Levites in their orders for the service of God in Jerusalem, as it is written in the book of Moses.

[19] The exiles observed the Passover on the fourteenth of the first month. [20] For the priests and the Levites had purified themselves together; all of them were pure. Then they slaughtered the Passover *lamb* for all the exiles, both for their brothers the priests and for themselves. [21] The sons of Israel who returned from exile and all those who had separated themselves from the impurity of the nations of the land to *join* them, to seek the LORD God of Israel, ate *the Passover.* [22] And they observed the Feast of Unleavened Bread seven days with joy, for the LORD had caused them to rejoice, and had turned the heart of the king of Assyria toward them to encourage them in the work of the house of God, the God of Israel.

6:22 turned the heart of the king of Assyria toward them. By turning the heart of the king in their favor by allowing them to complete the rebuilding, God encouraged His people. They understood the verse, "The king's heart is…in the hand of the LORD" (Pr 21:1) better through this ordeal. The title "King of Assyria" was held by every king who succeeded the great Neo-Assyrian Empire regardless of what country they may have come from.

Psalm 87:1–7

A Psalm of the sons of Korah. A Song.

H is foundation is in the
  holy mountains.
[2] The LORD loves the gates of Zion
  More than all the *other*
    dwelling places of Jacob.
[3] Glorious things are spoken of you,
  O city of God. *Selah*
[4] "I shall mention Rahab and Babylon
  among those who know Me;
  Behold, Philistia and Tyre
    with Ethiopia;
  'This one was born there.'"
[5] But of Zion it shall be said, "This one
  and that one were born in her";

And the Most High Himself
  will establish her.
[6] The LORD will count when He
  registers the peoples,
  "This one was born there." *Selah*
[7] Then those who sing as well
  as those who play the
    flutes *shall say,*
  "All my springs *of joy* are
    in you."

Proverbs 21:19–20

[19] It is better to live in a desert
  land
  Than with a contentious
    and vexing woman.
[20] There is precious treasure and oil
  in the dwelling of the wise,
  But a foolish man swallows it up.

Acts 23:1–15

23 Paul, looking intently at the Council, said, "Brethren, I have lived my life with a perfectly good conscience before God up to this day." [2] The high priest Ananias commanded those standing beside him to strike him on the mouth. [3] Then Paul said to him, "God is going to strike you, you whitewashed wall! Do you sit to try me according to the Law, and in violation of the Law order me to be struck?" [4] But the bystanders said,

23:2 high priest Ananias. Not the Annas of the Gospels, this man was one of Israel's cruelest and most corrupt High Priests. His pro-Roman policies alienated him from the Jewish people, who murdered him at the outset of the revolt against Rome (A.D. 66). **commanded… to strike him.** An illegal act in keeping with Ananias' brutal character. The verb translated "strike" is used of the mob's beating of Paul (21:32) and the Roman soldiers' beating of Jesus (Mt 27:30). It was no mere slap on the face, but a vicious blow.

23:3 whitewashed wall! See Ezekiel 13:10–16; Matthew 23:27. **in violation of the Law.** Outraged by the High Priest's flagrant violation of Jewish law, Paul flared up in anger. When Jesus was similarly struck in violation of the law, He reacted by calmly asking the reason for the blow (Jn 18:23). Paul's reaction was wrong, as he would shortly admit (v. 5). Although an evil man, Ananias still held a God-ordained office, and was to be granted the respect that position demanded.

"Do you revile God's high priest?" ⁵And Paul said, "I was not aware, brethren, that he was high priest; for it is written, 'You shall not speak evil of a ruler of your people.'"

⁶But perceiving that one group were Sadducees and the other Pharisees, Paul *began* crying out in the Council, "Brethren, I am a Pharisee, a son of Pharisees; I am on trial for the hope and resurrection of the dead!" ⁷As he said this, there occurred a dissension between the Pharisees and Sadducees, and the assembly was divided. ⁸For the Sadducees say that there is no resurrection, nor an angel, nor a spirit, but the Pharisees acknowledge them all. ⁹And there occurred

23:7 a dissension. There were major social, political, and theological differences between the Sadducees and Pharisees. By raising the issue of the resurrection, Paul appealed to the Pharisees for support on perhaps the most important theological difference. Since the resurrection of Jesus Christ is also the central theme of Christianity, this was no cynical ploy on Paul's part to divide the Sanhedrin over a trivial point of theology.

a great uproar; and some of the scribes of the Pharisaic party stood up and *began* to argue heatedly, saying, "We find nothing wrong with this man; suppose a spirit or an angel has spoken to him?" ¹⁰And as a great dissension was developing, the commander was afraid Paul would be torn to pieces by them and ordered the troops to go down and take him away from them by force, and bring him into the barracks.

¹¹But on the night *immediately* following, the Lord stood at his side and said, "Take courage; for as you have solemnly witnessed to My cause at Jerusalem, so you must witness at Rome also."

¹²When it was day, the Jews formed a conspiracy and bound themselves under an oath, saying that they would neither eat nor drink until they had killed Paul. ¹³There were more than forty who formed this plot. ¹⁴They came to the chief priests and the elders and said, "We have bound ourselves under a solemn oath to taste nothing until we have killed Paul. ¹⁵Now therefore, you and the Council notify the commander to bring him down to you, as though you were going to determine his case by a more thorough investigation; and we for our part are ready to slay him before he comes near *the place.*"

DAY 22: How does Psalm 87 describe God's love for Jerusalem?

This psalm describes the Lord's love for Jerusalem and exalts this city as the religious center of the world in the coming messianic kingdom (Ps 48). Though the nations of the world (even including some of Israel's former enemies) will worship the Lord then, Israel will still be the favored nation (Is. 2:2–4; 19:23–25; 45:22–25; 56:6–8; Zec 8:20–23; 14:16–19).

"His foundation is in the holy mountains" (v. 1). "His foundation" means "His founded city," namely Jerusalem, located in the hill country of Judea. "The LORD loves the gates of Zion" (v. 2). Zion is a poetic description of Jerusalem, seemingly used by the Old Testament writers when special spiritual and religious significance was being attached to the city. Though God certainly loved other cities in Israel, He did not choose any of them to be His worship center. The gates represent the access of the potential worshiper into the city where he could come into a special worshiping relationship with God. "More than all the other dwelling places of Jacob." The other cities in Israel were not chosen by God to be the place of His special dwelling.

"Glorious things are spoken of you, O city of God" (v. 3). Jerusalem was God's city because their God met His people in praise and offerings. "I shall mention Rahab and Babylon" (v. 4). Rahab was a monster of ancient pagan mythology and symbolized Egypt in the Old Testament (Ps 89:10; Is. 30:7; 51:9). Two of the superpowers of the ancient world, fierce enemies of Israel, will one day worship the Lord in Zion (Is. 19:19–25). "Philistia…Tyre…Ethiopia" (Ps 87:4). Three more Gentile nations, ancient enemies of Israel, whose descendants will worship the Lord in Jerusalem (Is. 14:28–32; 18:1–7). This multinational worship is pictured as a great joy to the Lord Himself. "This one was born there" (Ps 87:6). To be born in Jerusalem will be noted as a special honor in the messianic kingdom (vv. 5–6; also Zec 8:20–23).

"All my springs of joy are in you" (v. 7). "Springs" is a metaphor for the source of joyful blessings. Eternal salvation, including the death and resurrection of Christ, is rooted in Jerusalem. The prophets also tell of a literal fountain flowing from the temple in Jerusalem which will water the surrounding land (Joel 3:18; Eze 47:1–12).

JULY 23

Ezra 7:1–8:36

7 Now after these things, in the reign of Artaxerxes king of Persia, *there went up* Ezra son of Seraiah, son of Azariah, son of Hilkiah, ² son of Shallum, son of Zadok, son of Ahitub, ³ son of Amariah, son of Azariah, son of Meraioth, ⁴ son of Zerahiah, son of Uzzi, son of Bukki, ⁵ son of Abishua, son of Phinehas, son of Eleazar, son of Aaron the chief priest. ⁶ This Ezra went up from Babylon, and he was a scribe skilled in the law of Moses, which the LORD God of Israel had given; and the king granted him all he requested because the hand of the LORD his God *was* upon him.

7:6 a scribe skilled in the law. Ezra's role as a scribe was critical to reinstate the nation since the leaders had to go back to the law and interpret it. This was no small task because many aspects of life had changed in the intervening 1,000 years since the law was first given. Tradition says Ezra had the law memorized and could write it from recall. **the hand of the LORD his God *was* upon him.** This refrain occurs throughout the books of Ezra and Nehemiah. Its resounding presence assures the reader that it was not by the shrewd leadership skills of a few men that Judah, with its temple and walls, was rebuilt in the midst of a powerful Medo-Persian Empire. Rather it was the sovereign hand of the wise and powerful King of the universe that allowed this to happen.

⁷ Some of the sons of Israel and some of the priests, the Levites, the singers, the gatekeepers and the temple servants went up to Jerusalem in the seventh year of King Artaxerxes.

⁸ He came to Jerusalem in the fifth month, which was in the seventh year of the king. ⁹ For on the first of the first month he began to go up from Babylon; and on the first of the fifth month he came to Jerusalem, because the good hand of his God *was* upon him. ¹⁰ For Ezra had set his heart to study the law of the LORD and to practice *it*, and to teach *His* statutes and ordinances in Israel.

¹¹ Now this is the copy of the decree which King Artaxerxes gave to Ezra the priest, the scribe, learned in the words of the commandments of the LORD and His statutes to Israel: ¹² "Artaxerxes, king of kings, to Ezra the priest, the scribe of the law of the God of heaven, perfect *peace*. And now ¹³ I have issued a

7:10 study...practice...teach. The pattern of Ezra's preparation is exemplary. He studied before he attempted to live a life of obedience, and he studied and practiced the law in his own life before he opened his mouth to teach that law. But the success of Ezra's leadership did not come from his strength alone, but most significantly because "the good hand of his God *was* upon him" (7:9).

decree that any of the people of Israel and their priests and the Levites in my kingdom who are willing to go to Jerusalem, may go with you. ¹⁴ Forasmuch as you are sent by the king and his seven counselors to inquire concerning Judah and Jerusalem according to the law of your God which is in your hand, ¹⁵ and to bring the silver and gold, which the king and his counselors have freely offered to the God of Israel, whose dwelling is in Jerusalem, ¹⁶ with all the silver and gold which you find in the whole province of Babylon, along with the freewill offering of the people and of the priests, who offered willingly for the house of their God which is in Jerusalem; ¹⁷ with this money, therefore, you shall diligently buy bulls, rams and lambs, with their grain offerings and their drink offerings and offer them on the altar of the house of your God which is in Jerusalem. ¹⁸ Whatever seems good to you and to your brothers to do with the rest of the silver and gold, you may do according to the will of your God. ¹⁹ Also the utensils which are given to you for the service of the house of your God, deliver in full before the God of Jerusalem. ²⁰ The rest of the needs for the house of your God, for which you may have occasion to provide, provide *for it* from the royal treasury.

²¹ "I, even I, King Artaxerxes, issue a decree to all the treasurers who are *in the provinces* beyond the River, that whatever Ezra the priest, the scribe of the law of the God of heaven, may require of you, it shall be done diligently, ²² *even* up to 100 talents of silver, 100 kors of wheat, 100 baths of wine, 100 baths of oil, and salt as needed. ²³ Whatever is commanded by the God of heaven, let it be done with zeal for the house of the God of heaven, so that there will not be wrath against the kingdom of the king and his sons. ²⁴ We also inform you that it is not allowed to impose tax, tribute or toll *on* any of the priests, Levites, singers, doorkeepers, Nethinim or servants of this house of God.

25 "You, Ezra, according to the wisdom of your God which is in your hand, appoint magistrates and judges that they may judge all the people who are in the province beyond the River, even all those who know the laws of your God; and you may teach anyone who is ignorant of them. 26 Whoever will not observe the law of your God and the law of the king, let judgment be executed upon him strictly, whether for death or for banishment or for confiscation of goods or for imprisonment."

27 Blessed be the LORD, the God of our fathers, who has put such a thing as this in the king's heart, to adorn the house of the LORD which is in Jerusalem, 28 and has extended lovingkindness to me before the king and his counselors and before all the king's mighty princes. Thus I was strengthened according to the hand of the LORD my God upon me, and I gathered leading men from Israel to go up with me.

8 Now these are the heads of their fathers' households and the genealogical enrollment of those who went up with me from Babylon in the reign of King Artaxerxes: 2 of the sons of Phinehas, Gershom; of the sons of Ithamar, Daniel; of the sons of David, Hattush; 3 of the sons of Shecaniah who was of the sons of Parosh, Zechariah and with him 150 males who were in the genealogical list; 4 of the sons of Pahath-moab, Eliehoenai the son of Zerahiah and 200 males with him; 5 of the sons of Zattu, Shecaniah, the son of Jahaziel and 300 males with him; 6 and of the sons of Adin, Ebed the son of Jonathan and 50 males with him; 7 and of the sons of Elam, Jeshaiah the son of Athaliah and 70 males with him; 8 and of the sons of Shephatiah, Zebadiah the son of Michael and 80 males with him; 9 of the sons of Joab, Obadiah the son of Jehiel and 218 males with him; 10 and of the sons of Bani, Shelomith, the son of Josiphiah and 160 males with him; 11 and of the sons of Bebai, Zechariah the son of Bebai and 28 males with him; 12 and of the sons of Azgad, Johanan the son of Hakkatan and 110 males with him; 13 and of the sons of Adonikam, the last ones, these being their names, Eliphelet, Jeuel and Shemaiah, and 60 males with them; 14 and of the sons of Bigvai, Uthai and Zabbud, and 70 males with them.

15 Now I assembled them at the river that runs to Ahava, where we camped for three days; and when I observed the people and the priests, I did not find any Levites there. 16 So I sent for Eliezer, Ariel, Shemaiah, Elnathan, Jarib, Elnathan, Nathan, Zechariah and Meshullam, leading men, and for Joiarib and Elnathan, teachers. 17 I sent them to Iddo the leading man at the place Casiphia; and I told them what to say to Iddo and his brothers, the temple servants at the place Casiphia, that is, to bring ministers to us for the house of our God. 18 According to the good hand of our God upon us they brought us a man of insight of the sons of Mahli, the son of Levi, the son of Israel, namely Sherebiah, and his sons and brothers, 18 men; 19 and Hashabiah and Jeshaiah of the sons of Merari, with his brothers and their sons, 20 men; 20 and 220 of the temple servants, whom David and the princes had given for the service of the Levites, all of them designated by name.

21 Then I proclaimed a fast there at the river of Ahava, that we might humble ourselves before our God to seek from Him a safe journey for us, our little ones, and all our possessions. 22 For I was ashamed to request from the king troops and horsemen to protect us from the enemy on the way, because we had said to the king, "The hand of our God is favorably disposed to all those who seek Him, but His power and His anger are against all those who forsake Him." 23 So we fasted and sought our God concerning this matter, and He listened to our entreaty.

8:21–23 I proclaimed a fast. They would soon begin the long journey. Such travel was dangerous, for the roads were frequented by thieves who robbed for survival. Even messengers traveled with caravans to ensure their safety. Ezra and the people did not want to confuse the king regarding their trust in God's protection so they entreated Him for safety with a prayerful fast. God honored their prayer of faith with His protection.

24 Then I set apart twelve of the leading priests, Sherebiah, Hashabiah, and with them ten of their brothers; 25 and I weighed out to them the silver, the gold and the utensils, the offering for the house of our God which the king and his counselors and his princes and all Israel present there had offered. 26 Thus I weighed into their hands 650 talents of silver, and silver utensils worth 100 talents, and 100 gold talents, 27 and 20 gold bowls worth 1,000 darics, and two utensils of fine shiny bronze, precious as gold. 28 Then I said to them, "You are holy to the LORD, and the utensils are holy; and the silver and the gold are a freewill offering to the LORD God of your fathers.

²⁹Watch and keep *them* until you weigh *them* before the leading priests, the Levites and the heads of the fathers' *households* of Israel at Jerusalem, *in* the chambers of the house of the LORD." ³⁰So the priests and the Levites accepted the weighed out silver and gold and the utensils, to bring *them* to Jerusalem to the house of our God.

³¹Then we journeyed from the river Ahava on the twelfth of the first month to go to Jerusalem; and the hand of our God was over us, and He delivered us from the hand of the enemy and the ambushes by the way. ³²Thus we came to Jerusalem and remained there three days. ³³On the fourth day the silver and the gold and the utensils were weighed out in the house of our God into the hand of Meremoth the son of Uriah the priest, and with him *was* Eleazar the son of Phinehas; and with them *were* the Levites, Jozabad the son of Jeshua and Noadiah the son of Binnui. ³⁴Everything *was* numbered and weighed, and all the weight was recorded at that time.

³⁵The exiles who had come from the captivity offered burnt offerings to the God of Israel: 12 bulls for all Israel, 96 rams, 77 lambs, 12 male goats for a sin offering, all as a burnt offering to the LORD. ³⁶Then they delivered the king's edicts to the king's satraps and to the governors *in the provinces* beyond the River, and they supported the people and the house of God.

Psalm 88:1-5

A Song. A Psalm of the sons of Korah.
For the choir director; according to Mahalath Leannoth. A Maskil of Heman the Ezrahite.

O LORD, the God of my salvation,
  I have cried out by day and
    in the night before You.
² Let my prayer come before You;
  Incline Your ear to my cry!
³ For my soul has had enough troubles,
  And my life has drawn near to Sheol.
⁴ I am reckoned among those
    who go down to the pit;
  I have become like a man
    without strength,
⁵ Forsaken among the dead,
  Like the slain who lie in the grave,

88:4 go down to the pit. "Pit" is one of several references to the grave in this psalm (see the dead, vv. 5, 10; Sheol, or the grave, vv. 3, 5, 11; Abaddon, v. 11).

Whom You remember no more,
And they are cut off from Your hand.

Proverbs 21:21-22

²¹ He who pursues righteousness
    and loyalty
  Finds life, righteousness and honor.
²² A wise man scales the
    city of the mighty
  And brings down the stronghold
    in which they trust.

Acts 23:16-35

¹⁶But the son of Paul's sister heard of their ambush, and he came and entered the barracks and told Paul. ¹⁷Paul called one of the centurions to him and said, "Lead this young

23:16 son of Paul's sister. The only clear reference in Scripture to Paul's family (for other possible references see Ro 16:7, 11, 21). Why he was in Jerusalem, away from the family home in Tarsus, is not known. Nor is it evident why he would want to warn his uncle, since Paul's family possibly disinherited him when he became a Christian (Php 3:8). **entered the barracks and told Paul.** Since Paul was not under arrest, but merely in protective custody, he was able to receive visitors.

man to the commander, for he has something to report to him." ¹⁸So he took him and led him to the commander and *said, "Paul the prisoner called me to him and asked me to lead this young man to you since he has something to tell you." ¹⁹The commander took him by the hand and stepping aside, *began* to inquire of him privately, "What is it that you have to report to me?" ²⁰And he said, "The Jews have agreed to ask you to bring Paul down tomorrow to the Council, as though they were going to inquire somewhat more thoroughly about him. ²¹So do not listen to them, for more than forty of them are lying in wait for him who have bound themselves under a curse not to eat or drink until they slay him; and now they are ready and waiting for the promise from you." ²²So the commander let the young man go, instructing him, "Tell no one that you have notified me of these things." ²³And he called to him two of the centurions and said, "Get two hundred soldiers ready by the third hour of the night to proceed to Caesarea, with seventy horsemen and two hundred spearmen." ²⁴*They were* also to provide mounts to put Paul on and bring him safely to Felix the governor. ²⁵ And he wrote a letter having this form:

²⁶ "Claudius Lysias, to the most excellent governor Felix, greetings. ²⁷ "When this man was arrested by the Jews and was about to be slain by them, I came up to them with the troops and rescued him, having learned that he was a Roman. ²⁸ And wanting to ascertain the charge for which they were accusing him, I brought him down to their Council; ²⁹ and I found him to be accused over questions about their Law, but under no accusation deserving death or imprisonment.

³⁰ "When I was informed that there would be a plot against the man, I sent him to you at once, also instructing his accusers to bring charges against him before you."

³¹ So the soldiers, in accordance with their orders, took Paul and brought him by night to Antipatris. ³² But the next day, leaving the horsemen to go on with him, they returned to the barracks. ³³ When these had come to Caesarea and delivered the letter to the governor, they also presented Paul to him. ³⁴ When he had read it, he asked from what province he was, and when he learned that he was from Cilicia, ³⁵ he said, "I will give you a hearing after your accusers arrive also," giving orders for him to be kept in Herod's Praetorium.

23:27 having learned that he was a Roman. Actually, Lysias did not find this out until after he arrested Paul (22:25–26). Lysias sought to portray himself in the best possible light before the governor. For that reason, he also neglected to mention his order to have Paul scourged (22:24), and his mistaken assumption that he was the notorious Egyptian assassin (21:38).

DAY 23: How can Luke's authorship of Acts be defended when his name is not mentioned in the book?

Lack of the author's name is not an unusual challenge in establishing the authorship of a Bible book. Many books of the Bible come to us without obvious human authorship. In most cases, however, internal and external clues lead us to reasonable confidence in identifying the author. One benefit created by initial anonymity involves recognizing that the Bible books originated by the inspiration of the Holy Spirit. It may take some effort to discover whom God used in writing one of those books, but the original Author is not in question.

The Gospel of Luke and Acts of the Apostles share numerous marks of common human authorship. They are addressed to the same person—Theophilus (Lk 1:3; Ac 1:1). They are parallel in style. The second book claims to be an extension of the first.

Luke was in a unique position to record Acts of the Apostles. He was Paul's close friend, traveling companion, and personal physician (Col 4:14). His work indicates that he was a careful researcher (Lk 1:1–4) and an accurate historian, displaying an intimate knowledge of Roman laws and customs. His records of the geography of Palestine, Asia Minor, and Italy offer flawless details.

In writing Acts, Luke drew on written sources (15:23–29; 23:26–30). He, also, no doubt, interviewed key figures, such as Peter, John, and others in the Jerusalem church. Paul's 2-year imprisonment at Caesarea (24:27) gave Luke ample opportunity to interview Philip and his daughters (important sources of information on the early days of the church). Finally, Luke's frequent use of the first-person plural pronouns "we" and "us" (16:10–17; 20:5–21:18; 27:1–28:16) reveals that he was an eyewitness to many of the events recorded in Acts.

JULY 24

Ezra 9:1–10:44

9 Now when these things had been completed, the princes approached me, saying, "The people of Israel and the priests and the Levites have not separated themselves from the peoples of the lands, according to their abominations, *those* of the Canaanites, the Hittites, the Perizzites, the Jebusites, the Ammonites, the Moabites, the Egyptians and the Amorites. ² For they have taken some of their daughters *as wives* for themselves and for their sons, so that the holy race has intermingled with the peoples of the lands; indeed, the hands of the princes and the rulers have been foremost in this unfaithfulness." ³ When I heard about this matter, I tore my garment and my robe, and pulled some of the hair

9:1 when these things had been completed. This refers to the implementation of the different trusts and duties committed to him. **priests...Levites.** As was the case before the Assyrian and Babylonian deportations, the spiritual leadership defaulted along with the people (Is 24:2; Jer 5:30–31; 6:13–15; Hos 4:9; Mal 2:1–9; 2Ti 4:2–4). **abominations.** The reason for this exclusiveness was to keep the people pure. In the first settlement, Israel was warned not to make covenants with the nations, which would result in intermarriages and inevitably the worship of foreign gods (Ex 34:10–17; Dt 7:1–5). To a great extent, the continual violation of this precipitated the 70-year exile from which they had just returned. Ezra found out it had happened again and called for immediate repentance. Nehemiah (Ne 13:23–27) and Malachi (Mal 2:14–16) later encountered the same sin. It is unthinkable that the Jews would so quickly go down the same disastrous path of idolatry. Neither wrath from God in the exile to Babylon, nor grace from God in the return was enough to keep them from defecting again.

9:5–15 Ezra's priestly prayer of intercession and confession is like Daniel's (Da 9:1–20) and Nehemiah's (Ne 1:4–11), in that he used plural pronouns that identified himself with the people's sin, even though he did not participate in it. The use of "we," "our" and "us" demonstrates Ezra's understanding that the sin of the few is sufficient to contaminate the many.

---

from my head and my beard, and sat down appalled. ⁴Then everyone who trembled at the words of the God of Israel on account of the unfaithfulness of the exiles gathered to me, and I sat appalled until the evening offering.

⁵But at the evening offering I arose from my humiliation, even with my garment and my robe torn, and I fell on my knees and stretched out my hands to the LORD my God; ⁶and I said, "O my God, I am ashamed and embarrassed to lift up my face to You, my God, for our iniquities have risen above our heads and our guilt has grown even to the heavens. ⁷Since the days of our fathers to this day we *have been* in great guilt, and on account of our iniquities we, our kings *and* our priests have been given into the hand of the kings of the lands, to the sword, to captivity and to plunder and to open shame, as *it is* this day. ⁸But now for a brief moment grace has been *shown* from the LORD our God, to leave us an escaped remnant and to give us a peg in His holy place, that our God may enlighten our eyes and grant us a little reviving in our bondage. ⁹For we are slaves; yet in our bondage our God has not forsaken us, but has extended lovingkindness to us in the sight of the kings of Persia, to give us reviving to raise up the house of our God, to restore its ruins and to give us a wall in Judah and Jerusalem.

¹⁰"Now, our God, what shall we say after this? For we have forsaken Your commandments, ¹¹which You have commanded by Your servants the prophets, saying, 'The land which you are entering to possess is an unclean land with the uncleanness of the peoples of the lands, with their abominations which have filled it from end to end *and* with their impurity. ¹²So now do not give your daughters to their sons nor take their daughters to your sons, and never seek their peace or their prosperity, that you may be strong and eat the good *things* of the land and leave *it* as an inheritance to your sons forever.' ¹³After all that has come upon us for our evil deeds and our great guilt, since You our God have requited *us* less than our iniquities *deserve,* and have given us an escaped remnant as this, ¹⁴shall we again break Your commandments and intermarry with the peoples who commit these abominations? Would You not be angry with us to the point of destruction, until there is no remnant nor any who escape? ¹⁵O LORD God of Israel, You are righteous, for we have been left an escaped remnant, as *it is* this day; behold, we are before You in our guilt, for no one can stand before You because of this."

10 Now while Ezra was praying and making confession, weeping and prostrating himself before the house of God, a very large assembly, men, women and children, gathered to him from Israel; for the people wept bitterly. ²Shecaniah the son of Jehiel, one of the sons of Elam, said to Ezra, "We have been unfaithful to our God and have

10:1 praying and making confession, weeping and prostrating. Ezra's contrite spirit before the people was evident and they joined him. These extreme expressions of contrition demonstrated the seriousness of the sin and the genuineness of their repentance.

married foreign women from the peoples of the land; yet now there is hope for Israel in spite of this. ³ So now let us make a covenant with our God to put away all the wives and their children, according to the counsel of my lord and of those who tremble at the commandment of our God; and let it be done according to the law. ⁴ Arise! For *this* matter is your responsibility, but we will be with you; be courageous and act."

⁵ Then Ezra rose and made the leading priests, the Levites and all Israel, take oath that they would do according to this proposal; so they took the oath. ⁶ Then Ezra rose from before the house of God and went into the chamber of Jehohanan the son of Eliashib. Although he went there, he did not eat bread nor drink water, for he was mourning over the unfaithfulness of the exiles. ⁷ They made a proclamation throughout Judah and Jerusalem to all the exiles, that they should assemble at Jerusalem, ⁸ and that whoever would not come within three days, according to the counsel of the leaders and the elders, all his possessions should be forfeited and he himself excluded from the assembly of the exiles.

⁹ So all the men of Judah and Benjamin assembled at Jerusalem within the three days. It was the ninth month on the twentieth of the month, and all the people sat in the open square *before* the house of God, trembling because of this matter and the heavy rain. ¹⁰ Then Ezra the priest stood up and said to them, "You have been unfaithful and have married foreign wives adding to the guilt of Israel. ¹¹ Now therefore, make confession to the LORD God of your fathers and do His will; and separate yourselves from the peoples of the land and from the foreign wives." ¹² Then all the assembly replied with a loud voice, "That's right! As you have said, so it is our duty to do. ¹³ But there are many people; it is the rainy season and we are not able to stand in the open. Nor *can* the task *be done* in one or two days, for we have transgressed greatly in this matter. ¹⁴ Let our leaders represent the whole assembly and let all those in our cities who have married foreign wives come at appointed times, together with the elders and judges of each city, until the fierce anger of our God on account of this matter is turned away from us." ¹⁵ Only Jonathan the son of Asahel and Jahzeiah the son of Tikvah opposed this, with Meshullam and Shabbethai the Levite supporting them.

¹⁶ But the exiles did so. And Ezra the priest selected men *who were* heads of fathers'

households for *each of* their father's households, all of them by name. So they convened on the first day of the tenth month to investigate the matter. ¹⁷ They finished *investigating* all the men who had married foreign wives by the first day of the first month.

¹⁸ Among the sons of the priests who had married foreign wives were found of the sons of Jeshua the son of Jozadak, and his brothers: Maaseiah, Eliezer, Jarib and Gedaliah. ¹⁹ They pledged to put away their wives, and being guilty, *they offered* a ram of the flock for their offense. ²⁰ Of the sons of Immer *there were* Hanani and Zebadiah; ²¹ and of the sons of Harim: Maaseiah, Elijah, Shemaiah, Jehiel and Uzziah; ²² and of the sons of Pashhur: Elioenai, Maaseiah, Ishmael, Nethanel, Jozabad and Elasah.

²³ Of Levites *there were* Jozabad, Shimei, Kelaiah (that is, Kelita), Pethahiah, Judah and Eliezer.

²⁴ Of the singers *there was* Eliashib; and of the gatekeepers: Shallum, Telem and Uri.

²⁵ Of Israel, of the sons of Parosh *there were* Ramiah, Izziah, Malchijah, Mijamin, Eleazar, Malchijah and Benaiah; ²⁶ and of the sons of Elam: Mattaniah, Zechariah, Jehiel, Abdi, Jeremoth and Elijah; ²⁷ and of the sons of Zattu: Elioenai, Eliashib, Mattaniah, Jeremoth, Zabad and Aziza; ²⁸ and of the sons of Bebai: Jehohanan, Hananiah, Zabbai *and* Athlai; ²⁹ and of the sons of Bani: Meshullam, Malluch and Adaiah, Jashub, Sheal *and* Jeremoth; ³⁰ and of the sons of Pahath-moab: Adna, Chelal, Benaiah, Maaseiah, Mattaniah, Bezalel, Binnui and Manasseh; ³¹ and *of* the sons of Harim: Eliezer, Isshijah, Malchijah, Shemaiah, Shimeon, ³² Benjamin, Malluch *and* Shemariah; ³³ of the sons of Hashum: Mattenai, Mattattah, Zabad, Eliphelet, Jeremai, Manasseh *and* Shimei; ³⁴ of the sons of Bani: Maadai, Amram, Uel, ³⁵ Benaiah, Bedeiah, Cheluhi, ³⁶ Vaniah, Meremoth, Eliashib, ³⁷ Mattaniah, Mattenai, Jaasu, ³⁸ Bani, Binnui, Shimei, ³⁹ Shelemiah, Nathan, Adaiah, ⁴⁰ Machnadebai, Shashai, Sharai, ⁴¹ Azarel, Shelemiah, Shemariah, ⁴² Shallum, Amariah *and* Joseph. ⁴³ Of the sons of Nebo *there were* Jeiel, Mattithiah, Zabad, Zebina, Jaddai, Joel *and* Benaiah. ⁴⁴ All these had married foreign wives, and some of them had wives *by whom* they had children.

Psalm 88:6–10

⁶   You have put me in the lowest pit,
    In dark places, in the depths.
⁷   Your wrath has rested upon me,
    And You have afflicted me with all
    Your waves.   *Selah*

88:7 all Your waves. Like the waves rolling onto the seashore, so God has directed trouble after trouble on the psalmist (v. 17).

8 You have removed my
acquaintances far from me;
You have made me an object
of loathing to them;
I am shut up and cannot go out.
9 My eye has wasted away
because of affliction;
I have called upon You
every day, O LORD;
I have spread out my hands
to You.

10 Will You perform wonders
for the dead?
Will the departed spirits rise
and praise You?   *Selah*

Proverbs 21:23–24

23 He who guards his mouth
and his tongue,
Guards his soul from troubles.
24 "Proud," "Haughty," "Scoffer,"
are his names,
Who acts with insolent pride.

Acts 24:1–27

24 After five days the high priest Ananias came down with some elders, with an attorney *named* Tertullus, and they brought charges to the governor against Paul. 2 After *Paul* had been summoned, Tertullus began to accuse him, saying *to the governor,*

"Since we have through you attained much peace, and since by your providence reforms are being carried out for this nation, 3 we acknowledge *this* in every way and everywhere, most excellent Felix, with

24:3 Felix. Governor of Judea from A.D. 52 to 59. Felix was a former slave whose brother (a favorite of Emperor Claudius) had obtained for him the position as governor. He was not highly regarded by the influential Romans of his day and accomplished little during his term as governor. He defeated the Egyptian and his followers, but his brutality angered the Jews and led to his ouster as governor by Emperor Nero two years after Paul's hearing (v. 27).

all thankfulness. 4 But, that I may not weary you any further, I beg you to grant us, by your kindness, a brief hearing. 5 For we have found this man a real pest and a fellow who stirs up dissension among all the Jews throughout the world, and a ringleader of the sect of the Nazarenes. 6 And he even tried to desecrate the temple; and then we arrested him. [We wanted to judge him according to our own Law. 7 But Lysias the commander came along, and with much violence took him out of our hands, 8 ordering his accusers to come before you.] By examining him yourself concerning all these matters you will be able to ascertain the things of which we accuse him." 9 The Jews also joined in the attack, asserting that these things were so.

10 When the governor had nodded for him to speak, Paul responded:

"Knowing that for many years you have been a judge to this nation, I cheerfully make my defense, 11 since you can take note of the fact that no more than twelve days ago I went up to Jerusalem to worship. 12 Neither in the temple, nor in the synagogues, nor in the city *itself* did they find me carrying on a discussion with anyone or causing a riot. 13 Nor can they prove to you *the charges* of which they now accuse me. 14 But this I admit to you, that according to the Way which they call a sect I do serve the God of our fathers, believing everything that is in accordance with the Law and that is written in the Prophets; 15 having a hope in God, which these men cherish themselves, that there shall certainly be a resurrection of both the righteous and the wicked. 16 In view of this, I also do my best to maintain always a blameless conscience *both* before God and before men. 17 Now after several years I came to bring alms to my nation and to present offerings; 18 in which they found me *occupied* in the temple, having been purified, without *any* crowd or uproar. But *there were* some Jews from Asia— 19 who ought to have been present before you and to make accusation, if they should have anything against me. 20 Or else let these men themselves tell what misdeed they found when I stood before the Council, 21 other than for this one statement which I shouted out while standing among them, 'For the resurrection of the dead I am on trial before you today.'"

22 But Felix, having a more exact knowledge about the Way, put them off, saying, "When Lysias the commander comes down, I will decide your case." 23 Then he gave orders to the centurion for him to be kept in custody and *yet* have *some* freedom, and not to

prevent any of his friends from ministering to him.

²⁴But some days later Felix arrived with Drusilla, his wife who was a Jewess, and sent for Paul and heard him *speak* about faith in Christ Jesus. ²⁵But as he was discussing righteousness, self-control and the judgment to come, Felix became frightened and said, "Go away for the present, and when I find time I will summon you." ²⁶At the same time too, he was hoping that money would be given him by Paul; therefore he also used to send for him quite often and converse with him. ²⁷But after two years had passed,

24:24 **Drusilla.** The youngest daughter of Agrippa I, and Felix's third wife. Felix, struck by her beauty, had lured her away from her husband. At the time of Paul's hearing, she was not yet 20 years old.

Felix was succeeded by Porcius Festus, and wishing to do the Jews a favor, Felix left Paul imprisoned.

24:25 **righteousness, self-control and the judgment.** God demands "righteousness" of all people, because of His holy nature (Mt 5:48; 1Pe 1:15–16). For men and women to conform to that absolute standard requires "self-control." The result of failing to exhibit self-control and to conform oneself to God's righteous standard is (apart from salvation) "judgment." **Felix became frightened.** Living with a woman he had lured away from her husband, Felix obviously lacked "righteousness" and "self-control." The realization that he faced "judgment" alarmed him, and he hastily dismissed Paul. **when I find time.** The moment of conviction passed, and Felix foolishly passed up his opportunity to repent (2Co 6:2).

DAY 24: How does Ezra's handling of the intermarriage situation fit into the overall pattern of biblical teaching?

Ezr 9 and 10 record a critical time in the reestablishment of the Jewish people in their homeland. In the years before Ezra arrived from Persia, many of the returned Jewish men intermarried with pagan women from the area. This practice reflects no circumstances like we find in the marriages of Rahab or Ruth, Gentiles who became believers in God. The pagan background of these women was not taken into account by their husbands. Ezra received this news as part of the report when he reached Jerusalem.

For Ezra, this was almost the worst possible news. Intermarriage with pagans had historically been a key in the repeated downfalls of the nation. These marriages were an act of disobedience. Ezra was overwhelmed with shame and distress over the situation (Ezr 9:3–4). His grief was open and convicting.

Eventually, the people themselves confessed their error and decided that those who had married pagan women would have to "put away" (divorce) these wives.

God had not changed His mind about divorce. Malachi, who lived in this time period, declared that God hates divorce (Mal 2:16).

Several important notes can be made about this passage in Ezra. It does not establish a norm about divorce. It is also easy to overlook the fact that while the solution of divorce was a group decision, each of these marriages was examined individually. Presumably, cases in which the women had become believers were treated differently than cases in which the women involved saw questions of faith as violation of the marriage agreement.

In the humility of the guilty and the care in confronting these issues, a great deal of God's mercy comes through. A strict interpretation of the law could have led to the stoning death of all involved. The eagerness to set things right opened the doorway for a solution, even though in some of the cases it involved the grief and sadness of divorce.

JULY 25

Nehemiah 1:1–2:20

1 The words of Nehemiah the son of Hacaliah.
Now it happened in the month Chislev, *in* the twentieth year, while I was in Susa the capitol, ²that Hanani, one of my brothers, and

some men from Judah came; and I asked them concerning the Jews who had escaped *and* had survived the captivity, and about Jerusalem. ³They said to me, "The remnant there in the province who survived the captivity are in great distress and reproach, and the wall of Jerusalem is broken down and its gates are burned with fire."

⁴When I heard these words, I sat down and wept and mourned for days; and I was fasting and praying before the God of heaven. ⁵I said, "I beseech You, O LORD God of heaven, the great and awesome God, who preserves the covenant and lovingk-

1:4 sat down and wept and mourned for days. Although Nehemiah was neither a prophet nor a priest, he had a deep sense of Jerusalem's significance to God and was greatly distressed that affairs there had not advanced the cause and glory of God.

indness for those who love Him and keep His commandments, ⁶let Your ear now be attentive and Your eyes open to hear the prayer of Your servant which I am praying before You now, day and night, on behalf of the sons of Israel Your servants, confessing the sins of the sons of Israel which we have sinned against You; I and my father's house have sinned. ⁷We have acted very corruptly against You and have not kept the commandments, nor the statutes, nor the ordinances which You commanded Your servant Moses. ⁸Remember the word which You commanded Your servant Moses, saying, 'If you are unfaithful I will scatter you among the peoples; ⁹but *if* you return to Me and keep My commandments and do them, though those of you who have been scattered were in the most remote part of the heavens, I will gather them from there and will bring them to the place where I have chosen to cause My name to dwell.' ¹⁰They are Your servants and Your people whom You redeemed by Your great power and by Your strong hand. ¹¹O Lord, I be-

1:11 cupbearer to the king. As an escort of the monarch at meals, the cupbearer had a unique advantage to petition the king. Not only did the king owe him his life, since the cupbearer tested all the king's beverages for possible poison, thus putting his own life at risk, but he also became a close confidant. God sovereignly used this relationship between a Gentile and Jew to deliver His people, such as He did with Joseph, Daniel, Esther, and Mordecai.

seech You, may Your ear be attentive to the prayer of Your servant and the prayer of Your servants who delight to revere Your name, and make Your servant successful today and grant him compassion before this man."

Now I was the cupbearer to the king.

2 And it came about in the month Nisan, in the twentieth year of King Artaxerxes, that wine *was* before him, and I took up the wine and gave it to the king. Now I had not been sad in his presence. ²So the king said to me, "Why is your face sad though you are not sick? This is nothing but sadness of heart."

2:2 very much afraid. He feared that either his countenance, his explanation, or his request would anger the king and thus lead to his death (Est 4:11 with 5:1–3).

Then I was very much afraid. ³I said to the king, "Let the king live forever. Why should my face not be sad when the city, the place of my fathers' tombs, lies desolate and its gates have been consumed by fire?" ⁴Then the king said to me, "What would you request?" So I prayed to the God of heaven. ⁵I said to the king, "If it please the king, and if your servant has found favor before you, send me to Judah, to the city of my fathers' tombs, that I may rebuild it." ⁶Then the king said to me, the queen sitting beside him, "How long will your journey be, and when will you return?" So it pleased the king to send me, and I gave him a definite time. ⁷And I said to the king, "If it please the king, let letters be given me for the governors *of the provinces* beyond the River, that they may allow me to pass through until I come to Judah, ⁸and a letter to Asaph the keeper of the king's forest, that he may give me timber to make beams for the gates of the fortress which is by the temple, for the wall of the city and for the house to which I will go." And the king granted *them* to me because the good hand of my God *was* on me.

⁹Then I came to the governors *of the provinces* beyond the River and gave them the king's letters. Now the king had sent with me officers of the army and horsemen. ¹⁰When Sanballat the Horonite and Tobiah the Ammonite official heard *about it*, it was very displeasing to them that someone had come to seek the welfare of the sons of Israel.

2:10 Sanballat...Tobiah. These men were probably also behind the opposition described in Ezra 4:7–23 which stopped the work in Jerusalem. Sanballat served as governor of Samaria (Horonaim being a town in Moab, he was probably a Moabite) and Tobiah of the region east of the Jordan. These district magistrates were leaders of Samaritan factions (chap. 6) to the north and east. They had lost any recourse to prevent Judah from rebuilding since God's people were authorized to fortify their settlement against attack from enemies such as these two officials. To overtly attack or oppose the Jews would be to oppose the Persian king.

---

¹¹ So I came to Jerusalem and was there three days. ¹² And I arose in the night, I and a few men with me. I did not tell anyone what my God was putting into my mind to do for Jerusalem and there was no animal with me except the animal on which I was riding. ¹³ So I went out at night by the Valley Gate in the direction of the Dragon's Well and *on* to the Refuse Gate, inspecting the walls of Jerusalem which were broken down and its gates which were consumed by fire. ¹⁴ Then I passed on to the Fountain Gate and the King's Pool, but there was no place for my mount to pass. ¹⁵ So I went up at night by the ravine and inspected the wall. Then I entered the Valley Gate again and returned. ¹⁶ The officials did not know where I had gone or what I had done; nor had I as yet told the Jews, the priests, the nobles, the officials or the rest who did the work.

¹⁷ Then I said to them, "You see the bad situation we are in, that Jerusalem is desolate and its gates burned by fire. Come, let us rebuild the wall of Jerusalem so that we will no longer be a reproach." ¹⁸ I told them how the hand of my God had been favorable to me and also about the king's words which he had spoken to me. Then they said, "Let us arise and build." So they put their hands to the good *work.* ¹⁹ But when Sanballat the Horonite and Tobiah the Ammonite official, and Geshem the Arab heard *it,* they mocked us and despised us and said, "What is this thing you are doing? Are you rebelling against the king?" ²⁰ So I answered them and said to them, "The God of heaven will give us success; therefore we His servants will arise and build, but you have no portion, right or memorial in Jerusalem."

Psalm 88:11–18

¹¹ Will Your lovingkindness be
  declared in the grave,
  Your faithfulness in Abaddon?
¹² Will Your wonders be made
  known in the darkness?
  And Your righteousness in the
  land of forgetfulness?

¹³ But I, O LORD, have cried
  out to You for help,
  And in the morning my prayer
  comes before You.
¹⁴ O LORD, why do You reject
  my soul?
  Why do You hide Your face
  from me?
¹⁵ I was afflicted and about to
  die from my youth on;
  I suffer Your terrors; I am
  overcome.
¹⁶ Your burning anger has
  passed over me;
  Your terrors have destroyed me.
¹⁷ They have surrounded me
  like water all day long;
  They have encompassed
  me altogether.
¹⁸ You have removed lover and
  friend far from me;
  My acquaintances are *in*
  darkness.

Proverbs 21:25–26

²⁵ The desire of the sluggard
  puts him to death,
  For his hands refuse to work;
²⁶ All day long he is craving,
  While the righteous gives and
  does not hold back.

Acts 25:1–27

25 Festus then, having arrived in the province, three days later went up to Jerusalem from Caesarea. ² And the chief priests and the leading men of the Jews brought charges against Paul, and they were urging him, ³ requesting a concession against Paul, that he might have him brought to Jerusalem (*at the same time,* setting an ambush to kill him on the way). ⁴ Festus then answered that Paul was being kept in custody at Caesarea and that he himself was about to leave shortly. ⁵ "Therefore," he *said, "let the influential men among you go there with me, and if there is anything wrong about the man, let them prosecute him."

⁶ After he had spent not more than eight or

ten days among them, he went down to Caesarea, and on the next day he took his seat on the tribunal and ordered Paul to be brought. [7] After Paul arrived, the Jews who had come down from Jerusalem stood around him, bringing many and serious charges against him which they could not prove, [8] while Paul said in his own defense, "I have committed no offense either against the Law of the Jews or against the temple or against Caesar." [9] But Festus, wishing to do the Jews a favor, answered Paul and said, "Are you willing to go up to Jerusalem and stand trial before me on these *charges?*" [10] But Paul said, "I am standing before Caesar's tribunal, where I ought to be tried. I have done no wrong to *the* Jews, as you also very well know. [11] If, then, I am a wrongdoer and have committed anything worthy of death, I do not refuse to die; but if none of those things is *true* of which these men accuse me, no one can hand me over to them. I appeal to Caesar." [12] Then when Festus had conferred with his council, he answered, "You have appealed to Caesar, to Caesar you shall go."

[13] Now when several days had elapsed, King Agrippa and Bernice arrived at Caesarea and paid their respects to Festus. [14] While they were spending many days there, Festus laid Paul's case before the king, saying, "There is a man who was left as a prisoner by Felix; [15] and when I was at Jerusalem, the chief priests and the elders of the Jews brought charges against him, asking for a sentence of condemnation against him. [16] I answered them that it is not the custom of the Romans to hand over any man before the accused meets his accusers face to face and has an opportunity to make his defense against the charges. [17] So after they had assembled here, I did not delay, but on the next day took my seat on the tribunal and ordered the man to be brought before me. [18] When the accusers stood up, they *began* bringing charges against him not of such crimes as I was expecting, [19] but they *simply* had some points of disagreement with him about their own religion and about a dead man, Jesus, whom Paul asserted to be alive. [20] Being at a loss how to investigate such matters, I asked whether he was willing to go to Jerusalem and there stand trial on these matters. [21] But when Paul appealed to be held in custody for the Emperor's decision, I ordered him to be kept in custody until I send him to Caesar." [22] Then Agrippa *said* to Festus, "I also would like to hear the man myself." "Tomorrow," he *said, "you shall hear him."

[23] So, on the next day when Agrippa came together with Bernice amid great pomp, and entered the auditorium accompanied by the commanders and the prominent men of the city, at the command of Festus, Paul was brought in. [24] Festus *said, "King Agrippa, and all you gentlemen here present with us, you see this man about whom all the people of the Jews appealed to me, both at Jerusalem and here, loudly declaring that he ought not to live any longer. [25] But I found that he had committed nothing worthy of death; and since he himself appealed to the Emperor, I decided to send him. [26] Yet I have nothing definite about him to write to my lord. Therefore I have brought him before you *all* and especially before you, King Agrippa, so that after the investigation has taken place, I may have something to write. [27] For it seems absurd to me in sending a prisoner, not to indicate also the charges against him."

25:13 King Agrippa. Herod Agrippa II, son of the Herod who killed James and imprisoned Peter (12:1). He was the last of the Herods, who play a prominent role in New Testament history. His great-uncle, Herod Antipas, was the Herod of the Gospels (Mk 6:14–29; Lk 3:1; 13:31–33; 23:7–12), while his great-grandfather, Herod the Great, ruled at the time Jesus was born (Mt 2:1–19; Lk 1:5). Though not the ruler of Judea, Agrippa was well versed in Jewish affairs (26:3). **Bernice.** Not Agrippa's wife, but his consort and sister. (Their sister, Drusilla, was married to the former governor, Felix). Their incestuous relationship was the talk of Rome, where Agrippa grew up. Bernice for a while became the mistress of Emperor Vespasian, then of his son, Titus, but always returned to her brother.

25:26 I have nothing definite. Since Festus did not understand the nature of the charges against Paul, he did not know what to write in his official report to Nero. For a provincial governor to send a prisoner to the emperor with no clear charges against him was foolish, if not dangerous. **especially before you, King Agrippa.** Festus hoped Herod's expertise in Jewish affairs (26:3) would enable him to make sense of the charges against Paul.

Like many biblical leaders, Nehemiah demonstrated an understanding of God's call over his life. Whether as cupbearer to a king or as the rebuilder of Jerusalem, Nehemiah pursued his goals with commitment, careful planning, strategic delegation, creative problem solving, focus on the task at hand, and a continual reliance on God, particularly regarding areas beyond his control. Each of the leadership qualities above can be illustrated from Nehemiah's successful completion of the effort to rebuild the walls of Jerusalem.

First, Nehemiah demonstrated his commitment by his interest and his deep concern over the condition of his fellow Jews in Judah. Next, Nehemiah prayed and planned. He claimed God's promise to bring His people back to the Promised Land, but he didn't assume that he would be part of God's action. He declared himself available (1:11; 2:5).

Even when he arrived in Jerusalem, Nehemiah personally inspected the need before he revealed his plans. Then he enlisted the help of the local leadership. He challenged them to take responsibility for the common good. He placed before them a very specific goal—to rebuild the wall. Workers were assigned to work on the wall where it ran closest to their own homes. That way they could see the benefit in having the protective barrier near where they lived.

As the work sped forward, Nehemiah did not allow himself to be distracted by attacks of various kings or tricks from enemies. He took threats seriously enough to arm the people but not so seriously that the work came to a halt. At every turn, we find Nehemiah conferring in prayer with God, placing every decision before the ultimate Decider. Nehemiah succeeded because he never lost sight of the true reasons for the work and the source of power with which to do the work.

JULY 26

Nehemiah 3:1–5:19

3 Then Eliashib the high priest arose with his brothers the priests and built the Sheep Gate; they consecrated it and hung its doors. They consecrated the wall to the Tower of the Hundred *and* the Tower of Hananel. ² Next to him the men of Jericho built, and next to them Zaccur the son of Imri built.

³ Now the sons of Hassenaah built the Fish Gate; they laid its beams and hung its doors with its bolts and bars. ⁴ Next to them Meremoth the son of Uriah the son of Hakkoz made repairs. And next to him Meshullam the son of Berechiah the son of Meshezabel made repairs. And next to him Zadok the son of Baana *also* made repairs. ⁵ Moreover, next to him the Tekoites made repairs, but their nobles did not support the work of their masters.

⁶ Joiada the son of Paseah and Meshullam the son of Besodeiah repaired the Old Gate; they laid its beams and hung its doors with its bolts and its bars. ⁷ Next to them Melatiah the Gibeonite and Jadon the Meronothite, the men of Gibeon and of Mizpah, also made repairs for the official seat of the governor *of the province* beyond the River. ⁸ Next to him Uzziel the son of Harhaiah of the goldsmiths made repairs. And next to him Hananiah, one of the perfumers, made repairs, and they restored Jerusalem as far as the Broad Wall. ⁹ Next to them Rephaiah the son of Hur, the official of half the district of Jerusalem, made repairs. ¹⁰ Next to them Jedaiah the son of Harumaph made repairs opposite his house. And next to him Hattush the son of Hashabneiah made repairs. ¹¹ Malchijah the son of Harim and Hasshub the son of Pahath-moab repaired another section and the Tower of Furnaces. ¹² Next to him Shallum the son of Hallohesh, the official of half the district of Jerusalem, made repairs, he and his daughters.

¹³ Hanun and the inhabitants of Zanoah repaired the Valley Gate. They built it and hung its doors with its bolts and its bars, and a thousand cubits of the wall to the Refuse Gate.

¹⁴ Malchijah the son of Rechab, the official of the district of Beth-haccherem repaired the Refuse Gate. He built it and hung its doors with its bolts and its bars.

¹⁵ Shallum the son of Col-hozeh, the official of the district of Mizpah, repaired the Fountain Gate. He built it, covered it and hung its doors with its bolts and its bars, and the wall of the Pool of Shelah at the king's garden as far as the steps that descend from the city of David. ¹⁶ After him Nehemiah the son of Azbuk, official of half the district of Beth-zur, made repairs as far as *a point* opposite the tombs of David, and as far as the artificial pool and the house of the mighty men. ¹⁷ After him the Levites carried out repairs *under* Rehum the son of Bani. Next to him Hashabiah, the official of half the district of Keilah, carried out repairs for his district. ¹⁸ After him their brothers carried out repairs *under* Bavvai the son of Henadad, official of *the*

other half of the district of Keilah. ¹⁹ Next to him Ezer the son of Jeshua, the official of Mizpah, repaired another section in front of the ascent of the armory at the Angle. ²⁰ After him Baruch the son of Zabbai zealously repaired another section, from the Angle to the doorway of the house of Eliashib the high priest. ²¹ After him Meremoth the son of Uriah the son of Hakkoz repaired another section, from the doorway of Eliashib's house even as far as the end of his house. ²² After him the priests, the men of the valley, carried out repairs. ²³ After them Benjamin and Hasshub carried out repairs in front of their house. After them Azariah the son of Maaseiah, son of Ananiah, carried out repairs beside his house. ²⁴ After him Binnui the son of Henadad repaired another section, from the house of Azariah as far as the Angle and as far as the corner. ²⁵ Palal the son of Uzai *made repairs* in front of the Angle and the tower projecting from the upper house of the king, which is by the court of the guard. After him Pedaiah the son of Parosh *made repairs.* ²⁶ The temple servants living in Ophel *made repairs* as far as the front of the Water Gate toward the east and the projecting tower. ²⁷ After them the Tekoites repaired another section in front of the great projecting tower and as far as the wall of Ophel.

²⁸ Above the Horse Gate the priests carried out repairs, each in front of his house. ²⁹ After them Zadok the son of Immer carried out repairs in front of his house. And after him Shemaiah the son of Shecaniah, the keeper of the East Gate, carried out repairs. ³⁰ After him Hananiah the son of Shelemiah, and Hanun the sixth son of Zalaph, repaired another section. After him Meshullam the son of Berechiah carried out repairs in front of his own quarters. ³¹ After him Malchijah, one of the goldsmiths, carried out repairs as far as the house of the temple servants and of the merchants, in front of the Inspection Gate and as far as the upper room of the corner. ³² Between the upper room of the corner and the Sheep Gate the goldsmiths and the merchants carried out repairs.

4 Now it came about that when Sanballat heard that we were rebuilding the wall, he became furious and very angry and mocked the Jews. ² He spoke in the presence of his brothers and the wealthy *men* of Samaria and said, "What are these feeble Jews doing? Are they going to restore *it* for themselves? Can they offer sacrifices? Can they finish in a day? Can they revive the stones from the dusty rubble even the burned ones?" ³ Now Tobiah the Ammonite *was* near him and he said, "Even what they are building—if a fox should jump on *it,* he would break their stone wall down!"

⁴ Hear, O our God, how we are despised! Return their reproach on their own heads and give them up for plunder in a land of captivity. ⁵ Do not forgive their iniquity and let not their sin be blotted out before You, for they have demoralized the builders.

⁶ So we built the wall and the whole wall was joined together to half its *height,* for the people had a mind to work.

⁷ Now when Sanballat, Tobiah, the Arabs, the Ammonites and the Ashdodites heard that the repair of the walls of Jerusalem went on, *and* that the breaches began to be closed, they were very angry. ⁸ All of them conspired together to come *and* fight against Jerusalem and to cause a disturbance in it. ⁹ But we prayed to our God, and because of them we set up a guard against them day and night.

¹⁰ Thus in Judah it was said,

"The strength of the burden
  bearers is failing,
Yet there is much rubbish;
And we ourselves are unable
To rebuild the wall."

¹¹ Our enemies said, "They will not know or see until we come among them, kill them and put a stop to the work." ¹² When the Jews who lived near them came and told us ten times, "They will come up against us from every place where you may turn," ¹³ then I stationed *men* in the lowest parts of the space behind the wall, the exposed places, and I stationed the people in families with their swords, spears and bows. ¹⁴ When I saw *their fear,* I rose and spoke to the nobles, the officials and the rest of the people: "Do not be afraid of them; remember the Lord who is great and awesome, and fight for your brothers, your sons, your daughters, your wives and your houses."

¹⁵ When our enemies heard that it was known to us, and that God had frustrated their plan, then all of us returned to the wall, each one to his work. ¹⁶ From that day on, half of my servants carried on the work while half of them held the spears, the shields, the bows and the breastplates; and the captains *were* behind the whole house of Judah. ¹⁷ Those who were rebuilding the wall and those who carried burdens took *their* load with one hand doing the work and the other holding a weapon. ¹⁸ As for the builders, each *wore* his sword girded at his side as he built, while the trumpeter *stood* near me. ¹⁹ I said to the nobles, the officials and the rest of the people, "The work is great and extensive, and we are separated on the wall far from one another. ²⁰ At whatever place you hear

the sound of the trumpet, rally to us there. Our God will fight for us."

²¹ So we carried on the work with half of them holding spears from dawn until the stars appeared. ²² At that time I also said to the people, "Let each man with his servant spend the night within Jerusalem so that they may be a guard for us by night and a laborer by day." ²³ So neither I, my brothers, my servants, nor the men of the guard who followed me, none of us removed our clothes, each *took* his weapon *even to* the water.

5 Now there was a great outcry of the people and of their wives against their Jewish brothers. ² For there were those who said, "We, our sons and our daughters are many; therefore let us get grain that we may eat and live." ³ There were others who said, "We are mortgaging our fields, our vineyards and our houses that we might get grain because of the famine." ⁴ Also there were those who said, "We have borrowed money for the king's tax *on* our fields and our vineyards. ⁵ Now our flesh is like the flesh of our brothers, our children like their children. Yet behold, we are forcing our sons and our daughters to be slaves, and some of our daughters are forced into bondage *already,* and we are helpless because our fields and vineyards belong to others."

⁶ Then I was very angry when I had heard their outcry and these words. ⁷ I consulted with myself and contended with the nobles and the rulers and said to them, "You are exacting usury, each from his brother!" Therefore, I held a great assembly against them. ⁸ I said to them, "We according to our ability have redeemed our Jewish brothers who were sold to the nations; now would you even sell your brothers that they may be sold to us?" Then they were silent and could not find a word *to say.* ⁹ Again I said, "The thing which you are doing is not good; should you not walk in the fear of our God because of the reproach of the nations, our enemies? ¹⁰ And likewise I, my brothers and my servants are lending them money and grain. Please, let us leave off this usury. ¹¹ Please, give back to them this very day their fields, their vineyards, their olive groves and their houses, also the hundredth *part* of the money and of the grain, the new wine and the oil that you are exacting from them." ¹² Then they said, "We will give *it* back and will require nothing from them; we will do exactly as you say." So I called the priests and took an oath from them that they would do according to this promise. ¹³ I also shook out the front of my garment and said, "Thus may God shake out every man from his house and from his possessions who does

not fulfill this promise; even thus may he be shaken out and emptied." And all the assembly said, "Amen!" And they praised the LORD. Then the people did according to this promise.

¹⁴ Moreover, from the day that I was appointed to be their governor in the land of Judah, from the twentieth year to the thirty-second year of King Artaxerxes, *for* twelve years, neither I nor my kinsmen have eaten the governor's food *allowance.* ¹⁵ But the former governors who were before me laid burdens on the people and took from them bread and wine besides forty shekels of silver; even their servants domineered the people. But I did not do so because of the fear of God. ¹⁶ I also applied myself to the work on this wall; we did not buy any land, and all my servants were gathered there for the work. ¹⁷ Moreover, *there were* at my table one hundred and fifty Jews and officials, besides those who came to us from the nations that were around us. ¹⁸ Now that which was prepared for each day was one ox *and* six choice sheep, also birds were prepared for me; and once in ten days all sorts of wine *were furnished* in abundance. Yet for all this I did not demand the governor's food *allowance,* because the servitude was heavy on this people. ¹⁹ Remember me, O my God, for good, *according to* all that I have done for this people.

Psalm 89:1–4

A Maskil of Ethan the Ezrahite.

I will sing of the lovingkindness
of the LORD forever;
  To all generations I will make known
  Your faithfulness with my
  mouth.
² For I have said, "Lovingkindness
  will be built up forever;
  In the heavens You will establish
  Your faithfulness."
³ "I have made a covenant
  with My chosen;
  I have sworn to David My servant,

89:3 covenant with My chosen. The Davidic Covenant, culminating in Messiah's reign, was established in 2 Samuel 7 (1Ki 8:23; 1Ch 17; 2Ch 21:7; Pss 110, 132). The covenant was in the form of a royal grant covenant as God, the Great King, chose David as His servant king. In this type of covenant, the person with whom the Lord established the covenant could violate the terms of the covenant and the Lord would still be obligated to maintain the covenant.

⁴ I will establish your seed forever
　And build up your throne
　　to all generations." 　　　*Selah*

89:4 seed forever...throne. The covenant with David was extended to his descendants. The throne promise guaranteed that the rightful heir to the throne would always be a descendant of David (see vv. 29, 36; see also 2Sa 7:13, 16, 18; Lk 1:31–33). The genealogies of Jesus qualify Him for the throne (Mt 1:1–17; Lk 3:23–38).

Proverbs 21:27

²⁷ The sacrifice of the wicked
　　is an abomination,
　How much more when he
　　brings it with evil intent!

Acts 26:1–32

26 Agrippa said to Paul, "You are permitted to speak for yourself." Then Paul stretched out his hand and *proceeded* to make his defense:

² "In regard to all the things of which I am accused by the Jews, I consider myself fortunate, King Agrippa, that I am about to make my defense before you today; ³ especially because you are an expert in all customs and questions among *the* Jews; therefore I beg you to listen to me patiently.

⁴ "So then, all Jews know my manner of life from my youth up, which from the beginning was spent among my *own* nation and at Jerusalem; ⁵ since they have known about me for a long time, if they are willing to testify, that I lived *as* a Pharisee according to the strictest sect of our religion. ⁶ And now I am standing trial for the hope of the promise made by God to our fathers; ⁷ *the promise* to which our twelve tribes hope to attain, as they earnestly serve *God* night and day. And for this hope, O King, I am being accused by Jews. ⁸ Why is it considered incredible among you *people* if God does raise the dead?

⁹ "So then, I thought to myself that I had to do many things hostile to the name of Jesus of Nazareth. ¹⁰ And this is just what I did in Jerusalem; not only did I lock up many of the saints in prisons, having received authority from the chief priests, but also when they were being put to death I cast my vote against them. ¹¹ And as I punished them often in all the synagogues, I tried to force them to blaspheme; and being furiously enraged at them, I kept pursuing them even to foreign cities.

¹² "While so engaged as I was journeying to Damascus with the authority and commission of the chief priests, ¹³ at midday, O King, I saw on the way a light from heaven, brighter than the sun, shining all around me and those who were journeying with me. ¹⁴ And when we had all fallen to the ground, I heard a voice saying to me in the Hebrew dialect, 'Saul, Saul, why are you persecuting Me? It is hard for you to kick against the goads.' ¹⁵ And I said, 'Who are You, Lord?' And the Lord said, 'I am Jesus whom you are persecuting. ¹⁶ But get up and stand on your feet; for this purpose I have appeared to you, to appoint you a minister and a witness not only to the things which you have seen, but also to the things in which I will appear to you; ¹⁷ rescuing you from the *Jewish* people and from the Gentiles, to whom I am sending you, ¹⁸ to open their eyes so that they may turn from darkness to light and from the dominion of Satan to God, that they may receive forgiveness of sins and an inheritance among those who have been sanctified by faith in Me.'

¹⁹ "So, King Agrippa, I did not prove disobedient to the heavenly vision, ²⁰ but *kept* declaring both to those of Damascus first, and *also* at Jerusalem and *then* throughout all the region of Judea, and *even* to the Gentiles, that they should repent and turn to God, performing deeds appropriate to repentance. ²¹ For this reason *some* Jews seized me in the temple and tried to put me to death. ²² So, having obtained help from God, I stand to this day testifying both to small and great, stating nothing but what the Prophets and Moses said was going to take place; ²³ that the Christ was to suffer, *and* that by reason of *His* resurrection from the dead He would be the first to proclaim light both to the *Jewish* people and to the Gentiles."

²⁴ While *Paul* was saying this in his defense, Festus *said in a loud voice, "Paul, you are out of your mind! *Your* great learning is driving

---

26:24 you are out of your mind! Festus was astonished that a learned scholar like Paul could actually believe that the dead would live again—something no intelligent Roman would accept. Unable to contain himself, he interrupted the proceedings, shouting that Paul's tremendous learning had driven him insane (Mk 3:21; Jn 8:48, 52; 10:20).

you mad." ²⁵ But Paul *said, "I am not out of my mind, most excellent Festus, but I utter words of sober truth. ²⁶ For the king knows about these matters, and I speak to him also with confidence, since I am persuaded that none of these things escape his notice; for this has not been done in a corner. ²⁷ King Agrippa, do you believe the Prophets? I know that you do." ²⁸ Agrippa *replied* to Paul, "In a short time you will persuade me to become a Christian." ²⁹ And Paul *said*, "I would wish to God, that whether in a short or long time, not only you, but also all who hear me this day, might become such as I am, except for these chains."

³⁰ The king stood up and the governor and Bernice, and those who were sitting with them, ³¹ and when they had gone aside, they *began* talking to one another, saying, "This man is not doing anything worthy of death or imprisonment." ³² And Agrippa said to Festus, "This man might have been set free if he had not appealed to Caesar."

26:26 none of these things escape his notice. The death of Jesus and the Christians' claim that He rose from the dead were common knowledge in Israel.

26:27 do you believe the Prophets? Paul's shrewd question put Herod in a dilemma. If he affirmed his belief in the prophets, he would also have to admit that what they taught about Jesus' death and resurrection was true—an admission that would make him appear foolish before his Roman friends. Yet to deny the prophets would outrage his Jewish subjects.

26:28 In a short time you will persuade me. Agrippa was saying, "Do you think you can convince me to become a Christian in such a short time?" Recognizing his dilemma, Agrippa parried Paul's question with one of his own.

DAY 26: Why did Nehemiah denounce the nobles and rulers?

In Nehemiah 5:1–5, the people were fatigued with hard labor, drained by the relentless harassment of enemies, poor and lacking the necessities of life, lacking tax money and borrowing for it, and working on the wall in the city rather than getting food from the country. On top of this came complaints against the terrible exploitation and extortion by the rich Jews who would not help, but forced people to sell their homes and children, while having no ability to redeem them back. Under normal conditions, the law offered the hope of releasing these young people through the remission of debts which occurred every 7 years or in the 50th year of Jubilee (Lv 25). The custom of redemption made it possible to "buy back" the enslaved individual at almost any time, but the desperate financial situation of those times made that appear impossible.

So Nehemiah "contended with the nobles and rulers" (v. 7). They had become the enemy from within. "Exacting usury." Usury can refer to normal interest or it can signify excessive interest. According to Mosaic Law, the Jews were forbidden to take interest from their brothers on the loan of money, food, or anything else. If the person was destitute, they should consider it a gift. If they could pay it back later, it was to be without interest (Lv 25:36–37; Dt 23:19–20). Such generosity marked the godly (Ps 15:5; Jer 15:10; Pr 28:8). Interest could be taken from foreigners (v. 20). Interest loans were known to exceed 50 percent at times in ancient nations. Such usury took advantage of people's desperation and was virtually impossible to repay, consuming their entire family assets and reducing the debtors to permanent slavery.

Nehemiah denounced with just severity the evil conduct of selling a brother by means of usury. He contrasted it with his own action of redeeming with his own money some of the Jewish exiles, who through debt had lost their freedom in Babylon (v. 8). Nehemiah set the example again by making loans, but not in exacting usury (v. 10). To remedy the evil that they had brought, those guilty of usury were to return the property they had confiscated from those who couldn't pay the loans back, as well as returning the interest they had charged (v. 11).

JULY 27

Nehemiah 6:1–7:73

6 Now when it was reported to Sanballat, Tobiah, to Geshem the Arab and to the rest of our enemies that I had rebuilt the wall, and *that* no breach remained in it, although at that time I had not set up the doors in the gates, ²then Sanballat and Geshem sent *a message* to me, saying, "Come, let us meet together at Chephirim in the plain of Ono." But they were planning to harm me. ³So I sent messengers to them, saying, "I am doing a great work and I cannot come down. Why should the work stop while I leave it and come down to you?" ⁴They sent *messages* to me four times in this manner, and I answered them in the same way. ⁵Then Sanballat sent his servant to me in the same manner a fifth time with an open letter in his hand. ⁶In it was

6:5 open letter. Official letters were typically rolled up and sealed with an official signet by the letter's sender or one of his assisting officials. An open or unsealed letter was not only a sign of disrespect and open criticism, but also suggested the information therein was public knowledge. The goal of this document was to intimidate Nehemiah into stopping the work.

written, "It is reported among the nations, and Gashmu says, that you and the Jews are planning to rebel; therefore you are rebuilding the wall. And you are to be their king, according to these reports. ⁷You have also appointed prophets to proclaim in Jerusalem concerning you, 'A king is in Judah!' And now it will be reported to the king according to these reports. So come now, let us take counsel together." ⁸Then I sent *a message* to him saying, "Such things as you are saying have not been done, but you are inventing them in your own mind." ⁹For all of them were *trying* to frighten us, thinking, "They will become discouraged with the work and it will not be done." But now, *O God,* strengthen my hands.

¹⁰When I entered the house of Shemaiah the son of Delaiah, son of Mehetabel, who was confined at home, he said, "Let us meet together in the house of God, within the temple, and let us close the doors of the temple, for they are coming to kill you, and they are coming to kill you at night." ¹¹But I said, "Should a man like me flee? And could

6:10 Shemaiah. When the open letter failed to intimidate Nehemiah into stopping the work and coming to a meeting, his enemies decided to try intimidation from within. They hired a false prophet (v. 12), Shemaiah, to lure Nehemiah into the Holy Place in the temple for refuge from a murder plot. To enter and shut himself in the Holy Place would have been a desecration of the house of God and would have caused people to question his reverence for God. Shemaiah was the son of a priest who was an intimate friend of Nehemiah. This plan would give them grounds to raise an evil report against Nehemiah, who was not a priest and had no right to go into the Holy Place (6:13). It could also make the people question his courage (v. 11).

one such as I go into the temple to save his life? I will not go in." ¹²Then I perceived that surely God had not sent him, but he uttered *his* prophecy against me because Tobiah and Sanballat had hired him. ¹³He was hired for this reason, that I might become frightened and act accordingly and sin, so that they might have an evil report in order that they could reproach me. ¹⁴Remember, O my God, Tobiah and Sanballat according to these works of theirs, and also Noadiah the prophetess and the rest of the prophets who were *trying* to frighten me.

¹⁵So the wall was completed on the twenty-fifth of *the month* Elul, in fifty-two days. ¹⁶When all our enemies heard *of it,* and all the nations surrounding us saw *it,* they lost their confidence; for they recognized that this work had been accomplished with the help of our God. ¹⁷Also in those days many letters went from the nobles of Judah to Tobiah, and Tobiah's *letters* came to them. ¹⁸For many in Judah were bound by oath to him because he was the son-in-law of Shecaniah the son of Arah, and his son Jehohanan had married

6:16 this work had been accomplished with the help of our God. While modern readers might be tempted to exalt the leadership qualities which brought the work to completion, Nehemiah's conclusion was seen through the eyes of his enemies, i.e., God works through faithful people, but it is God who works. This is a change from the attitudes indicated in 4:1 and 5:9.

the daughter of Meshullam the son of Berechiah. ¹⁹Moreover, they were speaking about his good deeds in my presence and reported my words to him. Then Tobiah sent letters to frighten me.

7 Now when the wall was rebuilt and I had set up the doors, and the gatekeepers and the singers and the Levites were appointed, ²then I put Hanani my brother, and Hananiah the commander of the fortress, in charge of Jerusalem, for he was a faithful man and feared God more than many. ³Then I said to them, "Do not let the gates of Jerusalem be opened until the sun is hot, and while they are standing *guard,* let them shut and bolt the doors. Also appoint guards from the inhabitants of Jerusalem, each at his post, and each in front of his own house." ⁴Now the city was large and spacious, but the people in it were few and the houses were not built.

⁵Then my God put it into my heart to assemble the nobles, the officials and the people to be enrolled by genealogies. Then I found the book of the genealogy of those who came up first in which I found the following record:

⁶These are the people of the province who came up from the captivity of the exiles whom Nebuchadnezzar the king of Babylon had carried away, and who returned to Jerusalem and Judah, each to his city, ⁷who came with Zerubbabel, Jeshua, Nehemiah, Azariah, Raamiah, Nahamani, Mordecai, Bilshan, Mispereth, Bigvai, Nehum, Baanah.

The number of men of the people of Israel: ⁸the sons of Parosh, 2,172; ⁹the sons of Shephatiah, 372; ¹⁰the sons of Arah, 652; ¹¹the sons of Pahath-moab of the sons of Jeshua and Joab, 2,818; ¹²the sons of Elam, 1,254; ¹³the sons of Zattu, 845; ¹⁴the sons of Zaccai, 760; ¹⁵the sons of Binnui, 648; ¹⁶the sons of Bebai, 628; ¹⁷the sons of Azgad, 2,322; ¹⁸the sons of Adonikam, 667; ¹⁹the sons of Bigvai, 2,067; ²⁰the sons of Adin, 655; ²¹the sons of Ater, of Hezekiah, 98; ²²the sons of Hashum, 328; ²³the sons of Bezai, 324; ²⁴the sons of Hariph, 112; ²⁵the sons of Gibeon, 95; ²⁶the men of Bethlehem and Netophah, 188; ²⁷the men of Anathoth, 128; ²⁸the men of Beth-azmaveth, 42; ²⁹the men of Kiriath-jearim, Chephirah and Beeroth, 743; ³⁰the men of Ramah and Geba, 621; ³¹the men of Michmas, 122; ³²the men of Bethel and Ai, 123; ³³the men of the other Nebo, 52; ³⁴the sons of the other Elam, 1,254; ³⁵the sons of Harim, 320; ³⁶the men of Jericho, 345; ³⁷the sons of Lod, Hadid and Ono, 721; ³⁸the sons of Senaah, 3,930.

³⁹The priests: the sons of Jedaiah of the house of Jeshua, 973; ⁴⁰the sons of Immer, 1,052; ⁴¹the sons of Pashhur, 1,247; ⁴²the sons of Harim, 1,017.

⁴³The Levites: the sons of Jeshua, of Kadmiel, of the sons of Hodevah, 74. ⁴⁴The singers: the sons of Asaph, 148. ⁴⁵The gatekeepers: the sons of Shallum, the sons of Ater, the sons of Talmon, the sons of Akkub, the sons of Hatita, the sons of Shobai, 138.

⁴⁶The temple servants: the sons of Ziha, the sons of Hasupha, the sons of Tabbaoth, ⁴⁷the sons of Keros, the sons of Sia, the sons of Padon, ⁴⁸the sons of Lebana, the sons of Hagaba, the sons of Shalmai, ⁴⁹the sons of Hanan, the sons of Giddel, the sons of Gahar, ⁵⁰the sons of Reaiah, the sons of Rezin, the sons of Nekoda, ⁵¹the sons of Gazzam, the sons of Uzza, the sons of Paseah, ⁵²the sons of Besai, the sons of Meunim, the sons of Nephushesim, ⁵³the sons of Bakbuk, the sons of Hakupha, the sons of Harhur, ⁵⁴the sons of Bazlith, the sons of Mehida, the sons of Harsha, ⁵⁵the sons of Barkos, the sons of Sisera, the sons of Temah, ⁵⁶the sons of Neziah, the sons of Hatipha.

⁵⁷The sons of Solomon's servants: the sons of Sotai, the sons of Sophereth, the sons of Perida, ⁵⁸the sons of Jaala, the sons of Darkon, the sons of Giddel, ⁵⁹the sons of Shephatiah, the sons of Hattil, the sons of Pochereth-hazzebaim, the sons of Amon.

⁶⁰All the temple servants and the sons of Solomon's servants *were* 392.

⁶¹These *were* they who came up from Tel-melah, Tel-harsha, Cherub, Addon and Immer; but they could not show their fathers' houses or their descendants, whether they were of Israel: ⁶²the sons of Delaiah, the sons of Tobiah, the sons of Nekoda, 642. ⁶³Of the priests: the sons of Hobaiah, the sons of Hakkoz, the sons of Barzillai, who took a wife of the daughters of Barzillai, the Gileadite, and was named after them. ⁶⁴These searched *among* their ancestral registration, but it could not be located; therefore they were considered unclean *and excluded* from the priesthood. ⁶⁵The governor said to them that they should not eat from the most holy things until a priest arose with Urim and Thummim.

⁶⁶The whole assembly together *was* 42,360, ⁶⁷besides their male and their female servants, of whom *there were* 7,337; and they had 245 male and female singers. ⁶⁸Their horses were 736; their mules, 245; ⁶⁹*their* camels, 435; *their* donkeys, 6,720.

⁷⁰Some from among the heads of fathers' *households* gave to the work. The governor gave to the treasury 1,000 gold drachmas, 50 basins, 530 priests' garments. ⁷¹Some of the

heads of fathers' *households* gave into the treasury of the work 20,000 gold drachmas and 2,200 silver minas. ⁷²That which the rest of the people gave was 20,000 gold drachmas and 2,000 silver minas and 67 priests' garments.

⁷³Now the priests, the Levites, the gatekeepers, the singers, some of the people, the temple servants and all Israel, lived in their cities.

And when the seventh month came, the sons of Israel *were* in their cities.

Psalm 89:5-10

⁵ The heavens will praise Your
    wonders, O LORD;
    Your faithfulness also in the
    assembly of the holy ones.
⁶ For who in the skies is
    comparable to the LORD?
    Who among the sons of the
    mighty is like the LORD,
⁷ A God greatly feared in the
    council of the holy ones,
    And awesome above all those
    who are around Him?
⁸ O LORD God of hosts, who is
    like You, O mighty LORD?
    Your faithfulness also surrounds You.
⁹ You rule the swelling of the sea;
    When its waves rise, You still them.
¹⁰ You Yourself crushed Rahab
    like one who is slain;
    You scattered Your enemies
    with Your mighty arm.

Proverbs 21:28

²⁸ A false witness will perish,
   But the man who listens *to the*
   truth will speak forever.

Acts 27:1-26

27 When it was decided that we would sail for Italy, they proceeded to deliver Paul and some other prisoners to a centurion of the Augustan cohort named Julius. ²And embarking in an Adramyttian ship, which was about to sail to the regions along the coast of Asia, we put out to sea accompanied by Aristarchus, a Macedonian of Thessalonica. ³The next day we put in at Sidon; and Julius treated Paul with consideration and allowed him to go to his friends and receive care. ⁴From there we put out to sea and sailed under the shelter of Cyprus because the winds were contrary. ⁵When we had sailed through the sea along the coast of Cilicia and Pamphylia, we landed at Myra in Lycia. ⁶There the

27:1 we. The use of the pronoun "we" marks the return of Paul's close friend Luke, who has been absent since 21:18. He had likely been living near Caesarea so he could care for Paul during his imprisonment. Now he rejoined the apostle for the journey to Rome. **centurion of the Augustan cohort.** A cohort (regiment) of that name was stationed in Judea during the reign of Agrippa II. Julius may have been on detached duty, performing such tasks as escorting important prisoners.

centurion found an Alexandrian ship sailing for Italy, and he put us aboard it. ⁷When we had sailed slowly for a good many days, and with difficulty had arrived off Cnidus, since the wind did not permit us *to go* farther, we sailed under the shelter of Crete, off Salmone; ⁸and with difficulty sailing past it we came to a place called Fair Havens, near which was the city of Lasea.

⁹When considerable time had passed and the voyage was now dangerous, since even the fast was already over, Paul *began* to admonish them, ¹⁰and said to them, "Men, I perceive that the voyage will certainly be with damage and great loss, not only of the cargo and the ship, but also of our lives."

27:10 voyage…with damage. Because of the lateness of the season, and the difficulties they had already experienced, Paul wisely counseled them to spend the winter at Fair Havens.

¹¹But the centurion was more persuaded by the pilot and the captain of the ship than by what was being said by Paul. ¹²Because the harbor was not suitable for wintering, the majority reached a decision to put out to sea from there, if somehow they could reach Phoenix, a harbor of Crete, facing southwest and northwest, and spend the winter *there*.

¹³When a moderate south wind came up, supposing that they had attained their purpose, they weighed anchor and *began* sailing along Crete, close *inshore*. ¹⁴But before very long there rushed down from the land a violent wind, called Euraquilo; ¹⁵and when the ship was caught *in it* and could not face the wind, we gave way *to it* and let ourselves be driven along. ¹⁶Running under the shelter of a small island called Clauda,

we were scarcely able to get the *ship's* boat under control. [17] After they had hoisted it up, they used supporting cables in undergirding the ship; and fearing that they might run aground on *the shallows* of Syrtis, they let down the sea anchor and in this way let themselves be driven along. [18] The next day as we were being violently storm-tossed, they began to jettison the cargo; [19] and on the third

27:17 used supporting cables in undergirding the ship. A procedure known as frapping. The cables, wrapped around the hull and winched tight, helped the ship endure the battering of the wind and waves. **Syrtis.** A region of sandbars and shoals off the coast of Africa, much feared as a graveyard of ships. **let down the sea anchor.** The sailors probably also took down the sails, since putting out an anchor with the sails up would be self-defeating.

day they threw the ship's tackle overboard with their own hands. [20] Since neither sun nor stars appeared for many days, and no small storm was assailing *us*, from then on all hope of our being saved was gradually abandoned.

[21] When they had gone a long time without food, then Paul stood up in their midst and said, "Men, you ought to have followed my advice and not to have set sail from Crete and incurred this damage and loss. [22] *Yet* now I urge you to keep up your courage, for there will be no loss of life among you, but *only* of the ship. [23] For this very night an angel of the God to whom I belong and whom I serve stood before me, [24] saying, 'Do not be afraid, Paul; you must stand before Caesar; and behold, God has granted you all those who are sailing with you.' [25] Therefore, keep up your courage, men, for I believe God that it will turn out exactly as I have been told. [26] But we must run aground on a certain island."

DAY 27: What parts of the Old Testament and what people were active in the events surrounding the return of the Jews from exile?

Five historical books (1 and 2 Chr., Ezra, Neh, and Esth) come from or cover events after the exile. Three prophetic books (Hag, Zech, and Mal) come from the same period. The term "postexilic" is often used to describe these books and people.

First and Second Chronicles provide a summary of history viewed from the final days of the exile. Ezra and Nehemiah journal the thrilling and trying days of the return to Judah and the rebuilding of the nation. Haggai and Zechariah were prophets active during the time recorded in Ezra 4–6 when the temple was under reconstruction. Malachi wrote and prophesied during Nehemiah's revisit to Persia (Ne 13:6).

Although part of the purpose of these books confirms God's continued covenant with the house of David and the unbroken kingly line, the emphasis shifts from royalty to other servants of God. A scribe, a cupbearer, and prophets become God's central agents. Even Esther, although a queen, had to rely on God rather than her position and power to accomplish God's role for her in preserving the Jews in Persia.

All of this sets the stage for the mixed expectations that surrounded the birth of Jesus, the fulfillment of God's covenant with David, God's personal involvement in the history of salvation.

JULY 28

Nehemiah 8:1–9:38

8 And all the people gathered as one man at the square which was in front of the Water Gate, and they asked Ezra the scribe to bring the book of the law of Moses which the LORD had given to Israel. [2] Then Ezra the priest brought the law before the assembly of men, women and all who *could* listen with understanding, on the first day of the seventh month. [3] He read from it before the square which was in front of the Water Gate from

early morning until midday, in the presence of men and women, those who could understand; and all the people were attentive to the book of the law. [4] Ezra the scribe stood at a wooden podium which they had made for the purpose. And beside him stood Mattithiah, Shema, Anaiah, Uriah, Hilkiah, and Maaseiah on his right hand; and Pedaiah, Mishael, Malchijah, Hashum, Hashbaddanah, Zechariah *and* Meshullam on his left hand. [5] Ezra opened the book in the sight of all the people for he was standing above all the people; and when he opened it, all the people stood up. [6] Then Ezra blessed the LORD the great God. And all the people answered, "Amen, Amen!" while lifting up their hands; then they bowed low and worshiped the LORD with *their* faces to the ground. [7] Also Jeshua, Bani, Sherebiah, Jamin, Akkub, Shabbethai, Hodiah, Maaseiah, Kelita, Azariah, Jozabad, Hanan, Pelaiah, the Levites, explained the law to the people while the people *remained* in their place. [8] They read from the book, from the law of God, translating to give the sense so that they understood the reading.

[9] Then Nehemiah, who was the governor, and Ezra the priest *and* scribe, and the Levites who taught the people said to all the people, "This day is holy to the LORD your God; do not mourn or weep." For all the people were weeping when they heard the words of the law. [10] Then he said to them, "Go, eat of the fat, drink of the sweet, and send portions to him who has nothing prepared; for this day is holy to our Lord. Do not be grieved, for the joy of the LORD is your strength." [11] So the Levites calmed all the people, saying, "Be still, for the day is holy; do not be grieved." [12] All the people went away to eat, to drink, to send portions and to celebrate a great festival, because they understood the words which had been made known to them.

[13] Then on the second day the heads of fathers' *households* of all the people, the priests and the Levites were gathered to Ezra the scribe that they might gain insight into the words of the law. [14] They found written in the law how the LORD had commanded through Moses that the sons of Israel should live in booths during the feast of the seventh month. [15] So they proclaimed and circulated a proclamation in all their cities and in Jerusalem, saying, "Go out to the hills, and bring olive branches and wild olive branches, myrtle branches, palm branches and branches of *other* leafy trees, to make booths, as it is written." [16] So the people went out and brought *them* and made booths for themselves, each on his roof, and in their courts and in the courts of the house of God, and in the square at the Water Gate and in the square at the Gate of Ephraim. [17] The entire assembly of those who had returned from the captivity made booths and lived in them. The sons of Israel had indeed not done so from the days of Joshua the son of Nun to that day. And there was great rejoicing. [18] He read from the book of the law of God daily, from the first day to the last day. And they celebrated the feast seven days, and on the eighth day *there was* a solemn assembly according to the ordinance.

9 Now on the twenty-fourth day of this month the sons of Israel assembled with fasting, in sackcloth and with dirt upon them. [2] The descendants of Israel separated themselves from all foreigners, and stood and confessed their sins and the iniquities of their fathers. [3] While they stood in their place, they read from the book of the law of the LORD their God for a fourth of the day; and for *another* fourth they confessed and worshiped the LORD their God. [4] Now on the Levites' platform stood Jeshua, Bani, Kadmiel, Shebaniah, Bunni, Sherebiah, Bani *and* Chenani, and they cried with a loud voice to the LORD their God.

[5] Then the Levites, Jeshua, Kadmiel, Bani, Hashabneiah, Sherebiah, Hodiah, Shebaniah *and* Pethahiah, said, "Arise, bless the LORD your God forever and ever!

O may Your glorious name be blessed
And exalted above all
   blessing and praise!
[6] "You alone are the LORD.
You have made the heavens,

9:1 this month. Tishri (Sept./Oct.), 445 B.C. (7:73b; 8:2). **with fasting, in sackcloth and with dirt.** The outward demonstration of deep mourning and heaviness of heart for their iniquity seems to have been done in the spirit of the Day of Atonement which was normally observed on the tenth day of the seventh month (Lv 16:1–34; 23:26–32).

9:2 separated themselves from all foreigners. This call for divorcing all lawful wives taken from among the heathen was needed, since the last time, prompted 13 years before by Ezra, had only been partially successful. Many had escaped the required action of divorce and kept their pagan wives. Perhaps new defaulters had appeared also, and were confronted for the first time with this necessary action of divorce. Nehemiah's efforts were successful in removing this evil mixture.

9:3 they stood...read...confessed and worshiped. The succession of events helped to reestablish the essential commitment of Israel to God and His law. They read for 3 hours about the sins of their fathers and for 3 more hours confessed that they had been partakers of similar evil deeds. In response to all of this, they worshiped.

The heaven of heavens
with all their host,
The earth and all that is on it,
The seas and all that is in them.
You give life to all of them
And the heavenly host bows
down before You.

7 "You are the LORD God,
Who chose Abram
And brought him out from
Ur of the Chaldees,
And gave him the name Abraham.

8 "You found his heart
faithful before You,
And made a covenant with him
To give *him* the land of the Canaanite,
Of the Hittite and the Amorite,
Of the Perizzite, the Jebusite
and the Girgashite—
To give *it* to his descendants.
And You have fulfilled Your promise,
For You are righteous.

9 "You saw the affliction of
our fathers in Egypt,
And heard their cry by the Red Sea.

10 "Then You performed signs and
wonders against Pharaoh,
Against all his servants and all
the people of his land;
For You knew that they acted
arrogantly toward them,
And made a name for Yourself
as *it is* this day.

11 "You divided the sea before them,
So they passed through the midst
of the sea on dry ground;
And their pursuers You
hurled into the depths,
Like a stone into raging waters.

12 "And with a pillar of cloud
You led them by day,
And with a pillar of fire by night
To light for them the way
In which they were to go.

13 "Then You came down on Mount Sinai,
And spoke with them from heaven;
You gave them just ordinances
and true laws,
Good statutes and commandments.

14 "So You made known to them
Your holy sabbath,
And laid down for them
commandments, statutes
and law,
Through Your servant Moses.

15 "You provided bread from heaven
for them for their hunger,

You brought forth water from a
rock for them for their thirst,
And You told them to enter
in order to possess
The land which You swore
to give them.

16 "But they, our fathers,
acted arrogantly;
They became stubborn and would not
listen to Your commandments.

17 "They refused to listen,
And did not remember Your
wondrous deeds which You
had performed among them;
So they became stubborn and
appointed a leader to return
to their slavery in Egypt.
But You are a God of forgiveness,
Gracious and compassionate,
Slow to anger and abounding
in lovingkindness;
And You did not forsake them.

18 "Even when they made for themselves
A calf of molten metal
And said, 'This is your God
Who brought you up from Egypt,'
And committed great blasphemies,

19 You, in Your great compassion,
Did not forsake them in
the wilderness;
The pillar of cloud did not
leave them by day,
To guide them on their way,
Nor the pillar of fire by night,
to light for them the way in
which they were to go.

20 "You gave Your good Spirit
to instruct them,
Your manna You did not
withhold from their mouth,
And You gave them water
for their thirst.

21 "Indeed, forty years You provided
for them in the wilderness
and they were not in want;
Their clothes did not wear out,
nor did their feet swell.

22 "You also gave them kingdoms
and peoples,
And allotted *them* to them
as a boundary.
They took possession of the land
of Sihon the king of Heshbon
And the land of Og the
king of Bashan.

23 "You made their sons numerous
as the stars of heaven,

And You brought them into the land
Which You had told their fathers
to enter and possess.
24 "So their sons entered and
possessed the land.
And You subdued before
them the inhabitants of the
land, the Canaanites,
And You gave them into their
hand, with their kings and
the peoples of the land,
To do with them as they desired.
25 "They captured fortified cities
and a fertile land.
They took possession of houses
full of every good thing,
Hewn cisterns, vineyards,
olive groves,
Fruit trees in abundance.
So they ate, were filled and grew fat,
And reveled in Your great goodness.

26 "But they became disobedient
and rebelled against You,
And cast Your law behind their
backs
And killed Your prophets who
had admonished them
So that they might return to You,
And they committed great
blasphemies.
27 "Therefore You delivered them into
the hand of their oppressors
who oppressed them,
But when they cried to You in
the time of their distress,
You heard from heaven,
and according to Your
great compassion
You gave them deliverers who
delivered them from the
hand of their oppressors.
28 "But as soon as they had rest, they
did evil again before You;
Therefore You abandoned them
to the hand of their enemies,
so that they ruled over them.
When they cried again to You,
You heard from heaven,
And many times You rescued them
according to Your compassion,
29 And admonished them in order to
turn them back to Your law.
Yet they acted arrogantly and did not
listen to Your commandments but
sinned against Your ordinances,
By which if a man observes
them he shall live.

And they turned a stubborn
shoulder and stiffened their
neck, and would not listen.
30 "However, You bore with
them for many years,
And admonished them by Your
Spirit through Your prophets,
Yet they would not give ear.
Therefore You gave them into the
hand of the peoples of the lands.
31 "Nevertheless, in Your great
compassion You did not make an
end of them or forsake them,
For You are a gracious and
compassionate God.

32 "Now therefore, our God, the great,
the mighty, and the awesome
God, who keeps covenant
and lovingkindness,
Do not let all the hardship seem
insignificant before You,
Which has come upon us, our
kings, our princes, our priests,
our prophets, our fathers
and on all Your people,
From the days of the kings
of Assyria to this day.
33 "However, You are just in all
that has come upon us;
For You have dealt faithfully, but
we have acted wickedly.
34 "For our kings, our leaders,
our priests and our fathers
have not kept Your law
Or paid attention to Your
commandments and Your
admonitions with which You
have admonished them.
35 "But they, in their own kingdom,
With Your great goodness
which You gave them,
With the broad and rich land
which You set before them,
Did not serve You or turn
from their evil deeds.
36 "Behold, we are slaves today,
And as to the land which You
gave to our fathers to eat of
its fruit and its bounty,
Behold, we are slaves in it.
37 "Its abundant produce is for
the kings
Whom You have set over us
because of our sins;
They also rule over our bodies
And over our cattle as they please,
So we are in great distress.

38 "Now because of all this
We are making an agreement
in writing;
And on the sealed document *are
the names of* our leaders, our
Levites *and* our priests."

Psalm 89:11-18

11 The heavens are Yours, the
earth also is Yours;
The world and all it contains,
You have founded them.
12 The north and the south, You
have created them;
Tabor and Hermon shout
for joy at Your name.
13 You have a strong arm;
Your hand is mighty, Your
right hand is exalted.
14 Righteousness and justice are the
foundation of Your throne;
Lovingkindness and truth
go before You.
15 How blessed are the people who
know the joyful sound!
O LORD, they walk in the light
of Your countenance.
16 In Your name they rejoice all
the day,
And by Your righteousness
they are exalted.
17 For You are the glory of
their strength,
And by Your favor our horn is
exalted.
18 For our shield belongs to the LORD,
And our king to the Holy
One of Israel.

Proverbs 21:29-31

29 A wicked man displays a bold face,
But as for the upright, he
makes his way sure.
30 There is no wisdom and
no understanding
And no counsel against the LORD.
31 The horse is prepared for
the day of battle,
But victory belongs to the LORD.

21:29 The wicked become obstinate, maintaining what suits them without regard for others or the truth, while good people proceed with integrity.

Acts 27:27-44

27 But when the fourteenth night came, as we were being driven about in the Adriatic Sea, about midnight the sailors *began* to surmise that they were approaching some land. 28 They took soundings and found *it to be* twenty fathoms; and a little farther on they took another sounding and found *it to be* fifteen fathoms. 29 Fearing that we might

27:27 fourteenth night. Since they sailed from Fair Havens (v. 13). **Adriatic Sea.** The central Mediterranean Sea, not the present Adriatic Sea located between Italy and Croatia. The modern Adriatic was known in Paul's day as the Gulf of Adria. *began* **to surmise.** The sailors probably heard the sound of waves breaking on a shore.

27:28 took soundings. With a weight attached to a length of rope they measured the depth of the sea. **twenty fathoms...fifteen fathoms.** 120 feet...90 feet. The decreasing depth of the water confirmed the ship was approaching land.

run aground somewhere on the rocks, they cast four anchors from the stern and wished for daybreak. 30 But as the sailors were trying to escape from the ship and had let down the *ship's* boat into the sea, on the pretense of intending to lay out anchors from the bow, 31 Paul said to the centurion and to the soldiers, "Unless these men remain in the ship, you yourselves cannot be saved." 32 Then the soldiers cut away the ropes of the *ship's* boat and let it fall away.

33 Until the day was about to dawn, Paul was encouraging them all to take some food, saying, "Today is the fourteenth day that you have been constantly watching and going without eating, having taken nothing. 34 Therefore I encourage you to take some food, for this is for your preservation, for not a hair from the head of any of you will perish." 35 Having said this, he took bread and gave thanks to God in the presence of all, and he broke it and began to eat. 36 All of them were encouraged and they themselves also took food. 37 All of us in the ship were two hundred and seventy-six persons. 38 When they had eaten enough, they *began* to lighten the ship by throwing out the wheat into the sea. 39 When day came, they could not recognize the land; but they did observe a bay with

a beach, and they resolved to drive the ship onto it if they could. ⁴⁰And casting off the anchors, they left them in the sea while at the same time they were loosening the ropes of the rudders; and hoisting the foresail to the wind, they were heading for the beach. ⁴¹But striking a reef where two seas met, they ran the vessel aground; and the prow stuck fast and remained immovable, but the stern *began* to be broken up by the force *of the waves.* ⁴²The soldiers' plan was to kill the prisoners, so that none *of them* would swim away and escape; ⁴³but the centurion, wanting to bring Paul safely through, kept

them from their intention, and commanded that those who could swim should jump overboard first and get to land, ⁴⁴and the rest *should follow,* some on planks, and others on various things from the ship. And so it happened that they all were brought safely to land.

27:42 The soldiers' plan was to kill the prisoners. Knowing they could face punishment or death if their prisoners escaped (12:19; 16:27).

DAY 28: How do repentance from sin and rejoicing go together?

In response to the people's request, Ezra brought the Law of the Lord to the people (Nehemiah 8:1). At this time, the Law was a scroll, as opposed to a text consisting of bound pages. Such a reading was required every 7 years at the Feast of Tabernacles (Dt 31:10–13), even though it had been neglected since the Babylonian captivity until this occasion.

From daybreak to noon, a period of at least 6 hours, the Law was read and explained. Other men, probably priests, stood with Ezra to show agreement, and all of the people stood, as well (Ne 8:5). This was in respect for God's Word, as though they were in the presence of God Himself. Some of the Levites assisted Ezra with the people's understanding of the Scripture by reading and explaining it (vv. 7–8). This may have involved translation for people who were only Aramaic speakers in exile, but more likely it means "to break down" the text into its parts so that the people could understand it. This was an exposition or explanation of the meaning and not just translation.

When the people heard and understood God's law, they wept (v. 9). Not tears of joy, but penitent sorrow (v. 10) came forth as they were grieved by conviction (v. 11) over the distressing manifestations of sin in transgressing the Lord's commands and the consequent punishments they had suffered in their captivity.

The event called for a holy day of worship to prepare them for the hard days ahead (12:43), so they were encouraged to rejoice. The words they had heard did remind them that God punishes sin, but also that God blesses obedience. That was reason to celebrate. "Do not be grieved, for the joy of the LORD is your strength" (8:10). They had not been utterly destroyed as a nation, in spite of their sin, and were, by God's grace, on the brink of a new beginning. That called for celebration.

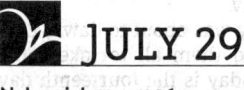

JULY 29

Nehemiah 10:1–11:36

10 Now on the sealed document *were the names of:* Nehemiah the governor, the son of Hacaliah, and Zedekiah, ²Seraiah, Azariah, Jeremiah, ³Pashhur, Amariah, Malchijah, ⁴Hattush, Shebaniah, Malluch, ⁵Harim, Meremoth, Obadiah, ⁶Daniel, Ginnethon, Baruch, ⁷Meshullam, Abijah, Mijamin, ⁸Maaziah, Bilgai, Shemaiah. These *were* the priests. ⁹And the Levites: Jeshua the son of Azaniah, Binnui of the sons of Henadad, Kadmiel; ¹⁰also their brothers Shebaniah, Hodiah, Kelita, Pelaiah, Hanan, ¹¹Mica, Rehob, Hashabiah, ¹²Zaccur, Sherebiah, Shebaniah, ¹³Hodiah, Bani, Beninu. ¹⁴The leaders of the people: Parosh,

Pahath-moab, Elam, Zattu, Bani, ¹⁵Bunni, Azgad, Bebai, ¹⁶Adonijah, Bigvai, Adin, ¹⁷Ater, Hezekiah, Azzur, ¹⁸Hodiah, Hashum, Bezai, ¹⁹Hariph, Anathoth, Nebai, ²⁰Magpiash, Meshullam, Hezir, ²¹Meshezabel, Zadok, Jaddua, ²²Pelatiah, Hanan, Anaiah, ²³Hoshea, Hananiah, Hasshub, ²⁴Hallohesh, Pilha, Shobek, ²⁵Rehum, Hashabnah, Maaseiah, ²⁶Ahiah, Hanan, Anan, ²⁷Malluch, Harim, Baanah.

²⁸Now the rest of the people, the priests, the Levites, the gatekeepers, the singers, the temple servants and all those who had separated themselves from the peoples of the lands to the law of God, their wives, their sons and their daughters, all those who had knowledge and understanding, ²⁹are joining with their kinsmen, their nobles, and are taking on themselves a curse and an oath to

10:28 who had separated themselves. These are those who 1) had followed the demand of Ezra and Nehemiah to divorce pagan spouses or 2) had been left in the land but never joined themselves to any heathen, thus remaining separate. Intermarriage with the nations had previously precipitated an influence in Israel which had culminated in Babylonian slavery, thus playing a major role in Israel's unfaithfulness to the covenant.

---

walk in God's law, which was given through Moses, God's servant, and to keep and to observe all the commandments of GOD our Lord, and His ordinances and His statutes; ³⁰ and that we will not give our daughters to the peoples of the land or take their daughters for our sons. ³¹ As for the peoples of the land who bring wares or any grain on the sabbath day to sell, we will not buy from them on the sabbath or a holy day; and we will forego *the crops* the seventh year and the exaction of every debt.

³² We also placed ourselves under obligation to contribute yearly one third of a shekel for the service of the house of our God: ³³ for the showbread, for the continual grain offering, for the continual burnt offering, the sabbaths, the new moon, for the appointed times, for the holy things and for the sin offerings to make atonement for Israel, and all the work of the house of our God.

³⁴ Likewise we cast lots for the supply of wood *among* the priests, the Levites and the people so that they might bring it to the house of our God, according to our fathers' households, at fixed times annually, to burn on the altar of the LORD our God, as it is written in the law; ³⁵ and that they might bring the first fruits of our ground and the first fruits

---

10:35–37 first fruits...firstborn...firstborn. These laws required the firstfruits of the ground (Ex 23:19; 34:26; Dt 26:2), the firstfruits of the trees (Lv 19:24; Nu 18:13), the firstborn sons redeemed by the estimated price of the priest (Nu 18:15), and the firstborn of the herds and flocks (Ex 13:12; Nu 18:15, 17). All of this was kept at the storehouses near the temple and distributed for the support of the priests and Levites. The Levites then gave a tenth of what they received to the priests (Nu 18:26).

---

of all the fruit of every tree to the house of the LORD annually, ³⁶ and bring to the house of our God the firstborn of our sons and of our cattle, and the firstborn of our herds and our flocks as it is written in the law, for the priests who are ministering in the house of our God. ³⁷ We will also bring the first of our dough, our contributions, the fruit of every tree, the new wine and the oil to the priests at the chambers of the house of our God, and the tithe of our ground to the Levites, for the Levites are they who receive the tithes in all the rural towns. ³⁸ The priest, the son of Aaron, shall be with the Levites when the Levites receive tithes, and the Levites shall bring up the tenth of the tithes to the house of our God, to the chambers of the storehouse. ³⁹ For the sons of Israel and the sons of Levi shall bring the contribution of the grain, the new wine and the oil to the chambers; there are the utensils of the sanctuary, the priests who are ministering, the gatekeepers and the singers. Thus we will not neglect the house of our God.

11 Now the leaders of the people lived in Jerusalem, but the rest of the people cast lots to bring one out of ten to live in Jerusalem, the holy city, while nine-tenths *remained* in the *other* cities. ² And the people blessed all the men who volunteered to live in Jerusalem.

³ Now these are the heads of the provinces who lived in Jerusalem, but in the cities of Judah each lived on his own property in their cities—the Israelites, the priests, the Levites, the temple servants and the descendants of Solomon's servants. ⁴ Some of the sons of Judah and some of the sons of Benjamin lived in Jerusalem. From the sons of Judah: Athaiah the son of Uzziah, the son of Zechariah, the son of Amariah, the son of Shephatiah, the son of Mahalalel, of the sons of Perez; ⁵ and Maaseiah the son of Baruch, the son of Colhozeh, the son of Hazaiah, the son of Adaiah, the son of Joiarib, the son of Zechariah, the son of the Shilonite. ⁶ All the sons of Perez who lived in Jerusalem were 468 able men.

⁷ Now these are the sons of Benjamin: Sallu the son of Meshullam, the son of Joed, the son of Pedaiah, the son of Kolaiah, the son of Maaseiah, the son of Ithiel, the son of Jeshaiah; ⁸ and after him Gabbai *and* Sallai, 928. ⁹ Joel the son of Zichri was their overseer, and Judah the son of Hassenuah was second in command of the city.

¹⁰ From the priests: Jedaiah the son of Joiarib, Jachin, ¹¹ Seraiah the son of Hilkiah, the son of Meshullam, the son of Zadok, the son of Meraioth, the son of Ahitub, the leader

of the house of God, [12] and their kinsmen who performed the work of the temple, 822; and Adaiah the son of Jeroham, the son of Pelaliah, the son of Amzi, the son of Zechariah, the son of Pashhur, the son of Malchijah, [13] and his kinsmen, heads of fathers' *households*, 242; and Amashsai the son of Azarel, the son of Ahzai, the son of Meshillemoth, the son of Immer, [14] and their brothers, valiant warriors, 128. And their overseer was Zabdiel, the son of Haggedolim.

[15] Now from the Levites: Shemaiah the son of Hasshub, the son of Azrikam, the son of Hashabiah, the son of Bunni; [16] and Shabbethai and Jozabad, from the leaders of the Levites, who were in charge of the outside work of the house of God; [17] and Mattaniah the son of Mica, the son of Zabdi, the son of Asaph, who was the leader in beginning the thanksgiving at prayer, and Bakbukiah, the second among his brethren; and Abda the son of Shammua, the son of Galal, the son of Jeduthun. [18] All the Levites in the holy city *were* 284.

[19] Also the gatekeepers, Akkub, Talmon and their brethren who kept watch at the gates, *were* 172. [20] The rest of Israel, of the priests *and* of the Levites, *were* in all the cities of Judah, each on his own inheritance. [21] But the temple servants were living in Ophel, and Ziha and Gishpa were in charge of the temple servants.

[22] Now the overseer of the Levites in Jerusalem was Uzzi the son of Bani, the son of Hashabiah, the son of Mattaniah, the son of Mica, from the sons of Asaph, who were the singers for the service of the house of God. [23] For *there was* a commandment from the king concerning them and a firm regulation for the song leaders day by day. [24] Pethahiah the son of Meshezabel, of the sons of Zerah the son of Judah, was the king's representative in all matters concerning the people.

[25] Now as for the villages with their fields, some of the sons of Judah lived in Kiriath-arba and its towns, in Dibon and its towns, and in Jekabzeel and its villages, [26] and in Jeshua, in Moladah and Beth-pelet, [27] and in Hazarshual, in Beersheba and its towns, [28] and in Ziklag, in Meconah and in its towns, [29] and in En-rimmon, in Zorah and in Jarmuth, [30] Zanoah, Adullam, and their villages, Lachish and its fields, Azekah and its towns. So they encamped from Beersheba as far as the valley of Hinnom. [31] The sons of Benjamin also *lived* from Geba *onward*, at Michmash and Aija, at Bethel and its towns, [32] at Anathoth, Nob, Ananiah, [33] Hazor, Ramah, Gittaim, [34] Hadid, Zeboim, Neballat, [35] Lod and Ono, the valley of craftsmen. [36] From the Levites, *some* divisions in Judah belonged to Benjamin.

Psalm 89:19-29

[19] Once You spoke in vision
to Your godly ones,
And said, "I have given help
to one who is mighty;
I have exalted one chosen
from the people.
[20] "I have found David My servant;
With My holy oil I have anointed him,
[21] With whom My hand will
be established;
My arm also will strengthen him.
[22] "The enemy will not deceive him,
Nor the son of wickedness afflict him.
[23] "But I shall crush his
adversaries before him,
And strike those who hate him.
[24] "My faithfulness and My
lovingkindness will be with him,
And in My name his horn
will be exalted.
[25] "I shall also set his hand on the sea
And his right hand on the rivers.
[26] "He will cry to Me, 'You are my
Father,
My God, and the rock of my salvation.'
[27] "I also shall make him *My* firstborn,
The highest of the kings of the earth.
[28] "My lovingkindness I will
keep for him forever,
And My covenant shall be
confirmed to him.
[29] "So I will establish his
descendants forever
And his throne as the days
of heaven.

89:27 *My* firstborn. The firstborn child was given a place of special honor and a double portion of the inheritance (Ge 27; 2Ki 2:9). However, in a royal grant covenant, a chosen person could be elevated to the level of firstborn sonship and thus have title to a perpetual gift involving dynastic succession (Ps 2:7). Though not actually the first, Israel was considered the firstborn among nations (Ex 4:22); Ephraim the younger was treated as the firstborn (Ge 48:13-20); and David was the firstborn among kings. In this latter sense of prominent favor, Christ can be called the firstborn over all creation (Col 1:15), in that He is given the preeminence over all created beings.

Proverbs 22:1–2

22 A *good* name is to be more desired than great wealth,
Favor is better than silver and gold.

² The rich and the poor have
a common bond,
The LORD is the maker of them all.

Acts 28:1–31

28 When they had been brought safely through, then we found out that the island was called Malta. ²The natives showed us extraordinary kindness; for because of the rain that had set in and because of the cold, they kindled a fire and received us all. ³But when Paul had gathered a bundle of sticks and laid them on the fire, a viper came out because of the heat and fastened itself on his hand. ⁴When the natives saw the creature hanging from his hand, they *began* saying to one another, "Undoubtedly this man is a murderer, and though he has been saved from the sea, justice has not allowed him to live." ⁵However he shook the creature off into the fire and suffered no harm. ⁶But they were expecting that he was about to swell up or suddenly fall down dead. But after they had waited a long time and had seen nothing unusual happen to him, they changed their minds and *began* to say that he was a god.

⁷Now in the neighborhood of that place were lands belonging to the leading man of the island, named Publius, who welcomed us and entertained us courteously three days. ⁸And it happened that the father of Publius was lying *in bed* afflicted with *recurrent* fever and dysentery; and Paul went in *to see* him and after he had prayed, he laid his hands on him and healed him. ⁹After this had hap-

28:8 afflicted with…fever and dysentery. The gastric fever (caused by a microbe found in goat's milk) that was common on Malta. Dysentery, often the result of poor sanitation, was widespread in the ancient world.

pened, the rest of the people on the island who had diseases were coming to him and getting cured. ¹⁰They also honored us with many marks of respect; and when we were setting sail, they supplied *us* with all we needed.

¹¹At the end of three months we set sail on an Alexandrian ship which had wintered at the island, and which had the Twin Brothers

for its figurehead. ¹²After we put in at Syracuse, we stayed there for three days. ¹³From there we sailed around and arrived at Rhegium, and a day later a south wind sprang up, and on the second day we came to Puteoli. ¹⁴There we found *some* brethren, and were invited to stay with them for seven days; and thus we came to Rome. ¹⁵And the brethren, when they heard about us, came from there as far as the Market of Appius and Three Inns to meet us; and when Paul saw them, he thanked God and took courage.

¹⁶When we entered Rome, Paul was allowed to stay by himself, with the soldier who was guarding him.

28:16 stay by himself…guarding. Possibly through Julius' intervention, Paul was allowed to live under guard in his own rented quarters (v. 30).

¹⁷After three days Paul called together those who were the leading men of the Jews, and when they came together, he *began* saying to them, "Brethren, though I had done nothing against our people or the customs of our fathers, yet I was delivered as a prisoner from Jerusalem into the hands of the Romans. ¹⁸And when they had examined me, they were willing to release me because there was no ground for putting me to death. ¹⁹But when the Jews objected, I was forced to appeal to Caesar, not that I had any accusation against my nation. ²⁰For this reason, therefore, I requested to see you and to speak with you, for I am wearing this chain for the sake of the hope of Israel." ²¹They said to him, "We have neither received letters from Judea concerning you, nor have any of the brethren come here and reported or spoken anything bad about you. ²²But we desire to hear from you what your views are; for concerning this sect, it is known to us that it is spoken against everywhere."

²³When they had set a day for Paul, they came to him at his lodging in large numbers; and he was explaining to them by solemnly testifying about the kingdom of God and trying to persuade them concerning Jesus, from both the Law of Moses and from the Prophets, from morning until evening. ²⁴Some were being persuaded by the things spoken, but others would not believe. ²⁵And when they did not agree with one another, they *began* leaving after Paul had spoken one *parting*

word, "The Holy Spirit rightly spoke through Isaiah the prophet to your fathers, ²⁶ saying,

'GO TO THIS PEOPLE AND SAY,
"YOU WILL KEEP ON HEARING, BUT
  WILL NOT UNDERSTAND;
AND YOU WILL KEEP ON SEEING,
  BUT WILL NOT PERCEIVE;
²⁷ FOR THE HEART OF THIS PEOPLE
  HAS BECOME DULL,
AND WITH THEIR EARS THEY
  SCARCELY HEAR,
AND THEY HAVE CLOSED THEIR EYES;
OTHERWISE THEY MIGHT SEE
  WITH THEIR EYES,
AND HEAR WITH THEIR EARS,
AND UNDERSTAND WITH THEIR
  HEART AND RETURN,
AND I WOULD HEAL THEM."'

²⁸ Therefore let it be known to you that this salvation of God has been sent to the Gentiles; they will also listen." ²⁹ [When he had spoken these words, the Jews departed, having a great dispute among themselves.]

³⁰ And he stayed two full years in his own rented quarters and was welcoming all who came to him, ³¹ preaching the kingdom of God and teaching concerning the Lord Jesus Christ with all openness, unhindered.

DAY 29: How does Nehemiah fit into the timeline of world history?

It is unclear how Nehemiah became King Artaxerxes' cupbearer, but the fact that Esther was the king's stepmother may have inclined the king to consider a Jew for such a trusted position. When Nehemiah carried out his mission to rebuild the walls of Jerusalem, the Persian Empire had been dominant for almost 100 years. King Cyrus's decree of repatriation given back in 539 B.C. had instigated a group of Jews to return to Israel under Zerubbabel. Their desperate state almost a century later spurred Nehemiah into action.

Ancient Egyptian documents (Elephantine papyri) dated around the 5th century B.C. independently confirm part of Nehemiah's account. Sanballat the governor of Samaria (2:19), Jehohanan (6:18; 12:23) and Nehemiah himself receive mention.

The events recorded in Nehemiah, along with Malachi's prophecies, make up the final inspired writings of the Old Testament. God chose to then remain silent for 400 years. That silence ended with the announcements of John the Baptist's and Jesus' births.

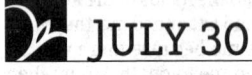

JULY 30

Nehemiah 12:1–13:31

12 Now these are the priests and the Levites who came up with Zerubbabel the son of Shealtiel, and Jeshua: Seraiah, Jeremiah, Ezra, ² Amariah, Malluch, Hattush, ³ Shecaniah, Rehum, Meremoth, ⁴ Iddo, Ginnethoi, Abijah, ⁵ Mijamin, Maadiah, Bilgah, ⁶ Shemaiah and Joiarib, Jedaiah, ⁷ Sallu, Amok, Hilkiah and Jedaiah. These were the heads of the priests and their kinsmen in the days of Jeshua.

⁸ The Levites *were* Jeshua, Binnui, Kadmiel, Sherebiah, Judah, *and* Mattaniah *who was* in charge of the songs of thanksgiving, he and his brothers. ⁹ Also Bakbukiah and Unni, their brothers, stood opposite them in *their* service divisions. ¹⁰ Jeshua became the father of Joiakim, and Joiakim became the father of Eliashib, and Eliashib became the father of Joiada, ¹¹ and Joiada became the father of Jonathan, and Jonathan became the father of Jaddua.

¹² Now in the days of Joiakim, the priests, the heads of fathers' *households* were: of Seraiah, Meraiah; of Jeremiah, Hananiah; ¹³ of Ezra, Meshullam; of Amariah, Jehohanan; ¹⁴ of Malluchi, Jonathan; of Shebaniah, Joseph; ¹⁵ of Harim, Adna; of Meraioth, Helkai; ¹⁶ of Iddo, Zechariah; of Ginnethon, Meshullam; ¹⁷ of Abijah, Zichri; of Miniamin, of Moadiah, Piltai; ¹⁸ of Bilgah, Shammua; of Shemaiah, Jehonathan; ¹⁹ of Joiarib, Mattenai; of Jedaiah, Uzzi; ²⁰ of Sallai, Kallai; of Amok, Eber; ²¹ of Hilkiah, Hashabiah; of Jedaiah, Nethanel.

²² As for the Levites, the heads of fathers' *households* were registered in the days of Eliashib, Joiada, and Johanan and Jaddua; so *were* the priests in the reign of Darius the Persian. ²³ The sons of Levi, the heads of fathers' *households,* were registered in the Book of the Chronicles up to the days of Johanan the son of Eliashib. ²⁴ The heads of the Levites *were* Hashabiah, Sherebiah and Jeshua the son of Kadmiel, with their brothers opposite them, to praise *and* give thanks, as prescribed by David the man of God, division corresponding to division. ²⁵ Mattaniah, Bakbukiah, Obadiah, Meshullam, Talmon *and* Akkub *were* gatekeepers keeping watch at the

storehouses of the gates. ²⁶ These *served* in the days of Joiakim the son of Jeshua, the son of Jozadak, and in the days of Nehemiah the governor and of Ezra the priest *and* scribe.

²⁷ Now at the dedication of the wall of Jerusalem they sought out the Levites from all their places, to bring them to Jerusalem so that they might celebrate the dedication with gladness, with hymns of thanksgiving and with songs *to the accompaniment* of cymbals, harps and lyres. ²⁸ So the sons of the singers were assembled from the district around Jerusalem, and from the villages of the Netophathites, ²⁹ from Beth-gilgal and from *their* fields in Geba and Azmaveth, for the singers had built themselves villages around Jerusalem. ³⁰ The priests and the Levites purified themselves; they also purified the people, the gates and the wall.

³¹ Then I had the leaders of Judah come up on top of the wall, and I appointed two great choirs, the first proceeding to the right on top of the wall toward the Refuse Gate. ³² Hoshaiah and half of the leaders of Judah followed them, ³³ with Azariah, Ezra, Meshullam, ³⁴ Judah, Benjamin, Shemaiah, Jeremiah, ³⁵ and some of the sons of the priests with trumpets; *and* Zechariah the son of Jonathan, the son of Shemaiah, the son of Mattaniah, the son of Micaiah, the son of Zaccur, the son of Asaph, ³⁶ and his kinsmen, Shemaiah, Azarel, Milalai, Gilalai, Maai, Nethanel, Judah *and* Hanani, with the musical instruments of David the man of God. And Ezra the scribe went before them. ³⁷ At the Fountain Gate they went directly up the steps of the city of David by the stairway of the wall above the house of David to the Water Gate on the east.

³⁸ The second choir proceeded to the left, while I followed them with half of the people on the wall, above the Tower of Furnaces, to the Broad Wall, ³⁹ and above the Gate of Ephraim, by the Old Gate, by the Fish Gate, the Tower of Hananel and the Tower of the Hundred, as far as the Sheep Gate; and they stopped at the Gate of the Guard. ⁴⁰ Then the two choirs took their stand in the house of God. So did I and half of the officials with me; ⁴¹ and the priests, Eliakim, Maaseiah, Miniamin, Micaiah, Elioenai, Zechariah and Hananiah, with the trumpets; ⁴² and Maaseiah, Shemaiah, Eleazar, Uzzi, Jehohanan, Malchijah, Elam and Ezer. And the singers sang, with Jezrahiah *their* leader, ⁴³ and on that day they offered great sacrifices and rejoiced because God had given them great joy, even the women and children rejoiced, so that the joy of Jerusalem was heard from afar.

⁴⁴ On that day men were also appointed over the chambers for the stores, the contributions, the first fruits and the tithes, to gather into them from the fields of the cities the portions required by the law for the priests and Levites; for Judah rejoiced over the priests and Levites who served. ⁴⁵ For they performed the worship of their God and the service of purification, together with the singers and the gatekeepers in accordance with the command of David *and* of his son Solomon. ⁴⁶ For in the days of David and Asaph, in ancient times, *there were* leaders of the singers, songs of praise and hymns of thanksgiving to God. ⁴⁷ So all Israel in the days of Zerubbabel and Nehemiah gave the portions due the singers and the gatekeepers as each day required, and set apart the consecrated *portion* for the Levites, and the Levites set apart the consecrated *portion* for the sons of Aaron.

13 On that day they read aloud from the book of Moses in the hearing of the people; and there was found written in it that no Ammonite or Moabite should ever enter the assembly of God, ² because they did not meet the sons of Israel with bread and water, but hired Balaam against them to curse them. However, our God turned the curse into a blessing. ³ So when they heard the law, they excluded all foreigners from Israel.

⁴ Now prior to this, Eliashib the priest, who was appointed over the chambers of the house of our God, being related to Tobiah, ⁵ had prepared a large room for him, where formerly they put the grain offerings, the frankincense, the utensils and the tithes of grain, wine and oil prescribed for the Levites, the singers and the gatekeepers, and the contributions for the priests. ⁶ But during all this *time* I was not in Jerusalem, for in the thirty-second year of Artaxerxes king of Babylon I had gone to the king. After some time, however, I asked leave from the king, ⁷ and I came to Jerusalem and learned about the evil that Eliashib had done for Tobiah, by preparing a room for him in the courts of the house of God. ⁸ It was very displeasing to me, so I threw all of Tobiah's household goods out of the room. ⁹ Then I gave an order and they cleansed the rooms; and I returned there the utensils of the house of God with the grain offerings and the frankincense.

¹⁰ I also discovered that the portions of the Levites had not been given *them,* so that the Levites and the singers who performed the service had gone away, each to his own field. ¹¹ So I reprimanded the officials and said, "Why

is the house of God forsaken?" Then I gathered them together and restored them to their posts. ¹²All Judah then brought the tithe of the grain, wine and oil into the storehouses. ¹³In charge of the storehouses I appointed Shelemiah the priest, Zadok the scribe, and Pedaiah of the Levites, and in addition to them was Hanan the son of Zaccur, the son of Mattaniah; for they were considered reliable, and it was their task to distribute to their kinsmen. ¹⁴Remember me for this, O my God, and do not blot out my loyal deeds which I have performed for the house of my God and its services.

¹⁵In those days I saw in Judah some who were treading wine presses on the sabbath, and bringing in sacks of grain and loading *them* on donkeys, as well as wine, grapes, figs and all kinds of loads, and they brought *them* into Jerusalem on the sabbath day. So I admonished *them* on the day they sold food. ¹⁶Also men of Tyre were living there *who* imported fish and all kinds of merchandise, and sold *them* to the sons of Judah on the sabbath, even in Jerusalem. ¹⁷Then I reprimanded the nobles of Judah and said to them, "What is this evil thing you are doing, by profaning the sabbath day? ¹⁸Did not your fathers do the same, so that our God brought on us and on this city all this trouble? Yet you are adding to the wrath on Israel by profaning the sabbath."

¹⁹It came about that just as it grew dark at the gates of Jerusalem before the sabbath, I commanded that the doors should be shut and that they should not open them until after the sabbath. Then I stationed some of my servants at the gates *so that* no load would enter on the sabbath day. ²⁰Once or twice the traders and merchants of every kind of merchandise spent the night outside Jerusalem. ²¹Then I warned them and said to them, "Why do you spend the night in front of the wall? If you do so again, I will use force against you." From that time on they did not come on the sabbath. ²²And I commanded the Levites that they should purify themselves and come as gatekeepers to sanctify the sabbath day. *For* this also remember me, O my God, and have compassion on me according to the greatness of Your lovingkindness.

²³In those days I also saw that the Jews had married women from Ashdod, Ammon *and* Moab. ²⁴As for their children, half spoke in the language of Ashdod, and none of them was able to speak the language of Judah, but the language of his own people. ²⁵So I contended with them and cursed them and struck some of them and pulled out their hair, and made them swear by God, "You shall not give your daughters to their sons, nor take of their daughters for your sons or for yourselves. ²⁶Did not Solomon king of Israel sin regarding these things? Yet among the many nations there was no king like him, and he was loved by his God, and God made him king over all Israel; nevertheless the foreign women caused even him to sin. ²⁷Do we then hear about you that you have committed all this great evil by acting unfaithfully against our God by marrying foreign women?" ²⁸Even one of the sons of Joiada, the son of Eliashib the high priest, was a son-in-law of Sanballat the Horonite, so I drove him away from me. ²⁹Remember them, O my God, because they have defiled the priesthood and the covenant of the priesthood and the Levites.

³⁰Thus I purified them from everything foreign and appointed duties for the priests and the Levites, each in his task, ³¹and *I arranged* for the supply of wood at appointed times and for the first fruits. Remember me, O my God, for good.

Psalm 89:30-37

³⁰ "If his sons forsake My law
    And do not walk in My judgments,
³¹ If they violate My statutes
    And do not keep My
      commandments,
³² Then I will punish their
    transgression with the rod
    And their iniquity with stripes.
³³ "But I will not break off My
      lovingkindness from him,
    Nor deal falsely in My faithfulness.
³⁴ "My covenant I will not violate,
    Nor will I alter the utterance
      of My lips.
³⁵ "Once I have sworn by My holiness;
    I will not lie to David.
³⁶ "His descendants shall endure
      forever
    And his throne as the sun before Me.
³⁷ "It shall be established
      forever like the moon,
    And the witness in the
      sky is faithful."   *Selah*

Proverbs 22:3-4

³ The prudent sees the evil
      and hides himself,
    But the naive go on, and
      are punished for it.
⁴ The reward of humility *and*
      the fear of the LORD
    Are riches, honor and life.

Romans 1:1–32

1 Paul, a bond-servant of Christ Jesus, called *as* an apostle, set apart for the gospel of God, ²which He promised beforehand through His prophets in the holy Scriptures, ³concerning His Son, who was born of a descendant of David according to the flesh, ⁴who was declared the Son of God with power by the resurrection from the dead, according to the Spirit of holiness, Jesus Christ our Lord, ⁵through whom we have received grace and apostleship to bring about *the* obedience of faith among all the Gentiles for His name's sake, ⁶among whom you also are the called of Jesus Christ;

⁷to all who are beloved of God in Rome, called *as* saints: Grace to you and peace from God our Father and the Lord Jesus Christ.

⁸First, I thank my God through Jesus Christ for you all, because your faith is being proclaimed throughout the whole world. ⁹For God, whom I serve in my spirit in the *preaching of the* gospel of His Son, is my witness *as to* how unceasingly I make mention of you, ¹⁰always in my prayers making request, if perhaps now at last by the will of God I may succeed in coming to you. ¹¹For I long to see you so that I may impart some spiritual gift to you, that you may be established; ¹²that is, that I may be encouraged together with you *while* among you, each of us by the other's faith, both yours and mine. ¹³I do not want you to be unaware, brethren, that often I have planned to come to you (and have been prevented so far) so that I may obtain some fruit among you also, even as among the rest of the Gentiles. ¹⁴I am under obligation both to Greeks and to barbarians, both to the wise and to the foolish. ¹⁵So, for my part, I am eager to preach the gospel to you also who are in Rome.

¹⁶For I am not ashamed of the gospel, for it is the power of God for salvation to everyone who believes, to the Jew first and also to the Greek. ¹⁷For in it *the* righteousness of God is revealed from faith to faith; as it is written, "BUT THE RIGHTEOUS *man* SHALL LIVE BY FAITH."

¹⁸For the wrath of God is revealed from heaven against all ungodliness and unrighteousness of men who suppress the truth in unrighteousness, ¹⁹because that which is known about God is evident within them; for God made it evident to them. ²⁰For since the creation of the world His invisible attributes, His eternal power and divine nature, have been clearly seen, being understood through what has been made, so that they are without excuse. ²¹For even though they knew God, they did not honor Him as God or give thanks,

1:17 BUT THE RIGHTEOUS *man* SHALL LIVE BY FAITH. Paul intends to prove that it has always been God's way to justify sinners by grace on the basis of faith alone. God established Abraham as a pattern of faith (4:22–25; Gal 3:6–7) and thus calls him the father of all who believe (4:11, 16). Elsewhere, Paul uses this same phrase to argue that no one has ever been declared righteous before God except by faith alone (Gal 3:11) and that true faith will demonstrate itself in action (Php 2:12–13). This expression emphasizes that true faith is not a single event, but a way of life—it endures. That endurance is called the perseverance of the saints (Col 1:22–23; Heb 3:12–14). One central theme of the story of Job is that no matter what Satan does, saving faith cannot be destroyed.

1:18 wrath of God. This is not an impulsive outburst of anger aimed capriciously at people whom God does not like. It is the settled, determined response of a righteous God against sin.

1:20 they are without excuse. God holds all men responsible for their refusal to acknowledge what He has shown them of Himself in His creation. Even those who have never had an opportunity to hear the gospel have received a clear witness about the existence and character of God—and have suppressed it. If a person will respond to the revelation he has, even if it is solely natural revelation, God will provide some means for that person to hear the gospel (Ac 8:26–39; 10:1–48; 17:27).

1:21 knew God. Man is conscious of God's existence, power, and divine nature through general revelation (vv. 19–20). **they did not honor Him.** Man's chief end is to glorify God (Lv 10:3; 1Ch 16:24–29; Ps 148; Ro 15:5–6), and Scripture constantly demands it (Ps 29:1–2; 1Co 10:31; Rev 4:11). To glorify Him is to honor Him, to acknowledge His attributes, and to praise Him for His perfections (Ex 34:5–7). It is to recognize His glory and extol Him for it. Failing to give Him glory is man's greatest affront to his Creator (Ac 12:22–23). **or give thanks.** They refused to acknowledge that every good thing they enjoyed came from God (Mt 5:45; Ac 14:15–17; 1Ti 6:17; Jas 1:17).

but they became futile in their speculations, and their foolish heart was darkened. ²²Professing to be wise, they became fools, ²³and exchanged the glory of the incorruptible God for an image in the form of corruptible man and of birds and four-footed animals and crawling creatures.

²⁴Therefore God gave them over in the lusts of their hearts to impurity, so that their bodies would be dishonored among them. ²⁵For they exchanged the truth of God for a lie, and worshiped and served the creature rather than the Creator, who is blessed forever. Amen.

²⁶For this reason God gave them over to degrading passions; for their women exchanged the natural function for that which is unnatural, ²⁷and in the same way also the men abandoned the natural function of the woman and burned in their desire toward one another, men with men committing indecent acts and receiving in their own persons the due penalty of their error.

²⁸And just as they did not see fit to acknowledge God any longer, God gave them over to a depraved mind, to do those things which are not proper, ²⁹being filled with all unrighteousness, wickedness, greed, evil; full of envy, murder, strife, deceit, malice; *they are* gossips, ³⁰slanderers, haters of God, insolent, arrogant, boastful, inventors of evil, disobedient to parents, ³¹without understanding, untrustworthy, unloving, unmerciful; ³²and although they know the ordinance of God, that those who practice such things are worthy of death, they not only do the same, but also give hearty approval to those who practice them.

DAY 30: How did Paul maintain his commitment to the gospel?

Paul tells us in Romans 1:16: "I am not ashamed of the gospel." He had been imprisoned in Philippi (Ac 16:23–24), chased out of Thessalonica (Ac 17:10), smuggled out of Berea (Ac 17:14), laughed at in Athens (Ac 17:32), regarded as a fool in Corinth (1Co 1:18, 23), and stoned in Galatia (Ac 14:19), but Paul remained eager to preach the gospel in Rome—the seat of contemporary political power and pagan religion. Neither ridicule, criticism, nor physical persecution could curb his boldness.

"For it is the power of God." The English word "dynamite" comes from this Greek word. Although the message may sound foolish to some (1Co 1:18), the gospel is effective because it carries with it the omnipotence of God. Only God's power is able to overcome man's sinful nature and give him new life (5:6; 8:3; John 1:12; 1Co 1:18, 23–25; 2:1–4; 4:20; 1Pe 1:23).

"The power of God for salvation." Used 5 times in Romans (the verb form occurs 8 times), this key word basically means "deliverance" or "rescue." The power of the gospel delivers people from lostness (Mt 18:11), from the wrath of God (Ro 5:9), from willful spiritual ignorance (Hos 4:6; 2Th 1:8), from evil self-indulgence (Lk 14:26), and from the darkness of false religion (Col 1:13; 1Pe 2:9). It rescues them from the ultimate penalty of their sin, i.e., eternal separation from God and eternal punishment (Rev 20:6).

"To everyone who believes." To trust, rely on, or have faith in. When used of salvation, this word usually occurs in the present tense ("is believing") which stresses that faith is not simply a one-time event, but an ongoing condition. True saving faith is supernatural, a gracious gift of God that He produces in the heart (Eph 2:8) and is the only means by which a person can appropriate true righteousness. Saving faith consists of 3 elements: 1) mental: the mind understands the gospel and the truth about Christ (10:14–17); 2) emotional: one embraces the truthfulness of those facts with sorrow over sin and joy over God's mercy and grace (6:17; 15:13); and 3) volitional: the sinner submits his will to Christ and trusts in Him alone as the only hope of salvation.

JULY 31

Esther 1:1–2:23

1 Now it took place in the days of Ahasuerus, the Ahasuerus who reigned from India to Ethiopia over 127 provinces, ²in those days as King Ahasuerus sat on his royal throne which *was* at the citadel in Susa, ³in the third year of his reign he gave a banquet for all his princes and attendants, the army *officers* of Persia and Media, the nobles and the princes of his provinces being in his presence. ⁴And he displayed the riches of his royal glory and the splendor of his great majesty for many days, 180 days.

⁵When these days were completed, the king gave a banquet lasting seven days for all the people who were present at the citadel in Susa, from the greatest to the least, in the court of the garden of the king's palace. ⁶*There were hangings of* fine white and violet linen held by cords of fine purple linen on silver rings and marble columns, *and* couches of gold and silver on a mosaic pavement of porphyry, marble, mother-of-pearl and precious stones. ⁷Drinks were served in golden vessels of various kinds, and the royal wine

was plentiful according to the king's bounty. [8] The drinking was *done* according to the law, there was no compulsion, for so the king had given orders to each official of his household that he should do according to the desires of each person. [9] Queen Vashti also gave a banquet for the women in the palace which belonged to King Ahasuerus.

1:9 Queen Vashti. Greek literature records her name as Amestris. She gave birth (ca. 483 B.C.) to Ahasuerus' third son, Artaxerxes, who later succeeded his father Ahasuerus on the throne (Ezr 7:1).

[10] On the seventh day, when the heart of the king was merry with wine, he commanded Mehuman, Biztha, Harbona, Bigtha, Abagtha, Zethar and Carkas, the seven eunuchs who served in the presence of King Ahasuerus, [11] to bring Queen Vashti before the king with *her* royal crown in order to display her beauty to the people and the princes, for she was beautiful. [12] But Queen Vashti refused to come at the king's command delivered by the eunuchs. Then the king became very angry and his wrath burned within him.

[13] Then the king said to the wise men who understood the times—for it was the custom of the king so *to speak* before all who knew law and justice [14] and were close to him: Carshena, Shethar, Admatha, Tarshish, Meres, Marsena and Memucan, the seven princes of Persia and Media who had access to the king's presence and sat in the first place in the kingdom— [15] "According to law, what is to be done with Queen Vashti, because she did not obey the command of King Ahasuerus *delivered* by the eunuchs?" [16] In the presence of the king and the princes, Memucan said, "Queen Vashti has wronged not only the king but *also* all the princes and all the peoples who are in all the provinces of King Ahasuerus. [17] For the queen's conduct will become known to all the women causing them to look with contempt on their husbands by saying, 'King Ahasuerus commanded Queen Vashti to be brought in to his presence, but she did not come.' [18] This day the ladies of Persia and Media who have heard of the queen's conduct will speak in *the same way* to all the king's princes, and there will be plenty of contempt and anger. [19] If it pleases the king, let a royal edict be issued by him and let it be written in the laws of Persia and Media so

that it cannot be repealed, that Vashti may no longer come into the presence of King Ahasuerus, and let the king give her royal position to another who is more worthy than she. [20] When the king's edict which he will make is heard throughout all his kingdom, great as it is, then all women will give honor to their husbands, great and small."

[21] *This* word pleased the king and the princes, and the king did as Memucan proposed. [22] So he sent letters to all the king's provinces, to each province according to its script and to every people according to their language, that every man should be the master in his own house and the one who speaks in the language of his own people.

2 After these things when the anger of King Ahasuerus had subsided, he remembered Vashti and what she had done and what had been decreed against her. [2] Then the king's attendants, who served him, said, "Let beautiful young virgins be sought for the king. [3] Let the king appoint overseers in all the provinces of his kingdom that they may gather every beautiful young virgin to the citadel of Susa, to the harem, into the custody of Hegai, the king's eunuch, who is in charge of the women; and let their cosmetics be given *them*. [4] Then let the young lady who pleases the king be queen in place of Vashti." And the matter pleased the king, and he did accordingly.

[5] *Now* there was at the citadel in Susa a Jew whose name was Mordecai, the son of Jair, the son of Shimei, the son of Kish, a Benjamite, [6] who had been taken into exile from

2:5 Mordecai. He was among the fourth generation of deported Jews. **Kish.** Mordecai's great grandfather who actually experienced the Babylonian deportation. After Babylon fell to Medo-Persia (ca. 539 B.C.), Jews were moved to other parts of the new kingdom. Kish represents a Benjamite family name that could be traced back (ca. 1100 B.C.) to Saul's father (1Sa 9:1).

Jerusalem with the captives who had been exiled with Jeconiah king of Judah, whom Nebuchadnezzar the king of Babylon had exiled. [7] He was bringing up Hadassah, that is Esther, his uncle's daughter, for she had no father or mother. Now the young lady was beautiful of form and face, and when her father and her mother died, Mordecai took her as his own daughter.

8 So it came about when the command and decree of the king were heard and many young ladies were gathered to the citadel of Susa into the custody of Hegai, that Esther was taken to the king's palace into the custody of Hegai, who was in charge of the women. 9 Now the young lady pleased him and found favor with him. So he quickly provided her with her cosmetics and food, gave her seven choice maids from the king's palace and transferred her and her maids to the best place in the harem. 10 Esther did not make known her people or her kindred, for Mordecai had instructed her that she should not make *them* known. 11 Every day Mordecai walked back and forth in front of the court of the harem to learn how Esther was and how she fared.

12 Now when the turn of each young lady came to go in to King Ahasuerus, after the end of her twelve months under the regulations for the women—for the days of their beautification were completed as follows: six months with oil of myrrh and six months with spices and the cosmetics for women—13 the young lady would go in to the king in this way: anything that she desired was given her to take with her from the harem to the king's palace. 14 In the evening she would go in and in the morning she would return to the second harem, to the custody of Shaashgaz, the king's eunuch who was in charge of the concubines. She would not again go in to the king unless the king delighted in her and she was summoned by name.

15 Now when the turn of Esther, the daughter of Abihail the uncle of Mordecai who had taken her as his daughter, came to go in to the king, she did not request anything except what Hegai, the king's eunuch who was in charge of the women, advised. And Esther found favor in the eyes of all who saw her. 16 So Esther was taken to King Ahasuerus to his royal palace in the tenth month which is the month Tebeth, in the seventh year of his reign.

17 The king loved Esther more than all the women, and she found favor and kindness with him more than all the virgins, so that he set the royal crown on her head and made her queen instead of Vashti. 18 Then the king gave a great banquet, Esther's banquet, for all his princes and his servants; he also made a holiday for the provinces and gave gifts according to the king's bounty.

19 When the virgins were gathered together the second time, then Mordecai was sitting at the king's gate. 20 Esther had not yet made known her kindred or her people, even as Mordecai had commanded her; for Esther did what Mordecai told her as she had done when under his care. 21 In those days, while Mordecai was sitting at the king's gate, Bigthan and Teresh, two of the king's officials from those who guarded the door, became angry and sought to lay hands on King Ahasuerus. 22 But the plot became known to Mordecai and he told Queen Esther, and Esther informed the king in Mordecai's name. 23 Now when the plot was investigated and found *to be so,* they were both hanged on a gallows; and it was written in the Book of the Chronicles in the king's presence.

Psalm 89:38-45

38 But You have cast off and rejected,
You have been full of wrath
against Your anointed.
39 You have spurned the covenant
of Your servant;
You have profaned his
crown in the dust.
40 You have broken down all
his walls;
You have brought his
strongholds to ruin.
41 All who pass along the
way plunder him;
He has become a reproach
to his neighbors.
42 You have exalted the right
hand of his adversaries;
You have made all his
enemies rejoice.
43 You also turn back the
edge of his sword
And have not made him
stand in battle.
44 You have made his splendor
to cease
And cast his throne to the
ground.
45 You have shortened the
days of his youth;
You have covered him
with shame.   *Selah*

Proverbs 22:5-6

5 Thorns *and* snares are in the
way of the perverse;
He who guards himself will
be far from them.
6 Train up a child in the
way he should go,
Even when he is old he will
not depart from it.

22:6 way he should go. There is only one right way, God's way, the way of life. That way is specified in great detail in Proverbs. Since it is axiomatic that early training secures life-long habits, parents must insist upon this way, teaching God's Word and enforcing it with loving discipline consistently throughout the child's upbringing

2:11 partiality. Literally "to receive a face," that is, to give consideration to someone simply because of his position, wealth, influence, popularity, or appearance. Because it is God's nature to be just, it is impossible for Him to be anything but impartial (Ac 10:34; Gal 2:6; Eph 6:7–8; Col 3:25; 1Pe 1:17).

Romans 2:1–29

2 Therefore you have no excuse, everyone of you who passes judgment, for in that which you judge another, you condemn yourself; for you who judge practice the same things. ² And we know that the judgment of God rightly falls upon those who practice such things. ³ But do you suppose this, O man, when you pass judgment on those who practice such things and do the same *yourself,* that you will escape the judgment of God? ⁴ Or do you think lightly of the riches of His kindness and tolerance and patience, not knowing that the kindness of God leads you to repentance? ⁵ But because of your stubbornness and unrepentant heart you are storing up wrath for yourself in the day of wrath and revelation of the righteous judgment of God, ⁶ who WILL RENDER TO EACH PERSON ACCORDING TO HIS DEEDS: ⁷ to those who by perseverance in doing good seek for glory and honor and immortality, eternal life; ⁸ but to those who are selfishly ambitious and do not obey the truth, but obey unrighteousness, wrath and indignation. ⁹ *There will be* tribulation and distress for every soul of man who does evil, of the Jew first and also of the Greek, ¹⁰ but glory and honor and peace to everyone who does good, to the Jew first and also to the Greek. ¹¹ For there is no partiality with God. ¹² For all who have sinned without the Law

will also perish without the Law, and all who have sinned under the Law will be judged by the Law; ¹³ for *it is* not the hearers of the Law *who* are just before God, but the doers of the Law will be justified. ¹⁴ For when Gentiles who do not have the Law do instinctively the things of the Law, these, not having the Law, are a law to themselves, ¹⁵ in that they show the work of the Law written in their hearts, their conscience bearing witness and their thoughts alternately accusing or else defending them, ¹⁶ on the day when, according to my gospel, God will judge the secrets of men through Christ Jesus.

¹⁷ But if you bear the name "Jew" and rely upon the Law and boast in God, ¹⁸ and know *His* will and approve the things that are essential, being instructed out of the Law, ¹⁹ and are confident that you yourself are a guide to the blind, a light to those who are in darkness, ²⁰ a corrector of the foolish, a teacher of the immature, having in the Law the embodiment of knowledge and of the truth, ²¹ you, therefore, who teach another, do you not teach yourself? You who preach that one shall not steal, do you steal? ²² You who say that one should not commit adultery, do you commit adultery? You who abhor idols, do you rob temples? ²³ You who boast in the Law, through your breaking the Law, do you dishonor God? ²⁴ For "THE NAME OF GOD IS BLASPHEMED AMONG THE GENTILES BECAUSE OF YOU," just as it is written.

²⁵ For indeed circumcision is of value if you practice the Law; but if you are a transgressor of the Law, your circumcision has become uncircumcision. ²⁶ So if the uncircumcised man keeps the requirements of the Law, will not his uncircumcision be regarded as circumcision? ²⁷ And he who is physically uncircumcised, if he keeps the Law, will he not judge you who though having the letter *of the Law* and circumcision are a transgressor of the Law? ²⁸ For he is not a Jew who is one outwardly, nor is circumcision that which is outward in the flesh. ²⁹ But he is a Jew who is one inwardly; and circumcision is that which is of the heart, by the Spirit, not by the letter; and his praise is not from men, but from God.

2:6–10 Although Scripture everywhere teaches that salvation is not on the basis of works, it consistently teaches that God's judgment is always on the basis of a person's deeds (Is 3:10–11; Jer 17:10; Jn 5:28–29; 1Co 3:8; 2Co 5:10; Gal 6:7–9; see Ro 14:12). Paul describes the deeds of two distinct groups: the redeemed (vv. 7, 10) and the unredeemed (vv. 8–9). The deeds of the redeemed are not the basis of their salvation but the evidence of it. They are not perfect and are prone to sin, but there is undeniable evidence of righteousness in their lives (Jas 2:14–20, 26).

DAY 31: Why isn't God directly mentioned in Esther?

The question naturally arises when reading the book. Even the usual clues about God's presence seem absent. No one refers to the Law of God, sacrifices, worship, or prayer. God does not appear to receive public or private recognition for the preservation of the Jews. When it comes to God, Esther seems strangely silent.

In fact, the silence is so obvious that it becomes an argument. Esther challenges the tendency to demand that God prove His power and presence. Must God be apparent? All too quickly we expect God to demonstrate in unmistakable ways His identity. Yet God has repeatedly resisted human ultimatums. God reveals Himself for His own purposes, not human requirements.

Throughout history, God has more readily operated behind the scenes than in plain sight. The Scriptures are filled with unusual circumstances in which God worked obviously. But Esther comes close to revealing God's standard procedure. God's fingerprints are all over Esther's story. His superficial absence points to a deeper presence. God chose to be subtle, but He was there. The events in Esther give us a model for hope when God works in less than obvious ways in our lives.

AUGUST 1

Esther 3:1–4:17

3 After these events King Ahasuerus promoted Haman, the son of Hammedatha the Agagite, and advanced him and established his authority over all the princes who *were* with him. ² All the king's servants who were at the king's gate bowed down and paid homage to Haman; for so the king had commanded concerning him. But Mordecai neither bowed down nor paid homage. ³ Then the king's servants who were at the king's gate said to Mordecai, "Why are you transgressing the king's command?" ⁴ Now it was when they had spoken daily to him and he would not listen to them, that they told Haman to see whether Mordecai's reason would stand; for he had told them that he

---

3:4 he was a Jew. It seems evident from Haman's fury and attempted genocide that there were strong anti-Semitic attitudes in Susa, which seems to explain Mordecai's reluctance to reveal his true ethnic background.

---

was a Jew. ⁵ When Haman saw that Mordecai neither bowed down nor paid homage to him, Haman was filled with rage. ⁶ But he disdained to lay hands on Mordecai alone, for they had told him *who* the people of Mordecai *were;* therefore Haman sought to destroy all the Jews, the people of Mordecai, who *were* throughout the whole kingdom of Ahasuerus.

⁷ In the first month, which is the month Nisan, in the twelfth year of King Ahasuerus, Pur, that is the lot, was cast before Haman from day to day and from month *to month,* until the twelfth month, that is the month Adar. ⁸ Then Haman said to King Ahasuerus, "There is a certain people scattered and dispersed among the peoples in all the provinces of your kingdom; their laws are different from *those* of all *other* people and they do not observe the king's laws, so it is not in the king's interest to let them remain. ⁹ If it is pleasing to the king, let it be decreed that they be destroyed, and I will pay ten thousand talents of silver into the hands of those who carry on the *king's* business, to put into the king's treasuries." ¹⁰ Then the king took his signet ring from his hand and gave it to Haman, the son of Hammedatha the Agagite, the enemy of the Jews. ¹¹ The king said to Haman, "The

silver is yours, and the people *also,* to do with them as you please."

¹² Then the king's scribes were summoned on the thirteenth day of the first month, and it was written just as Haman commanded to the king's satraps, to the governors who were over each province and to the princes of each people, each province according to its script, each people according to its language, being written in the name of King Ahasuerus and sealed with the king's signet ring. ¹³ Letters were sent by couriers to all the king's provinces to destroy, to kill and to annihilate all the Jews, both young and old, women and children, in one day, the thirteenth *day* of the twelfth month, which is the month Adar, and to seize their possessions as plunder. ¹⁴ A copy of the edict to be issued as law in every province was published to all the peoples so that they should be ready for this day. ¹⁵ The couriers went out impelled by the king's command while the decree was issued at the citadel in Susa; and while the king and Haman sat down to drink, the city of Susa was in confusion.

4 When Mordecai learned all that had been done, he tore his clothes, put on sackcloth and ashes, and went out into the midst of the city and wailed loudly and bitterly. ² He went as far as the king's gate, for no one was to enter the king's gate clothed in sackcloth. ³ In each and every province where the command and decree of the king came, there was great mourning among the Jews, with fasting, weeping and wailing; and many lay on sackcloth and ashes.

⁴ Then Esther's maidens and her eunuchs came and told her, and the queen writhed in great anguish. And she sent garments to clothe Mordecai that he might remove his sackcloth from him, but he did not accept *them.* ⁵ Then Esther summoned Hathach from the king's eunuchs, whom the king had appointed to attend her, and ordered him *to go* to Mordecai to learn what this *was* and why it *was.* ⁶ So Hathach went out to Mordecai to the city square in front of the king's gate. ⁷ Mordecai told him all that had happened to him, and the exact amount of money that Haman had promised to pay to the king's treasuries for the destruction of the Jews. ⁸ He also gave him a copy of the text of the edict which had been issued in Susa for their destruction, that he might show Esther and inform her, and to order her to go in to the king to implore his favor and to plead with him for her people.

⁹ Hathach came back and related Mordecai's words to Esther. ¹⁰ Then Esther spoke to Hathach and ordered him *to reply* to Mordecai:

[11] "All the king's servants and the people of the king's provinces know that for any man or woman who comes to the king to the inner court who is not summoned, he has but one law, that he be put to death, unless the king holds out to him the golden scepter so that he may live. And I have not been summoned to come to the king for these thirty days." [12] They related Esther's words to Mordecai.

[13] Then Mordecai told *them* to reply to Esther, "Do not imagine that you in the king's palace can escape any more than all the Jews. [14] For if you remain silent at this time, relief and deliverance will arise for the Jews from another place and you and your father's house will perish. And who knows whether you have not attained royalty for such a time as this?"

4:14 relief and deliverance. Mordecai exhibited a healthy faith in God's sovereign power to preserve His people. He may have remembered the Lord's promise to Abraham (Ge 12:3; 17:1–8). **you...will perish.** Mordecai indicated that Esther would not escape the sentence or be overlooked because of her prominence (4:13). **such a time as this.** Mordecai indirectly appealed to God's providential timing.

[15] Then Esther told *them* to reply to Mordecai, [16] "Go, assemble all the Jews who are found in Susa, and fast for me; do not eat or drink for three days, night or day. I and my maidens also will fast in the same way. And thus I will go in to the king, which is not according to the law; and if I perish, I perish." [17] So Mordecai went away and did just as Esther had commanded him.

Psalm 89:46–52

[46] How long, O LORD?
Will You hide Yourself forever?
Will Your wrath burn like fire?
[47] Remember what my span of life is;
For what vanity You have created
all the sons of men!
[48] What man can live and not see death?
Can he deliver his soul from
the power of Sheol? *Selah*
[49] Where are Your former
lovingkindnesses, O Lord,
Which You swore to David
in Your faithfulness?
[50] Remember, O Lord, the reproach
of Your servants;

89:46 hide Yourself forever? By God's seeming refusal to answer prayer and restore the Davidic kingship, it seemed as though God was hiding Himself. Of course, the discipline of disobedient kings had been foretold (v. 32). According to the prophets, God would eventually restore Israel and the Davidic throne in an earthly kingdom (Hos 3:4–5). Never in the Old Testament is there a sense that this Davidic promise would be fulfilled by Christ with a spiritual and heavenly reign.

How I bear in my bosom the *reproach*
of all the many peoples,
[51] With which Your enemies have
reproached, O LORD,
With which they have reproached
the footsteps of Your anointed.

[52] Blessed be the LORD forever!
Amen and Amen.

Proverbs 22:7–8

[7] The rich rules over the poor,
And the borrower *becomes*
the lender's slave.
[8] He who sows iniquity will reap vanity,
And the rod of his fury will perish.

Romans 3:1–31

3 Then what advantage has the Jew? Or what is the benefit of circumcision? [2] Great in every respect. First of all, that they were entrusted with the oracles of God. [3] What then? If some did not believe, their unbelief will not nullify the faithfulness of God, will it? [4] May it never be! Rather, let God be found

3:2 oracles. This Greek word is *logion*, a diminutive form of the common New Testament word *logos*, which is normally translated "word." These are important sayings or messages, especially supernatural ones. Here Paul uses the word to encompass the entire OT—the Jews received the very words of the true God (Dt 4:1–2; 6:1–2; see Mk 12:24; Lk 16:29; Jn 5:39). The Jews had a great advantage in having the OT, because it contained the truth about salvation (2Ti 3:15) and about the gospel in its basic form (Gal 3:8). When Paul said "preach the word" (2Ti 4:2), he meant the "utterances (or oracles) of God" (1Pe 4:11) recorded in Scripture.

true, though every man *be found* a liar, as it is written,

"THAT YOU MAY BE JUSTIFIED
IN YOUR WORDS,
AND PREVAIL WHEN YOU ARE JUDGED."

⁵ But if our unrighteousness demonstrates the righteousness of God, what shall we say? The God who inflicts wrath is not unrighteous, is He? (I am speaking in human terms.) ⁶ May it never be! For otherwise, how will God judge the world? ⁷ But if through my lie the truth of God abounded to His glory, why am I also still being judged as a sinner? ⁸ And why not *say* (as we are slanderously reported and as some claim that we say), "Let us do evil that good may come"? Their condemnation is just.

⁹ What then? Are we better than they? Not at all; for we have already charged that both Jews and Greeks are all under sin; ¹⁰ as it is written,

"THERE IS NONE RIGHTEOUS,
NOT EVEN ONE;
¹¹ THERE IS NONE WHO UNDERSTANDS,
THERE IS NONE WHO SEEKS FOR GOD;
¹² ALL HAVE TURNED ASIDE, TOGETHER
THEY HAVE BECOME USELESS;
THERE IS NONE WHO DOES GOOD,
THERE IS NOT EVEN ONE."
¹³ "THEIR THROAT IS AN OPEN GRAVE,

3:11 none who understands. Man is unable to comprehend the truth of God or grasp His standard of righteousness (Pss 14:2; 53:3; 1Co 2:14). Sadly, his spiritual ignorance does not result from a lack of opportunity (1:19–20; 2:15), but is an expression of his depravity and rebellion (Eph 4:18). **none who seeks.** This verse clearly implies that the world's false religions are fallen man's attempts to escape the true God—not to seek Him. Man's natural tendency is to seek his own interests (Php 2:21), but his only hope is for God to seek him (Jn 6:37, 44). It is only as a result of God's work in the heart that anyone seeks Him (Ps 16:8; Mt 6:33).

WITH THEIR TONGUES THEY
KEEP DECEIVING,"
"THE POISON OF ASPS IS
UNDER THEIR LIPS";
¹⁴ "WHOSE MOUTH IS FULL OF
CURSING AND BITTERNESS";
¹⁵ "THEIR FEET ARE SWIFT TO SHED BLOOD,
¹⁶ DESTRUCTION AND MISERY
ARE IN THEIR PATHS,
¹⁷ AND THE PATH OF PEACE THEY
HAVE NOT KNOWN."
¹⁸ "THERE IS NO FEAR OF GOD
BEFORE THEIR EYES."

¹⁹ Now we know that whatever the Law says, it speaks to those who are under the Law, so that every mouth may be closed and all the world may become accountable to God; ²⁰ because by the works of the Law no flesh will be justified in His sight; for through the Law *comes* the knowledge of sin.

²¹ But now apart from the Law *the* righteousness of God has been manifested, being witnessed by the Law and the Prophets, ²² even *the* righteousness of God through faith in Jesus Christ for all those who believe; for there is no distinction; ²³ for all have sinned and fall short of the glory of God, ²⁴ being justified as a gift by His grace through the redemption which is in Christ Jesus; ²⁵ whom God displayed publicly as a propitiation in His blood through faith. *This was* to demonstrate His righteousness, because in the forbearance of God He passed over the sins previously committed; ²⁶ for the demonstration, *I say*, of His righteousness at the present time, so that He would be just and the justifier of the one who has faith in Jesus.

²⁷ Where then is boasting? It is excluded. By what kind of law? Of works? No, but by a law of faith. ²⁸ For we maintain that a man is justified by faith apart from works of the Law. ²⁹ Or is God *the God* of Jews only? Is He not *the God* of Gentiles also? Yes, of Gentiles also, ³⁰ since indeed God who will justify the circumcised by faith and the uncircumcised through faith is one.

³¹ Do we then nullify the Law through faith? May it never be! On the contrary, we establish the Law.

DAY 1: As sinners, how are we justified before God?

In Romans 3:24, the verb "justified" is a legal or forensic term that comes from the Greek word for "righteous" and means "to declare righteous." This verdict includes pardon from the guilt and penalty of sin and the imputation of Christ's righteousness to the believer's account, which provides for the positive righteousness man needs to be accepted by God. God declares a sinner righteous solely on the basis of the merits of Christ's righteousness. God imputed a believer's sin to Christ's account in His sacrificial death (Is. 53:4–5; 1Pe 2:24), and He imputes

Christ's perfect obedience to God's law to Christians (5:19; 1Co 1:30; 2Co 5:21; Php 3:9). The sinner receives this gift of God's grace by faith alone (3:22, 25; 4:1-25). Sanctification, the work of God by which He makes righteous those whom He has already justified, is distinct from justification but without exception always follows it (8:30).

"Being justified as a gift by His grace through the redemption which is in Christ Jesus." Justification is a gracious gift God extends to the repentant, believing sinner, wholly apart from human merit or work. The imagery behind the Greek word for "redemption" comes from the ancient slave market. It meant paying the necessary ransom to obtain the prisoner's or slave's release. The only adequate payment to redeem sinners from sin's slavery and its deserved punishment was "in Christ Jesus" (1Ti 2:6; 1Pe 1:18-19) and was paid to God to satisfy His justice.

"Whom God displayed publicly as a propitiation in His blood" (v. 25). This great sacrifice was not accomplished in secret, but God publicly displayed His Son on Calvary for all to see. Crucial to the significance of Christ's sacrifice, a propitiation carries the idea of appeasement or satisfaction—in this case Christ's violent death satisfied the offended holiness and wrath of God against those for whom Christ died (Is. 53:11; Col 2:11-14). The Hebrew equivalent of this word was used to describe the mercy seat—the cover to the ark of the covenant—where the high priest sprinkled the blood of the slaughtered animal on the Day of Atonement to make atonement for the sins of the people. In pagan religions, it is the worshiper—not the god—who is responsible to appease the wrath of the offended deity. But in reality, man is incapable of satisfying God's justice apart from Christ, except by spending eternity in hell.

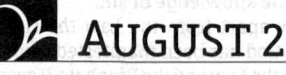 AUGUST 2

Esther 5:1-6:14

5 Now it came about on the third day that Esther put on her royal robes and stood in the inner court of the king's palace in front of the king's rooms, and the king was sitting on his royal throne in the throne room, opposite the entrance to the palace. ² When the king saw Esther the queen standing in the court, she obtained favor in his sight; and the king extended to Esther the golden scepter which *was* in his hand. So Esther came near and touched the top of the scepter. ³ Then the king said to her, "What is *troubling* you, Queen Esther? And what is your request? Even to half of the kingdom it shall be given to you." ⁴ Esther said, "If it pleases the king, may the king and Haman come this day to the banquet that I have prepared for him." ⁵ Then the king said, "Bring Haman quickly that we may do as Esther desires." So the king and Haman came to the banquet which Esther had prepared. ⁶ As they drank their wine at the banquet, the king said to Esther, "What is your petition, for it shall be granted to you. And what is your request? Even to half of the kingdom it shall be done." ⁷ So Esther replied, "My petition and my request is: ⁸ if I have found favor in the sight of the king, and if it pleases the king to grant my petition and do what I request, may the king and Haman come to the banquet which I will prepare for them, and tomorrow I will do as the king says."

⁹ Then Haman went out that day glad and pleased of heart; but when Haman saw Mordecai in the king's gate and that he did not stand up or tremble before him, Haman was filled with anger against Mordecai. ¹⁰ Haman controlled himself, however, went to his house and sent for his friends and his wife Zeresh. ¹¹ Then Haman recounted to them the glory of his riches, and the number of his sons, and every *instance* where the king had magnified him and how he had promoted him above the princes and servants of the king. ¹² Haman also said, "Even Esther the queen let no one but me come with the king to the banquet which she had prepared; and tomorrow also I am invited by her with the king. ¹³ Yet all of this does not satisfy me every time I see Mordecai the Jew sitting at the king's gate." ¹⁴ Then Zeresh his wife and all his friends said to him, "Have a gallows fifty cubits high made and in the morning ask the king to have Mordecai hanged on it; then go joyfully with the king to the banquet." And the advice pleased Haman, so he had the gallows made.

6 During that night the king could not sleep so he gave an order to bring the book of records, the chronicles, and they were read

6:1 the book. Five years had intervened since Mordecai's loyal, but as yet unrewarded, act (2:23). At exactly the proper moment, God providentially intervened so that the king suffered insomnia, called for the book of records, read of Mordecai's unrewarded deeds 5 years past, and then desired to reward him (Da 6:18).

before the king. [2] It was found written what Mordecai had reported concerning Bigthana and Teresh, two of the king's eunuchs who were doorkeepers, that they had sought to lay hands on King Ahasuerus. [3] The king said, "What honor or dignity has been bestowed on Mordecai for this?" Then the king's servants who attended him said, "Nothing has been done for him." [4] So the king said, "Who is in the court?" Now Haman had just entered the outer court of the king's palace in order to speak to the king about hanging Mordecai on the gallows which he had prepared for him. [5] The king's servants said to him, "Behold, Haman is standing in the court." And the king said, "Let him come in." [6] So Haman came in and the king said to him, "What is to be done for the man whom the king desires to honor?" And Haman said to himself, "Whom would the king desire to honor more than me?" [7] Then Haman said to the king, "For the man whom the king desires to honor, [8] let them bring a royal robe which the king has worn, and the horse on which the king has ridden, and on whose head a royal crown has been placed; [9] and let the robe and the horse be handed over to one of the king's most noble princes and let them array the man whom the king desires to honor and lead him on horseback through the city square, and proclaim before him, 'Thus it shall be done to the man whom the king desires to honor.'"

[10] Then the king said to Haman, "Take quickly the robes and the horse as you have said, and do so for Mordecai the Jew, who is sitting at the king's gate; do not fall short in anything of all that you have said." [11] So Haman took the robe and the horse, and arrayed Mordecai, and led him *on horseback* through the city square, and proclaimed before him, "Thus it shall be done to the man whom the king desires to honor."

[12] Then Mordecai returned to the king's gate. But Haman hurried home, mourning, with *his* head covered. [13] Haman recounted to Zeresh his wife and all his friends everything that had happened to him. Then his wise men

6:13 you have begun to fall. Neither divine prophecy (Ex 17:14) nor biblical history (1Sa 15:8–9) stood in Haman's favor. Haman's entourage seemed to have some knowledge of this biblical history.

and Zeresh his wife said to him, "If Mordecai, before whom you have begun to fall, is of Jewish origin, you will not overcome him, but will surely fall before him."

[14] While they were still talking with him, the king's eunuchs arrived and hastily brought Haman to the banquet which Esther had prepared.

Psalm 90:1–6

A Prayer of Moses, the man of God.

L ord, You have been our dwelling
　　place in all generations.
[2] Before the mountains were
　　born
　Or You gave birth to the
　　earth and the world,
　Even from everlasting to
　　everlasting, You are God.

[3] You turn man back into
　　dust
　And say, "Return, O children
　　of men."

90:Title Moses, the man of God. Moses the prophet (Dt 18:15–22) was unique in that the Lord knew him "face to face" (Dt 34:10–12). "Man of God" (Dt 33:1) is a technical term used over 70 times in the OT, always referring to one who spoke for God. It is used of Timothy in the New Testament (1Ti 6:11; 2Ti 3:17).

90:3 You turn man back into dust. Though different from the "dust" of Genesis 3:19, this phrase is no doubt a reference to that passage. Humanity lives under a sovereign decree of death and cannot escape it.

[4] For a thousand years in Your
　　sight
　Are like yesterday when it
　　passes by,
　Or *as* a watch in the night.
[5] You have swept them away
　　like a flood, they fall
　　asleep;
　In the morning they are
　　like grass which sprouts
　　anew.
[6] In the morning it flourishes
　　and sprouts anew;
　Toward evening it fades
　　and withers away.

Proverbs 22:9

9 He who is generous will be blessed,
For he gives some of his
food to the poor.

Romans 4:1–25

4 What then shall we say that Abraham, our forefather according to the flesh, has found? ²For if Abraham was justified by works, he has something to boast about, but not before God. ³For what does the Scripture say? "ABRAHAM BELIEVED GOD, AND IT WAS CREDITED TO HIM AS RIGHTEOUSNESS." ⁴Now to the one who works, his wage is not

4:3 A quotation of Genesis 15:6, one of the clearest statements in all Scripture about justification. **BELIEVED.** Abraham was a man of faith (1:16; 4:18–21; Gal 3:6–7, 9; Heb 11:8–10). But faith is not a meritorious work. It is never the ground of justification—it is simply the channel through which it is received, and it, too, is a gift. **CREDITED.** See vv. 5–6, 8–11, 22–24. Used in both financial and legal settings, this Greek word, which occurs 9 times in chap. 4 alone, means to take something that belongs to someone and credit it to another's account. It is a one-sided transaction—Abraham did nothing to accumulate it; God simply credited it to him. God took His own righteousness and credited it to Abraham as if it were actually his. This God did because Abraham believed in Him.

credited as a favor, but as what is due. ⁵But to the one who does not work, but believes in Him who justifies the ungodly, his faith is credited as righteousness, ⁶just as David also speaks of the blessing on the man to whom God credits righteousness apart from works:

7 "BLESSED ARE THOSE WHOSE
LAWLESS DEEDS HAVE
BEEN FORGIVEN,
AND WHOSE SINS HAVE BEEN
COVERED.
8 "BLESSED IS THE MAN WHOSE
SIN THE LORD WILL NOT
TAKE INTO ACCOUNT."

⁹Is this blessing then on the circumcised, or on the uncircumcised also? For we say, "FAITH WAS CREDITED TO ABRAHAM AS RIGHTEOUSNESS." ¹⁰How then was it credited? While he was circumcised, or uncircumcised? Not while circumcised, but while uncircum-

cised; ¹¹and he received the sign of circumcision, a seal of the righteousness of the faith which he had while uncircumcised, so that he might be the father of all who believe without being circumcised, that righteousness might be credited to them, ¹²and the father of circumcision to those who not only are of the circumcision, but who also follow in the steps of the faith of our father Abraham which he had while uncircumcised.

4:11–12 the father of all who believe. Racially, Abraham is the father of all Jews (circumcised); spiritually, he is the father of both believing Jews (v. 12) and believing Gentiles (uncircumcised; v. 11).

¹³For the promise to Abraham or to his descendants that he would be heir of the world was not through the Law, but through the righteousness of faith. ¹⁴For if those who are of the Law are heirs, faith is made void and the promise is nullified; ¹⁵for the Law brings about wrath, but where there is no law, there also is no violation.

¹⁶For this reason *it is* by faith, in order that *it may be* in accordance with grace, so that the promise will be guaranteed to all the descendants, not only to those who are of the Law, but also to those who are of the faith of Abraham, who is the father of us all, ¹⁷(as it is written, "A FATHER OF MANY NATIONS HAVE I MADE YOU") in the presence of Him whom he believed, *even* God, who gives life to the dead and calls into being that which does not exist. ¹⁸In hope against hope he believed, so that he might become a father of many nations according to that which had been spoken, "SO SHALL YOUR DESCENDANTS BE." ¹⁹Without becoming weak in faith he contemplated his own body, now as good as dead since he was about a hundred years old, and the deadness of Sarah's womb; ²⁰yet, with respect to the promise of God, he did not waver in unbelief but grew strong in faith, giving glory to God, ²¹and being fully assured that what God had promised, He was able also to perform. ²²Therefore IT WAS ALSO CREDITED TO HIM AS RIGHTEOUSNESS. ²³Now not for his sake only was it written that it was credited to him, ²⁴but for our sake also, to whom it will be credited, as those who believe in Him who raised Jesus our Lord from the dead, ²⁵*He* who was delivered over because of our transgressions, and was raised because of our justification.

DAY 2: Why do Esther and Mordecai appear so secular in their lifestyles?

In contrast to their near contemporaries Ezra, Nehemiah, and Daniel, the central people in Esther seem worldly. The lack of references to God is most obvious in Esther and Mordecai's conversations. Are these all subtle indications that Esther and Mordecai were people whose faith had little or no effect on their daily lives?

The Book of Esther does not settle this question. There are several important factors, however, that might hold us back from jumping to conclusions about Esther and Mordecai. Primary among these is the fact that the book has a limited scope. Only a few key events are recorded. Few if any details of the inner life of either main character are revealed. Yet the integrity of their actions ought to incline us toward giving them the benefit of the doubt when it comes to faith (4:13–16).

Here are a few other considerations regarding this question: 1) While Mordecai's caution about announcing his and Esther's heritage publicly might be questioned, it must also be pointed out that others were also cautious about this same matter (Ne 2:1–8 makes no mention of God in Nehemiah's conversation with Artaxerxes); 2) Public events such as Passover had fallen out of practice during the captivity, meaning that there were fewer occasions in which faith was practiced in the open (this doesn't mean however that the Jews were not a marked people, since they could be identified for the purpose of Haman's law); 3) When it was appropriate, Esther did openly identify her Jewish heritage (7:3–4). These considerations do not remove the charge that Esther and Mordecai seem less devoted to God than, for example, Daniel. But the fact that God did work out His purposes in their lives comes through clearly in the book.

AUGUST 3

Esther 7:1–8:17

7 Now the king and Haman came to drink *wine* with Esther the queen. ² And the king said to Esther on the second day also as they drank their wine at the banquet, "What is your petition, Queen Esther? It shall be granted you. And what is your request? Even to half of the kingdom it shall be done." ³ Then Queen Esther replied, "If I have found favor in your sight, O king, and if it pleases the king, let my life be given me as my petition, and my people as my request; ⁴ for we have been sold, I and my people, to be destroyed, to be killed and to be annihilated. Now if we had only been sold as slaves, men and women, I would have remained silent, for the trouble would not be commensurate with the annoyance to the king." ⁵ Then King Ahasuerus asked Queen Esther, "Who is he, and where is he, who would presume to do thus?" ⁶ Esther said, "A foe and an enemy is this wicked Haman!" Then Haman became terrified before the king and queen. ⁷ The king arose in his anger from drinking wine *and went* into the palace garden; but Haman stayed to beg for his life from Queen Esther, for he saw that harm had been determined against him by the king. ⁸ Now when the king returned from the palace garden into the place where they were drinking wine, Haman was falling on the couch where Esther was. Then the king said, "Will he even assault the queen with me in the house?" As the word went out of the king's mouth, they covered Haman's face. ⁹ Then Harbonah, one of the eunuchs who *were* before the king said, "Behold indeed, the gallows standing at Haman's house fifty cubits high, which Haman made for Mordecai who spoke good on behalf of the king!" And the king said, "Hang him on it." ¹⁰ So they hanged Haman on the gallows which he had prepared for Mordecai, and the king's anger subsided.

8 On that day King Ahasuerus gave the house of Haman, the enemy of the Jews, to Queen Esther; and Mordecai came before the king, for Esther had disclosed what he was to her. ² The king took off his signet ring which he had taken away from Haman, and gave it to Mordecai. And Esther set Mordecai over the house of Haman.

8:1 the house of Haman. Property of a traitor by Persian custom returned to the king. In this case, he gave it to his queen, Esther, who put Mordecai over it (8:2). The outcome for Haman's wife Zeresh and his wise men is unknown (5:14; 6:12–13). Haman's 10 sons later died (9:7–10).

³ Then Esther spoke again to the king, fell at his feet, wept and implored him to avert the evil *scheme* of Haman the Agagite and his plot which he had devised against the Jews. ⁴ The king extended the golden scepter to Esther. So Esther arose and stood before the king. ⁵ Then she said, "If it pleases the king and if I

have found favor before him and the matter *seems* proper to the king and I am pleasing in his sight, let it be written to revoke the letters devised by Haman, the son of Hammedatha the Agagite, which he wrote to destroy the Jews who are in all the king's provinces. ⁶ For how can I endure to see the calamity which will befall my people, and how can I endure to see the destruction of my kindred?" ⁷ So King Ahasuerus said to Queen Esther and to Mordecai the Jew, "Behold, I have given the house of Haman to Esther, and him they have hanged on the gallows because he had stretched out his hands against the Jews. ⁸ Now you write to the Jews as you see fit, in the king's name, and seal *it* with the king's signet ring; for a decree which is written in the name of the king and sealed with the king's signet ring may not be revoked."

⁹ So the king's scribes were called at that time in the third month (that is, the month Sivan), on the twenty-third day; and it was written according to all that Mordecai commanded to the Jews, the satraps, the governors and the princes of the provinces which *extended* from India to Ethiopia, 127 provinces, to every province according to its script, and to every people according to their language as well as to the Jews according to their script and their language. ¹⁰ He wrote in the name of King Ahasuerus, and sealed it with the king's signet ring, and sent letters by couriers on horses, riding on steeds sired by the royal stud. ¹¹ In them the king granted the Jews who were in each and every city *the right* to assemble and to defend their lives, to destroy, to kill and to annihilate the entire army of any people or province which might attack them, including children and women, and to plunder their spoil, ¹² on one day in all the provinces of King Ahasuerus, the thirteenth *day* of the twelfth month (that is, the month Adar). ¹³ A copy of the edict to be issued as law in each and every province was published to all the peoples, so that the Jews would be ready for this day to avenge themselves on their enemies. ¹⁴ The couriers, hastened and impelled by the king's command, went out, riding on the royal steeds; and the decree was given out at the citadel in Susa.

¹⁵ Then Mordecai went out from the presence of the king in royal robes of blue and white, with a large crown of gold and a garment of fine linen and purple; and the city of Susa shouted and rejoiced. ¹⁶ For the Jews there was light and gladness and joy and honor. ¹⁷ In each and every province and in each and every city, wherever the king's com-

mandment and his decree arrived, there was gladness and joy for the Jews, a feast and a holiday. And many among the peoples of the land became Jews, for the dread of the Jews had fallen on them.

8:17 many...peoples...Jews. The population realized that the God of the Jews greatly exceeded anything that the pantheon of Persian deities could offer (Ex 15:14–16; Ps 105:38; Ac 5:11), especially in contrast to their recent defeat by the Greeks.

Psalm 90:7–17

⁷ For we have been consumed
    by Your anger
And by Your wrath we have
    been dismayed.
⁸ You have placed our
    iniquities before You,
Our secret *sins* in the light
    of Your presence.
⁹ For all our days have
    declined in Your fury;
We have finished our years like a sigh.
¹⁰ As for the days of our life, they
    contain seventy years,
Or if due to strength, eighty years,
Yet their pride is *but* labor
    and sorrow;
For soon it is gone and we fly away.
¹¹ Who understands the
    power of Your anger
And Your fury, according to
    the fear that is due You?
¹² So teach us to number our days,
That we may present to You
    a heart of wisdom.

¹³ Do return, O LORD; how
    long *will it be*?
And be sorry for Your servants.
¹⁴ O satisfy us in the morning
    with Your lovingkindness,
That we may sing for joy and
    be glad all our days.

90:12 number our days. Evaluate the use of time in light of the brevity of life. **heart of wisdom.** Wisdom repudiates autonomy and focuses on the Lord's sovereignty and revelation.

¹⁵ Make us glad according to the
days You have afflicted us,
And the years we have seen evil.
¹⁶ Let Your work appear to Your servants
And Your majesty to their children.
¹⁷ Let the favor of the Lord
our God be upon us;
And confirm for us the
work of our hands;
Yes, confirm the work of our hands.

90:17 the favor of the Lord. The Lord's favor implies His delight and approval. **confirm the work of our hands.** By God's mercy and grace, one's life can have value, significance, and meaning (1Co 15:58).

Proverbs 22:10–11

¹⁰ Drive out the scoffer, and
contention will go out,
Even strife and dishonor will
cease.
¹¹ He who loves purity of heart
And whose speech is gracious,
the king is his friend.

Romans 5:1–21

5 Therefore, having been justified by faith, we have peace with God through our Lord Jesus Christ, ² through whom also we have obtained our introduction by faith into this grace in which we stand; and we exult in hope of the glory of God. ³ And not only this, but we also exult in our tribulations, knowing that tribulation brings about perseverance; ⁴ and perseverance, proven character; and proven character, hope; ⁵ and hope does not disappoint, because the love of God has been

5:3 tribulations. A word used for pressure, like that of a press squeezing the fluid from olives or grapes. Here they are not the normal pressures of living (8:35), but the inevitable troubles that come to followers of Christ because of their relationship with Him (Mt 5:10–12; Jn 15:20; 2Co 4:17; 1Th 3:3; 2Ti 3:12; 1Pe 4:19). Such difficulties produce rich spiritual benefits (vv. 3–4). **perseverance.** Sometimes translated "patience," this word refers to endurance, the ability to remain under tremendous weight and pressure without succumbing (15:5; Col 1:22–23; 2Th 1:4; Rev 14:12).

5:4 proven character. The Greek word simply means "proof." It was used of testing metals to determine their purity. Here the proof is Christian character (Jas 1:12). Christians can glory in tribulations because of what those troubles produce.

5:5 love of God...poured out. God's love for us (v. 8) has been lavishly poured out to the point of overflowing within our hearts. Paul moves from the objective aspects of our security in Christ to the internal, more subjective. God has implanted within our hearts evidence that we belong to Him in that we love the One who first loved us. **Spirit who was given.** A marvelous testimony to God's love for us.

poured out within our hearts through the Holy Spirit who was given to us.

⁶ For while we were still helpless, at the right time Christ died for the ungodly. ⁷ For one will hardly die for a righteous man; though perhaps for the good man someone would dare even to die. ⁸ But God demonstrates His own love toward us, in that while we were yet sinners, Christ died for us. ⁹ Much more then, having now been justified by His blood, we shall be saved from the wrath *of God* through Him. ¹⁰ For if while we were enemies we were reconciled to God through the death of His Son, much more, having been reconciled, we shall be saved by His life. ¹¹ And not only this, but we also exult in God through our Lord Jesus Christ, through whom we have now received the reconciliation.

¹² Therefore, just as through one man sin entered into the world, and death through sin, and so death spread to all men, because all sinned— ¹³ for until the Law sin was in the world, but sin is not imputed when there is no law. ¹⁴ Nevertheless death reigned from Adam until Moses, even over those who had not sinned in the likeness of the offense of Adam, who is a type of Him who was to come.

¹⁵ But the free gift is not like the transgression. For if by the transgression of the one the many died, much more did the grace of God and the gift by the grace of the one Man, Jesus Christ, abound to the many. ¹⁶ The gift is not like *that which came* through the one who sinned; for on the one hand the judgment *arose* from one *transgression* resulting in condemnation, but on the other hand the free gift *arose* from many transgressions resulting in justification. ¹⁷ For if by the transgression of the one, death reigned through

the one, much more those who receive the abundance of grace and of the gift of righteousness will reign in life through the One, Jesus Christ.

[18] So then as through one transgression there resulted condemnation to all men, even so through one act of righteousness there resulted justification of life to all men. [19] For as through the one man's disobedience the many were made sinners, even so through the obedience of the One the many will be made righteous. [20] The Law came in so that the transgression would increase; but where sin increased, grace abounded all the more, [21] so that, as sin reigned in death, even so grace would reign through righteousness to eternal life through Jesus Christ our Lord.

DAY 3: What are the results of being justified by faith?

Having proven that God justifies sinners on the basis of faith alone, Paul now counters the notion that, although believers receive salvation by faith, they will preserve it by good works (Ro 5:1–11). He argues that they are bound eternally to Jesus Christ, preserved by His power and not by human effort (Is. 11:5; Ps 36:5; La 3:23; Eph 1:18–20; 2Ti 2:13; Heb 10:23). "Having been justified by faith" (v. 1). The Greek construction—and its English translation—underscores that justification is a one-time legal declaration with continuing results, not an ongoing process. "We have peace with God." Not a subjective, internal sense of calm and serenity, but an external, objective reality. God has declared Himself to be at war with every human being because of man's sinful rebellion against Him and His laws (v. 10; 1:18; 8:7; Ex 22:24; Dt 32:21–22; Ps 7:11; Jn 3:36; Eph 5:6). But the first great result of justification is that the sinner's war with God is ended forever (Col 1:21–22). Scripture refers to the end of this conflict as a person's being reconciled to God (vv. 10–1; 2Co 5:18–20).

"Through whom also we have obtained our introduction by faith" (v. 2). Used only twice elsewhere in the New Testament (Eph 2:18; 3:12), this word always refers to the believer's access to God through Jesus Christ. What was unthinkable to the Old Testament Jew is now available to all who come (Jer 32:38, 40; Heb 4:16; 10:19–22; Mt 27:51). "Grace in which we stand." This refers to the permanent, secure position believers enjoy in God's grace (v. 10; 8:31–34; Jn 6:37; Php 1:6; 2Ti 1:12; Jude v. 24). "And we exult in hope of the glory of God." Unlike the English word "hope," the New Testament word contains no uncertainty. It speaks of something that is certain, but not yet realized. The believer's ultimate destiny is to share in the very glory of God (8:29–30; Jn 17:22; 2Co 3:18; Php 3:20–21; 1Jn 3:1–2), and that hope will be realized because Christ Himself secures it (1Ti 1:1). Without the clear and certain promises of the Word of God, the believer would have no basis for hope (15:4; Ps 119:81,114; Eph 2:12; Jer 14:8).

AUGUST 4

Esther 9:1–10:3

9 Now in the twelfth month (that is, the month Adar), on the thirteenth day when the king's command and edict were about to be executed, on the day when the enemies of the Jews hoped to gain the mastery over

9:1 twelfth month. During the period Feb.–Mar. Here is a powerful statement with regard to God's providential preservation of the Jewish race in harmony with God's unconditional promise to Abraham (Ge 17:1–8). This providential deliverance stands in contrast to God's miraculous deliverance of the Jews from Egypt; yet in both cases the same end had been accomplished by the supernatural power of God.

them, it was turned to the contrary so that the Jews themselves gained the mastery over those who hated them. [2] The Jews assembled in their cities throughout all the provinces of King Ahasuerus to lay hands on those who sought their harm; and no one could stand before them, for the dread of them had fallen on all the peoples. [3] Even all the princes of the provinces, the satraps, the governors and those who were doing the king's business assisted the Jews, because the dread of Mordecai had fallen on them. [4] Indeed, Mordecai was great in the king's house, and his fame spread throughout all the provinces; for the man Mordecai became greater and greater. [5] Thus the Jews struck all their enemies with the sword, killing and destroying; and they did what they pleased to those who hated them. [6] At the citadel in Susa the Jews killed and destroyed five hundred men, [7] and Parshandatha, Dalphon, Aspatha, [8] Poratha, Adalia, Aridatha, [9] Parmashta, Arisai, Aridai and Vaizatha, [10] the ten sons of Haman the son of Hammedatha, the Jews' enemy; but they did not lay their hands on the plunder.

[11] On that day the number of those who were killed at the citadel in Susa was reported to the king. [12] The king said to Queen Esther, "The Jews have killed and destroyed five hundred men and the ten sons of Haman at the citadel in Susa. What then have they done in the rest of the king's provinces! Now what is your petition? It shall even be granted you. And what is your further request? It shall also be done." [13] Then said Esther, "If it pleases the king, let tomorrow also be granted to the Jews who are in Susa to do according to the edict of today; and let Haman's ten sons be hanged on the gallows." [14] So the king commanded that it should be done so; and an edict was issued in Susa, and Haman's ten sons were hanged. [15] The Jews who were in Susa assembled also on the fourteenth day of the month Adar and killed three hundred men in Susa, but they did not lay their hands on the plunder.

[16] Now the rest of the Jews who *were* in the king's provinces assembled, to defend their lives and rid themselves of their enemies, and kill 75,000 of those who hated them; but they did not lay their hands on the plunder. [17] *This was done* on the thirteenth day of the month Adar, and on the fourteenth day they rested and made it a day of feasting and rejoicing. [18] But the Jews who were in Susa assembled on the thirteenth and the fourteenth of the same month, and they rested on the fifteenth day and made it a day of feasting and rejoicing. [19] Therefore the Jews of the rural areas, who live in the rural towns, make the fourteenth day of the month Adar *a* holiday for rejoicing and feasting and sending portions *of food* to one another.

[20] Then Mordecai recorded these events, and he sent letters to all the Jews who were in all the provinces of King Ahasuerus, both near and far, [21] obliging them to celebrate the fourteenth day of the month Adar, and the fifteenth day of the same month, annually, [22] because on those days the Jews rid themselves of their enemies, and *it was a* month which was turned for them from sorrow into gladness and from mourning into a holiday; that they should make them days of feasting and rejoicing and sending portions *of food* to one another and gifts to the poor.

[23] Thus the Jews undertook what they had started to do, and what Mordecai had written to them. [24] For Haman the son of Hammedatha, the Agagite, the adversary of all the Jews, had schemed against the Jews to destroy them

and had cast Pur, that is the lot, to disturb them and destroy them. [25] But when it came to the king's attention, he commanded by letter that his wicked scheme which he had devised against the Jews, should return on his own head and that he and his sons should be hanged on the gallows. [26] Therefore they called these days Purim after the name of Pur. And because of the instructions in this letter, both what they had seen in this regard and what had happened to them, [27] the Jews established and made a custom for themselves and for their descendants and for all those who allied themselves with them, so that they would not fail to celebrate these two days according to their regulation and according to their appointed time annually. [28] So these days were to be remembered and celebrated throughout every generation, every family, every province and every city; and these days of Purim were not to fail from among the Jews, or their memory fade from their descendants.

[29] Then Queen Esther, daughter of Abihail, with Mordecai the Jew, wrote with full authority to confirm this second letter about Purim. [30] He sent letters to all the Jews, to the 127 provinces of the kingdom of Ahasuerus, *namely,* words of peace and truth, [31] to establish these days of Purim at their appointed times, just as Mordecai the Jew and Queen Esther had established for them, and just as they had established for themselves and for their descendants with instructions for their times of fasting and their lamentations. [32] The command of Esther established these customs for Purim, and it was written in the book.

10 Now King Ahasuerus laid a tribute on the land and on the coastlands of the sea. [2] And all the accomplishments of his authority and strength, and the full account of the greatness of Mordecai to which the king advanced him, are they not written in the

10:3 Mordecai...was second. Mordecai joined the top echelon of Jewish international statesmen like Joseph, who ranked second in the Egyptian dynasty (Ge 41:37–45), and Daniel, who succeeded in both the Babylonian (Da 2:46–49; 5:29) and Medo-Persian Empires (Da 6:28). **spoke for the welfare.** Less than 10 years later (ca. 465 B.C.), Ahasuerus was assassinated. There are no further details concerning Esther and Mordecai. What Mordecai did for less than a decade on behalf of Israel, Jesus Christ will do for all eternity as the Prince of Peace (Is 9:6–7; Zec 9:9–10)

Book of the Chronicles of the Kings of Media and Persia? ³ For Mordecai the Jew was second *only* to King Ahasuerus, and great among the Jews and in favor with his many kinsmen, one who sought the good of his people and one who spoke for the welfare of his whole nation.

Psalm 91:1–6

He who dwells in the shelter
of the Most High
Will abide in the shadow
of the Almighty.

91:1 shelter of the Most High. An intimate place of divine protection. The use of "Most High" for God emphasizes that no threat can ever overpower Him. **shadow of the Almighty.** In a land where the sun can be oppressive and dangerous, a "shadow" was understood as a metaphor for care and protection.

2 I will say to the LORD, "My
refuge and my fortress,
My God, in whom I trust!"
3 For it is He who delivers you from
the snare of the trapper
And from the deadly pestilence.
4 He will cover you with His pinions,
And under His wings you
may seek refuge;
His faithfulness is a shield
and bulwark.

5 You will not be afraid of
the terror by night,
Or of the arrow that flies by day;
6 Of the pestilence that
stalks in darkness,
Or of the destruction that
lays waste at noon.

Proverbs 22:12

12 The eyes of the LORD
preserve knowledge,
But He overthrows the words
of the treacherous man.

Romans 6:1–23

6 What shall we say then? Are we to continue in sin so that grace may increase? ² May it never be! How shall we who died to sin still live in it? ³ Or do you not know that all of us who have been baptized into Christ Jesus have been baptized into His death? ⁴ Therefore we have been buried with Him

6:3 baptized into Christ Jesus. This does not refer to water baptism. Paul is actually using the word "baptized" in a metaphorical sense, as we might in saying someone was immersed in his work, or underwent his baptism of fire when experiencing some trouble. All Christians have, by placing saving faith in Him, been spiritually immersed into the person of Christ, that is, united and identified with Him (1Co 6:17; 10:2; Gal 3:27; 1Pe 3:21; 1Jn 1:3; Ac 2:38). Certainly water baptism pictures this reality, which is the purpose—to show the transformation of the justified. **into His death.** This means that immersion or identification is specifically with Christ's death and resurrection, as the apostle will explain (6:4–7).

through baptism into death, so that as Christ was raised from the dead through the glory of the Father, so we too might walk in newness of life. ⁵ For if we have become united with *Him* in the likeness of His death, certainly we shall also be *in the likeness* of His resurrection, ⁶ knowing this, that our old self was crucified with *Him,* in order that our body of sin might be done away with, so that we would no longer be slaves to sin; ⁷ for he who has died is freed from sin.

⁸ Now if we have died with Christ, we believe that we shall also live with Him, ⁹ knowing that Christ, having been raised from the dead, is never to die again; death no longer is master over Him. ¹⁰ For the death that He died, He died to sin once for all; but the life that He lives, He lives to God. ¹¹ Even so consider yourselves to be dead to sin, but alive to God in Christ Jesus.

¹² Therefore do not let sin reign in your mortal body so that you obey its lusts, ¹³ and do not go on presenting the members of your body to sin *as* instruments of unrighteousness; but present yourselves to God as those alive from the dead, and your members *as* instruments of righteousness to God. ¹⁴ For sin shall not be master over you, for you are not under law but under grace.

¹⁵ What then? Shall we sin because we are not under law but under grace? May it never be! ¹⁶ Do you not know that when you present yourselves to someone *as* slaves for obedience, you are slaves of the one whom you obey, either of sin resulting in death, or of obedience resulting in righteousness? ¹⁷ But thanks be to God that though you were slaves of sin, you became obedient from the heart to that form of teaching to which you were com-

mitted, [18] and having been freed from sin, you became slaves of righteousness. [19] I am speaking in human terms because of the weakness of your flesh. For just as you presented your members as slaves to impurity and to lawlessness, resulting in *further* lawlessness, so now present your members as slaves to righteousness, resulting in sanctification.

[20] For when you were slaves of sin, you were free in regard to righteousness. [21] Therefore what benefit were you then deriving from the things of which you are now ashamed? For the outcome of those things is death. [22] But now having been freed from sin and enslaved to God, you derive your benefit, resulting in sanctification, and the outcome, eternal life. [23] For the wages of sin is death, but the free gift of God is eternal life in Christ Jesus our Lord.

DAY 4: In verses such as Romans 5:12 and 6:23, to what kind of death is Paul referring?

The word "death" has three distinct manifestations in biblical terminology: 1) spiritual death or separation from God (Eph 1:1–2, 4, 18); 2) physical death (Heb 9:27); and 3) eternal death (also called the second death), which includes not only eternal separation from God, but eternal torment in the lake of fire (Rev 20:11–15).

When sin entered the human race through Adam, all these aspects of death came with it. Adam was not originally subject to death; but through his sin, death became a grim certainty for him and his posterity. The "death" referred to in Romans 6:23 includes the first and third descriptions above. That verse establishes two inexorable absolutes: 1) spiritual death and eternal separation from God make up the paycheck for every person's slavery to sin; and 2) eternal life is a free gift God gives undeserving sinners who believe in His Son (Eph 2:8–9).

AUGUST 5

Job 1:1–2:13

1 There was a man in the land of Uz whose name was Job; and that man was blameless, upright, fearing God and turning away from evil. [2] Seven sons and three daughters were born to him. [3] His possessions also were 7,000 sheep, 3,000 camels, 500 yoke of oxen, 500 female donkeys, and very many servants; and that man was the greatest of all the men of the east. [4] His sons used to go and hold a feast in the house of each one on his day, and they would send and invite their three sisters to eat and drink with them. [5] When the days of feasting had completed their cycle, Job would send and consecrate them, rising up early in the morning and offering burnt offerings *according to* the number of them all; for Job said, "Perhaps my sons have sinned and cursed God in their hearts." Thus Job did continually.

[6] Now there was a day when the sons of God came to present themselves before the LORD, and Satan also came among them. [7] The LORD said to Satan, "From where do you come?" Then Satan answered the LORD and said, "From roaming about on the earth and walking around on it." [8] The LORD said to Satan, "Have you considered My servant Job? For there is no one like him on the earth, a blameless and upright man, fearing God and turning away from evil." [9] Then Satan answered the LORD, "Does Job fear God for nothing? [10] Have You not made a hedge about him and his house and all that he has, on every side? You have blessed the work of his hands, and his possessions have increased in the land. [11] But put forth Your hand now and touch all that he has; he will surely curse You to Your face." [12] Then the LORD said to Satan, "Behold, all that he has is in your power, only do not put forth your hand on him." So Satan departed from the presence of the LORD.

1:6 sons of God. Job's life is about to be caught up in heavenly strategies as the scene moves from earth to heaven, where God is holding council with His heavenly court. Neither Job nor his friends ever knew about this. The angelic host (38:7; Pss 29:1; 89:7; Da 3:25) came to God's throne to render account of their ministry throughout the earth and heaven (1Ki 22:19–22). Like a Judas among the apostles, Satan was with the angels. **Satan.** Emboldened by the success he had with the unfallen Adam in paradise (Ge 3:6–12, 17–19), he was confident that the fear of God in Job, one of a fallen race, would not stand his tests. And he had fallen himself (Is 14:12). As opposed to a personal name, Satan as a title means "adversary," in either a personal or judicial sense. This demon is the ultimate spiritual adversary of all time and has been accusing the righteous throughout the ages (Rev 12:10).

1:1—2:13 This section identifies the main persons and sets the stage for the drama to follow. **Uz.** Job's home was a walled city with gates (29:7–8), where he held a position of great respect. The city was in the land of Uz in northern Arabia, adjacent to Midian, where Moses lived for 40 years (Ex 2:15). **Job.** The story begins on earth with Job as the central figure. He was a rich man with 7 sons and 3 daughters, in his middle years with a grown family. He was good, a family man, rich, and widely known. **blameless…upright,…feared God… shunned evil.** 1:8. Job was not perfect or without sin (6:24; 7:21; 9:20). However, it appears from the language that he had put his trust in God for redemption and faithfully lived a God-honoring, sincere life of integrity and consistency personally, maritally (2:10), and parentally (1:4–5).

---

¹³Now on the day when his sons and his daughters were eating and drinking wine in their oldest brother's house, ¹⁴a messenger came to Job and said, "The oxen were plowing and the donkeys feeding beside them, ¹⁵and the Sabeans attacked and took them. They also slew the servants with the edge of the sword, and I alone have escaped to tell you." ¹⁶While he was still speaking, another also came and said, "The fire of God fell from heaven and burned up the sheep and the servants and consumed them, and I alone have escaped to tell you." ¹⁷While he was still speaking, another also came and said, "The Chaldeans formed three bands and made a raid on the camels and took them and slew the servants with the edge of the sword, and I alone have escaped to tell you." ¹⁸While he was still speaking, another also came and said, "Your sons and your daughters were eating and drinking wine in their oldest brother's house, ¹⁹and behold, a great wind came from across the wilderness and struck the four corners of the house, and it fell on the young people and they died, and I alone have escaped to tell you."

²⁰Then Job arose and tore his robe and shaved his head, and he fell to the ground and worshiped. ²¹He said,

> "Naked I came from my
>   mother's womb,
> And naked I shall return there.
> The LORD gave and the
>   LORD has taken away.
> Blessed be the name of the LORD."

²²Through all this Job did not sin nor did he blame God.

2 Again there was a day when the sons of God came to present themselves before the LORD, and Satan also came among them to present himself before the LORD. ²The LORD said to Satan, "Where have you come from?" Then Satan answered the LORD and said, "From roaming about on the earth and walking around on it." ³The LORD said to Satan, "Have you considered My servant Job? For there is no one like him on the earth, a blameless and upright man fearing God and turning away from evil. And he still holds fast his integrity, although you incited Me against him to ruin him without cause." ⁴Satan answered

---

2:3 **he still holds fast his integrity.** God affirmed that Job had won round one. **without cause.** God uses the same expression the adversary used in Job 1: "for nothing" (1:9) and "without cause" (2:3). The message behind God's turn of words is that the adversary is the guilty party in this case, not Job who had suffered all the disaster without any personal cause. He had done nothing to incur the pain and loss, though it was massive. The issue was purely a matter of conflict between God and Satan. This is a crucial statement, because when Job's friends tried to explain why all the disasters had befallen him, they always put the blame on Job. Grasping this assessment from God—that Job had not been punished for something, but suffered for nothing related to him personally—is a crucial key to the story. Sometimes suffering is caused by divine purposes unknowable to us.

---

the LORD and said, "Skin for skin! Yes, all that a man has he will give for his life. ⁵However, put forth Your hand now, and touch his bone and his flesh; he will curse You to Your face." ⁶So the LORD said to Satan, "Behold, he is in your power, only spare his life."

⁷Then Satan went out from the presence of the LORD and smote Job with sore boils from the sole of his foot to the crown of his head. ⁸And he took a potsherd to scrape himself while he was sitting among the ashes.

⁹Then his wife said to him, "Do you still hold fast your integrity? Curse God and die!" ¹⁰But he said to her, "You speak as one of the foolish women speaks. Shall we indeed accept good from God and not accept adversity?" In all this Job did not sin with his lips.

¹¹Now when Job's three friends heard of all

this adversity that had come upon him, they came each one from his own place, Eliphaz the Temanite, Bildad the Shuhite and Zophar the Naamathite; and they made an appointment together to come to sympathize with him and comfort him. ¹²When they lifted up their eyes at a distance and did not recognize him, they raised their voices and wept. And each of them tore his robe and they threw dust over their heads toward the sky. ¹³Then they sat down on the ground with him for seven days and seven nights with no one speaking a word to him, for they saw that *his* pain was very great.

Psalm 91:7–13

⁷ A thousand may fall at your side
And ten thousand at your right hand,
But it shall not approach you.
⁸ You will only look on with your eyes
And see the recompense
of the wicked.
⁹ For you have made the
LORD, my refuge,
Even the Most High, your
dwelling place.
¹⁰ No evil will befall you,
Nor will any plague come
near your tent.
¹¹ For He will give His angels
charge concerning you,
To guard you in all your ways.
¹² They will bear you up in their hands,
That you do not strike your
foot against a stone.
¹³ You will tread upon the
lion and cobra,
The young lion and the serpent
you will trample down.

Proverbs 22:13–14

¹³ The sluggard says, "There
is a lion outside;
I will be killed in the streets!"
¹⁴ The mouth of an adulteress
is a deep pit;
He who is cursed of the
LORD will fall into it.

Romans 7:1–25

7 Or do you not know, brethren (for I am speaking to those who know the law), that the law has jurisdiction over a person as long as he lives? ²For the married woman is bound by law to her husband while he is living; but if her husband dies, she is released from the law concerning the husband. ³So then, if while

her husband is living she is joined to another man, she shall be called an adulteress; but if her husband dies, she is free from the law, so that she is not an adulteress though she is joined to another man.

⁴Therefore, my brethren, you also were made to die to the Law through the body of Christ, so that you might be joined to another, to Him who was raised from the dead, in order that we might bear fruit for God. ⁵For while we were in the flesh, the sinful passions, which were *aroused* by the Law, were at work in the members of our body to bear fruit for death. ⁶But now we have been released from the Law, having died to that by which we were bound, so that we serve in newness of the Spirit and not in oldness of the letter.

7:6 released from the Law. Not freedom to do what God's law forbids (6:1, 15; 8:4; see 3:31), but freedom from the spiritual liabilities and penalties of God's law. Because we died in Christ when He died, the law with its condemnation and penalties no longer has jurisdiction over us (vv. 1–3). **serve.** This is the verb form of the word for "bond-servant," but here it is parallel to being slaves of righteousness (6:22), emphasizing that this service is not voluntary. Not only is the believer able to do what is right, he will do what is right. **newness of the Spirit.** A new state of mind which the Spirit produces, characterized by a new desire and ability to keep the law of God. **oldness of the letter.** The external, written law code that produced only hostility and condemnation.

⁷What shall we say then? Is the Law sin? May it never be! On the contrary, I would not have come to know sin except through the Law; for I would not have known about coveting if the Law had not said, "You shall not covet." ⁸But sin, taking opportunity through the commandment, produced in me coveting of every kind; for apart from the Law sin *is* dead. ⁹I was once alive apart from the Law; but when the commandment came, sin became alive and I died; ¹⁰and this commandment, which was to result in life, proved to result in death for me; ¹¹for sin, taking an opportunity through the commandment, deceived me and through it killed me. ¹²So then, the Law is holy, and the commandment is holy and righteous and good.

¹³Therefore did that which is good become *a cause of* death for me? May it never be! Rather it was sin, in order that it might be

shown to be sin by effecting my death through that which is good, so that through the commandment sin would become utterly sinful.

¹⁴ For we know that the Law is spiritual, but I am of flesh, sold into bondage to sin. ¹⁵ For what I am doing, I do not understand; for I am not practicing what I *would* like to do, but I am doing the very thing I hate. ¹⁶ But if I do the very thing I do not want *to do*, I agree with the Law, *confessing* that the Law is good. ¹⁷ So now, no longer am I the one doing it, but sin which dwells in me. ¹⁸ For I know that nothing good dwells in me, that is, in my flesh; for the willing is present in me, but the doing of the good *is* not. ¹⁹ For the good that I want, I do not do, but I practice the very evil that I do not want. ²⁰ But if I am doing the very thing I do not want, I am no longer the one doing it, but sin which dwells in me.

²¹ I find then the principle that evil is present in me, the one who wants to do good. ²² For I joyfully concur with the law of God in the inner man, ²³ but I see a different law in the members of my body, waging war against the law of my mind and making me a prisoner of the law of sin which is in my members. ²⁴ Wretched man that I am! Who will set me free from the body of this death? ²⁵ Thanks be to God through Jesus Christ our Lord! So then, on the one hand I myself with my mind am serving the law of God, but on the other, with my flesh the law of sin.

DAY 5: In Romans 7:7-25, is Paul describing his own experience as a believer or unbeliever?

Paul uses the personal pronoun "I" throughout this passage, using his own experience as an example of what is true of unredeemed humanity (7:7-12) and of true Christians (7:13-25). Some interpret this chronicle of Paul's inner conflict as describing his life before Christ. They point out that Paul describes the person as "sold into bondage to sin" (7:14), as having "nothing good" in him (7:18), and as a "wretched man" trapped in a "body of this death" (7:24). Those descriptions seem to contradict Paul's earlier description of the believer (6:2, 6-7, 11, 17-18, 22).

It is correct, however, to understand Paul here to be speaking about a believer. This person desires to obey God's law and hates sin (7:15, 19, 21). He is humble, recognizing that nothing good dwells in his humanness (7:18). He sees sin in himself, but not as all that is there (7:17, 20-22). And he serves Jesus Christ with his mind (7:25). Paul has already established that none of those attitudes ever describe the unsaved (1:18-21, 32; 3:10-20). Paul's use of the present tense verbs in 7:14-25 strongly supports the idea that he was describing his current experience as a Christian.

Even those who agree that Paul was speaking as a genuine believer, however, still find room for disagreement. Some see a carnal, fleshly Christian under the influence of old habits. Others see a legalistic Christian, frustrated by his feeble attempts in his own power to please God by keeping the Mosaic Law. But the personal pronoun "I" refers to the apostle Paul, a standard of spiritual health and maturity. This leads to the conclusion that Paul, in 7:7-25, must be describing all Christians—even the most spiritual and mature—who, when they honestly evaluate themselves against the righteous standard of God's law, realize how far short they fall. Notice, particularly, Paul's honesty and transparency in the four laments (7:14-17, 18-20, 21-23, 24-25).

AUGUST 6

Job 3:1-4:21

3 Afterward Job opened his mouth and cursed the day of his *birth*. ² And Job said,

³ "Let the day perish on which
    I was to be born,
And the night *which* said,
    'A boy is conceived.'
⁴ "May that day be darkness;
    Let not God above care
      for it,
    Nor light shine on it.

⁵ "Let darkness and black gloom claim it;
    Let a cloud settle on it;
    Let the blackness of the day terrify it.
⁶ "*As for* that night, let darkness seize it;
    Let it not rejoice among the
      days of the year;
    Let it not come into the
      number of the months.
⁷ "Behold, let that night be barren;
    Let no joyful shout enter it.
⁸ "Let those curse it who curse the day,
    Who are prepared to rouse Leviathan.
⁹ "Let the stars of its twilight be darkened;
    Let it wait for light but have none,
    And let it not see the breaking dawn;

¹⁰ Because it did not shut the opening
of my *mother's* womb,
Or hide trouble from my eyes.

¹¹ "Why did I not die at birth,
Come forth from the
womb and expire?
¹² "Why did the knees receive me,
And why the breasts, that
I should suck?
¹³ "For now I would have lain
down and been quiet;
I would have slept then, I
would have been at rest,
¹⁴ With kings and *with*
counselors of the earth,
Who rebuilt ruins for themselves;
¹⁵ Or with princes who had gold,
Who were filling their
houses *with* silver.
¹⁶ "Or like a miscarriage which is
discarded, I would not be,
As infants that never saw light.
¹⁷ "There the wicked cease from raging,
And there the weary are at rest.
¹⁸ "The prisoners are at ease together;
They do not hear the voice
of the taskmaster.
¹⁹ "The small and the great are there,
And the slave is free from his master.

²⁰ "Why is light given to him who suffers,
And life to the bitter of soul,
²¹ Who long for death, but there is none,
And dig for it more than for
hidden treasures,
²² Who rejoice greatly,
And exult when they find the grave?
²³ *"Why is light given* to a man
whose way is hidden,
And whom God has hedged in?
²⁴ "For my groaning comes at
the sight of my food,
And my cries pour out like water.
²⁵ "For what I fear comes upon me,
And what I dread befalls me.
²⁶ "I am not at ease, nor am I quiet,
And I am not at rest, but
turmoil comes."

3:25–26 what I fear. Not a particular thing but a generic classification of suffering. The very worst fear that anyone could have was coming to pass in Job's life, and he is experiencing severe anxiety, fearing more.

4 Then Eliphaz the Temanite answered,

² "If one ventures a word with you,
will you become impatient?
But who can refrain from speaking?
³ "Behold you have admonished many,
And you have strengthened
weak hands.
⁴ "Your words have helped the
tottering to stand,
And you have strengthened
feeble knees.
⁵ "But now it has come to you,
and you are impatient;
It touches you, and you are dismayed.
⁶ "Is not your fear *of God*
your confidence,
And the integrity of your
ways your hope?

⁷ "Remember now, who *ever*
perished being innocent?
Or where were the upright destroyed?

4:7 who *ever* perished being innocent? Eliphaz, recognizing Job's "fear *of God*" and "integrity" (v. 6), was likely encouraging Job at the outset by saying he wouldn't die because he was innocent of any deadly iniquity, but must be guilty of some serious sin because he was reaping such anger from God. This was a moral universe and moral order was at work, he thought. He had oversimplified God's pattern of retribution. This simple axiom, "the righteous will prosper and the wicked will suffer," does not always hold up in human experience. It is true that plowing and sowing iniquity reap judgment, so Eliphaz was partially right (Gal 6:7–9; 1Pe 3:12), but not everything we reap in life is the result of something we have sown (2Co 12:7–10). Eliphaz was replacing theology with simplistic logic. To say that wherever there is suffering, it is the result of sowing sin is wrong (Ex 4:11; Jn 9:1–3).

⁸ "According to what I have seen,
those who plow iniquity
And those who sow trouble
harvest it.
⁹ "By the breath of God they perish,
And by the blast of His anger
they come to an end.
¹⁰ "The roaring of the lion and the
voice of the *fierce* lion,
And the teeth of the young
lions are broken.

11 "The lion perishes for lack of prey,
And the whelps of the
lioness are scattered.

12 "Now a word was brought
to me stealthily,
And my ear received a whisper of it.

13 "Amid disquieting thoughts from
the visions of the night,
When deep sleep falls on men,

14 Dread came upon me, and trembling,
And made all my bones shake.

15 "Then a spirit passed by my face;
The hair of my flesh bristled up.

16 "It stood still, but I could not
discern its appearance;
A form *was* before my eyes;
There was silence, then
I heard a voice:

17 'Can mankind be just before God?
Can a man be pure before his Maker?

18 'He puts no trust even in His
servants;
And against His angels
He charges error.

19 'How much more those who
dwell in houses of clay,
Whose foundation is in the dust,
Who are crushed before the moth!

20 'Between morning and evening
they are broken in pieces;
Unobserved, they perish forever.

21 'Is not their tent-cord plucked
up within them?
They die, yet without wisdom.'

Psalm 91:14-16

14 "Because he has loved Me,
therefore I will deliver him;
I will set him *securely* on high,
because he has known
My name.

15 "He will call upon Me, and
I will answer him;
I will be with him in trouble;
I will rescue him and honor him.

16 "With a long life I will satisfy him
And let him see My salvation."

91:14 he has loved Me. God Himself is the speaker in this section (vv. 14–16) and He describes the blessing He gives to those who know and love Him. The word for "loved" means a "deep longing" for God, or a "clinging" to God.

Proverbs 22:15

15 Foolishness is bound up in
the heart of a child;
The rod of discipline will
remove it far from him.

Romans 8:1-17

8 Therefore there is now no condemnation for those who are in Christ Jesus. 2 For the law of the Spirit of life in Christ Jesus has set you free from the law of sin and of death. 3 For what the Law could not do, weak

8:1 Therefore. The result or consequence of the truth just taught. Normally, it marks the conclusion of the verses immediately preceding it. But here it introduces the staggering results of Paul's teaching in the first 7 chapters: that justification is by faith alone on the basis of God's overwhelming grace. **no condemnation.** Occurring only 3 times in the NT, all in Romans (5:16, 18), "condemnation" is used exclusively in judicial settings as the opposite of justification. It refers to a verdict of guilty and the penalty that verdict demands. No sin a believer can commit—past, present, or future—can be held against him, since the penalty was paid by Christ and righteousness was imputed to the believer. And no sin will ever reverse this divine legal decision. **those…in Christ Jesus.** I.e., every true Christian; to be in Christ means to be united with Him.

as it was through the flesh, God *did:* sending His own Son in the likeness of sinful flesh and *as an offering* for sin, He condemned sin in the flesh, 4 so that the requirement of the Law might be fulfilled in us, who do not walk according to the flesh but according to the Spirit. 5 For those who are according to the flesh set their minds on the things of the flesh, but those who are according to the Spirit, the things of the Spirit. 6 For the mind set on the flesh is death, but the mind set on the Spirit is life and peace, 7 because the mind set on the flesh is hostile toward God; for it does not subject itself to the law of God, for it is not even able *to do so,* 8 and those who are in the flesh cannot please God.

9 However, you are not in the flesh but in the Spirit, if indeed the Spirit of God dwells in you. But if anyone does not have the Spirit of Christ, he does not belong to Him. 10 If Christ is in you, though the body is dead because of sin, yet the spirit is alive because of righteousness. 11 But if the Spirit of Him who raised Jesus from the

dead dwells in you, He who raised Christ Jesus from the dead will also give life to your mortal bodies through His Spirit who dwells in you.

¹² So then, brethren, we are under obligation, not to the flesh, to live according to the flesh— ¹³ for if you are living according to the flesh, you must die; but if by the Spirit you are putting to death the deeds of the body, you will live. ¹⁴ For all who are being led by the Spirit of God, these are sons of God. ¹⁵ For you have not received a spirit of slavery leading to fear again, but you have received a spirit of adoption as sons by which we cry out, "Abba! Father!" ¹⁶ The Spirit Himself testifies with our spirit that we are children of God, ¹⁷ and if children, heirs also, heirs of God and fellow heirs with Christ, if indeed we suffer with *Him* so that we may also be glorified with *Him*.

8:15 spirit of slavery…to fear. Because of their life of sin, unregenerate people are slaves to their fear of death (Heb 2:14–15), and to their fear of final punishment (1Jn 4:18). **spirit of adoption.** Not primarily a reference to the transaction by which God adopts us (Eph 1:5; Gal 4:5–7), , but to a Spirit-produced awareness of the rich reality that God has made us His children, and, therefore, that we can come before Him without fear or hesitation as our beloved Father. It includes the confidence that we are truly sons of God. **Abba!** An informal, Aram. term for Father that conveys a sense of intimacy. Like the Eng. terms "Daddy" or "Papa," it connotes tenderness, dependence, and a relationship free of fear or anxiety (Mk 14:36).

DAY 6: What kind of relationship does Satan have with God in the Book of Job?

Satan may be God's sworn enemy, but they are not equals. Satan is a creature; God is the Creator. Satan was an angel unwilling to serve in his exalted role, and he rebelled against God.

The continual conflict between Satan and God is illustrated when Satan states that righteous people remain faithful to God only because of what they get. They trust in God only as long as God is nice to them. Satan challenged God's claims of Job's righteousness by calling it untested, if not questionable. Apparently Satan was convinced that he could destroy Job's faith in God by inflicting suffering on him.

Satan suffered another defeat as God demonstrated through Job's life that saving faith can't be destroyed no matter how much trouble the believer suffers or how incomprehensible and undeserved the suffering seems.

After failing to destroy Job, Satan disappears from the story. He remains God's defeated enemy, still raging against God's inevitable triumph.

AUGUST 7

Job 5:1–6:30

5 "Call now, is there anyone
who will answer you?
And to which of the holy
ones will you turn?
² "For anger slays the foolish man,
And jealousy kills the simple.
³ "I have seen the foolish taking root,
And I cursed his abode immediately.
⁴ "His sons are far from safety,
They are even oppressed in the gate,
And there is no deliverer.
⁵ "His harvest the hungry devour
And take it to a *place of* thorns,
And the schemer is eager
for their wealth.
⁶ "For affliction does not
come from the dust,
Nor does trouble sprout
from the ground,

⁷ For man is born for trouble,
As sparks fly upward.

⁸ "But as for me, I would seek God,
And I would place my
cause before God;
⁹ Who does great and
unsearchable things,
Wonders without number.
¹⁰ "He gives rain on the earth
And sends water on the fields,
¹¹ So that He sets on high
those who are lowly,
And those who mourn are
lifted to safety.
¹² "He frustrates the plotting
of the shrewd,
So that their hands cannot
attain success.
¹³ "He captures the wise by their
own shrewdness,
And the advice of the cunning
is quickly thwarted.

¹⁴ "By day they meet with darkness,
And grope at noon as in the night.
¹⁵ "But He saves from the sword
of their mouth,
And the poor from the
hand of the mighty.
¹⁶ "So the helpless has hope,
And unrighteousness must
shut its mouth.

¹⁷ "Behold, how happy is the man
whom God reproves,
So do not despise the discipline
of the Almighty.

5:17 happy is the man whom God reproves.
Eliphaz put a positive spin on his advice by
telling Job that enviable or desirable is the situation of the one God cares enough to chasten.
"If only Job admitted his sin, he could be happy
again" was the advice.

¹⁸ "For He inflicts pain, and gives relief;
He wounds, and His hands *also* heal.
¹⁹ "From six troubles He will deliver you,
Even in seven evil will not touch you.
²⁰ "In famine He will redeem
you from death,
And in war from the power
of the sword.
²¹ "You will be hidden from the
scourge of the tongue,
And you will not be afraid of
violence when it comes.
²² "You will laugh at violence and famine,
And you will not be afraid
of wild beasts.
²³ "For you will be in league with
the stones of the field,
And the beasts of the field will
be at peace with you.
²⁴ "You will know that your tent is secure,
For you will visit your abode
and fear no loss.
²⁵ "You will know also that your
descendants will be many,
And your offspring as the
grass of the earth.
²⁶ "You will come to the grave
in full vigor,
Like the stacking of grain
in its season.
²⁷ "Behold this; we have investigated
it, *and* so it is.
Hear it, and know for yourself."

6 Then Job answered,

² "Oh that my grief were
actually weighed
And laid in the balances together
with my calamity!
³ "For then it would be heavier
than the sand of the seas;
Therefore my words have been rash.
⁴ "For the arrows of the Almighty
are within me,
Their poison my spirit drinks;
The terrors of God are
arrayed against me.
⁵ "Does the wild donkey bray
over *his* grass,
Or does the ox low over his fodder?
⁶ "Can something tasteless be
eaten without salt,
Or is there any taste in the
white of an egg?
⁷ "My soul refuses to touch *them*;
They are like loathsome food to me.

⁸ "Oh that my request might
come to pass,
And that God would grant my longing!
⁹ "Would that God were
willing to crush me,
That He would loose His
hand and cut me off!
¹⁰ "But it is still my consolation,
And I rejoice in unsparing pain,
That I have not denied the
words of the Holy One.

6:10 the words of the Holy One. Job had not
been avoiding the revelation of God that he
had received. The commands of the Holy One
were precious to him and he had lived by them.
This was confusing to him, as he couldn't find
any sinful source for his suffering. He would
rejoice in his pain if he knew it would soon
lead to death, but he couldn't see any hope
for death or deliverance in himself (vv. 11–13).

¹¹ "What is my strength, that
I should wait?
And what is my end, that
I should endure?
¹² "Is my strength the strength of stones,
Or is my flesh bronze?
¹³ "Is it that my help is not within me,
And that deliverance is
driven from me?

¹⁴ "For the despairing man *there should
be* kindness from his friend;
So that he does not forsake the
fear of the Almighty.
¹⁵ "My brothers have acted
deceitfully like a wadi,
Like the torrents of wadis
which vanish,
¹⁶ Which are turbid because of ice
And into which the snow melts.
¹⁷ "When they become waterless,
they are silent,
When it is hot, they vanish
from their place.
¹⁸ "The paths of their course wind along,
They go up into nothing and perish.
¹⁹ "The caravans of Tema looked,
The travelers of Sheba hoped for them.
²⁰ "They were disappointed for
they had trusted,
They came there and were
confounded.
²¹ "Indeed, you have now become such,
You see a terror and are afraid.
²² "Have I said, 'Give me *something*,'
Or, 'Offer a bribe for me
from your wealth,'
²³ Or, 'Deliver me from the hand
of the adversary,'
Or, 'Redeem me from the
hand of the tyrants'?
²⁴ "Teach me, and I will be silent;
And show me how I have erred.
²⁵ "How painful are honest words!
But what does your argument prove?
²⁶ "Do you intend to reprove *my* words,
When the words of one in despair
belong to the wind?
²⁷ "You would even cast *lots*
for the orphans
And barter over your friend.
²⁸ "Now please look at me,
And *see* if I lie to your face.
²⁹ "Desist now, let there be no injustice;
Even desist, my righteousness
is yet in it.
³⁰ "Is there injustice on my tongue?
Cannot my palate discern calamities?

Psalm 92:1–7

A Psalm, a Song for the Sabbath day.

It is good to give thanks to the LORD
And to sing praises to Your
name, O Most High;
² To declare Your lovingkindness
in the morning
And Your faithfulness by night,

³ With the ten-stringed lute
and with the harp,
With resounding music upon the lyre.
⁴ For You, O LORD, have made me
glad by what You have done,
I will sing for joy at the
works of Your hands.
⁵ How great are Your works, O LORD!
Your thoughts are very deep.
⁶ A senseless man has no knowledge,
Nor does a stupid man
understand this:
⁷ That when the wicked
sprouted up like grass
And all who did iniquity flourished,
It *was only* that they might be
destroyed forevermore.

Proverbs 22:16

¹⁶ He who oppresses the poor to
make more for himself
Or who gives to the rich, *will*
only *come to* poverty.

22:16 These two vices reflect the same selfish
attitude: withholding from the poor to keep
what one has and giving to the rich to induce
them to give one more. Both are unacceptable
to God and incur punishment.

Romans 8:18–39

¹⁸ For I consider that the sufferings of this
present time are not worthy to be compared
with the glory that is to be revealed to us.
¹⁹ For the anxious longing of the creation
waits eagerly for the revealing of the sons
of God. ²⁰ For the creation was subjected to
futility, not willingly, but because of Him
who subjected it, in hope ²¹ that the creation
itself also will be set free from its slavery to
corruption into the freedom of the glory of
the children of God. ²² For we know that the
whole creation groans and suffers the pains
of childbirth together until now. ²³ And not
only this, but also we ourselves, having the
first fruits of the Spirit, even we ourselves
groan within ourselves, waiting eagerly for
our adoption as sons, the redemption of our
body. ²⁴ For in hope we have been saved, but
hope that is seen is not hope; for who hopes
for what he *already* sees? ²⁵ But if we hope
for what we do not see, with perseverance
we wait eagerly for it.
²⁶ In the same way the Spirit also helps our

weakness; for we do not know how to pray as we should, but the Spirit Himself intercedes for *us* with groanings too deep for words; 27 and He who searches the hearts knows what the mind of the Spirit is, because He intercedes for the saints according to *the will of* God.

28 And we know that God causes all things to work together for good to those who love God, to those who are called according to *His* purpose. 29 For those whom He foreknew, He also predestined *to become* conformed to the image of His Son, so that He would be the firstborn among many brethren; 30 and these whom He predestined, He also called; and these whom He called, He also justified; and these whom He justified, He also glorified.

31 What then shall we say to these things? If God *is* for us, who *is* against us? 32 He who did not spare His own Son, but delivered Him over for us all, how will He not also with Him freely give us all things? 33 Who will bring a charge against God's elect? God is the one who justifies; 34 who is the one who condemns? Christ Jesus is He who died, yes, rather who was raised, who is at the right hand of God, who also intercedes for us. 35 Who will separate us from the love of Christ? Will tribulation, or distress, or persecution, or famine, or nakedness, or peril, or sword? 36 Just as it is written,

"FOR YOUR SAKE WE ARE BEING PUT
TO DEATH ALL DAY LONG;

WE WERE CONSIDERED AS SHEEP
TO BE SLAUGHTERED."

37 But in all these things we overwhelmingly conquer through Him who loved us. 38 For I am convinced that neither death, nor life, nor angels, nor principalities, nor things present, nor things to come, nor powers, 39 nor height, nor depth, nor any other created thing, will be able to separate us from the love of God, which is in Christ Jesus our Lord.

8:35-39 This list of experiences and persons that can't separate the believer from God's love in Christ was not just theory to Paul. It was rather personal testimony from one who had personally survived assaults from these entities and emerged triumphant.

8:35 the love of Christ. Not our love for Christ, but His love for us (Jn 13:1), specifically here as He demonstrated it in salvation (1Jn 4:9-10). **tribulation.** Here the word probably refers to the kind of adversity common to all men. **distress.** This refers to being strictly confined in a narrow, difficult place or being helplessly hemmed in by one's circumstances. **persecution.** Suffering inflicted on us by men because of our relationship with Christ (Mt 5:10-12).

DAY 7: Explain the process Paul refers to in Romans 8:28–30 and 9:6-29.

With these words, God reveals in human terms His divine role in the process of salvation. Paul's description offends the human spirit because it minimizes our role. Yet only those who see their own helplessness in the face of sin can come to see how gracious God has been in acting and choosing ahead of time. We never surprise God; He always anticipates us! "But God demonstrates His own love toward us, in that while we were yet sinners, Christ died for us" (Ro 5:8).

The term "foreknew" (8:29) does not simply refer to God's omniscience—that in eternity past He knew who would come to Christ. Rather, it speaks of a predetermined choice by God to set His love on us and establish an intimate relationship. The term "choice" (9:11) refers to the same action on God's part (1Pe 1:1–2, 20). Salvation is not initiated by human choice. Even faith is a gift of God (Ro 1:16; Jn 6:37; Eph 2:8–9).

The term "predestined" (8:29) literally means "to mark out, appoint, or determine beforehand." Those God chooses, He destines for His chosen end—that is, likeness to His Son (Eph 1:4–5, 11). The goal of God's predestined purpose for His own is that they would be made like Jesus Christ.

The reality and security of our standing with God rests ultimately in His character and decision, not ours. Paul summarized his teaching about the believer's security in Christ with a thundering litany of questions and answers that haunt believers. They reach their peak with "Who will separate us from the love of Christ?" (8:35). Paul's answer is an almost poetic expression of praise for God's grace in bringing salvation to completion for all who are chosen and believe—it is a hymn of security.

AUGUST 8

Job 7:1–8:22

7 "Is not man forced to labor on earth,
And *are not* his days like the
days of a hired man?

2 "As a slave who pants for the shade,
And as a hired man who eagerly
waits for his wages,

3 So am I allotted months of vanity,
And nights of trouble are
appointed me.

4 "When I lie down I say,
'When shall I arise?'
But the night continues,
And I am continually
tossing until dawn.

5 "My flesh is clothed with worms
and a crust of dirt,
My skin hardens and runs.

6 "My days are swifter than a
weaver's shuttle,
And come to an end without hope.

7 "Remember that my life is *but* breath;
My eye will not again see good.

8 "The eye of him who sees me
will behold me no longer;
Your eyes *will be* on me,
but I will not be.

9 "When a cloud vanishes, it is gone,
So he who goes down to Sheol
does not come up.

10 "He will not return again to his house,
Nor will his place know him anymore.

11 "Therefore I will not
restrain my mouth;
I will speak in the anguish
of my spirit,
I will complain in the
bitterness of my soul.

12 "Am I the sea, or the sea monster,
That You set a guard over me?

13 "If I say, 'My bed will comfort me,
My couch will ease my complaint,'

14 Then You frighten me with dreams
And terrify me by visions;

15 So that my soul would
choose suffocation,
Death rather than my pains.

16 "I waste away; I will not live forever.
Leave me alone, for my days
are *but* a breath.

17 "What is man that You magnify him,
And that You are concerned
about him,

18 That You examine him every morning
And try him every moment?

19 "Will You never turn Your
gaze away from me,
Nor let me alone until I
swallow my spittle?

7:19 until I swallow my spittle. This strange
statement was an Arabic proverb, indicating a
brief moment. Job was asking for a moment "to
catch his breath," or in the case of the proverb,
"swallow my spittle."

20 "Have I sinned? What have
I done to You,
O watcher of men?
Why have You set me as
Your target,
So that I am a burden to myself?

21 "Why then do You not pardon
my transgression
And take away my iniquity?
For now I will lie down in
the dust;
And You will seek me,
but I will not be."

8 Then Bildad the Shuhite answered,

2 "How long will you say these
things,
And the words of your mouth
be a mighty wind?

3 "Does God pervert justice?
Or does the Almighty pervert
what is right?

4 "If your sons sinned against Him,
Then He delivered them into the
power of their transgression.

5 "If you would seek God
And implore the compassion
of the Almighty,

8:3 Almighty pervert what is right. Bildad
took Job's claims for innocence and applied
them to his simplistic notion of retribution.
He concluded that Job was accusing God of
injustice when God must be meting out justice
to Job. Job tried to avoid outright accusations
of this sort, but the evidence led Bildad to this
conclusion because he had no knowledge of
the heavenly facts.

⁶ If you are pure and upright,
   Surely now He would rouse
     Himself for you
   And restore your righteous estate.
⁷ "Though your beginning
     was insignificant,
   Yet your end will increase greatly.

⁸ "Please inquire of past generations,
   And consider the things searched
     out by their fathers.
⁹ "For we are *only* of yesterday
     and know nothing,
   Because our days on earth
     are as a shadow.
¹⁰ "Will they not teach you *and*
     tell you,
   And bring forth words
     from their minds?

¹¹ "Can the papyrus grow up
     without a marsh?
   Can the rushes grow without
     water?
¹² "While it is still green *and*
     not cut down,
   Yet it withers before any
     other plant.
¹³ "So are the paths of all who
     forget God;
   And the hope of the
     godless will perish,
¹⁴ Whose confidence is fragile,
   And whose trust a spider's web.
¹⁵ "He trusts in his house, but
     it does not stand;
   He holds fast to it, but it
     does not endure.
¹⁶ "He thrives before the sun,
   And his shoots spread out
     over his garden.
¹⁷ "His roots wrap around a rock pile,
   He grasps a house of stones.
¹⁸ "If he is removed from his place,
   Then it will deny him, *saying,*
     'I never saw you.'
¹⁹ "Behold, this is the joy of His way;
   And out of the dust others will spring.
²⁰ "Lo, God will not reject *a*
     man of integrity,
   Nor will He support the evildoers.
²¹ "He will yet fill your mouth
     with laughter
   And your lips with shouting.
²² "Those who hate you will be
     clothed with shame,
   And the tent of the wicked
     will be no longer."

Psalm 92:8–15

⁸ But You, O LORD, are on high forever.
⁹ For, behold, Your enemies, O LORD,
   For, behold, Your enemies will perish;
   All who do iniquity will be scattered.

¹⁰ But You have exalted my horn
     like *that of* the wild ox;
   I have been anointed with fresh oil.

92:10 my horn...anointed with fresh oil. This figure is based on a practice of making an animal's horns gleam by rubbing oil on them. Thus God, in effect, had invigorated the psalmist (Pss 23:5; 133:2).

¹¹ And my eye has looked
     exultantly upon my foes,
   My ears hear of the evildoers
     who rise up against me.
¹² The righteous man will flourish
     like the palm tree,
   He will grow like a cedar
     in Lebanon.
¹³ Planted in the house of the LORD,
   They will flourish in the
     courts of our God.
¹⁴ They will still yield fruit in old age;
   They shall be full of sap
     and very green,
¹⁵ To declare that the LORD is
     upright;
   He is my rock, and there is no
     unrighteousness in Him.

Proverbs 22:17–21

¹⁷ Incline your ear and hear the
     words of the wise,
   And apply your mind to
     my knowledge;
¹⁸ For it will be pleasant if you
     keep them within you,
   That they may be ready on
     your lips.
¹⁹ So that your trust may be
     in the LORD,
   I have taught you today,
     even you.
²⁰ Have I not written to you
     excellent things
   Of counsels and knowledge,
²¹ To make you know the certainty
     of the words of truth
   That you may correctly answer
     him who sent you?

Romans 9:1-13

9 I am telling the truth in Christ, I am not lying, my conscience testifies with me in the Holy Spirit, ²that I have great sorrow and unceasing grief in my heart. ³For I could wish that I myself were accursed, *separated* from Christ for the sake of my brethren, my kinsmen according to the flesh, ⁴who are Israelites, to whom belongs the adoption as sons, and the glory and the covenants and the giving of the Law and the *temple* service and the promises, ⁵whose are the fathers, and from whom is the Christ according to the flesh, who is over all, God blessed forever. Amen.

⁶But *it is* not as though the word of God has failed. For they are not all Israel who are *descended* from Israel; ⁷nor are they all children because they are Abraham's descendants, but: "THROUGH ISAAC YOUR DESCENDANTS WILL BE NAMED." ⁸That is, it is not the children of the flesh who are children of God, but the children of the promise are regarded as descendants. ⁹For this is the word of promise: "AT THIS TIME I WILL COME, AND SARAH SHALL HAVE A SON." ¹⁰And not only this, but there was Rebekah also, when she had conceived *twins* by one man, our father Isaac; ¹¹for though *the twins* were not yet born and had not done anything good or bad, so that God's purpose according to *His* choice would stand, not because of works but because of Him who calls, ¹²it was said to her, "THE OLDER WILL SERVE THE YOUNGER." ¹³Just as it is written, "JACOB I LOVED, BUT ESAU I HATED."

9:4 Israelites. The descendants of Abraham through Jacob, whose name God changed to Israel (Ge 32:28). **adoption.** Not in the sense of providing salvation to every person born a Jew, but sovereignly selecting an entire nation to receive His special calling, covenant, and blessing and to serve as His witness nation (Ex 4:22; 19:6; Hos 11:1; Is 46:3-4). **glory.** The glory cloud (Shekinah) that pictured God's presence in the Old Testament (Ex 16:10; 24:16-17; 29:42-43; Lv 9:23). His glory was supremely present in the Holy of Holies in both the tabernacle and the temple, which served as the throne room of Yahweh, Israel's King (Ex 25:22; 40:34; 1Ki 8:11). **covenants.** A covenant is a legally binding promise, agreement, or contract. Three times in the New Testament the word "covenants" is used in the plural (Gal 4:24; Eph 2:12). All but one of God's covenants with man are eternal and unilateral—that is, God promised to accomplish something based on His own character and not on the response or actions of the promised beneficiary. The 6 biblical covenants include: 1) the covenant with Noah (Ge 9:8-17); 2) the covenant with Abraham (Ge 12:1-3); 3) the covenant of law given through Moses at Sinai (Ex 19-31; see Dt 29-30); 4) the priestly covenant (Nu 25:10-13); 5) the covenant of an eternal kingdom through David's greatest Son (2Sa 7:8-16); and 6) the New Covenant (Jer 31:31-34; Eze 37:26; see Heb 8:6-13). All but the Mosaic Covenant are eternal and unilateral. It is neither, since Israel's sin abrogated it and it has been replaced by the New Covenant (Heb 8:7-13).

DAY 8: Describe what Job was going through?

In Job 7:1, he said, "Is not man forced to labor on earth?" He felt like a slave under tyranny of his master, longing for relief and reward (vv. 1-2); he was sleepless (v. 3-4); he was loathsome because of worms and scabs, dried filth and new running sores (v. 5); he was like a weaver's shuttle, tossed back and forth (v. 6); he was like a breath or cloud that comes and goes on its way to death (vv. 7-10). In this discourse, Job attempted to reconcile in his own mind what God was doing.

Job's Living Death

1. Painful boils from head to toe (2:7, 13; 30:17)
2. Severe itching/irritation (2:7-8)
3. Great grief (2:13)
4. Lost appetite (3:24; 6:6-7)
5. Agonizing discomfort (3:24)
6. Insomnia (7:4)
7. Worm- and dust-infested flesh (7:5)
8. Continual oozing of boils (7:5)
9. Hallucinations (7:14)
10. Decaying skin (13:28)
11. Shriveled up (16:8; 17:7; 19:20)
12. Severe halitosis (19:17)
13. Teeth fell out (19:20)
14. Relentless pain (30:17)
15. Skin turned black (30:30)
16. Raging fever (30:30)
17. Dramatic weight loss (33:21)

AUGUST 9

Job 9:1–10:22

9 Then Job answered,

2 "In truth I know that this is so;
But how can a man be in the
right before God?

3 "If one wished to dispute with Him,
He could not answer Him once
in a thousand *times*.

4 "Wise in heart and mighty in strength,
Who has defied Him without harm?

5 "*It is God* who removes the
mountains, they know not *how*,
When He overturns them
in His anger;

6 Who shakes the earth out of its place,
And its pillars tremble;

7 Who commands the sun not to shine,
And sets a seal upon the stars;

8 Who alone stretches out the heavens
And tramples down the
waves of the sea;

9 Who makes the Bear, Orion
and the Pleiades,
And the chambers of the south;

10 Who does great things,
unfathomable,
And wondrous works
without number.

11 "Were He to pass by me, I
would not see Him;
Were He to move past *me*, I
would not perceive Him.

12 "Were He to snatch away, who
could restrain Him?
Who could say to Him, 'What
are You doing?'

13 "God will not turn back His anger;
Beneath Him crouch the
helpers of Rahab.

14 "How then can I answer Him,
And choose my words before Him?

15 "For though I were right, I
could not answer;
I would have to implore the
mercy of my judge.

16 "If I called and He answered me,
I could not believe that He was
listening to my voice.

17 "For He bruises me with a tempest
And multiplies my wounds
without cause.

18 "He will not allow me to get my breath,
But saturates me with bitterness.

9:15–20 though I were right. He means here,
not sinless, but having spiritual integrity, i.e.,
a pure heart to love, serve, and obey God. He
was affirming again that his suffering was not
due to sins he was not willing to confess. Even
at that, God found something to condemn him
for, he felt, making it hopeless, then, to contend
with God.

19 "If *it is a matter* of power, behold,
He is the strong one!
And if *it is a matter* of justice,
who can summon Him?

20 "Though I am righteous, my
mouth will condemn me;
Though I am guiltless, He
will declare me guilty.

21 "I am guiltless;
I do not take notice of myself;
I despise my life.

22 "It is *all* one; therefore I say,
'He destroys the guiltless
and the wicked.'

23 "If the scourge kills suddenly,
He mocks the despair of the innocent.

24 "The earth is given into the
hand of the wicked;
He covers the faces of its judges.
If *it is* not *He*, then who is it?

25 "Now my days are swifter
than a runner;
They flee away, they see no good.

26 "They slip by like reed boats,
Like an eagle that swoops on its prey.

27 "Though I say, 'I will forget
my complaint,
I will leave off my *sad* countenance
and be cheerful,'

28 I am afraid of all my pains,
I know that You will not acquit me.

29 "I am accounted wicked,
Why then should I toil in vain?

30 "If I should wash myself with snow
And cleanse my hands with lye,

31 Yet You would plunge me into the pit,
And my own clothes would
abhor me.

32 "For *He is* not a man as I am
that I may answer Him,
That we may go to court together.

33 "There is no umpire between us,
Who may lay his hand upon us both.

34 "Let Him remove His rod from me,
And let not dread of Him terrify me.

9:32 That we may go to court together. Job acknowledged that, as a mere man, he had no right to call on God to declare his innocence or to contend with God over his innocence. Job was not arguing that he was sinless, but he didn't believe he had sinned to the extent that he deserved his severe suffering. Job held on to the same simplistic system of retribution as that of his accusers, which said that suffering was always caused by sin. And he knew he was not sinless, but he couldn't identify any unconfessed or unrepented sins. "Where is mercy?" he wondered.

9:33–35 no umpire between us. A court official who sees both sides clearly, as well as the source of disagreement, so as to bring resolution was not found. Where was an advocate, an arbitrator, an umpire, or a referee? Was there no one to remove God's rod and call for justice?

---

35 "*Then* I would speak and not fear Him;
But I am not like that in myself.

10 "I loathe my own life;
I will give full vent to my complaint;
I will speak in the bitterness
of my soul.
2 "I will say to God, 'Do not condemn me;
Let me know why You
contend with me.
3 'Is it right for You indeed to oppress,
To reject the labor of Your hands,
And to look favorably on the
schemes of the wicked?
4 'Have You eyes of flesh?
Or do You see as a man sees?
5 'Are Your days as the days
of a mortal,
Or Your years as man's years,
6 That You should seek for my guilt
And search after my sin?
7 'According to Your knowledge
I am indeed not guilty,
Yet there is no deliverance
from Your hand.

8 'Your hands fashioned and
made me altogether,
And would You destroy me?
9 'Remember now, that You
have made me as clay;
And would You turn me
into dust again?
10 'Did You not pour me out like milk
And curdle me like cheese;

11 Clothe me with skin and flesh,
And knit me together with
bones and sinews?
12 'You have granted me life
and lovingkindness;
And Your care has preserved my spirit.
13 'Yet these things You have
concealed in Your heart;
I know that this is within You:
14 If I sin, then You would
take note of me,
And would not acquit me of my guilt.
15 'If I am wicked, woe to me!
And if I am righteous, I dare
not lift up my head.
I am sated with disgrace and
conscious of my misery.
16 'Should *my head* be lifted up, You
would hunt me like a lion;
And again You would show
Your power against me.
17 'You renew Your witnesses against me
And increase Your anger toward me;
Hardship after hardship is with me.

18 'Why then have You brought
me out of the womb?
Would that I had died and
no eye had seen me!
19 'I should have been as though
I had not been,
Carried from womb to tomb.'
20 "Would He not let my few days alone?
Withdraw from me that I
may have a little cheer
21 Before I go—and I shall not return—
To the land of darkness
and deep shadow,
22 The land of utter gloom
as darkness *itself,*
Of deep shadow without order,
And which shines as the darkness."

Psalm 93:1–5

The LORD reigns, He is
clothed with majesty;
The LORD has clothed and girded
Himself with strength;
Indeed, the world is firmly
established, it will not be moved.
2 Your throne is established
from of old;
You are from everlasting.

3 The floods have lifted up, O LORD,
The floods have lifted up their voice,
The floods lift up their
pounding waves.

⁴ More than the sounds of
many waters,
Than the mighty breakers
of the sea,
The LORD on high is mighty.
⁵ Your testimonies are fully
confirmed;
Holiness befits Your house,
O LORD, forevermore.

Proverbs 22:22-23

²² Do not rob the poor
because he is poor,
Or crush the afflicted at the gate;
²³ For the LORD will plead their case
And take the life of those
who rob them.

Romans 9:14-33

¹⁴ What shall we say then? There is no injustice with God, is there? May it never be! ¹⁵ For He says to Moses, "I WILL HAVE MERCY ON WHOM I HAVE MERCY, AND I WILL HAVE COMPASSION ON WHOM I HAVE COMPASSION." ¹⁶ So then it *does* not *depend* on the man who wills or the man who runs, but on God who has mercy. ¹⁷ For the Scripture says to Pharaoh, "FOR THIS VERY PURPOSE I RAISED YOU UP, TO DEMONSTRATE MY POWER IN YOU, AND THAT MY NAME MIGHT BE PROCLAIMED THROUGHOUT THE WHOLE EARTH." ¹⁸ So then He has mercy on whom He desires, and He hardens whom He desires.

¹⁹ You will say to me then, "Why does He still find fault? For who resists His will?" ²⁰ On the contrary, who are you, O man, who answers back to God? The thing molded will not say to the molder, "Why did you make me like this," will it? ²¹ Or does not the potter have a right over the clay, to make from the same lump one vessel for honorable use

9:20-21 Using the familiar Old Testament analogy of the potter (Is 64:6-8; Jer 18:3-16), Paul argues that it is as irrational, and far more arrogant, for men to question God's choice of certain sinners for salvation, as for a piece of pottery to question the purposes of the potter.

and another for common use? ²² What if God, although willing to demonstrate His wrath and to make His power known, endured with much patience vessels of wrath prepared for destruction? ²³ And *He did so* to make known the riches of His glory upon vessels

9:22-23 These verses are not intended to identify the origin of evil or explain fully why God has allowed it, but they do provide 3 reasons He has permitted its presence and contamination: 1) to demonstrate His wrath; 2) to make His power known; and 3) to put the riches of His glorious mercy on display. No one is treated unfairly; some receive the justice they earn and deserve (6:23), others graciously receive mercy.

of mercy, which He prepared beforehand for glory, ²⁴ *even* us, whom He also called, not from among Jews only, but also from among Gentiles. ²⁵ As He says also in Hosea,

"I WILL CALL THOSE WHO WERE NOT
MY PEOPLE, 'MY PEOPLE,'
AND HER WHO WAS NOT
BELOVED, 'BELOVED.'"
²⁶ "AND IT SHALL BE THAT
IN THE PLACE WHERE IT WAS SAID
TO THEM, 'YOU ARE NOT
MY PEOPLE,'
THERE THEY SHALL BE CALLED
SONS OF THE LIVING GOD."

²⁷ Isaiah cries out concerning Israel, "THOUGH THE NUMBER OF THE SONS OF ISRAEL BE LIKE THE SAND OF THE SEA, IT IS THE REMNANT THAT WILL BE SAVED; ²⁸ FOR THE LORD WILL EXECUTE HIS WORD ON THE EARTH, THOROUGHLY AND QUICKLY." ²⁹ And just as Isaiah foretold,

"UNLESS THE LORD OF SABAOTH
HAD LEFT TO US A POSTERITY,
WE WOULD HAVE BECOME LIKE
SODOM, AND WOULD HAVE
RESEMBLED GOMORRAH."

³⁰ What shall we say then? That Gentiles, who did not pursue righteousness, attained righteousness, even the righteousness which is by faith; ³¹ but Israel, pursuing a law of righteousness, did not arrive at *that* law. ³² Why? Because *they did* not *pursue it* by faith, but as though *it were* by works. They stumbled over the stumbling stone, ³³ just as it is written,

"BEHOLD, I LAY IN ZION A STONE OF
STUMBLING AND A ROCK
OF OFFENSE,
AND HE WHO BELIEVES IN HIM
WILL NOT BE DISAPPOINTED."

Of course, no human being is truly righteous or innocent. The Bible clearly states that all have sinned (Ro 3:23). And all sinners deserve to be punished, eternally. That's what makes God's grace so amazing!

In understanding that truth, however, it must be admitted that on a relative human scale, righteous and innocent people exist. That is, some people are more moral and virtuous than others and some are more innocent. Consider, for example, a person who strives to live out the Golden Rule, or another who gives generously to the poor. And certainly most consider small children to have a naive innocence. So this question could be rephrased: "Why do little children and people who live exemplary lives suffer?"

This question reveals the assumption that there is a direct connection between righteousness and innocence on the one hand and pain-free living on the other. There may be a connection, but it is not direct. Indeed, sin eventually does lead to suffering, but suffering is not an infallible indicator of sin. Job's friends could not see beyond this point. For them, a person's suffering was always an effect whose only cause could be that person's sin.

The righteous and the innocent do indeed suffer for a variety of reasons: 1) Sometimes righteous actions in a sinful world involve suffering—as when a righteous person sacrifices his or her life for another; 2) Sometimes the sins of others involve the righteous in suffering—a child may be deeply hurt as a result of his or her parent's actions; 3) The righteous and innocent are not exempt from the painful situations which arise in life in an imperfect and sinful world—like toothaches and smashed fingers; and 4) People sometimes suffer for no specific reason that can be clarified. Job is a perfect illustration of this last experience.

AUGUST 10

Job 11:1–12:25

11 Then Zophar the Naamathite answered,

2 "Shall a multitude of words
    go unanswered,
And a talkative man be acquitted?
3 "Shall your boasts silence men?
    And shall you scoff and none rebuke?
4 "For you have said, 'My
    teaching is pure,
And I am innocent in your eyes.'
5 "But would that God might speak,
    And open His lips against you,
6 And show you the secrets of wisdom!
    For sound wisdom has two sides.
Know then that God forgets
    a part of your iniquity.

7 "Can you discover the depths of God?
    Can you discover the limits
    of the Almighty?
8 "They are high as the heavens,
    what can you do?
Deeper than Sheol, what
    can you know?
9 "Its measure is longer than
    the earth
And broader than the sea.
10 "If He passes by or shuts up,
    Or calls an assembly, who
    can restrain Him?

11 "For He knows false men,
    And He sees iniquity without
    investigating.
12 "An idiot will become intelligent
    When the foal of a wild
    donkey is born a man.

13 "If you would direct your heart right
    And spread out your hand to Him,
14 If iniquity is in your hand,
    put it far away,
And do not let wickedness
    dwell in your tents;
15 Then, indeed, you could lift up your
    face without *moral* defect,
And you would be steadfast
    and not fear.
16 "For you would forget *your* trouble,
    As waters that have passed by,
    you would remember *it*.
17 "Your life would be brighter
    than noonday;
Darkness would be like the morning.
18 "Then you would trust,
    because there is hope;
And you would look around
    and rest securely.
19 "You would lie down and none
    would disturb *you*,
And many would entreat your favor.
20 "But the eyes of the wicked will fail,
    And there will be no escape for them;
    And their hope is to
    breathe their last."

12 Then Job responded,

2 "Truly then you are the people,
And with you wisdom will die!
3 "But I have intelligence as well as you;
I am not inferior to you.
And who does not know
such things as these?
4 "I am a joke to my friends,
The one who called on God
and He answered him;
The just *and* blameless *man* is a joke.

12:2–4 you are the people...with you wisdom will die! Job responded with cutting sarcasm directed at his know-it-all friends (v. 2) and then reminded them that he understood the principles of which they had spoken (v. 3), but they were irrelevant to his situation. On top of that, he despaired at the pain of becoming a derision to his friends, though he was innocent (v. 4).

---

5 "He who is at ease holds
calamity in contempt,
As prepared for those whose feet slip.
6 "The tents of the destroyers prosper,
And those who provoke
God are secure,
Whom God brings into their power.

7 "But now ask the beasts, and
let them teach you;
And the birds of the heavens,
and let them tell you.
8 "Or speak to the earth, and
let it teach you;
And let the fish of the sea
declare to you.
9 "Who among all these does not know
That the hand of the LORD
has done this,
10 In whose hand is the life of
every living thing,
And the breath of all mankind?
11 "Does not the ear test words,
As the palate tastes its food?
12 "Wisdom is with aged men,
With long life is understanding.

13 "With Him are wisdom and might;
To Him belong counsel and
understanding.
14 "Behold, He tears down, and
it cannot be rebuilt;

He imprisons a man, and
there can be no release.
15 "Behold, He restrains the
waters, and they dry up;
And He sends them out, and
they inundate the earth.
16 "With Him are strength and
sound wisdom,
The misled and the misleader
belong to Him.
17 "He makes counselors walk barefoot
And makes fools of judges.
18 "He loosens the bond of kings
And binds their loins with a girdle.
19 "He makes priests walk barefoot
And overthrows the secure ones.
20 "He deprives the trusted ones of speech
And takes away the discernment
of the elders.
21 "He pours contempt on nobles
And loosens the belt of the strong.
22 "He reveals mysteries from
the darkness
And brings the deep
darkness into light.
23 "He makes the nations great,
then destroys them;
He enlarges the nations, then
leads them away.
24 "He deprives of intelligence the
chiefs of the earth's people
And makes them wander
in a pathless waste.
25 "They grope in darkness with no light,
And He makes them stagger
like a drunken man.

Psalm 94:1–11

O LORD, God of vengeance,
God of vengeance, shine forth!
2 Rise up, O Judge of the earth,
Render recompense to the proud.
3 How long shall the wicked, O LORD,
How long shall the wicked exult?
4 They pour forth *words,* they
speak arrogantly;
All who do wickedness
vaunt themselves.

94:1 God of vengeance. Vengeance from God is not in the sense of uncontrolled vindictiveness, but in the sense of just retribution by the eternal Judge for trespasses against His law. **shine forth!** Make an appearance; he may even be asking for a theophany (Pss 50:2; 80:1).

---

5 They crush Your people, O LORD,
  And afflict Your heritage.
6 They slay the widow and the stranger
  And murder the orphans.
7 They have said, "The LORD
    does not see,
  Nor does the God of Jacob pay heed."

8 Pay heed, you senseless
    among the people;
  And when will you understand,
    stupid ones?
9 He who planted the ear,
    does He not hear?
  He who formed the eye,
    does He not see?
10 He who chastens the nations,
    will He not rebuke,
  Even He who teaches
    man knowledge?
11 The LORD knows the thoughts of man,
  That they are a *mere* breath.

Proverbs 22:24–25

24 Do not associate with a
    man *given* to anger;
  Or go with a hot-tempered man,
25 Or you will learn his ways
  And find a snare for yourself.

Romans 10:1–21

10 Brethren, my heart's desire and my prayer to God for them is for *their* salvation. ²For I testify about them that they have a zeal for God, but not in accordance with knowledge. ³For not knowing about God's righteousness and seeking to establish their own, they did not subject themselves to the righteousness of God. ⁴For Christ is the end of the law for righteousness to everyone who believes.

⁵For Moses writes that the man who

10:4 Christ is the end of the law. Although the Greek word translated "end" can mean either "fulfillment" or "termination," this is not a reference to Christ's having perfectly fulfilled the law through His teaching (Mt 5:17–18) or through His sinless life (2Co 5:21). Instead, as the second half of the verse shows, Paul means that belief in Christ as Lord and Savior ends the sinner's futile quest for righteousness through his imperfect attempts to save himself by efforts to obey the law (3:20–22; Is 64:6; Col 2:13–14).

practices the righteousness which is based on law shall live by that righteousness. ⁶But the righteousness based on faith speaks as follows: "DO NOT SAY IN YOUR HEART, 'WHO WILL ASCEND INTO HEAVEN?' (that is, to bring Christ down), ⁷or 'WHO WILL DESCEND INTO THE ABYSS?' (that is, to bring Christ up from the dead)." ⁸But what does it say? "THE WORD IS NEAR YOU, IN YOUR MOUTH AND IN YOUR HEART"—that is, the word of faith which we are preaching, ⁹that if you confess with your mouth Jesus *as* Lord, and believe in your heart that God raised Him from the dead, you will be saved; ¹⁰for with the heart

10:9 confess...Jesus *as* Lord. Not a simple acknowledgment that He is God and the Lord of the universe, since even demons acknowledge that to be true (Jas 2:19). This is the deep personal conviction, without reservation, that Jesus is that person's own master or sovereign. This phrase includes repenting from sin, trusting in Jesus for salvation, and submitting to Him as Lord. This is the volitional element of faith. **God raised Him from the dead.** Christ's resurrection was the supreme validation of His ministry (Jn 2:18–21). Belief in it is necessary for salvation because it proved that Christ is who He claimed to be and that the Father had accepted His sacrifice in the place of sinners (4:24; see Ac 13:32–33; 1Pe 1:3–4). Without the resurrection, there is no salvation (1Co 15:14–17).

a person believes, resulting in righteousness, and with the mouth he confesses, resulting in salvation. ¹¹For the Scripture says, "WHOEVER BELIEVES IN HIM WILL NOT BE DISAPPOINTED." ¹²For there is no distinction between Jew and Greek; for the same *Lord* is Lord of all, abounding in riches for all who call on Him; ¹³for "WHOEVER WILL CALL ON THE NAME OF THE LORD WILL BE SAVED."

¹⁴How then will they call on Him in whom they have not believed? How will they believe in Him whom they have not heard? And how will they hear without a preacher? ¹⁵How will they preach unless they are sent? Just as it is written, "HOW BEAUTIFUL ARE THE FEET OF THOSE WHO BRING GOOD NEWS OF GOOD THINGS!"

¹⁶However, they did not all heed the good news; for Isaiah says, "LORD, WHO HAS BELIEVED OUR REPORT?" ¹⁷So faith *comes* from hearing, and hearing by the word of Christ.

¹⁸But I say, surely they have never heard, have they? Indeed they have;

> "THEIR VOICE HAS GONE OUT
> INTO ALL THE EARTH,
> AND THEIR WORDS TO THE
> ENDS OF THE WORLD."

[19] But I say, surely Israel did not know, did they? First Moses says,

> "I WILL MAKE YOU JEALOUS BY THAT
> WHICH IS NOT A NATION,
> BY A NATION WITHOUT
> UNDERSTANDING WILL I ANGER YOU."

[20] And Isaiah is very bold and says,

> "I WAS FOUND BY THOSE WHO
> DID NOT SEEK ME,
> I BECAME MANIFEST TO THOSE
> WHO DID NOT ASK FOR ME."

[21] But as for Israel He says, "ALL THE DAY LONG I HAVE STRETCHED OUT MY HANDS TO A DISOBEDIENT AND OBSTINATE PEOPLE."

DAY 10: How was Zophar's argument right and wrong regarding Job's situation?

In Job 11:1–20, Zophar the Naamathite stepped in to interrogate Job. He chose to pound Job with the same law of retaliation. Job must repent, he said, not understanding the reality. He was indignant at Job's protests of innocence. And he moved the allegations against Job to a new level. Not only was Job guilty and unrepentant, he was also an empty talker (vv. 2–3). In fact, Job's long-winded defense of his innocence and God's apparent injustice was sin worthy of rebuke, in Zophar's mind.

In v. 4, Zophar claimed that Job had said, "I am innocent in your eyes." Job never claimed sinlessness; in fact, he acknowledged that he had sinned (7:21; 13:26). But he still maintained his innocence of any great transgression or attitude of unrepentance, affirming his sincerity and integrity as a man of faith and obedience to God. This claim infuriated Zophar (v. 5).

Zophar was correct that Job would have been much wiser if he had only known the unknowable secrets of God (v. 6). In this case, the scene in heaven between God and Satan would have clarified everything. But Job couldn't know the secret wisdom of God (vv. 7–9). Zophar should have applied his point to himself. If God's wisdom was so deep, high, long, and broad, how was it that he could understand it and have all the answers? Like his friends, Zophar thought he understood God and reverted to the same law of retaliation, the sowing and reaping principle, to again indict Job. He implied that Job was wicked (vv. 10–11) and thought he was wise, though actually he was out of control as if he were a "wild donkey" man (v. 12).

Zophar set out 4 steps of Job's repentance in vv. 13–14: 1) devote your heart to God; 2) stretch your hands to Him in prayer for forgiveness; 3) put your sin far away; and 4) don't allow any sin in your tent. If Job did these things, he would be blessed (vv. 15–19). If Job didn't repent, he would die (v. 20). Zophar was right that the life of faith in God is based on penitence and obedience. He was right that God blesses His people with hope, security, and peace. But, like his friends, he was wrong in not understanding that God allows unpredictable and seemingly unfair suffering for reasons not known to us. He was wrong in presuming that the answer for Job was repentance.

AUGUST 11

Job 13:1–14:22

13 "Behold, my eye has seen all *this*,
My ear has heard and understood it.
[2] "What you know I also know;
I am not inferior to you.

[3] "But I would speak to the Almighty,
And I desire to argue with God.
[4] "But you smear with lies;
You are all worthless physicians.
[5] "O that you would be completely silent,
And that it would become
your wisdom!

[6] "Please hear my argument
And listen to the contentions
of my lips.
[7] "Will you speak what is unjust
for God,
And speak what is deceitful for Him?
[8] "Will you show partiality for Him?
Will you contend for God?
[9] "Will it be well when He
examines you?
Or will you deceive Him as
one deceives a man?
[10] "He will surely reprove you
If you secretly show partiality.
[11] "Will not His majesty terrify you,
And the dread of Him fall on you?

12 "Your memorable sayings are
proverbs of ashes,
Your defenses are defenses of clay.

13 "Be silent before me so
that I may speak;
Then let come on me what may.

14 "Why should I take my
flesh in my teeth
And put my life in my hands?

15 "Though He slay me,
I will hope in Him.
Nevertheless I will argue my
ways before Him.

13:15 Though He slay me, I will hope in Him.
Job assured his accusers that his convictions
were not self-serving, because he was ready to
die trusting God. But still he would defend his
innocence before God and was confident that
he was truly saved and not a hypocrite (v. 16).

16 "This also will be my salvation,
For a godless man may not
come before His presence.

17 "Listen carefully to my speech,
And let my declaration *fill* your ears.

18 "Behold now, I have prepared my case;
I know that I will be vindicated.

19 "Who will contend with me?
For then I would be silent and die.

20 "Only two things do not do to me,
Then I will not hide from Your face:

21 Remove Your hand from me,
And let not the dread of You terrify me.

22 "Then call, and I will answer;
Or let me speak, then reply to me.

23 "How many are my iniquities and sins?
Make known to me my
rebellion and my sin.

24 "Why do You hide Your face
And consider me Your enemy?

25 "Will You cause a driven
leaf to tremble?
Or will You pursue the dry chaff?

13:23 How many are my iniquities and sins?
Job wanted to know how many so that he could
determine if his measure of suffering matched
the severity of his sin, and he could then repent
for sins he was unaware of.

26 "For You write bitter things against me
And make me to inherit the
iniquities of my youth.

27 "You put my feet in the stocks
And watch all my paths;
You set a limit for the soles of my feet,

28 While I am decaying like
a rotten thing,
Like a garment that is moth-eaten.

14 "Man, who is born of woman,
Is short-lived and full of turmoil.

2 "Like a flower he comes
forth and withers.
He also flees like a shadow
and does not remain.

3 "You also open Your eyes on him
And bring him into judgment
with Yourself.

4 "Who can make the clean
out of the unclean?
No one!

5 "Since his days are determined,
The number of his months is with You;
And his limits You have set
so that he cannot pass.

6 "Turn Your gaze from him
that he may rest,
Until he fulfills his day
like a hired man.

7 "For there is hope for a tree,
When it is cut down, that it
will sprout again,
And its shoots will not fail.

8 "Though its roots grow
old in the ground
And its stump dies in the dry soil,

9 At the scent of water it will flourish
And put forth sprigs like a plant.

10 "But man dies and lies prostrate.
Man expires, and where is he?

11 "*As* water evaporates from the sea,
And a river becomes parched
and dried up,

12 So man lies down and does not rise.
Until the heavens are no longer,
He will not awake nor be
aroused out of his sleep.

13 "Oh that You would hide me in Sheol,
That You would conceal me until
Your wrath returns *to You*,
That You would set a limit for
me and remember me!

14 "If a man dies, will he live *again?*
All the days of my struggle I will wait
Until my change comes.

¹⁵ "You will call, and I will answer You;
You will long for the work
of Your hands.
¹⁶ "For now You number my steps,
You do not observe my sin.
¹⁷ "My transgression is sealed
up in a bag,
And You wrap up my iniquity.
¹⁸ "But the falling mountain
crumbles away,
And the rock moves from its place;
¹⁹ Water wears away stones,
Its torrents wash away the
dust of the earth;
So You destroy man's hope.
²⁰ "You forever overpower him
and he departs;
You change his appearance
and send him away.
²¹ "His sons achieve honor, but
he does not know it;
Or they become insignificant,
but he does not perceive it.
²² "But his body pains him,
And he mourns only for himself."

Psalm 94:12–19

¹² Blessed is the man whom
You chasten, O LORD,
And whom You teach out of Your law;
¹³ That You may grant him relief
from the days of adversity,
Until a pit is dug for the wicked.
¹⁴ For the LORD will not
abandon His people,
Nor will He forsake His inheritance.
¹⁵ For judgment will again be righteous,
And all the upright in
heart will follow it.
¹⁶ Who will stand up for me
against evildoers?
Who will take his stand for me
against those who do wickedness?

94:14 will not abandon His people. God has a permanent commitment to His people, Israel, established through a covenant based on His abiding love (Ge 15; Jer 12:15; Mic 7:18). This important truth serves as a doctrinal basis for Pss 93–100 and was intended to encourage the nation during difficult times. Paul refers to this in Romans 11:1 as he assures the future salvation of Israel.

¹⁷ If the LORD had not been my help,
My soul would soon have dwelt
in the abode of silence.
¹⁸ If I should say, "My foot has
slipped,"
Your lovingkindness, O LORD,
will hold me up.
¹⁹ When my anxious thoughts
multiply within me,
Your consolations delight
my soul.

Proverbs 22:26–27

²⁶ Do not be among those
who give pledges,
Among those who become
guarantors for debts.
²⁷ If you have nothing with which
to pay,
Why should he take your
bed from under you?

Romans 11:1–16

11 I say then, God has not rejected His people, has He? May it never be! For I too am an Israelite, a descendant of Abraham, of the tribe of Benjamin. ² God has not rejected His people whom He foreknew. Or

11:1 rejected. To thrust away from oneself. The form of the question in the Greek text expects a negative answer. Despite Israel's disobedience (9:1–13; 10:14–21), God has not rejected His people (1Sa 12:22; 1Ki 6:13; Pss 89:31–37; 94:14; Is 49:15; 54:1–10; Jer 33:19–26). **May it never be!** The strongest form of negation in Greek.

do you not know what the Scripture says in the passage about Elijah, how he pleads with God against Israel? ³ "Lord, THEY HAVE KILLED YOUR PROPHETS, THEY HAVE TORN DOWN YOUR ALTARS, AND I ALONE AM LEFT, AND THEY ARE SEEKING MY LIFE." ⁴ But what is the divine response to him? "I HAVE KEPT for Myself SEVEN THOUSAND MEN WHO HAVE NOT BOWED THE KNEE TO BAAL." ⁵ In the same way then, there has also come to be at the present time a remnant according to God's gracious choice. ⁶ But if it is by grace, it is no longer on the basis of works, otherwise grace is no longer grace.

⁷ What then? What Israel is seeking, it has not obtained, but those who were chosen obtained it, and the rest were hardened; ⁸ just as it is written,

"GOD GAVE THEM A SPIRIT OF STUPOR,
EYES TO SEE NOT AND EARS
TO HEAR NOT,
DOWN TO THIS VERY DAY."

⁹ And David says,

"LET THEIR TABLE BECOME A
SNARE AND A TRAP,
AND A STUMBLING BLOCK AND
A RETRIBUTION TO THEM.
¹⁰ "LET THEIR EYES BE DARKENED
TO SEE NOT,
AND BEND THEIR BACKS FOREVER."

¹¹ I say then, they did not stumble so as to fall, did they? May it never be! But by their transgression salvation *has come* to the Gentiles, to make them jealous. ¹² Now if their transgression is riches for the world and their failure is riches for the Gentiles, how much more will their fulfillment be! ¹³ But I am speaking to you who are Gentiles. Inasmuch then as I am an apostle of Gentiles, I magnify my ministry, ¹⁴ if somehow I might move to jealousy my fellow countrymen and

11:17 branches were broken off. Some, but not all, of the branches of Israel were removed; God always preserved a believing remnant (vv. 3–4). **a wild olive…grafted in.** Olives were an important crop in the ancient world. Although trees often lived for hundreds of years, individual branches eventually stopped producing olives. When that happened, branches from younger trees were grafted in to restore productivity. Paul's point is that the old, unproductive branches (Israel) were broken off and branches from a wild olive tree (Gentiles) were grafted in. **rich root.** Once grafted in, Gentiles partake of the richness of God's covenant blessings as the spiritual heirs of Abraham (4:11; Gal 3:29). **the olive tree.** The place of divine blessing; God's covenant of salvation made with Abraham (Ge 12:1–3; 15:1–21; 17:1–27).

save some of them. ¹⁵ For if their rejection is the reconciliation of the world, what will *their* acceptance be but life from the dead? ¹⁶ If the first piece *of dough* is holy, the lump is also; and if the root is holy, the branches are too.

DAY 11: What kind of relationship did Job have with God?

Job's biography begins with a 4-part description of his character: "blameless, upright, fearing God and turning away from evil" (1:1). He prayed for his children and was concerned about their relationship with God (v. 5). He was successful and wealthy—the stereotype of a blessed man. In fact, God adds His own glowing approval of Job, using the same traits that open the book (v. 8).

Faced with the sudden, crushing loss of everything—children, servants, herds—Job's initial response was to grieve and recognize God's sovereignty. "'The LORD gave and the LORD has taken away. Blessed be the name of the Lord.' Through all this Job did not sin nor did he blame God" (vv. 21–22).

Under the harsh judgments of his friends, Job eventually struggled to understand why God seemed unwilling to settle matters. Once God did speak, at least part of Job's problem becomes clear—he confused a relationship with God with familiarity with God. The Lord did not rebuke Job's faith or sincerity; instead, God questioned Job's insistence on an answer for his difficulties. By allowing Job to hear just a little of the extent of his ignorance, God showed Job that there was a great deal of knowledge he would never understand. As a creature, Job simply had no right to demand an answer from his Creator. Job's final words are filled with humility and repentance: "I have heard of You by the hearing of the ear; but now my eye sees You; therefore I retract, and I repent in dust and ashes." (42:5–6).

Job spent his last days enjoying the same kind of relationship he had earlier with God. He prayed for his friends and raised another family of godly children. He lived a full life.

AUGUST 12

Job 15:1–16:22

15 Then Eliphaz the Temanite responded,

² "Should a wise man answer
with windy knowledge

And fill himself with the east wind?
³ "Should he argue with useless
talk,
Or with words which are
not profitable?
⁴ "Indeed, you do away with
reverence
And hinder meditation before God.

5 "For your guilt teaches your mouth,
   And you choose the language
      of the crafty.
6 "Your own mouth condemns
      you, and not I;
   And your own lips testify against you.

7 "Were you the first man to be born,
   Or were you brought forth
      before the hills?
8 "Do you hear the secret counsel of God,
   And limit wisdom to yourself?
9 "What do you know that
      we do not know?
   What do you understand
      that we do not?
10 "Both the gray-haired and the
      aged are among us,
   Older than your father.
11 "Are the consolations of God
      too small for you,
   Even the word *spoken*
      gently with you?
12 "Why does your heart carry you away?
   And why do your eyes flash,
13 That you should turn your
      spirit against God
   And allow *such* words to go
      out of your mouth?
14 "What is man, that he should be pure,
   Or he who is born of a woman,
      that he should be righteous?
15 "Behold, He puts no trust
      in His holy ones,
   And the heavens are not
      pure in His sight;
16 How much less one who is
      detestable and corrupt,
   Man, who drinks iniquity like water!

15:14–16 A strong statement with regard to the sinfulness of man (Ro 3:23), which attacked Job's claim to righteousness. Verse 15 refers to holy angels who fell and brought impurity into the heavens (Rev 12:1–4). The truth is accurate, that all men are sinners—but irrelevant in Job's case, because his suffering was not due to any sin.

---

17 "I will tell you, listen to me;
   And what I have seen I
      will also declare;
18 What wise men have told,
   And have not concealed
      from their fathers,

19 To whom alone the land was given,
   And no alien passed among them.
20 "The wicked man writhes
      in pain all *his* days,
   And numbered are the years
      stored up for the ruthless.
21 "Sounds of terror are in his ears;
   While at peace the destroyer
      comes upon him.
22 "He does not believe that he will
      return from darkness,
   And he is destined for the sword.
23 "He wanders about for food,
      saying, 'Where is it?'
   He knows that a day of
      darkness is at hand.
24 "Distress and anguish terrify him,
   They overpower him like a
      king ready for the attack,
25 Because he has stretched out
      his hand against God
   And conducts himself arrogantly
      against the Almighty.
26 "He rushes headlong at Him
   With his massive shield.
27 "For he has covered his
      face with his fat
   And made his thighs heavy with flesh.
28 "He has lived in desolate cities,
   In houses no one would inhabit,
   Which are destined to become ruins.
29 "He will not become rich, nor
      will his wealth endure;
   And his grain will not bend
      down to the ground.
30 "He will not escape from darkness;
   The flame will wither his shoots,
   And by the breath of His
      mouth he will go away.
31 "Let him not trust in emptiness,
      deceiving himself;
   For emptiness will be his reward.
32 "It will be accomplished
      before his time,
   And his palm branch will
      not be green.
33 "He will drop off his unripe
      grape like the vine,
   And will cast off his flower
      like the olive tree.
34 "For the company of the
      godless is barren,
   And fire consumes the
      tents of the corrupt.
35 "They conceive mischief and
      bring forth iniquity,
   And their mind prepares
      deception."

16

Then Job answered,

2 "I have heard many such things;
Sorry comforters are you all.
3 "Is there no limit to windy words?
Or what plagues you that you answer?
4 "I too could speak like you,
If I were in your place.
I could compose words against you
And shake my head at you.
5 "I could strengthen you
with my mouth,
And the solace of my lips
could lessen your pain.
6 "If I speak, my pain is not lessened,
And if I hold back, what has left me?
7 "But now He has exhausted me;
You have laid waste all my company.
8 "You have shriveled me up,
It has become a witness;
And my leanness rises up against me,
It testifies to my face.
9 "His anger has torn me and
hunted me down,
He has gnashed at me with His teeth;
My adversary glares at me.
10 "They have gaped at me
with their mouth,
They have slapped me on the
cheek with contempt;
They have massed themselves
against me.
11 "God hands me over to ruffians
And tosses me into the
hands of the wicked.
12 "I was at ease, but He shattered me,
And He has grasped me by the
neck and shaken me to pieces;
He has also set me up as His target.
13 "His arrows surround me.
Without mercy He splits
my kidneys open;
He pours out my gall on the ground.
14 "He breaks through me with
breach after breach;
He runs at me like a warrior.
15 "I have sewed sackcloth over my skin
And thrust my horn in the dust.
16 "My face is flushed from weeping,
And deep darkness is on my eyelids,
17 Although there is no violence
in my hands,
And my prayer is pure.
18 "O earth, do not cover my blood,
And let there be no resting
place for my cry.

19 "Even now, behold, my
witness is in heaven,
And my advocate is on high.
20 "My friends are my scoffers;
My eye weeps to God.
21 "O that a man might plead with God
As a man with his neighbor!
22 "For when a few years are past,
I shall go the way of no return.

Psalm 94:20–23

20 Can a throne of destruction
be allied with You,
One which devises mischief by decree?
21 They band themselves together
against the life of the righteous
And condemn the innocent to death.
22 But the LORD has been my stronghold,
And my God the rock of my refuge.
23 He has brought back their
wickedness upon them
And will destroy them in their evil;
The LORD our God will destroy them.

Proverbs 22:28–29

28 Do not move the ancient boundary
Which your fathers have set.

29 Do you see a man skilled in his work?
He will stand before kings;
He will not stand before obscure men.

Romans 11:17–36

17 But if some of the branches were broken off, and you, being a wild olive, were grafted in among them and became partaker with them of the rich root of the olive tree, 18 do not be arrogant toward the branches; but if you are arrogant, remember that it is not you who supports the root, but the root supports you. 19 You will say then, "Branches were broken off so that I might be grafted in." 20 Quite right, they were broken off for their unbelief, but you stand by your faith. Do not be conceited, but fear; 21 for if God did not spare the natural branches, He will not spare

11:20 unbelief...faith. Branches were broken off and others grafted in based solely on the issue of faith, not race, ethnicity, social or intellectual background, or external morality. Salvation is ever and always by faith alone (1:16–17; Eph 2:8–9). **fear.** (See 1Co 10:12; 2Co 13:5.) God will judge the apostate church (Rev 2:15–16; 3:16) just as surely as He judged apostate Israel.

you, either. ²²Behold then the kindness and severity of God; to those who fell, severity, but to you, God's kindness, if you continue in His kindness; otherwise you also will be cut off. ²³And they also, if they do not continue in their unbelief, will be grafted in, for God is able to graft them in again. ²⁴For if you were

11:22 Behold then the kindness and severity. All of God's attributes work in harmony; there is no conflict between His goodness and love, and His justice and wrath. Those who accept His gracious offer of salvation experience His goodness (2:4); those who reject it experience His severity (2:5). **those who fell.** The unbelieving Jews described in vv. 12–21. "Fell" translates a Greek word meaning "to fall so as to be completely ruined." Those who reject God's offer of salvation bring upon themselves utter spiritual ruin. **if you continue.** Genuine saving faith always perseveres (Jn 8:31; 15:5–6; Col 1:22–23; Heb 3:12–14; 4:11; 1Jn 2:19). **cut off.** God will deal swiftly and severely with those who reject Him.

cut off from what is by nature a wild olive tree, and were grafted contrary to nature into a cultivated olive tree, how much more will these who are the natural *branches* be grafted into their own olive tree?

²⁵For I do not want you, brethren, to be uninformed of this mystery—so that you will not be wise in your own estimation—that a partial hardening has happened to Israel until the fullness of the Gentiles has come in; ²⁶and so all Israel will be saved; just as it is written,

"THE DELIVERER WILL COME FROM ZION,
HE WILL REMOVE UNGODLINESS
FROM JACOB."
²⁷"THIS IS MY COVENANT WITH THEM,
WHEN I TAKE AWAY THEIR SINS."

²⁸From the standpoint of the gospel they are enemies for your sake, but from the standpoint of *God's* choice they are beloved for the sake of the fathers; ²⁹for the gifts and the calling of God are irrevocable. ³⁰For just as you once were disobedient to God, but now have been shown mercy because of their disobedience, ³¹so these also now have been disobedient, that because of the mercy shown to you they also may now be shown mercy. ³²For God has shut up all in disobedience so that He may show mercy to all.

³³Oh, the depth of the riches both of the wisdom and knowledge of God! How unsearchable are His judgments and unfathomable His ways! ³⁴For WHO HAS KNOWN THE MIND OF THE LORD, OR WHO BECAME HIS counselor? ³⁵Or WHO HAS FIRST GIVEN TO HIM THAT IT MIGHT BE PAID BACK TO HIM AGAIN? ³⁶For from Him and through Him and to Him are all things. To Him *be* the glory forever. Amen.

11:33 wisdom. See Psalm 104:24; Daniel 2:20; Ephesians 3:10; Revelation 7:12. **knowledge.** God's omniscience (1Sa 2:3; 1Ki 8:39; Pss 44:21; 147:5). **judgments.** God's purposes or decrees, which are beyond human understanding (Ps 36:6). **ways.** The methods God chooses to accomplish His purposes (Job 5:9; 9:10; 26:14).

DAY 12: How did Job's friends fail him?

"I have heard many such things; sorry comforters are you all" (Job 16:1). Job's friends had come to comfort him. In spite of 7 blissful days of silence at the outset, their mission had failed miserably, and their comfort had turned into more torment for Job. What started out as Eliphaz's sincere efforts to help Job understand his dilemma had turned into rancor and sarcasm. In the end, their haranguing had heightened the frustrations of all parties involved. If the matter were reversed and Job was comforter to his friends, he would never treat them as they have treated him. He would have strengthened and comforted them.

"His anger has torn me and hunted me down, He has gnashed at me with His teeth" (v. 9). "I was at ease, but He shattered me" (v. 12). These poignant thoughts from Job lamented his suffering as severe judgment from God, who had worn him out, withered his strength, and chewed him up by severe scrutiny ("glares at me," v. 9). Job refers to God as "my adversary," who had shattered, shaken, shot at, and sliced him (vv. 12–14).

He had no one to turn to in his sorrow, except God (v. 19), who was silent and had not vindicated him. "My friends are my scoffers" (v. 20), when they should have comforted him. "O that a man might plead with God" (v. 21). The pleading would be for a verdict of innocence on behalf of a friend or neighbor in a court setting before the judge/king. God anticipated the need of an advocate, and He has provided One in the Person of the Lord Jesus Christ (1Ti 2:5; 1Jn 2:1–2).

AUGUST 13

Job 17:1–18:21

17 "My spirit is broken, my days
are extinguished,
The grave is *ready* for me.

2 "Surely mockers are with me,
And my eye gazes on
their provocation.

3 "Lay down, now, a pledge for
me with Yourself;
Who is there that will be
my guarantor?

4 "For You have kept their heart
from understanding,
Therefore You will not exalt *them*.

5 "He who informs against friends
for a share *of the spoil*,
The eyes of his children
also will languish.

6 "But He has made me a
byword of the people,
And I am one at whom men spit.

7 "My eye has also grown dim
because of grief,
And all my members are as
a shadow.

8 "The upright will be appalled at this,
And the innocent will stir up
himself against the godless.

9 "Nevertheless the righteous
will hold to his way,
And he who has clean hands will
grow stronger and stronger.

10 "But come again all of you now,
For I do not find a wise
man among you.

11 "My days are past, my plans
are torn apart,
Even the wishes of my heart.

12 "They make night into day, *saying,*
'The light is near,' in the
presence of darkness.

13 "If I look for Sheol as my home,
I make my bed in the darkness;

14 If I call to the pit, 'You are
my father';
To the worm, 'my mother
and my sister';

15 Where now is my hope?
And who regards my hope?

16 "Will it go down with me
to Sheol?
Shall we together go down
into the dust?"

18 Then Bildad the Shuhite responded,

2 "How long will you hunt for words?
Show understanding and
then we can talk.

3 "Why are we regarded as beasts,
As stupid in your eyes?

4 "O you who tear yourself
in your anger—
For your sake is the earth
to be abandoned,
Or the rock to be moved
from its place?

5 "Indeed, the light of the
wicked goes out,
And the flame of his fire
gives no light.

6 "The light in his tent is darkened,
And his lamp goes out above him.

7 "His vigorous stride is shortened,
And his own scheme
brings him down.

8 "For he is thrown into the
net by his own feet,
And he steps on the webbing.

9 "A snare seizes *him* by the heel,
And a trap snaps shut on him.

10 "A noose for him is hidden
in the ground,
And a trap for him on the path.

11 "All around terrors frighten him,
And harry him at every step.

12 "His strength is famished,
And calamity is ready at his side.

13 "His skin is devoured by disease,
The firstborn of death
devours his limbs.

14 "He is torn from the security
of his tent,
And they march him before
the king of terrors.

15 "There dwells in his tent
nothing of his;
Brimstone is scattered on
his habitation.

16 "His roots are dried below,
And his branch is cut off above.

17 "Memory of him perishes
from the earth,
And he has no name abroad.

18 "He is driven from light into darkness,
And chased from the inhabited world.

19 "He has no offspring or posterity
among his people,
Nor any survivor where he sojourned.

20 "Those in the west are
appalled at his fate,

And those in the east are
seized with horror.
21 "Surely such are the dwellings
of the wicked,
And this is the place of him
who does not know God."

Psalm 95:1–5

O come, let us sing for joy
to the LORD,
Let us shout joyfully to the
rock of our salvation.
2 Let us come before His presence
with thanksgiving,
Let us shout joyfully to
Him with psalms.
3 For the LORD is a great God
And a great King above all gods,
4 In whose hand are the
depths of the earth,
The peaks of the mountains
are His also.
5 The sea is His, for it was
He who made it,
And His hands formed the
dry land.

95:1 rock of our salvation. This metaphor for
God was especially appropriate in this psalm,
which refers (vv. 8–9) to the water that came
from the rock in the wilderness (Ex 17:1–7; Nu
20:1–13; 1Co 10:4).

95:3 a great King above all gods. This is a
poetic way of denying the existence of other
gods (96:5), which existed only as statues, not
persons (Jer 10:1–10).

95:4 depths of the earth. This refers to the
depths of the seas, valleys, and caverns, and
contrasts with the hills. The point (v. 5) is that
God was not a local god like the imaginary
gods of the heathens, usually put up in high
places, but the universal Creator and Ruler of
the whole earth.

Proverbs 23:1–3

23 When you sit down to
dine with a ruler,
Consider carefully what is
before you,
2 And put a knife to your throat
If you are a man of *great* appetite.
3 Do not desire his delicacies,
For it is deceptive food.

Romans 12:1–21

12 Therefore I urge you, brethren, by the
mercies of God, to present your bodies
a living and holy sacrifice, acceptable to God,
which is your spiritual service of worship.
2 And do not be conformed to this world,
but be transformed by the renewing of
your mind, so that you may prove what the will
of God is, that which is good and acceptable
and perfect.
3 For through the grace given to me I say
to everyone among you not to think more

12:1 present your bodies a living…sacrifice.
Under the Old Covenant, God accepted the sacrifices of dead animals. But because of Christ's
ultimate sacrifice, the Old Testament sacrifices
are no longer of any effect (Heb 9:11–12). For
those in Christ, the only acceptable worship is to
offer themselves completely to the Lord. Under
God's control, the believer's yet-unredeemed
body can and must be yielded to Him as an
instrument of righteousness. **spiritual service.**
In light of all the spiritual riches believers enjoy
solely as the fruit of God's mercies (Ro 11:33,
36), it logically follows that they owe God their
highest form of service. Understood here is the
idea of priestly, spiritual service, which was such
an integral part of Old Testament worship.

12:2 do not be conformed. "Conformed" refers
to assuming an outward expression that does
not reflect what is really inside, a kind of mas-
querade or act. The word's form implies that
Paul's readers were already allowing this to happen and must stop. **this world.** Better translated
"age," which refers to the system of beliefs, values—or the spirit of the age—at any time current
in the world. This sum of contemporary thinking and values forms the moral atmosphere of
our world and is always dominated by Satan
(2Co 4:4). **transformed.** The Greek word, from
which the Eng. word "metamorphosis" comes,
connotes a change in outward appearance.
Matthew uses the same word to describe the
Transfiguration (Mt 17:2). Just as Christ briefly
and in a limited way displayed outwardly His
inner, divine nature and glory at the Transfiguration, Christians should outwardly manifest
their inner, redeemed natures, not once, however, but daily (2Co 3:18; Eph 5:18). **renewing
of your mind.** That kind of transformation can
occur only as the Holy Spirit changes our thinking through consistent study and meditation
of Scripture (Ps 119:11; see Col 1:28; 3:10, 16; Php
4:8). The renewed mind is one saturated with
and controlled by the Word of God.

highly of himself than he ought to think; but to think so as to have sound judgment, as God has allotted to each a measure of faith. ⁴For just as we have many members in one body and all the members do not have the same function, ⁵so we, who are many, are one body in Christ, and individually members one of another. ⁶Since we have gifts that differ according to the grace given to us, *each of us is to exercise them accordingly:* if prophecy, according to the proportion of his faith; ⁷if service, in his serving; or he who teaches, in his teaching; ⁸or he who exhorts, in his exhortation; he who gives, with liberality; he who leads, with diligence; he who shows mercy, with cheerfulness.

⁹*Let* love *be* without hypocrisy. Abhor what is evil; cling to what is good. ¹⁰*Be* devoted to one another in brotherly love; give preference to one another in honor; ¹¹not lagging behind in diligence, fervent in spirit, serving the Lord; ¹²rejoicing in hope, persevering in tribulation, devoted to prayer, ¹³contributing to the needs of the saints, practicing hospitality.

¹⁴Bless those who persecute you; bless and do not curse. ¹⁵Rejoice with those who rejoice, and weep with those who weep. ¹⁶Be of the same mind toward one another; do not be haughty in mind, but associate with the lowly. Do not be wise in your own estimation. ¹⁷Never pay back evil for evil to anyone. Respect what is right in the sight of all men. ¹⁸If possible, so far as it depends on you, be at peace with all men. ¹⁹Never take your own revenge, beloved, but leave room for the wrath *of God,* for it is written, "VENGEANCE IS MINE, I WILL REPAY," says the Lord. ²⁰"BUT IF YOUR ENEMY IS HUNGRY, FEED HIM, AND IF HE IS THIRSTY, GIVE HIM A DRINK; FOR IN SO DOING YOU WILL HEAP BURNING COALS ON HIS HEAD." ²¹Do not be overcome by evil, but overcome evil with good.

DAY 13: How has God gifted believers to fulfill His purposes?

Romans 12:6–8 describes the general categories of spiritual gifts. These come to us "according to the grace given"—undeserved and unmerited. The gift itself (1Co 12:4), the specific way in which it is used (1Co 12:5), and the spiritual results (1Co 12:6) are all sovereignly chosen by the Spirit completely apart from personal merit (1Co 12:11).

"Prophecy." This Greek word means "speaking forth" and does not necessarily include prediction of the future or any other mystical or supernatural aspects. Although some prophets in Acts did make predictions of future events (11:27–28; 21:10–11), others made no predictions but spoke the truth of God to encourage and strengthen their hearers (15:32; vv. 22–31). The evidence does suggest, however, that in the first century, before the New Testament was complete and the sign gifts had ceased (1Co 13:8; 2Co 12:12; Heb 2:3, 4), this word may have had both nonrevelatory and revelatory facets. In its nonrevelatory sense, the word "prophecy" simply identifies the skill of public proclamation of the word of God (1Co 14:3, 24–25; 1Pe 4:11). "According to the proportion of his faith." Literally, "the faith," or the fully revealed message or body of Christian faith (Jude 3; 2Ti 4:2). The preacher must be careful to preach the same message the apostles delivered.

"Service" (v. 7). From the same Greek word as "deacon" comes from, it refers to those who serve. This gift, similar to the gift of helps (1Co 12:28), has broad application to include every kind of practical help (Ac 20:35; 1Co 12:28). "Teaching." The ability to interpret, clarify, systematize, and explain God's truth clearly (Ac 18:24–25; 2Ti 2:2). Pastors must have the gift of teaching (1Ti 3:2; Titus 1:9; 1Ti 4:16); but many mature, qualified laymen also have this gift. This differs from preaching (prophecy), not in content, but in the unique skill for public proclamation.

"Exhortation" (v. 8). The gift which enables a believer to effectively call others to obey and follow God's truth. It may be used negatively to admonish and correct regarding sin (2Ti 4:2) or positively to encourage, comfort, and strengthen struggling believers (2Co 1:3–5; Heb 10:24–25). "Gives, with liberality." This denotes the sacrificial sharing and giving of one's resources and self to meet the needs of others (2Co 8:3–5, 9; 11; Eph 4:28). The believer who gives with a proper attitude does not do so for thanks and personal recognition, but to glorify God (Mt 6:2; Ac 2:44–45; 4:37–5:11; 2Co 8:2–5). "Leads." Literally, "standing before." Paul calls this gift "administrations" (1Co 12:28), a word that means "to guide" and is used of the person who steers a ship (Ac 27:11; Rev 18:17). Again, the church's leaders must exercise this gift, but it is certainly not limited to them. "Shows mercy, with cheerfulness." One who actively shows sympathy and sensitivity to those in suffering and sorrow and who has both the willingness and the resources to help lessen their afflictions. Frequently, this gift accompanies the gift of exhortation. This attitude is crucial to ensure that the gift of mercy becomes a genuine help, not a discouraging commiseration with those who are suffering (Pr 14:21, 31; Lk 4:18–19).

AUGUST 14

Job 19:1–20:29

19 Then Job responded,

2 "How long will you torment me
And crush me with words?

3 "These ten times you have insulted me;
You are not ashamed to wrong me.

4 "Even if I have truly erred,
My error lodges with me.

5 "If indeed you vaunt
yourselves against me
And prove my disgrace to me,

6 Know then that God has wronged me
And has closed His net around me.

7 "Behold, I cry, 'Violence!'
but I get no answer;
I shout for help, but there
is no justice.

8 "He has walled up my way so
that I cannot pass,
And He has put darkness
on my paths.

9 "He has stripped my honor from me
And removed the crown
from my head.

10 "He breaks me down on every
side, and I am gone;
And He has uprooted my
hope like a tree.

11 "He has also kindled His
anger against me
And considered me as His enemy.

12 "His troops come together,
And build up their way against me
And camp around my tent.

13 "He has removed my brothers
far from me,
And my acquaintances are
completely estranged from me.

14 "My relatives have failed,
And my intimate friends
have forgotten me.

15 "Those who live in my house and my
maids consider me a stranger.
I am a foreigner in their sight.

16 "I call to my servant, but he
does not answer;
I have to implore him with my mouth.

17 "My breath is offensive to my wife,
And I am loathsome to
my own brothers.

18 "Even young children despise me;
I rise up and they speak against me.

19 "All my associates abhor me,
And those I love have
turned against me.

20 "My bone clings to my skin
and my flesh,
And I have escaped *only* by
the skin of my teeth.

21 "Pity me, pity me, O you my friends,
For the hand of God has struck me.

22 "Why do you persecute
me as God *does,*
And are not satisfied with my flesh?

23 "Oh that my words were written!
Oh that they were inscribed in a book!

24 "That with an iron stylus and lead
They were engraved in
the rock forever!

25 "As for me, I know that my
Redeemer lives,
And at the last He will take
His stand on the earth.

26 "Even after my skin is destroyed,
Yet from my flesh I shall see God;

27 Whom I myself shall behold,
And whom my eyes will
see and not another.
My heart faints within me!

28 "If you say, 'How shall we
persecute him?'
And 'What pretext for a case
against him can we find?'

29 "*Then* be afraid of the sword
for yourselves,

19:20 skin of my teeth. This was the origin of a common slang phrase, referring to skin that is thin and fragile. The idea is that he had escaped death by a very slim margin. The loss of all his family and the abuse of his friends were added to the terror of God-forsakenness that had gripped him.

19:23–29 At the point of Job's greatest despair, his faith appeared at its highest as he confidently affirmed that God was his Redeemer. He wanted that confidence in the record for all to know (vv. 23–24). Job wished that the activities of his life were put into words and "engraved in the rock," so all would know that he had not sinned to the magnitude of his suffering. God granted his prayer. God was his Redeemer (Ex 6:6; Pss 19:14; 72:14; Is 43:14; 47:4; 49:26; Jer 50:34), who would vindicate him in that last day of judgment on the earth when justice was finally done (Jer 12:1–3; Jn 5:25, 29; Rev 20:11–15).

For wrath *brings* the
punishment of the sword,
So that you may know
there is judgment."

20 Then Zophar the Naamathite answered,

2 "Therefore my disquieting
thoughts make me respond,
Even because of my inward
agitation.
3 "I listened to the reproof
which insults me,
And the spirit of my understanding
makes me answer.
4 "Do you know this from of old,
From the establishment
of man on earth,
5 That the triumphing of the
wicked is short,
And the joy of the godless
momentary?
6 "Though his loftiness reaches
the heavens,
And his head touches the clouds,
7 He perishes forever like
his refuse;
Those who have seen him
will say, 'Where is he?'
8 "He flies away like a dream, and
they cannot find him;
Even like a vision of the night
he is chased away.
9 "The eye which saw him
sees him no longer,
And his place no longer
beholds him.
10 "His sons favor the poor,
And his hands give back his
wealth.
11 "His bones are full of his youthful
vigor,
But it lies down with him in
the dust.

12 "Though evil is sweet in his mouth
And he hides it under his tongue,
13 *Though* he desires it and
will not let it go,
But holds it in his mouth,
14 *Yet* his food in his stomach is
changed
To the venom of cobras within him.
15 "He swallows riches,
But will vomit them up;
God will expel them from his belly.
16 "He sucks the poison of cobras;
The viper's tongue slays him.

17 "He does not look at the streams,
The rivers flowing with
honey and curds.
18 "He returns what he has attained
And cannot swallow *it;*
As to the riches of his trading,
He cannot even enjoy *them.*
19 "For he has oppressed *and*
forsaken the poor;
He has seized a house which
he has not built.

20 "Because he knew no quiet
within him,
He does not retain anything
he desires.
21 "Nothing remains for him to
devour,
Therefore his prosperity
does not endure.
22 "In the fullness of his plenty
he will be cramped;
The hand of everyone who suffers
will come *against* him.
23 "When he fills his belly,
God will send His fierce anger
on him
And will rain *it* on him
while he is eating.
24 "He may flee from the iron
weapon,
But the bronze bow will pierce him.
25 "It is drawn forth and comes
out of his back,
Even the glittering point
from his gall.
Terrors come upon him,
26 Complete darkness is held in
reserve for his treasures,
And unfanned fire will devour him;
It will consume the
survivor in his tent.
27 "The heavens will reveal his iniquity,
And the earth will rise
up against him.
28 "The increase of his house will depart;
His possessions will flow away
in the day of His anger.
29 "This is the wicked man's
portion from God,
Even the heritage decreed
to him by God."

Psalm 95:6–11

6 Come, let us worship and
bow down,
Let us kneel before the
LORD our Maker.

7 For He is our God,
And we are the people of His pasture
and the sheep of His hand.
Today, if you would hear His voice,
8 Do not harden your hearts,
as at Meribah,
As in the day of Massah
in the wilderness,
9 "When your fathers tested Me,
They tried Me, though they
had seen My work.

95:9 tested Me. This is a reference to the same event (v. 8), also called "Massah" (translated "testing"), when God brought water out of the rock (Ex 17:7; Dt 6:16; 9:22; 33:8). The writer to the Hebrews applies the principle of this event to his readers, suggesting that their inclination to doubt the Lord and return to Judaism was parallel with their fathers' inclination to doubt the Lord and go back to Egypt.

10 "For forty years I loathed
that generation,
And said they are a people
who err in their heart,
And they do not know My ways.
11 "Therefore I swore in My anger,
Truly they shall not enter
into My rest."

Proverbs 23:4–5

4 Do not weary yourself to gain wealth,
Cease from your consideration *of it.*
5 When you set your eyes
on it, it is gone.
For *wealth* certainly
makes itself wings
Like an eagle that flies
toward the heavens.

23:4–5 Rather than wearing oneself out pursuing wealth, pursue the wisdom of God and what glorifies Him, and He will bless with prosperity as He chooses.

Romans 13:1–14

13 Every person is to be in subjection to the governing authorities. For there is no authority except from God, and those which exist are established by God. 2 Therefore whoever resists authority has opposed the ordinance of God; and they who have opposed will receive condemnation upon themselves. 3 For rulers are not a cause of fear for good behavior, but for evil. Do you want to have no fear of authority? Do what is good and you will have praise from the same; 4 for it is a minister of God to you for good. But if you do what is evil, be afraid; for it does not bear the sword for nothing; for it is a minister of God, an avenger who brings wrath on the one who practices evil. 5 Therefore it is necessary to be in subjection, not only because of wrath, but also for conscience' sake. 6 For because of this you also pay taxes, for *rulers* are servants of God, devoting themselves to this very thing. 7 Render to all what is due them: tax to whom tax *is* due; custom to whom custom; fear to whom fear; honor to whom honor.

8 Owe nothing to anyone except to love one another; for he who loves his neighbor has fulfilled *the* law. 9 For this, "YOU SHALL NOT COMMIT ADULTERY, YOU SHALL NOT MURDER, YOU SHALL NOT STEAL, YOU SHALL NOT COVET," and if there is any other commandment, it is summed up in this saying, "YOU SHALL LOVE YOUR NEIGHBOR AS YOURSELF." 10 Love does no wrong to a neighbor; therefore love is the fulfillment of *the* law.

11 *Do* this, knowing the time, that it is already the hour for you to awaken from sleep; for now salvation is nearer to us than when we believed. 12 The night is almost gone, and the day is near. Therefore let us lay aside the deeds of darkness and put on the armor of light. 13 Let us behave properly as in the day, not in carousing and drunkenness, not in sexual promiscuity and sensuality, not in strife and jealousy. 14 But put on the Lord Jesus Christ, and make no provision for the flesh in regard to *its* lusts.

13:14 But put on the Lord Jesus Christ. This phrase summarizes sanctification, the continuing spiritual process in which those who have been saved by faith are transformed into His image and likeness (2Co 3:18; Gal 4:19; Php 3:13–14; Col 2:7; 1Jn 3:2–3). The image Paul uses to describe that process is taking off and putting on clothing, which is symbolic of thoughts and behavior. **no provision.** This word has the basic meaning of planning ahead or forethought. Most sinful behavior results from wrong ideas and lustful desires we allow to linger in our minds (Jas 1:14–15).

DAY 14: How should a Christian respond to the government?

In Romans 13:1, Paul says, "Every person is to be in subjection to the governing authorities." This Greek word was used of a soldier's absolute obedience to his superior officer. Scripture makes one exception to this command: when obedience to civil authority would require disobedience to God's word (Ex 1:17; Da 3:16–18; 6:7, 10; Ac 4:19–20; 5:28–29). Every position of civil authority without regard to competency, morality, reasonableness, or any other caveat (1Th 4:11–12; 1Ti 2:1–2; Titus 3:1–2). "For there is no authority except from God." Since He alone is the sovereign ruler of the universe (Pss 62:11; 103:19; 1Ti 6:15), He has instituted 4 authorities on earth: 1) the government over all citizens; 2) the church over all believers; 3) the parents over all children; and 4) the masters over all employees. Human government's authority is "established" and is defined by God. He instituted human government to reward good and to restrain sin in an evil, fallen world.

Since all government is God-ordained, disobedience is rebellion against God (v. 2) and will be met with judgment. Not God's judgment, but punishment from the government for breaking the law. Even the most wicked, godless governments act as a deterrent to crime. Peaceful, law-abiding citizens need not fear the authorities. Few governments will harm those who obey their laws. In fact, governments usually commend such people.

"For because of this you also pay taxes" (v. 6). The Greek word referred specifically to taxes paid by individuals, particularly those living in a conquered nation to their foreign rulers—which makes the tax even more onerous. That tax was usually a combined income and property tax. In this context, however, Paul uses the term in the broadest possible sense to speak of all kinds of taxes. Jesus explicitly taught that taxes are to be paid—even to the pagan Roman government (Mt 22:17–21). He also set an example by willingly paying the temple tax (Mt 17:24–27). "Render to all what is due" (v. 7). "Render" translates a Greek word signifying the payment of something owed—not a voluntary contribution—and is reinforced by the word "due." The apostle reiterates that paying taxes is mandatory.

AUGUST 15

Job 21:1–22:30

21 Then Job answered,

2 "Listen carefully to my speech,
   And let this be your *way*
      of consolation.
3 "Bear with me that I may speak;
   Then after I have spoken,
      you may mock.
4 "As for me, is my complaint to man?
   And why should I not be impatient?
5 "Look at me, and be astonished,
   And put *your* hand over *your* mouth.
6 "Even when I remember,
   I am disturbed,
   And horror takes hold of my flesh.
7 "Why do the wicked *still* live,
   Continue on, also become
      very powerful?
8 "Their descendants are established
   with them in their sight,
   And their offspring before
      their eyes,
9 "Their houses are safe from fear,
   And the rod of God is not on them.
10 "His ox mates without fail;
   His cow calves and does not abort.

11 "They send forth their little
      ones like the flock,
   And their children skip about.
12 "They sing to the timbrel and harp
   And rejoice at the sound of the flute.
13 "They spend their days in prosperity,
   And suddenly they go down
      to Sheol.
14 "They say to God, 'Depart from us!
   We do not even desire the
      knowledge of Your ways.
15 'Who is the Almighty, that
      we should serve Him,
   And what would we gain if
      we entreat Him?'
16 "Behold, their prosperity is
      not in their hand;
   The counsel of the wicked
      is far from me.

17 "How often is the lamp of
      the wicked put out,
   Or does their calamity fall on them?
   Does God apportion destruction
      in His anger?
18 "Are they as straw before the wind,
   And like chaff which the
      storm carries away?
19 "*You say,* 'God stores away a
      man's iniquity for his sons.'

Let God repay him so that
he may know *it*.
20 "Let his own eyes see his decay,
And let him drink of the
wrath of the Almighty.
21 "For what does he care for his
household after him,
When the number of his
months is cut off?
22 "Can anyone teach God knowledge,
In that He judges those on high?
23 "One dies in his full strength,
Being wholly at ease and satisfied;
24 His sides are filled out with fat,
And the marrow of his bones is moist,
25 While another dies with a bitter soul,
Never even tasting *anything* good.
26 "Together they lie down in the dust,
And worms cover them.

27 "Behold, I know your thoughts,
And the plans by which you
would wrong me.
28 "For you say, 'Where is the
house of the nobleman,
And where is the tent, the dwelling
places of the wicked?'
29 "Have you not asked wayfaring men,
And do you not recognize
their witness?
30 "For the wicked is reserved for
the day of calamity;
They will be led forth at
the day of fury.
31 "Who will confront him
with his actions,
And who will repay him for
what he has done?
32 "While he is carried to the grave,
Men will keep watch over *his* tomb.
33 "The clods of the valley will
gently cover him;
Moreover, all men will
follow after him,
While countless ones *go* before him.
34 "How then will you vainly
comfort me,
For your answers remain
full of falsehood?"

22 Then Eliphaz the Temanite responded,

2 "Can a vigorous man be of use to God,
Or a wise man be useful to himself?
3 "Is there any pleasure to the
Almighty if you are righteous,
Or profit if you make your
ways perfect?

4 "Is it because of your reverence
that He reproves you,
That He enters into judgment
against you?
5 "Is not your wickedness great,
And your iniquities without end?
6 "For you have taken pledges of
your brothers without cause,
And stripped men naked.
7 "To the weary you have given
no water to drink,
And from the hungry you
have withheld bread.
8 "But the earth belongs to
the mighty man,
And the honorable man dwells in it.
9 "You have sent widows away empty,
And the strength of the orphans
has been crushed.
10 "Therefore snares surround you,
And sudden dread terrifies you,
11 Or darkness, so that you cannot see,
And an abundance of
water covers you.

12 "Is not God *in* the height of heaven?
Look also at the distant stars,
how high they are!
13 "You say, 'What does God know?
Can He judge through the
thick darkness?
14 'Clouds are a hiding place for
Him, so that He cannot see;
And He walks on the vault of heaven.'
15 "Will you keep to the ancient path
Which wicked men have trod,
16 Who were snatched away
before their time,
Whose foundations were
washed away by a river?
17 "They said to God, 'Depart from us!'
And 'What can the Almighty
do to them?'
18 "Yet He filled their houses
with good *things*;
But the counsel of the wicked
is far from me.
19 "The righteous see and are glad,
And the innocent mock them,
20 *Saying*, 'Truly our adversaries
are cut off,
And their abundance the
fire has consumed.'

21 "Yield now and be at peace with Him;
Thereby good will come to you.
22 "Please receive instruction
from His mouth

And establish His words
in your heart.
²³ "If you return to the Almighty,
you will be restored;
If you remove unrighteousness
far from your tent,
²⁴ And place *your* gold in the dust,
And *the gold of* Ophir among
the stones of the brooks,
²⁵ Then the Almighty will be
your gold
And choice silver to you.
²⁶ "For then you will delight
in the Almighty
And lift up your face to God.
²⁷ "You will pray to Him, and
He will hear you;
And you will pay your vows.
²⁸ "You will also decree a thing, and
it will be established for you;
And light will shine on your ways.
²⁹ "When you are cast down, you
will speak with confidence,
And the humble person He will save.
³⁰ "He will deliver one who
is not innocent,
And he will be delivered through
the cleanness of your hands."

Psalm 96:1–6

Sing to the LORD a new song;
Sing to the LORD, all the earth.
² Sing to the LORD, bless His name;
Proclaim good tidings of His
salvation from day to day.
³ Tell of His glory among the nations,
His wonderful deeds among
all the peoples.
⁴ For great is the LORD and
greatly to be praised;
He is to be feared above all gods.
⁵ For all the gods of the
peoples are idols,
But the LORD made the heavens.

96:1 a new song. This new song was intended for the future inauguration of the millennial rule of the Lord over the earth (Pss 144:9; 149:1; Rev 5:9; 14:3).

96:3 His glory...nations. The glory of the Lord is more than just His majestic splendor. It includes all of the reasons for admiring and praising Him, such as His acts of creation (Ps 19:2) and redemption (v. 2).

⁶ Splendor and majesty are before Him,
Strength and beauty are
in His sanctuary.

Proverbs 23:6–8

⁶ Do not eat the bread of a selfish man,
Or desire his delicacies;
⁷ For as he thinks within
himself, so he is.
He says to you, "Eat and drink!"
But his heart is not with you.
⁸ You will vomit up the morsel
you have eaten,
And waste your compliments.

Romans 14:1–23

14 Now accept the one who is weak in faith, *but* not for *the purpose of* passing judgment on his opinions. ² One person has faith that he may eat all things, but he who is weak eats vegetables *only*. ³ The one who eats is not to regard with contempt the one who does not eat, and the one who does not eat is not to judge the one who eats, for God has accepted him. ⁴ Who are you to judge the servant of another? To his own master he stands or falls; and he will stand, for the Lord is able to make him stand.

⁵ One person regards one day above another, another regards every day *alike*. Each person must be fully convinced in his own mind. ⁶ He who observes the day, observes it for the Lord, and he who eats, does so for the Lord, for he gives thanks to God; and he who eats not, for the Lord he does not eat, and gives thanks to God. ⁷ For not one of us lives for himself, and not one dies for himself; ⁸ for if we live, we live for the Lord, or if we die, we die for the Lord; therefore whether we live or die, we are the Lord's. ⁹ For to this end Christ died and lived again, that He might be Lord both of the dead and of the living.

¹⁰ But you, why do you judge your brother? Or you again, why do you regard your brother with contempt? For we will all stand before the judgment seat of God. ¹¹ For it is written,

"As I live, says the Lord, every
knee shall bow to Me,
And every tongue shall
give praise to God."

¹² So then each one of us will give an account of himself to God.

¹³ Therefore let us not judge one another anymore, but rather determine this—not to put an obstacle or a stumbling block in a brother's way. ¹⁴ I know and am convinced in the Lord Jesus that nothing is unclean

in itself; but to him who thinks anything to be unclean, to him it is unclean. ¹⁵ For if because of food your brother is hurt, you are no longer walking according to love. Do not destroy with your food him for whom Christ died. ¹⁶ Therefore do not let what is for you a good thing be spoken of as evil; ¹⁷ for the kingdom of God is not eating and drinking, but righteousness and peace and joy in the Holy Spirit. ¹⁸ For he who in this way serves Christ is acceptable to God and approved by men. ¹⁹ So then we pursue the things which make

14:15 hurt. The Greek word refers to causing pain or distress. A weak believer may be hurt when he sees a brother do something he believes is sinful. But still worse, the strong believer may cause his weaker brother to violate his own conscience (1Co 8:8–13). **love.** Love will ensure that the strong Christian is sensitive and understanding of his brother's weaknesses (1Co 8:8–13). **destroy.** This refers to complete devastation. In the NT, it is often used to indicate eternal damnation (Mt 10:28; Lk 13:3; Jn 3:16; Ro 2:12). In this context, however, it refers to a serious devastation of one's spiritual growth (Mt 18:3, 6, 14).

14:17 kingdom of God. The sphere of salvation where God rules in the hearts of those He has saved. **eating and drinking.** Non-essentials and external observances. **righteousness.** Holy, obedient living (Eph 6:14; Php 1:11). **peace.** The loving tranquillity, produced by the Spirit, that should characterize believers' relationships with God and one another (Gal 5:22). **joy in the Holy Spirit.** Another part of the Spirit's fruit, this describes an abiding attitude of praise and thanksgiving regardless of circumstances, which flows from one's confidence in God's sovereignty (Gal 5:22; 1Th 1:6).

for peace and the building up of one another. ²⁰ Do not tear down the work of God for the sake of food. All things indeed are clean, but they are evil for the man who eats and gives offense. ²¹ It is good not to eat meat or to drink wine, or *to do anything* by which your brother stumbles. ²² The faith which you have, have as your own conviction before God. Happy is he who does not condemn himself in what he approves. ²³ But he who doubts is condemned if he eats, because *his eating is* not from faith; and whatever is not from faith is sin.

DAY 15: How is unity maintained within the church when there is so much diversity?

Reading through Romans 14:1–12, it is clear that the diversity of the church displays Christ's power to bring together dissimilar people in genuine unity. Yet Satan often works on man's unredeemed flesh to create division and threaten that unity. The threat to unity Paul addresses in this passage arises when mature (strong) believers—both Jews and Gentiles—conflict with immature (weak) believers. The strong Jewish believers understood their freedom in Christ and realized the ceremonial requirements of the Mosaic Law were no longer binding. The mature Gentiles understood that idols are not gods and, therefore, that they could eat meat that had been offered to them. But in both cases the weaker brothers' consciences were troubled, and they were even tempted to violate their consciences, become more legalistic under the feelings of guilt, or even to sin. Knowing that the mature Jews and Gentiles would be able to understand these struggles, Paul addresses most of his comments to them.

The secret to unity begins with the willingness to "accept the one who is weak in faith" (v. 1). The Greek word refers to personal and willing acceptance of another. This characterizes those believers who are unable to let go of the religious ceremonies and rituals of their past. The weak Jewish believer had difficulty abandoning the rites and prohibitions of the Old Covenant; he felt compelled to adhere to dietary laws, observe the Sabbath, and offer sacrifices in the temple. The weak Gentile believer had been steeped in pagan idolatry and its rituals; he felt that any contact with anything remotely related to his past, including eating meat that had been offered to a pagan deity and then sold in the marketplace, tainted him with sin. Both had very sensitive consciences in these areas and were not yet mature enough to be free of those convictions.

Neither one should "regard with contempt . . . judge" the other (v. 3). "Despise" indicates a contempt for someone as worthless, who deserves only disdain and abhorrence. "Judge" is equally strong and means "to condemn." Paul uses them synonymously: The strong hold the weak in contempt as legalistic and self-righteous; the weak judge the strong to be irresponsible at best and perhaps depraved. "To his own master he stands or falls" (v. 4). How Christ evaluates each believer is what matters, and His judgment does not take into account religious tradition or personal preference.

AUGUST 16

Job 23:1–25:6

23 Then Job replied,

2 "Even today my complaint is
rebellion;
His hand is heavy despite
my groaning.
3 "Oh that I knew where I
might find Him,
That I might come to His seat!
4 "I would present *my* case before Him
And fill my mouth with arguments.
5 "I would learn the words *which*
He would answer,
And perceive what He
would say to me.
6 "Would He contend with me by
the greatness of *His* power?
No, surely He would pay
attention to me.
7 "There the upright would
reason with Him;
And I would be delivered
forever from my Judge.

8 "Behold, I go forward but
He is not *there*,
And backward, but I cannot
perceive Him;
9 When He acts on the left, I
cannot behold *Him;*
He turns on the right, I
cannot see Him.
10 "But He knows the way I take;
When He has tried me, I shall
come forth as gold.
11 "My foot has held fast to His path;
I have kept His way and
not turned aside.
12 "I have not departed from the
command of His lips;
I have treasured the words
of His mouth more than
my necessary food.
13 "But He is unique and who
can turn Him?
And *what* His soul desires,
that He does.
14 "For He performs what is
appointed for me,
And many such *decrees* are with Him.
15 "Therefore, I would be dismayed
at His presence;
When I consider, I am
terrified of Him.

16 "*It is* God *who* has made
my heart faint,
And the Almighty *who*
has dismayed me,
17 But I am not silenced by the darkness,
Nor deep gloom *which* covers me.

24 "Why are times not stored
up by the Almighty,
And why do those who know
Him not see His days?
2 "Some remove the landmarks;
They seize and devour flocks.
3 "They drive away the donkeys
of the orphans;
They take the widow's ox for
a pledge.
4 "They push the needy aside
from the road;
The poor of the land are made to
hide themselves altogether.
5 "Behold, as wild donkeys
in the wilderness
They go forth seeking food
in their activity,
As bread for *their* children
in the desert.
6 "They harvest their fodder in the field
And glean the vineyard of the wicked.
7 "They spend the night naked,
without clothing,
And have no covering
against the cold.
8 "They are wet with the mountain rains
And hug the rock for
want of a shelter.
9 "Others snatch the orphan
from the breast,
And against the poor they
take a pledge.
10 "They cause *the poor* to go about
naked without clothing,
And they take away the sheaves
from the hungry.
11 "Within the walls they produce oil;
They tread wine presses but thirst.
12 "From the city men groan,
And the souls of the wounded cry out;
Yet God does not pay
attention to folly.
13 "Others have been with those
who rebel against the light;
They do not want to know its ways
Nor abide in its paths.
14 "The murderer arises at dawn;
He kills the poor and the needy,
And at night he is as a thief.

¹⁵ "The eye of the adulterer
waits for the twilight,
Saying, 'No eye will see me.'
And he disguises his face.
¹⁶ "In the dark they dig into houses,
They shut themselves up by day;
They do not know the light.
¹⁷ "For the morning is the same to
him as thick darkness,
For he is familiar with the
terrors of thick darkness.

¹⁸ "They are insignificant on the
surface of the water;
Their portion is cursed on the earth.
They do not turn toward
the vineyards.
¹⁹ "Drought and heat consume
the snow waters,
So does Sheol *those who* have sinned.
²⁰ "A mother will forget him;
The worm feeds sweetly till he
is no longer remembered.
And wickedness will be
broken like a tree.
²¹ "He wrongs the barren woman
And does no good for the widow.

24:18-21 Again Job referred to the opinions of his counselors, saying that, if their view were correct, all the wicked should be experiencing punishment. But it is obvious they were not.

²² "But He drags off the valiant
by His power;
He rises, but no one has
assurance of life.
²³ "He provides them with security,
and they are supported;
And His eyes are on their ways.
²⁴ "They are exalted a little while,
then they are gone;
Moreover, they are brought low and
like everything gathered up;
Even like the heads of grain
they are cut off.
²⁵ "Now if it is not so, who can
prove me a liar,
And make my speech worthless?"

25 Then Bildad the Shuhite answered,

² "Dominion and awe belong to Him
Who establishes peace in His heights.
³ "Is there any number to His troops?

And upon whom does His
light not rise?
⁴ "How then can a man be just with God?
Or how can he be clean who
is born of woman?
⁵ "If even the moon has no brightness
And the stars are not
pure in His sight,
⁶ How much less man, *that* maggot,
And the son of man, *that* worm!"

Psalm 96:7-10

⁷ Ascribe to the LORD, O families
of the peoples,
Ascribe to the LORD glory
and strength.
⁸ Ascribe to the LORD the
glory of His name;
Bring an offering and come
into His courts.
⁹ Worship the LORD in holy attire;
Tremble before Him, all the earth.
¹⁰ Say among the nations,
"The LORD reigns;
Indeed, the world is firmly
established, it will not be moved;
He will judge the peoples with equity."

96:10 firmly established. Instead of the continuance of international chaos in human history, the world will be settled and efficiently managed by the Messiah in the millennial kingdom (Ps 2; Mic 4:1-5). **judge the peoples with equity.** Not only will the Lord establish international peace and stability in the future messianic kingdom, but He will also rule the world with impeccable justice (v. 13; Is 11:1-5).

Proverbs 23:9

⁹ Do not speak in the hearing of a fool,
For he will despise the
wisdom of your words.

Romans 15:1-21

15 Now we who are strong ought to bear the weaknesses of those without strength and not *just* please ourselves. ² Each of us is to please his neighbor for his good, to his edification. ³ For even Christ did not please Himself; but as it is written, "THE REPROACHES OF THOSE WHO REPROACHED YOU FELL ON ME." ⁴ For whatever was written in earlier times was written for our instruction, so that through perseverance and the encouragement of the Scriptures we might have hope.

15:1 to bear. The word means "to pick up and carry a weight." It is used of carrying a pitcher of water (Mk 14:13), of carrying a man (Ac 21:35), and figuratively of bearing an obligation (Ac 15:10). The strong are not to simply tolerate the weaknesses of their weaker brothers; they are to help the weak shoulder their burdens by showing loving and practical consideration for them (Gal 6:2; see 1Co 9:19–22; Php 2:2–4).

[5] Now may the God who gives perseverance and encouragement grant you to be of the same mind with one another according to Christ Jesus, [6] so that with one accord you may with one voice glorify the God and Father of our Lord Jesus Christ.

[7] Therefore, accept one another, just as Christ also accepted us to the glory of God. [8] For I say that Christ has become a servant to the circumcision on behalf of the truth of God to confirm the promises *given* to the fathers, [9] and for the Gentiles to glorify God for His mercy; as it is written,

> "THEREFORE I WILL GIVE PRAISE TO
> YOU AMONG THE GENTILES,
> AND I WILL SING TO YOUR NAME."

[10] Again he says,

> "REJOICE, O GENTILES,
> WITH HIS PEOPLE."

[11] And again,

> "PRAISE THE LORD ALL YOU
> GENTILES,
> AND LET ALL THE PEOPLES
> PRAISE HIM."

[12] Again Isaiah says,

> "THERE SHALL COME THE ROOT
> OF JESSE,
> AND HE WHO ARISES TO RULE
> OVER THE GENTILES,
> IN HIM SHALL THE GENTILES
> HOPE."

[13] Now may the God of hope fill you with all joy and peace in believing, so that you will abound in hope by the power of the Holy Spirit.

[14] And concerning you, my brethren, I myself also am convinced that you yourselves are full of goodness, filled with all knowledge and able also to admonish one another. [15] But I have written very boldly to you on some points so as to remind you again, because of the grace that was given me from God, [16] to be a minister of Christ Jesus to the Gentiles, ministering as a priest the gospel of God, so that *my* offering of the Gentiles may become acceptable, sanctified by the Holy Spirit. [17] Therefore in Christ Jesus I have found reason for boasting in things pertaining to God. [18] For I will not presume to speak of anything except what Christ has accomplished through me, resulting in the obedience of the Gentiles by word and deed, [19] in the power of signs and wonders, in the power of the Spirit; so that from Jerusalem and round about as far as Illyricum I have fully preached the gospel of Christ. [20] And thus I aspired to preach the gospel, not where Christ was *already* named, so that I would not build on another man's foundation; [21] but as it is written,

> "THEY WHO HAD NO NEWS
> OF HIM SHALL SEE,
> AND THEY WHO HAVE NOT HEARD
> SHALL UNDERSTAND."

DAY 16: How does Paul exemplify a "minister of Christ Jesus"?

Paul calls himself a "minister of Christ Jesus to the Gentiles" in Romans 15:16. "Minister" was a general Greek term used of public officials. But in the New Testament it is used most often of those who serve God in some form of public worship (e.g., Php 2:17; Heb 1:7, 14; 8:1, 2, 6), including that of a priest (Lk 1:23). Although Paul's practice was always to present the gospel to the Jews first in every city he visited, his primary apostolic calling was to the Gentiles (11:13; Ac 9:15). Having referred to himself as a minister, a word with priestly overtones, Paul explains that his priestly ministry is to present to God an offering of a multitude of Gentile converts.

"In Christ Jesus I have found reason for boasting in things pertaining to God" (v. 17). Paul never boasted in his accomplishments as an apostle, but only in what Christ had accomplished through him (1Co 1:27–29, 31; 2Co 10:13–17; 12:5, 9; Gal 6:14; 1Ti 1:12–16). In Paul's case, his preaching was accompanied with "signs and wonders" (v. 19). God used them to authenticate true preaching and teaching. "From Jerusalem and round about as far as Illyricum I have fully preached the gospel of Christ." The region that roughly corresponds to the former European country of Yugoslavia, spanning some 1,400 miles.

Paul's goal was to reach those who had never heard the gospel (v. 20)—the primary function of a New Testament evangelist (Eph 4:11). But for pastor-teachers, building on the foundation laid by such an evangelist is the crucial part of their ministry (1Co 3:6).

AUGUST 17

Job 26:1–14

26 Then Job responded,

2 "What a help you are to the weak!
How you have saved the arm
without strength!
3 "What counsel you have given
to one without wisdom!
What helpful insight you have
abundantly provided!
4 "To whom have you uttered words?
And whose spirit was
expressed through you?

5 "The departed spirits tremble
Under the waters and
their inhabitants.
6 "Naked is Sheol before Him,
And Abaddon has no covering.
7 "He stretches out the north
over empty space
And hangs the earth on nothing.
8 "He wraps up the waters in His clouds,
And the cloud does not
burst under them.
9 "He obscures the face of the full moon
And spreads His cloud over it.
10 "He has inscribed a circle on
the surface of the waters
At the boundary of light
and darkness.
11 "The pillars of heaven tremble
And are amazed at His rebuke.
12 "He quieted the sea with His power,
And by His understanding
He shattered Rahab.

26:7 hangs the earth on nothing. A statement that is accurate, given in ancient time, before scientific verification. This indicates the divine authorship of Scripture.

26:10 a circle. This describes the earth as a circular globe, another scientifically accurate statement at a time when many thought the world was flat.

13 "By His breath the heavens are cleared;
His hand has pierced the
fleeing serpent.
14 "Behold, these are the
fringes of His ways;
And how faint a word we hear
of Him!
But His mighty thunder, who
can understand?"

26:13 His breath. See 33:4. The Holy Spirit, described here as God's "breath," worked mightily in creation (Ge 1:2). **the fleeing serpent.** This is figurative language for the idea that God brought all constellations into subjection under His authority (26:12). "Serpent" could be translated "crooked" and refer to any wayward stars or planets being brought under control by His mighty power.

Psalm 96:11–13

11 Let the heavens be glad, and
let the earth rejoice;
Let the sea roar, and all it contains;
12 Let the field exult, and all that is in it.
Then all the trees of the
forest will sing for joy
13 Before the LORD, for He is coming,
For He is coming to judge the earth.
He will judge the world
in righteousness
And the peoples in His faithfulness.

96:13 He is coming. The rule of the Lord described in this psalm is not the present universal kingdom (Ps 93), but one which will be established when Christ returns to earth.

Proverbs 23:10–12

10 Do not move the ancient boundary
Or go into the fields of the fatherless,
11 For their Redeemer is strong;
He will plead their case against you.
12 Apply your heart to discipline
And your ears to words of knowledge.

23:11 Redeemer. In a normal situation the near kinsman would rescue the one who had fallen upon hard times (Lv 25:25; Ru 2:20; 3:12–13; 4:1–12) or avenge in the case of a murder (Nu 35:19). "Redeemer" is applied to God as the Savior of His people (e.g., Ge 48:16; Ex 6:6; Job 19:25; Ps 19:14; Is 41:14; 43:14; 44:24) since the helpless had no voice.

Romans 15:22–33

²² For this reason I have often been prevented from coming to you; ²³ but now, with no further place for me in these regions, and since I have had for many years a longing to come to you ²⁴ whenever I go to Spain—for I hope to see you in passing, and to be helped on my way there by you, when I have first enjoyed your company for a while— ²⁵ but now, I am going to Jerusalem serving the saints. ²⁶ For Macedonia and Achaia have been pleased to make a contribution for the poor among the saints in Jerusalem. ²⁷ Yes, they were pleased *to do so,* and they are indebted to them. For if the Gentiles have shared in their spiritual things, they are indebted to minister to them also in material things. ²⁸ Therefore, when I have finished this, and have put my seal on this fruit of theirs, I will go on by way of you to Spain. ²⁹ I know that when I come to you, I will come in the fullness of the blessing of Christ.

³⁰ Now I urge you, brethren, by our Lord Jesus Christ and by the love of the Spirit, to strive together with me in your prayers to God for me, ³¹ that I may be rescued from those who are disobedient in Judea, and *that* my service for Jerusalem may prove acceptable to the saints; ³² so that I may come to you in joy by the will of God and find *refreshing* rest in your company. ³³ Now the God of peace be with you all. Amen.

DAY 17: Who was Paul the apostle, and why does he seem to have two names?

Paul (Greek name) the apostle was also known as Saul, which was his Hebrew name. Along with his double name, Paul was also able to exercise dual citizenship as a Jewish descendant from the tribe of Benjamin (Php 3:5) and as a Roman (Ac 16:37; 22:25). Paul was born about the time of Christ's birth, in Tarsus, located in modern Turkey (Ac 9:11).

Young Saul spent much of his early life in Jerusalem as a student of the celebrated rabbi (teacher) Gamaliel (Ac 22:3). Like his father before him, Paul was a Pharisee (Ac 23:6), a member of the strictest Jewish sect (Php 3:5). He actively resisted those who followed Jesus. His first appearance in Scripture occurs in Acts 7:58 as he observed the martyrdom of Stephen.

Miraculously converted while on his way to Damascus (about A.C. 33–34) to persecute Christians, Paul immediately began proclaiming the gospel (Ac 9:20). After narrowly escaping Damascus (Ac 9:23–25; 2Co 11:32–33), Paul spent three years in the wilderness (Gal 1:17–18). During those years, he received much of his doctrine as direct revelation from the Lord (Gal 1:11–12).

More than any other individual, Paul was responsible for the spread of Christianity throughout the Roman Empire. He made three missionary journeys along the north side of the Mediterranean Sea, tirelessly preaching the gospel he had once tried to destroy (Ac 26:9). Eventually he was arrested in Jerusalem (Ac 21:27–31), appealed for a hearing before Caesar, and finally reached Rome (chaps. 27–28). Later, he was released for a short time of ministry then arrested again and martyred at Rome in about A.C. 65–67.

Though physically unimpressive (2Co 10:10; Gal 4:14), Paul possessed an inner strength granted him through the Holy Spirit's power (Php 4:13). The grace of God proved sufficient to provide for his every need (2Co 12:9–10), enabling this noble servant of Christ to successfully finish his spiritual race (2Ti 4:7).

AUGUST 18

Job 27:1–28:28

27 Then Job continued his discourse and said,

² "As God lives, who has taken
　　away my right,
　And the Almighty, who has
　　embittered my soul,

³ For as long as life is in me,
　And the breath of God is
　　in my nostrils,

⁴ My lips certainly will not
　　speak unjustly,
　Nor will my tongue mutter
　　deceit.

⁵ "Far be it from me that I should
　　declare you right;
　Till I die I will not put away
　　my integrity from me.

6 "I hold fast my righteousness
    and will not let it go.
My heart does not reproach
    any of my days.

7 "May my enemy be as the wicked
    And my opponent as the unjust.
8 "For what is the hope of the
    godless when he is cut off,
When God requires his life?
9 "Will God hear his cry
    When distress comes upon him?
10 "Will he take delight in the Almighty?
    Will he call on God at all times?
11 "I will instruct you in the
    power of God;
What is with the Almighty
    I will not conceal.
12 "Behold, all of you have seen *it;*
    Why then do you act foolishly?

13 "This is the portion of a
    wicked man from God,
And the inheritance *which* tyrants
    receive from the Almighty.
14 "Though his sons are many, they
    are destined for the sword;
And his descendants will not
    be satisfied with bread.
15 "His survivors will be buried
    because of the plague,
And their widows will not
    be able to weep.
16 "Though he piles up silver like dust
    And prepares garments as
    plentiful as the clay,
17   He may prepare *it,* but the
    just will wear *it*
And the innocent will
    divide the silver.
18 "He has built his house like
    the spider's web,
Or as a hut *which* the
    watchman has made.
19 "He lies down rich, but never again;
    He opens his eyes, and it is no longer.
20 "Terrors overtake him like a flood;
    A tempest steals him
    away in the night.
21 "The east wind carries him
    away, and he is gone,
For it whirls him away from his place.
22 "For it will hurl at him
    without sparing;
He will surely try to flee
    from its power.
23 "*Men* will clap their hands at him
    And will hiss him from his place.

28 "Surely there is a mine for silver
    And a place where they refine gold.
2 "Iron is taken from the dust,
    And copper is smelted from rock.
3 "*Man* puts an end to darkness,
    And to the farthest limit
    he searches out
The rock in gloom and deep shadow.
4 "He sinks a shaft far from habitation,
    Forgotten by the foot;
They hang and swing to and
    fro far from men.
5 "The earth, from it comes food,
    And underneath it is
    turned up as fire.
6 "Its rocks are the source of sapphires,
    And its dust *contains* gold.
7 "The path no bird of prey knows,
    Nor has the falcon's eye
    caught sight of it.
8 "The proud beasts have not trodden it,
    Nor has the *fierce* lion passed over it.
9 "He puts his hand on the flint;
    He overturns the mountains
    at the base.
10 "He hews out channels
    through the rocks,
And his eye sees anything precious.
11 "He dams up the streams
    from flowing,
And what is hidden he brings
    out to the light.

12 "But where can wisdom be found?
    And where is the place of
    understanding?
13 "Man does not know its value,
    Nor is it found in the land
    of the living.
14 "The deep says, 'It is not in me';
    And the sea says, 'It is not with me.'
15 "Pure gold cannot be given
    in exchange for it,
Nor can silver be weighed as its price.
16 "It cannot be valued in the
    gold of Ophir,
In precious onyx, or sapphire.
17 "Gold or glass cannot equal it,
    Nor can it be exchanged for
    articles of fine gold.
18 "Coral and crystal are not
    to be mentioned;
And the acquisition of wisdom
    is above *that of* pearls.
19 "The topaz of Ethiopia cannot equal it,
    Nor can it be valued in pure gold.
20 "Where then does wisdom come
    from?

And where is the place of
understanding?
²¹ "Thus it is hidden from the
eyes of all living
And concealed from the
birds of the sky.
²² "Abaddon and Death say,
'With our ears we have
heard a report of it.'

²³ "God understands its way,
And He knows its place.
²⁴ "For He looks to the ends of the earth
And sees everything under
the heavens.
²⁵ "When He imparted weight
to the wind
And meted out the waters
by measure,
²⁶ When He set a limit for the rain
And a course for the thunderbolt,
²⁷ Then He saw it and declared it;
He established it and also
searched it out.
²⁸ "And to man He said, 'Behold, the
fear of the Lord, that is wisdom;
And to depart from evil is
understanding.'"

Psalm 97:1–6

The LORD reigns, let the earth rejoice;
Let the many islands be glad.
² Clouds and thick darkness
surround Him;
Righteousness and justice are the
foundation of His throne.
³ Fire goes before Him
And burns up His adversaries
round about.
⁴ His lightnings lit up the world;
The earth saw and trembled.

⁵ The mountains melted like wax
at the presence of the LORD,
At the presence of the Lord
of the whole earth.
⁶ The heavens declare His
righteousness,
And all the peoples have
seen His glory.

Proverbs 23:13–14

¹³ Do not hold back discipline
from the child,
Although you strike him with
the rod, he will not die.
¹⁴ You shall strike him with the rod
And rescue his soul from Sheol.

Romans 16:1–27

16 I commend to you our sister Phoebe, who is a servant of the church which is at Cenchrea; ²that you receive her in the Lord in a manner worthy of the saints, and that you help her in whatever matter she may have need of you; for she herself has also been a helper of many, and of myself as well.

³Greet Prisca and Aquila, my fellow workers in Christ Jesus, ⁴who for my life risked their own necks, to whom not only do I give thanks, but also all the churches of the Gentiles; ⁵also *greet* the church that is in their house. Greet Epaenetus, my beloved, who is the first convert to Christ from Asia. ⁶Greet Mary, who has worked hard for you. ⁷Greet Andronicus and Junias, my kinsmen and my fellow prisoners, who are outstanding among the apostles, who also were in Christ before me. ⁸Greet Ampliatus, my beloved in the Lord. ⁹Greet Urbanus, our fellow worker in Christ, and Stachys my beloved. ¹⁰Greet Apelles, the approved in Christ. Greet those who are of the *household* of Aristobulus. ¹¹Greet Herodion,

97:1 many islands. Refers to all the continents as well as islands of the world (Is 42:10; Da 2:34–35, 44; Zec 14:9).

97:2 Clouds and thick darkness. Such a description emphasizes the terrifying effect of the Lord's presence, both in the past (Ex 19:16–18), and in the future day of the Lord (Joel 2:2; Zep 1:15; Mt 24:29–30).

97:3 burns up His adversaries. The Lord will utterly destroy His enemies in the future day of the Lord (Zec 14:12).

16:1 Phoebe. Means "bright and radiant," which aptly fits Paul's brief description of her personality and Christian character. **servant.** The term from which we get "deacon" and "deaconess" (1Ti 3:10–12). In the early church, women servants cared for sick believers, the poor, strangers, and those in prison. They instructed the women and children (Titus 2:3–5). Whether Phoebe had an official title or not, she had the great responsibility of delivering this letter to the Roman church. When they had served faithfully and become widowed and destitute, such women were to be cared for by the church (1Ti 5:3–16).

my kinsman. Greet those of the *household* of Narcissus, who are in the Lord. [12] Greet Tryphaena and Tryphosa, workers in the Lord. Greet Persis the beloved, who has worked hard in the Lord. [13] Greet Rufus, a choice man in the Lord, also his mother and mine. [14] Greet Asyncritus, Phlegon, Hermes, Patrobas, Hermas and the brethren with them. [15] Greet Philologus and Julia, Nereus and his sister, and Olympas, and all the saints who are with them. [16] Greet one another with a holy kiss. All the churches of Christ greet you.

16:16 holy kiss. Kissing of friends on the forehead, cheek, or beard was common in the Old Testament. The Jews in the New Testament church carried on the practice, and it became especially precious to new believers, who were often outcasts from their own families because of their faith, because of the spiritual kinship it signified.

[17] Now I urge you, brethren, keep your eye on those who cause dissensions and hindrances contrary to the teaching which you learned, and turn away from them. [18] For such men are slaves, not of our Lord Christ but of their own appetites; and by their smooth and flattering speech they deceive the hearts of the unsuspecting. [19] For the report of your obedience has reached to all; therefore I am rejoicing over you, but I want you to be wise

in what is good and innocent in what is evil. [20] The God of peace will soon crush Satan under your feet.

The grace of our Lord Jesus be with you. [21] Timothy my fellow worker greets you, and *so do* Lucius and Jason and Sosipater, my kinsmen.

[22] I, Tertius, who write this letter, greet you in the Lord.

[23] Gaius, host to me and to the whole church, greets you. Erastus, the city treasurer greets you, and Quartus, the brother. [24] [The grace of our Lord Jesus Christ be with you all. Amen.]

[25] Now to Him who is able to establish you according to my gospel and the preaching of Jesus Christ, according to the revelation of the mystery which has been kept secret for long ages past, [26] but now is manifested, and by the Scriptures of the prophets, according to the commandment of the eternal God, has been made known to all the nations, *leading* to obedience of faith; [27] to the only wise God, through Jesus Christ, be the glory forever. Amen.

16:26 Scriptures of the prophets...made known. God had told Israel that He would not only call her to righteousness, but appoint her as a light (of the gospel) to the nations (Ge 12:3; Ex 19:6; Is 42:6; 49:6, 22; 53:11; 60:3–5; Jer 31:31, 33; 1Pe 1:10).

DAY 18: What wise conclusion did Job come to regarding his debate with his friends?

Job said to his friends, "I will instruct you in the power of God" (27:11). Job had pinpointed the issue between him and his friends. They disagreed on the outworking of God's retribution. They agreed that God was powerful, wise, and sovereign. But because Job knew there was no cherished sin in his life that would bring upon him such intense suffering, Job was forced to conclude that the simplistic notion that all suffering comes from sin and all righteousness is rewarded, was wrong. At the outset, Job himself probably believed as the comforters still did, but he had seen that his friends' limitation of God's action was drastically in need of revision; in fact, it was nonsense.

"God understands its way, and He knows its place" (28:23). These are perhaps the most important thoughts in the chapter for the debates. Job and his friends have probed God's wisdom for 3 court rounds and basically have arrived nowhere near the truth. Finally, Job made the point clearly that the divine wisdom necessary to explain his suffering was inaccessible to man. Only God knew all about it, because He knows everything (v. 24). True wisdom belongs to the One who is the Almighty Creator (vv. 25–26). One can only know it if He declares it to him (Dt 29:29).

"Behold, the fear of the Lord, that is wisdom" (28:28). Job had made the connection that the others would not. While the specific features of God's wisdom may not be revealed to us, the alpha and omega of wisdom is to revere God and avoid sin (Ps 111:10; Pr 1:7; 9:10; Ecc 12:13–14), leaving the unanswered questions to Him in trusting submission. All we can do is trust and obey (Ecc 12:13), and that is enough wisdom. One may never know the reasons for life's sufferings.

AUGUST 19

Job 29:1–30:31

29 And Job again took up his discourse and said,

2 "Oh that I were as in months gone by,
As in the days when God
watched over me;

3 When His lamp shone over my head,
And by His light I walked
through darkness;

4 As I was in the prime of my days,
When the friendship of God
was over my tent;

5 When the Almighty was yet with me,
And my children were around me;

29:5 When the Almighty was yet with me. Job felt abandoned by God. But God would demonstrate to Job, by addressing his criticisms, that God was with him all throughout this ordeal.

6 When my steps were bathed in butter,
And the rock poured out for
me streams of oil!

7 "When I went out to the
gate of the city,
When I took my seat in the square,

8 The young men saw me
and hid themselves,
And the old men arose *and* stood.

9 "The princes stopped talking
And put *their* hands on their
mouths;

10 The voice of the nobles was
hushed,
And their tongue stuck to
their palate.

11 "For when the ear heard, it
called me blessed,
And when the eye saw, it
gave witness of me,

12 Because I delivered the poor
who cried for help,
And the orphan who had no helper.

13 "The blessing of the one ready
to perish came upon me,
And I made the widow's
heart sing for joy.

14 "I put on righteousness,
and it clothed me;
My justice was like a robe
and a turban.

29:12–13 poor…orphan…one ready to perish… widow's. All over the ancient Near Eastern world, a man's virtue was measured by his treatment of the weakest and most vulnerable members of society. If he protected and provided for this group, he was respected as being a noble man. These things, which Job had done, his accusers said he must not have done or he wouldn't be suffering (22:1–11).

15 "I was eyes to the blind
And feet to the lame.

16 "I was a father to the needy,
And I investigated the case
which I did not know.

17 "I broke the jaws of the wicked
And snatched the prey from his teeth.

18 "Then I thought, 'I shall die in my nest,
And I shall multiply *my*
days as the sand.

19 'My root is spread out to the waters,
And dew lies all night on my branch.

20 'My glory is *ever* new with me,
And my bow is renewed in my hand.'

21 "To me they listened and waited,
And kept silent for my counsel.

22 "After my words they did
not speak again,
And my speech dropped on them.

23 "They waited for me as for the rain,
And opened their mouth as
for the spring rain.

24 "I smiled on them when
they did not believe,
And the light of my face they
did not cast down.

25 "I chose a way for them
and sat as chief,
And dwelt as a king
among the troops,
As one who comforted the
mourners.

30 "But now those younger
than I mock me,
Whose fathers I disdained to put
with the dogs of my flock.

2 "Indeed, what *good was* the
strength of their hands to me?
Vigor had perished from them.

3 "From want and famine they
are gaunt
Who gnaw the dry ground by
night in waste and desolation,

4 Who pluck mallow by the bushes,
And whose food is the root
of the broom shrub.
5 "They are driven from the community;
They shout against them
as *against* a thief,
6 So that they dwell in dreadful valleys,
In holes of the earth and of the rocks.
7 "Among the bushes they cry out;
Under the nettles they are
gathered together.
8 "Fools, even those without a name,
They were scourged from the land.

9 "And now I have become their taunt,
I have even become a
byword to them.
10 "They abhor me *and* stand
aloof from me,
And they do not refrain from
spitting at my face.
11 "Because He has loosed His
bowstring and afflicted me,
They have cast off the
bridle before me.
12 "On the right hand their brood arises;
They thrust aside my feet and
build up against me their
ways of destruction.
13 "They break up my path,
They profit from my destruction;
No one restrains them.
14 "As *through* a wide breach they come,
Amid the tempest they roll on.
15 "Terrors are turned against me;
They pursue my honor as the wind,
And my prosperity has passed
away like a cloud.

16 "And now my soul is poured
out within me;
Days of affliction have seized me.
17 "At night it pierces my
bones within me,
And my gnawing *pains* take
no rest.
18 "By a great force my garment
is distorted;
It binds me about as the
collar of my coat.
19 "He has cast me into the mire,
And I have become like
dust and ashes.
20 "I cry out to You for help, but
You do not answer me;
I stand up, and You turn Your
attention against me.
21 "You have become cruel to me;

With the might of Your hand
You persecute me.
22 "You lift me up to the wind
and cause me to ride;
And You dissolve me in a storm.
23 "For I know that You will
bring me to death
And to the house of meeting
for all living.

24 "Yet does not one in a heap of
ruins stretch out *his* hand,
Or in his disaster therefore
cry out for help?
25 "Have I not wept for the one
whose life is hard?
Was not my soul grieved
for the needy?
26 "When I expected good,
then evil came;
When I waited for light,
then darkness came.
27 "I am seething within and
cannot relax;
Days of affliction confront me.
28 "I go about mourning
without comfort;
I stand up in the assembly
and cry out for help.
29 "I have become a brother to jackals
And a companion of ostriches.
30 "My skin turns black on me,
And my bones burn with fever.
31 "Therefore my harp is turned
to mourning,
And my flute to the sound
of those who weep.

Psalm 97:7–12

7 Let all those be ashamed who
serve graven images,
Who boast themselves of idols;
Worship Him, all you gods.
8 Zion heard *this* and was glad,
And the daughters of Judah
have rejoiced
Because of Your judgments, O LORD.
9 For You are the LORD Most
High over all the earth;
You are exalted far above all gods.

10 Hate evil, you who love the LORD,
Who preserves the souls
of His godly ones;
He delivers them from the
hand of the wicked.
11 Light is sown *like seed*
for the righteous

And gladness for the upright in heart.
¹² Be glad in the LORD, you
righteous ones,
And give thanks to His holy name.

Proverbs 23:15–16

¹⁵ My son, if your heart is wise,
My own heart also will be glad;
¹⁶ And my inmost being will rejoice
When your lips speak what is right.

1 Corinthians 1:1–31

1 Paul, called *as* an apostle of Jesus Christ by the will of God, and Sosthenes our brother, ² To the church of God which is at Corinth, to those who have been sanctified in Christ Jesus, saints by calling, with all who in every place call on the name of our Lord Jesus Christ, their *Lord* and ours: ³ Grace to you and peace from God our Father and the Lord Jesus Christ.

⁴ I thank my God always concerning you for the grace of God which was given you in Christ Jesus, ⁵ that in everything you were enriched in Him, in all speech and all knowledge, ⁶ even as the testimony concerning Christ was confirmed in you, ⁷ so that you are not lacking in any gift, awaiting eagerly the revelation of our Lord Jesus Christ, ⁸ who will also confirm you to the end, blameless in the day of our Lord Jesus Christ. ⁹ God is faithful, through whom you were called into fellowship with His Son, Jesus Christ our Lord.

¹⁰ Now I exhort you, brethren, by the name of our Lord Jesus Christ, that you all agree and that there be no divisions among you, but that you be made complete in the same mind and in the same judgment. ¹¹ For I have been informed concerning you, my brethren, by Chloe's *people,* that there are quarrels among you. ¹² Now I mean this, that each one of you is saying, "I am of Paul," and "I of Apollos," and "I of Cephas," and "I of Christ." ¹³ Has Christ been divided? Paul was not crucified for you, was he? Or were you baptized in the name of Paul? ¹⁴ I thank God that I baptized none of you except Crispus and Gaius, ¹⁵ so that no one would say you were baptized in my name. ¹⁶ Now I did baptize also the household of Stephanas; beyond that, I do not know whether I baptized any other. ¹⁷ For Christ did not send me to baptize, but to preach the gospel, not in cleverness of speech, so that the cross of Christ would not be made void.

¹⁸ For the word of the cross is foolishness to those who are perishing, but to us who

1:10 all agree. Paul is emphasizing the unity of doctrine in the local assembly of believers, not the spiritual unity of His universal church. Doctrinal unity, clearly and completely based on Scripture, must be the foundation of all church life (Jn 17:11, 21–23; Ac 2:46–47). Both weak commitment to doctrine and commitment to disunity of doctrine will severely weaken a church and destroy the true unity. In its place, there can be only shallow sentimentalism or superficial harmony. **made complete.** The basic idea is that of putting back together something that was broken or separated so it is no longer divided. The term is used in both the New Testament and in classical Greek to speak of mending such things as nets, broken bones or utensils, torn garments, and dislocated joints. **same mind... same judgment.** See Philippians 3:15–16. The demand is for unity internally in their individual minds and externally in decisions made among themselves—unified in truth by beliefs, convictions, standards, and in behavior by applied principles of living (Ac 4:32; Eph 4:3). The only source of such unity is God's Word which establishes the standard of truth on which true unity rests.

1:13 Has Christ been divided? No human leader, not even an apostle, should be given the loyalty that belongs only to the Lord. Such elevation of leaders leads only to contention, disputes, and a divided church. Christ is not divided and neither is His body, the church. Paul depreciates his worth in comparison to the Lord Jesus.

1:18 word of the cross. God's total revelation, i.e., the gospel in all its fullness, which centers in the incarnation and crucifixion of Christ (2:2); the entire divine plan and provision for the redemption of sinners, which is the theme of all Scripture, is in view. **foolishness.** Translates the word from which "moron" is derived. **perishing...being saved.** Every person is either in the process of salvation (though not completed until the redemption of the body; see Ro 8:23; 13:11) or the process of destruction. One's response to the cross of Christ determines which. To the Christ-rejectors who are in the process of being destroyed (Eph 2:1–2) the gospel is nonsense. To those who are believers it is powerful wisdom.

are being saved it is the power of God. ¹⁹ For it is written,

"I WILL DESTROY THE WISDOM
OF THE WISE,
AND THE CLEVERNESS OF THE
CLEVER I WILL SET ASIDE."

²⁰Where is the wise man? Where is the scribe? Where is the debater of this age? Has not God made foolish the wisdom of the world? ²¹For since in the wisdom of God the world through its wisdom did not *come to* know God, God was well-pleased through the foolishness of the message preached to save those who believe. ²²For indeed Jews ask for signs and Greeks search for wisdom; ²³but we preach Christ crucified, to Jews a stumbling block and to Gentiles foolishness, ²⁴but to those who are the called, both Jews and Greeks, Christ the power of God and the wisdom of God. ²⁵Because the foolishness of God is wiser than men, and the weakness of God is stronger than men.

²⁶For consider your calling, brethren, that there were not many wise according to the flesh, not many mighty, not many noble; ²⁷but God has chosen the foolish things of the world to shame the wise, and God has chosen the weak things of the world to shame the things which are strong, ²⁸and the base things of the world and the despised God has chosen, the things that are not, so that He may nullify the things that are, ²⁹so that no man may boast before God. ³⁰But by His doing you are in Christ Jesus, who became to us wisdom from God, and righteousness and sanctification, and redemption, ³¹so that, just as it is written, "LET HIM WHO BOASTS, BOAST IN THE LORD."

DAY 19: Describe the church in Corinth.

The church in Corinth was founded by Paul on his second missionary journey (Ac 18:1ff.). As usual, his ministry began in the synagogue, where he was assisted by two Jewish believers, Priscilla and Aquila, with whom he lived for a while and who were fellow tradesmen. Soon after, Silas and Timothy joined them, and Paul began preaching even more intensely in the synagogue. When most of the Jews resisted the gospel, he left the synagogue, but not before Crispus, the leader of the synagogue, his family, and many other Corinthians were converted (Ac 18:5–8).

After ministering in Corinth for over a year and a half (Ac 18:11), Paul was brought before a Roman tribunal by some of the Jewish leaders. Because the charges were strictly religious and not civil, the proconsul, Gallio, dismissed the case. Shortly thereafter, Paul took Priscilla and Aquila with him to Ephesus. From there he returned to Israel (vv. 18–22).

Unable to fully break with the culture from which it came, the church at Corinth was exceptionally factional, showing its carnality and immaturity. After the gifted Apollos had ministered in the church for some time, a group of his admirers established a clique and had little to do with the rest of the church. Another group developed that was loyal to Paul, another claimed special allegiance to Peter (Cephas), and still another to Christ alone (see 1:10–13; 3:1–9).

The most serious problem of the Corinthian church was worldliness, an unwillingness to divorce the culture around them. Most of the believers could not consistently separate themselves from their old, selfish, immoral, and pagan ways. It became necessary for Paul to write to correct this, as well as to command the faithful Christians not only to break fellowship with the disobedient and unrepentant members, but to put those members out of the church (5:9–13).

☽ AUGUST 20

Job 31:1–32:22

31 ¹"I have made a covenant
with my eyes;
How then could I gaze at a virgin?
²"And what is the portion
of God from above
Or the heritage of the
Almighty from on high?
³"Is it not calamity to the unjust
And disaster to those who
work iniquity?
⁴"Does He not see my ways
And number all my steps?

⁵"If I have walked with falsehood,
And my foot has hastened
after deceit,
⁶Let Him weigh me with
accurate scales,
And let God know my integrity.
⁷"If my step has turned from the way,
Or my heart followed my eyes,
Or if any spot has stuck to my hands,
⁸Let me sow and another eat,
And let my crops be uprooted.
⁹"If my heart has been enticed
by a woman,
Or I have lurked at my
neighbor's doorway,

10 May my wife grind for another,
And let others kneel down over her.

11 "For that would be a lustful crime;
Moreover, it would be an iniquity
punishable by judges.

12 "For it would be fire that
consumes to Abaddon,
And would uproot all my increase.

13 "If I have despised the claim of
my male or female slaves
When they filed a complaint
against me,

14 What then could I do when God arises?
And when He calls me to account,
what will I answer Him?

15 "Did not He who made me in
the womb make him,
And the same one fashion
us in the womb?

16 "If I have kept the poor
from *their* desire,
Or have caused the eyes of
the widow to fail,

17 Or have eaten my morsel alone,
And the orphan has not shared it

18 (But from my youth he grew up
with me as with a father,
And from infancy I guided her),

19 If I have seen anyone perish
for lack of clothing,
Or that the needy had no covering,

20 If his loins have not thanked me,
And if he has not been warmed
with the fleece of my sheep,

21 If I have lifted up my hand
against the orphan,
Because I saw I had support
in the gate,

22 Let my shoulder fall from the socket,
And my arm be broken
off at the elbow.

23 "For calamity from God is
a terror to me,
And because of His majesty
I can do nothing.

24 "If I have put my confidence *in* gold,
And called fine gold my trust,

25 If I have gloated because my
wealth was great,
And because my hand had
secured *so* much;

26 If I have looked at the sun
when it shone
Or the moon going in splendor,

27 And my heart became secretly enticed,

And my hand threw a kiss
from my mouth,

28 That too would have been an
iniquity *calling for* judgment,
For I would have denied God above.

29 "Have I rejoiced at the
extinction of my enemy,
Or exulted when evil befell him?

30 "No, I have not allowed
my mouth to sin
By asking for his life in a curse.

31 "Have the men of my tent not said,
'Who can find one who has not
been satisfied with his meat'?

32 "The alien has not lodged outside,
For I have opened my doors
to the traveler.

33 "Have I covered my
transgressions like Adam,
By hiding my iniquity in my bosom,

34 Because I feared the great multitude,
And the contempt of families
terrified me,
And kept silent and did not
go out of doors?

35 "Oh that I had one to hear me!
Behold, here is my signature;
Let the Almighty answer me!
And the indictment which my
adversary has written,

31:35 the indictment which my adversary has written. Job wished that God, the perfect Prosecutor who knows the allegations perfectly, had written a book that would have revealed God's will and wisdom and the reasons for Job's pain. This would have cleared him of all charges by his friends.

---

36 Surely I would carry it
on my shoulder,
I would bind it to myself like a crown.

37 "I would declare to Him the
number of my steps;
Like a prince I would approach Him.

38 "If my land cries out against me,
And its furrows weep together;

39 If I have eaten its fruit without
money,
Or have caused its owners
to lose their lives,

40 Let briars grow instead of wheat,
And stinkweed instead of barley."

The words of Job are ended.

32 Then these three men ceased answering Job, because he was righteous in his own eyes. ² But the anger of Elihu the son of Barachel the Buzite, of the family of Ram burned; against Job his anger burned because he justified himself before God. ³ And his anger burned against his three friends because they had found no answer, and yet had condemned Job. ⁴ Now Elihu had waited to speak to Job because they were years older than he. ⁵ And when Elihu saw that there was no answer in the mouth of the three men his anger burned.

⁶ So Elihu the son of Barachel the Buzite spoke out and said,

"I am young in years and you are old;
Therefore I was shy and afraid
to tell you what I think.
⁷ "I thought age should speak,
And increased years should
teach wisdom.
⁸ "But it is a spirit in man,
And the breath of the Almighty
gives them understanding.
⁹ "The abundant *in years*
may not be wise,
Nor may elders understand justice.
¹⁰ "So I say, 'Listen to me,
I too will tell what I think.'

¹¹ "Behold, I waited for your words,
I listened to your reasonings,
While you pondered what to say.
¹² "I even paid close attention to you;
Indeed, there was no one
who refuted Job,
Not one of you who
answered his words.
¹³ "Do not say,
'We have found wisdom;
God will rout him, not man.'
¹⁴ "For he has not arranged *his*
words against me,
Nor will I reply to him with
your arguments.

¹⁵ "They are dismayed, they
no longer answer;
Words have failed them.
¹⁶ "Shall I wait, because they
do not speak,
Because they stop *and* no
longer answer?
¹⁷ "I too will answer my share,
I also will tell my opinion.
¹⁸ "For I am full of words;

The spirit within me constrains me.
¹⁹ "Behold, my belly is like
unvented wine,
Like new wineskins it is
about to burst.
²⁰ "Let me speak that I may get relief;
Let me open my lips and answer.
²¹ "Let me now be partial to no one,
Nor flatter *any* man.
²² "For I do not know how to flatter,
Else my Maker would soon
take me away.

Psalm 98:1-3

A Psalm.

O sing to the LORD a new song,
For He has done wonderful things,
His right hand and His holy arm
have gained the victory for Him.
² The LORD has made known
His salvation;
He has revealed His righteousness
in the sight of the nations.
³ He has remembered His
lovingkindness and His
faithfulness to the house of Israel;
All the ends of the earth have seen
the salvation of our God.

98:1 right hand…holy arm. These are symbols of power. **the victory.** The Lord is often pictured in the Old Testament as a divine warrior (Ex 15:2–3; Pss 18; 68:1–8; Is 59:15ff.). According to the prophets, Christ will begin His millennial reign following His victory over the nations of the world which will gather against Israel in the end times (Zec 14:1–15; Rev 19:11–21).

Proverbs 23:17-18

¹⁷ Do not let your heart envy sinners,
But *live* in the fear of the
LORD always.
¹⁸ Surely there is a future,
And your hope will not be cut off.

23:18 there is a future. Anyone who might envy sinners needs to know that their prosperity is brief. They will die ("be cut off"); then there will be a time when all iniquities will be dealt with and divine justice will prevail (Ps 37:28–38). The righteous will live forever.

1 Corinthians 2:1–16

2 And when I came to you, brethren, I did not come with superiority of speech or of wisdom, proclaiming to you the testimony of God. ² For I determined to know nothing among you except Jesus Christ, and Him crucified. ³ I was with you in weakness and in fear and in much trembling, ⁴ and my message and my preaching were not in persuasive words of wisdom, but in demonstration of the Spirit and of power, ⁵ so that your faith would not rest on the wisdom of men, but on the power of God.

⁶ Yet we do speak wisdom among those who are mature; a wisdom, however, not of this age nor of the rulers of this age, who are passing away; ⁷ but we speak God's wisdom in a mystery, the hidden *wisdom* which God predestined before the ages to our glory; ⁸ *the wisdom* which none of the rulers of this age has understood; for if they had understood

it they would not have crucified the Lord of glory; ⁹ but just as it is written,

"THINGS WHICH EYE HAS NOT
    SEEN AND EAR HAS NOT
    HEARD,
AND *which* HAVE NOT ENTERED
    THE HEART OF MAN,
ALL THAT GOD HAS PREPARED
    FOR THOSE WHO LOVE HIM."

¹⁰ For to us God revealed *them* through the Spirit; for the Spirit searches all things, even the depths of God. ¹¹ For who among men knows the *thoughts* of a man except the spirit of the man which is in him? Even so the *thoughts* of God no one knows except the Spirit of God. ¹² Now we have received, not the spirit of the world, but the Spirit who is from God, so that we may know the things freely given to us by God, ¹³ which things we also speak, not in words taught by human wisdom, but in those taught by the Spirit, combining spiritual *thoughts* with spiritual *words.*

¹⁴ But a natural man does not accept the things of the Spirit of God, for they are foolishness to him; and he cannot understand them, because they are spiritually appraised. ¹⁵ But he who is spiritual appraises all things, yet he himself is appraised by no one. ¹⁶ For WHO HAS KNOWN THE MIND OF THE LORD, THAT HE WILL INSTRUCT HIM? But we have the mind of Christ.

2:7 mystery. This term does not refer to something puzzling, but to truth known to God before time, which He has kept secret until the appropriate time for Him to reveal it. **to our glory.** The truth God established before time and revealed in the New Testament wisdom of the gospel is the truth that God will save and glorify sinners.

DAY 20: How do we receive spiritual truth?

From 1 Corinthians 2:10–16, it is clear that the wisdom that saves, which man's wisdom can't know, is revealed to us by God. He makes it known by revelation, inspiration, and illumination. Revelation (vv. 10–11) and inspiration (vv. 12–13) were given to those who wrote the Bible. Illumination (vv. 14–16) is given to all believers who seek to know and understand that divinely written truth. In each case, the Holy Spirit is the divine agent doing the work (2Pe 1:21).

"God revealed them" (v. 10). By the Holy Spirit, God disclosed His saving truth (Mt 11:25; 13:10–13). The Spirit alone was qualified because He knows all that God knows, Himself being God. "To us." As with the "we's" in vv. 6–7 and vv. 12–13, Paul is, first of all, speaking of himself, and, in a sense, of believers who have been given the Word as recorded by the apostles and their associates who wrote the New Testament.

"We have received" (v. 12). The "we" and "us" refer to the apostles and other writers of the Word of God. The means was inspiration (2Ti 3:16; 2Pe 1:20–21), by which God freely gave the gift of His Word. It was this process of inspiration that turned the spiritual thoughts into spiritual words (v. 13) to give life (Mt 4:4).

"But a natural man does not accept the things of the Spirit of God" (v. 14). This refers to the unconverted, who lack supernatural life and wisdom. "Because they are spiritually appraised." Through illumination of the Word, the Holy Spirit provides His saints the capacity to discern divine truth, which the spiritually dead are unable to comprehend (Jn 5:37–39; 1Jn 2:20, 27). The doctrine of illumination does not mean we know everything (Dt 29:29), that we do not need teachers (Eph 4:11–12), or that understanding does not require hard work (2Ti 2:15).

AUGUST 21

Job 33:1–34:37

33 "However now, Job, please
hear my speech,
And listen to all my words.

2 "Behold now, I open my mouth,
My tongue in my mouth speaks.

3 "My words are *from the*
uprightness of my heart,
And my lips speak
knowledge sincerely.

4 "The Spirit of God has made me,
And the breath of the
Almighty gives me life.

5 "Refute me if you can;
Array yourselves before
me, take your stand.

6 "Behold, I belong to God like you;
I too have been formed out of the clay.

7 "Behold, no fear of me
should terrify you,
Nor should my pressure
weigh heavily on you.

8 "Surely you have spoken
in my hearing,
And I have heard the sound
of *your* words:

9 'I am pure, without transgression;
I am innocent and there
is no guilt in me.

10 'Behold, He invents pretexts
against me;
He counts me as His enemy.

11 'He puts my feet in the stocks;
He watches all my paths.'

12 "Behold, let me tell you, you
are not right in this,
For God is greater than man.

13 "Why do you complain against Him
That He does not give an
account of all His doings?

14 "Indeed God speaks once,
Or twice, *yet* no one notices it.

15 "In a dream, a vision of the night,
When sound sleep falls on men,
While they slumber in their beds,

16 Then He opens the ears of men,
And seals their instruction,

17 That He may turn man aside
from his conduct,
And keep man from pride;

18 He keeps back his soul from the pit,
And his life from passing
over into Sheol.

19 "Man is also chastened with
pain on his bed,
And with unceasing complaint
in his bones;

20 So that his life loathes bread,
And his soul favorite food.

21 "His flesh wastes away from sight,
And his bones which were
not seen stick out.

22 "Then his soul draws near to the pit,
And his life to those who
bring death.

23 "If there is an angel *as*
mediator for him,
One out of a thousand,
To remind a man what
is right for him,

24 Then let him be gracious
to him, and say,
'Deliver him from going
down to the pit,
I have found a ransom';

25 Let his flesh become fresher
than in youth,
Let him return to the days
of his youthful vigor;

26 Then he will pray to God, and
He will accept him,
That he may see His face with joy,
And He may restore His
righteousness to man.

27 "He will sing to men and say,
'I have sinned and perverted
what is right,
And it is not proper for me.

28 'He has redeemed my soul
from going to the pit,
And my life shall see the light.'

29 "Behold, God does all these
oftentimes with men,

30 To bring back his soul from the pit,
That he may be enlightened
with the light of life.

31 "Pay attention, O Job, listen to me;
Keep silent, and let me speak.

32 "*Then* if you have anything
to say, answer me;
Speak, for I desire to justify you.

33 "If not, listen to me;
Keep silent, and I will teach
you wisdom."

34 Then Elihu continued and said,

2 "Hear my words, you wise men,
And listen to me, you who know.

3 "For the ear tests words
  As the palate tastes food.
4 "Let us choose for ourselves
    what is right;
  Let us know among ourselves
    what is good.
5 "For Job has said, 'I am righteous,
  But God has taken away my right;
6 Should I lie concerning my right?
  My wound is incurable, *though I
    am* without transgression.'
7 "What man is like Job,
  Who drinks up derision like water,
8 Who goes in company with
    the workers of iniquity,
  And walks with wicked men?
9 "For he has said, 'It profits
    a man nothing
  When he is pleased with God.'

10 "Therefore, listen to me, you
    men of understanding.
  Far be it from God to do wickedness,
  And from the Almighty to do wrong.
11 "For He pays a man according
    to his work,
  And makes him find it
    according to his way.
12 "Surely, God will not act wickedly,
  And the Almighty will not
    pervert justice.
13 "Who gave Him authority
    over the earth?
  And who has laid *on Him*
    the whole world?
14 "If He should determine to do so,
  If He should gather to Himself
    His spirit and His breath,
15 All flesh would perish together,
  And man would return to dust.

16 "But if *you have* understanding,
    hear this;
  Listen to the sound of my words.
17 "Shall one who hates justice rule?
  And will you condemn the
    righteous mighty One,
18 Who says to a king, 'Worthless one,'
  To nobles, 'Wicked ones';
19 Who shows no partiality to princes
  Nor regards the rich above the poor,
  For they all are the work
    of His hands?
20 "In a moment they die,
    and at midnight
  People are shaken and pass away,
  And the mighty are taken
    away without a hand.

21 "For His eyes are upon the
    ways of a man,
  And He sees all his steps.
22 "There is no darkness or deep shadow
  Where the workers of iniquity
    may hide themselves.
23 "For He does not *need to*
    consider a man further,
  That he should go before
    God in judgment.
24 "He breaks in pieces mighty
    men without inquiry,
  And sets others in their place.
25 "Therefore He knows their works,
  And He overthrows *them*
    in the night,
  And they are crushed.
26 "He strikes them like the wicked
    In a public place,
27 Because they turned aside
    from following Him,
  And had no regard for
    any of His ways;
28 So that they caused the cry of
    the poor to come to Him,
  And that He might hear the
    cry of the afflicted—
29 When He keeps quiet, who
    then can condemn?
  And when He hides His face,
    who then can behold Him,
  That is, in regard to both
    nation and man?—
30 "So that godless men would
    not rule
  Nor be snares of the people.

34:1-37 Elihu addressed Job and his accusers. His approach was to quote Job directly (vv. 5–9), then respond to his complaints, but at times he misinterpreted Job's remarks, and at other times he put the words of the accusers in Job's mouth. The most obvious example of the latter wrongdoing was in saying that Job claimed to be sinlessly perfect (v. 6). Job never claimed that; in fact, Job acknowledged his sin (7:21; 13:26). Elihu didn't know it, but God had pronounced Job innocent (1:8; 2:3). In answer to Job's complaints that God seemed unjust, Elihu reminded Job that God was too holy to do anything wrong (v. 10), fair in dealing with people (vv. 11–12), powerful (vv. 13–14), just (vv. 17–18), impartial (vv. 19–20), omniscient (vv. 21–22), the Judge of all (v. 23), and the Sovereign who does what He wills to prevent evil (vv. 24–30).

31 "For has anyone said to God,
'I have borne *chastisement;*
I will not offend *anymore;*
32 Teach me what I do not see;
If I have done iniquity,
I will not do it again'?
33 "Shall He recompense on your terms,
because you have rejected *it?*
For you must choose, and not I;
Therefore declare what you know.
34 "Men of understanding will say to me,
And a wise man who hears me,
35 'Job speaks without knowledge,
And his words are without wisdom.
36 'Job ought to be tried to the limit,
Because he answers like wicked men.
37 'For he adds rebellion to his sin;
He claps his hands among us,
And multiplies his words
against God.' "

Psalm 98:4-9

4 Shout joyfully to the LORD,
all the earth;
Break forth and sing for joy
and sing praises.
5 Sing praises to the LORD with the lyre,
With the lyre and the
sound of melody.
6 With trumpets and the
sound of the horn
Shout joyfully before the
King, the LORD.

7 Let the sea roar and all it contains,
The world and those who dwell in it.
8 Let the rivers clap their hands,
Let the mountains sing
together for joy

98:4 Shout joyfully. A great cheer, greeting and welcoming a king (Zec 9:9; Mt 21:4-9). **Break forth.** The idea is that of an eruption of praise which could not be contained (Is 14:7; 44:23; 55:12).

98:8 rivers clap their hands. Different parts of nature are pictured as rejoicing in this universal scene of joy (Is 35:1-2; Ro 8:19-21).

---

9 Before the LORD, for He is
coming to judge the earth;
He will judge the world
with righteousness
And the peoples with equity.

Proverbs 23:19-21

19 Listen, my son, and be wise,
And direct your heart in the way.
20 Do not be with heavy
drinkers of wine,
Or with gluttonous eaters of meat;
21 For the heavy drinker and the
glutton will come to poverty,
And drowsiness will clothe
one with rags.

1 Corinthians 3:1-23

3 And I, brethren, could not speak to you as to spiritual men, but as to men of flesh, as to infants in Christ. 2 I gave you milk to drink, not solid food; for you were not yet able *to receive it.* Indeed, even now you are not yet able, 3 for you are still fleshly. For since there is jealousy and strife among you, are you not fleshly, and are you not walking like mere men? 4 For when one says, "I am of Paul," and another, "I am of Apollos," are you not *mere* men?

5 What then is Apollos? And what is Paul? Servants through whom you believed, even as the Lord gave *opportunity* to each one. 6 I planted, Apollos watered, but God was causing the growth. 7 So then neither the one who plants nor the one who waters is anything, but God who causes the growth. 8 Now he who plants and he who waters are one; but each will receive his own reward according to his own labor. 9 For we are God's fellow workers; you are God's field, God's building.

10 According to the grace of God which was given to me, like a wise master builder I laid a foundation, and another is building on it. But each man must be careful how he builds on it. 11 For no man can lay a foundation other than the one which is laid, which is Jesus Christ. 12 Now if any man builds on the foundation with gold, silver, precious stones, wood, hay, straw, 13 each man's work will become evident; for the day will show it because it is to be

3:12 if any man builds. This is, first of all, in reference to the evangelists and pastors (v. 9), and then to all believers who are called to build the church through faithful ministry. **gold, silver, precious stones.** His quality materials represent dedicated, spiritual service to build the church. **wood, hay, straw.** Inferior materials implying shallow activity with no eternal value. They do not necessarily refer to activities that are evil.

3:13 the day. Refers to the time of the Judgment Seat of Christ (2Co 5:10). **revealed with fire.** The fire of God's discerning judgment (Job 23:10; Zec 13:9; 1Pe 1:17–18; Rev 3:18). Second Corinthians 5:10 indicates that the wood, hay, and straw are "worthless" things that don't stand the test of judgment fire (Col 2:18).

revealed with fire, and the fire itself will test the quality of each man's work. ¹⁴ If any man's work which he has built on it remains, he will receive a reward. ¹⁵ If any man's work is burned up, he will suffer loss; but he himself will be saved, yet so as through fire. ¹⁶ Do you not know that you are a temple of God and *that* the Spirit of God dwells in you? ¹⁷ If any man destroys the temple of God, God will destroy him, for the temple of God is holy, and that is what you are.

¹⁸ Let no man deceive himself. If any man among you thinks that he is wise in this age, he must become foolish, so that he may become wise. ¹⁹ For the wisdom of this world is foolishness before God. For it is written, "*He is* THE ONE WHO CATCHES THE WISE IN THEIR CRAFTINESS"; ²⁰ and again, "THE LORD KNOWS THE REASONINGS of the wise, THAT THEY ARE USELESS." ²¹ So then let no one boast in men. For all things belong to you, ²² whether Paul or Apollos or Cephas or the world or life or death or things present or things to come; all things belong to you, ²³ and you belong to Christ; and Christ belongs to God.

DAY 21: What does it mean to be "of flesh"?

The cause of problems in the Corinthian church was more than external, worldly influence. It was also internal carnality (1Co 3:1). The pressures of the world were combined with the weakness of the flesh. Although Corinthian believers were no longer "natural," they were not "spiritual" (fully controlled by the Holy Spirit). In fact, they were carnal, or "of flesh" (controlled by the fallen flesh). Though all believers have the Holy Spirit (Ro 8:9), they still battle the fallen flesh (Ro 7:14–25; 8:23).

Paul calls them "infants in Christ." The carnality of those believers was indicative of their immaturity. They had no excuse for not being mature, since Paul implied that he should have been able to write to them as mature, in light of all he had taught them (v. 2). He could only feed them with "milk" (v. 2). Not a reference to certain doctrines, but to the more easily digestible truths of doctrine that were given to new believers. "Solid food" is the deeper features of the doctrines of Scripture. The difference is not in the kind of truth, but degree of depth. Spiritual immaturity makes one unable to receive the richest truths.

Carnality produces the attitude of envy, a severe form of selfishness, which produces the action of strife and the subsequent divisions (v. 3). They end up acting as "mere men." Apart from the will of Spirit, hence carnal, not spiritual. Factionalism was the divisive product of carnality, aligning themselves with "Paul...Apollos" (v. 4). Paul reminds them that all the human instruments God uses to produce salvation life are equally considered and rewarded for their willingness to be used by God. But all the glory goes to Him, who alone saves. Because of that, the silly favoritism is condemned (vv. 5–8).

AUGUST 22

Job 35:1–36:33

35 Then Elihu continued and said,

² "Do you think this is
  according to justice?
 Do you say, 'My righteousness
  is more than God's'?
³ "For you say, 'What advantage
  will it be to You?
 What profit will I have, more
  than if I had sinned?'

⁴ "I will answer you,
  And your friends with you.
⁵ "Look at the heavens and see;
  And behold the clouds—they
   are higher than you.
⁶ "If you have sinned, what do you
   accomplish against Him?
 And if your transgressions are
   many, what do you do
   to Him?
⁷ "If you are righteous, what
   do you give to Him,
 Or what does He receive
   from your hand?

8 "Your wickedness is for a
  man like yourself,
And your righteousness is
  for a son of man.

9 "Because of the multitude of
  oppressions they cry out;
They cry for help because of
  the arm of the mighty.

10 "But no one says, 'Where
  is God my Maker,
Who gives songs in the night,

11 Who teaches us more than
  the beasts of the earth
And makes us wiser than the
  birds of the heavens?'

12 "There they cry out, but He
  does not answer
Because of the pride of
  evil men.

13 "Surely God will not listen
  to an empty cry,
Nor will the Almighty
  regard it.

14 "How much less when you say
  you do not behold Him,
The case is before Him, and
  you must wait for Him!

15 "And now, because He has not
  visited in His anger,
Nor has He acknowledged
  transgression well,

16 So Job opens his mouth
  emptily;
He multiplies words
  without knowledge."

35:1–16 Elihu again referred to Job's complaints, first of all his thinking that there
appeared to be no advantage to being righteous (v. 3), which Job had said, as recorded
in 21:15 and 34:9. The first part of his answer is
that Job gained nothing by sinning or not sinning because God was so high that nothing
men do affects Him (vv. 5–7). It only affects
other men (v. 8). Job had also complained
that God did not answer his prayers when
he cried under this oppression (24:12; 30:20).
Elihu coldly gave 3 reasons why Job's prayers
had not been heard: pride (vv. 10, 12), wrong
motives (v. 13), and lack of patient trust (v. 14).
Again, all this theoretical talk missed Job's
predicament completely because he was
righteous. Elihu was no more help than the
other counselors.

---

36 Then Elihu continued and said,

2 "Wait for me a little, and
  I will show you
That there is yet more to be
  said in God's behalf.

3 "I will fetch my knowledge from afar,
And I will ascribe righteousness
  to my Maker.

4 "For truly my words are not false;
One who is perfect in
  knowledge is with you.

5 "Behold, God is mighty but
  does not despise any;
He is mighty in strength
  of understanding.

6 "He does not keep the wicked alive,
But gives justice to the afflicted.

7 "He does not withdraw His eyes
  from the righteous;
But with kings on the throne
He has seated them forever,
  and they are exalted.

8 "And if they are bound in fetters,
And are caught in the
  cords of affliction,

9 Then He declares to them their work
And their transgressions, that they
  have magnified themselves.

10 "He opens their ear to instruction,
And commands that they
  return from evil.

11 "If they hear and serve Him,
They will end their days in prosperity
And their years in pleasures.

12 "But if they do not hear, they
  shall perish by the sword
And they will die without knowledge.

13 "But the godless in heart lay up anger;
They do not cry for help
  when He binds them.

14 "They die in youth,
And their life perishes among
  the cult prostitutes.

15 "He delivers the afflicted
  in their affliction,
And opens their ear in
  time of oppression.

16 "Then indeed, He enticed you
  from the mouth of distress,
Instead of it, a broad place
  with no constraint;
And that which was set on your
  table was full of fatness.

17 "But you were full of judgment
  on the wicked;
Judgment and justice take hold of you.

36:15 opens their ear in *time of* oppression.
This was a new insight and perhaps the most helpful thing Elihu said. He went beyond all that had been said about God's using suffering to chasten and bring repentance. He was saying that God used suffering to open men's ears, to draw them to Himself. But as long as Job kept complaining, he was turning to iniquity rather than drawing near to God in his suffering (vv. 16–21).

---

18 "*Beware* that wrath does not
    entice you to scoffing;
And do not let the greatness of
    the ransom turn you aside.
19 "Will your riches keep you
    from distress,
Or all the forces of *your* strength?
20 "Do not long for the night,
    When people vanish in their place.
21 "Be careful, do not turn to evil,
    For you have preferred
    this to affliction.
22 "Behold, God is exalted in His power;
    Who is a teacher like Him?
23 "Who has appointed Him His way,
    And who has said, 'You
    have done wrong'?
24 "Remember that you should
    exalt His work,
Of which men have sung.
25 "All men have seen it;
    Man beholds from afar.
26 "Behold, God is exalted, and
    we do not know *Him;*
The number of His years
    is unsearchable.
27 "For He draws up the drops
    of water,
They distill rain from the mist,
28 Which the clouds pour down,
    They drip upon man abundantly.
29 "Can anyone understand the
    spreading of the clouds,
The thundering of His pavilion?
30 "Behold, He spreads His
    lightning about Him,
And He covers the depths
    of the sea.
31 "For by these He judges peoples;
    He gives food in abundance.
32 "He covers *His* hands with
    the lightning,
And commands it to strike the mark.

33 "Its noise declares His presence;
    The cattle also, concerning
    what is coming up.

Psalm 99:1–9

The LORD reigns, let the
    peoples tremble;
He is enthroned *above* the
    cherubim, let the earth shake!
2 The LORD is great in Zion,
    And He is exalted above
    all the peoples.
3 Let them praise Your great
    and awesome name;
Holy is He.
4 The strength of the King loves
    justice;
You have established equity;
You have executed justice and
    righteousness in Jacob.
5 Exalt the LORD our God
    And worship at His footstool;
Holy is He.

6 Moses and Aaron were
    among His priests,
And Samuel was among those
    who called on His name;
They called upon the LORD
    and He answered them.
7 He spoke to them in the
    pillar of cloud;
They kept His testimonies
    And the statute that He
    gave them.
8 O LORD our God, You answered
    them;
You were a forgiving God to them,
    And *yet* an avenger of their
    evil deeds.
9 Exalt the LORD our God
    And worship at His holy hill,
For holy is the LORD our God.

99:5 His footstool. In general, this is a metaphor for the temple in Jerusalem (Is 60:13; La 2:1); but more specifically, for the ark of the covenant (1Ch 28:2). Footstools were included with the thrones of the kings of Israel (2Ch 9:18).

99:9 His holy hill. This is the hill in Jerusalem where the temple was (Pss 15:1; 24:3), and where it will be located in the future messianic kingdom (Is 24:23).

Proverbs 23:22–25

22 Listen to your father who begot you,
And do not despise your
mother when she is old.
23 Buy truth, and do not sell *it,*
Get wisdom and instruction
and understanding.

23:23 Buy truth. Obtain the truth at all costs. Then never relinquish it at any price.

24 The father of the righteous
will greatly rejoice,
And he who sires a wise son
will be glad in him.
25 Let your father and your
mother be glad,
And let her rejoice who
gave birth to you.

1 Corinthians 4:1–21

4 Let a man regard us in this manner, as servants of Christ and stewards of the mysteries of God. 2 In this case, moreover, it is required of stewards that one be found trustworthy. 3 But to me it is a very small thing that I may be examined by you, or by *any* human court; in fact, I do not even examine myself. 4 For I am conscious of nothing against myself, yet I am not by this acquitted; but the one who examines me is the Lord. 5 Therefore do not go on passing judgment before the time, *but wait* until the Lord comes who will both bring to light the things hidden in the darkness and disclose the motives of *men's* hearts; and then each man's praise will come to him from God.

6 Now these things, brethren, I have figuratively applied to myself and Apollos for your sakes, so that in us you may learn not to exceed what is written, so that no one of you will become arrogant in behalf of one against the other. 7 For who regards you as superior? What do you have that you did not receive? And if you did receive it, why do you boast as if you had not received it?

8 You are already filled, you have already become rich, you have become kings without us; and indeed, *I* wish that you had become kings so that we also might reign with you. 9 For, I think, God has exhibited us apostles

4:8 filled…rich…reign. In a severe rebuke, Paul heaps on false praise, sarcastically suggesting that those Corinthians who were self-satisfied had already achieved spiritual greatness. They were similar to the Laodiceans (Rev 3:17). **reign.** Yet, Paul genuinely wished it really were the coronation time of the Millennium, so that they all might share in the glory of the Lord.

last of all, as men condemned to death; because we have become a spectacle to the world, both to angels and to men. 10 We are fools for Christ's sake, but you are prudent in Christ; we are weak, but you are strong; you are distinguished, but we are without honor. 11 To this present hour we are both hungry and thirsty, and are poorly clothed, and are roughly treated, and are homeless; 12 and we toil, working with our own hands; when we are reviled, we bless; when we are persecuted, we endure; 13 when we are slandered, we try to conciliate; we have become as the scum of the world, the dregs of all things, *even* until now.

14 I do not write these things to shame you, but to admonish you as my beloved children. 15 For if you were to have countless tutors in Christ, yet *you would* not *have* many fathers, for in Christ Jesus I became your father through the gospel. 16 Therefore I exhort you, be imitators of me. 17 For this reason I have sent to you Timothy, who is my beloved and faithful child in the Lord, and he will remind you of my ways which are in Christ, just as I teach everywhere in every church. 18 Now some have become arrogant, as though I were not coming to you. 19 But I will come to you soon, if the Lord wills, and I shall find out, not the words of those who are arrogant but their power. 20 For the kingdom of God does not consist in words but in power. 21 What do you desire? Shall I come to you with a rod, or with love and a spirit of gentleness?

DAY 22: How did Paul want to be regarded by the Corinthians?

"Let a man regard us in this manner, as servants of Christ and stewards of the mysteries of God" (1Co 4:1). Paul wanted everyone to view him and his fellow ministers only as the humble messengers God ordained them to be (3:9, 22). "Servants." Paul expresses his humility by using a word literally meaning "under rowers," referring to the lowest, most menial, and most despised galley slaves, who rowed on the bottom tier of a ship. "Stewards." Paul defines his responsibilities as an apostle by using a word originally referring to a person entrusted with and responsible for his master's entire household: e.g., buildings, fields, finances, food, other servants, and sometimes even children of the owner. "Mysteries of God." "Mystery" is used in the New Testament to refer to divine revelation previously hidden. Here the word is used in its broadest sense as God's fully revealed truth in the New Testament. It was all that truth which Paul had to oversee and dispense as God's servant and steward.

The most essential quality of a servant or steward is obedient loyalty to his master (vv. 2, 17; 7:25; Mt 24:45–51; Col 1:7; 4:7). Because of that, Paul said that "it is a very small thing that I may be examined by you, or by any human court" (v. 3). Paul is not being arrogant or saying that he is above fellow ministers, other Christians, or even certain unbelievers. He is saying that a human verdict on his life is not the one that matters, even if it was his own.

"For I am conscious of nothing against myself, yet I am not by this acquitted" (v. 4). Paul was not aware of any unconfessed or habitual sin in his own life, but his limited understanding assumed that his was not the final verdict. Paul's own sincere evaluation of his life did not acquit him of all failures to be faithful. The Lord is the ultimate and only qualified Judge of any man's obedience and faithfulness (2Ti 2:15). Since final rewards will be based not just on outward service but on inward devotion (10:31), only God can give the praise each deserves. He "will both bring to light the things hidden in the darkness...motives of men's hearts" (v. 5).

AUGUST 23

Job 37:1–38:41

37 "At this also my heart trembles,
And leaps from its place.
2 "Listen closely to the thunder
of His voice,
And the rumbling that goes
out from His mouth.
3 "Under the whole heaven
He lets it loose,
And His lightning to the
ends of the earth.
4 "After it, a voice roars;
He thunders with His majestic voice,
And He does not restrain the
lightnings when His voice is heard.
5 "God thunders with His
voice wondrously,
Doing great things which we
cannot comprehend.
6 "For to the snow He says,
'Fall on the earth,'
And to the downpour and
the rain, 'Be strong.'
7 "He seals the hand of every man,
That all men may know His work.
8 "Then the beast goes into its lair
And remains in its den.
9 "Out of the south comes the storm,
And out of the north the cold.
10 "From the breath of God ice is made,
And the expanse of the
waters is frozen.
11 "Also with moisture He loads
the thick cloud;
He disperses the cloud
of His lightning.

12 "It changes direction, turning
around by His guidance,
That it may do whatever
He commands it
On the face of the inhabited earth.
13 "Whether for correction,
or for His world,
Or for lovingkindness, He
causes it to happen.

14 "Listen to this, O Job,
Stand and consider the
wonders of God.
15 "Do you know how God
establishes them,
And makes the lightning of
His cloud to shine?
16 "Do you know about the layers
of the thick clouds,
The wonders of one perfect
in knowledge,
17 You whose garments are hot,
When the land is still because
of the south wind?
18 "Can you, with Him, spread
out the skies,
Strong as a molten mirror?
19 "Teach us what we shall say to Him;
We cannot arrange *our case*
because of darkness.
20 "Shall it be told Him that
I would speak?
Or should a man say that he
would be swallowed up?

21 "Now men do not see the light
which is bright in the skies;
But the wind has passed
and cleared them.

22 "Out of the north comes
   golden *splendor;*
   Around God is awesome majesty.
23 "The Almighty—we cannot find Him;
   He is exalted in power
   And He will not do violence to justice
   and abundant righteousness.
24 "Therefore men fear Him;
   He does not regard any who
   are wise of heart."

38 Then the LORD answered Job out of
the whirlwind and said,

2 "Who is this that darkens counsel
   By words without knowledge?
3 "Now gird up your loins like a man,
   And I will ask you, and
   you instruct Me!
4 "Where were you when I laid the
   foundation of the earth?
   Tell *Me,* if you have understanding,
5 Who set its measurements?
   Since you know.
   Or who stretched the line on it?

38:1 the LORD. Yahweh, the covenant Lord, was
the name used for God in the book's prologue,
where the reader was introduced to Job and his
relationship with God. However, in chaps. 3–37,
the name Yahweh is not used. God is called El
Shaddai, God the Almighty. In this book that
change becomes a way of illustrating that God
has been detached and distant. The relationship is restored in rich terms as God reveals
Himself to Job using His covenant name. **out of
the whirlwind.** Job had repeatedly called God
to court in order to verify his innocence. God
finally came to interrogate Job on some of the
comments he had made to his own accusers.
God was about to be Job's vindicator, but He
first brought Job to a right understanding of
Himself.

38:3 I will ask you. God silenced Job's presumption in constantly wanting to ask the questions
of God, by becoming Job's questioner. It must
be noted that God never told Job about the
reason for his pain, about the conflict between
Himself and Satan, which was the reason for
Job's suffering. He never gave Job any explanation at all about the circumstances of his
trouble. He did one thing in all He said. He
asked Job if he was as eternal, great, powerful,
wise, and perfect as God. If not, Job would
have been better off to be quiet and trust Him.

6 "On what were its bases sunk?
   Or who laid its cornerstone,
7 When the morning stars sang together
   And all the sons of God
   shouted for joy?

8 "Or *who* enclosed the sea with doors
   When, bursting forth, it went
   out from the womb;
9 When I made a cloud its garment
   And thick darkness its
   swaddling band,
10 And I placed boundaries on it
   And set a bolt and doors,
11 And I said, 'Thus far you shall
   come, but no farther;
   And here shall your proud
   waves stop'?

12 "Have you ever in your life
   commanded the morning,
   And caused the dawn to
   know its place,
13 That it might take hold of
   the ends of the earth,
   And the wicked be shaken out of it?
14 "It is changed like clay *under* the seal;
   And they stand forth like a garment.
15 "From the wicked their
   light is withheld,
   And the uplifted arm is broken.

16 "Have you entered into the
   springs of the sea
   Or walked in the recesses of the deep?
17 "Have the gates of death been
   revealed to you,
   Or have you seen the gates
   of deep darkness?
18 "Have you understood the
   expanse of the earth?
   Tell *Me,* if you know all this.

19 "Where is the way to the
   dwelling of light?
   And darkness, where is its place,
20 That you may take it to its territory
   And that you may discern
   the paths to its home?
21 "You know, for you were born then,
   And the number of your days is great!
22 "Have you entered the
   storehouses of the snow,
   Or have you seen the
   storehouses of the hail,
23 Which I have reserved for
   the time of distress,
   For the day of war and battle?

²⁴ "Where is the way that the
light is divided,
Or the east wind scattered
on the earth?

²⁵ "Who has cleft a channel for the flood,
Or a way for the thunderbolt,
²⁶ To bring rain on a land
without people,
On a desert without a man in it,
²⁷ To satisfy the waste and desolate land
And to make the seeds of
grass to sprout?
²⁸ "Has the rain a father?
Or who has begotten the
drops of dew?
²⁹ "From whose womb has come the ice?
And the frost of heaven, who
has given it birth?
³⁰ "Water becomes hard like stone,
And the surface of the deep
is imprisoned.

³¹ "Can you bind the chains
of the Pleiades,
Or loose the cords of Orion?
³² "Can you lead forth a
constellation in its season,
And guide the Bear with
her satellites?
³³ "Do you know the ordinances
of the heavens,
Or fix their rule over the earth?

³⁴ "Can you lift up your voice
to the clouds,
So that an abundance of
water will cover you?
³⁵ "Can you send forth lightnings
that they may go
And say to you, 'Here we are'?
³⁶ "Who has put wisdom in the
innermost being
Or given understanding to the mind?
³⁷ "Who can count the clouds by wisdom,
Or tip the water jars of the heavens,
³⁸ When the dust hardens into a mass
And the clods stick together?

³⁹ "Can you hunt the prey for the lion,
Or satisfy the appetite of
the young lions,
⁴⁰ When they crouch in *their* dens
And lie in wait in *their* lair?
⁴¹ "Who prepares for the raven
its nourishment
When its young cry to God
And wander about without food?

Psalm 100:1–5

A Psalm for Thanksgiving.

Shout joyfully to the LORD,
all the earth.
² Serve the LORD with gladness;
Come before Him with joyful singing.
³ Know that the LORD Himself is God;
It is He who has made us,
and not we ourselves;
We are His people and the
sheep of His pasture.

100:3 Know. In the sense of experiencing and being completely assured of the truth. **the LORD Himself is God.** A confession that Israel's covenant God, Jehovah, is the only true God. **made us.** Though God's actual creation of every human being is understood here, this phrase seems to refer to God's making and blessing Israel as a nation (Dt 32:6, 15; Ps 95:6; Is 29:22–23; 44:2). **His people…His pasture.** The shepherd image is often ascribed to the king of Israel, as well as to the Lord (Ps 78:70–72; Is 44:28; Jer 10:21; Zec 10:3; 11:4–17). The figure suggests intimate care (Lk 15:3–6). According to the New Testament, the Lord is also the Shepherd of saints in the church age (Jn 10:16).

⁴ Enter His gates with thanksgiving
And His courts with praise.
Give thanks to Him, bless His name.
⁵ For the LORD is good;
His lovingkindness is everlasting
And His faithfulness to
all generations.

Proverbs 23:26–28

²⁶ Give me your heart, my son,
And let your eyes delight in my ways.
²⁷ For a harlot is a deep pit
And an adulterous woman
is a narrow well.
²⁸ Surely she lurks as a robber,
And increases the faithless
among men.

1 Corinthians 5:1–13

5 It is actually reported that there is immorality among you, and immorality of such a kind as does not exist even among the Gentiles, that someone has his father's wife. ²You have become arrogant and have not mourned instead, so that the one who had done this deed would be removed from your midst.

5:1 immorality. This sin was so vile that even the church's pagan neighbors were doubtless scandalized by it. The Corinthians had rationalized or minimized this sin which was common knowledge, even though Paul had written them before about it (v. 9). The Greek for "immorality" is the root of the Eng. word "pornography." **his father's wife.** The man's stepmother, with whom having sexual relations bore the same sinful stigma as if between him and his natural mother. Incest was punishable by death in the Old Testament (Lv 18:7–8, 29; see Dt 22:30) and was both uncommon ("does not exist") and illegal under Roman law.

³ For I, on my part, though absent in body but present in spirit, have already judged him who has so committed this, as though I were present. ⁴ In the name of our Lord Jesus, when you are assembled, and I with you in spirit, with the power of our Lord Jesus, ⁵ I have decided to deliver such a one to Satan for the destruction of his flesh, so that his spirit may be saved in the day of the Lord Jesus.

⁶ Your boasting is not good. Do you not know that a little leaven leavens the whole lump of dough? ⁷ Clean out the old leaven so that you may be a new lump, just as you are in fact unleavened. For Christ our Passover also has been sacrificed. ⁸ Therefore let us celebrate the feast, not with old leaven, nor with the leaven of malice and wickedness, but with the unleavened bread of sincerity and truth.

⁹ I wrote you in my letter not to associate with immoral people; ¹⁰ I did not at all mean with the immoral people of this world, or with the covetous and swindlers, or with idolaters, for then you would have to go out of the world. ¹¹ But actually, I wrote to you not to associate with any so-called brother if he is an immoral person, or covetous, or an idolater, or a reviler, or a drunkard, or a swindler—not even to eat with such a one. ¹² For what have I to do with judging outsiders? Do you not judge those who are within the church? ¹³ But those who are outside, God judges. REMOVE THE WICKED MAN FROM AMONG YOURSELVES.

DAY 23: Why doesn't God answer all of Job's (and our) questions?

This question assumes that if God answered all our questions, it would be easier to believe. This is not true. Trust goes beyond answers. Sometimes, questions become a way to avoid trust.

Take, for example, a little girl invited to jump off the stairs into her father's waiting hands. She asks, "Will you catch me, Daddy?" He answers, "Yes, I will!" She may jump or she may proceed to ask endless versions of her first question. If she does jump, it will be more because of whom she knows her father to be than because of his answer to one of her questions. The fact that she jumps does not mean that she has run out of fears or questions; it means that her trust is greater than her fears or questions.

In the end, we must trust God more than our capacity to understand God's ways. The lesson from Job's experience does not forbid us from asking questions. Often these questions will lead us to the reasons for our suffering. But Job's experience also warns us that we may not be able to understand all our suffering all the time, or even any of it some of the time.

God doesn't answer all of our questions because we are simply unable to understand many of His answers.

AUGUST 24

Job 39:1–40:24

39 ¹ "Do you know the time the mountain goats give birth?
Do you observe the calving of the deer?
² "Can you count the months they fulfill,
Or do you know the time they give birth?
³ "They kneel down, they bring forth their young,
They get rid of their labor pains.

⁴ "Their offspring become strong,
they grow up in the open field;
They leave and do not return to them.

⁵ "Who sent out the wild donkey free?
And who loosed the bonds of the swift donkey,
⁶ To whom I gave the wilderness for a home
And the salt land for his dwelling place?
⁷ "He scorns the tumult of the city,
The shoutings of the driver he does not hear.

8 "He explores the mountains
for his pasture
And searches after every green thing.
9 "Will the wild ox consent to serve you,
Or will he spend the night
at your manger?
10 "Can you bind the wild ox in
a furrow with ropes,
Or will he harrow the
valleys after you?
11 "Will you trust him because
his strength is great
And leave your labor to him?
12 "Will you have faith in him that
he will return your grain
And gather *it from* your
threshing floor?

13 "The ostriches' wings flap joyously
With the pinion and plumage of love,
14 For she abandons her eggs to the earth
And warms them in the dust,
15 And she forgets that a foot
may crush them,
Or that a wild beast may
trample them.
16 "She treats her young cruelly,
as if *they* were not hers;
Though her labor be in vain,
she is unconcerned;
17 Because God has made her
forget wisdom,
And has not given her a share
of understanding.
18 "When she lifts herself on high,
She laughs at the horse and his rider.

19 "Do you give the horse *his* might?
Do you clothe his neck with a mane?
20 "Do you make him leap like the locust?
His majestic snorting is terrible.
21 "He paws in the valley, and
rejoices in *his* strength;
He goes out to meet the weapons.
22 "He laughs at fear and is not dismayed;
And he does not turn back
from the sword.
23 "The quiver rattles against him,
The flashing spear and javelin.
24 "With shaking and rage he
races over the ground,
And he does not stand still at
the voice of the trumpet.
25 "As often as the trumpet
sounds he says, 'Aha!'
And he scents the battle from afar,
And the thunder of the captains
and the war cry.

26 "Is it by your understanding
that the hawk soars,
Stretching his wings
toward the south?
27 "Is it at your command that
the eagle mounts up
And makes his nest on high?
28 "On the cliff he dwells and lodges,
Upon the rocky crag, an
inaccessible place.
29 "From there he spies out food;
His eyes see *it* from afar.
30 "His young ones also suck up blood;
And where the slain are,
there is he."

40 Then the LORD said to Job,

2 "Will the faultfinder contend
with the Almighty?
Let him who reproves God answer it."

3 Then Job answered the LORD and said,

4 "Behold, I am insignificant;
what can I reply to You?
I lay my hand on my mouth.
5 "Once I have spoken, and I
will not answer;
Even twice, and I will add
nothing more."

6 Then the LORD answered Job out of the
storm and said,

7 "Now gird up your loins like a man;
I will ask you, and you instruct Me.
8 "Will you really annul My judgment?
Will you condemn Me that
you may be justified?
9 "Or do you have an arm like God,
And can you thunder with
a voice like His?

10 "Adorn yourself with
eminence and dignity,
And clothe yourself with
honor and majesty.
11 "Pour out the overflowings
of your anger,
And look on everyone who is
proud, and make him low.
12 "Look on everyone who is
proud, *and* humble him,
And tread down the wicked
where they stand.
13 "Hide them in the dust together;
Bind them in the hidden *place*.

¹⁴ "Then I will also confess to you,
   That your own right hand
      can save you.

¹⁵ "Behold now, Behemoth, which
      I made as well as you;
   He eats grass like an ox.

¹⁶ "Behold now, his strength in his loins
   And his power in the
      muscles of his belly.

¹⁷ "He bends his tail like a cedar;
   The sinews of his thighs
      are knit together.

¹⁸ "His bones are tubes of bronze;
   His limbs are like bars of iron.

40:15-24 Behemoth. While this is a generic term used commonly in the Old Testament for large cattle or land animals, the description in this passage suggests an extraordinary creature. The hippopotamus has been suggested by the details in the passage (vv. 19-24). However, the short tail of a hippo is hardly consistent with v. 17, where tail could be translated "trunk." It could refer to an elephant, who could be considered "first" or chief of God's creatures whom only He can control (v. 19). Some believe God is describing His most impressive creation of land animals, the dinosaur species, which fit all the characteristics.

¹⁹ "He is the first of the ways of God;
   Let his maker bring near his sword.

²⁰ "Surely the mountains bring him food,
   And all the beasts of the
      field play there.

²¹ "Under the lotus plants he lies down,
   In the covert of the reeds
      and the marsh.

²² "The lotus plants cover
      him with shade;
   The willows of the brook
      surround him.

²³ "If a river rages, he is not alarmed;
   He is confident, though the
      Jordan rushes to his mouth.

²⁴ "Can anyone capture him
      when he is on watch,
   With barbs can anyone
      pierce *his* nose?

Psalm 101:1-4

A Psalm of David.

I will sing of lovingkindness
   and justice,
To You, O LORD, I will sing praises.

² I will give heed to the blameless way.
   When will You come to me?
I will walk within my house in
   the integrity of my heart.

101:2 blameless way. As the king goes, so go his followers (v. 6). **When will You come to me?** This is not an eschatological expectation, but rather a personal expression of David's need for God's immanent involvement in his earthly kingship. **my house.** The king first starts with his own personal life (v. 7), and then looks beyond to his kingdom (vv. 5, 8).

³ I will set no worthless thing
      before my eyes;
   I hate the work of those
      who fall away;
   It shall not fasten its grip on me.

⁴ A perverse heart shall
      depart from me;
   I will know no evil.

Proverbs 23:29-30

²⁹ Who has woe? Who has sorrow?
   Who has contentions? Who
      has complaining?
   Who has wounds without cause?
   Who has redness of eyes?

³⁰ Those who linger long over wine,
   Those who go to taste mixed wine.

23:30 mixed wine. Lingering long at the wine is indicative of constant drinking, so as to induce drunkenness (1Ti 3:3; Titus 1:7). Searching for more to drink indicates the same pursuit.

1 Corinthians 6:1-20

6 Does any one of you, when he has a case against his neighbor, dare to go to law before the unrighteous and not before the saints? ² Or do you not know that the saints will judge the world? If the world is judged by you, are you not competent to *constitute* the smallest law courts? ³ Do you not know that we will judge angels? How much more matters of this life? ⁴ So if you have law courts dealing with matters of this life, do you appoint them as judges who are of no account in the church? ⁵ I say *this* to your shame. *Is it so, that* there is not among you one wise man who will be able to decide between his brethren,

6:2 judge the world. Because Christians will assist Christ to judge the world in the millennial kingdom (Rev 2:26–27; 3:21; see Da 7:22), they are more than qualified with the truth, the Spirit, the gifts, and the resources they presently have in Him to settle small matters that come up among themselves in this present life.

⁶ but brother goes to law with brother, and that before unbelievers?

⁷ Actually, then, it is already a defeat for you, that you have lawsuits with one another. Why not rather be wronged? Why not rather be defrauded? ⁸ On the contrary, you yourselves wrong and defraud. *You do* this even to *your* brethren.

⁹ Or do you not know that the unrighteous will not inherit the kingdom of God? Do not be deceived; neither fornicators, nor idolaters, nor adulterers, nor effeminate, nor homosexuals, ¹⁰ nor thieves, nor *the* covetous, nor drunkards, nor revilers, nor swindlers, will inherit the kingdom of God. ¹¹ Such were some of you; but you were washed, but you were sanctified, but you were justified in the name of the Lord Jesus Christ and in the Spirit of our God.

¹² All things are lawful for me, but not all things are profitable. All things are lawful for me, but I will not be mastered by anything. ¹³ Food is for the stomach and the stomach is for food, but God will do away with both

of them. Yet the body is not for immorality, but for the Lord, and the Lord is for the body. ¹⁴ Now God has not only raised the Lord, but will also raise us up through His power. ¹⁵ Do you not know that your bodies are members of Christ? Shall I then take away the members of Christ and make them members of a prostitute? May it never be! ¹⁶ Or do you not know that the one who joins himself to a prostitute is one body *with her*? For He says, "THE TWO SHALL BECOME ONE FLESH." ¹⁷ But the one who joins himself to the Lord is one spirit *with Him*. ¹⁸ Flee immorality. Every *other* sin that a man commits is outside the body, but the immoral man sins against his own body. ¹⁹ Or do you not know that your body is a temple of the Holy Spirit who is in you, whom you have from God, and that you are not your own? ²⁰ For you have been bought with a price: therefore glorify God in your body.

6:15 members. The believer's body is not only for the Lord here and now (v. 14) but is of the Lord, a part of His body, the church (Eph 1:22–23). The Christian's body is a spiritual temple in which the Spirit of Christ lives (12:3; Jn 7:38–39; 20:22; Ac 1:8; Ro 8:9; 2Co 6:16); therefore, when a believer commits a sexual sin, it involves Christ with a harlot. All sexual sin is harlotry. **May it never be!** These words translate the strongest Greek negative—"this should never be so."

DAY 24: Who does Paul list among those who will not inherit God's kingdom?

First Corinthians 6:9–10 provides a list of people who will "not inherit the kingdom." The kingdom is the spiritual sphere of salvation where God rules as king over all who belong to Him by faith. All believers are in that spiritual kingdom yet are waiting to enter into the full inheritance of it in the age to come. While believers can and do commit these sins, they do not characterize them as an unbroken life pattern. When they do, it demonstrates that the person is not in God's kingdom. True believers who do sin, repent of that sin and seek to gain the victory over it (Ro 7:14–25).

"Fornicators." All who indulge in sexual immorality, but particularly unmarried persons. "Idolaters." Those who worship any false god or follow any false religious system. "Adulterers." Married persons who indulge in sexual acts outside their marriage. "Effeminate…homosexuals." These terms refer to those who exchange and corrupt normal male-female sexual roles and relations. Transvestism, sex changes, and other gender perversions are included (Ge 1:27; Dt 22:5). Sodomites (another term for homosexuals) are so-called because the sin of male-male sex dominated the city of Sodom (Ge 18:20; 19:4–5). This sinful perversion is condemned always, in any form, by Scripture (Lv 18:22; 20:13; Ro 1:26–27; 1Ti 1:10).

"Thieves…covetous." Both are guilty of the same basic sin of greed. Those who are covetous desire what belongs to others; thieves actually take it. "Revilers." People who try to destroy others with words. "Swindlers." Swindlers and embezzlers who steal indirectly, taking unfair advantage of others for their own financial gain.

Paul reminds the Corinthians that "such were some of you" (v. 11). Though not all Christians have been guilty of all those particular sins, every Christian is equally an ex-sinner, since Christ came to save sinners (Mt 9:13; Ro 5:20).

AUGUST 25

Job 41:1–42:17

41 "Can you draw out Leviathan
    with a fishhook?
  Or press down his tongue
    with a cord?
2 "Can you put a rope in his nose
  Or pierce his jaw with a hook?

41:1 Leviathan. This term appears in 4 other Old Testament texts (Job 3:8; Pss 74:14; 104:26; Is 27:1). In each case Leviathan refers to some mighty creature who can overwhelm man but who is no match for God. Since this creature lives in the sea among ships (Ps 104:26), some form of sea monster, possibly an ancient dinosaur, is in view. Some feel it was a crocodile, which had scaly hide (v. 15), terrible teeth (v. 14), and speed in the water (v. 32). But crocodiles are not sea creatures, and clearly this one was (v. 31). Some have thought it was a killer whale or a great white shark, because he is the ultimate killer beast over all other proud beasts (v. 34).

3 "Will he make many
    supplications to you,
  Or will he speak to you soft words?
4 "Will he make a covenant with you?
  Will you take him for a
    servant forever?
5 "Will you play with him as with a bird,
  Or will you bind him for
    your maidens?
6 "Will the traders bargain over him?
  Will they divide him among
    the merchants?
7 "Can you fill his skin with harpoons,
  Or his head with fishing spears?
8 "Lay your hand on him;
  Remember the battle; you
    will not do it again!
9 "Behold, your expectation is false;
  Will you be laid low even
    at the sight of him?
10 "No one is so fierce that he
    dares to arouse him;
  Who then is he that can
    stand before Me?
11 "Who has given to Me that I
    should repay *him*?
  Whatever is under the whole
    heaven is Mine.

12 "I will not keep silence
    concerning his limbs,
  Or his mighty strength, or
    his orderly frame.
13 "Who can strip off his outer armor?
  Who can come within his double mail?
14 "Who can open the doors of his face?
  Around his teeth there is terror.
15 "*His* strong scales are *his* pride,
  Shut up *as with* a tight seal.
16 "One is so near to another
  That no air can come between them.
17 "They are joined one to another;
  They clasp each other and
    cannot be separated.
18 "His sneezes flash forth light,
  And his eyes are like the
    eyelids of the morning.
19 "Out of his mouth go burning
    torches;
  Sparks of fire leap forth.
20 "Out of his nostrils smoke
    goes forth
  As *from* a boiling pot and
    burning rushes.
21 "His breath kindles coals,
  And a flame goes forth
    from his mouth.
22 "In his neck lodges strength,
  And dismay leaps before him.
23 "The folds of his flesh are
    joined together,
  Firm on him and immovable.
24 "His heart is as hard as a stone,
  Even as hard as a lower millstone.
25 "When he raises himself up,
    the mighty fear;
  Because of the crashing
    they are bewildered.
26 "The sword that reaches
    him cannot avail,
  Nor the spear, the dart or the javelin.
27 "He regards iron as straw,
  Bronze as rotten wood.
28 "The arrow cannot make him flee;
  Slingstones are turned into
    stubble for him.
29 "Clubs are regarded as stubble;
  He laughs at the rattling of the javelin.
30 "His underparts are *like*
    sharp potsherds;
  He spreads out *like* a threshing
    sledge on the mire.
31 "He makes the depths boil like a pot;
  He makes the sea like a jar of ointment.
32 "Behind him he makes a wake to shine;
  One would think the deep
    to be gray-haired.

33 "Nothing on earth is like him,
One made without fear.
34 "He looks on everything that is high;
He is king over all the sons of pride."

42

Then Job answered the LORD and said,

2 "I know that You can do all things,
And that no purpose of Yours
can be thwarted.
3 'Who is this that hides counsel
without knowledge?'
Therefore I have declared that
which I did not understand,
Things too wonderful for me,
which I did not know.
4 'Hear, now, and I will speak;
I will ask You, and You instruct me.'
5 "I have heard of You by the
hearing of the ear;
But now my eye sees You;
6 Therefore I retract,
And I repent in dust and ashes."

42:1–6 Job's confession and repentance took place finally. He still did not know why he suffered so profoundly, but he was done complaining, questioning, and challenging God's wisdom and justice. He was reduced to such utter humility, crushed beneath the weight of God's greatness, that all he could do was repent for his insolence. Without answers to all of his questions, Job quietly bowed in humble submission before his Creator and admitted that God was sovereign (Is 14:24; 46:8–11). Most importantly for the message of the book, Job was still diseased and without his children and possessions, and God had not changed anything (except for the humbling of the heart of His servant). Satan had been proven completely wrong in the charges he brought against Job and in thinking he could destroy true saving faith; Job's companions were completely wrong in the charges they brought against him; but most critically, Job himself was completely wrong in the charges he had raised against God. He expressed his own sorrowful regret that he had not just accepted God's will without such ignorant complaints and questions.

42:5 have heard...now my eye sees You. At last, Job said he understood God whom he had seen with the eyes of faith. He had never so well grasped the greatness, majesty, sovereignty, and independence of God as he did at that moment.

7 It came about after the LORD had spoken these words to Job, that the LORD said to Eliphaz the Temanite, "My wrath is kindled against you and against your two friends, because you have not spoken of Me what is right as My servant Job has. 8 Now therefore, take for yourselves seven bulls and seven rams, and go to My servant Job, and offer up a burnt offering for yourselves, and My servant Job will pray for you. For I will accept him so that I may not do with you *according to your* folly, because you have not spoken of Me what is right, as My servant Job has." 9 So Eliphaz the Temanite and Bildad the Shuhite *and* Zophar the Naamathite went and did as the LORD told them; and the LORD accepted Job.

10 The LORD restored the fortunes of Job when he prayed for his friends, and the LORD increased all that Job had twofold. 11 Then all his brothers and all his sisters and all who had known him before came to him, and they ate bread with him in his house; and they consoled him and comforted him for all the adversities that the LORD had brought on him. And each one gave him one piece of money, and each a ring of gold. 12 The LORD blessed the latter *days* of Job more than his beginning; and he had 14,000 sheep and 6,000 camels and 1,000 yoke of oxen and 1,000 female donkeys. 13 He had seven sons and three daughters. 14 He named the first Jemimah, and the second Keziah, and the third Keren-happuch. 15 In all the land no women were found so fair as Job's daughters; and their father gave them inheritance among their brothers. 16 After this, Job lived 140 years, and saw his sons and his grandsons, four generations. 17 And Job died, an old man and full of days.

Psalm 101:5–8

5 Whoever secretly slanders his
neighbor, him I will destroy;
No one who has a haughty look and
an arrogant heart will I endure.

6 My eyes shall be upon the
faithful of the land, that
they may dwell with me;
He who walks in a blameless way is
the one who will minister to me.

7 He who practices deceit shall
not dwell within my house;
He who speaks falsehood shall not
maintain his position before me.

8 Every morning I will destroy
all the wicked of the land,
So as to cut off from the city of the
LORD all those who do iniquity.

Proverbs 23:31–35

³¹ Do not look on the wine
    when it is red,
When it sparkles in the cup,
When it goes down smoothly;
³² At the last it bites like a serpent
And stings like a viper.
³³ Your eyes will see strange things
And your mind will utter
    perverse things.
³⁴ And you will be like one who lies
    down in the middle of the sea,
Or like one who lies down
    on the top of a mast.
³⁵ "They struck me, *but* I did
    not become ill;
They beat me, *but* I did not
    know *it.*
When shall I awake?
I will seek another drink."

1 Corinthians 7:1–16

7 Now concerning the things about which you wrote, it is good for a man not to touch a woman. ² But because of immoralities, each man is to have his own wife, and each woman is to have her own husband. ³ The husband must fulfill his duty to his wife, and likewise also the wife to her husband. ⁴ The wife does not have authority over her own body, but the husband *does;* and likewise also the husband does not have authority over his own body, but the wife *does.* ⁵ Stop depriving one another, except by agreement for a time, so that you may devote yourselves to prayer, and come together again so that Satan will not tempt you because of your lack of self-control. ⁶ But this I say by way of concession,

7:2 immoralities. There is a great danger of sexual sin when single (Mt 19:12). Marriage is God's only provision for sexual fulfillment. Marriage should not be reduced simply to that, however. Paul has a much higher view and articulates it in Ephesians 5:22–23. He is, here, stressing the issue of sexual sin for people who are single.

7:5 depriving. This command may indicate that this kind of deprivation was going on among believers, perhaps reacting to the gross sexual sins of their past and wanting to leave all that behind. Husbands and wives may abstain temporarily from sexual activity, but only when they mutually agree to do so for intercession, as a part of their fasting. **come together again.** Sexual intercourse is to be soon renewed after the spiritual interruption. **so that Satan will not tempt.** See 1Th 3:5. After the agreed-upon "time" of abstinence, sexual desires intensify and a spouse becomes more vulnerable to sinful desire.

not of command. ⁷ Yet I wish that all men were even as I myself am. However, each man has his own gift from God, one in this manner, and another in that.

⁸ But I say to the unmarried and to widows that it is good for them if they remain even as I. ⁹ But if they do not have self-control, let them marry; for it is better to marry than to burn *with passion.*

¹⁰ But to the married I give instructions, not I, but the Lord, that the wife should not leave her husband ¹¹ (but if she does leave, she must remain unmarried, or else be reconciled to her husband), and that the husband should not divorce his wife.

¹² But to the rest I say, not the Lord, that if any brother has a wife who is an unbeliever, and she consents to live with him, he must not divorce her. ¹³ And a woman who has an unbelieving husband, and he consents to live with her, she must not send her husband away. ¹⁴ For the unbelieving husband is sanctified through his wife, and the unbelieving wife is sanctified through her believing husband; for otherwise your children are unclean, but now they are holy. ¹⁵ Yet if the unbelieving one leaves, let him leave; the brother or the sister is not under bondage in such *cases,* but God has called us to peace. ¹⁶ For how do you know, O wife, whether you will save your husband? Or how do you know, O husband, whether you will save your wife?

DAY 25: How does Paul address the issue of divorce for the Corinthian church?

Paul taught about divorce in the context of answering a number of questions that the church had sent to him. The first of those questions had to do with marriage, an area of trouble due to the moral corruption of the surrounding culture that tolerated fornication, adultery, homosexuality, polygamy, and concubinage.

The apostle reminded the believers that his teaching was based on what Jesus had already made clear during His earthly ministry (Mt 5:31, 32; 19:5–8). Jesus Himself based His teaching on the previously revealed word of God (Ge 2:24; Mal 2:16).

Paul's departure point for teaching affirmed God's prohibition of divorce. He wrote that in cases where a Christian has already divorced another Christian except for adultery (1Co 7:10–11), neither partner is free to marry another person. They should reconcile or at least remain unmarried.

Paul then added some helpful direction on the issue of marital conflicts created in cases where one spouse becomes a believer (vv. 12–16). First, the believing spouse lives under orders to make the best of the marriage, seeking to win his or her spouse to Christ. If the unbelieving spouse decides to end the marriage, Paul's response is "let him leave" (v. 15). This term refers to divorce (vv. 10–11). When an unbelieving spouse cannot tolerate the partner's faith and wants a divorce, it is best to let that happen in order to preserve peace in the family (12:18). Therefore, the bond of marriage is broken only by death (7:2), adultery (Mt 19:9), or an unbeliever's departure.

When the bond of marriage is broken in any of those ways, a Christian is free to marry another believer (Ro 7:15). Throughout Scripture, whenever legitimate divorce occurs, remarriage is an assumed option. When divorce is permitted, so is remarriage.

In general, conversion and obedience to Christ should lead us to greater faithfulness and commitment in every relationship. This extended passage (vv. 1–24) plainly repeats the basic principle that Christians should willingly accept the marital condition and social situations into which God has placed them and be content to serve Him there until He leads them elsewhere.

AUGUST 26

Ecclesiastes 1:1–2:26

1 The words of the Preacher, the son of David, king in Jerusalem.

2 "Vanity of vanities," says the Preacher,
"Vanity of vanities! All is vanity."

3 What advantage does man
    have in all his work
Which he does under the sun?

4 A generation goes and a
    generation comes,
But the earth remains forever.

5 Also, the sun rises and the sun sets;
And hastening to its place
    it rises there *again*.

6 Blowing toward the south,
Then turning toward the north,
The wind continues swirling along;
And on its circular courses
    the wind returns.

7 All the rivers flow into the sea,
Yet the sea is not full.
To the place where the rivers flow,
There they flow again.

8 All things are wearisome;
Man is not able to tell *it*.
The eye is not satisfied with seeing,
Nor is the ear filled with hearing.

9 That which has been is
    that which will be,
And that which has been done
    is that which will be done.
So there is nothing new
    under the sun.

10 Is there anything of which
    one might say,
"See this, it is new"?
Already it has existed for ages
Which were before us.

11 There is no remembrance
    of earlier things;
And also the later things
    which will occur,
There will be for them no
    remembrance
Among those who will
    come later *still*.

12 I, the Preacher, have been king over Israel in Jerusalem. 13 And I set my mind to seek and explore by wisdom concerning all that has been done under heaven. *It* is a grievous task *which* God has given to the sons of men to be afflicted with. 14 I have seen all the works which have been done under the sun, and

1:13 wisdom. Solomon's use of the term, in typical Hebrew fashion, is more practical than philosophical and implies more than knowledge. It carries notions of ability for proper behavior, success, common sense, and wit. **grievous task.** Man's search to understand is at times difficult, yet God-given (2:26; 3:10; 5:16–19; 6:2; 8:11, 15; 9:9; 12:11). **God.** The covenant name, Lord, is never used in Ecclesiastes. However, "God" is found almost 40 times. The emphasis is more on God's sovereignty in creation and providence than His covenant relationship through redemption.

behold, all is vanity and striving after wind. [15] What is crooked cannot be straightened and what is lacking cannot be counted.

[16] I said to myself, "Behold, I have magnified and increased wisdom more than all who were over Jerusalem before me; and my mind has observed a wealth of wisdom and knowledge." [17] And I set my mind to know wisdom and to know madness and folly; I realized that this also is striving after wind. [18] Because in much wisdom there is much grief, and increasing knowledge *results in* increasing pain.

2 I said to myself, "Come now, I will test you with pleasure. So enjoy yourself." And behold, it too was futility. [2] I said of laughter, "It is madness," and of pleasure, "What does it accomplish?" [3] I explored with my mind *how* to stimulate my body with wine while my mind was guiding *me* wisely, and how to take hold of folly, until I could see what good there is for the sons of men to do under heaven the few years of their lives. [4] I enlarged my works: I built houses for myself, I planted vineyards for myself; [5] I made gardens and parks for myself and I planted in them all kinds of fruit trees; [6] I made ponds of water for myself from which to irrigate a forest of growing trees. [7] I bought male and female slaves and I had homeborn slaves. Also I possessed flocks and herds larger than all who preceded me in Jerusalem. [8] Also, I collected for myself silver and gold and the treasure of kings and provinces. I provided for myself male and female singers and the pleasures of men—many concubines.

[9] Then I became great and increased more than all who preceded me in Jerusalem. My wisdom also stood by me. [10] All that my eyes desired I did not refuse them. I did not withhold my heart from any pleasure, for my heart was pleased because of all my labor and this was my reward for all my labor. [11] Thus I considered all my activities which my hands had done and the labor which I had exerted, and behold all was vanity and striving after wind and there was no profit under the sun.

[12] So I turned to consider wisdom, madness and folly; for what *will* the man *do* who will come after the king *except* what has already been done? [13] And I saw that wisdom excels folly as light excels darkness. [14] The wise man's eyes are in his head, but the fool walks in darkness. And yet I know that one fate befalls them both. [15] Then I said to myself, "As is the fate of the fool, it will also befall me. Why then have I been extremely wise?" So I said to myself, "This too is vanity." [16] For there is no lasting remembrance of the wise man *as* with the fool, inasmuch as *in* the coming days all will be forgotten. And how the wise man and the fool alike die! [17] So I hated life, for the work which had been done under the sun was grievous to me; because everything is futility and striving after wind.

[18] Thus I hated all the fruit of my labor for which I had labored under the sun, for I must leave it to the man who will come after me. [19] And who knows whether he will be a wise man or a fool? Yet he will have control over all the fruit of my labor for which I have labored by acting wisely under the sun. This too is vanity. [20] Therefore I completely despaired of all the fruit of my labor for which I had labored under the sun. [21] When there is a man who has labored with wisdom, knowledge and skill, then he gives his legacy to one who has not labored with them. This too is vanity and a great evil. [22] For what does a man get in all his labor and in his striving with which he labors under the sun? [23] Because all his days his task is painful and grievous; even at night his mind does not rest. This too is vanity.

[24] There is nothing better for a man *than* to eat and drink and tell himself that his labor is good. This also I have seen that it is from the hand of God. [25] For who can eat and who can have enjoyment without Him? [26] For to a person who is good in His sight He has given wisdom and knowledge and joy, while to the sinner He has given the task of gathering and collecting so that he may give to one who is good in God's sight. This too is vanity and striving after wind.

Psalm 102:1–11

A Prayer of the Afflicted when he is faint and pours out his complaint before the LORD.

Hear my prayer, O LORD!
And let my cry for help come
to You.
[2] Do not hide Your face from me
in the day of my distress;
Incline Your ear to me;
In the day when I call
answer me quickly.
[3] For my days have been
consumed in smoke,
And my bones have been
scorched like a hearth.
[4] My heart has been smitten like
grass and has withered away,
Indeed, I forget to eat my bread.
[5] Because of the loudness
of my groaning
My bones cling to my flesh.

⁶ I resemble a pelican of
    the wilderness;
  I have become like an owl
    of the waste places.
⁷ I lie awake,
  I have become like a lonely
    bird on a housetop.

⁸ My enemies have reproached
    me all day long;
  Those who deride me have
    used my *name* as a curse.
⁹ For I have eaten ashes like bread
  And mingled my drink with weeping
¹⁰ Because of Your indignation
    and Your wrath,
  For You have lifted me up
    and cast me away.
¹¹ My days are like a lengthened shadow,
  And I wither away like grass.

102:10–11 a lengthened shadow. The time of sunset is used to describe the psalmist's desperate sense that his life will end shortly because God has punished him by withdrawing His presence and strength.

Proverbs 24:1–2

24 Do not be envious of evil men,
    Nor desire to be with them;
² For their minds devise violence,
    And their lips talk of trouble.

1 Corinthians 7:17–40

¹⁷ Only, as the Lord has assigned to each one, as God has called each, in this manner let him walk. And so I direct in all the churches. ¹⁸ Was any man called *when he was already* circumcised? He is not to become uncircumcised. Has anyone been called in uncircumcision? He is not to be circumcised. ¹⁹ Circumcision is nothing, and uncircumcision is nothing, but *what matters is* the keeping of the commandments of God. ²⁰ Each man must remain in that condition in which he was called.

²¹ Were you called while a slave? Do not worry about it; but if you are able also to become free, rather do that. ²² For he who was called in the Lord while a slave, is the Lord's freedman; likewise he who was called while free, is Christ's slave. ²³ You were bought with a price; do not become slaves of men. ²⁴ Brethren, each one is to remain with God in that *condition* in which he was called.

²⁵ Now concerning virgins I have no command of the Lord, but I give an opinion as one who by the mercy of the Lord is trustworthy. ²⁶ I think then that this is good in view of the present distress, that it is good for a man to remain as he is. ²⁷ Are you bound to a wife? Do not seek to be released. Are you released from a wife? Do not seek a wife. ²⁸ But if you marry, you have not sinned; and if a virgin marries, she has not sinned. Yet such will have trouble in this life, and I am trying to spare you. ²⁹ But this I say, brethren, the time has been shortened, so that from now on those who have wives should be as though they had none; ³⁰ and those who weep, as though they did not weep; and those who rejoice, as though they did not rejoice; and those who buy, as though they did not possess; ³¹ and those who use the world, as though they did not make full use of it; for the form of this world is passing away.

³² But I want you to be free from concern. One who is unmarried is concerned about the things of the Lord, how he may please the Lord; ³³ but one who is married is concerned about the things of the world, how he may please his wife, ³⁴ and *his interests* are divided. The woman who is unmarried, and the virgin, is concerned about the things of the Lord, that she may be holy both in body and spirit; but one who is married is concerned about the things of the world, how she may please

---

7:25–40 Having already established that both marriage and singleness are good and right before the Lord (vv. 1–9), and for the person who has the gift of singleness (v. 7), that state has many practical advantages, Paul continued to answer the questions about which the Corinthians had written him. Paul gives 6 reasons for never marrying, in relationship to the downside of marriage, but remaining single (virgins): 1) pressure from the system (vv. 25–27); 2) problems of the flesh (v. 28); 3) passing of the world (vv. 29–31); 4) preoccupations of marriage (vv. 32–35); 5) promises from fathers (vv. 36–38); and 6) permanency of marriage (vv. 39–40).

7:26 present distress. An unspecified, current calamity. Perhaps Paul anticipated the imminent Roman persecutions which began within 10 years after this epistle was written. **remain as he is.** Persecution is difficult enough for a single person to endure, but problems and pain are multiplied for those who are married, especially if they have children.

7:33-34 how he may please his wife...husband. Here is a basic and expected principle for a good marriage—each seeking to please the other.

her husband. ³⁵ This I say for your own benefit; not to put a restraint upon you, but to promote what is appropriate and *to secure* undistracted devotion to the Lord.

³⁶ But if any man thinks that he is acting unbecomingly toward his virgin *daughter,* if she is past her youth, and if it must be so, let him do what he wishes, he does not sin; let her marry. ³⁷ But he who stands firm in his heart, being under no constraint, but has authority over his own will, and has decided this in his own heart, to keep his own virgin *daughter,* he will do well. ³⁸ So then both he who gives his own virgin *daughter* in marriage does well, and he who does not give her in marriage will do better.

³⁹ A wife is bound as long as her husband lives; but if her husband is dead, she is free to be married to whom she wishes, only in the Lord. ⁴⁰ But in my opinion she is happier if she remains as she is; and I think that I also have the Spirit of God.

DAY 26: How does the author's declaration that "all is vanity" relate to the message of Ecclesiastes?

By stating one of his conclusions in the opening lines, the author of Ecclesiastes challenges readers to pay attention. The word translated "vanity" is used in at least three ways throughout the book. In each case, the term refers to the nature and value of human activity "under the sun":

1. "Vanity" refers to the "fleeting" nature of human accomplishments that James later described as like a vapor (Jas 4:14).
2. "Vanity" can mean "futile" or "meaningless," which points to the cursed condition of the universe and the debilitating effects it has on human earthly experience.
3. "Vanity" can represent "incomprehensible" or "enigmatic," which gives consideration to life's unanswerable questions. Solomon found that the word applied to his entire experiment.

While the context in each of the 37 appearances of "vanity" helps determine the particular meaning Solomon had in mind, his most frequent usage conveyed the idea of "incomprehensible" or "unknowable." He was expressing the human limits when faced with the mysteries of God's purposes. Solomon's final conclusion to "fear God and keep His commandments" (12:13-14) represents more than the book's summary; it states the only hope of the good life and the only reasonable response of faith and obedience to the sovereign God. God precisely superintends all activities under the sun, each in its time according to His perfect plan, while He discloses only as much as His perfect wisdom dictates. All people remain accountable. Those who refuse to take God and His Word seriously are doomed to lives of the severest vanity.

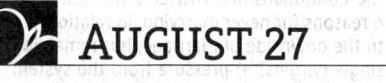

AUGUST 27

Ecclesiastes 3:1-22

3 There is an appointed time for everything. And there is a time for every event under heaven—

² A time to give birth and a time to die;
A time to plant and a time to
uproot what is planted.
³ A time to kill and a time to heal;
A time to tear down and a
time to build up.
⁴ A time to weep and a time to laugh;
A time to mourn and a time
to dance.

⁵ A time to throw stones and a
time to gather stones;
A time to embrace and a time
to shun embracing.
⁶ A time to search and a time
to give up as lost;

3:1-8 an appointed time. Not only does God fix the standard and withhold or dispense satisfaction (2:26), but He also appoints "times." Earthly pursuits are good in their proper place and time, but unprofitable when pursued as the chief goal (vv. 9-10).

A time to keep and a time
   to throw away.
7 A time to tear apart and a
    time to sew together;
  A time to be silent and
    a time to speak.
8 A time to love and a time
    to hate;
  A time for war and a time
    for peace.

9 What profit is there to the worker from that in which he toils? 10 I have seen the task which God has given the sons of men with which to occupy themselves. 11 He has made everything appropriate in its time. He has also set eternity in their heart, yet so that man will not find out the work which God has done from the beginning even to the end.

3:11 everything. Every activity or event for which a culmination point may be fixed. **appropriate.** The phrase echoes "God saw...it was good" (Ge 1:31). Even in a cursed universe, activity should not be meaningless. Its futility lies in the fickle satisfaction of man and his failure to trust the wisdom of sovereign God. **set eternity in their heart.** God made men for His eternal purpose, and nothing in post-Fall time can bring them complete satisfaction.

---

12 I know that there is nothing better for them than to rejoice and to do good in one's lifetime; 13 moreover, that every man who eats and drinks sees good in all his labor—it is the gift of God. 14 I know that everything God does will remain forever; there is nothing to add to it and there is nothing to take from it, for God has so worked that men should fear Him. 15 That which is has been already and that which will be has already been, for God seeks what has passed by.

16 Furthermore, I have seen under the sun that in the place of justice there is wickedness and in the place of righteousness there is wickedness. 17 I said to myself, "God will judge both the righteous man and the wicked man," for a time for every matter and for every deed is there. 18 I said to myself concerning the sons of men, "God has surely tested them in order for them to see that they are but beasts." 19 For the fate of the sons of men and the fate of beasts is the same. As one dies so dies the other; indeed, they all have the same breath and there is no advantage for man over beast,

for all is vanity. 20 All go to the same place. All came from the dust and all return to the dust. 21 Who knows that the breath of man ascends upward and the breath of the beast descends downward to the earth? 22 I have seen that nothing is better than that man should be happy in his activities, for that is his lot. For who will bring him to see what will occur after him?

Psalm 102:12–17

12 But You, O LORD, abide forever,
    And Your name to all generations.
13 You will arise *and* have
    compassion on Zion;
  For it is time to be gracious to her,
  For the appointed time has come.
14 Surely Your servants find
    pleasure in her stones
    And feel pity for her dust.
15 So the nations will fear the
    name of the LORD
  And all the kings of the
    earth Your glory.
16 For the LORD has built up Zion;
    He has appeared in His glory.
17 He has regarded the prayer
    of the destitute
  And has not despised their
    prayer.

Proverbs 24:3–4

3 By wisdom a house is built,
    And by understanding it is
    established;
4 And by knowledge the rooms
    are filled
  With all precious and pleasant
    riches.

1 Corinthians 8:1–13

8 Now concerning things sacrificed to idols, we know that we all have knowledge. Knowledge makes arrogant, but love edifies. 2 If anyone supposes that he knows anything, he has not yet known as he ought to know; 3 but if anyone loves God, he is known by Him.

4 Therefore concerning the eating of things sacrificed to idols, we know that there is no such thing as an idol in the world, and that there is no God but one. 5 For even if there are so-called gods whether in heaven or on earth, as indeed there are many gods and many lords, 6 yet for us there is *but* one God, the Father, from whom are all things and we *exist* for Him; and one Lord, Jesus Christ, by whom are all things, and we *exist* through Him.

8:1 things sacrificed to idols. The Greeks and Romans were polytheistic (worshiping many gods) and polydemonistic (believing in many evil spirits). They believed that evil spirits would try to invade human beings by attaching themselves to food before it was eaten, and that the spirits could be removed only by the food's being sacrificed to a god. The sacrifice was meant not only to gain favor with the god, but also to cleanse the meat from demonic contamination. Such decontaminated meat was offered to the gods as a sacrifice. That which was not burned on the altar was served at wicked pagan feasts. What was left was sold in the market. After conversion, believers resented eating such food bought out of idol markets, because it reminded sensitive Gentile believers of their previous pagan lives and the demonic worship. **we all have knowledge.** Paul and mature believers knew better than to be bothered by such food offered once to idols and then sold in the marketplace. They knew the deities did not exist and that evil spirits did not contaminate the food. **love edifies.** Knowledge mingled with love prevents a believer from exercising freedoms that offend weaker believers and, rather, builds the others up in truth and wisdom (13:1–4).

⁷However not all men have this knowledge; but some, being accustomed to the idol until now, eat *food* as if it were sacrificed to an idol; and their conscience being weak is de-

filed. ⁸But food will not commend us to God; we are neither the worse if we do not eat, nor the better if we do eat. ⁹But take care that this liberty of yours does not somehow become a stumbling block to the weak. ¹⁰For if someone sees you, who have knowledge, dining in an idol's temple, will not his conscience, if he is weak, be strengthened to eat things sacrificed to idols? ¹¹For through your knowledge he who is weak is ruined, the brother for whose sake Christ died. ¹²And so, by sinning against the brethren and wounding their conscience when it is weak, you sin against Christ. ¹³Therefore, if food causes my brother to stumble, I will never eat meat again, so that I will not cause my brother to stumble.

8:7 conscience…is defiled. The consciences of some newer converts were still accusing them strongly with regard to allowing them to eat idol food without feeling spiritually corrupted and guilty. They still imagined that idols were real and evil. A defiled conscience is one that has been violated, bringing fear, shame, and guilt.

8:12 you sin against Christ. A strong warning that causing a brother or sister in Christ to stumble is more than simply an offense against that person; it is a serious offense against the Lord Himself.

DAY 27: In Ecclesiastes, what reflections does Solomon give on Genesis?

Toward the end of his life, the penitent King Solomon pondered life in the wake of the Fall and the outworking of man's sin. Solomon drew the following conclusions, possibly from his own study of Genesis:

1. God created the heavens and earth with laws of design and regularity (Ecc 1:2–7; 3:1–8; Ge 1:1–31; 8:22).
2. Man is created from dust and returns to dust (Ecc 3:20; 12:7; Ge 2:7; 3:19).
3. God placed in man His life-giving breath (Ecc 12:7; Ge 2:7).
4. As God ordained it, marriage is one of life's most enjoyable blessings (Ecc 9:9; Ge 2:18–25).
5. Divine judgment results from the Fall (Ecc 3:14–22; 11:9; 12:14; Ge 2:17; 3:1–19).
6. The effect of the curse on creation is "vanity," i.e., futility (Ecc 1:5–8; Ge 3:17–19).
7. Labor after the Fall is difficult and yields little profit (Ecc 1:3, 13; 2:3; 3:9–11; Ge 3:17–19).
8. Death overcomes all creatures after the Fall (Ecc 8:8; 9:4–5; Ge 2:17; 3:19).
9. After the Fall, man's heart is desperately wicked (Ecc 7:20, 29; 8:11; 9:3; Ge 3:22; 6:5; 8:21).
10. God withholds certain knowledge and wisdom from man for His wise, but unspoken, reasons (Ecc 6:12; 8:17; Ge 3:22).

AUGUST 28

Ecclesiastes 4:1–6:12

4 Then I looked again at all the acts of oppression which were being done under the sun. And behold *I saw* the tears of the oppressed and *that* they had no one to comfort *them;* and on the side of their oppressors was power, but they had no one to comfort *them.* ² So I congratulated the dead who are already dead more than the living who are still living. ³ But better *off* than both of them is the one who has never existed, who has never seen the evil activity that is done under the sun.

⁴ I have seen that every labor and every skill which is done is *the result of* rivalry between a man and his neighbor. This too is vanity and striving after wind. ⁵ The fool folds his hands and consumes his own flesh. ⁶ One hand full of rest is better than two fists full of labor and striving after wind.

⁷ Then I looked again at vanity under the sun. ⁸ There was a certain man without a dependent, having neither a son nor a brother, yet there was no end to all his labor. Indeed, his eyes were not satisfied with riches *and he never asked,* "And for whom am I laboring and depriving myself of pleasure?" This too is vanity and it is a grievous task.

⁹ Two are better than one because they have a good return for their labor. ¹⁰ For if either of them falls, the one will lift up his companion. But woe to the one who falls when there is not another to lift him up. ¹¹ Furthermore, if two lie down together they keep warm, but how can one be warm *alone?* ¹² And if one can overpower him who is alone, two can resist him. A cord of three *strands* is not quickly torn apart.

¹³ A poor yet wise lad is better than an old and foolish king who no longer knows *how* to receive instruction. ¹⁴ For he has come out of prison to become king, even though he was born poor in his kingdom. ¹⁵ I have seen all the living under the sun throng to the side of the second lad who replaces him. ¹⁶ There is no end to all the people, to all who were before them, and even the ones who will come later will not be happy with him, for this too is vanity and striving after wind.

5 Guard your steps as you go to the house of God and draw near to listen rather than to offer the sacrifice of fools; for they do not know they are doing evil. ² Do not be hasty in word or impulsive in thought to bring up a matter in the presence of God. For God is in heaven and you are on the earth; therefore let your words be few. ³ For the dream comes through much effort and the voice of a fool through many words.

⁴ When you make a vow to God, do not be late in paying it; for *He takes* no delight in fools. Pay what you vow! ⁵ It is better that you should not vow than that you should vow and not pay. ⁶ Do not let your speech cause you to sin and do not say in the presence of the messenger *of God* that it was a mistake. Why should God be angry on account of your voice and destroy the work of your hands? ⁷ For in many dreams and in many words there is emptiness. Rather, fear God.

⁸ If you see oppression of the poor and denial of justice and righteousness in the province, do not be shocked at the sight; for one official watches over another official, and there are higher officials over them. ⁹ After all, a king who cultivates the field is an advantage to the land.

¹⁰ He who loves money will not be satisfied with money, nor he who loves abundance *with its* income. This too is vanity. ¹¹ When good things increase, those who consume them increase. So what is the advantage to their owners except to look on? ¹² The sleep of the working man is pleasant, whether he eats little or much; but the full stomach of the rich man does not allow him to sleep.

¹³ There is a grievous evil *which* I have seen under the sun: riches being hoarded by their owner to his hurt. ¹⁴ When those riches were lost through a bad investment and he had fathered a son, then there was nothing to support him. ¹⁵ As he had come naked from his mother's womb, so will he return as he came. He will take nothing from the fruit of his labor that he can carry in his hand. ¹⁶ This also is a grievous evil—exactly as a man is born, thus will he die. So what is the advantage to him who toils for the wind? ¹⁷ Throughout his life *he* also eats in darkness with great vexation, sickness and anger.

¹⁸ Here is what I have seen to be good and fitting: to eat, to drink and enjoy oneself in all one's labor in which he toils under the sun *during* the few years of his life which God has given him; for this is his reward. ¹⁹ Furthermore, as for every man to whom God has given riches and wealth, He has also empowered him to eat from them and to receive his reward and rejoice in his labor; this is the gift of God. ²⁰ For he will not often consider the years of his life, because God keeps him occupied with the gladness of his heart.

6 There is an evil which I have seen under the sun and it is prevalent among men— ² a man to whom God has given riches and wealth and honor so that his soul lacks

6:2 God has not empowered him to eat. The Lord gives and takes away for His own purposes. So, the blessings of God cannot be assumed or taken for granted. But they should be enjoyed with thankfulness while they are available.

nothing of all that he desires; yet God has not empowered him to eat from them, for a foreigner enjoys them. This is vanity and a severe affliction. ³If a man fathers a hundred *children* and lives many years, however many they be, but his soul is not satisfied with good things and he does not even have a *proper* burial, *then* I say, "Better the miscarriage than he, ⁴for it comes in futility and goes into obscurity; and its name is covered in obscurity. ⁵It never sees the sun and it never knows *anything;* it is better off than he. ⁶Even if the *other* man lives a thousand years twice and does not enjoy good things—do not all go to one place?"

⁷All a man's labor is for his mouth and yet the appetite is not satisfied. ⁸For what advantage does the wise man have over the fool? What *advantage* does the poor man have, knowing *how* to walk before the living? ⁹What the eyes see is better than what the soul desires. This too is futility and a striving after wind.

¹⁰Whatever exists has already been named, and it is known what man is; for he cannot dispute with him who is stronger than he is. ¹¹For there are many words which increase futility. What *then* is the advantage to a man? ¹²For who knows what is good for a man during *his* lifetime, *during* the few years of his futile life? He will spend them like a shadow. For who can tell a man what will be after him under the sun?

Psalm 102:18-28

¹⁸ This will be written for the
generation to come,
That a people yet to be created
may praise the LORD.

¹⁹ For He looked down from
His holy height;
From heaven the LORD
gazed upon the earth,

²⁰ To hear the groaning of the prisoner,
To set free those who were
doomed to death,

²¹ That *men* may tell of the name
of the LORD in Zion
And His praise in Jerusalem,

²² When the peoples are gathered together,
And the kingdoms, to serve the LORD.

²³ He has weakened my
strength in the way;
He has shortened my days.

²⁴ I say, "O my God, do not take me
away in the midst of my days,
Your years are throughout
all generations.

²⁵ "Of old You founded the earth,
And the heavens are the
work of Your hands.

²⁶ "Even they will perish, but You endure;
And all of them will wear
out like a garment;
Like clothing You will change them
and they will be changed.

²⁷ "But You are the same,
And Your years will not
come to an end.

²⁸ "The children of Your servants
will continue,
And their descendants will be
established before You."

102:25-27 Eternal God created the heavens and earth, which will one day perish (v. 26). Hebrews 1:10-12 applies this passage to the Lord Jesus Christ, who is superior to the angels because: 1) He is eternal, while they had a beginning; and 2) He created, but they were created. This passage clearly affirms the eternality and deity of Christ. The unchangeable God will outlast His creation, even into the new creation (Mal 3:6; Jas 1:17; 2Pe 3; Rev 21-22).

Proverbs 24:5-6

⁵ A wise man is strong,
And a man of knowledge
increases power.

⁶ For by wise guidance you
will wage war,
And in abundance of counselors
there is victory.

1 Corinthians 9:1-27

9 Am I not free? Am I not an apostle? Have I not seen Jesus our Lord? Are you not my work in the Lord? ²If to others I am not an apostle, at least I am to you; for you are the seal of my apostleship in the Lord.

³My defense to those who examine me is this: ⁴Do we not have a right to eat and drink? ⁵Do we not have a right to take along a believing wife, even as the rest of the apostles and the brothers of the Lord and Cephas? ⁶Or do only Barnabas and I not have a right to refrain from

working? ⁷Who at any time serves as a soldier at his own expense? Who plants a vineyard and does not eat the fruit of it? Or who tends a flock and does not use the milk of the flock? ⁸I am not speaking these things according to human judgment, am I? Or does not the Law also say these things? ⁹For it is written in the Law of Moses, "YOU SHALL NOT MUZZLE THE OX WHILE HE IS THRESHING." God is not concerned about oxen, is He? ¹⁰Or is He speaking altogether for our sake? Yes, for our sake it was written, because the plowman ought to plow in hope, and the thresher *to thresh* in hope of sharing *the crops.* ¹¹If we sowed spiritual things in you, is it too much if we reap material things from you? ¹²If others share the right over you, do we not more? Nevertheless, we did not use this right, but we endure all things so that we will cause no hindrance to the gospel of Christ. ¹³Do you not know that those who perform sacred services eat the *food* of the temple, *and* those who attend regularly to the altar have their share from the altar? ¹⁴So also the Lord directed those who proclaim the gospel to get their living from the gospel.

¹⁵But I have used none of these things. And I am not writing these things so that it will be done so in my case; for it would be better for me to die than have any man make my boast an empty one. ¹⁶For if I preach the gospel, I have nothing to boast of, for I am under compulsion; for woe is me if I do not preach the gospel. ¹⁷For if I do this voluntarily, I have a reward; but if against my will, I have a stewardship entrusted to me. ¹⁸What then is my reward? That, when I preach the gospel, I may offer the gospel without charge, so as not to make full use of my right in the gospel.

¹⁹For though I am free from all *men*, I have made myself a slave to all, so that I may win more. ²⁰To the Jews I became as a Jew, so that I might win Jews; to those who are under the Law, as under the Law though not being myself under the Law, so that I might win those who are under the Law; ²¹to those who are without law, as without law, though not being without the law of God but under the law of Christ, so that I might win those who are without law. ²²To the weak I became weak, that I might win the weak; I have become all things to all men, so that I may by all means save some. ²³I do all things for the sake of the gospel, so that I may become a fellow partaker of it.

²⁴Do you not know that those who run in a race all run, but *only* one receives the prize? Run in such a way that you may win. ²⁵Everyone who competes in the games exercises self-control in all things. They then *do it* to receive a perishable wreath, but we an imperishable. ²⁶Therefore I run in such a way, as not without aim; I box in such a way, as not beating the air; ²⁷but I discipline my body and make it my slave, so that, after I have preached to others, I myself will not be disqualified.

9:24 race. The Greeks enjoyed two great athletic events, the Olympic games and the Isthmian games, and because the Isthmian events were held in Corinth, believers there were quite familiar with this analogy of running to win.

9:26 not without aim. Four times he has mentioned his goal of winning people to salvation (vv. 19, 22). **beating the air.** Paul changes the metaphor to boxing to illustrate the point that he was no shadow boxer, just waving his arms without effect (1Ti 1:18).

DAY 28: How is Jesus Christ seen in the Psalms?		
Psalms	**New Testament Quote**	**Significance**
2:1–12	Acts 4:25–26; 13:33; Heb 1:5; 5:5	Incarnation, Crucifixion, Resurrection
8:3–8	1Co 15:27–28; Eph 1:22; Heb 2:5–10	Creation
16:8–11	Acts 2:24–31; 13:35–37	Death, Resurrection
22:1–31	Mt 27:35–46; John 19:23–24; Heb 2:12; 5:5	Incarnation, Crucifixion, Resurrection
40:6–8	Heb 10:5–9	Incarnation
41:9	John 13:18, 21	Betrayal
45:67	Heb 1:8–9	Deity
68:18	Eph 4:8	Ascension, Enthronement
69:20–21, 25	Mt 27:34, 48; Acts 1:15–20	Betrayal, Crucifixion
72:6–17	—	Millennial Kingship
78:1–2, 15	Mt 13:35; 1Co 10:4	Theophany, Earthly Teaching Ministry

89:3–37	Acts 2:30	Millennial Kingship
102:25–27	Heb 1:10–12	Creation, Eternality
109:6–19	Acts 1:15–20	Betrayal
110:1–7	Mt 22:43–45; Acts. 2:33–35; Heb 1:13; 5:6–10; 6:20; 7:24	Deity, Ascension, Heavenly Priesthood, Millennial Kingship
118:22–23	Mt 21:42; Mark 12:10–11; Luke 20:17; Acts 4:8–12; 1Pe 2:7	Rejection as Savior
132:12–18	Acts 2:30	Millennial Kingship

AUGUST 29

Ecclesiastes 7:1–29

7 A good name is better than
  a good ointment,
  And the day of one's death is better
  than the day of one's birth.

2 It is better to go to a house
  of mourning
  Than to go to a house of feasting,
  Because that is the end of every man,
  And the living takes it to heart.

3 Sorrow is better than laughter,
  For when a face is sad a
  heart may be happy.

4 The mind of the wise is in the
  house of mourning,
  While the mind of fools is in
  the house of pleasure.

5 It is better to listen to the
  rebuke of a wise man
  Than for one to listen to
  the song of fools.

6 For as the crackling of thorn
  bushes under a pot,
  So is the laughter of the fool;
  And this too is futility.

7 For oppression makes a
  wise man mad,
  And a bribe corrupts the heart.

8 The end of a matter is better
  than its beginning;
  Patience of spirit is better than
  haughtiness of spirit.

9 Do not be eager in your
  heart to be angry,
  For anger resides in the
  bosom of fools.

10 Do not say, "Why is it that
  the former days were
  better than these?"
  For it is not from wisdom that
  you ask about this.

11 Wisdom along with an
  inheritance is good
  And an advantage to those
  who see the sun.

12 For wisdom is protection just
  as money is protection,
  But the advantage of knowledge
  is that wisdom preserves the
  lives of its possessors.

13 Consider the work of God,
  For who is able to straighten
  what He has bent?

14 In the day of prosperity be happy,
  But in the day of adversity consider—
  God has made the one as
  well as the other
  So that man will not discover
  anything that will be after him.

15 I have seen everything during my lifetime of futility; there is a righteous man who perishes in his righteousness and there is a wicked man who prolongs his life in his wickedness. 16 Do not be excessively righteous and do not be overly wise. Why should you ruin yourself? 17 Do not be excessively wicked and do not be a fool. Why should you die before your time? 18 It is good that you grasp one thing and also not let go of the other; for the one who fears God comes forth with both of them.

19 Wisdom strengthens a wise man more than ten rulers who are in a city. 20 Indeed, there is not a righteous man on earth who continually does good and who never sins. 21 Also, do not take seriously all words which are spoken, so that you will not hear your servant cursing you. 22 For you also have realized that you likewise have many times cursed others.

23 I tested all this with wisdom, and I said, "I will be wise," but it was far from me. 24 What has been is remote and exceedingly mysterious. Who can discover it? 25 I directed my mind to know, to investigate and to seek wisdom and an explanation, and to know the evil of folly and the foolishness of madness. 26 And I discovered more bitter than death the woman whose heart is snares and nets, whose hands are chains. One who is pleasing to God will escape from her, but the sinner will be captured by her.

²⁷"Behold, I have discovered this," says the Preacher, "*adding* one thing to another to find an explanation, ²⁸which I am still seeking but have not found. I have found one man among a thousand, but I have not found a woman among all these. ²⁹Behold, I have found only this, that God made men upright, but they have sought out many devices."

Psalm 103:1-5

A Psalm of David.

Bless the LORD, O my soul,
And all that is within me,
bless His holy name.
² Bless the LORD, O my soul,
And forget none of His benefits;
³ Who pardons all your iniquities,
Who heals all your diseases;
⁴ Who redeems your life from
the pit,
Who crowns you with
lovingkindness and
compassion;
⁵ Who satisfies your years
with good things,
So that your youth is renewed
like the eagle.

103:2 forget none of His benefits. These earthly gifts from God included: 1) forgiveness of sin (v. 3), 2) recovery from sickness (v. 3), 3) deliverance from death (v. 4), 4) abundant lovingkindness and mercy (v. 4), and 5) food to sustain life (v. 5).

103:5 youth is renewed like the eagle. The mysterious way of the long-lived eagle symbolized strength and speed (Ex 19:4; Jer 48:40), which also characterizes human youth. As a general rule, a person blessed of God will grow weak and slow down less rapidly than otherwise (see Is 40:29-31, which uses the same language).

Proverbs 24:7-9

⁷ Wisdom is *too* exalted for
a fool,
He does not open his
mouth in the gate.

⁸ One who plans to do evil,
Men will call a schemer.
⁹ The devising of folly is sin,
And the scoffer is an
abomination to men.

1 Corinthians 10:1-13

10 For I do not want you to be unaware, brethren, that our fathers were all under the cloud and all passed through the sea; ²and all were baptized into Moses in the cloud and in the sea; ³and all ate the same spiritual food; ⁴and all drank the same spiritual drink, for they were drinking from a spiritual rock which followed them; and the rock was Christ. ⁵Nevertheless, with most of

10:4 a spiritual rock. The Jews had a legend that the actual rock Moses struck followed them throughout their wilderness wanderings, providing water for them. Paul says they have a Rock providing all they need, but it is Christ. Rock (*petra*) refers to a massive cliff, not simply a large stone or boulder, signifying the preincarnate Messiah (Christ), who protected and sustained His people.

them God was not well-pleased; for they were laid low in the wilderness.

⁶Now these things happened as examples for us, so that we would not crave evil things as they also craved. ⁷Do not be idolaters, as

10:6 examples for us. They died in the wilderness because of their failure of self-discipline and consequent indulgence of every desire. Four major sins characterized them: idolatry (v. 7); sexual immorality (v. 8); testing God (v. 9); and complaining (v. 10).

some of them were; as it is written, "THE PEOPLE SAT DOWN TO EAT AND DRINK, AND STOOD UP TO PLAY." ⁸Nor let us act immorally, as some of them did, and twenty-three thousand fell in one day. ⁹Nor let us try the Lord, as some of them did, and were destroyed by the serpents. ¹⁰Nor grumble, as some of them did, and were destroyed by the destroyer. ¹¹Now these things happened to them as an example, and they were written for our instruction, upon whom the ends of the ages have come. ¹²Therefore let him who thinks he stands take heed that he does not fall. ¹³No temptation has overtaken you but such as is common to man; and God is faithful, who will not allow you to be tempted beyond what you are able, but with the temptation will provide the way of escape also, so that you will be able to endure it.

>
> Solomon balanced his enjoyment theme with repeated reminders of divine judgment. Even the best moments in life ought not to cut a person off from awareness of God as Provider to whom all will give an account. Solomon declared that the possibility of enjoyment was based on faith (Ecc 2:24–26).
>
> Part of Ecclesiastes reports the king's experiment in trying to enjoy life without regard for the fear of God's judgment. Solomon discovered that such an effort was in vain. In the end, he came to grasp the importance of obedience.
>
> The tragic results of Solomon's personal experience, coupled with the insight of extraordinary wisdom, make Ecclesiastes a book from which all believers can receive warnings and lessons in their faith (2:1–26). This book demonstrates that a person who sees each day of existence, labor, and basic provision as a gift from God, and accepts whatever God gives, will actually live an abundant life. However, anyone who seeks to be satisfied apart from God will live with futility regardless of personal successes.

AUGUST 30

Ecclesiastes 8:1–10:20

8 Who is like the wise man and who knows the interpretation of a matter? A man's wisdom illumines him and causes his stern face to beam.

² I say, "Keep the command of the king because of the oath before God. ³ Do not be in a hurry to leave him. Do not join in an evil matter, for he will do whatever he pleases." ⁴ Since the word of the king is authoritative, who will say to him, "What are you doing?"

⁵ He who keeps a *royal* command experiences no trouble, for a wise heart knows the proper time and procedure. ⁶ For there is a proper time and procedure for every delight, though a man's trouble is heavy upon him. ⁷ If no one knows what will happen, who can tell him when it will happen? ⁸ No man has authority to restrain the wind with the wind, or authority over the day of death; and there is no discharge in the time of war, and evil will not deliver those who practice it. ⁹ All this I have seen and applied my mind to every deed that has been done under the sun wherein a man has exercised authority over *another* man to his hurt.

¹⁰ So then, I have seen the wicked buried, those who used to go in and out from the holy place, and they are *soon* forgotten in the city where they did thus. This too is futility. ¹¹ Because the sentence against an evil deed is not executed quickly, therefore the hearts of the sons of men among them are given fully to do evil. ¹² Although a sinner does evil a hundred *times* and may lengthen his *life*, still I know that it will be well for those who fear God, who fear Him openly. ¹³ But it will

not be well for the evil man and he will not lengthen his days like a shadow, because he does not fear God.

¹⁴ There is futility which is done on the earth, that is, there are righteous men to whom it happens according to the deeds of the wicked. On the other hand, there are evil men to whom it happens according to the deeds of the righteous. I say that this too is futility. ¹⁵ So I commended pleasure, for there is nothing good for a man under the sun except to eat and to drink and to be merry, and this will stand by him in his toils *throughout* the days of his life which God has given him under the sun.

8:15 pleasure. In no way does Solomon commend unbridled, rampant indulgence in sin, which is implied in Christ's account of the man whose barns were full. That man may have justified his sin by quoting this passage (Lk 12:19). His focus here is on the resolve to enjoy life in the face of the injustice which surrounded him.

¹⁶ When I gave my heart to know wisdom and to see the task which has been done on the earth (even though one should never sleep day or night), ¹⁷ and I saw every work of God, *I concluded* that man cannot discover the work which has been done under the sun. Even though man should seek laboriously, he will not discover; and though the wise man should say, "I know," he cannot discover.

9 For I have taken all this to my heart and explain it that righteous men, wise men, and their deeds are in the hand of God. Man does not know whether *it will be* love or hatred; anything awaits him.

² It is the same for all. There is one fate for the righteous and for the wicked; for the good, for the clean and for the unclean; for the man who offers a sacrifice and for the one who does not sacrifice. As the good man is, so is the sinner; as the swearer is, so is the one who is afraid to swear. ³ This is an evil in all that is done under the sun, that there is one fate for all men. Furthermore, the hearts of the sons of men are full of evil and insanity is in their hearts throughout their lives. Afterwards they *go* to the dead. ⁴ For whoever is joined with all the living, there is hope; surely a live dog is better than a dead lion. ⁵ For the living know they will die; but the dead do not know anything, nor have they any longer a reward, for their memory is forgotten. ⁶ Indeed their love, their hate and their zeal have already perished, and they will no longer have a share in all that is done under the sun.

⁷ Go *then,* eat your bread in happiness and drink your wine with a cheerful heart; for God has already approved your works. ⁸ Let your clothes be white all the time, and let not oil be lacking on your head. ⁹ Enjoy life with the woman whom you love all the days of your fleeting life which He has given to you under the sun; for this is your reward in life and in your toil in which you have labored under the sun.

¹⁰ Whatever your hand finds to do, do *it* with *all* your might; for there is no activity or planning or knowledge or wisdom in Sheol where you are going.

¹¹ I again saw under the sun that the race is not to the swift and the battle is not to the warriors, and neither is bread to the wise nor wealth to the discerning nor favor to men of ability; for time and chance overtake them all. ¹² Moreover, man does not know his time: like fish caught in a treacherous net and birds trapped in a snare, so the sons of men are ensnared at an evil time when it suddenly falls on them.

¹³ Also this I came to see as wisdom under the sun, and it impressed me. ¹⁴ There was a small city with few men in it and a great king came to it, surrounded it and constructed large siegeworks against it. ¹⁵ But there was found in it a poor wise man and he delivered the city by his wisdom. Yet no one remembered that poor man. ¹⁶ So I said, "Wisdom is better than strength." But the wisdom of the poor man is despised and his words are not heeded. ¹⁷ The words of the wise heard in quietness are *better* than the shouting of a ruler among fools. ¹⁸ Wisdom is better than weapons of war, but one sinner destroys much good.

10 Dead flies make a perfumer's oil stink, so a little foolishness is weightier than wisdom *and* honor. ² A wise man's heart *directs him* toward the right, but the foolish man's heart *directs him* toward the left. ³ Even when the fool walks along the road, his sense is lacking and he demonstrates to everyone *that* he is a fool. ⁴ If the ruler's temper rises against you, do not abandon your position, because composure allays great offenses.

⁵ There is an evil I have seen under the sun, like an error which goes forth from the ruler— ⁶ folly is set in many exalted places while rich men sit in humble places. ⁷ I have seen slaves *riding* on horses and princes walking like slaves on the land.

⁸ He who digs a pit may fall into it, and a serpent may bite him who breaks through a wall. ⁹ He who quarries stones may be hurt by them, and he who splits logs may be endangered by them. ¹⁰ If the axe is dull and he does not sharpen *its* edge, then he must exert more strength. Wisdom has the advantage of giving success. ¹¹ If the serpent bites before being charmed, there is no profit for

10:10 Wisdom…giving success. A little wisdom will ease the efforts of life. Even though life's experiences often don't turn out the way one would have hoped, wise living usually produces a good outcome. This is a very important conclusion for Solomon's testing of wisdom.

the charmer. ¹² Words from the mouth of a wise man are gracious, while the lips of a fool consume him; ¹³ the beginning of his talking is folly and the end of it is wicked madness. ¹⁴ Yet the fool multiplies words. No man knows what will happen, and who can tell him what will come after him? ¹⁵ The toil of a fool *so* wearies him that he does not *even* know how to go to a city. ¹⁶ Woe to you, O land, whose king is a lad and whose princes feast in the morning. ¹⁷ Blessed are you, O land, whose king is of nobility and whose princes eat at the appropriate time—for strength and not for drunkenness. ¹⁸ Through indolence the rafters sag, and through slackness the house leaks. ¹⁹ *Men* prepare a meal for enjoyment, and wine makes life merry, and money is the answer to everything. ²⁰ Furthermore, in your bedchamber do not curse a king, and in your sleeping rooms do not curse a rich man, for a bird of the heavens will carry the sound and the winged creature will make the matter known.

Psalm 103:6–14

⁶ The LORD performs righteous deeds
And judgments for all who
are oppressed.
⁷ He made known His ways
to Moses,
His acts to the sons of Israel.
⁸ The LORD is compassionate
and gracious,
Slow to anger and abounding
in lovingkindness.
⁹ He will not always strive
with us,
Nor will He keep *His anger*
forever.
¹⁰ He has not dealt with us
according to our sins,
Nor rewarded us according
to our iniquities.
¹¹ For as high as the heavens
are above the earth,
So great is His lovingkindness
toward those who fear Him.
¹² As far as the east is from
the west,
So far has He removed our
transgressions from us.
¹³ Just as a father has compassion
on *his* children,
So the LORD has compassion
on those who fear Him.
¹⁴ For He Himself knows our frame;
He is mindful that we are
but dust.

Proverbs 24:10–12

¹⁰ If you are slack in the day
of distress,
Your strength is limited.

¹¹ Deliver those who are being
taken away to death,
And those who are staggering to
slaughter, Oh hold *them* back.
¹² If you say, "See, we did not
know this,"
Does He not consider *it* who
weighs the hearts?

24:12 He...who weighs the hearts. God is the One who knows the truth about the motives of the heart and the excuses for failing to do what is right (Jas 4:17). **render to man according to his work.** See v. 29; Job 34:11; Jeremiah 25:14; 50:29.

And does He not know *it*
who keeps your soul?
And will He not render to man
according to his work?

1 Corinthians 10:14–33

¹⁴Therefore, my beloved, flee from idolatry. ¹⁵I speak as to wise men; you judge what I say. ¹⁶Is not the cup of blessing which we bless a sharing in the blood of Christ? Is not the bread which we break a sharing in the body of Christ? ¹⁷Since there is one bread,

10:16 cup of blessing. The proper name given to the third cup during the Passover Feast. At the last Passover with the disciples, Jesus used the third cup as the symbol of His blood shed for sin. That cup became the one used to institute the Lord's Supper. He set the cup apart as a token of salvation blessing before passing it to the 12. **a sharing.** This word means "to have in common, to participate and have partnership with." The same Greek word is used in 1:9; 2 Corinthians 8:4; Philippians 2:1; 3:10. Commemorating the Lord's Supper was a regular and cherished practice in the early church, by which believers remembered their Savior's death and celebrated their common salvation and eternal life which reflected their perfect spiritual oneness. **the blood of Christ.** A vivid phrase used to represent Christ's sacrificial death and full atoning work. **the bread.** This symbolized our Lord's body as the cup symbolized His blood. Both point to His death as a sacrifice for the salvation of men.

we who are many are one body; for we all partake of the one bread. ¹⁸Look at the nation Israel; are not those who eat the sacrifices sharers in the altar? ¹⁹What do I mean then? That a thing sacrificed to idols is anything, or that an idol is anything? ²⁰No, but *I say* that the things which the Gentiles sacrifice, they

10:19–20 Idols and the things sacrificed to them have no spiritual nature or power in themselves (8:4, 8), but they do represent the demonic. If pagan worshipers believe an idol was a god, demons act out the part of the imagined god (2Th 2:9–11). There is not a true god in the idol, but there is a satanic spiritual force (Dt 32:17; Ps 106:37).

sacrifice to demons and not to God; and I do not want you to become sharers in demons. ²¹You cannot drink the cup of the Lord and the cup of demons; you cannot partake of the table of the Lord and the table of demons. ²²Or do we provoke the Lord to jealousy? We are not stronger than He, are we?

²³All things are lawful, but not all things are profitable. All things are lawful, but not all things edify. ²⁴Let no one seek his own *good,* but that of his neighbor. ²⁵Eat anything that is sold in the meat market without asking questions for conscience' sake; ²⁶ FOR THE EARTH IS THE LORD'S, AND ALL IT CONTAINS. ²⁷If one of the unbelievers invites you and you want to go, eat anything that is set before you without asking questions for conscience' sake. ²⁸But if anyone says to you, "This is meat sacrificed to idols," do not eat *it,* for the sake of the one who informed *you,* and for conscience' sake; ²⁹I mean not your own

conscience, but the other *man's;* for why is my freedom judged by another's conscience? ³⁰If I partake with thankfulness, why am I slandered concerning that for which I give thanks?

³¹Whether, then, you eat or drink or whatever you do, do all to the glory of God. ³²Give no offense either to Jews or to Greeks or to the church of God; ³³just as I also please all men in all things, not seeking my own profit but the *profit* of the many, so that they may be saved.

10:23–30 Paul gives 4 principles for Christian liberty: 1) edification over gratification (v. 23); 2) others over self (v. 24); 3) liberty over legalism (vv. 25–27); and 4) condescension over condemnation (vv. 28–30).

DAY 30: What are the different kinds of Psalms?

The Psalms cover the full breadth of human experience. Some express in general terms while others express in very specific terms the shifting events of life. There's a psalm for almost any kind of day.

One way to categorize the Psalms groups them by five general types:

1. Wisdom Psalms—instructions for wise living (1; 37; 119)
2. Lamentation Psalms—meditations on the pangs of life (3; 17; 120)
3. Penitential Psalms—meditations on the pangs of sin (51)
4. Kingship Psalms—meditations on God's sovereign rule (2; 21; 144)
5. Thanksgiving Psalms—praise and worship offered to God (19; 32; 111)

AUGUST 31

Ecclesiastes 11:1–12:14

11 Cast your bread on the surface of the waters, for you will find it after many days. ²Divide your portion to seven, or even to eight, for you do not know what misfortune may occur on the earth. ³If the clouds are full, they pour out rain upon the earth; and whether a tree falls toward the south or toward the north, wherever the tree falls, there it lies. ⁴He who watches the wind will not sow and he who looks at the clouds will not reap. ⁵Just as you do not know the path of the wind and how bones *are formed* in the womb of the pregnant woman, so you do not know the activity of God who makes all things.

⁶Sow your seed in the morning and do not be idle in the evening, for you do not know whether morning or evening sowing will succeed, or whether both of them alike will be good.

⁷The light is pleasant, and *it is* good for the eyes to see the sun. ⁸Indeed, if a man should live many years, let him rejoice in them all, and let him remember the days of darkness, for they will be many. Everything that is to come *will be* futility.

⁹Rejoice, young man, during your childhood, and let your heart be pleasant during the days of young manhood. And follow the impulses of your heart and the desires of your eyes. Yet know that God will bring you to judgment for all these things. ¹⁰So, remove grief and anger from your heart and put away pain from your body, because childhood and the prime of life are fleeting.

12 Remember also your Creator in the days of your youth, before the evil days come and the years draw near when you will say, "I have no delight in them"; ²before the sun and the light, the moon and the stars are darkened, and clouds return after the rain; ³in the day that the watchmen of the house tremble, and mighty men stoop, the grinding ones stand idle because they are few, and those who look through windows grow dim; ⁴and the doors on the street are shut as the sound of the grinding mill is low, and one will arise at the sound of the bird, and all the daughters of song will sing softly. ⁵Furthermore, men are afraid of a high place and of terrors on the road; the almond tree blossoms, the grasshopper drags himself along, and the caperberry is ineffective. For man goes to his eternal home while mourners go about in the street. ⁶*Remember Him* before the silver cord is broken and the golden bowl is crushed, the pitcher by the well is shattered and the wheel at the cistern is crushed; ⁷then the dust will return to the earth as it was, and the spirit will return to God who gave it. ⁸"Vanity of vanities," says the Preacher, "all is vanity!"

⁹In addition to being a wise man, the Preacher also taught the people knowledge; and he pondered, searched out and arranged many proverbs. ¹⁰The Preacher sought to find delightful words and to write words of truth correctly.

¹¹The words of wise men are like goads, and masters of *these* collections are like well-driven nails; they are given by one Shepherd. ¹²But beyond this, my son, be warned: the writing of many books is endless, and excessive devotion *to books* is wearying to the body.

¹³The conclusion, when all has been heard, *is:* fear God and keep His commandments, because this *applies to* every person. ¹⁴For God will bring every act to judgment, everything which is hidden, whether it is good or evil.

Psalm 103:15-22

15 As for man, his days are like
      grass;
   As a flower of the field,
      so he flourishes.
16 When the wind has passed
      over it, it is no more,
   And its place acknowledges
      it no longer.
17 But the lovingkindness of the LORD
      is from everlasting to everlasting
      on those who fear Him,
   And His righteousness to
      children's children,
18 To those who keep His covenant
   And remember His precepts
      to do them.

19 The LORD has established His
      throne in the heavens,
   And His sovereignty rules over all.

103:17-18 the lovingkindness of the LORD. Those who appeal to God's mercy by proper fear (v. 17) and obedience (v. 18) will overcome the shortness of physical life with eternal life. Luke 1:50 quotes Psalms 103:17.

103:19 His throne in the heavens. From everlasting to everlasting God has always ruled over all things (Pss 11:4; 47:1-9; 148:8-13). This universal kingdom is to be distinguished from God's mediatorial kingdom on earth.

20 Bless the LORD, you His angels,
   Mighty in strength, who
      perform His word,
   Obeying the voice of His word!
21 Bless the LORD, all you His hosts,
   You who serve Him, doing His will.
22 Bless the LORD, all you works of His,
   In all places of His dominion;
   Bless the LORD, O my soul!

Proverbs 24:13-14

13 My son, eat honey, for it is good,
   Yes, the honey from the comb
      is sweet to your taste;
14 Know *that* wisdom is thus
      for your soul;
   If you find *it,* then there
      will be a future,
   And your hope will not be cut off.

1 Corinthians 11:1-16

11 Be imitators of me, just as I also am of Christ.

²Now I praise you because you remember me in everything and hold firmly to the traditions, just as I delivered them to you. ³But I want you to understand that Christ is the head of every man, and the man is the head of a woman, and God is the head of Christ. ⁴Every man who has *something* on his head while praying or prophesying disgraces his head. ⁵But every woman who has her head uncovered while praying or prophesying disgraces her head, for she is one and the same as the woman whose head is shaved. ⁶For if a woman does not cover her head, let her also have her hair cut off; but if it is disgraceful for a woman to have her hair cut off or her head shaved, let her cover her head. ⁷For a man ought not to have his head covered, since he is the image and glory of God; but the woman is the glory of man. ⁸For man does not originate from woman, but woman from

11:4 *something* **on his head...disgraces.** Literally "having down from head" is probably a reference to men wearing a head covering, which seems to have been a local custom. Jews began wearing head coverings during the fourth century A.D., although some may already have been wearing them in New Testament times. Apparently, Corinthian men were doing the same, and Paul informs them that it is a disgrace. Paul is not stating a universal law from God, but acknowledging a local custom, which did reflect divine principle. In that society, a man's uncovered head was a sign of his authority over women, who were to have their heads covered. For a man to cover his head was to suggest a reversal of proper roles.

11:5 woman...while praying or prophesying. Paul makes clear directives that women are not to lead or speak in the services of the church (14:34; 1Ti 2:12), but they may pray and proclaim the truth to unbelievers, as well as teaching children and other women (1Ti 5:16; Titus 2:3–4). Wherever and whenever women do pray and proclaim the Word appropriately, they must do so maintaining a proper distinction from men. **uncovered.** In the culture of Corinth, a woman's covered head while ministering or worshiping was a symbol to signify a subordinate relationship to her husband. The apostle is not laying down an absolute law for women to wear veils or coverings in all churches for all time, but is declaring that the symbols of the divinely established male and female roles are to be genuinely honored in every culture. As in the case of meat offered to idols (chaps. 8–9), there is nothing spiritual about wearing or not wearing a covering. But manifesting rebellion against God's order was wrong. **disgraces her head.** "Head" may refer to her own self being disgraced by refusing to conform to recognized symbols of submission, or to her husband, who is disgraced by her behavior.

man; 9 for indeed man was not created for the woman's sake, but woman for the man's sake. 10 Therefore the woman ought to have *a symbol of* authority on her head, because of the angels. 11 However, in the Lord, neither is woman independent of man, nor is man independent of woman. 12 For as the woman originates from the man, so also the man *has his birth* through the woman; and all things originate from God. 13 Judge for yourselves: is it proper for a woman to pray to God *with her head* uncovered? 14 Does not even nature itself teach you that if a man has long hair, it is a dishonor to him, 15 but if a woman has long hair, it is a glory to her? For her hair is given to her for a covering. 16 But if one is inclined to be contentious, we have no other practice, nor have the churches of God.

DAY 31: How does Solomon balance enjoyment in life with the coming judgment?

In Ecclesiastes 11:9—12:8, Solomon crystallizes the book's message. Death is imminent and with it comes retribution. Enjoyment and judgment, though strange partners, come together in this section because both clamor for man's deepest commitment. Surprisingly, one does not win out over the other. In a world created for enjoyment but damaged by sin, judgment and enjoyment/pleasure are held in tension. With too much pleasure, judgment stands as a threatening force; with too much judgment, enjoyment suffers. In the final analysis, both are prominent themes of life that are resolved in our relationship to God, the primary issue of life and this book.

"Rejoice...judgment" (11:9). The two terms seem to cancel out the other. How can this be explained? Enjoy life but do not commit iniquity. The balance that is called for ensures that enjoyment is not reckless, sinful abandonment. Pleasure is experienced in faith and obedience, for as Solomon has said repeatedly, one can only receive true satisfaction as a gift from God.

"Fear God" (12:13–14). Solomon's final word on the issues raised in this book, as well as life itself, focuses on one's relationship to God. All of the concern for a life under the sun, with its pleasures and uncertainties, was behind Solomon. Such things seemed comparatively irrelevant to him as he faced the end of his life. But death, in spite of the focused attention he had given to it in Ecclesiastes, was not the greatest equalizer. Judgment/retribution is the real equalizer as Solomon saw it, for God will bring every person's every act to judgment. Unbelievers will stand at the Great White Throne judgment (Rev 20:11–15) and believers before Christ at the Bema judgment (1Co 3:10–15; 2Co 5:9–10). When all is said and done, the certainty and finality of retribution give life the meaning for which David's ofttimes foolish son had been searching. Whatever may be one's portion in life, accountability to the God, whose ways are often mysterious, is both eternal and irrevocable.

SEPTEMBER 1

Song of Solomon 1:1–2:17

1 The Song of Songs, which is Solomon's.

2 "May he kiss me with the
 kisses of his mouth!
 For your love is better than wine.
3 "Your oils have a pleasing fragrance,
 Your name is *like* purified oil;
 Therefore the maidens love you.
4 "Draw me after you *and* let
 us run *together!*
 The king has brought me
 into his chambers."

"**We** will rejoice in you and be glad;
 We will extol your love
 more than wine.
 Rightly do they love you."

5 "I am black but lovely,
 O daughters of Jerusalem,
 Like the tents of Kedar,
 Like the curtains of Solomon.
6 "Do not stare at me because
 I am swarthy,
 For the sun has burned me.
 My mother's sons were
 angry with me;
 They made me caretaker
 of the vineyards,
 But I have not taken care of
 my own vineyard.
7 "Tell me, O you whom my
 soul loves,
 Where do you pasture *your flock,*
 Where do you make *it* lie
 down at noon?
 For why should I be like one
 who veils herself
 Beside the flocks of your
 companions?"

8 "If you yourself do not know,
 Most beautiful among women,
 Go forth on the trail of the flock
 And pasture your young goats
 By the tents of the shepherds.

9 "To me, my darling, you are like
 My mare among the
 chariots of Pharaoh.
10 "Your cheeks are lovely
 with ornaments,
 Your neck with strings
 of beads."

11 "We will make for you
 ornaments of gold
 With beads of silver."

12 "While the king was at his table,
 My perfume gave forth its fragrance.
13 "My beloved is to me a pouch of myrrh
 Which lies all night between
 my breasts.
14 "My beloved is to me a cluster
 of henna blossoms
 In the vineyards of Engedi."

15 "How beautiful you are, my darling,
 How beautiful you are!
 Your eyes are *like* doves."

16 "How handsome you are, my beloved,
 And so pleasant!
 Indeed, our couch is luxuriant!
17 "The beams of our houses are cedars,
 Our rafters, cypresses.

2 "I am the rose of Sharon,
 The lily of the valleys."

2 "Like a lily among the thorns,
 So is my darling among the
 maidens."

3 "Like an apple tree among
 the trees of the forest,
 So is my beloved among
 the young men.
 In his shade I took great
 delight and sat down,
 And his fruit was sweet to my taste.
4 "He has brought me to
 his banquet hall,
 And his banner over me is love.
5 "Sustain me with raisin cakes,
 Refresh me with apples,
 Because I am lovesick.
6 "Let his left hand be under my head
 And his right hand embrace me."

7 "I adjure you, O daughters
 of Jerusalem,
 By the gazelles or by the
 hinds of the field,
 That you do not arouse or
 awaken *my* love
 Until she pleases."

8 "Listen! My beloved!
 Behold, he is coming,
 Climbing on the mountains,
 Leaping on the hills!

2:7 I adjure you. This refrain, which is repeated before the wedding (3:5) and also afterward (8:4), explicitly expresses her commitment to a chaste life before and during marriage. She invites accountability to the daughters of Jerusalem.

9 "My beloved is like a gazelle
or a young stag.
Behold, he is standing
behind our wall,
He is looking through the windows,
He is peering through the lattice.

10 "My beloved responded and said to me,
'Arise, my darling, my beautiful one,
And come along.
11 'For behold, the winter is past,
The rain is over *and* gone.
12 'The flowers have *already*
appeared in the land;
The time has arrived for
pruning *the vines,*
And the voice of the turtledove
has been heard in our land.
13 'The fig tree has ripened its figs,
And the vines in blossom have
given forth *their* fragrance.
Arise, my darling, my beautiful one,
And come along!'"

14 "O my dove, in the clefts
of the rock,
In the secret place of the
steep pathway,
Let me see your form,
Let me hear your voice;
For your voice is sweet,
And your form is lovely."

15 "Catch the foxes for us,
The little foxes that are
ruining the vineyards,
While our vineyards are in
blossom."

16 "My beloved is mine, and I am his;
He pastures *his flock* among
the lilies.
17 "Until the cool of the day when
the shadows flee away,
Turn, my beloved, and
be like a gazelle
Or a young stag on the
mountains of Bether."

Psalm 104:1-9

B less the LORD, O my soul!
O LORD my God, You are very great;
You are clothed with
splendor and majesty,
2 Covering Yourself with
light as with a cloak,
Stretching out heaven like
a *tent* curtain.
3 He lays the beams of His upper
chambers in the waters;
He makes the clouds His chariot;
He walks upon the wings of the wind;
4 He makes the winds His messengers,
Flaming fire His ministers.

104:4 winds...Flaming fire. Hebrews 1:7 attributes these characteristics to angels describing their swiftness and destructiveness as God's instruments of judgment.

5 He established the earth
upon its foundations,
So that it will not totter
forever and ever.
6 You covered it with the deep
as with a garment;
The waters were standing
above the mountains.
7 At Your rebuke they fled,
At the sound of Your thunder
they hurried away.
8 The mountains rose; the
valleys sank down
To the place which You
established for them.
9 You set a boundary that they
may not pass over,
So that they will not return
to cover the earth.

Proverbs 24:15-16

15 Do not lie in wait, O wicked
man, against the dwelling
of the righteous;
Do not destroy his resting place;
16 For a righteous man falls seven
times, and rises again,
But the wicked stumble in
time of calamity.

1 Corinthians 11:17-34

17 But in giving this instruction, I do not praise you, because you come together not for the better but for the worse. 18 For, in the first

place, when you come together as a church, I hear that divisions exist among you; and in part I believe it. ¹⁹For there must also be factions among you, so that those who are approved may become evident among you. ²⁰Therefore when you meet together, it is not to eat the Lord's Supper, ²¹for in your eating each one takes his own supper first; and one is hungry and another is drunk. ²²What! Do you not have houses in which to eat and drink? Or do you despise the church of God and shame those who have nothing? What shall I say to you? Shall I praise you? In this I will not praise you.

²³For I received from the Lord that which I also delivered to you, that the Lord Jesus in the night in which He was betrayed took bread; ²⁴and when He had given thanks, He broke it and said, "This is My body, which is for you; do this in remembrance of Me." ²⁵In the same way He took the cup also after supper, saying, "This cup is the new covenant in My blood; do this, as often as you drink it, in remembrance of Me." ²⁶For as often as you eat this bread and drink the cup, you proclaim the Lord's death until He comes.

11:17–34 The early church love feasts (Jude 12) usually closed with observance of the Lord's Supper. The worldly, fleshly church at Corinth had turned those sacred meals into gluttonous, drunken revelries. Beyond that, wealthy believers brought ample food and drink for themselves but refused to share, letting their poorer brethren go away hungry (v. 21).

²⁷Therefore whoever eats the bread or drinks the cup of the Lord in an unworthy manner, shall be guilty of the body and the blood of the Lord. ²⁸But a man must examine himself, and in so doing he is to eat of the bread and drink of the cup. ²⁹For he who eats and drinks, eats and drinks judgment to himself if he does not judge the body rightly. ³⁰For this reason many among you are weak and sick, and a number sleep. ³¹But if we judged ourselves rightly, we would not be judged. ³²But when we are judged, we are disciplined by the Lord so that we will not be condemned along with the world.

³³So then, my brethren, when you come together to eat, wait for one another. ³⁴If anyone is hungry, let him eat at home, so that you will not come together for judgment. The remaining matters I will arrange when I come.

11:27 in an unworthy manner. I.e., ritualistically, indifferently, with an unrepentant heart, a spirit of bitterness, or any other ungodly attitude. **guilty.** To come to the Lord's Table clinging to one's sin does not only dishonor the ceremony, but it also dishonors His body and blood, treating lightly the gracious sacrifice of Christ for us. It is necessary to set all sin before the Lord (v. 28), then partake, so as not to mock the sacrifice for sin, by holding on to it.

11:30 sleep. I.e., are dead. The offense was so serious that God put the worst offenders to death, an extreme but effective form of church purification (Lk 13:1–5; Ac 5:1–11; 1Jn 5:16).

DAY 1: What is the central theme of the Song of Solomon?

Solomon, who reigned over the united kingdom 40 years (971-931 B.C.), appears 7 times by name in this book (1:1, 5; 3:7, 9, 11; 8:11–12). In view of his writing skills, musical giftedness (1Ki 4:32), and the authorial, not dedicatory, sense of 1:1, this piece of Scripture could have been penned at any time during Solomon's reign. Knowing that this portion of Scripture comprises one song by one author, it is best taken as a unified piece of poetic, Wisdom literature rather than a series of love poems without a common theme or author.

Two people dominate this true-life, dramatic love song. Solomon, whose kingship is mentioned 5 times (1:4, 12; 3:9, 11; 7:5), appears as "the beloved" in some translations. The Shulamite maiden (6:13) remains obscure; most likely she was a resident of Shunem, 3 miles north of Jezreel in lower Galilee. Some suggest she is Pharaoh's daughter (1Ki 3:1), although the Song provides no evidence for this conclusion. Others favor Abishag, the Shunammite who cared for King David (1Ki 1:1–4, 15). An unknown maiden from Shunem, whose family had possibly been employed by Solomon (8:11), seems most reasonable. She would have been Solomon's first wife (Ecc 9:9), before he sinned by adding 699 other wives and 300 concubines (1Ki 11:3).

In contrast to the two distorted extremes of ascetic abstinence and lustful perversion outside of marriage, Solomon's ancient love song exalts the purity of marital affection and romance. It parallels and enhances other portions of Scripture which portray God's plan for marriage, including the beauty and sanctity of sexual intimacy between husband and wife. The

Song rightfully stands alongside other classic Scripture passages which expand on this theme (Ge 2:24; Ps 45; Pr 5:15–23; 1Co 7:1–5; 13:1–8; Eph 5:18–33; Col 3:18–19; 1Pe 3:1–7). Hebrews 13:4 captures the heart of this song: "Marriage is to be held in honor among all, and the marriage bed is to be undefiled; for fornicators and adulterers God will judge."

SEPTEMBER 2

Song of Solomon 3:1–4:16

3 "On my bed night after
   night I sought him
Whom my soul loves;
I sought him but did not find him.
² 'I must arise now and go
      about the city;
In the streets and in the squares
I must seek him whom my soul loves.'
I sought him but did not find him.
³ "The watchmen who make the
      rounds in the city found me,
And I said, 'Have you seen him
   whom my soul loves?'
⁴ "Scarcely had I left them
When I found him whom
   my soul loves;
I held on to him and would
   not let him go
Until I had brought him to
   my mother's house,
And into the room of her
   who conceived me."

⁵ "I adjure you, O daughters
   of Jerusalem,
By the gazelles or by the
   hinds of the field,
That you will not arouse
   or awaken *my* love
Until she pleases."

⁶ "What is this coming up
   from the wilderness
Like columns of smoke,

3:5 As in 2:7, the beloved knows that the intensity of her love for Solomon cannot yet be experienced until the wedding, so she invites the daughters of Jerusalem to keep her accountable regarding sexual purity. Up to this point, the escalating desire of the Shulammite for Solomon has been expressed in veiled and delicate ways as compared to the explicit and open expressions which follow, as would be totally appropriate for a married couple (4:1ff.).

Perfumed with myrrh
   and frankincense,
With all scented powders
   of the merchant?
⁷ "Behold, it is the *traveling*
   couch of Solomon;
Sixty mighty men around it,
Of the mighty men of Israel.
⁸ "All of them are wielders of the sword,
Expert in war;
Each man has his sword at his side,
Guarding against the
   terrors of the night.
⁹ "King Solomon has made for
   himself a sedan chair
From the timber of Lebanon.
¹⁰ "He made its posts of silver,
Its back of gold
And its seat of purple fabric,
With its interior lovingly fitted out
By the daughters of Jerusalem.
¹¹ "Go forth, O daughters of Zion,
And gaze on King Solomon
   with the crown
With which his mother
   has crowned him
On the day of his wedding,
And on the day of his
   gladness of heart."

4 "How beautiful you are, my darling,
How beautiful you are!
Your eyes are *like* doves
   behind your veil;
Your hair is like a flock of goats
That have descended from
   Mount Gilead.
² "Your teeth are like a flock
   of *newly* shorn ewes
Which have come up from
   their washing,
All of which bear twins,
And not one among them
   has lost her young.
³ "Your lips are like a scarlet thread,
And your mouth is lovely.
Your temples are like a slice
   of a pomegranate
Behind your veil.
⁴ "Your neck is like the tower
   of David,
Built with rows of stones

On which are hung a
thousand shields,
All the round shields of
the mighty men.
5 "Your two breasts are like two fawns,
Twins of a gazelle
Which feed among the lilies.
6 "Until the cool of the day
When the shadows flee away,
I will go my way to the
mountain of myrrh
And to the hill of frankincense.

7 "You are altogether beautiful,
my darling,
And there is no blemish in you.
8 "*Come* with me from
Lebanon, *my* bride,
May you come with me
from Lebanon.
Journey down from the
summit of Amana,
From the summit of Senir
and Hermon,
From the dens of lions,
From the mountains of leopards.
9 "You have made my heart beat
faster, my sister, *my* bride;
You have made my heart beat faster
with a single *glance* of your eyes,
With a single strand of your necklace.
10 "How beautiful is your love,
my sister, *my* bride!
How much better is your
love than wine,
And the fragrance of your oils
Than all *kinds* of spices!
11 "Your lips, *my* bride, drip honey;
Honey and milk are under
your tongue,
And the fragrance of your garments
is like the fragrance of Lebanon.
12 "A garden locked is my
sister, *my* bride,
A rock garden locked, a
spring sealed up.
13 "Your shoots are an orchard
of pomegranates
With choice fruits, henna
with nard plants,
14 Nard and saffron, calamus
and cinnamon,
With all the trees of frankincense,
Myrrh and aloes, along with
all the finest spices.
15 "*You are* a garden spring,
A well of fresh water,
And streams *flowing* from Lebanon."

16 "Awake, O north *wind,*
And come, *wind of* the south;
Make my garden breathe
out *fragrance,*
Let its spices be wafted abroad.
May my beloved come into
his garden
And eat its choice fruits!"

Psalm 104:10–23

10 He sends forth springs in the valleys;
They flow between the mountains;
11 They give drink to every
beast of the field;
The wild donkeys quench their thirst.
12 Beside them the birds of
the heavens dwell;
They lift up *their* voices
among the branches.
13 He waters the mountains from
His upper chambers;
The earth is satisfied with
the fruit of His works.

14 He causes the grass to
grow for the cattle,
And vegetation for the labor
of man,
So that he may bring forth
food from the earth,
15 And wine which makes
man's heart glad,
So that he may make *his*
face glisten with oil,
And food which sustains man's heart.
16 The trees of the LORD drink their fill,
The cedars of Lebanon
which He planted,
17 Where the birds build their nests,
And the stork, whose home
is the fir trees.

18 The high mountains are
for the wild goats;
The cliffs are a refuge for
the shephanim.
19 He made the moon for the seasons;
The sun knows the place of its setting.
20 You appoint darkness and
it becomes night,
In which all the beasts of the
forest prowl about.
21 The young lions roar after their prey
And seek their food from God.
22 *When* the sun rises they withdraw
And lie down in their dens.
23 Man goes forth to his work
And to his labor until evening.

Proverbs 24:17-18

¹⁷ Do not rejoice when your enemy falls,
And do not let your heart be
glad when he stumbles;
¹⁸ Or the LORD will see *it*
and be displeased,
And turn His anger away from him.

1 Corinthians 12:1-31

12 Now concerning spiritual *gifts,* brethren, I do not want you to be unaware. ²You know that when you were pagans, *you were* led astray to the mute idols, however you were led. ³Therefore I make known to you that no one speaking by the Spirit of God says, "Jesus is accursed"; and no one can say, "Jesus is Lord," except by the Holy Spirit.

⁴Now there are varieties of gifts, but the same Spirit. ⁵And there are varieties of ministries, and the same Lord. ⁶There are varieties of effects, but the same God who works all things in all *persons.* ⁷But to each one is given the manifestation of the Spirit for

12:1 spiritual *gifts.* The NASB translators italicized "*gifts*" to indicate that the word is not in the original but is implied by the context (vv. 4, 9, 28, 30-31; 14:1). The Greek literally means "pertaining to the Spirit," referring to that which has spiritual qualities or characteristics or is under some form of spiritual control. Spiritual gifts are divine enablements for ministry that the Holy Spirit gives in some measure to all believers and that are to be completely under His control and used for the building of the church to Christ's glory (Ro 12:4-8). These had to be distinguished from the mystical experiences called "ecstasy" (supernatural, sensuous communion with a deity) and "enthusiasm" (divination, dreams, revelations, visions) that were found in the pagan religions of Corinth.

12:2 pagans. That is, Gentiles (1Th 4:5; 1Pe 2:12). **led astray.** Incredibly, some church members were mimicking certain dramatic and bizarre practices of the mystery religions in which they had been formerly involved. The practice of ecstasy, considered to be the highest expression of religious experience, involved supposed supernatural interaction with a deity, induced through frenzied hypnotic chants and ceremonies. The practice frequently included drunkenness (Eph 5:18) and sexual orgies, to which the devotees willfully yielded themselves to be led into gross sin.

12:3 accursed. This is the most severe kind of condemnation. Some of the Corinthians were fleshly and given over to ecstasies that were controlled by demons. In that condition, they actually claimed to be prophesying or teaching in the Spirit while demonically blaspheming the name of the Lord whom they were supposed to be worshiping. They had been judging the use of gifts on the basis of experience and not content. Satan always assaults the person of Christ. It is possible that the curser of Christ was a Gentile claiming to be a Christian, but holding to a philosophy that all matter was evil, including the human Jesus (i.e., pre-gnosticism). They might have said that the Christ spirit left the human Jesus before His death, and therefore Jesus died a cursed death as a mere man. **Jesus is Lord.** The validity of any speaking exercise is determined by the truthfulness of it. If the speaker affirms the lordship of Jesus, it is the truth from the Holy Spirit. What a person believes and says about Jesus Christ is the test of whether he speaks from the Holy Spirit. He always leads people to Christ's lordship (2:8-14; Jn 15:26; 1Jn 5:6-8).

the common good. ⁸For to one is given the word of wisdom through the Spirit, and to another the word of knowledge according to the same Spirit; ⁹to another faith by the same Spirit, and to another gifts of healing by the one Spirit, ¹⁰and to another the effecting of miracles, and to another prophecy, and to another the distinguishing of spirits, to another *various* kinds of tongues, and to another interpretation of tongues. ¹¹But one and the same Spirit works all these things, distributing to each one individually just as He wills.

¹²For even as the body is one and *yet* has many members, and all the members of the body, though they are many, are one body, so also is Christ. ¹³For by one Spirit we were all baptized into one body, whether Jews or Greeks, whether slaves or free, and we were all made to drink of one Spirit.

¹⁴For the body is not one member, but many. ¹⁵If the foot says, "Because I am not a hand, I am not *a part* of the body," it is not for this reason any the less *a part* of the body. ¹⁶And if the ear says, "Because I am not an eye, I am not *a part* of the body," it is not for this reason any the less *a part* of the body. ¹⁷If the whole body were an eye, where would the hearing be? If the whole were hearing, where would the sense of smell be? ¹⁸But now God has placed the members, each one of them, in

the body, just as He desired. [19] If they were all one member, where would the body be? [20] But now there are many members, but one body. [21] And the eye cannot say to the hand, "I have no need of you"; or again the head to the feet, "I have no need of you." [22] On the contrary, it is much truer that the members of the body which seem to be weaker are necessary; [23] and those *members* of the body which we deem less honorable, on these we bestow more abundant honor, and our less presentable members become much more presentable, [24] whereas our more presentable members have no need *of it*. But God has *so* composed the body, giving more abundant honor to that *member* which lacked, [25] so that there may be no division in the body, but *that* the mem-bers may have the same care for one another. [26] And if one member suffers, all the members suffer with it; if *one* member is honored, all the members rejoice with it.

[27] Now you are Christ's body, and individu-ally members of it. [28] And God has appointed in the church, first apostles, second proph-ets, third teachers, then miracles, then gifts of healings, helps, administrations, *various* kinds of tongues. [29] All are not apostles, are they? All are not prophets, are they? All are not teachers, are they? All are not *workers of* miracles, are they? [30] All do not have gifts of healings, do they? All do not speak with tongues, do they? All do not interpret, do they? [31] But earnestly desire the greater gifts.

And I show you a still more excellent way.

DAY 2: How does Paul's teaching in 1 Corinthians help resolve the controversy over the sign gifts discussed in chapters 12–14?

Three chapters in this letter are devoted to the subject of spiritual gifts in the church. Paul knew that the subject was controversial but vital to a healthy church. The atmosphere of false religions that abounded in Corinth caused counterfeit spiritual manifestations that had to be confronted. Paul informed the church and challenged the believers in Corinth to regulate their behavior by the truth and the Spirit.

The categories of giftedness in these verses do not refer to natural talents, skills, or abilities. Believers and unbelievers alike possess such resources. No, these gifts are sovereignly and supernaturally bestowed by the Holy Spirit on all believers (12:7, 11), enabling them to spiritu-ally edify each other effectively and thus honor the Lord.

The varieties of spiritual gifts fall roughly into two general types: 1) speaking gifts, and 2) serving gifts (12:8–10; Ro 12:6–8; 1Pe 4:10–11). The speaking or verbal gifts (prophecy, knowl-edge, wisdom, teaching, and exhortation) and the serving, nonverbal gifts (leadership, helps, giving, mercy, faith, and discernment) are all permanent and will operate throughout the church age. Their purpose is to build up the church and glorify God. The list here and in Romans 12:3–8 is best seen as representative of categories of giftedness from which the Holy Spirit draws to give each believer whatever kind or combination of kinds He chooses (12:11). Some believers may be gifted in similar ways to others but are personally unique because the Spirit suits each grace gift to the individual.

SEPTEMBER 3

Song of Solomon 5:1–6:13

5 "I have come into my garden,
   my sister, *my* bride;
I have gathered my myrrh
   along with my balsam.
I have eaten my honeycomb
   and my honey;
I have drunk my wine and my milk.
Eat, friends;
Drink and imbibe deeply, O lovers."

[2] "I was asleep but my heart was awake.
A voice! My beloved was knocking:
'Open to me, my sister, my darling,

My dove, my perfect one!
For my head is drenched with dew,
My locks with the damp
   of the night.'

5:1 I have. While the guests feasted, the cou-ple consummated their marriage (Ge 29:23; Dt 22:13–21) and Solomon announced the blessing (Ge 2:25). **Eat, friends.** Given the intimate and private nature of sexual union, it seems diffi-cult to understand anyone but God speaking these words (Pr 5:21). This is the divine affir-mation of sexual love between husband and wife as holy and beautiful.

3 "I have taken off my dress,
How can I put it on *again*?
I have washed my feet,
How can I dirty them *again*?

4 "My beloved extended his hand
through the opening,
And my feelings were
aroused for him.

5 "I arose to open to my beloved;
And my hands dripped with myrrh,
And my fingers with liquid myrrh,
On the handles of the bolt.

6 "I opened to my beloved,
But my beloved had turned
away *and* had gone!
My heart went out *to him* as he spoke.
I searched for him but I
did not find him;
I called him but he did
not answer me.

7 "The watchmen who make the
rounds in the city found me,
They struck me *and* wounded me;
The guardsmen of the walls took
away my shawl from me.

8 "I adjure you, O daughters
of Jerusalem,
If you find my beloved,
As to what you will tell him:
For I am lovesick."

9 "What kind of beloved is your beloved,
O most beautiful among women?
What kind of beloved is your beloved,
That thus you adjure us?"

10 "My beloved is dazzling and ruddy,
Outstanding among ten thousand.

11 "His head is *like* gold, pure gold;
His locks are *like* clusters of dates
And black as a raven.

12 "His eyes are like doves
Beside streams of water,
Bathed in milk,
And reposed in *their* setting.

13 "His cheeks are like a bed of balsam,
Banks of sweet-scented herbs;
His lips are lilies
Dripping with liquid myrrh.

14 "His hands are rods of gold
Set with beryl;
His abdomen is carved ivory
Inlaid with sapphires.

15 "His legs are pillars of alabaster
Set on pedestals of pure gold;
His appearance is like Lebanon
Choice as the cedars.

16 "His mouth is *full of* sweetness.

And he is wholly desirable.
This is my beloved and
this is my friend,
O daughters of Jerusalem."

6 "Where has your beloved gone,
O most beautiful among women?
Where has your beloved turned,
That we may seek him with you?"

2 "My beloved has gone down
to his garden,
To the beds of balsam,
To pasture *his flock* in the gardens
And gather lilies.

3 "I am my beloved's and my
beloved is mine,
He who pastures *his flock*
among the lilies."

4 "You are as beautiful as
Tirzah, my darling,
As lovely as Jerusalem,
As awesome as an army
with banners.

5 "Turn your eyes away from me,
For they have confused me;
Your hair is like a flock of goats
That have descended from Gilead.

6 "Your teeth are like a flock of ewes
Which have come up from
their washing,
All of which bear twins,
And not one among them
has lost her young.

7 "Your temples are like a slice
of a pomegranate
Behind your veil.

8 "There are sixty queens and
eighty concubines,
And maidens without number;

9 *But* my dove, my perfect
one, is unique:
She is her mother's only *daughter;*
She is the pure *child* of the
one who bore her.
The maidens saw her and
called her blessed,
The queens and the concubines *also,*
and they praised her, *saying,*

10 'Who is this that grows like the dawn,
As beautiful as the full moon,
As pure as the sun,
As awesome as an army
with banners?'

11 "I went down to the orchard
of nut trees

To see the blossoms of the valley,
To see whether the vine had budded
Or the pomegranates had bloomed.
¹² "Before I was aware, my soul set me
Over the chariots of my noble people."

¹³ "Come back, come back,
    O Shulammite;
Come back, come back, that
    we may gaze at you!"

"Why should you gaze at
    the Shulammite,
As at the dance of the two
    companies?

Psalm 104:24-30

²⁴ O LORD, how many are Your works!
    In wisdom You have made them all;
    The earth is full of Your possessions.
²⁵ There is the sea, great and broad,
    In which are swarms without number,
    Animals both small and great.
²⁶ There the ships move along,
    And Leviathan, which You have
        formed to sport in it.
²⁷ They all wait for You
    To give them their food in due
        season.
²⁸ You give to them, they gather
    it up;
    You open Your hand, they are
        satisfied with good.
²⁹ You hide Your face, they
        are dismayed;
    You take away their spirit,
        they expire
    And return to their dust.
³⁰ You send forth Your Spirit,
        they are created;
    And You renew the face
        of the ground.

Proverbs 24:19-20

¹⁹ Do not fret because of evildoers
    Or be envious of the wicked;
²⁰ For there will be no future
        for the evil man;
    The lamp of the wicked
        will be put out.

1 Corinthians 13:1-13

13 If I speak with the tongues of men and of angels, but do not have love, I have become a noisy gong or a clanging cymbal. ²If I have *the gift of* prophecy, and know all mysteries and all knowledge; and if I have

13:1-13 Spiritual gifts were present in Corinth (1:7); right doctrine was even in place (11:2); but love was absent. This led to the quarrels and exhibitions of selfishness and pride that plagued the church—notably in the area of spiritual gifts. Instead of selfishly and jealously desiring showy gifts which they don't have, believers should pursue the greatest thing of all—love for one another. This chapter is considered by many the greatest literary passage ever penned by Paul. It is central to his earnestly dealing with spiritual gifts (chaps. 12-14), because after discussing the endowment of gifts (chap. 12) and before presenting the function of gifts (chap. 14), he addresses the attitude necessary in all ministry in the church (chap. 13).

13:1 tongues of men. That this gift was actual languages is established in Acts 2:1-13, affirmed in this text by Paul's calling it "of men"—clearly a reference to human language. This was the gift which the Corinthians prized so highly, abused so greatly, and counterfeited so disastrously. God gave the ability to speak in a language not known to the speaker, as a sign with limited function. **tongues...of angels.** The apostle was writing in general hypothetical terms. There is no biblical teaching of any special angelic language that people could learn to speak. **love.** Self-giving love that is more concerned with giving than receiving (Jn 3:16; see 14:1; Mt 5:44-45; Jn 13:1, 34-35; 15:9; Ro 5:10; Eph 2:4-7; Php 2:2; Col 3:14; Heb 10:24). The word was not admired and thus seldom used in ancient Greek literature, but it is common in the New Testament. Without love, no matter how linguistically gifted one is to speak his own language, other languages, or even (hypothetically) the speech of angels, his speech is noise only. In New Testament times, rites honoring the pagan deities Cybele, Bacchus, and Dionysius included ecstatic noises accompanied by gongs, cymbals, and trumpets. Unless the speech of the Corinthians was done in love, it was no better than the gibberish of pagan ritual.

all faith, so as to remove mountains, but do not have love, I am nothing. ³And if I give all my possessions to feed *the poor,* and if I surrender my body to be burned, but do not have love, it profits me nothing.

⁴Love is patient, love is kind *and* is not jealous; love does not brag *and* is not arrogant, ⁵does not act unbecomingly; it does not seek its own, is not provoked, does not take into

account a wrong *suffered*, ⁶ does not rejoice in unrighteousness, but rejoices with the truth; ⁷ bears all things, believes all things, hopes all things, endures all things.

⁸ Love never fails; but if *there are gifts of* prophecy, they will be done away; if *there are* tongues, they will cease; if *there is* knowledge, it will be done away. ⁹ For we know in part and we prophesy in part; ¹⁰ but when the perfect comes, the partial will be done away. ¹¹ When I was a child, I used to speak like a child, think like a child, reason like a child; when I became a man, I did away with childish things. ¹² For now we see in a mirror dimly, but then face to face; now I know in part, but then I will know fully just as I also have been fully known. ¹³ But now faith, hope, love, abide these three; but the greatest of these is love.

13:4–7 In the previous comments (vv. 1–3), the focus is on the emptiness produced when love is absent from ministry. In these verses, the fullness of love is described, in each case by what love does. Love is action, not abstraction. Positively, love is patient with people and gracious to them with generosity. Negatively, love never envies, or brags, or is arrogant, since that is the opposite of selfless service to others. Never rude or overbearing, love never wants its own way, is not irritated or angered in personal offense, and finds no pleasure in someone else's sin, even the sin of an enemy. On the positive side again, love is devoted to truth in everything. With regard to "all things" within God's righteous and gracious will, love protects, believes, hopes, and endures what others reject.

DAY 3: What about interpretations of Song of Solomon that allergorize it to mean God's love for Israel or Christ's love for the church?

The Song has suffered strained interpretations over the centuries by those who use the "allegorical" method of interpretation, claiming that this song has no actual historical basis, but rather that it depicts God's love for Israel and/or Christ's love for the church. The misleading idea from hymnology that Christ is the rose of Sharon and the lily of the valleys results from this method (2:1). The "typological" variation admits the historical reality, but concludes that it ultimately pictures Christ's bridegroom love for His bride the church.

A more satisfying way to approach Solomon's Song is to take it at face value and interpret it in the normal historical sense, understanding the frequent use of poetic imagery to depict reality. To do so understands that Solomon recounts phases of his relationship with the Shulamite: 1) his own days of courtship, 2) the early days of his first marriage, followed by 3) the maturing of this royal couple through the good and bad days of life. The Song of Solomon expands on the ancient marriage instructions of Genesis 2:24, thus providing spiritual music for a lifetime of marital harmony. It is given by God to demonstrate His intention for the romance and loveliness of marriage, the most precious of human relations and "the grace of life" (1Pe 3:7).

SEPTEMBER 4

Song of Solomon 7:1–8:14

7 "How beautiful are your
    feet in sandals,
O prince's daughter!
The curves of your hips
    are like jewels,
The work of the hands of an artist.

² "Your navel is *like* a round goblet
Which never lacks mixed wine;
Your belly is like a heap of wheat
Fenced about with lilies.

³ "Your two breasts are like two fawns,
Twins of a gazelle.

⁴ "Your neck is like a tower of ivory,
Your eyes *like* the pools in Heshbon
By the gate of Bath-rabbim;

Your nose is like the tower
    of Lebanon,
Which faces toward Damascus.

⁵ "Your head crowns you like Carmel,
And the flowing locks of your
    head are like purple threads;
The king is captivated by *your* tresses.

⁶ "How beautiful and how
    delightful you are,
My love, with *all* your charms!

⁷ "Your stature is like a palm tree,
And your breasts are *like its*
    clusters.

⁸ "I said, 'I will climb the palm tree,
I will take hold of its fruit stalks.'
Oh, may your breasts be like
    clusters of the vine,
And the fragrance of your
    breath like apples,

9 And your mouth like the best wine!"

"It goes *down* smoothly
for my beloved,
Flowing gently *through* the lips
of those who fall asleep.

10 "I am my beloved's,
And his desire is for me.
11 "Come, my beloved, let us go
out into the country,
Let us spend the night in the villages.
12 "Let us rise early *and go*
to the vineyards;
Let us see whether the
vine has budded
And its blossoms have opened,
And whether the pomegranates
have bloomed.
There I will give you my love.
13 "The mandrakes have given
forth fragrance;
And over our doors are
all choice *fruits,*
Both new and old,
Which I have saved up for
you, my beloved.

8 "Oh that you were like a brother to me
Who nursed at my mother's breasts.
If I found you outdoors, I
would kiss you;
No one would despise me, either.
2 "I would lead you *and* bring you
Into the house of my mother,
who used to instruct me;
I would give you spiced wine
to drink from the juice of
my pomegranates.
3 "Let his left hand be under
my head
And his right hand embrace me."
4 "I want you to swear, O daughters
of Jerusalem,
Do not arouse or awaken *my* love
Until she pleases."

5 "Who is this coming up
from the wilderness
Leaning on her beloved?"

"Beneath the apple tree I
awakened you;
There your mother was
in labor with you,
There she was in labor *and*
gave you birth.

6 "Put me like a seal over your heart,
Like a seal on your arm.
For love is as strong as death,
Jealousy is as severe as Sheol;
Its flashes are flashes of fire,
The *very* flame of the LORD.
7 "Many waters cannot quench love,
Nor will rivers overflow it;
If a man were to give all the
riches of his house for love,
It would be utterly despised."

8:6–7 For love. This represents the 1 Corinthians 13:1–8 of the Old Testament. Four qualities of love appear: 1) love is unyielding in marriage, as death is to life; 2) love is intense like the brightest flame, perhaps as bright as the glory of the Lord; 3) love is invincible or unquenchable, even when flooded by difficulty; and 4) love is so priceless that it cannot be bought, only given away.

8 "We have a little sister,
And she has no breasts;
What shall we do for our sister
On the day when she is spoken for?
9 "If she is a wall,
We will build on her a
battlement of silver;
But if she is a door,
We will barricade her with
planks of cedar."

10 "I was a wall, and my breasts
were like towers;
Then I became in his eyes as
one who finds peace.
11 "Solomon had a vineyard
at Baal-hamon;
He entrusted the vineyard
to caretakers.
Each one was to bring a thousand
shekels of silver for its fruit.
12 "My very own vineyard is
at my disposal;
The thousand *shekels* are
for you, Solomon,
And two hundred are for those
who take care of its fruit."
13 "O you who sit in the gardens,
My companions are listening
for your voice—
Let me hear it!"

¹⁴ "Hurry, my beloved,
And be like a gazelle or a
young stag
On the mountains of spices."

Psalm 104:31-35

³¹ Let the glory of the LORD
endure forever;
Let the LORD be glad in
His works;
³² He looks at the earth, and it
trembles;
He touches the mountains,
and they smoke.
³³ I will sing to the LORD
as long as I live;
I will sing praise to my God
while I have my being.
³⁴ Let my meditation be
pleasing to Him;
As for me, I shall be glad
in the LORD.
³⁵ Let sinners be consumed
from the earth
And let the wicked be no more.
Bless the LORD, O my soul.
Praise the LORD!

Proverbs 24:21-22

²¹ My son, fear the LORD and
the king;
Do not associate with those
who are given to change,
²² For their calamity will rise
suddenly,
And who knows the ruin *that*
comes from both of them?

24:21 the king. Loyalty to the king is proper because he is the agent of the Lord's wisdom (Dt 17:14-20; Ro 13:1-7). That loyalty includes having no part with rebels who seek to subvert or overthrow him ("change"). Peter draws on this verse in his call to good citizenship in 1 Peter 1:17; 2:17.

1 Corinthians 14:1-19

14 Pursue love, yet desire earnestly spiritual *gifts,* but especially that you may prophesy. ² For one who speaks in a tongue does not speak to men but to God; for no one understands, but in *his* spirit he speaks mysteries. ³ But one who prophesies speaks to men for edification and exhortation and consolation. ⁴ One who speaks in a tongue ed-

14:1 Pursue love. A command for every believer. Because lovelessness was a root spiritual problem in the Corinthian church, the godly love just described should have been sought after by them with particular determination and diligence. **desire...spiritual *gifts*.** Love does not preclude the use of these enablements. Since Paul has addressed not desiring showy gifts (12:31) and not elevating one over the other (12:14-25), some might think it best to set them all aside for unity's sake. Spiritual gifts, on the other hand, are sovereignly bestowed by God on each believer and necessary for the building of the church (12:1-10). Desire for them, in this context, is in reference to their use collectively and faithfully in His service—not a personal yearning to have an admired gift that one did not possess. As a congregation, the Corinthians should be wanting the full expression of all the gifts to be exercised. "You" is plural, emphasizing the corporate desire of the church. **especially...prophesy.** This spiritual gift was desirable in the life of the church to serve in a way that tongues cannot, namely, by edifying the entire church (v. 5).

ifies himself; but one who prophesies edifies the church. ⁵ Now I wish that you all spoke in tongues, but *even* more that you would prophesy; and greater is one who prophesies than one who speaks in tongues, unless he interprets, so that the church may receive edifying.

⁶ But now, brethren, if I come to you speaking in tongues, what will I profit you unless I speak to you either by way of revelation or of knowledge or of prophecy or of teaching? ⁷ Yet *even* lifeless things, either flute or harp, in producing a sound, if they do not produce a distinction in the tones, how will it be known what is played on the flute or on the harp? ⁸ For if the bugle produces an indistinct sound, who will prepare himself for battle? ⁹ So also you, unless you utter by the tongue speech that is clear, how will it be known what is spoken? For you will be speaking into the air. ¹⁰ There are, perhaps, a great many kinds of languages in the world, and no *kind* is without meaning. ¹¹ If then I do not know the meaning of the language, I will be to the one who speaks a barbarian, and the one who speaks will be a barbarian to me. ¹² So also you, since you are zealous of spiritual *gifts,* seek to abound for the edification of the church.

¹³ Therefore let one who speaks in a

tongue pray that he may interpret. ¹⁴ For if I pray in a tongue, my spirit prays, but my mind is unfruitful. ¹⁵ What is *the outcome* then? I will pray with the spirit and I will pray with the mind also; I will sing with the spirit and I will sing with the mind also. ¹⁶ Otherwise if you bless in the spirit *only,* how will the one who fills the place of the ungifted say the "Amen" at your giving of thanks, since he does not know what you are saying? ¹⁷ For you are giving thanks well enough, but the other person is not edified. ¹⁸ I thank God, I speak in tongues more than you all; ¹⁹ however, in the church I desire to speak five words with my mind so that I may instruct others also, rather than ten thousand words in a tongue.

14:18 I speak in tongues more than you all. Paul emphasized that by writing all of this, he was not condemning genuine tongues (plural); nor, as some may have thought to accuse him, was he envious of a gift he did not possess. At that point, he stopped speaking hypothetically about counterfeit tongue-speaking. He actually had more occasions to use the true gift than all of them (though we have no record of a specific instance). He knew the true gift and had used it properly. It is interesting, however, that the New Testament makes no mention of Paul's actually exercising that gift. Nor does Paul in his own writings make mention of a specific use of it by any Christian.

DAY 4: What was at the heart of Paul's concern for the use of the gift of tongues in the church in Corinth?

In the section of 1 Corinthians 14:2–39, although it is not indicated consistently in some translations, the distinction between the singular tongue and the plural tongues is foundational to the proper interpretation of this chapter. Paul seems to use the singular to distinguish the counterfeit gift of pagan gibberish and the plural to indicate the genuine gift of a foreign language (v. 2). It was perhaps in recognition of that, that the King James Version (KJV) translators added consistently the word "unknown" before every singular form (see vv. 2, 4, 13–14, 19, 27). The implications of that distinction will be noted as appropriate. Against the backdrop of carnality and counterfeit ecstatic speech learned from the experience of the pagans, Paul covers 3 basic issues with regard to speaking in languages by the gift of the Holy Spirit: 1) its position, inferior to prophecy (vv. 1–19); 2) its purpose, a sign to unbelievers not believers (vv. 20–25); and 3) its procedure, systematic, limited, and orderly (vv. 26–40).

"He who speaks in a tongue" (v. 2). This is singular, indicating that it refers to the false gibberish of the counterfeit pagan ecstatic speech. The singular is used because gibberish can't be plural; there are not various kinds of nonlanguage. There are, however, various languages; hence, when speaking of the true gift of language, Paul uses the plural to make the distinction (vv. 6, 18, 22–23, 29). The only exception is in vv. 27–28, where it refers to a single person speaking a single genuine language. "No one understands . . . in his spirit he speaks mysteries." The carnal Corinthians using the counterfeit ecstatic speech of paganism were not interested in being understood, but in making a dramatic display. The spirit by which they spoke was not the Holy Spirit, but their own human spirit or some demon. And the mysteries they declared were the type associated with the pagan mystery religions, which was espoused to be the depths that only the initiated few were privileged to know and understand. Those mysteries were totally unlike the ones mentioned in Scripture (e.g., Mt 13:11; Eph 3:9), which are divine revelations of truths previously hidden (12:7; Eph 3:3–6). "Does not speak to men but to God." This is better translated, "to a god." The Greek text has no definite article. Their gibberish was worship of pagan deities. The Bible records no incident of any believer ever speaking to God in any other than normal human language.

SEPTEMBER 5

Isaiah 1:1–2:22

1 The vision of Isaiah the son of Amoz concerning Judah and Jerusalem, which he saw during the reigns of Uzziah, Jotham, Ahaz *and* Hezekiah, kings of Judah.

² Listen, O heavens, and hear, O earth;
  For the LORD speaks,
"Sons I have reared and brought up,
  But they have revolted against Me.
³ "An ox knows its owner,
  And a donkey its master's manger,
  But Israel does not know,
  My people do not understand."

4 Alas, sinful nation,
People weighed down with iniquity,
Offspring of evildoers,
Sons who act corruptly!
They have abandoned the LORD,
They have despised the
Holy One of Israel,
They have turned away from Him.

5 Where will you be stricken again,
As you continue in *your* rebellion?
The whole head is sick
And the whole heart is faint.

6 From the sole of the foot
even to the head
There is nothing sound in it,
Only bruises, welts and raw wounds,
Not pressed out or bandaged,
Nor softened with oil.

7 Your land is desolate,
Your cities are burned with fire,
Your fields—strangers are devouring
them in your presence;
It is desolation, as overthrown
by strangers.

8 The daughter of Zion is left like
a shelter in a vineyard,
Like a watchman's hut in
a cucumber field, like
a besieged city.

9 Unless the LORD of hosts
Had left us a few survivors,
We would be like Sodom,
We would be like Gomorrah.

10 Hear the word of the LORD,
You rulers of Sodom;
Give ear to the instruction
of our God,
You people of Gomorrah.

11 "What are your multiplied
sacrifices to Me?"
Says the LORD.
"I have had enough of burnt
offerings of rams
And the fat of fed cattle;
And I take no pleasure in the blood
of bulls, lambs or goats.

1:11 I have had enough...take no pleasure. God found all sacrifices meaningless and even abhorrent if the offerer failed in obedience to His laws. Rebellion is equated to the sin of witchcraft and stubbornness to iniquity and idolatry.

12 "When you come to appear before Me,
Who requires of you this
trampling of My courts?
13 "Bring your worthless
offerings no longer,
Incense is an abomination to Me.
New moon and sabbath, the
calling of assemblies—
I cannot endure iniquity and
the solemn assembly.
14 "I hate your new moon *festivals*
and your appointed feasts,
They have become a burden to Me;
I am weary of bearing *them*.

1:14 I hate. It is impossible to doubt the Lord's total aversion toward hypocritical religion. Other practices God hates include robbery for burnt offering (61:8), serving other gods (Jer 44:4), harboring evil against a neighbor and love for a false oath (Zec 8:16), divorce (Mal 2:16), and the one who loves violence (Ps 11:5).

15 "So when you spread out
your hands *in prayer*,
I will hide My eyes from you;
Yes, even though you
multiply prayers,
I will not listen.
Your hands are covered with blood.

16 "Wash yourselves, make
yourselves clean;
Remove the evil of your
deeds from My sight.
Cease to do evil,
17 Learn to do good;
Seek justice,
Reprove the ruthless,
Defend the orphan,
Plead for the widow.

18 "Come now, and let us
reason together,"
Says the LORD,
"Though your sins are as scarlet,
They will be as white as snow;
Though they are red like crimson,
They will be like wool.
19 "If you consent and obey,
You will eat the best of the land;
20 But if you refuse and rebel,
You will be devoured by the sword."
Truly, the mouth of the
LORD has spoken.

1:18 scarlet...crimson. The two colors speak of the guilt of those whose hands were "covered with blood" (v. 15). Being covered with blood speaks of extreme iniquity and perversity (59:3; Eze 9:9–10; 23:37, 45). **white as snow... like wool.** Snow and wool are substances that are naturally white, and therefore portray what is clean, the blood-guilt (v. 15) having been removed (Ps 51:7). Isaiah was a prophet of grace, but forgiveness is not unconditional. It comes through repentance as v. 19 indicates.

21 How the faithful city has
  become a harlot,
 She *who* was full of justice!
 Righteousness once lodged in her,
 But now murderers.
22 Your silver has become dross,
 Your drink diluted with water.
23 Your rulers are rebels
 And companions of thieves;
 Everyone loves a bribe
 And chases after rewards.
 They do not defend the orphan,
 Nor does the widow's plea
  come before them.

24 Therefore the Lord GOD of hosts,
 The Mighty One of Israel, declares,
 "Ah, I will be relieved of
  My adversaries
 And avenge Myself on My foes.
25 "I will also turn My hand against you,
 And will smelt away your
  dross as with lye
 And will remove all your alloy.
26 "Then I will restore your
  judges as at the first,
 And your counselors as
  at the beginning;
 After that you will be called
  the city of righteousness,
 A faithful city."

27 Zion will be redeemed with justice
 And her repentant ones
  with righteousness.
28 But transgressors and sinners
  will be crushed together,
 And those who forsake the
  LORD will come to an end.
29 Surely you will be ashamed of the
  oaks which you have desired,
 And you will be embarrassed at the
  gardens which you have chosen.

30 For you will be like an oak
  whose leaf fades away
 Or as a garden that has no water.
31 The strong man will become tinder,
 His work also a spark.
 Thus they shall both burn together
 And there will be none
  to quench *them*.

2 The word which Isaiah the son of Amoz
 saw concerning Judah and Jerusalem.

2 Now it will come about that
 In the last days
 The mountain of the
  house of the LORD
 Will be established as the
  chief of the mountains,
 And will be raised above the hills;
 And all the nations will stream to it.
3 And many peoples will come and say,
 "Come, let us go up to the
  mountain of the LORD,
 To the house of the God of Jacob;
 That He may teach us
  concerning His ways
 And that we may walk in His paths."
 For the law will go forth from Zion
 And the word of the LORD
  from Jerusalem.
4 And He will judge between
  the nations,
 And will render decisions
  for many peoples;
 And they will hammer their swords
  into plowshares and their
  spears into pruning hooks.
 Nation will not lift up sword
  against nation,
 And never again will they learn war.

5 Come, house of Jacob, and let us
  walk in the light of the LORD.
6 For You have abandoned Your
  people, the house of Jacob,
 Because they are filled *with
  influences* from the east,
 And *they are* soothsayers
  like the Philistines,
 And they strike *bargains* with
  the children of foreigners.
7 Their land has also been filled
  with silver and gold
 And there is no end to their
  treasures;
 Their land has also been
  filled with horses
 And there is no end to their chariots.

8 Their land has also been
  filled with idols;
They worship the work of their hands,
That which their fingers have made.
9 So the *common* man has
  been humbled
And the man *of importance*
  has been abased,
But do not forgive them.
10 Enter the rock and hide in the dust
From the terror of the LORD and
  from the splendor of His majesty.
11 The proud look of man will be abased
And the loftiness of man
  will be humbled,
And the LORD alone will be
  exalted in that day.

12 For the LORD of hosts will
  have a day *of reckoning*
Against everyone who is
  proud and lofty
And against everyone
  who is lifted up,
That he may be abased.
13 And *it will be* against all the
  cedars of Lebanon that
  are lofty and lifted up,
Against all the oaks of Bashan,
14 Against all the lofty mountains,
Against all the hills that are lifted up,
15 Against every high tower,
Against every fortified wall,
16 Against all the ships of Tarshish
And against all the beautiful craft.
17 The pride of man will be humbled
And the loftiness of men
  will be abased;
And the LORD alone will be
  exalted in that day,
18 But the idols will completely vanish.
19 *Men* will go into caves of the rocks
And into holes of the ground
Before the terror of the LORD
And the splendor of His majesty,
When He arises to make
  the earth tremble.

2:19 caves of the rocks...holes of the ground.
Revelation 6:12, 15–16 uses this passage and
2:21 to describe man's flight from the terrors
of tribulation during the period before Christ's
personal return to earth. This shows that the
final fulfillment of this prophecy will be during
Daniel's 70th week.

20 In that day men will cast away
  to the moles and the bats
Their idols of silver and
  their idols of gold,
Which they made for
  themselves to worship,
21 In order to go into the caverns of the
  rocks and the clefts of the cliffs
Before the terror of the LORD and
  the splendor of His majesty,
When He arises to make
  the earth tremble.
22 Stop regarding man, whose breath
  of life is in his nostrils;
For why should he be esteemed?

Psalm 105:1-6

Oh give thanks to the LORD,
  call upon His name;
Make known His deeds
  among the peoples.
2 Sing to Him, sing praises to Him;
Speak of all His wonders.
3 Glory in His holy name;
Let the heart of those who
  seek the LORD be glad.
4 Seek the LORD and His strength;
Seek His face continually.
5 Remember His wonders
  which He has done,
His marvels and the judgments
  uttered by His mouth,
6 O seed of Abraham, His servant,
O sons of Jacob, His chosen ones!

Proverbs 24:23-25

23 These also are sayings of the wise.
To show partiality in
  judgment is not good.
24 He who says to the wicked,
  "You are righteous,"
Peoples will curse him,
  nations will abhor him;
25 But to those who rebuke the
  wicked will be delight,
And a good blessing will
  come upon them.

1 Corinthians 14:20-40

20 Brethren, do not be children in your
thinking; yet in evil be infants, but in your
thinking be mature. 21 In the Law it is written, "BY MEN OF STRANGE TONGUES AND BY
THE LIPS OF STRANGERS I WILL SPEAK TO THIS
PEOPLE, AND EVEN SO THEY WILL NOT LISTEN
TO ME," says the Lord. 22 So then tongues are
for a sign, not to those who believe but to
unbelievers; but prophecy *is for a sign*, not to

unbelievers but to those who believe. ²³ Therefore if the whole church assembles together and all speak in tongues, and ungifted men or unbelievers enter, will they not say that you are mad? ²⁴ But if all prophesy, and an unbeliever or an ungifted man enters, he is convicted by all, he is called to account by all; ²⁵ the secrets of his heart are disclosed; and so he will fall on his face and worship God, declaring that God is certainly among you.

²⁶ What is *the outcome* then, brethren? When you assemble, each one has a psalm, has a teaching, has a revelation, has a tongue, has an interpretation. Let all things be done for edification. ²⁷ If anyone speaks in a tongue, *it should be* by two or at the most three, and *each* in turn, and one must interpret; ²⁸ but if there is no interpreter, he must keep silent in the church; and let him speak to himself and to God. ²⁹ Let two or three prophets speak, and let the others pass judgment. ³⁰ But if a revelation is made to another who is seated, the first one must keep silent. ³¹ For you can all prophesy one by one, so that all may learn and all may be exhorted; ³² and the spirits of prophets are subject to prophets; ³³ for God is not *a God* of confusion but of peace, as in all the churches of the saints.

³⁴ The women are to keep silent in the

14:33 confusion. Here is the key to the whole chapter. The church at worship before God should reflect His character and nature because He is a God of peace and harmony, order and clarity, not strife and confusion (Ro 15:33; 2Th 3:16; Heb 13:20). **as in all the churches.** This phrase does not belong in v. 33, but at the beginning of v. 34, as a logical introduction to a universal principle for churches.

churches; for they are not permitted to speak, but are to subject themselves, just as the Law also says. ³⁵ If they desire to learn anything, let them ask their own husbands at home; for it is improper for a woman to speak in church. ³⁶ Was it from you that the word of God *first* went forth? Or has it come to you only?

³⁷ If anyone thinks he is a prophet or spiritual, let him recognize that the things which I write to you are the Lord's commandment. ³⁸ But if anyone does not recognize *this,* he is not recognized.

³⁹ Therefore, my brethren, desire earnestly to prophesy, and do not forbid to speak in tongues. ⁴⁰ But all things must be done properly and in an orderly manner.

DAY 5: Who was Isaiah the prophet?

Isaiah, the son of Amoz, ministered in and around Jerusalem as a prophet to Judah during the reigns of 4 kings of Judah: Uzziah (called "Azariah" in 2 Kings), Jotham, Ahaz, and Hezekiah (1:1), from ca. 739 to 686 B.C. He evidently came from a family of some rank, because he had easy access to the king (7:3) and intimacy with a priest (8:2). He was married and had two sons who bore symbolic names: "Shear-Jashub" ("a remnant shall return," 7:3) and "Maher-Shalal-Hash-Baz" ("hasting to the spoil, hurrying to the prey," 8:3). When called by God to prophesy, in the year of King Uzziah's death (ca. 739 B.C.), he responded with a cheerful readiness, though he knew from the beginning that his ministry would be one of fruitless warning and exhortation (6:9–13). Having been reared in Jerusalem, he was an appropriate choice as a political and religious counselor to the nation.

Isaiah was a contemporary of Hosea and Micah. His writing style has no rival in its versatility of expression, brilliance of imagery, and richness of vocabulary. The early church father Jerome likened him to Demosthenes, the legendary Greek orator. His writing features a range of 2,186 different words, compared to 1,535 in Ezekiel, 1,653 in Jeremiah, and 2,170 in the Psalms. Second Chronicles 32:32 records that he wrote a biography of King Hezekiah, also. The prophet lived until at least 681 B.C. when he penned the account of Sennacherib's death (37:38). Tradition has it that he met his death under King Manasseh (ca. 695–642 B.C.) by being cut in two with a wooden saw (Heb 11:37).

SEPTEMBER 6

Isaiah 3:1–4:6

3 For behold, the Lord GOD of hosts is going to remove from Jerusalem and Judah

Both supply and support, the
   whole supply of bread
And the whole supply of water;
² The mighty man and the warrior,
The judge and the prophet,
The diviner and the elder,

3 The captain of fifty and the
   honorable man,
The counselor and the expert artisan,
And the skillful enchanter.
4 And I will make mere lads
   their princes,
And capricious children
   will rule over them,
5 And the people will be oppressed,
Each one by another, and each
   one by his neighbor;
The youth will storm against the elder
And the inferior against
   the honorable.
6 When a man lays hold of his brother
   in his father's house, *saying,*
"You have a cloak, you
   shall be our ruler,
And these ruins will be
   under your charge,"
7 He will protest on that day, saying,
"I will not be *your* healer,
For in my house there is
   neither bread nor cloak;
You should not appoint me
   ruler of the people."
8 For Jerusalem has stumbled
   and Judah has fallen,
Because their speech and their
   actions are against the LORD,
To rebel against His
   glorious presence.

3:8 Jerusalem...Judah. The fall of Jerusalem in 586 B.C. was only a partial fulfillment of this prophecy. The final fulfillment awaits the times just prior to Christ's second coming. **against the LORD.** The root of Zion's problem surfaces: overt rebellion against the Lord. The people sinned shamelessly; they made no effort to conceal it (3:9).

9 The expression of their faces
   bears witness against them,
And they display their sin like Sodom;
They do not *even* conceal *it.*
Woe to them!
For they have brought evil
   on themselves.
10 Say to the righteous that *it*
   will go well *with them,*
For they will eat the fruit
   of their actions.
11 Woe to the wicked! *It will*
   go badly *with him,*

For what he deserves will
   be done to him.
12 O My people! Their oppressors
   are children,
And women rule over them.
O My people! Those who guide
   you lead *you* astray
And confuse the direction
   of your paths.

13 The LORD arises to contend,
And stands to judge the people.
14 The LORD enters into judgment
   with the elders and
   princes of His people,
"It is you who have devoured
   the vineyard;
The plunder of the poor
   is in your houses.
15 "What do you mean by
   crushing My people
And grinding the face of the poor?"
Declares the Lord GOD of hosts.

16 Moreover, the LORD said, "Because
   the daughters of Zion are proud
And walk with heads held high
   and seductive eyes,
And go along with mincing steps
And tinkle the bangles on their feet,
17 Therefore the Lord will afflict the scalp
   of the daughters of Zion with scabs,
And the LORD will make
   their foreheads bare."

18 In that day the Lord will take away the beauty of *their* anklets, headbands, crescent ornaments, 19 dangling earrings, bracelets, veils, 20 headdresses, ankle chains, sashes, perfume boxes, amulets, 21 finger rings, nose rings, 22 festal robes, outer tunics, cloaks, money purses, 23 hand mirrors, undergarments, turbans and veils.

24 Now it will come about that
   instead of sweet perfume
   there will be putrefaction;
Instead of a belt, a rope;
Instead of well-set hair, a
   plucked-out scalp;
Instead of fine clothes, a
   donning of sackcloth;
And branding instead of beauty.
25 Your men will fall by the sword
And your mighty ones in battle.
26 And her gates will lament and mourn,
And deserted she will sit
   on the ground.

4 For seven women will take hold of one man in that day, saying, "We will eat our own bread and wear our own clothes, only let us be called by your name; take away our reproach!"

² In that day the Branch of the LORD will be beautiful and glorious, and the fruit of the earth *will be* the pride and the adornment of the survivors of Israel. ³ It will come about

4:2 Branch. This messianic title occurs also in Jeremiah 23:5; 33:15; Zechariah 3:8; 6:12. The thought behind the title relates to 2 Samuel 23:5, that of growth. The life of the Branch will bear spiritual fruit (Jn 15:4–5).

that he who is left in Zion and remains in Jerusalem will be called holy—everyone who is recorded for life in Jerusalem. ⁴When the Lord has washed away the filth of the daughters of Zion and purged the bloodshed of Jerusalem from her midst, by the spirit of judgment and the spirit of burning, ⁵then the LORD will create over the whole area of Mount Zion and over her assemblies a cloud by day, even smoke, and the brightness of a flaming fire by night; for over all the glory will be a canopy. ⁶There will be a shelter to *give* shade from the heat by day, and refuge and protection from the storm and the rain.

Psalm 105:7–22

7 He is the LORD our God;
His judgments are in all the earth.

8 He has remembered His
covenant forever,
The word which He commanded
to a thousand generations,

105:8 a thousand generations. A reference to an exceedingly long time (a generation is normally 40 years) which would encompass the remainder of human history, i.e., forever (Dt 7:9; 1Ch 16:15).

9 *The covenant* which He
made with Abraham,
And His oath to Isaac.

10 Then He confirmed it to
Jacob for a statute,
To Israel as an everlasting covenant,

11 Saying, "To you I will give
the land of Canaan
As the portion of your inheritance,"

12 When they were only a few
men in number,
Very few, and strangers in it.

13 And they wandered about
from nation to nation,
From *one* kingdom to another people.

14 He permitted no man to
oppress them,
And He reproved kings for
their sakes:

15 "Do not touch My anointed ones,
And do My prophets no harm."

16 And He called for a famine
upon the land;
He broke the whole staff of bread.

17 He sent a man before them,
Joseph, *who* was sold as a slave.

18 They afflicted his feet with fetters,
He himself was laid in irons;

19 Until the time that his
word came to pass,
The word of the LORD tested him.

20 The king sent and released him,
The ruler of peoples, and set him free.

21 He made him lord of his house
And ruler over all his possessions,

22 To imprison his princes at will,
That he might teach his
elders wisdom.

Proverbs 24:26–27

26 He kisses the lips
Who gives a right answer.

27 Prepare your work outside
And make it ready for
yourself in the field;
Afterwards, then, build your house.

1 Corinthians 15:1–28

15 Now I make known to you, brethren, the gospel which I preached to you, which also you received, in which also you stand, ² by which also you are saved, if you hold fast the word which I preached to you, unless you believed in vain.

³ For I delivered to you as of first importance what I also received, that Christ died for our sins according to the Scriptures, ⁴ and that He was buried, and that He was raised on the third day according to the Scriptures, ⁵ and that He appeared to Cephas, then to the twelve. ⁶ After that He appeared to more than five hundred brethren at one time, most of

15:5-7 The testimony of eyewitnesses, recorded in the NT, was added to support the reality of the resurrection. These included: 1) John and Peter together (Jn 20:19-20), but probably also separately before (Lk 24:34); 2) the 12 (Jn 20:19-20; Lk 24:36; Ac 1:22); 3) the 500, only referred to here, had all seen the risen Christ (Mt 28:9; Mk 16:9, 12, 14; Lk 24:31-39; Jn 21:1-23); 4) James, either one of the two so-named apostles (son of Zebedee or son of Alphaeus; Mk 3:17-18) or even James the half-brother of the Lord, the author of the epistle by that name and the key leader in the Jerusalem church (Ac 15:13-21); and 5) the apostles (Jn 20:19-29). Such unspecified appearances occurred over a 40-day period (Ac 1:3) to all the apostles.

whom remain until now, but some have fallen asleep; ⁷ then He appeared to James, then to all the apostles; ⁸ and last of all, as to one untimely born, He appeared to me also. ⁹ For I am the least of the apostles, and not fit to be called an apostle, because I persecuted the church of God. ¹⁰ But by the grace of God I am what I am, and His grace toward me did not prove vain; but I labored even more than all of them, yet not I, but the grace of God with me. ¹¹ Whether then *it was* I or they, so we preach and so you believed.

¹² Now if Christ is preached, that He has been raised from the dead, how do some among you say that there is no resurrection of the dead? ¹³ But if there is no resurrection of the dead, not even Christ has been raised; ¹⁴ and if Christ has not been raised, then our preaching is vain, your faith also is vain. ¹⁵ Moreover we are even found *to be* false witnesses of God, because we testified against God that He raised Christ, whom He did not raise, if in fact the dead are not raised. ¹⁶ For if the dead are not raised, not even Christ has been raised; ¹⁷ and if Christ has not been raised, your faith is worthless; you are still in your sins. ¹⁸ Then those also who have fallen asleep in Christ have perished. ¹⁹ If we have

hoped in Christ in this life only, we are of all men most to be pitied.

²⁰ But now Christ has been raised from the dead, the first fruits of those who are asleep. ²¹ For since by a man *came* death, by a man also *came* the resurrection of the dead. ²² For as in Adam all die, so also in Christ all will be made alive. ²³ But each in his own order: Christ the first fruits, after that those who are Christ's at His coming, ²⁴ then *comes* the end, when He hands over the kingdom to the God and Father, when He has abolished all rule and all authority and power. ²⁵ For He must reign until He has put all His enemies under His feet. ²⁶ The last enemy that will be abolished is death. ²⁷ For HE HAS PUT ALL THINGS IN SUBJECTION UNDER HIS FEET. But when He says, "All things are put in subjection," it is evident that He is excepted who put all things in subjection to Him. ²⁸ When all things are subjected to Him, then the Son Himself also will be subjected to the One who subjected all things to Him, so that God may be all in all.

15:25 all His enemies under His feet. This figure comes from the common practice of kings always sitting enthroned above their subjects, so that when the subjects bowed or kneeled, they were lower than the sovereign's feet. With enemies, the monarch might put his foot on the neck of a conquered ruler, symbolizing that enemy's total subjugation. In the millennial kingdom, Christ's foes will be in subjection to Him.

15:26-27 last enemy...death. Christ has broken the power of Satan, who held the power of death (Heb 2:14), at the cross. But Satan will not be permanently divested of his weapon of death until the end of the Millennium (Rev 20:1-10). At that point, having fulfilled completely the prophecy of Psalms 8:6 (v. 27a), Christ then will deliver the kingdom to His Father, and the eternal glory of Revelation 21-22 will begin.

DAY 6: What difference would it make if the Resurrection of Christ never really happened?

"How do some among you say that there is no resurrection of the dead?" (1Co 15:12). The Corinthian Christians believed in Christ's resurrection, or else they could not have been Christians (Jn 6:44; 11:25; Ac 4:12; 2Co 4:14; 1Th 4:16). But some had particular difficulty accepting and understanding the resurrection of believers. Some of this confusion was a result of their experiences with pagan philosophies and religions. A basic tenet of much of ancient Greek philosophy was dualism, which taught that everything physical was intrinsically evil; so the idea of a resurrected body was repulsive and disgusting (Ac 17:32). In addition, perhaps some Jews in the Corinthian church formerly may have been influenced by the Sadducees, who did not believe in the resurrection even though it is taught in the Old Testament (Job 19:26; Pss 16:8–11; 17:15; Da 12:2). On the other hand, New Testament teaching in the words of our Lord Himself was extensive on the resurrection (Jn 5:28–29; 6:44; 11:25; 14:19), and it was the theme of the apostolic preaching (Ac 4:1–2). In spite of that clarity, the church at Corinth was in doubt about the resurrection.

In vv. 13–19, Paul gives 6 disastrous consequences if there were no resurrection: 1) preaching Christ would be senseless (v. 14); 2) faith in Christ would be useless (v. 14); 3) all the witnesses and preachers of the resurrection would be liars (v. 15); 4) no one would be redeemed from sin (v. 17); 5) all former believers would have perished (v. 18); and 6) Christians would be the most pitiable people on earth (v. 19).

SEPTEMBER 7

Isaiah 5:1–6:13

5 Let me sing now for my well-beloved
  A song of my beloved
    concerning His vineyard.
  My well-beloved had a
    vineyard on a fertile hill.
² He dug it all around,
    removed its stones,
  And planted it with the choicest vine.
  And He built a tower in
    the middle of it
  And also hewed out a wine vat in it;
  Then He expected *it* to
    produce *good* grapes,
  But it produced *only* worthless ones.

5:2 *good* grapes…worthless ones. The owner made every conceivable provision for the vine's productivity and protection, illustrating the Lord's purely gracious choice of Israel. Justifiably, He expected a good yield from His investment, but the vine's produce was "sour berries," inedible and fit only for dumping.

³ "And now, O inhabitants of
    Jerusalem and men of Judah,
  Judge between Me and My vineyard.
⁴ "What more was there to do for My
    vineyard that I have not done in it?
  Why, when I expected *it* to
    produce *good* grapes did it
    produce worthless ones?
⁵ "So now let Me tell you what I am
    going to do to My vineyard:
  I will remove its hedge and
    it will be consumed;
  I will break down its wall and it
    will become trampled ground.
⁶ "I will lay it waste;
    It will not be pruned or hoed,

But briars and thorns will come up.
  I will also charge the clouds
    to rain no rain on it."

⁷ For the vineyard of the LORD of
    hosts is the house of Israel
  And the men of Judah His
    delightful plant.
  Thus He looked for justice,
    but behold, bloodshed;
  For righteousness, but behold,
    a cry of distress.

⁸ Woe to those who add house to
    house *and* join field to field,
  Until there is no more room,
  So that you have to live alone
    in the midst of the land!
⁹ In my ears the LORD of hosts *has
    sworn,* "Surely, many houses
    shall become desolate,
  Even great and fine ones,
    without occupants.
¹⁰ "For ten acres of vineyard will
    yield *only* one bath *of wine,*
  And a homer of seed will yield
    but an ephah of grain."
¹¹ Woe to those who rise early in
    the morning that they may
    pursue strong drink,
  Who stay up late in the evening
    that wine may inflame them!
¹² Their banquets are *accompanied*
    by lyre and harp, by tambourine
    and flute, and by wine;
  But they do not pay attention
    to the deeds of the LORD,
  Nor do they consider the
    work of His hands.

¹³ Therefore My people go into exile
    for their lack of knowledge;
  And their honorable men
    are famished,
  And their multitude is
    parched with thirst.

¹⁴ Therefore Sheol has enlarged
its throat and opened its
mouth without measure;
And Jerusalem's splendor, her
multitude, her din *of revelry*
and the jubilant within
her, descend *into it.*
¹⁵ So the *common* man will be
humbled and the man of
importance abased,
The eyes of the proud also
will be abased.
¹⁶ But the LORD of hosts will be
exalted in judgment,
And the holy God will show
Himself holy in righteousness.
¹⁷ Then the lambs will graze
as in their pasture,
And strangers will eat in the
waste places of the wealthy.

¹⁸ Woe to those who drag iniquity
with the cords of falsehood,
And sin as if with cart ropes;
¹⁹ Who say, "Let Him make speed,
let Him hasten His work,
that we may see *it;*
And let the purpose of the Holy
One of Israel draw near
And come to pass, that
we may know *it!*"
²⁰ Woe to those who call evil
good, and good evil;
Who substitute darkness for light
and light for darkness;
Who substitute bitter for sweet
and sweet for bitter!
²¹ Woe to those who are wise
in their own eyes
And clever in their own sight!
²² Woe to those who are heroes
in drinking wine
And valiant men in mixing
strong drink,
²³ Who justify the wicked for a bribe,
And take away the rights of the
ones who are in the right!

²⁴ Therefore, as a tongue of fire
consumes stubble
And dry grass collapses
into the flame,
So their root will become like rot and
their blossom blow away as dust;
For they have rejected the law
of the LORD of hosts
And despised the word of
the Holy One of Israel.

²⁵ On this account the anger of the LORD
has burned against His people,
And He has stretched out His
hand against them and
struck them down.
And the mountains quaked, and
their corpses lay like refuse in
the middle of the streets.
For all this His anger is not spent,
But His hand is still stretched out.

²⁶ He will also lift up a standard
to the distant nation,
And will whistle for it from
the ends of the earth;
And behold, it will come
with speed swiftly.
²⁷ No one in it is weary or stumbles,
None slumbers or sleeps;
Nor is the belt at its waist
undone,
Nor its sandal strap broken.
²⁸ Its arrows are sharp and all
its bows are bent;
The hoofs of its horses seem
like flint and its *chariot*
wheels like a whirlwind.
²⁹ Its roaring is like a lioness, and
it roars like young lions;
It growls as it seizes the prey
And carries *it* off with no
one to deliver *it.*
³⁰ And it will growl over it in that
day like the roaring of the sea.
If one looks to the land, behold,
there is darkness *and* distress;
Even the light is darkened
by its clouds.

6 In the year of King Uzziah's death I saw
the Lord sitting on a throne, lofty and
exalted, with the train of His robe filling the
temple. ²Seraphim stood above Him, each
having six wings: with two he covered his
face, and with two he covered his feet, and
with two he flew. ³And one called out to another and said,

"Holy, Holy, Holy, is the LORD of hosts,
The whole earth is full of His glory."

⁴And the foundations of the thresholds trembled at the voice of him who called out, while
the temple was filling with smoke. ⁵Then I
said,

"Woe is me, for I am ruined!
Because I am a man of unclean lips,

And I live among a people
of unclean lips;
For my eyes have seen the
King, the LORD of hosts."

⁶ Then one of the seraphim flew to me with a burning coal in his hand, which he had taken from the altar with tongs. ⁷ He touched my mouth *with it* and said, "Behold, this has touched your lips; and your iniquity is taken away and your sin is forgiven." ⁸ Then I heard the voice of the Lord, saying, "Whom shall I send, and who will go for Us?" Then I said, "Here am I. Send me!" ⁹ He said, "Go, and tell this people:

'Keep on listening, but
do not perceive;
Keep on looking, but do
not understand.'
¹⁰ "Render the hearts of this
people insensitive,
Their ears dull,
And their eyes dim,
Otherwise they might see
with their eyes,
Hear with their ears,
Understand with their hearts,
And return and be healed."

¹¹ Then I said, "Lord, how long?" And He answered,

"Until cities are devastated *and*
without inhabitant,
Houses are without people
And the land is utterly desolate,
¹² The LORD has removed men
far away,
And the forsaken places are many
in the midst of the land.
¹³ "Yet there will be a tenth portion
in it,
And it will again be *subject*
to burning,
Like a terebinth or an oak
Whose stump remains
when it is felled.
The holy seed is its stump."

Psalm 105:23-36

²³ Israel also came into Egypt;
Thus Jacob sojourned in
the land of Ham.
²⁴ And He caused His people
to be very fruitful,
And made them stronger
than their adversaries.

²⁵ He turned their heart to
hate His people,
To deal craftily with His
servants.
²⁶ He sent Moses His servant,
And Aaron, whom He had chosen.
²⁷ They performed His wondrous
acts among them,
And miracles in the land
of Ham.
²⁸ He sent darkness and made
it dark;
And they did not rebel
against His words.
²⁹ He turned their waters into blood
And caused their fish to die.
³⁰ Their land swarmed with frogs
Even in the chambers of their
kings.
³¹ He spoke, and there came
a swarm of flies
And gnats in all their territory.
³² He gave them hail for rain,
And flaming fire in their land.
³³ He struck down their vines
also and their fig trees,
And shattered the trees
of their territory.
³⁴ He spoke, and locusts came,
And young locusts, even
without number,
³⁵ And ate up all vegetation
in their land,
And ate up the fruit of their
ground.
³⁶ He also struck down all the
firstborn in their land,
The first fruits of all their vigor.

Proverbs 24:28-29

²⁸ Do not be a witness against your
neighbor without cause,
And do not deceive with
your lips.
²⁹ Do not say, "Thus I shall do to
him as he has done to me;
I will render to the man
according to his work."

1 Corinthians 15:29-58

²⁹ Otherwise, what will those do who are baptized for the dead? If the dead are not raised at all, why then are they baptized for them? ³⁰ Why are we also in danger every hour? ³¹ I affirm, brethren, by the boasting in you which I have in Christ Jesus our Lord, I die daily. ³² If from human motives I fought with wild beasts at Ephesus, what does it profit

15:29 This difficult verse has numerous possible interpretations. Other Scripture passages, however, clarify certain things which it does *not* mean. It does not teach, for example, that a dead person can be saved by another person's being baptized on his behalf, because baptism never has a part in a person's salvation (Eph 2:8; see Ro 3:28; 4:3; 6:3–4). A reasonable view seems to be that "those...who are baptized" refers to living believers who give outward testimony to their faith in baptism by water because they were first drawn to Christ by the exemplary lives, faithful influence, and witness of believers who had subsequently died. Paul's point is that if there is no resurrection and no life after death, then why are people coming to Christ to follow the hope of those who have died?

15:42b–44 Focusing directly on the resurrection body, Paul gives 4 sets of contrasts to show how the new body will differ from the present one (v. 54; Php 3:20–21): 1) no more sickness and death ("perishable *body*"); 2) no more shame because of sin ("dishonor"); 3) no more frailty in temptation ("weakness"); and 4) no more limits to the time/space sphere ("natural").

earthy, so also are those who are earthy; and as is the heavenly, so also are those who are heavenly. ⁴⁹ Just as we have borne the image of the earthy, we will also bear the image of the heavenly.

⁵⁰ Now I say this, brethren, that flesh and blood cannot inherit the kingdom of God; nor does the perishable inherit the imperishable. ⁵¹ Behold, I tell you a mystery; we will not all sleep, but we will all be changed, ⁵² in a moment, in the twinkling of an eye, at the last trumpet; for the trumpet will sound, and the dead will be raised imperishable, and we will

me? If the dead are not raised, LET US EAT AND DRINK, FOR TOMORROW WE DIE. ³³ Do not be deceived: "Bad company corrupts good morals." ³⁴ Become sober-minded as you ought, and stop sinning; for some have no knowledge of God. I speak *this* to your shame.

³⁵ But someone will say, "How are the dead raised? And with what kind of body do they come?" ³⁶ You fool! That which you sow does not come to life unless it dies; ³⁷ and that which you sow, you do not sow the body which is to be, but a bare grain, perhaps of wheat or of something else. ³⁸ But God gives it a body just as He wished, and to each of the seeds a body of its own. ³⁹ All flesh is not the same flesh, but there is one *flesh* of men, and another flesh of beasts, and another flesh of birds, and another of fish. ⁴⁰ There are also heavenly bodies and earthly bodies, but the glory of the heavenly is one, and the *glory* of the earthly is another. ⁴¹ There is one glory of the sun, and another glory of the moon, and another glory of the stars; for star differs from star in glory.

⁴² So also is the resurrection of the dead. It is sown a perishable *body,* it is raised an imperishable *body;* ⁴³ it is sown in dishonor, it is raised in glory; it is sown in weakness, it is raised in power; ⁴⁴ it is sown a natural body, it is raised a spiritual body. If there is a natural body, there is also a spiritual *body.* ⁴⁵ So also it is written, "The first MAN, Adam, BECAME A LIVING SOUL." The last Adam *became* a life-giving spirit. ⁴⁶ However, the spiritual is not first, but the natural; then the spiritual. ⁴⁷ The first man is from the earth, earthy; the second man is from heaven. ⁴⁸ As is the

15:52 twinkling of an eye. This was Paul's way of showing how brief the "moment" will be. The Greek word for "twinkling" refers to any rapid movement. Since the eye can move more rapidly than any other part of our visible bodies, it seems to well illustrate the sudden transformation of raptured believers. **trumpet will sound.** To herald the end of the church era when all believers will be removed from the earth at the rapture (1Th 4:16). **dead...raised.** According to 1 Thessalonians 4:16, they are first and the living saints follow.

be changed. ⁵³ For this perishable must put on the imperishable, and this mortal must put on immortality. ⁵⁴ But when this perishable will have put on the imperishable, and this mortal will have put on immortality, then will come about the saying that is written, "DEATH IS SWALLOWED UP in victory. ⁵⁵ O DEATH, WHERE IS YOUR VICTORY? O DEATH, WHERE IS YOUR STING?" ⁵⁶ The sting of death is sin, and the power of sin is the law; ⁵⁷ but thanks be to God, who gives us the victory through our Lord Jesus Christ.

⁵⁸ Therefore, my beloved brethren, be steadfast, immovable, always abounding in the work of the Lord, knowing that your toil is not *in* vain in the Lord.

DAY 7: Describe Isaiah's vision of heaven.

In Isaiah 6:1, Isaiah says that he "saw the Lord sitting on a throne, lofty and exalted." The prophet became unconscious of the outside world and with his inner eye saw what God revealed to him. This experience recalls the experience of John's prophetic vision in Revelation 4:1–11. The throne was greatly elevated, emphasizing the Most High God. His "train" refers to the hem or fringe of the Lord's glorious robe that filled the temple. Though Isaiah may have been at the earthly temple, this describes a vision which transcends the earthly. The throne of God is in the heavenly temple (Rev 4:1–6; 5:1–7; 11:19; 15:5–8).

The seraphim above the throne (v. 2) are an order of angelic creatures who bear a similarity to the 4 living creatures of Revelation 4:6, which in turn resemble the cherubim of Ezekiel 10:1ff. "Six wings." Two wings covered the faces of the seraphim because they dared not gaze directly at God's glory. Two covered their feet, acknowledging their lowliness even though engaged in divine service. With two they flew in serving the One on the throne. Thus, 4 wings related to worship, emphasizing the priority of praise.

"One called out to another and said, 'Holy, Holy, Holy" (v. 3). The seraphs were speaking to each other in antiphonal praise. The primary thrust of the 3-fold repetition of God's holiness is to emphasize God's separateness from and independence of His fallen creation, though it implies secondarily that God is 3 Persons. The earth is the worldwide display of His immeasurable glory, perfections, and attributes as seen in creation (Ro 1:20). Fallen man has nevertheless refused to glorify Him as God (Ro 1:23). "foundations of the thresholds trembled . . . smoke" (v. 4). The shaking and smoke symbolize God's holiness as it relates to His wrath and judgment (Ex 19:16–20; Rev 15:8).

Isaiah's vision made him painfully aware of his sin and broke him; in this way God has prepared him for his cleansing and his commission. "Woe is me...I am a man of unclean lips" (v. 5). If the lips are unclean, so is the heart. This vision of God's holiness vividly reminded the prophet of his own unworthiness which deserved judgment. Job (Job 42:6) and Peter (Lk 5:8) came to the same realization about themselves when confronted with the presence of the Lord (Eze 1:28–2:7; Rev 1:17). The hot coal taken from the altar of incense in heaven (Rev 8:3–5) is emblematic of God's purifying work (v. 6). Repentance is painful. Spiritual cleansing for special service to the Lord, not salvation, is in view (v. 8).

 # SEPTEMBER 8

Isaiah 7:1–8:22

7 Now it came about in the days of Ahaz, the son of Jotham, the son of Uzziah, king of Judah, that Rezin the king of Aram and Pekah the son of Remaliah, king of Israel, went up to Jerusalem to *wage* war against it, but could not conquer it. ²When it was reported to the house of David, saying, "The Arameans have camped in Ephraim," his heart and the hearts of his people shook as the trees of the forest shake with the wind.

³Then the LORD said to Isaiah, "Go out now to meet Ahaz, you and your son Shear-jashub, at the end of the conduit of the upper pool, on the highway to the fuller's field, ⁴and say to him, 'Take care and be calm, have no fear and do not be fainthearted because of these two stubs of smoldering firebrands, on account of the fierce anger of Rezin and Aram and the son of Remaliah. ⁵Because Aram, *with* Ephraim and the son of Remaliah, has planned evil against you, saying, ⁶"Let us go up against Judah and terrorize it, and make for ourselves a breach in its walls and set up the son of Tabeel as king in the midst of it," ⁷thus says the Lord GOD: "It shall not stand nor shall it come to pass. ⁸For the head of Aram is Damascus and the head of Damascus is Rezin (now within another 65 years Ephraim will be shattered, *so that it is* no longer a people), ⁹and the head of Ephraim is Samaria and the head of Samaria is the son of Remaliah. If you will not believe, you surely shall not last."'"

¹⁰Then the LORD spoke again to Ahaz, saying, ¹¹"Ask a sign for yourself from the LORD your God; make *it* deep as Sheol or high as heaven." ¹²But Ahaz said, "I will not ask, nor will I test the LORD!" ¹³Then he said, "Listen now, O house of David! Is it too slight a thing for you to try the patience of men, that you will try the patience of my God as well? ¹⁴Therefore the Lord Himself will give you a sign: Behold, a virgin will be with child and bear a son, and she will call His name Immanuel. ¹⁵He will eat curds and honey at the time He knows *enough* to refuse evil and choose good. ¹⁶For before the boy will know *enough* to refuse evil and choose good, the land whose two kings you dread will be forsaken. ¹⁷The LORD will bring on you, on

your people, and on your father's house such days as have never come since the day that Ephraim separated from Judah, the king of Assyria."

18 In that day the LORD will whistle for the fly that is in the remotest part of the rivers of Egypt and for the bee that is in the land of Assyria. 19 They will all come and settle on the steep ravines, on the ledges of the cliffs, on all the thorn bushes and on all the watering places.

7:18 fly...bee. Egypt was full of flies, and Assyria was a country noted for beekeeping. These insects represented the armies from the powerful countries which the Lord would summon to overrun Judah and take the people into exile.

20 In that day the Lord will shave with a razor, hired from regions beyond the Euphrates (*that is,* with the king of Assyria), the head and the hair of the legs; and it will also remove the beard.

21 Now in that day a man may keep alive a heifer and a pair of sheep; 22 and because of the abundance of the milk produced he will eat curds, for everyone that is left within the land will eat curds and honey.

23 And it will come about in that day, that every place where there used to be a thousand vines, *valued* at a thousand *shekels* of silver, will become briars and thorns. 24 *People* will come there with bows and arrows because all the land will be briars and thorns. 25 As for all the hills which used to be cultivated with the hoe, you will not go there for fear of briars and thorns; but they will become a place for pasturing oxen and for sheep to trample.

8 Then the LORD said to me, "Take for yourself a large tablet and write on it in ordinary letters: Swift is the booty, speedy is the prey. 2 And I will take to Myself faithful witnesses for testimony, Uriah the priest and Zechariah the son of Jeberechiah." 3 So I approached the prophetess, and she conceived and gave birth to a son. Then the LORD said to me, "Name him Maher-shalal-hash-baz; 4 for before the boy knows how to cry out 'My father' or 'My mother,' the wealth of Damascus and the spoil of Samaria will be carried away before the king of Assyria."

5 Again the LORD spoke to me further, saying,

6 "Inasmuch as these people
    have rejected the gently
    flowing waters of Shiloah
And rejoice in Rezin and
    the son of Remaliah;
7 Now therefore, behold, the Lord
    is about to bring on them
    the strong and abundant
    waters of the Euphrates,
Even the king of Assyria
    and all his glory;
And it will rise up over all its
    channels and go over all its banks.
8 "Then it will sweep on into Judah, it
    will overflow and pass through,
It will reach even to the neck;
And the spread of its wings
    will fill the breadth of your
    land, O Immanuel.

9 "Be broken, O peoples, and
    be shattered;
And give ear, all remote
    places of the earth.
Gird yourselves, yet be shattered;
Gird yourselves, yet be shattered.
10 "Devise a plan, but it will be thwarted;
State a proposal, but it will not stand,
For God is with us."

8:10 God is with us. The Hebrew is *Immanuel.* The name of the virgin's child (7:14) guaranteed the eventual triumph of the faithful remnant of Israel.

11 For thus the LORD spoke to me with mighty power and instructed me not to walk in the way of this people, saying,

12 "You are not to say, '*It is* a
    conspiracy!'
In regard to all that this people
    call a conspiracy,
And you are not to fear what they
    fear or be in dread of *it.*
13 "It is the LORD of hosts whom
    you should regard as holy.
And He shall be your fear,
And He shall be your dread.
14 "Then He shall become a sanctuary;
But to both the houses of
    Israel, a stone to strike and
    a rock to stumble over,
And a snare and a trap for the
    inhabitants of Jerusalem.

[15] "Many will stumble over them,
Then they will fall and be broken;
They will even be snared and caught."

[16] Bind up the testimony, seal the law among my disciples. [17] And I will wait for the LORD who is hiding His face from the house of Jacob; I will even look eagerly for Him. [18] Behold, I and the children whom the LORD has given me are for signs and wonders in Israel from the LORD of hosts, who dwells on Mount Zion.

[19] When they say to you, "Consult the mediums and the spiritists who whisper and mutter," should not a people consult their God? *Should they consult* the dead on behalf of the

8:19 *consult* the dead. People of Isaiah's day were using spiritualists to communicate with the dead as King Saul did through the medium at En-dor (1Sa 28:8–19). The law strictly forbade such consultations (Lv 19:26; Dt 18:10–11).

living? [20] To the law and to the testimony! If they do not speak according to this word, it is because they have no dawn. [21] They will pass through the land hard-pressed and famished, and it will turn out that when they are hungry, they will be enraged and curse their king and their God as they face upward. [22] Then they will look to the earth, and behold, distress and darkness, the gloom of anguish; and *they will be* driven away into darkness.

Psalm 105:37–45

[37] Then He brought them out
with silver and gold,
And among His tribes there was
not one who stumbled.
[38] Egypt was glad when they departed,
For the dread of them had
fallen upon them.
[39] He spread a cloud for a covering,
And fire to illumine by night.
[40] They asked, and He brought quail,
And satisfied them with the
bread of heaven.
[41] He opened the rock and
water flowed out;
It ran in the dry places *like* a river.
[42] For He remembered His holy word
With Abraham His servant;
[43] And He brought forth His
people with joy,
His chosen ones with a joyful shout.

[44] He gave them also the
lands of the nations,
That they might take possession of
the fruit of the peoples' labor,
[45] So that they might keep His statutes
And observe His laws,
Praise the LORD!

Proverbs 24:30–34

[30] I passed by the field of
the sluggard
And by the vineyard of the
man lacking sense,
[31] And behold, it was completely
overgrown with thistles;
Its surface was covered with
nettles,
And its stone wall was broken
down.
[32] When I saw, I reflected upon it;
I looked, *and* received instruction.
[33] "A little sleep, a little slumber,
A little folding of the hands to rest,"
[34] Then your poverty will
come *as* a robber
And your want like an armed man.

1 Corinthians 16:1–24

16 Now concerning the collection for the saints, as I directed the churches of Galatia, so do you also. [2] On the first day of every week each one of you is to put aside and save,

16:1 collection. An offering for destitute believers in the overpopulated, famine stricken city of Jerusalem (v. 3; see Ac 11:28). Paul had previously solicited funds from the churches of Galatia, Macedonia, and Achaia (Ro 15:26; see Lk 10:25–37; 2Co 8:1–5; 9:12–15; Gal 6:10; 1Jn 3:17).

16:2 as he may prosper. No required amount or percentage for giving to the Lord's work is specified in the New Testament. All giving to the Lord is to be freewill giving and completely discretionary (Lk 6:38; 2Co 9:6–8). This is not to be confused with the Old Testament required giving of 3 tithes (Lv 27:30; Nu 18:21–26; Dt 14:28–29; Mal 3:8–10) which totaled about 23 percent annually to fund the national government of Israel, take care of public festivals, and provide welfare. Modern parallels to the Old Testament tithe are found in the taxation system of countries (Ro 13:6). Old Testament giving to God was not regulated as to amount (Ex 25:1–2; 35:21; 36:6; Pr 3:9–10; 11:24).

as he may prosper, so that no collections be made when I come. ³When I arrive, whomever you may approve, I will send them with letters to carry your gift to Jerusalem; ⁴and if it is fitting for me to go also, they will go with me.

⁵But I will come to you after I go through Macedonia, for I am going through Macedonia; ⁶and perhaps I will stay with you, or even spend the winter, so that you may send me on my way wherever I may go. ⁷For I do not wish to see you now *just* in passing; for I hope to remain with you for some time, if the Lord permits. ⁸But I will remain in Ephesus until Pentecost; ⁹for a wide door for effective *service* has opened to me, and there are many adversaries.

¹⁰Now if Timothy comes, see that he is with you without cause to be afraid, for he is doing the Lord's work, as I also am. ¹¹So

16:9 many adversaries. Perhaps no New Testament church had such fierce opposition as the one in Ephesus. In spite of that opposition, the door for the gospel was open wide (see 2Co 2:12-13 where Paul also had an open door, but no heart to remain and preach), and Paul stayed. At the end of the experience of opposition described in 2 Corinthians 1:8-10, he wrote 1 Corinthians.

let no one despise him. But send him on his way in peace, so that he may come to me; for I expect him with the brethren.

¹²But concerning Apollos our brother, I encouraged him greatly to come to you with the brethren; and it was not at all *his* desire to come now, but he will come when he has opportunity.

¹³Be on the alert, stand firm in the faith, act like men, be strong. ¹⁴Let all that you do be done in love.

¹⁵Now I urge you, brethren (you know the household of Stephanas, that they were the first fruits of Achaia, and that they have devoted themselves for ministry to the saints), ¹⁶that you also be in subjection to such men and to everyone who helps in the work and labors. ¹⁷I rejoice over the coming of Stephanas and Fortunatus and Achaicus, because they have supplied what was lacking on your part. ¹⁸For they have refreshed my spirit and yours. Therefore acknowledge such men.

¹⁹The churches of Asia greet you. Aquila and Prisca greet you heartily in the Lord, with the church that is in their house. ²⁰All the brethren greet you. Greet one another with a holy kiss.

²¹The greeting is in my own hand—Paul. ²²If anyone does not love the Lord, he is to be accursed. Maranatha. ²³The grace of the Lord Jesus be with you. ²⁴My love be with you all in Christ Jesus. Amen.

DAY 8: From Isaiah 7 and 8, list a few of the many prophecies from Isaiah that were fulfilled in the New Testament.

In Isaiah 7:14, since Ahaz refused to choose a sign, the Lord chose His own sign, whose implementation would occur far beyond Ahaz's lifetime. "A virgin." This prophecy reached forward to the virgin birth of the Messiah, as the New Testament notes (Mt 1:23). The Hebrew word refers to an unmarried woman and means "virgin" (Ge 24:43; Pr 30:19; SS 1:3; 6:8), so the birth of Isaiah's own son (8:3) could not have fully satisfied the prophecy. "Shall call His name Immanuel." The title, applied to Jesus in Matthew 1:23, means "GOD WITH US."

Isaiah 8:14. "Sanctuary...stone to strike." Isaiah found encouragement in the Lord as his holy place of protection from his accusers. The New Testament applies this verse to corporate Israel in her ongoing rejection of Jesus as Messiah (Lk 2:34; Ro 9:32-33; 1Pe 2:8). "Both the houses of Israel." They will be collapsed until the return of the Messiah to the earth restores them.

Isaiah 8:15. "Many will stumble." Another prediction anticipated the stumbling of Israel, which included her rejection of her Messiah at His first advent (Lk 20:18; Ro 9:32; 28:16).

Isaiah 8:17. "Wait for...look eagerly." The speaker is Isaiah whose disposition was to await the Lord's deliverance, the national salvation promised the faithful remnant (40:31; 49:23).

Isaiah 8:18. "I and the children." In their historical setting, the words refer to Isaiah and his two sons, whose names had prophetic significance (i.e., as "signs and wonders"). In Hebrews 2:13, these verses emphasize the point that Christ had fully identified Himself with mankind by taking a human nature. And He demonstrated the reality of His human nature by His reliance upon God during His earthly sojourn.

SEPTEMBER 9

Isaiah 9:1–10:34

9 But there will be no *more* gloom for her who was in anguish; in earlier times He treated the land of Zebulun and the land of Naphtali with contempt, but later on He shall make *it* glorious, by the way of the sea, on the other side of Jordan, Galilee of the Gentiles.

2 The people who walk in darkness
Will see a great light;
Those who live in a dark land,
The light will shine on them.

3 You shall multiply the nation,
You shall increase their gladness;
They will be glad in Your presence
As with the gladness of harvest,
As men rejoice when they
divide the spoil.

4 For You shall break the yoke
of their burden and the
staff on their shoulders,
The rod of their oppressor, as
at the battle of Midian.

5 For every boot of the booted
warrior in the *battle* tumult,
And cloak rolled in blood, will be
for burning, fuel for the fire.

6 For a child will be born to us,
a son will be given to us;
And the government will
rest on His shoulders;

9:6 child…son. These terms elaborate further on Immanuel, the child to be born to the virgin (7:14). The virgin's child will also be the royal Son of David, with rights to the Davidic throne (9:7; see Mt 1:21; Lk 1:31–33; 2:7, 11). **government.** In fulfillment of this verse and Psalms 2:9, the Son will rule the nations of the world (Rev 2:27; 19:15). **Wonderful Counselor.** In contrast to Ahaz, this King will implement supernatural wisdom in discharging His office (2Sa 16:23; 1Ki 3:28). **Mighty God.** As a powerful warrior, the Messiah will accomplish the military exploits mentioned in 9:3–5 (10:21; Dt 10:17; Ne 9:32). **Eternal Father.** The Messiah will be a Father to His people eternally. As Davidic King, He will compassionately care for and discipline them (40:11; 63:16; 64:8; Pss 68:5–6; 103:13; Pr 3:12). **Prince of Peace.** The government of Immanuel will procure and perpetuate peace among the nations of the world (2:4; 11:6–9; Mic 4:3).

And His name will be called
Wonderful Counselor, Mighty God,
Eternal Father, Prince of Peace.

7 There will be no end to the increase
of *His* government or of peace,
On the throne of David and
over his kingdom,
To establish it and to uphold it
with justice and righteousness
From then on and forevermore.
The zeal of the LORD of hosts
will accomplish this.

9:7 throne of David. The virgin's Son will be the rightful heir to David's throne and will inherit the promises of the Davidic Covenant (2Sa 7:12–16; see Ps 89:1–37; Mt 1:1).

8 The Lord sends a message
against Jacob,
And it falls on Israel.

9 And all the people know *it,*
That is, Ephraim and the
inhabitants of Samaria,
Asserting in pride and in
arrogance of heart:

10 "The bricks have fallen down,
But we will rebuild with
smooth stones;
The sycamores have been cut down,
But we will replace *them* with cedars."

11 Therefore the LORD raises against
them adversaries from Rezin
And spurs their enemies on,

12 The Arameans on the east and
the Philistines on the west;
And they devour Israel
with gaping jaws.
In *spite of* all this, His anger
does not turn away
And His hand is still stretched out.

13 Yet the people do not turn back
to Him who struck them,
Nor do they seek the LORD of hosts.

14 So the LORD cuts off head
and tail from Israel,
Both palm branch and
bulrush in a single day.

15 The head is the elder and
honorable man,
And the prophet who teaches
falsehood is the tail.

16 For those who guide this people
are leading *them* astray;

And those who are guided by them
 are brought to confusion.
¹⁷ Therefore the Lord does not take
 pleasure in their young men,
Nor does He have pity on their
 orphans or their widows;
For every one of them is
 godless and an evildoer,
And every mouth is speaking
 foolishness.
In *spite of* all this, His anger
 does not turn away
And His hand is still stretched out.

¹⁸ For wickedness burns like a fire;
It consumes briars and thorns;
It even sets the thickets of
 the forest aflame
And they roll upward in a
 column of smoke.
¹⁹ By the fury of the LORD of hosts
 the land is burned up,
And the people are like
 fuel for the fire;
No man spares his brother.
²⁰ They slice off *what is* on the right
 hand but *still* are hungry,
And they eat *what is* on the left
 hand but they are not satisfied;
Each of them eats the flesh
 of his own arm.
²¹ Manasseh *devours* Ephraim,
 and Ephraim Manasseh,
And together they are against Judah.
In *spite of* all this, His anger
 does not turn away
And His hand is still stretched out.

10 Woe to those who enact evil
 statutes
And to those who constantly
 record unjust decisions,
² So as to deprive the needy of justice
And rob the poor of My
 people of *their* rights,
So that widows may be their spoil
And that they may plunder
 the orphans.
³ Now what will you do in the
 day of punishment,
And in the devastation which
 will come from afar?
To whom will you flee for help?
And where will you leave
 your wealth?
⁴ Nothing *remains* but to crouch
 among the captives
Or fall among the slain.

In *spite of* all this, His anger
 does not turn away
And His hand is still stretched out.

⁵ Woe to Assyria, the rod of My anger
And the staff in whose hands
 is My indignation,
⁶ I send it against a godless nation
And commission it against
 the people of My fury
To capture booty and to seize
 plunder,
And to trample them down
 like mud in the streets.
⁷ Yet it does not so intend,
Nor does it plan so in its heart,
But rather it is its purpose to destroy
And to cut off many nations.
⁸ For it says, "Are not my
 princes all kings?
⁹ "Is not Calno like Carchemish,
 Or Hamath like Arpad,
 Or Samaria like Damascus?
¹⁰ "As my hand has reached to the
 kingdoms of the idols,
 Whose graven images *were*
 greater than those of
 Jerusalem and Samaria,
¹¹ Shall I not do to Jerusalem
 and her images
Just as I have done to Samaria
 and her idols?"

¹² So it will be that when the Lord has completed all His work on Mount Zion and on Jerusalem, *He will say,* "I will punish the fruit of the arrogant heart of the king of Assyria and the pomp of his haughtiness." ¹³ For he has said,

"By the power of my hand and
 by my wisdom I did *this,*
For I have understanding;
And I removed the boundaries
 of the peoples
And plundered their treasures,
And like a mighty man I brought
 down *their* inhabitants,
¹⁴ And my hand reached to the riches
 of the peoples like a nest,
And as one gathers abandoned
 eggs, I gathered all the earth;
And there was not one that
 flapped its wing or opened
 its beak or chirped."
¹⁵ Is the axe to boast itself over the
 one who chops with it?

Is the saw to exalt itself over
the one who wields it?
That would be like a club
wielding those who lift it,
Or like a rod lifting *him*
who is not wood.
16 Therefore the Lord, the GOD of
hosts, will send a wasting disease
among his stout warriors;
And under his glory a fire will be
kindled like a burning flame.
17 And the light of Israel will become
a fire and his Holy One a flame,
And it will burn and devour
his thorns and his briars
in a single day.
18 And He will destroy the glory of
his forest and of his fruitful
garden, both soul and body,
And it will be as when a sick
man wastes away.
19 And the rest of the trees of his forest
will be so small in number
That a child could write them down.

20 Now in that day the remnant of Israel,
and those of the house of Jacob who have
escaped, will never again rely on the one who
struck them, but will truly rely on the LORD,
the Holy One of Israel.

21 A remnant will return, the remnant
of Jacob, to the mighty God.
22 For though your people, O Israel,
may be like the sand of the sea,
Only a remnant within
them will return;
A destruction is determined,
overflowing with righteousness.

23 For a complete destruction, one that is decreed, the Lord GOD of hosts will execute in
the midst of the whole land.
24 Therefore thus says the Lord GOD of
hosts, "O My people who dwell in Zion, do
not fear the Assyrian who strikes you with
the rod and lifts up his staff against you, the
way Egypt *did.* 25 For in a very little while My
indignation *against you* will be spent and My
anger *will be directed* to their destruction."
26 The LORD of hosts will arouse a scourge
against him like the slaughter of Midian at
the rock of Oreb; and His staff will be over
the sea and He will lift it up the way *He did*
in Egypt. 27 So it will be in that day, that his
burden will be removed from your shoulders
and his yoke from your neck, and the yoke will
be broken because of fatness.

28 He has come against Aiath,
He has passed through
Migron;
At Michmash he deposited
his baggage.
29 They have gone through
the pass, *saying,*
"Geba will be our lodging place."
Ramah is terrified, and Gibeah
of Saul has fled away.
30 Cry aloud with your voice,
O daughter of Gallim!
Pay attention, Laishah *and*
wretched Anathoth!
31 Madmenah has fled.
The inhabitants of Gebim
have sought refuge.
32 Yet today he will halt at Nob;
He shakes his fist at the mountain
of the daughter of Zion,
the hill of Jerusalem.

33 Behold, the Lord, the GOD of
hosts, will lop off the boughs
with a terrible crash;
Those also who are tall in
stature will be cut down
And those who are lofty
will be abased.
34 He will cut down the thickets of
the forest with an iron *axe,*
And Lebanon will fall by
the Mighty One.

Psalm 106:1–5

Praise the LORD!
Oh give thanks to the LORD,
for He is good;
For His lovingkindness is
everlasting.
2 Who can speak of the mighty
deeds of the LORD,
Or can show forth all His
praise?
3 How blessed are those
who keep justice,
Who practice righteousness
at all times!

4 Remember me, O LORD, in *Your*
favor toward Your people;
Visit me with Your salvation,
5 That I may see the prosperity
of Your chosen ones,
That I may rejoice in the
gladness of Your nation,
That I may glory with
Your inheritance.

Proverbs 25:1–2

25 These also are proverbs of Solomon which the men of Hezekiah, king of Judah, transcribed.

² It is the glory of God to
　conceal a matter,
But the glory of kings is to
　search out a matter.

2 Corinthians 1:1–24

1 Paul, an apostle of Christ Jesus by the will of God, and Timothy *our* brother,

To the church of God which is at Corinth with all the saints who are throughout Achaia: ²Grace to you and peace from God our Father and the Lord Jesus Christ.

³Blessed *be* the God and Father of our Lord Jesus Christ, the Father of mercies and God of all comfort, ⁴who comforts us in all our affliction so that we will be able to comfort those who are in any affliction with the comfort with which we ourselves are comforted

---

1:4 affliction. This term refers to crushing pressure, because in Paul's life and ministry there was always something attempting to weaken him, restrict or confine his ministry, or even crush out his life. But no matter what confronted him, Paul knew God would sustain and strengthen him (12:9–10; Rom. 8:31–38; Phil. 1:6)). **that we will be able to comfort.** Comfort from God is not an end in itself. Its purpose is that believers also might be comforters. Having humiliated and convicted the Corinthians, God used Paul to return to them with a strengthening message after he himself had received divine strengthening (6:1–13; 12:6–11; Lk 22:31–32).

---

by God. ⁵For just as the sufferings of Christ are ours in abundance, so also our comfort is abundant through Christ. ⁶But if we are afflicted, it is for your comfort and salvation; or if we are comforted, it is for your comfort, which is effective in the patient enduring of the same sufferings which we also suffer; ⁷and our hope for you is firmly grounded, knowing that as you are sharers of our sufferings, so also you are *sharers* of our comfort.

⁸For we do not want you to be unaware, brethren, of our affliction which came *to us* in Asia, that we were burdened excessively, beyond our strength, so that we despaired even of life; ⁹indeed, we had the sentence of death within ourselves so that we would not

---

1:8 affliction which came *to us* in Asia. This was a recent occurrence (following the writing of 1 Corinthians) that happened in or around the city of Ephesus. The details of this situation are not known. **despaired even of life.** Paul faced something that was beyond human survival and was extremely discouraging because he believed it threatened to end his ministry prematurely. The Greek word for "despaired" literally means "no passage," the total absence of an exit (2Ti 4:6). The Corinthians were aware of what had happened to Paul, but they did not realize the utter severity of it, or what God was doing through those circumstances.

1:9 the sentence of death. The word for "sentence" is a technical term that indicated the passing of an official resolution, in this case the death sentence. Paul was so absolutely sure he was going to die for the gospel that he had pronounced the sentence upon himself. **not trust in ourselves, but in God.** God's ultimate purpose for Paul's horrible extremity. The Lord took him to the point at which he could not fall back on any intellectual, physical, or emotional human resource (12:9–10). **who raises the dead.** A Jewish descriptive term for God used in synagogue worship language. Paul understood that trust in God's power to raise the dead was the only hope of rescue from his extreme circumstances.

---

trust in ourselves, but in God who raises the dead; ¹⁰who delivered us from so great a *peril of* death, and will deliver *us,* He on whom we have set our hope. And He will yet deliver us, ¹¹you also joining in helping us through your prayers, so that thanks may be given by many persons on our behalf for the favor bestowed on us through *the prayers of* many.

¹²For our proud confidence is this: the testimony of our conscience, that in holiness and godly sincerity, not in fleshly wisdom but in the grace of God, we have conducted ourselves in the world, and especially toward you. ¹³For we write nothing else to you than what you read and understand, and I hope you will understand until the end; ¹⁴just as you also partially did understand us, that we are your reason to be proud as you also are ours, in the day of our Lord Jesus.

¹⁵In this confidence I intended at first to come to you, so that you might twice receive a blessing; ¹⁶that is, to pass your way into Macedonia, and again from Macedonia to come to you, and by you to be helped on my journey to

Judea. [17] Therefore, I was not vacillating when I intended to do this, was I? Or what I purpose, do I purpose according to the flesh, so that with me there will be yes, yes and no, no *at the same time?* [18] But as God is faithful, our word to you is not yes and no. [19] For the Son of God, Christ Jesus, who was preached among you by us—by me and Silvanus and Timothy—was not yes and no, but is yes in Him. [20] For as many as are the promises of God, in Him they are yes; therefore also through Him is our Amen to the glory of God through us. [21] Now He who establishes us with you in Christ and anointed us is God, [22] who also sealed us and gave *us* the Spirit in our hearts as a pledge.

[23] But I call God as witness to my soul, that to spare you I did not come again to Corinth. [24] Not that we lord it over your faith, but are workers with you for your joy; for in your faith you are standing firm.

DAY 9: Why did Paul write a second book to the Corinthians?

Paul's association with the church of Corinth began on his second missionary journey (Ac 18:1–18), when he spent 18 months (Ac 18:11) ministering there. After leaving Corinth, Paul heard of immorality in the Corinthian church and wrote a letter (since lost) to confront that sin, referred to in 1 Corinthians 5:9. During his ministry in Ephesus, he received further reports of trouble in the Corinthian church in the form of divisions among them (1Co 1:11). In addition, the Corinthians wrote Paul a letter (1Co 7:1), asking for clarification of some issues. Paul responded by writing the letter known as 1 Corinthians. Planning to remain at Ephesus a little longer (1Co 16:8–9), Paul sent Timothy to Corinth (1Co 4:17; 16:10–11). Disturbing news reached the apostle (possibly from Timothy) of further difficulties at Corinth, including the arrival of self-styled false apostles.

To create the platform to teach their false gospel, the false apostles began by assaulting the character of Paul. They had to convince the people to turn from Paul to them if they were to succeed in preaching demon doctrine. Temporarily abandoning the work at Ephesus, Paul went immediately to Corinth. The visit (known as the "painful visit"; see 2Co 2:1) was not a successful one from Paul's perspective—someone in the Corinthian church even openly insulted him (2:5–8, 10; 7:12). Saddened by the Corinthians' lack of loyalty to defend him, seeking to spare them further reproof (1:23), and perhaps hoping time would bring them to their senses, Paul returned to Ephesus. From Ephesus, Paul wrote what is known as the "severe letter" (see 2:4) and sent it with Titus to Corinth (7:5–16). Leaving Ephesus after the riot sparked by Demetrius (Ac 19:23—20:1), Paul went to Troas to meet Titus (2:12–13). But Paul was so anxious for news of how the Corinthians had responded to the "severe letter" that he could not minister there though the Lord had opened the door (2:12; 7:5). So he left for Macedonia to look for Titus (2:13). To Paul's immense relief and joy, Titus met him with the news that the majority of the Corinthians had repented of their rebellion against Paul (7:7). Wise enough to know that some rebellious attitudes still smoldered under the surface and could erupt again, Paul wrote the Corinthians the letter called 2 Corinthians. In this letter, though the apostle expressed his relief and joy at their repentance (7:8–16), his main concern was to defend his apostleship (chaps. 1–7), exhort the Corinthians to resume preparations for the collection for the poor at Jerusalem (chaps. 8–9), and confront the false apostles head on (chaps. 10–13). He then went to Corinth, as he had written (12:14; 13:1–2). The Corinthians' participation in the Jerusalem offering (Ro 15:26) implies that Paul's third visit to that church was successful.

✝ SEPTEMBER 10

Isaiah 11:1–12:6

11 Then a shoot will spring from
the stem of Jesse,
And a branch from his
roots will bear fruit.
[2] The Spirit of the LORD
will rest on Him,
The spirit of wisdom and
understanding,
The spirit of counsel and
strength,

The spirit of knowledge and
the fear of the LORD.
[3] And He will delight in the
fear of the LORD,
And He will not judge by
what His eyes see,
Nor make a decision by
what His ears hear;
[4] But with righteousness He
will judge the poor,
And decide with fairness for
the afflicted of the earth;
And He will strike the earth
with the rod of His mouth,

11:1 stem…roots. With the Babylonian captivity of 586 B.C., the Davidic dynasty appeared as decimated as the Assyrian army. A major difference between the two was the life remaining in the stump and roots of the Davidic line. That life was to manifest itself in new growth in the form of the Rod and Branch. **Jesse.** Jesse was David's father through whose line the messianic king was to come (Ru 4:22; 1Sa 16:1, 12–13). **branch.** This is a title for the Messiah (see 4:2).

11:2 The Spirit of the LORD. As the Spirit of the Lord came upon David when he was anointed king (1Sa 16:13; Ps 51:11), so He will rest upon David's descendant, Christ, who will rule the world. **Spirit…the LORD…Him.** This verse refers to the 3 persons of the Holy Trinity (see 6:3). **wisdom and understanding…counsel and strength…knowledge…fear of the LORD.** These are Spirit-imparted qualifications that will enable the Messiah to rule justly and effectively.

11:10 in that day. The time of universal peace will come in the future reign of the Lord. **a signal for the peoples.** The Root of Jesse will also attract non-Jews who inhabit the future kingdom (49:6; 52:10; 60:3; 66:18). Paul saw God's ministry to Gentiles during the church age as an additional implication of this verse (Ro 15:12).

11 Then it will happen on that day that the Lord
Will again recover the second time with His hand
The remnant of His people, who will remain,
From Assyria, Egypt, Pathros, Cush, Elam, Shinar, Hamath,
And from the islands of the sea.
12 And He will lift up a standard for the nations
And assemble the banished ones of Israel,
And will gather the dispersed of Judah
From the four corners of the earth.
13 Then the jealousy of Ephraim will depart,
And those who harass Judah will be cut off;
Ephraim will not be jealous of Judah,
And Judah will not harass Ephraim.
14 They will swoop down on the slopes of the Philistines on the west;
Together they will plunder the sons of the east;
They will possess Edom and Moab,
And the sons of Ammon will be subject to them.
15 And the LORD will utterly destroy The tongue of the Sea of Egypt;
And He will wave His hand over the River
With His scorching wind;
And He will strike it into seven streams
And make men walk over dry-shod.
16 And there will be a highway from Assyria
For the remnant of His people who will be left,
Just as there was for Israel
In the day that they came up out of the land of Egypt.

And with the breath of His lips He will slay the wicked.
5 Also righteousness will be the belt about His loins,
And faithfulness the belt about His waist.

6 And the wolf will dwell with the lamb,
And the leopard will lie down with the young goat,
And the calf and the young lion and the fatling together;
And a little boy will lead them.
7 Also the cow and the bear will graze,
Their young will lie down together,
And the lion will eat straw like the ox.
8 The nursing child will play by the hole of the cobra,
And the weaned child will put his hand on the viper's den.
9 They will not hurt or destroy in all My holy mountain,
For the earth will be full of the knowledge of the LORD
As the waters cover the sea.

10 Then in that day
The nations will resort to the root of Jesse,
Who will stand as a signal for the peoples;
And His resting place will be glorious.

12 Then you will say on that day,
"I will give thanks to You,
O LORD;
For although You were
angry with me,
Your anger is turned away,
And You comfort me.
2 "Behold, God is my salvation,
I will trust and not be afraid;
For the LORD GOD is my
strength and song,
And He has become my
salvation."
3 Therefore you will joyously
draw water
From the springs of salvation.
4 And in that day you will say,
"Give thanks to the LORD,
call on His name.
Make known His deeds
among the peoples;
Make *them* remember that
His name is exalted."
5 Praise the LORD in song, for He
has done excellent things;
Let this be known throughout
the earth.
6 Cry aloud and shout for joy,
O inhabitant of Zion,
For great in your midst is the
Holy One of Israel.

Psalm 106:6–18

6 We have sinned like our fathers,
We have committed iniquity, we
have behaved wickedly.
7 Our fathers in Egypt did not
understand Your wonders;
They did not remember Your
abundant kindnesses,
But rebelled by the sea, at
the Red Sea.
8 Nevertheless He saved them
for the sake of His name,
That He might make His
power known.
9 Thus He rebuked the Red
Sea and it dried up,
And He led them through
the deeps, as through
the wilderness.
10 So He saved them from the
hand of the one who hated *them,*
And redeemed them from
the hand of the enemy.
11 The waters covered their
adversaries;
Not one of them was left.

12 Then they believed His words;
They sang His praise.
13 They quickly forgot His works;
They did not wait for His counsel,
14 But craved intensely in
the wilderness,
And tempted God in the desert.
15 So He gave them their request,
But sent a wasting disease
among them.
16 When they became envious
of Moses in the camp,
And of Aaron, the holy
one of the LORD,
17 The earth opened and
swallowed up Dathan,
And engulfed the company
of Abiram.
18 And a fire blazed up in
their company;
The flame consumed the
wicked.

Proverbs 25:3–5

3 *As* the heavens for height and
the earth for depth,
So the heart of kings is
unsearchable.
4 Take away the dross from
the silver,
And there comes out a
vessel for the smith;
5 Take away the wicked before
the king,
And his throne will be established
in righteousness.

2 Corinthians 2:1–17

2 But I determined this for my own sake,
that I would not come to you in sorrow
again. 2 For if I cause you sorrow, who then
makes me glad but the one whom I made
sorrowful? 3 This is the very thing I wrote
you, so that when I came, I would not have
sorrow from those who ought to make me
rejoice; having confidence in you all that
my joy would be *the joy* of you all. 4 For out
of much affliction and anguish of heart I
wrote to you with many tears; not so that
you would be made sorrowful, but that you
might know the love which I have especially
for you.

5 But if any has caused sorrow, he has
caused sorrow not to me, but in some degree—in order not to say too much—to all of
you. 6 Sufficient for such a one is this punish-

2:2 Although Paul was sensitive to the Corinthians' pain and sadness from the past confrontation, because of his commitment to purity he would confront them again if necessary. "The one whom I made sorrowful" refers to one convicted by his sin. In particular, there was apparently on Paul's last visit a man in the church who confronted him with the accusations taken from the false teachers. The church had not dealt with that man in Paul's defense, and Paul was deeply grieved over that lack of loyalty. The only thing that would bring Paul joy would be repentance from such a one and any who agreed with him, and Paul had been waiting for it.

finding Titus my brother; but taking my leave of them, I went on to Macedonia.

¹⁴ But thanks be to God, who always leads us in triumph in Christ, and manifests through us the sweet aroma of the knowledge of Him in every place. ¹⁵ For we are a fragrance of Christ to God among those who are being saved and among those who are perishing; ¹⁶ to the one an aroma from death to death, to the other an aroma from life to life. And who is adequate for these things? ¹⁷ For we are not like many, peddling the word of God, but as from sincerity, but as from God, we speak in Christ in the sight of God.

ment which *was inflicted* by the majority, ⁷ so that on the contrary you should rather forgive and comfort *him,* otherwise such a one might be overwhelmed by excessive sorrow. ⁸ Wherefore I urge you to reaffirm *your* love for him. ⁹ For to this end also I wrote, so that I might put you to the test, whether you are obedient in all things. ¹⁰ But one whom you forgive anything, I *forgive* also; for indeed what I have forgiven, if I have forgiven anything, *I did it* for your sakes in the presence of Christ, ¹¹ so that no advantage would be taken of us by Satan, for we are not ignorant of his schemes.

¹² Now when I came to Troas for the gospel of Christ and when a door was opened for me in the Lord, ¹³ I had no rest for my spirit, not

2:17 not like many. Or, "not as the majority." This specifically refers to the false teachers in Corinth and to the many other teachers and philosophers of that day who operated by human wisdom (1Co 1:19-20). **peddling.** From a Greek verb that means "to corrupt," this word came to refer to corrupt hucksters, or con men who by their cleverness and deception were able to sell as genuine an inferior product that was only a cheap imitation. The false teachers in the church were coming with clever, deceptive rhetoric to offer a degraded, adulterated message that mixed paganism and Jewish tradition. They were dishonest men seeking personal profit and prestige at the expense of gospel truth and people's souls.

DAY 10: What was Paul's rationale for forgiveness?

Second Corinthians 2:5-11 is one of the best texts in all of Scripture on the godly motivation for forgiveness. Paul said, "If any has caused sorrow" (v. 5). The Greek construction of this clause assumes the condition to be true—Paul is acknowledging the reality of the offense and its ongoing effect, not on him, but on the church. With this deflection of any personal vengeance, he sought to soften the charge against the penitent offender and allow the church to deal with the man and those who were with him objectively, apart from Paul's personal anguish or offense.

"This punishment...inflicted by the majority" (v. 6). This indicates that the church in Corinth had followed the biblical process in disciplining the sinning man (Mt 18:15-20; 2Th 3:6, 14). The Greek word for "punishment," used frequently in secular writings but only here in the New Testament, denoted an official legal penalty or commercial sanction that was enacted against an individual or group (city, nation). "Sufficient." The process of discipline and punishment was enough. Now it was time to show mercy because the man had repented (Mt 18:18, 23-35; Gal 6:1-2; Eph 4:32; Col 3:13; Heb 12:11).

"You should rather forgive and comfort him" (v. 7). It was time to grant forgiveness so the man's joy would be restored (Ps 51:12, 14; Is 42:2, 3). Paul knew there was—and is—no place in the church for man-made limits on God's grace, mercy, and forgiveness toward repentant sinners. Such restrictions could only rob the fellowship of the joy of unity (Mt 18:34-35; Mk 11:25-26). "Wherefore I urge you to reaffirm your love for him."

✒ SEPTEMBER 11

Isaiah 13:1–14:32

13 The oracle concerning Babylon which Isaiah the son of Amoz saw.

2 Lift up a standard on the bare hill,
Raise your voice to them,
Wave the hand that they may
enter the doors of the nobles.
3 I have commanded My
consecrated ones,
I have even called My
mighty warriors,
My proudly exulting ones,
To *execute* My anger.
4 A sound of tumult on the mountains,
Like that of many people!
A sound of the uproar of kingdoms,
Of nations gathered together!
The LORD of hosts is mustering
the army for battle.
5 They are coming from a far country,
From the farthest horizons,
The LORD and His instruments
of indignation,
To destroy the whole land.
6 Wail, for the day of the LORD is near!
It will come as destruction
from the Almighty.
7 Therefore all hands will fall limp,
And every man's heart will melt.
8 They will be terrified,
Pains and anguish will
take hold of *them;*
They will writhe like a
woman in labor,
They will look at one another
in astonishment,
Their faces aflame.
9 Behold, the day of the LORD is coming,
Cruel, with fury and burning anger,
To make the land a desolation;
And He will exterminate
its sinners from it.
10 For the stars of heaven and
their constellations
Will not flash forth their light;
The sun will be dark when it rises
And the moon will not shed its light.
11 Thus I will punish the
world for its evil
And the wicked for their iniquity;
I will also put an end to the
arrogance of the proud
And abase the haughtiness
of the ruthless.

12 I will make mortal man
scarcer than pure gold
And mankind than the gold of Ophir.
13 Therefore I will make the
heavens tremble,
And the earth will be shaken
from its place
At the fury of the LORD of hosts
In the day of His burning anger.
14 And it will be that like a
hunted gazelle,
Or like sheep with none
to gather *them,*
They will each turn to his own people,
And each one flee to his own land.
15 Anyone who is found will
be thrust through,
And anyone who is captured
will fall by the sword.
16 Their little ones also will
be dashed to pieces
Before their eyes;
Their houses will be plundered
And their wives ravished.

17 Behold, I am going to stir up
the Medes against them,
Who will not value silver or
take pleasure in gold.
18 And *their* bows will mow
down the young men,
They will not even have compassion
on the fruit of the womb,
Nor will their eye pity children.
19 And Babylon, the beauty of kingdoms,
the glory of the Chaldeans' pride,
Will be as when God overthrew
Sodom and Gomorrah.
20 It will never be inhabited or lived in
from generation to generation;
Nor will the Arab pitch *his* tent there,
Nor will shepherds make *their*
flocks lie down there.
21 But desert creatures will
lie down there,
And their houses will be full of owls;
Ostriches also will live there, and
shaggy goats will frolic there.
22 Hyenas will howl in their
fortified towers
And jackals in their luxurious palaces.
Her *fateful* time also will soon come
And her days will not be prolonged.

14 When the LORD will have compassion on Jacob and again choose Israel, and settle them in their own land, then strangers will join them and attach themselves to the house of Jacob. ²The peoples will take them along and bring them to their place, and the house of Israel will possess them as an inheritance in the land of the LORD as male servants and female servants; and they will take their captors captive and will rule over their oppressors.

³And it will be in the day when the LORD gives you rest from your pain and turmoil and harsh service in which you have been enslaved, ⁴that you will take up this taunt against the king of Babylon, and say,

"How the oppressor has ceased,
And how fury has ceased!
⁵ "The LORD has broken the
staff of the wicked,
The scepter of rulers
⁶ Which used to strike the peoples in
fury with unceasing strokes,
Which subdued the nations in anger
with unrestrained persecution.
⁷ "The whole earth is at rest *and* is quiet;
They break forth into shouts of joy.
⁸ "Even the cypress trees rejoice
over you, *and* the cedars
of Lebanon, *saying,*
'Since you were laid low, no *tree*
cutter comes up against us.'
⁹ "Sheol from beneath is excited over
you to meet you when you come;
It arouses for you the spirits of the
dead, all the leaders of the earth;
It raises all the kings of the
nations from their thrones.
¹⁰ "They will all respond and say to you,
'Even you have been made weak as we,
You have become like us.
¹¹ 'Your pomp *and* the music
of your harps
Have been brought down to Sheol;
Maggots are spread out *as*
your bed beneath you
And worms are your covering.'
¹² "How you have fallen from heaven,
O star of the morning,
son of the dawn!
You have been cut down to the earth,
You who have weakened the nations!
¹³ "But you said in your heart,
'I will ascend to heaven;
I will raise my throne above
the stars of God,
And I will sit on the mount
of assembly
In the recesses of the north.
¹⁴ 'I will ascend above the
heights of the clouds;
I will make myself like the Most High.'

14:12–14 fallen from heaven…make myself like the Most High. Jesus' use of v. 12 to describe Satan's fall (Lk 10:18; see Rev 12:8–10) has led many to see more than a reference to the king of Babylon. Just as the Lord addressed Satan in His words to the serpent (Ge 3:14–15), this inspired dirge speaks to the king of Babylon and to the devil who energized him. See Ezekiel 28:12–17 for similar language to the king of Tyre and Satan behind him.

14:12 heaven. The scene suddenly shifts from the underworld to heaven to emphasize the unbridled pride of the king and Satan energizing him. **star of the morning.** Tradition of the time saw the stars as representing gods battling among themselves for places of preeminence.

14:13–14 I will. Five "I wills" emphasize the arrogance of the king of Babylon, and of Satan, from whom he takes his cue.

¹⁵ "Nevertheless you will be
thrust down to Sheol,
To the recesses of the pit.
¹⁶ "Those who see you will gaze
at you,
They will ponder over you,
saying,
'Is this the man who made
the earth tremble,
Who shook kingdoms,
¹⁷ Who made the world like
a wilderness
And overthrew its cities,
Who did not allow his
prisoners to *go* home?'
¹⁸ "All the kings of the nations
lie in glory,
Each in his own tomb.
¹⁹ "But you have been cast
out of your tomb
Like a rejected branch,
Clothed with the slain who are
pierced with a sword,
Who go down to the stones
of the pit
Like a trampled corpse.
²⁰ "You will not be united with
them in burial,
Because you have ruined
your country,
You have slain your people.
May the offspring of evildoers
not be mentioned forever.

²¹ "Prepare for his sons a
place of slaughter
Because of the iniquity
of their fathers.
They must not arise and take
possession of the earth
And fill the face of the
world with cities."

²² "I will rise up against them," declares the LORD of hosts, "and will cut off from Babylon name and survivors, offspring and posterity," declares the LORD. ²³ "I will also make it a possession for the hedgehog and swamps of water, and I will sweep it with the broom of destruction," declares the LORD of hosts. ²⁴ The LORD of hosts has sworn saying, "Surely, just as I have intended so it has happened, and just as I have planned so it will stand, ²⁵ to break Assyria in My land, and I will trample him on My mountains. Then his yoke will be removed from them and his burden removed from their shoulder. ²⁶ This is the plan devised against the whole earth; and this is the hand that is stretched out against all the nations. ²⁷ For the LORD of hosts has planned, and who can frustrate *it*? And as for His stretched-out hand, who can turn it back?"

²⁸ In the year that King Ahaz died this oracle came:

²⁹ "Do not rejoice, O Philistia,
all of you,
Because the rod that struck
you is broken;
For from the serpent's root a
viper will come out,
And its fruit will be a flying
serpent.
³⁰ "Those who are most helpless
will eat,
And the needy will lie
down in security;
I will destroy your root with
famine,
And it will kill off your survivors.
³¹ "Wail, O gate; cry, O city;
Melt away, O Philistia, all of you;
For smoke comes from the north,
And there is no straggler in
his ranks.
³² "How then will one answer the
messengers of the nation?
That the LORD has founded
Zion,
And the afflicted of His
people will seek refuge in it."

Psalm 106:19–23

¹⁹ They made a calf in Horeb
And worshiped a molten image.
²⁰ Thus they exchanged their glory
For the image of an ox that
eats grass.
²¹ They forgot God their Savior,
Who had done great things in Egypt,
²² Wonders in the land of Ham
And awesome things by the Red Sea.
²³ Therefore He said that He
would destroy them,
Had not Moses His chosen one
stood in the breach before Him,
To turn away His wrath from
destroying *them*.

Proverbs 25:6–7

⁶ Do not claim honor in the
presence of the king,
And do not stand in the
place of great men;
⁷ For it is better that it be said
to you, "Come up here,"
Than for you to be placed lower
in the presence of the prince,
Whom your eyes have seen.

25:6-7 In the royal court as in all of life, self-seeking and pride bring a person down. Do not intrude into such a place, for the elevating of the humble is honorable, but the humbling of the proud is disgraceful (Lk 14:8–10; Jas 4:7–10).

2 Corinthians 3:1–18

3 Are we beginning to commend ourselves again? Or do we need, as some, letters of commendation to you or from you? ²You are our letter, written in our hearts, known and read by all men; ³being manifested that you are a letter of Christ, cared for by us, written not with ink but with the Spirit of the living God, not on tablets of stone but on tablets of human hearts.

⁴ Such confidence we have through Christ toward God. ⁵ Not that we are adequate in ourselves to consider anything as *coming* from ourselves, but our adequacy is from God, ⁶ who also made us adequate *as* servants of a new covenant, not of the letter but of the Spirit; for the letter kills, but the Spirit gives life.

⁷ But if the ministry of death, in letters engraved on stones, came with glory, so that the

sons of Israel could not look intently at the face of Moses because of the glory of his face, fading *as* it was, ⁸ how will the ministry of the Spirit fail to be even more with glory? ⁹ For if the ministry of condemnation has glory, much more does the ministry of righteousness abound in glory. ¹⁰ For indeed what had glory, in this case has no glory because of the glory that surpasses *it*. ¹¹ For if that which fades away *was* with glory, much more that which remains *is* in glory.

¹² Therefore having such a hope, we use great boldness in *our* speech, ¹³ and *are* not like Moses, *who* used to put a veil over his face so that the sons of Israel would not look intently at the end of what was fading away. ¹⁴ But their minds were hardened; for until this very day at the reading of the old covenant the same veil remains unlifted, because it is removed in Christ. ¹⁵ But to this day whenever Moses is read, a veil lies over their heart; ¹⁶ but whenever a person turns to the Lord, the veil is taken away. ¹⁷ Now the Lord is the Spirit, and where the Spirit of the Lord is, *there* is liberty. ¹⁸ But we all, with unveiled face, beholding as in a mirror the glory of the Lord, are being transformed into the same image from glory to glory, just as from the Lord, the Spirit.

3:18 we all. Not just Moses, or prophets, apostles, and preachers, but all believers. **with unveiled face.** Believers in the New Covenant have nothing obstructing their vision of Christ and His glory as revealed in the Scripture. **beholding as in a mirror.** Paul's emphasis here is not so much on the reflective capabilities of the mirror as it is on the intimacy of it. A person can bring a mirror right up to his face and get an unobstructed view. Mirrors in Paul's day were polished metal, and thus offered a far from perfect reflection. Though the vision is unobstructed and intimate, believers do not see a perfect representation of God's glory now, but will one day (1Co 13:12). **being transformed.** A continual, progressive transformation. **into the same image.** As they gaze at the glory of the Lord, believers are continually being transformed into Christlikeness. The ultimate goal of the believer is to be like Christ (Ro 8:29; Php 3:12–14; 1Jn 3:2), and by continually focusing on Him the Spirit transforms the believer more and more into His image. **from glory to glory.** From one level of glory to another level of glory—from one level of manifesting Christ to another. This verse describes progressive sanctification. The more believers grow in their knowledge of Christ, the more He is revealed in their lives (Php 3:12–14).

DAY 11: What credentials of his apostleship did Paul give to the Corinthians?

Because Paul did not want to allow the false teachers to accuse him of being proud, he began his defense in 2 Corinthians 3:1 by posing two questions rather than making any overt claims. "Are we beginning to commend ourselves again?" The Greek word for "commend" means "to introduce." Thus Paul was asking the Corinthians if he needed to reintroduce himself, as if they had never met, and prove himself once more. The form of the question demanded a negative answer. "Or do we need, as some, letters of commendation to you or from you?" The false teachers also accused Paul of not possessing the appropriate documents to prove his legitimacy. Such letters were often used to introduce and authenticate someone to the first-century churches (1Co 16:3, 10–11). The false teachers undoubtedly arrived in Corinth with such letters, which they may have forged (Ac 15:1, 5) or obtained under false pretenses from prominent members of the Jerusalem church. Paul's point was that he did not need secondhand testimony when the Corinthians had firsthand proof of his sincere and godly character, as well as the truth of his message that regenerated them.

"You are our letter, written in our hearts" (v. 2). An affirmation of Paul's affection for the believers in Corinth—he held them close to his heart. "Known and read by all men." The transformed lives of the Corinthians were Paul's most eloquent testimonial, better than any secondhand letter. Their changed lives were like an open letter that could be seen and read by all men as a testimony to Paul's faithfulness and the truth of his message.

"You are a letter of Christ" (v. 3). The false teachers did not have a letter of commendation signed by Christ, but Paul had the Corinthian believers' changed lives as proof that Christ had transformed them. "Written not with ink." Paul's letter was no human document written with ink that can fade. It was a living one. "Spirit of the living God." Paul's letter was alive, written by Christ's divine, supernatural power through the transforming work of the Holy Spirit (1Co 2:4–5; 1Th 1:5). "Tablets of stone." A reference to the Ten Commandments. "Tablets of human hearts." More than just writing His Law on stone, God was writing His Law on the hearts of those people He transformed. The false teachers claimed external adherence to the Mosaic Law as the basis of salvation, but the transformed lives of the Corinthians proved that salvation was an internal change wrought by God in the heart.

SEPTEMBER 12

Isaiah 15:1–16:14

15

The oracle concerning Moab.

Surely in a night Ar of Moab is
   devastated *and* ruined;
Surely in a night Kir of Moab is
   devastated *and* ruined.

2 They have gone up to the temple
   and *to* Dibon, *even* to the
   high places to weep.
Moab wails over Nebo and Medeba;
Everyone's head is bald *and*
   every beard is cut off.

3 In their streets they have girded
   themselves with sackcloth;
On their housetops and
   in their squares
Everyone is wailing,
   dissolved in tears.

4 Heshbon and Elealeh also
   cry out,
Their voice is heard all
   the way to Jahaz;
Therefore the armed men
   of Moab cry aloud;
His soul trembles within him.

5 My heart cries out for Moab;
His fugitives are as far as Zoar
   and Eglath-shelishiyah,
For they go up the ascent
   of Luhith weeping;
Surely on the road to Horonaim
   they raise a cry of distress
   over *their* ruin.

6 For the waters of Nimrim
   are desolate.
Surely the grass is withered,
   the tender grass died out,
There is no green thing.

7 Therefore the abundance
   which they have acquired
   and stored up
They carry off over the
   brook of Arabim.

8 For the cry of distress has gone
   around the territory of Moab,
Its wail *goes* as far as Eglaim and
   its wailing even to Beer-elim.

9 For the waters of Dimon
   are full of blood;
Surely I will bring added
   woes upon Dimon,
A lion upon the fugitives of
   Moab and upon the
   remnant of the land.

16

Send the *tribute* lamb to
   the ruler of the land,
From Sela by way of the
   wilderness to the mountain
   of the daughter of Zion.

2 Then, like fleeing birds *or*
   scattered nestlings,
The daughters of Moab will be
   at the fords of the Arnon.

3 "Give *us* advice, make a decision;
Cast your shadow like
   night at high noon;
Hide the outcasts, do not
   betray the fugitive.

4 "Let the outcasts of Moab
   stay with you;
Be a hiding place to them
   from the destroyer."
For the extortioner has come to an
   end, destruction has ceased,
Oppressors have completely
   disappeared from the land.

5 A throne will even be established
   in lovingkindness,
And a judge will sit on it in
   faithfulness in the tent of David;
Moreover, he will seek justice
And be prompt in righteousness.

6 We have heard of the pride of
   Moab, an excessive pride;
Even of his arrogance,
   pride, and fury;
His idle boasts are false.

7 Therefore Moab will wail;
   everyone of Moab will wail.
You will moan for the raisin
   cakes of Kir-hareseth
As those who are utterly stricken.

8 For the fields of Heshbon
   have withered, the vines
   of Sibmah *as well;*
The lords of the nations have
   trampled down its choice clusters
Which reached as far as Jazer *and*
   wandered to the deserts;
Its tendrils spread themselves
   out *and* passed over the sea.

9 Therefore I will weep bitterly for
   Jazer, for the vine of Sibmah;

16:9 I will weep bitterly. Isaiah displayed genuine emotion over the destruction of so rich an agricultural resource. This reflected the Lord's response too.

I will drench you with my tears,
O Heshbon and Elealeh;
For the shouting over your
summer fruits and your
harvest has fallen away.
¹⁰ Gladness and joy are taken away
from the fruitful field;
In the vineyards also there will be no
cries of joy or jubilant shouting,
No treader treads out wine
in the presses,
For I have made the shouting
to cease.
¹¹ Therefore my heart intones
like a harp for Moab
And my inward feelings
for Kir-hareseth.
¹² So it will come about when
Moab presents himself,
When he wearies himself
upon *his* high place
And comes to his sanctuary to pray,
That he will not prevail.

¹³ This is the word which the LORD spoke earlier concerning Moab. ¹⁴ But now the LORD speaks, saying, "Within three years, as a hired man would count them, the glory of Moab will be degraded along with all *his* great population, and *his* remnant will be very small *and* impotent."

Psalm 106:24–31

²⁴ Then they despised the pleasant land;
They did not believe in His word,
²⁵ But grumbled in their tents;
They did not listen to the
voice of the LORD.
²⁶ Therefore He swore to them
That He would cast them
down in the wilderness,
²⁷ And that He would cast their
seed among the nations
And scatter them in the lands.

²⁸ They joined themselves
also to Baal-peor,
And ate sacrifices offered to the dead.
²⁹ Thus they provoked *Him* to
anger with their deeds,
And the plague broke out
among them.
³⁰ Then Phinehas stood up
and interposed,
And so the plague was stayed.
³¹ And it was reckoned to him
for righteousness,
To all generations forever.

106:28 Baal-peor. Refers to Baal, a god of the Moabites, whose worship occurred at the location of the mountain called Peor (Nu 23:28). **sacrifices offered to the dead.** This most likely refers to sacrifices made to lifeless idols (1Th 1:9). Israel should have been worshiping "the living God" (Dt 5:26; 1Sa 17:26, 36; Pss 42:2; 84:2; Jer 10:3–10; Da 6:20, 26).

106:31 reckoned to him for righteousness. This was a just and rewardable action, evidencing faith in God. As with Abraham (see Ge 15:6 and Ro 4:3; Gal 3:6; Jas 2:23), so it was also with Phinehas. The everlasting covenant of perpetual priesthood through Aaron, from the house of Levi, was first made by God in Leviticus 24:8–9. This covenant was reaffirmed in Numbers 18:8, 19. In this text, the covenant is further specified to be through the line of faithful Phinehas.

Proverbs 25:8–10

⁸ Do not go out hastily to
argue *your case;*
Otherwise, what will you
do in the end,
When your neighbor humiliates you?
⁹ Argue your case with your
neighbor,
And do not reveal the
secret of another,
¹⁰ Or he who hears *it* will reproach you,
And the evil report about you
will not pass away.

2 Corinthians 4:1–18

4 Therefore, since we have this ministry, as we received mercy, we do not lose heart, ² but we have renounced the things hidden because of shame, not walking in craftiness or adulterating the word of God, but by the manifestation of truth commending ourselves to every man's conscience in the sight of God. ³ And even if our gospel is veiled, it is veiled to those who are perishing, ⁴ in whose case the god of this world has blinded the minds of the unbelieving so that they might not see the light of the gospel of the glory of Christ, who is the image of God. ⁵ For we do not preach ourselves but Christ Jesus as Lord, and ourselves as your bond-servants for Jesus' sake. ⁶ For God, who said, "Light shall shine out of darkness," is the One who has shone in our hearts to give the Light of the knowledge of the glory of God in the face of Christ.
⁷ But we have this treasure in earthen

vessels, so that the surpassing greatness of the power will be of God and not from ourselves; ⁸ we are afflicted in every way, but not crushed; perplexed, but not despairing; ⁹ persecuted, but not forsaken; struck down, but not destroyed; ¹⁰ always carrying about in the body the dying of Jesus, so that the life of Jesus also may be manifested in our body. ¹¹ For we who live are constantly being delivered over to death for Jesus' sake, so that the life of Jesus also may be manifested in our mortal flesh. ¹² So death works in us, but life in you.

¹³ But having the same spirit of faith, according to what is written, "I BELIEVED, THEREFORE I SPOKE," we also believe, therefore we also speak, ¹⁴ knowing that He who raised the Lord Jesus will raise us also with Jesus and will present us with you. ¹⁵ For all things are for your sakes, so that the grace which is spreading to more and more people may cause the giving of thanks to abound to the glory of God.

¹⁶ Therefore we do not lose heart, but though our outer man is decaying, yet our inner man is being renewed day by day. ¹⁷ For momentary, light affliction is producing for us an eternal weight of glory far beyond all comparison, ¹⁸ while we look not at the things which are seen, but at the things which are not seen; for the things which are seen are temporal, but the things which are not seen are eternal.

4:16 our outer man is decaying. The physical body is in the process of decay and will eventually die. On the surface Paul was referring to the normal aging process, but with the added emphasis that his lifestyle sped up that process. While not an old man, Paul wore himself out in ministry, both in the effort and pace he maintained, plus the number of beatings and attacks he absorbed from his enemies (6:4–10; 11:23–27). **inner man.** The soul of every believer i.e., the new creation—the eternal part of the believer (Eph 4:24; Col 3:10). **being renewed.** The growth and maturing process of the believer is constantly occurring. While the physical body is decaying, the inner self of the believer continues to grow and mature into Christlikeness (Eph 3:16–20).

4:17 momentary, light affliction. The Greek word for "light" means "a weightless trifle" and "affliction" refers to intense pressure. From a human perspective, Paul's own testimony lists a seemingly unbearable litany of sufferings and persecutions he endured throughout his life (11:23–33), yet he viewed them as weightless and lasting for only a brief moment. **eternal weight of glory.** The Greek word for "weight" refers to a heavy mass. For Paul, the future glory he would experience with the Lord far outweighed any suffering he experienced in this world (Ro 8:17–18; 1Pe 1:6–7).

DAY 12: Why do people not respond to the gospel?

Paul said, "If our gospel is veiled, it is veiled to those who are perishing" (2Co 4:3). The false teachers accused Paul of preaching an antiquated message. So Paul showed that the problem was not with the message or the messenger, but with the hearers headed for hell (1Co 2:14). The preacher cannot persuade people to believe; only God can do that.

"The god of this world has blinded the minds" (v. 4). Satan (Mt 4:8; Jn 12:31; 14:30; 16:11; Eph 2:2; 2Ti 2:26; 1Jn 5:19) is the god of this world—the current world mind-set expressed by the ideals, opinions, goals, hopes, and views of the majority of people. It encompasses the world's philosophies, education, and commerce. Satan blinds men to God's truth through the world system he has created. Without a godly influence, man left to himself will follow that system, which panders to the depravity of unbelievers and deepens their moral darkness (Mt 13:19). Ultimately, it is God who allows such blindness (Jn 12:40).

"For we do not preach ourselves but Christ Jesus" (v. 5). The false teachers accused Paul of preaching for his own benefit, yet they were the ones guilty of doing so. In contrast, Paul was always humble (12:5, 9; 1Co 2:3); he never promoted himself, but always preached Christ Jesus as Lord (1Co 2:2). "For God, who said, "Light shall shine out of darkness," is the One who has shone in our hearts to give the Light of the knowledge of the glory of God" (v. 6). A direct reference to God as Creator, who commanded physical light into existence (Ge 1:3). The same God who created physical light in the universe is the same God who must create supernatural light in the soul and usher believers from the kingdom of darkness to His kingdom of light (Col 1:13). That means to know that Christ is God incarnate. To be saved, one must understand that the glory of God shone in Jesus Christ.

SEPTEMBER 13

Isaiah 17:1–18:7

17 The oracle concerning Damascus.

"Behold, Damascus is about to be
  removed from being a city
And will become a fallen ruin.
2 "The cities of Aroer are forsaken;
  They will be for flocks to lie down in,
  And there will be no one
    to frighten *them*.
3 "The fortified city will disappear
    from Ephraim,
  And sovereignty from Damascus
  And the remnant of Aram;
  They will be like the glory
    of the sons of Israel,"
Declares the LORD of hosts.

4 Now in that day the glory
    of Jacob will fade,
  And the fatness of his flesh
    will become lean.
5 It will be even like the reaper
    gathering the standing grain,
  As his arm harvests the ears,
  Or it will be like one gleaning
    ears of grain
  In the valley of Rephaim.
6 Yet gleanings will be left in it like
    the shaking of an olive tree,
  Two *or* three olives on the
    topmost bough,
  Four *or* five on the branches
    of a fruitful tree,
  Declares the LORD, the God of Israel.
7 In that day man will have
    regard for his Maker
  And his eyes will look to the
    Holy One of Israel.
8 He will not have regard for the
    altars, the work of his hands,
  Nor will he look to that which
    his fingers have made,
  Even the Asherim and incense stands.
9 In that day their strong cities will be
    like forsaken places in the forest,
  Or like branches which
    they abandoned before
    the sons of Israel;
  And the land will be a desolation.
10 For you have forgotten the
    God of your salvation
  And have not remembered
    the rock of your refuge.
  Therefore you plant delightful plants

And set them with vine slips
    of a strange *god*.
11 In the day that you plant *it*
    you carefully fence *it* in,
  And in the morning you bring
    your seed to blossom;
  But the harvest will *be* a heap
  In a day of sickliness and
    incurable pain.

12 Alas, the uproar of many peoples
  Who roar like the roaring
    of the seas,
  And the rumbling of nations
  Who rush on like the rumbling
    of mighty waters!
13 The nations rumble on like the
    rumbling of many waters,
  But He will rebuke them and
    they will flee far away,
  And be chased like chaff in the
    mountains before the wind,
  Or like whirling dust before
    a gale.
14 At evening time, behold,
    there is terror!
  Before morning they are no more.
  Such *will be* the portion of
    those who plunder us
  And the lot of those who pillage us.

18 Alas, oh land of whirring wings
  Which lies beyond the rivers
    of Cush,
2 Which sends envoys by the sea,
  Even in papyrus vessels on the
    surface of the waters.
  Go, swift messengers, to a
    nation tall and smooth,
  To a people feared far and wide,
  A powerful and oppressive
    nation
  Whose land the rivers divide.
3 All you inhabitants of the world
    and dwellers on earth,
  As soon as a standard is raised on
    the mountains, you will see *it*,
  And as soon as the trumpet is
    blown, you will hear *it*.

4 For thus the LORD has told me,

"I will look from My dwelling
    place quietly
  Like dazzling heat in the
    sunshine,
  Like a cloud of dew in the
    heat of harvest."

18:4 I will look from My dwelling place quietly. The Lord will wait patiently until the appropriate time to intervene in human affairs, until sunshine and dew have built to an opportune climactic moment.

⁵ For before the harvest, as soon
   as the bud blossoms
And the flower becomes
   a ripening grape,
Then He will cut off the sprigs
   with pruning knives
And remove *and* cut away the
   spreading branches.
⁶ They will be left together for
   mountain birds of prey,
And for the beasts of the earth;
And the birds of prey will spend
   the summer *feeding* on them,
And all the beasts of the earth
   will spend harvest time on
   them.
⁷ At that time a gift of homage
   will be brought to the LORD
   of hosts
From a people tall and smooth,
Even from a people feared
   far and wide,
A powerful and oppressive
   nation,
Whose land the rivers divide—
To the place of the name
   of the LORD of hosts,
   even Mount Zion.

Psalm 106:32–39

³² They also provoked *Him* to
   wrath at the waters of
   Meribah,
So that it went hard with
   Moses on their account;
³³ Because they were rebellious
   against His Spirit,
He spoke rashly with his lips.

³⁴ They did not destroy the
   peoples,
As the LORD commanded them,
³⁵ But they mingled with the
   nations
And learned their practices,
³⁶ And served their idols,
Which became a snare to them.
³⁷ They even sacrificed their sons
   and their daughters to the demons,
³⁸ And shed innocent blood,
The blood of their sons and
   their daughters,
Whom they sacrificed to
   the idols of Canaan;
And the land was polluted
   with the blood.
³⁹ Thus they became unclean
   in their practices,
And played the harlot in their deeds.

Proverbs 25:11–12

¹¹ *Like* apples of gold in settings
   of silver
Is a word spoken in right
   circumstances.
¹² *Like* an earring of gold and an
   ornament of fine gold
Is a wise reprover to a listening
   ear.

2 Corinthians 5:1–21

5 For we know that if the earthly tent which is our house is torn down, we have a building from God, a house not made with hands, eternal in the heavens. ²For indeed in this *house* we groan, longing to be clothed with our dwelling from heaven, ³inasmuch as we, having put it on, will not be found naked. ⁴For indeed while we are in this tent, we groan, being burdened, because we do not want to be unclothed but to be clothed, so that what is mortal will be swallowed up by life. ⁵Now He who prepared us for this very purpose is God, who gave to us the Spirit as a pledge.

⁶Therefore, being always of good courage, and knowing that while we are at home in the body we are absent from the Lord— ⁷for we walk by faith, not by sight— ⁸we are of good courage, I say, and prefer rather to be absent from the body and to be at home with the Lord. ⁹Therefore we also have as our ambition, whether at home or absent, to be pleasing to Him. ¹⁰For we must all appear before the judgment seat of Christ, so that each one may be recompensed for his deeds in the body, according to what he has done, whether good or bad.

¹¹Therefore, knowing the fear of the Lord, we persuade men, but we are made manifest to God; and I hope that we are made manifest also in your consciences. ¹²We are not again commending ourselves to you but *are* giving you an occasion to be proud of us, so that you will have *an answer* for those who take pride in appearance and not in heart. ¹³For if we are beside ourselves, it is for God; if we are of sound mind, it is

5:10 This describes the believer's deepest motivation and highest aim in pleasing God—the realization that every Christian is inevitably and ultimately accountable to Him. **the judgment seat of Christ.** "Judgment seat" metaphorically refers to the place where the Lord will sit to evaluate believers' lives for the purpose of giving them eternal rewards. It was an elevated platform where victorious athletes (e.g., during the Olympics) went to receive their crowns. The term is also used in the New Testament to refer to the place of judging, as when Jesus stood before Pontius Pilate (Mt 27:19; Jn 19:13), but here the reference is definitely from the athletic analogy. Corinth had such a platform where both athletic rewards and legal justice were dispensed (Ac 18:12–16), so the Corinthians understood Paul's reference. **deeds in the body.** Actions which happened during the believer's time of earthly ministry. This does not include sins, since their judgment took place at the cross (Eph 1:7). Paul was referring to all those activities believers do during their lifetimes, which relate to their eternal reward and praise from God. What Christians do in their temporal bodies will, in His eyes, have an impact for eternity (Ro 12:1–2; Rev 22:12). **whether good or bad.** These Greek terms do not refer to moral good and moral evil. Matters of sin have been completely dealt with by the death of the Savior. Rather, Paul was comparing worthwhile, eternally valuable activities with useless ones.

---

for you. ¹⁴ For the love of Christ controls us, having concluded this, that one died for all, therefore all died; ¹⁵ and He died for all, so that they who live might no longer live for themselves, but for Him who died and rose again on their behalf.

¹⁶ Therefore from now on we recognize no one according to the flesh; even though we have known Christ according to the flesh, yet now we know *Him in this way* no longer. ¹⁷ Therefore if anyone is in Christ, *he is* a new creature; the old things passed away; behold, new things have come. ¹⁸ Now all *these* things are from God, who reconciled us to Himself through Christ and gave us the ministry of reconciliation, ¹⁹ namely, that God was in Christ reconciling the world to Himself, not counting their trespasses against them, and He has committed to us the word of reconciliation.

²⁰ Therefore, we are ambassadors for Christ, as though God were making an appeal

5:19 God was in Christ. God by His own will and design used His Son, the only acceptable and perfect sacrifice, as the means to reconcile sinners to Himself. **reconciling the world.** God initiates the change in the sinner's status in that He brings him from a position of alienation to a state of forgiveness and right relationship with Himself. This again is the essence of the gospel. The word "world" should not be interpreted in any universalistic sense, which would say that everyone will be saved, or even potentially reconciled. "World" refers rather to the entire sphere of mankind or humanity (Titus 2:11; 3:4), the category of beings to whom God offers reconciliation—people from every ethnic group, without distinction. The intrinsic merit of Christ's reconciling death is infinite, and the offer is unlimited. However, actual atonement was made only for those who believe (Jn 10:11, 15; 17:9; Ac 13:48; 20:28; Ro 8:32–33; Eph 5:25).

5:21 Here Paul summarized the heart of the gospel, explaining how sinners can be reconciled to God through Jesus Christ. These 15 Greek words express the doctrines of imputation and substitution like no other single verse. **who knew no sin.** Jesus Christ, the sinless Son of God (Gal 4:4–5; see Lk 23:4, 14, 22, 47; Jn 8:46; Heb 4:15; 7:26; 1Pe 1:19; 2:22–24; 3:18; Rev 5:2–10). **sin on our behalf.** God the Father, using the principle of imputation, treated Christ as if He were a sinner though He was not, and had Him die as a substitute to pay the penalty for the sins of those who believe in Him (Is 53:4–6; Gal 3:10–13; 1Pe 2:24). On the cross, He did not become a sinner (as some suggest), but remained as holy as ever. He was treated as if He were guilty of all the sins ever committed by all who would ever believe, though He committed none. The wrath of God was exhausted on Him and the just requirement of God's law met for those for whom He died. **the righteousness of God.** Another reference to justification and imputation. The righteousness that is credited to the believer's account is the righteousness of Jesus Christ, God's Son. As Christ was not a sinner, but was treated as if He were, so believers who have not yet been made righteous (until glorification) are treated as if they were righteous.

---

through us; we beg you on behalf of Christ, be reconciled to God. ²¹ He made Him who knew no sin *to be* sin on our behalf, so that we might become the righteousness of God in Him.

Paul uses the term "in Christ" when he writes about various aspects of our relationship with Jesus Christ as Lord and Savior. These two words comprise a brief but profound statement of the inexhaustible significance of the believer's redemption (salvation), which includes the following:

1. The believer's security in Christ, who bore in His body God's judgment against sin.
2. The believer's acceptance in (through) Christ with whom God alone is well pleased.
3. The believer's future assurance in Him who is the resurrection to eternal life and the sole guarantor of the believer's inheritance in heaven.
4. The believer's participation in the divine nature of Christ, the everlasting Word (2Pe 1:4).

All of the changes that Christ brings to the believer's life result in a state that can be rightly called "a new creature." The terms describe something created at a qualitatively new level of excellence. They parallel other biblical concepts like regeneration and new birth (Jn 3:3; Eph 2:1–3; Titus 3:5; 1Pe 1:23; 1Jn 2:29; 3:9; 5:4). The expression includes the Christian's forgiveness of sins paid for in Christ's substitutionary death (Gal 6:15; Eph 4:24).

 # SEPTEMBER 14

Isaiah 19:1–20:6

19 The oracle concerning Egypt.

Behold, the LORD is riding on a swift
    cloud and is about to come to Egypt;
The idols of Egypt will tremble
    at His presence,
And the heart of the Egyptians
    will melt within them.
2 "So I will incite Egyptians
    against Egyptians;
And they will each fight
    against his brother and each
    against his neighbor,
City against city *and* kingdom
    against kingdom.
3 "Then the spirit of the Egyptians will
    be demoralized within them;
And I will confound their strategy,
So that they will resort to idols
    and ghosts of the dead
And to mediums and spiritists.
4 "Moreover, I will deliver the
    Egyptians into the hand
    of a cruel master,
And a mighty king will rule over them,"
    declares the Lord GOD of hosts.

5 The waters from the sea will dry up,
    And the river will be parched and dry.
6 The canals will emit a stench,
The streams of Egypt will
    thin out and dry up;
The reeds and rushes will rot away.
7 The bulrushes by the Nile, by
    the edge of the Nile

And all the sown fields by the Nile
Will become dry, be driven
    away, and be no more.
8 And the fishermen will lament,
And all those who cast a line
    into the Nile will mourn,
And those who spread nets on
    the waters will pine away.
9 Moreover, the manufacturers of
    linen made from combed flax
And the weavers of white cloth
    will be utterly dejected.
10 And the pillars *of Egypt*
    will be crushed;
All the hired laborers will
    be grieved in soul.

11 The princes of Zoan are mere fools;
The advice of Pharaoh's wisest
    advisers has become stupid.
How can you *men* say to Pharaoh,
"I am a son of the wise, a son
    of ancient kings"?
12 Well then, where are your wise men?
Please let them tell you,
And let them understand
    what the LORD of hosts
Has purposed against Egypt.
13 The princes of Zoan have
    acted foolishly,
The princes of Memphis are
    deluded;
Those who are the cornerstone
    of her tribes
Have led Egypt astray.
14 The LORD has mixed within
    her a spirit of distortion;
They have led Egypt astray
    in all that it does,

As a drunken man staggers
in his vomit.
15 There will be no work for Egypt
Which *its* head or tail, *its* palm
branch or bulrush, may do.

16 In that day the Egyptians will become like women, and they will tremble and be in dread because of the waving of the hand of the LORD of hosts, which He is going to wave over them. 17 The land of Judah will become a terror to Egypt; everyone to whom it is mentioned will be in dread of it, because of the purpose of the LORD of hosts which He is purposing against them.

18 In that day five cities in the land of Egypt will be speaking the language of Canaan and swearing *allegiance* to the LORD of hosts; one will be called the City of Destruction.

19 In that day there will be an altar to the LORD in the midst of the land of Egypt, and

19:18 five cities. Humanly speaking, the chances of even one Egyptian city turning to the Lord were remote, but divinely speaking, there will be 5 times that many. **language of Canaan.** Egypt is to speak the language of Judah. Not only are they to fear Judah (v. 17), they are also to convert to Judah's form of worship. **swearing *allegiance* to the LORD of hosts.** Egypt will "in that day" turn to God in a dramatic way. This prophecy anticipates the personal reign of the Davidic King on earth.

a pillar to the LORD near its border. 20 It will become a sign and a witness to the LORD of hosts in the land of Egypt; for they will cry to the LORD because of oppressors, and He will send them a Savior and a Champion, and He will deliver them. 21 Thus the LORD will make Himself known to Egypt, and the Egyptians will know the LORD in that day. They will even worship with sacrifice and offering, and will make a vow to the LORD and perform it. 22 The LORD will strike Egypt, striking but healing; so they will return to the LORD, and He will respond to them and will heal them.

23 In that day there will be a highway from Egypt to Assyria, and the Assyrians will come into Egypt and the Egyptians into Assyria, and the Egyptians will worship with the Assyrians. 24 In that day Israel will be the third *party* with Egypt and Assyria, a blessing in the midst of the earth, 25 whom the LORD of hosts has blessed, saying, "Blessed is Egypt My peo-

19:25 My people...the work of My hands. Elsewhere Scripture uses these epithets to speak only of Israel (10:24; 29:23; 43:6–7; 45:11; 60:21; 64:8; Pss 100:3; 110:3; 138:8; Jer 11:4; Hos 1:10; 2:23). In the future kingdom, Israel is to be God's instrument for drawing other nations into His fold.

ple, and Assyria the work of My hands, and Israel My inheritance."

20 In the year that the commander came to Ashdod, when Sargon the king of Assyria sent him and he fought against Ashdod and captured it, 2 at that time the LORD spoke through Isaiah the son of Amoz, saying, "Go and loosen the sackcloth from your hips and take your shoes off your feet." And he did so, going naked and barefoot. 3 And the LORD said, "Even as My servant Isaiah has gone naked and barefoot three years as a sign and token against Egypt and Cush, 4 so the king of Assyria will lead away the captives of Egypt and the exiles of Cush, young and old, naked and barefoot with buttocks uncovered, to the shame of Egypt. 5 Then they will be dismayed and ashamed because of Cush their hope and Egypt their boast. 6 So the inhabitants of this coastland will say in that day, 'Behold, such is our hope, where we fled for help to be delivered from the king of Assyria; and we, how shall we escape?'"

Psalm 106:40–48

40 Therefore the anger of the LORD
was kindled against His people
And He abhorred His inheritance.
41 Then He gave them into the
hand of the nations,
And those who hated them
ruled over them.
42 Their enemies also oppressed them,
And they were subdued
under their power.
43 Many times He would deliver them;
They, however, were rebellious
in their counsel,
And *so* sank down in their iniquity.

44 Nevertheless He looked
upon their distress
When He heard their cry;
45 And He remembered His
covenant for their sake,
And relented according to the
greatness of His lovingkindness.

⁴⁶ He also made them *objects*
of compassion
In the presence of all their captors.

⁴⁷ Save us, O LORD our God,
And gather us from among
the nations,
To give thanks to Your holy name
And glory in Your praise.

⁴⁸ Blessed be the LORD, the God of Israel,
From everlasting even to everlasting.
And let all the people say, "Amen."
Praise the LORD!

Proverbs 25:13

¹³ Like the cold of snow in
the time of harvest
Is a faithful messenger to
those who send him,
For he refreshes the soul
of his masters.

2 Corinthians 6:1–18

6 And working together *with Him,* we also
urge you not to receive the grace of God
in vain— ² for He says,

"AT THE ACCEPTABLE TIME I
LISTENED TO YOU,
AND ON THE DAY OF SALVATION
I HELPED YOU."

Behold, now is "THE ACCEPTABLE TIME," behold, now is "THE DAY OF SALVATION"— ³ giving
no cause for offense in anything, so that the
ministry will not be discredited, ⁴ but in everything commending ourselves as servants
of God, in much endurance, in afflictions, in
hardships, in distresses, ⁵ in beatings, in imprisonments, in tumults, in labors, in sleeplessness, in hunger, ⁶ in purity, in knowledge,

6:2 Paul emphasized his point by quoting Isaiah 49:8. He was passionately concerned that
the Corinthians adhere to the truth because it
was God's time to save, and they were messengers for helping to spread that message. **now is
"THE DAY OF SALVATION."** Paul applied Isaiah's
words to the present situation. There is a time
in God's economy when He listens to sinners
and responds to those who are repentant—and
it was and is that time (Pr 1:20–23; Is 55:6; Heb
3:7–8; 4:7). However, there will also be an end
to that time (Ge 6:3; Pr 1:24–33; Jn 9:4), which
is why Paul's exhortation was so passionate.

in patience, in kindness, in the Holy Spirit,
in genuine love, ⁷ in the word of truth, in the
power of God; by the weapons of righteousness for the right hand and the left, ⁸ by glory

6:7 in the word of truth. The Scriptures, the
revealed Word of God (Col 1:5; Jas 1:18). During
his entire ministry, Paul never operated beyond
the boundaries of the direction and guidance
of divine revelation. **in the power of God.**
Paul did not rely on his own strength when
he ministered (1Co 1:18; 2:1–3; Ro 1:16). **by the
weapons of righteousness.** Paul did not fight
Satan's kingdom with human resources, but
with spiritual virtue (10:3–5; Eph 6:10–18). **the
right hand…the left.** Paul had both offensive
tools, such as the sword of the Spirit, and de-
fensive tools, such as the shield of faith and the
helmet of salvation, at his disposal.

and dishonor, by evil report and good report;
regarded as deceivers and yet true; ⁹ as unknown yet well-known, as dying yet behold,
we live; as punished yet not put to death, ¹⁰ as
sorrowful yet always rejoicing, as poor yet
making many rich, as having nothing yet
possessing all things.

¹¹ Our mouth has spoken freely to you,
O Corinthians, our heart is opened wide.
¹² You are not restrained by us, but you are
restrained in your own affections. ¹³ Now in
a like exchange—I speak as to children—open
wide *to us* also.

¹⁴ Do not be bound together with unbelievers;
for what partnership have righteousness and
lawlessness, or what fellowship has light with
darkness? ¹⁵ Or what harmony has Christ with
Belial, or what has a believer in common with an
unbeliever? ¹⁶ Or what agreement has the temple of God with idols? For we are the temple of
the living God; just as God said,

"I WILL DWELL IN THEM AND
WALK AMONG THEM;
AND I WILL BE THEIR GOD, AND
THEY SHALL BE MY PEOPLE.
¹⁷ "Therefore, COME OUT FROM
THEIR MIDST AND BE
SEPARATE," says the Lord.
"AND DO NOT TOUCH WHAT IS UNCLEAN;
And I will welcome you.
¹⁸ "And I will be a father to you,
And you shall be sons and
daughters to Me,"
Says the Lord Almighty.

DAY 14: What did Paul mean by warning believers to not become "bound together with unbelievers"?

Paul's use of this phrase in 2 Corinthians 6:14 is an illustration taken from Old Testament prohibitions to Israel regarding the work-related joining together of two different kinds of livestock (Dt 22:10). By this analogy, Paul taught that it is not right to join together in common spiritual enterprise with unbelievers—a relationship that would be detrimental to the Christian's testimony within the body of Christ. It is impossible under such an arrangement for things to be done to God's glory (1Co 5:9–13; 6:15–18; 10:7–21; Jas 4:4; 1Jn 2:15). This was especially important for the Corinthians because of the threats from the false teachers and the surrounding pagan idolatry. But this command does not mean believers should end all associations with unbelievers. That would defy the purpose for which God saved believers and left them on earth (Mt 28:19–20; 1Co 9:19–23).

"Or what harmony has Christ with Belial?" (v. 15). An ancient name for Satan, the utterly worthless one (Dt 13:13). This contrasts sharply with Jesus Christ, the worthy One with whom believers are to be in fellowship. "Or what agreement has the temple of God with idols?" (v. 16). The temple of God (true Christianity) and idols (idolatrous, demonic false religions) are utterly incompatible. "We are the temple of the living God." Believers individually are spiritual houses (5:1) in which the Spirit of Christ dwells. "Just as God said." Paul supported his statement by referring to a blend of Old Testament texts (Lv 26:11–12; Jer 24:7; 31:33; Eze 37:26–27; Hos 2:2–3).

Paul drew from Isaiah 52:11 and elaborated on the command to be spiritually separated. It is not only irrational and sacrilegious but disobedient to be bound together with unbelievers. When believers are saved, they are to disengage themselves from all forms of false religion and make a clean break from all sinful habits and old idolatrous patterns. "BE SEPARATE." This is a command for believers to be as Christ was (Heb 7:26).

SEPTEMBER 15

Isaiah 21:1–22:25

21 The oracle concerning the wilderness of the sea.

As windstorms in the
Negev sweep on,
It comes from the wilderness,
from a terrifying land.
2 A harsh vision has been shown
to me;
The treacherous one *still* deals
treacherously, and the
destroyer *still* destroys.
Go up, Elam, lay siege, Media;
I have made an end of all the
groaning she has caused.
3 For this reason my loins
are full of anguish;
Pains have seized me like the
pains of a woman in labor.
I am so bewildered I cannot hear,
so terrified I cannot see.
4 My mind reels, horror
overwhelms me;
The twilight I longed for has been
turned for me into trembling.
5 They set the table, they spread out
the cloth, they eat, they drink;
"Rise up, captains, oil the shields,"

6 For thus the Lord says to me,

"Go, station the lookout, let him
report what he sees.
7 "When he sees riders,
horsemen in pairs,
A train of donkeys, a train of camels,
Let him pay close attention,
very close attention."

8 Then the lookout called,

"O Lord, I stand continually by
day on the watchtower,
And I am stationed every
night at my guard post.
9 "Now behold, here comes a troop
of riders, horsemen in pairs."
And one said, "Fallen,
fallen is Babylon;

21:9 Fallen, fallen is Babylon. The watchman proclaimed the tragic end of mighty Babylon, which initially fell to the Assyrians in 689 B.C. and again to the Persians in 539 B.C. Yet Isaiah's prediction looked forward to the ultimate fall of the great enemy of God, as verified by John's citation of this verse in Revelation 14:8; 18:2 (Jer 50:2; 51:8, 49).

And all the images of her gods
are shattered on the ground."
¹⁰ O my threshed *people,* and my
afflicted of the threshing floor!
What I have heard from
the LORD of hosts,
The God of Israel, I make
known to you.

¹¹ The oracle concerning Edom.

One keeps calling to me from Seir,
"Watchman, how far gone is the night?
Watchman, how far gone
is the night?"
¹² The watchman says,
"Morning comes but also night.
If you would inquire, inquire;
Come back again."

¹³ The oracle about Arabia.

In the thickets of Arabia you
must spend the night,
O caravans of Dedanites.
¹⁴ Bring water for the thirsty,
O inhabitants of the land of Tema,
Meet the fugitive with bread.
¹⁵ For they have fled from the swords,
From the drawn sword, and
from the bent bow
And from the press of battle.

¹⁶ For thus the Lord said to me, "In a year, as
a hired man would count it, all the splendor
of Kedar will terminate; ¹⁷ and the remainder of
the number of bowmen, the mighty men of
the sons of Kedar, will be few; for the LORD
God of Israel has spoken."

22 The oracle concerning the valley of
vision.

What is the matter with you
now, that you have all gone
up to the housetops?
² You who were full of noise,
You boisterous town, you
exultant city;
Your slain were not slain
with the sword,
Nor did they die in battle.
³ All your rulers have fled
together,
And have been captured
without the bow;
All of you who were found were
taken captive together,
Though they had fled far away.

22:1 valley of vision. This referred to Israel,
since God often revealed Himself to Jerusalem
in visions. However, the unrepentant inhabitants displayed a marked lack of vision in their
oblivion to the destruction that awaited them.
What is the matter with you…? The prophet
reproached the people for celebrating with
wild parties when they should have been in
deep repentance because of their sins. Apparently he anticipated a condition that arose in
conjunction with Jerusalem's fall to the Babylonians in 586 B.C. But similar incursions by the
Assyrians in either 711 or 701 B.C., from which
the Lord delivered the city, had prompted the
revelry among the people.

⁴ Therefore I say, "Turn your
eyes away from me,
Let me weep bitterly,
Do not try to comfort me
concerning the destruction of
the daughter of my people."
⁵ For the Lord GOD of hosts has a day of
panic, subjugation and confusion
In the valley of vision,
A breaking down of walls
And a crying to the mountain.
⁶ Elam took up the quiver
With the chariots, infantry
and horsemen;
And Kir uncovered the shield.
⁷ Then your choicest valleys
were full of chariots,
And the horsemen took up fixed
positions at the gate.
⁸ And He removed the
defense of Judah.
In that day you depended on the
weapons of the house
of the forest,
⁹ And you saw that the breaches
In the *wall* of the city of
David were many;
And you collected the waters
of the lower pool.
¹⁰ Then you counted the
houses of Jerusalem
And tore down houses to
fortify the wall.
¹¹ And you made a reservoir
between the two walls
For the waters of the old pool.
But you did not depend on
Him who made it,
Nor did you take into consideration
Him who planned it long ago.

12 Therefore in that day the Lord
GOD of hosts called *you* to
weeping, to wailing,
To shaving the head and to
wearing sackcloth.
13 Instead, there is gaiety and gladness,
Killing of cattle and
slaughtering of sheep,
Eating of meat and drinking of wine:
"Let us eat and drink, for
tomorrow we may die."

22:13 Let us eat and drink, for tomorrow we may die. Paul cites the same philosophy (1Co 15:32): If there is no resurrection, enjoyment in this life is all that matters. It utterly disregards God's eternal values.

14 But the LORD of hosts revealed
Himself to me,
"Surely this iniquity shall
not be forgiven you
Until you die," says the
Lord GOD of hosts.

15 Thus says the Lord GOD of hosts,

"Come, go to this steward,
To Shebna, who is in charge
of the *royal* household,
16 'What right do you have here,
And whom do you have here,
That you have hewn a tomb
for yourself here,
You who hew a tomb on the height,
You who carve a resting place
for yourself in the rock?
17 'Behold, the LORD is about to
hurl you headlong, O man.
And He is about to grasp you firmly
18 *And* roll you tightly like a ball,
To be cast into a vast country;
There you will die
And there your splendid
chariots will be,
You shame of your master's house.'
19 "I will depose you from your office,
And I will pull you down
from your station.
20 "Then it will come about in that day,
That I will summon My servant
Eliakim the son of Hilkiah,
21 And I will clothe him with your tunic
And tie your sash securely about him.
I will entrust him with your authority,

And he will become a father to
the inhabitants of Jerusalem
and to the house of Judah.
22 "Then I will set the key of the house
of David on his shoulder,
When he opens no one will shut,
When he shuts no one will open.

22:22 key of the house of David. This authority to admit or refuse admittance into the king's presence evidenced the king's great confidence in Eliakim. Jesus applied this terminology to Himself as one who could determine who would enter His future Davidic kingdom (Rev 3:7).

23 "I will drive him *like* a peg
in a firm place,
And he will become a throne
of glory to his father's
house.

24 So they will hang on him all the glory of his father's house, offspring and issue, all the least of vessels, from bowls to all the jars. 25 In that day," declares the LORD of hosts, "the peg driven in a firm place will give way; it will even break off and fall, and the load hanging on it will be cut off, for the LORD has spoken."

Psalm 107:1–9

Oh give thanks to the LORD,
for He is good,
For His lovingkindness is
everlasting.
2 Let the redeemed of the LORD
say *so*,
Whom He has redeemed from
the hand of the adversary
3 And gathered from the lands,
From the east and from the west,
From the north and from
the south.

4 They wandered in the wilderness
in a desert region;
They did not find a way to
an inhabited city.
5 *They were* hungry and thirsty;
Their soul fainted within them.
6 Then they cried out to the
LORD in their trouble;
He delivered them out of
their distresses.

⁷ He led them also by a straight way,
  To go to an inhabited city.
⁸ Let them give thanks to the LORD
  for His lovingkindness,
  And for His wonders to
  the sons of men!
⁹ For He has satisfied the
  thirsty soul,
  And the hungry soul He has
  filled with what is good.

Proverbs 25:14-16

¹⁴ *Like* clouds and wind
  without rain
  Is a man who boasts of
  his gifts falsely.
¹⁵ By forbearance a ruler
  may be persuaded,
  And a soft tongue breaks
  the bone.
¹⁶ Have you found honey? Eat
  only what you need,
  That you not have it in
  excess and vomit it.

2 Corinthians 7:1-16

7 Therefore, having these promises, beloved, let us cleanse ourselves from all defilement of flesh and spirit, perfecting holiness in the fear of God.
² Make room for us *in your hearts;* we wronged no one, we corrupted no one, we took advantage of no one. ³ I do not speak to condemn you, for I have said before that you are in our hearts to die together and to live together. ⁴ Great is my confidence in you; great is my boasting on your behalf. I am filled with comfort; I am overflowing with joy in all our affliction.
⁵ For even when we came into Macedonia our flesh had no rest, but we were afflicted on every side: conflicts without, fears within. ⁶ But God, who comforts the depressed, comforted us by the coming of Titus; ⁷ and not only by his coming, but also by the comfort with which he was comforted in you, as he reported to us your longing, your mourning, your zeal for me; so that I rejoiced even more. ⁸ For though I caused you sorrow by my letter, I do not regret it; though I did regret it—*for* I see that that letter caused you sorrow, though only for a while— ⁹ I now rejoice, not that you were made sorrowful, but that you were made sorrowful to *the point of* repentance; for you were made sorrowful according to *the will of* God, so that you might not suffer loss in anything through us. ¹⁰ For the sorrow that is according to the

7:1 these promises. The Old Testament promises Paul quoted in 6:16-18. Scripture often encourages believers to action based on God's promises (Ro 12:1; 2Pe 1:3). **let us cleanse ourselves.** The form of this Greek verb indicates that this is something each Christian must do in his own life. **defilement.** This Greek word, which appears only here in the NT, was used in the Greek Old Testament to refer to religious defilement, or unholy alliances with idols, idol feasts, temple prostitutes, sacrifices, and festivals of worship. **flesh and spirit.** False religion panders to the human appetites, represented by both "flesh and spirit." While some believers for a time might avoid succumbing to fleshly sins associated with false religion, the Christian who exposes his mind to false teaching cannot avoid contamination by the devilish ideologies and blasphemies that assault the purity of divine truth and blaspheme God's name. **perfecting holiness.** The Greek word for "perfecting" means "to finish" or "to complete" (8:6). "Holiness" refers to separation from all that would defile both the body and the mind. Complete or perfect holiness was embodied only in Christ, thus believers are to pursue Him (3:18; Lv 20:26; Mt 5:48; Ro 8:29; Php 3:12-14; 1Jn 3:2-3).

will of God produces a repentance without regret, *leading* to salvation, but the sorrow of the world produces death. ¹¹ For behold what earnestness this very thing, this godly sorrow, has produced in you: what vindication of yourselves, what indignation, what fear, what longing, what zeal, what avenging of wrong! In everything you demonstrated yourselves to be innocent in the matter. ¹² So although I wrote to you, *it was* not for the sake of the offender nor for the sake of the one offended, but that your earnestness on our behalf might be made known to you in the sight of God. ¹³ For this reason we have been comforted.

And besides our comfort, we rejoiced even much more for the joy of Titus, because his spirit has been refreshed by you all. ¹⁴ For if in anything I have boasted to him about you, I was not put to shame; but as we spoke all things to you in truth, so also our boasting before Titus proved to be *the* truth. ¹⁵ His affection abounds all the more toward you, as he remembers the obedience of you all, how you received him with fear and trembling. ¹⁶ I rejoice that in everything I have confidence in you.

DAY 15: What are the characteristics of true repentance?

Paul's first letter to the Corinthians produced a sorrow in the believers that led them to repent of their sins (2Co 7:9). "Repentance" refers to the desire to turn from sin and restore one's relationship to God. "The sorrow that is according to the will of God produces a repentance without regret, leading to salvation" (v. 10). "Sorrow" refers to the sorrow that is according to the will of God and produced by the Holy Spirit. True repentance cannot occur apart from such a genuine sorrow over one's sin. Repentance is at the very heart of and proves one's salvation: unbelievers repent of their sin initially when they are saved, and then as believers, repent of their sins continually to keep the joy and blessing of their relationship to God.

Verse 11 provides a look at how genuine repentance will manifest itself in one's attitudes. "Earnestness." Also translated, "diligence" or "eagerness." It is the initial reaction of true repentance to eagerly and aggressively pursue righteousness. This is an attitude that ends indifference to sin and complacency about evil and deception. "What vindication of yourselves." A desire to clear one's name of the stigma that accompanies sin. The repentant sinner restores the trust and confidence of others by making his genuine repentance known. "Indignation." Often associated with righteous indignation and holy anger. Repentance leads to anger over one's sin and displeasure at the shame it has brought on the Lord's name and His people. "Fear." This is reverence toward God, who is the One most offended by sin. Repentance leads to a healthy fear of the One who chastens and judges sin. "Vehement desire." This could be translated "yearning," or "a longing for," and refers to the desire of the repentant sinner to restore the relationship with the one who was sinned against. "Zeal." This refers to loving someone or something so much that one hates anyone or anything that harms the object of this love. "Avenging of wrong." This refers to the desire to see justice done. The repentant sinner no longer tries to protect himself; he wants to see the sin avenged no matter what it might cost him. "To be innocent in the matter." The essence of repentance is an aggressive pursuit of holiness, which was characteristic of the Corinthians. The Greek word for "innocent" means "pure" or "holy." They demonstrated the integrity of their repentance by their purity.

SEPTEMBER 16

Isaiah 23:1–24:23

23 The oracle concerning Tyre.

Wail, O ships of Tarshish,
    For *Tyre* is destroyed, without
        house *or* harbor;
    It is reported to them from
        the land of Cyprus.
² Be silent, you inhabitants
        of the coastland,
    You merchants of Sidon;
    Your messengers crossed the sea

23:1 Tyre. A Phoenician seaport on the Mediterranean Sea, located about 35 miles north of Mt. Carmel and 28 miles west of Mt. Hermon, Tyre supplied lumber for King Solomon's temple (1Ki 5:1, 7–12) and sailors for his navy (1Ki 9:26–27). **destroyed.** Tyre was under siege 5 times between this prophecy and 332 B.C. Only the last of these attacks (in 332 B.C., by Alexander the Great) completely leveled and subdued the city. Ezekiel prophesied this destruction in Ezekiel 26:3—27:36.

³ And *were* on many waters.
    The grain of the Nile, the harvest
        of the River was her revenue;
    And she was the market of nations.
⁴ Be ashamed, O Sidon;
    For the sea speaks, the stronghold
        of the sea, saying,
    "I have neither travailed
        nor given birth,
    I have neither brought up young
        men *nor* reared virgins."
⁵ When the report *reaches* Egypt,
    They will be in anguish at
        the report of Tyre.
⁶ Pass over to Tarshish;
    Wail, O inhabitants of the
        coastland.
⁷ Is this your jubilant *city*,
    Whose origin is from antiquity,
    Whose feet used to carry her to
        colonize distant places?
⁸ Who has planned this against
        Tyre, the bestower of crowns,
    Whose merchants were princes,
    whose traders were the
        honored of the earth?
⁹ The LORD of hosts has planned it,
    to defile the pride of all beauty,

To despise all the honored
of the earth.
10 Overflow your land like the Nile,
O daughter of Tarshish,
There is no more restraint.
11 He has stretched His hand
out over the sea,
He has made the kingdoms tremble;
The LORD has given a command
concerning Canaan to
demolish its strongholds.

12 He has said, "You shall exult
no more, O crushed virgin
daughter of Sidon.
Arise, pass over to Cyprus; even
there you will find no rest."

13 Behold, the land of the Chaldeans—this is
the people *which* was not; Assyria appointed
it for desert creatures—they erected their
siege towers, they stripped its palaces, they
made it a ruin.

14 Wail, O ships of Tarshish,
For your stronghold is destroyed.

15 Now in that day Tyre will be forgotten for
seventy years like the days of one king. At the
end of seventy years it will happen to Tyre as
in the song of the harlot:

16 Take *your* harp, walk about the city,
O forgotten harlot;
Pluck the strings skillfully,
sing many songs,
That you may be remembered.

17 It will come about at the end of seventy
years that the LORD will visit Tyre. Then she
will go back to her harlot's wages and will
play the harlot with all the kingdoms on the
face of the earth. 18 Her gain and her harlot's
wages will be set apart to the LORD; it will
not be stored up or hoarded, but her gain will
become sufficient food and choice attire for
those who dwell in the presence of the LORD.

24 Behold, the LORD lays the earth waste,
devastates it, distorts its surface and
scatters its inhabitants. 2 And the people will
be like the priest, the servant like his master,
the maid like her mistress, the buyer like the
seller, the lender like the borrower, the creditor like the debtor. 3 The earth will be completely laid waste and completely despoiled,
for the LORD has spoken this word. 4 The
earth mourns *and* withers, the world fades
and withers, the exalted of the people of the
earth fade away. 5 The earth is also polluted
by its inhabitants, for they transgressed laws,
violated statutes, broke the everlasting covenant. 6 Therefore, a curse devours the earth,
and those who live in it are held guilty. Therefore, the inhabitants of the earth are burned,
and few men are left.

7 The new wine mourns,
The vine decays,
All the merry-hearted sigh.
8 The gaiety of tambourines ceases,
The noise of revelers stops,
The gaiety of the harp ceases.
9 They do not drink wine with song;
Strong drink is bitter to
those who drink it.
10 The city of chaos is broken down;
Every house is shut up so
that none may enter.
11 There is an outcry in the streets
concerning the wine;
All joy turns to gloom.
The gaiety of the earth is banished.
12 Desolation is left in the city
And the gate is battered to ruins.
13 For thus it will be in the midst of
the earth among the peoples,
As the shaking of an olive tree,
As the gleanings when the
grape harvest is over.
14 They raise their voices,
they shout for joy;
They cry out from the
west concerning the
majesty of the LORD.
15 Therefore glorify the LORD in
the east,
The name of the LORD,
the God of Israel,
In the coastlands of the sea.
16 From the ends of the earth
we hear songs, "Glory to
the Righteous One,"
But I say, "Woe to me! Woe
to me! Alas for me!
The treacherous deal
treacherously,
And the treacherous deal
very treacherously."
17 Terror and pit and snare
Confront you, O inhabitant
of the earth.
18 Then it will be that he who
flees the report of disaster
will fall into the pit,
And he who climbs out of the pit
will be caught in the snare;

24:18 windows above. In Noah's day, God judged with a flood (Ge 7:11). He will judge again from heaven, but not with a flood. See Revelation 6:13–14; 8:3–13; 16:1–21. **foundations of the earth.** Unparalleled earthquakes will mark the future visitation during and after the fulfillment of Daniel's 70-week prophecy (13:13; Mt 24:7; Rev 6:12, 14; 8:5; 11:19; 16:18).

For the windows above are
opened, and the foundations
of the earth shake.
19 The earth is broken asunder,
The earth is split through,
The earth is shaken violently.
20 The earth reels to and fro
like a drunkard
And it totters like a shack,
For its transgression is heavy upon it,
And it will fall, never to rise again.
21 So it will happen in that day,
That the LORD will punish the
host of heaven on high,
And the kings of the earth on earth.
22 They will be gathered together
Like prisoners in the dungeon,
And will be confined in prison;
And after many days they
will be punished.
23 Then the moon will be abashed
and the sun ashamed,
For the LORD of hosts will reign on
Mount Zion and in Jerusalem,
And *His* glory will be
before His elders.

24:23 moon...abashed...sun ashamed. In the eternal state after Christ's millennial reign, the glory of God and of the Lamb will replace the sun and moon as sources of light (Rev 21:23). **reign...in Jerusalem.** In Revelation 11:15–17; 19:6, 16 (Lk 1:31–33), John confirmed this clear prophecy of Messiah's future earthly reign in Jerusalem.

Psalm 107:10–22

10 There were those who dwelt
in darkness and in the
shadow of death,
Prisoners in misery and chains,
11 Because they had rebelled
against the words of God

And spurned the counsel
of the Most High.
12 Therefore He humbled their
heart with labor;
They stumbled and there
was none to help.
13 Then they cried out to the
LORD in their trouble;
He saved them out of their distresses.
14 He brought them out of darkness
and the shadow of death
And broke their bands apart.
15 Let them give thanks to the LORD
for His lovingkindness,
And for His wonders to
the sons of men!
16 For He has shattered gates of bronze
And cut bars of iron asunder.

17 Fools, because of their rebellious way,
And because of their iniquities,
were afflicted.
18 Their soul abhorred all kinds of food,
And they drew near to the
gates of death.
19 Then they cried out to the
LORD in their trouble;
He saved them out of their distresses.
20 He sent His word and healed them,
And delivered *them* from
their destructions.
21 Let them give thanks to the LORD
for His lovingkindness,
And for His wonders to
the sons of men!
22 Let them also offer sacrifices
of thanksgiving,
And tell of His works with
joyful singing.

Proverbs 25:17

17 Let your foot rarely be in
your neighbor's house,
Or he will become weary of
you and hate you.

2 Corinthians 8:1–24

8 Now, brethren, we *wish to* make known to you the grace of God which has been given in the churches of Macedonia, 2 that in a great ordeal of affliction their abundance of joy and their deep poverty overflowed in the wealth of their liberality. 3 For I testify that according to their ability, and beyond their ability, *they gave* of their own accord, 4 begging us with much urging for the favor of participation in the support of the saints, 5 and *this,* not as we had expected, but they

first gave themselves to the Lord and to us by the will of God. ⁶So we urged Titus that as he had previously made a beginning, so he would also complete in you this gracious work as well.

⁷But just as you abound in everything, in faith and utterance and knowledge and in all earnestness and in the love we inspired in you, *see* that you abound in this gracious work also. ⁸I am not speaking *this* as a command, but as proving through the earnestness of others the sincerity of your love also. ⁹For you know the grace of our Lord Jesus Christ, that though He was rich, yet for your sake He became poor, so that you through His poverty might become rich. ¹⁰I give *my*

8:9 though He was rich. A reference to the eternality and pre-existence of Christ. As the second person of the Trinity, Christ is as rich as God is rich. He owns everything and possesses all power, authority, sovereignty, glory, honor, and majesty (Is 9:6; Mic 5:2; Jn 1:1; 8:58; 10:30; 17:5; Col 1:15–18; 2:9; Heb 1:3). **He became poor.** A reference to Christ's incarnation (Jn 1:14; Ro 1:3; 8:3; Gal 4:4; Col 1:20; 1Ti 3:16; Heb 2:7). He laid aside the independent exercise of all His divine prerogatives, left His place with God, took on human form, and died on a cross like a common criminal (Php 2:5–8). **that you... might become rich.** Believers become spiritually rich through the sacrifice and impoverishment of Christ (Php 2:5–8). They become rich in salvation, forgiveness, joy, peace, glory, honor, and majesty (1Co 1:4–5; 3:22; Eph 1:3; 1Pe 1:3–4). They become joint heirs with Christ (Ro 8:17).

opinion in this matter, for this is to your advantage, who were the first to begin a year ago not only to do *this*, but also to desire to do *it*. ¹¹But now finish doing it also, so that just as *there was* the readiness to desire it, so *there may be* also the completion of it by your ability. ¹²For if the readiness is present, it is acceptable according to what *a person* has, not according to what he does not have. ¹³For *this* is not for the ease of others *and* for your affliction, but by way of equality—

8:12 readiness. Paul spoke of a readiness and eagerness to give. God is most concerned with the heart attitude of the giver, not the amount he gives (9:7; Mk 12:41–44). **according to what *a person* has.** Whatever a person has is the resource out of which he should give. That is why there are no set amounts or percentages for giving anywhere stated in the New Testament. The implication is that if one has much, he can give much; if he has little, he can give only little (9:6). **not according to what he does not have.** Believers do not need to go into debt to give, nor lower themselves to a poverty level. God never asks believers to impoverish themselves. The Macedonians received a special blessing of grace from God to give the way they did.

¹⁴at this present time your abundance *being a supply* for their need, so that their abundance also may become *a supply* for your need, that there may be equality; ¹⁵as it is written, "HE WHO *gathered* MUCH DID NOT HAVE TOO MUCH, AND HE WHO *gathered* LITTLE HAD NO LACK."

¹⁶But thanks be to God who puts the same earnestness on your behalf in the heart of Titus. ¹⁷For he not only accepted our appeal, but being himself very earnest, he has gone to you of his own accord. ¹⁸We have sent along with him the brother whose fame in *the things of* the gospel *has spread* through all the churches; ¹⁹and not only *this*, but he has also been appointed by the churches to travel with us in this gracious work, which is being administered by us for the glory of the Lord Himself, and *to show* our readiness, ²⁰taking precaution so that no one will discredit us in our administration of this generous gift; ²¹for we have regard for what is honorable, not only in the sight of the Lord, but also in the sight of men. ²²We have sent with them our brother, whom we have often tested and found diligent in many things, but now even more diligent because of *his* great confidence in you. ²³As for Titus, *he is* my partner and fellow worker among you; as for our brethren, *they are* messengers of the churches, a glory to Christ. ²⁴Therefore openly before the churches, show them the proof of your love and of our reason for boasting about you.

DAY 16: How did the Macedonians exemplify freewill giving?

The generosity of the churches of Macedonia that Paul addresses in 2 Corinthians 8:1 was motivated by God's grace. Paul did not merely commend those churches for a noble human work, but instead gave the credit to God for what He did through them. Paul's reference was to the churches at Philippi, Thessalonica, and Berea (Ac 17:11). This was basically an impoverished province that had been ravaged by many wars and, even then, was being plundered by Roman authority and commerce.

In spite of their difficult circumstances, the churches' joy rose above their pain because of their devotion to the Lord and the causes of His kingdom. It was through the "their abundance of joy" (v. 2) that it was given despite their "deep poverty." "Poverty" refers to the most severe type of economic deprivation, the kind that caused a person to become a beggar. "Wealth of their liberality." The Greek word for "liberality" can be translated "generosity" or "sincerity." It is the opposite of duplicity or being double-minded. The Macedonian believers were rich in their single-minded, selfless generosity to God and to others.

In v. 3, Paul highlighted 3 elements of the Macedonians' giving which summed up the concept of freewill giving: 1) "according to their ability." Giving is proportionate—God sets no fixed amount or percentage and expects His people to give based on what they have (Lk 6:38; 1Co 16:2); 2) "beyond their ability." Giving is sacrificial. God's people are to give according to what they have, yet it must be in proportions that are sacrificial (Mt 6:25–34; Mk 12:41–44; Php 4:19); and 3) "freely willing"—literally "one who chooses his own course of action." Giving is voluntary—God's people are not to give out of compulsion, manipulation, or intimidation. Freewill giving has always been God's plan (9:6; Ge 4:2–4; 8:20; Ex 25:1–2; 35:4–5, 21–22; 36:5–7; Nu 18:12; Dt 16:10, 17; 1Ch 29:9; Pr 3:9–10; 11:24; Lk 19:1–8). Freewill giving is not to be confused with tithing, which related to the national taxation system of Israel (Lv 27:30) and is paralleled in the New Testament and the present by paying taxes (Mt 22:21; Ro 13:6–7).

SEPTEMBER 17

Isaiah 25:1–26:21

25 O LORD, You are my God;
I will exalt You, I will give
thanks to Your name;
For You have worked wonders,
Plans *formed* long ago, with
perfect faithfulness.
2 For You have made a city into
a heap,
A fortified city into a ruin;
A palace of strangers is
a city no more,
It will never be rebuilt.
3 Therefore a strong people
will glorify You;
Cities of ruthless nations
will revere You.
4 For You have been a defense
for the helpless,
A defense for the needy
in his distress,
A refuge from the storm, a
shade from the heat;
For the breath of the ruthless
Is like a *rain* storm *against* a wall.
5 Like heat in drought, You subdue
the uproar of aliens;
Like heat by the shadow of a cloud,
the song of the ruthless is
silenced.

6 The LORD of hosts will prepare
a lavish banquet for all
peoples on this mountain;

A banquet of aged wine, choice
pieces with marrow,
And refined, aged wine.
7 And on this mountain He will
swallow up the covering
which is over all peoples,
Even the veil which is stretched
over all nations.
8 He will swallow up death for all time,
And the Lord GOD will wipe
tears away from all faces,
And He will remove the reproach of
His people from all the earth;
For the LORD has spoken.
9 And it will be said in that day,
"Behold, this is our God for whom we
have waited that He might
save us.
This is the LORD for whom
we have waited;

25:8 swallow up death. God will swallow up death, which itself functions as a swallower of human beings (5:14; Pr 1:12). Paul notes the fulfillment of this promise in the resurrection of believers (1Co 15:54). **wipe tears away.** The Lord God will remove the sorrow associated with death (65:19). Revelation alludes to the tender action of this verse twice—once in 7:17 to describe the bliss of the redeemed in heaven, and once in 21:4 to describe ideal conditions in the New Jerusalem. **remove the reproach.** Israel will be the head of the nations and no longer the tail (Dt 28:13).

Let us rejoice and be glad
in His salvation."
10 For the hand of the LORD will
rest on this mountain,
And Moab will be trodden
down in his place
As straw is trodden down in the
water of a manure pile.
11 And he will spread out his
hands in the middle of it
As a swimmer spreads out
his hands to swim,
But *the Lord* will lay low his
pride together with the
trickery of his hands.
12 The unassailable fortifications of
your walls He will bring down,
Lay low *and* cast to the ground,
even to the dust.

26

In that day this song will be sung in
the land of Judah:

"We have a strong city;
He sets up walls and
ramparts for security.
2 "Open the gates, that the righteous
nation may enter,
The one that remains faithful.
3 "The steadfast of mind You will
keep in perfect peace,
Because he trusts in You.

26:3 **perfect peace...trusts in You.** A fixed
disposition of trust in the Lord brings a peace
that the wicked can never know (48:22; 57:21).
Such reliance precludes double-mindedness
(Jas 1:6–8) and serving two masters (Mt 6:24).

4 "Trust in the LORD forever,
For in GOD the LORD, *we have*
an everlasting Rock.
5 "For He has brought low those
who dwell on high, the
unassailable city;
He lays it low, He lays it low to the
ground, He casts it to the dust.
6 "The foot will trample it,
The feet of the afflicted, the
steps of the helpless."

7 The way of the righteous
is smooth;
O Upright One, make the path
of the righteous level.

8 Indeed, *while following* the way
of Your judgments, O LORD,
We have waited for You eagerly;
Your name, even Your memory,
is the desire of *our* souls.
9 At night my soul longs for You,
Indeed, my spirit within me
seeks You diligently;
For when the earth experiences
Your judgments
The inhabitants of the world
learn righteousness.
10 *Though* the wicked is shown favor,
He does not learn righteousness;
He deals unjustly in the
land of uprightness,
And does not perceive the
majesty of the LORD.

11 O LORD, Your hand is lifted up
yet they do not see it.
They see *Your* zeal for the people
and are put to shame;
Indeed, fire will devour Your enemies.
12 LORD, You will establish peace for us,
Since You have also performed
for us all our works.
13 O LORD our God, other masters
besides You have ruled us;
But through You alone we
confess Your name.
14 The dead will not live, the
departed spirits will not rise;
Therefore You have punished
and destroyed them,
And You have wiped out all
remembrance of them.
15 You have increased the
nation, O LORD,
You have increased the nation,
You are glorified;
You have extended all the
borders of the land.

26:15 **have increased the nation.** With prophetic certainty from the perspective of Israel's
future restoration, Isaiah saw the expansion of
Israel's borders as an accomplished fact.

16 O LORD, they sought You in
distress;
They could only whisper a prayer,
Your chastening was upon them.
17 As the pregnant woman approaches
the time to give birth,

She writhes *and* cries out
    in her labor pains,
Thus were we before You, O LORD.
¹⁸ We were pregnant, we
    writhed *in labor,*
We gave birth, as it seems,
    only to wind.
We could not accomplish
    deliverance for the earth,
Nor were inhabitants of
    the world born.
¹⁹ Your dead will live;
    Their corpses will rise.
You who lie in the dust, awake
    and shout for joy,
For your dew *is as* the
    dew of the dawn,
And the earth will give birth
    to the departed spirits.

²⁰ Come, my people, enter
    into your rooms
And close your doors behind you;
Hide for a little while
Until indignation runs *its* course.
²¹ For behold, the LORD is about to
    come out from His place
To punish the inhabitants of the
    earth for their iniquity;
And the earth will reveal
    her bloodshed
And will no longer cover
    her slain.

Psalm 107:23–32

²³ Those who go down to
    the sea in ships,
Who do business on great waters;
²⁴ They have seen the works
    of the LORD,
And His wonders in the deep.
²⁵ For He spoke and raised
    up a stormy wind,
Which lifted up the waves of the sea.
²⁶ They rose up to the heavens, they
    went down to the depths;
Their soul melted away
    in *their* misery.
²⁷ They reeled and staggered
    like a drunken man,
And were at their wits' end.
²⁸ Then they cried to the LORD
    in their trouble,
And He brought them out
    of their distresses.
²⁹ He caused the storm to be still,
So that the waves of the
    sea were hushed.

³⁰ Then they were glad because
    they were quiet,
So He guided them to their
    desired haven.
³¹ Let them give thanks to the LORD
    for His lovingkindness,
And for His wonders to
    the sons of men!
³² Let them extol Him also in the
    congregation of the people,
And praise Him at the
    seat of the elders.

Proverbs 25:18–19

¹⁸ *Like* a club and a sword
    and a sharp arrow
Is a man who bears false witness
    against his neighbor.
¹⁹ *Like* a bad tooth and an
    unsteady foot
Is confidence in a faithless
    man in time of trouble.

2 Corinthians 9:1–15

9 For it is superfluous for me to write to you about this ministry to the saints; ² for I know your readiness, of which I boast about you to the Macedonians, *namely,* that Achaia has been prepared since last year, and your zeal has stirred up most of them. ³ But I have sent the brethren, in order that our boasting about you may not be made empty in this case, so that, as I was saying, you may be prepared; ⁴ otherwise if any Macedonians come with me and find you unprepared, we—not to speak of you—will be put to shame by this confidence. ⁵ So I thought it necessary to urge the brethren that they would go on ahead to you and arrange beforehand your previously promised bountiful gift, so that the same would be ready as a bountiful gift and not affected by covetousness.

⁶ Now this *I say,* he who sows sparingly will also reap sparingly, and he who sows bountifully will also reap bountifully. ⁷ Each one *must do* just as he has purposed in his heart, not grudgingly or under compulsion, for God loves a cheerful giver. ⁸ And God is able to make all grace abound to you, so that always having all sufficiency in everything, you may have an abundance for every good deed; ⁹ as it is written,

"HE SCATTERED ABROAD, HE
    GAVE TO THE POOR,
HIS RIGHTEOUSNESS
    ENDURES FOREVER."

921

9:12 ministry of this service. The Greek word translated "ministry" is a priestly word from which we get "liturgy." Paul viewed the entire collection project as a spiritual, worshipful enterprise that was primarily being offered to God to glorify Him. **supplying the needs of the saints.** The Greek word for "supplying" is a doubly intense term that could be rendered "really, fully supplying." This indicates the Jerusalem church had an extremely great need. Many residents of Jerusalem had undoubtedly lost their jobs in the waves of persecution that came after the martyrdom of Stephen (Ac 8:1). However, the Corinthians were wealthy enough (they had not yet suffered persecution and deprivation like the Macedonians) to help meet the huge need with a generous monetary gift.

¹⁰ Now He who supplies seed to the sower and bread for food will supply and multiply your seed for sowing and increase the harvest of your righteousness; ¹¹ you will be enriched in everything for all liberality, which through

us is producing thanksgiving to God. ¹² For the ministry of this service is not only fully supplying the needs of the saints, but is also overflowing through many thanksgivings to God. ¹³ Because of the proof given by this ministry, they will glorify God for your obedience to your confession of the gospel of Christ and for the liberality of your contribution to them and to all, ¹⁴ while they also, by prayer on your behalf, yearn for you because of the surpassing grace of God in you. ¹⁵ Thanks be to God for His indescribable gift!

9:15 Paul summarized his discourse by comparing the believer's act of giving with what God did in giving Jesus Christ (Ro 8:32), "His indescribable gift." God buried His Son and reaped a vast harvest of those who put their faith in the resurrected Christ (Jn 12:24). That makes it possible for believers to joyfully, sacrificially, and abundantly sow and reap. As they give in this manner, they show forth Christ's likeness (Jn 12:25–26; Eph 5:1–2).

DAY 17: What does God look for in our financial giving?

"He who sows sparingly will also reap sparingly, and he who sows bountifully will also reap bountifully" (2Co 9:6). The simple, self-evident agrarian principle—which Paul applied to Christian giving—that the harvest is directly proportionate to the amount of seed sown (Pr 11:24–25; 19:17; Lk 6:38; Gal 6:7). When a generous believer gives by faith and trust in God, with a desire to produce the greatest possible blessing, that person will receive that kind of a harvest of blessing (Pr 3:9–10; 28:27; Mal 3:10). God gives a return on the amount one invests with Him (Lk 6:38).

"Each one must do just as he has purposed in his heart" (v. 7). The term translated "purposed" indicates a premeditated, predetermined plan of action that is done from the heart voluntarily, but not impulsively. "Grudgingly." Literally, "with grief," "sorrow," or "sadness," which indicates an attitude of depression, regret, and reluctance that accompanies something done strictly out of a sense of duty and obligation, but not joy. "Compulsion." This refers to external pressure and coercion, quite possibly accompanied by legalism. Believers are not to give based on the demands of others or according to any arbitrary standards or set amounts. "God loves a cheerful giver." God has a unique, special love for those who are happily committed to generous giving. The Greek word for "cheerful" is the word from which we get "hilarious," which suggests that God loves a heart that is enthusiastically thrilled with the pleasure of giving.

God possesses an infinite amount of grace, and He gives it lavishly, without holding back (v. 8–9). Here "grace" does not refer to spiritual graces but to money and material needs. When the believer generously—and wisely—gives of his material resources, God graciously replenishes them so he always has plenty and will not be in need (2Ch 31:10). "Always having all sufficiency." In secular Greek philosophy, this was the proud contentment of self-sufficiency that supposedly led to true happiness. Paul sanctifies the secular term and says that God, not man, will supply everything needed for real happiness and contentment (Php 4:19). "May have an abundance for every good deed." God gives back lavishly to generous, cheerful givers, not so they may satisfy selfish, nonessential desires, but so they may meet the variety of needs others have (Dt 15:10–11).

SEPTEMBER 18

Isaiah 27:1–28:29

27 In that day the LORD will punish
Leviathan the fleeing serpent,
With His fierce and great
and mighty sword,
Even Leviathan the twisted serpent;
And He will kill the dragon
who *lives* in the sea.

2 In that day,
"A vineyard of wine, sing of it!
3 "I, the LORD, am its keeper;
I water it every moment.
So that no one will damage it,
I guard it night and day.
4 "I have no wrath.
Should someone give Me briars
and thorns in battle,
Then I would step on them, I
would burn them completely.
5 "Or let him rely on My protection,
Let him make peace with Me,
Let him make peace with Me."
6 In the days to come Jacob
will take root,
Israel will blossom and sprout,
And they will fill the whole
world with fruit.

7 Like the striking of Him who has
struck them, has He struck them?
Or like the slaughter of His slain,
have they been slain?
8 You contended with them
by banishing them, by
driving them away.
With His fierce wind He has
expelled *them* on the day
of the east wind.
9 Therefore through this Jacob's
iniquity will be forgiven;
And this will be the full price of
the pardoning of his sin:
When he makes all the altar stones
like pulverized chalk stones;
When Asherim and incense
altars will not stand.
10 For the fortified city is isolated,
A homestead forlorn and
forsaken like the desert;
There the calf will graze,
And there it will lie down and
feed on its branches.
11 When its limbs are dry,
they are broken off;

Women come *and* make
a fire with them,
For they are not a people
of discernment,
Therefore their Maker will not
have compassion on them.
And their Creator will not
be gracious to them.

12 In that day the LORD will start *His* threshing from the flowing stream of the Euphrates to the brook of Egypt, and you will be gathered up one by one, O sons of Israel. 13 It will come about also in that day that a great trumpet will be blown, and those who were perishing in the land of Assyria and who were scattered in the land of Egypt will come and worship the LORD in the holy mountain at Jerusalem.

28 Woe to the proud crown of the
drunkards of Ephraim,
And to the fading flower of
its glorious beauty,
Which is at the head of
the fertile valley
Of those who are overcome
with wine!
2 Behold, the Lord has a strong
and mighty *agent;*
As a storm of hail, a tempest
of destruction,
Like a storm of mighty
overflowing waters,
He has cast *it* down to the
earth with *His* hand.
3 The proud crown of the drunkards
of Ephraim is trodden under
foot.
4 And the fading flower of
its glorious beauty,
Which is at the head of
the fertile valley,
Will be like the first-ripe fig
prior to summer,
Which one sees,
And as soon as it is in his hand,
He swallows it.
5 In that day the LORD of hosts will
become a beautiful crown
And a glorious diadem to the
remnant of His people;
6 A spirit of justice for him
who sits in judgment,
A strength to those who repel
the onslaught at the gate.
7 And these also reel with wine and
stagger from strong drink:

The priest and the prophet
reel with strong drink,
They are confused by wine, they
stagger from strong drink;
They reel while having visions,
They totter *when rendering* judgment.
8 For all the tables are full of filthy
vomit, without a *single clean* place.

9 "To whom would He teach knowledge,
And to whom would He
interpret the message?
Those *just* weaned from milk?
Those *just* taken from the breast?
10 "For *He says,*
'Order on order, order on order,
Line on line, line on line,
A little here, a little there.'"
11 Indeed, He will speak to this people
Through stammering lips
and a foreign tongue,
12 He who said to them, "Here is
rest, give rest to the weary,"
And, "Here is repose," but
they would not listen.
13 So the word of the LORD
to them will be,
"Order on order, order on order,
Line on line, line on line,
A little here, a little there,"
That they may go and stumble
backward, be broken, snared
and taken captive.

14 Therefore, hear the word of
the LORD, O scoffers,
Who rule this people who
are in Jerusalem,
15 Because you have said, "We have
made a covenant with death,
And with Sheol we have made a pact.
The overwhelming scourge will
not reach us when it passes by,
For we have made falsehood our
refuge and we have concealed
ourselves with deception."

16 Therefore thus says the Lord GOD,

"Behold, I am laying in Zion a
stone, a tested stone,
A costly cornerstone *for* the
foundation, firmly placed.
He who believes *in it* will
not be disturbed.
17 "I will make justice the measuring line
And righteousness the level;
Then hail will sweep away
the refuge of lies

28:16 cornerstone *for* the foundation. The Lord God contrasted the only sure refuge with the false refuge of relying on foreigners (v. 15). This directly prophesied the coming of the Messiah (Mt 21:42; Mk 12:10; Lk 20:17; Ac 4:11; Ro 9:33; Eph 2:20; 1Pe 2:6–8; see 8:14–15; Ps 118:22). **disturbed.** The Hebrew word is "hurry." The Greek Old Testament interprets this Hebrew verb for "hurry" in the sense of "put to shame," furnishing the basis of the New Testament citations of this verse (Ro 9:33; 10:11; 1Pe 2:6).

And the waters will overflow
the secret place.
18 "Your covenant with death
will be canceled,
And your pact with Sheol
will not stand;
When the overwhelming
scourge passes through,
Then you become its trampling *place.*
19 "As often as it passes through,
it will seize you;
For morning after morning it
will pass through, *anytime*
during the day or night,
And it will be sheer terror to
understand what it means."
20 The bed is too short on
which to stretch out,
And the blanket is too small
to wrap oneself in.
21 For the LORD will rise up as
at Mount Perazim,
He will be stirred up as in
the valley of Gibeon,
To do His task, His unusual task,
And to work His work, His
extraordinary work.
22 And now do not carry on as scoffers,
Or your fetters will be made stronger;
For I have heard from the
Lord GOD of hosts
Of decisive destruction
on all the earth.

23 Give ear and hear my voice,
Listen and hear my words.
24 Does the farmer plow
continually to plant seed?
Does he *continually* turn and
harrow the ground?
25 Does he not level its surface
And sow dill and scatter cummin
And plant wheat in rows,

28:23 Give ear. The parable of a farmer underlined the lessons of judgment threats in vv. 18–22. As the farmer does his different tasks, each in the right season and proportion, so God adopts His measures to His purposes: now mercy, then judgment; punishing sooner, then later. His purpose was not to destroy His people, any more than the farmer's object in his threshing or plowing is to destroy his crop.

Barley in its place and rye
within its area?
26 For his God instructs and
teaches him properly.
27 For dill is not threshed with
a threshing sledge,
Nor is the cartwheel driven
over cummin;
But dill is beaten out with a rod,
and cummin with a club.
28 *Grain for* bread is crushed,
Indeed, he does not continue
to thresh it forever.
Because the wheel of *his* cart and
his horses *eventually* damage *it,*
He does not thresh it longer.
29 This also comes from the
LORD of hosts,
Who has made *His* counsel wonderful
and *His* wisdom great.

Psalm 107:33–43

33 He changes rivers into a wilderness
And springs of water into
a thirsty ground;
34 A fruitful land into a salt waste,
Because of the wickedness of
those who dwell in it.
35 He changes a wilderness
into a pool of water
And a dry land into springs
of water;
36 And there He makes the
hungry to dwell,
So that they may establish
an inhabited city,
37 And sow fields and plant vineyards,
And gather a fruitful harvest.
38 Also He blesses them and
they multiply greatly,
And He does not let their
cattle decrease.

39 When they are diminished
and bowed down

Through oppression,
misery and sorrow,
40 He pours contempt upon princes
And makes them wander
in a pathless waste.
41 But He sets the needy securely on
high away from affliction,
And makes *his* families like a flock.
42 The upright see it and are glad;
But all unrighteousness
shuts its mouth.
43 Who is wise? Let him give
heed to these things,
And consider the lovingkindnesses
of the LORD.

Proverbs 25:20

20 *Like* one who takes off a garment on
a cold day, *or like* vinegar on soda,
Is he who sings songs to
a troubled heart.

25:20 vinegar on soda. Pouring vinegar on an alkali (e.g., baking soda) produces a reaction like boiling or turning tranquility into agitation. So is the effect of singing joyful songs without sympathy to the sorrowful.

---

2 Corinthians 10:1–18

10 Now I, Paul, myself urge you by the meekness and gentleness of Christ—I who am meek when face to face with you, but bold toward you when absent! 2 I ask that when I am present I *need* not be bold with the confidence with which I propose to be courageous against some, who regard us as if we walked according to the flesh. 3 For though we walk in the flesh, we do not war according to the flesh, 4 for the weapons of our warfare are not of the flesh, but divinely powerful for the destruction of fortresses. 5 *We are* destroying speculations and every lofty thing raised up against the knowledge of God, and *we are* taking every thought captive to the obedience of Christ, 6 and we are ready to punish all disobedience, whenever your obedience is complete.

7 You are looking at things as they are outwardly. If anyone is confident in himself that he is Christ's, let him consider this again within himself, that just as he is Christ's, so also are we. 8 For even if I boast somewhat further about our authority, which the Lord gave for building you up and not for destroying you, I will not be put to shame, 9 for I do not

10:4 our warfare. The motif of the Christian life as warfare is a common one in the New Testament (6:7; Eph 6:10–18; 1Ti 1:18; 2Ti 2:3–4; 4:7). **of the flesh.** Human. **fortresses.** The metaphor would have been readily understandable to the Corinthians since Corinth, like most ancient cities, had a fortress (on top of a hill south of the city) in which its residents could take refuge. The formidable spiritual strongholds manned by the forces of hell can be demolished only by spiritual weapons wielded by godly believers—singularly the "sword of the Spirit" (Eph 6:17), since only the truth of God's Word can defeat satanic falsehoods. This is the true spiritual warfare. Believers are not instructed in the New Testament to assault demons or Satan, but to assault error with the truth. That is our battle (Jn 17:17; Heb 4:12).

10:5 speculations. Thoughts, ideas, reasonings, philosophies, and false religions are the ideological forts in which men barricade themselves against God and the gospel (1Co 3:20). **every thought captive.** Emphasizes the total destruction of the fortresses of human and satanic wisdom and the rescuing of those inside from the damning lies that had enslaved them.

wish to seem as if I would terrify you by my letters. [10] For they say, "His letters are weighty and strong, but his personal presence is unimpressive and his speech contemptible." [11] Let such a person consider this, that what we are in word by letters when absent, such persons *we are* also in deed when present.

[12] For we are not bold to class or compare ourselves with some of those who commend themselves; but when they measure themselves by themselves and compare themselves with themselves, they are without understanding. [13] But we will not boast beyond *our* measure, but within the measure of the sphere which God apportioned to us as a measure, to reach even as far as you. [14] For we are not overextending ourselves, as if we did not reach to you, for we were the first to come even as far as you in the gospel of Christ; [15] not boasting beyond *our* measure, *that is,* in other men's labors, but with the hope that as your faith grows, we will be, within our sphere, enlarged even more by you, [16] so as to preach the gospel even to the regions beyond you, *and* not to boast in what has been accomplished in the sphere of another. [17] But HE WHO BOASTS IS TO BOAST IN THE LORD. [18] For it is not he who commends himself that is approved, but he whom the Lord commends.

DAY 18: Why does the tone of 2 Corinthians change so abruptly between 9:15 and 10:1?

Even a casual reader usually notices the abrupt change in tone that occurs between the ninth and tenth chapters. This apparent difference has prompted various explanations of the relationship between chapters 1–9 and 10–13.

Some argue that chapters 10–13 were originally part of the "severe letter" (2:4), and hence belong chronologically before chapters 1–9. Chapters 10–13 cannot, however, have been written before chapters 1–9, since they refer to Titus's visit as a past event (12:18; 8:6). Further, the offender whose defiance of Paul prompted the "severe letter" (2:5–8) is nowhere mentioned in chapters 10–13.

Others agree that chapters 10–13 belong after chapters 1–9, but believe they form a separate letter. They assume that Paul, after sending chapters 1–9 to the Corinthians, received reports of new trouble at Corinth and wrote chapters 10–13 in response. A variation of this view is that Paul paused in his writing of 2 Corinthians after chapters 1–9, then heard bad news from Corinth before he resumed writing chapters 10–13. This view preserves the unity of 2 Corinthians; however, Paul does not mention anywhere in chapters 10–13 that he received any fresh news from Corinth.

The best interpretation views 2 Corinthians as a unified letter, with chapters 1–9 addressed to the repentant majority (2:6) and chapters 10–13 to the minority still influenced by the false teachers. The support for this view is that: 1) there is no historical evidence (from Greek manuscripts, the writings of the church fathers, or early translations) that chapters 10–13 ever circulated as a separate letter—all Greek manuscripts have them following chapters 1–9; 2) the differences in tone between chapters 10–13 and 1–9 have been exaggerated (11:11; 12:14 with 6:11; 7:2); and 3) chapters 10–13 form the logical conclusion to chapters 1–9, as Paul prepared the Corinthians for his promised visit (1:15–16; 2:1–3).

SEPTEMBER 19

Isaiah 29:1–24

29 Woe, O Ariel, Ariel the city
where David *once* camped!
Add year to year, observe *your*
feasts on schedule.

2 I will bring distress to Ariel,
And she will be *a city of*
lamenting and mourning;
And she will be like an Ariel to me.

3 I will camp against you
encircling *you,*
And I will set siegeworks against you,
And I will raise up battle
towers against you.

4 Then you will be brought low;
From the earth you will speak,
And from the dust *where*
you are prostrate
Your words *will come.*
Your voice will also be like that
of a spirit from the ground,
And your speech will whisper
from the dust.

5 But the multitude of your enemies
will become like fine dust,
And the multitude of the
ruthless ones like the chaff
which blows away;
And it will happen instantly, suddenly.

6 From the LORD of hosts you will
be punished with thunder and
earthquake and loud noise,
With whirlwind and tempest and
the flame of a consuming fire.

7 And the multitude of all the nations
who wage war against Ariel,
Even all who wage war against
her and her stronghold,
and who distress her,
Will be like a dream, a
vision of the night.

8 It will be as when a hungry
man dreams—
And behold, he is eating;
But when he awakens, his
hunger is not satisfied,
Or as when a thirsty man dreams—
And behold, he is drinking,
But when he awakens,
behold, he is faint
And his thirst is not quenched.
Thus the multitude of all
the nations will be
Who wage war against Mount Zion.

9 Be delayed and wait,
Blind yourselves and be blind;
They become drunk, but
not with wine,
They stagger, but not
with strong drink.

10 For the LORD has poured over
you a spirit of deep sleep,
He has shut your eyes, the prophets;
And He has covered your
heads, the seers.

29:10 spirit of deep sleep. Because Israel refused to hear her true prophets initially, their ability to hear has been impaired. God gave them up judicially to their own hardness of heart. Paul applied this verse specifically to the general condition of Israel's blindness during the age of the church (Ro 11:8). **prophets… seers.** False prophets and seers have blinded their listeners with their false prophecies.

11 The entire vision will be to you like the words of a sealed book, which when they give it to the one who is literate, saying, "Please read this," he will say, "I cannot, for it is sealed." 12 Then the book will be given to the one who is illiterate, saying, "Please read this." And he will say, "I cannot read." 13 Then the Lord said,

"Because this people draw
near with their words
And honor Me with their lip service,
But they remove their
hearts far from Me,
And their reverence for Me consists
of tradition learned *by rote,*

29:13 hearts far from Me. Empty ritualism does not bring closeness to God. Jesus used this verse to describe the Judaism of His day (Mt 15:7–9; Mk 7:6–7).

14 Therefore behold, I will once again
deal marvelously with this
people, wondrously marvelous;
And the wisdom of their
wise men will perish,
And the discernment of their
discerning men will be
concealed."

¹⁵ Woe to those who deeply hide
 their plans from the LORD,
And whose deeds are *done*
 in a dark place,
And they say, "Who sees us?"
 or "Who knows us?"
¹⁶ You turn *things* around!
Shall the potter be considered
 as equal with the clay,
That what is made would say to its
 maker, "He did not make me";
Or what is formed say to him
 who formed it, "He has
 no understanding"?

¹⁷ Is it not yet just a little while
Before Lebanon will be turned
 into a fertile field,
And the fertile field will be
 considered as a forest?
¹⁸ On that day the deaf will
 hear words of a book,
And out of *their* gloom and darkness
 the eyes of the blind will see.
¹⁹ The afflicted also will increase
 their gladness in the LORD,
And the needy of mankind will
 rejoice in the Holy One of Israel.
²⁰ For the ruthless will come to an end
 and the scorner will be finished,
Indeed all who are intent on
 doing evil will be cut off;
²¹ Who cause a person to be
 indicted by a word,
And ensnare him who
 adjudicates at the gate,
And defraud the one in the right
 with meaningless arguments.

²² Therefore thus says the LORD, who redeemed Abraham, concerning the house of Jacob:

"Jacob shall not now be ashamed,
 nor shall his face now turn pale;
²³ But when he sees his children, the
 work of My hands, in his midst,
They will sanctify My name;
Indeed, they will sanctify
 the Holy One of Jacob
And will stand in awe of
 the God of Israel.
²⁴ "Those who err in mind will
 know the truth,
And those who criticize will
 accept instruction.

Psalm 108:1–6

A Song, a Psalm of David.

My heart is steadfast, O God;
 I will sing, I will sing praises,
 even with my soul.
² Awake, harp and lyre;
 I will awaken the dawn!
³ I will give thanks to You, O LORD,
 among the peoples,
And I will sing praises to You
 among the nations.
⁴ For Your lovingkindness is
 great above the heavens,
And Your truth *reaches* to the skies.
⁵ Be exalted, O God, above the heavens,
And Your glory above all the earth.
⁶ That Your beloved may be delivered,
Save with Your right hand,
 and answer me!

Proverbs 25:21–22

²¹ If your enemy is hungry,
 give him food to eat;
And if he is thirsty, give
 him water to drink;
²² For you will heap burning
 coals on his head,
And the LORD will reward you.

29:22 redeemed Abraham. God delivered Abraham from his pagan background when He brought him from beyond the Euphrates River into the land of Canaan (Jos 24:2–3). Paul elaborates on this theme in Romans 4:1–22. **not now be ashamed.** Israel in her history had frequently suffered disgrace, but the personal presence of the Messiah is to change that (45:17; 49:23; 50:7; 54:4). After the salvation of Israel in the end time, the children of Jacob will no longer cause their forefathers to blush over their wickedness.

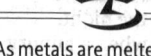

25:21–22 As metals are melted by placing fiery coals on them, so is the heart of an enemy softened by such kindness. Contrast the coals of judgment in Psalms 140:10. Paul quotes this proverb in Romans 12:20.

2 Corinthians 11:1–15

11 I wish that you would bear with me in a little foolishness; but indeed you are bearing with me. ² For I am jealous for you with a godly jealousy; for I betrothed you to one husband, so that to Christ I might present

you *as* a pure virgin. ³ But I am afraid that, as the serpent deceived Eve by his craftiness, your minds will be led astray from the simplicity and purity *of devotion* to Christ. ⁴ For if one comes and preaches another Jesus whom we have not preached, or you receive a different spirit which you have not received, or a different gospel which you have not accepted, you bear *this* beautifully. ⁵ For I consider myself not in the least inferior to the most eminent apostles. ⁶ But even if I am unskilled in speech, yet I am not *so* in knowledge; in fact, in every way we have made *this* evident to you in all things.

⁷ Or did I commit a sin in humbling myself so that you might be exalted, because I preached the gospel of God to you without charge? ⁸ I robbed other churches by taking wages *from them* to serve you; ⁹ and when I was present with you and was in need, I was not a burden to anyone; for when the brethren came from Macedonia they fully supplied my need, and in everything I kept myself from being a burden to you, and will continue to do so. ¹⁰ As the truth of Christ is in me, this boasting of mine will not be stopped in the regions of Achaia. ¹¹ Why? Because I do not love you? God knows I *do!*

¹² But what I am doing I will continue to do, so that I may cut off opportunity from those who desire an opportunity to be regarded just as we are in the matter about which they are boasting. ¹³ For such men are false apostles, deceitful workers, disguising themselves as apostles of Christ. ¹⁴ No wonder, for even Satan disguises himself as an angel of light.

11:7 without charge. Greek culture measured the importance of a teacher by the fee he could command. The false apostles therefore accused Paul of being a counterfeit, since he refused to charge for his services (1Co 9:1–15). They convinced the Corinthians to be offended by Paul's refusal to accept support from them, offering that as evidence that he did not love them (v. 11). Paul's resort to manual labor to support himself (Ac 18:1–3) also embarrassed the Corinthians, who felt such work to be beneath the dignity of an apostle. With biting irony Paul asked his accusers how foregoing his right to support could possibly be a sin. In fact, by refusing support he had humbled himself so they could be exalted; i.e., lifted out of their sin and idolatry.

11:13–15 No longer speaking with veiled irony or defending himself, Paul bluntly and directly exposed the false apostles for what they were—emissaries of Satan. Not only was their claim to apostleship false, so also was their doctrine. As satanic purveyors of false teaching, they were under the curse of Galatians 1:8–9. Paul's forceful language may seem harsh, but it expressed the godly jealousy he felt for the Corinthians. Paul was unwilling to sacrifice truth for the sake of unity.

¹⁵ Therefore it is not surprising if his servants also disguise themselves as servants of righteousness, whose end will be according to their deeds.

DAY 19: Why was Paul so emotional about the Corinthians' spiritual welfare?

In 2 Corinthians 11:2, Paul said, "I am jealous for you with a godly jealousy." Paul was concerned to the point of jealousy, a zeal for their spiritual purity. Jealousy inspired by zeal for God's causes, and thus similar to God's own jealousy for His holy name and His people's loyalty (Ex 20:5; 34:14; Dt 4:24; 5:9; 6:15; 32:16, 21; Jos 24:19; Ps 78:58; Eze 39:25; Na 1:2). "I betrothed you to one husband." As their spiritual father (12:14; 1Co 4:15; 9:1–2), Paul portrayed the Corinthians like a daughter, whom he betrothed to Jesus Christ (at their conversion). "To Christ…a pure virgin." Having betrothed or pledged the Corinthians to Christ, Paul wanted them to be pure until the marriage day finally arrived (Rev 19:7).

Paul compared the danger facing the Corinthian church to Eve's deception by Satan (v. 3). He feared the Corinthians, like Eve, would fall prey to satanic lies and have their minds corrupted. The tragic result would be the abandonment of their simple devotion to Christ in favor of the sophisticated error of the false apostles. Paul's allusion to Genesis 3 implies that the false apostles were Satan's emissaries—a truth that he later made explicit (vv. 13–15).

The false apostles came into the Corinthian church from the outside—just as Satan did into the Garden (v. 4). It is likely that they were Palestinian Jews (v. 22; Ac 6:1) who allegedly sought to bring the Corinthians under the sway of the Jerusalem church. They were in a sense Judaizers, seeking to impose Jewish customs on the Corinthians. Unlike the Judaizers who plagued the Galatian churches (Gal 5:2), however, the false apostles at Corinth apparently did not insist that the Corinthians be circumcised. Nor did they practice a rigid legalism; in fact, they apparently encouraged licentiousness (12:21). Their fascination with rhetoric and oratory (10:10) suggests they had been influenced by Greek culture and philosophy.

Though their teaching may have differed from the Galatian Judaizers, it was just as deadly. "Another Jesus…a different spirit…a different gospel" (v. 4). Paul's quarrel with the false apostles was not personal, but doctrinal. Those who adulterated the true gospel received Paul's strongest condemnation (Gal 1:6–9). Paul's fear that the Corinthians would embrace the damning lies of the false apostles prompted his jealous concern for them.

SEPTEMBER 20

Isaiah 30:1–32:20

30 "Woe to the rebellious children,"
  declares the LORD,
"Who execute a plan, but not Mine,
And make an alliance, but
  not of My Spirit,
In order to add sin to sin;

30:1 not Mine…not of My Spirit. Hezekiah's advisers urged him to turn to the Egyptians, not to God, for help against the invading Assyrians. Isaiah denounced this reliance on Egypt rather than God, who had forbidden such alliances.

2 Who proceed down to Egypt
  Without consulting Me,
  To take refuge in the
    safety of Pharaoh
  And to seek shelter in the
    shadow of Egypt!
3 "Therefore the safety of Pharaoh
    will be your shame
  And the shelter in the shadow
    of Egypt, your humiliation.
4 "For their princes are at Zoan
  And their ambassadors
    arrive at Hanes.
5 "Everyone will be ashamed because of
    a people who cannot profit them,
  Who are not for help or profit, but
    for shame and also for reproach."

6 The oracle concerning the beasts of the Negev.

  Through a land of distress
    and anguish,
  From where come lioness and
    lion, viper and flying serpent,
  They carry their riches on the
    backs of young donkeys
  And their treasures on
    camels' humps,
  To a people who cannot profit them;

7 Even Egypt, whose help is
    vain and empty.
  Therefore, I have called her
  "Rahab who has been exterminated."
8 Now go, write it on a
    tablet before them
  And inscribe it on a scroll,
  That it may serve in the time to come
  As a witness forever.
9 For this is a rebellious
    people, false sons,
  Sons who refuse to listen
  To the instruction of the LORD;
10 Who say to the seers, "You
    must not see visions";
  And to the prophets, "You must not
    prophesy to us what is right,
  Speak to us pleasant words,
  Prophesy illusions.
11 "Get out of the way, turn
    aside from the path,
  Let us hear no more about
    the Holy One of Israel."

12 Therefore thus says the Holy One of Israel,

  "Since you have rejected this word
  And have put your trust in oppression
    and guile, and have relied on them,
13 Therefore this iniquity will be to you
  Like a breach about to fall,
  A bulge in a high wall,
  Whose collapse comes
    suddenly in an instant,
14 Whose collapse is like the
    smashing of a potter's jar,
  So ruthlessly shattered
  That a sherd will not be found
    among its pieces
  To take fire from a hearth
  Or to scoop water from a cistern."

15 For thus the Lord GOD, the Holy One of Israel, has said,

  "In repentance and rest
    you will be saved,
  In quietness and trust is
    your strength."
  But you were not willing,

¹⁶ And you said, "No, for we
    will flee on horses,"
Therefore you shall flee!
"And we will ride on swift
    horses,"
Therefore those who pursue
    you shall be swift.
¹⁷ One thousand *will flee* at the
    threat of one *man;*
You will flee at the threat
    of five,
Until you are left as a flag
    on a mountain top
And as a signal on a hill.

¹⁸ Therefore the LORD longs to
    be gracious to you,
And therefore He waits on high
    to have compassion on you.
For the LORD is a God of justice;
How blessed are all those
    who long for Him.

¹⁹ O people in Zion, inhabitant in Jerusalem, you will weep no longer. He will surely be gracious to you at the sound of your cry; when He hears it, He will answer you. ²⁰ Although the Lord has given you bread of privation and water of oppression, *He,* your Teacher will no longer hide Himself, but your eyes will behold your Teacher. ²¹ Your ears will hear a word behind you, "This is the way, walk in it," whenever you turn to the right or to the left. ²² And you will defile your graven images overlaid with silver, and your molten images plated with gold. You will scatter them as an impure thing, *and* say to them, "Be gone!"

²³ Then He will give *you* rain for the seed which you will sow in the ground, and bread *from* the yield of the ground, and it will be rich and plenteous; on that day your livestock will graze in a roomy pasture. ²⁴ Also the oxen and the donkeys which work the ground will eat salted fodder, which has been winnowed with shovel and fork. ²⁵ On every lofty mountain and on every high hill there will be streams running with water on the day of the great slaughter, when the towers fall. ²⁶ The light of the moon will be as the light of the sun, and the light of the sun will be seven times *brighter,* like the light of seven days, on the day the LORD binds up the fracture of His people and heals the bruise He has inflicted.

²⁷ Behold, the name of the LORD
    comes from a remote place;

Burning is His anger and
    dense is *His* smoke;
His lips are filled with indignation
And His tongue is like a
    consuming fire;
²⁸ His breath is like an
    overflowing torrent,
Which reaches to the neck,
To shake the nations back
    and forth in a sieve,
And to *put* in the jaws of the
    peoples the bridle which
    leads to ruin.
²⁹ You will have songs as in the night
    when you keep the festival,
And gladness of heart as when
    one marches to *the*
    sound of the flute,
To go to the mountain of the
    LORD, to the Rock of Israel.
³⁰ And the LORD will cause His voice
    of authority to be heard,
And the descending of His arm
    to be seen in fierce anger,
And *in* the flame of a consuming
    fire
In cloudburst, downpour
    and hailstones.
³¹ For at the voice of the LORD
    Assyria will be terrified,
When He strikes with the rod.
³² And every blow of the rod
    of punishment,
Which the LORD will lay on him,
Will be with *the music of*
    tambourines and lyres;
And in battles, brandishing
    weapons, He will fight them.
³³ For Topheth has long been ready,
Indeed, it has been prepared
    for the king.
He has made it deep and large,
A pyre of fire with plenty of wood;
The breath of the LORD, like a torrent
    of brimstone, sets it afire.

30:33 Topheth. Literally a place of abomination. Idolatrous Israel had burned to death human victims in this valley just south of Jerusalem, an area sometimes called the Valley of Hinnom (2Ki 23:10). Later it became known as Gehenna, the place of refuse for the city, with constantly burning fires, symbolizing hell. The defeat was to be so complete that the fire burns continually.

31 Woe to those who go down
    to Egypt for help
And rely on horses,
And trust in chariots because
    they are many
And in horsemen because
    they are very strong,
But they do not look to the Holy One
    of Israel, nor seek the LORD!
² Yet He also is wise and
    will bring disaster
And does not retract His words,
But will arise against the
    house of evildoers
And against the help of the
    workers of iniquity.
³ Now the Egyptians are
    men and not God,
And their horses are flesh
    and not spirit;
So the LORD will stretch out His hand,
And he who helps will stumble
And he who is helped will fall,
And all of them will come
    to an end together.

⁴ For thus says the LORD to me,
"As the lion or the young lion
    growls over his prey,
Against which a band of
    shepherds is called out,
And he will not be terrified at their
    voice nor disturbed at their noise,
So will the LORD of hosts come
    down to wage war on Mount
    Zion and on its hill."
⁵ Like flying birds so the LORD of
    hosts will protect Jerusalem.
He will protect and deliver *it;*
He will pass over and rescue *it.*

⁶ Return to Him from whom you have
deeply defected, O sons of Israel. ⁷ For in that
day every man will cast away his silver idols
and his gold idols, which your sinful hands
have made for you as a sin.

⁸ And the Assyrian will fall by
    a sword not of man,
And a sword not of man
    will devour him.
So he will not escape the sword,
And his young men will
    become forced laborers.
⁹ "His rock will pass away
    because of panic,
And his princes will be terrified
    at the standard,"

Declares the LORD, whose
    fire is in Zion and whose
    furnace is in Jerusalem.

32 Behold, a king will reign righteously
    And princes will rule justly.
² Each will be like a refuge
    from the wind
And a shelter from the storm,
Like streams of water in
    a dry country,
Like the shade of a huge rock
    in a parched land.
³ Then the eyes of those who
    see will not be blinded,
And the ears of those who
    hear will listen.
⁴ The mind of the hasty will
    discern the truth,
And the tongue of the stammerers
    will hasten to speak clearly.
⁵ No longer will the fool
    be called noble,
Or the rogue be spoken
    of *as* generous.
⁶ For a fool speaks nonsense,
And his heart inclines
    toward wickedness:
To practice ungodliness and to
    speak error against the LORD,
To keep the hungry person
    unsatisfied
And to withhold drink
    from the thirsty.
⁷ As for a rogue, his weapons are evil;
He devises wicked schemes
To destroy *the* afflicted with slander,
Even though *the* needy one
    speaks what is right.
⁸ But the noble man devises
    noble plans;
And by noble plans he stands.

⁹ Rise up, you women who are at ease,
And hear my voice;
Give ear to my word,
You complacent daughters.
¹⁰ Within a year and *a few* days
You will be troubled,
    O complacent *daughters;*
For the vintage is ended,
And the *fruit* gathering will not come.
¹¹ Tremble, you *women* who are
    at ease;
Be troubled, you complacent
    daughters;
Strip, undress and put
    sackcloth on *your* waist,

12 Beat your breasts for the
 pleasant fields, for the fruitful
 vine,
13 For the land of my people *in
 which* thorns *and* briars
 shall come up;
 Yea, for all the joyful houses
 and for the jubilant city.
14 Because the palace has been
 abandoned, the populated
 city forsaken.
 Hill and watch-tower have
 become caves forever,
 A delight for wild donkeys,
 a pasture for flocks;
15 Until the Spirit is poured out
 upon us from on high,
 And the wilderness becomes
 a fertile field,
 And the fertile field is
 considered as a forest.
16 Then justice will dwell in
 the wilderness
 And righteousness will abide
 in the fertile field.
17 And the work of righteousness
 will be peace,
 And the service of righteousness,
 quietness and confidence
 forever.
18 Then my people will live in
 a peaceful habitation,
 And in secure dwellings and in
 undisturbed resting places;
19 And it will hail when the
 forest comes down,
 And the city will be utterly
 laid low.
20 How blessed will you be, you
 who sow beside all waters,
 Who let out freely the ox
 and the donkey.

Psalm 108:7-13

7 God has spoken in His holiness:
 "I will exult, I will portion
 out Shechem
 And measure out the
 valley of Succoth.
8 "Gilead is Mine, Manasseh
 is Mine;
 Ephraim also is the helmet
 of My head;
 Judah is My scepter.
9 "Moab is My washbowl;
 Over Edom I shall throw
 My shoe;
 Over Philistia I will shout aloud."
10 Who will bring me into
 the besieged city?
 Who will lead me to Edom?
11 Have not You Yourself,
 O God, rejected us?
 And will You not go forth with
 our armies, O God?
12 Oh give us help against the
 adversary,
 For deliverance by man is
 in vain.
13 Through God we will do valiantly,
 And it is He who shall tread
 down our adversaries.

Proverbs 25:23-24

23 The north wind brings forth
 rain,
 And a backbiting tongue, an
 angry countenance.
24 It is better to live in a
 corner of the roof
 Than in a house shared with
 a contentious woman.

2 Corinthians 11:16-33

16 Again I say, let no one think me foolish; but if *you do,* receive me even as foolish, so that I also may boast a little. 17 What I am saying, I am not saying as the Lord would, but as in foolishness, in this confidence of boasting. 18 Since many boast according to the flesh, I will boast also. 19 For you, being *so* wise, tolerate the foolish gladly. 20 For you tolerate it if anyone enslaves you, anyone devours you, anyone takes advantage of you, anyone exalts himself, anyone hits you in the face. 21 To *my* shame I *must* say that we have been weak *by comparison.*

But in whatever respect anyone *else* is bold—I speak in foolishness—I am just as bold myself. 22 Are they Hebrews? So am I. Are they Israelites? So am I. Are they descendants of Abraham? So am I. 23 Are they servants of Christ?—I speak as if insane—I more so; in far more labors, in far more imprisonments,

11:19–21 These verses contain some of the most scathing sarcasm Paul ever penned, demonstrating the seriousness of the situation at Corinth and revealing the jealous concern of a godly pastor. Paul did not view his disagreement with the false apostles as a mere academic debate; the souls of the Corinthians and the purity of the gospel were at stake.

beaten times without number, often in danger of death. ²⁴ Five times I received from the Jews thirty-nine *lashes.* ²⁵ Three times I was beaten with rods, once I was stoned, three times I was shipwrecked, a night and a day I have spent in the deep. ²⁶ *I have been* on frequent journeys, in dangers from rivers, dangers from robbers, dangers from *my* countrymen, dangers from the Gentiles, dangers in the city, dangers in the wilderness, dangers on the sea, dangers among false brethren; ²⁷ *I have been* in labor and hardship, through many sleepless nights, in hunger and thirst, often without food, in cold and exposure. ²⁸ Apart from *such* external things, there is the daily pressure on me *of* concern for all the churches. ²⁹ Who is weak without my being weak? Who is led into sin without my intense concern?

³⁰ If I have to boast, I will boast of what pertains to my weakness. ³¹ The God and Father of the Lord Jesus, He who is blessed forever, knows that I am not lying. ³² In Damascus the ethnarch under Aretas the king was guarding the city of the Damascenes in order to seize me, ³³ and I was let down in a basket through a window in the wall, and *so* escaped his hands.

11:20 enslaves you. The Greek verb translated by this phrase appears elsewhere in the New Testament only in Galatians 2:4, where it speaks of the Galatians' enslavement by the Judaizers. The false apostles had robbed the Corinthians of their freedom in Christ (Gal 5:1). **devours you.** Or "preys upon you." This probably refers to the false teachers' demands for financial support (the same verb appears in Luke 20:47 where Jesus denounces the Pharisees for devouring widows' houses). **takes advantage of you.** This is translated "I took you in by deceit" in 12:16. The false apostles were attempting to catch the Corinthians like fish in a net (Lk 5:5–6). **exalts himself.** This refers to one who is presumptuous, puts on airs, acts arrogantly, or lords it over people (1Pe 5:3). **hits you in the face.** The false apostles may have physically abused the Corinthians, but the phrase is more likely used in a metaphorical sense (1Co 9:27) to speak of the false teachers' humiliation of the Corinthians. To strike someone on the face was a sign of disrespect and contempt (1Ki 22:24; Lk 22:64; Ac 23:2).

DAY 20: What had being a minister of Christ cost the apostle Paul?

Contrasting his ministry to the false apostles in 2 Corinthians 11:23, Paul spoke of "far more labors, in far more imprisonments, beaten times without number, often in danger of death." This is a general summation of Paul's sufferings for the gospel. The next few verses give specific examples, many of which are not found in Acts.

"Thirty-nine lashes" (v. 24). Deuteronomy 25:1–3 set 40 as the maximum number that could legally be administered. In Paul's day the Jews reduced that number by one to avoid accidentally going over the maximum. Jesus warned that His followers would receive such beatings (Mt 10:17).

"Beaten with rods" (v. 25). Refers to Roman beatings with flexible sticks tied together (Ac 16:22–23). "Once I was stoned"—at Lystra (Ac 14:19–20). "Three times I was shipwrecked." Not including the shipwreck on his journey as a prisoner to Rome (Ac 27), which had not yet taken place. Paul had been on several sea voyages up to this time, giving ample opportunity for the 3 shipwrecks to have occurred. "A night and a day I have spent in the deep." At least one of the shipwrecks was so severe that Paul spent an entire day floating on the wreckage, waiting to be rescued.

"In dangers" (v. 26). Those connected with his frequent travels. "Rivers" and "robbers" posed a serious danger to travelers in the ancient world. Paul's journey from Perga to Pisidian Antioch (Ac 13:14), for example, required him to travel through the robber-infested Taurus Mountains and to cross two dangerous, flood-prone rivers. Paul was frequently in danger from his own "countrymen" (Ac 9:23, 29; 13:45; 14:2, 19; 17:5; 18:6, 12–16; 20:3, 19; 21:27–32) and, less often, from "Gentiles" (Ac 16:16–40; 19:23–20:1). "False brethren." Those who appeared to be Christians, but were not, such as the false apostles (v. 13) and the Judaizers (Gal 2:4).

And far worse than the occasional physical suffering Paul endured—weariness and toil, sleeplessness, hunger, thirst, fastings, and cold—was the constant, daily burden of concern for the churches that he felt (v. 28). Those who were "weak" (Ro 14; 1Co 8) in faith or were "led into sin" caused him intense emotional pain.

SEPTEMBER 21

Isaiah 33:1–34:17

33 Woe to you, O destroyer,
While you were not destroyed;
And he who is treacherous,
while *others* did not deal
treacherously with him.
As soon as you finish destroying,
you will be destroyed;
As soon as you cease to deal
treacherously, *others* will deal
treacherously with you.

2 O LORD, be gracious to us; we
have waited for You.
Be their strength every morning,
Our salvation also in the
time of distress.

3 At the sound of the tumult
peoples flee;
At the lifting up of Yourself
nations disperse.

4 Your spoil is gathered *as the*
caterpillar gathers;
As locusts rushing about
men rush about on it.

5 The LORD is exalted, for
He dwells on high;
He has filled Zion with justice
and righteousness.

6 And He will be the stability
of your times,
A wealth of salvation, wisdom
and knowledge;
The fear of the LORD is his treasure.

7 Behold, their brave men
cry in the streets,
The ambassadors of peace
weep bitterly.

8 The highways are desolate,
the traveler has ceased,
He has broken the covenant, he
has despised the cities,
He has no regard for man.

9 The land mourns *and* pines away,
Lebanon is shamed *and* withers;
Sharon is like a desert plain,
And Bashan and Carmel
lose *their foliage.*

10 "Now I will arise," says the LORD,
"Now I will be exalted, now
I will be lifted up.

11 "You have conceived chaff, you
will give birth to stubble;
My breath will consume
you like a fire.

12 "The peoples will be burned to lime,

Like cut thorns which are
burned in the fire.

13 "You who are far away, hear
what I have done;
And you who are near,
acknowledge My might."

14 Sinners in Zion are terrified;
Trembling has seized the godless.
"Who among us can live with
the consuming fire?
Who among us can live with
continual burning?"

15 He who walks righteously and
speaks with sincerity,
He who rejects unjust gain
And shakes his hands so that
they hold no bribe;
He who stops his ears from
hearing about bloodshed
And shuts his eyes from
looking upon evil;

16 He will dwell on the heights,
His refuge will be the
impregnable rock;
His bread will be given *him,*
His water will be sure.

17 Your eyes will see the King
in His beauty;
They will behold a far-distant land.

33:17 King in His beauty. The prophecy moves
beyond Hezekiah in his sackcloth, oppressed
by his enemy, to Messiah in His beauty. Seeing
Him in glory is another reward of the righteous.
The near-future deliverance from Sennacherib
anticipates a more distant wonder when the
Messiah will sit on His throne.

18 Your heart will meditate on terror:
"Where is he who counts?
Where is he who weighs?
Where is he who counts the towers?"

19 You will no longer see a fierce
people,
A people of unintelligible speech
which no one comprehends,
Of a stammering tongue which
no one understands.

20 Look upon Zion, the city of
our appointed feasts;
Your eyes will see Jerusalem, an
undisturbed habitation,
A tent which will not be folded;

Its stakes will never be pulled up,
Nor any of its cords be torn apart.

²¹ But there the majestic *One,*
the LORD, will be for us
A place of rivers *and* wide canals
On which no boat with oars will go,
And on which no mighty
ship will pass—

²² For the LORD is our judge,
The LORD is our lawgiver,
The LORD is our king;
He will save us—

²³ Your tackle hangs slack;
It cannot hold the base of
its mast firmly,
Nor spread out the sail.
Then the prey of an abundant
spoil will be divided;
The lame will take the plunder.

²⁴ And no resident will say, "I am sick";
The people who dwell there will
be forgiven *their* iniquity.

34 Draw near, O nations, to hear;
and listen, O peoples!
Let the earth and all it contains
hear, and the world and all
that springs from it.

² For the LORD'S indignation is
against all the nations,
And *His* wrath against
all their armies;
He has utterly destroyed them,
He has given them over to slaughter.

³ So their slain will be thrown out,
And their corpses will give
off their stench,
And the mountains will be
drenched with their blood.

⁴ And all the host of heaven
will wear away,
And the sky will be rolled
up like a scroll;
All their hosts will also wither away
As a leaf withers from the vine,
Or as *one* withers from the fig tree.

⁵ For My sword is satiated in heaven,
Behold it shall descend for
judgment upon Edom
And upon the people whom I
have devoted to destruction.

⁶ The sword of the LORD is
filled with blood,
It is sated with fat, with the
blood of lambs and goats,
With the fat of the kidneys of rams.
For the LORD has a sacrifice
in Bozrah

And a great slaughter in
the land of Edom.

⁷ Wild oxen will also fall with them
And young bulls with strong ones;
Thus their land will be
soaked with blood,
And their dust become
greasy with fat.

⁸ For the LORD has a day of vengeance,
A year of recompense for
the cause of Zion.

⁹ Its streams will be turned into pitch,
And its loose earth into brimstone,
And its land will become
burning pitch.

¹⁰ It will not be quenched night or day;
Its smoke will go up forever.
From generation to generation
it will be desolate;
None will pass through it
forever and ever.

¹¹ But pelican and hedgehog
will possess it,
And owl and raven will dwell in it;
And He will stretch over it
the line of desolation
And the plumb line of emptiness.

¹² Its nobles—there is no one there
Whom they may proclaim king—
And all its princes will be nothing.

¹³ Thorns will come up in its
fortified towers,
Nettles and thistles in its
fortified cities;
It will also be a haunt of jackals
And an abode of ostriches.

¹⁴ The desert creatures will
meet with the wolves,
The hairy goat also will cry to its kind;
Yes, the night monster
will settle there
And will find herself a resting place.

¹⁵ The tree snake will make its
nest and lay *eggs* there,
And it will hatch and gather
them under its protection.
Yes, the hawks will be gathered there,
Every one with its kind.

¹⁶ Seek from the book of the LORD, and read:

Not one of these will be missing;
None will lack its mate.
For His mouth has commanded,
And His Spirit has gathered them.

¹⁷ He has cast the lot for them,
And His hand has divided
it to them by line.

936

They shall possess it forever;
From generation to generation
they will dwell in it.

Psalm 109:1–5

For the choir director. A Psalm of David.

O God of my praise,
Do not be silent!
2 For they have opened the wicked
and deceitful mouth against me;
They have spoken against me
with a lying tongue.
3 They have also surrounded me
with words of hatred,
And fought against me without cause.
4 In return for my love they
act as my accusers;
But I am *in* prayer.
5 Thus they have repaid
me evil for good
And hatred for my love.

Proverbs 25:25–26

25 *Like* cold water to a weary soul,
So is good news from a distant land.
26 *Like* a trampled spring
and a polluted well
Is a righteous man who gives
way before the wicked.

25:26 trampled spring. The righteous one who sins muddies the water for the wicked who see him and for whom he should serve as an example of righteousness (Ps 17:5).

2 Corinthians 12:1–21

12 Boasting is necessary, though it is not profitable; but I will go on to visions and revelations of the Lord. 2 I know a man in Christ who fourteen years ago—whether in the body I do not know, or out of the body I do not know, God knows—such a man was caught up to the third heaven. 3 And I know how such a man—whether in the body or apart from the body I do not know, God knows— 4 was caught up into Paradise and heard inexpressible words, which a man is not permitted to speak. 5 On behalf of such a man I will boast; but on my own behalf I will not boast, except in regard to *my* weaknesses. 6 For if I do wish to boast I will not be foolish, for I will be speaking the truth; but I refrain *from this,* so that no one will credit me with more than he sees *in* me or hears from me. 7 Because of the surpassing greatness of the revelations, for

12:2–4 Since it took place 14 years before the writing of 2 Corinthians, the specific vision Paul relates cannot be identified with any incident recorded in Acts. It probably took place between his return to Tarsus from Jerusalem (Ac 9:30) and the start of his missionary journeys (Ac 13:1–3). **caught up to the third heaven... caught up into Paradise.** Paul was not describing two separate visions; "the third heaven" and "Paradise" are the same place (Rev 2:7, which says the tree of life is in Paradise, with Rev 22:14, which says it is in heaven). The first heaven is the earth's atmosphere (Ge 8:2; Dt 11:11; 1Ki 8:35); the second is interplanetary and interstellar space (Ge 15:5; Ps 8:3; Is 13:10); and the third is the abode of God (1Ki 8:30; 2Ch 30:27; Ps 123:1).

this reason, to keep me from exalting myself, there was given me a thorn in the flesh, a messenger of Satan to torment me—to keep me from exalting myself! 8 Concerning this I implored the Lord three times that it might leave me. 9 And He has said to me, "My grace is sufficient for you, for power is perfected in weakness." Most gladly, therefore, I will rather boast about my weaknesses, so that the power of Christ may dwell in me. 10 Therefore I am well content with weaknesses, with insults, with distresses, with persecutions, with difficulties, for Christ's sake; for when I am weak, then I am strong.

11 I have become foolish; you yourselves

12:8 I implored...three times. Paul, longing for relief from this painful hindrance to his ministry, went to his Lord, begging Him (the use of the definite article with "Lord" shows Paul's prayer was directed to Jesus) to remove it. The demons are only subject to His authority. The 3-fold repetition of Paul's request parallels that of Jesus in Gethsemane (Mk 14:32–41). Both Paul and Jesus had their requests denied, but were granted grace to endure their ordeals.

12:9 My grace is sufficient for you. The present tense of the verb translated "is sufficient" reveals the constant availability of divine grace. God would not remove the thorn, as Paul had requested, but would continually supply him with grace to endure it (1Co 15:10; Php 4:13; Col 1:29). **power is perfected in weakness.** See 4:7–11. The weaker the human instrument, the more clearly God's grace shines forth.

compelled me. Actually I should have been commended by you, for in no respect was I inferior to the most eminent apostles, even though I am a nobody. [12] The signs of a true apostle were performed among you with all perseverance, by signs and wonders and miracles. [13] For in what respect were you treated as inferior to the rest of the churches, except that I myself did not become a burden to you? Forgive me this wrong!

[14] Here for this third time I am ready to come to you, and I will not be a burden to you; for I do not seek what is yours, but you; for children are not responsible to save up for *their* parents, but parents for *their* children. [15] I will most gladly spend and be expended for your souls. If I love you more, am I to be loved less? [16] But be that as it may, I did not burden you myself; nevertheless, crafty fellow that I am, I took you in by deceit. [17] *Certainly* I have not taken advantage of you through any of those whom I have sent to you, have I? [18] I urged Titus *to go,* and I sent the brother with him. Titus did not take any advantage of you, did he? Did we not conduct ourselves in the same spirit *and walk* in the same steps?

[19] All this time you have been thinking that we are defending ourselves to you. *Actually,* it is in the sight of God that we have been speaking in Christ; and all for your upbuilding, beloved. [20] For I am afraid that perhaps when I come I may find you to be not what I wish and may be found by you to be not what you wish; that perhaps *there will be* strife, jealousy, angry tempers, disputes, slanders, gossip, arrogance, disturbances; [21] I am afraid that when I come again my God may humiliate me before you, and I may mourn over many of those who have sinned in the past and not repented of the impurity, immorality and sensuality which they have practiced.

DAY 21: To what was Paul referring by the term "thorn in the flesh"?

Paul began his account about the "thorn in the flesh" by indicating the reason it was given to him—"To keep me from exalting myself!" The assault was painful, but purposeful. As with Job, Satan was the immediate cause, but God was the ultimate cause. God was allowing Satan to bring this severe trouble in the church for the purpose of humbling Paul who, having had so many revelations, including a trip to heaven and back, would have been proud.

Paul's use of the word "messenger" (Greek, *angellos,* or angel) from Satan suggests the "thorn in the flesh" (literally, "a stake for the flesh") was a demon, not a physical illness. Of the 188 uses of the Greek word *angellos* in the New Testament, at least 180 are in reference to angels. This angel was from Satan, a demon afflicting Paul.

Possibly, the best explanation for this demon was that he was indwelling the ringleader of the Corinthian conspiracy, the leader of the false apostles. Through them he was tearing up Paul's beloved church and thus driving a painful stake through Paul. Further support for this view comes from the context of chapters 10–13, which is one of fighting adversaries (the false prophets). The verb translated "torment" always refers to ill treatment from other people (Mt 26:67; Mk 14:65; 1Co 4:11; 1Pe 2:20). Finally, the Old Testament describes Israel's personal opponents as thorns (Nu 33:55; Jos 23:13; Jdg 2:3; Eze 28:24).

SEPTEMBER 22

Isaiah 35:1–36:22

35 The wilderness and the
　　desert will be glad,
　And the Arabah will rejoice
　　and blossom;
　Like the crocus
[2]　It will blossom profusely
　And rejoice with rejoicing
　　and shout of joy.
　The glory of Lebanon will
　　be given to it,
　The majesty of Carmel and Sharon.
　They will see the glory of the LORD,
　The majesty of our God.

[3]　Encourage the exhausted, and
　　strengthen the feeble.
[4]　Say to those with anxious heart,
　　"Take courage, fear not.
　Behold, your God will come
　　with vengeance;
　The recompense of God will
　　come,
　But He will save you."
[5]　Then the eyes of the blind
　　will be opened
　And the ears of the deaf
　　will be unstopped.
[6]　Then the lame will leap like
　　a deer,
　And the tongue of the mute
　　will shout for joy.

For waters will break forth
    in the wilderness
And streams in the Arabah.
7   The scorched land will become a pool
And the thirsty ground
    springs of water;
In the haunt of jackals,
    its resting place,
Grass *becomes* reeds and rushes.
8   A highway will be there, a roadway,
And it will be called the
    Highway of Holiness.
The unclean will not travel on it,
But it *will* be for him who
    walks *that* way,
And fools will not wander *on it.*

35:6 lame…shout. God's restoration in the millennial age is to include physical restoration to the afflicted. Jesus' first coming gave a foretaste of that future day (Mt 11:5; 12:22; Mk 7:37; Lk 7:21; Ac 3:8).

35:8 Highway of Holiness. This refers to the way leading the redeemed back to Jerusalem, the throne of Messiah, literally and spiritually. Christ Himself is to be the leader on that way, called in 40:3, the "way for the LORD."

9   No lion will be there,
Nor will any vicious beast go up on it;
These will not be found there.
But the redeemed will walk *there,*
10   And the ransomed of the
    LORD will return
And come with joyful
    shouting to Zion,
With everlasting joy upon their heads.
They will find gladness and joy,
And sorrow and sighing will flee away.

36

Now in the fourteenth year of King Hezekiah, Sennacherib king of Assyria came up against all the fortified cities of Judah and seized them. 2 And the king of Assyria sent Rabshakeh from Lachish to Jerusalem to King Hezekiah with a large army. And he stood by the conduit of the upper pool on the highway of the fuller's field. 3 Then Eliakim the son of Hilkiah, who was over the household, and Shebna the scribe, and Joah the son of Asaph, the recorder, came out to him.

4 Then Rabshakeh said to them, "Say now to Hezekiah, 'Thus says the great king, the king of Assyria, "What is this confidence that you have? 5 I say, 'Your counsel and strength for the war are only empty words.' Now on whom do you rely, that you have rebelled against me? 6 Behold, you rely on the staff of this crushed reed, *even* on Egypt, on which if a man leans, it will go into his hand and pierce it. So is Pharaoh king of Egypt to all who rely on him. 7 But if you say to me, 'We trust in the LORD our God,' is it not He whose high places and whose altars Hezekiah has taken away and has said to Judah and to Jerusalem, 'You shall worship before this altar'? 8 Now therefore, come make a bargain with my master the king of Assyria, and I will give you two thousand horses, if you are able on your part to set riders on them. 9 How then can you repulse one official of the least of my master's servants and rely on Egypt for chariots and for horsemen? 10 Have I now come up without the LORD'S approval against this land to destroy it? The LORD said to me, 'Go up against this land and destroy it.'"'"

36:10 The LORD said. Rabshakeh's boastful claim of the authority from Judah's God for his mission may have been a ploy on his part to get a surrender, but it aligned with Isaiah's prophecy that the Assyrians would be His instrument to punish His people (8:7–8; 10:5–6). The Assyrians may have heard this from partisans or may not have known this, but Judah did.

11 Then Eliakim and Shebna and Joah said to Rabshakeh, "Speak now to your servants in Aramaic, for we understand *it;* and do not speak with us in Judean in the hearing of the people who are on the wall." 12 But Rabshakeh said, "Has my master sent me only to your master and to you to speak these words, *and* not to the men who sit on the wall, *doomed* to eat their own dung and drink their own urine with you?"

13 Then Rabshakeh stood and cried with a loud voice in Judean and said, "Hear the words of the great king, the king of Assyria. 14 Thus says the king, 'Do not let Hezekiah deceive you, for he will not be able to deliver you; 15 nor let Hezekiah make you trust in the LORD, saying, "The LORD will surely deliver us, this city will not be given into the hand of the king of Assyria." 16 Do not listen to Hezekiah,' for thus says the king of Assyria, 'Make your peace with me and come out to me, and eat each of his vine and each of his fig tree and drink each of the waters of his own cistern, 17 until I come and take you away to a land like your

own land, a land of grain and new wine, a land of bread and vineyards. ¹⁸ *Beware* that Hezekiah does not mislead you, saying, "The LORD will deliver us." Has any one of the gods of the nations delivered his land from the hand of the king of Assyria? ¹⁹ Where are the gods of Hamath and Arpad? Where are the gods of Sepharvaim? And when have they delivered Samaria from my hand? ²⁰ Who among all the gods of these lands have delivered their land from my hand, that the LORD would deliver Jerusalem from my hand?'"

²¹ But they were silent and answered him not a word; for the king's commandment was, "Do not answer him." ²² Then Eliakim the son of Hilkiah, who was over the household, and Shebna the scribe and Joah the son of Asaph, the recorder, came to Hezekiah with their clothes torn and told him the words of Rabshakeh.

Psalm 109:6-13

⁶ Appoint a wicked man
   over him,
And let an accuser stand
   at his right hand.
⁷ When he is judged, let him
   come forth guilty,
And let his prayer become sin.
⁸ Let his days be few;
   Let another take his office.
⁹ Let his children be fatherless
   And his wife a widow.
¹⁰ Let his children wander
      about and beg;
   And let them seek *sustenance* far
      from their ruined homes.
¹¹ Let the creditor seize all that
      he has,
   And let strangers plunder the
      product of his labor.
¹² Let there be none to extend
      lovingkindness to him,
   Nor any to be gracious to his
      fatherless children.
¹³ Let his posterity be cut off;
   In a following generation let
      their name be blotted out.

Proverbs 25:27-28

²⁷ It is not good to eat much
      honey,
   Nor is it glory to search out
      one's own glory.
²⁸ *Like* a city that is broken into
      and without walls
   Is a man who has no control
      over his spirit.

25:28 city that is broken. Such are exposed and vulnerable to the incursion of evil thoughts and successful temptations.

2 Corinthians 13:1-14

13 This is the third time I am coming to you. EVERY FACT IS TO BE CONFIRMED BY THE TESTIMONY OF TWO OR THREE WITNESSES. ²I have previously said when present the second time, and though now absent I say in advance to those who have sinned in the past and to all the rest *as well,* that if I come again I will not spare *anyone,* ³since you are seeking for proof of the Christ who speaks in me, and who is not weak toward you, but mighty in you. ⁴For indeed He was crucified because of weakness, yet He lives because of the power of God. For we also are weak in Him, yet we will live with Him because of the power of God *directed* toward you.

⁵Test yourselves *to see* if you are in the faith; examine yourselves! Or do you not recognize this about yourselves, that Jesus Christ is in you—unless indeed you fail the test? ⁶But I trust that you will realize that we ourselves do not fail the test. ⁷Now we pray to God that you do no wrong; not that we ourselves may appear approved, but that you may do what is right, even though we may appear unapproved. ⁸For we can do nothing against the truth, but *only* for the truth. ⁹For we rejoice when we ourselves are weak but you are strong; this we also pray for, that you be made complete. ¹⁰For this reason I am writing these things while absent, so that when present I *need* not use severity, in accordance with the authority which the Lord gave me for building up and not for tearing down.

¹¹Finally, brethren, rejoice, be made complete, be comforted, be like-minded, live in peace; and the God of love and peace will be with you. ¹²Greet one another with a holy kiss. ¹³All the saints greet you.

¹⁴The grace of the Lord Jesus Christ, and the love of God, and the fellowship of the Holy Spirit, be with you all.

13:12 a holy kiss. A sign of greeting in biblical times (Mt 26:49; Lk 7:45), much like the modern handshake. For Christians, it further expressed brotherly love and unity (Ro 16:16; 1Co 16:20; 1Th 5:26; 1Pe 5:14).

In 2 Corinthians 12:20, 21, it is clear that when he visited them, Paul did not want to find the Corinthians in the same sorry spiritual condition as on his last visit (the "painful visit," 2:1). If he found that they were not what he wished (i.e., still practicing the sins he listed), they would find him not as they wished—he would have had to discipline them (13:2). To find the Corinthians still living in unrepentant sin would both humiliate and sadden Paul. This warning (and the one in 13:2) was designed to prevent that from happening.

"I will not spare" (v. 2). Paul informed the Corinthians that he would deal biblically with any sin he found in Corinth. Those Corinthians still seeking proof that Paul was a genuine apostle would have it when he arrived (v. 3). They may have gotten more than they bargained for, however, for Paul was going to use his apostolic authority and power to deal with any sin and rebellion he found there. Christ's power was to be revealed through Paul against the sinning Corinthians (1Co 11:30–32). Paul was to come to Corinth armed with the irresistible power of the risen, glorified Christ (v. 4).

In vv. 5, 6, the Greek grammar places great emphasis on the pronouns "yourselves" and "you." Paul turned the tables on his accusers. Instead of presuming to evaluate his apostleship, they needed to test the genuineness of their faith (Jas 2:14–26). He pointed out the incongruity of the Corinthians' believing (as they did) that their faith was genuine and his apostleship false. Paul was their spiritual father (1Co 4:15). If his apostleship was counterfeit, so was their faith. The genuineness of their salvation was proof of the genuineness of his apostleship.

SEPTEMBER 23

Isaiah 37:1–38:22

37 And when King Hezekiah heard *it*, he tore his clothes, covered himself with sackcloth and entered the house of the LORD. ² Then he sent Eliakim who was over the household with Shebna the scribe and the elders of the priests, covered with sackcloth, to Isaiah the prophet, the son of Amoz. ³ They said to him, "Thus says Hezekiah, 'This day is a day of distress, rebuke and rejection; for children have come to birth, and there is no strength to deliver. ⁴ Perhaps the LORD your God will hear the words of Rabshakeh, whom his master the king of Assyria has sent to reproach the living God, and will rebuke the words which the LORD your God has heard. Therefore, offer a prayer for the remnant that is left.'"

⁵ So the servants of King Hezekiah came to Isaiah. ⁶ Isaiah said to them, "Thus you shall say to your master, 'Thus says the LORD, "Do not be afraid because of the words that you have heard, with which the servants of the king of Assyria have blasphemed Me. ⁷ Behold, I will put a spirit in him so that he will hear a rumor and return to his own land. And I will make him fall by the sword in his own land."'"

⁸ Then Rabshakeh returned and found the king of Assyria fighting against Libnah, for he had heard that the king had left Lachish. ⁹ When he heard *them* say concerning Tirhakah king of Cush, "He has come out to fight against you," and when he heard *it* he sent messengers to Hezekiah, saying, ¹⁰ "Thus you shall say to Hezekiah king of Judah, 'Do not let your God in whom you trust deceive you, saying, "Jerusalem will not be given into the hand of the king of Assyria." ¹¹ Behold, you have heard what the kings of Assyria have done to all the lands, destroying them completely. So will you be spared? ¹² Did the gods of those nations which my fathers have destroyed deliver them, *even* Gozan and Haran and Rezeph and the sons of Eden who *were* in Telassar? ¹³ Where is the king of Hamath, the king of Arpad, the king of the city of Sepharvaim, *and of* Hena and Ivvah?'"

¹⁴ Then Hezekiah took the letter from the hand of the messengers and read it, and he went up to the house of the LORD and spread it out before the LORD. ¹⁵ Hezekiah prayed to the LORD saying, ¹⁶ "O LORD of hosts, the God of Israel, who is enthroned *above* the cherubim, You are the God, You alone, of all the kingdoms of the earth. You have made heaven and earth. ¹⁷ Incline Your ear, O LORD, and hear; open Your eyes, O LORD, and see; and listen to all the words of Sennacherib, who sent *them* to reproach the living God. ¹⁸ Truly, O LORD, the kings of Assyria have devastated all the countries and their lands, ¹⁹ and have cast their gods into the fire, for they were not gods but the work of men's hands, wood and stone. So they have destroyed them. ²⁰ Now, O LORD our God, deliver us from his hand that all the kingdoms of the earth may know that You alone, LORD, are God."

²¹ Then Isaiah the son of Amoz sent *word* to Hezekiah, saying, "Thus says the LORD, the

God of Israel, 'Because you have prayed to Me about Sennacherib king of Assyria, [22] this is the word that the LORD has spoken against him:

> "She has despised you
>   and mocked you,
> The virgin daughter of Zion;
> She has shaken *her* head
>   behind you,
> The daughter of Jerusalem!

[23] "Whom have you reproached
>   and blasphemed?
> And against whom have
>   you raised *your* voice
> And haughtily lifted up your eyes?
> Against the Holy One of Israel!

[24] "Through your servants you
>   have reproached the Lord,
> And you have said, 'With my
>   many chariots I came up to the
>   heights of the mountains,
> To the remotest parts of Lebanon;
> And I cut down its tall cedars
>   *and* its choice cypresses.
> And I will go to its highest
>   peak, its thickest forest.

[25] 'I dug *wells* and drank waters,
> And with the sole of my
>   feet I dried up
> All the rivers of Egypt.'

[26] "Have you not heard?
> Long ago I did it,
> From ancient times I planned it.
> Now I have brought it to pass,
> That you should turn fortified
>   cities into ruinous heaps.

[27] "Therefore their inhabitants
>   were short of strength,
> They were dismayed and
>   put to shame;
> They were *as* the vegetation
>   of the field and *as* the
>   green herb,
> *As* grass on the housetops is
>   scorched before it is grown up.

[28] "But I know your sitting down
> And your going out and
>   your coming in
> And your raging against Me.

[29] "Because of your raging against Me
> And because your arrogance
>   has come up to My ears,
> Therefore I will put My
>   hook in your nose
> And My bridle in your lips,
> And I will turn you back by the
>   way which you came.

37:29 hook in your nose...bridle in your lips. In judging Sennacherib, the Lord treated him as an obstinate animal with a ring in his nose and/or a bridle in his mouth. Some ancient sources indicate that captives were led before a king by a cord attached to a hook or ring through the upper lip and nose. Thus, he was to be brought back to his own country.

[30] "Then this shall be the sign for you: you will eat this year what grows of itself, in the second year what springs from the same, and in the third year sow, reap, plant vineyards and eat their fruit. [31] The surviving remnant of the house of Judah will again take root downward and bear fruit upward. [32] For out of Jerusalem will go forth a remnant and out of Mount Zion survivors. The zeal of the LORD of hosts will perform this.'"

[33] "Therefore, thus says the LORD concerning the king of Assyria, 'He will not come to this city or shoot an arrow there; and he will not come before it with a shield, or throw up a siege ramp against it. [34] By the way that he came, by the same he will return, and he will not come to this city,' declares the LORD. [35] 'For I will defend this city to save it for My own sake and for My servant David's sake.'"

[36] Then the angel of the LORD went out and struck 185,000 in the camp of the Assyrians; and when men arose early in the morning, behold, all of these were dead. [37] So Sennacherib king of Assyria departed and returned *home* and lived at Nineveh. [38] It came about as he was worshiping in the house of Nisroch his god, that Adrammelech and Sharezer his sons killed him with the sword; and they escaped into the land of Ararat. And Esarhaddon his son became king in his place.

37:36 the angel of the LORD. This was Isaiah's only use of a title that is frequent in the OT, one referring to the Lord Himself. **struck.** Secular records also mention this massive slaughter of Assyrian troops, without noting its supernatural nature, of course (Ex 12:12, 29).

38 In those days Hezekiah became mortally ill. And Isaiah the prophet the son of Amoz came to him and said to him, "Thus says the LORD, 'Set your house in order, for you shall die and not live.'" [2] Then Hezekiah turned his face to the wall and prayed to the LORD, ³ and said, "Remember now, O LORD, I beseech You, how I have walked before You in truth and with a whole heart, and have done what is good in Your sight." And Hezekiah wept bitterly.

⁴ Then the word of the LORD came to Isaiah, saying, ⁵ "Go and say to Hezekiah, 'Thus says the LORD, the God of your father David, "I have heard your prayer, I have seen your tears; behold, I will add fifteen years to your life. ⁶ I will deliver you and this city from the hand of the king of Assyria; and I will defend this city."'

⁷ "This shall be the sign to you from the LORD, that the LORD will do this thing that He has spoken: ⁸ Behold, I will cause the shadow on the stairway, which has gone down with the sun on the stairway of Ahaz, to go back ten steps." So the sun's *shadow* went back ten steps on the stairway on which it had gone down.

⁹ A writing of Hezekiah king of Judah after his illness and recovery:

¹⁰ I said, "In the middle of my life
I am to enter the gates of Sheol;
I am to be deprived of the
rest of my years."

¹¹ I said, "I will not see the LORD,
The LORD in the land of the living;
I will look on man no more among
the inhabitants of the world.

¹² "Like a shepherd's tent my dwelling
is pulled up and removed
from me;
As a weaver I rolled up my life.
He cuts me off from the loom;
From day until night You
make an end of me.

¹³ "I composed *my soul* until morning.
Like a lion—so He breaks
all my bones,
From day until night You
make an end of me.

¹⁴ "Like a swallow, *like* a
crane, so I twitter;
I moan like a dove;
My eyes look wistfully to the heights;
O Lord, I am oppressed,
be my security.

¹⁵ "What shall I say?
For He has spoken to me, and
He Himself has done it;
I will wander about all my
years because of the
bitterness of my soul.

¹⁶ "O Lord, by *these* things *men* live,
And in all these is the life of my spirit;
O restore me to health and let
me live!

¹⁷ "Lo, for *my own* welfare I
had great bitterness;
It is You who has kept my soul
from the pit of nothingness,
For You have cast all my sins
behind Your back.

¹⁸ "For Sheol cannot thank You,
Death cannot praise You;
Those who go down to the
pit cannot hope for
Your faithfulness.

¹⁹ "It is the living who give thanks
to You, as I do today;
A father tells his sons about
Your faithfulness.

²⁰ "The LORD will surely save me;
So we will play my songs on
stringed instruments
All *the* days of our life at the
house of the LORD."

²¹ Now Isaiah had said, "Let them take a cake of figs and apply it to the boil, that he may recover." ²² Then Hezekiah had said, "What is the sign that I shall go up to the house of the LORD?"

Psalm 109:14–20

¹⁴ Let the iniquity of his fathers be
remembered before the LORD,
And do not let the sin of his
mother be blotted out.

¹⁵ Let them be before the
LORD continually,
That He may cut off their
memory from the earth;

¹⁶ Because he did not remember
to show lovingkindness,
But persecuted the afflicted
and needy man,
And the despondent in heart,
to put *them* to death.

¹⁷ He also loved cursing, so
it came to him;
And he did not delight in blessing,
so it was far from him.

¹⁸ But he clothed himself with
cursing as with his garment,
And it entered into his body like water
And like oil into his bones.

¹⁹ Let it be to him as a garment with
which he covers himself,
And for a belt with which he
constantly girds himself.

20 Let this be the reward of my
accusers from the LORD,
And of those who speak evil
against my soul.

Proverbs 26:1

26 Like snow in summer and
like rain in harvest,
So honor is not fitting for a fool.

Galatians 1:1–24

1 Paul, an apostle (not *sent* from men nor through the agency of man, but through Jesus Christ and God the Father, who raised Him from the dead), ²and all the brethren who are with me,

To the churches of Galatia:

³Grace to you and peace from God our Father and the Lord Jesus Christ, ⁴who gave Himself for our sins so that He might rescue us from this present evil age, according to the will of our God and Father, ⁵to whom *be* the glory forevermore. Amen.

⁶I am amazed that you are so quickly deserting Him who called you by the grace of Christ, for a different gospel; ⁷which is *really* not another; only there are some who are disturbing you and want to distort the gospel of Christ. ⁸But even if we, or an angel from heaven, should preach to you a gospel contrary to what we have preached to you, he is to be accursed! ⁹As we have said before, so I say again now, if any man is preaching to you a gospel contrary to what you received, he is to be accursed!

¹⁰For am I now seeking the favor of men, or of God? Or am I striving to please men? If I were still trying to please men, I would not be a bond-servant of Christ.

¹¹For I would have you know, brethren, that the gospel which was preached by me is not according to man. ¹²For I neither received it from man, nor was I taught it, but *I received it* through a revelation of Jesus Christ.

¹³For you have heard of my former manner of life in Judaism, how I used to persecute the church of God beyond measure and tried to destroy it; ¹⁴and I was advancing in Judaism beyond many of my contemporaries among my countrymen, being more extremely zealous for my ancestral traditions. ¹⁵But when God, who had set me apart *even* from my mother's womb and called me through His grace, was pleased ¹⁶to reveal His Son in me so that I might preach Him among the Gentiles, I did not immediately consult with flesh and blood, ¹⁷nor did I go up to Jerusalem to those who were apostles before me; but I

1:12 neither received it from man, nor was I taught it. In contrast to the Judaizers, who received their religious instruction from rabbinic tradition. Most Jews did not study the actual Scriptures; instead, they used human interpretations of Scripture as their religious authority and guide. Many of their traditions not only were not taught in Scripture but also contradicted it (Mk 7:13). **through a revelation.** This refers to the unveiling of something previously kept secret—in this case, Jesus Christ. While he knew about Christ, Paul subsequently met Him personally on the road to Damascus and received the truth of the gospel from Him (Ac 9:1–16).

went away to Arabia, and returned once more to Damascus.

¹⁸Then three years later I went up to Jerusalem to become acquainted with Cephas, and stayed with him fifteen days. ¹⁹But I did not see any other of the apostles except James, the Lord's brother. ²⁰(Now in what I am writing to you, I assure you before God that I am not lying.) ²¹Then I went into the regions of Syria and Cilicia. ²²I was *still* unknown by sight to the churches of Judea which were in Christ; ²³but only, they kept hearing, "He who once persecuted us is now preaching the faith which he once tried to destroy." ²⁴And they were glorifying God because of me.

1:17 Jerusalem…Arabia…Damascus. Rather than immediately travel to Jerusalem to be instructed by the apostles, Paul instead went to Nabatean Arabia, a wilderness desert that stretched east of Damascus down to the Sinai peninsula. After being prepared for ministry by the Lord, he returned to minister in nearby Damascus.

1:18 three years. The approximate time from Paul's conversion to his first journey to Jerusalem. During those years he made a visit to Damascus and resided in Arabia, under the instruction of the Lord. This Jerusalem visit is discussed in Acts 9:26–30. **up to Jerusalem.** Travelers in Israel always speak of going up to Jerusalem because of its higher elevation. **Cephas.** The apostle Peter, who was the personal companion of the Lord and the most powerful spokesman in the early years of the Jerusalem church (Ac 1–12).

DAY 23: What was so shocking to Paul about the Galatians?

That the Galatians were "deserting Him" (1:6). The Greek word was used of military desertion, which was punishable by death. The form of this Greek verb indicates that the Galatian believers were voluntarily deserting grace to pursue the legalism taught by the false teachers. "So quickly." This Greek word can mean either "easily" or "soon" and sometimes both. No doubt both senses characterized the Galatians' response to the false teachers' heretical doctrines. "Called you." This could be translated, "Who called you once and for all" (2Th 2:13–14; 2Ti 1:8–9; 1Pe 1:15) and refers to God's effectual call to salvation. "Grace of Christ." God's free and sovereign act of mercy in granting salvation through the death and resurrection of Christ, totally apart from any human work or merit. "Different gospel." The Judaizers' perversion of the true gospel. They added the requirements, ceremonies, and standards of the Old Covenant as necessary prerequisites to salvation.

"Some who are disturbing you" (v. 7). The Greek word is translated "disturb" and means "to shake back and forth," meaning to agitate or stir up. Here, it refers to the deep emotional disturbance the Galatian believers experienced. "Distort." To turn something into its opposite. By adding law to the gospel of Christ, the false teachers were effectively destroying grace, turning the message of God's undeserved favor toward sinners into a message of earned and merited favor. "The gospel of Christ." The good news of salvation by grace alone through faith alone in Christ alone.

Throughout history God has devoted certain objects, individuals, and groups of people to destruction or to be "accursed" (Jos 6:17, 18; 7:1, 25–26). Here the Judaizers are identified as members of this infamous company. "But even if we, or an angel from heaven" (v. 8). Paul's point is hypothetical, calling on the most unlikely examples for false teaching—himself and holy angels. The Galatians should receive no messenger, regardless of how impeccable his credentials, if his doctrine of salvation differs in the slightest degree from God's truth revealed through Christ and the apostles. "Accursed." The translation of the familiar Greek word *anathama,* which refers to devoting someone to destruction in eternal hell (Ro 9:3; 1Co 12:3; 16:22).

SEPTEMBER 24

Isaiah 39:1–40:31

39 At that time Merodach-baladan son of Baladan, king of Babylon, sent letters and a present to Hezekiah, for he heard that he had been sick and had recovered. ² Hezekiah was pleased, and showed them *all* his treasure house, the silver and the gold and the spices and the precious oil and his whole armory and all that was found in his treasuries. There was nothing in his house nor in all his dominion that Hezekiah did not show them. ³ Then Isaiah the prophet came to King Hezekiah and said to him, "What did these men say, and from where have they come to you?" And Hezekiah said, "They have come to me from a far country, from Babylon." ⁴ He said, "What have they seen in your house?" So Hezekiah answered, "They have seen all that is in my house; there is nothing among my treasuries that I have not shown them."

⁵ Then Isaiah said to Hezekiah, "Hear the word of the LORD of hosts, ⁶ 'Behold, the days are coming when all that is in your house and all that your fathers have laid up in store to this day will be carried to Babylon; nothing will be left,' says the LORD. ⁷ 'And *some* of your sons who will issue from you, whom you will beget, will be taken away, and they will become officials in the palace of the king of Babylon.'" ⁸ Then Hezekiah said to Isaiah, "The word of the LORD which you have spoken is good." For he thought, "For there will be peace and truth in my days."

40 "Comfort, O comfort My people," says your God.
² "Speak kindly to Jerusalem;
And call out to her, that her warfare has ended,
That her iniquity has been removed,
That she has received of the LORD'S hand
Double for all her sins."

40:1–2 Comfort...comfort. The prophecy addressed God's prophets, instructing them to emphasize the theme of comfort to a captive people in a foreign land many miles from their home city of Jerusalem. God has good plans for great blessing to Israel in the future because they are His covenant people, who are never to be permanently cast away (Ro 11:2).

3 A voice is calling,
"Clear the way for the LORD
in the wilderness;
Make smooth in the desert a
highway for our God.
4 "Let every valley be lifted up,
And every mountain and
hill be made low;
And let the rough ground
become a plain,
And the rugged terrain
a broad valley;

40:3–4 Clear the way. The remnant of Israel could remove obstacles from the coming Messiah's path through repentance from their sins. John the Baptist reminded his listeners of this necessity (Mt 3:2), as did Jesus (Mt 4:17; Mk 1:15). These verses reflect the custom of some eastern monarchs to send heralds before them to clear away obstacles, make causeways, straighten crooked roads and valleys, and level hills (45:1–2). John had the task of getting people ready for Messiah's arrival.

5 Then the glory of the LORD
will be revealed,
And all flesh will see *it* together;
For the mouth of the LORD
has spoken."
6 A voice says, "Call out."
Then he answered, "What
shall I call out?"
All flesh is grass, and all its loveliness
is like the flower of the field.
7 The grass withers, the flower fades,
When the breath of the
LORD blows upon it;
Surely the people are grass.
8 The grass withers, the flower fades,
But the word of our God
stands forever.

9 Get yourself up on a high mountain,
O Zion, bearer of good news,
Lift up your voice mightily,
O Jerusalem, bearer of good news;
Lift *it* up, do not fear.
Say to the cities of Judah,
"Here is your God!"
10 Behold, the Lord GOD will
come with might,
With His arm ruling for Him.
Behold, His reward is with Him
And His recompense before Him.

11 Like a shepherd He will tend His flock,
In His arm He will gather the lambs
And carry *them* in His bosom;
He will gently lead the nursing *ewes*.

12 Who has measured the waters
in the hollow of His hand,
And marked off the heavens
by the span,
And calculated the dust of the
earth by the measure,
And weighed the mountains
in a balance
And the hills in a pair of scales?
13 Who has directed the
Spirit of the LORD,
Or as His counselor has
informed Him?
14 With whom did He consult and
who gave Him understanding?
And *who* taught Him in the path of
justice and taught Him knowledge
And informed Him of the
way of understanding?

40:13–14 directed the Spirit of the LORD. Isaiah pointed to the incomparable wisdom of God. Paul alluded to this verse in connection with God's wisdom in dealing with Jews and Gentiles (Ro 11:34) and with God's impartation of wisdom to the spiritual believer (1Co 2:16).

15 Behold, the nations are like
a drop from a bucket,
And are regarded as a speck
of dust on the scales;
Behold, He lifts up the
islands like fine dust.
16 Even Lebanon is not enough to burn,
Nor its beasts enough for
a burnt offering.
17 All the nations are as
nothing before Him,
They are regarded by Him as less
than nothing and meaningless.

18 To whom then will you liken God?
Or what likeness will you
compare with Him?
19 *As for* the idol, a craftsman casts it,
A goldsmith plates it with gold,
And a silversmith *fashions*
chains of silver.
20 He who is too impoverished
for *such* an offering

Selects a tree that does not rot;
He seeks out for himself a
  skillful craftsman
To prepare an idol that will not totter.

²¹ Do you not know? Have
  you not heard?
Has it not been declared to you
  from the beginning?
Have you not understood from
  the foundations of the earth?
²² It is He who sits above the
  circle of the earth,
And its inhabitants are
  like grasshoppers,
Who stretches out the
  heavens like a curtain
And spreads them out like
  a tent to dwell in.
²³ He *it is* who reduces rulers
  to nothing,
Who makes the judges of the
  earth meaningless.
²⁴ Scarcely have they been planted,
Scarcely have they been sown,
Scarcely has their stock taken
  root in the earth,
But He merely blows on
  them, and they wither,
And the storm carries them
  away like stubble.
²⁵ "To whom then will you liken Me
That I would be *his* equal?"
  says the Holy One.
²⁶ Lift up your eyes on high
And see who has created these *stars,*
The One who leads forth
  their host by number,
He calls them all by name;
Because of the greatness of
  His might and the
  strength of *His* power,
Not one *of them* is missing.
²⁷ Why do you say, O Jacob,
  and assert, O Israel,
"My way is hidden from the LORD,
And the justice due me escapes
  the notice of my God"?
²⁸ Do you not know? Have
  you not heard?
The Everlasting God, the LORD, the
  Creator of the ends of the earth
Does not become weary or tired.
His understanding is inscrutable.
²⁹ He gives strength to the weary,
And to *him who* lacks might
  He increases power.

40:28 Does not become weary or tired. God was not too weak to act on their behalf, nor was fatigue an obstacle for the Creator in caring for His people (vv. 29–30). Though even the young and strong become tired and fall, the Ancient of Days never does. **inscrutable.** To the human mind, God's wisdom is not fully comprehensible in how He chooses to fulfill His promises to deliver Israel. Paul saw a further illustration of this truth in God's plan for the final restoration of Israel (Ro 11:33; Is 40:13).

³⁰ Though youths grow weary and tired,
And vigorous young men
  stumble badly,
³¹ Yet those who wait for the LORD
Will gain new strength;
They will mount up *with*
  wings like eagles,
They will run and not get tired,
They will walk and not become weary.

40:31 wait for the LORD. There is a general principle here that patient, praying believers are blessed by God with strength in their trials (2Co 12:8–10). The Lord also expected His people to be patient and await His coming in glory at the end to fulfill the promises of national deliverance, when believing Israel would become stronger than they had ever been.

Psalm 109:21-25

²¹ But You, O GOD, the Lord, deal *kindly*
  with me for Your name's sake;
Because Your lovingkindness
  is good, deliver me;
²² For I am afflicted and needy,
And my heart is wounded within me.
²³ I am passing like a shadow
  when it lengthens;
I am shaken off like the locust.
²⁴ My knees are weak from fasting,
And my flesh has grown
  lean, without fatness.
²⁵ I also have become a
  reproach to them;
When they see me, they
  wag their head.

Proverbs 26:2

² Like a sparrow in *its* flitting, like
  a swallow in *its* flying,

So a curse without cause
does not alight.

Galatians 2:1–21

2 Then after an interval of fourteen years I went up again to Jerusalem with Barnabas, taking Titus along also. ² It was because of a revelation that I went up; and I submitted to them the gospel which I preach among the Gentiles, but *I did so* in private to those who were of reputation, for fear that I might be running, or had run, in vain. ³ But not even Titus, who was with me, though he was a Greek, was compelled to be circumcised. ⁴ But *it was* because of the false brethren secretly brought in, who had sneaked in to spy out our liberty which we have in Christ Jesus, in order to bring us into bondage. ⁵ But we did not yield in subjection to them for even an hour, so that the truth of the gospel would remain with you. ⁶ But from those who were of high reputation (what they were makes no difference to me; God shows no partiality)—well, those who were of reputation contributed nothing to me. ⁷ But on the contrary, seeing that I had been entrusted with the gospel to the uncircumcised, just as Peter *had been* to the circumcised ⁸ (for He who effectually worked for Peter in *his* apostleship to the circumcised effectually worked for me also to the Gentiles), ⁹ and recognizing the grace that had been given to me, James and Cephas and John, who were reputed to be pillars, gave to me and Barnabas the right hand of fellowship, so that we *might go* to the Gentiles and they to the circumcised. ¹⁰ *They* only *asked* us to remember the poor—the very thing I also was eager to do.

¹¹ But when Cephas came to Antioch, I opposed him to his face, because he stood condemned. ¹² For prior to the coming of certain men from James, he used to eat with the Gentiles; but when they came, he *began* to withdraw and hold himself aloof, fearing the party of the circumcision. ¹³ The rest of the Jews joined him in hypocrisy, with the result that even Barnabas was carried away by their hypocrisy. ¹⁴ But when I saw that they were not straightforward about the truth of the gospel, I said to Cephas in the presence of all, "If you, being a Jew, live like the Gentiles and not like the Jews, how *is it that* you compel the Gentiles to live like Jews?

¹⁵ "We *are* Jews by nature and not sinners from among the Gentiles; ¹⁶ nevertheless knowing that a man is not justified by the works of the Law but through faith in Christ Jesus, even we have believed in Christ Jesus, so that we may be justified by faith in Christ and not by the works of the Law; since by the works of the Law no flesh will be justified. ¹⁷ But if, while seeking to be justified in Christ, we ourselves have also been found sinners, is Christ then a minister of sin? May it never be! ¹⁸ For if I rebuild what I have *once* destroyed, I prove myself to be a transgressor. ¹⁹ For through the Law I died to the Law, so that I might live to God. ²⁰ I have been crucified with Christ; and it is no longer I who live, but Christ lives in me; and the *life* which I now live in the flesh I live by faith in the Son of God, who loved me and gave Himself up for me. ²¹ I do not nullify the grace of God, for if righteousness *comes* through the Law, then Christ died needlessly."

2:20 I have been crucified with Christ. When a person trusts in Christ for salvation, he spiritually participates with the Lord in His crucifixion and His victory over sin and death. **no longer I who live, but Christ lives in me.** The believer's old self is dead, having been crucified with Christ (Ro 6:3, 5). The believer's new self has the privilege of the indwelling Christ empowering him and living through him (Ro 8:9–10). **gave Himself up for me.** The manifestation of Christ's love for the believer through His sacrificial death on the cross (Jn 10:17–18; Ro 5:6–8; Eph 5:25–30).

DAY 24: What led Paul to confront Peter with his hypocrisy?

It took place in the first Gentile church, which was at Antioch, where we are told that Peter "stood condemned" (Gal 2:11). Peter had been in Antioch for some time, eating with Gentiles. When Judaizers came, pretending to be sent by James (v. 12), they lied, giving false claims of support from the apostles. Peter had already given up all Mosaic ceremony (Ac 10:9–22); nevertheless, he "began to withdraw." The Greek term refers to strategic military withdrawal. The verb's form may imply that Peter's withdrawal was gradual and deceptive. To eat with the Judaizers and decline invitations to eat with the Gentiles, which he had previously done, meant that Peter was affirming the very dietary restrictions he knew God had abolished (Ac 10:15) and thus striking a blow at the gospel of grace. "Fearing the party of the circumcision"—the true motivation behind Peter's defection. He was afraid of losing popularity with the legalistic, Judaizing segment of people in the church, even though they were self-righteous hypocrites promoting a heretical doctrine.

The Jewish believers in Antioch followed Peter's example and "joined him in hypocrisy" (v. 13). This Greek word refers to an actor who wore a mask to depict a mood or certain character. In the spiritual sense, it refers to someone who masks his true character by pretending to be something he is not (Mt 6:1–6). They were committed to the gospel of grace but pretended to accept Jewish legalism. By withdrawing from the Gentile Christians, Peter and the other Jewish believers were not walking in line, "straightforward," with God's Word (v. 14). Before his gradual withdrawal, Peter regularly had fellowship and ate with the Gentiles, thus modeling the ideal of Christian love and liberty between Jew and Gentile. By his Judaizing mandate, he was declaring theirs was the right way.

Paul's rebuke of Peter in vv. 15–16 serves as one of the most dynamic statements in the New Testament on the absolute and unwavering necessity of the doctrine of justification by grace through faith. Peter's apparent repentance acknowledged Paul's apostolic authority and his own submission to the truth (2Pe 3:15–16).

SEPTEMBER 25

Isaiah 41:1–42:25

41 "Coastlands, listen to Me in silence,
And let the peoples gain
new strength;
Let them come forward,
then let them speak;
Let us come together for judgment.

2 "Who has aroused one from the east
Whom He calls in righteousness
to His feet?
He delivers up nations before him
And subdues kings.
He makes them like dust
with his sword,
As the wind-driven chaff
with his bow.

3 "He pursues them, passing
on in safety,
By a way he had not been
traversing with his feet.

4 "Who has performed and
accomplished *it*,
Calling forth the generations
from the beginning?

41:4 first...last. He existed before history and will exist after it (44:6; 48:12; Rev 1:17; 2:8; 22:13). **I am He.** It is legitimate to translate the two Hebrew words thus represented by "I am" (see also 42:8; 43:10, 13; 46:4), a messianic title appropriated by Jesus frequently as explicit testimony to His deity (e.g., Mk 13:6; 14:62; Lk 21:8; Jn 8:28, 58; 13:19). The title comes originally from the Lord's self-revelation to Moses in Exodus 3:14.

'I, the LORD, am the first, and
with the last. I am He.'"

5 The coastlands have seen
and are afraid;
The ends of the earth tremble;
They have drawn near
and have come.

6 Each one helps his neighbor
And says to his brother, "Be strong!"

7 So the craftsman encourages
the smelter,
And he who smooths *metal*
with the hammer *encourages*
him who beats the anvil,
Saying of the soldering, "It is good";
And he fastens it with nails,
So that it will not totter.

8 "But you, Israel, My servant,
Jacob whom I have chosen,
Descendant of Abraham My friend,

9 You whom I have taken from
the ends of the earth,
And called from its remotest parts
And said to you, 'You are My servant,
I have chosen you and
not rejected you.

10 'Do not fear, for I am with you;
Do not anxiously look about
you, for I am your God.
I will strengthen you, surely
I will help you,
Surely I will uphold you with
My righteous right hand.'

11 "Behold, all those who are
angered at you will be
shamed and dishonored;
Those who contend with you will
be as nothing and will perish.

12 "You will seek those who quarrel
with you, but will not find them,

Those who war with you will be
as nothing and non-existent.
13 "For I am the LORD your God, who
upholds your right hand,
Who says to you, 'Do not
fear, I will help you.'
14 "Do not fear, you worm Jacob,
you men of Israel;
I will help you," declares the
LORD, "and your Redeemer
is the Holy One of Israel.
15 "Behold, I have made you a
new, sharp threshing sledge
with double edges;
You will thresh the mountains
and pulverize *them,*
And will make the hills like chaff.
16 "You will winnow them, and the
wind will carry them away,
And the storm will scatter them;
But you will rejoice in the LORD,
You will glory in the Holy
One of Israel.

17 "The afflicted and needy are seeking
water, but there is none,
And their tongue is parched
with thirst;
I, the LORD, will answer them Myself,
As the God of Israel I will
not forsake them.
18 "I will open rivers on the bare heights
And springs in the midst
of the valleys;
I will make the wilderness
a pool of water
And the dry land fountains of water.
19 "I will put the cedar in the wilderness,
The acacia and the myrtle
and the olive tree;
I will place the juniper in the desert
Together with the box tree
and the cypress,
20 That they may see and recognize,
And consider and gain insight as well,
That the hand of the LORD
has done this,
And the Holy One of Israel
has created it.

21 "Present your case," the LORD says.
"Bring forward your strong
arguments,"
The King of Jacob says.
22 Let them bring forth and declare to
us what is going to take place;
As for the former *events,*
declare what they *were,*

That we may consider them
and know their outcome.
Or announce to us what is coming;
23 Declare the things that are
going to come afterward,
That we may know that you
are gods;
Indeed, do good or evil, that we
may anxiously look about
us and fear together.
24 Behold, you are of no account,
And your work amounts to nothing;
He who chooses you is
an abomination.

25 "I have aroused one from the
north, and he has come;
From the rising of the sun he
will call on My name;
And he will come upon
rulers as *upon* mortar,
Even as the potter treads clay."
26 Who has declared *this* from the
beginning, that we might know?
Or from former times, that we
may say, "*He is* right!"?
Surely there was no one
who declared,
Surely there was no one
who proclaimed,
Surely there was no one who
heard your words.
27 "Formerly *I said* to Zion,
'Behold, here they are.'
And to Jerusalem, 'I will give a
messenger of good news.'
28 "But when I look, there is no one,
And there is no counselor
among them
Who, if I ask, can give an answer.
29 "Behold, all of them are false;
Their works are worthless,
Their molten images are
wind and emptiness.

42 "Behold, My Servant, whom I uphold;
My chosen one *in whom*
My soul delights.
I have put My Spirit upon Him;
He will bring forth justice
to the nations.
2 "He will not cry out or raise *His voice,*
Nor make His voice heard
in the street.
3 "A bruised reed He will not break
And a dimly burning wick He
will not extinguish;
He will faithfully bring forth justice.

4 "He will not be disheartened
  or crushed
Until He has established
  justice in the earth;
And the coastlands will wait
  expectantly for His law."

5 Thus says God the LORD,

Who created the heavens and
  stretched them out,
Who spread out the earth
  and its offspring,
Who gives breath to the people on it
And spirit to those who walk in it,

6 "I am the LORD, I have called
  You in righteousness,
I will also hold You by the hand
  and watch over You,
And I will appoint You as a
  covenant to the people,
As a light to the nations,

7 To open blind eyes,
To bring out prisoners
  from the dungeon
And those who dwell in
  darkness from the prison.

8 "I am the LORD, that is My name;
I will not give My glory to another,
Nor My praise to graven images.

9 "Behold, the former things
  have come to pass,
Now I declare new things;
Before they spring forth I
  proclaim *them* to you."

10 Sing to the LORD a new song,
Sing His praise from the
  end of the earth!
You who go down to the sea,
  and all that is in it.
You islands, and those who
  dwell on them.

11 Let the wilderness and its
  cities lift up *their voices,*
The settlements where
  Kedar inhabits.
Let the inhabitants of Sela
  sing aloud,
Let them shout for joy from the
  tops of the mountains.

12 Let them give glory to the LORD
And declare His praise in
  the coastlands.

13 The LORD will go forth like
  a warrior,
He will arouse *His* zeal
  like a man of war.

He will utter a shout, yes, He
  will raise a war cry.
He will prevail against His enemies.

14 "I have kept silent for a long time,
I have kept still and restrained Myself.
Now like a woman in
  labor I will groan,
I will both gasp and pant.

15 "I will lay waste the
  mountains and hills
And wither all their vegetation;
I will make the rivers into coastlands
And dry up the ponds.

16 "I will lead the blind by a way
  they do not know,
In paths they do not know
  I will guide them.
I will make darkness into
  light before them
And rugged places into plains.
These are the things I will do,
And I will not leave them undone."

17 They will be turned back *and*
  be utterly put to shame,
Who trust in idols,
Who say to molten images,
"You are our gods."

18 Hear, you deaf!
And look, you blind, that you may see.

19 Who is blind but My servant,
Or so deaf as My messenger
  whom I send?
Who is so blind as he that
  is at peace *with Me,*
Or so blind as the servant
  of the LORD?

20 You have seen many things, but
  you do not observe *them;*
Your ears are open, but none hears.

21 The LORD was pleased for His
  righteousness' sake
To make the law great and glorious.

22 But this is a people plundered
  and despoiled;
All of them are trapped in caves,
Or are hidden away in prisons;
They have become a prey with
  none to deliver *them,*
And a spoil, with none to
  say, "Give *them* back!"

23 Who among you will give ear to this?
Who will give heed and
  listen hereafter?

24 Who gave Jacob up for spoil,
  and Israel to plunderers?

Was it not the LORD, against
whom we have sinned,
And in whose ways they were
not willing to walk,
And whose law they did not obey?
²⁵ So He poured out on him
the heat of His anger
And the fierceness of battle;
And it set him aflame all around,
Yet he did not recognize *it;*
And it burned him, but he
paid no attention.

Psalm 109:26–31

²⁶ Help me, O LORD my God;
Save me according to Your
lovingkindness.
²⁷ And let them know that
this is Your hand;
You, LORD, have done it.
²⁸ Let them curse, but You bless;
When they arise, they
shall be ashamed,
But Your servant shall be glad.
²⁹ Let my accusers be clothed
with dishonor,
And let them cover themselves with
their own shame as with a robe.

³⁰ With my mouth I will give thanks
abundantly to the LORD;
And in the midst of many
I will praise Him.
³¹ For He stands at the right
hand of the needy,
To save him from those
who judge his soul.

Proverbs 26:3–4

³ A whip is for the horse, a
bridle for the donkey,
And a rod for the back of fools.
⁴ Do not answer a fool
according to his folly,
Or you will also be like him.

Galatians 3:1–29

3 You foolish Galatians, who has bewitched you, before whose eyes Jesus Christ was publicly portrayed *as* crucified? ²This is the only thing I want to find out from you: did you receive the Spirit by the works of the Law, or by hearing with faith? ³Are you so foolish? Having begun by the Spirit, are you now being perfected by the flesh? ⁴Did you suffer so many things in vain—if indeed it was in vain? ⁵So then, does He who provides you with the Spirit and works miracles among

3:1 foolish. This refers not to lack of intelligence, but to lack of obedience (Lk 24:25; 1Ti 6:9; Titus 3:3). Paul expressed his shock, surprise, and outrage at the Galatians' defection. **who.** The Judaizers, the Jewish false teachers who were plaguing the Galatian churches. **bewitched.** Charmed or misled by flattery and false promises. The term suggests an appeal to the emotions by the Judaizers. **publicly portrayed.** The Greek word describes the posting of official notices in public places. Paul's preaching had publicly displayed the true gospel of Jesus Christ before the Galatians. **crucified.** The crucifixion of Christ was a onetime historical fact with continuing results into eternity. Christ's sacrificial death provides eternal payment for believers' sins (Heb 7:25) and does not need to be supplemented by any human works.

3:2 did you receive the Spirit...? The answer to Paul's rhetorical question is obvious. The Galatians had received the Spirit when they were saved (Ro 8:9; 1Co 12:13; 1Jn 3:24; 4:13), not through keeping the law, but through saving faith granted when hearing the gospel (Ro 10:17). The hearing *of* faith is actually hearing *with* faith. Paul appealed to the Galatians' own salvation to refute the Judaizers' false teaching that keeping the law is necessary for salvation.

3:3 Are you so foolish? Incredulous at how easily the Galatians had been duped, Paul asked a second rhetorical question, again rebuking them for their foolishness. **begun by the Spirit...by the flesh.** The notion that sinful, weak, fallen human nature could improve on the saving work of the Holy Spirit was ludicrous to Paul.

you, do it by the works of the Law, or by hearing with faith?
⁶Even so Abraham BELIEVED GOD, AND IT WAS RECKONED TO HIM AS RIGHTEOUSNESS. ⁷Therefore, be sure that it is those who are of faith who are sons of Abraham. ⁸The Scripture, foreseeing that God would justify the Gentiles by faith, preached the gospel beforehand to Abraham, *saying,* "ALL THE NATIONS WILL BE BLESSED IN YOU." ⁹So then those who are of faith are blessed with Abraham, the believer.
¹⁰For as many as are of the works of the Law are under a curse; for it is written, "CURSED IS EVERYONE WHO DOES NOT ABIDE BY ALL THINGS WRITTEN IN THE BOOK OF THE LAW, TO PERFORM THEM." ¹¹Now that no one is

justified by the Law before God is evident; for, "THE RIGHTEOUS MAN SHALL LIVE BY FAITH." [12] However, the Law is not of faith; on the contrary, "HE WHO PRACTICES THEM SHALL LIVE BY THEM." [13] Christ redeemed us from the curse of the Law, having become a curse for us— for it is written, "CURSED IS EVERYONE WHO HANGS ON A TREE"— [14] in order that in Christ Jesus the blessing of Abraham might come to the Gentiles, so that we would receive the promise of the Spirit through faith.

[15] Brethren, I speak in terms of human relations: even though it is *only* a man's covenant, yet when it has been ratified, no one sets it aside or adds conditions to it. [16] Now the promises were spoken to Abraham and to his seed. He does not say, "And to seeds," as *referring* to many, but *rather* to one, "And to your seed," that is, Christ. [17] What I am saying is this: the Law, which came four hundred and thirty years later, does not invalidate a covenant previously ratified by God, so as to nullify the promise. [18] For if the inheritance is based on law, it is no longer based on a promise; but God has granted it to Abraham by means of a promise.

[19] Why the Law then? It was added because of transgressions, having been ordained through angels by the agency of a mediator, until the seed would come to whom the promise had been made. [20] Now a mediator is not for one *party only;* whereas God is *only* one. [21] Is the Law then contrary to the promises of God? May it never be! For if a law had been given which was able to impart life, then righteousness would indeed have been based on law. [22] But the Scripture has shut up everyone under sin, so that the promise by faith in Jesus Christ might be given to those who believe.

[23] But before faith came, we were kept in custody under the law, being shut up to the faith which was later to be revealed. [24] Therefore the Law has become our tutor *to lead us* to Christ, so that we may be justified by faith. [25] But now that faith has come, we are no longer under a tutor. [26] For you are all sons of God through faith in Christ Jesus. [27] For all of you who were baptized into Christ have clothed yourselves with Christ. [28] There is neither Jew nor Greek, there is neither slave nor free man, there is neither male nor female; for you are all one in Christ Jesus. [29] And if you belong to Christ, then you are Abraham's descendants, heirs according to promise.

3:28 you are all one in Christ Jesus. All those who are one with Jesus Christ are one with one another. This verse does not deny that God has designed racial, social, and sexual distinctions among Christians, but it affirms that those do not imply spiritual inequality before God. Nor is this spiritual equality incompatible with the God-ordained roles of headship and submission in the church, society, and at home. Jesus Christ, though fully equal with the Father, assumed a submissive role during His incarnation (Php 2:5–8).

DAY 25: Who is the "Servant" of Isaiah 42?

Others deserve the title "my servant" (v. 1), but this personal Servant of the Lord is the Messiah, who was chosen (Lk 9:35; 1Pe 1:20; Rev 13:8) because the Lord delights in Him (Mt 3:17; 17:5) and puts His Spirit upon Him (11:2; 59:21; Mt 3:16; Lk 4:18). "He will bring forth justice to the nations." At His Second Coming, Christ will rule over a kingdom in which justice prevails throughout the world. The millennial kingdom is not for Israel alone, though the Messiah will reign on the throne of David in Jerusalem, and Israel will be the glorious people. In fact, all the nations of the world will experience the righteousness and justice of the Messiah King.

"He will not cry out...in the street" (v. 2). The quiet and submissive demeanor of Christ at His first advent fulfilled this prophecy (Mt 11:28–30; 1Pe 2:23). "A bruised reed...a dimly burning wick" (v. 3). The Servant will bring comfort and encouragement to the weak and oppressed (Mt 12:18–20). "Until He has established justice in the earth" (v. 4). Isaiah looked beyond the First Coming of Christ to His Second Coming. Jesus fulfilled vv. 1–3 at His First Coming and will fulfill vv. 1b, 4 at His Second Coming, when He rules the earth in perfect justice with "a rod of iron" (Ps 2:8–9; Rev 2:27).

"I am the LORD...will appoint You as a covenant to the people" (v. 6). The Servant is a covenant in that He personifies and provides the blessings of salvation to God's people Israel. He is the Mediator of a better covenant than the one with Moses, i.e., the New Covenant (Jer 31:31–34; Heb 8:6, 10–12). "As a light to the nations." Simeon saw the beginning of this fulfillment at Christ's First Coming (Lk 2:32). He came as the Messiah of Israel, yet the Savior of the world, who revealed Himself to a non-Jewish immoral woman by the well in Samaria (Jn 4:25–26) and commanded His followers to preach the gospel of salvation to everyone in the world (Mt 28:19–20).

Certainly the church, made up mostly of Gentiles grafted into the trunk of blessing (Ro 9:24–30; 11:11–24), fulfills this promise, as does the future kingdom on earth when the Servant will use Israel to shine and enlighten all the nations of the earth (49:6; 19:24).

SEPTEMBER 26

Isaiah 43:1–44:28

43 But now, thus says the LORD,
your Creator, O Jacob,
And He who formed you, O Israel,
"Do not fear, for I have redeemed you;
I have called you by name;
you are Mine!

2 "When you pass through the
waters, I will be with you;
And through the rivers, they
will not overflow you.
When you walk through the fire,
you will not be scorched,
Nor will the flame burn you.

3 "For I am the LORD your God,
The Holy One of Israel, your Savior;
I have given Egypt as your ransom,
Cush and Seba in your place.

4 "Since you are precious in My sight,
Since you are honored and I love you,
I will give other men in your
place and other peoples in
exchange for your life.

5 "Do not fear, for I am with you;
I will bring your offspring
from the east,
And gather you from the west.

6 "I will say to the north, 'Give
them up!'
And to the south, 'Do not
hold them back.'
Bring My sons from afar
And My daughters from the
ends of the earth,

7 Everyone who is called by My name,
And whom I have created
for My glory,
Whom I have formed, even
whom I have made."

8 Bring out the people who are blind,
even though they have eyes,
And the deaf, even though
they have ears.

9 All the nations have
gathered together
So that the peoples may
be assembled.
Who among them can declare this
And proclaim to us the former things?

Let them present their witnesses
that they may be justified,
Or let them hear and say, "It is true."

10 "You are My witnesses,"
declares the LORD,
"And My servant whom I have chosen,
So that you may know and believe Me
And understand that I am He.
Before Me there was no God formed,
And there will be none after Me.

11 "I, even I, am the LORD,
And there is no savior besides Me.

12 "It is I who have declared and
saved and proclaimed,
And there was no strange
god among you;
So you are My witnesses,"
declares the LORD,
"And I am God.

13 "Even from eternity I am He,
And there is none who can
deliver out of My hand;
I act and who can reverse it?"

14 Thus says the LORD your Redeemer, the
Holy One of Israel,

"For your sake I have sent to
Babylon,
And will bring them all
down as fugitives,
Even the Chaldeans, into the
ships in which they rejoice.

15 "I am the LORD, your Holy One,
The Creator of Israel, your King."

16 Thus says the LORD,

Who makes a way through the sea
And a path through the
mighty waters,

17 Who brings forth the chariot
and the horse,
The army and the mighty man
(They will lie down together
and not rise again;
They have been quenched and
extinguished like a wick):

18 "Do not call to mind the former things,
Or ponder things of the past.

19 "Behold, I will do something new,
Now it will spring forth;
Will you not be aware of it?

I will even make a roadway
   in the wilderness,
Rivers in the desert.
²⁰ "The beasts of the field will glorify Me,
   The jackals and the ostriches,
Because I have given waters
   in the wilderness
And rivers in the desert,
   To give drink to My chosen people.
²¹ "The people whom I formed for Myself
   Will declare My praise.

²² "Yet you have not called
   on Me, O Jacob;
But you have become weary
   of Me, O Israel.
²³ "You have not brought to Me the
   sheep of your burnt offerings,
Nor have you honored Me
   with your sacrifices.
I have not burdened you
   with offerings,
Nor wearied you with incense.
²⁴ "You have bought Me not sweet
   cane with money,
Nor have you filled Me with
   the fat of your sacrifices;
Rather you have burdened
   Me with your sins,
You have wearied Me with
   your iniquities.

²⁵ "I, even I, am the one who wipes
   out your transgressions
   for My own sake,
And I will not remember your sins.

43:25 I, even I…will not remember your sins.
This verse is probably the high point of grace in
the Old Testament. In spite of Israel's utter unworthiness, the Lord in His grace has devised
a way that He can forgive their sins and grant
righteousness, without compromising His holiness. This He would accomplish through the
work of His Servant (53:6). In spite of her failures, Israel will always be God's chosen people.

---

²⁶ "Put Me in remembrance, let us
   argue our case together;
State your *cause,* that you
   may be proved right.
²⁷ "Your first forefather sinned,
   And your spokesmen have
   transgressed against Me.

²⁸ "So I will pollute the princes
   of the sanctuary,
And I will consign Jacob to the
   ban and Israel to revilement.

44 "But now listen, O Jacob, My servant,
   And Israel, whom I have chosen:
² Thus says the LORD who made you
   And formed you from the
   womb, who will help you,
'Do not fear, O Jacob My servant;
   And you Jeshurun whom
   I have chosen.
³ 'For I will pour out water
   on the thirsty *land*
And streams on the dry ground;
I will pour out My Spirit
   on your offspring
And My blessing on your
   descendants;
⁴ And they will spring up
   among the grass
Like poplars by streams of water.'
⁵ "This one will say, 'I am the LORD'S';
   And that one will call on
   the name of Jacob;
And another will write *on* his
   hand, 'Belonging to the LORD,'
And will name Israel's
   name with honor.

⁶ "Thus says the LORD, the King of Israel
and his Redeemer, the LORD of hosts:

'I am the first and I am the last,
   And there is no God besides Me.
⁷ 'Who is like Me? Let him
   proclaim and declare it;
Yes, let him recount it to Me in order,
From the time that I established
   the ancient nation.
And let them declare to them
   the things that are coming
And the events that are
   going to take place.
⁸ 'Do not tremble and do not be afraid;
Have I not long since announced
   it to you and declared *it?*
And you are My witnesses.
Is there any God besides Me,
Or is there any *other* Rock?
I know of none.'"

⁹ Those who fashion a graven image are all
of them futile, and their precious things are
of no profit; even their own witnesses fail to
see or know, so that they will be put to shame.
¹⁰ Who has fashioned a god or cast an idol to

no profit? [11] Behold, all his companions will be put to shame, for the craftsmen themselves are mere men. Let them all assemble themselves, let them stand up, let them tremble, let them together be put to shame.

[12] The man shapes iron into a cutting tool and does his work over the coals, fashioning it with hammers and working it with his strong arm. He also gets hungry and his strength fails; he drinks no water and becomes weary. [13] *Another* shapes wood, he extends a measuring line; he outlines it with red chalk. He works it with planes and outlines it with a compass, and makes it like the form of a man, like the beauty of man, so that it may sit in a house. [14] Surely he cuts cedars for himself, and takes a cypress or an oak and raises *it* for himself among the trees of the forest. He plants a fir, and the rain makes it grow. [15] Then it becomes *something* for a man to burn, so he takes one of them and warms himself; he also makes a fire to bake bread. He also makes a god and worships it; he makes it a graven image and falls down before it. [16] Half of it he burns in the fire; over *this* half he eats meat as he roasts a roast and is satisfied. He also warms himself and says, "Aha! I am warm, I have seen the fire." [17] But the rest of it he makes into a god, his graven image. He falls down before it and worships; he also prays to it and says, "Deliver me, for you are my god."

[18] They do not know, nor do they understand, for He has smeared over their eyes so that they cannot see and their hearts so that they cannot comprehend. [19] No one recalls, nor is there knowledge or understanding to say, "I have burned half of it in the fire and also have baked bread over its coals. I roast meat and eat *it*. Then I make the rest of it into an abomination, I fall down before a block of wood!" [20] He feeds on ashes; a deceived heart has turned him aside. And he cannot deliver himself, nor say, "Is there not a lie in my right hand?"

[21] "Remember these things, O Jacob,
     And Israel, for you are My servant;
I have formed you, you
     are My servant,
O Israel, you will not be
     forgotten by Me.
[22] "I have wiped out your transgressions
     like a thick cloud
And your sins like a heavy mist.
Return to Me, for I have
     redeemed you."
[23] Shout for joy, O heavens, for
     the LORD has done *it!*

Shout joyfully, you lower
     parts of the earth;
Break forth into a shout of
     joy, you mountains,
O forest, and every tree in it;
For the LORD has redeemed Jacob
And in Israel He shows
     forth His glory.

[24] Thus says the LORD, your Redeemer, and the one who formed you from the womb,

"I, the LORD, am the maker
     of all things,
Stretching out the heavens by Myself
And spreading out the earth all alone,
[25] Causing the omens of boasters to fail,
     Making fools out of diviners,
     Causing wise men to draw back
     And turning their knowledge
          into foolishness,
[26] Confirming the word of His servant
     And performing the purpose
          of His messengers.
     It is I who says of Jerusalem,
          'She shall be inhabited!'
     And of the cities of Judah,
          'They shall be built,'
     And I will raise up her ruins *again.*
[27] "*It is I* who says to the depth of
          the sea, 'Be dried up!'
     And I will make your rivers dry,
[28] "*It is I* who says of Cyrus,
          '*He is* My shepherd!
     And he will perform all My desire.'
     And he declares of Jerusalem,
          'She will be built,'
     And of the temple, 'Your
          foundation will be laid.'"

44:28 Cyrus...My shepherd. The prophecy—given a century and a half before Cyrus lived and became king of Persia—predicted God's use of the Persian king to gather the faithful remnant of Israel back to the land. In this role, Cyrus prefigured the Lord's Servant, who will shepherd the sheep of Israel in their final re-gathering (Mic 5:4). The title "shepherd" applied to kings as leaders of God's people (2Sa 5:2; Jer 3:15). In Acts 13:22, Paul compares David to the standard of Cyrus' obedience. **Jerusalem...the temple.** In 538 B.C. Cyrus decreed the rebuilding of the temple (Ezr 1:1-2; 6:3), thus fulfilling Isaiah's prophecy. The returning Jews completed the work in 516 B.C. (Ezr 6:15).

Psalm 110:1–7

A Psalm of David.

The LORD says to my Lord:
"Sit at My right hand
  Until I make Your enemies a
    footstool for Your feet."
2 The LORD will stretch forth Your
    strong scepter from Zion, *saying,*
  "Rule in the midst of Your enemies."
3 Your people will volunteer freely
    in the day of Your power;
  In holy array, from the
    womb of the dawn,
  Your youth are to You *as* the dew.

4 The LORD has sworn and will
    not change His mind,
  "You are a priest forever
  According to the order of Melchizedek."
5 The Lord is at Your right hand;
  He will shatter kings in the
    day of His wrath.
6 He will judge among the nations,
  He will fill *them* with corpses,
  He will shatter the chief men
    over a broad country.
7 He will drink from the brook
    by the wayside;
  Therefore He will lift up *His* head.

Proverbs 26:5–9

5 Answer a fool as his folly *deserves,*
  That he not be wise in his own eyes.
6 He cuts off *his own* feet *and*
    drinks violence
  Who sends a message by
    the hand of a fool.
7 *Like* the legs *which* are
    useless to the lame,
  So is a proverb in the mouth of fools.
8 Like one who binds a stone in a sling,
  So is he who gives honor to a fool.
9 *Like* a thorn *which* falls into
    the hand of a drunkard,
  So is a proverb in the mouth of fools.

Galatians 4:1–31

4 Now I say, as long as the heir is a child, he does not differ at all from a slave although he is owner of everything, ² but he is under guardians and managers until the date set by the father. ³ So also we, while we were children, were held in bondage under the elemental things of the world. ⁴ But when the fullness of the time came, God sent forth His Son, born of a woman, born under the Law, ⁵ so that He might redeem those who were under the Law, that we might receive

4:4 the fullness of the time. In God's timetable, when the exact religious, cultural, and political conditions demanded by His perfect plan were in place, Jesus came into the world. **God sent forth His Son.** As a father set the time for the ceremony of his son becoming of age and being released from the guardians, managers, and tutors, so God sent His Son at the precise moment to bring all who believe out from under bondage to the law—a truth Jesus repeatedly affirmed (Jn 5:30, 36–37; 6:39, 44, 57; 8:16, 18, 42; 12:49; 17:21, 25; 20:21). That the Father sent Jesus into the world teaches His preexistence as the eternal second member of the Trinity. **born of a woman.** This emphasizes Jesus' full humanity, not merely His virgin birth (Is 7:14; Mt 1:20–25). Jesus had to be fully God for His sacrifice to be of the infinite worth needed to atone for sin. But, He also had to be fully man so He could take upon Himself the penalty of sin as the substitute for man. See Luke 1:32, 35; John 1:1, 14, 18. **under the Law.** Like all men, Jesus was obligated to obey God's law. Unlike anyone else, however, He perfectly obeyed that law (Jn 8:46; 2Co 5:21; Heb 4:15; 7:26; 1Pe 2:22; 1Jn 3:5). His sinlessness made Him the unblemished sacrifice for sins, who perfectly obeyed God in everything. That perfect righteousness is what is imputed to those who believe in Him.

---

the adoption as sons. ⁶ Because you are sons, God has sent forth the Spirit of His Son into our hearts, crying, "Abba! Father!" ⁷ Therefore you are no longer a slave, but a son; and if a son, then an heir through God.

⁸ However at that time, when you did not know God, you were slaves to those which by nature are no gods. ⁹ But now that you have come to know God, or rather to be known by God, how is it that you turn back again to the weak and worthless elemental things, to which you desire to be enslaved all over again? ¹⁰ You observe days and months and

4:5 those...under the Law. Guilty sinners who are under the law's demands and its curses and in need of a Savior. **the adoption as sons.** "Adoption" is the act of bringing someone who is the offspring of another into one's own family. Since unregenerate people are by nature children of the devil, the only way they can become God's children is by spiritual adoption (Ro 8:15, 23; Eph 1:5).

seasons and years. ¹¹ I fear for you, that perhaps I have labored over you in vain.

¹² I beg of you, brethren, become as I *am*, for I also *have become* as you *are*. You have done me no wrong; ¹³ but you know that it was because of a bodily illness that I preached the gospel to you the first time; ¹⁴ and that which was a trial to you in my bodily condition you did not despise or loathe, but you received me as an angel of God, as Christ Jesus *Himself*. ¹⁵ Where then is that sense of blessing you had? For I bear you witness that, if possible, you would have plucked out your eyes and given them to me. ¹⁶ So have I become your enemy by telling you the truth? ¹⁷ They eagerly seek you, not commendably, but they wish to shut you out so that you will seek them. ¹⁸ But it is good always to be eagerly sought in a commendable manner, and not only when I am present with you. ¹⁹ My children, with whom I am again in labor until Christ is formed in you— ²⁰ but I could wish to be present with you now and to change my tone, for I am perplexed about you.

²¹ Tell me, you who want to be under law, do you not listen to the law? ²² For it is written that Abraham had two sons, one by the bondwoman and one by the free woman. ²³ But the son by the bondwoman was born according to the flesh, and the son by the free woman through the promise. ²⁴ This is allegorically speaking, for these *women* are two covenants: one *proceeding* from Mount Sinai bearing children who are to be slaves; she is Hagar. ²⁵ Now this Hagar is Mount Sinai in Arabia and corresponds to the present Jerusalem, for she is in slavery with her children. ²⁶ But the Jerusalem above is free; she is our mother. ²⁷ For it is written,

> "REJOICE, BARREN WOMAN
>   WHO DOES NOT BEAR;
> BREAK FORTH AND SHOUT, YOU
>   WHO ARE NOT IN LABOR;
> FOR MORE NUMEROUS ARE THE
>   CHILDREN OF THE DESOLATE
> THAN OF THE ONE WHO
>   HAS A HUSBAND."

²⁸ And you brethren, like Isaac, are children of promise. ²⁹ But as at that time he who was born according to the flesh persecuted him *who was born* according to the Spirit, so it is now also. ³⁰ But what does the Scripture say?

> "CAST OUT THE BONDWOMAN
>   AND HER SON,
> FOR THE SON OF THE BONDWOMAN
>   SHALL NOT BE AN HEIR WITH
>   THE SON OF THE FREE WOMAN."

³¹ So then, brethren, we are not children of a bondwoman, but of the free woman.

DAY 26: How does Psalm 110 exalt Jesus Christ?

This psalm contains one of the most exalted prophetic portions of Scripture presenting Jesus Christ as both a holy king and a royal high priest—something that no human monarch of Israel ever experienced. It, along with Psalm 118, is by far the most quoted psalm in the New Testament (Mt 22:44; 26:64; Mk 12:36; 14:62; Lk 20:42–43; 22:69; Ac 2:34–35; Heb 1:13; 5:6; 7:17, 21; 10:13). While portraying the perfect king, the perfect high priest, and the perfect government, Psalm 110 declares Christ's current role in heaven as the resurrected Savior (110:1) and His future role on earth as the reigning Monarch (110:2–7). This psalm is decidedly messianic and millennial in content. Jesus Christ (Mt 22:43–44) verifies the Davidic authorship.

"The LORD said to my Lord" (v. 1). Refers to the divine/human King of Israel—the Lord Jesus Christ. Christ's humanity descended from David, which is demanded by the Davidic promise of 2 Samuel 7:12. Using this passage, Christ also declared His deity in the Gospels (Mt 22:44; Mk 12:36; Lk 20:42–43) by arguing that only God could have been lord to King David. "My right hand." God the Father invited God the Son in His ascension to sit at the place of honor in the heavenly throne room (Acts 2:22–36; Heb 10:10–12). "Your enemies a footstool." Footstool was an ancient Near Eastern picture of absolute victory portraying the idea that one's enemy was now underfoot (Pss 8:6–7; 47:3; Is 66:1; 1Co 15:27).

"You are a priest" (v. 4). The first time in the history of Israel when a king simultaneously served as high priest. Christ (a.k.a. "Branch," Is 4:2; Jer 23:5, 6; Zec 3:8; 6:12–13) will build the temple at which the world will worship God (2Sa 7:13; Is 2:2–4; Eze 40–48). "Forever." Christ represents the final and foremost high priest in the history of Israel. "The order of Melchizedek." This high priest could not be of Aaron's lineage in that he would not be eternal, not be of Judah, not be a king, and not be of the New Covenant (Jer 31:31–33; Heb 8–9). Melchizedek, which means "king of righteousness," served as the human priest/king of Salem in Genesis 14:17-20 and provides a picture of the order of Christ's priesthood (Heb 5:6; 7:17, 21).

SEPTEMBER 27

Isaiah 45:1–46:13

45 Thus says the LORD to
Cyrus His anointed,
Whom I have taken by the right hand,
To subdue nations before him
And to loose the loins of kings;
To open doors before him so

45:1 His anointed. This word is the one translated from the Hebrew by the transliteration 52:15 "Messiah." It is the word used for the messianic Redeemer King in Psalm 2:2 and Daniel 9:25–26, but here refers to Cyrus, as the king set apart by God's providence for divine purposes. Though not a worshiper of the Lord, the Persian monarch played an unusual role as Israel's shepherd (44:28) and God's anointed judge on nations.

that gates will not be shut:
2 "I will go before you and make
the rough places smooth;
I will shatter the doors of bronze
and cut through their iron bars.
3 "I will give you the treasures
of darkness
And hidden wealth of secret
places,
So that you may know that it is I,
The LORD, the God of Israel, who
calls you by your name.
4 "For the sake of Jacob My servant,
And Israel My chosen *one*,
I have also called you by your name;
I have given you a title of honor
Though you have not known Me.
5 "I am the LORD, and there is
no other;
Besides Me there is no God.
I will gird you, though you
have not known Me;
6 That men may know from the
rising to the setting of the sun
That there is no one besides Me.
I am the LORD, and there is
no other,
7 The One forming light and
creating darkness,
Causing well-being and
creating calamity;
I am the LORD who does all these.

8 "Drip down, O heavens, from above,
And let the clouds pour
down righteousness;
Let the earth open up and
salvation bear fruit,
And righteousness spring up with it.
I, the LORD, have created it.

9 "Woe to *the one* who quarrels
with his Maker—
An earthenware vessel among
the vessels of earth!
Will the clay say to the potter,
'What are you doing?'
Or the thing you are making
say, 'He has no hands'?
10 "Woe to him who says to a father,
'What are you begetting?'
Or to a woman, 'To what are
you giving birth?' "

11 Thus says the LORD, the Holy One of Israel, and his Maker:

"Ask Me about the things to
come concerning My sons,
And you shall commit to Me
the work of My hands.
12 "It is I who made the earth, and
created man upon it.
I stretched out the heavens
with My hands
And I ordained all their host.
13 "I have aroused him in righteousness
And I will make all his ways
smooth;
He will build My city and will
let My exiles go free,
Without any payment or reward,"
says the LORD of hosts.

14 Thus says the LORD,

"The products of Egypt and the
merchandise of Cush
And the Sabeans, men of stature,
Will come over to you and
will be yours;
They will walk behind you, they
will come over in chains
And will bow down to you;
They will make supplication to you:
'Surely, God is with you, and
there is none else,
No other God.' "
15 Truly, You are a God who
hides Himself,
O God of Israel, Savior!

16 They will be put to shame and
    even humiliated, all of them;
    The manufacturers of idols will go
    away together in humiliation.
17 Israel has been saved by the LORD
    With an everlasting salvation;
    You will not be put to shame
    or humiliated
    To all eternity.

18 For thus says the LORD, who created the heavens (He is the God who formed the earth and made it, He established it *and* did not create it a waste place, *but* formed it to be inhabited),

"I am the LORD, and there is none else.
19 "I have not spoken in secret,
    In some dark land;
    I did not say to the offspring of Jacob,
    'Seek Me in a waste place';
    I, the LORD, speak righteousness,
    Declaring things that are upright.

20 "Gather yourselves and come;
    Draw near together, you
        fugitives of the nations;
    They have no knowledge,
    Who carry about their wooden idol
    And pray to a god who cannot save.
21 "Declare and set forth *your case;*
    Indeed, let them consult together.
    Who has announced this
        from of old?
    Who has long since declared it?
    Is it not I, the LORD?
    And there is no other God besides Me,
    A righteous God and a Savior;
    There is none except Me.
22 "Turn to Me and be saved, all
        the ends of the earth;
    For I am God, and there is no other.

45:21 Who has announced this from of old? The Lord's case to prove He is the only true God is unanswerable; only He foretold the captivity of Judah and the deliverance from that captivity, as well as other future events that happened just as He had predicted. **there is no other...There is none.** The Lord restated the truth expressed by Moses in Deuteronomy 4:35. The scribe who asked Jesus about the greatest commandment cited this same principle in agreeing with Jesus' answer to his question (Mk 12:32).

23 "I have sworn by Myself,
    The word has gone forth from
        My mouth in righteousness
    And will not turn back,
    That to Me every knee will bow, every
    tongue will swear *allegiance.*

45:23 every knee will bow. In the kingdom age, all nations will worship the one true God of Israel. A further meaning, justified by the NT, applies this verse to believers' accountability to God when He evaluates their works (Ro 14:11). In assigning the words another meaning, Paul relates the words to the coming universal acknowledgment that "Jesus Christ is Lord, to the glory of God the Father" (Php 2:10–11).

24 "They will say of Me, 'Only in the LORD
        are righteousness and strength.'
    Men will come to Him,
    And all who were angry at Him
    will be put to shame.
25 "In the LORD all the offspring of Israel
    Will be justified and will glory."

46 Bel has bowed down,
    Nebo stoops over;
    Their images are *consigned* to
        the beasts and the cattle.
    The things that you carry
        are burdensome,
    A load for the weary *beast.*
2 They stooped over, they have
        bowed down together;
    They could not rescue the burden,
    But have themselves gone
        into captivity.

3 "Listen to Me, O house of Jacob,
    And all the remnant of the
        house of Israel,
    You who have been borne
        by Me from birth
    And have been carried
        from the womb;
4 Even to *your* old age I
        will be the same,
    And even to *your* graying
        years I will bear *you!*
    I have done *it,* and I will carry *you;*
    And I will bear *you* and I
        will deliver *you.*

5 "To whom would you liken Me
    And make Me equal and compare Me,

That we would be alike?
6 "Those who lavish gold from the purse
And weigh silver on the scale
Hire a goldsmith, and he
makes it *into* a god;
They bow down, indeed
they worship it.
7 "They lift it upon the shoulder
and carry it;
They set it in its place and
it stands *there*.
It does not move from its place.
Though one may cry to it,
it cannot answer;
It cannot deliver him
from his distress.

8 "Remember this, and be assured;
Recall it to mind, you transgressors.
9 "Remember the former
things long past,
For I am God, and there is no other;
I am God, and there is no one like Me,
10 Declaring the end from
the beginning,
And from ancient times things
which have not been done,
Saying, 'My purpose will
be established,
And I will accomplish all
My good pleasure';
11 Calling a bird of prey from the east,
The man of My purpose
from a far country.
Truly I have spoken; truly I
will bring it to pass.
I have planned *it, surely* I will do it.

12 "Listen to Me, you stubborn-minded,
Who are far from righteousness.
13 "I bring near My righteousness,
it is not far off;
And My salvation will not delay.
And I will grant salvation in Zion,
And My glory for Israel.

Psalm 111:1–6

Praise the LORD!
I will give thanks to the LORD
with all *my* heart,
In the company of the upright
and in the assembly.
2 Great are the works of the LORD;
They are studied by all who
delight in them.
3 Splendid and majestic is His work,
And His righteousness
endures forever.

4 He has made His wonders
to be remembered;
The LORD is gracious and
compassionate.
5 He has given food to those
who fear Him;
He will remember His
covenant forever.
6 He has made known to His people
the power of His works,
In giving them the heritage
of the nations.

Proverbs 26:10

10 *Like* an archer who wounds everyone,
So is he who hires a fool or who
hires those who pass by.

Galatians 5:1–26

5 It was for freedom that Christ set us free;
therefore keep standing firm and do not
be subject again to a yoke of slavery.

2 Behold I, Paul, say to you that if you receive
circumcision, Christ will be of no benefit to
you. 3 And I testify again to every man who receives circumcision, that he is under obligation
to keep the whole Law. 4 You have been severed
from Christ, you who are seeking to be justified
by law; you have fallen from grace. 5 For we
through the Spirit, by faith, are waiting for the
hope of righteousness. 6 For in Christ Jesus neither circumcision nor uncircumcision means
anything, but faith working through love.

7 You were running well; who hindered you
from obeying the truth? 8 This persuasion *did*
not *come* from Him who calls you. 9 A little
leaven leavens the whole lump *of dough.* 10 I

5:1 free. Deliverance from the curse that the
law pronounces on the sinner who has been
striving unsuccessfully to achieve his own righteousness (3:13, 22–26; 4:1–7), but who has now
embraced Christ and the salvation granted to
him by grace. **keep standing firm.** Stay where
you are, Paul asserts, because of the benefit
of being free from law and the flesh as a way
of salvation and the fullness of blessing by
grace. **subject again.** Better translated "to be
burdened by" or "to be oppressed by" because
of its connection with a yoke. **yoke of slavery.**
"Yoke" refers to the apparatus used to control a
domesticated animal. The Jews thought of the
"yoke of the law" as a good thing, the essence
of true religion. Paul argued that for those who
pursued it as a way of salvation, the law was
a yoke of slavery.

5:6 neither circumcision nor uncircumcision means anything. Nothing done or not done in the flesh, even religious ceremony, makes any difference in one's relationship to God. What is external is immaterial and worthless, unless it reflects genuine internal righteousness (Ro 2:25–29). **faith working through love.** Saving faith proves its genuine character by works of love. The person who lives by faith is internally motivated by love for God and Christ (Mt 22:37–40), which supernaturally issues forth in reverent worship, genuine obedience, and self-sacrificing love for others.

have confidence in you in the Lord that you will adopt no other view; but the one who is disturbing you will bear his judgment, whoever he is. [11] But I, brethren, if I still preach circumcision, why am I still persecuted? Then the stumbling block of the cross has been abolished. [12] I wish that those who are troubling you would even mutilate themselves.

[13] For you were called to freedom, brethren; only *do* not *turn* your freedom into an opportunity for the flesh, but through love serve one another. [14] For the whole Law is fulfilled in one word, in the *statement,* "You shall love your neighbor as yourself." [15] But if you bite and devour one another, take care that you are not consumed by one another.

[16] But I say, walk by the Spirit, and you will not carry out the desire of the flesh. [17] For the flesh sets its desire against the Spirit, and the Spirit against the flesh; for these are in opposition to one another, so that you may not do the things that you please. [18] But if you are led by the Spirit, you are not under the Law. [19] Now the deeds of the flesh are evident, which are: immorality, impurity, sensuality, [20] idolatry, sorcery, enmities, strife, jealousy, outbursts of anger, disputes, dissensions, factions, [21] envying, drunkenness, carousing, and things like these, of which I forewarn you, just as I have forewarned you, that those who practice such things will not inherit the kingdom of God. [22] But the fruit of the Spirit is love, joy, peace, patience, kindness, goodness, faithfulness, [23] gentleness, self-control; against such things there is no law. [24] Now those who belong to Christ Jesus have crucified the flesh with its passions and desires.

[25] If we live by the Spirit, let us also walk by the Spirit. [26] Let us not become boastful, challenging one another, envying one another.

DAY 27: Describe the fruit of the Spirit.

The fruit of the Spirit are the godly attitudes that characterize the lives of only those who belong to God by faith in Christ and possess the Spirit of God. The Spirit produces fruit which consists of 9 characteristics or attitudes that are inextricably linked with each other and are commanded of believers throughout the New Testament.

"Love." One of several Greek words for love, *agape,* is the love of choice, referring not to an emotional affection, physical attraction, or a familial bond, but to respect, devotion, and affection that leads to willing, self-sacrificial service (Jn 15:13; Ro 5:8; 1Jn 3:16–17). "Joy." A happiness based on unchanging divine promises and eternal spiritual realities. It is the sense of well-being experienced by one who knows all is well between himself and the Lord (1Pe 1:8). Joy is not the result of favorable circumstances, and even occurs when those circumstances are the most painful and severe (Jn 16:20–22). Joy is a gift from God, and as such, believers are not to manufacture it but to delight in the blessing they already possess (Ro 14:17; Php 4:4). "Peace." The inner calm that results from confidence in one's saving relationship with Christ. The verb form denotes binding together and is reflected in the expression "having it all together." Like joy, peace is not related to one's circumstances (Jn 14:27; Ro 8:28; Php 4:6–7, 9).

"Patience." This refers to the ability to endure injuries inflicted by others and the willingness to accept irritating or painful situations (Eph 4:2; Col 3:12; 1Ti 1:15–16). "Kindness." Tender concern for others, reflected in a desire to treat others gently, just as the Lord treats all believers (Mt 11:28–29; 19:13–14; 2Ti 2:24). "Goodness." Moral and spiritual excellence manifested in active kindness (Ro 5:7). Believers are commanded to exemplify goodness (6:10; 2Th 1:11). "Faithfulness." Loyalty and trustworthiness (La 3:22; Php 2:7–9; 1Th 5:24; Rev 2:10).

"Gentleness." Better translated "meekness." It is a humble and gentle attitude that is patiently submissive in every offense, while having no desire for revenge or retribution. In the New Testament, it is used to describe 3 attitudes: submission to the will of God (Col 3:12), teachability (Jas 1:21), and consideration of others (Eph 4:2). "Self-control." This refers to restraining passions and appetites (1Co 9:25; 2Pe 1:5–6). "No law." When a Christian walks by the Spirit and manifests His fruit, he needs no external law to produce the attitudes and behavior that please God (Ro 8:4).

SEPTEMBER 28

Isaiah 47:1–48:22

47 "Come down and sit in the dust,
O virgin daughter of Babylon;
Sit on the ground without a throne,
O daughter of the Chaldeans!
For you shall no longer be
called tender and delicate.

2 "Take the millstones and grind meal.
Remove your veil, strip off the skirt,
Uncover the leg, cross the rivers.

3 "Your nakedness will be uncovered,
Your shame also will be exposed;
I will take vengeance and
will not spare a man."

4 Our Redeemer, the LORD of
hosts is His name,
The Holy One of Israel.

5 "Sit silently, and go into darkness,
O daughter of the Chaldeans,
For you will no longer be called
The queen of kingdoms.

6 "I was angry with My people,
I profaned My heritage
And gave them into your hand.
You did not show mercy to them,
On the aged you made your
yoke very heavy.

7 "Yet you said, 'I will be a
queen forever.'
These things you did not consider
Nor remember the outcome of them.

8 "Now, then, hear this, you sensual one,
Who dwells securely,
Who says in your heart,
'I am, and there is no one besides me.
I will not sit as a widow,
Nor know loss of children.'

9 "But these two things will come
on you suddenly in one day:
Loss of children and widowhood.
They will come on you in full measure
In spite of your many sorceries,
In spite of the great power
of your spells.

10 "You felt secure in your
wickedness and said,
'No one sees me,'
Your wisdom and your knowledge,
they have deluded you;
For you have said in your heart,
'I am, and there is no one besides me.'

11 "But evil will come on you
Which you will not know
how to charm away;

And disaster will fall on you
For which you cannot atone;
And destruction about which
you do not know
Will come on you suddenly.

12 "Stand *fast* now in your spells
And in your many sorceries
With which you have labored
from your youth;
Perhaps you will be able to profit,
Perhaps you may cause trembling.

13 "You are wearied with your
many counsels;
Let now the astrologers,
Those who prophesy by the stars,
Those who predict by the new moons,
Stand up and save you from
what will come upon you.

14 "Behold, they have become
like stubble,
Fire burns them;
They cannot deliver themselves
from the power of the flame;
There will be no coal to warm by
Nor a fire to sit before!

15 "So have those become to you with
whom you have labored,
Who have trafficked with
you from your youth;
Each has wandered in his own way;
There is none to save you.

48 "Hear this, O house of Jacob,
who are named Israel
And who came forth from
the loins of Judah,
Who swear by the name of the LORD
And invoke the God of Israel,
But not in truth nor in righteousness.

2 "For they call themselves
after the holy city
And lean on the God of Israel;
The LORD of hosts is His name.

3 "I declared the former things
long ago
And they went forth from My
mouth, and I proclaimed them.
Suddenly I acted, and they
came to pass.

4 "Because I know that you
are obstinate,
And your neck is an iron sinew
And your forehead bronze,

5 Therefore I declared *them*
to you long ago,
Before they took place I
proclaimed *them* to you,

So that you would not say, 'My
   idol has done them,
And my graven image and my molten
   image have commanded them.'
6 "You have heard; look at all this.
And you, will you not declare it?
I proclaim to you new things
   from this time,
Even hidden things which
   you have not known.

48:6 new things. From this point onward, the prophecies of Messiah's first and second coming and the restoration of Israel have a new distinctiveness. Babylon becomes the Babylon of Revelation (v. 20), and God uses Isaiah to communicate truths about the messianic kingdom on earth and the new heavens and new earth that follow it (e.g., 11:1–5; 65:17). Verse 7 indicates that God had never before revealed these features about the future.

7 "They are created now and
   not long ago;
And before today you have
   not heard them,
So that you will not say,
   'Behold, I knew them.'
8 "You have not heard, you
   have not known.
Even from long ago your ear
   has not been open,
Because I knew that you would
   deal very treacherously;
And you have been called
   a rebel from birth.
9 "For the sake of My name
   I delay My wrath,
And *for* My praise I restrain
   it for you,
In order not to cut you off.
10 "Behold, I have refined you,
   but not as silver;
I have tested you in the
   furnace of affliction.
11 "For My own sake, for My
   own sake, I will act;
For how can *My name* be profaned?
And My glory I will not
   give to another.

12 "Listen to Me, O Jacob, even
   Israel whom I called;
I am He, I am the first, I
   am also the last.

48:10–11 refined…tested. Since Isaiah's time, Israel's testings have included the Babylonian captivity and present worldwide dispersion from her land; unlike silver purged in the furnace, the purging of Israel is not complete, and they are not refined. But God keeps up the afflictions until they are, so His name is not defamed through the destruction of Israel. The nation will be purged (Zec 13:1). God's plan is such that He alone, not man or man-made idols, will receive credit for Israel's salvation (42:8; Ro 11:25–27, 33–36). The adversaries of God are never to be given legitimate reasons for scoffing at God and His work.

13 "Surely My hand founded the earth,
And My right hand spread
   out the heavens;
When I call to them, they
   stand together.
14 "Assemble, all of you, and listen!
Who among them has
   declared these things?
The LORD loves him; he will
   carry out His good
   pleasure on Babylon,
And His arm *will be against*
   the Chaldeans.
15 "I, even I, have spoken; indeed
   I have called him,
I have brought him, and He will
   make his ways successful.
16 "Come near to Me, listen to this:
From the first I have not
   spoken in secret,
From the time it took
   place, I was there.
And now the Lord GOD has
   sent Me, and His Spirit."

17 Thus says the LORD, your Redeemer, the Holy One of Israel,

"I am the LORD your God, who
   teaches you to profit,
Who leads you in the way
   you should go.
18 "If only you had paid attention
   to My commandments!
Then your well-being would
   have been like a river,
And your righteousness like
   the waves of the sea.
19 "Your descendants would have
   been like the sand,
And your offspring like its grains;

Their name would never be cut off
or destroyed from My presence."

²⁰ Go forth from Babylon! Flee
from the Chaldeans!
Declare with the sound of joyful
shouting, proclaim this,
Send it out to the end of the earth;
Say, "The LORD has redeemed
His servant Jacob."
²¹ They did not thirst when He led
them through the deserts.
He made the water flow out
of the rock for them;
He split the rock and the
water gushed forth.
²² "There is no peace for the
wicked," says the LORD.

Psalm 111:7–10

⁷ The works of His hands are
truth and justice;
All His precepts are sure.
⁸ They are upheld forever and ever;
They are performed in truth
and uprightness.
⁹ He has sent redemption to His people;
He has ordained His covenant forever;
Holy and awesome is His name.
¹⁰ The fear of the LORD is the
beginning of wisdom;
A good understanding have all those
who do *His commandments;*
His praise endures forever.

Proverbs 26:11–12

¹¹ Like a dog that returns to its vomit
Is a fool who repeats his folly.
¹² Do you see a man wise
in his own eyes?
There is more hope for a
fool than for him.

Galatians 6:1–18

6 Brethren, even if anyone is caught in any
trespass, you who are spiritual, restore
such a one in a spirit of gentleness; *each one*
looking to yourself, so that you too will not
be tempted. ² Bear one another's burdens,
and thereby fulfill the law of Christ. ³ For if
anyone thinks he is something when he is
nothing, he deceives himself. ⁴ But each one
must examine his own work, and then he will
have *reason for* boasting in regard to himself
alone, and not in regard to another. ⁵ For each
one will bear his own load.

⁶ The one who is taught the word is to share
all good things with the one who teaches *him.*

⁷ Do not be deceived, God is not mocked; for
whatever a man sows, this he will also reap.
⁸ For the one who sows to his own flesh will
from the flesh reap corruption, but the one
who sows to the Spirit will from the Spirit reap
eternal life. ⁹ Let us not lose heart in doing

6:8 sows to his own flesh. Here it means pandering to the flesh's evil desires. **corruption.** From the Greek word for degeneration, as in decaying food. Sin always corrupts and, when left unchecked, always makes a person progressively worse in character (Ro 6:23). **sows to the Spirit.** To walk by the Holy Spirit. **eternal life.** This expression describes not only a life that endures forever but, primarily, the highest quality of living that one can experience (Ps 51:12; Jn 10:10; Eph 1:3, 18).

good, for in due time we will reap if we do not
grow weary. ¹⁰ So then, while we have opportunity, let us do good to all people, and especially
to those who are of the household of the faith.

¹¹ See with what large letters I am writing
to you with my own hand. ¹² Those who desire to make a good showing in the flesh try
to compel you to be circumcised, simply so
that they will not be persecuted for the cross
of Christ. ¹³ For those who are circumcised do
not even keep the Law themselves, but they
desire to have you circumcised so that they
may boast in your flesh. ¹⁴ But may it never be
that I would boast, except in the cross of our
Lord Jesus Christ, through which the world
has been crucified to me, and I to the world.
¹⁵ For neither is circumcision anything, nor uncircumcision, but a new creation. ¹⁶ And those
who will walk by this rule, peace and mercy
be upon them, and upon the Israel of God.

¹⁷ From now on let no one cause trouble for
me, for I bear on my body the brand-marks
of Jesus.

¹⁸ The grace of our Lord Jesus Christ be
with your spirit, brethren. Amen.

6:10 opportunity. This Greek word refers to a distinct, fixed time period, rather than occasional moments. Paul's point is that the believer's entire life provides the unique privilege by which he can serve others in Christ's name. **especially...the household of the faith.** Our love for fellow Christians is the primary test of our love for God.

DAY 28: How do we restore a believer overtaken in sin?

In Galatians 6:1, Paul addresses the situation where someone is overtaken in a sin, which may imply the person was actually seen committing the sin or that he was caught or snared by the sin itself. Those believers who are walking in the Spirit, filled with the Spirit, and evidencing the fruit of the Spirit are to "restore such a one." This is sometimes used metaphorically of settling disputes or arguments. It means "to mend" or "repair" and was used of setting a broken bone or repairing a dislocated limb (Heb 12:12–13; Ro 15:1; 1Th 5:14). The basic process of restoration is outlined in Matthew 18:15-20. "In a spirit of gentleness; each one looking to yourself, so that you too will not be tempted." The Greek form strongly emphasizes a continual, diligent attentiveness.

"Bear one another's burdens, and thereby fulfill the law of Christ" (v. 2). "Burdens" are extra heavy loads, which here represent difficulties or problems people have trouble dealing with. "Bear" connotes carrying something with endurance. The law of love which fulfills the entire law (Jn 13:34; Ro 13:8, 10).

"But each one must examine his own work" (v. 4). Literally, "to approve something after testing it." Believers first must be sure their lives are right with God before giving spiritual help to others (Mt 7:3–5). "Have reason for boasting in regard to himself alone." If a believer rejoices or boasts, it should be only boasting in the Lord for what God has done in him (2Co 10:12–18), not for what he supposedly has accomplished compared to other believers.

"For each one will bear his own load" (v. 5). This is not a contradiction to v. 2. "Load" has no connotation of difficulty; it refers to life's routine obligations and each believer's ministry calling (Mt 11:30; 1Co 3:12–15; 2Co 5:10). God requires faithfulness in meeting those responsibilities.

SEPTEMBER 29

Isaiah 49:1–50:11

49 Listen to Me, O islands,
And pay attention, you
peoples from afar.
The LORD called Me from
the womb;
From the body of My mother
He named Me.
2 He has made My mouth
like a sharp sword,
In the shadow of His hand
He has concealed Me;
And He has also made Me
a select arrow,
He has hidden Me in His quiver.
3 He said to Me, "You are
My Servant, Israel,
In Whom I will show My glory."
4 But I said, "I have toiled in vain,
I have spent My strength for
nothing and vanity;
Yet surely the justice *due* to
Me is with the LORD,
And My reward with My God."

5 And now says the LORD, who
formed Me from the womb
to be His Servant,
To bring Jacob back to Him,
so that Israel might be
gathered to Him

(For I am honored in the
sight of the LORD,
And My God is My strength),
6 He says, "It is too small a thing that
You should be My Servant
To raise up the tribes of
Jacob and to restore the
preserved ones of Israel;
I will also make You a light
of the nations
So that My salvation may reach
to the end of the earth."
7 Thus says the LORD, the Redeemer
of Israel *and* its Holy One,
To the despised One,
To the One abhorred by the nation,
To the Servant of rulers,
"Kings will see and arise,
Princes will also bow down,
Because of the LORD who is
faithful, the Holy One of Israel
who has chosen You."

8 Thus says the LORD,
"In a favorable time I have
answered You,
And in a day of salvation
I have helped You;
And I will keep You and give You
for a covenant of the people,
To restore the land, to make *them*
inherit the desolate heritages;
9 Saying to those who are
bound, 'Go forth,'

49:8 favorable time...day of salvation. Messiah is represented as asking for the grace of God to be given to sinners. God gives His favorable answer in a time of grace (61:1) when salvation's day comes to the world (Gal 4:4–5; Heb 4:7). At His appointed time in the future, the Lord will, by His Servant, accomplish the final deliverance of Israel. Paul applied these words to his ministry of proclaiming the gospel of God's grace to all people (2Co 6:2). **a covenant of the people.** When the Lord saves and regathers Israel, they will return to the land, to which Joshua brought their ancestors after their exit from Egypt, now restored and glorious (44:26; Jos 13:1–8).

To those who are in darkness,
  'Show yourselves.'
Along the roads they will feed,
And their pasture *will be*
  on all bare heights.
¹⁰ "They will not hunger or thirst,
  Nor will the scorching heat or
    sun strike them down;
For He who has compassion
  on them will lead them
And will guide them to
  springs of water.
¹¹ "I will make all My mountains a road,
And My highways will be raised up.
¹² "Behold, these will come from afar;
And lo, these *will come* from the
  north and from the west,
And these from the land of Sinim."
¹³ Shout for joy, O heavens!
  And rejoice, O earth!
Break forth into joyful
  shouting, O mountains!
For the LORD has comforted
  His people
And will have compassion
  on His afflicted.

¹⁴ But Zion said, "The LORD
  has forsaken me,
And the Lord has forgotten me."
¹⁵ "Can a woman forget her nursing child
And have no compassion on
  the son of her womb?
Even these may forget, but
  I will not forget you.
¹⁶ "Behold, I have inscribed you on
  the palms *of My hands;*
Your walls are continually before Me.
¹⁷ "Your builders hurry;

Your destroyers and devastators
  Will depart from you.
¹⁸ "Lift up your eyes and look around;
  All of them gather together,
    they come to you.
As I live," declares the LORD,
"You will surely put on all of them as
  jewels and bind them on as a bride.
¹⁹ "For your waste and desolate places
  and your destroyed land—
Surely now you will be too
  cramped for the inhabitants,
And those who swallowed
  you will be far away.
²⁰ "The children of whom you were
  bereaved will yet say in your ears,
'The place is too cramped for me;
  Make room for me that
    I may live *here.'*
²¹ "Then you will say in your heart,
'Who has begotten these for me,
Since I have been bereaved
  of my children
And am barren, an exile
  and a wanderer?
And who has reared these?
Behold, I was left alone;
From where did these come?'"

²² Thus says the Lord GOD,

"Behold, I will lift up My
  hand to the nations
And set up My standard
  to the peoples;
And they will bring your
  sons in *their* bosom,
And your daughters will be
  carried on *their* shoulders.
²³ "Kings will be your guardians,
  And their princesses your nurses.
They will bow down to you with
  their faces to the earth
And lick the dust of your feet;
And *you* will know that
  I am the LORD;
Those who hopefully wait for Me
  will not be put to shame.

²⁴ "Can the prey be taken from
  the mighty man,
Or the captives of a tyrant
  be rescued?"
²⁵ Surely, thus says the LORD,

"Even the captives of the mighty
  man will be taken away,

And the prey of the tyrant
will be rescued;
For I will contend with the one
who contends with you,
And I will save your sons.
²⁶ "I will feed your oppressors
with their own flesh,
And they will become drunk
with their own blood as
with sweet wine;
And all flesh will know that I,
the LORD, am your Savior
And your Redeemer, the
Mighty One of Jacob."

50 Thus says the LORD,

"Where is the certificate of divorce
By which I have sent your
mother away?
Or to whom of My creditors
did I sell you?
Behold, you were sold for
your iniquities,
And for your transgressions your
mother was sent away.
² "Why was there no man when I came?
When I called, why was there
none to answer?
Is My hand so short that
it cannot ransom?
Or have I no power to deliver?
Behold, I dry up the sea
with My rebuke,
I make the rivers a wilderness;
Their fish stink for lack of water
And die of thirst.
³ "I clothe the heavens with blackness
And make sackcloth their covering."

⁴ The Lord GOD has given Me
the tongue of disciples,
That I may know how to sustain
the weary one with a word.
He awakens Me morning by morning,
He awakens My ear to
listen as a disciple.
⁵ The Lord GOD has opened My ear;
And I was not disobedient
Nor did I turn back.
⁶ I gave My back to those who strike Me,
And My cheeks to those who
pluck out the beard;
I did not cover My face from
humiliation and spitting.
⁷ For the Lord GOD helps Me,
Therefore, I am not disgraced;
Therefore, I have set My face like flint,

50:6 My back...My cheeks...My face. The Servant remained obedient though provoked to rebel by excessively vile treatment. Jesus fulfilled this prophecy by remaining submissive to the Father's will (Mt 26:67; 27:26, 30; Mk 14:65; 15:19; Lk 22:63; Jn 18:22).

50:7 set My face like flint. So sure was He of the Lord God's help that He resolutely determined to remain unswayed by whatever hardship might await Him (Eze 3:8–9). Jesus demonstrated this determination in setting His face to go to Jerusalem to be crucified (Lk 9:51).

And I know that I will
not be ashamed.
⁸ He who vindicates Me is near;
Who will contend with Me?
Let us stand up to each other;
Who has a case against Me?
Let him draw near to Me.
⁹ Behold, the Lord GOD helps Me;
Who is he who condemns Me?
Behold, they will all wear
out like a garment;
The moth will eat them.
¹⁰ Who is among you that
fears the LORD,
That obeys the voice of His
servant,
That walks in darkness
and has no light?
Let him trust in the name of the
LORD and rely on his God.
¹¹ Behold, all you who kindle
a fire,
Who encircle yourselves
with firebrands,
Walk in the light of your fire
And among the brands you
have set ablaze.
This you will have from
My hand:
You will lie down in torment.

Psalm 112:1–4

P raise the LORD!
How blessed is the man
who fears the LORD,
Who greatly delights in His
commandments.
² His descendants will be
mighty on earth;
The generation of the upright
will be blessed.

³ Wealth and riches are in his
house,
And his righteousness
endures forever.
⁴ Light arises in the darkness
for the upright;
He is gracious and compassionate
and righteous.

Proverbs 26:13-15

¹³ The sluggard says, "There
is a lion in the road!
A lion is in the open square!"
¹⁴ *As* the door turns on its hinges,
So *does* the sluggard on his bed.
¹⁵ The sluggard buries his
hand in the dish;
He is weary of bringing it
to his mouth again.

Ephesians 1:1-23

1 Paul, an apostle of Christ Jesus by the will of God,

To the saints who are at Ephesus and *who are* faithful in Christ Jesus: ² Grace to you and peace from God our Father and the Lord Jesus Christ.

³ Blessed *be* the God and Father of our Lord Jesus Christ, who has blessed us with every spiritual blessing in the heavenly *places* in Christ, ⁴ just as He chose us in Him before the foundation of the world, that we would be holy and blameless before Him. In love ⁵ He predestined us to adoption as sons through Jesus Christ to Himself, according to the kind intention of His will, ⁶ to the praise of the glory of His grace, which He freely bestowed on us in the Beloved. ⁷ In Him we have redemption through His blood, the forgiveness of our trespasses, according to the riches of His grace ⁸ which He lavished on us. In all wisdom and insight ⁹ He made known to us the mystery of His will, according to His kind intention which He purposed in Him ¹⁰ with a view to an administration suitable to the fullness of the times, *that is,* the summing up of all things in Christ, things in the heavens and things on the earth. In Him ¹¹ also we have obtained an inheritance, having been predestined according to His purpose who works all things after the counsel of His will, ¹² to the end that we who were the first to hope in Christ would be to the praise of His glory. ¹³ In Him, you also, after listening to the message of truth, the gospel of your salvation—having also believed, you were sealed in Him with the Holy Spirit of promise, ¹⁴ who is given as a pledge of our inheritance, with a view to

1:13-14 sealed...with the Holy Spirit. God's own Spirit comes to indwell the believer and secures and preserves his eternal salvation. The sealing of which Paul speaks refers to an official mark of identification placed on a letter, contract, or other document. That document was thereby officially under the authority of the person whose stamp was on the seal. Four primary truths are signified by the seal: 1) security (Da 6:17; Mt 27:62-66); 2) authenticity (1Ki 21:6-16); 3) ownership (Jer 32:10); and 4) authority (Est 8:8-12). The Holy Spirit is given by God as His pledge of the believer's future inheritance in glory (2Co 1:21).

the redemption of *God's own* possession, to the praise of His glory.

¹⁵ For this reason I too, having heard of the faith in the Lord Jesus which *exists* among you and your love for all the saints, ¹⁶ do not cease giving thanks for you, while making mention *of you* in my prayers; ¹⁷ that the God of our Lord Jesus Christ, the Father of glory, may give to you a spirit of wisdom and of revelation in the knowledge of Him. ¹⁸ *I pray that* the eyes of your heart may be enlightened, so that you will know what is the hope of His calling, what are the riches of the glory of His inheritance in the saints, ¹⁹ and what is the surpassing greatness of His power toward us who believe. *These are* in accordance with the working of the strength of His might ²⁰ which He brought about in Christ, when He raised Him from the dead and seated Him at His right hand in the heavenly *places,* ²¹ far above all rule and authority and power and dominion, and every name that is named, not only in this age but also in the one to come. ²² And He put all things in subjection under His feet, and gave Him as head over all things to the church, ²³ which is His body, the fullness of Him who fills all in all.

1:19-20 surpassing greatness of His power. God's great power, that very power which raised Jesus from the dead and lifted Him by ascension back to glory to take His seat at God's right hand, is given to every believer at the time of salvation and is always available (Ac 1:8; Col 1:29). Paul therefore did not pray that God's power be given to believers, but that they be aware of the power they already possessed in Christ and use it (3:20).

DAY 29: Why does Paul use the word "mystery" so often in his letter to the Ephesians?

Paul actually uses the word "mystery" six times in this letter (1:9; 3:3, 4, 9; 5:32; 6:19). By comparison, the word appears twice in Romans, once in 1 Corinthians, four times in Colossians, once in 1 Timothy, and nowhere else. Contrary to our use of "mystery" as a series of clues to be figured out, Paul's use of the word points to mystery as a heretofore unrevealed truth that has been made clear. The word "mystery" preserves the sense that the revealed truth has such awesome implications that it continues to amaze and humble those who accept it.

Ephesians introduces various aspects of the "mystery." Paul explained his use of the word in 3:4-6 by saying, "that the Gentiles are fellow heirs and fellow members of the body, and fellow partakers of the promise in Christ Jesus through the gospel." When the unsearchable riches of Christ are preached among the Gentiles, one result is an understanding of the "administration of the mystery" (3:9). And when God's plan for human marriage is used to explain the unique relationship between Christ and His bride, the church, Paul reminded his readers that the real subject is a great mystery (5:32). And finally, Paul asked the Ephesians to pray for him that he would be able "make known with boldness the mystery of the gospel" (6:19). The gospel is not mysterious because it is hard to understand. It is mysterious because it is unexpected, unmerited, and free. Though Paul didn't use the word in this passage, his summary of the mystery for the Ephesians can be found in 2:8-9: "For by grace you have been saved through faith; and that not of yourselves, it is the gift of God; not as a result of works, so that no one may boast."

SEPTEMBER 30

Isaiah 51:1–52:15

51 "Listen to me, you who
pursue righteousness,
Who seek the LORD:
Look to the rock from which
you were hewn
And to the quarry from
which you were dug.

2 "Look to Abraham your father
And to Sarah who gave
birth to you in pain;
When *he was but* one I called him,
Then I blessed him and
multiplied him."

3 Indeed, the LORD will comfort Zion;
He will comfort all her waste places.
And her wilderness He will
make like Eden,
And her desert like the
garden of the LORD;
Joy and gladness will be found in her,
Thanksgiving and sound of a melody.

4 "Pay attention to Me, O My people,
And give ear to Me, O My nation;
For a law will go forth from Me,
And I will set My justice for
a light of the peoples.

5 "My righteousness is near, My
salvation has gone forth,
And My arms will judge the peoples;
The coastlands will wait for Me,
And for My arm they will
wait expectantly.

6 "Lift up your eyes to the sky,
Then look to the earth beneath;
For the sky will vanish like smoke,
And the earth will wear
out like a garment
And its inhabitants will
die in like manner;
But My salvation will be forever,
And My righteousness will not wane.

51:6 sky will vanish...earth will wear out. This begins to take place in the time of tribulation (Rev 6:12–14; 8:12–13; 16:8–10, 21), setting the stage, along with the earthly judgments on land, sea, and fresh water (Rev 6:14; 8:6–11; 16:3–5), for a renewed earth during the Millennium. The actual "uncreation" or destruction of the present universe, of which Peter wrote (2Pe 3:10–13), occurs at the end of Christ's millennial reign on the earth, when a new heaven and a new earth will replace the present creation (2Pe 3:10; Rev 21:1).

7 "Listen to Me, you who know
righteousness,
A people in whose heart is My law;
Do not fear the reproach of man,
Nor be dismayed at their revilings.

8 "For the moth will eat them
like a garment,
And the grub will eat them
like wool.
But My righteousness will be forever,
And My salvation to all generations."

9 Awake, awake, put on strength,
   O arm of the LORD;
   Awake as in the days of old, the
      generations of long ago.
   Was it not You who cut
      Rahab in pieces,
   Who pierced the dragon?
10 Was it not You who dried up the sea,
   The waters of the great deep;
   Who made the depths of
      the sea a pathway
   For the redeemed to cross over?
11 So the ransomed of the
      LORD will return
   And come with joyful
      shouting to Zion,
   And everlasting joy *will
   be* on their heads.
   They will obtain gladness and joy,
   And sorrow and sighing
      will flee away.

12 "I, even I, am He who comforts you.
   Who are you that you are
      afraid of man who dies
   And of the son of man who
      is made like grass,
13 That you have forgotten the
      LORD your Maker,
   Who stretched out the heavens
   And laid the foundations of the earth,
   That you fear continually all
      day long because of the
      fury of the oppressor,
   As he makes ready to destroy?
   But where is the fury of
      the oppressor?

14 The exile will soon be set free, and will not die
in the dungeon, nor will his bread be lacking.
15 For I am the LORD your God, who stirs up the
sea and its waves roar (the LORD of hosts is His
name). 16 I have put My words in your mouth
and have covered you with the shadow of My
hand, to establish the heavens, to found the
earth, and to say to Zion, 'You are My people.'"

17 Rouse yourself! Rouse yourself!
      Arise, O Jerusalem,
   You who have drunk from the LORD'S
      hand the cup of His anger;
   The chalice of reeling you have
      drained to the dregs.
18 There is none to guide her among
      all the sons she has borne,
   Nor is there one to take her
      by the hand among all the
      sons she has reared.

19 These two things have befallen you;
   Who will mourn for you?
   The devastation and destruction,
      famine and sword;
   How shall I comfort you?
20 Your sons have fainted,
   They lie *helpless* at the
      head of every street,
   Like an antelope in a net,
   Full of the wrath of the LORD,
   The rebuke of your God.

21 Therefore, please hear
      this, you afflicted,
   Who are drunk, but not with wine:
22 Thus says your Lord, the
      LORD, even your God
   Who contends for His people,
   "Behold, I have taken out of your
      hand the cup of reeling,
   The chalice of My anger;
   You will never drink it again.
23 "I will put it into the hand
      of your tormentors,
   Who have said to you, 'Lie down
      that we may walk over *you.*'
   You have even made your
      back like the ground
   And like the street for those
      who walk over *it.*"

52 Awake, awake,
   Clothe yourself in your
      strength, O Zion;
   Clothe yourself in your
      beautiful garments,
   O Jerusalem, the holy city;
   For the uncircumcised
      and the unclean
   Will no longer come into you.
2 Shake yourself from the dust,
      rise up,
   O captive Jerusalem;
   Loose yourself from the chains
      around your neck,
   O captive daughter of Zion.

3 For thus says the LORD, "You were sold
for nothing and you will be redeemed without money." 4 For thus says the Lord GOD, "My
people went down at the first into Egypt to
reside there; then the Assyrian oppressed
them without cause. 5 Now therefore, what
do I have here," declares the LORD, "seeing
that My people have been taken away without
cause?" *Again* the LORD declares, "Those who
rule over them howl, and My name is continually blasphemed all day long. 6 Therefore My

people shall know My name; therefore in that day I am the one who is speaking, 'Here I am.'"

7 How lovely on the mountains
   Are the feet of him who
       brings good news,
   Who announces peace
   And brings good news of happiness,
   Who announces salvation,
   And says to Zion, "Your God reigns!"

8 Listen! Your watchmen lift
       up *their* voices,
   They shout joyfully together;
   For they will see with their own eyes
   When the LORD restores Zion.

9 Break forth, shout joyfully
       together,
   You waste places of Jerusalem;
   For the LORD has comforted
       His people,
   He has redeemed Jerusalem.

10 The LORD has bared His holy arm
   In the sight of all the nations,
   That all the ends of the earth
       may see
   The salvation of our God.

11 Depart, depart, go out from there,
   Touch nothing unclean;
   Go out of the midst of her,
       purify yourselves,
   You who carry the vessels
       of the LORD.

12 But you will not go out in haste,
   Nor will you go as fugitives;
   For the LORD will go before you,
   And the God of Israel *will
       be* your rear guard.

13 Behold, My servant will prosper,
   He will be high and lifted up
       and greatly exalted.

14 Just as many were astonished
       at you, *My people,*
   So His appearance was marred
       more than any man
   And His form more than
       the sons of men.

52:14 His appearance was marred. The Servant must undergo inhuman cruelty to the point that He no longer looks like a human being. His appearance is so awful that people look at Him in astonishment (53:2–3; Ps 22:6; Mt 26:67; 27:30; Jn 19:3).

15 Thus He will sprinkle many nations,
   Kings will shut their mouths
       on account of Him;
   For what had not been told
       them they will see,
   And what they had not heard
       they will understand.

52:15 sprinkle many nations. The verb can have the sense of causing them to spring up in astonishment. They are electrified—startled, so much so that they are left speechless. The context best supports this understanding of "startle." **shut their mouths.** At His exaltation, human leaders in the highest places will be speechless and in awe before the once-despised Servant (Ps 2). When He takes His throne, they will see the unfolding of power and glory such as they have never heard. Paul applied the principle in this verse to his apostolic mission of preaching the gospel of Christ where Christ was yet unknown (Ro 15:21).

Psalm 112:5–10

5 It is well with the man who
       is gracious and lends;
   He will maintain his cause
       in judgment.

6 For he will never be shaken;
   The righteous will be
       remembered forever.

7 He will not fear evil tidings;
   His heart is steadfast,
       trusting in the LORD.

8 His heart is upheld, he will
       not fear,
   Until he looks *with satisfaction*
       on his adversaries.

9 He has given freely to the poor,
   His righteousness endures
       forever;
   His horn will be exalted in honor.

10 The wicked will see it and be vexed,
   He will gnash his teeth
       and melt away;
   The desire of the wicked
       will perish.

Proverbs 26:16

16 The sluggard is wiser in his
       own eyes
   Than seven men who can
       give a discreet answer.

Ephesians 2:1–22

2 And you were dead in your trespasses and sins, ²in which you formerly walked according to the course of this world, according to the prince of the power of the air, of the spirit that is now working in the sons of

2:1 dead in your trespasses and sins. A sobering reminder of the total sinfulness and lostness from which believers have been redeemed. "In" indicates the realm or sphere in which unregenerate sinners exist. They are not dead because of sinful acts that have been committed, but because of their sinful nature (Mt 12:35; 15:18–19).

disobedience. ³Among them we too all formerly lived in the lusts of our flesh, indulging the desires of the flesh and of the mind, and were by nature children of wrath, even as the rest. ⁴But God, being rich in mercy, because of His great love with which He loved us, ⁵even when we were dead in our transgressions, made us alive together with Christ (by grace you have been saved), ⁶and raised us up with Him, and seated us with Him in the heavenly *places* in Christ Jesus, ⁷so that in the ages to come He might show the surpassing riches of His grace in kindness toward us in Christ Jesus. ⁸For by grace you have been saved through faith; and that not of yourselves, *it is* the gift of God; ⁹not as a result of works, so that no one may boast. ¹⁰For we are His workmanship, created in Christ Jesus for good works, which God prepared beforehand so that we would walk in them.
¹¹Therefore remember that formerly you, the Gentiles in the flesh, who are called "Un-

circumcision" by the so-called "Circumcision," *which is* performed in the flesh by human hands— ¹²remember that you were at that time separate from Christ, excluded from the commonwealth of Israel, and strangers to the covenants of promise, having no hope and without God in the world. ¹³But now in Christ Jesus you who formerly were far off have been brought near by the blood of Christ. ¹⁴For He Himself is our peace, who made both *groups into* one and broke down the barrier of the dividing wall, ¹⁵by abolishing in His flesh the enmity, *which is* the Law of commandments *contained* in ordinances, so that in Himself He might make the two into one new man, *thus* establishing peace, ¹⁶and might reconcile them both in one body to God through the cross, by it having put to death the enmity. ¹⁷AND HE CAME AND PREACHED PEACE TO YOU WHO WERE FAR AWAY, AND PEACE TO THOSE WHO WERE NEAR; ¹⁸for through Him we both have our access in one Spirit to the Father. ¹⁹So then you are no longer strangers and aliens, but you are fellow citizens with the saints, and are of God's household, ²⁰having been built on the foundation of the apostles and prophets, Christ Jesus Himself being the corner *stone,* ²¹in whom the whole building, being fitted together, is growing into a holy temple in the Lord, ²²in whom you also are being built together into a dwelling of God in the Spirit.

2:21 a holy temple in the Lord. Every new believer is a new stone in Christ's temple, the church, Christ's body of believers (1Pe 2:5). Christ's building of His church will not be complete until every person who will believe in Him has done so (2Pe 3:9).

DAY 30: How were Gentiles brought into the family of God?

Historically, the Gentiles (the "uncircumcision") experienced two types of alienation. The first was social, resulting from the animosity that had existed between Jews and Gentiles for thousands of years. Jews considered Gentiles to be outcasts, objects of derision and reproach. The second and more significant type of alienation was spiritual, because Gentiles as a people were cut off from God in 5 different ways (Eph 2:11–12): 1) they were "separate from Christ," the Messiah, having no Savior and Deliverer and without divine purpose or destiny. 2) They were "excluded from the commonwealth of Israel." God's chosen people, the Jews, were a nation whose supreme King and Lord was God Himself, and from whose unique blessing and protection they benefitted. 3) Gentiles were "strangers to the covenants of promise," not able to partake of God's divine covenants in which He promised to give His people a land, a priesthood, a people, a nation, a kingdom, and a King—and to those who believe in Him, eternal life and heaven. 4) They had "no hope" because they had been given no divine promise. 5) They were "without God in the world." While Gentiles had many gods, they did not recognize the true God because they did not want Him.

"But now in Christ Jesus you who formerly were far off have been brought near by the blood of Christ" (v. 13). "Far off" was a common term in rabbinical writings used to describe Gentiles, those who were apart from the true God (Is 57:19; Ac 2:39). Every person who trusts in Christ alone for salvation, Jew or Gentile, is brought into spiritual union and intimacy with God. This is the reconciliation of 2 Corinthians 5:18-21. The atoning work accomplished by Christ's death on the cross washes away the penalty of sin and ultimately even its presence. "He Himself" (v. 14). Through His death, Christ abolished Old Testament ceremonial laws, feasts, and sacrifices which uniquely separated Jews from Gentiles. God's moral law (as summarized in the Ten Commandments and written on the hearts of all men, Ro 2:15) was not abolished but subsumed in the New Covenant, however, because it reflects His own holy nature (Mt 5:17-19).

OCTOBER 1

Isaiah 53:1–54:17

53 Who has believed our message?
And to whom has the arm of
the LORD been revealed?

2 For He grew up before Him
like a tender shoot,
And like a root out of parched ground;
He has no *stately* form or majesty
That we should look upon Him,
Nor appearance that we should
be attracted to Him.

3 He was despised and
forsaken of men,
A man of sorrows and
acquainted with grief;
And like one from whom
men hide their face
He was despised, and we
did not esteem Him.

4 Surely our griefs He Himself bore,
And our sorrows He carried;
Yet we ourselves esteemed
Him stricken,
Smitten of God, and afflicted.

5 But He was pierced through
for our transgressions,
He was crushed for our iniquities;
The chastening for our
well-being *fell* upon Him,
And by His scourging
we are healed.

6 All of us like sheep have gone astray,
Each of us has turned to his own way;
But the LORD has caused
the iniquity of us all
To fall on Him.

7 He was oppressed and He was afflicted,
Yet He did not open His mouth;
Like a lamb that is led to slaughter,
And like a sheep that is silent
before its shearers,
So He did not open His mouth.

8 By oppression and judgment
He was taken away;
And as for His generation,
who considered
That He was cut off out of
the land of the living
For the transgression of my people,
to whom the stroke *was due?*

9 His grave was assigned
with wicked men,
Yet He was with a rich
man in His death,
Because He had done no violence,
Nor was there any deceit in His mouth.

10 But the LORD was pleased
To crush Him, putting *Him* to grief;
If He would render Himself
as a guilt offering,
He will see *His* offspring,
He will prolong *His* days,
And the good pleasure of the LORD
will prosper in His hand.

11 As a result of the anguish of His soul,
He will see *it and* be satisfied;
By His knowledge the Righteous One,
My Servant, will justify the many,
As He will bear their iniquities.

12 Therefore, I will allot Him a
portion with the great,
And He will divide the booty
with the strong;
Because He poured out
Himself to death,
And was numbered with
the transgressors;

53:6 All of us...Each of us...us all. Every person has sinned (Ro 3:9, 23), but the Servant has sufficiently shouldered the consequences of sin and the righteous wrath deserved by sinners (1Ti 2:5–6; 4:10; 1Jn 2:2). The manner in which God laid our iniquity on Him was that God treated Him as if He had committed every sin ever committed by every person who would ever believe, though He was perfectly innocent of any sin. God did so to Him, so that wrath being spent and justice satisfied, God could then give to the account of sinners who believe the righteousness of Christ, treating them as if they had done only the righteous acts of Christ. In both cases, this is substitution.

53:10 the LORD was pleased. Though the Servant did not deserve to die, it was the Lord's will for Him to do so (Mt 26:39; Lk 22:42; Jn 12:27; Ac 2:23). **a guilt offering.** Fulfilled by the Servant as the Lamb of God (v. 7; Jn 1:29). Christ is the Christian's Passover (1Co 5:7). This conclusively eliminates the error that Christ's atonement provides present-day healing for those who pray in faith. His death was an atonement for sin, not sickness. **see His offspring... prolong His days.** To see His offspring, the Servant must rise from the dead. He will do this and live to reign forever.

Yet He Himself bore the sin of many,
And interceded for the transgressors.

54 "Shout for joy, O barren one, you
who have borne no *child;*
Break forth into joyful shouting
and cry aloud, you who
have not travailed;
For the sons of the desolate one
will be more numerous
Than the sons of the married
woman," says the LORD.
2 "Enlarge the place of your tent;
Stretch out the curtains of your
dwellings, spare not;
Lengthen your cords
And strengthen your pegs.
3 "For you will spread abroad to
the right and to the left.
And your descendants will
possess nations
And will resettle the desolate cities.
4 "Fear not, for you will not
be put to shame;
And do not feel humiliated, for
you will not be disgraced;
But you will forget the
shame of your youth,
And the reproach of your widowhood
you will remember no more.
5 "For your husband is your Maker,
Whose name is the LORD of hosts;
And your Redeemer is the
Holy One of Israel,
Who is called the God
of all the earth.
6 "For the LORD has called you,
Like a wife forsaken and
grieved in spirit,
Even like a wife of *one's* youth
when she is rejected,"
Says your God.
7 "For a brief moment I forsook you,
But with great compassion
I will gather you.
8 "In an outburst of anger
I hid My face from you for a moment,
But with everlasting lovingkindness
I will have compassion on you,"
Says the LORD your Redeemer.

9 "For this is like the days of Noah to Me,
When I swore that the waters of Noah
Would not flood the earth again;
So I have sworn that I will
not be angry with you
Nor will I rebuke you.

10 "For the mountains may be removed
and the hills may shake,
But My lovingkindness will not
be removed from you,
And My covenant of peace
will not be shaken,"
Says the LORD who has
compassion on you.

11 "O afflicted one, storm-tossed,
and not comforted,
Behold, I will set your
stones in antimony,
And your foundations I will
lay in sapphires.
12 "Moreover, I will make your
battlements of rubies,
And your gates of crystal,
And your entire wall of
precious stones.
13 "All your sons will be taught
of the LORD;
And the well-being of your
sons will be great.
14 "In righteousness you will
be established;
You will be far from oppression,
for you will not fear;
And from terror, for it will
not come near you.
15 "If anyone fiercely assails *you*
it will not be from Me.
Whoever assails you will
fall because of you.
16 "Behold, I Myself have created the
smith who blows the fire of coals
And brings out a weapon for its work;
And I have created the
destroyer to ruin.
17 "No weapon that is formed
against you will prosper;
And every tongue that accuses you
in judgment you will condemn.
This is the heritage of the
servants of the LORD,
And their vindication is from
Me," declares the LORD.

Psalm 113:1–4

Praise the LORD!
Praise, O servants of the LORD,
Praise the name of the LORD.
2 Blessed be the name of the LORD
From this time forth and forever.
3 From the rising of the sun to its setting
The name of the LORD is to be praised.
4 The LORD is high above all nations;
His glory is above the heavens.

Proverbs 26:17-19

17 *Like* one who takes a dog by the ears
   Is he who passes by *and* meddles
      with strife not belonging to him.
18 Like a madman who throws
   Firebrands, arrows and death,
19 So is the man who deceives
      his neighbor,
   And says, "Was I not joking?"

Ephesians 3:1-21

3 For this reason I, Paul, the prisoner of Christ Jesus for the sake of you Gentiles— 2 if indeed you have heard of the stewardship of God's grace which was given to me for you; 3 that by revelation there was made known to me the mystery, as I wrote before in brief. 4 By referring to this, when you read you can understand my insight into the mystery of Christ, 5 which in other generations was not made known to the sons of men, as it has now been revealed to His holy apostles and prophets in the Spirit; 6 *to be specific,* that the Gentiles are fellow heirs and fellow members of the body, and fellow partakers of the promise in Christ Jesus through the gospel, 7 of which I was made a minister, according to the gift of God's grace which was given to me according to the working of His power. 8 To me, the very least of all saints, this grace was given, to preach to the Gentiles the unfathomable riches of Christ, 9 and to bring to light what is the administration of the mystery which for ages has been hidden in God who created all things; 10 so that the manifold wisdom of God might now be made known through the church to the rulers and the authorities in the heavenly *places.* 11 *This was* in accordance with the eternal purpose which He carried out in Christ Jesus our Lord, 12 in whom we have boldness and confident access through faith in Him. 13 Therefore I ask you not to lose heart at my tribulations on your behalf, for they are your glory.

14 For this reason I bow my knees before the Father, 15 from whom every family in heaven and on earth derives its name, 16 that He would grant you, according to the riches of His glory, to be strengthened with power through His Spirit in the inner man, 17 so that Christ may dwell in your hearts through faith; *and* that you, being rooted and grounded in love, 18 may be able to comprehend with all the saints what is the breadth and length and height and depth, 19 and to know the love of Christ which surpasses knowledge, that you may be filled up to all the fullness of God.

20 Now to Him who is able to do far more abundantly beyond all that we ask or think, according to the power that works within us, 21 to Him *be* the glory in the church and in Christ Jesus to all generations forever and ever. Amen.

3:19 to know the love of Christ. Not the love believers have for Christ, but the love of and from Christ that He places in their hearts before they can truly and fully love Him or anyone else (Ro 5:5). **which surpasses knowledge.** Knowledge of Christ's love is far beyond the capability of human reason and experience. It is only known by those who are God's children (Php 4:7). **filled up to all the fullness of God.** To be so strong spiritually, so compelled by divine love, that one is totally dominated by the Lord with nothing left of self. Human comprehension of the fullness of God is impossible, because even the most spiritual and wise believer cannot completely grasp the full extent of God's attributes and characteristics—His power, majesty, wisdom, love, mercy, patience, kindness, and everything He is and does. But believers can experience the greatness of God in their lives as a result of total devotion to Him. Note the fullness of God, here; the fullness of Christ in 4:13; and the fullness of the Spirit in 5:18.

DAY 1: How explicit does Isaiah 53 get regarding the Messiah?

Isaiah begins in v. 1 by saying, "Who has believed our message?" The question implied that, in spite of these and other prophecies, only a few would recognize the Servant when He appeared. This anticipation found literal fulfillment at Christ's First Advent. Israel did not welcome Him at His First Advent (Jn 1:9-11; 12:38). Paul applied the same prophecy to the world at large (Ro 10:16). At His First Coming, the nation did not recognize the mighty, incarnate power of God in the Person of Jesus, their Deliverer.

Yet Messiah Jesus was observed carefully by God ("before Him," v. 2), who ordered every minute circumstance of His life. "Parched ground...no...appearance that we should be attracted to Him." The Servant will arise in lowly conditions and wear none of the usual emblems of royalty, making His true identity visible only to the discerning eye of faith.

"Despised...forsaken...despised" (v. 3). The prophet foresees the hatred and rejection by mankind toward the Messiah/Servant, who suffered not only external abuse, but also internal grief over those He came to save. "We did not esteem." By using the first person, the prophet spoke for his unbelieving nation's aversion to a crucified Messiah and their lack of respect for the incarnate Son of God.

"Surely our griefs He Himself bore, and our sorrows He carried" (v. 4). Isaiah was saying that the Messiah would bear the consequences of the sins of men, namely the griefs and sorrows of life, though incredibly the Jews who watched Him die thought He was being punished by God for His own sins. Matthew found an analogical fulfillment of these words in Jesus' healing ministry (Mt 8:16–17), because sickness results from sin for which the Servant paid with His life. In eternity, all sickness will be removed, so ultimately it is included in the benefits of the atonement.

"He was pierced through for our transgressions...crushed for our iniquities" (v. 5). The Servant suffered not for His own sin, since He was sinless (Heb 4:15; 7:26), but as the substitute for sinners. The emphasis here is on Christ being the substitute recipient of God's wrath on sinners (2Co 5:21; Gal 1:3–4; Heb 10:9–10). "Chastening for our well-being." He suffered the chastisement of God in order to procure our peace with God. "By His scourging we are healed." The stripe that caused His death has brought salvation to those for whose sins He died. Peter confirms this in 1 Peter 2:24.

 # OCTOBER 2

Isaiah 55:1–56:12

55 "Ho! Every one who thirsts,
  come to the waters;
And you who have no money
  come, buy and eat.
Come, buy wine and milk
Without money and without cost.
2 "Why do you spend money
  for what is not bread,
And your wages for what
  does not satisfy?
Listen carefully to Me, and
  eat what is good,
And delight yourself
  in abundance.
3 "Incline your ear and come to Me.
  Listen, that you may live;
And I will make an everlasting
  covenant with you,
According to the faithful
  mercies shown to David.
4 "Behold, I have made him a
  witness to the peoples,

A leader and commander
  for the peoples.
5 "Behold, you will call a nation
  you do not know,
And a nation which knows
  you not will run to you,
Because of the LORD your God,
  even the Holy One of Israel;
For He has glorified you."

6 Seek the LORD while He may be found;
  Call upon Him while He is near.
7 Let the wicked forsake his way
And the unrighteous man
  his thoughts;
And let him return to the LORD,
And He will have compassion on him,
And to our God,
For He will abundantly pardon.

55:6–7 Here is one of the clearest Old Testament invitations to salvation now and kingdom blessing later. It gives an excellent example of how people were saved during the Old Testament period. Salvation grace and mercy were available to the soul that was willing to 1) seek the Lord (Dt 4:29; 2Ch 15:4) and 2) call on Him while He is still available (65:1; Ps 32:6; Pr 8:17; Mt 25:1–13). Such true seeking in faith is accompanied by repentance, which is described as forsaking ways and thoughts and turning from sinful living to the Lord. A sinner must come, believing in God, recognizing his sin and desiring forgiveness and deliverance from that sin. At the same time he must recognize his own inability to be righteous or to satisfy God and cast himself on God's mercy. It is then that he receives a complete pardon. His sin has been covered by the substitution of the Messiah in his place (chap. 53).

55:1 Every one. The Servant's redemptive work and glorious kingdom are for the benefit of all who are willing to come (53:6). The prophet invites his readers to participate in the benefits obtained by the suffering of the Servant in chap. 53 and described in chap. 54. **no money... Without money...without cost.** Benefits in the Servant's kingdom will be free because of His redemptive work (53:6, 8, 11; Eph 2:8–9). **wine and milk.** Symbols for abundance, satisfaction, and prosperity (SS 5:1; Joel 3:18).

8 "For My thoughts are not
      your thoughts,
    Nor are your ways My ways,"
      declares the LORD.
9 "For *as* the heavens are
      higher than the earth,
    So are My ways higher than your ways
    And My thoughts than your thoughts.
10 "For as the rain and the snow
      come down from heaven,
    And do not return there without
      watering the earth
    And making it bear and sprout,
    And furnishing seed to the sower
      and bread to the eater;
11 So will My word be which goes
      forth from My mouth;
    It will not return to Me empty,
    Without accomplishing what I desire,
    And without succeeding *in the
      matter* for which I sent it.
12 "For you will go out with joy
    And be led forth with peace;
    The mountains and the hills
      will break forth into shouts
      of joy before you,
    And all the trees of the field
      will clap *their* hands.
13 "Instead of the thorn bush the
      cypress will come up,
    And instead of the nettle the
      myrtle will come up,
    And it will be a memorial to the LORD,
    For an everlasting sign which
      will not be cut off."

56 Thus says the LORD,
    "Preserve justice and do
      righteousness,
    For My salvation is about to come
    And My righteousness to be revealed.
2 "How blessed is the man
      who does this,
    And the son of man who
      takes hold of it;
    Who keeps from profaning
      the sabbath,
    And keeps his hand from
      doing any evil."
3 Let not the foreigner who has
      joined himself to the LORD say,
    "The LORD will surely separate
      me from His people."
    Nor let the eunuch say, "Behold,
      I am a dry tree."
4 For thus says the LORD,
    "To the eunuchs who keep
      My sabbaths,

And choose what pleases Me,
    And hold fast My covenant,
5 To them I will give in My house and
      within My walls a memorial,
    And a name better than that
      of sons and daughters;
    I will give them an everlasting
      name which will not be cut off.

6 "Also the foreigners who join
      themselves to the LORD,
    To minister to Him, and to love
      the name of the LORD,
    To be His servants, every one who
      keeps from profaning the sabbath
    And holds fast My covenant;
7 Even those I will bring to
      My holy mountain
    And make them joyful in
      My house of prayer.
    Their burnt offerings and
      their sacrifices will be
      acceptable on My altar;
    For My house will be called a house
      of prayer for all the peoples."
8 The Lord GOD, who gathers the
      dispersed of Israel, declares,
    "Yet *others* I will gather to them,
      to those *already* gathered."

9 All you beasts of the field,
    All you beasts in the forest,
    Come to eat.
10 His watchmen are blind,
    All of them know nothing.
    All of them are mute dogs
      unable to bark,
    Dreamers lying down, who
      love to slumber;
11 And the dogs are greedy,
      they are not satisfied.
    And they are shepherds who
      have no understanding;
    They have all turned
      to their own way,
    Each one to his unjust gain,
      to the last one.
12 "Come," *they say,* "let us get wine, and
      let us drink heavily of strong drink;
    And tomorrow will be like
      today, only more so."

Psalm 113:5–9

5 Who is like the LORD our God,
    Who is enthroned on high,
6 Who humbles Himself to behold
    The things that are in heaven
      and in the earth?

979

⁷ He raises the poor from the dust
   And lifts the needy from the ash heap,
⁸ To make *them* sit with princes,
   With the princes of His people.
⁹ He makes the barren woman
   abide in the house
   As a joyful mother of children.
   Praise the LORD!

113:9 the barren woman. Sarah (Ge 21:2), Rebekah (Ge 25:21), and Rachel (Ge 30:23) would be the most significant since the outcome of the Abrahamic Covenant depended on these childless women being blessed by God to be mothers.

Proverbs 26:20–21

²⁰ For lack of wood the fire goes out,
   And where there is no whisperer,
   contention quiets down.
²¹ *Like* charcoal to hot embers
   and wood to fire,
   So is a contentious man
   to kindle strife.

Ephesians 4:1–32

4 Therefore I, the prisoner of the Lord, implore you to walk in a manner worthy of the calling with which you have been called, ²with all humility and gentleness, with patience, showing tolerance for one another in love, ³being diligent to preserve the unity of the Spirit in the bond of peace. ⁴*There is* one body and one Spirit, just as also you were called in one hope of your calling; ⁵one Lord, one faith, one baptism, ⁶one God and Father of all who is over all and through all and in all.

⁷But to each one of us grace was given according to the measure of Christ's gift. ⁸Therefore it says,

"WHEN HE ASCENDED ON HIGH,
HE LED CAPTIVE A HOST OF CAPTIVES,
AND HE GAVE GIFTS TO MEN."

⁹(Now this *expression*, "He ascended," what does it mean except that He also had descended into the lower parts of the earth? ¹⁰He who descended is Himself also He who ascended far above all the heavens, so that He might fill all things.) ¹¹And He gave some *as* apostles, and some *as* prophets, and some *as* evangelists, and some *as* pastors and teachers, ¹²for the equipping of the saints for the work of service, to the building up of the body of

4:12 equipping. This refers to restoring something to its original condition, or its being made fit or complete. In this context, it refers to leading Christians from sin to obedience. Scripture is the key to this process (Jn 15:3). **saints.** All who believe in Jesus Christ. **the work of service.** The spiritual service required of every Christian, not just of church leaders (1Co 15:58). **the building up of the body of Christ.** The spiritual edification, nurturing, and development of the church (Ac 20:32).

4:14 carried about by every wind of doctrine. Spiritually immature believers who are not grounded in the knowledge of Christ through God's Word are inclined to uncritically accept every sort of beguiling doctrinal error and fallacious interpretation of Scripture promulgated by deceitful, false teachers in the church. They must learn discernment (1Th 5:21–22). See 3:1; 4:20. The New Testament is replete with warnings of such danger (Ac 20:30–31; Ro 16:17–18; Gal 1:6–7; 1Ti 4:1–7; 2Ti 2:15–18; 2Pe 2:1–3).

Christ; ¹³until we all attain to the unity of the faith, and of the knowledge of the Son of God, to a mature man, to the measure of the stature which belongs to the fullness of Christ. ¹⁴As a result, we are no longer to be children, tossed here and there by waves and carried about by every wind of doctrine, by the trickery of men, by craftiness in deceitful scheming; ¹⁵but speaking the truth in love, we are to grow up in all *aspects* into Him who is the head, *even* Christ, ¹⁶from whom the whole body, being fitted and held together by what every joint supplies, according to the proper working of each individual part, causes the growth of the body for the building up of itself in love.

¹⁷So this I say, and affirm together with the Lord, that you walk no longer just as the Gentiles also walk, in the futility of their mind, ¹⁸being darkened in their understanding, excluded from the life of God because of the ignorance that is in them, because of the hardness of their heart; ¹⁹and they, having become callous, have given themselves over to sensuality for the practice of every kind of impurity with greediness. ²⁰But you did not learn Christ in this way, ²¹if indeed you have heard Him and have been taught in Him, just as truth is in Jesus, ²²that, in reference to your former manner of life, you lay aside the old self, which is being corrupted in accordance with the lusts of deceit, ²³and that you be renewed in the spirit of your mind, ²⁴and put on the new self, which

in *the likeness of* God has been created in righteousness and holiness of the truth.

²⁵Therefore, laying aside falsehood, SPEAK TRUTH EACH ONE *of you* WITH HIS NEIGHBOR, for we are members of one another. ²⁶BE ANGRY, AND *yet* DO NOT SIN; do not let the sun go down on your anger, ²⁷and do not give the devil an opportunity. ²⁸He who steals must steal no longer; but rather he must labor, performing with his own hands what is good, so that he will have *something* to share with one who has need. ²⁹Let no unwholesome word proceed from your mouth, but only such *a word* as is good for edification according to the need *of the moment,* so that it will give grace to those who hear. ³⁰Do not grieve the Holy Spirit of God, by whom you were sealed for the day of redemption. ³¹Let all bitterness and wrath and anger and clamor and slander be put away from you, along with all malice. ³²Be kind to one another, tender-hearted, forgiving each other, just as God in Christ also has forgiven you.

DAY 2: Define the spiritually gifted men Christ calls to serve His church in Ephesians 4:11.

"Apostles." A term used particularly of the 12 disciples who had seen the risen Christ (Ac 1:22), including Matthias, who replaced Judas. Later, Paul was uniquely set apart as the apostle to the Gentiles (Gal 1:15–17) and was numbered with the other apostles. Those apostles were chosen directly by Christ, so as to be called "apostles of Christ" (Gal 1:1; 1Pe 1:1). They were given 3 basic responsibilities: 1) to lay the foundation of the church (2:20); 2) to receive, declare, and write God's Word (3:5; Ac 11:28; 21:10–11); and 3) to give confirmation of that Word through signs, wonders, and miracles (2Co 12:12; Ac 8:6–7). The term "apostle" is used in more general ways of other men in the early church, such as Barnabas (Ac 14:4), Silas, Timothy, and others (Ro 16:7; Php 2:25). They are called "apostles of the churches" (2Co 8:23) rather than "apostles of Jesus Christ" like the 13. They were not self-perpetuating nor was any apostle who died replaced.

"Prophets." Not ordinary believers who had the gift of prophecy but specially commissioned men in the early church. The office of prophet seems to have been exclusively for work within a local congregation. They were not "sent ones" as were the apostles (Ac 13:1), but, as with the apostles, their office ceased with the completion of the New Testament. They sometimes spoke practical direct revelation for the church from God (Ac 11:21–28) or expounded revelation already given (implied in Ac 13:1). Their messages were to be judged by other prophets for validity (1Co 14:32) and had to conform to the teaching of the apostles (v. 37). Those two offices were replaced by the evangelists and teaching pastors.

"Evangelists." Men who proclaim the good news of salvation in Jesus Christ to unbelievers. The related verb translated "to preach the gospel" is used 54 times and the related noun translated "gospel" is used 76 times in the New Testament.

"Pastors and teachers." This phrase is best understood in context as a single office of leadership in the church. The Greek word translated "and" can mean "in particular" (1Ti 5:17). The normal meaning of pastor is "shepherd," so the two functions together define the teaching shepherd. He is identified as one who is under the "great Pastor" Jesus (Heb 13:20–21; 1Pe 2:25). One who holds this office is also called an "elder" (Titus 1:5–9) and "overseer" (1Ti 3:1–7).

OCTOBER 3

Isaiah 57:1–58:14

57 The righteous man perishes, and
　　no man takes it to heart;
And devout men are taken away,
　　while no one understands.
For the righteous man is
　　taken away from evil,
² He enters into peace;
　　They rest in their beds,
　　Each one who walked in
　　　　his upright way.
³ "But come here, you sons of a sorceress,
　　Offspring of an adulterer
　　　　and a prostitute.

⁴ "Against whom do you jest?
　　Against whom do you open
　　　　wide your mouth
　　And stick out your tongue?
　　Are you not children of rebellion,
　　Offspring of deceit,
⁵ *Who* inflame yourselves
　　　　among the oaks,
　　Under every luxuriant tree,
　　Who slaughter the children
　　　　in the ravines,
　　Under the clefts of the crags?
⁶ "Among the smooth *stones*
　　　　of the ravine
　　Is your portion, they are your lot;
　　Even to them you have poured
　　　　out a drink offering,

You have made a grain offering.
Shall I relent concerning these things?

7 "Upon a high and lofty mountain
You have made your bed.
You also went up there
to offer sacrifice.

8 "Behind the door and the doorpost
You have set up your sign;
Indeed, far removed from Me, you
have uncovered yourself,
And have gone up and made
your bed wide.
And you have made an agreement
for yourself with them,
You have loved their bed,
You have looked on *their* manhood.

9 "You have journeyed to
the king with oil
And increased your perfumes;
You have sent your envoys
a great distance
And made *them* go down to Sheol.

10 "You were tired out by the
length of your road,
Yet you did not say, 'It is hopeless.'
You found renewed strength,
Therefore you did not faint.

11 "Of whom were you worried
and fearful
When you lied, and did
not remember Me
Nor give *Me* a thought?
Was I not silent even for a long time
So you do not fear Me?

12 "I will declare your righteousness
and your deeds,
But they will not profit you.

13 "When you cry out, let your
collection *of idols* deliver you.
But the wind will carry all of them up,
And a breath will take *them away.*
But he who takes refuge in Me
will inherit the land
And will possess My holy mountain."

14 And it will be said,
"Build up, build up, prepare the way,
Remove *every* obstacle out of
the way of My people."

15 For thus says the high
and exalted One
Who lives forever, whose name is Holy,
"I dwell *on* a high and holy place,
And *also* with the contrite
and lowly of spirit
In order to revive the spirit of the lowly
And to revive the heart of the contrite.

16 "For I will not contend forever,
Nor will I always be angry;
For the spirit would grow
faint before Me,
And the breath *of those*
whom I have made.

17 "Because of the iniquity of his unjust
gain I was angry and struck him;
I hid *My face* and was angry,
And he went on turning away,
in the way of his heart.

18 "I have seen his ways, but
I will heal him;
I will lead him and restore comfort
to him and to his mourners,

19 Creating the praise of the lips.
Peace, peace to him who is far
and to him who is near,"
Says the LORD, "and I will heal him."

20 But the wicked are like
the tossing sea,
For it cannot be quiet,
And its waters toss up refuse and mud.

21 "There is no peace," says my
God, "for the wicked."

58 "Cry loudly, do not hold back;
Raise your voice like a trumpet,
And declare to My people
their transgression
And to the house of Jacob their sins.

2 "Yet they seek Me day by day and
delight to know My ways,
As a nation that has done
righteousness
And has not forsaken the
ordinance of their God.
They ask Me *for* just decisions,
They delight in the nearness of God.

3 'Why have we fasted and
You do not see?
Why have we humbled ourselves
and You do not notice?'
Behold, on the day of your fast
you find *your* desire,
And drive hard all your workers.

4 "Behold, you fast for contention
and strife and to strike
with a wicked fist.
You do not fast like *you do* today to
make your voice heard on high.

5 "Is it a fast like this which I choose, a
day for a man to humble himself?
Is it for bowing one's head like a reed
And for spreading out sackcloth
and ashes as a bed?
Will you call this a fast, even an
acceptable day to the LORD?

58:3–7 Why…? The people complained when God did not recognize their religious actions, but God responded that their fastings had been only half-hearted. Hypocritical fasting resulted in contention, quarreling, and pretense, excluding the possibility of genuine prayer to God. Fasting consisted of more than just an outward ritual and a mock repentance. It involved penitence over sin and consequent humility, disconnecting from sin and oppression of others, feeding the hungry, and acting humanely toward those in need.

6 "Is this not the fast which I choose,
　To loosen the bonds of wickedness,
　To undo the bands of the yoke,
　And to let the oppressed go free
　And break every yoke?
7 "Is it not to divide your bread
　　with the hungry
　And bring the homeless
　　poor into the house;
　When you see the naked, to cover him;
　And not to hide yourself
　　from your own flesh?
8 "Then your light will break
　　out like the dawn,
　And your recovery will
　　speedily spring forth;
　And your righteousness
　　will go before you;
　The glory of the LORD will
　　be your rear guard.
9 "Then you will call, and the
　　LORD will answer;
　You will cry, and He will
　　say, 'Here I am.'
　If you remove the yoke
　　from your midst,
　The pointing of the finger and
　　speaking wickedness,
10 And if you give yourself
　　to the hungry
　And satisfy the desire of the afflicted,
　Then your light will rise in darkness
　And your gloom *will
　　become* like midday.
11 "And the LORD will continually
　　guide you,
　And satisfy your desire in
　　scorched places,
　And give strength to your bones;
　And you will be like a watered garden,
　And like a spring of water
　　whose waters do not fail.

12 "Those from among you will
　　rebuild the ancient ruins;
　You will raise up the age-old
　　foundations;
　And you will be called the
　　repairer of the breach,
　The restorer of the streets
　　in which to dwell.

13 "If because of the sabbath,
　　you turn your foot
　From doing your *own* pleasure
　　on My holy day,
　And call the sabbath a delight, the
　　holy *day* of the LORD honorable,
　And honor it, desisting from
　　your *own* ways,
　From seeking your *own* pleasure
　And speaking *your own* word,
14 Then you will take delight
　　in the LORD,
　And I will make you ride on
　　the heights of the earth;
　And I will feed you *with* the
　　heritage of Jacob your father,
　For the mouth of the LORD
　　has spoken."

58:14 take delight in the LORD. Repentant people walking in fellowship with the Lord experience satisfaction of soul (Ps 37:4). Their satisfaction will not come from material goods.

Psalm 114:1–8

When Israel went forth from Egypt,
　The house of Jacob from a
　　people of strange language,
2 Judah became His sanctuary,
　Israel, His dominion.

3 The sea looked and fled;
　The Jordan turned back.
4 The mountains skipped like rams,
　The hills, like lambs.
5 What ails you, O sea, that you flee?
　O Jordan, that you turn back?
6 O mountains, that you
　　skip like rams?
　O hills, like lambs?

7 Tremble, O earth, before the Lord,
　Before the God of Jacob,
8 Who turned the rock into
　　a pool of water,
　The flint into a fountain of water.

Proverbs 26:22

²² The words of a whisperer are
   like dainty morsels,
And they go down into the
   innermost parts of the body.

Ephesians 5:1-14

5 Therefore be imitators of God, as beloved children; ² and walk in love, just as Christ also loved you and gave Himself up for us, an offering and a sacrifice to God as a fragrant aroma.

³ But immorality or any impurity or greed must not even be named among you, as is proper among saints; ⁴ and *there must be no* filthiness and silly talk, or coarse jesting, which are not fitting, but rather giving of thanks. ⁵ For this you know with certainty, that no immoral or impure person or covetous man, who is an idolater, has an inheritance in the kingdom of Christ and God.

⁶ Let no one deceive you with empty words, for because of these things the wrath of God comes upon the sons of disobedience. ⁷ Therefore do not be partakers with them; ⁸ for you were formerly darkness, but now you are Light in the Lord; walk as children of Light ⁹ (for the fruit of the Light *consists* in all goodness and righteousness and truth), ¹⁰ trying to learn what is pleasing to the Lord. ¹¹ Do not participate in the unfruitful deeds of darkness, but instead even expose them; ¹² for it is disgraceful even to speak of the things which are done by them in secret. ¹³ But all things become visible when they are exposed by the light, for everything that becomes visible is light. ¹⁴ For this reason it says,

"Awake, sleeper,
And arise from the dead,
And Christ will shine on you."

DAY 3: What should the standard be for a Christian's life?

"Be imitators of God," says Paul in Ephesians 5:1. The Christian has no greater calling or purpose than that of imitating his Lord. That is the very purpose of sanctification, growing in likeness to the Lord while serving Him on earth (Mt 5:48). The Christian life is designed to reproduce godliness as modeled by the Savior and Lord, Jesus Christ, in whose image believers have been recreated through the new birth (Ro 8:29; 2Co 3:18; 1Pe 1:14-16). As God's dear children, believers are to become more and more like their heavenly Father (Mt 5:48; 1Pe 1:15-16).

"And walk in love, just as Christ also loved you and gave Himself up for us" (v. 2). The Lord is the supreme example in His self-sacrificing love for lost sinners (4:32; Ro 5:8-10). He took human sin upon Himself and gave up His very life that men might be redeemed from their sin. They are henceforth to be imitators of His great love in the newness and power of the Holy Spirit, who enables them to demonstrate divine love. "A fragrant aroma." Christ's offering of Himself for fallen man pleased and glorified His heavenly Father, because it demonstrated in the most complete and perfect way God's sovereign, perfect, unconditional, and divine kind of love.

In absolute contrast to God's holiness and love, such sins as "immorality…greed" (v. 3), by which Satan seeks to drive God's children as far away as possible from His image and will, are so godless that the world should never have reason even to suspect their presence in Christians. The 3 inappropriate sins of the tongue (v. 4) include any speech that is obscene and degrading or foolish and dirty, as well as suggestive and immoral wit. All such are destructive of holy living and godly testimony and should be confessed, forsaken, and replaced by open expressions of thankfulness to God (Col 3:8).

✒ OCTOBER 4

Isaiah 59:1-60:22

59 Behold, the LORD'S hand
   is not so short
That it cannot save;
Nor is His ear so dull
That it cannot hear.
² But your iniquities have made
   a separation between
   you and your God,
And your sins have hidden *His* face
   from you so that He does not hear.
³ For your hands are defiled with blood
And your fingers with iniquity;
Your lips have spoken falsehood,
Your tongue mutters wickedness.
⁴ No one sues righteously and
   no one pleads honestly.
They trust in confusion
   and speak lies;
They conceive mischief and
   bring forth iniquity.

5 They hatch adders' eggs and
   weave the spider's web;
He who eats of their eggs dies,
And *from* that which is crushed
   a snake breaks forth.

6 Their webs will not become clothing,
Nor will they cover themselves
   with their works;
Their works are works of iniquity,
And an act of violence is
   in their hands.

7 Their feet run to evil,
And they hasten to shed
   innocent blood;
Their thoughts are thoughts
   of iniquity,
Devastation and destruction
   are in their highways.

8 They do not know the way of peace,
And there is no justice in their tracks;
They have made their paths crooked,
Whoever treads on them
   does not know peace.

9 Therefore justice is far from us,
And righteousness does
   not overtake us;
We hope for light, but
   behold, darkness,
For brightness, but we
   walk in gloom.

10 We grope along the wall
   like blind men,
We grope like those who
   have no eyes;
We stumble at midday as
   in the twilight,
Among those who are vigorous
   we are like dead men.

11 All of us growl like bears,
And moan sadly like doves;
We hope for justice, but
   there is none,
For salvation, *but* it is far from us.

12 For our transgressions are
   multiplied before You,
And our sins testify against us;
For our transgressions are with us,
And we know our iniquities:

13 Transgressing and denying the LORD,
And turning away from our God,
Speaking oppression and revolt,
Conceiving *in* and uttering from
   the heart lying words.

14 Justice is turned back,
And righteousness stands far away;
For truth has stumbled in the street,
And uprightness cannot enter.

15 Yes, truth is lacking;
And he who turns aside from
   evil makes himself a prey.

Now the LORD saw,
And it was displeasing in His sight
   that there was no justice.

16 And He saw that there was no man,
And was astonished that there
   was no one to intercede;
Then His own arm brought
   salvation to Him,
And His righteousness upheld Him.

17 He put on righteousness
   like a breastplate,
And a helmet of salvation
   on His head;
And He put on garments of
   vengeance for clothing
And wrapped Himself with
   zeal as a mantle.

59:15–16 the LORD saw...no one to intercede.
The Lord was aware of Israel's tragic condition and of the absence of anyone to intervene
on His behalf. The Lord took it on Himself to
change Israel's condition through the intervention of His Suffering Servant (53:12).

**59:17 righteousness like a breastplate...hel-
met of salvation.** Figuratively speaking, the
Lord armed Himself for the deliverance of His
people and for taking vengeance on enemies
who would seek His destruction. Paul drew
on this terminology in describing a believer's
spiritual preparation for warding off the attacks
of Satan (Eph 6:14, 17; 1Th 5:8).

---

18 According to *their* deeds,
   so He will repay,
Wrath to His adversaries,
   recompense to His enemies;
To the coastlands He will
   make recompense.

19 So they will fear the name of
   the LORD from the west
And His glory from the
   rising of the sun,
For He will come like a
   rushing stream
Which the wind of the LORD drives.

20 "A Redeemer will come to Zion,
And to those who turn from
   transgression in Jacob,"
   declares the LORD.

21 "As for Me, this is My covenant with them," says the LORD: "My Spirit which is upon you, and My words which I have put in your mouth shall not depart from your mouth, nor from the mouth of your offspring, nor from the mouth of your offspring's offspring," says the LORD, "from now and forever."

60

"Arise, shine; for your light has come,
And the glory of the LORD
   has risen upon you.
2 "For behold, darkness will
   cover the earth
And deep darkness the peoples;
But the LORD will rise upon you
And His glory will appear upon you.
3 "Nations will come to your light,
And kings to the brightness
   of your rising.

4 "Lift up your eyes round about and see;
They all gather together,
   they come to you.
Your sons will come from afar,
And your daughters will be
   carried in the arms.
5 "Then you will see and be radiant,
And your heart will thrill and rejoice;
Because the abundance of the
   sea will be turned to you,
The wealth of the nations
   will come to you.
6 "A multitude of camels will cover you,
The young camels of
   Midian and Ephah;
All those from Sheba will come;
They will bring gold and
   frankincense,
And will bear good news of
   the praises of the LORD.
7 "All the flocks of Kedar will be
   gathered together to you,
The rams of Nebaioth will
   minister to you;
They will go up with
   acceptance on My altar,
And I shall glorify My glorious house.
8 "Who are these who fly like a cloud
And like the doves to their lattices?
9 "Surely the coastlands will wait for Me;
And the ships of Tarshish
   will come first,
To bring your sons from afar,
Their silver and their gold with them,
For the name of the LORD your God,
And for the Holy One of Israel
   because He has glorified you.

10 "Foreigners will build up your walls,
And their kings will minister to you;
For in My wrath I struck you,
And in My favor I have had
   compassion on you.
11 "Your gates will be open continually;
They will not be closed day or night,
So that *men* may bring to you
   the wealth of the nations,
With their kings led in procession.
12 "For the nation and the kingdom which
   will not serve you will perish,
And the nations will be utterly ruined.
13 "The glory of Lebanon
   will come to you,
The juniper, the box tree and
   the cypress together,
To beautify the place of
   My sanctuary;
And I shall make the place
   of My feet glorious.
14 "The sons of those who afflicted
   you will come bowing to you,
And all those who despised
   you will bow themselves at
   the soles of your feet;
And they will call you the
   city of the LORD,
The Zion of the Holy One of Israel.

15 "Whereas you have been
   forsaken and hated
With no one passing through,
I will make you an everlasting pride,
A joy from generation to generation.
16 "You will also suck the milk of nations
And suck the breast of kings;
Then you will know that I, the
   LORD, am your Savior
And your Redeemer, the
   Mighty One of Jacob.
17 "Instead of bronze I will bring gold,
And instead of iron I will bring silver,
And instead of wood, bronze,
And instead of stones, iron.
And I will make peace your
   administrators
And righteousness your overseers.
18 "Violence will not be heard
   again in your land,
Nor devastation or destruction
   within your borders;
But you will call your walls salvation,
   and your gates praise.
19 "No longer will you have the
   sun for light by day,
Nor for brightness will the
   moon give you light;

But you will have the LORD
for an everlasting light,
And your God for your glory.
²⁰ "Your sun will no longer set,
Nor will your moon wane;
For you will have the LORD
for an everlasting light,
And the days of your
mourning will be over.
²¹ "Then all your people *will be* righteous;
They will possess the land forever,
The branch of My planting,
The work of My hands,
That I may be glorified.
²² "The smallest one will become a clan,
And the least one a mighty nation.
I, the LORD, will hasten it in its time."

60:19 No longer...have the sun...everlasting light. Isaiah, looking beyond the millennial kingdom, sees a view of the new Jerusalem following the Millennium (Rev 21:23; 22:5). His prophetic perspective did not allow him to distinguish the eternal phase of the future kingdom from the temporal one, just as the Old Testament prophets could not distinguish between the first and second advent of Christ (1Pe 1:10–11).

Psalm 115:1–8

Not to us, O LORD, not to us,
But to Your name give glory
Because of Your lovingkindness,
because of Your truth.
² Why should the nations say,
"Where, now, is their God?"
³ But our God is in the heavens;
He does whatever He pleases.
⁴ Their idols are silver and gold,
The work of man's hands.
⁵ They have mouths, but
they cannot speak;
They have eyes, but they cannot see;
⁶ They have ears, but they cannot hear;
They have noses, but they
cannot smell;
⁷ They have hands, but
they cannot feel;
They have feet, but they cannot walk;
They cannot make a sound
with their throat.
⁸ Those who make them will
become like them,
Everyone who trusts in them.

Proverbs 26:23

²³ *Like* an earthen vessel overlaid
with silver dross
Are burning lips and a wicked heart.

26:23 earthen vessel overlaid. A cheap veneer of silver over a common clay pot hiding its commonness and fragility is like the deception spoken by evil people. This thought is expanded in vv. 24–28.

Ephesians 5:15–33

¹⁵ Therefore be careful how you walk, not as unwise men but as wise, ¹⁶ making the most of your time, because the days are evil. ¹⁷ So then do not be foolish, but understand what the will of the Lord is. ¹⁸ And do not get drunk with wine, for that is dissipation, but be filled with the Spirit, ¹⁹ speaking to one another in psalms and hymns and spiritual songs, singing and making melody with your heart to the Lord; ²⁰ always giving thanks for all things in the name of our Lord Jesus Christ to God, even the Father; ²¹ and be subject to one another in the fear of Christ.

²² Wives, *be subject* to your own husbands, as to the Lord. ²³ For the husband is the head of the wife, as Christ also is the head of the church, He Himself *being* the Savior of the body. ²⁴ But as the church is subject to Christ, so also the wives *ought to be* to their husbands in everything.

²⁵ Husbands, love your wives, just as Christ also loved the church and gave Himself up

5:18 but be filled with the Spirit. True communion with God is not induced by drunkenness, but by the Holy Spirit. Paul is not speaking of the Holy Spirit's indwelling (Ro 8:9) or the baptism by Christ with the Holy Spirit (1Co 12:13), because every Christian is indwelt and baptized by the Spirit at the time of salvation. He is rather giving a command for believers to live continually under the influence of the Spirit by letting the Word control them, pursuing pure lives, confessing all known sin, dying to self, surrendering to God's will, and depending on His power in all things. Being filled with the Spirit is living in the conscious presence of the Lord Jesus Christ, letting His mind, through the Word, dominate everything that is thought and done. Being filled with the Spirit is the same as walking in the Spirit.

for her, 26 so that He might sanctify her, having cleansed her by the washing of water with the word, 27 that He might present to Himself the church in all her glory, having no spot or wrinkle or any such thing; but that she would be holy and blameless. 28 So husbands ought also to love their own wives as their own bodies. He who loves his own wife loves himself; 29 for no one ever hated his own flesh, but nourishes and cherishes it, just as Christ also *does* the church, 30 because we are members of His body. 31 FOR THIS REASON A MAN SHALL LEAVE HIS FATHER AND MOTHER AND SHALL BE JOINED TO HIS WIFE, AND THE TWO SHALL BECOME ONE FLESH. 32 This mystery is great; but I am speaking with reference to Christ and the church. 33 Nevertheless, each individual among you also is to love his own wife even as himself, and the wife must *see to it* that she respects her husband.

DAY 4: How do the principles of submission and love in Ephesians 5:21–33 work in a marriage?

The section that begins with a call to wise living (5:15) leads up to Paul's general counsel about submission (5:21). This last verse serves to introduce the next section (5:22–6:9), which spells out the godly expectations for various relationships. Here Paul stated unequivocally that every Spirit-filled Christian is to be a humble, submissive Christian. This is foundational to all the relationships in this section. No believer is inherently superior to any other believer. In their standing before God, all believers are equal in every way (3:28).

Having established the foundational principle of submission (5:21), Paul applied it first to the wife. The command is unqualified and applicable to every Christian wife, no matter what her own abilities, education, knowledge of Scripture, spiritual maturity, or any other qualities might be in relation to those of her husband. The submission is not the husband's to command but for the wife to willingly and lovingly offer. The phrase "your own husbands" limits the wife's submission to the one man whom God has placed over her.

The Spirit-filled wife recognizes that her husband's role in giving leadership is not only God-ordained but also a reflection of Christ's own loving, authoritative headship of the church. As the Lord delivered His church from the dangers of sin, death, and hell, so the husband provides for, protects, preserves, and loves his wife, leading her to blessing as she submits (Titus 1:4; 2:13; 3:6).

Paul has much more to say to the man who has been placed in the role of authority within marriage. That authority comes with supreme responsibilities for husbands in regard to their wives. Husbands are to love their wives with the same sacrificial love that Christ has for His church. Christ gave everything He had, including His own life, for the sake of His church, and that is the standard of sacrifice for a husband's love of his wife.

The clarity of God's guidelines makes it certain that problems in marriage must always be traced in both directions so that each partner clearly understands his or her roles and responsibilities. Failure to love is just as often the source of marital trouble as failure to submit.

OCTOBER 5

Isaiah 61:1–62:12

61 The Spirit of the Lord
GOD is upon me,
Because the LORD has anointed me
To bring good news to the afflicted;
He has sent me to bind up
the brokenhearted,
To proclaim liberty to captives
And freedom to prisoners;
2 To proclaim the favorable
year of the LORD
And the day of vengeance
of our God;
To comfort all who mourn,

61:1–2a The Spirit...favorable year of the LORD. The Servant of the Lord (42:1) will be the ultimate Preacher and the Redeemer of Israel who rescues them. Jesus speaks of the initial fulfillment of this promise, referring it to His ministry of providing salvation's comfort to the spiritually oppressed (Lk 4:18–19). He says specifically, "Today this Scripture has been fulfilled in your hearing" (Lk 4:21). The Jews who were saved during Christ's ministry, and those being saved during this church age, still do not fulfill the promise of the salvation of the nation to come in the end time (Zec 12:10—13:1; Ro 11:25–27).

3 To grant those who mourn *in* Zion,
Giving them a garland instead of ashes,
The oil of gladness instead
of mourning,
The mantle of praise instead of
a spirit of fainting.
So they will be called oaks
of righteousness,
The planting of the LORD, that
He may be glorified.

4 Then they will rebuild
the ancient ruins,
They will raise up the
former devastations;
And they will repair the ruined cities,
The desolations of many generations.

5 Strangers will stand and
pasture your flocks,
And foreigners will be your farmers
and your vinedressers.

6 But you will be called the
priests of the LORD;
You will be spoken of *as*
ministers of our God.
You will eat the wealth of nations,
And in their riches you will boast.

7 Instead of your shame *you will
have a* double *portion,*
And *instead of* humiliation they will
shout for joy over their portion.
Therefore they will possess a
double *portion* in their land,
Everlasting joy will be theirs.

8 For I, the LORD, love justice,
I hate robbery in the burnt offering;
And I will faithfully give them
their recompense
And make an everlasting
covenant with them.

9 Then their offspring will be
known among the nations,
And their descendants in the
midst of the peoples.
All who see them will recognize them
Because they are the offspring
whom the LORD has blessed.

10 I will rejoice greatly in the LORD,
My soul will exult in my God;
For He has clothed me with
garments of salvation,
He has wrapped me with a
robe of righteousness,
As a bridegroom decks
himself with a garland,
And as a bride adorns herself
with her jewels.

61:10 clothed me...wrapped me. Here is the Old Testament picture of imputed righteousness, the essential heart of the New Covenant. When a penitent sinner recognizes he can't achieve his own righteousness by works (Ro 3:19–22; 2Co 5:21; Php 3:8–9), and repents and calls on the mercy of God, the Lord covers him with His own divine righteousness by grace through his faith.

11 For as the earth brings
forth its sprouts,
And as a garden causes the things
sown in it to spring up,
So the Lord GOD will cause
righteousness and praise
To spring up before all the nations.

62 For Zion's sake I will not keep silent,
And for Jerusalem's sake I
will not keep quiet,
Until her righteousness goes
forth like brightness,
And her salvation like a
torch that is burning.

2 The nations will see your
righteousness,
And all kings your glory;
And you will be called by a new name
Which the mouth of the
LORD will designate.

3 You will also be a crown of beauty
in the hand of the LORD,
And a royal diadem in the
hand of your God.

4 It will no longer be said to
you, "Forsaken,"
Nor to your land will it any
longer be said, "Desolate";
But you will be called, "My
delight is in her,"
And your land, "Married";
For the LORD delights in you,
And *to Him* your land will be married.

5 For *as* a young man marries a virgin,
So your sons will marry you;
And *as* the bridegroom
rejoices over the bride,
So your God will rejoice over you.

6 On your walls, O Jerusalem, I
have appointed watchmen;
All day and all night they
will never keep silent.
You who remind the LORD, take
no rest for yourselves;

7 And give Him no rest until
   He establishes
   And makes Jerusalem a
   praise in the earth.
8 The LORD has sworn by His right
   hand and by His strong arm,
   "I will never again give your grain
   as food for your enemies;
   Nor will foreigners drink your new
   wine for which you have labored."
9 But those who garner it will eat
   it and praise the LORD;
   And those who gather it will drink
   it in the courts of My sanctuary.
10 Go through, go through the gates,
   Clear the way for the people;
   Build up, build up the highway,
   Remove the stones, lift up a
   standard over the peoples.
11 Behold, the LORD has proclaimed
   to the end of the earth,
   Say to the daughter of Zion, "Lo,
   your salvation comes;
   Behold His reward is with Him, and
   His recompense before Him."
12 And they will call them,
   "The holy people,
   The redeemed of the LORD";
   And you will be called, "Sought
   out, a city not forsaken."

Psalm 115:9–13

9 O Israel, trust in the LORD;
   He is their help and their shield.
10 O house of Aaron, trust in the LORD;
   He is their help and their shield.
11 You who fear the LORD,
   trust in the LORD;
   He is their help and their shield.
12 The LORD has been mindful
   of us; He will bless *us*;
   He will bless the house of Israel;
   He will bless the house of Aaron.
13 He will bless those who fear the LORD,
   The small together with the great.

Proverbs 26:24–26

24 He who hates disguises *it* with his lips,
   But he lays up deceit in his heart.
25 When he speaks graciously,
   do not believe him,
   For there are seven abominations
   in his heart.
26 *Though his* hatred covers
   itself with guile,
   His wickedness will be revealed
   before the assembly.

Ephesians 6:1–24

6 Children, obey your parents in the Lord,
for this is right. [2] HONOR YOUR FATHER AND
MOTHER (which is the first commandment with
a promise), [3] SO THAT IT MAY BE WELL WITH YOU,
AND THAT YOU MAY LIVE LONG ON THE EARTH.

[4] Fathers, do not provoke your children
to anger, but bring them up in the discipline
and instruction of the Lord.

[5] Slaves, be obedient to those who are your
masters according to the flesh, with fear and
trembling, in the sincerity of your heart, as
to Christ; [6] not by way of eyeservice, as men-
pleasers, but as slaves of Christ, doing the
will of God from the heart. [7] With good will
render service, as to the Lord, and not to men,
[8] knowing that whatever good thing each one
does, this he will receive back from the Lord,
whether slave or free.

[9] And masters, do the same things to them,
and give up threatening, knowing that both
their Master and yours is in heaven, and there
is no partiality with Him.

[10] Finally, be strong in the Lord and in the
strength of His might. [11] Put on the full armor
of God, so that you will be able to stand firm
against the schemes of the devil. [12] For our
struggle is not against flesh and blood, but
against the rulers, against the powers, against
the world forces of this darkness, against the
spiritual *forces* of wickedness in the heavenly
places. [13] Therefore, take up the full armor of
God, so that you will be able to resist in the evil
day, and having done everything, to stand firm.
[14] Stand firm therefore, HAVING GIRDED YOUR
LOINS WITH TRUTH, and HAVING PUT ON THE
BREASTPLATE OF RIGHTEOUSNESS, [15] and having
shod YOUR FEET WITH THE PREPARATION OF THE
GOSPEL OF PEACE; [16] in addition to all, taking up
the shield of faith with which you will be able to
extinguish all the flaming arrows of the evil *one*.
[17] And take THE HELMET OF SALVATION, and the
sword of the Spirit, which is the word of God.
[18] With all prayer and petition pray at all

**6:10 be strong in the Lord and in the strength
of His might.** Ultimately, Satan's power over
Christians is already broken, and the great war
is won through Christ's crucifixion and resurrection, which forever conquered the power of
sin and death (Ro 5:18–21; 1Co 15:56–57; Heb
2:14). However, in life on earth, battles of temptation go on regularly. The Lord's power, the
strength of His Spirit, and the force of biblical
truth are required for victory.

6:13 Therefore, take up the full armor of God. Paul again emphasized the necessity of the Christian's appropriating God's full spiritual armor by obedience in taking it up, or putting it on (v. 11). The first 3 pieces of armor (girdle, breastplate, and shoes/boots, vv. 14–15) were worn continually on the battlefield; the last 3 (shield, helmet, and sword, vv. 16–17) were kept ready for use when actual fighting began. **the evil day.** Since the fall of man, every day has been evil, a condition that will persist until the Lord returns and establishes His own righteous kingdom on earth. **having done everything, to stand firm.** Standing firm against the enemy without wavering or falling is the goal.

times in the Spirit, and with this in view, be on the alert with all perseverance and petition for all the saints, [19] and *pray* on my behalf, that utterance may be given to me in the opening of my mouth, to make known with boldness the mystery of the gospel, [20] for which I am an ambassador in chains; that in *proclaiming* it I may speak boldly, as I ought to speak.

[21] But that you also may know about my circumstances, how I am doing, Tychicus, the beloved brother and faithful minister in the Lord, will make everything known to you. [22] I have sent him to you for this very purpose, so that you may know about us, and that he may comfort your hearts.

[23] Peace be to the brethren, and love with faith, from God the Father and the Lord Jesus Christ. [24] Grace be with all those who love our Lord Jesus Christ with incorruptible *love*.

DAY 5: Why does Paul insist in Ephesians 6:10–17 that Christians must be prepared for spiritual battle?

The true believer described in chapters 1–3, who lives the Spirit-controlled life described in 4:1–6:9, can be sure to encounter spiritual warfare. So Paul closed his letter with warnings about upcoming battles and instructions about victorious living. The Lord provides His saints with sufficient armor to combat and defeat the adversary. Ephesians 6:10–13 briefly sets forth the basic truths regarding the believer's necessary spiritual preparation as well as truths about the enemy, the battle, and the victory. Verses 14–17 specify the six most necessary pieces of spiritual armor with which God equips His children to resist and overcome Satan's assaults. The spiritual equipment parallels the standard military equipment worn by soldiers in Paul's day:

1. Belt of truth—The soldier wore a tunic of loose-fitting clothing. Since ancient combat was largely hand-to-hand, the tunic was a potential hindrance and danger. The belt cinched up the loose material. The belt that pulls together all the spiritual loose ends is "truth" or, better, "truthfulness."
2. Breastplate of righteousness—A tough, sleeveless piece of leather or heavy material covered the soldier's full torso, protecting his heart and other vital organs. Because righteousness, or holiness, is such a distinctive characteristic of God Himself, it is easy to understand why it is the Christian's chief protection against Satan and his schemes.
3. Boots of the gospel—Roman soldiers wore boots with nails in them to grip the ground in combat. The gospel of peace pertains to the good news that through Christ believers are at peace with God, and He is on their side (Ro 5:6–10).
4. Shield of faith—This Greek word usually refers to the large shield that protected the soldier's entire body. The believer's continual trust in God's Word and promise is "in addition to all" absolutely necessary to protect him or her from temptations to every sort of sin.
5. Helmet of salvation—The helmet protected the head, always a major target in battle. This passage is speaking to those who are already saved; therefore, it does not refer to attaining salvation. Rather, since Satan seeks to destroy a believer's assurance of salvation with his weapons of doubt and discouragement, the believer must be as conscious of his or her confident status in Christ as he or she would be aware of a helmet on the head.
6. Sword of the Spirit—A sword was the soldier's only weapon. In the same way, God's Word is the only weapon that a believer needs, infinitely more powerful than any of Satan's devices.

OCTOBER 6

Isaiah 63:1–64:12

63 Who is this who comes from Edom,
With garments of glowing
colors from Bozrah,
This One who is majestic
in His apparel,
Marching in the greatness
of His strength?
"It is I who speak in righteousness,
mighty to save."

2 Why is Your apparel red,
And Your garments like the one
who treads in the wine press?

3 "I have trodden the wine trough alone,
And from the peoples there
was no man with Me.
I also trod them in My anger
And trampled them in My wrath;
And their lifeblood is sprinkled
on My garments,
And I stained all My raiment.

4 "For the day of vengeance
was in My heart,
And My year of redemption has come.

5 "I looked, and there was no one to help,
And I was astonished and there
was no one to uphold;
So My own arm brought
salvation to Me,
And My wrath upheld Me.

6 "I trod down the peoples in My anger
And made them drunk in My wrath,
And I poured out their
lifeblood on the earth."

7 I shall make mention of the
lovingkindnesses of the LORD,
the praises of the LORD,
According to all that the
LORD has granted us,
And the great goodness toward
the house of Israel,
Which He has granted them
according to His compassion
And according to the abundance
of His lovingkindnesses.

8 For He said, "Surely, they
are My people,
Sons who will not deal falsely."
So He became their Savior.

9 In all their affliction He was afflicted,
And the angel of His
presence saved them;
In His love and in His mercy
He redeemed them,

63:7–8 lovingkindnesses…lovingkindnesses.
All the plurals in this verse imply that language is inadequate to recite all the goodness and undeserved mercies God has showered on the nation time after time because of His everlasting covenant with them. By His elective choice, they became His people and He their Savior (43:1, 3); this guarantees that they will not always be false, but someday true and faithful to God because of His sovereign election of them.

And He lifted them and carried
them all the days of old.

10 But they rebelled
And grieved His Holy Spirit;
Therefore He turned Himself to
become their enemy,
He fought against them.

11 Then His people remembered
the days of old, of Moses.
Where is He who brought them
up out of the sea with the
shepherds of His flock?
Where is He who put His Holy
Spirit in the midst of them,

12 Who caused His glorious arm to
go at the right hand of Moses,
Who divided the waters before
them to make for Himself
an everlasting name,

13 Who led them through the depths?
Like the horse in the wilderness,
they did not stumble;

14 As the cattle which go down
into the valley,
The Spirit of the LORD
gave them rest.
So You led Your people,
To make for Yourself
a glorious name.

15 Look down from heaven and
see from Your holy and
glorious habitation;
Where are Your zeal and
Your mighty deeds?
The stirrings of Your heart
and Your compassion are
restrained toward me.

16 For You are our Father, though
Abraham does not know us
And Israel does not recognize us.
You, O LORD, are our Father,
Our Redeemer from of
old is Your name.

992

17 Why, O LORD, do You cause us
    to stray from Your ways
And harden our heart
    from fearing You?
Return for the sake of Your servants,
    the tribes of Your heritage.
18 Your holy people possessed Your
    sanctuary for a little while,
Our adversaries have
    trodden *it* down.
19 We have become *like* those over
    whom You have never ruled,
Like those who were not
    called by Your name.

64 Oh, that You would rend the
    heavens *and* come down,
That the mountains might
    quake at Your presence—
2 As fire kindles the brushwood, *as*
    fire causes water to boil—
To make Your name known
    to Your adversaries,
That the nations may tremble
    at Your presence!
3 When You did awesome things
    which we did not expect,
You came down, the mountains
    quaked at Your presence.
4 For from days of old they have not
    heard or perceived by ear,
Nor has the eye seen a
    God besides You,
Who acts in behalf of the one
    who waits for Him.
5 You meet him who rejoices in
    doing righteousness,
Who remembers You
    in Your ways.
Behold, You were angry,
    for we sinned,
We continued in them a long time;
And shall we be saved?
6 For all of us have become like
    one who is unclean,
And all our righteous deeds
    are like a filthy garment;
And all of us wither like a leaf,
And our iniquities, like the
    wind, take us away.
7 There is no one who calls
    on Your name,
Who arouses himself to
    take hold of You;
For You have hidden Your
    face from us
And have delivered us into the
    power of our iniquities.

8 But now, O LORD, You
    are our Father,
We are the clay, and
    You our potter;
And all of us are the work
    of Your hand.
9 Do not be angry beyond
    measure, O LORD,
Nor remember iniquity forever;
Behold, look now, all of us
    are Your people.
10 Your holy cities have become
    a wilderness,
Zion has become a wilderness,
Jerusalem a desolation.
11 Our holy and beautiful house,
Where our fathers praised You,
Has been burned *by* fire;
And all our precious things
    have become a ruin.
12 Will You restrain Yourself at
    these things, O LORD?
Will You keep silent and afflict
    us beyond measure?

64:11 burned *by* fire...become a ruin. Through
prophetic revelation Isaiah uttered these words
many years before the fall of Jerusalem and the
destruction of the temple in 586 B.C. Yet, he
lamented over the fallen state as though it
had already occurred. God's people were in
desperate straits and their prayers urgent and
persistent: "How can You stand by when Your
people and Your land are so barren?"

Psalm 115:14–18

14 May the LORD give you increase,
    You and your children.
15 May you be blessed of the LORD,
    Maker of heaven and earth.
16 The heavens are the heavens
    of the LORD,
But the earth He has given
    to the sons of men.
17 The dead do not praise the LORD,
Nor *do* any who go down into silence;
18 But as for us, we will bless the LORD
From this time forth and forever.
Praise the LORD!

Proverbs 26:27

27 He who digs a pit will fall into it,
    And he who rolls a stone, it
    will come back on him.

Philippians 1:1–30

1 Paul and Timothy, bond-servants of Christ Jesus,

To all the saints in Christ Jesus who are in Philippi, including the overseers and deacons: [2] Grace to you and peace from God our Father and the Lord Jesus Christ.

[3] I thank my God in all my remembrance of you, [4] always offering prayer with joy in my every prayer for you all, [5] in view of your participation in the gospel from the first day until now. [6] *For I am* confident of this very thing, that He who began a good work in you will perfect it until the day of Christ Jesus. [7] For it is only right for me to feel this way about you all, because I have you in my heart, since both in my imprisonment and in the defense and confirmation of the gospel, you all are partakers of grace with me. [8] For God is my witness, how I long for you all with the affection of Christ Jesus. [9] And this I pray, that your love may abound still more and more in real knowledge and all discernment, [10] so that you may approve the things that are excellent, in order to be sincere and blameless until the day of Christ; [11] having been filled with the fruit of righteousness which *comes* through Jesus Christ, to the glory and praise of God.

[12] Now I want you to know, brethren, that my circumstances have turned out for the greater progress of the gospel, [13] so that my imprisonment in *the cause of* Christ has become well known throughout the whole praetorian guard and to everyone else, [14] and that most of the brethren, trusting in the Lord because of my imprisonment, have far more courage to speak the word of God without fear. [15] Some, to be sure, are preaching Christ even from envy and strife, but some also from good will; [16] the latter *do it* out of love, knowing that I am appointed for the defense of the gospel; [17] the former proclaim Christ out of selfish ambition rather than from pure motives, thinking to cause me distress in my imprisonment. [18] What then? Only that in every way, whether in pretense or in truth, Christ is proclaimed; and in this I rejoice.

1:18 I rejoice...will rejoice. Paul's joy was not tied to his circumstances or his critics (Ps 4:7–8; Ro 12:12; 2Co 6:10). He was glad when the gospel was proclaimed with authority, no matter who received credit. He endured the unjust accusations without bitterness at his accusers. Rather, he rejoiced that they preached Christ, even in a pretense of godliness.

Yes, and I will rejoice, [19] for I know that this will turn out for my deliverance through your prayers and the provision of the Spirit of Jesus Christ, [20] according to my earnest expectation and hope, that I will not be put to shame in anything, but *that* with all boldness, Christ will even now, as always, be exalted in my body, whether by life or by death. [21] For to me, to live is Christ and to die is gain. [22] But if *I am* to live *on* in the flesh, this *will mean* fruitful labor for me; and I do not know which to choose. [23] But I am hard-pressed from both *directions,* having the desire to depart and be with Christ, for *that* is very much better; [24] yet to remain on in the flesh is more necessary for your sake. [25] Convinced of this, I know that I will remain and continue with you all for your progress and joy in the faith, [26] so that your proud confidence in me may abound in Christ Jesus through my coming to you again.

[27] Only conduct yourselves in a manner worthy of the gospel of Christ, so that whether I come and see you or remain absent, I will hear of you that you are standing firm in one spirit, with one mind striving together for the faith of the gospel; [28] in no way alarmed by *your* opponents—which is a sign of destruction for them, but of salvation for you, and that *too,* from God. [29] For to you it has been granted for Christ's sake, not only to believe in Him, but also to suffer for His sake, [30] experiencing the same conflict which you saw in me, and now hear *to be* in me.

DAY 6: What was Paul's prayer for the Philippians?

"That your love may abound still more and more in real knowledge" (1:9). This is from the Greek word that describes genuine, full, or advanced knowledge. Biblical love is not an empty sentimentalism but is anchored deeply in the truth of Scripture and regulated by it. "Discernment." The English word "aesthetic" comes from this Greek word, which speaks of moral perception, insight, and the practical application of knowledge. Love is not blind, but perceptive, and it carefully scrutinizes to distinguish between right and wrong.

"That you may approve the...excellent" (v. 10). "Approve" in classical Greek described the assaying of metals or the testing of money for authenticity. "Excellent" means "to differ." Believers need the ability to distinguish those things that are truly important so they can establish the right priorities. "Sincere and blameless." "Sincere" means "genuine" and may have originally meant "tested by sunlight." In the ancient world, dishonest pottery dealers filled cracks in their inferior products with wax before glazing and painting them, making worthless pots difficult to distinguish from expensive ones. The only way to avoid being defrauded was to hold the pot to the sun, making the wax-filled cracks obvious. Dealers marked their fine pottery that could withstand "sun testing" as *sine cera*—"Without wax." "Blameless" can be translated "without offense," referring to relational integrity. Christians are to live lives of true integrity that do not cause others to sin.

"Having been filled with the fruit of righteousness" (v. 11). This is better translated, "the fruit righteousness produces." "Which comes through Jesus Christ." This speaks of the salvation transformation provided by our Lord and His ongoing work of power through His Spirit in us. "To the glory and praise of God." The ultimate end of all Paul's prayers was that God be glorified.

⤳ OCTOBER 7

Isaiah 65:1–66:24

65 "I permitted Myself to be sought
    by those who did not ask *for Me;*
I permitted Myself to be found by
    those who did not seek Me.
I said, 'Here am I, here am I,'
To a nation which did not
    call on My name.
2 "I have spread out My hands all day
    long to a rebellious people,
Who walk *in* the way which
    is not good, following
    their own thoughts,
3 A people who continually
    provoke Me to My face,
Offering sacrifices in gardens and
    burning incense on bricks;
4 Who sit among graves and spend
    the night in secret places;
Who eat swine's flesh,
And the broth of unclean
    meat is *in* their pots.
5 "Who say, 'Keep to yourself,
    do not come near me,
For I am holier than you!'
These are smoke in My nostrils,
A fire that burns all the day.
6 "Behold, it is written before Me,
    I will not keep silent, but I will repay;
I will even repay into their bosom,

⤳

65:1 not ask...not seek...not call. Though Israel sought the Lord, they did so only superficially. They did not genuinely seek Him. The New Testament assigns an additional sense to the words in Romans 10:20, applying them to Gentiles who find Him through the work of His sovereign grace.

7 Both their own iniquities and
    the iniquities of their fathers
    together," says the LORD.
"Because they have burned
    incense on the mountains
And scorned Me on the hills,
Therefore I will measure their
    former work into their bosom."

8 Thus says the LORD,

"As the new wine is found
    in the cluster,
And one says, 'Do not destroy
    it, for there is benefit in it,'
So I will act on behalf
    of My servants
In order not to destroy all of them.
9 "I will bring forth offspring
    from Jacob,
And an heir of My mountains
    from Judah;
Even My chosen ones
    shall inherit it,
And My servants will dwell there.
10 "Sharon will be a pasture
    land for flocks,
And the valley of Achor a
    resting place for herds,
For My people who seek Me.
11 "But you who forsake the LORD,
Who forget My holy mountain,
Who set a table for Fortune,
And who fill *cups* with mixed
    wine for Destiny,
12 I will destine you for the sword,
And all of you will bow down
    to the slaughter.
Because I called, but you
    did not answer;
I spoke, but you did not hear.
And you did evil in My sight
And chose that in which
    I did not delight."

13 Therefore, thus says the Lord GOD,
"Behold, My servants will eat,
but you will be hungry.
Behold, My servants will drink, but
you will be thirsty.
Behold, My servants will rejoice,
but you will be put to shame.
14 "Behold, My servants will shout
joyfully with a glad heart,
But you will cry out with a heavy heart,
And you will wail with a broken spirit.
15 "You will leave your name for a
curse to My chosen ones,
And the Lord GOD will slay you.
But My servants will be called
by another name.
16 "Because he who is blessed in the earth
Will be blessed by the God of truth;
And he who swears in the earth
Will swear by the God of truth;
Because the former troubles
are forgotten,
And because they are hidden
from My sight!

17 "For behold, I create new
heavens and a new earth;
And the former things will not be
remembered or come to mind.
18 "But be glad and rejoice forever
in what I create;
For behold, I create Jerusalem
for rejoicing
And her people for gladness.
19 "I will also rejoice in Jerusalem
and be glad in My people;
And there will no longer
be heard in her
The voice of weeping and
the sound of crying.
20 "No longer will there be in it an
infant who lives but a few days,
Or an old man who does
not live out his days;
For the youth will die at the
age of one hundred
And the one who does not reach
the age of one hundred
Will be thought accursed.
21 "They will build houses
and inhabit them;
They will also plant vineyards and
eat their fruit.
22 "They will not build and
another inhabit,
They will not plant and another eat;
For as the lifetime of a tree, so will
be the days of My people,

And My chosen ones will wear
out the work of their hands.
23 "They will not labor in vain,
Or bear children for calamity;
For they are the offspring of
those blessed by the LORD,
And their descendants with them.

24 It will also come to pass that before they
call, I will answer; and while they are still
speaking, I will hear. 25 The wolf and the lamb
will graze together, and the lion will eat straw
like the ox; and dust will be the serpent's food.
They will do no evil or harm in all My holy
mountain," says the LORD.

66 Thus says the LORD,

"Heaven is My throne and the
earth is My footstool.
Where then is a house you
could build for Me?
And where is a place that I may rest?
2 "For My hand made all these things,
Thus all these things came into
being," declares the LORD.
"But to this one I will look,
To him who is humble and
contrite of spirit, and who
trembles at My word.

3 "But he who kills an ox is like
one who slays a man;
He who sacrifices a lamb is like the
one who breaks a dog's neck;
He who offers a grain offering is
like one who offers swine's blood;
He who burns incense is like the
one who blesses an idol.
As they have chosen
their own ways,
And their soul delights in
their abominations,

66:1–2 Isaiah began the final summary of his
prophecy with a reminder that God is not looking for a temple of stone, since as Creator of
all things, the whole universe is His dwelling
place. Stephen cited this passage before the
Sanhedrin to point out their error in limiting
God to a temple made with hands (Ac 7:49–50).
On the contrary, God is looking for a heart to
dwell in, a heart that is tender and broken,
not one concerned with the externalities of
religion. God is looking to dwell in the heart
of a person who takes His Word seriously.

⁴ So I will choose their punishments
   And will bring on them
      what they dread.
   Because I called, but no one answered;
   I spoke, but they did not listen.
   And they did evil in My sight
   And chose that in which
      I did not delight."
⁵ Hear the word of the LORD, you
      who tremble at His word:
   "Your brothers who hate you, who
      exclude you for My name's sake,
   Have said, 'Let the LORD be glorified,
      that we may see your joy.'
   But they will be put to shame.
⁶ "A voice of uproar from the city,
      a voice from the temple,
   The voice of the LORD who is rendering
      recompense to His enemies.

⁷ "Before she travailed, she
      brought forth;
   Before her pain came, she
      gave birth to a boy.
⁸ "Who has heard such a thing?
      Who has seen such things?
   Can a land be born in one day?
   Can a nation be brought
      forth all at once?
   As soon as Zion travailed, she
      also brought forth her sons.
⁹ "Shall I bring to the point of birth and
      not give delivery?" says the LORD.
   "Or shall I who gives delivery shut
      the womb?" says your God.
¹⁰ "Be joyful with Jerusalem and rejoice
      for her, all you who love her;
   Be exceedingly glad with her, all
      you who mourn over her,
¹¹ That you may nurse and be satisfied
      with her comforting breasts,
   That you may suck and be delighted
      with her bountiful bosom."
¹² For thus says the LORD, "Behold, I
      extend peace to her like a river,
   And the glory of the nations like
      an overflowing stream;
   And you will be nursed, you
      will be carried on the hip
      and fondled on the knees.
¹³ "As one whom his mother comforts,
      so I will comfort you;
   And you will be comforted
      in Jerusalem."
¹⁴ Then you will see this, and
      your heart will be glad,
   And your bones will flourish
      like the new grass;

   And the hand of the LORD will be
      made known to His servants,
   But He will be indignant
      toward His enemies.
¹⁵ For behold, the LORD will come in fire
   And His chariots like the whirlwind,
   To render His anger with fury,
   And His rebuke with flames of fire.
¹⁶ For the LORD will execute
      judgment by fire
   And by His sword on all flesh,
   And those slain by the
      LORD will be many.
¹⁷ "Those who sanctify and purify
      themselves to go to the gardens,
   Following one in the center,
   Who eat swine's flesh, detestable
      things and mice,
   Will come to an end altogether,"
      declares the LORD.

¹⁸ "For I know their works and their
thoughts; the time is coming to gather all
nations and tongues. And they shall come
and see My glory. ¹⁹ I will set a sign among
them and will send survivors from them to
the nations: Tarshish, Put, Lud, Meshech, Tubal
and Javan, to the distant coastlands that have
neither heard My fame nor seen My glory.
And they will declare My glory among the
nations. ²⁰ Then they shall bring all your brethren from all the nations as a grain offering to
the LORD, on horses, in chariots, in litters, on
mules and on camels, to My holy mountain
Jerusalem," says the LORD, "just as the sons
of Israel bring their grain offering in a clean
vessel to the house of the LORD. ²¹ I will also
take some of them for priests and for Levites,"
says the LORD.

²² "For just as the new heavens
      and the new earth
   Which I make will endure before
      Me," declares the LORD,
   "So your offspring and your
      name will endure.
²³ "And it shall be from new
      moon to new moon
   And from sabbath to sabbath,
   All mankind will come to bow down
      before Me," says the LORD.
²⁴ "Then they will go forth and look
   On the corpses of the men
   Who have transgressed against Me.
   For their worm will not die
   And their fire will not be quenched;
   And they will be an abhorrence
      to all mankind."

Psalm 116:1–4

I love the LORD, because He hears
My voice *and* my supplications.

2 Because He has inclined His ear to me,
Therefore I shall call upon
Him as long as I live.

3 The cords of death encompassed me
And the terrors of Sheol
came upon me;
I found distress and sorrow.

4 Then I called upon the
name of the LORD:
"O LORD, I beseech You, save my life!"

Proverbs 26:28

28 A lying tongue hates those it crushes,
And a flattering mouth works ruin.

Philippians 2:1–30

2 Therefore if there is any encouragement
in Christ, if there is any consolation of
love, if there is any fellowship of the Spirit, if
any affection and compassion, 2 make my joy
complete by being of the same mind, maintaining the same love, united in spirit, intent
on one purpose. 3 Do nothing from selfishness
or empty conceit, but with humility of mind
regard one another as more important than
yourselves; 4 do not *merely* look out for your
own personal interests, but also for the interests of others. 5 Have this attitude in yourselves
which was also in Christ Jesus, 6 who, although
He existed in the form of God, did not regard
equality with God a thing to be grasped, 7 but
emptied Himself, taking the form of a bond-
servant, *and* being made in the likeness of
men. 8 Being found in appearance as a man,
He humbled Himself by becoming obedient
to the point of death, even death on a cross.
9 For this reason also, God highly exalted

2:2 make my joy complete. Paul's joy was tied
to concern for the unity of believers (Heb 13:17).
same mind. The Greek word means "think the
same way." This exhortation is not optional or
obscure, but is repeated throughout the New
Testament (Ro 15:5; 1Co 1:10; 2Co 13:11–13). **same
love.** Believers are to love others in the body of
Christ equally—not because they are all equally
attractive, but by showing the same kind of
sacrificial, loving service to all that was shown
to them by Christ. **united in spirit.** This is perhaps a term specially coined by Paul. It literally
means "one-souled" and describes people who
are knit together in harmony, having the same
desires, passions, and ambitions.

2:6 He existed in the form of God. Paul affirms
that Jesus eternally has been God. The usual
Greek word for "existed" or "being" is not used
here. Instead, Paul chose another term that
stresses the essence of a person's nature—
his continuous state or condition. Paul also
could have chosen one of two Greek words for
"form," but he chose the one that specifically
denotes the essential, unchanging character of
something—what it is in and of itself. The fundamental doctrine of Christ's deity has always
encompassed these crucial characteristics (Jn
1:1, 3–4, 14; 8:58; Col 1:15–17; Heb 1:3). **equality
with God.** The Greek word for "equality" defines
things that are exactly the same in size, quantity,
quality, character, and number. In every sense,
Jesus is equal to God and constantly claimed
to be so during His earthly ministry (Jn 5:18;
10:33, 38; 14:9; 20:28; Heb 1:1–3). **grasped.** The
Greek word originally meant "a thing seized
by robbery." It eventually came to mean anything clutched, embraced, or prized, and thus
is sometimes translated "held onto." Though
Christ had all the rights, privileges, and honors
of deity—which He was worthy of and could
never be disqualified from—His attitude was not
to cling to those things or His position but to be
willing to give them up for a season.

Him, and bestowed on Him the name which
is above every name, 10 so that at the name of
Jesus EVERY KNEE WILL BOW, of those who are
in heaven and on earth and under the earth,
11 and that every tongue will confess that Jesus
Christ is Lord, to the glory of God the Father.

12 So then, my beloved, just as you have
always obeyed, not as in my presence only,
but now much more in my absence, work out
your salvation with fear and trembling; 13 for
it is God who is at work in you, both to will
and to work for *His* good pleasure.

14 Do all things without grumbling or disputing; 15 so that you will prove yourselves to
be blameless and innocent, children of God
above reproach in the midst of a crooked and
perverse generation, among whom you appear
as lights in the world, 16 holding fast the word
of life, so that in the day of Christ I will have
reason to glory because I did not run in vain
nor toil in vain. 17 But even if I am being poured
out as a drink offering upon the sacrifice and
service of your faith, I rejoice and share my
joy with you all. 18 You too, *I urge you,* rejoice
in the same way and share your joy with me.

19 But I hope in the Lord Jesus to send
Timothy to you shortly, so that I also may be

encouraged when I learn of your condition. ²⁰ For I have no one *else* of kindred spirit who will genuinely be concerned for your welfare. ²¹ For they all seek after their own interests, not those of Christ Jesus. ²² But you know of his proven worth, that he served with me in the furtherance of the gospel like a child *serving* his father. ²³ Therefore I hope to send him immediately, as soon as I see how things *go* with me; ²⁴ and I trust in the Lord that I myself also will be coming shortly. ²⁵ But I thought it necessary to send to you Epaphroditus, my brother and fellow worker and fellow soldier, who is also your messenger and minister to my need; ²⁶ because he was longing for you all and was distressed because you had heard that he was sick. ²⁷ For indeed he was sick to the point of death, but God had mercy on him, and not on him only but also on me, so that I would not have sorrow upon sorrow. ²⁸ Therefore I have sent him all the more eagerly so that when you see him again you may rejoice and I may be less concerned *about you.* ²⁹ Receive him then in the Lord with all joy, and hold men like him in high regard; ³⁰ because he came close to death for the work of Christ, risking his life to complete what was deficient in your service to me.

DAY 7: How did Christ humble Himself for our salvation?

In Philippians 2:7, Paul writes that Christ "emptied Himself." This was a self-renunciation, not an emptying Himself of Deity nor an exchange of Deity for humanity. Jesus did, however, renounce or set aside His privileges in several areas: 1) heavenly glory—while on earth He gave up the glory of a face-to-face relationship with God (Jn 17:5); 2) independent authority—during His Incarnation Christ completely submitted Himself to the will of His Father (Mt 26:39; Jn 5:30); 3) divine prerogatives—He set aside the voluntary display of His divine attributes and submitted Himself to the Spirit's direction (Mt 24:36; Jn 1:45–49); 4) eternal riches—while on earth Christ was poor and owned very little (2Co 8:9); and 5) a favorable relationship with God—He felt the Father's wrath for human sin while on the cross (Mt 27:46; 2Co 5:21).

"Taking the form of a bond-servant" (v. 7). Again, Paul uses the Greek word "form," which indicates exact essence. As a true servant, Jesus submissively did the will of His Father (Is 52:13–14). "being made in the likeness of men." Christ became more than God in a human body, but He took on all the essential attributes of humanity (Lk 2:52; Gal 4:4; Col 1:22). He became the God-Man: fully God and fully man.

"Being found in appearance as a man" (v. 8). Christ's humanity is described from the viewpoint of those who saw Him. Paul is implying that, although He outwardly looked like a man, there was much more to Him (His deity) than many people recognized naturally (Jn 6:42; 8:48). "He humbled Himself." After the humbling of incarnation, Jesus further humbled Himself in that He subjected Himself to persecution and suffering (Is 53:7; Mt 26:62–64; Mk 14:60–61; 1Pe 2:23). "Obedient…death." Beyond even persecution, Jesus went to the lowest point or furthest extent in His humiliation in dying as a criminal, following God's plan for Him. "A cross." Even further humiliation was His because Jesus' death was not by ordinary means, but was accomplished by crucifixion—the cruelest, most excruciating, most degrading form of death ever devised.

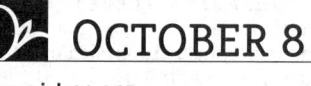

OCTOBER 8

Jeremiah 1:1–2:37

1 The words of Jeremiah the son of Hilkiah, of the priests who were in Anathoth in the land of Benjamin, ² to whom the word of the LORD came in the days of Josiah the son of Amon, king of Judah, in the thirteenth year of his reign. ³ It came also in the days of Jehoiakim the son of Josiah, king of Judah, until the end of the eleventh year of Zedekiah the son of Josiah, king of Judah, until the exile of Jerusalem in the fifth month.

⁴ Now the word of the LORD came to me saying,

⁵ "Before I formed you in the
    womb I knew you,
And before you were born
    I consecrated you;
I have appointed you a
    prophet to the nations."
⁶ Then I said, "Alas, Lord GOD!
Behold, I do not know how to speak,
Because I am a youth."

1:5 Before I formed you. This is not reincarnation; it is God's all-knowing cognizance of Jeremiah and sovereign plan for him before he was conceived (see Paul's similar realization, Gal 1:15).

7 But the LORD said to me,
"Do not say, 'I am a youth,'
Because everywhere I send
    you, you shall go,
And all that I command
    you, you shall speak.
8 "Do not be afraid of them,
For I am with you to deliver you,"
    declares the LORD.

9 Then the LORD stretched out His hand and touched my mouth, and the LORD said to me,

"Behold, I have put My words
    in your mouth.
10 "See, I have appointed you this
    day over the nations and
    over the kingdoms,
To pluck up and to break down,
To destroy and to overthrow,
To build and to plant."

11 The word of the LORD came to me saying, "What do you see, Jeremiah?" And I said, "I see a rod of an almond tree." 12 Then the LORD said to me, "You have seen well, for I am watching over My word to perform it."

13 The word of the LORD came to me a second time saying, "What do you see?" And I said, "I see a boiling pot, facing away from the north." 14 Then the LORD said to me, "Out of the north the evil will break forth on all the inhabitants of the land. 15 For, behold, I am calling all the families of the kingdoms of the north," declares the LORD; "and they will come and they will set each one his throne at the entrance of the gates of Jerusalem, and against all its walls round about and against all the cities of Judah. 16 I will pronounce My judgments on them concerning all their wickedness, whereby they have forsaken Me and have offered sacrifices to other gods, and worshiped the works of their own hands. 17 Now, gird up your loins and arise, and speak to them all which I command you. Do not be dismayed before them, or I will dismay you before them. 18 Now behold, I have made you today as a fortified city and as a pillar of iron and as walls of bronze against the whole land, to the kings of Judah, to its princes, to its priests and to the people of the land. 19 They will fight against you, but they will not overcome you, for I am with you to deliver you," declares the LORD.

2 Now the word of the LORD came to me saying, 2 "Go and proclaim in the ears of Jerusalem, saying, 'Thus says the LORD,

"I remember concerning you the
    devotion of your youth,
The love of your betrothals,
Your following after Me
    in the wilderness,
Through a land not sown.
3 "Israel was holy to the LORD,
The first of His harvest.
All who ate of it became guilty;
Evil came upon them,"
    declares the LORD.'"

4 Hear the word of the LORD, O house of Jacob, and all the families of the house of Israel. 5 Thus says the LORD,

"What injustice did your
    fathers find in Me,
That they went far from Me
And walked after emptiness
    and became empty?
6 "They did not say, 'Where is the LORD
Who brought us up out of
    the land of Egypt,
Who led us through the wilderness,
Through a land of deserts
    and of pits,
Through a land of drought
    and of deep darkness,
Through a land that no one crossed
And where no man dwelt?'
7 "I brought you into the fruitful land
To eat its fruit and its good things.
But you came and defiled My land,
And My inheritance you
    made an abomination.
8 "The priests did not say,
    'Where is the LORD?'
And those who handle the
    law did not know Me;
The rulers also transgressed
    against Me,
And the prophets prophesied by Baal
And walked after things
    that did not profit.

9 "Therefore I will yet contend with
    you," declares the LORD,
"And with your sons' sons
    I will contend.
10 "For cross to the coastlands
    of Kittim and see,
And send to Kedar and
    observe closely
And see if there has been
    such a thing as this!
11 "Has a nation changed gods
When they were not gods?

But My people have
changed their glory
For that which does not profit.

12 "Be appalled, O heavens, at this,
And shudder, be very desolate,"
declares the LORD.

13 "For My people have
committed two evils:
They have forsaken Me,
The fountain of living waters,
To hew for themselves cisterns,
Broken cisterns
That can hold no water.

14 "Is Israel a slave? Or is he a
homeborn servant?
Why has he become a prey?

15 "The young lions have roared at him,
They have roared loudly.
And they have made his land a waste;
His cities have been destroyed,
without inhabitant.

16 "Also the men of Memphis
and Tahpanhes
Have shaved the crown of your head.

17 "Have you not done this to yourself
By your forsaking the LORD your God
When He led you in the way?

18 "But now what are you doing
on the road to Egypt,
To drink the waters of the Nile?
Or what are you doing on
the road to Assyria,
To drink the waters of the Euphrates?

19 "Your own wickedness will correct you,
And your apostasies will reprove you;
Know therefore and see that
it is evil and bitter
For you to forsake the LORD your God,
And the dread of Me is not in you,"
declares the Lord GOD of hosts.

20 "For long ago I broke your yoke
And tore off your bonds;
But you said, 'I will not serve!'
For on every high hill
And under every green tree
You have lain down as a harlot.

21 "Yet I planted you a choice vine,
A completely faithful seed.
How then have you turned
yourself before Me
Into the degenerate shoots
of a foreign vine?

22 "Although you wash yourself with lye
And use much soap,
The stain of your iniquity is before
Me," declares the Lord GOD.

23 "How can you say, 'I am not defiled,
I have not gone after the Baals'?
Look at your way in the valley!
Know what you have done!
You are a swift young camel
entangling her ways,

24 A wild donkey accustomed
to the wilderness,
That sniffs the wind in her passion.
In the time of her heat who
can turn her away?
All who seek her will not
become weary;
In her month they will find her.

25 "Keep your feet from being unshod
And your throat from thirst;
But you said, 'It is hopeless!
No! For I have loved strangers,
And after them I will walk.'

26 "As the thief is shamed when
he is discovered,
So the house of Israel is shamed;
They, their kings, their princes
And their priests and their prophets,

27 Who say to a tree, 'You
are my father,'
And to a stone, 'You gave me birth.'
For they have turned their back to Me,
And not their face;
But in the time of their
trouble they will say,
'Arise and save us.'

28 "But where are your gods
Which you made for yourself?
Let them arise, if they can save you
In the time of your trouble;
For according to the number
of your cities
Are your gods, O Judah.

29 "Why do you contend with Me?
You have all transgressed against
Me," declares the LORD.

30 "In vain I have struck your sons;
They accepted no chastening.
Your sword has devoured
your prophets
Like a destroying lion.

31 "O generation, heed the
word of the LORD.
Have I been a wilderness to Israel,
Or a land of thick darkness?
Why do My people say, 'We
are free to roam;
We will no longer come to You'?

32 "Can a virgin forget her ornaments,
Or a bride her attire?

Yet My people have forgotten Me
Days without number.
33 "How well you prepare your way
To seek love!
Therefore even the wicked women
You have taught your ways.
34 "Also on your skirts is found
The lifeblood of the innocent poor;
You did not find them breaking in.
But in spite of all these things,
35 Yet you said, 'I am innocent;
Surely His anger is turned
away from me.'
Behold, I will enter into
judgment with you
Because you say, 'I have not sinned.'
36 "Why do you go around so much
Changing your way?
Also, you will be put to
shame by Egypt
As you were put to shame by Assyria.
37 "From this place also you will go out
With your hands on your head;
For the LORD has rejected
those in whom you trust,
And you will not prosper with them."

Psalm 116:5–14

5 Gracious is the LORD, and righteous;
Yes, our God is compassionate.
6 The LORD preserves the simple;
I was brought low, and He saved me.
7 Return to your rest, O my soul,
For the LORD has dealt
bountifully with you.
8 For You have rescued my
soul from death,
My eyes from tears,
My feet from stumbling.
9 I shall walk before the LORD
In the land of the living.
10 I believed when I said,
"I am greatly afflicted."
11 I said in my alarm,
"All men are liars."

12 What shall I render to the LORD
For all His benefits toward me?
13 I shall lift up the cup of salvation
And call upon the name of the LORD.
14 I shall pay my vows to the LORD,
Oh may it be in the presence
of all His people.

Proverbs 27:1

27 Do not boast about tomorrow,
For you do not know what a
day may bring forth.

Philippians 3:1–21

3 Finally, my brethren, rejoice in the Lord. To write the same things *again* is no trouble to me, and it is a safeguard for you.

2 Beware of the dogs, beware of the evil workers, beware of the false circumcision; 3 for we are the *true* circumcision, who worship in the Spirit of God and glory in Christ Jesus and put no confidence in the flesh, 4 although I myself might have confidence even in the flesh. If anyone else has a mind to put confidence in the flesh, I far more: 5 circumcised the eighth day, of the nation of Israel, of the tribe of Benjamin, a Hebrew of Hebrews; as to the Law, a Pharisee; 6 as to zeal, a persecutor of the church; as to the righteousness which is in the Law, found blameless.

3:2 dogs. During the first century, dogs roamed the streets and were essentially wild scavengers. Because dogs were such filthy animals, the Jews loved to refer to Gentiles as dogs. Yet here Paul refers to Jews, specifically the Judaizers, as dogs to describe their sinful, vicious, and uncontrolled character. **evil workers.** The Judaizers prided themselves on being workers of righteousness. Yet Paul described their works as evil, since any attempt to please God by one's own efforts and draw attention away from Christ's accomplished redemption is the worst kind of wickedness. **false circumcision.** In contrast to the Greek word for "circumcision," which means "to cut around," this term means "to cut down (off)" or "to mutilate." Like the prophets of Baal (1Ki 18:28) and pagans who mutilated their bodies in their frenzied rituals, which were forbidden in the Old Testament (Lv 19:28; 21:5; Dt 14:1; Is 15:2; Hos 7:14), the Judaizers' circumcision was, ironically, no spiritual symbol; it was merely physical mutilation.

7 But whatever things were gain to me, those things I have counted as loss for the sake of Christ. 8 More than that, I count all things to be loss in view of the surpassing value of knowing Christ Jesus my Lord, for whom I have suffered the loss of all things, and count them but rubbish so that I may gain Christ, 9 and may be found in Him, not having a righteousness of my own derived from *the* Law, but that which is through faith in Christ, the righteousness which *comes* from God on the basis of faith, 10 that I may know Him and the power of His resurrection and the fellowship of His sufferings, being conformed to His death; 11 in order that I may attain to the resurrection from the dead.

3:7 whatever things were gain…have counted as loss. The Greek word for "gain" is an accounting term that means "profit." The Greek word for "loss" also is an accounting term, used to describe a business loss. Paul used the language of business to describe the spiritual transaction that occurred when Christ redeemed him. All his Jewish religious credentials that he thought were in his profit column were actually worthless and damning (Lk 18:9-14). Thus, he put them in his loss column when he saw the glories of Christ.

3:8 knowing Christ Jesus. To "know" Christ is not simply to have intellectual knowledge about Him; Paul used the Greek verb that means to know "experientially" or "personally" (Jn 10:27; 17:3; 2Co 4:6; 1Jn 5:20). It is equivalent to shared life with Christ. It also corresponds to a Hebrew word used of God's knowledge of His people (Am 3:2) and their knowledge of Him in love and obedience (Jer 31:34; Hos 6:3; 8:2). **rubbish.** The Greek word refers to garbage or waste and can even be translated "dung" or "manure."

¹²Not that I have already obtained *it* or have already become perfect, but I press on so that I may lay hold of that for which also I was laid hold of by Christ Jesus. ¹³Brethren, I do not regard myself as having laid hold of *it* yet; but one thing *I do:* forgetting what *lies* behind and reaching forward to what *lies* ahead, ¹⁴I press on toward the goal for the prize of the upward call of God in Christ Jesus. ¹⁵Let us therefore, as many as are perfect, have this attitude; and if in anything you have a different attitude, God will reveal that also to you; ¹⁶however, let us keep living by that same *standard* to which we have attained.

¹⁷Brethren, join in following my example, and observe those who walk according to the pattern you have in us. ¹⁸For many walk, of whom I often told you, and now tell you even weeping, *that they are* enemies of the cross of Christ, ¹⁹whose end is destruction, whose god is *their* appetite, and *whose* glory is in their shame, who set their minds on earthly things. ²⁰For our citizenship is in heaven, from which also we eagerly wait for a Savior, the Lord Jesus Christ; ²¹who will transform the body of our humble state into conformity with the body of His glory, by the exertion of the power that He has even to subject all things to Himself.

DAY 8: Who was the prophet Jeremiah?

Jeremiah, who served as both a priest and a prophet, was the son of a priest named Hilkiah. He was from the small village of Anathoth (1:1), today called Anata, about 3 miles northeast of Jerusalem. As an object lesson to Judah, Jeremiah remained unmarried (16:1-4). He was assisted in ministry by a scribe named Baruch, to whom Jeremiah dictated and who copied and had custody over the writings compiled from the prophet's messages (36:4, 32; 45:1). Jeremiah has been known as "the weeping prophet" (9:1; 13:17; 14:17), living a life of conflict because of his predictions of judgment by the invading Babylonians. He was threatened, tried for his life, put in stocks, forced to flee from Jehoiakim, publicly humiliated by a false prophet, and thrown into a pit.

Jeremiah carried out a ministry directed mostly to his own people in Judah, but which expanded to other nations at times. He appealed to his countrymen to repent and avoid God's judgment via an invader (chaps. 7; 26). Once invasion was certain after Judah refused to repent, he pled with them not to resist the Babylonian conqueror in order to prevent total destruction (chap. 27). He also called on delegates of other nations to heed his counsel and submit to Babylon (chap. 27), and he predicted judgments from God on various nations (25:12-38; chaps. 46-51).

The dates of his ministry, which spanned 5 decades, are from the Judean king Josiah's thirteenth year, noted in 1:2 (627 B.C.), to beyond the fall of Jerusalem to Babylon in 586 B.C. (chaps. 39-40; 52). After 586 B.C., Jeremiah was forced to go with a fleeing remnant of Judah to Egypt (chaps. 43-44).

OCTOBER 9

Jeremiah 3:1–4:31

3 *God* says, "If a husband
divorces his wife
And she goes from him
And belongs to another man,
Will he still return to her?
Will not that land be
completely polluted?
But you are a harlot *with*
many lovers;
Yet you turn to Me,"
declares the LORD.

2 "Lift up your eyes to the bare
heights and see;
Where have you not been violated?
By the roads you have sat for them
Like an Arab in the desert,
And you have polluted a land
With your harlotry and with
your wickedness.

3 "Therefore the showers have
been withheld,
And there has been no spring rain.
Yet you had a harlot's forehead;
You refused to be ashamed.

4 "Have you not just now called to Me,
'My Father, You are the
friend of my youth?

5 'Will He be angry forever?
Will He be indignant to the end?'
Behold, you have spoken
And have done evil things,
And you have had your way."

6 Then the LORD said to me in the days of Josiah the king, "Have you seen what faithless Israel did? She went up on every high hill and under every green tree, and she was a harlot there. 7 I thought, 'After she has done all these things she will return to Me'; but she did not return, and her treacherous sister Judah saw it. 8 And I saw that for all the adulteries of faithless Israel, I had sent her away and given her a writ of divorce, yet her treacherous sister Judah did not fear; but she went and was a harlot also. 9 Because of the lightness of her harlotry, she polluted the land and committed adultery with stones and trees. 10 Yet in spite of all this her treacherous sister Judah did not return to Me with all her heart, but rather in deception," declares the LORD.

11 And the LORD said to me, "Faithless Israel has proved herself more righteous than treacherous Judah. 12 Go and proclaim these words toward the north and say,

'Return, faithless Israel,'
declares the LORD;
'I will not look upon you in anger.
For I am gracious,' declares the LORD;
'I will not be angry forever.

13 'Only acknowledge your iniquity,
That you have transgressed
against the LORD your God
And have scattered your
favors to the strangers
under every green tree,
And you have not obeyed My
voice,' declares the LORD.

14 'Return, O faithless sons,'
declares the LORD;
'For I am a master to you,
And I will take you one from a
city and two from a family,
And I will bring you to Zion.'

3:14 I am a master to you. God pictured His covenant relationship with Israel as a marriage, and pleaded with mercy for Judah to repent and return. He will take her back. See Hosea's restoration of Gomer as a picture of God taking back His wicked, adulterous people.

15 "Then I will give you shepherds after My own heart, who will feed you on knowledge and understanding. 16 It shall be in those days when you are multiplied and increased in the land," declares the LORD, "they will no longer say, 'The ark of the covenant of the LORD.' And it will not come to mind, nor will they remember it, nor will they miss *it,* nor will it be made again. 17 At that time they will call Jerusalem 'The Throne of the LORD,' and all the nations will be gathered to it, to Jerusalem, for the name of the LORD; nor will they walk anymore after the stubbornness of their evil heart. 18 In those days the house of Judah will walk with the house of Israel, and they will come together from the land of the north to the land that I gave your fathers as an inheritance.

19 "Then I said,

'How I would set you among My sons
And give you a pleasant land,
The most beautiful inheritance
of the nations!'
And I said, 'You shall call
Me, My Father,
And not turn away from
following Me.'

20 "Surely, as a woman treacherously
　　departs from her lover,
　So you have dealt
　　treacherously with Me,
　O house of Israel," declares the LORD.

21 A voice is heard on the bare heights,
　The weeping *and* the supplications
　　of the sons of Israel;
　Because they have perverted their way,
　They have forgotten the
　　LORD their God.
22 "Return, O faithless sons,
　I will heal your faithlessness."
　"Behold, we come to You;
　For You are the LORD our God.
23 "Surely, the hills are a deception,
　A tumult *on* the mountains.
　Surely in the LORD our God
　Is the salvation of Israel.

24 "But the shameful thing has consumed the labor of our fathers since our youth, their flocks and their herds, their sons and their daughters. 25 Let us lie down in our shame, and let our humiliation cover us; for we have sinned against the LORD our God, we and our fathers, from our youth even to this day. And we have not obeyed the voice of the LORD our God."

4 "If you will return, O Israel,"
　　declares the LORD,
　"*Then* you should return to Me.
　And if you will put away your
　　detested things from My presence,
　And will not waver,
2 　And you will swear, 'As
　　the LORD lives,'
　In truth, in justice and in
　　righteousness;
　Then the nations will bless
　　themselves in Him,
　And in Him they will glory."

3 For thus says the LORD to the men of Judah and to Jerusalem,

　"Break up your fallow ground,
　And do not sow among thorns.
4 　"Circumcise yourselves to the LORD
　And remove the foreskins
　　of your heart,
　Men of Judah and inhabitants
　　of Jerusalem,
　Or else My wrath will go forth like fire
　And burn with none to quench it,
　Because of the evil of your deeds."

4:4 Circumcise. This surgery (Ge 17:10–14) was to cut away flesh that could hold disease in its folds and could pass the disease on to wives. It was important for the preservation of God's people physically. But it was also a symbol of the need for the heart to be cleansed from sin's deadly disease. The really essential surgery needed to happen on the inside, where God calls for taking away fleshly things that keep the heart from being spiritually devoted to Him and from true faith in Him and His will. Jeremiah later expanded on this theme (31:31–34)

5 　Declare in Judah and proclaim
　　in Jerusalem, and say,
　"Blow the trumpet in the land;
　Cry aloud and say,
　'Assemble yourselves, and let us go
　Into the fortified cities.'
6 　"Lift up a standard toward Zion!
　Seek refuge, do not stand *still*,
　For I am bringing evil from the north,
　And great destruction.
7 　"A lion has gone up from his thicket,
　And a destroyer of nations has set out;
　He has gone out from his place
　To make your land a waste.
　Your cities will be ruins
　Without inhabitant.
8 　"For this, put on sackcloth,
　Lament and wail;
　For the fierce anger of the LORD
　Has not turned back from us."

9 "It shall come about in that day," declares the LORD, "that the heart of the king and the heart of the princes will fail; and the priests will be appalled and the prophets will be astounded."
10 Then I said, "Ah, Lord GOD! Surely You have utterly deceived this people and Jerusalem, saying, 'You will have peace'; whereas a sword touches the throat."
11 In that time it will be said to this people and to Jerusalem, "A scorching wind from the bare heights in the wilderness in the direction of the daughter of My people—not to winnow and not to cleanse, 12 a wind too strong for this—will come at My command; now I will also pronounce judgments against them.

13 "Behold, he goes up like clouds,
　And his chariots like the whirlwind;
　His horses are swifter than eagles.
　Woe to us, for we are ruined!"

14 Wash your heart from
   evil, O Jerusalem,
That you may be saved.
How long will your wicked thoughts
Lodge within you?
15 For a voice declares from Dan,
And proclaims wickedness
   from Mount Ephraim.
16 "Report *it* to the nations, now!
Proclaim over Jerusalem,
'Besiegers come from a far country,
And lift their voices against
   the cities of Judah.
17 'Like watchmen of a field they are
   against her round about,
Because she has rebelled against
Me,' declares the LORD.
18 "Your ways and your deeds
Have brought these things to you.
This is your evil. How bitter!
How it has touched your heart!"

19 My soul, my soul! I am in
   anguish! Oh, my heart!
My heart is pounding in me;
I cannot be silent,
Because you have heard, O my soul,
The sound of the trumpet,
The alarm of war.
20 Disaster on disaster is proclaimed,
For the whole land is devastated;
Suddenly my tents are devastated,
My curtains in an instant.
21 How long must I see the standard
And hear the sound of the trumpet?
22 "For My people are foolish,
They know Me not;
They are stupid children
And have no understanding.
They are shrewd to do evil,
But to do good they do not know."

23 I looked on the earth, and behold,
   it was formless and void;
And to the heavens, and
   they had no light.
24 I looked on the mountains, and
   behold, they were quaking,
And all the hills moved to and fro.
25 I looked, and behold, there
   was no man,
And all the birds of the
   heavens had fled.
26 I looked, and behold, the fruitful
   land was a wilderness,
And all its cities were pulled down
Before the LORD, before
   His fierce anger.

27 For thus says the LORD,
"The whole land shall
   be a desolation,
Yet I will not execute a
   complete destruction.
28 "For this the earth shall mourn
And the heavens above be dark,
Because I have spoken, I
   have purposed,
And I will not change My mind,
   nor will I turn from it."
29 At the sound of the horseman and
   bowman every city flees;
They go into the thickets and
   climb among the rocks;
Every city is forsaken,
And no man dwells in them.
30 And you, O desolate one,
   what will you do?
Although you dress in scarlet,
Although you decorate *yourself*
   with ornaments of gold,
Although you enlarge your
   eyes with paint,
In vain you make yourself beautiful.
Your lovers despise you;
They seek your life.
31 For I heard a cry as of a
   woman in labor,
The anguish as of one giving
   birth to her first child,
The cry of the daughter of
   Zion gasping for breath,
Stretching out her hands, *saying,*
"Ah, woe is me, for I faint
   before murderers."

Psalm 116:15–19

15 Precious in the sight of the LORD
Is the death of His godly ones.
16 O LORD, surely I am Your servant,
I am Your servant, the son
   of Your handmaid,
You have loosed my bonds.
17 To You I shall offer a sacrifice
   of thanksgiving,
And call upon the name of the LORD.
18 I shall pay my vows to the LORD,
Oh *may it be* in the presence of
   all His people,
19 In the courts of the LORD'S house,
In the midst of you, O Jerusalem.
Praise the LORD!

Proverbs 27:2

2 Let another praise you, and
   not your own mouth;
A stranger, and not your own lips.

Philippians 4:1-23

4 Therefore, my beloved brethren whom I long *to see,* my joy and crown, in this way stand firm in the Lord, my beloved.

² I urge Euodia and I urge Syntyche to live in harmony in the Lord. ³ Indeed, true companion, I ask you also to help these women who have shared my struggle in *the cause of* the gospel, together with Clement also and the rest of my fellow workers, whose names are in the book of life.

⁴ Rejoice in the Lord always; again I will say, rejoice! ⁵ Let your gentle *spirit* be known to all men. The Lord is near. ⁶ Be anxious for nothing, but in everything by prayer and supplication with thanksgiving let your requests be made known to God. ⁷ And the peace of God, which surpasses all comprehension, will guard your hearts and your minds in Christ Jesus.

⁸ Finally, brethren, whatever is true, whatever is honorable, whatever is right, whatever is pure, whatever is lovely, whatever is of good repute, if there is any excellence and if anything worthy of praise, dwell on these things. ⁹ The things you have learned and received and heard and seen in me, practice these things, and the God of peace will be with you.

¹⁰ But I rejoiced in the Lord greatly, that now at last you have revived your concern for me; indeed, you were concerned *before,* but you lacked opportunity. ¹¹ Not that I speak from want, for I have learned to be content in whatever circumstances I am. ¹² I know how to get along with humble means, and I also know how to live in prosperity; in any and every circumstance I have learned the secret of being filled and going hungry, both of having abundance and suffering need. ¹³ I can do all things through Him who strengthens me. ¹⁴ Nevertheless, you have done well to share *with me* in my affliction.

¹⁵ You yourselves also know, Philippians, that at the first preaching of the gospel, after I left Macedonia, no church shared with me in the matter of giving and receiving but you alone; ¹⁶ for even in Thessalonica you sent *a gift* more than once for my needs. ¹⁷ Not that I seek the gift itself, but I seek for the profit which increases to your account. ¹⁸ But I have received everything in full and have an abundance; I am amply supplied, having received from Epaphroditus what you have sent, a fragrant aroma, an acceptable sacrifice, well-pleasing to God. ¹⁹ And my God will supply all your needs according to His riches in glory in Christ Jesus. ²⁰ Now to our God and Father *be* the glory forever and ever. Amen.

²¹ Greet every saint in Christ Jesus. The brethren who are with me greet you. ²² All the saints greet you, especially those of Caesar's household.

²³ The grace of the Lord Jesus Christ be with your spirit.

4:12 humble means…prosperity. Paul knew how to get along with humble means (food, clothing, daily necessities) and how to live in prosperity. **being filled and going hungry.** The Greek word translated "being filled" was used of feeding and fattening animals. Paul knew how to be content when he had plenty to eat and when he was deprived of enough to eat.

4:13 I can do all things. Paul uses a Greek verb that means "to be strong" or "to have strength" (Ac 19:16, 20; Jas 5:16). He had strength to withstand "all things" (vv. 11–12), including both difficulty and prosperity in the material world. **through Him who strengthens me.** The Greek word for strengthen means "to put power in." Because believers are in Christ (Gal 2:20), He infuses them with His strength to sustain them until they receive some provision (Eph 3:16–20; 2Co 12:10).

4:4 Rejoice in the Lord. Paul's familiar theme throughout the epistle, which has already been heard in chapters 1 and 2. "In the Lord" signifies the sphere in which the believers' joy exists a sphere unrelated to the circumstances of life, but related to an unassailable, unchanging relationship to the sovereign Lord.

DAY 9: How do we keep the peace of God in our lives?

Paul tells us to "be anxious for nothing" (Php 4:6). Fret and worry indicate a lack of trust in God's wisdom, sovereignty, or power. Delighting in the Lord and meditating on His Word are a great antidote to anxiety (Ps 1:2). "In everything by prayer and supplication with thanksgiving… requests." All difficulties are within God's purposes. Gratitude to God accompanies all true prayer.

"And the peace of God" (v. 7). Inner calm or tranquility is promised to the believer who has a thankful attitude based on an unwavering confidence that God is able and willing to do what is best for His children (Ro 8:28). "Which surpasses all comprehension." This refers to the divine origin of peace. It transcends human intellect, analysis, and insight. "Will guard." A military term meaning "to keep watch over." God's peace guards believers from anxiety, doubt, fear, and distress. "Your hearts and your minds." Paul was not making a distinction between the two—he was giving a comprehensive statement referring to the whole inner person. Because of the believer's union with Christ, He guards his inner being with His peace.

And believers are to think on what is true (v. 8), what is found in God (2Ti 2:25), in Christ (Eph 4:20–21), in the Holy Spirit (Jn 16:13), and in God's Word (Jn 17:17). They are to think on what is worthy of respect, whatever is worthy of awe and adoration, i.e., the sacred as opposed to the profane. The believer is to think in harmony with God's divine standard of holiness and on what is morally clean and undefiled. Believers are to focus on whatever is lovely, "pleasing" or "amiable," and that which is highly regarded or thought well of. If they follow the truth of God proclaimed, along with the example of that truth lived by Paul before them, "the God of peace will be with [them]" (v. 9). God is peace (Ro 16:20; Eph 2:14), makes peace with sinners through Christ (2Co 5:18–20), and gives perfect peace in trouble (v. 7).

OCTOBER 10

Jeremiah 5:1–6:30

5 "Roam to and fro through the
streets of Jerusalem,
And look now and take note.
And seek in her open squares,
If you can find a man,
If there is one who does
justice, who seeks truth,
Then I will pardon her.
2 "And although they say, 'As
the LORD lives,'
Surely they swear falsely."
3 O LORD, do not Your eyes
look for truth?
You have smitten them,
But they did not weaken;
You have consumed them,
But they refused to take correction.
They have made their faces
harder than rock;
They have refused to repent.

4 Then I said, "They are only the poor,
They are foolish;
For they do not know the
way of the LORD
Or the ordinance of their God.
5 "I will go to the great
And will speak to them,
For they know the way of the LORD
And the ordinance of their God."
But they too, with one accord,
have broken the yoke
And burst the bonds.
6 Therefore a lion from the
forest will slay them,
A wolf of the deserts will destroy them,
A leopard is watching their cities.
Everyone who goes out of them
will be torn in pieces,

Because their transgressions
are many,
Their apostasies are numerous.

7 "Why should I pardon you?
Your sons have forsaken Me
And sworn by those who
are not gods.
When I had fed them to the full,
They committed adultery
And trooped to the harlot's house.
8 "They were well-fed lusty horses,
Each one neighing after
his neighbor's wife.
9 "Shall I not punish these *people*,"
declares the LORD,
"And on a nation such as this
Shall I not avenge Myself?

10 "Go up through her vine
rows and destroy,
But do not execute a
complete destruction;
Strip away her branches,
For they are not the LORD'S.
11 "For the house of Israel and
the house of Judah
Have dealt very treacherously
with Me," declares the LORD.

5:10 not the LORD's. The people, depicted as vine branches to be destroyed (11:16–17), did not genuinely know the Lord in a saving relationship, but had forsaken Him and given allegiance to other gods. The description of having eyes but not seeing, and ears but not hearing (v. 21) is used by Isaiah (6:9) and Jesus Christ (Mt 13:13) for such false professors as these branches. Jesus also referred to false branches in John 15:2, 6 which were burned.

¹² They have lied about the LORD
And said, "Not He;
Misfortune will not come on us,
And we will not see sword or famine.
¹³ "The prophets are *as* wind,
And the word is not in them.
Thus it will be done to them!"

¹⁴ Therefore, thus says the
LORD, the God of hosts,
"Because you have spoken this word,
Behold, I am making My words
in your mouth fire
And this people wood, and it
will consume them.
¹⁵ "Behold, I am bringing a nation
against you from afar, O house
of Israel," declares the LORD.
"It is an enduring nation,
It is an ancient nation,
A nation whose language
you do not know,
Nor can you understand
what they say.
¹⁶ "Their quiver is like an open grave,
All of them are mighty men.
¹⁷ "They will devour your harvest
and your food;
They will devour your sons and
your daughters;
They will devour your flocks
and your herds;
They will devour your vines and
your fig trees;
They will demolish with the
sword your fortified cities
in which you trust.

¹⁸ "Yet even in those days," declares the LORD, "I will not make you a complete destruction. ¹⁹ It shall come about when they say, 'Why has the LORD our God done all these things to us?' then you shall say to them, 'As you have forsaken Me and served foreign gods in your land, so you will serve strangers in a land that is not yours.'

²⁰ "Declare this in the house of Jacob
And proclaim it in Judah, saying,
²¹ 'Now hear this, O foolish and
senseless people,
Who have eyes but do not see;
Who have ears but do not hear.
²² 'Do you not fear Me?'
declares the LORD.
'Do you not tremble in My presence?
For I have placed the sand as
a boundary for the sea,

An eternal decree, so it
cannot cross over it.
Though the waves toss, yet
they cannot prevail;
Though they roar, yet they
cannot cross over it.
²³ 'But this people has a stubborn
and rebellious heart;
They have turned aside
and departed.
²⁴ 'They do not say in their heart,
"Let us now fear the LORD our God,
Who gives rain in its season,
Both the autumn rain and
the spring rain,
Who keeps for us
The appointed weeks of the harvest."
²⁵ 'Your iniquities have
turned these away,
And your sins have withheld
good from you.
²⁶ 'For wicked men are found
among My people,
They watch like fowlers lying in wait;
They set a trap,
They catch men.
²⁷ 'Like a cage full of birds,
So their houses are full of deceit;
Therefore they have become
great and rich.
²⁸ 'They are fat, they are sleek,
They also excel in deeds
of wickedness;
They do not plead the cause,
The cause of the orphan, that
they may prosper;
And they do not defend the
rights of the poor.
²⁹ 'Shall I not punish these *people?*'
declares the LORD,
'On a nation such as this
Shall I not avenge Myself?'

³⁰ "An appalling and horrible thing
Has happened in the land:
³¹ The prophets prophesy falsely,
And the priests rule on
their *own* authority;
And My people love it so!
But what will you do at the end of it?

6 "Flee for safety, O sons of Benjamin,
From the midst of Jerusalem!
Now blow a trumpet in Tekoa
And raise a signal over
Beth-haccerem;
For evil looks down from the north,
And a great destruction.

2 "The comely and dainty one, the
daughter of Zion, I will cut off.
3 "Shepherds and their flocks
will come to her,
They will pitch *their* tents around her,
They will pasture each in his place.
4 "Prepare war against her;
Arise, and let us attack at noon.
Woe to us, for the day declines,
For the shadows of the
evening lengthen!
5 "Arise, and let us attack by night
And destroy her palaces!"
6 For thus says the LORD of hosts,
"Cut down her trees
And cast up a siege against Jerusalem.
This is the city to be punished,
In whose midst there is
only oppression.
7 "As a well keeps its waters fresh,
So she keeps fresh her wickedness.
Violence and destruction
are heard in her;
Sickness and wounds are
ever before Me.
8 "Be warned, O Jerusalem,
Or I shall be alienated from you,
And make you a desolation,
A land not inhabited."

9 Thus says the LORD of hosts,
"They will thoroughly glean as the
vine the remnant of Israel;
Pass your hand again like
a grape gatherer
Over the branches."
10 To whom shall I speak
and give warning
That they may hear?
Behold, their ears are closed
And they cannot listen.
Behold, the word of the LORD has
become a reproach to them;
They have no delight in it.
11 But I am full of the wrath of the LORD;
I am weary with holding *it* in.
"Pour *it* out on the children in the street
And on the gathering of
young men together;
For both husband and wife
shall be taken,
The aged and the very old.
12 "Their houses shall be turned
over to others,
Their fields and their wives together;
For I will stretch out My hand
Against the inhabitants of the
land," declares the LORD.

13 "For from the least of them even
to the greatest of them,
Everyone is greedy for gain,
And from the prophet
even to the priest
Everyone deals falsely.
14 "They have healed the brokenness
of My people superficially,
Saying, 'Peace, peace,'
But there is no peace.
15 "Were they ashamed because of the
abomination they have done?
They were not even ashamed at all;
They did not even know how to blush.
Therefore they shall fall
among those who fall;
At the time that I punish them,
They shall be cast down,"
says the LORD.

6:14 Peace, peace. Wicked leaders among the prophets and priests (v. 13) proclaimed peace falsely and gave weak and brief comfort. They provided no true healing from the spiritual wound, not having discernment to deal with the sin and its effects (v. 15). The need was to return to obedience (v. 16).

16 Thus says the LORD,
"Stand by the ways and see and
ask for the ancient paths,
Where the good way is, and walk in it;
And you will find rest for your souls.
But they said, 'We will not walk *in it.'*
17 "And I set watchmen over you, *saying,*
'Listen to the sound of the trumpet!'
But they said, 'We will not listen.'
18 "Therefore hear, O nations,
And know, O congregation,
what is among them.
19 "Hear, O earth: behold, I am bringing
disaster on this people,
The fruit of their plans,
Because they have not
listened to My words,
And as for My law, they
have rejected it also.
20 "For what purpose does frankincense
come to Me from Sheba
And the sweet cane from
a distant land?
Your burnt offerings are
not acceptable
And your sacrifices are not
pleasing to Me."

21 Therefore, thus says the LORD,
"Behold, I am laying stumbling
blocks before this people.
And they will stumble against them,
Fathers and sons together;
Neighbor and friend will perish."

22 Thus says the LORD,
"Behold, a people is coming
from the north land,
And a great nation will be
aroused from the remote
parts of the earth.

23 "They seize bow and spear;
They are cruel and have no mercy;
Their voice roars like the sea,
And they ride on horses,
Arrayed as a man for the battle
Against you, O daughter of Zion!"

24 We have heard the report of it;
Our hands are limp.
Anguish has seized us,
Pain as of a woman in childbirth.

25 Do not go out into the field
And do not walk on the road,
For the enemy has a sword,
Terror is on every side.

26 O daughter of my people,
put on sackcloth
And roll in ashes;
Mourn as for an only son,
A lamentation most bitter.
For suddenly the destroyer
Will come upon us.

27 "I have made you an assayer and
a tester among My people,
That you may know and
assay their way."

28 All of them are stubbornly rebellious,
Going about as a talebearer.
They are bronze and iron;
They, all of them, are corrupt.

29 The bellows blow fiercely,
The lead is consumed by the fire;
In vain the refining goes on,
But the wicked are not separated.

30 They call them rejected silver,
Because the LORD has rejected them.

Psalm 117:1–2

P raise the LORD, all nations;
Laud Him, all peoples!

2 For His lovingkindness is
great toward us,
And the truth of the LORD
is everlasting.
Praise the LORD!

Proverbs 27:3–4

3 A stone is heavy and the sand weighty,
But the provocation of a fool is
heavier than both of them.

4 Wrath is fierce and anger is a flood,
But who can stand before jealousy?

Colossians 1:1–29

1 Paul, an apostle of Jesus Christ by the will
of God, and Timothy our brother,

2 To the saints and faithful brethren in Christ who are at Colossae: Grace to you and peace from God our Father.

3 We give thanks to God, the Father of our Lord Jesus Christ, praying always for you, 4 since we heard of your faith in Christ Jesus and the love which you have for all the saints; 5 because of the hope laid up for you in heaven, of which you previously heard in the word of truth, the gospel 6 which has come to you, just as in all the world also it is constantly bearing fruit and increasing, even as it has been doing in you also since the day you heard of it and understood the grace of God in truth; 7 just as you learned it from Epaphras, our beloved fellow bond-servant, who is a faithful servant of Christ on our behalf, 8 and he also informed us of your love in the Spirit.

9 For this reason also, since the day we heard of it, we have not ceased to pray for you and to ask that you may be filled with the knowledge of His will in all spiritual wisdom and understanding, 10 so that you will walk in a manner worthy of the Lord, to please Him in all respects, bearing fruit in every good work and increasing in the knowledge of God; 11 strengthened with all power, according to His glorious might, for the attaining of all steadfastness and patience; joyously 12 giving thanks to the Father, who has qualified us to share in the inheritance of the saints in Light. 13 For He rescued us from the domain of darkness, and transferred us to the kingdom of His beloved Son, 14 in whom we have redemption, the forgiveness of sins.

15 He is the image of the invisible God, the firstborn of all creation. 16 For by Him all things were created, both in the heavens and on earth, visible and invisible, whether thrones or dominions or rulers or authorities—all things have been created through Him and for Him. 17 He is before all things, and in Him all things hold together. 18 He is also head of the body, the church; and He is the beginning, the firstborn from the dead, so that He Himself will come to have first place in everything. 19 For it was the Father's good pleasure for all the fullness

1:12 qualified us. The Greek word for "qualified" means "to make sufficient," "to empower," or "to authorize." God qualifies us only through the finished work of the Savior. Apart from God's grace through Jesus Christ, all people would be qualified only to receive His wrath. **inheritance.** Literally "for the portion of the lot." Each believer will receive his own individual portion of the total divine inheritance, an allusion to the partitioning of Israel's inheritance in Canaan (Nu 26:52–56; 33:51–54; Jos 14:1–2). **in Light.** Scripture represents "light" intellectually as divine truth (Ps 119:130) and morally as divine purity (Eph 5:8–14; 1Jn 1:5). The saints' inheritance exists in the spiritual realm of truth and purity where God Himself dwells (1Ti 6:16). Light, then, is a synonym for God's kingdom.

1:19 all the fullness. A term likely used by those in the Colossian heresy to refer to divine powers and attributes they believed were divided among various emanations. Paul countered that by asserting that the fullness of deity—all the divine powers and attributes—was not spread out among created beings, but completely dwelt in Christ alone.

---

to dwell in Him, [20] and through Him to reconcile all things to Himself, having made peace through the blood of His cross; through Him, I say, whether things on earth or things in heaven.

[21] And although you were formerly alienated and hostile in mind, engaged in evil deeds, [22] yet He has now reconciled you in His fleshly body through death, in order to present you before Him holy and blameless and beyond reproach— [23] if indeed you continue in

1:27 Gentiles…Christ in you. The Old Testament predicted the coming of the Messiah and that the Gentiles would partake of salvation (Is 42:6; 45:21–22; 49:6; 52:10; 60:1–3; Pss 22:27; 65:5; 98:2–3), but it did not reveal that the Messiah would actually live in each member of His redeemed church, made up mostly of Gentiles. That believers, both Jew and Gentile, now possess the surpassing riches of the indwelling Christ is the glorious revealed. **the hope of glory.** The indwelling Spirit of Christ is the guarantee to each believer of future glory (Ro 8:11; Eph 1:13–14; 1Pe 1:3–4).

---

the faith firmly established and steadfast, and not moved away from the hope of the gospel that you have heard, which was proclaimed in all creation under heaven, and of which I, Paul, was made a minister.

[24] Now I rejoice in my sufferings for your sake, and in my flesh I do my share on behalf of His body, which is the church, in filling up what is lacking in Christ's afflictions. [25] Of this church I was made a minister according to the stewardship from God bestowed on me for your benefit, so that I might fully carry out the preaching of the word of God, [26] that is, the mystery which has been hidden from the past ages and generations, but has now been manifested to His saints, [27] to whom God willed to make known what is the riches of the glory of this mystery among the Gentiles, which is Christ in you, the hope of glory. [28] We proclaim Him, admonishing every man and teaching every man with all wisdom, so that we may present every man complete in Christ. [29] For this purpose also I labor, striving according to His power, which mightily works within me.

DAY 10: How does Colossians 1:15–16 define Christ as God?

The Greek word for "image" means "copy" or "likeness." Jesus Christ is the perfect image—the exact likeness—of God and is in the very form of God (Php 2:6; Jn 1:14; 14:9) and has been so from all eternity. By describing Jesus in this manner, Paul emphasizes that He is both the representation and manifestation of God. Thus, He is fully God in every way (2:9; Jn 8:58; 10:30–33; Heb 1:8).

"The firstborn of all creation." The Greek word for "firstborn" can refer to one who was born first chronologically, but most often refers to preeminence in position or rank (Heb 1:6; Ro 8:29). In both Greek and Jewish culture, the firstborn was the ranking son who had received the right of inheritance from his father, whether he was born first or not. It is used of Israel who, not being the first nation, was however the preeminent nation (Ex 4:22; Jer 31:9). Firstborn in this context clearly means highest in rank, not first created (Ps 89:27; Rev 1:5) for several reasons:

1. Christ cannot be both "first begotten" and "only begotten" (Jn 1:14, 18; 3:16, 18; 1Jn 4:9);
2. when the "firstborn" is one of a class, the class is in the plural form (v. 18; Ro 8:29), but "creation," the class here, is in a singular form;

3. if Paul was teaching that Christ was a created being, he was agreeing with the heresy he was writing to refute; and

4. it is impossible for Christ to be both created and the Creator of everything (v. 16).

Thus Jesus is the firstborn in the sense that He has the preeminence (v. 18) and possesses the right of inheritance "of all creation" (Heb 1:2; Rev 5:1–7, 13). He existed before the creation and is exalted in rank above it.

The false teachers had incorporated into their heresy the worship of angels, including the lie that Jesus was one of them, merely a spirit created by God and inferior to Him. Paul rejected that and made it clear that angels, whatever their rank, whether holy or fallen, are mere creatures, and their Creator is none other than the preeminent One, the Lord Savior, Jesus Christ (v. 16). The purpose of His catalog of angelic ranks is to show the immeasurable superiority of Christ over any being the false teachers might suggest.

OCTOBER 11

Jeremiah 7:1–8:22

7 The word that came to Jeremiah from the LORD, saying, ² "Stand in the gate of the LORD'S house and proclaim there this word and say, 'Hear the word of the LORD, all you of Judah, who enter by these gates to worship the LORD!'" ³ Thus says the LORD of hosts, the God of Israel, "Amend your ways and your deeds, and I will let you dwell in this place. ⁴ Do not trust in deceptive words, saying, 'This is the temple of the LORD, the temple of the LORD, the temple of the LORD.' ⁵ For if you truly amend your ways and your deeds, if you truly practice justice between a man and his neighbor, ⁶ if you do not oppress the alien, the orphan, or the widow, and do not shed innocent blood in this place, nor walk after other gods to your own ruin, ⁷ then I will let you dwell in this place, in the land that I gave to your fathers forever and ever.

⁸ "Behold, you are trusting in deceptive words to no avail. ⁹ Will you steal, murder, and commit adultery and swear falsely, and offer sacrifices to Baal and walk after other gods

that you have not known, ¹⁰ then come and stand before Me in this house, which is called by My name, and say, 'We are delivered!'—that you may do all these abominations? ¹¹ Has this house, which is called by My name, become a den of robbers in your sight? Behold, I, even I, have seen *it*," declares the LORD.

¹² "But go now to My place which was in Shiloh, where I made My name dwell at the first, and see what I did to it because of the wickedness of My people Israel. ¹³ And now, because you have done all these things," declares the LORD, "and I spoke to you, rising up early and speaking, but you did not hear, and I called you but you did not answer, ¹⁴ therefore, I will do to the house which is called by My name, in which you trust, and to the place which I gave you and your fathers, as I did to Shiloh. ¹⁵ I will cast you out of My sight, as I have cast out all your brothers, all the offspring of Ephraim.

¹⁶ "As for you, do not pray for this people, and do not lift up cry or prayer for them, and do not intercede with Me; for I do not hear you. ¹⁷ Do you not see what they are doing in the cities of Judah and in the streets of Jerusalem? ¹⁸ The children gather wood, and the fathers kindle the fire, and the women knead dough to make cakes for the queen of heaven; and *they* pour out drink offerings to other gods in order to spite Me. ¹⁹ Do they spite Me?" declares the LORD. "Is it not themselves *they spite*, to their own shame?" ²⁰ Therefore

7:1 The word that came. This was Jeremiah's first temple sermon (v. 2); another is found in chap. 26. God was aroused against the sins He names (vv. 6, 19), especially at His temple becoming a den of robbers (v. 11). The point of this message, however, was that if Israel would repent, even at this late hour, God would still keep the conqueror from coming (vv. 3, 7). They must reject lies such as the false hope that peace is certain, based on the reasoning that the Lord would never bring calamity on His own temple (v. 4). They must turn from their sins (v. 3, 5, 9), and end their hypocrisy (v. 10).

7:18 the queen of heaven. The Jews were worshiping Ishtar, an Assyrian and Babylonian goddess also called Ashtoreth and Astarte, the wife of Baal or Molech. Because these deities symbolized generative power, their worship involved prostitution.

thus says the Lord GOD, "Behold, My anger and My wrath will be poured out on this place, on man and on beast and on the trees of the field and on the fruit of the ground; and it will burn and not be quenched."

²¹Thus says the LORD of hosts, the God of Israel, "Add your burnt offerings to your sacrifices and eat flesh. ²²For I did not speak to your fathers, or command them in the day that I brought them out of the land of Egypt, concerning burnt offerings and sacrifices. ²³But this is what I commanded them, saying, 'Obey My voice, and I will be your God, and you will be My people; and you will walk in all the way which I command you, that it may be well with you.' ²⁴Yet they did not obey or incline their ear, but walked in *their own* counsels *and* in the stubbornness of their evil heart, and went backward and not forward. ²⁵Since the day that your fathers came out of the land of Egypt until this day, I have sent you all My servants the prophets, daily rising early and sending *them.* ²⁶Yet they did not listen to Me or incline their ear, but stiffened their neck; they did more evil than their fathers.

7:22 I did not…command. Bible writers sometimes use apparent negation to make a comparative emphasis. What God commanded His people at the Exodus was not so much the offerings, as it was the heart obedience which prompted the offerings. See this comparative sense used elsewhere.

²⁷"You shall speak all these words to them, but they will not listen to you; and you shall call to them, but they will not answer you. ²⁸You shall say to them, 'This is the nation that did not obey the voice of the LORD their God or accept correction; truth has perished and has been cut off from their mouth.

²⁹'Cut off your hair and cast *it* away,
And take up a lamentation
    on the bare heights;
For the LORD has rejected
    and forsaken
The generation of His wrath.'

³⁰For the sons of Judah have done that which is evil in My sight," declares the LORD, "they have set their detestable things in the house which is called by My name, to defile it. ³¹They have built the high places of Topheth, which

is in the valley of the son of Hinnom, to burn their sons and their daughters in the fire, which I did not command, and it did not come into My mind.

³²"Therefore, behold, days are coming," declares the LORD, "when it will no longer be called Topheth, or the valley of the son of Hinnom, but the valley of the Slaughter; for they will bury in Topheth because there is no *other* place. ³³The dead bodies of this people will be food for the birds of the sky and for the beasts of the earth; and no one will frighten *them away.* ³⁴Then I will make to cease from the cities of Judah and from the streets of Jerusalem the voice of joy and the voice of gladness, the voice of the bridegroom and the voice of the bride; for the land will become a ruin.

8 "At that time," declares the LORD, "they will bring out the bones of the kings of Judah and the bones of its princes, and the bones of the priests and the bones of the prophets, and the bones of the inhabitants of Jerusalem from their graves. ²They will spread them out to the sun, the moon and to all the host of heaven, which they have loved and which they have served, and which they have gone after and which they have sought, and which they have worshiped. They will not be gathered or buried; they will be as dung on the face of the ground. ³And death will be chosen rather than life by all the remnant that remains of this evil family, that remains in all the places to which I have driven them," declares the LORD of hosts. ⁴"You shall say to them, 'Thus says the LORD,

"Do *men* fall and not get up again?
    Does one turn away and not repent?
⁵ "Why then has this people, Jerusalem,
    Turned away in continual apostasy?
    They hold fast to deceit,
    They refuse to return.
⁶ "I have listened and heard,
    They have spoken what is not right;
    No man repented of his wickedness,
    Saying, 'What have I done?'
    Everyone turned to his course,
    Like a horse charging into the battle.
⁷ "Even the stork in the sky
    Knows her seasons;
    And the turtledove and the
        swift and the thrush
    Observe the time of their migration;
    But My people do not know
    The ordinance of the LORD.
⁸ "How can you say, 'We are wise,
    And the law of the LORD is with us'?

But behold, the lying pen of the scribes
Has made *it* into a lie.
9 "The wise men are put to shame,
They are dismayed and caught;
Behold, they have rejected
    the word of the LORD,
And what kind of wisdom
    do they have?
10 "Therefore I will give their
    wives to others,
Their fields to new owners;
Because from the least
    even to the greatest
Everyone is greedy for gain;
From the prophet even to the priest
Everyone practices deceit.
11 "They heal the brokenness
    of the daughter of My
    people superficially,
Saying, 'Peace, peace,'
But there is no peace.
12 "Were they ashamed because of the
    abomination they had done?
They certainly were not ashamed,
And they did not know how to blush;
Therefore they shall fall
    among those who fall;
At the time of their punishment
    they shall be brought down,"
Says the LORD.

13 "I will surely snatch them away,"
    declares the LORD;
"There will be no grapes on the vine
And no figs on the fig tree,
And the leaf will wither;
And what I have given them
    will pass away."'"
14 Why are we sitting still?
Assemble yourselves, and let us
    go into the fortified cities
And let us perish there,
Because the LORD our God
    has doomed us
And given us poisoned water to drink,
For we have sinned against the LORD.
15 *We* waited for peace, but
    no good *came;*
For a time of healing, but
    behold, terror!
16 From Dan is heard the
    snorting of his horses;
At the sound of the neighing
    of his stallions
The whole land quakes;
For they come and devour the
    land and its fullness,
The city and its inhabitants.

17 "For behold, I am sending
    serpents against you,
Adders, for which there is no charm,
And they will bite you,"
    declares the LORD.
18 My sorrow is beyond healing,
My heart is faint *within me!*
19 Behold, listen! The cry of the daughter
    of my people from a distant land:
"Is the LORD not in Zion? Is her
    King not within her?"
"Why have they provoked Me
    with their graven images,
    with foreign idols?"
20 "Harvest is past, summer is ended,
And we are not saved."
21 For the brokenness of the daughter
    of my people I am broken;
I mourn, dismay has
    taken hold of me.
22 Is there no balm in Gilead?
Is there no physician there?
Why then has not the health
    of the daughter of my
    people been restored?

Psalm 118:1–4

Give thanks to the LORD,
    for He is good;
For His lovingkindness is everlasting.
2 Oh let Israel say,
    "His lovingkindness is everlasting."
3 Oh let the house of Aaron say,
    "His lovingkindness is everlasting."
4 Oh let those who fear the LORD say,
    "His lovingkindness is everlasting."

Proverbs 27:5–6

5 Better is open rebuke
    Than love that is concealed.
6 Faithful are the wounds of a friend,
    But deceitful are the kisses
    of an enemy.

Colossians 2:1–23

2 For I want you to know how great a
struggle I have on your behalf and for
those who are at Laodicea, and for all those
who have not personally seen my face, 2 that
their hearts may be encouraged, having been
knit together in love, and *attaining* to all the
wealth that comes from the full assurance of
understanding, *resulting* in a true knowledge
of God's mystery, *that is,* Christ *Himself,* 3 in
whom are hidden all the treasures of wisdom
and knowledge. 4 I say this so that no one will
delude you with persuasive argument. 5 For

even though I am absent in body, nevertheless I am with you in spirit, rejoicing to see your good discipline and the stability of your faith in Christ. ⁶Therefore as you have received Christ Jesus the Lord, *so* walk in Him, ⁷having been firmly rooted *and now* being built up in Him and established in your faith, just as you were instructed, *and* overflowing with gratitude.

⁸See to it that no one takes you captive through philosophy and empty deception, according to the tradition of men, according to the elementary principles of the world, rather than according to Christ. ⁹For in Him all the fullness of Deity dwells in bodily form, ¹⁰and in Him you have been made complete, and He is the head over all rule and authority; ¹¹and in Him you were also circumcised with a circumcision made without hands, in the removal of the body of the flesh by the circumcision of Christ; ¹²having been buried with Him in baptism, in which you were also raised up with Him through faith in the working of God, who raised Him from the dead. ¹³When you were dead in your transgressions and the uncircumcision of your flesh, He made you alive together with Him, having forgiven us all our transgressions, ¹⁴having canceled out the certificate of debt consisting of decrees against us, which was hostile to us; and He has taken it out of the way, having nailed it to the cross. ¹⁵When He had disarmed the rulers and authorities, He made a public display of them, having triumphed over them through Him.

¹⁶Therefore no one is to act as your judge in regard to food or drink or in respect to a festival or a new moon or a Sabbath day— ¹⁷things which are a *mere* shadow of what is to come; but the substance belongs to Christ. ¹⁸Let no one keep defrauding you of your prize by delighting in self-abasement and the worship of the angels, taking his stand on *visions* he

has seen, inflated without cause by his fleshly mind, ¹⁹and not holding fast to the head, from whom the entire body, being supplied and held together by the joints and ligaments, grows with a growth which is from God.

²⁰If you have died with Christ to the elementary principles of the world, why, as if you were living in the world, do you submit yourself to decrees, such as, ²¹"Do not handle, do not taste, do not touch!" ²²(which all *refer to* things destined to perish with use)—in accordance with the commandments and teachings of men? ²³These are matters which have, to be sure, the appearance of wisdom in self-made religion and self-abasement and severe treatment of the body, *but are* of no value against fleshly indulgence.

2:14 canceled out the certificate of debt. This refers to the handwritten certificate of debt by which a debtor acknowledged his indebtedness. All people (Ro 3:23) owe God an unpayable debt for violating His law (Gal 3:10; Jas 2:10; see Mt 18:23–27), and are thus under sentence of death (Ro 6:23). Paul graphically compares God's forgiveness of believers' sins to wiping ink off a parchment. Through Christ's sacrificial death on the cross, God has totally erased our certificate of indebtedness and made our forgiveness complete. **nailed it to the cross.** This is another metaphor for forgiveness. The list of the crimes of a crucified criminal was nailed to the cross with that criminal to declare the violations he was being punished for (as in the case of Jesus, as noted in Mt 27:37). Believers' sins were all put to Christ's account, nailed to His cross as He paid the penalty in their place for them all, thus satisfying the just wrath of God against crimes requiring punishment in full.

DAY 11: What were the false teachers trying to do to the Colossians?

"See to it that no one takes you captive," Paul warns in Colossians 2:8. Here is a term for robbery. False teachers who are successful in getting people to believe lies rob them of truth, salvation, and blessing. "Through philosophy and empty deception." "Philosophy" ("love of wisdom") appears only here in the New Testament. The word referred to more than merely the academic discipline, but described any theory about God, the world, or the meaning of life. Those embracing the Colossian heresy used it to describe the supposed higher knowledge they claimed to have attained. Paul, however, equates the false teachers' philosophy with "empty deception"; that is, with worthless deception. "According to the elementary principles of the world." Far from being advanced, profound knowledge, the false teachers' beliefs were simplistic and immature like all the rest of the speculations, ideologies, philosophies, and psychologies the fallen satanic and human system invents.

"For in Him all the fullness of Deity dwells in bodily form" (v. 9). Christ possesses the fullness of the divine nature and attributes. In Greek philosophical thought, matter was evil; spirit was good. Thus, it was unthinkable that God would ever take on a human body. Paul refutes that false teaching by stressing the reality of Christ's Incarnation. Jesus was not only fully God, but fully human as well. "And in Him you have been made complete" (v. 10). Believers are complete in Christ, both positionally by the imputed perfect righteousness of Christ and the complete sufficiency of all heavenly resources for spiritual maturity. "He is the head over all rule and authority." Jesus Christ is the creator and ruler of the universe and all its spiritual beings, not a lesser being emanating from God as the Colossian errorists maintained.

OCTOBER 12

Jeremiah 9:1–10:25

9 Oh that my head were waters
And my eyes a fountain of tears,
That I might weep day and night
For the slain of the daughter
of my people!
2 Oh that I had in the desert
A wayfarers' lodging place;
That I might leave my people
And go from them!
For all of them are adulterers,
An assembly of treacherous men.

9:1 waters…tears. Jeremiah cared so deeply that he longed for the relief of flooding tears or a place of retreat to be free of the burden of Judah's sins for a while.

3 "They bend their tongue
like their bow;
Lies and not truth prevail
in the land;
For they proceed from
evil to evil,
And they do not know Me,"
declares the LORD.
4 "Let everyone be on guard
against his neighbor,
And do not trust any brother;
Because every brother
deals craftily,
And every neighbor goes
about as a slanderer.
5 "Everyone deceives his neighbor
And does not speak the truth,
They have taught their
tongue to speak lies;
They weary themselves
committing iniquity.
6 "Your dwelling is in the
midst of deceit;
Through deceit they refuse to
know Me," declares the LORD.

7 Therefore thus says the LORD of hosts,

"Behold, I will refine them
and assay them;
For what *else* can I do, because of
the daughter of My people?
8 "Their tongue is a deadly arrow;
It speaks deceit;
With his mouth one speaks
peace to his neighbor,
But inwardly he sets an
ambush for him.
9 "Shall I not punish them for these
things?" declares the LORD.
"On a nation such as this
Shall I not avenge Myself?
10 "For the mountains I will take up
a weeping and wailing,
And for the pastures of the
wilderness a dirge,
Because they are laid waste so
that no one passes through,
And the lowing of the
cattle is not heard;
Both the birds of the sky and the
beasts have fled; they are gone.
11 "I will make Jerusalem a heap of ruins,
A haunt of jackals;
And I will make the cities of Judah a
desolation, without inhabitant."

12 Who is the wise man that may understand this? And *who is* he to whom the mouth of the LORD has spoken, that he may declare it? Why is the land ruined, laid waste like a desert, so that no one passes through? 13 The LORD said, "Because they have forsaken My law which I set before them, and have not obeyed My voice nor walked according to it, 14 but have walked after the stubbornness of their heart and after the Baals, as their fathers taught them," 15 therefore thus says the LORD of hosts, the God of Israel, "behold, I will feed them, this people, with wormwood and give them poisoned water to drink. 16 I will scatter them among the nations, whom neither they nor their fathers have known; and I will send the sword after them until I have annihilated them."

¹⁷Thus says the LORD of hosts,

"Consider and call for the mourning
    women, that they may come;
And send for the wailing women,
    that they may come!
¹⁸ "Let them make haste and take
    up a wailing for us,
That our eyes may shed tears
And our eyelids flow with water.
¹⁹ "For a voice of wailing is
    heard from Zion,
'How are we ruined!
We are put to great shame,
For we have left the land,
Because they have cast down
    our dwellings.'"
²⁰ Now hear the word of the
    LORD, O you women,
And let your ear receive the
    word of His mouth;
Teach your daughters wailing,
And everyone her neighbor a dirge.
²¹ For death has come up
    through our windows;
It has entered our palaces
To cut off the children from the streets,
The young men from the
    town squares.
²² Speak, "Thus says the LORD,
'The corpses of men will fall like
    dung on the open field,
And like the sheaf after the reaper,
But no one will gather *them*.'"

²³Thus says the LORD, "Let not a wise man
boast of his wisdom, and let not the mighty
man boast of his might, let not a rich man
boast of his riches; ²⁴but let him who boasts
boast of this, that he understands and knows
Me, that I am the LORD who exercises lovingkindness, justice and righteousness on earth;
for I delight in these things," declares the LORD.
²⁵ "Behold, the days are coming," declares
the LORD, "that I will punish all who are circumcised and yet uncircumcised— ²⁶Egypt
and Judah, and Edom and the sons of Ammon,
and Moab and all those inhabiting the desert
who clip the hair on their temples; for all the
nations are uncircumcised, and all the house
of Israel are uncircumcised of heart."

10 Hear the word which the LORD speaks
to you, O house of Israel. ²Thus says
the LORD,

"Do not learn the way of the nations,
And do not be terrified by the
    signs of the heavens

Although the nations are
    terrified by them;
³ For the customs of the
    peoples are delusion;
Because it is wood cut from the forest,
The work of the hands of a
    craftsman with a cutting tool.
⁴ "They decorate *it* with silver
    and with gold;
They fasten it with nails
    and with hammers
So that it will not totter.
⁵ "Like a scarecrow in a cucumber
    field are they,
And they cannot speak;
They must be carried,
Because they cannot walk!
Do not fear them,
For they can do no harm,
Nor can they do any good."

⁶ There is none like You, O LORD;
You are great, and great is
    Your name in might.
⁷ Who would not fear You,
    O King of the nations?
Indeed it is Your due!
For among all the wise
    men of the nations
And in all their kingdoms,
There is none like You.

10:7 King. God, who sovereignly created and
controls all things (see vv. 12, 16; Dt 4:35), is
alone the eternal, living God (Pss 47, 145) worthy of trust. By contrast, earthly idols have to be
fashioned by men (v. 9), and will perish (v. 15).

⁸ But they are altogether
    stupid and foolish
In their discipline of delusion—
    their idol is wood!
⁹ Beaten silver is brought
    from Tarshish,
And gold from Uphaz,
The work of a craftsman and of
    the hands of a goldsmith;
Violet and purple are their clothing;
They are all the work of skilled men.
¹⁰ But the LORD is the true God;
He is the living God and the
    everlasting King.
At His wrath the earth quakes,
And the nations cannot
    endure His indignation.

11 Thus you shall say to them, "The gods that did not make the heavens and the earth will perish from the earth and from under the heavens."

12 It is He who made the
earth by His power,
Who established the world
by His wisdom;
And by His understanding He has
stretched out the heavens.

13 When He utters His voice, there is a
tumult of waters in the heavens,
And He causes the clouds to ascend
from the end of the earth;
He makes lightning for the rain,
And brings out the wind
from His storehouses.

14 Every man is stupid, devoid
of knowledge;
Every goldsmith is put to
shame by his idols;
For his molten images are deceitful,
And there is no breath in them.

15 They are worthless, a
work of mockery;
In the time of their punishment
they will perish.

16 The portion of Jacob is not like these;
For the Maker of all is He,
And Israel is the tribe of
His inheritance;
The LORD of hosts is His name.

17 Pick up your bundle from the ground,
You who dwell under siege!

18 For thus says the LORD,
"Behold, I am slinging out the
inhabitants of the land
At this time,
And will cause them distress,
That they may be found."

19 Woe is me, because of my injury!
My wound is incurable.
But I said, "Truly this is a sickness,
And I must bear it."

20 My tent is destroyed,
And all my ropes are broken;
My sons have gone from
me and are no more.
There is no one to stretch
out my tent again
Or to set up my curtains.

21 For the shepherds have become stupid
And have not sought the LORD;
Therefore they have not prospered,
And all their flock is scattered.

22 The sound of a report!
Behold, it comes—
A great commotion out of
the land of the north—
To make the cities of Judah
A desolation, a haunt of jackals.

23 I know, O LORD, that a man's
way is not in himself,
Nor is it in a man who walks
to direct his steps.

24 Correct me, O LORD, but with justice;
Not with Your anger, or You
will bring me to nothing.

25 Pour out Your wrath on the
nations that do not know You
And on the families that do
not call Your name;
For they have devoured Jacob;
They have devoured him
and consumed him
And have laid waste his habitation.

Psalm 118:5–9

5 From my distress I called
upon the LORD;
The LORD answered me and
set me in a large place.

6 The LORD is for me; I will not fear;
What can man do to me?

7 The LORD is for me among
those who help me;
Therefore I will look with satisfaction
on those who hate me.

8 It is better to take refuge in the LORD
Than to trust in man.

9 It is better to take refuge in the LORD
Than to trust in princes.

Proverbs 27:7

7 A sated man loathes honey,
But to a famished man any
bitter thing is sweet.

Colossians 3:1–25

3 Therefore if you have been raised up with Christ, keep seeking the things above, where Christ is, seated at the right hand of God. 2 Set your mind on the things above, not on the things that are on earth. 3 For you have died and your life is hidden with Christ in God. 4 When Christ, who is our life, is revealed, then you also will be revealed with Him in glory.

5 Therefore consider the members of your earthly body as dead to immorality, impurity, passion, evil desire, and greed, which amounts to idolatry. 6 For it is because of these

3:2 Set your mind. This can also be translated "think," or "have this inner disposition." As a compass points north, the believer's entire disposition should point itself toward the things of heaven. Heavenly thoughts can only come by understanding heavenly realities from Scripture (Ro 8:5; 12:2; Php 1:23; 4:8; 1Jn 2:15–17).

3:20 in all things. The only limit on a child's obedience is when parents demand something contrary to God's Word. For example, some children will act contrary to their parents' wishes even in coming to Christ (Lk 12:51–53; 14:26).

things that the wrath of God will come upon the sons of disobedience, [7] and in them you also once walked, when you were living in them. [8] But now you also, put them all aside: anger, wrath, malice, slander, *and* abusive speech from your mouth. [9] Do not lie to one another, since you laid aside the old self with its *evil* practices, [10] and have put on the new self who is being renewed to a true knowledge according to the image of the One who created him— [11] *a renewal* in which there is no *distinction between* Greek and Jew, circumcised and uncircumcised, barbarian, Scythian, slave and freeman, but Christ is all, and in all.

[12] So, as those who have been chosen of God, holy and beloved, put on a heart of compassion, kindness, humility, gentleness and patience; [13] bearing with one another, and forgiving each other, whoever has a complaint against anyone; just as the Lord forgave you, so also should you. [14] Beyond all these things *put on* love, which is the perfect bond of unity. [15] Let the peace of Christ rule in your hearts, to which indeed you were called

in one body; and be thankful. [16] Let the word of Christ richly dwell within you, with all wisdom teaching and admonishing one another with psalms *and* hymns *and* spiritual songs, singing with thankfulness in your hearts to God. [17] Whatever you do in word or deed, *do* all in the name of the Lord Jesus, giving thanks through Him to God the Father.

[18] Wives, be subject to your husbands, as is fitting in the Lord. [19] Husbands, love your wives and do not be embittered against them. [20] Children, be obedient to your parents in all things, for this is well-pleasing to the Lord. [21] Fathers, do not exasperate your children, so that they will not lose heart.

[22] Slaves, in all things obey those who are your masters on earth, not with external service, as those who *merely* please men, but with sincerity of heart, fearing the Lord. [23] Whatever you do, do your work heartily, as for the Lord rather than for men, [24] knowing that from the Lord you will receive the reward of the inheritance. It is the Lord Christ whom you serve. [25] For he who does wrong will receive the consequences of the wrong which he has done, and that without partiality.

DAY 12: What should a believer's relationship be to the Word of God?

In Colossians 3:16, Paul says to "let the word of Christ richly dwell within you." This is Scripture, the Holy Spirit inspired Scripture, the word of revelation He brought into the world. "Dwell" means "to live in" or "to be at home," and "richly" may be more fully rendered "abundantly or extravagantly rich." Scripture should permeate every aspect of the believer's life and control every thought, word, and deed (Ps 119:11; Mt 13:9; Php 2:16; 2Ti 2:15). This concept is parallel to being filled with the Spirit in Ephesians 5:18 since the results of each are the same. In Ephesians 5:18, the power and motivation for all the effects is the filling of the Holy Spirit; here it is the word richly dwelling. Those two realities are really one. The Holy Spirit fills the life controlled by His Word. This emphasizes that the filling of the Spirit is not some ecstatic or emotional experience, but a steady controlling of the life by obedience to the truth of God's Word.

"Teaching and admonishing one another in psalms and hymns and spiritual songs" (v. 16). The early church sang the Psalms. Old Testament psalms put to music, primarily, but the term was used also of vocal music in general. "Hymns"—perhaps songs of praise distinguished from the Psalms which exalted God, in that they focused on the Lord Jesus Christ. "Spiritual songs"— probably songs of personal testimony expressing truths of the grace of salvation in Christ. "With thankfulness in your hearts to God"—not just public, but private. The Lord Himself is both the source and the object of the believer's song-filled heart. That such music pleases God can be seen in the account of the temple dedication, when the singing so honored the Lord that His glory came down (2Ch 5:12, 14).

OCTOBER 13

Jeremiah 11:1–12:17

11 The word which came to Jeremiah from the LORD, saying, ² "Hear the words of this covenant, and speak to the men of Judah and to the inhabitants of Jerusalem; ³ and say to them, 'Thus says the LORD, the God of Israel, "Cursed is the man who does not heed the words of this covenant ⁴ which I commanded your forefathers in the day that I brought them out of the land of Egypt, from the iron furnace, saying, 'Listen to My voice, and do according to all which I command you; so you shall be My people, and I will be your God,' ⁵ in order to confirm the oath which I swore to your forefathers, to give them a land flowing with milk and honey, as *it is* this day." ' " Then I said, "Amen, O LORD."

⁶ And the LORD said to me, "Proclaim all these words in the cities of Judah and in the streets of Jerusalem, saying, 'Hear the words of this covenant and do them. ⁷ For I solemnly warned your fathers in the day that I brought them up from the land of Egypt, even to this day, warning persistently, saying, "Listen to My voice." ⁸ Yet they did not obey or incline their ear, but walked, each one, in the stubbornness of his evil heart; therefore I brought on them all the words of this covenant, which I commanded *them* to do, but they did not.' "

⁹ Then the LORD said to me, "A conspiracy has been found among the men of Judah and among the inhabitants of Jerusalem. ¹⁰ They have turned back to the iniquities of their ancestors who refused to hear My words, and they have gone after other gods to serve them; the house of Israel and the house of Judah have broken My covenant which I made with their fathers." ¹¹ Therefore thus says the LORD, "Behold I am bringing disaster on them which they will not be able to escape; though they will cry to Me, yet I will not listen to them. ¹² Then the cities of Judah and the inhabitants of Jerusalem will go and cry to the gods to whom they burn incense, but they surely will not save them in the time of their disaster. ¹³ For your gods are as many as your cities, O Judah; and as many as the streets of Jerusalem are the altars you have set up to the shameful thing, altars to burn incense to Baal.

¹⁴ "Therefore do not pray for this people, nor lift up a cry or prayer for them; for I will not listen when they call to Me because of their disaster.

¹⁵ "What right has My beloved
in My house
When she has done many vile deeds?
Can the sacrificial flesh take away
from you your disaster,
So *that* you can rejoice?"
¹⁶ The LORD called your name,
"A green olive tree, beautiful
in fruit and form";
With the noise of a great tumult
He has kindled fire on it,
And its branches are worthless.

11:15 My beloved. A phrase showing God's sensitive regard for His relationship to Israel as a nation (2:2; 12:7). It does not carry the assumption, however, that every individual is spiritually saved (5:10a). **vile deeds.** Shameful idolatry that defiled all that befits true temple worship, such as the examples in Ezekiel 8:6–13. These were gross violations of the first 3 commandments (Ex 20:2–7). **sacrificial flesh.** In some way, they corrupted the animal sacrifices by committing sin which they enjoyed.

¹⁷ The LORD of hosts, who planted you, has pronounced evil against you because of the evil of the house of Israel and of the house of Judah, which they have done to provoke Me by offering up sacrifices to Baal.

¹⁸ Moreover, the LORD made it
known to me and I knew it;
Then You showed me their deeds.
¹⁹ But I was like a gentle lamb
led to the slaughter;
And I did not know that they had
devised plots against me, *saying,*
"Let us destroy the tree with its fruit,
And let us cut him off from
the land of the living,
That his name be remembered
no more."
²⁰ But, O LORD of hosts, who
judges righteously,
Who tries the feelings and the heart,
Let me see Your vengeance on them,
For to You have I committed my cause.

²¹ Therefore thus says the LORD concerning the men of Anathoth, who seek your life, saying, "Do not prophesy in the name of the LORD, so that you will not die at our hand"; ²² therefore, thus says the LORD of hosts, "Behold, I am about to punish them! The young men will die

by the sword, their sons and daughters will die by famine; 23 and a remnant will not be left to them, for I will bring disaster on the men of Anathoth—the year of their punishment."

12 Righteous are You, O LORD, that I
would plead *my* case with You;
Indeed I would discuss matters
of justice with You:
Why has the way of the
wicked prospered?
Why are all those who deal
in treachery at ease?

2 You have planted them, they
have also taken root;
They grow, they have even
produced fruit.
You are near to their lips
But far from their mind.

3 But You know me, O LORD;
You see me;
And You examine my heart's
attitude toward You.
Drag them off like sheep
for the slaughter
And set them apart for a
day of carnage!

4 How long is the land to mourn
And the vegetation of the
countryside to wither?
For the wickedness of those
who dwell in it,
Animals and birds have
been snatched away,
Because *men* have said, "He will
not see our latter ending."

5 "If you have run with footmen
and they have tired you out,
Then how can you compete
with horses?
If you fall down in a land of peace,
How will you do in the
thicket of the Jordan?

12:5 If you have run. The Lord replied to Jeremiah telling him that if he grew faint with lesser trials and felt like quitting, what would he do when the battle got even harder? **thicket of the Jordan.** The river in flood stage overflowed its banks into a plain that grew up as a thicket. The point is that Jeremiah needed to be ready to deal with tougher testings, pictured by the invader's overwhelming the land like a flood, or posing high danger as in the Jordan thicket where concealed wild animals could terrify a person.

6 "For even your brothers and the
household of your father,
Even they have dealt
treacherously with you,
Even they have cried aloud after you.
Do not believe them, although they
may say nice things to you."

7 "I have forsaken My house,
I have abandoned My inheritance;
I have given the beloved of My soul
Into the hand of her enemies.

8 "My inheritance has become to Me
Like a lion in the forest;
She has roared against Me;
Therefore I have come to hate her.

9 "Is My inheritance like a speckled
bird of prey to Me?
Are the birds of prey against
her on every side?
Go, gather all the beasts of the field,
Bring them to devour!

10 "Many shepherds have
ruined My vineyard,
They have trampled down My field;
They have made My pleasant field
A desolate wilderness.

11 "It has been made a desolation,
Desolate, it mourns before Me;
The whole land has been
made desolate,
Because no man lays it to heart.

12 "On all the bare heights in
the wilderness
Destroyers have come,
For a sword of the LORD is devouring
From one end of the land
even to the other;
There is no peace for anyone.

13 "They have sown wheat and
have reaped thorns,
They have strained themselves
to no profit.
But be ashamed of your harvest
Because of the fierce anger
of the LORD."

14 Thus says the LORD concerning all My wicked neighbors who strike at the inheritance with which I have endowed My people Israel, "Behold I am about to uproot them from their land and will uproot the house of Judah from among them. 15 And it will come about that after I have uprooted them, I will again have compassion on them; and I will bring them back, each one to his inheritance and each one to his land. 16 Then if they will really learn the ways of My people, to swear

by My name, 'As the LORD lives,' even as they taught My people to swear by Baal, they will be built up in the midst of My people. [17] But if they will not listen, then I will uproot that nation, uproot and destroy it," declares the LORD.

Psalm 118:10–14

[10] All nations surrounded me;
    In the name of the LORD I will
      surely cut them off.
[11] They surrounded me, yes,
    they surrounded me;
    In the name of the LORD I will
      surely cut them off.
[12] They surrounded me like bees;
    They were extinguished
      as a fire of thorns;
    In the name of the LORD I will
      surely cut them off.
[13] You pushed me violently so
    that I was falling,
    But the LORD helped me.
[14] The LORD is my strength and song,
    And He has become my salvation.

Proverbs 27:8

[8] Like a bird that wanders from her nest,
    So is a man who wanders
      from his home.

Colossians 4:1–18

4 Masters, grant to your slaves justice and fairness, knowing that you too have a Master in heaven.

[2] Devote yourselves to prayer, keeping alert in it with *an attitude of* thanksgiving; [3] praying at the same time for us as well, that God will open up to us a door for the word, so that we may speak forth the mystery of Christ, for which I have also been imprisoned; [4] that I may make it clear in the way I ought to speak.

[5] Conduct yourselves with wisdom toward outsiders, making the most of the opportunity. [6] Let your speech always be with grace,

4:2 Devote yourselves. The Greek word for "devote" means "to be courageously persistent" or "to hold fast and not let go" and refers here to persistent prayer (Ac 1:14; Ro 12:12; Eph 6:18; 1Th 5:17; see Lk 11:5–10; 18:1–8). **keeping alert.** In its most general sense this means to stay awake while praying. But Paul has in mind the broader implication of staying alert for specific needs about which to pray, rather than being vague and unfocused.

4:6 with grace. To speak what is spiritual, wholesome, fitting, kind, sensitive, purposeful, complimentary, gentle, truthful, loving, and thoughtful. **seasoned with salt.** Just as salt not only flavors, but prevents corruption, the Christian's speech should act not only as a blessing to others, but as a purifying influence within the decaying society of the world.

as though seasoned with salt, so that you will know how you should respond to each person.

[7] As to all my affairs, Tychicus, *our* beloved brother and faithful servant and fellow bondservant in the Lord, will bring you information. [8] *For* I have sent him to you for this very purpose, that you may know about our circumstances and that he may encourage your hearts; [9] and with him Onesimus, *our* faithful and beloved brother, who is one of your *number.* They will inform you about the whole situation here.

[10] Aristarchus, my fellow prisoner, sends you his greetings; and *also* Barnabas's cousin Mark (about whom you received instructions; if he comes to you, welcome him); [11] and *also* Jesus who is called Justus; these are the only fellow workers for the kingdom of God who are from the circumcision, and they have proved to be an encouragement to me. [12] Epaphras, who is one of your number, a bondslave of Jesus Christ, sends you his greetings, always laboring earnestly for you in his prayers, that you may stand perfect and fully assured in all the will of God. [13] For I testify for him that he has a deep concern for you and for those who are in Laodicea and Hierapolis. [14] Luke, the beloved physician, sends you his greetings, and *also* Demas. [15] Greet the brethren who are in Laodicea and also Nympha and the church that is in her house. [16] When this letter is read among you, have it also read in the church of the Laodiceans; and you, for your part read my letter *that is coming* from Laodicea. [17] Say to Archippus, "Take heed to the ministry which you have received in the Lord, that you may fulfill it."

[18] I, Paul, write this greeting with my own hand. Remember my imprisonment. Grace be with you.

4:18 with my own hand. Paul usually dictated his letters to an amanuensis (recording secretary), but would often add his own greeting in his own writing at the end of his letters (1Co 16:21; Gal 6:11; 2Th 3:17; Phm 19).

DAY 13: What were the Prison Epistles, and what prison was Paul in when he wrote them?

Four of Paul's letters are grouped as the Prison Epistles: Ephesians, Philippians, Colossians, and Philemon. Each of them includes clear internal references to the writer's prison surroundings (Eph 3:1; 4:1; 6:20; Php 1:7, 13–14, 17; Col 4:3, 10, 18; Phm 1, 9–10, 13, 23). The similarities between the details of Paul's imprisonment given in Acts and in the Prison Epistles support the traditional position that the letters were written from Rome. Among these details are: 1) Paul was guarded by soldiers (Ac 28:16; Php 1:13, 14); 2) Paul was permitted to receive visitors (Ac 28:30; Php 4:18); and 3) Paul had the opportunity to preach the gospel (Ac 28:31; Eph 6:18–20; Php 1:12–14; Col 4:2—4).

Caesarea and Ephesus have also been suggested as Paul's possible location when he wrote at least some of these letters. Paul was imprisoned in Caesarea for two years (Ac 24:27), but his opportunities to receive visitors and proclaim the gospel were severely limited during that time (Ac 23:35). The Prison Epistles express Paul's hope for a favorable verdict (Php 1:25; 2:24; Phm 23). In Caesarea, however, Paul's only hope for release was either to bribe Felix (Ac 24:26) or agree to stand trial at Jerusalem under Festus (Ac 25:9). In the Prison Epistles, Paul expected the decision in his case to be final (Php 1:20–23; 2:17, 23). That could not have been true at Caesarea, since Paul could and did appeal his case to the emperor.

Ephesus has been the other suggested location. Most of the same difficulties faced by the Caesarea suggestion face those who support Ephesus. The most telling argument against Ephesus as the point of origin for the Prison Epistles, however, is that there is no evidence that Paul was ever imprisoned at Ephesus.

In light of the serious difficulties faced by both the Caesarean and Ephesian views, no reason remains for rejecting the traditional view that Paul wrote the Prison Epistles from Rome while awaiting a hearing before the emperor on his appeal for justice as a Roman citizen.

 OCTOBER 14

Jeremiah 13:1–14:22

13 Thus the LORD said to me, "Go and buy yourself a linen waistband and put it around your waist, but do not put it in water." ² So I bought the waistband in accordance with the word of the LORD and put it around my waist. ³ Then the word of the LORD came to me a second time, saying, ⁴ "Take the waistband that you have bought, which is around your waist, and arise, go to the Euphrates and hide it there in a crevice of the rock." ⁵ So I went and hid it by the Euphrates, as the LORD had

13:1 a linen waistband. One of several signs Jeremiah enacted to illustrate God's message involved putting on a linen waistband (generally the inner garment against the skin). This depicted Israel's close intimacy with God in the covenant, so that they could glorify Him (v. 11). **do not put it in water.** Signified the moral filth of the nation. Buried and allowed time to rot (v. 7), the waistband pictured Israel as useless to God because of sin (v. 10). Hiding it by the Euphrates (v. 6) pointed to the land of Babylon, where God would exile Israel to deal with her pride (v. 9).

commanded me. ⁶ After many days the LORD said to me, "Arise, go to the Euphrates and take from there the waistband which I commanded you to hide there." ⁷ Then I went to the Euphrates and dug, and I took the waistband from the place where I had hidden it; and lo, the waistband was ruined, it was totally worthless.

⁸ Then the word of the LORD came to me, saying, ⁹ "Thus says the LORD, 'Just so will I destroy the pride of Judah and the great pride of Jerusalem. ¹⁰ This wicked people, who refuse to listen to My words, who walk in the stubbornness of their hearts and have gone after other gods to serve them and to bow down to them, let them be just like this waistband which is totally worthless. ¹¹ For as the waistband clings to the waist of a man, so I made the whole household of Israel and the whole household of Judah cling to Me,' declares the LORD, 'that they might be for Me a people, for renown, for praise and for glory; but they did not listen.'

¹² "Therefore you are to speak this word to them, 'Thus says the LORD, the God of Israel, "Every jug is to be filled with wine." ' And when they say to you, 'Do we not very well know that every jug is to be filled with wine?' ¹³ then say to them, 'Thus says the LORD, "Behold I am about to fill all the inhabitants of this land—the kings that sit for David on his throne, the priests, the prophets and all the

inhabitants of Jerusalem—with drunkenness!
¹⁴ I will dash them against each other, both the
fathers and the sons together," declares the
LORD. "I will not show pity nor be sorry nor
have compassion so as not to destroy them."'"

15 Listen and give heed, do
    not be haughty,
For the LORD has spoken.
16 Give glory to the LORD your God,
Before He brings darkness
And before your feet stumble
On the dusky mountains,
And while you are hoping for light
He makes it into deep darkness,
And turns *it* into gloom.
17 But if you will not listen to it,
My soul will sob in secret
    for *such* pride;
And my eyes will bitterly weep
And flow down with tears,
Because the flock of the LORD
    has been taken captive.
18 Say to the king and the queen mother,
"Take a lowly seat,
For your beautiful crown
Has come down from your head."
19 The cities of the Negev have
    been locked up,
And there is no one to open *them;*
All Judah has been carried into exile,
Wholly carried into exile.

20 "Lift up your eyes and see
Those coming from the north.
Where is the flock that was given you,
Your beautiful sheep?
21 "What will you say when He
    appoints over you—
And you yourself had taught them—
Former companions to be
    head over you?
Will not pangs take hold of you
Like a woman in childbirth?
22 "If you say in your heart,
'Why have these things
    happened to me?'
Because of the magnitude
    of your iniquity
Your skirts have been removed
And your heels have been exposed.
23 "Can the Ethiopian change his skin
Or the leopard his spots?
Then you also can do good
Who are accustomed to doing evil.
24 "Therefore I will scatter them
    like drifting straw
To the desert wind.

25 "This is your lot, the portion
    measured to you
From Me," declares the LORD,
"Because you have forgotten Me
And trusted in falsehood.
26 "So I Myself have also stripped
    your skirts off over your face,
That your shame may be seen.
27 "As for your adulteries and
    your *lustful* neighings,
The lewdness of your prostitution
On the hills in the field,
I have seen your abominations.
Woe to you, O Jerusalem!
How long will you remain unclean?"

14 That which came as the word of the
LORD to Jeremiah in regard to the
drought:

2 "Judah mourns
And her gates languish;
They sit on the ground in mourning,
And the cry of Jerusalem
    has ascended.
3 "Their nobles have sent their
    servants for water;
They have come to the cisterns
    and found no water.
They have returned with
    their vessels empty;
They have been put to shame
    and humiliated,
And they cover their heads.
4 "Because the ground is cracked,
For there has been no
    rain on the land;
The farmers have been put to shame,
They have covered their heads.
5 "For even the doe in the field has given
    birth only to abandon *her young,*
Because there is no grass.
6 "The wild donkeys stand on
    the bare heights;
They pant for air like jackals,
Their eyes fail
For there is no vegetation.
7 "Although our iniquities
    testify against us,
O LORD, act for Your name's sake!
Truly our apostasies have been many,
We have sinned against You.
8 "O Hope of Israel,
Its Savior in time of distress,
Why are You like a stranger
    in the land
Or like a traveler who has pitched
    his *tent* for the night?

9 "Why are You like a man dismayed,
Like a mighty man who cannot save?
Yet You are in our midst, O LORD,
And we are called by Your name;
Do not forsake us!"

10 Thus says the LORD to this people, "Even so they have loved to wander; they have not kept their feet in check. Therefore the LORD does not accept them; now He will remember their iniquity and call their sins to account." 11 So the LORD said to me, "Do not pray for the welfare of this people. 12 When they fast, I am not going to listen to their cry; and when they offer burnt offering and grain offering, I am not going to accept them. Rather I am going to make an end of them by the sword, famine and pestilence."

13 But, "Ah, Lord GOD!" I said, "Look, the prophets are telling them, 'You will not see the sword nor will you have famine, but I will give you lasting peace in this place.'" 14 Then the LORD said to me, "The prophets are proph-esying falsehood in My name. I have neither sent them nor commanded them nor spoken to them; they are prophesying to you a false vision, divination, futility and the deception of their own minds. 15 Therefore thus says the LORD concerning the prophets who are prophesying in My name, although it was not I who sent them—yet they keep saying, 'There will be no sword or famine in this land'—by sword and famine those prophets shall meet their end! 16 The people also to whom they are prophesying will be thrown out into the streets of Jerusalem because of the famine and the sword; and there will be no one to bury them—*neither* them, *nor* their wives, nor their sons, nor their daughters—for I will pour out their *own* wickedness on them.

17 "You will say this word to them,
'Let my eyes flow down with
tears night and day,
And let them not cease;
For the virgin daughter of my
people has been crushed
with a mighty blow,
With a sorely infected wound.
18 'If I go out to the country,
Behold, those slain with the sword!
Or if I enter the city,
Behold, diseases of famine!
For both prophet and priest
Have gone roving about in the
land that they do not know.'"

19 Have You completely rejected Judah?
Or have You loathed Zion?

Why have You stricken us so that
we are beyond healing?
We waited for peace, but
nothing good *came;*
And for a time of healing,
but behold, terror!
20 We know our wickedness, O LORD,
The iniquity of our fathers, for
we have sinned against You.
21 Do not despise *us,* for Your
own name's sake;
Do not disgrace the throne
of Your glory;
Remember *and* do not annul
Your covenant with us.
22 Are there any among the idols of
the nations who give rain?
Or can the heavens grant showers?
Is it not You, O LORD our God?
Therefore we hope in You,
For You are the one who has
done all these things.

Psalm 118:15-20

15 The sound of joyful shouting
and salvation is in the
tents of the righteous;
The right hand of the LORD
does valiantly.
16 The right hand of the LORD is exalted;
The right hand of the LORD
does valiantly.
17 I will not die, but live,
And tell of the works of the LORD.
18 The LORD has disciplined me severely,
But He has not given me
over to death.

19 Open to me the gates of
righteousness;
I shall enter through them, I shall
give thanks to the LORD.
20 This is the gate of the LORD;
The righteous will enter through it.

118:19 gates of righteousness. Most likely a fig-urative reference, i.e., spiritual gates through which the righteous pass (Ps 100:4), rather than to the gates of the temple.

118:20 the gate. This points to the entryway which leads to the presence of the Lord. Jesus may have had this psalm in mind when He taught about "the narrow gate" in Matthew 7:13-14.

Proverbs 27:9

9   Oil and perfume make
       the heart glad,
     So a man's counsel is
       sweet to his friend.

1 Thessalonians 1:1–10

1 Paul and Silvanus and Timothy,
     To the church of the Thessalonians in
God the Father and the Lord Jesus Christ:
Grace to you and peace.

² We give thanks to God always for all of
you, making mention of you in our prayers;
³ constantly bearing in mind your work of
faith and labor of love and steadfastness of
hope in our Lord Jesus Christ in the presence
of our God and Father, ⁴ knowing, brethren
beloved by God, *His* choice of you; ⁵ for our
gospel did not come to you in word only,
but also in power and in the Holy Spirit
and with full conviction; just as you know
what kind of men we proved to be among
you for your sake. ⁶ You also became imitators of us and of the Lord, having received
the word in much tribulation with the joy
of the Holy Spirit, ⁷ so that you became an
example to all the believers in Macedonia
and in Achaia. ⁸ For the word of the Lord has
sounded forth from you, not only in Macedonia and Achaia, but also in every place
your faith toward God has gone forth, so
that we have no need to say anything. ⁹ For
they themselves report about us what kind
of a reception we had with you, and how
you turned to God from idols to serve a living and true God, ¹⁰ and to wait for His Son
from heaven, whom He raised from the dead,
that is Jesus, who rescues us from the wrath
to come.

1:6 imitators. The Thessalonians had become
third-generation mimics of Christ. Christ is the
first; Paul is the second; and the Thessalonians
are the third (1Co 4:16; 11:1). **joy of the Holy
Spirit.** Joy in the midst of suffering evidenced
the reality of their salvation, which included the
indwelling Holy Spirit (1Co 3:16; 6:19).

DAY 14: Why was Paul writing to the Thessalonians?

Paul had originally traveled 100 miles from Philippi via Amphipolis and Apollonia to Thessalonica on his second missionary journey (A.D. 50; Ac 16:1–18:22). As his custom was upon arrival,
he sought out the synagogue in which to teach the local Jews the gospel (Ac 17:1–2). On that
occasion, he dialogued with them from the Old Testament concerning Christ's death and resurrection in order to prove that Jesus of Nazareth was truly the promised Messiah (Ac 17:2–3).
Some Jews believed and soon after, Hellenistic proselytes and some wealthy women of the
community also were converted (Ac 17:4).

Because of their effective ministry, the Jews had Paul's team evicted from the city
(Ac 17:5–9), so they went south to evangelize Berea (Ac 17:10). There Paul had a similar experience to Thessalonica with conversions followed by hostility, so the believers sent Paul
away. He headed for Athens, while Silvanus and Timothy remained in Berea (Ac 17:11–14).
They rejoined Paul in Athens (Ac 17:15–16 with 1Th 3:1), from which Timothy was later dis-
patched back to Thessalonica (3:2). Apparently, Silas afterwards traveled from Athens to
Philippi while Paul journeyed on alone to Corinth (Ac 18:1). It was after Timothy and Silvanus
rejoined Paul in Corinth (Ac 18:5) that he wrote 1 Thessalonians in response to Timothy's
good report of the church.

Paul undoubtedly had multiple reasons for writing, all coming out of his supreme concern
for the flock from which he had been separated. Some of Paul's purposes clearly included:
1) encouraging the church (1:2–10); 2) answering false allegations (2:1–12); 3) comforting the
persecuted flock (2:13–16); 4) expressing his joy in their faith (2:17–3:13); 5) reminding them of
the importance of moral purity (4:1–8); 6) condemning the sluggard lifestyle (4:9–12); 7) correcting a wrong understanding of prophetic events (4:13–5:11); 8) defusing tensions within the
flock (5:12–15); and 9) exhorting the flock in the basics of Christian living (5:16–22).

OCTOBER 15

Jeremiah 15:1–16:21

15 Then the LORD said to me, "Even though Moses and Samuel were to stand before Me, My heart would not be with this people; send them away from My presence and let them go! ²And it shall be that when they say to you, 'Where should we go?' then you are to tell them, 'Thus says the LORD:

"Those *destined* for death, to death;
And those *destined* for the
sword, to the sword;
And those *destined* for
famine, to famine;
And those *destined* for
captivity, to captivity."'

³I will appoint over them four kinds *of doom*," declares the LORD: "the sword to slay, the dogs to drag off, and the birds of the sky and the beasts of the earth to devour and destroy. ⁴I will make them an object of horror among all the kingdoms of the earth because of Manasseh, the son of Hezekiah, the king of Judah, for what he did in Jerusalem.

5 "Indeed, who will have pity
on you, O Jerusalem,
Or who will mourn for you,
Or who will turn aside to ask
about your welfare?
6 "You who have forsaken Me,"
declares the LORD,
"You keep going backward.
So I will stretch out My hand
against you and destroy you;
I am tired of relenting!
7 "I will winnow them with
a winnowing fork
At the gates of the land;
I will bereave *them* of children,
I will destroy My people;
They did not repent of their ways.
8 "Their widows will be more
numerous before Me
Than the sand of the seas;
I will bring against them, against
the mother of a young man,
A destroyer at noonday;
I will suddenly bring down on her
Anguish and dismay.
9 "She who bore seven *sons* pines away;
Her breathing is labored.
Her sun has set while it was yet day;
She has been shamed and humiliated.

15:1–9 It was ineffective at this point to intercede for the nation. Even prayers by Moses (Nu 14:11–25) and Samuel (1Sa 12:19–25), eminent in intercession, would not defer judgment, where unrepentance persists. Chief among things provoking judgment was the intense sin of King Manasseh (695–642 B.C.). Noted in v. 4., this provocation is recounted in 2 Kings 21:1–18, see 2 Kings 23:26, which says the Lord did not relent from His anger because of this.

So I will give over their
survivors to the sword
Before their enemies,"
declares the LORD.

10 Woe to me, my mother, that
you have borne me
As a man of strife and a man of
contention to all the land!
I have not lent, nor have men
lent money to me,
Yet everyone curses me.
11 The LORD said, "Surely I will set
you free for *purposes of* good;
Surely I will cause the enemy to
make supplication to you
In a time of disaster and
a time of distress.

12 "Can anyone smash iron,
Iron from the north, or bronze?
13 "Your wealth and your treasures
I will give for booty without cost,
Even for all your sins
And within all your borders.
14 "Then I will cause your
enemies to bring *it*
Into a land you do not know;
For a fire has been kindled
in My anger,
It will burn upon you."

15 You who know, O LORD,
Remember me, take notice of me,
And take vengeance for me
on my persecutors.
Do not, in view of Your
patience, take me away;
Know that for Your sake I
endure reproach.
16 Your words were found
and I ate them,
And Your words became for me a
joy and the delight of my heart;

For I have been called by Your name,
O LORD God of hosts.

¹⁷ I did not sit in the circle
    of merrymakers,
    Nor did I exult.
Because of Your hand *upon*
    me I sat alone,
For You filled me with indignation.

¹⁸ Why has my pain been perpetual
    And my wound incurable,
        refusing to be healed?
    Will You indeed be to me like
        a deceptive *stream*
    With water that is unreliable?

¹⁹ Therefore, thus says the LORD,
    "If you return, then I will restore you—
    Before Me you will stand;
    And if you extract the precious
        from the worthless,
    You will become My spokesman.
    They for their part may turn to you,
    But as for you, you must
        not turn to them.

²⁰ "Then I will make you to this people
    A fortified wall of bronze;
    And though they fight against you,
    They will not prevail over you;
    For I am with you to save you
    And deliver you," declares the LORD.

²¹ "So I will deliver you from the
    hand of the wicked,
    And I will redeem you from
        the grasp of the violent."

16 The word of the LORD also came to me saying, ² "You shall not take a wife for yourself nor have sons or daughters in this place." ³ For thus says the LORD concerning the sons and daughters born in this place, and concerning their mothers who bear them, and their fathers who beget them in this land: ⁴ "They will die of deadly diseases, they will not be lamented or buried; they will be as dung on the surface of the ground and come to an end by sword and famine, and their carcasses will become food for the birds of the sky and for the beasts of the earth."

16:2 You shall not take a wife. Since destruction and exile are soon to fall on Judah, the prophet must not have a wife and family. God's kindness will keep him from anxiety over them in the awful situation of suffering and death (v. 4).

---

⁵ For thus says the LORD, "Do not enter a house of mourning, or go to lament or to console them; for I have withdrawn My peace from this people," declares the LORD, "*My* lovingkindness and compassion. ⁶ Both great men and small will die in this land; they will not be buried, they will not be lamented, nor will anyone gash himself or shave his head for them. ⁷ Men will not break *bread* in mourning for them, to comfort anyone for the dead, nor give them a cup of consolation to drink for anyone's father or mother. ⁸ Moreover you shall not go into a house of feasting to sit with them to eat and drink." ⁹ For thus says the LORD of hosts, the God of Israel: "Behold, I am going to eliminate from this place, before your eyes and in your time, the voice of rejoicing and the voice of gladness, the voice of the groom and the voice of the bride.

¹⁰ "Now when you tell this people all these words, they will say to you, 'For what reason has the LORD declared all this great calamity against us? And what is our iniquity, or what is our sin which we have committed against the LORD our God?' ¹¹ Then you are to say to them, '*It is* because your forefathers have forsaken Me,' declares the LORD, 'and have followed other gods and served them and bowed down to them; but Me they have forsaken and have not kept My law. ¹² You too have done evil, *even* more than your forefathers; for behold, you are each one walking according to the stubbornness of his own evil heart, without listening to Me. ¹³ So I will hurl you out of this land into the land which you have not known, neither you nor your fathers; and there you will serve other gods day and night, for I will grant you no favor.'

¹⁴ "Therefore behold, days are coming," declares the LORD, "when it will no longer be said, 'As the LORD lives, who brought up the sons of Israel out of the land of Egypt,' ¹⁵ but, 'As the LORD lives, who brought up the sons of Israel from the land of the north and from all the countries where He had banished them.' For I will restore them to their own land which I gave to their fathers.

¹⁶ "Behold, I am going to send for many fishermen," declares the LORD, "and they will fish for them; and afterwards I will send for many hunters, and they will hunt them from every mountain and every hill and from the clefts of the rocks. ¹⁷ For My eyes are on all their ways; they are not hidden from My face, nor is their iniquity concealed from My eyes. ¹⁸ I will first doubly repay their iniquity and

their sin, because they have polluted My land; they have filled My inheritance with the carcasses of their detestable idols and with their abominations."

19 O LORD, my strength and
my stronghold,
And my refuge in the day of distress,
To You the nations will come
From the ends of the earth and say,
"Our fathers have inherited
nothing but falsehood,
Futility and things of no profit."
20 Can man make gods for himself?
Yet they are not gods!

21 "Therefore behold, I am going
to make them know—
This time I will make them know
My power and My might;
And they shall know that My
name is the LORD."

Psalm 118:21–24

21 I shall give thanks to You, for
You have answered me,
And You have become
my salvation.
22 The stone which the
builders rejected
Has become the chief corner *stone*.
23 This is the LORD'S doing;
It is marvelous in our eyes.
24 This is the day which the
LORD has made;
Let us rejoice and be glad in it.

118:22 stone...builders rejected...chief corner *stone*. Peter identified the chief cornerstone in the New Testament as Christ (Ac 4:11; 1Pe 2:7). In the parable of the vineyard (Mt 21:42; Mk 12:10–11; Lk 20:17), the rejected son of the vineyard owner is likened to the rejected stone which became the chief cornerstone. Christ was that rejected stone. Jewish leaders were pictured as builders of the nation. Now, this passage in v. 22 has a historical basis which is paralleled in its major features by analogy with the rejection of Christ who came to deliver/save the nation. Moses' experience, as a type of Christ, pictured Christ's rejection. On at least 3 occasions Moses ("stone") was rejected by the Jews ("builders") as their God sent the deliverer ("chief corner *stone*"). For examples see Exodus 2:11–15; Exodus 14:10–14; 16:1–20.

Proverbs 27:10

10 Do not forsake your own friend
or your father's friend,
And do not go to your brother's house
in the day of your calamity;
Better is a neighbor who is near
than a brother far away.

1 Thessalonians 2:1–20

2 For you yourselves know, brethren, that our coming to you was not in vain, 2 but after we had already suffered and been mistreated in Philippi, as you know, we had the boldness in our God to speak to you the gospel of God amid much opposition. 3 For our exhortation does not *come* from error or impurity or by way of deceit; 4 but just as we have been approved by God to be entrusted with the gospel, so we speak, not as pleasing men, but God who examines our hearts. 5 For we never came with flattering speech, as you know, nor with a pretext for greed—God is witness— 6 nor did we seek glory from men, either from you or from others, even though as apostles of Christ we might have asserted our authority. 7 But we proved to be gentle among you, as a nursing *mother* tenderly cares for her own children. 8 Having so fond an affection for you, we were well-pleased to impart to you not only the gospel of God but also our own lives, because you had become very dear to us.

9 For you recall, brethren, our labor and hardship, *how* working night and day so as not to be a burden to any of you, we proclaimed to you the gospel of God. 10 You are witnesses, and *so is* God, how devoutly and uprightly and blamelessly we behaved toward you believers; 11 just as you know how we *were* exhorting and encouraging and imploring each one of you as a father *would* his own children, 12 so that you would walk in a manner worthy of the God who calls you into His own kingdom and glory.

13 For this reason we also constantly thank God that when you received the word of God

2:7–8 gentle...as a nursing *mother*. Paul may have had in mind Moses' portrayal of himself as a nursing mother to Israel (Nu 11:12). He used the same tender picture with the Corinthians (2Co 12:14–15) and the Galatians (Gal 4:19). Paul's affection for the Thessalonians was like that felt by a mother willing to sacrifice her life for her child as was Christ who was willing to give up His own life for those who would be born again into the family of God (Mt 20:28).

which you heard from us, you accepted *it* not *as* the word of men, but *for* what it really is, the word of God, which also performs its work in you who believe. ¹⁴ For you, brethren, became imitators of the churches of God in Christ Jesus that are in Judea, for you also endured the same sufferings at the hands of your own countrymen, even as they *did* from the Jews, ¹⁵ who both killed the Lord Jesus and the prophets, and drove us out. They are not pleasing to God, but hostile to all men, ¹⁶ hindering us from speaking to the Gentiles so that they may be saved; with the result that they always fill up the measure of their sins. But wrath has come upon them to the utmost.

¹⁷ But we, brethren, having been taken away from you for a short while—in person, not in spirit—were all the more eager with great desire to see your face. ¹⁸ For we wanted to come to you—I, Paul, more than once—and *yet* Satan hindered us. ¹⁹ For who is our hope or joy or crown of exultation? Is it not even you, in the presence of our Lord Jesus at His coming? ²⁰ For you are our glory and joy.

DAY 15: What is the effect of the Word of God working in a person's life?

"We also constantly thank God," Paul said, "that when you received the word of God which you heard from us, you accepted it not as the word of men, but for what it really is, the word of God" (1Th 2:13). Paul's message from God is equated with the Old Testament (Mk 7:13). It was the message taught by the apostles (Ac 4:31; 6:2). Peter preached it to the Gentiles (Ac 11:1). It was the word Paul preached on his first missionary journey (Ac 13:5, 7, 44, 48–49), his second (Ac 16:32; 17:13; 18:11), and his third (Ac 19:10).

"Which also performs its work in you who believe." The work of God's Word includes:

saving (Ro 10:17; 1Pe 1:23);
teaching and training (2Ti 3:16–17);
guiding (Ps 119:105);
counseling (Ps 119:24);
reviving (Ps 119:154);
restoring (Ps 19:7);
warning and rewarding (Ps 19:11);
nourishing (1Pe 2:2);
judging (Heb 4:12);

sanctifying (Jn 17:17);
freeing (Jn 8:31–32);
enriching (Col 3:16);
protecting (Ps 119:11);
strengthening (Ps 119:28);
making wise (Ps 119:17–100);
rejoicing the heart (Ps 19:8);
and prospering (Jos 1:8–9).

OCTOBER 16

Jeremiah 17:1–18:23

17 The sin of Judah is written
    down with an iron stylus;
    With a diamond point it is engraved
      upon the tablet of their heart
    And on the horns of their altars,
²   As they remember their children,
    So they *remember* their altars
      and their Asherim
    By green trees on the high hills.
³   O mountain of Mine in
      the countryside,
    I will give over your wealth and
      all your treasures for booty,
    Your high places for sin
      throughout your borders.
⁴   And you will, even of yourself,
      let go of your inheritance
    That I gave you;
    And I will make you serve
      your enemies

17:1 The sin of Judah. Reasons for the judgment continue here: 1) idolatry (vv. 1–4), 2) relying on the flesh (v. 5), and 3) dishonesty in amassing wealth (v. 11). **iron stylus.** The names of idols were engraved on the horns of their altars with such a tool. The idea is that Judah's sin was permanent, etched in them as if into stone. How much different to have God's word written on the heart.

In the land which you
    do not know;
For you have kindled a
    fire in My anger
Which will burn forever.

⁵   Thus says the LORD,
"Cursed is the man who
    trusts in mankind
And makes flesh his strength,
And whose heart turns
    away from the LORD.

6 "For he will be like a bush in the desert
And will not see when
prosperity comes,
But will live in stony wastes
in the wilderness,
A land of salt without inhabitant.
7 "Blessed is the man who
trusts in the LORD
And whose trust is the LORD.
8 "For he will be like a tree
planted by the water,
That extends its roots by a stream
And will not fear when
the heat comes;
But its leaves will be green,
And it will not be anxious
in a year of drought
Nor cease to yield fruit.
9 "The heart is more deceitful
than all else
And is desperately sick;
Who can understand it?
10 "I, the LORD, search the heart,
I test the mind,
Even to give to each man
according to his ways,
According to the results of his deeds.
11 "As a partridge that hatches
eggs which it has not laid,
So is he who makes a
fortune, but unjustly;
In the midst of his days it
will forsake him,
And in the end he will be a fool."
12 A glorious throne on high
from the beginning
Is the place of our sanctuary.
13 O LORD, the hope of Israel,
All who forsake You will
be put to shame.
Those who turn away on earth
will be written down,
Because they have forsaken
the fountain of living
water, even the LORD.
14 Heal me, O LORD, and I will be healed;
Save me and I will be saved,
For You are my praise.
15 Look, they keep saying to me,
"Where is the word of the LORD?
Let it come now!"
16 But as for me, I have not hurried away
from *being* a shepherd after You,
Nor have I longed for the woeful day;
You Yourself know that the
utterance of my lips

Was in Your presence.
17 Do not be a terror to me;
You are my refuge in the
day of disaster.
18 Let those who persecute me be
put to shame, but as for me,
let me not be put to shame;
Let them be dismayed, but let
me not be dismayed.
Bring on them a day of disaster,
And crush them with
twofold destruction!

19 Thus the LORD said to me, "Go and stand in the public gate, through which the kings of Judah come in and go out, as well as in all the gates of Jerusalem; 20 and say to them, 'Listen to the word of the LORD, kings of Judah, and all Judah and all inhabitants of Jerusalem who come in through these gates: 21 Thus says the LORD, "Take heed for yourselves, and do not carry any load on the sabbath day or bring anything in through the gates of Jerusalem. 22 You shall not bring a load out of your houses on the sabbath day nor do any work, but keep the sabbath day holy, as I commanded your forefathers. 23 Yet they did not listen or incline their ears, but stiffened their necks in order not to listen or take correction.

24 "But it will come about, if you listen attentively to Me," declares the LORD, "to bring no load in through the gates of this city on the sabbath day, but to keep the sabbath day holy by doing no work on it, 25 then there will come in through the gates of this city kings and princes sitting on the throne of David, riding in chariots and on horses, they and their princes, the men of Judah and the inhabitants of Jerusalem, and this city will be inhabited forever. 26 They will come in from the cities of Judah and from the environs of Jerusalem, from the land of Benjamin, from the lowland, from the hill country and from the Negev, bringing burnt offerings, sacrifices, grain offerings and incense, and bringing sacrifices of thanksgiving to the house of the LORD. 27 But if you do not listen to Me to keep the sabbath day holy by not carrying a load and coming in through the gates of Jerusalem on the sabbath day, then I will kindle a fire in its gates and it will devour the palaces of Jerusalem and not be quenched."'"

18 The word which came to Jeremiah from the LORD saying, 2 "Arise and go down to the potter's house, and there I will announce My words to you." 3 Then I went down to the potter's house, and there he was, making something on the wheel. 4 But the

18:2–6 potter's house. God sent Jeremiah to a potter, who gave him an illustration by shaping a vessel. The prophet secured a vessel and used it for his own illustration (19:1ff.). Jeremiah watched the potter at his wheel. The soft clay became misshapen, but the potter shaped it back into a good vessel. God will so do with Judah if she repents.

vessel that he was making of clay was spoiled in the hand of the potter; so he remade it into another vessel, as it pleased the potter to make.

⁵Then the word of the LORD came to me saying, ⁶"Can I not, O house of Israel, deal with you as this potter *does*?" declares the LORD. "Behold, like the clay in the potter's hand, so are you in My hand, O house of Israel. ⁷At one moment I might speak concerning a nation or concerning a kingdom to uproot, to pull down, or to destroy *it*; ⁸if that nation against which I have spoken turns from its evil, I will relent concerning the calamity I planned to bring on it. ⁹Or at another moment I might speak concerning a nation or concerning a kingdom to build up or to plant *it*; ¹⁰if it does evil in My sight by not obeying My voice, then I will think better of the good with which I had promised to bless it. ¹¹So now then, speak to the men of Judah and against the inhabitants of Jerusalem saying, 'Thus says the LORD, "Behold, I am fashioning calamity against you and devising a plan against you. Oh turn back, each of you from his evil way, and reform your ways and your deeds."' ¹²But they will say, 'It's hopeless! For we are going to follow our own plans, and each of us will act according to the stubbornness of his evil heart.'

18:12 It's hopeless! Jeremiah brought them to the point where they actually stated their condition honestly. The prophet's threats were useless because they were so far gone—abandoned to their sins and the penalty. All hypocrisy was abandoned in favor of honesty, without repentance. Repentance was not in Israel (as v. 18; 19:15). This explains a seeming paradox: that Israel can repent and avert judgment, yet Jeremiah is not to pray for Israel (7:16; 11:14). It would do no good to pray for their change since they steeled themselves against any change.

¹³"Therefore thus says the LORD,
'Ask now among the nations,
Who ever heard the like of this?
The virgin of Israel
Has done a most appalling thing.
¹⁴'Does the snow of Lebanon forsake
the rock of the open country?
Or is the cold flowing water *from* a
foreign *land* ever snatched away?
¹⁵'For My people have forgotten Me,
They burn incense to worthless gods
And they have stumbled
from their ways,
From the ancient paths,
To walk in bypaths,
Not on a highway,
¹⁶To make their land a desolation,
An object of perpetual hissing;
Everyone who passes by it
will be astonished
And shake his head.
¹⁷'Like an east wind I will scatter them
Before the enemy;
I will show them My back
and not *My* face
In the day of their calamity.'"

¹⁸Then they said, "Come and let us devise plans against Jeremiah. Surely the law is not going to be lost to the priest, nor counsel to the sage, nor the *divine* word to the prophet! Come on and let us strike at him with *our* tongue, and let us give no heed to any of his words."

¹⁹ Do give heed to me, O LORD,
And listen to what my
opponents are saying!
²⁰ Should good be repaid with evil?
For they have dug a pit for me.
Remember how I stood before You
To speak good on their behalf,
So as to turn away Your
wrath from them.
²¹ Therefore, give their children
over to famine
And deliver them up to the
power of the sword;
And let their wives become
childless and widowed.
Let their men also be smitten to death,
Their young men struck down
by the sword in battle.
²² May an outcry be heard
from their houses,
When You suddenly bring
raiders upon them;
For they have dug a pit to capture me
And hidden snares for my feet.

²³ Yet You, O LORD, know
All their deadly designs against me;
Do not forgive their iniquity
Or blot out their sin from Your sight.
But may they be overthrown
before You;
Deal with them in the time
of Your anger!

Psalm 118:25–29

²⁵ O LORD, do save, we beseech You;
O LORD, we beseech You,
do send prosperity!
²⁶ Blessed is the one who comes
in the name of the LORD;
We have blessed you from
the house of the LORD.
²⁷ The LORD is God, and He
has given us light;
Bind the festival sacrifice with
cords to the horns of the altar.
²⁸ You are my God, and I give
thanks to You;
You are my God, I extol You.
²⁹ Give thanks to the LORD,
for He is good;
For His lovingkindness is everlasting.

Proverbs 27:11–12

¹¹ Be wise, my son, and make
my heart glad,
That I may reply to him
who reproaches me.
¹² A prudent man sees evil
and hides himself,
The naive proceed *and*
pay the penalty.

1 Thessalonians 3:1–13

3 Therefore when we could endure *it* no longer, we thought it best to be left behind
at Athens alone, ²and we sent Timothy, our
brother and God's fellow worker in the gospel
of Christ, to strengthen and encourage you
as to your faith, ³ so that no one would be disturbed by these afflictions; for you yourselves
know that we have been destined for this.
⁴For indeed when we were with you, we *kept*
telling you in advance that we were going to
suffer affliction; and so it came to pass, as you

know. ⁵For this reason, when I could endure
it no longer, I also sent to find out about your
faith, for fear that the tempter might have
tempted you, and our labor would be in vain.

⁶But now that Timothy has come to us
from you, and has brought us good news of
your faith and love, and that you always think
kindly of us, longing to see us just as we also
long to see you, ⁷for this reason, brethren, in
all our distress and affliction we were comforted about you through your faith; ⁸for now
we *really* live, if you stand firm in the Lord.
⁹For what thanks can we render to God for
you in return for all the joy with which we
rejoice before our God on your account, ¹⁰as
we night and day keep praying most earnestly
that we may see your face, and may complete
what is lacking in your faith?

¹¹Now may our God and Father Himself
and Jesus our Lord direct our way to you;
¹²and may the Lord cause you to increase
and abound in love for one another, and for
all people, just as we also *do* for you; ¹³so that
He may establish your hearts without blame
in holiness before our God and Father at the
coming of our Lord Jesus with all His saints.

3:2 strengthen...encourage...your faith. This
was a common ministry concern and practice
of Paul (Ac 14:22; 15:32; 18:23). Paul's concern
did not focus on health, wealth, self-esteem,
or ease of life, but rather the spiritual quality
of life. Their faith was of supreme importance
in Paul's mind as evidenced by 5 mentions in
vv. 1–10. Faith includes the foundation of the
body of doctrine (Jude 3) and their believing response to God in living out that truth (Heb 11:6).

3:5 the tempter. Satan had already been characterized as a hinderer (2:18) and now as a tempter
in the sense of trying/testing for the purpose of
causing failure (Mt 4:3; 1Co 7:5; Jas 1:12–18). Paul
was not ignorant of Satan's schemes (2Co 2:11;
11:23) nor vulnerable to his methods (Eph 6:11),
so Paul took action to counterattack Satan's
expected maneuver and to assure that all his
efforts were not useless.

DAY 16: What was Paul's prayer for the Thessalonians?

"Now may our God...direct our way to you" (1Th 3:11). Paul knew that Satan had hindered his
return (2:18). Even though Timothy had visited and returned with a good report, Paul still felt
the urgency to see his spiritual children again. Paul followed the biblical admonition of the
Psalms (Ps 37:1–5) and Proverbs (Pr 3:5–6) to entrust difficult situations to God.

"May the Lord cause you to increase and abound in love for one another" (v. 12). With over

30 positive and negative "one anothers" in the New Testament, love appears by far most frequently (4:9; Ro 12:10; 13:8; 2Th 1:3; 1Pe 1:22; 1Jn 3:11, 23; 4:7, 11; 2Jn 5). It is the overarching term that includes all of the other "one anothers." Its focus is on believers in the church. "And for all." In light of the fact that God loved the world and sent His Son to die for human sin, believers who were loved when they were unlovely (Ro 5:8) are to love unbelievers (Mt 5:43–44). Other New Testament commands concerning all men include pursuing peace (Ro 12:18), doing good (Gal 6:10), being patient (Php 4:5), praying (1Ti 2:1), showing consideration (Titus 3:2), and honoring (1Pe 2:17).

"So that He may establish your hearts without blame in holiness before our God." Paul prayed that there would be no grounds of accusation because of unholiness. "At the coming of our Lord Jesus Christ with all His saints." Since this exact term is not used elsewhere in the New Testament of angels but is commonly used for believers, it is best to understand the coming of the Lord to rapture all His church and take them to heaven to enjoy His presence.

OCTOBER 17

Jeremiah 19:1–20:18

19 Thus says the LORD, "Go and buy a potter's earthenware jar, and *take* some of the elders of the people and some of the senior priests. ²Then go out to the valley of Ben-hinnom, which is by the entrance of the potsherd gate, and proclaim there the words that I tell you, ³and say, 'Hear the word of the LORD, O kings of Judah and inhabitants of Jerusalem: thus says the LORD of hosts, the God of Israel, "Behold I am about to bring a calamity upon this place, at which the ears of everyone that hears of it will tingle. ⁴Because they have forsaken Me and have made this an alien place and have burned sacrifices in it to other gods, that neither they nor their forefathers nor the kings of Judah had *ever* known, and *because* they have filled this place with the blood of the innocent ⁵and have built the high places of Baal to burn their sons in the fire as burnt offerings to Baal, a thing which I never commanded or spoke of, nor did it *ever* enter My mind; ⁶therefore, behold, days are coming," declares the LORD, "when this place will no longer be called Topheth or the valley of Ben-hinnom, but rather the valley of Slaughter. ⁷I will make void the counsel of Judah and Jerusalem in this place, and I will cause them to fall by the sword before their enemies and by the hand of those who seek their life; and I will give over their carcasses as food for the birds of the sky and the beasts of the earth. ⁸I will also make this city a desolation and an *object of* hissing; everyone who passes by it will be astonished and hiss because of all its disasters. ⁹I will make them eat the flesh of their sons and the flesh of their daughters, and they will eat one another's flesh in the siege and in the distress with which their enemies and those who seek their life will distress them."'

¹⁰"Then you are to break the jar in the sight of the men who accompany you ¹¹and say to them, 'Thus says the LORD of hosts, "Just so will I break this people and this city, even as one breaks a potter's vessel, which cannot again be repaired; and they will bury in Topheth because there is no *other* place for burial. ¹²This is how I will treat this place and its inhabitants," declares the LORD, "so as to make this city like Topheth. ¹³The houses of Jerusalem and the houses of the kings of Judah will be defiled like the place Topheth, because of all the houses on whose rooftops they burned sacrifices to all the heavenly host and poured out drink offerings to other gods."'"

¹⁴Then Jeremiah came from Topheth, where the LORD had sent him to prophesy; and he stood in the court of the LORD'S house and said to all the people: ¹⁵"Thus says the LORD of hosts, the God of Israel, 'Behold, I am about to bring on this city and all its towns the entire calamity that I have declared against it, because they have stiffened their necks so as not to heed My words.'"

20 When Pashhur the priest, the son of Immer, who was chief officer in the house of the LORD, heard Jeremiah prophesying these things, ²Pashhur had Jeremiah the prophet beaten and put him in the stocks that were at the upper Benjamin Gate, which was by the house of the LORD. ³On the next

20:2 had Jeremiah...beaten. He or others acting on his authority delivered 40 lashes (Dt 25:3) to the prophet. **put him in the stocks.** Hands, feet, and neck were fastened in holes, bending the body to a distorted posture, causing excruciating pain. **upper Benjamin Gate.** The northern gate of the upper temple court.

day, when Pashhur released Jeremiah from the stocks, Jeremiah said to him, "Pashhur is not the name the LORD has called you, but rather Magor-missabib. ⁴For thus says the LORD, 'Behold, I am going to make you a terror to yourself and to all your friends; and while your eyes look on, they will fall by the sword of their enemies. So I will give over all Judah to the hand of the king of Babylon, and he will carry them away as exiles to Babylon and will slay them with the sword. ⁵I will also give over all the wealth of this city, all its produce and all its costly things; even all the treasures of the kings of Judah I will give over to the hand of their enemies, and they will plunder them, take them away and bring them to Babylon. ⁶And you, Pashhur, and all who live in your house will go into captivity; and you will enter Babylon, and there you will die and there you will be buried, you and all your friends to whom you have falsely prophesied.'"

7 O LORD, You have deceived
   me and I was deceived;
   You have overcome me and prevailed.
   I have become a laughingstock
       all day long;
   Everyone mocks me.
8 For each time I speak, I cry aloud;
   I proclaim violence and destruction,
   Because for me the word of
       the LORD has resulted
   In reproach and derision all day long.
9 But if I say, "I will not remember Him
   Or speak anymore in His name,"
   Then in my heart it becomes
       like a burning fire
   Shut up in my bones;
   And I am weary of holding *it* in,
   And I cannot endure *it*.
10 For I have heard the
       whispering of many,
   "Terror on every side!
   Denounce *him;* yes, let us
       denounce him!"
   All my trusted friends,
   Watching for my fall, say:
   "Perhaps he will be deceived, so that
       we may prevail against him
   And take our revenge on him."
11 But the LORD is with me like
       a dread champion;
   Therefore my persecutors will
       stumble and not prevail.
   They will be utterly ashamed,
       because they have failed,
   With an everlasting disgrace
       that will not be forgotten.

12 Yet, O LORD of hosts, You
       who test the righteous,
   Who see the mind and the heart;
   Let me see Your vengeance on them;
   For to You I have set forth my cause.
13 Sing to the LORD, praise the LORD!
   For He has delivered the
       soul of the needy one
   From the hand of evildoers.

14 Cursed be the day when I was born;
   Let the day not be blessed when
       my mother bore me!
15 Cursed be the man who
       brought the news
   To my father, saying,
   "A baby boy has been born to you!"
   And made him very happy.
16 But let that man be like the cities
   Which the LORD overthrew
       without relenting,
   And let him hear an outcry
       in the morning
   And a shout of alarm at noon;
17 Because he did not kill
       me before birth,
   So that my mother would
       have been my grave,
   And her womb ever pregnant.
18 Why did I ever come forth
       from the womb
   To look on trouble and sorrow,
   So that my days have been
       spent in shame?

Psalm 119:1–8

א ALEPH.

H ow blessed are those whose
   way is blameless,
   Who walk in the law of the LORD.
2 How blessed are those who
       observe His testimonies,
   Who seek Him with all *their* heart.
3 They also do no unrighteousness;
   They walk in His ways.
4 You have ordained Your precepts,
   That we should keep *them* diligently.
5 Oh that my ways may be established
   To keep Your statutes!
6 Then I shall not be ashamed
   When I look upon all Your
       commandments.
7 I shall give thanks to You with
       uprightness of heart,
   When I learn Your righteous
       judgments.
8 I shall keep Your statutes;
   Do not forsake me utterly!

119:1–176 This longest of psalms and chapters in the Bible stands as the "Mt. Everest" of the Psalter. It joins Pss 1 and 19 in exalting God's Word. The author is unknown for certain, although David, Daniel, or Ezra have reasonably been suggested. The psalmist apparently wrote while under some sort of serious duress as comes through in many verses. This is an acrostic psalm (Pss 9–10, 25, 34, 37, 111–112, 145) composed of 22 sections, each containing 8 lines. All 8 lines of the first section start with the first letter of the Hebrew alphabet; thus the psalm continues until all 22 letters have been used in order. The 8 different terms referring to Scripture occurring throughout the psalm are: 1) law, 2) testimonies, 3) precepts, 4) statutes, 5) commandments, 6) judgments, 7) word, and 8) ordinances. From before sunrise to beyond sunset, the Word of God dominated the psalmist's life, e.g., 1) before dawn (v. 147), 2) daily (v. 97), 3) 7 times daily (v. 164), 4) nightly (vv. 55, 148), and 5) at midnight (v. 62).

Proverbs 27:13

¹³ Take his garment when he becomes
    surety for a stranger;
  And for an adulterous woman
    hold him in pledge.

1 Thessalonians 4:1–18

4 Finally then, brethren, we request and exhort you in the Lord Jesus, that as you received from us *instruction* as to how you ought to walk and please God (just as you actually do walk), that you excel still more. ² For you know what commandments we gave you by *the authority of* the Lord Jesus. ³ For this is the will of God, your sanctification; *that is,* that you abstain from sexual immorality; ⁴ that each of you know how to possess his own vessel in sanctification and honor, ⁵ not in lustful passion, like the Gentiles who do not know God; ⁶ *and* that no man transgress and defraud his brother in the matter because the Lord is *the* avenger in all these things, just as we also told you before and solemnly warned *you.* ⁷ For God has not called us for the purpose of impurity, but in sanctification. ⁸ So, he who rejects *this* is not rejecting man but the God who gives His Holy Spirit to you.

⁹ Now as to the love of the brethren, you have no need for *anyone* to write to you, for you yourselves are taught by God to love one another; ¹⁰ for indeed you do practice it toward all the brethren who are in all Macedonia. But we urge you, brethren, to excel still more, ¹¹ and to make it your ambition to lead a quiet life and attend to your own business and work with your hands, just as we commanded you, ¹² so that you will behave properly toward outsiders and not be in any need.

¹³ But we do not want you to be uninformed, brethren, about those who are asleep, so that you will not grieve as do the rest who have no hope. ¹⁴ For if we believe that Jesus died and rose again, even so God will bring with Him those who have fallen asleep in Jesus. ¹⁵ For this we say to you by the word of the Lord, that we who are alive and remain until the coming of the Lord, will not precede those who have fallen asleep. ¹⁶ For the Lord Himself will descend from heaven with a shout, with the voice of *the* archangel and with the trumpet of God, and the dead in Christ will rise first. ¹⁷ Then we who are alive and remain will be caught up together with them in the clouds to meet the Lord in the air, and so we shall always be with the Lord. ¹⁸ Therefore comfort one another with these words.

4:13 those who are asleep. Sleep is the familiar New Testament euphemism for death which describes the appearance of the deceased. It describes the dead body, not the soul (2Co 5:1–9; Php 1:23). Sleep is used of Jarius' daughter (Mt 9:24) whom Jesus raised from the dead and Stephen who was stoned to death (Ac 7:60; see Jn 11:11; 1Co 7:39; 15:6, 18, 51; 2Pe 3:4). Those who sleep are identified in v. 16 as "the dead in Christ." The people, in ignorance, had come to the conclusion that those who die miss the Lord's return, and they were grieved over their absence at such a glorious event. Thus the departure of a loved one brought great anguish to the soul.

4:18 comfort one another. The primary purpose of this passage is not to teach a scheme of prophecy, but rather to provide encouragement to those Christians whose loved ones have died. The comfort here is based on the following: 1) the dead will be resurrected and will participate in the Lord's coming for His own; 2) when Christ comes the living will be reunited forever with their loved ones; and 3) they all will be with the Lord eternally (v. 17).

DAY 17: How does Paul describe the return of Jesus Christ in 1 Thessalonians 4:15–16?

It is clear the Thessalonians had come to believe in and hope for the reality of their Savior's return (1:3, 9–10; 2:19; 5:1–2). They were living in expectation of that coming, eagerly awaiting Christ. First Thessalonians 4:13 indicates they were even agitated about some things that might affect their participation in it. They knew Christ's return was the climactic event in redemptive history and didn't want to miss it. The major question they had was: "What happens to the Christians who die before He comes? Do they miss His return?" Clearly, they had an imminent view of Christ's return, and Paul had left the impression it could happen in their lifetime. Their confusion came as they were being persecuted, an experience they thought they were to be delivered from by the Lord's return (3:3–4).

Paul answers by saying "the Lord Himself will descend from heaven with a shout" (v. 16). This fulfills the pledge of John 14:1–3 (Ac 1:11). Until then He remains in heaven (1:10; Heb 1:1–3). "With the voice of the archangel." Perhaps it is Michael, the archangel, whose voice is heard as he is identified with Israel's resurrection in Daniel 12:1–3. At that moment, the dead rise first. They will not miss the Rapture but will be the first participants. "And with the trumpet of God." This trumpet is illustrated by the trumpet of Exodus 19:16–19, which called the people out of the camp to meet God. It will be a trumpet of deliverance (Zep 1:16; Zec 9:14).

After the dead come forth, their spirits, already with the Lord (2Co 5:8; Php 1:23), now being joined to resurrected new bodies, the living Christians will be raptured, "caught up" (v. 17). This passage along with John 14:1–3 and 1 Corinthians 15:51–52 form the biblical basis for "the Rapture" of the church.

OCTOBER 18

Jeremiah 21:1–22:30

21 The word which came to Jeremiah from the LORD when King Zedekiah sent to him Pashhur the son of Malchijah, and Zephaniah the priest, the son of Maaseiah, saying, 2 "Please inquire of the LORD on our behalf, for Nebuchadnezzar king of Babylon is warring against us; perhaps the LORD will deal with us according to all His wonderful acts, so that *the enemy* will withdraw from us."

3 Then Jeremiah said to them, "You shall say to Zedekiah as follows: 4 'Thus says the LORD God of Israel, "Behold, I am about to turn back the weapons of war which are in your hands, with which you are warring against the king of Babylon and the Chaldeans who are besieging you outside the wall; and I will gather them into the center of this city. 5 I Myself will war against you with an outstretched hand and a mighty arm, even in anger and wrath and great indignation. 6 I will also strike down the inhabitants of this city, both man and beast; they will die of a great pestilence. 7 Then afterwards," declares the LORD, "I will give over Zedekiah king of Judah and his servants and the people, even those who survive in this city from the pestilence, the sword and the famine, into the hand of Nebuchadnezzar king of Babylon, and into the hand of their foes and into the hand of those who seek their lives; and he will strike them down with the edge of the sword. He will not spare them nor have pity nor compassion."'

8 "You shall also say to this people, 'Thus says the LORD, "Behold, I set before you the way of life and the way of death. 9 He who dwells in this city will die by the sword and by famine and by pestilence; but he who goes out and falls away to the Chaldeans who are besieging you will live, and he will have his own life as booty. 10 For I have set My face against this city for harm and not for good," declares the LORD. "It will be given into the hand of the king of Babylon and he will burn it with fire."'

11 "Then *say* to the household of the king of Judah, 'Hear the word of the LORD, 12 O house of David, thus says the LORD:

"Administer justice every morning;
And deliver the *person* who
  has been robbed from the
  power of *his* oppressor,
That My wrath may not
  go forth like fire
And burn with none to extinguish *it*,
Because of the evil of their deeds.

13 "Behold, I am against you,
  O valley dweller,
O rocky plain," declares the LORD,
"You men who say, 'Who will
  come down against us?
Or who will enter into
  our habitations?'

¹⁴ "But I will punish you according
  to the results of your deeds,"
    declares the LORD,
  "And I will kindle a fire in its forest
  That it may devour all its environs."'"

22 Thus says the LORD, "Go down to the house of the king of Judah, and there speak this word ²and say, 'Hear the word of the LORD, O king of Judah, who sits on David's throne, you and your servants and your people who enter these gates. ³Thus says the LORD, "Do justice and righteousness, and deliver the one who has been robbed from the power of *his* oppressor. Also do not mistreat *or* do violence to the stranger, the orphan, or the widow; and do not shed innocent blood in this place. ⁴For if you men will indeed perform this thing, then kings will enter the gates of this house, sitting in David's place on his throne, riding in chariots and on horses, *even the king* himself and his servants and his people. ⁵But if you will not obey these words, I swear by Myself," declares the LORD, "that this house will become a desolation."'" ⁶For thus says the LORD concerning the house of the king of Judah:

"You are *like* Gilead to Me,
Like the summit of Lebanon;
Yet most assuredly I will make
  you like a wilderness,
Like cities which are not inhabited.
⁷ "For I will set apart destroyers
    against you,
  Each with his weapons;
  And they will cut down
    your choicest cedars
  And throw *them* on the fire.

⁸ "Many nations will pass by this city; and they will say to one another, 'Why has the LORD done thus to this great city?' ⁹Then they will answer, 'Because they forsook the covenant of the LORD their God and bowed down to other gods and served them.'"

¹⁰ Do not weep for the dead
    or mourn for him,
  But weep continually for the
    one who goes away;
  For he will never return
  Or see his native land.

¹¹ For thus says the LORD in regard to Shallum the son of Josiah, king of Judah, who became king in the place of Josiah his father, who went forth from this place, "He will never return there; ¹²but in the place where they led him captive, there he will die and not see this land again.

¹³ "Woe to him who builds his house
    without righteousness
  And his upper rooms without
    justice,
  Who uses his neighbor's
    services without pay
  And does not give him his wages,
¹⁴ Who says, 'I will build myself
    a roomy house
  With spacious upper rooms,
  And cut out its windows,
  Paneling *it* with cedar and
    painting *it* bright red.'
¹⁵ "Do you become a king because
    you are competing in cedar?
  Did not your father eat and drink
  And do justice and righteousness?
  Then it was well with him.
¹⁶ "He pled the cause of the
    afflicted and needy;
  Then it was well.
  Is not that what it means
    to know Me?"
  Declares the LORD.
¹⁷ "But your eyes and your heart
  Are *intent* only upon your
    own dishonest gain,
  And on shedding innocent blood
  And on practicing oppression
    and extortion."

¹⁸ Therefore thus says the LORD in regard to Jehoiakim the son of Josiah, king of Judah,

"They will not lament for him:
'Alas, my brother!' or, 'Alas, sister!'
They will not lament for him:
'Alas for the master!' or, 'Alas
  for his splendor!'
¹⁹ "He will be buried with a
    donkey's burial,
  Dragged off and thrown out
    beyond the gates of Jerusalem.

22:18–19 Jehoiakim. Ruling from 609 to 598 B.C., he was also wicked in taxing the people (2Ki 23:35) and making them build his splendid palace without pay, violating God's law in Leviticus 19:13 and Deuteronomy 24:14–15. He was slain in Babylon's second siege and his corpse dishonored, being left like a dead donkey on the ground for scavengers to feed on.

²⁰ "Go up to Lebanon and cry out,
    And lift up your voice in Bashan;
    Cry out also from Abarim,
    For all your lovers have been crushed.
²¹ "I spoke to you in your prosperity;
    But you said, 'I will not listen!'
    This has been your practice
        from your youth,
    That you have not obeyed My voice.
²² "The wind will sweep away
        all your shepherds,
    And your lovers will go into captivity;
    Then you will surely be
        ashamed and humiliated
    Because of all your wickedness.
²³ "You who dwell in Lebanon,
    Nested in the cedars,
    How you will groan when
        pangs come upon you,
    Pain like a woman in childbirth!

²⁴ "As I live," declares the LORD, "even though
Coniah the son of Jehoiakim king of Judah were
a signet *ring* on My right hand, yet I would pull
you off; ²⁵ and I will give you over into the hand
of those who are seeking your life, yes, into
the hand of those whom you dread, even into
the hand of Nebuchadnezzar king of Babylon
and into the hand of the Chaldeans. ²⁶ I will
hurl you and your mother who bore you into
another country where you were not born, and
there you will die. ²⁷ But as for the land to which
they desire to return, they will not return to it.

²⁸ "Is this man Coniah a despised,
        shattered jar?
    Or is he an undesirable vessel?
    Why have he and his descendants
        been hurled out
    And cast into a land that
        they had not known?
²⁹ "O land, land, land,
    Hear the word of the LORD!

³⁰ Thus says the LORD,

    'Write this man down childless,
    A man who will not prosper in his days;
    For no man of his descendants
        will prosper
    Sitting on the throne of David
    Or ruling again in Judah.'"

Psalm 119:9–16

ב BETH.

⁹ How can a young man
        keep his way pure?
    By keeping *it* according to Your word.

¹⁰ With all my heart I have sought You;
    Do not let me wander from
        Your commandments.
¹¹ Your word I have treasured
        in my heart,
    That I may not sin against You.
¹² Blessed are You, O LORD;
    Teach me Your statutes.
¹³ With my lips I have told of
    All the ordinances of Your mouth.
¹⁴ I have rejoiced in the way
        of Your testimonies,
    As much as in all riches.
¹⁵ I will meditate on Your precepts
    And regard Your ways.
¹⁶ I shall delight in Your statutes;
    I shall not forget Your word.

Proverbs 27:14

¹⁴ He who blesses his friend with a
        loud voice early in the morning,
    It will be reckoned a curse to him.

1 Thessalonians 5:1–28

5 Now as to the times and the epochs, brethren, you have no need of anything to be
written to you. ² For you yourselves know full
well that the day of the Lord will come just
like a thief in the night. ³ While they are saying, "Peace and safety!" then destruction will
come upon them suddenly like labor pains
upon a woman with child, and they will not
escape. ⁴ But you, brethren, are not in darkness, that the day would overtake you like a
thief; ⁵ for you are all sons of light and sons
of day. We are not of night nor of darkness;
⁶ so then let us not sleep as others do, but let
us be alert and sober. ⁷ For those who sleep
do their sleeping at night, and those who get
drunk get drunk at night. ⁸ But since we are
of *the* day, let us be sober, having put on the
breastplate of faith and love, and as a helmet, the hope of salvation. ⁹ For God has not
destined us for wrath, but for obtaining salvation through our Lord Jesus Christ, ¹⁰ who died
for us, so that whether we are awake or asleep,
we will live together with Him. ¹¹ Therefore
encourage one another and build up one another, just as you also are doing.

¹² But we request of you, brethren, that
you appreciate those who diligently labor
among you, and have charge over you in the
Lord and give you instruction, ¹³ and that you
esteem them very highly in love because of
their work. Live in peace with one another.
¹⁴ We urge you, brethren, admonish the unruly, encourage the fainthearted, help the
weak, be patient with everyone. ¹⁵ See that

5:12 appreciate. This means that the people are to know their pastors well enough to have an intimate appreciation for them and to respect them because of their value. The work of pastors is summarized in a 3-fold description which includes: 1) laboring, working to the point of exhaustion; 2) overseeing, literally standing before the flock to lead them in the way of righteousness; and 3) instructing in the truths of God's Word.

---

no one repays another with evil for evil, but always seek after that which is good for one another and for all people. ¹⁶ Rejoice always; ¹⁷ pray without ceasing; ¹⁸ in everything give thanks; for this is God's will for you in Christ Jesus. ¹⁹ Do not quench the Spirit; ²⁰ do not despise prophetic utterances. ²¹ But examine everything *carefully;* hold fast to that which is good; ²² abstain from every form of evil.

²³ Now may the God of peace Himself sanctify you entirely; and may your spirit and soul and body be preserved complete, without blame at the coming of our Lord

5:19 quench. The fire of God's Spirit is not to be doused with sin. Believers are also instructed to not grieve the Holy Spirit (Eph 4:30), but to be controlled by the Holy Spirit (Eph 5:18) and to walk by the Holy Spirit (Gal 5:16).

5:23 God...sanctify you. Only God (Ro 15:33; 16:20; Php 4:9; Heb 13:20) "Himself" can separate us from sin to holiness "entirely." **spirit and soul and body.** This comprehensive reference makes the term "complete" more emphatic. By using spirit and soul, Paul was not indicating that the immaterial part of man could be divided into two substances (Heb 4:12). The two words are used interchangeably throughout Scripture (Heb 6:19; 10:39; 1Pe 2:11; 2Pe 2:8).

Jesus Christ. ²⁴ Faithful is He who calls you, and He also will bring it to pass.

²⁵ Brethren, pray for us.

²⁶ Greet all the brethren with a holy kiss. ²⁷ I adjure you by the Lord to have this letter read to all the brethren.

²⁸ The grace of our Lord Jesus Christ be with you.

DAY 18: When Paul refers to the "day of the Lord" in 1 Thessalonians 5:2, what does he mean?

There are 19 indisputable uses of "the day of the Lord" in the Old Testament and 4 in the New Testament (Ac 2:20; 2Th 2:2; 2Pe 3:10). The Old Testament prophets used "day of the Lord" to describe near historical judgments (Is 13:6–22; Eze 30:2–19; Joel 1:15; 3:14; Am 5:18–20; Zep 1:14–18) or far eschatological divine judgments (Joel 2:30–32; Zec 14:1; Mal 4:1, 5). Six times it is referred to as the "day of doom" and 4 times as the "day of vengeance." The New Testament calls it a day of "wrath," a day of "visitation," and the "Great Day of God, the Almighty" (Rev 16:14). These are terrifying judgments from God (Joel 2:30–31; 2Th 1:7–10) for the overwhelming sinfulness of the world.

The future "day of the Lord" which unleashes God's wrath falls into two parts: 1) the end of the 7-year tribulation period (Rev 19:11–21), and 2) the end of the Millennium. These two are actually 1,000 years apart, and Peter refers to the end of the 1,000-year period in connection with the final "day of the Lord" (2Pe 3:10; Rev 20:7–15). Here, Paul refers to that aspect of the "day of the Lord," which concludes the Tribulation period. When Paul uses the phrase "a thief in the night," it is never used to refer to the Rapture of the church. It is used of Christ's coming in judgment on the day of the Lord at the end of the 7-year Tribulation which is distinct from the Rapture of the church, and it is used of the judgment which concludes the Millennium (2Pe 3:10). As a thief comes unexpectedly and without warning, so will the day of the Lord come in both its final phases.

OCTOBER 19

Jeremiah 23:1–24:10

23 "Woe to the shepherds who are destroying and scattering the sheep of My pasture!" declares the LORD. ²Therefore thus says the LORD God of Israel concerning the shepherds who are tending My people: "You have scattered My flock and driven them away, and have not attended to them; behold, I am about to attend to you for the evil of your deeds," declares the LORD. ³"Then I Myself will gather the remnant of My flock out of all the countries where I have driven them and bring them back to their pasture, and they will be fruitful and multiply. ⁴I will also raise up shepherds over them and they will tend them; and they will not be afraid any longer, nor be terrified, nor will any be missing," declares the LORD.

⁵ "Behold, *the* days are coming,"
    declares the LORD,
"When I will raise up for David
    a righteous Branch;
And He will reign as king and act wisely
And do justice and righteousness
    in the land.
⁶ "In His days Judah will be saved,
    And Israel will dwell securely;
And this is His name by which
    He will be called,
'The LORD our righteousness.'

23:3–4 I…will gather. God pledged to restore exiled Israelites to their ancient soil. The land in view was literally Israel, being contrasted with all the other countries (v. 3), thus assuring that the regathering would be as literal as the scattering. The restoration of Judah from Babylon is referred to in language which in its fullness can only refer to the final restoration of God's people ("out of all the countries," and v. 8), under Messiah. "Nor will any be missing" indicates that no one will be missing or detached. These are prophecies not yet fulfilled.

23:4 shepherds…will tend them. Zerubbabel, Ezra, Nehemiah, and others were small fulfillments compared to the consummate shepherding of the Messiah Jesus.

23:5 Branch. The Messiah is pictured as a branch (literally "shoot") out of David's family tree (33:15–16; Is 4:2; 11:1–5; Zec 3:8; 6:12–13), who will rule over God's people in the future.

⁷"Therefore behold, *the* days are coming," declares the LORD, "when they will no longer say, 'As the LORD lives, who brought up the sons of Israel from the land of Egypt,' ⁸but, 'As the LORD lives, who brought up and led back the descendants of the household of Israel from *the* north land and from all the countries where I had driven them.' Then they will live on their own soil."

⁹ As for the prophets:
    My heart is broken within me,
    All my bones tremble;
    I have become like a drunken man,
    Even like a man overcome with wine,
    Because of the LORD
    And because of His holy words.
¹⁰ For the land is full of adulterers;
    For the land mourns
        because of the curse.
    The pastures of the wilderness
        have dried up.
    Their course also is evil
    And their might is not right.
¹¹ "For both prophet and
        priest are polluted;
    Even in My house I have found their
        wickedness," declares the LORD.
¹² "Therefore their way will be like
        slippery paths to them,
    They will be driven away into the
        gloom and fall down in it;
    For I will bring calamity upon them,
    The year of their punishment,"
        declares the LORD.

¹³ "Moreover, among the prophets of
        Samaria I saw an offensive thing:
    They prophesied by Baal and led
        My people Israel astray.
¹⁴ "Also among the prophets
        of Jerusalem I have seen
        a horrible thing:
    The committing of adultery
        and walking in falsehood;
    And they strengthen the
        hands of evildoers,
    So that no one has turned back
        from his wickedness.
    All of them have become
        to Me like Sodom,
    And her inhabitants like Gomorrah.

¹⁵Therefore thus says the LORD of hosts concerning the prophets,

    'Behold, I am going to feed
        them wormwood

And make them drink poisonous water,
For from the prophets of Jerusalem
Pollution has gone forth
into all the land.'"

¹⁶ Thus says the LORD of hosts,
"Do not listen to the words
of the prophets who are
prophesying to you.
They are leading you into futility;
They speak a vision of their
own imagination,
Not from the mouth of the LORD.
¹⁷ "They keep saying to those
who despise Me,
'The LORD has said, "You
will have peace"';
And as for everyone who walks in the
stubbornness of his own heart,
They say, 'Calamity will not
come upon you.'
¹⁸ "But who has stood in the
council of the LORD,
That he should see and
hear His word?
Who has given heed to His
word and listened?
¹⁹ "Behold, the storm of the LORD
has gone forth in wrath,
Even a whirling tempest;
It will swirl down on the
head of the wicked.
²⁰ "The anger of the LORD
will not turn back
Until He has performed and carried
out the purposes of His heart;
In the last days you will
clearly understand it.
²¹ "I did not send these prophets,
But they ran.
I did not speak to them,
But they prophesied.
²² "But if they had stood in My council,
Then they would have announced
My words to My people,
And would have turned them
back from their evil way
And from the evil of their deeds.

²³ "Am I a God who is near,"
declares the LORD,
"And not a God far off?
²⁴ "Can a man hide himself
in hiding places
So I do not see him?"
declares the LORD.
"Do I not fill the heavens and the
earth?" declares the LORD.

²⁵ "I have heard what the prophets have said who prophesy falsely in My name, saying, 'I had a dream, I had a dream!' ²⁶ How long? Is there anything in the hearts of the prophets who prophesy falsehood, even these prophets of the deception of their own heart, ²⁷ who intend to make My people forget My name by their dreams which they relate to one another, just as their fathers forgot My name because of Baal? ²⁸ The prophet who has a dream may relate his dream, but let him who has My word speak My word in truth. What does straw have in common with grain?" declares the LORD. ²⁹ "Is not My word like fire?" declares the LORD, "and like a hammer which shatters a rock? ³⁰ Therefore behold, I am against the prophets," declares the LORD, "who steal My words from each other. ³¹ Behold, I am against the prophets," declares the LORD, "who use their tongues and declare, 'The Lord declares.' ³² Behold, I am against those who have prophesied false dreams," declares the LORD, "and related them and led My people astray by their falsehoods and reckless boasting; yet I did not send them or command them, nor do they furnish this people the slightest benefit," declares the LORD.

23:29 like fire…hammer. God's Word has irresistible qualities to prevail over the deception in the shepherds' false messages.

³³ "Now when this people or the prophet or a priest asks you saying, 'What is the oracle of the LORD?' then you shall say to them, 'What oracle?' The LORD declares, 'I will abandon you.' ³⁴ Then as for the prophet or the priest or the people who say, 'The oracle of the LORD,' I will bring punishment upon that man and his household. ³⁵ Thus will each of you say to his neighbor and to his brother, 'What has the LORD answered?' or, 'What has the LORD spoken?' ³⁶ For you will no longer remember the oracle of the LORD, because every man's own word will become the oracle, and you have perverted the words of the living God, the LORD of hosts, our God. ³⁷ Thus you will say to that prophet, 'What has the LORD answered you?' and, 'What has the LORD spoken?' ³⁸ For if you say, 'The oracle of the LORD!' surely thus says the LORD, 'Because you said this word, "The oracle of the LORD!" I have also sent to you, saying, "You shall not say, 'The oracle of the LORD!'"' ³⁹ Therefore behold, I will surely

forget you and cast you away from My presence, along with the city which I gave you and your fathers. ⁴⁰ I will put an everlasting reproach on you and an everlasting humiliation which will not be forgotten."

24 After Nebuchadnezzar king of Babylon had carried away captive Jeconiah the son of Jehoiakim, king of Judah, and the officials of Judah with the craftsmen and smiths from Jerusalem and had brought them to Babylon, the LORD showed me: behold, two baskets of figs set before the temple of the LORD! ² One basket had very good figs, like first-ripe figs, and the other basket had very bad figs which could not be eaten due to rottenness. ³ Then the LORD said to me, "What do you see, Jeremiah?" And I said, "Figs, the good figs, very good; and the bad *figs,* very bad, which cannot be eaten due to rottenness."

⁴ Then the word of the LORD came to me, saying, ⁵ "Thus says the LORD God of Israel, 'Like these good figs, so I will regard as good the captives of Judah, whom I have sent out of this place *into* the land of the Chaldeans. ⁶ For I will set My eyes on them for good, and I will bring them again to this land; and I will build them up and not overthrow them, and I will plant them and not pluck them up. ⁷ I will give them a heart to know Me, for I am the LORD; and they will be My people, and I will be their God, for they will return to Me with their whole heart.

⁸ 'But like the bad figs which cannot be eaten due to rottenness—indeed, thus says the LORD—so I will abandon Zedekiah king of Judah and his officials, and the remnant of Jerusalem who remain in this land and the ones who dwell in the land of Egypt. ⁹ I will make them a terror *and an* evil for all the kingdoms of the earth, as a reproach and a proverb, a taunt and a curse in all places where I will scatter them. ¹⁰ I will send the sword, the famine and the pestilence upon them until they are destroyed from the land which I gave to them and their forefathers.'"

Psalm 119:17–24

ג GIMEL.

¹⁷ Deal bountifully with Your servant,
   That I may live and keep Your word.
¹⁸ Open my eyes, that I may behold
   Wonderful things from Your law.
¹⁹ I am a stranger in the earth;
   Do not hide Your commandments
      from me.
²⁰ My soul is crushed with longing
   After Your ordinances at all times.

119:18 Open my eyes. Perhaps this is the supreme prayer that a student of Scripture could speak since it confesses the student's inadequacy and the Divine Author's sufficiency (vv. 98–99, 105, 130).

²¹ You rebuke the arrogant, the cursed,
   Who wander from Your
      commandments.
²² Take away reproach and
      contempt from me,
   For I observe Your testimonies.
²³ Even though princes sit
      and talk against me,
   Your servant meditates
      on Your statutes.
²⁴ Your testimonies also
      are my delight;
   They are my counselors.

Proverbs 27:15–16

¹⁵ A constant dripping on a
      day of steady rain
   And a contentious woman are alike;
¹⁶ He who would restrain her
      restrains the wind,
   And grasps oil with his right hand.

2 Thessalonians 1:1–12

1 Paul and Silvanus and Timothy,
   To the church of the Thessalonians in God our Father and the Lord Jesus Christ: ² Grace to you and peace from God the Father and the Lord Jesus Christ.

³ We ought always to give thanks to God for you, brethren, as is *only* fitting, because your faith is greatly enlarged, and the love of each one of you toward one another grows *ever* greater; ⁴ therefore, we ourselves speak proudly of you among the churches of God for your perseverance and faith in the midst of all your persecutions and afflictions which you endure. ⁵ *This is* a plain indication of God's righteous judgment so that you will be considered worthy of the kingdom of God, for which indeed you are suffering. ⁶ For after all it is *only* just for God to repay with affliction those who afflict you, ⁷ and *to give* relief to you who are afflicted and to us as well when the Lord Jesus will be revealed from heaven with His mighty angels in flaming fire, ⁸ dealing out retribution to those who do not know God and to those who do not obey the gospel of our Lord Jesus. ⁹ These will pay the penalty of eternal destruction,

away from the presence of the Lord and from the glory of His power, ¹⁰when He comes to be glorified in His saints on that day, and to be marveled at among all who have believed— for our testimony to you was believed. ¹¹To this end also we pray for you always, that our God will count you worthy of your calling, and fulfill every desire for goodness and the work of faith with power, ¹²so that the name of our Lord Jesus will be glorified in you, and you in Him, according to the grace of our God and *the* Lord Jesus Christ.

DAY 19: What should a believer's attitude be toward suffering?

In 2 Thessalonians 1:4, Paul speaks of the "perseverance and faith" of the Thessalonians. Nowhere was their growth in faith and love more evident than in the way they patiently and faithfully endured hostilities and suffering from the enemies of Christ. Although there was no need to speak, since the Thessalonians' lives spoke clearly enough (1Th 1:8), Paul's joy before the Lord over their perseverance bubbled up.

Having a right attitude toward suffering (v. 5) is essential, and that required attitude is concern for the kingdom of God. They were not self-centered but concentrated on God's kingdom. Their focus was not on personal comfort, fulfillment, and happiness, but on the glory of God and the fulfillment of His purposes. They were not moaning about the injustice of their persecutions. Rather, they were patiently enduring the sufferings they did not deserve (v. 4). This very attitude was "a plain indication" or positive proof that God's wise process of purging, purifying, and perfecting through suffering was working to make His beloved people worthy of the kingdom (2:12) by being perfected (Jas 1:2-4; 1Pe 5:10).

For believers, afflictions are to be expected (1Th 3:3) as they live and develop Christian character in a satanic world. Suffering is not to be thought of as evidence that God has forsaken them, but as evidence that He is with them, perfecting them (Mt 5:10; Ro 8:18; 2Co 12:10). So the Thessalonians demonstrated that their salvation, determined by faith alone in the Lord Jesus Christ, was genuine because they, like Christ, were willing to suffer on account of God and His kingdom. They suffered unjustly as objects of man's wrath against Christ and His kingdom (Ac 5:41; Php 3:10; Col 1:24).

 # OCTOBER 20

Jeremiah 25:1–26:24

25 The word that came to Jeremiah concerning all the people of Judah, in the fourth year of Jehoiakim the son of Josiah, king of Judah (that was the first year of Nebuchadnezzar king of Babylon), ²which Jeremiah the prophet spoke to all the people of Judah and to all the inhabitants of Jerusalem, saying, ³"From the thirteenth year of Josiah the son of Amon, king of Judah, even to this day, these twenty-three years the word of the LORD has come to me, and I have spoken to you again and again, but you have not listened. ⁴And the LORD has sent to you all His servants the prophets again and again, but you have not listened nor inclined your ear to hear, ⁵saying, 'Turn now everyone from his evil way and from the evil of your deeds, and dwell on the land which the LORD has given to you and your forefathers forever and ever; ⁶and do not go after other gods to serve them and to worship them, and do not provoke Me to anger with the work of your hands, and I will do you no harm.' ⁷Yet you have not listened to Me," declares the LORD, "in order that you might provoke Me to anger with the work of your hands to your own harm.

⁸"Therefore thus says the LORD of hosts, 'Because you have not obeyed My words, ⁹behold, I will send and take all the families of the north,' declares the LORD, 'and *I will send* to Nebuchadnezzar king of Babylon, My servant, and will bring them against this land and against its inhabitants and against all these nations round about; and I will utterly destroy them and make them a horror and a hissing, and an everlasting desolation. ¹⁰Moreover, I will take from them the voice of joy and the voice of gladness, the voice of the bridegroom and the voice of the bride, the sound of the millstones and the light of the lamp. ¹¹This whole land will be a desolation and a horror, and these nations will serve the king of Babylon seventy years.

¹²'Then it will be when seventy years are completed I will punish the king of Babylon and that nation,' declares the LORD, 'for their iniquity, and the land of the Chaldeans; and I will make it an everlasting desolation. ¹³I will bring upon that land all My words which I have pronounced against it, all that is written

25:11 seventy years. Here is the first specific statement on the length of the exile. This period probably began in the fourth year of Jehoiakim, when Jerusalem was first captured and the temple treasures were taken. It ends with the decree of Cyrus to let the Jews return, spanning from ca. 605/04 B.C. to 536/35 B.C. The exact number of Sabbath years is 490 years, the period from Saul to the Babylonian captivity. This was retribution for their violation of the Sabbath law (Lv 26:34–35; 2Ch 36:21).

in this book which Jeremiah has prophesied against all the nations. ¹⁴(For many nations and great kings will make slaves of them, even them; and I will recompense them according to their deeds and according to the work of their hands.)'"

¹⁵For thus the LORD, the God of Israel, says to me, "Take this cup of the wine of wrath from My hand and cause all the nations to whom I send you to drink it. ¹⁶They will drink and stagger and go mad because of the sword that I will send among them."

¹⁷Then I took the cup from the LORD'S hand and made all the nations to whom the LORD sent me drink it: ¹⁸Jerusalem and the cities of Judah and its kings *and* its princes, to make them a ruin, a horror, a hissing and a curse, as it is this day; ¹⁹Pharaoh king of Egypt, his servants, his princes and all his people; ²⁰and all the foreign people, all the kings of the land of Uz, all the kings of the land of the Philistines (even Ashkelon, Gaza, Ekron and the remnant of Ashdod); ²¹Edom, Moab and the sons of Ammon; ²²and all the kings of Tyre, all the kings of Sidon and the kings of the coastlands which are beyond the sea; ²³and Dedan, Tema, Buz and all who cut the corners *of their hair;* ²⁴and all the kings of Arabia and all the kings of the foreign people who dwell in the desert; ²⁵and all the kings of Zimri, all the kings of Elam and all the kings of Media; ²⁶and all the kings of the north, near and far, one with another; and all the kingdoms of the earth which are upon the face of the ground, and the king of Sheshach shall drink after them.

²⁷"You shall say to them, 'Thus says the LORD of hosts, the God of Israel, "Drink, be drunk, vomit, fall and rise no more because of the sword which I will send among you."' ²⁸And it will be, if they refuse to take the cup from your hand to drink, then you will say to them, 'Thus says the LORD of hosts: "You shall

surely drink! ²⁹For behold, I am beginning to work calamity in *this* city which is called by My name, and shall you be completely free from punishment? You will not be free from punishment; for I am summoning a sword against all the inhabitants of the earth," declares the LORD of hosts.'

³⁰"Therefore you shall prophesy against them all these words, and you shall say to them,

'The LORD will roar from on high
And utter His voice from
   His holy habitation;
He will roar mightily against His fold.
He will shout like those who
   tread *the* grapes,
Against all the inhabitants
   of the earth.
³¹ 'A clamor has come to the
   end of the earth,
Because the LORD has a
   controversy with the nations.
He is entering into judgment
   with all flesh;
As for the wicked, He has given them
   to the sword,' declares the LORD."

³² Thus says the LORD of hosts,
"Behold, evil is going forth
   From nation to nation,
And a great storm is being stirred up
   From the remotest parts of the earth.

³³"Those slain by the LORD on that day will be from one end of the earth to the other. They will not be lamented, gathered or buried; they will be like dung on the face of the ground.

³⁴ "Wail, you shepherds, and cry;
And wallow *in ashes,* you
   masters of the flock;
For the days of your slaughter and
   your dispersions have come,
And you will fall like a choice vessel.
³⁵ "Flight will perish from the shepherds,
And escape from the
   masters of the flock.
³⁶ *Hear* the sound of the cry
   of the shepherds,
And the wailing of the
   masters of the flock!
For the LORD is destroying
   their pasture,
³⁷ And the peaceful folds
   are made silent
Because of the fierce
   anger of the LORD.

38 "He has left His hiding
place like the lion;
For their land has become a horror
Because of the fierceness of
the oppressing *sword*
And because of His fierce anger."

26 In the beginning of the reign of Jehoiakim the son of Josiah, king of Judah, this word came from the LORD, saying, 2 "Thus says the LORD, 'Stand in the court of the LORD'S house, and speak to all the cities of Judah who have come to worship *in* the LORD'S house all the words that I have commanded you to speak to them. Do not omit a word! 3 Perhaps they will listen and everyone will turn from his evil way, that I may repent of the calamity which I am planning to do to them because of the evil of their deeds.' 4 And you will say to them, 'Thus says the LORD, "If you will not listen to Me, to walk in My law which I have set before you, 5 to listen to the words of My servants the prophets, whom I have been sending to you again and again, but you have not listened; 6 then I will make this house like Shiloh, and this city I will make a curse to all the nations of the earth."'"

7 The priests and the prophets and all the people heard Jeremiah speaking these words in the house of the LORD. 8 When Jeremiah finished speaking all that the LORD had commanded *him* to speak to all the people, the priests and the prophets and all the people seized him, saying, "You must die! 9 Why have you prophesied in the name of the LORD saying, 'This house will be like Shiloh and this city will be desolate, without inhabitant'?" And all the people gathered about Jeremiah in the house of the LORD.

10 When the officials of Judah heard these things, they came up from the king's house to the house of the LORD and sat in the entrance of the New Gate of the LORD'S *house.* 11 Then the priests and the prophets spoke to the officials and to all the people, saying, "A death sentence for this man! For he has prophesied against this city as you have heard in your hearing."

12 Then Jeremiah spoke to all the officials and to all the people, saying, "The LORD sent me to prophesy against this house and against this city all the words that you have heard. 13 Now therefore amend your ways and your deeds and obey the voice of the LORD your God; and the LORD will change His mind about the misfortune which He has pronounced against you. 14 But as for me, behold, I am in your hands; do with me as is

26:12 Jeremiah spoke. Leaders and people threatened to kill him (v. 8). The prophet defended himself while in extreme danger. He did not compromise, but displayed tremendous spiritual courage. He was ready to die (v. 14), yet warned the crowd that God would hold the guilty accountable (v. 15).

good and right in your sight. 15 Only know for certain that if you put me to death, you will bring innocent blood on yourselves, and on this city and on its inhabitants; for truly the LORD has sent me to you to speak all these words in your hearing."

16 Then the officials and all the people said to the priests and to the prophets, "No death sentence for this man! For he has spoken to us in the name of the LORD our God." 17 Then some of the elders of the land rose up and spoke to all the assembly of the people, saying, 18 "Micah of Moresheth prophesied in the days of Hezekiah king of Judah; and he spoke to all the people of Judah, saying, 'Thus the LORD of hosts has said,

"Zion will be plowed *as* a field,
And Jerusalem will become ruins,
And the mountain of the house as
the high places of a forest."'

19 Did Hezekiah king of Judah and all Judah put him to death? Did he not fear the LORD and entreat the favor of the LORD, and the LORD changed His mind about the misfortune which He had pronounced against them? But we are committing a great evil against ourselves."

20 Indeed, there was also a man who prophesied in the name of the LORD, Uriah the son of Shemaiah from Kiriath-jearim; and he prophesied against this city and against this land words similar to all those of Jeremiah. 21 When King Jehoiakim and all his mighty men and all the officials heard his words, then the king sought to put him to death; but Uriah heard *it,* and he was afraid and fled and went to Egypt. 22 Then King Jehoiakim sent men to Egypt: Elnathan the son of Achbor and *certain* men with him *went* into Egypt. 23 And they brought Uriah from Egypt and led him to King Jehoiakim, who slew him with a sword and cast his dead body into the burial place of the common people.

24 But the hand of Ahikam the son of Shaphan was with Jeremiah, so that he was

not given into the hands of the people to put him to death.

Psalm 119:25–32

ד DALETH.

25 My soul cleaves to the dust;
   Revive me according to Your word.
26 I have told of my ways, and
      You have answered me;
   Teach me Your statutes.
27 Make me understand the
      way of Your precepts,
   So I will meditate on Your wonders.
28 My soul weeps because of grief;
   Strengthen me according
      to Your word.
29 Remove the false way from me,
   And graciously grant me Your law.
30 I have chosen the faithful way;
   I have placed Your ordinances
      before me.
31 I cling to Your testimonies;
   O LORD, do not put me to shame!
32 I shall run the way of Your
      commandments,
   For You will enlarge my heart.

Proverbs 27:17

17 Iron sharpens iron,
   So one man sharpens another.

27:17 Iron sharpens iron. The benefits of intellectual and theological discussion encourage joy through a keener mind and the improvement of good character which the face will reveal.

2 Thessalonians 2:1–17

2 Now we request you, brethren, with regard to the coming of our Lord Jesus Christ and our gathering together to Him, ²that you not be quickly shaken from your composure or be disturbed either by a spirit or a message or a letter as if from us, to the effect that the day of the Lord has come. ³Let no one in any way deceive you, for *it will not come* unless the apostasy comes first, and the man of lawlessness is revealed, the son of destruction, ⁴who opposes and exalts himself above every so-called god or object of worship, so that he takes his seat in the temple of God, displaying himself as being God. ⁵Do you not remember that while I was still with you, I was telling you these things? ⁶And you know what restrains him now, so that in his time he will be revealed. ⁷For the mystery of

lawlessness is already at work; only he who now restrains *will do so* until he is taken out of the way. ⁸Then that lawless one will be revealed whom the Lord will slay with the breath of His mouth and bring to an end by the appearance of His coming; ⁹*that is,* the one whose coming is in accord with the activity of Satan, with all power and signs and false wonders, ¹⁰and with all the deception of wickedness for those who perish, because they did not receive the love of the truth so as to be saved. ¹¹For this reason God will send upon them a deluding influence so that they will believe what is false, ¹²in order that they all may be judged who did not believe the truth, but took pleasure in wickedness.

¹³But we should always give thanks to God for you, brethren beloved by the Lord, because God has chosen you from the beginning for salvation through sanctification by the Spirit and faith in the truth. ¹⁴It was for this He called you through our gospel, that you may gain the glory of our Lord Jesus Christ. ¹⁵So then, brethren, stand firm and hold to the traditions which you were taught, whether by word *of mouth* or by letter from us.

¹⁶Now may our Lord Jesus Christ Himself and God our Father, who has loved us and given us eternal comfort and good hope by grace, ¹⁷comfort and strengthen your hearts in every good work and word.

2:7 the mystery of lawlessness. This is the spirit of lawlessness already prevalent in society (1Jn 3:4; 5:17), but still a mystery in that it is not fully revealed as it will be in the one who so blatantly opposes God that he blasphemously assumes the place of God on earth, which God has reserved for Jesus Christ. The spirit of such a man is already in operation (1Jn 2:18; 4:3), but the man who fully embodies that spirit has not come. **taken out of the way.** This refers not to spatial removal (therefore it could not be the rapture of the church) but rather "a stepping aside." The idea is "out of the way," not gone. This restraint will be in place until the Antichrist is revealed, at the midpoint of the Tribulation, leaving him 42 months to reign (Da 7:25; Rev 13:5).

2:9–10 the one. This "lawless one" will do mighty acts pointing to himself as supernaturally empowered. His whole operation will be deceptive, luring the world to worship him and be damned. The career of the coming lawless one is more fully described in Revelation 13:1–18.

DAY 20: What is the "apostasy," or falling away that Paul speaks of in 2 Thessalonians 2:3-4?

The day of the Lord cannot occur until a deliberate abandonment of a formerly professed position, allegiance, or commitment occurs (the term was used to refer to military, political, or religious rebellion). Some have suggested, on questionable linguistic evidence, that this refers to a "departure" in the sense of the Rapture. Context, however, points to a religious defection, which is further described in v. 4. The language indicates a specific event, not general apostasy which exists now and always will. Rather, Paul has in mind the apostasy. This is an event which is clearly and specifically identifiable and unique, the consummate act of rebellion, an event of final magnitude. The key to identifying the event is to identify the main person, which Paul does, calling him the "man of sin." Some texts have "man of lawlessness." But there is no real difference in meaning since sin equals lawlessness (1Jn 3:4). This is the one who is called "the prince who is to come" (Da 9:26) and "the little horn" (see Da 7:8), whom John calls "the beast" (Rev 13:2-10, 18) and most known as the Antichrist. The context and language clearly identify a real person in future times who actually does the things prophesied of him in Scripture. He is also called "the son of destruction," or perdition, a term used of Judas Iscariot (Jn 17:12).

"The apostasy" is the abomination of desolation that takes place at the midpoint of the Tribulation spoken of in Daniel 9:27; 11:31 and Matthew 24:15. This man is not Satan, although Satan is the force behind him (v. 9) and he has motives like the desires of the devil (Is 14:13-14). Paul is referring to the very act of ultimate apostasy which reveals the final Antichrist and sets the course for the events that usher in the day of the Lord. Apparently, he will be seen as supportive of religion so that God and Christ will not appear as his enemies until the apostasy. He exalts himself and opposes God by moving into the temple, the place for worship of God, declaring himself to be God and demanding the worship of the world. In this act of satanic self-deification, he commits the great apostasy in defiance of God.

OCTOBER 21

Jeremiah 27:1–28:17

27 In the beginning of the reign of Zedekiah the son of Josiah, king of Judah, this word came to Jeremiah from the LORD, saying— [2] thus says the LORD to me—"Make for yourself bonds and yokes and put them on your neck, [3] and send word to the king of Edom, to the king of Moab, to the king of the sons of Ammon, to the king of Tyre and to the king of Sidon by the messengers who come to Jerusalem to Zedekiah king of Judah. [4] Command them *to go* to their masters, saying, 'Thus says the LORD of hosts, the God of Israel, thus you shall say to your masters, [5] "I have made the earth, the men and the beasts which are on the face of the earth by My great power and by My outstretched arm, and I will give it to the one who is pleasing in My sight. [6] Now I have given all these lands into the hand of Nebuchadnezzar king of Babylon, My servant, and I have given him also the wild animals of the field to serve him. [7] All the nations shall serve him and his son and his grandson until the time of his own land comes; then many nations and great kings will make him their servant.

[8] "It will be, *that* the nation or the kingdom which will not serve him, Nebuchadnezzar king of Babylon, and which will not put its neck under the yoke of the king of Babylon, I will punish that nation with the sword, with famine and with pestilence," declares the LORD, "until I have destroyed it by his hand. [9] But as for you, do not listen to your prophets, your diviners, your dreamers, your soothsayers or your sorcerers who speak to you, saying, 'You will not serve the king of Babylon.' [10] For they prophesy a lie to you in order to remove you far from your land; and I will drive you out and you will perish. [11] But the nation which will bring its neck under the yoke of the king of Babylon and serve him, I will let remain on its land," declares the LORD, "and they will till it and dwell in it." '"

[12] I spoke words like all these to Zedekiah king of Judah, saying, "Bring your necks under the yoke of the king of Babylon and serve him

27:8 yoke of...Babylon. The point of the object lesson is simple. Any nation that will serve Babylon willingly may stay in their own land, but nations that will not submit voluntarily to Babylon will suffer destruction. Consequently, Judah should submit and not be removed from the land (vv. 9–18).

and his people, and live! ¹³Why will you die, you and your people, by the sword, famine and pestilence, as the LORD has spoken to that nation which will not serve the king of Babylon? ¹⁴So do not listen to the words of the prophets who speak to you, saying, 'You will not serve the king of Babylon,' for they prophesy a lie to you; ¹⁵for I have not sent them," declares the LORD, "but they prophesy falsely in My name, in order that I may drive you out and that you may perish, you and the prophets who prophesy to you."

¹⁶Then I spoke to the priests and to all this people, saying, "Thus says the LORD: Do not listen to the words of your prophets who prophesy to you, saying, 'Behold, the vessels of the LORD'S house will now shortly be brought again from Babylon'; for they are prophesying a lie to you. ¹⁷Do not listen to them; serve the king of Babylon, and live! Why should this city become a ruin? ¹⁸But if they are prophets, and if the word of the LORD is with them, let them now entreat the LORD of hosts that the vessels which are left in the house of the LORD, in the house of the king of Judah and in Jerusalem may not go to Babylon. ¹⁹For thus says the LORD of hosts concerning the pillars, concerning the sea, concerning the stands and concerning the rest of the vessels that are left in this city, ²⁰which Nebuchadnezzar king of Babylon did not take when he carried into exile Jeconiah the son of Jehoiakim, king of Judah, from Jerusalem to Babylon, and all the nobles of Judah and Jerusalem. ²¹Yes, thus says the LORD of hosts, the God of Israel, concerning the vessels that are left in the house of the LORD and in the house of the king of Judah and in Jerusalem, ²²'They will be carried to Babylon and they will be there until the day I visit them,' declares the LORD. 'Then I will bring them back and restore them to this place.'"

28 Now in the same year, in the beginning of the reign of Zedekiah king of Judah, in the fourth year, in the fifth month, Hananiah the son of Azzur, the prophet, who was from Gibeon, spoke to me in the house of the LORD in the presence of the priests and all the people, saying, ²"Thus says the LORD of hosts, the God of Israel, 'I have broken the yoke of the king of Babylon. ³Within two years I am going to bring back to this place all the vessels of the LORD'S house, which Nebuchadnezzar king of Babylon took away from this place and carried to Babylon. ⁴I am also going to bring back to this place Jeconiah the son of Jehoiakim, king of Judah, and all the exiles of Judah who went to Babylon,' declares the

28:2-3 I have broken the yoke. The false prophet, of the kind Jeremiah warned of in 27:14-16, boldly predicted victory over Babylon and the return of the temple vessels within two years. In actuality, Babylon achieved its third and final step in conquering Judah 11 years later (586 B.C.) as in chaps. 39-40, 52.

LORD, 'for I will break the yoke of the king of Babylon.'"

⁵Then the prophet Jeremiah spoke to the prophet Hananiah in the presence of the priests and in the presence of all the people who were standing in the house of the LORD, ⁶and the prophet Jeremiah said, "Amen! May the LORD do so; may the LORD confirm your words which you have prophesied to bring back the vessels of the LORD'S house and all the exiles, from Babylon to this place. ⁷Yet hear now this word which I am about to speak in your hearing and in the hearing of all the people! ⁸The prophets who were before me and before you from ancient times prophesied against many lands and against great kingdoms, of war and of calamity and of pestilence. ⁹The prophet who prophesies of peace, when the word of the prophet comes to pass, then that prophet will be known as one whom the LORD has truly sent."

¹⁰Then Hananiah the prophet took the yoke from the neck of Jeremiah the prophet and broke it. ¹¹Hananiah spoke in the presence of all the people, saying, "Thus says the LORD, 'Even so will I break within two full years the yoke of Nebuchadnezzar king of Babylon from the neck of all the nations.'" Then the prophet Jeremiah went his way.

¹²The word of the LORD came to Jeremiah after Hananiah the prophet had broken the yoke from off the neck of the prophet Jeremiah, saying, ¹³"Go and speak to Hananiah, saying, 'Thus says the LORD, "You have broken the yokes of wood, but you have made instead of them yokes of iron." ¹⁴For thus says the LORD of hosts, the God of Israel, "I have put a yoke of iron on the neck of all these nations, that they may serve Nebuchadnezzar king of Babylon; and they will serve him. And I have also given him the beasts of the field."'" ¹⁵Then Jeremiah the prophet said to Hananiah the prophet, "Listen now, Hananiah, the LORD has not sent you, and you have made this people trust in a lie. ¹⁶Therefore thus says the LORD, 'Behold, I am about to remove you from the face of the earth. This year you are going

to die, because you have counseled rebellion against the LORD.'"

17 So Hananiah the prophet died in the same year in the seventh month.

Psalm 119:33-40

ה HE.

33 Teach me, O LORD, the way
of Your statutes,
And I shall observe it to the end.
34 Give me understanding, that
I may observe Your law
And keep it with all *my* heart.
35 Make me walk in the path of
Your commandments,
For I delight in it.
36 Incline my heart to Your testimonies
And not to *dishonest* gain.
37 Turn away my eyes from
looking at vanity,
And revive me in Your ways.
38 Establish Your word to Your servant,
As that which produces
reverence for You.
39 Turn away my reproach
which I dread,
For Your ordinances are good.
40 Behold, I long for Your precepts;
Revive me through Your
righteousness.

119:39 good. The very attributes of God (v. 68) become the characteristics of Scripture: 1) trustworthy (v. 42); 2) true (vv. 43, 142, 151, 160); 3) faithful (v. 86); 4) unchangeable (v. 89); 5) eternal (vv. 90, 152); 6) light (v. 105); and 7) pure (v. 140).

Proverbs 27:18

18 He who tends the fig tree
will eat its fruit,
And he who cares for his
master will be honored.

2 Thessalonians 3:1-18

3 Finally, brethren, pray for us that the word of the Lord will spread rapidly and be glorified, just as *it did* also with you; 2 and that we will be rescued from perverse and evil men; for not all have faith. 3 But the Lord is faithful,

3:1 pray for us. Paul frequently enlisted prayer support from the churches for his ministry (Ro 15:30–32; Eph 6:18–19; Col 4:2–3; 1Th 5:25; Phm 22). In particular, he asked them to pray that the word of God would continue to spread rapidly as it had been already (Ac 6:7; 12:24; 13:44–49), and be received with the honor it deserved.

and He will strengthen and protect you from the evil *one*. 4 We have confidence in the Lord concerning you, that you are doing and will *continue to* do what we command. 5 May the Lord direct your hearts into the love of God and into the steadfastness of Christ.

6 Now we command you, brethren, in the name of our Lord Jesus Christ, that you keep away from every brother who leads an unruly life and not according to the tradition which you received from us. 7 For you yourselves know how you ought to follow our example, because we did not act in an undisciplined manner among you, 8 nor did we eat anyone's bread without paying for it, but with labor and hardship we *kept* working night and day so that we would not be a burden to any of you; 9 not because we do not have the right *to this*, but in order to offer ourselves as a model for you, so that you would follow our example. 10 For even when we were with you, we used to give you this order: if anyone is not willing to work, then he is not to eat, either. 11 For we hear that some among you are leading an undisciplined life, doing no work at all, but acting like busybodies. 12 Now such persons we command and exhort in the Lord Jesus Christ to work in quiet fashion and eat their own bread. 13 But as for you, brethren, do not grow weary of doing good.

14 If anyone does not obey our instruction in this letter, take special note of that person and do not associate with him, so that he will be put to shame. 15 Yet do not regard him as an enemy, but admonish him as a brother.

16 Now may the Lord of peace Himself continually grant you peace in every circumstance. The Lord be with you all!

17 I, Paul, write this greeting with my own hand, and this is a distinguishing mark in every letter; this is the way I write. 18 The grace of our Lord Jesus Christ be with you all.

DAY 21: How does Paul's teaching on church discipline in 2 Thessalonians 3:6-15 fit with other major biblical passages on this subject?

Paul addressed a particular issue of church discipline with the Thessalonians in 3:6-15. Helpful parallel passages that should be consulted in studying this one include Matthew 18:15-20, 1 Corinthians 5:1-13, Galatians 6:1-5, and 1 Timothy 5:19-20.

This passage (3:6-15) gives specific direction on the nature of the church's response to someone who deliberately refuses to follow God's Word, expecting to benefit from fellowship with God's people while being unwilling to participate in a meaningful way. Paul's directions were not mere suggestions, but rather they carried the weight and authority of a judge's court order which the apostle delivered and enforced (vv. 4, 6, 10, 12). In Paul's words, "If anyone is not willing to work, then he is not to eat, either" (3:10). These were fellow believers acting in a parasitic way, sapping the generosity of other believers. Paul had already addressed this pattern in his first letter (1Th 4:11). If there were any questions, Paul called them to imitate him (v. 7; 1Th 1:6) because he imitated Christ (1Co 4:16; 11:1; Eph 5:1).

This passage offers an emphatic command, a personal confrontation, and a compassionate caution. First, vv. 6 and 14 instruct the rest of the church to "keep away" and "not associate" with such a person. In other words, Paul was commanding the church to disfellowship blatantly disobedient Christians in order to bring shame (v. 14) and, hopefully, repentance. Second, Paul was giving the sluggards a direct command to "work in quiet fashion and eat their own bread" (v. 12), removing any excuse that they had not been warned about discipline. Third, Paul added two crucial words of caution. He reminded the believers that genuinely needy people deserved help. He urged them, "Do not grow weary of doing good" (v. 13). He also cautioned them to limit their disciplinary withdrawal. "Do not regard him as an enemy, but admonish him as a brother" (v. 15). While an unrepentant pattern of sin should be handled decisively, they should continually remember that the person being disciplined is a brother or sister in the Lord. All further warnings to this person about his or her sin should be done with love and concern, praying for this fellow believer's restoration.

The goal for any prescription for church discipline must be the restoration of the sinning person. If successful, Jesus said that "you have won your brother" (Mt 18:15). The idea is not merely to punish the offender or to shun him completely, but to remove him as a detrimental influence from the fellowship of the church, and henceforth to regard him as an evangelistic prospect rather than a brother. Ultimately, the sin for which he is excommunicated is a hard-hearted impenitence.

OCTOBER 22

Jeremiah 29:1-30:24

29 Now these are the words of the letter which Jeremiah the prophet sent from Jerusalem to the rest of the elders of the exile, the priests, the prophets and all the people whom Nebuchadnezzar had taken into exile from Jerusalem to Babylon. ²(This was after King Jeconiah and the queen mother, the court officials, the princes of Judah and Jerusalem, the craftsmen and the smiths had departed from Jerusalem.) ³ *The letter was sent* by the hand of Elasah the son of Shaphan, and Gemariah the son of Hilkiah, whom Zedekiah king of Judah sent to Babylon to Nebuchadnezzar king of Babylon, saying, ⁴ "Thus says the LORD of hosts, the God of Israel, to all the exiles whom I have sent into exile from Jerusalem to Babylon, ⁵ 'Build houses and live *in them;* and plant gardens and eat their produce. ⁶ Take wives and become the fathers of sons and daughters, and take wives for your sons and give your daughters to husbands, that they may bear sons and daughters; and multiply there and do not decrease. ⁷ Seek the welfare of the city where I have sent you into exile, and pray to the LORD on its behalf; for in its welfare you will have welfare.' ⁸ For thus says the LORD of hosts, the God of Israel, 'Do not let your prophets who are in your midst and your diviners deceive you, and do not listen to the dreams which they dream. ⁹ For they prophesy falsely to you in My name; I have not sent them,' declares the LORD.

¹⁰ "For thus says the LORD, 'When seventy years have been completed for Babylon, I will visit you and fulfill My good word to you, to bring you back to this place. ¹¹ For I know the plans that I have for you,' declares the LORD, 'plans for welfare and not for calamity to give you a future and a hope. ¹² Then you will call upon Me and come and pray to Me, and I will

listen to you. [13] You will seek Me and find *Me* when you search for Me with all your heart. [14] I will be found by you,' declares the LORD, 'and I will restore your fortunes and will gather you from all the nations and from all the places where I have driven you,' declares the LORD, 'and I will bring you back to the place from where I sent you into exile.'

29:14 I will be found by you. The Lord would answer their prayer by returning the Jews to their land, see Daniel's example and God's response (Da 9:4–27). Fulfillment would occur in the era of Ezra and Nehemiah, and beyond this in even fuller measure after the Second Advent of their Messiah (Da 2:35, 45; 7:13–14, 27; 12:1–3, 13).

[15] "Because you have said, 'The LORD has raised up prophets for us in Babylon'— [16] for thus says the LORD concerning the king who sits on the throne of David, and concerning all the people who dwell in this city, your brothers who did not go with you into exile— [17] thus says the LORD of hosts, 'Behold, I am sending upon them the sword, famine and pestilence, and I will make them like split-open figs that cannot be eaten due to rottenness. [18] I will pursue them with the sword, with famine and with pestilence; and I will make them a terror to all the kingdoms of the earth, to be a curse and a horror and a hissing, and a reproach among all the nations where I have driven them, [19] because they have not listened to My words,' declares the LORD, 'which I sent to them again and again by My servants the prophets; but you did not listen,' declares the LORD. [20] You, therefore, hear the word of the LORD, all you exiles, whom I have sent away from Jerusalem to Babylon.

[21] "Thus says the LORD of hosts, the God of Israel, concerning Ahab the son of Kolaiah and concerning Zedekiah the son of Maaseiah, who are prophesying to you falsely in My name, 'Behold, I will deliver them into the hand of Nebuchadnezzar king of Babylon, and he will slay them before your eyes. [22] Because of them a curse will be used by all the exiles from Judah who are in Babylon, saying, "May the LORD make you like Zedekiah and like Ahab, whom the king of Babylon roasted in the fire, [23] because they have acted foolishly in Israel, and have committed adultery with their neighbors' wives and have spoken words in My name falsely, which I did not command them; and I am He who knows and am a witness," declares the LORD.'"

[24] To Shemaiah the Nehelamite you shall speak, saying, [25] "Thus says the LORD of hosts, the God of Israel, 'Because you have sent letters in your own name to all the people who are in Jerusalem, and to Zephaniah the son of Maaseiah, the priest, and to all the priests, saying, [26] "The LORD has made you priest instead of Jehoiada the priest, to be the overseer in the house of the LORD over every madman who prophesies, to put him in the stocks and in the iron collar, [27] now then, why have you not rebuked Jeremiah of Anathoth who prophesies to you? [28] For he has sent to us in Babylon, saying, 'The exile will be long; build houses and live in them and plant gardens and eat their produce.'"'"

[29] Zephaniah the priest read this letter to Jeremiah the prophet. [30] Then came the word of the LORD to Jeremiah, saying, [31] 'Send to all the exiles, saying, 'Thus says the LORD concerning Shemaiah the Nehelamite, "Because Shemaiah has prophesied to you, although I did not send him, and he has made you trust in a lie," [32] therefore thus says the LORD, "Behold, I am about to punish Shemaiah the Nehelamite and his descendants; he will not have anyone living among this people, and he will not see the good that I am about to do to My people," declares the LORD, "because he has preached rebellion against the LORD."'"

30 The word which came to Jeremiah from the LORD, saying, [2] "Thus says the LORD, the God of Israel, 'Write all the words which I have spoken to you in a book. [3] For behold, days are coming,' declares the LORD, 'when I will restore the fortunes of My people Israel and Judah.' The LORD says, 'I will also bring them back to the land that I gave to their forefathers and they shall possess it.'"

[4] Now these are the words which the LORD spoke concerning Israel and concerning Judah:

[5] "For thus says the LORD,

'I have heard a sound of terror,
Of dread, and there is no peace.
[6] 'Ask now, and see
If a male can give birth.
Why do I see every man
With his hands on his loins, as
a woman in childbirth?
And *why* have all faces turned pale?
[7] 'Alas! for that day is great,
There is none like it;
And it is the time of Jacob's distress,
But he will be saved from it.

30:7 time of Jacob's distress. This period of unprecedented difficulty for Israel, as the verse defines, is set in a context of Israel's final restoration. It is best equated with the time of tribulation (vv. 8–9) just before Christ's Second Advent, mentioned elsewhere (Da 12:1; Mt 24:21–22) and described in detail by Revelation 6–19.

8 'It shall come about on that day,' declares the LORD of hosts, 'that I will break his yoke from off their neck and will tear off their bonds; and strangers will no longer make them their slaves. 9 But they shall serve the LORD their God and David their king, whom I will raise up for them.

10 'Fear not, O Jacob My servant,'
    declares the LORD,
  'And do not be dismayed, O Israel;
  For behold, I will save you from afar
  And your offspring from the
    land of their captivity.
  And Jacob will return and will
    be quiet and at ease,
  And no one will make him afraid.
11 'For I am with you,' declares
    the LORD, 'to save you;
  For I will destroy completely
    all the nations where I
    have scattered you,
  Only I will not destroy
    you completely.
  But I will chasten you justly
  And will by no means leave
    you unpunished.'

12 "For thus says the LORD,
  'Your wound is incurable
  And your injury is serious.
13 'There is no one to plead your cause;
  No healing for your sore,
  No recovery for you.
14 'All your lovers have forgotten you,
  They do not seek you;
  For I have wounded you with
    the wound of an enemy,
  With the punishment of a cruel one,
  Because your iniquity is great
  And your sins are numerous.
15 'Why do you cry out over your injury?
  Your pain is incurable.
  Because your iniquity is great
  And your sins are numerous,
  I have done these things to you.

16 'Therefore all who devour
    you will be devoured;
  And all your adversaries, every one
    of them, will go into captivity;
  And those who plunder you
    will be for plunder,
  And all who prey upon you
    I will give for prey.
17 'For I will restore you to health
  And I will heal you of your
    wounds,' declares the LORD,
  'Because they have called you
    an outcast, saying:
  "It is Zion; no one cares for her."'

18 "Thus says the LORD,
  'Behold, I will restore the fortunes
    of the tents of Jacob
  And have compassion on
    his dwelling places;
  And the city will be
    rebuilt on its ruin,
  And the palace will stand
    on its rightful place.
19 'From them will proceed
    thanksgiving
  And the voice of those
    who celebrate;
  And I will multiply them and
    they will not be diminished;
  I will also honor them and they
    will not be insignificant.
20 'Their children also will
    be as formerly,
  And their congregation shall
    be established before Me;
  And I will punish all their oppressors.
21 'Their leader shall be one of them,
  And their ruler shall come
    forth from their midst;
  And I will bring him near and
    he shall approach Me;
  For who would dare to risk his life to
    approach Me?' declares the LORD.
22 'You shall be My people,
  And I will be your God.'"

23 Behold, the tempest of the LORD!
  Wrath has gone forth,
  A sweeping tempest;
  It will burst on the head of the wicked.
24 The fierce anger of the LORD
    will not turn back
  Until He has performed and
    until He has accomplished
  The intent of His heart;
  In the latter days you will
    understand this.

Psalm 119:41-48

ו VAV.

41 May Your lovingkindnesses
     also come to me, O LORD,
   Your salvation according
     to Your word;

42 So I will have an answer for
     him who reproaches me,
   For I trust in Your word.

43 And do not take the word of truth
     utterly out of my mouth,
   For I wait for Your ordinances.

44 So I will keep Your law continually,
   Forever and ever.

45 And I will walk at liberty,
   For I seek Your precepts.

46 I will also speak of Your
     testimonies before kings
   And shall not be ashamed.

47 I shall delight in Your commandments,
   Which I love.

48 And I shall lift up my hands to
     Your commandments,
   Which I love;
   And I will meditate on Your statutes.

Proverbs 27:19

19 As in water face *reflects* face,
   So the heart of man *reflects* man.

1 Timothy 1:1-20

1 Paul, an apostle of Christ Jesus according
to the commandment of God our Savior,
and of Christ Jesus, *who is* our hope,

² To Timothy, *my* true child in *the* faith:
Grace, mercy *and* peace from God the Father
and Christ Jesus our Lord.

³ As I urged you upon my departure for
Macedonia, remain on at Ephesus so that you
may instruct certain men not to teach strange
doctrines, ⁴ nor to pay attention to myths and
endless genealogies, which give rise to mere
speculation rather than *furthering* the administration of God which is by faith. ⁵ But the goal
of our instruction is love from a pure heart and
a good conscience and a sincere faith. ⁶ For
some men, straying from these things, have

1:4 myths and endless genealogies. Legends
and fanciful stories manufactured from elements of Judaism (v. 7; see Titus 1:14), which
probably dealt with allegorical or fictitious interpretations of Old Testament genealogical
lists. In reality, they were "doctrines of demons"
(4:1), posing as God's truth (4:7).

turned aside to fruitless discussion, ⁷ wanting
to be teachers of the Law, even though they do
not understand either what they are saying or
the matters about which they make confident
assertions.

⁸ But we know that the Law is good, if one
uses it lawfully, ⁹ realizing the fact that law is
not made for a righteous person, but for those
who are lawless and rebellious, for the ungodly
and sinners, for the unholy and profane, for
those who kill their fathers or mothers, for
murderers ¹⁰ and immoral men and homosexuals and kidnappers and liars and perjurers,
and whatever else is contrary to sound teaching, ¹¹ according to the glorious gospel of the
blessed God, with which I have been entrusted.

¹² I thank Christ Jesus our Lord, who has
strengthened me, because He considered
me faithful, putting me into service, ¹³ even
though I was formerly a blasphemer and a
persecutor and a violent aggressor. Yet I was
shown mercy because I acted ignorantly in
unbelief; ¹⁴ and the grace of our Lord was
more than abundant, with the faith and love
which are *found* in Christ Jesus. ¹⁵ It is a trustworthy statement, deserving full acceptance,
that Christ Jesus came into the world to save
sinners, among whom I am foremost *of all.*
¹⁶ Yet for this reason I found mercy, so that

1:8 the Law is good. The Greek word for "good"
can be translated "useful." The law is good or
useful because it reflects God's holy will and
righteous standard (Ps 19:7; Ro 7:12), which
accomplishes its purpose in showing sinners
their sin (Ro 3:19) and their need for a Savior
(Gal 3:24). The law forces people to recognize
that they are guilty of disobeying God's commands, and it thereby condemns every person
and sentences them to hell.

1:13 I acted ignorantly in unbelief. Paul was
neither a Jewish apostate nor a Pharisee who
clearly understood Jesus' teaching and still
rejected Him. He was a zealous, fastidious
Jew trying to earn his salvation, thus lost and
damned. His plea of ignorance was not a claim
to innocence nor an excuse denying his guilt.
It was simply a statement indicating that he
did not understand the truth of Christ's gospel
and was honestly trying to protect his religion.
His willing repentance when confronted by
Christ (Ro 7:9; Php 3:8-9) is evidence that he
had not understood the ramifications of his
actions—he truly thought he was doing God
a service (Ac 26:9).

in me as the foremost, Jesus Christ might demonstrate His perfect patience as an example for those who would believe in Him for eternal life. [17] Now to the King eternal, immortal, invisible, the only God, *be* honor and glory forever and ever. Amen.

[18] This command I entrust to you, Timothy, *my* son, in accordance with the prophecies previously made concerning you, that by them you fight the good fight, [19] keeping faith and a good conscience, which some have rejected and suffered shipwreck in regard to their faith. [20] Among these are Hymenaeus and Alexander, whom I have handed over to Satan, so that they will be taught not to blaspheme.

DAY 22: Who is Timothy?

Timothy received his name, which means "one who honors God," from his mother (Eunice) and grandmother (Lois), devout Jews who became believers in the Lord Jesus Christ (2Ti 1:5) and taught Timothy the Old Testament Scriptures from his childhood (2Ti 3:15). His father was a Greek (Ac 16:1) who may have died before Timothy met Paul.

Timothy was from Lystra (Ac 16:1-3), a city in the Roman province of Galatia (part of modern Turkey). Paul led Timothy to Christ (1:2, 18; 1Co 4:17; 2Ti 1:2), undoubtedly during his ministry in Lystra on his first missionary journey (Ac 14:6-23). When he revisited Lystra on his second missionary journey, Paul chose Timothy to accompany him (Ac 16:1-3). Although Timothy was very young (probably in his late teens or early twenties, since about 15 years later Paul referred to him as a young man; 4:12), he had a reputation for godliness (Ac 16:2). Timothy was to be Paul's disciple, friend, and colaborer for the rest of the apostle's life, ministering with him in Berea (Ac 17:14), Athens (Ac 17:15), Corinth (Ac 18:5; 2Co 1:19), and accompanying him on his trip to Jerusalem (Ac 20:4). He was with Paul in his first Roman imprisonment and went to Philippi (2:19-23) after Paul's release. In addition, Paul frequently mentions Timothy in his epistles. Paul often sent Timothy to churches as his representative (1Co 4:17; 16:10; Php 2:19; 1Th 3:2), and 1 Timothy finds him on another assignment, serving as pastor of the church at Ephesus (1:3).

OCTOBER 23

Jeremiah 31:1–32:44

31 "At that time," declares the LORD, "I will be the God of all the families of Israel, and they shall be My people."

2 Thus says the LORD,
"The people who survived the sword
Found grace in the wilderness—
Israel, when it went to find its rest."
3 The LORD appeared to him
from afar, *saying,*
"I have loved you with an
everlasting love;
Therefore I have drawn you
with lovingkindness.
4 "Again I will build you and
you will be rebuilt,
O virgin of Israel!
Again you will take up
your tambourines,
And go forth to the dances
of the merrymakers.
5 "Again you will plant vineyards
On the hills of Samaria;
The planters will plant
And will enjoy *them.*

6 "For there will be a day when watchmen
On the hills of Ephraim call out,
'Arise, and let us go up *to* Zion,
To the LORD our God.'"

7 For thus says the LORD,
"Sing aloud with gladness for Jacob,
And shout among the chief
of the nations;
Proclaim, give praise and say,
'O LORD, save Your people,
The remnant of Israel.'
8 "Behold, I am bringing them
from the north country,
And I will gather them from the
remote parts of the earth,
Among them the blind and the lame,
The woman with child and she who
is in labor with child, together;
A great company, they
will return here.
9 "With weeping they will come,
And by supplication I will lead them;
I will make them walk by
streams of waters,
On a straight path in which
they will not stumble;
For I am a father to Israel,
And Ephraim is My firstborn."

10 Hear the word of the LORD, O nations,
And declare in the coastlands afar off,
And say, "He who scattered
Israel will gather him
And keep him as a shepherd
keeps his flock."
11 For the LORD has ransomed Jacob
And redeemed him from the hand of
him who was stronger than he.
12 "They will come and shout for
joy on the height of Zion,
And they will be radiant over
the bounty of the LORD—
Over the grain and the new
wine and the oil,
And over the young of the
flock and the herd;
And their life will be like a
watered garden,
And they will never languish again.
13 "Then the virgin will rejoice
in the dance,
And the young men and
the old, together,
For I will turn their mourning into joy
And will comfort them and give
them joy for their sorrow.
14 "I will fill the soul of the priests
with abundance,
And My people will be satisfied with
My goodness," declares the LORD.

15 Thus says the LORD,
"A voice is heard in Ramah,
Lamentation *and* bitter weeping.
Rachel is weeping for her children;
She refuses to be comforted
for her children,
Because they are no more."

16 Thus says the LORD,

"Restrain your voice from weeping
And your eyes from tears;
For your work will be rewarded,"
declares the LORD,
"And they will return from
the land of the enemy.
17 "There is hope for your future,"
declares the LORD,
"And *your* children will return
to their own territory.
18 "I have surely heard Ephraim grieving,
'You have chastised me, and
I was chastised,
Like an untrained calf;
Bring me back that I may be restored,
For You are the LORD my God.

19 'For after I turned back, I repented;
And after I was instructed,
I smote on *my* thigh;
I was ashamed and also humiliated
Because I bore the reproach
of my youth.'
20 "Is Ephraim My dear son?
Is he a delightful child?
Indeed, as often as I have
spoken against him,
I certainly *still* remember him;
Therefore My heart yearns for him;
I will surely have mercy on
him," declares the LORD.

21 "Set up for yourself roadmarks,
Place for yourself guideposts;
Direct your mind to the highway,
The way by which you went.
Return, O virgin of Israel,
Return to these your cities.
22 "How long will you go here and there,
O faithless daughter?
For the LORD has created a
new thing in the earth—
A woman will encompass a man."

23 Thus says the LORD of hosts, the God of Israel, "Once again they will speak this word in the land of Judah and in its cities when I restore their fortunes,

'The LORD bless you, O abode
of righteousness,
O holy hill!'

24 Judah and all its cities will dwell together in it, the farmer and they who go about with flocks. 25 For I satisfy the weary ones and refresh everyone who languishes." 26 At this I awoke and looked, and my sleep was pleasant to me.

27 "Behold, days are coming," declares the LORD, "when I will sow the house of Israel and the house of Judah with the seed of man and with the seed of beast. 28 As I have watched over them to pluck up, to break down, to overthrow, to destroy and to bring disaster, so I will watch over them to build and to plant," declares the LORD.

29 "In those days they will not say again,
'The fathers have eaten sour grapes,
And the children's teeth
are set on edge.'

30 But everyone will die for his own iniquity; each man who eats the sour grapes, his teeth will be set on edge.

³¹ "Behold, days are coming," declares the LORD, "when I will make a new covenant with the house of Israel and with the house of Judah, ³² not like the covenant which I made with their fathers in the day I took them by the hand to bring them out of the land of Egypt, My covenant which they broke, although I was a husband to them," declares the LORD. ³³ "But this is the covenant which I will make with the house of Israel after those days," declares the LORD, "I will put My law within them and on their heart I will write it; and I will be their God, and they shall be My people. ³⁴ They will not teach again, each man his neighbor and each man his brother, saying, 'Know the LORD,' for they will all know Me, from the least of them to the greatest of them," declares the LORD, "for I will forgive their iniquity, and their sin I will remember no more."

³⁵ Thus says the LORD,
Who gives the sun for light by day
And the fixed order of the moon
    and the stars for light by night,
Who stirs up the sea so
    that its waves roar;
The LORD of hosts is His name:
³⁶ "If this fixed order departs
From before Me," declares the LORD,
"Then the offspring of Israel
    also will cease
From being a nation
    before Me forever."
³⁷ Thus says the LORD,
"If the heavens above can be measured
And the foundations of the
    earth searched out below,
Then I will also cast off all
    the offspring of Israel
For all that they have done,"
    declares the LORD.

³⁸ "Behold, days are coming," declares the LORD, "when the city will be rebuilt for the LORD from the Tower of Hananel to the Corner Gate. ³⁹ The measuring line will go out farther straight ahead to the hill Gareb; then it will turn to Goah. ⁴⁰ And the whole valley of the dead bodies and of the ashes, and all the fields as far as the brook Kidron, to the corner of the Horse Gate toward the east, shall be holy to the LORD; it will not be plucked up or overthrown anymore forever."

32 The word that came to Jeremiah from the LORD in the tenth year of Zedekiah king of Judah, which was the eighteenth year of Nebuchadnezzar. ² Now at that time the army of the king of Babylon was besieging Jerusalem, and Jeremiah the prophet was shut up in the court of the guard, which *was in* the house of the king of Judah, ³ because Zedekiah king of Judah had shut him up, saying, "Why do you prophesy, saying, 'Thus says the LORD, "Behold, I am about to give this city into the hand of the king of Babylon, and he will take it; ⁴ and Zedekiah king of Judah will not escape out of the hand of the Chaldeans, but he will surely be given into the hand of the king of Babylon, and he will speak with him face to face and see him eye to eye; ⁵ and he will take Zedekiah to Babylon, and he will be there until I visit him," declares the LORD. "If you fight against the Chaldeans, you will not succeed" '?"

⁶ And Jeremiah said, "The word of the LORD came to me, saying, ⁷ 'Behold, Hanamel the son of Shallum your uncle is coming to you, saying, "Buy for yourself my field which is at Anathoth, for you have the right of redemption to buy *it*." ' ⁸ Then Hanamel my uncle's son came to me in the court of the guard according to the word of the LORD and said to me, 'Buy my field, please, that is at Anathoth, which is in the land of Benjamin; for you have the right of possession and the redemption is yours; buy *it* for yourself.' Then I knew that this was the word of the LORD.

⁹ "I bought the field which was at Anathoth from Hanamel my uncle's son, and I weighed out the silver for him, seventeen shekels of silver. ¹⁰ I signed and sealed the deed, and called in witnesses, and weighed out the silver on the scales. ¹¹ Then I took the deeds of purchase, both the sealed *copy containing* the terms and conditions and the open *copy;* ¹² and I gave the deed of purchase to Baruch the son of Neriah, the son of Mahseiah, in the sight of Hanamel my uncle's *son* and in the sight of the witnesses who signed the deed of purchase, before all the Jews who were sitting in the court of the guard. ¹³ And I commanded Baruch in their presence, saying, ¹⁴ 'Thus says the LORD of hosts, the God of Israel, "Take these deeds, this sealed deed of purchase and this open deed, and put them in an earthenware jar, that they may last a long time." ¹⁵ For thus says the LORD of hosts, the God of Israel, "Houses and fields and vineyards will again be bought in this land." '

¹⁶ "After I had given the deed of purchase to Baruch the son of Neriah, then I prayed to the LORD, saying, ¹⁷ 'Ah Lord GOD! Behold, You have made the heavens and the earth by Your great power and by Your outstretched arm! Nothing is too difficult for You, ¹⁸ who shows lovingkindness to thousands, but repays the iniquity of fathers into the bosom of their children after them, O great and mighty God. The

32:14 Take these deeds. Title deeds to the land, kept for security reasons in a pottery jar, would attest in a future day to one's claim of possession. Men of Anathoth did return to Jerusalem from Babylon (Ezr 2:23). Also, some of the poor of the land, left by the Babylonians (chap. 39), could have included certain inhabitants of Anathoth. In a still future day, God will be able (vv. 17, 27) to make this land good to a resurrected Jeremiah and confirm to the right people that they are the prophet/priest's descendants.

LORD of hosts is His name; ¹⁹ great in counsel and mighty in deed, whose eyes are open to all the ways of the sons of men, giving to everyone according to his ways and according to the fruit of his deeds; ²⁰ who has set signs and wonders in the land of Egypt, *and* even to this day both in Israel and among mankind; and You have made a name for Yourself, as at this day. ²¹ You brought Your people Israel out of the land of Egypt with signs and with wonders, and with a strong hand and with an outstretched arm and with great terror; ²² and gave them this land, which You swore to their forefathers to give them, a land flowing with milk and honey. ²³ They came in and took possession of it, but they did not obey Your voice or walk in Your law; they have done nothing of all that You commanded them to do; therefore You have made all this calamity come upon them. ²⁴ Behold, the siege ramps have reached the city to take it; and the city is given into the hand of the Chaldeans who fight against it, because of the sword, the famine and the pestilence; and what You have spoken has come to pass; and behold, You see *it.* ²⁵ You have said to me, O Lord GOD, "Buy for yourself the field with money and call in witnesses"—although the city is given into the hand of the Chaldeans.' "

²⁶ Then the word of the LORD came to Jeremiah, saying, ²⁷ "Behold, I am the LORD, the God of all flesh; is anything too difficult for Me?" ²⁸ Therefore thus says the LORD, "Behold, I am about to give this city into the hand of the Chaldeans and into the hand of Nebuchadnezzar king of Babylon, and he will take it. ²⁹ The Chaldeans who are fighting against this city will enter and set this city on fire and burn it, with the houses where *people* have offered incense to Baal on their roofs and poured out drink offerings to other gods to provoke Me to anger. ³⁰ Indeed the sons of Israel and the sons of Judah have been doing only evil in My sight from their youth; for the sons of Israel have been only provoking Me to anger by the work of their hands," declares the LORD. ³¹ "Indeed this city has been to Me *a provocation of* My anger and My wrath from the day that they built it, even to this day, so that it should be removed from before My face, ³² because of all the evil of the sons of Israel and the sons of Judah which they have done to provoke Me to anger—they, their kings, their leaders, their priests, their prophets, the men of Judah and the inhabitants of Jerusalem. ³³ They have turned *their* back to Me and not *their* face; though *I* taught them, teaching again and again, they would not listen and receive instruction. ³⁴ But they put their detestable things in the house which is called by My name, to defile it. ³⁵ They built the high places of Baal that are in the valley of Ben-hinnom to cause their sons and their daughters to pass through *the fire* to Molech, which I had not commanded them nor had it entered My mind that they should do this abomination, to cause Judah to sin.

³⁶ "Now therefore thus says the LORD God of Israel concerning this city of which you say, 'It is given into the hand of the king of Babylon by sword, by famine and by pestilence.' ³⁷ Behold, I will gather them out of all the lands to which I have driven them in My anger, in My wrath and in great indignation; and I will bring them back to this place and make them dwell in safety. ³⁸ They shall be My people, and I will be their God; ³⁹ and I will give them one heart and one way, that they may fear Me always, for their own good and for *the good of* their children after them. ⁴⁰ I will make an everlasting covenant with them that I will not turn away from them, to do them good; and I will put the fear of Me in their hearts so that they will not turn away from Me. ⁴¹ I will rejoice over them to do them good and will faithfully plant them in this land with all My heart and with all My soul. ⁴² For thus says the LORD, 'Just as I brought all this great disaster on this people, so I am going to bring on them all the good that I am promising them. ⁴³ Fields will be bought in this land of which you say, "It is a desolation, without man or beast; it is given into the hand of the Chaldeans." ⁴⁴ Men will buy fields for money, sign and seal deeds, and call in witnesses in the land of Benjamin, in the environs of Jerusalem, in the cities of Judah, in the cities of the hill country, in the cities of the lowland and in the cities of the Negev; for I will restore their fortunes,' declares the LORD."

Psalm 119:49-56

ז ZAYIN.

⁴⁹ Remember the word to Your servant,
In which You have made me hope.
⁵⁰ This is my comfort in my affliction,
That Your word has revived me.
⁵¹ The arrogant utterly deride me,
Yet I do not turn aside from Your law.
⁵² I have remembered Your ordinances
from of old, O LORD,
And comfort myself.
⁵³ Burning indignation has seized
me because of the wicked,
Who forsake Your law.
⁵⁴ Your statutes are my songs
In the house of my pilgrimage.
⁵⁵ O LORD, I remember Your
name in the night,
And keep Your law.
⁵⁶ This has become mine,
That I observe Your precepts.

Proverbs 27:20

²⁰ Sheol and Abaddon are
never satisfied,
Nor are the eyes of man ever satisfied.

27:20 Sheol and Abaddon. Man's desires are never filled up. They are as insatiable as the place of eternal punishment which never overfills.

1 Timothy 2:1-15

2 First of all, then, I urge that entreaties *and* prayers, petitions *and* thanksgivings, be made on behalf of all men, ² for kings and all who are in authority, so that we may lead a tranquil and quiet life in all godliness and dignity. ³ This is good and acceptable in the sight of God our Savior, ⁴ who desires all men to be saved and to come to the knowledge of the truth. ⁵ For there is one God, *and* one mediator also between God and men, *the* man Christ Jesus, ⁶ who gave Himself as a ransom for all, the testimony *given* at the proper time. ⁷ For this I was appointed a preacher and an apostle (I am telling the truth, I am not lying) as a teacher of the Gentiles in faith and truth.

2:1 entreaties. The Greek word is from a root that means "to lack," "to be deprived," or "to be without." Thus this kind of prayer occurs because of a need. The lost have a great need for salvation, and believers should always be asking God to meet that need. **petitions.** This word comes from a root meaning "to fall in with someone," or "to draw near so as to speak intimately." The verb from which this word derives is used of Christ's and the Spirit's intercession for believers (Ro 8:26; Heb 7:25). Paul's desire is for the Ephesian Christians to have compassion for the lost, to understand the depths of their pain and misery, and to come intimately to God pleading for their salvation.

2:9 adorn...proper clothing. The Greek word for "adorn" means "to arrange," "to put in order," or "to make ready." A woman is to arrange herself appropriately for the worship service, which includes wearing decent clothing which reflects a properly adorned chaste heart. **modestly and discreetly.** "Modestly" refers to modesty mixed with humility, which carries the underlying idea of shame. It can also refer to a rejection of anything dishonorable to God, or refer to grief over sin. "Discreetly" basically refers to self-control over sexual passions. Godly women hate sin and control their passions so as not to lead another into sin.

⁸ Therefore I want the men in every place to pray, lifting up holy hands, without wrath and dissension. ⁹ Likewise, *I want* women to adorn themselves with proper clothing, modestly and discreetly, not with braided hair and gold or pearls or costly garments, ¹⁰ but rather by means of good works, as is proper for women making a claim to godliness. ¹¹ A woman must quietly receive instruction with entire submissiveness. ¹² But I do not allow a woman to teach or exercise authority over a man, but to remain quiet. ¹³ For it was Adam who was first created, *and* then Eve. ¹⁴ And *it was* not Adam *who* was deceived, but the woman being deceived, fell into transgression. ¹⁵ But *women* will be preserved through the bearing of children if they continue in faith and love and sanctity with self-restraint.

DAY 23: What is the "New Covenant" in Jeremiah 31:31-34?

God announced here the coming establishment of a New Covenant with His people. This covenant will be different from the one "I made with their fathers in the day I took them by the hand to bring them out of the land of Egypt, My covenant which they broke." The New Covenant is given in these terms: "I will put My law within them and on their heart I will write it; and I will be their God, and they shall be My people."

The fulfillment of this New Covenant was to individuals, as well as to Israel as a nation (v. 36; Ro 11:16–27). It is set 1) in the framework of a reestablishment in their land (vv. 38–40 and chaps. 30–33) and 2) in the time after the ultimate difficulty (30:7).

In principle, this covenant, also announced by Jesus Christ (Lk 22:20), began to be exercised with spiritual aspects realized for Jewish and Gentile believers in the church era (1Co 11:25; Heb 8:7–13; 9:15; 10:14–17; 12:24; 13:20). It has already begun to take effect with "a remnant according to God's gracious choice" (Ro 11:5). The New Covenant will be also realized by the people of Israel in the last days, including the regathering to their ancient land, Palestine (chaps. 30–33). The streams of the Abrahamic, Davidic, and New Covenants find their confluence in the millennial kingdom ruled over by the Messiah.

OCTOBER 24

Jeremiah 33:1–34:22

33 Then the word of the LORD came to Jeremiah the second time, while he was still confined in the court of the guard, saying, ² "Thus says the LORD who made *the earth,* the LORD who formed it to establish it, the LORD is His name, ³ 'Call to Me and I will answer you, and I will tell you great and mighty things, which you do not know.' ⁴ For thus says the LORD God of Israel concerning the houses of this city, and concerning the houses of the kings of Judah which are broken down *to make a defense* against the siege ramps and against the sword, ⁵ 'While *they* are coming to fight with the Chaldeans and to fill them with the corpses of men whom I have slain in My anger and in My wrath, and I have hidden My face from this city because of all their wickedness: ⁶ Behold, I will bring to it health and healing, and I will heal them; and I will reveal to them an abundance of peace and truth. ⁷ I will restore the fortunes of Judah and the fortunes of Israel and will rebuild them as they were at first. ⁸ I will cleanse them from all their iniquity by which they have sinned against Me, and I will pardon all their iniquities by which they have sinned against Me and by which they have transgressed against Me. ⁹ It will be to Me a name of joy, praise and glory before all the nations of the earth which will hear of all the good that I do for them, and they will fear and tremble because of all the good and all the peace that I make for it.'

¹⁰ "Thus says the LORD, 'Yet again there will be heard in this place, of which you say, "It is a waste, without man and without beast," *that is,* in the cities of Judah and in the streets of Jerusalem that are desolate, without man and without inhabitant and without beast, ¹¹ the voice of joy and the voice of gladness, the voice of the bridegroom and the voice of the bride, the voice of those who say,

"Give thanks to the LORD of hosts,
For the LORD is good,
For His lovingkindness
is everlasting";

and of those who bring a thank offering into the house of the LORD. For I will restore the fortunes of the land as they were at first,' says the LORD.

¹² "Thus says the LORD of hosts, 'There will again be in this place which is waste, without man or beast, and in all its cities, a habitation of shepherds who rest their flocks. ¹³ In the cities of the hill country, in the cities of the lowland, in the cities of the Negev, in the land of Benjamin, in the environs of Jerusalem and in the cities of Judah, the flocks will again pass under the hands of the one who numbers them,' says the LORD.

¹⁴ 'Behold, days are coming,' declares the LORD, 'when I will fulfill the good word which I have spoken concerning the house of Israel and the house of Judah. ¹⁵ In those days and at that time I will cause a righteous Branch of David to spring forth; and He shall execute justice and righteousness on the earth. ¹⁶ In those days Judah will be saved and Jerusalem will dwell in safety; and this is *the name* by which she will be called: the LORD is our righteousness.' ¹⁷ For thus says the LORD, 'David shall never lack a man to sit on the throne of the house of Israel; ¹⁸ and the Levitical priests shall never lack a man before Me to offer burnt offerings, to burn grain offerings and to prepare sacrifices continually.'"

¹⁹ The word of the LORD came to Jeremiah, saying, ²⁰ "Thus says the LORD, 'If you

33:15 a righteous Branch. This is the Messiah King in David's lineage. He is the King whose reign immediately follows the second coming when He appears in power (Da 2:35, 45; 7:13–14, 27; Mt 16:27–28; 24:30; 26:64).

can break My covenant for the day and My covenant for the night, so that day and night will not be at their appointed time, ²¹then My covenant may also be broken with David My servant so that he will not have a son to reign on his throne, and with the Levitical priests, My ministers. ²²As the host of heaven cannot be counted and the sand of the sea cannot be measured, so I will multiply the descendants of David My servant and the Levites who minister to Me.'"

²³And the word of the LORD came to Jeremiah, saying, ²⁴"Have you not observed what this people have spoken, saying, 'The two families which the LORD chose, He has rejected them'? Thus they despise My people, no longer are they as a nation in their sight. ²⁵Thus says the LORD, 'If My covenant for day and night stand not, and the fixed patterns of heaven and earth I have not established, ²⁶then I would reject the descendants of Jacob and David My servant, not taking from his descendants rulers over the descendants of Abraham, Isaac and Jacob. But I will restore their fortunes and will have mercy on them.'"

34 The word which came to Jeremiah from the LORD, when Nebuchadnezzar king of Babylon and all his army, with all the kingdoms of the earth that were under his dominion and all the peoples, were fighting against Jerusalem and against all its cities, saying, ²"Thus says the LORD God of Israel, 'Go and speak to Zedekiah king of Judah and say to him: "Thus says the LORD, 'Behold, I am giving this city into the hand of the king of Babylon, and he will burn it with fire. ³You will not escape from his hand, for you will surely be captured and delivered into his hand; and you will see the king of Babylon eye to eye, and he will speak with you face to face, and you will go to Babylon.'"' ⁴Yet hear the word of the LORD, O Zedekiah king of Judah! Thus says the LORD concerning you, 'You will not die by the sword. ⁵You will die in peace; and as spices were burned for your fathers, the former kings who were before you, so they will burn spices for you; and they will lament for you, "Alas, lord!"' For I have spoken the word," declares the LORD.

⁶Then Jeremiah the prophet spoke all these words to Zedekiah king of Judah in Jerusalem ⁷when the army of the king of Babylon was fighting against Jerusalem and against all the remaining cities of Judah, that is, Lachish and Azekah, for they alone remained as fortified cities among the cities of Judah.

⁸The word which came to Jeremiah from the LORD after King Zedekiah had made a covenant with all the people who were in Jerusalem to proclaim release to them: ⁹that each man should set free his male servant and each man his female servant, a Hebrew man or a Hebrew woman; so that no one should keep them, a Jew his brother, in bondage. ¹⁰And all the officials and all the people obeyed who had entered into the covenant that each man should set free his male servant and each man his female servant, so that no one should keep them any longer in bondage; they obeyed, and set them free. ¹¹But afterward they turned around and took back the male servants and the female servants whom they had set free, and brought them into subjection for male servants and for female servants.

¹²Then the word of the LORD came to Jeremiah from the LORD, saying, ¹³"Thus says the LORD God of Israel, 'I made a covenant with your forefathers in the day that I brought them out of the land of Egypt, from the house of bondage, saying, ¹⁴"At the end of seven years each of you shall set free his Hebrew brother who has been sold to you and has served you six years, you shall send him out free from you; but your forefathers did not obey Me or incline their ear to Me. ¹⁵Although recently you had turned and done what is right in My sight, each man proclaiming release to his neighbor, and you had made a covenant before Me in the house which is called by My name. ¹⁶Yet you turned and profaned My name, and each man took back his male servant and each man his female servant whom you had set free according to their desire, and you brought them into subjection to be your male servants and female servants."'

¹⁷"Therefore thus says the LORD, 'You have not obeyed Me in proclaiming release each man to his brother and each man to his neighbor. Behold, I am proclaiming a release to you,' declares the LORD, 'to the sword, to the pestilence and to the famine; and I will make you a terror to all the kingdoms of the earth. ¹⁸I will give the men who have transgressed My covenant, who have not fulfilled the words of the covenant which they made before Me, when they cut the calf in two and passed between its parts— ¹⁹the officials of Judah and the officials of Jerusalem, the court officers and the priests and all the people of the land who passed between the parts of the calf— ²⁰I will give them into the hand of their enemies and into the hand of those who seek their life. And their dead bodies will be food for the birds of the sky and the

34:18, 21 cut the calf in two. God will give the guilty over to death before the conqueror, for they denied the covenant ratified by blood (v. 21). In this custom, as in Genesis 15:8–17, two parties laid out parts of a sacrifice on two sides, then walked between the parts. By that symbolic action each pledged to fulfill his promise, agreeing in effect, "May my life (represented by the blood) be poured out if I fail to honor my part."

beasts of the earth. ²¹ Zedekiah king of Judah and his officials I will give into the hand of their enemies and into the hand of those who seek their life, and into the hand of the army of the king of Babylon which has gone away from you. ²² Behold, I am going to command,' declares the LORD, 'and I will bring them back to this city; and they will fight against it and take it and burn it with fire; and I will make the cities of Judah a desolation without inhabitant.'"

Psalm 119:57–64

ח HETH.

⁵⁷ The LORD is my portion;
I have promised to
keep Your words.
⁵⁸ I sought Your favor
with all *my* heart;
Be gracious to me according
to Your word.
⁵⁹ I considered my ways
And turned my feet to
Your testimonies.
⁶⁰ I hastened and did not delay
To keep Your commandments.
⁶¹ The cords of the wicked
have encircled me,
But I have not forgotten Your law.
⁶² At midnight I shall rise to
give thanks to You
Because of Your righteous ordinances.
⁶³ I am a companion of all
those who fear You,
And of those who keep Your precepts.
⁶⁴ The earth is full of Your
lovingkindness, O LORD;
Teach me Your statutes.

Proverbs 27:21

²¹ The crucible is for silver and
the furnace for gold,
And each *is tested* by the
praise accorded him.

3:1 aspires…desires. Two different Greek words are used. The first means "to reach out after." It describes external action, not internal motive. The second means "a strong passion," and refers to an inward desire. Taken together, these two words aptly describe the type of man who belongs in the ministry—one who outwardly pursues it because he is driven by a strong internal desire. **overseer.** The word identifies the men who are responsible to lead the church (5:17; 1Th 5:12; Heb 13:7). In the New Testament the words "elder," "overseer," and "pastor" are used interchangeably to describe the same men (Ac 20:17, 28; Titus 1:5–9; 1Pe 5:1–2). Pastors are responsible to lead (5:17), preach and teach (5:17), help the spiritually weak (1Th 5:12–14), care for the church (1Pe 5:1–2), and ordain other leaders (4:14).

1 Timothy 3:1–16

3 It is a trustworthy statement: if any man aspires to the office of overseer, it is a fine work he desires *to do.* ² An overseer, then, must be above reproach, the husband of one wife, temperate, prudent, respectable, hospitable, able to teach, ³ not addicted to wine or pugnacious, but gentle, peaceable, free from the love of money. ⁴ *He must be* one who manages his own household well, keeping his children under control with all dignity ⁵ (but if a man does not know how to manage his own household, how will he take care of the church of God?), ⁶ *and* not a new convert, so that he will not become conceited and fall into the condemnation incurred by the devil. ⁷ And he must have a good reputation with those outside *the church,* so that he will not fall into reproach and the snare of the devil.

⁸ Deacons likewise *must be* men of dignity, not double-tongued, or addicted to much wine

3:6 not a new convert…not become conceited. Putting a new convert into a leadership role would tempt him to pride. Elders, therefore, are to be drawn from the spiritually mature men of the congregation. **fall into the condemnation incurred by the devil.** Satan's condemnation was due to pride over his position. It resulted in his fall from honor and authority. The same kind of fall and judgment could easily happen to a new and weak believer put in a position of spiritual leadership.

or fond of sordid gain, ⁹but holding to the mystery of the faith with a clear conscience. ¹⁰These men must also first be tested; then let them serve as deacons if they are beyond reproach. ¹¹Women *must* likewise *be* dignified, not malicious gossips, but temperate, faithful in all things. ¹²Deacons must be husbands of *only* one wife, *and* good managers of *their* children and their own households. ¹³For those who have served well as deacons obtain for themselves a high standing and great confidence in the faith that is in Christ Jesus.

¹⁴I am writing these things to you, hoping to come to you before long; ¹⁵but in case I am delayed, *I write* so that you will know how one ought to conduct himself in the household of God, which is the church of the living God, the pillar and support of the truth. ¹⁶By common confession, great is the mystery of godliness:

3:8 Deacons. From a word group meaning "to serve." Originally referring to menial tasks such as waiting on tables (Ac 6:1–4), "deacon" came to denote any service in the church. Deacons serve under the leadership of elders, helping them exercise oversight in the practical matters of church life. Scripture defines no official or specific responsibilities for deacons; they are to do whatever the elders assign them or whatever spiritual ministry is necessary.

He who was revealed in the flesh,
Was vindicated in the Spirit,
Seen by angels,
Proclaimed among the nations,
Believed on in the world,
Taken up in glory.

DAY 24: What does it mean for an elder to be "the husband of one wife"?

In 1 Timothy 3:2, the Greek is literally a "one-woman man." This says nothing about marriage or divorce (v. 4). The issue is not the elder's marital status but his moral and sexual purity. This qualification heads the list, because it is in this area that leaders are most prone to fail. Various interpretations of this qualification have been offered. Some see it as a prohibition against polygamy—an unnecessary injunction since polygamy was not common in Roman society and clearly forbidden by Scripture (Ge 2:24), the teaching of Jesus (Mt 19:5, 6; Mk 10:6–9), and Paul (Eph 5:31). A polygamist could not even have been a church member, let alone a church leader. Others see this requirement as barring those who remarried after the death of their wives. But, as already noted, the issue is sexual purity, not marital status. Further, the Bible encourages remarriage after widowhood (5:14; 1Co 7:39). Some believe that Paul here excludes divorced men from church leadership. That again ignores the fact that this qualification does not deal with marital status. Nor does the Bible prohibit all remarriage after divorce (Mt 5:31–32; 19:9; 1Co 7:15). Finally, some think that this requirement excludes single men from church leadership. But if that were Paul's intent, he would have disqualified himself (1Co 7:8).

A "one-woman man" is one totally devoted to his wife, maintaining singular devotion, affection, and sexual purity in both thought and deed. To violate this is to forfeit blamelessness and no longer be "above reproach" (Titus 1:6–7).

OCTOBER 25

Jeremiah 35:1–36:32

35 The word which came to Jeremiah from the LORD in the days of Jehoiakim the son of Josiah, king of Judah, saying, ²"Go to the house of the Rechabites and speak to them, and bring them into the house of the LORD, into one of the chambers, and give them wine to drink." ³Then I took Jaazaniah the son of Jeremiah, son of Habazziniah, and his brothers and all his sons and the whole house of the Rechabites, ⁴and I brought them into the house of the LORD, into the chamber of the sons of Hanan the son of

Igdaliah, the man of God, which was near the chamber of the officials, which was above the chamber of Maaseiah the son of Shallum, the doorkeeper. ⁵Then I set before the men of the house of the Rechabites pitchers full of wine and cups; and I said to them, "Drink wine!" ⁶But they said, "We will not drink wine, for Jonadab the son of Rechab, our father, commanded us, saying, 'You shall not drink wine, you or your sons, forever. ⁷You shall not build a house, and you shall not sow seed and you shall not plant a vineyard or own one; but in tents you shall dwell all your days, that you may live many days in the land where you sojourn.' ⁸We have obeyed the voice of Jonadab the son of Rechab, our father, in all

that he commanded us, not to drink wine all our days, we, our wives, our sons or our daughters, ⁹nor to build ourselves houses to dwell in; and we do not have vineyard or field or seed. ¹⁰We have only dwelt in tents, and have obeyed and have done according to all that Jonadab our father commanded us. ¹¹But when Nebuchadnezzar king of Babylon came up against the land, we said, 'Come and let us go to Jerusalem before the army of the Chaldeans and before the army of the Arameans.' So we have dwelt in Jerusalem."

¹²Then the word of the LORD came to Jeremiah, saying, ¹³"Thus says the LORD of hosts, the God of Israel, 'Go and say to the men of Judah and the inhabitants of Jerusalem, "Will you not receive instruction by listening to My words?" declares the LORD. ¹⁴"The words of Jonadab the son of Rechab, which he commanded his sons not to drink wine, are observed. So they do not drink wine to this day, for they have obeyed their father's command. But I have spoken to you again and again; yet you have not listened to Me. ¹⁵Also I have sent to you all My servants the prophets, sending them again and again, saying: 'Turn now every man from his evil way and amend your deeds, and do not go after other gods to worship them. Then you will dwell in the land which I have given to you and to your forefathers; but you have not inclined your ear or listened to Me. ¹⁶Indeed, the sons of Jonadab the son of Rechab have observed the command of their father which he commanded them, but this people has not listened to Me.'" ¹⁷Therefore thus says the LORD, the God of hosts, the God of Israel, 'Behold, I am bringing on Judah and on all the inhabitants of Jerusalem all the disaster that I have pronounced against them; because I spoke to them but they did not listen, and I have called them but they did not answer.'"

¹⁸Then Jeremiah said to the house of the Rechabites, "Thus says the LORD of hosts, the God of Israel, 'Because you have obeyed the command of Jonadab your father, kept all his commands and done according to all that he commanded you; ¹⁹therefore thus says the LORD of hosts, the God of Israel, "Jonadab the son of Rechab shall not lack a man to stand before Me always."'"

36 In the fourth year of Jehoiakim the son of Josiah, king of Judah, this word came to Jeremiah from the LORD, saying, ²"Take a scroll and write on it all the words which I have spoken to you concerning Israel and concerning Judah, and concerning all the nations, from the day I first spoke to you, from the days of Josiah, even to this day. ³Perhaps the house of Judah will hear all the calamity which I plan to bring on them, in order that every man will turn from his evil way; then I will forgive their iniquity and their sin."

⁴Then Jeremiah called Baruch the son of Neriah, and Baruch wrote on a scroll at the dictation of Jeremiah all the words of the LORD which He had spoken to him. ⁵Jeremiah commanded Baruch, saying, "I am restricted; I cannot go into the house of the LORD. ⁶So you go and read from the scroll which you have written at my dictation the words of the LORD to the people in the LORD's house on a fast day. And also you shall read them to all the people of Judah who come from their cities. ⁷Perhaps their supplication will come before the LORD, and everyone will turn from his evil way, for great is the anger and the wrath that the LORD has pronounced against this people." ⁸Baruch the son of Neriah did according to all that Jeremiah the prophet commanded him, reading from the book the words of the LORD in the LORD's house.

36:4 Baruch wrote. Jeremiah's recording secretary wrote the prophet's messages and penned them a second time after the first scroll was burned (36:32). He also read the messages in the temple (v. 10) and in the palace (v. 15). Later, Jehudi read a small part of the first scroll before King Jehoiakim (vv. 21–23).

⁹Now in the fifth year of Jehoiakim the son of Josiah, king of Judah, in the ninth month, all the people in Jerusalem and all the people who came from the cities of Judah to Jerusalem proclaimed a fast before the LORD. ¹⁰Then Baruch read from the book the words of Jeremiah in the house of the LORD in the chamber of Gemariah the son of Shaphan the scribe, in the upper court, at the entry of the New Gate of the LORD's house, to all the people.

¹¹Now when Micaiah the son of Gemariah, the son of Shaphan, had heard all the words of the LORD from the book, ¹²he went down to the king's house, into the scribe's chamber. And behold, all the officials were sitting there—Elishama the scribe, and Delaiah the son of Shemaiah, and Elnathan the son of Achbor, and Gemariah the son of Shaphan, and Zedekiah the son of Hananiah, and all the other officials. ¹³Micaiah declared to them all the words that he had heard when Baruch read from the book to the people. ¹⁴Then all

the officials sent Jehudi the son of Nethaniah, the son of Shelemiah, the son of Cushi, to Baruch, saying, "Take in your hand the scroll from which you have read to the people and come." So Baruch the son of Neriah took the scroll in his hand and went to them. ¹⁵They said to him, "Sit down, please, and read it to us." So Baruch read it to them. ¹⁶When they had heard all the words, they turned in fear one to another and said to Baruch, "We will surely report all these words to the king." ¹⁷And they asked Baruch, saying, "Tell us, please, how did you write all these words? *Was it* at his dictation?" ¹⁸Then Baruch said to them, "He dictated all these words to me, and I wrote them with ink on the book." ¹⁹Then the officials said to Baruch, "Go, hide yourself, you and Jeremiah, and do not let anyone know where you are."

²⁰So they went to the king in the court, but they had deposited the scroll in the chamber of Elishama the scribe, and they reported all the words to the king. ²¹Then the king sent Jehudi to get the scroll, and he took it out of the chamber of Elishama the scribe. And Jehudi read it to the king as well as to all the officials who stood beside the king. ²²Now the king was sitting in the winter house in the ninth month, with *a fire* burning in the brazier before him. ²³When Jehudi had read three or four columns, *the king* cut it with a scribe's knife and threw *it* into the fire that was in the brazier, until all the scroll was consumed in the fire that was in the brazier. ²⁴Yet the king and all his servants who heard all these words were not afraid, nor did they rend their garments. ²⁵Even though Elnathan and Delaiah and Gemariah pleaded with the king not to burn the scroll, he would not listen to them. ²⁶And the king commanded Jerahmeel the king's son, Seraiah the son of Azriel, and Shelemiah the son of Abdeel to seize Baruch the scribe and Jeremiah the prophet, but the LORD hid them.

²⁷Then the word of the LORD came to Jeremiah after the king had burned the scroll and the words which Baruch had written at the dictation of Jeremiah, saying, ²⁸"Take again another scroll and write on it all the former words that were on the first scroll which Jehoiakim the king of Judah burned. ²⁹And concerning Jehoiakim king of Judah you shall say, 'Thus says the LORD, "You have burned this scroll, saying, 'Why have you written on it that the king of Babylon will certainly come and destroy this land, and will make man and beast to cease from it?' " ³⁰Therefore thus says the LORD concerning Jehoiakim king of Judah, "He shall have no one to sit on the throne of David, and his dead body shall be cast out to the heat of the day and the frost of the night. ³¹I will also punish him and his descendants and his servants for their iniquity, and I will bring on them and the inhabitants of Jerusalem and the men of Judah all the calamity that I have declared to them—but they did not listen." ' "

³²Then Jeremiah took another scroll and gave it to Baruch the son of Neriah, the scribe, and he wrote on it at the dictation of Jeremiah all the words of the book which Jehoiakim king of Judah had burned in the fire; and many similar words were added to them.

Psalm 119:65–72

ט TETH.

⁶⁵ You have dealt well
  with Your servant,
 O LORD, according to Your word.
⁶⁶ Teach me good discernment
  and knowledge,
 For I believe in Your
  commandments.
⁶⁷ Before I was afflicted I went astray,
 But now I keep Your word.
⁶⁸ You are good and do good;
 Teach me Your statutes.
⁶⁹ The arrogant have forged
  a lie against me;
 With all *my* heart I will
  observe Your precepts.
⁷⁰ Their heart is covered with fat,
 But I delight in Your law.
⁷¹ It is good for me that I was afflicted,
 That I may learn Your statutes.
⁷² The law of Your mouth is better to me
 Than thousands of gold
  and silver *pieces.*

36:23 cut it. As often as Jehudi read "three or four columns," the king cut it up, doing so all the way through the whole scroll because he rejected the message (v. 29). Jehoiakim is the king who sent men to Egypt (chap. 26) to bring back God's faithful prophet, Uriah, so that he could execute him.

Proverbs 27:22

²² Though you pound a fool in a
  mortar with a pestle along
  with crushed grain,
 Yet his foolishness will not
  depart from him.

1 Timothy 4:1–16

4 But the Spirit explicitly says that in later times some will fall away from the faith, paying attention to deceitful spirits and doctrines of demons, ² by means of the hypocrisy of liars seared in their own conscience as with a branding iron, ³ *men* who forbid marriage *and advocate* abstaining from foods which God has created to be gratefully shared in by those who believe and know the truth. ⁴ For everything created by God is good, and nothing is to be rejected if it is received with gratitude; ⁵ for it is sanctified by means of the word of God and prayer.

4:6 nourished…words of the faith…sound doctrine. Continual feeding on the truths of Scripture is essential to the spiritual health of all Christians (2Ti 3:16–17), but especially of spiritual leaders like Timothy. Only by reading the Word, studying it, meditating on it, and mastering its contents can a pastor fulfill his mandate (2Ti 2:15). Timothy had been doing so since childhood (2Ti 3:15), and Paul urged him to continue (see v. 16; 2Ti 3:14). "Words of the faith" is a general reference to Scripture, God's revealed truth. "Sound doctrine" indicates the theology Scripture teaches.

4:1 the Spirit explicitly says. Paul repeats to Timothy the warning he had given many years earlier to the Ephesian elders (Ac 20:29–30). The Holy Spirit through the Scriptures has repeatedly warned of the danger of apostasy (Mt 24:4–12; Ac 20:29–30; 2Th 2:3–12; Heb 3:12; 5:11—6:8; 10:26–31; 2Pe 3:3; 1Jn 2:18; Jude 18). **in later times.** The period from the first coming of Christ until His return (Ac 2:16–17; Heb 1:1–2; 9:26; 1Pe 1:20; 1Jn 2:18). Apostasy will exist throughout that period, reaching a climax shortly before Christ returns (Mt 24:12). **fall away from the faith.** Those who fall prey to the false teachers will abandon the Christian faith. The Greek word for "fall away" is the source of the Eng. word "apostatize," and refers to someone moving away from an original position. These are professing or nominal Christians who associate with those who truly believe the gospel, but defect after believing lies and deception, thus revealing their true nature as unconverted. **deceitful spirits.** Those demonic spirits, either directly or through false teachers, who have wandered away from the truth and lead others to do the same. **doctrines of demons.** Not teaching about demons, but false teaching that originates from them. To sit under such teaching is to hear lies from the demonic realm (Eph 6:12; Jas 3:15; 2Jn 7–11). The influence of demons will reach its peak during the Tribulation (2Th 2:9; Rev 9:2–11; 16:14; 20:2–3, 8, 10). Satan and demons constantly work the deceptions that corrupt and pervert God's Word.

⁶ In pointing out these things to the brethren, you will be a good servant of Christ Jesus, *constantly* nourished on the words of the faith and of the sound doctrine which you have been following. ⁷ But have nothing to do with worldly fables fit only for old women. On the other hand, discipline yourself for the purpose of godliness; ⁸ for bodily discipline is only of little profit, but godliness is profitable for all things, since it holds promise for the present life and *also* for the *life* to come. ⁹ It is a trustworthy statement deserving full acceptance. ¹⁰ For it is for this we labor and strive, because we have fixed our hope on the living God, who is the Savior of all men, especially of believers.

¹¹ Prescribe and teach these things. ¹² Let no one look down on your youthfulness, but *rather* in speech, conduct, love, faith *and* purity, show yourself an example of those who believe. ¹³ Until I come, give attention to the *public* reading *of Scripture,* to exhortation and teaching. ¹⁴ Do not neglect the spiritual gift within you, which was bestowed on you through prophetic utterance with the laying on of hands by the presbytery. ¹⁵ Take pains with these things; be *absorbed* in them, so that your progress will be evident to all. ¹⁶ Pay close attention to yourself and to your teaching; persevere in these things, for as you do this you will ensure salvation both for yourself and for those who hear you.

DAY 25: What specific instructions did Paul give Timothy that would apply to a young person?

A young person seeking to live as a disciple of Jesus Christ can find essential guidelines in 4:12–16, where Paul listed five areas (verse 12) in which Timothy was to be an example to the church:

1. In "speech" or word—see also Matthew 12:34–37; Ephesians 4:25, 29, 31.
2. In "conduct" or righteous living—see also Titus 2:10; 1 Peter 1:15; 2:12; 3:16.

3. In "love" or self-sacrificial service for others—see also John 15:13.
4. In "faith" or faithfulness or commitment, not belief—see also 1 Corinthians 4:2.
5. In "purity" and particularly sexual purity—see also 4:2.

The verses that follow hold several other building blocks to a life of discipleship:

1. Timothy was to be involved in the public reading, study, and application of Scripture (v. 13).
2. Timothy was to diligently use his spiritual gift that others had confirmed and affirmed in a public way (v. 14).
3. Timothy was to be committed to a process of progress in his walk with Christ (v. 15).
4. Timothy was to "pay careful attention to yourself and to your teaching" (v. 16).

The priorities of a godly leader should be summed up in Timothy's personal holiness and public teaching. All of Paul's exhortations in vv. 6–16 fit into one or the other of those two categories. By careful attention to his own godly life and faithful preaching of the Word, Timothy would continue to be the human instrument God would use to bring the gospel and to save some who heard him. Though salvation is God's work, it is His pleasure to do it through human instruments.

OCTOBER 26

Jeremiah 37:1–38:28

37 Now Zedekiah the son of Josiah whom Nebuchadnezzar king of Babylon had made king in the land of Judah, reigned as king in place of Coniah the son of Jehoiakim. ² But neither he nor his servants nor the people of the land listened to the words of the LORD which He spoke through Jeremiah the prophet.

³ Yet King Zedekiah sent Jehucal the son of Shelemiah, and Zephaniah the son of Maaseiah, the priest, to Jeremiah the prophet, saying, "Please pray to the LORD our God on our behalf." ⁴ Now Jeremiah was *still* coming in and going out among the people, for they had not *yet* put him in the prison. ⁵ Meanwhile, Pharaoh's army had set out from Egypt; and when the Chaldeans who had been besieging Jerusalem heard the report about them, they lifted the *siege* from Jerusalem.

⁶ Then the word of the LORD came to Jeremiah the prophet, saying, ⁷ "Thus says the LORD God of Israel, 'Thus you are to say to the king of Judah, who sent you to Me to inquire of Me: "Behold, Pharaoh's army which has come out for your assistance is going to return to its own land of Egypt. ⁸ The Chaldeans will also return and fight against this city, and they will capture it and burn it with fire." ⁹ Thus says the LORD, 'Do not deceive yourselves, saying, "The Chaldeans will surely go away from us," for they will not go. ¹⁰ For even if you had defeated the entire army of Chaldeans who were fighting against you, and there were *only* wounded men left among

them, each man in his tent, they would rise up and burn this city with fire.'"

¹¹ Now it happened when the army of the Chaldeans had lifted *the siege* from Jerusalem because of Pharaoh's army, ¹² that Jeremiah went out from Jerusalem to go to the land of Benjamin in order to take possession of *some* property there among the people. ¹³ While he was at the Gate of Benjamin, a captain of the guard whose name was Irijah, the son of Shelemiah the son of Hananiah was there; and he arrested Jeremiah the prophet, saying, "You are going over to the Chaldeans!" ¹⁴ But Jeremiah said, "A lie! I am not going over to the Chaldeans"; yet he would not listen to him. So Irijah arrested Jeremiah and brought him to the officials. ¹⁵ Then the officials were angry at Jeremiah and beat him, and they put him in jail in the house of Jonathan the scribe, which they had made into the prison. ¹⁶ For Jeremiah had come into the dungeon, that is, the vaulted cell; and Jeremiah stayed there many days.

¹⁷ Now King Zedekiah sent and took him *out;* and in his palace the king secretly asked him and said, "Is there a word from the LORD?" And Jeremiah said, "There is!" Then he said, "You will be given into the hand of the king of Babylon!" ¹⁸ Moreover Jeremiah said to King Zedekiah, "*In* what *way* have I sinned against you, or against your servants, or against this people, that you have put me in prison? ¹⁹ Where then are your prophets who prophesied to you, saying, 'The king of Babylon will not come against you or against this land'? ²⁰ But now, please listen, O my lord the king; please let my petition come before you and do not make me return to the house of Jonathan the scribe, that I may not die there."

21 Then King Zedekiah gave commandment, and they committed Jeremiah to the court of the guardhouse and gave him a loaf of bread daily from the bakers' street, until all the bread in the city was gone. So Jeremiah remained in the court of the guardhouse.

38 Now Shephatiah the son of Mattan, and Gedaliah the son of Pashhur, and Jucal the son of Shelemiah, and Pashhur the son of Malchijah heard the words that Jeremiah was speaking to all the people, saying, 2 "Thus says the LORD, 'He who stays in this city will die by the sword and by famine and by pestilence, but he who goes out to the Chaldeans will live and have his *own* life as booty and stay alive.' 3 Thus says the LORD, 'This city will certainly be given into the hand of the army of the king of Babylon and he will capture it.'" 4 Then the officials said to the king, "Now let this man be put to death, inasmuch as he is discouraging the men of war who are left in this city and all the people, by speaking such words to them; for this man is not seeking the well-being of this people but rather their harm." 5 So King Zedekiah said, "Behold, he is in your hands; for the king can *do* nothing against you." 6 Then they took Jeremiah and cast him into the cistern *of* Malchijah the king's son, which was in the court of the guardhouse; and they let Jeremiah down with ropes. Now in the cistern there was no water but only mud, and Jeremiah sank into the mud. 7 But Ebed-melech the Ethiopian, a eunuch, while he was in the king's palace, heard that they had put Jeremiah into the cistern. Now the king was sitting in the Gate of Benjamin; 8 and Ebed-melech went out from the king's palace and spoke to the king, saying, 9 "My lord the king, these men have acted wickedly in all that they have done to Jeremiah the prophet whom they have cast into the cistern; and he will die right where he is because of the famine, for there is no more bread in the city." 10 Then the king commanded Ebed-melech the Ethiopian, saying, "Take thirty men from here under your authority and bring up Jeremiah the prophet from the cistern before he dies." 11 So Ebed-melech took the men under his authority and went into the king's palace to *a place* beneath the storeroom and took from

there worn-out clothes and worn-out rags and let them down by ropes into the cistern to Jeremiah. 12 Then Ebed-melech the Ethiopian said to Jeremiah, "Now put these worn-out clothes and rags under your armpits under the ropes"; and Jeremiah did so. 13 So they pulled Jeremiah up with the ropes and lifted him out of the cistern, and Jeremiah stayed in the court of the guardhouse.

14 Then King Zedekiah sent and had Jeremiah the prophet brought to him at the third entrance that is in the house of the LORD; and the king said to Jeremiah, "I am going to ask you something; do not hide anything from me." 15 Then Jeremiah said to Zedekiah, "If I tell you, will you not certainly put me to death? Besides, if I give you advice, you will not listen to me." 16 But King Zedekiah swore to Jeremiah in secret saying, "As the LORD lives, who made this life for us, surely I will not put you to death nor will I give you over to the hand of these men who are seeking your life."

17 Then Jeremiah said to Zedekiah, "Thus says the LORD God of hosts, the God of Israel, 'If you will indeed go out to the officers of the king of Babylon, then you will live, this city will not be burned with fire, and you and your household will survive. 18 But if you will not go out to the officers of the king of Babylon, then this city will be given over to the hand of the Chaldeans; and they will burn it with fire, and you yourself will not escape from their hand.'" 19 Then King Zedekiah said to Jeremiah, "I dread the Jews who have gone over to the Chaldeans, for they may give me over into their hand and they will abuse me." 20 But Jeremiah said, "They will not give you over. Please obey the LORD in what I am saying to you, that it may go well with you and you may live. 21 But if you keep refusing to go out, this is the word which the LORD has shown me: 22 'Then behold, all of the women who have been left in the palace of the king of Judah are going to be brought out to the officers of the king of Babylon; and those women will say,

"Your close friends
Have misled and overpowered you;
While your feet were sunk in the mire,
They turned back."

23 They will also bring out all your wives and your sons to the Chaldeans, and you yourself will not escape from their hand, but will be seized by the hand of the king of Babylon, and this city will be burned with fire.'"

24 Then Zedekiah said to Jeremiah, "Let no man know about these words and you will

38:6 no water but only mud. The murderous princes (v. 4) would let God's spokesman die of thirst, hunger, hypothermia, or suffocation if he sank too deeply into the bottom of the cistern.

not die. ²⁵ But if the officials hear that I have talked with you and come to you and say to you, 'Tell us now what you said to the king and what the king said to you; do not hide *it* from us and we will not put you to death,' ²⁶ then you are to say to them, 'I was presenting my petition before the king, not to make me return to the house of Jonathan to die there.'" ²⁷ Then all the officials came to Jeremiah and questioned him. So he reported to them in accordance with all these words which the king had commanded; and they ceased speaking with him, since the conversation had not been overheard. ²⁸ So Jeremiah stayed in the court of the guardhouse until the day that Jerusalem was captured.

Psalm 119:73–80

ᵀ YODH.

⁷³ Your hands made me and
fashioned me;
Give me understanding, that I may
learn Your commandments.
⁷⁴ May those who fear You
see me and be glad,
Because I wait for Your word.
⁷⁵ I know, O LORD, that Your
judgments are righteous,
And that in faithfulness You
have afflicted me.
⁷⁶ O may Your lovingkindness
comfort me,
According to Your word
to Your servant.
⁷⁷ May Your compassion come to
me that I may live,
For Your law is my delight.
⁷⁸ May the arrogant be ashamed, for
they subvert me with a lie;
But I shall meditate on Your precepts.
⁷⁹ May those who fear You turn to me,
Even those who know
Your testimonies.
⁸⁰ May my heart be blameless
in Your statutes,
So that I will not be ashamed.

Proverbs 27:23–27

²³ Know well the condition
of your flocks,
And pay attention to your herds;
²⁴ For riches are not forever,
Nor does a crown *endure*
to all generations.
²⁵ *When* the grass disappears,
the new growth is seen,
And the herbs of the mountains
are gathered in,

²⁶ The lambs *will be* for your clothing,
And the goats *will bring*
the price of a field,
²⁷ And *there will be* goats' milk
enough for your food,
For the food of your household,
And sustenance for your maidens.

1 Timothy 5:1–25

5 Do not sharply rebuke an older man, but *rather* appeal to *him* as a father, *to* the younger men as brothers, ² the older women as mothers, *and* the younger women as sisters, in all purity.

³ Honor widows who are widows indeed; ⁴ but if any widow has children or grandchildren, they must first learn to practice piety in regard to their own family and to make some return to their parents; for this is acceptable in the sight of God. ⁵ Now she who is a widow indeed and who has been left alone, has fixed her hope on God and continues in entreaties and prayers night and day. ⁶ But she who gives herself to wanton pleasure is dead even while she lives. ⁷ Prescribe these things as well, so that they may be above reproach. ⁸ But if anyone does not provide for his own, and especially for those of his household, he has denied the faith and is worse than an unbeliever.

5:3 Honor. "To show respect or care," "to support," or "to treat graciously." Although it includes meeting all kinds of needs, Paul had in mind here not only this broad definition, but primarily financial support (Ex 20:12; Mt 15:1–6; 27:9). **widows indeed.** Not all widows are truly alone and without resources. Financial support from the church is mandatory only for widows who have no means to provide for their daily needs.

⁹ A widow is to be put on the list only if she is not less than sixty years old, *having been* the wife of one man, ¹⁰ having a reputation for good works; *and* if she has brought up children, if she has shown hospitality to strangers, if she has washed the saints' feet, if she has assisted those in distress, *and* if she has devoted herself to every good work. ¹¹ But refuse *to put* younger widows *on the list,* for when they feel sensual desires in disregard of Christ, they want to get married, ¹² *thus* incurring condemnation, because they have set aside their previous pledge. ¹³ At the same time they also learn *to be* idle, as they go around from house to house; and not merely

idle, but also gossips and busybodies, talking about things not proper *to mention*. ¹⁴ Therefore, I want younger *widows* to get married, bear children, keep house, *and* give the enemy no occasion for reproach; ¹⁵ for some have already turned aside to follow Satan. ¹⁶ If any woman who is a believer has *dependent* widows, she must assist them and the church must not be burdened, so that it may assist those who are widows indeed.

¹⁷ The elders who rule well are to be considered worthy of double honor, especially those who work hard at preaching and teaching. ¹⁸ For the Scripture says, "You shall not muzzle the ox while he is threshing," and "The laborer is worthy of his wages." ¹⁹ Do not receive an accusation against an elder except on the basis of two or three witnesses. ²⁰ Those who continue in sin, rebuke in the presence of all, so that the rest also will be fearful *of sinning*. ²¹ I solemnly charge you in the presence of God and of Christ Jesus and of *His* chosen angels, to maintain these *principles* without bias, doing nothing in a *spirit of* partiality. ²² Do not lay hands upon anyone *too* hastily and thereby share *responsibility for* the sins of others; keep yourself free from sin.

²³ No longer drink water *exclusively*, but use a little wine for the sake of your stomach and your frequent ailments.

²⁴ The sins of some men are quite evident, going before them to judgment; for others, their *sins* follow after. ²⁵ Likewise also, deeds that are good are quite evident, and those which are otherwise cannot be concealed.

5:17 elders. This identifies the "overseer" (3:1) or bishop, who is also called pastor (Eph 4:11). **rule well.** Elders are spiritual rulers in the church. **double honor.** Elders who serve with greater commitment, excellence, and effort should have greater acknowledgment from their congregations. This expression does not mean such men should receive exactly twice as much remuneration as others, but because they have earned such respect they should be paid more generously. **especially.** Means "chiefly" or "particularly." Implicit is the idea that some elders will work harder than others and be more prominent in ministry. **work hard.** Literally "work to the point of fatigue or exhaustion." The Greek word stresses the effort behind the work more than the amount of work. **preaching and teaching.** The first emphasizes proclamation, along with exhortation and admonition, and calls for a heart response to the Lord. The second is an essential fortification against heresy and puts more stress on instruction.

5:23 No longer drink water *exclusively*. "Water" in the ancient world was often polluted and carried many diseases. Therefore, Paul urged Timothy not to risk illness, not even for the sake of a commitment to abstinence from wine. Apparently, Timothy avoided wine, so as not to place himself in harm's way. **use a little wine…ailments.** Paul wanted Timothy to use wine which, because of fermentation, acted as a disinfectant to protect his health problems due to the harmful effects of impure water.

DAY 26: Why should elders be chosen very carefully?

Paul cautions Timothy: "Do not lay hands upon anyone too hastily" (1Ti 5:22). This regards the ceremony that affirmed a man's suitability for and acceptance into public ministry as an elder/pastor/overseer. This came from the Old Testament practice of laying hands on a sacrificial animal to identify with it (Ex 29:10, 15, 19). "Hastily" refers to proceeding with this ceremony without a thorough investigation and preparation period to be certain of the man's qualifications (as in 3:1–7). "Thereby share responsibility for the sins of others." This refers to the sin of hasty ordination, which makes those responsible culpable for the man's sin of serving as an unqualified elder and, thus, misleading people. "Keep yourself free from sin." Some versions translate this as "pure." Paul wanted Timothy, by not participating in the recognition of unqualified elders, to remain untainted by others' sins. The church desperately needed qualified spiritual leaders, but the selection had to be carefully executed.

In v. 24, Paul adds that "sins of some men are quite evident." The sins of some men are manifest for all to see, thus disqualifying them out of hand for service as elders. "Going before them to judgment." The known sins of the unqualified announce those men's guilt and unfitness before all. "Judgment" refers to the church's process for determining men's suitability to serve as elders. "For others, their sins follow after." The sins of other candidates for elder will come to light in time, perhaps even during the scrutiny of the evaluation process.

The same is true of good works (v. 25). Some are evident; others come to light later. Time and truth go hand in hand. The whole emphasis in this instruction regarding choosing elders, according to the qualifications of 3:1–7, is to be patient, fair, impartial, and pure (vv. 21–25). Such an approach will yield the right choices.

OCTOBER 27

Jeremiah 39:1–40:16

39 Now when Jerusalem was captured in the ninth year of Zedekiah king of Judah, in the tenth month, Nebuchadnezzar king of Babylon and all his army came to Jerusalem and laid siege to it; ²in the eleventh year of Zedekiah, in the fourth month, in the ninth *day* of the month, the city *wall* was breached. ³Then all the officials of the king of Babylon came in and sat down at the Middle Gate: Nergal-sar-ezer, Samgar-nebu, Sar-sekim the Rab-saris, Nergal-sar-ezer *the* Rab-mag, and all the rest of the officials of the king of Babylon. ⁴When Zedekiah the king of Judah and all the men of war saw them, they fled and went out of the city at night by way of the king's garden through the gate between the two walls; and he went out toward the Arabah. ⁵But the army of the Chaldeans pursued them and overtook Zedekiah in the plains of Jericho; and they seized him and brought him up to Nebuchadnezzar king of Babylon at Riblah in the land of Hamath, and he passed sentence on him. ⁶Then the king of Babylon slew the sons of Zedekiah before his eyes at Riblah; the king of Babylon also slew all the nobles of Judah. ⁷He then blinded Zedekiah's eyes and bound him in fetters of bronze to bring him to Babylon. ⁸The Chaldeans also burned with fire the king's palace and the houses of the people, and they broke down the walls of Jerusalem. ⁹As for the rest of the people who were left in the city, the deserters who had gone over to him and the rest of the people who remained, Nebuzaradan the captain of the bodyguard carried *them* into exile in Babylon. ¹⁰But some of the poorest people who had nothing, Nebuzaradan the captain of the bodyguard left behind in the land of Judah, and gave them vineyards and fields at that time.

¹¹Now Nebuchadnezzar king of Babylon gave orders about Jeremiah through Nebuzaradan the captain of the bodyguard, saying, ¹²"Take him and look after him, and do nothing harmful to him, but rather deal with him just as he tells you." ¹³So Nebuzaradan the captain of the bodyguard sent *word*, along with Nebushazban the Rab-saris, and Nergal-sar-ezer the Rab-mag, and all the leading officers of the king of Babylon; ¹⁴they even sent and took Jeremiah out of the court of the guardhouse and entrusted him to Gedaliah, the son of Ahikam, the son of Shaphan, to take him home. So he stayed among the people.

¹⁵Now the word of the LORD had come to Jeremiah while he was confined in the court of the guardhouse, saying, ¹⁶"Go and speak to Ebed-melech the Ethiopian, saying, 'Thus says the LORD of hosts, the God of Israel, "Behold, I am about to bring My words on this city for disaster and not for prosperity; and they will take place before you on that day. ¹⁷But I will deliver you on that day," declares the LORD, "and you will not be given into the hand of the men whom you dread. ¹⁸For I will certainly rescue you, and you will not fall by the sword; but you will have your *own* life as booty, because you have trusted in Me," declares the LORD.'"

40 The word which came to Jeremiah from the LORD after Nebuzaradan captain of the bodyguard had released him from Ramah, when he had taken him bound in chains among all the exiles of Jerusalem and Judah who were being exiled to Babylon. ²Now the captain of the bodyguard had taken Jeremiah and said to him, "The LORD your God promised this calamity against this place; ³and the LORD has brought *it* on and done just as He promised. Because you *people* sinned against the LORD and did not listen to His voice, therefore this thing has happened to you. ⁴But now, behold, I am freeing you today from the chains which are on your hands. If you would prefer to come with me to Babylon, come *along,* and I will look after you; but if you would prefer not to come with me to Babylon, never mind. Look, the whole land is before you; go wherever it seems good and right for you to go." ⁵As Jeremiah was still not going back, *he said,* "Go on back then to Gedaliah the son of Ahikam, the son of Shaphan, whom the king of Babylon has appointed over the cities of Judah, and stay with him among the people; or else go anywhere it seems right for you to go." So the captain of the bodyguard gave him a ration and a gift and let him go. ⁶Then Jeremiah went to Mizpah to Gedaliah the son of Ahikam and stayed with him among the people who were left in the land.

⁷Now all the commanders of the forces that were in the field, they and their men, heard that the king of Babylon had appointed Gedaliah the son of Ahikam over the land and that he had put him in charge of the men, women and children, those of the poorest of the land who had not been exiled to Babylon. ⁸So they came to Gedaliah at Mizpah, along with Ishmael the son of Nethaniah, and Johanan and Jonathan the sons of Kareah, and Seraiah the son of Tanhumeth, and the sons of Ephai the Netophathite, and Jezaniah the son of the Maacathite, *both* they and their men. ⁹Then

Gedaliah the son of Ahikam, the son of Shaphan, swore to them and to their men, saying, "Do not be afraid of serving the Chaldeans; stay in the land and serve the king of Babylon, that it may go well with you. ¹⁰Now as for me, behold, I am going to stay at Mizpah to stand *for you* before the Chaldeans who come to us; but as for you, gather in wine and summer fruit and oil and put *them* in your *storage* vessels, and live in your cities that you have taken over." ¹¹Likewise, also all the Jews who were in Moab and among the sons of Ammon and in Edom and who were in all the *other* countries, heard that the king of Babylon had left a remnant for Judah, and that he had appointed over them Gedaliah the son of Ahikam, the son of Shaphan. ¹²Then all the Jews returned from all the places to which they had been driven away and came to the land of Judah, to Gedaliah at Mizpah, and gathered in wine and summer fruit in great abundance.

¹³Now Johanan the son of Kareah and all the commanders of the forces that were in the field came to Gedaliah at Mizpah ¹⁴and said to him, "Are you well aware that Baalis the king of the sons of Ammon has sent Ishmael the son of Nethaniah to take your life?" But Gedaliah the son of Ahikam did not believe them. ¹⁵Then Johanan the son of Kareah spoke secretly to Gedaliah in Mizpah, saying, "Let me go and kill Ishmael the son of Nethaniah, and not a man will know! Why should he take your life, so that all the Jews who are gathered to you would be scattered and the remnant of Judah would perish?" ¹⁶But Gedaliah the son of Ahikam said to Johanan the son of Kareah, "Do not do this thing, for you are telling a lie about Ishmael."

Psalm 119:81–88

 כ KAPH.

⁸¹ My soul languishes for Your salvation;
I wait for Your word.
⁸² My eyes fail *with longing*
for Your word,
While I say, "When will
You comfort me?"
⁸³ Though I have become like a
wineskin in the smoke,
I do not forget Your statutes.

119:83 a wineskin in the smoke. Just as smoke will dry out, stiffen, and crack a wineskin, thus making it useless, so the psalmist's affliction has debilitated him.

⁸⁴ How many are the days
of Your servant?
When will You execute judgment
on those who persecute me?
⁸⁵ The arrogant have dug pits for me,
Men who are not in accord
with Your law.
⁸⁶ All Your commandments are faithful;
They have persecuted me
with a lie; help me!
⁸⁷ They almost destroyed me on earth,
But as for me, I did not
forsake Your precepts.
⁸⁸ Revive me according to
Your lovingkindness,
So that I may keep the
testimony of Your mouth.

Proverbs 28:1

28 The wicked flee when no
one is pursuing,
But the righteous are bold as a lion.

28:1 A guilty conscience imagines accusers everywhere (Nu 32:23; Ps 53:5), while a clear conscience has boldness to face everyone.

1 Timothy 6:1–21

6 All who are under the yoke as slaves are to regard their own masters as worthy of all honor so that the name of God and *our* doctrine will not be spoken against. ²Those who have believers as their masters must not be disrespectful to them because they are brethren, but must serve them all the more, because those who partake of the benefit are believers and beloved. Teach and preach these *principles*.

³If anyone advocates a different doctrine and does not agree with sound words, those of our Lord Jesus Christ, and with the doctrine conforming to godliness, ⁴he is conceited *and*

6:3 Paul identifies 3 characteristics of false teachers: 1) they "advocate a different doctrine"—a different teaching that contradicts God's revelation in Scripture; 2) they do "not agree with sound words"—they do not accept sound, healthy teaching, specifically the teaching contained in Scripture (2Pe 3:16); and 3) they reject "doctrine conforming to godliness"—teaching not based on Scripture will always result in an unholy life. Instead of godliness, false teachers will be marked by sin.

understands nothing; but he has a morbid interest in controversial questions and disputes about words, out of which arise envy, strife, abusive language, evil suspicions, ⁵and constant friction between men of depraved mind and deprived of the truth, who suppose that godliness is a means of gain. ⁶But godliness *actually* is a means of great gain when accompanied by contentment. ⁷For we have brought nothing into the world, so we cannot take anything out of it either. ⁸If we have food and covering, with these we shall be content. ⁹But those who want to get rich fall into temptation and a snare and many foolish and harmful desires which plunge men into ruin and destruction. ¹⁰For the love of money is a root of all sorts of evil, and some by longing for it have wandered away from the faith and pierced themselves with many griefs.

¹¹But flee from these things, you man of God, and pursue righteousness, godliness, faith, love, perseverance *and* gentleness. ¹²Fight the good fight of faith; take hold of the eternal life to which you were called, and you made the good confession in the presence of many witnesses. ¹³I charge you in the presence of God, who gives life to all things, and of Christ Jesus, who testified the good confession before Pontius Pilate, ¹⁴that you keep the commandment without stain or reproach until the appearing of our Lord Jesus Christ, ¹⁵which He will bring about at the proper time—He who is the blessed and only Sovereign, the King of kings and Lord of lords, ¹⁶who alone possesses immortality and dwells in unapproachable light, whom no man has seen or can see. To Him *be* honor and eternal dominion! Amen.

¹⁷Instruct those who are rich in this present world not to be conceited or to fix their hope on the uncertainty of riches, but on God, who richly supplies us with all things to enjoy.

¹⁸*Instruct them* to do good, to be rich in good works, to be generous and ready to share, ¹⁹storing up for themselves the treasure of a good foundation for the future, so that they may take hold of that which is life indeed.

²⁰O Timothy, guard what has been entrusted to you, avoiding worldly *and* empty chatter *and* the opposing arguments of what is falsely called "knowledge"— ²¹which some have professed and thus gone astray from the faith.

Grace be with you.

6:12 Fight the good fight of faith. The Greek word for "fight" gives us the Eng. word "agonize," and was used in both military and athletic endeavors to describe the concentration, discipline, and extreme effort needed to win. The "good fight of faith" is the spiritual conflict with Satan's kingdom of darkness in which all men of God are necessarily involved. **take hold of the eternal life.** Paul is here admonishing Timothy to "get a grip" on the reality of the matters associated with eternal life, so that he would live and minister with a heavenly and eternal perspective (Php 3:20; Col 3:2). **to which you were called.** Refers to God's effectual, sovereign call of Timothy to salvation. **good confession.** Timothy's public confession of faith in the Lord Jesus Christ, which likely occurred at his baptism and again when he was ordained to the ministry (4:14; 2Ti 1:6).

6:17–19 Paul counsels Timothy what to teach those who are rich in material possessions, those who have more than the mere essentials of food, clothing, and shelter. Paul does not condemn such people, nor command them to get rid of their wealth. He does call them to be good stewards of their God-given resources (Dt 8:18; 1Sa 2:7; 1Ch 29:12).

DAY 27: How can a believer find genuine contentment?

In 1 Timothy 6:6, the Greek word for "contentment" means "self-sufficiency" and was used by Stoic philosophers to describe a person who was unflappable and unmoved by external circumstances. Christians are to be satisfied and sufficient and not to seek for more than what God has already given them. He is the source of true contentment (2Co 3:5; 9:8; Php 4:11–13, 19).

"Have food and covering...be content" (v. 8). The basic necessities of life are what ought to make Christians content. Paul does not condemn having possessions as long as God graciously provides them (v. 17). He does, however, condemn a self-indulgent desire for money, which results from discontentment.

"Those who want to get rich fall into temptation" (v. 9). "Want," or desire, refers to a settled wish born of reason and clearly describes those guilty of greed. The form of the Greek verb for "fall" indicates that those who have such a desire are continually falling into temptation. Greedy people are compulsive—they are continually trapped in sins by their consuming desire to acquire more. "Into ruin and destruction." Such greed may lead these people to suffer the tragic end of destruction and hell. These terms refer to the eternal punishment of the wicked.

"For the love of money" (v. 10). Literally, "affection for silver." In the context, this sin applies to false teachers specifically, but the principle is true universally. Money itself is not evil since it is a gift from God (Dt 8:18). Paul condemns only the love of it (Mt 6:24), which is so characteristic of false teachers (1Pe 5:2; 2Pe 2:1–3, 15). "Some…have wandered away from the faith." From the body of Christian truth. Gold has replaced God for these apostates, who have turned away from pursuing the things of God in favor of money.

OCTOBER 28

Jeremiah 41:1–42:22

41 In the seventh month Ishmael the son of Nethaniah, the son of Elishama, of the royal family and *one* of the chief officers of the king, along with ten men, came to Mizpah to Gedaliah the son of Ahikam. While they were eating bread together there in Mizpah, ² Ishmael the son of Nethaniah and the ten men who were with him arose and struck down Gedaliah the son of Ahikam, the son of Shaphan, with the sword and put to death the one whom the king of Babylon had appointed over the land. ³ Ishmael also struck down all the Jews who were with him, *that is* with Gedaliah at Mizpah, and the Chaldeans who were found there, the men of war.

⁴ Now it happened on the next day after the killing of Gedaliah, when no one knew about *it,* ⁵ that eighty men came from Shechem, from Shiloh, and from Samaria with their beards shaved off and their clothes torn and their bodies gashed, having grain offerings and incense in their hands to bring to the house of the LORD. ⁶ Then Ishmael the son of Nethaniah went out from Mizpah to meet them, weeping as he went; and as he met them, he said to them, "Come to Gedaliah the son of Ahikam!" ⁷ Yet it turned out that as soon as they came inside the city, Ishmael the son of Nethaniah and the men that were with him slaughtered them *and cast them* into the cistern. ⁸ But ten men who were found among them said to Ishmael, "Do not put us to death; for we have stores of wheat, barley, oil and honey hidden in the field." So he refrained and did not put them to death along with their companions.

⁹ Now as for the cistern where Ishmael had cast all the corpses of the men whom he had struck down because of Gedaliah, it was the one that King Asa had made on account of Baasha, king of Israel; Ishmael the son of Nethaniah filled it with the slain. ¹⁰ Then Ishmael took captive all the remnant of the people who were in Mizpah, the king's

daughters and all the people who were left in Mizpah, whom Nebuzaradan the captain of the bodyguard had put under the charge of Gedaliah the son of Ahikam; thus Ishmael the son of Nethaniah took them captive and proceeded to cross over to the sons of Ammon.

¹¹ But Johanan the son of Kareah and all the commanders of the forces that were with him heard of all the evil that Ishmael the son of Nethaniah had done. ¹² So they took all the men and went to fight with Ishmael the son of Nethaniah and they found him by the great pool that is in Gibeon. ¹³ Now as soon as all the people who were with Ishmael saw Johanan the son of Kareah and the commanders of the forces that were with him, they were glad. ¹⁴ So all the people whom Ishmael had taken captive from Mizpah turned around and came back, and went to Johanan the son of Kareah. ¹⁵ But Ishmael the son of Nethaniah escaped from Johanan with eight men and went to the sons of Ammon. ¹⁶ Then Johanan the son of Kareah and all the commanders of the forces that were with him took from Mizpah all the remnant of the people whom he had recovered from Ishmael the son of Nethaniah, after he had struck down Gedaliah the son of Ahikam, *that is,* the men who were soldiers, *the* women, *the* children, and *the* eunuchs, whom he had brought back from Gibeon. ¹⁷ And they went and stayed in Geruth Chimham, which is beside Bethlehem, in order to proceed into Egypt ¹⁸ because of the Chaldeans; for they were afraid of them, since Ishmael the son of Nethaniah had struck down Gedaliah the son of Ahikam, whom the king of Babylon had appointed over the land.

42 Then all the commanders of the forces, Johanan the son of Kareah, Jezaniah the son of Hoshaiah, and all the people both small and great approached ² and said to Jeremiah the prophet, "Please let our petition come before you, and pray for us to the LORD your God, *that is* for all this remnant; because we are left *but* a few out of many, as your own eyes *now* see us, ³ that the LORD your God may tell us the way in which we should walk and the thing that we should do." ⁴Then Jeremiah the prophet said to them, "I have heard you. Behold, I am going to pray to the LORD your God in accordance with your words; and I will tell you the whole message which the LORD will answer you. I will not keep back a word from you." ⁵Then they said to Jeremiah, "May the LORD be a true and faithful witness against us if we do not act in accordance with the whole message with which the LORD your God will send you to us. ⁶Whether it is pleasant or unpleasant, we will listen to the voice of the LORD our God to whom we are sending you, so that it may go well with us when we listen to the voice of the LORD our God."

⁷Now at the end of ten days the word of the LORD came to Jeremiah. ⁸Then he called for Johanan the son of Kareah and all the commanders of the forces that were with him, and for all the people both small and great, ⁹and said to them, "Thus says the LORD the God of Israel, to whom you sent me to present your petition before Him: ¹⁰'If you will indeed stay in this land, then I will build you up and not tear you down, and I will plant you and not uproot you; for I will relent concerning the calamity that I have inflicted on you. ¹¹Do not be afraid of the king of Babylon, whom you are now fearing; do not be afraid of him,' declares the LORD, 'for I am with you to save you and deliver you from his hand. ¹²I will also show you compassion, so that he will have compassion on you and restore you to your own soil. ¹³But if you are going to say, "We will not stay in this land," so as not to listen to the voice of the LORD your God, ¹⁴saying, "No, but we will go to the land of Egypt, where we will not see war or hear the sound of a trumpet or hunger for bread, and we will stay there"; ¹⁵then in that case listen to the word of the LORD, O remnant of Judah. Thus says the LORD of hosts, the God of Israel, "If you really set your mind to enter Egypt and go in to reside there, ¹⁶then the sword, which you are afraid of, will overtake you there in the land of Egypt; and the famine, about which you are anxious, will follow closely after you there in Egypt, and you will die there. ¹⁷So all the men who set their mind to go to Egypt to reside there will die by the sword, by famine and by pestilence; and they will have no survivors or refugees from the calamity that I am going to bring on them."'"

¹⁸For thus says the LORD of hosts, the God of Israel, "As My anger and wrath have been poured out on the inhabitants of Jerusalem, so My wrath will be poured out on you when you enter Egypt. And you will become a curse, an object of horror, an imprecation and a reproach; and you will see this place no more." ¹⁹The LORD has spoken to you, O remnant of Judah, "Do not go into Egypt!" You should clearly understand that today I have testified against you. ²⁰For you have only deceived yourselves; for it is you who sent me to the LORD your God, saying, "Pray for us to the LORD our God; and whatever the LORD our God says, tell us so, and we will do it." ²¹So I have told you today, but you have not obeyed the LORD your God, even in whatever He has sent me to tell you. ²²Therefore you should now clearly understand that you will die by the sword, by famine and by pestilence, in the place where you wish to go to reside.

Psalm 119:89–96

ל LAMEDH.

⁸⁹ Forever, O LORD,
   Your word is settled in heaven.
⁹⁰ Your faithfulness continues
   throughout all generations;
  You established the earth,
   and it stands.
⁹¹ They stand this day according
   to Your ordinances,
  For all things are Your servants.
⁹² If Your law had not been my delight,
  Then I would have perished
   in my affliction.
⁹³ I will never forget Your precepts,
  For by them You have revived me.
⁹⁴ I am Yours, save me;
  For I have sought Your precepts.
⁹⁵ The wicked wait for me
   to destroy me;
  I shall diligently consider
   Your testimonies.
⁹⁶ I have seen a limit to all perfection;
  Your commandment is
   exceedingly broad.

Proverbs 28:2

² By the transgression of a land
   many are its princes,
  But by a man of understanding
   and knowledge, so it endures.

28:2 many are its princes. Unrighteousness in a nation produces political instability, with many vying for power, thus the tenure of each leader is shortened. Wisdom promotes social order and long rule.

2 Timothy 1:1–18

1 Paul, an apostle of Christ Jesus by the will of God, according to the promise of life in Christ Jesus,

² To Timothy, my beloved son: Grace, mercy *and* peace from God the Father and Christ Jesus our Lord.

³ I thank God, whom I serve with a clear conscience the way my forefathers did, as I constantly remember you in my prayers night and day, ⁴ longing to see you, even as I recall your tears, so that I may be filled with joy. ⁵ For I am mindful of the sincere faith within you, which first dwelt in your grandmother Lois and your mother Eunice, and I am sure that *it is* in you as well. ⁶ For this reason I remind you to kindle afresh the gift of God which is in you through the laying on of my hands. ⁷ For God has not given us a spirit of timidity, but of power and love and discipline.

1:4 recall your tears. Paul perhaps remembered this occurring at their latest parting, which occurred after a short visit to Ephesus, following the writing of 1 Timothy, and prior to Paul's arrest at Troas and his second imprisonment in Rome. Years before, Paul had a similar parting with the elders at Ephesus (Ac 20:36–38).

1:7 a spirit of timidity. The Greek word, which can also be translated "fear," denotes a cowardly, shameful fear caused by a weak, selfish character. The threat of Roman persecution, which was escalating under Nero, the hostility of those in the Ephesian church who resented Timothy's leadership, and the assaults of false teachers with their sophisticated systems of deceptions may have been overwhelming Timothy. But if he was fearful, it didn't come from God. **power.** Positively, God has already given believers all the spiritual resources they need for every trial and threat (Mt 10:19–20). Divine power—effective, productive spiritual energy—belongs to believers (Eph 1:18–20; 3:20; see Zec 4:6). **love.** This kind of love centers on pleasing God and seeking others' welfare before one's own (Ro 14:8; Gal 5:22, 25; Eph 3:19; 1Pe 1:22; 1Jn 4:18). **discipline.** Refers to a self-controlled and properly prioritized mind. This is the opposite of fear and cowardice that cause disorder and confusion. Focusing on the sovereign nature and perfect purposes of our eternal God allows believers to control their lives with godly wisdom and confidence in every situation.

⁸ Therefore do not be ashamed of the testimony of our Lord or of me His prisoner, but join with *me* in suffering for the gospel according to the power of God, ⁹ who has saved us and called us with a holy calling, not according to our works, but according to His own purpose and grace which was granted us in Christ Jesus from all eternity, ¹⁰ but now has been revealed by the appearing of our Savior Christ Jesus, who abolished death and brought life and immortality to light through the gospel, ¹¹ for which I was appointed a preacher and an apostle and a teacher. ¹² For this reason I also suffer these things, but I am not ashamed; for I know whom I have believed and I am convinced that He is able to guard what I have entrusted to Him until that day. ¹³ Retain the standard of sound words which you have heard from me, in the faith and love which are in Christ Jesus. ¹⁴ Guard, through the Holy Spirit who dwells in us, the treasure which has been entrusted to *you.*

¹⁵ You are aware of the fact that all who are in Asia turned away from me, among whom are Phygelus and Hermogenes. ¹⁶ The Lord grant mercy to the house of Onesiphorus, for he often refreshed me and was not ashamed of my chains; ¹⁷ but when he was in Rome, he eagerly searched for me and found me— ¹⁸ the Lord grant to him to find mercy from the Lord on that day—and you know very well what services he rendered at Ephesus.

1:12 I also suffer. Paul had no fear of persecution and death from preaching the gospel in a hostile setting, because he was so confident God had sealed his future glory and blessing. **know whom I have believed.** "Know" describes the certainty of Paul's intimate, saving knowledge—the object of which was God Himself. The form of the Greek verb translated "I have believed" refers to something that began in the past and has continuing results. This knowing is equal to "the knowledge of the truth" (3:7; 1Ti 2:4). **He is able to guard. what I have entrusted.** Paul's life in time and eternity had been given to his Lord. He lived with unwavering confidence and boldness because of the revealed truth about God's power and faithfulness, and his own experience of an unbreakable relationship to the Lord (Ro 8:31–39). **that day.** Also called "day of Christ," when believers will stand before the judgment seat and be rewarded.

DAY 28: Why did Paul write 2 Timothy?

Paul was released from his first Roman imprisonment for a short period of ministry during which he wrote 1 Timothy and Titus. Second Timothy, however, finds Paul once again in a Roman prison (1:16; 2:9), apparently rearrested as part of Nero's persecution of Christians. Unlike Paul's confident hope of release during his first imprisonment (Php 1:19, 25-26; 2:24; Phm 22), this time he had no such hopes (4:6-8). In his first imprisonment in Rome (ca. A.D. 60-62), before Nero had begun the persecution of Christians (A.D. 64), he was only under house arrest and had opportunity for much interaction with people and ministry (Ac 28:16-31). At this time, 5 or 6 years later (ca. A.D. 66-67), however, he was in a cold cell (4:13), in chains (2:9), and with no hope of deliverance (4:6).

Abandoned by virtually all of those close to him for fear of persecution (1:15; 4:9-12, 16) and facing imminent execution, Paul wrote to Timothy, urging him to hasten to Rome for one last visit with the apostle (4:9, 21). Whether Timothy made it to Rome before Paul's execution is not known. According to tradition, Paul was not released from this second Roman imprisonment but suffered the martyrdom he had foreseen (4:6).

In this letter, Paul, aware the end was near, passed the nonapostolic mantle of ministry to Timothy (2:2) and exhorted him to continue faithful in his duties (1:6), hold on to sound doctrine (1:13-14), avoid error (2:15-18), accept persecution for the gospel (2:3-4; 3:10-12), put his confidence in the Scripture, and preach it relentlessly (3:15-4:5).

 # OCTOBER 29

Jeremiah 43:1-44:30

43 But as soon as Jeremiah, whom the LORD their God had sent, had finished telling all the people all the words of the LORD their God—that is, all these words— ²Azariah the son of Hoshaiah, and Johanan the son of Kareah, and all the arrogant men said to Jeremiah, "You are telling a lie! The LORD our God has not sent you to say, 'You are not to enter Egypt to reside there'; ³ but Baruch the son of Neriah is inciting you against us to give us over into the hand of the Chaldeans, so they will put us to death or exile us to Babylon." ⁴So Johanan the son of Kareah and all the commanders of the forces, and all the people, did not obey the voice of the LORD to stay in the land of Judah. ⁵But Johanan the son of Kareah and all the commanders of the forces took the entire remnant of Judah who had returned from all the nations to which they had been driven away, in order to reside in the land of Judah— ⁶the men, the women, the children, the king's daughters and every person that Nebuzaradan the captain of the bodyguard had left with Gedaliah the son of Ahikam and grandson of Shaphan, together with Jeremiah the prophet and Baruch the son of Neriah— ⁷and they entered the land of Egypt (for they did not obey the voice of the LORD) and went in as far as Tahpanhes.

⁸Then the word of the LORD came to Jeremiah in Tahpanhes, saying, ⁹ "Take *some* large stones in your hands and hide them in the

43:1-7 as soon as Jeremiah...had finished telling. The incorrigible, disobedient leaders accused him of deceit and forced Jeremiah and the remnant to go to Egypt, despite the fact that all his prophecies regarding Babylon had come to pass. In so doing, they went out of God's protection into His judgment, as all who are disobedient to His Word do.

mortar in the brick *terrace* which is at the entrance of Pharaoh's palace in Tahpanhes, in the sight of some *of the* Jews; ¹⁰ and say to them, 'Thus says the LORD of hosts, the God of Israel, "Behold, I am going to send and get Nebuchadnezzar the king of Babylon, My servant, and I am going to set his throne *right* over these stones that I have hidden; and he will spread his canopy over them. ¹¹ He will also come and strike the land of Egypt; those who are *meant* for death *will be given over* to death, and those for captivity to captivity, and those for the sword to the sword. ¹² And I shall set fire to the temples of the gods of Egypt, and he will burn them and take them captive. So he will wrap himself with the land of Egypt as a shepherd wraps himself with his garment, and he will depart from there safely. ¹³ He will also shatter the obelisks of Heliopolis, which is in the land of Egypt; and the temples of the gods of Egypt he will burn with fire." '"

44 The word that came to Jeremiah for all the Jews living in the land of Egypt, those who were living in Migdol, Tahpanhes,

Memphis, and the land of Pathros, saying, [2] "Thus says the LORD of hosts, the God of Israel, 'You yourselves have seen all the calamity that I have brought on Jerusalem and all the cities of Judah; and behold, this day they are in ruins and no one lives in them, [3] because of their wickedness which they committed so as to provoke Me to anger by continuing to burn sacrifices *and* to serve other gods whom they had not known, *neither* they, you, nor your fathers. [4] Yet I sent you all My servants the prophets, again and again, saying, "Oh, do not do this abominable thing which I hate." [5] But they did not listen or incline their ears to turn from their wickedness, so as not to burn sacrifices to other gods. [6] Therefore My wrath and My anger were poured out and burned in the cities of Judah and in the streets of Jerusalem, so they have become a ruin and a desolation as it is this day. [7] Now then thus says the LORD God of hosts, the God of Israel, "Why are you doing great harm to yourselves, so as to cut off from you man and woman, child and infant, from among Judah, leaving yourselves without remnant, [8] provoking Me to anger with the works of your hands, burning sacrifices to other gods in the land of Egypt, where you are entering to reside, so that you might be cut off and become a curse and a reproach among all the nations of the earth? [9] Have you forgotten the wickedness of your fathers, the wickedness of the kings of Judah, and the wickedness of their wives, your own wickedness, and the wickedness of your wives, which they committed in the land of Judah and in the streets of Jerusalem? [10] But they have not become contrite even to this day, nor have they feared nor walked in My law or My statutes, which I have set before you and before your fathers." '

[11] "Therefore thus says the LORD of hosts, the God of Israel, 'Behold, I am going to set My face against you for woe, even to cut off all Judah. [12] And I will take away the remnant of Judah who have set their mind on entering the land of Egypt to reside there, and they will all meet their end in the land of Egypt; they will fall by the sword *and* meet their end by famine. Both small and great will die by the sword and famine; and they will become a curse, an object of horror, an imprecation and a reproach. [13] And I will punish those who live in the land of Egypt, as I have punished Jerusalem, with the sword, with famine and with pestilence. [14] So there will be no refugees or survivors for the remnant of Judah who have entered the land of Egypt to reside there and then to return to the land of Judah, to which they are longing to return and live; for none will return except *a few* refugees.' "

[15] Then all the men who were aware that their wives were burning sacrifices to other gods, along with all the women who were standing by, *as* a large assembly, including all the people who were living in Pathros in the land of Egypt, responded to Jeremiah, saying, [16] "As for the message that you have spoken to us in the name of the LORD, we are not going to listen to you! [17] But rather we will certainly carry out every word that has proceeded from our mouths, by burning sacrifices to the queen of heaven and pouring out drink offerings to her, just as we ourselves, our forefathers, our kings and our princes did in the cities of Judah and in the streets of Jerusalem; for *then* we had plenty of food and were well off and saw no misfortune. [18] But since we stopped burning sacrifices to the queen of heaven and pouring out drink offerings to her, we have lacked everything and have met our end by the sword and by famine." [19] "And," *said the women,* "when we were burning sacrifices to the queen of heaven and were pouring out drink offerings to her, was it without our husbands that we made for her *sacrificial* cakes in her image and poured out drink offerings to her?"

[20] Then Jeremiah said to all the people, to the men and women—even to all the people who were giving him *such* an answer—saying, [21] "As for the smoking sacrifices that you burned in the cities of Judah and in the streets of Jerusalem, you and your forefathers, your kings and your princes, and the people of the land, did not the LORD remember them and did not *all this* come into His mind? [22] So the LORD was no longer able to endure *it,* because of the evil of your deeds, because of the abominations which you have committed; thus your land has become a ruin, an object of horror and a curse, without an inhabitant, as *it is* this day. [23] Because you have burned sacrifices and have sinned against the LORD and not obeyed the voice of the LORD or walked in His law, His statutes or His testimonies, therefore this calamity has befallen you, as *it has* this day."

[24] Then Jeremiah said to all the people, including all the women, "Hear the word of the LORD, all Judah who are in the land of Egypt, [25] thus says the LORD of hosts, the God of Israel, as follows: 'As for you and your wives, you have spoken with your mouths and fulfilled *it* with your hands, saying, "We will certainly

perform our vows that we have vowed, to burn sacrifices to the queen of heaven and pour out drink offerings to her." Go ahead and confirm your vows, and certainly perform your vows!' ²⁶ Nevertheless hear the word of the LORD, all Judah who are living in the land of Egypt, 'Behold, I have sworn by My great name,' says the LORD, 'never shall My name be invoked again by the mouth of any man of Judah in all the land of Egypt, saying, "As the Lord GOD lives." ²⁷ Behold, I am watching over them for harm and not for good, and all the men of Judah who are in the land of Egypt will meet their end by the sword and by famine until they are completely gone. ²⁸ Those who escape the sword will return out of the land of Egypt to the land of Judah few in number. Then all the remnant of Judah who have gone to the land of Egypt to reside there will know whose word will stand, Mine or theirs. ²⁹ This will be the sign to you,' declares the LORD, 'that I am going to punish you in this place, so that you may know that My words will surely stand against you for harm.' ³⁰ Thus says the LORD, 'Behold, I am going to give over Pharaoh Hophra king of Egypt to the hand of his enemies, to the hand of those who seek his life, just as I gave over Zedekiah king of Judah to the hand of Nebuchadnezzar king of Babylon, who was his enemy and was seeking his life.'"

Psalm 119:97–104

מ MEM.

⁹⁷ O how I love Your law!
    It is my meditation all the day.
⁹⁸ Your commandments make me
        wiser than my enemies,
    For they are ever mine.
⁹⁹ I have more insight than
        all my teachers,
    For Your testimonies are
        my meditation.
¹⁰⁰ I understand more than the aged,
    Because I have observed
        Your precepts.
¹⁰¹ I have restrained my feet
        from every evil way,
    That I may keep Your word.
¹⁰² I have not turned aside from
        Your ordinances,
    For You Yourself have taught me.
¹⁰³ How sweet are Your words
        to my taste!
    Yes, sweeter than honey to my mouth!
¹⁰⁴ From Your precepts I get
        understanding;
    Therefore I hate every false way.

Proverbs 28:3

³ A poor man who oppresses the lowly
  Is *like* a driving rain which
      leaves no food.

28:3 oppresses the lowly. When the poor come to power and oppress their own, it is as bad as a destructive storm washing the fields clean instead of watering the crop.

2 Timothy 2:1–26

2 You therefore, my son, be strong in the grace that is in Christ Jesus. ² The things which you have heard from me in the presence of many witnesses, entrust these to faithful men who will be able to teach others also. ³ Suffer hardship with *me,* as a good soldier of Christ Jesus. ⁴ No soldier in active service entangles himself in the affairs of everyday life, so that he may please the one who enlisted him as a soldier. ⁵ Also if anyone competes as an athlete, he does not win the prize unless he competes according to the rules. ⁶ The hard-working farmer ought to be the first to receive his share of the crops. ⁷ Consider what I say, for the Lord will give you understanding in everything.

2:2 faithful men who will be able to teach others. Timothy was to take the divine revelation he had learned from Paul and teach it to other faithful men—men with proven spiritual character and giftedness, who would in turn pass on those truths to another generation. From Paul to Timothy to faithful men to others encompasses four generations of godly leaders. That process of spiritual reproduction, which began in the early church, is to continue until the Lord returns.

⁸ Remember Jesus Christ, risen from the dead, descendant of David, according to my gospel, ⁹ for which I suffer hardship even to imprisonment as a criminal; but the word of God is not imprisoned. ¹⁰ For this reason I endure all things for the sake of those who are chosen, so that they also may obtain the salvation which is in Christ Jesus *and* with *it* eternal glory. ¹¹ It is a trustworthy statement:

For if we died with Him, we
    will also live with Him;

2:8 Remember Jesus Christ. The supreme model of a faithful teacher (v. 2), soldier (vv. 3-4), athlete (v. 5), and farmer (v. 6). Timothy was to follow His example in teaching, suffering, pursuing the prize, and planting the seeds of truth for a spiritual harvest. **risen from the dead.** The resurrection of Christ is the central truth of the Christian faith (1Co 15:3-4, 17, 19). By it, God affirmed the perfect redemptive work of Jesus Christ. **descendant of David.** As David's descendant, Jesus is the rightful heir to his throne (Lk 1:32-33). The Lord's humanity is stressed.

---

12 If we endure, we will also
    reign with Him;
    If we deny Him, He also will deny us;
13 If we are faithless, He
    remains faithful, for He
    cannot deny Himself.

14 Remind *them* of these things, and solemnly charge *them* in the presence of God not to wrangle about words, which is useless *and leads* to the ruin of the hearers. 15 Be diligent to present yourself approved to God as a workman who does not need to be ashamed, accurately handling the word of truth. 16 But avoid worldly *and* empty chatter, for it will lead to further ungodliness, 17 and their talk will spread like gangrene. Among them are Hymenaeus and Philetus, 18 *men* who have gone astray from the truth saying that the resurrection has already taken place, and they upset the faith of some. 19 Nevertheless, the firm foundation of God stands, having this seal, "The Lord knows those who are His," and, "Everyone who names the name of the Lord is to abstain from wickedness."

20 Now in a large house there are not only gold and silver vessels, but also vessels of wood and of earthenware, and some to honor and some to dishonor. 21 Therefore, if anyone cleanses himself from these *things,* he will be a vessel for honor, sanctified, useful to the Master, prepared for every good work. 22 Now flee from youthful lusts and pursue righteousness, faith, love *and* peace, with those who call on the Lord from a pure heart. 23 But refuse foolish and ignorant speculations, knowing that they produce quarrels. 24 The Lord's bondservant must not be quarrelsome, but be kind to all, able to teach, patient when wronged, 25 with gentleness correcting those who are in opposition, if perhaps God may grant them repentance leading to the knowledge of the truth, 26 and they may come to their senses *and escape* from the snare of the devil, having been held captive by him to do his will.

DAY 29: How is the Christian life compared to being a soldier, an athlete, and a farmer?

"Suffer hardship with me, as a good soldier" (2Ti 2:3). The metaphor of the Christian life as warfare (against the evil world system, the believer's sinful human nature, and Satan) is a familiar one in the New Testament (2Co 10:3-5; Eph 6:10-20; 1Th 4:8; 1Ti 1:18; 4:7; 6:12). Here Paul is dealing with the conflict against the hostile world and the persecution. "No soldier in active service entangles himself" (v. 4). Just as a soldier called to duty is completely severed from the normal affairs of civilian life, so also must the good soldier of Jesus Christ refuse to allow the things of the world to distract him (Jas 4:4; 1Jn 2:15-17).

"If anyone competes as an athlete" (v. 5). The Greek verb expresses the effort and determination needed to compete successfully in an athletic event (1Co 9:24). This is a useful picture of spiritual effort and untiring pursuit of the victory to those familiar with events such as the Olympic Games and the Isthmian Games (held in Corinth). "Win...rules." All an athlete's hard work and discipline will be wasted if he or she fails to compete according to the rules. This is a call to obey the Word of God in the pursuit of spiritual victory.

"The hard-working farmer" (v. 6). "Hard-working" is from a Greek verb meaning "to labor to the point of exhaustion." Ancient farmers worked long hours of backbreaking labor under all kinds of conditions with the hope that their physical effort would be rewarded by a good harvest. Paul is urging Timothy not to be lazy or indolent but to labor intensely (Col 1:28-29) with a view to the harvest.

☙ OCTOBER 30

Jeremiah 45:1-46:28

45 *This is* the message which Jeremiah the prophet spoke to Baruch the son of Neriah, when he had written down these words in a book at Jeremiah's dictation, in the fourth year of Jehoiakim the son of Josiah, king of Judah, saying: ² "Thus says the LORD the God of Israel to you, O Baruch: ³ 'You said, "Ah, woe is me! For the LORD has added sorrow to my pain; I am weary with my groaning and have found no rest."' ⁴ Thus you are to say to him, 'Thus says the LORD, "Behold, what I have built I am about to tear down, and what I have planted I am about to uproot, that is, the whole land." ⁵ But you, are you seeking great things for yourself? Do not seek *them;* for behold, I am going to bring disaster on all flesh,' declares the LORD, 'but I will give your life to you as booty in all the places where you may go.'"

❧

45:3 woe is me! Baruch felt anxiety as his own cherished plans of a bright future were apparently dashed; even death became a darkening peril (v. 5). Also, he was possibly pressed by human questionings about God carrying through with such calamity (v. 4). Jeremiah spoke to encourage him (v. 2).

45:5 are you seeking great things...? Baruch had his expectations far too high, and that made the disasters harder to bear. It is enough that he be content just to live. Jeremiah, who once also complained, learned by his own suffering to encourage complainers.

---

46 That which came as the word of the LORD to Jeremiah the prophet concerning the nations.

² To Egypt, concerning the army of Pharaoh Neco king of Egypt, which was by the Euphrates River at Carchemish, which Nebuchadnezzar king of Babylon defeated in the fourth year of Jehoiakim the son of Josiah, king of Judah:

³ "Line up the shield and buckler,
And draw near for the battle!
⁴ "Harness the horses,
And mount the steeds,
And take your stand with helmets *on!*
Polish the spears,
Put on the scale-armor!

⁵ "Why have I seen *it?*
They are terrified,
They are drawing back,
And their mighty men are defeated
And have taken refuge in flight,
Without facing back;
Terror is on every side!"
Declares the LORD.
⁶ Let not the swift man flee,
Nor the mighty man escape;
In the north beside the river Euphrates
They have stumbled and fallen.
⁷ Who is this that rises like the Nile,
Like the rivers whose
waters surge about?
⁸ Egypt rises like the Nile,
Even like the rivers whose
waters surge about;
And He has said, "I will rise
and cover *that* land;
I will surely destroy the city
and its inhabitants."
⁹ Go up, you horses, and drive
madly, you chariots,
That the mighty men may
march forward:
Ethiopia and Put, that
handle the shield,
And the Lydians, that handle
and bend the bow.
¹⁰ For that day belongs to the
Lord GOD of hosts,
A day of vengeance, so as to
avenge Himself on His foes;
And the sword will devour
and be satiated
And drink its fill of their blood;
For there will be a slaughter for
the Lord GOD of hosts,
In the land of the north by
the river Euphrates.
¹¹ Go up to Gilead and obtain balm,
O virgin daughter of Egypt!
In vain have you multiplied remedies;
There is no healing for you.
¹² The nations have heard
of your shame,
And the earth is full of
your cry *of distress;*
For one warrior has stumbled
over another,
And both of them have
fallen down together.

¹³ *This is* the message which the LORD spoke to Jeremiah the prophet about the coming of Nebuchadnezzar king of Babylon to smite the land of Egypt:

¹⁴ "Declare in Egypt and
proclaim in Migdol,
Proclaim also in Memphis
and Tahpanhes;
Say, 'Take your stand and
get yourself ready,
For the sword has devoured
those around you.'
¹⁵ "Why have your mighty ones
become prostrate?
They do not stand because the
LORD has thrust them down.
¹⁶ "They have repeatedly stumbled;
Indeed, they have fallen
one against another.
Then they said, 'Get up!
And let us go back
To our own people and our native land
Away from the sword of the oppressor.'
¹⁷ "They cried there, 'Pharaoh king
of Egypt *is but* a big noise;
He has let the appointed time pass by!'
¹⁸ "As I live," declares the King
Whose name is the LORD of hosts,
"Surely one shall come *who looms up*
like Tabor among the mountains,
Or like Carmel by the sea.
¹⁹ "Make your baggage ready for exile,
O daughter dwelling in Egypt,
For Memphis will become
a desolation;
It will even be burned down
and bereft of inhabitants.
²⁰ "Egypt is a pretty heifer,
But a horsefly is coming from
the north—it is coming!
²¹ "Also her mercenaries in her midst
Are like fattened calves,
For even they too have turned back
and have fled away together;
They did not stand *their ground.*
For the day of their calamity
has come upon them,
The time of their punishment.
²² "Its sound moves along like a serpent;
For they move on like an army
And come to her as
woodcutters with axes.
²³ "They have cut down her forest,"
declares the LORD;
"Surely it will no *more* be found,
Even though they are *now* more
numerous than locusts
And are without number.
²⁴ "The daughter of Egypt has
been put to shame,
Given over to the power of the
people of the north."

²⁵ The LORD of hosts, the God of Israel, says, "Behold, I am going to punish Amon of Thebes, and Pharaoh, and Egypt along with her gods and her kings, even Pharaoh and those who trust in him. ²⁶ I shall give them over to the power of those who are seeking their lives, even into the hand of Nebuchadnezzar king of Babylon and into the hand of his officers. Afterwards, however, it will be inhabited as in the days of old," declares the LORD.

²⁷ "But as for you, O Jacob My
servant, do not fear,
Nor be dismayed, O Israel!
For, see, I am going to save
you from afar,
And your descendants from the
land of their captivity;
And Jacob will return and
be undisturbed
And secure, with no one
making *him* tremble.
²⁸ "O Jacob My servant, do not
fear," declares the LORD,
"For I am with you.
For I will make a full end
of all the nations
Where I have driven you,
Yet I will not make a
full end of you;
But I will correct you properly
And by no means leave
you unpunished."

Psalm 119:105–112

ℶ NUN.

¹⁰⁵ Your word is a lamp to my feet
And a light to my path.
¹⁰⁶ I have sworn and I will confirm it,
That I will keep Your
righteous ordinances.
¹⁰⁷ I am exceedingly afflicted;
Revive me, O LORD, according
to Your word.
¹⁰⁸ O accept the freewill offerings
of my mouth, O LORD,
And teach me Your ordinances.
¹⁰⁹ My life is continually in my hand,
Yet I do not forget Your law.
¹¹⁰ The wicked have laid a snare for me,
Yet I have not gone astray
from Your precepts.
¹¹¹ I have inherited Your
testimonies forever,
For they are the joy of my heart.
¹¹² I have inclined my heart to
perform Your statutes
Forever, *even* to the end.

Proverbs 28:4

4 Those who forsake the law
    praise the wicked,
But those who keep the law
    strive with them.

2 Timothy 3:1-17

3 But realize this, that in the last days difficult times will come. ² For men will be lovers of self, lovers of money, boastful, arrogant,
revilers, disobedient to parents, ungrateful,
unholy, ³ unloving, irreconcilable, malicious
gossips, without self-control, brutal, haters
of good, ⁴ treacherous, reckless, conceited,
lovers of pleasure rather than lovers of God,
⁵ holding to a form of godliness, although they
have denied its power; Avoid such men as
these. ⁶ For among them are those who enter
into households and captivate weak women
weighed down with sins, led on by various
impulses, ⁷ always learning and never able to
come to the knowledge of the truth. ⁸ Just as
Jannes and Jambres opposed Moses, so these
men also oppose the truth, men of depraved

mind, rejected in regard to the faith. ⁹ But they
will not make further progress; for their folly
will be obvious to all, just as Jannes's and
Jambres's folly was also.

¹⁰ Now you followed my teaching, conduct,
purpose, faith, patience, love, perseverance,
¹¹ persecutions, *and* sufferings, such as happened to me at Antioch, at Iconium *and* at
Lystra; what persecutions I endured, and out
of them all the Lord rescued me! ¹² Indeed,
all who desire to live godly in Christ Jesus
will be persecuted. ¹³ But evil men and im-
postors will proceed *from bad* to worse, deceiving and being deceived. ¹⁴ You, however,
continue in the things you have learned and
become convinced of, knowing from whom
you have learned *them,* ¹⁵ and that from childhood you have known the sacred writings
which are able to give you the wisdom that
leads to salvation through faith which is in
Christ Jesus. ¹⁶ All Scripture is inspired by
God and profitable for teaching, for reproof,
for correction, for training in righteousness;
¹⁷ so that the man of God may be adequate,
equipped for every good work.

3:1 the last days. This phrase refers to this
age, the time since the first coming of the
Lord Jesus. **difficult times.** "Difficult" is used
to describe the savage nature of two demon-
possessed men (Mt 8:28). The word for "times"
had to do with epochs, rather than clock or
calendar time. Such savage, dangerous eras or
epochs will increase in frequency and severity
as the return of Christ approaches (v. 13). The
church age is fraught with these dangerous
movements accumulating strength as the
end nears.

3:8 Jannes and Jambres. Although their names
are not mentioned in the Old Testament, they
were likely two of the Egyptian magicians that
opposed Moses (Ex 7:11, 22; 8:7, 18-19; 9:11).
According to Jewish tradition, they pretended
to become Jewish proselytes, instigated the
worship of the golden calf, and were killed with
the rest of the idolaters (Ex 32). Paul's choice
of them as examples may indicate the false
teachers at Ephesus were practicing deceiving
signs and wonders.

DAY 30: How does 2 Timothy 3:16 describe Scripture?

"All Scripture"—both Old Testament and New Testament Scripture are included (2Pe 3:15-16,
which identify New Testament writings as Scripture). "Is inspired by God." Literally,
"breathed out by God" or "God-breathed." Sometimes God told the Bible writers the exact
words to say (Jer 1:9), but more often He used their minds, vocabularies, and experiences
to produce His own infallible, inerrant Word (1Th 2:13; Heb 1:1; 2Pe 1:20-21). It is important to
note that inspiration applies only to the original autographs of Scripture, not the Bible writers; there are no inspired Scripture writers, only inspired Scripture. So identified is God with
His Word that when Scripture speaks, God speaks (Ro 9:17; Gal 3:8). Scripture is called "the
oracles of God" (Ro 3:2; see also 1Pe 4:11) and cannot be altered (Jn 10:35; Mt 5:17-18; Lk 16:17;
Rev 22:18-19).
  "And profitable for teaching." The divine instruction or doctrinal content of both the Old
Testament and the New Testament (2:15; Ac 20:18, 20-21, 27; 1Co 2:14-16; Col 3:16; 1Jn 2:20, 24,
27). The Scripture provides the comprehensive and complete body of divine truth necessary
for life and godliness. "For reproof." Rebuke for wrong behavior or wrong belief. The Scripture
exposes sin (Heb 4:12-13) that can then be dealt with through confession and repentance. "For
correction." The restoration of something to its proper condition. The word appears only here
in the New Testament but was used in extrabiblical Greek of righting a fallen object or helping

back to their feet those who had stumbled. Scripture not only rebukes wrong behavior but also points the way back to godly living. "For training in righteousness." Scripture provides positive training ("training" originally referred to training a child) in godly behavior, not merely rebuke and correction of wrong behavior (Ac 20:32; 1Ti 4:6; 1Pe 2:1–2).

OCTOBER 31

Jeremiah 47:1–48:47

47 That which came as the word of the LORD to Jeremiah the prophet concerning the Philistines, before Pharaoh conquered Gaza. [2] Thus says the LORD:

"Behold, waters are going to
rise from the north
And become an overflowing
torrent,
And overflow the land
and all its fullness,
The city and those who live in it;
And the men will cry out,
And every inhabitant of
the land will wail.
[3] "Because of the noise of
the galloping hoofs
of his stallions,
The tumult of his chariots, *and*
the rumbling of his wheels,
The fathers have not turned
back for *their* children,
Because of the limpness
of *their* hands,
[4] On account of the day
that is coming
To destroy all the Philistines,
To cut off from Tyre and Sidon
Every ally that is left;
For the LORD is going to
destroy the Philistines,
The remnant of the
coastland of Caphtor.
[5] "Baldness has come upon Gaza;
Ashkelon has been ruined.
O remnant of their valley,
How long will you gash yourself?
[6] "Ah, sword of the LORD,
How long will you not be quiet?
Withdraw into your sheath;
Be at rest and stay still.
[7] "How can it be quiet,
When the LORD has
given it an order?
Against Ashkelon and
against the seacoast—
There He has assigned it."

48 Concerning Moab. Thus says the LORD of hosts, the God of Israel,

"Woe to Nebo, for it has
been destroyed;
Kiriathaim has been put to
shame, it has been captured;
The lofty stronghold has been
put to shame and shattered.
[2] "There is praise for Moab no longer;
In Heshbon they have devised
calamity against her:
'Come and let us cut her off
from *being* a nation!'
You too, Madmen, will be silenced;
The sword will follow after you.
[3] "The sound of an outcry
from Horonaim,
'Devastation and great destruction!'
[4] "Moab is broken,
Her little ones have sounded
out a cry *of distress.*
[5] "For by the ascent of Luhith
They will ascend with
continual weeping;
For at the descent of Horonaim
They have heard the anguished
cry of destruction.
[6] "Flee, save your lives,
That you may be like a juniper
in the wilderness.
[7] "For because of your trust in your
own achievements and treasures,
Even you yourself will be captured;
And Chemosh will go off into exile
Together with his priests
and his princes.
[8] "A destroyer will come to every city,
So that no city will escape;
The valley also will be ruined
And the plateau will be destroyed,
As the LORD has said.
[9] "Give wings to Moab,
For she will flee away;
And her cities will become
a desolation,
Without inhabitants in them.
[10] "Cursed be the one who does the
LORD'S work negligently,
And cursed be the one who restrains
his sword from blood.

¹¹ "Moab has been at ease
    since his youth;
He has also been undisturbed,
    like wine on its dregs,
And he has not been emptied
    from vessel to vessel,
Nor has he gone into exile.
Therefore he retains his flavor,
And his aroma has not changed.

¹² Therefore behold, the days are coming,"
declares the LORD, "when I will send to him
those who tip *vessels,* and they will tip him
over, and they will empty his vessels and shatter his jars. ¹³ And Moab will be ashamed of
Chemosh, as the house of Israel was ashamed
of Bethel, their confidence.

48:11–12 This winemaking imagery is vivid. In
the production of sweet wine, the juice was left
in a wineskin until the sediment or dregs settled onto the bottom. Then it was poured into
another skin until more dregs were separated.
This process continued until the dregs were all
removed and a pure, sweet wine obtained. Moab
was not taken from suffering to suffering so that
her bitter dregs would be removed through the
purging of pain. Thus the nation was settled into
the thickness and bitterness of its own sin. Judgment from God was coming to smash them.

---

¹⁴ "How can you say, 'We are
    mighty warriors,
And men valiant for battle'?
¹⁵ "Moab has been destroyed and men
    have gone up to his cities;
His choicest young men have also
    gone down to the slaughter,"
Declares the King, whose name
    is the LORD of hosts.
¹⁶ "The disaster of Moab will soon come,
And his calamity has
    swiftly hastened.
¹⁷ "Mourn for him, all you who
    live around him,
Even all of you who know his name;
Say, 'How has the mighty
    scepter been broken,
A staff of splendor!'
¹⁸ "Come down from your glory
And sit on the parched ground,
O daughter dwelling in Dibon,
For the destroyer of Moab has
    come up against you,
He has ruined your strongholds.

¹⁹ "Stand by the road and keep watch,
    O inhabitant of Aroer;
Ask him who flees and
    her who escapes
    And say, 'What has happened?'
²⁰ "Moab has been put to shame,
    for it has been shattered.
Wail and cry out;
Declare by the Arnon
That Moab has been destroyed.

²¹ "Judgment has also come upon the
plain, upon Holon, Jahzah and against Mephaath, ²² against Dibon, Nebo and Beth-
diblathaim, ²³ against Kiriathaim, Beth-gamul
and Beth-meon, ²⁴ against Kerioth, Bozrah and
all the cities of the land of Moab, far and near.
²⁵ The horn of Moab has been cut off and his
arm broken," declares the LORD. ²⁶ "Make him
drunk, for he has become arrogant toward
the LORD; so Moab will wallow in his vomit,
and he also will become a laughingstock.
²⁷ Now was not Israel a laughingstock to you?
Or was he caught among thieves? For each
time you speak about him you shake *your
head in scorn.*

²⁸ "Leave the cities and dwell
    among the crags,
O inhabitants of Moab,
And be like a dove that nests
Beyond the mouth of the chasm.
²⁹ "We have heard of the pride of
    Moab—he *is* very proud—
Of his haughtiness, his
    pride, his arrogance and
    his self-exaltation.
³⁰ "I know his fury," declares the LORD,
    "But it is futile;
His idle boasts have
    accomplished nothing.
³¹ "Therefore I will wail for Moab,
Even for all Moab will I cry out;
I will moan for the men of Kir-heres.
³² "More than the weeping for Jazer
I will weep for you, O vine of Sibmah!
Your tendrils stretched across the sea,
They reached to the sea of Jazer;
Upon your summer fruits and
    your grape harvest
The destroyer has fallen.
³³ "So gladness and joy are taken away
From the fruitful field, even
    from the land of Moab.
And I have made the wine to
    cease from the wine presses;
No one will tread *them* with shouting,
The shouting will not be shouts *of joy.*

³⁴ From the outcry at Heshbon even to Elealeh, even to Jahaz they have raised their voice, from Zoar even to Horonaim *and to* Eglath-shelishiyah; for even the waters of Nimrim will become desolate. ³⁵ I will make an end of Moab," declares the LORD, "the one who offers *sacrifice* on the high place and the one who burns incense to his gods.

³⁶ "Therefore My heart wails for Moab like flutes; My heart also wails like flutes for the men of Kir-heres. Therefore they have lost the abundance it produced. ³⁷ For every head is bald and every beard cut short; there are gashes on all the hands and sackcloth on the loins. ³⁸ On all the housetops of Moab and in its streets there is lamentation everywhere; for I have broken Moab like an undesirable vessel," declares the LORD. ³⁹ "How shattered it is! *How* they have wailed! How Moab has turned his back—he is ashamed! So Moab will become a laughingstock and an object of terror to all around him."

⁴⁰ For thus says the LORD:
"Behold, one will fly swiftly like an eagle
And spread out his wings
    against Moab.
⁴¹ "Kerioth has been captured
And the strongholds have been seized,
So the hearts of the mighty
    men of Moab in that day
Will be like the heart of a
    woman in labor.
⁴² "Moab will be destroyed
    from *being* a people
Because he has become arrogant
    toward the LORD.
⁴³ "Terror, pit and snare are
    coming upon you,
O inhabitant of Moab,"
    declares the LORD.
⁴⁴ "The one who flees from the terror
Will fall into the pit,
And the one who climbs
    up out of the pit
Will be caught in the snare;
For I shall bring upon her,
    even upon Moab,
The year of their punishment,"
    declares the LORD.

⁴⁵ "In the shadow of Heshbon
The fugitives stand without strength;
For a fire has gone forth
    from Heshbon
And a flame from the midst of Sihon,
And it has devoured the
    forehead of Moab

And the scalps of the riotous revelers.
⁴⁶ "Woe to you, Moab!
The people of Chemosh
    have perished;
For your sons have been
    taken away captive
And your daughters into captivity.
⁴⁷ "Yet I will restore the fortunes of Moab
In the latter days," declares the LORD.

Thus far the judgment on Moab.

Psalm 119:113–120

ס SAMEKH.

¹¹³ I hate those who are double-minded,
    But I love Your law.
¹¹⁴ You are my hiding place
    and my shield;
    I wait for Your word.
¹¹⁵ Depart from me, evildoers,
    That I may observe the
        commandments of my God.
¹¹⁶ Sustain me according to Your
        word, that I may live;
    And do not let me be
        ashamed of my hope.
¹¹⁷ Uphold me that I may be safe,
    That I may have regard for
        Your statutes continually.
¹¹⁸ You have rejected all those who
        wander from Your statutes,
    For their deceitfulness is useless.
¹¹⁹ You have removed all the wicked
        of the earth *like* dross;
    Therefore I love Your testimonies.
¹²⁰ My flesh trembles for fear of You,
    And I am afraid of Your judgments.

Proverbs 28:5

⁵ Evil men do not understand justice,
    But those who seek the LORD
        understand all things.

2 Timothy 4:1–22

4 I solemnly charge *you* in the presence of God and of Christ Jesus, who is to judge the living and the dead, and by His appearing and His kingdom: ² preach the word; be ready in season *and* out of season; reprove, rebuke, exhort, with great patience and instruction. ³ For the time will come when they will not endure sound doctrine; but *wanting* to have their ears tickled, they will accumulate for themselves teachers in accordance to their own desires, ⁴ and will turn away their ears from the truth and will turn aside to myths. ⁵ But you, be sober in all things, endure hardship, do the work of an evangelist, fulfill your ministry.

⁶For I am already being poured out as a drink offering, and the time of my departure has come. ⁷I have fought the good fight, I have finished the course, I have kept the faith; ⁸in the future there is laid up for me the crown of righteousness, which the Lord, the righteous Judge, will award to me on that day; and not only to me, but also to all who have loved His appearing.

⁹Make every effort to come to me soon; ¹⁰for Demas, having loved this present world, has deserted me and gone to Thessalonica; Crescens *has gone* to Galatia, Titus to Dalmatia. ¹¹Only Luke is with me. Pick up Mark and bring him with you, for he is useful to me for service. ¹²But Tychicus I have sent to Ephesus. ¹³When you come bring the cloak which I left at Troas with Carpus, and the books, especially the parchments. ¹⁴Alexander the coppersmith did me much harm; the Lord will repay him according to his deeds. ¹⁵Be on guard against him yourself, for he vigorously opposed our teaching.

¹⁶At my first defense no one supported me, but all deserted me; may it not be counted against them. ¹⁷But the Lord stood with me and strengthened me, so that through me the proclamation might be fully accomplished, and that all the Gentiles might hear; and I was rescued out of the lion's mouth. ¹⁸The Lord will rescue me from every evil deed, and will bring me safely to His heavenly kingdom; to Him *be* the glory forever and ever. Amen.

¹⁹Greet Prisca and Aquila, and the household of Onesiphorus. ²⁰Erastus remained at Corinth, but Trophimus I left sick at Miletus.

4:2 the word. The entire written Word of God, His complete revealed truth as contained in the Bible (3:15–16; Ac 20:27). **be ready.** The Greek word has a broad range of meanings, including suddenness or forcefulness. Here the form of the verb suggests the complementary ideas of urgency, preparedness, and readiness. It was used of a soldier prepared to go into battle or a guard who was continually alert for any surprise attack—attitudes which are imperative for a faithful preacher. **in season** *and* **out of season.** The faithful preacher must proclaim the Word when it is popular and/or convenient, and when it is not; when it seems suitable to do so, and when it seems not. The dictates of popular culture, tradition, reputation, acceptance, or esteem in the community (or in the church) must never alter the true preacher's commitment to proclaim God's Word. **reprove, rebuke.** The negative side of preaching the Word (the "reproof" and "correction"; see 3:16). The Greek word for "reprove" refers to correcting behavior or false doctrine by using careful biblical argument to help a person understand the error of his actions. The Greek word for "rebuke" deals more with correcting the person's motives by convicting him of his sin and leading him to repentance.

²¹Make every effort to come before winter. Eubulus greets you, also Pudens and Linus and Claudia and all the brethren.

²²The Lord be with your spirit. Grace be with you.

DAY 31: Describe how Paul recaps his life in 2 Timothy 4:6–8.

"For I am already being poured out as a drink offering" (v. 6). Meaning his death was imminent. In the Old Testament sacrificial system, a drink offering was the final offering that followed the burnt and grain offerings prescribed for the people of Israel (Nu 15:1–16). Paul saw his coming death as his final offering to God in a life that had already been full of sacrifices to Him. "My departure" speaks of Paul's death. The Greek word essentially refers to the loosening of something, such as the mooring ropes of a ship or the ropes of a tent; thus, it eventually acquired the secondary meaning of "departure."

"I have fought...have finished...have kept" (v. 7). The form of the 3 Greek verbs indicates completed action with continuing results. Paul saw his life as complete—he had been able to accomplish through the Lord's power all that God called him to do. He was a soldier, an athlete, and a guardian. "The faith." The truths and standards of the revealed Word of God.

"There is laid up for me the crown of righteousness" (v. 8). The Greek word for "crown" literally means "surrounding," and it was used of the plaited wreaths or garlands placed on the heads of dignitaries and victorious military officers or athletes. Linguistically, "of righteousness" can mean either that righteousness is the source of the crown or that righteousness is the nature of the crown. The crown represents eternal righteousness received through the imputed righteousness of Christ at salvation (Ro 4:6, 11). The Holy Spirit works practical righteousness (sanctification) in the believer throughout his lifetime of struggle with sin (Ro 6:13, 19; 8:4). But only when the struggle is complete will the Christian receive Christ's righteousness perfected in him (glorification) when he enters heaven (Gal 5:5).

NOVEMBER 1

Jeremiah 49:1–50:46

49 Concerning the sons of Ammon. Thus says the LORD:

"Does Israel have no sons?
Or has he no heirs?
Why then has Malcam taken
possession of Gad
And his people settled in its cities?
2 "Therefore behold, the days are
coming," declares the LORD,
"That I will cause a trumpet
blast of war to be heard
Against Rabbah of the
sons of Ammon;
And it will become a desolate heap,
And her towns will be set on fire.
Then Israel will take possession
of his possessors,"
Says the LORD.
3 "Wail, O Heshbon, for Ai has
been destroyed!
Cry out, O daughters of Rabbah,
Gird yourselves with
sackcloth and lament,
And rush back and forth
inside the walls;
For Malcam will go into exile
Together with his priests
and his princes.
4 "How boastful you are
about the valleys!
Your valley is flowing *away*,
O backsliding daughter
Who trusts in her treasures, *saying*,
'Who will come against me?'
5 "Behold, I am going to bring
terror upon you,"
Declares the Lord GOD of hosts,
"From all *directions* around you;
And each of you will be
driven out headlong,
With no one to gather the
fugitives together.
6 "But afterward I will restore
The fortunes of the sons of Ammon,"
Declares the LORD.

7 Concerning Edom.
Thus says the LORD of hosts,
"Is there no longer any
wisdom in Teman?
Has good counsel been lost
to the prudent?
Has their wisdom decayed?

8 "Flee away, turn back, dwell
in the depths,
O inhabitants of Dedan,
For I will bring the disaster
of Esau upon him
At the time I punish him.
9 "If grape gatherers came to you,
Would they not leave gleanings?
If thieves *came* by night,
They would destroy *only*
until they had enough.
10 "But I have stripped Esau bare,
I have uncovered his hiding places
So that he will not be able
to conceal himself;
His offspring has been destroyed
along with his relatives
And his neighbors, and he is no more.
11 "Leave your orphans behind,
I will keep *them* alive;
And let your widows trust in Me."

12 For thus says the LORD, "Behold, those who were not sentenced to drink the cup will certainly drink *it*, and are you the one who will be completely acquitted? You will not be acquitted, but you will certainly drink *it*. 13 For I have sworn by Myself," declares the LORD, "that Bozrah will become an object of horror, a reproach, a ruin and a curse; and all its cities will become perpetual ruins."

14 I have heard a message
from the LORD,
And an envoy is sent among
the nations, *saying*,
"Gather yourselves together
and come against her,
And rise up for battle!"
15 "For behold, I have made you
small among the nations,
Despised among men.
16 "As for the terror of you,
The arrogance of your heart
has deceived you,
O you who live in the
clefts of the rock,
Who occupy the height of the hill.
Though you make your nest
as high as an eagle's,
I will bring you down from
there," declares the LORD.

17 "Edom will become an object of horror; everyone who passes by it will be horrified and will hiss at all its wounds. 18 Like the overthrow of Sodom and Gomorrah with its neighbors," says the LORD, "no one will live there,

nor will a son of man reside in it. ¹⁹Behold, one will come up like a lion from the thickets of the Jordan against a perennially watered pasture; for in an instant I will make him run away from it, and whoever is chosen I shall appoint over it. For who is like Me, and who will summon Me *into court?* And who then is the shepherd who can stand against Me?"

²⁰Therefore hear the plan of the LORD which He has planned against Edom, and His purposes which He has purposed against the inhabitants of Teman: surely they will drag them off, *even* the little ones of the flock; surely He will make their pasture desolate because of them. ²¹The earth has quaked at the noise of their downfall. There is an outcry! The noise of it has been heard at the Red Sea. ²²Behold, He will mount up and swoop like an eagle and spread out His wings against Bozrah; and the hearts of the mighty men of Edom in that day will be like the heart of a woman in labor.

²³ Concerning Damascus.
"Hamath and Arpad are put to shame,
For they have heard bad news;
They are disheartened.
There is anxiety by the sea,
It cannot be calmed.
²⁴ "Damascus has become helpless;
She has turned away to flee,
And panic has gripped her;
Distress and pangs have
taken hold of her
Like a woman in childbirth.
²⁵ "How the city of praise has
not been deserted,
The town of My joy!
²⁶ "Therefore, her young men
will fall in her streets,
And all the men of war will
be silenced in that day,"
declares the LORD of hosts.
²⁷ "I will set fire to the wall of Damascus,
And it will devour the fortified
towers of Ben-hadad."

²⁸ Concerning Kedar and the kingdoms of Hazor, which Nebuchadnezzar king of Babylon defeated. Thus says the LORD,

"Arise, go up to Kedar
And devastate the men of the east.
²⁹ "They will take away their
tents and their flocks;
They will carry off for themselves
Their tent curtains, all their
goods and their camels,

And they will call out to one
another, 'Terror on every side!'
³⁰ "Run away, flee! Dwell in the depths,
O inhabitants of Hazor,"
declares the LORD;
"For Nebuchadnezzar king of Babylon
has formed a plan against you
And devised a scheme against you.
³¹ "Arise, go up against a nation
which is at ease,
Which lives securely,"
declares the LORD.
"It has no gates or bars;
They dwell alone.
³² "Their camels will become plunder,
And their many cattle for booty,
And I will scatter to all the
winds those who cut the
corners *of their hair;*
And I will bring their disaster from
every side," declares the LORD.
³³ "Hazor will become a haunt of jackals,
A desolation forever;
No one will live there,
Nor will a son of man reside in it."

³⁴That which came as the word of the LORD to Jeremiah the prophet concerning Elam, at the beginning of the reign of Zedekiah king of Judah, saying:

³⁵ "Thus says the LORD of hosts,
'Behold, I am going to break
the bow of Elam,
The finest of their might.
³⁶ 'I will bring upon Elam the four winds
From the four ends of heaven,
And will scatter them to
all these winds;
And there will be no nation
To which the outcasts of
Elam will not go.
³⁷ 'So I will shatter Elam before
their enemies
And before those who seek their lives;
And I will bring calamity upon them,
Even My fierce anger,'
declares the LORD,
'And I will send out the
sword after them
Until I have consumed them.
³⁸ 'Then I will set My throne in Elam
And destroy out of it king and princes,'
Declares the LORD.
³⁹ 'But it will come about in the last days
That I will restore the
fortunes of Elam,'"
Declares the LORD.

50 The word which the LORD spoke concerning Babylon, the land of the Chaldeans, through Jeremiah the prophet:

2 "Declare and proclaim
among the nations.
Proclaim it and lift up a standard.
Do not conceal *it but* say,
'Babylon has been captured,
Bel has been put to shame,
Marduk has been shattered;
Her images have been put to shame,
her idols have been shattered.'

3 For a nation has come up against her out of the north; it will make her land an object of horror, and there will be no inhabitant in it. Both man and beast have wandered off, they have gone away!

4 "In those days and at that time," declares the LORD, "the sons of Israel will come, *both* they and the sons of Judah as well; they will go along weeping as they go, and it will be the LORD their God they will seek. 5 They will ask for the way to Zion, *turning* their faces in its direction; they will come that they may join themselves to the LORD *in* an everlasting covenant that will not be forgotten.

6 "My people have become lost sheep;
Their shepherds have
led them astray.
They have made them turn
aside *on* the mountains;
They have gone along from
mountain to hill
And have forgotten their
resting place.
7 "All who came upon them
have devoured them;
And their adversaries have
said, 'We are not guilty,
Inasmuch as they have sinned
against the LORD *who is* the
habitation of righteousness,
Even the LORD, the hope
of their fathers.'

8 "Wander away from the
midst of Babylon
And go forth from the land
of the Chaldeans;
Be also like male goats at
the head of the flock.
9 "For behold, I am going to arouse
and bring up against Babylon
A horde of great nations from
the land of the north,
And they will draw up *their*
battle lines against her;
From there she will be taken captive.
Their arrows will be like
an expert warrior
Who does not return empty-handed.
10 "Chaldea will become plunder;
All who plunder her will have
enough," declares the LORD.

11 "Because you are glad, because
you are jubilant,
O you who pillage My heritage,
Because you skip about like
a threshing heifer
And neigh like stallions,
12 Your mother will be greatly ashamed,
She who gave you birth
will be humiliated.
Behold, *she will be* the
least of the nations,
A wilderness, a parched land
and a desert.
13 "Because of the indignation of the
LORD she will not be inhabited,
But she will be completely desolate;
Everyone who passes by
Babylon will be horrified
And will hiss because of
all her wounds.
14 "Draw up your battle lines against
Babylon on every side,
All you who bend the bow;
Shoot at her, do not be sparing
with *your* arrows,
For she has sinned against the LORD.
15 "Raise your battle cry against
her on every side!
She has given herself up, her
pillars have fallen,
Her walls have been torn down.
For this is the vengeance of the LORD:
Take vengeance on her;
As she has done *to others*,
so do to her.
16 "Cut off the sower from Babylon
And the one who wields the
sickle at the time of harvest;
From before the sword
of the oppressor
They will each turn back
to his own people
And they will each flee
to his own land.

17 "Israel is a scattered flock, the lions have driven *them* away. The first one *who* devoured him was the king of Assyria, and this last one

who has broken his bones is Nebuchadnezzar king of Babylon. [18] Therefore thus says the LORD of hosts, the God of Israel: 'Behold, I am going to punish the king of Babylon and his land, just as I punished the king of Assyria. [19] And I will bring Israel back to his pasture and he will graze on Carmel and Bashan, and his desire will be satisfied in the hill country of Ephraim and Gilead. [20] In those days and at that time,' declares the LORD, 'search will be made for the iniquity of Israel, but there will be none; and for the sins of Judah, but they will not be found; for I will pardon those whom I leave as a remnant.'

[21] "Against the land of Merathaim,
    go up against it,
And against the inhabitants of Pekod.
Slay and utterly destroy them,"
    declares the LORD,
"And do according to all that I
    have commanded you.
[22] "The noise of battle is in the land,
And great destruction.
[23] "How the hammer of the whole earth
Has been cut off and broken!
How Babylon has become
An object of horror among
    the nations!

50:23 hammer of the whole earth. The description was of Babylon's former conquering force, and God's breaking the "hammer" He had once used. The fact that God used Babylon as His executioner was no commendation of that nation (Hab 1:6–7).

[24] "I set a snare for you and you were
    also caught, O Babylon,
While you yourself were not aware;
You have been found and also seized
Because you have engaged in
    conflict with the LORD."
[25] The LORD has opened His armory
And has brought forth the
    weapons of His indignation,
For it is a work of the
    Lord GOD of hosts
In the land of the Chaldeans.
[26] Come to her from the
    farthest border;
Open up her barns,
Pile her up like heaps
And utterly destroy her,
Let nothing be left to her.

[27] Put all her young bulls to the sword;
Let them go down to the slaughter!
Woe be upon them, for
    their day has come,
The time of their punishment.

[28] There is a sound of fugitives and
    refugees from the land of Babylon,
To declare in Zion the vengeance
    of the LORD our God,
Vengeance for His temple.

[29] "Summon many against Babylon,
All those who bend the bow:
Encamp against her on every side,
Let there be no escape.
Repay her according to her work;
According to all that she has
    done, *so* do to her;
For she has become arrogant
    against the LORD,
Against the Holy One of Israel.
[30] "Therefore her young men
    will fall in her streets,
And all her men of war will
    be silenced in that day,"
    declares the LORD.
[31] "Behold, I am against you,
    O arrogant one,"
Declares the Lord GOD of hosts,
"For your day has come,
The time when I will punish you.
[32] "The arrogant one will
    stumble and fall
With no one to raise him up;
And I will set fire to his cities
And it will devour all his environs."

[33] Thus says the LORD of hosts,
"The sons of Israel are oppressed,
And the sons of Judah as well;
And all who took them captive
    have held them fast,
They have refused to let them go.
[34] "Their Redeemer is strong, the
    LORD of hosts is His name;
He will vigorously plead their case
So that He may bring rest to the earth,
But turmoil to the inhabitants
    of Babylon.
[35] "A sword against the Chaldeans,"
    declares the LORD,
"And against the inhabitants
    of Babylon
And against her officials
    and her wise men!
[36] "A sword against the oracle priests,
    and they will become fools!

A sword against her mighty men,
and they will be shattered!
37 "A sword against their horses
and against their chariots
And against all the foreigners
who are in the midst of her,
And they will become women!
A sword against her treasures,
and they will be plundered!
38 "A drought on her waters, and
they will be dried up!
For it is a land of idols,
And they are mad over
fearsome idols.

39 "Therefore the desert creatures
will live *there* along
with the jackals;
The ostriches also will live in it,
And it will never again be inhabited
Or dwelt in from generation
to generation.
40 "As when God overthrew Sodom
And Gomorrah with its neighbors,"
declares the LORD,
"No man will live there,
Nor will *any* son of man reside in it.

41 "Behold, a people is coming
from the north,
And a great nation and many kings
Will be aroused from the
remote parts of the earth.
42 "They seize *their* bow and javelin;
They are cruel and have no mercy.
Their voice roars like the sea;
And they ride on horses,
Marshalled like a man for the battle
Against you, O daughter of Babylon.
43 "The king of Babylon has heard
the report about them,
And his hands hang limp;
Distress has gripped him,
Agony like a woman in childbirth.

44 "Behold, one will come up like a lion
from the thicket of the Jordan to a perennially
watered pasture; for in an instant I will make
them run away from it, and whoever is chosen
I will appoint over it. For who is like Me, and
who will summon Me *into court?* And who
then is the shepherd who can stand before
Me?" 45 Therefore hear the plan of the LORD
which He has planned against Babylon, and
His purposes which He has purposed against
the land of the Chaldeans: surely they will
drag them off, *even* the little ones of the flock;
surely He will make their pasture desolate
because of them. 46 At the shout, "Babylon has
been seized!" the earth is shaken, and an outcry is heard among the nations.

Psalm 119:121–128

ע AYIN.
121 I have done justice
and righteousness;
Do not leave me to my oppressors.
122 Be surety for Your servant for good;
Do not let the arrogant oppress me.
123 My eyes fail *with longing*
for Your salvation
And for Your righteous word.
124 Deal with Your servant according
to Your lovingkindness
And teach me Your statutes.
125 I am Your servant; give
me understanding,
That I may know Your testimonies.
126 It is time for the LORD to act,
For they have broken Your law.
127 Therefore I love Your
commandments
Above gold, yes, above fine gold.
128 Therefore I esteem right all *Your*
precepts concerning everything,
I hate every false way.

Proverbs 28:6

6 Better is the poor who walks
in his integrity
Than he who is crooked
though he be rich.

Titus 1:1–16

1 Paul, a bond-servant of God and an apostle
of Jesus Christ, for the faith of those chosen
of God and the knowledge of the truth which
is according to godliness, 2 in the hope of eternal life, which God, who cannot lie, promised
long ages ago, 3 but at the proper time manifested, *even* His word, in the proclamation
with which I was entrusted according to the
commandment of God our Savior,

1:1 bond-servant. Paul pictures himself as the
most menial slave of New Testament times,
indicating his complete and willing servitude
to the Lord, by whom all believers have been
"bought with a price" (1Co 6:20; see 1Pe 1:18–19).
This is the only time Paul referred to himself
as a "bond-servant of God" (Ro 1:1; Gal 1:10;
Php 1:1). He was placing himself alongside Old
Testament men of God (Rev 15:3).

⁴To Titus, my true child in a common faith: Grace and peace from God the Father and Christ Jesus our Savior.

⁵For this reason I left you in Crete, that you would set in order what remains and appoint elders in every city as I directed you, ⁶namely, if any man is above reproach, the husband of one wife, having children who believe, not accused of dissipation or rebellion. ⁷For the overseer must be above reproach as God's steward, not self-willed, not quick-tempered, not addicted to wine, not pugnacious, not fond of sordid gain, ⁸but hospitable, loving what is good, sensible, just, devout, self-controlled, ⁹holding fast the faithful word which is in accordance with the teaching, so that he will be able both to exhort in sound doctrine and to refute those who contradict.

¹⁰For there are many rebellious men, empty talkers and deceivers, especially those of the circumcision, ¹¹who must be silenced because they are upsetting whole families, teaching things they should not *teach* for the sake of sordid gain. ¹²One of themselves, a prophet of their own, said, "Cretans are always liars, evil beasts, lazy gluttons." ¹³This testimony is true. For this reason reprove them severely so that they may be sound in the faith, ¹⁴not paying attention to Jewish myths and commandments of men who turn away from the truth. ¹⁵To the pure, all things are pure; but to those who are defiled and

1:12 a prophet. Epimenides, the highly esteemed sixth century B.C. Greek poet and native of Crete, had characterized his own people as the dregs of Greek culture. Elsewhere, Paul also quoted pagan sayings (Ac 17:28; 1Co 15:33). This quote is directed at the false teachers' character.

1:14 myths and commandments of men. Paul reemphasized (v. 10, "those of the circumcision") that most of the false teachers were Jewish. They taught the same kind of externalism and unscriptural laws and traditions that both Isaiah and Jesus railed against (Is 29:13; Mt 15:1–9; Mk 7:5–13).

1:15 defiled. The outwardly despicable things that those men practiced (vv. 10–12) were simply reflections of their inner corruption. See Matthew 15:15–20. **mind...conscience.** If the mind is defiled, it cannot accurately inform the conscience, so conscience cannot warn the person. When conscience is accurately and fully infused with God's truth, it functions as the warning system God designed.

unbelieving, nothing is pure, but both their mind and their conscience are defiled. ¹⁶They profess to know God, but by *their* deeds they deny *Him,* being detestable and disobedient and worthless for any good deed.

DAY 1: Who was Titus, and what was his role in the church?

Although Luke did not mention Titus by name in the Book of Acts, it seems probable that Titus, a Gentile (Gal 2:3), met and may have been led to faith in Christ by Paul (Titus 1:4) before or during the apostle's first missionary journey. Later, Titus ministered for a period of time with Paul on the Island of Crete and was left behind to continue and strengthen the work (1:5). After Artemas or Tychicus (3:12) arrived to direct the ministry there, Paul wanted Titus to join him in the city of Nicopolis, in the province of Achaia in Greece, and stay through the winter (3:12).

Because of his involvement with the church at Corinth during Paul's third missionary journey, Titus is mentioned 9 times in 2 Corinthians, where Paul refers to him as "my brother" (2:13) and "my partner and fellow worker" (8:23). The young elder was already familiar with Judaizers, false teachers in the church, who among other things insisted that all Christians, Gentile as well as Jew, were bound by the Mosaic Law. Titus had accompanied Paul and Barnabas years earlier to the Council of Jerusalem where that heresy was the subject (Ac 15; Gal 2:1–5).

Crete, one of the largest islands in the Mediterranean Sea, measuring 160 miles long by 35 miles at its widest, lying south of the Aegean Sea, had been briefly visited by Paul on his voyage to Rome (Ac 27). He returned there for ministry and later left Titus to continue the work, much as he left Timothy at Ephesus (1Ti 1:3), while he went on to Macedonia. He most likely wrote to Titus in response to a letter from Titus or a report from Crete.

NOVEMBER 2

Jeremiah 51:1–52:34

51 Thus says the LORD:

"Behold, I am going to arouse
against Babylon
And against the inhabitants
of Leb-kamai
The spirit of a destroyer.

2 "I will dispatch foreigners to Babylon
that they may winnow her
And may devastate her land;
For on every side they will
be opposed to her
In the day of *her* calamity.

3 "Let not him who bends
his bow bend *it,*
Nor let him rise up in his scale-armor;
So do not spare her young men;
Devote all her army to destruction.

4 "They will fall down slain in the
land of the Chaldeans,
And pierced through in their streets."

5 For neither Israel nor Judah
has been forsaken
By his God, the LORD of hosts,
Although their land is full of guilt
Before the Holy One of Israel.

6 Flee from the midst of Babylon,
And each of you save his life!
Do not be destroyed in
her punishment,
For this is the LORD'S time
of vengeance;
He is going to render
recompense to her.

7 Babylon has been a golden cup
in the hand of the LORD,
Intoxicating all the earth.
The nations have drunk of her wine;
Therefore the nations are going mad.

8 Suddenly Babylon has fallen
and been broken;
Wail over her!
Bring balm for her pain;
Perhaps she may be healed.

51:8 Suddenly...fallen. The focus was first on
Babylon's sudden fall on one night in 539 B.C.
(Da 5:30). The far view looks at the destruction
of the final Babylon near the Second Advent
when it will be absolutely sudden (Rev 18).

---

9 We applied healing to Babylon,
but she was not healed;
Forsake her and let us each
go to his own country,
For her judgment has
reached to heaven
And towers up to the very skies.

10 The LORD has brought about
our vindication;
Come and let us recount in Zion
The work of the LORD our God!

11 Sharpen the arrows, fill the quivers!
The LORD has aroused the spirit
of the kings of the Medes,
Because His purpose is against
Babylon to destroy it;
For it is the vengeance of the LORD,
vengeance for His temple.

12 Lift up a signal against the
walls of Babylon;
Post a strong guard,
Station sentries,
Place men in ambush!
For the LORD has both
purposed and performed
What He spoke concerning the
inhabitants of Babylon.

13 O you who dwell by many waters,
Abundant in treasures,
Your end has come,
The measure of your end.

14 The LORD of hosts has
sworn by Himself:
"Surely I will fill you with a
population like locusts,
And they will cry out with
shouts of victory over you."

15 *It is* He who made the
earth by His power,
Who established the world
by His wisdom,
And by His understanding He
stretched out the heavens.

16 When He utters His voice, *there is* a
tumult of waters in the heavens,
And He causes the clouds to ascend
from the end of the earth;
He makes lightning for the rain
And brings forth the wind
from His storehouses.

17 All mankind is stupid,
devoid of knowledge;
Every goldsmith is put to
shame by his idols,
For his molten images are deceitful,
And there is no breath in them.

¹⁸ They are worthless, a
work of mockery;
In the time of their punishment
they will perish.
¹⁹ The portion of Jacob is not like these;
For the Maker of all is He,
And of the tribe of His inheritance;
The LORD of hosts is His name.
²⁰ *He says,* "You are My war-club,
My weapon of war;
And with you I shatter nations,
And with you I destroy kingdoms.
²¹ "With you I shatter the
horse and his rider,
And with you I shatter the
chariot and its rider,
²² And with you I shatter
man and woman,
And with you I shatter old man
and youth,
And with you I shatter young
man and virgin,
²³ And with you I shatter the
shepherd and his flock,
And with you I shatter the
farmer and his team,
And with you I shatter
governors and prefects.

51:15–19 He who made the earth. God's almighty power and wisdom in creation are evidences of His superiority to all idols (vv. 17–18),
who along with their worshipers will all be
destroyed by His mighty power (vv. 15–16, 19),
as in Babylon's case.

²⁴ "But I will repay Babylon and all the in-
habitants of Chaldea for all their evil that they
have done in Zion before your eyes," declares
the LORD.

²⁵ "Behold, I am against you,
O destroying mountain,
Who destroys the whole earth,"
declares the LORD,
"And I will stretch out My
hand against you,
And roll you down from the crags,
And I will make you a burnt
out mountain.
²⁶ "They will not take from you
even a stone for a corner
Nor a stone for foundations,
But you will be desolate forever,"
declares the LORD.

²⁷ Lift up a signal in the land,
Blow a trumpet among the nations!
Consecrate the nations against her,
Summon against her the kingdoms
of Ararat, Minni and Ashkenaz;
Appoint a marshal against her,
Bring up the horses like
bristly locusts.
²⁸ Consecrate the nations against her,
The kings of the Medes,
Their governors and
all their prefects,
And every land of their dominion.
²⁹ So the land quakes and writhes,
For the purposes of the LORD
against Babylon stand,
To make the land of Babylon
A desolation without inhabitants.
³⁰ The mighty men of Babylon
have ceased fighting,
They stay in the strongholds;
Their strength is exhausted,
They are becoming *like* women;
Their dwelling places are set on fire,
The bars of her *gates* are broken.
³¹ One courier runs to meet another,
And one messenger to meet another,
To tell the king of Babylon
That his city has been captured
from end *to end;*
³² The fords also have been seized,
And they have burned the
marshes with fire,
And the men of war are terrified.

³³ For thus says the LORD of
hosts, the God of Israel:
"The daughter of Babylon is
like a threshing floor
At the time it is stamped firm;
Yet in a little while the time of
harvest will come for her."

³⁴ "Nebuchadnezzar king of Babylon has
devoured me *and* crushed me,
He has set me down *like*
an empty vessel;
He has swallowed me
like a monster,
He has filled his stomach
with my delicacies;
He has washed me away.
³⁵ "May the violence *done* to me and
to my flesh be upon Babylon,"
The inhabitant of Zion will say;
And, "May my blood be upon the
inhabitants of Chaldea,"
Jerusalem will say.

36 Therefore thus says the LORD,

"Behold, I am going to plead your case
And exact full vengeance for you;
And I will dry up her sea
And make her fountain dry.
37 "Babylon will become a heap of
ruins, a haunt of jackals,
An object of horror and hissing,
without inhabitants.
38 "They will roar together
like young lions,
They will growl like lions' cubs.
39 "When they become heated up, I
will serve them their banquet
And make them drunk, that
they may become jubilant
And may sleep a perpetual sleep
And not wake up," declares the LORD.
40 "I will bring them down like
lambs to the slaughter,
Like rams together with male goats.

41 "How Sheshak has been captured,
And the praise of the whole
earth been seized!
How Babylon has become an object
of horror among the nations!
42 "The sea has come up over Babylon;
She has been engulfed with
its tumultuous waves.
43 "Her cities have become an
object of horror,
A parched land and a desert,
A land in which no man lives
And through which no
son of man passes.
44 "I will punish Bel in Babylon,
And I will make what he has
swallowed come out of his mouth;
And the nations will no
longer stream to him.
Even the wall of Babylon
has fallen down!

45 "Come forth from her
midst, My people,
And each of you save yourselves
From the fierce anger of the LORD.
46 "Now so that your heart
does not grow faint,
And you are not afraid at the report
that will be heard in the land—
For the report will come one year,
And after that another report
in another year,
And violence will be in the land
With ruler against ruler—

47 Therefore behold, days are coming
When I will punish the
idols of Babylon;
And her whole land will
be put to shame
And all her slain will
fall in her midst.
48 "Then heaven and earth and
all that is in them
Will shout for joy over Babylon,
For the destroyers will come
to her from the north,"
Declares the LORD.

49 Indeed Babylon is to fall for
the slain of Israel,
As also for Babylon the slain of
all the earth have fallen.
50 You who have escaped the sword,
Depart! Do not stay!
Remember the LORD from afar,
And let Jerusalem come
to your mind.
51 We are ashamed because we
have heard reproach;
Disgrace has covered our faces,
For aliens have entered
The holy places of the LORD'S house.

52 "Therefore behold, the days are
coming," declares the LORD,
"When I will punish her idols,
And the mortally wounded will
groan throughout her land.
53 "Though Babylon should
ascend to the heavens,
And though she should fortify
her lofty stronghold,
From Me destroyers will come
to her," declares the LORD.

54 The sound of an outcry from Babylon,
And of great destruction from
the land of the Chaldeans!
55 For the LORD is going to
destroy Babylon,
And He will make her loud
noise vanish from her.
And their waves will roar
like many waters;
The tumult of their voices
sounds forth.
56 For the destroyer is coming
against her, against Babylon,
And her mighty men will be captured,
Their bows are shattered;
For the LORD is a God of recompense,
He will fully repay.

⁵⁷ "I will make her princes and
    her wise men drunk,
Her governors, her prefects
    and her mighty men,
That they may sleep a perpetual
    sleep and not wake up,"
Declares the King, whose name
    is the LORD of hosts.

⁵⁸ Thus says the LORD of hosts,

"The broad wall of Babylon will
    be completely razed
And her high gates will be set on fire;
So the peoples will toil for nothing,
And the nations become
    exhausted only for fire."

⁵⁹ The message which Jeremiah the prophet commanded Seraiah the son of Neriah, the grandson of Mahseiah, when he went with Zedekiah the king of Judah to Babylon in the fourth year of his reign. (Now Seraiah was quartermaster.) ⁶⁰ So Jeremiah wrote in a single scroll all the calamity which would come upon Babylon, that is, all these words which have been written concerning Babylon. ⁶¹ Then Jeremiah said to Seraiah, "As soon as you come to Babylon, then see that you read all these words aloud, ⁶² and say, 'You, O LORD, have promised concerning this place to cut it off, so that there will be nothing dwelling in it, whether man or beast, but it will be a perpetual desolation.' ⁶³ And as soon as you finish reading this scroll, you will tie a stone to it and throw it into the middle of the Euphrates, ⁶⁴ and say, 'Just so shall Babylon sink down and not rise again because of the calamity that I am going to bring upon her; and they will become exhausted.'" Thus far are the words of Jeremiah.

52

Zedekiah was twenty-one years old when he became king, and he reigned eleven years in Jerusalem; and his mother's name was Hamutal the daughter of Jeremiah of Libnah. ² He did evil in the sight of the LORD like all that Jehoiakim had done. ³ For through the anger of the LORD this came about in Jerusalem and Judah until He cast them out from His presence. And Zedekiah rebelled against the king of Babylon. ⁴ Now it came about in the ninth year of his reign, on the tenth day of the tenth month, that Nebuchadnezzar king of Babylon came, he and all his army, against Jerusalem, camped against it and built a siege wall all around it. ⁵ So the city was under siege until the eleventh year of King Zedekiah. ⁶ On the ninth day of the fourth month the famine was so severe in the city that there was no food for the people of the land. ⁷ Then the city was broken into, and all the men of war fled and went forth from the city at night by way of the gate between the two walls which was by the king's garden, though the Chaldeans were all around the city. And they went by way of the Arabah. ⁸ But the army of the Chaldeans pursued the king and overtook Zedekiah in the plains of Jericho, and all his army was scattered from him. ⁹ Then they captured the king and brought him up to the king of Babylon at Riblah in the land of Hamath, and he passed sentence on him. ¹⁰ The king of Babylon slaughtered the sons of Zedekiah before his eyes, and he also slaughtered all the princes of Judah in Riblah. ¹¹ Then he blinded the eyes of Zedekiah; and the king of Babylon bound him with bronze fetters and brought him to Babylon and put him in prison until the day of his death.

¹² Now on the tenth day of the fifth month, which was the nineteenth year of King Nebuchadnezzar, king of Babylon, Nebuzaradan the captain of the bodyguard, who was in the service of the king of Babylon, came to Jerusalem. ¹³ He burned the house of the LORD, the king's house and all the houses of Jerusalem; even every large house he burned with fire. ¹⁴ So all the army of the Chaldeans who were with the captain of the guard broke down all the walls around Jerusalem. ¹⁵ Then Nebuzaradan the captain of the guard carried away into exile some of the poorest of the people, the rest of the people who were left in the city, the deserters who had deserted to the king of Babylon and the rest of the artisans. ¹⁶ But Nebuzaradan the captain of the guard left some of the poorest of the land to be vinedressers and plowmen.

¹⁷ Now the bronze pillars which belonged to the house of the LORD and the stands and the bronze sea, which were in the house of the LORD, the Chaldeans broke in pieces and carried all their bronze to Babylon. ¹⁸ They also took away the pots, the shovels, the snuffers, the basins, the pans and all the bronze vessels which were used in temple service. ¹⁹ The captain of the guard also took away the bowls, the firepans, the basins, the pots, the lampstands, the pans and the drink offering bowls, what was fine gold and what was fine silver. ²⁰ The two pillars, the one sea, and the twelve bronze bulls that were under the sea, and the stands, which King Solomon had made for the house of the LORD—the bronze of all these vessels was beyond weight. ²¹ As for the pillars, the

height of each pillar *was* eighteen cubits, and it *was* twelve cubits in circumference and four fingers in thickness, *and* hollow. 22 Now a capital of bronze was on it; and the height of each capital was five cubits, with network and pomegranates upon the capital all around, all of bronze. And the second pillar was like these, including pomegranates. 23 There were ninety-six exposed pomegranates; all the pomegranates *numbered* a hundred on the network all around.

24 Then the captain of the guard took Seraiah the chief priest and Zephaniah the second priest, with the three officers of the temple. 25 He also took from the city one official who was overseer of the men of war, and seven of the king's advisers who were found in the city, and the scribe of the commander of the army who mustered the people of the land, and sixty men of the people of the land who were found in the midst of the city. 26 Nebuzaradan the captain of the guard took them and brought them to the king of Babylon at Riblah. 27 Then the king of Babylon struck them down and put them to death at Riblah in the land of Hamath. So Judah was led away into exile from its land.

28 These are the people whom Nebuchadnezzar carried away into exile: in the seventh year 3,023 Jews; 29 in the eighteenth year of Nebuchadnezzar 832 persons from Jerusalem; 30 in the twenty-third year of Nebuchadnezzar, Nebuzaradan the captain of the guard carried into exile 745 Jewish people; there were 4,600 persons in all.

31 Now it came about in the thirty-seventh year of the exile of Jehoiachin king of Judah, in the twelfth month, on the twenty-fifth of the month, that Evil-merodach king of Babylon, in the *first* year of his reign, showed favor to Jehoiachin king of Judah and brought him out of prison. 32 Then he spoke kindly to him and set his throne above the thrones of the kings who *were* with him in Babylon. 33 So Jehoiachin changed his prison clothes, and had his meals in the king's presence regularly all the days of his life. 34 For his allowance, a regular allowance was given him by the king of Babylon, a daily portion all the days of his life until the day of his death.

Psalm 119:129–136

 פ PE.

129 Your testimonies are wonderful;
    Therefore my soul observes them.
130 The unfolding of Your
        words gives light;
    It gives understanding to the simple.
131 I opened my mouth wide and panted,
    For I longed for Your commandments.
132 Turn to me and be gracious to me,
    After Your manner with those
        who love Your name.
133 Establish my footsteps in Your word,
    And do not let any iniquity
        have dominion over me.
134 Redeem me from the
        oppression of man,
    That I may keep Your precepts.
135 Make Your face shine upon
        Your servant,
    And teach me Your statutes.
136 My eyes shed streams of water,
    Because they do not keep Your law.

Proverbs 28:7–8

7 He who keeps the law is
    a discerning son,
   But he who is a companion of
    gluttons humiliates his father.
8 He who increases his wealth
    by interest and usury
   Gathers it for him who is
    gracious to the poor.

Titus 2:1–15

2 But as for you, speak the things which are fitting for sound doctrine. 2 Older men are to be temperate, dignified, sensible, sound in faith, in love, in perseverance.

3 Older women likewise are to be reverent in their behavior, not malicious gossips nor enslaved to much wine, teaching what is good, 4 so that they may encourage the young women to love their husbands, to love their children, 5 *to be* sensible, pure, workers at home, kind, being subject to their own husbands, so that the word of God will not be dishonored.

6 Likewise urge the young men to be sensible; 7 in all things show yourself to be an example of good deeds, *with* purity in doctrine,

2:4 encourage the young women. Their own examples of godliness (v. 3) give older women the right and the credibility to instruct younger women in the church. The obvious implication is that older women must exemplify the virtues (vv. 4–5) that they "encourage." **love their husbands.** Like the other virtues mentioned here, this one is unconditional. It is based on God's will, not on a husband's worthiness. The Greek word *phileō* emphasizes affection.

dignified, [8] sound in speech which is beyond reproach, so that the opponent will be put to shame, having nothing bad to say about us.

[9] *Urge* bondslaves to be subject to their own

2:9 bondslaves. The term applies generally to all employees, but direct reference is to slaves—men, women, and children who, in the Roman Empire and in much of the ancient world, were owned by their masters. They had few, if any, civil rights and often were accorded little more dignity or care than domestic animals. The New Testament nowhere condones or condemns the practice of slavery, but it everywhere teaches that freedom from the bondage of sin is infinitely more important than freedom from any human bondage a person may have to endure (see Ro 6:22). **subject to... masters...well-pleasing.** Paul clearly teaches that, even in the most servile of circumstances, believers are "to be subject" and seek to please those for whom they work, whether their "masters" are believers or unbelievers, fair or unfair, kind or cruel. How much more obligated are believers to respect and obey employers for whom they work voluntarily! As with wives' obedience to their husbands (v. 5), the only exception would involve a believer's being required to disobey God's Word.

masters in everything, to be well-pleasing, not argumentative, [10] not pilfering, but showing all good faith so that they will adorn the doctrine of God our Savior in every respect.

[11] For the grace of God has appeared, bringing salvation to all men, [12] instructing us to deny ungodliness and worldly desires and to live sensibly, righteously and godly in the present age, [13] looking for the blessed hope and the appearing of the glory of our great God and Savior, Christ Jesus, [14] who gave Himself for us to redeem us from every lawless deed, and to purify for Himself a people for His own possession, zealous for good deeds.

[15] These things speak and exhort and reprove with all authority. Let no one disregard you.

2:14 redeem...purify. Another expression (v. 12) summarizes the dual effect of salvation (regeneration and sanctification). To "redeem" is to release someone held captive, on the payment of a ransom. The price was Christ's blood paid to satisfy God's justice. **a people for His own possession.** People who are special by virtue of God's decree and confirmed by the grace of salvation which they have embraced (1Co 6:19–20; 1Pe 2:9). **zealous.** Good works are the product, not the means, of salvation (Eph 2:10).

DAY 2: How does the Book of Titus indicate that the message was intended for more than just Titus and the Christians on Crete?

Titus 2:11–13 presents the heart of Paul's letter to Titus. The apostle had already emphasized that God's sovereign purpose in calling out elders (1:5) and in commanding His people to live righteously (vv. 1–10) is to provide the witness that brings God's plan and purpose of salvation to fulfillment. Paul condensed the saving plan of God into 3 realities: 1) salvation from the penalty (v. 11); 2) salvation from the power (v. 12); and 3) salvation from the presence of sin (v. 13).

As Paul described the "grace of God...bringing salvation" (v. 11), he was not simply referring to the divine attribute of grace, but Jesus Christ Himself, grace incarnate, God's supremely gracious gift to fallen mankind (Jn 1:14). The term "all men" does not teach universal salvation. "All men" is used as "man" in 3:4 to refer to humanity in general, as a category, not to every individual. Jesus Christ made a sufficient sacrifice to cover every sin of everyone who believes (Jn 3:16–18; 1Ti 2:5–6; 4:10; 1Jn 2:2). Paul makes clear in the opening words of this letter to Titus that salvation becomes effective only through "the faith of those chosen of God" (1:1). Paul was well aware that the gospel had universal implications. Out of all humanity, only those who believe will be saved (Jn 1:12; 3:16; 5:24, 38, 40; 6:40; 10:9; Ro 10:9–17).

NOVEMBER 3

Lamentations 1:1–2:22

1 How lonely sits the city
That was full of people!
She has become like a widow

Who was once great among
  the nations!
She who was a princess
  among the provinces
Has become a forced laborer!
[2] She weeps bitterly in the night
  And her tears are on her cheeks;

She has none to comfort her
Among all her lovers.
All her friends have dealt
   treacherously with her;
They have become her enemies.

3 Judah has gone into exile
   under affliction
And under harsh servitude;
She dwells among the nations,
But she has found no rest;
All her pursuers have overtaken her
In the midst of distress.

4 The roads of Zion are in mourning
Because no one comes to
   the appointed feasts.
All her gates are desolate;
Her priests are groaning,
Her virgins are afflicted,
And she herself is bitter.

5 Her adversaries have
   become her masters,
Her enemies prosper;
For the LORD has caused her grief
Because of the multitude of
   her transgressions;
Her little ones have gone away
As captives before the adversary.

6 All her majesty
Has departed from the
   daughter of Zion;
Her princes have become like deer
That have found no pasture;
And they have fled without strength
Before the pursuer.

7 In the days of her affliction
   and homelessness
Jerusalem remembers all
   her precious things
That were from the days of old,
When her people fell into the
   hand of the adversary
And no one helped her.
The adversaries saw her,
They mocked at her ruin.

8 Jerusalem sinned greatly,
Therefore she has become
   an unclean thing.
All who honored her despise her
Because they have seen her nakedness;
Even she herself groans
   and turns away.

9 Her uncleanness was in her skirts;
She did not consider her future.
Therefore she has fallen astonishingly;
She has no comforter.
"See, O LORD, my affliction,
For the enemy has
   magnified himself!"

10 The adversary has stretched
   out his hand
Over all her precious things,
For she has seen the nations
   enter her sanctuary,
The ones whom You commanded
That they should not enter
   into Your congregation.

11 All her people groan seeking bread;
They have given their precious
   things for food
To restore their lives themselves.
"See, O LORD, and look,
For I am despised."

12 "Is it nothing to all you who
   pass this way?
Look and see if there is any
   pain like my pain
Which was severely dealt out to me,
Which the LORD inflicted on the
   day of His fierce anger.

13 "From on high He sent fire
   into my bones,
And it prevailed *over them.*
He has spread a net for my feet;
He has turned me back;
He has made me desolate,
Faint all day long.

14 "The yoke of my transgressions
   is bound;
By His hand they are knit together.
They have come upon my neck;
He has made my strength fail.
The Lord has given me into the hands
Of *those against whom* I am
   not able to stand.

15 "The Lord has rejected all
   my strong men
In my midst;
He has called an appointed
   time against me
To crush my young men;
The Lord has trodden *as in* a wine press
The virgin daughter of Judah.

16 "For these things I weep;
My eyes run down with water;
Because far from me is a comforter,
One who restores my soul.
My children are desolate
Because the enemy has prevailed."

17 Zion stretches out her hands;
There is no one to comfort her;
The LORD has commanded
   concerning Jacob
That the ones round about him
   should be his adversaries;
Jerusalem has become an
   unclean thing among them.

¹⁸ "The LORD is righteous;
For I have rebelled against
His command;
Hear now, all peoples,
And behold my pain;
My virgins and my young men
Have gone into captivity.
¹⁹ "I called to my lovers, *but*
they deceived me;
My priests and my elders
perished in the city
While they sought food to restore
their strength themselves.
²⁰ "See, O LORD, for I am in distress;
My spirit is greatly troubled;
My heart is overturned within me,
For I have been very rebellious.
In the street the sword slays;
In the house it is like death.
²¹ "They have heard that I groan;
There is no one to comfort me;
All my enemies have heard
of my calamity;
They are glad that You have done *it*.
Oh, that You would bring the day
which You have proclaimed,
That they may become like me.
²² "Let all their wickedness
come before You;
And deal with them as You
have dealt with me
For all my transgressions;
For my groans are many and
my heart is faint."

1:21–22 bring the day. A prayer that God will likewise bring other ungodly people into judgment, especially Babylon (3:64–66; 4:21–22). Such prayers are acceptable against the enemies of God (Ps 109:14–15).

2 How the Lord has covered
the daughter of Zion
With a cloud in His anger!
He has cast from heaven to earth
The glory of Israel,
And has not remembered
His footstool
In the day of His anger.
² The Lord has swallowed up;
He has not spared
All the habitations of Jacob.
In His wrath He has thrown down
The strongholds of the
daughter of Judah;

He has brought *them* down
to the ground;
He has profaned the kingdom
and its princes.
³ In fierce anger He has cut off
All the strength of Israel;
He has drawn back His right hand
From before the enemy.
And He has burned in Jacob
like a flaming fire
Consuming round about.
⁴ He has bent His bow like an enemy;
He has set His right hand
like an adversary
And slain all that were
pleasant to the eye;
In the tent of the daughter of Zion
He has poured out His wrath like fire.
⁵ The Lord has become like an enemy.
He has swallowed up Israel;
He has swallowed up all its palaces,
He has destroyed its strongholds
And multiplied in the
daughter of Judah
Mourning and moaning.
⁶ And He has violently treated His
tabernacle like a garden *booth;*
He has destroyed His appointed
meeting place.
The LORD has caused to be forgotten
The appointed feast and
sabbath in Zion,
And He has despised king and priest
In the indignation of His anger.
⁷ The Lord has rejected His altar,
He has abandoned His sanctuary;
He has delivered into the
hand of the enemy
The walls of her palaces.
They have made a noise in
the house of the LORD
As in the day of an appointed feast.
⁸ The LORD determined to destroy
The wall of the daughter of Zion.
He has stretched out a line,
He has not restrained His
hand from destroying,
And He has caused rampart
and wall to lament;
They have languished together.
⁹ Her gates have sunk into the ground,
He has destroyed and
broken her bars.
Her king and her princes are
among the nations;
The law is no more.
Also, her prophets find
No vision from the LORD.

10 The elders of the daughter of Zion
  Sit on the ground, they are silent.
  They have thrown dust on their heads;
  They have girded themselves
      with sackcloth.
  The virgins of Jerusalem
  Have bowed their heads to the ground.
11 My eyes fail because of tears,
  My spirit is greatly troubled;
  My heart is poured out on the earth
  Because of the destruction of
      the daughter of my people,
  When little ones and infants faint
  In the streets of the city.
12 They say to their mothers,
  "Where is grain and wine?"
  As they faint like a wounded man
  In the streets of the city,
  As their life is poured out
  On their mothers' bosom.
13 How shall I admonish you?
  To what shall I compare you,
  O daughter of Jerusalem?
  To what shall I liken you
      as I comfort you,
  O virgin daughter of Zion?
  For your ruin is as vast as the sea;
  Who can heal you?
14 Your prophets have seen for you
  False and foolish *visions;*
  And they have not exposed
      your iniquity
  So as to restore you from captivity,
  But they have seen for you false
      and misleading oracles.
15 All who pass along the way
  Clap their hands *in derision* at you;
  They hiss and shake their heads
  At the daughter of Jerusalem,
  "Is this the city of which they said,
  'The perfection of beauty,
  A joy to all the earth'?"
16 All your enemies
  Have opened their mouths
      wide against you;
  They hiss and gnash *their* teeth.
  They say, "We have swallowed *her* up!
  Surely this is the day for
      which we waited;
  We have reached *it,* we have seen *it.*"
17 The LORD has done what
      He purposed;
  He has accomplished His word
  Which He commanded
      from days of old.
  He has thrown down without sparing,
  And He has caused the enemy
      to rejoice over you;

He has exalted the might of
    your adversaries.
18 Their heart cried out to the Lord,
  "O wall of the daughter of Zion,
  Let *your* tears run down like
      a river day and night;
  Give yourself no relief,
  Let your eyes have no rest.
19 "Arise, cry aloud in the night
  At the beginning of the
      night watches;
  Pour out your heart like water
  Before the presence of the Lord;
  Lift up your hands to Him
  For the life of your little ones
  Who are faint because of hunger
  At the head of every street."
20 See, O LORD, and look!
  With whom have You dealt thus?
  Should women eat their offspring,
  The little ones who were
      born healthy?
  Should priest and prophet be slain
  In the sanctuary of the Lord?

2:20 See, O LORD, and look! The chapter closes by placing the issue before God. **women eat their offspring.** Hunger became so desperate in the 18-month siege that women resorted to the unbelievable—even eating their children (4:10; Lv 26:29; Dt 28:53, 56–57; Jer 19:9).

---

21 On the ground in the streets
  Lie young and old;
  My virgins and my young men
  Have fallen by the sword.
  You have slain *them* in the
      day of Your anger,
  You have slaughtered, not sparing.
22 You called as in the day of
      an appointed feast
  My terrors on every side;
  And there was no one who
      escaped or survived
  In the day of the LORD'S anger.
  Those whom I bore and reared,
  My enemy annihilated them.

Psalm 119:137–144

צ TSADHE.
137 Righteous are You, O LORD,
  And upright are Your judgments.
138 You have commanded Your
      testimonies in righteousness
  And exceeding faithfulness.

¹³⁹ My zeal has consumed me,
　Because my adversaries have
　　forgotten Your words.
¹⁴⁰ Your word is very pure,
　Therefore Your servant loves it.
¹⁴¹ I am small and despised,
　Yet I do not forget Your precepts.
¹⁴² Your righteousness is an
　　everlasting righteousness,
　And Your law is truth.
¹⁴³ Trouble and anguish have
　　come upon me,
　Yet Your commandments
　　are my delight.
¹⁴⁴ Your testimonies are
　　righteous forever;
　Give me understanding
　　that I may live.

Proverbs 28:9–10

⁹ He who turns away his ear
　from listening to the law,
　Even his prayer is an abomination.
¹⁰ He who leads the upright
　astray in an evil way
　Will himself fall into his own pit,
　But the blameless will inherit good.

Titus 3:1–15

3 Remind them to be subject to rulers, to authorities, to be obedient, to be ready for every good deed, ²to malign no one, to be peaceable, gentle, showing every consideration for all men. ³For we also once

3:1–11 In his closing remarks, Paul admonished Titus to remind believers under his care of their attitudes toward: 1) the unsaved rulers (v. 1) and people in general (v. 2); 2) their previous state as unbelievers lost in sin (v. 3); 3) of their gracious salvation through Jesus Christ (vv. 4–7); 4) of their righteous testimony to the unsaved world (v. 8); 5) and of their responsibility to oppose false teachers and factious members within the church (vv. 9–11). All of these matters are essential to effective evangelism.

3:3 ourselves. It is not that every believer has committed every sin listed here, but rather that before salvation every life is characterized by such sins. That sobering truth should make believers humble in dealing with the unsaved, even those who are grossly immoral and ungodly. If it weren't for God's grace to His own, they would all be wicked.

were foolish ourselves, disobedient, deceived, enslaved to various lusts and pleasures, spending our life in malice and envy, hateful, hating one another. ⁴But when the kindness of God our Savior and *His* love for mankind appeared, ⁵He saved us, not on the basis of deeds which we have done in righteousness, but according to His mercy, by the washing of regeneration and renewing by the Holy Spirit, ⁶whom He poured out upon us richly through Jesus Christ our Savior, ⁷so that being justified by His grace we would be made heirs according to *the* hope of eternal life. ⁸This is a trustworthy statement; and concerning these things I want you to speak confidently, so that those who have believed God will be careful to engage in good deeds. These things are good and profitable for men. ⁹But avoid foolish controversies and genealogies and strife and disputes about the Law, for they are unprofitable and worthless. ¹⁰Reject a factious man after a first and second warning, ¹¹knowing that such a man is perverted and is sinning, being self-condemned.

¹²When I send Artemas or Tychicus to you, make every effort to come to me at Nicopolis, for I have decided to spend the winter there. ¹³Diligently help Zenas the lawyer and Apollos on their way so that nothing is lacking for them. ¹⁴Our people must also learn to engage in good deeds to meet pressing needs, so that they will not be unfruitful.

¹⁵All who are with me greet you. Greet those who love us in *the* faith.

Grace be with you all.

DAY 3: What is the Book of Lamentations about?

The prophetic seeds of Jerusalem's destruction were sown through Joshua 800 years in advance (Jos 23:15–16). Now, for over 40 years, Jeremiah had prophesied of coming judgment and been scorned by the people for preaching doom (ca. 645–605 B.C.). When that judgment came on the disbelieving people from Nebuchadnezzar and the Babylonian army, Jeremiah still responded with great sorrow and compassion toward his suffering and obstinate people. Lamentations relates closely to the Book of Jeremiah, describing the anguish over Jerusalem's receiving God's judgment for unrepentant sins. In the book that bears his name, Jeremiah had predicted the calamity in chapters 1–29. In Lamentations, he concentrates in more detail on the bitter suffering and heartbreak that was felt over Jerusalem's devastation (Ps 46:4–5). So critical was Jerusalem's destruction that the facts are recorded in 4 separate Old Testament chapters: 2 Kings 25; Jeremiah 39:1–11; 52; and 2 Chronicles 36:11–21.

All 154 verses have been recognized by the Jews as a part of their sacred canon. Along with Ruth, Esther, Song of Solomon, and Ecclesiastes, Lamentations is included among the Old Testament books of the Megilloth, or "five scrolls," which were read in the synagogue on special occasions. Lamentations is read on the ninth of Ab (July/Aug.) to remember the date of Jerusalem's destruction by Nebuchadnezzar. Interestingly, this same date later marked the destruction of Herod's temple by the Romans in A.D. 70.

NOVEMBER 4

Lamentations 3:1–5:22

3 I am the man who has seen affliction
Because of the rod of His wrath.

2 He has driven me and made me walk
In darkness and not in light.

3 Surely against me He has
turned His hand
Repeatedly all the day.

4 He has caused my flesh and
my skin to waste away,
He has broken my bones.

5 He has besieged and encompassed
me with bitterness and hardship.

6 In dark places He has made me dwell,
Like those who have long been dead.

7 He has walled me in so that
I cannot go out;
He has made my chain heavy.

8 Even when I cry out and call for help,
He shuts out my prayer.

9 He has blocked my ways
with hewn stone;
He has made my paths crooked.

10 He is to me like a bear lying in wait,
Like a lion in secret places.

11 He has turned aside my ways
and torn me to pieces;
He has made me desolate.

12 He bent His bow
And set me as a target for the arrow.

13 He made the arrows of His quiver
To enter into my inward parts.

14 I have become a laughingstock
to all my people,
Their *mocking* song all the day.

15 He has filled me with bitterness,
He has made me drunk
with wormwood.

16 He has broken my teeth with gravel;
He has made me cower in the dust.

17 My soul has been rejected from peace;
I have forgotten happiness.

18 So I say, "My strength has perished,
And *so has* my hope from the LORD."

19 Remember my affliction
and my wandering, the
wormwood and bitterness.

20 Surely my soul remembers
And is bowed down within me.

21 This I recall to my mind,
Therefore I have hope.

22 The LORD'S lovingkindnesses
indeed never cease,
For His compassions never fail.

23 *They* are new every morning;
Great is Your faithfulness.

24 "The LORD is my portion,"
says my soul,
"Therefore I have hope in Him."

25 The LORD is good to those
who wait for Him,
To the person who seeks Him.

26 *It is* good that he waits silently
For the salvation of the LORD.

3:8 He shuts out my prayer. God's nonresponse to Jeremiah's prayers was not because Jeremiah was guilty of personal sin (Ps 66:18); rather, it was due to Israel's perpetual sin without repentance (Jer 19:15). God's righteousness to judge that sin must pursue its course (Jer 7:16; 11:14). Jeremiah knew that, yet prayed, wept (vv. 48–51), and longed to see repentance.

3:22–24 His compassions never fail. As bleak as the situation of judgment had become, God's covenant lovingkindness was always present (vv. 31–32), and His incredible faithfulness always endured so that Judah would not be destroyed forever (Mal 3:6).

27 *It is* good for a man that
    he should bear
    The yoke in his youth.
28 Let him sit alone and be silent
    Since He has laid *it* on him.
29 Let him put his mouth in the dust,
    Perhaps there is hope.
30 Let him give his cheek to the smiter,
    Let him be filled with reproach.
31 For the Lord will not reject forever,
32 For if He causes grief,
    Then He will have compassion
    According to His abundant
        lovingkindness.
33 For He does not afflict willingly
    Or grieve the sons of men.
34 To crush under His feet
    All the prisoners of the land,
35 To deprive a man of justice
    In the presence of the Most High,
36 To defraud a man in his lawsuit—
    Of these things the Lord
        does not approve.
37 Who is there who speaks
    and it comes to pass,
    Unless the Lord has commanded *it?*
38 *Is it* not from the mouth
    of the Most High
    That both good and ill go forth?

39 Why should *any* living
    mortal, or *any* man,
    Offer complaint in view of his sins?
40 Let us examine and probe our ways,
    And let us return to the LORD.
41 We lift up our heart and hands
    Toward God in heaven;
42 We have transgressed and rebelled,
    You have not pardoned.
43 You have covered *Yourself* with anger
    And pursued us;
    You have slain *and* have not spared.
44 You have covered Yourself
    with a cloud
    So that no prayer can pass through.
45 *You have made us mere*
    offscouring and refuse
    In the midst of the peoples.
46 All our enemies have opened
    their mouths against us.
47 Panic and pitfall have befallen us,
    Devastation and destruction;
48 My eyes run down with
    streams of water
    Because of the destruction of
    the daughter of my people.
49 My eyes pour down unceasingly,
    Without stopping,

50 Until the LORD looks down
    And sees from heaven.
51 My eyes bring pain to my soul
    Because of all the daughters
    of my city.
52 My enemies without cause
    Hunted me down like a bird;
53 They have silenced me in the pit
    And have placed a stone on me.
54 Waters flowed over my head;
    I said, "I am cut off!"
55 I called on Your name, O LORD,
    Out of the lowest pit.
56 You have heard my voice,
    "Do not hide Your ear from
        my *prayer for* relief,
    From my cry for help."
57 You drew near when I called on You;
    You said, "Do not fear!"
58 O Lord, You have pleaded
    my soul's cause;
    You have redeemed my life.
59 O LORD, You have seen
    my oppression;
    Judge my case.
60 You have seen all their vengeance,
    All their schemes against me.
61 You have heard their
    reproach, O LORD,
    All their schemes against me.
62 The lips of my assailants
    and their whispering
    Are against me all day long.
63 Look on their sitting and their rising;
    I am their mocking song.
64 You will recompense them, O LORD,
    According to the work
    of their hands.
65 You will give them hardness of heart,
    Your curse will be on them.
66 You will pursue them in anger
    and destroy them
    From under the heavens of the LORD!

4 How dark the gold has become,
    How the pure gold has changed!
    The sacred stones are poured out
    At the corner of every street.
2 The precious sons of Zion,
    Weighed against fine gold,
    How they are regarded
    as earthen jars,
    The work of a potter's hands!
3 Even jackals offer the breast,
    They nurse their young;
    But the daughter of my people
    has become cruel
    Like ostriches in the wilderness.

⁴ The tongue of the infant cleaves
To the roof of its mouth
    because of thirst;
The little ones ask for bread,
But no one breaks *it* for them.
⁵ Those who ate delicacies
Are desolate in the streets;
Those reared in purple
Embrace ash pits.
⁶ For the iniquity of the
    daughter of my people
Is greater than the sin of Sodom,
Which was overthrown
    as in a moment,
And no hands were turned
    toward her.
⁷ Her consecrated ones were
    purer than snow,
They were whiter than milk;
They were more ruddy *in*
    body than corals,
Their polishing *was like* lapis lazuli.
⁸ Their appearance is blacker than soot,
They are not recognized in the streets;
Their skin is shriveled on their bones,
It is withered, it has
    become like wood.
⁹ Better are those slain with the sword
Than those slain with hunger;
For they pine away, being stricken
For lack of the fruits of the field.
¹⁰ The hands of compassionate women
Boiled their own children;
They became food for them
Because of the destruction of
    the daughter of my people.
¹¹ The LORD has accomplished
    His wrath,
He has poured out His fierce anger;
And He has kindled a fire in Zion
Which has consumed its foundations.
¹² The kings of the earth did not believe,
Nor *did* any of the inhabitants
    of the world,
That the adversary and the enemy
Could enter the gates of Jerusalem.
¹³ Because of the sins of her prophets
And the iniquities of her priests,
Who have shed in her midst
The blood of the righteous;
¹⁴ They wandered, blind, in the streets;
They were defiled with blood
So that no one could touch
    their garments.
¹⁵ "Depart! Unclean!" they
    cried of themselves.
"Depart, depart, do not touch!"
So they fled and wandered;

Men among the nations said,
"They shall not continue
    to dwell *with us*."
¹⁶ The presence of the LORD
    has scattered them,
He will not continue to regard them;
They did not honor the priests,
They did not favor the elders.
¹⁷ Yet our eyes failed,
Looking for help was useless;
In our watching we have watched
For a nation that could not save.
¹⁸ They hunted our steps
So that we could not walk
    in our streets;
Our end drew near,
Our days were finished
For our end had come.
¹⁹ Our pursuers were swifter
Than the eagles of the sky;
They chased us on the mountains,
They waited in ambush for
    us in the wilderness.
²⁰ The breath of our nostrils,
    the LORD'S anointed,
Was captured in their pits,
Of whom we had said,
    "Under his shadow
We shall live among the nations."
²¹ Rejoice and be glad,
    O daughter of Edom,
Who dwells in the land of Uz;
But the cup will come around
    to you as well,
You will become drunk and
    make yourself naked.
²² *The punishment* of your
    iniquity has been completed,
    O daughter of Zion;
He will exile you no longer.
But He will punish your iniquity,
    O daughter of Edom,
He will expose your sins!

5 Remember, O LORD, what
    has befallen us;
Look, and see our reproach!
² Our inheritance has been
    turned over to strangers,
Our houses to aliens.
³ We have become orphans
    without a father,
Our mothers are like widows.
⁴ We have to pay for our drinking water,
Our wood comes *to us* at a price.
⁵ Our pursuers are at our necks;
We are worn out, there
    is no rest for us.

6 We have submitted to Egypt *and*
Assyria to get enough bread.
7 Our fathers sinned, *and* are no more;
It is we who have borne
their iniquities.
8 Slaves rule over us;
There is no one to deliver
us from their hand.
9 We get our bread at the
risk of our lives
Because of the sword in
the wilderness.
10 Our skin has become as
hot as an oven,
Because of the burning
heat of famine.
11 They ravished the women in Zion,
The virgins in the cities of Judah.
12 Princes were hung by their hands;
Elders were not respected.
13 Young men worked at the
grinding mill,
And youths stumbled under
loads of wood.
14 Elders are gone from the gate,
Young men from their music.
15 The joy of our hearts has ceased;
Our dancing has been turned
into mourning.
16 The crown has fallen from our head;
Woe to us, for we have sinned!
17 Because of this our heart is faint,
Because of these things
our eyes are dim;
18 Because of Mount Zion
which lies desolate,
Foxes prowl in it.

19 You, O LORD, rule forever;
Your throne is from generation
to generation.
20 Why do You forget us forever?
Why do You forsake us so long?
21 Restore us to You, O LORD, that
we may be restored;
Renew our days as of old,
22 Unless You have utterly rejected us
And are exceedingly angry with us.

Psalm 119:145–152

ᵖ QOPH.

145 I cried with all my heart;
answer me, O LORD!
I will observe Your statutes.
146 I cried to You; save me
And I shall keep Your testimonies.
147 I rise before dawn and cry for help;
I wait for Your words.

148 My eyes anticipate the night watches,
That I may meditate on Your word.
149 Hear my voice according to
Your lovingkindness;
Revive me, O LORD, according
to Your ordinances.
150 Those who follow after
wickedness draw near;
They are far from Your law.
151 You are near, O LORD,
And all Your commandments are truth.
152 Of old I have known from
Your testimonies
That You have founded them forever.

Proverbs 28:11

11 The rich man is wise in his own eyes,
But the poor who has understanding
sees through him.

Philemon 1–25

Paul, a prisoner of Christ Jesus, and Timothy
our brother,

To Philemon our beloved *brother* and fellow worker, ²and to Apphia our sister, and to Archippus our fellow soldier, and to the church in your house: ³Grace to you and peace from God our Father and the Lord Jesus Christ.

---

1 prisoner of Christ Jesus. At the time of writing, Paul was a prisoner in Rome. Paul was imprisoned for the sake of and by the sovereign will of Christ (Eph 3:1; 4:1; 6:19–20; Php 1:13; Col 4:3). By beginning with his imprisonment and not his apostolic authority, Paul made this letter a gentle and singular appeal to a friend. A reminder of Paul's severe hardships was bound to influence Philemon's willingness to do the comparatively easy task Paul was about to request.

---

4 I thank my God always, making mention of you in my prayers, ⁵because I hear of your love and of the faith which you have toward the Lord Jesus and toward all the saints; ⁶and *I pray* that the fellowship of your faith may become effective through the knowledge of every good thing which is in you for Christ's sake. ⁷For I have come to have much joy and comfort in your love, because the hearts of the saints have been refreshed through you, brother.

⁸Therefore, though I have enough confidence in Christ to order you *to do* what is proper, ⁹yet for love's sake I rather appeal *to*

you—since I am such a person as Paul, the aged, and now also a prisoner of Christ Jesus— ¹⁰I appeal to you for my child Onesimus, whom I have begotten in my imprisonment, ¹¹who formerly was useless to you, but now is useful both to you and to me. ¹²I have sent him back to you in person, that is, *sending my very heart*, ¹³whom I wished to keep with me, so that on your behalf he might minister to me in my imprisonment for the gospel; ¹⁴but without your consent I did not want to do anything, so that your goodness would not be, in effect, by compulsion but of your own free will. ¹⁵For perhaps he was for this reason separated *from you* for a while, that you would have him back forever, ¹⁶no longer as a slave, but more than a slave, a beloved brother, especially to me, but how much more to you, both in the flesh and in the Lord.

¹⁷If then you regard me a partner, accept him as *you would* me. ¹⁸But if he has wronged you in any way or owes you anything, charge that to my account; ¹⁹I, Paul, am writing this with my own hand, I will repay it (not to mention to you that you owe to me even your own self as well). ²⁰Yes, brother, let me benefit from you in the Lord; refresh my heart in Christ.

²¹Having confidence in your obedience, I write to you, since I know that you will do even more than what I say.

²²At the same time also prepare me a lodging, for I hope that through your prayers I will be given to you.

²³Epaphras, my fellow prisoner in Christ Jesus, greets you, ²⁴*as do* Mark, Aristarchus, Demas, Luke, my fellow workers.

²⁵The grace of the Lord Jesus Christ be with your spirit.

16 more than a slave, a beloved brother. Paul did not call for Onesimus' freedom (1Co 7:20-22), but that Philemon would receive his slave now as a fellow-believer in Christ (Eph 6:9; Col 4:1; 1Ti 6:2). Christianity never sought to abolish slavery, but rather to make the relationships within it just and kind. **in the flesh.** In this physical life (Php 1:22), as they worked together. **in the Lord.** The master and slave were to enjoy spiritual oneness and fellowship as they worshiped and ministered together.

DAY 4: What is the background for the Book of Philemon?

Philemon had been saved under Paul's ministry, probably at Ephesus (v. 19), several years earlier. Wealthy enough to have a large house (v. 2), Philemon also owned at least one slave, a man named Onesimus (literally, "useful"; a common name for slaves). Onesimus was not a believer at the time he stole some money (v. 18) from Philemon and ran away. Like countless thousands of other runaway slaves, Onesimus fled to Rome, seeking to lose himself in the imperial capital's teeming and nondescript slave population. Through circumstances not recorded in Scripture, Onesimus met Paul in Rome and became a Christian.

The apostle quickly grew to love the runaway slave (vv. 12, 16) and longed to keep Onesimus in Rome (v. 13), where he was providing valuable service to Paul in his imprisonment (v. 11). But by stealing and running away from Philemon, Onesimus had both broken Roman law and defrauded his master. Paul knew those issues had to be dealt with and decided to send Onesimus back to Colosse. It was too hazardous for him to make the trip alone (because of the danger of slavecatchers), so Paul sent him back with Tychicus, who was returning to Colosse with the Epistle to the Colossians (Col 4:7-9). Along with Onesimus, Paul sent Philemon this beautiful personal letter, urging him to forgive Onesimus and welcome him back to service as a brother in Christ (vv. 15-17).

NOVEMBER 5

Ezekiel 1:1–2:10

1 Now it came about in the thirtieth year, on the fifth *day* of the fourth month, while I was by the river Chebar among the exiles, the heavens were opened and I saw visions of God. ² (On the fifth of the month in the fifth year of King Jehoiachin's exile, ³the word of the LORD came expressly to Ezekiel the priest, son of Buzi, in the land of the Chaldeans by the river Chebar; and there the hand of the LORD came upon him.)

⁴As I looked, behold, a storm wind was coming from the north, a great cloud with fire flashing forth continually and a bright light around it, and in its midst something like glowing metal in the midst of the fire. ⁵Within it there were figures resembling four

1:4 storm wind...fire. Judgment on Judah in a further and totally devastating phase (beyond the 597 B.C. deportation) is to come out of the north and did come from Babylon in 588–586 (as Jer 39–40). Its terror is depicted by a fiery "storm wind" emblematic of God's judgments and the golden brightness signifying dazzling glory.

---

living beings. And this was their appearance: they had human form. ⁶Each of them had four faces and four wings. ⁷Their legs were straight and their feet were like a calf's hoof, and they gleamed like burnished bronze. ⁸Under their wings on their four sides *were* human hands. As for the faces and wings of the four of them, ⁹their wings touched one another; *their faces* did not turn when they moved, each went straight forward. ¹⁰As for the form of their faces, *each* had the face of a man; all four had the face of a lion on the right and the face of a bull on the left, and all four had the face of an eagle. ¹¹Such were their faces. Their wings were spread out above; each had two touching another *being,* and two covering their bodies. ¹²And each went straight forward; wherever the spirit was about to go, they would go, without turning as they went. ¹³In the midst of the living beings there was something that looked like burning coals of fire, like torches darting back and forth among the living beings. The fire was bright, and lightning was flashing from the fire. ¹⁴And the living beings ran to and fro like bolts of lightning.

¹⁵Now as I looked at the living beings, behold, there was one wheel on the earth beside the living beings, for *each of* the four of them. ¹⁶The appearance of the wheels and their workmanship *was* like sparkling beryl, and all four of them had the same form, their appearance and workmanship *being* as if one wheel were within another. ¹⁷Whenever they moved, they moved in any of their four directions without turning as they moved. ¹⁸As

1:16 as if one wheel were within another. This depicted the gigantic (v. 15, "on the earth" and "lofty," v. 18) energy of the complicated revolutions of God's massive judgment machinery bringing about His purposes with unerring certainty.

---

for their rims they were lofty and awesome, and the rims of all four of them were full of eyes round about. ¹⁹Whenever the living beings moved, the wheels moved with them. And whenever the living beings rose from the earth, the wheels rose *also.* ²⁰Wherever the spirit was about to go, they would go in that direction. And the wheels rose close beside them; for the spirit of the living beings *was* in the wheels. ²¹Whenever those went, these went; and whenever those stood still, these stood still. And whenever those rose from the earth, the wheels rose close beside them; for the spirit of the living beings *was* in the wheels.

²²Now over the heads of the living beings *there was* something like an expanse, like the awesome gleam of crystal, spread out over their heads. ²³Under the expanse their wings *were stretched out* straight, one toward the other; each one also had two wings covering its body on the one side and on the other. ²⁴I also heard the sound of their wings like the sound of abundant waters as they went, like the voice of the Almighty, a sound of tumult like the sound of an army camp; whenever they stood still, they dropped their wings. ²⁵And there came a voice from above the expanse that was over their heads; whenever they stood still, they dropped their wings.

²⁶Now above the expanse that was over their heads there was something resembling a throne, like lapis lazuli in appearance; and on that which resembled a throne, high up, *was* a figure with the appearance of a man. ²⁷Then I noticed from the appearance of His loins and upward something like glowing metal that looked like fire all around within it, and from the appearance of His loins and downward I saw something like fire; and *there was* a radiance around Him. ²⁸As the appearance of the rainbow in the clouds on a rainy day, so *was* the appearance of the surrounding radiance. Such *was* the appearance of the likeness of the glory of the LORD. And when I saw *it,* I fell on my face and heard a voice speaking.

2 Then He said to me, "Son of man, stand on your feet that I may speak with you!" ²As He spoke to me the Spirit entered me and set me on my feet; and I heard *Him* speaking to me. ³Then He said to me, "Son of man, I am sending you to the sons of Israel, to a rebellious people who have rebelled against Me; they and their fathers have transgressed against Me to this very day. ⁴I am sending you to them who are stubborn and obstinate children, and you shall say to them, 'Thus

2:2 the Spirit entered me. What God commands a servant to do (v. 1), He gives power to fulfill by His Spirit (3:14; Zec 4:6). This pictures the selective empowering by the Holy Spirit to enable an individual for special service to the Lord, which occurred frequently in the Old Testament. (For examples see 11:5; 37:1; Numbers 24:2; Judges 3:10; 6:34; 11:29; 13:25; 1 Samuel 10:10; 16:13–14; 19:20; 2 Chronicles 15:1; Luke 4:18.)

says the Lord GOD.' ⁵ As for them, whether they listen or not—for they are a rebellious house—they will know that a prophet has been among them. ⁶ And you, son of man, neither fear them nor fear their words, though thistles and thorns are with you and you sit on scorpions; neither fear their words nor be dismayed at their presence, for they are a rebellious house. ⁷ But you shall speak My words to them whether they listen or not, for they are rebellious.

⁸ "Now you, son of man, listen to what I am speaking to you; do not be rebellious like that rebellious house. Open your mouth and eat what I am giving you." ⁹ Then I looked, and behold, a hand was extended to me; and lo, a scroll *was* in it. ¹⁰ When He spread it out before me, it was written on the front and back, and written on it were lamentations, mourning and woe.

Psalm 119:153–160

ר RESH.

¹⁵³ Look upon my affliction
   and rescue me,
   For I do not forget Your law.
¹⁵⁴ Plead my cause and redeem me;
   Revive me according
      to Your word.
¹⁵⁵ Salvation is far from the wicked,
   For they do not seek Your statutes.
¹⁵⁶ Great are Your mercies, O LORD;
   Revive me according to
      Your ordinances.
¹⁵⁷ Many are my persecutors
      and my adversaries,
   Yet I do not turn aside from
      Your testimonies.
¹⁵⁸ I behold the treacherous
      and loathe *them,*
   Because they do not keep Your word.
¹⁵⁹ Consider how I love Your precepts;
   Revive me, O LORD, according
      to Your lovingkindness.

¹⁶⁰ The sum of Your word is truth,
   And every one of Your
      righteous ordinances
   is everlasting.

Proverbs 28:12

¹² When the righteous triumph,
      there is great glory,
   But when the wicked rise,
      men hide themselves.

Hebrews 1:1–14

1 God, after He spoke long ago to the fathers in the prophets in many portions and in many ways, ² in these last days has spoken to us in His Son, whom He appointed heir of all things, through whom also He made the world. ³ And He is the radiance of His glory and the exact representation of His nature, and upholds all things by the word of His power. When He had made purification of sins, He sat down at the right hand of the Majesty on high, ⁴ having become as much better than the angels, as He has inherited a more excellent name than they.

1:2 last days. Jews understood the "last days" to mean the time when Messiah (Christ) would come (Nu 24:14; Jer 33:14–16; Mic 5:1–2; Zec 9:9, 16). The fulfillment of the messianic prophecies commenced with the advent of the Messiah. Since He came, it has been the "last days" (1Co 10:11; Jas 5:3; 1Pe 1:20; 4:7; 1Jn 2:18). In the past God gave revelation through His prophets, but in these times, beginning with the Messiah's advent, God spoke the message of redemption through the Son. **heir.** Everything that exists will ultimately come under the control of the Son of God, the Messiah. This "inheritance" is the full extension of the authority which the Father has given to the Son (Da 7:13–14; Mt 28:18), as the "firstborn." **world.** The word can also be translated "ages." It refers to time, space, energy, and matter—the entire universe and everything that makes it function (Jn 1:3).

⁵ For to which of the angels did He ever say,

"You are My Son,
   Today I have begotten You"?

And again,

"I will be a Father to Him
   And He shall be a Son to Me"?

⁶And when He again brings the firstborn into the world, He says,

"AND LET ALL THE ANGELS OF
GOD WORSHIP HIM."

⁷And of the angels He says,

"WHO MAKES HIS ANGELS WINDS,
AND HIS MINISTERS A FLAME OF FIRE."

⁸But of the Son *He says,*

"YOUR THRONE, O GOD, IS
FOREVER AND EVER,
AND THE RIGHTEOUS SCEPTER IS
THE SCEPTER OF HIS KINGDOM.

1:8–9 *He says.* Quoting from Psalms 45:6–7, the writer argues for the deity and the lordship of the Son over creation (v. 3). The text is all the more significant since the declaration of the Son's deity is presented as the words of the Father Himself (Is 9:6; Jer 23:5–6; Jn 5:18; Titus 2:13; 1Jn 5:20). It is clear that the writer of Hebrews had the 3 messianic offices in mind: Prophet (v. 1), Priest (v. 3), and King (vv. 3, 8). Induction into those 3 offices required anointing (v. 9). The title Messiah (Christ) means "anointed one" (Is 61:1–3; Lk 4:16–21).

⁹ "YOU HAVE LOVED RIGHTEOUSNESS
AND HATED LAWLESSNESS;
THEREFORE GOD, YOUR GOD,
HAS ANOINTED YOU
WITH THE OIL OF GLADNESS
ABOVE YOUR COMPANIONS."

¹⁰And,

"YOU, LORD, IN THE BEGINNING LAID
THE FOUNDATION OF THE EARTH,
AND THE HEAVENS ARE THE
WORKS OF YOUR HANDS;
¹¹ THEY WILL PERISH, BUT YOU REMAIN;
AND THEY ALL WILL BECOME
OLD LIKE A GARMENT,
¹² AND LIKE A MANTLE YOU
WILL ROLL THEM UP;
LIKE A GARMENT THEY WILL
ALSO BE CHANGED.
BUT YOU ARE THE SAME,
AND YOUR YEARS WILL NOT
COME TO AN END."

¹³But to which of the angels has He ever said,

"SIT AT MY RIGHT HAND,
UNTIL I MAKE YOUR ENEMIES
A FOOTSTOOL FOR YOUR FEET"?

¹⁴Are they not all ministering spirits, sent out to render service for the sake of those who will inherit salvation?

DAY 5: To which Hebrews was this book written?

Although the author and the original recipients of this letter are unknown, the title, dating as early as the second century A.D., had been "To the Hebrews." The title certainly fits the content. The epistle exudes a Jewish mind-set. References to Hebrew history and religion abound. And since no particular Gentile or pagan practice gains any attention in the book, the church has kept the traditional title.

A proper interpretation of this epistle requires the recognition that it addresses 3 distinct groups of Hebrews:

1. Hebrew Christians who suffered rejection and persecution by fellow Jews (10:32–34), although none as yet had been martyred (12:4). The letter was written to give them encouragement and confidence in Christ, their Messiah and High Priest. They were an immature group of believers who were tempted to hold on to the symbolic and spiritually powerless rituals and traditions of Judaism.
2. Jewish unbelievers who were intellectually convinced of the basic truths of the gospel but who had not placed their faith in Jesus Christ as their own Savior and Lord. They were intellectually persuaded but spiritually uncommitted. These unbelievers are addressed in such passages as 2:1–3; 6:4–6; 10:26–29; and 12:15–17.
3. Jewish unbelievers who were attracted by the gospel and the Person of Christ but who had reached no final conviction about Him. Chapter 9 is largely devoted to them.

NOVEMBER 6

Ezekiel 3:1–4:17

3 Then He said to me, "Son of man, eat what you find; eat this scroll, and go, speak to the house of Israel." ² So I opened my mouth, and He fed me this scroll. ³ He said to me, "Son of man, feed your stomach and fill your body with this scroll which I am giving you." Then I ate it, and it was sweet as honey in my mouth.

⁴ Then He said to me, "Son of man, go to the house of Israel and speak with My words to them. ⁵ For you are not being sent to a people of unintelligible speech or difficult language, *but* to the house of Israel, ⁶ nor to many peoples of unintelligible speech or difficult language, whose words you cannot understand. But I have sent you to them who should listen to you; ⁷ yet the house of Israel will not be willing to listen to you, since they are not willing to listen to Me. Surely the whole house of Israel is stubborn and obstinate. ⁸ Behold, I have made your face as hard as their faces and your forehead as hard as their foreheads. ⁹ Like emery harder than flint I have made your forehead. Do not be afraid of them or be dismayed before them, though they are a rebellious house." ¹⁰ Moreover, He said to me, "Son of man, take into your heart all My words which I will speak to you and listen closely. ¹¹ Go to the exiles, to the sons of your people, and speak to them and tell them, whether they listen or not, 'Thus says the Lord GOD.'"

¹² Then the Spirit lifted me up, and I heard a great rumbling sound behind me, "Blessed be the glory of the LORD in His place." ¹³ And I *heard* the sound of the wings of the living beings touching one another and the sound of the wheels beside them, even a great rumbling sound. ¹⁴ So the Spirit lifted me up

3:8–9 I have made your face…hard. What God commands ("Do not be afraid") He gives sufficiency to do ("I have made"), so God will enable the prophet to live up to his name (which means "strengthened by God"). See 2:2; 3:14, 24; Isaiah 41:10; Jeremiah 1:8, 17.

3:9 rebellious. It is sad to observe that the exile and affliction did not make the Jews more responsive to God; rather, they were hardened by their sufferings. God gave Ezekiel a "hardness" to surpass the people and sustain his ministry as prophet to the exiles.

and took me away; and I went embittered in the rage of my spirit, and the hand of the LORD was strong on me. ¹⁵ Then I came to the exiles who lived beside the river Chebar at Tel-abib, and I sat there seven days where they were living, causing consternation among them.

¹⁶ At the end of seven days the word of the LORD came to me, saying, ¹⁷ "Son of man, I have appointed you a watchman to the house of Israel; whenever you hear a word from My mouth, warn them from Me. ¹⁸ When I say to the wicked, 'You will surely die,' and you do not warn him or speak out to warn the wicked from his wicked way that he may live, that wicked man shall die in his iniquity, but his blood I will require at your hand. ¹⁹ Yet if you have warned the wicked and he does not turn from his wickedness or from his wicked way, he shall die in his iniquity; but you have delivered yourself. ²⁰ Again, when a righteous man turns away from his righteousness and commits iniquity, and I place an obstacle before him, he will die; since you have not warned him, he shall die in his sin, and his righteous deeds which he has done shall not be remembered; but his blood I will require at your hand. ²¹ However, if you have warned the righteous man that the righteous should not sin and he does not sin, he shall surely live because he took warning; and you have delivered yourself."

3:17 a watchman. This role was spiritually analogous to the role of watchmen on a city wall, vigilant to spot the approach of an enemy and warn the residents to muster a defense. The prophet gave timely warnings of approaching judgment. The work of a watchman is vividly set forth in 2 Samuel 18:24–27 and 2 Kings 9:17–20.

²² The hand of the LORD was on me there, and He said to me, "Get up, go out to the plain, and there I will speak to you." ²³ So I got up and went out to the plain; and behold, the glory of the LORD was standing there, like the glory which I saw by the river Chebar, and I fell on my face. ²⁴ The Spirit then entered me and made me stand on my feet, and He spoke with me and said to me, "Go, shut yourself up in your house. ²⁵ As for you, son of man, they will put ropes on you and bind you with them so that you cannot go out among them. ²⁶ Moreover, I will make your tongue stick to the roof of your mouth so that you will be

mute and cannot be a man who rebukes them, for they are a rebellious house. [27] But when I speak to you, I will open your mouth and you will say to them, 'Thus says the Lord GOD.' He who hears, let him hear; and he who refuses, let him refuse; for they are a rebellious house.

4 "Now you son of man, get yourself a brick, place it before you and inscribe a city on it, Jerusalem. [2] Then lay siege against it, build a siege wall, raise up a ramp, pitch camps and place battering rams against it all around. [3] Then get yourself an iron plate and set it up as an iron wall between you and the city, and set your face toward it so that it is under siege, and besiege it. This is a sign to the house of Israel.

[4] "As for you, lie down on your left side and lay the iniquity of the house of Israel on it; you shall bear their iniquity for the number of days that you lie on it. [5] For I have assigned you a number of days corresponding to the years of their iniquity, three hundred and ninety days; thus you shall bear the iniquity of the house of Israel. [6] When you have completed these, you shall lie down a second time, *but* on your right side and bear the iniquity of the house of Judah; I have assigned it to you for forty days, a day for each year. [7] Then you shall set your face toward the siege of Jerusalem with your arm bared and prophesy against it. [8] Now behold, I will put ropes on you so that you cannot turn from one side to the other until you have completed the days of your siege.

[9] "But as for you, take wheat, barley, beans, lentils, millet and spelt, put them in one vessel and make them into bread for yourself; you shall eat it according to the number of the days that you lie on your side, three hundred and ninety days. [10] Your food which you eat *shall be* twenty shekels a day by weight; you shall eat it from time to time. [11] The water you drink shall be the sixth part of a hin by measure; you shall drink it from time to time. [12] You shall eat it as a barley cake, having baked *it* in their sight over human dung." [13] Then the LORD said, "Thus will the sons of Israel eat their bread unclean among the nations where I will banish them." [14] But I said, "Ah, Lord GOD! Behold, I have never been defiled; for from my youth until now I have never eaten what died of itself or was torn by beasts, nor has any unclean meat ever entered my mouth." [15] Then He said to me, "See, I will give you cow's dung in place of human dung over which you will prepare your bread." [16] Moreover, He said to me, "Son of man, behold, I am going to break the staff of bread in Jerusalem, and they will eat bread by weight and with anxiety, and drink water by measure and in horror, [17] because bread and water will be scarce; and they will be appalled with one another and waste away in their iniquity.

Psalm 119:161–168

ש SHIN.

[161] Princes persecute me without cause,
But my heart stands in
awe of Your words.
[162] I rejoice at Your word,
As one who finds great spoil.
[163] I hate and despise falsehood,
But I love Your law.
[164] Seven times a day I praise You,
Because of Your righteous ordinances.
[165] Those who love Your law
have great peace,
And nothing causes
them to stumble.
[166] I hope for Your salvation, O LORD,
And do Your commandments.
[167] My soul keeps Your testimonies,
And I love them exceedingly.
[168] I keep Your precepts and
Your testimonies,
For all my ways are before You.

Proverbs 28:13

[13] He who conceals his transgressions
will not prosper,
But he who confesses and forsakes
them will find compassion.

Hebrews 2:1–18

2 For this reason we must pay much closer attention to what we have heard, so that we do not drift away *from it.* [2] For if the word spoken through angels proved unalterable, and every transgression and disobedience received a just penalty, [3] how will we escape if we neglect so great a salvation? After it was at the first spoken through the Lord, it was confirmed to us by those who heard, [4] God also testifying with them, both by signs and wonders and by various miracles and by gifts of the Holy Spirit according to His own will.

[5] For He did not subject to angels the world to come, concerning which we are speaking. [6] But one has testified somewhere, saying,

"WHAT IS MAN, THAT YOU
REMEMBER HIM?
OR THE SON OF MAN, THAT YOU
ARE CONCERNED ABOUT HIM?

2:4 signs...wonders...miracles...gifts. The supernatural powers demonstrated by Jesus and by His apostles were the Father's divine confirmation of the gospel of Jesus Christ, His Son (Jn 10:38; Ac 2:22; Ro 15:19; 1Co 14:22; 2Co 12:12). This authentication of the message was the purpose of such miraculous deeds. **the Holy Spirit.** The epistle's first reference to the Holy Spirit refers in passing to His ministry of confirming the message of salvation by means of miraculous gifts. Mentioned elsewhere in the epistle are the Holy Spirit's involvement in the revelation of Scripture (3:7; 10:15), in teaching (9:8), in pre-salvation operations (6:4, perhaps His convicting work; 10:29, common grace), and in ministry to Christ (9:14).

7 "YOU HAVE MADE HIM FOR A LITTLE
    WHILE LOWER THAN THE ANGELS;
  YOU HAVE CROWNED HIM WITH
    GLORY AND HONOR,
  AND HAVE APPOINTED HIM OVER
    THE WORKS OF YOUR HANDS;
8 YOU HAVE PUT ALL THINGS IN
    SUBJECTION UNDER HIS FEET."

For in subjecting all things to him, He left nothing that is not subject to him. But now we do not yet see all things subjected to him. 9 But we do see Him who was made for a little while lower than the angels, *namely,* Jesus, because of the suffering of death crowned with glory and honor, so that by the grace of God He might taste death for everyone.

10 For it was fitting for Him, for whom are all things, and through whom are all things, in bringing many sons to glory, to perfect the author of their salvation through sufferings. 11 For both He who sanctifies and those who are sanctified are all from one *Father;* for which reason He is not ashamed to call them brethren, 12 saying,

"I WILL PROCLAIM YOUR NAME
  TO MY BRETHREN,
IN THE MIDST OF THE CONGREGATION
  I WILL SING YOUR PRAISE."

13 And again,

"I WILL PUT MY TRUST IN HIM."

And again,

"BEHOLD, I AND THE CHILDREN
  WHOM GOD HAS GIVEN ME."

14 Therefore, since the children share in flesh and blood, He Himself likewise also partook of the same, that through death He might render powerless him who had the power of death, that is, the devil, 15 and might free those who through fear of death were subject to slavery all their lives. 16 For assuredly He does not give help to angels, but He gives help to the descendant of Abraham. 17 Therefore, He had to be made like His brethren in all things, so that He might become a merciful and faithful high priest in things pertaining to God, to make propitiation for the sins of the people. 18 For since He Himself was tempted in that which He has suffered, He is able to come to the aid of those who are tempted.

2:14 share...partook. The Greek word for "partook" means fellowship, communion, or partnership. "Share" means to take hold of something that is not related to one's own kind. The Son of God was not by nature "flesh and blood," but took upon Himself that nature for the sake of providing redemption for mankind. **death... power of death.** This is the ultimate purpose of the incarnation: Jesus came to earth to die. By dying, He was able to conquer death in His resurrection (Jn 14:19). By conquering death, He rendered Satan powerless against all who are saved. Satan's using the power of death is subject to God's will (Job 2:6).

2:17 propitiation. The word means "to conciliate" or "satisfy." Christ's work of propitiation is related to His high priestly ministry. By His partaking of a human nature, Christ demonstrated His mercy to mankind and His faithfulness to God by satisfying God's requirement for sin and thus obtaining for His people full forgiveness.

DAY 6: How can we know whether Ezekiel's language is descriptive of a literal event or symbolic of an idea or principle?

Ezekiel's life offered his audience a sequence of experiences and actions that became teachable moments. Some of these were scenes in visions that held special significance. For example, the first three chapters of the book report extended visions in which the prophet saw a whirlwind, heavenly creatures, and an edible scroll. He also received his call to the prophetic ministry.

In addition, Ezekiel carried out certain unusual or highly symbolic actions that were intended to picture a message or convey a warning. In 4:1-3, the prophet was directed to carve on a clay tablet and then use an iron plate as a sign about the danger facing Jerusalem. Other acted-out sermons followed: symbolic sleeping postures (4:4-8), siege bread making and baking (4:9-17), and haircutting and burning (5:1-4). God instructed Ezekiel to respond even to the tragedies in his life in such a way that a message was communicated to the people. The prophet learned of his wife's impending death but was told by God that his loss would provide an important lesson the people needed to hear. Just as Ezekiel was not allowed to mourn, the people would not be allowed to mourn when they finally faced the "death" of Jerusalem. "Thus Ezekiel will be a sign to you; according to all that he has done you will do; when it comes, then you will know that I am the Lord GOD" (Eze 24:24).

The unique nature of Ezekiel's approach creates a striking contrast between the clarity of his message and the willful rejection of that message by the people. His ministry removed every excuse.

NOVEMBER 7

Ezekiel 5:1–6:14

5 "As for you, son of man, take a sharp sword; take and use it *as* a barber's razor on your head and beard. Then take scales for weighing and divide the hair. ²One third you shall burn in the fire at the center of the city, when the days of the siege are completed. Then you shall take one third and strike *it* with the sword all around the city, and one third you shall scatter to the wind; and I will unsheathe a sword behind them. ³Take also a few in number from them and bind them in the edges of your *robes.* ⁴Take again some of them and throw them into the fire and burn them in the fire; from it a fire will spread to all the house of Israel.

⁵ "Thus says the Lord GOD, 'This is Jerusalem; I have set her at the center of the nations, with lands around her. ⁶But she has rebelled against My ordinances more wickedly than the nations and against My statutes more than the lands which surround her; for they have rejected My ordinances and have not walked

5:1-4 a barber's razor. The sign in shaving his hair illustrated the severe humiliation to come at the hand of enemies, emphasizing calamities to three segments of Jerusalem due to the Babylonian conquest. Some were punished by fire, i.e., plague and famine (v. 12), others died by the enemy's sword, and some were dispersed and pursued by death (v. 12). A small part of his hair clinging to his garment (v. 3) depicted a remaining remnant, some of whom were subject to further calamity (v. 4; see 6:8; Jer 41-44).

in My statutes.' ⁷Therefore, thus says the Lord GOD, 'Because you have more turmoil than the nations which surround you *and* have not walked in My statutes, nor observed My ordinances, nor observed the ordinances of the nations which surround you,' ⁸therefore, thus says the Lord GOD, 'Behold, I, even I, am against you, and I will execute judgments among you in the sight of the nations. ⁹And because of all your abominations, I will do among you what I have not done, and the like of which I will never do again. ¹⁰Therefore, fathers will eat *their* sons among you, and sons will eat their fathers; for I will execute judgments on you and scatter all your remnant to every wind. ¹¹So as I live,' declares the Lord GOD, 'surely, because you have defiled My sanctuary with all your detestable idols and with all your abominations, therefore I will also withdraw, and My eye will have no pity and I will not spare. ¹²One third of you will die by plague or be consumed by famine among you, one third will fall by the sword around you, and one third I will scatter to every wind, and I will unsheathe a sword behind them.

¹³ 'Thus My anger will be spent and I will satisfy My wrath on them, and I will be appeased; then they will know that I, the LORD, have spoken in My zeal when I have spent My wrath upon them. ¹⁴Moreover, I will make you a desolation and a reproach among the nations which surround you, in the sight of all who pass by. ¹⁵So it will be a reproach, a reviling, a warning and an object of horror to the nations who surround you when I execute judgments against you in anger, wrath and raging rebukes. I, the LORD, have spoken. ¹⁶When I send against them the deadly arrows of famine which were for the destruction of those whom I will send to destroy you, then I will also intensify the famine

upon you and break the staff of bread. ¹⁷ Moreover, I will send on you famine and wild beasts, and they will bereave you of children; plague and bloodshed also will pass through you, and I will bring the sword on you. I, the LORD, have spoken.'"

6 And the word of the LORD came to me saying, ² "Son of man, set your face toward the mountains of Israel, and prophesy against them ³ and say, 'Mountains of Israel, listen to the word of the Lord GOD! Thus says the Lord GOD to the mountains, the hills, the ravines and the valleys: "Behold, I Myself am going to bring a sword on you, and I will destroy your high places. ⁴ So your altars will become desolate and your incense altars will be smashed; and I will make your slain fall in front of your idols. ⁵ I will also lay the dead bodies of the sons of Israel in front of their idols; and I will scatter your bones around your altars. ⁶ In all your dwellings, cities will become waste and the high places will be desolate, that your altars may become waste and desolate, your idols may be broken and brought to an end, your incense altars may be cut down, and your works may be blotted out. ⁷ The slain will fall among you, and you will know that I am the LORD.

6:7 you will know that I am the LORD. This clause recurs in vv. 10, 13–14 and 60 times elsewhere in the book. It shows that the essential reason for judgment is the violation of the character of God. This is repeatedly acknowledged in Leviticus 18–26, where the motive for all obedience to God's law is the fact that He is the Lord God.

⁸ "However, I will leave a remnant, for you will have those who escaped the sword among the nations when you are scattered among the countries. ⁹ Then those of you who escape will remember Me among the nations to which they will be carried captive, how I have been hurt by their adulterous hearts which turned away from Me, and by their eyes which played the harlot after their idols; and they will loathe themselves in their own sight for the evils which they have committed, for all their abominations. ¹⁰ Then they will know that I am the LORD; I have not said in vain that I would inflict this disaster on them."'

¹¹ "Thus says the Lord GOD, 'Clap your hand, stamp your foot and say, "Alas, because of all the evil abominations of the house of Israel, which will fall by sword, famine and plague! ¹² He who is far off will die by the plague, and he who is near will fall by the sword, and he who remains and is besieged will die by the famine. Thus will I spend My wrath on them. ¹³ Then you will know that I am the LORD, when their slain are among their idols around their altars, on every high hill, on all the tops of the mountains, under every green tree and under every leafy oak—the places where they offered soothing aroma to all their idols. ¹⁴ So throughout all their habitations I will stretch out My hand against them and make the land more desolate and waste than the wilderness toward Diblah; thus they will know that I am the LORD."'"

Psalm 119:169–176

ת TAV.

¹⁶⁹ Let my cry come before You, O LORD;
Give me understanding
according to Your word.
¹⁷⁰ Let my supplication
come before You;
Deliver me according to Your word.
¹⁷¹ Let my lips utter praise,
For You teach me Your statutes.
¹⁷² Let my tongue sing of Your word,
For all Your commandments
are righteousness.
¹⁷³ Let Your hand be ready to help me,
For I have chosen Your precepts.
¹⁷⁴ I long for Your salvation, O LORD,
And Your law is my delight.
¹⁷⁵ Let my soul live that it
may praise You,
And let Your ordinances help me.
¹⁷⁶ I have gone astray like a lost
sheep; seek Your servant,
For I do not forget Your
commandments.

Proverbs 28:14

¹⁴ How blessed is the man
who fears always,
But he who hardens his heart
will fall into calamity.

Hebrews 3:1–19

3 Therefore, holy brethren, partakers of a heavenly calling, consider Jesus, the Apostle and High Priest of our confession; ² He was faithful to Him who appointed Him, as Moses also was in all His house. ³ For He has been counted worthy of more glory than Moses, by just so much as the builder of the house has more honor than the house. ⁴ For every

3:1 consider. The writer asks for the readers' complete attention and diligent observation of the superiority of Jesus Christ. **Apostle and High Priest.** An apostle is a "sent one" who has the rights, power, and authority of the one who sends him. Jesus was sent to earth by the Father (Jn 3:17, 34; 5:36–38; 8:42). The topic of the High Priesthood of Christ, which was begun in 2:17–18 and is mentioned again here, will be taken up again in greater detail in 4:14–10:18. Meanwhile, the writer presents the supremacy of Christ to Moses (vv. 1–6), to Joshua (4:8), and to all other national heroes and Old Testament preachers whom Jews held in high esteem. Jesus Himself spoke of His superiority to Moses in the same context in which He spoke of His being sent by the Father (Jn 5:36–38, 45–47; see Lk 16:29–31). Moses had been sent by God to deliver His people from historical Egypt and its bondage (Ex 3:10). Jesus was sent by God to deliver His people from spiritual Egypt and its bondage (2:15). **of our confession.** Christ is the center of our confession of faith in the gospel, both in creed and public testimony. The term is used again in 4:14 and 10:23. In all 3 uses in Hebrews there is a sense of urgency. Surely, the readers would not give up Christ, whom they had professed, and reject what He had done for them, if they could understand the superiority of His person and work.

house is built by someone, but the builder of all things is God. ⁵ Now Moses was faithful in all His house as a servant, for a testimony of those things which were to be spoken later; ⁶ but Christ *was faithful* as a Son over His house—whose house we are, if we hold fast our confidence and the boast of our hope firm until the end.

⁷ Therefore, just as the Holy Spirit says,

"TODAY IF YOU HEAR HIS VOICE,
⁸ DO NOT HARDEN YOUR HEARTS AS
    WHEN THEY PROVOKED ME,
  AS IN THE DAY OF TRIAL IN
    THE WILDERNESS,
⁹ WHERE YOUR FATHERS TRIED
    Me BY TESTING *Me*,
  AND SAW MY WORKS FOR FORTY YEARS.
¹⁰ "THEREFORE I WAS ANGRY WITH
    THIS GENERATION,
  AND SAID, 'THEY ALWAYS GO
    ASTRAY IN THEIR HEART,
  AND THEY DID NOT KNOW MY WAYS';
¹¹ AS I SWORE IN MY WRATH,
  'THEY SHALL NOT ENTER MY REST.' "

¹² Take care, brethren, that there not be in any one of you an evil, unbelieving heart that falls away from the living God. ¹³ But encourage one another day after day, as long as it is *still* called "Today," so that none of you will be hardened by the deceitfulness of sin. ¹⁴ For we have become partakers of Christ, if we hold fast the beginning of our assurance firm until the end, ¹⁵ while it is said,

"TODAY IF YOU HEAR HIS VOICE,
  DO NOT HARDEN YOUR HEARTS, AS
    WHEN THEY PROVOKED ME."

¹⁶ For who provoked *Him* when they had heard? Indeed, did not all those who came out of Egypt *led* by Moses? ¹⁷ And with whom was He angry for forty years? Was it not with those who sinned, whose bodies fell in the wilderness? ¹⁸ And to whom did He swear that they would not enter His rest, but to those who were disobedient? ¹⁹ *So* we see that they were not able to enter because of unbelief.

DAY 7: What are the central warnings for believers in the Book of Hebrews?

Beyond its value as a doctrinal treatise, this book is intensely practical in its application to everyday living. The writer himself even refers to his letter as a "word of exhortation" (13:22). Exhortations designed to stir the readers into action are found throughout the text. Those exhortations are given in the form of 6 warnings:

1. Warning against drifting from "what we have heard" (2:1–4)
2. Warning against disbelieving the "VOICE" of God (3:7–14)
3. Warning against degenerating from "the elementary principles" of Christ (5:11–6:20)
4. Warning against despising "the knowledge of the truth" (10:26–39)
5. Warning against devaluing "the grace of God" (12:15–17)
6. Warning against departing from Him "who is speaking" (12:25–29)

For example, when the writer warns of the danger of drifting (2:1), he uses some vivid nautical terms. The phrase "much closer attention" refers to mooring a ship by securing it to a dock.

The second phrase "drift away" was often used of a ship that had been allowed to drift past the harbor. The warning is to secure oneself to the truth of the gospel in such a way as to not pass by the only harbor of salvation. The alternate tendency toward apathy points to those who make a shipwreck of their lives.

NOVEMBER 8

Ezekiel 7:1–8:18

7 Moreover, the word of the LORD came to me saying, ² "And you, son of man, thus says the Lord GOD to the land of Israel, 'An end! The end is coming on the four corners of the land. ³ Now the end is upon you, and I will send My anger against you; I will judge you according to your ways and bring all your abominations upon you. ⁴ For My eye will have no pity on you, nor will I spare *you,* but I will bring your ways upon you, and your abominations will be among you; then you will know that I am the LORD!'

⁵ "Thus says the Lord GOD, 'A disaster, unique disaster, behold it is coming! ⁶ An end is coming; the end has come! It has awakened against you; behold, it has come! ⁷ Your doom has come to you, O inhabitant of the land. The time has come, the day is near—tumult rather than joyful shouting on the mountains. ⁸ Now I will shortly pour out My wrath on you and spend My anger against you; judge you according to your ways and bring on you all your abominations. ⁹ My eye will show no pity nor will I spare. I will repay you according to your ways, while your abominations are in your midst; then you will know that I, the LORD, do the smiting.

¹⁰ 'Behold, the day! Behold, it is coming! *Your* doom has gone forth; the rod has budded, arrogance has blossomed. ¹¹ Violence has grown into a rod of wickedness. None of them *shall remain,* none of their people, none of their wealth, nor anything eminent among them. ¹² The time has come, the day has arrived. Let not the buyer rejoice nor the seller mourn; for wrath is against all their multitude. ¹³ Indeed, the seller will not regain what he sold as long as they *both* live; for the vision regarding all their multitude will not be averted, nor will any of them maintain his life by his iniquity.

¹⁴ 'They have blown the trumpet and made everything ready, but no one is going to the battle, for My wrath is against all their multitude. ¹⁵ The sword is outside and the plague and the famine are within. He who is in the field will die by the sword; famine and the plague will also consume those in the city. ¹⁶ Even when their survivors escape, they will be on the mountains like doves of the valleys, all of them mourning, each over his own iniquity. ¹⁷ All hands will hang limp and all knees will become *like* water. ¹⁸ They will gird themselves with sackcloth and shuddering will overwhelm them; and shame *will be* on all faces and baldness on all their heads. ¹⁹ They will fling their silver into the streets and their gold will become an abhorrent thing; their silver and their gold will not be able to deliver them in the day of the wrath of the LORD. They cannot satisfy their appetite nor can they fill their stomachs, for their iniquity has become an occasion of stumbling. ²⁰ They transformed the beauty of His ornaments into pride, and they made the images of their abominations *and* their detestable things with it; therefore I will make it an abhorrent thing to them. ²¹ I will give it into the hands of the foreigners as plunder and to the wicked of the earth as spoil, and they will profane it. ²² I will also turn My face from them, and they will profane My secret place; then robbers will enter and profane it.

²³ 'Make the chain, for the land is full of bloody crimes and the city is full of violence. ²⁴ Therefore, I will bring the worst of the nations, and they will possess their houses. I will also make the pride of the strong ones cease, and their holy places will be profaned. ²⁵ When anguish comes, they will seek peace, but there will be none. ²⁶ Disaster will come upon disaster and rumor will be *added* to rumor; then they will seek a vision from a prophet, but the law will be lost from the priest and counsel from the elders. ²⁷ The king will mourn, the prince will be clothed with horror, and the hands of the people of the land will tremble. According to their conduct I will deal with them, and by their judgments I will judge them. And they will know that I am the LORD.'"

8 It came about in the sixth year, on the fifth *day* of the sixth month, as I was sitting in my house with the elders of Judah sitting before me, that the hand of the Lord GOD fell on me there. ² Then I looked, and behold, a likeness as the appearance of a man; from His loins and downward *there was* the

appearance of fire, and from His loins and upward the appearance of brightness, like the appearance of glowing metal. ³He stretched out the form of a hand and caught me by a lock of my head; and the Spirit lifted me up between earth and heaven and brought me in the visions of God to Jerusalem, to the entrance of the north gate of the inner *court*, where the seat of the idol of jealousy, which provokes to jealousy, was *located*. ⁴And behold, the glory of the God of Israel *was* there, like the appearance which I saw in the plain.

8:3 the visions of God. Ezekiel 8–11 deals with details conveyed only to Ezekiel in visions. Ezekiel's trip to Jerusalem was in spirit only, while his body physically remained in his house. In visions, he went to Jerusalem, and in visions he returned to Babylon (11:24). After God finished the visions, Ezekiel told his home audience what he had seen. The visions are not a description of deeds done in the past in Israel, but a survey of Israel's current condition, as they existed at that very time. **the seat… idol of jealousy.** God represents to Ezekiel the image of an idol (Dt 4:16) in the entrance to the inner court of the temple. It is called "the idol of jealousy" because it provoked the Lord to jealousy (5:13; 16:38; 36:6; 38:19; Ex 20:5).

⁵Then He said to me, "Son of man, raise your eyes now toward the north." So I raised my eyes toward the north, and behold, to the north of the altar gate *was* this idol of jealousy at the entrance. ⁶And He said to me, "Son of man, do you see what they are doing, the great abominations which the house of Israel are committing here, so that I would be far from My sanctuary? But yet you will see still greater abominations." ⁷Then He brought me to the entrance of the court, and when I looked, behold, a hole in the wall. ⁸He said to me, "Son of man, now dig through the wall." So I dug through the wall, and behold, an entrance. ⁹And He said to me, "Go in and see the wicked abominations that they are committing here." ¹⁰So I entered and looked, and behold, every form of creeping things and beasts *and* detestable things, with all the idols of the house of Israel, were carved on the wall all around. ¹¹Standing in front of them were seventy elders of the house of Israel, with Jaazaniah the son of Shaphan standing among them, each man with his censer in his hand and the fragrance

of the cloud of incense rising. ¹²Then He said to me, "Son of man, do you see what the elders of the house of Israel are committing in the dark, each man in the room of his carved images? For they say, 'The LORD does not see us; the LORD has forsaken the land.'" ¹³And He said to me, "Yet you will see still greater abominations which they are committing."

¹⁴Then He brought me to the entrance of the gate of the LORD'S house which *was* toward the north; and behold, women were sitting there weeping for Tammuz. ¹⁵He said to me, "Do you see *this*, son of man? Yet you will see still greater abominations than these."

8:14 weeping for Tammuz. Yet a greater abomination than the secret cult was Israel's engaging in the Babylonian worship of Tammuz or Dumuzi (Duzu), beloved of Ishtar, the god of spring vegetation. Vegetation burned in the summer, died in the winter, and came to life in the spring. The women mourned over the god's demise in July and longed for his revival. The fourth month of the Hebrew calendar still bears the name Tammuz. With the worship of this idol were connected the basest immoralities.

¹⁶Then He brought me into the inner court of the LORD'S house. And behold, at the entrance to the temple of the LORD, between the porch and the altar, *were* about twenty-five men with their backs to the temple of the LORD and their faces toward the east; and they were prostrating themselves eastward toward the sun. ¹⁷He said to me, "Do you see *this*, son of man? Is it too light a thing for the house of Judah to commit the abominations which they have committed here, that they have filled the land with violence and provoked Me repeatedly? For behold, they are putting the twig to their nose. ¹⁸Therefore, I indeed will deal in wrath. My eye will have no pity nor will I spare; and though they cry in My ears with a loud voice, yet I will not listen to them."

Psalm 120:1–7

A Song of Ascents.

In my trouble I cried to the LORD,
  And He answered me.
² Deliver my soul, O LORD,
    from lying lips,
  From a deceitful tongue.
³ What shall be given to you, and
    what more shall be done to you,
  You deceitful tongue?

⁴ Sharp arrows of the warrior,
With the *burning* coals of
the broom tree.

⁵ Woe is me, for I sojourn in Meshech,
For I dwell among the tents of Kedar!
⁶ Too long has my soul had its dwelling
With those who hate peace.
⁷ I am *for* peace, but when I speak,
They are for war.

120:4 Sharp arrows…coals. Lies and false accusations are likened to 1) the pain/injury inflicted in battle by arrows, and 2) the pain of being burned with charcoal made from the wood of a broom tree (a desert bush that grows 10 to 15 ft. high).

Proverbs 28:15

¹⁵ *Like* a roaring lion and a rushing bear
Is a wicked ruler over a poor people.

Hebrews 4:1–16

4 Therefore, let us fear if, while a promise remains of entering His rest, any one of you may seem to have come short of it. ² For indeed we have had good news preached to us, just as they also; but the word they heard did not profit them, because it was not united by faith in those who heard. ³ For we who have believed enter that rest, just as He has said,

"As I swore in My wrath,
They shall not enter My rest,"

although His works were finished from the foundation of the world. ⁴ For He has said somewhere concerning the seventh *day:* "And God rested on the seventh day from all His works"; ⁵ and again in this *passage,* "They shall not enter My rest." ⁶ Therefore, since it remains for some to enter it, and those who formerly had good news preached to them failed to enter because of disobedience, ⁷ He again fixes a certain day, "Today," saying through David after so long a time just as has been said before,

"Today if you hear His voice,
Do not harden your hearts."

⁸ For if Joshua had given them rest, He would not have spoken of another day after that. ⁹ So there remains a Sabbath rest for the people of God. ¹⁰ For the one who has entered His rest has himself also rested from his works, as God did from His. ¹¹ Therefore let us be diligent to enter that rest, so that no one will fall, through *following* the same example of disobedience. ¹² For the word of God is living and active and sharper than any two-edged sword, and piercing as far as the division of soul and spirit, of both joints and marrow, and able to judge the thoughts and intentions of the heart. ¹³ And there is no creature hidden from His sight, but all things are open and laid bare to the eyes of Him with whom we have to do.

¹⁴ Therefore, since we have a great high priest who has passed through the heavens, Jesus the Son of God, let us hold fast our confession. ¹⁵ For we do not have a high priest who cannot sympathize with our weaknesses, but One who has been tempted in all things as *we are, yet* without sin. ¹⁶ Therefore let us draw near with confidence to the throne of grace, so that we may receive mercy and find grace to help in time of need.

4:12 two-edged sword. While the Word of God is comforting and nourishing to those who believe, it is a tool of judgment and execution for those who have not committed themselves to Jesus Christ. Some of the Hebrews were merely going through the motions of belonging to Christ. Intellectually, they were at least partly persuaded, but inside they were not committed to Him. God's Word would expose their shallow beliefs and even their false intentions (1Sa 16:7; 1Pe 4:5). **division of soul and spirit.** These terms do not describe two separate entities (any more than "thoughts and intentions" do) but are used as one might say "heart and soul" to express fullness (Lk 10:27; Ac 4:32; 1Th 5:23). Elsewhere these two terms are used interchangeably to describe man's immaterial self, his eternal inner person.

DAY 8: What does Hebrews 4:14–16 teach about prayer?

Just as the high priest under the Old Covenant passed through 3 areas (the outer court, the Holy Place, and the Holy of Holies) to make the atoning sacrifice, Jesus passed through 3 heavens (the atmospheric heaven, the stellar heaven, and God's abode; 2Co 12:2–4) after making the perfect, final sacrifice (v. 14). Once a year on the Day of Atonement the high priest of Israel would enter the Holy of Holies to make atonement for the sins of the people (Lv 16). That tabernacle was but a limited copy of the heavenly reality (8:1–5). When Jesus entered into the heavenly Holy of Holies, having accomplished redemption, the earthly facsimile was replaced by the reality of heaven itself. Freed from that which is earthly, the Christian faith is characterized by the heavenly (3:1; Eph 1:3; 2:6; Php 3:20; Col 1:5; 1Pe 1:4).

And Jesus as our High Priest was "tempted in all things as we are, yet without sin" (v. 15). Jesus became fully capable of understanding and sympathizing with His human brethren.

"Therefore let us draw near with confidence to the throne of grace" (v. 16). Most ancient rulers were unapproachable by anyone but their highest advisers (Est 4:11). In contrast, the Holy Spirit calls for all to come confidently before God's throne to receive mercy and grace through Jesus Christ. The ark of the covenant was viewed as the place on earth where God sat enthroned between the cherubim (2Ki 19:15; Jer 3:16–17). Oriental thrones included a footstool—yet another metaphor for the ark (Ps 132:7). It was at the throne of God that Christ made atonement for sins, and it is there that grace is dispensed to believers for all the issues of life (2Co 4:15; 9:8; 12:9; Eph 1:7; 2:7).

NOVEMBER 9

Ezekiel 9:1–10:22

9 Then He cried out in my hearing with a loud voice saying, "Draw near, O executioners of the city, each with his destroying weapon in his hand." ² Behold, six men came from the direction of the upper gate which faces north, each with his shattering weapon in his hand; and among them was a certain man clothed in linen with a writing case at his loins. And they went in and stood beside the bronze altar.

³ Then the glory of the God of Israel went up from the cherub on which it had been, to the threshold of the temple. And He called to the man clothed in linen at whose loins was the writing case. ⁴ The LORD said to him, "Go through the midst of the city, *even* through the midst of Jerusalem, and put a mark on the foreheads of the men who sigh and groan over all the abominations which are being committed in its midst." ⁵ But to the others He said in my hearing, "Go through the city after him and strike; do not let your

---

9:3 the glory…went up. The glory of God departs before the destruction of the city and temple. The gradual departure of God from His temple is depicted in stages: the glory resides in the temple's Most Holy Place, between the wings of the cherubs on each side of the ark of the covenant over the mercy seat, then leaves to the front door (9:3; 10:4), later to the east gate by the outer wall (10:18–19), and finally to the Mt. of Olives to the east, having fully departed (11:22–23). The glory will return in the future kingdom of Messiah (43:2–7).

---

eye have pity and do not spare. ⁶ Utterly slay old men, young men, maidens, little children, and women, but do not touch any man on whom is the mark; and you shall start from My sanctuary." So they started with the elders who *were* before the temple. ⁷ And He said to them, "Defile the temple and fill the courts with the slain. Go out!" Thus they went out and struck down *the people* in the city. ⁸ As they were striking *the people* and I *alone* was left, I fell on my face and cried out saying, "Alas, Lord GOD! Are You destroying the whole remnant of Israel by pouring out Your wrath on Jerusalem?"

⁹ Then He said to me, "The iniquity of the house of Israel and Judah is very, very great, and the land is filled with blood and the city is full of perversion; for they say, 'The LORD has forsaken the land, and the LORD does not see!' ¹⁰ But as for Me, My eye will have no pity nor will I spare, but I will bring their conduct upon their heads."

¹¹ Then behold, the man clothed in linen at whose loins was the writing case reported, saying, "I have done just as You have commanded me."

10 Then I looked, and behold, in the expanse that was over the heads of the cherubim something like a sapphire stone, in appearance resembling a throne, appeared above them. ² And He spoke to the man clothed in linen and said, "Enter between the whirling wheels under the cherubim and fill your hands with coals of fire from between the cherubim and scatter *them* over the city." And he entered in my sight.

³ Now the cherubim were standing on the right side of the temple when the man entered, and the cloud filled the inner court. ⁴ Then the glory of the LORD went up from the cherub to the threshold of the temple, and the temple was filled with the cloud and the court was filled with the brightness of

10:2 fill...with coals. God specifies that the marking angel (9:2, 11) reach into the war machine and fill his hands with fiery coals in the presence of the angels of chap. 1. These coals picture the fires of judgment which God's angels are to "scatter" on Jerusalem. In Isaiah 6, "a coal" was used for the purification of the prophet; here coals were for the destruction of the wicked (Heb 12:29). Fire did destroy Jerusalem in 586 B.C.

10:9–17 wheels beside the cherubim. This whole section is similar to 1:4–21. Four wheels on God's chariot mingled with the 4 angels (1:15–21) coordinated with one another in precision, and each with a different one of the cherubim. All looked so much alike that it was as if one wheel blended entirely with another (v. 10). As their appearance was so unified, their action was in unison, and instant (v. 11). The cherubim had bodies like men, and their chariot wheels were full of eyes, denoting full perception both to see the sinners and their fitting judgment. The color tarshish, or beryl, is a sparkling yellow or gold.

the glory of the LORD. ⁵Moreover, the sound of the wings of the cherubim was heard as far as the outer court, like the voice of God Almighty when He speaks.

⁶It came about when He commanded the man clothed in linen, saying, "Take fire from between the whirling wheels, from between the cherubim," he entered and stood beside a wheel. ⁷Then the cherub stretched out his hand from between the cherubim to the fire which was between the cherubim, took *some* and put *it* into the hands of the one clothed in linen, who took *it* and went out. ⁸The cherubim appeared to have the form of a man's hand under their wings.

⁹Then I looked, and behold, four wheels beside the cherubim, one wheel beside each cherub; and the appearance of the wheels *was* like the gleam of a Tarshish stone. ¹⁰As for their appearance, all four of them had the same likeness, as if one wheel were within another wheel. ¹¹When they moved, they went in *any of* their four directions without turning as they went; but they followed in the direction which they faced, without turning as they went. ¹²Their whole body, their backs, their hands, their wings and the wheels were full of eyes all around, the wheels belonging to all four of them. ¹³The wheels were called in my hearing, the whirling wheels. ¹⁴And each one had four faces. The first face *was* the face of a cherub, the second face *was* the face of a man, the third the face of a lion, and the fourth the face of an eagle.

¹⁵Then the cherubim rose up. They are the living beings that I saw by the river Chebar. ¹⁶Now when the cherubim moved, the wheels would go beside them; also when the cherubim lifted up their wings to rise from the ground, the wheels would not turn from beside them. ¹⁷When the cherubim stood still, the wheels would stand still; and when they rose up, the wheels would rise with them, for the spirit of the living beings *was* in them.

¹⁸Then the glory of the LORD departed from the threshold of the temple and stood over the cherubim. ¹⁹When the cherubim departed, they lifted their wings and rose up from the earth in my sight with the wheels beside them; and they stood still at the entrance of the east gate of the LORD'S house, and the glory of the God of Israel hovered over them.

²⁰These are the living beings that I saw beneath the God of Israel by the river Chebar; so I knew that they *were* cherubim. ²¹Each one had four faces and each one four wings, and beneath their wings *was* the form of human hands. ²²As for the likeness of their faces, they were the same faces whose appearance I had seen by the river Chebar. Each one went straight ahead.

Psalm 121:1–8

A Song of Ascents.

I will lift up my eyes to the mountains;
From where shall my help come?
² My help *comes* from the LORD,
Who made heaven and earth.
³ He will not allow your foot to slip;
He who keeps you will not slumber.
⁴ Behold, He who keeps Israel
Will neither slumber nor sleep.
⁵ The LORD is your keeper;
The LORD is your shade on
your right hand.
⁶ The sun will not smite you by day,
Nor the moon by night.
⁷ The LORD will protect
you from all evil;
He will keep your soul.
⁸ The LORD will guard your going
out and your coming in
From this time forth and forever.

Proverbs 28:16

¹⁶ A leader who is a great oppressor
lacks understanding,
But he who hates unjust gain
will prolong *his* days.

Hebrews 5:1–14

5 For every high priest taken from among
men is appointed on behalf of men in
things pertaining to God, in order to offer
both gifts and sacrifices for sins; ² he can deal
gently with the ignorant and misguided, since
he himself also is beset with weakness; ³ and
because of it he is obligated to offer *sacrifices*
for sins, as for the people, so also for himself.
⁴ And no one takes the honor to himself, but
receives it when he is called by God, even as
Aaron was.

⁵ So also Christ did not glorify Himself so
as to become a high priest, but He who said
to Him,

"You are My Son,
Today I have begotten You";

⁶ just as He says also in another *passage,*

"You are a priest forever
According to the order
of Melchizedek."

⁷ In the days of His flesh, He offered up both
prayers and supplications with loud crying
and tears to the One able to save Him from
death, and He was heard because of His piety.
⁸ Although He was a Son, He learned obedi-
ence from the things which He suffered. ⁹ And
having been made perfect, He became to all
those who obey Him the source of eternal

salvation, ¹⁰ being designated by God as a high
priest according to the order of Melchizedek.
¹¹ Concerning him we have much to say,
and *it is* hard to explain, since you have become dull of hearing. ¹² For though by this
time you ought to be teachers, you have need
again for someone to teach you the elementary principles of the oracles of God, and you
have come to need milk and not solid food.
¹³ For everyone who partakes *only* of milk is
not accustomed to the word of righteousness,
for he is an infant. ¹⁴ But solid food is for the
mature, who because of practice have their
senses trained to discern good and evil.

5:11 dull. The Hebrews' spiritual lethargy and
slow response to gospel teaching prevented
additional teaching at this time. This is a reminder that failure to appropriate the truth
of the gospel produces stagnation in spiritual
advancement and the inability to understand
or assimilate additional teaching (Jn 16:12).
Such a situation exists also among the Gentiles
who have received revelatory truth (natural or
general revelation) from God in the creation
(Ro 1:18–20). Rejection of that revelation results in a process of hardening (Ro 1:21–32).
The Hebrews had not only received the same
general revelation, they had also received special revelation consisting of the Old Testament
Scriptures (Ro 9:4), the Messiah Himself (Ro
9:5), and the teaching of the apostles (2:3–4).
Until the Hebrews obeyed the revelation they
had received and obtained eternal salvation
(v. 8), additional teaching about the Messiah's Melchizedekian priesthood would be of
no profit to them.

DAY 9: Why does it say that Jesus "learned obedience"?

The context of Hebrews 5:7 makes it clear that "in the days of His flesh, He" refers back to Christ,
the main subject in v. 5. In Gethsemane, Jesus agonized and wept, but committed Himself to
do the Father's will in accepting the cup of suffering which would bring His death (Mt 26:38–
46; Lk 22:44–45). Anticipating bearing the burden of judgment for sin, Jesus felt its fullest pain
and grief (Is 52:14; 53:3–5, 10). Though He bore the penalty in silence and did not seek to deliver
Himself from it (Is 53:7), He did cry out from the agony of the fury of God's wrath poured on His
perfectly holy and obedient Person (Mt 27:46; 2Co 5:21). Jesus asked to be saved from remaining
in death, i.e., to be resurrected (Ps 16:9–10).

"Although He was a Son, He learned obedience from the things which He suffered" (v. 8).
Christ did not need to suffer in order to conquer or correct any disobedience. In His deity (as the
Son of God), He understood obedience completely. As the incarnate Lord, He humbled Himself
to learn (Lk 2:52). He learned obedience for the same reasons He bore temptation: to confirm
His humanity and experience its sufferings to the fullest (2:10; Lk 2:52; Php 2:8). Christ's obedience was also necessary so that He could fulfill all righteousness (Mt 5:13) and thus prove to be
the perfect sacrifice to take the place of sinners (1Pe 3:18). He was the perfectly righteous One,
whose righteousness would be imputed to sinners (Ro 3:24–26).

"And having been perfect, He became to all those who obey Him the source of eternal salvation" (v. 9). Because of the perfect righteousness of Jesus Christ and His perfect sacrifice for sin, He became the cause of salvation. True salvation evidences itself in obedience to Christ, from the initial obedience to the gospel command to repent and believe (Ac 5:32; Ro 1:5; 2Th 1:8; 1Pe 1:2, 22; 4:17) to a life pattern of obedience to the Word (Ro 6:16).

NOVEMBER 10

Ezekiel 11:1–12:28

11 Moreover, the Spirit lifted me up and brought me to the east gate of the LORD'S house which faced eastward. And behold, *there were* twenty-five men at the entrance of the gate, and among them I saw Jaazaniah son of Azzur and Pelatiah son of Benaiah, leaders of the people. ² He said to me, "Son of man, these are the men who devise iniquity and give evil advice in this city, ³ who say, '*The time* is not near to build houses. This *city* is the pot and we are the flesh.' ⁴ Therefore, prophesy against them, son of man, prophesy!"

⁵ Then the Spirit of the LORD fell upon me, and He said to me, "Say, 'Thus says the LORD, "So you think, house of Israel, for I know your thoughts. ⁶ You have multiplied your slain in this city, filling its streets with them." ⁷ Therefore, thus says the Lord GOD, "Your slain whom you have laid in the midst of the city are the flesh and this *city* is the pot; but I will bring you out of it. ⁸ You have feared a sword; so I will bring a sword upon you," the Lord GOD declares. ⁹ "And I will bring you out of the midst of the city and deliver you into the hands of strangers and execute judgments against you. ¹⁰ You will fall by the sword. I will judge you to the border of Israel; so you shall know that I am the LORD. ¹¹ This *city* will not be a pot for you, nor will you be flesh in the midst of it, *but* I will judge you to the border of Israel. ¹² Thus you will know that I am the LORD; for you have not walked in My statutes nor have you executed My ordinances, but have acted according to the ordinances of the nations around you." ' "

¹³ Now it came about as I prophesied, that Pelatiah son of Benaiah died. Then I fell on my face and cried out with a loud voice and said, "Alas, Lord GOD! Will You bring the remnant of Israel to a complete end?"

¹⁴ Then the word of the LORD came to me, saying, ¹⁵ "Son of man, your brothers, your relatives, your fellow exiles and the whole house of Israel, all of them, *are those* to whom the inhabitants of Jerusalem have said, 'Go far from the LORD; this land has been given us

as a possession.' ¹⁶ Therefore say, 'Thus says the Lord GOD, "Though I had removed them far away among the nations and though I had scattered them among the countries, yet I was a sanctuary for them a little while in the countries where they had gone."' ¹⁷ Therefore say, 'Thus says the Lord GOD, "I will gather you from the peoples and assemble you out of the countries among which you have been scattered, and I will give you the land of Israel."' ¹⁸ When they come there, they will remove all its detestable things and all its abominations from it. ¹⁹ And I will give them one heart, and put a new spirit within them. And I will take the heart of stone out of their flesh and give them a heart of flesh, ²⁰ that they may walk in My statutes and keep My ordinances and do them. Then they will be My people, and I shall be their God. ²¹ But as for those whose hearts go after their detestable things and abominations, I will bring their conduct down on their heads," declares the Lord GOD.

²² Then the cherubim lifted up their wings with the wheels beside them, and the glory of the God of Israel hovered over them. ²³ The glory of the LORD went up from the midst of the city and stood over the mountain which is east of the city. ²⁴ And the Spirit lifted me up and brought me in a vision by the Spirit of God to the exiles in Chaldea. So the vision that I had seen left me. ²⁵ Then I told the exiles all the things that the LORD had shown me.

12 Then the word of the LORD came to me, saying, ² "Son of man, you live in the midst of the rebellious house, who have eyes to see but do not see, ears to hear but do not hear; for they are a rebellious house. ³ Therefore, son of man, prepare for yourself baggage for exile and go into exile by day in their sight; even go into exile from your place to another place in their sight. Perhaps they will understand though they are a rebellious house. ⁴ Bring your baggage out by day in their sight, as baggage for exile. Then you will go out at evening in their sight, as those going into exile. ⁵ Dig a hole through the wall in their sight and go out through it. ⁶ Load *the baggage* on *your* shoulder in their sight *and* carry *it* out in the dark. You shall cover your face so that you cannot see the land, for I have set you as a sign to the house of Israel."

12:3 prepare...for exile. This dramatic object lesson by the prophet called for carrying belongings out in a stealthy way as an act that depicted baggage packed for exile, just the bare necessities. His countrymen carried out such baggage when they went into captivity or sought to escape during Babylon's takeover of Jerusalem (vv. 7, 11). Some attempting to escape were caught as in a net, like King Zedekiah who was overtaken, blinded, and forced into exile. Verse 7 indicates that Ezekiel actually did what he was told.

⁷ I did so, as I had been commanded. By day I brought out my baggage like the baggage of an exile. Then in the evening I dug through the wall with my hands; I went out in the dark *and* carried *the baggage* on *my* shoulder in their sight.

⁸ In the morning the word of the LORD came to me, saying, ⁹ "Son of man, has not the house of Israel, the rebellious house, said to you, 'What are you doing?' ¹⁰ Say to them, 'Thus says the Lord GOD, "This burden *concerns* the prince in Jerusalem as well as all the house of Israel who are in it."' ¹¹ Say, 'I am a sign to you. As I have done, so it will be done to them; they will go into exile, into captivity.' ¹² The prince who is among them will load *his baggage* on *his* shoulder in the dark and go out. They will dig a hole through the wall to bring *it* out. He will cover his face so that he can not see the land with *his* eyes. ¹³ I will also spread My net over him, and he will be caught in My snare. And I will bring him to Babylon in the land of the Chaldeans; yet he will not see it, though he will die there. ¹⁴ I will scatter to every wind all who are around him, his helpers and all his troops; and I will draw out a sword after them. ¹⁵ So they will know that I am the LORD when I scatter them among the nations and spread them among the countries. ¹⁶ But I will spare a few of them from the sword, the famine and the pestilence that they may tell all their abominations among the nations where they go, and may know that I am the LORD."

¹⁷ Moreover, the word of the LORD came to me saying, ¹⁸ "Son of man, eat your bread with trembling and drink your water with quivering and anxiety. ¹⁹ Then say to the people of the land, 'Thus says the Lord GOD concerning the inhabitants of Jerusalem in the land of Israel, "They will eat their bread with anxiety and drink their water with horror, because their land will be stripped of its fullness on account of the violence of all who live in it. ²⁰ The inhabited cities will be laid waste and the land will be a desolation. So you will know that I am the LORD."'"

²¹ Then the word of the LORD came to me, saying, ²² "Son of man, what is this proverb you *people* have concerning the land of Israel, saying, 'The days are long and every vision fails'? ²³ Therefore say to them, 'Thus says the Lord GOD, "I will make this proverb cease so that they will no longer use it as a proverb in Israel." But tell them, "The days draw near as well as the fulfillment of every vision. ²⁴ For there will no longer be any false vision or flattering divination within the house of Israel. ²⁵ For I the LORD will speak, and whatever word I speak will be performed. It will no longer be delayed, for in your days, O rebellious house, I will speak the word and perform it,"' declares the Lord GOD.'"

12:22 this proverb. Delay had given the people the false impression that the stroke of judgment would never come. In fact, a saying had become popular, no doubt developed by false prophets who caused the people to reject Ezekiel's visions and prophecies (v. 27) and gave "false vision or flattering divination" (vv. 23–24).

²⁶ Furthermore, the word of the LORD came to me, saying, ²⁷ "Son of man, behold, the house of Israel is saying, 'The vision that he sees is for many years *from now,* and he prophesies of times far off.' ²⁸ Therefore say to them, 'Thus says the Lord GOD, "None of My words will be delayed any longer. Whatever word I speak will be performed,"'" declares the Lord GOD.

Psalm 122:1–5

A Song of Ascents, of David.

I was glad when they said to me,
"Let us go to the house of the LORD."
² Our feet are standing
Within your gates, O Jerusalem,
³ Jerusalem, that is built
As a city that is compact together;
⁴ To which the tribes go up, even
the tribes of the LORD—
An ordinance for Israel—
To give thanks to the
name of the LORD.
⁵ For there thrones were
set for judgment,
The thrones of the house of David.

Proverbs 28:17-18

¹⁷ A man who is laden with the
  guilt of human blood
Will be a fugitive until death;
  let no one support him.
¹⁸ He who walks blamelessly
  will be delivered,
But he who is crooked will
  fall all at once.

Hebrews 6:1-20

6 Therefore leaving the elementary teaching about the Christ, let us press on to maturity, not laying again a foundation of repentance from dead works and of faith toward God, ² of instruction about washings and laying on of hands, and the resurrection of the dead and eternal judgment. ³ And this we will do, if God permits. ⁴ For in the case of those who have once been enlightened and have tasted of the heavenly gift and have been made partakers of the Holy Spirit, ⁵ and have tasted the good word of God and the powers of the age to come, ⁶ and *then* have fallen away, it is impossible to renew them again to repentance, since they again crucify to themselves the Son of God and put Him to open shame. ⁷ For ground that drinks the rain which often falls on it and brings forth vegetation useful to those for whose sake it is also tilled, receives a blessing from God; ⁸ but if it yields thorns and thistles, it is worthless and close to being cursed, and it ends up being burned.

⁹ But, beloved, we are convinced of better

6:1 leaving. This "leaving" does not mean to despise or abandon the basic doctrines. They are the place to start, not stop. They are the gate of entrance on the road to salvation in Christ. **elementary teaching about the Christ.** As "the oracles of God" in 5:12 refers to the OT, so does this phrase. The writer is referring to basic Old Testament teaching that prepared the way for Messiah—the beginning teaching about Christ. This Old Testament "teaching" includes the 6 features listed in vv. 1-2. **press on to maturity.** Salvation by faith in Messiah Jesus. The verb is passive, so as to indicate "let us be carried to salvation." That is not a matter of learners being carried by teachers, but both being carried forward by God. The writer warns his Jewish readers that there is no value in stopping with the Old Testament basics and repeating ("laying again") what was only intended to be foundational.

6:4 enlightened. They had received instruction in biblical truth which was accompanied by intellectual perception. Understanding the gospel is not the equivalent of regeneration (10:26, 32). In John 1:9 it is clear that enlightening is not the equivalent of salvation. **tasted of the heavenly gift.** Tasting in the figurative sense in the New Testament refers to consciously experiencing something (2:9). The experience might be momentary or continuing. Christ's "tasting" of death (2:9) was obviously momentary and not continuing or permanent. All men experience the goodness of God, but that does not mean they are all saved (Mt 5:45; Ac 17:25). Many Jews during the Lord's earthly ministry experienced the blessings from heaven He brought—in healings and deliverance from demons, as well as eating the food He created miraculously (Jn 6). Whether the gift refers to Christ (Jn 6:51; 2Co 9:15) or to the Holy Spirit (Ac 2:38; 1Pe 1:12), experiencing either one was not the equivalent of salvation (Jn 16:8; Ac 7:51).

things concerning you, and things that accompany salvation, though we are speaking in this way. ¹⁰ For God is not unjust so as to forget your work and the love which you have shown toward His name, in having ministered and in still ministering to the saints. ¹¹ And we desire that each one of you show the same diligence so as to realize the full assurance of hope until the end, ¹² so that you will not be sluggish, but imitators of those who through faith and patience inherit the promises.

¹³ For when God made the promise to Abraham, since He could swear by no one greater, He swore by Himself, ¹⁴ saying, "I WILL SURELY BLESS YOU AND I WILL SURELY MULTIPLY YOU." ¹⁵ And so, having patiently waited, he obtained the promise. ¹⁶ For men swear by one greater *than themselves,* and with them an oath *given* as confirmation is an end of every dispute. ¹⁷ In the same way God, desiring even more to show to the heirs of the promise the unchangeableness of His purpose, interposed with an oath, ¹⁸ so that by two unchangeable things in which it is impossible for God to lie, we who have taken refuge would have strong encouragement to take hold of the hope set before us. ¹⁹ This hope we have as an anchor of the soul, a *hope* both sure and steadfast and one which enters within the veil, ²⁰ where Jesus has entered as a forerunner for us, having become a high priest forever according to the order of Melchizedek.

The phrase "once being enlightened" is often taken to refer to Christians. The accompanying warning, then, is taken to indicate the danger of losing their salvation if they "have fallen away" and "again crucify to themselves the Son of God." But the immediate context has no mention of their being saved. They are not described with any terms that apply only to believers (such as holy, born again, righteous, or saints).

The interpretive problem arises from inaccurately identifying the spiritual condition of the ones being addressed. In this case, they were unbelievers who had been exposed to God's redemptive truth and, perhaps, had made a profession of faith but had not exercised genuine saving faith. Another passage (10:26) addresses the same issue. The subject here is people who come in contact with the gospel but are spiritually unchanged by it. Apostate Christians are Christians in name only, not genuine believers who are often incorrectly thought to lose their salvation because of their sins.

There is no possibility of these verses referring to someone losing their salvation. Many Scripture passages make unmistakably clear that salvation is eternal (see, e.g., Jn 10:27–29; Ro 8:35, 38–39; Php 1:6; 1Pe 1:4–5). Those who want to make this passage mean that believers can lose salvation will have to admit that it would then also make the point that one could never get it back again.

NOVEMBER 11

Ezekiel 13:1–14:23

13 Then the word of the LORD came to me saying, ² "Son of man, prophesy against the prophets of Israel who prophesy, and say to those who prophesy from their own inspiration, 'Listen to the word of the LORD! ³ Thus says the Lord GOD, "Woe to the foolish prophets who are following their own spirit and have seen nothing. ⁴ O Israel, your prophets have been like foxes among ruins. ⁵ You have not gone up into the breaches, nor did you build the wall around the house of Israel to stand in the battle on the day of the LORD. ⁶ They see falsehood and lying divination who are saying, 'The LORD declares,' when the LORD has not sent them; yet they hope for the fulfillment of *their* word. ⁷ Did you not see a false vision and speak a lying divination when you said, 'The LORD declares,' but it is not I who have spoken?" ' "

⁸ Therefore, thus says the Lord GOD, "Because you have spoken falsehood and seen a lie, therefore behold, I am against you," declares the Lord GOD. ⁹ "So My hand will be against the prophets who see false visions and utter lying divinations. They will have no place in the council of My people, nor will they be written down in the register of the house of Israel, nor will they enter the land of Israel, that you may know that I am the Lord GOD. ¹⁰ It is definitely because they have misled My people by saying, 'Peace!' when there is no peace. And when anyone builds a wall, behold, they

13:10–11 builds a wall. False prophets had lulled the people into false security. Phony "peace" promises, while sin continued on the brink of God's judgment, was a way, so to speak, of erecting a defective "wall" and whitewashing it to make it look good. Such an unsafe "wall" was doomed to collapse (v. 11) when God would bring His storm, picturing the invaders' assault (v. 11).

plaster it over with whitewash; ¹¹ *so* tell those who plaster *it* over with whitewash, that it will fall. A flooding rain will come, and you, O hailstones, will fall; and a violent wind will break out. ¹² Behold, when the wall has fallen, will you not be asked, 'Where is the plaster with which you plastered *it?*' " ¹³ Therefore, thus says the Lord GOD, "I will make a violent wind break out in My wrath. There will also be in My anger a flooding rain and hailstones to consume *it* in wrath. ¹⁴ So I will tear down the wall which you plastered over with whitewash and bring it down to the ground, so that its foundation is laid bare; and when it falls, you will be consumed in its midst. And you will know that I am the LORD. ¹⁵ Thus I will spend My wrath on the wall and on those who have plastered it over with whitewash; and I will say to you, 'The wall is gone and its plasterers are gone, ¹⁶ *along with* the prophets of Israel who prophesy to Jerusalem, and who see visions of peace for her when there is no peace,' declares the Lord GOD.

[17] "Now you, son of man, set your face against the daughters of your people who are prophesying from their own inspiration. Prophesy against them [18] and say, 'Thus says the Lord GOD, "Woe to the women who sew *magic* bands on all wrists and make veils for the heads of *persons* of every stature to hunt down lives! Will you hunt down the lives of My people, but preserve the lives *of others* for yourselves? [19] For handfuls of barley and fragments of bread, you have profaned Me to My people to put to death some who should not die and to keep others alive who should not live, by your lying to My people who listen to lies." '

[20] Therefore, thus says the Lord GOD, "Behold, I am against your *magic* bands by which you hunt lives there as birds and I will tear them from your arms; and I will let them go, even those lives whom you hunt as birds. [21] I will also tear off your veils and deliver My people from your hands, and they will no longer be in your hands to be hunted; and you will know that I am the LORD. [22] Because you disheartened the righteous with falsehood when I did not cause him grief, but have encouraged the wicked not to turn from his wicked way *and* preserve his life, [23] therefore, you women will no longer see false visions or practice divination, and I will deliver My people out of your hand. Thus you will know that I am the LORD."

14 Then some elders of Israel came to me and sat down before me. [2] And the word of the LORD came to me, saying, [3] "Son of man, these men have set up their idols in their hearts and have put right before their faces the stumbling block of their iniquity. Should I be consulted by them at all? [4] Therefore speak to them and tell them, 'Thus says the Lord GOD, "Any man of the house of Israel who sets up his idols in his heart, puts right before his face the stumbling block of his iniquity, and *then* comes to the prophet, I the LORD will be brought to give him an answer in the matter in view of the multitude of his idols, [5] in order to lay hold of the hearts of the house of Israel who are estranged from Me through all their idols." '

[6] "Therefore say to the house of Israel, 'Thus says the Lord GOD, "Repent and turn away from your idols and turn your faces away from all your abominations. [7] For anyone of the house of Israel or of the immigrants who stay in Israel who separates himself from Me, sets up his idols in his heart, puts right before his face the stumbling block of his iniquity, and *then* comes to the prophet to inquire of Me for himself, I the LORD will be brought to answer him in My own person. [8] I will set My face against that man and make him a sign and a

proverb, and I will cut him off from among My people. So you will know that I am the LORD.

[9] "But if the prophet is prevailed upon to speak a word, it is I, the LORD, who have prevailed upon that prophet, and I will stretch out My hand against him and destroy him from among My people Israel. [10] They will bear *the punishment of* their iniquity; as the iniquity of the inquirer is, so the iniquity of the prophet will be, [11] in order that the house of Israel may no longer stray from Me and no longer defile themselves with all their transgressions. Thus they will be My people, and I shall be their God," ' declares the Lord GOD."

[12] Then the word of the LORD came to me saying, [13] "Son of man, if a country sins against Me by committing unfaithfulness, and I stretch out My hand against it, destroy its supply of bread, send famine against it and cut off from it both man and beast, [14] even *though* these three men, Noah, Daniel and Job were in its midst, by their *own* righteousness they could *only* deliver themselves," declares the Lord GOD. [15] "If I were to cause wild beasts to pass through the land and they depopulated it, and it became desolate so that no one would pass through it because of the beasts, [16] though these three men were in its midst, as I live," declares the Lord GOD, "they could not deliver either *their* sons or *their* daughters. They alone would be delivered, but the country would be desolate. [17] Or *if* I should bring a sword on that country and say, 'Let the sword pass through the country and cut off man and beast from it,' [18] even *though* these three men were in its midst, as I live," declares the Lord GOD, "they could not deliver either *their* sons or *their* daughters, but they alone would be delivered. [19] Or *if* I should send a plague against

14:14–20 Noah, Daniel and Job. Jeremiah 7:16 and 15:1–4 provide a close parallel to this passage. According to Jeremiah, even Moses and Samuel, well known for their power in intercessory prayer, would not prevail to deliver Jerusalem and the people. The 3 Old Testament heroes mentioned in this section exhibited power in intercession on behalf of others (Ge 6:18; Job 42:7–10; Da 1–2) at strategic points in redemptive history, and even they could not deliver anyone but themselves if they were there praying earnestly. Even the presence and prayers of the godly could not stop the coming judgment. Genesis 18:22–32 and Jer 5:1–4 provide rare exceptions to the principle that one man's righteousness is no protection for others.

that country and pour out My wrath in blood on it to cut off man and beast from it, [20] even *though* Noah, Daniel and Job were in its midst, as I live," declares the Lord GOD, "they could not deliver either *their* son or *their* daughter. They would deliver only themselves by their righteousness."

[21] For thus says the Lord GOD, "How much more when I send My four severe judgments against Jerusalem: sword, famine, wild beasts and plague to cut off man and beast from it! [22] Yet, behold, survivors will be left in it who will be brought out, *both* sons and daughters. Behold, they are going to come forth to you and you will see their conduct and actions; then you will be comforted for the calamity which I have brought against Jerusalem for everything which I have brought upon it. [23] Then they will comfort you when you see their conduct and actions, for you will know that I have not done in vain whatever I did to it," declares the Lord GOD.

Psalm 122:6–9

[6] Pray for the peace of Jerusalem:
"May they prosper who love you.
[7] "May peace be within your walls,
And prosperity within your palaces."
[8] For the sake of my brothers
and my friends,
I will now say, "May peace
be within you."
[9] For the sake of the house of
the LORD our God,
I will seek your good.

Proverbs 28:19

[19] He who tills his land will
have plenty of food,
But he who follows empty *pursuits*
will have poverty in plenty.

Hebrews 7:1–28

7 For this Melchizedek, king of Salem, priest of the Most High God, who met Abraham as he was returning from the slaughter of the kings and blessed him, [2] to whom also Abraham apportioned a tenth part of all *the spoils,* was first of all, by the translation *of his name,* king of righteousness, and then also king of Salem, which is king of peace. [3] Without father, without mother, without genealogy, having neither beginning of days nor end of life, but made like the Son of God, he remains a priest perpetually.

[4] Now observe how great this man was to whom Abraham, the patriarch, gave a tenth of the choicest spoils. [5] And those indeed of the sons of Levi who receive the priest's office have commandment in the Law to collect a tenth from the people, that is, from their brethren, although these are descended from Abraham. [6] But the one whose genealogy is not traced from them collected a tenth from Abraham and blessed the one who had the promises. [7] But without any dispute the lesser is blessed by the greater. [8] In this case mortal men receive tithes, but in that case one *receives them,* of whom it is witnessed that he lives on. [9] And, so to speak, through Abraham even Levi, who received tithes, paid tithes, [10] for he was still in the loins of his father when Melchizedek met him.

[11] Now if perfection was through the Levitical priesthood (for on the basis of it the people received the Law), what further need *was there* for another priest to arise according to the order of Melchizedek, and not be designated according to the order of Aaron? [12] For when the priesthood is changed, of necessity there takes place a change of law also. [13] For the one concerning whom these things are spoken belongs to another tribe, from which no one has officiated at the altar. [14] For it is evident that our Lord was descended from Judah, a tribe with reference to which Moses spoke nothing concerning priests. [15] And this is clearer still, if another priest arises according to the likeness of Melchizedek, [16] who has become *such* not on the basis of a law of physical requirement, but according to the power of an indestructible life. [17] For it is attested *of Him,*

"YOU ARE A PRIEST FOREVER
ACCORDING TO THE ORDER
OF MELCHIZEDEK."

[18] For, on the one hand, there is a setting aside of a former commandment because of its weakness and uselessness [19] (for the Law made nothing perfect), and on the other hand there is a bringing in of a better hope, through which we draw near to God. [20] And

7:19 the Law made nothing perfect. The law saved no one (Ro 3:19–20); rather it cursed everyone (Gal 3:10–13). **draw near to God.** This is the key phrase in this passage. Drawing near to God is the essence of Christianity as compared with the Levitical system, which kept people outside His presence. As believer priests, we are all to draw near to God—that is a characteristic of priesthood (Ex 19:22; Mt 27:51).

inasmuch as *it was* not without an oath ²¹(for they indeed became priests without an oath, but He with an oath through the One who said to Him,

"THE LORD HAS SWORN
AND WILL NOT CHANGE HIS MIND,
'YOU ARE A PRIEST FOREVER'");

²²so much the more also Jesus has become the guarantee of a better covenant.

²³The *former* priests, on the one hand, existed in greater numbers because they were prevented by death from continuing, ²⁴but Jesus, on the other hand, because He continues forever, holds His priesthood permanently. ²⁵Therefore He is able also to save forever those who draw near to God through Him, since He always lives to make intercession for them.

²⁶For it was fitting for us to have such a high priest, holy, innocent, undefiled, separated from sinners and exalted above the heavens; ²⁷who does not need daily, like those

high priests, to offer up sacrifices, first for His own sins and then for the *sins* of the people, because this He did once for all when He offered up Himself. ²⁸For the Law appoints men as high priests who are weak, but the word of the oath, which came after the Law, *appoints* a Son, made perfect forever.

7:25 forever. Virtually the same concept as was expressed in "perfection" (v. 11) and "make perfect" (v. 19). The Greek term is used only here and in Luke 13:11 (the woman's body could not be straightened completely). **intercession.** The word means "to intercede on behalf of another." It was used to refer to bringing a petition to a king on behalf of someone. The High Priestly intercessory prayer of Christ in John 17 is an example. Since rabbis assigned intercessory powers to angels, perhaps the people were treating angels as intercessors. The writer makes it clear that only Christ is the intercessor (1Ti 2:5).

DAY 11: Who was Melchizedek, and why was he so important?

Melchizedek shows up abruptly and briefly in the Old Testament, but his special role in Abraham's life makes him a significant figure. He is mentioned again in Psalm 110:4, the passage under consideration in Hebrews 4:14–7:28. As the king of Salem and priest of the Most High God in the time of Abraham, Melchizedek offered a historical precedent for the role of king-priest (Ge 14:18–20), filled perfectly by Jesus Christ.

By using the two Old Testament references to Melchizedek, the writer (7:1–28) explains the superiority of Christ's priesthood by reviewing Melchizedek's unique role as a type of Christ and his superiority to the Levitical high priesthood. The Levitical priesthood was hereditary, but Melchizedek's was not. Through Abraham's honor, Melchizedek's rightful role was established. The major ways in which the Melchizedekan priesthood was superior to the Levitical priesthood are these:

1. The receiving of tithes (7:2–10), as when Abraham the ancestor of the Levites gave Melchizedek a tithe of the spoils.
2. The giving of the blessing (7:1, 6–7), as when Abraham accepted Melchizedek's blessing.
3. The continual replacement of the Levitical priesthood (7:11–19), which passed down from father to son.
4. The perpetuity of the Melchizedekan priesthood (7:3, 8, 16–17, 20–28), since the record about his priesthood does not record his death.

NOVEMBER 12

Ezekiel 15:1–16:63

15 Then the word of the LORD came to me, saying, ² "Son of man, how is the wood of the vine *better* than any wood of a branch which is among the trees of the forest? ³ Can wood be taken from it to make anything, or can *men* take a peg from it on which to hang any vessel? ⁴ If it has been put into the fire for fuel, *and* the fire has consumed both of its

15:1–3 Then the word...came. Israel, often symbolized by a vine (17:6–10; Ge 49:22; Jer 2:21), had become useful for nothing. Failing to do the very thing God set her apart to do—bear fruit—she no longer served any purpose and was useless (v. 2). Other trees can be used for construction of certain things, but a fruitless vine is useless (v. 3). It has no value. In every age the people of God have their value in their fruitfulness.

ends and its middle part has been charred, is it *then* useful for anything? [5] Behold, while it is intact, it is not made into anything. How much less, when the fire has consumed it and it is charred, can it still be made into anything! [6] Therefore, thus says the Lord GOD, 'As the wood of the vine among the trees of the forest, which I have given to the fire for fuel, so have I given up the inhabitants of Jerusalem; [7] and I set My face against them. *Though* they have come out of the fire, yet the fire will consume them. Then you will know that I am the LORD, when I set My face against them. [8] Thus I will make the land desolate, because they have acted unfaithfully,'" declares the Lord GOD.

16 Then the word of the LORD came to me, saying, [2] "Son of man, make known to Jerusalem her abominations [3] and say, 'Thus says the Lord GOD to Jerusalem, "Your origin and your birth are from the land of the Canaanite, your father was an Amorite and your mother a Hittite. [4] As for your birth, on the day you were born your navel cord was not cut, nor were you washed with water for cleansing; you were not rubbed with salt or even wrapped in cloths. [5] No eye looked with pity on you to do any of these things for you, to have compassion on you. Rather you were thrown out into the open field, for you were abhorred on the day you were born.

[6] "When I passed by you and saw you squirming in your blood, I said to you *while you were* in your blood, 'Live!' Yes, I said to you *while you were* in your blood, 'Live!' [7] I made you numerous like plants of the field. Then you grew up, became tall and reached the age for fine ornaments; *your* breasts were formed and your hair had grown. Yet you were naked and bare.

[8] "Then I passed by you and saw you, and behold, you were at the time for love; so I spread My skirt over you and covered your nakedness. I also swore to you and entered into a covenant with you so that you became Mine," declares the Lord GOD. [9] "Then I bathed you with water, washed off your blood from

16:8 the time for love. This refers to the marriageable state. Spreading his "skirt" was a custom of espousal (Ru 3:9) and indicates that God entered into a covenant with the young nation at Mt. Sinai (Ex 19:5–8). Making a covenant signifies marriage, the figure of God's relation to Israel (Jer 2:2; 3:1ff.; Hos 2:2–23).

you and anointed you with oil. [10] I also clothed you with embroidered cloth and put sandals of porpoise skin on your feet; and I wrapped you with fine linen and covered you with silk. [11] I adorned you with ornaments, put bracelets on your hands and a necklace around your neck. [12] I also put a ring in your nostril, earrings in your ears and a beautiful crown on your head. [13] Thus you were adorned with gold and silver, and your dress was of fine linen, silk and embroidered cloth. You ate fine flour, honey and oil; so you were exceedingly beautiful and advanced to royalty. [14] Then your fame went forth among the nations on account of your beauty, for it was perfect because of My splendor which I bestowed on you," declares the Lord GOD.

[15] "But you trusted in your beauty and played the harlot because of your fame, and you poured out your harlotries on every passer-by who might be *willing*. [16] You took some of your clothes, made for yourself high places of various colors and played the harlot on them, which should never come about nor happen. [17] You also took your beautiful jewels *made* of My gold and of My silver, which I had given you, and made for yourself male images that you might play the harlot with them. [18] Then you took your embroidered cloth and covered them, and offered My oil and My incense before them. [19] Also My bread which I gave you, fine flour, oil and honey with which I fed you, you would offer before them for a soothing aroma; so it happened," declares the Lord GOD. [20] "Moreover, you took your sons and daughters whom you had borne to Me and sacrificed them to idols to be devoured. Were your harlotries so small a matter? [21] You slaughtered My children and offered them up to idols by causing them to pass through *the fire*. [22] Besides all your abominations and harlotries you did not remember the days of your youth, when you were naked and bare and squirming in your blood.

[23] "Then it came about after all your wickedness ('Woe, woe to you!' declares the Lord GOD), [24] that you built yourself a shrine and made yourself a high place in every square. [25] You built yourself a high place at the top of every street and made your beauty abominable, and you spread your legs to every passer-by to multiply your harlotry. [26] You also played the harlot with the Egyptians, your lustful neighbors, and multiplied your harlotry to make Me angry. [27] Behold now, I have stretched out My hand against you and diminished your rations. And I delivered you up to the desire of those who hate you, the

daughters of the Philistines, who are ashamed of your lewd conduct. [28] Moreover, you played the harlot with the Assyrians because you were not satisfied; you played the harlot with them and still were not satisfied. [29] You also multiplied your harlotry with the land of merchants, Chaldea, yet even with this you were not satisfied." '"

[30] "How languishing is your heart," declares the Lord GOD, "while you do all these things, the actions of a bold-faced harlot. [31] When you built your shrine at the beginning of every street and made your high place in every square, in disdaining money, you were not like a harlot. [32] You adulteress wife, who takes strangers instead of her husband! [33] Men give gifts to all harlots, but you give your gifts to all your lovers to bribe them to come to you from every direction for your harlotries. [34] Thus you are different from those women in your harlotries, in that no one plays the harlot as you do, because you give money and no money is given you; thus you are different."

[35] Therefore, O harlot, hear the word of the LORD. [36] Thus says the Lord GOD, "Because your lewdness was poured out and your nakedness uncovered through your harlotries with your lovers and with all your detestable idols, and because of the blood of your sons which you gave to idols, [37] therefore, behold, I will gather all your lovers with whom you took pleasure, even all those whom you loved *and* all those whom you hated. So I will gather them against you from every direction and expose your nakedness to them that they may see all your nakedness. [38] Thus I will judge you like women who commit adultery or shed blood are judged; and I will bring on you the blood of wrath and jealousy. [39] I will also give you into the hands of your lovers, and they will tear down your shrines, demolish your high places, strip you of your clothing, take away your jewels, and will leave you naked and bare. [40] They will incite a crowd against you and they will stone you and cut you to pieces with their swords. [41] They will burn your houses with fire and execute judgments on you in the sight of many women. Then I will stop you from playing the harlot, and you will also no longer pay your lovers. [42] So I will calm My fury against you and My jealousy will depart from you, and I will be pacified and angry no more. [43] Because you have not remembered the days of your youth but have enraged Me by all these things, behold, I in turn will bring your conduct down on your own head," declares the Lord GOD, "so that

you will not commit this lewdness on top of all your *other* abominations.

[44] "Behold, everyone who quotes proverbs will quote *this* proverb concerning you, saying, 'Like mother, like daughter.' [45] You are the daughter of your mother, who loathed her husband and children. You are also the sister of your sisters, who loathed their husbands and children. Your mother was a Hittite and your father an Amorite. [46] Now your older sister is Samaria, who lives north of you with her daughters; and your younger sister, who lives south of you, is Sodom with her daughters. [47] Yet you have not merely walked in their ways or done according to their abominations; but, as if that were too little, you acted more corruptly in all your conduct than they. [48] As I live," declares the Lord GOD, "Sodom, your sister and her daughters have not done as you and your daughters have done. [49] Behold, this was the guilt of your sister Sodom: she and her daughters had arrogance, abundant food and careless ease, but she did not help the poor and needy. [50] Thus they were haughty and committed abominations before Me. Therefore I removed them when I saw *it.* [51] Furthermore, Samaria did not commit half of your sins, for you have multiplied your abominations more than they. Thus you have made your sisters appear righteous by all your abominations which you have committed. [52] Also bear your disgrace in that you have made judgment favorable for your sisters. Because of your sins in which you acted more abominably than they, they are more in the right than you. Yes, be also ashamed and bear your disgrace, in that you made your sisters appear righteous.

[53] "Nevertheless, I will restore their captivity, the captivity of Sodom and her daughters, the captivity of Samaria and her daughters, and along with them your own captivity, [54] in order that you may bear your humiliation and feel ashamed for all that you have done when you become a consolation to them. [55] Your sisters, Sodom with her daughters and Samaria with her daughters, will return to their former state, and you with your daughters will *also* return to your former state. [56] As *the name of* your sister Sodom was not heard from your lips in your day of pride, [57] before your wickedness was uncovered, so now you have become the reproach of the daughters of Edom and of all who are around her, of the daughters of the Philistines—those surrounding *you* who despise you. [58] You have borne *the penalty of* your lewdness and abominations," the LORD declares. [59] For thus says

the Lord GOD, "I will also do with you as you have done, you who have despised the oath by breaking the covenant.

⁶⁰ "Nevertheless, I will remember My covenant with you in the days of your youth, and I will establish an everlasting covenant with you. ⁶¹ Then you will remember your ways and be ashamed when you receive your sisters, *both* your older and your younger; and I will give them to you as daughters, but not because of your covenant. ⁶² Thus I will establish My covenant with you, and you shall know that I am the LORD, ⁶³ so that you may remember and be ashamed and never open your mouth anymore because of your humiliation, when I have forgiven you for all that you have done," the Lord GOD declares.

16:60 I will remember My covenant. God is gracious and He always finds a covenant basis on which He can exercise His grace. The Lord will remember the Abrahamic Covenant (Ge 12:1ff.) made with Israel in her youth. Restoration will be by grace, not merit. **an everlasting covenant.** This is the New Covenant, which is unconditional, saving, and everlasting (37:26; Is 59:21; 61:8; Jer 31:31–34; Heb 8:6–13). The basis of God's grace will not be the Mosaic Covenant, which the Jews could never fulfill, even with the best intentions (Ex 24:1ff.). When God establishes His eternal covenant, Israel will know that God is the Lord because of His grace.

Psalm 123:1–4

A Song of Ascents.

To You I lift up my eyes,
    O You who are enthroned
        in the heavens!
² Behold, as the eyes of servants *look*
        to the hand of their master,
    As the eyes of a maid to the
        hand of her mistress,
    So our eyes *look* to the
        LORD our God,
    Until He is gracious to us.

³ Be gracious to us, O LORD,
        be gracious to us,
    For we are greatly filled
        with contempt.
⁴ Our soul is greatly filled
    With the scoffing of those
        who are at ease,
    And with the contempt of the proud.

Proverbs 28:20

²⁰ A faithful man will abound
        with blessings,
    But he who makes haste to be
        rich will not go unpunished.

Hebrews 8:1–13

8 Now the main point in what has been said *is this:* we have such a high priest, who has taken His seat at the right hand of the throne of the Majesty in the heavens, ² a minister in the sanctuary and in the true tabernacle, which the Lord pitched, not man. ³ For every high priest is appointed to offer both gifts and sacrifices; so it is necessary that this *high priest* also have something to offer. ⁴ Now if He were on earth, He would not be a priest at all, since there are those who offer the gifts according to the Law; ⁵ who serve a copy and shadow of the heavenly things, just as Moses was warned *by God* when he was about to erect the tabernacle; for, "SEE," He says, "THAT YOU MAKE all things ACCORDING TO THE PATTERN WHICH WAS SHOWN YOU ON THE MOUNTAIN." ⁶ But now He has obtained a more excellent ministry, by as much as He is also the mediator of a better covenant, which has been enacted on better promises. ⁷ For if that first *covenant* had been faultless, there would have been no occasion sought for a second. ⁸ For finding fault with them, He says,

8:5 The quote is from Exodus 25:40. **copy and shadow.** This does not mean that there are actual buildings in heaven which were copied in the tabernacle, but rather that the heavenly realities were adequately symbolized and represented in the earthly tabernacle model.

"BEHOLD, DAYS ARE COMING,
        SAYS THE LORD,
    WHEN I WILL EFFECT
        A NEW COVENANT
    WITH THE HOUSE OF ISRAEL AND
        WITH THE HOUSE OF JUDAH;
⁹ NOT LIKE THE COVENANT WHICH I
        MADE WITH THEIR FATHERS
    ON THE DAY WHEN I TOOK
        THEM BY THE HAND
    TO LEAD THEM OUT OF THE
        LAND OF EGYPT;
    FOR THEY DID NOT CONTINUE
        IN MY COVENANT,
    AND I DID NOT CARE FOR
        THEM, SAYS THE LORD.

¹⁰ "For this is the covenant that I will
   make with the house of Israel
After those days, says the Lord:
I will put My laws into their minds,
And I will write them
   on their hearts.
And I will be their God,
And they shall be My people.
¹¹ "And they shall not teach
   everyone his fellow citizen,
And everyone his brother,
   saying, 'Know the Lord,'

For all will know Me,
From the least to the
   greatest of them.
¹² "For I will be merciful to
   their iniquities,
And I will remember their
   sins no more."

¹³ When He said, "A new *covenant*," He has made the first obsolete. But whatever is becoming obsolete and growing old is ready to disappear.

DAY 12: Who was the prophet Ezekiel?

If the "thirtieth year" of Ezekiel 1:1 refers to Ezekiel's age, he was 25 when taken captive and 30 when called into ministry. Thirty was the age when priests commenced their office, so it was a notable year for Ezekiel. His ministry began in 593/92 B.C. and extended at least 22 years until 571/70 B.C. (25:17). He was a contemporary of both Jeremiah (who was about 20 years older) and Daniel (who was the same age), whom he names in 14:14, 20; 28:3 as an already well-known prophet. Like Jeremiah (Jer 1:1) and Zechariah (Zec 1:1 with Ne 12:16), Ezekiel was both a prophet and a priest (1:3). Because of his priestly background, he was particularly interested in and familiar with the temple details. So God used him to write much about them (8:1–11:25; 40:1–47:12).

Ezekiel and his wife (who is mentioned in 24:15–27) were among 10,000 Jews taken captive to Babylon in 597 B.C. (2Ki 24:11–18). They lived in Tel Abib (3:15) on the bank of the Chebar River, probably southeast of Babylon. Domestically, Ezekiel and the 10,000 lived more as colonists than captives, being permitted to farm tracts of land under somewhat favorable conditions (Jer 29). Ezekiel even had his own house (3:24; 20:1). Ezekiel writes of his wife's death in exile (Eze 24:18), but the book does not mention Ezekiel's death, which rabbinical tradition suggests occurred at the hands of an Israelite prince whose idolatry he rebuked around 560 B.C.

Prophetically, false prophets deceived the exiles with assurances of a speedy return to Judah (13:3, 16; Jer 29:1). From 593 to 585 B.C., Ezekiel warned that their beloved Jerusalem would be destroyed and their exile prolonged, so there was no hope of immediate return. In 585 B.C., an escapee from Jerusalem, who had evaded the Babylonians, reached Ezekiel with the first news that the city had fallen in 586 B.C., about 6 months earlier (33:21). That dashed the false hopes of any immediate deliverance for the exiles, so the remainder of Ezekiel's prophecies related to Israel's future restoration to its homeland and the final blessings of the messianic kingdom.

 # NOVEMBER 13

Ezekiel 17:1–18:32

17 Now the word of the LORD came to me saying, ² "Son of man, propound a riddle and speak a parable to the house of Israel, ³ saying, 'Thus says the Lord GOD, "A great eagle with great wings, long pinions and a full plumage of many colors came to Lebanon and took away the top of the cedar. ⁴ He plucked off the topmost of its young twigs and brought it to a land of merchants; he set it in a city of traders. ⁵ He also took some of the seed of the land and planted it in fertile soil. He placed *it* beside abundant waters; he set it *like* a willow. ⁶ Then it sprouted and became a low, spreading vine with its branches turned toward him, but its roots remained under it.

So it became a vine and yielded shoots and sent out branches.

⁷ "But there was another great eagle with great wings and much plumage; and behold, this vine bent its roots toward him and sent out its branches toward him from the beds where it was planted, that he might water it. ⁸ It was planted in good soil beside abundant waters, that it might yield branches and bear fruit *and* become a splendid vine."' ⁹ Say, 'Thus says the Lord GOD, "Will it thrive? Will he not pull up its roots and cut off its fruit, so that it withers—so that all its sprouting leaves wither? And neither by great strength nor by many people can it be raised from its roots *again.* ¹⁰ Behold, though it is planted, will it thrive? Will it not completely wither as soon as the east wind strikes it—wither on the beds where it grew?"'"

¹¹Moreover, the word of the LORD came to me, saying, ¹²"Say now to the rebellious house, 'Do you not know what these things *mean?*' Say, 'Behold, the king of Babylon came to Jerusalem, took its king and princes and brought them to him in Babylon. ¹³He took one of the royal family and made a covenant with him, putting him under oath. He also took away the mighty of the land, ¹⁴that the kingdom might be in subjection, not exalting itself, *but* keeping his covenant that it might continue. ¹⁵But he rebelled against him by sending his envoys to Egypt that they might give him horses and many troops. Will he succeed? Will he who does such things escape? Can he indeed break the covenant and escape? ¹⁶As I live,' declares the Lord GOD, 'Surely in the country of the king who put him on the throne, whose oath he despised and whose covenant he broke, in Babylon he shall die. ¹⁷Pharaoh with *his* mighty army and great company will not help him in the war, when they cast up ramps and build siege walls to cut off many lives. ¹⁸Now he despised the oath by breaking the covenant, and behold, he pledged his allegiance, yet did all these things; he shall not escape.'" ¹⁹Therefore, thus says the Lord GOD, "As I live, surely My oath which he despised and My covenant which he broke, I will inflict on his head. ²⁰I will spread My net over him, and he will be caught in My snare. Then I will bring him to Babylon and enter into judgment with him there *regarding* the unfaithful act which he has committed against Me. ²¹All the choice men in all his troops will fall by the sword, and the survivors will be scattered to every wind; and you will know that I, the LORD, have spoken."

²²Thus says the Lord GOD, "I will also take *a sprig* from the lofty top of the cedar and set *it* out; I will pluck from the topmost of its young twigs a tender one and I will plant *it* on a high and lofty mountain. ²³On the high

17:22–23 *a sprig* **from the lofty top.** This is messianic prophecy stating that God will provide the Messiah from the royal line of David ("the cedar") and establish Him in His kingdom (like a "mountain," see Da 2:35, 44–45). He will be "*a sprig*" reigning in the height of success. "Sprig," or "branch," is a name for Messiah (34:23–24; 37:24–25; Is 4:2; Jer 23:5; 33:15; Zec 3:8; 6:12). Messiah will be "a tender one" (v. 22) growing into a "stately cedar" (v. 23). Under His kingdom rule, all nations will be blessed and Israel restored.

mountain of Israel I will plant it, that it may bring forth boughs and bear fruit and become a stately cedar. And birds of every kind will nest under it; they will nest in the shade of its branches. ²⁴All the trees of the field will know that I am the LORD; I bring down the high tree, exalt the low tree, dry up the green tree and make the dry tree flourish. I am the LORD; I have spoken, and I will perform *it.*"

18 Then the word of the LORD came to me, saying, ²"What do you mean by using this proverb concerning the land of Israel, saying,

'The fathers eat the sour grapes,
But the children's teeth
   are set on edge'?

³As I live," declares the Lord GOD, "you are surely not going to use this proverb in Israel anymore. ⁴Behold, all souls are Mine; the soul of the father as well as the soul of the son is Mine. The soul who sins will die.

18:4 The soul who sins will die. God played no favorites, but was fair in holding each individual accountable for his own sin. The death is physical death which, for many, results in eternal death.

⁵"But if a man is righteous and practices justice and righteousness, ⁶and does not eat at the mountain *shrines* or lift up his eyes to the idols of the house of Israel, or defile his neighbor's wife or approach a woman during her menstrual period— ⁷if a man does not oppress anyone, but restores to the debtor his pledge, does not commit robbery, *but* gives his bread to the hungry and covers the naked with clothing, ⁸if he does not lend *money* on interest or take increase, *if* he keeps his hand from iniquity *and* executes true justice between man and man, ⁹*if* he walks in My statutes and My ordinances so as to deal faithfully—he is righteous *and* will surely live," declares the Lord GOD.

¹⁰"Then he may have a violent son who sheds blood and who does any of these things to a brother ¹¹(though he himself did not do any of these things), that is, he even eats at the mountain *shrines,* and defiles his neighbor's wife, ¹²oppresses the poor and needy, commits robbery, does not restore a pledge, but lifts up his eyes to the idols *and* commits abomination, ¹³he lends *money* on interest

and takes increase; will he live? He will not live! He has committed all these abominations, he will surely be put to death; his blood will be on his own head.

¹⁴ "Now behold, he has a son who has observed all his father's sins which he committed, and observing does not do likewise. ¹⁵ He does not eat at the mountain *shrines* or lift up his eyes to the idols of the house of Israel, or defile his neighbor's wife, ¹⁶ or oppress anyone, or retain a pledge, or commit robbery, *but* he gives his bread to the hungry and covers the naked with clothing, ¹⁷ he keeps his hand from the poor, does not take interest or increase, *but* executes My ordinances, and walks in My statutes; he will not die for his father's iniquity, he will surely live. ¹⁸ As for his father, because he practiced extortion, robbed *his* brother and did what was not good among his people, behold, he will die for his iniquity.

¹⁹ "Yet you say, 'Why should the son not bear the punishment for the father's iniquity?' When the son has practiced justice and righteousness and has observed all My statutes and done them, he shall surely live. ²⁰ The person who sins will die. The son will not bear the punishment for the father's iniquity, nor will the father bear the punishment for the son's iniquity; the righteousness of the righteous will be upon himself, and the wickedness of the wicked will be upon himself.

²¹ "But if the wicked man turns from all his sins which he has committed and observes all My statutes and practices justice and righteousness, he shall surely live; he shall not die. ²² All his transgressions which he has committed will not be remembered against him; because of his righteousness which he has practiced, he will live. ²³ Do I have any pleasure in the death of the wicked," declares the Lord GOD, "rather than that he should turn from his ways and live?

²⁴ "But when a righteous man turns away from his righteousness, commits iniquity and does according to all the abominations that a wicked man does, will he live? All his righteous deeds which he has done will not be remembered for his treachery which he has committed and his sin which he has committed; for them he will die. ²⁵ Yet you say, 'The way of the Lord is not right.' Hear now, O house of Israel! Is My way not right? Is it not your ways that are not right? ²⁶ When a righteous man turns away from his righteousness, commits iniquity and dies because of it, for his iniquity which he has committed he will die. ²⁷ Again, when a wicked man turns away from his wickedness which he

has committed and practices justice and righteousness, he will save his life. ²⁸ Because he considered and turned away from all his transgressions which he had committed, he shall surely live; he shall not die. ²⁹ But the house of Israel says, 'The way of the Lord is not right.' Are My ways not right, O house of Israel? Is it not your ways that are not right?

³⁰ "Therefore I will judge you, O house of Israel, each according to his conduct," declares the Lord GOD. "Repent and turn away from all your transgressions, so that iniquity may not become a stumbling block to you. ³¹ Cast away from you all your transgressions which you have committed and make yourselves a new heart and a new spirit! For why will you die, O house of Israel? ³² For I have no pleasure in the death of anyone who dies," declares the Lord GOD. "Therefore, repent and live."

Psalm 124:1–8

A Song of Ascents, of David.

"**H**ad it not been the LORD
who was on our side,"
Let Israel now say,
² "Had it not been the LORD
who was on our side
When men rose up against us,
³ Then they would have
swallowed us alive,
When their anger was
kindled against us;
⁴ Then the waters would
have engulfed us,
The stream would have
swept over our soul;
⁵ Then the raging waters would
have swept over our soul."

⁶ Blessed be the LORD,
Who has not given us to be
torn by their teeth.
⁷ Our soul has escaped as a bird out
of the snare of the trapper;
The snare is broken and
we have escaped.
⁸ Our help is in the name of the LORD,
Who made heaven and earth.

Proverbs 28:21

²¹ To show partiality is not good,
Because for a piece of bread
a man will transgress.

Hebrews 9:1–28

9 Now even the first *covenant* had regulations of divine worship and the earthly sanctuary. ² For there was a tabernacle prepared, the outer one, in which *were* the lampstand and the table and the sacred bread; this is called the holy place. ³Behind the second veil there was a tabernacle which is called the Holy of Holies, ⁴having a golden altar of incense and the ark of the covenant covered on all sides with gold, in which was a golden jar holding the manna, and Aaron's rod which budded, and the tables of the covenant; ⁵and above it *were* the cherubim of glory overshadowing the mercy seat; but of these things we cannot now speak in detail.

⁶Now when these things have been so prepared, the priests are continually entering the outer tabernacle performing the divine worship, ⁷but into the second, only the high priest *enters* once a year, not without *taking* blood, which he offers for himself and for the sins of the people committed in ignorance. ⁸The Holy Spirit *is* signifying this, that the way into the holy place has not yet been disclosed while the outer tabernacle is still standing, ⁹which *is* a symbol for the present time. Accordingly both gifts and sacrifices are offered which cannot make the worshiper perfect in conscience, ¹⁰since they *relate* only to food and drink and various washings, regulations for the body imposed until a time of reformation.

9:8 The Levitical system did not provide any direct access into God's presence for His people. Rather, it kept them away. Nearness had to be provided by another way (v. 12). This is the primary lesson which the Holy Spirit taught concerning the tabernacle. It teaches how inaccessible God is apart from the death of Jesus Christ. **Holy Spirit.** By the Spirit-inspired instruction given for the Holiest of All, He was indicating that there was no way to God in the ceremonial system. Only Christ could open the way (Jn 14:6).

¹¹But when Christ appeared *as* a high priest of the good things to come, *He entered* through the greater and more perfect tabernacle, not made with hands, that is to say, not of this creation; ¹²and not through the blood of goats and calves, but through His own blood, He entered the holy place once for all, having obtained eternal redemption. ¹³For if the blood of goats and bulls and the ashes of a heifer sprinkling those who have been defiled sanctify for the cleansing of the flesh, ¹⁴how much more will the blood

of Christ, who through the eternal Spirit offered Himself without blemish to God, cleanse your conscience from dead works to serve the living God?

¹⁵For this reason He is the mediator of a new covenant, so that, since a death has taken place for the redemption of the transgressions that were *committed* under the first covenant, those who have been called may receive the promise of the eternal inheritance. ¹⁶For where a covenant is, there must of necessity be the death of the one who made it. ¹⁷For a covenant is valid *only* when men are dead, for it is never in force while the one who made it lives. ¹⁸Therefore even the first *covenant* was not inaugurated without blood. ¹⁹For when every commandment had been spoken by Moses to all the people according to the Law, he took the blood of the calves and the goats, with water and scarlet wool and hyssop, and sprinkled both the book itself and all the people, ²⁰saying, "This is the blood of the covenant which God commanded you." ²¹And in the same way he sprinkled both the tabernacle and all the vessels of the ministry with the blood. ²²And according to the Law, *one may* almost *say*, all things are cleansed with blood, and without shedding of blood there is no forgiveness.

²³Therefore it was necessary for the copies of the things in the heavens to be cleansed with these, but the heavenly things themselves with better sacrifices than these. ²⁴For Christ did not enter a holy place made with hands, a *mere* copy of the true one, but into heaven itself, now to appear in the presence of God for us; ²⁵nor was it that He would offer Himself often, as the high priest enters the holy place year by year with blood that is not his own. ²⁶Otherwise, He would have

9:27 to die once. This is a general rule for all mankind. There have been very rare exceptions (e.g., Lazarus died twice; see Jn 11:43–44). Those, like Lazarus, who were raised from the dead by a miraculous act of our Lord were not resurrected to a glorified body and unending life. They only experienced resuscitation. Another exception will be those who don't die even once, but who will be "caught up...to meet the Lord in the air" (1Th 4:17; see Enoch, Ge 5:24; Elijah, 2Ki 2:11). **judgment.** A general term encompassing the judgment of all people, believers (2Co 5:10) and unbelievers (Rev 20:11–15).

needed to suffer often since the foundation of the world; but now once at the consummation of the ages He has been manifested to put away sin by the sacrifice of Himself. [27] And inasmuch as it is appointed for men to die once and after this *comes* judgment, [28] so Christ also, having been offered once to bear the sins of many, will appear a second time for salvation without *reference to* sin, to those who eagerly await Him.

DAY 13: Why does Hebrews have so much about blood, including a statement such as "without shedding of blood there is no forgiveness" (9:22)?

Beginning with 9:7, the writer examined the significance of the blood of sacrifice. This term is especially central to 9:1–10:18 where the passage identifies the deaths of Old Testament sacrifices with the death of Christ (9:12–14). Note, however, that this shedding of blood in and of itself was an insufficient sacrifice. Christ had not only to shed His blood, but He also had to die—10:10 indicates that He gave His body as a sacrificial offering. Without His death, His blood had no saving value.

The expression, then, "blood of Christ" (9:14) refers not simply to the fluid but to the whole atoning sacrificial work of Christ in His death. Blood is used as a substitute word for death (see, e.g., Mt 23:30, 35; 27:6, 8, 24–25; Jn 6:54–56; Ac 18:6; 20:26). By reviewing the significance of the blood sacrifices in the Old Testament, the writer was pointing to a pattern of lessons that prepared the world to understand the necessity of Christ's death. The emphatic phrase "without shedding of blood there is no forgiveness" (9:22) simply repeats the lesson that sin creates a debt that must be paid by someone. "It is the blood by reason of the life that makes atonement" (Lv 17:11). The phraseology is reminiscent of Christ's words, "For this is My blood of the covenant, which is poured out for many for forgiveness of sins" (Mt 26:28). Remission means forgiveness in these verses—forgiveness for the sinner and payment of the debt. Christ's death (blood) provides the remission.

NOVEMBER 14

Ezekiel 19:1–20:49

19 "As for you, take up a lamentation for the princes of Israel [2] and say,

'What was your mother?
A lioness among lions!
She lay down among young lions,
She reared her cubs.
[3] 'When she brought up
one of her cubs,
He became a lion,
And he learned to tear *his* prey;
He devoured men.
[4] 'Then nations heard about him;
He was captured in their pit,
And they brought him with hooks
To the land of Egypt.
[5] 'When she saw, as she waited,
That her hope was lost,
She took another of her cubs
And made him a young lion.
[6] 'And he walked about
among the lions;
He became a young lion,
He learned to tear *his* prey;
He devoured men.
[7] 'He destroyed their fortified towers
And laid waste their cities;

And the land and its fullness
were appalled
Because of the sound of his roaring.
[8] 'Then nations set against him
On every side from *their* provinces,
And they spread their net over him;
He was captured in their pit.
[9] 'They put him in a cage with hooks
And brought him to the
king of Babylon;
They brought him in hunting nets
So that his voice would
be heard no more
On the mountains of Israel.
[10] 'Your mother was like a vine
in your vineyard,
Planted by the waters;
It was fruitful and full of branches
Because of abundant waters.
[11] 'And it had strong branches *fit*
for scepters of rulers,
And its height was raised
above the clouds
So that it was seen in its height
with the mass of its branches.
[12] 'But it was plucked up in fury;
It was cast down to the ground;
And the east wind dried up its fruit.
Its strong branch was torn off
So that it withered;
The fire consumed it.

¹³ 'And now it is planted in
the wilderness,
In a dry and thirsty land.
¹⁴ 'And fire has gone out
from *its* branch;
It has consumed its shoots *and* fruit,
So that there is not in it
a strong branch,
A scepter to rule.'"

This is a lamentation, and has become a lamentation.

20 Now in the seventh year, in the fifth *month,* on the tenth of the month, certain of the elders of Israel came to inquire of the LORD, and sat before me. ² And the word of the LORD came to me saying, ³ "Son of man, speak to the elders of Israel and say to them, 'Thus says the Lord GOD, "Do you come to inquire of Me? As I live," declares the Lord GOD, "I will not be inquired of by you."' ⁴ Will you judge them, will you judge them, son of man? Make them know the abominations of their fathers; ⁵ and say to them, 'Thus says the Lord GOD, "On the day when I chose Israel and swore to the descendants of the house of Jacob and made Myself known to them in the land of Egypt, when I swore to them, saying, I am the LORD your God, ⁶ on that day I swore to them, to bring them out from the land of Egypt into a land that I had selected for them, flowing with milk and honey, which is the glory of all lands. ⁷ I said to them, 'Cast away, each of you, the detestable things of his eyes, and do not defile yourselves with the idols of Egypt; I am the LORD your God.' ⁸ But they rebelled against Me and were not willing to listen to Me; they did not cast away the detestable things of their eyes, nor did they forsake the idols of Egypt.

Then I resolved to pour out My wrath on them, to accomplish My anger against them in the midst of the land of Egypt. ⁹ But I acted for the sake of My name, that it should not be profaned in the sight of the nations among whom they *lived,* in whose sight I made Myself known to them by bringing them out of the land of Egypt. ¹⁰ So I took them out of the land of Egypt and brought them into the wilderness. ¹¹ I gave them My statutes and informed them of My ordinances, by which, if a man observes them, he will live. ¹² Also I gave them My sabbaths to be a sign between Me and them, that they might know that I am the LORD who sanctifies them. ¹³ But the house of Israel rebelled against Me in the wilderness. They did not walk in My statutes and

they rejected My ordinances, by which, if a man observes them, he will live; and My sabbaths they greatly profaned. Then I resolved to pour out My wrath on them in the wilderness, to annihilate them. ¹⁴ But I acted for the sake of My name, that it should not be profaned in the sight of the nations, before whose sight I had brought them out. ¹⁵ Also I swore to them in the wilderness that I would not bring them into the land which I had given them, flowing with milk and honey, which is the glory of all lands, ¹⁶ because they rejected My ordinances, and as for My statutes, they did not walk in them; they even profaned My sabbaths, for their heart continually went after their idols. ¹⁷ Yet My eye spared them rather than destroying them, and I did not cause their annihilation in the wilderness.

¹⁸ "I said to their children in the wilderness, 'Do not walk in the statutes of your fathers or keep their ordinances or defile yourselves with their idols. ¹⁹ I am the LORD your God; walk in My statutes and keep My ordinances and observe them. ²⁰ Sanctify My sabbaths; and they shall be a sign between Me and you, that you may know that I am the LORD your God.' ²¹ But the children rebelled against Me; they did not walk in My statutes, nor were they careful to observe My ordinances, by which, *if* a man observes them, he will live; they profaned My sabbaths. So I resolved to pour out My wrath on them, to accomplish My anger against them in the wilderness. ²² But I withdrew My hand and acted for the sake of My name, that it should not be profaned in the sight of the nations in whose sight I had brought them out. ²³ Also I swore to them in the wilderness that I would scatter them among the nations and disperse them among the lands, ²⁴ because they had not observed My ordinances, but had rejected My statutes and had profaned My sabbaths, and their eyes were on the idols of their fathers. ²⁵ I also gave them statutes that were not good and ordinances by which they could not live; ²⁶ and I pronounced them unclean because of their gifts, in that they caused all their firstborn to pass through *the fire* so that I might make them desolate, in order that they might know that I am the LORD."'

²⁷ "Therefore, son of man, speak to the house of Israel and say to them, 'Thus says the Lord GOD, "Yet in this your fathers have blasphemed Me by acting treacherously against Me. ²⁸ When I had brought them into the land which I swore to give to them, then they saw every high hill and every leafy tree, and they offered there their sacrifices and

there they presented the provocation of their offering. There also they made their soothing aroma and there they poured out their drink offerings. ²⁹ Then I said to them, 'What is the high place to which you go?' So its name is called Bamah to this day."' ³⁰ Therefore, say to the house of Israel, 'Thus says the Lord GOD, "Will you defile yourselves after the manner of your fathers and play the harlot after their detestable things? ³¹ When you offer your gifts, when you cause your sons to pass through the fire, you are defiling yourselves with all your idols to this day. And shall I be inquired of by you, O house of Israel? As I live," declares the Lord GOD, "I will not be inquired of by you. ³² What comes into your mind will not come about, when you say: 'We will be like the nations, like the tribes of the lands, serving wood and stone.'

³³ "As I live," declares the Lord GOD, "surely with a mighty hand and with an outstretched arm and with wrath poured out, I shall be king over you. ³⁴ I will bring you out from the peoples and gather you from the lands where you are scattered, with a mighty hand and with an outstretched arm and with wrath poured out; ³⁵ and I will bring you into the wilderness of the peoples, and there I will enter into judgment with you face to face. ³⁶ As I entered into judgment with your fathers in the wilderness of the land of Egypt, so I will enter into judgment with you," declares the Lord GOD. ³⁷ "I will make you pass under the rod, and I will bring you into the bond of the covenant; ³⁸ and I will purge from you the rebels and those who transgress against Me; I will bring them out of the land where they sojourn, but they will not enter the land of Israel. Thus you will know that I am the LORD.

³⁹ "As for you, O house of Israel," thus says the Lord GOD, "Go, serve everyone his idols; but later you will surely listen to Me, and My holy name you will profane no longer with

20:37 pass under the rod. God used a shepherd figure here, apt since He was their Great Shepherd (34:11–13; Jer 23:5–8). As a shepherd, God brings His sheep home to their fold (Jer 33:13), has them file in, separating sheep from goats (Mt 25), passing under His shepherd's rod to be noted and checked for injury. He will bring them into the bond of the New Covenant by giving them His Spirit with life (36:24–27; 37:14; 39:29). This is Israel's final salvation (Ro 11:26–33).

20:39 If they persist in their stubborn idolatry, God will allow them to follow it to their doom. He would also rather have them as out-and-out idolaters rather than hypocritical patronizers of His worship as they had been (Am 5:21–26).

your gifts and with your idols. ⁴⁰ For on My holy mountain, on the high mountain of Israel," declares the Lord GOD, "there the whole house of Israel, all of them, will serve Me in the land; there I will accept them and there I will seek your contributions and the choicest of your gifts, with all your holy things. ⁴¹ As a soothing aroma I will accept you when I bring you out from the peoples and gather you from the lands where you are scattered; and I will prove Myself holy among you in the sight of the nations. ⁴² And you will know that I am the LORD, when I bring you into the land of Israel, into the land which I swore to give to your forefathers. ⁴³ There you will remember your ways and all your deeds with which you have defiled yourselves; and you will loathe yourselves in your own sight for all the evil things that you have done. ⁴⁴ Then you will know that I am the LORD when I have dealt with you for My name's sake, not according to your evil ways or according to your corrupt deeds, O house of Israel," declares the Lord GOD.'"

⁴⁵ Now the word of the LORD came to me, saying, ⁴⁶ "Son of man, set your face toward Teman, and speak out against the south and prophesy against the forest land of the Negev, ⁴⁷ and say to the forest of the Negev, 'Hear the word of the LORD: thus says the Lord GOD, "Behold, I am about to kindle a fire in you, and it will consume every green tree in you, as well as every dry tree; the blazing flame will not be quenched and the whole surface from south to north will be burned by it. ⁴⁸ All flesh will see that I, the LORD, have kindled it; it shall not be quenched."'" ⁴⁹ Then I said, "Ah Lord GOD! They are saying of me, 'Is he not *just* speaking parables?'"

Psalm 125:1–5

A Song of Ascents.

Those who trust in the LORD
  Are as Mount Zion, which cannot
    be moved but abides forever.
² As the mountains surround
    Jerusalem,
  So the LORD surrounds His people
  From this time forth and forever.

3 For the scepter of wickedness shall not
  rest upon the land of the righteous,
So that the righteous will not put
  forth their hands to do wrong.

4 Do good, O LORD, to those
  who are good
And to those who are upright
  in their hearts.
5 But as for those who turn aside
  to their crooked ways,
The LORD will lead them away
  with the doers of iniquity.
Peace be upon Israel.

Proverbs 28:22

22 A man with an evil eye
  hastens after wealth
And does not know that want
  will come upon him.

Hebrews 10:1–18

10 For the Law, since it has *only* a shadow
of the good things to come *and* not the
very form of things, can never, by the same
sacrifices which they offer continually year
by year, make perfect those who draw near.
2 Otherwise, would they not have ceased to
be offered, because the worshipers, having
once been cleansed, would no longer have
had consciousness of sins? 3 But in those *sacrifices* there is a reminder of sins year by year.
4 For it is impossible for the blood of bulls and
goats to take away sins. 5 Therefore, when He
comes into the world, He says,

"SACRIFICE AND OFFERING YOU
  HAVE NOT DESIRED,
BUT A BODY YOU HAVE
  PREPARED FOR ME;
6 IN WHOLE BURNT OFFERINGS
  AND *sacrifices* FOR SIN YOU
  HAVE TAKEN NO PLEASURE.
7 "THEN I SAID, 'BEHOLD, I HAVE COME
  (IN THE SCROLL OF THE BOOK
  IT IS WRITTEN OF ME)
  TO DO YOUR WILL, O GOD.'"

10:5–6 YOU HAVE NOT DESIRED. God was not
pleased with sacrifices given by a person who
did not give them out of a sincere heart (Ps
51:17; Is 1:11; Jer 6:20; Hos 6:6; Am 5:21–25). To
sacrifice only as a ritual, without obedience,
was a mockery and worse than no sacrifice at
all (Is 1:11–18).

8 After saying above, "SACRIFICES AND OF-
FERINGS AND WHOLE BURNT OFFERINGS AND
sacrifices FOR SIN YOU HAVE NOT DESIRED, NOR
HAVE YOU TAKEN PLEASURE *in them*" (which
are offered according to the Law), 9 then He
said, "BEHOLD, I HAVE COME TO DO YOUR WILL."
He takes away the first in order to establish
the second. 10 By this will we have been sanctified through the offering of the body of Jesus
Christ once for all.

10:10 sanctified. "Sanctify" means to "make
holy," to be set apart from sin for God (1Th
4:3). When Christ fulfilled the will of God, He
provided for the believer a continuing, permanent condition of holiness (Eph 4:24; 1Th 3:13).
This is the believer's positional sanctification
as opposed to the progressive sanctification
that results from daily walking by the will of
God (Ro 6:19; 12:1–2; 2Co 7:1). **body.** Refers to His
atoning death, as the term "blood" has been
used to do (9:7, 12, 14, 18, 22). Mention of the
body of Christ in such a statement is unusual
in the NT, but it is logically derived from the
quotation from Psalms 40:6.

11 Every priest stands daily ministering
and offering time after time the same sacrifices, which can never take away sins; 12 but
He, having offered one sacrifice for sins for
all time, SAT DOWN AT THE RIGHT HAND OF
GOD, 13 waiting from that time onward UNTIL
HIS ENEMIES BE MADE A FOOTSTOOL FOR HIS
FEET. 14 For by one offering He has perfected
for all time those who are sanctified. 15 And
the Holy Spirit also testifies to us; for after
saying,

16 "THIS IS THE COVENANT THAT I
  WILL MAKE WITH THEM
  AFTER THOSE DAYS,
  SAYS THE LORD:
I WILL PUT MY LAWS UPON
  THEIR HEART,
AND ON THEIR MIND I WILL
  WRITE THEM,"

He then says,

17 "AND THEIR SINS AND THEIR
  LAWLESS DEEDS
I WILL REMEMBER NO MORE."

18 Now where there is forgiveness of these
things, there is no longer *any* offering for sin.

DAY 14: What was the problem with the Old Testament sacrificial system?

"For the Law, since it has only a shadow of the good things to come and not the very form of things" (Heb 10:1). The Greek term translated "shadow" refers to a pale reflection, as contrasted with a sharp, distinct one. The term behind "very form," on the other hand, indicates an exact and distinct replica (Col 2:17). "Can never...make perfect those who draw near." This term is used repeatedly in Hebrews to refer to salvation. As much as those living under the law desired to approach God, the Levitical system provided no way to enter His holy presence (Pss 15:1; 16:11; 24:3–4).

If sin had really been overpowered by that system of sacrifices, the Old Testament believers' consciences would have been cleansed from condemning guilt (v. 2). There was not freedom of conscience under the Old Covenant. The Old Testament sacrifices not only could not remove sin, but their constant repetition was a constant reminder of that deficiency (v. 3). The promise of the New Covenant was that the sin would be removed and even God would "REMEMBER" their sins "NO MORE" (8:12, quoting Jer 31:34).

"For it is impossible for the blood of bulls and goats to take away sins" (v. 4). The Levitical system was not designed by God to remove or forgive sins. It was preparatory for the coming of the Messiah (Gal 3:24) in that it made the people expectant (1Pe 1:10). It revealed the seriousness of their sinful condition, in that even temporary covering required the death of an animal. It revealed the reality of God's holiness and righteousness by indicating that sin had to be covered. Finally, it revealed the necessity of full and complete forgiveness so that God could have desired fellowship with His people.

NOVEMBER 15

Ezekiel 21:1–22:31

21 And the word of the LORD came to me saying, ² "Son of man, set your face toward Jerusalem, and speak against the sanctuaries and prophesy against the land of Israel; ³ and say to the land of Israel, 'Thus says the LORD, "Behold, I am against you; and I will draw My sword out of its sheath and cut off from you the righteous and the wicked. ⁴ Because I will cut off from you the righteous and the wicked, therefore My sword will go forth from its sheath against all flesh from south *to* north. ⁵ Thus all flesh will know that I, the LORD, have drawn My sword out of its sheath. It will not return to *its sheath* again."' ⁶ As for you, son of man, groan with breaking heart and bitter grief, groan in their sight. ⁷ And when they say to you, 'Why do you groan?' you shall say, 'Because of the news that is coming; and every heart will melt, all hands will be feeble, every spirit will faint and all knees will be weak as water. Behold, it comes and it will happen,' declares the Lord GOD."

⁸ Again the word of the LORD came to me, saying, ⁹ "Son of man, prophesy and say, 'Thus says the LORD.' Say,

'A sword, a sword sharpened
And also polished!
¹⁰ 'Sharpened to make a slaughter,
Polished to flash like lightning!'

Or shall we rejoice, the rod of My son despising every tree? ¹¹ It is given to be polished, that it may be handled; the sword is sharpened and polished, to give it into the hand of the slayer. ¹² Cry out and wail, son of man; for it is against My people, it is against all the officials of Israel. They are delivered over to the sword with My people, therefore strike *your* thigh. ¹³ For *there is* a testing; and what if even the rod which despises will be no more?" declares the Lord GOD.

¹⁴ "You therefore, son of man, prophesy and clap *your* hands together; and let the sword be doubled the third time, the sword for the slain. It is the sword for the great one slain, which surrounds them, ¹⁵ that *their* hearts may melt, and many fall at all their gates. I have given the glittering sword. Ah! It is made *for striking* like lightning, it is wrapped up *in readiness* for slaughter. ¹⁶ Show yourself sharp, go to the right; set yourself; go to the left, wherever your edge is appointed. ¹⁷ I will also clap My hands together, and I will appease My wrath; I, the LORD, have spoken."

¹⁸ The word of the LORD came to me saying, ¹⁹ "As for you, son of man, make two ways for the sword of the king of Babylon to come; both of them will go out of one land. And make a signpost; make it at the head of the way to the city. ²⁰ You shall mark a way for the sword to come to Rabbah of the sons of Ammon, and to Judah into fortified Jerusalem. ²¹ For the king of Babylon stands at the parting of the way, at the head of the two ways, to use divination; he shakes the arrows,

he consults the household idols, he looks at the liver. ²² Into his right hand came the divination, 'Jerusalem,' to set battering rams, to open the mouth for slaughter, to lift up the voice with a battle cry, to set battering rams against the gates, to cast up ramps, to build a siege wall. ²³ And it will be to them like a false divination in their eyes; they have *sworn* solemn oaths. But he brings iniquity to remembrance, that they may be seized.

²⁴ "Therefore, thus says the Lord GOD, 'Because you have made your iniquity to be remembered, in that your transgressions are uncovered, so that in all your deeds your sins appear—because you have come to remembrance, you will be seized with the hand. ²⁵ And you, O slain, wicked one, the prince of Israel, whose day has come, in the time of the punishment of the end,' ²⁶ thus says the Lord GOD, 'Remove the turban and take off the crown; this *will* no longer *be* the same. Exalt that which is low and abase that which is high. ²⁷ A ruin, a ruin, a ruin, I will make it. This also will be no more until He comes whose right it is, and I will give it *to Him.*'

21:27 until He comes. The 3-fold mention of "ruin" expresses the severest degree of unsettled and chaotic conditions. Israel was to experience severe instability and even the kingly privilege will not be Israel's again until the coming of the Messiah, "whose right it is" (Ge 49:10). God will give the kingship to Him (Jer 23:5–8), the greater "David" (Eze 37:24). His "right" is that perfect combination of priestly and royal offices (Heb 5–7).

²⁸ "And you, son of man, prophesy and say, 'Thus says the Lord GOD concerning the sons of Ammon and concerning their reproach,' and say: 'A sword, a sword is drawn, polished for the slaughter, to cause it to consume, that it may be like lightning— ²⁹ while they see for you false visions, while they divine lies for you—to place you on the necks of the wicked who are slain, whose day has come, in the time of the punishment of the end. ³⁰ Return *it* to its sheath. In the place where you were created, in the land of your origin, I will judge you. ³¹ I will pour out My indignation on you; I will blow on you with the fire of My wrath, and I will give you into the hand of brutal men, skilled in destruction. ³² You will be fuel for the fire; your blood will be in the midst of the land. You will not be remembered, for I, the LORD, have spoken.'"

22 Then the word of the LORD came to me, saying, ² "And you, son of man, will you judge, will you judge the bloody city? Then cause her to know all her abominations. ³ You shall say, 'Thus says the Lord GOD, "A city shedding blood in her midst, so that her time will come, and that makes idols, contrary to her *interest,* for defilement! ⁴ You have become guilty by the blood which you have shed, and defiled by your idols which you have made. Thus you have brought your day near and have come to your years; therefore I have made you a reproach to the nations and a mocking to all the lands. ⁵ Those who are near and those who are far from you will mock you, you of ill repute, full of turmoil.

⁶ "Behold, the rulers of Israel, each according to his power, have been in you for the purpose of shedding blood. ⁷ They have treated father and mother lightly within you. The alien they have oppressed in your midst; the fatherless and the widow they have wronged in you. ⁸ You have despised My holy things and profaned My sabbaths. ⁹ Slanderous men have been in you for the purpose of shedding blood, and in you they have eaten at the mountain *shrines.* In your midst they have committed acts of lewdness. ¹⁰ In you they have uncovered *their* fathers' nakedness; in you they have humbled her who was unclean in her menstrual impurity. ¹¹ One has committed abomination with his neighbor's wife and another has lewdly defiled his daughter-in-law. And another in you has humbled his sister, his father's daughter. ¹² In you they have taken bribes to shed blood; you have taken interest and profits, and you have injured your neighbors for gain by oppression, and you have forgotten Me," declares the Lord GOD.

¹³ "Behold, then, I smite My hand at your dishonest gain which you have acquired and at the bloodshed which is among you. ¹⁴ Can your heart endure, or can your hands be strong in the days that I will deal with you? I, the LORD, have spoken and will act. ¹⁵ I will scatter you among the nations and I will disperse you through the lands, and I will consume your uncleanness from you. ¹⁶ You will profane yourself in the sight of the nations, and you will know that I am the LORD."'"

¹⁷ And the word of the LORD came to me, saying, ¹⁸ "Son of man, the house of Israel has become dross to Me; all of them are bronze and tin and iron and lead in the furnace; they are the dross of silver. ¹⁹ Therefore, thus says the Lord GOD, 'Because all of you have become dross, therefore, behold, I am going to gather

you into the midst of Jerusalem. ²⁰As they gather silver and bronze and iron and lead and tin into the furnace to blow fire on it in order to melt *it*, so I will gather *you* in My anger and in My wrath and I will lay you *there* and melt you. ²¹I will gather you and blow on you with the fire of My wrath, and you will be melted in the midst of it. ²²As silver is melted in the furnace, so you will be melted in the midst of it; and you will know that I, the LORD, have poured out My wrath on you.'"

²³And the word of the LORD came to me, saying, ²⁴"Son of man, say to her, 'You are a land that is not cleansed or rained on in the day of indignation.' ²⁵There is a conspiracy of her prophets in her midst like a roaring lion tearing the prey. They have devoured lives; they have taken treasure and precious things; they have made many widows in the midst of her. ²⁶Her priests have done violence to My law and have profaned My holy things; they have made no distinction between the holy and the profane, and they have not taught the difference between the unclean and the clean; and they hide their eyes from My sabbaths, and I am profaned among them. ²⁷Her princes within her are like wolves tearing the prey, by shedding blood *and* destroying lives in order to get dishonest gain. ²⁸Her prophets have smeared whitewash for them, seeing false visions and divining lies for them, saying, 'Thus says the Lord GOD,' when the LORD has not spoken. ²⁹The people of the land have practiced oppression and committed robbery, and they have wronged the poor and needy and have oppressed the sojourner without justice. ³⁰I searched for a man among them who would build up the wall and stand in the gap before Me for the land, so that I would not destroy it; but I found no one. ³¹Thus I have poured out My indignation on them;

❧

22:30 I searched for a man. Ezekiel and Jeremiah were faithful, but apart from them God sought a man capable of advocacy for Israel when its sin had gone so far. But no one could lead the people to repentance and draw the nation back from the brink of the judgment that came in 586 B.C. (Jer 7:26, 34; 19:15). Only God's Messiah, God Himself, will have the character and the credentials sufficient to do what no man can do, intercede for Israel (Is 59:16–19; 63:5; Rev 5). He was rejected by them in His earthly ministry, so the effects of this judgment continue today, until they turn to Him in faith (Zec 12:10; 13:1).

I have consumed them with the fire of My wrath; their way I have brought upon their heads," declares the Lord GOD.

Psalm 126:1–6

A Song of Ascents.

When the LORD brought back
the captive ones of Zion,
We were like those who dream.
² Then our mouth was filled
with laughter
And our tongue with joyful shouting;
Then they said among the nations,
"The LORD has done great
things for them."
³ The LORD has done great
things for us;
We are glad.

⁴ Restore our captivity, O LORD,
As the streams in the South.
⁵ Those who sow in tears shall
reap with joyful shouting.
⁶ He who goes to and fro weeping,
carrying *his* bag of seed,
Shall indeed come again with
a shout of joy, bringing
his sheaves *with him*.

Proverbs 28:23

²³ He who rebukes a man will
afterward find *more* favor
Than he who flatters with the tongue.

Hebrews 10:19–39

¹⁹Therefore, brethren, since we have confidence to enter the holy place by the blood of Jesus, ²⁰by a new and living way which He inaugurated for us through the veil, that is, His flesh, ²¹and since *we have* a great priest over the house of God, ²²let us draw near with a sincere heart in full assurance of faith, having our hearts sprinkled *clean* from an evil conscience and our bodies washed with pure water. ²³Let us hold fast the confession of our hope without wavering, for He who promised is faithful; ²⁴and let us consider how to stimulate one another to love and good deeds, ²⁵not forsaking our own assembling together, as is the habit of some, but encouraging *one another*; and all the more as you see the day drawing near.

²⁶For if we go on sinning willfully after receiving the knowledge of the truth, there no longer remains a sacrifice for sins, ²⁷but a terrifying expectation of judgment and THE FURY OF A FIRE WHICH WILL CONSUME THE ADVERSARIES. ²⁸Anyone who has set aside the

10:20 new. In Greek, this word originally meant "newly slain," but was understood as "recent" when the epistle was written. The way is new because the covenant is new. It is not a way provided by the Levitical system. **living way.** Though it is the path of eternal life, it was not opened by Christ's sinless life—it required His death. The Hebrews were invited to embark on this way which is characterized by the eternal life of the Son of God who loved them and gave Himself for them (Jn 14:6; Gal 2:20). The Christian faith was known as "the Way" among the Jews of Jerusalem (Ac 9:2) as well as among the Gentiles (Ac 19:23). Those receiving this epistle understood quite clearly that the writer was inviting them to become Christians—to join those who had been persecuted for their faith. True believers in their midst were even then suffering persecution, and those who had not committed themselves to the Way were asked to become targets of the same persecution.

Law of Moses dies without mercy on *the testimony of* two or three witnesses. ²⁹ How much severer punishment do you think he will deserve who has trampled under foot the Son of God, and has regarded as unclean the blood of the covenant by which he was sanctified, and has insulted the Spirit of grace? ³⁰ For we know Him who said, "Vengeance is Mine, I will repay." And again, "The Lord will judge His people." ³¹ It is a terrifying thing to fall into the hands of the living God.

³² But remember the former days, when, after being enlightened, you endured a great conflict of sufferings, ³³ partly by being made a public spectacle through reproaches and tribulations, and partly by becoming sharers with those who were so treated. ³⁴ For you showed sympathy to the prisoners and accepted joyfully the seizure of your property, knowing that you have for yourselves a better possession and a lasting one. ³⁵ Therefore, do not throw away your confidence, which has a great reward. ³⁶ For you have need of endurance, so that when you have done the will of God, you may receive what was promised.

³⁷ For yet in a very little while,
He who is coming will come,
    and will not delay.
³⁸ But My righteous one
    shall live by faith;
And if he shrinks back, My soul
    has no pleasure in him.

³⁹ But we are not of those who shrink back to destruction, but of those who have faith to the preserving of the soul.

DAY 15: How do we draw near to God?

"Let us draw near with a sincere heart" (Heb 10:22). Based on what had been written, this was the heart of the invitation to those in the assembly who had not come to Christ. The same invitation is found in the first New Testament book to be written (Jas 4:8), where James reveals the corollary of drawing near to God: God will draw near to you. Asaph taught that it is a good thing to draw near to God (Ps 73:28). The full restoration of Israel to God's blessing is dependent upon their drawing near to Him (Jer 30:18–22). In other words, it is an eschatological invitation coming to them "in these last days" (Heb 1:2). This verse describes the prerequisites for entering the presence of God (Ps 15): sincerity, security, salvation, and sanctification. The Greek term behind "sincere" carries the ideas of being genuine and without ulterior motive (Jer 24:7; Mt 15:8). This one thing these particular Hebrews lacked: genuine commitment to Christ.

"In full assurance of faith." Utter confidence in the promises of God is intended by the phrase. Such confidence will result in heartfelt assurance or security which will allow them to persevere through the coming trials. This is the first of a familiar triad: faith, hope (v. 23), and love (v. 24). "Having our hearts sprinkled...with pure water." The imagery in this verse is taken from the sacrificial ceremonies of the Old Covenant, where blood was sprinkled as a sign of cleansing, and the priests were continually washing themselves and the sacred vessels in basins of clear water. "Washed with pure water" does not refer to Christian baptism, but to the Holy Spirit's purifying one's life by means of the Word of God (Eph 5:25–26; Titus 3:5). This is purely a New Covenant picture (Jer 31:33; Eze 36:25–26).

NOVEMBER 16

Ezekiel 23:1–24:27

23 The word of the LORD came to me again, saying, ²"Son of man, there were two women, the daughters of one mother; ³ and they played the harlot in Egypt. They played the harlot in their youth; there their breasts were pressed and there their virgin bosom was handled. ⁴Their names were Oholah the elder and Oholibah her sister. And they became Mine, and they bore sons and daughters. And *as for* their names, Samaria is Oholah and Jerusalem is Oholibah.

⁵"Oholah played the harlot while she was Mine; and she lusted after her lovers, after the Assyrians, *her* neighbors, ⁶ who were clothed in purple, governors and officials, all of them desirable young men, horsemen riding on horses. ⁷She bestowed her harlotries on them, all of whom *were* the choicest men of Assyria; and with all whom she lusted after, with all their idols she defiled herself. ⁸ She did not forsake her harlotries from *the time in* Egypt; for in her youth men had lain with her, and they handled her virgin bosom and poured out their lust on her. ⁹Therefore, I gave her into the hand of her lovers, into the hand of the Assyrians, after whom she lusted. ¹⁰They uncovered her nakedness; they took her sons and her daughters, but they slew her with the sword. Thus she became a byword among women, and they executed judgments on her.

¹¹"Now her sister Oholibah saw *this,* yet she was more corrupt in her lust than she, and her harlotries were more than the harlotries of her sister. ¹²She lusted after the Assyrians, governors and officials, the ones near, magnificently dressed, horsemen riding on horses, all of them desirable young men. ¹³I saw that she had defiled herself; they both took the same way. ¹⁴So she increased her harlotries. And she saw men portrayed on the wall, images of the Chaldeans portrayed with vermilion, ¹⁵ girded with belts on their loins, with flowing turbans on their heads, all of them looking like officers, like the Babylonians *in* Chaldea, the land of their birth. ¹⁶When she saw them she lusted after them and sent messengers to them in Chaldea. ¹⁷The Babylonians came to her to the bed of love and defiled her with their harlotry. And when she had been defiled by them, she became disgusted with them. ¹⁸ She uncovered her harlotries and uncovered her nakedness; then I became disgusted with her, as I had become disgusted with her sister. ¹⁹Yet she multiplied her harlotries, remembering the days of her youth, when she played the harlot in the land of Egypt. ²⁰ She lusted after their paramours, whose flesh is *like* the flesh of donkeys and whose issue is *like* the issue of horses. ²¹Thus you longed for the lewdness of your youth, when the Egyptians handled your bosom because of the breasts of your youth.

²²"Therefore, O Oholibah, thus says the Lord GOD, 'Behold I will arouse your lovers against you, from whom you were alienated, and I will bring them against you from every side: ²³the Babylonians and all the Chaldeans, Pekod and Shoa and Koa, *and* all the Assyrians with them; desirable young men, governors and officials all of them, officers and men of renown, all of them riding on horses. ²⁴They will come against you with weapons, chariots and wagons, and with a company of peoples. They will set themselves against you on every side with buckler and shield and helmet; and I will commit the judgment to them, and they will judge you according to their customs. ²⁵I will set My jealousy against you, that they may deal with you in wrath. They will remove your nose and your ears; and your survivors will fall by the sword. They will take your sons and your daughters; and your survivors will be consumed by the fire. ²⁶They will also strip you of your clothes and take away your beautiful jewels. ²⁷Thus I will make your lewdness and your harlotry *brought* from the land of Egypt to cease from you, so that you will not lift up your eyes to them or remember Egypt anymore.' ²⁸For thus says the Lord GOD, 'Behold, I will give you into the hand of those whom you hate, into the hand of those from whom you were alienated. ²⁹They will deal with you in hatred, take all your property, and leave you naked and bare. And the nakedness of your harlotries will be uncovered, both your lewdness and your harlotries. ³⁰These things will be done to you because you have played the harlot with the nations, because you have defiled yourself with their idols. ³¹You have walked in the way of your sister; therefore I will give her cup into your hand.' ³²Thus says the Lord GOD,

'You will drink your sister's cup,
Which is deep and wide.
You will be laughed at and
    held in derision;
It contains much.
³³ 'You will be filled with
    drunkenness and sorrow,
The cup of horror and desolation,
The cup of your sister Samaria.

³⁴ 'You will drink it and drain it.
    Then you will gnaw its fragments
    And tear your breasts;

for I have spoken,' declares the Lord GOD. ³⁵ Therefore, thus says the Lord GOD, 'Because you have forgotten Me and cast Me behind your back, bear now the *punishment* of your lewdness and your harlotries.'"

³⁶ Moreover, the LORD said to me, "Son of man, will you judge Oholah and Oholibah? Then declare to them their abominations. ³⁷ For they have committed adultery, and blood is on their hands. Thus they have committed adultery with their idols and even caused their sons, whom they bore to Me, to pass through *the fire* to them as food. ³⁸ Again, they have done this to Me: they have defiled My sanctuary on the same day and have profaned My sabbaths. ³⁹ For when they had slaughtered their children for their idols, they entered My sanctuary on the same day to profane it; and lo, thus they did within My house.

⁴⁰ "Furthermore, they have even sent for men who come from afar, to whom a messenger was sent; and lo, they came—for whom you bathed, painted your eyes and decorated yourselves with ornaments; ⁴¹ and you sat on a splendid couch with a table arranged before it on which you had set My incense and My oil. ⁴² The sound of a carefree multitude was with her; and drunkards were brought from the wilderness with men of the common sort. And they put bracelets on the hands of the women and beautiful crowns on their heads.

⁴³ "Then I said concerning her who was worn out by adulteries, 'Will they now commit adultery with her when she is *thus*?' ⁴⁴ But they went in to her as they would go in to a harlot. Thus they went in to Oholah and to Oholibah, the lewd women. ⁴⁵ But they, righteous men, will judge them with the judgment of adulteresses and with the judgment of women who shed blood, because they are adulteresses and blood is on their hands.

⁴⁶ "For thus says the Lord GOD, 'Bring up a company against them and give them over to terror and plunder. ⁴⁷ The company will stone them with stones and cut them down with their swords; they will slay their sons and their daughters and burn their houses with fire. ⁴⁸ Thus I will make lewdness cease from the land, that all women may be admonished and not commit lewdness as you have done. ⁴⁹ Your lewdness will be requited upon you, and you will bear the penalty of *worshiping* your idols; thus you will know that I am the Lord GOD.'"

24 And the word of the LORD came to me in the ninth year, in the tenth month, on the tenth of the month, saying, ² "Son of man, write the name of the day, this very day. The king of Babylon has laid siege to Jerusalem this very day. ³ Speak a parable to the rebellious house and say to them, 'Thus says the Lord GOD,

"Put on the pot, put *it* on and
    also pour water in it;
⁴ Put in it the pieces,
    Every good piece, the thigh
      and the shoulder;
    Fill *it* with choice bones.
⁵ "Take the choicest of the flock,
    And also pile wood under the pot.
    Make it boil vigorously.
    Also seethe its bones in it."

⁶ 'Therefore, thus says the Lord GOD,

"Woe to the bloody city,
    To the pot in which there is rust
    And whose rust has
      not gone out of it!
    Take out of it piece after piece,
    Without making a choice.
⁷ "For her blood is in her midst;
    She placed it on the bare rock;
    She did not pour it on the ground
    To cover it with dust.
⁸ "That it may cause wrath to come
      up to take vengeance,
    I have put her blood
      on the bare rock,
    That it may not be covered."

⁹ Therefore, thus says the Lord GOD,

"Woe to the bloody city!
    I also will make the pile great.
¹⁰ "Heap on the wood, kindle the fire,
    Boil the flesh well
    And mix in the spices,
    And let the bones be burned.
¹¹ "Then set it empty on its coals
    So that it may be hot
    And its bronze may glow
    And its filthiness may be melted in it,
    Its rust consumed.
¹² "She has wearied *Me* with toil,
    Yet her great rust has not
      gone from her;
    Let her rust *be* in the fire!
¹³ "In your filthiness is lewdness.
    Because I *would* have cleansed you,
    Yet you are not clean,

You will not be cleansed from
your filthiness again
Until I have spent My wrath on you.

¹⁴I, the LORD, have spoken; it is coming and I will act. I will not relent, and I will not pity and I will not be sorry; according to your ways and according to your deeds I will judge you," declares the Lord GOD.'"

¹⁵And the word of the LORD came to me saying, ¹⁶"Son of man, behold, I am about to take from you the desire of your eyes with a blow; but you shall not mourn and you shall not weep, and your tears shall not come. ¹⁷Groan silently; make no mourning for the dead. Bind on your turban and put your shoes on your feet, and do not cover *your* mustache and do not eat the bread of men." ¹⁸So I spoke to the people in the morning, and in the evening my wife died. And in the morning I did as I was commanded. ¹⁹The people said to me, "Will you not tell us what these things that you are doing mean for us?" ²⁰Then I said to them, "The word of the LORD came to me saying, ²¹'Speak to the house of Israel, "Thus says the Lord GOD, 'Behold, I am about to profane My sanctuary, the pride of your power, the desire of your eyes and the delight of your soul; and your sons and your daughters whom you have left behind will fall by the sword. ²²You will do as I have done; you will not cover *your* mustache and you will not eat the bread of men. ²³Your turbans will be on your heads and your shoes on your feet. You will not mourn and you will not weep, but you will rot away in your iniquities and you will groan to one another. ²⁴Thus Ezekiel will be a sign to you; according to all that he has done you will do; when it comes, then you will know that I am the Lord GOD.'"

²⁵'As for you, son of man, will *it* not be on the day when I take from them their stronghold, the joy of their pride, the desire of their eyes and their heart's delight, their sons and their daughters, ²⁶that on that day he who escapes

24:16–27 Ezekiel's wife died as a sign to Israel. All personal sorrow was eclipsed in the universal calamity. Just as Ezekiel was not to mourn the death of his wife (v. 17), so Israel was not to mourn the death of her families (vv. 19–24). Though the text emphasizes how precious his wife was, the "desire of [his] eyes" (v. 16), he was obedient and submitted to God's will. He became a heartbreaking sign to his people.

will come to you with information for *your* ears? ²⁷On that day your mouth will be opened to him who escaped, and you will speak and be mute no longer. Thus you will be a sign to them, and they will know that I am the LORD.'"

Psalm 127:1–5

A Song of Ascents, of Solomon.

Unless the LORD builds the house,
They labor in vain who build it;
Unless the LORD guards the city,
The watchman keeps awake in vain.
² It is vain for you to rise up early,
To retire late,
To eat the bread of painful labors;
For He gives to His beloved
even in his sleep.

³ Behold, children are a
gift of the LORD,
The fruit of the womb is a reward.
⁴ Like arrows in the hand of a warrior,
So are the children of one's youth.
⁵ How blessed is the man whose
quiver is full of them;
They will not be ashamed
When they speak with their
enemies in the gate.

127:3 gift...reward. Children are a blessing from the Lord. There are overtones of God's promise to Abraham to make his offspring like the dust of the earth and the stars of heaven (Ge 13:16; 15:5).

Proverbs 28:24

²⁴ He who robs his father or his mother
And says, "It is not a transgression,"
Is the companion of a man
who destroys.

Hebrews 11:1–16

11 Now faith is the assurance of *things* hoped for, the conviction of things not seen. ²For by it the men of old gained approval.

³By faith we understand that the worlds were prepared by the word of God, so that what is seen was not made out of things which are visible. ⁴By faith Abel offered to God a better sacrifice than Cain, through which he obtained the testimony that he was righteous, God testifying about his gifts, and through faith, though he is dead, he still speaks. ⁵By

faith Enoch was taken up so that he would not see death; AND HE WAS NOT FOUND BECAUSE GOD TOOK HIM UP; for he obtained the witness that before his being taken up he was pleasing to God. ⁶And without faith it is impossible to please *Him,* for he who comes to God must believe that He is and *that* He is a rewarder of those who seek Him. ⁷By faith Noah, being warned *by God* about things not yet seen, in reverence prepared an ark for the salvation of his household, by which he condemned the world, and became an heir of the righteousness which is according to faith.

⁸By faith Abraham, when he was called, obeyed by going out to a place which he was to receive for an inheritance; and he went out, not knowing where he was going. ⁹By faith he

11:6 impossible to please. Enoch pleased God because he had faith. Without such faith it is not possible for anyone to "walk with God" or "please *Him*" (10:38). **He is.** The emphasis here is on "He," the true God. Genuine faith does not simply believe that *a* divine being exists, but that the God of Scripture is the *only* real and true God who exists. Not believing that God exists is equivalent to calling Him a liar (1Jn 5:10). **rewarder.** A person must believe not only that the true God exists, but also that He will reward men's faith in Him with forgiveness and righteousness, because He has promised to do so (10:35; Ge 15:1; Dt 4:29; 1Ch 28:9; Ps 58:11; Is 40:10).

lived as an alien in the land of promise, as in a foreign *land,* dwelling in tents with Isaac and Jacob, fellow heirs of the same promise; ¹⁰for he was looking for the city which has foundations, whose architect and builder is God. ¹¹By faith even Sarah herself received ability to conceive, even beyond the proper time of life, since she considered Him faithful who had promised. ¹²Therefore there was born even of one man, and him as good as dead at that, *as many descendants* AS THE STARS OF HEAVEN IN NUMBER, AND INNUMERABLE AS THE SAND WHICH IS BY THE SEASHORE.

¹³All these died in faith, without receiving the promises, but having seen them and having welcomed them from a distance, and having confessed that they were strangers and exiles on the earth. ¹⁴For those who say such things make it clear that they are seeking a country of their own. ¹⁵And indeed if they had been thinking of that *country* from which they went out, they would have had opportunity to return. ¹⁶But as it is, they desire a better *country,* that is, a heavenly one. Therefore God is not ashamed to be called their God; for He has prepared a city for them.

11:13–16 strangers and exiles. Their faith was patient and endured great hardships because they believed God had something better. They had no desire to go back to Ur, but did long for heaven (Job 19:25–26; Ps 27:4).

DAY 16: Why are so many Old Testament people listed in chapter 11?

The eleventh chapter of Hebrews offers a moving account of faithful Old Testament saints who remain models of faith. The chapter has received such titles as "The Saint's Hall of Fame," "The Honor Roll of Old Testament Saints," and "Heroes of the Faith." Their lives attest to the value of living by faith. They compose the "cloud of witnesses" (12:1) who give powerful testimony to the Hebrews that they should come to faith in Christ.

This passage begins with an emphatic statement about the nature of faith. Faith involves the most solid possible conviction—the God-given present assurance of a future reality. True faith is not based on empirical evidence but on divine assurance and is a gift of God (Eph 2:8).

The names, accomplishments, and sufferings described in this chapter illustrate the range of faithfulness in the lives of saints. Some experienced great success in this world; whereas others suffered great affliction. The point is that they all courageously and uncompromisingly followed God, regardless of the earthly outcome. They placed their trust in Him and in His promises (see 6:12; 2Ti 3:12).

NOVEMBER 17

Ezekiel 25:1–26:21

25 And the word of the LORD came to me saying, ² "Son of man, set your face toward the sons of Ammon and prophesy against them, ³ and say to the sons of Ammon, 'Hear the word of the Lord GOD! Thus says the Lord GOD, "Because you said, 'Aha!' against My sanctuary when it was profaned, and against the land of Israel when it was made desolate, and against the house of Judah when they went into exile, ⁴ therefore, behold, I am going to give you to the sons of the east for a possession, and they will set their encampments among you and make their dwellings among you; they will eat your fruit and drink your milk. ⁵ I will make Rabbah a pasture for camels and the sons of Ammon a resting place for flocks. Thus you will know that I am the LORD." ⁶ For thus says the Lord GOD, "Because you have clapped your hands and stamped your feet and rejoiced with all the scorn of your soul against the land of Israel, ⁷ therefore, behold, I have stretched out My hand against you and I will give you for spoil to the nations. And I will cut you off from the peoples and make you perish from the lands; I will destroy you. Thus you will know that I am the LORD."

⁸ 'Thus says the Lord GOD, "Because Moab and Seir say, 'Behold, the house of Judah is like all the nations,' ⁹ therefore, behold, I am going to deprive the flank of Moab of *its* cities, of its cities which are on its frontiers, the glory of the land, Beth-jeshimoth, Baal-meon and Kiriathaim, ¹⁰ and I will give it for a possession along with the sons of Ammon to the sons of the east, so that the sons of Ammon will not be remembered among the nations. ¹¹ Thus I will execute judgments on Moab, and they will know that I am the LORD."

¹² 'Thus says the Lord GOD, "Because Edom has acted against the house of Judah by taking vengeance, and has incurred grievous guilt, and avenged themselves upon them," ¹³ therefore thus says the Lord GOD, "I will also stretch out My hand against Edom and cut off man and beast from it. And I will lay it waste; from Teman even to Dedan they will fall by the sword. ¹⁴ I will lay My vengeance on Edom by the hand of My people Israel. Therefore, they will act in Edom according to My anger and according to My wrath; thus they will know My vengeance," declares the Lord GOD.

¹⁵ 'Thus says the Lord GOD, "Because the Philistines have acted in revenge and have taken vengeance with scorn of soul to destroy with everlasting enmity," ¹⁶ therefore thus says the Lord GOD, "Behold, I will stretch out My hand against the Philistines, even cut off the Cherethites and destroy the remnant of the seacoast. ¹⁷ I will execute great vengeance on them with wrathful rebukes; and they will know that I am the LORD when I lay My vengeance on them." ' "

26 Now in the eleventh year, on the first of the month, the word of the LORD came to me saying, ² "Son of man, because Tyre has said concerning Jerusalem, 'Aha, the gateway of the peoples is broken; it has opened to me. I shall be filled, *now that* she is laid waste,' ³ therefore thus says the Lord GOD, 'Behold, I am against you, O Tyre, and I will bring up many nations against you, as the sea brings up its waves. ⁴ They will destroy the walls of Tyre and break down her towers; and I will scrape her debris from her and make her a bare rock. ⁵ She will be a place for the spreading of nets in the midst of the sea, for I have spoken,' declares the Lord GOD, 'and she will become spoil for the nations. ⁶ Also her daughters who are on the mainland will be slain by the sword, and they will know that I am the LORD.' "

⁷ For thus says the Lord GOD, "Behold, I will bring upon Tyre from the north Nebuchadnezzar king of Babylon, king of kings, with horses, chariots, cavalry and a great army. ⁸ He will slay your daughters on the mainland with the sword; and he will make siege walls against you, cast up a ramp against you and raise up a large shield against you. ⁹ The blow of his battering rams he will direct against your walls, and with his axes he will break down your towers. ¹⁰ Because of the multitude of his horses, the dust *raised by* them will cover you; your walls will shake at the noise of cavalry and wagons and chariots when he enters your gates as men enter a city that is breached. ¹¹ With the hoofs of his horses he will trample all your streets. He will slay your people with the sword; and your strong pillars will come down to the ground. ¹² Also they will make a spoil of your riches and a prey of your merchandise, break down your walls and destroy your pleasant houses, and throw your stones and your timbers and your debris into the water. ¹³ So I will silence the sound of your songs, and the sound of your harps will be heard no more. ¹⁴ I will make you a bare rock; you will be a place for the spreading of nets. You will be built no more, for I the LORD have spoken," declares the Lord GOD.

[15] Thus says the Lord GOD to Tyre, "Shall not the coastlands shake at the sound of your fall when the wounded groan, when the slaughter occurs in your midst? [16] Then all the princes of the sea will go down from their thrones, remove their robes and strip off their embroidered garments. They will clothe themselves with trembling; they will sit on the ground, tremble every moment and be appalled at you. [17] They will take up a lamentation over you and say to you,

'How you have perished,
  O inhabited one,
From the seas, O renowned city,
Which was mighty on the sea,
She and her inhabitants,
Who imposed her terror
On all her inhabitants!
[18] 'Now the coastlands will tremble
On the day of your fall;
Yes, the coastlands which are by the sea
Will be terrified at your passing.'"

[19] For thus says the Lord GOD, "When I make you a desolate city, like the cities which are not inhabited, when I bring up the deep over you and the great waters cover you, [20] then I will bring you down with those who go down to the pit, to the people of old, and I will make you dwell in the lower parts of the earth, like the ancient waste places, with those who go down to the pit, so that you will not be inhabited; but I will set glory in the land of the living. [21] I will bring terrors on you and you will be no more; though you will be sought, you will never be found again," declares the Lord GOD.

Psalm 128:1-6

A Song of Ascents.

How blessed is everyone
  who fears the LORD,
Who walks in His ways.
[2] When you shall eat of the
  fruit of your hands,
  You will be happy and it
  will be well with you.

128:1 who fears the LORD. A good working definition is provided by the parallel line, "Who walks in His ways." Fathers (Ps 128:1, 4), mothers (Pr 31:30), and children (Ps 34:11) are to fear the Lord. This psalm may have been the basis for Jesus' illustration of the two builders (Mt 7:24–27).

[3] Your wife shall be like a fruitful vine
  Within your house,
  Your children like olive plants
  Around your table.
[4] Behold, for thus shall the
  man be blessed
  Who fears the LORD.

[5] The LORD bless you from Zion,
  And may you see the prosperity of
    Jerusalem all the days of your life.
[6] Indeed, may you see your
    children's children.
  Peace be upon Israel!

Proverbs 28:25

[25] An arrogant man stirs up strife,
  But he who trusts in the
    LORD will prosper.

Hebrews 11:17-40

[17] By faith Abraham, when he was tested, offered up Isaac, and he who had received the promises was offering up his only begotten *son*; [18] *it was he* to whom it was said, "IN ISAAC YOUR DESCENDANTS SHALL BE CALLED." [19] He considered that God is able to raise *people* even from the dead, from which he also received him back as a type. [20] By faith Isaac blessed Jacob and Esau, even regarding things to come. [21] By faith Jacob, as he was dying, blessed each of the sons of Joseph, and worshiped, *leaning* on the top of his staff. [22] By faith Joseph, when he was dying, made mention of the exodus of the sons of Israel, and gave orders concerning his bones.

[23] By faith Moses, when he was born, was hidden for three months by his parents, because they saw he was a beautiful child; and they were not afraid of the king's edict. [24] By faith Moses, when he had grown up, refused to be called the son of Pharaoh's daughter, [25] choosing rather to endure ill-treatment with the people of God than to enjoy the passing pleasures of sin, [26] considering the reproach

11:19 even from the dead. Believing that God's promise regarding Isaac was unconditional, Abraham came to the conclusion that God would fulfill that promise even if it required raising Isaac from the dead (Ge 22:5). type. The word is the same as in 9:9, which is the basis for the Eng. word "parable." Abraham received Isaac back from the dead, as it were, even though Isaac had not been slain.

of Christ greater riches than the treasures of Egypt; for he was looking to the reward. ²⁷ By faith he left Egypt, not fearing the wrath of the king; for he endured, as seeing Him who is unseen. ²⁸ By faith he kept the Passover and the sprinkling of the blood, so that he who destroyed the firstborn would not touch them. ²⁹ By faith they passed through the Red Sea as though *they were passing* through dry land; and the Egyptians, when they attempted it, were drowned.

³⁰ By faith the walls of Jericho fell down after they had been encircled for seven days. ³¹ By faith Rahab the harlot did not perish along with those who were disobedient, after she had welcomed the spies in peace.

³² And what more shall I say? For time will fail me if I tell of Gideon, Barak, Samson, Jephthah, of David and Samuel and the prophets, ³³ who by faith conquered kingdoms, performed *acts of* righteousness, obtained

promises, shut the mouths of lions, ³⁴ quenched the power of fire, escaped the edge of the sword, from weakness were made strong, became mighty in war, put foreign armies to flight. ³⁵ Women received *back* their dead by resurrection; and others were tortured, not accepting their release, so that they might obtain a better resurrection; ³⁶ and others experienced mockings and scourgings, yes, also chains and imprisonment. ³⁷ They were stoned, they were sawn in two, they were tempted, they were put to death with the sword; they went about in sheepskins, in goatskins, being destitute, afflicted, ill-treated ³⁸ (men of whom the world was not worthy), wandering in deserts and mountains and caves and holes in the ground.

³⁹ And all these, having gained approval through their faith, did not receive what was promised, ⁴⁰ because God had provided something better for us, so that apart from us they would not be made perfect.

DAY 17: How did faith shape the life of Moses?

In Hebrews 11:24, we are told that "By faith, Moses, when he had grown up," refused the fame he could have in Egypt if he would have capitalized on his position as the adopted son of Pharaoh's daughter (Ex 2:10). "Choosing rather to endure ill-treatment with the people of God" (v. 25). Moses would have sinned had he refused to take on the responsibility God gave him regarding Israel, and he had a clear and certain conviction that "God would deliver them by his hand" (Ac 7:25). Moses repudiated the pleasures of Egypt.

"Considering the reproach of Christ greater riches than the treasures of Egypt" (v. 26). Moses suffered reproach for the sake of Christ in the sense that he identified with the Messiah's people in their suffering (v. 25). In addition, Moses identified himself with the Messiah because of his own role as leader and prophet (12:2; Dt 18:15; Pss 69:9; 89:51). Moses knew of the sufferings and glory of the Messiah (Jn 5:46; Ac 26:22–23; 1Pe 1:10–12).

"By faith he left Egypt" (v. 27). Moses left Egypt for the first time when he fled for his life after killing the Egyptian slave master (Ex 2:14–15). That time he did fear Pharaoh's wrath. On the second occasion, he turned his back on Egypt and all that it represented. This leaving was not for fear of Pharaoh, so it is the one in view here. "Seeing Him who is unseen." Moses' faith was such that he responded to God's commands as though God were standing visibly before him. This was the basis for his loyalty to God, and it should be a believer's example for loyalty (2Co 4:16–18).

NOVEMBER 18

Ezekiel 27:1–28:26

27 Moreover, the word of the LORD came to me saying, ² "And you, son of man, take up a lamentation over Tyre; ³ and say to Tyre, who dwells at the entrance to the sea, merchant of the peoples to many coastlands, 'Thus says the Lord GOD,

"O Tyre, you have said, 'I am
        perfect in beauty.'
⁴ "Your borders are in the
        heart of the seas;

Your builders have perfected
        your beauty.
⁵ "They have made all *your* planks
        of fir trees from Senir;
They have taken a cedar from
        Lebanon to make a mast for you.
⁶ "Of oaks from Bashan they
        have made your oars;
With ivory they have inlaid
        your deck of boxwood from
        the coastlands of Cyprus.
⁷ "Your sail was of fine embroidered
        linen from Egypt
So that it became your
        distinguishing mark;

Your awning was blue and purple
from the coastlands of Elishah.
⁸ "The inhabitants of Sidon and
Arvad were your rowers;
Your wise men, O Tyre, were
aboard; they were your pilots.
⁹ "The elders of Gebal and her
wise men were with you
repairing your seams;
All the ships of the sea and their
sailors were with you in order
to deal in your merchandise.

¹⁰ "Persia and Lud and Put were in your army, your men of war. They hung shield and helmet in you; they set forth your splendor. ¹¹ The sons of Arvad and your army were on your walls, *all* around, and the Gammadim were in your towers. They hung their shields on your walls *all* around; they perfected your beauty. ¹² "Tarshish was your customer because of the abundance of all *kinds* of wealth; with silver, iron, tin and lead they paid for your wares. ¹³ Javan, Tubal and Meshech, they were your traders; with the lives of men and vessels of bronze they paid for your merchandise. ¹⁴ Those from Beth-togarmah gave horses and war horses and mules for your wares. ¹⁵ The sons of Dedan were your traders. Many coastlands were your market; ivory tusks and ebony they brought as your payment. ¹⁶ Aram was your customer because of the abundance of your goods; they paid for your wares with emeralds, purple, embroidered work, fine linen, coral and rubies. ¹⁷ Judah and the land of Israel, they were your traders; with the wheat of Minnith, cakes, honey, oil and balm they paid for your merchandise. ¹⁸ Damascus was your customer because of the abundance of your goods, because of the abundance of all *kinds* of wealth, because of the wine of Helbon and white wool. ¹⁹ Vedan and Javan paid for your wares from Uzal; wrought iron, cassia and sweet cane were among your merchandise. ²⁰ Dedan traded with you in saddlecloths for riding. ²¹ Arabia and all the princes of Kedar, they were your customers for lambs, rams and goats; for these they were your customers. ²² The traders of Sheba and Raamah, they traded with you; they paid for your wares with the best of all *kinds* of spices, and with all *kinds* of precious stones and gold. ²³ Haran, Canneh, Eden, the traders of Sheba, Asshur *and* Chilmad traded with you. ²⁴ They traded with you in choice garments, in clothes of blue and embroidered work, and in carpets of many colors *and* tightly wound cords,

which were among your merchandise. ²⁵ The ships of Tarshish were the carriers for your merchandise.

And you were filled and
were very glorious
In the heart of the seas.

²⁶ "Your rowers have brought you
Into great waters;
The east wind has broken you
In the heart of the seas.
²⁷ "Your wealth, your wares,
your merchandise,
Your sailors and your pilots,
Your repairers of seams, your
dealers in merchandise
And all your men of war
who are in you,
With all your company that
is in your midst,
Will fall into the heart of the seas
On the day of your overthrow.
²⁸ "At the sound of the cry of your pilots
The pasture lands will shake.
²⁹ "All who handle the oar,
The sailors *and* all the
pilots of the sea
Will come down from their ships;
They will stand on the land,
³⁰ And they will make their
voice heard over you
And will cry bitterly.
They will cast dust on their heads,
They will wallow in ashes.
³¹ "Also they will make themselves
bald for you
And gird themselves with sackcloth;
And they will weep for you
in bitterness of soul
With bitter mourning.
³² "Moreover, in their wailing they will
take up a lamentation for you
And lament over you:
'Who is like Tyre,
Like her who is silent in the
midst of the sea?
³³ 'When your wares went
out from the seas,
You satisfied many peoples;
With the abundance of your wealth
and your merchandise
You enriched the kings of earth.
³⁴ 'Now that you are broken by the seas
In the depths of the waters,
Your merchandise and all
your company
Have fallen in the midst of you.

35 'All the inhabitants of the coastlands
    Are appalled at you,
    And their kings are horribly afraid;
    They are troubled in countenance.
36 'The merchants among the
      peoples hiss at you;
    You have become terrified
    And you will cease to be forever.'"'"

28 The word of the LORD came again to me, saying, 2 "Son of man, say to the leader of Tyre, 'Thus says the Lord GOD,

"Because your heart is lifted up
    And you have said, 'I am a god,
    I sit in the seat of gods
    In the heart of the seas';
    Yet you are a man and not God,
    Although you make your heart
      like the heart of God—
3 Behold, you are wiser than Daniel;
    There is no secret that is
      a match for you.
4 "By your wisdom and understanding
    You have acquired riches for yourself
    And have acquired gold and
      silver for your treasuries.
5 "By your great wisdom, by your trade
    You have increased your riches
    And your heart is lifted up
      because of your riches—
6 Therefore thus says the Lord GOD,

'Because you have made your heart
    Like the heart of God,
7 Therefore, behold, I will bring
      strangers upon you,
    The most ruthless of the nations.
    And they will draw their swords
    Against the beauty of your wisdom
    And defile your splendor.
8 'They will bring you down to the pit,
    And you will die the death
      of those who are slain
    In the heart of the seas.
9 'Will you still say, "I am a god,"
    In the presence of your slayer,
    Though you are a man and not God,
    In the hands of those who wound you?
10 'You will die the death of
      the uncircumcised
    By the hand of strangers,
    For I have spoken!' declares
      the Lord GOD!"'"

11 Again the word of the LORD came to me saying, 12 "Son of man, take up a lamentation

28:12 the seal of perfection. The Lord led Ezekiel to address the king as the one to be judged, but clearly the power behind him was Satan. This phrase must be associated with Satan as one perfect in angelic beauty before he rebelled against God. But, it can also relate to "perfection" in the same context of Tyre's enterprise, topmost in its trade to the ancient world (27:3–4, 11), glorious in her seafaring efforts (27:24), and the crowning city (Is 23:8), i.e., "perfect" as Jerusalem also is said to be (16:14; La 2:15). **Full of wisdom.** This referred to Satan's wisdom as an angel and to Tyre's wisdom (skill) in trade (27:8–9; 28:4).

over the king of Tyre and say to him, 'Thus says the Lord GOD,

"You had the seal of perfection,
    Full of wisdom and perfect
      in beauty.
13 "You were in Eden, the
      garden of God;
    Every precious stone was
      your covering:
    The ruby, the topaz and
      the diamond;
    The beryl, the onyx and the jasper;
    The lapis lazuli, the turquoise
      and the emerald;
    And the gold, the workmanship
      of your settings and sockets,
    Was in you.
    On the day that you were created
    They were prepared.
14 "You were the anointed
      cherub who covers,
    And I placed you *there.*
    You were on the holy
      mountain of God;
    You walked in the midst of
      the stones of fire.
15 "You were blameless in your ways
    From the day you were created
    Until unrighteousness
      was found in you.
16 "By the abundance of your trade
    You were internally filled
      with violence,
    And you sinned;
    Therefore I have cast
      you as profane
    From the mountain of God.
    And I have destroyed you,
      O covering cherub,
    From the midst of the stones of fire.

¹⁷ "Your heart was lifted up
  because of your beauty;
You corrupted your wisdom by
  reason of your splendor.
I cast you to the ground;
I put you before kings,
That they may see you.
¹⁸ "By the multitude of your iniquities,
In the unrighteousness
  of your trade
You profaned your sanctuaries.
Therefore I have brought fire
  from the midst of you;
It has consumed you,
And I have turned you to
  ashes on the earth
In the eyes of all who see you.
¹⁹ "All who know you
  among the peoples
Are appalled at you;
You have become terrified
And you will cease to be forever." ' "

28:1–19 This section concerning the king of Tyre is similar to Isaiah 14:3–23 referring to the king of Babylon. In both passages, some of the language best fits Satan. Most likely, both texts primarily describe the human king who is being used by Satan, much like Peter when Jesus said to him, "Get behind Me, Satan!" (Mt 16:23). The judgment can certainly apply to Satan also.

---

²⁰ And the word of the LORD came to me saying, ²¹ "Son of man, set your face toward Sidon, prophesy against her ²² and say, 'Thus says the Lord GOD,

  "Behold, I am against
    you, O Sidon,
  And I will be glorified
    in your midst.
  Then they will know that I am
    the LORD when I execute
    judgments in her,
  And I will manifest My
    holiness in her.
²³ "For I will send pestilence to her
  And blood to her streets,
  And the wounded will
    fall in her midst
  By the sword upon her
    on every side;
  Then they will know that
    I am the LORD.

²⁴ And there will be no more for the house of Israel a prickling brier or a painful thorn from any round about them who scorned them; then they will know that I am the Lord GOD."

²⁵ 'Thus says the Lord GOD, "When I gather the house of Israel from the peoples among whom they are scattered, and will manifest My holiness in them in the sight of the nations, then they will live in their land which I gave to My servant Jacob. ²⁶ They will live in it securely; and they will build houses, plant vineyards and live securely when I execute judgments upon all who scorn them round about them. Then they will know that I am the LORD their God." ' "

Psalm 129:1–4

A Song of Ascents.

" **M** any times they have persecuted
    me from my youth up,"
  Let Israel now say,
² "Many times they have
    persecuted me from
    my youth up;
  Yet they have not prevailed
    against me.
³ "The plowers plowed
    upon my back;
  They lengthened their furrows."
⁴ The LORD is righteous;
  He has cut in two the cords
    of the wicked.

Proverbs 28:26

²⁶ He who trusts in his own
    heart is a fool,
  But he who walks wisely
    will be delivered.

Hebrews 12:1–29

12 Therefore, since we have so great a cloud of witnesses surrounding us, let us also lay aside every encumbrance and the sin which so easily entangles us, and let us run with endurance the race that is set before us, ² fixing our eyes on Jesus, the author and perfecter of faith, who for the joy set before Him endured the cross, despising the shame, and has sat down at the right hand of the throne of God.

³ For consider Him who has endured such hostility by sinners against Himself, so that you will not grow weary and lose heart. ⁴ You have not yet resisted to the point of shedding blood in your striving against sin; ⁵ and you have forgotten the exhortation which is addressed to you as sons,

12:4 shedding blood. None of the Hebrews had experienced such intense exhaustion or persecution that it brought them to death or martyrdom. Since Stephen (Ac 7:60), James (Ac 12:1), and others (Ac 9:1; 22:4; 26:10) had faced martyrdom in Jerusalem, it would appear to rule out that city as the residence of this epistle's recipients.

> "MY SON, DO NOT REGARD LIGHTLY
> THE DISCIPLINE OF THE LORD,
> NOR FAINT WHEN YOU ARE
> REPROVED BY HIM;
> 6 FOR THOSE WHOM THE LORD
> LOVES HE DISCIPLINES,
> AND HE SCOURGES EVERY SON
> WHOM HE RECEIVES."

7 It is for discipline that you endure; God deals with you as with sons; for what son is there whom *his* father does not discipline? 8 But if you are without discipline, of which all have become partakers, then you are illegitimate children and not sons. 9 Furthermore, we had earthly fathers to discipline us, and we respected them; shall we not much rather be subject to the Father of spirits, and live? 10 For they disciplined us for a short time as seemed best to them, but He *disciplines us* for *our* good, so that we may share His holiness. 11 All discipline for the moment seems not to be joyful, but sorrowful; yet to those who have been trained by it, afterwards it yields the peaceful fruit of righteousness.

12 Therefore, strengthen the hands that are weak and the knees that are feeble, 13 and make straight paths for your feet, so that *the limb* which is lame may not be put out of joint, but rather be healed.

14 Pursue peace with all men, and the sanctification without which no one will see the

12:14 Pursue...sanctification. In this epistle, it is explained as 1) a drawing near to God with full faith and a cleansed conscience (10:14, 22), and 2) a genuine acceptance of Christ as the Savior and sacrifice for sin, bringing the sinner into fellowship with God. Unbelievers will not be drawn to accept Christ if believers' lives do not demonstrate the qualities God desires, including peace and holiness (Jn 13:35; 1Ti 4:3; 1Pe 1:16).

Lord. 15 See to it that no one comes short of the grace of God; that no root of bitterness springing up causes trouble, and by it many be defiled; 16 that *there be* no immoral or godless person like Esau, who sold his own birthright for a *single* meal. 17 For you know that even afterwards, when he desired to inherit the blessing, he was rejected, for he found no place for repentance, though he sought for it with tears.

18 For you have not come to *a mountain* that can be touched and to a blazing fire, and to darkness and gloom and whirlwind, 19 and to the blast of a trumpet and the sound of words which *sound was such that* those who heard begged that no further word be spoken to them. 20 For they could not bear the command, "IF EVEN A BEAST TOUCHES THE MOUNTAIN, IT WILL BE STONED." 21 And so terrible was the sight, *that* Moses said, "I AM FULL OF FEAR and trembling." 22 But you have come to Mount Zion and to the city of the living God, the heavenly Jerusalem, and to myriads of angels, 23 to the general assembly and church of the firstborn who are enrolled in heaven, and to God, the Judge of all, and to the spirits of *the* righteous made perfect, 24 and to Jesus, the mediator of a new covenant, and to the sprinkled blood, which speaks better than *the blood* of Abel.

25 See to it that you do not refuse Him who is speaking. For if those did not escape when they refused him who warned *them* on earth, much less *will* we *escape* who turn away from Him who *warns* from heaven. 26 And His voice shook the earth then, but now He has promised, saying, "YET ONCE MORE I WILL SHAKE NOT ONLY THE EARTH, BUT ALSO THE HEAVEN." 27 This *expression*, "Yet once more," denotes the removing of those things which can be shaken, as of created things, so that those things which cannot be shaken may remain. 28 Therefore, since we receive a kingdom which cannot be shaken, let us show gratitude, by which we may offer to God an acceptable service with reverence and awe; 29 for our God is a consuming fire.

12:29 consuming fire. See Deuteronomy 4:24. God's law given at Sinai prescribed many severe punishments, but the punishment is far worse for those who reject His offer of salvation through His own Son, Jesus Christ (Lk 3:16–17).

DAY 18: How does Hebrews 12:1 represent a crucial transition for its readers?

"Therefore, since we have so great a cloud of witnesses surrounding us." This is a very crucial transition word offering an emphatic conclusion to the section which began in 10:19. The deceased people of chapter 11 give witness to the value and blessing of living by faith. Motivation for running "the race" is not in the possibility of receiving praise from "observing" heavenly saints. Rather, the runner is inspired by the godly examples those saints set during their lives. The great crowd are not comprised of spectators but rather are ones whose past life of faith encourages others to live that way (11:2, 4–5, 33, 39).

"Let us run with endurance the race that is set before us." The reference is to those Hebrews who had made a profession of Christ but had not gone all the way to full faith. They had not yet begun the race, which starts with salvation. The writer has invited them to accept salvation in Christ and join the race. "Lay aside every encumbrance." Different from the "sin" mentioned next, this refers to the main encumbrance weighing down the Hebrews which was the Levitical system with its stifling legalism. The athlete would strip away every piece of unnecessary clothing before competing in the race. The outward things emphasized by the Levitical system not only impede, they "entangle." "And sin." In this context, this focuses first on the particular sin of unbelief—refusing to turn away from the Levitical sacrifices to the perfect sacrifice, Jesus Christ (Jn 16:8–11), as well as other sins cherished by the unbeliever. The athletic metaphor presents the faith-filled life as a demanding, grueling effort. The English word "agony" is derived from the Greek word used here for "endurance."

"Fixing our eyes on" (v. 2). They were to fix their eyes on Jesus as the object of faith and salvation (11:26–27; Ac 7:55–56; Php 3:8). "The author...of faith." The term means originator or preeminent example. "The perfecter...of faith." The term "perfecter" has the idea of carrying through to perfect completion (Jn 19:30). Jesus persevered so that He might receive the joy of accomplishment of the Father's will and exaltation (1:9; Ps 16:9–11; Lk 10:21–24).

NOVEMBER 19

Ezekiel 29:1–30:26

29 In the tenth year, in the tenth *month,* on the twelfth of the month, the word of the LORD came to me saying, ² "Son of man, set your face against Pharaoh king of Egypt and prophesy against him and against all Egypt. ³ Speak and say, 'Thus says the Lord GOD,

"Behold, I am against you,
Pharaoh king of Egypt,
The great monster that lies in
the midst of his rivers,
That has said, 'My Nile is mine,
and I myself have made *it.*'
⁴ "I will put hooks in your jaws
And make the fish of your rivers
cling to your scales.
And I will bring you up out of
the midst of your rivers,
And all the fish of your rivers
will cling to your scales.
⁵ "I will abandon you to the wilderness,
you and all the fish of your rivers;
You will fall on the open field;
you will not be brought
together or gathered.

I have given you for food to
the beasts of the earth and
to the birds of the sky.
⁶ "Then all the inhabitants of Egypt
will know that I am the LORD,
Because they have been *only* a staff
made of reed to the house of Israel.
⁷ "When they took hold of
you with the hand,
You broke and tore all their hands;
And when they leaned on you,
You broke and made all
their loins quake."

⁸ 'Therefore thus says the Lord GOD, "Behold, I will bring upon you a sword and I will cut off from you man and beast. ⁹ The land of Egypt will become a desolation and waste. Then they will know that I am the LORD.

Because you said, 'The Nile is mine, and I have made *it,*' ¹⁰ therefore, behold, I am against you and against your rivers, and I will make the land of Egypt an utter waste and desolation, from Migdol *to* Syene and even to the border of Ethiopia. ¹¹ A man's foot will not pass through it, and the foot of a beast will not pass through it, and it will not be inhabited for forty years. ¹² So I will make the land of Egypt a desolation in the midst of desolated lands. And her cities, in the midst of cities that are laid waste, will be desolate forty years; and I will scatter the Egyptians among the nations and disperse them among the lands."

13 'For thus says the Lord GOD, "At the end of forty years I will gather the Egyptians from the peoples among whom they were scattered. 14 I will turn the fortunes of Egypt and make them return to the land of Pathros, to the land of their origin, and there they will be a lowly kingdom. 15 It will be the lowest of the kingdoms, and it will never again lift itself up above the nations. And I will make them so small that they will not rule over the nations. 16 And it will never again be the confidence of the house of Israel, bringing to mind the iniquity of their having turned to Egypt. Then they will know that I am the Lord GOD." '"

17 Now in the twenty-seventh year, in the first *month,* on the first of the month, the word of the LORD came to me saying, 18 "Son of man, Nebuchadnezzar king of Babylon made his army labor hard against Tyre; every head was made bald and every shoulder was rubbed bare. But he and his army had no wages from Tyre for the labor that he had performed against it." 19 Therefore thus says the Lord GOD, "Behold, I will give the land of Egypt to Nebuchadnezzar king of Babylon. And he will carry off her wealth and capture her spoil and seize her plunder; and it will be wages for his army. 20 I have given him the land of Egypt *for* his labor which he performed, because they acted for Me," declares the Lord GOD.

21 "On that day I will make a horn sprout for the house of Israel, and I will open your mouth in their midst. Then they will know that I am the LORD."

29:21 I will make a horn sprout. God caused Israel's power to return and restored her authority as the power in an animal's horn (1Sa 2:1). Though other nations subdued her, her latter end in messianic times will be blessed. **I will open your mouth.** Most likely this refers to the day when Ezekiel's writings would be understood by looking back at their fulfillment. His muteness had already ceased in 586/585 B.C. when Jerusalem fell (33:21–22).

---

30 The word of the LORD came again to me saying, 2 "Son of man, prophesy and say, 'Thus says the Lord GOD,

"Wail, 'Alas for the day!'
3 "For the day is near,
  Even the day of the LORD is near;
  It will be a day of clouds,
  A time *of doom* for the nations.
4 "A sword will come upon Egypt,
  And anguish will be in Ethiopia;
  When the slain fall in Egypt,
  They take away her wealth,
  And her foundations are torn down.

5 Ethiopia, Put, Lud, all Arabia, Libya and the people of the land that is in league will fall with them by the sword."

6 'Thus says the LORD,
  "Indeed, those who support
    Egypt will fall
  And the pride of her power
    will come down;
  From Migdol *to* Syene
  They will fall within her
    by the sword,"
  Declares the Lord GOD.
7 "They will be desolate
  In the midst of the desolated lands;
  And her cities will be
  In the midst of the
    devastated cities.
8 "And they will know that
    I am the LORD,
  When I set a fire in Egypt
  And all her helpers are broken.

9 On that day messengers will go forth from Me in ships to frighten secure Ethiopia; and anguish will be on them as on the day of Egypt; for behold, it comes!"

10 'Thus says the Lord GOD,

  "I will also make the hordes
    of Egypt cease
  By the hand of Nebuchadnezzar
    king of Babylon.
11 "He and his people with him,
  The most ruthless of the nations,
  Will be brought in to destroy the land;
  And they will draw their
    swords against Egypt
  And fill the land with the slain.
12 "Moreover, I will make the
    Nile canals dry
  And sell the land into the
    hands of evil men.
  And I will make the land desolate
  And all that is in it,
  By the hand of strangers; I
    the LORD have spoken."

13 'Thus says the Lord GOD,

"I will also destroy the idols
And make the images cease
   from Memphis.
And there will no longer be a
   prince in the land of Egypt;
And I will put fear in the
   land of Egypt.
14 "I will make Pathros desolate,
Set a fire in Zoan
And execute judgments on Thebes.
15 "I will pour out My wrath on Sin,
The stronghold of Egypt;
I will also cut off the
   hordes of Thebes.
16 "I will set a fire in Egypt;
Sin will writhe in anguish,
Thebes will be breached
And Memphis *will have*
   distresses daily.
17 "The young men of On
   and of Pi-beseth
Will fall by the sword,
And the women will
   go into captivity.
18 "In Tehaphnehes the day will be dark
When I break there the
   yoke bars of Egypt.
Then the pride of her power
   will cease in her;
A cloud will cover her,
And her daughters will
   go into captivity.
19 "Thus I will execute
   judgments on Egypt,
And they will know that
   I am the LORD."'"

20 In the eleventh year, in the first *month,* on the seventh of the month, the word of the LORD came to me saying, 21 "Son of man, I have broken the arm of Pharaoh king of Egypt; and, behold, it has not been bound up for healing or wrapped with a bandage, that it may be strong to hold the sword. 22 There-fore thus says the Lord GOD, 'Behold, I am against Pharaoh king of Egypt and will break his arms, both the strong and the broken; and I will make the sword fall from his hand. 23 I will scatter the Egyptians among the nations and disperse them among the lands. 24 For I will strengthen the arms of the king of Bab-ylon and put My sword in his hand; and I will break the arms of Pharaoh, so that he will groan before him with the groanings of a wounded man. 25 Thus I will strengthen the arms of the king of Babylon, but the arms of

Pharaoh will fall. Then they will know that I am the LORD, when I put My sword into the hand of the king of Babylon and he stretches it out against the land of Egypt. 26 When I scatter the Egyptians among the nations and disperse them among the lands, then they will know that I am the LORD.'"

Psalm 129:5–8

5 May all who hate Zion
   Be put to shame and
      turned backward;
6 Let them be like grass upon
      the housetops,
   Which withers before it grows up;
7 With which the reaper does
      not fill his hand,
   Or the binder of sheaves his bosom;
8 Nor do those who pass by say,
   "The blessing of the LORD
      be upon you;
   We bless you in the name
      of the LORD."

Proverbs 28:27

27 He who gives to the poor
      will never want,
    But he who shuts his eyes
      will have many curses.

Hebrews 13:1–25

13 Let love of the brethren continue. 2 Do not neglect to show hospitality to strangers, for by this some have entertained angels without knowing it. 3 Remember the prisoners, as though in prison with them, *and* those who are ill-treated, since you yourselves also are in the body. 4 Marriage *is to be held* in honor among all, and the *marriage* bed *is to be* undefiled; for fornicators and adulterers God will judge. 5 *Make sure that* your character is free from the love of money, being content with what you have; for He Himself has said, "I WILL NEVER DESERT YOU, NOR WILL I EVER FORSAKE YOU," 6 so that we confidently say,

13:4 in honor. God highly honors marriage, which He instituted at creation (Ge 2:24); but some people in the early church considered celibacy to be holier than marriage, an idea Paul strongly denounces in 1 Timothy 4:3. Sexual activity in a marriage is pure, but any sexual activity outside marriage brings one under divine judgment. **God will judge.** God prescribes serious consequences for sexual immorality.

"THE LORD IS MY HELPER, I
WILL NOT BE AFRAID.
WHAT WILL MAN DO TO ME?"

⁷Remember those who led you, who spoke the word of God to you; and considering the result of their conduct, imitate their faith. ⁸Jesus Christ *is* the same yesterday and today and forever. ⁹Do not be carried away by varied and strange teachings; for it is good for the heart to be strengthened by grace, not by foods, through which those who were so occupied were not benefited. ¹⁰We have an altar from which those who serve the tabernacle have no right to eat. ¹¹For the bodies of those animals whose blood is brought into the holy place by the high priest *as an offering* for sin, are burned outside the camp. ¹²Therefore Jesus also, that He might sanctify the people through His own blood, suffered outside the gate. ¹³So, let us go out to Him outside the camp, bearing His reproach. ¹⁴For here we do not have a lasting city, but we are seeking *the city* which is to come. ¹⁵Through Him then, let us continually offer up a sacrifice of praise to God, that is, the fruit of lips that give thanks to His name. ¹⁶And do not neglect doing good and sharing, for with such sacrifices God is pleased.

¹⁷Obey your leaders and submit *to them,* for they keep watch over your souls as those who will give an account. Let them do this with joy and not with grief, for this would be unprofitable for you. ¹⁸Pray for us, for we are sure that we have a good conscience, desiring to conduct ourselves honorably in all things. ¹⁹And I urge *you* all the more to do this, so that I may be restored to you the sooner.

²⁰Now the God of peace, who brought up from the dead the great Shepherd of the sheep through the blood of the eternal covenant, *even* Jesus our Lord, ²¹equip you in every good thing to do His will, working in us that which is pleasing in His sight, through Jesus Christ, to whom *be* the glory forever and ever. Amen.

²²But I urge you, brethren, bear with this word of exhortation, for I have written to you briefly. ²³Take notice that our brother Timothy has been released, with whom, if he comes soon, I will see you. ²⁴Greet all of your leaders and all the saints. Those from Italy greet you.

²⁵Grace be with you all.

13:17 your leaders. The pastors/elders of the church exercise the very authority of Christ when they preach, teach, and apply Scripture (Ac 20:28; 1Th 5:12–13). They serve the church on behalf of Christ and must give Him an account of their faithfulness. These may include both secular and spiritual leaders. Even those who do not acknowledge God are nevertheless ordained and used by Him (Ro 13:1, 4). **joy.** The church is responsible to help its leaders do their work with satisfaction and delight.

13:21 equip you. This is not the Greek word for "perfect" or "perfection" used throughout Hebrews to indicate salvation but is a word which is translated "prepared" in 10:5 and 11:3. It refers to believers being edified. The verb has the idea of equipping by means of adjusting, shaping, mending, restoring, or preparing (11:3; 1Co 1:10; 2Co 13:11; 2Ti 3:17).

DAY 19: Did the writer of Hebrews actually think Christians might entertain angels (13:2)?

The last chapter of the epistle focuses on some of the essential practical ethics of Christian living. These ethics help portray the true gospel to the world, encourage others to believe in Christ, and bring glory to God. The first of these is love for fellow believers (Jn 13:35). Although the primary reference would be to Christians, the writer must have had emotions similar to those of the apostle Paul when it came to considering his fellow Hebrews (see Ro 9:3–4).

"Do not neglect to show hospitality to strangers, for by this some have entertained angels without knowing it" (v. 2). The second grace needing development was the extension of love to those who were strangers (Ro 12:3; 1Ti 3:2). Hospitality in the ancient world often included putting up a guest overnight or longer. This is hardest to do when experiencing a time of persecution. The Hebrews would not know whether a guest would prove to be a spy or a fellow believer being pursued. To bring up "angels" was not given as the ultimate motivation for hospitality but to reveal that one never knows how far-reaching an act of kindness might be (Mt 25:40, 45). This is exactly what happened to Abraham and Sarah (Ge 18:1–3), Lot (Ge 19:1–2), Gideon (Jdg 6:11–24), and Manoah (Jdg 13:6–20).

NOVEMBER 20

Ezekiel 31:1–32:32

31 In the eleventh year, in the third *month,* on the first of the month, the word of the LORD came to me saying, ² "Son of man, say to Pharaoh king of Egypt and to his hordes,

'Whom are you like in your greatness?
³ 'Behold, Assyria *was* a
cedar in Lebanon
With beautiful branches
and forest shade,
And very high,
And its top was among the clouds.
⁴ 'The waters made it grow, the
deep made it high.
With its rivers it continually extended
all around its planting place,
And sent out its channels to
all the trees of the field.
⁵ 'Therefore its height was loftier
than all the trees of the field
And its boughs became many
and its branches long
Because of many waters as
it spread them out.
⁶ 'All the birds of the heavens
nested in its boughs,
And under its branches all the
beasts of the field gave birth,
And all great nations lived
under its shade.
⁷ 'So it was beautiful in its greatness,
in the length of its branches;
For its roots extended to many waters.
⁸ 'The cedars in God's garden
could not match it;
The cypresses could not
compare with its boughs,
And the plane trees could not
match its branches.
No tree in God's garden could
compare with it in its beauty.
⁹ 'I made it beautiful with the
multitude of its branches,
And all the trees of Eden,
which were in the garden of
God, were jealous of it.

¹⁰ 'Therefore thus says the Lord GOD, "Because it is high in stature and has set its top among the clouds, and its heart is haughty in its loftiness, ¹¹ therefore I will give it into the hand of a despot of the nations; he will thoroughly deal with it. According to its

wickedness I have driven it away. ¹² Alien tyrants of the nations have cut it down and left it; on the mountains and in all the valleys its branches have fallen and its boughs have been broken in all the ravines of the land. And all the peoples of the earth have gone down from its shade and left it. ¹³ On its ruin all the birds of the heavens will dwell, and all the beasts of the field will be on its *fallen* branches ¹⁴ so that all the trees by the waters may not be exalted in their stature, nor set their top among the clouds, nor their well-watered mighty ones stand *erect* in their height. For they have all been given over to death, to the earth beneath, among the sons of men, with those who go down to the pit."

¹⁵ 'Thus says the Lord GOD, "On the day when it went down to Sheol I caused lamentations; I closed the deep over it and held back its rivers. And *its* many waters were stopped up, and I made Lebanon mourn for it, and all the trees of the field wilted away on account of it. ¹⁶ I made the nations quake at the sound of its fall when I made it go down to Sheol with those who go down to the pit; and all the well-watered trees of Eden, the choicest and best of Lebanon, were comforted in the earth beneath. ¹⁷ They also went down with it to Sheol to those who were slain by the sword; and those who were its strength lived under its shade among the nations.

¹⁸ "To which among the trees of Eden are you thus equal in glory and greatness? Yet you will be brought down with the trees of Eden to the earth beneath; you will lie in the midst of the uncircumcised, with those who were slain by the sword. So is Pharaoh and all his hordes!" ' declares the Lord GOD."

31:2–18 Whom are you like...? Ezekiel filled this chapter with a metaphor/analogy comparing Egypt to a huge tree that dominates a forest to a king/nation that dominates the world (17:22–24; Da 4:1–12, 19–27). He reasoned that just as a strong tree like Assyria (v. 3) fell (ca. 609 B.C.), so will Egypt (ca. 568 B.C.). If the Egyptians tend to be proud and feel invincible, let them remember how powerful Assyria had fallen already.

32 In the twelfth year, in the twelfth *month,* on the first of the month, the word of the LORD came to me saying, ² "Son of man, take up a lamentation over Pharaoh king of Egypt and say to him,

'You compared yourself to a
    young lion of the nations,
Yet you are like the monster in the seas;
And you burst forth in your rivers
And muddied the waters
    with your feet
And fouled their rivers.'"

³ Thus says the Lord GOD,

"Now I will spread My net over you
With a company of many peoples,
And they shall lift you up in My net.

⁴ "I will leave you on the land;
I will cast you on the open field.
And I will cause all the birds of
    the heavens to dwell on you,
And I will satisfy the beasts of the
    whole earth with you.

⁵ "I will lay your flesh on the mountains
And fill the valleys with your refuse.

⁶ "I will also make the land drink
    the discharge of your blood
As far as the mountains,
And the ravines will be full of you.

⁷ "And when I extinguish you,
I will cover the heavens and
    darken their stars;
I will cover the sun with a cloud
And the moon will not give its light.

⁸ "All the shining lights in the heavens
I will darken over you
And will set darkness on your land,"
Declares the Lord GOD.

⁹ "I will also trouble the hearts of many peoples when I bring your destruction among the nations, into lands which you have not known. ¹⁰ I will make many peoples appalled at you, and their kings will be horribly afraid of you when I brandish My sword before them; and they will tremble every moment, every man for his own life, on the day of your fall."

¹¹ For thus says the Lord GOD, "The sword of the king of Babylon will come upon you. ¹² By the swords of the mighty ones I will cause your hordes to fall; all of them are tyrants of the nations,

And they will devastate
    the pride of Egypt,
And all its hordes will be destroyed.

¹³ "I will also destroy all its cattle
    from beside many waters;
And the foot of man will not
    muddy them anymore
And the hoofs of beasts will
    not muddy them.

¹⁴ "Then I will make their waters settle
And will cause their rivers
    to run like oil,"
Declares the Lord GOD.

¹⁵ "When I make the land of
    Egypt a desolation,
And the land is destitute of
    that which filled it,
When I smite all those who live in it,
Then they shall know that
    I am the LORD.

¹⁶ This is a lamentation and they shall chant it. The daughters of the nations shall chant it. Over Egypt and over all her hordes they shall chant it," declares the Lord GOD.

¹⁷ In the twelfth year, on the fifteenth of the month, the word of the LORD came to me saying, ¹⁸ "Son of man, wail for the hordes of Egypt and bring it down, her and the daughters of the powerful nations, to the nether world, with those who go down to the pit;

¹⁹ 'Whom do you surpass in beauty?
    Go down and make your bed
        with the uncircumcised.'

²⁰ They shall fall in the midst of those who are slain by the sword. She is given over to the sword; they have drawn her and all her hordes away. ²¹ The strong among the mighty ones shall speak of him and his helpers from the midst of Sheol, 'They have gone down, they lie still, the uncircumcised, slain by the sword.'

²² "Assyria is there and all her company; her graves are round about her. All of them are slain, fallen by the sword, ²³ whose graves are set in the remotest parts of the pit and her company is round about her grave. All of them are slain, fallen by the sword, who spread terror in the land of the living.

²⁴ "Elam is there and all her hordes around her grave; all of them slain, fallen by the sword, who went down uncircumcised to the lower parts of the earth, who instilled their terror in the land of the living and bore their disgrace with those who went down to the pit. ²⁵ They have made a bed for her among the slain with all her hordes. Her graves are around it, they are all uncircumcised, slain by the sword (although their terror was instilled in the land of the living), and they bore their disgrace with those who go down to the pit; they were put in the midst of the slain.

²⁶ "Meshech, Tubal and all their hordes are there; their graves surround them. All of them were slain by the sword uncircumcised,

though they instilled their terror in the land of the living. ²⁷ Nor do they lie beside the fallen heroes of the uncircumcised, who went down to Sheol with their weapons of war and whose swords were laid under their heads; but the punishment for their iniquity rested on their bones, though the terror of *these* heroes *was once* in the land of the living. ²⁸ But in the midst of the uncircumcised you will be broken and lie with those slain by the sword.

²⁹ "There also is Edom, its kings and all its princes, who for *all* their might are laid with those slain by the sword; they will lie with the uncircumcised and with those who go down to the pit.

³⁰ "There also are the chiefs of the north, all of them, and all the Sidonians, who in spite of the terror resulting from their might, in shame went down with the slain. So they lay down uncircumcised with those slain by the sword and bore their disgrace with those who go down to the pit.

³¹ "These Pharaoh will see, and he will be comforted for all his hordes slain by the sword, *even* Pharaoh and all his army," declares the Lord GOD. ³² "Though I instilled a terror of him in the land of the living, yet he will be made to lie down among *the* uncircumcised *along* with those slain by the sword, *even* Pharaoh and all his hordes," declares the Lord GOD.

Psalm 130:1-4

A Song of Ascents.

Out of the depths I have
  cried to You, O LORD.
² Lord, hear my voice!
  Let Your ears be attentive
  To the voice of my supplications.
³ If You, LORD, should mark iniquities,
  O Lord, who could stand?
⁴ But there is forgiveness with You,
  That You may be feared.

Proverbs 28:28

²⁸ When the wicked rise, men
  hide themselves;
  But when they perish, the
  righteous increase.

James 1:1-27

1 James, a bond-servant of God and of the Lord Jesus Christ,

To the twelve tribes who are dispersed abroad: Greetings.

² Consider it all joy, my brethren, when you encounter various trials, ³ knowing that the testing of your faith produces endurance.

⁴ And let endurance have *its* perfect result, so that you may be perfect and complete, lacking in nothing.

⁵ But if any of you lacks wisdom, let him ask of God, who gives to all generously and without reproach, and it will be given to him. ⁶ But he must ask in faith without any doubting, for the one who doubts is like the surf of the sea, driven and tossed by the wind. ⁷ For that man ought not to expect that he will receive anything from the Lord, ⁸ *being* a double-minded man, unstable in all his ways.

1:6 ask in faith. Prayer must be offered with confident trust in a sovereign God (Heb 11:1). **without any doubting.** This refers to having one's thinking divided within himself, not merely because of mental indecision but an inner moral conflict or distrust in God. **surf of the sea.** The person who doubts God's ability or willingness to provide this wisdom is like the billowing, restless sea, moving back and forth with its endless tides, never able to settle (Jos 24:15; 1Ki 18:21; Rev 3:16).

⁹ But the brother of humble circumstances is to glory in his high position; ¹⁰ and the rich man *is to glory* in his humiliation, because like flowering grass he will pass away. ¹¹ For the sun rises with a scorching wind and withers the grass; and its flower falls off and the beauty of its appearance is destroyed; so too the rich man in the midst of his pursuits will fade away.

¹² Blessed is a man who perseveres under trial; for once he has been approved, he will receive the crown of life which *the Lord* has promised to those who love Him. ¹³ Let no one say when he is tempted, "I am being tempted by God"; for God cannot be tempted by evil, and He Himself does not tempt anyone. ¹⁴ But each one is tempted when he is carried away and enticed by his own lust. ¹⁵ Then when lust has conceived, it gives birth to sin; and when sin is accomplished, it brings forth death. ¹⁶ Do not be deceived, my beloved brethren. ¹⁷ Every good thing given and every perfect gift is from above, coming down from the Father of lights, with whom there is no variation or shifting shadow. ¹⁸ In the exercise of His will He brought us forth by the word of truth, so that we would be a kind of first fruits among His creatures.

¹⁹ *This* you know, my beloved brethren. But everyone must be quick to hear, slow to speak *and* slow to anger; ²⁰ for the anger of man does not achieve the righteousness of God.

²¹Therefore, putting aside all filthiness and *all* that remains of wickedness, in humility receive the word implanted, which is able to save your souls. ²²But prove yourselves doers of the word, and not merely hearers who delude themselves. ²³For if anyone is a hearer of the word and not a doer, he is like a man who looks at his natural face in a mirror; ²⁴for *once* he has looked at himself and gone away, he has immediately forgotten what kind of person he was. ²⁵But one who looks intently at the perfect law, the *law* of liberty, and abides by it, not having become a forgetful hearer but an effectual doer, this man will be blessed in what he does.

²⁶If anyone thinks himself to be religious, and yet does not bridle his tongue but deceives his *own* heart, this man's religion is worthless. ²⁷Pure and undefiled religion in the sight of *our* God and Father is this: to visit orphans and widows in their distress, *and* to keep oneself unstained by the world.

1:14 carried away. This Greek word was used to describe wild game being lured into traps. Just as animals can be drawn to their deaths by attractive baits, temptation promises people something good, which is actually harmful. **enticed.** A fishing term that means "to capture" or "to catch with bait" (2Pe 2:14, 18). It is a parallel to "carried away." **his own lust.** This refers to the strong desire of the human soul to enjoy or acquire something to fulfill the flesh. Man's fallen nature has the propensity to strongly desire whatever sin will satisfy it (Ro 7:8–25). "His own" describes the individual nature of lust—it is different for each person as a result of inherited tendencies, environment, upbringing, and personal choices. The Greek grammar also indicates that this "lust" is the direct agent or cause of one's sinning.

DAY 20: How can James expect Christians to "consider it all joy" when they face difficulties and trials (1:2)?

The Greek word for "consider" may also be translated "count" or "evaluate." The natural human response to trials is not to rejoice; therefore the believer must make a conscious commitment to face them with joy. "Trials" connote troubles or things that break the pattern of peace, comfort, joy, and happiness in someone's life. The verb form of this word means "to put someone or something to the test," with the purpose of discovering that person's nature or that thing's quality. God brings such tests to prove—and increase—the strength and quality of one's faith and to demonstrate its validity (vv. 2–12). Every trial becomes a test of faith designed to strengthen. If the believer fails the test by wrongly responding, that test then becomes a temptation or a solicitation to evil.

"Knowing that the testing of your faith produces endurance" (v. 3). This means "proof" or "proving." This testing produces "endurance" or "perseverance." Through tests, a Christian will learn to withstand and even cherish the benefit of the pressure of a trial until God removes it at His appointed time.

"Let endurance have its perfect result" (v. 4). This is not a reference to sinless perfection (3:2), but to spiritual maturity (1Jn 2:14). The testing of faith drives believers to deeper communion and greater trust in Christ—qualities that in turn produce a stable, godly, and righteous character. "That you may be…complete." From a compound Greek word that means "all the portions whole."

NOVEMBER 21

Ezekiel 33:1–34:31

33 And the word of the LORD came to me, saying, ²"Son of man, speak to the sons of your people and say to them, 'If I bring a sword upon a land, and the people of the land take one man from among them and make him their watchman, ³and he sees the sword coming upon the land and blows on the trumpet and warns the people, ⁴then he who hears the sound of the trumpet and does not take warning, and a sword comes and takes him away, his blood will be on his *own*

33:4 his blood…on his *own* head. Once the watchman did his duty, the responsibility passed to each person. Each person is accountable for his own response to God's warnings, whether to die in judgment or to live as one who heeded and repented. Ezekiel had been a very faithful and obedient "watchman."

---

head. ⁵He heard the sound of the trumpet but did not take warning; his blood will be on himself. But had he taken warning, he would have delivered his life. ⁶But if the watchman sees the sword coming and does not blow the trumpet and the people are not warned, and a sword comes and takes a person from them, he is taken away in his iniquity; but his blood I will require from the watchman's hand.'

⁷"Now as for you, son of man, I have appointed you a watchman for the house of Israel; so you will hear a message from My mouth and give them warning from Me. ⁸When I say to the wicked, 'O wicked man, you will surely die,' and you do not speak to warn the wicked from his way, that wicked man shall die in his iniquity, but his blood I will require from your hand. ⁹But if you on your part warn a wicked man to turn from his way and he does not turn from his way, he will die in his iniquity, but you have delivered your life.

33:2–9 watchman. Such men as Jeremiah and Ezekiel (3:16–21) were spiritual watchmen (33:7–9), warning that God would bring a sword on His people so that they had opportunity to prepare and be safe. This analogy came from the custom of putting guards on the city wall watching for the approach of danger, then trumpeting the warning.

¹⁰"Now as for you, son of man, say to the house of Israel, 'Thus you have spoken, saying, "Surely our transgressions and our sins are upon us, and we are rotting away in them; how then can we survive?"' ¹¹Say to them, 'As I live!' declares the Lord GOD, 'I take no pleasure in the death of the wicked, but rather that the wicked turn from his way and live. Turn back, turn back from your evil ways! Why then will you die, O house of Israel?' ¹²And you, son of man, say to your fellow citizens, 'The righteousness of a righteous man will not deliver him in the day of his transgression, and as for the wickedness of the wicked, he will not stumble because of it in the day when he turns from his wickedness; whereas a righteous man will not be able to live by his righteousness on the day when he commits sin.' ¹³When I say to the righteous he will surely live, and he *so* trusts in his righteousness that he commits iniquity, none of his righteous deeds will be remembered; but in that same iniquity of his which he has committed he will die. ¹⁴But when I say to the wicked, 'You will surely die,' and he turns from his sin and practices justice and righteousness, ¹⁵*if a* wicked man restores a pledge, pays back what he has taken by

robbery, walks by the statutes which ensure life without committing iniquity, he shall surely live; he shall not die. ¹⁶None of his sins that he has committed will be remembered against him. He has practiced justice and righteousness; he shall surely live.

¹⁷"Yet your fellow citizens say, 'The way of the Lord is not right,' when it is their own way that is not right. ¹⁸When the righteous turns from his righteousness and commits iniquity, then he shall die in it. ¹⁹But when the wicked turns from his wickedness and practices justice and righteousness, he will live by them. ²⁰Yet you say, 'The way of the Lord is not right.' O house of Israel, I will judge each of you according to his ways."

²¹Now in the twelfth year of our exile, on the fifth of the tenth month, the refugees from Jerusalem came to me, saying, "The city has been taken." ²²Now the hand of the LORD had been upon me in the evening, before the refugees came. And He opened my mouth at the time *they* came to me in the morning; so my mouth was opened and I was no longer speechless.

²³Then the word of the LORD came to me saying, ²⁴"Son of man, they who live in these waste places in the land of Israel are saying, 'Abraham was *only* one, yet he possessed the land; so to us who are many the land has been given as a possession.' ²⁵Therefore say to them, 'Thus says the Lord GOD, "You eat *meat* with the blood *in it,* lift up your eyes to your idols as you shed blood. Should you then possess the land? ²⁶You rely on your sword, you commit abominations and each of you defiles his neighbor's wife. Should you then possess the land?"' ²⁷Thus you shall say to them, 'Thus says the Lord GOD, "As I live, surely those who are in the waste places will fall by the sword, and whoever is in the open field I will give to the beasts to be devoured, and those who are in the strongholds and in the caves will die of pestilence. ²⁸I will make the land a desolation and a waste, and the pride of her power will cease; and the mountains of Israel will be desolate so that no one will pass through. ²⁹Then they will know that I am the LORD, when I make the land a desolation and a waste because of all their abominations which they have committed."'

³⁰"But as for you, son of man, your fellow citizens who talk about you by the walls and in the doorways of the houses, speak to one another, each to his brother, saying, 'Come now and hear what the message is which comes forth from the LORD.' ³¹They come to

you as people come, and sit before you *as* My people and hear your words, but they do not do them, for they do the lustful desires *expressed* by their mouth, *and* their heart goes after their gain. [32] Behold, you are to them like a sensual song by one who has a beautiful voice and plays well on an instrument; for they hear your words but they do not practice them. [33] So when it comes to pass—as surely it will—then they will know that a prophet has been in their midst."

34 Then the word of the LORD came to me saying, [2] "Son of man, prophesy against the shepherds of Israel. Prophesy and say to those shepherds, 'Thus says the Lord GOD, "Woe, shepherds of Israel who have been feeding themselves! Should not the shepherds feed the flock? [3] You eat the fat and clothe yourselves with the wool, you slaughter the fat *sheep* without feeding the flock. [4] Those who are sickly you have not strengthened, the diseased you have not healed, the broken you have not bound up, the scattered you have not brought back, nor have you sought for the lost; but with force and with severity you have dominated them. [5] They were scattered for lack of a shepherd, and they became food for every beast of the field and were scattered. [6] My flock wandered through all the mountains and on every high hill; My flock was scattered over all the surface of the earth, and there was no one to search or seek *for them.*"'"

[7] Therefore, you shepherds, hear the word of the LORD: [8] "As I live," declares the Lord GOD, "surely because My flock has become a prey, My flock has even become food for all the beasts of the field for lack of a shepherd, and My shepherds did not search for My flock, but *rather* the shepherds fed themselves and did not feed My flock; [9] therefore, you shepherds, hear the word of the LORD: [10] 'Thus says the Lord GOD, "Behold, I am against the shepherds, and I will demand My sheep from them and make them cease from feeding sheep. So the shepherds will not feed themselves anymore, but I will deliver My flock from their mouth, so that they will not be food for them."'"

[11] For thus says the Lord GOD, "Behold, I Myself will search for My sheep and seek them out. [12] As a shepherd cares for his herd in the day when he is among his scattered sheep, so I will care for My sheep and will deliver them from all the places to which they were scattered on a cloudy and gloomy day. [13] I will bring them out from the peoples and gather them from the countries and bring them to their own land; and I will feed them on the mountains of Israel, by the streams, and in all the inhabited places of the land. [14] I will feed them in a good pasture, and their grazing ground will be on the mountain heights of Israel. There they will lie down on good grazing ground and feed in rich pasture on the mountains of Israel. [15] I will feed My flock and I will lead them to rest," declares the Lord GOD. [16] "I will seek the lost, bring back the scattered, bind up the broken and strengthen the sick; but the fat and the strong I will destroy. I will feed them with judgment.

[17] "As for you, My flock, thus says the Lord GOD, 'Behold, I will judge between one sheep and another, between the rams and the male goats. [18] Is it too slight a thing for you that you should feed in the good pasture, that you must tread down with your feet the rest of your pastures? Or that you should drink of the clear waters, that you must foul the rest with your feet? [19] As for My flock, they must eat what you tread down with your feet and drink what you foul with your feet!'"

[20] Therefore, thus says the Lord GOD to them, "Behold, I, even I, will judge between the fat sheep and the lean sheep. [21] Because you push with side and with shoulder, and thrust at all the weak with your horns until you have scattered them abroad, [22] therefore, I will deliver My flock, and they will no longer be a prey; and I will judge between one sheep and another.

[23] "Then I will set over them one shepherd, My servant David, and he will feed them; he will feed them himself and be their shepherd. [24] And I, the LORD, will be their God, and My servant David will be prince among them; I the LORD have spoken.

[25] "I will make a covenant of peace with them and eliminate harmful beasts from the land so that they may live securely in the wilderness and sleep in the woods. [26] I will make them and the places around My hill a blessing. And I will cause showers to come down in their season; they will be showers of blessing. [27] Also the tree of the field will yield its fruit and the earth will yield its increase, and they will be secure on their land. Then they will know that I am the LORD, when I have broken the bars of their yoke and have delivered them from the hand of those who enslaved them. [28] They will no longer be a prey to the nations, and the beasts of the earth will not devour them; but they will live securely, and no one will make *them* afraid. [29] I will establish for them a renowned planting place, and they will not again be victims of

famine in the land, and they will not endure the insults of the nations anymore. ³⁰Then they will know that I, the LORD their God, am with them, and that they, the house of Israel, are My people," declares the Lord GOD. ³¹"As for you, My sheep, the sheep of My pasture, you are men, and I am your God," declares the Lord GOD.

Psalm 130:5-8

5 I wait for the LORD, my
soul does wait,
And in His word do I hope.
6 My soul *waits* for the Lord
More than the watchmen
for the morning;
Indeed, more than the watchmen
for the morning.
7 O Israel, hope in the LORD;
For with the LORD there
is lovingkindness,
And with Him is abundant
redemption.
8 And He will redeem Israel
From all his iniquities.

Proverbs 29:1

29 A man who hardens *his* neck
after much reproof
Will suddenly be broken
beyond remedy.

James 2:1-26

2 My brethren, do not hold your faith in our glorious Lord Jesus Christ with *an attitude of* personal favoritism. ²For if a man comes into your assembly with a gold ring and dressed in fine clothes, and there

2:1 your faith. This refers not to the act of believing, but to the entire Christian faith (Jude 3), which has as its central focus Jesus Christ. **our glorious Lord.** Christ is the One who reveals the glory of God (Jn 1:14; 2Co 4:4-6; Heb 1:1-3). In His incarnation, He showed only impartiality (Mt 22:16)—for example, consider the non-elite people included in His genealogy, His choice of the humble village of Nazareth as His residence for 30 years, and His willingness to minister in Galilee and Samaria, both regions held in contempt by Israel's leaders. **favoritism.** Originally, this word referred to raising someone's face or elevating the person, but it came to refer to exalting someone strictly on a superficial, external basis, such as appearance, race, wealth, rank, or social status.

also comes in a poor man in dirty clothes, ³and you pay special attention to the one who is wearing the fine clothes, and say, "You sit here in a good place," and you say to the poor man, "You stand over there, or sit down by my footstool," ⁴have you not made distinctions among yourselves, and become judges with evil motives? ⁵Listen, my beloved brethren: did not God choose the poor of this world *to be* rich in faith and heirs of the kingdom which He promised to those who love Him? ⁶But you have dishonored the poor man. Is it not the rich who oppress you and personally drag you into court? ⁷Do they not blaspheme the fair name by which you have been called?

⁸If, however, you are fulfilling the royal law according to the Scripture, "YOU SHALL LOVE YOUR NEIGHBOR AS YOURSELF," you are doing well. ⁹But if you show partiality, you are committing sin *and* are convicted by the law as transgressors. ¹⁰For whoever keeps the whole law and yet stumbles in one *point,* he has become guilty of all. ¹¹For He who said, "DO NOT COMMIT ADULTERY," also said, "DO NOT COMMIT MURDER." Now if you do not commit adultery, but do commit murder, you have become a transgressor of the law. ¹²So speak and so act as those who are to be judged by *the* law of liberty. ¹³For judgment *will be* merciless to one who has shown no mercy; mercy triumphs over judgment.

2:8 royal law. This is better translated "sovereign law." The idea is that this law is supreme or binding. **LOVE YOUR NEIGHBOR AS YOURSELF.** This sovereign law (quoted from Lv 19:18), when combined with the command to love God (Dt 6:4-5), summarizes all the Law and the Prophets (Mt 22:36-40; Ro 13:8-10). James is not advocating some kind of emotional affection for oneself—self-love is clearly a sin (2Ti 3:2). Rather, the command is to pursue meeting the physical health and spiritual well-being of one's neighbors (all within the sphere of our influence; Lk 10:30-37) with the same intensity and concern as one does naturally for oneself (Php 2:3-4).

¹⁴What use is it, my brethren, if someone says he has faith but he has no works? Can that faith save him? ¹⁵If a brother or sister is without clothing and in need of daily food, ¹⁶and one of you says to them, "Go in peace, be warmed and be filled," and yet you do not

give them what is necessary for *their* body, what use is that? [17] Even so faith, if it has no works, is dead, *being* by itself.

[18] But someone may *well* say, "You have faith and I have works; show me your faith without the works, and I will show you my faith by my works." [19] You believe that God is one. You do well; the demons also believe, and shudder. [20] But are you willing to recognize, you foolish fellow, that faith without works is useless? [21] Was not Abraham our father justified by works when he offered up Isaac his son on the altar? [22] You see that faith was working with his works, and as a result of the works, faith was perfected; [23] and the Scripture was fulfilled which says, "AND ABRAHAM BELIEVED GOD, AND IT WAS RECKONED TO HIM AS RIGHTEOUSNESS," and he was called the friend of God. [24] You see that a man is justified by works and not by faith alone. [25] In the same

2:19 You believe that God is one. A clear reference to the passage most familiar to his Jewish readers: the *Shema* (Dt 6:4–5), the most basic doctrine of the Old Testament. **demons also believe.** Even fallen angels affirm the oneness of God and tremble at its implications. Demons are essentially orthodox in their doctrine (Mt 8:29–30; Mk 5:7; Lk 4:41; Ac 19:15). But orthodox doctrine by itself is no proof of saving faith. They know the truth about God, Christ, and the Spirit, but hate it and Them.

way, was not Rahab the harlot also justified by works when she received the messengers and sent them out by another way? [26] For just as the body without *the* spirit is dead, so also faith without works is dead.

DAY 21: If salvation is by faith in Christ alone, how can James write "faith without works is useless" (2:20)?

"But are you willing to recognize, you foolish fellow, that faith without works is useless?" Literally, "empty, defective." The objector's claim of belief is fraudulent, and his faith is a sham. James is not contrasting two methods of salvation (faith versus works). Instead, he contrasts two kinds of faith: living faith that saves and dead faith that does not (1Jn 3:7–10).

"Was not Abraham our father justified by works?" (v. 21). This does not contradict Paul's clear teaching that Abraham was justified before God by grace alone through faith alone (Ro 3:20; 4:1–25; Gal 3:6, 11). For several reasons, James cannot mean that Abraham was constituted righteous before God because of his own good works: 1) James already stressed that salvation is a gracious gift (1:17–18); 2) in the middle of this disputed passage (v. 23), James quoted Genesis 15:6, which forcefully claims that God credited righteousness to Abraham solely on the basis of his faith (Ro 1:17; 3:24; 4:1–25); and 3) the work that James said justified Abraham was his offering up of Isaac (Ge 22:9, 12), an event that occurred many years after he first exercised faith and was declared righteous before God (Ge 12:1–7; 15:6). Instead, Abraham's offering of Isaac demonstrated the genuineness of his faith and the reality of his justification before God. James is emphasizing the vindication before others of a man's claim to salvation. James's teaching perfectly complements Paul's writings; salvation is determined by faith alone (Eph 2:8–9) and demonstrated by faithfulness to obey God's will alone (Eph 2:10).

"And as a result of the works, faith was perfected" (v. 22). This refers to bringing something to its end or to its fullness. Just as a fruit tree has not arrived at its goal until it bears fruit, faith has not reached its end until it demonstrates itself in a righteous life.

NOVEMBER 22

Ezekiel 35:1–36:38

35 Moreover, the word of the LORD came to me, saying, [2] "Son of man, set your face against Mount Seir, and prophesy against it [3] and say to it, 'Thus says the Lord GOD,

"Behold, I am against you, Mount Seir,
And I will stretch out My
hand against you

And make you a desolation
and a waste.
[4] "I will lay waste your cities
And you will become a desolation.
Then you will know that
I am the LORD.

[5] Because you have had everlasting enmity and have delivered the sons of Israel to the power of the sword at the time of their calamity, at the time of the punishment of the end, [6] therefore as I live," declares the Lord

GOD, "I will give you over to bloodshed, and bloodshed will pursue you; since you have not hated bloodshed, therefore bloodshed will pursue you. ⁷I will make Mount Seir a waste and a desolation and I will cut off from it the one who passes through and returns. ⁸I will fill its mountains with its slain; on your hills and in your valleys and in all your ravines those slain by the sword will fall. ⁹I will make you an everlasting desolation and your cities will not be inhabited. Then you will know that I am the LORD.

¹⁰ "Because you have said, 'These two nations and these two lands will be mine, and we will possess them,' although the LORD was there, ¹¹therefore as I live," declares the Lord GOD, "I will deal *with you* according to your anger and according to your envy which you showed because of your hatred against them; so I will make Myself known among them when I judge you. ¹²Then you will know that I, the LORD, have heard all your revilings which you have spoken against the mountains of Israel saying, 'They are laid desolate; they are given to us for food.' ¹³And you have spoken arrogantly against Me and have multiplied your words against Me; I have heard *it*." ¹⁴Thus says the Lord GOD, "As all the earth rejoices, I will make you a desolation. ¹⁵As you rejoiced over the inheritance of the house of Israel because it was desolate, so I will do to you. You will be a desolation, O Mount Seir, and all Edom, all of it. Then they will know that I am the LORD."'

36 "And you, son of man, prophesy to the mountains of Israel and say, 'O mountains of Israel, hear the word of the LORD. ²Thus says the Lord GOD, "Because the enemy has spoken against you, 'Aha!' and, 'The everlasting heights have become our possession,' ³therefore prophesy and say, 'Thus says the Lord GOD, "For good reason they have made you desolate and crushed you from every side, that you would become a possession of the rest of the nations and you have been taken up in the talk and the whispering of the people." ' " ⁴Therefore, O mountains of Israel, hear the word of the Lord GOD. Thus says the Lord GOD to the mountains and to the hills, to the ravines and to the valleys, to the desolate wastes and to the forsaken cities which have become a prey and a derision to the rest of the nations which are round about, ⁵therefore thus says the Lord GOD, "Surely in the fire of My jealousy I have spoken against the rest of the nations, and against all Edom, who appropriated My land for themselves as a

36:1 This chapter presents the prerequisite regeneration which Israel must experience before they can nationally enter into the promised blessings. This chapter must be understood to speak of a literal Israel, a literal land, and a literal regeneration, leading to a literal kingdom under Messiah. **prophesy to the mountains.** See vv. 1, 4, 6, 8. Ezekiel addresses Israel's mountains, as symbolic of the whole nation. He promises: 1) to give these mountains again to dispersed Israel (v. 12); 2) to cause fruit to grow on them (v. 8); 3) to rebuild cities and to multiply people there (v. 10); and 4) to bless in a greater way than in the past (v. 11). This promise can only be fulfilled in future millennial blessing to Israel that she has not yet experienced, because it includes the salvation of the New Covenant (vv. 25–27, 29, 31, 33).

possession with wholehearted joy *and* with scorn of soul, to drive it out for a prey." ⁶Therefore prophesy concerning the land of Israel and say to the mountains and to the hills, to the ravines and to the valleys, "Thus says the Lord GOD, 'Behold, I have spoken in My jealousy and in My wrath because you have endured the insults of the nations.' ⁷Therefore thus says the Lord GOD, 'I have sworn that surely the nations which are around you will themselves endure their insults. ⁸But you, O mountains of Israel, you will put forth your branches and bear your fruit for My people Israel; for they will soon come. ⁹For, behold, I am for you, and I will turn to you, and you will be cultivated and sown. ¹⁰I will multiply men on you, all the house of Israel, all of it; and the cities will be inhabited and the waste places will be rebuilt. ¹¹I will multiply on you man and beast; and they will increase and be fruitful; and I will cause you to be inhabited as you were formerly and will treat you better than at the first. Thus you will know that I am the LORD. ¹²Yes, I will cause men—My people Israel—to walk on you and possess you, so that you will become their inheritance and never again bereave them of children.'

¹³ "Thus says the Lord GOD, 'Because they say to you, "You are a devourer of men and have bereaved your nation of children," ¹⁴therefore you will no longer devour men and no longer bereave your nation of children,' declares the Lord GOD. ¹⁵I will not let you hear insults from the nations anymore, nor will you bear disgrace from the peoples

any longer, nor will you cause your nation to stumble any longer," declares the Lord GOD.'"

¹⁶Then the word of the LORD came to me saying, ¹⁷"Son of man, when the house of Israel was living in their own land, they defiled it by their ways and their deeds; their way before Me was like the uncleanness of a woman in her impurity. ¹⁸Therefore I poured out My wrath on them for the blood which they had shed on the land, because they had defiled it with their idols. ¹⁹Also I scattered them among the nations and they were dispersed throughout the lands. According to their ways and their deeds I judged them. ²⁰When they came to the nations where they went, they profaned My holy name, because it was said of them, 'These are the people of the LORD; yet they have come out of His land.' ²¹But I had concern for My holy name, which the house of Israel had profaned among the nations where they went.

²²"Therefore say to the house of Israel, 'Thus says the Lord GOD, "It is not for your sake, O house of Israel, that I am about to act, but for My holy name, which you have profaned among the nations where you went. ²³I will vindicate the holiness of My great name which has been profaned among the nations, which you have profaned in their midst. Then the nations will know that I am the LORD," declares the Lord GOD, "when I prove Myself holy among you in their sight. ²⁴For I will take you from the nations, gather you from all the lands and bring you into your own land. ²⁵Then I will sprinkle clean water on you, and you will be clean; I will cleanse you from all your filthiness and from all your idols. ²⁶Moreover, I will give you a new heart and put a new spirit within you; and I will remove the heart of stone from your flesh and give you a heart of flesh. ²⁷I will put My Spirit within you and cause you to walk in My statutes, and you will be careful to observe My ordinances. ²⁸You will live in the land that I gave to your forefathers; so you will

36:25-27 I will cleanse you. Along with the physical reality of a return to the land, God pledged spiritual renewal: 1) cleansing from sin; 2) a new heart of the New Covenant (Jer 31:31–34); 3) a new spirit or disposition inclined to worship Him; and 4) His Spirit dwelling in them, enabling them to walk in obedience to His word. This has not happened, because Israel has not trusted Jesus Christ as Messiah and Savior, but it will before the kingdom of Messiah (Zec 12–14; Ro 11:25–27; Rev 11:13).

be My people, and I will be your God. ²⁹Moreover, I will save you from all your uncleanness; and I will call for the grain and multiply it, and I will not bring a famine on you. ³⁰I will multiply the fruit of the tree and the produce of the field, so that you will not receive again the disgrace of famine among the nations. ³¹Then you will remember your evil ways and your deeds that were not good, and you will loathe yourselves in your own sight for your iniquities and your abominations. ³²I am not doing *this* for your sake," declares the Lord GOD, "let it be known to you. Be ashamed and confounded for your ways, O house of Israel!"

36:25-31 What was figuratively described in v. 25 is explained as literal in vv. 26–27. The gift of the "new heart" signifies the new birth, which is regeneration by the Holy Spirit (11:18–20). The "heart" stands for the whole nature. The "spirit" indicates the governing power of the mind which directs thought and conduct. A "heart of stone" is stubborn and self-willed. A "heart of flesh" is pliable and responsive. The evil inclination is removed and a new nature replaces it. This is New Covenant character as in Jeremiah 31:31–34.

³³'Thus says the Lord GOD, "On the day that I cleanse you from all your iniquities, I will cause the cities to be inhabited, and the waste places will be rebuilt. ³⁴The desolate land will be cultivated instead of being a desolation in the sight of everyone who passes by. ³⁵They will say, 'This desolate land has become like the garden of Eden; and the waste, desolate and ruined cities are fortified *and* inhabited.' ³⁶Then the nations that are left round about you will know that I, the LORD, have rebuilt the ruined places *and* planted that which was desolate; I, the LORD, have spoken and will do it."

³⁷'Thus says the Lord GOD, "This also I will let the house of Israel ask Me to do for them: I will increase their men like a flock. ³⁸Like the flock for sacrifices, like the flock at Jerusalem during her appointed feasts, so will the waste cities be filled with flocks of men. Then they will know that I am the LORD."'"

Psalm 131:1-3
A Song of Ascents, of David.

O LORD, my heart is not proud,
  nor my eyes haughty;
Nor do I involve myself
  in great matters,
Or in things too difficult for me.

² Surely I have composed and
    quieted my soul;
Like a weaned child *rests*
    against his mother,
My soul is like a weaned
    child within me.
³ O Israel, hope in the LORD
From this time forth and forever.

Proverbs 29:2–3

² When the righteous increase,
    the people rejoice,
But when a wicked man
    rules, people groan.
³ A man who loves wisdom
    makes his father glad,
But he who keeps company with
    harlots wastes *his* wealth.

James 3:1–18

3 Let not many *of you* become teachers, my brethren, knowing that as such we will incur a stricter judgment. ² For we all stumble in many *ways*. If anyone does not stumble in what he says, he is a perfect man, able to bridle the whole body as well. ³ Now if we put the bits into the horses' mouths so that they will obey us, we direct their entire body as well. ⁴ Look at the ships also, though they are so great and are driven by strong winds, are still directed by a very small rudder wherever the inclination of the pilot desires. ⁵ So also the tongue is a small part of the body, and *yet* it boasts of great things.

See how great a forest is set aflame by such a small fire! ⁶ And the tongue is a fire, the *very* world of iniquity; the tongue is set among our members as that which defiles the entire body, and sets on fire the course of *our* life, and is set on fire by hell. ⁷ For every species of beasts and birds, of reptiles and creatures of the sea, is tamed and has been tamed by the human race. ⁸ But no one can tame the tongue; *it is* a restless evil *and* full of deadly poison. ⁹ With it we bless *our* Lord and Father, and

3:6 tongue is a fire. Like fire, the tongue's sinful words can spread destruction rapidly, or as its accompanying smoke, those words can permeate and ruin everything around it. **defiles.** This means "to pollute or contaminate" (Mk 7:20; Jude 23). **the course of *our* life.** Better translated "the circle of life," this underscores that the tongue's evil can extend beyond the individual to affect everything in his sphere of influence. **hell.** A translation of the Greek word *gehenna* (or valley of Hinnom). In Christ's time this valley that lay southwest of Jerusalem's walls served as the city dump and was known for its constantly burning fire. Jesus used that place to symbolize the eternal place of punishment and torment (Mk 9:43, 45). To James "hell" conjures up not just the place but the satanic host that will some day inherit it—they use the tongue as a tool for evil.

with it we curse men, who have been made in the likeness of God; ¹⁰ from the same mouth come *both* blessing and cursing. My brethren, these things ought not to be this way. ¹¹ Does a fountain send out from the same opening *both* fresh and bitter *water*? ¹² Can a fig tree, my brethren, produce olives, or a vine produce figs? Nor *can* salt water produce fresh.

¹³ Who among you is wise and understanding? Let him show by his good behavior his deeds in the gentleness of wisdom. ¹⁴ But if you have bitter jealousy and selfish ambition in your heart, do not be arrogant and *so* lie against the truth. ¹⁵ This wisdom is not that which comes down from above, but is earthly, natural, demonic. ¹⁶ For where jealousy and selfish ambition exist, there is disorder and every evil thing. ¹⁷ But the wisdom from above is first pure, then peaceable, gentle, reasonable, full of mercy and good fruits, unwavering, without hypocrisy. ¹⁸ And the seed whose fruit is righteousness is sown in peace by those who make peace.

DAY 22: How does James explain the difference between the two kinds of wisdom in the world (3:13–18)?

The term "wise" in v. 13 is the common Greek word for speculative knowledge and philosophy, but the Hebrews infused it with the much richer meaning of skillfully applying knowledge to the matter of practical living. This passage points out that two groups of people can be called wise; but in each case, the source of wisdom and the character of the "wise" are entirely opposite.

"Wisdom from above" (v. 17) includes the following characteristics: 1) pure. This refers to spiritual integrity and moral sincerity. Every genuine Christian has this kind of heart motivation (Pss 24:3–4; 51:7; Mt 5:8; Ro 7:22–23; Heb 12:14); 2) peaceable. Means "peace loving" or "peace promoting" (Mt 5:9); 3) gentle. This word is difficult to translate, but most nearly means a character trait of sweet reasonableness. Such a person will submit to all kinds of mistreatment and difficulty with an attitude of kind, courteous, patient humility, without any thought of hatred or revenge (Mt 5:10–11); 4) willing to yield. The original term described someone who was teachable, compliant, easily persuaded, and who willingly submitted to military discipline or moral and legal standards. For believers, it defines obedience to God's standards (Mt 5:3–5); 5) full of mercy. The gift of showing concern for those who suffer pain and hardship, and the ability to forgive quickly (Mt 5:7; Ro 12:8); 6) without partiality. The Greek word occurs only here in the New Testament and denotes a consistent, unwavering person who is undivided in his commitment and conviction and does not make unfair distinctions.

NOVEMBER 23

Ezekiel 37:1–38:23

37 The hand of the LORD was upon me, and He brought me out by the Spirit of the LORD and set me down in the middle of the valley; and it was full of bones. ² He caused me to pass among them round about, and behold, *there were* very many on the surface of the valley; and lo, *they were* very dry. ³ He said to me, "Son of man, can these bones live?" And I answered, "O Lord GOD, You know." ⁴ Again He said to me, "Prophesy over these bones and say to them, 'O dry bones, hear the word of the LORD.' ⁵ Thus says the Lord GOD to these bones, 'Behold, I will cause breath to enter you that you may come to life. ⁶ I will put sinews on you, make flesh grow back on you, cover you with skin and put breath in you that you may come alive; and you will know that I am the LORD.'"

⁷ So I prophesied as I was commanded; and as I prophesied, there was a noise, and behold, a rattling; and the bones came together, bone to its bone. ⁸ And I looked, and behold, sinews were on them, and flesh grew and skin covered them; but there was no breath in them.

37:3 can these bones live? The many dry bones (v. 2) picture the nation Israel (v. 11) as apparently dead in their dispersion, and waiting for national resurrection. The people knew about the doctrine of individual resurrection, otherwise this prophecy would have had no meaning (1Ki 17; 2Ki 4; 13:21; Is 25:8; 26:19; Da 12:2; Hos 13:14).

37:4–6 Prophesy over these bones. Ezekiel is to proclaim God's pledge to reassemble Israelites from various parts of the world and restore the nation of Israel to life (v. 5) and give them His Spirit (v. 14) in true salvation and spiritual life. Clearly, God is promising the resurrection of the nation of Israel and its spiritual regeneration (36:25–27).

⁹ Then He said to me, "Prophesy to the breath, prophesy, son of man, and say to the breath, 'Thus says the Lord GOD, "Come from the four winds, O breath, and breathe on these slain, that they come to life."'" ¹⁰ So I prophesied as He commanded me, and the breath came into them, and they came to life and stood on their feet, an exceedingly great army.

¹¹ Then He said to me, "Son of man, these bones are the whole house of Israel; behold, they say, 'Our bones are dried up and our hope has perished. We are completely cut off.' ¹² Therefore prophesy and say to them, 'Thus says the Lord GOD, "Behold, I will open your graves and cause you to come up out of your graves, My people; and I will bring you into the land of Israel. ¹³ Then you will know that I am the LORD, when I have opened your graves and caused you to come up out of your graves, My people. ¹⁴ I will put My Spirit within you and you will come to life, and I will place you on your own land. Then you will know that I, the LORD, have spoken and done it," declares the LORD.'"

¹⁵ The word of the LORD came again to me saying, ¹⁶ "And you, son of man, take for yourself one stick and write on it, 'For Judah and for the sons of Israel, his companions'; then take another stick and write on it, 'For Joseph, the stick of Ephraim and all the house of Israel, his companions.' ¹⁷ Then join them for yourself one to another into one stick, that they may become one in your hand. ¹⁸ When the sons of your people speak to you saying, 'Will you not declare to us what you mean by these?' ¹⁹ say to them, 'Thus says the Lord GOD, "Behold, I will take the stick of Joseph, which is in the hand of Ephraim, and the tribes of Israel, his companions; and I will put them with it, with the stick of Judah, and make them one stick, and they will be one in My hand."' ²⁰ The sticks on which you write will be in your hand before their eyes. ²¹ Say to them, 'Thus says the Lord GOD, "Behold, I will take the sons of Israel from among the nations where they have gone, and I will gather them from every side and bring them into their

own land; ²²and I will make them one nation in the land, on the mountains of Israel; and one king will be king for all of them; and they will no longer be two nations and no longer be divided into two kingdoms. ²³They will no longer defile themselves with their idols, or with their detestable things, or with any of their transgressions; but I will deliver them from all their dwelling places in which they have sinned, and will cleanse them. And they will be My people, and I will be their God.

²⁴"My servant David will be king over them, and they will all have one shepherd; and they will walk in My ordinances and keep My statutes and observe them. ²⁵They will live on the land that I gave to Jacob My servant, in which your fathers lived; and they will live on it, they, and their sons and their sons' sons, forever; and David My servant will be their prince forever. ²⁶I will make a covenant of peace with them; it will be an everlasting covenant with them. And I will place them and multiply them, and will set My sanctuary in their midst forever. ²⁷My dwelling place also will be with them; and I will be their God, and they will be My people. ²⁸And the nations will know that I am the LORD who sanctifies Israel, when My sanctuary is in their midst forever."'"

38 And the word of the LORD came to me saying, ²"Son of man, set your face toward Gog of the land of Magog, the prince of Rosh, Meshech and Tubal, and prophesy against him ³and say, 'Thus says the Lord GOD, "Behold, I am against you, O Gog, prince of Rosh, Meshech and Tubal. ⁴I will turn you about and put hooks into your jaws, and I will bring you out, and all your army, horses and horsemen, all of them splendidly attired, a great company *with* buckler and shield, all of them wielding swords; ⁵Persia, Ethiopia and Put with them, all of them *with* shield and helmet; ⁶Gomer with all its troops; Beth-togarmah *from* the remote parts of the north with all its troops—many peoples with you.

⁷"Be prepared, and prepare yourself, you and all your companies that are assembled about you, and be a guard for them. ⁸After many days you will be summoned; in the latter years you will come into the land that is restored from the sword, *whose inhabitants* have been gathered from many nations to the mountains of Israel which had been a continual waste; but its people were brought out from the nations, and they are living securely, all of them. ⁹You will go up, you will come like a storm; you will be like a cloud covering the land, you and all your troops, and many peoples with you."

¹⁰'Thus says the Lord GOD, "It will come about on that day, that thoughts will come into your mind and you will devise an evil plan, ¹¹and you will say, 'I will go up against the land of unwalled villages. I will go against those who are at rest, that live securely, all of them living without walls and having no bars or gates, ¹²to capture spoil and to seize plunder, to turn your hand against the waste places which are *now* inhabited, and against the people who are gathered from the nations, who have acquired cattle and goods, who live at the center of the world.' ¹³Sheba and Dedan and the merchants of Tarshish with all its villages will say to you, 'Have you come to capture spoil? Have you assembled your company to seize plunder, to carry away silver and gold, to take away cattle and goods, to capture great spoil?'"'

¹⁴"Therefore prophesy, son of man, and say to Gog, 'Thus says the Lord GOD, "On that day when My people Israel are living securely, will you not know *it?* ¹⁵You will come from your place out of the remote parts of the north, you and many peoples with you, all of them riding on horses, a great assembly and a mighty army; ¹⁶and you will come up against My people Israel like a cloud to cover the land. It shall come about in the last days that I will bring you against My land, so that the nations may know Me when I am sanctified through you before their eyes, O Gog."

¹⁷'Thus says the Lord GOD, "Are you the one of whom I spoke in former days through My servants the prophets of Israel, who prophesied in those days for *many* years that I would bring you against them? ¹⁸It will come about on that day, when Gog comes against the land of Israel," declares the Lord GOD, "that My fury will mount up in My anger. ¹⁹In My zeal and in My blazing wrath I declare *that* on that day there will surely be a great earthquake in the land of Israel. ²⁰The fish of the sea, the birds of the heavens, the beasts of the field, all the creeping things that creep on the earth, and all the men who are on the face of the earth will shake at My presence; the mountains also will be thrown down, the steep pathways will collapse and every wall will fall to the ground. ²¹I will call for a sword against him on all My mountains," declares the Lord GOD. "Every man's sword will be against his brother. ²²With pestilence and with blood I will enter into judgment with him; and I will rain on him and on his troops, and on the many peoples who are with him, a torrential rain, with hailstones, fire and brimstone. ²³I will magnify Myself, sanctify

Myself, and make Myself known in the sight of many nations; and they will know that I am the LORD."'

Psalm 132:1-9

A Song of Ascents.

Remember, O LORD, on David's behalf,
All his affliction;
2 How he swore to the LORD
And vowed to the Mighty
One of Jacob,
3 "Surely I will not enter my house,
Nor lie on my bed;
4 I will not give sleep to my eyes
Or slumber to my eyelids,
5 Until I find a place for the LORD,
A dwelling place for the
Mighty One of Jacob."

6 Behold, we heard of it in Ephrathah,
We found it in the field of Jaar.
7 Let us go into His dwelling place;
Let us worship at His footstool.
8 Arise, O LORD, to Your resting place,
You and the ark of Your strength.
9 Let Your priests be clothed
with righteousness,
And let Your godly ones sing for joy.

Proverbs 29:4

4 The king gives stability to
the land by justice,
But a man who takes bribes
overthrows it.

James 4:1-17

4 What is the source of quarrels and conflicts among you? Is not the source your pleasures that wage war in your members? ²You lust and do not have; *so* you commit murder. You are envious and cannot obtain; *so* you fight and quarrel. You do not have because you do not ask. ³You ask and do not receive, because you ask with wrong motives, so that you may spend *it* on your pleasures. ⁴You adulteresses, do you not know that friendship with the world is hostility toward God? Therefore whoever wishes to be a friend of the world makes himself an enemy of God. ⁵Or do you think that the Scripture speaks to no purpose: "He jealously desires the Spirit which He has made to dwell in us"? ⁶But He gives a greater grace. Therefore *it* says, "GOD IS OPPOSED TO THE PROUD, BUT GIVES GRACE TO THE HUMBLE." ⁷Submit therefore to God. Resist

4:4 friendship. Appearing only here in the NT, the Greek word describes love in the sense of a strong emotional attachment. Those with a deep and intimate longing for the things of the world give evidence that they are not redeemed (1Jn 2:15–17). **hostility toward God.** The necessary corollary to friendship with the world. The sobering truth that unbelievers are God's enemies is taught throughout Scripture (Dt 32:41–43; Pss 21:8; 68:21; 72:9; 110:1–2; Is 42:13; Na 1:2, 8; Lk 19:27; Ro 5:10; 8:5–7; 1Co 15:25).

4:6 greater grace. The only ray of hope in man's spiritual darkness is the sovereign grace of God, which alone can rescue man from his propensity to lust for evil things. That God gives "greater grace" shows that His grace is greater than the power of sin, the flesh, the world, and Satan (Ro 5:20). The Old Testament quote (from Pr 3:34; see 1Pe 5:5) reveals who obtains God's grace—the humble, not the proud enemies of God. The word "HUMBLE" does not define a special class of Christians, but encompasses all believers (Is 57:15; 66:2; Mt 18:3–4).

the devil and he will flee from you. ⁸Draw near to God and He will draw near to you. Cleanse your hands, you sinners; and purify your hearts, you double-minded. ⁹Be miserable and mourn and weep; let your laughter be turned into mourning and your joy to gloom. ¹⁰Humble yourselves in the presence of the Lord, and He will exalt you.

¹¹Do not speak against one another, brethren. He who speaks against a brother or judges his brother, speaks against the law and judges the law; but if you judge the law, you are not a doer of the law but a judge *of it.* ¹²There is *only* one Lawgiver and Judge, the One who is able to save and to destroy; but who are you who judge your neighbor?

¹³Come now, you who say, "Today or tomorrow we will go to such and such a city, and spend a year there and engage in business and make a profit." ¹⁴Yet you do not know what your life will be like tomorrow. You are *just* a vapor that appears for a little while and then vanishes away. ¹⁵Instead, *you ought* to say, "If the Lord wills, we will live and also do this or that." ¹⁶But as it is, you boast in your arrogance; all such boasting is evil. ¹⁷Therefore, to one who knows *the* right thing to do and does not do it, to him it is sin.

DAY 23: What do the 10 commands that fill James 4:7-10 have to do with grace?

These verses contain a series of 10 commands that prepare a person to receive saving grace. These commands delineate a person's response to God's gracious offer of salvation and reveal what it means to be humble. Each command uses a Greek imperative to define the expected action:

1. "Submit...to God" (v. 7)—James used the word to describe a willing, conscious submission to God's authority as sovereign ruler of the universe.
2. "Resist the devil" (v. 7)—those who consciously take their stand against Satan and transfer their allegiance to God will find that Satan "will flee from" them; he is a defeated foe.
3. "Draw near to God" (v. 8)—pursue an intimate love relationship with God (Php 3:10).
4. "Cleanse your hands" (v. 8)—the added term "sinners" addresses the unbelievers' need to recognize and confess their sin (5:20).
5. "Purify your hearts" (v. 8)—cleansing the hands symbolizes external behavior; this phrase refers to the inner thoughts, motives, and desires of the heart (Ps 24:3-4).
6. "Be miserable" (v. 9)—to be afflicted and wretched. This is the state of those truly broken over their sin (Mt 5:4).
7. "Mourn" (v. 9)—the internal experience of brokenness over sin (Ps 51:17; Mt 5:4).
8. "Weep" (v. 9)—the outward manifestation of inner sorrow over sin (Mk 14:72).
9. Grieve without laughter or joy (v. 9)—the signs of denial; the flippant laughter of those foolishly indulging in worldly pleasures without regard to God, life, death, sin, judgment, or holiness.
10. "Humble yourselves" (v. 10)—this final command sums up the preceding 9. The word "humble" comes from a word meaning "to make oneself low." Those conscious of being in the presence of the majestic, infinitely holy God are humble (Is 6:5).

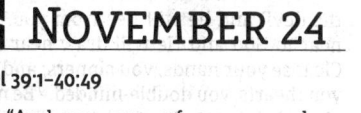

NOVEMBER 24

Ezekiel 39:1-40:49

39 "And you, son of man, prophesy against Gog and say, 'Thus says the Lord GOD, "Behold, I am against you, O Gog, prince of Rosh, Meshech and Tubal; ² and I will turn you around, drive you on, take you up from the remotest parts of the north and bring you against the mountains of Israel. ³ I will strike your bow from your left hand and dash down your arrows from your right hand. ⁴ You will fall on the mountains of Israel, you and all your troops and the peoples who are with you; I will give you as food to every kind of predatory bird and beast of the field. ⁵ You will fall on the open field; for it is I who have spoken," declares the Lord GOD. ⁶ "And I will send fire upon Magog and those who inhabit the coastlands in safety; and they will know that I am the LORD.

⁷ "My holy name I will make known in the midst of My people Israel; and I will not let My holy name be profaned anymore. And the nations will know that I am the LORD, the Holy One in Israel. ⁸ Behold, it is coming and it shall be done," declares the Lord GOD. "That is the day of which I have spoken.

⁹ "Then those who inhabit the cities of Israel will go out and make fires with the weap-

ons and burn *them,* both shields and bucklers, bows and arrows, war clubs and spears, and for seven years they will make fires of them. ¹⁰ They will not take wood from the field or gather firewood from the forests, for they will make fires with the weapons; and they will take the spoil of those who despoiled them and seize the plunder of those who plundered them," declares the Lord GOD.

¹¹ "On that day I will give Gog a burial ground there in Israel, the valley of those who pass by east of the sea, and it will block off those who would pass by. So they will bury Gog there with all his horde, and they will call *it* the valley of Hamon-gog. ¹² For seven months the house of Israel will be burying them in order to cleanse the land. ¹³ Even all the people of the land will bury *them;* and it will be to their renown *on* the day that I glorify Myself," declares the Lord GOD. ¹⁴ "They will set apart men who will constantly pass through the land, burying those who were passing through, even those left on the surface of the ground, in order to cleanse it. At the end of seven months they will make a search. ¹⁵ As those who pass through the land pass through and anyone sees a man's bone, then he will set up a marker by it until the buriers have buried it in the valley of Hamon-gog. ¹⁶ And even *the* name of *the* city will be Hamonah. So they will cleanse the land."'

17 "As for you, son of man, thus says the Lord GOD, 'Speak to every kind of bird and to every beast of the field, "Assemble and come, gather from every side to My sacrifice which I am going to sacrifice for you, as a great sacrifice on the mountains of Israel, that you may eat flesh and drink blood. 18 You will eat the flesh of mighty men and drink the blood of the princes of the earth, as *though they were* rams, lambs, goats and bulls, all of them fatlings of Bashan. 19 So you will eat fat until you are glutted, and drink blood until you are drunk, from My sacrifice which I have sacrificed for you. 20 You will be glutted at My table with horses and charioteers, with mighty men and all the men of war," declares the Lord GOD.

21 "And I will set My glory among the nations; and all the nations will see My judgment which I have executed and My hand which I have laid on them. 22 And the house of Israel will know that I am the LORD their God from that day onward. 23 The nations will know that the house of Israel went into exile for their iniquity because they acted treacherously against Me, and I hid My face from them; so I gave them into the hand of their adversaries, and all of them fell by the sword. 24 According to their uncleanness and according to their transgressions I dealt with them, and I hid My face from them." ' "

25 Therefore thus says the Lord GOD, "Now I will restore the fortunes of Jacob and have mercy on the whole house of Israel; and I will be jealous for My holy name. 26 They will forget their disgrace and all their treachery which they perpetrated against Me, when they live securely on their *own* land with no one to make *them* afraid. 27 When I bring them back from the peoples and gather them from the lands of their enemies, then I shall be sanctified through them in the sight of the many nations. 28 Then they will know that I am the LORD their God because I made them go into exile among the nations, and then gathered them *again* to their own land; and I will leave none of them there any longer. 29 I will not hide My face from them any longer, for I will have poured out My Spirit on the house of Israel," declares the Lord GOD.

40 In the twenty-fifth year of our exile, at the beginning of the year, on the tenth of the month, in the fourteenth year after the city was taken, on that same day the hand of the LORD was upon me and He brought me there. 2 In the visions of God He brought me into the land of Israel and set me on a very high mountain, and on it to the south *there*

was a structure like a city. 3 So He brought me there; and behold, there was a man whose appearance was like the appearance of bronze, with a line of flax and a measuring rod in his hand; and he was standing in the gateway. 4 The man said to me, "Son of man, see with your eyes, hear with your ears, and give attention to all that I am going to show you; for you have been brought here in order to show *it* to you. Declare to the house of Israel all that you see."

5 And behold, there was a wall on the outside of the temple all around, and in the man's hand was a measuring rod of six cubits, *each of which was* a cubit and a handbreadth. So he measured the thickness of the wall, one rod; and the height, one rod. 6 Then he went to the gate which faced east, went up its steps and measured the threshold of the gate, one rod in width; and the other threshold *was* one rod in width. 7 The guardroom *was* one rod long and one rod wide; and *there were* five cubits between the guardrooms. And the threshold of the gate by the porch of the gate facing inward *was* one rod. 8 Then he measured the porch of the gate facing inward, one rod. 9 He measured the porch of the gate, eight cubits; and its side pillars, two cubits. And the porch of the gate was faced inward. 10 The guardrooms of the gate toward the east *numbered* three on each side; the three of them had the same measurement. The side pillars also had the same measurement on each side. 11 And he measured the width of the gateway, ten cubits, and the length of the gate, thirteen cubits. 12 *There was* a barrier *wall* one cubit *wide* in front of the guardrooms on each side; and the guardrooms *were* six cubits *square* on each side. 13 He measured the gate from the roof of the one guardroom to the roof of the other, a width of twenty-five cubits from *one* door to *the* door opposite. 14 He made the side pillars sixty cubits *high;* the gate *extended* round about to the side pillar of the courtyard. 15 *From* the front of the entrance gate to the front of the inner porch of the gate *was* fifty cubits. 16 *There were* shuttered windows *looking* toward the guardrooms, and toward their side pillars within the gate all around, and likewise for the porches. And *there were* windows all around inside; and on *each* side pillar *were* palm tree ornaments.

17 Then he brought me into the outer court, and behold, *there were* chambers and a pavement made for the court all around; thirty chambers faced the pavement. 18 The pavement (*that is,* the lower pavement) *was* by the side of the gates, corresponding to the length

of the gates. ¹⁹Then he measured the width from the front of the lower gate to the front of the exterior of the inner court, a hundred cubits on the east and on the north.

²⁰*As for* the gate of the outer court which faced the north, he measured its length and its width. ²¹It had three guardrooms on each side; and its side pillars and its porches had the same measurement as the first gate. Its length *was* fifty cubits and the width twenty-five cubits. ²²Its windows and its porches and its palm tree ornaments *had* the same measurements as the gate which faced toward the east; and it was reached by seven steps, and its porch *was* in front of them. ²³The inner court had a gate opposite the gate on the north as well as *the gate* on the east; and he measured a hundred cubits from gate to gate.

²⁴Then he led me toward the south, and behold, there was a gate toward the south; and he measured its side pillars and its porches according to those same measurements. ²⁵The gate and its porches had windows all around like those other windows; the length *was* fifty cubits and the width twenty-five cubits. ²⁶*There were* seven steps going up to it, and its porches *were* in front of them; and it had palm tree ornaments on its side pillars, one on each side. ²⁷The inner court had a gate toward the south; and he measured from gate to gate toward the south, a hundred cubits.

²⁸Then he brought me to the inner court by the south gate; and he measured the south gate according to those same measurements. ²⁹Its guardrooms also, its side pillars and its porches *were* according to those same measurements. And the gate and its porches had windows all around; it *was* fifty cubits long and twenty-five cubits wide. ³⁰*There were* porches all around, twenty-five cubits long and five cubits wide. ³¹Its porches *were* toward the outer court; and palm tree ornaments *were* on its side pillars, and its stairway *had* eight steps.

³²He brought me into the inner court toward the east. And he measured the gate according to those same measurements. ³³Its guardrooms also, its side pillars and its porches *were* according to those same measurements. And the gate and its porches had windows all around; it *was* fifty cubits long and twenty-five cubits wide. ³⁴Its porches *were* toward the outer court; and palm tree ornaments *were* on its side pillars, on each side, and its stairway *had* eight steps.

³⁵Then he brought me to the north gate; and he measured *it* according to those same measurements, ³⁶*with* its guardrooms, its side pillars and its porches. And the gate

had windows all around; the length *was* fifty cubits and the width twenty-five cubits. ³⁷Its side pillars *were* toward the outer court; and palm tree ornaments *were* on its side pillars on each side, and its stairway had eight steps.

³⁸A chamber with its doorway was by the side pillars at the gates; there they rinse the burnt offering. ³⁹In the porch of the gate *were* two tables on each side, on which to slaughter the burnt offering, the sin offering and the guilt offering. ⁴⁰On the outer side, as one went up to the gateway toward the north, *were* two tables; and on the other side of the porch of the gate *were* two tables. ⁴¹Four tables *were* on each side next to the gate; *or,* eight tables on which they slaughter *sacrifices.* ⁴²For the burnt offering *there were* four tables of hewn stone, a cubit and a half long, a cubit and a half wide and one cubit high, on which they lay the instruments with which they slaughter the burnt offering and the sacrifice. ⁴³The double hooks, one handbreadth in length, were installed in the house all around; and on the tables *was* the flesh of the offering.

⁴⁴From the outside to the inner gate were chambers for the singers in the inner court, *one of* which was at the side of the north gate, with its front toward the south, and one at the side of the south gate facing toward the north. ⁴⁵He said to me, "This is the chamber which faces toward the south, *intended* for the priests who keep charge of the temple; ⁴⁶but the chamber which faces toward the north is for the priests who keep charge of the altar. These are the sons of Zadok, who from the sons of Levi come near to the LORD to minister to Him." ⁴⁷He measured the court, a *perfect* square, a hundred cubits long and a hundred cubits wide; and the altar was in front of the temple.

⁴⁸Then he brought me to the porch of the temple and measured *each* side pillar of the porch, five cubits on each side; and the width of the gate was three cubits on each side. ⁴⁹The length of the porch *was* twenty cubits and the width eleven cubits; and at the stairway by which it was ascended *were* columns belonging to the side pillars, one on each side.

Psalm 132:10–18

¹⁰ For the sake of David Your servant,
　Do not turn away the face
　　of Your anointed.
¹¹ The LORD has sworn to David
　A truth from which He
　　will not turn back:
　"Of the fruit of your body I will
　　set upon your throne.

132:10 A prayer that God's promise and favor would not be withheld from David's descendants on the throne of Judah. **Your anointed.** As David had been anointed king (1Sa 16:13), so a greater King had been anointed, namely Christ, but not yet seated on the throne (Is 61:1; Lk 4:18–19).

---

¹² "If your sons will keep My covenant
And My testimony which
I will teach them,
Their sons also shall sit upon
your throne forever."

¹³ For the LORD has chosen Zion;
He has desired it for His habitation.
¹⁴ "This is My resting place forever;
Here I will dwell, for I have desired it.
¹⁵ "I will abundantly bless her provision;
I will satisfy her needy with bread.
¹⁶ "Her priests also I will clothe
with salvation,
And her godly ones will
sing aloud for joy.
¹⁷ "There I will cause the horn of
David to spring forth;
I have prepared a lamp
for Mine anointed.
¹⁸ "His enemies I will clothe with shame,
But upon himself his
crown shall shine."

Proverbs 29:5

⁵ A man who flatters his neighbor
Is spreading a net for his steps.

James 5:1–20

5 Come now, you rich, weep and howl for your miseries which are coming upon you. ² Your riches have rotted and your garments have become moth-eaten. ³ Your gold and your silver have rusted; and their rust will be a witness against you and will consume your flesh like fire. It is in the last days that you have stored up your treasure! ⁴ Behold, the pay of the laborers who mowed your fields, *and* which has been withheld by you, cries out *against you;* and the outcry of those who did the harvesting has reached the ears of the Lord of Sabaoth. ⁵ You have lived luxuriously on the earth and led a life of wanton pleasure; you have fattened your hearts in a day of slaughter. ⁶ You have condemned and put to death the righteous *man;* he does not resist you.

5:7 patient. The word emphasizes patience with people (1Th 5:14), not trials or circumstances (as in 1:3). Specifically, James has in mind patience with the oppressive rich. **the coming.** The second coming of Christ. Realizing the glory that awaits them at Christ's return should motivate believers to patiently endure mistreatment (Ro 8:18). **the early and late rains.** The "early" rain falls in Israel during October and November and softens the ground for planting. The "late" rain falls in March and April, immediately before the spring harvest. Just as the farmer waits patiently from the early rain to the latter for his crop to ripen, so must Christians patiently wait for the Lord's return (Gal 6:9; 2Ti 4:8; Titus 2:13).

---

⁷ Therefore be patient, brethren, until the coming of the Lord. The farmer waits for the precious produce of the soil, being patient about it, until it gets the early and late rains. ⁸ You too be patient; strengthen your hearts, for the coming of the Lord is near. ⁹ Do not complain, brethren, against one another, so that you yourselves may not be judged; behold, the Judge is standing right at the door. ¹⁰ As an example, brethren, of suffering and patience, take the prophets who spoke in the name of the Lord. ¹¹ We count those blessed who endured. You have heard of the endurance of Job and have seen the outcome of the Lord's dealings, that the Lord is full of compassion and *is* merciful. ¹² But above all, my brethren, do not swear, either by heaven or by earth or with any other oath; but your yes is to be yes, and your no, no, so that you may not fall under judgment. ¹³ Is anyone among you suffering? *Then* he must pray. Is anyone cheerful? He is to sing praises. ¹⁴ Is anyone among you sick? *Then* he must call for the elders of the church and they are to pray over him, anointing him with

5:14 anointing him with oil. Literally "rubbing him with oil": 1) possibly this is a reference to ceremonial anointing (Lv 14:18; Mk 6:13); 2) on the other hand, James may have had in mind medical treatment of believers physically bruised and battered by persecution. Perhaps it is better to understand the anointing in a metaphorical sense of the elders' encouraging, comforting, and strengthening the believer.

oil in the name of the Lord; ¹⁵ and the prayer offered in faith will restore the one who is sick, and the Lord will raise him up, and if he has committed sins, they will be forgiven him. ¹⁶ Therefore, confess your sins to one another, and pray for one another so that you may be healed. The effective prayer of a righteous man can accomplish much. ¹⁷ Elijah was a man with a nature like ours, and he prayed earnestly that it would not rain, and it did not rain on the earth for three years and six months. ¹⁸ Then he prayed again, and the sky poured rain and the earth produced its fruit.

¹⁹ My brethren, if any among you strays from the truth and one turns him back, ²⁰ let him know that he who turns a sinner from the error of his way will save his soul from death and will cover a multitude of sins.

5:14–15 sick. James directs those who are "sick," meaning weakened by their suffering to call for the elders of the church for strength, support, and prayer.

5:15 prayer offered in faith. The prayer offered on their behalf by the elders. **restore the... sick.** Deliver them from their suffering because they have been weakened by their infirmity, not from their sin, which was confessed. **committed sins...be forgiven.** Not by the elders, since God alone can forgive sins (Is 43:25; Da 9:9; Mk 2:7). That those who are suffering called for the elders implies they had a contrite, repentant heart, and that part of their time with the overseers would involve confessing their sins to God.

DAY 24: What warning does James give to the rich?

In James 5:1, he begins: "Come now, you rich, weep and howl for your miseries which are coming upon you." James condemns them not for being wealthy, but for misusing their resources. Unlike the believing rich in Timothy's congregation (1Ti 6:17–19), these are the wicked wealthy who profess Christian faith and have associated themselves with the church, but whose real god is money.

"Behold, the pay...which has been withheld" (v. 4). The rich had gained some of their wealth by oppressing and defrauding their day laborers—a practice strictly forbidden in the Old Testament (Lv 19:13; Dt 24:14–15). The One who hears the cries of the defrauded laborers, James warns, is the Lord of hosts, the commander of the armies of heaven (angels). The Bible teaches that angels will be involved in the judgment of unbelievers (Mt 13:39–41, 49; 16:27; 25:31; 2Th 1:7–8).

"You have lived luxuriously on the earth" (v. 5). After robbing their workers to accumulate their wealth, the rich indulged themselves in an extravagant lifestyle. "Pleasure" has the connotation of wanton pleasure. "Luxury" leads to vice when a person becomes consumed with the pursuit of pleasure, since a life without self-denial soon becomes out of control in every area. Like fattened cattle ready to be slaughtered, the rich that James condemns had indulged themselves to the limit.

"You have condemned...put to death the righteous" (v. 6). This describes the next step in the sinful progression of the rich. Hoarding led to fraud, which led to self-indulgence. Finally, that overindulgence has consumed the rich to the point that they will do anything to sustain their lifestyle. "Condemned" comes from a word meaning "to sentence." The implication is that the rich were using the courts to commit judicial murder (2:6).

NOVEMBER 25

Ezekiel 41:1–42:20

41 Then he brought me to the nave and measured the side pillars; six cubits wide on each side *was* the width of the side pillar. ² The width of the entrance *was* ten cubits and the sides of the entrance *were* five cubits on each side. And he measured the length of the nave, forty cubits, and the width, twenty cubits. ³ Then he went inside and measured each side pillar of the door-way, two cubits, and the doorway, six cubits *high;* and the width of the doorway, seven cubits. ⁴ He measured its length, twenty cubits, and the width, twenty cubits, before the nave; and he said to me, "This is the most holy *place.*"

⁵ Then he measured the wall of the temple, six cubits; and the width of the side chambers, four cubits, all around about the house on every side. ⁶ The side chambers were in three stories, one above another, and thirty in each story; and the side chambers extended to the wall which *stood* on their inward side

all around, that they might be fastened, and not be fastened into the wall of the temple *itself.* 7 The side chambers surrounding the temple were wider at each successive story. Because the structure surrounding the temple went upward by stages on all sides of the temple, therefore the width of the temple *increased* as it went higher; and thus one went up from the lowest *story* to the highest by way of the second *story.* 8 I saw also that the house had a raised platform all around; the foundations of the side chambers were a full rod of six long cubits *in height.* 9 The thickness of the outer wall of the side chambers *was* five cubits. But the free space between the side chambers belonging to the temple 10 and the *outer* chambers *was* twenty cubits in width all around the temple on every side. 11 The doorways of the side chambers toward the free space *consisted of* one doorway toward the north and another doorway toward the south; and the width of the free space *was* five cubits all around.

12 The building that *was* in front of the separate area at the side toward the west *was* seventy cubits wide; and the wall of the building *was* five cubits thick all around, and its length *was* ninety cubits.

13 Then he measured the temple, a hundred cubits long; the separate area with the building and its walls *were* also a hundred cubits long. 14 Also the width of the front of the temple and *that of* the separate areas along the east *side* totaled a hundred cubits.

15 He measured the length of the building along the front of the separate area behind it, with a gallery on each side, a hundred cubits; *he* also *measured* the inner nave and the porches of the court. 16 The thresholds, the latticed windows and the galleries round about their three stories, opposite the threshold, were paneled with wood all around, and *from* the ground to the windows (but the windows were covered), 17 over the entrance, and to the inner house, and on the outside, and on all the wall all around inside and outside, by measurement. 18 It was carved with cherubim and palm trees; and a palm tree was between cherub and cherub, and every cherub had two faces, 19 a man's face toward the palm tree on one side and a young lion's face toward the palm tree on the other side; they were carved on all the house all around. 20 From the ground to above the entrance cherubim and palm trees were carved, as well as *on* the wall of the nave.

21 The doorposts of the nave were square; as for the front of the sanctuary, the appearance of one doorpost was like that of the other. 22 The altar *was* of wood, three cubits high and its length two cubits; its corners, its base and its sides *were* of wood. And he said to me, "This is the table that is before the LORD." 23 The nave and the sanctuary each had a double door. 24 Each of the doors had two leaves, two swinging leaves; two *leaves* for one door and two leaves for the other. 25 Also there were carved on them, on the doors of the nave, cherubim and palm trees like those carved on the walls; and *there was* a threshold of wood on the front of the porch outside. 26 *There were* latticed windows and palm trees on one side and on the other, on the sides of the porch; thus *were* the side chambers of the house and the thresholds.

42 Then he brought me out into the outer court, the way toward the north; and he brought me to the chamber which *was* opposite the separate area and opposite the building toward the north. 2 Along the length, *which was* a hundred cubits, *was* the north door; the width *was* fifty cubits. 3 Opposite the twenty *cubits* which belonged to the inner court, and opposite the pavement which belonged to the outer court, *was* gallery corresponding to gallery in three stories. 4 Before the chambers *was* an inner walk ten cubits wide, a way of one *hundred* cubits; and their openings *were* on the north. 5 Now the upper chambers *were* smaller because the galleries took more *space* away from them than from the lower and middle ones in the building. 6 For they *were* in three stories and had no pillars like the pillars of the courts; therefore *the upper chambers* were set back from the ground upward, more than the lower and middle ones. 7 As for the outer wall by the side of the chambers, toward the outer court facing the chambers, its length *was* fifty cubits. 8 For the length of the chambers which *were* in the outer court *was* fifty cubits; and behold, *the length of those* facing the temple *was* a hundred cubits. 9 Below these chambers *was* the entrance on the east side, as one enters them from the outer court.

10 In the thickness of the wall of the court toward the east, facing the separate area and facing the building, *there were* chambers. 11 The way in front of them *was* like the appearance of the chambers which *were* on the north, according to their length so was their width, and all their exits *were* both according to their arrangements and openings. 12 Corresponding to the openings of the chambers which were toward the south was an opening

at the head of the way, the way in front of the wall toward the east, as one enters them. ¹³Then he said to me, "The north chambers *and* the south chambers, which are opposite the separate area, they are the holy chambers where the priests who are near to the LORD shall eat the most holy things. There they shall lay the most holy things, the grain offering, the sin offering and the guilt offering; for the place is holy. ¹⁴When the priests enter, then they shall not go out into the outer court from the sanctuary without laying there their garments in which they minister, for they are holy. They shall put on other garments; then they shall approach that which is for the people."

¹⁵Now when he had finished measuring the inner house, he brought me out by the way of the gate which faced toward the east and measured it all around. ¹⁶He measured on the east side with the measuring reed five hundred reeds by the measuring reed. ¹⁷He measured on the north side five hundred reeds by the measuring reed. ¹⁸On the south side he measured five hundred reeds with the measuring reed. ¹⁹He turned to the west side *and* measured five hundred reeds with the measuring reed. ²⁰He measured it on the four sides; it had a wall all around, the length five hundred and the width five hundred, to divide between the holy and the profane.

Psalm 133:1–3

A Song of Ascents, of David.

B ehold, how good and
     how pleasant it is
   For brothers to dwell
     together in unity!
² It is like the precious oil
     upon the head,
   Coming down upon the beard,
   Even Aaron's beard,
   Coming down upon the
     edge of his robes.
³ It is like the dew of Hermon
   Coming down upon the
     mountains of Zion;
   For there the LORD commanded
     the blessing—life forever.

133:2 oil upon. Most likely refers to the anointing of Aaron as High Priest of the nation (Ex 29:7; 30:30), which would picture a rich spiritual blessing as a first priority.

Proverbs 29:6

⁶ By transgression an evil
     man is ensnared,
   But the righteous sings and rejoices.

1 Peter 1:1–25

1 Peter, an apostle of Jesus Christ,
   To those who reside as aliens, scattered throughout Pontus, Galatia, Cappadocia, Asia, and Bithynia, who are chosen ²according to the foreknowledge of God the Father, by the sanctifying work of the Spirit, to obey Jesus Christ and be sprinkled with His blood: May grace and peace be yours in the fullest measure.

³Blessed be the God and Father of our Lord Jesus Christ, who according to His great mercy has caused us to be born again to a living hope through the resurrection of Jesus Christ from the dead, ⁴to *obtain* an inheritance *which is* imperishable and undefiled and will not fade away, reserved in heaven for you, ⁵who are protected by the power of God through faith for a salvation ready to be revealed in the last time. ⁶In this you greatly rejoice, even though now for a little while, if necessary, you have been distressed by various trials, ⁷so that the proof of your faith, *being* more precious than gold which is perishable, even though tested by fire, may be found to result in praise and glory and honor at the revelation of Jesus Christ; ⁸and though you have not seen Him, you love Him, and though you

1:4 inheritance. Peter showed those persecuted Christians how to look past their troubles to their eternal inheritance. Life, righteousness, joy, peace, perfection, God's presence, Christ's glorious companionship, rewards, and all else God has planned is the Christian's heavenly inheritance (v. 5; Mt 25:34; Ac 26:18; Eph 1:11; Col 1:12; Heb 9:15; also Pss 16:5; 23; 26; 72; La 3:24). According to Ephesians 1:14, the indwelling Holy Spirit is the resident guarantee of that inheritance. **imperishable.** The inheritance is not subject to passing away, nor liable to decay. The word was used in secular Greek of something that was unravaged by an invading army (see Mt 6:19–21). **undefiled.** This word means unpolluted, unstained with evil. The undefiled inheritance of the Christian is in marked contrast to an earthly inheritance, all of which is corrupted and defiled. **will not fade away.** "Fading" was often used of flowers that wither and decay. Though earthly inheritances eventually fade away, the eternal inheritance of a Christian has no decaying elements.

1:7 proof of your faith. God's purpose in allowing trouble is to test the reality of one's faith. But the benefit of such a testing, or "fire," is immediately for the Christian, not God. When a believer comes through a trial still trusting the Lord, he is assured that his faith is genuine (Ge 22:1-12; Job 1:20-22). **revelation of Jesus Christ.** The revelation or unveiling of Christ refers to His second coming, particularly focusing on the time when He comes to call and reward His redeemed people (v. 13; 4:13; 1Co 1:7), i.e., the Rapture (1Th 4:13-18).

do not see Him now, but believe in Him, you greatly rejoice with joy inexpressible and full of glory, 9 obtaining as the outcome of your faith the salvation of your souls.

10 As to this salvation, the prophets who prophesied of the grace that *would come* to you made careful searches and inquiries, 11 seeking to know what person or time the Spirit of Christ within them was indicating as He predicted the sufferings of Christ and the glories to follow. 12 It was revealed to them that they were not serving themselves, but you, in these things which now have been announced to you through those who preached the gospel to you by the Holy Spirit sent from heaven—things into which angels long to look. 13 Therefore, prepare your minds for action, keep sober *in spirit*, fix your hope completely on the grace to be brought to you at the revelation of Jesus Christ. 14 As obedient children, do not be conformed to the former lusts *which*

were yours in your ignorance, 15 but like the Holy One who called you, be holy yourselves also in all *your* behavior; 16 because it is written, "YOU SHALL BE HOLY, FOR I AM HOLY."

17 If you address as Father the One who impartially judges according to each one's work, conduct yourselves in fear during the time of your stay *on earth;* 18 knowing that you were not redeemed with perishable things like silver or gold from your futile way of life inherited from your forefathers, 19 but with precious blood, as of a lamb unblemished and spotless, *the blood* of Christ. 20 For He was foreknown before the foundation of the world, but has appeared in these last times for the sake of you 21 who through Him are believers in God, who raised Him from the dead and gave Him glory, so that your faith and hope are in God.

22 Since you have in obedience to the truth purified your souls for a sincere love of the brethren, fervently love one another from the heart, 23 for you have been born again not of seed which is perishable but imperishable, *that is,* through the living and enduring word of God. 24 For,

"ALL FLESH IS LIKE GRASS,
AND ALL ITS GLORY LIKE THE
  FLOWER OF GRASS.
THE GRASS WITHERS,
AND THE FLOWER FALLS OFF,
25 BUT THE WORD OF THE LORD
  ENDURES FOREVER."

And this is the word which was preached to you.

DAY 25: Why did Peter write his first epistle?

When the city of Rome burned, the Romans believed that their emperor, Nero, had set the city on fire, probably because of his incredible lust to build. In order to build more, he had to destroy what already existed.

The Romans were totally devastated. Their culture, in a sense, went down with the city. All the religious elements of their life were destroyed—their great temples, shrines, and even their household idols were burned up. This had great religious implications because it made them believe that their deities had been unable to deal with this conflagration and were also victims of it. The people were homeless and hopeless. Many had been killed. Their bitter resentment was severe, so Nero realized that he had to redirect the hostility.

The emperor's chosen scapegoat was the Christians, who were already hated because they were associated with Jews, and because they were seen as being hostile to the Roman culture. Nero spread the word quickly that the Christians had set the fires. As a result, a vicious persecution against Christians began, and soon spread throughout the Roman Empire, touching places north of the Taurus mountains, like Pontus, Galatia, Cappadocia, Asia, and Bithynia (1:1), and impacting the Christians, whom Peter calls "aliens." These "aliens" were probably Gentiles, for the most part (1:14, 18; 2:9-10; 4:3), possibly led to Christ by Paul and his associates and established on Paul's teachings. But they needed spiritual strengthening because of their sufferings. Thus, the apostle Peter, under the inspiration of the Holy Spirit, wrote this epistle to strengthen them.

NOVEMBER 26

Ezekiel 43:1–44:31

43 Then he led me to the gate, the gate facing toward the east; ²and behold, the glory of the God of Israel was coming from the way of the east. And His voice was like the sound of many waters; and the earth shone with His glory. ³And *it was* like the appearance of the vision which I saw, like the vision which I saw when He came to destroy the city. And the visions *were* like the vision which I saw by the river Chebar; and I fell on my face. ⁴And the glory of the LORD came into the house by the way of the gate facing toward the east. ⁵And the Spirit lifted me up and brought me into the inner court; and behold, the glory of the LORD filled the house.

⁶Then I heard one speaking to me from the house, while a man was standing beside me. ⁷He said to me, "Son of man, *this is* the place of My throne and the place of the soles of My feet, where I will dwell among the sons of Israel forever. And the house of Israel will not again defile My holy name, neither they nor their kings, by their harlotry and by the corpses of their kings when they die, ⁸by setting their threshold by My threshold and their door post beside My door post, with *only* the wall between Me and them. And they have defiled My holy name by their abominations which they have committed. So I have consumed them in My anger. ⁹Now let them put away their harlotry and the corpses of their kings far from Me; and I will dwell among them forever.

¹⁰"As for you, son of man, describe the temple to the house of Israel, that they may be ashamed of their iniquities; and let them measure the plan. ¹¹If they are ashamed of all that they have done, make known to them the design of the house, its structure, its exits, its entrances, all its designs, all its statutes, and all its laws. And write *it* in their sight, so that they may observe its whole design and all its statutes and do them. ¹²This is the law of the house: its entire area on the top of the mountain all around *shall be* most holy. Behold, this is the law of the house.

¹³"And these are the measurements of the altar by cubits (the cubit being a cubit and a handbreadth): the base *shall be* a cubit and the width a cubit, and its border on its edge round about one span; and this *shall be* the height of the base of the altar. ¹⁴From the base on the ground to the lower ledge *shall be* two cubits and the width one cubit; and

from the smaller ledge to the larger ledge *shall be* four cubits and the width one cubit. ¹⁵The altar hearth *shall be* four cubits; and from the altar hearth shall extend upwards four horns. ¹⁶Now the altar hearth *shall be* twelve *cubits* long by twelve wide, square in its four sides. ¹⁷The ledge *shall be* fourteen *cubits* long by fourteen wide in its four sides, the border around it *shall be* half a cubit and its base *shall be* a cubit round about; and its steps shall face the east."

¹⁸And He said to me, "Son of man, thus says the Lord GOD, 'These are the statutes for the altar on the day it is built, to offer burnt offerings on it and to sprinkle blood on it. ¹⁹You shall give to the Levitical priests who are from the offspring of Zadok, who draw near to Me to minister to Me,' declares the Lord GOD, 'a young bull for a sin offering. ²⁰You shall take some of its blood and put it on its four horns and on the four corners of the ledge and on the border round about; thus you shall cleanse it and make atonement for it. ²¹You shall also take the bull for the sin offering, and it shall be burned in the appointed place of the house, outside the sanctuary.

²²'On the second day you shall offer a male goat without blemish for a sin offering, and they shall cleanse the altar as they cleansed *it* with the bull. ²³When you have finished cleansing *it*, you shall present a young bull without blemish and a ram without blemish from the flock. ²⁴You shall present them before the LORD, and the priests shall throw salt on them, and they shall offer them up as a burnt offering to the LORD. ²⁵For seven days you shall prepare daily a goat for a sin offering; also a young bull and a ram from the flock, without blemish, shall be prepared. ²⁶For seven days they shall make atonement for the altar and purify it; so shall they consecrate it. ²⁷When they have completed the days, it shall be that on the eighth day and onward, the priests shall offer your burnt offerings on the altar, and your peace offerings; and I will accept you,' declares the Lord GOD."

44 Then He brought me back by the way of the outer gate of the sanctuary, which faces the east; and it was shut. ²The LORD said to me, "This gate shall be shut; it shall not be opened, and no one shall enter by it, for the LORD God of Israel has entered by it; therefore it shall be shut. ³As for the prince, he shall sit in it as prince to eat bread before the LORD; he shall enter by way of the porch of the gate and shall go out by the same way."

⁴Then He brought me by way of the north gate to the front of the house; and I looked,

and behold, the glory of the LORD filled the house of the LORD, and I fell on my face. ⁵The LORD said to me, "Son of man, mark well, see with your eyes and hear with your ears all that I say to you concerning all the statutes of the house of the LORD and concerning all its laws; and mark well the entrance of the house, with all exits of the sanctuary. ⁶You shall say to the rebellious ones, to the house of Israel, 'Thus says the Lord GOD, "Enough of all your abominations, O house of Israel, ⁷when you brought in foreigners, uncircumcised in heart and uncircumcised in flesh, to be in My sanctuary to profane it, *even* My house, when you offered My food, the fat and the blood; for they made My covenant void—*this* in addition to all your abominations. ⁸And you have not kept charge of My holy things yourselves, but you have set *foreigners* to keep charge of My sanctuary."

⁹'Thus says the Lord GOD, "No foreigner uncircumcised in heart and uncircumcised in flesh, of all the foreigners who are among the sons of Israel, shall enter My sanctuary. ¹⁰But the Levites who went far from Me when Israel went astray, who went astray from Me after their idols, shall bear the punishment for their iniquity. ¹¹Yet they shall be ministers in My sanctuary, having oversight at the gates of the house and ministering in the house; they shall slaughter the burnt offering and the sacrifice for the people, and they shall stand before them to minister to them. ¹²Because they ministered to them before their

44:5–9 mark well the entrance. Since the Lord's glory fills the temple, it is sanctified (v. 4), and God is particular about what kind of people worship there. Sins of the past, as in chaps. 8–11, must not be repeated, and if they are they will exclude their perpetrators from the temple. Only the circumcised in heart may enter (Dt 30:6; Jer 4:4; Ro 2:25–29), whether of Israel or another nation (vv. 7, 9). Many other peoples than Jews will go into the kingdom in unresurrected bodies, because they have believed in Jesus Christ and were ready for His coming. They will escape His deadly judgment and populate and reproduce in the 1,000-year kingdom. Such circumcision pertains to a heart which is sincere about removing sin and being devoted to the Lord (Jer 29:13). In the Millennium, a Jew with an uncircumcised heart will be considered a foreigner (v. 9). "Uncircumcised in flesh" refers to sinners and "foreigners" identifies rejecters of the true God.

idols and became a stumbling block of iniquity to the house of Israel, therefore I have sworn against them," declares the Lord GOD, "that they shall bear *the punishment for* their iniquity. ¹³And they shall not come near to Me to serve as a priest to Me, nor come near to any of My holy things, to the things that are most holy; but they will bear their shame and their abominations which they have committed. ¹⁴Yet I will appoint them to keep charge of the house, of all its service and of all that shall be done in it.

¹⁵"But the Levitical priests, the sons of Zadok, who kept charge of My sanctuary when the sons of Israel went astray from Me, shall come near to Me to minister to Me; and they shall stand before Me to offer Me the fat and the blood," declares the Lord GOD. ¹⁶"They shall enter My sanctuary; they shall come near to My table to minister to Me and keep My charge. ¹⁷It shall be that when they enter at the gates of the inner court, they shall be clothed with linen garments; and wool shall not be on them while they are ministering in the gates of the inner court and in the house. ¹⁸Linen turbans shall be on their heads and linen undergarments shall be on their loins; they shall not gird themselves with *anything which makes them* sweat. ¹⁹When they go out into the outer court, into the outer court to the people, they shall put off their garments in which they have been ministering and lay them in the holy chambers; then they shall put on other garments so that they will not transmit holiness to the people with their garments. ²⁰Also they shall not shave their heads, yet they shall not let their locks grow long; they shall only trim *the hair of* their heads. ²¹Nor shall any of the priests drink wine when they enter the inner court. ²²And they shall not marry a widow or a divorced woman but shall take virgins from the offspring of the house of Israel, or a widow who is the widow of a priest. ²³Moreover, they shall teach My people *the difference* between the holy and the profane, and cause them to discern between the unclean and the clean. ²⁴In a dispute they shall take their stand to judge; they shall judge it according to My ordinances. They shall also keep My laws and My statutes in all My appointed feasts and sanctify My sabbaths. ²⁵They shall not go to a dead person to defile *themselves;* however, for father, for mother, for son, for daughter, for brother, or for a sister who has not had a husband, they may defile themselves. ²⁶After he is cleansed, seven days shall elapse for him. ²⁷On the day that he goes into the sanctuary, into the inner

court to minister in the sanctuary, he shall offer his sin offering," declares the Lord GOD.

²⁸ "And it shall be with regard to an inheritance for them, *that* I am their inheritance; and you shall give them no possession in Israel—I am their possession. ²⁹ They shall eat the grain offering, the sin offering and the guilt offering; and every devoted thing in Israel shall be theirs. ³⁰ The first of all the first fruits of every kind and every contribution of every kind, from all your contributions, shall be for the priests; you shall also give to the priest the first of your dough to cause a blessing to rest on your house. ³¹ The priests shall not eat any bird or beast that has died a natural death or has been torn to pieces.

Psalm 134:1-3
A Song of Ascents.

Behold, bless the LORD, all
  servants of the LORD,
Who serve by night in the
  house of the LORD!
2 Lift up your hands to the sanctuary
  And bless the LORD.
3 May the LORD bless you from Zion,
  He who made heaven and earth.

Proverbs 29:7

7 The righteous is concerned for
    the rights of the poor,
  The wicked does not understand
    such concern.

1 Peter 2:1-25

2 Therefore, putting aside all malice and all deceit and hypocrisy and envy and all slander, ² like newborn babies, long for the pure milk of the word, so that by it you may grow in respect to salvation, ³ if you have tasted the kindness of the Lord.

2:2 long for the pure milk of the word. Spiritual growth is always marked by a craving for and a delight in God's Word with the intensity with which a baby craves milk (Job 23:12; Pss 1:1-2; 19:7-11; 119:16, 24, 35, 47-48, 72, 92, 97, 103, 111, 113, 127, 159, 167, 174; Jer 15:16). A Christian develops a desire for the truth of God's Word by: 1) remembering his life's source (1:25; see Is 55:10-11; Jn 15:3; Heb 4:12); 2) eliminating sin from his life (v. 1); 3) admitting his need for God's truth (v. 2, "like newborn babies"; see Mt 4:4); 4) pursuing spiritual growth (v. 2, "by it you may grow"); and 5) surveying his blessings (v. 3, "kindness of the Lord").

⁴ And coming to Him as to a living stone which has been rejected by men, but is choice and precious in the sight of God, ⁵ you also, as living stones, are being built up as a spiritual house for a holy priesthood, to offer up spiritual sacrifices acceptable to God through Jesus Christ. ⁶ For *this* is contained in Scripture:

"Behold, I lay in Zion a choice
  stone, a precious corner *stone*,
And he who believes in Him
  will not be disappointed."

⁷ This precious value, then, is for you who believe; but for those who disbelieve,

"The stone which the
  builders rejected,
This became the very corner *stone*,"

⁸ and,

"A stone of stumbling and
  a rock of offense";

for they stumble because they are disobedient to the word, and to this *doom* they were also appointed.

⁹ But you are a chosen race, a royal priesthood, a holy nation, a people for *God's* own possession, so that you may proclaim the excellencies of Him who has called you out of darkness into His marvelous light; ¹⁰ for you once were not a people, but now you are the people of God; you had not received mercy, but now you have received mercy.

¹¹ Beloved, I urge you as aliens and strangers to abstain from fleshly lusts which wage war against the soul. ¹² Keep your behavior

2:11 abstain from fleshly lusts. Perhaps more literally "hold yourself away from fleshly lusts." In order to have an impact on the world for God, Christians must be disciplined in an inward and private way by avoiding the desires of the fallen nature (see Gal 5:19-21, where "fleshly lusts" include much more than sexual temptations). **which wage war against the soul.** "War," i.e., to carry on a military campaign. Fleshly lusts are personified as if they were an army of rebels or guerrillas who incessantly search out and try to destroy the Christian's joy, peace and usefulness (4:2-3).

excellent among the Gentiles, so that in the thing in which they slander you as evildoers, they may because of your good deeds, as they observe *them*, glorify God in the day of visitation.

¹³ Submit yourselves for the Lord's sake to every human institution, whether to a king as the one in authority, ¹⁴ or to governors as sent by him for the punishment of evildoers and the praise of those who do right. ¹⁵ For such is the will of God that by doing right you may

---

2:13 Submit yourselves. "Submit" is a military term meaning "to arrange in military fashion under the commander," "to put oneself in an attitude of submission." As citizens in the world and under civil law and authority, God's people are to live in a humble, submissive way in the midst of any hostile, godless, slandering society (vv. 21–23; Pr 24:21; Jer 29:4–14; Mt 22:21; Ro 13:1ff., 1Ti 2:1; Heb 10:32–34). **for the Lord's sake.** Though the Christian's true citizenship is in heaven (Php 3:20) he still must live as an obedient citizen in this world so that God will be honored and glorified. Rebellious conduct by a Christian brings dishonor on Christ.

---

silence the ignorance of foolish men. ¹⁶ *Act* as free men, and do not use your freedom as a covering for evil, but *use it* as bondslaves of God. ¹⁷ Honor all people, love the brotherhood, fear God, honor the king.

¹⁸ Servants, be submissive to your masters with all respect, not only to those who are good and gentle, but also to those who are unreasonable. ¹⁹ For this *finds* favor, if for the sake of conscience toward God a person bears up under sorrows when suffering unjustly. ²⁰ For what credit is there if, when you sin and are harshly treated, you endure it with patience? But if when you do what is right and suffer *for it* you patiently endure it, this *finds* favor with God. ²¹ For you have been called for this purpose, since Christ also suffered for you, leaving you an example for you to follow in His steps, ²² WHO COMMITTED NO SIN, NOR WAS ANY DECEIT FOUND IN HIS MOUTH; ²³ and while being reviled, He did not revile in return; while suffering, He uttered no threats, but kept entrusting *Himself* to Him who judges righteously; ²⁴ and He Himself bore our sins in His body on the cross, so that we might die to sin and live to righteousness; for by His wounds you were healed. ²⁵ For you were continually straying like sheep, but now you have returned to the Shepherd and Guardian of your souls.

DAY 26: How are Christians described in 1 Peter 2:9?

Believers there are described as a "CHOSEN RACE." Peter uses Old Testament concepts to emphasize the privileges of New Testament Christians (Dt 7:6–8). In strong contrast to the disobedient who are appointed by God to wrath (v. 8), Christians are chosen by God to salvation (1:2).

They are also called a "royal PRIESTHOOD." The concept of a kingly priesthood is drawn from Exodus 19:6. Israel temporarily forfeited this privilege because of its apostasy and because its wicked leaders executed the Messiah. At the present time, the church is a royal priesthood united with the royal priest, Jesus Christ. A royal priesthood is not only a priesthood that belongs to and serves the king but is also a priesthood which exercises rule. This will ultimately be fulfilled in Christ's future kingdom (1Co 6:1–4; Rev 5:10; 20:6).

And they are described as a "HOLY NATION." Another allusion to Exodus 19:6 (Lv 19:2; 20:26; Dt 7:6; Is 62:12). Tragically, Israel temporarily forfeited the great privilege of being the unique people of God through unbelief. Until Israel's future acceptance of its Messiah, God has replaced the nation with the church. "A PEOPLE FOR God's OWN POSSESSION." This combines phraseology found in Exodus 19:5; Isaiah 43:21; Malachi 3:17. "That you may proclaim the excellencies of Him who has called." To "proclaim" means to tell forth, to tell something not otherwise known. "Excellencies " are praises, virtues, eminent qualities.

NOVEMBER 27

Ezekiel 45:1–46:24

45 "And when you divide by lot the land for inheritance, you shall offer an allotment to the LORD, a holy portion of the land; the length shall be the length of 25,000

cubits, and the width shall be 20,000. It shall be holy within all its boundary round about. ² Out of this there shall be for the holy place a square round about five hundred by five hundred *cubits,* and fifty cubits for its open space round about. ³ From this area you shall measure a length of 25,000 *cubits* and a width of 10,000 *cubits;* and in it shall be the sanctuary, the most holy place. ⁴It shall be the holy portion of the land; it shall be for the priests, the ministers of the sanctuary, who come near to minister to the LORD, and it shall be a place for their houses and a holy place for the sanctuary. ⁵An area 25,000 cubits in length and 10,000 in width shall be for the Levites, the ministers of the house, and for their possession cities to dwell in.

⁶"You shall give the city possession of an area 5,000 cubits wide and 25,000 cubits long, alongside the allotment of the holy portion; it shall be for the whole house of Israel.

⁷"The prince shall have land on either side of the holy allotment and the property of the city, adjacent to the holy allotment and the property of the city, on the west side toward the west and on the east side toward the east, and in length comparable to one of the portions, from the west border to the east border. ⁸This shall be his land for a possession in Israel; so My princes shall no longer oppress My people, but they shall give the rest of the land to the house of Israel according to their tribes."

⁹'Thus says the Lord GOD, "Enough, you princes of Israel; put away violence and destruction, and practice justice and righteousness. Stop your expropriations from My people," declares the Lord GOD.

¹⁰"You shall have just balances, a just ephah and a just bath. ¹¹The ephah and the bath shall be the same quantity, so that the bath will contain a tenth of a homer and the ephah a tenth of a homer; their standard shall be according to the homer. ¹²The shekel shall be twenty gerahs; twenty shekels, twenty-five shekels, and fifteen shekels shall be your maneh.

45:9–12 The leaders of the land are urged to be thoroughly honest in their commercial dealings. This warning shows that there will be sin in the Millennium. The believing Jews who entered the 1,000-year reign of Christ on earth and inherited the promised kingdom will be fully human and capable of such sins. There also will be children who do not necessarily believe, as the final rebellion against King Messiah and His temple proves (Rev 20:7–9).

---

¹³"This is the offering that you shall offer: a sixth of an ephah from a homer of wheat; a sixth of an ephah from a homer of barley; ¹⁴and the prescribed portion of oil (namely, the bath of oil), a tenth of a bath from each kor (which is ten baths or a homer, for ten baths are a homer); ¹⁵and one sheep from each flock of two hundred from the watering places of Israel—for a grain offering, for a burnt offering and for peace offerings, to make atonement for them," declares the Lord GOD. ¹⁶"All the people of the land shall give to this offering for the prince in Israel. ¹⁷It shall be the prince's part to provide the burnt offerings, the grain offerings and the drink offerings, at the feasts, on the new moons and on the sabbaths, at all the appointed feasts of the house of Israel; he shall provide the sin offering, the grain offering, the burnt offering and the peace offerings, to make atonement for the house of Israel."

¹⁸'Thus says the Lord GOD, "In the first month, on the first of the month, you shall take a young bull without blemish and cleanse the sanctuary. ¹⁹The priest shall take some of the blood from the sin offering and put it on the door posts of the house, on the four corners of the ledge of the altar and on the posts of the gate of the inner court. ²⁰Thus you shall do on the seventh day of the month for everyone who goes astray or is naive; so you shall make atonement for the house.

²¹"In the first month, on the fourteenth day of the month, you shall have the Passover, a feast of seven days; unleavened bread shall be eaten. ²²On that day the prince shall provide for himself and all the people of the land a bull for a sin offering. ²³During the seven days of the feast he shall provide as a burnt offering to the LORD seven bulls and seven rams without blemish on every day of the seven days, and a male goat daily for a sin offering. ²⁴He shall provide as a grain offering an ephah with a bull, an ephah with a ram and a hin of oil with an ephah. ²⁵In the seventh month, on the fifteenth day of the month, at the feast, he shall provide like this, seven days for the sin offering, the burnt offering, the grain offering and the oil."

46 'Thus says the Lord GOD, "The gate of the inner court facing east shall be shut the six working days; but it shall be opened on the sabbath day and opened on the day of the new moon. ²The prince shall enter by way of the porch of the gate from outside and stand by the post of the gate. Then the priests shall provide his burnt offering and his peace offerings, and he shall worship at the threshold of the gate and then go out; but the gate shall not be shut until the evening. ³The people of the land shall also worship at the doorway of that gate before the LORD on the sabbaths and on the new moons. ⁴The burnt offering which the prince shall offer to the LORD on the sabbath day shall be six lambs without blemish and a ram without blemish; ⁵and the grain offering shall be an ephah with the ram, and the grain offering with the lambs as much as he is able to give, and a hin of oil with an ephah. ⁶On the day of the new moon *he shall offer* a young bull without blemish, also six lambs and a ram, *which* shall be without blemish. ⁷And he shall provide a grain offering, an ephah with the bull and an ephah with the ram, and with the lambs as much as he is able, and a hin of oil with an ephah. ⁸When the prince enters, he shall go in by way of the porch of the gate and go out by the same way. ⁹But when the people of the land come before the LORD at the appointed feasts, he who enters by way of the north gate to worship shall go out by way of the south gate. And he who enters by way of the south gate shall go out by way of the north gate. No one shall return by way of the gate by which he entered but shall go straight out. ¹⁰When they go in, the prince shall go in among them; and when they go out, he shall go out.

¹¹ "At the festivals and the appointed feasts the grain offering shall be an ephah with a bull and an ephah with a ram, and with the lambs as much as one is able to give, and a hin of oil with an ephah. ¹²When the prince provides a freewill offering, a burnt offering, or peace offerings *as* a freewill offering to the LORD, the gate facing east shall be opened for him. And he shall provide his burnt offering and his peace offerings as he does on the sabbath day. Then he shall go out, and the gate shall be shut after he goes out.

¹³ "And you shall provide a lamb a year old without blemish for a burnt offering to the LORD daily; morning by morning you shall provide it. ¹⁴Also you shall provide a grain offering with it morning by morning, a sixth of an ephah and a third of a hin of oil to moisten the fine flour, a grain offering to the LORD continually by a perpetual ordinance. ¹⁵Thus they shall provide the lamb, the grain offering and the oil, morning by morning, for a continual burnt offering."

¹⁶ 'Thus says the Lord GOD, "If the prince gives a gift *out of* his inheritance to any of his sons, it shall belong to his sons; it is their possession by inheritance. ¹⁷But if he gives a gift from his inheritance to one of his servants, it shall be his until the year of liberty; then it shall return to the prince. His inheritance *shall be* only his sons'; it shall

belong to them. ¹⁸The prince shall not take from the people's inheritance, thrusting them out of their possession; he shall give his sons inheritance from his own possession so that My people will not be scattered, anyone from his possession." ' "

¹⁹Then he brought me through the entrance, which *was* at the side of the gate, into the holy chambers for the priests, which faced north; and behold, there *was* a place at the extreme rear toward the west. ²⁰He said to me, "This is the place where the priests shall boil the guilt offering and the sin offering *and* where they shall bake the grain offering, in order that they may not bring *them* out into the outer court to transmit holiness to the people."

²¹Then he brought me out into the outer court and led me across to the four corners of the court; and behold, in every corner of the court *there was* a *small* court. ²²In the four corners of the court *there were* enclosed courts, forty *cubits* long and thirty wide; these four in the corners *were* the same size. ²³ *There was* a row of *masonry* round about in them, around the four of them, and boiling places were made under the rows round about. ²⁴Then he said to me, "These are the boiling places where the ministers of the house shall boil the sacrifices of the people."

Psalm 135:1–7

Praise the LORD!
Praise the name of the LORD;
Praise *Him,* O servants of the LORD,
2   You who stand in the
    house of the LORD,
  In the courts of the house of our God!
3   Praise the LORD, for the LORD is good;
  Sing praises to His name,
    for it is lovely.
4   For the LORD has chosen
    Jacob for Himself,
  Israel for His own possession.

5   For I know that the LORD is great
  And that our Lord is above all gods.
6   Whatever the LORD pleases, He does,
  In heaven and in earth, in the
    seas and in all deeps.
7   He causes the vapors to ascend
    from the ends of the earth;
  Who makes lightnings for the rain,
  Who brings forth the wind
    from His treasuries.

Proverbs 29:8

8   Scorners set a city aflame,
  But wise men turn away anger.

1 Peter 3:1–22

3 In the same way, you wives, be submissive to your own husbands so that even if any *of them* are disobedient to the word, they may be won without a word by the behavior of their wives, ²as they observe your chaste and respectful behavior. ³Your adornment must not be *merely* external—braiding the hair, and wearing gold jewelry, or putting on dresses; ⁴but *let it be* the hidden person of the heart, with the imperishable quality of a gentle and quiet spirit, which is precious in the sight of God. ⁵For in this way in former times the holy women also, who hoped in God, used to adorn themselves, being submissive to their own husbands; ⁶just as Sarah obeyed Abraham, calling him lord, and you have become her children if you do what is right without being frightened by any fear.

3:1 In the same way. In chap. 2, Peter taught that living successfully as a Christian in a hostile world would require relating properly in two places: the civil society (2:13–17), and the workplace (2:18–25). At the start of this chapter, he added two more places: the family (vv. 1–7) and the local church (vv. 8–9). **be submissive.** Peter insisted that if Christians are to be a witness for their Lord, they must submit not only to the civil, but also to the social order which God has designed. **own husbands.** Women are not inferior to men in any way, any more than submissive Christians are inferior to pagan rulers or non-Christian bosses (Gal 3:28). But wives have been given a role which puts them in submission to the headship which resides in their own husbands (1Co 11:1–9; Eph 5:22; Col 3:18; Titus 2:4–5).

⁷You husbands in the same way, live with *your wives* in an understanding way, as with someone weaker, since she is a woman; and show her honor as a fellow heir of the grace of life, so that your prayers will not be hindered.

⁸To sum up, all of you be harmonious, sympathetic, brotherly, kindhearted, and humble in spirit; ⁹not returning evil for evil or insult for insult, but giving a blessing instead; for you were called for the very purpose that you might inherit a blessing. ¹⁰For,

"THE ONE WHO DESIRES LIFE, TO
  LOVE AND SEE GOOD DAYS,
MUST KEEP HIS TONGUE FROM EVIL AND
  HIS LIPS FROM SPEAKING DECEIT.

3:7 husbands in the same way. Submission is the responsibility of a Christian husband as well (Eph 5:21). Though not submitting to his wife as a leader, a believing husband must submit to the loving duty of being sensitive to the needs, fears, and feelings of his wife. In other words, a Christian husband needs to subordinate his needs to hers, whether she is a Christian or not. Peter specifically notes consideration, chivalry, and companionship. **someone weaker.** While she is fully equal in Christ and not inferior spiritually because she is a woman (Gal 3:28), she is physically weaker, and in need of protection, provision, and strength from her husband. **fellow heir of the grace of life.** Here the "grace of life" is not salvation, but marriage—the best relationship earthly life has to offer. The husband must cultivate companionship and fellowship with his wife, Christian or not (Ecc 9:9).

¹¹ "HE MUST TURN AWAY FROM
    EVIL AND DO GOOD;
  HE MUST SEEK PEACE AND PURSUE IT.
¹² "FOR THE EYES OF THE LORD ARE
    TOWARD THE RIGHTEOUS,
  AND HIS EARS ATTEND TO
    THEIR PRAYER,
  BUT THE FACE OF THE LORD IS
    AGAINST THOSE WHO DO EVIL."

¹³Who is there to harm you if you prove zealous for what is good? ¹⁴But even if you should suffer for the sake of righteousness, you are blessed. AND DO NOT FEAR THEIR INTIMIDATION, AND DO NOT BE TROUBLED, ¹⁵but sanctify Christ as Lord in your hearts, always

3:15 sanctify Christ as Lord in your hearts. The meaning is "set apart in your hearts Christ as Lord." The heart is the sanctuary in which He prefers to be worshiped. Live in submissive communion with the Lord Jesus, loving and obeying Him—and you have nothing to fear. **always *being* ready to make a defense.** The Eng. word "apologetics" comes from the Greek word here translated "defense." Peter is using the word in an informal sense (Php 1:16–17) and is insisting that the believer must understand what he believes and why one is a Christian, and then be able to articulate one's beliefs humbly, thoughtfully, reasonably, and biblically. **the hope that is in you.** Salvation with its anticipation of eternal glory.

being ready to make a defense to everyone who asks you to give an account for the hope that is in you, yet with gentleness and reverence; [16] and keep a good conscience so that in the thing in which you are slandered, those who revile your good behavior in Christ will be put to shame. [17] For it is better, if God should will it so, that you suffer for doing what is right rather than for doing what is wrong. [18] For Christ also died for sins once for all, *the* just for *the* unjust, so that He might bring us to God, having been put to death in the flesh, but made alive in the spirit; [19] in which also He went and made proclamation to the spirits *now* in prison, [20] who once were disobedient, when the patience of God kept waiting in the days of Noah, during the construction of the ark, in which a few, that is, eight persons, were brought safely through *the* water. [21] Corresponding to that, baptism now saves you—not the removal of dirt from the flesh, but an appeal to God for a good conscience—through the resurrection of Jesus Christ, [22] who is at the right hand of God, having gone into heaven, after angels and authorities and powers had been subjected to Him.

DAY 27: How does Peter use familiar terms such as spirit, abyss, flood, and baptism in 1 Peter 3:18–22?

This passage proves to be one of the most difficult texts in the New Testament to translate and interpret. The line between Old Testament allusions and New Testament applications gets blurred. Peter's overall purpose of this passage, which was to encourage his readers in their suffering, must be kept in mind during interpretation. The apostle repeatedly reminded them that even Christ suffered unjustly because it was God's will (vv. 17–18) and accomplished God's purposes.

Therefore, although Jesus experienced a violent physical execution that terminated His earthly life when He was "put to death in the flesh" (v. 18; Heb 5:7), nevertheless He was "made alive in the spirit" (v. 18). This is not a reference to the Holy Spirit, but to Jesus' true inner life, His own spirit. Contrasted with His flesh (humanness) which was dead for three days, His spirit (Deity) remained alive, literally "in spirit" (see Lk 23:46).

Part of God's purpose in Christ's death involved His activities between His death and resurrection. His living spirit went to the demon spirits bound in the Abyss and proclaimed victory in spite of death. Peter further explained that the Abyss is inhabited by bound demons that have been there since the time of Noah. They were sent there because they overstepped the limits of God's tolerance with their wickedness. Not even 120 years of Noah's example and preaching had stemmed the tide of wickedness in his time (Ge 6:1–8). Thus, God bound these demons permanently in the Abyss until their final sentencing.

Peter's analogy spotlights the ministry of Jesus Christ in saving us as surely as the ark saved Noah's family. He is not referring to water baptism here but to a figurative immersion in Christ that keeps us safe from the flood of God's sure judgment. The resurrection of Christ demonstrates God's acceptance of Christ's substitutionary death for the sins of those who believe (Ac 2:30–31; Ro 1:4). God's judgment fell on Christ just as the judgment of the floodwaters fell on the ark. The believer who is in Christ is thus in the ark of safety that will sail over the waters of judgment into eternal glory (Ro 6:1–4).

NOVEMBER 28

Ezekiel 47:1–48:35

47 Then he brought me back to the door of the house; and behold, water was flowing from under the threshold of the house toward the east, for the house faced east. And the water was flowing down from under, from the right side of the house, from south of the altar. [2] He brought me out by way of the north gate and led me around on the outside to the outer gate by way of *the gate* that faces east. And behold, water was trickling from the south side.

[3] When the man went out toward the east with a line in his hand, he measured a thousand cubits, and he led me through the water, water *reaching* the ankles. [4] Again he measured a thousand and led me through the water, water *reaching* the knees. Again he measured a thousand and led me through *the water*, water *reaching* the loins. [5] Again he measured a thousand; *and it was* a river that I could not ford, for the water had risen, *enough* water to swim in, a river that could not be forded. [6] He said to me, "Son of man, have you seen *this?*" Then he brought me back to the bank of the river. [7] Now when I had returned, behold, on the bank of the river

there *were* very many trees on the one side and on the other. [8] Then he said to me, "These waters go out toward the eastern region and go down into the Arabah; then they go toward the sea, being made to flow into the sea, and the waters *of the sea* become fresh. [9] It will come about that every living creature which swarms in every place where the river goes, will live. And there will be very many fish, for these waters go there and *the others* become fresh; so everything will live where the river goes. [10] And it will come about that fishermen will stand beside it; from Engedi to Eneglaim there will be a place for the spreading of nets. Their fish will be according to their kinds, like the fish of the Great Sea, very many. [11] But its swamps and marshes will not become fresh; they will be left for salt. [12] By the river on its bank, on one side and on the other, will grow all *kinds of* trees for food. Their leaves will not wither and their fruit will not fail. They will bear every month because their water flows from the sanctuary, and their fruit will be for food and their leaves for healing."

[13] Thus says the Lord GOD, "This *shall be* the boundary by which you shall divide the land for an inheritance among the twelve tribes of Israel; Joseph *shall have* two portions. [14] You shall divide it for an inheritance, each one equally with the other; for I swore to give it to your forefathers, and this land shall fall to you as an inheritance.

[15] "This *shall be* the boundary of the land: on the north side, from the Great Sea *by* the way of Hethlon, to the entrance of Zedad; [16] Hamath, Berothah, Sibraim, which is between the border of Damascus and the border of Hamath; Hazer-hatticon, which is by the border of Hauran. [17] The boundary shall extend from the sea *to* Hazar-enan *at* the border of Damascus, and on the north toward the north is the border of Hamath. This is the north side.

[18] "The east side, from between Hauran, Damascus, Gilead and the land of Israel, *shall be* the Jordan; from the *north* border to the eastern sea you shall measure. This is the east side.

[19] "The south side toward the south *shall extend* from Tamar as far as the waters of Meribath-kadesh, to the brook *of Egypt and* to the Great Sea. This is the south side toward the south.

[20] "The west side *shall be* the Great Sea, from the *south* border to a point opposite Lebo-hamath. This is the west side.

[21] "So you shall divide this land among yourselves according to the tribes of Israel.

[22] You shall divide it by lot for an inheritance among yourselves and among the aliens who stay in your midst, who bring forth sons in your midst. And they shall be to you as the native-born among the sons of Israel; they shall be allotted an inheritance with you among the tribes of Israel. [23] And in the tribe with which the alien stays, there you shall give *him* his inheritance," declares the Lord GOD.

48 "Now these are the names of the tribes: from the northern extremity, beside the way of Hethlon to Lebo-hamath, *as far as* Hazar-enan *at* the border of Damascus, toward the north beside Hamath, running from east to west, Dan, one *portion*. [2] Beside the border of Dan, from the east side to the west side, Asher, one *portion*. [3] Beside the border of Asher, from the east side to the west side, Naphtali, one *portion*. [4] Beside the border of Naphtali, from the east side to the west side, Manasseh, one *portion*. [5] Beside the border of Manasseh, from the east side to the west side, Ephraim, one *portion*. [6] Beside the border of Ephraim, from the east side to the west side, Reuben, one *portion*. [7] Beside the border of Reuben, from the east side to the west side, Judah, one *portion*.

[8] "And beside the border of Judah, from the east side to the west side, shall be the allotment which you shall set apart, 25,000 *cubits* in width, and in length like one of the portions, from the east side to the west side; and the sanctuary shall be in the middle of it. [9] The allotment that you shall set apart to the LORD *shall be* 25,000 *cubits* in length and 10,000 in width. [10] The holy allotment shall be for these, *namely* for the priests, toward the north 25,000 *cubits in length*, toward the west 10,000 in width, toward the east 10,000 in width, and toward the south 25,000 in length; and the sanctuary of the LORD shall be in its midst. [11] *It shall be* for the priests who are sanctified of the sons of Zadok, who have kept My charge, who did not go astray when the sons of Israel went astray as the Levites went astray. [12] It shall be an allotment to them from the allotment of the land, a most holy place, by the border of the Levites. [13] Alongside the border of the priests the Levites *shall have* 25,000 *cubits* in length and 10,000 in width. The whole length *shall be* 25,000 *cubits* and the width 10,000. [14] Moreover, they shall not sell or exchange any of it, or alienate this choice *portion* of land; for it is holy to the LORD.

[15] "The remainder, 5,000 *cubits* in width and 25,000 in length, shall be for common use

for the city, for dwellings and for open spaces; and the city shall be in its midst. 16 These *shall be* its measurements: the north side 4,500 *cubits,* the south side 4,500 *cubits,* the east side 4,500 *cubits,* and the west side 4,500 *cubits.* 17 The city shall have open spaces: on the north 250 *cubits,* on the south 250 *cubits,* on the east 250 *cubits,* and on the west 250 *cubits.* 18 The remainder of the length alongside the holy allotment shall be 10,000 *cubits* toward the east and 10,000 toward the west; and it shall be alongside the holy allotment. And its produce shall be food for the workers of the city. 19 The workers of the city, out of all the tribes of Israel, shall cultivate it. 20 The whole allotment *shall be* 25,000 by 25,000 *cubits;* you shall set apart the holy allotment, a square, with the property of the city.

21 "The remainder *shall be* for the prince, on the one side and on the other of the holy allotment and of the property of the city; in front of the 25,000 *cubits* of the allotment toward the east border and westward in front of the 25,000 toward the west border, alongside the portions, *it shall be* for the prince. And the holy allotment and the sanctuary of the house shall be in the middle of it. 22 Exclusive of the property of the Levites and the property of the city, *which* are in the middle of that which belongs to the prince, *everything* between the border of Judah and the border of Benjamin shall be for the prince.

23 "As for the rest of the tribes: from the east side to the west side, Benjamin, one *portion.* 24 Beside the border of Benjamin, from the east side to the west side, Simeon, one *portion.* 25 Beside the border of Simeon, from the east side to the west side, Issachar, one *portion.* 26 Beside the border of Issachar, from the east side to the west side, Zebulun, one *portion.* 27 Beside the border of Zebulun, from the east side to the west side, Gad, one *portion.* 28 And beside the border of Gad, at the south side toward the south, the border shall be from Tamar to the waters of Meribath-kadesh, to the brook *of Egypt,* to the Great Sea. 29 This is the land which you shall divide by lot to the tribes of Israel for an inheritance, and these are their *several* portions," declares the Lord GOD.

30 "These are the exits of the city: on the north side, 4,500 *cubits* by measurement, 31 shall be the gates of the city, named for the tribes of Israel, three gates toward the north: the gate of Reuben, one; the gate of Judah, one; the gate of Levi, one. 32 On the east side, 4,500 *cubits,* shall be three gates: the gate of Joseph, one; the gate of Benjamin, one; the gate of Dan, one. 33 On the south side, 4,500 *cubits* by measurement, shall be three gates: the gate of Simeon, one; the gate of Issachar, one; the gate of Zebulun, one. 34 On the west side, 4,500 *cubits, shall be* three gates: the gate of Gad, one; the gate of Asher, one; the gate of Naphtali, one. 35 *The city shall be* 18,000 *cubits* round about; and the name of the city from *that* day *shall be,* 'The LORD is there.'"

48:35 the name. The city is called YHWH Shammah, "The LORD Is there." The departed glory of God (chaps. 8–11) has returned (44:1–2), and His dwelling, the temple, is in the very center of the district given over to the Lord. With this final note, all of the unconditional promises which God had made to Israel in the Abrahamic Covenant (Ge 12); the Priestly Covenant (Nu 25); the Davidic Covenant (2Sa 7); and the New Covenant (Jer 31) have been fulfilled. So this final verse provides the consummation of Israel's history—the returned presence of God!

Psalm 135:8–14

8 He smote the firstborn of Egypt,
Both of man and beast.
9 He sent signs and wonders
into your midst, O Egypt,
Upon Pharaoh and all his servants.
10 He smote many nations
And slew mighty kings,
11 Sihon, king of the Amorites,
And Og, king of Bashan,
And all the kingdoms of Canaan;
12 And He gave their land as a heritage,
A heritage to Israel His people.
13 Your name, O LORD, is everlasting,
Your remembrance, O LORD,
throughout all generations.
14 For the LORD will judge His people
And will have compassion
on His servants.

Proverbs 29:9

9 When a wise man has a controversy
with a foolish man,
The foolish man either rages or
laughs, and there is no rest.

29:9 controversy. A fool may respond to wisdom with anger or laughter, but in either case, no agreement can be reached.

1 Peter 4:1-19

4 Therefore, since Christ has suffered in the flesh, arm yourselves also with the same purpose, because he who has suffered in the flesh has ceased from sin, ² so as to live the rest of the time in the flesh no longer for the lusts of men, but for the will of God. ³ For the time already past is sufficient *for you* to have carried out the desire of the Gentiles, having pursued a course of sensuality, lusts, drunkenness, carousing, drinking parties and abominable idolatries. ⁴ In *all* this, they are surprised that you do not run with *them* into the same excesses of dissipation, and they malign *you;* ⁵ but they will give account to Him who is ready to judge the living and the dead. ⁶ For the gospel has for this purpose been preached even to those who are dead, that though they are judged in the flesh as men, they may live in the spirit according to *the will* of God.

⁷ The end of all things is near; therefore, be of sound judgment and sober *spirit* for the purpose of prayer. ⁸ Above all, keep fervent in your love for one another, because love covers a multitude of sins. ⁹ Be hospitable to one another without complaint. ¹⁰ As each one has received a *special* gift, employ it in serving one another as good stewards of the manifold grace of God. ¹¹ Whoever speaks, *is to do so* as one who is speaking the utterances of God; whoever serves *is to do so* as one who is serving by the strength which God supplies; so that in all things God may be glorified through Jesus Christ, to whom belongs the glory and dominion forever and ever. Amen.

¹² Beloved, do not be surprised at the fiery ordeal among you, which comes upon you for your testing, as though some strange thing were happening to you; ¹³ but to the degree that you share the sufferings of Christ, keep on rejoicing, so that also at the revelation of His glory you may rejoice with exultation. ¹⁴ If you are reviled for the name of Christ, you are blessed, because the Spirit of glory and of God rests on you. ¹⁵ Make sure that none of you suffers as a murderer, or thief, or evildoer, or a troublesome meddler; ¹⁶ but if *anyone suffers* as a Christian, he is not to be ashamed, but is to glorify God in this name. ¹⁷ For *it is* time for judgment to begin with the household of God; and if *it begins* with us first, what *will be* the outcome for those who do not obey the gospel of God? ¹⁸ AND IF IT IS WITH DIFFICULTY THAT THE RIGHTEOUS IS SAVED, WHAT WILL BECOME OF THE GODLESS MAN AND THE SINNER? ¹⁹ Therefore, those also who suffer according to the will of God shall entrust their souls to a faithful Creator in doing what is right.

4:12 the fiery ordeal. Peter probably wrote this letter shortly before or after the burning of Rome, and at the beginning of the horrors of a 200-year period of Christian persecution. Peter explains that 4 attitudes are necessary in order to be triumphant in persecution: 1) expect it (v. 12); 2) rejoice in it (vv. 13-14); 3) evaluate its cause (vv. 15-18); and 4) entrust it to God (v. 19). **some strange thing were happening.** "Happening" means "to fall by chance." A Christian must not think that his persecution is something that happened accidentally. God allowed it and designed it for the believer's testing, purging, and cleansing.

4:9 Be hospitable to one another. The Greek word means "love of strangers." Love is intensely practical, not just emotional. In Peter's day, love included opening one's home and caring for other needy Christians, such as traveling preachers. It also included opening one's home for church services. Scripture also teaches that Christians should be hospitable to strangers (Ex 22:21; Dt 14:28-29; Heb 13:1-2).

DAY 28: What did Peter mean when he said "the end of all things is near" (1Pe 4:7)?

The Greek word for "end" is never used in the New Testament as a chronological end, as if something simply stops. Instead, the word means a consummation, a goal achieved, a result attained, or a realization. Having emphasized triumphant suffering through death, Peter here begins to emphasize triumphant suffering through the Second Coming of Christ (1:3; 2:12), which is the goal of all things. He is calling believers to live obediently and expectantly in the light of Christ's return. "Is near." The idea is that of a process consummated with a resulting nearness, i.e., "imminent." Peter is reminding the readers of this letter that the return of Jesus Christ could be at any moment (Ro 13:12; 1Th 1:10; James 5:7-8; Rev 22:20).

"Be of sound judgment and sober spirit." This implies here to not be swept away by emotions or passions, thus maintaining a proper eternal perspective on life. The doctrine of the imminent return of Christ should not turn the Christian into a zealous fanatic who does nothing but wait for it to occur. Instead, it should lead the believer into a watchful pursuit of holiness. Moreover, a watchful attitude creates a pilgrim mentality (2:11). It reminds the Christian that he is a citizen of heaven only sojourning on earth. It should also remind him that he will face the record of his service to God and be rewarded for what stands the test at the judgment seat of Christ, which follows the return of Christ to rapture His church. "Sober spirit for the purpose of prayer." A mind victimized by emotion and passion, out of control, or knocked out of balance by worldly lusts and pursuits, is a mind that cannot know the fullness of holy communion in prayer with God (3:7). A mind fixed on His return is purified (1Jn 3:3) and enjoys the fullness of fellowship with the Lord.

NOVEMBER 29

Daniel 1:1–2:49

1 In the third year of the reign of Jehoiakim king of Judah, Nebuchadnezzar king of Babylon came to Jerusalem and besieged it. ² The Lord gave Jehoiakim king of Judah into his hand, along with some of the vessels of the house of God; and he brought them to the land of Shinar, to the house of his god, and he brought the vessels into the treasury of his god.

³ Then the king ordered Ashpenaz, the chief of his officials, to bring in some of the sons of Israel, including some of the royal family and of the nobles, ⁴ youths in whom was no defect, who were good-looking, showing intelligence in every *branch of* wisdom, endowed with understanding and discerning knowledge, and who had ability for serving in the king's court; and *he ordered him* to teach them the literature and language of the Chaldeans. ⁵ The king appointed for them a daily ration from the king's choice food and from the wine which he drank, and *appointed* that they should be educated three years, at the end of which they were to enter the king's personal service. ⁶ Now among them from the sons of Judah were Daniel, Hananiah, Mishael and Azariah. ⁷ Then the commander of the officials assigned *new* names to them; and to Daniel he assigned *the name* Belteshazzar, to Hananiah Shadrach, to Mishael Meshach and to Azariah Abed-nego.

⁸ But Daniel made up his mind that he would not defile himself with the king's choice food or with the wine which he drank; so he sought *permission* from the commander of the officials that he might not defile himself. ⁹ Now God granted Daniel favor and compassion in the sight of the commander of the officials, ¹⁰ and the commander of the officials said to Daniel, "I am afraid of my lord the king, who has appointed your food and your drink; for why should he see your faces looking more haggard than the youths

1:8 Daniel made up his mind. The pagan food and drink were devoted to idols. To indulge was to be understood as honoring these deities. Daniel "made up his mind" not to engage in compromise by being untrue to God's call of commitment (Ex 34:14–15). Also, foods that God's law prohibited (Lv 11) were items that pagans consumed; to partake entailed direct compromise (Da 1:12). Moses took this stand (Heb 11:24–26), as did the psalmist (Ps 119:115), and Jesus (Heb 7:26).

who are your own age? Then you would make me forfeit my head to the king." ¹¹ But Daniel said to the overseer whom the commander of the officials had appointed over Daniel, Hananiah, Mishael and Azariah, ¹² "Please test your servants for ten days, and let us be given some vegetables to eat and water to drink. ¹³ Then let our appearance be observed in your presence and the appearance of the youths who are eating the king's choice food; and deal with your servants according to what you see." ¹⁴ So he listened to them in this matter and tested them for ten days. ¹⁵ At the end of ten days their appearance seemed better and they were fatter than all the youths who had been eating the king's choice food. ¹⁶ So the overseer continued to withhold their choice food and the wine they were to drink, and kept giving them vegetables.

¹⁷ As for these four youths, God gave them knowledge and intelligence in every *branch of* literature and wisdom; Daniel even understood all *kinds of* visions and dreams.

¹⁸ Then at the end of the days which the king had specified for presenting them, the commander of the officials presented them before Nebuchadnezzar. ¹⁹ The king talked with them, and out of them all not one was found like Daniel, Hananiah, Mishael and Azariah; so they entered the king's personal service. ²⁰ As for every matter of wisdom and understanding about which the king

consulted them, he found them ten times better than all the magicians *and* conjurers who *were* in all his realm. [21] And Daniel continued until the first year of Cyrus the king.

2 Now in the second year of the reign of Nebuchadnezzar, Nebuchadnezzar had dreams; and his spirit was troubled and his sleep left him. [2] Then the king gave orders to call in the magicians, the conjurers, the sorcerers and the Chaldeans to tell the king his dreams. So they came in and stood before the king. [3] The king said to them, "I had a dream and my spirit is anxious to understand the dream."

[4] Then the Chaldeans spoke to the king in Aramaic: "O king, live forever! Tell the dream to your servants, and we will declare the interpretation." [5] The king replied to the Chaldeans, "The command from me is firm: if you do not make known to me the dream and its interpretation, you will be torn limb from limb and your houses will be made a rubbish heap. [6] But if you declare the dream and its interpretation, you will receive from me gifts and a reward and great honor; therefore declare to me the dream and its interpretation." [7] They answered a second time and said, "Let the king tell the dream to his servants, and we will declare the interpretation." [8] The king replied, "I know for certain that you are bargaining for time, inasmuch as you have seen that the command from me is firm, [9] that if you do not make the dream known to me, there is only one decree for you. For you have agreed together to speak lying and corrupt words before me until the situation is changed; therefore tell me the dream, that I may know that you can declare to me its interpretation." [10] The Chaldeans answered the king and said, "There is not a man on earth who could declare the matter for the king, inasmuch as no great king or ruler has *ever* asked anything like this of any magician, conjurer or Chaldean. [11] Moreover, the thing which the king demands is difficult, and there is no one else who could declare it to the king except gods, whose dwelling place is not with *mortal* flesh."

[12] Because of this the king became indignant and very furious and gave orders to destroy all the wise men of Babylon. [13] So the decree went forth that the wise men should be slain; and they looked for Daniel and his friends to kill *them*.

[14] Then Daniel replied with discretion and discernment to Arioch, the captain of the king's bodyguard, who had gone forth to slay the wise men of Babylon; [15] he said to Arioch, the king's commander, "For what reason is the decree from the king *so* urgent?" Then Arioch informed Daniel about the matter. [16] So Daniel went in and requested of the king that he would give him time, in order that he might declare the interpretation to the king.

[17] Then Daniel went to his house and informed his friends, Hananiah, Mishael and Azariah, about the matter, [18] so that they might request compassion from the God of heaven concerning this mystery, so that Daniel and his friends would not be destroyed with the rest of the wise men of Babylon. [19] Then the mystery was revealed to Daniel in a night vision. Then Daniel blessed the God of heaven; [20] Daniel said,

"Let the name of God be blessed
    forever and ever,
For wisdom and power
    belong to Him.
[21] "It is He who changes the
    times and the epochs;
He removes kings and
    establishes kings;
He gives wisdom to wise men
And knowledge to men of
    understanding.
[22] "It is He who reveals the profound
    and hidden things;
He knows what is
    in the darkness,
And the light dwells with Him.
[23] "To You, O God of my fathers, I
    give thanks and praise,
For You have given me
    wisdom and power;
Even now You have made known to
    me what we requested of You,
For You have made known to
    us the king's matter."

[24] Therefore, Daniel went in to Arioch, whom the king had appointed to destroy the wise men of Babylon; he went and spoke to him as follows: "Do not destroy the wise men of Babylon! Take me into the king's presence, and I will declare the interpretation to the king."

[25] Then Arioch hurriedly brought Daniel into the king's presence and spoke to him as follows: "I have found a man among the exiles from Judah who can make the interpretation known to the king!" [26] The king said to Daniel, whose name was Belteshazzar, "Are you able to make known to me the dream which I have seen and its interpretation?" [27] Daniel answered before the king and said, "As for the

mystery about which the king has inquired, neither wise men, conjurers, magicians *nor* diviners are able to declare *it* to the king. ²⁸ However, there is a God in heaven who reveals mysteries, and He has made known to King Nebuchadnezzar what will take place in the latter days. This was your dream and the visions in your mind *while* on your bed. ²⁹ As for you, O king, *while* on your bed your thoughts turned to what would take place in the future; and He who reveals mysteries has made known to you what will take place. ³⁰ But as for me, this mystery has not been revealed to me for any wisdom residing in me more than *in* any *other* living man, but for the purpose of making the interpretation known to the king, and that you may understand the thoughts of your mind.

³¹ "You, O king, were looking and behold, there was a single great statue; that statue, which was large and of extraordinary splendor, was standing in front of you, and its appearance was awesome. ³² The head of that statue *was made* of fine gold, its breast and its arms of silver, its belly and its thighs of bronze, ³³ its legs of iron, its feet partly of iron and partly of clay. ³⁴ You continued looking until a stone was cut out without hands, and it struck the statue on its feet of iron and clay and crushed them. ³⁵ Then the iron, the clay, the bronze, the silver and the gold were crushed all at the same time and became like chaff from the summer threshing floors; and the wind carried them away so that not a trace of them was found. But the stone that struck the statue became a great mountain and filled the whole earth.

³⁶ "This *was* the dream; now we will tell its interpretation before the king. ³⁷ You, O king, are the king of kings, to whom the God of heaven has given the kingdom, the power, the strength and the glory; ³⁸ and wherever the sons of men dwell, *or* the beasts of the field, or the birds of the sky, He has given *them* into your hand and has caused you to rule over them all. You are the head of gold. ³⁹ After you there will arise another kingdom inferior to you, then another third kingdom of bronze, which will rule over all the earth. ⁴⁰ Then there will be a fourth kingdom as strong as iron; inasmuch as iron crushes and shatters all things, so, like iron that breaks in pieces, it will crush and break all these in pieces. ⁴¹ In that you saw the feet and toes, partly of potter's clay and partly of iron, it will be a divided kingdom; but it will have in it the toughness of iron, inasmuch as you saw the iron mixed with common clay. ⁴² As

the toes of the feet *were* partly of iron and partly of pottery, *so* some of the kingdom will be strong and part of it will be brittle. ⁴³ And in that you saw the iron mixed with common clay, they will combine with one another in the seed of men; but they will not adhere to one another, even as iron does not combine with pottery. ⁴⁴ In the days of those kings the God of heaven will set up a kingdom which will never be destroyed, and *that* kingdom will not be left for another people; it will crush and put an end to all these kingdoms, but it will itself endure forever. ⁴⁵ Inasmuch as you saw that a stone was cut out of the mountain without hands and that it crushed the iron, the bronze, the clay, the silver and the gold, the great God has made known to the king what will take place in the future; so the dream is true and its interpretation is trustworthy."

2:36-45 we will tell its interpretation. Five empires in succession would rule over Israel, here pictured by parts of a statue (body). In Daniel 7, the same empires are represented by 4 great beasts. These empires are Babylon, Medo-Persia, Greece, Rome, and the later revived Rome, each one differentiated from the previous as indicated by the declining quality of the metal. A stone picturing Christ (Lk 20:18) at His second coming (as the Son of Man also does in Da 7:13-14) will destroy the fourth empire in its final phase with catastrophic suddenness (2:34-35, 44-45). Christ's total shattering of Gentile power will result in the establishment of His millennial kingdom, the ultimate empire, and then continuing on eternally (2:44; 7:27).

⁴⁶ Then King Nebuchadnezzar fell on his face and did homage to Daniel, and gave orders to present to him an offering and fragrant incense. ⁴⁷ The king answered Daniel and said, "Surely your God is a God of gods and a Lord of kings and a revealer of mysteries, since you have been able to reveal this mystery." ⁴⁸ Then the king promoted Daniel and gave him many great gifts, and he made him ruler over the whole province of Babylon and chief prefect over all the wise men of Babylon. ⁴⁹ And Daniel made request of the king, and he appointed Shadrach, Meshach and Abed-nego over the administration of the province of Babylon, while Daniel *was* at the king's court.

Psalm 135:15–21

15 The idols of the nations are
    but silver and gold,
    The work of man's hands.
16 They have mouths, but
    they do not speak;
    They have eyes, but they do not see;
17 They have ears, but they do not hear,
    Nor is there any breath at
    all in their mouths.
18 Those who make them
    will be like them,
    Yes, everyone who trusts in them.

19 O house of Israel, bless the LORD;
    O house of Aaron, bless the LORD;
20 O house of Levi, bless the LORD;
    You who revere the LORD,
    bless the LORD.
21 Blessed be the LORD from Zion,
    Who dwells in Jerusalem.
    Praise the LORD!

Proverbs 29:10

10 Men of bloodshed hate
    the blameless,
    But the upright are
    concerned for his life.

1 Peter 5:1–14

5 Therefore, I exhort the elders among you, as *your* fellow elder and witness of the sufferings of Christ, and a partaker also of the glory that is to be revealed, ² shepherd the flock of God among you, exercising oversight not under compulsion, but voluntarily, according to *the will of* God; and not for sordid gain, but with eagerness; ³ nor yet as lording it over those allotted to your charge, but proving to be examples to the flock. ⁴ And when the Chief Shepherd appears, you will receive the unfading crown of glory. ⁵ You younger men, likewise, be subject to *your* elders; and

5:6 under the mighty hand of God. This is an Old Testament symbol of the power of God working in the experience of men, always accomplishing His sovereign purpose (Ex 3:19–20; Job 30:20–21; Eze 20:33, 37; Mic 6:8). The readers of Peter's letter were not to fight the sovereign hand of God, even when it brought them through testings. One of the evidences of lack of submission and humility is impatience with God in His work of humbling believers. **exalt you at the proper time.** God will lift up the suffering, submissive believers in His wisely appointed time (see Job 42).

all of you, clothe yourselves with humility toward one another, for GOD IS OPPOSED TO THE PROUD, BUT GIVES GRACE TO THE HUMBLE. ⁶ Therefore humble yourselves under the mighty hand of God, that He may exalt you at the proper time, ⁷ casting all your anxiety on Him, because He cares for you. ⁸ Be of sober *spirit,* be on the alert. Your adversary, the devil, prowls around like a roaring lion, seeking someone to devour. ⁹ But resist him, firm in *your* faith, knowing that the same experiences of suffering are being accomplished by your brethren who are in the world. ¹⁰ After you have suffered for a little while, the God of all grace, who called you to His eternal glory in Christ, will Himself perfect, confirm, strengthen *and* establish you. ¹¹ To Him *be* dominion forever and ever. Amen.

¹² Through Silvanus, our faithful brother (for so I regard *him*), I have written to you briefly, exhorting and testifying that this is the true grace of God. Stand firm in it! ¹³ She who is in Babylon, chosen together with you, sends you greetings, and *so does* my son, Mark. ¹⁴ Greet one another with a kiss of love.
    Peace be to you all who are in Christ.

DAY 29: How are pastors to care for their congregations?

First Peter 5:2 gives this exhortation to the elders: "Shepherd the flock of God." After the motivation (v. 1) comes the exhortation (vv. 2–4). Since the primary objective of shepherding is feeding, or teaching, every elder must be able to teach (Jn 21:15–17; 1Ti 3:2; Titus 1:9). Involved with the feeding of the flock is also protecting the flock (Ac 20:28–30). In both duties, it must be remembered that the flock belongs to God, not to the pastor. God entrusts some of His flock to the pastor of a church to lead, care for, and feed (v. 3).

"Not under compulsion, but voluntarily." Specifically, Peter may be warning the elders against a first danger—laziness. The divine calling (1Co 9:16), along with the urgency of the task (Ro 1:15), should prevent laziness and indifference. "Not for sordid gain." False teachers are always motivated by a second danger, money, and use their power and position to rob people of their own wealth (2Pe 2:1–3). Scripture is clear that churches should pay their shepherds well (1Co 9:7–14; 1Ti 5:17–18); but a desire for undeserved money must never be a motive for ministers to serve (1Ti 3:3; 6:9–11; 2Ti 2:4; Titus 1:7; 2Pe 2:3; see also Jer 6:13; 8:10; Mic 3:11; Mal 1:10).

"Nor yet as lording it over" (v. 3). This is the third major temptation for a pastor: demagoguery. In this context, "lording" means to dominate someone or some situation. It implies leadership by manipulation and intimidation. Rather, true spiritual leadership is by example (1Ti 4:12).

NOVEMBER 30

Daniel 3:1–4:37

3 Nebuchadnezzar the king made an image of gold, the height of which *was* sixty cubits *and* its width six cubits; he set it up on the plain of Dura in the province of Babylon. ²Then Nebuchadnezzar the king sent *word* to assemble the satraps, the prefects and the governors, the counselors, the treasurers, the judges, the magistrates and all the rulers of the provinces to come to the dedication of the image that Nebuchadnezzar the king had set up. ³Then the satraps, the prefects and the governors, the counselors, the treasurers, the judges, the magistrates and all the rulers of the provinces were assembled for the dedication of the image that Nebuchadnezzar the king had set up; and they stood before the image that Nebuchadnezzar had set up. ⁴Then the herald loudly proclaimed: "To you the command is given, O peoples, nations and *men of every* language, ⁵that at the moment you hear the sound of the horn, flute, lyre, trigon, psaltery, bagpipe and all kinds of music, you are to fall down and worship the golden image that Nebuchadnezzar the king has set up. ⁶But whoever does not fall down and worship shall immediately be cast into the

3:1 image of gold. The statue, which the king arrogantly made, represented himself as an expression of his greatness and glory and reflected the dream where he was the head of gold (2:38). It was not necessarily made of solid gold, but more likely would have been overlaid with gold, like many objects found in the ruins of Babylon. The word for "image" usually means a human form. The height of the figure was about 90 ft. and the width 9 ft.; it would have been comparable in height to date palms found in that area. The self-deifying statue of the king need not have been grotesquely thin in proportion to the height since a massive base could have contributed to the height. This established the worship of Nebuchadnezzar and the nation under his power, in addition to the other gods.

midst of a furnace of blazing fire." ⁷Therefore at that time, when all the peoples heard the sound of the horn, flute, lyre, trigon, psaltery, bagpipe and all kinds of music, all the peoples, nations and *men of every* language fell down *and* worshiped the golden image that Nebuchadnezzar the king had set up.

⁸For this reason at that time certain Chaldeans came forward and brought charges against the Jews. ⁹They responded and said to Nebuchadnezzar the king: "O king, live forever! ¹⁰You, O king, have made a decree that every man who hears the sound of the horn, flute, lyre, trigon, psaltery, and bagpipe and all kinds of music, is to fall down and worship the golden image. ¹¹But whoever does not fall down and worship shall be cast into the midst of a furnace of blazing fire. ¹²There are certain Jews whom you have appointed over the administration of the province of Babylon, *namely* Shadrach, Meshach and Abed-nego. These men, O king, have disregarded you; they do not serve your gods or worship the golden image which you have set up."

¹³Then Nebuchadnezzar in rage and anger gave orders to bring Shadrach, Meshach and Abed-nego; then these men were brought before the king. ¹⁴Nebuchadnezzar responded and said to them, "Is it true, Shadrach, Meshach and Abed-nego, that you do not serve my gods or worship the golden image that I have set up? ¹⁵Now if you are ready, at the moment you hear the sound of the horn, flute, lyre, trigon, psaltery and bagpipe and all kinds of music, to fall down and worship the image that I have made, *very well*. But if you do not worship, you will immediately be cast into the midst of a furnace of blazing fire; and what god is there who can deliver you out of my hands?"

3:15 what god…? The king's challenge would return to embarrass him. The true God was able to deliver, just as He was able to reveal a dream and its meaning. Nebuchadnezzar had earlier called him "a God of gods" (2:47), but having let that fade from his attention, he soon would be shocked and humiliated when God took up his challenge (3:28–29).

¹⁶ Shadrach, Meshach and Abed-nego replied to the king, "O Nebuchadnezzar, we do not need to give you an answer concerning this matter. ¹⁷ If it be *so*, our God whom we serve is able to deliver us from the furnace of blazing fire; and He will deliver us out of your hand, O king. ¹⁸ But *even* if *He does* not, let it be known to you, O king, that we are not going to serve your gods or worship the golden image that you have set up."

¹⁹ Then Nebuchadnezzar was filled with wrath, and his facial expression was altered toward Shadrach, Meshach and Abed-nego. He answered by giving orders to heat the furnace seven times more than it was usually heated. ²⁰ He commanded certain valiant warriors who *were* in his army to tie up Shadrach, Meshach and Abed-nego in order to cast *them* into the furnace of blazing fire. ²¹ Then these men were tied up in their trousers, their coats, their caps and their *other* clothes, and were cast into the midst of the furnace of blazing fire. ²² For this reason, because the king's command *was* urgent and the furnace had been made extremely hot, the flame of the fire slew those men who carried up Shadrach, Meshach and Abed-nego. ²³ But these three men, Shadrach, Meshach and Abed-nego, fell into the midst of the furnace of blazing fire *still* tied up.

²⁴ Then Nebuchadnezzar the king was astounded and stood up in haste; he said to his high officials, "Was it not three men we cast bound into the midst of the fire?" They replied to the king, "Certainly, O king." ²⁵ He said, "Look! I see four men loosed *and* walking *about* in the midst of the fire without harm, and the appearance of the fourth is like a son of *the* gods!" ²⁶ Then Nebuchadnezzar came near to the door of the furnace of blazing fire; he responded and said, "Shadrach, Meshach and Abed-nego, come out, you servants of the Most High God, and come here!" Then Shadrach, Meshach and Abed-nego came out of the midst of the fire. ²⁷ The satraps, the prefects, the governors and the king's high officials gathered around *and* saw in regard to these men that the fire had no effect on the bodies of these men nor was the hair of their head singed, nor were their trousers damaged, nor had the smell of fire *even* come upon them.

²⁸ Nebuchadnezzar responded and said, "Blessed be the God of Shadrach, Meshach and Abed-nego, who has sent His angel and delivered His servants who put their trust in Him, violating the king's command, and yielded up their bodies so as not to serve or worship any god except their own God. ²⁹ Therefore I make a decree that any people, nation or tongue that speaks anything offensive against the God of Shadrach, Meshach and Abed-nego shall be torn limb from limb and their houses reduced to a rubbish heap, inasmuch as there is no other god who is able to deliver in this way." ³⁰ Then the king caused Shadrach, Meshach and Abed-nego to prosper in the province of Babylon.

4 Nebuchadnezzar the king to all the peoples, nations, and *men of every* language that live in all the earth: "May your peace abound! ² It has seemed good to me to declare the signs and wonders which the Most High God has done for me.

³ "How great are His signs
And how mighty are His wonders!
His kingdom is an
everlasting kingdom
And His dominion is from
generation to generation.

⁴ "I, Nebuchadnezzar, was at ease in my house and flourishing in my palace. ⁵ I saw a dream and it made me fearful; and *these* fantasies *as I lay* on my bed and the visions in my mind kept alarming me. ⁶ So I gave orders to bring into my presence all the wise men of Babylon, that they might make known to me the interpretation of the dream. ⁷ Then the magicians, the conjurers, the Chaldeans and the diviners came in and I related the dream to them, but they could not make its interpretation known to me. ⁸ But finally Daniel came in before me, whose name is Belteshazzar according to the name of my god, and in whom is a spirit of the holy gods; and I related the dream to him, *saying,* ⁹ 'O Belteshazzar, chief of the magicians, since I know that a spirit of the holy gods is in you and no mystery baffles you, tell *me* the visions of my dream which I have seen, along with its interpretation.

¹⁰ 'Now *these were* the visions in my mind *as I lay* on my bed: I was looking, and behold, *there was* a tree in the midst of the earth and its height *was* great.

¹¹ 'The tree grew large and
became strong
And its height reached to the sky,
And it *was* visible to the end
of the whole earth.
¹² 'Its foliage *was* beautiful and
its fruit abundant,
And in it *was* food for all.

The beasts of the field found
    shade under it,
And the birds of the sky
    dwelt in its branches,
And all living creatures fed
    themselves from it.

¹³ 'I was looking in the visions in my mind *as I lay* on my bed, and behold, an *angelic* watcher, a holy one, descended from heaven.

¹⁴ 'He shouted out and
    spoke as follows:
"Chop down the tree and
    cut off its branches,
Strip off its foliage and
    scatter its fruit;
Let the beasts flee from under it
And the birds from its branches.
¹⁵ "Yet leave the stump with its
    roots in the ground,
But with a band of iron and
    bronze *around it*
In the new grass of the field;
And let him be drenched with
    the dew of heaven,
And let him share with the beasts
    in the grass of the earth.
¹⁶ "Let his mind be changed
    from *that of* a man
And let a beast's mind
    be given to him,
And let seven periods of
    time pass over him.
¹⁷ "This sentence is by the decree
    of the *angelic* watchers
And the decision is a command
    of the holy ones,
In order that the living may know
That the Most High is ruler over
    the realm of mankind,
And bestows it on whom He wishes
And sets over it the lowliest of men."

¹⁸ This is the dream *which* I, King Nebuchadnezzar, have seen. Now you, Belteshazzar, tell *me* its interpretation, inasmuch as none of the wise men of my kingdom is able to make known to me the interpretation; but you are able, for a spirit of the holy gods is in you.'

¹⁹ "Then Daniel, whose name is Belteshazzar, was appalled for a while as his thoughts alarmed him. The king responded and said, 'Belteshazzar, do not let the dream or its interpretation alarm you.' Belteshazzar replied, 'My lord, *if only* the dream applied to those who hate you and its interpretation to your adversaries! ²⁰ The tree that you saw, which became large and grew strong, whose height reached to the sky and was visible to all the earth ²¹ and whose foliage *was* beautiful and its fruit abundant, and in which *was* food for all, under which the beasts of the field dwelt and in whose branches the birds of the sky lodged— ²² it is you, O king; for you have become great and grown strong, and your majesty has become great and reached to the sky and your dominion to the end of the earth. ²³ In that the king saw an *angelic* watcher, a holy one, descending from heaven and saying, "Chop down the tree and destroy it; yet leave the stump with its roots in the ground, but with a band of iron and bronze *around it* in the new grass of the field, and let him be drenched with the dew of heaven, and let him share with the beasts of the field until seven periods of time pass over him," ²⁴ this is the interpretation, O king, and this is the decree of the Most High, which has come upon my lord the king: ²⁵ that you be driven away from mankind and your dwelling place be with the beasts of the field, and you be given grass to eat like cattle and be drenched with the dew of heaven; and seven periods of time will pass over you, until you recognize that the Most High is ruler over the realm of mankind and bestows it on whomever He wishes. ²⁶ And in that it was commanded to leave the stump with the roots of the tree, your kingdom will be assured to you after you recognize that *it is* Heaven *that* rules. ²⁷ Therefore, O king, may my advice be pleasing to you: break away now from your sins by *doing* righteousness and from your iniquities by showing mercy to *the* poor, in case there may be a prolonging of your prosperity.'

²⁸ "All *this* happened to Nebuchadnezzar the king. ²⁹ Twelve months later he was walking on the *roof of* the royal palace of Babylon. ³⁰ The king reflected and said, 'Is this not Babylon the great, which I myself have built as a royal residence by the might of my power and for the glory of my majesty?' ³¹ While the word *was* in the king's mouth, a voice came from heaven, *saying,* 'King Nebuchadnezzar, to you it is declared: sovereignty has been removed from you, ³² and you will be driven away from mankind, and your dwelling place *will be* with the beasts of the field. You will be given grass to eat like cattle, and seven periods of time will pass over you until you recognize that the Most High is ruler over the realm of mankind and bestows it on whomever He wishes.' ³³ Immediately the word concerning Nebuchadnezzar was fulfilled; and he was driven away from mankind and

began eating grass like cattle, and his body was drenched with the dew of heaven until his hair had grown like eagles' *feathers* and his nails like birds' *claws*.

³⁴"But at the end of that period, I, Nebuchadnezzar, raised my eyes toward heaven and my reason returned to me, and I blessed the Most High and praised and honored Him who lives forever;

> For His dominion is an
> everlasting dominion,
> And His kingdom *endures* from
> generation to generation.
³⁵ "All the inhabitants of the earth
> are accounted as nothing,
> But He does according to His
> will in the host of heaven
> And *among* the inhabitants of earth;
> And no one can ward off His hand
> Or say to Him, 'What
> have You done?'

³⁶At that time my reason returned to me. And my majesty and splendor were restored to me for the glory of my kingdom, and my counselors and my nobles began seeking me out; so I was reestablished in my sovereignty, and surpassing greatness was added to me. ³⁷Now I, Nebuchadnezzar, praise, exalt and honor the King of heaven, for all His works are true and His ways just, and He is able to humble those who walk in pride."

Psalm 136:1–9

G̲ive thanks to the LORD,
> for He is good,
> For His lovingkindness is everlasting.
² Give thanks to the God of gods,
> For His lovingkindness is everlasting.
³ Give thanks to the Lord of lords,
> For His lovingkindness is everlasting.
⁴ To Him who alone does
> great wonders,
> For His lovingkindness is everlasting;
⁵ To Him who made the
> heavens with skill,
> For His lovingkindness is everlasting;
⁶ To Him who spread out the
> earth above the waters,
> For His lovingkindness is everlasting;
⁷ To Him who made
> *the* great lights,
> For His lovingkindness is everlasting:
⁸ The sun to rule by day,
> For His lovingkindness is everlasting,
⁹ The moon and stars to rule by night,
> For His lovingkindness is everlasting.

Proverbs 29:11

¹¹ A fool always loses his temper,
> But a wise man holds it back.

2 Peter 1:1–21

1̲ Simon Peter, a bond-servant and apostle of Jesus Christ,

To those who have received a faith of the same kind as ours, by the righteousness of our God and Savior, Jesus Christ: ² Grace and peace be multiplied to you in the knowledge of God and of Jesus our Lord; ³ seeing that His divine power has granted to us everything pertaining to life and godliness, through the true knowledge of Him who called us by His own glory and excellence. ⁴ For by these He has granted to us His precious and magnificent promises, so that by them you may become partakers of *the* divine nature, having escaped the corruption that is in the world by lust. ⁵ Now for this very reason also, applying all diligence, in your faith supply moral excellence, and in *your* moral excellence, knowledge, ⁶ and in *your* knowledge, self-control, and in *your* self-control, perseverance, and in *your* perseverance, godliness, ⁷ and in *your* godliness, brotherly kindness, and in *your* brotherly kindness, love. ⁸ For if these *qualities* are yours and are increasing, they render you neither useless nor unfruitful in the true knowledge of our Lord Jesus Christ. ⁹ For he who lacks these *qualities* is blind *or* short-sighted, having forgotten *his* purification from his former sins. ¹⁰ Therefore, brethren, be all the more diligent to make certain about His calling and choosing you; for as long as you practice these things, you will never stumble; ¹¹ for in this way the entrance into the eternal kingdom of our Lord and Savior Jesus Christ will be abundantly supplied to you.

¹²Therefore, I will always be ready to remind you of these things, even though you *already* know *them,* and have been established

---

1:4 partakers of *the* divine nature. This expression is not different from the concepts of being born again, born from above (Jn 3:3; Jas 1:18; 1Pe 1:23), being in Christ (Ro 8:1), or being the home of the Trinity (Jn 14:17–23). The precious promises of salvation result in becoming God's children in the present age (Jn 1:12; Ro 8:9; Gal 2:20; Col 1:27), and thereby sharing in God's nature by the possession of His eternal life.

in the truth which is present with *you*. [13] I consider it right, as long as I am in this *earthly* dwelling, to stir you up by way of reminder, [14] knowing that the laying aside of my *earthly* dwelling is imminent, as also our Lord Jesus Christ has made clear to me. [15] And I will also be diligent that at any time after my departure you will be able to call these things to mind.

[16] For we did not follow cleverly devised tales when we made known to you the power and coming of our Lord Jesus Christ, but we were eyewitnesses of His majesty. [17] For when He received honor and glory from God the Father, such an utterance as this was made to Him by the Majestic Glory, "This is My beloved Son with whom I am well-pleased"— [18] and we ourselves heard this utterance made from heaven when we were with Him on the holy mountain.

[19] *So* we have the prophetic word *made* more sure, to which you do well to pay attention as to a lamp shining in a dark place, until the day dawns and the morning star arises in your hearts. [20] But know this first of all, that no prophecy of Scripture is *a matter* of one's own interpretation, [21] for no prophecy was ever made by an act of human will, but men moved by the Holy Spirit spoke from God.

1:21 by an act of human will. As Scripture is not of human origin, neither is it the result of human will. The emphasis in the phrase is that no part of Scripture was ever at any time produced because men wanted it so. The Bible is not the product of human effort. The prophets, in fact, sometimes wrote what they could not fully understand (1Pe 1:10–11), but were nonetheless faithful to write what God revealed to them. **moved by the Holy Spirit.** Grammatically, this means that they were continually carried or borne along by the Spirit of God (Lk 1:70; Ac 27:15, 17). The Holy Spirit thus is the divine author and originator, the producer of the Scriptures. In the Old Testament alone, the human writers refer to their writings as the words of God over 3800 times (e.g., Jer 1:4; see 3:2; Ro 3:2; 1Co 2:10). Though the human writers of Scripture were active rather than passive in the process of writing Scripture, God the Holy Spirit superintended them so that, using their own individual personalities, thought processes, and vocabulary, they composed and recorded without error the exact words God wanted written. The original copies of Scripture are therefore inspired, i.e., God-breathed (2Ti 3:16) and inerrant, i.e., without error (Jn 10:34–35; 17:17; Titus 1:2). Peter defined the process of inspiration which created an inerrant original text (Pr 30:5; 1Co 14:36; 1Th 2:13).

DAY 30: Who was the fourth person in the fiery furnace of Daniel 3:19–25?

The delivery of Shadrach, Meshach, and Abed-Nego from the flames was an astonishing, miraculous event. The furnace was real, and the flames were hot. The guards who carried the young men close enough to cast them in the furnace were killed. Why complicate this miracle with a fourth person in the furnace? Because the king himself noticed the discrepancy between the number he had thrown into the flames and the number he saw strolling about. The truth usually includes unexpected complications.

The king concluded the fourth person was a heavenly being. He identified the visitor in two different ways: 1) "like a son of the gods" (3:25); 2) "angel" (3:28). When he commanded the three friends to exit the furnace, the king did not extend an invitation to God's special servant.

Viewed from the context of all of Scripture, the fourth person could possibly have been the Second Person of the Godhead (Jesus Christ) in a preincarnate appearance. For other similar Old Testament instances, see Exodus 3:2, Joshua 5:13–15, and Judges 6:11ff. While the term "angel" is used in these reports, the person had a special connection with the Lord. He wasn't an angel, but the Angel of the Lord. His presence may be startling, but He does not have the stunning and awe-inspiring appearance of an angel. The king saw four men in the furnace. The one who appeared miraculously he identified as the Son of God. It may well have been an inspired exclamation.

⚘ DECEMBER 1

Daniel 5:1–6:28

5 Belshazzar the king held a great feast for a thousand of his nobles, and he was drinking wine in the presence of the thousand. ²When Belshazzar tasted the wine, he gave orders to bring the gold and silver vessels which Nebuchadnezzar his father had taken out of the temple which *was* in Jerusalem, so that the king and his nobles, his wives and his concubines might drink from them. ³Then they brought the gold vessels that had been taken out of the temple, the house of God which *was* in Jerusalem; and the king and his nobles, his wives and his concubines drank from them. ⁴They drank the wine and praised the gods of gold and silver, of bronze, iron, wood and stone.

⁵Suddenly the fingers of a man's hand emerged and began writing opposite the lampstand on the plaster of the wall of the king's palace, and the king saw the back of the hand that did the writing. ⁶Then the king's face grew pale and his thoughts alarmed him, and his hip joints went slack and his knees began knocking together. ⁷The king called aloud to bring in the conjurers, the Chaldeans and the diviners. The king spoke and said to the wise men of Babylon, "Any man who can read this inscription and explain its interpretation to me shall be clothed with purple and have a necklace of gold around his neck, and have authority as third *ruler* in the kingdom." ⁸Then all the king's wise men came in, but they could not read the inscription or make known its interpretation to the king. ⁹Then King Belshazzar was greatly alarmed, his face grew *even* paler, and his nobles were perplexed.

¹⁰The queen entered the banquet hall because of the words of the king and his nobles; the queen spoke and said, "O king, live forever! Do not let your thoughts alarm you or your face be pale. ¹¹There is a man in your kingdom in whom is a spirit of the holy gods; and in the days of your father, illumination, insight and wisdom like the wisdom of the gods were found in him. And King Nebuchadnezzar, your father, your father the king, appointed him chief of the magicians, conjurers, Chaldeans *and* diviners. ¹²*This was* because an extraordinary spirit, knowledge and insight, interpretation of dreams, explanation of enigmas and solving of difficult problems were found in this Daniel, whom the king named Belteshazzar. Let Daniel now be summoned and he will declare the interpretation."

¹³Then Daniel was brought in before the king. The king spoke and said to Daniel, "Are you that Daniel who is one of the exiles from Judah, whom my father the king brought from Judah? ¹⁴Now I have heard about you that a spirit of the gods is in you, and that illumination, insight and extraordinary wisdom have been found in you. ¹⁵Just now the wise men *and* the conjurers were brought in before me that they might read this inscription and make its interpretation known to me, but they could not declare the interpretation of the message. ¹⁶But I personally have heard about you, that you are able to give interpretations and solve difficult problems. Now if you are able to read the inscription and make its interpretation known to me, you will be clothed with purple and *wear* a necklace of gold around your neck, and you will have authority as the third *ruler* in the kingdom."

¹⁷Then Daniel answered and said before the king, "Keep your gifts for yourself or give your rewards to someone else; however, I will read the inscription to the king and make the interpretation known to him. ¹⁸O king, the Most High God granted sovereignty, grandeur, glory and majesty to Nebuchadnezzar your father. ¹⁹Because of the grandeur which He bestowed on him, all the peoples, nations and *men of every* language feared and trembled before him; whomever he wished he killed and whomever he wished he spared alive; and whomever he wished he elevated and whomever he wished he humbled. ²⁰But when his heart was lifted up and his spirit became so proud that he behaved arrogantly, he was deposed from his royal throne and *his* glory was taken away from him. ²¹He was also driven away from mankind, and his heart was made like *that of* beasts, and his dwelling place *was* with the wild donkeys. He was given grass to eat like cattle, and his body was drenched with the dew of heaven until he recognized that the Most High God is ruler over the realm of mankind and *that* He sets over it whomever He wishes. ²²Yet you, his son, Belshazzar, have not humbled your heart, even though you knew all this, ²³but you have exalted yourself against the Lord of heaven; and they have brought the vessels of His house before you, and you and your nobles, your wives and your concubines have been drinking wine from them; and you have praised the gods of silver and gold, of bronze, iron, wood and stone, which do not see, hear or understand. But the God in whose hand are your life-breath and all your ways, you have

not glorified. ²⁴Then the hand was sent from Him and this inscription was written out.

²⁵"Now this is the inscription that was written out:

'MENĒ, MENĒ, TEKĒL, UPHARSIN.'

²⁶This is the interpretation of the message: 'MENĒ'—God has numbered your kingdom and put an end to it. ²⁷'TEKĒL'—you have been weighed on the scales and found deficient. ²⁸'PERĒS'—your kingdom has been divided and given over to the Medes and Persians."

²⁹Then Belshazzar gave orders, and they clothed Daniel with purple and *put* a necklace of gold around his neck, and issued a proclamation concerning him that he *now* had authority as the third *ruler* in the kingdom.

³⁰That same night Belshazzar the Chaldean king was slain. ³¹So Darius the Mede received the kingdom at about the age of sixty-two.

5:25-29 MENĒ, MENĒ. This means "counted," or "appointed," and is doubled for stronger emphasis. TEKĒL means "weighed" or "assessed," by the God who weighs actions (1Sa 2:3; Ps 62:9). PERĒS denotes "divided," i.e., to the Medes and Persians. UPHARSIN in v. 25 is the plural of PERĒS, possibly emphasizing the parts in the division. The "U" prefix on PHARSIN has the idea of the English "and."

6 It seemed good to Darius to appoint 120 satraps over the kingdom, that they would be in charge of the whole kingdom, ²and over them three commissioners (of whom Daniel was one), that these satraps might be accountable to them, and that the king might not suffer loss. ³Then this Daniel began distinguishing himself among the commissioners and satraps because he possessed an extraordinary spirit, and the king planned to appoint him over the entire kingdom. ⁴Then the commissioners and satraps began trying to find a ground of accusation against Daniel in regard to government affairs; but they could find no ground of accusation or *evidence of* corruption, inasmuch as he was faithful, and no negligence or corruption was *to be* found in him. ⁵Then these men said, "We will not find any ground of accusation against this Daniel unless we find *it* against him with regard to the law of his God."

⁶Then these commissioners and satraps came by agreement to the king and spoke

6:3 an extraordinary spirit. Daniel, over 80, had enjoyed God's blessing throughout his life (1:20-21; 2:49; 4:8; 5:12). **over the entire kingdom.** Daniel was the favorite of the king. He had experience, wisdom, a sense of history, leadership, a good reputation, ability, attitude, and revelation from the God of heaven. Apparently, God wanted him in the place of influence to encourage and assist in the Jews' return to Judah, since the return was made in Cyrus' first year (539–537 B.C.), right before the lions' den incident. From the record of Ezra 1 and 6, all the basic elements of the return appear: 1) the temple was to be rebuilt with the cost paid from Cyrus' treasury; 2) all Jews who visited could return, and those who stayed were urged to assist financially; and 3) the gold and silver vessels stolen from the temple by Nebuchadnezzar were to be taken back. To account for such favor toward the Jews, it is easy to think of Daniel not only influencing Cyrus to write such a decree, but even formulating it for him.

to him as follows: "King Darius, live forever! ⁷All the commissioners of the kingdom, the prefects and the satraps, the high officials and the governors have consulted together that the king should establish a statute and enforce an injunction that anyone who makes a petition to any god or man besides you, O king, for thirty days, shall be cast into the lions' den. ⁸Now, O king, establish the injunction and sign the document so that it may not be changed, according to the law of the Medes and Persians, which may not be revoked." ⁹Therefore King Darius signed the document, that is, the injunction.

¹⁰Now when Daniel knew that the document was signed, he entered his house (now in his roof chamber he had windows open toward Jerusalem); and he continued kneeling on his knees three times a day, praying and giving thanks before his God, as he had been doing previously. ¹¹Then these men came by agreement and found Daniel making petition and supplication before his God. ¹²Then they approached and spoke before the king about the king's injunction, "Did you not sign an injunction that any man who makes a petition to any god or man besides you, O king, for thirty days, is to be cast into the lions' den?" The king replied, "The statement is true, according to the law of the Medes and Persians, which may not be revoked." ¹³Then they answered and spoke before the king, "Daniel, who is one of the exiles from Judah, pays no

attention to you, O king, or to the injunction which you signed, but keeps making his petition three times a day."

¹⁴Then, as soon as the king heard this statement, he was deeply distressed and set *his* mind on delivering Daniel; and even until sunset he kept exerting himself to rescue him. ¹⁵Then these men came by agreement to the king and said to the king, "Recognize, O king, that it is a law of the Medes and Persians that no injunction or statute which the king establishes may be changed."

¹⁶Then the king gave orders, and Daniel was brought in and cast into the lions' den. The king spoke and said to Daniel, "Your God whom you constantly serve will Himself deliver you." ¹⁷A stone was brought and laid over the mouth of the den; and the king sealed it with his own signet ring and with the signet rings of his nobles, so that nothing would be changed in regard to Daniel. ¹⁸Then the king went off to his palace and spent the night fasting, and no entertainment was brought before him; and his sleep fled from him.

¹⁹Then the king arose at dawn, at the break of day, and went in haste to the lions' den. ²⁰When he had come near the den to Daniel, he cried out with a troubled voice. The king spoke and said to Daniel, "Daniel, servant of the living God, has your God, whom you constantly serve, been able to deliver you from the lions?" ²¹Then Daniel spoke to the king, "O king, live forever! ²²My God sent His angel and shut the lions' mouths and they have not harmed me, inasmuch as I was found innocent before Him; and also toward you, O king, I have committed no crime." ²³Then the king was very pleased and gave orders for Daniel to be taken up out of the den. So Daniel was taken up out of the den and no injury whatever was found on him, because he had trusted in his God. ²⁴The king then gave orders, and they brought those men who had maliciously accused Daniel, and they cast them, their children and their wives into the lions' den; and they had not reached the bottom of the den before the lions overpowered them and crushed all their bones.

²⁵Then Darius the king wrote to all the peoples, nations and *men of every* language who were living in all the land: "May your peace abound! ²⁶I make a decree that in all the dominion of my kingdom men are to fear and tremble before the God of Daniel;

For He is the living God and
    enduring forever,

And His kingdom is one which
    will not be destroyed,
And His dominion *will be* forever.
²⁷"He delivers and rescues and
    performs signs and wonders
In heaven and on earth,
Who has *also* delivered Daniel
    from the power of the lions."

²⁸So this Daniel enjoyed success in the reign of Darius and in the reign of Cyrus the Persian.

Psalm 136:10-26

¹⁰ To Him who smote the Egyptians
    in their firstborn,
    For His lovingkindness is everlasting,
¹¹ And brought Israel out
    from their midst,
    For His lovingkindness is everlasting,
¹² With a strong hand and an
    outstretched arm,
    For His lovingkindness is everlasting.
¹³ To Him who divided the
    Red Sea asunder,
    For His lovingkindness is everlasting,
¹⁴ And made Israel pass through
    the midst of it,
    For His lovingkindness is everlasting;
¹⁵ But He overthrew Pharaoh and
    his army in the Red Sea,
    For His lovingkindness is everlasting.
¹⁶ To Him who led His people
    through the wilderness,
    For His lovingkindness is everlasting;
¹⁷ To Him who smote great kings,
    For His lovingkindness is everlasting,
¹⁸ And slew mighty kings,
    For His lovingkindness is everlasting:
¹⁹ Sihon, king of the Amorites,
    For His lovingkindness is everlasting,
²⁰ And Og, king of Bashan,
    For His lovingkindness is everlasting,
²¹ And gave their land as a heritage,
    For His lovingkindness is everlasting,
²² Even a heritage to Israel His servant,
    For His lovingkindness is everlasting.
²³ Who remembered us in
    our low estate,
    For His lovingkindness is everlasting,
²⁴ And has rescued us from
    our adversaries,
    For His lovingkindness is everlasting;
²⁵ Who gives food to all flesh,
    For His lovingkindness is everlasting.
²⁶ Give thanks to the God of heaven,
    For His lovingkindness is everlasting.

Proverbs 29:12–13

¹² If a ruler pays attention to falsehood,
All his ministers *become* wicked.
¹³ The poor man and the oppressor
have this in common:
The LORD gives light to
the eyes of both.

2 Peter 2:1–22

2 But false prophets also arose among
the people, just as there will also be
false teachers among you, who will secretly
introduce destructive heresies, even denying
the Master who bought them, bringing swift
destruction upon themselves. ² Many will follow their sensuality, and because of them the
way of the truth will be maligned; ³ and in
their greed they will exploit you with false
words; their judgment from long ago is not
idle, and their destruction is not asleep.

⁴ For if God did not spare angels when they
sinned, but cast them into hell and committed
them to pits of darkness, reserved for judgment; ⁵ and did not spare the ancient world, but
preserved Noah, a preacher of righteousness,
with seven others, when He brought a flood
upon the world of the ungodly; ⁶ and *if* He condemned the cities of Sodom and Gomorrah to
destruction by reducing *them* to ashes, having
made them an example to those who would
live ungodly *lives* thereafter; ⁷ and *if* He rescued righteous Lot, oppressed by the sensual
conduct of unprincipled men ⁸ (for by what
he saw and heard *that* righteous man, while
living among them, felt *his* righteous soul tormented day after day by *their* lawless deeds),
⁹ *then* the Lord knows how to rescue the godly
from temptation, and to keep the unrighteous
under punishment for the day of judgment,
¹⁰ and especially those who indulge the flesh
in *its* corrupt desires and despise authority.

Daring, self-willed, they do not tremble
when they revile angelic majesties, ¹¹ whereas
angels who are greater in might and power do
not bring a reviling judgment against them
before the Lord. ¹² But these, like unreasoning animals, born as creatures of instinct to
be captured and killed, reviling where they
have no knowledge, will in the destruction of
those creatures also be destroyed, ¹³ suffering
wrong as the wages of doing wrong. They count
it a pleasure to revel in the daytime. They are
stains and blemishes, reveling in their deceptions, as they carouse with you, ¹⁴ having eyes
full of adultery that never cease from sin, en-
ticing unstable souls, having a heart trained in
greed, accursed children; ¹⁵ forsaking the right
way, they have gone astray, having followed

**2:11 angels who are greater in might and
power.** A reference to the holy angels, who are
greater in power than human beings. **do not
bring a reviling judgment.** Unlike false teachers who are defiant toward higher powers, the
holy angels so revere their Lord that they will
not speak insults against any authority. Even
the archangel, Michael, recognizing the great
presence and power of Satan, refused to speak
evil of him (Jude 8–9), but called on the Lord to
do so. No believer should be so boldly foolish
as to mock or command the power of supernatural demons, especially Satan.

the way of Balaam, the *son* of Beor, who loved
the wages of unrighteousness; ¹⁶ but he received a rebuke for his own transgression,
for a mute donkey, speaking with a voice of a
man, restrained the madness of the prophet.

¹⁷ These are springs without water and
mists driven by a storm, for whom the black
darkness has been reserved. ¹⁸ For speaking
out arrogant *words* of vanity they entice
by fleshly desires, by sensuality, those who
barely escape from the ones who live in error,
¹⁹ promising them freedom while they themselves are slaves of corruption; for by what a
man is overcome, by this he is enslaved. ²⁰ For
if, after they have escaped the defilements of
the world by the knowledge of the Lord and
Savior Jesus Christ, they are again entangled
in them and are overcome, the last state has
become worse for them than the first. ²¹ For it
would be better for them not to have known
the way of righteousness, than having known
it, to turn away from the holy commandment
handed on to them. ²² It has happened to them
according to the true proverb, "A DOG RETURNS
TO ITS OWN VOMIT," and, "A sow, after washing,
returns to wallowing in the mire."

2:19 promising them freedom. False teachers promise those "trying to escape" the
struggles of life the very freedom they seek.
slaves of corruption. The false teachers can't
deliver the freedom they promise, because
they themselves are enslaved to the very corruption which people are trying to escape.
overcome…enslaved. Whoever puts himself,
in the name of freedom, into the hands of a
false teacher, who is a prisoner himself, also
becomes a prisoner. Bondage to corruption
awaits all followers of false teachers.

DAY 1: Who were the false teachers that Peter describes in 2 Peter 2:1?

Peter described false teachers in detail in this chapter so that Christians would always recognize their characteristics and methods. The greatest sin of Christ-rejecters and the most damning work of Satan is misrepresentation of the truth and its consequent deception. Nothing is more wicked than for someone to claim to speak for God to the salvation of souls when in reality he speaks for Satan to the damnation of souls.

Peter says they will be from "among the people." "The people" is used in the New Testament of Israel (Ac 26:17, 23). Peter's point, though, is that Satan has always endeavored to infiltrate groups of believers with the deceptions of false teachers (Jn 8:44). Since Eve, he has been in the deceit business (2Co 11:3-4). The false teachers parade themselves as Christian pastors, teachers, and evangelists and "secretly introduce destructive heresies." "Heresies" means self-designed religious lies which lead to division and faction (1Co 11:19; Gal 5:20). The Greek word for "destructive" basically means damnation. This word is used 6 times in this letter and always speaks of final damnation (vv. 1-3; 3:7, 16). This is why it is so tragic when a church makes a virtue out of the toleration of unscriptural teachings and ideas in the name of love and unity (2Th 3:14; 1Ti 4:1-5; Titus 3:9-11).

"Denying the Master." This phrase exposes the depth of the crime and guilt of the false teachers. This unusual Greek word for "Master" appears 10 times in the New Testament and means one who has supreme authority, whether human authority or divine authority. Peter here warns that false prophets deny the sovereign lordship of Jesus Christ. Though their heresies may include the denial of the virgin birth, deity, bodily resurrection, and Second Coming of Christ, the false teachers' basic error is that they will not submit their lives to the rule of Christ. All false religions have an erroneous Christology.

DECEMBER 2

Daniel 7:1–8:27

7 In the first year of Belshazzar king of Babylon Daniel saw a dream and visions in his mind *as he lay* on his bed; then he wrote the dream down *and* related the *following* summary of it. ² Daniel said, "I was looking in my vision by night, and behold, the four winds of heaven were stirring up the great sea. ³ And four great beasts were coming up from the sea, different from one another. ⁴ The first *was* like a lion and had *the* wings of an eagle. I kept looking until its wings were plucked, and it was lifted up from the ground and made to stand on two feet like a man; a human mind also was given to it. ⁵ And behold, another beast, a second one, resembling a bear. And it was raised up on one side, and three ribs *were* in its mouth between its teeth; and thus they said to it, 'Arise, devour much meat!' ⁶ After this I kept looking, and behold, another one, like a leopard, which had on its back four wings of a bird; the beast also had four heads, and dominion was given to it. ⁷ After this I kept looking in the night visions, and behold, a fourth beast, dreadful and terrifying and extremely strong; and it had large iron teeth. It devoured and crushed and trampled down the remainder with its feet; and it was different from all the beasts that were before it, and it had ten horns. ⁸ While I was contemplating the horns, behold, another horn, a little one, came up among them, and three of the first horns were pulled out by the roots before it; and behold, this horn possessed eyes like the eyes of a man and a mouth uttering great *boasts*.

⁹ "I kept looking
Until thrones were set up,
And the Ancient of Days took *His* seat;
His vesture *was* like white snow
And the hair of His head
    like pure wool.
His throne *was* ablaze with flames,
Its wheels *were* a burning fire.
¹⁰ "A river of fire was flowing
And coming out from before Him;
Thousands upon thousands
    were attending Him,
And myriads upon myriads
    were standing before Him;
The court sat,
And the books were opened.

¹¹ Then I kept looking because of the sound of the boastful words which the horn was speaking; I kept looking until the beast was slain, and its body was destroyed and given to the burning fire. ¹² As for the rest of the beasts, their dominion was taken away, but an extension of life was granted to them for an appointed period of time.

¹³ "I kept looking in the night visions,
And behold, with the clouds of heaven
One like a Son of Man was coming,
And He came up to the
Ancient of Days
And was presented before Him.
¹⁴ "And to Him was given dominion,
Glory and a kingdom,
That all the peoples, nations and
men of every language
Might serve Him.
His dominion is an
everlasting dominion
Which will not pass away;
And His kingdom is one
Which will not be destroyed.

¹⁵ "As for me, Daniel, my spirit was distressed within me, and the visions in my mind kept alarming me. ¹⁶ I approached one of those who were standing by and began asking him the exact meaning of all this. So he told me and made known to me the interpretation of these things: ¹⁷ 'These great beasts, which are four in number, are four kings who will arise from the earth. ¹⁸ But the saints of the Highest One will receive the kingdom and possess the kingdom forever, for all ages to come.'

¹⁹ "Then I desired to know the exact meaning of the fourth beast, which was different from all the others, exceedingly dreadful, with its teeth of iron and its claws of bronze, and which devoured, crushed and trampled down the remainder with its feet, ²⁰ and the meaning of the ten horns that were on its head and the other horn which came up, and before which three of them fell, namely, that horn which had eyes and a mouth uttering great boasts and which was larger in appearance than its associates. ²¹ I kept looking, and that horn was waging war with the saints and overpowering them ²² until the Ancient of Days came and judgment was passed in favor of the saints of the Highest One, and the time arrived when the saints took possession of the kingdom.

²³ "Thus he said: 'The fourth beast will be a fourth kingdom on the earth, which will be different from all the other kingdoms and will devour the whole earth and tread it down and crush it. ²⁴ As for the ten horns, out of this kingdom ten kings will arise; and another will arise after them, and he will be different from the previous ones and will subdue three kings. ²⁵ He will speak out against the Most High and wear down the saints of the Highest One, and he will intend to make alterations in times and in law; and they will

be given into his hand for a time, times, and half a time. ²⁶ But the court will sit for judgment, and his dominion will be taken away, annihilated and destroyed forever. ²⁷ Then the sovereignty, the dominion and the greatness of all the kingdoms under the whole heaven will be given to the people of the saints of the Highest One; His kingdom will be an everlasting kingdom, and all the dominions will serve and obey Him.'

²⁸ "At this point the revelation ended. As for me, Daniel, my thoughts were greatly alarming me and my face grew pale, but I kept the matter to myself."

8 In the third year of the reign of Belshazzar the king a vision appeared to me, Daniel, subsequent to the one which appeared to me previously. ² I looked in the vision, and while I was looking I was in the citadel of Susa, which is in the province of Elam; and I looked in the vision and I myself was beside the Ulai Canal. ³ Then I lifted my eyes and looked, and behold, a ram which had two horns was standing in front of the canal. Now the two horns were long, but one was longer than the other, with the longer one coming up last. ⁴ I saw the ram butting westward, northward, and southward, and no other beasts could stand before him nor was there anyone to rescue from his power, but he did as he pleased and magnified himself.

8:3–9 This imagery unfolded historically. The ram pictures the Medo-Persian Empire, as a whole, its two horns standing for the two entities (the Medes and the Persians) that merged into one. The history of this empire is briefly noted in v. 4, as it is seen conquering from the east to the west, south, and north, under Cyrus, as predicted also by Isaiah 150 years earlier (Is 45:1–7). The longer horn, which appeared last, represents Persia. The goat (v. 5) represents Greece with its great horn Alexander, who with his army of 35,000, moved with such speed that he is pictured as not even touching the ground. The broken horn is Alexander in his death; the 4 horns are generals who became kings over 4 sectors of the Grecian empire after Alexander (7:6). The small horn is Antiochus Epiphanes, who rose from the third empire to rule the Syrian division in 175–164 B.C. and is the same king dominant in 11:21–35. See 7:8, 24–26 where a similar "little horn" clearly represents the final Antichrist. The reason both are described as "little horns" is because one prefigures the other.

⁵While I was observing, behold, a male goat was coming from the west over the surface of the whole earth without touching the ground; and the goat *had* a conspicuous horn between his eyes. ⁶He came up to the ram that had the two horns, which I had seen standing in front of the canal, and rushed at him in his mighty wrath. ⁷I saw him come beside the ram, and he was enraged at him; and he struck the ram and shattered his two horns, and the ram had no strength to withstand him. So he hurled him to the ground and trampled on him, and there was none to rescue the ram from his power. ⁸Then the male goat magnified *himself* exceedingly. But as soon as he was mighty, the large horn was broken; and in its place there came up four conspicuous *horns* toward the four winds of heaven.

⁹Out of one of them came forth a rather small horn which grew exceedingly great toward the south, toward the east, and toward the Beautiful *Land*. ¹⁰It grew up to the host of heaven and caused some of the host and some of the stars to fall to the earth, and it trampled them down. ¹¹It even magnified *itself* to be equal with the Commander of the host; and it removed the regular sacrifice from Him, and the place of His sanctuary was thrown down. ¹²And on account of transgression the host will be given over *to the horn* along with the regular sacrifice; and it will fling truth to the ground and perform *its will* and prosper. ¹³Then I heard a holy one speaking, and another holy one said to that particular one who was speaking, "How long will the vision *about* the regular sacrifice apply, while the transgression causes horror, so as to allow both the holy place and the host to be trampled?" ¹⁴He said to me, "For 2,300 evenings *and* mornings; then the holy place will be properly restored."

¹⁵When I, Daniel, had seen the vision, I sought to understand it; and behold, standing before me was one who looked like a man. ¹⁶And I heard the voice of a man between *the banks of* Ulai, and he called out and said, "Gabriel, give this *man* an understanding of the vision." ¹⁷So he came near to where I was standing, and when he came I was frightened and fell on my face; but he said to me, "Son of man, understand that the vision pertains to the time of the end." ¹⁸Now while he was talking with me, I sank into a deep sleep with my face to the ground; but he touched me and made me stand upright. ¹⁹He said, "Behold, I am going to let you know what will occur at the final period of the indignation, for *it* pertains to the

appointed time of the end. ²⁰The ram which you saw with the two horns represents the kings of Media and Persia. ²¹The shaggy goat *represents* the kingdom of Greece, and the large horn that is between his eyes is the first king. ²²The broken *horn* and the four *horns that* arose in its place *represent* four kingdoms *which* will arise from *his* nation, although not with his power.

²³ "In the latter period of their rule,
When the transgressors
  have run *their course,*
A king will arise,
Insolent and skilled in intrigue.
²⁴ "His power will be mighty, but
  not by his *own* power,
And he will destroy to an
  extraordinary degree
And prosper and perform *his will;*
He will destroy mighty men
  and the holy people.
²⁵ "And through his shrewdness
He will cause deceit to succeed
  by his influence;
And he will magnify
  himself in his heart,
And he will destroy many
  while *they are* at ease.
He will even oppose the
  Prince of princes,
But he will be broken without
  human agency.
²⁶ "The vision of the evenings
  and mornings
Which has been told is true;
But keep the vision secret,
For *it* pertains to many
  days *in the future.*"

²⁷Then I, Daniel, was exhausted and sick for days. Then I got up *again* and carried on the king's business; but I was astounded at the vision, and there was none to explain *it.*

Psalm 137:1–6

By the rivers of Babylon,
  There we sat down and wept,
When we remembered Zion.
² Upon the willows in the midst of it
We hung our harps.
³ For there our captors
  demanded of us songs,
And our tormentors mirth, *saying,*
"Sing us one of the songs of Zion."

⁴ How can we sing the LORD'S song
In a foreign land?

137:1 **the rivers of Babylon.** The Tigris and Euphrates Rivers. **we...wept.** They even wept when the exile was over and the second temple was being built (Ezr 3:12), so deep was their sorrow. **Zion.** The dwelling place of God on earth (Pss 9:11; 76:2) which was destroyed by the Babylonians (2Ch 36:19; Pss 74:6–8; 79:1; Is 64:10–11; Jer 52:12–16; La 2:4, 6–9).

5 If I forget you, O Jerusalem,
   May my right hand forget *her skill.*
6 May my tongue cling to the
      roof of my mouth
   If I do not remember you,
   If I do not exalt Jerusalem
   Above my chief joy.

Proverbs 29:14

14 If a king judges the poor with truth,
    His throne will be established forever.

2 Peter 3:1–18

3 This is now, beloved, the second letter I am writing to you in which I am stirring up your sincere mind by way of reminder, [2] that you should remember the words spoken beforehand by the holy prophets and the commandment of the Lord and Savior *spoken* by your apostles. [3] Know this first of all, that in the last days mockers will come with *their* mocking, following after their own lusts, [4] and saying, "Where is the promise of His coming? For *ever* since the fathers fell asleep, all continues just as it was from the beginning of creation." [5] For when they maintain this, it escapes their notice that by the word of God *the* heavens existed long ago and *the*

3:3 Know this first. "First" here means the pre-eminent matter, not the first in a list. Peter's priority in this section of his letter is to warn Christians about how the false teachers would try to deny this judgment and steal the hope of believers. **in the last days.** This phrase refers to that entire period of time from the arrival of the Messiah to His return (Ac 2:17; Gal 4:4; 2Ti 3:1; Heb 1:2; Jas 5:3; 1Pe 1:20; 1Jn 2:18–19; Jude 18). The entire age will be marked by saboteurs of the Christian truth and especially the hope of Christ's return. **mockers will come.** False teachers argue against the second coming of Christ or any teaching of Scripture through ridicule (Is 5:19; Jude 18).

earth was formed out of water and by water, [6] through which the world at that time was destroyed, being flooded with water. [7] But by His word the present heavens and earth are being reserved for fire, kept for the day of judgment and destruction of ungodly men.

[8] But do not let this one *fact* escape your notice, beloved, that with the Lord one day is like a thousand years, and a thousand years like one day. [9] The Lord is not slow about His promise, as some count slowness, but is patient toward you, not wishing for any to perish but for all to come to repentance. [10] But the day of the Lord will come like a thief, in which the heavens will pass away with a roar and the elements will be destroyed with intense heat, and the earth and its works will be burned up.

[11] Since all these things are to be destroyed in this way, what sort of people ought you to be in holy conduct and godliness, [12] looking for and hastening the coming of the day of God, because of which the heavens will be destroyed by burning, and the elements will melt with intense heat! [13] But according to His promise we are looking for new heavens and a new earth, in which righteousness dwells.

[14] Therefore, beloved, since you look for these things, be diligent to be found by Him in peace, spotless and blameless, [15] and regard the patience of our Lord *as* salvation; just as also our beloved brother Paul, according to the wisdom given him, wrote to you, [16] as also in all *his* letters, speaking in them of these things, in which are some things hard to understand, which the untaught and unstable distort, as *they do* also the rest of the Scriptures, to their own destruction. [17] You therefore, beloved, knowing this beforehand, be on your guard so that you are not carried away by the error of unprincipled men and fall from your own steadfastness, [18] but grow in the grace and knowledge of our Lord and Savior Jesus Christ. To Him *be* the glory, both now and to the day of eternity. Amen.

3:15b–16 hard to understand. Since Paul had (by the time Peter wrote) written all his letters and died, the readers of 2 Peter would have already received letters about future events from Paul. Some of Paul's explanations were difficult (not impossible) to interpret. Nevertheless, Peter uses Paul as a support for his teaching.

DAY 2: How can we answer those who doubt Daniel's authorship because his prophecies are so astonishingly accurate?

Confidence in the divine origin of Scripture does not rely on blind faith. There are reasonable explanations and acceptable corroborating evidence that point to the trustworthiness of the Bible. Daniel's use of what is now called Imperial Aramaic in writing the book points to an early date. The Dead Sea Scrolls offer evidence that also pushes back the date for Daniel.

When accurate prophecy and possible miracles are discounted by definition as unacceptable, proving Daniel's value becomes challenging. But the problem has little to do with lack of evidence and much to do with willful unbelief. Skeptical interpreters, unwilling to acknowledge supernatural prophecies in Daniel that came to pass (over 100 in chapter 11 alone that were fulfilled), attempt to replace miraculous foresight with simple observation. They assume that the writer of Daniel was actually living in the time of Antiochus and reported current events in prophetic form. That is, the writer wrote as though he was predicting certain events, when, in reality, he was writing after the events had occurred. For scholars like these, no amount of fulfilled prophecy will be enough to convince them. They actually become a reminder to believers that people are not argued into the kingdom of God. The most compelling evidence as well as the most resistant people both need the assistance of God's Spirit in arriving at genuine faith.

 # DECEMBER 3

Daniel 9:1–10:21

9 In the first year of Darius the son of Ahasuerus, of Median descent, who was made king over the kingdom of the Chaldeans— ² in the first year of his reign, I, Daniel, observed in the books the number of the years which was *revealed as* the word of the LORD to Jeremiah the prophet for the completion of the desolations of Jerusalem, *namely,* seventy years. ³ So I gave my attention to the Lord God to seek *Him by* prayer and supplications, with fasting, sackcloth and ashes. ⁴ I prayed to the LORD my God and confessed and said, "Alas, O Lord, the great and awesome God, who keeps His covenant and lovingkindness for those who love Him and keep His commandments, ⁵ we have sinned, committed iniquity, acted wickedly and rebelled, even turning aside from Your commandments and ordinances. ⁶ Moreover, we have not listened to Your servants the prophets, who spoke in Your name to our kings, our princes, our fathers and all the people of the land.

⁷ "Righteousness belongs to You, O Lord, but to us open shame, as it is this day—to the men of Judah, the inhabitants of Jerusalem and all Israel, those who are nearby and those who are far away in all the countries to which You have driven them, because of their unfaithful deeds which they have committed against You. ⁸ Open shame belongs to us, O Lord, to our kings, our princes and our fathers, because we have sinned against You. ⁹ To the Lord our God *belong* compassion and forgiveness, for we have rebelled against Him; ¹⁰ nor have we obeyed the voice of the LORD our God, to walk in His teachings which He set before us through His servants the prophets. ¹¹ Indeed all Israel has transgressed Your law and turned aside, not obeying Your voice; so the curse has been poured out on us, along with the oath which is written in the law of Moses the servant of God, for we have sinned against Him. ¹² Thus He has confirmed His words which He had spoken against us and against our rulers who ruled us, to bring on us great calamity; for under the whole heaven there has not been done *anything* like what was done to Jerusalem. ¹³ As it is written in the law of Moses, all this calamity has come on us; yet we have not sought the favor of the LORD our God by turning from our iniquity and giving attention to Your truth. ¹⁴ Therefore the LORD has kept the calamity in store and brought it on us; for the LORD our God is righteous with respect to all His deeds which He has done, but we have not obeyed His voice.

¹⁵ "And now, O Lord our God, who have brought Your people out of the land of Egypt with a mighty hand and have made a name for Yourself, as it is this day—we have sinned, we have been wicked. ¹⁶ O Lord, in accordance with all Your righteous acts, let now Your anger and Your wrath turn away from Your city Jerusalem, Your holy mountain; for because of our sins and the iniquities of our fathers, Jerusalem and Your people *have become* a reproach to all those around us. ¹⁷ So now, our God, listen to the prayer of Your servant and to his supplications, and for Your sake, O Lord, let Your face shine on Your desolate sanctuary. ¹⁸ O my God, incline Your ear and hear! Open Your eyes and see our desolations

and the city which is called by Your name; for we are not presenting our supplications before You on account of any merits of our own, but on account of Your great compassion. ¹⁹ O Lord, hear! O Lord, forgive! O Lord, listen and take action! For Your own sake, O my God, do not delay, because Your city and Your people are called by Your name."

²⁰ Now while I was speaking and praying, and confessing my sin and the sin of my people Israel, and presenting my supplication before the LORD my God in behalf of the holy mountain of my God, ²¹ while I was still speaking in prayer, then the man Gabriel, whom I had seen in the vision previously, came to me in *my* extreme weariness about the time of the evening offering. ²² He gave *me* instruction and talked with me and said, "O Daniel, I have now come forth to give you insight with understanding. ²³ At the beginning of your supplications the command was issued, and I have come to tell *you*, for you are highly esteemed; so give heed to the message and gain understanding of the vision.

²⁴ "Seventy weeks have been decreed for your people and your holy city, to finish the transgression, to make an end of sin, to make atonement for iniquity, to bring in everlasting righteousness, to seal up vision and prophecy and to anoint the most holy *place*. ²⁵ So you are to know and discern *that* from the issuing of a decree to restore and rebuild Jerusalem until Messiah the Prince *there will be* seven weeks and sixty-two weeks; it will be built again, with plaza and moat, even in times of distress. ²⁶ Then after the sixty-two weeks the Messiah will be cut off and have nothing, and

9:24–26 Seventy weeks…from…until. These are weeks of years, whereas weeks of days are described in a different way (10:2–3). The time spans from the Persian Artaxerxes' decree to rebuild Jerusalem, ca. 445 B.C. (Ne 2:1–8), to the Messiah's kingdom. This panorama includes: 1) 7 weeks or 49 years, possibly closing Nehemiah's career in the rebuilding of Jerusalem as well as the end of the ministry of Malachi and the close of the OT; 2) 62 weeks or 434 more years for a total of 483 years to the first advent of Messiah. This was fulfilled at the triumphal entry on 10 Nisan, A.D. 30 (Mt 21:1–11). The Messiah will be "cut off," (a common reference to death); and 3) the final 7 years or 70th week of the time of Antichrist (v. 27). Roman people, from whom the Antichrist will come, will "destroy the city" of Jerusalem and its temple in A.D. 70.

the people of the prince who is to come will destroy the city and the sanctuary. And its end *will come* with a flood; even to the end there will be war; desolations are determined. ²⁷ And he will make a firm covenant with the many for one week, but in the middle of the week he will put a stop to sacrifice and grain offering; and on the wing of abominations *will come* one who makes desolate, even until a complete destruction, one that is decreed, is poured out on the one who makes desolate."

10 In the third year of Cyrus king of Persia a message was revealed to Daniel, who was named Belteshazzar; and the message was true and *one of* great conflict, but he understood the message and had an understanding of the vision.

² In those days, I, Daniel, had been mourning for three entire weeks. ³ I did not eat any tasty food, nor did meat or wine enter my mouth, nor did I use any ointment at all until the entire three weeks were completed. ⁴ On the twenty-fourth day of the first month, while I was by the bank of the great river, that is, the Tigris, ⁵ I lifted my eyes and looked, and behold, there was a certain man dressed in linen, whose waist was girded with *a belt of* pure gold of Uphaz. ⁶ His body also *was* like beryl, his face had the appearance of lightning, his eyes were like flaming torches, his arms and feet like the gleam of polished bronze, and the sound of his words like the sound of a tumult. ⁷ Now I, Daniel, alone saw the vision, while the men who were with me did not see the vision; nevertheless, a great dread fell on them, and they ran away to hide themselves. ⁸ So I was left alone and saw this great vision; yet no strength was left in me, for my natural color turned to a deathly pallor, and I retained no strength. ⁹ But I heard the sound of his words; and as soon as I heard the sound of his words, I fell into a deep sleep on my face, with my face to the ground.

¹⁰ Then behold, a hand touched me and set me trembling on my hands and knees. ¹¹ He said to me, "O Daniel, man of high esteem, understand the words that I am about to tell you and stand upright, for I have now been sent to you." And when he had spoken this word to me, I stood up trembling. ¹² Then he said to me, "Do not be afraid, Daniel, for from the first day that you set your heart on understanding *this* and on humbling yourself before your God, your words were heard, and I have come in response to your words. ¹³ But the prince of the kingdom of Persia was withstanding me for twenty-one days; then behold, Michael, one of the chief princes,

10:13 prince of...Persia. The 3 week delay was due to an evil angel opposing Gabriel in heavenly warfare (Rev 16:12–14). This angel was specially anointed with Persian power in an effort to thwart the work of God. This tells us that Satan engages in heavenly warfare to influence generations and nations against God and His people (Eph 6:10ff.). **Michael.** This is the chief angel of heaven (10:21; 12:1; Jude 9; Rev 12:7). Michael remained to assure that the Jews would be free to return to their land.

---

came to help me, for I had been left there with the kings of Persia. [14] Now I have come to give you an understanding of what will happen to your people in the latter days, for the vision pertains to the days yet *future*."

[15] When he had spoken to me according to these words, I turned my face toward the ground and became speechless. [16] And behold, one who resembled a human being was touching my lips; then I opened my mouth and spoke and said to him who was standing before me, "O my lord, as a result of the vision anguish has come upon me, and I have retained no strength. [17] For how can such a servant of my lord talk with such as my lord? As for me, there remains just now no strength in me, nor has any breath been left in me."

[18] Then *this* one with human appearance touched me again and strengthened me. [19] He said, "O man of high esteem, do not be afraid. Peace be with you; take courage and be courageous!" Now as soon as he spoke to me, I received strength and said, "May my lord speak, for you have strengthened me." [20] Then he said, "Do you understand why I came to you? But I shall now return to fight against the prince of Persia; so I am going forth, and behold, the prince of Greece is about to come. [21] However, I will tell you what is inscribed in the writing of truth. Yet there is no one who stands firmly with me against these *forces* except Michael your prince.

10:21 writing of truth. God's plan of certain and true designs for men and nations, which He can reveal according to His discretion (11:2; Is 46:9–11). **except Michael.** The angel with Michael intended to handle the demons of Persia and Greece. This actually forms the heavenly basis for the earthly unfolding of history in 11:2–35.

Psalm 137:7–9

[7] Remember, O LORD, against
  the sons of Edom
The day of Jerusalem,
Who said, "Raze it, raze it
To its very foundation."
[8] O daughter of Babylon, you
  devastated one,
How blessed will be the
  one who repays you
With the recompense with
  which you have repaid us.
[9] How blessed will be the
  one who seizes and dashes
  your little ones
Against the rock.

Proverbs 29:15

[15] The rod and reproof
  give wisdom,
But a child who gets
  his own way brings
  shame to his mother.

1 John 1:1–10

1 What was from the beginning, what we have heard, what we have seen with our eyes, what we have looked at and touched with our hands, concerning the Word of Life— [2] and the life was manifested, and we have seen and testify and proclaim to you the eternal life, which was with the Father and was manifested to us— [3] what we have seen and heard we proclaim to you also, so that you too may have fellowship with us; and indeed our fellowship is with the Father, and with His Son Jesus Christ. [4] These things we write, so that our joy may be made complete.

[5] This is the message we have heard from Him and announce to you, that God is Light, and in Him there is no darkness at all. [6] If we say that we have fellowship with Him and *yet* walk in the darkness, we lie and not practice the truth; [7] but if we walk in the

---

1:2–3 manifested...seen...testify...heard... proclaim. John dramatically reemphasizes through repetition of these terms in vv. 2–3 (v. 1) the authority of his own personal experience as an eyewitness of Jesus' life. Such repetition pointedly reminds his readers that John's personal testimony refutes the false teachers who boasted arrogantly and wrongly about the Christ they had never seen or known.

Light as He Himself is in the Light, we have fellowship with one another, and the blood of Jesus His Son cleanses us from all sin. [8] If we say that we have no sin, we are deceiving ourselves and the truth is not in us. [9] If we confess our sins, He is faithful and righteous to forgive us our sins and to cleanse us from all unrighteousness. [10] If we say that we have not sinned, we make Him a liar and His word is not in us.

DAY 3: Contrast how the lives of true believers and false teachers differ.

In 1 John 1:7, a genuine Christian walks habitually in the light (truth and holiness), not in darkness (falsehood and sin). Their walk also results in cleansing from sin as the Lord continually forgives His own. Since those walking in the light share in the character of God, they will be habitually characterized by His holiness (3Jn 11), indicating their true fellowship with Him (Jas 1:27). A genuine Christian does not walk in darkness but only in the light (2Co 6:14; Eph 5:8; Col 1:12–13).

Not only did the false teachers walk in darkness (v. 8), but they went so far as to deny totally the existence of a sin nature in their lives. If someone never admits to being a sinner, salvation cannot result. Not only did the false teachers make false claims to fellowship and disregard sin (v. 6), they are also characterized by deceit regarding sinlessness (Ecc 7:20; Ro 3:23).

In the lives of genuine believers, a continual confession of sin is an indication of genuine salvation (v. 9). While the false teachers would not admit their sin, the genuine Christian admitted and forsook it (Ps 32:3–5; Pr 28:13). The term "confess" means to say the same thing about sin as God does—to acknowledge His perspective about sin. While v. 7 is from God's perspective, v. 9 is from the Christian's perspective. Confession of sin characterizes genuine Christians, and God continually cleanses those who are confessing (v. 7). Rather than focusing on confession for every single sin as necessary, John has especially in mind here a settled recognition and acknowledgment that one is a sinner in need of cleansing and forgiveness (Eph 4:32; Col 2:13).

DECEMBER 4

Daniel 11:1–12:13

11 "In the first year of Darius the Mede, I arose to be an encouragement and a protection for him. [2] And now I will tell you the truth. Behold, three more kings are going to arise in Persia. Then a fourth will gain far more riches than all *of them;* as soon as he becomes strong through his riches, he will arouse the whole *empire* against the realm of Greece. [3] And a mighty king will arise, and he will rule with great authority and do as he pleases. [4] But as soon as he has arisen, his kingdom will be broken up and parceled out toward the four points of the compass, though not to his *own* descendants, nor according to his authority which he wielded, for his sovereignty will be uprooted and *given* to others besides them.

[5] "Then the king of the South will grow strong, along with *one* of his princes who will gain ascendancy over him and obtain dominion; his domain *will be* a great dominion *indeed.* [6] After some years they will form an alliance, and the daughter of the king of the South will come to the king of the North to carry out a peaceful arrangement. But she will not retain her position of power, nor will he remain with his power, but she will be given up, along with those who brought her in and the one who sired her as well as he who supported her in *those* times. [7] But one of the descendants of her line will arise in his place, and he will come against *their* army and enter the fortress of the king of the North, and he will deal with them and display *great* strength. [8] Also their gods with their metal images *and* their precious vessels of silver and gold he will take into captivity to Egypt, and he on his part will refrain from *attacking* the king of the North for *some* years. [9] Then the latter will enter the realm of the king of the South, but will return to his *own* land.

11:2–45 As in 8:3–26, this prophecy sweeps all the way from the history of spiritual conflict in Israel (11:2–35) to the tribulation (vv. 36–42) when Michael aids in fully delivering Israel (12:1). The detail of this history is so minute and accurate, so confirmed by history, that unbelieving critics have, without evidence, insisted that it was actually written 400 years later than Daniel, after it had happened, which would make the prophet a deceiver. The prophecy actually looks ahead from Daniel to the final Antichrist.

¹⁰ "His sons will mobilize and assemble a multitude of great forces; and one of them will keep on coming and overflow and pass through, that he may again wage war up to his *very* fortress. ¹¹ The king of the South will be enraged and go forth and fight with the king of the North. Then the latter will raise a great multitude, but *that* multitude will be given into the hand of the *former.* ¹² When the multitude is carried away, his heart will be lifted up, and he will cause tens of thousands to fall; yet he will not prevail. ¹³ For the king of the North will again raise a greater multitude than the former, and after an interval of some years he will press on with a great army and much equipment.

¹⁴ "Now in those times many will rise up against the king of the South; the violent ones among your people will also lift themselves up in order to fulfill the vision, but they will fall down. ¹⁵ Then the king of the North will come, cast up a siege ramp and capture a well-fortified city; and the forces of the South will not stand *their ground,* not even their choicest troops, for there will be no strength to make a stand. ¹⁶ But he who comes against him will do as he pleases, and no one will *be able to* withstand him; he will also stay *for a time* in the Beautiful Land, with destruction in his hand. ¹⁷ He will set his face to come with the power of his whole kingdom, bringing with him a proposal of peace which he will put into effect; he will also give him the daughter of women to ruin it. But she will not take a stand *for him* or be on his side. ¹⁸ Then he will turn his face to the coastlands and capture many. But a commander will put a stop to his scorn against him; moreover, he will repay him for his scorn. ¹⁹ So he will turn his face toward the fortresses of his own land, but he will stumble and fall and be found no more.

²⁰ "Then in his place one will arise who will send an oppressor through the Jewel of *his* kingdom; yet within a few days he will be shattered, though not in anger nor in battle. ²¹ In his place a despicable person will arise, on whom the honor of kingship has not been conferred, but he will come in a time of tranquility and seize the kingdom by intrigue. ²² The overflowing forces will be flooded away before him and shattered, and also the prince of the covenant. ²³ After an alliance is made with him he will practice deception, and he will go up and gain power with a small *force of* people. ²⁴ In a time of tranquility he will enter the richest *parts* of the realm, and he will accomplish what his fathers never did, nor his ancestors; he will

distribute plunder, booty and possessions among them, and he will devise his schemes against strongholds, but *only* for a time. ²⁵ He will stir up his strength and courage against the king of the South with a large army; so the king of the South will mobilize an extremely large and mighty army for war; but he will not stand, for schemes will be devised against him. ²⁶ Those who eat his choice food will destroy him, and his army will overflow, but many will fall down slain. ²⁷ As for both kings, their hearts will be *intent* on evil, and they will speak lies *to each other* at the same table; but it will not succeed, for the end is still *to come* at the appointed time. ²⁸ Then he will return to his land with much plunder; but his heart will be *set* against the holy covenant, and he will take action and *then* return to his *own* land.

²⁹ "At the appointed time he will return and come into the South, but this last time it will not turn out the way it did before. ³⁰ For ships of Kittim will come against him; therefore he will be disheartened and will return and become enraged at the holy covenant and take action; so he will come back and show regard for those who forsake the holy covenant. ³¹ Forces from him will arise, desecrate the sanctuary fortress, and do away with the regular sacrifice. And they will set up the abomination of desolation. ³² By smooth *words* he will turn to godlessness those who act wickedly toward the covenant, but the people who know their God will display strength and take action. ³³ Those who have insight among the people will give understanding to the many;

11:31 desecrate the sanctuary. Antiochus' soldiers, no doubt working with apostate Jews, guarded the temple, halting all worship, while others attacked the city on the Sabbath and slaughtered men, women, and children. Soldiers desecrated Israel's temple, banned circumcision and daily sacrifices (1 Macc. 1:44–54), and sacrificed a pig on the altar. The Syrians on Chislev (Dec. 15, 167 B.C.) even imposed an idol statue in honor of the Olympian god Zeus into the temple. Jews called it "the abomination of desolation," i.e., emptying or ruining for Jewish worship. **abomination of desolation.** Antiochus' soldiers profaned God's temple by spreading sow's broth on the altar and banning daily sacrifices (8:14) as described in 1 Macc. 1:44–54. Both Daniel and Jesus said this was only a preview of the abomination that would happen later under the final Antichrist (9:27; Mt 24:15).

yet they will fall by sword and by flame, by captivity and by plunder for *many* days. ³⁴ Now when they fall they will be granted a little help, and many will join with them in hypocrisy. ³⁵ Some of those who have insight will fall, in order to refine, purge and make them pure until the end time; because *it is* still *to come* at the appointed time.

³⁶ "Then the king will do as he pleases, and he will exalt and magnify himself above every god and will speak monstrous things against the God of gods; and he will prosper until the indignation is finished, for that which is decreed will be done. ³⁷ He will show no regard for the gods of his fathers or for the desire of women, nor will he show regard for any *other* god; for he will magnify himself above *them* all. ³⁸ But instead he will honor a god of fortresses, a god whom his fathers did not know; he will honor *him* with gold, silver, costly stones and treasures. ³⁹ He will take action against the strongest of fortresses with *the help of* a foreign god; he will give great honor to those who acknowledge *him* and will cause them to rule over the many, and will parcel out land for a price.

⁴⁰ "At the end time the king of the South will collide with him, and the king of the North will storm against him with chariots, with horsemen and with many ships; and he will enter countries, overflow *them* and pass through. ⁴¹ He will also enter the Beautiful Land, and many *countries* will fall; but these will be rescued out of his hand: Edom, Moab and the foremost of the sons of Ammon. ⁴² Then he will stretch out his hand against *other* countries, and the land of Egypt will not escape. ⁴³ But he will gain control over the hidden treasures of gold and silver and over all the precious things of Egypt; and Libyans and Ethiopians *will follow* at his heels. ⁴⁴ But rumors from the East and from the North will disturb him, and he will go forth with great wrath to destroy and annihilate many. ⁴⁵ He will pitch the tents of his royal pavilion between the seas and the beautiful Holy Mountain; yet he will come to his end, and no one will help him.

12 "Now at that time Michael, the great prince who stands *guard* over the sons of your people, will arise. And there will be a time of distress such as never occurred since there was a nation until that time; and at that time your people, everyone who is found written in the book, will be rescued. ² Many of those who sleep in the dust of the ground will awake, these to everlasting life, but the others to disgrace *and* everlasting contempt.

³ Those who have insight will shine brightly like the brightness of the expanse of heaven, and those who lead the many to righteousness, like the stars forever and ever. ⁴ But as for you, Daniel, conceal these words and seal up the book until the end of time; many will go back and forth, and knowledge will increase."

⁵ Then I, Daniel, looked and behold, two others were standing, one on this bank of the river and the other on that bank of the river. ⁶ And one said to the man dressed in linen, who was above the waters of the river, "How long *will it be* until the end of *these* wonders?" ⁷ I heard the man dressed in linen, who was above the waters of the river, as he raised his right hand and his left toward heaven, and swore by Him who lives forever that it would be for a time, times, and half *a time;* and as soon as they finish shattering the power of the holy people, all these *events* will be completed. ⁸ As for me, I heard but could not understand; so I said, "My lord, what *will be* the outcome of these *events?*" ⁹ He said, "Go *your way,* Daniel, for *these* words are concealed and sealed up until the end time. ¹⁰ Many will be purged, purified and refined, but the wicked will act wickedly; and none of the wicked will understand, but those who have insight will understand. ¹¹ From the time that the regular sacrifice is abolished and the abomination of desolation is set up, *there will be* 1,290 days. ¹² How blessed is he who keeps waiting and attains to the 1,335 days! ¹³ But as for you, go *your way* to the end; then you will enter into rest and rise *again* for your allotted portion at the end of the age."

Psalm 138:1-3

A Psalm of David.

I will give You thanks with
　all my heart;
I will sing praises to You
　before the gods.
² I will bow down toward
　Your holy temple
And give thanks to Your name
　for Your lovingkindness
　and Your truth;
For You have magnified Your word
　according to all Your name.
³ On the day I called, You answered me;
　You made me bold with
　strength in my soul.

Proverbs 29:16

¹⁶ When the wicked increase,
　transgression increases;
But the righteous will see their fall.

1 John 2:1–29

2 My little children, I am writing these things to you so that you may not sin. And if anyone sins, we have an Advocate with the Father, Jesus Christ the righteous; ²and He Himself is the propitiation for our sins; and not for ours only, but also for *those of* the whole world.

³By this we know that we have come to know Him, if we keep His commandments. ⁴The one who says, "I have come to know Him," and does not keep His commandments, is a liar, and the truth is not in him; ⁵but whoever keeps His word, in him the love of God has truly been perfected. By this we know that we are in Him: ⁶the one who says he abides in Him ought himself to walk in the same manner as He walked.

⁷Beloved, I am not writing a new commandment to you, but an old commandment which you have had from the beginning; the old commandment is the word which you have heard. ⁸On the other hand, I am writing a new commandment to you, which is true in Him and in you, because the darkness is passing away and the true Light is already shining. ⁹The one who says he is in the Light and *yet* hates his brother is in the darkness until now. ¹⁰The one who loves his brother abides in the Light and there is no cause for stumbling in him. ¹¹But the one who hates his brother is in the darkness and walks in the darkness, and does not know where he is going because the darkness has blinded his eyes.

¹²I am writing to you, little children, because your sins have been forgiven you for His name's sake. ¹³I am writing to you, fathers, because you know Him who has been from the beginning. I am writing to you, young men, because you have overcome the evil one. I have written to you, children, because you know the Father. ¹⁴I have written to you, fathers, because you know Him who has been from the beginning. I have written to you, young men, because you are strong, and the word of God abides in you, and you have overcome the evil one.

¹⁵Do not love the world nor the things in the world. If anyone loves the world, the love of the Father is not in him. ¹⁶For all that is in the world, the lust of the flesh and the lust of the eyes and the boastful pride of life, is not from the Father, but is from the world. ¹⁷The world is passing away, and *also* its lusts; but the one who does the will of God lives forever.

¹⁸Children, it is the last hour; and just as you heard that antichrist is coming, even now

2:16 all that is in the world. While the world's philosophies and ideologies and much that it offers may appear attractive and appealing, that is deception. Its true and pervasive nature is evil, harmful, ruinous, and satanic. Its deadly theories are raised up against the knowledge of God and hold the souls of men captive (2Co 10:3–5). **lust.** John uses the term negatively here for a strong desire for evil things. **flesh.** The term refers to the sin nature of man; the rebellious self dominated by sin and in opposition to God (Ro 7:15–25; 8:2–8; Gal 5:19–21). Satan uses the evil world system to incite the flesh. **eyes.** Satan uses the eyes as a strategic avenue to incite wrong desires (Jos 7:20–21; 2Sa 11:2; Mt 5:27–29). Satan's temptation of Eve involved being attracted to something beautiful in appearance, but the result was spiritual death (Ge 3:6 "a delight to the eyes"). **pride of life.** The phrase has the idea of arrogance over one's circumstances, which produced haughtiness or exaggeration, parading what one possessed to impress other people (Jas 4:16).

---

many antichrists have appeared; from this we know that it is the last hour. ¹⁹They went out from us, but they were not *really* of us; for if they had been of us, they would have remained with us; but *they went out,* so that it would be shown that they all are not of us. ²⁰But you have an anointing from the Holy One, and you all know. ²¹I have not written to you because you do not know the truth, but because you do know it, and because no lie is of the truth. ²²Who is the liar but the one who denies that Jesus is the Christ? This is the antichrist, the one who denies the Father and the Son. ²³Whoever denies the Son does not have the Father; the one who confesses

2:19 They went out from us…they were not *really* of us. The first characteristic mentioned of antichrists, i.e., false teachers and deceivers (vv. 22–26), is that they depart from the faithful. They arise from within the church and depart from true fellowship and lead people out with them. The verse also places emphasis on the doctrine of the perseverance of the saints. Those genuinely born again endure in faith and fellowship and the truth (1Co 11:19; 2Ti 2:12). The ultimate test of true Christianity is endurance (Mk 13:13; Heb 3:14). The departure of people from the truth and the church is their unmasking.

the Son has the Father also. ²⁴As for you, let that abide in you which you heard from the beginning. If what you heard from the beginning abides in you, you also will abide in the Son and in the Father. ²⁵This is the promise which He Himself made to us: eternal life.

²⁶These things I have written to you concerning those who are trying to deceive you. ²⁷As for you, the anointing which you received from Him abides in you, and you have no need for anyone to teach you; but as His anointing teaches you about all things, and is true and is not a lie, and just as it has taught you, you abide in Him.

²⁸Now, little children, abide in Him, so that when He appears, we may have confidence and not shrink away from Him in shame at His coming. ²⁹If you know that He is righteous, you know that everyone also who practices righteousness is born of Him.

DAY 4: How does 1 John help us understand some of the destructive teaching that attacked Christianity in the first century?

Paul, Peter, and John all faced early forms of a system of false teaching that later became known as Gnosticism. That term (derived from the Greek word "knowledge") refers to the habit that gnostics had of claiming an elevated knowledge, a higher truth known only to those in on the deep things. Those initiated into this mystical knowledge of truth had a higher internal authority than Scripture. This resulted in a chaotic situation in which the gnostics tried to judge divine revelation by human ideas rather than judging human ideas by divine revelation (1Jn 2:15–17).

Philosophically, the heresy relied on a distortion of Platonism. It advocated a dualism in which matter was inherently evil and spirit was good. One of the direct errors of this heresy involved attributing some form of deity to Christ but denying His true humanity, supposedly to preserve Him from evil (which they concluded He would be if He actually came in the flesh). Such a view destroys not only the true humanity of Jesus, but also the atonement work of Christ. Jesus must not only have been truly God, but also the truly human (physically real) man who actually suffered and died upon the cross in order to be the acceptable substitutionary sacrifice for sin (Heb 2:14–17). The biblical view of Jesus affirms His complete humanity, as well as His full deity.

The gnostic heresy, even in John's day, featured two basic forms: 1) Docetism; and 2) the error of Cerinthus. Docetism (from a Greek word that means, "to appear") asserted that Jesus' physical body was not real but only "seemed" to be physical. John forcefully and repeatedly affirmed the physical reality of Jesus. He reminded his readers that he was an eyewitness to Him ("heard," "seen," "touched," "Jesus Christ has come in the flesh"; 1Jn 1:1–4; 4:2–3). The other form of early Gnosticism was traced back to Cerinthus by the early church apologist Irenaeus. Cerinthus taught that Christ's "spirit" descended on the human Jesus at His baptism but left Him shortly before His crucifixion. John asserted that the Jesus who was baptized at the beginning of His ministry was the same Person who was crucified on the cross (1Jn 5:6).

John does not directly specify the early gnostic beliefs, but his arguments offer clear clues about his targets. Further, John's wisdom was to avoid direct attacks on rapidly shifting heresies, but to provide a timely, positive restatement of the fundamentals of the faith that would provide timeless truth and answers for later generations of Christians.

DECEMBER 5

Hosea 1:1–2:23

1 The word of the LORD which came to Hosea the son of Beeri, during the days of Uzziah, Jotham, Ahaz *and* Hezekiah, kings of Judah, and during the days of Jeroboam the son of Joash, king of Israel.

²When the LORD first spoke through Hosea, the LORD said to Hosea, "Go, take to yourself a wife of harlotry and *have* children of harlotry; for the land commits flagrant harlotry, forsaking the LORD." ³So he went and took Gomer the daughter of Diblaim, and she conceived and

1:2 children of harlotry. This points to the future unfaithfulness of their mother. The children were possibly not fathered by Hosea. That Hosea's marriage to Gomer was to depict God's marriage to Israel is clearly set forth and becomes the key to the theme of the book.

bore him a son. ⁴And the LORD said to him, "Name him Jezreel; for yet a little while, and I will punish the house of Jehu for the bloodshed of Jezreel, and I will put an end to the kingdom of the house of Israel. ⁵On that day I will break the bow of Israel in the valley of Jezreel."

⁶Then she conceived again and gave birth to a daughter. And the LORD said to him, "Name her Lo-ruhamah, for I will no longer have compassion on the house of Israel, that I would ever forgive them. ⁷But I will have compassion on the house of Judah and deliver them by the LORD their God, and will not deliver them by bow, sword, battle, horses or horsemen."

⁸When she had weaned Lo-ruhamah, she conceived and gave birth to a son. ⁹And the LORD said, "Name him Lo-ammi, for you are not My people and I am not your God."

10 Yet the number of the sons of Israel
    Will be like the sand of the sea,
    Which cannot be measured
        or numbered;
    And in the place
    Where it is said to them,
    "You are not My people,"
    It will be said to them,
    "You are the sons of the living God."
11 And the sons of Judah and
        the sons of Israel will be
        gathered together,
    And they will appoint for
        themselves one leader,
    And they will go up from the land,
    For great will be the day of Jezreel.

2 Say to your brothers, "Ammi," and to your
  sisters, "Ruhamah."

2 "Contend with your mother, contend,
    For she is not my wife, and I
        am not her husband;
    And let her put away her
        harlotry from her face
    And her adultery from
        between her breasts,
3 Or I will strip her naked
    And expose her as on the day
        when she was born.
    I will also make her like a wilderness,
    Make her like desert land
    And slay her with thirst.
4 "Also, I will have no compassion
        on her children,
    Because they are children of harlotry.
5 "For their mother has
        played the harlot;
    She who conceived them
        has acted shamefully.
    For she said, 'I will go after my lovers,
    Who give me my bread and my water,
    My wool and my flax, my
        oil and my drink.'

6 "Therefore, behold, I will hedge
        up her way with thorns,
    And I will build a wall against her so
        that she cannot find her paths.
7 "She will pursue her lovers, but
        she will not overtake them;
    And she will seek them, but
        will not find them.
    Then she will say, 'I will go
        back to my first husband,
    For it was better for me
        then than now!'
8 "For she does not know that it
        was I who gave her the grain,
        the new wine and the oil,
    And lavished on her silver and gold,
    Which they used for Baal.
9 "Therefore, I will take back My
        grain at harvest time
    And My new wine in its season.
    I will also take away My
        wool and My flax
    Given to cover her nakedness.
10 "And then I will uncover her lewdness
        In the sight of her lovers,
    And no one will rescue her
        out of My hand.
11 "I will also put an end to all her gaiety,
    Her feasts, her new moons,
        her sabbaths
    And all her festal assemblies.
12 "I will destroy her vines and fig trees,
    Of which she said, 'These are my wages
    Which my lovers have given me.'
    And I will make them a forest,
    And the beasts of the field
        will devour them.
13 "I will punish her for the
        days of the Baals
    When she used to offer
        sacrifices to them
    And adorn herself with her
        earrings and jewelry,
    And follow her lovers, so that she
        forgot Me," declares the LORD.
14 "Therefore, behold, I will allure her,
    Bring her into the wilderness
    And speak kindly to her.
15 "Then I will give her her
        vineyards from there,
    And the valley of Achor
        as a door of hope.
    And she will sing there as in
        the days of her youth,
    As in the day when she came
        up from the land of Egypt.

16 "It will come about in that day,"
   declares the LORD,
   "That you will call Me Ishi
   And will no longer call Me Baali.
17 "For I will remove the names of
   the Baals from her mouth,
   So that they will be mentioned
   by their names no more.
18 "In that day I will also make
   a covenant for them
   With the beasts of the field,
   The birds of the sky
   And the creeping things
   of the ground.
   And I will abolish the bow, the
   sword and war from the land,
   And will make them lie
   down in safety.
19 "I will betroth you to Me forever;
   Yes, I will betroth you to Me in
   righteousness and in justice,
   In lovingkindness and in compassion,
20 And I will betroth you to
   Me in faithfulness.
   Then you will know the LORD.

2:19–20 I will betroth you. Repeated 3 times, the term emphasizes the intensity of God's restoring love for the nation. In that day, Israel will no longer be thought of as a prostitute. Israel brings nothing to the marriage; God makes all the promises and provides all the dowry. These verses are recited by every orthodox Jew as he places the phylacteries on his hand and forehead (Dt 11:18). The regeneration/conversion of the nation is much like that of an individual (2Co 5:16–19).

21 "It will come about in that
   day that I will respond,"
   declares the LORD.
   "I will respond to the heavens, and
   they will respond to the earth,
22 And the earth will respond
   to the grain, to the new
   wine and to the oil,
   And they will respond to Jezreel.
23 "I will sow her for Myself in the land.
   I will also have compassion
   on her who had not
   obtained compassion,
   And I will say to those who
   were not My people,
   'You are My people!'
   And they will say, 'You are my God!'"

Psalm 138:4–6

4 All the kings of the earth will
   give thanks to You, O LORD,
   When they have heard the
   words of Your mouth.
5 And they will sing of the
   ways of the LORD,
   For great is the glory of the LORD.
6 For though the LORD is exalted,
   Yet He regards the lowly,
   But the haughty He knows from afar.

Proverbs 29:17

17 Correct your son, and he will
   give you comfort;
   He will also delight your soul.

1 John 3:1–24

3 See how great a love the Father has bestowed on us, that we would be called children of God; and *such* we are. For this reason the world does not know us, because it did not know Him. 2 Beloved, now we are children of God, and it has not appeared as yet what we will be. We know that when He appears, we will be like Him, because we will see Him just as He is. 3 And everyone who has this hope *fixed* on Him purifies himself, just as He is pure.

3:3 purifies himself, just as He is pure. This is the key verse to 2:28—3:3 and introduces the fifth feature of the believer's hope in this section. Living in the reality of Christ's return makes a difference in a Christian's behavior. Since Christians someday will be like Him, a desire should grow within the Christian to become like Him now. That was Paul's passion, expressed in Philippians 3:12–14. That calls for a purifying of sin, in which we play a part (2Co 7:1; 1Ti 5:22; 1Pe 1:22).

4 Everyone who practices sin also practices lawlessness; and sin is lawlessness. 5 You know that He appeared in order to take away sins; and in Him there is no sin. 6 No one who abides in Him sins; no one who sins has seen Him or knows Him. 7 Little children, make sure no one deceives you; the one who practices righteousness is righteous, just as He is righteous; 8 the one who practices sin is of the devil; for the devil has sinned from the beginning. The Son of God appeared for this purpose, to destroy the works of the devil. 9 No one who is born of God practices

sin, because His seed abides in him; and he cannot sin, because he is born of God. [10] By this the children of God and the children of the devil are obvious: anyone who does not practice righteousness is not of God, nor the one who does not love his brother.

[11] For this is the message which you have heard from the beginning, that we should love one another; [12] not as Cain, *who* was of the evil one and slew his brother. And for what reason did he slay him? Because his deeds were evil, and his brother's were righteous.

[13] Do not be surprised, brethren, if the world hates you. [14] We know that we have passed out of death into life, because we love the brethren. He who does not love abides in death. [15] Everyone who hates his brother is a murderer; and you know that no murderer has eternal life abiding in him. [16] We know love by this, that He laid down His life for us; and we ought to lay down our lives for the brethren. [17] But whoever has the world's goods, and sees his brother in need and closes his heart against him, how does the love of God abide in him? [18] Little children, let us not love with word or with tongue, but in deed and truth. [19] We will know by this that we are of the truth, and will assure our heart before Him [20] in whatever our heart condemns us; for God is greater than our heart and knows all things. [21] Beloved, if our heart does not condemn us, we have

3:16 We know love by this. With this phrase, John introduces the standard of love that is reflected in genuine Christianity. It becomes the measuring stick for every expression of love (v. 18). John presents the third characteristic of Satan's children in terms of their lack of love. Satan's children are marked by indifference toward others' needs. **He laid down His life for us.** This expression is unique to John (Jn 10:11, 15, 17–18; 13:37–38; 15:13) and speaks of divesting oneself of something. Christian love is self-sacrificing and giving. Christ's giving up His life for believers epitomized the true nature of Christian love (Jn 15:12–13; Php 2:5–8; 1Pe 2:19–23). **we ought to lay down our lives for the brethren.** God calls Christians to that same standard of love for one another as He had for us.

confidence before God; [22] and whatever we ask we receive from Him, because we keep His commandments and do the things that are pleasing in His sight.

[23] This is His commandment, that we believe in the name of His Son Jesus Christ, and love one another, just as He commanded us. [24] The one who keeps His commandments abides in Him, and He in him. We know by this that He abides in us, by the Spirit whom He has given us.

DAY 5: What 4 reasons does John give for why believers cannot habitually practice sin (1Jn 3:4–10)?

This passage begins with the phrase "Whoever practices sin" (v. 4). "Practices" translates a Greek verb that conveys the idea of habitual practice. Although genuine Christians have a sin nature (1:8) and do behave sinfully, their confession of sin (1:9; 2:1) and acceptance of forgiveness prevent sin from becoming the unbroken pattern of their lives (Jn 8:31, 34–36; Ro 6:11; 2Jn 9). God builds a certain growing awareness about sin that provides 4 effective reasons why true Christians cannot habitually practice sin:

1. Genuine Christians cannot practice sin because sin is incompatible with the law of God, which they love (3:4; Ps 119:34, 77, 97; Ro 7:12, 22); whereas habitual sin betrays the ultimate sense of rebellion—living as if there were no law or ignoring what laws exist (Jas 4:17)—in short, lawlessness.
2. Genuine Christians cannot practice sin because sin is incompatible with the work of Christ (3:5). Christ died to sanctify (make holy) the believer (2Co 5:21; Eph 5:25–27). Habitual sin contradicts Christ's work of breaking the dominion of sin in the believer's life (Ro 6:1–15).
3. Genuine Christians cannot practice sin because Christ came to destroy the works of the arch-sinner, Satan (3:8). The devil is still operating, but he has been defeated, and in Christ we escape his tyranny. The day will come when all of Satan's activity will cease in the universe, and he will be sent to hell forever (Rev 20:10).
4. Genuine Christians cannot practice sin because sin is incompatible with the ministry of the Holy Spirit, who has imparted a new nature to the believer (3:9; Jn 3:5–8). This new nature shuns sin and exhibits the habitual character of righteousness produced by the Holy Spirit (Gal 5:22–24).

DECEMBER 6

Hosea 3:1–4:19

3 Then the LORD said to me, "Go again, love a woman *who* is loved by *her* husband, yet an adulteress, even as the LORD loves the sons of Israel, though they turn to other gods and love raisin cakes." ²So I bought her for myself for fifteen *shekels* of silver and a homer and a half of barley. ³Then I said to her, "You shall stay with me for many days. You shall not play the harlot, nor shall you have a man; so I will also be toward you." ⁴For the sons of Israel will remain for many days without king or prince, without sacrifice or *sacred* pillar and without ephod or household idols. ⁵Afterward the sons of Israel will return and seek the LORD their God and David their king; and they will come trembling to the LORD and to His goodness in the last days.

3:1 Go again, love. Having been previously separated, Hosea was commanded to pursue his estranged wife Gomer, thereby illustrating God's unquenchable love for faithless Israel. **raisin cakes.** Eaten as a part of special occasions (2Sa 6:19), they may have been used in idolatrous ceremonies, possibly as an aphrodisiac (SS 2:5).

3:2 bought her. Probably from a slave auction, Hosea purchased Gomer for 15 shekels of silver and 1 1/2 homers of barley. Together, the total may have equaled 30 pieces of silver, the price paid for a common slave (Ex 21:32). Barley was the offering of one accused of adultery (Nu 5:15).

4 Listen to the word of the
   LORD, O sons of Israel,
For the LORD has a case against
   the inhabitants of the land,
Because there is no faithfulness
   or kindness
Or knowledge of God in the land.
² *There is* swearing, deception,
   murder, stealing and adultery.
They employ violence, so that
   bloodshed follows bloodshed.
³ Therefore the land mourns,
And everyone who lives
   in it languishes
Along with the beasts of the field
   and the birds of the sky,
And also the fish of the sea disappear.

⁴ Yet let no one find fault, and
   let none offer reproof;
For your people are like those
   who contend with the priest.
⁵ So you will stumble by day,
And the prophet also will
   stumble with you by night;
And I will destroy your mother.
⁶ My people are destroyed for
   lack of knowledge.
Because you have rejected
   knowledge,
I also will reject you from
   being My priest.
Since you have forgotten
   the law of your God,
I also will forget your children.

⁷ The more they multiplied, the
   more they sinned against Me;
I will change their glory into shame.
⁸ They feed on the sin of My people
And direct their desire
   toward their iniquity.
⁹ And it will be, like
   people, like priest;
So I will punish them
   for their ways
And repay them for their deeds.
¹⁰ They will eat, but not have enough;
They will play the harlot,
   but not increase,
Because they have stopped
   giving heed to the LORD.

¹¹ Harlotry, wine and new wine take
   away the understanding.
¹² My people consult their wooden
   idol, and their *diviner's*
   wand informs them;
For a spirit of harlotry has
   led *them* astray,
And they have played the harlot,
   departing from their God.
¹³ They offer sacrifices on the
   tops of the mountains
And burn incense on the hills,
Under oak, poplar and terebinth,
Because their shade is pleasant.
Therefore your daughters
   play the harlot
And your brides commit adultery.
¹⁴ I will not punish your daughters
   when they play the harlot
Or your brides when they
   commit adultery,
For *the men* themselves go
   apart with harlots

And offer sacrifices with
temple prostitutes;
So the people without
understanding are ruined.

15 Though you, Israel, play the harlot,
Do not let Judah become guilty;
Also do not go to Gilgal,
Or go up to Beth-aven
And take the oath:
"As the LORD lives!"
16 Since Israel is stubborn
Like a stubborn heifer,
Can the LORD now pasture them
Like a lamb in a large field?
17 Ephraim is joined to idols;
Let him alone.
18 Their liquor gone,
They play the harlot continually;
Their rulers dearly love shame.
19 The wind wraps them in its wings,
And they will be ashamed
because of their sacrifices.

Psalm 138:7–8

7 Though I walk in the midst of
trouble, You will revive me;
You will stretch forth Your hand
against the wrath of my enemies,
And Your right hand will save me.
8 The LORD will accomplish
what concerns me;
Your lovingkindness, O LORD,
is everlasting;
Do not forsake the works
of Your hands.

Proverbs 29:18

18 Where there is no vision, the
people are unrestrained,
But happy is he who keeps the law.

29:18 no vision. This proverb looks both to the lack of the Word (i.e., 1Sa 3:1) and the lack of hearing the Word (Am 8:11–12), which lead to lawless rebellion (Ex 32:25; Lv 13:45; Nu 5:18). The proverb then contrasts the joy and glory of a lawful society (28:14; Mal 4:4).

1 John 4:1-21

4 Beloved, do not believe every spirit, but test the spirits to see whether they are from God, because many false prophets have gone out into the world. 2 By this you know the Spirit of God: every spirit that confesses

4:1 do not believe every spirit. The mention of the Holy Spirit in 3:24 prompts John to inform his readers that other spirits exist, i.e., demonic spirits, who produce false prophets and false teachers to propagate their false doctrine (1Ti 4:1–2). Christians are to have a healthy skepticism regarding any teaching, unlike some among John's congregations who were too open minded to anyone claiming a new teaching regarding the faith. Christians are to be like the Bereans who, as students of the Word, examined the Scriptures to determine truth and error (Ac 17:11–12). **test.** The word "test" is a metallurgist's term used for assaying metals to determine their purity and value. Christians must test any teaching with a view to approving or disapproving it, rigorously comparing any teaching to the Scripture. **the spirits... many false prophets.** By juxtaposing "spirits" with "false prophets," John reminds his readers that behind human teachers who propagate false doctrine and error are demons inspired by Satan. Human false prophets and teachers are the physical expressions of demonic, spiritual sources (Mt 7:15; Mk 13:22).

that Jesus Christ has come in the flesh is from God; 3 and every spirit that does not confess Jesus is not from God; this is the *spirit* of the antichrist, of which you have heard that it is coming, and now it is already in the world. 4 You are from God, little children, and have overcome them; because greater is He who is in you than he who is in the world. 5 They are from the world; therefore they speak *as* from the world, and the world listens to them. 6 We are from God; he who knows God listens to us; he who is not from God does not listen to us. By this we know the spirit of truth and the spirit of error.

7 Beloved, let us love one another, for love is from God; and everyone who loves is born of God and knows God. 8 The one who does not love does not know God, for God is love. 9 By this the love of God was manifested in us, that God has sent His only begotten Son into the world so that we might live through Him. 10 In this is love, not that we loved God, but that He loved us and sent His Son *to be* the propitiation for our sins. 11 Beloved, if God so loved us, we also ought to love one another. 12 No one has seen God at any time; if we love one another, God abides in us, and His love is perfected in us. 13 By this we know that we abide in Him and He in us, because He has given us of His Spirit. 14 We have seen and

testify that the Father has sent the Son *to be* the Savior of the world.

¹⁵Whoever confesses that Jesus is the Son of God, God abides in him, and he in God. ¹⁶We have come to know and have believed the love which God has for us. God is love, and the one who abides in love abides in God, and God abides in him. ¹⁷By this, love is perfected with us, so that we may have confidence in the day of judgment; because as He is, so also are we in this world. ¹⁸There is no fear in love; but perfect love casts out fear, because fear involves punishment, and the one who fears is not perfected in love. ¹⁹We love, because He first loved us. ²⁰If someone says, "I love God," and hates his brother, he is a liar; for the one who does not love his brother whom he has seen, cannot love God whom he has not seen. ²¹And this commandment we have from Him, that the one who loves God should love his brother also.

4:17 love is perfected with us. John is not suggesting sinless perfection, but rather mature love marked by confidence in the face of judgment. Confidence is a sign that love is mature. **as He is, so also are we.** Jesus was God's Son in whom He was well pleased on earth; we also are God's children (3:11) and the objects of His gracious goodness. If Jesus called God Father, so may we, since we are accepted in the Beloved (Eph 1:6). In v. 18, the same truth is stated negatively. The love that builds confidence also banishes fears. We love God and reverence Him, but we do not love God and come to Him in love, and at the same time, hide from Him in terror (Ro 8:14–15; 2Ti 1:7). Fear involves torment or punishment, a reality the sons of God will never experience, because they are forgiven.

DAY 6: What are the 5 reasons that John gives us for why believers love?

In stark contrast to the self-centered and destructive philosophies and practices of the false teachers, John unfolds the powerful reasons why Christians practice love. In 1 John 4:7-21, the apostle includes 5 such reasons:

1. Christians habitually practice love because God, who indwells them, is the essence of love. The Gnostics believed that God was immaterial spirit and light, but never defined the source of love as coming from His inmost being. As God is Spirit (Jn 4:24), light (1:5), and a consuming fire (Heb 12:9), so He is love (4:7–8). Love is inherent in all He is and does. Even His judgment and wrath are perfectly harmonized with His love.
2. Christians habitually practice love because they desire to imitate the supreme example of God's sacrificial love in sending His Son for us (4:9).
3. Christians habitually practice love because love is the heart of Christian witness (4:12). Nobody can see God loving since He is invisible. Jesus no longer is in the world to manifest the love of God. The only demonstration of God's love in this age is the church. That testimony is critical (Jn 13:35; 2Co 5:18–20).
4. Christians habitually practice love because love is the Christian's assurance (4:13–16; 3:21). Love banishes self-condemnation. When a Christian recognizes in his life the manifestation of love in actions, it results in confidence about his relationship with God.
5. Christians habitually practice love because love is the Christian's confidence in judgment (4:17–20; 3:16–23). Confidence is a sign that love is mature. This is not to suggest sinless perfection in a Christian's life, but rather a habitual practice of love marked by confidence in the face of judgment. Christians love, not in order to escape judgment, but because they have escaped judgment.

DECEMBER 7

Hosea 5:1–6:11

5 Hear this, O priests!
Give heed, O house of Israel!
Listen, O house of the king!
For the judgment applies to you,
For you have been a snare at Mizpah
And a net spread out on Tabor.

² The revolters have gone
    deep in depravity,
But I will chastise all of them.
³ I know Ephraim, and Israel is
    not hidden from Me;
For now, O Ephraim, you
    have played the harlot,
Israel has defiled itself.
⁴ Their deeds will not allow them
To return to their God.

For a spirit of harlotry is within them,
And they do not know the LORD.

5 Moreover, the pride of Israel
testifies against him,
And Israel and Ephraim
stumble in their iniquity;
Judah also has stumbled with them.

6 They will go with their
flocks and herds
To seek the LORD, but they
will not find *Him;*
He has withdrawn from them.

7 They have dealt treacherously
against the LORD,
For they have borne
illegitimate children.
Now the new moon will devour
them with their land.

8 Blow the horn in Gibeah,
The trumpet in Ramah.
Sound an alarm at Beth-aven:
"Behind you, Benjamin!"

9 Ephraim will become a desolation
in the day of rebuke;
Among the tribes of Israel I
declare what is sure.

10 The princes of Judah have become
like those who move a boundary;
On them I will pour out My
wrath like water.

11 Ephraim is oppressed,
crushed in judgment,
Because he was determined to
follow *man's* command.

12 Therefore I am like a
moth to Ephraim
And like rottenness to the
house of Judah.

13 When Ephraim saw his sickness,
And Judah his wound,
Then Ephraim went to Assyria
And sent to King Jareb.
But he is unable to heal you,
Or to cure you of your wound.

14 For I *will be* like a lion to Ephraim
And like a young lion to
the house of Judah.
I, even I, will tear to pieces
and go away,
I will carry away, and there
will be none to deliver.

15 I will go away *and* return
to My place
Until they acknowledge their
guilt and seek My face;
In their affliction they will
earnestly seek Me.

6 "Come, let us return to the LORD.
For He has torn *us,* but
He will heal us;
He has wounded *us,* but He
will bandage us.

2 "He will revive us after two days;
He will raise us up on the third day,
That we may live before Him.

3 "So let us know, let us press
on to know the LORD.
His going forth is as certain
as the dawn;
And He will come to us like the rain,
Like the spring rain
watering the earth."

4 What shall I do with you, O Ephraim?
What shall I do with you, O Judah?
For your loyalty is like a morning cloud
And like the dew which
goes away early.

5 Therefore I have hewn *them* in
pieces by the prophets;
I have slain them by the
words of My mouth;
And the judgments on you are
like the light that goes forth.

6 For I delight in loyalty
rather than sacrifice,
And in the knowledge of God
rather than burnt offerings.

7 But like Adam they have
transgressed the covenant;
There they have dealt
treacherously against Me.

8 Gilead is a city of wrongdoers,
Tracked with bloody *footprints.*

9 And as raiders wait for a man,
So a band of priests murder
on the way to Shechem;
Surely they have committed crime.

10 In the house of Israel I have
seen a horrible thing;
Ephraim's harlotry is there,
Israel has defiled itself.

11 Also, O Judah, there is a harvest
appointed for you,
When I restore the fortunes
of My people.

Psalm 139:1–6

For the choir director. A Psalm of David.

O LORD, You have searched
me and known *me.*

2 You know when I sit down
and when I rise up;
You understand my
thought from afar.

139:1 searched me. As it has been in David's life, he prays later that it will continue to be (vv. 23–24). David understands that nothing inside of him can be hidden from God.

3 You scrutinize my path and
   my lying down,
   And are intimately acquainted
   with all my ways.
4 Even before there is a word
   on my tongue,
   Behold, O LORD, You know it all.
5 You have enclosed me
   behind and before,
   And laid Your hand upon me.
6 *Such* knowledge is too
   wonderful for me;
   It is *too* high, I cannot attain to it.

Proverbs 29:19

19 A slave will not be instructed
   by words *alone*;
   For though he understands,
   there will be no response.

1 John 5:1–21

5 Whoever believes that Jesus is the Christ is born of God, and whoever loves the Father loves the *child* born of Him. 2 By this we know that we love the children of God, when we love God and observe His commandments. 3 For this is the love of God, that we keep His commandments; and His commandments are not burdensome. 4 For whatever is born of God overcomes the world; and this is the victory that has overcome the world— our faith.

5 Who is the one who overcomes the world, but he who believes that Jesus is the Son of God? 6 This is the One who came by water and blood, Jesus Christ; not with the water only, but with the water and with the blood. It is the Spirit who testifies, because the Spirit is the truth. 7 For there are three that testify: 8 the Spirit and the water and the blood; and the three are in agreement. 9 If we receive the testimony of men, the testimony of God is greater; for the testimony of God is this, that He has testified concerning His Son. 10 The one who believes in the Son of God has the testimony in himself; the one who does not believe God has made Him a liar, because he has not believed in the testimony that God has given concerning His Son. 11 And the testimony is this, that God has

5:4 overcomes. John clearly defines who these overcomers are: they are all who believe that Jesus is God's Son, and all that means. The overcomers are believers—all of them (2:13). The word for "overcomes" or "overcomer" comes from a Greek word meaning "to conquer," "to have victory," "to have superiority" or "conquering power." The word reflects a genuine superiority that leads to overwhelming success. The victory is demonstrable; it involves overthrowing an enemy so that the victory is seen by all. Jesus also used this word to describe Himself (Jn 16:33). Because of believers' union with Christ, they too partake in His victory (Ro 8:37; 2Co 2:14). The word "overcomes" in the original language conveys the idea that the believer has continual victory over the world.

given us eternal life, and this life is in His Son. 12 He who has the Son has the life; he who does not have the Son of God does not have the life.

13 These things I have written to you who believe in the name of the Son of God, so that you may know that you have eternal life. 14 This is the confidence which we have before Him, that, if we ask anything according to His will, He hears us. 15 And if we know that He hears us *in* whatever we ask, we know that we have the requests which we have asked from Him.

16 If anyone sees his brother committing a sin not *leading* to death, he shall ask and *God* will for him give life to those who commit sin not *leading* to death. There is a sin *leading*

5:13 These things. This has reference to all that John has written in his letter. **that you may know that you have eternal life.** Assurance of eternal life constitutes the first Christian certainty. While John wrote his gospel to bring unbelievers to faith (Jn 20:31), he wrote the epistle to give believers confidence that they possessed eternal life. The false brethren's departure left John's congregations shaken (2:19). He assured those who remained that since they adhered to the fundamentals of the faith (a proper view of Christ, obedience, love), their salvation was sure. **eternal life.** This does not refer primarily to a period of time but a person (v. 20; Jn 17:3). Eternal life is a relationship with the person of Jesus Christ and possessing His nature (as in vv. 11–12).

to death; I do not say that he should make request for this. ¹⁷All unrighteousness is sin, and there is a sin not *leading* to death.

¹⁸We know that no one who is born of God sins; but He who was born of God keeps him, and the evil one does not touch him. ¹⁹We know that we are of God, and that the whole world lies in *the power of* the evil one. ²⁰And we know that the Son of God has come, and has given us understanding so that we may know Him who is true; and we are in Him who is true, in His Son Jesus Christ. This is the true God and eternal life.

²¹Little children, guard yourselves from idols.

5:21 guard yourselves from idols. John contrasts the term "idols" with "the true God" of v. 20. He has reference here to the false teachers who withdrew from the brotherhood with which they had been formerly associated (2:19). Their false beliefs and practices are the idols from which the readers are commanded to protect themselves. The false teachers upheld the world's philosophy as superior to God's revelation as demonstrated in their perversion of basic Christian teaching. In closing, John once again highlights the importance of adherence to the fundamentals of the faith.

DAY 7: What are the 3 characteristics of an overcomer?

"Whoever believes that Jesus is the Christ is born of God" (1Jn 5:1). Saving faith is the first characteristic of an overcomer. The term "believes" conveys the idea of continuing faith, making the point that the mark of genuine believers is that they continue in faith throughout their life. Saving belief is not simply intellectual acceptance, but wholehearted dedication to Jesus Christ that is permanent. The object of the believer's faith is Jesus, particularly that He is the promised Messiah or "Anointed One" whom God sent to be the Savior from sin. Whoever places faith in Jesus Christ as the only Savior has been born again and, as a result, is an overcomer (v. 5). To be "born of God" is a reference to the new birth and is the same word that Jesus used in John 3:7. The tense of the Greek verb indicates that ongoing faith is the result of the new birth and, therefore, the evidence of the new birth. The sons of God will manifest the reality that they have been born again by continuing to believe in God's Son, the Savior. The new birth brings us into a permanent faith relationship with God and Christ.

"And whoever loves the Father loves the child born of Him" (v. 1). Love is the second characteristic of the overcomer. The overcomer not only believes in God but loves both God and fellow believers. The moral test is again in view.

"By this we know that we love the children of God, when we love God and observe His commandments" (v. 2). John repeats this phrase twice in these 2 verses. Obedience is the third characteristic of an overcomer. In these verses, John weaves faith, love, and obedience all together inextricably. They exist mutually in a dynamic relationship—as the genuine proof of love is obedience, so the genuine proof of faith is love. The word "keep" conveys the idea of constant obedience (Jn 8:31–32; 14:15, 21; 15:10).

DECEMBER 8

Hosea 7:1–8:14

7 When I would heal Israel,
The iniquity of Ephraim is uncovered,
And the evil deeds of Samaria,
For they deal falsely;
The thief enters in,
Bandits raid outside,
² And they do not consider
in their hearts
That I remember all their wickedness.
Now their deeds are all around them;
They are before My face.
³ With their wickedness they
make the king glad,
And the princes with their lies.

⁴ They are all adulterers,
Like an oven heated by the baker
Who ceases to stir up *the fire*
From the kneading of the
dough until it is leavened.
⁵ On the day of our king, the princes
became sick with the heat of wine;
He stretched out his hand
with scoffers,
⁶ For their hearts are like an oven
As they approach their plotting;
Their anger smolders all night,
In the morning it burns
like a flaming fire.
⁷ All of them are hot like an oven,
And they consume their rulers;
All their kings have fallen.
None of them calls on Me.

7:4–7 The civil leaders' evil lust burned so passionately all night that the prophet repeatedly described it like a consuming oven (vv. 4, 6–7), so hot that the baker could forego stirring the fire during the entire night and still have adequate heat for baking the next morning.

8 Ephraim mixes himself
    with the nations;
Ephraim has become a
    cake not turned.
9 Strangers devour his strength,
Yet he does not know *it;*
Gray hairs also are
    sprinkled on him,
Yet he does not know *it.*
10 Though the pride of Israel
    testifies against him,
Yet they have not returned
    to the LORD their God,
Nor have they sought
    Him, for all this.
11 So Ephraim has become like a
    silly dove, without sense;
They call to Egypt, they
    go to Assyria.
12 When they go, I will spread
    My net over them;
I will bring them down like
    the birds of the sky.
I will chastise them in accordance
    with the proclamation
    to their assembly.
13 Woe to them, for they have
    strayed from Me!
Destruction is theirs, for they
    have rebelled against Me!
I would redeem them, but they
    speak lies against Me.
14 And they do not cry to Me
    from their heart
When they wail on their beds;
For the sake of grain and new wine
    they assemble themselves,
They turn away from Me.
15 Although I trained *and*
    strengthened their arms,
Yet they devise evil against Me.
16 They turn, *but* not upward,
They are like a deceitful bow;
Their princes will fall by the sword
Because of the insolence
    of their tongue.
This *will be* their derision
    in the land of Egypt.

8 *Put* the trumpet to your lips!
Like an eagle *the enemy comes*
    against the house of the LORD,
Because they have transgressed
    My covenant
And rebelled against My law.
2 They cry out to Me,
"My God, we of Israel know You!"
3 Israel has rejected the good;
The enemy will pursue him.
4 They have set up kings,
    but not by Me;
They have appointed princes,
    but I did not know *it.*
With their silver and gold they have
    made idols for themselves,
That they might be cut off.
5 He has rejected your calf,
    O Samaria, *saying,*
"My anger burns against them!"
How long will they be
    incapable of innocence?
6 For from Israel is even this!
A craftsman made it, so it is not God;
Surely the calf of Samaria will
    be broken to pieces.
7 For they sow the wind
And they reap the whirlwind.
The standing grain has no heads;
It yields no grain.
Should it yield, strangers
    would swallow it up.

8 Israel is swallowed up;
They are now among the nations
Like a vessel in which
    no one delights.
9 For they have gone up to Assyria,
Like a wild donkey all alone;
Ephraim has hired lovers.
10 Even though they hire *allies*
    among the nations,
Now I will gather them up;
And they will begin to diminish
Because of the burden of
    the king of princes.

11 Since Ephraim has multiplied
    altars for sin,
They have become altars
    of sinning for him.
12 Though I wrote for him ten
    thousand *precepts* of My law,
They are regarded as a strange thing.
13 As for My sacrificial gifts,
They sacrifice the flesh and eat *it,*
But the LORD has taken no
    delight in them.

Now He will remember their iniquity,
And punish *them* for their sins;
They will return to Egypt.
14 For Israel has forgotten his
  Maker and built palaces;
And Judah has multiplied
  fortified cities,
But I will send a fire on its
  cities that it may consume
  its palatial dwellings.

Psalm 139:7–12

7 Where can I go from Your Spirit?
  Or where can I flee from
  Your presence?
8 If I ascend to heaven, You are there;
  If I make my bed in Sheol,
  behold, You are there.
9 If I take the wings of the dawn,
  If I dwell in the remotest
  part of the sea,
10 Even there Your hand will lead me,
  And Your right hand will
  lay hold of me.
11 If I say, "Surely the darkness
  will overwhelm me,
  And the light around me
  will be night,"
12 Even the darkness is not dark to You,
  And the night is as bright as the day.
  Darkness and light are alike *to* You.

139:9 the wings of the dawn. In conjunction with "the remotest part of the sea," David uses this literary figure to express distance.

Proverbs 29:20

20 Do you see a man who is
  hasty in his words?
  There is more hope for a
  fool than for him.

2 John 1–13

The elder to the chosen lady and her children, whom I love in truth; and not only I, but also all who know the truth, ²for the sake of the truth which abides in us and will be with us forever: ³ Grace, mercy *and* peace will be with us, from God the Father and from Jesus Christ, the Son of the Father, in truth and love.

⁴I was very glad to find *some* of your children walking in truth, just as we have received commandment *to do* from the Father. ⁵ Now I ask you, lady, not as though I

1 The elder. John uses this title to emphasize his advanced age, his spiritual authority over the congregations in Asia Minor, and the strength of his own personal eyewitness testimony to the life of Jesus and all that He taught (vv. 4–6). **the chosen lady and her children.** Some think that this phrase refers metaphorically to a particular local church, while "her children" would refer to members of the congregation. The more natural understanding in context, however, is that it refers to a particular woman and her children (i.e., offspring) who were well known to John. **whom I love in truth.** The basis of Christian hospitality is the truth (vv. 1–3). John accentuates the need for truth by repeating the term "truth" 5 times in the opening 4 verses. Truth refers to the basics or fundamentals of the faith that John has discussed in 1 John, as well as the truths expressed in 2 John 4–6. Truth is the necessary condition of unity and, as a result, the basis of hospitality.

---

were writing to you a new commandment, but the one which we have had from the beginning, that we love one another. ⁶And this is love, that we walk according to His commandments. This is the commandment, just as you have heard from the beginning, that you should walk in it.

⁷For many deceivers have gone out into the world, those who do not acknowledge Jesus Christ *as* coming in the flesh. This is the deceiver and the antichrist. ⁸Watch yourselves, that you do not lose what we have accomplished, but that you may receive a full reward. ⁹Anyone who goes too far and does not abide in the teaching of Christ, does not have God; the one who abides in the teaching, he has both the Father and the Son. ¹⁰If anyone comes to you and does not bring this

10 do not receive him into *your* house... not give him a greeting. John's prohibition is not a case of entertaining people who disagree on minor matters. These false teachers were carrying on a regular campaign to destroy the basic, fundamental truths of Christianity. Complete disassociation from such heretics is the only appropriate course of action for genuine believers. No benefit or aid of any type (not even a greeting) is permissible. Believers should aid only those who proclaim the truth (vv. 5–8).

teaching, do not receive him into *your* house, and do not give him a greeting; [11]for the one who gives him a greeting participates in his evil deeds.

[12]Though I have many things to write to you, I do not want to *do so* with paper and ink; but I hope to come to you and speak face to face, so that your joy may be made full.

[13]The children of your chosen sister greet you.

DAY 8: Why is it so important to John to "acknowledge Jesus Christ as coming in the flesh" (2Jn 7)?

John's purpose was to strengthen Christians to resist the tide of heresy that was rising against the church. Much of this false teaching was an early form of Gnosticism.

The gnostic idea that matter was evil and only spirit was good led to the idea that either the body should be treated harshly, a form of asceticism (Col 2:21–23), or that sin committed in the body had no connection or effect on one's spirit. In other words, the false teaching sought to drive a wedge between body and soul. This is why it often maintained that Jesus could not have been God and man at the same time.

The result of this error in teaching was compounded when some, including John's opponents, concluded that sins committed in the physical body did not matter. Absolute indulgence in immorality was permissible. One could deny sin even existed (1Jn 1:8–10) and disregard God's law (1Jn 3:4).

As a bulwark against this heresy, John lifted the confession that "Jesus Christ [came] in the flesh" (v. 7). What Christians do in their physical life is directly connected with what they do in their spiritual life. John emphasized the need for obedience to God's laws, for he defined the true love for God as obedience to His commandments (1Jn 5:3). Jesus, in His human living, offered the perfect example of that kind of love.

DECEMBER 9

Hosea 9:1–10:15

9 Do not rejoice, O Israel, with
  exultation like the nations!
 For you have played the harlot,
  forsaking your God.
 You have loved *harlots'* earnings
  on every threshing floor.
[2] Threshing floor and wine
  press will not feed them,
 And the new wine will fail them.
[3] They will not remain in
  the LORD's land,
 But Ephraim will return to Egypt,
 And in Assyria they will
  eat unclean *food.*
[4] They will not pour out drink
  offerings of wine to the LORD,
 Their sacrifices will
  not please Him.
 Their bread will be like
  mourners' bread;
 All who eat of it will be defiled,
 For their bread will be for
  themselves *alone;*
 It will not enter the house
  of the LORD.
[5] What will you do on the day of
  the appointed festival

 And on the day of the
  feast of the LORD?
[6] For behold, they will go
  because of destruction;
 Egypt will gather them up,
  Memphis will bury them.
 Weeds will take over their
  treasures of silver;
 Thorns *will be* in their tents.
[7] The days of punishment have come,
 The days of retribution have come;
 Let Israel know *this!*
 The prophet is a fool,
 The inspired man is demented,
 Because of the grossness
  of your iniquity,
 And *because* your hostility is *so* great.
[8] Ephraim *was* a watchman
  with my God, a prophet;
 Yet the snare of a bird catcher
  is in all his ways,
 And there is *only* hostility in
  the house of his God.

9:7–8 The prophets were God's inspired messengers and watchmen (Eze 3:17; 33:1–7), yet Israel considered them fools and madmen.

9 They have gone deep in depravity
As in the days of Gibeah;
He will remember their iniquity,
He will punish their sins.

10 I found Israel like grapes
in the wilderness;
I saw your forefathers as the earliest
fruit on the fig tree in its first *season*.
But they came to Baal-peor and
devoted themselves to shame,
And they became as detestable
as that which they loved.

11 As for Ephraim, their glory
will fly away like a bird—
No birth, no pregnancy
and no conception!

12 Though they bring up their children,
Yet I will bereave them until
not a man is left.
Yes, woe to them indeed when
I depart from them!

13 Ephraim, as I have seen,
Is planted in a pleasant
meadow like Tyre;
But Ephraim will bring out his
children for slaughter.

14 Give them, O LORD—what will You give?
Give them a miscarrying
womb and dry breasts.

15 All their evil is at Gilgal;
Indeed, I came to hate them there!
Because of the wickedness of their deeds
I will drive them out of My house!
I will love them no more;
All their princes are rebels.

16 Ephraim is stricken, their
root is dried up,
They will bear no fruit.
Even though they bear children,
I will slay the precious
ones of their womb.

17 My God will cast them away
Because they have not listened to Him;
And they will be wanderers
among the nations.

10 Israel is a luxuriant vine;
He produces fruit for himself.
The more his fruit,
The more altars he made;
The richer his land,
The better he made the *sacred* pillars.

2 Their heart is faithless;
Now they must bear their guilt.
The LORD will break down their altars
And destroy their *sacred* pillars.

3 Surely now they will say,
"We have no king,
For we do not revere the LORD.
As for the king, what can he do for us?"

4 They speak *mere* words,
With worthless oaths they
make covenants;
And judgment sprouts like poisonous
weeds in the furrows of the field.

5 The inhabitants of Samaria will fear
For the calf of Beth-aven.
Indeed, its people will mourn for it,
And its idolatrous priests
will cry out over it,
Over its glory, since it has
departed from it.

6 The thing itself will be
carried to Assyria
As tribute to King Jareb;
Ephraim will be seized with shame
And Israel will be ashamed
of its own counsel.

7 Samaria will be cut off *with* her king
Like a stick on the surface of the water.

8 Also the high places of Aven, the
sin of Israel, will be destroyed;
Thorn and thistle will grow
on their altars;
Then they will say to the mountains,
"Cover us!" And to the hills, "Fall on us!"

10:8 Cover us!...Fall on us! The captivity would
be so severe that the people would pray for the
mountains and hills to fall on them, similar to
the last days (Lk 23:30; Rev 6:16).

9 From the days of Gibeah you
have sinned, O Israel;
There they stand!
Will not the battle against the sons of
iniquity overtake them in Gibeah?

10 When it is My desire, I will
chastise them;
And the peoples will be
gathered against them
When they are bound for
their double guilt.

11 Ephraim is a trained heifer
that loves to thresh,
But I will come over her fair
neck *with a yoke*;
I will harness Ephraim,
Judah will plow, Jacob will
harrow for himself.

¹² Sow with a view to righteousness,
Reap in accordance with kindness;
Break up your fallow ground,
For it is time to seek the LORD
Until He comes to rain
righteousness on you.
¹³ You have plowed wickedness,
you have reaped injustice,
You have eaten the fruit of lies.
Because you have trusted in your
way, in your numerous warriors,
¹⁴ Therefore a tumult will arise
among your people,
And all your fortresses
will be destroyed,
As Shalman destroyed Beth-arbel
on the day of battle,
When mothers were dashed in
pieces with *their* children.
¹⁵ Thus it will be done to you at Bethel
because of your great wickedness.
At dawn the king of Israel will
be completely cut off.

Psalm 139:13-16

¹³ For You formed my inward parts;
You wove me in my mother's womb.
¹⁴ I will give thanks to You, for I am
fearfully and wonderfully made;
Wonderful are Your works,
And my soul knows it very well.
¹⁵ My frame was not hidden from You,
When I was made in secret,
And skillfully wrought in the
depths of the earth;
¹⁶ Your eyes have seen my
unformed substance;
And in Your book were all written
The days that were ordained *for me,*
When as yet there was not one of them.

139:13 formed…wove. By virtue of the divinely designed period of pregnancy, God providentially watches over the development of the child while yet in the mother's womb.

139:16 Your book. This figure of speech likens God's mind to a book of remembrance. **not one of them.** God sovereignly ordained David's life before he was conceived.

Proverbs 29:21

²¹ He who pampers his slave
from childhood
Will in the end find him to be a son.

3 John 1-15

The elder to the beloved Gaius, whom I love in truth. ²Beloved, I pray that in all respects you may prosper and be in good health, just as your soul prospers. ³For I was very glad when brethren came and testified to your truth, *that is,* how you are walking in truth. ⁴I have no greater joy than this, to hear of my children walking in the truth.

4 I have no greater joy. John's personal affection for Gaius radiated especially from his personal conduct (Lk 6:46). **my children.** The word "my" is emphatic in the original. John's heart delighted in the proper conduct of his spiritual children in the faith. Those who walk (conduct) in the truth (belief) have integrity; there is no dichotomy between professing and living. He had strong fatherly affection for them (1Co 4:14-16; 1Th 2:11; 3:1-10).

⁵Beloved, you are acting faithfully in whatever you accomplish for the brethren, and especially *when they are* strangers; ⁶and they have testified to your love before the church. You will do well to send them on their way in a manner worthy of God. ⁷For they went out for the sake of the Name, accepting nothing from the Gentiles. ⁸Therefore we ought to support such men, so that we may be fellow workers with the truth.

⁹I wrote something to the church; but Diotrephes, who loves to be first among them, does not accept what we say. ¹⁰For this reason, if I come, I will call attention to his deeds which he does, unjustly accusing us with wicked words; and not satisfied with this, he himself does not receive the brethren, either, and he forbids those who desire to do so and puts *them* out of the church.

¹¹Beloved, do not imitate what is evil, but what is good. The one who does good is of God; the one who does evil has not seen God. ¹²Demetrius has received a *good* testimony from everyone, and from the truth itself; and we add our testimony, and you know that our testimony is true.

¹³I had many things to write to you, but I am not willing to write *them* to you with pen and ink; ¹⁴but I hope to see you shortly, and we will speak face to face.

¹⁵Peace *be* to you. The friends greet you. Greet the friends by name.

DAY 9: What was the problem with Diotrephes in 3 John vv. 9–10?

John apparently had written a previous letter to the church (v. 9), perhaps on the subject of hospitality, but it was lost. Perhaps Diotrephes never read it to the church because he rejected John's authority (vv. 9–10). "Diotrephes, who loves to be first among them." This phrase conveys the idea of someone who is selfish, self-centered, and self-seeking. The language suggests a self-promoting demagogue, who served no one, but wanted all to serve only him. Diotrephes' actions directly contradict Jesus' and the New Testament's teaching on servant leadership in the church (Mt 20:20–28; Php 2:5–11; 1Ti 3:3; 1Pe 5:3). "Diotrephes...does not accept what we say." Diotrephes modeled the opposite of kindness and hospitality to God's servants, even denying John's apostolic authority over the local congregation, and as a result, denying the revelation of God that came through that authority. His pride endeavored to supplant the rule of Christ through John in the church. Diotrephes' character was the very opposite of the gentle and loving Gaius who readily showed hospitality.

"If I come, I will call attention to his deeds" (v. 10). John's apostolic authority meant that Diotrephes had to answer for his behavior. The apostle did not overlook this usurping of Christ's place in the church. Verse 10 indicates that Diotrephes was guilty of 4 things: 1) "unjustly accusing against us." Also translated as "prating," which comes from a word meaning "to bubble up" and has the idea of useless, empty jabber, i.e., talking nonsense. The charges against John were completely unjustified; 2) "with wicked words." Not only were Diotrephes' charges false, they were evil; 3) "does not receive the brethren." He not only slandered John but also deliberately defied other believers; and 4) "puts them out of the church." The original language indicates that Diotrephes' habit was to excommunicate those who resisted his authority. To accept John's authority (v. 9), as well as being hospitable to the traveling ministers, directly threatened the authority that Diotrephes coveted.

DECEMBER 10

Hosea 11:1–12:14

11 When Israel *was* a youth I loved him,
And out of Egypt I called My son.
2   The more they called them,
The more they went from them;
They kept sacrificing to the Baals
And burning incense to idols.
3   Yet it is I who taught
Ephraim to walk,
I took them in My arms;
But they did not know that
I healed them.
4   I led them with cords of a man,
with bonds of love,
And I became to them as one who
lifts the yoke from their jaws;
And I bent down *and* fed them.

11:1 In tender words reminiscent of the Exodus from Egypt (Ex 4:22–23), the Lord reassured Israel of His intense love for her. His compassion for her was aroused (Is 12:1; 40:1–2; 49:13; Jer 31:10–14; Zec 1:12–17). See Matthew 2:15 for Matthew's analogical use of this verse in relationship to Jesus Christ.

5   They will not return to
the land of Egypt;
But Assyria—he will be their king
Because they refused to return *to* Me.
6   The sword will whirl
against their cities,
And will demolish their gate bars
And consume *them* because
of their counsels.
7   So My people are bent on
turning from Me.
Though they call them to
the One on high,
None at all exalts *Him*.

8   How can I give you up, O Ephraim?
How can I surrender you, O Israel?
How can I make you like Admah?
How can I treat you like Zeboiim?
My heart is turned over within Me,
All My compassions are kindled.
9   I will not execute My fierce anger;
I will not destroy Ephraim again.
For I am God and not man, the
Holy One in your midst,
And I will not come in wrath.
10   They will walk after the LORD,
He will roar like a lion;
Indeed He will roar
And *His* sons will come
trembling from the west.

11 They will come trembling
   like birds from Egypt
   And like doves from the
   land of Assyria;
   And I will settle them in their
   houses, declares the LORD.

12 Ephraim surrounds Me with lies
   And the house of Israel with deceit;
   Judah is also unruly against God,
   Even against the Holy One
   who is faithful.

12 Ephraim feeds on wind,
   And pursues the east
   wind continually;
   He multiplies lies and violence.
   Moreover, he makes a
   covenant with Assyria,
   And oil is carried to Egypt.

2 The LORD also has a
   dispute with Judah,
   And will punish Jacob
   according to his ways;
   He will repay him according
   to his deeds.

3 In the womb he took his
   brother by the heel,
   And in his maturity he
   contended with God.

4 Yes, he wrestled with the
   angel and prevailed;
   He wept and sought His favor.
   He found Him at Bethel
   And there He spoke with us,

5 Even the LORD, the God of hosts,
   The LORD is His name.

6 Therefore, return to your God,
   Observe kindness and justice,
   And wait for your God continually.

7 A merchant, in whose hands
   are false balances,
   He loves to oppress.

8 And Ephraim said, "Surely
   I have become rich,
   I have found wealth for myself;
   In all my labors they
   will find in me
   No iniquity, which *would be* sin."

9 But I *have been* the LORD your
   God since the land of Egypt;
   I will make you live in tents again,
   As in the days of the
   appointed festival.

10 I have also spoken to the prophets,
   And I gave numerous visions,
   And through the prophets
   I gave parables.

11 Is there iniquity *in* Gilead?
   Surely they are worthless.
   In Gilgal they sacrifice bulls,
   Yes, their altars are like
   the stone heaps
   Beside the furrows of the field.

12 Now Jacob fled to the land of Aram,
   And Israel worked for a wife,
   And for a wife he kept *sheep*.

13 But by a prophet the LORD
   brought Israel from Egypt,
   And by a prophet he was kept.

14 Ephraim has provoked to bitter anger;
   So his Lord will leave his
   bloodguilt on him
   And bring back his reproach to him.

Psalm 139:17-24

17 How precious also are Your
   thoughts to me, O God!
   How vast is the sum of them!

18 If I should count them, they
   would outnumber the sand.
   When I awake, I am still with You.

19 O that You would slay the
   wicked, O God;
   Depart from me, therefore,
   men of bloodshed.

20 For they speak against You wickedly,
   And Your enemies take
   Your name in vain.

21 Do I not hate those who
   hate You, O LORD?
   And do I not loathe those who
   rise up against You?

22 I hate them with the utmost hatred;
   They have become my enemies.

23 Search me, O God, and
   know my heart;
   Try me and know my
   anxious thoughts;

24 And see if there be any
   hurtful way in me,
   And lead me in the everlasting way.

Proverbs 29:22

22 An angry man stirs up strife,
   And a hot-tempered man
   abounds in transgression.

Jude 1-25

Jude, a bond-servant of Jesus Christ, and
brother of James,
To those who are the called, beloved in God
the Father, and kept for Jesus Christ: 2 May

mercy and peace and love be multiplied to you.

3 Beloved, while I was making every effort to write you about our common salvation, I felt the necessity to write to you appealing that you contend earnestly for the faith which was once for all handed down to the saints. 4 For certain persons have crept in unnoticed, those who were long beforehand marked out for this condemnation, ungodly persons who turn the grace of our God into licentiousness and deny our only Master and Lord, Jesus Christ.

3 contend earnestly. While the salvation of those to whom he wrote was not in jeopardy, false teachers preaching and living out a counterfeit gospel were misleading those who needed to hear the true gospel. Jude wrote this urgent imperative for Christians to wage war against error in all forms and fight strenuously for the truth, like a soldier who has been entrusted with a sacred task of guarding a holy treasure (1Ti 6:12; 2Ti 4:7). **the faith.** This is the whole body of revealed salvation truth contained in the Scriptures (Gal 1:23; Eph 4:5, 13; Php 1:27; 1Ti 4:1). See v. 20. Here is a call to know sound doctrine (Eph 4:14; Col 3:16; 1Pe 2:2; 1Jn 2:12–14), to be discerning in sorting out truth from error (1Th 5:20–22), and to be willing to confront and attack error (2Co 10:3–5; Php 1:7, 27; 1Ti 1:18; 6:12; 2Ti 1:13; 4:7–8; Titus 1:13). **once for all handed down.** God's revelation was delivered once as a unit, at the completion of the Scripture, and is not to be edited by either deletion or addition (Dt 4:2; 12:32; Pr 30:6; Rev 22:18–19). Scripture is complete, sufficient, and finished; therefore it is fixed for all time. Nothing is to be added to the body of the inspired Word because nothing else is needed.

5 Now I desire to remind you, though you know all things once for all, that the Lord, after saving a people out of the land of Egypt, subsequently destroyed those who did not believe. 6 And angels who did not keep their own domain, but abandoned their proper abode, He has kept in eternal bonds under darkness for the judgment of the great day, 7 just as Sodom and Gomorrah and the cities around them, since they in the same way as these indulged in gross immorality and went after strange flesh, are exhibited as an example in undergoing the punishment of eternal fire. 8 Yet in the same way these men, also by dreaming, defile the flesh, and reject authority, and revile angelic majesties. 9 But Michael the archangel, when he disputed with the devil and argued about the body of Moses, did not dare pronounce against him a railing judgment, but said, "The Lord rebuke you!" 10 But these men revile the things which they do not understand; and the things which they know by instinct, like unreasoning animals, by these things they are destroyed. 11 Woe to them! For they have gone the way of Cain, and for pay they have rushed headlong into the error of Balaam, and perished in the rebellion of Korah. 12 These are the men who are hidden reefs in your love feasts when they feast with you without fear, caring for themselves; clouds without water, carried along by winds; autumn trees without fruit, doubly dead, uprooted; 13 wild waves of the sea, casting up their own shame like foam; wandering stars, for whom the black darkness has been reserved forever.

13 wild waves. Apostates promise powerful ministry, but are quickly exposed as wreakers of havoc and workers of worthless shame (Is 57:20). **wandering stars.** This most likely refers to a meteor or shooting star which has an uncontrolled moment of brilliance and then fades away forever into nothing. Apostates promise enduring spiritual direction, but deliver a brief, aimless, and worthless flash.

14 It was also about these men that Enoch, in the seventh generation from Adam, prophesied, saying, "Behold, the Lord came with many thousands of His holy ones, 15 to execute judgment upon all, and to convict all the ungodly of all their ungodly deeds which they have done in an ungodly way, and of all the harsh things which ungodly sinners have spoken against Him." 16 These are grumblers, finding fault, following after their own lusts; they speak arrogantly, flattering people for the sake of gaining an advantage.

17 But you, beloved, ought to remember the words that were spoken beforehand by the apostles of our Lord Jesus Christ, 18 that they were saying to you, "In the last time there will be mockers, following after their own ungodly lusts." 19 These are the ones who cause divisions, worldly-minded, devoid of the Spirit. 20 But you, beloved, building yourselves up on your most holy faith, praying in the Holy Spirit, 21 keep yourselves in the love of God, waiting anxiously for the mercy of our Lord Jesus Christ to eternal life. 22 And have mercy on some, who are

doubting; ²³save others, snatching them out of the fire; and on some have mercy with fear, hating even the garment polluted by the flesh.

²⁴Now to Him who is able to keep you from stumbling, and to make you stand in the presence of His glory blameless with great joy, ²⁵to the only God our Savior, through Jesus Christ our Lord, be glory, majesty, dominion and authority, before all time and now and forever. Amen.

DAY 10: Who was Jude, and why did he write his letter?

Although Jude (Judas) was a common name in Palestine (at least 8 are named in the New Testament), the author of Jude generally has been accepted as Jude, Christ's half-brother. He is to be differentiated from the apostle Judas, the son of James (Lk 6:16; Ac 1:13). Several lines of thought lead to this conclusion: 1) Jude's appeal to being the "brother of James," the leader of the Jerusalem Council (Ac 15) and another half-brother of Jesus (v. 1; Gal 1:19); 2) Jude's salutation being similar to James's (Jas 1:1); and 3) Jude's not identifying himself as an apostle (v. 1), but rather distinguishing between himself and the apostles (v. 17).

Jude lived at a time when Christianity was under severe political attack from Rome and aggressive spiritual infiltration from gnostic like apostates and libertines who sowed abundant seed for a gigantic harvest of doctrinal error. It could be that this was the forerunner to full-blown Gnosticism which the apostle John would confront over 25 years later in his epistles. Except for John, who lived at the close of the century, all of the other apostles had been martyred; and Christianity was thought to be extremely vulnerable. Thus, Jude called the church to fight, in the midst of intense spiritual warfare, for the truth.

Jude is the only New Testament book devoted exclusively to confronting apostasy, meaning defection from the true, biblical faith (vv. 3, 17). Apostates are described elsewhere in 2 Thessalonians 2:10; Hebrews 10:29; 2 Peter 2:1–22; 1Jn 2:18–23. He wrote to condemn the apostates and to urge believers to contend for the faith. He called for discernment on the part of the church and a rigorous defense of biblical truth. He followed the earlier examples of: 1) Christ (Mt 7:15ff.; 16:6–12; 24:11ff; Rev 2–3); 2) Paul (Ac 20:29–30; 1Ti 4:1; 2Ti 3:1–5; 4:3–4); 3) Peter (2Pe 2:–2; 3:3–4); and 4) John (1Jn 4:1–6; 2Jn 6–11).

DECEMBER 11

Hosea 13:1–14:9

13 When Ephraim spoke, there was trembling.
He exalted himself in Israel,
But through Baal he did wrong and died.

² And now they sin more and more,
And make for themselves molten images,
Idols skillfully made from their silver,
All of them the work of craftsmen.
They say of them, "Let the men who sacrifice kiss the calves!"

³ Therefore they will be like the morning cloud
And like dew which soon disappears,
Like chaff which is blown away from the threshing floor
And like smoke from a chimney.

⁴ Yet I have been the LORD your God
Since the land of Egypt;
And you were not to know any god except Me,
For there is no savior besides Me.

⁵ I cared for you in the wilderness,
In the land of drought.

⁶ As they had their pasture, they became satisfied,
And being satisfied, their heart became proud;
Therefore they forgot Me.

⁷ So I will be like a lion to them;
Like a leopard I will lie in wait by the wayside.

⁸ I will encounter them like a bear robbed of her cubs,
And I will tear open their chests;
There I will also devour them like a lioness,
As a wild beast would tear them.

⁹ It is your destruction, O Israel,
That you are against Me, against your help.

¹⁰ Where now is your king
That he may save you in all your cities,
And your judges of whom you requested,
"Give me a king and princes"?

¹¹ I gave you a king in My anger
And took him away in My wrath.

12 The iniquity of Ephraim is bound up;
His sin is stored up.
13 The pains of childbirth
come upon him;
He is not a wise son,
For it is not the time that he should
delay at the opening of the womb.
14 Shall I ransom them from
the power of Sheol?
Shall I redeem them from death?
O Death, where are your thorns?
O Sheol, where is your sting?
Compassion will be hidden
from My sight.

13:14 Placing the strong affirmation of deliverance so abruptly after a denunciation intensified the wonder of His unrequited love (11:8–9; Lv 26:44). This can apply to God's restoration of Israel from Assyria, and in future times from all the lands of the dispersion, preserving them and bringing them back to their land for the kingdom of Messiah (Eze 37). It also speaks of the time of personal resurrection as in Daniel 12:2–3. Repentant Israelites will be restored to the land and even raised from death to glory. Paul uses this text in 1 Corinthians 15:55 (quoting the LXX) to celebrate the future resurrection of the church. The Messiah's great victory over death and the grave is the firstfruits of the full harvest to come, when all believers will likewise experience the power of His resurrection.

---

15 Though he flourishes
among the reeds,
An east wind will come,
The wind of the LORD coming
up from the wilderness;
And his fountain will become dry
And his spring will be dried up;
It will plunder *his* treasury of
every precious article.
16 Samaria will be held guilty,
For she has rebelled against her God.
They will fall by the sword,
Their little ones will be
dashed in pieces,
And their pregnant women
will be ripped open.

14 Return, O Israel, to the
LORD your God,
For you have stumbled because
of your iniquity.

2 Take words with you and
return to the LORD.
Say to Him, "Take away all iniquity
And receive *us* graciously,
That we may present the
fruit of our lips.
3 "Assyria will not save us,
We will not ride on horses;
Nor will we say again, 'Our god,'
To the work of our hands;
For in You the orphan finds mercy."

4 I will heal their apostasy,
I will love them freely,
For My anger has turned
away from them.
5 I will be like the dew to Israel;
He will blossom like the lily,
And he will take root like *the
cedars of* Lebanon.
6 His shoots will sprout,
And his beauty will be
like the olive tree
And his fragrance like *the
cedars of* Lebanon.
7 Those who live in his shadow
Will again raise grain,
And they will blossom
like the vine.
His renown *will be* like the
wine of Lebanon.

8 O Ephraim, what more have
I to do with idols?
It is I who answer and
look after you.
I am like a luxuriant cypress;
From Me comes your fruit.

9 Whoever is wise, let him
understand these things;
Whoever is discerning, let
him know them.
For the ways of the LORD are right,
And the righteous will walk in them,
But transgressors will
stumble in them.

Psalm 140:1–5

For the choir director. A Psalm of David.

Rescue me, O LORD, from evil men;
Preserve me from violent men
2 Who devise evil things in *their* hearts;
They continually stir up wars.
3 They sharpen their tongues
as a serpent;
Poison of a viper is under
their lips.   *Selah*

⁴ Keep me, O LORD, from the
    hands of the wicked;
Preserve me from violent men
Who have purposed to
    trip up my feet.
⁵ The proud have hidden a trap
    for me, and cords;
They have spread a net
    by the wayside;
They have set snares for me.   *Selah*

Proverbs 29:23

²³ A man's pride will bring him low,
But a humble spirit
    will obtain honor.

Revelation 1:1-20

1 The Revelation of Jesus Christ, which God gave Him to show to His bond-servants, the things which must soon take place; and He sent and communicated *it* by His angel to His bond-servant John, ² who testified to the word of God and to the testimony of Jesus Christ, *even* to all that he saw. ³ Blessed is he who reads and those who hear the words of the prophecy, and heed the things which are written in it; for the time is near.

⁴ John to the seven churches that are in Asia: Grace to you and peace, from Him who is and who was and who is to come, and from the seven Spirits who are before His throne, ⁵ and from Jesus Christ, the faithful witness, the firstborn of the dead, and the ruler of the kings of the earth. To Him who loves us and released us from our sins by His blood— ⁶ and He has made us *to be* a kingdom, priests to His God and Father—to Him *be* the glory and the

1:4 seven churches that are in Asia. Asia Minor, equivalent to modern Turkey, was composed of 7 postal districts. At the center of those districts were 7 key cities which served as central points for the dissemination of information. It is to the churches in those cities that John writes. **who is and who was and who is to come.** God's eternal presence is not limited by time. He has always been present and will come in the future. **the seven Spirits.** There are two possible meanings: 1) a reference to Isaiah's prophecy concerning the 7-fold ministry of the Holy Spirit (Is 11:2); or 2) more likely, it is a reference to the lampstand with 7 lamps (a menorah) in Zechariah—also a description of the Holy Spirit (4:5; 5:6; Zec 4:1–10). In either case, 7 is the number of completeness, so John is identifying the fullness of the Holy Spirit.

dominion forever and ever. Amen. ⁷ BEHOLD, HE IS COMING WITH THE CLOUDS, and every eye will see Him, even those who pierced Him; and all the tribes of the earth will mourn over Him. So it is to be. Amen.

⁸ "I am the Alpha and the Omega," says the Lord God, "who is and who was and who is to come, the Almighty."

⁹ I, John, your brother and fellow partaker in the tribulation and kingdom and perseverance *which are* in Jesus, was on the island called Patmos because of the word of God and the testimony of Jesus. ¹⁰ I was in the Spirit on the Lord's day, and I heard behind me a loud voice like *the sound* of a trumpet, ¹¹ saying, "Write in a book what you see, and send *it* to the seven churches: to Ephesus and to Smyrna and to Pergamum and to Thyatira and to Sardis and to Philadelphia and to Laodicea."

1:10 in the Spirit. This was not a dream. John was supernaturally transported out of the material world awake—not sleeping—to an experience beyond the normal senses. The Holy Spirit empowered his senses to perceive revelation from God (Ac 10:11). **Lord's day.** This phrase appears in many early Christian writings and refers to Sunday, the day of the Lord's resurrection. Some have suggested this phrase refers to "the day of the Lord," but the context doesn't support that interpretation. **loud voice.** Throughout Revelation, a loud sound or voice indicates the solemnity of what God is about to reveal.

¹² Then I turned to see the voice that was speaking with me. And having turned I saw seven golden lampstands; ¹³ and in the middle of the lampstands I *saw* one like a son of man, clothed in a robe reaching to the feet, and girded across His chest with a golden sash. ¹⁴ His head and His hair were white like white wool, like snow; and His eyes were like a flame of fire. ¹⁵ His feet *were* like burnished bronze, when it has been made to glow in a furnace, and His voice *was* like the sound of many waters. ¹⁶ In His right hand He held seven stars, and out of His mouth came a sharp two-edged sword; and His face was like the sun shining in its strength.

¹⁷ When I saw Him, I fell at His feet like a dead man. And He placed His right hand on me, saying, "Do not be afraid; I am the first and the last, ¹⁸ and the living One; and I was

1:17 fell at His feet. A common response to seeing the awesome glory of the Lord (Ge 17:3; Nu 16:22; Is 6:1–8; Eze 1:28; Ac 9:4). **first and the last.** Jesus Christ applies this Old Testament name for Yahweh (22:13; Is 41:4; 44:6; 48:12) to Himself, clearly claiming to be God. Idols will come and go. He was before them, and He will remain after them.

dead, and behold, I am alive forevermore, and I have the keys of death and of Hades. [19]Therefore write the things which you have seen, and the things which are, and the things which will take place after these things. [20]As for the mystery of the seven stars which you saw in My right hand, and the seven golden lampstands: the seven stars are the angels of the seven churches, and the seven lampstands are the seven churches.

DAY 11: What is the background for the Book of Revelation?

Revelation begins with John, the last surviving apostle and an old man, in exile on the small barren island of Patmos, located in the Aegean Sea southwest of Ephesus. The Roman authorities had banished him there because of his faithful preaching of the gospel (1:9). While on Patmos, John received a series of visions that laid out the future history of the world.

When he was arrested, John was in Ephesus, ministering to the church there and in the surrounding cities. Seeking to strengthen those congregations, he could no longer minister to them in person and, following the divine command (1:11), John addressed Revelation to them (1:4). The churches had begun to feel the effects of persecution; at least one man—probably a pastor—had already been martyred (2:13), and John himself had been exiled. But the storm of persecution was about to break in full fury upon the 7 churches so dear to the apostle's heart (2:10). To those churches, Revelation provided a message of hope: God is in sovereign control of all the events of human history; and though evil often seems pervasive and wicked men all-powerful, their ultimate doom is certain. Christ will come in glory to judge and rule.

Unlike most books of the Bible, Revelation contains its own title: "The Revelation of Jesus Christ" (1:1). "Revelation" (Greek, *apokalupsis*) means "an uncovering," "an unveiling," or "a disclosure." In all its uses, "revelation" refers to something or someone, once hidden, becoming visible. What this book reveals or unveils is Jesus Christ in glory. Truths about Him and His final victory, that the rest of Scripture merely allude to, become clearly visible through revelation about Jesus Christ.

DECEMBER 12

Joel 1:1–3:21

1 The word of the LORD that came to Joel, the son of Pethuel:

[2] Hear this, O elders,
　And listen, all inhabitants of the land.
　Has *anything like* this
　　happened in your days
　Or in your fathers' days?
[3] Tell your sons about it,
　And *let* your sons *tell* their sons,
　And their sons the next generation.

[4] What the gnawing locust has left,
　　the swarming locust has eaten;
　And what the swarming locust
　　has left, the creeping
　　locust has eaten;
　And what the creeping locust
　　has left, the stripping
　　locust has eaten.

1:2 Hear...listen. The gravity of the situation demanded the undivided focus of their senses, emphasizing the need to make a conscious, purposeful decision in the matter. The terminology was commonly used in "lawsuit" passages (Is 1:2; Hos 4:1), intimating that Israel was found guilty and that the present judgment was her "sentence." **elders...all inhabitants.** The former term refers to the civil and religious leaders, who, in light of their position, were exhorted to lead by example the entire population toward repentance.

[5] Awake, drunkards, and weep;
　And wail, all you wine drinkers,
　On account of the sweet wine
　That is cut off from your mouth.
[6] For a nation has invaded
　　my land,
　Mighty and without number;
　Its teeth are the teeth of a lion,
　And it has the fangs of a lioness.

7 It has made my vine a waste
And my fig tree splinters.
It has stripped them bare
and cast *them* away;
Their branches have become white.

8 Wail like a virgin girded with sackcloth
For the bridegroom of her youth.

9 The grain offering and the
drink offering are cut off
From the house of the LORD.
The priests mourn,
The ministers of the LORD.

10 The field is ruined,
The land mourns;
For the grain is ruined,
The new wine dries up,
Fresh oil fails.

11 Be ashamed, O farmers,
Wail, O vinedressers,
For the wheat and the barley;
Because the harvest of the
field is destroyed.

12 The vine dries up
And the fig tree fails;
The pomegranate, the palm
also, and the apple tree,
All the trees of the field dry up.
Indeed, rejoicing dries up
From the sons of men.

13 Gird yourselves *with sackcloth*
And lament, O priests;
Wail, O ministers of the altar!
Come, spend the night in sackcloth
O ministers of my God,
For the grain offering and
the drink offering
Are withheld from the
house of your God.

14 Consecrate a fast,
Proclaim a solemn assembly;
Gather the elders
And all the inhabitants of the land
To the house of the LORD your God,
And cry out to the LORD.

15 Alas for the day!
For the day of the LORD is near,
And it will come as destruction
from the Almighty.

16 Has not food been cut off
before our eyes,
Gladness and joy from the
house of our God?

17 The seeds shrivel under their clods;
The storehouses are desolate,
The barns are torn down,
For the grain is dried up.

18 How the beasts groan!
The herds of cattle wander aimlessly
Because there is no pasture for them;
Even the flocks of sheep suffer.

19 To You, O LORD, I cry;
For fire has devoured the
pastures of the wilderness
And the flame has burned up
all the trees of the field.

20 Even the beasts of the
field pant for You;
For the water brooks are dried up
And fire has devoured the
pastures of the wilderness.

2 Blow a trumpet in Zion,
And sound an alarm on
My holy mountain!
Let all the inhabitants of
the land tremble,
For the day of the LORD is coming;
Surely it is near,

2 A day of darkness and gloom,
A day of clouds and thick darkness.
As the dawn is spread over
the mountains,
So there is a great and mighty people;
There has never been *anything* like it,
Nor will there be again after it
To the years of many generations.

3 A fire consumes before them
And behind them a flame burns.
The land is like the garden
of Eden before them
But a desolate wilderness
behind them,
And nothing at all escapes them.

4 Their appearance is like the
appearance of horses;
And like war horses, so they run.

5 With a noise as of chariots
They leap on the tops of
the mountains,
Like the crackling of a flame of
fire consuming the stubble,
Like a mighty people
arranged for battle.

6 Before them the people are in anguish;
All faces turn pale.

7 They run like mighty men,
They climb the wall like soldiers;
And they each march in line,
Nor do they deviate from their paths.

8 They do not crowd each other,
They march everyone in his path;
When they burst through
the defenses,
They do not break ranks.

9 They rush on the city,
They run on the wall;
They climb into the houses,
They enter through the
windows like a thief.
10 Before them the earth quakes,
The heavens tremble,
The sun and the moon grow dark
And the stars lose their brightness.
11 The LORD utters His voice
before His army;
Surely His camp is very great,
For strong is he who carries
out His word.
The day of the LORD is indeed
great and very awesome,
And who can endure it?
12 "Yet even now," declares the LORD,
"Return to Me with all your heart,
And with fasting, weeping
and mourning;
13 And rend your heart and
not your garments."
Now return to the LORD your God,
For He is gracious and
compassionate,
Slow to anger, abounding
in lovingkindness
And relenting of evil.
14 Who knows whether He will
not turn and relent
And leave a blessing behind Him,
Even a grain offering and
a drink offering
For the LORD your God?
15 Blow a trumpet in Zion,
Consecrate a fast, proclaim
a solemn assembly,
16 Gather the people, sanctify
the congregation,
Assemble the elders,
Gather the children and the
nursing infants.
Let the bridegroom come
out of his room
And the bride out of her
bridal chamber.
17 Let the priests, the LORD'S ministers,
Weep between the porch
and the altar,
And let them say, "Spare
Your people, O LORD,
And do not make Your
inheritance a reproach,
A byword among the nations.
Why should they among
the peoples say,
'Where is their God?'"

18 Then the LORD will be
zealous for His land
And will have pity on His people.
19 The LORD will answer and
say to His people,
"Behold, I am going to send you
grain, new wine and oil,
And you will be satisfied
in full with them;
And I will never again make you a
reproach among the nations.
20 "But I will remove the northern
army far from you,
And I will drive it into a parched
and desolate land,
And its vanguard into
the eastern sea,
And its rear guard into
the western sea.
And its stench will arise and its
foul smell will come up,
For it has done great things."

21 Do not fear, O land, rejoice
and be glad,
For the LORD has done great things.
22 Do not fear, beasts of the field,
For the pastures of the wilderness
have turned green,
For the tree has borne its fruit,
The fig tree and the vine
have yielded in full.
23 So rejoice, O sons of Zion,
And be glad in the LORD your God;
For He has given you the early
rain for your vindication.
And He has poured down
for you the rain,
The early and latter rain as before.
24 The threshing floors will
be full of grain,
And the vats will overflow with
the new wine and oil.
25 "Then I will make up to
you for the years
That the swarming
locust has eaten,
The creeping locust, the stripping
locust and the gnawing locust,
My great army which I
sent among you.
26 "You will have plenty to eat
and be satisfied
And praise the name of
the LORD your God,
Who has dealt wondrously with you;
Then My people will never
be put to shame.

27 "Thus you will know that I am
    in the midst of Israel,
And that I am the LORD your God,
And there is no other;
And My people will never
    be put to shame.

28 "It will come about after this
That I will pour out My Spirit
    on all mankind;
And your sons and daughters
    will prophesy,
Your old men will dream dreams,
Your young men will see visions.

2:28 after this. The abundance of material blessings would be followed by the outpouring of spiritual blessings. When coupled with the other temporal phrases within the passage ("in those days" [v. 29] and "before the great and awesome day of the LORD comes" [v. 31]), the term points to a Second Advent fulfillment time frame. **all mankind.** Since the context is "your sons and daughters," "all mankind" best refers to the house of Israel only. The nations are the recipients of God's wrath, not the effusion of His Spirit (3:2, 9ff.).

---

29 "Even on the male and female servants
    I will pour out My Spirit in those days.
30 "I will display wonders in the
    sky and on the earth,
Blood, fire and columns of smoke.
31 "The sun will be turned into darkness
And the moon into blood
Before the great and awesome
    day of the LORD comes.
32 "And it will come about that whoever
    calls on the name of the LORD
Will be delivered;
For on Mount Zion and in Jerusalem
There will be those who escape,
As the LORD has said,
Even among the survivors
    whom the LORD calls.

3 "For behold, in those days
    and at that time,
When I restore the fortunes of
    Judah and Jerusalem,
2 I will gather all the nations
And bring them down to the
    valley of Jehoshaphat.
Then I will enter into judgment
    with them there

On behalf of My people and
    My inheritance, Israel,
Whom they have scattered
    among the nations;
And they have divided up My land.
3 "They have also cast
    lots for My people,
Traded a boy for a harlot
And sold a girl for wine
    that they may drink.

4 Moreover, what are you to Me, O Tyre, Sidon and all the regions of Philistia? Are you rendering Me a recompense? But if you do recompense Me, swiftly and speedily I will return your recompense on your head. 5 Since you have taken My silver and My gold, brought My precious treasures to your temples, 6 and sold the sons of Judah and Jerusalem to the Greeks in order to remove them far from their territory, 7 behold, I am going to arouse them from the place where you have sold them, and return your recompense on your head. 8 Also I will sell your sons and your daughters into the hand of the sons of Judah, and they will sell them to the Sabeans, to a distant nation," for the LORD has spoken.

9 Proclaim this among the nations:
    Prepare a war; rouse
        the mighty men!
Let all the soldiers draw near,
    let them come up!
10 Beat your plowshares into swords
And your pruning hooks into spears;
Let the weak say, "I am
    a mighty man."
11 Hasten and come, all you
    surrounding nations,
And gather yourselves there.
Bring down, O LORD, Your
    mighty ones.
12 Let the nations be aroused
And come up to the valley
    of Jehoshaphat,
For there I will sit to judge
All the surrounding nations.
13 Put in the sickle, for the
    harvest is ripe.
Come, tread, for the wine press is full;
The vats overflow, for their
    wickedness is great.
14 Multitudes, multitudes in
    the valley of decision!
For the day of the LORD is near
    in the valley of decision.
15 The sun and moon grow dark
And the stars lose their brightness.

16 The LORD roars from Zion
   And utters His voice from Jerusalem,
   And the heavens and the
      earth tremble.
   But the LORD is a refuge
      for His people
   And a stronghold to
      the sons of Israel.
17 Then you will know that I am the
      LORD your God,
   Dwelling in Zion, My holy mountain.
   So Jerusalem will be holy,
   And strangers will pass
      through it no more.

18 And in that day
   The mountains will drip
      with sweet wine,
   And the hills will flow with milk,
   And all the brooks of Judah
      will flow with water;
   And a spring will go out from
      the house of the LORD
   To water the valley of Shittim.
19 Egypt will become a waste,
   And Edom will become a
      desolate wilderness,
   Because of the violence done
      to the sons of Judah,
   In whose land they have
      shed innocent blood.
20 But Judah will be inhabited forever
   And Jerusalem for all generations.
21 And I will avenge their blood
      which I have not avenged,
   For the LORD dwells in Zion.

Psalm 140:6–13

6 I said to the LORD, "You are my God;
   Give ear, O LORD, to the voice
      of my supplications.
7 "O GOD the Lord, the strength
      of my salvation,
   You have covered my head
      in the day of battle.
8 "Do not grant, O LORD, the
      desires of the wicked;
   Do not promote his *evil* device, *that*
      they *not* be exalted.   *Selah*

9 "As for the head of those
      who surround me,
   May the mischief of their
      lips cover them.
10 "May burning coals fall upon them;
   May they be cast into the fire,
   Into deep pits from which
      they cannot rise.

11 "May a slanderer not be
      established in the earth;
   May evil hunt the violent
      man speedily."
12 I know that the LORD will maintain
      the cause of the afflicted
   And justice for the poor.
13 Surely the righteous will give
      thanks to Your name;
   The upright will dwell in
      Your presence.

Proverbs 29:24

24 He who is a partner with a
      thief hates his own life;
   He hears the oath but tells nothing.

Revelation 2:1–29

2 "To the angel of the church in Ephesus
   write:
   The One who holds the seven stars in His
right hand, the One who walks among the
seven golden lampstands, says this:
   2 'I know your deeds and your toil and
perseverance, and that you cannot tolerate
evil men, and you put to the test those who
call themselves apostles, and they are not,
and you found them *to be* false; 3 and you
have perseverance and have endured for My
name's sake, and have not grown weary. 4 But
I have *this* against you, that you have left your
first love. 5 Therefore remember from where
you have fallen, and repent and do the deeds
you did at first; or else I am coming to you and
will remove your lampstand out of its place—
unless you repent. 6 Yet this you do have, that
you hate the deeds of the Nicolaitans, which
I also hate. 7 He who has an ear, let him hear
what the Spirit says to the churches. To him
who overcomes, I will grant to eat of the tree
of life which is in the Paradise of God.'
   8 "And to the angel of the church in Smyrna
write:
   The first and the last, who was dead, and
has come to life, says this:

2:4 left your first love. To be a Christian is to
love the Lord Jesus Christ (Jn 14:21, 23; 1Co 16:22).
But the Ephesians' passion and fervor for Christ
had become cold, mechanical orthodoxy. Their
doctrinal and moral purity, their undiminished
zeal for the truth, and their disciplined service
were no substitute for the love for Christ they
had forsaken.

2:8 Smyrna. Smyrna means "myrrh," the substance used for perfume and often for anointing a dead body for aromatic purposes. Called the crown of Asia, this ancient city (modern Izmir, Turkey) was the most beautiful in Asia Minor and a center of science and medicine. Always on the winner's side in the Roman wars, Smyrna's intense loyalty to Rome resulted in a strong emperor-worship cult. Fifty years after John's death, Polycarp, the pastor of the church in Smyrna, was burned alive at the age of 86 for refusing to worship Caesar. A large Jewish community in the city also proved hostile to the early church.

9 'I know your tribulation and your poverty (but you are rich), and the blasphemy by those who say they are Jews and are not, but are a synagogue of Satan. ¹⁰ Do not fear what you are about to suffer. Behold, the devil is about to cast some of you into prison, so that you will be tested, and you will have tribulation for ten days. Be faithful until death, and I will give you the crown of life. ¹¹ He who has an ear, let him hear what the Spirit says to the churches. He who overcomes will not be hurt by the second death.'

¹² "And to the angel of the church in Pergamum write:

The One who has the sharp two-edged sword says this:

¹³ 'I know where you dwell, where Satan's throne is; and you hold fast My name, and did not deny My faith even in the days of Antipas, My witness, My faithful one, who was killed among you, where Satan dwells. ¹⁴ But I have a few things against you, because you have there some who hold the teaching of Balaam, who kept teaching Balak to put a stumbling block

2:13 where Satan's throne is. The headquarters of satanic opposition and a Gentile base for false religions. On the acropolis in Pergamum was a huge, throne-shaped altar to Zeus. In addition, Asklepios, the god of healing, was the god most associated with Pergamum. His snake-like form is still the medical symbol today. The famous medical school connected to his temple mingled medicine with superstition. One prescription called for the worshiper to sleep on the temple floor, allowing snakes to crawl over his body and infuse him with their healing power.

before the sons of Israel, to eat things sacrificed to idols and to commit *acts of* immorality. ¹⁵ So you also have some who in the same way hold the teaching of the Nicolaitans. ¹⁶ Therefore repent; or else I am coming to you quickly, and I will make war against them with the sword of My mouth. ¹⁷ He who has an ear, let him hear what the Spirit says to the churches. To him who overcomes, to him I will give *some* of the hidden manna, and I will give him a white stone, and a new name written on the stone which no one knows but he who receives it.'

¹⁸ "And to the angel of the church in Thyatira write:

The Son of God, who has eyes like a flame of fire, and His feet are like burnished bronze, says this:

¹⁹ 'I know your deeds, and your love and faith and service and perseverance, and that your deeds of late are greater than at first. ²⁰ But I have *this* against you, that you tolerate the woman Jezebel, who calls herself a prophetess, and she teaches and leads My bond-servants astray so that they commit *acts of* immorality and eat things sacrificed to idols. ²¹ I gave her time to repent, and she does not want to repent of her immorality. ²² Behold, I will throw her on a bed *of sickness,* and those who commit adultery with her into great tribulation, unless they repent of her deeds. ²³ And I will kill her children with pestilence, and all the churches will know that I am He who searches the minds and hearts; and I will give to each one of you according to your deeds. ²⁴ But I say to you, the rest who are in Thyatira, who do not hold this teaching, who have not known the deep things of Satan, as they call them—I place no other burden on you. ²⁵ Nevertheless what you have, hold fast until I come. ²⁶ He who overcomes, and he who keeps My deeds until the end, TO HIM I WILL GIVE AUTHORITY OVER THE NATIONS; ²⁷ AND HE SHALL RULE THEM WITH A ROD OF IRON, AS THE VESSELS OF THE POTTER ARE BROKEN TO PIECES, as I also have received *authority* from My Father; ²⁸ and I will give him the morning star. ²⁹ He who has an ear, let him hear what the Spirit says to the churches.'

2:24 the deep things of Satan. This unbelievable libertinism and license was the fruit of pre-gnostic teaching that one was free to engage and explore the sphere of Satan and participate in evil with the body without harming the spirit.

DAY 12: Who was the prophet Joel, and what was he writing about?

The author identified himself only as "Joel the son of Pethuel" (1:1). The prophecy provides little else about the man. Even the name of his father is not mentioned elsewhere in the Old Testament. Although he displayed a profound zeal for the temple sacrifices (1:9; 2:13–16), his familiarity with pastoral and agricultural life and his separation from the priests (1:13–14; 2:17) suggest he was not a Levite. Extrabiblical tradition records that he was from the tribe of Reuben, from the town of Bethom or Bethharam, located northeast of the Dead Sea on the border of Reuben and Gad. The context of the prophecy, however, hints that he was a Judean from the Jerusalem vicinity, since the tone of a stranger is absent.

The theme of Joel is the day of the Lord. It permeates all parts of Joel's message, making it the most sustained treatment in the entire Old Testament (1:15; 3:14). The phrase is employed 19 times by 8 different Old Testament authors (Is 2:12; 13:6, 9; Eze 13:5; 30:3; Joel 1:15; 2:1, 11, 31; 3:14; Am 5:18 [2x],20; Obad v. 15; Zep 1:7, 14 [2x]; Zec 14:1; Mal 4:5). The phrase does not have reference to a chronological time period, but to a general period of wrath and judgment uniquely belonging to the Lord. It is exclusively the day which unveils His character—mighty, powerful, and holy, thus terrifying His enemies. The day of the Lord does not always refer to an eschatological event; on occasion it has a near historical fulfillment, as seen in Ezekiel 13:5, where it speaks of the Babylonian conquest and destruction of Jerusalem. As is common in prophecy, the near fulfillment is a historic event upon which to comprehend the more distant, eschatological fulfillment.

DECEMBER 13

Amos 1:1–3:15

1 The words of Amos, who was among the sheepherders from Tekoa, which he envisioned in visions concerning Israel in the days of Uzziah king of Judah, and in the days of Jeroboam son of Joash, king of Israel, two years before the earthquake.

2 He said,
"The LORD roars from Zion
And from Jerusalem He
utters His voice;
And the shepherds' pasture
grounds mourn,
And the summit of Carmel dries up."

3 Thus says the LORD,
"For three transgressions of
Damascus and for four
I will not revoke its *punishment,*
Because they threshed Gilead with
implements of sharp iron.
4 "So I will send fire upon the
house of Hazael
And it will consume the
citadels of Ben-hadad.
5 "I will also break the *gate*
bar of Damascus,
And cut off the inhabitant
from the valley of Aven,
And him who holds the
scepter, from Beth-eden;

So the people of Aram will
go exiled to Kir,"
Says the LORD.

6 Thus says the LORD,
"For three transgressions of
Gaza and for four
I will not revoke its *punishment,*
Because they deported an
entire population
To deliver *it* up to Edom.
7 "So I will send fire upon
the wall of Gaza
And it will consume her citadels.
8 "I will also cut off the inhabitant
from Ashdod,
And him who holds the
scepter, from Ashkelon;
I will even unleash My
power upon Ekron,
And the remnant of the
Philistines will perish,"
Says the Lord GOD.

9 Thus says the LORD,
"For three transgressions of
Tyre and for four
I will not revoke its *punishment,*
Because they delivered up an
entire population to Edom
And did not remember *the*
covenant of brotherhood.
10 "So I will send fire upon
the wall of Tyre
And it will consume her citadels."

¹¹ Thus says the LORD,
"For three transgressions of
    Edom and for four
I will not revoke its *punishment,*
Because he pursued his
    brother with the sword,
While he stifled his compassion;
His anger also tore continually,
And he maintained his
    fury forever.
¹² So I will send fire upon Teman
    And it will consume the
    citadels of Bozrah."

¹³ Thus says the LORD,
"For three transgressions of the
    sons of Ammon and for four
I will not revoke its *punishment,*
Because they ripped open the
    pregnant women of Gilead
In order to enlarge their borders.
¹⁴ So I will kindle a fire on
    the wall of Rabbah
And it will consume her citadels
Amid war cries on the
    day of battle,
And a storm on the day of tempest.
¹⁵ Their king will go into exile,
    He and his princes together,"
    says the LORD.

2 Thus says the LORD,
"For three transgressions of
    Moab and for four
I will not revoke its *punishment,*
Because he burned the bones of
    the king of Edom to lime.
² So I will send fire upon Moab
    And it will consume the
    citadels of Kerioth;
And Moab will die amid tumult,
With war cries and the
    sound of a trumpet.
³ I will also cut off the judge
    from her midst
And slay all her princes with
    him," says the LORD.

⁴ Thus says the LORD,
"For three transgressions of
    Judah and for four
I will not revoke its *punishment,*
Because they rejected the
    law of the LORD
And have not kept His statutes;
Their lies also have led them astray,
Those after which their
    fathers walked.

⁵ So I will send fire upon Judah
    And it will consume the
    citadels of Jerusalem."

⁶ Thus says the LORD,
"For three transgressions of
    Israel and for four
I will not revoke its *punishment,*
Because they sell the
    righteous for money
And the needy for a pair of sandals.
⁷ These who pant after the *very*
    dust of the earth on the
    head of the helpless
Also turn aside the way
    of the humble;
And a man and his father
    resort to the same girl
In order to profane My holy name.
⁸ On garments taken as
    pledges they stretch out
    beside every altar,
And in the house of their God
    they drink the wine of those
    who have been fined.

⁹ Yet it was I who destroyed the
    Amorite before them,
Though his height *was* like
    the height of cedars
And he *was* strong as the oaks;
I even destroyed his fruit above
    and his root below.
¹⁰ It was I who brought you up
    from the land of Egypt,
And I led you in the
    wilderness forty years
That you might take possession
    of the land of the Amorite.
¹¹ Then I raised up some of your
    sons to be prophets
And some of your young
    men to be Nazirites.
Is this not so, O sons of Israel?"
    declares the LORD.
¹² But you made the Nazirites
    drink wine,
And you commanded the
    prophets saying, 'You
    shall not prophesy!'
¹³ Behold, I am weighted
    down beneath you
As a wagon is weighted down
    when filled with sheaves.
¹⁴ Flight will perish from the swift,
    And the stalwart will not
    strengthen his power,
Nor the mighty man save his life.

¹⁵ "He who grasps the bow will
not stand *his ground,*
The swift of foot will not escape,
Nor will he who rides the
horse save his life.
¹⁶ "Even the bravest among the
warriors will flee naked in
that day," declares the LORD.

3 Hear this word which the LORD has spoken against you, sons of Israel, against the entire family which He brought up from the land of Egypt:

² "You only have I chosen among
all the families of the earth;
Therefore I will punish you
for all your iniquities."
³ Do two men walk together
unless they have made
an appointment?
⁴ Does a lion roar in the forest
when he has no prey?
Does a young lion growl
from his den unless he has
captured *something?*
⁵ Does a bird fall into a trap
on the ground when
there is no bait in it?
Does a trap spring up from
the earth when it captures
nothing at all?
⁶ If a trumpet is blown in a city
will not the people tremble?
If a calamity occurs in a city
has not the LORD done it?
⁷ Surely the Lord GOD does nothing
Unless He reveals His secret counsel
To His servants the prophets.
⁸ A lion has roared! Who will not fear?
The Lord GOD has spoken!
Who can but prophesy?

⁹ Proclaim on the citadels in Ashdod and on the citadels in the land of Egypt and say, "Assemble yourselves on the mountains of Samaria and see *the* great tumults within her and *the* oppressions in her midst. ¹⁰ But they do not know how to do what is right," declares the LORD, "these who hoard up violence and devastation in their citadels." ¹¹ Therefore, thus says the Lord GOD,

"An enemy, even one
surrounding the land,
Will pull down your
strength from you
And your citadels will be looted."

¹² Thus says the LORD,

"Just as the shepherd snatches
from the lion's mouth a couple
of legs or a piece of an ear,
So will the sons of Israel dwelling
in Samaria be snatched away—
With *the* corner of a bed and
the cover of a couch!
¹³ "Hear and testify against
the house of Jacob,"
Declares the Lord GOD, the
God of hosts.
¹⁴ "For on the day that I punish
Israel's transgressions,
I will also punish the
altars of Bethel;
The horns of the altar
will be cut off
And they will fall to the ground.
¹⁵ "I will also smite the winter
house together with the
summer house;
The houses of ivory will also perish
And the great houses will
come to an end,"
Declares the LORD.

Psalm 141:1–4

A Psalm of David.

O LORD, I call upon You; hasten to me!
Give ear to my voice
when I call to You!
² May my prayer be counted
as incense before You;
The lifting up of my hands as
the evening offering.
³ Set a guard, O LORD, over my mouth;
Keep watch over the door of my lips.
⁴ Do not incline my heart to
any evil thing,
To practice deeds of wickedness
With men who do iniquity;
And do not let me eat of
their delicacies.

Proverbs 29:25

²⁵ The fear of man brings a snare,
But he who trusts in the
LORD will be exalted.

Revelation 3:1–22

3 "To the angel of the church in Sardis write: He who has the seven Spirits of God and the seven stars, says this: 'I know your deeds, that you have a name that you are alive, but you are dead. ² Wake up, and strengthen the things that remain, which were about to die;

for I have not found your deeds completed in the sight of My God. ³So remember what you have received and heard; and keep *it*, and repent. Therefore if you do not wake up, I will come like a thief, and you will not know at what hour I will come to you. ⁴But you have a few people in Sardis who have not soiled their garments; and they will walk with Me in white, for they are worthy. ⁵He who overcomes will thus be clothed in white garments; and I will not erase his name from the book of life, and I will confess his name before My Father and before His angels. ⁶He who has an ear, let him hear what the Spirit says to the churches.'

⁷"And to the angel of the church in Philadelphia write:

He who is holy, who is true, who has the key of David, who opens and no one will shut, and who shuts and no one opens, says this:

⁸'I know your deeds. Behold, I have put before you an open door which no one can shut, because you have a little power, and have kept My word, and have not denied My name. ⁹Behold, I will cause *those* of the synagogue of Satan, who say that they are Jews and are not, but lie—I will make them come and bow down at your feet, and *make them* know that I have loved you. ¹⁰Because you have kept the word of My perseverance, I also will keep you from the hour of testing, that *hour* which is about to come upon the whole world, to test those who dwell on the earth. ¹¹I am coming quickly; hold fast what

3:10 keep you from the hour of testing. Christ's description—an event still future that for a short time severely tests the whole world—must refer to the time of tribulation, the 7-year period before Christ's earthly kingdom is consummated, featuring the unleashing of divine wrath in judgments expressed as seals, trumpets, and bowls. This period is described in detail throughout chaps. 6–19. The latter half is called "the great tribulation" (7:14; Mt 24:21) and is identified as to time in 11:2–3; 12:6, 14; 13:5. The verb "keep" is followed by a preposition whose normal meaning is "from" or "out of"—this phrase, "keep...from" supports the pretribulational rapture of the church. This period is the same as Daniel's 70th week (Da 9:24–27) and "the time of Jacob's distress" (Jer 30:7).

you have, so that no one will take your crown. ¹²He who overcomes, I will make him a pillar in the temple of My God, and he will not go out from it anymore; and I will write on him the name of My God, and the name of the city of My God, the new Jerusalem, which comes down out of heaven from My God, and My new name. ¹³He who has an ear, let him hear what the Spirit says to the churches.'

¹⁴"To the angel of the church in Laodicea write:

The Amen, the faithful and true Witness, the Beginning of the creation of God, says this:

¹⁵'I know your deeds, that you are neither cold nor hot; I wish that you were cold or hot. ¹⁶So because you are lukewarm, and neither hot nor cold, I will spit you out of My mouth. ¹⁷Because you say, "I am rich, and have become wealthy, and have need of nothing," and you do not know that you are wretched and miserable and poor and blind and naked, ¹⁸I advise you to buy from Me gold refined by fire so that you may become rich, and white garments so that you may clothe yourself, and *that* the shame of your nakedness will not be revealed; and eye salve to anoint your eyes so that you may see. ¹⁹Those whom I love, I reprove and discipline; therefore be zealous and repent. ²⁰Behold, I stand at the door and knock; if anyone hears My voice and opens the door, I will come in to him and will dine with him, and he with Me. ²¹He who overcomes, I will grant to him to sit down with Me on My throne, as I also overcame and sat down with My Father on His throne. ²²He who has an ear, let him hear what the Spirit says to the churches.'"

3:16 lukewarm. I.e., tepid. Nearby Hierapolis was famous for its hot springs, and Colossae for its cold, refreshing mountain stream. But Laodicea had dirty, tepid water that flowed for miles through an underground aqueduct. Visitors, unaccustomed to it, immediately spat it out. The church at Laodicea was neither cold, openly rejecting Christ, nor hot, filled with spiritual zeal. Instead, its members were lukewarm, hypocrites professing to know Christ, but not truly belonging to Him (Mt 7:21ff.). **I will spit you out of My mouth.** Just like the dirty, tepid water of Laodicea, these self-deceived hypocrites sickened Christ.

Amos was from Tekoa, a small village 10 miles south of Jerusalem. He was the only prophet to give his occupation before declaring his divine commission. He was not of priestly or noble descent but worked as a "sheepherder" (1:1; 2Ki 3:4) and a "grower of sycamore figs" (7:14) and was a contemporary of Jonah (2Ki 14:25), Hosea (Hos 1:1), and Isaiah (Is 1:1).

Amos was a Judean prophet called to deliver a message primarily to the northern tribes of Israel (7:15). Politically, it was a time of prosperity under the long and secure reign of Jeroboam II who, following the example of his father Joash (2Ki 13:25), significantly "restored the border of Israel" (2Ki 14:25). It was also a time of peace with both Judah (5:5) and her more distant neighbors. The ever-present menace of Assyria was subdued earlier that century because of Nineveh's repentance at the preaching of Jonah (Jon 3:10). Spiritually, however, it was a time of rampant corruption and moral decay (4:1; 5:10–13; 2Ki 14:24).

Amos addresses Israel's two primary sins: 1) an absence of true worship and 2) a lack of justice. In the midst of their ritualistic performance of worship, they were not pursuing the Lord with their hearts (4:4–5; 5:4–6) nor following His standard of justice with their neighbors (5:10–13; 6:12). This apostasy, evidenced by continual, willful rejection of the prophetic message of Amos, is promised divine judgment. Because of His covenant, however, the Lord will not abandon Israel altogether, but will bring future restoration to the righteous remnant (9:7–15).

DECEMBER 14

Amos 4:1–5:27

4 Hear this word, you cows of
  Bashan who are on the
  mountain of Samaria,
Who oppress the poor, who
  crush the needy,
Who say to your husbands, "Bring
  now, that we may drink!"
2 The Lord GOD has sworn
  by His holiness,
"Behold, the days are coming upon you
When they will take you away
  with meat hooks,
And the last of you with fish hooks.
3 "You will go out *through*
  breaches *in the walls,*
Each one straight before her,
And you will be cast to Harmon,"
  declares the LORD.

4 "Enter Bethel and transgress;
In Gilgal multiply transgression!
Bring your sacrifices every morning,
Your tithes every three days.
5 "Offer a thank offering also from
  that which is leavened,
And proclaim freewill offerings,
  make them known.
For so you love *to do,* you
  sons of Israel,"
Declares the Lord GOD.

6 "But I gave you also cleanness
  of teeth in all your cities

And lack of bread in all your places,
  Yet you have not returned to
  Me," declares the LORD.
7 "Furthermore, I withheld
  the rain from you
While *there were* still three
  months until harvest.
Then I would send rain on one city
And on another city I would
  not send rain;
One part would be rained on,
While the part not rained
  on would dry up.
8 "So two or three cities would stagger
  to another city to drink water,
But would not be satisfied;
Yet you have not returned to
  Me," declares the LORD.
9 "I smote you with scorching
  wind and mildew;
And the caterpillar was devouring
Your many gardens and vineyards,
  fig trees and olive trees;
Yet you have not returned to
  Me," declares the LORD.
10 "I sent a plague among you after
  the manner of Egypt;
I slew your young men by the sword
  along with your captured horses,
And I made the stench of your
  camp rise up in your nostrils;
Yet you have not returned to
  Me," declares the LORD.
11 "I overthrew you, as God overthrew
  Sodom and Gomorrah,
And you were like a firebrand
  snatched from a blaze;

Yet you have not returned to
Me," declares the LORD.
12 "Therefore thus I will do to you, O Israel;
Because I will do this to you,
Prepare to meet your God, O Israel."
13 For behold, He who forms mountains
and creates the wind
And declares to man what
are His thoughts,
He who makes dawn into darkness
And treads on the high
places of the earth,
The LORD God of hosts is His name.

5 Hear this word which I take up for
you as a dirge, O house of Israel:
2 She has fallen, she will not rise again—
The virgin Israel.
She lies neglected on her land;
There is none to raise her up.

3 For thus says the Lord GOD,

"The city which goes forth
a thousand *strong*
Will have a hundred left,
And the one which goes forth
a hundred *strong*
Will have ten left to the house of Israel."

4 For thus says the LORD to the house of
Israel,

"Seek Me that you may live.
5 "But do not resort to Bethel
And do not come to Gilgal,
Nor cross over to Beersheba;
For Gilgal will certainly
go into captivity
And Bethel will come to trouble.
6 "Seek the LORD that you may live,
Or He will break forth like a
fire, O house of Joseph,
And it will consume with none
to quench *it* for Bethel,
7 *For* those who turn justice
into wormwood
And cast righteousness
down to the earth."
8 He who made the Pleiades and Orion
And changes deep darkness
into morning,
Who also darkens day *into* night,
Who calls for the waters of the sea
And pours them out on the
surface of the earth,
The LORD is His name.

9 It is He who flashes forth *with*
destruction upon the strong,
So that destruction comes
upon the fortress.
10 They hate him who reproves
in the gate,
And they abhor him who
speaks *with* integrity.
11 Therefore because you impose
heavy rent on the poor
And exact a tribute of
grain from them,
Though you have built houses
of well-hewn stone,
Yet you will not live in them;
You have planted pleasant
vineyards, yet you will
not drink their wine.
12 For I know your transgressions are
many and your sins are great,
You who distress the righteous
and accept bribes
And turn aside the poor in the gate.
13 Therefore at such a time the
prudent person keeps silent,
for it is an evil time.
14 Seek good and not evil,
that you may live;
And thus may the LORD God
of hosts be with you,
Just as you have said!
15 Hate evil, love good,
And establish justice in the gate!
Perhaps the LORD God of hosts
May be gracious to the
remnant of Joseph.

16 Therefore thus says the LORD God of
hosts, the Lord,

"There is wailing in all the plazas,
And in all the streets they
say, 'Alas! Alas!'
They also call the farmer to mourning
And professional mourners
to lamentation.
17 "And in all the vineyards
there is wailing,
Because I will pass through the
midst of you," says the LORD.
18 Alas, you who are longing for
the day of the LORD,
For what purpose *will* the day
of the LORD *be* to you?
It *will be* darkness and not light;

¹⁹ As when a man flees from a lion
And a bear meets him,
Or goes home, leans his
hand against the wall
And a snake bites him.
²⁰ *Will* not the day of the LORD *be*
darkness instead of light,
Even gloom with no brightness in it?

²¹ "I hate, I reject your festivals,
Nor do I delight in your
solemn assemblies.
²² "Even though you offer up to Me burnt
offerings and your grain offerings,
I will not accept *them;*
And I will not *even* look at the peace
offerings of your fatlings.
²³ "Take away from Me the
noise of your songs;
I will not even listen to the
sound of your harps.
²⁴ "But let justice roll down like waters
And righteousness like an
ever-flowing stream.

²⁵ "Did you present Me with sacrifices and grain offerings in the wilderness for forty years, O house of Israel? ²⁶ You also carried along Sikkuth your king and Kiyyun, your images, the star of your gods which you made for yourselves. ²⁷ Therefore, I will make you go into exile beyond Damascus," says the LORD, whose name is the God of hosts.

5:25-26 In addition to worshiping the Lord in the wilderness, Israel also worshiped other gods, carrying along "Sikkuth (or 'tabernacle') your king (or 'Molech') and Kiyyun, your images." Molech worship included the astrological worship of Saturn and the host of heaven and the actual sacrificing of children (2Ki 17:16–17). Warned against Molech worship (Dt 18:9–13), Israel nevertheless pursued all facets of it, continuing with Solomon (1Ki 11:7) and his descendants (1Ki 12:28; 2Ki 17:16–17; Jer 32:35) until Josiah (2Ki 23:10). Stephen recited Amos 5:25–27 when he recounted the sins of Israel in Ac 7:42–43.

Psalm 141:5-10

⁵ Let the righteous smite me in
kindness and reprove me;
It is oil upon the head;
Do not let my head refuse it,
For still my prayer is against
their wicked deeds.

⁶ Their judges are thrown down
by the sides of the rock,
And they hear my words,
for they are pleasant.
⁷ As when one plows and
breaks open the earth,
Our bones have been scattered
at the mouth of Sheol.

⁸ For my eyes are toward You,
O GOD, the Lord;
In You I take refuge; do not
leave me defenseless.
⁹ Keep me from the jaws of the trap
which they have set for me,
And from the snares of those
who do iniquity.
¹⁰ Let the wicked fall into
their own nets,
While I pass by safely.

Proverbs 29:26

²⁶ Many seek the ruler's favor,
But justice for man *comes*
from the LORD.

Revelation 4:1-11

4 After these things I looked, and behold, a door *standing* open in heaven, and the first voice which I had heard, like *the sound* of a trumpet speaking with me, said, "Come up here, and I will show you what must take place after these things." ² Immediately I was in the Spirit; and behold, a throne was standing in heaven, and One sitting on the throne. ³ And He who was sitting *was* like a jasper stone and a sardius in appearance; and *there was* a rainbow around the throne, like an emerald in appearance. ⁴ Around the throne *were* twenty-four thrones; and upon the thrones *I saw* twenty-four elders sitting, clothed in white garments, and golden crowns on their heads. ⁵ Out from the throne come flashes of lightning and sounds and peals of thunder. And *there were* seven lamps of fire burning before the throne, which are the seven Spirits of God; ⁶ and before the throne *there was something* like a sea of glass, like crystal; and in the center and around the throne, four living creatures full of eyes in front and behind. ⁷ The first creature *was* like a lion, and the second creature like a calf, and the third creature had a face like that of a man, and the fourth creature *was* like a flying eagle. ⁸ And the four living creatures, each one of them having six wings, are full of eyes around and within; and day and night they do not cease to say,

4:4 twenty-four elders. Their joint rule with Christ, their white garments, and their golden crowns all seem to indicate that these 24 represent the redeemed (vv. 9–11; 5:5–14; 7:11–17; 11:16–18; 14:3; 19:4). The question is which redeemed? Not Israel, since the nation is not yet saved, glorified, and coronated. That is still to come at this point in the events of the end. Their resurrection and glory will come at the end of the 7-year tribulation time (Da 12:1–3). Tribulation saints aren't yet saved (7:9–10). Only one group will be complete and glorified at that point—the church. Here elders represent the church, which sings the song of redemption (5:8–10). They are the overcomers who have their crowns and live in the place prepared for them, where they have gone with Jesus (Jn 14:1–4).

"Holy, holy, holy *is* the Lord God, the Almighty, who was and who is and who is to come."

⁹And when the living creatures give glory and honor and thanks to Him who sits on the throne, to Him who lives forever and ever, ¹⁰ the twenty-four elders will fall down before Him who sits on the throne, and will worship Him who lives forever and ever, and will cast their crowns before the throne, saying,

¹¹ "Worthy are You, our Lord and our God, to receive glory and honor and power; for You created all things, and because of Your will they existed, and were created."

DAY 14: Are there different approaches to interpreting the Book of Revelation?

No other New Testament book poses more serious and difficult interpretive challenges than Revelation. The book's vivid imagery and striking symbolism have produced 4 main interpretive approaches:

The *preterist* approach interprets Revelation as a description of first-century events in the Roman Empire. This view conflicts with the book's own often repeated claim to be prophecy (1:3; 22:7, 10, 18–19). It is impossible to see all the events in Revelation as already fulfilled. The Second Coming of Christ, for example, obviously did not take place in the first century.

The *historicist* approach views Revelation as a panoramic view of church history from apostolic times to the present—seeing in the symbolism such events as the barbarian invasions of Rome, the rise of the Roman Catholic Church, the emergence of Islam, and the French Revolution. This interpretive method robs Revelation of any meaning for those to whom it was written. It also ignores the time limitations the book itself places on the unfolding events (11:2; 12:6, 14; 13:5). Historicism has produced many different—and often conflicting—interpretations of the actual historical events contained in Revelation.

The *idealist* approach interprets Revelation as a timeless depiction of the cosmic struggle between the forces of good and evil. In this view, the book contains neither historical allusions nor predictive prophecy. This view also ignores Revelation's prophetic character and, if carried to its logical conclusion, severs the book from any connection with actual historical events. Revelation then becomes merely a collection of stories designed to teach spiritual truth.

The *futurist* approach insists that the events of chapters 6–22 are yet future and that those chapters literally and symbolically depict actual people and events yet to appear on the world scene. It describes the events surrounding the Second Coming of Jesus Christ (chaps. 6–19), the Millennium and final judgment (chap. 20), and the eternal state (chaps. 21–22). Only this view does justice to Revelation's claim to be prophecy and interprets the book by the same grammatical-historical method as chapters 1–3 and the rest of Scripture.

DECEMBER 15

Amos 6:1–7:17

6 Woe to those who are at ease in Zion
And to those who *feel* secure in
   the mountain of Samaria,
The distinguished men of the
   foremost of nations,
To whom the house of Israel comes.

² Go over to Calneh and look,
And go from there to
   Hamath the great,
Then go down to Gath of
   the Philistines.
Are they better than these kingdoms,
Or is their territory greater than yours?
³ Do you put off the day of calamity,
And would you bring near
   the seat of violence?

⁴ Those who recline on beds of ivory
And sprawl on their couches,
And eat lambs from the flock
And calves from the midst of the stall,
⁵ Who improvise to the
sound of the harp,
And like David have composed
songs for themselves,
⁶ Who drink wine from sacrificial bowls
While they anoint themselves
with the finest of oils,
Yet they have not grieved
over the ruin of Joseph.
⁷ Therefore, they will now go into
exile at the head of the exiles,
And the sprawlers' banqueting
will pass away.

⁸ The Lord GOD has sworn by
Himself, the LORD God of
hosts has declared:
"I loathe the arrogance of Jacob,
And detest his citadels;
Therefore I will deliver up *the*
city and all it contains."

⁹And it will be, if ten men are left in one house, they will die. ¹⁰Then one's uncle, or his undertaker, will lift him up to carry out *his* bones from the house, and he will say to the one who is in the innermost part of the house, "Is anyone else with you?" And that one will say, "No one." Then he will answer, "Keep quiet. For the name of the LORD is not to be mentioned." ¹¹For behold, the LORD is going to command that the great house be smashed to pieces and the small house to fragments.

6:10 undertaker. Literally "one who burns him." This could refer to cremation, demanded by the excessive number killed and because of fear of epidemics. With rare exceptions (1Sa 31:12), corpses were buried in ancient Israel. **name of the LORD is not to be mentioned.** Previously welcomed as a friend, the Lord came in judgment as a foe; survivors would not want to invoke His name out of fear.

¹² Do horses run on rocks?
Or does one plow them with oxen?
Yet you have turned
justice into poison
And the fruit of righteousness
into wormwood,

¹³ You who rejoice in Lodebar,
And say, "Have we not by
our *own* strength taken
Karnaim for ourselves?"
¹⁴ "For behold, I am going to raise
up a nation against you,
O house of Israel," declares
the LORD God of hosts,
"And they will afflict you from
the entrance of Hamath
To the brook of the Arabah."

7 Thus the Lord GOD showed me, and behold, He was forming a locust-swarm when the spring crop began to sprout. And behold, the spring crop *was* after the king's mowing. ²And it came about, when it had finished eating the vegetation of the land, that I said,

"Lord GOD, please pardon!
How can Jacob stand,
For he is small?"
³ The LORD changed His
mind about this.
"It shall not be," said the LORD.

⁴Thus the Lord GOD showed me, and behold, the Lord GOD was calling to contend *with them* by fire, and it consumed the great deep and began to consume the farm land. ⁵Then I said,

"Lord GOD, please stop!
How can Jacob stand, for he is small?"
⁶ The LORD changed His
mind about this.
"This too shall not be," said
the Lord GOD.

⁷Thus He showed me, and behold, the Lord was standing by a vertical wall with a plumb line in His hand. ⁸The LORD said to me, "What do you see, Amos?" And I said, "A plumb line." Then the Lord said,

"Behold I am about to put a plumb line
In the midst of My people Israel.
I will spare them no longer.
⁹ "The high places of Isaac
will be desolated
And the sanctuaries of
Israel laid waste.
Then I will rise up against the house
of Jeroboam with the sword."

¹⁰Then Amaziah, the priest of Bethel, sent *word* to Jeroboam king of Israel, say-

ing, "Amos has conspired against you in the midst of the house of Israel; the land is unable to endure all his words. ¹¹For thus Amos says, 'Jeroboam will die by the sword and Israel will certainly go from its land into exile.'" ¹²Then Amaziah said to Amos, "Go, you seer, flee away to the land of Judah and there eat bread and there do your prophesying! ¹³But no longer prophesy at Bethel, for it is a sanctuary of the king and a royal residence."

¹⁴Then Amos replied to Amaziah, "I am not a prophet, nor am I the son of a prophet; for I am a herdsman and a grower of sycamore figs. ¹⁵But the LORD took me from following the flock and the LORD said to me, 'Go prophesy to My people Israel.' ¹⁶Now hear the word of the LORD: you are saying, 'You shall not prophesy against Israel nor shall you speak against the house of Isaac.' ¹⁷Therefore, thus says the LORD, 'Your wife will become a harlot in the city, your sons and your daughters will fall by the sword, your land will be parceled up by a *measuring* line and you yourself will die upon unclean soil. Moreover, Israel will certainly go from its land into exile.'"

Psalm 142:1–7

Maskil of David, when he was
in the cave. A Prayer.

I cry aloud with my voice to the LORD;
I make supplication with my
voice to the LORD.
² I pour out my complaint
before Him;
I declare my trouble before Him.
³ When my spirit was
overwhelmed within me,
You knew my path.
In the way where I walk
They have hidden a trap for me.
⁴ Look to the right and see;
For there is no one who regards me;
There is no escape for me;
No one cares for my soul.

⁵ I cried out to You, O LORD;
I said, "You are my refuge,
My portion in the land of the living.
⁶ "Give heed to my cry,
For I am brought very low;
Deliver me from my persecutors,
For they are too strong for me.
⁷ "Bring my soul out of prison,
So that I may give thanks
to Your name;
The righteous will surround me,
For You will deal bountifully with me."

142:1–7 Under the same circumstances as Psalms 57 (according to the superscription), David recounted his desperate days hiding in the cave of Adullam (1Sa 22:1) while Saul sought him to take his life (1Sa 18–24). It appears that David's situation, for the moment at least, seems hopeless without God's intervention. Psalm 91 provides the truths that bring the solution.

Proverbs 29:27

²⁷ An unjust man is abominable
to the righteous,
And he who is upright in the way
is abominable to the wicked.

Revelation 5:1–14

5 I saw in the right hand of Him who sat on the throne a book written inside and on the back, sealed up with seven seals. ²And I saw a strong angel proclaiming with a loud voice, "Who is worthy to open the book and to break its seals?" ³And no one in heaven or on the earth or under the earth was able to open the book or to look into it. ⁴Then I *began* to weep greatly because no one was found worthy to open the book or to look into it; ⁵and one of the elders *said to me, "Stop weeping; behold, the Lion that is from the tribe of Judah, the Root of David, has overcome so as to open the book and its seven seals."

⁶And I saw between the throne (with the four living creatures) and the elders a Lamb standing, as if slain, having seven horns and seven eyes, which are the seven Spirits of God, sent out into all the earth. ⁷And He came and took the book out of the right hand of Him

5:1 written inside and on the back. This is typical of various kinds of contracts in the ancient world, including deeds, marriage contracts, rental and lease agreements, and wills. The inside of the scroll contained all the details of the contract, and the outside—or back—contained a summary of the document. In this case it almost certainly is a deed—the title deed to the earth (Jer 32:7ff.) **sealed up with seven seals.** Romans sealed their wills 7 times—on the edge at each roll—to prevent unauthorized entry. Hebrew title deeds required a minimum of 3 witnesses and 3 separate seals, with more important transactions requiring more witnesses and seals.

who sat on the throne. [8]When He had taken the book, the four living creatures and the twenty-four elders fell down before the Lamb, each one holding a harp and golden bowls full of incense, which are the prayers of the saints. [9]And they *sang a new song, saying,

"Worthy are You to take the book and to break its seals; for You were slain, and purchased for God with Your blood *men* from every tribe and tongue and people and nation. [10]You have made them *to be* a kingdom and priests to our God; and they will reign upon the earth."

[11]Then I looked, and I heard the voice of many angels around the throne and the living creatures and the elders; and the number of them was myriads of myriads, and thousands of thousands, [12]saying with a loud voice,

"Worthy is the Lamb that was slain to receive power and riches and wisdom and might and honor and glory and blessing."

[13]And every created thing which is in heaven and on the earth and under the earth and on the sea, and all things in them, I heard saying,

"To Him who sits on the throne, and to the Lamb, *be* blessing and honor and glory and dominion forever and ever."

[14]And the four living creatures kept saying, "Amen." And the elders fell down and worshiped.

DAY 15: Describe the worship in Revelation 5.

"The four living creatures and the twenty-four elders fell down before the Lamb, each one holding a harp" (v. 8). These ancient stringed instruments not only accompanied the songs of God's people (1Ch 25:6; Ps 33:2), but also accompanied prophecy (1Sa 10:5). The 24 elders, representative of the redeemed church, played their harps in praise and in a symbolic indication that all the prophets had said was about to be fulfilled. "Each one holding…bowls full of incense, which are the prayers of the saints." These golden, wide-mouth saucers were common in the tabernacle and temple. Incense was a normal part of the Old Testament ritual. Priests stood twice daily before the inner veil of the temple and burned incense so that the smoke would carry into the Holy of Holies and be swept into the nostrils of God. That symbolized the people's prayers rising to Him. Specifically, these prayers represent all that the redeemed have ever prayed concerning ultimate and final redemption. This becomes a major theme throughout the book (11:17–18; 13:7, 9–10; 14:12; 16:6; 17:6; 18:20, 24; 19:8; 20:9).

"And they sang a new song" (v. 9). The Old Testament is filled with references to a new song that flows from a heart that has experienced God's redemption or deliverance (14:3; Pss 33:3; 96:1; 144:9). This new song anticipates the final, glorious redemption that God is about to begin. "For You were slain, and purchased for God with Your blood." The sacrificial death of Christ on behalf of sinners made Him worthy to take the scroll.

DECEMBER 16

Amos 8:1–9:15

8 Thus the Lord GOD showed me, and behold, *there was* a basket of summer fruit. [2]He said, "What do you see, Amos?" And I said, "A basket of summer fruit." Then the LORD said to me, "The end has come for My people Israel. I will spare them no longer. [3]The songs of the palace will turn to wailing in that day," declares the Lord GOD. "Many *will be* the corpses; in every place they will cast them forth in silence."

[4]Hear this, you who trample the needy, to do away with the humble of the land, [5]saying,

"When will the new moon be over, So that we may sell grain, And the sabbath, that we may open the wheat *market,* To make the bushel smaller and the shekel bigger, And to cheat with dishonest scales,
[6] So as to buy the helpless for money And the needy for a pair of sandals, And *that* we may sell the refuse of the wheat?"

[7] The LORD has sworn by the pride of Jacob, "Indeed, I will never forget any of their deeds.

8 "Because of this will not the land quake
    And everyone who dwells
        in it mourn?
    Indeed, all of it will rise
        up like the Nile,
    And it will be tossed about
    And subside like the Nile of Egypt.

9 "It will come about in that day,"
        declares the Lord GOD,
    "That I will make the sun
        go down at noon
    And make the earth dark
        in broad daylight.

10 "Then I will turn your festivals
        into mourning
    And all your songs into lamentation;
    And I will bring sackcloth
        on everyone's loins
    And baldness on every head.
    And I will make it like *a time of*
        mourning for an only son,
    And the end of it will be
        like a bitter day.

11 "Behold, days are coming,"
        declares the Lord GOD,
    "When I will send a famine
        on the land,
    Not a famine for bread or
        a thirst for water,
    But rather for hearing the
        words of the LORD.

12 "People will stagger from sea to sea
    And from the north even to the east;
    They will go to and fro to seek
        the word of the LORD,
    But they will not find *it*.

13 "In that day the beautiful virgins
    And the young men will
        faint from thirst.

14 "*As for* those who swear by
        the guilt of Samaria,
    Who say, 'As your god lives, O Dan,'
    And, 'As the way of Beersheba lives,'
    They will fall and not rise again."

9 I saw the Lord standing beside the altar,
    and He said,

    "Smite the capitals so that the
        thresholds will shake,
    And break them on the
        heads of them all!
    Then I will slay the rest of
        them with the sword;
    They will not have a fugitive
        who will flee,
    Or a refugee who will escape.

2 "Though they dig into Sheol,
    From there will My hand take them;
    And though they ascend to heaven,
    From there will I bring them down.

3 "Though they hide on the
        summit of Carmel,
    I will search them out and
        take them from there;
    And though they conceal
        themselves from My sight
        on the floor of the sea,
    From there I will command the
        serpent and it will bite them.

4 "And though they go into captivity
        before their enemies,
    From there I will command the
        sword that it slay them,
    And I will set My eyes against them
        for evil and not for good."

5 The Lord GOD of hosts,
    The One who touches the
        land so that it melts,
    And all those who dwell in it mourn,
    And all of it rises up like the Nile
    And subsides like the Nile of Egypt;

6 The One who builds His upper
        chambers in the heavens
    And has founded His vaulted
        dome over the earth,
    He who calls for the waters of the sea
    And pours them out on the
        face of the earth,
    The LORD is His name.

7 "Are you not as the sons
        of Ethiopia to Me,
    O sons of Israel?" declares the LORD.
    "Have I not brought up Israel
        from the land of Egypt,
    And the Philistines from Caphtor
        and the Arameans from Kir?

8 "Behold, the eyes of the Lord GOD
        are on the sinful kingdom,
    And I will destroy it from
        the face of the earth;
    Nevertheless, I will not totally
        destroy the house of Jacob,"
    Declares the LORD.

9 "For behold, I am commanding,
    And I will shake the house of
        Israel among all nations
    As *grain* is shaken in a sieve,
    But not a kernel will fall to the ground.

10 "All the sinners of My people
        will die by the sword,
    Those who say, 'The calamity will
        not overtake or confront us.'

11 "In that day I will raise up the
    fallen booth of David,
And wall up its breaches;
I will also raise up its ruins
And rebuild it as in the days of old;
12 That they may possess the
    remnant of Edom
And all the nations who are
    called by My name,"
Declares the LORD who does this.

13 "Behold, days are coming,"
    declares the LORD,
"When the plowman will
    overtake the reaper
And the treader of grapes
    him who sows seed;
When the mountains will
    drip sweet wine
And all the hills will be dissolved.
14 "Also I will restore the captivity
    of My people Israel,
And they will rebuild the ruined
    cities and live *in them;*
They will also plant vineyards
    and drink their wine,
And make gardens and eat their fruit.
15 "I will also plant them on their land,
And they will not again be
    rooted out from their land
Which I have given them,"
Says the LORD your God.

**9:15 they will not again be rooted out from
their land.** The ultimate fulfillment of God's
land promise to Abraham (Ge 12:7; 15:7; 17:8)
will occur during Christ's millennial reign on
earth (Joel 2:26–27).

Psalm 143:1–6

A Psalm of David.

Hear my prayer, O LORD,
    Give ear to my supplications!
Answer me in Your faithfulness,
    in Your righteousness!
2 And do not enter into judgment
    with Your servant,
For in Your sight no man
    living is righteous.
3 For the enemy has
    persecuted my soul;
He has crushed my life to the ground;
He has made me dwell in
    dark places, like those who
    have long been dead.

4 Therefore my spirit is
    overwhelmed within me;
My heart is appalled within me.

5 I remember the days of old;
I meditate on all Your doings;
I muse on the work
    of Your hands.
6 I stretch out my hands to You;
My soul *longs* for You,
    as a parched land.   *Selah*

Proverbs 30:1–4

30 The words of Agur the son of Jakeh,
the oracle.
The man declares to Ithiel, to Ithiel and
Ucal:

2 Surely I am more stupid
    than any man,
And I do not have the
    understanding of a man.
3 Neither have I learned wisdom,
Nor do I have the knowledge
    of the Holy One.
4 Who has ascended into
    heaven and descended?
Who has gathered the
    wind in His fists?
Who has wrapped the waters
    in His garment?
Who has established all the
    ends of the earth?
What is His name or
    His son's name?
Surely you know!

30:1–33 The words of Agur. This is a collection
of proverbs written by an unknown sage who
was likely a student of wisdom at the time of
Solomon (1Ki 4:30–31). Agur reflects humility
(vv. 1–4), a deep hatred for arrogance (vv. 7–9),
and a keen theological mind (vv. 5–6).

30:4 Who….What…? These questions can be
answered only by revelation from God. A man
can know the "what" about creative wisdom
through observation of the physical world
and its inner workings but cannot know the
"who." The "who" can be known only when
God reveals Himself, which He has in Scripture. This is the testimony and conclusion of
Job (Job 42:1–6), Solomon (Ecc 12:1–14), Isaiah
(Is 40:12–17; 46:8–11; 66:18–19), and Paul (Ro
8:18–39). **His son's name.** Jesus Christ. See
John 1:1–18.

Revelation 6:1-17

6 Then I saw when the Lamb broke one of the seven seals, and I heard one of the four living creatures saying as with a voice of thunder, "Come." ²I looked, and behold, a white horse, and he who sat on it had a bow; and a crown was given to him, and he went out conquering and to conquer.

6:1 the seven seals. In chap. 5, Christ was the only One found worthy to open the little scroll—the title deed to the universe. As He breaks the 7 seals that secure the scroll, each seal unleashes a new demonstration of God's judgment on the earth in the future tribulation period. These seal judgments include all the judgments to the end. The seventh seal contains the 7 trumpets; the seventh trumpet contains the 7 bowls.

---

³When He broke the second seal, I heard the second living creature saying, "Come." ⁴And another, a red horse, went out; and to him who sat on it, it was granted to take peace from the earth, and that *men* would slay one another; and a great sword was given to him. ⁵When He broke the third seal, I heard the third living creature saying, "Come." I looked, and behold, a black horse; and he who sat on it had a pair of scales in his hand. ⁶And I heard *something* like a voice in the center of the four living creatures saying, "A quart of wheat for a denarius, and three quarts of barley for a denarius; and do not damage the oil and the wine." ⁷When the Lamb broke the fourth seal, I heard the voice of the fourth living crea-

ture saying, "Come." ⁸I looked, and behold, an ashen horse; and he who sat on it had the name Death; and Hades was following with him. Authority was given to them over a fourth of the earth, to kill with sword and with famine and with pestilence and by the wild beasts of the earth.

⁹When the Lamb broke the fifth seal, I saw underneath the altar the souls of those who had been slain because of the word of God, and because of the testimony which they had maintained; ¹⁰and they cried out with a loud voice, saying, "How long, O Lord, holy and true, will You refrain from judging and avenging our blood on those who dwell on the earth?" ¹¹And there was given to each of them a white robe; and they were told that they should rest for a little while longer, until *the number of* their fellow servants and their brethren who were to be killed even as they had been, would be completed also.

¹²I looked when He broke the sixth seal, and there was a great earthquake; and the sun became black as sackcloth *made* of hair, and the whole moon became like blood; ¹³and the stars of the sky fell to the earth, as a fig tree casts its unripe figs when shaken by a great wind. ¹⁴The sky was split apart like a scroll when it is rolled up, and every mountain and island were moved out of their places. ¹⁵Then the kings of the earth and the great men and the commanders and the rich and the strong and every slave and free man hid themselves in the caves and among the rocks of the mountains; ¹⁶and they *said to the mountains and to the rocks, "Fall on us and hide us from the presence of Him who sits on the throne, and from the wrath of the Lamb; ¹⁷for the great day of their wrath has come, and who is able to stand?"

DAY 16: How does Amos 9:11 relate to the Jerusalem Council of Acts 15?

In Amos 9:11, the Lord promised that He "will raise up the fallen booth of David." At the Jerusalem Council, convened to discuss whether Gentiles should be allowed into the church without requiring circumcision, James quotes this passage (Ac 15:15-16) to support Peter's report of how God had "concerned Himself about taking from among the Gentiles a people for His name" (Ac 15:14). Some have thus concluded that the passage was fulfilled in Jesus, the greater Son of David, through whom the dynasty of David was reestablished. The Acts reference, however, is best seen as an illustration of Amos's words and not the fulfillment. The temporal allusions to a future time ("In that day," 9:11), when Israel will "possess the remnant of Edom and all the nations" (9:12), when the Lord "will plant them on their land, and they will not again be rooted out from their land which I have given them" (9:15), all make it clear that the prophet is speaking of Messiah's return at the Second Advent to sit upon the throne of David (Is 9:7), not the establishment of the church by the apostles.

DECEMBER 17

Obadiah 1–21

The vision of Obadiah. Thus says the Lord GOD concerning Edom—

> We have heard a report
>   from the LORD,
> And an envoy has been sent
>   among the nations *saying,*
> "Arise and let us go against
>   her for battle"—

---

1 The vision. The prophetic word often came from God in the form of a vision (Hab 1:1). **Thus says the Lord GOD.** Although the background of the prophet is obscure, the source of his message is not. It was supernaturally given by God, and was not motivated by unholy vengeance. **Edom.** Descendants of Esau (Ge 25:30; 36:1ff.), the Edomites settled in the region south of the Dead Sea. **Arise...go against her.** The prophet heard of a God-ordained international plot to overthrow Edom. The selfish motives of Edom's enemies were divinely controlled by the Lord's "envoy" to serve His sovereign purposes (Ps 104:4).

> 2 "Behold, I will make you small
>   among the nations;
> You are greatly despised.
> 3 "The arrogance of your heart
>   has deceived you,
> You who live in the clefts of the rock,
> In the loftiness of your
>   dwelling place,
> Who say in your heart,
> 'Who will bring me down to earth?'
> 4 "Though you build high like the eagle,
> Though you set your nest
>   among the stars,
> From there I will bring you
>   down," declares the LORD.
> 5 "If thieves came to you,
> If robbers by night—
> O how you will be ruined!—
> Would they not steal *only*
>   until they had enough?
> If grape gatherers came to you,
> Would they not leave *some* gleanings?
> 6 "O how Esau will be ransacked,
> *And* his hidden treasures
>   searched out!

> 7 "All the men allied with you
> Will send you forth to the border,
> And the men at peace with you
> Will deceive you and overpower you.
> *They who eat* your bread
> Will set an ambush for you.
> (There is no understanding in him.)
> 8 "Will I not on that day,"
>   declares the LORD,
> "Destroy wise men from Edom
> And understanding from the
>   mountain of Esau?
> 9 "Then your mighty men will
>   be dismayed, O Teman,
> So that everyone may be cut off from
>   the mountain of Esau by slaughter.

> 10 "Because of violence to
>   your brother Jacob,
> You will be covered *with* shame,
> And you will be cut off forever.
> 11 "On the day that you stood aloof,
> On the day that strangers
>   carried off his wealth,
> And foreigners entered his gate
> And cast lots for Jerusalem—
> You too were as one of them.
> 12 "Do not gloat over your brother's day,
> The day of his misfortune.
> And do not rejoice over
>   the sons of Judah
> In the day of their destruction;
> Yes, do not boast
> In the day of *their* distress.
> 13 "Do not enter the gate of My people
> In the day of their disaster.
> Yes, you, do not gloat over
>   their calamity
> In the day of their disaster.
> And do not loot their wealth
> In the day of their disaster.
> 14 "Do not stand at the fork of the road
> To cut down their fugitives;
> And do not imprison their survivors
> In the day of their distress.

> 15 "For the day of the LORD draws
>   near on all the nations.
> As you have done, it will
>   be done to you.
> Your dealings will return
>   on your own head.
> 16 "Because just as you drank on
>   My holy mountain,
> All the nations will drink continually.
> They will drink and swallow
> And become as if they
>   had never existed.

¹⁷ "But on Mount Zion there will
    be those who escape,
And it will be holy.
And the house of Jacob will
    possess their possessions.
¹⁸ "Then the house of Jacob will be a fire
And the house of Joseph a flame;
But the house of Esau *will
    be* as stubble.
And they will set them on fire
    and consume them,
So that there will be no survivor
    of the house of Esau,"
For the LORD has spoken.
¹⁹ Then *those of* the Negev will
    possess the mountain of Esau,
And *those of* the Shephelah
    the Philistine *plain;*
Also, possess the territory
    of Ephraim and the
    territory of Samaria,
And Benjamin *will possess* Gilead.
²⁰ And the exiles of this host
    of the sons of Israel,
Who are *among* the Canaanites
    as far as Zarephath,
And the exiles of Jerusalem
    who are in Sepharad
Will possess the cities
    of the Negev.
²¹ The deliverers will ascend Mount Zion
To judge the mountain of Esau,
And the kingdom will be the LORD'S.

Psalm 143:7–12

⁷ Answer me quickly, O LORD,
    my spirit fails;
Do not hide Your face from me,
Or I will become like those
    who go down to the pit.
⁸ Let me hear Your lovingkindness
    in the morning;
For I trust in You;
Teach me the way in which
    I should walk;
For to You I lift up my soul.
⁹ Deliver me, O LORD, from
    my enemies;
I take refuge in You.

¹⁰ Teach me to do Your will,
For You are my God;
Let Your good Spirit lead
    me on level ground.
¹¹ For the sake of Your name,
    O LORD, revive me.
In Your righteousness bring
    my soul out of trouble.

¹² And in Your lovingkindness,
    cut off my enemies
And destroy all those who
    afflict my soul,
For I am Your servant.

Proverbs 30:5

⁵ Every word of God is tested;
    He is a shield to those who
    take refuge in Him.

Revelation 7:1–17

7 After this I saw four angels standing at the
four corners of the earth, holding back the
four winds of the earth, so that no wind would
blow on the earth or on the sea or on any tree.
² And I saw another angel ascending from the
rising of the sun, having the seal of the living
God; and he cried out with a loud voice to the
four angels to whom it was granted to harm
the earth and the sea, ³ saying, "Do not harm
the earth or the sea or the trees until we have
sealed the bond-servants of our God on their
foreheads."
    ⁴ And I heard the number of those who
were sealed, one hundred and forty-four
thousand sealed from every tribe of the sons
of Israel:

7:4 One hundred and forty-four thousand. A
missionary corps of redeemed Jews who are
instrumental in the salvation of many Jews and
Gentiles during the Tribulation (vv. 9–17). They
will be the firstfruits of a new redeemed Israel
(v. 4; Zec 12:10). Finally, Israel will be the witness
nation she refused to be in the Old Testament.
every tribe of the sons of Israel. By sovereign
election, God will seal 12,000 from each of the
12 tribes, promising His protection while they
accomplish their mission.

⁵ from the tribe of Judah, twelve
thousand *were* sealed, from the tribe
of Reuben twelve thousand, from the
tribe of Gad twelve thousand,
⁶ from the tribe of Asher twelve
thousand, from the tribe of Naphtali
twelve thousand, from the tribe of
Manasseh twelve thousand,
⁷ from the tribe of Simeon twelve
thousand, from the tribe of Levi
twelve thousand, from the tribe of
Issachar twelve thousand,
⁸ from the tribe of Zebulun twelve
thousand, from the tribe of Joseph

twelve thousand, from the tribe of Benjamin, twelve thousand *were* sealed.

⁹After these things I looked, and behold, a great multitude which no one could count, from every nation and *all* tribes and peoples and tongues, standing before the throne and before the Lamb, clothed in white robes, and palm branches *were* in their hands; ¹⁰and they cry out with a loud voice, saying,

"Salvation to our God who sits on the throne, and to the Lamb." ¹¹And all the angels were standing around the throne and *around* the elders and the four living creatures; and they fell on their faces before the throne and worshiped God, ¹²saying,

"Amen, blessing and glory and wisdom and thanksgiving and honor and power and might, *be* to our God forever and ever. Amen."

¹³Then one of the elders answered, saying to me, "These who are clothed in the white robes, who are they, and where have they come from?" ¹⁴I said to him, "My lord, you know." And he said to me, "These are the ones who come out of the great tribulation, and they have washed their robes and made them white in the blood of the Lamb. ¹⁵For this reason, they are before the throne of God; and they serve Him day and night in His temple; and He who sits on the throne will spread His tabernacle over them. ¹⁶They will hunger no longer, nor thirst anymore; nor will the sun beat down on them, nor any heat; ¹⁷for the Lamb in the center of the throne will be their shepherd, and will guide them to springs of the water of life; and God will wipe every tear from their eyes."

7:1–17 Chapter 7 forms a parenthesis between the sixth seal (6:12–17) and the seventh seal (8:1) and answers the question posed at the end of chap. 6. Two distinct groups will survive the divine fury: 1) 144,000 Jewish evangelists on earth (vv. 1–8) and 2) their converts in heaven (vv. 9–17).

DAY 17: Who make up the "great multitude" of Revelation 7:9?

While the tribulation period will be a time of judgment, it will also be a time of unprecedented redemption (v. 14; 6:9–11; 20:4; Is 11:10; Mt 24:14). This is noted in v. 9 with the "great multitude which no one could count, from every nation and all tribes and peoples and tongues, standing before the throne and before the Lamb."

John is told that "These are the ones who come out of the great tribulation" (v. 14). These people didn't go with the raptured church, since they were not yet saved. During the 7-year period, they will be saved, martyred, and enter heaven. Though it is a time of unparalleled judgment, it is also a time of unparalleled grace in salvation (Mt 24:12–14). "And they have washed their robes and made them white in the blood of the Lamb" (Rev 7:14). Salvation's cleansing is in relationship to the atoning sacrifice of Christ (1:5; 5:9; Ro 3:24–25; 5:9).

"For this reason, they are before the throne of God; and they serve Him day and night in His temple" (v. 15). This refers to the heavenly throne of God. During the Millennium, there will also be a temple on earth—a special holy place where God dwells in a partially restored, but still fallen universe (see Eze 40–48). In the final, eternal state with its new heavens and new earth, there is no temple; God Himself, who will fill all, will be its temple (21:22). "And He who sits on the throne will spread His tabernacle over them." The preferred reading is that He "will spread His tabernacle over them." God's presence will become their canopy of shelter to protect them from all the terrors of a fallen world and the indescribable horrors they have experienced on the earth during the time of tribulation.

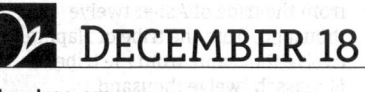

DECEMBER 18

Jonah 1:1–4:11

1 The word of the LORD came to Jonah the son of Amittai saying, ²"Arise, go to Nineveh the great city and cry against it, for their wickedness has come up before Me." ³But Jonah rose up to flee to Tarshish from the presence of the LORD. So he went down to Joppa, found a ship which was going to Tarshish, paid the fare and went down into it to go with them to Tarshish from the presence of the LORD.

⁴The LORD hurled a great wind on the sea and there was a great storm on the sea so that the ship was about to break up. ⁵Then the sailors became afraid and every man cried to

1:3 But Jonah rose up to flee to Tarshish. This is the only recorded instance of a prophet refusing God's commission (Jer 20:7–9). The location of Tarshish, known for its wealth (Ps 72:10; Jer 10:9; Eze 27:12, 25), is uncertain. The Greek historian Herodotus identified it with Tartessus, a merchant city in southern Spain. The prophet went as far west in the opposite direction as possible, showing his reluctance to bring salvation blessing to Gentiles. **from the presence of the LORD.** While no one can escape from the Lord's omnipresence (Ps 139:7–12), it is thought that the prophet was attempting to flee His manifest presence in the temple at Jerusalem (Ge 4:16; Jon 2:4).

1:17 a great fish. The species of fish is uncertain; the Hebrew word for whale is not here employed. God sovereignly prepared (literally, "appointed") a great fish to rescue Jonah. Apparently, Jonah sank into the depth of the sea before the fish swallowed him (2:3, 5–6).

his god, and they threw the cargo which was in the ship into the sea to lighten *it* for them. But Jonah had gone below into the hold of the ship, lain down and fallen sound asleep. ⁶ So the captain approached him and said, "How is it that you are sleeping? Get up, call on your god. Perhaps *your* god will be concerned about us so that we will not perish."

⁷ Each man said to his mate, "Come, let us cast lots so we may learn on whose account this calamity *has struck* us." So they cast lots and the lot fell on Jonah. ⁸ Then they said to him, "Tell us, now! On whose account *has* this calamity *struck* us? What is your occupation? And where do you come from? What is your country? From what people are you?" ⁹ He said to them, "I am a Hebrew, and I fear the LORD God of heaven who made the sea and the dry land."

¹⁰ Then the men became extremely frightened and they said to him, "How could you do this?" For the men knew that he was fleeing from the presence of the LORD, because he had told them. ¹¹ So they said to him, "What should we do to you that the sea may become calm for us?"—for the sea was becoming increasingly stormy. ¹² He said to them, "Pick me up and throw me into the sea. Then the sea will become calm for you, for I know that on account of me this great storm *has come* upon you." ¹³ However, the men rowed *desperately* to return to land but they could not, for the sea was becoming *even* stormier against them. ¹⁴ Then they called on the LORD and said, "We earnestly pray, O LORD, do not let us perish on account of this man's life and do not put innocent blood on us; for You, O LORD, have done as You have pleased."

¹⁵ So they picked up Jonah, threw him into the sea, and the sea stopped its raging. ¹⁶ Then the men feared the LORD greatly, and they offered a sacrifice to the LORD and made vows.

¹⁷ And the LORD appointed a great fish to swallow Jonah, and Jonah was in the stomach of the fish three days and three nights.

2 Then Jonah prayed to the LORD his God from the stomach of the fish, ² and he said,

"I called out of my distress
    to the LORD,
    And He answered me.
I cried for help from the
    depth of Sheol;
You heard my voice.
³ "For You had cast me into the deep,
    Into the heart of the seas,
    And the current engulfed me.
All Your breakers and billows
    passed over me.
⁴ "So I said, 'I have been expelled
    from Your sight.
Nevertheless I will look again
    toward Your holy temple.'
⁵ "Water encompassed me to
    the point of death.
The great deep engulfed me,
Weeds were wrapped
    around my head.
⁶ "I descended to the roots
    of the mountains.
The earth with its bars *was*
    around me forever,
But You have brought up
    my life from the pit,
    O LORD my God.
⁷ "While I was fainting away,
    I remembered the LORD,
And my prayer came to You,
    Into Your holy temple.
⁸ "Those who regard vain idols
    Forsake their faithfulness,
⁹ But I will sacrifice to You
    With the voice of thanksgiving.
    That which I have vowed I will pay.
    Salvation is from the LORD."

¹⁰ Then the LORD commanded the fish, and it vomited Jonah up onto the dry land.

3 Now the word of the LORD came to Jonah the second time, saying, ² "Arise, go to Nineveh the great city and proclaim to it the proclamation which I am going to tell you." ³ So Jonah arose and went to Nineveh according to the word of the LORD. Now Nineveh was an exceedingly great city, a three days' walk. ⁴ Then Jonah began to go through the city one day's walk; and he cried out and said, "Yet forty days and Nineveh will be overthrown."

⁵ Then the people of Nineveh believed in God; and they called a fast and put on sackcloth from the greatest to the least of them. ⁶ When the word reached the king of Nineveh, he arose from his throne, laid aside his robe from him, covered *himself* with sackcloth and sat on the ashes. ⁷ He issued a proclamation and it said, "In Nineveh by the decree of the king and his nobles: Do not let man, beast, herd, or flock taste a thing. Do not let them eat or drink water. ⁸ But both man and beast must be covered with sackcloth; and let men call on God earnestly that each may turn from his wicked way and from the violence which is in his hands. ⁹ Who knows, God may turn and relent and withdraw His burning anger so that we will not perish."

¹⁰ When God saw their deeds, that they turned from their wicked way, then God relented concerning the calamity which He had declared He would bring upon them. And He did not do *it*.

4 But it greatly displeased Jonah and he became angry. ² He prayed to the LORD and said, "Please LORD, was not this what I said while I was still in my *own* country? Therefore in order to forestall this I fled to Tarshish, for I knew that You are a gracious and compassionate God, slow to anger and abundant in lovingkindness, and one who relents concerning calamity. ³ Therefore now, O LORD, please take my life from me, for death is better to me than life." ⁴ The LORD said, "Do you have good reason to be angry?"

4:1–2 Jonah, because of his rejection of Gentiles and distaste for their participation in salvation, was displeased at God's demonstration of mercy towards the Ninevites, thereby displaying the real reason for his original flight to Tarshish. From the very beginning, Jonah had clearly understood the gracious character of God (1Ti 2:4; 2Pe 3:9). He had received pardon, but he didn't want Nineveh to know God's mercy (see a similar attitude in Lk 15:25ff.).

⁵ Then Jonah went out from the city and sat east of it. There he made a shelter for himself and sat under it in the shade until he could see what would happen in the city. ⁶ So the LORD God appointed a plant and it grew up over Jonah to be a shade over his head to deliver him from his discomfort. And Jonah was extremely happy about the plant. ⁷ But God appointed a worm when dawn came the next day and it attacked the plant and it withered. ⁸ When the sun came up God appointed a scorching east wind, and the sun beat down on Jonah's head so that he became faint and begged with *all* his soul to die, saying, "Death is better to me than life."

⁹ Then God said to Jonah, "Do you have good reason to be angry about the plant?" And he said, "I have good reason to be angry, even to death." ¹⁰ Then the LORD said, "You had compassion on the plant for which you did not work and *which* you did not cause to grow, which came up overnight and perished overnight. ¹¹ Should I not have compassion on Nineveh, the great city in which there are more than 120,000 persons who do not know *the difference* between their right and left hand, as well as many animals?"

Psalm 144:1–8

A Psalm of David.

B lessed be the LORD, my rock,
   Who trains my hands for war,
   And my fingers for battle;
² My lovingkindness and my fortress,
   My stronghold and my deliverer,
   My shield and He in whom
      I take refuge,
   Who subdues my people under me.
³ O LORD, what is man, that You
      take knowledge of him?
   Or the son of man, that
      You think of him?
⁴ Man is like a mere breath;
   His days are like a passing shadow.

⁵ Bow Your heavens, O LORD,
      and come down;
   Touch the mountains, that
      they may smoke.
⁶ Flash forth lightning and scatter them;
   Send out Your arrows and
      confuse them.
⁷ Stretch forth Your hand from on high;
   Rescue me and deliver me
      out of great waters,
   Out of the hand of aliens
⁸ Whose mouths speak deceit,
   And whose right hand is a
      right hand of falsehood.

Proverbs 30:6–9

6   Do not add to His words
    Or He will reprove you, and
      you will be proved a liar.

7   Two things I asked of You,
    Do not refuse me before I die:
8   Keep deception and lies
      far from me,
    Give me neither poverty nor riches;
    Feed me with the food
      that is my portion,
9   That I not be full and deny *You*
    and say, "Who is the LORD?"
    Or that I not be in want and steal,
    And profane the name of my God.

Revelation 8:1–13

8 When the Lamb broke the seventh seal, there was silence in heaven for about half an hour. 2 And I saw the seven angels who stand before God, and seven trumpets were given to them.

3 Another angel came and stood at the altar, holding a golden censer; and much incense was given to him, so that he might add it to the prayers of all the saints on the golden altar which was before the throne. 4 And the smoke of the incense, with the prayers of the saints, went up before God out of the angel's hand. 5 Then the angel took the censer and filled it with the fire of the altar, and threw it to the earth; and there followed peals of thunder and sounds and flashes of lightning and an earthquake.

6 And the seven angels who had the seven trumpets prepared themselves to sound them.

7 The first sounded, and there came hail and fire, mixed with blood, and they were thrown to the earth; and a third of the earth was burned up, and a third of the trees were burned up, and all the green grass was burned up.

8 The second angel sounded, and *something* like a great mountain burning with fire was thrown into the sea; and a third of the sea became blood, 9 and a third of the creatures which were in the sea and had life, died; and a third of the ships were destroyed.

10 The third angel sounded, and a great star fell from heaven, burning like a torch, and it fell on a third of the rivers and on the springs of waters. 11 The name of the star is called Wormwood; and a third of the waters became wormwood, and many men died from the waters, because they were made bitter.

12 The fourth angel sounded, and a third of the sun and a third of the moon and a third of the stars were struck, so that a third of them would be darkened and the day would not shine for a third of it, and the night in the same way.

13 Then I looked, and I heard an eagle flying in midheaven, saying with a loud voice, "Woe, woe, woe to those who dwell on the earth, because of the remaining blasts of the trumpet of the three angels who are about to sound!"

DAY 18: Why did Jonah run from his mission to Nineveh?

Jonah, though a prophet of Israel, is not remembered for his ministry in Israel, which could explain why the Pharisees erringly claimed in Jesus' day that no prophet had come from Galilee (Jn 7:52). Rather, the book relates the account of his call to preach repentance to Nineveh and his refusal to go. Nineveh, the capital of Assyria and infamous for its cruelty, was a historical nemesis of Israel and Judah. The focus of this book is on that Gentile city, which was founded by Nimrod, great-grandson of Noah (Ge 10:6–12). Perhaps the largest city in the ancient world (1:2; 3:2–3; 4:11), it was nevertheless destroyed about 150 years after the repentance of the generation in the time of Jonah's visit (612 B.C.), as Nahum prophesied (Na 1:1ff.).

Israel's political distaste for Assyria, coupled with a sense of spiritual superiority as the recipient of God's covenant blessing, produced a recalcitrant attitude in Jonah toward God's request for missionary service. Jonah was sent to Nineveh in part to shame Israel by the fact that a pagan city repented at the preaching of a stranger, whereas Israel would not repent though preached to by many prophets. He was soon to learn that God's love and mercy extends to all of His creatures (4:2, 10–11), not just His covenant people (Ge 9:27; 12:3; Lv 19:33–34; 1Sa 2:10; Is 2:2; Joel 2:28–32).

DECEMBER 19

Micah 1:1–3:12

1 The word of the LORD which came *to* Micah of Moresheth in the days of Jotham, Ahaz *and* Hezekiah, kings of Judah, which he saw concerning Samaria and Jerusalem.

2 Hear, O peoples, all of you;
  Listen, O earth and all it contains,
  And let the Lord GOD be a
    witness against you,
  The Lord from His holy temple.
3 For behold, the LORD is coming
    forth from His place.
  He will come down and tread on
    the high places of the earth.
4 The mountains will melt under Him
  And the valleys will be split,
  Like wax before the fire,
  Like water poured down a steep place.
5 All this is for the rebellion of Jacob
  And for the sins of the
    house of Israel.
  What is the rebellion of Jacob?
  Is it not Samaria?
  What is the high place of Judah?
  Is it not Jerusalem?
6 For I will make Samaria a heap of
    ruins in the open country,
  Planting places for a vineyard.
  I will pour her stones down
    into the valley
  And will lay bare her foundations.
7 All of her idols will be smashed,
  All of her earnings will be
    burned with fire
  And all of her images I
    will make desolate,
  For she collected *them* from
    a harlot's earnings,
  And to the earnings of a
    harlot they will return.
8 Because of this I must
    lament and wail,
  I must go barefoot and naked;
  I must make a lament like the jackals
  And a mourning like the ostriches.
9 For her wound is incurable,
  For it has come to Judah;
  It has reached the gate of my people,
  Even to Jerusalem.
10 Tell it not in Gath,
  Weep not at all.
  At Beth-le-aphrah roll
    yourself in the dust.

11 Go on your way, inhabitant of
    Shaphir, in shameful nakedness.
  The inhabitant of Zaanan
    does not escape.
  The lamentation of Beth-ezel: "He
    will take from you its support."
12 For the inhabitant of Maroth
  Becomes weak waiting for good,
  Because a calamity has come
    down from the LORD
  To the gate of Jerusalem.
13 Harness the chariot to the
    team of horses,
  O inhabitant of Lachish—
  She was the beginning of sin
  To the daughter of Zion—
  Because in you were found
  The rebellious acts of Israel.
14 Therefore you will give parting gifts
  On behalf of Moresheth-gath;
  The houses of Achzib *will*
    become a deception
  To the kings of Israel.
15 Moreover, I will bring on you
  The one who takes possession,
  O inhabitant of Mareshah.
  The glory of Israel will enter Adullam.
16 Make yourself bald and
    cut off your hair,
  Because of the children of your delight;
  Extend your baldness like the eagle,
  For they will go from you into exile.

2 Woe to those who scheme iniquity,
  Who work out evil on their beds!
  When morning comes, they do it,
  For it is in the power of their hands.
2 They covet fields and then seize *them*,
  And houses, and take *them* away.
  They rob a man and his house,
  A man and his inheritance.

3 Therefore thus says the LORD,

  "Behold, I am planning against
    this family a calamity
  From which you cannot
    remove your necks;
  And you will not walk haughtily,
  For it will be an evil time.
4 "On that day they will take up
    against you a taunt
  And utter a bitter lamentation *and* say,
  'We are completely destroyed!
  He exchanges the portion of my people;
  How He removes it from me!
  To the apostate He apportions
    our fields.'

5 "Therefore you will have no one
  stretching a measuring line
  For you by lot in the
  assembly of the LORD.

6 'Do not speak out,' *so* they speak out.
  But if they do not speak out
  concerning these things,
  Reproaches will not be turned back.
7 "Is it being said, O house of Jacob:
  'Is the Spirit of the LORD impatient?
  Are these His doings?'
  Do not My words do good
  To the one walking uprightly?

2:7 Spirit of the LORD. God responded to the evil prophets that their message affirming sin in the nation was inconsistent with the Holy Spirit and His true message to Micah (3:8). God's words do reward the righteous, but they also rebuke those engaging in evil deeds.

8 "Recently My people have
  arisen as an enemy—
  You strip the robe off
  the garment
  From unsuspecting passers-by,
  From those returned from war.
9 "The women of My
  people you evict,
  Each *one* from her
  pleasant house.
  From her children you take
  My splendor forever.
10 "Arise and go,
  For this is no place of rest
  Because of the uncleanness that
  brings on destruction,
  A painful destruction.

2:6–11 False prophets, commanding Micah to cease prophesying, would certainly not prophesy against the people's evildoing; they would not confront them with the divine standard of holiness. Rather, their false message (v. 7) had stopped the mouths of the true prophets and had permitted the rulers to engage in social atrocities (vv. 8–9), leading the people to destruction (v. 10). They didn't want true prophecies; therefore, they got what they wanted (Is 30:10). It is best to understand that Micah speaks in v. 6 and God in vv. 7–11.

11 "If a man walking after
  wind and falsehood
  Had told lies *and said,*
  'I will speak out to you concerning
  wine and liquor,'
  He would be spokesman
  to this people.
12 "I will surely assemble all
  of you, Jacob,
  I will surely gather the
  remnant of Israel.
  I will put them together like
  sheep in the fold;
  Like a flock in the midst of its pasture
  They will be noisy with men.
13 "The breaker goes up before them;
  They break out, pass through
  the gate and go out by it.
  So their king goes on before them,
  And the LORD at their head."

3 And I said,

"Hear now, heads of Jacob
  And rulers of the house of Israel.
  Is it not for you to know justice?
2 "You who hate good and love evil,
  Who tear off their skin from them
  And their flesh from their bones,
3 Who eat the flesh of my people,
  Strip off their skin from them,
  Break their bones
  And chop *them* up as for the pot
  And as meat in a kettle."
4 Then they will cry out to the LORD,
  But He will not answer them.
  Instead, He will hide His face
  from them at that time
  Because they have practiced
  evil deeds.

5 Thus says the LORD concerning the prophets who lead my people astray;

When they have *something*
  to bite with their teeth,
They cry, "Peace,"
But against him who puts
  nothing in their mouths
They declare holy war.
6 Therefore *it will be* night for
  you—without vision,
  And darkness for you—
  without divination.
  The sun will go down on the prophets,
  And the day will become
  dark over them.

7 The seers will be ashamed
And the diviners will be embarrassed.
Indeed, they will all cover
   their mouths
Because there is no answer from God.
8 On the other hand I am
   filled with power—
With the Spirit of the LORD—
And with justice and courage
To make known to Jacob
   his rebellious act,
Even to Israel his sin.
9 Now hear this, heads of
   the house of Jacob
And rulers of the house of Israel,
Who abhor justice
And twist everything that is straight,
10 Who build Zion with bloodshed
And Jerusalem with violent injustice.
11 Her leaders pronounce
   judgment for a bribe,
Her priests instruct for a price
And her prophets divine for money.
Yet they lean on the LORD saying,
"Is not the LORD in our midst?
Calamity will not come upon us."
12 Therefore, on account of you
Zion will be plowed as a field,
Jerusalem will become
   a heap of ruins,
And the mountain of the temple *will*
   become high places of a forest.

Psalm 144:9–15

9 I will sing a new song to You, O God;
Upon a harp of ten strings I
   will sing praises to You,
10 Who gives salvation to kings,
Who rescues David His servant
   from the evil sword.
11 Rescue me and deliver me out
   of the hand of aliens,
Whose mouth speaks deceit
And whose right hand is a
   right hand of falsehood.

12 Let our sons in their youth be
   as grown-up plants,
And our daughters as corner pillars
   fashioned as for a palace;
13 Let our garners be full, furnishing
   every kind of produce,
And our flocks bring forth thousands
   and ten thousands in our fields;
14 Let our cattle bear
Without mishap and without loss,
Let there be no outcry
   in our streets!

15 How blessed are the people
   who are so situated;
How blessed are the people
   whose God is the LORD!

Proverbs 30:10

10 Do not slander a slave to his master,
Or he will curse you and you
   will be found guilty.

Revelation 9:1–21

9 Then the fifth angel sounded, and I saw a star from heaven which had fallen to the earth; and the key of the bottomless pit was given to him. 2 He opened the bottomless pit, and smoke went up out of the pit, like the smoke of a great furnace; and the sun and the air were darkened by the smoke of the pit. 3 Then out of the smoke came locusts upon the earth, and power was given them, as the scorpions of the earth have power. 4 They were told not to hurt the grass of the earth, nor any green thing, nor any tree, but only the men who do not have the seal of God on their foreheads. 5 And they were not permitted to kill anyone, but to torment for five months; and their torment was like the torment of a scorpion when it stings a man. 6 And in those days men will seek death and will not find it; they will long to die, and death flees from them.

7 The appearance of the locusts was like horses prepared for battle; and on their heads appeared to be crowns like gold, and their faces were like the faces of men. 8 They had hair like the hair of women, and their teeth

---

9:3 locusts. A grasshopper-like insect that descends in swarms so thick they can obscure the sun and strip bare all vegetation. In the 1950s a locust swarm devoured every growing thing for several hundred thousand square miles in the Middle East. These are not normal locusts, however, but specially prepared ones that are merely the outward form of demons, who, like locusts, will bring swarming desolation (Joel 2:1–5). "Like" appears several times in John's description; he finds it difficult to describe what he sees in a way the reader can understand. **scorpions.** An arachnid that inhabits warm, dry regions and has an erect tail tipped with a venomous stinger. A scorpion's victim often rolls on the ground in agony, foams at the mouth, and grinds his teeth in pain. The demons in locust form are able to inflict the physical—and perhaps spiritual—pain like the scorpion (v. 5).

were like *the teeth* of lions. ⁹They had breastplates like breastplates of iron; and the sound of their wings was like the sound of chariots, of many horses rushing to battle. ¹⁰They have tails like scorpions, and stings; and in their tails is their power to hurt men for five months. ¹¹They have as king over them, the angel of the abyss; his name in Hebrew is Abaddon, and in the Greek he has the name Apollyon.

¹²The first woe is past; behold, two woes are still coming after these things.

¹³Then the sixth angel sounded, and I heard a voice from the four horns of the golden altar which is before God, ¹⁴one saying to the sixth angel who had the trumpet, "Release the four angels who are bound at the great river Euphrates." ¹⁵And the four angels, who had been prepared for the hour and day and month and year, were released, so that they would kill a third of mankind. ¹⁶The number of the armies of the horsemen was two hundred million; I heard the number of them. ¹⁷And this is how I saw in the vision the horses and those who sat on them: *the riders* had breastplates *the color* of fire and of hyacinth and of brimstone; and the heads of the horses are like the heads of lions; and out of their mouths proceed

9:11 Abaddon...Apollyon. Although locusts normally have no king (Pr 30:27), these demonic creatures do. His name in both Hebrew and Greek means "destroyer." There is a hierarchy of power among the demons, just as among the holy angels. Apparently, "the angel of the abyss" is one of Satan's most trusted leaders or possibly Satan himself.

fire and smoke and brimstone. ¹⁸A third of mankind was killed by these three plagues, by the fire and the smoke and the brimstone which proceeded out of their mouths. ¹⁹For the power of the horses is in their mouths and in their tails; for their tails are like serpents and have heads, and with them they do harm.

²⁰The rest of mankind, who were not killed by these plagues, did not repent of the works of their hands, so as not to worship demons, and the idols of gold and of silver and of brass and of stone and of wood, which can neither see nor hear nor walk; ²¹and they did not repent of their murders nor of their sorceries nor of their immorality nor of their thefts.

DAY 19: Who was the prophet Micah, and what was his message?

The first verse establishes Micah as the author. Beyond that, little is known about him. His parentage is not given, but his name suggests a godly heritage. He traces his roots to the town of Moresheth (1:1, 14), located in the foothills of Judah, approximately 25 miles southwest of Jerusalem, on the border of Judah and Philistia, near Gath. From a productive agricultural area, he was like Amos, a country resident removed from the national politics and religion yet chosen by God (3:8) to deliver a message of judgment to the princes and people of Jerusalem.

Primarily, Micah proclaimed a message of judgment to a people persistently pursuing evil. Similar to other prophets (Hos 4:1; Am 3:1), Micah presented his message in lawsuit/courtroom terminology (1:2; 6:1, 2). The prophecy is arranged in 3 oracles or cycles, each beginning with the admonition to "hear" (1:2; 3:1; 6:1). Within each oracle, he moves from doom to hope-doom because they have broken God's law given at Sinai; hope because of God's unchanging covenant with their forefathers (7:20). One-third of the book targets the sins of his people; another third looks at the punishment of God to come; and another third promises hope for the faithful after the judgment. Thus, the theme of the inevitability of divine judgment for sin is coupled together with God's immutable commitment to His covenant promises. The combination of God's 1) absolute consistency in judging sin and 2) unbending commitment to His covenant through the remnant of His people provides the hearers with a clear disclosure of the character of the Sovereign of the universe. Through divine intervention, He will bring about both judgment on sinners and blessing on those who repent.

DECEMBER 20

Micah 4:1–5:15

4 And it will come about in the last days
That the mountain of the
  house of the LORD
Will be established as the
  chief of the mountains.
It will be raised above the hills,
And the peoples will stream to it.

4:1 In a reversal of 3:12, Micah shifted from impending judgment to prophecies of the future millennial kingdom ("the last days") in which Mt. Zion (v. 2), the center of Messiah's coming earthly kingdom, shall be raised both spiritually and physically (Zec 14:9–10). This discussion continues to 5:15.

2 Many nations will come and say,
"Come and let us go up to the
  mountain of the LORD
And to the house of the God of Jacob,
That He may teach us about His ways
And that we may walk in His paths."
For from Zion will go forth the law,
Even the word of the LORD
  from Jerusalem.
3 And He will judge between
  many peoples
And render decisions for
  mighty, distant nations.
Then they will hammer their
  swords into plowshares
And their spears into pruning hooks;
Nation will not lift up sword
  against nation,
And never again will they
  train for war.
4 Each of them will sit under his vine
And under his fig tree,
With no one to make *them* afraid,
For the mouth of the LORD
  of hosts has spoken.
5 Though all the peoples walk
Each in the name of his god,
As for us, we will walk
In the name of the LORD our
  God forever and ever.

6 "In that day," declares the LORD,
"I will assemble the lame
And gather the outcasts,
Even those whom I have afflicted.

7 "I will make the lame a remnant
And the outcasts a strong nation,
And the LORD will reign over
  them in Mount Zion
From now on and forever.
8 "As for you, tower of the flock,
Hill of the daughter of Zion,
To you it will come—
Even the former dominion will come,
The kingdom of the daughter
  of Jerusalem.

9 "Now, why do you cry out loudly?
Is there no king among you,
Or has your counselor perished,
That agony has gripped you like
  a woman in childbirth?
10 "Writhe and labor to give birth,
Daughter of Zion,
Like a woman in childbirth;
For now you will go out of the city,
Dwell in the field,
And go to Babylon.
There you will be rescued;
There the LORD will redeem you
From the hand of your enemies.
11 "And now many nations have
  been assembled against you
Who say, 'Let her be polluted,
And let our eyes gloat over Zion.'
12 "But they do not know the
  thoughts of the LORD,
And they do not understand
  His purpose;
For He has gathered them like
  sheaves to the threshing floor.
13 "Arise and thresh, daughter of Zion,
For your horn I will make iron
And your hoofs I will make bronze,
That you may pulverize
  many peoples,
That you may devote to the
  LORD their unjust gain
And their wealth to the
  Lord of all the earth.

5 "Now muster yourselves in
  troops, daughter of troops;
They have laid siege against us;
With a rod they will smite the
  judge of Israel on the cheek.
2 "But as for you, Bethlehem Ephrathah,
Too little to be among the
  clans of Judah,
From you One will go forth for
  Me to be ruler in Israel.
His goings forth are from long ago,
From the days of eternity."

3 Therefore He will give them
  up until the time
When she who is in labor
  has borne a child.
Then the remainder of His brethren
Will return to the sons of Israel.
4 And He will arise and
  shepherd *His flock*
In the strength of the LORD,
In the majesty of the name
  of the LORD His God.
And they will remain,
Because at that time
  He will be great
To the ends of the earth.
5 This One will be *our* peace.

When the Assyrian invades our land,
When he tramples on our citadels,
Then we will raise against him
Seven shepherds and eight
  leaders of men.
6 They will shepherd the land of
  Assyria with the sword,
The land of Nimrod at its entrances;
And He will deliver *us*
  from the Assyrian
When he attacks our land
And when he tramples our territory.

7 Then the remnant of Jacob
Will be among many peoples
Like dew from the LORD,
Like showers on vegetation
Which do not wait for man
Or delay for the sons of men.
8 The remnant of Jacob
Will be among the nations,
Among many peoples
Like a lion among the
  beasts of the forest,
Like a young lion among
  flocks of sheep,
Which, if he passes through,
Tramples down and tears,
And there is none to rescue.
9 Your hand will be lifted up
  against your adversaries,
And all your enemies will be cut off.

10 "It will be in that day,"
  declares the LORD,
"That I will cut off your horses
  from among you
And destroy your chariots.
11 "I will also cut off the cities
  of your land
And tear down all your fortifications.

12 "I will cut off sorceries
  from your hand,
And you will have
  fortune-tellers no more.
13 "I will cut off your carved images
And your *sacred* pillars from
  among you,
So that you will no longer bow down
To the work of your hands.
14 "I will root out your Asherim
  from among you
And destroy your cities.
15 "And I will execute vengeance
  in anger and wrath
On the nations which
  have not obeyed."

Psalm 145:1–9

A Psalm of Praise, of David.

I will extol You, my God, O King,
  And I will bless Your name
  forever and ever.
2 Every day I will bless You,
  And I will praise Your name
  forever and ever.
3 Great is the LORD, and
  highly to be praised,
  And His greatness is unsearchable.
4 One generation shall praise
  Your works to another,
  And shall declare Your mighty acts.
5 On the glorious splendor
  of Your majesty
  And on Your wonderful
  works, I will meditate.
6 Men shall speak of the power
  of Your awesome acts,
  And I will tell of Your greatness.
7 They shall eagerly utter the memory
  of Your abundant goodness
  And will shout joyfully of
  Your righteousness.

8 The LORD is gracious and merciful;
  Slow to anger and great
  in lovingkindness.
9 The LORD is good to all,
  And His mercies are over
  all His works.

Proverbs 30:11–14

11 There is a kind of *man* who
  curses his father
  And does not bless his mother.
12 There is a kind who is pure
  in his own eyes,
  Yet is not washed from
  his filthiness.

¹³ There is a kind—oh how
   lofty are his eyes!
And his eyelids are raised
   in arrogance.
¹⁴ There is a kind of *man* whose
   teeth are *like* swords
And his jaw teeth *like* knives,
To devour the afflicted from the earth
And the needy from among men.

30:11–14 There is a kind. These proverbs condemn various forms of unwise behavior and are connected with this common phrase which points to the fact that certain sins can uniquely permeate a whole society or time period.

Revelation 10:1–11

10 I saw another strong angel coming down out of heaven, clothed with a cloud; and the rainbow was upon his head, and his face was like the sun, and his feet like pillars of fire; ² and he had in his hand a little book which was open. He placed his right foot on the sea and his left on the land; ³ and he cried out with a loud voice, as when a lion roars; and when he had cried out, the seven peals of thunder uttered their voices. ⁴When the seven peals of thunder had spoken, I was about to write; and I heard a voice from heaven saying, "Seal up the things which the seven peals of thunder have spoken and do not write them." ⁵ Then the angel whom I saw standing on the sea and on the land lifted up his right hand to heaven, ⁶ and swore by Him who lives forever and ever, WHO CREATED

10:1 another strong angel. Many commentators understand this to be Jesus Christ. But the Greek word translated "another" means one of the same kind, that is, a created being. This is not one of the 7 angels responsible for sounding the trumpets (8:2), but one of the highest ranking in heaven, filled with splendor, greatness, and strength (5:2; 8:3; 18:1). **rainbow.** Perhaps God included this to remind John, that even in judgment, He will always remember His Noahic Covenant and protect His own. **feet like pillars of fire.** This angel's feet and legs indicate the firm resolve with which he will execute the day of the Lord.

HEAVEN AND THE THINGS IN IT, AND THE EARTH AND THE THINGS IN IT, AND THE SEA AND THE THINGS IN IT, that there will be delay no longer, ⁷ but in the days of the voice of the seventh angel, when he is about to sound, then the mystery of God is finished, as He preached to His servants the prophets.

⁸ Then the voice which I heard from heaven, *I heard* again speaking with me, and saying, "Go, take the book which is open in the hand of the angel who stands on the sea and on the land." ⁹ So I went to the angel, telling him to give me the little book. And he *said to me, "Take it and eat it; it will make your stomach bitter, but in your mouth it will be sweet as honey." ¹⁰ I took the little book out of the angel's hand and ate it, and in my mouth it was sweet as honey; and when I had eaten it, my stomach was made bitter. ¹¹And they *said to me, "You must prophesy again concerning many peoples and nations and tongues and kings."

DAY 20: Is the Bethlehem of Micah 5:2-4 the birthplace of Christ?

"But as for you, Bethlehem Ephrathah, too little to be among the clans of Judah, from you One will go forth for Me to be ruler in Israel" (v. 2). This town south of Jerusalem was the birthplace of David and later Jesus Christ (1Sa 16; Mt 2:5; Lk 2:4–7). The name "Bethlehem" means "house of bread" because the area was a grain-producing region in Old Testament times. The name "Ephrathah" ("fruitful") differentiates it from the Galilean town by the same name. The town, known for her many vineyards and olive orchards, was small in size but not in honor. "His goings forth are from long ago, from the days of eternity." This speaks of eternal God's incarnation in the Person of Jesus Christ. It points to His millennial reign as King of kings (Is 9:6).

"Therefore He will give them up until the time when she who is in labor has borne a child" (v. 3). A reference to the interval between Messiah's rejection at His First Advent and His Second Advent, during the times of the Gentiles when Israel rejects Christ and is under the domination of enemies. Regathering of the "remainder of His brethren" did not occur at the First Advent but is slated for the Second Advent (Is 10:20–22; 11:11–16). Nor can "return" speak of Gentiles, since it cannot be said that they "returned" to the Lord. Rather, the context of 5:3–4 is millennial and cannot be made to fit the First Advent. Thus, "she who is in labor" must denote the nation of Israel (Rev 12:1–6).

Verse 4 clearly depicts the millennial rule of Christ, sitting upon the throne of David (Is 6:1–3).

DECEMBER 21

Micah 6:1–7:20

6 Hear now what the LORD is saying,
"Arise, plead your case before
the mountains,
And let the hills hear your voice.

2 "Listen, you mountains, to the
indictment of the LORD,
And you enduring foundations
of the earth,
Because the LORD has a case
against His people;
Even with Israel He will dispute.

3 "My people, what have I done to you,
And how have I wearied
you? Answer Me.

4 "Indeed, I brought you up
from the land of Egypt
And ransomed you from
the house of slavery,
And I sent before you Moses,
Aaron and Miriam.

5 "My people, remember now
What Balak king of Moab counseled
And what Balaam son of
Beor answered him,
And from Shittim to Gilgal,
So that you might know the
righteous acts of the LORD."

6 With what shall I come to the LORD
And bow myself before
the God on high?
Shall I come to Him with
burnt offerings,
With yearling calves?

7 Does the LORD take delight
in thousands of rams,
In ten thousand rivers of oil?
Shall I present my firstborn
for my rebellious acts,
The fruit of my body for
the sin of my soul?

8 He has told you, O man, what is good;
And what does the LORD require of you
But to do justice, to love kindness,
And to walk humbly with your God?

6:6–7 Micah, as though speaking on behalf of the people, asked rhetorically how, in light of God's faithfulness toward them, they could continue their hypocrisy by being outwardly religious but inwardly sinful.

6:8 Micah's terse response (v. 8) indicated they should have known the answer to the rhetorical question. Spiritual blindness had led them to offer everything except the one thing He wanted—a spiritual commitment of the heart from which right behavior would ensue (Dt 10:12–19; Mt 22:37–39). This theme is often represented in the Old Testament (1Sa 15:22; Is 1:11–20; Jer 7:21–23; Hos 6:6; Am 5:15).

9 The voice of the LORD will
call to the city—
And it is sound wisdom to
fear Your name:
"Hear, O tribe. Who has
appointed its time?

10 "Is there yet a man in the
wicked house,
Along with treasures
of wickedness
And a short measure
that is cursed?

11 "Can I justify wicked scales
And a bag of deceptive weights?

12 "For the rich men of *the* city
are full of violence,
Her residents speak lies,
And their tongue is deceitful
in their mouth.

13 "So also I will make *you* sick,
striking you down,
Desolating *you* because of your sins.

14 "You will eat, but you will
not be satisfied,
And your vileness will be
in your midst.
You will *try to* remove
for safekeeping,
But you will not preserve *anything,*
And what you do preserve I
will give to the sword.

15 "You will sow but you will not reap.
You will tread the olive but will
not anoint yourself with oil;
And the grapes, but you
will not drink wine.

16 "The statutes of Omri
And all the works of the house
of Ahab are observed;
And in their devices you walk.
Therefore I will give you
up for destruction
And your inhabitants for derision,
And you will bear the
reproach of My people."

7 Woe is me! For I am
Like the fruit pickers, like
    the grape gatherers.
There is not a cluster of grapes to eat,
Or a first-ripe fig *which* I crave.

2 The godly person has perished
    from the land,
And there is no upright
    person among men.
All of them lie in wait for bloodshed;
Each of them hunts the
    other with a net.

3 Concerning evil, both hands do it well.
The prince asks, also the
    judge, for a bribe,
And a great man speaks the
    desire of his soul;
So they weave it together.

4 The best of them is like a briar,
The most upright like a thorn hedge.
The day when you post
    your watchmen,
Your punishment will come.
Then their confusion will occur.

5 Do not trust in a neighbor;
Do not have confidence in a friend.
From her who lies in your bosom
Guard your lips.

6 For son treats father contemptuously,
Daughter rises up against her mother,
Daughter-in-law against
    her mother-in-law;
A man's enemies are the men
    of his own household.

7 But as for me, I will watch
    expectantly for the LORD;
I will wait for the God of my salvation.
My God will hear me.

8 Do not rejoice over me, O my enemy.
Though I fall I will rise;
Though I dwell in darkness, the
    LORD is a light for me.

9 I will bear the indignation of the LORD
Because I have sinned against Him,
Until He pleads my case and
    executes justice for me.
He will bring me out to the light,
And I will see His righteousness.

10 Then my enemy will see,
And shame will cover her
    who said to me,
"Where is the LORD your God?"
My eyes will look on her;
At that time she will be
    trampled down
Like mire of the streets.

11 *It will be* a day for building
    your walls.
On that day will your
    boundary be extended.

12 It *will be* a day when they
    will come to you
From Assyria and the cities of Egypt,
From Egypt even to the Euphrates,
Even from sea to sea and
    mountain to mountain.

13 And the earth will become desolate
    because of her inhabitants,
On account of the fruit of their deeds.

14 Shepherd Your people
    with Your scepter,
The flock of Your possession
Which dwells by itself in
    the woodland,
In the midst of a fruitful field.
Let them feed in Bashan and Gilead
As in the days of old.

15 "As in the days when you came
    out from the land of Egypt,
I will show you miracles."

16 Nations will see and be ashamed
Of all their might.
They will put *their* hand
    on *their* mouth,
Their ears will be deaf.

17 They will lick the dust like a serpent,
Like reptiles of the earth.
They will come trembling
    out of their fortresses;
To the LORD our God they
    will come in dread
And they will be afraid before You.

18 Who is a God like You, who
    pardons iniquity
And passes over the rebellious act of
    the remnant of His possession?
He does not retain His anger forever,
Because He delights in
    unchanging love.

19 He will again have compassion on us;
He will tread our iniquities
    under foot.
Yes, You will cast all their sins
Into the depths of the sea.

20 You will give truth to Jacob
And unchanging love to Abraham,
Which You swore to our forefathers
From the days of old.

Psalm 145:10–16

10 All Your works shall give
    thanks to You, O LORD,
And Your godly ones shall bless You.

¹¹ They shall speak of the glory
of Your kingdom
And talk of Your power;

¹² To make known to the sons of
men Your mighty acts
And the glory of the majesty
of Your kingdom.

¹³ Your kingdom is an
everlasting kingdom,
And Your dominion *endures*
throughout all generations.

¹⁴ The LORD sustains all who fall
And raises up all who are
bowed down.

¹⁵ The eyes of all look to You,
And You give them their
food in due time.

¹⁶ You open Your hand
And satisfy the desire of
every living thing.

Proverbs 30:15

¹⁵ The leech has two daughters,
"Give," "Give."
There are three things that
will not be satisfied,
Four that will not say, "Enough":

Revelation 11:1–19

11 Then there was given me a measuring rod like a staff; and someone said, "Get up and measure the temple of God and the altar, and those who worship in it. ² Leave out the court which is outside the temple and do not measure it, for it has been given to the nations; and they will tread under foot the holy city for forty-two months. ³ And I will grant *authority* to my two witnesses, and they will prophesy for twelve hundred and sixty days, clothed in sackcloth." ⁴ These are the two olive trees and the two lampstands that stand before the Lord of the earth. ⁵ And if anyone wants to harm them, fire flows out of their mouth and devours their enemies; so if anyone wants to harm them, he must be killed in this way. ⁶ These have the power to shut up the sky, so that rain will not fall during the days of their prophesying; and they have power over the waters to turn them into blood, and to strike the earth with every plague, as often as they desire.

⁷ When they have finished their testimony, the beast that comes up out of the abyss will make war with them, and overcome them and kill them. ⁸ And their dead bodies *will lie* in the street of the great city which mystically

11:7 the beast. The first of 36 references to this person in Revelation, who is none other than the Antichrist (see chap. 13). That he will ascend out of the bottomless pit indicates that his power is satanic. **kill them.** Their ministry completed, God will withdraw the two witnesses' supernatural protection. The beast will then be able to accomplish what many had died trying to do.

is called Sodom and Egypt, where also their Lord was crucified. ⁹ Those from the peoples and tribes and tongues and nations *will* look at their dead bodies for three and a half days, and will not permit their dead bodies to be laid in a tomb. ¹⁰ And those who dwell on the earth *will* rejoice over them and celebrate; and they will send gifts to one another, because these two prophets tormented those who dwell on the earth.

¹¹ But after the three and a half days, the breath of life from God came into them, and they stood on their feet; and great fear fell upon those who were watching them. ¹² And they heard a loud voice from heaven saying to them, "Come up here." Then they went up into heaven in the cloud, and their enemies watched them. ¹³ And in that hour there was a great earthquake, and a tenth of the city fell; seven thousand people were killed in the earthquake, and the rest were terrified and gave glory to the God of heaven.

¹⁴ The second woe is past; behold, the third woe is coming quickly.

¹⁵ Then the seventh angel sounded; and there were loud voices in heaven, saying,

"The kingdom of the world has become *the kingdom* of our Lord and of His Christ; and He will reign forever and ever." ¹⁶ And the twenty-four elders, who sit on their thrones

11:13 earthquake. God punctuates the ascension of His prophets with a shattering earthquake. The destruction and loss of life may be primarily among the leaders of the Antichrist's forces. **the rest.** This refers to the Jews still living, who will not yet have come to faith in Christ. **gave glory to the God of heaven.** A genuine experience of the salvation of Jews (Lk 17:18–19), in contrast to those who blaspheme and refuse to glorify God (16:9). This makes a key fulfilment of Zechariah's prophecy (12:10; 13:1) and Paul's (Ro 11:25–27).

before God, fell on their faces and worshiped God, [17]saying,

"**We** give You thanks, O Lord God, the Almighty, who are and who were, because You have taken Your great power and have begun to reign. [18]And the nations were enraged, and Your wrath came, and the time *came* for the dead to be judged, and *the time* to reward Your bond-servants the prophets and the saints and those who fear Your name, the small and the great, and to destroy those who destroy the earth."

[19]And the temple of God which is in heaven was opened; and the ark of His covenant appeared in His temple, and there were flashes of lightning and sounds and peals of thunder and an earthquake and a great hailstorm.

DAY 21: Who are the "two witnesses" of Revelation 11?

In v. 3, John is told that "I will grant authority to my two witnesses." These individuals are granted special power and authority by God to preach a message of judgment and salvation during the second half of the Tribulation. The Old Testament required 2 or more witnesses to confirm testimony (Dt 17:6; 19:15; Mt 18:16; Jn 8:17; Heb 10:28), and these 2 prophets will be the culmination of God's testimony to Israel: a message of judgment from God and of His gracious offer of the gospel to all who will repent and believe. "They will prophesy for twelve hundred and sixty days," which is 42 months or 3 1/2 years, "clothed in sackcloth." Coarse, rough cloth made from goat or camel hair. Wearing garments made from it expressed penitence, humility, and mourning. The witnesses are mourning because of the wretched wickedness of the world, God's judgment on it, and the desecration of the temple and the holy city by the Antichrist.

The imagery in v. 4 is drawn from Zechariah 3–4. Zechariah's vision had both a near fulfillment (the rebuilding of the temple by Joshua and Zerubbabel) and a far future fulfillment (the 2 witnesses, whose ministry points toward Israel's final restoration in the Millennium). "Two olive trees and the two lampstands." Olive oil was commonly used in lamps; together the olive trees and lampstands symbolize the light of spiritual revival. The 2 witnesses' preaching will spark a revival, just as Joshua's and Zerubbabel's did in Israel after the Babylonian captivity.

While it is impossible to be dogmatic about the identity of these 2 witnesses, several observations from vv. 5–6 suggest they might be Moses and Elijah: 1) like Moses, they strike the earth with plagues, and like Elijah, they have the power to keep it from raining; 2) Jewish tradition expected both Moses (Dt 18:15–18) and Elijah (Mal 4:5–6) to return in the future (Jn 1:21); 3) both Moses and Elijah were present at the Transfiguration, the preview of Christ's Second Coming; 4) both Moses and Elijah used supernatural means to provoke repentance; 5) Elijah was taken up alive into heaven, and God buried Moses' body where it would never be found; and 6) the length of the drought the 2 witnesses bring (3 1/2 years) is the same as that brought by Elijah (Jas 5:17).

❧ DECEMBER 22

Nahum 1:1–3:19

1 The oracle of Nineveh. The book of the vision of Nahum the Elkoshite.

[2] A jealous and avenging
   God is the LORD;
The LORD is avenging and wrathful.
The LORD takes vengeance
   on His adversaries,
And He reserves wrath for His enemies.
[3] The LORD is slow to anger
   and great in power,
And the LORD will by no means
   leave *the guilty* unpunished.
In whirlwind and storm is His way,
And clouds are the dust
   beneath His feet.

[4] He rebukes the sea and makes it dry;
   He dries up all the rivers.
Bashan and Carmel wither;
   The blossoms of Lebanon wither.
[5] Mountains quake because of Him
   And the hills dissolve;
Indeed the earth is upheaved
   by His presence,
The world and all the
   inhabitants in it.
[6] Who can stand before
   His indignation?
Who can endure the burning
   of His anger?
His wrath is poured out like fire
And the rocks are broken up by Him.
[7] The LORD is good,
   A stronghold in the day of trouble,
And He knows those who
   take refuge in Him.

8 But with an overflowing flood
   He will make a complete
      end of its site,
   And will pursue His enemies
      into darkness.

9 Whatever you devise
      against the LORD,
   He will make a complete end of it.
   Distress will not rise up twice.

10 Like tangled thorns,
   And like those who are drunken
      with their drink,
   They are consumed
   As stubble completely withered.

11 From you has gone forth
   One who plotted evil
      against the LORD,
   A wicked counselor.

1:11 wicked counselor. The phrase, literally, "counselor of Belial," suggests Satanic influence on the leadership, identified as the king of Assyria (3:18). Specific reference could be to Ashurbanipal (669–633 B.C.) or more likely to Sennacherib (705–681 B.C.), who invaded Judah in 701 B.C. and of whom Isaiah speaks in similar language (Is 10:7).

12 Thus says the LORD,

"Though they are at full *strength*
   and likewise many,
Even so, they will be cut
   off and pass away.
Though I have afflicted you,
   I will afflict you no longer.

13 "So now, I will break his yoke
      bar from upon you,
   And I will tear off your shackles."

14 The LORD has issued a command
      concerning you:
   "Your name will no longer
      be perpetuated.
   I will cut off idol and image
   From the house of your gods.
   I will prepare your grave,
   For you are contemptible."

15 Behold, on the mountains the feet
      of him who brings good news,
   Who announces peace!
   Celebrate your feasts, O Judah;
   Pay your vows.

For never again will the wicked
   one pass through you;
He is cut off completely.

2 The one who scatters has
   come up against you.
Man the fortress, watch the road;
Strengthen your back, summon
   all *your* strength.

2 For the LORD will restore
      the splendor of Jacob
   Like the splendor of Israel,
   Even though devastators
      have devastated them
   And destroyed their vine branches.

3 The shields of his mighty
      men are *colored* red,
   The warriors are dressed in scarlet,
   The chariots are *enveloped*
      in flashing steel
   When he is prepared *to march*,
   And the cypress *spears*
      are brandished.

4 The chariots race madly
      in the streets,
   They rush wildly in the squares,
   Their appearance is like torches,
   They dash to and fro like
      lightning flashes.

5 He remembers his nobles;
   They stumble in their march,
   They hurry to their wall,
   And the mantelet is set up.

6 The gates of the rivers are opened
   And the palace is dissolved.

7 It is fixed:
   She is stripped, she is carried away,
   And her handmaids are moaning
      like the sound of doves,
   Beating on their breasts.

8 Though Nineveh *was* like a pool of
      water throughout her days,
   Now they are fleeing;
   "Stop, stop,"
   But no one turns back.

9 Plunder the silver!
   Plunder the gold!
   For there is no limit to the treasure—
   Wealth from every kind of
      desirable object.

10 She is emptied! Yes, she is
      desolate and waste!
   Hearts are melting and
      knees knocking!
   Also anguish is in the whole body
   And all their faces are grown pale!

11 Where is the den of the lions
And the feeding place of
the young lions,
Where the lion, lioness and
lion's cub prowled,
With nothing to disturb *them*?
12 The lion tore enough for his cubs,
Killed *enough* for his lionesses,
And filled his lairs with prey
And his dens with torn flesh.

13 "Behold, I am against you," declares the LORD of hosts. "I will burn up her chariots in smoke, a sword will devour your young lions; I will cut off your prey from the land, and no longer will the voice of your messengers be heard."

3 Woe to the bloody city, completely
full of lies *and* pillage;
Her prey never departs.
2 The noise of the whip,
The noise of the rattling of the wheel,
Galloping horses
And bounding chariots!

3:1 bloody city. The first accusation was a charge well documented in history. Assyria proved to be an unusually cruel, bloodthirsty nation. **lies.** Assyria employed falsehood and treachery to subdue her enemies (2Ki 18:28–32). **pillage.** Preying upon her victims, she filled her cities with the goods of other nations.

3 Horsemen charging,
Swords flashing, spears gleaming,
Many slain, a mass of corpses,
And countless dead bodies—
They stumble over the dead bodies!
4 *All* because of the many
harlotries of the harlot,
The charming one, the
mistress of sorceries,
Who sells nations by her harlotries
And families by her sorceries.
5 "Behold, I am against you,"
declares the LORD of hosts;
"And I will lift up your skirts
over your face,
And show to the nations
your nakedness
And to the kingdoms your disgrace.
6 "I will throw filth on you
And make you vile,
And set you up as a spectacle.

7 "And it will come about that
all who see you
Will shrink from you and say,
'Nineveh is devastated!
Who will grieve for her?'
Where will I seek comforters for you?"

8 Are you better than No-amon,
Which was situated by the
waters of the Nile,
With water surrounding her,
Whose rampart *was* the sea,
Whose wall *consisted* of the sea?
9 Ethiopia was *her* might,
And Egypt too, without limits.
Put and Lubim were
among her helpers.
10 Yet she became an exile,
She went into captivity;
Also her small children were
dashed to pieces
At the head of every street;
They cast lots for her honorable men,
And all her great men were
bound with fetters.
11 You too will become drunk,
You will be hidden.
You too will search for a
refuge from the enemy.
12 All your fortifications are fig
trees with ripe fruit—
When shaken, they fall into
the eater's mouth.
13 Behold, your people are
women in your midst!
The gates of your land are opened
wide to your enemies;
Fire consumes your gate bars.
14 Draw for yourself water for the siege!
Strengthen your fortifications!
Go into the clay and tread the mortar!
Take hold of the brick mold!
15 There fire will consume you,
The sword will cut you down;
It will consume you as the locust *does*.

Multiply yourself like the
creeping locust,
Multiply yourself like the
swarming locust.
16 You have increased your traders
more than the stars of heaven—
The creeping locust strips
and flies away.
17 Your guardsmen are like the
swarming locust.
Your marshals are like hordes
of grasshoppers

Settling in the stone walls
    on a cold day.
The sun rises and they flee,
And the place where they
    are is not known.
¹⁸ Your shepherds are sleeping,
    O king of Assyria;
Your nobles are lying down.
Your people are scattered
    on the mountains
And there is no one to regather *them*.
¹⁹ There is no relief for your breakdown,
Your wound is incurable.
All who hear about you
Will clap *their* hands over you,
For on whom has not your
    evil passed continually?

Psalm 145:17-21

¹⁷ The LORD is righteous in all His ways
And kind in all His deeds.
¹⁸ The LORD is near to all
    who call upon Him,
To all who call upon Him in truth.
¹⁹ He will fulfill the desire of
    those who fear Him;
He will also hear their cry
    and will save them.
²⁰ The LORD keeps all who love Him,
But all the wicked He will destroy.
²¹ My mouth will speak the
    praise of the LORD,
And all flesh will bless His holy
    name forever and ever.

Proverbs 30:16

¹⁶ Sheol, and the barren womb,
Earth that is never satisfied
    with water,
And fire that never says, "Enough."

Revelation 12:1-17

12 A great sign appeared in heaven: a woman clothed with the sun, and the moon under her feet, and on her head a crown of twelve stars; ² and she was with child; and she *cried out, being in labor and in pain to give birth. ³ Then another sign appeared in heaven: and behold, a great red dragon having seven heads and ten horns, and on his heads *were* seven diadems. ⁴ And his tail *swept away a third of the stars of heaven and threw them to the earth. And the dragon stood before the woman who was about to give birth, so that when she gave birth he might devour her child. ⁵ And she gave birth to a son, a male *child,* who is to rule all the nations with a rod of iron; and her child was caught up

12:3 great red dragon. The woman's mortal enemy is Satan, who appears as a dragon 13 times in this book (v. 9; 20:2). Red speaks of bloodshed (Jn 8:44). **seven heads...ten horns...seven diadems.** Figurative language depicting Satan's domination of 7 past worldly kingdoms and 10 future kingdoms (Da 7:7, 20, 24). Satan has and will rule the world until the seventh trumpet blows (11:15). He has inflicted relentless pain on Israel (Da 8:24), desiring to kill the woman before she could bring forth the child that would destroy him.

to God and to His throne. ⁶ Then the woman fled into the wilderness where she *had a place prepared by God, so that there she would be nourished for one thousand two hundred and sixty days.

⁷ And there was war in heaven, Michael and his angels waging war with the dragon. The dragon and his angels waged war, ⁸ and they were not strong enough, and there was no longer a place found for them in heaven. ⁹ And the great dragon was thrown down, the serpent of old who is called the devil and Satan, who deceives the whole world; he was thrown down to the earth, and his angels were thrown down with him. ¹⁰ Then I heard a loud voice in heaven, saying,

"Now the salvation, and the power, and the kingdom of our God and the authority of His Christ have come, for the accuser of our brethren has been thrown down, he who accuses them before our God day and night.

12:9 dragon was thrown down...to the earth. Satan and his demons were cast out of heaven at the time of their original rebellion, but still have access to it (Job 1:6; 2:1). That access will then be denied, and they will be forever barred from heaven. **devil and Satan.** See 20:2. "Devil" comes from a Greek verb meaning "to slander" or "to falsely accuse." He is a malignant liar (Jn 8:44; 1Jn 3:8). His accusations against believers (v. 10) are unsuccessful because of Christ our Advocate (1Jn 2:1). Satan, meaning "adversary," or "enemy," appears especially in Job and the gospels. **deceives the whole world.** As he has throughout human history, Satan will deceive people during the Tribulation (13:14; 20:3; Jn 8:44). After his temporary release from the bottomless pit at the end of the Millennium, he will briefly resume his deceitful ways (20:8, 10).

[11] And they overcame him because of the blood of the Lamb and because of the word of their testimony, and they did not love their life even when faced with death. [12] For this reason, rejoice, O heavens and you who dwell in them. Woe to the earth and the sea, because the devil has come down to you, having great wrath, knowing that he has *only* a short time."

[13] And when the dragon saw that he was thrown down to the earth, he persecuted the woman who gave birth to the male *child*. [14] But the two wings of the great eagle were given to the woman, so that she could fly into the wilderness to her place, where she *was nourished for a time and times and half a time, from the presence of the serpent. [15] And the serpent poured water like a river out of his mouth after the woman, so that he might cause her to be swept away with the flood. [16] But the earth helped the woman, and the earth opened its mouth and drank up the river which the dragon poured out of his mouth. [17] So the dragon was enraged with the woman, and went off to make war with the rest of her children, who keep the commandments of God and hold to the testimony of Jesus.

DAY 22: Who was the prophet Nahum, and how was his message related to the prophet Jonah?

The significance of the writing prophets was not their personal lives; it was their message. Thus, background information about the prophet from within the prophecy is rare. Occasionally one of the historical books will shed additional light. In the case of Nahum, nothing is provided except that he was an Elkoshite (1:1), referring either to his birthplace or his place of ministry. Attempts to identify the location of Elkosh have been unsuccessful. Suggestions include Al Qosh, situated in northern Iraq (thus Nahum would have been a descendant of the exiles taken to Assyria in 722 B.C.), Capernaum ("town of Nahum"), or a location in southern Judah (1:15). His birthplace or locale is not significant to the interpretation of the book.

Nahum forms a sequel to the Book of Jonah, who prophesied over a century earlier. Jonah recounts the remission of God's promised judgment toward Nineveh, while Nahum depicts the later execution of God's judgment. Nineveh was proud of her invulnerable city, with her walls reaching 100 feet high and with a moat 150 feet wide and 60 feet deep. But Nahum established the fact that the sovereign God (1:2–5) would bring vengeance upon those who violated His law (1:8, 14; 3:5–7). The same God had a retributive judgment against evil which is also redemptive, bestowing His loving kindnesses upon the faithful (1:7, 12–13, 15; 2:2). The prophecy brought comfort to Judah and all who feared the cruel Assyrians. Nahum said Nineveh would end "with an overflowing flood" (1:8); and it happened when the Tigris River overflowed to destroy enough of the walls to let the Babylonians through. Nahum also predicted that the city would be hidden (3:11). After its destruction in 612 B.C., the site was not rediscovered until 1842 A.D.

DECEMBER 23

Habakkuk 1:1–3:19

1 The oracle which Habakkuk the prophet saw.

2 How long, O LORD, will I call for help,
And You will not hear?
I cry out to You, "Violence!"
Yet You do not save.

3 Why do You make me see iniquity,
And cause *me* to look on wickedness?
Yes, destruction and violence
are before me;
Strife exists and contention arises.

4 Therefore the law is ignored
And justice is never upheld.
For the wicked surround the righteous;
Therefore justice comes out perverted.

5 "Look among the nations! Observe!
Be astonished! Wonder!
Because *I am* doing something
in your days—
You would not believe if
you were told.

6 "For behold, I am raising
up the Chaldeans,
That fierce and impetuous people
Who march throughout the earth
To seize dwelling places
which are not theirs.

7 "They are dreaded and feared;
Their justice and authority
originate with themselves.

8 "Their horses are swifter than leopards
And keener than wolves
in the evening.
Their horsemen come galloping,
Their horsemen come from afar;

They fly like an eagle swooping
down to devour.
9 "All of them come for violence.
Their horde of faces *moves* forward.
They collect captives like sand.
10 "They mock at kings
And rulers are a laughing
matter to them.
They laugh at every fortress
And heap up rubble to capture it.
11 "Then they will sweep through
like the wind and pass on.
But they will be held guilty,
They whose strength is their god."

12 Are You not from everlasting,
O LORD, my God, my Holy One?
We will not die.
You, O LORD, have appointed
them to judge;
And You, O Rock, have established
them to correct.
13 *Your* eyes are too pure to approve evil,
And You can not look on
wickedness *with favor.*
Why do You look with favor
On those who deal treacherously?
Why are You silent when the
wicked swallow up
Those more righteous than they?
14 *Why* have You made men
like the fish of the sea,
Like creeping things without
a ruler over them?
15 *The Chaldeans* bring all of
them up with a hook,
Drag them away with their net,
And gather them together
in their fishing net.
Therefore they rejoice and are glad.
16 Therefore they offer a
sacrifice to their net
And burn incense to their fishing net;
Because through these things
their catch is large,
And their food is plentiful.
17 Will they therefore empty their net
And continually slay nations
without sparing?

2 I will stand on my guard post
And station myself on the rampart;
And I will keep watch to see
what He will speak to me,
And how I may reply when
I am reproved.
2 Then the LORD answered me and said,
"Record the vision

And inscribe *it* on tablets,
That the one who reads it may run.
3 "For the vision is yet for the
appointed time;
It hastens toward the goal
and it will not fail.
Though it tarries, wait for it;
For it will certainly come,
it will not delay.
4 "Behold, as for the proud one,
His soul is not right within him;
But the righteous will live by his faith.
5 "Furthermore, wine betrays
the haughty man,
So that he does not stay at home.
He enlarges his appetite like Sheol,
And he is like death, never satisfied.
He also gathers to himself all nations
And collects to himself all peoples.

2:4 the righteous will live by his faith. In contrast to the proud, the righteous will be truly preserved through his faithfulness to God. This is the core of God's message to/through Habakkuk. Both the aspect of justification by faith, as noted by Paul's usage in Romans 1:17 and Galatians 3:11, as well as the aspect of sanctification by faith, as employed by the writer of Hebrews (10:38), reflect the essence of Habakkuk; no conflict exists. The emphasis in both Habakkuk and the New Testament references goes beyond the act of faith to include the continuity of faith. Faith is not a one-time act, but a way of life. The true believer, declared righteous by God, will persevere in faith as the pattern of his life (Col 1:22–23; Heb 3:12–14).

6 "Will not all of these take up a
taunt-song against him,
Even mockery *and* insinuations
against him
And say, 'Woe to him who
increases what is not his—
For how long—
And makes himself rich with loans?'
7 "Will not your creditors
rise up suddenly,
And those who collect
from you awaken?
Indeed, you will become
plunder for them.
8 "Because you have looted many nations,
All the remainder of the
peoples will loot you—

Because of human bloodshed and
    violence done to the land,
To the town and all its inhabitants.

9 "Woe to him who gets evil
        gain for his house
    To put his nest on high,
    To be delivered from the
        hand of calamity!
10 "You have devised a shameful
        thing for your house
    By cutting off many peoples;
    So you are sinning against yourself.
11 "Surely the stone will cry
        out from the wall,
    And the rafter will answer it
        from the framework.

12 "Woe to him who builds a
        city with bloodshed
    And founds a town with violence!
13 "Is it not indeed from the
        LORD of hosts
    That peoples toil for fire,
    And nations grow weary
        for nothing?
14 "For the earth will be filled
    With the knowledge of the
        glory of the LORD,
    As the waters cover the sea.

15 "Woe to you who make your
        neighbors drink,
    Who mix in your venom even
        to make them drunk
    So as to look on their nakedness!
16 "You will be filled with disgrace
        rather than honor.
    Now you yourself drink and
        expose your own nakedness.
    The cup in the LORD'S right hand
        will come around to you,
    And utter disgrace will come
        upon your glory.
17 "For the violence done to Lebanon
        will overwhelm you,
    And the devastation of its beasts
        by which you terrified them,
    Because of human bloodshed and
        violence done to the land,
    To the town and all its inhabitants.

18 "What profit is the idol when
        its maker has carved it,
    Or an image, a teacher of falsehood?
    For its maker trusts in his
        own handiwork
    When he fashions speechless idols.

19 "Woe to him who says to a
        piece of wood, 'Awake!'
    To a mute stone, 'Arise!'
    And that is your teacher?
    Behold, it is overlaid with
        gold and silver,
    And there is no breath at all inside it.
20 "But the LORD is in His holy temple.
    Let all the earth be silent before Him."

3 A prayer of Habakkuk the prophet, accord-
    ing to Shigionoth.

2 LORD, I have heard the report
        about You and I fear.
    O LORD, revive Your work in
        the midst of the years,
    In the midst of the years
        make it known;
    In wrath remember mercy.

3 God comes from Teman,
    And the Holy One from
        Mount Paran.   Selah
    His splendor covers the heavens,
    And the earth is full of His praise.
4 His radiance is like the sunlight;
    He has rays flashing
        from His hand,
    And there is the hiding
        of His power.
5 Before Him goes pestilence,
    And plague comes after Him.
6 He stood and surveyed the earth;
    He looked and startled the nations.
    Yes, the perpetual mountains
        were shattered,
    The ancient hills collapsed.
    His ways are everlasting.
7 I saw the tents of Cushan
        under distress,
    The tent curtains of the land of
        Midian were trembling.

8 Did the LORD rage against the rivers,
    Or was Your anger against the rivers,
    Or was Your wrath against the sea,
    That You rode on Your horses,
    On Your chariots of salvation?
9 Your bow was made bare,
    The rods of chastisement
        were sworn.   Selah
    You cleaved the earth with rivers.
10 The mountains saw
        You and quaked;
    The downpour of waters swept by.
    The deep uttered forth its voice,
    It lifted high its hands.

11 Sun *and* moon stood in their places;
  They went away at the light
    of Your arrows,
  At the radiance of Your gleaming spear.
12 In indignation You marched
    through the earth;
  In anger You trampled the nations.
13 You went forth for the
    salvation of Your people,
  For the salvation of Your anointed.
  You struck the head of the
    house of the evil
  To lay him open from thigh to neck.
                                    Selah
14 You pierced with his own spears
  The head of his throngs.
  They stormed in to scatter us;
  Their exultation *was* like those
  Who devour the oppressed in secret.
15 You trampled on the sea
    with Your horses,
  On the surge of many waters.

16 I heard and my inward
    parts trembled,
  At the sound my lips quivered.
  Decay enters my bones,
  And in my place I tremble.
  Because I must wait quietly
    for the day of distress,
  For the people to arise *who*
    will invade us.
17 Though the fig tree should not blossom
  And there be no fruit on the vines,
  Though the yield of the
    olive should fail
  And the fields produce no food,
  Though the flock should be
    cut off from the fold
  And there be no cattle in the stalls,
18 Yet I will exult in the LORD,
  I will rejoice in the God
    of my salvation.
19 The Lord GOD is my strength,
  And He has made my feet
    like hinds' *feet,*
  And makes me walk on
    my high places.

For the choir director, on my stringed instruments.

Psalm 146:1–10

Praise the LORD!
  Praise the LORD, O my soul!
2 I will praise the LORD while I live;
  I will sing praises to my God
    while I have my being.

3 Do not trust in princes,
  In mortal man, in whom
    there is no salvation.
4 His spirit departs, he
    returns to the earth;
  In that very day his thoughts perish.
5 How blessed is he whose help
    is the God of Jacob,
  Whose hope is in the LORD his God,
6 Who made heaven and earth,
  The sea and all that is in them;
  Who keeps faith forever;
7 Who executes justice for
    the oppressed;
  Who gives food to the hungry.
  The LORD sets the prisoners free.

8 The LORD opens *the eyes of* the blind;
  The LORD raises up those
    who are bowed down;
  The LORD loves the righteous;
9 The LORD protects the strangers;
  He supports the fatherless
    and the widow,
  But He thwarts the way of the wicked.
10 The LORD will reign forever,
  Your God, O Zion, to all generations.
  Praise the LORD!

Proverbs 30:17

17 The eye that mocks a father
  And scorns a mother,
  The ravens of the valley
    will pick it out,
  And the young eagles will eat it.

30:17 eye that mocks. This proverb vividly speaks to the tragic results of disregarding parental respect and authority and the destruction it brings. **ravens…young eagles.** These birds scavenge the unburied corpse of a child who dies prematurely because of rebellion. See 1 Samuel 17:44; 1 Kings 14:11; Jeremiah 16:4; Ezekiel 29:5; 39:7.

Revelation 13:1–18

13 And the dragon stood on the sand of the seashore.
  Then I saw a beast coming up out of the sea, having ten horns and seven heads, and on his horns *were* ten diadems, and on his heads *were* blasphemous names. 2 And the beast which I saw was like a leopard, and his feet were like *those* of a bear, and his mouth like the mouth of a lion. And the dragon gave him

13:3 his fatal wound was healed. This statement could refer to one of the kingdoms that was destroyed and revived (i.e., the Roman Empire). But more likely it refers to a fake death and resurrection enacted by the Antichrist, as part of his lying deception (vv. 12, 14; 17:8, 11; 2Th 2:9). **earth was amazed.** People in the world will be astounded and fascinated when Antichrist appears to rise from the dead. His charisma, brilliance, and attractive but deluding powers will cause the world to follow him unquestioningly (v. 14; 2Th 2:8–12).

his power and his throne and great authority. ³ I saw one of his heads as if it had been slain, and his fatal wound was healed. And the whole earth was amazed *and followed* after the beast; ⁴ they worshiped the dragon because he gave his authority to the beast; and they worshiped the beast, saying, "Who is like the beast, and who is able to wage war with him?" ⁵ There was given to him a mouth speaking arrogant words and blasphemies, and authority to act for forty-two months was given to him. ⁶ And he opened his mouth in blasphemies against God, to blaspheme His name and His tabernacle, *that is,* those who dwell in heaven.

⁷ It was also given to him to make war with the saints and to overcome them, and authority over every tribe and people and tongue and nation was given to him. ⁸ All who dwell on the earth will worship him, *everyone* whose name has not been written from the foundation of the world in the book of life of the Lamb who has been slain. ⁹ If anyone has an ear, let him hear. ¹⁰ If anyone *is destined* for captivity, to captivity he goes; if anyone kills with the sword, with the sword he must be killed. Here is the perseverance and the faith of the saints.

¹¹ Then I saw another beast coming up out of the earth; and he had two horns like a lamb and he spoke as a dragon. ¹² He exercises all the authority of the first beast in his presence. And he makes the earth and those who dwell in it to worship the first beast, whose fatal wound was healed. ¹³ He performs great signs, so that he even makes fire come down out of heaven to the earth in the presence of men. ¹⁴ And he deceives those who dwell on the earth because of the signs which it was given him to perform in the presence of the beast, telling those who dwell on the earth to make an image to the beast who *had the wound of the sword and has come to life. ¹⁵ And it was given to him to give breath to the image of the beast, so that the image of the beast would even speak and cause as many as do not worship the image of the beast to be killed. ¹⁶ And he causes all, the small and the great, and the rich and the poor, and the free men and the slaves, to be given a mark on their right hand or on their forehead, ¹⁷ and *he provides* that no one will be able to buy or to sell, except the one who has the mark, *either* the name of the beast or the number of his name. ¹⁸ Here is wisdom. Let him who has understanding calculate the number of the beast, for the number is that of a man; and his number is six hundred and sixty-six.

13:18 his number is six hundred and sixty-six. This is the essential number of a man. The number 6 falls one short of God's perfect number, 7, and thus represents human imperfection. Antichrist, the most powerful human the world will ever know, will still be a man, i.e., a 6. The ultimate in human and demonic power is a 6, not perfect, as God is. The 3-fold repetition of the number is intended to reiterate and underscore man's identity. When Antichrist is finally revealed, there will be some way to identify him with this basic number of a man, or his name may have the numerical equivalent of 666. (In many languages, including Hebrew, Greek, and Latin, letters have numerical equivalents.) Because this text reveals very little about the meaning of 666, it is unwise to speculate beyond what is said.

DAY 23: Who was Habakkuk, and where did his questions for God take him?

As with many of the Minor Prophets, nothing is known about the prophet except that which can be inferred from the book. In the case of Habakkuk, internal information is virtually nonexistent, making conclusions about his identity and life conjectural. His simple introduction as "Habakkuk the prophet" may imply that he needed no introduction since he was a well-known prophet of his day. It is certain that he was a contemporary of Jeremiah, Ezekiel, Daniel, and Zephaniah.

The opening verses reveal a historical situation similar to the days of Amos and Micah. Justice had essentially disappeared from the land. Violence and wickedness were pervasive, existing unchecked. In the midst of these dark days, the prophet cried out for divine intervention (1:2–4). God's response, that He was sending the Chaldeans to judge Judah (1:5–11), creates an even greater theological dilemma for Habakkuk: Why didn't God purge His people and restore their righteousness? How could God use the Chaldeans to judge a people more righteous than they (1:12–2:1)? God's answer that He would judge the Chaldeans, also (2:2–20), did not fully satisfy the prophet's theological quandary; in fact, it only intensified it. In Habakkuk's mind, the issue crying for resolution is no longer God's righteous response toward evil (or lack thereof), but the vindication of God's character and covenant with His people (1:13). Like Job, the prophet argued with God; and through that experience, he achieved a deeper understanding of God's sovereign character and a firmer faith in Him (Job 42:5–6; Is 55:8–9). Ultimately, Habakkuk realized that God was not to be worshiped merely because of the temporal blessings He bestowed, but for His own sake (3:17–19).

DECEMBER 24

Zephaniah 1:1–3:20

1 The word of the LORD which came to Zephaniah son of Cushi, son of Gedaliah, son of Amariah, son of Hezekiah, in the days of Josiah son of Amon, king of Judah:

2 "I will completely remove all *things*
From the face of the earth,"
   declares the LORD.
3 "I will remove man and beast;
I will remove the birds of the sky
And the fish of the sea,
And the ruins along
   with the wicked;
And I will cut off man from
   the face of the earth,"
   declares the LORD.
4 "So I will stretch out My
   hand against Judah
And against all the inhabitants
   of Jerusalem.
And I will cut off the remnant
   of Baal from this place,
And the names of the idolatrous
   priests along with the priests.
5 "And those who bow down on the
   housetops to the host of heaven,
And those who bow down
   and swear to the LORD and
   yet swear by Milcom,
6 And those who have turned back
   from following the LORD,
And those who have not sought
   the LORD or inquired of Him."

7 Be silent before the Lord GOD!
For the day of the LORD is near,
For the LORD has prepared
   a sacrifice,
He has consecrated His guests.

8 "Then it will come about
   on the day of the
   LORD'S sacrifice
That I will punish the princes,
   the king's sons
And all who clothe themselves
   with foreign garments.
9 "And I will punish on that
   day all who leap on the
   temple threshold,
Who fill the house of their lord
   with violence and deceit.
10 "On that day," declares the LORD,
"There will be the sound of a
   cry from the Fish Gate,
A wail from the Second Quarter,
And a loud crash from the hills.
11 "Wail, O inhabitants of the Mortar,
For all the people of Canaan
   will be silenced;
All who weigh out silver will
   be cut off.
12 "It will come about at that time
That I will search Jerusalem
   with lamps,
And I will punish the men
Who are stagnant in spirit,
Who say in their hearts,
'The LORD will not do good or evil!'

1:8 the princes...king's sons. Judgment began with the royal house. Lacking commitment to God's covenant, they had adopted the customs and idolatrous practices of the heathen. Since Josiah was only 8 years old when he assumed rulership (ca. 640 B.C.), the reference would not be to his sons but to the princes of the royal house or to the children of the king who would be ruling when the prophecy was fulfilled (2Ki 25:7; Jer 39:6).

13 "Moreover, their wealth will
  become plunder
And their houses desolate;
Yes, they will build houses
  but not inhabit *them,*
And plant vineyards but not
  drink their wine."

14 Near is the great day of the LORD,
Near and coming very quickly;
Listen, the day of the LORD!
In it the warrior cries out bitterly.

15 A day of wrath is that day,
A day of trouble and distress,
A day of destruction
  and desolation,
A day of darkness and gloom,
A day of clouds and thick darkness,

16 A day of trumpet and battle cry
Against the fortified cities
And the high corner towers.

17 I will bring distress on men
So that they will walk like the blind,
Because they have sinned
  against the LORD;
And their blood will be
  poured out like dust
And their flesh like dung.

18 Neither their silver nor their gold
Will be able to deliver them
On the day of the LORD'S wrath;
And all the earth will be devoured
In the fire of His jealousy,
For He will make a complete end,
Indeed a terrifying one,
Of all the inhabitants of the earth.

2 Gather yourselves together,
    yes, gather,
O nation without shame,

2 Before the decree takes effect—
The day passes like the chaff—
Before the burning anger of the
  LORD comes upon you,
Before the day of the LORD'S
  anger comes upon you.

3 Seek the LORD,
All you humble of the earth
Who have carried out
  His ordinances;
Seek righteousness, seek humility.
Perhaps you will be hidden
In the day of the LORD'S anger.

4 For Gaza will be abandoned
And Ashkelon a desolation;
Ashdod will be driven out at noon
And Ekron will be uprooted.

5 Woe to the inhabitants
  of the seacoast,
The nation of the Cherethites!
The word of the LORD
  is against you,
O Canaan, land of the Philistines;
And I will destroy you
So that there will be no inhabitant.

6 So the seacoast will be pastures,
With caves for shepherds
  and folds for flocks.

7 And the coast will be
For the remnant of the
  house of Judah,
They will pasture on it.
In the houses of Ashkelon they
  will lie down at evening;
For the LORD their God
  will care for them
And restore their fortune.

8 "I have heard the taunting of Moab
And the revilings of the
  sons of Ammon,
With which they have
  taunted My people
And become arrogant
  against their territory.

9 "Therefore, as I live," declares
  the LORD of hosts,
The God of Israel,
"Surely Moab will be like Sodom
And the sons of Ammon
  like Gomorrah—
A place possessed by
  nettles and salt pits,
And a perpetual desolation.
The remnant of My people
  will plunder them
And the remainder of My
  nation will inherit them."

10 This they will have in return for their pride,
because they have taunted and become arrogant against the people of the LORD of hosts.
11 The LORD will be terrifying to them, for He
will starve all the gods of the earth; and all
the coastlands of the nations will bow down
to Him, everyone from his *own* place.

12 "You also, O Ethiopians, will
  be slain by My sword."

13 And He will stretch out His
  hand against the north
And destroy Assyria,
And He will make Nineveh
  a desolation,
Parched like the wilderness.

14 Flocks will lie down in her midst,
All beasts which range in herds;
Both the pelican and the hedgehog
Will lodge in the tops of her pillars;
Birds will sing in the window,
Desolation *will be* on the threshold;
For He has laid bare the cedar work.
15 This is the exultant city
Which dwells securely,
Who says in her heart,
"I am, and there is no one besides me."
How she has become a desolation,
A resting place for beasts!
Everyone who passes by her will hiss
And wave his hand *in contempt.*

3 Woe to her who is rebellious
        and defiled,
The tyrannical city!
2 She heeded no voice,
She accepted no instruction.
She did not trust in the LORD,
She did not draw near to her God.
3 Her princes within her
        are roaring lions,
Her judges are wolves at evening;
They leave nothing for the morning.
4 Her prophets are reckless,
        treacherous men;
Her priests have profaned
        the sanctuary.
They have done violence to the law.
5 The LORD is righteous within her;
He will do no injustice.
Every morning He brings
        His justice to light;
He does not fail.
But the unjust knows no shame.
6 "I have cut off nations;
Their corner towers are in ruins.
I have made their streets desolate,
With no one passing by;
Their cities are laid waste,
Without a man, without an inhabitant.
7 "I said, 'Surely you will revere Me,
Accept instruction.'
So her dwelling will not be cut off
According to all that I have
        appointed concerning her.
But they were eager to
        corrupt all their deeds.

8 "Therefore wait for Me,"
        declares the LORD,
"For the day when I rise
        up as a witness.
Indeed, My decision is to
        gather nations,

3:8 The prophet transitions from the historical invasion of Judah by Babylon to the future day of the Lord. He speaks of the Great Tribulation, when the Lord will gather all the nations for judgment (Joel 3:1–2, 12–17; Zec 12:2–3; 14:2; Mt 24:21). The faithful remnant, presumably the meek of 2:1–3, are exhorted to wait in trust for Him to carry out His judgment.

To assemble kingdoms,
To pour out on them My indignation,
All My burning anger;
For all the earth will be devoured
By the fire of My zeal.
9 "For then I will give to the
        peoples purified lips,
That all of them may call on
        the name of the LORD,
To serve Him shoulder to shoulder.
10 "From beyond the rivers of Ethiopia
My worshipers, My dispersed ones,
Will bring My offerings.
11 "In that day you will feel no shame
Because of all your deeds
By which you have rebelled against Me;
For then I will remove
        from your midst
Your proud, exulting ones,
And you will never again be haughty
On My holy mountain.
12 "But I will leave among you
A humble and lowly people,
And they will take refuge in
        the name of the LORD.
13 "The remnant of Israel
        will do no wrong
And tell no lies,
Nor will a deceitful tongue
Be found in their mouths;
For they will feed and lie down
With no one to make them tremble."

14 Shout for joy, O daughter of Zion!
Shout *in triumph,* O Israel!
Rejoice and exult with all *your* heart,
O daughter of Jerusalem!
15 The LORD has taken away *His*
        judgments against you,
He has cleared away your enemies.
The King of Israel, the LORD,
        is in your midst;
You will fear disaster no more.
16 In that day it will be said to Jerusalem:
"Do not be afraid, O Zion;
Do not let your hands fall limp.

17 "The LORD your God is
    in your midst,
    A victorious warrior.
    He will exult over you with joy,
    He will be quiet in His love,
    He will rejoice over you
        with shouts of joy.
18 "I will gather those who grieve
        about the appointed feasts—
    They came from you, O Zion;
    The reproach of exile is a
        burden on them.
19 "Behold, I am going to deal
        at that time
    With all your oppressors,
    I will save the lame
    And gather the outcast,
    And I will turn their shame
        into praise and renown
    In all the earth.
20 "At that time I will bring you in,
    Even at the time when I
        gather you together;
    Indeed, I will give you
        renown and praise
    Among all the peoples of the earth,
    When I restore your fortunes
        before your eyes,"
    Says the LORD.

Psalm 147:1-6

Praise the LORD!
    For it is good to sing praises
        to our God;
    For it is pleasant and
        praise is becoming.
2   The LORD builds up Jerusalem;
    He gathers the outcasts of Israel.
3   He heals the brokenhearted
    And binds up their wounds.
4   He counts the number of the stars;
    He gives names to all of them.
5   Great is our Lord and
        abundant in strength;
    His understanding is infinite.
6   The LORD supports the afflicted;
    He brings down the wicked
        to the ground.

Proverbs 30:18-19

18   There are three things which
        are too wonderful for me,
    Four which I do not understand:
19   The way of an eagle in the sky,
    The way of a serpent on a rock,
    The way of a ship in the
        middle of the sea,
    And the way of a man with a maid.

Revelation 14:1-20

14 Then I looked, and behold, the Lamb was standing on Mount Zion, and with Him one hundred and forty-four thousand, having His name and the name of His Father written on their foreheads. 2 And I heard a voice from heaven, like the sound of many waters and like the sound of loud thunder, and the voice which I heard was like the sound of harpists playing on their harps. 3 And they *sang a new song before the throne and before the four living creatures and the elders; and no one could learn the song except the one hundred and forty-four thousand who had been purchased from the earth. 4 These are the ones who have not been defiled with women, for they have kept themselves chaste. These are the ones who follow the Lamb wherever He goes. These have been purchased from among men as first fruits to God and to the Lamb. 5 And no lie was found in their mouth; they are blameless.

6 And I saw another angel flying in midheaven, having an eternal gospel to preach to those who live on the earth, and to every nation and tribe and tongue and people; 7 and he said with a loud voice, "Fear God, and give Him glory, because the hour of His judgment has come; worship Him who made the heaven and the earth and sea and springs of waters."

8 And another angel, a second one, followed, saying, "Fallen, fallen is Babylon the great, she who has made all the nations drink of the wine of the passion of her immorality."

9 Then another angel, a third one, followed them, saying with a loud voice, "If anyone

---

14:8 fallen is Babylon. Lack of response to the first angel's message causes a second angel to pronounce this judgment. Babylon refers to the entire worldwide political, economic, and religious kingdom of Antichrist. (See 16:17-19 for details of this fall.) The original city of Babylon was the birthplace of idolatry where the residents built the Tower of Babel, a monument to rebelliousness and false religion. Such idolatry was subsequently spread when God confounded man's language and scattered them around the world (Ge 11:1-9). **wine of the passion of her immorality.** This pictures Babylon causing the world to become intoxicated with her pleasures and enter an orgy of rebellion, hatred, and idolatry toward God. Fornication is spiritual prostitution to Antichrist's false system, which will fall for such iniquity.

worships the beast and his image, and receives a mark on his forehead or on his hand, [10] he also will drink of the wine of the wrath of God, which is mixed in full strength in the cup of His anger; and he will be tormented with fire and brimstone in the presence of the holy angels and in the presence of the Lamb. [11] And the smoke of their torment goes up forever and ever; they have no rest day and night, those who worship the beast and his image, and whoever receives the mark of his name." [12] Here is the perseverance of the saints who keep the commandments of God and their faith in Jesus.

[13] And I heard a voice from heaven, saying, "Write, 'Blessed are the dead who die in the Lord from now on!'" "Yes," says the Spirit, "so that they may rest from their labors, for their deeds follow with them."

[14] Then I looked, and behold, a white cloud, and sitting on the cloud *was* one like a son of man, having a golden crown on His head and a sharp sickle in His hand. [15] And another angel came out of the temple, crying out with a loud voice to Him who sat on the cloud, "Put in your sickle and reap, for the hour to reap has come, because the harvest of the earth is ripe." [16] Then He who sat on the cloud swung His sickle over the earth, and the earth was reaped.

[17] And another angel came out of the temple which is in heaven, and he also had a sharp sickle. [18] Then another angel, the one who has power over fire, came out from the altar; and he called with a loud voice to him who had the sharp sickle, saying, "Put in your sharp sickle and gather the clusters from the vine of the earth, because her grapes are ripe." [19] So the angel swung his sickle to the earth and gathered *the clusters from* the vine of the earth, and threw them into the great wine press of the wrath of God. [20] And the wine press was trodden outside the city, and blood came out from the wine press, up to the horses' bridles, for a distance of two hundred miles.

14:19 wine press. This vivid imagery signifies a horrendous slaughter or bloodbath (Is 63:2–3; La 1:15; Joel 3:13). Here it refers to the slaughter of all the enemies of God who are still alive, facing the destruction at Armageddon, the final battle against God's enemies, staged on the Plain of Esdraelon. The bloody imagery comes from the fresh juice of stomped grapes splattering and running down a trough from the upper vat to the lower vat of a stone winepress.

DAY 24: What is known about Zephaniah, and what was his message for Judah?

Little is known about the author, Zephaniah. Three other Old Testament individuals share his name. He traces his genealogy back 4 generations to King Hezekiah (ca. 715–686 B.C.), standing alone among the prophets descended from royal blood (1:1). Royal genealogy would have given him the ear of Judah's king, Josiah, during whose reign he preached.

The prophet himself dates his message during the reign of Josiah (640–609 B.C.). The moral and spiritual conditions detailed in the book (1:4–6; 3:1–7) seem to place the prophecy prior to Josiah's reforms, when Judah was still languishing in idolatry and wickedness. It was in 628 B.C. that Josiah tore down all the altars to Baal, burned the bones of false prophets, and broke the carved idols (2Ch 34:3–7); and in 622 B.C., the Book of the Law was found (2Ch 34:8—35:19). Consequently, Zephaniah most likely prophesied from 635 to 625 B.C. and was a contemporary of Jeremiah.

Zephaniah's message on the day of the Lord warned Judah that the final days were near, through divine judgment at the hands of Nebuchadnezzar, ca. 605–586 B.C. (1:4-13). Yet, it also looks beyond to the far fulfillment in the judgments of Daniel's 70th week (1:18; 3:8). The expression "day of the Lord" is employed by the author more often than by any other Old Testament writer and is described as a day that is near (1:7), and as a day of wrath, trouble, distress, devastation, desolation, darkness, gloominess, clouds, thick darkness, trumpet, and alarm (1:15-16, 18). Yet even within these oracles of divine wrath, the prophet exhorted the people to seek the Lord, offering a shelter in the midst of judgment (2:3) and proclaiming the promise of eventual salvation for His believing remnant (2:7; 3:9-20).

DECEMBER 25

Haggai 1:1–2:23

1 In the second year of Darius the king, on the first day of the sixth month, the word of the LORD came by the prophet Haggai to Zerubbabel the son of Shealtiel, governor of Judah, and to Joshua the son of Jehozadak, the high priest, saying, ² "Thus says the LORD of hosts, 'This people says, "The time has not come, *even* the time for the house of the LORD to be rebuilt."'" ³ Then the word of the LORD came by Haggai the prophet, saying, ⁴ "Is it time for you yourselves to dwell in your paneled houses while this house *lies* desolate?" ⁵ Now therefore, thus says the LORD of hosts, "Consider your ways! ⁶ You have sown much, but harvest little; *you* eat, but *there is* not *enough* to be satisfied; *you* drink, but *there is* not *enough* to become drunk; *you* put on clothing, but no one is warm *enough;* and he who earns, earns wages *to put* into a purse with holes."

⁷ Thus says the LORD of hosts, "Consider your ways! ⁸ Go up to the mountains, bring wood and rebuild the temple, that I may be pleased with it and be glorified," says the LORD. ⁹ "*You* look for much, but behold, *it comes* to little; when you bring *it* home, I blow it *away.* Why?" declares the LORD of hosts, "Because of My house which *lies* desolate, while each of you runs to his own house. ¹⁰ Therefore, because of you the sky has withheld its dew and the earth has withheld its produce. ¹¹ I called for a drought on the land, on the mountains, on the grain, on the new wine, on the oil, on what the ground produces, on men, on cattle, and on all the labor of your hands."

¹² Then Zerubbabel the son of Shealtiel, and Joshua the son of Jehozadak, the high priest, with all the remnant of the people, obeyed the voice of the LORD their God and the words of Haggai the prophet, as the LORD their God had sent him. And the people showed reverence for the LORD. ¹³ Then Haggai, the messenger of the LORD, spoke by the commission of the LORD to the people saying, "'I am with you,' declares the LORD." ¹⁴ So the LORD stirred up the spirit of Zerubbabel the son of Shealtiel, governor of Judah, and the spirit of Joshua the son of Jehozadak, the high priest, and the spirit of all the remnant of the people; and they came and worked on the house of the LORD of hosts, their God, ¹⁵ on the twenty-fourth day of the sixth month in the second year of Darius the king.

1:13 I am with you. The people were oppressed by hostilities from without and famine from within. The Lord responded to their genuine repentance and obedience, assuring them of His presence with them. This should have evoked a memory of God's Word to Joshua and the returning people centuries before (Jos 1:5).

2 On the twenty-first of the seventh month, the word of the LORD came by Haggai the prophet saying, ² "Speak now to Zerubbabel the son of Shealtiel, governor of Judah, and to Joshua the son of Jehozadak, the high priest, and to the remnant of the people saying, ³ 'Who is left among you who saw this temple in its former glory? And how do you see it now? Does it not seem to you like nothing in comparison? ⁴ But now take courage, Zerubbabel,' declares the LORD, 'take courage also, Joshua son of Jehozadak, the high priest, and all you people of the land take courage,' declares the LORD, 'and work; for I am with you,' declares the LORD of hosts. ⁵ 'As for the promise which I made you when you came out of Egypt, My Spirit is abiding in your midst; do not fear!' ⁶ For thus says the LORD of hosts, 'Once more in a little while, I am going to shake the heavens and the earth, the sea also and the dry land. ⁷ I will shake all the nations; and they will come with the wealth of all nations, and I will fill this house with glory,' says the LORD of hosts. ⁸ 'The silver is Mine and the gold is Mine,' declares the LORD of hosts. ⁹ 'The latter glory of this house will be greater than the former,' says the LORD

2:7 wealth of all nations. While some view the phrase as referring to Jerusalem (e.g., Ezr 6:3–9), it seems preferable to see a reference here to the Messiah, the Deliverer for whom all the nations ultimately long. **I will fill this house with glory.** There is no Scripture to indicate that God's glory ever did come to Zerubbabel's temple, as the first temple was filled with the Shekinah glory (1Ki 8:10–11; 2Ch 5:13–14). However, His glory will fill the millennial temple (Eze 43:5). This glorification cannot refer to Christ's physical presence in Herod's temple, for the events of vv. 6–9 cannot be accounted for historically. The context speaks of the establishment of His earthly, Davidic, millennial kingdom and His presence in the temple during that kingdom.

of hosts, 'and in this place I will give peace,' declares the LORD of hosts."

¹⁰ On the twenty-fourth of the ninth *month,* in the second year of Darius, the word of the LORD came to Haggai the prophet, saying, ¹¹ "Thus says the LORD of hosts, 'Ask now the priests *for* a ruling: ¹² If a man carries holy meat in the fold of his garment, and touches bread with this fold, or cooked food, wine, oil, or any *other* food, will it become holy?'" And the priests answered, "No." ¹³ Then Haggai said, "If one who is unclean from a corpse touches any of these, will *the latter* become unclean?" And the priests answered, "It will become unclean." ¹⁴ Then Haggai said, "'So is this people. And so is this nation before Me,' declares the LORD, 'and so is every work of their hands; and what they offer there is unclean. ¹⁵ But now, do consider from this day onward: before one stone was placed on another in the temple of the LORD, ¹⁶ from that time *when* one came to a *grain* heap of twenty *measures,* there would be only ten; and *when* one came to the wine vat to draw fifty measures, there would be *only* twenty. ¹⁷ I smote you *and* every work of your hands with blasting wind, mildew and hail; yet you *did* not *come back* to Me,' declares the LORD. ¹⁸ 'Do consider from this day onward, from the twenty-fourth day of the ninth *month;* from the day when the temple of the LORD was founded, consider: ¹⁹ Is the seed still in the barn? Even including the vine, the fig tree, the pomegranate and the olive tree, it has not borne *fruit.* Yet from this day on I will bless *you.'"*

²⁰ Then the word of the LORD came a second time to Haggai on the twenty-fourth *day* of the month, saying, ²¹ "Speak to Zerubbabel governor of Judah, saying, 'I am going to shake the heavens and the earth. ²² I will overthrow the thrones of kingdoms and destroy the power of the kingdoms of the nations; and I will overthrow the chariots and their riders, and the horses and their riders will go down, everyone by the sword of another.' ²³ 'On that day,' declares the LORD of hosts, 'I will take you, Zerubbabel, son of Shealtiel, My servant,' declares the LORD, 'and I will make you like a signet *ring,* for I have chosen you,'" declares the LORD of hosts.

Psalm 147:7–11

⁷ Sing to the LORD with thanksgiving;
    Sing praises to our God on the lyre,
⁸ Who covers the heavens with clouds,
    Who provides rain for the earth,
    Who makes grass to grow
        on the mountains.

⁹ He gives to the beast its food,
    And to the young ravens
        which cry.
¹⁰ He does not delight in the
        strength of the horse;
    He does not take pleasure
        in the legs of a man.
¹¹ The LORD favors those
        who fear Him,
    Those who wait for His
        lovingkindness.

Proverbs 30:20

²⁰ This is the way of an
        adulterous woman:
    She eats and wipes her mouth,
    And says, "I have done no wrong."

Revelation 15:1–8

15 Then I saw another sign in heaven, great and marvelous, seven angels who had seven plagues, *which are* the last, because in them the wrath of God is finished. ² And I saw something like a sea of glass mixed with fire, and those who had been victorious over the beast and his image and the number of his name, standing on the sea of glass, holding harps of God. ³ And they *sang the song of Moses, the bond-servant of God, and the song of the Lamb, saying,

"Great and marvelous
    are Your works,
    O Lord God, the Almighty;
    Righteous and true are Your ways,
    King of the nations!

15:3 song of Moses. Sung by the people of Israel immediately after their passage through the Red Sea and their deliverance from the Egyptian armies (Ex 15:1–21; see Dt 32:1–43), this was a song of victory and deliverance that the redeemed who overcome Antichrist and his system will readily identify with. **song of the Lamb.** See 5:8–14. These two songs celebrate two great redemptive events: 1) deliverance of Israel by God from Egypt through Moses; and 2) deliverance of sinners by God from sin through Christ. **Great and marvelous are Your works.** This statement from the song of the Lamb extols God's powerful works in creation as He providentially upholds the universe (Ps 139:14). **Almighty.** God is omnipotent (Am 4:13). **King of the nations!** God is sovereign over the redeemed of every nation (Jer 10:7).

⁴ "Who will not fear, O Lord, and
glorify Your name?
For You alone are holy;
For ALL THE NATIONS WILL COME
AND WORSHIP BEFORE YOU,
FOR YOUR RIGHTEOUS ACTS
HAVE BEEN REVEALED."

⁵ After these things I looked, and the temple of the tabernacle of testimony in heaven was opened, ⁶ and the seven angels who had the seven plagues came out of the temple, clothed in linen, clean *and* bright, and girded around their chests with golden sashes. ⁷ Then one of the four living creatures gave to the seven angels seven golden bowls full of the wrath of God, who lives forever and ever. ⁸ And the temple was filled with smoke from the glory of God and from His power; and no one was able to enter the temple until the seven plagues of the seven angels were finished.

DAY 25: What is the primary message of the Book of Haggai?

In 538 B.C., as a result of the proclamation of Cyrus the Persian (Ezr 1:1–4), Israel was allowed to return from Babylon to her homeland under the civil leadership of Zerubbabel and the spiritual guidance of Joshua the high priest (Ezr 3:2). About 50,000 Jews returned. In 536 B.C., they began to rebuild the temple (Ezr 3:1–4:5); but opposition from neighbors and indifference by the Jews caused the work to be abandoned (Ezr 4:1–24). Sixteen years later Haggai and Zechariah were commissioned by the Lord to stir up the people to 1) not only rebuild the temple, but also to 2) reorder their spiritual priorities (Ezr 5:1–6:22). As a result, the temple was completed 4 years later (ca. 516 B.C.; Ezr 6:15).

The primary theme is the rebuilding of God's temple, which had been lying in ruins since its destruction by Nebuchadnezzar in 586 B.C. By means of 5 messages from the Lord, Haggai exhorted the people to renew their efforts to build the house of the Lord. He motivated them by noting that the drought and crop failures were caused by misplaced spiritual priorities (1:9–11).

But to Haggai, the rebuilding of the temple was not an end in itself. The temple represented God's dwelling place, His manifest presence with His chosen people. The destruction of the temple by Nebuchadnezzar followed the departure of God's dwelling glory (Eze 8–11). To the prophet, the rebuilding of the temple invited the return of God's presence to their midst. Using the historical situation as a springboard, Haggai reveled in the supreme glory of the ultimate messianic temple yet to come (2:7), encouraging them with the promise of even greater peace (2:9), prosperity (2:19), divine rulership (2:21–22), and national blessing (2:23) during the Millennium.

 DECEMBER 26

Zechariah 1:1–3:10

1 In the eighth month of the second year of Darius, the word of the LORD came to Zechariah the prophet, the son of Berechiah, the son of Iddo saying, ² "The LORD was very angry with your fathers. ³ Therefore say to them, 'Thus says the LORD of hosts, "Return to Me," declares the LORD of hosts, "that I may return to you," says the LORD of hosts. ⁴ "Do not be like your fathers, to whom the former prophets proclaimed, saying, 'Thus says the LORD of hosts, "Return now from your evil ways and from your evil deeds."' But they did not listen or give heed to Me," declares the LORD. ⁵ "Your fathers, where are they? And the prophets, do they live forever? ⁶ But did not My words and My statutes, which I commanded My servants the prophets, overtake your fathers? Then they repented and said, 'As the LORD of hosts purposed to do to us in accordance with our ways and our deeds, so He has dealt with us.'"'

⁷ On the twenty-fourth day of the eleventh month, which is the month Shebat, in the second year of Darius, the word of the LORD came to Zechariah the prophet, the son of Berechiah, the son of Iddo, as follows: ⁸ I saw at night, and behold, a man was riding on a red horse, and he was standing among the myrtle trees which were in the ravine, with red, sorrel and white horses behind him. ⁹ Then I said, "My lord, what are these?" And the angel who was speaking with me said to me, "I will show you what these are." ¹⁰ And the man who was standing among the myrtle trees answered and said, "These are those whom the LORD has sent to patrol the earth." ¹¹ So they answered the angel of the LORD who was standing among the myrtle trees and said, "We have patrolled the earth, and behold, all the earth is peaceful and quiet." ¹² Then the angel of the LORD said, "O LORD of hosts, how long will You have no compas-

sion for Jerusalem and the cities of Judah, with which You have been indignant these seventy years?" ¹³ The LORD answered the angel who was speaking with me with gracious words, comforting words. ¹⁴ So the angel who was speaking with me said to me, "Proclaim, saying, 'Thus says the LORD of hosts, "I am exceedingly jealous for Jerusalem and Zion. ¹⁵ But I am very angry with the nations who are at ease; for while I was only a little angry, they furthered the disaster." ¹⁶ Therefore thus says the LORD, "I will return to Jerusalem with compassion; My house will be built in it," declares the LORD of hosts, "and a measuring line will be stretched over Jerusalem."' ¹⁷ Again, proclaim, saying, 'Thus says the LORD of hosts, "My cities will again overflow with prosperity, and the LORD will again comfort Zion and again choose Jerusalem."'"

¹⁸ Then I lifted up my eyes and looked, and behold, *there were* four horns. ¹⁹ So I said to the angel who was speaking with me, "What are these?" And he answered me, "These are the horns which have scattered Judah, Israel and Jerusalem." ²⁰ Then the LORD showed me four craftsmen. ²¹ I said, "What are these coming to do?" And he said, "These are the horns which have scattered Judah so that no man lifts up his head; but these *craftsmen* have come to terrify them, to throw down the horns of the nations who have lifted up *their* horns against the land of Judah in order to scatter it."

2 Then I lifted up my eyes and looked, and behold, *there was* a man with a measuring line in his hand. ² So I said, "Where are you going?" And he said to me, "To measure Jerusalem, to see how wide it is and how long it is." ³ And behold, the angel who was speaking with me was going out, and another angel was coming out to meet him, ⁴ and said to him, "Run, speak to that young man, saying, 'Jerusalem will be inhabited without walls because of the multitude of men and cattle within it. ⁵ For I,' declares the LORD, 'will be a wall of fire around her, and I will be the glory in her midst.'"

⁶ "Ho there! Flee from the land of the north," declares the LORD, "for I have dispersed you as the four winds of the heavens," declares the LORD. ⁷ "Ho, Zion! Escape, you who are living with the daughter of Babylon." ⁸ For thus says the LORD of hosts, "After glory He has sent me against the nations which plunder you, for he who touches you, touches the apple of His eye. ⁹ For behold, I will wave My hand over them so that they will be plunder for their slaves. Then you will know that the LORD of

hosts has sent Me. ¹⁰ Sing for joy and be glad, O daughter of Zion; for behold I am coming and I will dwell in your midst," declares the LORD. ¹¹ "Many nations will join themselves to the LORD in that day and will become My people. Then I will dwell in your midst, and you will know that the LORD of hosts has sent Me to you. ¹² The LORD will possess Judah as His portion in the holy land, and will again choose Jerusalem.

¹³ "Be silent, all flesh, before the LORD; for He is aroused from His holy habitation."

3 Then he showed me Joshua the high priest standing before the angel of the LORD, and Satan standing at his right hand to accuse him. ² The LORD said to Satan, "The LORD rebuke you, Satan! Indeed, the LORD who has chosen Jerusalem rebuke you! Is this not a brand plucked from the fire?" ³ Now Joshua was clothed with filthy garments and standing before the angel. ⁴ He spoke and said to those who were standing before him, saying, "Remove the filthy garments from him." Again he said to him, "See, I have taken your iniquity away from you and will clothe you with festal robes." ⁵ Then I said, "Let them put a clean turban on his head." So they put a clean turban on his head and clothed him with garments, while the angel of the LORD was standing by.

3:1 Satan. This could also be translated "adversary" and thus the person's identity would be unknown. However, because the activity of accusation is so in keeping with Satan (Job 1–2; Rev 12:10), his identification is preferable. The malicious adversary stands in the presence of the Lord to proclaim Israel's sins and their unworthiness of God's favor. The situation is crucial: if Joshua is vindicated, Israel is accepted; if Joshua is rejected, Israel is rejected. The entire plan of God for the nation was revealed in the outcome. Israel's hopes would either be destroyed or confirmed.

⁶ And the angel of the LORD admonished Joshua, saying, ⁷ "Thus says the LORD of hosts, 'If you will walk in My ways and if you will perform My service, then you will also govern My house and also have charge of My courts, and I will grant you free access among these who are standing *here.* ⁸ Now listen, Joshua the high priest, you and your friends who are sitting in front of you—indeed they are men who are a symbol, for behold, I am going to

bring in My servant the Branch. ⁹ For behold, the stone that I have set before Joshua; on one stone are seven eyes. Behold, I will engrave an inscription on it,' declares the LORD of hosts, 'and I will remove the iniquity of that land in one day. ¹⁰ In that day,' declares the LORD of hosts, 'every one of you will invite his neighbor to *sit* under *his* vine and under *his* fig tree.'"

3:9 the stone. Here is another reference to Messiah. In Psalm 118:22–23; Isaiah 8:13–15; 28:16; Daniel 2:35, 45; Matthew 21:42; Ephesians 2:19–22; 1 Peter 2:6–8, He is a rejected stone, a stone of stumbling, a stone of refuge, a destroying stone, and a foundation stone. Here He is the precious foundation stone, with "seven eyes" symbolic of His omniscience and infinite intelligence (4:10; Is 11:2; Col 2:3; Rev 5:6). The engraving may be a reference to the cornerstone of the temple building, on which will be engraved an inscription attesting to the Divine Builder and the purpose for which the building was erected. As such, it is closely tied to the removal of "the iniquity of that land in one day," symbolized by the removal of filthy garments in v. 4. The phrase looks to the future day when there will be cleansing and forgiveness for the nation as a whole (12:10—13:1; Ro 11:25–27), made possible through Christ's redemptive provision at Calvary.

Psalm 147:12–20

¹² Praise the LORD, O Jerusalem!
  Praise your God, O Zion!
¹³ For He has strengthened the
    bars of your gates;
  He has blessed your
    sons within you.
¹⁴ He makes peace in your borders;
  He satisfies you with the
    finest of the wheat.
¹⁵ He sends forth His command
    to the earth;
  His word runs very swiftly.
¹⁶ He gives snow like wool;
  He scatters the frost like ashes.
¹⁷ He casts forth His ice as fragments;
  Who can stand before His cold?
¹⁸ He sends forth His word
    and melts them;
  He causes His wind to blow
    and the waters to flow.
¹⁹ He declares His words to Jacob,
  His statutes and His
    ordinances to Israel.

²⁰ He has not dealt thus with any nation;
  And as for His ordinances, they
    have not known them.
  Praise the LORD!

Proverbs 30:21–23

²¹ Under three things the earth quakes,
  And under four, it cannot bear up:
²² Under a slave when he becomes king,
  And a fool when he is
    satisfied with food,
²³ Under an unloved woman
    when she gets a husband,
  And a maidservant when she
    supplants her mistress.

Revelation 16:1–21

16 Then I heard a loud voice from the temple, saying to the seven angels, "Go and pour out on the earth the seven bowls of the wrath of God."

² So the first *angel* went and poured out his bowl on the earth; and it became a loathsome and malignant sore on the people who had the mark of the beast and who worshiped his image.

³ The second *angel* poured out his bowl into the sea, and it became blood like *that* of a dead man; and every living thing in the sea died.

⁴ Then the third *angel* poured out his bowl into the rivers and the springs of waters; and they became blood. ⁵ And I heard the angel of the waters saying, "Righteous are You, who are and who were, O Holy One, because You judged these things; ⁶ for they poured out the blood of saints and prophets, and You have given them blood to drink. They deserve it." ⁷ And I heard the altar saying, "Yes, O Lord God, the Almighty, true and righteous are Your judgments."

⁸ The fourth *angel* poured out his bowl upon the sun, and it was given to it to scorch men with fire. ⁹ Men were scorched with fierce heat; and they blasphemed the name of God who has the power over these plagues, and they did not repent so as to give Him glory.

16:5 who are and who were. This phrase expresses God's eternality (1:4, 8; 4:8; 11:17). Verse 6 says that the eternal God will judge justly because they have killed the believers and preachers of the gospel (6:9–11; 7:9–17; 11:18; 17:6; 18:20). This slaughter will have no parallel in history (Mt 24:21) and neither will the vengeance of God (Ro 12:19–21).

¹⁰Then the fifth *angel* poured out his bowl on the throne of the beast, and his kingdom became darkened; and they gnawed their tongues because of pain, ¹¹and they blasphemed the God of heaven because of their pains and their sores; and they did not repent of their deeds.

¹²The sixth *angel* poured out his bowl on the great river, the Euphrates; and its water was dried up, so that the way would be prepared for the kings from the east. ¹³And I saw *coming* out of the mouth of the dragon and out of the mouth of the beast and out of the mouth of the false prophet, three unclean spirits like frogs; ¹⁴for they are spirits of demons, performing signs, which go out to the kings of the whole world, to gather them together for the war of the great day of God, the Almighty. ¹⁵("Behold, I am coming like a thief. Blessed is the one who stays awake and keeps his clothes, so that he will not walk about naked and men will not see his shame.") ¹⁶And they gathered them together to the place which in Hebrew is called Har-Magedon.

¹⁷Then the seventh *angel* poured out his bowl upon the air, and a loud voice came out of the temple from the throne, saying, "It is done." ¹⁸And there were flashes of lightning and sounds and peals of thunder; and there was a great earthquake, such as there had not been since man came to be upon the earth, so great an earthquake *was it, and* so mighty. ¹⁹The great city was split into three parts, and the cities of the nations fell. Babylon the great was remembered before God, to give her the cup of the wine of His fierce wrath. ²⁰And every island fled away, and the mountains were not found. ²¹And huge hailstones, about one hundred pounds each, *came down from heaven upon men; and men blasphemed God because of the plague of the hail, because its plague *was extremely severe.

16:16 Har-Magedon. The Hebrew name for Mt. Megiddo, 60 miles north of Jerusalem. The battle will rage on the nearby plains, site of Barak's victory over the Canaanites (Jdg 4), and Gideon's victory over the Midianites (Jdg 7). Napoleon called this valley the greatest battlefield he had ever seen. But the Battle of Armageddon will not be limited to the Megiddo plains—it will encompass the length of Palestine.

DAY 26: What was Zechariah's relationship to Haggai?

Like Jeremiah and Ezekiel, Zechariah was also a priest (Ne 12:12-16). According to tradition, he was a member of the Great Synagogue, a council of 120 originated by Nehemiah and presided over by Ezra. This council later developed into the ruling elders of the nation, called the Sanhedrin. He was born in Babylon and joined his grandfather, Iddo, in the group of exiles who first returned to Jerusalem under the leadership of Zerubbabel and Joshua the high priest (Ne 12:4). Because he is occasionally mentioned as the son of his grandfather (Ezr 5:1; 6:14; Ne 12:16), it is thought that his father, Berechiah, died at an early age before he could succeed his father into the priesthood.

Zechariah joined Haggai in rousing the people from their indifference, challenging them to resume the building of the temple. Haggai's primary purpose was to rebuild the temple. His preaching has a tone of rebuke for the people's indifference, sin, and lack of trust in God. He was used to start the revival, while Zechariah was used to keep it going strong with a more positive emphasis, calling the people to repentance and reassuring them regarding future blessings. Zechariah sought to encourage the people to build the temple in view of the promise that someday the Messiah would come to inhabit it. The people were not just building for the present, but with the future hope of the Messiah in mind. He encouraged the people, still downtrodden by the Gentile powers (1:8-12), with the reality that the Lord remembers His covenant promises to them and that He would restore and bless them. Thus, the name of the book (which means "The Lord remembers") contains in seed form the theme of the prophecy.

DECEMBER 27

Zechariah 4:1—6:15

4 Then the angel who was speaking with me returned and roused me, as a man who is awakened from his sleep. ²He said to me, "What do you see?" And I said, "I see, and behold, a lampstand all of gold with its bowl on the top of it, and its seven lamps on it with seven spouts belonging to each of the lamps which are on the top of it; ³also two olive trees by it, one on the right side of the bowl and the other on its left side." ⁴Then I said to the angel who was speaking with me saying, "What are these, my lord?" ⁵So the angel who was speaking with me answered and said to me, "Do you not know what these are?" And I said, "No, my lord." ⁶Then he said to me, "This is the word of the LORD to Zerubbabel saying, 'Not by might nor by power, but by My Spirit,' says the LORD of hosts. ⁷'What are you, O great mountain? Before Zerubbabel *you will become* a plain; and he will bring forth the top stone with shouts of "Grace, grace to it!"'"

⁸Also the word of the LORD came to me, saying, ⁹"The hands of Zerubbabel have laid the foundation of this house, and his hands will finish *it*. Then you will know that the LORD of hosts has sent me to you. ¹⁰For who has despised the day of small things? But these seven will be glad when they see the plumb line in the hand of Zerubbabel—*these are* the eyes of the LORD which range to and fro throughout the earth."

¹¹Then I said to him, "What are these two olive trees on the right of the lampstand and on its left?" ¹²And I answered the second time and said to him, "What are the two olive branches which are beside the two golden pipes, which empty the golden *oil* from themselves?" ¹³So he answered me, saying, "Do you not know what these are?" And I said, "No,

4:10 the day of small things. Though the rebuilding of a temple smaller than Solomon's may have been discouraging to some (Ezr 3:12; Hag 2:3), the Lord announced that His pleasure was upon this work, and that His omniscient care was watching over and taking pleasure in its completion. He said in effect, "Don't despise what God is pleased with." This was only a picture of the glorious restoration when Messiah comes to reign. That temple will make all others pale by comparison (Eze 40–48).

my lord." ¹⁴Then he said, "These are the two anointed ones who are standing by the Lord of the whole earth."

5 Then I lifted up my eyes again and looked, and behold, *there was* a flying scroll. ²And he said to me, "What do you see?" And I answered, "I see a flying scroll; its length is twenty cubits and its width ten cubits." ³Then he said to me, "This is the curse that is going forth over the face of the whole land; surely everyone who steals will be purged away according to the writing on one side, and everyone who swears will be purged away according to the writing on the other side. ⁴I will make it go forth," declares the LORD of hosts, "and it will enter the house of the thief and the house of the one who swears falsely by My name; and it will spend the night within that house and consume it with its timber and stones."

⁵Then the angel who was speaking with me went out and said to me, "Lift up now your eyes and see what this is going forth." ⁶I said, "What is it?" And he said, "This is the ephah going forth." Again he said, "This is their appearance in all the land ⁷(and behold, a lead cover was lifted up); and this is a woman sitting inside the ephah." ⁸Then he said, "This is Wickedness!" And he threw her down into the middle of the ephah and cast the lead weight on its opening. ⁹Then I lifted up my eyes and looked, and there two women were coming out with the wind in their wings; and they had wings like the wings of a stork, and they lifted up the ephah between the earth and the heavens. ¹⁰I said to the angel who was speaking with me, "Where are they taking the ephah?" ¹¹Then he said to me, "To build a temple for her in the land of Shinar; and when it is prepared, she will be set there on her own pedestal."

6 Now I lifted up my eyes again and looked, and behold, four chariots were coming forth from between the two mountains; and the mountains *were* bronze mountains. ²With the first chariot *were* red horses, with the second chariot black horses, ³with the third chariot white horses, and with the fourth chariot strong dappled horses. ⁴Then I spoke and said to the angel who was speaking with me, "What are these, my lord?" ⁵The angel replied to me, "These are the four spirits of heaven, going forth after standing before the Lord of all the earth, ⁶with one of which the black horses are going forth to the north country; and the white ones go forth after them, while the dappled ones go forth to the south country. ⁷When the strong ones went

out, they were eager to go to patrol the earth." And He said, "Go, patrol the earth." So they patrolled the earth. [8] Then He cried out to me and spoke to me saying, "See, those who are going to the land of the north have appeased My wrath in the land of the north."

[9] The word of the LORD also came to me, saying, [10] "Take an offering from the exiles, from Heldai, Tobijah and Jedaiah; and you go the same day and enter the house of Josiah the son of Zephaniah, where they have arrived from Babylon. [11] Take silver and gold, make an ornate crown and set it on the head of Joshua the son of Jehozadak, the high priest. [12] Then say to him, 'Thus says the LORD of hosts, "Behold, a man whose name is Branch, for He will branch out from where He is; and He will build the temple of the LORD. [13] Yes, it is He who will build the temple of the LORD, and He who will bear the honor and sit and rule on His throne. Thus, He will be a priest on His throne, and the counsel of peace will be between the two offices."' [14] Now the crown will become a reminder in the temple of the LORD to Helem, Tobijah, Jedaiah and Hen the son of Zephaniah. [15] Those who are far off will come and build the temple of the LORD." Then you will know that the LORD of hosts has sent me to you. And it will take place if you completely obey the LORD your God.

6:12–15 In this brief section, 8 facts are given about Messiah, the Branch: 1) He will come from Israel (v. 12); 2) He will build the millennial temple (vv. 12b, 13a); 3) He will be glorious (v. 13); 4) He will be king and priest (v. 13); 5) He makes peace (v. 13); 6) He opens the kingdom to Gentiles (v. 15a); 7) He will corroborate God's Word (v. 15b); and 8) He demands obedience (v. 15c). This, as always, is the essential matter. After Israel believes, the Messiah will come to set up His kingdom (12:10—13:1; 14:9–21). Faith and cleansing must come first.

Psalm 148:1–6

Praise the LORD!
Praise the LORD from the heavens;
Praise Him in the heights!
[2] Praise Him, all His angels;
Praise Him, all His hosts!
[3] Praise Him, sun and moon;
Praise Him, all stars of light!
[4] Praise Him, highest heavens,
And the waters that are
above the heavens!

[5] Let them praise the name of the LORD,
For He commanded and
they were created.
[6] He has also established them
forever and ever;
He has made a decree which
will not pass away.

Proverbs 30:24–28

[24] Four things are small on the earth,
But they are exceedingly wise:
[25] The ants are not a strong people,
But they prepare their food
in the summer;
[26] The shephanim are not mighty people,
Yet they make their houses in the rocks;
[27] The locusts have no king,
Yet all of them go out in ranks;
[28] The lizard you may grasp
with the hands,
Yet it is in kings' palaces.

30:24–28 Four things are small. These verses picture 4 creatures which survive due to natural instinct. The wisdom seen in each of these reveals the beauty of the wise Creator and His creation (Ps 8:3–9) and becomes a model for the principle that labor, diligence, organization, planning, and resourcefulness are better than strength, thus implying the superiority of wisdom over might.

Revelation 17:1–18

17 Then one of the seven angels who had the seven bowls came and spoke with me, saying, "Come here, I will show you the judgment of the great harlot who sits on many waters, [2] with whom the kings of the earth committed acts of immorality, and those who dwell on the earth were made drunk with the wine of her immorality." [3] And he carried me away in the Spirit into a wilderness; and I saw a woman sitting on a scarlet beast, full of blasphemous names, having seven heads and ten horns. [4] The woman was clothed in purple and scarlet, and adorned with gold and precious stones and pearls, having in her hand a gold cup full of abominations and of the unclean things of her immorality, [5] and on her forehead a name was written, a mystery,

"BABYLON THE GREAT,
THE MOTHER OF HARLOTS
AND OF THE ABOMINATIONS
OF THE EARTH."

17:5 forehead. It was customary for Roman prostitutes to wear a headband with their name on it (Jer 3:3) parading their wretchedness for all to see. The harlot's forehead is emblazoned with a 3-fold title descriptive of the world's final false religious system. **mystery.** A New Testament mystery is truth once hidden, but in the New Testament revealed. Spiritual Babylon's true identity is yet to be revealed. Thus, the precise details of how it will be manifested in the world are not yet known. **BABYLON THE GREAT.** This Babylon is distinct from the historical, geographical city of Babylon (which still existed in John's day). The details of John's vision cannot be applied to any historical city (14:8). **MOTHER OF HARLOTS.** All false religion stems ultimately from Babel, or Babylon (Ge 11).

⁶And I saw the woman drunk with the blood of the saints, and with the blood of the witnesses of Jesus. When I saw her, I wondered greatly. ⁷And the angel said to me, "Why do you wonder? I will tell you the mystery of the woman and of the beast that carries her, which has the seven heads and the ten horns.

⁸"The beast that you saw was, and is not, and is about to come up out of the abyss and go to destruction. And those who dwell on the earth, whose name has not been written in the book of life from the foundation of the world, will wonder when they see the beast, that he was and is not and will come. ⁹Here is the mind which has wisdom. The seven heads are seven mountains on which the woman sits, ¹⁰and they are seven kings; five have fallen, one is, the other has not yet come; and when he comes, he must remain a little while. ¹¹The beast which was and is not, is himself also an eighth and is one of the seven, and he goes to destruction. ¹²The ten horns which you saw are ten kings who have not yet received a kingdom, but they receive authority as kings with the beast for one hour. ¹³These have one purpose, and they give their power and authority to the beast. ¹⁴These will wage war against the Lamb, and the Lamb will overcome them, because He is Lord of lords and King of kings, and those who are with Him are the called and chosen and faithful."

¹⁵And he *said to me, "The waters which you saw where the harlot sits, are peoples and multitudes and nations and tongues. ¹⁶And the ten horns which you saw, and the beast, these will hate the harlot and will make her desolate and naked, and will eat her flesh and will burn her up with fire. ¹⁷For God has put it in their hearts to execute His purpose by having a common purpose, and by giving their kingdom to the beast, until the words of God will be fulfilled. ¹⁸The woman whom you saw is the great city, which reigns over the kings of the earth."

DAY 27: What is God's word to inspire Zerubbabel to act on His promise?

Zechariah 4:6 states: "This is the word of the LORD to Zerubbabel." The purpose of the vision was to encourage Zerubbabel to complete the temple rebuilding, to assure him of divine enablement for that venture and the endless supply for the future glory of the Messiah's kingdom and temple. The lampstand pictured Israel fully supplied by God to be His light then and in the future. It must be noted that the church has temporarily taken this role presently (Eph 5:8, 9; Rev 1:12–13, 20), until Israel's salvation and restoration to covenant blessing and usefulness.

"'Not by might nor by power, but by My Spirit.'" Neither human might, wealth, or physical stamina would be sufficient to complete the work. Only an abundant supply of the power of the Holy Spirit, pictured by the "bowl" (v. 2), would enable him to carry out the task and enable Israel in the Messiah's kingdom to be a light again to the world by the operation of the Spirit (Eze 36:24).

"What are you, O great mountain? Before Zerubbabel you will become a plain" (v. 7). Because the outcome is guaranteed (vv. 6, 9), any mountainlike opposition will be leveled by God to become like a flat surface. No obstacle will be able to stop the completion of the temple in Zerubbabel's time or in the final kingdom of the Messiah (Eze 40–48). "He will bring forth the top stone." The final stone of the building will be put into place, signifying its completion. "With shouts of 'Grace, grace to it!'" This blessing signifying shouts of joy and thanksgiving came to pass (Ezr 3:11–13) over the completion of the temple. Contrast this attitude with that of the people seeing the unfinished temple (Hag 2:3).

DECEMBER 28

Zechariah 7:1–9:17

7 In the fourth year of King Darius, the word of the LORD came to Zechariah on the fourth *day* of the ninth month, *which is* Chislev. ² Now *the town of* Bethel had sent Sharezer and Regemmelech and their men to seek the favor of the LORD, ³ speaking to the priests who belong to the house of the LORD of hosts, and to the prophets, saying, "Shall I weep in the fifth month and abstain, as I have done these many years?" ⁴ Then the word of the LORD of hosts came to me, saying, ⁵ "Say to all the people of the land and to the priests, 'When you fasted and mourned in the fifth and seventh months these seventy years, was it actually for Me that you fasted? ⁶ When you eat and drink, do you not eat for yourselves and do you not drink for yourselves? ⁷ Are not *these* the words which the LORD proclaimed by the former prophets, when Jerusalem was inhabited and prosperous along with its cities around it, and the Negev and the foothills were inhabited?'"

⁸ Then the word of the LORD came to Zechariah saying, ⁹ "Thus has the LORD of hosts said, 'Dispense true justice and practice kindness and compassion each to his brother; ¹⁰ and do not oppress the widow or the orphan, the stranger or the poor; and do not devise evil in your hearts against one another.' ¹¹ But they refused to pay attention and turned a stubborn shoulder and stopped their ears from hearing. ¹² They made their hearts *like* flint so that they could not hear the law and the words which the LORD of hosts had sent by His Spirit through the former prophets; therefore great wrath came from the LORD of hosts. ¹³ And just as He called and they would not listen, so they called and I would not listen," says the LORD of hosts; ¹⁴ "but I scattered them with a storm wind among all the nations whom they have not known. Thus the land is desolated behind them so that no one went back and forth, for they made the pleasant land desolate."

8 Then the word of the LORD of hosts came, saying, ² "Thus says the LORD of hosts, 'I am exceedingly jealous for Zion, yes, with great wrath I am jealous for her.' ³ Thus says the LORD, 'I will return to Zion and will dwell in the midst of Jerusalem. Then Jerusalem will be called the City of Truth, and the mountain of the LORD of hosts *will be called* the Holy Mountain.' ⁴ Thus says the LORD of hosts, 'Old men and old women will again sit in the streets of Jerusalem, each man with his staff in his hand because of age. ⁵ And the streets of the city will be filled with boys and girls playing in its streets.' ⁶ Thus says the LORD of hosts, 'If it is too difficult in the sight of the remnant of this people in those days, will it also be too difficult in My sight?' declares the LORD of hosts. ⁷ Thus says the LORD of hosts, 'Behold, I am going to save My people from the land of the east and from the land of the west; ⁸ and I will bring them *back* and they will live in the midst of Jerusalem; and they shall be My people, and I will be their God in truth and righteousness.'

⁹ "Thus says the LORD of hosts, 'Let your hands be strong, you who are listening in these days to these words from the mouth of the prophets, *those* who *spoke* in the day that the foundation of the house of the LORD of hosts was laid, to the end that the temple might be built. ¹⁰ For before those days there was no wage for man or any wage for animal; and for him who went out or came in there was no peace because of his enemies, and I set all men one against another. ¹¹ But now I will not treat the remnant of this people as in the former days,' declares the LORD of hosts. ¹² 'For *there will be* peace for the seed: the vine will yield its fruit, the land will yield its produce and the heavens will give their dew; and I will cause the remnant of this people to inherit all these *things*. ¹³ It will come about that just as you were a curse among the nations, O house of Judah and house of Israel, so I will save you that you may become a blessing. Do not fear; let your hands be strong.'

¹⁴ "For thus says the LORD of hosts, 'Just as I purposed to do harm to you when your fathers provoked Me to wrath,' says the LORD of hosts, 'and I have not relented, ¹⁵ so I have again purposed in these days to do good to Jerusalem and to the house of Judah. Do not fear! ¹⁶ These are the things which you should do: speak the truth to one another; judge with truth and judgment for peace in your gates. ¹⁷ Also let none of you devise evil in your heart against another, and do not love perjury; for all these are what I hate,' declares the LORD."

¹⁸ Then the word of the LORD of hosts came to me, saying, ¹⁹ "Thus says the LORD of hosts, 'The fast of the fourth, the fast of the fifth, the fast of the seventh and the fast of the tenth *months* will become joy, gladness, and cheerful feasts for the house of Judah; so love truth and peace.'

²⁰ "Thus says the LORD of hosts, '*It will* yet *be* that peoples will come, even the inhabitants of many cities. ²¹ The inhabitants of one will go to another, saying, "Let us go at once to entreat the favor of the LORD, and to seek

the LORD of hosts; I will also go." ²² So many peoples and mighty nations will come to seek the LORD of hosts in Jerusalem and to entreat the favor of the LORD.' ²³ Thus says the LORD of hosts, 'In those days ten men from all the nations will grasp the garment of a Jew, saying, "Let us go with you, for we have heard that God is with you."'"

9 The burden of the word of the LORD is against the land of Hadrach, with Damascus as its resting place (for the eyes of men, especially of all the tribes of Israel, are toward the LORD),

2 And Hamath also, which borders on it;
  Tyre and Sidon, though
    they are very wise.
3 For Tyre built herself a fortress
  And piled up silver like dust,
  And gold like the mire of the streets.
4 Behold, the Lord will dispossess her
  And cast her wealth into the sea;
  And she will be consumed with fire.
5 Ashkelon will see *it* and be afraid.
  Gaza too will writhe in great pain;
  Also Ekron, for her expectation
    has been confounded.
  Moreover, the king will
    perish from Gaza,
  And Ashkelon will not be inhabited.
6 And a mongrel race will
    dwell in Ashdod,
  And I will cut off the pride
    of the Philistines.
7 And I will remove their blood
    from their mouth
  And their detestable things
    from between their teeth.
  Then they also will be a
    remnant for our God,
  And be like a clan in Judah,
  And Ekron like a Jebusite.
8 But I will camp around My
    house because of an army,

9:1–8 This oracle features a series of judgments announced against the nations surrounding Israel (vv. 1–7), with deliverance promised for His people (v. 8). Most understand this to be a prophecy of the famous Greek conqueror, Alexander the Great's victories, given approximately 200 years before he marched through Israel. He provides an analogy of Christ returning to judge the nations and save Israel at the end of the Great Tribulation (Mt 24:21).

Because of him who passes
    by and returns;
And no oppressor will pass
    over them anymore,
For now I have seen with My eyes.
9 Rejoice greatly, O daughter of Zion!
  Shout *in triumph*, O daughter
    of Jerusalem!
  Behold, your king is coming to you;
  He is just and endowed
    with salvation,
  Humble, and mounted on a donkey,
  Even on a colt, the foal of a donkey.
10 I will cut off the chariot
    from Ephraim
  And the horse from Jerusalem;
  And the bow of war will be cut off.
  And He will speak peace
    to the nations;
  And His dominion will be
    from sea to sea,
  And from the River to the
    ends of the earth.
11 As for you also, because of the
    blood of *My* covenant with you,
  I have set your prisoners free
    from the waterless pit.
12 Return to the stronghold,
    O prisoners who have the hope;
  This very day I am declaring that
    I will restore double to you.
13 For I will bend Judah as My bow,
  I will fill the bow with Ephraim.
  And I will stir up your sons, O Zion,
    against your sons, O Greece;
  And I will make you like a
    warrior's sword.
14 Then the LORD will appear over them,
  And His arrow will go
    forth like lightning;
  And the Lord GOD will
    blow the trumpet,
  And will march in the storm
    winds of the south.
15 The LORD of hosts will defend them.
  And they will devour and trample
    on the sling stones;
  And they will drink *and* be
    boisterous as with wine;
  And they will be filled like
    a *sacrificial* basin,
  Drenched like the corners of the altar.
16 And the LORD their God will
    save them in that day
  As the flock of His people;
  For *they are as* the stones of a crown,
  Sparkling in His land.

17 For what comeliness and
beauty *will be* theirs!
Grain will make the young men
flourish, and new wine the virgins.

Psalm 148:7-14

7 Praise the LORD from the earth,
Sea monsters and all deeps;
8 Fire and hail, snow and clouds;
Stormy wind, fulfilling His word;
9 Mountains and all hills;
Fruit trees and all cedars;
10 Beasts and all cattle;
Creeping things and winged fowl;
11 Kings of the earth and all peoples;
Princes and all judges of the earth;
12 Both young men and virgins;
Old men and children.

13 Let them praise the name of the LORD,
For His name alone is exalted;
His glory is above earth and heaven.
14 And He has lifted up a horn
for His people,
Praise for all His godly ones;
Even for the sons of Israel, a
people near to Him.
Praise the LORD!

148:14 a horn. Refers in general to the strength and prosperity of the nation, which became the cause of praise for Israel. This suggests that Israel will enjoy better times than in the past, e.g., during David's and Solomon's reigns or after returning from the Babylonian Captivity. **a people near to Him.** See also "My chosen people" (Is 43:20) and "His own possession" (Ps 135:4).

Proverbs 30:29-31

29 There are three things which
are stately in *their* march,
Even four which are stately
when they walk:
30 The lion *which* is mighty among beasts
And does not retreat before any,

30:29-31 three things...stately in *their* march...four. The 3 creatures and the king all picture wise, stately, and orderly deportment. Each offers a glimpse of the Creator's power and wisdom (Job 38:1—42:6) and illustrates the dignity and confidence of those who walk wisely.

31 The strutting rooster, the
male goat also,
And a king *when his* army is with him.

Revelation 18:1-24

18 After these things I saw another angel coming down from heaven, having great authority, and the earth was illumined with his glory. ²And he cried out with a mighty voice, saying, "Fallen, fallen is Babylon the great! She has become a dwelling place of demons and a prison of every unclean spirit, and a prison of every unclean and hateful bird. ³For all the nations have drunk of the wine of the passion of her immorality, and the kings of the earth have committed *acts of* immorality with her, and the merchants of the earth have become rich by the wealth of her sensuality."

⁴I heard another voice from heaven, saying, "Come out of her, my people, so that you will not participate in her sins and receive of her plagues; ⁵for her sins have piled up as high as heaven, and God has remembered her iniquities. ⁶Pay her back even as she has paid, and give back *to her* double according to her deeds; in the cup which she has mixed, mix twice as much for her. ⁷To the degree that she glorified herself and lived sensuously, to the same degree give her torment and mourning; for she says in her heart, 'I SIT *AS* A QUEEN AND I AM NOT A WIDOW, and will never see mourning.' ⁸For this reason in one day her plagues will come, pestilence and mourning and famine, and she will be burned up with fire; for the Lord God who judges her is strong.

⁹"And the kings of the earth, who committed *acts of* immorality and lived sensuously with her, will weep and lament over her when they see the smoke of her burning, ¹⁰standing at a distance because of the fear of her torment, saying, 'Woe, woe, the great city, Babylon, the strong city! For in one hour your judgment has come.'

¹¹"And the merchants of the earth weep and mourn over her, because no one buys their cargoes any more— ¹²cargoes of gold and silver and precious stones and pearls and fine linen and purple and silk and scarlet, and every *kind of* citron wood and every article of ivory and every article *made* from very costly wood and bronze and iron and marble, ¹³and cinnamon and spice and incense and perfume and frankincense and wine and olive oil and fine flour and wheat and cattle and sheep, and *cargoes* of horses and chariots and slaves and human lives. ¹⁴The fruit you long

for has gone from you, and all things that were luxurious and splendid have passed away from you and *men* will no longer find them. ¹⁵ The merchants of these things, who became rich from her, will stand at a distance because of the fear of her torment, weeping and mourning, ¹⁶ saying, 'Woe, woe, the great city, she who was clothed in fine linen and purple and scarlet, and adorned with gold and precious stones and pearls; ¹⁷ for in one hour such great wealth has been laid waste!' And every shipmaster and every passenger and sailor, and as many as make their living by the sea, stood at a distance, ¹⁸ and were crying out as they saw the smoke of her burning, saying, 'What *city* is like the great city?' ¹⁹ And they threw dust on their heads and were crying out, weeping and mourning, saying, 'Woe, woe, the great city, in which all who had ships at sea became rich by her wealth, for in one hour she has been laid waste!' ²⁰ Rejoice over her, O heaven, and you saints and apostles and prophets, because God has pronounced judgment for you against her."

²¹ Then a strong angel took up a stone like a great millstone and threw it into the sea, saying, "So will Babylon, the great city, be thrown down with violence, and will not be found any longer. ²² And the sound of harpists and musicians and flute-players and trumpeters will not be heard in you any longer; and no craftsman of any craft will be found in you any longer; and the sound of a mill will not be heard in you any longer; ²³ and the light of a lamp will not shine in you any longer; and the voice of the bridegroom and bride will not be heard in you any longer; for your merchants were the great men of the earth, because all the nations were deceived by your sorcery. ²⁴ And in her was found the blood of prophets and of saints and of all who have been slain on the earth."

18:24 blood of prophets and of saints. The religious and commercial/political systems embodied in Babylon will commit unspeakable atrocities against God's people (6:10; 11:7; 13:7, 15; 17:6; 19:2). God will avenge that slaughter of His people (19:2).

DAY 28: If Zechariah 9:9 refers to the First Advent of Christ, how does v. 10 relate to that?

"Behold, your king is coming to you…mounted on a donkey" (v. 9). Unlike Alexander the Great, this King comes riding on a donkey (Jer 17:25). This was fulfilled at Christ's Triumphal Entry into Jerusalem (Mt 21:1–5; Jn 12:12–16). The Jews should have been looking for someone from the line of David (2Sa 7; 1Ch 17). Four elements in this verse describe the Messiah's character: 1) He is King; 2) He is just; 3) He brings salvation; and 4) He is humble.

Zechariah moves to the Second Advent of Christ and the establishment of His universal kingdom in v. 10. "His dominion will be from sea to sea." Not characterized by bloodshed, the Messiah's rule will be a kingdom of peace in which weapons of warfare will be destroyed or converted to peaceful uses (Is 2:4; 9:5–7; 11:1–10; Mic 5:2, 10–15), and peace spreads from the Euphrates River (the terminus of civilization) to the world.

The two advents of Christ are here compressed as though they were one as in Isaiah 61:1–3 (Lk 4:16, 21). Verse 9 refers to His First Coming and v. 10 is His Second. Old Testament prophets didn't see the great time period between the two comings. The church age was a "mystery" hidden from them (Eph 3:1–9; Col 1:27).

DECEMBER 29

Zechariah 10:1–12:14

10 Ask rain from the LORD at the
   time of the spring rain—
   The LORD who makes the storm clouds;
   And He will give them showers of rain,
      vegetation in the field to *each* man.
   ² For the teraphim speak iniquity,
      And the diviners see lying visions
   And tell false dreams;
      They comfort in vain.

Therefore *the people* wander like sheep,
   They are afflicted, because
      there is no shepherd.
³ "My anger is kindled against
      the shepherds,
   And I will punish the male goats;
   For the LORD of hosts has visited
      His flock, the house of Judah,
   And will make them like His
      majestic horse in battle.
⁴ "From them will come the cornerstone,
   From them the tent peg,
   From them the bow of battle,

From them every ruler, *all*
of them together.
5 "They will be as mighty men,
Treading down *the enemy*
in the mire of the
streets in battle;
And they will fight, for the
LORD *will be* with them;
And the riders on horses
will be put to shame.
6 "I will strengthen the
house of Judah,
And I will save the house of Joseph,
And I will bring them back,
Because I have had
compassion on them;
And they will be as though I
had not rejected them,
For I am the LORD their God
and I will answer them.
7 "Ephraim will be like a mighty man,
And their heart will be glad
as if *from* wine;
Indeed, their children will
see *it* and be glad,
Their heart will rejoice in the LORD.
8 "I will whistle for them to
gather them together,
For I have redeemed them;
And they will be as numerous
as they were before.
9 "When I scatter them
among the peoples,
They will remember Me
in far countries,
And they with their children
will live and come back.
10 "I will bring them back from
the land of Egypt
And gather them from Assyria;
And I will bring them into the
land of Gilead and Lebanon
Until no *room* can be
found for them.
11 "And they will pass through
the sea *of* distress
And He will strike the
waves in the sea,
So that all the depths of the
Nile will dry up;
And the pride of Assyria
will be brought down
And the scepter of
Egypt will depart.
12 "And I will strengthen
them in the LORD,
And in His name they will
walk," declares the LORD.

11 Open your doors, O Lebanon,
That a fire may feed on your cedars.
2 Wail, O cypress, for the
cedar has fallen,
Because the glorious *trees*
have been destroyed;
Wail, O oaks of Bashan,
For the impenetrable forest
has come down.
3 There is a sound of the
shepherds' wail,
For their glory is ruined;
There is a sound of the
young lions' roar,
For the pride of the Jordan is ruined.

4 Thus says the LORD my God, "Pasture the flock *doomed* to slaughter. 5 Those who buy them slay them and go unpunished, and *each of* those who sell them says, 'Blessed be the LORD, for I have become rich!' And their own shepherds have no pity on them. 6 For I will no longer have pity on the inhabitants of the land," declares the LORD; "but behold, I will cause the men to fall, each into another's power and into the power of his king; and they will strike the land, and I will not deliver *them* from their power."

7 So I pastured the flock *doomed* to slaughter, hence the afflicted of the flock. And I took for myself two staffs: the one I called Favor and the other I called Union; so I pastured the flock. 8 Then I annihilated the three shepherds in one month, for my soul was impatient with them, and their soul also was weary of me. 9 Then I said, "I will not pasture you. What is to die, let it die, and what is to be annihilated, let it be annihilated; and let those who are left eat one another's flesh." 10 I took my staff Favor and cut it in pieces, to break my covenant which I had made with all the peoples. 11 So it was broken on that day, and thus the afflicted of the flock who were watching me realized that it was the word of the LORD. 12 I said to them, "If it is good in your sight, give *me* my wages; but if not, never mind!" So they weighed out thirty *shekels* of silver as my wages. 13 Then the LORD said to me, "Throw it to the potter, *that* magnificent price at which I was valued by them." So I took the thirty *shekels* of silver and threw them to the potter in the house of the LORD. 14 Then I cut in pieces my second staff Union, to break the brotherhood between Judah and Israel.

15 The LORD said to me, "Take again for yourself the equipment of a foolish shepherd. 16 For behold, I am going to raise up a shepherd in the land who will not care for the perishing,

seek the scattered, heal the broken, or sustain the one standing, but will devour the flesh of the fat *sheep* and tear off their hoofs.

¹⁷ "Woe to the worthless shepherd
Who leaves the flock!
A sword will be on his arm
And on his right eye!
His arm will be totally withered
And his right eye will be blind."

12 The burden of the word of the LORD concerning Israel.

Thus declares the LORD who stretches out the heavens, lays the foundation of the earth, and forms the spirit of man within him, ² "Behold, I am going to make Jerusalem a cup that causes reeling to all the peoples around; and when the siege is against Jerusalem, it will also be against Judah. ³ It will come about in that day that I will make Jerusalem a heavy stone for all the peoples; all who lift it will be severely injured. And all the nations of the earth will be gathered against it. ⁴ In that day," declares the LORD, "I will strike every horse with bewilderment and his rider with madness. But I will watch over the house of Judah, while I strike every horse of the peoples with blindness. ⁵ Then the clans of Judah will say in their hearts, 'A strong support for us are the inhabitants of Jerusalem through the LORD of hosts, their God.'

⁶ "In that day I will make the clans of Judah like a firepot among pieces of wood and a flaming torch among sheaves, so they will consume on the right hand and on the left all the surrounding peoples, while the inhabitants of Jerusalem again dwell on their own sites in Jerusalem. ⁷ The LORD also will save the tents of Judah first, so that the glory of the house of David and the glory of the inhabitants of Jerusalem will not be magnified above Judah. ⁸ In that day the LORD will defend the inhabitants of Jerusalem, and the one who is feeble among them in that day will be like David, and the house of David *will be* like God, like the angel of the LORD before them. ⁹ And in that day I will set about to destroy all the nations that come against Jerusalem.

¹⁰ "I will pour out on the house of David and on the inhabitants of Jerusalem, the Spirit of grace and of supplication, so that they will look on Me whom they have pierced; and they will mourn for Him, as one mourns for an only son, and they will weep bitterly over Him like the bitter weeping over a firstborn. ¹¹ In that day there will be great mourning in Jerusalem, like the mourning of Hadadrimmon

12:10 I will pour. God, in His own perfect time and by His own power, will sovereignly act to save Israel. This was prophesied by other prophets (Eze 39:29; Joel 2:28–32), and by the apostle Paul (Ro 11:25–27). **Spirit of grace and of supplication.** The Holy Spirit is so identified because He brings saving grace and because that grace produces sorrow that will result in repentant prayer to God for forgiveness (Mt 5:4; Heb 10:29). **look on Me whom they have pierced.** Israel's repentance will come because they look to Jesus, the One whom they rejected and crucified (Is 53:5; Jn 19:37), in faith at the Second Advent (Ro 11:25–27). When God says they pierced "Me," He is certainly affirming the incarnation of deity—Jesus was God.

in the plain of Megiddo. ¹² The land will mourn, every family by itself; the family of the house of David by itself and their wives by themselves; the family of the house of Nathan by itself and their wives by themselves; ¹³ the family of the house of Levi by itself and their wives by themselves; the family of the Shimeites by itself and their wives by themselves; ¹⁴ all the families that remain, every family by itself and their wives by themselves.

Psalm 149:1-4

Praise the LORD!
Sing to the LORD a new song,
And His praise in the congregation of the godly ones.
² Let Israel be glad in his Maker;
Let the sons of Zion rejoice in their King.
³ Let them praise His name with dancing;
Let them sing praises to Him with timbrel and lyre.
⁴ For the LORD takes pleasure in His people;
He will beautify the afflicted ones with salvation.

Proverbs 30:32-33

³² If you have been foolish in exalting yourself
Or if you have plotted *evil, put your* hand on your mouth.
³³ For the churning of milk produces butter,
And pressing the nose brings forth blood;
So the churning of anger produces strife.

Revelation 19:1–21

19 After these things I heard something like a loud voice of a great multitude in heaven, saying,

"Hallelujah! Salvation and glory and power belong to our God; ² BECAUSE HIS JUDGMENTS ARE TRUE AND RIGHTEOUS; for He has judged the great harlot who was corrupting the earth with her immorality, and HE HAS AVENGED THE BLOOD OF HIS BOND-SERVANTS ON HER." ³ And a second time they said, "Hallelujah! HER SMOKE RISES UP FOREVER AND EVER." ⁴ And the twenty-four elders and the four living creatures fell down and worshiped God who sits on the throne saying, "Amen. Hallelujah!" ⁵ And a voice came from the throne, saying,

"Give praise to our God, all you His bond-servants, you who fear Him, the small and the great." ⁶ Then I heard *something* like the voice of a great multitude and like the sound of many waters and like the sound of mighty peals of thunder, saying,

"Hallelujah! For the Lord our God, the Almighty, reigns. ⁷ Let us rejoice and be glad and give the glory to Him, for the marriage of the Lamb has come and His bride has made herself ready." ⁸ It was given to her to clothe herself in fine linen, bright *and* clean; for the fine linen is the righteous acts of the saints.

⁹ Then he *said to me, "Write, 'Blessed are those who are invited to the marriage supper of the Lamb.'" And he *said to me, "These are true words of God." ¹⁰ Then I fell at his feet to worship him. But he *said to me, "Do not do that; I am a fellow servant of yours and your brethren who hold the testimony of Jesus; worship God. For the testimony of Jesus is the spirit of prophecy."

¹¹ And I saw heaven opened, and behold, a white horse, and He who sat on it *is* called Faithful and True, and in righteousness He judges and wages war. ¹² His eyes *are* a flame of fire, and on His head *are* many diadems; and He has a name written *on Him* which no one knows except Himself. ¹³ *He is* clothed with a robe dipped in blood, and His name is called The Word of God. ¹⁴ And the armies which are in heaven, clothed in fine linen, white *and* clean, were following Him on white horses. ¹⁵ From His mouth comes a sharp sword, so that with it He may strike down the nations, and He will rule them with a rod of iron; and He treads the wine press of the fierce wrath of God, the Almighty. ¹⁶ And on His robe and on His thigh He has a name written,

"KING OF KINGS, AND LORD OF LORDS."

¹⁷ Then I saw an angel standing in the sun, and he cried out with a loud voice, saying to all the birds which fly in midheaven, "Come, assemble for the great supper of God, ¹⁸ so that you may eat the flesh of kings and the flesh of commanders and the flesh of mighty men and the flesh of horses and of those who sit on them and the flesh of all men, both free men and slaves, and small and great."

19:11 heaven opened. The One who ascended to heaven (Ac 1:9–11) and had been seated at the Father's right hand (Heb 8:1; 10:12; 1Pe 3:22) will return to take back the earth from the usurper and establish His kingdom (5:1–10). The nature of this event shows how it differs from the Rapture. At the Rapture, Christ meets His own in the air—in this event He comes with them to earth. At the Rapture, there is no judgment; in this event it is all judgment. This event is preceded by blackness—the darkened sun, moon gone out, stars fallen, smoke—then lightning and blinding glory as Jesus comes. Such details are not included in Rapture passages (Jn 14:1–3; 1Th 4:13–18). **white horse.** In the Roman triumphal processions, the victorious general rode his white war horse up the Via Sacra to the temple of Jupiter on the Capitoline Hill. Jesus' first coming was in humiliation on a colt (Zec 9:9). John's vision portrays Him as the conqueror on His warhorse, coming to destroy the wicked, to overthrow the Antichrist, to defeat Satan, and to take control of the earth (2Co 2:14). **Faithful and True.** True to His word, Jesus will return to earth (Mt 24:27–31). **wages war.** This startling statement, appearing only here and 2:16, vividly portrays the holy wrath of God against sinners (Ps 7:11). God's patience will be exhausted with sinful, rebellious mankind.

19:20 beast was seized, and...the false prophet. In an instant, the world's armies are without their leaders. The beast is Antichrist (13:1–4); the false prophet is his religious cohort (13:11–17). **thrown alive.** The bodies of the beast and the false prophet will be transformed, and they will be banished directly to the lake of fire (Da 7:11)—the first of countless millions of unregenerate men (20:15) and fallen angels (Mt 25:41) to arrive in that dreadful place. That these two still appear there 1,000 years later (20:10) refutes the false doctrine of annihilationism. **lake of fire.** The final hell, the place of eternal punishment for all unrepentant rebels, angelic or human (20:10, 15).

¹⁹ And I saw the beast and the kings of the earth and their armies assembled to make war against Him who sat on the horse and against His army. ²⁰ And the beast was seized, and with him the false prophet who performed the signs in his presence, by which he deceived those who had received the mark of the beast and those who worshiped his image; these two were thrown alive into the lake of fire which burns with brimstone. ²¹ And the rest were killed with the sword which came from the mouth of Him who sat on the horse, and all the birds were filled with their flesh.

DAY 29: What is the "marriage of the Lamb" in Revelation 19:7–9 about?

Hebrew weddings consisted of 3 phases: 1) betrothal (often when the couple were children); 2) presentation (the festivities, often lasting several days, that preceded the ceremony); and 3) the ceremony (the exchanging of vows). The church was betrothed to Christ by His sovereign choice in eternity past (Eph 1:4; Heb 13:20) and will be presented to Him at the Rapture (Jn 14:1–3; 1Th 4:13–18). The final supper will signify the end of the ceremony. This symbolic meal will take place at the establishment of the millennial kingdom and last throughout that 1,000-year period (21:2). While the term "bride" often refers to the church, and does so here (see 2Co 11:2; Eph 5:22–24), it ultimately expands to include all the redeemed of all ages.

"It was given to her to clothe herself in fine linen…the righteous acts of the saints" (v. 8). Not Christ's imputed righteousness granted to believers at salvation, but the practical results of that righteousness in believers' lives, i.e., the outward manifestation of inward virtue.

"Blessed are those who are invited to the marriage supper of the Lamb" (v. 9). This is not the bride (the church) but the guests. The bride doesn't get invited; she invites. These are those saved before Pentecost, all the faithful believers saved by grace through faith up to the birth of the church (Ac 2:1ff.). Though they are not the bride, they still are glorified and reign with Christ in the millennial kingdom. It is really differing imagery rather than differing reality. The guests also will include tribulation saints and believers alive in earthly bodies in the kingdom. The church is the bride, pure and faithful—never a harlot, like Israel was (see Hos 2). So the church is the bride during the presentation feast in heaven, then comes to earth for the celebration of the final meal (the Millennium). After that event, the new order comes and the marriage is consummated (21:1–2).

DECEMBER 30

Zechariah 13:1–14:21

13 "In that day a fountain will be opened for the house of David and for the inhabitants of Jerusalem, for sin and for impurity.

² "It will come about in that day," declares the LORD of hosts, "that I will cut off the names of the idols from the land, and they will no longer be remembered; and I will also remove the prophets and the unclean spirit from the land. ³ And if anyone still prophesies, then his father and mother who gave birth to him will say to him, 'You shall not live, for you have spoken falsely in the name of the LORD'; and his father and mother who gave birth to him will pierce him through when he prophesies. ⁴ Also it will come about in that day that the prophets will each be ashamed of his vision when he prophesies, and they will not put on a hairy robe in order to deceive; ⁵ but he will say, 'I am not a prophet; I am a tiller of the ground, for a man sold me as a slave in my youth.' ⁶ And one will say to him, 'What are these wounds between your arms?' Then he will say, '*Those* with which I was wounded in the house of my friends.'

⁷ "Awake, O sword, against My Shepherd,
And against the man, My Associate,"
Declares the LORD of hosts.
"Strike the Shepherd that the
sheep may be scattered;
And I will turn My hand
against the little ones.
⁸ "It will come about in all the land,"
Declares the LORD,
"That two parts in it will be
cut off *and* perish;
But the third will be left in it.
⁹ "And I will bring the third
part through the fire,
Refine them as silver is refined,
And test them as gold is tested.
They will call on My name,
And I will answer them;
I will say, 'They are My people,'
And they will say, 'The
LORD is my God.'"

13:7 My Shepherd…My Associate. God spoke of the True Shepherd, that mighty Man who is His intimate associate, thus He identified Christ as His co-equal, affirming the deity of Christ (Jn 1:1; 10:30; 14:9). **Strike the Shepherd.** In 11:17, it was the worthless shepherd who was to be struck; now it is the Good Shepherd (12:10) whose death was designed by God from before the foundation of the world (Is 53:10; Ac 2:23; 1Pe 1:18–20). **sheep…scattered.** Jesus applies this prophecy to the disciples who defected from Him after His arrest (Mt 26:56; Mk 14:50), including Peter's denial (Mt 26:33–35, 69–75). **the little ones.** The same as the "afflicted of the flock" (11:7). The reference is to the remnant of believers, among the Jews, who were faithful to the Messiah after His crucifixion. Turning God's hand "against" them could mean they would suffer persecution, which they did (Jn 15:18, 20; 16:2; Jas 1:1), or it could be translated "upon" and refer to God's protection of the faithful.

14 Behold, a day is coming for the LORD when the spoil taken from you will be divided among you. ²For I will gather all the nations against Jerusalem to battle, and the city will be captured, the houses plundered, the women ravished and half of the city exiled, but the rest of the people will not be cut off from the city. ³Then the LORD will go forth and fight against those nations, as when He fights on a day of battle. ⁴In that day His feet will stand on the Mount of Olives, which is in front of Jerusalem on the east; and the Mount of Olives will be split in its middle from east to west by a very large valley, so that half of the mountain will move toward

14:3–4 His feet will stand on the Mount of Olives. To prevent the eradication of His remnant, the Lord will personally intervene to fight against the gathered nations. Just as He fought for His people in the past, so He will do in the future as the ultimate Warrior-King. Jesus will literally return to the Mt. of Olives, located east of the Kidron Valley, just as the angels announced at His ascension (Ac 1:11). When He does, there will be a tremendous topographical upheaval (perhaps an earthquake), a phenomenon not uncommon when God announces His coming in judgment (Mic 1:2–4; Na 1:5; Rev 16:18–21). The reaction of people is given in Revelation 6:15–17.

the north and the other half toward the south. ⁵You will flee by the valley of My mountains, for the valley of the mountains will reach to Azel; yes, you will flee just as you fled before the earthquake in the days of Uzziah king of Judah. Then the LORD, my God, will come, *and* all the holy ones with Him!

⁶In that day there will be no light; the luminaries will dwindle. ⁷For it will be a unique day which is known to the LORD, neither day nor night, but it will come about that at evening time there will be light.

⁸And in that day living waters will flow out of Jerusalem, half of them toward the eastern sea and the other half toward the western sea; it will be in summer as well as in winter.

⁹And the LORD will be king over all the earth; in that day the LORD will be *the only* one, and His name *the only* one.

¹⁰All the land will be changed into a plain from Geba to Rimmon south of Jerusalem; but Jerusalem will rise and remain on its site from Benjamin's Gate as far as the place of the First Gate to the Corner Gate, and from the Tower of Hananel to the king's wine presses. ¹¹People will live in it, and there will no longer be a curse, for Jerusalem will dwell in security.

¹²Now this will be the plague with which the LORD will strike all the peoples who have gone to war against Jerusalem; their flesh will rot while they stand on their feet, and their eyes will rot in their sockets, and their tongue will rot in their mouth. ¹³It will come about in that day that a great panic from the LORD will fall on them; and they will seize one another's hand, and the hand of one will be lifted against the hand of another. ¹⁴Judah also will fight at Jerusalem; and the wealth of all the surrounding nations will be gathered, gold and silver and garments in great abundance. ¹⁵So also like this plague will be the plague on the horse, the mule, the camel, the donkey and all the cattle that will be in those camps.

¹⁶Then it will come about that any who are left of all the nations that went against Jerusalem will go up from year to year to worship the King, the LORD of hosts, and to celebrate the Feast of Booths. ¹⁷And it will be that whichever of the families of the earth does not go up to Jerusalem to worship the King, the LORD of hosts, there will be no rain on them. ¹⁸If the family of Egypt does not go up or enter, then no *rain will fall* on them; it will be the plague with which the LORD smites the nations who do not go up to celebrate the Feast of Booths. ¹⁹This will be the punishment of Egypt, and the punishment of

all the nations who do not go up to celebrate the Feast of Booths.

²⁰ In that day there will *be inscribed* on the bells of the horses,

"HOLY TO THE LORD."

And the cooking pots in the LORD'S house will be like the bowls before the altar. ²¹ Every cooking pot in Jerusalem and in Judah will be holy to the LORD of hosts; and all who sacrifice will come and take of them and boil in them. And there will no longer be a Canaanite in the house of the LORD of hosts in that day.

Psalm 149:5–9

⁵ Let the godly ones exult in glory;
   Let them sing for joy on their beds.
⁶ *Let* the high praises of God
   be in their mouth,
   And a two-edged sword in their hand,
⁷ To execute vengeance on the nations
   And punishment on the peoples,
⁸ To bind their kings with chains
   And their nobles with fetters of iron,
⁹ To execute on them the
   judgment written;
   This is an honor for all
   His godly ones.
   Praise the LORD!

Proverbs 31:1–9

31 The words of King Lemuel, the oracle which his mother taught him:

² What, O my son?
   And what, O son of my womb?
   And what, O son of my vows?
³ Do not give your strength to women,
   Or your ways to that which
   destroys kings.
⁴ It is not for kings, O Lemuel,
   It is not for kings to drink wine,
   Or for rulers to desire strong drink,
⁵ For they will drink and forget
   what is decreed,
   And pervert the rights of
   all the afflicted.
⁶ Give strong drink to him
   who is perishing,
   And wine to him whose life is bitter.
⁷ Let him drink and forget his poverty
   And remember his trouble no more.
⁸ Open your mouth for the mute,
   For the rights of all the unfortunate.
⁹ Open your mouth, judge righteously,
   And defend the rights of the
   afflicted and needy.

Revelation 20:1–15

20 Then I saw an angel coming down from heaven, holding the key of the abyss and a great chain in his hand. ²And he laid hold of the dragon, the serpent of old, who is the devil and Satan, and bound him for a thousand years; ³ and he threw him into the abyss, and shut *it* and sealed *it* over him, so that he would not deceive the nations any longer, until the thousand years were completed; after these things he must be released for a short time.

⁴ Then I saw thrones, and they sat on them, and judgment was given to them. And I *saw* the souls of those who had been beheaded because of their testimony of Jesus and because of the word of God, and those who had not worshiped the beast or his image, and had not received the mark on their forehead and on their hand; and they came to life and reigned with Christ for a thousand years. ⁵ The rest of the dead did not come to life until the thousand years were completed. This is the first resurrection. ⁶ Blessed and holy is the one who has a part in the first resurrection; over these the second death has no power, but they will be priests of God and of Christ and will reign with Him for a thousand years.

⁷ When the thousand years are completed, Satan will be released from his prison, ⁸ and will come out to deceive the nations which are in the four corners of the earth, Gog and Magog, to gather them together for the war; the number of them is like the sand of the seashore. ⁹ And they came up on the broad plain of the earth and surrounded the camp of the saints and the beloved city, and fire came down from heaven and devoured them. ¹⁰ And the devil who deceived them was thrown into

20:5 first resurrection. Scripture teaches two kinds of resurrections: the "resurrection of life" and the "resurrection of judgment" (Jn 5:29; see Da 12:2; Ac 24:15). The first kind of resurrection is described as "the resurrection of the righteous" (Lk 14:14), the resurrection of "those who are Christ's at His coming" (1Co 15:23), and the "better resurrection" (Heb 11:35). It includes only the redeemed of the church age (1Th 4:13–18), the Old Testament (Da 12:2), and the Tribulation (v. 4). They will enter the kingdom in resurrection bodies, along with believers who survived the Tribulation. The second kind of resurrection, then, will be the resurrection of the unconverted who will receive their final bodies suited for torment in hell.

the lake of fire and brimstone, where the beast and the false prophet are also; and they will be tormented day and night forever and ever. ¹¹Then I saw a great white throne and Him who sat upon it, from whose presence earth and heaven fled away, and no place was found for them. ¹²And I saw the dead, the great and the small, standing before the throne, and books were opened; and another book was opened, which is *the book* of life; and the dead were judged from the things which were written in the books, according to their deeds. ¹³And the sea gave up the dead which were in it, and death and Hades gave up the dead which were in them; and they were judged, every one *of them* according to their deeds. ¹⁴Then death and Hades were thrown into the lake of fire. This is the second death, the lake of fire. ¹⁵And if anyone's name was not found written in the book of life, he was thrown into the lake of fire.

20:12 standing before the throne. In a judicial sense, as guilty, condemned prisoners before the bar of divine justice. There are no living sinners left in the destroyed universe since all sinners were killed and all believers glorified. **books.** These books record every thought, word, and deed of sinful men—all recorded by divine omniscience. They will provide the evidence for eternal condemnation. *book of* **life.** It contains the names of all the redeemed (Da 12:1). **judged...according to their deeds.** Their thoughts (Lk 8:17; Ro 2:16), words (Mt 12:37), and actions (Mt 16:27) will be compared to God's perfect, holy standard (Mt 5:48; 1Pe 1:15–16) and will be found wanting (Ro 3:23). This also implies that there are degrees of punishment in hell (Mt 10:14–15; 11:22; Mk 12:38–40; Lk 12:47–48; Heb 10:29).

DAY 30: What is the Millennium?

In Revelation 20:2, Satan is bound for a "thousand years." This is the first of 6 references to the length of the millennial kingdom (vv. 3, 4, 5, 6, 7). There are 3 main views of the duration and nature of this period:

1. Premillennialism sees this as a literal 1,000-year period during which Jesus Christ, in fulfillment of numerous Old Testament prophecies (e.g., 2Sa 7:12–16; Ps 2; Is 11:6–12; 24:23; Hos 3:4–5; Joel 3:9–21; Am 9:8–15; Mic 4:1–8; Zep 3:14–20; Zec 14:1–11; Mt 24:29–31, 36–44), reigns on the earth. Using the same general principles of interpretation for both prophetic and nonprophetic passages leads most naturally to Premillennialism. Another strong argument supporting this view is that so many biblical prophecies have already been literally fulfilled, suggesting that future prophecies will likewise be fulfilled literally.
2. Postmillennialism understands the reference to a 1,000-year period as only symbolic of a golden age of righteousness and spiritual prosperity. It will be ushered in by the spread of the gospel during the present church age and brought to completion when Christ returns. According to this view, references to Christ's reign on earth primarily describe His spiritual reign in the hearts of believers in the church.
3. Amillennialism understands the 1,000 years to be merely symbolic of a long period of time. This view interprets Old Testament prophecies of a Millennium as being fulfilled spiritually now in the church (either on earth or in heaven) or as references to the eternal state. Using the same literal, historical, grammatical principles of interpretation so as to determine the normal sense of language, one is left with the inescapable conclusion that Christ will return and reign in a real kingdom on earth for 1,000 years. There is nothing in the text to render the conclusion that "a thousand years" is symbolic.

DECEMBER 31

Malachi 1:1–4:6

1 The oracle of the word of the LORD to Israel through Malachi.

²"I have loved you," says the LORD. But you say, "How have You loved us?" "*Was* not Esau Jacob's brother?" declares the LORD. "Yet I have loved Jacob; ³but I have hated Esau, and I have made his mountains a desolation and *appointed* his inheritance for the jackals of the wilderness." ⁴Though Edom says, "We have been beaten down, but we will return and build up the ruins"; thus says the LORD of hosts, "They may build, but I will tear down; and *men* will call them the wicked territory, and the people toward whom the LORD is indignant forever." ⁵Your eyes will see this and you will say, "The LORD be magnified beyond the border of Israel!"

⁶"'A son honors *his* father, and a servant

his master. Then if I am a father, where is My honor? And if I am a master, where is My respect?' says the LORD of hosts to you, O priests who despise My name. But you say, 'How have we despised Your name?' ⁷ You are presenting defiled food upon My altar. But you say, 'How have we defiled You?' In that you say, 'The table of the LORD is to be despised.' ⁸ But when you present the blind for sacrifice, is it not evil? And when you present the lame and sick, is it not evil? Why not offer it to your governor? Would he be pleased with you? Or would he receive you kindly?" says the LORD of hosts. ⁹ "But now will you not entreat God's favor, that He may be gracious to us? With such an offering on your part, will He receive any of you kindly?" says the LORD of hosts. ¹⁰ "Oh that there were one among you who would shut the gates, that you might not uselessly kindle *fire on* My altar! I am not pleased with you," says the LORD of hosts, "nor will I accept an offering from you. ¹¹ For from the rising of the sun even to its setting, My name *will be* great among the nations, and in every place incense is going to be offered to My name, and a grain offering *that is* pure; for My name *will be* great among the nations," says the LORD of hosts. ¹² "But you are profaning it, in that you say, 'The table of the Lord is defiled, and as for its fruit, its food is to be despised.' ¹³ You also say, 'My, how tiresome it is!' And you disdainfully sniff at it," says the LORD of hosts, "and you bring what was taken by robbery and *what is* lame or sick; so you bring the offering! Should I receive that from your hand?" says the LORD. ¹⁴ "But cursed be the swindler who has a male in his flock and vows it, but sacrifices a blemished animal to the Lord, for I am a great King," says the LORD of hosts, "and My name is feared among the nations."

2 "And now this commandment is for you, O priests. ² If you do not listen, and if you do not take it to heart to give honor to My name," says the LORD of hosts, "then I will send the curse upon you and I will curse your blessings; and indeed, I have cursed them *already,* because you are not taking *it* to heart. ³ Behold, I am going to rebuke your offspring, and I will spread refuse on your faces, the refuse of your feasts; and you will be taken away with it. ⁴ Then you will know that I have sent this commandment to you, that My covenant may continue with Levi," says the LORD of hosts. ⁵ "My covenant with him was *one of* life and peace, and I gave them to him *as an object of* reverence; so he revered Me and stood in awe of My name. ⁶ True instruction

was in his mouth and unrighteousness was not found on his lips; he walked with Me in peace and uprightness, and he turned many back from iniquity. ⁷ For the lips of a priest should preserve knowledge, and men should seek instruction from his mouth; for he is the messenger of the LORD of hosts. ⁸ But as for you, you have turned aside from the way; you have caused many to stumble by the instruction; you have corrupted the covenant of Levi," says the LORD of hosts. ⁹ "So I also have made you despised and abased before all the people, just as you are not keeping My ways but are showing partiality in the instruction.

¹⁰ "Do we not all have one father? Has not one God created us? Why do we deal treacherously each against his brother so as to profane the covenant of our fathers? ¹¹ Judah has dealt treacherously, and an abomination has been committed in Israel and in Jerusalem; for Judah has profaned the sanctuary of the LORD which He loves and has married the daughter of a foreign god. ¹² *As* for the man who does this, may the LORD cut off from the tents of Jacob *everyone* who awakes and answers, or who presents an offering to the LORD of hosts.

¹³ "This is another thing you do: you cover the altar of the LORD with tears, with weeping and with groaning, because He no longer regards the offering or accepts *it with* favor from your hand. ¹⁴ Yet you say, 'For what reason?' Because the LORD has been a witness between you and the wife of your youth, against whom you have dealt treacherously, though she is your companion and your wife by covenant. ¹⁵ But not one has done *so* who has a remnant of the Spirit. And what did *that* one *do* while he was seeking a godly offspring? Take heed then to your spirit, and let no one deal treacherously against the wife of your youth. ¹⁶ For I hate divorce," says the LORD, the God of Israel, "and him who covers his garment with wrong," says the LORD of hosts. "So take heed to your spirit, that you do not deal treacherously."

¹⁷ You have wearied the LORD with your words. Yet you say, "How have we wearied *Him?*" In that you say, "Everyone who does evil is good in the sight of the LORD, and He delights in them," or, "Where is the God of justice?"

3 "Behold, I am going to send My messenger, and he will clear the way before Me. And the Lord, whom you seek, will suddenly come to His temple; and the messenger of the covenant, in whom you delight, behold, He is coming," says the LORD of hosts.

3:1 My messenger. It was a custom of the Near Eastern kings to send messengers before them to remove obstacles to their visit. Employing a wordplay on the name of Malachi, "the Lord's messenger," the Lord Himself announced He was sending one who would "clear the way before Me." This is the voice of one "calling" in the wilderness (Is 40:3) and the Elijah of 4:5 who comes before the Lord. The New Testament clearly identifies him as John the Baptist (Mt 3:3; 11:10, 14; 17:12ff.; Mk 1:2; Lk 1:17; 7:26–27; Jn 1:23).

² "But who can endure the day of His coming? And who can stand when He appears? For He is like a refiner's fire and like fullers' soap. ³ He will sit as a smelter and purifier of silver, and He will purify the sons of Levi and refine them like gold and silver, so that they may present to the LORD offerings in righteousness. ⁴ Then the offering of Judah and Jerusalem will be pleasing to the LORD as in the days of old and as in former years.

⁵ "Then I will draw near to you for judgment; and I will be a swift witness against the sorcerers and against the adulterers and against those who swear falsely, and against those who oppress the wage earner in his wages, the widow and the orphan, and those who turn aside the alien and do not fear Me," says the LORD of hosts. ⁶ "For I, the LORD, do not change; therefore you, O sons of Jacob, are not consumed.

⁷ "From the days of your fathers you have turned aside from My statutes and have not kept *them*. Return to Me, and I will return to you," says the LORD of hosts. "But you say, 'How shall we return?'

⁸ "Will a man rob God? Yet you are robbing Me! But you say, 'How have we robbed You?' In tithes and offerings. ⁹ You are cursed with a curse, for you are robbing Me, the whole nation *of you!* ¹⁰ Bring the whole tithe into the storehouse, so that there may be food in My house, and test Me now in this," says the LORD of hosts, "if I will not open for you the windows of heaven and pour out for you a blessing until it overflows. ¹¹ Then I will rebuke the devourer for you, so that it will not destroy the fruits of the ground; nor will your vine in the field cast *its grapes,*" says the LORD of hosts. ¹² "All the nations will call you blessed, for you shall be a delightful land," says the LORD of hosts.

¹³ "Your words have been arrogant against Me," says the LORD. "Yet you say, 'What have we spoken against You?' ¹⁴ You have said, 'It is vain to serve God; and what profit is it that we have kept His charge, and that we have walked in mourning before the LORD of hosts? ¹⁵ So now we call the arrogant blessed; not only are the doers of wickedness built up but they also test God and escape.'"

¹⁶ Then those who feared the LORD spoke to one another, and the LORD gave attention and heard *it,* and a book of remembrance was written before Him for those who fear the LORD and who esteem His name. ¹⁷ "They will be Mine," says the LORD of hosts, "on the day that I prepare *My* own possession, and I will spare them as a man spares his own son who serves him." ¹⁸ So you will again distinguish between the righteous and the wicked, between one who serves God and one who does not serve Him.

4 "For behold, the day is coming, burning like a furnace; and all the arrogant and every evildoer will be chaff; and the day that is coming will set them ablaze," says the LORD of hosts, "so that it will leave them neither root nor branch." ² "But for you who fear My name, the sun of righteousness will rise with healing in its wings; and you will go forth and skip about like calves from the stall. ³ You will tread down the wicked, for they will be ashes under the soles of your feet on the day which I am preparing," says the LORD of hosts.

4:2 sun of righteousness. While the wicked will be devoured by the heat of His wrath, those who fear Him will feel His warmth with healing in His "light" (Is 30:26; 60:1, 3). The reference is to the Messiah, "the LORD our righteousness" (Ps 84:11; Jer 23:5–6; 1Co 1:30). **healing.** The reference should not be limited to the physical recovery from the harm done by the wicked (3:5). This sickness is inextricably linked with sin, with healing coming only through the suffering of the Servant (Ps 103:3; Is 53:5; 57:18–19; 1Pe 2:24).

⁴ "Remember the law of Moses My servant, *even the* statutes and ordinances which I commanded him in Horeb for all Israel.

⁵ "Behold, I am going to send you Elijah the prophet before the coming of the great and terrible day of the LORD. ⁶ He will restore the hearts of the fathers to *their* children and the hearts of the children to their fathers, so that I will not come and smite the land with a curse."

Psalm 150:1–6

Praise the LORD!
Praise God in His sanctuary;
Praise Him in His mighty expanse.
2 Praise Him for His mighty deeds;
Praise Him according to His
excellent greatness.

3 Praise Him with trumpet sound;
Praise Him with harp and lyre.
4 Praise Him with timbrel and dancing;
Praise Him with stringed
instruments and pipe.
5 Praise Him with loud cymbals;
Praise Him with resounding cymbals.
6 Let everything that has breath
praise the LORD.
Praise the LORD!

Proverbs 31:10–31

10 An excellent wife, who can find?
For her worth is far above jewels.
11 The heart of her husband trusts in her,
And he will have no lack of gain.
12 She does him good and not evil
All the days of her life.
13 She looks for wool and flax
And works with her hands in delight.
14 She is like merchant ships;
She brings her food from afar.
15 She rises also while it is still night
And gives food to her household
And portions to her maidens.
16 She considers a field and buys it;
From her earnings she
plants a vineyard.
17 She girds herself with strength
And makes her arms strong.
18 She senses that her gain is good;
Her lamp does not go out at night.
19 She stretches out her hands
to the distaff,
And her hands grasp the spindle.
20 She extends her hand to the poor,
And she stretches out her
hands to the needy.
21 She is not afraid of the snow
for her household,
For all her household are
clothed with scarlet.
22 She makes coverings for herself;
Her clothing is fine linen and purple.
23 Her husband is known in the gates,
When he sits among the
elders of the land.
24 She makes linen garments
and sells *them,*
And supplies belts to the tradesmen.

25 Strength and dignity are her clothing,
And she smiles at the future.
26 She opens her mouth in wisdom,
And the teaching of kindness
is on her tongue.
27 She looks well to the ways
of her household,
And does not eat the
bread of idleness.
28 Her children rise up and bless her;
Her husband *also,* and he
praises her, *saying:*
29 "Many daughters have done nobly,
But you excel them all."
30 Charm is deceitful and beauty is vain,
But a woman who fears the
LORD, she shall be praised.
31 Give her the product of her hands,
And let her works praise
her in the gates.

31:10–31 This poem offers a beautiful description of the excellent wife as defined by a wife and mother (v. 1). Spiritual and practical wisdom plus moral virtues mark the character of this woman in contrast to the immoral women of v. 3. While the scene here is of a wealthy home and the customs of the ancient Near East, the principles apply to every family. They are set forth as the prayer of every mother for the future wife of her son, and literarily arranged with each of the 22 verses beginning with the 22 letters of the Hebrew alphabet in consecutive order.

Revelation 21:1–22:21

21 Then I saw a new heaven and a new earth; for the first heaven and the first earth passed away, and there is no longer *any* sea. 2 And I saw the holy city, new Jerusalem, coming down out of heaven from God, made ready as a bride adorned for her husband. 3 And I heard a loud voice from the throne, saying, "Behold, the tabernacle of God is among men, and He will dwell among them, and they shall be His people, and God Himself will be among them, 4 and He will wipe away every tear from their eyes; and there will no longer be *any* death; there will no longer be *any* mourning, or crying, or pain; the first things have passed away."

5 And He who sits on the throne said, "Behold, I am making all things new." And He *said, "Write, for these words are faithful and true." 6 Then He said to me, "It is done. I am the

rod, fifteen hundred miles; its length and width and height are equal. [17] And he measured its wall, seventy-two yards, *according to* human measurements, which are *also* angelic *measurements*. [18] The material of the wall was jasper; and the city was pure gold, like clear glass. [19] The foundation stones of the city wall were adorned with every kind of precious stone. The first foundation stone was jasper; the second, sapphire; the third, chalcedony; the fourth, emerald; [20] the fifth, sardonyx; the sixth, sardius; the seventh, chrysolite; the eighth, beryl; the ninth, topaz; the tenth, chrysoprase; the eleventh, jacinth; the twelfth, amethyst. [21] And the twelve gates were twelve pearls; each one of the gates was a single pearl. And the street of the city was pure gold, like transparent glass.

[22] I saw no temple in it, for the Lord God the Almighty and the Lamb are its temple. [23] And the city has no need of the sun or of the moon to shine on it, for the glory of God has illumined it, and its lamp *is* the Lamb. [24] The nations will walk by its light, and the kings of the earth will bring their glory into it. [25] In the daytime (for there will be no night there) its gates will never be closed; [26] and they will bring the glory and the honor of the nations into it; [27] and nothing unclean, and no one who practices abomination and lying, shall ever come into it, but only those whose names are written in the Lamb's book of life.

22 Then he showed me a river of the water of life, clear as crystal, coming from the throne of God and of the Lamb, [2] in the middle of its street. On either side of the river was the tree of life, bearing twelve *kinds of* fruit, yielding its fruit every month; and the leaves of the tree were for the healing of the nations. [3] There will no longer be any curse; and the throne of God and of the Lamb will be in it, and His bond-servants will serve Him; [4] they will see His face, and His name *will be* on their foreheads. [5] And there will no longer be *any* night; and they will not have need of the light of a lamp nor the light of the sun, because the Lord God will illumine them; and they will reign forever and ever.

[6] And he said to me, "These words are faithful and true"; and the Lord, the God of the spirits of the prophets, sent His angel to show to His bond-servants the things which must soon take place.

[7] "And behold, I am coming quickly. Blessed is he who heeds the words of the prophecy of this book."

[8] I, John, am the one who heard and saw these things. And when I heard and saw, I

21:2 new Jerusalem. This is the capital city of heaven, a place of perfect holiness. It is seen "coming down out of heaven," indicating it already existed; but it descends into the new heavens and new earth from its place on high. This is the city where the saints will live (Jn 14:1–3). **bride.** An important New Testament metaphor for the church (Mt 25:1–13; Eph 5:25–27). John's imagery here extends from the third part of the Jewish wedding, the ceremony. Believers (the bride) in the New Jerusalem come to meet Christ (the bridegroom) in the final ceremony of redemptive history (19:7). The whole city, occupied by all the saints, is called the bride, so that all saints must be finally included in the bride imagery and bridal blessing. God has brought home a bride for His beloved Son. All the saints live with Christ in the Father's house (a promise made before the church began; Jn 14:2).

Alpha and the Omega, the beginning and the end. I will give to the one who thirsts from the spring of the water of life without cost. [7] He who overcomes will inherit these things, and I will be his God and he will be My son. [8] But for the cowardly and unbelieving and abominable and murderers and immoral persons and sorcerers and idolaters and all liars, their part *will be* in the lake that burns with fire and brimstone, which is the second death."

[9] Then one of the seven angels who had the seven bowls full of the seven last plagues came and spoke with me, saying, "Come here, I will show you the bride, the wife of the Lamb." [10] And he carried me away in the Spirit to a great and high mountain, and showed me the holy city, Jerusalem, coming down out of heaven from God, [11] having the glory of God. Her brilliance was like a very costly stone, as a stone of crystal-clear jasper. [12] It had a great and high wall, with twelve gates, and at the gates twelve angels; and names *were* written on them, which are *the names* of the twelve tribes of the sons of Israel. [13] *There were* three gates on the east and three gates on the north and three gates on the south and three gates on the west. [14] And the wall of the city had twelve foundation stones, and on them *were* the twelve names of the twelve apostles of the Lamb.

[15] The one who spoke with me had a gold measuring rod to measure the city, and its gates and its wall. [16] The city is laid out as a square, and its length is as great as the width; and he measured the city with the

fell down to worship at the feet of the angel who showed me these things. ⁹ But he *said to me, "Do not do that. I am a fellow servant of yours and of your brethren the prophets and of those who heed the words of this book. Worship God."

¹⁰ And he *said to me, "Do not seal up the words of the prophecy of this book, for the time is near. ¹¹ Let the one who does wrong, still do wrong; and the one who is filthy, still be filthy; and let the one who is righteous, still practice righteousness; and the one who is holy, still keep himself holy."

¹² "Behold, I am coming quickly, and My reward is with Me, to render to every man according to what he has done. ¹³ I am the Alpha and the Omega, the first and the last, the beginning and the end."

¹⁴ Blessed are those who wash their robes, so that they may have the right to the tree of life, and may enter by the gates into the city. ¹⁵ Outside are the dogs and the sorcerers and the immoral persons and the murderers and the idolaters, and everyone who loves and practices lying.

¹⁶ "I, Jesus, have sent My angel to testify to you these things for the churches. I am the root and the descendant of David, the bright morning star."

¹⁷ The Spirit and the bride say, "Come." And let the one who hears say, "Come." And let the one who is thirsty come; let the one who wishes take the water of life without cost.

¹⁸ I testify to everyone who hears the words of the prophecy of this book: if anyone adds to them, God will add to him the plagues which are written in this book; ¹⁹ and if anyone takes away from the words of the book of this prophecy, God will take away his part from the tree of life and from the holy city, which are written in this book.

²⁰ He who testifies to these things says, "Yes, I am coming quickly." Amen. Come, Lord Jesus.

²¹ The grace of the Lord Jesus be with all. Amen.

DAY 31: What is the Book of Malachi about?

Only 50,000 exiles had returned to Judah from Babylon (538–536 B.C.). The temple had been rebuilt under the leadership of Zerubbabel (516 B.C.) and the sacrificial system renewed. Ezra had returned in 458 B.C., followed by Nehemiah in 445 B.C. After being back in the land of Palestine for only a century, the ritual of the Jews' religious routine led to hard-heartedness toward God's great love for them and to widespread departure from His law by both people and priest. Malachi rebuked and condemned these abuses, forcefully indicting the people and calling them to repentance. When Nehemiah returned from Persia the second time (ca. 424 B.C.), he vigorously rebuked them for these abuses in the temple and priesthood, for the violation of the Sabbath rest, and for the unlawful divorce of their Jewish wives so they could marry Gentile women (Ne 13).

As over two millennia of Old Testament history since Abraham concluded, none of the glorious promises of the Abrahamic, Davidic, and New Covenants had been fulfilled in their ultimate sense. Although there had been a few high points in Israel's history, e.g., Joshua, David, and Josiah, the Jews had seemingly lost all opportunity to receive God's favor. Less than 100 years after returning from captivity, they had already sunk to a depth of sin that exceeded the former iniquities which brought on the Assyrian and Babylonian deportations. Beyond this, the long-anticipated Messiah had not arrived and did not seem to be in sight.

So, Malachi wrote the capstone prophecy of the Old Testament in which he delivered God's message of judgment on Israel for their continuing sin and God's promise that one day in the future, when the Jews would repent, the Messiah would be revealed and God's covenant promises would be fulfilled. There were over 400 years of divine silence, with only Malachi's words ringing condemnation in their ears, before another prophet arrived with a message from God. That was John the Baptist preaching, "Repent, for the kingdom of heaven is at hand" (Mt 3:2). Messiah had come.

A Note Regarding the Type

This Bible was set in the Zondervan NASB Typeface, commissioned by Zondervan, a division of HarperCollins Christian Publishing, and designed in Aarhus, Denmark, by Klaus E. Krogh and Heidi Rand Sørensen of 2K/DENMARK. The typeface design takes inspiration from clear, readable Aramaic lettering to inscriptions of the Second Temple period. The design pays homage to the NASB's rich heritage of word-for-word translation and its faithfulness to the original biblical languages. The result is a distinctive Bible typeface that is uncompromisingly beautiful, clear, and readable at any size.

A Note Regarding the Type

This Bible was set in the Zondervan NASB Typeface, commissioned by Zondervan, a division of HarperCollins Christian Publishing, and designed in Aarhus, Denmark, by Klaus E. Krogh and Heidi Rand Sørensen of 2K/DENMARK. The typeface design takes inspiration from clear, distinct Aramaic limestone inscriptions of the Second Temple period. The design pays homage to the NASB's rich heritage of word-for-word translation and its faithfulness to the original biblical languages. The result is a distinctive Bible typeface that is uncompromisingly beautiful, clear, and readable at any size.